P9-ASK-933

Voices of
MULTICULTURAL AMERICA

Voices of MULTICULTURAL AMERICA

Notable Speeches Delivered by African, Asian, Hispanic and Native Americans, 1790–1995

Deborah Gillan Straub,
Editor

An ITP Information/Reference Group Company

NEW YORK • LONDON • BONN • BOSTON • DETROIT
MADRID • MELBOURNE • MEXICO CITY • PARIS
SINGAPORE • TOKYO • TORONTO • WASHINGTON
ALBANY NY • BELMONT CA • CINCINNATI OH

GALE RESEARCH STAFF

Allison K. McNeill, *Developmental Editor*
Andrea Kovacs, Jessica Proctor and Camille Killens, *Contributing Editors*
Lawrence W. Baker, *Managing Editor*

Mary Beth Trimper, *Production Director*
Evi Seoud, *Assistant Production Manager*
Shanna P. Heilveil, *Production Assistant*

Mary Krzewinski, *Art Director*
Cynthia Baldwin, *Product Design Manager*
Barbara J. Yarrow, *Graphic Services Manager*
Pamela Hayes, *Photography Coordinator*
Willie Mathis, *Camera Operator*

Maria L. Franklin, *Text Permissions Associate*
Susan Brohman, *Picture Permissions Assistant*

Front cover images: Malcolm X, *UPI/Bettmann*; César Chávez, *AP/Wide World Photos*; Chief Joseph and Smohalla, *Courtesy of Library of Congress*; Helen Zia, *Courtesy of Helen Zia*

Library of Congress Cataloging-in-Publication Data

Voices of Multicultural America: Notable Speeches Delivered by African, Asian, Hispanic, and Native Americans, 1790-1995 / [edited by] Deborah G. Straub.
p. cm.
Includes bibliographical references and index.
ISBN 0-8103-9378-6 (alk. paper)
1. Speeches, addresses, etc., American. 2. American prose literature–Minority authors. 3. American prose literature–Afro-American authors. 4. American prose literature–Asian American authors. 5. American prose literature–Hispanic American authors. 6. American prose literature–Indian authors. 7. Ethnic groups–United States. 8. Minorities–United States. I. Straub, Deborah Gillan.
PS663.M55V64 1996 95-31473
815.008'0920693–dc20 CIP

∞™ This book is printed on acid-free paper that meets the minimum requirements of American National Standard for Information Sciences—Permanence Paper for Printed Library Materials, ANSI Z39.48-1984.

ISBN 0-8103-9378-6
Printed in the United States of America
10 9 8 7 6 5 4 3 2

Contents

Highlights

Voices of Multicultural America compiles more than 230 noteworthy and compelling speeches delivered by over 130 prominent African Americans, Asian Americans, Hispanic Americans, and Native Americans from the late 1700s through early 1995. Included in one comprehensive volume are:

Arthur Ashe	Malcolm X
Dolores Huerta	Toni Morrison
César Chávez	Susette LaFlesche
Wilma Mankiller	Russell Means
Jesse Jackson	Bette Bao Lord
Sitting Bull	Chief Seattle
David Henry Hwang	Federico Peña, and many more

More than just a volume of speeches, *Voices of Multicultural America* brings to life the people and events surrounding each speech with colorful narratives preceding and often concluding every speech. Users gain an historical background for each speech, as well as learn the significance or impact of each speech. Other important features include:

- Over 230 speeches reprinted in their entirety whenever possible
- Over 100 photos
- Introduction compiled by experts in the field of oratory and cultural traditions in each ethnic group
- Ethnicity Index which allows access to speechmakers by ethnic or tribal affiliation
- Speech Category Index which allows access to speeches by topic or type of speech
- Keyword Index of names, events, locations, etc.
- Timeline of important U.S. events to help place speeches within an historical context

Preface

O the orator's joys!
To inflate the chest, to roll the thunder of the voice
out from the ribs and throat,
To make the people rage, weep, hate, desire, with
yourself,
To lead America—to quell America with a great tongue.
—Walt Whitman, "Calamus: A Song of Joys," from *Leaves of Grass*

Endowed with the ability to evoke a wide range of emotions and influence both thought and action, the orator has played a pivotal role throughout history. This is especially true in the United States, where the spoken word has helped shape both foreign and domestic policy ever since the nation was founded over 200 years ago.

All too often, though, speechmakers who have been excluded from full participation in American society by virtue of their gender or race have also received scant attention in print. *Voices of Multicultural America* aims to remedy that oversight by collecting in a single source some of the most important and interesting speeches delivered by African Americans, Native Americans, Hispanic Americans, and Asian Americans from the late 1700s to early 1995. The editor recognizes that the aforementioned ethnic distinctions may not be specific enough to suit everyone, but the intent is to emphasize the all-encompassing nature of the book's coverage.

SELECTING THE SPEECHMAKERS

The more than 130 speechmakers profiled in *Voices of Multicultural America* were chosen from a list of nearly 300 candidates in myriad fields of endeavor. An advisory board then reviewed the list, noting their selections and suggesting the names of other people they considered appropriate for inclusion. For purposes of this volume, those individuals who enjoy considerable recognition within their own ethnic communities and in American society at large were eligible. In a few instances, the advisors also identified specific speeches they deemed particularly worthy of inclusion.

The advisors' choices thus yielded a wide variety of potential listees, many of whom you will find profiled in the pages of *Voices of Multicultural America*. While this first edition is by no means exhaustive in its contents, due in part to space limitations and the availability of material, it features over 230 speeches by African Americans, Native Americans, Hispanic Americans, and Asian Americans whose names will be familiar to many students and general readers. The events that occasioned these speeches run the gamut from conventions and commencement ceremonies to political rallies and debates on the floor of the United States Congress. Also included are Nobel Prize lectures, statements delivered before government and judicial bodies, and eulogies. The topics discussed are equally diverse—civil rights, education, health care, race relations, the environment, economic development, politics, and the arts, to name only a few.

COMPILATION METHODS AND ENTRY FORMAT

The editor obtained tapes and transcripts of speeches from a number of different sources. Newspapers, periodicals, college and university archives, government documents, speech and literary anthologies (most long out of print), biographies, and autobiographies all proved especially fruitful. In the case of many living listees, the editor contacted them directly to secure material from their own files. While not every potential entrant was able to accommodate such a request, some two dozen speechmakers submitted transcripts of their favorite or most important speeches, which now appear exclusively in *Voices of Multicultural America.*

Much more than just a compilation of speeches, each entry in *Voices of Multicultural America* begins with a biographical sketch of the listee that furnishes key information regarding the person's childhood, education, career, and other significant events in his or her life culled from autobiographies, biographies, essay collections, newspapers, and magazines. Sketches continue by setting the stage for the speech that follows, such as placing it in its historical context or noting its connection to the person's field of endeavor or philosophical outlook. Finally comes a mention of the occasion on which the speech was delivered, including the date and the location. If an entry contains more than one speech, they appear in chronological order according to the dates on which they were delivered; each has its own introduction.

The speeches themselves are, whenever possible, published *in their entirety,* not excerpted as they often are in other sources. In a number of instances, audience reactions and comments from others present are also included in brackets within the speech, even though such information does not typically appear as part of most speech transcriptions. Bracketed information is also sometimes provided by the editor to identify a person or explain a situation not evident from the original speech.

Following many speeches is a brief concluding paragraph that summarizes what happened in the wake of the speechmaker's remarks, or may simply bring the reader up to date on the speechmaker's life. All entries end with a "Sources" section directing readers to more information on the speechmaker and his or her speeches.

SPECIAL FEATURES ENHANCE VOLUME

In addition to the biographical sketches that accompany each entry, *Voices of Multicultural America* features:

- An **Introduction,** consisting of four separate essays, which provides brief overviews of oratory traditions among African Americans, Native Americans, Hispanic Americans, and Asian Americans. Written by specialists in fields as diverse as communications, literature, and history, the essays reflect on the role of oratory in each culture through the years and describe specific characteristics of style and content that you will recognize as you read certain speeches. Each essayist also looks at the kinds of social and cultural barriers many of the people profiled in this volume have had to surmount in a nation that has not always granted them a public forum;
- An **expanded table of contents** includes a brief descriptor of each speechmaker as well as birth and death dates;
- An **Ethnicity Index** enables readers to identify a listee according to his or her ancestral homeland or, in the case of Native Americans, tribal affiliation;
- A **Speech Category Index** makes quick and easy work of your search for a speech on a particular topic;
- A **Timeline** to help place a speechmaker or a speech against the backdrop of other major U.S. events;
- **Over 100 photographs** help link names with faces;
- The **Keyword Index** lists key places, events, awards, institutions, and people cited in each entry.

AN INDISPENSABLE RESOURCE FOR ALL

With its broad coverage, informative biographical sketches, complete speech texts, and wide variety of indexes, *Voices of Multicultural America* will fulfill the needs of many different kinds of users. A student might turn to it to analyze the mechanics of a particular speech, to provide documentation for a report, or to identify a speech suitable to memorize and deliver in competition. Others involved in preparing their own speeches, articles, or books might find in its pages an interesting quote or a bit of inspiration. And for the casual reader with an interest in history or current events, *Voices of Multicultural America* offers a fascinating look at the people and ideas that have shaped the world in which we live.

ACKNOWLEDGMENTS

The editor wishes to thank the following people who served as advisors on this project: Wil A. Linkugel, Professor of Communication Studies, University of Kansas, Lawrence, Kansas; Rhonda Rios Kravitz, Head of Access Services, Library, California State University, Sacramento, California; Jeanette J. Smith, Regional Coordinator, Julia Davis Branch, St. Louis Public Library, St. Louis, Missouri; Suzanne Lo, Branch Manager, Asian Branch, Oakland Public Library, Oakland, California; Hilda K. Weisburg, Media Specialist, Sayreville War Memorial High School, Parlin, New Jersey.

SUGGESTIONS ARE WELCOME

The editor and publisher welcome your comments and suggestions for future editions of *Voices of Multicultural America.* Please send comments or suggestions to:

Editor
Voices of Multicultural America
Gale Research Inc.
835 Penobscot Building
Detroit, MI 48226
Toll-free: 1-800-347-GALE

Deborah Gillan Straub
September 1995

Introduction

To enhance your appreciation of the many different speeches and speechmakers included in this first edition of *Voices of Multicultural America,* the four essays that follow provide brief overviews of oratory traditions among African Americans, Native Americans, Hispanic Americans, and Asian Americans.

TRADITIONS IN AFRICAN AMERICAN ORATORY

In the American tradition, there is a fundamental assumption that everyone has freedom of speech and the right to be heard in the public forum as guaranteed by the First Amendment to the Constitution. Imagine, then, the plight of some people in the United States who historically did not have freedom of speech—African Americans. Because many of them were slaves from the seventeenth century until the Emancipation Proclamation freed them in 1863, they were not regarded as citizens. The U.S. Supreme Court reinforced this view in 1857 when it ruled that the Constitution had been written only for whites. Thus, as noncitizens without freedom of speech, blacks had to earn their "voice" in American society.

The roots of African American oratory can be traced back to oral African culture. In that environment, the human voice as well as drums were used to send messages, which another speaker or drummer would then respond to immediately. Both the original message and the answer were often quite creative and reflected the African religious belief in the spirit world.

Once in America, Africans continued their creative ways of communicating. During the time of slavery, these methods included field chants, hollers, and music, much of which had double or hidden meanings. This prevented the masters from knowing the true message, lest the slaves be punished for plotting against them.

Free blacks in the North, on the other hand, enjoyed freedom of speech to a degree their enslaved brothers in the South never could. Thus it was in the North that we heard speakers such as Frederick Douglass and Sojourner Truth. While some of these orators (such as Truth) could neither read nor write, they nevertheless spoke with passion and, more often than not, with strong religious conviction.

Given her reputation as an eloquent and persuasive speaker, Sojourner Truth is a good example of what has made so many African American orators effective—their delivery, their style, and their voice tones. Truth spoke in deep, sonorous tones and projected a sense of confidence. There was also a spiritual quality in her oratory that is common among many African American orators, including Martin Luther King, Jr., and Jesse Jackson. They all give the impression that God is on their side, a practice known as mythication.

While Sojourner Truth most notably reflects the spiritualist tradition in African American oratory, she was unique in other ways that have implications for how we understand African American oratory today. First, she was a woman; second, she was African American; third, she was illiterate; and fourth, she was poor. As a black woman who spoke before white audiences, she recognized the social distance between women and men and between African American women and white women. For her, race, gender, and class were barriers to be surmounted. Addressing these very same barriers in more recent times are African American women orators such as Fannie Lou Hamer and Shirley Chisholm.

While the written public record provides us with a fair amount of information about what the early black orators in the North had to say in their speeches, it is only in recent years that technology has allowed us to capture fully the interactive dynamics that typically occur between African American orators and their audiences. When both the speaker and his or her audience are black (and occasionally in racially-mixed groups as well), there is almost always a spontaneous verbal exchange that takes place known as call-response. This lively verbal interplay is unique to the African American oratorical tradition and has roots that extend back to Africa. Many of the early black orators were preachers, and their congregations continued the African tradition of providing an immediate response to the message. These responses were both verbal and nonverbal, such as saying "Amen," "Hallelujah," or "Thank you, Lord," or waving one's hands or standing and pointing toward the preacher. In this way, the congregation affirmed the messenger and created collective harmony with him or her and with the Holy Spirit.

Today, call-response is a way of uniting the orator and the audience, making the communication between them circular rather than one-way. The orator does not consider the verbal and nonverbal feedback from the audience as an interruption. In fact, many African American orators solicit this kind of feedback to determine whether they are reaching their audience, asking questions such as "Is anybody with me?" or "Can I get a witness?" The audience gives an immediate response ("Right on," "Make it plain," "Go 'head," "Take your time"), and this in turn affirms the messenger and urges him or her on to greater oratorical heights.

In addition to documenting this colorful tradition, modern technology has also helped preserve the accuracy of black oratory. Accuracy is always a concern when orators speak without a written text or when the written text is not saved. For example, since Sojourner Truth did not write down her speeches, there is now some question as to the accuracy of the existing printed texts.

The importance of technology in establishing accuracy is also evident when oratory contains a combination of prepared written text and extemporaneous speech, as in Martin Luther King, Jr.'s "I Have a Dream" speech. Audio and video recordings allow us to pinpoint when King dispensed with the text and began to speak extemporaneously. Such recordings also play a vital role in helping us to hear the moving musical qualities of his voice as he emphasized the many metaphors within his speech.

While Sojourner Truth and Martin Luther King, Jr., represent the extremes of literacy in African American oratory, each was effective due to their mastery of language and their ethos. Like many African American orators in U.S. history, they felt an urgency to give voice to the needs of their people.

Dorthy L. Pennington
Associate Professor
University of Kansas
Lawrence, Kansas

SPEAKING IN/OF NATIVE AMERICA

Reaching reliable generalizations when speaking of oratorical tradition in Native America is exceedingly difficult for two very important reasons. First, much of what comes down to us as Native American oratory was preserved by people who had, at best, a modest understanding of the speaker's language—rather like asking an English-speaking student who has just completed her first year of French to serve as the translator of one of Charles de Gaulle's speeches. (Christopher Columbus's journals are filled with what various Native Americans supposedly said, for instance, even though no one in Columbus's group had a working knowledge of the languages they encountered.) Then, too, among many of the translators we find either or both of two major biases: a desire to make Native American speakers "sound" more like someone of European extraction or a need to make Native American speakers "sound" like savages who didn't deserve an audience among "civilized" people.

Second, there is no such thing as "Native American culture." Films, television shows, books, advertisements, school mascots, and humor of all sorts consistently have created the impression that Native Americans belong to a single, monolithic culture in which all "Indians" look, act, and speak pretty much the same. Yet it makes no more sense to think of Native Americans as belonging to a single culture than it does to speak of Europeans as belonging to a single culture. In fact, in some ways it makes considerably *less* sense. Europeans were hugely influenced by the spread of Christianity, by the promulgation of Latin, and by a widespread reverence for Greece and Rome. Among Native Americans, contrary to popular belief, there is no single religion, no single reference-language, and no single sociocultural literary tradition.

One consequence of all this is that people who speak of *the* Native American culture, *the* Native American religion, *the* Native American worldview, or *the* Native American anything else do considerably more damage than good. It is worth bearing in mind, then, that the Native American speeches that follow are not representative—not because *Voices of Multicultural America* is flawed or its editor incompetent, but because no single volume can possibly represent all of the oratorical traditions of Native America.

With these points in mind, we nevertheless can make some useful observations that hold fairly well for many of the hundreds of Native American cultures, particularly prior to the twentieth century and particularly among contemporary traditionalists in Native America. We may begin with two communicative precepts: first, that breath is sacred, and second, that the communicative well-being of the tribe must take priority over all other communicative commitments.

Because breath is sacred, Native Americans generally have maintained an oral rather than a literary tradition. Until the resurgence of Native American organizations in the 1950s, Native American languages were falling rapidly into disuse. Since the 1950s, however, Native Americans have been working hard and long to revitalize their languages, which has led to a new vitality for Native American speaking.

Structurally, Native American cultures generally are horizontal (where people are considered equals) rather than vertical (where people are considered either dominant or subordinate). Therefore, anyone is entitled to speak insofar as they actually have something important to say. Older speakers—if they are also wiser speakers—typically were and are given greater respect than younger, less experienced speakers. This was and is true of women as well, for contrary to popular belief, women in most Native American cultures are not second-class citizens and have therefore always been the equals of men in all areas, including speechmaking.

Regardless of who is speaking, however, shorter speeches—speeches that get to the point—typically are preferable to long-winded, flowery speeches. Notice that this runs contrary to typical media portrayals, where "Indians" seem to go on and on about "cherry blossoms" and "the autumn moon" and such.

From these generalizations about Native American oratory spring a number of guiding principles. Some of the more obvious ones include:

- never lie;
- always communicate *with;*
- always and only communicate through the sacred principles of life;
- always and only permit one person to speak at a time, provide a period of silence following the speaker's speech to permit the speaker's revisions and/or amendments, and permit no shouting or interruptions;
- always and only speak to educate or persuade and never to confront;
- always preserve the principle that sharing is a requirement of life;
- always remember that gratitude can be shown only in deeds and never in words;
- always preserve the horizontal, egalitarian social environment, and never think someone less worthy than yourself;
- learn by doing rather than saying;
- always acknowledge leadership that is fostered by responsibility and never leadership that wields power;
- always speak when you have something to say and never otherwise;

- always demonstrate respect for the other—both human and nonhuman, both living and dead—and for the relationship that communication establishes;
- always protect the communicative rights of all tribal members;
- always remember that one's duty to the children of others is no less than one's duty to one's self; and
- always remember that conflict requires understanding, which is growth, rather than resolution, which is death.

As you read through the speeches that follow, please bear the above points in mind as much as possible. Also try to remember that [Native Americans] are not all the same [but] that we have the same kinds of thoughts, hopes, fears, concerns, and dreams as anyone else.

Dr. Richard Morris
Professor of Communication Studies
Northern Illinois University
DeKalb, Illinois

TRADITIONS IN HISPANIC AMERICAN ORATORY

Eloquence of expression has become ingrained in Hispanic culture through education and oral tradition since the emergence of the Spanish language in the Middle Ages. Much of the university curriculum at that time consisted of lecture and oral debate in Latin, and this tradition passed into Spanish when it became the official tongue of Spain during the Renaissance. Spanish subsequently became the language of governmental, educational and religious institutions throughout Spain's colonies in the Americas.

Educational methodology in Hispanic countries has been criticized for relying too much on oral recitation. But few outsiders have understood the value that the culture places on the oral performance itself and on improvisation. The product of an Hispanic education is expected to be able to compose and deliver extemporaneously a beautiful, enlightening and precise speech on any topic. The same is true in folk culture, where improvisation and elegance of expression have always ranked very high in the creation of epics, songs and stories. Hispanic audiences of all kinds—students in university classes, townsfolk at a patriotic celebration or churchgoers listening to a sermon—have typically expected and delighted in long compositions that reflect in both style and content the weightiness of the subjects under discussion.

It is in the political realm, however, that Hispanics have produced their most memorable and celebrated oratory. What may be considered the golden age of Spanish oratory occurred during the nineteenth century, when Spain's colonies in the New World began seeking their freedom. The powerful speeches of Venezuela's Simón Bolívar, Argentina's José San Martín, Mexico's Benito Juárez and scores of others who led independence movements and founded republics live on in legend and in history, and they are still studied throughout the Americas as examples of both literature and oratory.

Hispanics in the United States not only inherited these oratorical traditions but participated in their development. Of course, those areas that were once part of Spanish America—Puerto Rico, Florida and the Southwest—were directly involved in the political discourse of Mexico and Spain.

But as early as the first decade of the nineteenth century, expatriates from Spain established themselves in New York, Philadelphia and Boston and used their oratorical prowess to raise funds for the effort to oust French invaders from the Iberian peninsula. Later, various Spanish American independence movements—particularly the century-long struggle to win freedom for Cuba and Puerto Rico—were financed and planned in part in New York, Philadelphia, Tampa, New Orleans and other cities.

Of all of the orators who have articulated the needs and aspirations of the Hispanic communities in the United States, probably the most famous was José Martí, the lawyer, poet and leader of the Cuban independence movement during the late nineteenth century. He spent much of his life in the United States working as a journalist and lining up support for his cause among members of Hispanic communities from New York to New Orleans. The topics of Martí's speeches ranged from the right of the Cuban people to self-determination to an examination of the cultural conflicts between Anglo Americans and Hispanics. He also spoke out against racism and prejudice in the United States and around the world. One of his most important speeches—one that has become mortar in the building of Latin American identity in this hemisphere, and which is reprinted in this volume—is "Nuestra America" (Our America), which he delivered in New York around 1891.

Like many of the important addresses given by Hispanic leaders in the United States, Martí's speeches were originally transcribed and published in local Spanish-language newspapers; some have since been reprinted in history books and textbooks. In general, however, Spanish-speaking orators in the United States have not been well served by schools, libraries, publishers, and other institutions. Most of the speeches Hispanic Americans have given over the last two centuries have been lost to us forever, sometimes because they were never recorded, and sometimes because librarians and archivists failed to save newspaper accounts of an address or the speaker's personal notes. Even publication in a Spanish-language newspaper did not guarantee that a speech would be preserved, for out of an estimated 4,000 Hispanic periodicals published in the U.S. between 1800 and 1960, only incomplete runs of some 1,300 have been located to date.

Despite the loss of this rich heritage, the spirit of José Martí and others like him live on in today's Hispanic expatriate and immigrant communities across the United States. It is a pattern that also repeats itself among public servants and the leaders of various civil rights organizations. The eloquent and forceful declaration of organizing principals for the community, the call for unity and solidarity, the appeal to divine or human rights for inspiration, and the motivation to take action all figure prominently in the speeches of activists such as Henry G. Cisneros and César Chávez.

As in most European cultures, women in Latin America historically were not encouraged to pursue higher education or participate in public life. Nevertheless, Hispanic culture is replete with the names of women who emerged as leaders in education, politics, unions, the arts and many other areas, and in doing so they became outstanding orators. While their accomplishments were modest given the patriarchal make-up of Hispanic society in general, their activism and public oratory help us to understand the contemporary leadership of such women as Nicaragua's Violeta Chamorro, Puerto Rico's Felisa Rincón de Guatier, and even Argentina's Evita Perón, all of whom became leaders of their people through their impassioned speechmaking. Today, Hispanic American women such as Nydia Velásquez of New York and

Ileana Ros-Lehtinen of Florida are establishing a new tradition of eloquence as members of the United States Congress.

Dr. Nicolás Kanellos
Professor and Founding Publisher of Arte Público Press
University of Houston
Houston, Texas

ASIAN PACIFIC AMERICANS AND PUBLIC ORAL DISCOURSE

Asian Pacific Americans are a diverse group. They include East Asians (Chinese, Japanese, Koreans), Southeast Asians (Filipinos, Vietnamese, Cambodians, Laotians, Thais, Indonesians, Malaysians), South Asians (Indians, Pakistanis, Bangladeshis, Sri Lankans), and Pacific Islanders (Hawaiians, Samoans, Guamanians). Besides their diverse origins and cultures, Asian Pacific Americans have a varied past in America. Hawaiians settled their island home possibly as early as the third century BC and were forcibly annexed by the United States in 1898. Filipino communities formed in North America as early as the 1760s. Chinese and Asian Indians were on the East Coast by the 1790s, and Chinese settled in Hawaii and California before 1850. However, the majority of Asian Americans have been in the United States only since 1965, when immigration laws that discriminated against them (as well as against Latinos) were lifted. That ethnic diversity gives an indication of how difficult it is to write about an "Asian Pacific American tradition" in public discourse.

In the face of those historical and cultural differences, a striking commonality about Asian Pacific American oral public discourse is its apparent absence. We find very little evidence of Asian Pacific American speechmaking. I suppose that we in America generally think about public speaking as an arena where leaders—mainly politicians and social and labor reformers—address audiences to move masses of people into action. Most Americans couldn't name an Asian Pacific American social movement or an Asian Pacific American leader. Part of this difficulty is due to the historical fact that Asians were legally barred from participating fully in American life from the time of their arrival to the 1950s.

What were some of those barriers? For one, most Asians weren't even permitted to become naturalized citizens until 1952. In addition, they were restricted in their work and housing opportunities, they were prohibited from joining labor unions, and their children were forced to attend segregated schools. Hawaiians lost most of their land and were encouraged to abandon their language and culture. Asian Pacific Americans thus were generally excluded from the life of the mainstream, from politics to labor to the social and cultural arenas.

But Asian Pacific Americans *did* participate in the American pageant, and within their own communities Asian Pacific American leaders galvanized social movements that involved large numbers of people. For instance, after having been removed from her throne by force of arms in 1898, Liliuokalani, the last Hawaiian monarch, argued the cause of Hawaiian independence. "Oh, honest Americans, as Christians hear me for my downtrodden people!" she pleaded. "Their form of government is as dear to them as yours is precious to you. Quite as warmly as you love your country, so they love theirs."

Beginning in 1901, the Reverend Wu P'an-chao (also known as Ng Poon Chew), a Christian minister and newspaper publisher in San Francisco, made several national tours during which he addressed English and Chinese-speaking audiences about the need for immigration reform and the Chinese contribution to American society. Another distinguished speaker of Chinese ancestry was Jinqin Xue, who had studied at the University of California, Berkeley, in 1902 as a sixteen-year-old. She went on to become a leading feminist in China, and when she revisited California, she appeared before hundreds of San Francisco Chinatown residents to discuss ending China's patriarchal system and advancing women's liberation.

Between 1908 and 1910, Taraknath Das, a self-described "itinerant preacher," devoted himself to "explaining the economic, educational, and political conditions to the masses of the people." He spoke to audiences in Canada and the United States urging India's independence from British colonialism and calling for an end to discriminatory laws against Asian Indians in North America.

Waka Yamada, a woman of Japanese ancestry who had been tricked into marriage and forced into prostitution around the turn of the century, escaped the brothels of Seattle and San Francisco to become a leading writer, social critic, and feminist in Japan. She returned to America in 1937 on a lecture tour of West Coast Japanese American communities, riveting listeners with her insights on politics, peace, and women's liberation.

By and large, however, precious little survives of what these pioneering leaders actually said and what the reactions of their listeners were. Hawaiians in particular comprise a largely silent people because Americans have too easily ignored their articulate and persistent voices. An oral culture before contact with Europeans and Americans, Hawaiians told stories of their past in chants and dances of the hula. Those were deemed "uncivilized" by Christian missionaries who tried to forbid and change the meanings of those traditions, but they survived and have seen a revitalization in the resurgence of Hawaiian culture and language since the 1960s.

Furthermore, we know of few instances in which Asian Americans addressed large numbers of Americans outside of their communities. Only since World War II and the African American civil rights movement of the 1960s have Asian Americans become a part of American politics in any significant way.

Asian Pacific America has therefore not been devoid of leaders or social movements—they have simply not been recognized or widely mentioned. Asian Pacific Americans organized and participated in labor unions, initiated civil rights suits that resulted in landmark Supreme Court decisions, engaged in feminist struggles against patriarchy, and formed societies for the liberation of colonized Asia. Ministers preached sermons, labor leaders mobilized masses of workers, and feminists and civil rights leaders testified in courts and lectured to audiences from Hawaii to New York.

Within their own communities, Asian Pacific Americans took part in lively and vigorous public discourse. Among those who did so were people such as American-educated Syngman Rhee, the first president of the Republic of Korea, and D.S. Saund, who gave public lectures on Indian independence while a student at the University of California, Berkeley, during the 1920s and who in 1956 became the first Asian American elected to the U.S. Congress. They in turn paved the way for contemporary civil rights, feminist, and political leaders such as Clifford I. Uyeda, Helen Zia, S.I. Hayakawa, Norman Y. Mineta, and Robert T. Matsui. Meanwhile, Asian Pacific Americans such as Hiram L. Fong, Spark M. Matsunaga, Daniel K. Inouye, Patsy Takemoto Mink, and Daniel K. Akaka have played key roles in transforming the political landscape of Hawaii in the last half of the twentieth century.

Asian Pacific American voices resonate throughout America's past and present, if we will only listen.

Dr. Gary Y. Okihiro
Director of Asian American Studies Program
and Professor of History
Cornell University
Ithaca, New York

Entrants

D

E

F

G

H

I

J

S

T

U

W

Y

Z

Ethnicity Index

AFRICAN AMERICAN

BOLIVIAN AMERICAN

CHEROKEE TRIBE

CHEYENNE NATION

CHINESE AMERICAN

CHIPPEWA TRIBE

CHIRICAHUA APACHE TRIBE

COMANCHE TRIBE

CUBAN AMERICAN

DUWAMISH TRIBE

FILIPINO AMERICAN

JAPANESE AMERICAN

KIOWA TRIBE

KOREAN

MENOMINEE TRIBE

MEXICAN AMERICAN

MOHAWK TRIBE

MUSCOGEE NATION

NEZ PERCE TRIBE

NORTHERN CHEYENNE TRIBE

OJIBWA TRIBE

OMAHA TRIBE

NATIVE HAWAIIAN

PONCA TRIBE

PUERTO RICAN

SALISH TRIBE

SAUK (SAC) TRIBE

SEMINOLE TRIBE

SENECA TRIBE

SIOUX TRIBE

SPANISH AMERICAN

SUQUAMISH TRIBE

Speech Category Index

CONGRESSIONAL RECORD SPEECHES

(see also TESTIMONY–CONGRESSIONAL)

CONSTITUTION, U.S.

CUBA

CULTURAL DIVERSITY (see MULTICULTURALISM)

CULTURAL VALUES

DEMONSTRATIONS (see PROTEST SPEECHES)

DESEGREGATION (see also DISCRIMINATION–RACIAL)

DISCRIMINATION–ETHNIC

DISCRIMINATION–RACIAL

DISTRICT OF COLUMBIA STATEHOOD

ECONOMIC ISSUES (see also LABOR ISSUES)

EDUCATION

EMPLOYMENT ISSUES (see also LABOR ISSUES)

LYNCHING

MARCHES (see PROTEST SPEECHES)

MASCOT/SPORTS TEAM NAMES ISSUE (see ETHNIC STEREOTYPING)

McCARTHYISM

MEDIA ETHICS/EXPLOITATION

MEXICAN AMERICAN LEGAL DEFENSE AND EDUCATIONAL FUND (MALDEF)

MIGRANT FARM WORKER ISSUES

MULTICULTURALISM

NATIONAL ASSOCIATION FOR THE ADVANCEMENT OF COLORED PEOPLE (NAACP)

NATIONAL PRESS CLUB SPEECHES

NATIONAL URBAN LEAGUE

NATION OF ISLAM

NATIVE AMERICAN POLICY, U.S.

NIAGARA MOVEMENT

NOBEL PRIZE SPEECHES

NONVIOLENT RESISTANCE

Credits

Grateful acknowledgment is made to the following sources whose works appear in this volume. Every effort has been made to trace copyright, but if omissions have been made, please contact the publisher:

Abernathy, Ralph David. From "They Didn't Know Who He Was" in *The Cry For Freedom: An Anthology of the Best That Has Been Said and Written on Civil Rights Since 1954*. Edited by Frank W. Hale, Jr. A. S. Barnes and Company, 1969. © 1969 by A. S. Barnes and Company, Inc./From "The Kerner Report: Promises and Realities" in *The Voice of Black America: Major Speeches by Negroes in the United States, 1797-1971*. Edited by Philip S. Foner. Simon and Schuster, 1972. Copyright © 1972 by Philip S. Foner. All rights reserved. Both reprinted by permission of the Literary Estate of Ralph David Abernathy.

Akwesasne Notes, v. 9, July 1977 for "Statement to Judge Paul Benson" by Leonard Peltier; v. 9, December 1977 for "There is Only One Color of Mankind That is Not Allowed to Participate in the International Community. And That Color is The Red" by Russell Means; v. 10, Summer 1978 for ". . . If Our Drum Was Ever Stilled, We Would Be Through as a Nation" by Clyde Bellecourt. All reprinted by permission of the publisher.

Bellecourt, Vernon. From "American Indian Movement" in *Contemporary Native American* Address. Edited by John R. Maestas. Brigham Young University, 1976. ©1976 by Brigham Young University. All rights reserved. Reprinted by permission of the publisher.

Black Hawk. From "Black Hawk's Farewell" in *Literature of the American Indian*. By Thomas E. Sanders and Walter W. Peek. Glencoe Press. Copyright © 1973 by Benziger Bruce & Glencoe, Inc. All rights reserved. Reprinted by permission of the publisher.

The Black Panther, v. 2, March 16, 1968 for "Political Struggle in America," by Eldridge Cleaver. Reprinted by permission of the author./ v. II, March 3, 1969 for "Message from Huey" by Huey Newton; v. 5, August 21, 1970 for a eulogy delivered on August 15, 1970, at the Revolutionary Funeral of Comrades Jonathan Jackson and William Christmas, St. Augustine Church, Oakland, CA. Both reprinted by permission of the Huey P. Newton Foundation.

Bonilla, Tony. From a speech delivered in February 1983, at the *National Meeting of Operation PUSH* in Chicago, IL. Reprinted by permission of the author.

Bonnin, Gertrude. From a speech delivered on December 14-15, 1928, addressed before the *Indian Rights Association on "Problem of Indian Administration"* in Atlantic City. Reprinted by permission of the Brigham Young University Archives.

Brown, Tony. In a speech delivered in August 1993, at the *Black Human Resources Conference.*

Bunche, Ralph J. From a lecture delivered on December 11, 1950, at the University of Oslo, in *Peace 1926-1950, Vol. 2.* Edited by Frederick W. Haberman. Elsevier Publishing Company, 1972. © The Nobel Foundation 1950. All rights reserved. Reprinted by permission of the publisher.

Carmichael, Stokely. From "Berkeley Speech" in *Stokely Speaks: Black Power Back to Pan-Africanism.*/ From "Free Huey" in *Stokely Speaks: Black Power Back to Pan-Africanism.* Random House, 1971. Both reprinted by permission of the author.

Carson, Ben. From a speech delivered on June 27, 1994, at the *Million Dollar Roundtable Convention,* in Dallas, TX. Reprinted by permission of the author.

Catholic Mind, October 1975 for "Saying 'Yes' to Man's Dignity" by Cesar Chavez. Reprinted by permission from the Cesar E. Chavez Foundation, P.O. Box 62, Keene, CA 93531, (805) 822-5571, ext. 256, chavezfdtn@igc.apc.org.

Chavez, Cesar. From a speech delivered on March 10, 1968, in *Cesar Chavez: The Rhetoric of Nonviolence.* By Winthrop Yinger. Exposition Press, 1975. © 1975 by Winthrop Yinger. All rights reserved./From a speech delivered in 1974, at the *Greater Washington Central Labor Council Luncheon.*/From an address delivered in 1991, before the *Building Industry Association of Northern California.* All reprinted by permission from the Cesar E. Chavez Foundation, P.O. Box 62, Keene, CA 93531, (805) 822-5571, ext. 256, chavezfdtn@igc.apc.org.

Chavez, Linda. In a speech delivered in October 1992, "Fostering Appreciation for Cultural Diversity: Recognizing America's Changing Complexion," at the *National Preservation Conference.* Reprinted by permission of the author.

Chisholm, Shirley. From "Economic Injustice in America Today," in *Representative American Speeches: 1971-1972.* Edited by Waldo W. Braden. H. W. Wilson, 1972./From "Women in Politics," in *Representative American Speeches: 1972-1973.* Edited by Waldo W. Braden. H. W. Wilson, 1973. Copyright © 1972, 1973 by The H. W. Wilson Company. Both reprinted by permission of the author.

Christian Social Action, v. 6, June 1993. Copyright © 1993 by the General Board of Church and Society of The United Methodist Church. Reprinted by permission of the publisher.

Cole, Johnnetta B. From a speech delivered on January 28, 1994, at the *National Science Foundation in Celebration of Martin Luther King Jr.'s Birthday* in Arlington, VA. Reprinted by permission of the author.

Delano Record, April 28, 1966, for "Speech at Capital Rally," by Dolores Huerta. Reprinted by permission of Dolores C. Huerta, United Farm Workers of America, AFL-CIO, P.O. Box 62, Keene, CA 93531.

Dove, Rita. In a speech delivered on March 17, 1994, "Who's Afraid of Poetry?" at the *National Press Club.* Reprinted by permission of the author.

Du Bois, W. E. B. From "We Claim Our Rights," in *A Documentary History of the Negro People of the United States, 1933-1945.* Edited by Herbert Aptheker. Citadel Press, 1951. Copyright 1951, renewed 1979 by Herbert Aptheker. Published by arrangement with Carol Publishing Group.

Edelman, Marian Wright. From *Representative American Speeches: 1987-1988.* Edited by Owen Peterson. H. W. Wilson, 1988. Copyright © 1988 by The H. W. Wilson Company. All rights reserved. Reprinted by permission of the author.

Escalante, Jaime. From a speech delivered during the summer of 1992 at the *Annual Meeting of the Million Dollar Round Table* in Chicago, IL.

Fernandez, Joseph A. In a speech delivered on September 7, 1993, to the *National Press Club.*

Freedomways, v. 5, Winter 1965; v. 7, Spring 1967. Copyright © 1965, 1967 by Freedomways Associates, Inc. Both reprinted by permission of Freedomways.

Garvey, Marcus. From a speech in *Philosophy and Opinions of Marcus Garvey.*/ From "The Principles of the Universal Negro Improvement Association" in *Philosophy and Opinions of Marcus Garvey.* Edited by Amy Jacques-Garvey. Arno Press, 1969. Both reprinted by permission of the Literary Estate of Marcus Garvey.

George, Chief Dan. From a speech delivered in 1967, in *Touch the Earth: A Self Portrait of Indian Existence.* By T. C. McLuhan. Outerbridge & Dienstfrey, 1971. Copyright © 1971 by T. C. McLuhan./ From "Brotherhood & Understanding" in *Contemporary Native American Address.* Edited by John R. Maestas. Brigham Young University, 1976. © 1976 by Brigham Young University. All rights reserved. Reprinted by permission of the publisher.

Geronimo. From "I Was Living Peaceably and Satisfied When People Began to Speak Bad of Me" (1886), in *The Truth About Geronimo.* By Britton Davis. Edited by M. M. Quaife. Yale University Press, 1929. Copyright, 1929 by Yale University Press. Renewed 1956 by Nathalie D. Connor. Reprinted by permission of the publisher.

Guinier, Lani. From "We Need a National Debate About Racial Justice," in *A Collection of Speeches From The NAACP's 84th Annual Convention,* July 10—15, 1993. NAACP, 1993. Reprinted by permission of the author.

Haley, Alex. From a speech delivered on January 30, 1992, at *Hope College* in Holland, MI.

Hamer, Fannie Lou. In a testimony delivered on August 22, 1964, before the Credential Committee, in Proceedings of the Democratic National Convention. Reprinted by permission of the publisher.

Haney, Michael. From a speech delivered on March 30, 1991, on the *International Indian Treaty Council before the United Nations Subcommission on the Prevention of Discrimination Against Minorities,* at the American Indian Community House in New York, NY. Reprinted by permission of the author.

Harjo, Suzan Shown. From a keynote address delivered on September 18, 1992, "Seeds of Change" at the *Fourth Annual Conference* in Santa Fe, NM. Reprinted by permission of the author.

Harris, LaDonna. From "Kerner Commission Paper" in *Native American Reader: Stories, Speeches and Poems.* Edited by Jerry D. Blanche. The Denali Press, 1990. Copyright © 1990 by Jerry D. Blanche. Reprinted by permission of the publisher.

Harvard Educational Review, v. 58, 1988. Copyright © 1988 by the President and Fellows of Harvard College. All rights reserved. Reprinted by permission of the publisher.

Hernandez, Antonia. From a speech delivered on November 18, 1994, to the *MALDEF Chapter* in Albuquerque, New Mexico./From a speech delivered on October 5, 1994, on "Are We Compassion Fatigued?" at the Temple Isaih in Los Angeles, CA. Both reprinted by permission of the author.

Hope, John. From a speech in *The Story of John Hope.* By Ridgely Torrence. Macmillan, 1948. Copyright 1948 by Ridgely Torrence. Renewed 1976 by Ellen W. Dunbar. All rights reserved. Reprinted with the permission of Macmillan Publishing Company.

Huerta, Dolores. From a keynote speech delivered on October 21, 1974, at the *Annual Convention of American Public Health Association* in New Orleans, LA. Reprinted by permission of the author.

Hwang, David Henry. From a lecture delivered on April 15, 1994, at the *Abramowitz Lecture Series, at Massachusetts Institute of Technology.* Reprinted by permission of the author.

Jackson, Jesse L. From *Straight from the Heart.* Edited by Roger D. Hatch and Frank E. Watkins. Fortress Press, 1987. Copyright © 1987 by Jesse L. Jackson. All rights reserved. Both used by permission of Augsburg Fortress.

Jeffries, Leonard. From a speech delivered on July 20, 1991, at the *Empire State Black Arts and Cultural Festival* in Albany, NY. Reprinted by permission of the author.

Jordan, Barbara. From "A New Beginning: A New Dedication," in *Representative American Speeches: 1976-1977.* Edited by Waldo W. Braden. H. W. Wilson, 1977.

Copyright © 1977 by The H. W. Wilson Company. Reprinted by permission of the author.

Jordan, Jr., Vernon E. From "Blacks and the Nixon Administration: The Next Four Years," in *Representative American Speeches: 1972–1973.* Edited by Waldo W. Braden. H. W. Wilson, 1973. Copyright © 1973 by The H. W. Wilson Company./ From *Representative American Speeches: 1979–1980.* Edited by Waldo W. Braden. H. W. Wilson, 1980. Copyright © 1980 by The H. W. Wilson Company. All rights reserved. Both reprinted by permission of the author.

King, Coretta Scott. From *My Life with Martin Luther King, Jr.* Holt, Rinehart and Winston, 1969. Copyright © 1969 by Coretta Scott King./In a speech delivered on April 8, 1993, at the *National Press Club.*/In a speech on January 17, 1994, *"The State of the Dream."* All reprinted by arrangement with Coretta Scott King, c/o Joan Daves Agency as agent for the proprietor.

King, Jr., Martin Luther. From "I Have a Dream" in *Rhetoric of Racial Revolt.*/ From "Love, Law and Civil Disobedience" in *Rhetoric of Racial Revolt.* Edited by Roy L. Hill. Golden Bell Press, 1964. © Copyright 1964, renewed 1992 Golden Bell Press./ From *A Testament of Hope: The Essential Writings of Martin Luther King, Jr.* Edited by James Melvin Washington. Harper & Row, 1986. Copyright © 1986 by Coretta Scott King, Executrix of the Estate of Martin Luther King, Jr. All rights reserved./From a speech delivered at Holt Street Baptist Church in *The Eyes on the Prize.* Edited by Clayborne Carson and others. Penguin Books, 1991. Copyright 1955, 1968 by Martin Luther King, Jr., and the Estate of Martin Luther King, Jr. Copyright © Blackside, Inc. 1991. All rights reserved. All reprinted by arrangement with The Heirs to the Estate of Martin Luther King, Jr., c/o Joan Daves Agency as agent for the proprietor.

Malcolm X. From *Malcolm X Speaks: Selected Speeches and Statements.* Edited by George Breitman. Pathfinder, 1965. Copyright © 1965, renewed 1993 by Betty Shabazz and Pathfinder Press. All rights reserved. All reprinted by permission of the publisher.

Mankiller, Wilma P. From "Inaugural Address" in *Native American Reader: Stories, Speeches and Poems.* Edited by Jerry D. Blanche. The Denali Press, 1990. Copyright © 1990 by Jerry D. Blanche. Reprinted by permission of the publisher./ From a speech delivered on September 3, 1994, at the *Cherokee Nation State of the Nation Address* in Tahlequah, OK. Reprinted by permission of the publisher

Liberation, January 1965 for "Nobel Prize Acceptance Speech (1964)" by Martin Luther King, Jr. Copyright 1964 by Martin Luther King, Jr. Renewed 1992 by Coretta Scott King. Reprinted by arrangement with The Heirs to the Estate of Martin Luther King, Jr., c/o Joan Daves Agency as agent for the proprietor.

Martinez, Vilma S. From a speech delivered on February 8, 1990, on Cultural Diversity and Academic Excellence: A Golden Opportunity, at the *UC All-University Faculty Conference,* at the Pala Mesa Resort Hotel. Reprinted by permission of the author.

Means, Russell. From "The State of Native America" in *Native American Reader: Stories, Speeches and Poems.* Edited by Jerry D. Blanche. The Denali Press, 1990. Copyright © 1990 by Jerry D. Blanche. Reprinted by permission of the publisher.

Mink, Patsy. From "Seeking a Link with the Past" in *Representative American Speeches: 1972–1973.* Edited by Waldo W. Braden. H. W. Wilson, 1972. Copyright © 1972 by The H. W. Wilson Company. Reprinted by permission of the author.

Natividad, Irene. From a keynote address delivered on March 7, 1991, at the symposium of the *National Museum of American History Smithsonian Institution* in Washington DC in Proceedings of Specializing in the Impossible: Women and Social Reform in America, 1890-1990 Conference. Reprinted by permission of the author.

Norton, Eleanor Holmes. From "In Pursuit of Equality in Academe: New Themes and Dissonant Chords" in *Individualizing the System: Current Issues in Higher Edition.* Edited by Dyckman W. Vermile. Jossey-Bass, 1976. Copyright 1976 by the American Association for Higher Education and Jossey-Bass Inc., Publisher. Reprinted by permission of the publisher.

Pensacola Journal, February 15, 1975. Reprinted by permission of the publisher.

Poussaint, Alvin F. From *The Fedele F. Fauri Memorial Lecture Series in Child Welfare*. The University of Michigan School of Social Work, 1987. Reprinted by permission of the publisher.

Powell, Colin L. In a commencement address on May 14, 1994, at *Howard University*. Reprinted by permission of the author.

Powell, Jr., Adam Clayton. From "Can There be Any Good Thing Come Out of Nazareth?" in *Rhetoric of Black Revolution*. By Arthur L. Smith. Allyn and Bacon, 1969. © Copyright 1969 by Allyn and Bacon, Inc. All rights reserved. Reprinted by permission of Arthur L. Smith.

Price, Hugh B. In a speech delivered on July 24, 1994, at the *National Urban League Convention*. Reprinted by permission of the author.

Randolph, A. Philip. From "The March on Washington Movement," in *Black Protest: History, Documents, and Analyses, 1619 to the Present*. Second edition. Edited by Joanne Grant. Fawcett Premier, 1968.

Ross, John. From "The Cherokee People Stand Upon New Ground" (1861) in *Indian Oratory: Famous Speeches by Noted Indian Chieftains*. By W. C. Vanderwerth. University of Oklahoma Press, 1971. Copyright © 1971 by the University of Oklahoma Press. Reprinted by permission of the publisher.

Rustin, Bayard. From "Toward Integration as a Goal" in *Representative American Speeches: 1968–1969*. Edited by Lester Thonssen. H. W. Wilson, 1969. Copyright © 1969 by The H. W. Wilson Company. Reprinted by permission of the author./ From *Down the Line: The Collected Writings of Bayard Rustin*. Quadrangle Books, 1971. Copyright ©1971 by Bayard Rustin. All rights reserved. Reprinted by permission of Random House, Inc.

Seattle, Chief. From "Chief Seattle's Speech," (version 2, revised by William Arrowsmith); "Chief Seattle Speech," (version 3, written by Ted Perry); "Chief Seattle's Speech," (version 4, from the Spokane Expo of 1974) in *Recovering the Word: Essays on Native American Literature*. Edited by Brian Swann and Arnold Krupat. University of California Press, 1987. Copyright © 1987 by The Regents of the University of California. All reprinted by permission of the publisher.

Sitting Bull. From a speech delivered in 1877 in *To Serve the Devil, Vol. 1*. By Paul Jacobs and Saul Landau. Vintage Books, 1971. Copyright ©1971 by Paul Jacobs and Saul Landau./From *The Way: An Anthology of American Literature*. Edited by Shirley Hill Witt and Stan Steiner. Alfred A. Knopf, 1972. Copyright © 1972 by Alfred A. Knopf, Inc. All rights reserved.

Smohalla. From "Smohalla Speaks" in *Literature of the American Indian*. By Thomas E. Sanders and Walter W. Peek. Glencoe Press. Copyright © 1973 by Benziger Bruce & Glencoe, Inc. All rights reserved. Reprinted by permission of the publisher.

Swimmer, Ross. In a speech "An Indian Crossroad." Reprinted by permission of the author.

Tecumseh. From "We Must Smoke the Same Pipe" in *Literature of the American Indian*. By Thomas E. Sanders and Walter W. Peek. Glencoe Press. Copyright © 1973 by Benziger Bruce & Glencoe, Inc. All rights reserved. Reprinted by permission of the publisher.

Trudell, John. From "Commitment" in *Contemporary Native American Address*. Edited by John R. Maestas. Brigham Young University, 1976. © 1976 by Brigham Young University. All rights reserved. Reprinted by permission of the publisher.

Turner, Henry McNeal. From *Respect Black: The Writings and Speeches of Henry McNeal Turner*. Edited by Edwin S. Redkey. Arno Press and The New York Times, 1971. Copyright © 1971 by Arno Press Inc. All rights reserved. Reprinted by permission of the Literary Estate of Henry McNeal Turner.

Uyeda, Clifford I. From a speech delivered on January 20, 1979, on "Why Redress for Japanese Americans," at the *Twin Cities JACL Chapter Installation Dinner* in Minneapolis, MN. Reprinted by permission of the author.

Vital Speeches of the Day, v. XXXVI, September 15, 1970. Reprinted by permission of the publisher./v. LIV, May 15, 1988 for "Politics and Public Policy: The

Hispanic Community" by Harry P. Pachon. Reprinted by permission of the publisher and the author.

West, Cornel. In a speech delivered on January 12, 1942, at *Calvin College*.

White, Walter. From a speech delivered on July 16, 1944, at *The Annual Meeting of the NAACP* in Chicago, IL.

Wilder, L. Douglas. From "I Am a Son of Virginia," in *Representative American Speeches: 1968-1969*. Edited by Lester Thonssen. The H. W. Wilson Company, 1969. Copyright © 1969 by The H. W. Wilson Company. Reprinted by permission of the author.

Worldview, April 1972. Reprinted by permission of the publisher.

Young, Jr., Whitney M. From "For Protest Plus 'Corrective Measures': Address to National Urban League Conference 1963" in *Negro Protest Thought in the Twentieth Century*. Edited by Francis L. Broderick and August Meier. Bobbs-Merrill, 1965. Copyright © 1965, renewed 1993 by Macmillan Publishing Company. Reprinted with the permission of Macmillan Publishing Company./ From "The Crisis of the Cities: The Danger of the Ghetto" in *Representative American Speeches: 1966-1967*. Edited by Lester Thonssen. H. W. Wilson, 1967. Copyright © 1967 by The H. W. Wilson Company./From "Agenda for the Future" (1965), in *The Negro Speaks: The Rhetoric of Contemporary Black Leaders*. Edited by Jamye Coleman Williams and McDonald Williams. Noble and Noble, 1970. Copyright © 1970 by Noble and Noble, Publishers, Inc. All rights reserved. Both reprinted by permission of the Literary Estate of the Whitney M. Young, Jr.

Yzaguirre, Raul. From a speech delivered in June 1994, at *Mercy College*, Dobbs Ferry, NY. Reprinted by permission of the author.

Zia, Helen. From a keynote address delivered on August 27, 1992, at the *Annual Convention of Asian American Journalists Association*. Copyright © 1992 by Helen Zia./ From a speech delivered on March 6, 1993, "Racism, Hate Crimes, and Pornography" at the *Equality and Harm Conference* in Chicago. Copyright © 1993 by Helen Zia./ From a speech delivered on January 29, 1994, at the *6th Annual Gay Asian Pacific Alliance* in San Francisco. Copyright © 1994 by Helen Zia. All reprinted with permission.

Images appearing in *Voices of Multicultural America* were received from the following sources:

AP/Wide World Photos: **pp. 3, 32, 54, 77, 112, 135, 182, 262, 276, 282, 322, 329, 357, 375, 469, 496, 538, 557, 621, 750, 893, 965, 979, 1185, 1220**; Courtesy of Daniel Akaka: **p. 16**; Reuters/Bettmann: **pp. 19, 128, 224, 246, 452, 548, 900, 934, 948, 972, 1172, 1282**; UPI/The Bettmann Archive: **pp. 27, 63, 1104, 1149**; The Bettmann Archive: **pp. 37, 48, 152, 290, 738, 1035, 1125, 1152, 1190, 1226**; The Granger Collection, New York: **pp. 72, 90, 97, 266, 398, 428, 508, 639, 670, 1050, 1080, 1132, 1179, 1207, 1232**; UPI/Bettmann Newsphotos: **pp. 172, 255, 595, 653, 930**; Courtesy of the Library of Congress: **pp. 195, 1111, 1130, 1258**; UPI/Bettmann: **pp. 216, 232, 344, 410, 422, 434, 457, 488, 518, 526, 614, 663, 683, 697, 753, 787, 800, 859, 865, 907, 918, 995, 1006, 1058, 1063, 1087, 1273, 1289, 1301, 1329, 1333**; Arte Publico Press: **p. 368**; Courtesy of Hiram Fong: **p. 383**; Courtesy of the U.S. Department of the Interior; photograph by Tami A. Heilemann: **p. 442**; Courtesy of Michael Haney: **p. 479**; Courtesy of David Henry Hwang: **p. 570**; Courtesy of Daniel K. Inouye: **p. 582**; Moorland-Spingarn Research Center/Howard University: **pp. 647, 1160**; Nebraska State Historical Society: **p. 732**; Courtesy of Vilma S. Martinez: **p. 822**; Courtesy of Robert T. Matsui: **p. 842**; Courtesy of Norman Mineta: **p. 876**; Courtesy of Patsy Mink: **p. 884**; Courtesy of Irene Natividad; photograph by Michael Geissinger: **p. 923**; Lou Jones Studio: **p. 1028**; Amon Carter Museum: **p. 1100**; Courtesy of Benno Friedman: **p. 1248**; Courtesy of Helen Zia: **p. 1333.**

Timeline

1754-63 French and Indian War.

1775-83 Revolutionary War.

1776 The Declaration of Independence is signed.

1787 The Continental Congress bans slavery in the Northwest Territory and declares that no land is to be taken from Indians without their consent.

The U.S. Constitution is approved and subsequently ratified by the states to take effect March 4, 1789.

1790 The first U.S. Naturalization Act allows only "free white persons" to become American citizens.

1791 The Bill of Rights (consisting of the first ten amendments to the Constitution) is ratified.

1793 Congress passes the first Fugitive Slave Law, making it a crime to hide an escaped slave or to interfere with his or her arrest.

1803 The U.S. negotiates the Louisiana Purchase with France.

1810-13 Shawnee chief **Tecumseh** tries to forge an alliance of several Indian tribes to resist white encroachment westward into the Great Lakes region.

1810 Hispanic colonists in New Spain (a territory encompassing Mexico as well as large portions of the present-day U.S. Southwest) proclaim their independence from Spain.

1812-15 War of 1812.

1820 Congress approves the Missouri Compromise.

1821 New Spain gains its independence and renames itself the Republic of Mexico.

The U.S. purchases Florida from Spain.

1824 The Bureau of Indian Affairs is established under the jurisdiction of the U.S. War Department.

1827 **Red Jacket** is ousted as chief of the Seneca nation for his outspoken opposition to the white man's religion and customs.

1830 Congress passes the Indian Removal Act. Indians living east of the Mississippi River are forced to give up their land and relocate west of the river. Many die of disease, exposure, and starvation along the way, prompting the Cherokee to name the route the "Trail of Tears."

1831 Nat Turner leads the most famous slave rebellion in American history. He is soon captured and hung.

1832 Sauk Chief **Black Hawk** surrenders.

Maria W. Miller Stewart becomes the first American-born woman to give a public speech.

1836 Anglo American settlers in Texas—by now in the majority—declare their independence from Mexico and form the Republic of Texas.

1843 At a national convention of black men held in Buffalo, New York, **Henry Highland Garnet** delivers a fiery speech urging slaves to revolt.

1845 The U.S. officially annexes Texas.

1846 The U.S. declares war on Mexico.

1847 The Oregon Trail opens, encouraging an increasing number of white settlers to head westward.

1848 War ends between the U.S. and Mexico. The Treaty of Guadalupe Hidalgo is signed between the two countries.

1848–49 The California gold rush begins.

1849 The Bureau of Indian Affairs is transferred from the War Department to the new Department of the Interior.

1850 Congress approves the Compromise of 1850, which outlaws the slave trade in Washington, D.C., allows it to continue throughout the South, and admits California to the Union as a free state.

1851 At a women's rights convention in Ohio, **Sojourner Truth** delivers her famous "Ain't I a Woman?" speech.

1852 **Frederick Douglass** delivers the powerful "Fourth of July Oration."

1854 The Kansas-Nebraska Act, which repeals the Missouri Compromise of 1820, is approved.

1857 The Supreme Court issues its *Dred Scott* decision, ruling that blacks cannot become citizens, that they have no rights under the Constitution, and that Congress has no power to prohibit slavery in any part of U.S. territory.

1861 Jefferson Davis is named president of the newly-formed Confederate States of America.

Civil War begins when Confederate forces attack a small group of Union soldiers at Fort Sumter off the coast of Charleston, South Carolina.

1862 Congress authorizes President Abraham Lincoln to accept blacks for service in the Union Army.

1863 President Lincoln issues the Emancipation Proclamation, freeing slaves in the states then at war against the Union.

1864 Several hundred peaceful Cheyenne men, women, and children are massacred by U.S. troops at Sand Creek, Colorado.

1865 Confederate General Robert E. Lee surrenders to Union General Ulysses S. Grant at Appomattox, Virginia, to end the Civil War.

President Lincoln is assassinated.

1865 President Johnson announces his Reconstruction program for reorganizing and rebuilding the southern states to prepare them for rejoining the Union.

Congress ratifies the 13th Amendment, which outlaws slavery in the U.S.

1868 The Cuban War for Independence forces many Cubans into exile, with most choosing to flee to Europe and the U.S.

Congress ratifies the 14th Amendment, which recognizes blacks as American citizens with certain constitutional guarantees. It also declares all people of Hispanic origin born in the U.S. as citizens.

1869 Congress establishes the Board of Indian Commissioners to oversee Indian affairs.

With a workforce consisting primarily of Chinese immigrants, the first transcontinental rail route across the U.S. is completed.

1870 Congress passes a Naturalization Act that excludes Chinese from citizenship and prohibits the wives of Chinese laborers from entering the country.

A nationwide economic recession prompts angry mobs in California and other western states to lash out violently against Chinese immigrants, who are blamed for taking away jobs from unemployed whites.

Congress ratifies the Fifteenth Amendment, which states that no male American citizen can be denied the right to vote.

1872 **P.B.S. Pinchback,** lieutenant governor of Louisiana, becomes the first black to serve as a state governor when he takes over briefly for the elected governor, then fighting impeachment. A year later, he is elected to the U.S. Senate, but members eventually vote to deny him his seat.

1874 The discovery of gold in the Dakotas attracts hordes of miners to the area, most of whom ignore treaties protecting Indian lands.

1875 Congress passes a civil rights bill (known as the Civil Rights Act of 1875) that outlaws discrimination in public places and on public transportation.

Blanche K. Bruce becomes the only black man to serve a full term in the Senate until the mid-twentieth century.

1876 In the Battle of the Little Bighorn, a contingent of Sioux and Cheyenne warriors defeat General George Armstrong Custer and his troops.

1877 With U.S. troops in pursuit, **Chief Joseph** of the Nez Perce leads his people from Oregon to the promise of safety and freedom in Canada until he is forced to surrender just a few miles from the border.

1878 The Ten Years' War ends between Spain and Cuba.

1880 A treaty between the U.S. and China allows the U.S. to restrict the immigration of Chinese laborers.

The buffalo are exterminated in the southern portion of the Great Plains.

1881 **Booker T. Washington** opens the Tuskegee Institute.

Sitting Bull and his followers surrender to U.S. troops.

1882 Congress passes the Chinese Exclusion Act, which prohibits Chinese laborers from entering the country and denies citizenship to those already in the U.S. Japanese immigrants soon begin to replace the Chinese as a source of cheap labor.

1883 The Supreme Court overturns the Civil Rights Act of 1875.

1885 The buffalo are virtually exterminated in the northern portion of the Great Plains.

1886 Apache chief **Geronimo** surrenders to U.S. troops.

1887 Congress passes the General Allotment Act (also known as the Dawes Act), which breaks up tribally-owned lands and parcels it out to individuals.

The earliest known version of **Chief Seattle's** famous speech is published in a Seattle newspaper.

1889 Indian Territory (present-day Oklahoma) is opened to white settlers.

1890 Sioux chief **Sitting Bull** is killed in an uprising.

U.S. troops massacre some 300 Sioux women, children, and elders at Wounded Knee in present-day South Dakota.

1892 The Chinese Exclusion Act is extended for another ten years.

The Cuban Revolutionary Party is created to organize the Cuban and Puerto Rican independence movements.

Ida B. Wells-Barnett launches an anti-lynching campaign with a series of scathing newspaper editorials.

1895 Led by **José Martí**, Cuban revolutionaries begin a war for independence from Spain.

Booker T. Washington delivers his "Atlanta Compromise" address.

1896 In *Yick Wo v. Hopkins,* the U.S. Supreme Court rules that a San Francisco safety ordinance enforced exclusively against Chinese violates the 14th Amendment.

The Supreme Court issues its *Plessy v. Ferguson* decision upholding the "separate but equal" doctrine regarding the use of public places and public transportation by blacks.

1897 Spain grants Cuba and Puerto Rico autonomy and home rule.

1898 Hawaii is annexed to the U.S.

1898-99 The Spanish-American War. In the end, Spain gives Puerto Rico and Guam to the U.S., and the U.S. agrees to pay Spain $20 million for the Philippines. Cuba achieves independence from Spain but remains under U.S. military control until 1902.

1900 Congress establishes a civilian government in Puerto Rico under which islanders can elect their own House of Representatives, but they are denied a vote in Washington.

1901 U.S. Representative **George H. White** of North Carolina delivers an impassioned farewell address to his colleagues upon leaving the House after two terms. More than twenty years pass before any other African Americans are elected to Congress.

1902 Congress indefinitely extends the provisions of the Chinese Exclusion Act.

1903 Korean laborers begin to arrive in Hawaii in large numbers and later move to the mainland, often to work on the railroad.

1905 The Niagara Movement, the forerunner of the National Association for the Advancement of Colored People (NAACP), is established.

1907 An attempt by the San Francisco School Board to segregate students of Japanese ancestry fails when President Theodore Roosevelt intervenes and forces the board to rescind its order.

President Roosevelt issues an Executive Order prohibiting Japanese immigrants from entering the mainland via Hawaii, Mexico, or Canada.

1908 The U.S. and Japan reach an agreement restricting the immigration of Japanese laborers.

1909 The National Association for the Advancement of Colored People (NAACP) is founded. **W.E.B. Du Bois** serves as editor of its official publication, the *Crisis*.

1910 Angel Island is set up to serve as a processing center for Asian immigrants, becoming the West Coast version of New York's Ellis Island.

The Supreme Court broadens the 1870 Naturalization Act to include Asians other than the Chinese.

The Mexican Revolution begins; thousands of people flee north, with most settling in the southwestern U.S.

The National Urban League is founded.

1914–18 World War I; the U.S. does not officially enter the conflict until 1917.

1915 **Booker T. Washington** dies.

1916 **Marcus Garvey** establishes a branch of his Universal Negro Improvement Association in New York City.

1917 Congress grants citizenship to all Puerto Ricans.

Congress passes the Immigration Act, which imposes a literacy requirement on all immigrants.

The Asiatic Barred Zone Act takes effect, prohibiting immigration from all of Asia and India.

1919 Led by **W.E.B. Du Bois,** the first Pan-African Congress meets in Paris.

Syngman Rhee flees Korea and establishes a government-in-exile in Hawaii.

1921 For the first time in its history, the U.S. imposes limits on the number of immigrants allowed to enter the country in a single year.

1922 The Supreme Court upholds the Naturalization Law prohibiting Asian immigrants from becoming citizens.

1923 **George Washington Carver** receives the NAACP's Spingarn Medal in recognition of his distinguished research in agricultural chemistry.

1924 The Immigration Act of 1924 (also known as the Quota Immigration Act or National Origins Act) is signed into law prohibiting the immigration of all Asian laborers.

Congress grants citizenship to all Native Americans in gratitude for their service during World War I.

1925 The U.S. Border Patrol is established.

1926 **Gertrude Simmons Bonnin** forms the National Council of American Indians and becomes its first president.

Mordecai Wyatt Johnson becomes the first black president of Howard University.

1928 The Institute for Government Research publishes the Meriam Report, a landmark study describing the deplorable living conditions among Native Americans.

1929 The Japanese American Citizens League (JACL) is founded with a focus on educational issues and civil rights.

The League of United Latin American Citizens (LULAC) is founded to secure greater opportunities for Mexican Americans.

The U.S. stock market crashes, marking the beginning of the Great Depression.

1931 **Walter F. White** becomes executive secretary of the NAACP.

1934 The Indian Reorganization Act (also known as the Wheeler-Howard Act) is signed into law, reversing the policies of the General Allotment Act and once again permitting tribal ownership of land.

Elijah Muhammad becomes head of the Black Muslims.

1936 President Roosevelt appoints **Mary McLeod Bethune** to his unofficial "Black Cabinet."

1939-45 World War II; the U.S. does not officially enter the conflict until the Japanese bomb Pearl Harbor on December 7, 1941.

1941 **A. Philip Randolph** calls off the massive March on Washington demonstration after President Roosevelt issues an executive order banning racial discrimination in the defense industry and in government training programs.

1942 President Roosevelt issues Executive Order 9066 authorizing the evacuation of Japanese American civilians from designated areas of the West Coast to detention camps.

1943 To help deal with the wartime labor shortage, the U.S. government reaches an agreement with the Mexican government to allow temporary workers known as *braceros* to enter the country.

Congress repeals the Chinese Exclusion Act, allowing the Chinese to become naturalized citizens and establishing a quota of 105 immigrants per year.

1944 Two all-Japanese American military units, the 100th Battalion and the 442nd Regimental Combat Team, are united and go on to serve with distinction in Europe as the most decorated unit in U.S. history. Future U.S. Senators **Spark Matsunaga** and **Daniel Inouye** are among those who receive citations for their battlefield heroics.

Adam Clayton Powell, Jr., is elected to the U.S. House of Representatives, making him the first black congressman from the East.

1945 Japanese Americans held in detention camps are allowed to return to the West Coast.

1948 The Japanese American Evacuation Claims Act, which enables former detainees to file claims against the government for their financial losses, is signed into law.

President Truman issues an executive order calling for equality of treatment and opportunity for all Americans in the armed forces, thus officially ending segregation and discrimination in the military.

The independent Republic of Korea is proclaimed following United Nations-supervised elections. **Syngman Rhee** is named president.

1950-53 Korean War

1950 Due in large part to the efforts of **Luis Muñoz-Marín,** Congress upgrades Puerto Rico's political status from protectorate to commonwealth.

1950 **Ralph Bunche** becomes the first black to win the Nobel Peace Prize.

1952-57 The Bureau of Indian Affairs launches a "relocation program" designed to improve the standard of living for reservation Indians and foster their assimilation into mainstream society by moving them into major U.S. cities.

1952 **Malcolm X** is paroled from prison and soon becomes a minister in the Nation of Islam.

The McCarran-Walter Immigration and Naturalization Act goes into effect. It establishes immigration quotas for Japanese and other Asians and grants naturalization and citizenship rights to Asians not born in the U.S.

1953 Congress approves the Termination Resolution, ending the special legal relationship between Indian governments and the federal government.

1954 The Supreme Court issues its *Hernández v. Texas* decision, which entitles Hispanics to the protection of the 14th Amendment. It is the first Mexican American discrimination case to reach the nation's highest court and the first argued by Mexican American attorneys.

The Supreme Court issues its landmark *Brown v. Board of Education of Topeka* decision overturning *Plessy v. Ferguson* and declaring racial segregation in public schools unconstitutional. Attorney **Thurgood Marshall** leads the NAACP legal team.

1954-58 Operation Wetback results in the deportation of nearly four million people of Mexican descent, often without hearings.

1955 **Roy Wilkins** becomes executive secretary of the NAACP.

Martin Luther King, Jr., launches the year-long Montgomery bus boycott after Rosa Parks is arrested for refusing to give up her seat on a city bus to a white person.

1957 The Southern Christian Leadership Conference (SCLC) is co-founded by **Martin Luther King, Jr.**; he serves as its first president.

Congress passes the Voting Rights Bill of 1957, the first major civil rights legislation since 1875.

Federal troops are sent to Little Rock, Arkansas, to stop local residents from interfering with the desegregation of a local public high school.

1959 In Cuba, revolutionary leader Fidel Castro assumes control after President Fulgencio Batista resigns and flees the country, touching off a wave of Cuban immigration to the U.S. that lasts until 1962.

Lorraine Hansberry's play *A Raisin in the Sun* becomes the first play by a black woman to open on Broadway.

Hawaii becomes the 50th state of the Union. Elected to represent Hawaii in Congress are **Hiram Fong** (the first Chinese American elected to the Senate), and **Daniel Inouye** (the first Japanese American elected to the House of Representatives).

1960 The Student Nonviolent Coordinating Committee (SNCC) is founded.

1961 U.S. severs diplomatic relations with Cuba.

Cuban exiles—aided by the U.S.—stage the Bay of Pigs invasion of Cuba.

Whitney M. Young, Jr. becomes executive director of the National Urban League.

1962 **César Chávez, Dolores Huerta,** and other activists form the National Farm Workers Association, later known as the United Farmworkers of America.

The Cuban Missile Crisis.

Daniel Inouye becomes the first Japanese American elected to the Senate, and **Spark Matsunaga** is elected to the House of Representatives.

1963 **Martin Luther King, Jr.**, delivers his "I Have a Dream" speech to a crowd of more than 200,000 assembled at the Lincoln Memorial for the massive March on Washington civil rights demonstration.

President John F. Kennedy is assassinated.

1964 Due to the efforts of Representative **Henry B. Gonzalez** of Texas and other legislators, the *bracero* program ends.

Congress ratifies the 24th Amendment, which outlaws the use of the poll tax to prevent people from voting.

Malcolm X drops out of the Nation of Islam to start his own movement.

Congress passes the Civil Rights Act of 1964. It prohibits discrimination in hiring and employment practices and paves the way for various affirmative action programs.

Congress passes the Tonkin Gulf Resolution, authorizing President Lyndon Johnson to take military action against North Vietnam.

Patsy Mink becomes the first Asian American woman elected to the House of Representatives.

Martin Luther King, Jr., receives the Nobel Peace Prize.

Fannie Lou Hamer co-founds the Mississippi freedom Democratic Party.

1965 **Malcolm X** is assassinated.

Fidel Castro allows Cubans with relatives in the U.S. to leave—but only if their relatives come and get them. The policy prompts many Cuban Americans in South Florida to set out by boat to pick up family members.

The Immigration Act of 1965 is approved, allowing for much higher levels of non-European immigration to the U.S., primarily from Latin America, the Caribbean, and Asia.

The SCLC launches a voter registration drive in Selma, Alabama, that escalates into a nationwide protest movement and culminates in the famous "Freedom March" from Selma to Montgomery and an address by the demonstration's leader, **Martin Luther King, Jr.**

Congress passes the Voting Rights Act of 1965.

Racial disturbances erupt in the Watts ghetto of Los Angeles.

1966–73 More than 250,000 Cubans emigrate to the U.S. under the terms of a special airlift program.

1966 **Stokely Carmichael** becomes head of the Student Nonviolent Coordinating Committee (SNCC).

Huey Newton and Bobby Seale establish the Black Panther Party. **Eldridge Cleaver** joins them and becomes the one of group's key spokesman.

1967 Race riots occur in Newark, Detroit, and several other U.S. cities.

The Supreme Court rules unconstitutional all laws prohibiting interracial marriage.

Thurgood Marshall is sworn in as the first black justice of the Supreme Court.

1968 **Martin Luther King, Jr.**, is assassinated.

The new head of the SCLC, **Ralph Abernathy**, leads a group of blacks, whites, Native Americans, and Mexican Americans on a march to Washington, D.C., known as the "Poor People's Campaign."

Presidential candidate Robert F. Kennedy dies one day after being shot and critically wounded.

College president **S.I. Hayakawa** takes a strong stand against student demonstrators at San Francisco State College and garners national attention.

The American Indian Movement (AIM) is founded by **Clyde Bellecourt**, Dennis Banks, and other activists. **Russell Means** joins soon thereafter.

The Kerner Commission releases the results of its investigation into the causes of the 1967 race riots, concluding that "white racism" was largely to blame.

The Indian Civil Rights Act is approved.

Shirley Chisholm wins a seat in the House of Representatives, becoming the first black woman ever to serve in Congress.

César Chávez undertakes the first of many fasts on behalf of the farm workers movement.

1969-71 Indians from many different tribes occupy Alcatraz Island to lay claim to the land and protest federal government policy toward Native Americans.

1969 U.S. troops begin to withdraw from Vietnam and elsewhere in Southeast Asia.

The Supreme Court rules that public school districts must end racial segregation immediately.

1970-76 Racial violence erupts in school districts across the U.S. as court-ordered desegregation plans are implemented.

1970 The Voting Rights Act of 1965 is extended until 1975.

LaDonna Harris founds Americans for Indian Opportunity.

1971 **Whitney M. Young, Jr.**, head of the National Urban League, drowns. He is replaced by **Vernon Jordan**, head of the United Negro College Fund.

The Supreme Court rules that busing students to achieve racial desegregation is constitutional.

1972 **Shirley Chisholm** becomes the first black and the first woman to seek the Democratic nomination for president.

Angela Davis is acquitted of murder, kidnapping, and conspiracy charges stemming from a 1970 courtroom shooting.

A group of about 500 Indians arrive in Washington, D.C., at the end of their Trail of Broken Treaties protest march, and some demonstrators—including a number of AIM activists—occupy the headquarters of the Bureau of Indian Affairs.

1973 U.S. military participation in the Vietnam War ends.

The Supreme Court rules in *Espinoza v. Farah Manufacturing Company* that nothing in the Civil Rights Act of 1964 prohibits discrimination on the basis of citizenship or alien status.

Some 200 Indians under AIM leadership occupy the hamlet of Wounded Knee on the Pine Ridge Reservation in South Dakota.

Marion Wright Edelman establishes the Children's Defense Fund.

1974 Congress passes the Equal Educational Opportunity Act.

After a series of hearings, the House Judiciary Committee—including **Barbara Jordan** of Texas—adopts three articles of impeachment against President Richard Nixon.

President Nixon resigns.

Norman Y. Mineta becomes the first Japanese American on the mainland to be elected to the House of Representatives.

1975 South Vietnam falls to the communist North. More than 140,000 refugees flee Southeast Asia. Many settle in the U.S.

A shoot-out on the Pine Ridge Indian Reservation leaves two FBI agents and one Indian dead. AIM activist **Leonard Peltier** is subsequently tried and convicted for the crime and sentenced to life in prison.

The Voting Rights Act of 1965 is extended for an additional seven years and specifically adds protection for Hispanic voters as well as for black voters.

Daniel "Chappie" James, Jr., becomes the first black to be promoted to the rank of four-star general in the U.S. armed forces.

1976 The Supreme Court rules that blacks and other minorities are entitled to retroactive job security.

S.I. Hayakawa becomes the first immigrant of Japanese ancestry elected to the Senate.

Representative **Barbara Jordan** delivers a rousing keynote address at the Democratic National Convention.

1977 **Alex Haley** is awarded a special Pulitzer Prize for *Roots*.

1978 Under the leadership of **Clifford I. Uyeda,** the Japanese American Citizens League (JACL) launches its national redress campaign for those people of Japanese ancestry who were evacuated and detained during World War II.

The Longest Walk, a protest march calling attention to the federal government's poor treatment of Indian people throughout history, begins at Alcatraz Island off the California coast and ends in Washington, D.C., with some 30,000 participants.

The Supreme Court issues its *Bakke* decision declaring racial and ethnic quota systems in college admissions unconstitutional.

The American Indian Religious Freedom Act is enacted.

Congress passes the Indian Child Welfare Act.

1980 More than 125,000 Cubans emigrate to the U.S. as part of the Mariel boat lift.

Jorge Mas Canosa co-founds the Cuban American National Foundation.

The Refugee Act of 1980 abandons the definition of "refugee" as someone who flees a communist country, thus opening the door for thousands to declare themselves refugees in order to enter the U.S.

Miami, Florida, is the scene of the most serious racial disturbances in the country since the riots of the 1960s.

1981 **Henry G. Cisneros** wins the San Antonio, Texas, mayoral election to become the first Hispanic head of a major U.S. city.

1982 In Detroit, two unemployed autoworkers who attribute auto industry layoffs to competition from Japan beat to death a young Chinese American man named Vincent Chin they mistake for Japanese. **Helen Zia** subsequently co-founds and serves as national spokesperson for American Citizens for Justice, a group dedicated to seeking justice for Chin and combatting anti-Asian prejudice.

1983 The Commission on Wartime Relocation and Internment of Civilians (CWRIC) issues a report criticizing the government's treatment of Japanese Americans during World War II and recommends that each detainee receive a compensatory payment of $20,000.

1986 The first national **Martin Luther King, Jr.,** holiday is celebrated.

1984 **Jesse Jackson** delivers a rousing address at the Democratic National Convention.

1987 **Wilma Mankiller** becomes the first woman elected principal chief of the Cherokee Nation.

Johnnetta B. Cole becomes the first black woman president of Spelman College.

Dr. **Ben Carson** performs the first successful separation of Siamese twins joined at the back of the head.

After impassioned speeches by Congressman **Robert T. Matsui** and others, the House of Representatives votes in favor of redress for Japanese Americans.

The Immigration Reform and Control Act, to curb illegal immigration, is signed in to law.

1988 With Senator **Spark Matsunaga** leading the way, the Senate votes in favor of redress for Japanese Americans.

Lauro F. Cavazos becomes the first Hispanic secretary of education.

Congress repeals the Termination Resolution of 1953.

Jesse Jackson places second behind Michael Dukakis in the delegate count to win the Democratic party's nomination for president of the United States.

President Ronald Reagan enacts the Civil Liberties Act of 1988 granting redress to Japanese Americans detained during World War II.

1989 **Colin Powell** becomes the first black chairman of the Joint Chiefs of Staff.

L. Douglas Wilder of Virginia becomes the nation's first black elected governor.

David Henry Hwang wins a Tony award for *M Butterfly*.

1990–91 Persian Gulf War.

1990 **Antonia Novello** becomes the first woman and the first Hispanic surgeon general of the U.S.

President George Bush signs into law the Native American Graves Protection and Repatriation Act.

Daniel K. Akaka becomes the first U.S. Senator of Native Hawaiian ancestry.

1991 In Los Angeles, the beating of black motorist Rodney King by four white policemen is captured on videotape and broadcast on network news programs, sparking an international outcry.

Thurgood Marshall retires from the Supreme Court.

Clarence Thomas is confirmed on the Supreme Court after controversial hearings during which University of Oklahoma law professor **Anita Hill** accuses him of sexual harassment.

The name of the Custer Battlefield National Monument is changed to Little Bighorn Battlefield National Monument.

1992 Tennis star **Arthur Ashe** confirms rumors that he is suffering from AIDS.

Racial violence erupts in Los Angeles after four white police officers are acquitted in the beating of black motorist Rodney King.

Carol Moseley-Braun of Illinois becomes the first black woman elected to the U.S. Senate; **Ben Nighthorse Campbell** becomes the first Native American elected to the Senate since 1929.

U.S. troops leave the Philippines, ending nearly a century of U.S. military presence there.

1993 Poet **Rita Dove** is named U.S. poet laureate.

President Bill Clinton withdraws the controversial nomination of **Lani Guinier** to head the civil rights division of the U.S. Justice Department.

Joycelyn Elders becomes the first black U.S. surgeon general.

Toni Morrison becomes the first black woman to win the Nobel Prize for literature.

Ada Deer becomes the first woman to head the Bureau of Indian Affairs.

César Chávez dies.

Henry G. Cisneros becomes U.S. Secretary of Housing and Urban Development.

Voters in Puerto Rico reject statehood.

Congress approves the North American Free Trade Agreement (NAFTA).

Federico Peña becomes U.S. Secretary of Transportation.

1994 Thousands of Cubans attempt to make their way to the U.S. on makeshift rafts and other unseaworthy vessels, sparking a refugee crisis in south Florida.

Clinton announces that he is ending the special status enjoyed by Cuban immigrants for 28 years, which granted them U.S. residency if they made it to American shores. Instead, they will be picked up at sea and detained at Guantánamo Bay.

The NAACP board of directors fires Executive Director **Benjamin Chavis.**

The U.S. and Cuba reach an agreement on the refugee issue. In return for Fidel Castro's pledge to discourage Cubans from trying to flee on rafts and other vessels, the U.S. promises to accept a minimum of 20,000 refugees a year through normal channels.

In the mid-term elections, the Republicans regain majorities in both the House of Representatives and the Senate for the first time in 40 years as voters reject Democratic incumbents.

California voters pass Proposition 187, which denies state education, medical, and welfare services to undocumented immigrants.

President Clinton fires Surgeon General **Joycelyn Elders.**

A new policy goes into effect that sends Cuban refugees picked up at sea back home. Angry Cuban Americans in Miami react with marches and other protests.

1995 Republicans in Congress begin work on the reforms and budget cuts proposed in their "Contract with America"; opponents such as **Jesse Jackson** and **Marian Wright Edelman** publicly condemn the "Contract" as especially devastating to the poor, children, and the elderly.

In two separate decisions written by Justice **Clarence Thomas,** the U.S. Supreme Court comes out in favor of sharply limiting federal affirmative-action programs and court-ordered school integration efforts.

The nomination of black physician Henry Foster for the post of U.S. surgeon general goes down to defeat in the Senate.

The Supreme Court declares unconstitutional the practice of using race as the major factor in drawing legislative districts.

Voices of
MULTICULTURAL AMERICA

Ralph David Abernathy

1926–1990

African American clergyman and civil rights activist

One of the most prominent figures of the civil rights movement was Ralph David Abernathy, who worked side by side with Martin Luther King, Jr., from the days of the Montgomery bus boycott in 1955 until King was felled by an assassin's bullet in 1968. Together the two men founded and led the powerful Southern Christian Leadership Conference (SCLC), which advocated assertive but nonviolent means to achieve racial equality. At the forefront of these activities was Abernathy, who was King's closest friend, trusted confidant, and loyal supporter during the long and often dangerous civil rights struggle.

An Alabama native and the grandson of a slave, Abernathy was born into a respected and civic-minded family that farmed a large parcel of land in the village of Linden. Young Ralph demonstrated more of an interest in reading and studying than in farming, however, so after serving in the U.S. Army during the last few months of World War II, he began attending Alabama State College in Montgomery. Ordained a Baptist minister in 1948, he continued his studies and received a bachelor's degree in mathematics in 1950. Abernathy then headed to Atlanta University to pursue a master's degree in sociology. His stay in the Georgia capital also included a stint as pastor at a local church, which brought him into contact with another young minister in town named Martin Luther King, Jr. Their shared interest in the fledgling civil rights movement provided the basis for a friendship that grew even stronger after King moved to Montgomery to become pastor of the Dexter Avenue Baptist Church in 1954. Waiting to welcome him was Abernathy, who had been serving as pastor of the city's First Baptist Church since 1951.

At that point in their lives, neither man was especially eager to become involved in civic affairs; Abernathy wanted to focus on his graduate studies, and King was busy trying to settle into his new church. But when seamstress Rosa Parks was arrested in December 1955 for violating segregation laws by refusing to give up her seat to a white man and move to the back of a city bus, both ministers took immediate action to organize and lead a protest. Over the next year, they each played leading roles in the successful boycott local blacks launched against the bus system—King as head and chief spokesman of what came to be known as the

Montgomery Improvement Association, and Abernathy as the man responsible for keeping participants interested but nonviolent.

This pattern continued with the founding of the Southern Christian Leadership Conference in 1957; King served as president, and Abernathy functioned as his top assistant in the position of secretary-treasurer and later as vice-president at large. Together they marched and demonstrated for voting rights and integration in dozens of towns and cities throughout the South during the 1960s, molding the SCLC into an organization that soon gained national recognition and respect for its nonviolent resistance to injustice. Perhaps their greatest triumph came in August 1963, when over 250,000 people participated in the famous March on Washington and listened as King delivered his stirring "I Have a Dream" speech on the steps of the Lincoln Memorial *(see page 704)**.*

After an assassin mortally wounded King on April 4, 1968, as he stood on the balcony of a Memphis motel, it was Abernathy who cradled his dying friend in his arms. He also delivered one of the principal eulogies at King's funeral and, as the slain civil rights leader had wished, he succeeded him as head of the SCLC, vowing to "prove beyond the shadow of a doubt that you can kill the dreamer but you cannot kill the dream." Abernathy also took over leadership of the Poor People's Campaign, a massive demonstration that King had been planning since December 1967. The idea quickly gained momentum in the weeks after his death, and in mid-May, several thousand unemployed blacks, whites, Latinos, and Native Americans converged on Washington, D.C. There they erected and occupied hundreds of tents and plywood shanties in an attempt to pressure Congress to take action against poverty. Abernathy and a number of other protesters were arrested when their permit to use the land expired but they refused to leave the spot they had christened "Resurrection City"; bad weather and a lack of cooking, bathing, and sanitation facilities drove the remaining demonstrators away by late June.

On January 15, 1969, still mourning the loss of his longtime friend and colleague, Abernathy addressed an audience at Atlanta's Ebenezer Baptist Church. The occasion that prompted his reflections was a special ceremony in honor of what would have been King's fortieth birthday. An excerpt from Abernathy's remarks that day is reprinted here from The Cry for Freedom: An Anthology of the Best That Has Been Said and Written on Civil Rights Since 1954, *edited by Frank W. Hale, Jr. (A.S. Barnes & Co., 1969).*

There is a traditional spiritual that is sung with as much familiarity and fervor at Christmas time as are the carols. The title of this spiritual is "Sweet Little Jesus Boy," and the words that follow are these: "Sweet Little Jesus Boy. They made Him be born in a manger. Sweet Little Jesus Boy. *They didn't know who He was."*

You have heard it from the choir lofts of Baptist and Protestant churches and Catholic cathedrals across the land. For me, and for many of you, it is a favorite. It is as familiar as "Silent Night" or "Joy to the World."

The question that comes to my mind at this hour is whether we really understand the meaning, significance and profundity of the story in this spiritual. The story is plain and simple. They made Jesus—the Prince of Peace, the Saviour of the world, the most moving and dynamic figure in history—be born in a manger, simply because *they did not know who He was.*

Just as Jesus came as the Saviour, on this day, January 15, forty years ago, Martin Luther King, Jr., came a few doors down the street as the saviour, the deliverer, the emancipator, the Moses to his people. *But we didn't know who he was.*

Ralph David Abernathy

Unlike Jesus, his birth did not take place in a manger, but he was born in a ghetto. But like Jesus, he was permitted to live on the earth only for a brief period, and like Jesus he was cut down while still in his thirties. Like Jesus, he was misunderstood, castigated, rebuked and even despised and rejected by his own because *we didn't know who he was.*

Like Jesus, he opposed the system of injustice and inequality, and stood in the courts of the Pharaohs and cried, "Let my people go." Like Jesus, he unstopped the ears of the deaf, he opened the eyes of the blind as he challenged the most powerful and unjust system in the world. Like Jesus, he fed the hungry, he worked to clothe the naked, he lived an unselfish life and he was concerned about "the least of these"—*but we didn't know who he was.*

Who did we think he was?

We thought he might be an ordinary Baptist preacher, well trained in theology and philosophy. We thought his days were to end at an old age when his eloquent and melodious baritone voice would still be lifting thousands to lofty peaks of inspiration.

Many people thought he was out of his mind when he led an army, not armed with guns or bricks or stones, fifty thousand strong in Montgomery, Alabama, in 1955, and said to his followers: "Love your enemies, pray for them that curse and despitefully use you." Some of us may have wondered about him when he led us without physical weapons in the battles of Albany, Georgia; St. Augustine, Florida; and Danville, Virginia. And we knew something must have been wrong with him when defenseless we stood before Bull Connor in Birmingham, facing vicious and hungry dogs, fire hoses and brutal policemen. Or when he journeyed into the Black Belt of Alabama—the worst area of oppression in the nation—and confronted the very embodiment of racism, Jim Clark, in Selma.

Some felt that he was merely a seeker of publicity, a preacher of that which he was unwilling to suffer for. Much of the nation felt, as expressed by a high and powerful government official, that he was the world's most notorious liar.

But in fact—*we didn't know who he was.*

And nine months and eleven days ago, on April 4, 1968, a man representing what I believe a conspiracy fired a bullet and stilled his heartbeat and silenced his physical voice, because *he didn't know who he was.*

In truth, who was Martin Luther King, Jr.?

He was, first of all, an emancipator. He was sent by God to fulfill the dreams expressed by the founding fathers of this nation in 1776. The founding document had said that this was a nation under God, a nation "dedicated to the proposition that all men are created equal, and that they are endowed by their Creator with certain inalienable rights, and among these are life, liberty and the pursuit of happiness." It was an inspired and glorious document, but in reality,

America was not such a nation, and America had written a lie.

The black man had been enslaved for 244 years in this nation, and when Martin Luther King, Jr., came, 100 years later, the black man was still oppressed and had lost all hope for fulfilling the dream of America.

But Dr. King came to declare that the nation must live by those beautiful words and pronouncements in the Declaration of Independence, and he became the emancipator of his people.

He was, secondly, the redeemer of the soul of America. As the redeemer he taught his people in Montgomery that their "feet may be tired, but their souls could be rested." He taught the nation that "an eye for an eye, and a tooth for a tooth," if followed to its ultimate conclusion, would only end in a totally blind and toothless society. He discovered that the most potent force for revolution and reform in America is nonviolence. He knew, as the eminent historian Arnold Toynbee has written, that if America is saved, it will be through the black man who can inject new dimensions of nonviolence into the veins of our civilization. Therefore, Dr. King both practiced and preached nonviolence, in his home, in his family, in our SCLC family and in all of our movements. On April 4, 1967, exactly one year before his assassination, he was striving to redeem the soul of America when he spoke to the Riverside Church in New York City and warned the nation that it must end the unjust and vicious war in Vietnam.

"I would gladly have given my life in exchange for his, and I would even give it today if I could bring him back."

Martin Luther King, Jr. was, finally, a "drum major for justice." He talked about this right here in Ebenezer Baptist Church last February 4. He said, "I have tried to love and serve humanity," and that was the way he wanted to be remembered—as a man loving and serving all people in the cause of justice. His last act was a mission in this cause. He went to Memphis, Tennessee, to lead a movement for poor garbage workers. They are the men who pick up the filth and clean the city—but they are scorned and abused and impoverished. They sent out the Macedonian call for help to a man who had earned the highest academic degree and had been awarded dozens of honorary degrees. They sent out the trumpet call to a man who had been entertained by kings and queens and been awarded the Nobel Prize for Peace. He did not ignore that call because it came from garbage workers. Rather, Dr. King went there to serve his brothers. He was in the front ranks in a campaign for equality. And he was not content with freedom for black people alone. He worked for freedom of all people. He worked for the Baptist and other Protestants, the Catholics, the Jews; yes, he worked for all believers as well as the unbelievers. He followed his "drum major instinct" to be out in front as the leader of a mighty parade with a mighty band, on the way to freedom's land.

It was my privilege and my honor to stand by the side of this great, beautiful and sensitive man. Like Gibran, I learned my lesson well: "to be close, but not too close, for the cyprus tree does not flourish in the shadow of the oak." I had to be near when needed, but never so near that I would be in the way and impede the progress of this twentieth-century prophet. I would gladly have given my life in exchange for his, and I would even give it today if I could bring him back. I would turn my eyes into a fountain of tears, I would mourn and grieve every day and night if this would do any good.

To the best of my ability, I worked with him. We went to jail together 19 times in 13 years. I prayed with him during the dark and lonely hours of the night. I was with him when he went atop Mount Pisgah's lofty heights, and like Elijah, he flung his mantle upon me and spoke with the authority of Moses and said: "Joshua take the children of Israel on across the Jordan into the land of Canaan."

So today I stand on January 15, his birthday, and I want to send him this birthday greeting:

To Martin Luther King, in the city called Heaven, in care of Jesus Christ the Saviour: Greetings and felicitations. Many years we celebrated your birthday with you in person. But today we must celebrate it with you physically removed. Even so, I know that you are here. I can feel your spirit in the air. During this period, many streets are being named for you, many scholarship funds are being established in your name, and monuments, statues, hospitals, schools and buildings are being erected in your honor.

Martin, I know that all of these are significant and important, and I praise those courageous persons who take steps in this direction. But, Martin, I know you. You were never interested in mortar, brick or stone. You always were interested in freeing the captives and setting at liberty them that are bruised, exalting the valleys, making low the hills and mountains, straightening the crooked, and creating a society with no gulf between the haves and have-nots.

Therefore, we in the Southern Christian Leadership Conference are determined to make January 15, your birthday, a legal and national holiday so that the wheels of industry and commerce will stop, banks and schools will close, and on this day each year the nation can pay tribute to you, our hero and the hero of black people and all men and women of good will throughout the world.

Martin, this is not an adequate gift for you on your birthday, for we admit that we are selfish in our gifts and we are so limited in what we can give you today for you gave all, even your life. The making of your birthday a legal and national holiday will be a gift to black and white America which enriches our heritage and strengthens our faith in the democratic process.

Also, Martin, you should know about the New Thrust in SCLC, for we feel that the greatest tribute we can pay you will be the continuation of your feeble and humble efforts to redeem the soul of America. So in our staff retreat in Frogmore, South Carolina, last week, we decided that we would make the following gifts to America, in keeping with your wishes:

Number One, we will help poor people get decent homes for their families. Incidentally, Martin, this will be done under the housing act that was passed because of our Poor People's Campaign.

Number Two, we will organize the poor workers of America—the garbage men, the hospital workers, the domestic workers and the millions of other hard-working poor people—so that they can gain their rightful incomes and security.

Number Three, we will work for economic development and freedom in the black community, not seeking riches for the few businessmen, but seeking a rich community for all.

Number Four, we will demand that America will provide the best modern education for all children, equipping them with the wondrous skills of technology and the beautiful wisdom of humanity and brotherhood.

Number Five, we will continue your quest for peace in the world, to save not only America but all mankind from destruction.

Number Six, we will mobilize and work with students and young people in all these endeavors. Martin, you always did love to be with young people, because you were young yourself. You saw in them the hope for America's salvation, and so do we, for we are going out among the young to enlist their support and participation at the high school, college and university levels.

Number Seven, we will work for political gains for poor people so that they will have true and honest representation in the councils of their governments. . . .

Everywhere, Martin, we will battle for the rights of all people, using the armor of nonviolence which you molded for us. And we know that you will be with us wherever we go—into the homes and churches of the poor, into the offices of the rich and powerful, into the streets and highways whenever it is necessary.

Finally, we have another gift. In remaining true to the principles of nonviolence, I call upon the forces of good will throughout this land to exert their total influence in seeing to it that the life of James Earl Ray, or whoever is proven to have pulled the trigger that felled our sainted and beloved leader, is spared.

> ***"Our society is sick, our nation is a sick nation, concentrated with violence, saturated with hate."***

I say, unto you today, it is needless to kill one man for the sins of millions. . . . For us to kill those that are truly guilty of taking Dr. King's life, we would *but* be guilty of mass murder perpetuating an atrocity no less than that of Adolf Hitler.

We must understand that the elimination of Earl Ray, or whoever killed Dr. King, does not deal with our major problem. This would only be dealing with the symptom of our major problem. Our job is to deal with the cause of our problem. Our problem is that our society is sick, our nation is a sick nation, concentrated with violence, saturated with hate. This sick system of ours is constantly conceiving, giving birth, nurturing and producing millions of Rays.

And, I say to the American system today, the true killer of Martin Luther King, Jr., a man who tried to teach everybody to love, one who gave his life in an effort to redeem your soul, one who tried to make the American dream a living reality: Don't go deeper into degradation by participating in the philosophy of genocide but change this system, get your soul right with God. Stop the hunger and the illiteracy perpetrated upon the poor. Stop these unjust wars, raise up no more assassins; instead, as God said, Let Justice raise up a nation that will obey. Yes, my friends, this evil system killed Dr. King and will kill many more of us unless we rid ourselves of a system that produces assassins, and instead redeem the soul of America.

These are gifts which we can not send to you, Martin, so we shall give them to the people you love.

I thought of sending you a flashlight, but where you are today there is no need of a light, for the sun never goes down. I thought of sending you a birthday cake today, but you are in a place where food never gives out for your Saviour and mine is the bread of life. I thought of sending you a color television set, but the stars and the moon now give you a sweeping telescopic view of the universe and there is nothing more colorful and beautiful than the sunset. I thought of other gifts, but the angels now await your command for any need imaginable.

And so we are giving our gifts to the people you love, the people to whom you gave the ultimate gift of your earthly life.

I must close now, Martin. But honesty impels me to admit that, "nights are long since you went away, I think of you, Martin, both night and day, my buddy, my buddy," your buddy misses you. . . . But you may be assured that I am going to tell the world who you were.

Less than two months after delivering this moving tribute, Abernathy participated in a conference at Georgetown University on the findings of the Kerner Commission, a special advisory panel appointed by President Lyndon Johnson to look into the reasons behind a series of racial disorders that had rocked the nation's cities during the summer of 1967. Members of the commission had concluded in their report (issued in March 1968) that "white racism" was the principal cause of the riots and that the United States was quickly splitting into two distinct communities, "one white, one black, separate and unequal." Abernathy, fearing that the report would be set aside and forgotten as had so many others in the past, seized the opportunity at Georgetown on March 5, 1969, to deliver his own pointed assessment of the situation and to issue a call for action. His speech, excerpts of which follow, is taken from The Voice of Black America: Major Speeches by Negroes in the United States, 1797–1971, *edited by Philip S. Foner (Simon & Schuster, 1972).*

Students of Georgetown University, members of the faculty, distinguished guests, ladies and gentlemen:

As your chairman of the committee organizing this symposium, Mr. T. Stephen Cheston, said when he invited me, "The Kerner Report will be remembered as one of the major documents in twentieth-century American history. It was comprehensive in its study, incisive in its analysis, and courageous in expressing its findings."

But today, one year after the release of the Kerner Report, I am deeply troubled by a question: Will that report be remembered by all Americans as a call to national action that will save America?

Unhappily, but in candor, I must say to you today that the answer thus far is that the Kerner Report is just another piece of paper gathering dust on a shelf littered with similarly hopeful and promising reports—reports that have been consistently, cynically, cruelly ignored by America.

Let me begin by reminding you of some of these reports. One report, if I may give it that term, was issued 193 years ago. It said in ringing words that were to shake the world for the next two centuries: "We hold these truths to be self-evident, that all men are created equal, that they are endowed by their Creator with certain unalienable rights, that among these are life, liberty, and the pursuit of happiness."

That document, the Declaration of Independence, held great promise, but the reality even today is that no one can pretend that all men are considered equal in America, and that millions of poor people are in fact denied their right to life, liberty and the pursuit of happiness.

The Constitution of the United States took effect 180 years ago, on March 4, 1787, and specifically stated an intention to establish justice, welfare and liberty for all. Yet that same Constitution upheld slavery and condemned my people to a life of injustice, insecurity and bondage.

One hundred and six years ago, in 1863, Lincoln issued the Emancipation Proclamation. The promise was an end to slavery, but what was the reality? The reality was that only the slaves in parts of the South unoccupied by Northern troops were set free as a military strategy to disrupt the Confederacy. But in Missouri, General Fremont was fired because he set the slaves free. And the reality also is that my people have been kept in virtual slavery—the slavery of segregation, discrimination and economic exploitation—ever since, in spite of the Emancipation and the Thirteenth Amendment, which was ratified abolishing slavery in 1865.

Next, in 1868, 101 years ago, the Fourteenth Amendment guaranteeing the right of *all people* to life, liberty and property, was ratified. What was the reality? The reality was, for example, in that same year, 40,000 black people in South Carolina were promised 400,000 acres of farm land. But do you think they ever got it? No! And the reality to this day is that we never did get our rights to life, liberty and property—not even our little 40 acres and a mule.

In 1870—99 years ago—the Fifteenth Amendment, guaranteeing the right to vote, was ratified. In 1890—79 years ago—Congress passed a bill providing for federal registrars in the South. In 1944—25 years ago—the Supreme Court outlawed the white primary election in Texas. But what happened to all these promises? The reality is that black people were denied the right to vote, and lily-white elections continued in fact, until we in the Southern Christian Leadership Conference put so much pressure on Congress with the Selma-to-Montgomery March that the Voting Rights Act was passed in 1965. Black people now vote in the South, but not without risking harassment, abuse and retaliation, because the Voting Rights Act is not adequately enforced. And another glaring gap between promise and reality is that the Voting Rights Act of 1965 expires in 1970. And another gap can be seen in the fact that last summer, in the national conventions of both major parties, black people and other poor people were systematically denied proportional representation in their state delegations.

When the Kerner Commission began its hearings, Dr. Kenneth Clark, a very distinguished scholar, pointed out some other promises and

"The Kerner Report is just another piece of paper gathering dust on a shelf littered with similarly hopeful and promising reports—reports that have been consistently, cynically, cruelly ignored by America."

realities. He recalled similar reports that had been issued with great fanfare and promise, but ignored in reality: reports on the Chicago riot of 1919, the Harlem riot of 1935, another Harlem riot in 1943, the McCone Commission on Watts three years ago.

We have had the promise of the Supreme Court's school desegregation order of 1954, fifteen years ago, and the reality of de facto segregation in the South *and* North. We have the promise of a new president saying he wants to "bring us together," but failing to make himself clear on whether he is going to keep our children apart.

We had the promises of many recent analyses of our racial and economic problems—including recommendations from established business leaders, the report of the White House Conference on Civil Rights, President Johnson's vision of a "Great Society," the repeated eloquent calls to action from my predecessor, Dr. Martin Luther King, Jr., and, finally, the Kerner Report.

And again, what are the realities? All of these studies and reports and calls have been turned aside. Instead of a Great Society, we have a nation gone mad in an evil, unwinnable war in Vietnam. Instead of reforms recommended by moderate business and political leaders, we have the same old subsidies and protections for the rich and oppression of the poor—what I call socialism for the rich and rugged free enterprise for the poor. Instead of investment in life-giving measures for peace and justice, we have investment in death-dealing war, assassination, and daily violence to poor people. Instead of meaningful action on the Kerner Report, one year later we only have another study of the Kerner Report.

Ladies and gentlemen, I am here today to tell you that *I am sick and tired of promises, and I am sick and tired of the realities of war, poverty and racism.* I am also here to tell you that the time has come for more action and fewer words.

I am also here to tell you that Ralph David Abernathy has his own promise to make and a new reality to create. I promise today that I am going to take action to make the recommendations of the Kerner Report, the Poor People's Campaign, and the dozens of other reports I have mentioned a living reality. I am going to confront this nation and the world with the reality of massive, ceaseless confrontation until America deals with the reality of her evils. I am going into the streets of our cities and the plantations of the Southland, and I will take every student, every housewife, every businessman, every working man, the old and young, the robust and the weak, black and white—everyone who believes in justice and who is willing to stand and march with me. I am tired of the promises of Kerner reports. I want the reality of action.

To find out what this nation must do, we need only turn to the Kerner Report. That report recommended, first of all, that full opportunities, rights and benefits be extended to *all* Americans in the areas of jobs, education, welfare and housing. The Kerner Commission disposed of the myths that America cannot afford these reforms and the myth that problems in jobs, education, welfare and housing do not exist. But let me just remind you of a few facts.

In the case of jobs, it was recently disclosed that the Johnson Administration suppressed a study which found that black workers are held down not so much by inadequate education as by racial discrimination, even among Negroes with superior education. And we all know that black men, particularly young black men, suffer from Depression-level unemployment rates. I say that we must follow the Kerner recommendation to create at least one million new jobs in the public sector and one million in the private sector during the next three years, and to enact massive recruiting and training programs for the poor. We must also have full enforcement of antidiscrimination laws, not the lip-service promises of the past. Did you know that the president signed an order three years ago which would remove defense contracts from companies which practice racial discrimination—and that not one single contract has been withheld, not even in the South?

To anyone who asks, can we afford to create these jobs? My answer is this: If Congress can raise its own pay by 40 percent in 1969, spend two and a half billion dollars a month on the war in Vietnam, give jobs to an army of political patronage workers, and build 1,710 ICBMs with nuclear bombs, then America can create the jobs that are so desperately needed.

In education, the Kerner Report stated that we must eliminate segregation and provide the best modern education for all, from preschool to college and vocational training. If you doubt the need for this, go into any black school in Washington, D.C., and see the terribly inadequate facilities, teachers and curriculum for black children. Or go into any white school and see the failure to teach the evils of racism, economic oppression and war. Or go to a public hospital and see poor people dying because we have not educated enough doctors, black or white.

If you ask, can we afford to educate our children? Check into the massive spending on schools in the affluent suburbs—for example, Montgomery County, Maryland, a few miles from this campus. I say, if Mr. Nixon can spend 15 times as much on guns and war as he does on education, the time has come to reduce the killing and escalate the teaching.

The Kerner Report recommended in the field of welfare and incomes that federal standards be adopted to insure full rights and benefits to all recipients, and that the United States of America, the richest country in history, should follow the example of all other industrialized and civilized nations by providing a guaranteed income.

When I talk about welfare, I think the very word "welfare" is a joke. As it exists today, the welfare system degrades and punishes people, it has no policy for helping people get out of the welfare cycle (which they desperately want to do), it denies most recipients as much as half of the benefits to which they are entitled by law, and it prevents hundreds of thousands of people eligible for welfare from getting any benefits at all. When I talk about income, I do not mean the family allowances proposed by Mr. Daniel Patrick Moynihan. The vast majority of people who would be helped by his scheme are not poor at all, and even the rich would get the allowances. I think the rich already receive too many tax advantages and government handouts. The poor should be guaranteed a decent annual income.

Once again, people ask: Can we afford a decent welfare system and a guaranteed income? My answer is that if we can pay Senator Eastland 13 thousand dollars a month *not* to grow food or fiber on his plantation, we can pay more than the nine dollars a month that a hungry child receives in welfare in the state of Mississippi. And if we can guarantee the incomes of retired congressmen and presidents, we can guarantee incomes to people who cannot get jobs and mothers of infants and old folks and sick people. If we can guarantee a few thousand cotton, tobacco and sugar farmers more subsidy payments than 40 million poor people get in the entire antipoverty program, we can have a guaranteed income for all. Finally, if we really believe in equality in America, we can ask ourselves why there is nothing close to equality of income for black people. Americans now receive 550 billion dollars in personal income each year. If black people make up 11 percent of the population—actually, the census does not count millions of us—but if we had even 11 percent of the income, we would be earning 60.5 billion dollars. But in reality, we receive only 27 billion.

In the field of housing, the Kerner Commission found that open-housing laws and building codes must be enforced, and we need massive housing programs for the poor—including Model Cities, rent supplements, and modern, decent low-cost housing. None of these things have been done. Earlier, I mentioned the many gaps between promises and realities in America. You may not know that one of these gaps has been in enforcing housing laws. Congress passed an open-housing law covering all housing in the nation in 1866-103 years ago.

It has never been enforced, even in spite of the open-housing act of 1968 and the Supreme Court's decision for open housing last summer. Similarly, existing housing programs have never really served poor and black people. More people have been made homeless by urban renewal than have been provided with new homes. Public-housing projects are prisons, where the occupants have no rights and are terrorized by rats. Privately owned slum housing is ruled by the human form of rats, the absentee slum landlord. Model Cities and rent supplements have never been fully funded, and the existing ceilings for these programs should be greatly increased.

Once again, it is asked: Can we afford decent housing? If we can subsidize the whole middle class of America with tax concessions for buying homes, then we can certainly provide housing for poor people. If we give free housing to military people, why not the poor? If we can talk piously about "law and order," how about starting by enforcing open-housing laws and cracking down on the crimes of slum landlords?

Those are my conclusions in reference to the Kerner Report's recommendations on jobs, education, welfare, income and housing.

> ***"I am tired of the promises of Kerner reports. I want the reality of action."***

I now turn briefly to its two other major recommendations.

The first is that black people and other poor and oppressed people should control their own lives and communities, so that the great frustrations of powerlessness will be removed. What is supposedly more traditional in America than local control? The majority of Americans enjoy a significant measure of control over their lives. Let us extend this to all. Let us give the poor—not mayors, governors and bureaucrats—control of the poverty program. Let us extend this to all. Let poor tenants control the management and upkeep of their homes. Let black businesses and services develop—not as in a phony "black capitalism" to make a few men rich, but as a kind of "black socialism" of cooperative efforts to serve the entire community. Let poor workers organize collectively into a powerful bargaining force. Let poor people unite for political control of their communities. Let the poor develop police protection in their own neighborhoods and eliminate the police state now imposed on the ghettos of America by the white power structure. And let the students of America demand, demonstrate, win, and exercise their rights to, an education that is not dehumanizing and oppressive, but humane and free and truthful. We need to close the generation gap in America, and the way to do it is not to beat students' heads, but to teach older people how to be young again.

The last objective stated by the Kerner Report was simply that we must have increased communication across racial lines "to destroy stereotypes, to halt polarization, to end distrust and hostility, and to create common ground for efforts toward goals of public order and social justice."

The need for this is so obvious that I need not elaborate on it except to say this: In the case of all of the Kerner Commission's recommendations, the important thing now is to *go ahead and do it.* I am confident that students and young people especially are ready, willing and able to seek the interracial communications we are talking about. Indeed, this process began among young people long ago, and it is continuing. I only urge you to accelerate this.

My other challenge to you today is to take action with me for the kinds of reforms suggested by the Kerner report. We must admit the white racism in America, just as the Kerner Commission did, and we must take action to end it.

No amount of talk, and certainly no report, will produce the changes we need in America.

I urge you to join me, the Southern Christian Leadership Conference, and many national, regional and local organizations of the rich and poor, young and old, in a new movement to save America. . . .

Despite his efforts to keep the SCLC in the vanguard of the civil rights struggle during the 1970s, Abernathy was never able to sustain the energy and effectiveness it had enjoyed under his predecessor's charismatic leadership. In 1977, he resigned from the organization to run for political office but fared poorly in the race to succeed Andrew Young as Atlanta's representative in the U.S. Congress. Abernathy then gradually withdrew from the civil rights movement to concentrate on his duties as a Baptist minister and as the founder and head of the Foundation for Economic Enterprises Development (FEED), which helped train blacks to take advantage of economic opportunities.

The distance between Abernathy and many other civil rights leaders continued to widen throughout the 1980s, particularly after he endorsed Ronald Reagan in the 1980 presidential campaign and then Jesse Jackson in the 1984 contest. Still more controversy erupted in the months just before his death in 1990, when Abernathy published an autobiography in which he provided details about a number of Martin Luther King, Jr.'s extramarital affairs. Many black leaders harshly criticized him for including such information in his book; a couple of the people he wrote about filed lawsuits. The strain took its toll on Abernathy, who had been suffering from various health problems for quite a few years. He died on April 17, 1990.

SOURCES

Books

Abernathy, Ralph David, *And the Walls Came Tumbling Down,* Harper & Row, 1989.

Foner, Philip S., editor, *The Voice of Black America: Major Speeches by Negroes in the United States, 1797-1971,* Simon & Schuster, 1972.

Hale, Frank W., Jr., editor, *The Cry for Freedom: An Anthology of the Best That Has Been Said and Written on Civil Rights Since 1954,* A.S. Barnes & Company, 1969.

Periodicals

Newsweek, "A Fight Among Dr. King's Faithful," October 23, 1989, p. 31.

People, "A Bitter Battle Erupts over the Last Hours of Martin Luther King," October 30, 1989, pp. 40-42.

Time, "Tattletale Memoir," October 23, 1989, p. 42.

Daniel K. Akaka

1924–

Chinese American/Native Hawaiian member of the U.S. Senate

Low-key, nonconfrontational, and totally devoted to advancing the interests of his fellow Hawaiians, Daniel K. Akaka is one of the U.S. Senate's hardest-working members as well as one of the least inclined to seek personal recognition for his efforts. He was born in Honolulu, the youngest of eight children in a family that constantly struggled to make ends meet. Yet Akaka recalls that his parents never hesitated to reach out and help others in need despite their own precarious circumstances, displaying a generosity of spirit that he believes formed the basis of his own lifelong commitment to public service.

Akaka also credits his parents with instilling in him the drive to get a good education, an option they themselves never had. Without one, they knew, the islands offered little in the way of employment except for the backbreaking labor required on the coffee and sugar plantations. So after graduating from a private boys' school in 1942, Akaka set about earning some money to go on to college. For several years during the mid-1940s he worked as a welder, first for the Hawaiian Electric Company and then for the U.S. Army Corps of Engineers. When his stint in the service ended in 1947, he enrolled at the University of Hawaii, earning his bachelor's degree in education in 1953 and a secondary-school teaching certificate the following year.

Throughout the rest of the 1950s, Akaka gained valuable experience as a teacher in rural and urban settings as well as in a military school. In 1960, he moved from the classroom into administration, serving as a vice-principal until 1963 and then as a principal from 1963 until 1968. During this same period, Akaka returned to the University of Hawaii and obtained his master's degree in education in 1966.

Akaka's growing reputation as leader in his field eventually led to his involvement in state politics. From 1969 until 1971, he was a program specialist in the Department of Education, followed by a three-year term as director of the Hawaii Office of Economic Opportunity. Then, in 1975, he went to work for newly-elected Governor George R. Ariyoshi as his special assistant for human resources after losing a bid in the Democratic primary election to be Ariyoshi's lieutenant governor.

In 1976, Akaka decided to take another stab at elective politics, this time as a Democratic candidate for the U.S. House of Representatives. He captured some eighty percent of the vote and easily won re-election seven more times before being appointed to fill the U.S. Senate seat left vacant by the 1990 death of Spark M. Matsunaga. Later that same year, Akaka was re-elected to the Senate in his own right, where he has continued to advance a liberal agenda despite facing strong opposition.

Although his positions have occasionally put him at odds with some of his colleagues—Republicans and Democrats alike—Akaka quietly yet firmly sticks to his guns while using what he calls "the spirit of Aloha" to foster an atmosphere that will bring people together rather than drive them apart. Considering that he is the first U.S. senator of Native Hawaiian ancestry, it is not surprising that he takes a strong interest in issues of particular import to Hawaii. He has, for example, supported sugar cane growers by opposing efforts to cut federal sugar subsidies, and in the devastating wake of Hurricane Iniki in 1992, he urged the Federal Emergency Management Agency (FEMA) to create a field office in the islands.

Akaka has also tried to right some historical wrongs. In 1993, he successfully persuaded his fellow legislators to sign a joint congressional resolution acknowledging the U.S. government's role in overthrowing Hawaii's native government in 1893 and formally apologizing to the Hawaiian people for that act. Also thanks to his efforts, bills have been signed into law commending Hawaiian civilians for their heroism in the days after the Japanese attack on Pearl Harbor in December 1941.

The environment is also of great concern to Akaka, who serves on the Senate Committee on Energy and Natural Resources. Eager to preserve the islands' delicate ecosystem, he has won passage of strict legislation safeguarding Hawaii against the introduction of potentially destructive plant and animal species. He has also succeeded in establishing a tropical forest recovery program for Hawaii and has managed to eliminate U.S. territories in the Pacific as possible sites for nuclear waste disposal.

In his role as chairman of the Subcommittee on Mineral Resources Development and Production of the Committee on Energy and Natural Resources, Akaka took a special interest in the use of technology to explore and mine the oceans. At a hearing he convened on the issue on November 4, 1993, he opened the session with a brief statement outlining why he felt it was time to increase mankind's understanding of what lies beneath the sea, from both a scientific and a commercial standpoint. (The ultimate goal of the hearing was to gather facts that could prove helpful when Akaka and his Senate colleagues tackled a general overhaul of mining laws that was scheduled to begin in 1994.) Akaka's remarks are reprinted here from Ocean Mining Technology: Hearing Before the Subcommittee on Mineral Resources Development and Production of the Committee on Energy and Natural Resources, United States Senate, *103rd Congress, 1st Session, U.S. Government Printing Office, 1994.*

Aloha, and good morning. The Energy Subcommittee on Mineral Resources Development and Production is in order, and today we will hear testimony on the status and future of ocean mining. In particular, we are interested in learning more about the development of technologies that could make ocean mining commercially feasible.

Such technologies would also have direct application in other disciplines, such as monitoring the ocean environment, pollution control, seafloor exploration, evaluation, and mapping, and other fields of scientific research and technology commercialization.

I should also point out that this technology will have direct application to undersea ordnance detection and removal. This is a major environmental problem for Kahoolawe, an island in Hawaii. Ever since the research vessel, H.M.S. *Challenger,* hoisted the first manganese nodules from the deep ocean during its epic voyage in 1873, there has been persistent and underlying curiosity about seabed minerals.

One hundred ten years later, another dramatic development occurred which will forever affect seabed research. In 1983, President Reagan established the 200-mile Exclusive Economic Zone [EEZ]. The U.S. EEZ is the largest territorial expansion in our history, larger than the Louisiana Purchase or the purchase of Alaska from Russia.

Our EEZ covers more than 2.5 billion acres, an area slightly greater than that of the United States. The U.S. EEZ is the largest under any nation's jurisdiction, and contains a resource base estimated in the trillions of dollars. It is a vast, new ocean frontier.

Because eighty-five percent of these waters are in the Pacific, Hawaii will play a central role in EEZ research and development. Unfortunately, our new frontier remains largely unexplored. After ten years, the United States has performed a detailed reconnaissance of less than five percent of our EEZ.

Every American schoolchild can recite President Kennedy's famous challenge to reach the moon before the decade of the 1960s ended. The success of our country's space program has become a source of great national pride. Far less attention—far less—has been given to the speech Kennedy gave that same year which challenged Americans to tap the ocean depths.

Well, we have reached the moon and our spacecraft have explored our solar system. Today, we know more about the surface of planets located millions of miles from Earth than we know about much of the ocean floor, which is the Earth's own basement. Our map of Venus is better than the map of our own EEZ.

Competitiveness is the buzzword of the moment in Washington. Perhaps the greatest field of opportunity for enhancing U.S. competitiveness lies in our oceans, but like any area of economic opportunity, the payoff will only come if we commit adequate resources and attention to the task.

Today's hearing will examine the current status and future potential of technology used to explore and mine the ocean. Mineral-rich oxides found as nodules and crusts on the deep seabeds and on seamounts are one important EEZ resource. Compared to land-base operations, mining of seabed minerals is not currently economical.

Investment in seabed exploration and the development of technologies to permit the efficient exploration of the oceans must be pursued as a long-term venture. Ocean technology continues to advance, but at an extremely slow pace, even though the potential payoffs associated with ocean technology development will be vast.

The Deep Seabed Hard Minerals Resources Act expires September 30, 1994. Reauthorization of this act offers an opportunity to examine the current state of technology necessary to survey, map, probe, sample, and monitor the deep seabed. The availability of this technology will directly affect the pace, location, and cost of EEZ exploration and development.

In addition to seabed mineral resources, the hearing will focus more broadly on advances in technology which can improve U.S. competitiveness and facilitate the rational development of ocean resources in an environmentally responsible manner. The testimony and recommendations received today will be used to craft legislation which applies to many areas of ocean resource development other than fisheries.

I welcome all of our distinguished witnesses and would like to express my sincere gratitude for their efforts to help educate Congress—and this is a major endeavor, and this is the beginning of it—to educate Congress about the importance of ocean technology development. . . .

Usually, we hear from administration witnesses first, but because of a schedule conflict I want to recognize Dr. Robert Ballard. Dr. Ballard, I know you have to catch a plane, and I am saying this for the others to know this morning, and so I would like to modify the sequence of witnesses and allow you to testify first. After your statement and a few questions, we will return to the panel of federal witnesses.

I am pleased to welcome a witness whose many accomplishments include the discovery of deep ocean hot vents which are host to previously unknown life systems, where creatures flourish without sunlight and feed on chemicals and heat generated by the Earth's magma.

He also founded the Jason Project, which has brought high-tech ocean adventure to millions of students, and I also understand that Dr. Ballard has made a comment that he is one of the few that has seen so much mud in a lifetime on the bottom of the ocean in his ventures. [Laughter.] Dr. Ballard, welcome to the committee.

[After a morning of testimony from Dr. Ballard and more than a half-dozen other expert witnesses, the hearing came to an end with some additional thoughts from Akaka.]

Let me close with a few observations.

Japan and the European Community appear to be outpacing us with their aggressive programs in ocean technology development. If this continues, we will lose important opportunities that could lead to new ocean industries, technology advances and job creation.

To avoid this, the United States needs to refocus its ocean policy toward technologies that are critical to the future ocean research and development. Effective management of our EEZ depends upon having better tools to survey, map, probe, sample, and monitor the seabed in an environmentally sound manner. At the same time, we must also get much more aggressive about establishing partnerships, as you have mentioned, among industry, government and academia, which concentrate on ocean R & D.

Other nations, and particularly Japan, have employed this technique with great success. Such partnerships are our best hope of restoring the United States to a position of leadership in the use and protection of our ocean resources. I hope the Clinton administration will seriously consider the benefits of supporting a technology development program as part of its overall restructuring of the federal government.

I will review the information gathered today, and will continue to closely follow the developments related to ocean technologies. With this information in hand—and thanks for all of your help—I will draft legislation to reauthorize the Seabed Mining Act in a way that fosters the technologies necessary to promote ocean research and development. We must provide our engineers and scientists with the tools and resources necessary to explore and economically develop our ocean resources.

Daniel K. Akaka

SOURCES

Ocean Mining Technology: Hearing Before the Subcommittee on Mineral Resources Development and Production of the Committee on Energy and Natural Resources, United States Senate, 103rd Congress, 1st Session, U.S. Government Printing Office, 1994.

Zia, Helen, and Susan Gall, eds., *Notable Asian Americans,* Gale Research, Detroit, 1995.

Arthur Ashe

1943–1993

African American professional tennis player, broadcaster, writer, and activist

One of the most talented and well-liked athletes of this century was Arthur Ashe, known and respected internationally not only for his skills on the tennis court but also for his dedication to a wide variety of human rights issues. Mild-mannered yet strong-willed, he almost singlehandedly took on the racial barriers that kept blacks out of professional tennis and conquered them with style, dignity, and the firm conviction that there was no place in the world for injustice. This sentiment carried over to his life outside tennis as well, where he was an outspoken champion of causes ranging from the anti-apartheid movement to the plight of Haitian refugees. But his last and probably most difficult fight was against an enemy he never dreamed of having to face—AIDS.

A native of Richmond, Virginia, Ashe was only about seven years old when a playground instructor noticed his unusual skill with a tennis racket and arranged for him to take lessons from Dr. Walter Johnson, an African American physician with an interest in developing the talents of promising young black players. He took the youngster under his wing and not only worked on his game but also taught him how to win without arrogance and lose without anger. It was a lesson that shaped Ashe's behavior for the rest of his life, both professionally and personally.

Ashe entered his first major competition in 1958, and by 1962 he was the fifth-ranked junior singles player in the country—the lone black star in a sport dominated by whites. He then headed off to the University of California at Los Angeles (UCLA) on a tennis scholarship. There he trained with coach J.D. Morgan and tennis star Pancho Gonzalez, becoming the first African American to be named to America's Davis Cup team and earning a reputation as one of the team's top singles players. After graduating from UCLA in 1966 with a degree in business administration, Ashe served two years in the U.S. Army while continuing to work on his tennis whenever possible. He reached the top of the amateur ranks in 1968 following victories at a series of 30 straight tournaments, including the U.S. Amateur Championship (which had not been won by an American since 1955) and the U.S. Open Championship (where he was the first black to win top honors). That same year and again the following year, he also made the semifinals at Wimbledon and led the U.S. Davis Cup team to victory.

As soon as his Army service ended in 1969, Ashe turned professional, and his next six years on the court were the best and busiest of his career. Consistently ranked among the top five players in the game, he won numerous important singles and doubles matches in worldwide competition. But his crowning achievement came in 1975 at Wimbledon, where he upset top-seeded Jimmy Connors for the men's singles title. This made him the first African American to win top honors at the prestigious All-England Open and the first to be ranked number one internationally. It was an especially satisfying victory for the 32-year-old Ashe, who was by that time considered to be past his prime.

Ashe kept playing throughout the rest of the 1970s, winning several more important tournaments before some minor health problems began taking their toll on his game. Then in mid-1979 he suffered a serious heart attack that eventually led to bypass surgery. When he still experienced chest pain after trying to ease his way back into tennis in early 1980, he knew it was time to quit the game he loved.

Ashe then turned his energies to a variety of other activities. He worked behind the scenes in tennis, promoting the sport (especially among inner-city youths) as a sort of "goodwill ambassador," serving as co-chairman of the player development committee of the U.S. Tennis Association, and trying to improve conditions for players as co-founder and head of the Association of Tennis Professionals. He also served as a television commentator for major matches and hosted his own syndicated tennis show.

In addition, Ashe was involved in many non-tennis projects. He contributed his time to charities such as the American Heart Association and the Children's Defense Fund. A passionate defender of human rights, he spoke out frequently on social and political issues, including racial discrimination and minority participation in college and professional athletics, South Africa's apartheid system, and the Haitian refugee problem. He was also a columnist for a number of magazines and newspapers, and in 1988, he published A Hard Road to Glory, *a much-praised, three-volume history of the black athlete in America.*

On April 8, 1992, however, Ashe's life took a sudden and dramatic turn when he publicly confirmed reports that he had AIDS. At a crowded press conference held in New York City, he faced the media and read the following statement. At times, his voice was so choked with emotion that his wife, Jeanne, had to step in and speak for him. His comments are reprinted here from Historic Documents of 1992, *Congressional Quarterly Inc., 1993.*

I thank all of you for coming on such short notice. Rumors and half-truths have been floating about concerning my medical condition since my heart attack on July 31, 1979. Most of you know I had my first heart bypass operation six months later on December 13, 1979. But beginning with my admittance to New York Hospital for brain surgery in September 1988, many of you heard that I had tested positive for HIV, the virus that causes AIDS. That was indeed the case. It was transmitted through a blood transfusion after my first or my second open-heart bypass operation in June, 1983. I have known since September 1988, that I had AIDS.

My right hand had lost all motor function and a biopsy of brain tissue removed detected the presence of toxoplasmosis, a marker for the AIDS virus which is relatively harmless in people with normally-functioning immune systems. Subsequent blood tests proved positive for HIV.

So, some may ask, why not admit it earlier? Why hide it? The answer is simple: any admis-

Arthur Ashe

sion of HIV infection at that time would have seriously, permanently, and, my wife, Jeanne, and I believed, unnecessarily infringed upon our family's right to privacy. Just as I am sure everyone in this room has some personal matter he or she would like to keep private, so did we. There was certainly no compelling medical or physical necessity to "go public" with my condition. I had it on good authority that my status was common knowledge in the medical community. However, I am truly grateful to all of you—medical and otherwise—who know but either didn't even ask me or never made it public. What I came to feel about a year ago was that there was a silent and unspoken conspiracy and complicity to assist me in maintaining my privacy.

This has meant a great deal to me, Jeanne and my daughter Camera (although she doesn't know it yet). She already knows that perfect strangers come up to daddy on the street and say "hi." Beginning tonight, Jeanne and I must teach her how to react to new, different, and sometimes cruel comments, that have little to do with reality.

Particularly for the sake of our family, Jeanne and I and some close friends have often talked about how long we could conceal this secret. Then, sometime last week, someone telephoned *USA Today* and told them. After several days of checking it out they decided to confront me with the rumors. It put me in the unenviable position of having to lie if I wanted to protect our privacy. *No one should have to make that choice.* I am sorry that I have been forced to make this revelation. I am not sick, and I can function very well in all that I have been involved in for the past three years. After all, I am not running for some office of public trust, nor do I have stockholders to account to. It is only that I fall under the dubious umbrella of "public figure."

As for my family, my wife and daughter are in excellent health and both are HIV-negative.

I have been an activist on many issues in the past—against apartheid, for education and the athlete, the need for better, faster change in tennis. I will continue with projects, and will certainly get involved with the AIDS crisis. I will be talking with several people and experts about how I might best help the cause. I have gained much insight in watching Magic Johnson weave his magic among school children, and I suspect we may join hands to work together.

The quality of one's life changes irrevocably when something like this becomes public. Reason and rational thought are too often waived out of fear, caution, or just plain ignorance. My family and I must now learn a new set of behavioral standards to function in the everyday world, and sadly, there really was no good reason for this to have to happen now. But, it has happened, and we will adjust and go forward.

Ashe's disclosure touched off an intense debate about a person's right to privacy versus the public's right to know. But as he admitted some months later, getting the truth out in the open also eliminated much of the strain he and his family and friends had been under while they struggled to keep his secret. In the weeks immediately after his announcement, Ashe—determined to remain as pro-

ductive as possible—assumed a leading a role in the fight against AIDS, crisscrossing the country in a virtual one-man campaign. He joined the boards of both the Harvard and the UCLA AIDS institutes, and in August 1992, he established his own Arthur Ashe Foundation for the Defeat of AIDS, making use of his connections in the international tennis community to garner support and publicity for the group's educational and fundraising efforts.

On February 5, 1993, Ashe entered the hospital after developing AIDS-related pneumonia. Despite initial signs that he was improving, he died the next day.

SOURCES

Books

Ashe, Arthur, and Neil Amdur, *Off the Court,* New American Library, 1981.

Ashe, Arthur, and Arnold Rampersad, *Days of Grace: A Memoir,* Knopf, 1993.

Historic Documents of 1992; Congressional Quarterly Inc., 1993.

Periodicals

Newsweek, "Arthur Ashe's Secret," April 20, 1992, pp. 62-63; "Lessons from a Friend," February 22, 1993, pp. 60-61.

People, "For Recovering Arthur Ashe, His Heart Attack May Not Be a Net Loss," September 17, 1979, pp. 86-89; "An Athlete Nearly Dying Young: A Tennis Champ Tells His History," September 21, 1981, pp. 113-114; "The Burden of Truth," April 20, 1992, pp. 50-51; "Seize the Day," June 8, 1992, pp. 42-44; "Man of Grace and Glory," February 22, 1993, pp. 68-72.

Time, "Fair Game?," April 20, 1992, pp. 74-75; "A Man of Fire and Grace," February 15, 1993, p. 70.

Sports Illustrated, "Service, But First a Smile," August 29, 1966, pp. 47-50; "It Couldn't Be a Heart Attack—But It Was," September 3, 1979, pp. 24-25; "Another Battle Joined," April 20, 1992, pp. 24-25; "Sportsman of the Year: The Eternal Example," December 21, 1992, pp. 16-27.

Clyde and Vernon Bellecourt

Native American activists of the Ojibwa tribe

Although their names and faces may not be as well known as those of some of their fellow Native American activists, brothers Clyde and Vernon Bellecourt both played crucial roles in the founding of the American Indian Movement (AIM), the most militant of the Indian protest groups during the 1960s and 1970s. They were born on the White Earth Reservation in Minnesota, members of a family of 14 that struggled against overwhelming poverty and racist attitudes that branded them as "dirty Indians." Both left the reservation as young men in search of what they hoped would be a somewhat better life in Minneapolis, but the so-called "red ghetto" they found there only heightened their sense of despair and frustration. Before long the Bellecourts turned to crime, attempting burglaries and armed robberies that landed them lengthy prison sentences.

By the early 1960s, Vernon was out on parole and working as a barber, a trade he had learned while in jail. (He eventually owned a beauty salon and later an import business specializing in gift items.) Clyde, however, was still doing time in Minnesota's Stillwater State Prison. Facing the possibility of having to spend many more years behind bars, he went on a hunger strike with the intention of staying on it until he died. Then one of his fellow inmates, another Ojibwa named Eddie Benton, began talking to him about their shared heritage and about the "Red Power" civil rights movement then making news on the West Coast. Resistant at first, Clyde eventually abandoned his hunger strike and worked actively with Benton to promote Indian awareness within the prison.

Released on parole in the mid-1960s, Clyde Bellecourt returned to Minneapolis, convinced by now that the federal government's supervision of the Indian people was slowly but surely destroying them and that they had to take charge of their own future in order to survive. His first inclination was to establish a rather traditional civil-rights association—one that worked within the system to secure full rights for Native Americans as citizens of the United States. But after a frustrating few years spent dealing with church groups and government agencies who showed little interest in supporting his efforts, Clyde came to the realization that "the system" cared little about the notion of Indian citizenship or independence.

So it was that in mid-1968, Clyde and a number of his supporters (including Eddie Benton and another ex-convict named Dennis Banks) founded a group they dubbed Concerned Indian Americans (CIA). However, the unacceptable acronym *resulting from this choice quickly prompted them to change the name to the American Indian Movement (AIM). Initially, AIM leaders focused their efforts on reaching out to Native Americans who, as a direct result of government policy during the 1950s, had been relocated from reservations to urban areas. (Making such a radical change in their lives had left many of these Indians confused and demoralized; the racism and discrimination they encountered at almost every turn made their situation even worse.) AIM members helped them deal with police harassment and obtain education, job training, housing, and health care. With the support of Minnesota's judicial system, they also set up a program that offered young Indians who had broken the law an alternative to prison; in addition, they worked with others who had already served time to keep them from ending up in prison again. And because they felt alcohol abuse was a major source of misery in the Indian community, AIM leaders strongly counseled against drinking and demanded sobriety from those who wanted to become involved in the movement. When Vernon Bellecourt—who was then enjoying a comfortable life in suburbia as a prosperous businessman—saw the difference AIM was beginning to make in Minneapolis among young Indian men and women in particular, he joined up, too.*

As AIM evolved over the next few years, it took on a much more radical look. Members allowed their hair to grow long, dressed in Indian attire, and carried weapons (presumably for self-defense). Nonviolent protest was out; direct confrontation became the rule. This threatening and dramatic style of protest often left AIM members at odds with reservation Indians, a generally more conservative group who faced a different set of problems than urban Indians. But it attracted national attention to their struggle and captured the imaginations of young Native Americans in a way no other activist group had ever been able to do.

During the early 1970s, the Bellecourts were involved in most of the major AIM demonstrations. On the eve of the November elections in 1972, for example, about five hundred Native Americans from all over the country arrived in Washington, D.C., to protest government Indian policy. Known as the Trail of Broken Treaties march, it was led primarily by AIM members; Clyde Bellecourt had helped draw up a list of 20 proposals for improving U.S.-Indian relations that the demonstrators planned to present to White House officials.

The proposals were soon forgotten, however, when the march took an unexpected turn. Frustrated by President Richard Nixon's refusal to meet with them, some of the activists occupied the offices of the Bureau of Indian Affairs. During their five-day standoff with authorities, they committed acts of vandalism and destruction that resulted in bad publicity for AIM and prompted the FBI to classify it as an "extremist" organization like the Black Panthers and the U.S. Communist party. Two months later, the Nixon administration officially rejected AIM's 20 proposals, which included demands for a separate government for Indians, the restoration of Indian lands, and the renegotiation of all treaties. Later, charges were filed (and eventually dismissed) against Clyde Bellecourt for his part in the march.

Clyde Bellecourt was also among the leaders of the famous Wounded Knee occupation, which began on South Dakota's Pine Ridge Reservation on February 27, 1973, after several hundred AIM members and sympathizers had gathered there to take a stand against the mistreatment of Indians. Their anger was focused in particular on the reservation's head administrator, Richard Wilson, whom some of the Sioux elders had accused of corruption and resorting to violence and intimidation. After AIM occupied Wounded Knee, federal marshals and FBI agents immediately moved in to re-establish government control. The resulting armed standoff lasted 71 days, ending only when federal negotiators promised to set up a meeting between Sioux elders and White House representatives. The meeting never took place, and once again AIM leaders, including Clyde Bellecourt, soon found themselves facing a variety of criminal charges. The evidence against him was so flimsy, however, that he never actually went to trial.

In the aftermath of Wounded Knee, AIM established a defense fund to help pay the legal fees of those who had been involved in the siege. The organization's leaders shouldered much of the responsibility for raising money, often by giving speeches and soliciting donations. On one such occasion in mid-1975, shortly after two FBI agents were shot and killed on the Pine Ridge Reservation in a confrontation with AIM members and supporters, Vernon Bellecourt gave the following talk in which he described the beginnings of the American Indian Movement and discussed its tactics and goals. His speech is reprinted from Contemporary Native American Address, *edited by John R. Maestas (Brigham Young University, 1976).*

The organization was formed in mid-1968 in the ghetto community of Minneapolis, Minnesota. It had to go back to the policy of the United States government which for many years, up until four months ago, was called *relocation.* It was an effort to train people in some area of trade or education to bring them into the mainstream. Generally, the program was ill-devised and ill-planned. In fact, it was never really successful because the program was designed to fail. They would never provide enough assistance. They would just provide enough to get them in the city and drop them off—only compounding the problem for Indian people.

Because of the inadequacy of those services provided under the law by the government, they were completely severed from Indian people when they went into urban areas trying to make that transition from a reservation environment into a city environment. For a lot of our people this has created some social problems. So the organization then started in Minneapolis, and when they looked around and saw that in spite of all the work that the various churches were doing in their missions, in spite of all the programs that were designed by the federal government, in spite of all the efforts of liberal do-gooders to do something for Indian people, they never at one time said, "Let's do it with you." They were always trying to do it for us and failed. The American Indian Movement recognized that we had to form to draw attention to these conditions, to start working on police-community relations in the community because Indian people were assaulted as a way of life by the police in Minneapolis and throughout this country.

We started creating programs directed towards the youth. We became advocates for legal services, alcoholic programs, drug addiction programs, etc. The American Indian Movement immediately took a strong role in the urban areas. Recognizing that an organization formed would have advocates for all Indian people and because of the philosophy of the Indian Movement and the growth and success it had, immediately several of our brothers in various reservations started opening up organizations, and today we have seventy-five or so chapters. We have six more forming. We will probably have about eighty chapters representing the Indian people in the near future.

The movement is solvent and has been able to break down tribalism, and we have representation from every tribe in our organization. We stand together as red people first and then we stand together as tribes and fuse together a strong coalition from the young people today who are once again identifying with their traditional religion. AIM is first of all the religious rebirth, a spiritual movement, and then, of course, comes the new Indian pride, new Indian dignity. And it has been described as an organization where the people have gone back to an old religion of their tribes, away from the confusion of the society that has made them slaves of unguided lives.

We strongly believe that the movement has been able to unite our young people. It has been able to unite them together with our traditionalness, our elders, our more respected leaders and with a conservative element in between the bureaucrats and the people who for some strange reason see us as a threat to their existence. Although we have never attacked Indian people we have always found out that they were not our enemy. We have defined the system. We know what the problems are. We are quite capable of dealing with them as we are dealing with them today.

We recognize in Wounded Knee, as with the case of the Bureau of Indian Affairs occupation during election week, that the primary purpose of the AIM has been as a catalytic organization that was going to focus not only national attention but international attention on what has become a national disgrace in this country, the conditions in which Indian people are forced to live. We did that in Washington, D.C., and,

"We stand together as red people first and then we stand together as tribes. . . ."

of course, we are doing it again at Wounded Knee. Now, we recognize that in addition to the confrontation that is taking place between the sovereign people at Wounded Knee and the government that AIM and other tribes represented there are not only confronting the bureaucratical impression of the United States government, the Department of Interior's Bureau of Indian Affairs, but most important we see that we are confronting the conscience of America and the conscience of the world.

Indian people, particularly the young people today who have taken a very active role in the AIM, have recognized that for close to 482 years the American Indians have tried to oppose western expansion of the European culture in our land which we recognize could survive and could go on by itself. But what they have tried to do is brainwash us into bringing our people into that mainstream and, in doing so, our people have become poor. We recognize that the efforts toward entering the so-called "mainstream" concept has not only failed our people but has also failed a lot of people in the country. We have exhausted our diplomatic efforts. We have negotiated. We have pleaded. Our people have been going to Washington for years and nothing changes, the conditions only get worse. So, what has happened in Wounded Knee is that a declaration of sovereignty was made. It is a start of a revolution among the Indian people today, not only a revolution that is taking place in our own existing tribal form of government on the reservations, but we recognize that we have to take a position of sovereignty in relationship to the treaties.

Sovereign treaties or congressionally ratified treaties were made with Indian nations as sovereign people, and it is really immoral, at this time, to suggest that in negotiating those treaties that we should play it by their ground rules within their judicial system and within their courts. We recognize that we have to deal with the treaties on the basis of a sovereign nation. The government in Pine Ridge has totally failed their people while the bureaucracy gets stronger and they buy more guns and police cars and build bigger buildings on the Bureau of Indian Affairs Agency.

Meanwhile, the reservation people are suffering with a forty-two-year life expectancy and still suffering from three times the national average in infant mortality rates and five times the national average suicide rate. Chronic ill-health and diseases that first appeared in the white world yet prevail in reservations. When we can see these kinds of conditions, we recognize that the system has totally failed us, and now we should have the right to pool our self-determination, our interpretation of which is total self-government. This is a whole new attitude being created at Wounded Knee, and it will continue to become a reality.

The term "revolution" which has become stereotyped now leads the people to believe that it is a violent revolution or that it is some type of thing where we are going to assassinate a lot of people. That is not what we are talking about. We are basically talking about a philosophical revolution which is really going to free our people. We see among the new generation, people who are willing to put meaning into those words of support instead of words of sympathy. We talk about revolution and we talk about a philosophical revolution brought about by political confrontation, and we term it as "confrontation politics." We recognize that, unfortunately, we live within a system and society in our country here where a society exists that can only respond to some kind of strong confrontation. We can see the success that we have already had in that area. The budget for the Bureau of Indian Affairs for the fiscal year 1974 has been increased by fifteen percent, so we can see that our efforts are already materializing and we are bringing a lot of new awareness for the first time in our lives.

There are a lot of responsible tribal leaders in this country. And I am not trying to throw them all into the same category, but we see in spite of the reservations that some of the people are being abused: They are poor; the conditions of poverty are getting worse, and we realize that we have to have some type of revolution to bring about these changes so that we can exist and survive as a society.

There have been two attempts by responsible Indian people in the Pine Ridge Reservation to remove their existing tribal chairman. They recognize that he has become a puppet of Washington and, in fact, never really an advocate of Indian people. They can see the leasing processes taking place over whole sections of land. These lands are being leased illegally, and transfers of land are taking place illegally by their leasing department. They have charged him with nepotism which involves hiring of all his relatives, etc. This is another bona fide complaint which the people have. They have indicated to us very strongly that they no longer want that kind of puppet government, and they want to cast it off. In doing so, the people and the AIM met with the traditional chief on the Pine Ridge Reservation.

It has always been our feeling that the American Indian Movement has been a traditional organization, going back to our traditional way of life, our traditional ties, values, standards, etc. The tribal form of government, as the government exists today, was set up by Washington some years back. The whole impression of their policy is being threatened, and, of course, this is why they are opposing any type of stand by the people up there. And so we are having meetings with the traditional chiefs. And the wishes of the overall people are to restore the government back to the chiefs who are in fact serving as advocates of their people.

This is what is happening so far as the issue on the Pine Ridge Reservation is concerned. We have recognized that in several of these non-Indian communities that the whole economy depends on the monies that Indian people spend in those communities. It is ironic that those same communities are the ones that are practicing racism against Indian people. Indian people are assaulted, arrested, charged with drunkenness when they aren't drunk so that they can post fines on them and get their money. They view the Indian people as a parasite living off the economy, and they abuse them. We can see what a complete double standard of justice we have in this country affecting the Indian people. We know that as many as one-third of the prisoners in this country are Indian men and woman. When we only represent 850,000 people, we have to definitely question the judicial system.

We found a case in Buffalo Gap where a man named Wesley Bad Heart Bull, a young Indian man, was accosted on the street. A fight broke out, and he defended himself. There was a threat made that "We'll get him." The next day they did and ran a knife into him and killed him. The murderer, who was non-Indian, was arrested and at the discretion of the county attorney (who it turned out was another racist) charged the man with second-degree manslaughter when all evidence pointed to at least a first-degree murder charge. He was immediately placed on bail at $5,000.

In another county, a man named Harold Whitehorn, Jr., an Indian man, was alleged to have been in the proximity of the area where a white woman was murdered. On the testimony of someone who was intoxicated at the time, the man was arrested and held for eighteen days without bond, completely contrary to the Bill of Rights where excessive bonds are prohibited. He was charged with first-degree murder. This is just an example of the double standards of justice.

At that time, our national field director, Dennis Banks, called a National Indian Rights Day at Custer, South Dakota, and asked that all concerned Indian people and chapters of our organization assemble in Custer. Once again, almost every one of the men that were there were arrested. (I think there were forty-six.) They all went to Custer to stand firm and confront the establishment in the area and tell them that no more were we going to tolerate this kind of injustice. Again, we were confronted. We went there unarmed. Again, we were assaulted by police and the whole world saw that fight on TV. We had to defend ourselves. So, Custer will no doubt become a memorial in this country to Indian resistance. Ironically, once again it all started at Custer, South Dakota, so we have had the occasion to deal with Custer twice in these last two centuries.

We have always recognized our credibility as a sovereignty. We have always recognized that several nations [tribes] have never given up the feeling of sovereignty. The United States government has never given up the feeling that we are sovereign people and have been subjected to tyranny and actually a conquered people. Because of this strong feeling of sovereignty, we always recognize that Indian people perhaps have had to fight to bring about social change in this country. If you really evaluate and look at the conditions we have to live in today, we can bring clear-cut indictment against the government and system along with an unconcerned society for allowing these conditions to exist and continue. We always recognize that we have a valid cause to also stand up the very same way that this country stood up in 1776 and wrote a document called a Declaration of Independence. We only have to read that document and ask ourselves if we don't understand what we are doing at Wounded Knee.

It is defined in the Declaration of Independence very clearly that when, for long periods of time, a government becomes a tyranny to the people, when it becomes abusive to people, committing indignities and continually suppressing them, you have not only a legal responsibility but a moral responsibility to change that form of government or attempt to destroy it. All we have said at Wounded Knee today is that we are trying to change that form of government. We are trying to bring about change, social change.

> ***"The American Indian Movement is a spiritual movement first and a political organization secondly."***

And with what happened today in this land, the civil rights movement just about died, and about that time, the Vietnam War, the longest undeclared war in history, as it is termed, came to an end. The people fail to see the longest undeclared war in history, and that is the war that has been going on against us for 482 years in our land and against our way of life. They cannot say they are not guilty of it considering the death rate, etc., that I quoted before. The conditions are worse.

We recognize the whole civil rights movement across this country has recognized that the American Indian people are going to take the lead as far as bringing about social change. We have had several national organizations who have indicated to us clearly that they could see in our efforts that we have rekindled the flame again in this land of bringing about justice for a change, to bring about truth where there hasn't been any.

We believe that we are going to be a primary force in the history of this country. Our prophecies told us that one day a man would come from the North, and his skin would be the color of death, and he would be here for a short while, and he would leave, and then again he would return and be here for a long time, and our people would suffer. But in the fifth generation after the second coming of the white man [Viking], small fires would crop up about our nations, and confrontations at Fort Lewis, Alcatraz—these are those small flames. The conditions are the same as they were when the white man came the second time to our land. People are fighting and children are fighting with their parents. Our prophecies tell us when trees would start dying from the top [pollution], a black cloud would settle, and there would be rioting, and the small fires would become one gigantic flame, and, at that time, the red people would stand once again in power. We can see the answer to our prophecy is coming true now.

This is the time we have to stand as a sovereign people. We have to stand and give direction to the society and our country which has been lost for the most part. We know that we can take that role and provide the truth, spirituality, freedom not only for the redman but for all people in this land and that is the role that the AIM is going to play. We have leaped up with Sioux medicine men, the holy men, the spiritual leaders who have been there all these years, hanging on to that which has rekindled the spirit amongst our people. We have been able to sit down with our Sioux brothers and so-called tribes of Indians who supposedly were enemies with one another. We have been able to completely overrule that problem by joining together spiritually.

The American Indian Movement is a spiritual movement first and a political organization secondly. It has been very good for us to see the outcome of this new awareness, the new pride that has been introduced to our young people. Every day young people are getting off alcohol and narcotics because of this new awareness. It is probably serving the same use with the whites. Now the movement is bringing them

Vernon Bellecourt

back to Christianity and spirituality, and we know that as far as Indian people are concerned, going back to our ways is the way we want to do it.

I am sure the government also recognizes the fact that we have this fuse in our hand right now, and they want to extinguish it.

The movement itself is going to continue in an effort to confront the conscience of American people. We are going to continue confronting the establishment. We are going to continue working within the system.

We recognize that in 1976 when this country is going to celebrate its 200th birthday, they will be celebrating in our backyard. And, by then, they had better have involved the host, or we are going to be very much concerned whether they are going to have a happy birthday or not.

We're going to work on and be involved in controversial issues, and in spite of all the criticism we are getting today, our movement is getting stronger because it is a movement of people wanting change. We recognize that Wounded Knee has become a memorial for freedom not only for Indian people but for all people for a better way of life. If that can be crushed, and this society allows it to be crushed, they are perhaps crushing an opportunity to really have peace in the world. We have recognized our spiritual leaders. And our old people tell us that the reason this government has never been able to find peace in the world is because they have never made peace with the sovereign people here. Until they make peace with the redman in our part of the universe, they will never find peace.

For thousands of years, ever since the time of creation, it has been our position that we were imbued by the Creator, the Great Spirit, with certain rights that could not be alienated by any foreign power, and certainly in this case, we can only see the United States government as a foreign power. The traditional people, the people on the reservations, have maintained their culture, language, spiritual ways, their way of life as much as they can within a contemporary society, of course. And their society has been really disrupted.

In 1934, the United States government, in order to impose a so-called process of government, patterned a government, after the United States government, on the reservations to impose leadership on people who went through their Bureau of Indian Affairs schools and other indoctrination so the mining interests could gain the resources of our land. They had to impose this kind of leadership. I think it only fair to say that within this alien form of government that has been imposed upon the people since 1934, passed by Congress without ratification by the tribe, forced upon them, that many tribal leaders have tried to function within that system. We have been honest, very sincere people, very much handicapped by government-Washington bureaucracy.

We have always maintained and respected the traditional hereditary chiefs. In their place the government has put puppets, people who have sold their own people out to the mining corporations who are now strip-mining vast lands that no one wanted at one time. We were forced at the point of a rifle. So, the traditional view is that we are a civilization, we are a sovereign people, we have our own form of government with imposed leadership. This is the difference, there is a split there. For years, the traditional form of government elected to ignore the elective process, and these people have gotten entrenched.

Through the fact the AIM has happened, we have provided an alternative voice, an alternative voice of action for Indian people. We have almost total support of the traditional people. Also the young people today can see what is happening. They have the vision as to what is happening to our nations and civilization. They see they are destroyed through practices of the Christian church, the anti-Indian concepts of education, and the federal bureaucracy. These are the three major enemies of the Indian people. We have identified them, and we know that in order to survive as a people we must go back to our lands. We must rebuild our tribal form of government, we must take control of our destiny and our future. We must control the Dick Wilsons across this country who are controlled by the Interior Department, the agency of government who has the trust, the protective status over our resources. This is the same agency of government that gives our leases to the mining companies, the strip-mining corporations, the power plants. And it is going to happen on the Cheyenne Reservation in Montana, and the Crow Agency Reservation. This is the enemy we have identified—the federal bureaucracy.

And so the traditional people cannot compromise. It is said by our leaders that we cannot hurt the sacred Mother Earth without hurting ourselves. We cannot compromise, we can no longer desecrate the earth if we are to survive as a people. We see the kinds of tribal government that's allied with the special interests, with the corporations of Washington government. We see these people along with whites, destroying the three basic elements of life: earth, air and water. They walk the path of destruction. We are saying, walk the path of destruction with the white people if you want to. But there are a lot of white people who realize that it is a fact and the truth, and they no longer want to walk the path to destruction. These are the people that we are appealing to.

I would like the people to understand that the AIM is not Dennis Banks and Russell Means and Vernon Bellecourt, or Leonard Crow Dog, but the American Indian Movement is the thousands and thousands of traditional, grass-roots elders on the reservations, the poor people who have had no voice, the poor people for whom nothing changes, but conditions continue to deteriorate. The American Indian Movement is the youth of our nation who have now seen that we must survive as a civilization, for if the redman is to perish, then, who deserves to live? This is what has been said by a woman by the name of Martha Graff, a traditional woman from Tonka City. She said that if the Great Spirit can be with us, who can be against us?

We have only to look at the information that has surfaced out of the socialist party, and, of course, the information has come out of CIA involvement. It has all been directly associated with the American Indian Movement and efforts to disrupt us.

Since Wounded Knee, all across the United States, on almost all reservations, and as I travel, people come up and tell me that almost every day the FBI has squads on reservations, interviewing and interrogating various people associated with the American Indian Movement in an effort to discourage these people from supporting our views. It is an effort to destroy the movement.

This is going on actively now and has been for two years on the Pine Ridge Reservation. The tribal chairman has his own vigilante squad, armed with automatic weapons most times, who have been spreading alcohol and drugs on the reservations. There have been up to forty unsolved murders of people who have been sympathetic or supporters of the American Indian Movement and through the urgings of the AIM, we have impaneled grand juries in South Dakota. This was a mistake because the grand jury system then is used as a political tool against Indian people. The only people that are getting indicted are people that are associated with the American Indian Movement. Yet, known killers and rapists, who have assaulted people on the reservations have not been indicted, and this is the kind of harassment that takes place. These latest warrants were out of one of these corrupt grand juries in South Dakota that brought the special squads of FBI agents on the reservations and eventually ended up in the shooting of a young Indian man. [The death of an

Indian man, Joe Killsright, was not mentioned when the press reported a shooting incident in which two FBI agents were also killed. Bellecourt felt that the incident in which two FBI agents were also killed occurred because of the continuing patterns of harassment by government officials at Pine Ridge.]

In order to put this into its proper perspective, we have to understand that the Bureau of Indian Affairs Police, along with the FBI, and we understand now that a State Highway Patrol Tactical Squad under the command of William Janklow (who ran on an election ticket to destroy the American Indian Movement and sided, of course, with anti-Indian racism in South Dakota) have mobilized probably a larger force than was even at Wounded Knee two years ago. The press for the most part has been censored. The information we have received is from direct sources, telephone conversations occurring last night and today. Much of the press, which is only getting the reports from the FBI office, would indicate to the American people that agents Ron Williams and Jack Coler are, in fact, martyrs, that they were innocent FBI agents who during the course of their duty, were gunned down without provocation. This is totally ridiculous.

One has to look at the fact that these two men are only part of a massive FBI force, that since Wounded Knee, not only on Pine Ridge but on other reservations all across this country, have been systematically interrogating, harassing, intimidating and in many cases, assaulting any native people that might share the philosophies of self-determination of the American Indian Movement.

Agent Ron Williams was the same agent who testified in the Wounded Knee trials of Dennis Banks and Russell Means, which everyone should know were dismissed by Federal Judge Fred Nichol on the basis of governmental misconduct. He very strongly criticized the FBI agents and their agency for questionable, if not illegal, acts of perjury. Ron Williams is the same agent that brought witness Louis Moves Camp into the courtroom in the closing days of the trial, encouraged this young man to perjure himself. He, in fact, did perjure himself on the witness stand. And the next involvement of Ron Williams was that he harbored Louis and did attempt to cover up a rape charge that was lodged against their key prosecution witness in Wisconsin.

These two men are only part of a force that has been on the Pine Ridge Reservation for two years now (since Wounded Knee) in an effort to turn off any kind of support for the American Indian Movement by the poor people on that reservation. They are the same force that has kept the imposed leadership of Dick Wilson and kept him in office on that reservation.

It is interesting to note the parallel. The fact that the United States government who supports the imposed leadership of Dick Wilson is the same United States government that supported the imposed leadership in Southeast Asia. The parallels are almost exact. The American Indian people have suffered under the worst form of colonialization, and the American Indian Movement is a struggle for self-determination and freedom and independence of people.

This is the root cause of what manifested—the killing of a young, eighteen-year-old man who was gunned down by agent Ron Williams (this comes from very reliable witnesses). In the ensuing gun battle these two murderers that had been disrupting homes on that reservation for some weeks were dispatched. The situation is at this time that because of the statements that I have heard from senators from South Dakota that a state of anarchy exists. It certainly has paved the way for the attorney general of that state to move in with his state Tactical Riot Squad to assume jurisdiction, and this has pretty much been the plot. They have illegally moved onto the reservation at Wagner, South Dakota, without jurisdiction, and, of course, we see it as another plot along with the FBI and the federal government to take control through state jurisdiction on those reservations.

This is a threat not only to the nations of South Dakota but of tribal leadership across this country. If it is allowed to happen here then, next, the government will be moving in on their reservations. There is a state of emergency that exists. We see the same kind of massive overreaction that we witnessed in Southeast Asia taking place right on the Pine Ridge Reservation against the sovereign people.

I think one of the major enemies of Indian people today is ignorance. We have an American society that has been kept ignorant about the facts of history. The educational system has polluted the minds of their children, either portraying us in an image of the proud and noble savage without any concern for the human suffering that continues today, or on the other hand, the John Wayne mentality or frontier mentality prevails in the minds of most Americans. They don't even care about Indian people. They either feel that we don't exist or we are museum pieces. And the whole concept has brought about a dehumanization of Indian people. Because of that, there is not the kind of broad concern that we have had for the violence in Vietnam. It is interesting to note the cultural conditioning fabric of the American white society. They do not even know that they are, in fact, racist against Indian people.

Indian people have been brutalized and murdered on reservations and off reservations for 483 years. We have termed it America's longest undeclared war, and the first time that FBI agents are shot, there is a sudden outcry across the country that they become martyrs. They become heroes in a sense. Now it provokes the FBI and the police authorities in this country for a massive crackdown on the people of Pine Ridge. This is our fear right now, and unless the American people become aware of what the facts are, become aware of the fact that we have a forty-three-year life expectancy, that infant mortality rates for 50,000 native people is five times the national average, that murders of Indians go unsolved, that the prisons of this country are ten-fifteen-twenty-thirty percent crammed with Indian people, until American people become aware of America's longest undeclared war, the war against native people, our lands, our ways of life, until they become aware of this, it is never going to change, and they will remain unconcerned.

"We have an American society that has been kept ignorant about the facts of history. . . . [Whites] do not even know that they are, in fact, racist against Indian people."

I think the thing that has to be considered by the people who are listening is how and why we have been tied up in the federal courts now for two years. First, they must realize that at Wounded Knee itself, we have brought about world attention by Indian people and non-Indians which is also very important. Our getting this attention is unfavorable to government bureaucracies.

One has to go back further to the Bureau of Indian Affairs seizure in Washington where we inadvertently occupied the Bureau building. At that time you must remember who was in power: Nixon, Haldeman, Erlichmann, Mitchell, and they started machinery against us through illegal wiretappings, disruption of the movement, provocateurs, and infiltrators. We just recently got word that the Rockefeller Commission (although we all know it's a cover-up) report indicates that the American Indian Movement is one of fourteen organizations whose phone calls are being monitored by the CIA, particularly European calls out of the country. This is a mass of conspiracy that was initiated in the White House and in the justice department, and the machinery has been put in motion, and now it continues against us.

We are now tied up in five different court rooms. We have the Wounded Knee Defense Committee defending Dennis Banks in the Custer cases. We have the Wounded Knee Defense Committee in Sioux Falls defending other people that are out of the Sioux Falls County Courthouse case where last year people refused to stand before a judge an the basis that they were beaten. We have the defense offices in Cedar Rapids, Iowa, defending and handling the appeal of Leonard Crow Dog. We are operating five offices dealing with five different courts, both federal and state, and this has been a tactic of the government to divide our resources. In fact, they have forced us into running out of money in defending ourselves.

Real help right now could come through awareness. People should become aware of what is going on in Pine Ridge, become aware of the American Indian Movement as a traditional, spiritual movement. We need funds as a reality to continue to fund our defense in the courts, and we would ask those that want to contribute to please contribute to the Wounded Knee Committee, P.O. Box 918, Council Bluffs, Iowa, and I think if they just send it to Wounded Knee Committee that anything would be deeply appreciated.

As for Clyde Bellecourt, after Wounded Knee he began to devote more of his time to AIM's "survival school" program. The purpose of these schools was twofold—to help Indian youngsters adjust to white society while preserving important features of their own culture and to counteract the distorted (and often negative) image of Indians common in many textbooks and in the popular media. Or, as Bellecourt himself once stated, "We wanted to teach our kids the truth about Indian people."

This sentiment was at the heart of a speech Clyde Bellecourt gave in Washington, D.C., on July 15, 1978, during a protest march known as The Longest Walk. The march had begun some five months earlier in San Francisco, and by the time it reached the nation's capital, it had grown to include demonstrators from the entire continent of North America. (Many celebrity activists were also in attendance, including Dick Gregory and Marlon Brando.) A notably peaceful—and even spiritual—event, it also ranks as one of the strongest displays of Indian unity in United States history. Bellecourt's remarks are reprinted here from Native American Reader: Stories, Speeches and Poems, *edited by Jerry D. Blanche (Denali Press, 1990).*

We want you to know that we are attempting to call attention to and to gain your support in turning back the anti-Indian attitude, the anti-Indian legislation, and the John Wayne mentality that exists among the media today. We are asking you to help us to stop these genocidal practices that are taking place against my people.

We'll stop nuclear power! We'll stop nuclear warfare around this world! We have the capability and the spiritual power. It is here, with us today!

We want you who have gathered here today to hear our story to know that it hasn't been easy. I joined this Sacred Walk, this spiritual march, in ceremonies that were taking place in Topeka, Kansas. We were aware at that time that the FBI, in collusion with the Community Relations Service of the United States Justice Department, had been in front of us and in back of us, flashing phony mug shots of supposed fugitives, criminals, people who escaped from jails. They were telling our support groups in front of us and in back of us that these were the type of people that were on the Walk.

The FBI has worked in every way possible. It parallels their efforts to destroy Martin Luther King, to destroy Malcolm X, to destroy the Black Panther Party, and to destroy the black civil rights movement in this country. But we have been able to overcome that through these sacred pipes, the sacred drum, and the ceremonies.

This is all we have left here. Our way of life. And it was told to us that if our drum was ever stilled, you too would be through as a nation.

In the Mormon religion that we have come in contact with throughout this march, they say among one part of that church that it is the Native people that will stand up. It is Native people that will offer survival to the rest of the world. It is Native people that will inherit this part of the world, this island. And these Mormon people that I talked to said that they too, in their scripture and their philosophy and their prophesies, knew that a great march was coming from the West, travelling East. No different from the prophesies of our great medicine men, our great spiritual leaders and holy men, that have passed on before us. They too talked about this generation.

They even identified the young people who came down from the North—from the East and the South and the West—that they would run ten, fifteen, twenty miles, long distances, each day to carry these sacred pipes. It was said that

Clyde Bellecourt

from among this generation, these young people you see gathered here today, would spring our leadership. The fifth generation is here among us. This is where our power is, and our strength. We are many great chiefs and great leaders, clan mothers, warriors, that have developed out of this spiritual walk and other occupations that have taken place for many, many years.

I would like to thank our younger brothers and sisters who have joined in to support our leadership. They support our chiefs that you see here among us. They support our women and they support our brothers and sisters who are in prisons and jails across this country.

In the state of Minnesota, we make up less than one half of one percent of the population, but ten percent of the inmate population is Indian and we do twenty percent of the time. We walk for our brothers and sisters and pray for our brothers and sisters who cannot be here with us today.

We walk also for our brother, Buddy Lamont, a Vietnam veteran who came home one of the most decorated warriors on the Pine Ridge Reservation. He came home and found the same armed forces that he fought with, surrounding his mother, his family, and his relatives on that reservation. We walk for this young warrior who came there and gave his life that we might live and that we might walk together again.

We walk for Pedro Bissonette, and Raymond Yellow Thunder, and the millions of Indian people who gave their lives that we might be given the opportunity to gather here to create, to build, to bring back the Old Ways, the ways of survival.

One of the greatest things I have seen coming out of this march is that I have had whole families come up to me from the ghettos that they have pushed us into through these relocation programs. They told me that they could not go back home after being on this walk, holding these sacred pipes. There is a deurbanization coming along. It will be for the survival of our youth and the survival of our unborn generations.

We ask each and every one of you to pray with us for the next four days. We want to meet your community, we want to talk to your people, and we want to change the image that has been portrayed by John Wayne, the media, and the history books. We want to portray the truth. We the Indian people, the Red Man of the Western Hemisphere, are the truth of the Western Hemisphere!

The Bellecourts are still very active in the movement to secure respect and justice for Native Americans. Most recently, they have been among those speaking out against sports teams that have Indian names or mascots (such as the Washington Redskins and the Atlanta Braves) on the grounds that the practice is racist and that it denigrates Native American people.

SOURCES

Books

Blanche, Jerry D., editor, *Native American Reader: Stories, Speeches and Poems,* Denali Press, 1990.

Maestas, John R., editor, *Contemporary Native American Address,* Brigham Young University, 1976.

Matthiessen, Peter, *In the Spirit of Crazy Horse,* Viking, 1983, new edition, 1991.

Nabokov, Peter, editor, *Native American Testimony: A Chronicle of Indian-White Relations from Prophecy to the Present, 1492-1992,* Penguin Books, 1991.

Voices from Wounded Knee, 1973: In the Words of the Participants, Akwesasne Notes, 1974.

Periodicals

Sporting News, "NFL Comes Under Protest," February 3, 1992, p. 13.

Mary McLeod Bethune

1875–1955

African American educator and civil rights activist

Mary McLeod Bethune—the founder and president of her own college, an advisor and friend to Franklin and Eleanor Roosevelt, and prominent clubwoman—was without a doubt one of the best-known and most respected women of the 20th century. She came of age at a time of great desperation and hardship for African Americans, and she personally had to overcome poverty and prejudice to make her dreams become reality. Her inspirational story was a familiar one to blacks as well as whites, for Bethune was an immensely popular speaker who lectured frequently before audiences large and small in towns and cities across the country. Employing a dignified yet very personable style that conveyed her energy, sincerity, and deep spirituality, she successfully used such public forums to advance the cause of racial harmony and equal opportunity.

A native of South Carolina, Bethune was the 15th of 17 children born to former slaves who farmed a small plot of land they purchased from their former owners after the Civil War. Barred from attending local public schools on account of her race, she received her elementary, secondary, and early college education at mission schools run by the Presbyterian Church. Bethune then continued her studies at Chicago's Moody Bible Institute with the idea of becoming a missionary but was rejected for such service in 1895 on the grounds that she was too young. So she began teaching instead, working at several small schools throughout the South before finally settling in Daytona Beach, Florida, in 1904.

There Bethune set about the daunting task of opening a school for the children of black construction workers who had been drawn to the area by the promise of steady employment on a major railroad project. The conditions she faced were dismal at best; most of her potential pupils lived amid squalor, crime, and the threat of racial violence, and few of their parents were interested in listening to her proposal. But she persevered and soon opened the Daytona Normal and Industrial School for Negro Girls. Its first home was a ramshackle old building that Bethune herself scrubbed and repaired with funds she raised by making pies, ice cream, and fried fish and selling the food to construction crews. Furniture and supplies were either homemade or salvaged from the garbage outside some of the city's resort hotels. Bethune also went door to door soliciting donations of all kinds from individuals, churches, clubs, and other groups.

In keeping with its founder's practical focus, the Daytona curriculum stressed basic knowledge of reading, writing, and arithmetic and vocational skills such as cooking and sewing. The school grew quickly in its first few years, and in 1907 Bethune purchased thirty-two acres of neighboring swamp and dump property, cleaned it up, and built several new buildings with secondhand material and labor provided by her students' fathers in exchange for tuition fees. Bolstered by slow but steady gains in enrollment, in 1928 the Daytona School merged with the Cookman Institute, a Jacksonville-based boys' school, to become Bethune-Cookman College.

Meanwhile, Bethune's vision and determination had brought her national prominence as an educator, particularly after she began approaching noted philanthropists and businessmen for badly-needed funding. She spent most of the 1930s in Washington, D.C., where she served as an advisor on minority affairs to President Franklin Roosevelt and worked closely with his wife, Eleanor, on a number of issues of interest to both women. In 1936, she took on an official government role as director of Negro affairs for the National Youth Administration, a position in which she supervised the development of recreational and vocational programs for young African Americans. During this same period, Bethune established and headed the National Council of Negro Women and worked with the National Association for the Advancement of Colored People, the National Urban League, and the Association for the Study of Negro Life and History. In addition, she was much in demand as a speaker and as a contributor to magazines and newspapers.

On June 30, 1933, Bethune met with members of the Chicago Women's Federation and delivered a speech on one of her favorite topics—the many achievements of black women. Her observations came at a time in history when years of dealing with Jim Crow laws and other repressive legislation had put African Americans on the defensive. To counter the racist images then so prevalent in society at large, many black women felt compelled to do all they could to convince others (especially white women) that they were decent and moral human beings who were worthy of respect. The following is an abridged version of Bethune's remarks taken from Black Women in White America: A Documentary History, *edited by Gerda Lerner (Pantheon Books, 1972).*

To Frederick Douglass is credited the plea that, "the Negro be not judged by the heights to which he is risen, but by the depths from which he has climbed." Judged on that basis, the Negro woman embodies one of the modern miracles of the New World.

One hundred years ago she was the most pathetic figure on the American continent. She was not a person, in the opinion of many, but a thing—a thing whose personality had no claim to the respect of mankind. She was a household drudge—a means for getting distasteful work done; she was an animated agricultural implement to augment the service of mules and plows in cultivating and harvesting the cotton crop. Then she was an automatic incubator, a producer of human live stock, beneath whose heart and lungs more potential laborers could be bred and nurtured and brought to the light of toilsome day.

Today she stands side by side with the finest manhood the race has been able to produce. Whatever the achievements of the Negro man in letters, business, art, pulpit, civic progress and moral reform, he cannot but share them with his sister of darker hue. Whatever glory belongs to the race for a development unprecedented in history for the given length of time, a full share belongs to the womanhood of the race. . . .

By the very force of circumstances, the part she has played in the progress of the race has

Mary McLeod Bethune

been of necessity, to a certain extent, subtle and indirect. She has not always been permitted a place in the front ranks where she could show her face and make her voice heard with effect.... [But] she has been quick to seize every opportunity which presented itself to come more and more into the open and strive directly for the uplift of the race and nation. In that direction, her achievements have been amazing....

Negro women have made outstanding contributions in the arts. Meta V.W. Fuller and May Howard Jackson are significant figures in fine arts development. Angelina Grimké, Georgia Douglass Johnson and Alice Dunbar Nelson are poets of note. Jessie Fausett has become famous as a novelist. In the field of music Anita Patti Brown, Lillian Evanti, Elizabeth Greenfield, Florence Cole-Talbert, Marian Anderson and Marie Selika stand out preeminently.

Very early in the post-emancipation period women began to show signs of ability to contribute to the business progress of the race. Maggie L. Walker, who is outstanding as the guiding spirit of the Order of Saint Luke ... in 1902 ... went before her Grand Council with a plan for a Saint Luke Penny Savings Bank. This organization started with a deposit of about eight thousand dollars and twenty-five thousand in paid-up capital, with Maggie L. Walker as the first woman bank president in America. For twenty-seven years she has held this place. Her bank has paid dividends to its stockholders; has served as a depository for gas and water accounts of the city of Richmond and has given employment to hundreds of Negro clerks, bookkeepers and office workers....

With America's great emphasis on the physical appearance, a Negro woman left her washtub and ventured into the field of facial beautification. From a humble beginning Madame C.J. Walker built a substantial institution that is a credit to American business in every way.

Mrs. Annie M. Malone is another pioneer in this field of successful business. The C.J. Walker Manufacturing Company and the Poro College do not confine their activities in the field of beautification, to race. They serve both races and give employment to both....

When the ballot was made available to the womanhood of America, the sister of darker hue was not slow to seize the advantage. In sections where the Negro could gain access to the voting booth, the intelligent, forward-looking element of the race's women have taken hold of political issues with an enthusiasm and mental acumen that might well set worthy examples for other groups. Oftimes she has led the struggle toward moral improvement and political record, and has compelled her reluctant brother to follow her determined lead. . . .

In time of war as in time of peace, the Negro woman has ever been ready to . . . [serve] . . . for her people's and the nation's good . . . during the recent World War . . . she . . . pleaded to go in the uniform of the Red Cross nurse and was denied the opportunity only on the basis of racial distinction.

Addie W. Hunton and Kathryn M. Johnson gave yeoman service with the American Expeditionary Forces . . . with the Y.M.C.A. group. . . .

Negro women have thrown themselves wholeheartedly into the organization of groups to direct the social uplift of their fellowmen . . . one of the greatest achievements of the race.

Perhaps the most outstanding individual social worker of our group today is Jane E. Hunter, founder and executive secretary of the Phillis Wheatley Association, Cleveland, Ohio.

In November, 1911, Miss Hunter, who had been a nurse in Cleveland for only a short time, recognizing the need for a Working Girls' Home, organized the Association and prepared to establish the work. Today the Association is housed in a magnificent structure of nine stories, containing one hundred thirty-five rooms, offices, parlors, a cafeteria and beauty parlor. It is not only a home for working girls but a recreational center and ideal hospice for the young Negro woman who is living away from home. It maintains an employment department and a fine, up-to-date camp. Branches of the activities of the main Phillis Wheatley are located in other sections of Cleveland, special emphasis being given to the recreational facilities for children and young women of the vicinities in which the branches are located.

In no field of modern social relationship has the hand of service and the influence of the Negro woman been felt more distinctly than in the Negro orthodox church. . . . It may be safely said that the chief sustaining force in support of the pulpit and the various phases of missionary enterprise has been the feminine element of the membership. The development of the Negro church since the Civil War has been another of the modern miracles. Throughout its growth the untiring effort, the unflagging enthusiasm, the sacrificial contribution of time, effort and cash earnings of the black woman have been the most significant factors, without which the modern Negro church would have no history worth the writing. . . .

Both before and since emancipation, by some rare gift, she has been able . . . to hold onto the fibres of family unity and keep the home one unimpaired whole. In recent years it has become increasingly the case where in many instances, the mother is the sole dependence of the home, and singlehanded, fights the wolf from the door, while the father submits unwillingly to enforced idleness and unavoidable unemployment. Yet in myriads of instances she controls home discipline with a tight rein and exerts a unifying influence that is the miracle of the century. . . .

The true worth of a race must be measured by the character of its womanhood. . . .

As the years have gone on the Negro woman has touched the most vital fields in the civilization of today. Wherever she has contributed she has left the mark of a strong character. The educational institutions she has established and directed have met the needs of her young people; her cultural development has concentrated itself into artistic presentation accepted and acclaimed by meritorious critics; she is successful as a poet and a novelist; she is shrewd in business and capable in politics; she recognizes the importance of uplifting her people through social, civic and religious activities; starting at the time when as a "mammy" she nursed the infants of the other race and taught him her meager store of truth, she has been a contributing factor of note to interracial relations.

Finally, through the past century she has made and kept her home intact—humble though it may have been in many instances. She has made and is making history.

Philosophically, Bethune in many ways bridged the gap between the conservatism of Booker T. Washington and the radicalism of W.E.B. Du Bois, two competing black leaders of the early twentieth century. Like Washington, she felt that it was essential for African Americans to obtain the kinds of job skills that would

bring them economic success. But she disagreed with the Tuskegee president on the subject of securing civil and social equality. Her position was more in line with that of Du Bois, who completely rejected the idea that blacks should wait patiently for whites to grant them their rights at some distant and undetermined future date. Bethune felt that both problems had to be tackled at once.

Displaying the skills of a diplomat, she learned to deal with whites on their terms without compromising her true beliefs, which were inclined to be somewhat more militant than she generally revealed in public to all-white or mixed-race audiences. In speaking to all black audiences, however, she took a stronger stance. In the following speech, delivered October 31, 1937, in Washington, D.C., at the annual meeting of the Association for the Study of Negro Life and History, Bethune challenged her listeners to make instilling race pride in young blacks a top priority. While this was a common theme in her addresses, her plea had a special urgency before this particular group. Also typical was her use of dramatic imagery to help make her point and establish a bond with her audience. Her remarks are reprinted here from the Journal of Negro History, *Volume 23, 1938.*

John Vandercook's *Black Majesty* tells the dramatic story of Jean Christophe, the black emperor of Haiti, and how he molded his empire with his bare hands out of the rugged cliffs and the unchained slaves of his native land. One night, in the midst of his Herculean struggles, Sir Home, his English adviser, accused him of building too fast and working his subjects like slaves until they were discontent. For a long moment Christophe was silent. . . . When he spoke, his full rich voice seemed suddenly old.

"You do not understand. . . ."

He stopped again, seemed to be struggling for words. Then he went on:

"My race is as old as yours. In Africa, they tell me, there are as many blacks as there are white men in Europe. In Saint Domingue, before we drove the French out, there were a hundred Negroes to every master. But we were your slaves. Except in Haiti, nowhere in the world have we resisted you. We have suffered, we have grown dull, and, like cattle under a whip, we have obeyed. Why? Because we have no pride! And we have no pride because we have nothing to remember. Listen!"

He lifted his hand. From somewhere behind them was coming a faint sound of drumming, a monotonous, weird melody that seemed to be born of the heart of the dark, rearing hills, that rose and fell and ran in pallid echoes under the moon. The King went on.

"It is a drum, Sir Home. Somewhere my people are dancing. It is almost all we have. The drum, laughter, love for one another, and our share of courage. But we have nothing white men can understand. You despise our dreams and kill the snakes and break the little sticks you think are our gods. Perhaps if we had something we could show you, if we had something we could show ourselves, you would respect us and we might respect ourselves."

"If we had even the names of our great men! If we could lay our hands"—he thrust his out—"on things we've made, monuments and towers and palaces, we might find our strength, gentlemen. While I live I shall try to build that pride we need, and build in terms white men as well as black can understand! I am thinking of the future, not of now. I will teach pride if my teaching breaks every back in my kingdom."

Today I would salute in homage that wise old emperor. I bring you again his vibrant message. Our people cry out all around us like children lost in the wilderness. Hemmed in by a careless world, we are losing our homes and our farms and our jobs. We see vast numbers of us on the land sunk into the degradation of peonage and virtual slavery. In the cities, our workers are barred from the unions, forced to "scab" and often to fight with their very lives for work. About us cling the ever-tightening tentacles of poor wages, economic insecurity, sordid homes, labor by women and children, broken homes, ill health, delinquency and crime.

Our children are choked by denied opportunity for health, for education, for work, for recreation, and thwarted with their ideals and ambitions still a-borning. We are scorned of men; they spit in our faces and laugh. We cry out in this awesome darkness. Like a clarion call, I invoke today again the booming voice of Jean Christophe:

"If we had something we could show you, if we had something we could show ourselves, you would respect us and we might respect ourselves. If we had even the names of our great men! If we could lay our hands on things we've made, monuments and towers and palaces, we might find our strength, gentlemen. . . ."

If our people are to fight their way up out of bondage we must arm them with the sword and the shield and the buckler of pride—belief in themselves and their possibilities, based upon a sure knowledge of the achievements of the past. That knowledge and that pride we must give them "if it breaks every back in the kingdom."

Through the scientific investigation and objective presentation of the facts of our history and our achievement to ourselves and to all men, our Association for the Study of Negro Life and History serves to tear the veil from our eyes and allow us to see clearly and in true perspective our rightful place among all men. Through accurate research and investigation, we serve so to supplement, correct, re-orient and annotate the story of world progress as to enhance the standing of our group in the eyes of all men. In the one hand, we bring pride to our own; in the other, we bear respect from the others.

> ***"If our people are to fight their way up out of bondage we must arm them with the sword and the shield and the buckler of pride—belief in themselves and their possibilities, based upon a sure knowledge of the achievements of the past."***

We must tell the story with continually accruing detail from the cradle to the grave. From the mother's knee and the fireside of the home, through the nursery, the kindergarten and the grade school, high school, college and university, through the technical journals, studies and bulletins of the Association, through newspaper, storybook and pictures, we must tell the thrilling story. When they learn the fairy tales of mythical king and queen and princess, we must let them hear, too, of the pharaohs and African kings and the brilliant pageantry of the Valley of the Nile; when they learn of Caesar and his legions, we must teach them of Hannibal and his Africans; when they learn of Shakespeare and Goethe, we must teach them of Pushkin and Dumas. When they read of Columbus, we must introduce the Africans who touched the shores of America before Europeans emerged from savagery; when they are thrilled by Nathan Hale, baring his breast and crying: "I have but one life to give for my country," we must make their hearts leap to see Crispus Attucks stand and fall for liberty on Boston Common with the red blood of freedom streaming down his breast. With the *Tragic Era* we give them *Black Reconstruction;* with Edison, we give them Jan Matzeliger; with John Dewey, we place Booker T. Washington; above the folk music of the cowboy and the hillbilly, we place the spiritual and the "blues"; when they boast of Maxfield Parrish, we show them E. Simms Campbell. Whatever man has done, we have done—and often, better. As we tell this story, as we present to the world the facts, our pride in racial achievement grows, and our respect in the eyes of all men heightens.

Certainly, too, it is our task to make plain to ourselves the great story of our rise in America from "less than the dust" to the heights of sound achievement. We must recount in accurate detail the story of how the Negro population has grown from a million in 1800 to almost 12 million in 1930. The Negro worker is today an indispensable part of American agriculture and industry. His labor has built the economic empires of cotton, sugar cane and tobacco; he furnishes nearly 12 percent of all American breadwinners, one-third of all servants, one-fifth of all farmers. In 1930, we operated 1,000,000 farms and owned 750,000 homes. Negroes operate today over 22,000 business establishments with over 27 million dollars in yearly receipts and payrolls of more than 5 million dollars. Negroes manufacture more than 60 different commodities. They spend annually for groceries over 2 billion dollars, a billion more for clothes, with total purchasing power in excess of 4 and one-half billion dollars. Negro churches have more than 5 million members in 42,500 organizations, owning 206 million dollars' worth of property and spending 43 million dollars a year. Some 360,000 Negroes served in the World War, with 150,000 of them going to France. Negroes are members of legislatures in 12 states; 3 or more states have black judges on the bench and a federal judge has recently been appointed to the Virgin Islands. Twenty-three Negroes have sat in Congress, and there is one member of the House at present. Under the "New Deal," a number of well qualified Negroes hold administrative posts.

Illiteracy has decreased from about 95 per cent in 1865 to only 16.3 per cent in 1930. In the very states that during the dark days of Reconstruction prohibited the education of Negroes by law, there are today over 2 million pupils in 25,000 elementary schools, 150,000 high school pupils in 2,000 high schools and 25,000 students in the more than 100 Negro colleges and universities. Some 116 Negroes have been elected to Phi Beta Kappa in white Northern colleges; over 60 have received the degree of Doctor of Philosophy from leading American universities and 97 Negroes are mentioned in *Who's Who in America*. It is the duty of our Association to tell the glorious story of our past and of our marvelous achievement in American life over almost insuperable obstacles.

From this history, our youth will gain confidence, self-reliance and courage. We shall thereby raise their mental horizon and give them a base from which to reach out higher and higher into the realm of achievement. And as we look about us today, we know that they must have this courage and self-reliance. We are beset on every side with heart-rending and fearsome difficulties.

Recently, in outlining to the president of the United States the position of the Negro in America, I saw fit to put it this way: "The great masses of Negro workers are depressed and unprotected in the lowest levels of agriculture and domestic service while black workers in industry are generally barred from the unions and grossly discriminated against. The housing and living conditions of the Negro masses are sordid and unhealthy; they live in constant terror of the mob, generally shorn of their constitutionally guaranteed right of suffrage, and humiliated by the denial of civil liberties. The great masses of Negro youth are offered only one-fifteenth the educational opportunity of the average American child."

These things also we must tell them, accurately, realistically and factually. The situation we face must be defined, reflected and evaluated. Then, armed with the pride and courage of his glorious tradition, conscious of his positive contribution to American life, and enabled to face clear-eyed and unabashed the actual situation before him, the Negro may gird his loins and go forth to battle to return "with their shields or on them." And so today I charge our Association for the Study of Negro Life and History to carry forward its great mission to arm us with the facts so that we may face the future with clear eyes and a sure vision. Our Association may say again with Emperor Jean Christophe: "While I live I shall try to build that pride we need, and build in terms white men as well as black can understand! I am thinking of the future, not of now. I will teach pride if my teaching breaks every back in my Kingdom."

Twelve years later, on October 29, 1949, Bethune addressed the same group, this time at their annual convention in New York City. On this occasion, she chose to look at African Americans "in retrospect and prospect." Having nearly reached the age of seventy-five, she reflected on the achievements of the past and looked forward with eagerness and optimism to still more changes she felt were just around the corner. Her speech is reprinted here from the Journal of Negro History, *Volume 35, 1950.*

A decade ago, or even five years ago, few would have predicted that the position of the Negro in world affairs would have attained its present significance. The world has been moving rapidly. Well might we pause, then, today to view the Negro in retrospect and prospect.

My splendid audience, here, will join with me in paying tribute to the builders of earlier days, who laid the foundation for today's advance. But we shall not stop over-long to praise our warriors, L'Ouverture and Peter Salem; our churchmen, Allen, Bryan and Garnet; our statesmen, Frederick Douglass and Grimké; or our educators, Booker T. Washington and Lucy Laney, for their greatest tribute, their greatest monument—the greatest monument to all our black heroes since the Negro first set foot in the New World—is the influence which you and I, my friends, are wielding in the world today.

Those of us who are a little older will recall that as we arrived at maturity and took our places as participants in the immediate world about us we quickly learned that we were regarded as a "problem." We spent our early years as adults with the term "Negro problem" dragging at our feet—slowing our steps.

Always we heard discussed the question of what the world's *controlling minority must do about us*. Always—in religion, in education, in employment, there it was—what must be done with the "Negro element?" The pattern of our education, for better or for worse, was worked out *for* us. Someone else decided what we should study, and, outside of the Negro denominations, where we should pray.

"Those of us who are a little older will recall that . . . we spent our early years as adults with the term 'Negro problem' dragging at our feet—slowing our steps."

We oldsters must take off our hats to ourselves, that through those trying years we did not lose sight of our objectives under the tremendous pressures exerted to induce us to accommodate ourselves to the acceptance of what was clearly illogical and untenable in human relations.

Out of the many fine developments of that period, that one fact stands out sharply—it was a period of pulling ourselves together; of girding our minds and our spirits for an aggressive struggle against the forces of reaction—of timorous people afraid of their future; afraid of their own form of government; afraid of their fellow men!

We recently went through a revival of the colonization projects and of panicky back-to-Africa proposals, with the Marcus Garvey movement gathering considerable strength among the frustrated of darker hue before it finally collapsed. We had already gone through the separate-as-the-fingers period in which paradoxically the growth of a great educational philosophy, paralleled in its initiation and development that of a less farsighted social philosophy of appeasement to separatists.

All this represented the thinking of those not yet grown up to the implications of a practicing democracy—to the implications of spiritual and social progress at a time when our country was assuming its place as a world power—was fast moving into position as *the greatest* of world powers!

This represented the days when we were outgrowing our twenties and thirties and forties—and some of us our fifties—when we began in larger numbers to pull to pieces this "Negro problem," this "color problem," to analyze its parts, to determine what manner of phenomenon was dogging our footsteps. We were determined to find out how much of this "problem," if any, was basic difference, and how much of it was suppression and inhibition and fear—and WHOSE!

These were the days when Negro leadership concluded at long last that what the Negro had to deal with, first and foremost, was not so much his own thinking as the stereotyped, nervous thinking of the world's non-colored minority! And with that conclusion the so-called "Negro problem" ceased to drag at our feet.

We took the pieces of that "problem" and spread them out on the conference table of the world. We looked at them dispassionately and objectively and said to the world:

"See here! Here is the difficulty! The difficulty is the hard, democratic way of life that you are unwilling to face; the way of life that is not for the self-satisfied or the indolent, or for the smug, or for the fearful who have faith only in themselves—but the only way that leads to peace, among neighbors or among nations."

And there came a period of transition in the world's thinking. The world began to worry about us—about what we "wanted"—which was a sign of progress. And we began to know more surely just what we wanted. It has been only five years since fourteen of us produced, on request, a volume of essays called *What the Negro Wants,* edited by our friend, Rayford W. Logan, and published by the University of North Carolina Press. In 344 pages of comment and analysis, eleven of which were mine, we succeeded in saying that we want precisely what everybody else wants, and find no good reason for being apologetic about it.

We were supposed to represent all shades of thought. What shade I was supposed to represent I do not know. But when we were all through itemizing our "wants" and laid them on the table, the only person remotely apologizing for that list was the publisher, and I doubt if his dissent convinced even himself of the value of further hedging!

How has "the Negro," as the term is used, arrived this close to unity? The answer might well be summarized in the reply of a leader who has retained his poise and objectivity, when asked for his opinion of a fellow Negro who had thrown his controls to the wind. It was simply a difference of reactions, he replied. We all want the same things. We all intend to get them. We've all been hurt, and the hurt affects us in different ways. That was a sensible, factual answer—a statement to which all citizens of the world must sooner or later face up. It reflects a healthy trend away from denunciation of those who have difficulty in functioning in the midst of racial pressures, and a growing will and desire to find a common denominator on which to base constructive, concerted action.

These hurts are sometimes very useful, and serve us better than we sometimes realize. They have drawn us together. They have drawn friends to us. They have made us organization-minded. They have solidified us and our organizations with the organizations of others, on an intelligently aggressive front.

The movement of the Negro worker from the farms of the South to industry, especially Northern industry, has increased his consciousness of the power of organization. He has been forced to observe the operation of unions—those which have excluded him as well as those which have welcomed him. He has watched his fellow workers bargaining for himself—on all fronts. He has learned that he, too, has resources of value. He has learned that when he offers his wares as an individual, he is a *peddler*. When he offers them as an organization, he is a *power!*

So, as the eyes of the Negro have opened to his own significance as a power, and the burden of his morale-destroying label as a "problem" has begun to fall away from him, his fellow Americans, his fellow citizens of the world, have begun to see the futility of attempting to keep him forever in bondage, in any kind of bondage, however polite the name by which it may be called—parallel culture, separate but equal, or racial integrity. And of the last mentioned it might be said that it is a theory practiced least by those who proclaim it most, with results in hybrid population which preclude argument!

We know that the franchise has not been extended solely from altruistic motives. But in an era of government by pressures, we have constantly improved our techniques in the application of pressures, and so have pushed back, steadily, the areas of unrepresentative government.

We may agree or disagree with any given cause or opinion, but the fact of growing unity

"The concept is rapidly gaining ground that [our] needs as first-class citizens are indistinguishable from the needs of any other first-class citizens, and that the objectives of all are identical."

of effort remains. Conscientious objectors picket the French Embassy to protest the imprisonment, in France, of another conscientious objector. There is a Negro among them. The steel workers bargain for increased benefits. There are many Negroes among them. The president of a great steel company comes out and talks with these workers, to get their views at first hand. Veterans, teachers, domestic workers, farm workers, university women, men and women of many interests, are united for service to humanity on many fronts. Negroes are a part of organizations representing all of these without racial distinction. And while there will be need for special effort by and with Negroes, to enable them to move fully and freely in the normal life of this country, which is *their* country, so long as any obstructions remain—the concept is rapidly gaining ground that their needs as first-class citizens are indistinguishable from the needs of any other first-class citizens, and that the objectives of all are identical.

All racial barriers, as such, may not fall, today or tomorrow, but they will not be able to stand long, before the determined advance of citizens of all races, shedding their cumbersome, outgrown racial complexes, in their march toward democratic living.

There have been some very interesting developments in this stretching out process. One of the most interesting has been the gradual disappearance of the one-spokesman concept. Negroes now listen with great respect, not to just one or two people who can "speak for" them, but to many people who speak with authority, not from pinnacles, but from vantage points gained by mingling, observing and working with the masses.

Consequently, their fellow citizens who are public servants, from the highest post in the land to the most obscure, also listen with respect, to a growing body of Negro leadership, which does not necessarily "think alike," on ways and means, but which holds with remarkable consistency to a common objective.

Trends in world affairs have broadened our vision of the world, and the world's vision of us, and have forced a larger measure of thinking upon the masses.

The terrible lessons of world conflict have educated all of us. The youth from our firesides, for whom we have worked and prayed and sacrificed, have gone to the ends of the earth to battle with other youth. *Where* did they go? For what *reason* did they go ? Will they have to go again? What influences are abroad in the world that keep the peoples of the world at one another's throats—that have made compulsory military service a normal expectancy for the youth of this generation? What can we do about these influences? What controls can we use?

And then the boys who lived to return to us—what were their observations and reactions to other parts of the world—to other peoples, some of whom we called "friends," some of whom we called "allies," some of whom we called "neutrals," and some of whom we called "enemies"—but all human beings, like ourselves, with special problems, about which, heretofore, we had not known too much, nor had been too much concerned?

It did something to us! It took us out of ourselves! We saw something bigger than we had before envisioned. Our thinking expanded and became less subjective. Our sphere of action broadened. We did not forget that we were Negroes, but the fact became less important, to us and to others.

The advent of the Atomic Age flattened out a great deal of race consciousness among all peoples. It eliminated at one sweep, the zones of "safe living"—the places where it was possible for one part of the world placidly to ignore any other part. Ideologies became more important than race. Mankind began regrouping itself around ideologies rather than around color. The mass of Negroes found in the democratic ideal, freedom to work out progress in an imperfect world.

The Negro press immediately recognized the scope of this enlarged interest, and met it by sending sage and seasoned writers to every corner of the globe to report their findings on social, economic and political functioning, in other world areas with heavily mixed populations.

Acceptance of our more cosmopolitan interests and growing economic strength is reflected in the advertising seen in publications slanted to Negro readers, and not infrequently in national publications slanted to all of Main Street. Negro mothers, Negro babies, Negro scientists, Negro skilled workers, Negro glamour girls, Negro athletes and entertainers greet one from advertisements promoting everything from baby food to automobiles—bidding for the dollars earned and spent by the darker brother.

This concession to our buying power did not just *happen*. It is the result of the skillful, persistent assembling and presentation of authentic data on the Negro by Negro advertising folk, to whom we may well take off our hats.

The concession to Negro buying power has been followed, and we say this advisedly, by concession to Negro thinking, power and influence through organizations in which Negroes have interest. In the academic world, administrators, teachers and taught have found that intellect, like disease, knows no barriers of race. Either it is there or it is not. If it is there, it should be available to all. To make it available to all, educational institutions in increasing numbers are seeking the best brains available in sciences, in the humanities, in the arts, to impart knowledge to those who seek it, regardless of the race of the scholar who possesses it.

In the academic world, the student, young or old—the serious seeker of truth and wisdom with which to live more adequately—is determinedly pushing aside the specious arguments of separation. He is saying that if he is to live successfully in a world of people whose origins are as varied as their complexions, he must know these people. In order to know them, he is seeking them out—seeking to enter schools known as "Negro schools." As many of us know, this is true in very many places even in the Deep South; and, contrary to superficial opinion, those who are applying are not "transplanted Yankees." For the most part they are sons and daughters of the South, girding themselves, understandingly for life in a changing world. At Howard University, in Washington, white students have registered this year from as far south as Houston, Texas, and as far north as Massachusetts—to learn and to learn to live.

Hardly any cause of consequence essays to go before the public, these days, without recognition of the influence of the Negro minority by acquisition of one or more Negro members on its staff to serve as liaison officers in contacts with special organizations.

A professional organization which has pointedly avoided Negroes in its membership, in spite of noteworthy achievements of Negroes in its field, suddenly becomes "Negro conscious" in the midst of a fight on social legislation of which it disapproves and hastily appoints a Negro to its directing body. It was an attempt to replace like color with like interests. And while the action will probably change few minds, its implications are food for thought—we are no longer PEDDLERS!

In the fight for civil rights led by the president of the United States, government has bowed to the inevitable. In some areas, it has bowed graciously; in other areas, grudgingly. But the few outposts that have undertaken to ignore or evade official directives, are clinging to another lost cause. "The Army," to quote one leading daily publication, "will continue to manufacture a Negro problem for itself, so long as it employs criteria of race rather than ability, anywhere along the line." And the same holds true for every branch of government and every phase of civilian life.

Without indulging in self-applause, we can very well turn for a brief moment at this point in our march forward and view, with a feeling of so-far-so-good, the gains we have made and held. As mature people we shall waste no time in over-admiration. Long stretches of the road to the full life we shall achieve still lie ahead. But we are traveling with our eyes open and our wits about us, and in traversing the unseen stretches ahead we shall have the benefit of techniques developed and proved in conquering the rough terrain behind.

As the Negro moves out in his newly-recognized capacity as a power to be reckoned with, it will be well to remember that not only courage but caution has a place in progress. The caution of which I speak does not mean fearfulness of new ideas, or of putting them into action. It means avoidance of the not-too-good American tendency of those too impatient, too emotion-swayed, or just too lazy-minded to weigh men and measures objectively, to brand, denounce and attack. We shall live more harmoniously if we learn to do without the cliches and shibboleths and catch-words which clutter and confuse our thinking.

I would caution that when the opportunity to advance a step presents itself, we should take that step and thank God for it, whether we consider the motive behind it to be dictated by love, by justice, or by expediency, provided only *that there is no booby-trap behind it!*

> ***"The one world toward which we are rapidly moving will not, I think, be a world of one race, or a world of one thought, but a world of mutual understanding, respect and tolerance . . ."***

The caution of which I speak would call for a more general facing of facts calmly and courageously. This great organization with which we are meeting, today, has pioneered, under the leadership of Carter Godwin Woodson, in providing us with many of the facts necessary to progress. My kind of caution would call for acceptance of the responsibility of being informed; for strengthening of moral character; for an increase in formal and informal education at the expense of personal sacrifice, as GI benefits wane. It would call for an increase in religion, not to "drown our sorrows," but to inspire our souls; not as an "opiate," but as a balance-wheel—as a recognition that mankind does not know all and will never know all, and does have and can rely upon a spiritual objective.

I firmly believe that the world is on its way toward greater unity, that this country is on its way to a fuller realization of democracy, and that the part of the Negro in both movements is one of increased strength and significance.

The one world toward which we are rapidly moving will not, I think, be a world of one race, or a world of one thought, but a world of mutual understanding, respect and tolerance, based on knowledge of ourselves and knowledge of our neighbors. In such a world as this we are entering, not race, but racial barriers will disappear, because in spite of DAR's, Gray Ladies, and other groups who avoid their fellow men, there will be too much work in the world to do for any group to waste time in building futile fences around the fears of economic or intellectual competition, or challenge to their self-assumed controls, which lead to their rigidity and keep them perpetually out of step with progress.

The progress of the world will call for the best that all of us have to give. And in giving it we shall continue to move on in the directions indicated by individual aptitudes and abilities, knowing that the world is gradually recovering from the long sickness of mind—the unbalance—which has heretofore kept its peoples living in little camps of isolation, intolerance and suspicion.

Whether or not possession of the atom bomb by this country or many countries will mean the end of civilization, only God knows. But I feel that we should daily rejoice in the certainty that it has caused many people to regard their neighbors—across the street and across the world—with a more friendly eye, and has marvelously stimulated fresh interest in the application of the Golden Rule.

I see no cause for discouragement, in viewing the years ahead. Democracy in this country is neither dead nor dying. As every mother knows, the pangs of childbirth are keenest just before the child is born. If our hurts are great, now; if our country is torn with controversy over the expansion of social responsibility, over the acceptance of civil rights, it is because a new and more powerful democracy is being born, to serve more greatly the people of all races, of this country, and of the world.

SOURCES

Books

Anderson, Judith, editor, *Outspoken Women: Speeches by American Women Reformers, 1635-1935,* Kendall/Hunt Publishing Company, 1984.

Boulware, Marcus H., *The Oratory of Negro Leaders: 1900-1968,* Negro Universities Press, 1969.

Halasa, Malu, *Mary McLeod Bethune,* Chelsea House, 1989.

Holt, Rackham, *Mary McLeod Bethune,* Doubleday, 1964.

Lerner, Gerda, editor, *Black Women in White America: A Documentary History,* Pantheon Books, 1972.

Periodicals

Ebony, "My Last Will and Testament," August, 1955, reprinted, November, 1990, pp. 128-134.

Journal of Negro History, "Clarifying Our Vision with the Facts," Volume 23, 1938, pp. 10-15; "The Negro in Retrospect and Prospect," Volume 35, 1950, pp. 9-19; "Mary McLeod Bethune," October, 1955, pp. 393-395.

Newsweek, "Faith in a Swampland," May 30, 1955, p. 47.

New York Times, May 19, 1955, p. 29.

Time, "Matriarch," July 22, 1946, p. 55.

Black Hawk (Ma-ka-tae-me-she-kia-kiah)

1767–1838

Native American chief of the Sauk (Sac) tribe

Black Hawk, whose lands stretched out on both sides of the Mississippi River around present-day Illinois and neighboring states, was one of a number of prominent Native American leaders who actively resisted the westward expansion of white settlements. Born in a Sauk village near the mouth of the Rock River in Illinois, he first distinguished himself as a warrior while still in his early teens and led his own war party at the age of only seventeen. Later, during the War of 1812, he allied himself with the British against the United States as part of his ongoing effort to undermine white migration. Black Hawk also worked for years to establish a loose coalition of other midwestern tribes threatened by America's growth in the hope that together they could mount a more successful challenge.

Claiming that Indians were usually pressured or tricked into signing away their lands (often while under the influence of alcohol furnished by whites), Black Hawk denounced each new treaty that allowed more settlers to move into Sauk territory. Despite his continued opposition, by 1831, after decades of conflict, most of his people had been forced west across the Mississippi into Iowa, where the less-fertile soil made farming more difficult. After watching the Sauks struggle to grow enough food to feed themselves, Black Hawk decided it was time to take back the land that had once been theirs.

In early April, 1832, the Sauk chief assembled his warriors for a special ceremony at which he delivered the following speech. Known as a spellbinding orator with the power to incite others to take action, Black Hawk tried to convince his listeners of the need to go to war against the whites by recalling the many ways in which they had hurt and deceived the Indian people. His words, as they were later recalled by a white prisoner who witnessed the event, are reprinted from W.C. Vanderwerth's Indian Oratory: Famous Speeches by Noted Indian Chieftains, *University of Oklahoma Press, 1971.*

Head-men, Chiefs, Braves and Warriors of the Sauks: For more than a hundred winters our nation was a powerful, happy and united people. The Great Spirit gave to us a territory, seven hundred miles in length, along the Mississippi, reaching from Prairie du Chien to the mouth of the Illinois river. This vast territory was composed of some of the finest and best land for the home and use of the Indian ever found in this country. The woods and prairies teemed with buffalo, moose, elk, bear and deer, with other game suitable to our enjoyment, while its lakes, rivers, creeks and ponds were alive with the very best kinds of fish, for our food. The islands in the Mississippi were our gardens, where the Great Spirit caused berries, plums and other fruits to grow in great abundance, while the soil, when cultivated, produced corn, beans, pumpkins and squash of the finest quality and largest quantities. Our children were never known to cry of hunger, and no stranger, red or white, was permitted to enter our lodges without finding food and rest. Our nation was respected by all who came in contact with it, for we had the ability as well as the courage to defend and maintain our rights of territory, person and property against the world. Then, indeed, was it an honor to be called a Sauk, for that name was a passport to our people traveling in other territories and among other nations. But an evil day befell us when we became a divided nation, and with that division our glory deserted us, leaving us with the hearts and heels of the rabbit in place of the courage and strength of the bear.

All this was brought about by the long guns, who now claim all our territory east of the Mississippi, including Saukenuk, our ancient village, where all of us were born, raised, lived, hunted, fished and loved, and near which are our corn lands, which have yielded abundant harvests for an hundred winters, and where sleep the bones of our sacred dead, and around which cluster our fondest recollections of heroism and noble deeds of charity done by our fathers, who were Sauks, not only in name, but in courage and action. I thank the Great Spirit for making me a Sauk, and the son of a great Sauk chief, and a lineal descendant of Nanamakee, the founder of our nation.

The Great Spirit is the friend and protector of the Sauks, and has accompanied me as your war chief upon the warpath against our enemies, and has given me skill to direct and you

Black Hawk

the courage to achieve a hundred victories over our enemies upon the warpath. All this occurred before we became a divided nation. We then had the courage and strength of the bear, but since the division our hearts and heels are like those of the rabbit and fawn. We have neither courage or confidence in our leaders or ourselves, and have fallen a prey to internal jealousies and petty strifes until we are no longer worth of the illustrious name we bear. In a word, we have become subjects of ridicule and badinage "there goes a cowardly Sauk." All this has resulted from the white man's accursed firewater united with our own tribal quarrels and personal jealousies. The Great Spirit created this country for the use and benefit of his red children, and placed them in full possession of it, and we were happy and contented. Why did he send the palefaces across the great ocean to take it from us? When they landed on our territory they were received as long-absent brothers whom the Great Spirit had returned to us. Food and rest were freely given them by our fathers, who treated them all the more kindly on account of their weak and helpless condition. Had our fathers the desire, they could have crushed the intruders out of existence with the same ease we kill the bloodsucking mosquitoes. Little did our fathers then think they were taking to their bosoms, and warming them to life, a lot of torpid, half-frozen and starving vipers, which in a few winters would fix their deadly fangs upon the very bosom that had nursed and cared for them when they needed help.

From the day when the palefaces landed upon our shores, they have been robbing us of our inheritance, and slowly, but surely, driving us back, back, back towards the setting sun, burning our villages, destroying our growing crops, ravishing our wives and daughters, beating our papooses with cruel sticks, and brutally murdering our people upon the most flimsy pretenses and trivial causes.

Upon our return to Saukenuk from our winter hunting grounds last spring, we found the palefaces in our lodges, and that they had torn down our fences and were plowing our corn lands and getting ready to plant their corn upon the lands which the Sauks have owned and cultivated for so many winters that our memory cannot go back to them. Nor is this all. They claim to own our lands and lodges by right of purchase from the cowardly and treacherous Quashquamme, nearly thirty winters ago, and drive us away from our lodges and fields with kicks of their cruel boots, accompanied with vile cursing and beating with sticks. When returning from an ill-fated day's hunt, wearied and hungry, with my feet stumbling with the weight of sixty-four winters, I was basely charged by two palefaces of killing their hogs, which I indignantly denied because the charges were false, but they told me I lied, and then they took my gun, powder-horn and bullet-pouch from me by violence, and beat me with a hickory stick until blood ran down my back like drops of falling rain, and my body was so lame and sore for a moon that I could not hunt or fish. They brought their accursed firewater to our village, making wolves of our braves and warriors, and the when we protested against the sale and destroyed their bad spirits, they came with a multitude on horseback, compelling us to flee across the Mississippi for our lives, and then they burned down our ancient village and turned their horses into our growing corn.

They are now running their plows through our graveyards, turning up the bones and ashes of our sacred dead, whose spirits are calling to us from the land of dreams for vengeance on the despoilers. Will the descendants of Nanamakee and our other illustrious dead stand idly by and suffer this sacrilege to be continued? Have they lost their strength and courage, and become squaws and papooses? The Great Spirit whispers in my ear, no! Then let us be again united as a nation and at once cross the Mississippi, rekindle our watchfires upon our ancient watchtower, and send forth the warwhoop of the again united Sauks, and our cousins, the Masquawkees, Pottawattamies, Ottawas, Chippewas, Winnebagos and Kickapoos, will unite with us in avenging our wrongs upon the white pioneers of Illinois.

"They are now running their plows through our graveyards, turning up the bones and ashes of our sacred dead, whose spirits are calling to us from the land of dreams for vengeance . . ."

When we recross the Mississippi with a strong army, the British Father will send us not only guns, tomahawks, spears, knives and ammunition in abundance, but he will also send us British soldiers to fight our battles for us. Then will the deadly arrow and fatal tomahawk hurtle through the air at the hearts and heads of the pale-faced invaders, sending their guilty spirits to the white man's place of endless punishment, and should we, while on the warpath, meet the Pauguk, our departing spirits will be led along that path which is strewn with beautiful flowers, laden with the fragrance of patriotism and heroism, which leads to the land of dreams, whence the spirit of our fathers are beckoning us on, to avenge their wrongs.

On April 5, 1832, soon after delivering this speech, Black Hawk led his supporters east across the Mississippi, ostensibly to plant some corn but also prepared to fight any whites who challenged their right to do so. They did not have to wait long; attacked by a hastily-assembled contingent of U.S. Army troops, the Sauk chief and his warriors battled back successfully and then headed north into Wisconsin, touching off what became known as the Black Hawk War. On July 21, they again confronted U.S. soldiers, this time a much larger and better-prepared group that killed many of the Sauk warriors over the following weeks. With his hoped-for escape route down the Mississippi blocked, Black Hawk found himself trapped in northern Wisconsin. On August 27, after being captured by some members of the Winnebago tribe, he reluctantly agreed to surrender. It is believed he made the following speech at the time he was turned over to U.S. government authorities in Prairie du Chien. The text is reprinted from Literature of the American Indian *by Thomas E. Sanders and Walter W. Peek, Glencoe Press, 1973.*

You have taken me prisoner with all my warriors. I am much grieved, for I expected, if I did not defeat you, to hold out much longer, and give you more trouble before I surrendered. I tried hard to bring you into ambush, but your last general understands Indian fighting. The first one was not so wise. When I saw that I could not beat you by Indian fighting, I determined to rush on you, and fight you face to face. I fought hard. But your guns were well aimed. The bullets flew like birds in the air, and whizzed by our ears like the wind through the trees in winter. My warriors fell around me; it began to look dismal. I saw my evil day at hand. The sun rose dim on us in the morning, and at night it sank in a dark cloud, and looked like a ball of fire. That was the last sun that shone on Black Hawk. His heart is dead, and no longer beats quick in his bosom. He is now a prisoner to the white men; they will do with him as they wish. But he can stand torture, and is not afraid of death. He is no coward. Black Hawk is an Indian.

"The white men do not scalp the head; but they do worse—they poison the heart. . . ."

He has done nothing for which an Indian ought to be ashamed. He has fought for his countrymen, the squaws and papooses, against white men, who came, year after year, to cheat them and take away their lands. You know the cause of our making war. It is known to all white men. They ought to be ashamed of it. The white men despise the Indians, and drive them from their homes. But the Indians are not deceitful. The white men speak bad of the Indian, and look at him spitefully. But the Indian does not tell lies; Indians do not steal.

An Indian who is as bad as the white men, could not live in our nation; he would be put to death, and eaten up by the wolves. The white men are bad schoolmasters; they carry false looks and deal in false actions; they smile in the face of the poor Indian to cheat him; they shake them by the hand to gain their confidence, to make them drunk, to deceive them, and ruin our wives. We told them to let us alone, and keep away from us; but they followed on and beset our paths, and they coiled themselves among us like the snake. They poisoned us by their touch. We were not safe. We lived in danger. We were becoming like them, hypocrites and liars, adulterers. Lazy drones, all talkers, and no workers.

We looked up to the Great Spirit. We went to our great father. We were encouraged. His great council gave us fair words and big promises; but we got no satisfaction. Things were growing worse. There were no deer in the forest. The opossum and beaver were fled; the springs were drying up, and our squaws and papooses without victuals to keep them from starving; we called a great council and built a large fire. The spirit of our fathers arose and spoke to us to avenge our wrongs or die. We all spoke before the council fire. It was warm and pleasant. We set up the war-whoop, and dug up the tomahawk; our knives were ready, and the heart of Black Hawk swelled high in his bosom when he led his warriors to battle. He is satisfied. He will go to the world of spirits contented. He has done his duty. His father will meet him there, and commend him.

Black Hawk is a true Indian, and disdains to cry like a woman. He feels for his wife, his children and friends. But he does not care for himself. He cares for his nation and the Indians. They will suffer. He laments their fate. The white men do not scalp the head; but they do worse—they poison the heart; it is not pure with them. His countrymen will not be scalped, but they will, in a few years, become like white men, so that you can't trust them, and there must be, as in the white settlements, nearly as many officers as men, to take care of them and keep them in order.

Farewell, my nation! Black Hawk tried to save you, and avenge your wrongs. He drank the blood of some of the whites. He has been taken prisoner, and his plans are stopped. He can do no more. He is near his end. His sun is setting, and he will rise no more. Farewell to Black Hawk.

Taken to Washington as a prisoner, Black Hawk met with President Andrew Jackson, who chided him for going to war against the whites. He was then sent on a tour of several major cities, including New York, Philadelphia, and Baltimore, so that he could see for himself how big and powerful his enemy truly was. While the exposure gave him celebrity status and led to the publication of his autobiography in 1833, it also had the desired effect of convincing him of the futility of struggling against the westward push of white civilization. Eventually, he and the rest of the Sauk people were relocated to a reservation near present-day Des Moines, Iowa. There Black Hawk died in 1838, stripped of his rank as chief as a result of the disastrous Black Hawk War. Later, his bones were unearthed and put on display in a local museum that was destroyed by fire in 1853.

SOURCES

Armstrong, Virginia Irving, compiler, *I Have Spoken: American History Through the Voices of the Indians,* Sage Books, 1971.

Black Hawk, *Life of Black Hawk* (reprint of 1833 autobiography), Dover, 1994.

Jones, Louis Thomas, *Aboriginal American Oratory: The Tradition of Eloquence Among the Indians of the United States,* Southwest Museum (Los Angeles), 1965.

McLuhan, T.C., *Touch the Earth: A Self-Portrait of Indian Existence,* Outerbridge & Dienstfrey, 1971.

Rosenstiel, Annette, *Red and White: Indian Views of the White Man, 1492-1982,* Universe Books, 1983.

Sanders, Thomas E., and Walter W. Peek, *Literature of the American Indian,* Glencoe Press, 1973.

Vanderwerth, W.C., *Indian Oratory: Famous Speeches by Noted Indian Chieftains,* University of Oklahoma Press, 1971.

Witt, Shirley Hill, and Stan Steiner, editors, *The Way: An Anthology of American Indian Literature,* Knopf, 1972.

Tony Bonilla

1936–

Mexican American attorney and civil rights activist

A native of Calvert, Texas, Tony Bonilla was just a child when he first experienced the sting of racial and ethnic prejudice. In his rural hometown, Hispanics and blacks lived and worked together, separated by a highway and a set of railroad tracks from the whites who shunned both groups. As a result, he developed a kinship with African Americans that in later years prompted him to work at forging alliances between Hispanics and blacks in a mutual quest for social, economic, and political justice.

After graduating from high school, Bonilla went on to Del Mar College on a football scholarship and earned his associate's degree. He then obtained his bachelor's degree at Baylor University in 1958 and his law degree at the University of Houston in 1960. A specialist in personal injury litigation, he has been in private practice for many years with one of his brothers and several other partners.

Outside the courtroom, Bonilla has devoted a great deal of his time to various political and civil rights causes. He served for three years in the Texas state legislature during the mid-1960s and since then has been appointed to several special posts in the state government, including the Coordinating Board for Texas Colleges and Universities, the Texas Constitutional Revision Committee, the Governor's Select Committee on Public Education, and the Advisory Committee on the Spanish-Speaking Population for the 1980 Census. But Bonilla has made his most significant mark in key roles with the League of United Latin American Citizens (LULAC) during the early 1970s and again in the early 1980s and, more recently, as the longtime president of the National Hispanic Leadership Conference.

As LULAC's executive director from 1972 until 1975 followed by a stint as its president from 1981 until 1983, Bonilla was a national spokesman for the Hispanic community on social, political, and civil rights issues, economic affairs, and education. He also broke new ground by fostering more cooperation between Hispanics and blacks in the belief that together they presented a much more potent political and social force for change. Working with him on many occasions was Jesse Jackson, who later expanded on their efforts to form the so-called "Rainbow Coalition" during his 1984 bid for the Democratic presidential nomination.

In February, 1983, Jackson's Operation PUSH organization presented Bonilla with an award for the many bridges he had built between LULAC and

Operation PUSH. At the ceremonies, which were held in Chicago during Harold Washington's historic campaign to become the city's first black mayor, Bonilla accepted the honor and then launched into a colorful and spirited assessment of the benefits of forming such coalitions. The following speech was transcribed from an audiotape provided by Bonilla.

Thank you very much, Reverend Jesse Jackson. And thank you, ladies and gentlemen, for your presence here this morning on this very historic occasion, for it is the first time in the history of our nation that any black group has taken time out to honor a Hispanic citizen of a national level.

I have a number of things to say to you this morning, and to share some thoughts that I've wrestled with over the past several months. But because we have such a distinguished visitor with us who *will* be the next mayor of this city, I wanted to introduce him first so that he could proceed to his other scheduled activities for today and then, with your permission, come back and give you my thoughts.

When I was last here, I said that we have to practice what we preach. And if we're going to talk about coalescing between blacks and Hispanics, then at some point, some point, we have to bite the bullet and show our commitment and take that first step to show the way to the rest of the black and Hispanic community in this nation that it *can* be done, that it *will* be done, and that it *must* be done.

After that endorsement, I received calls from some friends in Chicago questioning my sanity. What am I doing getting involved in Chicago politics? And how could I join Jesse Jackson, Harold Washington, and others in this endeavor? In fact, at least one of them suggested that I call in sick! Well, I *ain't* sick! And I *ain't* crazy!

We know, ladies and gentlemen, brothers and sisters, when we're getting ripped off. And it's happening here in Chicago. And if we ever want to change, now's the time to do it.

Therefore, I'd like to present to you—with a reassurance to you, Mayor Byrne—that I made an endorsement to support Harold Washington for mayor. That that commitment is firm. That that commitment is irrevocable. And that we are asking our Hispanic, our black, and other people of goodwill to join us in getting political, economic freedom for our people.

Tony Bonilla

[Bonilla then introduced Harold Washington and, after a brief pause in the proceedings, resumed his speech.]

Thank you very much again, Reverend Jesse, and you, ladies and gentlemen, for your very warm reception. We know we're at the PUSH headquarters when they send us notes to move a Toyota and not a Cadillac!

I want to acknowledge the presence from California of Dr. Jésus Chavaria, who is the publisher of the *Hispanic Business* magazine. He is committed to the goal of getting corporate parity and not charity, and I wanted you to take a bow, Jésus Chavaria. Back here in the back? You know, Jésus, it looks bad for an Hispanic to be in a black church and sitting on the back row!

First thing you know, they're gonna start calling us backsliders.

I also want to acknowledge the presence of Bob and Linda Alvarado. Bob is the national president of the Contractor's Association, and they want a piece of the action, too.

When Jesse came to California, he brought Mike with him. Where is Mike? Stand up, Mike—everybody look at you one more time. Mike has been a big help to us. And I said, "Well, if he can bring his Hispanic friends with him, I ought to at least be able to bring my black friends with me." So I brought with me my closest, personal friend, who is a former professional football player with the Buffalo Bills—Cookie Gilchrist and Jack Kemp were in the same backfield, and he was the starting halfback—Bobby Smith. You look at Bobby now, you'd think he used to play tackle!

I also have with us Dr. Sal Gómez, an MD, who's come all the way from California to be with us.

And we have from Texas, the national director of publicity, Leo Barrera.

We have Hispanics here from not only California and Colorado and Texas, but Indiana and Wisconsin and other points in between because they see this as an historic day. And I think, in order to put things in proper perspective, perhaps I should share a little story with you about a fisherman who used to like to go out to the lake in south Texas. And he used to like to take sticks of dynamite with him when he'd row out there in his boat. He'd light up the stick of dynamite and throw it into the lake and kill a bunch of fish—they'd just come right on up and he'd get his net, scoop 'em right up, and put 'em into his boat. Had a fine way of fishin'.

One day, he decided to invite his cousin to go with him. They rowed out there into the middle of the lake. He lit the stick of dynamite and threw it into the water, and the fish came up. He scooped 'em up and put 'em into his boat.

His cousin looked at him. And he said to the fisherman, "You know, I'm a game warden. And it's interesting the way you catch these fish, but it's illegal. And I'm gonna have to take you in, 'cause you've violated the law."

So the fisherman looked at him. He lit another stick of dynamite and handed it to him, and he says, "D'you wanna fish or d'you wanna talk?"

So today what I want to do is do a little fishin' and talkin'.

When I came to Chicago a couple of weeks ago and made an appearance here, people said, "Who is Tony Bonilla? Who does he think—coming into Chicago and messin' in internal politics here? And what's he talkin' about dealing with blacks? Blacks are our enemies!"

And I said to myself—and perhaps the first thing I should do is tell the people here, the multitudes gathered here and those listening on the radio, that Tony Bonilla was born in Calvert, Texas. That Calvert, Texas, had a highway that ran right through the heart of the city and a railroad track that ran parallel to it. And all the blacks and Hispanics lived on one side of the track. And all the whites lived on the other side of the track. So I was raised with the black people.

When I was a senior in high school, in my hometown, I couldn't get a haircut in the white-owned barber shop. In fact, my barber was a black. My first girlfriend was a black. I picked cotton with the blacks. We hauled watermelons together. We chopped cotton together.

My dad was a Mexican national, as was my mother. And they came to this country not knowing how to read, write, or speak the English language. They worked like slaves seven days a week from sunup to sundown. And ladies and gentlemen, brothers and sisters, it was the black community in my hometown of Calvert that made it possible for all eight children to go to college, for four of us to become lawyers, for two of them to become schoolteachers, and for two of them to go into business. So I've never forgotten my roots. I'm *supposed* to be here today, Jesse Jackson. And Jesse and I are *supposed* to work together. The Lord's spirit is among us. And we know that. And there is no stopping us.

Someone shared a story with me recently. Talked about the man who was asleep. And in his sleep, he had a dream. And his whole life came upon the scene. He saw himself walking with the Master on the beach. They were walking together throughout his life. And as he looked back over his life, he noticed that there were two sets of footprints. And the Lord was always with him. But as he neared the end of his life in his dream, he saw, in looking back, that there were some times when there was only one set of footprints. And that really concerned him and he says in his sleep, "Master, Master, it worries me that during the time that I was weakest, during the time that I was the most troubled, hungry, when I was perturbed and fighting with myself and needed help, there was only one set of footprints in the sand. It troubles me, Master, that I don't see two sets of footprints."

The Master says to him, "My son, my son, I would not forget you. I love you. It was during the time that you saw that one set of footprints—that you were weak and hungry and tired and needed help—that you only see one set of footprints, my son, because that's when I was carrying you."

What we feel in LULAC and what we feel in PUSH sometimes is we travel across the country with a heavy burden of helping people whose rights have been denied, whose heads have been beaten. It's been our burden to carry our people and only leave one set of footprints sometime.

As we travel across the country, we find our people on board a boat with no rudder. The sails are down, and the boat is floating in a sea of confusion. We don't condemn those on board that boat—we condemn the system that left us no rudder. We don't condemn our people, but the system that encourages division and confusion. You know, the system may provide us housing for our bodies but not for our souls.

So we pray, then, for understanding among our people. To learn to look at things not just from the standpoint of our own neighborhoods, but to look at a much broader picture from the standpoint of what's right for the country and our people who live in that country. To look at things not just for today and right now, but to look for the needs and concerns of the future generations of our people. To look at things not just as they are, but to look at things as how they ought to be. And it's up to us—PUSH and LULAC, black and Hispanic—to provide our own rudders, to lift up our own sails, and to steer our boat to the tranquil sea of opportunity.

When you pick up the *Chicago* magazine and they say, "The New Majority—How Will Blacks and Hispanics Vote?" you know we've arrived because they're worried about what we're gonna do. And they *ought* to be worried!

PUSH and LULAC got together and decided to look at a few figures. We found out that when you start thinkin', talkin', about 39,700 of the top positions in city government—and by the way, Jesse, you gave me one in Spanish, man. Give me one in English! I can *read* Spanish, but I can *understand* English better! What this study shows, brothers and sisters, and we just looked at a few—yeah, they don't even say I'm bilingual, they say I'm bi-illiterate, can't speak in any language! What this study shows—and we only looked at eleven departments—39,000 jobs. We've been shortchanged.

You know how many Hispanics work, on the average, for the city of Chicago? Four percent. Seventeen percent population, four percent. It's *disgusting!*

You know how many blacks usually work for the city on the average? Twenty percent. If you look at the statistics, then, of the highest-paying jobs in the city, the statistics get worse and not better.

In fact, the highest number of Hispanics and blacks are working in the positions that pay nineteen thousand [dollars] or less, Reverend Jesse. You get to the positions that pay thirty-five, forty thousand—those good, nice, sweet positions—and you will not find us there by a very large number.

And it's just not employment, which is so basic. We're also talkin' about contract procurement and services. In '79, '80, '81, the city let 1.4 billion dollars in contacts. And the minorities, the minorities—they won't even tell us which minorities, black or Hispanic, they lumped us together then—and they said, "Minorities got 860,000 of 1.4 billion dollars." They're doin' us a big favor, takin' care of their friends in high places.

And we look at those statistics and if you look at the jobs, it should be balanced. We have forty percent black population, seventeen percent Hispanic population—there ought to be forty percent of the jobs in the city for blacks, seventeen percent for Hispanics. If you look at those statistics, we've been robbed out of a hundred and sixty million dollars! If you look at the statistics in procurement and services, Hispanics should be having two hundred million dollars in contracts based on our seventeen percent. And blacks should be having somewhere around five or six hundred million dollars in contracts.

So those people in the Hispanic and black community who are supporting the other candidates, you'd better start thinkin' twice!

When we hear the politicians talk, we're reminded of the old Elvis Presley tune. You know, when they run for office, they always say, "Love me tender, love me true, never let me go." Is that right? As soon as the election's over, they put the flip side on and say, "You ain't nothin' but a hound dog."

Well, we're gonna have our own song! Our song's gonna be, "We ain't gonna play that game no more." And if there hasn't been one written, I want somebody to write it.

What does all this mean to us? Maybe I can relate it more in a biblical sense since we're in God's house and there are some ministers here and God-fearing people who are listening and in the audience. We all know the story about the prodigal son—the father who had his two sons, and one of 'em wanted all his money and wanted to take off. And he got all his money. He went off and had a good time. Went out to the best country club, we can assume. Had all kind of pretty women. Lived a wicked way, it says in the Bible. Then he lost it all. Ended up going back to feed the swine. He got to thinkin' about it. "Hey, this ain't no good. My servants back home with my daddy are doin' better than I am. I'd better go home." So what he did, then, he went back home, and we know the rest of the story—that the father killed a fatted calf and had a big feast. People asked him why, and he said, "Because my son was lost and he's been found." What we're saying, then, to our people is it's time our people came home.

Blacks and Hispanics who have been denied economic opportunity—gotta come home. Blacks and Hispanics who do not enjoy political freedom must come home. Blacks and Hispanics who are successful, who rub elbows with the big politicians and belong to the best clubs, have forgotten their roots—they've got to come home. Hispanics and blacks who have received token appointments when there are much bigger plums to pluck from that tree of opportunity—got to come home. Hispanics and blacks who have become wealthy because our people have made them wealthy have got to come home. Hispanics and blacks who are fightin' each other, even today as I stand here, have got to stop fightin' and come home. When they come home, we can have our *own* feast.

You know what Jesse said? He said, "Tony, they've been givin' us a ham all this time and we're entitled to the whole hog!" And when he told me that, he said, "You know, Tony, a hog has two hams, and I believe two shoulders and four feet." Jesse never did mention the head. Well, I want you to know, *we* want the head, because that's what we make tamales from!

When you look at the candidates for mayor who fed us these crumbs for the past many years—people fightin' each other to decide who wants to be the fair-haired buddy of the candidate, the mayor in power. You think in terms of how we've been kicked on, stepped over. We say, today, to those who are listenin'—hopefully, Mayor Byrne and Richard Daley [are] both listenin'—I know Harold is. As far as we're concerned, Richard Daley represents a relic of the past. Mayor Byrne represents the evil of the present. And Harold Washington represents the hope of the future.

People ask, "Why do you care about what happens in Chicago?" And we say, "Because Chicago is a mirror of America. Chicago sets the tone for the way people react toward blacks and Hispanics. If they can divide us by drivin' a wedge between us in Chicago, they'll do it in Los Angeles. They'll do it in Miami. They'll do it all over the world, all over the country." You see, we recognize that in Chicago—Chicago is the straw, as Reggie Jackson says, that stirs the drink.

So it's important for us to be here. And to remind the people that the machine has dominated us for too long. We've given you these statistics and it shows clearly that the machine is denying us economic opportunity. One of the machine candidates has already suggested that our people go back to Mexico. Well, I tell you, if he wants us to go back to Mexico, we don't have to go no further than Colorado 'cause that's all ours anyway!

But you know what's happening, brothers and sisters. When you hear this man say to us, "Go back to Mexico," I'm waiting for the mayor of this great city in America to stand up and say, "I censure you for making a racist statement against seventeen percent of our population." I'm waiting for Richard Daley to say it. Because we can't have that kind of attitude running the government that's supposed to be our friend.

It took a lawsuit in federal court to get us—to try to get us—integration because the machine stood in the way. It took a lawsuit in fed-

> ***"One of the candidates has already suggested that our people go back to Mexico. I tell you, if he wants us to go back to Mexico, we don't have to go no further than Colorado 'cause that's all ours anyway!"***

eral court to try to get us representation at the city council level because the machine stood in the way of equal representation for blacks and Hispanics. It was the machine that kept Juan Soliz off the ballot, and it was the machine that led the fight to defeat him when he *did* get on the ballot. Stand up, Juan. Juan didn't forget. His memory's not short. And he's with Harold Washington.

You see, the danger is that what happens in Chicago spills over. Just this week, the Justice Department announced that they're filing suit against Cicero because of discrimination in housing and employment. There's going to be a lot more Ciceros if we don't stay united.

So you see, then, when people criticize me for endorsing Harold Washington, I'm here to say that Harold Washington has got my support throughout this campaign. There are some, in all candor, who say LULAC cannot endorse candidates. Well, LULAC can't. And LULAC hasn't said a word about endorsing Harold Washington—Tony Bonilla is. It'll be Tony Bonilla out there knockin' on doors. It'll be Tony Bonilla speakin' on radio and sending this message in Spanish, to our people, so they'll know.

What we then need, ladies and gentlemen, brothers and sisters, is more truth and love and trust and understanding. 'Cause see, people right this very moment are having meetings and scratchin' their heads saying, "How we gonna divide those people? We can't have them workin' together. That represents fifty-seven percent of the population of this city."

We've got to look back at history to see what happened. El Cid, a Spanish hero, went against the wishes of his king to try to bring the Moors and the Christians together for a united Spain, and he did it through truth and love. It was truth and love that helped Gandhi get independence for India. It was truth and love that helped Dr. Martin Luther King, Jr., conquer Montgomery. And there's going to be truth and love that will help Hispanics and blacks in the city of Chicago gain economic and political freedom.

Let me close, if I may, with a story.

There was a family out here in Kansas that made it a practice of going out and having their yearly picnic. And they were right next to a wheat field. And their little girl got lost in the wheat field. So all the people scattered out when they found out this little girl was lost and went in different directions lookin' for this little girl, and they couldn't find her. Finally, somebody came up and said, "Why don't we join hands and walk through this wheat field together, and maybe we can find her?" So what they did, then, they joined hands and they walked through that wheat field of Kansas and they found the little girl. And when they found the little girl, the father kneeled down, held her in his arms, and saw that it was too late. He looked up at the crowd gathered around him and said, "If only we had joined hands earlier!"

We don't want nobody sayin' that about blacks and Hispanics. Because we're here today to join hands. And we're gonna walk through the wheat field at Chicago! We're gonna bring hope where there's despair! Love where there's hate! Understanding where there's misunderstanding! Justice where there's injustice! Education where there's unequal education opportunities! Housing where there's indecent housing! And as we walk across Chicago holding hands, we're gonna be able to say, we're gonna be able to say, "We *shall* overcome! We *have* overcome! We're *gonna* overcome!" We can join hands right now with Jesse Jackson!

In 1983, Bonilla and several others founded the National Hispanic Leadership Conference (NHLC), a "think tank" that brings together leaders from the Hispanic community and encourages their participation in the economic, political, and social affairs of the mainstream society. The NHLC also fosters cooperation between the Hispanic community and other minorities as well as with various Latin American nations. As the group's president almost since it began, Bonilla has directed projects that address a wide range of concerns. On the subject of drug abuse, for example, he and the NHLC have set up prevention programs in the Hispanic community and have tried to tackle the problem at its source by discuss-

ing possible solutions with local leaders in drug-producing countries. Bonilla has also worked closely with his friend Jesse Jackson and other civil rights leaders to negotiate agreements with major U.S. corporations that will result in the hiring of more minorities and the development of more appropriate marketing strategies. Most recently, the NHLC has been trying to increase minority participation in the news media.

SOURCES

Tardiff, Joseph C., and L. Mpho Mabunda, eds., *Dictionary of Hispanic Biography,* Gale Research, Detroit, 1995.

Gertrude Simmons Bonnin (Zitkala-Sa, Red Bird)

1876–1938

Native American activist and writer of the Sioux tribe

One of the most outspoken voices raised on behalf of Native Americans during the early twentieth century was that of Gertrude Simmons Bonnin, a granddaughter of the famous Sioux chief Sitting Bull. As a writer, she produced a number of essays and short stories that established her as a significant figure in Indian literature. Her enduring legacy, however, is that of a reformer and activist devoted to improving the lives of Native Americans both on and off the reservation. Calling upon her skills as an orator, Bonnin made numerous appearances before government officials in Washington and ordinary citizens throughout the nation to draw attention to the plight of Indians trapped in poverty and despair.

Bonnin was born to an Indian mother and a white father at the Yankton Sioux Agency in South Dakota. She spent her early childhood on the reservation, immersed in traditional Sioux ways. But when she was about eight, she left to attend a Quaker missionary school for Indians located in Wabash, Indiana. After a difficult and unhappy adjustment period, young Gertrude finally settled in and completed a three-year term, then returned home for four years before going back for another three-year course of study. Following her graduation in 1895, she went on to Earlham College in Richmond, Indiana, earning recognition as the winner of a state-wide oratory contest.

After leaving college in 1897, Gertrude Simmons, as she was then known, secured a teaching position at Pennsylvania's Carlisle Indian School. While the time she spent there was not pleasant, she did manage to make some contacts in the eastern literary establishment that enabled her to begin publishing some of her work (under her Sioux name, Zitkala-Sa, or Red Bird) in such well-known magazines as Harper's *and* Atlantic Monthly. *In 1899, she resigned from the Carlisle faculty and enrolled at the New England Conservatory of Music in Boston to study violin. Free to pursue her writing and her music in a cultural milieu she enjoyed, she was happier than she had been in many years. (In 1901, she even published her first full-length book, a collection of Indian legends.) But she still felt somewhat torn between two worlds, and she very much wanted to do something for those she had left behind on the reservation.*

Returning to South Dakota around 1902, Gertrude met and married a fellow

Yankton Sioux, Raymond T. Bonnin, who worked for the Indian Service. They soon moved to the Uintah and Ouray Reservation in Utah, where Gertrude worked as a clerk and a teacher. During this same period, she also became involved with the Society of American Indians, an Indian reform organization founded in 1911 at Ohio State University. The first group of its kind to be established and managed solely by Indians, it operated on the principle that assimilation was ultimately the best course for the country's Native American population. To that end, the Society focused its efforts not only on government reforms but on activities such as increasing Indian employment in the Indian Service (the federal agency charged with managing Indian affairs), codifying laws pertaining to Indians, achieving Indian citizenship, opening the courts to all just claims regarding land settlements between Indians and the government, and preserving Indian history.

In 1916, Bonnin was elected secretary of the Society of American Indians, and not long after, she and her husband moved to Washington, D.C. From her new base in the nation's capital, which she would call home for the rest of her life, she continued to serve as secretary of the Society (until 1919) and editor of its major publication, American Indian Magazine. *She also joined forces with a number of other organizations spearheading Indian rights and reform, including the American Indian Defense Association and the Indian Rights Association. In addition, she began lecturing extensively from coast to coast, speaking to women's clubs and other groups on Indian affairs and lobbying for Indian citizenship. Her work on behalf of the latter met with success in 1924 with the passage of the Indian Citizenship Bill.*

Both Bonnin and her husband devoted a great deal of their time to meeting with officials of the federal government on behalf of individual Indians and tribes. They also testified before various congressional committees on a wide variety of issues. Many of their findings were the result of their own investigations and travels throughout the country visiting reservations and noting the need for improvements in areas such as health care, education, conservation of natural resources, and preserving Indian cultural traditions.

In 1926, following the disbanding of the Society of American Indians, the Bonnins formed the National Council of American Indians (NCAI). Like the Society, the NCAI was made up exclusively of Native Americans; Gertrude Bonnin served as its president. Its focus was also on reform, and to that end, Bonnin directed her energies toward lobbying for Indian legislation in Congress and calling attention to the deficiencies of the Indian Service.

This spirit that motivated these efforts finally prompted some government officials to take a closer look at the Indian Service. In 1928, U.S. Secretary of the Interior Hubert Work commissioned a group of scholars to study living conditions among Native Americans, focusing in particular on economic activity, education, health, and the federal government's administrative policies and practices. Under the direction of Dr. Lewis Meriam, the Institute for Government Research conducted an exhaustive survey and published the results in a landmark report entitled The Problem of Indian Administration, *more commonly known as the Meriam Report. Its description of the "deplorable" state of life on the reservations—the high death rate among all age groups, the failure of the educational system, the widespread poverty and malnutrition—focused national attention of the plight of Native Americans and increased pressure on the government to take immediate action.*

In mid-December 1928, Bonnin voiced her thoughts on the findings of the Meriam Report at a meeting of the Indian Rights Association in Atlantic City, New

Jersey. The text of the following speech was furnished by the Harold B. Lee Library at Brigham Young University, which houses the Gertrude Simmons Bonnin Collection.

The opportunity to speak today in a conference discussing the report of the Indian survey made by the Institute for Government Research is appreciated by this Indian speaker.

At the outset, permit me to explain that I did not learn English in the government Indian schools. I attended Earlham College, Richmond, Indiana. A brief sketch of my activities is given in *Who's Who in the Nation's Capital,* 1927.

I have the honor to be president of the National Council of American Indians, an all-Indian organization based upon citizenship rights granted by Congress June 2, 1924.

Before that, Indians were jailed if they held meetings without permission from a superintendent.

The National Council of American Indians was created by the Indians themselves and I was elected to office, which carries no pay whatsoever. I devote my whole time to its work and never have I sought any personal benefit.

The Indian's American citizenship has been dearly bought by repeated self sacrifices, until his unsurpassed loyalty and volunteer service in the World War won this recognition from Congress.

Many times, standing by the grave of the Unknown Soldier, I have felt that it may be an Indian boy, who bravely fought and heroically died for the principles of democracy, who lies there now.

Positively, no one on earth can honestly challenge the American Indian's loyalty to the government of the United States, though this government has waged more wars upon its Indian wards than any other nation against its own subordinate peoples.

There is a distinction between "government" and "servants of the government." Whenever an Indian complains of unfaithful servants of the government and the maladministration of his affairs, he is heralded as "disloyal to the government" from certain quarters. This is untrue.

This preliminary is made necessary today in refutation of false charges uttered on the floor of the House by Congressman Crampton of Michigan on December 11, 1928, against the National Council of American Indians. Mr. Crampton inserted in the *Congressional Record* a portion of a letter, which he misquoted as follows:

Gertrude Simmons Bonnin

> *According to an Indian's statement and from my own personal observations, the Indians are very poor and hungry. They have no voice in their affairs. They are neglected. Whether sick or well, whether young or old, most of them or nearly all of them live in bad houses, wearing rags, and with little or no food. Their complaints to government officials go unheeded. Agents' offices are locked against the Indians most of the time.*

And so forth ad nauseam.

Mr. Crampton described it as the "character of propaganda used to poison the judgment of the country against their own government."

Yet before Mr. Crampton concludes his speech defending the Indian Bureau and the Budget Bureau for lack of adequate appropriations, and denying the disgraceful condition of Indian affairs, he contradicts himself. He agrees with me and with the report of the Institute for Government Research in their first sentence, which says: "An overwhelming majority of the Indians are poor, even extremely poor." Mr. Crampton falls into this agreement unwittingly in trying to refute the report that children in government schools are underfed.

He said:

> *I have never seen any evidence of the children suffering from lack of food or from an undesirable character of food. Quite the contrary. It is true that oftentimes children will be seen in these schools who give evidence of lack of proper nutrition, but you must remember where these children have come from—the primitive sort of homes they come from to the schools.*

The "primitive sort of homes"—that is exactly what I had in mind. The congressman admits these homes are bad and that food is lacking, and therefore, Indians young and old are hungry and sick.

The subcommittee of the Senate Indian Affairs Committee is holding hearings right now, and sworn testimony reveals horrible conditions—rotten meat, full of maggots, and spoiled flour which mice and cats had defiled, are fed to children in government schools. Sworn statements amply show that the report of the Institute for Government Research could all be transformed into the superlative degree and not begin to tell the whole story of Indian exploitation.

Had it been possible, these hearings of the Senate investigating committee should have been printed and read at this conference, together with this discussion of the report of the Institute for Government Research. We would all be convinced beyond any doubt as to the accuracy of this survey report under discussion. Printed reports of these hearings should be made available to the public—the American people. They have a right to know the facts if, as Mr. Crampton said, in justifying the Budget Bureau's cuts in Indian appropriations, increased appropriations would mean higher taxes upon the American people. Let the people know the facts, if this is a government "of the people, for the people, by the people."

As an Indian, speaking earnestly for the very life of my race, I must say that this report by the Institute for Government Research, *The Problem of Indian Administration,* is all too true, although I do not always concur in their conclusions, which tend to minimize the responsibility of the Bureau.

On pages 11-12 the report says:

> *The survey staff finds itself obliged to say frankly and unequivocally that the provisions for the care of the Indian children in boarding schools are grossly inadequate.*
>
> *The outstanding deficiency is in the diet furnished the Indian children, many of whom are below normal health. The diet is deficient in quantity, quality and variety. The effort has been made to feed the children on a per capita of eleven cents a day, plus what can be produced on the school farm, including the dairy. At a few, very few schools, the farm and dairy are sufficiently productive to be a highly important factor in raising the standard of the diet, but even at the best schools these sources do not fully meet the requirements for the health and development of the children. At the worst schools the situation is serious in the extreme. The major diseases of the Indians are tuberculosis and trachoma. Tuberculosis unquestionably can best be combated by a preventive, curative diet and proper living conditions, and a considerable amount of evidence suggests that the same may prove true of trachoma. The great protective foods are milk and fruit and vegetables, particularly fresh green vegetables. The diet of Indian children in boarding schools is generally notably lacking in these preventive foods. Although the Indian Service has established a quart of milk a day per pupil as the standard, it has been able to achieve this standard in very few schools. At the special school for children suffering from trachoma, now in operation at Fort Defiance, Arizona, milk is not a part of the normal diet. The little produced is mainly consumed in the hospital where children acutely ill are sent. It may be seriously questioned whether the Indian Service could do very much better than it does without more adequate appropriations.*

I do not agree with this concluding sentence, which minimizes the Bureau's actual responsibility by blaming Congress for inadequate appropriations.

For more than eleven years I have lived in Washington, D.C., and I have learned through attending congressional committee hearings and pending Indian legislation that it is the Indian Bureau that drafts these appropriations bills. In fact, all other bills affecting Indians are also referred to the Indian Bureau for its approval or disapproval. The American Congress is dependent for its information upon the Indian Bureau. What "compromises" are made in congressional committees behind closed doors is another chapter.

In the printed hearings on Indian appropriations by the House Indian Affairs Committee, Volume 1, page 806, year 1919, the assistant commissioner, Mr. Meritt, is quoted as follows:

> *After the next year (i.e., beginning 1921) I think there should be a gradual decrease of the appropriations carried in the Indian Bill, and the only sure way for bringing about that decrease would be for Congress to arbitrarily direct that there be a decrease of appropriations for, say, a period of four years, of five percent per year.... I do not believe that the Indian Service would be very materially hurt and it would result in saving the government approximately $750,000 a year.*

Bear in mind, this was before President Coolidge's economy program. There was no Budget Bureau in existence in 1919.

During the three last consecutive summers I have visited many Indian reservations, keeping my information on Indian conditions up to date. This past summer I went with Captain Bonnin, who was doing field investigation work for the Senate Indian Affairs Committee, authorized by the King Resolution No. 79. Incidentally, the Indian Bureau opposed the passage of this resolution. I will here tell you an observation of my own.

The Indian Bureau superintendents in the field have been holding meetings this summer, discussing this same report of the Institute for Government Research before us now. Their purpose was to refute and disprove the things contained in it! Subordinate employees have been approached and told they should be "loyal" to the government when asked to refute statements in the report. At peril of losing their jobs, some of them refused to deny the facts.

I repeat, "There is a distinction to be made between the government and the government's servants." On Indian reservations, subordinate employees as well as the Indians are called "disloyal" to the government by their superintendents when one of them dares to report existing evils. On the contrary, any American citizen who can help to bring efficiency into the federal machinery is "loyal to the government," though it may mean the dismissal of inefficient employees—a real housecleaning in the Indian Service.

In addition to this pernicious activity among Indian Bureau superintendents trying to refute things told in the report of the Institute for Government Research, there are circulated misleading articles emanating from the Bureau. Recently I casually picked up from the reading table of a hotel a current magazine—the November, 1928, issue of the *National Republic.* On page 34 is the caption "Education of the Indians"; the subhead states "Graduates of Government Indian Schools Are Doing Successful Work in All Walks of Life."

The pictures used are from the government Indian school, Haskell Institute. This is considered one of the best schools. But the article is upon the entire Indian field. The article, therefore, is entirely misleading.

To show you the Bureau's own attitude toward its Indian schools, I quote from it:

> *Health promoting activities are given a prominent place in the conduct of the schools. The health of the pupil is the first purpose, and daily routine of the boarding school as to diet, bathing, exercise, sleep, periodical weighing and examination of pupils, and supervised nursing supplied by Indian girls, furnishes an organized system throughout the year for the protection of health and the formation of health habits. The value of a sufficient supply of milk daily is emphasized and an endeavor made to provide plenty for the schools....*

It does not tell the American public, as a matter of fact, how miserably this endeavor fails to actually supply the necessary milk. This kind of a presentation of Indian matters is not conducive to having Congress make larger appropriations. Congress as a whole is dependent upon the Indian Bureau for its information, just as the American public is. Both Congress and the American people are wilfully misled about the actual conditions of Indian want and hopeless destitution. The stubborn fact remains, just as told in the report of the Institute for Government Research made to the Secretary of the Interior about a year ago, particularly on pages 11 and 12, and supported by sworn testimony before the Senate Indian Committee and the Red Cross report.

> *The diet is deficient in quantity, quality and variety. The effort has been made to feed the children on a per capita of eleven cents a day, plus what can be produced on the school farm,*

including the dairy. At a few, very few schools, the farm and dairy are sufficiently productive to be a highly important factor in raising the standard of the diet, but even at the best schools these sources do not fully meet the requirements for the health and development of the children. At the worst schools the situation is serious in the extreme.

A superintendent who questioned the accuracy of the report on the eleven cents per child per day spent for food in government schools was invited to figure it out, which he did while I looked on. Much to his own surprise, he had to admit the survey staff of the Institute for Government Research knew their business and their report was correct.

The tabulations of Assistant Commissioner, Mr. Meritt, which Mr. Crampton put in the *Congressional Record* (December 11, 1928), denying the 11-cents-a-day-for-food-per-child report and showing it to be 20.4 cents instead, is only paper-talk, just like the menus placarded in the schools showing what the children ought to have, but in actual fact do not get because of lack of the materials.

In the printed hearings of the House Appropriations Committee in 1922, on page 328, Mr. Meritt said: "We favor keeping subsistence down to the lowest possible point."

He was speaking of rations to old and indigent Indians and orphans.

I have visited Indian homes during my three summer visits. They are extremely poor. They have scarcely any food in their hovels. They complain to me of starving.

This summer I went to see a proud Indian chief who was sick. Before I reached the hut I heard men and women crying aloud. I stepped into the open door. The Indian was dead. They were washing the body, ready for burial. The corpse was only skin and bones. These grief-stricken Indians, with tears streaming down their faces, came to shake hands with me. Utterly hopeless, they cried as only heartbroken humans cry, until I, too, wept with them.

The government doctor arrived. I asked him what disease caused the death of the old Indian. He replied that he had no disease, but simply starved to death.

There was a time, long ago, when Indians shared their food with the hungry, but that day is past. Now all Indians are too poor. They have nothing to divide. There is starvation.

On page 262 of the report of the Institute for Government Research, referring to the Red Cross survey of 1924, there appears the following: "It may be said in passing that the findings of the Red Cross report correspond very closely to those of the present survey as they relate to the same reservations."

This Red Cross survey of 1924 had been kept in the secret archives of the Indian Bureau these four years and has been refused to members of Congress who asked to see it. The evil conditions reported in the Red Cross survey remain unchanged, four years later.

Withholding reported facts of bad conditions in Indian affairs, the Bureau is broadcasting through the American press, and Congressman Crampton through the *Congressional Record,* about *how much* the Indians have been helped and benefitted; how the Indian population has increased; how well they are fed and housed!

In the *Native American* of December 1, 1928, published at the Leupp Indian School, Arizona, Assistant Commissioner Meritt has an article which he addressed to the Navajos, telling them about their "increase in population" and "their wealth derived from oil leases" under the administration of Commissioner Burke; but nowhere did Mr. Meritt tell, as a matter of fact, that under the same policy of the Bureau, the whole Navajo Indians are today suffering fast-approaching blindness! Nor does he mention the heated battles fought by true friends of the Navajos, which defeated the Bureau policy and its endorsement of bills H.R. 9133 and S. 3159, under former Secretary Fall.

Those Bureau bills, had they passed, would have had the following effects:

(1) To deprive the "Executive Order" reservation Indians of 37 1/2% of their oil revenue, giving it to the states;

(2) To exempt the oil companies from the production tax;

(3) To provide a congressional declaration against the Indian claim of vested rights in 22,500,000 acres—two-thirds of the undivided reservation area.

These atrocious misuses of huge federal machinery against the Indian wards of the government are sugar-coated to fool the American public. The National Council of American Indians was one of the organizations that dared to defend the rights of the Navajo people and all other Indian tribes who occupied "Executive Order" reservations.

If the high officials of the Indian Bureau continually fail to insist upon adequate congressional appropriations, are they ignorant of the actual suffering on the reservations? If not, they must be incompetent. If, on the other hand, these officials of the government prove unfaithful to their charge in "compromises" that would legislate away the wards' interests, knowing it means the ultimate destruction of helpless human beings—young and old—then they are criminals. In either case, a housecleaning is imperative.

I am desperately concerned for the life of my race while these countless investigations, revealing un-Christian exploitation of government wards, are made from time to time, only to lodge under lock and key in the Indian Bureau. How long—oh, how long!—shall this cruel practice continue?

The Indian race is starving—not only physically, but mentally and morally. It is a dire tragedy. The government Indian schools are not on a par with the American schools of today. The so-called "Indian Graduates from Government Schools" cannot show any credentials that would be accepted by any business house. They are unable to pass the Civil Service examinations. The proviso in Indian treaties that educated Indians, wherever qualified, be given preference in Indian Service employment is rendered meaningless. Indians are kept ignorant and "incompetent" to cope with the world's trained workers, because they are not sufficiently educated in the government schools.

Secretary Work, in his annual report, 1928, page 13, states: "There is not an Indian school in the United States that is strictly a high school."

I quote this in refutation of the glowing propaganda in the November, 1928, issue of the *National Republic* and Mr. Crampton's speech in the *Congressional Record,* previously mentioned.

The topic of Indian education has already been discussed by others, but I am obliged to make a passing comment upon it.

The Secretary of the Interior in his report on education of Indians says in part (on page 13) as follows:

> *No complete high-school courses were taught for them until 1921 and then only at one school. In 1925, three such courses were added; one was added in 1926 and a fifth in 1927. The increase during the last three years in the number of pupils—junior and senior grades—has been by 1,178 in the former and by 526 in the latter. There are only six institutions maintained by the federal government where Indians may receive a high school education. Elementary and junior high-school courses are also taught in these institutions, the senior high-school grades constitute only one department. There is not an Indian school in the United States that is strictly a high school. Contrast these conditions with the educational advantages offered the white population.*

Then he gives facts and figures. On page 15 of his report he says:

> *As the inadequacy of the educational system for the Indians was one of the reasons for the department's request for the survey and report, the following summary of the findings of the investigators on this subject is of especial interest:*
>
> *The survey staff finds itself obliged to say frankly and unequivocally that the provisions for the care of the Indian children in boarding schools are grossly inadequate.*
>
> *The diet is deficient in quality, quantity and variety.*
>
> *The great protective foods are milk and fruit and vegetables, particularly fresh green vegetables. The diet of Indian children is generally notably lacking in these foods.*
>
> *The boarding schools are overcrowded materially beyond their capacities.*
>
> *The medical attention rendered the boarding school children is not up to a reasonable standard.*
>
> *The medical attention given children in day schools maintained by the government is also below a reasonable standard.*
>
> *The boarding schools are supported in part by the labor of students.*
>
> *The service is notably weak in personnel trained and experienced in educational work with families and communities.*

Now these are some of the things of which I have complained in the past, and as a result I am referred to by Indian Bureau officials and congressmen as being an agitator and disloyal to the government; they even infer that I am dishonest and living off of the Indians. Such statements are grossly untrue and unjust. The sole purpose in making any criticism has been with a view that the evils pointed out by me might be corrected.

The Secretary of the Interior's report contained these statements. It is evident that he regards them as of sufficient importance to incorporate them in his report. He further states that "this subject is of especial interest."

In this same report, on page 34, he deals with "Negro Education" and states as follows:

One of the more important activities of the department has been a comprehensive study of Negro colleges and universities throughout the United States. This study was conducted by the Bureau of Education. Its purpose was to ascertain the present status of Negro higher education and to recommend means for its improvement and development.

The results show marked progress and an extraordinary demand among the Negro people of the country for college and university education. Of the 79 institutions included in the Bureau's survey, 77 were doing college work as compared with 31 institutions ten years ago. The enrollment of Negro students in those institutions totaled 13,860 as compared with 2,132 in 1917, a gain of 550 percent. For every 10,000 Negroes in the United States 15 are attending college, as against 90 for every 10,000 whites.

With five exceptions, the colleges included in the study were located in Southern states, indicating a widespread sentiment in the South in favor of Negro higher education. Twenty-two of the institutions were operated by states and supported through public taxation. The Bureau's study also shows that the Negroes, themselves, have not been remiss in providing higher education, 17 of their colleges being owned, administered, and financed entirely by members of their race.

It will be noted that 17 of their colleges are owned and financed by members of the Negro race.

Indian funds might have been better used for higher education and colleges for Indians instead of building steel bridges, highways and expensive but worthless irrigation systems under Indian Bureau management.

Attention is also directed to the statement that "One of the more important activities of the department has been a comprehensive study of Negro colleges and universities throughout the United States. This study was conducted by the Bureau of Education. Its purpose was to ascertain the present status of Negro higher education and to recommend means for its improvement and development."

The Negroes are not wards of the government. Neither have they any treaty agreements with the United States for their education, as the Indians have. Yet means for educational development are sought for them. Why not extend such activities to the Indians?

In conclusion, I quote Major Frank Knox, who said at the close of his investigation of three reservations in Colorado and Utah in 1925: "The reform which good business methods, efficient administration and an adequate protection of Indian rights requires cannot come from within the Bureau. It must come from without."

Too often employees in the Indian Service are Indian-haters and they are discourteous to Indians in their daily routine.

Above all things let there be this proviso written large in the government's new Indian policy—"That no expert or subordinate shall be employed who has racial prejudice against the Indian people."

The problem of Indian administration cannot be solved by mere increased appropriations unless coincidentally a new personnel is had in the Indian Service, and a new Indian policy which will provide court review of the guardian's handling of Indian funds and property, including natural resources estimated at a billion and a half.

While it did not bring about major improvements, the Meriam Report did exert some influence on government policies regarding Native Americans during the administrations of Herbert Hoover (1928-33) and his successor, Franklin D. Roosevelt (1933-45). Hoover, for example, appointed two leading members of the Indian Rights Association as commissioner and assistant commissioner of the Bureau of Indian Affairs. As part of his Depression-era reforms, Roosevelt pushed for the Indian Reorganization Act of 1934 and its promised "Indian New Deal,"

which granted Indians more self-government and the right to keep observing their own cultural ceremonies and other events.

As for Bonnin, she remained active in the reform movement throughout the 1930s. She continued lobbying Congress, particularly on behalf of the Sioux and the Utes, and frequently lectured across the United States, often appearing in native dress to dramatize her message. While she devoted less time to her writing, she renewed her interest in music and even composed an Indian opera entitled Sun Dance. *After her death in 1938 at the age of only sixty-one, Bonnin was buried in Arlington National Cemetery.*

SOURCES

Books

Bonnin, Gertrude Simmons, *Old Indian Legends* (reprint of original 1901 edition), University of Nebraska Press, 1985.

———, *American Indian Stories* (reprint of original 1921 edition), University of Nebraska Press, 1985.

Gridley, Marion E., *American Indian Women,* Hawthorn Books, 1974.

Jones, Louis Thomas, *Aboriginal American Oratory: The Tradition of Eloquence Among the Indians of the United States,* Southwest Museum (Los Angeles), 1965.

Periodicals

American Indian Quarterly, "Gertrude Simmons Bonnin, 1876-1938: 'Americanize the First Americans,'" winter, 1988, pp. 27-40.

Journal of the West, "Twentieth Century Indian Leaders: Brokers and Providers," July, 1984, pp. 3-6.

New York Times, January 27, 1938. p. 21.

Other

Gertrude Simmons Bonnin Collection, Harold B. Lee Library, Brigham Young University.

Joseph Brant (Thayendanega)

1742–1807

Native American chief of the Mohawk tribe

One of the best known Indian leaders of the American colonial period was Joseph Brant, a Mohawk chief and major spokesman for the League of Six Nations, a powerful confederation of six Iroquois tribes whose original territory spanned present-day New York State and southeastern Ontario. Brant himself was the son of a full-blooded Mohawk chief and a woman who some historians believe might have been half European. He lost his father at an early age and took the surname of his stepfather upon his mother's remarriage. Later, after his sister married a British colonial official, Joseph went to live with them in Lebanon, Connecticut. There he attended a local Christian school and became fluent in both spoken and written English.

As a young adult, Brant—a convert to the Anglican faith—prepared translations of various religious texts (including parts of the Bible) and served as a missionary to the Mohawk people. He also worked as an interpreter and diplomat for the British in their dealings with various Iroquois tribes. In addition, he lent his support to Great Britain during the French and Indian War (1754–63) and during confrontations with the Ottawa chief Pontiac, thus expanding the Iroquois confederation's sphere of influence while at the same time maintaining the delicate balance of power between British and French interests in the colonies.

In 1774, Brant became secretary to the British superintendent of Indian affairs. The following year, he made his first trip to England, where he was presented at court. He also posed in Native American dress for formal portraits by the painters George Romney and Benjamin West.

During the American Revolution, Brant again allied himself with the British, who commissioned him an officer in their army. (As a result, he is often referred to in historical accounts of the time as Captain Brant.) He served with distinction as both a soldier and a diplomat, devising military strategy, leading numerous Indian raids on white settlements as far west as the Ohio Valley, and persuading as many of his fellow Iroquois as possible to fight for the British. After the war, Brant led the Mohawks to safety in Canada, establishing a new home on land the British granted to him near present-day Brantford, Ontario. There he spent the rest of his life acting as a mediator between the Indians, the British, and the Americans as they struggled to reach a compromise that would allow them to live together in peace.

On April 21, 1794, for example, a special council meeting between Indians and whites took place in an Onondaga village on Buffalo Creek, New York. In attendance were Brant, who spoke for the Iroquois confederation, Colonel John Butler, representing England's King George III, and General Israel Chapin, appearing on behalf of the new American government. Addressing the whites, Brant called on his fellow negotiators to be straightforward and honest in their dealings with the Indian people as they tried to resolve disputes over various peace terms and territorial boundaries proposed since the end of the war. His remarks are reprinted from W.C. Vanderwerth's Indian Oratory: Famous Speeches by Noted Indian Chieftains *(University of Oklahoma Press, 1971).*

Brothers: You, of the United States, listen to what we are going to say to you; you, likewise, the King.

Brothers: We are very happy to see you, Colonel Butler and General Chapin, sitting side by side, with the intent of hearing what we have to say. We wish to do no business but what is done open and aboveboard.

Brother: You, of the United States, make your mind easy, on account of the long time your president's speech has been under our consideration; when we received it, we told you it was a business of importance, and required some time to be considered of.

Brother: The answer you have brought us is not according to what we expected, which was the reason for our long delay; the business would have been done with expedition, had the United States agreed to our proposals. We would then have collected our associates, and repaired to Venango, the place you proposed for meeting us.

Joseph Brant

Brother: It is not now in our power to accept your invitation; provided we were to go, you would conduct the business, as you might think proper; this has been the case at all the treaties held, from time to time, by your commissioners.

Brother: At the first treaty, after the conclusion of the war between you and Great Britain, at Fort Stanwix, your commissioners conducted the business as it to them seemed best; they pointed out a line of division, and then confirmed it; after this, they held out that our country was ceded to them by the King; this confused the chiefs who attended there, and prevented them from making any reply to the contrary; still holding out, if we did not consent to it, their warriors were at their back, and that we would get no further protection from Great Britain. [In 1784, the Iroquois confederation had signed a treaty at Fort Stanwix granting to the United States all of the land west of the Niagara River.]

This has ever been held out to us, by the commissioners from Congress; at all the treaties held with us since the peace, at Fort McIntosh, at Rocky River, and every other meeting held, the idea was still the same.

Brother: This has been the case from time to time. Peace has not taken place, because you have held up these ideas, owing to which much mischief has been done to the southward.

Brother: We, the Six Nations, have been exerting ourselves to keep peace since the conclusion of the war; we think it would be best for both parties; we advised the confederate nations to request a meeting, about halfway between us and the United States, in order that such steps might be taken as would bring about a peace; this request was made, and Congress appointed commissioners to meet us at Muskingum, which we agreed to, a boundary line was then proposed by us, and refused by Governor [Arthur] St. Clair [of the Northwest Territory], one of your commissioners. The Wyandots, a few Delawares, and some others, met the commissioners, though not authorized, and confirmed the lines of what was not their property, but a common to all nations.

Brothers: The idea we all held out at our council, at Lower Sandusky, held for the purpose of forming our confederacy, and to adopt measures that would be for the general welfare of our Indian nations, or people of our color; owing to those steps taken by us, the United States held out, that when we went to the westward to transact our private business, that we went with an intention of taking an active part in the troubles subsisting between them and our western brethren; this never has been the case. We have ever wished for the friendship of the United States.

Brother: We think you must be fully convinced, from our perseverance last summer, as your commissioners saw, that we were anxious for a peace between us. The exertions that we, the Six Nations, have made towards the accomplishing this desirable end, is the cause of the western nations being somewhat dubious as to our sincerity. After we knew their doubts, we still persevered; and, last fall, we pointed out methods to be taken, and sent them, by you, to Congress; this we certainly expected would have proved satisfactory to the United States; in that case we should have more than ever exerted ourselves, in order that the offers we made should be confirmed by our confederacy, and by them strictly adhered to.

Brother: Our proposals have not met with the success from Congress that we expected; this still leaves us in a similar situation to what we were when we first entered on the business.

Brother: You must recollect the number of chiefs who have, at divers times, waited on Congress; they have pointed out the means to be taken, and held out the same language, uniformly, at one time as another; that was, if you would withdraw your claim to the boundary line, and lands within the line, as offered by us; had this been done, peace would have taken place; and, unless this still be done, we see no other method of accomplishing it.

Brother: We have borne everything patiently for this long time past; we have done everything we could consistently do with the welfare of our nations in general—notwithstanding the many advantages that have been taken of us, by individuals making purchases from us, the Six Nations, whose fraudulent conduct towards us Congress never has taken notice of, nor in any wise seen us rectified, nor made our minds easy. This is the case to the present day; our patience is now entirely worn out; you see the difficulties we labor under, so that we cannot at present rise from our seats and attend

"We are of the same opinion with the people of the United States; you consider yourselves as independent people; we . . . look upon ourselves as equally independent. . . ."

your council at Venango, agreeable to your invitation. The boundary line we pointed out, we think is a just one, although the United States claim lands west of that line; the trifle that has been paid by the United States can be no object in comparison to what a peace would be.

Brother: We are of the same opinion with the people of the United States; you consider yourselves as independent people; we, as the original inhabitants of this country, and sovereigns of the soil, look upon ourselves as equally independent, and free as any other nation or nations. This country was given to us by the Great Spirit above; we wish to enjoy it, and have our passage along the lake, within the line we have pointed out.

Brother: The great exertions we have made, for this number of years, to accomplish a peace, and have not been able to obtain it; our patience, as we have already observed, is exhausted, and we are discouraged from persevering any longer. We, therefore, throw ourselves under the protection of the Great Spirit above, who, we hope, will order all things for the best. We have told you our patience is worn out; but not so far, but that we wish for peace, and, whenever we hear that pleasing sound, we shall pay attention to it.

SOURCES

Jones, Louis Thomas, *Aboriginal American Oratory: The Tradition of Eloquence Among the Indians of the United States,* Southwest Museum (Los Angeles), 1965.

Kelsay, Isabel Thompson, *Joseph Brant, 1743-1807: Man of Two Worlds,* [Syracuse], 1984.

Rosenstiel, Annette, *Red and White: Indian Views of the White Man, 1492-1982,* Universe Books, 1983.

Vanderwerth, W.C., *Indian Oratory: Famous Speeches by Noted Indian Chieftains,* University of Oklahoma Press, 1971.

Van Every, Dale, *A Company of Heroes: The American Frontier, 1775-1783,* Ayer, 1976.

Witt, Shirley Hill, and Stan Steiner, *The Way: An Anthology of American Indian Literature,* Knopf, 1972.

Tony Brown

1933–

African American television commentator, journalist, entrepreneur, and activist

"The only color of freedom is green." So says Tony Brown, host of public television's longest-running minority affairs program and perhaps the most vocal and visible leader of those who believe that achieving economic self-sufficiency will be the salvation of the black community. For virtually his entire life, Brown has challenged blacks to determine their own future, pointedly noting the folly of relying on government handouts and white liberal guilt to make a true and lasting difference in their status. Instead, he maintains, only by fostering black self-reliance will this nation solve its racial problems and become more competitive and more productive in the global marketplace.

Born in Charleston, West Virginia, Brown was raised by a family friend and her daughter. Even as a youngster, he was very much aware that money and education were the keys to improving not only his lot in life but that of his entire community as well. So whenever he was not busy with his school work, he was thinking up ways to earn a little cash. One of his earliest ventures was collecting and selling soda pop bottles, which in turn enabled him to finance a small poultry farm that supplied his neighbors with eggs and chickens.

After serving in the U.S. Army for two years during the mid-1950s, Brown attended Wayne State University in Detroit, earning a bachelor's degree in sociology and psychology in 1959 and a master's degree in psychiatric social work in 1961. But his career in social work was brief; he soon found himself drawn to the communications industry instead, first as a drama critic and city editor for a Detroit newspaper and then as a writer, producer, and host for several community affairs programs on a local public television station. During this same period, Brown was also active in the civil rights movement in Detroit.

Before long, his work captured the attention of executives at the Corporation for Public Broadcasting. In 1970, they hired him to produce and host "Black Journal," an award-winning minority affairs program based in New York that was broadcast on public television stations across the country. Brown immediately set out to revamp the content and philosophy of the show to reflect its national scope and his own strong commitment to portraying the positive side of the black community. The changes initially sparked criticism from those who had been satisfied with the program's noncontroversial mix of interviews, commentaries, documentaries, and other features that examined the American scene from a black point of view. But within a year, the new, more provocative "Black Journal" had become so popular that it was expanded from a monthly to a weekly show.

Brown's hard-hitting approach to the issues eventually began to anger many of those in the political and media establishment, blacks as well as whites. His continued attacks against what he felt was racism in public television also won him few fans and in the mid-1970s nearly cost him the funding he needed to continue his program. So, in 1977, he took it into commercial syndication as "Tony Brown's Journal." Five years later, unhappy with the number of stations and broadcast times that syndication offered, he moved the show back to public television, where it remains today.

Throughout his career, Brown has aggressively championed the importance of black economic empowerment. He is sharply critical of those who think that more government programs and increased public assistance are keys to improving the lives of African Americans. Instead, he insists that blacks must create businesses and invest in their own communities to achieve true equality and that it is up to the blacks who have enjoyed success to help those who have not.

Brown himself has practiced what he preaches. Beginning in 1971, for example, he served as the founding dean of the School of Communications at Howard University, where his priority was to train black students for successful careers in the communications industry. In 1980, he organized a national celebration known as "Black College Day" to draw attention to the need to promote and support historically black colleges in the United States. And in 1985, he established the Council for the Economic Development of Black Americans, which sponsors the "Buy Freedom" campaign and its nationwide drive to create new jobs and businesses by encouraging blacks to patronize black establishments.

A dynamic and forceful advocate for his beliefs, Brown is an immensely popular speaker at banquets, conferences, seminars, business expositions, corporate meetings, and schools. At one such event—the Black Human Resources Conference, held in Washington, D.C., in August 1993—he discussed some of his latest ideas on cultural diversity and the need for everyone to learn to live and work together to prosper in an increasingly competitive world. His speech is transcribed from an audiotape available from Tony Brown Productions, Inc.

I'd like to thank you so much for having the opportunity to address you. I think particularly it's quite propitious or opportunistic that I speak with you during the early stages of your formation. When you are thinking out, cognitively, what your mission is. And to that extent, I would like to offer my suggestions.

If I may, I'd like to go back to the end of World War II. At the end of World War II, the United States controlled all of the major resources that give a nation competitive advantage. We had a monopoly on capital. We had a monopoly on our ability to feed not only our nation but the world. We had a monopoly on *human* capital. Those countries that were devastated in Europe sent us the best brains. Wernher von Braun brought us the V-2 rocket which created our space program. We had a monopoly on technology. Because every time we'd bomb the factory in Berlin, a factory in Detroit became more valuable. So we had the world in our hands.

And what did America do? America used that opportunity to convince itself that we were invincible and superior because we were Ameri-

Tony Brown

cans. And because we felt all we had to do was to put "Made in USA" on a garment, the rest of the world would flock to it. All we had to do was to say, "This is from America," and the world would love it. So we went to play golf. We bought second homes. We created junk bonds. We found ways not to create wealth, but to create greed.

And we today, ladies and gentlemen, are at the bottom of the barrel in *any* index of competition, globally, you want to find. We are fourteenth and fifteenth in education. Our schools are a *disgrace* by any standards. We have less wealth than small countries such as Finland. First-world capital is in third-world countries, so they can put up a factory in Indonesia as quick as you can put up a factory in Chicago. They now have technology. We created most of the computer chips, but we import nineteen out of twenty-one we need from [the] Japanese. We created the computer chip and the transistor, but the Japanese sell them to us. You look at America from any way you want, and we are a declining power.

Now I will not get around and I don't want to be partisan, but what is happening to us economically, ladies and gentlemen, is disastrous. What you are seeing is the elimination of the middle class in this country. And what you are seeing globally is one economy and two groups of people—the haves and the have-nots. You're not seeing a world being formed around blacks and whites. You're seeing a world being formed around those who have and those who don't. And those who *don't* have are people who are not skilled in technology. And the variable in which country is going to be the most competitive is human resources or human capital.

The reason that we are at the bottom technologically and competitively is our workers are not as smart as the Japanese and the Germans. That's why we don't make cars as well as they make cars. When IBM hires workers in Vermont to make one million-byte computer chips, they must first teach American workers Algebra 1. They don't take Algebra 1 when they go to work in Japan. They got it in high school. As a matter of fact, in twelve years—because they go to school more days than we do—they have four years' more education and of a quality greater than ours. So we are losing the battle because of our underdeveloped human resources or human capital.

Now as all of you know, there are three forms of wealth. One form of wealth is your money. You know about that. Your second form of wealth is your socialization, your social capital—your ability to put on the right suit, the right dress, to say, know the right words, to be on time for an interview, to sell yourself. You got that through your socialization process. Your third and most important form of wealth is your human capital. That's the totality of your formal education and your experience on the job.

Now of the three, the greater wealth is your human capital. A person can open up a business, go bankrupt, open up a business next year, and make a few million dollars *if* that person has social and human capital. But if that person does not have social and human capital, no matter how much financial capital they have, they will never succeed. So in effect, social and human capital, but human capital more so than any other form, creates financial wealth. Now that, ladies and gentlemen, takes us to where we are as black Americans.

The reason that America failed and is failing is because America is not competitive. And the definition of competition is, one, to be a person or group that will sacrifice and change. And that's what America refused to do after World War II. Germany and Japan, because they lost World War II, changed and sacrificed. Of course, when you lose, you have no choice. And as a result of changing and sacrificing, they now dominate the world.

Everybody in this room is well educated. And

you're well educated because you have postponed immediate gratification and you've changed and you've sacrificed. Your positions, corporately, depend on your ability to change and sacrifice. To subsume your individual needs to the greater good.

As a matter of fact, a very loose working definition of cultural diversity is simply a corporate environment in which individuals meet their own needs in the context of corporate advantage. To the extent to which you can create advantage for your corporate entity, and the corporation meet your individual needs, is the extent to which cultural diversity will be a reality.

Cultural diversity is *not* affirmative action. Those of you in this room will oversee the demise and death of affirmative action, because affirmative action won't be needed. We are moving toward a time in which all you're going to need, in spite of your gender or your race, is human capital.

Corporate America cannot afford not to bring women and nonwhites into the work force. Although I will say to you, many of these nonwhites will not be American born. So don't think that this is going to be a new affirmative action program or a new preference program. Technology has eliminated preference. Whatever happened to us, I'm sorry. And I don't believe that anybody is going to ever pay us, but I do believe that we are moving toward a work force composition in which the demographics will necessitate white people helping nonwhite people in order for white people to feed their families.

"The worst thing that can happen to blacks—and it's happening to some of us—is that we've bought into racism."

I have never believed in integration, and I never will believe in it. I never believed anybody was going to melt and turn white. And I never believed that white people were going to be truly, *genuinely* interested in nonwhite people. So I have never believed that anything but competition is going to make us equal.

They will come to you and give you all of the Democratic lies you can hear, the Republicans will give you all of the Republican lies you can hear. You can believe that the right white man with the right white wife in the White House is going to change your status. You can believe in Santa Claus if you want to.

But I am here to tell you if you don't take your resources—collectively, because individually they don't mean a thing—if you don't use your resources *collectively* as a group of people, you cannot have what another group of people have who use their resources collectively. It's very simple, and some of us have to get over this, "I don't like you and I don't like her." You may not like me, and I may not particularly care for you, but you and I'd better get one thing straight—we're all we've got.

And as far as black people and white people are concerned, we've got to get over the nonsense of one race dominating the other race. Because you only dominate a group at your own expense. The worst thing that can happen to blacks—and it's happening to some of us—is that we've bought into racism. And we think in order to eliminate white racism, we've got to create a black racism. Racism can't work because you can't prove you're superior. Because you're not. So don't get in the bag that somebody else is trying to get out of.

What is destroying this country now is a group of people have convinced themselves they can do something better than everybody else, and they can't perform. So they've become very neurotic. In some instances, very pathological. And you really don't want that.

What you *really* want is the ability to compete and have what you want. What you really want is to be free, and you must understand, first of all, that freedom is internal. Your external reality is the result of your internal reality, and only when you change within can your external reality change. No government can change your reality. They all lie. All governments have two functions—they collect taxes and they spend taxes, and they lie in between those two.

So I'm going to ask black America to change and to sacrifice. I'm going to ask you and I in this room, the best trained, the best educated, the most affluent blacks in the history of America, to change and sacrifice, because what you and I are doing is not right. What you and I are doing is not working.

The affirmative action that you and I promote is not affirmative action, it's class action. And you and I are helping members of our group like you and me. You can't find another group in this country where you have rich Jews and poor Jews, rich Koreans and poor Koreans, rich Cubans and poor Cubans. You've got a good distribution in every other ethnic and racial group but the black community. Black people like you and I who make over $50,000 a year are growing at a faster rate than whites who make over $50,000 a year. Living right beside a whole underclass that is growing exponentially. Now how in the world does that happen? There's only one way it *can* happen. It can only happen when a group doesn't focus on the group, it focuses on a group in the group. And you and I are the group.

When we get a $5000, $10,000 scholarship, who gets the scholarship? The daughter of the son of the woman who's a rocket scientist married to a doctor who's got eight degrees and PhDs in biophysics! *That's* who gets the money! So you and I and our little girls and boys do well, don't they? I had a lady say to me, "Oh, my little girl's sixteen, and she's studying the classics, and she plays the piano and the violin and she's ballet and she's a. . . ." I said, "That's *so* wonderful. But who's she going to marry?" I said, "Oh, Woody Jones is standing out on the corner beating up particles, dangling participles, killing germs. Who's she going to marry?" We all live in a vacuum? You can't live in a situation—you know, can you imagine, you go out and get a good promotion and a nice salary and go home to have a party by *yourself?* You gotta have somebody with you. We can't think, ladies and gentlemen, that affirmative action is for me and you! And that's essentially what we think. Because that's who we take care of.

Let me tell you what affirmative action is. You want to know what affirmative action is? Affirmative action is best described in the holy Bible, reverend. And it's the story of the prodigal son. The father getting his wisdom when the son came back home, gave all of the resources of the family unit to the son coming back. He didn't give anything to those who stayed there, because in his wisdom, he knew if he could strengthen the weakest link in the chain, he could strengthen the family unit. That's affirmative action.

Now you want to see another classical example of affirmative action? Look at the National Basketball League. At the end of the season, when they draft the best new player, what team gets the best new player? The *worst* team. Why in the world would you give the best new player—that seven-foot-nine guy who makes five hundred points a game—why would you put him on the worst team? Because if you put him on the worst team, you'll strengthen the league. Because on any given day or night, any team can defeat any other team. Therefore, we'll have more spectators. If we have more spectators, because we like a more competitive sport, the owners will make more money because the networks make more money, and the owners will pay the players more money, and the fans are happy. So is it not win-win, and isn't it win-win because we helped the worst team in the league?

Do you know in the black community, if we adopted affirmative action on a need base, you know who we would first give something to? The young man you passed out on the corner, sixteen years old, selling dope. Killing himself, destroying his world, and eliminating his soul. He is out there peddling death. But have you ever watched him work? He doesn't have a pen and paper, because he can't read and write. Doesn't have a calculator, because he doesn't know how to use one. But a customer comes up, one of his 150 customers from the suburbs, and he knows all of them by name. He knows what brand of death they buy. And when they buy 14 and 1/2 and 3/4 ounces of grams of death at $14 and 16 millimeters in a half, he can compute it in his head in about two seconds. He is a veritable genius. That's who *we* should look for for affirmative action.

You and I don't have to worry about being successful. You're neurotic if you're in this room worried about being successful. You are *already* successful. How many more shoes can you wear? All of us are overweight. No matter how thin you are, you eat too much. You've got too much of everything. And in our minds, you know why we do this? Because we are *afraid.* Fear, ladies and gentlemen, is the first cousin of the ego which tells your soul not to grow. Because if you tell the truth, they will destroy you.

We don't live in the future, and we don't live in the past. We live in the *present.* You never have lived in the past, and you never *will* live in the future. Every day of your life will be in the present. Why in the world are you afraid of what's not there? People say, "Oh, let's get in touch with our emotions." No, let's get *out* of touch with our feelings. Your feelings are making you afraid!

This is precisely the way they constructed slavery. To make the African afraid, fearful twenty-four hours a day. Any time of day or night, someone could come in and do anything they wanted to do with you. So we got afraid. And the fear is a part of our community. It is as integral to our personality as any other behavior trait. And the reason, ladies and gentlemen, we don't have what other groups have is we are afraid to have what they have because they've told us if we have it, we'll do something wrong.

The bottom line is, if we don't go inside of ourselves and see ourselves for what we are, we are never going to have what other people have. I don't care how many petitions we make, and I don't care how many other folks protest this phony love of us. The bottom line is, if you want to see who succeeds in America, go back and understand the first lie you learned.

Before they taught you how to read and write, they taught you this was a melting pot. And it is the biggest lie ever told. You are not going to melt. Now I don't want to frighten anybody in here, but if you were born black, that's the way you're going to die. So I simply suggest that you get in touch with reality. And whatever's sitting in that seat with you *is* your reality. That's all you have to do.

> ***"The bottom line is, if we don't go inside of ourselves and see ourselves for what we are, we are never going to have what other people have."***

The bottom line is, when other groups come here—isn't it striking that the Vietnamese came here in 1979 not speaking one word of English, and they now dominate every honor science society in America? Isn't it amazing that in twenty-five years the Cubans took Miami, southern Florida, elected a governor? [That] the Cubans have more money in one Cuban bank in Miami than the blacks have in the nine largest black banks combined? Isn't it amazing that black West Indians and Haitians, who come from the poorest country in the western hemisphere, and Africans who have migrated here in the last ten years now have a per capita family income higher than the native-born black American? And [that] black West Indians earn ten percent more than the average white American? And [that] black West Indians are better educated than the average white American? Isn't it amazing that these groups—black, brown, yellow, polka dot and whatever it is—come here and in ten years come here and do better than we're doing?

Now just be objective, get out of being black, be objective about it. They *have* to be doing something we're not doing, don't they? Now maybe we don't know what it is. But they're doing something, and you know what they're doing? They all have one thing in common—they love what they are. They use pride in their heritage as a basis of economic, social, political, and educational achievement. That's precisely what we're not doing. In our community, we're even debating being African. Nobody else is debating being a Jew, a Pole, a Frenchman, or a German. We're debating being an African!

Now how in the world do you think we're going to compete with other folks who *use* culture as a basis of success? Now why is culture important, Tony? You wouldn't be important if you lived in Japan because you got one culture. But it's important in a multicultural society in which everybody is organized around some community interest. And to the extent to which the *community* benefits, is the extent to which the individual opportunities are created.

Jackie Robinson was *not* the first black who was capable of playing in the major leagues, baseball. He was the first black who had the *opportunity* to play in the major leagues, and he got there because the influence and affluence of the black community had reached such a level, they had no choice because blacks were spending too much money going to baseball games. They *had* to have blacks. Blacks saved the sport. It was just a matter of choosing *one* of us. Not the best, but one of us. Jackie Robinson is *not* an example of outstanding individual merit, although he was an outstanding man; he is the result of the black community's progress.

And every job you and I in this room have was created by black folks in the streets of Watts, Detroit, and Newark, New Jersey. Everything you and I have, I have been on national television for one reason only, and that is there were enough black people in this country to *demand* that somebody black be on, and enough blacks who watch me to keep me on. And if I do not remember that's my source, then I will lose whatever I've got and I will have no potential.

Your potential in corporate America is to serve the interests of corporate America. That's your job. You are not there to serve black people. But *if* you do not serve black people, you will not be effective in your job. Because you do know the study I have referred to, the Hudson Study, [in the] year 2000 the work force will be over fifty percent female and nonwhite. Not because of discriminatory patterns against white men, but because there weren't enough white men born in the sixties and fifties. You do know that if corporate America does not bring in women and nonwhites, it cannot remain competitive, because there's nothing left in the labor share but women and nonwhites. Therefore, if they must bring in women and nonwhites, they must have you there to help them do it.

You are not there because of affirmative action, you are there, ladies and gentlemen, because the learning curve of corporate America is way ahead of the rest of us. They know more about cultural diversity than everybody in this room put together. And don't you think for one second they don't. They know they are the end users of the public school system in this country. And they know if the school systems and human capital dry up, they don't have a ghost of a chance. And they can only go so far offshore. They can't grow. This is their base. And they have to protect their base. Which means they have to relate to people they haven't related to before.

But it's not a matter of coming in and bringing an Indian in to show the white folks how to dance, and a black person to come in and show them the boogaloo and all that other nonsense. That is *not* cultural diversity. Cultural diversity is learning how to help your corporate interest while you help your people. And to the extent to which you help your people, you're going to help your corporate interest. They cannot be separated in a society in which we are going to dominate the work force.

And I'd like to say this to the women. You talk a lot about the glass ceiling. Understand one thing, just be real practical. Look at the demographics of this country. Women *must* dominate American society. There is no other alternative. Stop talking about the glass ceiling. You *own* the damn glass! And in case you didn't get that point, understand this: a woman's place is in the house . . . and the senate. And it is up to you, my sisters, to decide where you want to be. It is not in the hands of anybody else. Those decisions can no longer be made by white men.

White men are going to be traumatized and are traumatized, particularly those in middle management. Top management in every company I know is all gung ho for cultural diversity. But the middle-management whites—men—tend to think they are going to be discriminated against. What they do not understand is if they don't get some other women and if they don't get some black people and some Hispanic people in those corporations, they are not even going to have a job. That's what they don't understand.

Black people are going to go through a traumatic period because we aren't going to have to fight racism. We won't know what to do. I mean, what in the world will we have seminars about if we can't talk about racism? "You mean, Tony, that they'll give me that job making $400,000 a year?" I said, "They'll give it to you and make it a million-four if you show them how to run that computer and increase sales by one percent." They don't care! These people, ladies and gentlemen, are at a sea change in history in which you have the greatest opportunity we've ever had. You notice that's the first time I've used racism since I've been up here? And in case there's somebody here who's disappointed they're not getting their good dose of how bad white people are, how hard it is to make it in America, let me apologize to you.

But I don't intend to talk about the predicament. I'm going to talk about the problem. You see, racism is not the problem, it's the predicament. In case you don't know the difference between a predicament and a problem, let me give you an example. My rent is due today. That is *not* the problem. That is the *predicament.* What I'm going to do about *paying* my rent is the problem. You see, racism is alive and well. You can see it anywhere you want every night at six o'clock on television. We don't need to discuss racism, we know it's there. We know the LAPD will treat you like a king. We don't need to discuss racism.

What we need to discuss is what are we going to *do* about racism. What we need to discuss is why is it that the black middle class, 350 national black organizations, spend $16 billion every summer in white hotels discussing white racism and black poverty. That's what we need to discuss.

We need to discuss why we're going to come here to Washington, D.C., next month to the Congressional Black Caucus legislative weekend and spend five hundred million dollars in five days—a hundred million dollars a day, a half billion dollars—at white hotels calling white people all kinds of names. At the fashion show, the biggest thing there at midnight after we're sitting there in ten-thousand-dollar—each table is ten thousand dollars. You got a three-thousand-dollar dress on, eight-hundred-dollar pair of shoes, four-hundred-dollar purse, eating buffalo wings, drinking Scotch whiskey and doing the electric slide. And then the speaker's going to get up at midnight and cuss Republicans, conservatives, and white folks every which way. And you're going to give him all the trophies you got. And the only thing you're going to do is to come here this year and plan next year's meeting.

It was *disgraceful* last year to see thirty black folks stand up in a meeting and give Bill Clinton $600,000 in thirty minutes. It was a *disgrace.* You've never seen thirty black people give anybody black $600,000 in the history of America. And all they're trying to do is to buy personal influence. "Put me in office." "Give me a donation." "Run me for president." "Make me famous." And therefore we'll help the black community.

You're *not* helping the black community. Michael Jackson's billions and billions of dollars don't help black people. Your money doesn't help black people, either. It's when you build up our institutions, our churches, our nonprofit organizations, when you help our young people get human capital, *that's* when you've helped the black community. You making more money is *not* helping black people.

We've got this twisted notion, somehow, when all of us like you and I get together and have a good time, we've advanced the black cause, we've helped ourselves. And let's put it in perspective, and there's nothing wrong with that. But if that's what you want to do, admit that's what you're doing. Don't pretend you're on some mission. Just do like everybody else does, go somewhere, drink a lot of whiskey, do a lot of boogalooing and have a nice time and go home. Don't call it a think tank. Don't call it some type of "We have a community service component." Just say what you are. Tell the world what you are about.

But if you indeed want to help our people, and if people like you *don't* help our people, they can't survive, because they have no resources. You and I, thirty percent of the black community, control eighty percent of its wealth and all of its education, all of its human capital. And if you and I don't change, and if you and I don't sacrifice, our people are dead. And that, ladies and gentlemen, is not a legal decision, it's a moral decision. That's between you and your God. That tells you what you want to do with your life. If you want to get in your position and get scared, and worry, and not be critical, and let any black person get away with anything, but you criticize any white person for anything, you are *not* being a moral human being. You're being a demagogue. If that's what we choose to be, so be it.

But if you want to have an effective national organization, commit yourself to our community, *not* to your careers. Your careers can only grow if our community grows. And if we die, you die with us. Because if corporate America doesn't need me and you and the little guy out on the corner selling dope or the little girl turning the trick, they don't need you, either.

And the common sense, ladies and gentlemen, is what we've been doing does not work. Because we've misled ourselves, and we've misled ourselves because we don't like ourselves, and we don't like ourselves because we don't understand what culture's all about.

Now I know somebody's thinking that guy's beating up that ol' black stuff again, that old culture. I've got a culture, "Hi, guy, I'm on the 'Today' show, I'm color-blind." Just let me say this to you, whatever is sitting in that seat with you is your culture. And your culture, ladies and gentlemen, tells you to do everything you do. I don't care if you deny it, I don't care if you try not to be what you are. You are what you are.

Let me give you an example, I spoke recently at a black church, and just before I got there, the preacher had been fired for some unspoken indiscretion. And he got up to tell his flock goodbye. Arrogant, unrepentant, he said, "Jesus brought me here and Jesus is taking me away." And about that time, the brothers and sisters slowly broke into "Oh, What a Friend We Have in Jesus."

Now in academic circles they call that call-and-response. You see, in the black community, when a black speaker is before a black audience, the audience helps the speaker deliver the message. "Uh huh, right on, brother, I hear you, now watch out, don't hurt nobody, uh huh." Now in the Euro-centered culture, the audience waits until the end of the message and politely punctuates it with applause. Neither culture is superior, we've just developed uniquely.

Then when you get blacks in a room, where you have a critical mass of whites, like at your annual dinner, you know, your professional thing, blacks tend to become culturally ambivalent. They don't know which culture to call on. And you watch them, like when it's time to laugh, they check the whites, "What do I do now . . . ?"

So, I say the next time you get in that situation, and you don't want your white friends to see you doing your "right on, baby, get down, um hmmm, I hear ya," you can just [gesture]. You see this is a non-oral "right on," you understand? You know where it comes from? When we lived near the railroad tracks. Yeah, when we were by the tracks and when it was safe to cross, we just [gestured].

Now nobody ever had a class and said, "Oh, little black Tony, this is how you get to be black." You just who you are. Now get it real straight, this speaker is grandmama's biscuits. I am my mama's switches. You ever get whipped with switches? They're like a blowtorch on your legs, right? Now today, they call it child abuse. I am Reverend Woods' sermons at the Methodist Church in Charleston, West Virginia, every Sunday morning when he told us, love God, love other people—including those who don't know how to love—get a little job, work hard, meet a nice lady or a nice guy, be a decent person, save your money and above all, get a good education. And in life, you'll have pretty much what you want. Don't worry about getting it all, life will be pretty good to you, if you have some sense of service.

And then I went to school, and I had Mrs. Norman, Mrs. Ruth S. Norman, my English teacher. She said, "Today we're going to read Shakespeare. We're going to particularly pay attention to Hamlet and we're going to focus on Polonius, the father's, advice to Laertes, the son, as he goes out into the world, when he said, 'This above all: to thine own self be true,/And it must follow, as the night the day,/Thou canst not then be false to any man.'"

That's all there is, ladies and gentlemen. There is no black and white in the world. You just live in a racist society, and that's all you know. There's only God and you, and whatever else anybody else tries to do really is not part of that equation. It's not a matter of how they see you, it's a matter of how you see yourselves.

And you want to get over racism? You can't fight racism because it's ignorance. You see, I never understand why blacks want to get rid of racism. I don't understand how you do it because people who are racist are pathological. Anybody who needs a entire group of folks to look down on is sick. I'm out in a mental hospital, a guy walks up to me and says, "Hey, man, I'm Napoleon." I say, "Have a nice day." There's nothing *I* can do for him. I mean, *I* can't cure anybody who's a racist.

But you see of all the positive influences I had in my life—Reverend Woods at the church, Mrs. Norman in school, all these wonderful people—the most important influence on me was my drunk Uncle Kenny. You got one. See, but my drunk Uncle Kenny was not always a drunk. At one time before he went off to fight World War II, he was a stand-up, good-looking young man. Marched off to Burma in his uniform looking great, went to Burma, lay in the swamps, fighting malaria, contracted malaria fighting the Japanese to make the world safe for democracy and make America safe for Americans, came back to his own home, could not get a job because he was black, picked up a bottle and became a drunk.

And in the latter years of his life, always in his tattered uniform, of which he was most proud, he admonished us, the children. He said, "I've come as far as I can come. I've passed the baton to you. I've taken all I can take. I couldn't handle any more. *You've* got to do it." He said, "You won't get all the way there, either, but you'll get further than I got." He said, "You have faith, because you're good and you're from a good stock."

You see, of all the good influences I had, my drunk Uncle Kenny made more sense to me than anybody. Because he transferred to me my legacy. He told me who and what I was and most of all he gave me faith. I learned to have faith through his failure. And you see, you never know, ladies and gentlemen, but your culture is always there.

I'll give you another example how culture automatically works. I was out in San Francisco, and I spoke to a black community group. These are plain old ordinary folks; nobody had ever been to college, so they were very intelligent, very logical. And they had this big, fancy banquet, downtown, the big, fancy hotel, first time they'd ever been down there. They were real pretty, with new dresses and suits, two thousand of them. You know, table 55, 922, 35, and I was at the podium, and I saw this one man walking from table to table. Everybody was calling him, he was all over the place. And I hit the brother next to me, and I said, "Who's that?" He said, "That's Scotty." I said, "What's he doing?" He said, "Scotty brought the hot sauce." Now *somehow* they knew the food wasn't going to be right. So Scotty brought the hot sauce. Now see you intelligent, well-educated, rich black folks, you'd pick a committee to figure it out, wouldn't you?

The bottom line, ladies and gentlemen, is there's something wonderful about you if you're ever able to go on automatic. You think about it. You think about being that queen or king that you are. Think about being that person. Think about just doing it as a natural part of your life. Rather than worrying about if anybody sees it they're going to do something to you. That's that fear. Ladies and gentlemen, do you know who you are? You are the sleeping giants of the universe. You are the kings and queens of the world.

A young black woman called me up and said, "Mr. Brown I'm twenty-two years old, I've got a PhD from Harvard and an MBA from Stanford. I can't make it in America." I said, "What's wrong, my sister?" She said, "They're taking quotas away from me. I can't make it without quotas." I said, "On behalf of *my* generation of blacks, let me apologize to you and your generation for what we've done to you."

You look exactly like Cleopatra, the woman who sat on the throne of Egypt. You look like Pythagoras, the man who gave the world mathematics. People in this room look exactly like the people who created the University of Timbuktu in Africa when people in Europe were living in caves. You look exactly like the man and woman who created mathematics and science and geometry and architecture. You *are* learning. And they have us so brainwashed as, quote, "poor and minority" that here we are seven years from the millennium begging white folks to bus us to their neighborhoods so we can get educated.

And one of the dumbest ideas in the world is busing. You get up real early in the morning and you get this little African, you put him or her on a yellow bus, ship him across town to sit next to this superior European, so these good white genes will jump in the little dummy's body and he'll learn to read, write, and count. Well, let me tell what's really dumb about busing. Busing is really dumb because only seventeen percent of white people finish college. Forty-six percent of Asian Americans finish college. So if you want to bus Tony Brown, you bus me to Chinatown!

The bottom line, ladies and gentlemen, is that everything has to do with the way you see yourself. Therefore, let me ask you a couple three questions about the way you see yourself. You've heard George Santayana's very famous statement, "He who does not understand history is doomed to repeat it." So let me ask you three American history questions. I know you don't know the words to the black national anthem. So let me ask you three others. Number one, name three African American heroes of the American Revolutionary War. Number two, what African American laid out our nation's capital, Washington, D.C., the city we're in? Number three, who chopped down the cherry tree and could not tell a lie?

Now if you only got number three, you probably received an "A" in high school history. And if you received an "A" in high school history, you are an expert in *his* story. Not history, *his* story. And *his* story is the glue that holds all of the lies together. If you've ever put the truth in the place of *his* story, in every history book, there wouldn't even be such a thing as a concept called racism.

You see, I love America. I love America because I know America's history. I know the first American to die in the Revolutionary War was a black man named Crispus Attucks. I know that a black scientific genius named Benjamin Banneker laid out our nation's capital when Pierre L'Enfant became upset with Jefferson and took the plans back to France. I know the first successful open heart surgery was performed by Dr. Daniel Hale Williams in Chicago in 1893. I know that Garrett A. Morgan invented the electric traffic signal—the stop sign—not to stop black people in black cars, but so we could *all* have a system of street safety. And Hank Aaron is not the all-time black home run hitter in baseball; Hank Aaron is *the* all-time home run hitter in baseball.

So if we may now, let us go back to the very beginning of civilization. *His* story said civilization began in Europe. It did not. In 711 AD, Moors—Africans—navigated from Africa with compasses, sailed across the water, conquered Spain, and took the bagpipes into Scotland when the Spaniards believed if you went too far out in the water, you fell off the end of the world. Aleksandr Sergeyevich Pushkin, a black Russian, created the syntax for the Russian language. Alexandre Dumas—you read *The Three Musketeers*—they told you he was a Frenchman. Did they tell you he was a *black* Frenchman? And a man named Beethoven, who played the piano at three and composed at six, was called a Moor for black. . . . And the citizens of Greece and Rome did *not* look like Charlton Heston and Kirk Douglas. You see, at one point, Europe is only fourteen miles from Africa. And you can't stay white that close to that many black people.

Now, if we may, let us go back to the very beginning of the human race. And I will apologize in a racist society for calling all of us human beings. But we *are* all human beings because all of us came from the cradle of civilization which is Africa, and it was one million years before one human being left the continent of Africa to go to Europe, the Far East, or Asia. Therefore, every human being who lives, who has lived, or who shall ever live is an African. You can call yourself anything you want. You can paint wings on a pig, but if you throw him off of a building, he still can't fly.

Now a white friend of mine said, "Come on, Tony, you've gone too far with all that ol' black stuff. After all, look at me. My white skin, blue eyes, and blonde hair—how in the world could I be of African descent?" I said, "Well, number one, the anthropologists and sociologists at the University of California at Berkeley have proven in a scientific study that all human life, all human beings on the planet earth, are descended from one woman who lived in southern Africa 120,000 years ago. Now that means that everybody who lives, no matter what they call themselves, is of the same derivation. And I'll say it another way. Everybody who lives, I'd like to say, 'Yo mama is black.'"

Now he just got outraged. "I don't understand that stuff man, you've gotten carried away." I said, "Well, let me explain it another way. You look like you look because you got your genes from your ancestors and your ancestors got their genes from the environment. It's called phenotype adaptation or the adaptation of the physical body to the human elements. You live in the northern part of Europe for long periods of time, the ultraviolet rays of the sun are very weak, therefore the skin does not need melanin, therefore the skin is so-called white. The nostrils in that part of the world develop long and narrow because the air is dry and cold. Take this physical type to the Sudan, 120° a day heat, the skin must become a so-called brown or black because it needs melanin to protect it from the ultraviolet rays of the sun. The nostrils will become wide to breathe the thick air, and the hair will become good, like mine." That is simple phenotype or physical adaptation.

The dumbest idea in the world is that one group is inferior or superior because of the absence or presence of melanin in the skin. God made your hair as curly, kinky, or straight as he chose. He placed your eyes the exact number of centimeters on either side of your nose. He made your nostrils wide for breathing, and your lips thick for kissing. When you look into the mirror, you look into the face of perfection. When you look into the mirror, you look into the face of God if you have the love and the beauty to see God when He or She looks back at you.

The bottom line, ladies and gentlemen, is when you go back to yourself, you will find out who the world and what the world is, and the world will understand who and what you are. And when you understand yourself, you will be most competitive. You'll be most competitive if you learn, ladies and gentlemen, that your culture is as good as anybody else's but not any better. You will be economically and politically and socially equal to other people when you understand that you cannot spend 95 percent of your money with other people and blame them for 100 percent of your problems. You will be politically and economically equal when you take the $300 billion that you, as black people, spend each year and instead of spending 95 percent of it with other people, spend 50 percent of it with yourselves and 50 percent of it with non-black people who support our community. Therefore, we will teach our dollar some sense and 100 percent of all our wealth will come back to us in some form. Now when you do that, you'll be equal to other people.

"The dumbest idea in the world is that one group is inferior or superior because of the absence or presence of melanin in the skin."

But you can't be equal to other people through programs of preference. Preference is always what somebody else has in excess that they have left over, and when times get tight, they take that back. Therefore, I like the old—I know you've heard it comes out of the Bible, sung best by Billie Holiday, "God bless the child that's got his own." And if you don't have your own, you're at somebody else's mercy. And if you don't take your money and understand that you have $300 billion as black people that you will spend this year. That's more money than the gross national product of Canada or Australia, more money than the gross national product of the fourteenth-richest nation in the world.

You are twelve percent of the population. There are thirty million of us that the Census Bureau can find. You are twelve percent of the population. You buy eighteen percent of the orange juice, twenty percent of the rice, twenty-six percent of Cadillac cars, ninety-nine percent of Florsheim shoes. Fifty-six percent of us own our own homes. Black teens buy forty percent of all records purchased. Blacks between twelve and twenty-four purchase over fifty percent of all tickets to movie theaters. You're twelve percent of the population and you drink twenty percent of the Scotch whiskey. If you took blacks out of America, Wall Street would collapse last week.

If you want to know how to stay in your own hotels, I've got a little plan up here, I've got some flyers that I'll give to you after I speak. It's real simple, I've done the math for you, it's all written down. If we would take of the $16 billion that we spent each year on conventions, put it in—take 3 billion of the 16, put it in a bank, the interest would be $400 million. Take the $400 million, split it into units of $20 million each, take each $20 million unit and buy a major hotel in each of the top 20 markets, where over 50 percent of the black population resides. Each hotel would do a minimum gross of $50 million. Fifty million times 20 hotels would give us a $3 billion cash flow. Therefore, we could hire and put blacks in business because a hotel is nothing but a mobile city. Everything human beings need, a hotel must buy and sell. Therefore, we could put all of our folks in every city in business. And we did that on the interest. The principal is still on deposit. We take the $3 billion on deposit and we leverage that times 10, so have $30 billion that we could use as a capital formation fund to fund every program we're on our knees begging the government and white people to do for us.

Now all we have to do is to do it. That, ladies and gentlemen, will require what? Us to change and us to sacrifice. Because nobody else is going to do it.

And let me make my final point about what nobody else can do. Nobody else can speak the English language the way we speak it. And, therefore, one of the greatest forms of discrimination in America is not being called bad names, but it's someone saying that your dialect is faulty, therefore your IQ is lower because you can't speak the English language the way Caucasians can.

Now let me tell you why you speak like you speak. You speak like you speak because your language, like all other groups who've come to this country—and everybody came to this country from somewhere else—your language, your so-called dialect, is simply the derivative of the residual of the language of your ancestors. And it's simply been modified by your experience, the history of your people and your region in the country.

A white woman saw me once and said, "Oh, Mr. Brown, I've seen you on television and you're so intelligent, but you have a southern accent." I said, "Yes, ma'am, if you'd been raised in Charleston, West Virginia, *you'd* have a southern accent." I *am* a southerner, that's why I *speak* like a southerner. If I weren't, I wouldn't speak this way.

The bottom line is, whatever's in that seat with you, whatever language you speak, is who you are. You can't be anything but your language, because your language is the accumulated experience of everything you've done and everything your people have done. Therefore, the way you speak is legitimate. That's why there are eleven discernible dialects in America.

Now if there are eleven discernible dialects in America, what is the so-called standard dialect? The standard dialect in any society is the language of the group with the most money and power. In America, that's the white Anglo-Saxon Protestants. If blacks had as much wealth as WASPs, Walter Cronkite would have to speak the way I speak to be on television, rather than me speaking the way he speaks to be on television.

But speaking of the way I speak, I am bidialectal. And I recommend that all blacks speak, read, and write the standard dialect very, very well. I recommend it highly for food, clothing, and shelter. Now when you get smart enough to spend fifty percent of your money in your own neighborhood and make your own people as rich and as wealthy and as happy as you make everybody else, then you can just stand at the cash register and grunt if you want to. But as long as you're giving everybody else ninety-five percent of your money, you must speak their language to get your j-o-b. Which is why I am bidialectal.

I have a movie I made a couple years ago, it's now on video, and it's being distributed, and I had to go to Hollywood to make a deal. So I went in to talk to the president of this company, who happened to be white. I didn't go in and say, "Hey, baby, what's happenin'?" I said, "Good morning, Mr. President, have a nice day." Makes him feel safe. I didn't go there to be his black experience. I went there for commercial reasons. Now a little later on tonight, when I'm with the tribe, I'll use a more colorful language. You ever see two black men greet one another? "How you doin'? How you doin'? What's happenin'? What's happenin'?" We *never* answer. I mean, I can look at him and tell he's catching hell, so we go right on into the conversation.

And then, if you think black folks are the only ones who do it, look at what they do in New York. What do they do in New York? They "paahk the caah." In "Baahstin they paahk the caah in the Haahvaahd Yaahd." That's called the post-vocalic "r." Words ending in "r" preceded by a vowel, they drop the "r." That tells you the history of the people in the Northeast. You go to Texas and ask for directions. What do they say? "Turn left, raaht here." You go to S-o-u-t-h Carolina, ask a brother where you are, he will tell you, "You are in 'Souse' Carolina." You go to a Chinese restaurant and order french fried rice, they will serve you "flench flied lice." Everybody speaks the English language through the filter of their cultural background. And that's all you can do.

For an example, if you don't think black people have a language, we do because we have a syntax. You ever heard black people say, *"be's* that way sometimes"? That's the continued "to be." See, the rule is when a black person says, "it *be's* that way sometimes," it's that way temporarily. But when "it *be* that way," it's that way *all* the time!

And then, if you notice how when we mix it up—I mean, beyond a shadow of a doubt, we are masters at communications arts. I mean, we mix the oral with the non-oral. I mean, we really get cute. I was at St. Louis University, a young brother was sitting next to me, he looked down at his buddy and said, "Hey, Charles, what's happenin'?" Charles responded. . . . He said, "I hear ya."

And then, all you've got to do, ladies and gentlemen, is to take a very good look around you. When you go home tonight, go to your room, wherever you go, turn on your television. Don't look at it, listen to it. What are you going to hear? *Your* music. *Your* music—James Brown, Ruth Brown, Charles Brown, all those old people that they said their music was evil, it's no good. Where is it? It's around, it's the music bed for every major commercial company in America. *Your* music. And *what* is your music? It's your fears, your faith, your love, your creativity, your history. That's your *culture.* And corporate America knows, and the world knows, and it cannot resist goodness. And when they see and hear your music, they feel *good,* because it's a universal message. And it comes out of your people, and it comes out of *you.* Ladies and gentlemen, simply recognize, consciously, who you are because the rest of the world already knows.

I'd like to say this in closing. Don't try to be evil to fight it. Redemption is found in the hearts of your enemy. God says, "Vengeance is mine." That's *not* your department. Your department is being the *best* that you can be. Your department is developing your own resources and developing our collective *human* capital as a community of people. You are the talented, you are the chosen. You are the best we've ever produced.

Don't be a demagogue and sit in the back of the room and listen to us come up and celebrate our ignorance. Saying that we've got to belong to only one party, saying that we've got to give our money away, saying we can't believe in ourselves, we've got to wait on a white person to do it, and then come up to the front of the room and celebrate us for our ignorance and get elected our leader. That's a demagogue.

Leadership is making your people come to the limits, the maximum, of which they're capable. It's about us telling our young people that this rap music is filthy, that it is degrading, that it is not only misogynist, it is evil. And if you're *not* willing to tell them that, you're going to be afraid of them, because they're growing at a faster rate than you are. If you don't challenge evil, you're simply a good German. And look it where it got Germany. If you're not going to come up here and be good and honest with us, stay in the back.

That's what leadership requires in our community. It doesn't require a bunch of pimps telling us to keep them in office so they can make deals and line their pockets. You're simply a part of the problem. And you are strategically placed. You are the bridge between our people, our desperate people, in a desperate situation, and the resources that cannot only aid your company, but it can also help rehabilitate our people. But *you* must be our spiritual motivators. And you must challenge us. And you, as a group, must challenge yourselves, to change and to sacrifice.

And in that context, I leave you with a challenge that comes from a poem [by Canadian writer John McCrae] called "[In] Flanders Field[s]." Flanders field is a graveyard in Europe in which many of the American dead from

World War I are buried. And the poem was written to remind those Americans who came back from that great war of the tremendous sacrifice that those dead men made. And it goes like this: "To you from failing hands we throw/ The torch; be yours to hold it high./If ye break faith with us who die/We shall not sleep, though poppies grow/In Flanders fields." God bless you.

SOURCES

Books

Brown, Tony, *No Black Lies, No White Lies, Only the Truth!*, Morrow, 1995.

Periodicals

Black Enterprise, January, 1974; "Tony Brown: Television's Civil Rights Crusader," September, 1979, p. 36; "The Price of Freedom," February, 1986, p. 28.

Chicago Tribune, January 8, 1989; February 9, 1990.

Detroit Free Press, "The Economics of a Movement," September 27, 1993, p. 4F.

Fortune, "PBS's Tony Brown Tunes in to GOP," November 4, 1991, p. 200.

New York Times, November 29, 1970.

Wall Street Journal, July 24, 1991; August 5, 1991; "America's Industrial Salvation: Team America," June 21, 1994, p. S16.

William Wells Brown

1815(?)–1884

African American novelist, playwright, and author of nonfiction

Although he is probably best known as the first African American to publish a novel, a play, and a travel book, William Wells Brown was also a noted lecturer whose chief interests were abolition and temperance. Born into slavery in Kentucky, he was taken to Missouri as an infant when his owner moved there. He spent the first twenty or so years of his life in and around the city of St. Louis as the property of three different masters, laboring at times as a house slave, a field hand, a tavern boy, and a jack-of-all-trades in the offices of the St. Louis Times, *in a doctor's office, and on board a Mississippi riverboat.*

In 1834, while accompanying his then-owner on a business trip to Cincinnati, William escaped and was befriended by an Ohio Quaker named Wells Brown, from whom the former slave took his new middle and last names. He then settled in Cleveland and from there moved on to Buffalo and eventually Farmington, New York, serving as a steward on various ships that sailed Lake Erie. Brown used his position to conduct many other former slaves to freedom in Canada via the Underground Railroad and devoted whatever free time he had left to a rigorous self-education program. He also became active in a temperance society in Buffalo and soon displayed a talent for public speaking.

In 1843, Brown began lecturing for the Western New York Anti-Slavery Society. Four years later, he was hired by the Massachusetts Anti-Slavery Society to lecture throughout New England. His subsequent relocation to Boston brought him into contact with a number of well-known abolitionists, including William Lloyd Garrison. Before long, Brown himself was a prominent figure in the national antislavery movement.

On November 4, 1847, members of the Female Anti-Slavery Society of Salem, Massachusetts, gathered to hear Brown speak on how slavery had affected the American people and how it had influenced the world's perception of the United States. An excerpt from his address, reprinted here from The Voice of Black America: Major Speeches by Negroes in the United States, 1797-1971, *edited by Philip S. Foner (Simon & Schuster, 1972), was originally published in pamphlet form in 1847 by the Massachusetts Anti-Slavery Society.*

. . . It is deplorable to look at the character of the American people, the character that has been given to them by the institution of slavery. The profession of the American people is far above the profession of the people of any other country. Here the people profess to carry out the principles of Christianity. The American people are a sympathizing people. They not only profess, but appear to be a sympathizing people to the inhabitants of the whole world. They sympathize with everything else but the American slave. When the Greeks were struggling for liberty, meetings were held to express sympathy. Now they are sympathizing with the poor downtrodden serfs of Ireland, and are sending their sympathy across the ocean to them.

But what will the people of the Old World think? Will they not look upon the American people as hypocrites? Do they not look upon your professed sympathy as nothing more than hypocrisy? You may hold your meetings and send your words across the ocean; you may ask Nicholas of Russia to take the chains from his poor downtrodden serfs, but they look upon it all as nothing but hypocrisy. Look at our twenty thousand fugitive slaves, running from under the stars and stripes, and taking refuge in the Canadas; *twenty thousand,* some leaving their wives, some their husbands, some leaving their children, some their brothers, and some their sisters—fleeing to take refuge in the Canadas. Wherever the stars and stripes are seen flying in the United States of America, they point him out as a slave.

If I wish to stand up and say, "I am a man," I must leave the land that gave me birth. If I wish to ask protection as a man, I must leave the American stars and stripes. Wherever the stars and stripes are seen flying upon American soil, I can receive no protection; I am a slave, a chattel, a thing. I see your liberty poles around in your cities. If tomorrow morning you are hoisting the stars and stripes upon one of your liberty poles, and I should see the man following me who claims my body and soul as his property, I might climb to the very top of your liberty pole, I might cut the cord that held your stars and stripes and bind myself with it as closely as I could to your liberty pole, I might talk of law and the Constitution, but nothing could save me unless there be public sentiment enough in Salem. I could not appeal to law or the Constitution; I could only appeal to public sentiment; and if public sentiment would not protect me, I must be carried back to the plantations of the South, there to be lacerated, there to drag the chains that I left upon the Southern soil a few years since.

William Wells Brown

This is deplorable. And yet the American slave *can* find a spot where he may be a man—but it is not under the American flag. Fellow citizens, I am the last to eulogize any country where they oppress the poor. I have nothing to say in behalf of England or any other country, any further than as they extend protection to mankind. I say that I honor England for protecting the black man. I honor every country that shall receive the American slave, that shall protect him, and that shall recognize him as a man.

I know that the United States will not do it; but I ask you to look at the efforts of other countries. Even the Bey of Tunis, a few years since, has decreed that there shall not be a slave in his dominions; and we see that the subject of liberty is being discussed throughout the world. People are looking at it; they are examining it; and it seems as though every country and every people and every government were doing something, excepting the United States. But Christian, democratic, republican America is doing nothing at all. It seems as though she would be the last. It seems as though she was determined to be the last to knock the chain from the limbs of the slave. Shall the American people be behind the people of the Old World? Shall they be behind those who are represented as almost living in the dark ages?

Shall every flap of England's flag
Proclaim that all around are free,
From farthest Ind to each blue crag
That beetles o'er the western sea?
And shall we scoff at Europe's kings,
When Freedom's fire is dimmed with us
And round our country's altar clings
The damning shade of Slavery's curse?

Shall we, I ask, shall the American people be the last? I am here, not for the purpose of condemning the character of the American people, but for the purpose of trying to protect or vindicate their character. I would to God that there were some feature that I could vindicate. There is no liberty here for me; there is no liberty for those with whom I am associated; there is no liberty for the American slave; and yet we hear a great deal about liberty! How do the people of the Old World regard the American people? Only a short time since, an American gentleman, in traveling through Germany, passed the window of a bookstore where he saw a number of pictures. One of them was a cut representing an American slave on his knees, with chains upon his limbs. Over him stood a white man, with a long whip; and underneath was written, "the latest specimen of American democracy." I ask my audience, Who placed that in the hands of those that drew it? It was the people of the United States. Slavery, as it is to be found in this country, has given the serfs of the Old World an opportunity of branding the American people as the most tyrannical people upon God's footstool.

Only a short time since, an American man-of-war was anchored in the bay opposite Liverpool. The English came down by the hundreds and thousands. The stars and stripes were flying; and there stood those poor persons that had never seen an American man-of-war, but had heard a great deal of American democracy. Some were eulogizing the American people; some were calling it the "land of the free and the home of the brave." And while they stood there, one of their number rose up, and pointing his fingers to the American flag, said:

United States, your banner wears
Two emblems,—one of fame;
Alas, the other that it bears,
Reminds us of your shame.
The white man's liberty entyped,
Stands blazoned by your stars;
But what's the meaning of your stripes?
They mean your Negro scars.

What put that in the mouth of that individual? It was the system of American slavery; it was the action of the American people; the inconsistency of the American people; their profession of liberty, and their practice in opposition to their profession.

"Slavery, as it is to be found in this country, has given the serfs of the Old World an opportunity of branding the American people as the most tyrannical people upon God's footstool."

In 1849, Brown left the United States to attend the International Peace Congress in Paris. He ended up staying abroad for five years, settling in England and working to gain British support for the American antislavery movement. Some of the friends he made during his stay eventually purchased his freedom so that upon his eventual return home he would not be subject to capture under the provisions of the Fugitive Slave Act of 1850.

It was while he was in England that Brown published his first work, an autobiography entitled the Narrative of William W. Brown, A Fugitive Slave, Written by Himself. *He soon followed it with a collection of poems,* The Anti-Slavery Harp, *and a travelogue,* Three Years in Europe; Or, Places I Have Seen and People I Have Met, *the first book of its kind ever published by an African American. In 1853 came the fictional work* Clotel; Or, The President's Daughter: A Narrative of Slave Life in the United States, *which is generally acknowledged to be the first novel ever written by an African American. In 1856, two years after he had returned to the United States, Brown wrote an antislavery play entitled* Experience; Or, How to Give a Northern Man a Backbone; *in 1858, it became the first drama published by an African American. Brown also authored several historical works, including* The Black Man: His Antecedents, His Genius, and His Achievements *and* My Southern Home; Or, The South and Its People.

In the years leading up to the Civil War and during the war itself, Brown continued to lecture on abolitionism. He also spoke out in support of allowing blacks to serve in the Union Army. At a meeting of the American Anti-Slavery Society in New York on May 6, 1862, he was one of several who addressed the gathering on this issue. A brief excerpt from his remarks follows; originally published in the antislavery newspaper the Liberator, *it is reprinted here from Volume 1 of* A Documentary History of the Negro People in the United States, *edited by Herbert Aptheker, 3rd paperbound ed., Citadel Press, 1965.*

... All I demand for the black man is, that the white people shall take their heels off his neck, and let him have a chance to rise by his own efforts. [Applause.] One of the first things that I heard when I arrived in the free states—and it was the strangest thing to me that I heard—was, that the slaves cannot take care of themselves. I came off without any education. Society did not take me up; I took myself up. [Laughter.] I did not ask society to take me up. All I asked of the white people was, to get out of the way, and give me a chance to come from the South to the North. That was all I asked, and I went to work with my own hands. And that is all I demand for my brethren of the South today—that they shall have an opportunity to exercise their own physical and mental abilities. Give them that, and I will leave the slaves to take care of themselves, and be satisfied with the result.

> ***"... the fidelity of the black people of this country to the cause of freedom is enough to put to shame every white man in the land who would think of driving us out of the country ..."***

Now, Mr. President, I think that the present contest has shown clearly that the fidelity of the black people of this country to the cause of freedom is enough to put to shame every white man in the land who would think of driving us out of the country, provided freedom shall be proclaimed. I remember well, when Mr. Lincoln's proclamation went forth, calling for the first 75,000 men, that among the first to respond to that call were the colored men. A meeting was held in Boston, crowded as I never saw a meeting before; meetings were held in Rhode Island and Connecticut, in New York and Philadelphia, and throughout the West, responding to the president's call. Although the colored men in many of the free states were disfranchised, abused, taxed without representation, their children turned out of the schools, nevertheless, they went on, determined to try to discharge their duty to the country, and to save it from the tyrannical power of the slaveholders of the South.

But the cry went forth—"We won't have the Negroes; we won't have anything to do with them; we won't fight with them; we won't have them in the army, nor about us." Yet scarcely had you got into conflict with the South, when you were glad to receive the news that contrabands brought. [Applause.] The first telegram announcing any news from the disaffected district commences with—"A contraband just in from Maryland tells us" so much. The last telegram, in today's paper, announces that a contraband tells us so much about Jefferson Davis and Mrs. Davis and the little Davises. [Laughter.] The nation is glad to receive the news from the contraband.

We have an old law with regard to the mails, that a Negro shall not touch the mails at all; and for fifty years the black man has not had the privilege of touching the mails of the United States with his little finger; but we are glad enough now to have the Negro bring the mail in his pocket! The first thing asked of a contraband is—"Have you got a newspaper?—what's the news?" And the news is greedily taken in, from the lowest officer or soldier in the army, up to the secretary of war. They have tried to keep the Negro out of the war, but they could not keep him out, and now they drag him in, with his news, and are glad to do so. General Wool says the contrabands have brought the most reliable news. Other generals say their information can be relied upon. The Negro is taken as a pilot to guide the fleet of General Burnside through the inlets of the South. [Applause.] The black man welcomes your armies and your fleets, takes care of your sick, is ready to do anything, from cooking up to shouldering a musket; and yet these would-be patriots and professed lovers of the land talk about driving the Negro out!

Once blacks were allowed to enlist in the Union Army following the Emancipation Proclamation, Brown worked as a recruiter for the famous 54th Regiment of Massachusetts. After the war, he began practicing medicine (which he had been studying on his own for quite some time) and continued to lecture, mostly on behalf of the temperance movement.

SOURCES

Aptheker, Herbert, editor, *A Documentary History of the Negro People in the United States,* Volume 1: *From Colonial Times through the Civil War,* 3rd paperbound edition, Citadel Press, 1965.

Farrison, William Edward, *William Wells Brown: Author and Reformer,* University of Chicago Press, 1969.

Foner, Philip S., editor, *The Voice of Black America: Major Speeches by Negroes in the United States, 1797-1971,* Simon & Schuster, 1972.

Blanche Kelso Bruce

1841–1898

African American educator, businessman, and politician

As the first African American to serve a full six-year term as a United States Senator, Blanche Kelso Bruce occupies a special niche in history. (In fact, it was not until the mid-twentieth century that another black could make the same claim.) As the only black in Congress during much of his term, he willingly assumed the role of spokesman for his race. And unlike most of his colleagues, he also stood up for other races he felt had been subject to mistreatment by the laws and customs of an indifferent—if not outright hostile—nation.

The youngest of eleven children, Bruce was the son of a Virginia slave woman named Polly and an unknown white man, probably his mother's master, Pettus Perkinson. (Bruce acquired his surname from the man who had owned his mother and ten siblings before he was born.) During the late 1840s, Perkinson moved his family and his slaves back and forth across several southern states, eventually settling in Missouri. There young Blanche served as the personal valet to his master's son, which gave him the opportunity to receive a basic education from the young man's tutor. Later, he toiled as a field hand, a factory worker, and as a printer's apprentice.

During the early days of the Civil War, Bruce escaped to freedom in Lawrence, Kansas, where he opened the state's first elementary school for blacks and continued his own education under the guidance of a minister. After Missouri's slaves were freed in January 1865, he returned home and briefly resumed his career as a schoolteacher and a printer's apprentice before heading off to attend Oberlin College in Ohio. His money only lasted a few months, however, so he was soon forced to take a job as a porter on a riverboat. Two years later, having heard that the state of Mississippi had much to offer to an ambitious young man such as himself, Bruce headed there in 1869. He quickly became involved in politics, serving first as supervisor of elections in Tallahatchie County and then as sergeant-at-arms in the state senate, sheriff and tax assessor in Bolivar County, and superintendent of education and alderman in the town of Floreyville. He also purchased a plantation that before long made him a wealthy and respected businessman as well.

In 1874, the Mississippi legislature elected Bruce to the United States Senate.

(He was the second black Mississippian to serve in that position; the first was Hiram Revels, who was in office for just over a year, from 1870–71.) His actual arrival in the Senate chamber was a much-publicized moment of high drama. When Bruce's fellow Mississippi senator, a white man, refused to honor custom and escort him to the swearing-in ceremony, Senator Roscoe Conkling of New York stepped forward, took the black legislator by the hand, and led him to the front of the room.

Bruce took office at a time when the Republican-led reform movement that had dominated national and local politics since the end of the Civil War was running out of steam, especially in the South. In the elections of 1875, Bruce's own home state was the scene of particularly flagrant misdeeds by white Democrats who resorted to fraud and intimidation to wrest control of the state from the Republicans. Their actions generated outrage and controversy in the halls of Congress, where Senator Oliver Morton of Indiana, acting on behalf of his Michigan counterpart, introduced a resolution proposing that a special committee be formed to investigate election practices in Mississippi. On March 31, 1876, Bruce stood before his colleagues in the Senate to underscore the seriousness of the problem and the need to take immediate action on Morton's resolution. His speech is reprinted here from the Congressional Record, *44th Congress, 1876.*

Mr. President, I had hoped that no occasion would arise to make it necessary for me again to claim the attention of the Senate until at least I had acquired a larger acquaintance with its methods of business and a fuller experience in public affairs; but silence at this time would be infidelity to my senatorial trust and unjust to both the people and the state I have the honor in part to represent.

The conduct of the late election in Mississippi affected not merely the fortunes of the partisans—as the same were necessarily involved in the defeat or success of the respective parties to the contest—but put in question and jeopardy the sacred rights of the citizen; and the investigation contemplated in the pending resolution has for its object not the determination of the question whether the offices shall be held and the public affairs of that state be administered by Democrats or Republicans, but the higher and more important end, the protection in all their purity and significance of the political rights of the people and the free institutions of the country. I believe the action sought is within the legitimate province of the Senate; but I shall waive a discussion of that phase of the question, and address myself to the consideration of the importance of the proposed investigation.

The demand of the substitute of the senator from Michigan proceeds upon the allegation that fraud and intimidation were practiced by the opposition in the late state election, so as not only to deprive many citizens of their political rights, but so far as practically to have defeated a fair expression of the will of a majority of the legal voters of the state of Mississippi, resulting in placing in power many men who do not represent the popular will.

The truth of the allegations relative to fraud and violence is strongly suggested by the very success claimed by the democracy. In 1873 the Republicans carried the state by 20,000 majority; in November last the opposition claimed to have carried it by 30,000; thus a Democratic gain of more than 50,000. Now, by what miraculous or extraordinary interposition was this brought about? I can conceive that a large state like New York, where free speech and free press operate upon intelligent masses—a state full of railroads, telegraphs, and newspapers—on the occasion of a great national contest, might furnish an illustration of such a thorough and general change in the political views of the people; but such a change of front is unnatural and highly improbable in a state like my own, with few railroads, and a widely scattered and sparse population. Under the most active and friendly canvass the voting masses could not have

Blanche Kelso Bruce

been so rapidly and thoroughly reached as to have rendered this result probable.

There was nothing in the character of the issues nor in the method of the canvass that would produce such an overwhelming revolution in the sentiments of the colored voters of the state as is implied in this pretended Democratic success. The Republicans—nineteen-twentieths of whom are colored—were not brought, through the press or public discussions, in contact with Democratic influences to such an extent as would operate a change in their political convictions, and there was nothing in Democratic sentiments nor in the proscriptive and violent temper of their leaders to justify such a change of political relations.

The evil practices so naturally suggested by this view of the question as probable will be found in many instances by the proposed investigation to have been actual. Not desiring to anticipate the work of the committee nor to weary senators with details, I instance the single county of Yazoo as illustrative of the effects of the outrages of which we complain. This county gave in 1873 a Republican majority of nearly two thousand. It was cursed with riot and bloodshed prior to the late election, and gave but seven votes for the Republican ticket, and some of these, I am credibly informed, were cast in derision by the Democrats, who declared that Republicans must have some votes in the county.

To illustrate the spirit that prevailed in that section, I read from the *Yazoo Democrat,* an influential paper published at its county seat:

Let unanimity of sentiment pervade the minds of men. Let invincible determination be depicted on every countenance. Send forth from our deliberative assembly of the eighteenth the soul-stirring announcement that Mississippians shall rule Mississippi though the heavens fall. Then will woe, irretrievable woe, betide the radical tatterdemalions. Hit them hip and thigh, everywhere and at all times.

Carry the election peaceably if we can, forcibly if we must.

Again:

There is no radical ticket in the field, and it is more than likely there will be none; for the leaders are not in this city, and dare not press their claims in this county.

Speaking of the troubles in Madison County, the *Yazoo City Democrat* for the 26th of October says:

Try the rope on such characters. It acts fairly on such characters here.

The evidence in hand and accessible will show beyond peradventure that in many parts of the State corrupt and violent influences were brought to bear upon the registrars of voters, thus materially affecting the character of the voting or poll lists; upon the inspectors of election, prejudicially and unfairly thereby changing the number of votes cast; and, finally, threats and violence were practiced directly upon the masses of voters in such measure and strength as to produce grave apprehensions for their personal safety and as to deter them from the exercise of their political franchises.

Lawless outbreaks have not been confined to any particular section of the country, but have prevailed in nearly every state at some period in its history. But the violence complained of and exhibited in Mississippi and other Southern states, pending a political canvass, is exceptional and peculiar. It is not the blow that the beggared miner strikes that he may give bread to his children, nor the stroke of the bondsman that he may win liberty for himself, nor the mad turbulence of the ignorant masses when their passions have been stirred by the appeals of the demagogue; but it is an attack by an aggressive, intelligent, white political organization upon inoffensive, law-abiding fellow citizens; a violent method for political supremacy, that seeks not the protection of the rights of the aggressors, but the destruction of the rights of the party assailed. Violence so unprovoked, inspired by such motives, and looking to such ends, is a spectacle not only discreditable to the country, but dangerous to the integrity of our free institutions.

I beg senators to believe that I refer to this painful and reproachful condition of affairs in my own state not in resentment, but with sentiments of profound regret and humiliation.

If honorable senators ask why such flagrant wrongs were allowed to go unpunished by a Republican state government, and unresented by a race claiming 20,000 majority of the voters, the answer is at hand. The civil officers of the state were unequal to meet and suppress the murderous violence that frequently broke out in different parts of the state, and the state executive found himself thrown for support upon a militia partially organized and poorly armed. When he attempted to perfect and call out this force and to use the very small appropriation that had been made for their equipment, he was met by the courts with an injunction against the use of the money, and by the proscriptive elements of the opposition with such fierce outcry and show of counter-force, that he became convinced a civil strife, a war of races, would be precipitated unless he staid his hand. As a last resort, the protection provided in the national Constitution for a state threatened with domestic violence was sought; but the national executive—from perhaps a scrupulous desire to avoid the appearance of interference by the federal authority with the internal affairs of that state—declined to accede to the request made for federal troops.

> ***"It will not accord with the laws of nature or history to brand the colored people as a race of cowards."***

It will not accord with the laws of nature or history to brand the colored people as a race of cowards. On more than one historic field, beginning in 1776 and coming down to the centennial year of the Republic, they have attested in blood their courage as well as love of liberty. I ask Senators to believe that no consideration of fear or personal danger has kept us quiet and forbearing under the provocations and wrongs that have so sorely tried our souls. But feeling kindly toward our white fellow citizens, appreciating the good purposes and offices of the better classes, and, above all, abhorring war of races, we determined to wait until such time as an appeal to the good sense and justice of the American people could be made.

A notable feature of the outrages alleged is that they have referred almost exclusively to the colored citizens of the state. Why is the colored voter to be proscribed? Why direct the attack upon him? While the methods of violence, resorted to for political purposes in the South, are foreign to the genius of our institutions as applied to citizens generally—and so much is conceded by even the opposition—yet they seem to think we are an exceptional class and citizens, rather by sufferance than right; and when pressed to account for their bitterness and proscription toward us they, with more or less boldness, allege incompetent and bad government as their justification before the public opinion of the country. Now, I declare that neither political incapacity nor venality are qualities of the masses of colored citizens. The emancipation of the colored race during the late civil strife was an expression alike of the magnanimity and needs of the nation; and the subsequent and early subtraction of millions of industrial values from the resources of the insurrectionary states and the presence of many thousand additional brave hearts and strong hands around the flag of the country vindicated the justice and wisdom of the measure.

The close of the war found four millions of freedmen, without homes or property, charged with the duty of self-support and with the oversight of their personal freedom, yet without civil and political rights! The problem presented by this condition of things was one of the gravest that has ever been submitted to the American people. Shall these liberated millions of a separate race, while retaining personal liberty, be deprived of political rights? The practical sense of the American people definitely settled this delicate and difficult question, and the demand for a more pronounced loyal element in the work of reconstruction in the lately rebellious states furnished an opportunity for the recognition of the political rights of the race, both in the interest of justice and good government.

The history of my race since enfranchisement, considered in connection with the difficulties that have environed us, will exhibit hopeful progress and attest that we have been neither ungrateful for the civil and political privileges received nor wanting in appreciation of the correspondingly weighty obligations imposed upon us.

[Bruce then presented a number of statistics from census data and other sources regarding marriage, churches, and occupations to demonstrate the stability and progress of Mississippi's black residents since 1865. He then resumed his speech.]

The data here adduced, though not exhaustive, is sufficiently full to indicate and illustrate the capacity and progress of this people in the directions specified, and the fuller statistics, derived from subsequent and later investigations, and exhibiting the operation of the more liberal and judicious legislation and administration introduced since 1870, will amply sustain the conclusion authorized by the facts I have adduced. I submit that the showing made, relative to the social, moral, and industrial condition of the Negro, is favorable, and proves that he is making commendable and hopeful advances in the qualities and acquisitions desirable as a citizen and member of society; and, in these directions, attest there is nothing to provoke or justify the suspicion and proscription with which he has been not infrequently met by some of his more highly favored white fellow citizens.

Again, we began our political career under the disadvantages of the inexperience in public affairs that generations of enforced bondage had entailed upon our race. We suffered also from the vicious leadership of some of the men whom our necessities forced us temporarily to accept. Consider further that the states of the South, where we were supposed to control by our majorities, were in an impoverished and semi-revolutionary condition—society demoralized, the industries of the country prostrated, the people sore, morbid, and sometimes turbulent, and no healthy controlling public opinion either existent or possible—consider all these conditions, and it will be seen that we began our political novitiate and formed the organic and statutory laws under great embarrassments.

Despite the difficulties and drawbacks suggested, the constitutions formed under colored majorities, whatever their defects may be, were improvements on the instruments they were designed to supersede; and the statutes framed, though necessarily defective because of the crude and varying social and industrial conditions upon which they were based, were more in harmony with the spirit of the age and the genius of our free institutions than the obsolete laws that they supplanted. Nor is there just or any sufficient grounds upon which to charge an oppressive administration of the laws.

The state debt proper is less than a half million dollars and the state taxes are light. Nor can complaint be reasonably made of the judiciary. The records of the supreme judicial tribunal of the state will show, in 1859-60, 266 decisions in cases of appeal from the lower courts, of which 169 were affirmed and 97 reversed. In 1872-73 the records show 328 decisions rendered in cases of appeal from below, of which 221 were affirmed and 107 reversed; and in 1876, of appeals from chancellors, appointed by Governor Ames, up to date, 41 decisions have been rendered, of which 33 were affirmed and 8 reversed. This exhibit, whether of legislation or administration, shows there has been no adequate provocation to revolution and no justification for violence in Mississippi. That we should have made mistakes, under the circumstances, in measures of both legislation and administration, was natural, and that we have had any success is both creditable and hopeful.

But if it can be shown that we have used the ballot either to abridge the rights of our fellow citizens or to oppress them; if it shall appear that we have ever used our newly acquired power as a sword of attack and not as a shield of defense, then we may with some show of propriety be charged with incapacity, dishonesty, or tyranny. But, even then, I submit that the corrective is in the hands of the people, and not of a favored class, and the remedy is in the honest exercise of the ballot, and not in fraud and violence.

Mr. President, do not misunderstand me; I do not hold that all the white people of the state of Mississippi aided and abetted the white-league organizations. There is in Mississippi a large and respectable element among the opposition who are not only honest in their recognition of the political rights of the colored citizen and deprecate the fraud and violence through which those rights have been assailed, but who would be glad to see the color line in politics abandoned and goodwill obtain and govern among all classes of her people. But the fact is to be regretted that this better class of citizens in many parts of the state is dominated by a turbulent and violent element of the opposition, known as the White League—a ferocious minority—and has thus far proved powerless to prevent the recurrence of the outrages it deprecates and deplores.

The uses of this investigation are various. It will be important in suggesting such action as may be found necessary not only to correct and repair the wrongs perpetrated, but to prevent their recurrence. But I will venture to assert that the investigation will be most beneficial in this, that it will largely contribute to the formation of a public sentiment that, while it restrains the vicious in their attacks upon the rights of the loyal, law-abiding voters of the South, will so energize the laws as to secure condign punishment to wrongdoers, and give a security to all classes, which will effectively and abundantly produce the mutual goodwill and confidence that constitute the foundations of the public prosperity.

We want peace and good order at the South; but it can only come by the fullest recognition of the rights of all classes. The opposition must concede the necessity of change, not only in the temper but in the philosophy of their party organization and management. The sober American judgment must obtain in the South as elsewhere in the Republic, that the only distinctions upon which parties can be safely organized and in harmony with our institutions are differences of opinions relative to principles and policy of government, and that differences of religion, nationality, or race can neither with safety nor propriety be permitted for a moment to enter into the party contests of the day. The unanimity with which the colored voters act with a party is not referable to any race prejudice on their part. On the contrary, they invite the political cooperation of their white brethren, and vote as a unit because proscribed as such. They deprecate the establishment of the color line by the opposition, not only because the act is unwise and wrong in principle, but because it isolates them from the white men of the South and forces them, in sheer self-protection and against their inclination, to act seemingly upon the basis of a race prejudice that they neither respect nor entertain. As a class they are free from prejudices, and have no uncharitable suspicions against their white fellow citizens, whether native born or settlers from the Northern states. They not only recognize the equality of citizenship and the right of every man to hold, without proscription, any position of honor and trust to which the confidence of the people may elevate him; but owing nothing to race, birth, or surroundings, they, above all other classes in the community, are interested to see prejudices drop out of both politics and the business of the country, and success in life proceed only upon the integrity and merit of the man who seeks it. They are also appreciative—felling and exhibiting the liveliest gratitude for counsel and help in their new career, whether they come from the men of the North or of the South. But withal, as they progress in intelligence and appreciation of the dignity of their prerogatives as citizens, they, as an evidence of growth, begin to realize the significance of the proverb, "When thou doest well for thyself, men shall praise thee"; and are disposed to exact the same protection and concession of rights that are conferred upon other citizens by the Constitution, and that, too, without humiliation involved in the enforced abandonment of their political convictions.

> ***"We want peace and good order at the South; but it can only come by the fullest recognition of the rights of all classes. The opposition must concede the necessity of change. . . ."***

We simply demand the practical recognition of the rights given us in the Constitution and laws, and ask from our white fellow citizens only the consideration and fairness that we so willingly extend to them. Let them generally realize and concede that citizenship imports to us what it does to them, no more and no less, and impress the colored people that a party defeat does not imperil their political franchise. Let them cease their attempts to coerce our political cooperation, and invite and secure it by a policy so fair and just as to commend itself to our judgment, and resort to no motive or measure to control us that self-respect would preclude their applying to themselves. When we can entertain opinions and select party affiliations without proscription, and cast our ballots as other citizens and without jeopardy to person or privilege, we can safely afford to be governed by the considerations that ordinarily determine the political action of American citizens. But we must be guaranteed in the unproscribed exercise of our honest convictions and be absolutely, from within or without, protected in the use of our ballot before we can either wisely or safely divide our vote. In union, not division, is strength, so long as White League proscription renders division of our vote impracticable by making a difference of opinion opprobrious and an antagonism in politics a crime. On the other hand, if we should, from considerations of fear, yield to the shotgun policy of our opponents, the White League might win a temporary success, but the ultimate result would be disastrous to both races, for they would first become aggressively turbulent, and we, as a class, would become servile, unreliable, and worthless.

It has been suggested, as the popular sentiment of the country, that the colored citizens must no longer expect special legislation for their benefit, nor exceptional interference by the national government for their protection. If this is true, if such is the judgment relative to our demands and needs, I venture to offset the suggestion, so far as it may be used as reason for a denial of the protection we seek, by the statement of another and more prevalent popular conviction. Back of this, and underlying the foundations of the Republic itself, there lies deep in the breasts of the patriotic millions of the country the conviction that the laws must be enforced, and life, liberty, and property must, alike to all for all, be protected. But I allege that we do not seek special action in our behalf, except to meet special danger, and only then such as all classes of citizens are entitled to receive under the Constitution. We do not ask the enactment of new laws, but only the enforcement of those that already exist.

The vicious and exceptional political action had by the White League in Mississippi has been repeated in other contests and in other states of the South, and the colored voters have been subjected therein to outrages upon their rights similar to those perpetrated in my own state at the recent election. Because violence has become so general a quality in the political canvasses of the South and my people the common sufferers in each instance, I have considered this subject more in detail than would, under other circumstances, have been either appropriate or necessary. As the proscription and violence toward the colored voters are special and almost exclusive, and seem to proceed upon the assumption that there is something exceptionally offensive and unworthy in them, I have felt, as the only representative of my race in the Senate of the United States, that I was placed, in some sort, upon the defensive, and I have consequently endeavored to show how aggravated and inexcusable were the wrongs worked upon us, and have sought to vindicate our title to both the respect and goodwill of the just people of the nation. The gravity of the issues involved has demanded great plainness of speech from me. But I have endeavored to present my views to the Senate with the moderation and deference inspired by the recollection that both my race and myself were once bondsmen, and are today debtors largely to the love and justice of a great people for the enjoyment of our personal and political liberty. While my antecedents and surroundings suggest modesty, there are some considerations that justify frankness, and even boldness of speech.

Mr. President, I represent, in an important sense, the interest of nearly a million of voters, constituting a new, hopeful, permanent, and influential political element, and large enough to affect in critical periods the fortunes of this great Republic; and the public safety and common weal alike demand that the integrity of this element should be preserved and its character improved. They number more than a million of producers, who, since their emancipation and outside of their contributions to the production of sugar, rice, tobacco, cereals, and the mechanical industries of the country, have furnished nearly forty million bales of cotton, which, at the ruling prices of the world's market, have yielded $2,000,000,000, a sum nearly equal to the national debt; producers who, at the accepted ratio that an able-bodied laborer earns, on an average $800 per year, annually bring to the aggregate of the nation's great bulk of values more than $800,000,000.

I have confidence, not only in my country and her institutions, but in the endurance, capacity and destiny of my people. We will, as opportunity offers and ability serves, seek our places, sometimes in the field of letters, arts, science, and the professions. More frequently mechanical pursuits will attract and elicit our efforts; more still of my people will find employment and livelihood as the cultivators of the soil. The bulk of this people—by surroundings, habits, adaptation, and choice—will continue to find their homes in the South, and constitute the masses of its yeomanry. We will there, probably of our own volition and more abundantly than in the past, produce the great staples that will contribute to the basis of foreign exchange, aid in giving the nation a balance of trade, and minister to the wants and comforts and build up the prosperity of the whole land. Whatever our ultimate position in the composite civilization of the Republic and whatever varying fortunes attend our career, we will not forget our instincts for freedom nor our love of country. Guided and guarded by a beneficent Providence, and living under the genial influence of liberal institutions, we have no apprehensions that we shall fail from the land from attrition with other races, or ignobly disappear from either the politics or industries of the country.

Mr. President, allow me here to say that, although many of us are uneducated in the schools, we are informed and advised as to our duties to the government, our state, and ourselves. Without class prejudice or animosities, with obedience to authority, as the lesson and love of peace and order as the passion of our lives, with scrupulous respect for the rights of others, and with the hopefulness of political youth, we are determined that the great government that gave us liberty, and rendered its gift valuable by giving us the ballot, shall not find us wanting in a sufficient response to any demand that humanity or patriotism may make upon us; and we ask such action as will not only protect us in the enjoyment of our constitutional rights, but will preserve the integrity of our republican institutions.

During his Senate career, Bruce took vigorous action on behalf of African Americans. Besides fighting for their voting rights, he introduced legislation demanding the desegregation of the armed forces and took other steps in support of equal treatment for black military personnel. In addition, he was an advocate of industrial education for African Americans and voted in favor of giving financial help to Southern blacks who wanted to migrate west during the so-called "Great Exodus" of the late 1870s. As chairman of a special Senate investigating committee, Bruce was also instrumental in straightening out the tangled affairs of the Freedmen's Bank, which had gone bankrupt in 1874 as a result of mismanagement.

Bruce did not limit himself to helping members of his own race, however. In 1878, for example, in what he described as a gesture of sympathy for another oppressed people, he voted against the Chinese Exclusion Act, which sought to prohibit Chinese laborers and their families from entering the United States. (The measure passed and was not repealed until 1943.) He was also critical of what he termed the government's "selfish" policy toward Native Americans, which was slowly but surely leading to their complete extermination. On April 7, 1880, Bruce stood up in Congress and announced his support of a bill that proposed a new strategy. Under the terms of the bill, the notion of tribal autonomy—even on the reservation—would undergo major changes. Reservation lands would be divided, and each head of a family would receive a plot to farm; after twenty-five years, the family would be granted full ownership of the land and full citizenship in the United States. In his address, reprinted here from the Congressional Record, *46th Congress, 1880, Bruce explained why he felt it was time for the government to deal with Native Americans in ways that would encourage their assimilation rather than their destruction.*

Mr. President, I shall support the pending bill, and without attempting a discussion of the specific features of the measure, I desire to submit a few remarks upon the general subject suggested by it.

Our Indian policy and administration seem to me to have been inspired and controlled by a stern selfishness, with a few honorable exceptions. Indian treaties have generally been made as the condition and instrument of acquiring the valuable territory occupied by the several Indian nations, and have been changed and revised from time to time as it became desirable that the steadily growing, irrepressible white races should secure more room for their growth and more lands for their occupancy; and wars, bounties, and beads have been used as auxiliaries for the purpose of temporary peace and security for the whites, and as the preliminary to further aggressions upon the red man's lands, with the ultimate view of his expulsion and extinction from the continent.

No set purpose has been evinced in adequate, sufficient measure to build him up, to civilize him, and to make him part of the great community of states. Whatever of occasional and spasmodic effort has been made for his redemption from savagery and his perpetuity as a race, has been only sufficient to supply that class of exceptions to the rule necessary to prove the selfishness of the policy that we allege to have been practiced toward him.

The political or governmental idea, underlying the Indian policy, is to maintain the paramount authority of the United States over the Indian Territory and over the Indian tribes, yet recognizing tribal independence and autonomy and a local government, un-American in structure and having no reference to the Constitution or laws of the United States, so far as the tribal governments affect the persons, lives, and rights of the members of the tribe alone. Currently with the maintenance of a policy thus based, under treaty obligations, the government of the United States contributes to the support, equipments, and comforts of these Indians, not only by making appropriations for food and raiment but by sustaining blacksmiths, mechanics, farmers, millers, and schools in the midst of the Indian reservations. This government also, in its treaties and its enforcement thereof, encourages and facilitates the missionary enterprises of the different churches which look to the Christianization and education of the Indians distributed throughout the public domain. The effort, under these circumstances, to preserve peace among the Indian tribes in their relations to each other and in their relations to the citizens of the United States becomes a very onerous and difficult endeavor, and has not heretofore produced results that have either satisfied the expectations and public sentiment of the country, vindicated the wisdom of the policy practiced toward this people, or honored the Christian institutions and civilizations of our great country.

We have in the effort to realize a somewhat intangible ideal, to wit, the preservation of Indian liberty and the administration and exercise of national authority, complicated an essentially difficult problem by surrounding it with needless and equivocal adjuncts; we have rendered a questionable policy more difficult of successful execution by basing it upon a political theory which is un-American in character, and which, in its very structure, breeds and perpetuates the difficulties sought to be avoided and overcome.

Our system of government is complex in that it recognizes a general and local jurisdiction, and seeks to subserve and protect the rights of the individual and of the different political communities and the great aggregates of society making up the nation, by a division of authority distributed among general and local agencies, which are required, like "the wheels within wheels" of Ezekiel's vision, to so move in their several appropriate spheres as shall not only prevent attrition and collision, but as shall secure unity in the system, in its fullest integrity, currently with the enjoyment of the largest liberty by the citizen.

Our system, I repeat, is complex, but it is nevertheless homogeneous. It is not incongruous; the general and local organisms belong to the same great class; they are both American, and they are moved by and respond to the same great impulse—the popular will of the American people.

Now, the political system that underlies our Indian policy is not only complex but it is incongruous, and one of the governments embraced in the system, ostensibly to secure the largest license and independence to the red race affected by the subject of this nondescript policy, is foreign in its character; the individuals and the system of laws are neither American. All the contradictions, the absurdities, and impossibilities developed and cropping out on the surface of our administration of Indian affairs are referable to this singular philosophy upon which, as a political theory, the Indian policy of the United States rests.

Now, sir, there must be a change in the Indian policy if beneficent, practical results are expected, and any change that gives promise of solving this red-race problem must be a change based upon an idea in harmony, and not at war with our free institutions. If the Indian is expected and required to respond to federal authority; if this people are expected to grow up into organized and well-ordered society; if they are to be civilized, in that the best elements of their natures are to be developed in the exercise of their best functions, so as to produce individual character and social groups characteristic of enlightened people; if this is to be done under our system, its ultimate realization requires an adoption of a political philosophy that shall make the Indians, as an individual and as a tribe, subjects of American law and beneficiaries of American institutions, by making them first American citizens, and clothing them, as rapidly as their advancement and location will permit, with the protective and ennobling prerogatives of such citizenship.

I favor the measure pending, because it is a step in the direction that I have indicated. You propose to give the Indian not temporary but permanent residence as a tribe, and not tribal location, but by a division of lands in severalty you secure to him the individual property rights which, utilized, will sustain life for himself and family better than his nomadic career. By this location you lay the foundation for that love of country essential to the patriotism and growth of a people, and by the distribution of lands to the individual, in severalty, you appeal to and develop that essential constitutional quality of humanity, the disposition to accumulate, upon which, when healthily and justly developed, depends the wealth, the growth, the power, the comfort, the refinement, and the glory of the nations of the earth.

> ***"[Americans] are beginning to reach the conscientious conviction that redemption and civilization are due to the Indian tribes of the U.S."***

The measure also, with less directness, but as a necessary sequence to the provisions that I have just characterized, proposes, as preliminary to bringing the red race under the operation of our laws, to present the best phases of civilized life. Having given the red man a habitat, having identified the individual as well as the tribe with his new home, by securing his individual interests and rights therein; having placed these people where law can reach them, govern them, and protect them, you propose a system of administration that shall bring them in contact not with the adventurer of the border, not a speculative Indian agent, not an armed blue-coated soldier, but with the American people, in the guise and fashion in which trade, commerce, arts—useful and attractive—in the panoply that loving peace supplies, and with the plenty and comforts that follow in the footsteps of peace, and for the first time in the Indian's history, he will see the industrial, commercial, comfortable side of the character of the American people, will find his contact and form his associations with the citizens of the great Republic, and not simply and exclusively its armed men—its instruments of justice and destruction. So much this measure, if it should be a type of the new policy, will do for the Indian; and the Indian problem—heretofore rendered difficult of solution because of the false philosophy underlying it and the unjust administration too frequently based upon it, a policy that has kept the Indian a fugitive and a vagabond, that has bred discontent, suspicion and hatred in the mind of the red man—will be settled, not immediately, in a day or a year, but it will be put in course of settlement, and the question will be placed where a successful issue will be secured beyond a peradventure.

Mr. President, the red race are not a numerous people in our land, not equaling probably a half million of souls, but they are the remnants of a great and multitudinous nation, and their hapless fortunes heretofore not only appeal to sympathy and to justice in any measures that we may take affecting them, but the vigor, energy, bravery, and integrity of this remnant entitle them to consideration on the merits of this question.

Our age has been signalized by the grand scientific and mechanical discoveries and inventions which have multiplied the productive forces of the world. The powers of nature has been harnessed to do the work of man, and every hour some new discovery contributes to swell the volume of the physical energies that make a people rich, prosperous, and happy. Yet, sir, in the midst of this affluence of physical energy and its utilization, human ingenuity and thought have already been directed to the conservation, to the economy against the waste, of the physical forces. The man is considered a public benefactor who can utilize waste fuel, who can convert to some practical end some physical energy still lost, to a percent, at least, through the imperfection of the machinery employed.

Now, sir, the Indian is a physical force; a half million of vigorous, physical, intellectual agents ready for the plastic hand of Christian civilization, living in a country possessing empires of untilled and uninhabited lands. The Indian tribes, viewed from this utilitarian standpoint, are worth preservation, conservation, utilization, and civilization, and I believe that we have reached a period when the public sentiment of the country demands such a modification in the Indian policy, in its purposes, and in its methods, as shall save and not destroy these people.

There is nothing in the matter of obstructions, as suggested by the opponents of this measure, to convince me that the new policy is either impracticable or visionary. As a people, our history is full of surmounted obstacles; we have been solving difficult problems for more than a hundred years; we have been settling material, moral, and great political questions that before our era had been unsolved, and the possible solution of which, even among the timid in our midst, was questioned.

The Indian is human, and no matter what his traditions or his habits, if you will locate him and put him in contact, and hold him in contact with the forces of our civilization, his fresh, rugged nature will respond, and the fruit of his endeavor, in his civilization and development, will be the more permanent and enduring because his nature is so strong and obdurate. When you have no longer made it necessary for him to be a vagabond and a fugitive; when you have allowed him to see the lovable and attractive side of our civilization as well as the stern military phase; when you have made the law apply to him as it does to others, so that the ministers of the law shall not only be the executors of its penalties but the administrators of its saving, shielding, protecting provisions, he will become trustful and reliable, and when he is placed in position in which not only to become an industrial force—to multiply his comforts and those of his people—but the honest, full sharer of the things he produces, savage life will lose its attractions and the hunter will become the herdsman, the herdsman in his turn the farmer, and the farmer the mechanic, and out of the industries and growth of the Indian homes will spring up commercial interests and men competent to foster and handle them.

The American people are beginning to reach the conscientious conviction that redemption and civilization are due to the Indian tribes of the United States, and the present popular purpose is not to exterminate them but to perpetuate them on this continent.

The Indian policy has never attracted so much attention as at the present time, and the public sentiment demands that the new departure on this question shall ultimate in measures, toward the wild tribes of America, that shall be Christian and righteous in their character. The destruction of this vigorous race, rather than their preservation and development, is coming to be considered not only an outrage against Christian civilization, but an economic wrong to the people of the United States; and the people of America demand that the measures and administration of government, relative to these people, shall proceed upon the wise and equitable principles that regulate the conduct of public affairs relative to every other race in the Republic, and when rightful conceptions obtain in the treatment of the red race, the Indian question, with its cost, anxieties and wars, will disappear.

SOURCES

Books

Christopher, Maurine, *America's Black Congressmen,* Crowell, 1971.

Congressional Record, 44th Congress, 1st Session, U.S. Government Printing Office, 1876, pp. 2101-2104; 46th Congress, 2nd Session, U.S. Government Printing Office, 1880, pp. 2195-2196.

Periodicals

Journal of Negro History, "A Negro Senator," July, 1922, pp. 243-256.

Negro History Bulletin, "Three Negro Senators of the United States: Hiram R. Revels, Blanche K. Bruce, and Edward W. Brooke," January, 1967, pp. 4-5, 12.

Ralph Bunche

1904–1971

African American diplomat

In 1950, an extraordinary American named Ralph Bunche became the first black ever awarded the Nobel Peace Prize. What he had managed to accomplish in his role as a United Nations mediator was nothing short of a miracle—peace between Jews and Arabs in the Middle East after several years of fierce fighting. Although the truce proved to be only temporary, it was a major accomplishment for the fledgling international organization. For the eternally optimistic Bunche, it also suggested that no human relations problem is beyond solution. It was this firm belief in the ability of nonviolent action to settle disputes that shaped his view of the world, both overseas and at home in the battle to secure civil rights for his fellow African Americans.

Bunche was born in Detroit and lived there until he was ten, when his mother's poor health prompted the family to move to Albuquerque, New Mexico, in search of a milder climate. Three years later, both of his parents died within just a few months of each other, and Bunche and his sister went to Los Angeles to live with their maternal grandmother, a strong-willed woman who demanded the best for (and from) her grandson. He did not let her down; an outstanding student, he finished at the top of his high school class and then went on to graduate with highest honors from the University of California at Los Angeles (UCLA) with a degree in international relations. He continued his studies at Harvard University, earning his master's in government in 1928. After spending four years in Washington, D.C., teaching at Howard University, Bunche returned to Harvard to work on his doctorate, which he received in 1934.

Over the next few years, Bunche completed postdoctoral work in colonial and racial problems at Northwestern University, the London School of Economics, and South Africa's Capetown University. He also served as co-director of the Institute of Race Relations at Swarthmore College and as a staff member of the Carnegie Corporation, during which time he worked closely with Swedish sociologist Gunnar Myrdal on gathering research for Myrdal's landmark study of race relations in the United States, An American Dilemma. *During the late 1930s, Bunche also returned to teaching at Howard, where he remained until World War II began and he entered government service instead. As an expert in colonial affairs, he held several important positions throughout the war years with the Office of Strategic*

Services (OSS) and the State Department and was thus one of the highest-ranking African Americans in the Roosevelt administration. He often functioned as the country's official representative at major international conferences. One of these was the 1945 meeting at which delegates from all over the world drafted the agreement that established a new organization known as the United Nations.

In 1946, Bunche joined the United Nations as director of its trusteeship department. In this post, he worked to protect the rights of people who lived in countries under colonial rule in parts of Asia, Africa, and the Middle East. It was a daunting task that became even more so in the immediate postwar years as many of these countries began seeking independence from the European powers that had dominated them for decades and sometimes centuries.

The situation was especially tense in the Middle East. The United Nations, responding in part to pressures to create a homeland for thousands of European Jews displaced by World War II, had recommended partitioning Palestine into separate Arab and Jewish states. This decision inflamed long-simmering hostilities between the two groups; Arabs in particular deeply resented having to give up any of their territory to people they viewed as outsiders. In 1947, civil war broke out. The fighting grew even more intense the following year after Israel was officially proclaimed the new Jewish state and neighboring Arab countries became involved. Meanwhile, United Nations mediators led by Sweden's Count Folke Bernadotte worked tirelessly behind the scenes to come up with a peaceful solution to the conflict.

But when Count Bernadotte was assassinated in September 1948, just four months after entering the fray, a new figure emerged to lead the negotiators: Ralph Bunche. A skilled diplomat whose optimism knew no bounds, he continued the talks for some eleven months until both parties finally agreed to a truce in late 1949. It was a victory for the United Nations as well as for Bunche, whose personal efforts were formally recognized in 1950 when he was awarded the Nobel Peace Prize—the first black ever to be so honored. On December 11 of that year, he stood in the auditorium of the University of Oslo and delivered his Nobel Lecture, in which he reflected on the prospect of peace being within reach of mankind. The full text of his speech is reprinted here from Volume 2 of Nobel Lectures: Peace, 1926-1950, *edited by Frederick W. Haberman (Elsevier, 1972). Bunche's actual spoken version was somewhat abridged.*

In this most anxious period of human history, the subject of peace, above every other, commands the solemn attention of all men of reason and good will. Moreover, on this particular occasion, marking the fiftieth anniversary of the Nobel Foundation, it is eminently fitting to speak of peace. No subject could be closer to my own heart, since I have the honor to speak as a member of the international secretariat of the United Nations.

In these critical times—times which test to the utmost the good sense, the forbearance, and the morality of every peace-loving people—it is not easy to speak of peace with either conviction or reassurance. True it is that statesmen the world over, exalting lofty concepts and noble ideals, pay homage to peace and freedom in a perpetual torrent of eloquent phrases. But the statesmen also speak darkly of the lurking threat of war; and the preparations for war ever intensity, while strife flares or threatens in many localities.

The words used by statesmen in our day no longer have a common meaning. Perhaps they never had. Freedom, democracy, human rights, international morality, peace itself, mean different things to different men. Words, in a constant flow of propaganda—itself an instrument of war—are employed to confuse, mislead, and debase the common man. Democracy is prostituted to dignify enslavement; freedom and equality are held good for some men but withheld from others by and in allegedly "democratic" societies; in "free" societies, so-called, individual human rights are severely denied: aggressive adventures are launched under the guise of "liberation." Truth and morality are subverted by propaganda, on the cynical assumption that truth is whatever propaganda can induce people to believe. Truth and morality, therefore, become gravely weakened as defenses against injustice and war. With what great insight did Voltaire, hating war enormously, declare: "War is the greatest of all crimes: and yet there is no aggressor who does not color his crime with the pretext of justice."

To the common man, the state of world affairs is baffling. All nations and peoples claim to be for peace. But never has peace been more continuously in jeopardy. There are no nations today, as in the recent past, insistently clamoring for *Lebensraum* under the duress of readiness to resort to war. Still the specter of war looms ominously. Never in human history have so many peoples experienced freedom. Yet human freedom itself is a crucial issue and is widely endangered. Indeed, by some peoples, it has already been gained and lost.

Peoples everywhere wish and long for peace and freedom in their simplest and clearest connotations: an end to armed conflict and to the suppression of the inalienable rights of man. In a single generation, the peoples of the world have suffered the profound anguish of two catastrophic wars; they have had enough of war. Who could doubt that the people of Norway—ever peaceful, still deeply wounded from an unprovoked, savage Nazi aggression—wish peace? Who could doubt that all of the peoples of Europe—whose towns and cities, whose peaceful countrysides, have been mercilessly ravaged; whose fathers and sons, mothers and daughters, have been slaughtered and maimed in tragic numbers—wish peace? Who could sincerely doubt that the peoples of the Western hemisphere—who, in the common effort to save the world from barbaric tyranny, came into the two world wars only reluctantly and at great sacrifice of human and material resources—wish peace? Who could doubt that the long-suffering masses of Asia and Africa wish peace? Who indeed, could be so unseeing as not to realize that in modern war victory is illusory; that the harvest of war can be only misery, destruction, and degradation?

If war should come, the peoples of the world would again be called upon to fight it, but they would not have willed it.

Statesmen and philosophers repeatedly have warned that some values—freedom, honor, self-respect—are higher than peace or life itself. This may be true. Certainly, very many would hold that the loss of human dignity and self-respect, the chains of enslavement, are too high a price even for peace. But the horrible realities of modern warfare scarcely afford even this fatal choice. There is only suicidal escape, not freedom, in the death and destruction of atomic war. This is mankind's great dilemma. The well-being and the hopes of the peoples of the world can never be served until peace—as well as freedom, honor and self-respect—is secure.

"Who . . . could be so unseeing as not to realize that in modern war victory is illusory; that the harvest of war can be only misery, destruction, and degradation?"

The ideals of peace on earth and the brotherhood of man have been expounded by philosophers from earliest times. If human relations were governed by the sagacity of the great philosophers, there would be little danger of war, for in their collective wisdom over the centuries they have clearly charted the course to free and peaceful living among men.

Throughout the ages, however, man has but little heeded the advice of the wise men. He has been—fatefully, if not willfully—less virtuous, less constant, less rational, less peaceful than he knows how to be, than he is fully capable of being. He has been led astray from the ways of peace and brotherhood by his addiction to concepts and attitudes of narrow nationalism, racial and religious bigotry, greed and lust for power. Despite this, despite the almost continuous state of war to which bad human relations have condemned him, he has made steady progress. In his scientific genius, man has wrought material miracles and has transformed his world.

He has harnessed nature and has developed great civilizations. But he has never learned very well how to live with himself. The values he has created have been predominantly materialistic; his spiritual values have lagged far behind. He has demonstrated little spiritual genius and has made little progress toward the realization of human brotherhood. In the contemporary atomic age, this could prove man's fatal weakness.

Alfred Nobel, a half-century ago, foresaw with prophetic vision that if the complacent mankind of his day could, with equanimity, contemplate war, the day would soon inevitably come when man would be confronted with the fateful alternative of peace or reversion to the Dark Ages. Man may well ponder whether he has not now reached that stage. Man's inventive genius has so far outreached his reason—not his capacity to reason but his willingness to apply reason—that the peoples of the world find themselves precariously on the brink of total disaster.

If today we speak of peace, we also speak of the United Nations, for in this era, peace and the United Nations have become inseparable. If the United Nations cannot ensure peace, there will be none. If war should come, it will be only because the United Nations has failed. But the United Nations need not fail. Surely, every man of reason must work and pray to the end that it will not fail.

In these critical days, it is a high privilege and a most rewarding experience to be associated with the United Nations—the greatest peace effort in human history. Those who work in and with the organization, perhaps inevitably, tend to develop a professional optimism with regard to the prospects for the United Nations and, therefore, to the prospects for peace. But there is also a sense of deep frustration, which flows from the knowledge that mankind could readily live in peace and freedom and good neighborliness if there were but a minimum of will to do so. There is the ever present, simple but stark truth that though the peoples long primarily for peace, they may be prodded by their leaders and governments into needless war, which may at worst destroy them, at best lead them once again to barbarism.

The United Nations strives to be realistic. It understands well the frailties of man. It is realized that if there is to be peace in the world, it must be attained through men and with man, in his nature and mores, just about as he now is. Intensive effort is exerted to reach the hearts and minds of men with the vital pleas for peace and human understanding, to the end that human attitudes and relations may be steadily improved. But this is a process of international education, or better, education for international living, and it is at best gradual. Men change their attitudes and habits slowly, and but grudgingly divorce their minds from fears, suspicions, and prejudices.

The United Nations itself is but a cross section of the world's peoples. It reflects, therefore, the typical fears, suspicions, and prejudices which bedevil human relations throughout the world. In the delegations from the sixty member states and in the international secretariat in which most of them are represented, may be found individual qualities of goodness and badness, honesty and subterfuge, courage and timorousness, internationalism and chauvinism. It could not be otherwise. Still, the activities of all are within the framework of a great international organization dedicated to the imperative causes of peace, freedom, and justice in the world.

The United Nations, inescapably, is an organization at once of great weakness and great strength.

Its powers of action are sharply limited by the exigencies of national sovereignties. With nationalism per se there may be no quarrel. But narrow, exclusively self-centered nationalism persists as the outstanding dynamic of world politics and is the prime obstacle to enduring peace. The international well-being, on the one hand, and national egocentrism, on the other, are inevitably at cross-purposes. The procedures and processes of the United Nations as a circumscribed international parliament are unavoidably complex and tedious.

The United Nations was established in the hope, if not on the assumption, that the five great powers would work harmoniously toward an increasingly better world order. The existing impasse between West and East and the resultant "cold war" were not foreseen by those who formulated the United Nations Charter in the spring of 1945 in the misleading, but understandably jubilant, atmosphere of war's triumphant end. Nevertheless, the United Nations has exhibited a fortunate flexibility which has enabled it to adjust to the regrettable circumstances of the discord among the great powers and to continue to function effectively.

Reflecting the hopes and aspirations of all peoples for peace, security, freedom, and justice, the foundations of the United Nations are firmly anchored, and its moral sanctions are strong. It is served by a fully competent international secretariat which is devoted to the high principles and purposes of the organization. At the head of this secretariat is the Secretary-General of the United Nations, Trygve Lie, a great son of Norway, and a man whose name will be writ large in the annals of world statesmanship and peacemaking. No living man has worked more persistently or courageously to save the world from the scourge of war than Trygve Lie.

In its short but turbulent five years, the United Nations, until the past few weeks, at least, has demonstrated a comforting ability to cope with every dangerous crisis that has erupted into violence or threatened to do so. It has never been easily done nor as well as might be hoped for, but the fact remains that it has been done. In these postwar years, the United Nations, in the interest of peace, has been called upon to eliminate the threat of local wars, to stop local wars already underway, and now in Korea, itself to undertake an international police action which amounts to full-scale war. Its record has been impressive. Its interventions have been directly responsible for checking and containing dangerous armed conflicts in Indonesia, Kashmir, and Palestine, and to only a lesser extent in Greece.

That the United Nations has been able to serve the cause of peace in this way has been due in large measure to the determination of its members to reject the use of armed force as an instrument of national policy, and to the new techniques of international intervention which it has employed. In each instance of a threat to the peace, the United Nations projects itself directly into the area of conflict by sending United Nations representatives to the area for the purpose of mediation and conciliation.

It was as the head of a United Nations mission of this kind that Count Folke Bernadotte went to Palestine in the spring of 1948. On his arrival in the Near East, he found the Arabs and Jews locked in a bitter, bloody, and highly emotional war in Palestine. He was armed only with the strong demand of the United Nations that in the interest of world peace the Palestine problem must be settled by peaceful means.

In one of the most brilliant individual feats of diplomatic history, Count Bernadotte, within two weeks of his arrival on the scene of conflict, had negotiated a four weeks' truce and the guns had ceased firing. In order to supervise that truce, he requested of the Secretary-General and promptly received an international team of civilian and military personnel, numbering some seven hundred men and women. The members of this compact and devoted United Nations "peace army" in Palestine, many of whom were from the Scandinavian countries and all of whom were unarmed, under the early leadership of Count Bernadotte wrote a heroic chapter in the cause of peacemaking. Their leader, Bernadotte himself, and ten others, gave their lives in this effort. The United Nations and the peace-loving world must ever be grateful to them.

We who had the privilege to serve under the leadership of Count Bernadotte revere his name. He was a great internationalist, a warmhearted humanitarian, a warrior of unflinching courage in the cause of peace, and a truly noble man. We who carried on after him were inspired by his self-sacrifice and were determined to pay him the one tribute which he would have appreciated above all others—the successful completion of the task which he had begun, the restoration of peace to Palestine.

In Korea, for the first, and it may be fervently hoped, the last time, the United Nations processes of peaceful intervention to settle disputes failed. They failed only because the North Korean regime stubbornly refused to afford them the chance to work and resorted to aggressive force as the means of attaining its ends. Confronted with this, the gravest challenge to its mandate to preserve the peace of the world, the United Nations had no reasonable alternative but to check aggressive national force with decisive international force. This it has attempted to do, and it was enabled to do so only by the firm resolve of the overwhelming majority of its members that the peace must be preserved and that aggression shall be struck down wherever undertaken or by whom.

By virtue of recent setbacks to United Nations forces in Korea, as a result of the injection of vast numbers of Chinese troops into the conflict, it becomes clear that this resolve of its members has not been backed by sufficient armed strength to ensure that the right shall prevail. In the future, it must be the forces of peace that are overwhelming.

But whatever the outcome of the present military struggle in Korea in which the United Nations and Chinese troops are now locked, Korea provides the lesson which can save peace and freedom in the world if nations and peoples will but learn that lesson, and learn it quickly. To make peace in the world secure, the United Nations must have readily at its disposal, as a result of firm commitments undertaken by all of its members, military strength of sufficient dimensions to make it certain that it can meet aggressive military force with international military force, speedily and conclusively.

If that kind of strength is made available to the United Nations—and under action taken by the General Assembly this fall it can be made available—in my view that strength will never again be challenged in war and therefore need never be employed.

But military strength will not be enough. The moral position of the United Nations must ever be strong and unassailable; it must stand steadfastly, always, for the right.

The international problems with which the United Nations is concerned are the problems of the interrelations of the peoples of the world. They are human problems. The United Nations is entitled to believe, and it does believe, that there are no insoluble problems of human relations and that there is none which cannot be solved by peaceful means. The United Nations—in Indonesia, Palestine, and Kashmir—has demonstrated convincingly that parties to the most severe conflict may be induced to abandon war as the method of settlement in favor of mediation and conciliation, at a merciful saving of untold lives and acute suffering.

Unfortunately, there may yet be some in the world who have not learned that today war can settle nothing, that aggressive force can never be enough, nor will it be tolerated. If this should be so, the pitiless wrath of the organized world must fall upon those who would endanger the peace for selfish ends. For in this advanced day, there is no excuse, no justification, for nations resorting to force except to repel armed attack.

> ***"The United Nations is entitled to believe, and it does believe, that there are no insoluble problems of human relations and that there is none which cannot be solved by peaceful means."***

The world and its peoples being as they are, there is no easy or quick or infallible approach to a secure peace. It is only by patient, persistent, undismayed effort, by trial and error, that peace can be won. Nor can it be won cheaply, as the taxpayer is learning. In the existing world tension, there will be rebuffs and setbacks, dangerous crises, and episodes of violence. But the United Nations, with unshakable resolution, in the future as in the past, will continue to man the dikes of peace. In this common purpose, all states, irrespective of size, are vital.

Ralph Bunche

The small nations, which constitute the overwhelming majority in its membership, are a great source of strength for the United Nations. Their desire for peace is deep seated and constant. The fear, suspicion, and conflict which characterize the relations among the great powers, and the resultant uncertainty, keep them and their peoples in a state of anxious tension and suspense. For the relations among the great powers will largely determine their future. A third world war would quickly engulf the smaller states, and many of them would again provide the battlefields. On many of them, now as before, the impact of war would be even more severe than upon the great powers. They in particular, therefore, support and often initiate measures designed to ensure that the United Nations shall be increasingly effective as a practical instrumentality for peace. In this regard, the Scandinavian countries contribute signally to the constructive effort of the United Nations.

One legacy of the recent past greatly handicaps the work of the United Nations. It can never realize its maximum potential for peace until the Second World War is fully liquidated. The impasse between West and East has prevented the great powers from concluding the peace treaties which would finally terminate that last war. It can be little doubted that the United Nations, if called upon, could afford valuable aid toward this end. At present, the United Nations must work for future peace in the unhappy atmosphere of an unconcluded great war, while precluded from rendering any assistance toward the liquidation of that war. These, obviously, are matters of direct and vital concern to all peace-loving nations, whatever their size.

At the moment, in view of the disturbing events in Korea and Indo-China, the attention of a fearful world is focused on Asia, seeking an answer to the fateful question "peace or war?" But the intrinsic importance of Europe in the world peace equation cannot be ignored. The peace of Europe, and therefore of the world, can never be secure so long as the problem of Germany remains unsolved.

In this regard, those who at the end of the last war were inclined to dismiss Europe as a vital factor in reckoning the future security and prosperity of the world, have had to revise their calculations. For Europe, grievously wounded though it was, has displayed a remarkable resiliency and has quickly regained its place in the orbit of world affairs.

But Europe, and the Western world generally, must become fully aware that the massive and restive millions of Asia and Africa are henceforth a new and highly significant factor in all peace calculations. These hitherto suppressed masses are rapidly awakening and are demanding, and are entitled to enjoy, a full share in the future fruits of peace, freedom, and security.

Very many of these millions are experiencing a newfound freedom. Many other millions are still in subject status as colonials. The aspirations and demands of those who have achieved freedom and those who seek it are the same: security, treatment as equals, and their rightful place in the brotherhood of nations.

It is truer today than when Alfred Nobel realized it a half-century ago, that peace cannot be achieved in a vacuum. Peace must be paced by human progress. Peace is no mere matter of men fighting or not fighting. Peace, to have meaning for many who have known only suffering in both peace and war, must be translated into bread or rice, shelter, health, and education, as well as freedom and human dignity—a steadily better life. If peace is to be secure, long-suffering and long-starved, forgotten peoples of the world, the underprivileged and the undernourished, must begin to realize without delay the promise of a new day and a new life.

In the world of today, Europe, like the rest of the West, is confronted with the urgent necessity of a new orientation—a global orientation. The prewar outlook is as obsolete as the prewar world. There must be an awakening to the incontestable fact that the far away, little known and little understood peoples of Asia and Africa, who constitute the majority of the world's population, are no longer passive and no longer to be ignored. The fury of the world ideological struggle swirls about them. Their vast numbers will prove a dominant factor in the future world pattern of life. They provide virgin soil for the growth of democracy, but the West must first learn how to approach them understandingly and how to win their trust and friendship. There is a long and unsavory history of western imperialism, suppression, and exploitation to be overcome, despite the undenied benefits which the West also brought to them. There must be an acceleration in the liquidation of colonialism. A friendly hand must be extended to the peoples who are laboring under the heavy burden of newly won independence, as well as to those who aspire to it. And in that hand must be tangible aid in generous quantity—funds, goods, foodstuffs, equipment, technical assistance.

There are great issues demanding resolution in the world: the clash of the rather loosely defined concepts and systems of capitalism and communism; the radically contrasting conceptions of democracy, posing extreme views of individualism against extreme views of statism; the widespread denials of human rights; the understandable impatience of many among some two hundred million colonial peoples for the early realization of their aspirations toward emancipation; and others.

But these are issues which in no sense may be considered as defying solution. The issue of capitalism versus communism is one of ideology which in the world of today cannot, in fact, be clearly defined. It cannot be clearly defined because there are not two worlds, one "capitalist" and one "communist." There is but one world—a world of sharp clashes, to be sure—with these two doctrines at the opposite ideological poles. In between these extremes are found many gradations of the two systems and ideologies.

There is room in the world for both capitalism and communism, and all gradations of them, providing only that neither system is set upon pursuing an aggressively imperialistic course.

The United Nations is opposed to imperialism of any kind, ideological or otherwise. The United Nations stands for the freedom and equality of all peoples, irrespective of race, religion, or ideology. It is for the peoples of every society to make their own choices with regard to ideologies, economic systems, and the relationship which is to prevail between the state and the individual. The United Nations is engaged in an historic effort to underwrite the rights of man. It is also attempting to give reassurance to the colonial peoples that their aspirations for freedom can be realized, if only gradually, by peaceful processes.

There can be peace and a better life for all man. Given adequate authority and support, the United Nations can ensure this. But the decision really rests with the peoples of the world. The United Nations belongs to the people. but it is not yet as close to them, as much a part of their conscious interest, as it must come to be. The United Nations must always be on the people's side. Where their fundamental rights and interests are involved, it must never act from mere expediency. At times, perhaps, it has done so, but never to its own advantage nor to that of the sacred causes of peace and freedom. If the peoples of the world are strong in their resolve and if they speak through the United Nations, they need never be confronted with the tragic alternatives of war or dishonorable appeasement, death, or enslavement.

Amidst the frenzy and irrationality of a topsy-turvy world, some simple truths would appear to be self-evident.

As Alfred Nobel finally discerned, people are never deterred from the folly of war by the stark terror of it. But it is nonetheless true that if in atomic war there would be survivors, there could be no victors. What, then, could war achieve which could not be better gained by peaceful means? There are, to be sure, vital differences and wide areas of conflict among the nations, but there is utterly none which could not be settled peacefully—by negotiation and mediation—given a genuine will for peace and even a modicum of mutual good faith.

But there would appear to be little hope that efforts to break the great power impasse could be very fruitful in the current atmosphere of fear, suspicion, and mutual recrimination. Fear, suspicion, and recrimination in the relations among nations tend to be dangerously self-compounding. They induce that national hysteria which, in its rejection of poise and rationality, can itself be the fatal prelude to war. A favorable climate for peaceful negotiation must be created and can only be created by painstaking, unremitting effort. Conflicting parties must be led to realize that the road to peace can never be traversed by threatening to fight at every bend, by merely being armed to the teeth, or by flushing every bush to find an enemy. An essential first step in a civilized approach to peace in these times would call for a moratorium on recrimination and reproach.

There are some in the world who are prematurely resigned to the inevitability of war. Among them are the advocates of the so-called "preventive war," who, in their resignation to war, wish merely to select their own time for initiating it. To suggest that war can prevent war is a base play on words and a despicable form of warmongering. The objective of any who sincerely believe in peace clearly must be to exhaust every honorable recourse in the effort to save the peace. The world has had ample evidence that war begets only conditions which beget further war.

In the final analysis, the acid test of a genuine will to peace is the willingness of disputing parties to expose their differences to the peaceful processes of the United Nations and to the bar of international public opinion which the United Nations reflects. It is only in this way that truth, reason, and justice may come to prevail over the shrill and blatant voice of propaganda; that a wholesome international morality can be cultivated.

It is worthy of emphasis that the United Nations exists not merely to preserve the peace but also to make change—even radical change—possible without violent upheaval. The United Nations has no vested interest in the status quo. It seeks a more secure world, a better world, a world of progress for all peoples. In the dynamic world society which is the objective of the United Nations, all peoples must have equality and equal rights. The rights of those who at any given time may be in the minority—whether for reasons of race, religion, or ideology—are as important as those of the majority, and the minorities must enjoy the same respect and protection. The United Nations does not seek a world cut after a single pattern, nor does it consider this desirable. The United Nations seeks only unity, not uniformity, out of the world's diversity.

There will be no security in our world, no release from agonizing tension, no genuine progress, no enduring peace, until, in Shelley's fine words, "reason's voice, loud as the voice of nature, shall have waked the nations."

Bunche's tireless efforts on behalf of world peace left him with less time than he would have liked to participate in the civil rights struggle in the United States. (In fact, some of the more militant black activists of his era, including Adam Clayton Powell, Jr., publicly criticized him for not playing a more prominent role.) Yet he was a staunch defender of the movement and frequently warned that America could not possibly hope to inspire trust and admiration abroad if it continued to oppress minorities at home. This was the very theme he touched upon in a commencement address he gave at Baltimore's Morgan State College (a historically black institution) on June 4, 1951. His remarks to the graduates are reprinted here from Vital Speeches of the Day, *August 15, 1951.*

This day belongs, or should belong, exclusively to those who are graduating. It is their day. What manner of commencement program could there be without them? This afternoon, at least, all roads lead to them.

For this reason, I am inclined to be rather diffident about commencement speeches unless they are made by the graduates themselves. I have a strong suspicion that the best commencement speeches are those that are never spoken.

The main business of the day here is the awarding of the degrees which these graduates have earned, and earned, I take it, the hard way. Indeed, this occasion is really a celebration—signaling the liberation of the graduates from the drudgery and discipline of the classroom. Because their joy at this liberation might understandably be excessive and overflowing, by tradition they must be enshrouded in these somber black robes and mortar boards. This might well serve to remind them that all is not joyful and carefree in the world beyond the academic cloister, and that the road ahead of them will be anything but easy—if, indeed, they need to be reminded.

Throughout the nation during this month of June, thousands of young men and women, graduates all and Americans all, will be attending commencement exercises similar to these. All of these thousands of graduates will be looking to the future with no little anxiety. They will have very much on their minds what may lie ahead for them—whether there will be peace or war; what their chances may be for a promising career in their chosen fields of endeavor; how they may profitably and usefully employ the knowledge and training they have acquired.

But the Negro graduates at such exercises, good and loyal Americans though they are, will have on their minds not only these thoughts, but some quite special ones, too, as they contemplate their future. This is inevitably so, because it is the great irony of our nation, a nation firmly dedicated to a democratic way of life, that a substantial proportion of its citizens must still overcome unjust and undemocratic racial handicaps, must surmount arbitrary obstacles of racial bigotry, in running the race of life. And this is so not because of any misdeeds, of any shortcomings, of any lack of industry, ability, or loyalty on the part of these citizens so handicapped. It is so only because they are Negroes, because of their color and race.

The conscience of every white American who believes in our Constitution, in our traditional way of life, in the sacred principles of equality and liberty handed down to us by our founding fathers, must experience acute pain when he thinks of this utterly indefensible situation in our supposedly enlightened age.

These graduates whom we honor today are to be doubly congratulated, for in coming this far they have had to meet not only the challenge of learning, they have had to learn over the handicaps of race—handicaps both economic and social.

And what has this meant and what will this mean for them? It means that all of them are fully acquainted with the Negro ghetto and the severe disadvantages it entails. They have had to endure the political and economic under privilege which is synonymous with a segregated, separate, ghetto existence. Much of their life has unfolded thus far behind a cruel curtain of segregation and discrimination.

They know that their country was founded upon the sacred principles of the inalienable rights of man and the equality of all men before God. But they have been told that for Negroes this means only a qualified equality—separate equality, a separate existence from the rest of the community. They know too well the humiliation, the degradation, the psychological stresses and strains, the personality warping, which are the inevitable end-products of that separation. No one knows better than they that the doctrine of "separate but equal" is a monstrous fiction, an unabashed lie. Every Negro knows this is so from his harsh experiences with separate schools for Negroes, separate residential areas for Negroes, separate railroad accommodations for Negroes, separate facilities of every kind.

Indeed, the very concept of segregation, the fundamental motivation of it, involves discrimination and inequality. Involuntary segregation means a status of inferiority for those segregated.

To what utterly ridiculous lengths the doctrine and practice of segregation may be carried has been graphically demonstrated recently in this very city of Baltimore. I understand that the local park board police only a few days ago refused to permit a tennis match to be played between two tennis clubs, one white and one Negro, because it was contrary to the board's policy to permit interracial matches. The members of the two clubs were prevented from playing the match under threat of arrest. Danger in a tennis match! What utter nonsense! Can there be anyone in this community ingenious enough to explain what harm could possibly be done to the community if tennis players of the two races, voluntarily wishing to do so, should play tennis together? What a strange doctrine it is that requires Negro taxpayers of Baltimore to play tennis on public courts only with Negroes, even though others may wish to play with them.

The practices and incidents of racial bigotry can only be intolerably offensive to every fair-minded and right-thinking American. They are costly to the nation in these dangerous times. They are costly because they raise serious doubts internally and externally—about the true nature of the American democratic way of life. Because they seriously question our sincerity in our democratic professions. Because they cannot fail to induce our friends abroad to doubt the genuineness of our democracy and to question our ability to treat nonwhite peoples anywhere as equals. They are, therefore, tremendously damaging to our international prestige and to our leadership in the free world. And they hand to our enemies a most effective propaganda weapon in the worldwide ideological struggle—the struggle for the confidence of the peoples of the world, the preponderance of whom are nonwhite.

The heavy costs of racial prejudice in the American society are today being paid by every American citizen—white and black alike. These costs in their totality are incalculable, but who can doubt the tremendous burden they impose? The security of our great nation, the way of life which is the source of our unparalleled national strength, are confronted with the most ominous challenge in our history. Never before have we so desperately needed our full strength and unity. But this is denied the nation only because some of our allegedly patriotic citizens insist upon continuing to indulge themselves in the social vice of racial prejudice. They are quite willing to do so even at the cost of impairing the unity of our people in our hour of gravest crisis; even though it means that one-tenth of the population remains underprivileged

"The practices and incidents of racial bigotry can only be intolerably offensive to every fair-minded and right-thinking American."

and properly resentful; even though the inevitable result must be a shameful wasting of one-tenth of our human resources, of our manpower, though we can ill afford to be wasteful in this crucial hour.

This, surely, is not patriotism, nor is it good sense. It is sickness, or madness, or both.

Who, in his good senses, could doubt for an instant what it would mean to the strength, the unity, and the prestige of our nation if the cancerous growth of racial bigotry in the society were to be expelled?

This is all the Negro asks—that he be freed from the bondage of racial prejudice. Nothing more. I lay no claim to leadership and I have no right whatsoever to act as a spokesman for some fifteen million Negro citizens. I have always been a strong individualist, and since there are already literally millions of self-anointed Negro leaders and spokesmen, far be it from me to join the crowd. But from long observation, I am sure I am right when I say the Negro American asks no special treatment from this society. He asks that nothing be given to him. He asks, or rather demands, only that he be permitted to enjoy what is rightfully his—his God-given, Constitution-guaranteed right to live and work and play in this society on the same basis as every other citizen. He seeks escape from the handicaps of race, for he has proved to the world that he is inferior to no people. He seeks escape, rather, from the handicaps, the indignities, the humiliations and slurs of arbitrary, undemocratic racial prejudice.

The Negro asks no right to go into anyone's home, to force himself on anyone in any way. He asks only that he, as an individual, be permitted freely to make his way in a free society on the same basis as every other individual citizen; to rise or fall as his merit dictates. If the society grants him that, and nothing short of that could ever be acceptable, the Negro problem is solved. This would in no way affect the right of any person in the society to have as little or as much to do with any Negro, many Negroes, or all Negroes as he pleases.

In short, the needs of the Negro citizen would be satisfied if old prejudices, like old soldiers, would just fade away.

Indeed, in my thinking the urgency of rapid progress toward solution of this grave national problem is less in terms of the interest of the Negro than the interest of the nation. The challenge already confronts us as a nation and the time in which we can prepare adequately to meet it is already alarmingly short.

I am not at all unmindful that the Negro citizen in the American society has made great progress, particularly in recent years. The barriers of segregation and discrimination are being beaten down, and in this effort the Negro has had much help from white Americans who believe in as well as profess democracy. I think it no exaggeration at all to say that no group of people in history has made as much progress in a comparable time as the Negro has made since his release from slavery. Moreover, I realize that this magnificent progress has been possible only because the Negro has been able to take increasing advantage of the opportunities for work, development, and struggle afforded by a society whose framework is free and democratic.

But the fact remains, nevertheless, that these graduates before us today, despite the fine training they have received here, will go out into the world and encounter unique obstacles in shaping their careers only because they are Negroes. They, unquestionably, are better off than similar graduates of ten, twenty, or fifty years ago, and today there are many more Negro graduates than ever before. That is good. Still, they will not enjoy their full rights as American citizens, and until Negro graduates and all other Negroes can do so the American society will be guilty of a terrible injustice.

These graduates, as you and I, must think of rights and privileges and opportunities as something to be enjoyed in one's life span or not at all. These benefits cannot be taken with one to the great beyond nor can they be enjoyed in the hereafter. I will be happy, of course, to be assured that my children or my grandchildren or my great-grandchildren will enjoy their full right of American citizenship at some distant date. But I wish to enjoy them, too, for the simple reason that as an American citizen I am fully entitled to do so, and because I need the benefit of them to make my way in our highly competitive society.

It is important that these Negro graduates bear in mind that though the Negro has made and is making great progress, very much remains to be done. The road immediately ahead will never be easy. The rate of progress will depend in large degree upon the preparation and ability, the determination, and the courage of these young Negroes. They must never relax in the struggle for full citizenship for the Negro, for the complete integration of American Negroes in the life of the nation. They must be ever alert.

In this regard there are certain truths which the Negro citizen must learn well and bear constantly in mind.

In a democratic society, and we are greatly privileged to live in one—the world being as it is these days—the Negro citizen like all other citizens must willingly and self-sacrificingly assume heavy responsibilities and obligations in return for the rights and freedoms which he may enjoy. Democracy gives no free rides. The Negro cannot be a good citizen if he concentrates exclusively on the problems of his group. All of the problems of his community and nation are his problems and the Negro must devote his intelligent interest and effort to them. Integration in the society is a two-way proposition. The more integrated the Negro becomes the heavier will his civic responsibilities become. Freedom is a blessing to be highly treasured; it is not license and should not be abused.

Because of discrimination, the Negro has much to complain of, but let us not fall into the fatal error of ascribing all of our failures to racial prejudice. The cry of discrimination must never be used as an alibi for lack of effort, preparation, and ability. We can never end discrimination by hiding behind it, or as I fear some Negroes do, by acquiring a vested interest in it.

> ***"... let us not fall into the fatal error of ascribing all of our failures to racial prejudice. The cry of discrimination must never be used as an alibi for lack of effort, preparation, and ability."***

It is well also to bear always in mind in this hard world that fate helps only those who help themselves. We are much stronger now than we were and we can utilize our own resources of ability and wealth to much better advantage than in earlier years. I wonder if we really do as much for ourselves as we might, if we are as united and resolved as we should be. I doubt very much, for example, that we give to our two leading organizations, the NAACP and the Urban League, which have accomplished so much for us, the support, monetary and otherwise, which they deserve. There are Negroes of considerable affluence in very many American communities—professional and businessmen—many of whom are not, by any means, giving the assistance which should be given. If they do not realize that despite the success they may have had they can never rise very far above their group, and that their own future is tied to the future of the Negro, they are fatally shortsighted. In my view, no Negro, however high he may have risen, is worth very much if he forgets his people and remains aloof from the unrelenting struggle for full Negro emancipation.

Let us also be aware of the unfortunate inclination of the Negro himself to tighten the bonds of the ghetto by ghetto thinking. Life in the ghetto tempts the Negro to make the Negro problem the pivotal point of his thinking, as though everything in the world revolves about this problem. This is racial provincialism of the worst kind, and can only retard the progress of the group. It develops a narrowness of mind and a racial egocentrism, which is bad for both the Negro and the society in which he lives.

The world does not revolve around the Negro and will not stand still for him. But the Negro may be sure that a large part of the world sympathizes with his aspirations for full equality.

I am reasonably optimistic about the future of race relations in America. The conscience of the nation quickens. An ever-increasing number of citizens, South as well as North, realize that our bad race relations are immensely damaging to the nation, and they are determined to do something about it. The forces of true democracy are strongly at work in our society and the force of democracy on the march is irresistible.

Indeed, I feel that the time has never been more propitious for effective results from a planned and concerted attack upon racial bigotry here. The time is ripe. What is greatly needed is a coordination of the efforts of the greatest possible number of Negro, interracial, and other organizations to the end that their resources and good will may achieve maximum impact. At present there is clearly too little planning and too much duplication of effort.

You graduates have no reason to be discouraged or pessimistic about the future before you. You can surmount the obstacles in your path if you are determined, courageous, and hardworking. Never be faint-hearted. Be resolute, but never bitter. Bitterness will serve only to warp your personality. Permit no one to dissuade you from pursuing the goals you set for yourselves. In this country, difficult as it may be for you compared with others of fairer skin, no achievement is beyond you. Do not fear to pioneer, to venture down new paths of endeavor. Demand and make good use of your rights, but never fail to discharge faithfully the obligations and responsibilities of good citizenship. Be good Americans.

You are to be congratulated on having journeyed this far. You will, I am sure, be valuable assets to your group, your community, and your nation. You will have much to do with the shaping of the nation's future.

I salute you and I wish you well.

Bunche never lost hope that there were peaceful solutions to the many conflicts raging at home and overseas. As he once explained, "I have a deep-seated bias against hate and intolerance. I have a bias against racial and religious bigotry. I have a bias against war, a bias for peace. I have a bias which leads me to believe that no problem of human relations is ever insoluble." Indeed, he devoted the remainder of his United Nations career after receiving the Nobel Prize to developing the organization's peacekeeping strategies while mediating disputes in hotspots such as the Congo (now known as Zaire), Cyprus, the Suez Canal, India, and Pakistan. In 1968, he was named under-secretary general of the United Nations, the highest rank ever held by an American.

When not involved in international politics, Bunche was often busy with various civil rights activities. He was a member of the board of directors of the NAACP, for example, and he participated in several major demonstrations led by Martin Luther King, Jr., including the 1963 March on Washington and the 1965 Selma-to-Montgomery March. Even as the civil rights struggle grew more militant, Bunche remained firmly opposed to violence and confrontation. On October 23, 1963, he spoke to a gathering at Tougaloo Southern Christian College in Tougaloo, Mississippi, in honor of United Nations Day. In his address, an excerpt of which is reprinted here from The Negro Speaks: The Rhetoric of Contemporary Black Leaders, *edited by Jamye Coleman Williams and McDonald Williams (Noble & Noble, 1970), he left no doubt where he stood both as a world-renowned diplomat and as an African American.*

. . . I warmly compliment Tougaloo College—its students, faculty, and administration—on the spirit and the broad vision which have led it to hold this observance. Indeed, I am told that Tougaloo College, for more than a decade, has been the only institution of higher education in the entire state of Mississippi to recognize United Nations Day and thereby keep alive the ideal and practical significance of the United Nations. That makes Tougaloo look good and the rest of the state look very bad, in a blind, provincial, and isolationist sense. But I suspect that not all the white citizens of Mississippi are so narrow-minded as that and so ignorant of our national interest in a small world and a nuclear age. On the contrary, I imagine that there are not a few white Mississippians who would like to feel free to take enlightened views on both world and racial affairs, but who are intimidated against doing so by the threats of the professional bigots of their communities. It is a great irony of the southern pattern of racial relations that the white citizens of the South, as well as Negroes, also are not free and, in general, dare not even follow the dictates of their consciences and their intelligence for fear of reprisal. That the Negro is content in this society is wishful thinking. Whites, I feel, would be relieved were all this racial tension over. I am glad to see this audience integrated.

Once I was invited to the University of Arkansas, but after I received the invitation, I realized it was segregated and wrote to cancel the reservation. However, the administration said this would not be the case.

I finally arrived in Fayetteville and spent two days, and they were the most inspiring and delightful days I've ever had. All of the meetings were integrated, the social affairs were integrated, and the atmosphere was excellent. So I was totally unprepared for what the professor in charge said to me as I was going to the airport to leave. He got chummy and said, "Ralph, now that it's all over, I must tell you how much trouble that letter of yours and our reply caused us," and I said, "Oh you're joking. I've been in racial situations all of my life and this was natural—there was no strain here"; and he said, "A few days before you were due here we were reviewing the correspondence with you, and we saw the assurance we had given you that the audience would be integrated, and one of the professors on the committee, who was a social scientist, said, 'Uh, huh, we're in trouble.'" Then I said, "What do you mean?" He said, "Well, the university is in a rural county, which is an almost white county. There are only a few Negroes in it, and they're cotton farmers, and they wouldn't come to hear Booker T. Washington much less Ralph Bunche!" And he said, "He'll get here, and he'll find an all white audience and figure he has been tricked." I said, "Yes, I might have done that, but what did you do?" He said, "Well, the only thing we could do; we sent out runners to Pine Bluff and Little Rock, which is two hundred miles over the Ozark Mountains, to round up Negroes to get them to come to hear you," and I told them I thought that this was extending democracy and integration just a little too far, because these Negroes who had to drive all this distance to hear me talk would probably hate me and integration for the rest of their lives. But I take it that wasn't necessary with regard to this part of the audience tonight which does not belong to the same tribe as I do.

In endorsing the United Nations today, I assure you, you are serving both the interests of this state and of the nation, because those interests are certainly identified with peace and goodwill among men. I doubt if there is any place in the world—including the Union of South Africa—where recognition of those basic principles of decency and amity which should everywhere govern the relations among peoples is as sorely needed as in this state of Mississippi. That is all this so-called race problem amounts to; in fact, despite all of the hysteria generated by some die-hard Negro haters, white citizens must treat black citizens decently, which, after all, is the only way the whites themselves can claim to be decent people. Prejudice and decency are utterly incompatible. . . .

I take my stand firmly and unflinchingly as an American. This is my country; my ancestors and I helped to build it. I say my color has nothing to do with it. I have a stake in this country, and I am determined that I and my children and their children will cash in on it. I am determined to fight therefore for what is mine. I want no one—Malcolm X or anyone else—to tell me to give up this fight because equality is unattainable and to look elsewhere, in some mythical, fanciful state of black men, for my salvation. I say that is surrender and escapism and I want none of it. . . .

I have come to Tougaloo tonight in response to your friendly invitation. It is much more important for me as a sort of missionary for the UN and for civil rights, to be here rather than at the UN ceremony in New York, where most everyone is already converted. Here, at least, I am in shouting distance of the heathens, who in this part of the world all seem to have pale faces. I have come as an American and as a Negro and also as an official of the UN organization, to talk with you about the United Nations. If, in my talk tonight, I have to deviate from the subject of the United Nations now and then to comment on the racial crisis in America, as I have already been doing, it is not because you and I would prefer to discuss race but only because the offenses against the Negro in this state of Mississippi are so flagrant that no one with any conscience and morality could fail to cry out against those injustices as crimes against humanity. . . .

Now what of the UN in 1963? The eighteenth annual session of the General Assembly is well underway. The most relaxed and encouraging atmosphere and the most promising beginning in the entire eighteen-year history of the UN prevails. This is very important, highly significant, and very vital to all of us of whatever race, creed, or color because this concerns the future of mankind. This concerns the question of whether or not there is to be peace or nuclear war or survival on this planet. That is why I say it is of as deep concern to every individual of whatever race in Mississippi as in the rest of the world. Nuclear weapons, the death and destruction of war, are color-blind, and in that context, there is complete equality among the races. The entire world will be living on borrowed time until peace is finally made secure, and if that is to be accomplished, it will be only the UN that can do it. At this time at the UN, the cold war has diminished. This is perhaps, in part, because of the agreement made last summer on banning nuclear weapons testing (except for underground tests). This certainly has been a major factor, and this, of course, has been made possible because of the position taken by communist China against the test ban, which has led to the split with the Soviet Union. There is a restrained optimism at the United Nations. No one thinks we are near the millennium. It is recognized that the basic West-East conflict is unresolved. It is recognized that the danger of nuclear war is ever present, but it is also recognized that there is less danger than there was even a year ago. There will be troubles —this is known—and there will be conflicts; but it is felt now that they all can be met and surmounted.

It is well for us to recall that just one year ago the world and the United Nations were confronted with actually the most dangerous situation since the end of World War II. The United States and the Soviet Union were plunging headlong toward direct military confrontation over Cuba (that is, Russian missiles and troops in Cuba). Then there was President Kennedy's rare statesmanship: unilateral action in the interest of national defense and also his appeal simultaneously to the United Nations. This was followed by Secretary General U Thant's direct appeal to President Kennedy and Chairman Khrushchev to which he got immediate and favorable response. And this action by the United Nations slowed things down, relaxed the tension of the crisis, eased it, making possible a better climate for the exchanges between the two heads of state, which finally ended the imminent threat of war over Cuba.

This is, in fact, a vital function of the United Nations, the function in threatening situations, of intervening, not with the idea of finding an immediate solution to the problem but of relaxing the tension, of getting communications started, getting a dialogue started, of slowing things down, of averting recourse through arms. Now, this affair of Cuba, although the most dangerous, was not by any means the first time the UN has had a big hand in averting major and probably nuclear war since 1946. It similarly intervened and saved the world from wars in Indonesia and in Kashmir in the dispute between India and Pakistan, which, indeed, is not yet settled and is being contained by the vital continued presence after all these years of UN military observers as a buffer in Kashmir. We never hear anything about it, but they have been out there since 1947. The war in Palestine was stopped by the United Nations' intervention. The war over Suez, which involved two of the big powers, France and the United Kingdom, was settled by the United Nations' intervention. The United Nations still maintains (now for over six years along the border between Egypt and Israel) an emergency force, a peace force of fifty-three hundred officers and men. The civil war in Lebanon was contained by direct UN intervention; but the biggest, the most expensive, the most difficult, and what promises to be the most successful intervention of all began in mid-July 1960 in the Congo, and it still continues with a much improved situation out there.

Ever since the Cuban crisis of last fall, the United Nations has had a major role in settling dangerous conflict situations between the Dutch and Indonesians over West Irian (New Guinea). It has helped achieve decisive results in maintaining the territorial integrity of the Congo. In just mentioning the Congo, I can't help recalling a personal experience I had out there. . . . At the beginning of that conflict, I had been sent out there before independence in 1960 by Dag Hammarskjöld to represent the UN at its independence, and then was told to stay on because it was feared that trouble might break out. I was to be there to be of such help as I could to the newly independent government. And sure enough, one week after independence was declared, trouble broke out because the large Congolese army of twenty-eight thousand well-trained, heavily armed men, all Africans, mutinied. They mutinied because they insisted upon Africanization. This army, after eighty years of Belgian control, was all black except for the officers. There wasn't a single African officer in the army, not even with the rank of lieutenant. And so, one week after independence, the soldiers mutinied, and you could hear them chanting in the streets of Leopoldville, chanting, "President Kasavubu is a black man, Prime Minister Lumumba is a black man, the members of the cabinet are all black men, the members of the Parliament are all black, but the officers in our army are all white," and so overnight they revolted, mutinied, chased the Belgian officers out, and then found themselves with an army with no officers and therefore no discipline. The whole country was tense, the Belgian settlers panicked and fled in hysteria, and we were all frightened silly in Leopoldville that day. I was particularly frightened because I scare easily anyway; and when I looked out my hotel window that morning, and I saw that those Congolese soldiers had already imbibed too much beer, obviously, that scared me even more. Three came to my room, and only one of them could speak a little French (the other two spoke only Lingala, neither English nor French), but from him I understood that they were arresting me because I was a Belgian paratrooper. Well, you know it's amazing what runs through your mind on an occasion of that kind. I just took it for granted I was a "goner," that they were going to take me out and stand me up against a wall and shoot me for being a Belgian paratrooper. I wrote my son that night, after I stopped shaking enough to be able to write, and I told him that what went through my mind at that time was this: "I am fifty-six years old, spent most of my adult life in a struggle for equality for my own group in America and for the independence of the states of Africa. I was once inducted into the Kikuyu Tribe in Kenya and given a tribal name Kanioki. And now, I find myself in the very heart of Africa, in the Congo, and my career is coming to an end for being mistaken for being a Belgian paratrooper. What greater irony could there be?" Well, they just took us downstairs and huddled us together and kept us huddled until they drank up all the beer in the hotel, and then they left us, and I was left free to carry on my career, but I will never forget that experience. . . .

The United Nations intervened in the Yemen controversy, in the course of this year, at the request of Saudi Arabia and the United Arab Republic. That situation is complex—it is not settled by any means; but we are sticking with it, and we are hoping that we can continue to keep it contained, so that it doesn't flare up at all. I was sent out there by U Thant in March, the strangest place I have ever been. You sort of go back two thousand years immediately—fantastic, actually. I flew by helicopter from Sanaa in Yemen, an Arab country on the coast of Aden. I went to Marab because there had been some fighting there, and also I had heard of it as the home of the Queen of Sheba. When we landed down there on the desert, we were greeted by a group of local tribal chiefs, in prebiblical dress, actually, but all carrying rifles and with ammunition slung over their shoulders. They started to welcome us; they formed a circle and put us into the middle of it, and the elder of the group pulled out a little piece of paper and began to read a word of greeting in Arabic and that went all right. The second one got started, but he had said but a few words, when all of a sudden, there was a tremendous commotion and babble, and they started brandishing rifles, curved knives, and so on. I got scared again, but I said to the interpreter, "What's it all about, what have I done?" He said, "Nothing, you just keep quiet, they are not denouncing you, they are appealing to you." I said, "What are they appealing to me about?" "Well," he said, "they claim that the British crossed the border, or some people crossed the border from the British territory the other day, and now you say you have come as their friend, and they are asking you to lead them in battle against the British." It took me a couple of hours to explain to them that as United Nations officials we are trying to stop wars, not start them. I might not have succeeded if the Egyptian officer had not brought out some boxes of Egyptian candy, beautifully wrapped in bright tinfoil, and the chiefs became interested and forgot about me leading them into battle.

Just Monday of this week, a UN mission left for South Vietnam—we hope that it will be helpful, and we are sure they will make a great effort in that situation. There has been, in the course of the years, as I have mentioned, the ban on testing nuclear weapons and also the ban on nuclear weapons in outer space. . . . There is continuing pressure on Portugal with regard to Angola and Mozambique and their freedom, and on the United Kingdom with regard to Southern Rhodesia. I can assure you that colonialism as an institution, in practice, will within a very few years become a thing of the past. This has been, in large part, because of the continuous pressing of the United Nations since 1946.

One of our hottest issues, the issue which comes from the committee in which I sit and which I left only this noon, is the question of apartheid, the racial policy of South Africa, which, of course, is the most overt form of racial separation to be found anywhere in the world. That's saying a lot when one is where we are now. This is a perennial problem of the General Assembly. One resolution has already been adopted in this session and that was by the most remarkable vote ever taken in the United Nations. It was a resolution denouncing apartheid and demanding that the political prisoners that have been taken by the Union of South Africa be released. There are 111 members of the United Nations. The vote in favor of this resolution, sponsored by the Africans and the Asians, was 106 member states for, only one member against, and that was the Union of South Africa itself. In other words, not only all the Africans and Asians and South Americans and Arabs voted for this, but so did the United States and the United Kingdom and France and all the European states. Aside from the four absences, this was the total membership of the UN. I can assure you that the United Nations is overwhelmingly and solidly against racial discrimination everywhere and in any form.

The UN officially does not concern itself with problems of race in the United States. It accepts these as a domestic matter, but there is no doubt that overwhelmingly the sympathy of the members of the UN, from all sections of the world and peoples of all colors, is for the American Negro in his heroic struggle for justice. The eyes of the world are focused on this problem, on what happens in the United States. This has a tremendous effect on the United States image abroad. I have always been confident that the Negro will win this struggle, but it is not the Negro, really, but the nation that must win it. There are still many obstacles and much trouble ahead which will require ever greater effort, persistence, courage, and sacrifice.

There is good reason for concern that among those elements in the country which are necessarily most responsible for a constructive effort to solve the racial problem—notably the white leadership in many of the communities of the South and only to a lesser extent in the North, and especially in our Congress—there is still, at this very late day, so little understanding and sense of urgency about the solution of this problem.

They seem to believe, or perhaps they only wishfully think, that the Negro's impatience, and its manifestations in the demonstrations and protests throughout the land, are a passing phenomenon and that the American communities can get over their racial crises by some token actions and gestures toward equality nicely wrapped in pious words.

I am confident in warning that such attitudes are grossly mistaken and that those who hold them are bound to experience a rude awakening. The impatience of the Negro about the lack of decisive and immediate progress—and that is the only kind of progress that can now have meaning in the removal of racial shackles—is increasing and will continue to increase until all of the racial shackles are removed. Moreover, Negro impatience, more and more, will be accompanied by that frustration which inevitably induces bitterness and leads to desperation and desperate acts. This could only mean increasing violence. Now if that stage is reached—and I solemnly hope there is enough sanity in our society to avoid it—it will no longer be a question of whether the white majority or the Negro minority wins or loses. It would then be the nation that would be bound to lose, and to lose disastrously.

It is not only in our individual interest but also in our nation's interest that every Negro must succeed in achieving the full status of an American. We are serving not ourselves but our country in seeking to realize the promise of our constitution for every American, irrespective of color.

Because of our stand, our faith, and our courage, we can be confident that there are no better Americans anywhere than we.

Bunche died in December 1971, about six months after a series of illnesses brought on by kidney failure forced him to retire from the United Nations.

SOURCES

Books

Bunche, Ralph, *A World View of Race*, Association in Negro Folk Education, 1936, reprinted, Kennikat, 1968.

Foner, Philip S., editor, *The Voice of Black America: Major Speeches by Negroes in the United States, 1797-1971*, Simon & Schuster, 1972.

Haberman, Frederick W., editor, *Nobel Lectures: Peace, 1926-1950*, Volume 2, Elsevier, 1972.

Hale, Frank W., Jr., editor, *The Cry for Freedom: An Anthology of the Best That Has Been Said and Written on Civil Rights Since 1954*, A.S. Barnes & Co., 1969.

Haskins, Jim, *Ralph Bunche: A Most Reluctant Hero*, Hawthorn, 1974.

Kugelmass, J. Alvin, *Ralph J. Bunche: Fighter for Peace*, Messner, 1962.

Mann, Peggy, *Ralph Bunche: UN Peacemaker*, Coward, McCann & Geoghegan, 1975.

Reid, Loren, editor, *American Public Address: Studies in Honor of Albert Craig Baird* (contains chapter entitled "Ralph Bunche: Negro Spokesman"), University of Missouri Press, 1961.

Urquhart, Brian, *Ralph Bunche: An American Life*, Norton, 1993.

Williams, Jamye Coleman, and McDonald Williams, editors, *The Negro Speaks: The Rhetoric of Contemporary Black Leaders*, Noble & Noble, 1970.

Periodicals

Nation, "Ralph Bunche," December 27, 1971.

Newsweek, "Never Did He Despair," October 11, 1971, pp. 44-49; "Ralph Bunche, 1904-1971," December 20, 1971, p. 33.

New York Times, December 10, 1971.

Time, "Man Without Color," December 20, 1971, pp. 34-39.

Vital Speeches of the Day, "The Barriers of Race Can Be Surmounted," July 1, 1949; "Freedom Is Blessing, Not a License," August 15, 1951; "The Road to Peace," August 15, 1954.

Yale Review, "Remembering Ralph Bunche," spring, 1987, pp. 448-451.

Ben Nighthorse Campbell

1933–

Native American artist, businessman, and U.S. Senator of the Northern Cheyenne tribe

In contrast to many of the rather staid figures who populate the chambers of the United States Senate, Ben Nighthorse Campbell stands out as an especially colorful and independent-minded free spirit in both his personal and professional life. The ponytailed politician usually sports a cowboy hat and boots, a bolo tie, and distinctive jewelry he designs and makes himself; his preferred mode of transportation is his Harley-Davidson, or, when he is back home on his ranch, his beloved horse, War Bonnet. On the Senate floor, where he views himself as a representative of all Native Americans, he has antagonized some of his colleagues at both ends of the political spectrum by voting in ways that reflect his self-described position as a social liberal and fiscal conservative. In his typically blunt and outspoken fashion, however, Campbell brushes aside any criticism. "I always say that if I have the right and the left both mad at me," he once remarked to a People *magazine reporter, "then I must be doing something right."*

Campbell was born in Auburn, California, of a mother who immigrated from Portugal and a father of Cheyenne, Apache, and Pueblo ancestry. (Campbell himself is an enrolled member of the Northern Cheyenne tribe.) Due to his parents' chronic ill health (his mother suffered from tuberculosis and his father was an alcoholic), he had a difficult and unsettled childhood marked by extreme poverty and sporadic stays in foster homes and orphanages. Campbell found some solace in expressing himself through art, however; using scrap materials he found in the garbage, he learned to work with metal and wood and by the age of twelve was creating pieces of jewelry.

A lackluster student who spent more time hanging out with the members of a gang he belonged to than attending class, Campbell dropped out of high school during his junior year and joined the Air Force. During his two-year stint, half of which he spent in South Korea, he earned his diploma and indulged a growing passion for judo. Upon his return home in 1953, he attended San Jose State University, from which he graduated with a bachelor's degree in physical education and fine arts in 1957. While there, Campbell also served as captain of the judo team, winning the Pacific Coast championship and becoming the youngest American ever to attain the rank of fourth-degree black belt.

Campbell spent the next two years as an elementary school teacher before quitting to move to Tokyo, Japan, so that he could continue his judo instruction and prepare to compete on an international level. Four grueling years of training helped him reach sixth-degree black belt status and win a gold medal in the 1963 Pan American Games in Brazil. The following year, he earned a spot on the U.S. Olympic judo team, but an injury dashed his hopes of capturing a medal.

Shortly after that, Campbell decided to call an end to his competitive career (at the time, he was ranked number four in the world) and return to teaching. However, he remained active in judo as an instructor and promoter until the early 1970s, when he withdrew from the sport to pursue another love instead—raising and training championship quarter horses.

Around the same time, Campbell also went into the jewelry business. Using metalworking techniques he had learned in Japan, he began creating unique necklaces, bracelets, rings, and other pieces that feature traditional Native American designs. Since then, his artistic skills have earned him more than two hundred awards. His "Painted Mesa" line is available nationally at prices ranging from a couple of hundred dollars to well over twenty thousand.

Campbell entered politics in 1982 when Democratic party leaders in his district drafted him to run for a seat in the Colorado house of representatives against a popular Republican. His tireless campaigning resulted in victory that year and in two subsequent elections. In 1986, Campbell traded on his popularity in the state legislature to win a seat in the U.S. House of Representatives. There he remained for the next six years, easily winning re-election twice in a very diverse district consisting of large blocs of Republican voters and Democratic-leaning Hispanic Americans.

Very early on, Campbell demonstrated that his agenda reflected the concerns of his constituents and not necessarily those of his party. As a member of committees that drafted legislation regarding small businesses, national parks and tourism, agriculture, and mining, he often voted in ways that did not please his fellow Democrats, such as when he came out against gun control and for a constitutional amendment to prohibit flag-burning. By the same token, his pro-choice stance did not sit well with conservative Republicans.

Campbell also tackled issues of particular interest to Native Americans. For example, he lent his support to the efforts to establish a Smithsonian-affiliated National Museum of the American Indian in Washington, D.C. He also helped draft and served as co-sponsor of the Indian Arts and Craft Act of 1990, which is intended to help protect artists and consumers from fraudulent "native" art. And noting that it was "the only battlefield I've ever heard of being named after the loser," he was instrumental in the fight to change the name of Montana's Custer National Battlefield Monument to the Little Bighorn National Battlefield Monument.

It was during his third and final term in the House that he delivered the following speech to the May 1991, graduates of Haskell Indian Nations University in Kansas. It is a variation of an address he has delivered on many other occasions to Native American youth on the topic of achieving success.

Today is the day you and your families have long looked forward to and is a turning point in your lives. For me it is particularly rewarding to know the dreams of the elders are being fulfilled. The philosopher Goethe once said, "Whatever you dream, follow it with action, because the boldness of action in making dreams come true has a magic, a power, and a genius in itself." Literature and philosophy were not my strong suits, but people of all races have recognized the importance of dreams—American Indians more than most.

Today is the day on which you begin making your dreams come true. What you dream, so once did I. In years to come, you will look back to a very special person in your lives (or perhaps several) who you will always remember as the person who encouraged those dreams. They may take credit for your successes, but blame the failure on no one.

To our graduating class today, I would suppose you have been deluged by time-worn phrases such as "commencement is the beginning" or "the future belongs to you" or equally abstract comments on your new venture. But no matter how many times your friends and teachers said the same thing to other graduating classes, they are sincere. They love you and are proud of you.

As a former teacher, I am proud of you, too. In part you are a product of the story of the American education system. That story is one of the great epochs of human learning. It is the story of goodness and sharing as well as greatness that has been heard around the world. Almost forty percent of all doctorate degrees conferred in the United States now go to foreign students who have heard that message. Many stay to become good citizens, others return to their own lands with a better understanding of America. Many of us can trace our own roots to countries from which they came. Our educational system has become the most important link in a world that grows ever smaller. The strength of our education system will determine whether this world will face a future of enlightenment or darkness.

If ever in the coming years you grow disillusioned with this nation, if ever you doubt that America holds a special place in all the long history of humankind, remember that we are still the center of the world for new skills and new ideas. We are still the stronghold for dissent, challenge, and experiment. We are a nation in which questioning is encouraged and protest is a constitutional right, and even though our national policy has a terrible record in dealing with American Indians, we must strive to improve.

Remember with pride that many of America's greatest accomplishments had their roots in traditional Indian life. From medicine to nutrition to the founding of our U.S. Constitution, our native people provided the source material and often the inspiration for this nation. Our institutions do not control us, and although your college days may be over, your education is not, nor will it ever be.

That time has come to move forward and take both the human and economic skills you have learned with you. Full well, you must remind yourselves that real success is not gauged by monetary measurements but by human measurements. It is the size of your heart that really counts, not the size of your wallet. Just as the history of a nation is not measured by its wealth but by its goodness. Let us hope that when you return to this institution for the graduation of your own son or daughter, you will not only do so in a world at peace, but will have been judged successfully by those human measurements that we commonly call "the Indian way" that is our cultural heritage to pass on to our children. Let us not forget that this good fortune has come to you because our elders have suffered and sacrificed, and that to preserve it, there will come times when you, too, must sacrifice.

> ***"From medicine to nutrition to the founding of our U.S. Constitution, our native people provided the source material and often the inspiration for this nation."***

We see in you such strength and hope, such buoyancy, such good will. Such straightforward and uncomplicated happiness that our Creator has already blessed you and that our people have already imprinted the love of peace and freedom in your hearts. Perhaps Thomas Jefferson would have agreed with Indian dreamers when he said, "I like the dreams of the future better than the history of the past."

As I think back to my own experiences since I graduated San Jose State about a hundred years ago, I can tell you that nothing is without risk. Success does not come through simplicities but through hard work and perseverance. You have been educated but not indoctrinated. Now you must go forward with equal shares of confidence and skepticism, full well knowing that you may pursue a profession not yet created. It is estimated that thirty percent of the jobs available in the year 2000 are not yet known, and ten percent of the jobs now available will be obsolete by that same year. What you have trained for, you may not do. Look at me; I majored in physical education and ended up making my living as an artist who raises cattle and is occasionally distracted by public office.

Not to worry about specifics, we have confidence you will rank wisdom ahead of book knowledge, truth ahead of technology. You will maintain high standards without being snooty and have convictions without being crabby. You will be principled without being prudish and show sympathy without being saccharin. And if you do all that very well, you will qualify for a full professorship or the priesthood.

For most of you, the grades you worked so hard for are now moot. Few people you meet will care. Old grades become like polished merit badges or Aunt Minnie's baby pictures. In the professional world, no one will ask you what grade you made in Psychology 1A or Accounting 302. What they will ask you is, "Can you do the job?" "How active are you in the community?" "To what associations do you subscribe?" And, "Do you get along with your fellows?" Those are now the goals on which you must concentrate.

No one can mandate success. No one can legislate that you reach your goals. There are no laws to make you excel, and to everything there is a cost. The cost of excellence is discipline; the cost of mediocrity is disappointment. But the cost of apathy is by far the greatest—the cost of apathy is failure.

I am convinced that what you do with your life is secondary to how well you do it. As a former Olympic team member, I used to think my goal should be how much weight I should lift up. Now I know it should be how many humans I can uplift. Surely, we all make mistakes. I've made more than I can remember. To that end I would say, remember the words of President Lincoln, who said, "I am not concerned that you fall, I am concerned that you arise."

Ben Nighthorse Campbell

Arise you can, lead you must. Succeed you will, because this land is your future. Your decisions will determine the world's future as well as the future of our Indian people.

Even though my age group has not done a very good job of finding common goals, we have confidence in your ability to learn from our mistakes and do better. Don't settle for doing as well, do better. Think of the mistakes we have made in caring for our air, our water, our Earth Mother. You must strive for a peaceful world and recognize in the great scheme of things that, although any darn fool can kill, not even the wisest man can give life back. We would have done better, but did not. You will do better because our failures have brought your goals into focus.

Think of what people can do with a focus and a goal. A poor girl becomes one of America's greatest educators and is given the Presidential Medal of Freedom—Annie Wauneka. A youngster born on the Pine Ridge Reservation who was given no chance to win becomes a world-famous Olympian—Billy Mills. A young Pueblo Indian blinded by an explosion in Vietnam becomes a world-famous sculptor—Michael Naranjo. They prove there are no secrets to success, but the common denominator is simply be the best you can be.

My friends, as I stand here as the last obstacle you must endure before going forward to your life's work, I want to describe the place in which some of the world's most meaningful decisions have been made. A place that most Americans know as the Hall of the People. A place where each person is heard, a process patterned after Indian council fires.

When I was elected to Congress, I had never been inside our Capitol building. When I was traveling with the U.S. Olympic team, I saw the Great Pyramids of Egypt and the Taj Mahal in India. I marvelled at the Coliseum in Rome and the Eiffel Tower in Paris. I saw people pay homage to the great Buddha in Kamakura and to the Christ on the mountain above Rio de Janeiro. I tell you truthfully that what you own in your Capitol easily equals any and all of the manmade treasures on this earth. And the reason it does is because all the brilliance, all the imagination and all the cumulative wisdom of mankind has a hand in developing our institutions. They are only two hundred years old, but they meld thousands of years of experience.

As you look around the chamber of the House, you realize how many human beings in history sowed and nurtured the seeds of freedom that have grown to maturity in this nation. The stone reliefs that surround the House chamber with the names of Blackstone, Solomon, Justinian, Croesus, Süleyman, Innocent, Jefferson, and Napoleon, to mention a few, are constant reminders that during their time on earth, each helped us mold the values of this nation. Surely Sitting Bull, Sequoia, and Chief Joseph could have been included in that august body of collective wisdom. I must admit that sometimes our decisions in Congress fly in the face of collective, conventional, or any other kind of wisdom, but we are still young as nations go.

I compare it to the magic place where I live near the ruins of Mesa Verde National Park in Colorado, where the ancient ones settled before Christ walked this earth and where they lived in harmony for nine hundred years, twice as long as America's post-Columbian history. Surely if they could do it, we can, too.

And that, my brothers and sisters, must be your objectives as you leave this place. I cannot tell you how much I believe that as we go into 1992, [the] anniversary of Columbus, the coming decade will be a major turning point in the history of our people. As my friends know, I never let an opportunity go by without encouraging Indian people to get involved in the political system. I am convinced that America, which has failed so miserably in fighting social evils from drugs to crime, from prostitution to hunger, *is ready* to learn values of traditional Native American ways. Native Americans cannot continue to live our insulated lifestyles if we are going to help lead this nation. We need to help lead this nation. We need not abandon our traditional values—that's what makes our people so unique in this nation—we need to affect public policy to recognize those values, and to do that, we must be involved in city, school board, county, state, and federal government. Run, help, question.

> ***"I am convinced that America . . . is ready to learn values of traditional Native American ways. Native Americans cannot continue to live our insulated lifestyles if we are going to help lead this nation."***

In closing, let me leave you with a Daniel Webster phrase that is inscribed in marble behind the speaker's chair in the House chamber and boldly proclaims to all who enter that chamber: "Let us develop the resources of our land, call forth its powers, build up its institutions, promote all its great interests and see whether we, also, in our day and generation, may not perform something worthy to be remembered." Young friends, do something to be remembered. Go forward, make your mark. Win some and lose some. Fight the good fight. Be proud of being Indian. But above all, do something to be remembered for.

In 1992, Campbell ran for the U.S. Senate and won, making him the first Native American to serve in that body since 1929. Since then, he has continued to display an independent streak, siding with Republicans in backing legislation to develop natural gas resources underneath land that is within his district and opposing the Clinton administration's efforts to raise fees for grazing, mining, and logging on federal property. Despite his past opposition to gun control, he cast the deciding vote in 1993 in favor of the controversial crime bill that banned most assault weapons, a decision that prompted hundreds of negative calls to his office, including some two dozen death threats. He has also tackled one of the major problems of the Indian community with his sponsorship of a bill to increase the public's awareness of Fetal Alcohol Syndrome and Fetal Alcohol Effect, incurable conditions that can result in severe damage to the mental and physical health of children whose mothers consume large amounts of alcohol during pregnancy. In addition, he introduced a bill that would force the Washington Redskins football team to change their name (which many Native Americans find offensive) in exchange for the privilege of leasing federal land for a new stadium in the nation's capital.

Perhaps the most notable statement Campbell has made on the Senate floor since taking office, however, came during the course of an emotional debate on racism that unexpectedly erupted on July 22, 1993. The trigger was a controversial amendment to some otherwise innocuous legislation regarding national and community service programs. Introduced by North Carolina Senator Jesse Helms (and seconded by South Carolina Senator Strom Thurmond), the amendment would have granted a congressional design patent to the emblem of the United Daughters of the Confederacy (UDC). Freshman Democrat Carol Moseley-Braun of Illinois, the first black woman ever elected to the Senate, passionately objected on the grounds that the UDC emblem—which featured the original Confederate flag encircled by a wreath—was an unacceptable and offensive tribute to slavery and racism. She argued that the Senate had no business giving such a painful symbol of the past what amounted to a stamp of approval *(see page 898)**.*

Campbell was one of several senators that day who spoke up in support of Moseley-Braun. At the height of the discussion, he asked to be given the opportunity to go on the record with his comments, which are reprinted here from the Congressional Record, *103rd Congress, 1st session, July 22, 1993, p. S9261.*

Let me say that I came over to the floor and voted a while ago with Carol Moseley-Braun, went back to my office, as many of us did, and was answering some mail and watching television and it sort of exploded in my office on television.

I just wanted to tell her in front of this body that I was so proud that she stood up and kind of took on this issue. She is an outstanding legislator, and I am very proud to be able to serve with her. And I guess as the only other so-called person of color in this body, perhaps I have some insight that some of my colleagues may not except Carol.

If I can ask her forgiveness, I would also say that I know there are some places in this country yet where American Indians are called "prairie niggers," which is about the most vulgar term I can think of, or calling any African American a name and certainly American Indians, too.

I know that some of my colleagues who did not support her in this last issue feel they were upholding tradition. I would point out to them that slavery was once a tradition, like killing Indians like animals was once a tradition. That did not make them right, and we sought, as a body, as a nation, to correct that. There are still remnants.

Unfortunately, too many of our children are taught anger and insensitivity, not love, patience, and tolerance, and we have a long way to go. I think probably some of the people who did not support Senator Braun did not do it out of malice. They did it out of some kind of a misguided idea that they were preserving some kind of tradition.

I had a couple of experiences when I ran for this body just last fall that reminded me you never get to a point in America where we are going to totally erase some of the roots of prejudices. In one place, in fact—I am a veteran of the Korean conflict and very proud of our country, proud of the fact I was in the Air Force and proud of the fact that I carried the flag of the 1964 Olympic games when Bill Bradley and I were teammates in 1964 in Tokyo. And yet when I was endorsed by a veterans group and they asked the VFW, of which I am a member in one town in my state, if I could be endorsed in that VFW, they said we are not letting any Indians be endorsed in this body.

The VFW certainly apologized for that and whoever said that as a specific person did not speak for the VFW, which is by and large a good, patriotic, wonderful group of Americans, and I am very supportive of them. But it does tell from firsthand experience that you never get away from that stuff. And maybe because of that kind of constant reminder, even when you are a senator, we develop maybe some raw nerves that other people do not have.

I wanted to point that out. That was only one of several things that happened to me just in the last year or so. But one thing is clear. Symbols are important in this country; otherwise what is that flag about that I said I once carried, and what is the Statue of Liberty about? They are meant to do several things. One is to uphold and uplift the spirits of people and to draw them together. But, clearly, other symbols, such as the swastika, were meant to symbolize a division and draw people apart.

> ***"I would point out to them that slavery was once a tradition, like killing Indians like animals was once a tradition. That did not make it right. . . ."***

That is what we are talking about. Do we want to validate and ratify symbols in this country through this body? And I think historically we have tried to say we want to validate and ratify those symbols which are positive and which point out to all of us that we are all Americans and have a common goal, perhaps a common background, and we need to work together and not validate those symbols that are going to divide us and made us enemies of each other.

I just want Carol Moseley-Braun to know that she is not alone in this fight. The history of this country has not been good to African Americans and perhaps not good to American Indians either. So I understand that sensitivity. . . . I thank the senator for the time.

After additional debate, the Senate voted 75-25 to reject the amendment.

In March 1995, Campbell shocked and angered many of his Democratic colleagues when he announced that he was switching political parties. According to the senator himself, he decided to join the Republican fold as a result of differences with the Democrats over the balanced-budget amendment to the constitution, federal land-use policies, term limits, and shabby treatment by Colorado party officials. Noting that the move was not done "out of vindictiveness or impulsiveness or anything of the sort," Campbell told reporters that after months of contemplation, "I can no longer represent the agenda that's put forth by the party, although I certainly agree with many of the things that Democrats stand for."

SOURCES

Books

Congressional Record, 103rd Congress, 1st session, July 22, 1993, p. S9261.

Viola, Herman J., *Ben Nighthorse Campbell: An American Warrior,* Orion Books, 1993.

Periodicals

Detroit Free Press, "Second Senator Defects to GOP," March 4, 1995, p. 5A.

Grand Rapids Press, "Colorado Senator Makes Switch to GOP," March 4, 1995, p. A2.

Indian Country Today, "Campbell Discusses Issues of Today," August 18, 1993.

Life, "A Gem of a Lawmaker," June, 1994, p. 108.

Newsweek, "How the West Was Lost," March 20, 1995, p. 31.

New Yorker, "Silver Lining," November 23, 1992, pp. 49-50.

People, "Rites of Victory," November 30, 1992, pp. 50-52.

Stokely Carmichael

(Kwame Touré)

1941–

African American political and social activist

During the mid- and late 1960s, Stokely Carmichael stood at the forefront of the black power movement, first as head of the Student Non-Violent Coordinating Committee (SNCC) and later as a key figure in the Black Panther Party. (He is, in fact, credited with coining the phrase "black power.") A militant offshoot of the mainstream civil rights struggle, the black power movement resurrected the themes of previous black nationalists—namely, the need for African Americans to take pride in their heritage and achievements ("black is beautiful") and to demand political, social, economic, and cultural independence from white institutions. But due to media coverage that often leaned toward sensationalism and exaggeration, the idea of "black power" generated suspicion and fear among those who equated it with black racial hatred and violence.

Carmichael was known as the movement's most effective and popular speaker as well as one of its most creative thinkers. A native of Trinidad, he moved to New York City with his family when he was eleven and grew up in the ghetto. While attending Howard University, he participated in the student sit-ins sponsored by the Congress of Racial Equality (CORE). After graduating in 1964, Carmichael joined SNCC and assumed the leadership position just two years later. He then moved quickly to change the moderate SNCC philosophy, rejecting the notion of nonviolent resistance and warning that black demonstrators would respond in kind if attacked by whites. He also banned white liberals from serving in key roles in the organization. Eventually, Carmichael left SNCC for the even more radical Black Panthers. His association with them was short-lived, however; dismayed by the group's overtures to white radicals, he resigned and moved to Africa in 1969 to work for the Pan-African movement under the name Kwame Touré.

On July 28, 1966, Carmichael gave a speech in which he explained the black power philosophy and outlined what African Americans needed to do to make the movement work. An excerpt from his remarks, which originally appeared in an SNCC publication entitled Notes and Comment, *is reprinted here from the book* Black Nationalism in America, *edited by John H. Bracey Jr., August Meier, and Elliott Rudwick (Bobbs-Merrill, 1970).*

This is 1966 and it seems to me that it's "time out" for nice words. It's time black people got together. We have to say things nobody else in this country is willing to say and find the strength internally and from each other to say the things that need to be said. We have to understand the lies this country has spoken about black people and we have to set the record straight. No one else can do that but black people.

I remember when I was in school they used to say, "If you work real hard, if you sweat, if you are ambitious, then you will be successful." I'm here to tell you that if that was true, black people would own this country, because we sweat more than anybody else in this country. We have to say to this country that you have lied to us. We picked your cotton for $2.00 a day, we washed your dishes, we're the porters in your bank and in your building, we are the janitors and the elevator men. We worked hard and all we get is a little pay and a hard way to go from you. We have to talk not only about what's going on here but what this country is doing across the world. When we start getting the internal strength to tell them what should be told and to speak the truth as it should be spoken, let them pick the sides and let the chips fall where they may.

"The only thing we own in this country is the color of our skins and we are ashamed of that because they made us ashamed. We have to stop being ashamed of being black."

Now, about what black people have to do and what has been done to us by white people. If you are born in Lowndes County, Alabama, Swillingchit, Mississippi, or Harlem, New York, and the color of your skin happens to be black you are going to catch it. The only reason we have to get together is the color of our skins. They oppress us because we are black and we are going to use that blackness to get out of the trick bag they put us in. Don't be ashamed of your color.

A few years ago, white people used to say, "Well, the reason they live in the ghetto is they are stupid, dumb, lazy, unambitious, apathetic, don't care, happy, contented," and the trouble was a whole lot of us believed that junk about ourselves. We were so busy trying to prove to white folks that we were everything they said we weren't that we got so busy being white we forgot what it was to be black. We are going to call our black brother's hand.

Now, after 1960, when we got moving, they couldn't say we were lazy and dumb and apathetic and all that anymore so they got sophisticated and started to play the dozens with us. They called conferences about our mamas and told us that's why we were where we were at. Some people were sitting up there talking with Johnson while he was talking about their mamas. I don't play the dozens with white folks. To set the record straight, the reason we are in the bag we are in isn't because of my mama, it's because of what they did to my mama. That's why I'm where I'm at. We have to put the blame where it belongs. The blame does not belong on the oppressed but on the oppressor, and that's where it is going to stay.

Don't let them scare you when you start opening your mouth—speak the truth. Tell them, "Don't blame us because we haven't ever had the chance to do wrong." They made sure that we have been so blocked-in we couldn't move until they said, "Move." Now there are a number of things we have to do. The only thing we own in this country is the color of our skins and we are ashamed of that because they made us ashamed. We have to stop being ashamed of being black. A broad nose, a thick lip and nappy hair is us and we are going to call that beautiful whether they like it or not. We are not going to fry our hair anymore but they can start wearing their hair natural to look like us.

We have to define how we are going to move, not how they say we can move. We have never been able to do that before. Everybody in this country jumps up and says, "I'm a friend of the civil rights movement. I'm a friend of the Negro." We haven't had the chance to say whether or not that man is stabbing us in the back or not. All those people who are calling us friends are nothing but treacherous enemies and we

Stokely Carmichael

can take care of our enemies but God deliver us from our "friends." The only protection we are going to have is from each other. We have to build a strong base to let them know if they touch one black man driving his wife to the hospital in Los Angeles, or one black man walking down a highway in Mississippi or if they take one black man who has a rebellion and put him in jail and start talking treason, we are going to disrupt this whole country.

We have to say, "Don't play jive and start writing poems after Malcolm is shot." We have to move from the point where the man left off and stop writing poems. We have to start supporting our own movement. If we can spend all that money to send a preacher to a Baptist convention in a Cadillac then we can spend money to support our own movement.

Now, let's get to what the white press has been calling riots. In the first place don't get confused with the words they use like "anti-white," "hate," "militant" and all that nonsense like "radical" and "riots." What's happening is rebellions not riots and the extremist element is not RAM. As a matter of fact RAM is a very reactionary group, reacting against the pressures white people are putting on them. The extremists in this country are the white people who force us to live the way we live. We have to define our own ethic. We don't have to (and don't make any apologies about it) obey any law that we didn't have a part to make, especially if that law was made to keep us where we are. We have the right to break it.

We have to stop apologizing for each other. We must tell our black brothers and sisters who go to college, "Don't take any job for IBM or Wall Street because you aren't doing anything for us. You are helping this country perpetuate its lies about how democracy rises in this country." They have to come back to the community, where they belong and use their skills to help develop us. We have to tell the doctors, "You can't go to college and come back and charge us $5.00 and $10.00 a visit. You have to charge us 50¢ and be thankful you get that." We have to tell our lawyers not to charge us what they charge but to be happy to take a case and plead it free of charge. We have to define success and tell them the food Ralph Bunche eats doesn't feed our hungry stomachs. We have to tell Ralph Bunche the only reason he is up there is so when we yell they can pull him out. We have to do that, nobody else can do that for us.

We have to talk about wars and soldiers and just what that means. A mercenary is a hired killer and any black man serving in this man's army is a black mercenary, nothing else. A mercenary fights for a country for a price but does not enjoy the rights of the country for which he is fighting. A mercenary will go to Vietnam to fight for free elections for the Vietnamese but doesn't have free elections in Alabama, Mississippi, Georgia, Texas, Louisiana, South Carolina and Washington, D.C. A mercenary goes to Vietnam and gets shot fighting for his country and they won't even bury him in his own hometown. He's a mercenary, that's all. We must find the strength so that when they start grabbing us to fight their war we say, "Hell no."

We have to talk about nonviolence among us, so that we don't cut each other on Friday nights and don't destroy each other but move to a point where we appreciate and love each other. That's the nonviolence that has to be talked about. The psychology the man has used on us has turned us against each other. He says nothing about the cutting that goes on Friday night but talk about raising one fingertip towards him and that's when he jumps up. We have to talk about nonviolence among us first.

We have to study black history but don't get fooled. You should know who John Hullett is, and Fannie Lou Hamer is, who Lerone Bennett is, who Max Stanford is, who Lawrence Landry is, who May Mallory is and who Robert Williams is. You have to know these people yourselves because you can't read about them in a book or in the press. You have to know what Mr. X said from his own lips not the *Chicago Sun-Times*. That responsibility is ours. The Muslims call themselves Muslims but the press calls them black Muslims. We have to call them Muslims and go to their mosque to find out what they are talking about firsthand and then we can talk about getting together. Don't let that man get up there and tell you, "Oh, you know those Muslims preach nothing but hate. You shouldn't be messing with them." "Yah, I don't mess with them, yah, I know they bad." The man's name is the Honorable Elijah Muhammad and he represents a great section of the black community. Honor him.

We have to go out and find our young blacks who are cutting and shooting each other and tell them they are doing the cutting and shooting to the wrong people. We have to bring them together and spend the time if we are not just shucking and jiving. This is 1966 and my grandmother used to tell me, "The time is far spent." We have to move this year.

There is a psychological war going on in this country and it's whether or not black people are going to be able to use the terms they want about their movement without white people's blessing. We have to tell them we are going to use the term "Black Power" and we are going to define it because Black Power speaks to us. We can't let them project Black Power because they can only project it from white power and we know what white power has done to us. We have to organize ourselves to speak from a position of strength and stop begging people to look kindly upon us. We are going to build a movement in this country based on the color of our skins that is going to free us from our oppressors and we have to do that ourselves.

We have got to understand what is going on in Lowndes County, Alabama, what it means, who is in it and what they are doing so if white people steal that election like they do all over this country then the eyes of black people all over this country will be focused there to let them know we are going to take care of business if they mess with us in Lowndes County. That responsibility lies on all of us, not just the civil rights workers and do-gooders.

If we talk about education we have to educate ourselves, not with Hegel or Plato or the missionaries who came to Africa with the Bible and we had the land and when they left we had the Bible and they had the land. We have to tell them the only way anybody eliminates poverty in this country is to give poor people money. You don't have to Headstart, Uplift and Upward-Bound them into your culture. Just give us the money you stole from us, that's all. We have to say to people in this country, "We don't really care about you. For us to get better, we don't have to go to white things. We can do it in our own community, ourselves if you didn't steal the resources that belong there." We have to understand the Horatio Alger lie and that the individualist, profit-concept nonsense will never work for us. We have to form cooperatives and use the profits to benefit our community. We can't tolerate their system.

When we form coalitions we must say on what grounds we are going to form them, not white people telling us how to form them. We must build strength and pride amongst ourselves. We must think politically and get power because we are the only people in this country that are powerless. We are the only people who have to protect ourselves from our protectors. We are the only people who want a man called Willis removed who is a racist, that have to lie down in the street and beg a racist named Daley to remove the racist named Willis. We have to build a movement so we can see Daley and say, "Tell Willis to get hat," and by the time we turn around he is gone. That's Black Power.

Everybody in this country is for "Freedom Now" but not everybody is for Black Power because we have got to get rid of some of the people who have white power. We have got to get us some Black Power. We don't control anything but what white people say we can control. We have to be able to smash any political machine in the country that's oppressing us and bring it to its knees. We have to be aware that if we keep growing and multiplying the way we do in ten years all the major cities are going to be ours. We have to know that in Newark, New Jersey, where we are sixty percent of the population, we went along with their stories about integrating and we got absorbed. All we have to show for it is three councilmen who are speaking for them and not for us. We have to organize ourselves to speak for each other. That's Black Power. We have to move to control the economics and politics of our community....

In October, 1966, Carmichael spoke at the Berkeley Black Power Conference in California. In his address to a largely white student audience, he discussed racism and how advocates of black power proposed ending it. The speech is taken from Carmichael's own Stokely Speaks: Black Power Back to Pan-Africanism *(Random House, 1971).*

It's a privilege and an honor to be in the white intellectual ghetto of the West. This is a student conference, as it should be, held on a campus, and we'll never be caught up in intellectual masturbation on the question of Black Power. That's a function of the people who are advertisers but call themselves reporters. Incidentally, for my friends and members of the press, my self-appointed white critics, I was reading Mr. Bernard Shaw two days ago, and I came across a very important quote that I think is most apropos to you. He says, "All criticism is an autobiography." Dig yourself. OK.

The philosophers Camus and Sartre raise the question of whether or not a man can condemn himself. The black existentialist philosopher who is pragmatic, Frantz Fanon, answered the question. He said that man could not. Camus and Sartre don't answer the question. We in SNCC tend to agree with Fanon—a man cannot condemn himself. If he did, he would then have to inflict punishment upon himself. An example is the Nazis. Any of the Nazi prisoners who, after he was caught and incarcerated, admitted that he committed crimes, that he killed all the many people he killed, had to commit suicide. The only ones able to stay alive were the ones who never admitted that they committed a crime against people—that is, the ones who rationalized that Jews were not human beings and deserved to be killed, or that they were only following orders. There's another, more recent example provided by the officials and the population—the white population—of Neshoba County, Mississippi (that's where Philadelphia is). They could not condemn Sheriff Rainey, his deputies, and the other fourteen men who killed three human beings [civil rights workers James Chaney, Andrew Goodman, and Michael Schwerner]. They could not because they elected Mr. Rainey to do precisely what he did; and condemning him would be condemning themselves.

In a much larger view, SNCC says that white America cannot condemn herself for her criminal acts against black America. So black people have done it—you stand condemned. The institutions that function in this country are clearly racist; they're built upon racism. The questions to be dealt with then are: How can black people inside this country move? How can white people who say they're not part of those institutions begin to move? And how then do we begin to clear away the obstacles that we have in this society, to make us live like human beings?

Several people have been upset because we've said that integration was irrelevant when initiated by blacks, and that in fact it was an insidious subterfuge for the maintenance of white supremacy. In the past six years or so, this country has been feeding us a "thalidomide drug of integration," and some Negroes have been walking down a dream street talking about sitting next to white people. That does not begin to solve the problem. We didn't go to Mississippi to sit next to Ross Barnett [former Governor of Mississippi], we did not go to sit next to Jim Clark [sheriff of Selma, Alabama], we went to get them out of our way. People ought to understand that; we were never fighting for the right to integrate, we were fighting against white supremacy. In order to understand white supremacy we must dismiss the fallacious notion that white people can give anybody his freedom. A man is born free. You may enslave a man after he is born free, and that is in fact what this country does. It enslaves blacks after they're born. The only thing white people can do is stop denying black people their freedom.

I maintain that every civil rights bill in this country was passed for white people, not for black people. For example, I am black. I know that. I also know that while I am black I am a human being. Therefore I have the right to go into any public place. White people didn't know that. Every time I tried to go into a public place they stopped me. So some boys had to write a bill to tell that white man, "He's a human being; don't stop him." That bill was for the white man, not for me. I knew I could vote all the time and that it wasn't a privilege but my right. Every time I tried I was shot, killed or jailed, beaten or economically deprived. So somebody had to write a bill to tell white people, "When a black man comes to vote, don't bother him." That bill was for white people. I know I can live anyplace I want to live. It is white people across this country who are incapable of allowing me to live where I want. You need a civil rights bill, not me. The failure of the civil rights bill isn't because of Black Power or because of the Student Nonviolent Coordinating Committee or because of the rebellions that are occurring in the major cities. That failure is due to the whites' incapacity to deal with their own problems inside their own communities.

And so in a sense we must ask, How is it that black people move? And what do we do? But the question in a much greater sense is, How can white people who are the majority, and who are responsible for making democracy work, make it work? They have failed miserably on this point. They have never made democracy work, be it inside the United States, Vietnam, South Africa, the Philippines, South America, Puerto Rico, or wherever America has been. We not only condemn the country for what it has done internally, but we must condemn it for what it does externally. We see this country trying to rule the world, and someone must stand up and start articulating that this country is not God, and that it cannot rule the world.

The white supremacist attitude, which you have either consciously or subconsciously, is running rampant through society today. For example, missionaries were sent to Africa with the attitude that blacks were automatically inferior. As a matter of fact, the first act the missionaries did when they got to Africa was to make us cover up our bodies, because they said it got them excited. We couldn't go bare-breasted any more because they got excited! When the missionaries came to civilize us because we were uncivilized, to educate us because we were uneducated, and to give us some literate studies because we were illiterate, they charged a price. The missionaries came with the Bible, and we had the land; when they left, they had the land, and we still have the Bible. That's been the rationalization for Western civilization as it moves across the world—stealing, plundering and raping everybody in its path. Their one rationalization is that the rest of the world is uncivilized and they are in fact civilized. But the West is un-civ-i-lized. And that still runs on today, you see, because now we have "modern-day missionaries," and they come into our ghettos—they Head Start, Upward Lift, Bootstrap, and Upward Bound us into white society. They don't want to face the real problem. A man is poor for one reason and one reason only—he does not have money. If you want to get rid of poverty, you give people money. And you ought not to tell me about people who don't work, and that you can't give people money if they don't work, because if that were true, you'd have to start stopping Rockefeller, Kennedy, Lyndon Baines Johnson, Lady Bird Johnson, the whole of Standard Oil, the Gulf Corporation, all of them, including probably a large number of the board of trustees of this university. The question, then, is not whether or not one can work; it's who has power to make his or her acts legitimate? That is all. In this country that power is invested in the hands of white people, and it makes their acts legitimate.

We are now engaged in a psychological struggle in this country about whether or not black people have the right to use the words they want to use without white people giving their sanction. We maintain the use of the words Black Power—let them address themselves to that. We are not going to wait for white people to sanction Black Power. We're tired of waiting; every time black people try to move in this country, they're forced to defend their position beforehand. It's time that white people do that. They ought to start defending themselves as to why they have oppressed and exploited us. A man was picked as a slave for one reason—the color of his skin. Black was automatically inferior, inhuman, and therefore fit for slavery, so the question of whether or not we are individually suppressed is nonsensical, and it's a downright lie. We are oppressed as a group because we are black, not because we are lazy or apathetic, not because we're stupid or we stink, not because we eat watermelon or have good rhythm. We are oppressed because we are black.

In order to escape that oppression we must wield the group power we have, not the individual power that this country sets as the criterion under which a man may come into it. That's what is called integration. "You do what I tell you to do and we'll let you sit at the table with us." Well, if you believe in integration, you can come live in Watts, send your children to the ghetto schools. Let's talk about that. If you believe in integration, then we're going to start adopting us some white people to live in our neighborhoods. So it is clear that this question is not one of integration or segregation. We cannot afford to be concerned about the six per cent of black children in this country whom you allow to enter white schools. We are going to be concerned about the ninety-four per cent. You ought to be concerned about them too. But are we willing to be concerned about the black people who will never get to Berkeley, never get to Harvard, and cannot get an education, the ones you'll never get a chance to rub shoulders with and say, "Why, he's almost as good as we are; he's not like the others"? The question is, How can white society begin to move to see black people as human beings? I am black, therefore I am. Not: I am black and I must go to college to prove myself. I am black, therefore I am. And don't deprive me of anything and say to me that you must go to college before you gain access to X, Y, and Z. That's only a rationalization for suppression.

The political parties of this country do not meet the needs of the people on a day-to-day basis. How can we build new political institutions that will become the political expressions of people? How can you build political institutions that will begin to meet the needs of Oakland, California? The need of Oakland, California, is not a thousand policemen with submachine guns. They need that least of all. How can we build institutions that will allow those people to function on a day-to-day basis, so that they can get decent jobs and have decent houses, and they can begin to participate in the policy and make the decisions that affect their lives? That's what they need, not Gestapo troops, because this is not 1942, and if you play like Nazis, we're not going to play Jew this time around. Get hip to that. Can white people move inside their own community and start tearing down racism where in fact it exists? It is you who live in Cicero and stopped us from living there. White people stopped us from moving into Grenada, Mississippi. White people make sure that we live in the ghettos of this country. White institutions do that. They must change. In order for America to really live on a basic principle of human relationships, a new society must be born. Racism must die. The economic exploitation by this country of non-white people around the world must also die.

There are several programs in the South where whites are trying to organize poor whites so they can begin to move around the question of economic exploitation and political disfranchisement. We've all heard the theory several times. But few people are willing to go into it. The question is, Can the white activist stop trying to be a Pepsi generation who comes alive in the black community, and be a man who's willing to move into the white community and start organizing where the organization is needed? Can he do that? Can the white activist disassociate himself from the clowns who waste time parrying with each other and start talking about the problems that are facing people in this state? You must start inside the white community. Our political position is that we don't think the Democratic Party represents the needs of black people. We know that it does not. If, in fact, white people believe that they're going to move inside that structure, how are they going to organize around a concept of whiteness based on true brotherhood and on stopping economic exploitation in order to form a coalition base for black people to hook up with? You cannot build a coalition

> *"This is not 1942, and if you play like Nazis, we're not going to play Jew this time around."*

based on national sentiment. If you want a coalition to address itself to real changes in this country, white people must start building those institutions inside the white community. And that's the real question facing the white activists today. Can they tear down the institutions that have put us all in the trick bag we've been into for the last hundreds of years? Frederick Douglass said that the youth should fight to be leaders today. God knows we need to be leaders today, because the men who run this country are sick. We must begin to start building those institutions and to fight to articulate our position, to fight to be able to control our universities (we need to be able to do that), to fight to control the basic institutions that perpetuate racism by destroying them and building new ones. That's the real question that faces us today, and it is a dilemma because most of us don't know how to work.

Most white activists run into the black community as an excuse. We cannot have white people working in the black community—on psychological grounds. The fact is that all black people question whether or not they are equal to whites, since every time they start to do something, white people are around showing them how to do it. If we are going to eliminate that for the generation that comes after us, then black people must be in positions of power, doing and articulating for themselves. That's not reverse racism; it is moving onto healthy ground; it is becoming what the philosopher Sartre says, an "antiracist racist." And this country can't understand that. What we have in SNCC is antiracist racism. We are against racists. If everybody who's white sees himself as racist and sees us against him, he's speaking from his own guilt.

We do not have the power in our hands to change the institution of war in this country—to begin to re-create it so that they learn to leave the Vietnamese people alone. The only power we have is the power to say, "Hell, no!" to the draft.

The war in Vietnam is illegal and immoral. The question is, What can we do to stop that war? What can we do to stop the people who, in the name of America, are killing babies, women, and children? We have to say to ourselves that there's a higher law than the law of a fool named [Dean] Rusk; there's a higher law than the law of a buffoon named Johnson. It's the law of each of us. We will not murder anybody who they say kill, and if we decide to kill, we're going to decide who it shall be. This country will only stop the war in Vietnam when the young men who are made to fight it begin to say, "Hell, no, we ain't going."

The peace movement has been a failure because it hasn't gotten off the college campuses where everybody has a 2S and is not afraid of being drafted anyway. The problem is how you can move out of that into the white ghettos of this country and articulate a position for those white youth who do not want to go. You cannot do that. It is sometimes ironic that many of the peace groups have begun to call SNCC violent and say they can no longer support us, when we are in fact the most militant organization for peace or civil rights or human rights against the war in Vietnam in this country today. There isn't one organization that has begun to meet our stand on the war in Vietnam. We not only say we are against the war in Vietnam; we are against the draft. No man has the right to take a man for two years and train him to be a killer. Any black man fighting in the war in Vietnam is nothing but a black mercenary. Any time a black man leaves the country where he can't vote to supposedly deliver the vote to somebody else, he's a black mercenary. Any time a black man leaves this country, gets shot in Vietnam on foreign ground, and returns home and you won't give him a burial place in his own homeland, he's a black mercenary. Even if I believed the lies of Johnson, that we're fighting to give democracy to the people in Vietnam, as a black man living in this country I wouldn't fight to give this to anybody. We have to use our bodies and our minds in the only way that we see fit. We must begin, as the philosopher Camus says, to come alive by saying "No." This country is a nation of thieves. It stole everything it has, beginning with black people. The U.S. cannot justify its existence as the policeman of the world any longer. The marines are at ready disposal to bring democracy, and if the Vietnamese don't want democracy, well then, "We'll just wipe them out, because they don't deserve to live if they won't have our way of life."

There is a more immediate question: What do you do on your campus? Do you raise questions about the hundred black students who were kicked off campus a couple of weeks ago? Eight hundred? And how does that question begin to move ? Do you begin to relate to people outside the ivory tower and university walls? Do you think you're capable of building those human relationships as the country now stands? You're fooling yourself. It is impossible for white and black people to talk about building a relationship based on humanity when the country is the way it is, when the institutions are clearly against us.

We have found all the myths of the country to be nothing but downright lies. We were told that if we worked hard we would succeed, and if that were true we would own this country lock, stock, and barrel. We have picked the cotton for nothing; we are the maids in the kitchens of liberal white people; we are the janitors, the porters, the elevator men; we sweep up your college floors. We are the hardest workers and the lowest paid. It is nonsensical for people to talk about human relationships until they are willing to build new institutions. Black people are economically insecure. White liberals are economically secure. Can you begin to build an economic coalition? Are the liberals willing to share their salaries with the economically insecure black people they so much love? Then if you're not, are you willing to start building new institutions that will provide economic security for black people? That's the question we want to deal with!

American students are perhaps the most politically unsophisticated students in the world. Across every country of the world, while we were growing up, students were leading the major revolutions of their countries. We have not been able to do that. They have been politically aware of their existence. In South America our neighbors have one every twenty-four hours just to remind us that they are politically aware. But we have been unable to grasp it because we've always moved in the field of morality and love while people have been politically jiving with our lives. You can't move morally against men like [Pat] Brown and [Ronald] Reagan. You can't move morally against Lyndon Baines Johnson because he is an immoral man. He doesn't know what it's all about. So you've got to move politically. We have to develop a political sophistication that doesn't parrot ("The two-party system is the best system in the world"). We have to raise questions about whether we need new types of political institutions in this country, and we in SNCC maintain that we need them now. Any time Lyndon Baines Johnson can head a party that has in it Bobby Kennedy, Wayne Morse, [James] Eastland, [George] Wallace, and all those other supposed-to-be-liberal cats, there's something wrong with that party. They're moving politically, not morally. If that party refuses to seat black people from Mississippi and goes ahead and seats racists like Eastland and his clique, it's clear to me that they're moving politically, and that one cannot begin to talk morality to people like that.

We must question the values of this society, and I maintain that black people are the best people to do that since we have been excluded from that society. We ought to think whether or not we want to become a part of that society. That's precisely what the Student Nonviolent Coordinating Committee is doing. We are raising questions about this country. I do not want to be a part of the American pie. The American pie means raping South Africa, beating Vietnam, beating South America, raping the Philippines, raping every country you've been in. I don't want any of your blood money. I don't want to be part of that system. We are the generation who has found this country to be a world power and the wealthiest country in the world. We must question whether or not we want this country to continue being the wealthiest country in the world at the price of raping everybody else. And because black people are saying we do not now want to become a part of you, we are called reverse racists. Ain't that a gas?

White society has caused the failure of nonviolence. I was always surprised at Quakers who came to Alabama and counseled me to be nonviolent, but didn't have the guts to tell James Clark to be nonviolent. That's where nonviolence needs to be preached—to Jim Clark, not to black people. White people should conduct their nonviolent schools in Cicero where they are needed, not among black people in Mississippi. Six-foot-two men kick little black children in Grenada—can you conduct nonviolent schools there? Can you name one black man today who has killed anybody white and is still alive? Even after a rebellion, when some black brothers throw bricks and bottles, ten thousand of them have to pay the price. When the white policeman comes in, anybody who's black is arrested because we all look alike.

The youth of this country must begin to raise those questions. We are going to have to change the foreign policy of this country. One of the problems with the peace movement is that it is too caught up in Vietnam, and if America pulled out the troops from Vietnam this week, next week you'd have to get another peace movement for Santo Domingo. We have to hook up with black people around the world; and that hookup must not only be psychological, but real. If South America were to rebel today, and black people were to shoot the hell out of all the white people there, as they should, Standard Oil would crumble tomorrow. If South Africa were to go today, Chase Manhattan Bank would crumble tomorrow. If Zimbabwe, which is called Rhodesia by white people, were to go tomorrow, General Electric would cave in on the East Coast. How do we stop those institutions that are so willing to fight against "Communist aggression" but close their eyes against racist oppression? We're not talking about a policy of aid or sending Peace Corps people in to teach people how to read and write and build houses while we steal their raw materials from them. Because that's all this country does. What underdeveloped countries need is information about how to become industrialized, so they can keep their raw materials where they have them, produce goods, sell them to this country for the price it's supposed to pay. Instead, America keeps selling goods back to them for a profit and keeps sending our modern-day missionaries there, calling them the sons of Kennedy. And if the youth are going to participate in that program, how do you begin to control the Peace Corps?

This country assumes that if someone is poor, they are poor because of their own individual blight, or because they weren't born on the right side of town, or they had too many children, or went in the army too early, or because their father was a drunk, or they didn't care about school—they made a mistake. That's a lot of nonsense. Poverty is well calculated in this country, and the reason why the poverty program won't work is because the calculators of poverty are administering it.

"The only time I hear people talk about nonviolence is when black people move to defend themselves against white people."

How can you, as the youth in this country, move to start carrying those things out? Move into the white community. We have developed a movement in the black community. The white activist has miserably failed to develop the movement inside of his community. Will white people have the courage to go into white communities and start organizing them? That's the question for the white activist. We won't get caught up in questions about power. This country knows what power is. It knows what Black Power is because it deprived black people of it for over four hundred years. White people associate Black Power with violence because of their own inability to deal with blackness. If we had said "Negro power" nobody would get scared. Everybody would support it. If we said power for colored people, everybody'd be for that, but it is the word "black" that bothers people in this country, and that's their problem, not mine. That's the lie that says anything black is bad.

You're all a college and university crowd. You've taken your basic logic course. You know about major premise, minor premise. People have been telling you anything all black is bad. Let's make that our major premise.

Major premise: Anything all black is bad.

Minor premise or particular premise: I am all black.

Therefore . . . I'm never going to be put in that bag; I'm all black and I'm all good. Anything all black is not necessarily bad. Anything all black is only bad when you use force to keep whites out. Now that's what white people have done in this country, and they're projecting their same fears and guilt on us, and we won't have it. Let them handle their own affairs and their own guilt. Let them find their own psychologists. We refuse to be the therapy for white society any longer. We have gone stark, raving mad trying to do it.

I look at Dr. King on television every single day, and I say to myself: "Now there is a man who's desperately needed in this country. There is a man full of love. There is a man full of mercy. There is a man full of compassion." But every time I see Lyndon on television, I say, "Martin, baby, you got a long way to go."

If we were to be real and honest, we would have to admit that most people in this country see things black and white. We live in a country that's geared that way. White people would have to admit that they are afraid to go into a black ghetto at night. They're afraid because they'd be "beat up," "lynched," "looted," "cut up," etc. It happens to black people inside the ghetto every day, incidentally. Since white people are afraid of that, they get a man to do it for them—a policeman. Figure his mentality. The first time a black man jumps, that white man's going to shoot him. Police brutality is going to exist on that level. The only time I hear people talk about nonviolence is when black people move to defend themselves against white people. Black people cut themselves every night in the ghetto—nobody talks about nonviolence. Lyndon Baines Johnson is busy bombing the hell out of Vietnam—nobody talks about nonviolence. White people beat up black people every day—nobody talks about nonviolence. But as soon as black people start to move, the double standard comes into being. You can't defend yourself. You show me a black man who advocates aggressive violence who would be able to live in this country. Show him to me. Isn't it hypocritical for Lyndon to talk about how you can't accomplish anything by looting and you must accomplish it by the legal ways? What does he know about legality? Ask [North Vietnamese leader] Ho Chi Minh.

We must wage a psychological battle on the right for black people to define themselves as they see fit, and organize themselves as they see fit. We don't know whether the white community will allow for that organizing, because once they do they must also allow for the organizing inside their own community. It doesn't make a difference, though—we're going to organize our way. The question is how we're going to facilitate those matters, whether it's going to be done with a thousand policemen with submachine guns, or whether it's going to be done in a context where it's allowed by white people warding off those policemen. Are white people who call themselves activists ready to move into the white communities on two counts, on building new political institutions to destroy the old ones that we have, and to move around the concept of white youth refusing to go into the army? If so, than we can start to build a new world. We must urge you to fight now to be the leaders of today, not tomorrow. This country is a nation of thieves. It stands on the brink of becoming a nation of murderers. We must stop it. We must stop it. We must stop it.

We are on the move for our liberation. We're tired of trying to prove things to white people. We are tired of trying to explain to white people that we're not going to hurt them. We are concerned with getting the things we want, the things we have to have to be able to function. The question is, Will white people overcome their racism and allow for that to happen in this country? If not, we have no choice but to say very clearly, "Move on over, or we're going to move on over you."

Two years later, a far more militant Carmichael spoke at a birthday benefit rally for fellow Black Panther Huey Newton, then in prison for killing a white policeman. By this time, he had rejected the possibility that black and white radicals might be able to work together. His emphasis instead was on broadening the struggle against racial oppression to include blacks from all over the world, and he looked to Africa as the homeland. In his speech, delivered February 17, 1968, in Oakland, California, Carmichael stressed the need for unity in the face of what he felt were white America's attempts to annihilate the black race. It is reprinted from Stokely Speaks: Black Power Back to Pan-Africanism *(Random House, 1971).*

We're here to celebrate Brother Huey P. Newton's birthday. We're not here to celebrate it as Huey Newton the individual, but as Huey Newton part and parcel of black people wherever we are in the world today. In talking about Brother Huey Newton tonight, we have to talk about the struggle of black people—not only in the United States but in the world today and how we become part and parcel of the struggle, how we move on so that our people will survive America.

We are not talking about politics tonight, we're not talking about economics tonight, we are talking about the survival of a race of people. That is all that is at stake.

Why is it necessary for us to talk about the survival of our people? Many of us feel—many of our generation feel—that the white folks are getting ready to commit genocide against us. Now, many people think that's a horrible thing to say, but as Brother Malcolm said, we should examine history.

The birth of this nation was conceived in the genocide of the red man. In order for this country to come about, the honky had to completely exterminate the red man, and he did it! And now he doesn't even feel sorry; he romanticizes it on television with cowboys and Indians. The question we must ask ourselves is, If he's capable of doing it to the red man, can he also do it to us?

Let us examine history some more. People say it is a horrible thing to say that white people would think about committing genocide against black people. Let us check our history. It is a fact that we built this country, nobody else. When this country started, economically it was an agricultural country. The cash crop on the world market was cotton. We picked the cotton! And we fought in the wars of this country. We built this country.

This country is becoming more and more technological, so that the need for black people is disappearing fast. When the need for black people disappears, so will we. The white man will consciously wipe us out.

"We're talking about survival—and brothers and sisters, we're going to survive America."

Let us check World War II. He will not do it unto his own. Notice who he dropped an atomic bomb on, some helpless yellow people in Hiroshima, some *helpless* yellow people. If you do not think he's *capable* of committing genocide against us, check out what he's doing to our brothers in Vietnam. We have to understand that we're talking about our survival—whether or not this beautiful race of people is going to survive on the earth.

Check out the white race. Wherever they have gone they have ruled, conquered, murdered, and plagued—whether they are the majority or the minority they *always* rule. Check out the pattern in which they move. They came to this country and didn't know a damn thing about it. The red man showed them how to adapt. He showed them how to grow corn. He showed them how to hunt. And when the Indians finished showing them *they wiped them out!*

The white man wasn't satisfied. He went to South America. The Aztec Indians said: "This is our silver, this is our copper, these are our metals, these are our statues. We built them for the beauty of our people." After the Indians showed their wealth to him, he took it and *he wiped them out!*

The white man went to Africa. Our ancestors said: "Dig, this is our way of life. We beat drums, we enjoy ourselves, we have gold, we make diamonds and stuff for our women." He took the gold, he made us slaves, and today he *runs* Africa. He went to Asia. The Chinese showed him everything they had. They showed him gunpowder. They said: "We use this for fireworks on our anniversaries, on our days of festivities." He took it, he made it a gun, and he conquered China.

We are talking about a certain type of superiority complex that exists in the white man wherever he is. That's what we have to understand today. So that everything else goes out the window, we talk about survival. They can cut all the junk about poverty programs, education, housing, welfare. We're talking about survival—and brothers and sisters, we're going to survive America.

We have to understand what is going on not only in this country but in the world, especially in Africa. Because we are an African people, we have *always* maintained our own value system.

Our people have resisted for 413 years in this wilderness. And they resisted so that *this* generation can carry out what must be done. We cannot fail our ancestors.

We resisted in every way you can point to. Take the English language. There are cats who come here from Italy, from Germany, from Poland, from France—in two generations they speak English perfectly. We have *never* spoken English perfectly. And that is because our people consciously resisted a language that did not belong to us. Never did, never will, anyhow they try to run it down our throat, we ain't gonna have it. We ain't gonna have it! You must understand that as a level of resistance. Anybody can speak that simple honky's language correctly. We have not done it because we have resisted.

Check out our way of life. No matter how hard he's tried, we still maintain a communal way of life in our community. We do not send old people to old people's homes—that's junk. We do not call children illegitimate; we take care of any child in our community. It is a level of resistance that we must begin to look for among our people. Pick up that thread and do what has to be done so that our people will survive.

Three things: first and foremost, the honky has been able to make us hate each other. He has channeled our love for each other into love for his country—*his* country. We must begin to develop—and this is the most important thing we can do as a people—*we must develop an undying love for our people, our people.* We must develop the undying love personified by Brother Huey P. Newton. Undying love for our people. If we do not do that, we will be wiped out. Our slogan will become: first, our people; then, and only then, me and you as individuals. Our people first.

Second, comes the slogan: Every Negro is a potential black man. We *will not* alienate him. And we must understand the concept of Negro and the concept of black man. We came to this country as black men and as Africans. It took us four hundred years to become Negroes. Understand that. It means that the concept of a black man is one who recognizes his cultural and historical roots. He recognizes that his African ancestors were the greatest warriors on the face of this earth.

Many of our people's minds have been whitewashed. If a Negro comes up to you and you turn your back on him, he's got to run to the honky. We're gonna take time and patience with our people, because they're *ours*. All of the Uncle Toms are ours. We're gonna sit down and we're gonna talk, and when they slap we're gonna bow. We're gonna *try* to bring them home; and if they don't come home, we gonna off them, that's all.

We have to recognize who our major enemy is. The major enemy is not your brother, flesh of your flesh and blood of your blood. The major enemy is the honky and his institutions of racism—*that* is the major enemy. And whenever anybody prepares for revolutionary warfare, you concentrate on the major enemy. We're not strong enough to fight each other and also fight him. We will not fight each other today. There will be no fights in the black community among black people, there will just be people who will be offed! There will be no fights, there will be no disruptions. We are going to be united.

Third, and most important, we must understand that for black people the question of community is not a question of geography, it is a question of color. If you live in Watts, if you live in Harlem, South Side Chicago, Detroit, West Philadelphia, Georgia, Mississippi, Alabama, wherever you go, the first place you go is to your people. Not to the land, but to your *people*. We must break down the concept that black people living inside the United States are black Americans. That's nonsense! We have brothers in Africa and Cuba, we have brothers in Latin America, we have brothers all over the world. And once we begin to understand that the concept "community" is simply one of "our people," it makes no difference where we are—we are with our people and therefore we are home.

Now then, survival. It is necessary to understand the moves of our enemy. The United States works on what we call the three Ms—the missionaries, the money, and the marines. That's precisely the way it's moved all over the world; it is the way it moves against *us*. They send the missionaries in—we send them out. They send the money in, with the poverty program—the Vietnamese and the Koreans are pulling the money out. The next thing comes the marines. Comes the marines. And if we're talking seriously, we get prepared for the marines. Now, even if some black people do not think that the white man is going to wipe us out completely, there won't be any harm being prepared just in case he decides to do it. So there'll be no harm in preparing ourselves for the marines.

"Even if some black people do not think that the white man is going to wipe us out completely, there won't be any harm being prepared just in case he decides to do it."

There are a lot of tactics we can learn. The VC are showing us the best way to get it done. And don't be afraid to say, yeah, you want the Vietnamese to defeat America 'cause they wrong from the jump. Don't get up there and play games with them! You ever see them on T.V.— "Well, actually, we were wrong going into Vietnam but we can't get out unless we save face." To save that honky's face, millions of Vietnamese have to die. That's a lot of junk. If you're wrong, say you're wrong and get out. Get out!

We have to then go down the programs that they run through our throats and see how they relate to us. The first one is the vote. They have a new thing now: "Black Power is the vote." The vote in this country is, has been, and always will be irrelevant to the lives of black people. That is a fact. We survived in Mississippi, Alabama, Georgia, Louisiana, Texas, South Carolina, North Carolina, Virginia, and Washington, D.C., without the vote. Two years ago, Julian Bond was elected by black people in Georgia. They took him off the seat, and there was no representation, but black people in Georgia are still surviving today. They took Adam Clayton Powell out of office, they had him out of office for a year and a half—black people in Harlem are still surviving. That should teach you the vote isn't anything but a honky's trick, nothing but a honky's trick.

If we talk about the vote today, we talk about it as one thing—*an organizing tool to bring our people together, nothing else*. It becomes a vehicle for organization, it cannot be anything else. To believe the vote is going to save you is to believe the way Brother Adam Clayton Powell did. He's in Bimini now.

That's what we have to understand. The second thing they ram down our throat is the poverty program. And you have to understand the poverty program. It is designed, number one, to split the black community, and number two, to split the black family. There is no doubt about its splitting the black community. We know all the people who've started fighting over the crumbs (because that's all the poverty program is—crumbs). If we'd leave the crumbs alone and organize, we could take the whole loaf. It belongs to us.

But what happens is that the poverty program sends a couple of hundred thousand dollars into the community and groups start fighting over that money. So, automatically you've got splits in the community. Watts is the best example that we have to date. It was the first one to get the poverty program after the rebellion and today it is the most divided black community in the country.

We have to recognize what the poverty program does. In any race of people the most instinctively revolutionary group are the youth. Because the youth are always willing to fight at the drop of a hat. In anybody's race. And the poverty program is aimed right at our youth—to stop them from fighting. That's all the poverty program is: stop rebellions—not take care of black people—stop the rebellions. How would you feel if you were a father, and your son, who you were supposed to be providing for, comes home with ninety dollars a week and you are still unemployed? What is the poverty program doing to our fathers? If they were concerned about the black community, if they believed the garbage they run down about the black family, they would give the jobs to our fathers, the breadwinners of our families, so we *could* have some respect for them.

But it is precisely because the poverty program is aimed at quelling our youth that they do that, and all the people who administer the poverty program won't even put their children in those programs that are supposed to be so good for us.

Let us move to education. And we must talk very clearly about this concept of education. Frantz Fanon said very clearly: "Education is nothing but the re-establishment and reinforcement of values and institutions of a given society."

All the brother's saying is that whatever this society says is right, when you go to school they are going to tell you it's right and you got to run it down. If you run it on down you get an A. If as your teacher I say to you, "Columbus discovered America in 1492," and you say, "No, Columbus didn't discover America in 1492, there were *Indians* here," I simply tell you that you flunk the course. So education doesn't mean what they say it means. We must begin to use education for our people.

And we must understand our communities. In our communities there are dope addicts, there are pimps, there are prostitutes, there are hustlers, there are teachers, there are maids, there are porters, there are preachers, there are gangsters. If I go to high school I want to learn how to be a good maid, a good porter, a good hustler, a good pimp, a good prostitute, a good preacher, a good teacher.

Education is supposed to prepare you to live in your community. That's what our community is like. If the educational system cannot do that, it must teach us how to change our community. It must do one or the other. The schools we send our children to do neither; they do something absolutely opposite. And when our youth, who are more intelligent than all those honkies on those school boards, drop out of that school because they recognize it's not going to help them, then we turn around and yell at them, dividing our community again. We have to understand that until we control an educational system that will teach us how to change our community, there's no need to send anybody to school. That's just a natural fact.

We have no alternative but to fight, whether we like it or not. On every level in this country black people have *got* to fight, *got* to fight, *got* to fight.

Let us move down and talk about organizing as a concept. We have the masses and the bourgeoisie in our community of black people. The bourgeoisie is very, very minute inside our community. We have to bring them home. We have to bring them home for many reasons. We must bring them home because they have technical skills that must be used for the benefit of their people, not for the benefit of this country that is against their people. We've got to bring them home. The way to bring our people home is by using patience, love, brotherhood, and unity—not force—love, patience, brotherhood and unity. We try and we try and we try. If they become a threat, we off them.

But we must begin to understand bringing them home in the context of forming a united front inside our community—a black united front that engulfs every sector, so that every facet and every person inside our community is working for the benefit of black people. And that is, for each other's survival. A lot of people in the bourgeoisie tell me they don't like Rap Brown when he says, "I'm gonna burn the country down." But every time Rap Brown says that, they get a poverty program.

A lot of people tell me that they don't like the Black Panthers for Self-Defense walking around with guns. But I tell you now, if the honkies in San Francisco off the fighters, who happen to be the Black Panthers for Self-Defense (there isn't anybody in this community prepared to fight right now), everybody gets offed. Everybody gets offed.

We need each other. We have to have each other for our survival. We need everyone from the revolutionaries to the conservatives—a Black United Front is what we're about, a Black United Front. Now there are some people who may not understand Brother Rap when he talks about forming alliances. He says we have to ally with Mexican-Americans, Puerto Ricans, and the dispossessed people of the earth. He doesn't mention poor whites. We must understand that. I will not deny that poor whites in this country are oppressed. But there are two types of oppression. One is exploitation, the other is colonization. And we have to understand the difference between them. Exploitation is when you exploit somebody of your own race. Colonization is when you exploit somebody of a different race. *We* are colonized, *they* are exploited.

If I am black and I am exploiting you who are also black, we have the same values, the same culture, the same language, the same society, the same institutions, so I do not have to destroy those institutions for you. But if you are of another race, if you have a different culture, different language, different values, I have to destroy all of those to make you bow to me. And that is the difference between poor black and poor white. Poor whites have their culture, have their values, have their institutions; ours have been completely destroyed.

We need alliances with people who are trying to rebuild their culture, trying to rebuild their history, trying to rebuild their dignity, with people who are fighting for their humanity. Poor white people are not fighting for their humanity, they're fighting for more money. There are a lot of poor white people in this country, and you haven't seen any of them rebel yet, have you? Why is it that black people are rebelling? Do you think it's only because of poor jobs? Don't believe that junk the honky is running down. It's not only poor jobs—it's a question of a people fighting for their culture and their nature, fighting for their *humanity*.

We have been so colonized that we are ashamed to say we hate, and that is the best example of a person who's colonized. You sit in your house, a honky walks in your house, beats you up, rapes your wife, beats up your child, and you don't have the humanity to say, "I hate you." You don't have it. That is how dehumanized we are. We are so dehumanized we cannot say, "Yes, we hate you for what you have done to us"—can't say it. And we are afraid to think beyond that point. Who do you think has more hatred pent up in them, white people for black people or black people for white people? Obviously the hatred has been more from white people for black people. What have we done to them for them to build up this hatred? Absolutely nothing! Yet we don't even want to hate them for what they've done to us. If hate should be justified, we have the best justification of all for hating honkies. But we have been so dehumanized, we're like a dog that the master can throw out the house, that the master can spit on, and whenever he calls, the dog comes running back. We are human beings and we have emotions. We're fighting for our humanity, and in regaining our humanity we recognize all the emotions that are in us. If you have love, you've got to have hate. You don't have one-sided emotions, that's a lot of junk. You always have two sides—hot, cold; white, black—everything goes—love, hate. If you don't have hate, you cannot differentiate love.

That brings us to the point about communism and socialism. The ideologies of communism and socialism speak to class structure, to people who oppress people from the top down to the bottom. We are not just facing exploitation. We are facing something much more important, because we are the victims of racism. In their present form neither communism nor socialism speak to the problem of racism. And to black people in this country, racism comes first, far more important than exploitation. No matter how much money you make in the black community, when you go into the white world you are still a nigger. The question of racism must be uppermost in our minds. How do we destroy those institutions that seek to keep us dehumanized? That is all we're talking about.

> ***"You don't have one-sided emotions. You always have two sides—hot, cold; white, black. If you don't have hate, you cannot differentiate love."***

Now, for white people who are exploited, the question of communism comes first, because they're exploited by their own people. If you were exploited by other black people, it would be a question of how we divide the profits. It is not that for us. It is a question of how we regain our humanity and begin to live as a people. We do not do that because of the effects of racism in this country. We must therefore consciously strive for an ideology which deals with racism first, and if we do that we recognize the necessity of hooking up with the nine hundred million black people in the world today.

If we recognize that, then our political situation must become international, it cannot be national. Honkies don't exploit us alone, they exploit the whole Third World—Asia, Africa, Latin America. They take advantage of Europe, but they don't colonize Europe, they colonize Asia, Africa, and Latin America. If we begin to understand that, then the problems America is heading for become uppermost in our minds.

The first one is the conflict in the Middle East. We must declare on whose side we stand. We can be for no one but the Arabs. There can be *no* doubt in our minds at all. We can be for no one but the Arabs because Israel belonged to the Arabs in 1917. The British gave it to a group of Zionists who went to Palestine, ran the Palestinian Arabs out with terrorist groups, organized the state of Israel and did not get anywhere until Hitler came along and they swelled the state in 1948. That country belonged to the Palestinians. Not only that, they're moving to take over Egypt. Egypt is our motherland—it's in Africa.

We do not understand the concept of love. Here are a group of Zionists who come anywhere they want to organize love and feeling for a place called Israel, which was created in 1948, and their youth are willing to go and fight for Israel. Egypt belongs to us since four thousand years ago, and we sit here supporting the Zionists. We have got to be for the Arabs. Period.

That means that we also move with the rest of the Third World and understand exactly what is going on. It is no coincidence that the honky who stole a heart out of our brother and put it into another devil, was brought here on nationwide T.V. Now, for those of the older generation who say I may be harsh because I said the "devil," let me give you a biblical quotation: "Beware that the devil will come telling you that he can give you back life after death." If that's not what they're doing I don't know what it is.

Just today the United States voted for South Africa to come into the Olympics, and black people here are debating whether black athletes should be part of the Olympics. That is not a debate. The question is final. There can be no black athletes with any dignity participating in that white nonsense.

Survival means that we organize politically, we organize consciously (that's what they call education; we call it black consciousness, because that speaks to us, education speaks to them), we organize economically, and we organize militarily. If we don't do that, if you don't have a gun in your hand, they can snatch the ballot from you. But if you have a gun, it's either them or us. The preparation of that fight on all levels must become conscious among our people. We are ahead of the Jews in Germany because we know what they're getting ready to do. They tell us every day in their *Esquire* magazines, they tell us on their televisions, they tell us with the fifteen thousand soldiers they're putting in the cities, they tell us with their tanks, they tell us with their Stoner guns, they tell us! We must wake up and tell them *we* are going to get them.

Wipe the questions of minority and technology out of your mind. Technology never decides a war, it is the will of a people that decides a war. Wipe out of your mind the fact that we do not have guns. The Vietnamese didn't have guns when they started, now they have American guns, American tanks, American everything. If they come to get us they will have to bring some. We are going to take the gun, and the tank, and the grenade! Unless we raise our minds to the level of consciousness where we have an undying love for our people, where we're willing to shed our blood like Huey Newton did for our people, we will not survive. There are many people who know that. All of the brothers sitting on the stage, all of the brothers around here know that when something goes down, we are the first ones offed. There's no question in any of our minds. Only thing going to stop us today is a bullet, and we are spittin' them back! The question is not whether or not we can move, but how this entire black community moves for survival in a world that's clearly heading for a color clash. That is what we must ask ourselves, the only question. We can do that only by organizing our people and orienting them toward an African ideology that speaks to our blackness—nothing else.

It's not a question of right or left, it's a question of black. You dig where we are coming from? We are coming from a black thing, from a *black* thing, that's where we are coming from. We can begin to pick up the threads of resistance that our ancestors laid down for us. And unless we begin to understand our people as a people, we will not do that, because they *will* split us and divide us. That means consciously we have to begin to *organize our people!* Nothing else! We have no time for them; all our sweat, all our blood, even our life must go to our people, nothing else. We have to understand this consciously. Our youth must be organized with a revolutionary prospectus. A revolutionary prospectus says that we're fighting a war of liberation. In order to fight a war of liberation, you need an ideology of nationalism. We do not have this country. The nationalism can be nothing but black nationalism. It is insane to think of anything else. Black nationalism must be our ideology. While blackness is necessary, it is not sufficient, so we must move on to consciously organize our communities. And we recognize today while we're organizing that we do not have the money to feed our people, so there's no use saying, "Organize, we can get you a job." We can't get them, they control them, that is a fact. That isn't a reason for you to sit down, it is only more reason for you to fight. That's more of an inspiration to fight so you *can* give them a job rather than to sit down and say the honkies have us on every end. They are not God. We are a beautiful race of people, we can do anything we want to do; all we have to do is get up, get up, get up and do it!

We have to discuss very coldly the question of rebellions. It is a fact that they're prepared to meet rebellions anywhere in the cities. Now, what's going to happen if one of our brothers gets offed? What happens if they go ahead and off Huey Newton? We must develop tactics where we do the maximum damage to them with minor damage to us. When we move into the arena, that means that this black community must be organized if Brother Huey Newton goes, and ten honky cops go, won't a black man in this community get up and open his mouth, because if he does, *he* goes too. That means that in organizing for the maximum damage against them and minor damage to us, we must be consciously aware of the fact that there will be people in our community who are going around doing just that. In our community, we see nothing, we hear nothing, we know nothing.

Now, the question of agents in our community is beginning to make us paranoid. We cannot become paranoid because what they can do is make us so afraid we won't move. So we're not going to do that. We're going to plan. Little groups will plan theirs, big groups will plan theirs. If an agent is found, there is no question; he is going to be offed in such a manner that any other black man who dares inform to the honky will have three thoughts before he even *talks* to a white man about reporting in our community.

Our people have demonstrated a willingness to fight. Our people have demonstrated the courage of our ancestors—to face tanks, guns, and police dogs with bricks and bottles. That is a courageous act! Since our people have demonstrated a willingness to fight, the question is how we can organize that fight so we win. If a major rebellion breaks out, our people may or may not become the losers, but if a small group was doing maximum damage, we remain on top. We remain on top. It is not a matter of *what* they might do, but only one of *how* and *when* they're going to do it. That is all. For us the question is not going to Vietnam any more, the question is how we can protect our brothers who do not go to Vietnam from going to jail so that when one brother says "Hell, no," there're enough people in that community around him, so that if they dare come in, they are going to face maximum damage in their community.

We are talking about survival. We are talking about a people whose entire culture, whose entire history, whose entire way of life have been destroyed. We're talking about a people who have produced in *this* year a generation of warriors who are going to restore to our people the humanity and the love that we have for each other. That's what we're talking about *today,* we are talking about becoming the executioners of our executioners. For example, you should give a lot of money to the Huey defense fund, because while some of that money will go for that court thing, the rest of the money's going for the executioners. If they execute Huey, the final execution rests in our hands.

It is simply a question of a people. They control everything. They make us fight, they make us steal, they judge us, they put us in prison, they parole us, they send us out, they pick us up again—where in God's name do we exercise any sense of dignity in this country? What in God's name do we control, except the church, whose ideology is set up to be compatible with the system that's against us? Where in God's name do we exercise any control as a people whose ancestors were the proudest people that walked the face of this earth? Everywhere the white man has gone he controls our people; in South Africa he steals the gold from our people, in the West Indies he steals the materials from our people, in South America, where he's scattered our people, he's raping us blind. He rapes us in America and in Nova Scotia. Where in God's name will we find a piece of earth that belongs to us so we can restore our humanity? Where will we find it unless this generation begins to organize to fight for it?

When this generation begins to fight, there can be no disruptive elements in our community. We will tolerate none. We put our lives on the line for anyone who fights for our people. Huey Newton fought for our people. Whether or not Huey Newton becomes free depends upon black people, nobody else. Other people may help, but the final decision on Brother Huey depends on *us.* He didn't lay down his life for other people, he laid it down for *us.* And if he did that, we must be willing to do the same, not only for him but for the generation that's going to follow us.

We must consciously organize every element in our community. That work must begin. People must be willing to give money to an organizer who is willing to spend twenty-four hours a day organizing. He cannot organize from the poverty program because they tell him what to do. But if black people are giving him the money, he can do anything for the benefit of black people. We have to run all the exploiters out of our community. That means that people have to consciously give money, by any means necessary. Ask yourself, if you were white, why would you want to be a cop in a black ghetto today when you know they are looking for you? Why, if you weren't sick in the mind and felt you were so superior that you had the right to rule, why would you want a lousy $5,000-a-year job when you are white and you can make it in this society? Would you want to be in their community if they were ready to off you, for $4,000, for $5,000, for $6,000 a year? We have to understand the politics of those honkies in our community. They are there to patrol and to control. Well, we are going to do the patrolling and controlling. We are building a concept of peoplehood. If the honkies get in our way, they will have to go. We are not concerned about their way of life, we are concerned about our *people.* We want to give our people the dignity and humanity that we once knew as a people, and if they get in our way, they're going to be offed. We're not concerned with their system. Let them have it. We want our way of life, and we're going to get it. We're going to get it or nobody's going to have any peace on this earth.

I want to read a statement that Brother Huey P. Newton wrote yesterday when I saw him in jail:

> *As the racist police escalate the war in our communities against black people, we reserve the right to self-defense and maximum retaliation.*

All of the things we spoke about tonight centered around Brother Huey P. Newton because all of the things we spoke about tonight exemplify what he was trying to do. There is no need for us to go to jail today for what we *say.* They did that to Brother Malcolm X, they just offed him for what he was saying. We have to progress as a race. Brother Huey may or may not have wiped out that honky, but at least it shows a progression, at least we're not getting offed for what we say; we're getting offed for what we *do*. Understand this concept: when they offed Brother Malcolm, we did nothing; if they off Brother Huey, we *must* retaliate. Do you think that any other race of people will let them off somebody, and the rest of them sit there? Where in God's name would you find a race of people like that?

In the last five years we have lost some of our best leaders—Lumumba, Malcolm X, Brother Kwame Nkrumah—and we do nothing. While they are murdering our leaders, they take our youth and send them to Vietnam and Korea. We are slowly getting wiped out. We must retaliate, we must fight for our humanity. It is our humanity that is at stake. It is not a question of dollars and cents. We will survive, because we have survived what *they* couldn't survive—that's a natural-born fact. We have survived. We survived through slavery, we survived through the Depression, we survived through World War II, we survived after World War II when they threw us out of the jobs in the North, we survived their Korean War. We are going to survive. Ain't no doubt about that in my mind, no doubt at all.

Our problem is to develop an undying love for our people. We must be willing to give our talents, our sweat, our blood, even our life for our people. We must develop the concept that every Negro is a potential black man. You do not alienate your potential allies. Let's bring our people *home*. Let's bring our people *home*.

We must understand the concept that for us the question of community is not geography, it is a question of us black people, wherever we are. We have to consciously become a part of the nine hundred million black people that are separated over this world. We are separated by *them*. We are blood of the same blood and flesh of the same flesh. We do not know who is our sister, who is our brother, or where we came from. They took us from Africa and they put thousands of miles of water between us, but they forgot—blood is thicker than water. We are coming together. We are an African people with an African ideology, and we are wandering in the United States. We are going to build a concept of peoplehood in this country or there will be no country.

Brothers and sisters, Brother Huey P. Newton belongs to *us*. He is flesh of our flesh, he is blood of our blood. He may be Mrs. Newton's baby, but he is our brother. We do not have to talk about what we're going to do if we're consciously preparing and consciously willing to back those who prepare!

All we say: Brother Huey will be set free—or else!

SOURCES

Books

Bracey, John H., Jr., August Meier, and Elliott Rudwick, editors, *Black Nationalism in America,* Bobbs-Merrill, 1970.

Carmichael, Stokely, *Stokely Speaks: Black Power Back to Pan-Africanism,* Random House, 1971.

Carmichael, Stokely, and Charles Hamilton, *Black Power: The Politics of Liberation in America,* Random House, 1967.

Carson, Clayborne, and others, editors, *The Eyes on the Prize Civil Rights Reader,* Penguin, 1991.

Foner, Philip S., editor, *The Voice of Black America: Major Speeches by Negroes in the United States, 1797–1971,* Simon & Schuster, 1972.

Holland, DeWitte, editor, *America in Controversy: History of American Public Address,* William C. Brown Company, 1973.

Johnson, Jacqueline, *Stokely Carmichael: The Story of Black Power,* Silver Burdett, 1990.

Lomas, Charles W., *The Agitator in American Society,* Prentice-Hall, 1968.

Scott, Robert L., and Wayne Brockriede, *The Rhetoric of Black Power,* Harper & Row, 1969.

Smith, Arthur L., and Stephen Robb, editors, *The Voice of Black Rhetoric: Selections,* Allyn & Bacon, 1971.

Williams, Jayme Coleman, and McDonald Williams, editors, *The Negro Speaks: The Rhetoric of Contemporary Black Leaders,* Noble & Noble, 1970.

Periodicals

Ebony, "Stokely Carmichael: Architect of Black Power," September, 1966.

Massachusetts Review, "Toward Black Liberation," September, 1966, pp. 639-651

New York Review of Books, September 22, 1966, pp. 5-8.

Saturday Review, "The Real Stokely Carmichael," July 9, 1966.

Other

"Black Americans: Stokely Carmichael" (audiocassette of interview on "Face the Nation" television program, June 19, 1966), Holt Information Systems, c. 1973.

"Stokely Carmichael" (audiocassette of interview, February, 1975), Pacifica Tape Library, 1975.

Ben Carson

1951–

African American neurosurgeon

In September 1987, a young black doctor in Baltimore made headlines worldwide when he successfully separated Siamese twins Patrick and Benjamin Binder, whose bodies were joined together in a tangled mass of blood vessels at the back of each of their heads. In other similar cases, attempts to perform such a complex operation had always ended in death or severe brain damage for at least one of the children involved. But the challenge of proving the conventional wisdom wrong intrigued Dr. Ben Carson, an easy-going, soft-spoken man known as "Gentle Ben" to his coworkers and patients. In truth, it was merely the latest in a number of challenges he has had to face on the road to becoming one of the world's foremost pediatric neurosurgeons.

Born and raised in Detroit except for a two-year period when he lived with relatives in Boston, Carson grew up in a single-parent household after his parents divorced when he was only eight years old. His mother, Sonya Carson, always had to struggle to provide for herself and her two young sons, both of whom at times seemed destined to follow the hopelessly self-destructive path of so many of their peers. Although very bright, they did poorly in school, and Ben in particular had a hair-trigger temper that often got him into serious trouble.

But thanks to Sonya Carson's persistence and a plan of action that included turning off the television and reading instead, the two boys slowly began to turn their lives around. Ben was fascinated by what he discovered in the pages of the books he checked out of the library and soon developed a passion for science that translated into a desire to become a doctor. By the time he reached seventh grade, he had zoomed to the top of his class academically. Around the same time, he also managed to conquer his temper after an argument with a friend took a potentially deadly turn. This life-changing event occurred when an enraged Ben lunged at another boy with a knife because he had changed stations on the radio they were listening to and then refused Ben's request to change back. The knife hit a metal belt buckle and snapped off; scared and shaken, both boys immediately ran home. Ben spent the next few hours praying and agonizing over how close he had come to injuring—or killing—his friend. Realizing that by harboring such anger he allowed others to have control over him, he vowed then and there never to give in to his temper again.

With his life at last on track, Carson continued to excel in high school and graduated third in his class. He then went on to Yale University on a scholarship and from there to medical school at the University of Michigan. After earning his degree, he was accepted into the prestigious residency program at Baltimore's Johns Hopkins Hospital, where he decided to specialize in neurosurgery. Carson then spent a year working as chief resident at a hospital in Australia. There the shortage of doctors in his specialty resulted in a very heavy workload and the opportunity to gain much more experience than he ever would have obtained had he stayed in the United States.

Soon after his return to Baltimore in 1984, the thirty-three-year-old Carson was named head of the department of pediatric neurosurgery at Johns Hopkins, making him the youngest doctor in the country to hold such a position. Since then, he has earned a reputation as a compassionate and innovative surgeon willing to take on the toughest cases, mostly (but not exclusively) those involving children with severe neurological disorders.

Carson is an enthusiastic fan of using modern technology to make the impossible possible; he was, for example, the first doctor to perform brain surgery on a fetus inside the womb. He has also achieved phenomenal success performing hemispherectomies, extremely risky operations in which half the brain is removed to stop the debilitating seizures caused by a rare and chronic form of encephalitis. (They had fallen out of favor with most doctors because so few patients survived.) In the case of the Binder Siamese twins, whose shared blood vessels seemingly doomed them to heavy blood loss (and probably death) during surgery, Carson spent several months coming up with an entirely new approach that borrowed from standard procedure in heart operations—stopping the babies' hearts, draining all of their blood, and then working quickly to separate them before restoring circulation.

The radical new method worked, and the doctor who was responsible soon found himself showered with media attention by those who were interested in knowing exactly how he had done it. They also wanted to hear a bit about Ben Carson the man, and before long news of his inspiring journey to the top of his profession had made him a bona fide celebrity.

Now in constant demand as a motivational speaker, Carson willingly shares the story of his life and of his formula for success with many different audiences across the country. For example, on June 27, 1994, in Dallas, Texas, he spoke at the annual meeting of the Million Dollar Round Table (MDRT), a group of life insurance agents who are among their industry's top performers in terms of sales and service. The address he delivered at the convention has been transcribed from an audiotape available through the MDRT.

Thank you. Thank you. It's a real pleasure to be here at the Million Dollar Round Table, and I want to thank you for inviting me. I've spoken in just about any venue you can imagine, from San Quentin Prison, to schools, to stadiums full of people, to the halls of the United States Senate. But you know, there's a special electricity here at this place, and the people that I've met are people who I feel are very similar to myself. But I have discovered that there is something very literal about the things that you say, because as I was preparing to come out, several people said to me, "Break a leg." Well, it's so dark back there I tripped on something, so I knew that I'd better be careful!

What you are doing and what this theme is—

"imagine"—is something that I think about all the time as a brain surgeon, because what do you imagine with? Your brain. That's how it's all done. I want you to think about what a brain surgeon does, what *I* do.

Now the week before last, I was in South Africa. I had been asked to come over there to help try to separate Siamese twins that were joined at the head. And this, of course, was a very complex endeavor. Well, it turned out that the surgical separation was extremely difficult technically but went very well. However, the twins did not survive, because they were something that had never been described before—they were . . . living off each other. One had the cardiac function for both, and one had the renal function for both. So even though we were able to separate them, they were unable to survive apart from each other, and they were in the process of dying together, because the one who had the cardiac function was rapidly deteriorating because he couldn't work hard enough for both of them. Nevertheless, we learned some very important things from that—things that will be very useful to the medical community as life goes on. And it brings up one of the themes in my life, one of the things I tell young people all the time—that there is no such thing as failure as long as you learn from it. You have to be able to take something away from every incident. That's why we have these complex brains which allow us to process information and to move ahead.

The reason I was asked to go to South Africa is because, as many of you may recall, in 1987, I was privileged to lead the seventy-member surgical team that successfully separated the Binder Siamese twins from West Germany, who are still alive. Many of you have probably seen me involved in intrauterine surgery on television, or hemispherectomies, or complex brain tumors, and the fact of the matter is, it's very interesting work.

Tomorrow I will be doing a fourteen-hour operation on a little girl who has multiple cysts in the spine. We're inventing a special type of device which is used with a micro-camera to go into her spine through all of these little . . . cysts and hopefully drain them, if it's God's will. That's one of three surgeries tomorrow that will probably last twelve to fourteen hours.

I say all that just to give you some perspective in terms of the kinds of things that I'm involved in. But you know, as a youngster, you probably never would have imagined it as I was sitting there in the hallways of Detroit's Receiving Hospital, or Boston's City Hospital, and I would hear over the PA system, "Dr. Jones! Dr. Jones to the emergency room!" He sounded *so* important! Or "Dr. Johnson! Dr. Johnson to the otolaryngology clinic!" I would sit there and I would imagine, I'd say, "One day, they're gonna say, 'Dr. Carson! Dr. Carson to the operating room!'" But of course nowadays they have beepers, so I still don't get to hear it!

I really got interested in medicine because I would listen to the mission stories in church, and they frequently featured missionary doctors. There were stories about how these people, at great personal sacrifice, would go out into the world and bring not only physical, but mental and spiritual healing to people. And I said, "What a *wonderful* thing! How could *anybody* do anything more *magnificent* than that?" I harbored that dream of being a missionary doctor from the age of eight until I was thirteen, when, having grown up in dire poverty, I decided I'd rather be rich.

So at that point, I wanted to be a psychiatrist. Now, I didn't *know* any psychiatrists, but at least on television they lived in these big, fancy houses with gates and fountains, and they drove Jaguars, and they had these big plush offices, and all they had to do was talk to crazy people all day! It seemed like I was doing that anyway, so I said, this will be a fantastic way to get very rich! I started reading *Psychology Today,* majored in psychology, did advanced psych when I went to medical school. That's when I started meeting a bunch of psychiatrists. And I don't think I need say more about *that*.

Now, actually, I should say some of my best friends are psychiatrists. There's nothing wrong with psychiatrists, it's just that I discovered that my concept of psychiatry had been gleaned from television. A lot of our young people glean their concepts of the world from television, and these are some of the most inaccurate portrayals imaginable to man. We have to be very careful about making sure that our young people really understand the world that they're going out into.

I think back—at age eight, my parents got divorced. My mother had only a third-grade education and the responsibility of trying to raise two young sons in inner-city Detroit with no money and very little hope. But she had some wisdom, and she decided we would move to Boston to live with her older sister and brother-in-law in one of the tenements in Boston. It was a typical tenement with large, multi-family dwellings, broken glass on the streets, boarded-up windows and doors, and gangs and sirens and murders.

But the thing that was most impressive to me were the roaches. They had very large, aggressive roaches. And not only would they crawl on your table, they'd crawl in your ear at nighttime, the little ones. More impressive than them were the rats. They had something there called water rats. Now these things were *monstrous*. In fact, the first time I saw one I thought it was a dog. They could move a garbage can by themselves.

While we were out there enjoying that environment, my mother was out working two—frequently three—jobs at a time trying to stay off of welfare. She didn't want to be on welfare, she wanted to be in control of her own life. She was a person who would never adopt what I call the "victim's mentality." I think that's one of the essential things that she was able to pass along to my brother and myself, and I frequently thank her for that. After working for a couple of years, she was, in fact, able to gain some degree of independence. We were able to move back to Detroit, still in a multi-family dwelling, still with significant wildlife, but nevertheless independent at that time.

"No one ever had to worry about getting the worst mark on anything as long as I was around. I was the safety net."

I was a fifth-grader. And I'll tell you, my idea of a good time was to goof off all day in school. My favorite subject was recess, and then to go home and play outside—baseball, football, basketball, kickball, throwing rocks at cars—whatever. And then when it was too dark, to go inside and watch TV till bedtime. As a result of that philosophy, I had no competition for last spot in my class. No one ever had to worry about getting the worst mark on anything as long as I was around. I was the safety net, you might say. I believed that I was stupid, and everybody else did.

I had a major philosophical disagreement with my math teacher, who seemed to think you needed to know the times tables. In my opinion, since they were printed on the back of the notebooks, why [should I] waste my time memorizing them? So you can imagine what kind of scores I used to get. In fact, I remember once I got a "D" in math, and the teacher was so pleased with me. She said, "Benjamin, on the whole, you're doing much better."

But my mother was very discouraged when she saw my fifth-grade report card at midterm and I was failing almost every subject. She didn't know what to do. My brother was also doing poorly. She prayed and she asked God to give her wisdom. What could she do to get her young sons to understand the importance of developing their minds intellectually so that they could have control of their own lives? And you know something? God gave her the wisdom, at least in her opinion. My brother and I didn't think it was all that wise, because it was to turn off the TV set, let us watch only two or three TV programs during the week, and with all that spare time, we had to read two books apiece from the Detroit Public Library *and* submit to her written book reports which she couldn't read—but we didn't know that. So, in fact, she had pulled a fast one on us, but we didn't know it.

I was kind of a rebellious fellow, so I said, well, I'm gonna get books that have a lot of pictures in them, and I'll just report on the pictures. But those pictures were so interesting, pretty soon I wanted to read the legend beneath the picture, and the page next to the picture. And the pictures became less important, and the reading became much *more* important.

I started reading about all kinds of things, and all kind of careers where people used their intellect—astronomers, astronauts, research chemists, surgeons, insurance salesmen—and I started saying, this is something that maybe *I* can do. I really got interested in animals, started reading all kinds of animal—I read every animal book in the Detroit Public Library. I remember the very first one I read was about a beaver. It was called *Chip, the Dam Builder*. If you ever have time, I suggest—it's a good book. Then I started reading about plants. But the thing that really grabbed my attention was rocks, because we lived near the railroad tracks. And what is there along the railroad tracks? Rocks! So I would collect little boxes of rocks, bring them home, get my geology books from the library, and compare the rocks with the pictures. Pretty soon I could identify virtually any rock, tell you where it came from, how it was formed. Still in the fifth grade, still the dummy in the class—nobody knew about this project.

And one day the fifth-grade science teacher

walked in, held up a big black shiny rock, [and] says, "Can *anybody* tell me what this is?" Well, as the dummy of the class, I *never* raised my hand. So I waited for one of the *smart* kids to raise their hand. And none of them did! So I waited for one of the *dumb* kids to raise their hand. And none of *them* did! I said, this is it, it's my big chance, and up went my hand. And *everybody* turned around, they looked, they were poking each other; this was something they'd never seen before—me with my hand up! The teacher called on me, and I said, "Mr. Jake, that's obsidian." There was silence in the room. Because it *sounded* good, and nobody knew whether it was right or wrong, and they didn't know whether they should be laughing, or whether they should be impressed. Finally, Mr. Jake said, "That's right! It *is* obsidian!" And I said, "You know, obsidian is formed after a volcanic eruption. The lava flows down, it hits the water, there's a super-cooling process, and the elements coalesce, and the air is forced out, and the surface glazes...." Everybody was *staring* at me! Their mouths were hanging open. They couldn't believe all this geological information spewing forth from the mouth of the dummy.

But *I* was perhaps the most amazed person because it dawned on me at that moment that I wasn't dumb after all. I said, Carson, the reason you knew those answers is because you were reading those books. I said, now suppose you read books about all your other subjects—science and math and history and geography and social studies—I said, couldn't you then know more than *all* these students who love to tease you? And I must say the idea appealed to me to the extent that no book was safe in my grasp. I read everything in sight. And within the space of a year-and-a-half, I went from no competition for last spot to no competition for first spot in my class.

Now this was much to the consternation of many of those students who used to tease me and call me a dummy. I remember there was one guy in particular who used to be the smartest guy in the class. His name was Steve. He was *exceedingly* obnoxious. He would always come up to you after a test and say, "What'd you get on your test? Lemme see your paper!" Then he'd say, "*I* got an A!" I walked up to him one day and I said, "Steve, how'd you do on the exam?" He poked out his chest, he said, "Oh, I got a 91." I said, "Gee, that's too bad! *I* got a 100!" And I said, "Next time, if you need help, let me know." Now, admittedly, this was a little bit obnoxious. But, gosh, did it feel good to say that to him!

Things *really* started rolling for me at that point. It's very important to understand that when I was in the fifth grade, and I took a test, I expected to get the lowest mark on it, and I generally did. When I was in the *seventh* grade, and I took a test, I expected to get the *highest* mark, and I generally did. I did *not* have a brain transplant in between. It tells you something about the human mind, the human capacity, and how to use it appropriately.

I am always disturbed when I hear people talking about what they *cannot* do, and how they have these negative attitudes. Because as a brain surgeon, I've studied this thing, and I realize how complex it is. How many people here remember what they had for breakfast today? Good! I'm glad to see there are still many functional brains out there!

Now let me tell you what your brain had to do—a very simple thing, and you were able to respond very quickly. This is how sophisticated your brain is....

[Speaking at a breakneck pace in one long, run-on sentence, Carson then launched into a technical description of the brain activity involved in processing the sound waves of his voice, understanding the meaning of his words, and directing the muscles to respond to his question with a raised hand.]

> ***"[In high school,] I ran into perhaps the worst thing a young person can run into—p-e-e-r-s. Negative peers. That stands for 'people who encourage errors, rudeness, and stupidity.' "***

That happens to be the *simplified* version of what your brain had to do, because I didn't want to get into all the coordinating and inhibitory influences—we'd have been here all day. But if your brain can do that and you barely have to think about it, can you imagine what the human mind is capable of when people put their mind to it?

You would've thought that maybe after I learned all these things I would be OK. But you see, then I went to high school. I was a straight-A student until I got to the tenth grade, and then I ran into perhaps the worst thing a young person can run into—it's called *peers*. Negative *peers*. P-e-e-r-s. That stands for "people who encourage errors, rudeness, and stupidity." That's what negative peers are. Unfortunately, we find them not only amongst young people but we find them amongst older people, too.

It was very interesting, because in every high school, you have two groups: you have your nerds and you have your cool guys. Now many of you were probably nerds. *I* was. You can always *tell* the difference. Because the cool guys are the ones who have the latest fashions, they know all the popular tunes, they can talk about all the movies, they have lettered in sports, they have a car, they have three chicks on each arm. The nerd, on the other hand—his clothes are clean, he carries books (even outside the school), he has these big, thick glasses, and he even understands his science experiments. And none of the girls want to be seen talking to him in public. I know you can identify with that!

But something happens. A few years go by. It's time to graduate from high school. Now the nerd wins a scholarship, goes off to college. The cool guy, with all his coolness, walks over to McDonald's and gets himself a job there. A few more years go by. The cool guy's still flipping hamburgers. The nerd has done very well, and there he is getting a signed contract with one of the Fortune 500 companies, and [he] takes that big signing bonus, first stop—he goes to the eye doctor. Gets rid of those thick glasses and gets a pair of contact lenses. Next stop—he goes to the tailor, gets himself some nice clothes. Next stop—he goes to the automobile dealer, gets himself a nice car. And then all those girls who wouldn't talk to him, they say, "Hey, don't I know you?" They won't talk to the guy at McDonald's anymore.

What I'm talking about here is delayed gratification. I'm talking about the ability to plan for the future. That's why we have these sophisticated minds. And that's what we use our imagination in order to do.

After I was able to learn these kinds of lessons, things went very well. I was able to go through high school, go to Yale University, on to the University of Michigan, to Johns Hopkins.

When I was chief resident at Johns Hopkins, we had the grand opening of the new neuroscience center. Hopkins is the modern birthplace of neurosurgery, so everybody who is *anybody* was there, including one of the fellows from Australia. He kept after me to come to Australia to be their senior registrar. I said, "Australia? You've got to be kidding me!" I mean, I didn't *say* that to him, but that's what I was thinking. I mean, where's Australia? You dig a hole in the earth from Baltimore, you come out in Australia. I don't wanna to go there! And plus I [had] heard all these things about, you know, it was worse than South Africa, they had a whites-only policy. So I said, forget about this mess.

But it seemed like every time I turned around there was someone there saying, "G'day, mate, how you doin'?" Australians *everywhere*. Every time we turned on the TV, there was a special on about Australia. I told my wife, "The Lord wants us to go there." So we packed up our belongings, off we went to Australia, and you know something? Interestingly enough, the biggest problem we had was keeping up with all the dinner invitations! People were enormously friendly.

The second biggest problem I had is every time I sat down to write on a chart or something, someone invariably would come up, and they would say, "Would you mind if I felt your hair?" They'd seen it on television and in magazines, and this was their big opportunity to feel the stuff. And I would say, "You can feel it, but it's gonna cost you ten bucks." But I would always get back at the Australians. I would say, "You know, I can't remember any of your names 'cause you guys all look alike."

But it was interesting—the reason the Lord wanted me to go there, I got so *much* experience. It was incredible, doing things. It was the only referral hospital in all of western Australia, so by the time I came back and joined the staff at Johns Hopkins, I knew how to do just about everything. So when the position of director of pediatric neurosurgery opened up, they gave me the position even at the age of thirty-three. People would come from all kinds of places with their young children to see Dr. Carson, chief of pediatric neurosurgery at Johns Hopkins. I would walk in the room and they would say, "When's Dr. Carson coming?" They couldn't imagine it was me. And I would say, "Well, I'm Dr. Carson," and they'd just about fall down and have a seizure—which is how I got interested in seizure surgery. *That's* not [really] how I got interested! But it *was* interesting to see the reactions.

I started doing all kinds of interesting things. But the reason I would do these operations—

the hemispherectomies, the intrauterine surgery, separation of Siamese twins—I would ask myself the question, "What happens if I *don't* do it?" And if the answer was they're going to die or something horrible, I would say, "You've got nothing to lose." The fact of the matter is, if you do your best and let God do the rest, you don't have to worry about what's going to happen.

That brings me to the close here of how I developed my philosophy for success in life. It's called "think big." Each one of those letters means something special.

The "t" is for talent, which God has given to every one of us—not just the ability to sing, dance, or throw a ball, but *intellectual* talent. We must learn to use that in our careers. We must learn to use that in our nation so that we will not be number twenty-one out of twenty-two nations, as the last survey demonstrated, in science and math. We can do better than that.

The "h" is for honesty, because if you lead a clean and honest life, you don't have to worry about skeletons in the closet. Because if you put them there, they will come back just when you don't want to see them. And if you always tell the truth, you don't have to worry about what you said three months ago, and you can concentrate on the task at hand.

The "i" is for insight, which comes from listening to people who've already gone where you're trying to go. Solomon, the wisest man who ever lived, said wise is the person who can learn from someone else's triumphs and mistakes. He said the person who cannot is a fool.

I have a particular affinity for Solomon. I think the Lord has a sense of humor, too, because my middle name is Solomon. He must have known that I was going to have this affinity for Solomon. When Solomon became the king of Israel, the first thing that he did that brought him a lot of fame was when two women came to him claiming the same baby, [and] he said, "Separate them." Well, *I* became very well known when I separated some babies also. So it's kind of interesting.

At any rate, the "n" is for nice. Be nice to people, because once they get over their suspicion of why you're being nice, they'll be nice to you, and you'll get a lot more done. And that includes not only people who look like you, it includes *everybody*.

In the United States of America, we're very lucky because we have a great deal of diversity. Some people tend to make that into a problem. But how many people here would go to an aquarium and pay money to get in if all the fish in there were the same? How many people would want a bouquet of flowers if they all looked alike? And how many people would want to get up in the morning if everybody looked like you? Think about it! The fact of the matter is, it would be bad if everybody even looked like *me,* and I'm not that bad looking! So I think we ought to consider it a great, wonderful thing that the Lord has done for us to give us this diversity. Let's not make it into a problem; let's make it into a strength.

"If you do your best and let God do the rest, you don't have to worry about what's going to happen."

The "k" is for knowledge. Knowledge is the thing that makes us into more valuable people. And the more of it you have, the more people need you, and when people need you, they pay you. There's a very good correlation there.

The "b" is for books, which is the mechanism for obtaining that knowledge. Because when you read, you have to put letters together to make them into words, so you learn how to spell. You have to take words together, put them into sentences, you learn grammar and syntax. And you have to take those sentences and use your imagination, you have to learn to imagine so you become a creative person.

The second "i" is for in-depth learning—learning for the sake of knowledge and understanding, *not* for the sake of taking a test, like superficial learners. They're people who cram, cram, cram before an exam. Sometimes they do OK, and three weeks later they know *nothing*. Of course, no one here knows any such person, but *that* is the reason that we're number twenty-one out of twenty-two. We can do better.

The last and most important letter, "g," is for God. We live in a society today in this country where people say, "You can't talk about God in public! That violates the separation of church and state." Well, I want to tell you something. The flag of our country, the United States of America—when we send our kids to school the first day, they learn the pledge of allegiance that says there's one nation, under *God*. You go into any court in our land and on the wall it says, "In God We Trust." Every coin in our pocket says "In God We Trust." Every bill in our wallet says "In God We Trust."

Now tell me something: if it's on our money, if it's in our creed, if it's on our courts, and we can't talk about it, what is that? That's schizophrenia. And that's the reason that we're having so many problems. People—we, those of us, those of you who've had the opportunity to reap the benefits of this land, who've had the opportunity to gain the education, to gain the insight, to use your imagination—we must be the ones to lead the rest of this nation, to lead the rest of this world, to "think big." And in so doing, I believe that this could be the greatest nation the world has ever known. Thank you very much.

SOURCES

Books

Carson, Ben, with Cecil B. Murphey, *Gifted Hands: The Ben Carson Story*, Zondervan, 1990.

Carson, Ben, *Think Big: Unleashing Your Potential for Excellence*, Zondervan, 1992.

Periodicals

Black Enterprise, "Merging Medicine with Technology," October, 1988, p. 70.

Christianity Today, "Surgeon on a Mission: With Prayer and Self-Discipline, Ben Carson Overcame Poverty to Become America's Leading Pediatric Neurosurgeon," May 27, 1991, pp. 24-26.

Ebony, "Surgical Superstar," January, 1988, pp. 52-58; "The Love That Changed My Life," May, 1990, p. 38.

People, "The Physician Who Healed Himself First," fall, 1991 (special issue), pp. 96-99.

Reader's Digest, "Ben Carson: Man of Miracles," April, 1990, pp. 71-75.

Other

Gifted Hands: The Ben Carson Story (video recording), Zondervan, 1992.

Gifted Hands (audio recording), Million Dollar Round Table Tape Cassette Program, 1994.

Think Big: Unleashing Your Potential for Excellence (audio recording), two cassettes, Audio Pages, 1992.

George Washington Carver

1864(?)–1943

African American educator and scientist

Most often remembered as the man who developed more than three hundred uses for the peanut, George Washington Carver was a skilled teacher and a creative thinker who attained the status of a folk hero during his own lifetime. His rise to fame occurred during an era of great disappointment and despair for many African Americans, who had seen their post-World War I hopes for a better life fade as racial discrimination and hostility increased. Out of this grim atmosphere emerged Carver, who was held up as an example (mostly in the white press) as a symbol of what blacks could achieve despite racism. Regarded as the foremost African American scientist of his day, he was a beloved figure among blacks as well as whites. At the heart of his appeal was his deep religious faith and his image as a gentle eccentric with a talent for explaining complex scientific principles in terms that ordinary people could appreciate.

Carver's early years gave little hint as to the course his life would eventually take. Born into slavery during the final months of the Civil War, he was orphaned as an infant and raised by a childless white couple on their farm in Missouri. Poor health kept him from doing any heavy outdoor work, so he did household chores and tended the family garden instead, displaying a particular talent for nurturing plants.

When he was about twelve, Carver left his rural home for a nearby town where he hoped to supplement the basic education he had already received. By his mid-teens, however, he had moved on to Kansas, thus beginning a period of restless wandering that lasted more than a dozen years and took him back and forth across several midwestern states. In 1890, he enrolled in Iowa's Simpson College with the intention of studying painting. After realizing that he would never be able to earn a living as an artist, he transferred to the agriculture program at Iowa State College, from which he graduated in 1894. Carver then began studying for his master's degree while teaching some biology courses. As news of his skills in the classroom spread among members of the academic community, he received many invitations to teach elsewhere, including a personal request from Booker T. Washington to head the new agricultural school at Alabama's Tuskegee Institute. Carver accepted Washington's offer and joined the faculty in 1896.

At Tuskegee, Carver had a wide variety of responsibilities. In addition to teaching and performing administrative duties as head of the agricultural school, he ran its experimental station, managed its two farms, and served for a while as its veterinarian. He also directed agricultural extension services throughout rural areas of the South, teaching poor farmers how to grow crops other than cotton without having to invest in expensive equipment, seeds, and fertilizers. In both the classroom and out in the field, he excelled as a teacher, emphasizing practical, hands-on work over book learning and instilling in his students a reverence for nature as a miraculous creation of God.

Carver was a dreamer at heart, and by the mid-1910s his shortcomings as an administrator had become evident. He then began to devote most of his time to public speaking (he was much in demand throughout the South) and to what was known as "creative chemistry," or research into products that could ultimately be marketed and sold. Partly out of necessity (financial resources were scarce at Tuskegee) and partly as a result of his own personal hatred of waste, Carver became a champion recycler who developed many ways in which material of all kinds could be turned into other useful items. Soon he began to attract national and even international recognition for his innovative laboratory work.

On January 21, 1921, Carver was asked to testify before the House Ways and Means Committee on behalf of the American peanut industry, which desperately wanted the government to help out Southern farmers by imposing a protective duty on cheap imported peanuts. The Tuskegee educator rose to the challenge with an entertaining demonstration of how important and versatile the peanut was, particularly the variety grown in the South. His presentation was so thorough and his manner so charming that he quickly won over the committee members, who encouraged him to continue past his allotted time. His testimony, as well as the responses it prompted from the various committee members, is reprinted here from the official government record of the hearing, Tariff Information, 1921: Comparison of Foreign Selling Prices & Landed Costs with American Selling Prices, *U.S. Govt. Printing Office 1921.*

Mr. Carver: Mr. Chairman, I have been asked by the United Peanut Growers' Association to tell you something about the possibility of the peanut and its possible extension. I come from Tuskegee, Alabama. I am engaged in agricultural research work, and I have given some attention to the peanut, but not as much as I expect to give. I have given a great deal of time to the sweet potato and allied southern crops. I am especially interested in southern crops and their possibilities, and the peanut comes in, I think, for one of the most remarkable crops that we are all acquainted with. It will tell us a number of things that we do not already know, and you will also observe that it has possibilities that we are just beginning to find out.

If I may have a little space here to put these things down, I should like to exhibit them to you. I am going to just touch a few high places here and there because in ten minutes you will tell me to stop.

This is the crushed cake, which has a great many possibilities. I simply call attention to that. The crushed cake may be used in all sorts of combinations—for flours and meals and breakfast foods and a great many things that I have not time to touch upon just now.

Then we have the hulls, which are ground and made into a meal for burnishing tin plate. It has a very important value in that direction, and more of it is going to be used as the tin-plate manufacturers understand its value.

Now there is a rather interesting confection.

This is another confection. It is peanuts covered with chocolate. As I passed through

Greensboro, South Carolina, I noticed in one of the stores that this was displayed on the market, and, as it is understood better, more of it is going to be made up into this form.

Here is a breakfast food. I am very sorry that you can not taste this, so I will taste it for you. [Laughter.]

Now, this is a combination and, by the way, one of the finest breakfast foods that you or anyone else has ever seen. It is a combination of the sweet potato and the peanut, and if you will pardon a little digression here I will state that the peanut and the sweet potato are twin brothers and can not and should not be separated. They are two of the greatest products that God has ever given us. They can be made into a perfectly balanced ration. If all of the other foodstuffs were destroyed—that is, vegetable foodstuffs were destroyed—a perfectly balanced ration with all of the nutriment in it could be made with the sweet potato and the peanut. From the sweet potato we get starches and carbohydrates, and from the peanut we get all the muscle-building properties.

Here is the original salted peanut, for which there is an increasing demand, and here is a very fine peanut bar. The peanut bar is coming into prominence in a way that very few of us recognize, and the manufacturers of this peanut bar have learned that it is a very difficult matter to get a binder for it, something to stick it together. That is found in the sweet potato syrup. The sweet potato syrup makes one of the best binders of anything yet found. So in comes the sweet potato again.

Then we have the peanut stock food. This is Number 1, which consists of the ground hay, ground into meal, much the same as our alfalfa hay, which has much of the same composition as our alfalfa hay, and we are going to use more of it just as soon as we find out its value. So that nothing about the peanut need to be thrown away.

Here is peanut meal Number 2. That can be used for making flours and confections and candies, and doughnuts, and Zu-Zus and ginger bread and all sorts of things of that kind.

Here is another kind of breakfast food. This is almost the equal of breakfast food Number 1. It will also have a considerable value in the market.

Here is a sample of peanut hearts. Now, it is not necessary for me to say that the peanut hearts must be removed from the peanut before many of the very fine articles of manufactured products can be made, such as peanut butter and various confections that go into candies and so forth. Now these peanut hearts are used for feeding pigeons. Pigeon growers claim that it is one of the very best foods that they have found.

Now here is an entirely new thing in the way of combinations. It is a new thing for making ice cream. It is a powder made largely from peanuts, with a little sweet potato injected into it to give it the necessary consistency. But it is far ahead of any flavoring yet found for ice cream. It is a very new product that is going to have considerable value.

You know the country now is alive looking for new things that can be put out in the dietary. Here is a meal, Number 1. That is used for very fine cooking and confections of various kinds. I will not attempt to tell you how it is made.

"The peanut and the sweet potato are twin brothers and can not and should not be separated. They are two of the greatest products that God has ever given us."

Here is another thing that is quite interesting. This consists of the little skins that come off of the peanut. These skins are used in a very great many ways. They are used for dyes. About thirty different dyes can be made from the skins, ranging from black to orange yellow. And in addition to that they contain a substance very similar to quinine, and they are using a good deal of this now as a substitute for quinine, and physicians find it is quite attractive. Just how far it is going to affect the medical profession it is difficult to say, but I am very much interested in it myself, because the more I work with it the more I find that it is interesting and has great possibilities.

Here is another type of breakfast food quite as attractive as the other two. It is ready to serve. All that is necessary is to use cream and sugar, and very little sugar; because it is quite sweet enough.

Here is breakfast food Number 5. That contains more protein than any of the others. One of them is a diabetic food. If any of you are suffering from that disease, you will find one of these breakfast foods very valuable, because it contains such a small amount of starch and sugar.

Here is a stock food that is quite as attractive as any now on the market. It consists of a combination of peanut meal and peanut hay, together with molasses, making a sweet food of it, and chinaberries. The chinaberry has a great many medicinal properties, such as saponin and mangrove, and many other of those peculiar complex bodies that make it an especially valuable product that we are going to use as soon as we find out its value. All kinds of stock eat them with relish, and thrive upon them, and when they are added to these other foodstuffs, it makes a tonic stock food. I have tried that out to a considerable extent on the school grounds, and I find that it is a very fine thing indeed.

Here is another breakfast food that has its value. I will not attempt to tell you, because there are several of these breakfast foods that I will not take the time to describe, because I suppose my ten minutes' time is about up. Of course I had to lose some time in getting these samples out.

Mr. Garner: I think this is very interesting. I think his time should be extended.

Mr. Carver: This is really the chinaberry. The other was not the chinaberry. It consists of a composition of ground peanuts and the peanut hay and the peanut bran, and so forth, made up into a balanced ration.

Now, a great many people do not know the chinaberry. I have been very much interested in it. In fact I dug up a bulletin here a few days ago and found out that an English gentleman had gone over into Morocco and was attracted by the great yield of chinaberries and had made rather an exhaustive analysis of them and was advocating their use. However, we in Alabama advocated the use of the chinaberry several years ago.

Mr. Rainey: Do we produce in this country the chinaberry?

Mr. Carver: Oh, yes.

Mr. Garner: Yes, a great deal of it.

Mr. Carver: And it is one crop that is infallible year after year. We understand that the chinaberry belongs to the same group of vegetation that the mahogany tree belongs to, and all of them have great medicinal properties.

Mr. Rainey: Do we import any chinaberries?

Mr. Carver: No, sir; we do not import any chinaberries, because we grow them in abundance here. Of course they are not used now.

Mr. Garner: They are not used to any great extent.

Mr. Carver: No, sir, they are not used to any great extent, but I am just as confident as that I stand here that they will be used as soon as we find out their value.

Mr Rainey: You don't need any tariff on them, do you?

Mr. Carver: No, sir; we don't need any tariff on them down there. We need to know their value and to profit by their value.

Mr. Rainey: The varied use of the peanut is increasing rapidly?

Mr. Carver: Yes, sir.

Mr. Rainey: It is an exceedingly valuable product, is it not?

Mr. Carver: We are just beginning to learn the value of the peanut.

Mr. Rainey: Is it not going to be such a valuable product that the more we have of them here the better we are off?

Mr. Carver: Well, that depends. It depends upon the problems that these gentlemen have brought before you.

Mr. Rainey: Could we get too much of them, they being so valuable for stock foods and everything else?

Mr. Carver: Well, of course, we would have to have protection for them. [Laughter.] That is, we could not allow other countries to come in and take our rights away from us. I wish to say here in all sincerity that America produces better peanuts than any other part of the world, as far as I have been able to test them out.

Mr. Rainey: Then we need not fear these inferior peanuts from abroad at all? They would not compete with our better peanuts?

Mr. Carver: Well, you know that is just about like everything else. You know that some people like oleomargarine just as well as butter, and some people like lard just as well as butter. So sometimes you have to protect a good thing.

Mr. Rainey: We have no tariff on oleomargarine.

Mr. Carver: I just used that as an illustration.

Mr. Rainey: But to still carry out your illustration further, oleomargarine is in competition with butter.

Mr. Carver: I believe that the dairy people want it there.

Mr. Rainey: They never asked for a tariff on oleomargarine.

Mr. Oldfield: But they did put a tax on butter.

Mr. Garner: And they did use the taxing power to put it out of business.

Mr. Carver: Oh, yes. Yes, sir. That is all the tariff means—to put the other fellow out of business. [Laughter.]

The Chairman: Go ahead, brother. Your time is unlimited.

Mr. Carver: Now, I want very hastily to bring before you another phase of the peanut industry which I think is well worth considering. Here a short time ago, or some months ago, we found how to extract milk from peanuts. Here is a bottle of milk that is extracted from peanuts. Now, it is absolutely impossible to tell that milk from cow's milk in looks and general appearance. This is normal milk. The cream rises on it the same as on cow's milk, and in fact it has much of the same composition as cow's milk.

Here is a bottle of full cream. That cream is very rich in fats, and can be used the same as the cream from cow's milk.

Mr. Oldfield: You made a mistake there, didn't you? You haven't got the milk mixed up, have you?

Mr. Carver: No, sir. I may have made a little mistake there, but nevertheless the result is the same. That is what I say. Number 1 might be Number 2, because I am running over them very hastily.

Mr. Oldfield: Don't you think we ought to put a tax on that peanut milk so as to keep it from competing with the dairy product?

Mr. Carver: No, sir. It is not going to specifically affect the dairy products. We don't mean that it shall affect dairy products, because it has a distinct value of its own, and can be put right alongside of the dairy products, and if it is—

Mr. Oldfield: Did you say it was used for the same purpose as dairy products?

Mr. Carver: It is used for the same purposes, yes, sir.

Mr. Oldfield: What is the reason it won't displace dairy products, then? Every time you use a pint of it will that not displace the dairy products?

Mr. Carver: We do not now make as much milk and butter as we need in the United States, and then there are some people that would choose dairy products rather than these, and vice versa. Some would take this rather than dairy products.

This one is made especially for ice cream making. It makes the most delicious ice cream that I have ever eaten.

Mr. Carew: How does it go in a punch?

Mr. Carver: Well, I will show you some punches. [Laughter.] Here is one with orange, and here is one with lemon, and here is one with cherry. Here is a bottle of buttermilk. This buttermilk is very rich in fats, and very delightful.

Mr. Hawley: Is that made from the peanut?

Mr. Carver: Made from the peanut milk; yes, sir.

These are derivatives from the buttermilk. That is, the peanut milk has about the same quantity of curds in it as the cow's milk has, and the whey settles out the same as it does from cow's milk, and leaves this clear curd. It has a distinctive flavor, and you can take it and use any flavoring you want, add any other flavor to it that you desire, and you have your punches and fruit juices, as you wish to call them.

That is another type of punch.

This is the evaporated milk. That is evaporated down much on the order of Borden's milk.

Now here is a very attractive product—an instant coffee. This is instant coffee. All that is necessary is take a teaspoonful of this and stir it into a cup of hot water, and you have your coffee, cream and sugar combined.

Here is a bottle of Worcestershire sauce. This Worcestershire sauce is built on a peanut basis, and you know the original Worcestershire sauce is built on a soybean basis, and I find that the peanut makes just as good a base for Worcestershire sauce as the soybean. So that it comes in for its measure of value in that direction.

Now here is the foundation for the Worcestershire sauce. That is a dry powder, ready for all of the various things that enter into the manufacture of Worcestershire sauce.

Now here is a very highly flavored sauce that imitates the Chinese sauce that enters into chop suey and the various Chinese confections that they are so very fond of.

Here is the dry coffee. Now peanuts make probably one of the finest coffees, of the cereal coffees, that can be made. It is far ahead of Postum. I suppose some of you gentlemen would, judging from what I heard you say awhile ago, look upon it just about the same as a person did at the fair where I had this, and he wanted to know what it tasted like. I told him it was better than any Postum he had ever drunk. He said, "Well, that is no recommendation for it." [Laughter.] Nevertheless, it does make a very fine coffee, imitating the cereal coffee.

Now here is a bottle of curds. Now, as I stated before, the peanut milk has about the same amount of curds that cow's milk has, and the curds can be taken out and made into the various fancy cheeses, the Neufchâtel and Edam, and any of those soft cheeses, and these curds now are ready to be resoftened and worked into these various fancy cheeses.

Of the oils, we have the oil Number 1, which is the first refined oil, and oil Number 2, which makes a very fine salad oil, and this one was made just before I came up here. I just finished that. This is taken directly from the milk itself, and has properties that the other oils do not have. It is a very beautifully colored oil, and I am looking forward to that with a great deal of interest, as it is a by-product from the manufacture of some of these other things taken, as I stated, directly from the milk.

Mr. Carew: Did you make all of the products yourself?

Mr. Carver: Yes, sir. They are made there in the research laboratory. That is what the research laboratory is for. The sweet potato products now number 107 up to date.

Mr. Garner: I did not catch that statement.

Mr. Carver: The sweet potato products number 107 up to date. I have not finished working with them yet. The peanut products are going to beat the sweet potato products by far. I have just begun with the peanut. So what is going to come of it, why, we do not know.

This is the very last thing. Now this is a pomade. That is, it is a face cream and will be attractive to the ladies, of course, because it is just as soft and just as fine as the famous almond cream, and it has the quality of vanishing as soon as put on. It carries a very high percentage of oil and three minutes after it is applied to the skin you can not tell that any has ever been put on at all, yet is a finer softener of the skin than almond cream, and it will take any perfume that one wishes. You can have rose or carnation or any of those fine perfumes.

So therefore the peanut is going to come in as very important in that direction. It is also going to be a fattening element, that is, for the massaging of infants that are anemic and run down. It is going to be quite the equal or above

George Washington Carver

the olive oil because, as I said before, it immediately vanishes into the skin, and is going to be a very attractive thing as soon as physicians find out its value.

Then we have here a bottle of ink. I find that the peanut makes a very fine quality of ink. This is a very interesting thing, indeed.

Then we have the peanut flakes or dried flakes. Now all that is necessary is to dissolve these in hot water, and you have your peanut milk again.

Then we have a relish here. This is relish Number 1, which is a combination of—well, various things. I will not attempt to tell you what it is. But it is a peanut relish.

And then here is a bottle of mock oysters. The peanut curds can be made into mock meat dishes so thoroughly that it is impossible to tell them from meat, and it is going to be very satisfactory in that direction. We are going to use less and less meat just as soon as science touches these various vegetable products, and teaches us how to use them. I remember years and years ago when the automobile first was being introduced how the people laughed and how they jeered and how they talked of the horses, about the impossibility of running them off the streets. I have been here two days, and I have not seen a single horse on your streets. They are automobiles. And now the same thing is true, or much the same thing is true about our vegetable products with reference to the meat business.

Mr. Rainey: You are going to ruin the livestock business?

Mr. Carver: No, sir, I don't think I am going to affect it very much, because we will use livestock in another way.

Here is another one of the fancy punches and fruit juices.

Now, gentlemen, I have a number of other things. I have probably twenty-five or thirty other things, including the various wood dyes and stains and all sorts of things, but if my time is up, I am going to stop.

Mr. Garner: I understood you to say that the properties of the peanut combined with the properties of the sweet potato was a balanced ration, and that you could destroy all other vegetable life and continue to sustain the human race?

Mr. Carver: Yes, sir. Because you can make up the necessary food elements there. Then, as I said before, in addition to that you have your vitamins. You know the war taught us many, many things we did not know before. We did not know anything about these vitamins, and we did not know anything about these various peculiar compounds which are brought out by the complex handling of these various products, and science has touched these things in a way that is bringing to life or bringing to light what was intended should be brought to light, and there is scarcely a vegetable product that we have not learned something about. Then again, if we think of how the peanut is used, it is the only thing that is universally used among civilized and uncivilized people, and all sorts of animals like it, and I do not know of a single case—that is, I mean normal—that complains because peanuts hurt them. I remember a little boy that we have in our town. Well, he is one of our professor's boys. He made up his Christmas budget, his Santa Claus budget. He started out with peanuts first, and then he would mention a horse, and then peanuts, and then a dog, and then peanuts, and peanuts were the beginning and the ending. He eats peanuts all the time. So that it is a natural diet that was intended that everybody should use. Then again, if you go to the first chapter of Genesis, we can interpret very clearly, I think, what God intended when he said, "Behold, I have given you every herb that bears seed upon the face of the earth, and every tree bearing a seed. To you it shall be meat." That is what he means about it. It shall be meat. There is everything there to strengthen and nourish and keep the body alive and healthy.

The Chairman: Mr. Carver, what school did you attend?

Mr. Carver: The last school I attended was the Agricultural College of Iowa—the Iowa Agricultural College. You doubtless remember Mr. Wilson, who served in the cabinet here so long, Secretary James Wilson. He was my instructor for six years.

Mr. Green: What research laboratory do you work in now?

Mr. Carver: At the Tuskegee Institute, Tuskegee, Alabama.

Mr. Carew: You have rendered the committee a great service.

Mr. Garner: I think he is entitled to the thanks of the committee. [Applause.]

Mr. Treadway: Did the institute send you here or did you come of your own volition?

Mr. Carver: The United Peanut Association of America, sir, asked me to come.

Mr. Treadway: In order to explain to us all this variety of uses of the peanut?

Mr. Carver: Yes, sir. You have seen, gentlemen, just about half of them. There is just about twice this many more.

Mr. Treadway: Well, come again and bring the rest.

The Chairman: We want to compliment you, sir, on the way you have handled your subject.

The many newspaper and magazine accounts of his appearance before the Ways and Means Committee soon made Carver a national celebrity. Various groups began clamoring for his services as a lecturer and spokesman, and throughout the rest of the 1920s and into the 1930s, he was showered with awards and lauded as

a genius. By the time of his death in 1943, Carver had ascended to near-mythic stature as the "Wizard of Tuskegee." Although historians now downplay the significance of his scientific discoveries (very few of them actually made it to the marketplace), they have begun to take a closer look at his accomplishments as a teacher and scientific popularizer. It is in that role, they say, that Carver revealed his true strengths as a man dedicated to helping poor Southern farmers—primarily black sharecroppers—improve their standard of living through a better understanding of agriculture.

SOURCES

Books

Adair, Gene, *George Washington Carver,* Chelsea House, 1989.

Holt, Rackham, *George Washington Carver: An American Biography,* revised edition, Doubleday, 1962.

McMurry, Linda O., *George Washington Carver: Scientist and Symbol,* Oxford University Press, 1981.

Tariff Information, 1921: Comparison of Foreign Selling Prices and Landed Costs with American Selling Prices (U.S. Congress, House Committee on Ways and Means), U.S. Government Printing Office, 1921.

Periodicals

Newsweek, January 18, 1943, pp. 75-76.

Time, "Black Leonardo," November 24, 1941, pp. 81-82; January 18, 1943, p. 89.

Lauro F. Cavazos

1927–

Mexican American educator and former U.S. government official

Lauro F. Cavazos, the first Hispanic American ever to serve in the cabinet of a United States president, is a Texas native whose ancestral roots in the area date back to the time when it was still under Mexico's control. He was born on the famous King Ranch in the southern part of the state, where his father, who was also named Lauro, worked for many years as a cattle foreman. Eager for his five children to obtain the best education possible, the elder Cavazos pulled them out of the ranch's tiny two-room schoolhouse (which had been built especially for the children of Hispanic workers) and managed to get them admitted to the all-Anglo elementary school in the nearby town of Kingsville.

At first, young Lauro—or Larry, as he was known—did not share his father's enthusiasm for education. After graduating from high school, he joined the Army and served during the last months of World War II rather than go on to college. At the end of his two-year stint, he headed home to Texas with the intention of becoming a commercial fisherman. That was not quite what the senior Cavazos had in mind for his oldest son, however, and his wishes finally prevailed when Larry agreed to enroll at Texas A & I University in Kingsville.

Cavazos later transferred to Texas Tech University, earning a bachelor's degree in zoology in 1949 and a master's degree in cytology in 1951. He then went on to complete his PhD in physiology at Iowa State University in 1954. He launched his academic career at the Medical College of Virginia, beginning as an instructor in anatomy in 1956. Cavazos was an associate professor of anatomy by the time he left Virginia in 1964 for a full professorship in the same field at the Tufts University School of Medicine in Boston. There he remained for the next sixteen years, joining the administrative ranks in 1975 when he was named dean of the medical school. Five years later, Cavazos resigned to return to his alma mater, Texas Tech, to become president of the university—the first Hispanic American and the first alumnus to serve in that capacity. In addition, he headed the medical school (known as the Health Sciences Center) and held the positions of professor of anatomy and professor of biological science.

Under his leadership, Texas Tech enhanced its standing in the academic community by improving its research programs (most notably in his own area of expertise, health sciences), trimming its budget while boosting its fundraising efforts, and attracting more Hispanic and black students. Cavazos was personally involved in many of these efforts, especially those that brought him into contact with young people, their parents, and educators. He made numerous visits to Texas public schools and worked with their administrators on dropout prevention and related issues, for example, and also spoke frequently before Hispanic groups to encourage adults to communicate the value of education to children.

But his presidency also saw its share of controversy. Recruiting violations by officials of the university's football program, for example, led the NCAA to impose a one-year probation. And in 1984, without consulting any faculty members, Cavazos suggested changes to the university's tenure policy—including regular performance reviews of tenured staff—that sparked outrage among Texas Tech professors. (Later that same year, eighty percent of them formally expressed their dismay in a no-confidence vote against him.) While his actions were not popular with the American Association of University Professors and its supporters, they garnered praise from some outsiders (including President Ronald Reagan) who admired his willingness to take on an established labor union. The dispute was finally settled in 1986 when Cavazos and the university faculty agreed to a modified tenure policy.

In the summer of 1988, President Reagan nominated Cavazos to replace William Bennett in the cabinet-level post of U.S. Secretary of Education. (This was actually the second time the president had approached Cavazos about the job; the first time was in 1980, but Cavazos quickly took himself out of the running because he had just arrived at Texas Tech.) Many saw the move as a blatant political maneuver to entice Hispanics—especially those in Texas, with its rich supply of electoral votes—to support Reagan's fellow Republican (and vice-president) George Bush in the 1988 presidential race against Michael Dukakis. Cavazos, a Democrat, downplayed such speculation and stressed that he had no intention of being a token. Indeed, few people questioned his qualifications for the job. Furthermore, his genial, low-key approach and commitment to consensus-building were welcome relief to some after the angry, combative rhetoric of his predecessor, Bennett, who regularly used his position to blast teachers, unions, and "elitism" at U.S. universities.

Confirmed by the Senate and sworn into office in September 1988, Cavazos immediately set out on a speaking tour of the Southwest, where his pro-education/stay-in-school message dovetailed nicely with Bush's oft-repeated pledge to make education a top priority in his administration if he were elected. Soon after Bush defeated Dukakis in November, he re-appointed Cavazos to the cabinet and vowed to increase federal spending on education and find ways to reward outstanding teachers and schools.

As secretary, Cavazos espoused the belief that America's ability to compete in the global marketplace relies on its ability to educate its citizens to their fullest potential. To that end, he championed programs to reduce the dropout rate and make education more accessible (financially or otherwise) to minorities and the disadvantaged. Recalling his own experience growing up in a household where he spoke Spanish with his mother and English with his father, he also came out as a strong advocate of bilingual education. (He felt that conducting some classes in a child's native language while helping him or her master English as quickly as possible would ease some of the adjustment and self-esteem problems such students often face.) In addition, Cavazos announced his plans to work closely with teachers and the education establishment to raise professional standards, hold educators responsible for improvements, develop innovative methods of instruction, and look at alternative ways to run schools. Above all, however, he stated again and again that parents must instill in their children a thirst for knowledge and an appreciation for the importance of education.

On May 19, 1989, Cavazos faced members of the Education Press Association at the National Press Club in Washington, D.C., to discuss the concept of school "choice," one of his major plans for restructuring the American educational system. According to this philosophy, parents should have the freedom to choose which public school they want their children to attend. This was a key element of the Bush administration's education policy, and it is still a popular concept among conservative Republicans in particular. Proponents argue that choice fosters market-type competition between schools that will result in across-the-board improvements in education; opponents counter that choice will lead to more segregation along socioeconomic lines considering that not all schools will be able to afford the programs, staff, and facilities that attract students. Cavazos's remarks on the subject are reprinted here from the June 15, 1989, issue of Vital Speeches of the Day.

It is a pleasure to join you today and share some thoughts and plans for education in the near future. This nation suffers from three deficits—a trade deficit, a budget deficit and an education deficit. All three of these deficits are linked and, I submit, that the trade and budget deficits will not be resolved until we overcome the education deficit.

One can quantitate the trade and budget deficits. It is done daily in Washington to the nearest million. I can quantitate the education deficit:

-27 million adults are illiterate

-28 percent of our students drop out of high school

-the national high school graduation rate is only 71.5 percent

-SAT and ACT scores have declined or remained static for the last three years

-U.S. students score low in math and science when compared to their peers in other industrialized nations.

By any measure one wishes to apply, we are failing or not making progress.

What is the solution? I believe that we must first have a national commitment to excellence in education and, second, we must restructure elementary and secondary education in this nation.

By restructuring, I mean developing and implementing strategies that will improve the educational process at the elementary and secondary school level. Some examples of restructuring include:

-curriculum reform that results in better education

-alternative certification of teachers and principals

-early childhood education to make every experience of young children a learning situation

-more educational decision authority for teachers and parents

-educational deregulation or cutting red tape

-choice

Again, a total restructuring and we must start now. Time is against us and for too long decisions on what is taught by our schools have been the exclusive province of professional educators. We have paid a high price for that exclusivity in lowered parental interest and a boring sameness among our schools. Again and again, scholars studying American education have bemoaned a widespread lack of parental concern and involvement in the education of their children and noted a remarkable national uniformity in the methods and organization of our schools.

But this is changing. Lately, we have begun to see glimmerings of a new level of diversity in American education, a diversity based on pro-

Lauro F. Cavasos

viding parents and students with an array of choices in both the form and substance of educational offerings. Whenever choice appears, commitment and involvement in education have been revitalized, and that revitalization sets the scene for a leap forward in achievement. It is that crucial next step, the provision of choice in education, that I would like to discuss with you today. I consider choice the cornerstone to restructuring elementary and secondary education in this country.

Why do I believe so strongly in choice in education? Because I believe in young people like Andre Lawrence and Chris Schaefer.

Andre is graduating from the Jose Feliciano School for the Performing Arts in East Harlem next month. This young man lives on the Lower East Side of Manhattan and must leave his home shortly after dawn each morning to catch the subway which takes him across the city to East Harlem. Andre could walk to a neighborhood school but it doesn't offer the curriculum that interests him and there are problems with drugs near the school. At the School for Performing Arts, he has grown academically and polished his considerable skills in music. And his musical talent would have gone untapped if he had not had a magnet school to attend. Thus, choice provided education and opportunity.

Chris Schaefer almost dropped out of school two years ago. To quote Chris, he was "sleepwalking through his classes" in his local high school, in a state of "educational depression." The choice reforms in Minnesota saved Chris as a student. With support from his mother, he enrolled at the Chisago-Pine Area Learning Center. In his new school, Chris developed his potential as a writer and his grades have improved.

Andre and Chris have had the advantage of choice in education. Working with their parents, they determined the school that would provide the best education for them.

Because of choice, we have seen remarkable changes in East Harlem. Test scores have risen and admission of students from East Harlem to the selective high schools in the city has climbed dramatically. It is axiomatic that good schools take care of and educate all students to their fullest potential. The blueprint is clear—all we need to do is to follow it to bring about positive change.

Minnesota has been putting the nation's most ambitious statewide choice program into effect since 1985. This program offers open enrollment across district lines, post-secondary options, and area learning centers, like the one Chris attends. The successes here have inspired

Iowa and Arkansas to enact open enrollment legislation, and it is reported that twenty-one states are considering choice programs.

All our young people should have the opportunities offered by choice that have benefited students like Andre and Chris. We must do away with ineffective conventional arrangements that only block reform.

It is expected that choice will promote school reform. Initially we tried to improve education by imposing regulations from the top down while leaving the basic structure of our schools untouched. Obviously, this has not worked.

In the current movement of reform, schools must be responsible to parents, students and teachers. To accomplish this, schools need the freedom to change and innovate.

Schools should remain accountable, of course, but accountable to parents, teachers and students as well as to central administrators.

In short, we must infuse our schools with the ingredients that are essential to any enterprise—entrepreneurship and accountability. Choice offers this opportunity.

The failings of our school system today affect all children, but none more severely than America's minority and disadvantaged young people. You are well aware of the tragic situation in some of our inner-city and rural schools where it is common for half or more of the minority students to drop out . . . and for those who do graduate to go out into the world unprepared for college and the workplace.

It's not enough to deplore the situation or to blame it on a supposed lack of money. We already spend more on our students than any major industrialized country in the world. No, as I emphasized earlier, I believe that we can no longer patch, adjust, tinker and complain. It is time to act. The solution is restructuring and the catalyst is choice.

No child, no matter his or her circumstances, should be compelled to attend a failing school, or one that does not meet their academic needs. Choice offers parents, students and teachers the opportunity to select the better schools if the neighborhood school is faulty or if it cannot satisfy educational requirements. Through choice, we can exercise the same kind of judgment in selecting schools that we take for granted in making other decisions.

Those who have benefited from choice are pleased with it. Yet, relatively few students have access to choice despite the benefits. This must be changed.

The president has called for "a second great wave of education reform" where choice is "perhaps the single most promising" idea. As David Kearns, the chairman of Xerox, says, "To be successful, the new agenda for school reform must be driven by competition and market discipline . . . the objective should be clear from the outset: complete restructuring. . . . The public schools must change if we are to survive."

Where choice is used, it works. Charles Glenn, the civil rights director for the Massachusetts Department of Education, says choice can promote equity, ". . . by creating conditions which encourage schools to become more effective . . . by allowing schools to specialize and thus to meet the needs of some students very well rather than all students at a level of minimum adequacy, and . . . by increasing the influence of parents over the education of their children in a way which is largely conflict free. We have become excited about the potential of choice for public education."

> *"We must infuse our schools with the ingredients that are essential to any enterprise—entrepreneurship and accountability."*

There are many reasons to be in concert with the innovations that choice can bring. This approach recognizes that there is no "one best way" for everyone. Children have different needs and learning modes. Teachers have different approaches. Parents have different philosophies. Choice allows schools to draw strength from diversity by developing different programs. It allows each school to excel.

And, choice does something more: it empowers parents by bringing them into the decision-making process. It encourages teachers and principals to become entrepreneurs and structure their curriculum and standards; students are encouraged to become learners with options that direct and capture their potential.

A free and productive society thrives on empowerment of the people. The American economy and our democracy are products of empowerment, and this approach can revitalize schools around the country.

For an example of choice across a broad front, we only need to look at the system of postsecondary education in this country. At the postsecondary level, schools compete for students, offering a variety of programs to satisfy distinct needs. We have a fine system of universities and colleges . . . some say the best in the world. The rector of a university in Russia who was on a tour of our higher education system recently observed that "American universities are not good because the United States is rich. America is rich because it has good universities." That's quite an endorsement. And students from all over the globe come to this country to attend our universities and colleges.

My point is basic . . . there are choices at the postsecondary level of education in this country and they have helped to produce the highest caliber educational system. I am convinced that the same approach can promote progress and success for our elementary and secondary schools.

There is one thing I want to make clear before going on. I have heard the criticism that choice would promote a two-tiered system of

> *"No citizen should attend a second-rate school in the United States of America."*

education, that is, one system for the fortunate and another for the disadvantaged. It is blind not to recognize that inequities already exist in our schools. It assumes that choice cannot be exercised in an effective and responsible manner by *all* parents and students to improve their situation. I say, enable all Americans to make choices in education. Furthermore, armed with the power of choice, parents can force inferior schools to *upgrade or close*. No citizen should attend a second-rate school in the United States of America.

President Bush and I are determined to use the power of choice to help restructure American education. The president, who visited a magnet school in Rochester, New York, just yesterday, has asked Congress to expand the federal magnet schools program in the Educational Excellence Act of 1989, and I strongly endorse that proposal. Among other issues, this measure also calls for alternative certification of teachers; recognizing Merit Schools, outstanding teachers and science scholars; and the funding of drug prevention programs.

In order to provide momentum in the national effort on choice in education, I am announcing several federal initiatives.

First, I will move immediately to convene four regional strategy meetings and invite teams of governors, legislators, state education chiefs, principals, teachers and parents to develop innovations to promote choice in their respective states.

Second, I am creating in our own office a special task force to promote, encourage and evaluate choice programs and report to me on a quarterly basis regarding our progress in those areas. Based on the findings of the task force, you will be hearing more from us on additional federal activities.

Third, I am today naming Jack Klenk of our staff as a Special Advisor on Choice Programs to work on the development of further initiatives.

Fourth, I am directing the Office of Educational Research and Improvement to identify choice as a major priority of grants to be awarded this year under the Secretary's Fund for Innovation in Education.

We are also aware of a special and critical obligation to see that the public has valid information at its disposal for making choices in education. I plan two immediate actions to fulfill that responsibility.

First, I am releasing two publications that distill the theory and practice of choice, and will release two others in the near future.

Choosing a School for Your Child is a practical guide for parents on how to select a school. Although this booklet is designed for parents, we believe it will also interest educators and policymakers. This publication will be translated into Spanish to ensure its widest distribution to the public. Parents can get these booklets free of charge through the Consumer Information Center.

The second book, *Educating Our Children: Parents and Schools Together,* is a report prepared for the president in January 1989 by the Working Group on the Parental Role in Education. It addresses the issue of parental involvement as a key factor in educating children.

Improving Schools and Empowering Parents: The White House Workshop on Choice in Educa-

tion will discuss that conference and provide background on the issue of choice. This booklet will be released this summer, along with *Parental Choice in Six Nations*.

At the request of the state of Minnesota, I am ordering the Department to conduct a three-year evaluation of the impact of that state's ambitious open-enrollment choice program. Governor Rudy Perpich's pioneering efforts in Minnesota provide an unparalleled laboratory for looking at what works and how it works in choice programs.

The American public education system was once the envy of the world. Our past successes were built on a recognition that parents, teachers, students and local school administrators must work together to educate our nation's children. We strayed from this solid principle some time ago and placed our trust in processes and institutions that distanced parents and students from their educational systems. The concept of choice returns the crucial element of parent and student involvement. This involvement revives the relationship between parent and teacher, parent and principal, parent and student, and parent and parent, thereby rekindling community concern for education in this great country.

"He is free who lives as he chooses," a Greek philosopher wrote nearly 2000 years ago. Americans today still hold firmly to that ancient but timeless ideal. To be an American means to have choices. Yet, ironically, we are often powerless to make one decision with a profound and enduring effect . . . where to send our children to school.

Thank you.

Less than a year after taking office, Cavazos found himself under fire from both conservatives and liberals for not acting quickly and decisively to take charge of his department and propose firm ideas and practical policies. In addition, Cavazos faced the dilemma of too many needs and too little money in the budget to deal with them. But his inexperience with Washington-style politics, his unfamiliarity with the needs of elementary and secondary schools, and his failure to rally public support for his few initiatives eventually proved to be his undoing. In December 1990, Cavazos resigned as Secretary of Education.

SOURCES

Books

Newsmakers: 1989 Cumulation, Gale Research, Detroit, 1990.

Periodicals

Hispanic, "From the King Ranch to Capitol Hill," August, 1990, p. 32.

National Review, "Shortest Education Presidency?" March 24, 1989, pp. 11-12; "To the Dark Tower Came," January 28, 1991, pp. 17-18.

New Republic, "Lauro's Themes," July 10, 1989, pp. 7-8.

Newsweek, "The Do-Nothing Education Secretary," October 2, 1989, p. 56; "A Summit for Schools," October 2, 1989, pp. 56-58.

Time, "'Please, Children, Do Not Leave,'" December 5, 1988, p. 80; "Go to the Rear of the Class," May 29, 1989, p. 76; "Cavazos Flunks Out," December 24, 1990, p. 64.

U.S. News and World Report, "The President's Worst Subject," August 6, 1990, pp. 46-48.

Vital Speeches of the Day, "Restructuring American Education Through Choice," June 15, 1989, pp. 514-516.

César Chávez

1927–1993

Mexican American labor leader and activist

By most measures, he was an unlikely leader—a soft-spoken, sad-eyed, grammar-school dropout who was small in stature and modest in both demeanor and dress. Yet as the founder of the United Farm Workers (UFW) union, César Chávez unquestionably did more to improve the lives of those who toiled in the produce fields of California and elsewhere than any other person before him. Described by a New York Times *reporter as "David taking on the Goliaths of agriculture," Chávez made skillful use of nonviolent protest tactics such as strikes, marches, boycotts, and fasts to challenge the power of growers and corporations. His efforts won him respect and support not only among the Mexican Americans who looked to him for help but also among scores of sympathizers the world over.*

Chávez's special link to the migrant workers had been forged during his childhood. Born near Yuma, Arizona, he spent his early years on the farm that his grandfather, an immigrant from Mexico, had bought when he settled in the area around 1880. The year César was ten, however, his circumstances changed dramatically; financially wiped out by the Depression, the Chávezes lost their land and their house and were forced to take to the road in search of work. Like thousands of others from across the country who had suffered a similar fate, the family headed to California. There they joined the ranks of those who followed the harvest from place to place, picking grapes, citrus fruits, and vegetables from dawn until dusk.

Such migrant laborers typically endured pitifully low wages and intolerable working conditions. More often than not, they were housed in tiny shacks made of tar-paper or sheet metal with no running water, no electricity, and no fuel for heat or for cooking. As members of an ethnic minority that locals looked down upon, they also faced discrimination and segregation on a daily basis. And because of their nomadic existence, migrant children had little hope of escaping from this cycle of poverty and prejudice.

In fact, young César's formal education essentially came to an end when he moved to California. He later recalled attending some sixty-five different elementary schools "for a day, a week or a few months" until he finally quit for good around the eighth grade. Not long after, he struck out on his own and found work in the vineyards near the town of Delano.

After serving in the U.S. Navy during World War II, Chávez returned to work in the fields. But he was beginning to think that he and his fellow Mexican Americans—especially veterans who had fought for their country—deserved to be treated more fairly. He even participated in a few labor protests that quickly fizzled in the face of the overwhelming power the growers exercised over their employees.

In the early 1950s, Chávez's hunger for action led him to join the Community Service Organization (CSO). Established by non-Hispanic liberals to empower Mexican Americans to help themselves, the CSO conducted voter-registration drives and sponsored numerous programs (mostly in urban areas) that offered poor and working-class people assistance with everyday needs such as housing and legal services. Although he started out as an unpaid volunteer, Chávez displayed a talent for recruiting new members and developing those with leadership ability. He eventually moved up the ranks, becoming the CSO's general director in 1958. At the same time, however, he was also growing increasingly frustrated at the lack of interest among his colleagues in organizing and empowering the rural poor—namely, the farm workers. Finally, Chávez realized that the farm workers had to create their own union if they ever expected to improve their lives. So, along with Dolores Huerta, a fellow CSO official who shared his views, he resigned and founded the National Farm Workers Association (NFWA) in Fresno in September 1962.

Over the next few years, Chávez spent as much of his time as possible trying to convince people to join his fledgling union. It was not an easy task, as previous organizers had discovered; most of the farm workers were illiterate, could barely afford to pay dues, and were easily bullied by the growers, many of whom threatened to fire anyone who became involved with a union. But at countless evening meetings across the agricultural heart of the state, Chávez shared his dream of mounting an aggressive but nonviolent "revolution." Slowly but surely, people signed up, and by 1965 the NFWA numbered about two thousand members.

That same year, the NFWA at last felt strong enough to take on some of the growers. In September, Chávez and his farm workers voted to combine forces with a group of Filipino grape-pickers in Delano who had gone on strike for higher wages. Fearing the loss of their harvest, two of the three grape growers involved quickly agreed to pay higher wages and allow their workers to join the union, but the third grower—which happened to be the largest—refused. So the strike continued and began to attract national attention to La Causa, *as the farm workers' struggle came to be known. With increasing moral and financial support from a number of major civil rights groups, liberal religious and political leaders, and various AFL-CIO-affiliated unions, Chávez decided to raise the stakes a bit higher: he asked Americans not to buy California table grapes unless they carried the union label.*

The strike and the boycott dragged on until 1970, but it was a time of tremendous growth for the union (which became an AFL-CIO affiliate in 1966 and changed its name to the United Farm Workers, or UFW) and international exposure for its charismatic leader. It was also during this same period that Chávez went on the first of several fasts he periodically undertook to dramatize the farm workers' plight and stress the nonviolent nature of their movement. Beginning on February 14, 1968, he refused all but water for the next twenty-five days. On March 10, he and about eight thousand of his supporters (including Senator Robert Kennedy, just a few days away from announcing his candidacy for the Democratic presidential nomination) gathered in a Delano park for a celebration to mark the end of the fast. By that time, Chávez was so weak and ill that he could not stand, hold up his head, or raise his voice above a whisper. He therefore designated two people to speak in his place, a UFW official in Spanish and a minister in English.

His statement was very brief but widely quoted and distributed; as Winthrop Yinger observes in his book César Chávez: The Rhetoric of Nonviolence *(Exposition Press, 1975), from which the following version of Chávez's words are taken, it "represent[s] a crystallization and refinement of his political, economic and theological ethic; a kind of 'credo' of the farm worker movement." Stylistically, too, the statement contains many of the elements typical of Chávez's longer speeches—a very simple, personal, and informal method of delivery, allusions to elements of everyday life as well as to religion and history, and motivational appeals to remain involved in* La Causa.

I have asked the Reverend James Drake to read this statement to you because my heart is so full and my body too weak to be able to say what I feel.

My warm thanks to all of you for coming today. Many of you have been here before, during the fast. Some have sent beautiful cards and telegrams and made offerings at the Mass. All of these expressions of your love have strengthened me and I am grateful.

We should all express our thanks to Senator Kennedy for his constant work on behalf of the poor, for his personal encouragement to me, and for taking the time to break bread with us today.

I do not want any of you to be deceived about the fast. The strict fast of water only which I undertook on February 16 ended after the twenty-first day because of the advice of our doctor, James McKnight, and other physicians. Since that time I have been taking liquids in order to prevent serious damage to my kidneys.

We are gathered here today not so much to observe the end of the fast but because we are a family bound together in a common struggle for justice. We are a union family celebrating our unity and the nonviolent nature of our movement. Perhaps in the future we will come together at other times and places to break bread and to renew our courage and to celebrate important victories.

The fast has had different meanings for different people. Some of you may still wonder about its meaning and importance. It was not intended as a pressure against any growers. For that reason we have suspended negotiations and arbitration proceedings and relaxed the militant picketing and boycotting of the strike during this period. I undertook this fast because my heart was filled with grief and pain for the sufferings of farm workers. The fast was first for me and then for all of us in this union. It was a fast for nonviolence and a call to sacrifice.

Our struggle is not easy. Those who oppose our cause are rich and powerful and they have many allies in high places. We are poor. Our allies are few. But we have something the rich do not own. We have our own bodies and spirits and the justice of our cause as our weapons.

When we are really honest with ourselves we must admit that our lives are all that really belong to us. So, it is how we use our lives that determines what kind of men we are. It is my deepest belief that only by giving our lives do we find life. I am convinced that the truest act of courage, the strongest act of manliness is to sacrifice ourselves for others in a totally nonviolent struggle for justice. To be a man is to suffer for others. God help us to be men!

The boycott proved to be a spectacular success, and in mid-1970, after incurring losses estimated in the millions of dollars, the last of the hold-outs among the grape-growers finally agreed to sign contracts. This was without a doubt the high point in the UFW's history; flush with victory, it began to expand its horizons into more ordinary activities such as establishing credit unions, offering medical and other forms of insurance, and lobbying legislators.

In other ways, however, the UFW was truly a unique organization in the history of the American labor movement. With its emphasis on family, ethnicity, and—perhaps most notably—religion, it was indeed more of a "cause" than a union; as its founder once noted, the UFW was out "to change the conditions of human life," to work on God's behalf to right the wrongs perpetrated against the poor and minorities. Chávez himself was a devout Roman Catholic, and from the very beginning of the farm workers' movement, his beliefs shaped the spirit and direction of his organizing efforts. This in turn led many priests, nuns, and other religious leaders to lend their support to the UFW and the man some people considered a "secular saint."

In March 1974, Chávez addressed the National Federation of Priests' Councils at the group's annual convention, held that year in San Francisco. The subject of his talk was "Saying 'Yes' to Man's Dignity," and in it he reflected on how the fight for social justice is often so much more—it is also a demand to be acknowledged as a human being worthy of respect. He also shared his thoughts on the many personal sacrifices involved in choosing a life of service and thanked those in attendance for their willingness to make such sacrifices. His comments are reprinted here from Catholic Mind: The Monthly Review of Christian Thought, *October 1975; they were originally published in* Chicago Studies, *summer, 1974.*

I am grateful to the priests of the United States for the continued support they have given the farm worker movement. I take this opportunity to thank particularly those priests and nuns who were with us last summer in Fresno. I understand that that experience represented the largest number of religious in jail on any one social issue in the history of our country. That kind of help is very special to us. It is the help of commitment and understanding; but, even more important, it is the help of one's body—it is the help of people getting into trouble because they are helping us. It is the kind of help that is respected and appreciated by all of us. For in our struggle to change, to bring about some dignity to man—and I say to the men, the women and the children who toil in the fields—we are seeing that, throughout the ages, little—but little—dignity has come to them.

In the days of the horse and buggy, the farm worker's dignity was equal to that of the beast. And today, in the day of mechanical harvesters, his dignity is equal to that of the machine. And, so, we ask ourselves: Is that saying "yes" to man's dignity?

When priests began organizing in recent years, they also were saying "yes" to their own dignity. For in former times the priests were known as clerics and functionaries; and today they are organized. We, too, in the farm movement, want to have our own federation, to be able to say "yes" to our own dignity. Saying "yes" to the farm worker's struggle is really saying "yes" to man's dignity because it is putting an ideal into action. We are blessed more than most men and most movements because we have had more men saying "yes" to our dignity in our struggle than most struggles in the history of this country have had. And I think that we have been said "yes" to by many people throughout the land because we are saying "yes" to our own dignity.

But saying "yes" to man's dignity is not something new. It has been happening in the entire history of man. Moses said "yes" to man's dignity. And so did the prophets, saints. In our lifetime Gandhi, King and others have said "yes" to man's dignity epitomized in Christ. Why do farm workers engage in similarly insurmountable odds against powerful forces—the growers, the Teamsters, those who oppose us? Why do we march and picket and face jailings, expose ourselves to physical violence, fasting and praying? I think that these things are done because we are saying "yes" to man's dignity.

Saying "yes" to man's dignity means getting into trouble. How many times when we say "yes" it becomes a controversy! And it becomes painful because in many cases the controversy starts—it originates—among our closest friends. Saying "yes" to man's dignity means saying no to fear.

The struggle to say "yes" to man's dignity is difficult. And we often wonder why it should not be as easy as sleeping, eating and walking. But it is not. There should not be a question about saying "yes" to justice. Why should there be even a second thought? How many times in our lives do we find that we know we are right and yet we are afraid to act? The saying "yes" in the struggle for the dignity of man cannot be bought with money. Although that struggle is endless, always there is the problem that, once you say "yes," you've got to continue saying "yes." The more you say "yes" to man's dignity the more demands there are. And I think that is the way it should be. When we say "yes" to man's dignity we are saying "yes" to life because that is really what life is all about.

FEAR AND FREEDOM

People who were in jail in Fresno for two weeks last summer were certainly very uncomfortable. But by their action they said "yes." And by their "yes" they stopped the arrests. They gave their bodies and they were in jail for two weeks. But they kept hundreds—God knows how many hundreds—of farm workers from going to jail. The way things stand now we may have to have more "yeses" to man's dignity this summer.

Saying "yes" to man's dignity is not only a Christian thing. We know some agnostics in our day who said some very profound things—simple but profound. Saul Alinsky, a most controversial man, said "yes" to men—to the dignity of man—always. He once said that you really aren't free until you accept death. Once you accept death you can overcome most things. You can overcome fear which will set you free then to struggle and to do God's work in this land. And, so, the fear of struggling, the fear of material insecurity, the fear of death many times may interfere with our duty to put ourselves on the line. The conflict with the obligation of service often becomes political controversy.

Strength comes from God, and if man is created in God's image, it should come from man. The problem we have then is that when you say "yes" to man's dignity and you get elected to public office, something strange happens. The power came from the people. No sooner is power acquired than the same man who got the power from the people begins to isolate himself—insulate himself—from people. Labor leaders have the same problem. The power comes from the people. There is a strange paradox here where we spend more time planning how not to be with people than the time we spend planning how to do the work. I understand that even some priests are not immune to this. It is that demand that we are afraid of, the demand that people know there is a good priest over there. We don't care what time or hour of the day or night it is: he'll say "yes." It is an awful thing, because that word spreads, and people come from all over and make demands. And the more he gives the more they will want.

It happens to us, too. There is a fear to put a limit. Twenty-two years ago I was working in a small community in Madeira, California, and I got myself caught in a very difficult situation. I was beginning to organize and beginning to be successful at it. The more I did, the more that was demanded of me. I was beginning to get very angry with myself and with people, because I wanted to have one Sunday off. And, after working about six months, I began to plan with my family—my wife and kids—that I was going to go to the park on that Sunday and have a picnic—and I didn't give a hoot who came. I was not going to give it up. I was just not going to be anybody's fool. I was going to take some time off. I was getting very, very upset about the whole idea. I don't mind working thirteen hours a day; but on Sunday I need a day

César Chávez

off. And I was having difficulties living in a situation with millions of problems of people, poor and exploited, finding someone, some organization that was beginning to deal with their problems.

So, on Sunday I wanted to get out of the house very early. I got the kids in the car, went to very early Mass, came back home—made the mistake of coming home to pick up the picnic basket—and there was a car there with a family. Could I help them ? Their son was in jail. And could I please help him? What I wanted them to do was to go away, because although I did not want to help them, I felt very, very guilty. I did not have the courage to say "no." So I went with them and spent most of the day trying to get that man out of jail. By the time I came back, there was no way in which I could go to the picnic—and I had spent another Sunday working.

I made up my mind that day. I told my wife that I can not continue this way. Either I get out of this work and do something else where I work forty hours a week; or, if I decide to stay here, I've got to decide that it is a pleasure to help people. And, if I cannot get that in me, really I'll be miserable the rest of my life. And I don't want to be miserable. So, I gave myself six months. That was thirteen years ago.

Saying "yes" to man's dignity when you teach means supporting them. Our union runs five or six clinics. There are nine people on the executive board of the union—seven Catholics, one Jew and one Protestant. The issues of abortion and the pill were before us. When we came to the executive board everyone said in one voice: "Oh, we don't want to get into that. We don't want to have abortions in our clinic, or the pill. We just can't have that." Easier said than done! Right away forty or fifty percent of the people working in those clinics began to rebel, and some left because we were saying "no." We thought we were saying "yes" to man's dignity by saying, "Let them live." On the other hand we were being told "no" because, if we say that, then we who are doctors and nurses can't stay here. We have to leave.

PATERNALISM

I was brought up with the liberal idea that farm workers were too poor to pay dues. And we know that, if we are going to build a movement, we have to build it ourselves, and we have to sacrifice to do it. But we did not want to ask the workers to do it because of our paternalism. Several years ago, I was confronted with the decision one winter evening. I went to a man's home who was, I remember, one month in arrears, and the second month coming up. I went to collect the $3.50—there were no contracts then, no benefits, just the idea of a union. And this man said: "I was just going to the store. I have a five-dollar bill. I will give you $3.50 if you come with me." I went to the store. He changed the five-dollar bill, gave me $3.50, and he bought $1.50 worth of groceries. I had his $3.50 in my pocket and I went home. I couldn't get over that. I couldn't sleep that night because I was asking myself: "Who am I to take $3.50 from this man for the dues, when he needed that money right last night to buy food?" But, then, saying "yes" to man's dignity means having hope. About four years later that same man was among the first workers to be hired when we got our first contract. I never forgot that. I went back to his home when he got his first paycheck. And what impressed me so much had not even made a little ripple in his memory. I reminded him, but he didn't remember. He, too, was saying "yes."

We have a duty to understand the difference between saying "yes" to man's dignity in terms of service or saying "yes" to man's dignity in terms of being a servant. I think being of service at our convenience is not really truly letting go. For, when a man says, "I will say 'yes' to man's dignity by being a servant," I think that that makes all the difference in the world—being of service on a certain day at a certain place or at a certain time as against being of service all the time, everywhere and to everyone. Fighting for social justice, it seems to me, is one of the most profound ways in which men can say "yes" to man's dignity. And keeping silent about these issues is probably one of the most effective ways of saying "no" to man's dignity. We don't say "yes" to man's dignity by thinking that prayer is an end to things instead of a means, that saying "yes" is all we have to do instead of saying "yes, here I am, here is my body." I think that saying "yes" to man's dignity really means sacrifice. There is no way on this earth in which one can say "yes" to man's dignity and know that one is going to be spared some sacrifice.

> ***"Fighting for social justice . . . is one of the most profound ways in which men can say 'yes' to man's dignity."***

To priests of America I am happy to say: You have said "yes" to us many times. And your saying "yes" to us has meant that other people have said "yes" to us, that countless numbers of people—probably into the hundreds of thousands or even millions—have said "yes" because you have said "yes" to us. And so, dear brothers, you are then the source of hope for us—the harvesters of love and the symbol of faith.

As Chávez mentioned in the previous speech, by the early 1970s the UFW was facing another foe—the Teamsters union. In an effort to dilute the strength of the UFW, some of the larger growers had invited the Teamsters to come in and organize workers. This touched off bitter and sometimes violent confrontations as the Teamsters made substantial gains at the expense of the UFW, often by illegally bringing in men, women, and children from Mexico to replace striking UFW members. On September 9, 1974, while the dispute still raged, Chávez was honored for his union activities at a Greater Washington (D.C.) Central Labor Council luncheon. In his address that day to fellow AFL-CIO leaders, reprinted here from a copy held in the archives of the Walter P. Reuther Library at Wayne State University in Detroit, he spoke of the ongoing efforts to settle the differences between the UFW and the Teamsters.

Thank you very much, Brother Apperson, Brother George Meany, Monsignor Higgins, Brothers and Sisters.

We are very happy to be here with you today to tell you that, in a very special way, we wish to thank Brother Meany for his support and personal interest in the outcome of the tremendously important struggle that is taking place in California and other places in the Southwest, which will determine, eventually, whether there is going to be a union for farm workers. We want to thank him and the Federation—and all of you—for your concern, your interest, and especially for you dedication in assisting us to bring about a fair solution to the conflict in California.

Throughout the great United States, the boycott is unfolding. Many central labor councils and many state federations are really in gear. To give you an example of what is happening, let me cite just two or three examples.

Detroit saw over five hundred trade unionists picketing, distributing leaflets, about two weeks ago.

There is a huge committee of trade unionists in Boston that gets together weekly to work on the boycott.

The support of the state federation in New Jersey is among the best.

In Ohio—throughout the various cities in Ohio—the support from the labor movement is excellent.

Several weeks ago, the Los Angeles County Federation of Labor got together and raised the money to buy signs to be placed on the buses—the public transportation buses. We are told that something like three hundred buses are carrying signs, "Boycott Lettuce—Boycott Grapes." We estimate that by now, at least half of the citizens of the Los Angeles area have seen that message.

The two hundred and fifty delegates to the Montana State AFL-CIO convention two weeks ago took up a collection for us and raised over six thousand dollars.

And so it goes—many other federations and labor councils are assisting us.

Today begins what we are calling "Week of International Boycott of Grapes and Lettuce." We say "international" because grapes and lettuce are sold not only in the United States, they are sold, in large quantities in Canada, in England, in Scandinavia and West Germany. And so we have to appeal to our friends in the labor movements over there, and to our friends, to assist us in bringing about a boycott everywhere the grapes and lettuce are being sold.

So today is the beginning of a week of action, a week of activities that will include press conferences, parades and demonstrations, picket lines and leafleting, religious services and fund-raising, to get the message of the boycott out to the public.

We have to keep reminding the people, keep it before the public, so that they will know that the growers refuse to either recognize a union or give the workers a chance to have an election, so that they can determine for themselves which union they want.

As long as they are against these two things, we must continue to strike and boycott. The boycott, as you know, is really an extension of the strike.

You know that the farm workers are not covered by legislation. You know that the farm workers in the places where we strike are at the mercy of the courts, and the awesome and total power that the growers have in small communities to get the courts to enjoin the union the moment there is a strike or the moment there is going to be a strike. Last year, in a period of less than sixty days, we were hit with sixty-nine injunctions. Right now, there are one hundred and two injunctions against our union.

The injunction is usually enforced by civil action. What they do in California is, the sheriff takes it upon himself and makes it a criminal action. The growers use the power of the district attorney and the sheriff's office to enjoin us, and enforce these injunctions—using the taxpayers' money—by making the injunction a criminal matter.

And then we have the "illegals." If the illegals were to be taken out of the places where we are now striking, the strike would be over tomorrow. If we could get the illegals out of the grape fields, if we could get the illegals out of the lettuce fields, the growers would have to come and meet with us within twenty-four hours. In the Delano area today, the growers are harvesting the grapes with about fifty percent of the workers that they normally need, and we estimate that about eighty-five percent, if not more, of the people working there are illegals—brand-new illegals—brought from Mexico within the last month or so.

A funny thing happened last Friday. As you know, we are striking against and boycotting the Gallo wine people. Last Friday, the people went on strike. These are the people that are supposed to be Teamster members—these are the people who are supposed to be strikebreakers. They went out on strike last Friday. There were 420 of them working there. We were able to get 150 or 155 U.S. citizens out on strike. Then we went back and talked to the illegals, and we were able to get about 200 of them to come out. That left between 80 and 100 people in the fields.

On Saturday, we had everyone out. This morning—before we came here, I called the office—this morning, they had 250 illegals—not the same illegals, but brand-new people. We went to the U.S. Immigration Service on Friday, and on Saturday, and this morning. We were told two things. We were told that they don't have enough personnel to do the work, and they also told us that they are not going to go into a struck field and take the illegals out, because they have to remain neutral. They've been telling that since last year. So we need to have pressure, we need to get to the U.S. congressmen and the U.S. senators and let them know what is happening, because that is the deciding factor.

We were attacked last year, this contract was stolen from us. But the concern, and the love, and the interest of the workers for our union is such that today, we have had more strikes this years than any other time in the history of our union, even though we lost those contacts and our membership was reduced by seventy percent.

If illegals were not there, we wouldn't have to have the boycott, we could win by ourselves. But we have sent wires and telephone calls and letters to General Chapman, and we haven't had one answer. We try to get Attorney General Saxbe to do something about it—no answer.

In Yuma, Arizona, which is just on this side of the Mexican border, 3,300 people work there picking lemons. They went out on strike, and they have been on strike now for two weeks tomorrow—every single worker, including irrigators, tractor drivers and pickers. Not one single lemon has been picked—not one—and it will be two weeks tomorrow. We haven't picketed, we don't need picket lines. But we have injunctions against us from the Yuma courts for having too many people out in the picket lines. That is how ridiculous things get.

We talked to the attorney that represents the growers and he said, "We are not worried, we are going to get people to do the job." So we tried to find where they were going to get the people. He said, "Well, where they usually come from."

So unless a great miracle happens, they will bring people from Mexico, just across the border—the orchards are just twenty yards from the border.

Last Friday, too, in the counties of Sutter, Yolo, Colusa, Sacramento and Solano—the five-county area that accounts for the growth of about seventy percent of all of the canning tomatoes in California—we went out on strike. The one great fear that the Teamsters have is that our union should be stopped—that our union should be terminated—because what would happen if the tomato workers went out on strike—what would happen to the canneries?

There was great expectation on the part of the workers. There was a bill proposed in California—a simple bill—to let the workers decide which union they wanted—a representation election bill. It had nothing to do with collective bargaining. The California State Federation of Labor and ourselves, we introduced a bill, and we didn't even go into collective bargaining because we thought we couldn't get it. So we said we would just go for a simple election bill.

We were able to get it through two committees of the Assembly. Finally, the whole Assembly voted for it, but when it got to the Senate, it was killed. There was tremendous pressure against the simple bill to let the people decide, by a vote, which union they wanted.

Who was campaigning against it?

The Chamber of Commerce, the Farm Bureau Federation and the Teamsters Union.

Brothers and Sisters, the boycott is having its impact, and unless great changes take place, we think that we are going to win. We are going to win, because of the concern of Brother Meany; we are going to win because of the help of the Federation; we are going to win because of the concern of all of you here.

And we are going to win because the workers have had a taste of what a union is. A group of workers who, for almost 100 years, have been struggling to have a union, when in 1970, as if by a miracle, they were able to have an idea—a taste of what a union can do for them, and even though they lost a union, they will never forget that experience. Because of that experience, we see today that we have tremendous support from the workers—their willingness to sacrifice, to go out there and struggle and do all the things that strikers must do to have a union. We see that kind of commitment.

A group of growers in Stockton, against whom we were striking in the tomatoes, were talking to one of our leaders. They said, "You know, we thought that when you lost the contracts last year, that was the end of the Farm Workers Union. But we are seeing now that nothing is going to stop the union until we sit down and negotiate with you." And our leader said, "Sure, and once you recognize a union, once you deal with us, then and only then will the strikes and boycotts end."

"We are going to win because the workers have had a taste of what a union is."

We think that the growers made a bad mistake in taking those contracts away from us. They were banking on essentially two or three things.

Number one, the biggest thing that they were banking on was that the AFL-CIO would never endorse our boycott. They were so sure of that, that when President Meany and the AFL-CIO executive council endorsed our boycott—that same day—I got reports from the people on the picket lines that the growers were walking around with long faces. One of the growers said, "You know, that endorsement is worth at least twenty million dollars."

The struggle continues. The workers continue to struggle and continue to have faith. They are no different than you and the men who built your unions—no different. They have the same ideals, the same goals, the same determination, and the same love to have a union.

We were in Coachella not long ago, and a group of kids on the picket lines asked to have a meeting with me. It was rather unusual, but I did it—I talked with them. They wanted to tell me a story that I want to leave with you, because this little story says a lot about how people feel.

It is about three men who were traveling in a car in the grape vineyards. Towards the late afternoon, the car broke down. They were from Los Angeles, and Coachella is about 120 miles from Los Angeles. Knowing that they would not be able to return to the city, they went to the nearest farmhouse and asked the farmer if he could put them up for the night. According to the story, one was a man from India—Hindu by religion—one was a rabbi, and the third man was a high Teamster official.

After a good supper, the farmer told them that he had failed to tell them that he did not have enough room for all three to sleep in the house, that two could stay in the house and one of them could stay in the barn.

So the visitor from India volunteered to go to the barn because it would be an experience for him to sleep one night in an American barn. So he went to the barn, the lights were turned out, and the people were getting ready to sleep when there was a knock on the door. The farmer got up and opened the door. The Hindu, the Indian, was at the door, and he said he was sorry, but he couldn't stay in the barn because there were cows there—because of his religion.

The rabbi heard this, and being ever thoughtful and concerned about people's religions and beliefs, said, "I'll go to the barn."

So the rabbi went to the barn. The lights were turned out and the farmer went back to bed. After a little while, there was a knock on the door. The farmer got up and opened the door. The rabbi was in the door. He said he couldn't stay in the barn because of his religion—there were pigs in the barn.

The Teamster, not caring, said, "I'm not afraid of animals." He jumped out of bed and went to the barn, and the rabbi went into the house. They closed the door and turned out the lights—the people wanted to sleep. Along about midnight, there was a tremendous racket—all kinds of noise at the front door. The farmer jumped out of bed and opened the door—and all the cows and all the pigs were at the front door.

The moral of that story is, not even the cows and pigs wanted the Teamsters in the fields, and you can imagine how the workers feel.

Thank you very much.

The rivalry between the UFW and the Teamsters was not resolved until 1977, when the two unions finally reached a settlement granting the UFW sole bargaining rights. This came on the heels of another significant victory—the 1975 passage in California of the Agricultural Labor Relations Act. This landmark piece of legislation was the first to recognize the right of farm workers to engage in collective bargaining. These successes, along with the farm-worker-friendly administration of Democratic Governor Jerry Brown, helped bring about a resurgence in the UFW's membership and influence during the late 1970s.

But the 1980s proved disastrous for the union. Beginning in 1983, the new Republican administration headed by Governor George Deukmejian tilted the balance of power toward the growers, many of whom had helped finance Deukmejian's campaign. Changes in the make-up of the state assembly also had a negative impact on legislation affecting farm workers. (Nationally, too, there was a shift toward a more conservative political agenda that did not favor unions in general or the farm workers' cause in particular.) In addition, California's economy went into a slump, depressing wages and prompting widespread unemployment.

Perhaps most damaging of all, however, was the fact that the UFW itself was in turmoil, plagued by internal dissent and organizational problems that drove away some of the very people who had been instrumental in the union's earlier triumphs. (A few who commented publicly about the disarray blamed it on Chávez's authoritarian style of leadership and unwillingness to accept criticism.) As a result, by the end of the decade, the UFW had lost most of its contracts and membership had dropped from its 1970s peak of nearly 100,000 to less than 20,000. Even a highly-publicized thirty-six-day fast Chávez undertook in 1988 to draw attention to careless pesticide use that he felt endangered farm workers and consumers alike failed to rekindle the old spark.

Despite these setbacks and his own increasingly frail health, Chávez continued to take the UFW's message to audiences across the country. His fund-raising efforts took him to college campuses, churches, union halls—wherever he thought he could find a sympathetic ear. One such occasion was on November 21, 1991, when he spoke to the Building Industry Association of Northern California at a meeting in San Jose. The primary focus of his talk was on the steps the UFW had taken to provide affordable housing for farm workers, an especially difficult task in California, where land and construction costs typically are among the highest in the nation. Yet as he pointed out in this and so many more of his speeches, what at first glance seems impossible is indeed possible if people are willing to be creative and flexible. The usual Chávez style is evident here as well—a very direct, simple, and personal approach totally lacking in flamboyance or fiery rhetoric, a reliance on many examples and facts to make his case, a fondness for folksy anecdotes, and an emphasis on the moral imperative to take action. His remarks are reprinted here from a copy of the text held in the archives of the Walter P. Reuther Library of Wayne State University in Detroit.

I always feel like I'm coming home when I visit San Jose. My family often called this place home when we became migrants after the bank foreclosed on my father's small Arizona farm during the late 1930s.

After World War II, we returned to San Jose, to a little house on Sharf Avenue in the tough eastside barrio they nicknamed *Sal Si Puedes*—which for those of you who are culturally deprived translates "get out if you can."

The nickname came about because it seemed as though the only way young men left Sal Si Puedes was to go off to jail, the military or the cemetery. A lot of people who lived in Sal Si Puedes were farm workers who scratched out a living in the orchards and vineyards that used to flourish on the outskirts of town.

I was one of *them*—working in the apricots in 1952, when I began my organizing career by starting up the first local chapter of the Community Service Organization, a civil rights/civic action group among the Hispanics that grew into the most militant and effective organization of its kind in the country.

Throughout California we registered people to vote and turned them out at the polls. We fought segregation. We battled police brutality—the roughing up of young guys and the breaking and entering without warrants. We opposed the forced removal of Hispanics to make way for urban renewal projects. We fought to improve the poor conditions that were so common in Sal Si Puedes and in other minority neighborhoods: the mean streets and walkways, the lack of street lights and traffic signals, the polluted creeks and horse pastures where kids played, the poor drainage, the overflowing cesspools, the amoebic dysentery.

"Farm labor in this state and nation is one shameful tale after another of hardship and exploitation. The wealth and plenty of California agribusiness has been built atop the suffering of these men, women and children."

Some things change and some things never do.

I understand San Jose recently named its first Hispanic chief of police—Louis Cobarruviaz, a twenty-six-year veteran of the force. And Hispanics have been elected to the city council and the board of supervisors.

My mother still lives on Sharf Avenue. But most of Sal Si Puedes is gone; it was taken years ago when they put in the freeway.

That neighborhood and many of those conditions may no longer exist in San Jose. But as we meet here this evening—only a short drive from this place—farm workers are living in caves and crude shacks, under trees and bridges, and in wretched farm labor camps.

In the Alameda Valley, right here in Santa Clara County, massive sanitation and safety violations were documented at two labor camps—including raw sewage on the ground.

Some workers in labor camps, who can't find space in crowded barracks, sleep out in the open—while farm labor contractors deduct money from their paychecks for *utility* expenses.

Many go without plumbing or electricity. They bathe in irrigation water that is laden with pesticides.

Entire migrant families are homeless—people living out of their cars near fields and vineyards or under stands of trees.

In Santa Clara and Monterey and San Benito counties—in the Central Valley and throughout California—these savage conditions are often the rule and not the exception.

Farm labor in this state and nation is one shameful tale after another of hardship and exploitation. The wealth and plenty of California agribusiness has been built atop the suffering of these men, women and children. It was true when my family and I were migrants in the '30s and '40s. It is true even more so today.

We created the United Farm Workers to battle these injustices; it's what we've done with our lives for the last twenty-nine years. It's why we have conducted strikes and marches and fasts and demonstrations. It's why we are once again asking the public to boycott California table grapes.

But we also recognize that many of the social problems plaguing farm workers stem from the denial of housing that is decent and affordable.

The fastest-growing population in California are the Hispanics.

The neediest segment of the Hispanic population are the farm workers.

What better place to go if you really want to build affordable, entry-level housing for the people who need it the most?

We have. And let me tell you—it *can* be done.

Through a nonprofit, tax-exempt organization—the National Farm Workers Service Center—we've begun an aggressive program to build single-family and rental housing in rural California for low-income farm workers, Hispanics, other minorities, and Anglo families.

Just because it's housing for farm workers and other low-income rural residents doesn't mean it has to be shabby or second-rate. All projects developed by the Service Center come with amenities not generally found in farm-worker housing: wall-to-wall carpeting, central heat and air, two-car garages, large lots, tile roofs, bay windows, garbage disposals, and dishwashers.

We insist on those amenities for the same reasons you and other home builders do: so the houses *we* build will appreciate at the same rate as *other* houses in the community.

Sometimes we've been frustrated by federal restrictions that place limits on these amenities. We're *not* interested in building projects that become instant ghettos. We *don't* accept federal bureaucrats who want to tell us that *our* houses have to be inferior to the houses offered to more *affluent* home-buyers—just because our homes are for farm workers and other low-income families.

Almost all of our projects seek out available state or local financial assistance. Our staff work with local redevelopment agencies to obtain help for land acquisition and infrastructure. We help families quality for modest grants that they often need to get into a home.

Sale prices at our 71-lot subdivision in Parlier, near Fresno, start at $49,900—for four models of three- and four-bedroom homes. At this project, for the first time, low-income families could personalize their homes—for example, by deciding on colors for carpets and paint.

We helped low-income home buyers in Parlier obtain below-market interest rates to lower monthly mortgage payments. In addition, we helped these families qualify for government grants to write down the costs of loans.

Under the state's Farm Worker Grant Program, low-income people who work in agriculture and need money for down payments can qualify for up to $15,000 in grants. With a $15,000 grant, a family that purchased a Service Center home for $49,500 would only need to qualify for a $34,000 mortgage. The state grant program was discontinued, although there is talk about reinstating it for next year.

We built the first single-family subdivision in twenty years in the West Fresno County town of Firebaugh—a 104-lot single-family subdivision with four floor plans and home buyer financial assistance. Most home buyers were local residents. But we also sold to some families from as far away as Oakland and Richmond that were willing to make the daily commute to their jobs.

Our 45-lot subdivision for low-income buyers in Avenal even includes front-yard landscaping.

Our 81-unit apartment complex in Parlier, our 106-unit complex in Fresno, and our 56-unit complex in Tehachapi all serve *very* low- to low-income families, many of them farm workers. In Fresno, ninety percent of our tenants earn far below the median income. Rents are also considerably below average. Yet the amenities, especially in Fresno, are on a par with higher-rent apartments. There are no vacancies.

The Padilla family is a typical example of what the Service Center has been able to achieve. Steve Padilla works in the area's grape and citrus fields. He, his wife and three children used to live in a small, rat- and cockroach-infested two-bedroom apartment. It had no carpeting or central heat and air.

His new residence is an apartment at the Service Center's La Paz Villa Apartments in Parlier. The Padillas live in a three-bedroom apartment with wall-to-wall carpeting, central heat and air, dishwasher and garbage disposal. The rent they pay at La Paz Villa is thirty percent *less* than what they paid for their previous apartment.

Many of the tenants in our apartment projects used to live in garages, labor camps and other substandard housing. A lot of them were affected by last December's freeze. Lack of jobs and a steady income are constant problems.

The Service Center works with its tenants, helping them stay in their housing—even when that means making arrangements for late rent payments.

The labor movement is working to create innovative programs that help working people own their own homes. Under a first-of-its-kind contract negotiated by the Boston Hotel and

Restaurant Employees Union, employers are paying five cents an hour into a joint trust fund. The fund will help hotel workers with new home purchases. Money will go to help make down payments, cover closing expenses or bank costs, or secure more favorable interest rates.

Before the housing trust fund could be set up, Congress had to amend the Taft-Hartley Act of 1947 so that employers could write off their contributions to the fund as tax deductions.

The national AFL-CIO has created the Union Member Mortgage program, which just began operating earlier this year. During the program's first six months, more than 1,200 union members obtained over $100 million in home mortgage financing commitments. More than 70,000 workers have phoned Union Member Mortgage's toll-free numbers for more information.

The program is funding refinancing of high-interest mortgages on present homes, purchases of new homes by union members who are "buying up," and new home purchases by first-time home buyers. It offers down payments as low as five percent, competitive interest rates, and financing through a wholly union-owned bank in New York. It helps first-time buyers by reducing the up-front cash needed to purchase a home.

> ***"Should all people be able to work for the day when they can purchase a home—unless their skin is brown or black, or they work on a farm or in a factory?"***

Housing is not the National Farm Workers Service Center's sole activity. The Service Center has sponsored economic development programs to help rural agricultural-based farm worker communities diversify and expand their tax bases. That, in turn, produces improvements in basic municipal services—such as fire and police protection—as well as new employment opportunities for local residents.

The first and most challenging economic development project was a 10,000-square-foot commercial center in Parlier.

Most of the existing retail in Parlier used to consist of bars and pool halls. There was no place to buy clothes, no neighborhood family-oriented shopping center in town. The commercial project developed by the Service Center features a number of small retailers, including a meat market, clothing store, and sit-down restaurant.

The Service Center is developing another, slightly larger commercial center. It is bringing in a flower shop, pizza parlor, auto parts store, and sit-down café.

Parlier is finally being promoted as a place where families can live and prosper. These economic development projects are changing the reputation of the town; other developers are bringing their own projects on line—they're coming to see Parlier as a place where they can build and be successful.

New housing and commercial projects are planned for farm worker areas in other parts of the state.

We're now working in Hollister with city officials and a nonprofit group representing more than 500 low-income families to develop a 105-lot single-family housing project in that San Benito County community.

A major obstacle to developing affordable housing in the Hollister area is the high cost of land. Land costs in the San Joaquin Valley are around $25,000 per acre. In Hollister, the average cost of land reaches $150,000 an acre.

One of the reasons land costs are being driven up is the high demand for housing created by out-of-town families—especially from Santa Clara and Monterey counties—that are seeking more affordable housing.

Added to the high cost of land are city and school fees, which exceed $14,000 for a 1,200 square-foot house.

These pre-development costs make the construction of affordable housing for low-income families unprofitable for traditional home builders and very difficult even for the nonprofit National Farm Workers Service Center.

Still, we're trying hard to come up with a creative plan that will produce a 105-unit subdivision for farm workers and other low-income people in Hollister.

The BIA has often made the point—quite correctly—that owning your own home is a dream that is being denied to more and more people in California.

Across the country, sixty-four percent of Americans are homeowners. If things continue as they are, the percentage of homeowners in the Bay Area may soon fall below fifty percent.

In today's housing market, only about ten percent of Bay Area residents can afford the median price of a home—which is tagged at $268,000. That means households earning more than $70,000 a year can't afford to buy homes.

Those statistics also mean that low- and moderate-income working-class people in urban communities were long ago frozen out of the home market. Most farm workers and other low-income residents in rural areas don't even have a chance to attain home ownership.

Home ownership has been the path to security and prosperity for tens of millions of people in this country. It is the way working men and women have built up wealth for themselves and their children. It is often what people have to show for years of sweat and sacrifice.

Should owning a home of your own be the dream *all* Americans can work toward—*except* farm workers and Hispanics and other working families, rural or urban?

Should home ownership be *everybody's* right—*except* farm workers and Hispanics and other working families?

Should *all* people be able to work for the day when they can purchase a home—*unless* their skin is brown or black, or they work on a farm or in a factory?

When I got out of the Navy at the end of World War II, home builders were universally respected because of the opportunities they helped bring to a whole generation of Americans. My family, and many others, never achieved home ownership because we were farm workers.

I want future generations of farm workers—the people of the land—to have what too many of us were denied: the right to own a decent home, a home of our own.

We're working toward that goal. I ask you to join us in that effort.

Thank you.

On April 23, 1993, Chávez—who had just ended a six-day fast—died in his sleep while in Arizona on business. His funeral procession, which began a few miles outside Delano and wound past farm fields before ending at the UFW compound in town, attracted some 35,000 mourners from around the world. While the union he left behind never became the nationwide organization he once dreamed of, it does have members in California, Florida, Texas, Arizona, and Washington. Yet it faces a rather uncertain future without its charismatic founder at the helm.

SOURCES

Books

Acuña, Rodolfo, *Occupied America: The Chicano's Struggle Toward Liberation,* Canfield Press, 1972.

Cortes, Carlos E., Arlin I. Ginsburg, Allan W.F. Green, and James A. Turner, *Three Perspectives on Ethnicity in America,* Putnam, 1976.

Daniel, Clete, *Bitter Harvest,* University of California Press, 1981.

Day, Mark, *Forty Acres: César Chávez and the Farm Workers,* Praeger, 1973.

Duffy, Bernard K., and Halford R. Ryan, editors, *American Orators of the Twentieth Century: Critical Studies and Sources,* Greenwood Press, 1987.

Dunne, John Gregory, *Delano,* Farrar, Straus, 1971.

Garcia, F. Chris, editor, *La Causa Politica: A Chicano Politics Reader,* University of Notre Dame Press, 1974.

Hammerback, John C., Richard J. Jensen, and Jose Angel Gutierrez, *A War of Words: Chicano Protest in the 1960s and 1970s,* Greenwood Press, 1985.

Levy, Jacques E., *César Chávez: Autobiography of La Causa,* Norton, 1975.

London, Joan, and Henry Anderson, *So Shall Ye Reap,* Crowell, 1970.

Matthiessen, Peter, *Sal Si Puedes: César Chávez and the New American Revolution,* Random House, 1969.

Meier, Matt S., and Feliciano Rivera, *The Chicanos: A History of Mexican Americans,* Hill & Wang, 1972.

Meister, Dick, and Anne Loftis, *A Long Time Coming: The Struggle to Unionize America's Farm Workers,* Macmillan, 1977.

Taylor, Ronald B., *Chávez and the Farm Workers,* Beacon Press, 1975.

Valdez, Luis, and Stan Steiner, editors, *Aztlan: An Anthology of Mexican American Literature,* Knopf, 1972.

Yinger, Winthrop, *César Chávez: The Rhetoric of Nonviolence,* Exposition Press, 1975.

Periodicals

Catholic Mind: The Monthly Review of Christian Thought, "Saying 'Yes' to Man's Dignity," October, 1975, pp. 43-47.

Christian Century, "Viva La Causa!" August 27, 1969, pp. 115-116; "Tilting with the System: An Interview with César Chávez," February 18, 1970, p. 206.

Detroit Free Press, "Farm Workers' Chávez Is Dead," April 24, 1993, p. 2A.

Grand Rapids Press, "Farm-Worker Organizer, Activist César Chávez, 66, Is Found Dead," April 24, 1993, p. A1; "Chávez Was an Inspiration to Farm Workers," April 25, 1993, p. A14; "Chávez's Last March is 35,000 Strong," April 30, 1993, p. A3; "Farmworker Gains Slide, Union Struggles for Survival Following Death of Chávez," July 25, 1993, p. A4; "United Farm Workers Remember Chávez with 350-Mile March," April 3, 1994, p. E2.

Hispanic, "Chávez Legacy," June, 1993, p. 14.

Look, "Nonviolence Still Works," April 1, 1969, p. 52.

Nation, "César's Ghost," July 26/August 2, 1993, pp. 130-135.

New Republic, "The Future of the United Farm Workers: Chávez Against the Wall," December 7, 1974, p. 13.

Newsweek, "César's Triumph," March 21, 1977, pp. 70-72; "A Secular Saint of the '60s," May 3, 1993, p. 68.

New York Times, "César Chávez, 66, Organizer of Union for Migrants, Dies," April 24, 1993.

People, "César Chávez Breaks His Longest Fast as His Followers Pray for an End to the Grapes of Wrath," September 5, 1988, pp. 52-54; "His Harvest Was Dignity," May 10, 1993, p. 71.

Time, "The Little Strike That Grew into *La Causa,*" July 4, 1979, p. 16.

Western Journal of Speech Communication, "The Rhetorical Worlds of César Chávez and Reies Tijerina," summer, 1980, pp. 166-176.

Dennis Chávez

1888–1962

Spanish American member of the U.S. Senate

The first Hispanic American to win a seat in the United States Senate, Dennis Chávez served his country and the Democratic party with distinction for nearly thirty years. Of vital interest to him during his long political career was the struggle against intolerance. During the 1940s and 1950s, he was one of the chief architects and supporters of fair employment practices legislation, which sought to eliminate racial, ethnic, and religious discrimination in the workplace. In Chávez's view, the implications of this fight went far beyond the borders of the United States into the realm of foreign policy. As he once declared to an audience in New York City, "World peace cannot become a reality unless men are able to exercise their basic rights without discrimination because of race or creed."

A native of New Mexico who was extremely proud of his Spanish heritage, Dionisio (later anglicized to "Dennis") Chávez was born on ranchland that had been in his family since 1769. The Chávezes were very poor, and young Dionisio was forced to drop out of school after completing the eighth grade so that he could go to work to help support his seven brothers and sisters. He continued reading and studying on his own, however, dreaming of the day when he might be able to follow in the footsteps of his idol, Thomas Jefferson.

In 1916, a window of opportunity opened for Chávez when he was hired to work as a Spanish-language interpreter in the U.S. Senate campaign of New Mexico politician A.A. Jones. This assignment later helped him secure a senate clerkship in Washington, D.C., where he decided to make the most of his time in the nation's capital. Although he had never even attended high school, Chávez passed a special entrance exam that allowed him to enter Georgetown University, from which he obtained a law degree in 1920. He then returned home to New Mexico with an eye toward launching his own political career.

Not long after setting up a law practice in Albuquerque, Chávez ran for and won a seat in New Mexico's House of Representatives. He served in that body throughout the 1920s until winning election to the U.S. House of Representatives in 1930 and again in 1932. In 1934, he made his first bid for the U.S. Senate. Although he lost in a close and especially bitter campaign, Chávez was appointed to the seat a year later after the man who had defeated him was killed in a plane crash. He won election to the post in his own right in 1936 and was returned to office four more times over the next twenty-six years, serving for most of that time as the Senate's only Hispanic American member. There he championed the interests of Mexican Americans, Native Americans, and Puerto Ricans in particular; he also took the lead in fostering better relations with Latin American nations.

In general, Chávez's reputation was that of a quiet and soft-spoken man who rarely engaged in debate with his colleagues—except when the subject was discrimination. This was especially true during the World War II years, when he sided with President Franklin Roosevelt's efforts to make jobs in the defense industry available to all regardless of race, ethnic background, or religion. In 1941, Roosevelt established the Fair Employment Practices Committee (FEPC) to monitor the training and hiring policies of companies and unions involved in defense production. Although its efforts to eliminate discrimination and segregation were severely hampered by a lack of funds, inadequate staffing, limited enforcement capabilities, and strong resistance across the South, the FEPC nevertheless represented a significant step in the ongoing battle for justice for America's minority citizens.

Chávez was one of the FEPC's most ardent supporters, and in May 1945, he gained subcommittee approval of a bill (S. 101) that would have created a permanent Fair Employment Practices Commission (also known by the acronym FEPC) to carry on the work of its predecessor as the nation shifted to a peacetime economy. A number of Southern senators delayed action on the bill, allowing it to languish throughout the rest of the year. A frustrated Chávez continued his lobbying efforts, however, urging Americans not to turn their backs on those who had risked their lives defending freedom and democracy so that all might share *equally in the victory. He shared his thoughts on the subject of intolerance and the implications of allowing it to flourish in a speech he delivered in Chicago on December 1, 1945. Two days later, Chávez stood before his Senate colleagues and asked for permission to enter his remarks into the* Congressional Record. *The following is thus reprinted from the* Congressional Record Appendix, *79th Congress, 1st Session, Volume 91, Part 13, U.S. Government Printing Office, 1945.*

Mr. Chairman, distinguished guests, ladies, and gentlemen, of all the issues confronting our country today, the issue of racial and religious discrimination is at once the most neglected and the most critical. There is no victory over Hitler and Tojo which by itself will erase the injustice of economic discrimination practiced against the minority groups among our people. Full employment without fair employment means the fastening of religious and racial minorities to the bottom rung of the economic ladder regardless of their education, abilities, and skills. Unemployment compensation will not break down the barrier of prejudice. There is nothing in the so-called GI bill of rights which will protect the returning two millions of minority veterans from the pattern of job discrimination which exists in this country.

We in this nation stand at a crossroads in history. Either we will take the road which will lead us past another goalpost of human progress or we will be forced into the path riddled with the pitfalls of human hatreds which led Europe into World War II. We shall not be permitted to stand still. Whichever road we take will be for you, the people, to choose.

Every great crisis in American history has thus far had the moral result of increased protection and increased liberty for the individual. This country's first great crisis—the American Revolution—gave us political and religious independence. The crisis which was the Civil War gave us freedom from bondage for all men

Dennis Chávez

and women. Out of the crisis of the First World War came women's suffrage. Out of this World War II, with all its terrifying implications, comes: What?

This present-day crisis must at least give us true democracy, and the kernel of that is equality of economic opportunity. We must pluck down from the thin air the Atlantic Charter's freedom from fear and freedom from want and ground those freedoms not on the government dole, but upon the right to work and the opportunity to work for every man and every woman according to his skill, his experience, and his ability.

This is no new ideal in the development of American life. It is common knowledge that the struggle for that ideal began when the first paths were cut through the virgin wilderness by the first settlers—victims of religious and economic persecution themselves—who came to these shores. The Pilgrims in Massachusetts, the English Catholics of Maryland, the French Huguenots of the Carolinas, the Scotch Presbyterians of Georgia, the Quakers of Pennsylvania, the Jews, the Irish, the Dutch, the Germans, and even the poverty-stricken debtors of the English prisons came to this country as to a refuge, to a haven of new, unshackled opportunity.

The translation into law of the new concepts of religious and economic liberty was not easily achieved any more than the enactment of fair-employment legislation will be easily won. Rigid religious conformity was woven into the law of some of the separate colonies, and rebellious sects were driven forth to found new colonies where religious freedom could flourish. At one point, Catholics and Jews were not allowed to vote. For many years people without property were denied the franchise. But the ideal of freedom was not to be downed, and when the crisis which precipitated the American Revolution came about, the cornerstone of liberty upon which our country was founded was given deathless voice in the Declaration of Independence:

> *We hold these truths to be self-evident, that all men are created equal, that they are endowed by their Creator with certain inalienable rights, that among these are life, liberty, and the pursuit of happiness. That to secure these rights, governments are instituted among men, deriving their just powers from among the consent of the governed. That whenever any form of government becomes destructive of these ends, it is the right of the people to alter or to abolish it, and to institute new government, laying its foundation on such principles and organizing its powers in such form, as to them shall seem most likely to effect their safety and happiness.*

These words of the great leader of humanistic democracy, Thomas Jefferson, have captured the philosophy of the American ideal. Indeed, they are reechoed and restated in the American creed—the Constitution's Bill of Rights. I often think, humbly, of the prophetic recognition Jefferson gave to the three basics from which this country draws so much of its strength—political independence, religious tolerance, and public education—when I remember the simple epitaph he ordered engraved upon his tombstone: "Here was buried Thomas Jefferson, author of the Declaration of Independence, of the Statute of Virginia for Religious Freedom, and Father of the University of Virginia."

The people's determination to cling to this heritage of the protection of human rights under law was challenged in the ratification of the Constitution itself when it was discovered that that original document failed to guarantee them. It was only after amendments, constituting the so-called Bill of Rights, were agreed to that the Constitution was finally adopted. It is no accident that the first of these amendments pledged this government's protection of the individual's freedom of worship, freedom of speech and of press, and "the right of the people peaceably to assemble and to petition the Government for a redress of grievance." Need I remind you that it is under that right you are now here assembled?

These were rights such as the Old World had never known, and the lack of which blocked the forward march of civilization. As this country flourished and grew strong on roots fed by all its people, in other lands struggling people took them for their own and mankind moved up and onward. Nevertheless, the freedom-loving people of this nation were not yet satisfied. They saw the horror, the injustice, and the inhumanity of the institution of slavery and rose against it. Then one of them, a Kentucky rail splitter, an Illinois and Indiana farmer, a country lawyer who was way ahead of his time, came and enunciated to the whole world that this country could not exist "half slave and half free." A great war which rocked the new nation was fought between the citizens of this country to decide that question. The answer was written in the thirteenth, fourteenth, and fifteenth amendments to our Constitution—this nation's second bill of rights.

These rights are now in our care to preserve and to strengthen for our children, and our children's children. How well our citizenry appreciated those rights and those freedoms was proved by their willingness to fight for them when they became endangered. Even during the memory of the living, two great wars have been fought. And while those wars were fought, it was proved conclusively that on the battlefield where suffering takes place, where men are mutilated, where men die, you do not see the attempts that are made in normal times within our own country to set aside those principles for which the soldier and the sailor have suffered.

"Even now, the ugly head of racial and religious prejudice shows itself too vividly to be ignored."

No discrimination was shown by the Japanese enemy in his treatment of the Negro or the Jew or the Mexican or the so-called Anglo-Saxon stock—he murdered them all irrespective of their religion, color, or politics. On the beachheads of Tarawa, Okinawa, or Guam there was no discrimination. Along the sandbanks of Anzio no discrimination was shown by the German or any other common enemy. But here in our own country by people who should know better, and do know better, discrimination at times becomes rampant. Even now, the ugly head of racial and religious prejudice shows itself too vividly to be ignored.

To outlaw the discriminatory employment practices stemming from racial and religious bigotry is the new task which must now engage us. We have seen, in wartime, the effectiveness of a Fair Employment Practice Committee. It gave hope and courage to those on the battlefields and new opportunities for those at home to test their mettle on the production lines. Aircraft plants were persuaded to upgrade Mexican-Americans; white workers to cooperate with colored workers. Government agencies accepted in new positions qualified minority workers referred by Civil Service. Trade unions policed their own nondiscrimination policy among their locals. Employers rearranged work schedules to permit Sabbatarians and orthodox Jews opportunity to observe religious customs. The theory of fair employment became a successful practice.

For that reason, some of us in Congress have determined that now we must have a basic law to carry out the purport of the Declaration of Independence and the Constitution. That is why Senate bill 101 and House bill 2232 were introduced. The bill to establish a permanent Fair Employment Practice Commission is designed to have but one function—to eliminate unfair employment practices based on discrimination on grounds of race, color, creed, national origin or ancestry. Under the bill, management continues free to set its own hiring, training, and upgrading practices: to adjust its internal plant policy; and to discharge according to any standard it may adopt so long as there is no arbitrary discrimination because of race, color, creed, national origin, or ancestry. In the same way, organized labor continues free to manage its internal affairs according to its own lights, except that it cannot deny any of the advantages or opportunities of union organization and collective bargaining to any person because of race, color, creed, national origin, or ancestry. The bill covers all federal agencies, firms having federal contracts, and firms in or affecting interstate commerce having six or more employees. The agency cannot enforce its own orders, but it is empowered to go to the courts to request enforcement when firms or unions coming under its jurisdiction refuse to discontinue discriminatory employment policies.

Of course, there are those who say, "Why not just investigate discrimination and educate those who persist in erecting barriers of prejudice?" But experience has shown that education is not enough. Even on the basic principles of nature and the Mosaic laws, murder is denounced, but nevertheless, every civilized nation in the world has laws against murder. We are instructed to love our fellow men, but we still take the precaution of establishing laws to protect them from fraud or violence.

It was my privilege to serve as chairman of the subcommittee which held hearings on S. 101. Representatives of every faith, every race, every walk of life testified on this measure. I think I lean to the side of conservatism when I estimate that sixty million Americans were represented in those hearings. That is an amazing expression of popular interest in any legislation. To me, the most encouraging thing that was developed at these hearings was that the representatives of all the different faiths of our American people—Protestant, Catholic, and Jewish—have been unanimous in coming before the Senate committee to plead for the enactment of the bill to establish a permanent Fair Employment Practice Commission with enforcement powers. The position of the church leadership on this question is very clear. So, too, has been the supporting role played by the two leading houses of labor—the American Federation of Labor and the Congress of Industrial Organizations.

After those hearings, the Senate Committee on Education and Labor recommended S. 101 to the full Senate for favorable action by a 12-to-6 vote. This bill is now high on the Senate calendar ready for debate and vote. It is also on the president's must-list of legislation, I think I am safe in saying that the majority of the Senate body is favorably disposed toward this legislation. What, then, keeps the bill from the Senate floor? Unfortunately, there are men in the Senate who are adamant and, I believe, mistaken in their opposition to the enactment of this measure. These senators, recognizing that the tide of human progress has out-paced them, would try to stem its onrush by the extreme tactic of filibustering the bill. To meet that kind of opposition we need not only a majority of senators to support the bill—we must have, in addition, the cloture vote of two-thirds of the entire Senate to successfully counterattack the threatened filibuster.

Because of the nature of these parliamentary obstacles, it is my considered opinion that only by efforts of an alert and vigilant people will we be able to get successful action on this legislation. In other words, this is the time to let your elected representatives in the Senate know of your wishes regarding their actions both on the bill and on cloture. The Senate is made up of men who will understand your concern once they are informed and who always give a sympathetic ear to the voting public. If there is one thing which is certain about the outcome of this struggle for equal job opportunity, it is that its success depends upon the people. This is a people's bill and a people's fight.

What we want most now is action. We know that practices growing out of discrimination and intolerance, which are thoroughly un-American, must not be allowed to continue. The American way of protecting human rights against such practices is by law. We have the backing of our president. We have the commitment of the Republican Party. Therefore, whether you are a Democrat or a Republican, you have the right and the responsibility to remind your leadership that these promises are yet to be fulfilled. You have it in your hands to get such a law. Make your voices heard.

In doing this you will be promoting Americanism. You will perform a service to your country by eradicating an evil that is foreign and un-American, an evil that smacks of the racial theories of Hitler and Goebbels and not of the four freedoms of the Atlantic Charter. You will be performing further service to our country by thus furnishing proof to fellow peoples throughout the world that we mean to live the letter and the spirit of our American creed and that our nation is sincere in championing the cause of the democracies and the rights of man.

We have just fought a great war to a successful conclusion. It would be a national disaster and humiliation if those who have fought valiantly abroad to defend the freedom and dignity of the individual against racial barbarism should now come home to find that the bringing of peace meant a wiping out of the antidiscrimination policy that we achieved in wartime. Today we stand embarked upon the task of reconversion for peace. Shall we reconvert to racial prejudice, national bigotry, and religious discrimination, or shall we reconvert to full peacetime employment based on the American principle of equality of human rights?

Let me give you an example of what I mean. During this war, 245 Congressional Medals of

Honor—the highest honor our nation can give its war heroes—were awarded. Six of these were given to servicemen who in ordinary times would be referred to as "these Mexicans." They were Joe Martinez, who died from Japanese bullets at Attu; Ysmael Vellegas, who gave his life at Luzon; Jose Calugas, who distinguished himself at Bataan; Joe Lopez, who saved his entire company in Belgium; Cleto Rodriguez, who with one other overcame three hundred Japanese soldiers at Manila; and Macario Garcia, who singlehanded[ly] assaulted two enemy machine-gun emplacements in Germany. Honors and awards of every description—the Distinguished Flying Cross, the Purple Heart, the Silver Star, the Air Medal, etc.—were given to members of all the minorities who make up the American people. Would it be their just due, when these heroes apply for a job, to have them turned down on account of the accident of their birth or their religious belief?

Do you remember the timeless words uttered by Lincoln at Gettysburg at the close of the Civil War? Let me repeat just two sentences to you, for they epitomize the spirit in which we must put our shoulders to the wheel if we are to move forward:

> *It is rather for us (the living) to be here dedicated to the great task remaining before us—that from these honored dead we take increased devotion to that cause for which they gave the last full measure of devotion—that we here highly resolve that these dead shall not had died in vain—that this nation, under God, shall have a new birth of freedom—and that government of the people, by the people, for the people shall not perish from the earth.*

Finally, on January 17, 1946, Chávez succeeded in introducing S. 101, the Fair Employment Practice Act, on the Senate floor. Again, he faced resistance from several Southern colleagues, among them James Eastland of Mississippi, who proposed sending the bill back to committee. In the discussion that ensued, Chávez offered a passionate response to critics of S. 101 and tried his best to push for immediate consideration. His remarks that day, including some pointed exchanges with fellow senators, are reprinted here from the Congressional Record, *79th Congress, 2nd Session, Volume 92, Part 1, U.S. Government Printing Office, 1946.*

Mr. Chávez: Two or three weeks ago the country heard the message of the president of United States. Regardless of what some Democrats may think, the country heard the president's message, and in it the president called attention to legislation which should be enacted. Among the legislation which the president had in mind was fair-employment-practice legislation, and in simple American words he definitely insisted that the Congress at least consider Senate bill 101, which has for its purpose the adoption of fair-employment practices.

One of the fine characteristics of the American is fair play. So far as Senate bill 101 is concerned, what other legislation of the type or kind which the president of the United States recalled to the mind of Congress and the nation could the Senate now take up and consider? Is any labor legislation before the Senate? No; it is in committee. Is any minimum-wage legislation before the Senate? No; it is in committee. Is any measure relating to the proposed loan to England before the Senate? No; it is in committee. Every other piece of legislation which has been suggested by the president is in committee. But here is a measure which is ready for consideration. Do we wish to waste the time of the Senate? I am in favor of this bill. If the Senate wishes to kill it, well and good. But I object to any maneuvering to keep this body from taking action by voting either "yea" or "nay" on proposed legislation, especially legislation of the character which has been recommended by the president of the United States, which was talked about and endorsed by the late President Roosevelt, which was approved by President Truman, which was discussed by him in his message to the people of the country, and which also was endorsed by both the great political parties of the United States. A year ago in June the Republicans came out pointblank to the effect that "We, the Republicans, are in favor of fair employment practice legislation." Perhaps, some were trying to "cover up." I have some complaints about Democrats, too; and I say God pity the Democratic senators who now are chairmen of committees unless the Democratic party keeps itself liberal and votes to enact legislation such as that proposed by the bill providing for the adoption of fair-employment practices. I know that unless we do so, the people will complain, as they will have a right to do, and the people will be resentful, as they will have a right to be, and the people will vote for a change. Unless a majority of the Democratic members of the Senate vote for this legislation, all these chairmanships, which now are in good hands, will be completely changed. So we see that the question is a two-sided one.

The main point is that fair-employment practices should be adopted in this country. What is wrong with fair-employment practices? We love to talk about liberality and about saving the world. We sent our boys to Europe, to China, and to the Pacific. The only decoration which thousands of them received was a white cross surmounting a grave. So we should look at the record; we should look at the casualty lists. On them there will be found the name of McGinty, an Irishman; the name of Michael, an Armenian; the name of Levine, a Jew; the name of Chávez, a Mexican; and the names of many others. But, despite that, some persons object to legislation by means of which justice would be done to the relatives of those who paid the supreme sacrifice in the war and generally to the American people who have made so many sacrifices.

So, Mr. President, what is wrong with the fair-employment-practice bill? The bill does not provide that because a man's name is Levine or Petachelli, he is entitled to a job. However, the bill does provide that a man cannot be kept from having a job because his name is Petachelli, or Garcia, or something else. It is most regrettable that some persons think that it was all well and good to use such men and call upon them to make the supreme sacrifice in foreign fields, to land on a deadly beach at Okinawa or Guam or elsewhere, but that they are not good enough to receive equal treatment in our country. I say to my colleagues that they had better place themselves in the correct position. Those boys did not die in vain. We must make sure that it can never be said that our boys who went all over the world and conquered many other nations in order to achieve freedom and victory, died in vain. The Democratic party owes them too much, the Congress owes them too much, ever to permit that to be said. Believe me, Mr. President, the American people are fair and just, and they wish to act fairly and justly. There is no reason why the fair-employment-practices bill should not be enacted. Both parties promised it.

Mr. President, what about those promises?

"We must make sure that it can never be said that our boys who went all over the world and conquered many other nations in order to achieve freedom and victory, died in vain."

Were they supposed to be made but not to be kept? I went to the convention which was held in Chicago. The senator from Mississippi and other senators went to Chicago, each to the convention of his own party. The conventions made pronouncements to the American people and upon the basis of those pronouncements the people had faith in what was promised. They either believed us or they did not believe us. They believed the Democratic party at the last election and they elected us as their representatives. We have a certain responsibility to perform. When the Democratic Convention acted in Chicago the position it took was good enough for me. On this question I do not think the Democratic party at Chicago was quite so honest as was the Republican party. If senators think that the proposed legislation is political, I assure them that it is not. It is not being offered in the interest of the Democratic party or in the interest of the Republican party. It is being offered in the interest of America, and in the interest of fairness and decency. If the Constitution is worth anything, if the Declaration of Independence is worth anything, if the boys who died on the field of battle did not die in vain, fair-employment practices are correct and necessary.

Mr. President, I will read from the report of the committee on this bill. I ask the Senate to listen to it and then tell me if there is anything wrong with this type of legislation, if there is any reason why all senators should not vote "yea" or "nay" on the proposition. The report begins as follows:

> *The Committee on Education and Labor, to whom were referred the bill (S. 101) to prohibit discrimination in employment because of race, creed, color, national origin, or ancestry, and the bill (S. 459) to establish a Fair Employment Practice Commission and to aid in eliminating discrimination in employment because of race, creed, color, national origin, or ancestry, after holding hearings and giving consideration to the two bills, report favorably on the former of these bills (S. 101) and recommend that it do pass.*

After listening for weeks and weeks to testimony both in behalf of and against the bill, an outstanding legislative committee which had been created by this body reported the bill favorably to the Senate.

I continue reading:

> *Inasmuch as this bill embodies all the objectives of S. 459 and also embodies powers of judicial enforcement and judicial review which the committee considers essential to any effective legislation in this field and which are entirely lacking in S. 459, no separate report on S. 459 is deemed necessary, and the following analysis is limited to the provisions of S. 101.*

What is the purpose of the bill?

> *This bill is designed to eliminate discrimination in all employment relations which fall under the jurisdiction or control of the federal government. It forbids discrimination in (a) federal employment—*

Is that fair? There are many governmental agencies in the city of Albuquerque. Is it fair for them to employ Grace Jones and refuse to employ Mary Smith? Is it fair to employ Edna So-and-So and refuse to employ the Antonelli girl? Is it fair to employ a girl who is supposed to be white and of Anglo-Saxon extraction and not employ a girl who might have a Jewish name?

Mr. Eastland: Mr. President, will the senator yield?

Mr. Chávez: Not for the moment. Is it fair, Mr. President, to employ only those who happen to be of one racial extraction? I do not find anything in the Constitution which says that only those whose ancestors happened to be from the British Isles may be Americans. The Constitution says nothing at all like that. I have known some pretty good Americans who were not of British extraction, and when the country was in the midst of an emergency, when the shooting started, we found the Levines, the Gallaghers, the Negroes, the Assyrians, the Jews, and others doing their part in the war effort.

Mr. Eastland: Mr. President, will the senator yield?

Mr. Chávez: Not at the moment. I am sorry. Very well, Mr. President, I continue reading:

> *It forbids discrimination in (a) federal employment, (b) employment under governmental contracts—*

Let us say that a large corporation receives a contract from the federal government. This bill would prohibit such corporation from being unfair to any person because of race, creed, national origin, or ancestry.

The purposes of the bill are outlined further as follows:

> *(c) employment in activities affecting interstate or foreign commerce which are subject to federal control in respect to labor relations. It applies equally to employers and to unions, forbidding discrimination by unions against members, employees, or employers.*

Mr. Johnston of South Carolina: Mr. President, will the senator yield?

The Presiding Officer: Does the senator from New Mexico yield to the senator from South Carolina?

Mr. Chávez: I yield for a question.

Mr. Johnston of South Carolina: How many persons does the senator employ in his office?

Mr. Chávez: I employ the full limit.

Mr. Johnston of South Carolina: Does the senator employ colored help in his office?

Mr. Chávez: I do not happen to have any colored employees.

Mr. Johnston of South Carolina: Does not the senator believe that if he employed colored help it would result in the creation of trouble in his office?

Mr. Chávez: I do not know whether it would

or not. However, I may say that I employ Mexicans, Italians, Greeks, and also Jews.

Mr. Johnston of South Carolina. If employers were forced to employ, for example, colored persons and require them to work alongside white persons, does not the senator believe that it would cause trouble?

Mr. Chávez: I do not know whether it would or not.

Mr. Johnston of South Carolina: If this bill were enacted into law, I assert that it would cause trouble, and perhaps riots right here in Washington and in other cities.

Mr. Chávez: I do not believe that it would cause any trouble.

Mr. Eastland: Mr. President, will the senator yield?

Mr. Chávez: I yield for a question.

Mr. Eastland: If I understand correctly the senator's bill, it provides that no discrimination may be exercised because of race, creed, or color.

Mr. Chávez: The senator is correct.

Mr. Eastland: In other words, the bill would provide for a certain number of jobs in this country to be held by persons who were Jews.

Mr. Chávez: It would not do that.

Mr. Eastland: It would prevent discrimination against them.

Mr. Chávez: The purpose of the bill is to prevent discrimination. However, the fact that a person who may be a Negro, for example, goes to a factory seeking employment, does not of itself entitle him to a job. All the bill does is to provide that he shall not be turned down merely because he happens to be a Negro.

Mr. Eastland: If this bill were enacted into law, the American government could go to a manufacturer and tell him that he must give employment to a certain number of Negroes. Am I correct?

Mr. Chávez: No; the bill does not contain anything like that at all. The bill would not become effective until after the manufacturer or the union had engaged in acts of discrimination.

Mr. Eastland: But the manufacturer would be punished, would he not, if he did not give employment to a Negro?

Mr. Chávez: All the bill provides is that if a Negro, a Jew, or a person of some other racial extraction goes to a manufacturer to seek employment, he may not be turned down because of his color, race, or religion.

Mr. Eastland: If the Congress of the United States has authority to say that no person shall be discriminated against in employment because of race, creed, or color, does not the senator believe that the Congress also has the constitutional authority to say that persons may be discriminated against because of race, creed, or color?

Mr. Chávez: That they may be discriminated against?

Mr. Eastland: Yes.

Mr. Chávez: I do not believe so. I do not think that the rights of people can be taken away from them merely because Congress happens to say so. We may create rights under the Constitution, but we cannot deprive anyone of his fundamental rights under the Constitution.

Mr. Eastland: Will the senator refer to the section of the Constitution which provides anything with reference to discrimination because of race, creed, or color?

Mr. Chávez: No; the Constitution is definite in the creation of rights. Those rights are enhanced by legislation in order to carry out the purpose of the Constitution. But, as a matter of fact, the rights come from the Constitution. What we do, as members of the Congress of the United States, must be within the limits of the Constitution.

Mr. Eastland: Does not the senator believe that under the Constitution an employer, as a contractor, has the right to contract with whomever he desires to engage as an employee in his business?

Mr. Chávez: I think he has.

Mr. Eastland: If that be true, then this bill is unconstitutional.

Mr. Chávez: Why?

Mr. Eastland: Because it interferes with the freedom of contract by the employer.

Mr. Chávez: That is a question of opinion. I believe so much in the Constitution, I am so devoted to it that I want it to apply to every human in this country. I do not want it to apply only to New Mexico. I want it to apply to New York, to Vermont, and even to Mississippi. I want it to apply there, too.

Mr. Eastland: It does apply to Mississippi. Mr. President, I understood that there would be some Communists—I read it in the *Daily Worker*—down from New York today, and I see the galleries are infested with them. If this is an American measure, it should be discussed before Americans in the galleries.

Mr. Chávez: It is going to be discussed—

Mr. Eastland: And not before a group of Communists who come to Washington and attempt to stampede the Senate of the United States into destroying the Constitution of our country.

Mr. Chávez: Mr. President, I do not know the make-up of the guests of this body. I do not know whether they are Communists, Socialists, Mississippi Democrats, or New Mexico Democrats.

Mr. Eastland: Mr. President, I referred to what I saw in the *Daily Worker*, which is the mouthpiece of the Communists.

Mr. Chávez: I do not know any Communists, but personally I am becoming tired of hearing men who are merely interested in human beings and in human rights accused of being Communists. In order not to be classed as a Communist, probably one would have to be satisfied with a wage of $15 or so a month. Then he would not be called a Communist; he would be an American. The guests of the Senate seem to me to have been behaving fairly well. I do not know whether they are on my side or the other side, nor do I care.

Mr. Aiken: Mr. President—

The Presiding Officer (Mr. McClellan in the chair): Does the senator from New Mexico yield to the senator from Vermont?

Mr. Chávez: I yield.

Mr. Aiken: I should like first to ask the senator from New Mexico whether he does not know that it is customary in some quarters to call a person a Communist if nothing else wrong with him can be found.

Mr. Chávez: That is correct.

Mr. Aiken: If he disagrees with the name-caller.

Mr. Chávez: I have been fighting for the so-called underprivileged all my days, because I was one of them. I was reared in that atmosphere, and I am proud of the chance I had in America under the government of the United States, and I want my fellow beings to have the same chance I had.

[Following some additional comments by Senator Aiken explaining that S. 101 would in no way require employers to hire a certain number of minorities, Chávez resumed his speech.]

Mr. Chávez: Mr. President, I read further from the report:

A board of five members, to be appointed by the president, with Senate ratification, and to be known as the Fair Employment Practice Commission, is created to administer the act. The federal courts are empowered, after appropriate judicial hearings, to enforce "cease and desist" orders found to have been properly issued by the Commission. The progress of the war to date—

This report was submitted before the war ended—

The progress of the war to date has focused world attention on the miracle of American war production, which, despite all obstacles and difficulties, speedily outstripped the war production of all the rest of the world. The United States could not have thus established itself as the "arsenal of democracy" if we had not adopted a national policy of full utilization of manpower without discrimination because of race, creed, color, national origin, or ancestry. We cannot afford to return, after the war, to a situation in which efficient workers are separated from their machines and condemned to unemployment and the manifold social evils which grow out of unemployment merely because of the color of their skin, their religion, or their ancestry. Several states have already enacted legislation to protect minorities within their borders. The federal government, in its own sphere, can do no less.

I do not care who gets the credit for passing the bill. I believe so thoroughly in its merits that I would be willing to pass it with Republican votes and let them get the credit. As I have heretofore stated, the bill is not intended to serve the Republican party or the Democratic party. It is intended to serve everyone in the United States, to insure justice and fair play. I read further from the report:

The federal government must not shrink from its responsibility in its own employment policies and in those fields of private employment which are constitutionally subject to federal control.

S. 101 is designed to promote in peace the same national harmony and efficiency we have achieved in war; to prevent, in the reconversion and postwar readjustment period—

We were trying to get ready before the war ended for the reconversion period—

to prevent, in the reconversion and postwar readjustment period, fears and injustices which led to mob violence and race riots in the years following World War I.

In my opinion the committee earned the

gratitude and the appreciation of the country for giving time and attention and thought in an attempt to avoid such problems as arose after the last war. Does anyone want race riots in St. Louis? Does anyone want a white man shooting a Negro, or a Negro shooting an Italian, or an Italian shooting someone else? I think it is our duty to pass legislation of such a character as will prevent that kind of condition.

I read further from the report:

To remove a serious obstacle to friendly relations with certain of the United Nations who have long been sensitive to the treatment accorded people of similar origin in this country; to give effect to our declarations for freedom from want and freedom from fear; to raise the standard of living and purchasing power of our people.

Because I happen to have been rather fortunate, and when I go home I have a fairly good meal, or, at any rate, plenty to eat, it does not make me happy to reflect that possibly there are thousands and millions throughout the country who do not have anything to eat. Others may feel happy, others may be content when there are poor people in this country as a result of discrimination. I cannot be contented with such a condition. It is not American. I read further from the report:

And finally, to confound our enemies who hope by dividing us class by class, race by race, group by group, to vitiate the victory that is at hand and to lay the basis for World War III.

Hitler believed in discrimination. We know what happened. He carried it to its finality. He believed in a superior race. He believed in a superior people and the power of might and dictatorship. I believe in the law. I prefer due process of law to paying tribute to any individual in this country.

I read further from the committee report:

Because we all subscribe to these objectives, it should be possible to approach this problem without political partisanship. The Republican Party, in its 1944 platform, proclaimed—

And this proclamation was made to the citizen who on election day would go to the polls and express his opinion as a free man—

We pledge the establishment by federal legislation of a permanent Fair Employment Practice Committee.

That, Mr. President, is what the Republican party said. I am proud of an American like Governor Dewey who took that pledge to heart, and notwithstanding he could contribute nothing to having enacted a federal law on the subject, he has contributed his share toward establishing a fair employment practice law in the State of New York. He did that, Mr. President. More power to him as an American.

I read further from the committee report.

Its standard-bearer, Governor Dewey, in his speech at Buffalo on October 31, 1944, announced: "We shall establish the Fair Employment Practice Committee as a permanent agency with full legal authority."

Let us now go to our side, the Democratic side. Where did we, the majority, who have the responsibility to the American people at the moment, stand?

Mr. Overton: Mr. President, will the senator yield to me for a question?

The Presiding Officer: Does the senator from New Mexico yield to the Senator from Louisiana?

Mr. Chávez: For a question, yes.

Mr. Overton: The senator hardly expects, does he, that the Republican party, which from the days of the War Between the States up to the present time, has been a true-hearted friend of the Negro, would take any other position than that taken by Mr. Dewey, as candidate for president of the United States?

Mr. Chávez: I do not know what were the motives of the members of the Republican party, but they certainly pledged themselves to the establishment by federal legislation of a permanent Fair Employment Practice Committee. Let us find out what our side did.

Mr. Overton: Before the Senator does that, let me ask him: Is it not passing strange that the Democratic party, whose strength and whose success in national politics is dependent upon the vote of the South, should take a contrary position?

Mr. Chávez: Of course, I do not try to approach and analyze this particular matter in that manner. I will say that to me the Negro is incidental, to me the Jew is incidental, to me the Irish are incidental. I am trying to approach the question only from the American point of view. To me it is not a question of racial origin; to me the question is: Are they Americans?

Mr. Overton: I will help the senator approach the question from that point of view.

Mr. Eastland: Mr. President, will the senator from New Mexico yield to me so I may ask the senator from Louisiana a question?

Mr. Chávez: I yield.

Mr. Eastland: Does not the senator from Louisiana think that the Negro voter makes a grave mistake in voting the Democratic ticket?

Mr. Overton: I certainly think so. I think that for a short term of political advantage the Negro made a very bad bargain. I think the Negro ought to have stood by, and I think the Negro today ought to stand by, the great party which has been the Negro's friend from the day of the Emancipation Proclamation by Abraham Lincoln up to the present time. I believe the Negro made a mistake when he yielded his friendship for the party which had stood by him through thick and thin in return for the aid which has been given to him during the last few years.

Mr. Eastland: The senator does not think the Democratic party is friendly to the Negro, does he?

Mr. Overton: Certainly not the backbone of the Democratic party.

Mr. Chávez: Mr. President, possibly—

Mr. Eastland: Mr. President—

Mr. Chávez: Mr. President, I have the floor. I refuse to yield at the moment. The fact that the Negro has voted the Democratic party in the last few elections made it possible to have such senators as our friends, the senators from Pennsylvania (Mr. Guffey and Mr. Myers), our friend the senator from Illinois (Mr. Lucas), our friend the senator from Indiana (Mr. Willis), and senators from other states. Were it not for the fact that the Negroes voted for them and that the Lucases and the Chávezes and Myers and the Guffeys were elected, so our party became the majority party, I am afraid the chairmanships of the standing committees of the Senate would be found to be in the possession of senators on the other side of the aisle.

Mr. Overton: Mr. President, will the senator yield to me?

Mr. Chávez: Yes.

Mr. Overton: In other words, if the senators from doubtful states who required the Negro vote in order that they might be elected to and maintain their seats in the Senate had not pursued the course they followed, the Democratic party would have remained what it ought to be, the white man's party?

Mr. Chávez: We were the white man's party for many years. From the Civil War up to the time of the election of Cleveland we were a white man's party but we did not have a president. Then as I recall, from 1896 until 1912 we also were a white man's party, but there was a Republican in the White House. The majority of senators were members of the party on the other side of the chamber. I am glad the Negroes can vote. Let me say to my friends that if the Negroes are good enough to die for their country, if they are good enough to be allowed to serve their country, to feel in their throats the points of the bayonets thrust by Japanese, and to have their lifeblood gush from their veins as a result, they are good enough to vote.

Mr. Eastland: Mr. President, will the senator yield for a question?

The Presiding Officer: Does the senator from New Mexico yield to the senator from Mississippi for a question?

Mr. Chávez: Yes.

Mr. Eastland: I shall have to ask the senator to excuse me. I wanted to make a statement of two sentences. I asked the senator if he would yield for a question. I made a mistake. I wanted to make a statement of two sentences. Will the senator yield for that purpose?

Mr. Chávez: No, Mr. President. Let me proceed. I want to obtain a vote on this bill quickly. Therefore I wish to proceed.

Mr. Eastland: I will say to the senator that my statement will have no connection whatever with the racial issue.

The Presiding Officer: Does the senator from New Mexico yield to the senator from Mississippi to make a statement?

Mr. Chávez: No, Mr. President, I do not yield. I feel so deeply concerning the merits of this matter that I do not want to take too much of the Senate's time.

Mr. Eastland: Mr. President—

Mr. Chávez: I want to get a vote on the measure possibly this afternoon if I can.

Mr. Eastland: Mr. President—

The Presiding Officer: The senator from New Mexico declines to yield.

Mr. Eastland: Mr. President, I want the American people to know that this maneuver effectively blocks consideration of antistrike legislation which is so necessary to save our country today.

Mr. Chávez: Mr. President, I have stated before, and I will repeat, that this bill has been on the Senate calendar since May of last year.

It is the only measure on which the senator can vote "yea" or "nay" this afternoon. He could not vote on labor legislation. He could not vote on legislation dealing with demobilization this afternoon. But if he gives us an opportunity, we will get the pending measure out of the way this afternoon, and then I shall join the senator from Mississippi—

Mr. Eastland: Mr. President, the senator knows, of course, that there is utterly no chance of a vote being had on this bill this afternoon. It is proposed to move to discharge the Committee on Education and Labor from consideration of a measure, and to take up antistrike legislation immediately, but the present maneuver blocks such action. The American people should know what is behind this matter.

Mr. Chávez: We can vote today on the pending bill. The senator from Mississippi can vote against it. We are not trying to delay the matter, but the president called the country's attention to the fact that he had recommended this bill. Defeat it if you must, but it is the only bill on which noses can be counted this afternoon. We are not delaying any other legislation. We are not delaying labor legislation. We are not delaying appropriation bills. But let me say to senators who are so serious in endeavoring to have passed legislation dealing with strikes we can be counted this afternoon on the pending measure.

After some additional attempts by his opponents to block action on S. 101, Chávez resumed his discussion of the subcommittee report recommending its passage. But his efforts proved to be in vain; Southern Democrats filibustered for eighteen days, until February 9, when a vote was taken to cut off debate. The motion failed to garner the support of a two-thirds majority (the results were forty-eight in favor and thirty-six opposed), prompting Chávez to withdraw the Fair Employment Practices Act from consideration. In doing so, he noted:

Mr. President, it took the crucifixion of Christ to redeem the world. It took intestinal fortitude to bring about the Declaration of Independence. It took ordinary American decency to bring about the Constitution of the United States. It took the death of Americans during the Civil War to find out that this was one country. It took this vote today to find out that a majority cannot have its will.

Mr. President, notwithstanding what has happened today and heretofore, America will go forward. This is only the beginning. Please believe me, this is one country, as Lincoln said. We cannot have it divided. We cannot have one country for the South and another country for the other states of the United States.

Despite such opposition from forces within his own party, Chávez continued to sound the call for an end to racial intolerance. On May 9, 1948, for example, he spoke before the Long Beach (New York) Forum on the serious international implications of the country's reluctance to enact antidiscrimination laws. His ad-

dress is reprinted here from the Congressional Record Appendix, *80th Congress, 2nd Session, Volume 94, Part 11, U.S. Government Printing Office, 1948.*

The topic for discussion this evening is racial discrimination. However, before taking up the subject, allow me to express appreciation to my good friend, Councilman Joe Ross, who has so cordially invited me to be here this evening and to speak on a subject which I deem to be of transcendental importance to all of us.

As I look over the audience I am reminded of the Chicago newspaper which spoke of New York editorial writers who refer to the United States as "we Anglo-Saxons" and suggested that they should see some of the Anglo-Saxons at Forty-seventh and South Parkway.

Needless to say, I am happy to be here. I feel at home in New York and its environs although I come from a sparsely populated state and one utterly unlike yours from the standpoint of population, industry, commerce, and geography. I enjoy the fast tempo of your life. I like to see the vast crowds, the thousands of eager faces showing strains of many races—all living, working, and playing, and together making the greatest city in the world.

> ***"I view national problems not as a Catholic, not as a descendant of the Spanish conquistadors, but solely and exclusively as an American."***

I am particularly glad to be in your lovely little city of Long Beach. The interest in national and world affairs expressed through this forum gives testimony to the progressive attitude and civic pride of your citizens and you are to be congratulated.

Most speakers try to be as circumspect as possible when handling a subject as delicate as racial discrimination. But the world situation today is so critical, the fate of western civilization is so precarious, and the future of our nation as a great power is so imperiled that we find circumspection out of order; it is time to speak out boldly—let the chips fall where they may. Discrimination endangers our country, and a threat to our national safety is a matter which vitally concerns us all, and it behooves us as good citizens to study and understand the problem. And if we find that racial discrimination presents such a threat to our safety, then we should immediately, with every ounce of resolution and determination at our command, seek to eradicate it from our way of life.

I can approach the problem with firsthand knowledge. I am a Catholic of Spanish descent and a representative of one of the larger racial minority groups. It is a racial minority which has been especially discriminated against in a country which we all know is predominantly Anglo-Saxon and Protestant. Still I feel I can approach the problem impartially because I view national problems not as a Catholic, not as a descendant of the Spanish conquistadors, but solely and exclusively as an American. Furthermore, though belonging to a minority group, I occupy, thanks to the electorate of my state and our democratic institutions, one of the highest offices our nation has to offer.

I feel deeply on the subject—there is already too much division in our country. Two weeks ago I led the fight against the granting of a federal charter to the Catholic War Veterans because I felt that our boys fought, bled, and died together in the last war as Americans—not as Catholics, not as Jews, not as Presbyterians—and in peace, veterans should be encouraged always to face the future as Americans. I am opposed to dividing them in times of peace into racial or religious groupings, as I am opposed to so dividing them in times of war.

Before discussing discrimination let us examine the credit side of the ledger. Our heritage of civil liberties is something we should be very proud of—our national record is a worthy one. The dignity of the individual is the core of this heritage and the welfare of the individual is the purpose and final goal and objective of our laws and institutions. We have a record three centuries long of constant striving to equalize opportunity for all men, and certainly no nation in history has ever offered better opportunity of achieving the ultimate goal of complete freedom and equality. It is true that we have fallen short of reaching the goal, but we all know the objective and we want to get there. For what we have accomplished we can take pride. Our heritage has permitted the election of a Smith, a Roosevelt, a Lehman, and a Dewey as the executive of this great state. In New Mexico at least half of the elected officials are of Spanish ancestry.

Unfortunately this is far from the case in the neighboring states of Texas, Arizona, and Colorado. There the record is not good. Perhaps the reason for this is because our laws and Constitution provide equal rights and equal opportunity under federal authority but no attention is given to the abuse of civil rights by individuals or by the states.

Discrimination is too widespread to need prove its existence—inequality of opportunity, segregation of individuals, abuse and mistreatment because of race and color is familiar to us all. The implications of discrimination, however, are not always so well known or understood. That an American citizen of Mexican descent in Arizona or Colorado may not occupy public office is a national disgrace. But what is more important at the moment is that such discrimination imperils relations with our sister republics of the Western Hemisphere at a time when pan-American solidarity is the cornerstone of national security.

Therefore, when Southern spokesmen tell us to mind our own business and let the South solve its own problems we can hurl back the answer with a vengeance—Bilboism in Mississippi concerns each and every American. [Theodore Bilbo was a U.S. senator from Mississippi with a reputation as a racist demagogue.] First because Bilboism is intrinsically wrong; second, because it is un-American and, third, because it jeopardizes our national security.

But let us retrace our steps for one moment—why do we have racial and religious bigotry in this country? The answer is simple. The population of the United States is composed of immigrants, or descendants of immigrants, who came to this country from all parts of the world. Every race, clime, and language is represented here. Basically the older population came from northern Europe and is predominantly Anglo-Saxon, white and Protestant. However, even in early days the French, the Germans, the Irish, and the Jews were represented and, of course, helpless shackled blacks from Africa soon joined them. Slavery was introduced in Virginia ten years before the Pilgrims landed at Plymouth, though strangely enough, these blacks were held like the indentured whites and could gain their freedom after the period of indenture. Following the Civil War and with the coming of the industrial revolution and the march of civilization westward a new flood of immigrants came to our country. They introduced the language, the customs, the religion, and even the dress of the countries of their origin.

Today, people representing every race known to man live in New York City. In Massachusetts we have Poles, French, Portuguese. There are Germans in Pennsylvania, Swedes, Norwegians, and Danes in the lake region and Italians and Greeks are scattered from one end of the country to the other. This conglomeration of races, languages, customs, and religions gave rise to countless differences and conflicts, most of which remain unsettled to this day. Until the problems created by the presence of minority groups are solved, the United States will to that extent be divided.

Negroes form our largest minority, closely followed by the Jews. Another great minority is represented by people who came to this country from our neighbor to the south—Mexico.

Wherever these newcomers have settled their poverty, ignorance, and low standard of living permitted exploitation by the older populations with whom they came in contact, and the latter were not reluctant to take advantage of the fact.

In time, with education, leaders arose among the exploited and pushed by universal yearning for advancement of the masses they sought to elevate themselves and their fellows and collided head-on with the entrenched interests of the older populations. Fanned by ignorance and greed the conflict inevitably becomes more acute in ratio to the extent of the profit obtained by the exploiting group.

The pattern was true when the Irish, the Poles, and the Italians, etc., were foreigners and so long as the so-called 100-percent American could keep them in the lower-wage-scale jobs. The pattern is true today in the case of the Negroes and Mexican-Americans.

Let us see how this works out in relation to the whole economic and social picture—let us examine the problem and see if we are interlopers in pressing for fair employment practices, as the Bilbos and Talmadges charge.

In World War II we were fighting to preserve our way of life and to defend western civilization. Hitler had loosed the demon hordes of pagan nihilism on civilization, and to our everlasting honor it became our glorious role in history to crush these hordes and destroy their master and his maniacal system. To do this we had to wage total war. Every sinew, every muscle, every last bit of energy and determination had to be expended in order to win the victory.

We all had a stake in that war. New Mexico had its entire National Guard fighting with its back to the wall at Bataan and Corregidor. Our men weren't asking for relief or rescue; they begged only for arms, medicine, and provisions. I wish that the congressional opponents of FEPC could ask the helpless hulks of men in New Mexico, the prisoners who survived the death march and the salt mines of Japan, if it was wise—not right, mind you—to keep the manpower represented by thirteen million Negroes and some two million Mexican-Americans out of the defense plants because of color or race.

> ***"Discrimination is un-American and cannot be a part of the American way of life."***

This is not idle talk. Let me tell you what happened. Early in the war, when the reserves of our manpower were reaching the point of exhaustion, a vast source of manpower remained untapped. The Negroes and the Mexican-Americans in our war plants were deprived undemocratically, unrealistically, and foolhardily of the opportunity to help win the war by contributing their labor and skill in defense-plant work. They could fight, but they couldn't work. The situation grew critical, production was lagging; finally, after considerable study, President Roosevelt by executive order established the Fair Employment Practices Commission, and at long last we began to utilize this important source of manpower.

In the last war the percentage of volunteers from New Mexico, Arizona, Colorado, and Texas was very high. A vast number were boys of Spanish or Mexican ancestry; they could bear arms, but their fathers, brothers, and sisters, under the system existing at the time, could not get jobs in war plants, or, if allowed to work, they could do only the most menial of tasks and at a discriminatory wage rate.

Discrimination is un-American and cannot be a part of the American way of life. It is contrary to our spirit of fair play.

Imagine the feelings of the Japanese-American, who fought so valiantly in Italy—we had no better troops, not excepting the Marines—fighting for democracy and all the while his country was gathering up his father, mother, and sisters and herding them like cattle into concentration camps.

Macario Garcia, of Texas, won the Congressional Medal of Honor. President Truman bestowed the decoration, and he told the young hero that he would rather have earned that medal than be president of the United States. Back home in Texas a week later, on his way to a Rotary Club luncheon to which he had been invited, this young man stopped at a drug store in Sugar Land to get a Coca-Cola—in the uniform of the country he loved and wearing its highest decoration—he was referred to a sign, "We don't serve Mexicans." When he protested the insult he was hit over the head with a baseball bat and was hurt so badly he could not proceed with his journey. Texas should be ashamed.

And the Negro who lay dying of wounds in New Guinea and asked that a grave marker be placed over him reading: "Here lies a black man who died fighting yellow men that white men might be free." Perhaps he could foresee the shocking massacre at Monroe, Georgia, when two helpless Negro couples were forcibly removed from a car by a lynch mob and shot down like dogs as they pleaded for their lives.

At Pando, Colorado, construction of a camp to train winter troops was started. Hundreds of employees were needed by the contractor. Workmen were recruited from all the surrounding areas, including New Mexico. About six hundred of these employees were Americans of Spanish extraction from New Mexico, Wyoming, Utah, Colorado, and Arizona. Most of them had sons in the service of the country. Many had sons who were prisoners of the Japanese in the Philippines. Someone complained that there were "too many Mexicans" working in the camp. Suddenly came an order dismissing everyone who bore a Spanish name. Better than six hundred persons were dismissed in one day. Juan P. Romero, of Rodarte, New Mexico, formerly a state representative from Taos

County, and a Republican, telephoned me about the situation. Senator Ed Johnson of Colorado was as horrified as I when he learned of the situation. Together we protested to the general staff and in three days every man went back to work and the matter was settled, except perhaps in the hearts of the men who had ordered the discriminatory firing in the first place. Unquestionably malice, prejudice, and ignorance still remained embedded in their hearts.

These things are wrong. I know that there are many among us who refer to the Italians as "Wops," to the Mexicans as "Greasers," to the Jews as "Yids," and the Irish as "Harps," but if we stop to consider how important it is that we be united now, we would forget our differences, forget that we are of Irish, Spanish, English, or Italian extraction and concentrate on being Americans.

Anyone who has observed the progress of Communist aggression since World War II will realize that the greatest aid to its progress has been disunity and political disorganization. Every nation engulfed by communism has previously been torn asunder by factionalism, confusion, and bitter internal controversy. We cannot afford racial differences in America.

We now realize the folly of having disarmed so soon after the end of World War II. We plan to build a great air force, to strengthen our ground forces, and to increase the striking power of our navy. We are waging a cold war against communism throughout the world. We are sending billions to Europe in an effort to rehabilitate those war-torn countries, to stabilize their economies and their governments, and if possible to weld them together into a political unit which will stand strong and steadfast against the onslaught from the east.

All this, however, will be useless if we try to fight communism with arms and dollars alone. Our best answer to communism is the living, working proof of democracy furnished by our divinely inspired institutions and system of government. As long as America offers the world a haven of hope for the oppressed and the weak, we will triumph over communism. To accomplish this we must have a deep-rooted conviction of the superiority of our institutions. Contrariwise, if under our system of government there is misery, suffering, want, oppression and discrimination, the weapons of communism are strengthened and sharpened.

Every slum, every lynching, every example of Jim Crowism is taken up by the Communist and used as an argument to advance his cause. Let us quit kidding ourselves. The Negro, the oriental, and the Mexican have cousins by the millions throughout the world. Their numbers may be few in this country by comparison with other racial groups, but every time a barber in Arizona refuses to serve a visiting Latin American from Mexico or Venezuela you can be sure that they hear about it in South America, and you can bet your bottom dollar that the Communist agents will make use of it as propaganda.

The Communist agents in China, in Korea, in Formosa, Indochina, the East Indies, and Japan are doubtless now exploiting the knowledge that under California laws the last wish of the dying Nisei hero is denied him—his parents cannot hold land willed them by their son: it escheats to the state.

And what about Latin America? We can't expect the nations of this hemisphere to break their necks to help us in the event of another war if we continue to mistreat their cousins in our own country.

Doubtless there are many who would say, "To hell with South America." But it is not as simple as that. Had it not been for the endless supply of raw materials which came from South America to feed our war industries, the end of World War II might well have been prolonged, or perhaps even different.

We are on the brink of war today. No thinking person wants war, but if we have war we cannot afford to be isolated from the rest of the world. If we face facts we must admit that the population of the world is not predominantly white. As a matter of fact, the yellow, brown, and black races far outnumber the white. These races are restless. The downtrodden millions in Indo-China, the East Indies, and Africa are striving even now to throw off the yoke of imperialism. We will need vital raw materials which these countries possess and without which it is impossible to wage modern war. We can't expect these races to be friendly and to assist us in war if at the same time we discriminate against groups of our own citizens because of race or color.

From a moral, ethical, and ethnological standpoint, there is absolutely no basis for discrimination. Given equal background, equal opportunity, equal schooling, most people in a given environment, though of different race or color, will tend in the long run to progress equally.

The Mexican-American Joe Martinez from Colorado, who won the Congressional Medal of Honor and a hero's grave on Attu loved his country just as much as Colin Kelly or John Bassilone.

I am quite sure we all agree that in the eyes of God all men are equal, and it matters not to God if a man be black, brown, yellow, or white.

In the dedication of the Fifth Marine Division graveyard at Iwo Jima, the division's Jewish chaplain, Rabbi Roland B. Gittlesohn, the Cleveland-born son of a Lithuanian immigrant, had this to say:

> *Here lie officers and men, Negroes and whites, rich men and poor. . . . Here are Protestants, Catholics, and Jews. . . . Here no man prefers another because of his color. Here there are no quotas of how many from each group are admitted or allowed. Theirs is the highest and purest democracy.*
>
> *Any man among us the living who . . . lifts his hand in hate against a brother, or thinks himself superior to those who happen to be in the minority, makes of this ceremony and of the bloody sacrifices it commemorates, an empty mockery. . . .*

I am not speaking academically. We are facing stern reality. This forum is composed of public-spirited citizens. You are interested in the outcome of the next presidential election. You are interested in the international situation. Being well-read persons, you know that President Truman by executive order created over a year ago a commission which had for its purpose the study of civil rights in the United States. In a report entitled *To Secure These Rights,* the president's committee outlined the minority problem in the United States, analyzed the civil rights which are most abused and which require the protection of the federal government. The committee recommended to the president the enactment of legislation enabling administrative institutions to protect these rights. In a vigorous message to Congress President Truman stood four-square on the recommendations of his committee. Immediately a hue and cry arose from the South. Threats of bolting and of withholding electoral votes filled the air. Leaving political implications aside, the president is right and the southerners are wrong on this issue.

From a practical standpoint it seems foolhardy that ten percent of our people should be permanently held down and prevented from using their energies in critical times. We are in a cold war up to our necks. A shooting war may be just around the corner, and whether we like it or not, we cannot afford to turn down the help of fifteen million people. The opponents of a civil-rights program are imperiling the security of our nation by persisting in their bigoted approach to this problem. The civilization which they love so much can well be endangered by their shortsightedness.

The State of New York is to be congratulated for its enlightened attitude toward minority problems. It is not easy, I know, to live with neighbors who are different from ourselves. As a matter of fact, where is the family that has no spats? I know in my own case that the Spanish-speaking people of New Mexico, from whom I spring, have had a tremendous struggle to adapt themselves to American ways of life, but they are winning the fight. Every day lawyers, doctors, dentists, nurses, and scientists of Spanish descent are taking their place as useful American citizens. They are proud of their heritage; they are proud that their ancestors came to New Mexico before the Anglo-Saxons; they are proud of their language; but above all, they are proud of being Americans.

Their pride in America must not be transformed into bitterness and disillusionment by discrimination and segregation. False doctrines of racial superiority properly belong in a Nazi state—not in America. Join then in a fight which concerns us all. Fight to provide the equality of freedom and opportunity that alone will make worthwhile the death of Joe Martinez, Colin Kelly, and John Bassilone.

I thank you.

Although new fair-employment-practices legislation surfaced again several times during the late 1940s, the 1950s, and early 1960s, it continued to meet strong resistance from Southern lawmakers; in many instances, bills never even reached the floor. Antidiscrimination measures were finally passed in 1964—two

years after Chávez died of cancer while serving his fifth term in office—as part of the landmark Civil Rights Act.

SOURCES

Books

Congressional Record, 79th Congress, 2nd Session, Volume 92, Part 1, U.S. Government Printing Office, 1946.

Congressional Record Appendix, 79th Congress, 1st Session, Volume 91, Part 13, U.S. Government Printing Office, 1945; 80th Congress, 2nd Session, Volume 94, Part 11, U.S. Government Printing Office, 1948.

Periodicals

New York Times, "Senator Chávez, 74, Is Dead in Capital," November 19, 1962.

Linda Chavez

1947–

Spanish American political leader and writer

A self-described "stubborn" person who frequently goes "against the grain," Linda Chavez has generated controversy among political liberals and some members of the Hispanic American community for challenging the conventional wisdom on topics such as affirmative action, bilingual education, and immigration policy. She also takes issue with efforts to foster multiculturalism at the expense of assimilation—especially if the government becomes involved in those efforts—because it tends to fragment rather than unite the country. As Chavez declares, "The more diverse we become racially and ethnically, the more important it is that we learn to tolerate differences—and also to celebrate what we all have in common."

Chavez was born in Albuquerque, New Mexico, to a mother of English and Irish ancestry and a father whose ancestors had lived in the same general area of the Southwest for nearly four hundred years after their arrival from Spain. When she was nine, she moved with her parents and younger sister to Denver, Colorado, and it was there that she encountered racial discrimination for the first time in her life. But she found the inspiration to overcome this obstacle in the words of her father, who encouraged her to be proud of her heritage and never use it as an excuse.

After graduating from high school, Chavez attended the University of Colorado, earning a bachelor's degree in 1970. She then went on to graduate school at the University of California in Los Angeles (UCLA) to pursue a degree in English literature. It was a time of tremendous social upheaval both on and off campus, and school administrators soon found themselves under pressure to establish a Chicano studies program. Over her protests that there wasn't enough material to develop an entire course in Chicano literature, Chavez was drafted to do so anyway.

But what she experienced during her brief tenure in academia soured her on liberal politics and helped shape her conservative philosophy. Her more radical students "didn't believe they had to read books at all, much less any book that was written by a non-Hispanic," she later recalled. Some literally turned their backs on her in protest; outside class, she endured acts of vandalism on her car and personal threats on her life after she failed those students who didn't complete the required course work. In addition, Chavez objected to the efforts of many of her fellow professors to "manipulate" these same kids into thinking that they didn't need to do *well to stay in school—all they had to do was demand that the rules be changed for them.*

Thoroughly disenchanted, Chavez left UCLA in 1972 and headed for Washington, D.C. There she spent several years working for a variety of liberal-leaning groups as she tried to sort out her true political beliefs; she even served six months at the Department of Health, Education, and Welfare during the Carter administration. It was while she was editor of the American Federation of Teachers publication American Educator, *however, that Chavez first caught the eye of capital-area conservatives who admired a series of articles she had written on the need to return to "traditional values" in the schools. This in turn led to an invitation in 1981 to serve as a consultant to the Reagan administration.*

This appointment proved to be only the first in a series of high-profile positions Chavez held throughout most of the 1980s. In 1983, for example, she became staff director of the U.S. Commission on Civil Rights, an ostensibly nonpartisan government agency charged with monitoring adherence to equal-protection laws. She immediately ruffled some feathers when she issued a memo calling for an end to the kinds of programs and practices typically favored by liberals (such as affirmative action) because they operate on the false assumption that "racism and sexism are ingrained in American society"; she also felt affirmative action demeans people by reducing them to an ethnic category. In addition, Chavez raised some eyebrows when she declared that "a general decline in academic standards coincided with the advent of affirmative action in higher education."

In 1985, Chavez became the highest-ranking woman in the Reagan administration when she accepted the post of director of the White House Office of Public Liaison, which called upon her to promote the president's policies among members of Congress and various public groups. (Around this same time, Chavez officially changed her party affiliation from Democrat to Republican.) She left her job ten months later and in 1986 ran for the office of U.S. senator from Maryland. In a bitter campaign that pitted conservative Republican Chavez (a married mother of three) as the "family values" candidate against liberal Democrat Barbara Mikulski (unmarried and childless), Chavez lost by a large margin.

Chavez then withdrew from public office but not from the spotlight as the head of U.S. English, a private organization that supports making English the official national language. She resigned about a year later, however, in protest against what she felt were the "anti-Hispanic" and "anti-Catholic" sentiments the founder of the group expressed in a memo that was made public.

Since then, Chavez has been affiliated with the Manhattan Institute, a conservative think-tank located in Washington, D.C. As senior fellow and head of the Center for the New American Community, she carries out the center's mission to "foster a renewed commitment to a common American civic culture and shared identity among the many diverse people who built this nation and live in it today." To that end, it sponsors conferences and speakers and produces a quarterly newsletter, the American Experiment.

Chavez herself contributes frequently to a variety of publications and is a weekly columnist in USA Today. *In 1991 she authored the book* Out of the Barrio: Toward a New Politics of Hispanic Assimilation *(Basic Books), which discusses topics such as bilingual education, voting rights, immigration policy, and affirmative action and emphasizes Hispanic progress and achievement rather than perpetuate what she believes are stereotypes about Hispanics as a poor and disadvantaged underclass. In fact, Chavez sees the current anti-immigration sentiment as a consequence of such images and attitudes. "If we are constantly telling everyone through our Hispanic leaders that we can't make it in America," she says, "well, then, we shouldn't be surprised when people say maybe we don't want so many of you here."*

In addition to appearing on radio and television news and public-affairs programs to discuss her views, Chavez is often called upon to share them in person with various groups. In October 1992, for instance, she spoke in Miami at the forty-sixth annual National Preservation Conference, an event sponsored by the National Trust for Historic Preservation. The theme of her talk was how to encourage appreciation for cultural diversity in the United States without sabotaging the ultimate goal of assimilation. Her speech is reprinted here from Historic Preservation Forum, *January/February 1993.*

The face of America is changing—becoming more diverse and complex than at any time in our history. We're no longer a white-and-black society struggling to integrate two major groups of people who have been in this country for nearly four hundred years, but a multiracial, multiethnic society in which newcomers are arriving in record numbers every day. The 1980s will be remembered as a period of one the highest levels of immigration in our nation's history. Some ten million persons immigrated to the United States in the last decade, a number as great as that of the peak decade, 1900 to 1910.

Unlike the immigrants of the early part of this century who were primarily from Europe, the great bulk of the last decade's immigrants—approximately eighty percent—were from Asia and Latin America. Much has been made of this phenomenon and many who favor restricting immigration suggest that these new Asian and Latin immigrants will be less successfully absorbed into the fabric of American society: "I know that earlier large waves of immigrants didn't 'overturn' America," says former Colorado governor Dick Lamm, "but there are . . . reasons to believe that today's migration is different from earlier flows."

But, in fact, when we look at one of these groups, we find that most Hispanics are assimilating the social, educational, economic, and language norms of this society despite the image of Hispanics portrayed in the media and perpetuated by Hispanic leaders. Let me just acquaint you with a few facts about the Hispanic population with which you may not be familiar:

-Mexican-origin men have the highest labor-force participation rates of any group, including non-Hispanic whites and Asians.

-U.S.-born Hispanics have rapidly moved into the middle class. The earnings of Mexican-American men are now roughly eighty percent of those of non-Hispanic white men.

-Mexican-Americans with thirteen to fifteen years of education earn, on an average, ninety-seven percent of the average earnings of non-Hispanic white males.

-Most differences in earnings between Hispanics and non-Hispanics can be explained by educational differences between the two groups, but at the secondary-school level, young Mexican-Americans are closing the gap with their non-Hispanic peers. Seventy-eight percent of second-generation Mexican-American men aged twenty-five to thirty-four have completed twelve years of school or more, compared with approximately ninety percent of comparable non-Hispanic whites.

-English proficiency is also key to earnings among Hispanics, but here, too, conventional wisdom about Hispanics is mostly invalid. The overwhelming majority of U.S.-born Hispanics are English-dominant, and one half of all third generation Mexican-Americans—like most other American ethnics—speak only one language: English.

-What's more, Hispanics, with the exception of Puerto Ricans, have marriage rates comparable to those of non-Hispanic whites.

Linda Chavez

> Three quarters of Mexican-origin, Cuban, and Central and South American Hispanics live in married-couple households. And nearly half own their own homes.

If these facts come as a surprise to you, it's largely because most of the analysis of Hispanics fails to note that nearly half of the adult Hispanic population is foreign-born. And like new immigrants of the past, Hispanic immigrants will take at least one generation to move up the economic ladder and into the cultural mainstream.

Perhaps a little history lesson is in order. The current period is not the time in our history during which we have viewed new immigrants with distrust and suspicion. We tend to forget that Italians, Greeks, Jews, Poles, and others—whom some people lump together as "Europeans"—were considered alien to the white Americans of the early twentieth century, most of whom were of British, German, or Scandinavian descent. As Thomas Sowell recounts in his book, *Ethnic America:*

> *The remarkable achievements—especially intellectual achievements—of later generations of Jews cannot simply be read back into the immigrants' generation. These children often had serious educational problems. A 1910 survey of a dozen cities found two thirds of the children of Polish Jews to be below the normal grade for their ages.*

Jews weren't the only group that suffered such educational disadvantages. More than half of the immigrants from southern Italy at the turn of the century could neither read nor write, nor could nearly forty percent of those from Lithuania. Nor were these "Europeans" insulated from prejudice and discrimination. For anyone who believes that immigrants of an earlier day lived in halcyon time of tolerance and acceptance among their fellow white European-descended Americans, I recommend a few hours of reading through the reports of the 1921 Dillingham Commission, which in 1924 ultimately recommended a quota system to keep out southern and eastern European immigrants and Asians.

The point is that immigrants have never had it particularly easy in this society, nor have they always been welcomed with open arms, despite Emma Lazarus's words on the base of the Statue of Liberty. Nonetheless, most of those who came here from other countries found the struggle worth the effort. And these groups did, by and large, succeed in America. Today, Italians, Jews, Poles, Greeks, and others of southern and eastern European background are virtually indistinguishable from so-called native-stock Americans on measure of earnings, status, and education. Even Chinese- and Japanese-Americans, who were subject to much greater discrimination than southern and eastern Europeans, have done exceedingly well and outperform most other groups on all indicators of social and economic success. But it took three generations for most of these groups to achieve this status. For Italian-Americans, for example, it took until 1970 before they achieved the same average educational attainment as other Americans—some sixty years after the peak of their immigration to the United States.

Is it possible, then, simply to mimic what we did in the past in treating this generation of newcomers? No. Let me concede that we did a great deal of wrong in the past, and immigrants succeeded in spite of, not because of, our mistakes. It would be neither compassionate nor legal to return to a system in which we put non-English-speaking children into public-school classrooms in which the instruction was entirely in English and expect those children to "sink or swim." In 1974 this approach was declared by the United States Supreme Court to violate our civil rights laws. Nor should we harken back to the "good old days" when Anglo conformity was the sole acceptable cultural model. But in trying to right past wrongs, we should be careful not to reverse ourselves 180 degrees by attempting to educate each group of immigrant children in their own native language and inculcate them in their own native culture. There is something wrong when two thirds of children from Spanish-speaking homes are taught to read in Spanish when they enter first grade in American public schools and three fourths are given Spanish oral-language development. If we insist on separate language instruction for all immigrant students—167 different languages are spoken in New York alone—we will close the door on integration, divide ourselves along cultural/linguistic lines, and thereby perpetuate inequalities rather than eradicate them. It seems to me that too often those who propose multicultural education are so obsessed with the excesses of Anglo conformity that they fail to see the benefits of a shared, common culture—not entirely white, Anglo-Saxon, and Protestant—but common nonetheless. And they fail to see the dangers in substituting one orthodoxy with another, no less rigid.

The more diverse we become racially and ethnically, the more important it is that we learn to tolerate differences—and also to celebrate what we all have in common. Whether we came to the United States voluntarily or involuntarily, we all choose to live here now. And more people want to live here than anywhere else in the world. No other country accepts as many immigrants as we do. Surely, even those who criticize our so-called Eurocentric society must admit that it has something to offer or there would not be such long lines of those waiting to get in—very few of them European, by the way. What is it we have that these Mexicans, Cambodians, Ethiopians, Filipinos, and others want? Two things primarily: economic opportunity and political freedom. The two, by the way, go hand in hand, and it is our legal and political institutions that protect both. Now it so happens that those political institutions did not, in fact, develop in Asia or Latin America or Africa or even throughout most of Europe. It happens that the framework for our political institutions comes from England. The basis for American jurisprudence comes from English common law—not from Spanish adaptations of Roman Law that governed most of Latin America, or from the legendary rulers of China or from the Hsia Dynasty or from Confucianism, or from the Ghanian Empire, the Kush state in Nubia, or from Mali. That is not to say that these others are not important civilizations deserving recognition in their own right, but it is to acknowledge the special importance to our particular political/legal system of the Magna Carta, habeas corpus, and trial by jury, all of which were handed down directly from England. Of course, not all of these concepts were totally indigenous to England; King Henry II adapted from the Franks the system of trial by jury to replace the oath, the ordeal, or the duel, which were used in both criminal and civil cases until the twelfth century.

> ***"Immigrants have never had it particularly easy in this society, nor have they always been welcomed with open arms. . . . Nonetheless, most . . . found the struggle worth the effort."***

In our zeal to tell the stories of other civilizations, to include the history of those whose ancestors came from places other than England, we should not attempt to rewrite the history of our own founding and our political antecedents. Nor should we blush at the thought that this political/institutional history now belongs to children who come here from Mexico, Vietnam, or Ghana or whose parents came from those countries. These children are now American children, and this is their political inheritance as much as it is the inheritance of the child of Italian or Greek or Russian roots, certainly every bit as much as it is the child of English roots. I believe that in our zeal to promote diversity we are forgetting that what makes this country virtually unique in the world is that we have forged an identity as a people even though most of us share very little in common in terms of our own personal histories. There is nothing wrong with holding onto personal history, but—given the incredible diversity of the country as a whole—it becomes increasingly difficult to expect the state to try to pass on that sense of personal history to each and every group. The most that can be expected, I think, is that we make sure that we recognize the contributions each group—once here—has made to the common history of this nation.

Is it possible to study the individual culture of the ancestors of each group represented in America? That depends on how superficial we're willing to be. I suppose it's possible to develop a dictionary of cultural literary of every major group and teach children to memorize a few facts and dates about each. Given our current success with children's learning to locate Arkansas on a map of the United States or China on a map of the world, or to tell in what half a century the Civil War was fought, or to name more than four past presidents of the United States, I don't know what hope there is that such a project would have any lasting benefit. But there are other problems with this approach as well. Who decides what represents the "history" of each of these groups? Take Hispanic children, for example. What do we teach them about the Mayas, the Aztecs, the Incas—all important civilizations, but from which relatively few Hispanics living in the United States are actually descended? And what about the history of Spain? Should Hispanic youngsters be reading Cervantes and Lope de Vega or *I, Rigoberta Menchu,* an oral autobiography of a Guatemalan Indian now memorialized in Dinesh D'Souza's new book, *Illiberal Education: The Politics of Race and Sex on Campus?*

> ***"In our zeal to promote diversity we are forgetting that what makes this country virtually unique in the world is that we have forged an identity as a people even though most of us share very little in common . . ."***

The issue is certainly no less complicated when it comes to African-Americans. In the name of multicultural education, many school systems have adopted an Afrocentric curriculum that mostly focuses on the contributions of ancient Egypt. There is no questions about the fact that Egypt is on the continent of Africa. But that is about all traditional Egyptologists and Afrocentric scholars can agree on. Is Egypt better understood as part of the broader thalassic culture of the Mediterranean, which also includes the Middle East and southern Europe? The Sahara, which separates Egypt from the continent to the south, remains even today a powerful cultural barrier. Are we to assume it was less so thousands of years ago? These issues are rarely addressed by Afrocentric curricula.

So if we cannot—and perhaps should not—try to teach each group its own individual history through multiple ethnocentric curricula, how do we try to deal with this increasingly diverse student population?

First, black, Hispanic, Asian, and American Indian children need the same basic skills that we take for granted that white children need. This is an obvious point, but one that seems sometimes to be forgotten when the subject of multicultural education is raised. All children in American public schools need to be taught to read, write, and speak standard English well. Their ability to master these skills will affect their life chances more than virtually anything else they learn—or fail to learn—in school.

Second, they need to be taught the basic math and science that will enable them to function in an increasingly complex technological society.

Third, they need a broad understanding of our form of government and its institutions. We live in a country in which we enjoy great freedom, but we also live in a country in which people are highly apathetic. If we hope to preserve democracy, our young people must develop a better appreciation for our heritage and be committed to preserving it. Somewhere along the way we have become reticent about instilling in our young an appreciation for democracy. If we expect to preserve our democratic way of life, we had better begin to develop that appreciation once again. And that means emphasizing the duties and responsibilities that go along with good citizenship.

Fourth, we need to teach our children the history of this nation. Here, we sometimes failed in the past to include the contributions made by all the groups that made up this nation. I said earlier that we shouldn't shy away from teaching the essentially English antecedents of our political and legal institutions. But neither should we forget that many who built this nation were neither English, nor white, nor male. There are many excellent histories to consult about the contribution of African-Americans: W.E.B. Du Bois, John Hope Franklin, Carter Woodson, to name only three historians of the black experience in America. There are fewer familiar texts to consult on the contributions of Mexican-Americans, Puerto Ricans, Chinese-Americans, and other Asians, but two books on Latinos I would recommend are *Hispanics in the United States* by Harry Pachón and Joan Moore and *The Puerto Ricans* by Father Joseph Fitzpatrick. Both are short but comprehensive.

Fifth, all American children need a better understanding of the world in which we live, an understanding that includes something of the history of other nations. They need a grounding in geography, which, if taught well, will also teach them why nations developed as they did. Rivers, seas, terrain, climate are all important to the development of culture and should be understood as such. Man's ancient struggle was one to comprehend and overcome the tyranny of nature. Of course, learning the language of another country is the best way to develop real depth in understanding that culture, and I would hope we would not ignore developing second-language proficiency in all of our students. In this respect, immigrant children will have an advantage.

These recommendations are not exhaustive. Nor are they geared only to the child who comes from a nonwhite, non-European background. These recommendations are suited to all of our children.

The American public school was created on the premise that it would be a common school, one for all children. It has not always lived up to that ideal—certainly not before 1954—but that does not mean we should abandon the ideal. The face of America is changing, but we should not give up on the idea that we are one people, one nation. Our efforts should be dedicated to making that ideal a reality.

Is there no place, then, for the preservation of language and culture for those among new immigrants—or any others in this society—who wish to retain aspects of their former traditions? Of course there is. Some would have us believe that assimilation means that every group will be stripped of what makes it unique and that the American character will be forged into a colorless alloy in an indifferent melting pot. But, of course, that is not what has happened in this country. As a trip into the heart of any American city will tell you, ethnic communities are alive and well, even as their inhabitants enjoy the fruits of social, political, and economic integration.

The question is not whether any ethnic group has the right to maintain its language, culture, and traditions, but whose responsibility it is to do so: Is it the individual's or the group's responsibility? Or should it be the responsibility of government to ensure that each group's separate traditions be maintained? This, of course, is the heart of the debate now raging in many circles—a debate in which I come down solidly on the side of personal responsibility. If Hispanics, Asians, Jews, Greeks, or the members of any other group wish to maintain their individual and unique cultures, languages, or traditions, it must be up to them to do so. Indeed, many groups have been quite successful in preserving their native languages and cultures within the United States. Chinese parents send their children to school on Saturday to learn Cantonese or Mandarin and the history of their ancestors. Jewish children frequently attend Hebrew classes and receive religious instruction that teaches them not only the tenets of their faith but also the history of their people. Greek Americans are among the most successful of any group in maintaining their language in the United States; according to the 1980 census a majority of Greek Americans say they still speak Greek in their homes at least occasionally.

Those Hispanics who wish to maintain their native language and culture—and polls show that a majority of Hispanic immigrants do—should follow the example of their fellow ethnic Americans by establishing their own cultural societies by which to do so. Frankly, given the tremendous diversity within the Hispanic community, the only successful way for each group to ensure that its members know its history and traditions is to undertake that education itself. If government is entrusted with the responsibility, it is likely to amalgamate and homogenize in ways that make the original culture virtually indecipherable. The government, after all, is capable of lumping all twenty-two million Hispanics in this nation into one category—a category that includes Cakchikel Indians from Guatemala, mestizos from Mexico, the descendants of Italian immigrants from Argentina, Japanese immigrants from Peru, Spaniards from Europe, and the descendants of colonists who settled the Southwest nearly four hundred years ago. Wouldn't it be better to entrust each of these very different groups with the responsibility of maintaining its own traditions without the interference—or assistance—of the government?

Some critics warn that the United States is in danger of fragmenting into competing racial and ethnic groups. Historian Arthur Schlesinger, Jr., has called it the "disuniting of America." No doubt, our task is more complicated today than at any time in the recent past. Nonetheless, I remain optimistic that we can—if we commit ourselves—successfully integrate the more than seventy million blacks, Hispanics, Asians, and American Indians into our society. That we can create a new *unum* out the many already here and the many more who are to come. But to do so will require the cooperation of us all—those who have been here for generations as well as those who are coming each day. It will require that each of us recognizes the covenant that exists between the old and the new: that we respect the rights of individuals to maintain what is unique in their ancestral heritages, but that we understand that our future is in forging a common identity of shared values and beliefs essential to the democratic ideal.

SOURCES

Books

Chavez, Linda, *Out of the Barrio: Toward a New Politics of Hispanic Assimilation,* Basic Books, 1991.

Periodicals

Commentary, "Hispanics Versus Their Leaders," October, 1991, pp. 47-49.

Forbes, "The Fracturing of America," March 30, 1992, pp. 74-75.

Hispanic, "Making People Mad," August, 1992, pp. 11-16.

Historic Preservation Forum, "Fostering Appreciation for Cultural Diversity," January/February, 1993, pp. 12-19.

New Republic, "Quitters," February 24, 1986, pp. 8-10.

People, "Barbara Mikulski and Linda Chavez Stage a Gloves-Off Battle in a Women-Only U.S. Senate Race," November 3, 1986, pp. 115-116.

Washington Monthly, "Linda Chavez and the Exploitation of Ethnic Identity," June, 1985, pp. 34-39.

Benjamin Chavis

1948–

African American religious and civil rights leader

When activist Benjamin Chavis became the new executive director of the National Association for the Advancement of Colored People (NAACP) in April 1993, the move was hailed as a major turning point in the history of the venerable civil rights organization. Indeed, the aggressive young minister wasted no time making good on his pledge to "accelerate the pace" of change in the ongoing effort to improve the quality of life for African Americans. But within months, Chavis's often-controversial initiatives had created an uproar both inside and outside the NAACP. And as the leadership crisis persisted into 1995, some observers were seriously questioning the group's prospects for long-term survival.

Chavis's involvement in the civil rights struggle began during his youth in Oxford, North Carolina. At the age of twelve, as a symbol of his initiation into manhood, he received his own NAACP membership card. Less than a year later, he stood up to local Jim Crow laws when he led a protest against his town's whites-only library and eventually won the right for blacks to use the facility. While still only in his mid-teens, Chavis joined the Southern Christian Leadership Conference (SCLC) and participated in the 1963 March on Washington, where Martin Luther King's "I Have a Dream" speech (see page 690) inspired him to devote his own life to the fight for civil rights.

After earning a bachelor's degree in chemistry from the University of North Carolina in 1969, Chavis then returned to his hometown to teach high school. But teaching bored him; before long he left for a job in Washington, D.C., with the Commission for Racial Justice, a Cleveland, Ohio-based human rights organization affiliated with the United Church of Christ. During this same period, he was also active with the NAACP, the Congress on Racial Equality (CORE), the SCLC, and the American Federation of State, County, and Municipal Employees (AFSCME).

In February 1971, Chavis went to Wilmington, North Carolina, to lend his support to local school desegregation efforts. Over the course of his visit, conflicts between black and white protesters gradually escalated into violence, culminating in the shooting deaths of a black student and a white man, an arson fire at a white-owned grocery store, and the deployment of National Guard troops. The following year, Chavis and nine students—dubbed the "Wilmington 10"—were indicted on conspiracy, assault, and arson charges in connection with the disturbances; Chavis was also charged with conspiracy to murder for the death of the white man. A jury consisting of two blacks and ten whites (some of whom were known to be members of the Ku Klux Klan) found Chavis guilty, and as the most prominent member of the group, he received the harshest sentence: thirty-four years in prison, later reduced to seventeen years.

In 1980, after several of the witnesses who had testified against Chavis admitted that they had made up their stories at the insistence of local law enforcement authorities, his conviction was overturned. (The United Church of Christ and Amnesty International, both of which considered him a political prisoner, were instrumental in securing his freedom.) By then, he had spent nearly five years in jail. Thanks to a special study-release program, however, he had been able to work toward his master's degree in divinity at Duke University. (He later earned a doctorate in theology from Howard University and a doctorate in philosophy from Union Theological Seminary.) He also wrote a book, Psalms from Prison, *and remained as active as possible in the struggle that had landed him in prison in the first place.*

Chavis spent the next thirteen years serving in various positions with the Commission on Racial Justice, rising to the rank of executive director and chief executive officer in 1985. Many of his activities centered around helping minorities and poor people wrongly convicted of crimes. But he also made a name for himself across the United States as the father of the "environmental racism" movement, which maintains that black neighborhoods are home to a disproportionate number of toxic waste dumps.

In February 1992, Benjamin Hooks announced his intention to step down as head of the NAACP after sixteen years in office. Jesse Jackson emerged as a favorite choice to succeed Hooks, but when he withdrew his name from consideration on April 7, 1993, Benjamin Chavis—who had promoted himself as the candidate who could unite the warring factions—moved to the top of the list. Two days later, the forty-five-year-old minister and activist was named the new executive director of the NAACP, making him the youngest person ever to serve in the post. Among the priorities he identified were boosting membership (especially among young people and other minorities), establishing closer ties with other black organizations in the United States and Africa, expanding the group's focus beyond civil rights activities, and securing its financial independence from corporate support through the creation of a one-hundred-million-dollar endowment.

Confident that he had been given a clear mandate to reinvigorate an organization many felt was out of touch with the average black American, Chavis "hit the ground running immediately after his appointment," as a reporter for Ebony *noted. Within days, for example, he traveled to South Central Los Angeles to be on hand when the verdicts were handed down in the civil rights trial of the four police officers charged with violating motorist Rodney King's civil rights. He then headed to Kansas City, where he hosted a "gang summit" and tried to persuade the young attendees to end their violent ways. In subsequent weeks he took part in a gay rights rally in Washington, met with the Congressional Black Caucus, testified on environmental waste at a hearing in Chicago, and delivered a well-received speech at the NAACP's annual Freedom Fund dinner in Detroit.*

Three months after taking office, Chavis was in Indianapolis to preside over the annual NAACP convention for the first time as executive director. On July 11, at the opening of the six-day gathering, he faced thousands of delegates and other guests and shared his ambitious dreams for the organization he had joined as a boy of twelve. Chavis opened his speech with a dramatic announcement about the NAACP's new endowment fund that prompted a standing ovation from the audience. The following text is reprinted from a copy of Chavis's remarks provided by the NAACP.

Mr. Chairman, Esteemed Members of the National Board of Directors of the National Association for the Advancement of Colored People, Delegates to this historic 84th Annual Convention, Members and Friends of the NAACP, Madame Attorney General, Ladies and Gentlemen, Sisters and Brothers:

Reginald F. Lewis was truly a great American, a great brother who made an outstanding contribution to national and international business and to the uplifting of all humanity. [Lewis, who died in January 1993, had been chairman of TLC Beatrice International, the nation's largest black-owned business.] As a reflection to his commitment to helping others, Mr. Lewis, as you have heard, established the Reginald F. Lewis Foundation.

In one of our last conversations early this year, Mr. Lewis shared with me his desire to assist the NAACP in moving forward into the twenty-first century. I am therefore honored and pleased to take this opportunity to make an historic announcement, and I will ask Dr. Gibson, the chairman of our national board, to join me at the podium at this time for this announcement.

We are pleased to announce the establishment of the *NAACP/Reginald F. Lewis Memorial Endowment.* The goal of this endowment is to raise a minimum of one hundred million dollars to ensure the long-term financial stability and security of the NAACP. We are further pleased to announce the receipt today of a two million-dollar commitment from the Reginald F. Lewis Foundation for the Endowment. Doc, stand with me for a moment.

We are honored to have present with us tonight Mr. Lewis's oldest daughter, Leslie N. Lewis, a junior at Harvard University and a member of the board of directors of TLC Beatrice International Holdings, Inc., and also a member of the board of directors of the Reginald F. Lewis Foundation.

Also present is Mr. Anthony Fugett, Mr. Lewis's brother and president and CEO of ASF Systems, Inc., and a member of the board of TLC Beatrice International Holdings Corporation as well as a member of the Chavis transition team into the NAACP.

And lastly, we are also pleased to have with us tonight another member of the board of the Reginald F. Lewis Foundation who is also his aunt (talk about family values)! Please greet Ms. Beverly Cooper, a member of the Foundation.

Now I don't want the press to be upset, because I am not going to read a written speech—so bear with me. I will try to speak slowly so that you can keep up. But the truth is that there was massive speculation. Some of us have said that we were going to try to get one million dollars between April and the time of our convention. Well, I hope that you all clearly hear that we have two million dollars for our endowment—two million.

The Lord moves in mysterious ways. I want to thank the attorney general. I don't know how Dan Quayle feels about this, but I had a good reception over at the State House from the lieutenant governor and was graciously welcomed by our sister, who is the great attorney general of this State of Indiana, and we want to thank you for the honor that you have bestowed upon me.

We are off to a great start. I feel good tonight, so I want for you all to loosen up. It's good to be at a convention, it's good to have sisters and brothers together. There has been a lot written about the NAACP lately. This time there are no fights, no divisions. Our ranks are together, we are moving forward, we are making progress, we are making a difference from coast to coast—on the east coast, on the west coast, in the north and in the south.

The NAACP is taking care of business in the name of the freedom struggle, and we are proud of it on this night. So I just feel good tonight.

Benjamin Chavis

The theme of our convention is "Passing the Torch—Preparing for a Better Tomorrow," and my remarks tonight will be focused on that theme.

For eighty-four years, the NAACP has stood the test of time as our nation's oldest and largest civil rights organization. The historical record confirms beyond the shadow of a doubt that the NAACP also has been one of the boldest, one of the most respected, one of the most aggressive, one of the most tenacious, and one of the most feared organizations in the world.

Yet the truth is we have also, on occasion, been one of the most misunderstood and maligned organizations, particularly by certain forces that are opposed to freedom, particularly by certain forces that are opposed to civil rights that would put a spin on the civil rights movement to try to superimpose illusions on our true image. And so we come tonight to acknowledge and to celebrate the fact that the NAACP continues to be a freedom-fighting organization.

Now sometimes when you use the language of the freedom movement, it makes some people who are opposed to freedom uncomfortable. So tonight, if I step on some toes, forgive me.

The quest for freedom has been long. The NAACP has a unique place in the leadership of the struggle for justice, freedom, and equality. We therefore affirm that we all stand an the shoulders of others. Thirty years ago in 1963 we all well remember that our state field secretary down in Mississippi was slain, was shot to death in the sight of his wife, in the sight of his children, solely because he dared to mobilize, he dared to organize African Americans for the right to vote. And yet, thirty years later, if the truth will be told, we still have to mobilize, we still have to organize to get the full right to vote, to get the full representation of our communities, of our constituencies.

The recent rulings by the Supreme Court seek to challenge whether or not we can have equal representation in the halls of Congress. I am so proud that on this day I can say without fear of contradiction we have the strongest chairman of the Congressional Black Caucus in its whole history, Kweisi Mfume. Kweisi Mfume, we are proud of you. And we at the NAACP intend to forge a strategic alliance with the Congressional Black Caucus. When the Congressional Black Caucus takes a stand on Capitol Hill, we will take a stand on our hill and in two thousand places throughout the United States of America.

It is about closing our ranks. We accept the torch, and we intend to run the race. Not just to mark time, but we intend to run the race to win the race for the benefit of our people who have been denied too long, who have been denied equal justice too long, who have been denied racial justice too long, who have been denied economic justice too long, who have been denied full justice too long.

Now I have to be careful because in tomorrow's *Time* magazine, even before I speak, they have already concluded that I am too radical for the NAACP. I got my membership card when I was twelve years old. . . . I thanked my mamma, I thanked my daddy for placing that card in my hands and for telling me one Sunday morning before we even had grace, they said, "Son, take this card, put it in your pocket, but also put it in your soul, put it in your life. . . . Stand up even as a child, don't bow down to injustice. . . ."

And I want to tell you, for a mamma and a daddy to tell their child to stand up—Lord have mercy! . . . If we would tell our children to stand up in 1993, do away with drugs, stand up in 1993, do away with fratricidal killing, stand up in 1993, tell our children not only to join the NAACP, tell our children to participate in resurrecting the life, revitalizing the life of the NAACP. Because if you revitalize the life of the NAACP, we help to revitalize the life of the community where the NAACP has a residence.

After all of the stones that have been thrown at the NAACP, we are still here. After eighty-four years let the word go out that as we look toward the twenty-first century, we are not going anywhere but up the mountain, down freedom road, winning more victories, making a difference in more lives. That's our tradition and that will be our future, so help us God.

I am going to say something. . . . From the very moment of my election, there have been attempts—this is a family meeting—there have been attempts to divide me from the chairman. I want to put it out so that everybody will hear it. There is a rigid solidarity between the executive director and the chairman of the board, there is no disunity. And people say, "Well, how can you deal with a strong chairman?" I want a strong chairman, a strong executive director. A strong chairman makes for a strong NAACP. And I want all of my branch presidents—all the branch presidents stand up—I want all of the branch presidents to be strong branch presidents, because as strong as you are, it enables our NAACP to be strong. All of our branch presidents, God bless you.

No national organization is any stronger than its local base. If you want to know where the strength of the NAACP is, go to our local branches. That's where the strength is. And by the grace of God we are going to use all of our strength, we are going to use the interest from the endowment over these many years into the future to strengthen our local base, to strengthen our outreach into the community, to strengthen our participation in the life of our beloved association.

I have come a long way to get here, be patient with me. I wish I could really take the time to tell you how it feels to have chains around your ankles, to have somebody strip-search you in the sight of your children, to have somebody put you in prison because you stand up for other people's children. But you know, through it all, like Nelson Mandela said yesterday to us,

"I have to be careful because . . . they have already concluded that I am too radical for the NAACP."

the forces of oppression only endure or only last as long as those who are oppressed will tolerate. And things in South Africa are changing, but they are changing because sisters and brothers in the ANC and sisters and brothers in the anti-apartheid movement in South Africa have sacrificed much.

When you saw this brother standing at this podium yesterday—seventy-one some years old, after being locked up for twenty-seven years in a South African dungeon, with the ability to stand before us and issue a clarion call to the people of South Africa and to the people of the world to bring a democratic transformation of that nation—it makes us all proud, but it also makes us understand that we too have a responsibility on this side of the ocean. Because if the truth was told there are still lingering vestiges of American apartheid, there are still lingering vestiges of racial discrimination in our land, and that is why the NAACP is in business to challenge racial discrimination.

And you will see going through this, the eighty-fourth annual convention, there is one theme among many themes, and it is a necessity for us as we move toward the twenty-first century to tackle the problem of economic inequity, of economic inequality. . . . And so we are asking all our branches, we are going to be discussing it at the national board of directors meeting this week, "What is it that we need to do?" You have heard about the historic Fair Share Agreement that we signed with Flagstar Corporation [owners of the Denny's restaurant chain], that we signed with Richardson Sports—and again I want to clarify that Dr. Gibson is going to talk in more depth about this tomorrow night—but since he and I are on the same page, I just want to share a little bit with you.

Our quest is not just to get us into the restaurant. Let me tell you a true story. When I was a boy in Oxford, North Carolina we could not go into the movies. I thought that they must have been showing something mighty powerful to keep us locked out, but now we can go in. But if you look at what's on the screen, what's on the screen is still segregated.

And so we have to not only now move to change the product and what is seen in most movies but we have to also start owning some of the movie houses, start owning some of the outlets for distribution. Now when I stayed in Los Angeles that first week after my selection while everybody waited for the verdict of the officers that had been accused of beating Rodney King, I stayed in the 'hood. And the constant refrain in Nickerson Gardens and Jordon Downs and Imperial Courts housing projects in South Central Los Angeles was the theme "jobs, jobs, jobs—we need jobs."

And we at the NAACP understand that we are not a social service organization, we are a social change organization, but in trying to create and bring about social change, sometimes it is necessary to exhibit the kind of social change methodology in life at the community level that we want the government and the state and others to abide by. The Fair Share Agreement with Flagstar is an example, it is not the totality but just a small example, because over the next seven years we are going to put over one billion dollars of economic benefit directly into the hands of African Americans, where they will own the franchises, where they will be controlling the marketing, where they will receive economic benefit.

But that does not mean that we will back off from our stance of being against discrimination. What it does mean is that where there is a Denny's or Hardee's or whatever the name of the restaurant, we are not only going to demand that we be treated fairly, but we are going to demand that we have equal access to owning businesses in our community.

And this subject about enterprise zones needs to be expanded. Right now, enterprise zones in South Central and other parts of the country have not really served our needs. We would rather have empowerment zones—zones where we become economically empowered in the communities where we live, in the communities where we work, rather than for outside interests to come in and exploit our work forces and take the capital and apply it outside of our communities. We want the benefit of our labor, the benefit of our work to stay in our communities so that our communities will get the economic uplift and benefit from it. So economic development, community development, is high on our agenda as we move toward the twenty-first century.

Now I am very pleased to say that we have a national housing corporation and in a few weeks—I see my friend from the *Baltimore Sun* here and I am going to say this very slowly—in a few weeks the NAACP is going to announce a joint venture in the City of Baltimore that will derive over six hundred units of housing for low income persons in the City of Baltimore through the work of our national housing corporation.

And does it mean that we are going into the housing business? It means that we will go into the business until we can find others to take it on right and show how it should be done. The answer is yes. If we have an opportunity to provide one house, we will do it. And in this case we will provide six hundred houses to low-income persons in the City of Baltimore. John Mance, a member of our national board of directors, heads up our national housing commission. John, where are you? Let the people see you. So I hope that tomorrow's story in the *Baltimore Sun* will have a little different spin than the one that we got a few weeks ago.

Secondly, when I talked about expanding the mission of the NAACP to other racial and ethnic communities, I was also talking about expanding the mission and the totality of the NAACP to the diversity that is within the African American community. Do you all know that we have diversity within us?

Now I know that I am getting ready to do something that you have never seen before. We have in our midst tonight a black Indian chief, and I am going to introduce him. But before I introduce him, let me just say what we are going to do. It turns out that there is a Native American tribe in the state of Connecticut that has land rights to most of the state. Now while we are talking about economic development and community development, I would hope that NAACP members in Connecticut don't get nervous when we are talking about opening up the NAACP to welcome home—come back home to the NAACP, our Native American sisters and brothers. He is not going to speak but I want you to see this brother, I want to introduce him. I am pleased to introduce the chief of the Golden Hero Tribe of the Pasquescat Indian Nation, Chief Quiet Hawk. Let's greet him. Give him an NAACP welcome—Chief Quiet Hawk. I told you this was going to be a historic convention.

Now, Brother Chairman Kweisi Mfume, some tribes get immediate recognition, some other tribes can't get an answer from the Bureau of Indian Affairs. Chief Quiet Hawk has had to go to court just to get some recognition. Now, we know why they do not want to give him recognition—because he has got title to the land. And so, Brother Chairman of the Congressional Black Caucus, the NAACP wants to work with the Congressional Black Caucus to aid our Indian brothers and sisters, not only to get recognition, but to get their land. Now you know the Lord moves in mysterious ways. We have heard that Bridgeport is about to go bankrupt. Well, we can help Bridgeport if you give us our land, give us our land, give us our land.

Economic development, economic empowerment, expanding the mission of the NAACP, it all works together. We are accepting the torch and we are going to run this race. We are going to run the race to win the race, not just to mark time in the race. Now you see I have to say that my vice-chairman, Benjamin Andrews, has been the instigator for this and another one of my national board members have brought to my attention that we have a postmaster general in Washington named Marvin Runyon. Marvin Runyon is a holdover. Marvin is a leftover from prior administrations. We are calling on President Clinton to help us remove the leftovers from the prior administration because Marvin Runyon, the postmaster general, has put on the hit list tens of thousands of African American workers.

We have enough unemployment. We do not need to lose the few jobs that we got, and so if we have to choose between keeping one man as postmaster general and losing tens of thousands of brothers' and sisters' jobs, we say bye-bye Mr. Postmaster General. Bye-bye, bye-bye, bye-bye.

Thirty years ago, a couple of months after the tragic assassination of Medgar Evers in Jackson, Mississippi, we assembled ourselves in Washington, D.C., for the historic March on Washington. It was the day that Martin Luther King, Jr., made his famous "I Have A Dream" speech. A month after the March on Washington, in Birmingham, Alabama, a bomb was placed in the Sixteenth Street Baptist Church and four of our little sisters in Sunday School were tragically murdered. And yet this is 1993, thirty years later, and while we have been here in Indianapolis, we have also planned for the Thirtieth Anniversary Memorial March on Washington.

Now my concept of having memorials is that we do something in the present that will signify and give dignity to our respect for what happened in the past. In other words, we are interested in doing something more than having a nostalgic replay of '63. What we want to have is to mobilize our constituencies, our branches, to come to Washington with a clear civil rights agenda, with a clear set of programs, public policy issues affecting every neighborhood, in every congressional district. Everyone knows why we are marching. See, marching is therapeutic. But the question is after the march is over—what do we do?

Because if you were to have a commemorative account of all of the marches that we have had, all of the marches that we have participated in, we would have to admit that we have some homework to do. And so as we plan this march, and as the NAACP repositions itself to provide leadership for the 1993 March on Washington, we have said in clear terms that as we mobilize our troops, our forces, our constituencies, we are marching to demand justice, we are marching for jobs, we are marching for health care. We are marching for an end to the kind of neglect of the urban centers that have gone on far too long. We are marching for our children. We are marching for ourselves. We are marching for the unborn generation.

But we are also marching to send a signal—not so much to the White House, because as a minister some of you have heard me say Capitol Hill is not the only hill from which cometh our help. There is a God somewhere and I know that this is Sunday night, but let me say to you that we will betray our Creator if we sit down and don't stand up and point out the inequities in our society. We will betray our faith in the God that has provided the bridges over the troubled waters and we shall turn it around now.

You see, one of the things about being the oldest and the largest, it may make you think that we have got to relax. But being the oldest and the largest means that we have the most responsibility. It means that we have the most determination to mobilize our constituencies so that we can make a difference. So when you see those banners and when you wear those buttons about marching on Washington is not just marching on Washington, it is marching on the state houses, it's marching on the municipal houses, it's marching around our houses to straighten out the lives in our communities.

We would be wrong to go to Washington to talk about jobs, justice and peace and then go back home and allow high unemployment and allow injustice to take place in our local communities. We must exhibit strength at home. And when you exhibit strength at home, then when we go to Washington, we have something to talk about.

"We will betray our Creator if we don't stand up and point out the inequities in our society."

Now as I move to my conclusion, I want to say once again how proud I am. There are other members of my family that I want to introduce.

First, I am proud that the first lady of the NAACP is sticking with me. She is sticking with me in a way that allows me to be out there on the cutting edge. It is not easy to be away from home ninety percent of the time and then to still get a smile when you come back home. I want to say that I have had the fullest support from my wife, and I am proud to introduce you to the first lady of the NAACP, Martha Rivera Chavis.

Now this won't take long, but I am proud of my family. I have six children and three grandchildren. I am recruiting members for the NAACP. You have got to practice what you preach.

My youngest son is asleep. His name is Franklin, he is three years old. I have a twenty-one-year-old daughter who is here—Renita. Renita, stand up. Thank you. She is a member of the Youth Council in Oxford, North Carolina. And my sister—one of my sisters—is here. She is a professor at St. Augustus College in Raleigh, North Carolina, chairman of the English department and Afro-American studies department, Dr. Helen Chavis-Otho.

I wanted you to know that we practice in the Chavis family in the national outreach. My sister was in graduate school at the University of Wisconsin and we had already talked about going to Africa in our house. And when my mother had found out that my sister had gone to Africa and gotten married, it put a test on these principles that we were talking about. And I am pleased to report that my family celebrated the fact that my sister went into the heart of the Sudan and found a strong African husband, Arnada Otho, from the Sudan.

And one of the things that we want to change is some of the foreign policy towards the Sudan. The United States for twelve years was on the wrong side. You know we just happen to be on the wrong side of all these issues, and that is why we have said that the NAACP must not only impact domestic policy, we must impact international policy. We live in a global community. What affects us in our communities here affects sisters and brothers from the Sudan to Soweto, from Rwanda to Zambia, all over Africa and in the Caribbean. And I am pleased to report to you that we have already gotten applications to open branches of the NAACP in Africa and the Caribbean. This is good news.

So we are going to be with the Golden Hero Tribe in Connecticut and we are going to be with the tribe in Sudan. We are going to be with the tribe in South Africa. We are going to be with the tribe in the 'hood. Wherever our people are, we are going to be together.

Now at the end of my remarks—Mr. Chairman, I am going to ask special permission—I want some brothers that have come out of the Detroit branch of the NAACP to come and perform a song that they have put together for the NAACP. And when you hear me talk about expanding the mission, when you hear me talking about bringing a new beat, about getting the torch and running the race to win, something about having the beat as you run the race to win, we got a song. The name of the song is "Come Back Home to the NAACP."

God bless you. May God keep you. May God bless the NAACP. "Come Back Home to the NAACP." God bless you.

It wasn't long, however, before the enthusiasm that reigned at the annual convention gave way to conflict, some of it stemming from infighting that had been going on for years between members of the board of directors. In addition, not everyone was comfortable with the "new" NAACP. Traditionalists were uneasy because they felt Chavis was trying to do too much, too fast; in many cases, they also disagreed philosophically with parts of his agenda. Of particular concern to people both inside and outside the organization were his overtures to street-gang members, Nation of Islam leader Louis Farrakhan, and various black militants and leftists in his attempt to forge closer bonds between all African Americans. Chavis also drew criticism for not informing board members of his decision to settle a sexual harassment lawsuit lodged against him by a former assistant and for other alleged instances of financial mismanagement that plunged the NAACP deep into debt.

By the time the NAACP met for its annual convention in July 1994, some members were angrily demanding that Chavis resign. Declaring that the charges against him were "a complete political ploy" intended to force him from office, he refused to step down, even after some local NAACP branches began to withhold money from the national organization pending an audit and a coalition of influential black professional women questioned his ability to lead. The furor reached a crescendo over the next few weeks, and on August 20, the NAACP board of directors voted to fire him.

Since then, a still-defiant Chavis—who described his ouster as a "lynching" and himself as a "freedom fighter" in the war over the very future of the civil rights movement—has taken steps to establish himself as the leader of a new coalition of black nationalists (including Louis Farrakhan) and Pan-Africanists known as the National African American Leadership Summit. Two days after his firing, he also filed a lawsuit against the NAACP in which he demanded his job back and claimed that the organization had ruined his reputation as a civil rights activist. A judge quickly rejected his request for reinstatement, and he and the NAACP came to an out-of-court agreement on severance issues.

The NAACP continues to wrestle with its desperate financial situation while it searches for a new executive director whose views will be more in line with its traditional integrationist approach. It took a step in that direction in February 1995, when longtime chairman William F. Gibson, a Chavis ally, was ousted and replaced by Myrlie Evers-Williams, the widow of slain civil rights leader Medgar Evers.

SOURCES

Black Enterprise, "Chavis to Lead NAACP into New Era," July, 1993, p. 17.

Crisis, "A New Beginning as Chavis Takes the Helm," April/May, 1993, pp. 24-26; "Productivity Highlights NAACP Confab in Indy," August/September, 1993, pp. 48-51.

Detroit Free Press, "NAACP Chooses Militant Minister," April 10, 1993; "NAACP Chief Looks Forward," April 19, 1993; "Chavis Breathes New Life into Civil Rights Agenda," July 11, 1993; "Chavis to Face Tough Crowd at NAACP Board Meeting," August 13, 1994; "Opposition to Chavis Increases," August 15, 1994; "NAACP Board Hunts New Leader, Tries to Stabilize After Firing Chavis," August 22, 1994; "Chavis Claims NAACP Ruined His Reputation," August 24, 1994; "Chavis Vows to Stand by Farrakhan," August 29,

1994; "Chavis, NAACP Settle Suit Over Firing," October 22, 1994.

Detroit News, "New NAACP Director Pushes 'New Agenda for a New Time,'" April 11, 1993; "NAACP Hopes New Director Will Bond Splintering Board," April 12, 1993, p. 6A; "NAACP Tries to Halt Internal Feud," April 13, 1994, p. 5A; "Chavis Striving to Revamp NAACP," April 28, 1994, p. 10; "NAACP Summit Focus Shifts to Chavis," June 12, 1994, p. 5A; "NAACP Source: Chavis Out," August 21, 1994; "Chavis Hints of a Lawsuit: 'I Just Want to Be Treated Fairly,'" August 22, 1994.

Ebony, June, 1979; "Ben Chavis: A New Director, a New Direction at the NAACP," July, 1993, pp. 76-80.

Grand Rapids Press, "NAACP's New Chief Quickly Sets Ambitious Program," April 11, 1993, p. A5; "Chavis Challenges NAACP Members as Convention Closes," July 16, 1993, p. 5A; "NAACP Chief Meets with Leftists," April 10, 1994, p. A23; "NAACP Rewrites Black Civil Rights Agenda," June 13, 1994, p. A3; "Black Leaders 'Get in Trenches,' Show Unity," June 14, 1994, p. A2; "NAACP Chief Chavis Vows to Stay on New Course," July 11, 1994, p. A2; "Politics Behind Lawsuit, Chavis Says," August 5, 1994, p. A3; "Chavis Fired as Leader of NAACP," August 21, 1994; "Chavis Rips NAACP Board After His Ouster," August 22, 1994, p. A3; "Chavis Vows to Continue Freedom Fight," August 25, 1994, p. A6; "NAACP Flounders in Financial Crisis," November 6, 1994, p. A2; "Ex-NAACP Director Creates New Group," June 4, 1995, p. A4.

Jet, "New NAACP Director Chavis Maps Strategies for Future," April 26, 1993.

Newsweek, "Getting Real at the NAACP: Can New Head Benjamin Chavis Bring Young Blacks Back into the Aging Organization?" June 14, 1993; "Grieving for the NAACP," June 27, 1994, p. 37; "Buying Silence, Paying a Price," August 8, 1994, pp. 21-22; "Trial by Fire at the NAACP," August 22, 1994, pp. 24-28; "The Fall of Benjamin Chavis," August 29, 1994, p. 27.

New York Times Magazine, "A Bridge Too Far?: Benjamin Chavis," June 12, 1994.

People, "Man in Motion: Benjamin Chavis Is Taking the NAACP into the Streets—and into Corporate Boardrooms," July 19, 1993; "An Uncivil War," September 5, 1994.

Time, "And the New NAACP Head Is . . . ," April 5, 1993, p. 13; "Process of Elimination," April 19, 1993, p. 17; "He's No Gentle Ben: The NAACP's New Leader Is Shaking Up the Stodgy Group," July 19, 1993, p. 33; "Playing Board Games," August 8, 1994, p. 28; "After the Revolution," August 29, 1994, p. 40.

U.S. News and World Report, "Chavis's Story: Eyes on the Next Prize," August 30, 1993.

Shirley Chisholm

1924–

African American politician and women's rights activist

In November 1968, Shirley Chisholm made history when she became the first black woman elected to the United States Congress as a representative from New York. A little more than three years later, on January 25, 1972, she made history once again when she became the first black and the first woman to announce her intention to seek the Democratic presidential nomination. Although these "firsts" by themselves form a considerable legacy, they are not her only accomplishments. As a politician and activist at both the state and national level, Chisholm has earned the respect and admiration of many for her efforts to improve the lives of women and children, especially those trapped in poverty.

A native of Brooklyn, New York, Chisholm spent most of her early childhood in the home of her maternal grandmother on the Caribbean island of Barbados while her parents struggled to establish themselves financially. There she attended the British-style schools until she was about ten, at which time she rejoined her parents in New York City and continued her education in the public school system. Chisholm later earned a bachelor's degree from Brooklyn College and a master's degree from Columbia University. A specialist in early childhood education, she then began teaching nursery school and eventually was promoted to director, a position she held for twenty years.

Chisholm first became active in politics during the early 1950s, working mostly behind the scenes for the local Democratic party. But by 1960, she had become a key figure in the struggle to defeat her district's well-entrenched political machine and secure new representation instead. Her own election to the New York State Assembly followed in 1964, and in 1968, she defeated Republican candidate James Farmer (the former national chairman of CORE) for a seat in the U.S. House of Representatives.

While serving at the state level, Chisholm had gained a reputation as a candid, feisty, and hard-working "maverick" who cherished her independence from the official party line. She burst upon the Washington scene in exactly the same way. In a dramatic break with precedent, she balked at being assigned to the House Agricultural Committee and demanded an alternate assignment that was more in line with her interests and the needs of her constituents. (She ended up on the Veterans' Affairs Committee and, later, the Education and Labor Committee.)

In her first speech before fellow members of the House of Representatives, delivered March 26, 1969, Chisholm made her feelings clear on the need for a change in national priorities. It is reprinted from the Congressional Record, *91st Congress, 1st session, U.S. Gov't Printing Office, 1969.*

Mr. Speaker, on the same day President Nixon announced he had decided the United States will not be safe unless we start to build a defense system against missiles, the Headstart program in the District of Columbia was cut back for the lack of money.

As a teacher, and as a woman, I do not think I will ever understand what kind of values can be involved in spending nine billion dollars—and more, I am sure—on elaborate, unnecessary and impractical weapons when several thousand disadvantaged children in the nation's capital get nothing.

When the new administration took office, I was one of the many Americans who hoped it would mean that our country would benefit from the fresh perspectives, the new ideas, the different priorities of a leader who had no part in the mistakes of the past. Mr. Nixon had said things like this: "If our cities are to be livable for the next generation, we can delay no longer in launching new approaches to the problems that beset them and to the tensions that tear them apart." And he said, "When you cut expenditures for education, what you are doing is shortchanging the American future."

But frankly, I have never cared too much what people say. What I am interested in is what they do. We have waited to see what the new administration is going to do. The pattern now is becoming clear.

Apparently launching those new programs can be delayed for a while, after all. It seems we have to get some missiles launched first.

Recently the new Secretary of Commerce spelled it out. The Secretary, Mr. Stans, told a reporter that the new administration is "pretty well agreed it must take time out from major social objectives" until it can stop inflation.

The new Secretary of Health, Education and Welfare, Robert Finch, came to the Hill to tell the House Education and Labor Committee that he thinks we should spend more on education, particularly in city schools. But, he said, unfortunately we cannot "afford" to, until we have reached some kind of honorable solution to the Vietnam war. I was glad to read that the distinguished Member from Oregon [Mrs. Green] asked Mr. Finch this: "With the crisis we have in education, and the crisis in our cities, can we wait to settle the war? Shouldn't it be the other way around? Unless we can meet the crisis in education, we really can't afford the war."

Shirley Chisholm

Secretary of Defense Melvin Laird came to Capitol Hill, too. His mission was to sell the antiballistic-missile insanity to the Senate. He was asked what the new administration is doing about the war. To hear him, one would have thought it was 1968, that the former Secretary of State was defending the former policies, that nothing had ever happened—a President had never decided not to run because he knew the nation would reject him, in despair over this tragic war we have blundered into. Mr. Laird talked of being prepared to spend at least two more years in Vietnam.

Two more years, two more years of hunger for Americans, of death for our best young men, of children here at home suffering the lifelong handicap of not having a good education when they are young. Two more years of high taxes, collected to feed the cancerous growth of a Defense Department budget that now consumes two thirds of our federal income.

Two more years of too little being done to fight our greatest enemies, poverty, prejudice and neglect, here in our own country. Two more years of fantastic waste in the Defense Department and of penny pinching on social programs. Our country cannot survive two more years, or four, of these kinds of policies. It must stop—this year—now.

Now, I am not a pacifist. I am deeply, unalterably opposed to this war in Vietnam. Apart from all the other considerations—and they are many—the main fact is that we cannot squander there the lives, the money, the energy that we need desperately here, in our cities, in our schools.

I wonder whether we cannot reverse our whole approach to spending. For years, we have given the military, the defense industry, a blank check. New weapons systems are dreamed up, billions are spent, and many times they are found to be impractical, inefficient, unsatisfactory, even worthless. What do we do then? We spend more money on them. But with social programs, what do we do? Take the Job Corps. Its failure has been mercilessly exposed and criticized. If it had been a military research and development project, they would have been covered up or explained away, and Congress would have been ready to pour more billions after those that had been wasted on it.

The case of Pride, Inc., is interesting. This vigorous, successful black organization, here in Washington, conceived and built by young inner-city men, has been ruthlessly attacked by its enemies in the government, in this Congress. At least six auditors from the General Accounting Office were put to work investigating Pride. They worked seven months and spent more than $100,000. They uncovered a fraud. It was something less than $2,100. Meanwhile, millions of dollars—billions of dollars, in fact—were being spent by the Department of Defense, and how many auditors and investigators were checking into their negotiated contracts? Five.

We Americans have come to feel that it is our mission to make the world free. We believe that we are the good guys, everywhere—in Vietnam, in Latin America, wherever we go. We believe we are the good guys at home, too. When the Kerner Commission told white America what black America had always known, that prejudice and hatred built the nation's slums, maintain them and profit by them, white America would not believe it. But it is true. Unless we start to fight and defeat the enemies of poverty and racism in our own country and make our talk of equality and opportunity ring true, we are exposed as hypocrites in the eyes of the world when we talk about making other people free.

I am deeply disappointed at the clear evidence that the number-one priority of the new administration is to buy more and more weapons of war, to return to the era of the cold war, to ignore the war we must fight here—the war that is not optional. There is only one way, I believe, to turn these policies around. The Congress can respond to the mandate that the American people have clearly expressed. They have said, "End this war. Stop the waste. Stop the killing. Do something for your own people first." We must find the money to "launch the new approaches," as Mr. Nixon said. We must force the administration to rethink its distorted, unreal scale of priorities. Our children, our jobless men, our deprived, rejected and starving fellow citizens must come first.

For this reason, I intend to vote "No" on every money bill that comes to the floor of this House that provides any funds for the Department of Defense. Any bill whatsoever, until the time comes when our values and priorities have been turned right side up again, until the monstrous waste and the shocking profits in the defense budget have been eliminated and our country starts to use its strength, its tremen-

"Unless we start to fight and defeat the enemies of poverty and racism in our own country and make our talk of equality and opportunity ring true, we are exposed as hypocrites in the eyes of the world when we talk about making other people free."

dous resources, for people and peace, not for profits and war.

It was Calvin Coolidge, I believe, who made the comment that "the Business of America is Business." We are now spending eighty billion dollars a year on defense—that is two-thirds of every tax dollar. At this time, gentlemen, the business of America is war, and it is time for a change.

*As a member of Congress, Chisholm worked tirelessly on issues involving women, children, education, and what she characterized as the government's neglect of minorities—*all *minorities, not just blacks. (She took very seriously her responsibility to represent* everyone *in her ethnically-diverse district, not just the black community.) In January 1972, she decided to take her message to a national audience as the first black and the first woman to run for the Democratic presidential nomination. In a speech she gave to students at the Newark (New Jersey) College of Engineering on April 15, 1972—one of many similar ones she delivered during her campaign that spring and summer—Chisholm examined the problem of economic injustice in America. It is reprinted from* Representative American Speeches: 1971-1972, *edited by Waldo W. Braden (Wilson, 1972).*

Political participation has been and continues to be the way individuals gain access to Government in this country. But . . . there has been a failure in the process of political participation—we all know this—and I think most of us are now aware that the failure has done its damage in Government, so that individuals in this country now feel powerless and out of control of their own lives. We have a Government that is remote. We have a Government that is responsive to other institutions that are equally remote: large corporations, conglomerates, powerful interest groups, and an uncaring or condescending financial establishment. We have a Government that has, in short, lost its credibility.

There are a lot of theories about why this Government of ours has lost touch with its own people. But if we were to wait until we had a total agreement about exactly what is wrong to try to make changes, we could all be sitting here for two or three centuries and we would still probably be without answers, no changes would have been made, and the problems would be worse.

We don't have time to sit and wait. We have to make an input. This is why you see me here in New Jersey today—a black woman from Brooklyn, New York—as a candidate for nomination to the United States presidency.

I have my own theory about what we can do to improve this United States Government. And my theory is easy to understand. We have to expand the base of political participation in this country so that the decisions made reflect the thinking of more than just a small segment of the population. For I believe that you cannot exclude over one half of the population—women—and one tenth of the population—black people—and exclude in addition the points of view represented by young people, poor people, the Spanish-speaking and other minorities—you cannot exclude all of these groups from influence over governmental decisions and social policy without finding that the Government is out of touch and that its policy is narrow and damaging to the majority of people it is intended to serve.

Let's take the American economy for an example of what I mean by "narrow and damaging" policy. Today, we have no economic bill of rights, and we need one. We must renegotiate the basic terms of our economic relationships in this society.

The American Indian knows that the capital he needs to start basic economic development in Indian communities is not available in significant amounts through public agencies of Government, yet he knows that without that capital he will continue to be exploited on and near reservations, in urban centers, and wherever he lives.

Ask him and he will tell you that the American economy denies his citizenship.

Ask the Chicano in East Los Angeles, in which thirty-five percent of the housing is substandard, whether President Nixon's announcement of a record two million housing starts in 1971 had anything to do with improvement of housing in East Los Angeles.

Or talk to the Spanish-speaking migrant worker in California, or Texas, about the abundance of good health and medical care which this Administration proclaims: That migrant worker knows that infant and maternal mortality among his or her people is 125 percent higher than the national rate; that influenza and pneumonia death rates are 200 percent higher than the national rate; that death from tuberculosis and infectious disease is 260 percent higher: And life expectancy itself for the migrant worker is 49 years—compared with 67.5 years for the members of the silent majority.

Talk to the young black man or woman in our urban areas.

In urban poverty neighborhoods the unemployment rate three years ago was almost six percent—on the average—and that is the figure which today the President's economic policies have bestowed on the entire nation—on the average. Yet today in the urban black ghetto unemployment averages twelve percent and rising! Is that where President Nixon plans to take the nation during the next four years? He has made this entire nation an unemployment disaster area comparable to conditions which existed only in ghettos three years ago.

In the city of Seattle the Nixon economic policy has created a whole new class of involuntary poor—middle-class Americans who five years ago never thought they would have to know what the bitter sting and emptiness of unemployment feels like.

I mention the systematic exclusion of the Indian, the Chicano, and the ghetto black from the American economy only as examples of a much broader and more disturbing pattern.

They are not the only ones who live outside the system. Children under sixteen comprise thirty-eight percent of the poor; and households headed by persons aged sixty-five and older make up twenty-three percent of all the poor in America today. Women, regardless of race or class, find themselves the victims of economic discrimination so consistently on the basis of their sex alone that they are uniting across a broad front to fight for basic economic equality.

The coalition women have formed—in which the white college graduate links arms with the black household domestic worker whose only education may be life itself—is the beginning of the union of the disenfranchised peoples of America. As the American labor movement discovered years ago there is no better or quicker way to bring people together than the common experience of economic injustice!

Economic injustice, however, is now no longer the exclusive possession of the poor.

> ***"Economic injustice is now no longer the exclusive possession of the poor."***

A union of the disenfranchised, a coalition of those who are on the outside of the American economy, will not be purely a union of racial minorities, the young, and women. For economic injustice has shown its ugly head in millions of American homes where five years ago it was unknown.

If unemployment is not enough, there is the question of interest rates on home loans, the price of food and clothing, the price of gasoline and heating oil, and the ever-increasing cost of everyday public transportation in city after city.

The Administration's sensational price control program, in the face of repeated and categorical statements by the President that he would never use such controls, was at best an effort to close the barn door after the horse of runaway inflation had long gone. In fact, the door was never even half closed.

I have been particularly concerned about the rent control aspect of Phase II. The rent controls were highly publicized by the Administration—so highly publicized in fact that they amounted to an open season on tenants by landlords who declared that the President had said, "Now is the time for a rent increase, so get it while you can."

Or look at food prices now that we're into Phase II. The Consumer Price Index for food showed an increase of four-tenths of a percent in December after the conclusion of Phase I controls: The December figure, according to a recent article entitled "Higher Prices Ahead for Groceries" in *U.S. News & World Report,* translates into a 4.8 percent annual increase in food prices—double the rate which occurred under Phase I.

And in some notable specific items, food prices skyrocketed immediately after the end of Phase I: tomatoes up fifty percent a pound from forty-three cents to sixty cents on the average; lettuce per head up from thirty-four to forty-seven cents, an increase of thirty-eight percent. Across the board, the cost of food in grocery stores went up 1.3 percent in December, twice what is usual for that month.

And Dr. Herbert Stein, chairman of the President's Council of Economic Advisers, states that he wouldn't be surprised if the "bulge" in prices would increase in the future. He did not mention the increases in other areas as well—the cost of new cars and gasoline during December for one.

The cost of living is first on all of our minds this important year. Yet the President has decided that it is a year for travel.

But I ask—when is he going to make a "Trip to Peking" in regard to the basic problems facing us in the United States this year? He is willing to go halfway 'round the world—yet he doesn't have time to walk ten blocks from the White House in Washington and look at the lives people are living under Phase II.

While the President was in Peking, almost twenty-one million Americans over sixty-five—roughly ten percent of our population—faced the rising costs of food and services with fixed incomes—fixed at a median of $2,800 a year if you are an old man, fixed at $1,400 a year if you happen to be an old woman. The most recent survey—published in 1970—showed that ninety percent of these citizens over sixty-five subsist on retirement benefits of which the bulk is Social Security payments.

In the President's State of the Union Message January 20 of this year he laid special emphasis on "action for the aging" and urged Congress to enact a five percent across-the-board increase in Social Security. That my friends is just two-tenths of a percent above the 4.8 percent increase in food prices we are now experiencing in Phase II.

And I think it is very significant that President Nixon lied to the American people when he spoke to the nation on January 20 and said that "our program of wage and price controls is working," and cited as evidence for that statement the fact that the Consumer Price Index, and I quote him again, ". . . which rose at a yearly rate of slightly over 6 percent during 1969 and the first half of 1970, rose at a rate of only 1.7 percent from August through November of 1971."

The next day, January 21, the White House released the figures which showed what the President deliberately omitted from his State of the Union Message: that during December 1971 and into the month of January consumer prices rose by 4.8 percent, well on their way back to the previous outrageous levels.

Older Americans know what these figures mean. They mean taking scarce funds from this month's meager food budget and putting it into clothing if it's winter; or they mean less for medical care or medicine these months in order to buy food.

But since the President has decided this year to try to turn our attention to his foreign policy grandstanding, I would say a few words about the impact of international economic decisions as they affect you and me.

Our economic bill of rights should set forth certain basic principles regarding foreign economic policy. If I am elected President, one of the first acts of my Administration would be high-level reconsideration of the relation between our international economic decisions and their impact, in particular, on the poor people of America.

Every day the President virtually by himself makes decisions on foreign trade, surcharges, tariffs, and balance of payments which have direct consequences on the lives of millions of Americans, but neither the Congress nor the American public share in a great many of those decisions.

As part of the President's Annual Economic Report, I would submit to the Congress an "Economic Impact Statement" similar to the environmental impact statements required now under Federal law. The Economic Impact Statement would show how, for example, foreign trade quotas or changes in tariff rates impact on various groups in our national economy at home. Today this is not done. President Nixon acts on the assumption that what is good for the international bankers and corporations on Wall Street will inevitably trickle down to the middle-class consumer and the unemployed person.

Yet the only things trickling down from this Administration are taxes and increased costs of goods and services.

Take for example the so-called value-added tax which the Nixon economists are now promoting. It is nothing other than a thinly disguised sales tax on a national level, designed to add taxes at each stage of the journey from manufacturer (or importer) to the consumer.

Now in theory, says the President, this spreads the tax load on that item and indeed it would if rigid price controls existed at the retail level, so that the item could not be increased in cost along the way. But what do you think will really happen? The pattern under Phase II is that costs, not savings, are being passed along to the consumer.

A sales tax is the enemy of the poor person. It is the enemy of the elderly couple who live on fixed income. And it is the enemy of the everyday American consumer, poor or not.

I am completely opposed to increasing the debt ceiling without basic tax reform. What we need in this country today is leadership which has the courage to call for income tax reform to put the burden where it must be placed, on those who can afford to pay.

It makes me sick to read every year the "honor roll" of all the wealthy Americans who avoided paying income taxes this year or last because of loopholes and special subsidies. Yet in the face of chronic and continuing inequities, the Administration suggests raising the debt ceiling while creating the value-added tax to bring in new revenues from the people at the bottom of the economic ladder.

I say the time to force tax reform is now, and the way to force it is to keep the lid on the debt ceiling and end the system of special privilege which is the tax system of this country today.

The American people don't need college degrees to understand the phony arithmetic of the Nixon economy. In 1971, individual citizen taxpayers paid in $86.2 billion in taxes, while corporations—which control ninety percent of the wealth of this nation—paid in $26.8 billion in income taxes.

In other words, you and I collectively paid in roughly $60 billion more than all the great corporations of this country.

Well, where did President Nixon put that money? He spent $77.6 billion on national defense, $3.5 billion on outer space, almost $20 billion on interest to pay off previous extensions of the debt limit, $12 billion on commerce and transportation, and about $20 billion on programs which are designed to help people get on their feet in our economy.

In the national defense budget, just under $19 billion was spent on procurement of hardware in 1971—in short, the corporations did not quite break even, they took a $7 billion loss in the speculative market on paying income taxes to the Federal Government. Of course, the corporations actually got back considerably more than the $26.8 billion they paid in taxes, when you look at the money in every sector of the budget which goes not to the citizen but to private producers of Government services.

In the last year we have seen a whole series of incredible Government welfare subsidies for the huge corporations: the supersonic transport, the C-5A giant aircraft, and most recently the President's endorsement of a multibillion expenditure on the space shuttle. A space shuttle to where? Mars, Jupiter, or Saturn?

I know a lot of Americans who would be glad to settle for better bus service from their home to their jobs, or from poor neighborhoods to areas of the city where jobs are to be found. Repeated studies of riots in urban ghettos show that lack of adequate transportation was a big factor in the discontent and bitterness which caused riot conditions to erupt, but President Nixon's answer is to build a space shuttle or an SST with precious public funds, to serve a tiny elite of the population or to stimulate the economy of a state or region by creating massive and useless technological public-works projects.

Why don't we get this country to work again at things which need to be done?

I would start with the construction and maintenance of a good subway system in every city over 250,000 population. Our city streets and basic public facilities are badly dilapidated in huge areas of inner cities—even in suburban areas for that matter: many cities have no public sidewalks, bad street lighting, poorly maintained public parks. And perhaps one of the biggest items of unfinished business is the rehabilitation of existing housing—this in itself would be a prime stimulus to the revitalization of our basic economy and job market.

I am fully aware that there are important aspects of the economy which are served by technological industry. For example, in Japan the best engineers and scientists perfected high-speed rail transportation which could be a model for this country. But we waste our best minds on outer space! And our slow train service between major cities is a disgrace to a society which thinks of itself as the most technologically advanced in the world.

We have come to the point where we have allowed our economic well-being to wither away and rot in order to support a few highly specialized and remote kinds of activity, much of it defense-oriented.

The price you and I have paid is not necessarily better protection at home or less involvement in foreign and distant wars, as the availability of this hardware seems to often beg for its use: The real price we pay is in shoddy consumer goods, rotting cities which can no longer pay their share of taxes, increased property taxes in suburban areas to pay for the declining revenue base in the older parts of cities, and collapse of school systems because taxpayers revolt and say they have had enough. And the basic reason, the underlying cause, of this cycle is the fundamental lack of balance in national priorities. If the priorities were set by the people for a change, some of this imbalance would be removed.

Although Chisholm emphasized again and again during her historic run for the Democratic presidential nomination that she was not just the candidate of black America or the candidate of women's groups but "the candidate of the people," she was cast in that role from the beginning and never managed to build a broad base of support. She was also never able to win over members of the Congressional Black Caucus, many of whom resented her as a self-serving upstart who undermined their efforts to promote black male politicians. (South Dakota Senator George McGovern went on to capture the nomination in July 1972, but he was soundly defeated by President Nixon in the November election.) In a speech she delivered on February 9, 1973, to delegates at the National Women's Political Caucus Convention in Houston, Texas, Chisholm analyzed her failed campaign and looked at the future of women in politics. It is reprinted from Representative American Speeches: 1972-1973, *edited by Waldo W. Braden (Wilson, 1973).*

When it was arranged that I should speak to you today, Liz Carpenter wrote me a note and suggested my speech should be, "Can a Woman Become President?" Knowing Liz, she probably thought this would be a wonderful occasion for me to exhort an audience of potential candidates to plan their own onslaughts on the pinnacle of elective office.

As I look back on the past year and a half, I think my campaign did help to break the barrier against women seeking the presidency and other elective offices but, my experiences also made me acutely aware of some of the problems women candidates face as well as particular problems which the women's movement, and especially the National Women's Political Caucus, must face up to.

One of my biggest problems was that my campaign was viewed as a symbolic gesture. While I realized that my campaign was an important rallying symbol for women and that my presence in the race forced the other candidates to deal with issues relating to women, my primary objective was to force people to accept me as a real viable candidate.

Although many have compared my race to that of [nineteenth-century reformer] Victoria Woodhull, I specifically rejected that comparison. Mrs. Woodhull was a feminist candidate running on a feminist party platform. I specifically rejected this feminist candidacy as I did the projection of myself into a black candidacy or an antiwar candidacy. I chose to run for the nomination of one of the major national parties.

I did this because I feel that the time for tokenism and symbolic gestures is past. Women need to plunge into the world of politics and battle it out toe to toe on the same ground as their male counterparts. If they do not do this, they will not succeed as a presidential candidate or in any other campaign for political office.

First and foremost, it is essential that you believe in yourself and your ability to handle the job you are seeking. If you don't, it is difficult to persuade others to support you. While pretty obvious to anyone who has run for office, I found that the press, the public, and even those in the women's movement found it difficult to understand this key point. Over and over in the campaign, I was asked, "But why are you running, Mrs. Chisholm?" Over and over I would reply, "Because I think I can do the job," "Because I think I am better than the rest of the candidates in the field."

One of the stumbling blocks I encountered was the fact that many people, including feminists, thought that since I "didn't have a chance" it was foolish to work for me.

For those who genuinely preferred another candidate, one can have no quarrel. But for those who thought I was the best candidate but chose to work for someone else because they viewed my campaign as hopeless, they will need to reexamine their thinking for truly, no woman will ever achieve the presidency as long as their potential supporters hold this view.

As the effect of the [George] Wallace phenomenon in this last election points out, a campaign becomes truly effective when those who believe in their candidate pull out all the stops.

One of the other most difficult problems I faced was that many of my wonderful women's movement supporters did not understand that I both wanted and needed to talk about issues other than equal rights, abortion and child care. As you know, I am a strong supporter of all of these issues but in a campaign, there is a great deal of other ground to cover. Senior citizens don't really give a hang about abortion and homosexuals are more concerned with their own situation than the status of the Equal Rights Amendment.

Further, and this is critical to the discussion we will enter into at this convention, different women view different segments of the women's movement agenda as priority items.

The movement has, for the most part, been led by educated white middle-class women. There is nothing unusual about this. Reform as movements are usually led by the better educated and better off. But, if the women's movement is to be successful you must recognize the broad variety of women there are and the depth and range of their interests and concerns. To black and Chicano women, picketing a restricted club or insisting on the title Ms. are not burning issues. They are more concerned about bread-and-butter items such as the extension of minimum wage, welfare reform and day care.

> ***"Women need to plunge into the world of politics and battle it out toe to toe on the same ground as their male counterparts."***

Further, they are not only women but women of color and thus are subject to additional and sometimes different pressures.

For example, the black experience in America has not been one of unbridled success for black men. Indeed, there have been times when discrimination and the economic situation were such that it was easier for a black woman to get a job than her husband. Because of this, anything that might be construed as anti-male will be viewed skeptically by a black woman.

Indeed this is a problem not only for black women but most women.

If this caucus is to have a real impact, we must have a broad base and appeal to the average woman.

Unfortunately, the movement is currently perceived as anti-male, anti-child, and anti-family.

Part of this is bad press. The media does not concentrate on the blue-haired lady in pearls testifying on behalf of the equal employment opportunities bill. It trains its eyes on the young girl shaking her fist and screaming obscenities at an abortion rally.

Part of it is that many of the leaders of the movement have downgraded traditional roles in their attempts to show abuses and to affirm the right of a woman to have a choice of roles to play.

Finally, there have been excesses. Not all sexual advances are sexist. Children are more than a pile of dirty diapers, and families, while they have often restricted women, have also provided warmth, security, and love.

If we are to succeed in uniting ourselves and in attracting the typical woman who is likely to be a housewife and mother who likes living in suburbia, we are going to have to make a concerted effort to articulate issues so that everyone will want to be identified with and active in the movement.

With this in mind, the function of the National Women's Political Caucus is not to be the cutting edge of the women's liberation movement but the big umbrella organization which provides the weight and muscle for those issues which the majority of women see as concerns.

One of the critical items on the convention agenda is to put the National Women's Political Caucus on a sound financial basis. I don't know if you realize it or not but most of the time the women in our national office have to pay for the privilege of being screamed at, accused of doing things without authorization, or not doing enough. Yet, in a real sense these gals are the Caucus. They get the mailings out, they do the nitty grittying of organizing meetings and conventions. Most of the time they work long hours and are lucky to get reimbursed for carfare. If we accuse others of ripping off and abusing women, we should begin by rectifying our own house.

It is time we rose above the cake sale mentality of financing. In this country we spend $6.4 billion on cosmetics. If we can spend that much on our faces, we can spend ten dollars a year for a membership fee—that is less than one dollar a month. Newsletters are also an enormous expense and should be put on some kind of paying basis.

Finally, we should set aside money to hire one full-time paid legislative lobbyist for the Caucus, and set up legislative lobbying leaders in every state and major subdivision. What is the point of having a National Women's Political Caucus and working at electing women to office if we ignore the simplest and most obvious methods of effecting this political process—that of lobbying? Without this we will lose everything we have gained. Right now the Equal Rights Amendment is stalled in the ratification process. Without effective lobbying, it will die after over a half a century of effort. The minimum wage bill, which affects a vast number of women was killed last year for a want of five votes to send it to conference committee. The National Women's Political Caucus could provide the margin of votes necessary for passage. After we passed a child care bill, the president vetoed it saying that day-care centers were destructive to families. The White House needs to know this is a vital issue for women all over America and that we disagree.

Another issue this convention must grapple with is the form and format of this organization and the composition of the new policy council. I, for one, believe that the Caucus will never be completely effective unless we develop a strong grass roots organization.

As I traveled around the country, I met hundreds of bright, capable, articulate women. These are the people who ought to be projected into the positions of authority and leadership.

We don't need any more of the "superstar" syndrome. Indeed, I am sure that Betty, Gloria, and Bella are as sick of seeing their faces as I am of seeing mine. What we need is to thrust new people into the limelight and to show the range and breadth of talent among women all over the nation.

I, therefore, propose that you do not place my name in nomination for the policy council and I hope that the others in the policy council, who are in the same position, will do likewise. This does not mean breaking our association with the Caucus. You can establish some sort of honorary advisory council or hall of fame or something and we can remain "on call" when we are needed but, what is necessary now are new faces.

In closing, I would like to make one observation: normally our meetings go on endlessly with much shouting, haranguing, grandstanding, and discussion of extraneous issues. Could we all try to be respectful and understanding of each other's views, concise, to the point, and mindful of the clock?

SOURCES

Braden, Waldo W., editor, *Representative American Speeches: 1971-1972,* Wilson, 1972.

———, editor, *Representative American Speeches: 1972-1973,* Wilson, 1973.

Brownmiller, Susan, *Shirley Chisholm: A Biography,* Doubleday, 1970.

Chisholm, Shirley, *Unbought and Unbossed,* Houghton, 1970.

———, *The Good Fight,* Harper, 1973.

Congressional Record, 91st Congress, 1st session, U.S. Gov't Printing Office, 1969.

Duffy, Bernard K. and Halford R. Ryan, editors, *American Orators of the Twentieth Century: Critical Studies and Sources,* Greenwood Press, 1987.

Haskins, James, *Fighting Shirley Chisholm,* Dial, 1975.

Henry G. Cisneros

1947–

Mexican American official of the U.S. government

During the early 1980s, a new face appeared on the national political scene—that of San Antonio Mayor Henry G. Cisneros. Charming, intelligent, and energetic, he was soon hailed as one of the brightest stars of the Democratic party for his progressive approach to tackling urban woes such as unemployment, crumbling downtowns, and fractured relations between whites and minorities. As Secretary of Housing and Urban Development (HUD) in the administration of President Bill Clinton, Cisneros is now trying to take his formula for success nationwide. Although he faces an uncertain future as the head of a department that some would like to abolish in light of its history of failure and inefficiency, he remains determined to transform HUD into a friend rather than an enemy of those who need its services most—the urban poor.

A native of the city he once served as mayor, Cisneros grew up in an atmosphere where both education and self-discipline were highly prized. His mother, Elvira, was the daughter of a Mexican printer, journalist, and intellectual who was forced to flee his native country in 1926 for political reasons; he then settled in San Antonio and became active in the community. Cisneros's father, George, a descendant of early Spanish settlers in the Southwest, spent his childhood as a migrant worker in Colorado and then joined the Army during World War II. Afterwards; he became a civilian administrator for the Army and rose to the rank of colonel in the reserve.

Although Henry spoke only Spanish when he first entered school (at home and in his middle-class San Antonio neighborhood, that was the language of choice), he was a quick learner and a good student who even then had a certain charisma, as his teachers later recalled. After graduating from high school, he enrolled at Texas A & M University with the intention of following his father's footsteps and becoming a military officer. Instead, Cisneros found himself drawn to the relatively new field of urban planning. He earned his bachelor's degree in the subject in 1968, then worked for several federal and city urban revitalization programs in and around his hometown while pursuing his master's degree, which he received in 1970. By this time, according to family members, the ambitious young man had already made up his mind that someday he was going to be mayor of San Antonio.

Cisneros then left Texas for Washington, D.C., where he began studying for his doctorate in urban administration at George Washington University. Meanwhile, he also secured a job as administrative assistant to the executive vice-president of the National League of Cities. In 1971, however, he landed a prestigious White House fellowship (granted to young people aspiring to careers in politics) that enabled him to work as an assistant to then-Secretary of Health, Education, and Welfare Elliot Richardson.

In 1972, Cisneros headed to Boston, where he spent the next two years pursuing a master's degree in public administration at Harvard University's John F. Kennedy School of Government. During this same period, he also completed doctoral studies at the Massachusetts Institute of Technology (MIT) and worked there as a teaching assistant. Turning down an offer to join the MIT faculty, Cisneros returned to San Antonio in 1974 and became an assistant professor at the University of Texas branch there. Soon afterward, he also completed work on his doctorate from George Washington University and officially received his degree in 1975.

Cisneros's return to his hometown also marked the beginning of his political career. For more than two decades, an organization of Anglo businessman known as the Good Government League (GGL) had exerted tremendous influence over San Antonio's political affairs. By the 1970s, however, their clout had begun to diminish as they lost Hispanic support to emerging grass-roots advocacy groups such as Communities Organized for Public Service (COPS). In 1975, the GGL was looking for a Hispanic candidate it could support in upcoming city council elections. Cisneros fit the bill, and the GGL added his name to their ticket. But he ran a fiercely independent campaign and was elected to the city council on his own merits. Only twenty-seven at the time, he was the youngest city councilman in San Antonio history.

From the start, Cisneros—a liberal who favors economic growth rather than more welfare as the key to solving social problems—devoted himself to building bridges between the conservative Anglo establishment and the growing Hispanic community, which had effectively been shut out of having any say in running San Antonio. While time-consuming and often frustrating (at any given time, leaders from one side or the other were angry with him for taking a stand they opposed), this approach was popular with voters and helped Cisneros win re-election to the city council in 1977 and again in 1979.

In 1980, Cisneros felt it was time to make a bid for the mayor's office. Emphasizing the theme he had promoted as a councilman—overcoming ethnic divisions to work together and foster economic growth that would benefit all of San Antonio—he captured the support of a majority of Anglo and Hispanic voters in the 1981 election, making him the first Hispanic to head a major U.S. city.

Once in office, Cisneros launched an all-out effort to fulfill the terms of his agenda, which called for diversifying the local economy by creating jobs in light manufacturing, high technology, medical services, and biosciences research. He met with tremendous success in attracting many new businesses to the area and was also able to convince local schools and colleges to develop programs that would teach students the skills needed to work in those new businesses. In addition, he boosted tourism by recruiting conventions and renovating the downtown area. Before long, Cisneros had garnered national recognition as a bold new political leader who was in touch with emerging economic trends and who acted on them rather than reacted to them.

Cisneros was elected to a second term in 1983 on a promise that he would focus more of his considerable energies on quality-of-life issues such as improving city services (especially on the Hispanic West Side, which had always been shortchanged) and building an arts center and sports stadium. Meanwhile, he enjoyed an even more prominent role on the national scene as an appointee of President Ronald Reagan to the National Bipartisan Commission on Central America. The following year, he was second on the list of Democratic presidential candidate Walter Mondale's choices for vice-president. And in 1985, Cisneros became president of the National League of Cities, another high-profile position. Yet this wildly popular politician continued to downplay speculation that he would make the leap to higher office and easily won re-election to the mayor's post in 1985 and again in 1987.

In 1989, Cisneros surprised and disappointed his supporters when he declined to run for governor (he was considered a front-runner) and instead announced he was quitting politics. The reasons were many, but most revolved around his family (in 1987, his wife had given birth to a son with severe health problems) and his need to earn more money in anticipation of sending his two older daughters to college. (In San Antonio, the office of mayor is largely a ceremonial post that pays only $50 plus expenses per council meeting; a city manager oversees daily operations. Nevertheless, Cisneros had always put in full-time hours as mayor while earning some additional income teaching and speaking before various groups.) To that end, he went into business as founder and chairman of the Cisneros Asset Management Company, a national fixed-income asset management firm for tax-exempt institutions.

In 1992, however, he again felt the pull of politics with the election of his friend and mentor Ann Richards as governor of Texas and Democrat Bill Clinton (for whom Cisneros had campaigned) as president of the United States. Both had plans for him; Richards wanted him to run for the U.S. Senate seat left vacant when Lloyd Bentsen of Texas joined the Clinton cabinet as Secretary of the Treasury, and Clinton wanted him in the cabinet as Secretary of Housing and Urban Development (HUD). Cisneros weighed both options carefully and decided to take the job he felt he had been training for all his life—heading up the agency where he might be able to help the poor, the ill-housed, and the homeless of the nation's cities.

On April 13, 1993, not long after taking over the reins at HUD, Cisneros addressed the National Press Club in Washington, D.C. In his speech, he reflected on the many problems facing America's urban areas and offered his perspective on what HUD needed to do to begin solving those problems. His remarks are reprinted here from a copy of his speech provided by HUD's Office of Public Affairs.

Gil, thank you very much and thank you, everyone, for the wonderful opportunity, the invitation to be with you today. It is a treat, an honor to be in this distinguished institution, and I can't tell you what a treat [it is] to be introduced by someone who can get through the introduction and actually pronounce my name correctly at the end of the process. That is a treat for me because it isn't always so. On one occasion in Washington I was introduced as "Henry Cisnerosis."

On another—and I'll admit it wasn't in Washington—I was introduced in a way that was so off the mark that I really couldn't understand how it might have occurred until a week later or so I was reading the style section of the local newspaper and came across an article that described a memory-jogging technique for remembering people's names. It said try to focus on a prominent feature on a person's face and associate it with their name and it will bring you somewhere. And then it dawned on me why I had been introduced as "Henry Cisnernose."

But the worst case of all, I must admit, happened in my own city. It was in San Antonio. I was mayor at the time. In those days I had to go over to the convention center to welcome groups several times a week, convention groups, and this particular group was a medical group. It was a Monday morning. They had been in medical symposia all weekend long and that was clear, because as the presenter became ready to actually make the presentation, the introduction, I noticed that the expression on his face could only be described as panic. It's very difficult to get through a whole introduction and never mention a person's name. He managed to do it until the moment of truth. He could avoid it no longer. He got his courage together. I noticed this was stressful for him. And he said, "Ladies and gentlemen, at this time would you please welcome Mayor Sclerosis."

So after you've been introduced as a disease, you do look forward to the details and Gil, you did a wonderful job.

I feel that I'm one of the luckiest people around—able to work on the things I believe in, serve our country and serve a president who believes in communities, has worked in communities and is intent on making a difference in our country, in partnership with communities.

President Clinton said to me in Little Rock, as we spent an hour during the transition period to talk about a position in his cabinet, at the conclusion of that one hour, he said, "I hope you don't mind—if you take this job, I'm going to be spending a lot of time in your area of work because these are the things that I believe in." I said, "Mr. President, not only do I not mind, but the more the president cares about things, the more the rest of the government will be attentive to them. So I welcome, absolutely welcome, any involvement that you will have."

I'm very proud today to be here as President Clinton's Secretary of Housing and Urban Development.

Like the president, all of us, you care about our country and its communities, about both their promise and their peril. We are inspired by the locally-inspired turnarounds, by the national promise of, say, Pittsburgh or Baltimore in the east, of Indianapolis and Omaha in the heartland, of Seattle and Salt Lake in the west.

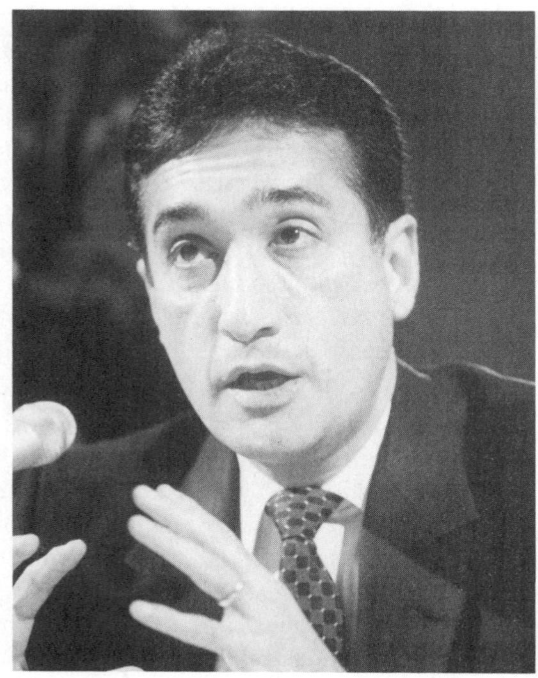

Henry G. Cisneros

But we've also seen the peril of heightened crime, of the plague of drugs, of fear on the faces of the elderly, of neighborhoods that have lost their life force, with churches closed, ball fields empty, downtown stores with empty windows, factories with weeds that have overgrown their parking lots in communities of all sizes, in all regions, made up of people of all incomes and ages and races.

For every example of civic cooperation such as the promise of Minneapolis-St. Paul, there is another, the peril, where leaders glare across at each other across a chasm of misunderstanding, even hatred, refusing to cooperate.

For every Portland, Oregon, the promise, striving to literally redesign its future, there is a community in peril that has surrendered to the larger forces of the global economy.

For every city such as Fort Worth, the promise of sustaining attractive, graceful, and life-enhancing neighborhoods, there's a community in peril where the elderly are afraid to walk to the corner store with their Social Security checks, where children peek out of windows to see if the drug pushers are still at the pay phone across the street.

For every city such as Tampa, meeting its promise by building homes, using the Community Development Block Grant program and matching it to the capital of commercial bankers, there is the peril of a city where the homeless look for a wind-free alcove, a sheltered stairwell, a steam exhaust pipe to sleep through the frozen night.

And for every community of promise, like Rockford, Illinois, where people have come together across traditional lines, there are those communities in peril where the slow burn of anger smolders, occasionally to flare into terrible intensity as in Los Angeles last spring.

The morning after the civil disturbances began in Los Angeles, I called Mayor Bradley and several members of the city council there and, in consultation with them, concluded that because it was not clear how extensive the civil disturbances might become in the Latino community of Los Angeles, that people like myself who might have a chance to do something should go, and so I did, was there by Thursday evening as the conflagration continued.

What I saw and smelled and felt makes it possible for me to speak to you today with greater clarity and certainty than ever. On a Los Angeles street that Thursday night the smoke was everywhere; it smelled of burning wire and plastic. The smoke was so thick that it obscured the lights of a helicopter circling directly overhead. Sirens screamed every few seconds as strike teams of fire engines, escorted by California highway patrol, convoys, literally convoys, of thirty vehicles with police, designed to protect the firemen as they would try to do their jobs at the next fire.

Pick-up trucks were pulled up next to electronics stores with the glass fronts bashed in, as men hurriedly loaded VCRs and television sets. One man told me he had just walked by a teenager around the corner. The young man had been shot in the head, lying arms wide, sprawled out on the city sidewalk, eyes open, staring straight up, dead.

It was the urban apocalypse in smoky smelly orange, an assault on all the senses, people wide-eyed, all-out fear just one more loud bang away.

Well, that was Los Angeles that Thursday night, but it could be another city in America some other night. No, you say, no way, Los Angeles is different. Well, Los Angeles is different—it's bigger, it's more diverse, it's rapper street-smart, its edges are sharper, cooler, tougher, maybe readier to take offense. No, you say, it couldn't happen in my city—not in Miami or Washington or Atlanta or Cleveland. Really? Not in Denver or Kansas City or Memphis or Houston or Philadelphia. Well, maybe yes, maybe no, maybe not the same form, maybe not the same intensity, maybe not the same flashpoint.

But the white-hot intensity of Los Angeles was the combustion of smoldering embers waiting to ignite. Like piles of dry wood with red coals underneath, other American cities can ignite, or maybe we'll call ourselves lucky and they'll just smolder away taking a human toll at a slower rate. Just smolder away.

Why are our cities smoldering? Well, perhaps it's a matter of isolation. Our cities and our neighborhoods have become more geographically segregated by race, class, and ethnicity. Fifty cities of more than 100,000 persons of population each now have populations that are better than majority African American, Hispanic and Asian. Among those cities with sixty percent of their population African American, Hispanic and Asian are Atlanta, Baltimore, Washington, D.C., Chicago, Detroit—Detroit is eighty percent minority; it's the most segregated city in the United States. White populations leave, some seeking the advantages of the suburbs, some fleeing the deteriorated crime-ridden city, and others escaping people, the minority populations themselves.

> ***"And for every community of promise . . . there are those communities in peril where the slow burn of anger smolders . . ."***

The result is desperation, distrust and poor populations left behind to fend for themselves in racial enclaves. And we ask—why are our cities smoldering?

Well, perhaps it's a loss of economic function amidst larger economic trends. Cities no longer play the same role that they did in the past, urban economies have been completely transformed from the manufacturing goods-producing engines of jobs that they once were, when thirty percent of the jobs in a community were in manufacturing, to the reality today of cities that offer finance and services jobs, ill-matched to the populations who live in the cities.

And we ask, why are our cities smoldering?

Perhaps it has to do with the new face of poverty. Geographically isolated, economically depressed, racially segregated, cities have become warehouses of the poor. We now have more than two million families who are poor despite having an adult member in the household working a full-time week. One out of every five children in America is born in poverty; one out of every three Latino children in the United States is born into poverty; and one out of every two African American children in the United States—fifty percent, flip a coin—is born in poverty. And we ask, why are our cities smoldering?

Perhaps it has to do with the isolation of neighborhoods and the way people are forced to live. The economic crisis of cities is exacerbated in poor neighborhoods so that low-income families don't have access to the necessities the rest of us take for granted.

When they want to cash a check, they're forced to go to check-cashing outlets which often charge gouging rates; when they want to shop for groceries, they may have to travel miles to a major supermarket; when their children go to school, they often go to dilapidated schools that are outright dangerous; when they go to health clinics, they sometimes have no substitute but the trauma center of the public hospital.

When urban experts review this litany of realities, they reserve their harshest criticism for the role of the federal government reinforcing and exacerbating these terrible trends. Perhaps the clearest observation that I can bring you after the first two months on the job is that the federal government itself must change its way of doing business.

Large public housing developments have concentrated the poorest of the poor in housing that is overly dense, poorly designed, badly built and located in isolated, segregated neighborhoods. The preference rules for tenants assure that those with the worst-case needs are concentrated in such public housing. And our income-targeting rules enable only very low-income families to be eligible for federal housing assistance, impeding any economic mixing, the kind of mixing that makes possible role models and working families mixed with our very poor.

Cost containment and other rules of the past decade have assured that when we do build subsidized housing, it looks like subsidized housing, making the location and the siting of affordable housing a near-impossible task because people don't want it in their neighborhoods.

Fair housing laws have been enforced with little vigor or commitment despite pervasive evidence of discrimination in both the rental and the mortgage markets.

Regulations governing the affordable housing activities of Fannie Mae and Freddie Mac—secondary market institutions, government-sponsored entities—have been virtually ignored. And there's a total lack of coordination between HUD and other federal organizations. Within HUD itself a crazy-quilt of despairing programs have emerged each supported by separate constituencies with little relation or connectedness.

So where do we go from here? Well, the magnitude of our urban problems and of our federal failures has helped paralyze the federal government and stifle innovative thinking. Yet the cost of doing nothing or doing something that responds to the wrong problem is vast, almost incalculable.

Los Angeles, in almost biblical terms, is a signpost, a guide post, a warning that America has to deal with its cities or its cities ultimately will seek vengeance. Over the past two months we've been engaged in an effort at HUD to set a framework for addressing the ills of urban America. It's not an urban policy, but a work in progress. And I regard today as a kind of progress report.

Our task has been to redefine our mission, ask what should HUD be doing in the 1990s, in the environment of urban America as we know it today? What are our priorities? What are our goals?

This has been an effort that we have attempted to make inclusive, bringing people together from across the department and from outside the department. And what has emerged after weeks of dialogue and interaction and listening and reflection is the beginnings of what I hope is a change in how we think about our cities and ourselves.

We've identified three themes, or values, which pull together what we stand for at HUD. They are, first, a commitment to the spirit of community; secondly, a commitment to economic lift and creating a ladder of opportunity; and, thirdly, a commitment to confront the behaviors that ravage our society—racism and the self-destructive patterns of life, behaviors which go to the heart of America's social contract of rights and responsibilities.

First, community. We hear that word "community" used in many ways. To some it means a physical place, to others it means a spirit of common bonds, to the new communitarians it means a specific consensus on how individual rights are balanced against the larger good.

But what does it mean for our nation's cities in modern terms, and their relationship with a large Washington bureaucracy? Well, we know what community is not. It's not streets darkened by the shadows of vacant shells of buildings, a street where no one goes without fear of sudden and vicious attack, and where no one will help. It's not public housing where children die in the crossfire of rival gangs, and where security guards crouch around staircases to avoid surprising the drug sentries with Uzis, posted at the end of the halls. It's not neighborhoods where everyone, young and old, 3-year-olds and 73-year-olds, are on their own. It's not decision-making where someone else—planners, architects, city officials, federal bureaucrats, housing authority managers—calls the tune.

What is community? It's a place where housing has been built with poor people that is as functional, as sturdy, as dignified, as attractive as in a nice suburb—in a central city neighborhood of Chattanooga, Tennessee, led by the Enterprise Foundation. It's a place where activists have gained the respect of the city government and turned the city's attentions to their priorities—children—and called their effort "A Chance for Every Child"—in Oakland, California. It's a place where church parishes have served as the focal point for Nehemiah housing in East Brooklyn, led by the Industrial Areas Foundation.

The common themes? Neighborhood organizing, strong institutions, local planning, and experts in partnership. And a government that respects community, that is organized to help communities, that facilitates the efforts of communities, that is not afraid to say that it will cost something, but not as much as we will pay for neglect, and that uses its resources where they matter the most.

It's important in a department like ours to recognize that the federal government, and certainly the five thousand people who work in the headquarters of HUD in Washington, never build one single building, one single house, with their hands. We must rely on people in communities—nonprofit organizations, community development corporations. The thrust of our efforts must be to create a department that enables communities to be masters of their own destinies, places where people can talk to each other and conduct a civic dialogue.

HUD can fund community development corporations, can build the capacity of neighborhood organizations, can insist that community plans are built into our most important programs, can reward communities that work strategically together by extending greater trust and flexibility to them. And HUD can remove barriers in existing programs with set-asides for community-based nonprofits. We can, we must, and we are reinventing HUD to support inclusive decision-making with communities at all levels of HUD programs.

Secondly, we must infuse in our programs a sense of upward lift. It's not good enough to concentrate on static policies that maintain people. We must infuse into everything we do, particularly the wide spectrum of HUD housing policies, a sense of lift. Our business is not just to create housing but to make of housing a platform from which we create opportunities for people, opportunities to go from homelessness to rental housing, from public housing to homeownership, opportunities to go from a public housing experience without a job, without training, without education, to self-sufficiency.

I had a sad experience the week before last in Atlanta. It began as one of those rare moments when you spend a moment at sunset with a family and just enjoy the beautiful afternoon breeze. Just as quickly, reality intruded.

I was walking through a housing project and across the street noticed a man, his wife and three little children, two little girls and a smaller little boy, maybe a year old. I walked across the street to visit with them, a heart-warming sight, taken, as I was, by the love shared among the family members.

And I talked to the man. He described his occupation. He's a roofer who works on commercial roofing projects. And then he said something that made me pause. He said, "I come by every afternoon to visit my family." He and his family are not separated, estranged, divorced, yet he explained to me he came by every afternoon after work, every afternoon, to visit his children, children he so obviously loves, affection he bestowed gently that afternoon, because the rules of public housing make it impossible for him to live in the unit with his family because their income would rise so quickly that they wouldn't be able to stay in that unit.

Now, that's the kind of circumstance, repeated too many times in our cities, where we've created Catch-22 rules and regulations that crush the lifting opportunities for people to make something of their lives. I've described one instance from public housing. You know of similar dysfunctions in other parts of our system of support and service that we must change in order to infuse a dimension of lift into our policies and programs, to reinforce training and upward mobility through family self-sufficiency, stimulate work incentives and reward initiative and savings for those living in public and assisted housing, redesign our voucher and certificate programs to give tenants greater choice, demonstrate the use of regional approaches to housing so that we can allocate our assistance on a broader basis than concentrated central city areas. These are examples of the things that we must do.

Third, and finally, let me say we at HUD must do an honest and truthful job of speaking to the most devastating division in American life, and that is race. Both sides of the racial divide must speak to each other truthfully across the chasm. We must speak about race and what it continues to do to American life. Denying people opportunity on the basis of nothing other than skin color—access to rental housing or to homeownership or to bank loans or insurance or the other essentials of being able to make it in American life—is wrong. These are what our testers find when they send two people out with exactly the same education and the same income, one white, one black, to rent an apartment. Same occupation, same income, and one is told that there's a unit for rent at $450 and the other is told that there is no unit for rent, that it was just rented, and all of this is caught on tape.

> ***"We've created Catch-22 rules and regulations that crush the lifting opportunities for people to make something of their lives."***

These are the circumstances of race in America. They're real. They exist. We don't like to acknowledge them. They create the circumstances that are impossible to overcome with governmental programs unless we engage the American people in broader discussion.

There are also other realities on the other side of the racial divide, another set of behaviors, those which have been bred by chronic subordination, those who have been bred by the isolation of ghetto life, those patterns of behavior that result in crime, result in dissolved families, that result in the reality of the wrongs perpetrated on children, the shortened childhoods that result in chronic and measurable depression and trauma in the lives of little children.

What we must do is work to change our own policies so that we can encourage people to see both sides of the contract that is rights and responsibilities—the right to an education but the responsibility to study, the right to decent and safe housing but the responsibility to maintain and improve it, the right to live in secure and safe communities but the responsibility to take a part in citizenship and improving them.

What can a federal department do? Well, it can identify and eliminate the structural and institutional barriers to equality of opportunity; it can fight crime and drugs and gangs and antisocial behavior, discourage teen pregnancy, create safe schools. But in order to do this a government must reinvent itself so that all of its arms and branches are working together, so that they make sense as they come together in a local community. That's what the president's initiatives about enterprise zones are about, to bring resources together in a particular piece of geography. And it's what we will continue to work on.

Well, I've said to you that this is a work in progress. We're beginning to identify the themes, the values of what we stand for. And this will result in policies and actions, policies designed to attack the vast separations spatially in American society, opening up and making it possible for people move from central city existences to suburban life even as we create better places for people to come back to the cities, as try to relate the destiny of the cities to the momentum of the larger national economy and as we work together to redesign government itself.

In the final analysis, we're all in this together, all Americans in all our communities, from Boston in the East to Santa Monica in Los Angeles in the west where the golden rays of the sun set, from the canyons of Manhattan to communities on the edge of the canyons of Arizona—all races, all incomes, this amalgam that is peoples and traditions and heritage.

Let me close my remarks by recalling the words of the American poet, Archibald MacLeish, who in his poem "A Letter the American

People" wrote this—and I will close with his thought. He said:

This, this is our land, this is our people,
This that is neither a land nor a race. We must reap
The wind here in the grass for our souls' harvest;
Here we must eat our salt or our bones starve.
Here we must live or live only as shadows.
This is our race, we that have none, that have had
Neither the old walls nor the voices around us,
This is our land, this is our ancient ground—
The raw earth, the mixed bloods and the strangers,
The different eyes, the wind, and the heart's change.
These we will not leave though the old call us.
This is our country-earth, our blood, our kind.
[Here we will live our years till the earth blind us—.]

We're all in this together—and we have a lot of work to do. Thank you very much for allowing me to come over and be part of your program.

Since taking office, Cisneros has won praise for his efforts as HUD secretary to literally reinvent an agency with a well-entrenched reputation as a quagmire of bureaucratic arrogance, corruption, and mismanagement. He has trimmed the staff and suggested program mergers or cuts, boosted morale, stimulated innovative ways of thinking, and given the department a new sense of purpose and direction—all while facing the prospect of huge budget cuts aimed at gutting the department or eliminating it entirely.

Besides trying to address the needs of the those entirely without homes by making it easier for cities to apply for federal aid, Cisneros has tackled the problems of crime and racial discrimination in public housing projects. For example, he has looked into ways to ban guns from all HUD buildings to enhance tenants' safety. He has also ordered the demolition of rundown or abandoned public housing complexes in more than twenty cities. In addition, he has instructed department staffers to settle more than a dozen anti-discrimination lawsuits in which local officials have tried to prevent blacks from moving into public housing located in all-white areas. In fact, one of Cisneros's top priorities is putting an end to the practice of concentrating all low-income people in inner-city projects by making housing available to them in all kinds of neighborhoods, including affluent suburban ones.

Unlike some of his predecessors, Cisneros has been frank about his frustrations with the secretary's role. He resents having so little leeway in instituting major changes because "most everything is a formula program, and you simply administer the formula," as he explained to a reporter for Time *magazine. "You can't move this massive machinery or relate it to massive machinery in other departments real easily. You move with concrete blocks tied to your arms and legs. I can't believe how gridlocked the system is, how it runs counter to common sense sometimes, how irrelevant it is to things that are happening out in the country."*

Cisneros's ultimate goal is very similar to the one he set for himself when he ran for city council in San Antonio—to break down the racial, social, and economic barriers that divide American cities and hasten their decline. "I truly believe in my heart the country is in trouble on this agenda," he told an interviewer during the summer of 1994. "Race. Class. Poverty. Cities. It is so clear when you try to understand the dynamics of what's happening in a city that people are making decisions of all kinds—housing patterns, school choice—based on race. I really think it's the great unresolved question of American life. And we can't fix our cities without addressing this question."

More recently, Cisneros has been forced to revisit a painful episode from his past. In July 1994, a former girlfriend filed suit against him, claiming that he had reneged on promise to pay her $4,000 a month in support money. While the affair itself was not news—Cisneros had publicly admitted to it in 1988 and acknowledged the problems it had caused in his marriage—the amount of money in question was. In late 1994, FBI agents who conducted background interviews with Cisneros after he was nominated to be HUD secretary indicated he had misled them about the payments, a revelation that prompted Attorney General Janet Reno to call for a Justice Department investigation. Responding to news of this decision in March 1995, Cisneros predicted that he would eventually be cleared of all wrongdoing and vowed to remain in his job "and fight for this department." Meanwhile, he reached an out-of-court settlement with his former girlfriend in May 1995.

SOURCES

Books

Cisneros, Henry G., *The Entrepreneurial City*, Ballinger, 1986.

———, editor, *Interwoven Destinies: The Cities and the Nation*, Norton, 1993.

Contemporary Newsmakers: 1987 Cumulation, Gale Research, Detroit, 1988.

Gillies, John, *Señor Alcalde: A Biography of Henry Cisneros*, Dillon Press, 1988.

Henry, Christopher E., *Henry Cisneros*, Chelsea House, 1995.

Peterson, Owen, editor, *Representative American Speeches: 1982-1983*, Wilson, 1983.

———, editor, *Representative American Speeches: 1985-1986*, Wilson, 1986.

Periodicals

Detroit Free Press, "HUD Secretary Builds Hope," August 3, 1994; "Independent Counsel to Probe Housing Secretary," March 15, 1995; "Vow to Stay Put Doesn't Surprise Cisneros' Friends," March 16, 1995; "Cisneros Gave GOP a Head Start on Cutting HUD, Hurting Poor" (column), March 19, 1995, p. 6F; "Cisneros Fights to Save Housing Agency as Many in Congress Reach for the Plug," April 7, 1995; "HUD Boss Cisneros Settles with Ex-Mistress," May 20, 1995, p. 2A.

Detroit News, "HUD Chief Proposes Major Cuts," December 15, 1994, p. 15A; "Cisneros Busily Reinvents HUD'S Public Housing Policy" (syndicated column by William Raspberry), January 9, 1995, p. 7A; "Cisneros Won't Quit Despite Probe," March 15, 1995, p. 5A.

Grand Rapids Press, "Red Tape Stifling HUD, Cisneros Says," May 3, 1994, p. A5.

Mother Jones, "Cisneros' Cross," March/April, 1993, pp. 11-12.

Nation's Cities Weekly, "Cisneros Warns of Big Changes in HUD Programs," December 19, 1994.

Newsweek, "San Antonio: Putting Family First," September 14, 1987, p. 8; ' "I Am Not Perfect,"' October 24, 1988, p. 25; "An Affair to Forget," September 26, 1994, p. 45.

New York Times, "Secretary Proposes Reshaping HUD to Save It," March 21, 1995, p. A19.

Time, " 'They Said I'd Get Used to It,' " December 6, 1993, p. 31.

U.S. News and World Report, "Fixing Disasters and Doing Penance," February 21, 1994, pp. 30-31.

Eldridge Cleaver

1935–

African American political and social activist

As minister of information for the Black Panther Party during the late 1960s, Eldridge Cleaver served as one of the movement's key spokesmen. Thanks to his bestselling collection of essays on his own life and black attitudes toward American society, Soul on Ice *(published in 1968), he was also its most widely-known leader.*

Cleaver was born near Little Rock, Arkansas, but later moved with his parents to Los Angeles, California. He spent much of the 1950s and early 1960s in various state prisons for crimes ranging from theft and drug dealing to assault with intent to kill for raping several white women. Eventually, he made up his mind to follow a different path. He finished his high school education in prison and concentrated on developing his writing skills. He then began writing the provocative essays that later brought him fame. Cleaver also converted to the Black Muslim faith, which he abandoned following the assassination of Malcolm X. (During the 1970s, while in self-imposed exile abroad to avoid imprisonment for violating the terms of his parole, he became a born-again Christian, a conversion chronicled in his book Soul on Fire.*) In 1967, he joined the Black Panther Party for Self-Defense, founded the previous year in Oakland, California, by black militants Bobby Seale and Huey Newton. Besides serving as the party's minister of information, Cleaver was editor of its newspaper,* The Black Panther. *In 1968, he ran for president of the United States on the Peace and Freedom party ticket.*

In his writings as well as in his speeches, Cleaver demonstrated his willingness to take the black revolution in new directions. Unlike many of his colleagues, for example, he supported the idea of forming a coalition with white radicals to challenge the forces of oppression, personified by the police. (One of the founding principles of the Black Panther Party centered around the right of blacks to defend themselves against police brutality.) He also advocated holding a vote—supervised by the United Nations—to determine whether blacks wanted to remain part of the United States. These and other causes he championed generated controversy both inside and outside the Black Panther Party.

In its issue of March 16, 1968, The Black Panther *included the text of a speech Cleaver had given outlining his views on the political struggle in America. It was later reprinted in the book* Rhetoric of Black Revolution, *by Arthur L. Smith (Allyn & Bacon, 1969), from which the following version was taken.*

I think the first thing we have to realize, really get into our minds, is that it is a reality when you hear people say that there's a "black colony" and a "white mother country." I think you really have to get that distinction clear in your minds in order to understand that there are two different sets of political dynamics functioning in this country. If you don't make that distinction, then a lot of the activities going on in this country will be nonsensical. For instance, if there's a homogeneous country and everyone here is a citizen of that country, when it comes to participating in the politics of this country, it makes a lot of sense to insist that black people participate in electoral politics and all the other forms of politics as we have known them. But if you accept the analysis that the black colony is separate and distinct from the mother country, then a lot of other forms of political struggle are indicated.

I think that most black revolutionaries or militants or what have you have generally accepted this distinction. A lot of people seem reluctant to accept this distinction. I know that in your education you were given to believe the melting pot theory, that people have come from all over the world and they've been put into this big pot and they've been melted into American citizens. In terms of the white immigrants who came to this country, this is more or less true. But in this stew that's been produced by these years and years of stirring the pot, you'll find that the black elements, the black components, have not blended well with the rest of the ingredients. And this is so because of the forms of oppression that have been generated—black people have been blocked out of this, and blocked out of that, and not allowed to participate in this, and excluded from that. This has created a psychology in black people where they have now turned all the negative exclusions to their advantage.

I mean the same things that were used to our disadvantage are now being turned around to our advantage. The whole thing about condemning blackness and developing an inferior image of everything black has now been turned completely around because I think the slogan of Black Power was a recognition of the change in the psychology of black people, that in fact they have seized upon their blackness and rallied around the elements or the points at which they were oppressed. They have turned the focal point of the oppression into the focal point of the struggle for national liberation.

Now, when people decide in their own minds that they are going to separate themselves from a country or from a political situation, a lot of dynamics and a lot of directions flow from that basic distinction. For example, people are talking these days about going to the United Nations and seeking membership in the United Nations for Afro-America. And when you look at the criteria for nationhood, you'll find that the only place that black people fall short in terms of this standard is the one where the land question comes up. They say that a nation is defined as a people sharing a common culture, a common language, a common history, and a common land situation. Now, that land question was a hang-up for a long time, simply because the black people in this country were dispersed throughout the population of the mother country. People couldn't begin to deal with the question of how to build a nation on someone else's land. It presents a very sticky problem.

In the history of the liberation struggle in this country, the two outstanding efforts that we remember in history were the Marcus Garvey movement and the Nation of Islam under Elijah Muhammad. I consider their fundamental mistake was that they projected goals that they were unable to fulfill. Marcus Garvey said that he was going to take black people back to Africa. In fact, he wasn't in a position to do that, technically speaking in terms of resources. It falls down to a question of resources, because I think that if Marcus Garvey had been able to come over here with enough ships and enough technical resources, he would have succeeded, because he did have a very tight grip on the minds and imaginations of black people, and he could have had enough of them with him to make his dream a reality. Elijah Muhammad said that he wanted to have a part of this coun-

Eldridge Cleaver

try, that he would accept some of these states. Well, the way he approached the question I think, was sure to doom it to be unfulfilled because he was asking the white power structure to give him several states. He offered no alternative means of obtaining these states other than come down from the sky and give them to us. Well, black people have been waiting for help to come from abroad and from the sky, from underground, and from anywhere, and it hasn't come. So that we began to feel that we were in a bag where nothing could happen.

The beautiful thing about the slogan Black Power was that it implemented the dictum laid down by Kwame Nkrumah, in which he said, "Seek ye first the political kingdom, and other things will be added unto you." It's very important to realize that in moving to gain power, you do not conceal or repudiate the land question, you hold it in abeyance. What you're saying is that we must first get ourselves organized, and then we can get some of this land. It's very important to realize that twenty million people or thirty million people, what have you—we're going to have to take a count because the government has been lying to us about everything else they do so we can assume that they are lying about that, so we can say that there might be thirty million, forty million, we might even be a majority, I don't know; but I am quite sure that there are more than the twenty million that the government wants to give us. But, we can say that it's possible to organize twenty million or thirty million people right here. Even though we are dispersed throughout the mother country, it is possible to set up political forms where we can have representatives in the full sense of the word, like ambassadors going to other countries.

You can see from the experience of Malcolm and from the experience of Stokely that governments around the world are hip enough to the political realities of our situation to recognize and to accept our representatives in every sense of the word. I mean, Stokely Carmichael, when he went to Havana, received the same respect, or maybe even a little more, as delegates from other countries. Black people recognize this and they know that there is a way through the international machinery to cope with the situation.

I think it's very important to realize that there is a way to move. So that today black people are talking about going to the United Nations, asking the United Nations for a UN-supervised plebiscite throughout the colony. Black people have never been able through any mechanism to express what their will is. People have come along and spoken in the name of black people; they have said that black people want to be integrated; they have said black people want to be separated; but no where at no time have black people been given the chance to register their own position. I think it's very important that we decide this once and for all, because as black people we are able to wage a campaign on this subject: do you want to be a part of

America, do you want to be integrated into America, or do you want to be separated from America, do you want to be a nation, do you want to have your ambassadors, your representatives seated in the United Nations, as a full member of the General Assembly, do you want to have your ambassadors accepted around the world? I think it would be very hard for the black people to say no, particularly when the argument of the government is going to be that black people don't need those things because they are already American citizens. Because then we come back and say, Well, if we're citizens, what about this, and what about that? And, at the very least, what it will do is to put tremendous pressure on the Babylonians, and they need all the pressure we can give them.

Now, a lot of people don't want to see this country and its structure basically change. They want to think the United States of America is an eternal entity. When you look at history, you'll find that great empires have had their boundaries changed, have had their political structures rearranged, and some of them, like Rome, lasted for five hundred, six hundred years, and the people thought nothing could ever destroy this. It's gone. The Egyptian Empire—all the empires as you look down through history, you will find that a day of reckoning came down and the whole situation was rearranged. Americans cannot envision a situation where the same thing could happen here. I think that black people have already envisioned that this, in fact, could happen, because if we were to get organized in this fashion and then be able to bring international leverage against the United States, we could have those questions decided in our favor in an international forum. I think that by then Mao Tse-tung would be at the UN, I think he would vote for us, I don't think he would sustain LBJ's argument. I think that Fidel Castro would vote for us. I think Charles de Gaulle may say something about that. I don't think he would just turn thumbs down on us, so that there are a lot of areas that we have to get into and explore. Now what that means is that there are realities out here today and will be in the future.

One thing about the coalition with the Peace and Freedom Party: we approached this whole thing from the point of view of international relations. We feel that our coalition is part of our foreign policy. That is how we look at it, that is how we are moving on it and thinking about it.

A lot of people feel just as Mike Parker said: We are endangering them as well as ourselves by coalescing with the white radicals, particularly here in Berkeley. Berkeley, as far as we can see, has a foul reputation among a lot of black cats, especially black cats associated with the NCNP. Bobby Seale, myself, and several other members of the Black Panther Party spent about a week in Los Angeles, and we were put through a lot of changes by black cats who didn't relate to the Peace and Freedom Party. They told us rather frankly that we had become tools of the white racists who had refused to accept the 50 percent bit in Chicago and they wanted to know what we were trying to do, were we trying to undercut what other blacks were trying to around the country? Our reply to that was that we had made a functional coalition with the Peace and Freedom Party and that we feel that we have 100 percent say-so over our affairs. I mean we don't allow Mike Parker and Bob Avakian to come in and dictate to us what is going to happen in terms of what we want to do. They have not tried to do that, and they are not going to try, and they had better not try. And in the same way, we do not come in and try to dictate to them what they are going to do, although we have been accused of that, but that is not the way it goes.

We recognize that we have a powerful interest in seeing a white radical movement develop into something that we can relate to. There are many things that we cannot do by ourselves. And then, there are many things that the white radical movement cannot do by itself. So we recognize that, and we are not going to be running around trying to stab each other in the back, or put each other in trickbags. It is not going to work from our point of view and we hope it won't work from your point of view because we have an interest in seeing that you develop a stable organization and a stable movement.

Now, one very important thing that we are working towards is how to unify the black population in this country within a national structure. The structure has to be inclusive enough to pull in all black people. In the past, when a new organization came on the scene, it sought to eliminate existing organizations. It was going to move every other organization out and it was going to take over and do this thing. We say that this is a mistake. What we have done is worked out a merger with SNCC. The Black Panther Party for Self-Defense and SNCC are going to merge into a functional organization that can move nationally. We are moving into a period now where the Black Panther Party for

Self-Defense has consolidated enough of a base to move things nationally. SNCC has already established national contact as well as international contact.

It is very important to realize that SNCC is composed virtually of black hippies, you might say, of black college students who have dropped out of the black middle class. And because that is their origin and that is where they came from, they cannot relate to the black brother on the block in a political fashion. They can relate to him, they can talk to him, they can communicate with him much better than, say, Roy Wilkins ever could. But, they are not able to move him en masse to the point where he could be organized and involved in political functions.

Now, the beauty and the genius of what Bobby Seale and Huey Newton have done is that they are able to move the last man on the totem pole. That is very important, because until that man can move, we really can't do that thing. SNCC has seen that the Black Panther Party is able to get to that man. So what they have done is made their apparatus available to us and there's no hangup; we can move into that. Most people don't know this, but a lot of the rhetoric you hear from Stokely Carmichael and Rap Brown these days, especially when Rap Brown first started speaking, was adopted precisely because they had come to the West Coast and spent a little time with the Black Panthers out here. That is very important, and if you see them you ask them to tell you about that, that they were greatly influenced by the Panthers. I mean that their lines were already moving in that direction because of the political pressures they were forced to deal with, but they hadn't yet made that step, they hadn't taken that leap. But coming out here and seeing the Panthers moving, seeing brothers carrying guns on the street, talking about the gun, violence, and revolution had a certain impact on their minds and they went back talking about that. So now we can say that SNCC—actually, I shouldn't even be going into this until February 17 at the Oakland Auditorium. This is when we are going to do this officially. I think it is very important that you be there so that you can see and hear for yourself what these people have to say, unless you want to depend on the newspapers, and you really don't want to get into that. So, let's just say that we are involved in trying to create models in the vanguard set so that people around the country will see how we can move.

Now, we have done two important things, I think. One, we have made this coalition with the Peace and Freedom Party; and two, we have merged with SNCC. When people look at that they can say that in the Era of Black Power, we have got to merge and merge into larger units until we have a national structure. In terms of our relationship with the white community, we can move with functional coalitions.

It is very important that we all hold up our end of the bargain—and don't think that by using us you can get away with something, because, in fact, you will only destroy what you are trying to build for yourself. Black people have only one way to protect themselves, particularly politically, and that is to be capable of implementing and inflicting a political consequence. If we cannot inflict a political consequence, then we will in fact become nothing. So, that if the Peace and Freedom Party ever tries to misuse us, we have to be in a position to hurt the Peace and Freedom Party. We have to keep the political relationship such that if we were to pull out of it, that would be very costly to the Peace and Freedom Party. We must maintain that, we must be able to inflict a consequence, and we intend to be able to do that, and it is very important that that happens. White radicals who are like the vanguard in the white community should recognize that and then move to help us get in that position—because without that you are not going to be able to convince people that they should even relate to this whole effort.

As Mike Parker said, we are also catching a lot of hell—the word is purgatory, rather, it is not hell—about this coalition. Because a lot of people have begun to feel that we can be trusted, they have taken a wait-and-see attitude to find out how this coalition comes down, to see if we, in fact, do become puppets. People all around the country are asking—if you could look at our mail or listen to our phone calls—you would know about all the people who have asked, "Hey, what is this you are doing out there? What do you think you're doing, man, explain that to me." We feel that we are able to explain that, and as I said, Bobby is going to be going on a nationwide tour and is going to be explaining that, I am going on a nationwide tour and other members of the Party are going to be going on these tours. We are going to be explaining it and SNCC is going to be explaining it, and I think that we are going to be able to do it. It is very important that the Peace and Freedom Party be able to relate to that, because when we move nationally we will have to talk about the Peace and Freedom Party and then they will have grounds for moving into areas that we have already organized. So it is going to become extremely important that we realize what we are doing. And the thing that we need from the white mother country is technical assistance—technical assistance to the colony, dig it?

I think we have a good thing going. I want to see it continue to develop and broaden and deepen because we are all involved in this and there is no way out. We have got to do it, because time is against us, a lot of people are against us, and I know that I am out of time, so I think I will cool it right here.

Cleaver's life since he returned to the United States from exile in 1975 has included numerous brushes with the law. In 1988, for example, he was convicted of burglary and put on probation. Later that same year, he was jailed for violating the terms of his probation after testing positive for cocaine use.

Cleaver entered a drug rehabilitation program in 1990 for what he said was an addiction to crack cocaine, and events since then suggest it is a problem with which he is still struggling. In 1992, he was arrested for possession of crack, but because police found the drug during an illegal search, the charges against him were eventually dropped. Two years later, he underwent surgery for a brain hemorrhage after he became ill while being booked for alleged public drunkenness and possession of cocaine and drug paraphernalia.

SOURCES

Books

Cleaver, Eldridge, *Soul on Ice*, McGraw, 1968.

———, *Soul on Fire*, Word Inc., 1978.

Foner, Philip S., editor, *The Black Panthers Speak*, Lippincott, 1970.

Holland, DeWitte, editor, *America in Controversy: History of American Public Address*, William C. Brown Company, 1973.

Scheer, Robert, editor, *Eldridge Cleaver: Post-Prison Writings and Speeches*, Random House, 1969.

Smith, Arthur L., *Rhetoric of Black Revolution*, Allyn & Bacon, 1969.

Smith, Arthur L., and Stephen Robb, editors, *The Voice of Black Rhetoric: Selections*, Allyn & Bacon, 1971.

Periodicals

Grand Rapids Press, "Ex-Black Panther Cleaver Mends After Brain Surgery," March 3, 1994, p. A7.

Johnnetta B. Cole

1936–

African American educator, anthropologist, and writer

Affectionately called "America's Sister President" in recognition of the fact that she is the first black woman president of historically black Spelman College, Johnnetta B. Cole has in just a few short years compiled an impressive record as a dynamic and inspirational leader. In addition to cementing Spelman's reputation for academic excellence, she has imbued the school with a renewed sense of commitment to goals that encompass more than just preparing for a career. As Cole declared when she assumed the presidency, "If we do nothing to improve our world, then we cannot call ourselves educated women."

A native of Jacksonville, Florida, Cole grew up as part of the city's black middle class. Her family was well known and well respected for both their business and civic activities, yet like everyone else in their community, they were forced to endure the strict segregationist laws then observed in the South. At the blacks-only school she attended, Cole compiled an outstanding academic record and graduated at the age of fifteen, then enrolled in an early entrance program at Fisk University, a predominantly black institution in Nashville, Tennessee.

Cole remained at Fisk for only a year, however, before transferring to Ohio's Oberlin College with the intention of focusing on science courses in preparation for medical school. Instead, she developed an interest in anthropology. After earning her bachelor's degree in 1957, she continued her studies at Northwestern University outside Chicago and received a master's degree in 1959. In 1967, after conducting two years of anthropological research in the West African nation of Liberia and completing her dissertation, Cole was awarded her PhD from Northwestern.

In 1969, Cole began her career in education as an assistant professor of anthropology at Washington State University, where she also helped create and eventually direct the school's black studies program. In 1970, she headed east to the University of Massachusetts in Amherst and a position as associate professor of Afro-American studies. She remained there for the next thirteen years, rising to the rank of full professor of both Afro-American studies and anthropology and serving for two years as associate provost of undergraduate education. In 1982, she produced her first book, a collection of introductory readings in anthropology.

Cole's next move was to Hunter College of the City University of New York, first as a visiting professor and then as a full professor of anthropology and head of the school's Latin American and Caribbean studies program. Cole has carried out anthropological fieldwork in Cuba, the Dominican Republic, Haiti, and other parts of the Caribbean. During her time at Hunter College, Cole published her second book, All-American Women: Lines That Divide, Ties That Bind.

When the presidency of Spelman College opened up in 1986, Cole—who had not given much thought to changing jobs because she enjoyed hers so much—went ahead and submitted an application. Her timing was fortuitous; in its 107-year history, the nation's oldest and most prestigious liberal arts school for black women had been led by white women and black men, but never a black woman, and Spelman officials were under pressure to remedy the situation. As they evaluated potential candidates, it soon became clear that Cole was the ideal choice—not only was she a black feminist, she was also an eminently qualified scholar with a solid background in black studies. Furthermore, as she demonstrated during a personal interview, she was unusually charismatic and energetic and displayed a strong sense of purpose that seemingly guaranteed the school would be revitalized under her leadership. In April 1987, Cole learned that the job was hers.

Since she officially took over the reins at Spelman in July 1987, Cole has indeed made a name for herself as one of the most vibrant and inspirational college administrators in the country. Her goal is to make Spelman a place where black women from around the world can receive not only a superb education but also the kind of nurturing that will help them become confident, self-motivated, and compassionate leaders in all fields of endeavor. She would also like to see the school become a major center for scholarship by and about black women.

To that end, Cole spends a great deal of her time engaged in raising funds for Spelman (an activity at which she has been tremendously successful), establishing ties with other schools and with businesses, and interacting with students past and present, whom she refers to as her "daughters." Her efforts have been rewarded in numerous ways. In 1988, for instance, entertainer Bill Cosby and his wife, Camille, announced their plans to donate twenty million dollars to Spelman, the single largest personal donation to a historically black institution. In 1992, Spelman again made headlines by becoming the first historically black institution to receive a number-one rating in U.S. News & World Report *magazine's annual "best colleges" issue. Also in 1992, Cole was chosen to serve as a member of President-elect Bill Clinton's transition team in the role of coordinator for education, labor, and the arts and humanities.*

Cole's high-profile activities on behalf of Spelman often include giving speeches. "Empowerment" is a favorite theme in her writings and in her lectures, and on January 28, 1994, it was the focus of a talk she gave to staff of the National Science Foundation (NSF) at a ceremony commemorating the birthday of Martin Luther King, Jr. A copy of the speech was furnished by Cole.

Sisters and Brothers All:

Over the years, Spelman College has participated in several programs sponsored by the National Science Foundation, and so I come to you today with knowledge of NSF's commitment to scientific research and the great service each of you makes to our nation. Spelman faculty have enjoyed a working relationship with many of you here at NSF. Of course, when we think of our colleagues at NSF, we think most readily of Dr. Luther Williams. As the former president of what is now Clark Atlanta University, we consider him to be a member of our Atlanta University Center family. We are proud of the work he has done over the years to increase educational opportunities for all students, and we are particularly grateful for his work on behalf of all of the folks who are traditionally underrepresented in the sciences.

We also want to commend each of you for carrying out a commitment to advancing excellence *and* equity in education. Your continued leadership in this area is needed now more than ever.

Today we come together in tribute to Dr. Martin Luther King, and to acknowledge what he stood for. Our brother Martin led a movement for peace and justice that fundamentally changed our nation. Indeed, our country has changed since the days when Sister Rosa Parks refused to move to the back of a bus and Brother Martin Luther King led nonviolent protests, marches, boycotts, and voter registration drives—singing all along, "Ain't gonna let nobody turn me round. . . ."

Thirty-five years after the Montgomery boycott, African Americans have made demonstrable progress. Growing up in the Jim Crow South of "Colored" and "White" water fountains, I know things have changed. As just one example, look at the political arena. The National Urban league reports that following the 1992 elections, the number of African American elected officials exceeded eight thousand. More than ninety percent of these officials will serve at the local levels of government. And, for the first time in our country's history, the number of sisters and brothers in Congress will reach forty—including Carol Moseley-Braun, the first African American woman in the U.S. Senate. Proving once again that women belong in the house and the senate, too.

Indeed, so many conditions have truly changed. But all has not changed for the better. In many places and for many people, the quality of their lives has declined, and conditions associated with racism, with sexism, with poverty, illiteracy, unemployment and poor housing, health and education, remain deplorable.

As we ponder these realities, listen to the words of our brother Martin. He once said: "America has been sincere and even ardent in welcoming some change. But too quickly apathy and disinterest rise to the surface when the next logical steps are to be taken. Laws are passed in a crisis mood. . . . The recording of the law in itself is treated as the reality of the reform." He went on to say that:

> *When millions of people have been cheated for centuries, restitution is a costly process. Inferior education, poor housing, unemployment, inadequate health care—each is a bitter component of the oppression that has been our heritage. Each will require billions of dollars to correct. Justice so long deferred has accumulated interest and its costs for this society will be substantial in financial as well as human terms.*

How accurately our brother Martin described matters of his day, how prophetically he spoke of what remains the plight of so many African Americans. The financial and human costs associated with complacency and continued deferral of equality have indeed reached exorbitant heights. During the 1980s and early part of the 1990s, our government's efforts to address the crises in inner cities and rural communities can be described as lethargic at best. The cost of our accrued inaction has often been the loss of life itself and the endangerment of our most valued resource—our children.

Just last week, the Children's Defense Fund (CDF) released a report that contains alarming information. In our nation, a gun takes the life of a child every two hours. That is the equivalent of our loosing a classroom full of children every two days. The report documents that homicide is now the leading cause of death for elementary and middle school children, ages 5 to 14.

In just one year, 1990, 560 American children ages 10 to 14 died from guns—twice the number of handgun deaths of citizens of all ages in Sweden, Switzerland, Japan, Canada, Great Britain, and Australia combined.

Over the course of the last twenty-five years, there have been 800,000 deaths in our nation from guns, and another 500,000 violent deaths by other means. In total, 1.3 million Americans have either killed themselves or others. This number triples the number of Americans killed in battle in all the foreign wars our nation fought in the twentieth century.

And how it pains me to say that these dismal numbers are disproportionately pronounced for African Americans. That is so because we are disproportionately poor, disproportionately the victims of covert and blatant racism.

Johnnetta B. Cole

For all of the '90s, homicide has been the leading cause of death for African American males *and* females between the ages of 14 and 35. Homicide is the second leading cause of death for African American children between the ages of 1 and 4. In her book, *Deadly Consequences,* Spelman alumna Dr. Deborah Prothrow-Stith shares with us the words of a woman whose two sons were shot in the same incident. One died, one did not. Hear her words:

> *The children who are dying are real kids. . . . They are real kids from real families. Some were doing foolish things, and some were just caught in the wrong place at the wrong time. But all kids have a right to make mistakes. All kids have a right to live. Somebody has to wake up and see that our children are dying. My child is dead, your child could be next.*

What would our brother Martin say about this state of affairs? Surely he would be shocked by the indifference so many of our children display toward life. He would be profoundly troubled by how they busy themselves dancing with death. Surely Brother Martin would be outraged by the fact that we adults—the persons who are charged with the responsibility of raising children—have been sleeping on our watch. Children do not come into the world raised; they must get raised. Without us, how sadly they raise themselves.

And children do not come into the world with guns set in their hands. When we fail to put books, musical instruments and the stuff of decent work in their hands, there is room for these instruments of destruction. There is an African proverb that says, "It takes a whole village to raise a child." I must tell you that in village after village in our America, folks have not been on the case.

There is another African proverb that I must now cite: "If you're sleeping on the floor, you can't fall off of the bed." We are on the floor when it comes to violence in our nation. And thank goodness there are signs that we are finally ready to get up!

I am encouraged by the leadership President Clinton and his administration are showing in trying to stop this madness whereby violence has become America's favorite entertainment and violence is now a frequent means for settling disputes.

Outside the administration, African American leaders are speaking up and speaking out on violence. Dr. Bill Cosby, Reverend Jesse Jackson, Congresswomen Maxine Waters and Eleanor Holmes Norton, Sister and Brother representatives of the Congressional Black Caucus are all saying ENOUGH! And folks in the motion picture industry have been enlisted in the campaign to save our children. But ultimate victory will depend on to what extent and how soon folks like you and I get involved.

I deeply believe that there is a special responsibility on the shoulders of those of us who are educators. At a time in our nation when so many families are unable to fulfill the roles they have traditionally played, and the ties that bind people into a sense of community have come apart, we educators have no choice but to work with others to provide the support, discipline, instruction and plain ole educating that every child needs—and really craves.

It is in the absence of all of that good stuff that they turn to gangs and guns and drugs. It is as if they are asking gangs to be their families, guns to substitute for dignity and self esteem, and drugs to take the place of love.

And once the inevitable happens, once crimes are committed and the young people are locked up, know that as long as we put them in jails and prisons and then release them without any improvement in their ability to hold a job—because they still can't read and write and are without marketable skills—as long as we do that, expect more holdups! People may well turn to crime to get what they see others with in flashy TV commercials. But more fundamentally, without education and training and meaningful employment, people will often commit crimes for the basic necessities of life.

Specifically, when it comes to our young African American children, we have got to do a massive job of life saving. Listen to this fact: today there are more college-age African American men in the cells of our jails and prisons than in the dormitories of our colleges and universities. Of course we must do all that is in our power to keep young people in school, because a child who drops out of school is three and one-half times more likely to have a criminal record than a child who has a high school education.

When it comes to educating African Americans, historically Black colleges and universities [HBCUs] play a very special role that we must protect. Today close to forty percent of all African American students who have completed college attended HBCUs. This is an impressive figure when you realize that these schools only enroll about seventeen percent of the total number of African American college students.

HBCUs were the undergraduate schools of the majority of professional Black Americans in all fields—from federal judges to librarians. Three quarters of all Black PhDs did their undergraduate work at HBCUs.

If given adequate federal assistance and an opportunity to work in greater partnership with federal agencies, I know HBCUs could have an even mightier impact on the very problems that haunt our nation.

The perilous conditions of our communities and changing demographics require that we move quickly to garner greater involvement of these schools. As you know, the United States Census Bureau predicts that by the year 2000, over sixty percent of the total population growth will be women and people of color. It is already the case that African Americans and Hispanics are the majority in almost all of our nation's large city school systems. As we look at these pipeline issues and the impending shortages of science and engineering personnel, we must take special care to address issues related to African American girls and women. When it comes to girls and women of color, there is a particularly intense situation. Today a young Black girl has only one chance in twenty-one thousand of ever getting a PhD in math, engineering or a physical science. She has two in five chances of dropping out of school before her high school graduation and one chance in five of having a baby before her twentieth birthday!

In a recent article published by Margaret E.M. Tolbert, formerly an employee of NSF, data are presented which documents that while minority women as an aggregate group show an overall increase in the percent of doctoral degrees earned in 1990 compared to 1980, there has been a decline in the number of African American women earning doctorates in science and engineering.

In the face of this stark reality there is a critical role that we play at Spelman. At Spelman College, thirty-eight percent of the students major in science, math and a dual degree program in engineering. The college ranks among the top ten U.S. institutions in terms of the number of African American students admitted to medical school. We rank second in the number of undergraduate degrees given to African Americans in mathematics. We rank fifth among American colleges and universities in the number of bachelor degrees conferred in the physical sciences to African Americans; and Spelman ranks seventh in the number of degrees given in the biological sciences.

> ***"I deeply believe that there is a special responsibility on the shoulders of those of us who are educators . . . to provide the support, discipline, instruction and plain ole educating that every child needs—and really craves."***

The amazing thing is that we are educating these future Black women scientists in a building constructed in 1925. Because our science facilities are cramped and outdated we are in a campaign to raise the funds to build a state-of-the-art science complex.

Understanding the unique and vital role Spelman has played and needs to play in helping our nation meet the challenge for women and minority scientists and engineers, we wish to work even closer in partnership with federal agencies such as NSF. I ask that you meet us halfway.

Research institutions and universities have been the primary recipients of federal support for scientific research and training. Liberal arts colleges, such as Spelman, are often excluded from such competitions. We need to reconfigure these funding patterns so that enhanced support can reach colleges, like Spelman, that are educating disproportionately high numbers of women and persons of color in science, math and engineering.

As I move toward closure, let me say quite explicitly that there are connections between the violence that is widespread in our nation and what it is that you do here at NSF, and that we do at Spelman.

There will never be a way to address our nation's need for top-notch scientists and engineers if we do not get guns out of our children's hands and get books, test tubes, and microscopes into their grasp.

There is so much that each of us here must do—as parents, as surrogate parents, as citizens who can vote, as community activists who can tutor and mentor and hug our nation's children.

And then, as educators at Spelman and other educational institutions, and as women and men of this National Science Foundation, we must take on the specific responsibility of making sure that our nation has top-notch women and folks of color in all fields of science and technology.

The time to forge a renewed sense of shared purpose is now. This is the time to fully address the issues associated with racism, sexism, poverty, violence, illiteracy and unemployment. This is the time to remove the barriers which keep some folks down, and which keep too many of us separate and unequal. In moving forward, we must proceed boldly. Let me change that: we must proceed fiercely as we attempt to breathe life into the principles Dr. King left with us. The nature of our effort was once graphically described by Dr. King when he said:

> *Human progress is neither automatic nor inevitable. Even a superficial look at history reveals that no social advance rolls in on the wheels of inevitability. Every step toward the goal of justice requires sacrifice, suffering, and struggle; the tireless exertions and passionate concern of dedicated individuals. Without persistent effort, time itself becomes an ally of the insurgent and primitive forces of irrational emotionalism and social destruction. This is no time for apathy or complacency. This is a time for vigorous and positive action.*

My brothers and sisters, we are in a great position to make tomorrow better than today. That is our job. Let's do it!

SOURCES

Books

Cole, Johnnetta B., *Conversations: Straight Talk with America's Sister President,* Doubleday, 1993.

Periodicals

Black Enterprise, "A Conversation with Spelman's 'Sister President,'" February, 1989, p. 28.

Ebony, " 'Sister' Presidents," February, 1988, pp. 82-88.

Essence, "Sister President," November, 1987, p. 35; "The 1989 Essence Awards," October, 1989, p. 60; "In the Limelight," July, 1990. p. 34.

Glamour, "Women of the Year," December, 1991.

McCall's, February, 1991.

Ms., "Sister President," October, 1987, pp. 58-61.

Nation, ". . . And Who's Out," January 18, 1993, p. 40.

New York Times, July 20, 1987; January 10, 1993.

New York Times Book Review, February 28, 1993, p. 28.

People, "Driving Home a Point," May 10, 1993, pp. 97-99.

Washington Post, November 11, 1989.

Working Woman, "The Inspiring Leader of Scholars (and Dollars)," June, 1989, pp. 68-74; "Sister President," November, 1991, p. 88.

Cornplanter
(Ki-on-twog-ky, John O'Beale)

1732(?)–1836

Native American chief of the Seneca tribe

A notable colonial-era Indian orator, Cornplanter was the son of a full-blooded Seneca woman and a white trader, most likely an Irishman named O'Beale or O'Bail. His exact birth date is unknown, but historians estimate that it was sometime between 1732 and 1740. The exact place is somewhat in doubt, too, although it was probably in New York State, home of the powerful Iroquois confederation known as the League of Six Nations to which the Seneca tribe belonged. Cornplanter grew up among his mother's family after his father left the area. As a result of his mixed heritage, however, he was known not only by his Indian name but also by the name O'Beale, which was sometimes spelled Obeale.

Cornplanter's first role was as a warrior, and it was in that capacity that he aided the French during the French and Indian War (1754–63). He later became an admirer of the British and even adopted their style of dress and mannerisms after making a trip to England. When confronted by enraged fellow Senecas upon his return home, however, he was forced to don more traditional apparel. His allegiance to the British nevertheless endured; he fully supported them during the Revolutionary War and led many raids against American troops.

In 1784, Cornplanter was among the Iroquois leaders who signed the Treaty of Fort Stanwix, which granted all of the land west of the Niagara River to the new United States. Not everyone in the confederation approved of the treaty, however; also unacceptable to some was Cornplanter's insistence that the Iroquois would be wise to learn American ways of farming and governing if they expected to survive. He nevertheless continued to reach out in peace and friendship to the leaders of the new nation and worked tirelessly to bring the concerns of the Indian people to the attention of government officials, including George Washington. At a meeting between the two men in 1790, Cornplanter confided to the country's first president that despite receiving assurances to the contrary, he feared the Iroquois would be subjected to future demands for more land.

As a representative of the Senecas, Cornplanter attended numerous councils. Most of these required him to travel to Philadelphia, the seat of colonial rule as well as of the fledgling U.S. government. At one council that convened there in 1790, for example, he spoke at length to a gathering on October 29 about the injustices his people had endured at the hands of unscrupulous whites. Near the close of his remarks, reprinted here from W.C. Vanderwerth's Indian Oratory: Famous Speeches by Noted Indian Chieftains *(University of Oklahoma Press, 1971), Cornplanter asked for help in ensuring that the Senecas would be treated fairly in the future. Of significance is his use of the deferential greeting "Father" rather than the more customary "Brother" and its implication of equality.*

The Fathers of the Quaker State, Obeale or Cornplanter returns thanks to God for the pleasure he has in meeting you this day with six of his people.

Fathers: Six years ago I had the pleasure of making peace with you, and at that time a hole was dug in the earth, and all contentions between my nation and you ceased and were buried there.

At a treaty then held at Fort Stanwix between the six nations of Indians and the Thirteen Fires, three friends from the Quaker State came to me and treated with me for the purchase of a large tract of land upon the northern boundary of Pennsylvania, extending from Tioga to Lake Erie for the use of their warriors. I agreed to sale of the same, and sold it to them for four thousand dollars. I begged of them to take pity on my nation and not buy it forever. They said they would purchase it forever, but that they would give me further one thousand dollars in goods when the leaves were ready to fall, and when I found that they were determined to have it, I agreed that they should have it. I then requested, as they were determined to have the land, to permit my people to have the game and hunt upon the same, which request they complied with, and promised me to have it put upon record, that I and my people should have that privilege.

Fathers: The six nations then requested that another talk might be held with the Thirteen Fires, which was agreed to, and a talk afterwards held between them at Muskingum. Myself with three of my chiefs attended punctually, and were much fatigued in endeavoring to procure the attendance of the other nations, but none of them came to the council fire except the Delawares and the Wyandots.

Fathers: At the same treaty the Thirteen Fires asked me on which side I would die, whether on their side, or the side on those nations who did not attend the council fire. I replied, "Listen to me, fathers of the Thirteen Fires, I hope you will consider how kind your fathers were treated by our fathers, the six nations, when they first came into this country, since which time you have become strong, insomuch, that I now call you fathers.

Cornplanter

In former days when you were young and weak, I used to call you brother, but now I call you father. Father, I hope you will take pity on your children, for now I inform you that I'll die on your side. Now, father, I hope you will make my bed strong.

Fathers of the Quaker State: I speak but little now, but will speak more when the Thirteen Fires meet. I will only inform you further, that when I had finished my talk with the Thirteen Fires, General Gibson, who was sent by the Quaker State, came to the fire, and said that the Quaker State had bought of the Thirteen Fires a tract of land extending from the northern boundary of Pennsylvania at Connewango River to Buffalo Creek on Lake Erie, and thence along the said lake to the northern boundary of Pennsylvania aforesaid. Hearing this I run to my father, and said to him, "Father, have you sold this land to the Quaker State?" And he said he did not know, it might have been done since he came there. I then disputed with Gibson and Butler, who was with him, about the same, and told them I would be satisfied if the line was run from Connewango River through Chatochque Lake to Lake Erie, for Gibson and Butler had told me that the Quaker State had purchased the land from the Thirteen Fires, but that notwithstanding the Quaker State had given to me one thousand dollars in fine prime goods which were ready for me and my people at Fort Pitt. We then agreed that the line should be run from Connewango River through Chatochque Lake into Lake Erie, and that one-half of the fish in Chatochque Lake should be mine and one-half theirs.

They then said as the Quaker State had purchased the whole from the Thirteen Fires, that the Thirteen Fires must pay back to the Quaker State the value of the remaining land. When I heard this my mind was at ease, and I was satisfied.

I then proposed to give a half mile square of land upon the line so agreed upon to a Mr. Hartzhorn, who was an ensign in General Harmar's army, out to a Mr. Britt, a cadet who acted as a clerk upon occasion, and who I well know by the name of Half-Town, for the purpose of their settling there to prevent any mischief being committed in future upon my people's lands. And I hoped that the Quaker State would in addition thereto give them another half mile square on their side of the line so agreed upon for the same purpose, expecting thereby that the line so agreed upon would be known with sufficient certainty and that no disputes would thereafter arise between my people and the Quaker State concerning it. I then went to my father of the Thirteen Fires and told him I was satisfied, and the coals being covered up, I said to my children, "You must take your course right through the woods to Fort Pitt." When I was leaving Muskingum, my own son, who remained a little while behind to warm himself at the fire, was robbed of a rifle by one of the white men, who I believe to have been a Yankee. Myself with Mr. Joseph Nicholson and a Mr. Morgan then traveled three days together through the wilderness, but the weather being very severe they were obliged to separate from me, and I sent some of my own people along with Mr. Nicholson and Mr. Morgan as guides to conduct them on to Wheelen.

After I had separated from Mr. Nicholson and Mr. Morgan, I had under my charge one hundred and seventy persons of my own nation, consisting of men, women and children to conduct through the wilderness through heaps of briars, and having lost our way, we, with great difficulty, reached Wheelen. When arrived there being out of provision, I requested of a Mr. Zanes to furnish me and my people with bacon and flour to the amount of seventeen dollars, to be paid for out of goods belonging to me and my people at Fort Pitt. Having obtained my request, I proceeded on my journey for Pittsburgh, and about ten miles from Wheelen my party were fired upon by three white people, and one of my people in the rear of my party received two shot through his blanket.

Fathers: It was a constant practice with me throughout the whole journey to take great care of my people, and not suffer them to commit any outrages or drink more than their necessities required. During the whole of my journey only one accident happened, which was owing to the kindness of the people of the town called Catfish, in the Quaker State, who, while I was talking with the head men of the town, gave to my people more liquor than was proper, and some of them got drunk, which obliged me to continue there with my people all night, and in the night my people were robbed of three rifles and one shotgun. And though every endeavor was used by the head men of the town upon complaint made to them to discover the perpetrators of the robbery, they could not be found; and on my people's complaining to me I told them it was their own fault by getting drunk.

Fathers: Upon my arrival at Fort Pitt I saw the goods which I had been informed of at Muskingum, and one hundred of the blankets were all moth-eaten and good for nothing. I was advised not to take the blankets, but the blankets which I and my people then had being all torn by the briars in our passage through the wilderness, we were under the necessity of taking them to keep ourselves warm. And what most surprised me was that after I had received the goods, they extinguished the fire and swept away the ashes, and having no interpreter there, I could talk with no one upon the subject. Feeling myself much hurt upon the occasion, I wrote a letter to you Fathers of the Quaker State complaining of the injury, but never received any answer. Having waited a considerable time, and having heard that my letter got lost, I wrote a second time to you Fathers of the Quaker State and then I received an answer.

I am very thankful to have received that answer, and as the answer entreated me to come and speak for myself, I thank God that I have this opportunity, I therefore speak to you as follows. I hope that you, the Fathers of the Quaker State, will fix some person at Fort Pitt to take care of me and my people. I wish, and it is the wish of my people if agreeable to you, that my present interpreter, Joseph Nicholson, may be the person, as I and my people have a confidence in him, and are satisfied that he will always exert himself to preserve peace and harmony between you and us. My reasons for wishing an interpreter to be placed there, are that oftentimes when my hunters and people come there, their canoes and other things are stolen, and they can obtain no redress, not having any person there on whom they can rely to interpret for them and see justice done to them.

Fathers of the Quaker State: About a year ago a young man, one of my tribe who lived among the Shawanese, was one of a party who had committed some outrages and stolen a quantity of skins the property of David Duncan, being at Fort Pitt, was seized by the white people there who would have put him into confinement and perhaps to death had not some of the chiefs of the Seneca Nation interfered and bound themselves to the said David Duncan, who insisted upon satisfaction, for payment of the sum of five hundred and thirty dollars for the said skins so stolen, upon which the young man aforesaid was released and delivered up to them.

"It is my wish and the wishes of my people to live peaceably and quietly with you and yours. . . ."

Fathers of the Quaker State: I wish now to acquaint you with what happened to one of my people about four years ago, four miles above Fort Pitt. A young man who was married to my wife's sister, when he was hunting, was murdered by a white man. There were three reasons for his being killed: In the first place he had a very fine riding horse; secondly, he was very richly dressed, and had about him a good deal of silver; and thirdly, he had with him a very fine rifle. The white man invited him to his house, to light from his horse, and as he was getting off his horse, his head being rather down, the white man struck him with a tomahawk on the head and killed him, and having plundered him dragged him into the river. Upon discovery of the murder, my people, with Mr. Nicholson and Mr. Duncan, had a great deal of trouble, and took a great deal of pains to find out the person who had committed the murder, and after three days' searching, they discovered him.

Father of the Quaker State: About five years ago, one of my chiefs, name Half-Town, was sent to Fort Pitt to deliver up into your hands your own flesh and blood who were taken in the war, and before he returned two horses were stolen from him by the white people. Now, Fathers, I will inform you of another accident which happened to my people last winter, fifteen miles below Fort Pitt. My nephew, with a hunting party, being there, was shot through the head in Mr. Nicholson's camp, the particulars of which Mr. Nicholson, who is here present, can inform you.

Well, Fathers, I beg of you once more not to let such bad people be 'longside of me. And, Fathers, you must not think I or any of my people are bad or wish evil to you and yours, nor must you blame us for mischiefs that have been committed by the other nations. Fathers, consider me and my people, and the many injuries we have sustained by the repeated robberies, and the murders and depredations committed by the whites against us.

It is my wish and the wishes of my people to live peaceably and quietly with you and yours, but the losses we have sustained require some compensation. I have, with the consent of my people, agreed to receive from you eight hundred and thirty dollars, as a satisfaction for all losses and injuries I and my people have sustained, and this being paid me by you, to enable me to satisfy such of my people as have sustained those losses and suffered those injuries, we shall, I hope, in future live peaceable together, and bury in the earth all ill will and enmity to each other.

Fathers of the Quaker State: I have now had the pleasure to meet you with six of my people. We have come a great way, by your desire, to talk with you and to show to you the many injuries my nation has sustained. It now remains with you to do with me and my people what you please, on account of the present trouble which I and my people have taken for your satisfaction, and in compliance with your request.

Fathers, having come this great way at your request, and as it is necessary for some of us to remain here to talk with the Thirteen Fires when they meet, I have concluded to send back four of my people, and to remain here myself with Half-Town and my interpreter, Mr. Nicholson, until that time, which I hope you will approve of. But should you not approve of it, I must be under the necessity of returning with the whole of my people, which will be attended with a considerable expense.

Fathers of the Quaker State: You have now got the most of our lands, and have taken the game upon the same. We have only the privilege of hunting and fishing thereon. I, therefore, would make this further request, that a store may be established at Fort Pitt for the accommodation of my people and the other nations when they go out to hunt; and where they may purchase goods at a reasonable price. For, believe me, Fathers, you yourselves would be frightened were you to know the extravagant prices we are obliged to pay for the goods we purchase.

There is a man, Esquire Wilkie, in Pittsburgh who has taken a great deal of pains to serve my people, and has pitied them; my people, when there, are very kindly treated by him, and give him a great deal of trouble, but he thinks nothing of it; he is the man my people wish should have charge of the store.

Fathers of the Quaker State: I have heard that you have been pleased to present to me a tract of land, but as yet I have not seen no writings for the same. Well, Fathers, if it is true that you have given me this tract of land, I can only thank you for the same, but I hope you will also give me tools and materials for working the same.

Fathers of the Quaker State: Five years ago, when I used to be with my present interpreter, Joseph Nicholson, he took care of me and my people. Considering his services and the difficulties he underwent in his journey from Muskingum to Fort Pitt, the Six Nations wished to have him seated upon a tract of land of six miles square, lying in the forks of Allegheny River, and Broken Straw creek, and accordingly patented the same to him, this being the place where the battle was fought between my people and yours, and where about thirty of my people were beaten by him and twenty-five of your people, and where he was shot through the thigh. Now, Fathers, it is my wish, and I tell you it is the wish of the whole Six Nations, in behalf of whom and myself, I request that you would grant and confirm to our brother and friend, the before-named Joseph Nicholson, the aforesaid tract of land, as described in our patent or grant to him.

This, Fathers, is all I have to say to the Quaker State, and I hope you will consider well all I have mentioned.

SOURCES

Armstrong, Virginia Irving, compiler, *I Have Spoken: American History Through the Voices of the Indians,* Sage Books, 1971.

Sanders, Thomas E., and Walter W. Peek, *Literature of the American Indian,* Glencoe Press, 1973.

Vanderwerth, W.C., *Indian Oratory: Famous Speeches by Noted Indian Chieftains,* University of Oklahoma Press, 1971.

Angela Davis

1944–

African American political and social activist and educator

At the height of her notoriety during the early 1970s, Angela Davis was one of the world's most recognizable symbols of militant resistance to the status quo. She first sparked headlines when she challenged a decision by the regents of the University of California at Los Angeles to dismiss her because she was a member of the Communist party. She then provoked even more controversy for her outspoken support of the Soledad Brothers, three black prison inmates charged with murdering a white guard. Her involvement in their case eventually landed her on the FBI's "Ten Most Wanted" list for the role she allegedly played in a deadly shootout outside a California courtroom. Before it all ended, Davis had become a worldwide cause célèbre *among those who were convinced she was being persecuted for her political beliefs rather than for any criminal acts.*

A native of Birmingham, Alabama, Davis displayed an activist bent even as a youngster when she participated in civil rights demonstrations and helped organize interracial study groups at school. With her parents' support and encouragement, she left the South at the age of fifteen to finish her secondary education at a progressive private school in New York's Greenwich Village. From there, she went on to Brandeis University, where she studied under well-known leftist political philosopher Herbert Marcuse. His condemnation of modern industrial society and his call to reform its repressive nature through revolutionary means left a strong impression on Davis.

After graduating with honors from Brandeis in 1965, Davis continued her course work in philosophy at Germany's Goethe University. But the more she watched from afar as racial and political turmoil escalated at home, the more impossible she found it to remain on the sidelines. Returning to the United States in 1967, she enrolled at the University of California in San Diego (where her mentor, Marcuse, had joined the faculty) and became active in a number of radical organizations, including the Black Students Council, the Student Nonviolent Coordinating Committee (SNCC), and the Che-Lumumba Club, an all-black faction of the Communist party. She officially joined the Communist party in 1968 after concluding that it espoused a world view that was most in tune with her own.

In early 1969, Davis accepted a teaching position in the philosophy depart-

ment at the University of California in Los Angeles. Although she was popular and respected among students as well as her fellow faculty members and even the administration, she was eyed with suspicion by the Board of Regents and then-Governor Ronald Reagan. They could not tolerate her affiliation with the Communist party and strongly objected to the passionate speeches she delivered outside the classroom in defense of various radical causes. At first, the regents tried to fire her, but their decision was overturned in court; they then waited until after the 1969-70 academic year and simply refused to renew her contract.

Davis then turned all her energies to the crusade that had figured so prominently in her dispute with UCLA: the Soledad Brothers Defense Committee. The so-called "brothers"—George Jackson, Fleeta Drumgo, and John Cluchette—were black inmates of California's Soledad Prison. (Jackson, the most famous member of the trio, was also one of the leaders of a Marxist revolutionary group made up of fellow prisoners.) In February 1970, they had been charged with murdering a white guard shortly after several black prisoners involved in a fistfight were killed by shots fired from a guard tower. Davis (and others) believed that the Soledad Brothers had been unjustly accused and were not murderers but victims of political and racial repression. However, her efforts to drum up support for the men and raise money to cover their legal expenses outraged many people who felt the Soledad Brothers were indeed criminals.

Within a few months, however, Davis's connection to the Soledad Brothers landed her in more serious trouble. On August 7, 1970, George Jackson's younger brother, Jonathan, went to the Marin County Courthouse in San Rafael, California, and walked into the room where a black inmate from San Quentin was on trial for a prison stabbing. Pulling out several guns he had hidden in his clothes, Jackson took over the courtroom and then gave weapons to the man on trial as well as to two other prisoners who were there to testify on his behalf. The group then fled the building with five hostages they allegedly planned to exchange for the release of the Soledad Brothers. But in the parking lot outside the courtroom, a gun battle erupted leaving Jackson, two of the inmates, and a judge dead and a district attorney critically wounded. After an investigation revealed that at least three of the guns in Jackson's possession were registered to Davis, federal authorities issued a warrant for her arrest.

Davis immediately went into hiding and spent the next two months on the run, ending up in New York City. It was there that FBI agents took her into custody on October 13, 1970, and then jailed her while awaiting approval to extradite her back to California.

In January 1971, Davis was extradited to California, where she was formally charged with murder, kidnapping, and conspiracy for her alleged role in the Marin County Courthouse shooting. Denied bail, she remained in jail for over a year until her case finally came to trial in early 1972. The proceedings were attended by black and white activists from all over the world who wanted to make sure she received a fair trial. On June 4, 1972, a jury of eleven whites and one Mexican American acquitted her of all charges.

Since regaining her freedom, Davis has returned to teaching, writing, and lecturing. Her most recent academic affiliations have been with San Francisco State University and the University of California at Santa Cruz, where, in 1995, she was awarded a prestigious Presidential Chair for a three-year project to expand feminist and ethnic studies at the school. She has remained active politically as well, running for vice-president on the Communist party ticket in 1980 and again in 1984. (She is no longer a member of the party, however.) Davis's interests now center largely around the issues facing black women in modern society, including health care, sexism, violence, and the need for them to claim their rightful place in the feminist movement. In June 1987, while in Atlanta, Georgia, to attend the tenth National Women's Studies Association Conference, Davis shared her thoughts on empowering African American women. Her keynote address, with some revisions, was later reprinted in the Harvard Educational Review, *August 1988.*

The concept of empowerment is hardly new to Afro-American women. For almost a century, we have been organized in bodies that have sought collectively to develop strategies that illuminate the way to economic and political power for ourselves and our communities. In the last decade of the nineteenth century, after having been repeatedly shunned by the racially homogeneous women's rights movement, Black women organized their own Club Movement. In 1895—five years after the founding of the General Federation of Women's Clubs, which consolidated a club movement reflecting concerns of middle-class White women—one hundred Black women from ten states met in the city of Boston, under the leadership of Josephine St. Pierre Ruffin, to discuss the creation of a national organization of Black women's clubs. As compared to their White counterparts, the Afro-American women issuing the call for this national club movement articulated principles that were more openly political in nature. They defined the primary function of their clubs as an ideological as well as an activist defense of Black women—and men—from the ravages of racism. When the meeting was convened, its participants emphatically declared that, unlike their White sisters, whose organizational policies were seriously tainted by racism, they envisioned their movement as one open to all women:

> *Our woman's movement is woman's movement in that it is led and directed by women for the good of women and men, for the benefit of all humanity, which is more than any one branch or section of it. We want, we ask the active interest of our men, and, too, we are not drawing the color line; we are women, American women, as intensely interested in all that pertains to us as such as all other American women; we are not alienating or withdrawing, we are only coming to the front, willing to join any others in the same work and cordially inviting and welcoming any others to join us.*

The following year, the formation of the National Association of Colored Women's Clubs was announced. The motto chosen by the Association was "Lifting As We Climb."

The nineteenth-century women's movement was also plagued by classism. Susan B. Anthony wondered why her outreach to working-class women on the issue of the ballot was so frequently met with indifference. She wondered why these women seemed to be much more concerned with improving their economic situation than with achieving the right to vote. As essential as political equality may have been to the larger campaign for women's rights, in the eyes of Afro-American and White working-class women it was not synonymous with emancipation. That the conceptualization of strategies for struggle was based on the peculiar condition of White women of the privileged classes rendered those strategies discordant with working-class women's perceptions of empowerment. It is not surprising that many of them told Ms. Anthony, "Women want bread, not the ballot." Eventually, of course, working-class White women, and Afro-American women as well, reconceptualized this struggle, defining the vote not as an end in itself—not as the panacea that would cure all the ills related to gender-based discrimination—but rather as an important weapon in the continuing fight for higher wages, better working conditions, and an end to the omnipresent menace of the lynch mob.

Today, as we reflect on the process of empowering Afro-American women, our most efficacious strategies remain those that are guided by the principle used by Black women in the club movement. We must strive to "lift as we climb." In other words, we must climb in such a way as to guarantee that all of our sisters, regardless of social class, and indeed all of our brothers, climb with us. This must be the essential dynamic of our quest for power—a principle that must not only determine our struggles as Afro-American women, but also govern all authentic struggles of dispossessed people. Indeed, the overall battle for equality can be profoundly enhanced by embracing this principle.

Afro-American women bring to the women's movement a strong tradition of struggle around issues that politically link women to the most crucial progressive causes. This is the meaning of the motto, "Lifting As We Climb." This approach reflects the often unspoken interests and aspirations of masses of women of all racial backgrounds. Millions of women today are concerned about jobs, working conditions, higher wages, and racist violence. They are concerned about plant closings, homelessness, and repressive immigration legislation. Women are concerned about homophobia, ageism, and discrimination against the physically challenged. We are concerned about Nicaragua and South Africa. And we share our children's dreams that tomorrow's world will be delivered from the threat of nuclear omnicide. These are some of the issues that should be made a part of the overall struggle for women's rights, if there is to be a serious commitment to the empowerment of women who, throughout history, have been rendered invisible. These are some of the issues we should consider if we wish to lift as we climb.

During this decade we have witnessed an exciting resurgence of the women's movement. If the first wave of the movement appeared in the 1840s, and the second wave in the 1960s, then we are approaching the crest of a third wave in the final days of the 1980s. When the feminist historians of the twenty-first century attempt to recapitulate the third wave, will they ignore the momentous contributions of Afro-American women, who have been leaders and activists in movements often confined to women of color, but whose accomplishments have invariably advanced the cause of White women as well? Will the exclusionary policies of the mainstream women's movement—from its inception to the present—which have often compelled Afro-American women to conduct their struggle for equality outside the ranks of that movement, continue to result in the systematic omission of our names from the roster of prominent leaders and activists of the women's movement? Will there continue to be two distinct continua of the women's movement, one visible and another invisible? One publicly acknowledged and another ignored except by the conscious progeny of the working-class women—Black, Latina, Native American, Asian, and White—who forged that hidden continuum? If this question is answered in the affirmative, it will mean that women's quest for equality will continue to be gravely deficient. The revolutionary potential of the women's movement still will not have been realized. The racist-inspired flaws of the first and second waves of the women's movement will have become the inherited flaws of the third wave.

How can we guarantee that this historical pattern is broken? As advocates of and activists for women's rights in the latter 1980s, we must begin to merge that double legacy and create a single continuum, one that solidly represents the aspirations of all women in our society. We must begin to create a revolutionary, multiracial women's movement that seriously addresses the main issues affecting poor and working-class women. In order to tap the potential for such a movement, we must further develop those sectors of the movement that are addressing seriously issues affecting poor and working-class women, such as jobs, pay equity, paid maternity leave, federally subsidized child care, protection from sterilization abuse, and subsidized abortions. Women of all racial and class backgrounds will greatly benefit from such an approach.

Creating a revolutionary women's movement will not be simple. For decades, White women activists have repeated the complaint that women of color frequently fail to respond to their appeals: "We invited them to our meetings, but they didn't come; We asked them to participate in our demonstration, but they didn't show; They just don't seem to be interested in women's studies." The process cannot be initiated merely by intensified efforts to attract Latina or Afro-American or Asian or Native American women into the existing organizations dominated by White women of the more privileged economic strata. The particular concerns of women of color must be included in the agenda.

An issue of special concern to Afro-American women is unemployment. Indeed, the most fundamental prerequisite for empowerment is the ability to earn an adequate living. The Reagan administration boasts that unemployment has leveled off, leaving only(!) 7.5 million people unemployed. However, Black people in general are twice as likely to be unemployed as White people, and Black teenagers are almost three times as likely to be unemployed as White teenagers. We must remember that these figures do not include the millions who hold part-time jobs, although they want and need full-time employment. A disproportionate number of these underemployed individuals are women. Neither do the figures reflect those who, out of utter frustration, have ceased to search for employment, nor those whose unemployment insurance has run out, nor those who have never had a job. Women on welfare are among those who are not counted as unemployed.

The AFL-CIO estimates that there are eighteen million people of working age without jobs. These still critical levels of unemployment, distorted and misrepresented by the Reagan administration, are fundamentally responsible for the impoverished status of Afro-American women, the most glaring evidence of which resides in the fact that women, together with their dependent children, constitute the fastest growing sector of the population of four million homeless in the United States. There can be no serious discussion of empowerment today if we do not embrace the plight of the homeless with an enthusiasm as passionate as that with which we embrace issues more immediately related to our own lives.

The United Nations declared 1987 to be the Year of Shelter for the Homeless, although only the developing countries were the initial focus of this resolution. Eventually it became clear that the United States is an "undeveloping country." Two-thirds of the four million homeless in this country are families, and forty percent of them are Afro-American. In some urban areas, as many as seventy percent of the homeless are Black. In New York City, for example, sixty percent of the homeless population is Black, twenty percent Latino, and twenty percent White. Presently, under New York's Work Incentive Program, homeless women and men are employed to clean toilets, wash graffiti from subway trains, and clean parks at wages of sixty-two cents an hour, a mere fraction of the minimum wage. In other words, the homeless are being compelled to provide slave labor for the government if they wish to receive assistance.

Black women scholars and professionals cannot afford to ignore the straits of our sisters who are acquainted with the immediacy of oppression in a way many of us are not. The process of empowerment cannot be simplistically defined in accordance with our own particular class interests. We must learn to lift as we climb.

If we are to elevate the status of our entire community as we scale the heights of empowerment, we must be willing to offer organized resistance to the proliferating manifestations of racist violence across the country. A virtual "race riot" took place on the campus of one of the most liberal educational institutions in this country some months ago. In the aftermath of the 1986 World Series, White students at the University of Massachusetts, Amherst, who were purportedly fans of the losing Boston Red Sox, vented their wrath on Black students, whom they perceived as a surrogate for the winning team, the New York Mets, because of the predominance of Black players on the New York team. When individuals in the crowd yelled "Black bitch" at a Black woman student, a Black man who hastened to defend her was seriously wounded and was rushed, unconscious, to the hospital. Another one of the many dramatic instances of racist harassment to occur on college campuses during this period was the burning of a cross in front of the Black Students Cultural Center at Purdue University. In December 1986, Michael Griffith, a young Black man, lost his life in what amounted to a virtual lynching by a mob of White youths in the Howard Beach, Queens, section of New York City. Not far from Atlanta, civil rights marchers were attacked on Dr. Martin Luther King's birthday by a mob led by the Ku Klux Klan. An especially outrageous instance in which racist violence was officially condoned was the acquittal of Bernhard Goetz, who, on his own admission, attempted to kill four Black youths because he *felt* threatened by them on a New York subway.

"Black women . . . cannot afford to ignore the straits of our sisters who are acquainted with the immediacy of oppression in a way many of us are not."

Black women have organized before to oppose racist violence. The birth of the Black Women's Club Movement at the end of the nineteenth century was in large part a response to the epidemic of lynching during that era. Leaders like Ida B. Wells and Mary Church Terrell recognized that Black women could not move toward empowerment if they did not radi-

Angela Davis

cally challenge the reign of lynch law in the land. Today, in the late 1980s, Afro-American women must actively take the lead in the movement against racist violence, as did our sister-ancestors almost a century ago. We must lift as we climb. As our ancestors organized for the passage of a federal anti-lynch law—and indeed involved themselves in the women's suffrage movement for the purpose of securing that legislation—we must today become activists in the effort to secure legislation declaring racism and anti-Semitism crimes. As extensive as publicized instances of racist violence may be at this time, many more racist-inspired crimes go unnoticed as a consequence of the failure of law enforcement to classify them specifically as such. A person scrawling swastikas or "KKK" on an apartment building may simply be charged—if criminal charges are brought at all—with defacing property or malicious mischief. Recently, a Ku Klux Klansman who burned a cross in front of a Black family's home was charged with "burning without a permit." We need federal and local laws against acts of racist and anti-Semitic violence. We must organize, lobby, march, and demonstrate in order to guarantee their passage.

As we organize, lobby, march, and demonstrate against racist violence, we who are women of color must be willing to appeal for multiracial unity in the spirit of our sister-ancestors. Like them we must proclaim: We do not draw the color line. The only line we draw is one based on our political principles. We know that empowerment for the masses of women in our country will never be achieved as long as we do not succeed in pushing back the tide of racism. It is not a coincidence that sexist-inspired violence—and, in particular, terrorist attacks on abortion clinics—has reached a peak during the same period in which racist violence has proliferated dramatically. Violent attacks on women's reproductive rights are nourished by these explosions of racism. The vicious anti-lesbian and anti-gay attacks are a part of the same menacing process. The roots of sexism and homophobia are found in the same economic and political institutions that serve as the foundation of racism in this country, and, more often than not, the same extremist circles that inflict violence on people of color are responsible for the eruptions of violence inspired by sexist and homophobic biases. Our political activism must clearly manifest our understanding of these connections.

We must always attempt to lift as we climb. Another urgent point on our political agenda—that of Afro-American as well as all progressive women—must be the repeal of the Simpson-Rodino Act: a racist law that spells repression for vast numbers of women and men who are undocumented immigrants in this country. Camouflaged as an amnesty program, the eligibility restrictions are so numerous that hundreds of thousands of people stand to be prosecuted and deported under its provisions. Amnesty is provided in a restricted way only for those who came to this country before 1982. Thus, vast numbers of Mexicans, who have recently crossed the border in an attempt to flee impoverishment generated by the unrestricted immigration of U.S. corporations into their country, are not eligible for citizenship. Salvadorans and other Central Americans who have escaped political persecution in their respective countries over the last few years will not be offered amnesty. We must organize, lobby, march, and demonstrate for a repeal of the Simpson-Rodino Act. We must lift as we climb.

When we as Afro-American women, when we as women of color, proceed to ascend toward empowerment, we lift up with us our brothers of color, our White sisters and brothers in the working class, and indeed all women who experience the effects of sexist oppression. Our activist agenda must encompass a wide range of demands. We must call for jobs and for the unionization of unorganized women workers, and, indeed, unions must be compelled to take on such issues as affirmative action, pay equity, sexual harassment on the job, and paid maternity leave. Black and Latina women are AIDS victims in disproportionately large numbers. We therefore have an urgent need to demand emergency funding for AIDS research. We must also oppose all instances of repressive mandatory AIDS testing and quarantining, as well as homophobic manipulations of the AIDS crisis. Effective strategies for the reduction of teenage pregnancy are needed, but we must beware of succumbing to propagandistic attempts to relegate to young single mothers the responsibility for our community's impoverishment.

In this unfortunate era of Reaganism, it should be clear that there are forces in our society that reap enormous benefits from the persistent, deepening oppression of women. Members of the Reagan administration include advocates for the most racist, sexist, and anti-working-class circles of contemporary monopoly capitalism. These corporations prop up apartheid in South Africa and profit from the spiraling arms race, while they propose the most vulgar and irrational forms of anti-Sovietism—invoking, for example, the "evil empire" image popularized by Ronald Reagan—as justifications for their omnicidal ventures. If we are not afraid to adopt a revolutionary stance, if, indeed, we wish to be radical in our quest for change, then we must get to the root of our oppression. After all, "radical" simply means grasping things at the root. Our agenda for women's empowerment must thus be unequivocal in its challenge to monopoly capitalism as a major obstacle to the achievement of equality.

I want to suggest, as I conclude, that we link our grassroots organizing, our essential involvement in electoral politics, and our involvement as activists in mass struggles with the long-range aim of fundamentally transforming the socioeconomic conditions that generate and persistently nourish the various forms of oppression we suffer. Let us learn from the strategies of our sisters in South Africa and Nicaragua. As Afro-American women, as women of color in general, as progressive women of all racial backgrounds, let us join our sisters *and* brothers across the globe who are attempting to forge a new socialist order—an order which will reestablish socioeconomic priorities so that the quest for monetary profit will never be permitted to take precedence over the real interests of human beings. This is not to say that our problems will magically dissipate with the advent of socialism. Rather, such a social order should provide us with the real opportunity to extend further our struggles, with the assurance that one day we will be able to redefine the basic elements of our oppression as useless refuse of the past.

SOURCES

Books

Davis, Angela Y., *Angela Davis: An Autobiography*, Random House, 1974.

———, *Women, Race, and Class*, Random House, 1981.

———, *Women, Culture, and Politics*, Random House, 1989.

Davis, Angela Y., and others, *If They Come in the Morning: Voices of Resistance*, Third Press, 1971.

Periodicals

Ebony, "Angela Davis: Radical of the '60s Changes with the Times," July, 1990.

Harvard Educational Review, "Radical Perspectives on Empowerment for Afro-American Women," August, 1988, pp. 348-353.

Muhammad Speaks, "Angela Davis: What's on Her Mind?" January 1, 1971, pp. 3-5.

New Statesman, "Revolution by Other Means" (interview), August 14, 1987, pp. 16-17.

Other

Angela Davis Speaks (recording), Folkways, 1971.

Ada Deer

1935–

Native American social worker, activist, and U.S. government official of the Menominee tribe

As the first woman ever to head the Bureau of Indian Affairs (BIA), Ada Deer has vowed to "shake things up" in the much-maligned federal agency. The task before her is a monumental one indeed, for the BIA has most often been characterized as a hotbed of bureaucratic mismanagement and corruption. With Deer's coming, however, there is a sense of heightened energy and commitment. Declaring that "the days of federal paternalism are over," she has announced her intention to fashion a new administration "based on the Indian values of caring, sharing, and respect." Given her background as a social worker and activist and the respect she commands among Native Americans, many believe that Deer may well succeed where others have tried and failed.

Born and raised on the Menominee Reservation in northeastern Wisconsin, Deer credits her mother with instilling in her a drive to do whatever she could to correct injustice in the world. It was her commitment to a life of service, in fact, that influenced her decision to pursue studies in social work at the University of Wisconsin in Madison. After graduating in 1957—an event that made her the first member of her tribe to earn a bachelor's degree from the university—Deer went on to reach another milestone in 1961 as the first Native American to obtain a master's degree in social work from Columbia University.

Throughout the late 1950s and 1960s, Deer held several different jobs in her chosen field, initially in New York City while she was still at Columbia and then in Minneapolis. In 1964, she accepted a post as community service coordinator with the BIA's Minneapolis office but resigned a few years later in frustration over the lack of interest BIA officials showed in her many suggestions for improvement.

Deer spent the rest of the 1960s and early 1970s in a variety of other social work positions, mostly in Minnesota and Wisconsin except for a brief period in 1968 when she helped train Native American Peace Corps volunteers in Puerto Rico. She was also active on behalf of issues related to women's rights and the environment. Beginning in 1971, she took the first steps toward earning a law degree when she attended the University of New Mexico's American Indian Law Program. Later, she enrolled in law school at the University of Wisconsin in Madison to continue her studies.

Around this same time, however, Deer was becoming increasingly preoccupied with a far more pressing matter—restoring federal recognition to the Menominee tribe. As part of its 1950s-era policy of forcing Indians to assimilate into mainstream white society, the United States government had decreed that the Menominees were no longer officially considered Indians. Thus, with the signing of the so-called Menominee Termination Act in 1954 (which was not fully implemented until 1961), the tribe lost the benefits they had been entitled to while their affairs were under federal control, including health care and education services and exemption from taxes; their reservation lands became a new county under the jurisdiction of the state of Wisconsin. By the end of the 1960s, the combined effects of poverty, health problems, racism, and mismanagement had left the tribe in a shambles economically, politically, and culturally.

Into this desperate situation stepped Deer and several others who felt that the only way to save the Menominees was to restore their status as a federally-recognized tribe. In 1970, they founded a political organization known as Determination of Rights and Unity for Menominee Shareholders, or DRUMS, which sought to address both the short-term and long-term needs of the community, including the repeal of the Termination Act. As vice-president and chief lobbyist of a DRUMS-affiliated group called the National Committee to Save the Menominee People and Forest, Deer spent the next few years relentlessly arguing the case for restoration before state and national legislators. Her efforts were finally rewarded in December 1973, when President Richard Nixon signed the Menominee restoration act into law. Not only was this event the crowning achievement of Deer's life, it was also the first time a Native American tribe had succeeded in convincing the federal government to reverse its Indian policy.

Afterwards, Deer was elected chief of the Menominee Restoration Committee, the interim government in charge of carrying out the tribe's transition back to reservation status and setting the course for its future. In 1977, believing that she had accomplished her goals and it was time for others to take over, she resigned from the committee to join the faculty of the University of Wisconsin in Madison, where she taught in both the School of Social Work and in the American Indian Studies Program.

In 1978, Deer entered elective politics with an unsuccessful bid to become the Democratic party's nominee for Wisconsin secretary of state; a second try for the same office in 1982 also met with failure. Ten years later, she entered the fray once again, this time in a race for a seat in the U.S. House of Representatives. While she scored a surprising come-from-behind victory in the primary over her well-known Democratic opponent, she was unable to turn that into a win against her Republican challenger in the general election.

Six months later, in May 1993, President Bill Clinton nominated Deer to serve as the Department of the Interior's assistant secretary for Indian affairs, the position that would put her in charge of the BIA. She was a popular choice among Native Americans and in the halls of Congress. At her confirmation hearing in Washington, D.C., that summer, Deer explained a little bit about her background and why she felt she was qualified to lead the troubled agency. Her testimony is reprinted here from Nomination of Ada Deer: Hearing Before the Committee on Indian Affairs, United States Senate, 103rd Congress, 1st Session, July 15, 1993, *U.S. Government Printing Office, 1993.*

Mr. Chairman, Mr. Vice-Chairman, and other distinguished members of the Senate Committee on Indian Affairs, my name is Ada Elizabeth Deer and I am proud to say I am an enrolled member of the Menominee Indian Tribe of Wisconsin. I would like to thank you for your time and courtesies shown me during our recent interviews and for the opportunity to appear before you today. I am honored that President Clinton and Secretary Babbitt have nominated me as the first woman to be Assistant Secretary for Indian Affairs. I embrace this administration's theme of change. I have dedicated my life to being an agent of change, as a Menominee, as a social worker and as a human being.

I come before you with rich and diverse experiences, including extensive travel in Indian country. I also have been enriched by many wonderful friends, some of whom I would like to acknowledge, for they have helped shape the person I am today. The late Philleo Nash, former BIA Commissioner, enlarged my vision and inspired me to work for the Bureau. The late Whitney Young, former executive director of the National Urban League, [whose] work and deeds truly exemplified what it meant to be a good social worker. Former HEW Secretary John Gardner lent me a deeper and richer understanding of what it means to be a public servant and what leadership embodies. And most importantly, LaDonna Harris, founder of Americans for Indian Opportunity, taught me that every challenge is an opportunity and that "No Indian problem exists. There is, instead, a basic human problem that involves Indians." Their collective wit, vision, and conviction reinforced in me that one person can make a difference!

Personally, you should know that forty years ago my tribe, the Menominee, was terminated; twenty years ago we were restored; and today I come before you as a true survivor of Indian policy.

I was born on the Menominee Indian Reservation in Wisconsin, a land of dense forests, a winding wild river, and streams and lakes that nourish the land, animals, and the people. I am an extension of this environment that has fostered my growth and enriched my vision. An appreciation and reverence for the land is fundamental to being Indian.

Our family of seven lived in a log cabin on the banks of the Wolf River. We had no running water or electricity. Yet, while all of the statistics said we were poor, I never felt poor in spirit. My mother, Constance Wood Deer, was the single greatest influence on my life. She instilled in me rich values which have shaped my lifetime commitment to service.

She was born into a Main Line family in Philadelphia. She was a nonconformist from the beginning. Her father was a minister, and had hand-picked a minister's son for her to marry. But my mother, instead, chose nursing school. Her first nursing job was in Appalachia and her next job was as a BIA nurse on the Rosebud Sioux Reservation in South Dakota. She rejected the Bureau's policies and procedures, and approached nursing with a deep appreciation for the culture and values of the people. At Rosebud, she wore moccasins, learned to ride horseback and even spoke some Lakota. I still run into people from Rosebud who knew of her.

Later, my mother was transferred to Menominee, where she met and married my father, Joe Deer. He was nearly a full-blood Menominee Indian with, as we say, just a squirt of French blood. I loved my family and as the oldest child caring for my siblings, Joe, Robert, Ferial and Connie. It was a labor of love in every way, especially considering the admirable people they have now become. All the while, my mother's idealism and dedication to social justice was infused in me.

My mother was a fierce crusader for Indian rights. She read Indian history and law and brooked no compromises. Many a tribal leader and lawyer would grow more than a little apprehensive upon her approach. Many would think "here comes Connie Deer and it looks like she has something on her mind." I am told that there are people who have said the same thing about her oldest daughter.

In time, I graduated from the University of Wisconsin, where I received a wonderful education and which was supported by a tribal scholarship. I then attended Columbia University and received a master's in social work. I was drawn to social work for it embodies many Indian values and it is dedicated to social justice and the elimination of discrimination. My mother often told me, "Ada, you were put on this earth, not for your own pleasure, but to help others."

Over time, my involvements grew. I became a founding director of Americans for Indian Opportunity and the American Indian Graduate Program. I was also appointed by the Senate to the American Indian Policy Review Commission. I was a client, a staff member, a board member, board chair, and finally, chair of the National Support Committee of the Native American Rights Fund. Over the years, I have also worked for many other Indian causes.

My interests and involvements are far ranging, essentially devoted to enhancing the human condition. I also have served on the boards of the Girl Scouts, Common Cause, Independent Sector, National Association of Social Work and other organizations. Later, I was appointed by both presidents Carter and Reagan to the President's Commission on White House Fellowships.

One of the most compelling times in my life, however, involved the termination and restoration of my tribe. Pardon my brief historical account, but an understanding of history is critical to understanding Indian policy.

Ada Deer

The leaders of my tribe had signed the Wolf River Treaty of 1854 guaranteeing the Menominees 250,000 acres of land—*and sovereignty over that land—forever*. This was not a gift. Under decisions from Chief Justice John Marshall through the current Supreme Court, the Menominees, like other tribes, owned their land and much more *before* the treaty era. We ceded most of our aboriginal land held by us for thousands of years, and in the treaties reserved—thus the term "reservation"—a small part of it. Our tribal leaders were sophisticated people. They insisted upon land, sovereignty, and federal trust protection from the onrushing settlers. In that time of crisis, one of the greatest collisions of cultures in the history of the world, our leaders relied upon those promises. Of course, promise after promise has been broken. By the end of the treaty making, in 1871, tribes held 140 million acres. But the non-Indians marching West wanted more, and so the General Allotment Act of 1887 was passed. Indian land was opened for homesteading on a wholesale basis and by the 1930s the tribal land base had dwindled to 50 million acres.

The next assault on our land and sovereignty was the termination policy of the 1950s. Termination was a misguided and now-discredited experiment that targeted several tribes, including mine. This policy completely abrogated the federal trust relationship. State jurisdiction was imposed on tribal members and land. My tribe literally went from being prosperous to being Wisconsin's newest, smallest and poorest county. Many terminated tribes saw their land sold off. My tribe land was held by a state-chartered tribal corporation. The termination act stripped us of our treaty-guaranteed exemption from taxation and our tribal leaders were forced to begin to sell off ancestral tribal land to pay the taxes.

By the 1960s, my people were in despair. Poverty had sunk to new depths and we faced the loss of our land, tribal identity, and culture. My own personal choice was clear. I had to leave law school, return to the reservation, and create a coalition of tribal leaders to reverse termination. The 1950s and 1960s were the low point for Indian people in our history on this continent.

At Menominee, we collectively discovered the kind of determination that human beings only find in times of impending destruction. Against all odds, we invented a new policy—restoration. Finally, after grueling work by more people than I could ever possibly thank, our coalition pushed the Menominee Restoration Act through Congress. This legislation is a vivid reminder of how great a government can be when it is large enough to admit and rectify its mistakes. It is also indicative of my tribe's spirit, tenacity, and ability to hold other sovereign entities accountable.

We have regained a sacred vision. Our vision is bright and clear throughout all of our homelands, whether at a First Salmon Ceremony in the Pacific Northwest, at a secret ritual deep in a Pueblo kiva, or at a Sun Dance in Sioux country.

My vision for the Bureau of Indian Affairs is to create a progressive federal/tribal partnership. First and foremost, the heart of Indian policy must be strong, effective tribal sovereignty. There is no reason for me or for any of you to be reluctant to support the permanency of tribal sovereignty any more than we would be reluctant to support the permanency of federal or state sovereignty. There are three kinds of sovereignty recognized in the United States Constitution—tribal, state, and federal. It is our moral obligation to ensure that these rights are supported vigorously. The role of the federal government should be to support and to implement tribally-inspired solutions to tribally-defined problems. The days of federal paternalism are over.

As Secretary Babbitt stated before this Committee, "Tribal sovereignty; the notion of the government-to-government relationship; recognizing that the best way to work in Indian country is to recognize the special responsibility of the federal government; and to acknowledge that the participation of the states, while important, must always be drawn through and coordinated with the dominant historic legal and constitutional trust relationship between tribes themselves and the federal government." This pledge by Secretary Babbitt shall be a guiding principle in my administration.

If our new partnership is to be effective, Indian policy must be coordinated closely between the Bureau of Indian Affairs, the Department of the Interior, other cabinet departments and the White House. To this end, Secretary Babbitt has reached an agreement with the White House Domestic Policy Council that it will assume an active role in coordinating administration policy initiatives to benefit American Indian people. If confirmed, I will work diligently to ensure that the Council has the full policy input of my office and that of Indian tribes.

I enthusiastically endorse greater self-determination for Indian tribes and the protection of treaty rights. Like many people in Indian country and in Congress, I am excited about the Department of the Interior's Self-Governance Demonstration Project. It is designed to empower tribes by allocating federal resources and responsibilities to those tribal governments willing to assume them.

As Secretary Babbitt has noted, "We must accelerate the trend toward self-governance so that we can reshape our role from paternal guardians to active engaged partners." I note, too, that not every Indian tribe will seek self-governance compacts and the Department must respect and honor its commitments to those tribal governments choosing different courses.

If confirmed, one of my highest priorities will be the publishing of the regulations implementing the 1988 Public Law 93-638 amendments. These regulations, now in draft form, must undergo a careful review to determine how to promote tribal self-determination in the contracting of federal programs.

No discussion of my goals for Indian affairs would be complete without noting the critical area of Native American religious freedom. I wholeheartedly endorse the process in which the Department of the Interior will convene working groups composed of Interior officials and Native American representatives, so that we can jointly discuss common approaches to S. 1021, the Native American Free Exercise of Religion Act.

"First and foremost, the heart of Indian policy must be strong, effective tribal sovereignty. . . . The days of federal paternalism are over."

If confirmed, I look forward to forging partnerships with tribes across the country and intend to visit Indian people where they live. One of my first visits shall be to Pine Ridge, for it is one of the poorest areas in the country. Collectively, we have a responsibility to reverse these devastating socioeconomic conditions that plague the Oglala Sioux and many other tribes. This task is daunting, though one we cannot afford to ignore.

There are many important areas I have not discussed with you today. These include education, health, housing, Indian child welfare protection, natural resource protection, trust funds, gaming and economic development to name just a few. These are all important to me and I look forward to working with each of you on these matters, should you confirm me.

Although Indians now constitute ninety percent of the employees in the Bureau of Indian Affairs, we must remember that the Bureau was created by non-Indians. It has not been a proactive Indian institution. I want to activate and to mobilize people in the Bureau so that they can be creative and forward-looking. I want the Indian values of sharing, caring, and respect incorporated into their day-to-day work. I want to help the BIA be a full partner in the effort to fulfill the Indian agenda developed in Indian country. The best way we can do this is for the tribes to decide what needs to be done and for the tribes to do it on their own terms, with our enthusiastic and constructive support.

The constellation of history is aligned in favor of Indian people. President Clinton ran for office on a platform that expressly supported tribal sovereignty. This Committee, under the vision and diligence of Senator Inouye and Senator McCain and with the active support of each of you, has been the most productive legislative body for justice for Indians in the history of this nation. Secretary Babbitt is the most committed and knowledgeable person on Indian issues ever to hold this critical office; his intellect, character, and commitment to public service are rare and compelling. He means it when he says that fulfilling the Indian trust relationship is his highest obligation. These times are notable, too, by the increasing number of women and the new approach toward policy at all levels of government.

So hope, healing, commitment and change are in the skies all around us and, if I am confirmed, they will be the hallmark of my administration. The time is right for a partnership to fulfill long-held promises and to address long-overdue injustices.

We think most of all about the future of our young people. On this summer's night tens of thousands of girls and boys across Indian country will go to sleep. Some in my Wisconsin homeland will hear the vibrant sounds I heard many years ago in the cabin where I grew up. Others will hear the wind in the Douglas fir trees at Warm Springs, the surging current of the great Missouri at Fort Peck, or the song of the canyon wren calling out from a redrock monument at Navajo. There is no reason why they cannot grow up to live in prosperity, in good health, with excellent educations, in clean environments, and immersed in their rich traditions.

In this new administration, if we work together, I am confident that we can eliminate the barriers of the past, and work with the tribes to embrace the challenges of the twenty-first century.

In closing, know that I bring a strong sense of history, vision, maturity, and compassion to the tasks before me.

Thank you very much.

The members of the Committee on Indian Affairs honored Deer's statement with a standing ovation, and the next day she was confirmed in the Senate on a voice vote and sworn into office. She hit the ground running, visiting many BIA offices and reservations throughout the country over the following months. At every stop, she challenged BIA employees and tribal leaders to contact her directly her about the problems they face and what solutions they have considered, declaring, "I want visionary thinking."

Deer's goals include seeing to it that Indians finally have the things she says "are basic to every human being"—namely, jobs, food, shelter, health care, and education. She has also come out in support of teaching young Native Americans their own languages and allowing them to observe their own cultural practices if they wish. A strong proponent of self-determination, she has pledged to continue the push toward shifting more power to the tribes in an effort to help them gain self-sufficiency. Meanwhile, a number of other critical policy issues are currently facing the BIA, among them expanding reservation gambling, granting mining and grazing rights and regulating hazardous waste disposal on tribal lands, ex-

tending federal recognition to certain tribes, and—perhaps most significantly—reorganizing the BIA itself to improve its efficiency and fiscal accountability. Deer, who lives by the motto "one person can make a difference," expects to make a major dent in those areas and more.

In late July 1994, a year after she took office, Deer was the featured speaker at an awards dinner held during the tenth annual conference of the Native American Journalists Association. The conference, which took place in Atlanta, Georgia, coincided with a larger gathering of minority journalists called Unity '94 Alliance. At a series of workshops, lectures, and discussion groups, attendees voiced their opinions on a variety of topics of professional interest, including how to combat ethnic stereotyping in the media. As a longtime social worker, Deer was all too familiar with the damage done to Indian self-esteem by distorted images of Native Americans in print and on film, so urging her listeners to do everything possible to remedy that became the focus of her address. It is reprinted here from a copy furnished by Deer.

~

Good evening. I want to thank you, the Native American Journalists Association, and the Unity '94 Alliance for inviting me to this historic event in Atlanta, Georgia, where the first Indian newspaper, the *Cherokee Phoenix,* was published in New Echota in 1828—not far from here.

By the way, it's nice to be in a state with Cherokee roots.

I know that as delegates to this convention, you are networking with other minority journalists—Asians, Hispanics, and Afro-Americans. You certainly have a full agenda working apart and together on common concerns such as media stereotyping in news coverage and the need to diversify America's newsrooms. I also appreciate the fact that each association is working on special issues pertinent to their particular community. In this regard, I applaud NAJA for taking a look at the issue of freedom of the press and Indian reservation newspapers.

Before I say any more, however, I'd like to acknowledge a few people tonight. First of all, congratulations to the Unity '94 Alliance, especially to its president, Paul DeMain, who also heads up NAJA. Most importantly, a thank-you to the NAJA board of directors—Ruth Denny, Nancy Butterfield, Agnes Jack, Gary Fife, Karen Lincoln, Tony Lone Fight, Minnie Two Shoes, and Susan Arkeketa. And of course, a special thank-you to Gordon Regguiniti, your executive director. This group was instrumental in helping the Alliance raise over one million dollars to put on this unprecedented event involving over five thousand journalists of color. Everyone now! Let's give these people their due.

I heard that back in 1984, when the original members of the then-Native American Press Association held its very first meeting on the Penn State campus, you met in a phone booth! But I'm only kidding. After all, it's no joke that NAJA—only ten years later—can now boast of over five hundred members. That's success!

This evening, many deserving NAJA members will be cited for their journalistic excellence. To that end, I'm happy to be able to remind you that several new categories are being presented. Among these, the Elias Boundinot Award [is] one of four "Milestone Awards," and it will undoubtedly set a new benchmark for excellence for native journalists. It is being given in memory of the editor of the *Cherokee Phoenix,* who was assassinated—murdered—for his news exposés on the forced removal of the Cherokee. This coveted award is to be presented to someone who not only contributed greatly to NAJA but who has shown the non-Indian world who native journalists are and what native journalism is about.

I now wish to comment on the exciting premiere of AIROS—the American Indian Radio on Satellite—at this historic conference. This new national public radio programming network will feature regularly scheduled shows on political and socioeconomic issues of concern to native peoples. Hopefully, this will help improve communications, news, and information exchanges between Indians, tribes, and communities. This, too, is yet another "milestone" for Indian Country. Thank you to the Corporation for Public Broadcasting and to the staff of AIROS.

As we gather at this banquet awards program in the beautiful Radisson Hotel to commemorate a decade of progress in the communications field for American Indians and other people of color and to pay tribute to past or current reporters who gave their life or lost a job so that the "truth" could be told, I'd like to share with you my thoughts about the problem of media stereotypes and what can be done about it.

Earlier this month, on July 4, the United States of America observed its 218th birthday. At such times, we think about the Founding Fathers such as Benjamin Franklin, Thomas Jefferson, and Thomas Paine. But rarely does one read news stories in daily papers [or] hear or see any mention on radio or television about the major contributions American Indians made to democracy and the federal government system we know today. This, my friends, is the type of uplifting and true story you as reporters can help to tell, not only to our own people, but to everyone. And I'm not talking about "advocacy journalism." What I am talking about is simply good factual reporting.

Let me elaborate. American democracy owes its distinctive character of debate and compromise to the principles and structure of American Indian civil government. You see, the Founding Fathers faced a major problem when it came time to invent a "new" nation, for they really had no blueprint for the type of government they envisioned. Many of them, however, had come to admire the Iroquois League, particularly Thomas Jefferson, Thomas Paine, and Benjamin Franklin.

Jefferson, author of the Declaration of Independence and framer for the U.S. Constitution, was so fascinated by the Indians and their form of self-rule that he advocated the University of Virginia (of which he was the founder) offer Indian studies. He was the first to propose a systematic, ethnological study of American Indians. Jefferson noted that Indian political leaders did not acquire their positions by heredity, but by election, although "outsiders" could be naturalized or adopted into the Indian nation. In such cases, even they could then be elected to tribal office. This was not the case in Europe, with its rigid class system based on family lines and nobility.

As for Thomas Paine, a Quaker and radical proponent of democracy, he, too, developed an interest in Indians. Paine viewed the Indians as models for how society might be organized. He was later to be the first to call for Independence from the British Crown in his famous pamphlet, *Common Sense*.

At the time the Europeans arrived in America, the Iroquois League was the most extensive [and] important political unit north of the Aztec civilization. Its beginnings predated the arrival of Columbus by hundreds of years. The sovereign nations represented in the League were the Mohawk, Onondaga, Seneca, Oneida, and Cayuga.

It was Iroquois Chief Canassatego in July of 1744 who suggested the colonists of Pennsylvania form a "union" much like the Iroquois had done. They would then be able to speak with one voice. Under the Iroquois form of government, certain chiefs were nominated by the women and confirmed by the tribal and league councils. No action could be taken without unanimous consent. This structure influenced many of the Founding Fathers, like Benjamin Franklin, who sought a plan of representative government for the colonies.

Some key political contributions of the Iroquois are the concept of a "caucus" and "electoral college." Contrary to popular belief, the word *caucus* comes from an Algonquian language, not from a Latin word. The caucus permits informal discussion about an issue. The model for an electoral college derived from the Iroquois League's "Grand Council." By the way, they did not allow slavery.

Prior to the War of 1812, some Indians and tribes were highly regarded by the early settlers. In fact, a large number of whites at this time traded their European lifestyles in to "go native." They were referred to as "Squaw Men." Only a few years after Virginia was settled, for example, more than forty male colonists and several Englishwomen had married Indians and gone off to live with the tribes.

During the colonial period Chief Tammany became very popular. He was head of the Lenni-Lenape (Delaware) and was the first to welcome William Penn when he arrived on October 27, 1682, to establish the colony of Pennsylvania. Chief Tammany helped the European settlers (much like Squanto and Powhatan) to survive in the North American environment. Indians like Chief Tammany came to symbolize freedom and liberty to the early settlers.

But after the American Revolution relations

became strained, especially when some Indian nations sided with the British during the War of 1812. In the years to follow, various Indians for different reasons fought against the Americans on the side of the Dutch, French or British. It's interesting that the change in perception of Indians from nobles to savages coincided with the start of the great trek westward and the opening of the plains and Pacific areas to settlers by the 1880s.

Since Hollywood or the film industry has played such a big role in promoting ethnic stereotypes and caricatures, mostly through Western cowboy pictures, it's interesting to note that actor John Wayne, who was a famous celluloid Indian fighter, once told an interviewer, "I don't feel we did wrong in taking this great country away from them. There were great numbers of people who needed new land, and the Indians were selfishly trying to keep it for themselves."

Also, I find it interesting that on holidays like Memorial Day, we seldom (if ever) hear about the major significant contributions American Indians have made to this country through the military. American Indians have fought in every war, including the American Revolutionary War. In fact, this demonstration of patriotism was one of the reasons that Congress decided to pass the Indian Citizenship Act of 1924. More than eight thousand Indians served in the Army during World War I. Most recently, we once again saw brave American Indian men and women participate in the Persian Gulf War. American Indians have received every award possible, including Congressional Medals of Honor. And it was the Navajo Marines, later called the CodeTalkers, who managed to outsmart the Japanese using their native language as a secret code in World War II. But again, this positive image of American Indians and their invaluable contributions to America remain "invisible" in the mainstream media channels of this country. In order to overcome media stereotypes of Indians, we must become proactive in educating the press and public about the "true history" and current conditions of native people.

I believe two recent events, among several others, have helped to change the image of the Indian community in the eyes of the press, the political establishment and the public. I'm happy to say I was able to play a role in both events. I'm referring to the historic White House Indian Policy Summit held in early May of this year. This event received positive publicity. Indians were portrayed as "pro-active" since tribal leaders had called for the meeting and set the agenda. Never before had a sitting president, as did Bill Clinton, have his entire cabinet present to hear first-hand what leaders from Indian Country had to say about key issues.

The second positive and pro-active happening was the National American Indian Listening Conference. Here again, media coverage was different in that Indians were shown as a political power to deal with. I enjoyed reading the press clips because of this. For example, the *Washington Post*'s Colman McCarthy in his May 7 column wrote about the White House meeting: "Rose Ann Abramson, member of the Shosone-Bannock tribes of southeastern Idaho, was one of over three hundred Native American leaders meeting with President Clinton. If it's accepted that tribes are sovereign nations—they are—then the people who lead them were meeting with Clinton, a fellow head of state, not Clinton, the Great White Father."

There are other examples of positive media accounts of these two exciting events, which goes to show you that the press is capable of being fair and factual. I think a great organiza-

"In order to overcome media stereotypes of Indians, we must become pro-active in educating the press and public about the 'true history' and current conditions of native people."

tion like yours could help expedite the media educational process by perhaps publishing a reporter's stylebook (along the lines of the Associated Press version) giving backgrounders on Indian issues, a historical timeline, and a list of terms deemed offensive to Indians. Certainly the more Indian reporters, editors, publishers, and filmmakers we can get placed in meaningful positions in the media industry, the better off we will be. I know that's why NAJA featured a jobs fair here, and I hope many aspiring Indian journalists will find work because of it.

In my position as Assistant Secretary for Indian Affairs [in the] Department of Interior, I find myself having to constantly "educate" reporters—and elected officials—about Indian history and contemporary issues, which, naturally, are always linked to the past. Therefore, I'm very aware of the need for us to tell our story to the non-Indian community in order to keep things in perspective and create better understanding. Certainly using all forms of media to do this is of paramount importance.

It is a time for "reconciliation and diversity" in our world. In the middle of an "Information Age," we can no longer afford the luxury of misinformation or mean-spirited ethnic stereotypes. In order to survive in our "new world order," we must seek to live together in harmony and peace, more so now than ever.

Thank you for inviting me to your tenth annual NAJA awards dinner.

SOURCES

Books

Deer, Ada, and R.E. Simon, Jr., *Speaking Out,* Children's Press Open Door Books, 1970.

Hardy, Gayle J., *American Women Civil Rights Activists: Biobibliographies of 68 Leaders, 1825-1992,* McFarland, 1993.

Katz, Jane B., editor, *I Am the Fire of Time: The Voices of Native American Women,* Dutton, 1977.

Malinowski, Sharon, ed., *Notable Native Americans,* Gale Research, Detroit, 1995.

Nomination of Ada Deer: Hearing Before the Committee on Indian Affairs, United States Senate, 103rd Congress, 1st Session, July 15, 1993, U.S. Government Printing Office, 1993.

Peroff, Nicholas C., *Menominee Drums: Tribal Termination and Restoration, 1954-1974,* University of Oklahoma Press, 1982.

Periodicals

Anchorage Daily News, "First Woman to Lead BIA Calls for Vision," August 31, 1993, p. B2.

Capital Times (Madison, Wisconsin), "Ada Deer Is Finally Given 'Heroine' Status," March 18, 1985, p. 2; "Ada Deer for Congress," August 27, 1992; "Deer Brings Fresh Outlook," August 10, 1993.

Chicago Tribune, "Woman Picked to Lead Indian Bureau," May 20, 1993, p. A1.

Christian Science Monitor, "Aiming to Make Electoral History," October 21, 1992.

Denver Post, "Female BIA Chief 'Shaking Agency Up,'" September 2, 1993, p. B2.

Indian Country Today, "Standing Ovation for Deer," July 21, 1993, p. A1; "Deer Calls for Help in BIA Shake-Up," September 8, 1993, p. A1.

Star Tribune (Minneapolis), "Dauntless Deer Shaking Up BIA," March 6, 1994.

Sunday Oregonian, "Woman Tapped to Lead BIA May Gain Fame But Enters Tough Game," May 23, 1993, p. A20.

Tundra Times, "Ada Deer: Native Values for BIA Management," September 8, 1993, p. 1.

Frederick Douglass

1817–1895

African American antislavery activist, journalist, and U.S. government official

Born into slavery on a plantation in Talbot County, Maryland, in 1817, Frederick Douglass spent much of his youth as a house servant in Baltimore. There he learned to read and write before he was sent back to the plantation to work as a field hand. The cruel treatment Douglass was then forced to endure only strengthened his determination to escape, and in 1838 he fled to freedom in New York City. He then made his way to Massachusetts, home of the well-known abolitionist William Lloyd Garrison and his Antislavery Society.

A brilliant thinker and forceful speaker whose message was enhanced by his striking physical appearance, Douglass quickly became the movement's chief spokesperson as well as the most influential black leader of the nineteenth century. In addition to his success as an orator, he received acclaim as founder and editor of the North Star *newspaper. In its pages, he not only crusaded against slavery but also championed equal rights for women and Native Americans, supported public education, and opposed the death penalty. As an advisor to Abraham Lincoln during the Civil War, Douglass urged the president to free all of the slaves and led the drive to allow blacks to serve in the army. After the war, he served the federal government in a variety of positions, including marshall of the District of Columbia and minister to Haiti and the Dominican Republic.*

Douglass's fame, however, sprang from his impassioned yet carefully reasoned arguments calling for an end to slavery. His speeches left no doubt as to the depth of his hatred for the system that had imprisoned him and his fellow blacks. Perhaps his strongest and most bitterly ironic condemnation came in an address he gave in Rochester, New York, on July 5, 1852, in honor of America's Independence Day. Often referred to as the Fourth of July Oration, it blasts the hypocrisy of a nation that celebrates freedom while enslaving millions. It is reprinted from Rhetoric of Black Revolution, *by Arthur L. Smith (Allyn & Bacon, 1969).*

Mr. President, Friends and Fellow Citizens:

He who could address this audience without a quailing sensation, has stronger nerves than I have. I do not remember ever to have appeared as a speaker before any assembly more shrinkingly, nor with greater distrust of my ability, than I do this day. A feeling has crept over me quite unfavorable to the exercise of my limited powers of speech. The task before me is one which requires much previous thought and study for its proper performance. I know that apologies of this sort are generally considered flat and unmeaning. I trust, however, that mine will not be so considered. Should I seem at ease, my appearance would much misrepresent me. The little experience I have had in addressing public meetings, in country school houses, avails me nothing on the present occasion.

The papers and placards say that I am to deliver a Fourth of July Oration. This certainly sounds large, and out of the common way, for me. It is true that I have often had the privilege to speak in this beautiful Hall, and to address many who now honor me with their presence. But neither their familiar faces, nor the perfect gage I think I have of Corinthian Hall seems to free me from embarrassment.

The fact is, ladies and gentlemen, the distance between this platform and the slave plantation, from which I escaped, is considerable—and the difficulties to be overcome in getting from the latter to the former are by no means slight. That I am here to-day is, to me, a matter of astonishment as well as of gratitude. You will not, therefore, be surprised, if in what I have to say I evince no elaborate preparation, nor grace my speech with any high sounding exordium. With little experience and with less learning, I have been able to throw my thoughts hastily and imperfectly together; and trusting to your patient and generous indulgence, I will proceed to lay them before you.

This, for the purpose of this celebration, is the Fourth of July. It is the birthday of your National Independence, and of your political freedom. This, to you, is what the Passover was to the emancipated people of God. It carries your minds back to the day, and to the act of your great deliverance; and to the signs, and to the wonders, associated with that act, and that day. This celebration also marks the beginning of another year of your national life; and reminds you that the Republic of America is now 76 years old. I am glad, fellow-citizens, that your nation is so young. Seventy-six years, though a good old age for a man, is but a mere speck in the life of a nation. Three score years and ten is the allotted time for individual men; but nations number their years by thousands. According to this fact, you are, even now, only in the beginning of your national career, still lingering in the period of childhood. I repeat, I am glad this is so. There is hope in the thought, and hope is much needed, under the dark clouds which lower above the horizon. The eye of the reformer is met with angry flashes, portending disastrous times; but his heart may well beat lighter at the thought that America is young, and that she is still in the impressible stage of her existence. May he not hope that high lessons of wisdom, of justice and of truth, will yet give direction to her destiny? Were the nation older, the patriot's heart might be sadder, and the reformer's brow heavier. Its future might be shrouded in gloom, and the hope of its prophets go out in sorrow. There is consolation in the thought that America is young. Great streams are not easily turned from channels, worn deep in the course of ages. They may sometimes rise in quiet and stately majesty, and inundate the land, refreshing and fertilizing the earth with their mysterious properties. They may also rise in wrath and fury, and bear away, on their angry waves, the accumulated wealth of years of toil and hardship. They, however, gradually flow back to the same old channel, and flow on as

Frederick Douglass

serenely as ever. But, while the river may not be turned aside, it may dry up, and leave nothing behind but the withered branch, and the unsightly rock, to howl in the abyss-sweeping wind, the sad tale of departed glory. As with rivers so with nations.

Fellow-citizens, I shall not presume to dwell at length on the associations that cluster about this day. The simple story of it is, that, 76 years ago, the people of this country were British subjects. The style and title of your "sovereign people" (in which you now glory) was not then born. You were under the British Crown. Your fathers esteemed the English Government as the home government; and England as the fatherland. This home government, you know, although a considerable distance from your home, did, in the exercise of its parental prerogatives, impose upon its colonial children, such restraints, burdens and limitations, as, in its mature judgment, it deemed wise, right and proper.

But your fathers, who had not adopted the fashionable idea of this day, of the infallibility of government, and the absolute character of its acts, presumed to differ from the home government in respect to the wisdom and the justice of some of those burdens and restraints. They went so far in their excitement as to pronounce the measures of government unjust, unreasonable, and oppressive, and altogether such as ought not to be quietly submitted to. I scarcely need say, fellow-citizens, that my opinion of those measures fully accords with that of your fathers. Such a declaration of agreement on my part would not be worth much to anybody. It would certainly prove nothing as to what part I might have taken had I lived during the great controversy of 1776. To say now that America was right, and England wrong, is exceedingly easy. Everybody can say it; the dastard, not less than the noble brave, can flippantly discant on the tyranny of England towards the American Colonies. It is fashionable to do so; but there was a time when, to pronounce against England, and in favor of the cause of the colonies, tried men's souls. They who did so were accounted in their day plotters of mischief, agitators and rebels, dangerous men. To side with the right against the wrong, with the weak against the strong, and with the oppressed against the oppressor! Here lies the merit, and the one which, of all others, seems unfashionable in our day. The cause of liberty may be stabbed by the men who glory in the deeds of your fathers. But, to proceed.

Feeling themselves harshly and unjustly treated, by the home government, your fathers, like men of honesty, and men of spirit, earnestly sought redress. They petitioned and remonstrated; they did so in a decorous, respectful, and loyal manner. Their conduct was wholly unexceptionable. This, however, did not answer the purpose. They saw themselves treated with sovereign indifference, coldness and scorn. Yet they persevered. They were not the men to look back.

As the sheet anchor takes a firmer hold, when the ship is tossed by the storm, so did the cause of your fathers grow stronger as it breasted the chilling blasts of kingly displeasure. The greatest and best of British statesmen admitted its justice, and the loftiest eloquence of the British Senate came to its support. But, with that blindness which seems to be the unvarying characteristic of tyrants, since Pharaoh and his hosts were drowned in the Red Sea, the British Government persisted in the exactions complained of.

The madness of this course, we believe, is admitted now, even by England; but we fear the lesson is wholly lost on our present rulers.

Oppression makes a wise man mad. Your fathers were wise men, and if they did not go mad, they became restive under this treatment. They felt themselves the victims of grievous wrongs, wholly incurable in their colonial capacity. With brave men there is always a remedy for oppression. Just here, the idea of a total separation of the colonies from the crown was born! It was a startling idea, much more so than we, at this distance of time, regard it. The timid and the prudent (as has been intimated) of that day were, of course, shocked and alarmed by it.

Such people lived then, had lived before, and will, probably, ever have a place on this planet; and their course, in respect to any great change (no matter how great the good to be attained, or the wrong to be redressed by it), may be calculated with as much precision as can be the course of the stars. They hate all changes, but silver, gold and copper change! Of this sort of change they are always strongly in favor.

These people were called Tories in the days of your fathers; and the appellation, probably, conveyed the same idea that is meant by a more modern, though a somewhat less euphonious term, which we often find in our papers, applied to some of our old politicians.

Their opposition to the then dangerous thought was earnest and powerful; but, amid all their terror and affrighted vociferations against it, the alarming and revolutionary idea moved on, and the country with it.

On the second of July, 1776, the old Continental Congress, to the dismay of the lovers of ease, and the worshippers of property, clothed that dreadful idea with all the authority of national sanction. They did so in the form of a resolution; and as we seldom hit upon resolutions, drawn up in our day, whose transparency is at all equal to this, it may refresh your minds and help my story if I read it.

> *Resolved, that these united colonies* are, *and of right, ought to be free and Independent States; that they are absolved from all allegiance to the British Crown; and that all political connection between them and the State of Great Britain* is, *and ought to be, dissolved.*

Citizens, your fathers made good that resolution. They succeeded; and to-day you reap the fruits of their success. The freedom gained is yours; and you, therefore, may properly celebrate this anniversary. The 4th of July is the first great fact in your nation's history—the very ring-bolt in the chain of your yet undeveloped destiny.

Pride and patriotism, not less than gratitude, prompt you to celebrate and to hold it in perpetual remembrance. I have said that the Declaration of Independence is the RING-BOLT to the chain of your nation's destiny; so indeed, I regard it. The principles contained in that instrument are saving principles. Stand by those principles, be true to them on all occasions, in all places, against all foes, and at whatever cost.

From the round top of your ship of state, dark and threatening clouds may be seen. Heavy billows, like mountains in the distance, disclose to the leeward huge forms of flinty rocks! That *bolt* drawn, that *chain* broken, and all is lost. *Cling to this day—cling to it,* and to its principles, with the grasp of a storm-tossed mariner to a spar at midnight.

The coming into being of a nation, in any circumstances, is an interesting event. But, besides general considerations, there were peculiar circumstances which make the advent of this republic an event of special attractiveness.

The whole scene, as I look back to it, was simple, dignified and sublime.

The population of the country, at the time, stood at the insignificant number of three millions. The country was poor in the munitions of war. The population was weak and scattered, and the country a wilderness unsubdued. There were then no means of concert and combination, such as exist now. Neither steam nor lightning had then been reduced to order and discipline. From the Potomac to the Delaware was a journey of many days. Under these, and innumerable other disadvantages, your fathers declared for liberty and independence and triumphed.

Fellow Citizens, I am not wanting in respect for the fathers of this republic. The signers of the Declaration of Independence were brave men. They were great men, too great enough to give frame to a great age. It does not often happen to a nation to raise, at one time, such a number of truly great men. The point from which I am compelled to view them is not, certainly, the most favorable; and yet I cannot contemplate their great deeds with less than admiration. They were statesmen, patriots and heroes, and for the good they did, and the principles they contended for, I will unite with you to honor their memory.

They loved their country better than their own private interests; and, though this is not the highest form of human excellence, all will concede that it is a rare virtue, and that when it is exhibited it ought to command respect. He who will, intelligently, lay down his life for his country is a man whom it is not in human nature to despise. Your fathers staked their lives, their fortunes, and their sacred honor, on the cause of their country. In their admiration of liberty, they lost sight of all other interests.

They were peace men; but they preferred revolution to peaceful submission to bondage. They were quiet men; but they did not shrink from agitating against oppression. They showed forbearance; but that they knew its limits. They believed in order; but not in the order of tyranny. With them, nothing was *"settled"* that was not right. With them, justice, liberty and humanity were *"final"*; not slavery and oppression. You may well cherish the memory of such men. They were great in their day and generation. Their solid manhood stands out the more as we contrast it with these degenerate times.

How circumspect, exact and proportionate were all their movements! How unlike the politicians of an hour! Their statesmanship looked beyond the passing moment, and stretched away in strength into the distant future. They seized upon eternal principles, and set a glorious example in their defence. Mark them!

Fully appreciating the hardships to be encountered, firmly believing in the right of their cause, honorably inviting the scrutiny of an onlooking world, reverently appealing to heaven to attest their sincerity, soundly comprehending the solemn responsibility they were about to assume, wisely measuring the terrible odds against them, your fathers, the fathers of this republic, did, most deliberately, under the inspiration of a glorious patriotism, and with a sublime faith in the great principles of justice and freedom, lay deep, the corner-stone of the national superstructure, which has risen and still rises in grandeur around you.

Of this fundamental work, this day is the anniversary. Our eyes are met with demonstrations of joyous enthusiasm. Banners and pennants wave exultingly on the breeze. The din of business, too, is hushed. Even mammon seems to have quitted his grasp on this day. The ear-piercing fife and the stirring drum unite their accents with the ascending peal of a thousand church bells. Prayers are made, hymns are sung, and sermons are preached in honor of this day; while the quick martial tramp of a great and multitudinous nation, echoed back by all the hills, valleys and mountains of a vast continent, bespeak the occasion one of thrilling and universal interest—a nation's jubilee.

Friends and citizens, I need not enter further into the causes which led to this anniversary. Many of you understand them better than I do. You could instruct me in regard to them. That is a branch of knowledge in which you feel, perhaps, a much deeper interest than your speaker. The causes which led to the separation of the colonies from the British crown have never lacked for a tongue. They have all been taught in your common schools, narrated at your firesides, unfolded from your pulpits, and thundered from your legislative halls, and are as familiar to you as household words. They form the staple of your national poetry and eloquence.

I remember, also, that as people, Americans are remarkably familiar with all facts which make in their own favor. This is esteemed by some as a national trait—perhaps a national weakness. It is a fact, that whatever makes for the wealth or for the reputation of Americans and can be had cheap(!) will be found by Americans. I shall not be charged with slandering Americans if I say I think the American side of any question may be safely left in American hands.

I leave, therefore, the great deeds of your fathers to other gentlemen whose claim to have been regularly descended will be less likely to be disputed than mine!

THE PRESENT

My business, if I have any here to-day, is with the present. The accepted time with God and His cause is the ever-living now.

Trust no future, however pleasant,
Let the dead past bury its dead;
Act, act in the living present,
Heart within, and God overhead.

We have to do with the past only as we can make it useful to the present and to the future. To all inspiring motives, to noble deeds which can be gained from the past, we are welcome. But now is the time, the important time. Your fathers have lived, died, and have done their work, and have done much of it well. You live and must die, and you must do your work. You have no right to enjoy a child's share in the labor of your fathers, unless your children are to be blest by your labors. You have no right to wear out and waste the hard-earned fame of your fathers to cover your indolence. Sydney Smith tells us that men seldom eulogize the wisdom and virtues of their fathers, but to excuse some folly or wickedness of their own. This truth is not a doubtful one. There were illustrations of it near and remote, ancient and modern. It was fashionable, hundreds of years ago, for the children of Jacob to boast, we have "Abraham to our father," when they had long lost Abraham's faith and spirit. That people contented themselves under the shadow of Abraham's great name, while they repudiated the deeds which made his name great. Need I remind you that a similar thing is being done all over this country to-day? Need I tell you that the Jews are not the only people who built the tombs of the prophets, and garnished the sepulchers of the righteous? Washington could not die till he had broken the chains of his slaves. Yet his monument is built up by the price of human blood, and the traders in the bodies and souls of men shout—"We have Washington to *our father.*"—Alas! that it should be so; yet so it is.

The evil that men do, lives after them,
The good is oft interred with
their bones.

Fellow-citizens, pardon me, allow me to ask, why am I called upon to speak here to-day? What have I, or those I represent, to do with your national independence? Are the great principles of political freedom and of natural justice, embodied in that Declaration of Independence, extended to us? And am I, therefore, called upon to bring our humble offering to the national altar, and to confess the benefits and express devout gratitude for the blessings resulting from your independence to us?

Would to God, both for your sakes and ours, that an affirmative answer could be truthfully returned to these questions! Then would my task be light, and my burden easy and delightful. For *who* is there so cold, that a nation's sympathy could not warm him? Who so obdurate and dead to the claims of gratitude, that would not thankfully acknowledge such priceless benefits? Who so stolid and selfish, that would not give his voice to swell the hallelujahs of a nation's jubilee, when the chains of servitude had been torn from his limbs? I am not that man. In a case like that, the dumb might eloquently speak, and the "lame man leap as an hart."

But such is not the state of the case. I say it with a sad sense of the disparity between us. I am not included within the pale of this glorious anniversary! Your high independence only reveals the immeasurable distance between us. The blessings in which you, this day, rejoice, are not enjoyed in common. The rich inheritance of justice, liberty, prosperity and independence, bequeathed by your fathers, is shared by you, not by me. The sunlight that brought light and healing to you, has brought stripes and death to me. This Fourth of July is *yours,* not *mine. You* may rejoice, *I* must mourn. To drag a man in fetters into the grand illuminated temple of liberty, and call upon him to join you in joyous anthems, were inhuman mockery and sacrilegious irony. Do you mean, citizens, to mock me, by asking me to speak today? If so, there is a parallel to your conduct. And let me warn you that it is dangerous to copy the example of a nation whose crimes, towering up to heaven, were thrown down by the breath of the Almighty, burying that nation in irrevocable ruin! I can to-day take up the plaintive lament of a peeled and woe-smitten people!

> ***"Fellow-citizens, pardon me, allow me to ask, why am I called upon to speak here to-day? What have I, or those I represent, to do with your national independence?"***

"By the rivers of Babylon, there we sat down. Yea! we wept when we remembered Zion. We hanged our harps upon the willows in the midst thereof. For there, they that carried us away captive, required of us a song; and they who wasted us required of us mirth, saying, Sing us one of the songs of Zion. How can we sing the Lord's song in a strange land? If I forget thee, O Jerusalem, let my right hand forget her cunning. If I do not remember thee, let my tongue cleave to the roof of my mouth."

Fellow-citizens, above your national, tumultuous joy, I hear the mournful wail of millions(!) whose chains, heavy and grievous yesterday, are, to-day, rendered more intolerable by the jubilee shouts that reach them. If I do forget, if I do not faithfully remember those bleeding children of sorrow this day, "may my right hand forget her cunning, and may my tongue cleave to the roof of my mouth!" To forget them, to pass lightly over their wrongs, and to chime in with the popular theme, would be treason most scandalous and shocking, and would make me a reproach before God and the world. My subject, then, fellow-citizens, is AMERICAN SLAVERY. I shall see this day and its popular characteristics from the slave's point of view. Standing there identified with the American bondman, making his wrongs mine, I do not hesitate to declare, with all my soul, that the character and conduct of this nation never looked blacker to me than on this 4th of July! Whether we turn to the declarations of the past, or to the professions of the present, the conduct of the nation seems equally hideous and revolting. America is false to the past, false to the present, and solemnly binds herself to be false to the future. Standing with God and the crushed and bleeding slave on this occasion, I will, in the name of humanity which is outraged, in the name of liberty which is fettered, in the name of the constitution and the Bible which are disregarded and trampled upon, dare to call in question and to denounce, with all the emphasis I can command, everything that serves to perpetuate slavery—the great sin and shame of America! "I will not equivocate; I will not excuse"; I will use the severest language I can command; and yet not one word shall escape me that any man, whose judgment is not blinded by prejudice, or who is not at heart a slaveholder, shall not confess to be right and just.

But I fancy I hear some one of my audience

say, "It is just in this circumstance that you and your brother abolitionists fail to make a favorable impression on the public mind. Would you argue more, and denounce less; would you persuade more, and rebuke less; your cause would be much more likely to succeed." But, I submit, where all is plain there is nothing to be argued. What point in the anti-slavery creed would you have me argue? On what branch of the subject do the people of this country need light? Must I undertake to prove that the slave is a man? That point is conceded already. Nobody doubts it. The slaveholders themselves acknowledge it in the enactment of laws for their government. They acknowledge it when they punish disobedience on the part of the slave. There are seventy-two crimes in the State of Virginia which, if committed by a black man (no matter how ignorant he be), subject him to the punishment of death; while only two of the same crimes will subject a white man to the like punishment. What is this but the acknowledgment that the slave is a moral, intellectual, and responsible being? The manhood of the slave is conceded. It is admitted in the fact that Southern statute books are covered with enactments forbidding, under severe fines and penalties, the teaching of the slave to read or to write. When you can point to any such laws in reference to the beasts of the field, then I may consent to argue the manhood of the slave. When the dogs in your streets, when the fowls of the air, when the cattle on your hills, when the fish of the sea, and the reptiles that crawl, shall be unable to distinguish the slave from a brute, *then* will I argue with you that the slave is a man!

For the present, it is enough to affirm the equal manhood of the Negro race. Is it not astonishing that, while we are ploughing, planting, and reaping, using all kinds of mechanical tools, erecting houses, constructing bridges, building ships, working in metals of brass, iron, copper, silver and gold; that, while we are reading, writing and ciphering, acting as clerks, merchants and secretaries, having among us lawyers, doctors, ministers, poets, authors, editors, orators and teachers; that, while we are engaged in all manner of enterprises common to other men, digging gold in California, capturing the whale in the Pacific, feeding sheep and cattle on the hill-side, living, moving, acting, thinking, planning, living in families as husbands, wives and children, and, above all, confessing and worshipping the Christian's God, and looking hopefully for life and immortality beyond the grave, we are called upon to prove that we are men!

Would you have me argue that man is entitled to liberty? that he is the rightful owner of his own body? You have already declared it. Must I argue the wrongfulness of slavery? Is that a question for Republicans? Is it to be settled by the rules of logic and argumentation, as a matter beset with great difficulty, involving a doubtful application of the principle of justice, hard to be understood? How should I look to-day, in the presence of Americans, dividing, and subdividing a discourse, to show that men have a natural right to freedom? Speaking of it relatively and positively, negatively and affirmatively. To do so, would be to make myself ridiculous, and to offer an insult to your understanding. There is not a man beneath the canopy of heaven that does not know that slavery is wrong *for him*.

What, am I to argue that it is wrong to make men brutes, to rob them of their liberty, to work them without wages, to keep them ignorant of their relations to their fellow men, to beat them with sticks, to flay their flesh with the lash, to load their limbs with irons, to hunt them with dogs, to sell them at auction, to sunder their families, to knock out their teeth, to burn their flesh, to starve them into obedience and submission to their masters? Must I argue that a system thus marked with blood, and stained with pollution, is *wrong?* No! I will not. I have better employment for my time and strength than such arguments would imply.

What, then, remains to be argued? Is it that slavery is not divine; that God did not establish it; that our doctors of divinity are mistaken? There is blasphemy in the thought. That which is inhuman, cannot be divine! *Who* can reason on such a proposition? They that can, may; I cannot. The time for such argument is passed.

At a time like this, scorching irony, not convincing argument, is needed. O! had I the ability, and could I reach the nation's ear, I would, to-day, pour out a fiery stream of biting ridicule, blasting reproach, withering sarcasm, and stern rebuke. For it is not light that is needed, but fire; it is not the gentle shower, but thunder. We need the storm, the whirlwind, and the earthquake. The feeling of the nation must be quickened; the conscience of the nation must be roused; the propriety of the nation must be startled; the hypocrisy of the nation must be exposed; and its crimes against God and man must be proclaimed and denounced.

What, to the American slave, is your 4th of

July? I answer; a day that reveals to him, more than all other days in the year, the gross injustice and cruelty to which he is the constant victim. To him, your celebration is a sham; your boasted liberty, an unholy license; your national greatness, swelling vanity; your sounds of rejoicing are empty and heartless; your denunciation of tyrants, brass fronted impudence; your shouts of liberty and equality, hollow mockery; your prayers and hymns, your sermons and thanksgivings, with all your religious parade and solemnity, are to Him, mere bombast, fraud, deception, impiety, and hypocrisy—a thin veil to cover up crimes which would disgrace a nation of savages. There is not a nation on the earth guilty of practices more shocking and bloody than are the people of the United States, at this very hour.

Go where you may, search where you will,

> ***"What, to the American slave, is your 4th of July? I answer; a day that reveals to him . . . the gross injustice and cruelty to which he is the constant victim."***

roam through all the monarchies and despotisms of the Old World, travel through South America, search out every abuse, and when you have found the last, lay your facts by the side of the everyday practices of this nation, and you will say with me, that, for revolting barbarity and shameless hypocrisy, America reigns without a rival.

THE INTERNAL SLAVE TRADE

Take the American slave-trade, which we are told by the papers, is especially prosperous just now. Ex-Senator [Thomas Hart] Benton [of Missouri] tells us that the price of men was never higher than now. He mentions the fact to show that slavery is in no danger. This trade is one of the peculiarities of American institutions. It is carried on in all the large towns and cities in one-half of this confederacy; and millions are pocketed every year by dealers in this horrid traffic. In several states this trade is a chief source of wealth. It is called (in contradistinction to the foreign slave-trade) *"the internal slave-trade."* It is, probably, called so, too, in order to divert from it the horror with which the foreign slave-trade is contemplated. That trade has long since been denounced by this government as piracy. It has been denounced with burning words from the high places of the nation as an execrable traffic. To arrest it, to put an end to it, this nation keeps a squadron, at immense cost, on the coast of Africa. Everywhere, in this country, it is safe to speak of this foreign slave-trade as a most inhuman traffic, opposed alike to the laws of God and of man. The duty to extirpate and destroy it, is admitted even by our DOCTORS OF DIVINITY. In order to put an end to it, some of these last have consented that their colored brethren (nominally free) should leave this country, and establish themselves on the western coast of Africa! It is, however, a notable fact that, while so much execration is poured out by Americans upon all those engaged in the foreign slave-trade, the men engaged in the slave-trade between the states pass without condemnation, and their business is deemed honorable.

Behold the practical operation of this internal slave-trade, the American slave-trade, sustained by American politics and American religion. Here you will see men and women reared like swine for the market. You know what is a swine-drover? I will show you a man-drover. They inhabit all our Southern states. They perambulate the country, and crowd the highways of the nation, with droves of human stock. You will see one of these human flesh jobbers, armed with pistol, whip, and bowie-knife, driving a company of a hundred men, women, and children, from the Potomac to the slave market at New Orleans. These wretched people are to be sold singly, or in lots, to suit purchasers. They are food for the cotton field and the deadly sugar-mill. Mark the sad procession, as it moves wearily along, and the inhuman wretch who drives them. Hear his savage yells and his blood-curdling oaths, as he hurries on his affrighted captives! There, see the old man with locks thinned and gray. Cast one glance, if you please, upon that young mother, whose shoulders are bare to the scorching sun, her briny tears falling on the brow of the babe in her arms. See, too, that girl of thirteen, weeping, *yes!* weeping, as she thinks of the mother from whom she has been torn! The drove moves tardily. Heat and sorrow have nearly consumed their strength; suddenly you hear a quick snap, like the discharge of a rifle; the fetters clank, and the chain rattles simultaneously; your ears are saluted with a scream, that seems to have torn its way to the center of your soul! The crack you heard was the sound of the slave-whip; the scream you heard was from the woman you saw with the babe. Her speed had faltered under the weight of her child and her chains! That gash on her shoulder tells her to move on. Follow this drove to New Orleans. Attend the auction; see men examined like horses; see the forms of women rudely and brutally exposed to the shocking gaze of American slave-buyers. See this drove sold and separated forever; and never forget the deep, sad sobs that arose from that scattered multitude. Tell me, citizens, WHERE, under the sun, you can witness a spectacle more fiendish and shocking. Yet this is but a glance at the American slave-trade, as it exists, at this moment, in the ruling part of the United States.

I was born amid such sights and scenes. To me the American slave-trade is a terrible reality. When a child, my soul was often pierced with a sense of its horrors. I lived on Philpot Street, Fell's Point, Baltimore, and have watched from the wharves the slave ships in the Basin, anchored from the shore, with their cargoes of human flesh, waiting for favorable winds to waft them down the Chesapeake. There was, at that time, a grand slave mart kept at the head of Pratt Street, by Austin Woldfolk. His agents were sent into every town and county in Maryland, announcing their arrival, through the papers, and on flaming *"hand-bills,"* headed CASH FOR NEGROES. These men were generally well dressed men, and very captivating in their manners; ever ready to drink, to treat, and to gamble. The fate of many a slave has depended upon the turn of a single card; and many a child has been snatched from the arms of its mother by bargains arranged in a state of brutal drunkenness.

The flesh-mongers gather up their victims by dozens, and drive them, chained, to the general depot at Baltimore. When a sufficient number has been collected here, a ship is chartered for the purpose of conveying the forlorn crew to Mobile, or to New Orleans. From the slave prison to the ship, they are usually driven in the darkness of night; for since the anti-slavery agitation, a certain caution is observed.

In the deep, still darkness of midnight, I have been aroused by the dead, heavy footsteps, and the piteous cries of the chained gangs that passed our door. The anguish of my boyish heart was intense; and I was often consoled, when speaking to my mistress in the morning, to hear her say that the custom was very wicked; that she hated to hear the rattle of the chains and the heart-rending cries. I was glad to find one who sympathized with me in my horror.

Fellow-citizens, this murderous traffic is, to-day, in active operation in this boasted republic. In the solitude of my spirit I see clouds of dust raised on the highways of the South; I see the bleeding footsteps; I hear the doleful wail of fettered humanity on the way to the slave-markets, where the victims are to be sold like *horses, sheep,* and *swine,* knocked off to the highest bidder. There I see the tenderest ties ruthlessly broken, to gratify the lust, caprice and rapacity of the buyers and sellers of men. My soul sickens at the sight.

Is this the land your Fathers loved,
The freedom which they toiled to win?
Is this the earth whereon they moved?
Are these the graves they slumber in?

But a still more inhuman, disgraceful, and scandalous state of things remains to be presented.

By an act of the American Congress, not yet two years old, slavery has been nationalized in its most horrible and revolting form. By that act, Mason and Dixon's line has been obliterated; New York has become as Virginia; and the power to hold, hunt, and sell men, women and children, as slaves, remains no longer a mere state institution, but is now an institution of the whole United States. The power is co-extensive with the star-spangled banner, and American Christianity. Where these go, may also go the merciless slave-hunter. Where these are, man is not sacred. He is a bird for the sportsman's gun. By that most foul and fiendish of all human decrees, the liberty and person of every man are put in peril. Your broad republican domain is hunting ground for *men. Not* for thieves and robbers, enemies of society, merely, but for men guilty of no crime. Your lawmakers have commanded all good citizens to engage in this hellish sport. Your President, your Secretary of State, your *lords, nobles,* and ecclesiastics enforce, as a duty you owe to your free and glorious country, and to your God, that you do this accursed thing. Not fewer than forty Americans have, within the past two years, been hunted down and, without a moment's warning, hurried away in chains, and consigned to slavery and excruciating torture. Some of these have had wives and children, dependent on them for bread; but of this, no account was made. The right of the hunter to his prey stands superior to the right of marriage, and to *all* rights in this republic, the rights of God included! For black men there is neither law nor justice, humanity nor religion. The Fugitive Slave *Law* makes MERCY TO THEM A CRIME; and bribes the judge who tries them. An American JUDGE GETS TEN DOLLARS FOR EVERY VICTIM HE CONSIGNS to slavery, and five, when he fails to do so. The oath of any two villains is sufficient, under this hell-black enactment, to send the most pious and exemplary black man into the remorseless jaws of slavery! His own testimony is nothing. He can bring no witnesses for himself. The minister of American justice is bound by the law to hear but *one* side; and *that* side is the side of the oppressor. Let this damning fact be perpetually told. Let it be thundered around the world that in tyrant-killing, king-hating, people-loving, democratic, Christian America the seats of justice are filled with judges who hold their offices under an open and palpable *bribe,* and are bound, in deciding the case of a man's liberty, *to hear only his accusers!*

In glaring violation of justice, in shameless disregard of the forms of administering law, in cunning arrangement to entrap the defenseless, and in diabolical intent this Fugitive Slave Law stands alone in the annals of tyrannical legislation. I doubt if there be another nation on the globe having the brass and the baseness to put such a law on the statute-book. If any man in this assembly thinks differently from me in this matter, and feels able to disprove my statements, I will gladly confront him at any suitable time and place he may select.

"For black men there is neither law nor justice, humanity nor religion."

RELIGIOUS LIBERTY

I take this law to be one of the grossest infringements of Christian liberty, and, if the churches and ministers of our country were not stupidly blind, or most wickedly indifferent, they, too, would so regard it.

At the very moment that they are thanking God for the enjoyment of civil and religious liberty, and for the right to worship God according to the dictates of their own consciences, they are utterly silent in respect to a law which robs religion of its chief significance and makes it utterly worthless to a world lying in wickedness. Did this law concern the *"mint, anise,* and *cummin"*—abridge the right to sing psalms, to partake of the sacrament, or to engage in any of the ceremonies of religion, it would be smitten by the thunder of a thousand pulpits. A general shout would go up from the church demanding *repeal, repeal, instant repeal!*—And it would go hard with that politician who presumed to solicit the votes of the people without inscribing this motto on his banner. Further, if this demand were not complied with, another Scotland would be added to the history of religious liberty, and the stern old convenanters would be thrown into the shade. A John Knox would be seen at every church door and heard from every pulpit, and Fillmore would have no more quarter than was shown by Knox to the beautiful, but treacherous, Queen Mary of Scotland. The fact that the church of our country (with fractional exceptions) does not esteem "the Fugitive Slave Law" as a declaration of war against religious liberty, implies that that church regards religion simply as a form of worship, an empty ceremony, and *not* a vital principle, requiring active benevolence, justice, love, and good will towards man. It esteems sacrifice above mercy; psalm-singing above right doing; solemn meetings above practical righteousness. A worship that can be conducted by persons who refuse to give shelter to the houseless, to give bread to the hungry, clothing to the naked, and who enjoin obedience to a law forbidding these acts of mercy is a curse, not a blessing to mankind. The Bible addresses all such persons as "scribes, pharisees, hypocrites, who pay tithe of *mint, anise,* and *cummin,* and have omitted the weightier matters of the law, judgment, mercy, and faith."

THE CHURCH RESPONSIBLE

But the church of this country is not only indifferent to the wrongs of the slave, it actually takes sides with the oppressors. It has made itself the bulwark of American slavery, and the shield of American slave-hunters. Many of its most eloquent Divines, who stand as the very lights of the church, have shamelessly given the sanction of religion and the Bible to the whole slave system. They have taught that man may, properly, be a slave; that the relation of master and slave is ordained of God; that to send back an escaped bondman to his master is clearly the duty of all the followers of the Lord Jesus Christ; and this horrible blasphemy is palmed off upon the world for Christianity.

For my part, I would say, welcome infidelity! welcome atheism! Welcome anything! In preference to the gospel, *as preached by those Divines!* They convert the very name of religion into an engine of tyranny and barbarous cruelty, and serve to confirm more infidels, in this age, than all the infidel writings of Thomas Paine, Voltaire, and Bolingbroke put together have done! These ministers make religion a cold and flinty-hearted thing, having neither principles of right action nor bowels of compassion. They strip the love of God of its beauty and leave the throne of religion a huge, horrible, repulsive form. It is a religion for oppressors, tyrants, man-stealers, and *thugs*. It is not that *"pure and undefiled religion"* which is from above, and which is *"first pure, then peaceable, easy to be entreated,* full of mercy and good fruits, *without partiality, and without hypocrisy."* But a religion which favors the rich against the poor; which exalts the proud above the humble; which divides mankind into two classes, tyrants and slaves; which says to the man in chains, *stay there;* and to the oppressor, *oppress on;* it is a religion which may be professed and enjoyed by all the robbers and enslavers of mankind; it makes God a respecter of persons, denies his fatherhood of the race, and tramples in the dust the great truth of the brotherhood of man. All this we affirm to be true of the popular church, and the popular worship of our land and nation—a religion, a church, and a worship which, on the authority of inspired wisdom, we pronounce to be an abomination in the sight of God. In the language of Isaiah, the American church might be well addressed, "Bring no more vain oblations; incense is an abomination unto me: the new moons and Sabbaths, the calling of assemblies, I cannot away with; it is iniquity, even the solemn meeting. Your new moons, and your appointed feasts my soul hateth. They are a trouble to me; I am weary to bear them; and when ye spread forth your hands I will hide mine eyes from you. Yea! when ye make many prayers, I will not hear. YOUR HANDS ARE FULL OF BLOOD; cease to do evil, learn to do well; seek judgment; relieve the oppressed; judge for the fatherless; plead for the widow."

The American church is guilty, when viewed in connection with what it is doing to uphold slavery; but it is superlatively guilty when viewed in its connection with its ability to abolish slavery.

The sin of which it is guilty is one of omission as well as of commission. Albert Barnes but uttered what the common sense of every man at all observant of the actual state of the case will receive as truth, when he declared that "There is no power out of the church that could sustain slavery an hour, if it were not sustained in it."

Let the religious press, the pulpit, the Sunday school, the conference meeting, the great ecclesiastical, missionary, Bible and tract associations of the land array their immense powers against slavery, and slave-holding; and the whole system of crime and blood would be scattered to the winds, and that they do not do this involves them in the most awful responsibility of which the mind can conceive.

In prosecuting the anti-slavery enterprise, we have been asked to spare the church, to spare the ministry; but *how,* we ask, could such a thing be done? We are met on the threshold of our efforts for the redemption of the slave, by the church and ministry of the country, in battle arrayed against us; and we are compelled to fight or flee. From what *quarter,* I beg to know, has proceeded a fire so deadly upon our ranks, during the last two years, as from the Northern pulpit? As the champions of oppressors, the chosen men of American theology have appeared—men honored for their so-called piety, and their real learning. The LORDS of Buffalo, the SPRINGS of New York, the LATHROPS of Auburn, the COXES and SPENCERS of Brooklyn, the GANNETS and SHARPS of Boston, the DEWEYS of Washington, and other great religious lights of the land have, in utter denial of the authority of *Him* by whom they professed to be called to the ministry, deliberately taught us, against the example of the Hebrews, and against the remonstrance of the Apostles, *"that we ought to obey man's law before the law of God."*

My spirit wearies of such blasphemy; and how such men can be supported, as the "standing types and representatives of Jesus Christ," is a mystery which I leave others to penetrate. In speaking of the American church, however, let it be distinctly understood that I mean the *great mass* of the religious organizations of our land. There are exceptions, and I thank God that there are. Noble men may be found, scattered all over these Northern states, of whom Henry Ward Beecher, of Brooklyn; Samuel J. May, of Syracuse; and my esteemed friend on the platform [Rev. R. R. Raymond], are shining examples; and let me say further, that, upon these men lies the duty to inspire our ranks with high religious faith and zeal, and to cheer us on in the great mission of the slave's redemption from his chains.

RELIGION IN ENGLAND AND RELIGION IN AMERICA

One is struck with the difference between the attitude of the American church towards the anti-slavery movement, and that occupied by the churches in England towards a similar movement in that country. There, the church, true to its mission of ameliorating, elevating and improving the condition of mankind, came forward promptly, bound up the wounds of the West Indian slave, and restored him to his liberty. There, the question of emancipation was a high religious question. It was demanded in the name of humanity, and according to the law of the living God. The Sharps, the Clarksons, the Wilberforces, the Buxtons, the Burchells, and the Knibbs were alike famous for their piety and for their philanthropy. The anti-slavery movement *there* was not an anti-church movement, for the reason that the church took its full share in prosecuting that movement: and the anti-slavery movement in this country will cease to be an anti-church movement, when the church of this country shall assume a favorable instead of a hostile position towards that movement.

Americans! Your republican politics, not less than your republican union, are flagrantly inconsistent. You boast of your love of liberty, your superior civilization, and your pure Christianity, which the whole political power of the nation (as embodied in the two great political parties) is solemnly pledged to support and perpetuate the enslavement of three millions of your countrymen. You hurl your anathemas at the crowned headed tyrants of Russia and Austria and pride yourselves on your democratic institutions, while you yourselves consent to be the mere *tools* and *body-guards* of the tyrants of Virginia and Carolina. You invite to your shores fugitives of oppression from abroad, honor them with banquets, greet them with ovations, cheer them, toast them, salute them, protect them, and pour out your money to them like water; but the fugitives from your own land you advertise, hunt, arrest, shoot, and kill. You glory in your refinement and your universal education; yet you maintain a system as barbarous and dreadful as ever stained the character of a nation—a system begun in avarice, supported in pride, and perpetuated in cruelty. You shed tears over fallen Hungary, and make the sad story of her wrongs the theme of your poets, statesmen, and orators, till your gallant sons are ready to fly to arms to vindicate her cause against the oppressor; but, in regard to the ten thousand wrongs of the American slave, you would enforce the strictest silence, and would hail him as an enemy of the nation who dares to make those wrongs the subject of public discourse! You are all on fire at the mention of liberty for France or for Ireland; but are as cold as an iceberg at the thought of liberty for the enslaved of America. You discourse eloquently on the dignity of labor; yet, you sustain a system which, in its very essence, casts a stigma upon labor. You can bare your bosom to the storm of British artillery to throw off a three-penny tax on tea; and yet wring the last hard earned farthing from the grasp of the black laborers of your country. You profess to believe "that, of one blood, God made all nations of men to dwell on the face of all the earth," and hath commanded all men, everywhere, to love one another; yet you notoriously hate (and glory in your hatred) all men whose skins are not colored like your own. You declare before the world, and are understood by the world to declare that you *"hold these truths to be self-evident, that all men are created equal; and are endowed by their Creator with certain inalienable rights; and that among these are, life, liberty, and the pursuit of happiness"*; and yet, you hold securely, in a bondage which, according to your own Thomas Jefferson, *"is worse than ages of that which your fathers rose in rebellion to oppose,"* a seventh part of the inhabitants of your country.

Fellow-citizens, I will not enlarge further on your national inconsistencies. The existence of slavery in this country brands your republicanism as a sham, your humanity as a base pretense, and your Christianity as a lie. It destroys your moral power abroad: it corrupts your politicians at home. It saps the foundation of religion; it makes your name a hissing and a bye-word to a mocking earth. It is the antagonistic force in your government, the only thing that seriously disturbs and endangers your *Union*. It fetters your progress; it is the enemy of improvement; the deadly foe of education; it fosters pride, it breeds insolence; it promotes vice; it shelters crime; it is a curse to the earth that supports it; and yet you cling to it as if it were the sheet anchor of all your hopes. Oh! Be warned! A horrible reptile is coiled up in your nation's bosom; the venomous creature is nursing at the tender breast of your youthful republic; *for the love of God, tear away,* and fling from you the hideous monster, and *let the weight of twenty millions crush and destroy it forever!*

THE CONSTITUTION

But it is answered in reply to all this, that precisely what I have now denounced is, in fact, guaranteed and sanctioned by the Constitution of the United States; that, the right to hold, and to hunt slaves is a part of that Constitution framed by the illustrious Fathers of this Republic.

Then, I dare to affirm, notwithstanding all I have said before, your fathers stooped, basely stooped:

To palter with us in a double sense:
And keep the word of promise to the ear,
But break it to the heart.

And instead of being the honest men I have before declared them to be, they were the veriest impostors that ever practiced on mankind. *This* is the inevitable conclusion, and from it there is no escape; but I differ from those who charge this baseness on the framers of the Constitution of the United States. *It is a slander upon their memory,* at least, so I believe. There is not time now to argue the constitutional question at length; nor have I the ability to discuss it as it ought to be discussed. The subject has been handled with masterly power by Lysander Spooner, Esq., by William Goodell, by Samuel E. Sewall, Esq., and last, though not least, by Gerritt Smith, Esq. These gentlemen have, as I think, fully and clearly vindicated the Constitution from any design to support slavery for an hour.

Fellow-citizens! There is no matter in respect to which the people of the North have allowed themselves to be so ruinously imposed upon as that of the pro-slavery character of the Constitution. In *that* instrument I hold there is neither warrant, license, nor sanction of the hateful thing; but interpreted, as it *ought* to be interpreted, the Constitution is a GLORIOUS LIBERTY DOCUMENT. Read its preamble, consider its purposes. Is slavery among them? Is it at the gateway? Or is it in the temple? It is neither. While I do not intend to argue this question on the present occasion, let me ask, if it be not somewhat singular that, if the Constitution were intended to be, by its framers and adopters, a slaveholding instrument, why neither *slavery, slaveholding,* nor *slave* can anywhere be found in it. What would be thought of an instrument, drawn up, *legally* drawn up, for the purpose of entitling the city of Rochester to a tract of land, in which no mention of land was made? Now, there are certain rules of interpretation for the proper understanding of all legal instruments. These rules are well established. They are plain, common-sense rules, such as you and I, and all of us, can understand and apply, without having passed years in the study of law. I scout the idea that the question of the constitutionality, or unconstitutionality of slavery, is not a question for the people. I hold that every American citizen has a right to form an opinion of the Constitution, and to propagate that opinion, and to use all honorable means to make his opinion the prevailing one. Without this right, the liberty of an American citizen would be as insecure as that of a Frenchman. Ex-Vice-President [George Mifflin] Dallas tells us that the Constitution is an object to which no American mind can be too attentive, and no American heart too devoted. He further says, the Constitution, in its words, is plain and intelligible, and is meant for the homebred, unsophisticated understandings of our fellow-citizens. Senator Berrien tells us that the Constitution is the fundamental law, that which controls all others. The charter of our liberties, which every citizen has a personal interest in understanding thoroughly. The testimony of Senator Breese, Lewis Cass, and many others that might be named, who are everywhere esteemed as sound lawyers, so regard the Constitution. I take it, therefore, that it is not presumption in a private citizen to form an opinion of that instrument.

Now, take the Constitution according to the plain reading, and I defy the presentation of a single pro-slavery clause in it. On the other hand, it will be found to contain principles and purposes, entirely hostile to the existence of slavery.

I have detained my audience entirely too long already. At some future period I will gladly avail myself of an opportunity to give this subject a full and fair discussion.

Allow me to say, in conclusion, notwithstanding the dark picture I have this day presented, of the state of the nation, I do not despair of this country. There are forces in operation which must inevitably work the downfall of slavery. *"The arm of the Lord is not shortened,"* and the doom of slavery is certain. I, therefore, leave off where I began, with *hope.* While drawing encouragement from "the Declaration of Independence," the great principles it contains, and the genius of American Institutions, my spirit is also cheered by the obvious tendencies of the age. Nations do not now stand in the same relation to each other that they did ages ago. No nation can now shut itself up from the surrounding world and trot round in the same old path of its fathers without interference. The time *was* when such could be done. Long established customs of hurtful character could formerly fence themselves in, and do their evil work with social impunity. Knowledge was then confined and enjoyed by the privileged few, and the multitude walked on in mental darkness. But a change has now come over the affairs of mankind. Walled cities and empires have become unfashionable. The arm of commerce has borne away the gates of the strong city. Intelligence is penetrating the darkest corners of the globe. It makes its pathway over and under the sea, as well as on the earth. Wind, steam, and lightning are its chartered agents. Oceans no longer divide, but link nations together. From Boston to London is now a holiday excursion. Space is comparatively annihilated. Thoughts expressed on one side of the Atlantic are distinctly heard on the other.

The far off and almost fabulous Pacific rolls in grandeur at our feet. The Celestial Empire, the mystery of ages, is being solved. The fiat of the Almighty, *"Let there be Light,"* has not yet spent its force. No abuse, no outrage whether in taste, sport or avarice, can now hide itself from the all-pervading light. The iron shoe, and crippled foot of China must be seen in contrast with nature. *Africa must rise and put on her yet unwoven garment. "Ethiopia shall stretch out her hand unto God."* In the fervent aspirations of William Lloyd Garrison, I say, and let every heart join in saying it:

God speed the year of jubilee
The wide world o'er!
When from their galling chains set free,
Th' oppress'd shall vilely bend the knee,
And wear the yoke of tyranny
Like brutes no more.
That year will come, and freedom's reign,
To man his plundered rights again
Restore.

God speed the day when human blood
Shall cease to flow!
In every clime be understood,
The claims of human brotherhood,
And each return for evil, good,
Not blow for blow;
That day will come all feuds to end,
And change into a faithful friend
Each foe.

God speed the hour, the glorious hour,
When none on earth
Shall exercise a lordly power,
Nor in a tyrant's presence cower;
But to all manhood's stature tower,
By equal birth!
That hour will come, to each, to all,
And from his prison-house, to thrall
Go forth.

Until that year, day, hour, arrive,
With head, and heart, and hand
I'll strive,
To break the rod, and rend the gyve,
The spoiler of his prey deprive–
So witness Heaven!
And never from my chosen post,
Whate'er the peril or the cost,
Be driven.

In late 1863 and early 1864, Douglass visited numerous towns and cities giving what some consider his most important wartime speech. Known as "The Mission of the War," it emphatically underscored his belief that the abolition of slavery was the single most important goal in the conflict between the North and the South. What follows is the major part of his remarks before the Women's Loyal League in New York City on January 13, 1864, as reported in the next day's New York Tribune. *It is reprinted from* The Voice of Black America: Major Speeches by Negroes in the United States, 1797-1971, *edited by Philip S. Foner (Simon & Schuster, 1972).*

Ladies and Gentlemen: By the mission of the war I mean nothing occult, arbitrary or difficult to be understood, but simply those great moral changes in the fundamental condition of the people, demanded by the situation of the country plainly involved in the nature of the war, and which, if the war is conducted in accordance with its true character, it is naturally and logically fitted to accomplish.

Speaking in the name of Providence, some men tell me that slavery is already dead, that it expired with the first shot at Sumter. This may be so, but I do not share the confidence with which it is asserted. In a grand crisis like this, we should all prefer to look facts sternly in the face and to accept their verdict whether it bless or blast us. I look for no miraculous destruction of slavery. The war looms before me simply as a great national opportunity, which may be improved to national salvation, or neglected to national ruin. I hope much from the bravery of our soldiers, but in vain is the might of armies if our rulers fail to profit by experience and refuse to listen to the suggestions of wisdom and justice. The most hopeful fact of the hour is that we are now in a salutary school—the school of affliction. If sharp and signal retribution, long protracted, wide-sweeping and overwhelming, can teach a great nation respect for the long-despised claims of justice, surely we shall be taught now and for all time to come. But if, on the other hand, this potent teacher, whose lessons are written in characters of blood and thundered to us from a hundred battlefields shall fail, we shall go down as we shall deserve to go down, as a warning to all other nations which shall come after us. It is not pleasant to contemplate the hour as one of doubt and danger. We naturally prefer the bright side, but when there is a dark side it is folly to shut our eyes to it or deny its existence.

I know that the acorn involves the oak, but I know also that the commonest accident may destroy its potential character and defeat its natural destiny. One wave brings its treasure from the briny deep, but another often sweeps it back to its primal depths. The saying that revolutions never go backward must be taken with limitations. The Revolution of 1848 was one of the grandest that ever dazzled a gazing world. It overturned the French throne, sent Louis Philippe into exile, shook every throne in Europe, and inaugurated a glorious Republic. Looking from a distance, the friends of democratic liberty saw in the convulsion the death of kingcraft in Europe and throughout the world. Great was their disappointment. Almost in the twinkling of an eye, the latent forces of despotism rallied. The Republic disappeared. Her noblest defenders were sent into exile, and the hopes of democratic liberty were blasted in the moment of their bloom. Politics and perfidy proved too strong for the principles of liberty and justice in that contest. I wish I could say that no such liabilities darken the horizon around us. But the same elements are plainly involved here as there. Though the portents are that we shall flourish, it is too much to say that we cannot fail and fall. Our destiny is to be taken out of our own hands. It is cowardly to shuffle our responsibilities upon the shoulders of Providence. I do not intend to argue but to state facts.

We are now wading into the third year of conflict with a fierce and sanguinary rebellion, one which, at the beginning of it, we were hopefully assured by one of our most sagacious and trusted political prophets would be ended in less than ninety days; a rebellion which, in its worst features, stands alone among rebellions a solitary and ghastly horror, without a parallel in the history of any nation, ancient or modern; a rebellion inspired by no love of liberty and by no hatred of oppression, as most other rebellions have been, and therefore utterly indefensible upon any moral or social grounds; a rebellion which openly and shamelessly sets at defiance the world's judgment of right and wrong, appeals from light to darkness, from intelligence to ignorance, from the ever-increasing prospects and blessings of a high and glorious civilization to the cold and withering blasts

> ***"The war looms before me simply as a great national opportunity, which may be improved to national salvation, or neglected to national ruin."***

of a naked barbarism; a rebellion which even at this unfinished stage of it counts the number of its slain not by thousands nor by tens of thousands, but by hundreds of thousands; a rebellion which in the destruction of human life and property has rivaled the earthquake, the whirlwind and the pestilence that walketh in darkness and wasteth at noonday. It has planted agony at a million hearthstones, thronged our streets with the weeds of mourning, filled our land with mere stumps of men, ridged our soil with two hundred thousand rudely formed graves and mantled it all over with the shadow of death. A rebellion which, while it has arrested the wheels of peaceful industry and checked the flow of commerce, has piled up a debt heavier than a mountain of gold to weigh down the necks of our children's children. There is no end to the mischief wrought. It has brought ruin at home, contempt abroad, has cooled our friends, heated our enemies and endangered our existence as a nation.

Now, for what is all this desolation, ruin, shame, suffering and sorrow? Can anybody want the answer? Can anybody be ignorant of the answer? It has been given a thousand times from this and other platforms. We all know it is slavery. Less than a half a million of Southern slaveholders—holding in bondage four million slaves—finding themselves outvoted in the effort to get possession of the United States government, in order to serve the interests of slavery, have madly resorted to the sword—have undertaken to accomplish by bullets what they failed to accomplish by ballots. That is the answer.

It is worthy of remark that secession was an afterthought with the rebels. Their aim was higher; secession was only their second choice. Who was going to fight for slavery in the Union? It was not separation, but subversion. It was not Richmond, but Washington. It was not the Confederate rag, but the glorious Star-Spangled Banner.

Whence came the guilty ambition equal to this atrocious crime. A peculiar education was necessary to this bold wickedness. Here all is plain again. Slavery—the peculiar institution—is aptly fitted to produce just such patriots, who first plunder and then seek to destroy their country. A system which rewards labor with stripes and chains, which robs the slave of his manhood and the master of all just consideration for the rights of his fellow man—has prepared the characters, male and female, that figure in this rebellion—and for all its cold-blooded and hellish atrocities. In all the most horrid details of torture, starvation and murder in the treatment of our prisoners, I behold the features of the monster in whose presence I was born, and that is slavery. From no sources less foul and wicked could such a rebellion come. I need not dwell here. The country knows the story by heart. But I am one of those who think this rebellion—inaugurated and carried on for a cause so unspeakably guilty and distinguished by barbarities which would extort a cry of shame from the painted savage—is quite enough for the whole lifetime of any one nation, though the lifetime should cover the space of a thousand years. We ought not to want a repetition of it. Looking at the matter from no higher ground than patriotism—setting aside the high considerations of justice, liberty, progress and civilization—the American people should resolve that this shall be the last slaveholding rebellion that shall ever curse this continent. Let the war cost more or cost little, let it be long or short, the work now begun should suffer no pause, no abatement, until it is done and done forever.

I know that many are appalled and disappointed by the apparently interminable character of this war. I am neither appalled nor disappointed without pretending to any higher wisdom than other men. I knew well enough and often said it: once let the North and South confront each other on the battlefield, and slavery and freedom be the inspiring motives of the respective sections, the contest will be fierce, long and sanguinary. Governor [Horatio] Seymour [of New York] charges us with prolonging the war, and I say the longer the better if it must be so—in order to put an end to the hell-black cause out of which the rebellion has risen.

Say not that I am indifferent to the horrors and hardships of the war. I am not indifferent. In common with the American people generally, I feel the prolongation of the war a heavy calamity, private as well as public. There are vacant spaces at my hearthstone which I shall rejoice to see filled again by the boys who once occupied them, but which cannot be thus filled while the war lasts, for they have enlisted "during the war."

But even from the length of this struggle, we who mourn over it may well enough draw some consolation when we reflect upon the vastness and grandeur of its mission. The world has witnessed many wars—and history records and perpetuates their memory—but the world has not seen a nobler and grander war than that which the loyal people of this country are now waging against the slaveholding rebels. The blow we strike is not merely to free a country or continent, but the whole world, from slavery; for when slavery fails here, it will fall everywhere. We have no business to mourn over our mission. We are writing the statutes of eternal justice and liberty in the blood of the worst of tyrants as a warning to all aftercomers. We should rejoice that there was normal life and health enough in us to stand in our appointed place, and do this great service for mankind.

It is true that the war seems long. But this very slow progress is an essential element of its effectiveness. Like the slow convalescence of some patients the fault is less chargeable to the medicine than to the deep-seated character of the disease. We were in a very low condition before the remedy was applied. The whole head was sick and the whole heart faint. Dr. Buchanan and his Democratic friends had given us up and were preparing to celebrate the nation's funeral. We had been drugged nearly to death by proslavery compromises. A radical change was needed in our whole system. Nothing is better calculated to effect the desired change than the slow, steady and certain progress of the war.

I know that this view of the case is not very consoling to the peace Democracy. I was not sent and am not come to console this breach of our political church. They regard this grand moral revolution in the mind and heart of the nation as the most distressing attribute of the war, and howl over it like certain characters of whom we read—who thought themselves tormented before their time.

Upon the whole, I like their mode of characterizing the war. They charge that it is no longer conducted upon Constitutional principles. The same was said by Breckinridge and Vallandigham. They charge that it is not waged to establish the Union as it was. The same idea has occurred to Jefferson Davis. They charge that this is a war for the subjugation of the South. In a word, that it is an Abolition war.

For one, I am not careful to deny this charge. But it is instructive to observe how this charge is brought and how it is met. Both warn us of danger. Why is this war fiercely denounced as an Abolition war? I answer, because the nation has long and bitterly hated Abolition and the enemies of the war confidently rely upon this hatred to serve the ends of treason. Why do the loyal people deny the charge? I answer, because they know that Abolition, though now a vast power, is still odious. Both the charge and the denial tell how the people hate and despise the only measure that can save the country.

An Abolition war! Well, let us thank the Democracy for teaching us this word. The charge in a comprehensive sense is most true, and it is a pity that it is true, but it would be a vast pity if it were not true. Would that it were more true than it is. When our government and people shall bravely avow this to be an Abolition war, then the country will be safe. Then our work will be fairly mapped out. Then the uplifted arm of the nation will swing unfettered to its work, and the spirit and power of the rebellion will be broken. Had slavery been abolished in the Border States at the very beginning of the war, as it ought to have been—had it been abolished in Missouri, as it would have been but for Presidential interference—there would now be no rebellion in the Southern states, for, instead of having to watch these Border States, as they have done, our armies would have marched in overpowering numbers directly upon the rebels and overwhelmed them. I now hold that a sacred regard for truth, as well as sound policy, makes it our duty to own and avow before heaven and earth that this war is, and of right ought to be, an Abolition war.

The abolition of slavery is the comprehensive and logical object of the war, for it includes everything else which the struggle involves. It is a war for the Union, a war for the Constitution, I admit; but it is logically such a war only in the sense that the greater includes the lesser. Slavery has proved itself the strong man of our national house. In every rebel state it proved itself stronger than the Union, stronger than the Constitution, and stronger than the Republican institutions. It overrode majorities, made no account of the ballot box, and had everything its own way. It is plain that this strong man must be bound and cast out of our house before Union, Constitution and Republican institutions can become possible. An Abolition war, therefore, includes Union, Constitution, Republican institutions, and all else that goes to make up the greatness and glory of our common country. On the other hand, exclude Abolition, and you exclude all else for which you are fighting.

The position of the Democratic party in relation to the war ought to surprise nobody. It is consistent with the history of the party for thirty years. Slavery, and only slavery, has been its recognized master during all that time. It early won for itself the title of being the natural ally of the South and of slavery. It has always been for peace or against peace, for war and against war, precisely as dictated by slavery. Ask why it was for the Florida War, and it answers, slavery. Ask why it was for the Mexican War, and it answers, slavery. Ask why it was for the annexation of Texas, and it answers, slavery. Ask why it was opposed to the habeas corpus when a Negro was the applicant, and it answers, slavery. Ask why it is now in favor of the habeas corpus, when rebels and traitors are the applicants for its benefits, and it answers, slavery. Ask why it was for mobbing down freedom of speech a few years ago, when that freedom was claimed by the Abolitionists, and it answers, slavery. Ask why it now asserts freedom of speech, when sympathizers with traitors claim that freedom, and again slavery is the answer. Ask why it denied the right of a state to protect itself against possible abuses of the Fugitive Slave Bill, and you have the same old answer. Ask why it now asserts the sovereignty of the states separately as against the states united, and again slavery is the answer. Ask why it was opposed to giving persons claimed as fugitive slaves a jury trial before returning them to slavery; ask why it is now in favor of giving jury trial to traitors before sending them to the forts for safekeeping; ask why it was for war at the beginning of the Rebellion; ask why it has attempted to embarrass and hinder the loyal government at every step of its progress, and you have but one answer, slavery.

The fact is, the party in question—I say nothing of individual men who were once members of it—has had but one vital and animating principle for thirty years, and that has been the same old horrible and hell-born principle of Negro slavery.

It has now assumed a saintly character. Its members would receive the benediction due to peacemakers. At one time they would stop bloodshed at the South by inaugurating bloody revolution at the North. The livery of peace is a beautiful livery, but in this case it is a stolen livery and sits badly on the wearer. These new apostles of peace call themselves Peace Democrats, and boast that they belong to the only party which can restore the country to peace. I neither dispute their title nor the pretensions founded upon it. The best that can be said of the peacemaking ability of this class of men is their bitterest condemnation. It consists in their known treachery to the loyal government. They have but to cross the rebel lines to be hailed by the traitors as countrymen, clansmen, kinsmen, and brothers beloved in a common conspiracy. . . .

Here is a part of the platform of principles upon which it seems to me every loyal man should take his stand at this hour:

First: That this war, which we are compelled to wage against slaveholding rebels and traitors, at untold cost of blood and treasure, shall be, and of right ought to be, an Abolition war.

Secondly: That we, the loyal people of the North and of the whole country, while determined to make this a short and final war, will offer no peace, accept no peace, consent to no peace, which shall not be to all intents and purposes an Abolition peace.

Thirdly: That we regard the whole colored population of the country, in the loyal as well as in the disloyal states, as our countrymen—valuable in peace as laborers, valuable in war as soldiers—entitled to all the rights, protection, and opportunities for achieving distinction enjoyed by any other class of our countrymen.

Fourthly: Believing that the white race has nothing to fear from fair competition with the black race, and that the freedom and elevation of one race are not to be purchased or in any manner rightfully subserved by the disfranchisement of another, we shall favor immediate and unconditional emancipation in all the states, invest the black man everywhere with the right to vote and to be voted for, and remove all discriminations against his rights on account of his color, whether as a citizen or as a soldier.

Ladies and gentlemen, there was a time when I hoped that events unaided by discussions would couple this rebellion and slavery in a common grave. But, as I have before intimated, the facts do still fall short of our hopes. The question as to what shall be done with slavery—and especially what shall be done with the Negro—threaten to remain open questions for some time yet.

It is true we have the Proclamation of January, 1863. It was a vast and glorious step in the right direction. But unhappily, excellent as that paper is—and much as it has accomplished temporarily—it settles nothing. It is still open to decision by courts, canons and Congresses. I have applauded that paper and do now applaud it, as a wise measure—while I detest the motive and principle upon which it is based. By it the holding and flogging of Negroes is the exclusive luxury of loyal men.

Our chief danger lies in the absence of all moral feeling in the utterances of our rulers. In his letter to Mr. [Horace] Greeley the President told the country virtually that the abolition or nonabolition of slavery was a matter of indifference to him. He would save the Union with slavery or without slavery. In his last Message he shows the same moral indifference, by saying as he does say that he had hoped that the rebellion could be put down without the abolition of slavery.

When the late Stephen A. Douglas uttered the sentiment that he did not care whether slavery were voted up or voted down in the territories, we thought him lost to all genuine feeling on the subject, and no man more than Mr. Lincoln denounced that sentiment as unworthy of the lips of any American statesman. But today, after nearly three years of a slaveholding rebellion, we find Mr. Lincoln uttering substantially the same heartless sentiments. Douglas wanted popular sovereignty; Mr. Lincoln wants the Union. Now did a warm heart and a high moral feeling control the utterance of the President, he would welcome, with joy unspeakable and full of glory, the opportunity afforded by the rebellion to free the country from the matchless crime and infamy. But policy, policy, everlasting policy, has robbed our statesmanship of all soul-moving utterances.

The great misfortune is and has been during all the progress of this war, that the government and loyal people have not understood and accepted its true mission. Hence we have been floundering in the depths of dead issues. Endeavoring to impose old and worn-out conditions upon new relations—putting new wines into old bottles, new cloth into old garments and thus making the rent worse than before.

Had we been wise we should have recognized the war at the outset as at once the signal and the necessity for a new order of social and political relations among the whole people. We could, like the ancients, discern the face of the sky, but not the signs of the times. Hence we have been talking of the importance of carrying on the war within the limits of a Constitution broken down by the very people in whose behalf the Constitution is pleaded! Hence we have from the first been deluding ourselves with the miserable dream that the old Union can be revived in the states where it has been abolished.

Now, we of the North have seen many strange things and may see many more; but that old Union, whose canonized bones we saw hearsed in death and inurned under the frowning battlements of Sumter, we shall never see again while the world standeth. The issue before us is a living issue. We are not fighting for the dead past, but for the living present and the glorious future. We are not fighting for the old Union, nor for anything like it, but for that which is ten thousand times more important; and that thing, crisply rendered, is national unity. Both sections have tried Union. It has failed.

The lesson for the statesmen at this hour is to discover and apply some principle of government which shall produce unity of sentiment, unity of idea, unity of object. Union without unity is, as we have seen, body without soul, marriage without love, a barrel without hoops, which falls at the first touch.

The statesmen of the South understood this matter earlier and better than the statesmen of the North. The dissolution of the Union on the old bases of compromise was plainly foreseen and predicted thirty years ago. Mr. Calhoun, and not Mr. Seward, is the original author of the doctrine of the irrepressible conflict. The South is logical and consistent. Under the teachings of their great leader they admit into their form of government no disturbing force. They have based their Confederacy squarely on their cornerstone. Their two great and all-commanding ideas are, first, that slavery is right, and second, that the slaveholders are a superior order or class. Around these two ideas their manners, morals, politics, religion and laws revolve. Slavery being right, all that is inconsistent with its entire security is necessarily wrong, and of course ought to be put down. There is no flaw in their logic.

> *"We are not fighting for the dead past, but for the living present and the glorious future."*

They first endeavored to make the federal government stand upon their accursed cornerstone; and we but barely escaped, as you well know, that calamity. Fugitive-slave laws, slavery-extension laws, and Dred Scott decisions were among the steps to get the nation squarely upon the cornerstone now chosen by the Confederate states. The loyal North is less definite in regard to the necessity of principles of national unity. Yet, unconsciously to ourselves, and against our own protestations, we are in reality, like the South, fighting for national unity—a unity of which the great principles of liberty and equality, and not slavery and class superiority, are the cornerstone.

Long before this rude and terrible war came to tell us of a broken Constitution and a dead Union, the better portion of the loyal people had outlived and outgrown what they had been taught to believe were the requirements of the old Union. We had come to detest the principle by which slavery had a strong representation in Congress. We had come to abhor the idea of being called upon to suppress slave insurrections. We had come to be ashamed of slave hunting, and being made the watchdogs of slaveholders, who were too proud to scent out and hunt down their slaves for themselves. We had so far outlived the old Union four years ago that we thought the little finger of the hero of Harpers Ferry of more value to the world struggling for liberty than all the first families of old Virginia put together.

What business, then, have we to be pouring out our treasure and shedding our best blood like water for that old worn-out, dead and buried Union, which had already become a calamity and a curse? The fact is, we are not fighting for any such thing, and we ought to come out under our own true colors, and let the South and the whole world know that we don't want and will not have anything analogous to the old Union.

What we now want is a country—a free country—a country not saddened by the footprints of a single slave—and nowhere cursed by the presence of a slaveholder. We want a country which shall not brand the Declaration of Independence as a lie. We want a country whose fundamental institutions we can proudly defend before the highest intelligence and civilization of the age. Hitherto we have opposed European scorn of our slavery with a blush of shame as our best defense. We now want a country in which the obligations of patriotism shall not conflict with fidelity to justice and liberty. We want a country, and are fighting for a country, which shall be free from sectional political parties—free from sectional religious denominations—free from sectional benevolent associations—free from every kind and description of sect, party, and combination of a sectional character. We want a country where men may assemble from any part of it, without prejudice to their interests or peril to their persons. We are in fact, and from absolute necessity, transplanting the whole South with the higher civilization of the North. The New England schoolhouse is bound to take the place of the Southern whipping post. Not because we love the Negro, but the nation; not because we prefer to do this, because we must or give up the contest and give up the country. We want a country, and are fighting for a country, where social intercourse and commercial relations shall neither be embarrassed nor embittered by the imperious exactions of an insolent slaveholding oligarchy, which required Northern merchants to sell their souls as a condition precedent to selling their goods. We want a country, and are fighting for a country, through the length and breadth of which the literature and learning of any section of it may float to its extremities unimpaired, and thus become the common property of all the people—a country in which no man shall be fined for reading a book, or imprisoned for selling a book—a country where no man may be imprisoned or flogged or sold for learning to read, or teaching a fellow mortal how to read. We want a country, and are fighting for a country, in any part of which to be called an American citizen shall mean as much as it did to be called a Roman citizen in the palmiest days of the Roman Empire.

We have heard much in other days of manifest destiny. I don't go all the lengths to which such theories are pressed, but I do believe that it is the manifest destiny of this war to unify and reorganize the institutions of the country, and that herein is the secret of the strength, the fortitude, the persistent energy—in a word, the sacred significance—of this war. Strike out the high ends and aims thus indicated, and the war would appear to the impartial eye of an onlooking world like better than a gigantic enterprise for shedding human blood.

A most interesting and gratifying confirmation of this theory of its mission is furnished in the varying fortunes of the struggle itself. Just in proportion to the progress made in taking upon itself the character I have ascribed to it has the war prospered and the rebellion lost ground.

Justice and humanity are often overpowered, but they are persistent and eternal forces, and fearful to contend against. Let but our rulers place the government fully within these trade winds of omnipotence, and the hand of death is upon the Confederate rebels. A war waged as ours seemed to be at first merely for power and empire, repels sympathy though supported by legitimacy. If Ireland should strike for independence tomorrow, the sympathy of this country would be with her, and I doubt if American statesmen would be more discreet in the expression of their opinions of the merits of the contest than British statesmen have been concerning the merits of ours. When we were merely fighting for the old Union the world looked coldly upon our government. But now the world begins to see something more than legitimacy, something more than national pride. It sees national wisdom aiming at national unity, and national justice breaking the chains of a long-enslaved people. It is this new complexion of our cause which warms our hearts and strengthens our hands at home, disarms our enemies and increases our friends abroad. It is this more than all else which has carried consternation into the bloodstained halls of the South. It has sealed the fiery and scornful lips of the Roebucks and Lindsays of England, and caused even the eloquent Mr. Gladstone to restrain the expression of his admiration for Jeff Davis and his rebel nation. It has placed the broad arrow of British suspicion on the prows of the rebel rams in the Mersey and performed a like service in France. It has driven Mason, the shameless man hunter, from London, where he never should have been allowed to stay for an hour, except as a bloodhound is tolerated in Regent Park for exhibition.

We have had, from the first, warm friends in England. We owe a debt of respect and gratitude to William Edward Forster, John Bright, Richard Cobden, and other British statesmen, in that they outran us in comprehending the high character of our struggle. They saw that this must be a war for human nature, and walked by faith to its defense while all was darkness about us—while we were yet conducting it in profound reverence for slavery.

I know we are not to be praised for this changed character of the war. We did our very best to prevent it. We had but one object at the beginning, and that was, as I have said, the restoration of the old Union; and for the first two years the war was kept to that object strictly, and you know full well and bitterly with what results. I will not stop here to blame and denounce the past; but I will say that the most of the blunders and disasters of the earlier part of the war might have been avoided had our armies and generals not repelled the only true friends the Union cause had in the rebel states. The Army of the Potomac took up an anti-Negro position from the first and has not entirely renounced it yet. The colored people told me a few days ago in Washington that they were the victims of the most brutal treatment by these Northern soldiers when they first came there. But let that pass. Few men, however great their wisdom, are permitted to see the end from the beginning. Events are mightier than our rulers, and these divine forces, with overpowering logic, have fixed upon this war, against the wishes of our government, the comprehensive character and mission I have ascribed to it. The collecting of revenue in the rebel ports, the repossession of a few forts and arsenals and other public property stolen by the rebels, have almost disappeared from the recollection of the people. The war has been a growing war in every sense of the word. It began weak and has risen strong. It began low and has risen high. It began narrow and has become broad. It began with few and now, behold, the country is full of armed men, ready, with courage and fortitude, to make the wisest and best idea of American statesmanship the law of the land.

Let, then, the war proceed in its strong, high and broad course till the rebellion is put down and our country is saved beyond the necessity of being saved again!

I have already hinted at our danger. Let me be a little more direct and pronounced.

The Democratic party, though defeated in the elections last fall, is still a power. It is the ready organized nucleus of a powerful proslavery and prorebel reaction. Though it has lost in members, it retains all the elements of its former power and malevolence.

That party has five very strong points in its favor, and its public men and journals know well how to take advantage of them.

First: There is the absence of any deep moral feeling among the loyal people against slavery itself, their feeling against it being on account of its rebellion against the government, and not because it is a stupendous crime against human nature.

Secondly: The vast expense of the war and the heavy taxes in money as well as men which the war requires for its prosecution. Loyalty has a strong back, but taxation has often broken it.

Thirdly: The earnest desire for peace which is shared by all classes except government contractors who are making money out of the war; a feeling which may be kindled to a flame by any serious reverses to our arms. It is silent in victory but vehement and dangerous in defeat.

Fourthly: And superior to all others, is the national prejudice and hatred toward all colored people of the country, a feeling which has done more to encourage the hopes of the rebels than all other powers beside.

Fifthly: An Abolitionist is an object of popular dislike. The guilty rebel who with broad blades and bloody hands seeks the life of the nation, is at this hour more acceptable to the Northern Democracy than an Abolitionist guilty of no crime. Whatever may be a man's abilities, virtue or service, the fact that he is an Abolitionist makes him an object of popular hate.

Upon these five strings the Democracy still have hopes of playing themselves into power, and not without reason. While our government has the meanness to ask Northern colored men to give up the comfort of home, endure untold hardships, peril health, limbs and life itself, in its defense, and then degrades them in the eyes of other soldiers, by offering them the paltry sum of seven dollars per month, and refuses to reward their valor with even the hope of promotion—the Democratic party may well enough presume upon the strength of popular prejudice for support.

While our Republican government at Washington makes color and not character the criterion of promotion in the Army and degrades colored commissioned officers at New Orleans below the rank to which even the rebel government had elevated them, I think we are in danger of a compromise with slavery.

> ***"Let but the little finger of slavery get back into this Union, and in one year you shall see its whole body again upon our backs."***

Our hopeful Republican friends tell me this is impossible—that the day of compromise with slavery is past. This may do for some men, but will not do for me.

The Northern people have always been remarkably confident of their own virtue. They are hopeful to the last. Twenty years ago we hoped that Texas could not be annexed; but if that could not be prevented we hoped that she would come in a free state. Thirteen years ago we were quite sure that no such abomination as the Fugitive Slave Bill could get itself on our national statute book; but when it got there we were equally sure that it never could be enforced. Four years ago we were sure that the slave states would not rebel, but if they did we were sure it would be a very short rebellion. I know that times have changed very rapidly, and that we have changed with them. Nevertheless, I know also we are the same old American people, and that what we have done once we may possibly do again. The leaven of compromise is among us. I repeat, while we have a Democratic party at the North trimming its sails to catch the Southern breeze in the next Presidential election, we are in danger of compromise. Tell me not of amnesties and oaths of allegiance. They are valueless in the presence of twenty hundred millions invested in human flesh. Let but the little finger of slavery get back into this Union, and in one year you shall see its whole body again upon our backs.

While a respectable colored man or woman can be kicked out of the commonest streetcar in New York where any white ruffian may ride unquestioned, we are in danger of a compromise with slavery. While the North is full of such papers as the New York *World, Express* and *Herald,* firing the nation's heart with hatred to Negroes and Abolitionists, we are in danger of a slaveholding peace. While the major part of antislavery profession is based upon devotion to the Union rather than hostility to slavery, there is danger of a slaveholding peace. Until we shall see the election of November next, and that it has resulted in the election of a sound antislavery man as President, we shall be in danger of a slaveholding compromise. Indeed, as long as slavery has any life in it anywhere in the country, we are in danger of such a compromise.

Then there is the danger arising from the impatience of the people on account of the prolongation of the war. I know the American people. They are an impulsive people, impatient of delay, clamorous for change, and often look for results out of all proportion to the means employed in attaining them.

You and I know that the mission of this war is national regeneration. We know and consider that a nation is not born in a day. We know that large bodies move slowly—and often seem to move thus when, could we perceive their actual velocity, we should be astonished at its greatness. A great battle lost or won is easily described, understood and appreciated, but the moral growth of a great nation requires reflection, as well as observation, to appreciate it. There are vast numbers of voters, who make no account of the moral growth of a great nation and who only look at the war as a calamity to be endured only so long as they have no power to arrest it. Now, this is just the sort of people whose votes may turn the scale against us in the last event.

Thoughts of this kind tell me that there never was a time when antislavery work was more needed than now. The day that shall see the rebels at our feet, their weapons flung away, will be the day of trial. We have need to prepare for that trial. We have long been saved a proslavery peace by the stubborn, unbending persistence of the rebels. Let them bend as they will bend, there will come the test of our sternest virtues.

I have now given, very briefly, some of the grounds of danger. A word as to the ground of hope. The best that can be offered is that we have made progress—vast and striking progress—within the last two years.

President Lincoln introduced his administration to the country as one which would faithfully catch, hold and return runaway slaves to their masters. He avowed his determination to protect and defend the slaveholder's right to plunder the black laborer of his hard earnings. Europe was assured by Mr. Seward that no slave should gain his freedom by this war. Both the President and the Secretary of State have made progress since then.

Our generals, at the beginning of the war, were horribly proslavery. They took to slave catching and slave killing like ducks to water. They are now very generally and very earnestly in favor of putting an end to slavery. Some of them, like Hunter and Butler, because they hate slavery on its own account, and others, because slavery is in arms against the government.

The rebellion has been a rapid educator. Congress was the first to respond to the instinctive judgment of the people, and fixed the broad brand of its reprobation upon slave hunting in shoulder straps. Then came very temperate talk about confiscation, which soon came to be pretty radical talk. Then came propositions for Border State, gradual, compensated, colonized emancipation. Then came the threat of a proclamation, and then came the Proclamation. Meanwhile the Negro had passed along from a loyal spade and pickax to a Springfield rifle.

Haiti and Liberia are recognized. Slavery is humbled in Maryland, threatened in Tennessee, stunned nearly to death in western Kentucky, and gradually melting away before our arms in the rebellious states.

The hour is one of hope as well as danger. But whatever may come to pass, one thing is clear: The principles involved in the contest, the necessities of both sections of the country, the obvious requirements of the age, and every suggestion of enlightened policy demand the utter extirpation of slavery from every foot of American soil, and the enfranchisement of the entire colored population of the country. Elsewhere we may find peace, but it will be a hollow and deceitful peace. Elsewhere we may find prosperity, but it will be a transient prosperity. Elsewhere we may find greatness and renown, but if these are based upon anything less substantial than justice they will vanish, for righteousness alone can permanently exalt a nation.

I end where I began—no war but an Abolition war; no peace but an Abolition peace; liberty for all, chains for none; the black man a soldier in war, a laborer in peace; a voter at the South as well as at the North; America his permanent home, and all Americans his fellow countrymen. Such, fellow citizens, is my idea of the mission of the war. If accomplished, our glory as a nation will be complete, our peace will flow like a river, and our foundations will be the everlasting rocks.

Although Reconstruction-era reforms had extended certain constitutional guarantees to blacks during the late 1860s and early 1870s, they became virtually meaningless following a series of Supreme Court challenges and newly-enacted state laws. By the 1880s, the call for change had been effectively silenced, and African Americans once again found themselves living under conditions comparable to those they had known as slaves—in some cases, even worse. On April 16, 1888, Douglass addressed a crowd that had gathered to celebrate the twenty-sixth

anniversary of emancipation in Washington, D.C. In a voice that often shook with emotion, he created a national sensation by angrily condemning the "so-called emancipation as a stupendous fraud." It ranks as one of the most impressive speeches he ever gave. It was published in the Washington National Republican *on April 17, 1888, and reprinted in* The Voice of Black America: Major Speeches by Negroes in the United States, 1797-1971 *(Simon & Schuster, 1972).*

Friends and fellow citizens: It has been my privilege to assist in several anniversary celebrations of the abolition of slavery in the District of Columbia, but I remember no occasion of this kind when I felt a deeper solicitude for the future welfare of our emancipated people than now.

The chief cause of anxiety is not in the condition of the colored people of the District of Columbia, though there is much that is wrong and unsatisfactory here, but the deplorable condition of the Negro in the Southern states. At no time since the abolition of slavery has there been more cause for alarm on this account than at this juncture in our history.

I have recently been in two of the Southern states—South Carolina and Georgia—and my impression from what I saw, heard and learned there is not favorable to my hopes for the race. I know this is a sad message to bring you on this twenty-sixth anniversary of freedom in the District of Columbia, but I know, too, that I have a duty to perform and that duty is to tell the truth, the whole truth, and nothing but the truth, and I should be unworthy to stand here, unworthy of the confidence of the colored people of this country, if I should from any considerations of policy withhold any fact or feature of the condition of the freedmen which the people of this country ought to know.

The temptation on anniversary occasions like this is to prophesy smooth things, to be joyful and glad, to indulge in the illusions of hope—to bring glad tidings on our tongues, and words of peace reveal. But while I know it is always easier to be the bearer of glad tidings than sad ones, while I know that hope is a powerful motive to exertion and high endeavor, while I know that people generally would rather look upon the bright side of their condition than to know the worst; there comes a time when it is best that the worst should be made known, and in my judgment that time, in respect to the condition of the colored people of the South, is now. There are times when neither hope nor fear should be allowed to control our speech. Cry aloud and spare not, is the word of wisdom as well as of Scripture. "Ye shall know the truth, and the truth shall make you free," applies to the body not less than the soul, to this world not less than the world to come. Outside the truth there is no solid foundation for any of us, and I assume that you who have invited me to speak, and you who have come to hear me speak, expect me to speak the truth as I understand the truth.

The truth at which we should get on this occasion respects the precise relation subsisting between the white and colored people of the South, or, in other words, between the colored people and the old master class of the South. We have need to know this and to take it to heart.

It is well said that "a people may lose its liberty in a day and not miss it in half a century," and that "the price of liberty is eternal vigilance." In my judgment, with my knowledge of what has already taken place in the South, these wise and wide-awake sentiments were never more apt and timely than now.

I have assisted in fighting one battle for the abolition of slavery, and the American people have shed their blood in defense of the Union and the Constitution, and neither I nor they should wish to fight this battle over again—and in order that we may not, we should look the facts in the face today and, if possible, nip the evil in the bud.

I have no taste for the role of an alarmist. If my wishes could be allowed to dictate my speech I would tell you something quite the reverse of what I now intend. I would tell you that everything is lovely with the Negro in the South; I would tell you that the rights of the Negro are respected, and that he has no wrongs to redress; I would tell you that he is honestly paid for his labor; that he is secure in his liberty; that he is tried by a jury of his peers when accused of crime; that he is no longer subject to lynch law; that he has freedom of speech; that the gates of knowledge are open to him; that he goes to the ballot box unmolested; that his vote is duly counted and given its proper weight in determining result; I would tell you that he is making splendid progress in the acquisition of knowledge, wealth and influence; I would tell you that his bitterest enemies have become his warmest friends; that the desire to make him a slave no longer exists anywhere in the South; that the Democratic party is a better friend to him than the Republican party, and that each party is competing with the other to see which can do the most to make his liberty a blessing to himself and to the country and the world. But in telling you all this I should be telling you what is absolutely false, and what you know to be false, and the only thing which would save such a story from being a lie would be its utter inability to deceive.

What is the condition of the Negro at the South at this moment? Let us look at it both in the light of facts and in the light of reason. To understand it we must consult nature as well as circumstances, the past as well as the present. No fact is more obvious than the fact that there is a perpetual tendency of power to encroach upon weakness, and of the crafty to take advantage of the simple. This is as natural as for smoke to ascend or water to run down. The love of power is one of the strongest traits in the Anglo-Saxon race. This love of power common to the white race has been nursed and strengthened at the South by slavery: accustomed during two hundred years to the unlimited possession and exercise of irresponsible power, the love of it has become stronger by habit. To assume that this feeling of pride and power has died out and disappeared from the South is to assume a miracle. Any man who tells you that it has died out or has ceased to be exercised and made effective, tells you that which is untrue and in the nature of things could not be true. Not only is the love of power there, but a talent for its exercise has been fully developed. This talent makes the old master class of the South not only the masters of the Negro, but the masters of Congress and, if not checked, will make them the masters of the nation.

It was something more than an empty boast in the old times, when it was said that one slave master was equal to three Northern men. Though this did not turn out to be true on the battlefield, it does seem to be true in the councils of the nation. In sight of all the nation these ambitious men of the South have dared to take possession of the government which they, with broad blades and bloody hands, sought to destroy; in sight of all the nation they have disregarded and trampled upon the Constitution, and organized parties on sectional lines. From the ramparts of the Solid South, with their 153 electoral votes in the Electoral College, they have dared to defy the nation to put a Republican in the Presidential chair for the next four years, as they once threatened the nation with civil war if it elected Abraham Lincoln. With this grip on the Presidential chair, with the House of Representatives in their hands, with the Supreme Court deciding every question in favor of the states, as against the powers of the federal government, denying to the government the right to protect the elective franchise of its own citizens, they may well feel themselves masters, not only of their former slaves, but of the whole situation. With these facts before us, tell me not that the Negro is safe in the possession of his liberty. Tell me not that power will not assert itself. Tell me not that they who despise the Constitution they have sworn to support will respect the rights of the Negro, whom they already despise. Tell me not that men who thus break faith with God will be scrupulous in keeping faith with the poor Negro laborer of the South. Tell me not that a people who have lived by the sweat of other men's faces, and thought themselves Christian gentlemen while doing it, will feel themselves bound by principles of justice to their former victims in their weakness. Such a pretense in face of facts is shameful, shocking and sickening. Yet there are men at the North who believe all this.

Well may it be said that Americans have no memories. We look over the House of Representatives and see the Solid South enthroned there. We listen with calmness to eulogies of the South and of the traitors, and forget Andersonville. We look over the Senate and see the Senator from South Carolina, and we forget Hamburg. We see Robert Smalls cheated out of his seat in Congress, and forget the *Planter,* and the service rendered by the colored troops in the late war for the Union.

Well, the nation may forget; it may shut its eyes to the past and frown upon any who may do otherwise, but the colored people of this country are bound to keep fresh a memory of the past till justice shall be done them in the present. When this shall be done we shall as readily as any other part of our respected citizens plead for an act of oblivion.

We are often confronted of late in the press and on the platform with the discouraging statement that the problem of the Negro as a free man and a citizen is not yet solved; that since his emancipation he has disappointed the best hopes of his friends and fulfilled the worst predictions of his enemies, and that he has shown himself unfit for the position assigned him by the mistaken statesmanship of the nation. It is said that physically, morally, socially and religiously he is in a condition vastly more deplorable than was his condition as a slave; that he has not proved himself so good a master to himself as his old master was to him; that he is gradually, but surely, sinking below the point of industry, good manners and civilization to which he attained in a state of slavery; that his industry is fitful; that his economy is wasteful; that his honesty is deceitful; that his morals are impure; that his domestic life is beastly; that his religion is fetishism, and his worship is simply emotional; and that, in a word, he is falling into a state of barbarism.

> *"I here and now denounce [the] so-called emancipation as a stupendous fraud. . . ."*

Such is the distressing description of the emancipated Negro as drawn by his enemies and as it is found reported in the journals of the South. Unhappily, however, it is a description not confined to the South. It has gone forth to the North. It has crossed the ocean; I met with it in Europe. And it has gone as far as the wings of the press and the power of speech can carry it. There is no measuring the injury inflicted upon the Negro by it. It cools our friends, heats our enemies, and turns away from us much of the sympathy and aid which we need and deserve to receive at the hands of our fellow men.

But now comes the question, Is this description of the emancipated Negro true? In answer to this question I must say, Yes and no. It is not true in all its lines and specifications and to the full extent of the ground it covers, but it certainly is true in many of its important features, and there is no race under heaven of which the same would not be equally true with the same antecedents and the same treatment which the Negro is receiving at the hands of this nation and the old master class, to which the Negro is still a subject.

I admit that the Negro, and especially the plantation Negro, the tiller of the soil, has made little progress from barbarism to civilization, and that he is in a deplorable condition since his emancipation. That he is worse off, in many respects, than when he was a slave, I am compelled to admit, but I contend that the fault is not his, but that of his heartless accusers. He is the victim of a cunningly devised swindle, one which paralyzes his energies, suppresses his ambition, and blasts all his hopes; and though he is nominally free he is actually a slave. I here and now denounce his so-called emancipation as a stupendous fraud—a fraud upon him, a fraud upon the world. It was not so meant by Abraham Lincoln; it was not so meant by the Republican party; but whether so meant or not, it is practically a lie, keeping the word of promise to the ear and breaking it to the heart.

Do you ask me why the Negro of the plantation has made so little progress, why his cupboard is empty, why he flutters in rags, why his children run naked, and why his wife hides herself behind the hut when a stranger is passing? I will tell you. It is because he is systematically and universally cheated out of his hard earnings. The same class that once extorted his labor under the lash now gets his labor by a mean, sneaking, and fraudulent device. That device is a trucking system which never permits him to see or to save a dollar of his hard earnings. He struggles and struggles, but, like a man in a morass, the more he struggles the deeper he sinks. The highest wages paid him is eight dollars a month, and this he receives only in orders on the store, which, in many cases, is owned by his employer. The scrip has purchasing power on that one store, and that one only. A blind man can see that the laborer is by this arrangement bound hand and foot, and is completely in the power of his employer. He can charge the poor fellow what he pleases and give what kind of goods he pleases, and he does both. His victim cannot go to another store and buy, and this the storekeeper knows. The only security the wretched Negro has under this arrangement is the conscience of the storekeeper—a conscience educated in the school of slavery, where the idea prevailed in theory and practice that the Negro had no rights which white men were bound to respect, an arrangement in which everything in the way of food or clothing, whether tainted meat or damaged cloth, is deemed good enough for the Negro. For these he is often made to pay a double price.

But this is not all, or the worst result of the system. It puts it out of the power of the Negro to save anything of what he earns. If a man gets an honest dollar for his day's work, he has a motive for laying it by and saving it for future emergency. It will be as good for use in the future and perhaps better a year hence than now, but this miserable scrip has in no sense the quality of a dollar. It is only good at one store and for a limited period. Thus the man who has it is tempted to get rid of it as soon as possible. It may be out of date before he knows it, or the storekeeper may move away and it may be left worthless on his hands.

But this is not the only evil involved in this satanic arrangement. It promotes dishonesty. The Negro sees himself paid but limited wages—far too limited to support himself and family, and that in worthless scrip—and he is tempted to fight the devil with fire. Finding himself systematically robbed he goes to stealing and as a result finds his liberty—such as it is—taken from him, and himself put to work for a master in a chain gang, and he comes out, if he ever gets out, a ruined man.

Every Northern man who visits the old master class, the landowners and landlords of the South, is told by the old slaveholders with a great show of virtue that they are glad that they are rid of slavery and would not have the slave system back if they could; that they are better off than they ever were before, and much more of the same tenor. Thus Northern men come home duped and go on a mission of duping others by telling the same pleasing story.

There are very good reasons why these people would not have slavery back if they could—reasons far more creditable to their cunning than to their conscience. With slavery they had some care and responsibility for the physical well-being of their slaves. Now they have as firm a grip on the freedman's labor as when he was a slave and without any burden of caring for his children or himself. The whole arrangement is stamped with fraud and is supported by hypocrisy, and I here and now, on this Emancipation Day: denounce it as a villainous swindle, and invoke the press, the pulpit and the lawmaker to assist in exposing it and blotting it out forever.

We denounce the imposition upon the working classes of England, and we do well, but in England this trucking system is abolished by law. It is a penal offense there, and it should be made so here. It should be made a crime to pay any man for his honest labor in any other than honest money. Until this is done in the Southern states the laborer of the South will be ground to the earth, and progress with him will be impossible. It is the duty of the Negro press to take up the subject. The Negro, where he may have a vote, should vote for no man who is not in favor of making this scrip and truck system unlawful.

I come now to another feature of Southern policy which bears hard and heavily on the Negro laborer and land renter. It is found in the landlord-and-tenant laws. I will read an extract to you from these laws that you may see how completely and rigidly the rights of the landlord are guarded and how entirely the tenant is in the clutches of the landlord:

REVISED CODE OF MISSISSIPPI

SEC. 1301. Every lessor of land shall have a lien on all the agricultural products of the leased premises, however and by whomsoever produced, to secure the payment of the rent and the market value of all advances made by him to his tenant for supplies for the tenant and others for whom he may contract.

SEC. 1304. When any landlord or lessor shall have just cause to suspect and shall verily believe that his tenant will remove his effects from the leased premises to any other place within or without the county before the rent or claims for supplies will fall due, so that no distress can be made, such landlord or lessor on making oath thereof, and of the amount the tenant is to pay, and at what time the same will fall due, and giving a bond as required in the preceding section, may, in like manner obtain an attachment against the goods and chattels of such tenant, and the officers making the distress shall give notice thereof and advertise the property distrained for sale, in the manner directed in the last preceding section, and if such tenant shall not, before the time appointed for such sale, give bond with sufficient security in double the amount of the rent, or other demand payable to the plaintiff, conditioned for the payment of said rent or other thing at the time it shall be due, with all cost, the goods distrained, or so much thereof as shall be necessary, shall be sold by the said officer at public sale to the highest bidder for cash, and out of the proceeds of the sale he shall pay to the plaintiff the amount due him, deducting interest for the time until the same shall become payable.

SEC. 1361. Said lien shall exist by virtue of the relation of the parties as employer and employee, and without any writing or recording.

SEC. 1362. Provides that any person who aids or assists in removing anything subject to these liens; without the consent of the landlord, shall, upon conviction, be punished by a fine of not more than $500, and be imprisoned in the county jail not more than six months, or by either such fine and imprisonment.

VOORHEE'S REVISED LAWS OF LOUISIANA 2D

SEC. 2165. Article 287 shall be so amended that a lessor may obtain a writ of provisional seizure even before the rent is due, and it shall be sufficient to entitle the lessor to the writ to swear to the amount which he claims, whether due or not due, and that he has good reasons to believe that the lessee will remove the furniture or property upon which he has a lien or privilege out of the premises, and that he may be, therefore, deprived of his lien.

LAWS OF FLORIDA—
M'CLELLAN'S DIGEST

SEC. I, chapter 137. All claims for rent shall be a lien on agricultural products raised on the land rented, and shall be superior to all other liens and claims, though of older date, and also a superior lien on all other property of the lessee or his sublessee, or assigns usually kept on the premises, over any lien acquired subsequently to such property having been bought on the premises leased.

CODE OF ALABAMA

SEC. 3055, chapter 6. Lien continues and attaches to crop of succeeding years. When the tenant fails to pay any part of such rent or advances, and continues his tenancy under the same landlord for the next succeeding year for which the original lien for advances, if any remain unpaid, shall continue on the articles advanced or property purchased with money advanced or obtained by barter in exchange for articles advanced, and for which a lien shall also attach to the crop of such succeeding year.

You have thus seen a specimen, and a fair specimen, of the landlord-and-tenant laws of several of the old slave states; you have thus seen how scrupulously and rigidly the rights of the landlords are guarded and protected by these laws; you have thus seen how completely the tenant is put at the mercy of the landlord; you have thus seen the bias, the motive, and intention of the legislators by whom these laws have been enacted, and by whom they have been administered; and now you are only to remember the sentiment in regard to the Negro, peculiar to the people of the South, and the character of the people against whom these laws are to be enforced, and the fact that no people are better than their laws, to have a perfectly just view of the whole situation.

To my mind these landlord-and-tenant laws are a disgrace and a scandal to American civilization. A more skillfully contrived device than these laws to crush out all aspiration, all hope of progress in the landless Negro could not well be devised. They sound to me like the grating hinges of a slave prison. They read like the inhuman bond of Shylock, stipulating for his pound of flesh. They environ the helpless Negro like the devilfish of Victor Hugo, and draw the blood from every pore. He may writhe and twist, and strain every muscle, but he is held and firmly bound in a strong, remorseless and deadly grasp, a grasp from which only death can free him. Floods may rise, droughts may scorch, the elements may destroy his crops, famine may come, but whatever else may happen, the greedy landlord must have from his tenant the uttermost farthing. Like the den of the lion, all toes in its path turn inward.

The case is aggravated when you think of the illiteracy and ignorance of the people who sign land leases. They are ignorant of the terms of the contract, ignorant of the requirements of the law, and are thus absolutely in the power of the landholder.

You have heard much, read much, and thought much of the flagrant injustice, the monstrous cruelty and oppression inflicted on the tenant class in Ireland. I have no disposition to underrate the hardships of that class. On the contrary, I deplore them. But knowing them as I do and deploring them as I do, I declare to you that the condition of the Irish tenant is merciful, tender and just, as compared with the American freedman. There are thousands in Ireland today who fix the price of their own rent, and thousands more for whom the government itself measures the amount of rent to be paid, not by the greed of the landlord, but by the actual value of the land and its productions, and by the ability of the tenant to pay.

But how is it with us? The tenant is left in the clutches of the landlord. No third party intervenes between the greed and power of one and the helplessness of the other. The landholder imposes his price, exacts his conditions, and the landless Negro must comply or starve. It is impossible to conceive of conditions more unfavorable to the welfare and prosperity of the laborer. It is often said that the law is merciful, but there is no mercy in this law.

Now let us sum up some of the points in the situation of the freedman. You will have seen how he is paid for his labor, how a full-grown man gets only eight dollars a month for his labor, out of which he has to feed, clothe and educate his children. You have seen how even this sum is reduced by the infamous truck system of payment. You have seen how easily he may be charged with one third more than the value of the goods that he buys. You have seen how easily he may be compelled to receive the poorest commodities at the highest prices. You have seen how he is never allowed to see or handle a dollar. You have seen how impossible it is for him to accumulate money or property. You have seen how completely he is chained to the locality in which he lives. You have seen, therefore, that having no money, he cannot travel or go anywhere to better his condition. You have seen by these laws that even on the premises which he rents he can own nothing, possess nothing. You have seen that he cannot sell a sheep, or a pig, or even a chicken without the consent of the landlord, whose claim to all he has is superior and paramount to all other claims whatsoever. You have seen all this and more, and I ask, in view of it all, How, in the name of human reason, could the Negro be expected to rise higher in the scale of morals, manner, religion and civilization than he has done during the twenty years of his freedom. Shame, eternal shame, on those writers and speakers who taunt, denounce and disparage the Negro because he is today found in poverty, rags and wretchedness.

But again, let us see what are the relations subsisting between the Negro and the state and national governments—what support, what assistance he has received from either of them. Take his relation to the national government and we shall find him a deserted, a defrauded, a swindled, and an outcast man—in law free, in fact a slave; in law a citizen, in fact an alien; in law a voter, in fact, a disfranchised man. In law, his color is no crime; in fact, his color exposes him to be treated as a criminal. Toward him every attribute of a just government is contradicted. For him, it is not a government of the people, by the people, and for the people. Toward him, it abandons the beneficent character of a government, and all that gives a government the right to exist. The true object for which governments are ordained among men is to protect the weak against the encroachments of the strong, to hold its strong arm of justice over all the civil relations of its citizens and to see that all have an equal chance in the race of life. Now, in the case of the Negro citizen, our national government does precisely the reverse of all this. Instead of protecting the weak against the encroachments of the strong, it tacitly protects the strong in its encroachments upon the weak. When the colored citizens of the South point to the fourteenth and fifteenth amendments of the Constitution for the protection of their civil and political rights, the Supreme Court of the United States turns them out of court and tells them they must look for justice at the hands of the states, well knowing that those states are, in effect, the very parties that deny them justice. Thus is the Negro citizen swindled. The government professes to give him citizenship and silently permits him to be divested of every attribute of citizenship. It demands allegiance, but denies protection. It taxes him as a citizen in peace, and compels him to bear arms and meet bullets in war. It imposes upon him all the burdens of citizenship and withholds from him all its benefits.

I know it is said that the general government is a government of limited powers. It was also once said that the national government could not coerce a state and it is generally said that this and that public measure is unconstitutional. But whenever an administration has had the will to do anything, it has generally found Constitutional power to do it. If the general government had the power to make black men citizens, it has the power to protect them in that citizenship. If it had the right to make them voters it has the right to protect them in the exercise of the elective franchise. If it has this right, and refuses to exercise it, it is a traitor to the citizen. If it has not this right, it is destitute of the fundamental quality of a government and ought to be hissed and hurried out of the sisterhood of government, a usurper, a sham, a delusion and a snare.

> *"How could the Negro be expected to rise higher in the scale of morals, manner, religion and civilization than he has done during the twenty years of his freedom[?]"*

On the other hand, if the fault is not in the structure of the government, but in the treachery and indifference of those who administer it, the American people owe it to themselves, owe it to the world, and to the Negro, to sweep from place and power those who are thus derelict in the discharge of their place in the government who will not enforce the Constitutional right of every class of American citizen.

I am a Republican. I believe in the Republican party. My political hopes for the future of the colored people are enforced in the character and composition, in the wisdom and justice, in the courage and fidelity of the Republican party. I am unable to see how any honest and intelligent colored man can be a Democrat or play fast and loose between the two parties. But while I am a Republican and believe in the party, I dare to tell that party the truth. In my judgment it can no longer repose on the history of its grand and magnificent achievements. It must not only stand abreast with the times, but must create the times. Its power and greatness consisted in this at the beginning. It was in advance of the times and made the times when it abolished the slave trade between the states, when it emancipated the slaves of the District of Columbia, when it stemmed the bloody tide of disunion, when it abolished slavery in all the states, when it made the Negro a soldier and a citizen, when it conceded to him the elective franchise; and now, in my judgment, the strength, success and glory of the Republican party will be found in its holding this advanced position. It must not stand still or take any step backward. Its mission is to lead, not to follow; to make circumstances, not to be made by them. It is held and firmly bound by every sentiment of justice and honor to make a living fact out of the dead letter of the Constitutional amendments. It must make the path of the black citizen to the ballot box as safe and smooth as that of the white citizen. It must make it impossible for a man like James Russell Lowell to say he sees no difference between the Democratic party and the Republican party. If it fails to do all this, I for one shall welcome the bolt which shall scatter it into a thousand fragments.

The supreme movement in the life of the Republican party is at hand. The question, to be or not to be, will be decided at Chicago, and I reverently trust in God that it may be decided rightly. If the platform it shall adopt shall be in accordance with its earlier antecedents; if the party shall have the courage in its maturity which it possessed and displayed in its infancy; if it shall express its determination to vindicate the honor and integrity of the Republic by stamping out the fraud, injustice and violence which make elections in the South a disgrace and scandal to the Republic, and place a man on that platform with a clear head, a clean hand and a heroic heart, the country will triumphantly elect him. If it, however, should fail to elect him, we shall have done our duty and shall still have under us a grand party of the future, certain of success.

I do not forget that there are other great interests beside the Negro to be thought of. The civil service is a great interest, protection to American industry is a great interest, the proper management of our finances so as to promote the business and prosperity of the country is a great interest; but the national honor—the redemption of our national pledge to the freedmen, the supremacy of the Constitution in the fullness of its spirit and in the completeness of its letter over all the states of the Union alike—is an incomparably greater interest than all others. It touches the soul of the nation, which against all things else should be preserved. Should all be lost but this, the nation would be like Chicago after the fire—more prosperous and beautiful than ever. But what I ask of the Republican party requires no sacrifice or postponement of the material interest of the country. I simply say to the Republican party: Those things ye ought to have done and not to have left the others undone, and the present is the time to enforce this lesson.

The time has come for a new departure as to the kind of man who is to be the standard-bearer of the Republican party. Events are our instructors. We have had enough of names, we now want things. We have had enough of good feeling, enough of shaking hands over the bloody chasm, enough of conciliation, enough of laudation of the bravery of our Southern brethren. We tried all that with President Hayes, of the purity of whose motives I have no shadow of doubt. His mistake was that he confided in the honor of the Confederates, who were without honor. He supposed that if left to themselves and thrown upon their honor they would obey the Constitution they had sworn to support and treat the colored citizens with justice and fairness at the ballot box. Time has proved the reverse of all this, and this fact should cure the Republican party of adopting in its platform any such soft policy or any such candidate. Let us have a candidate this time of pronounced opinions and, above all, a backbone....

There has been no show of federal power in

the borders of the South for a dozen years. Its people have been left to themselves. Northern men have even refrained from going among them in election times to discuss the claims of public men, or the wisdom of public measures. They have had the field all to themselves, and we all now know just what has come of it, and the eyes of the leaders of the Republican party are, I trust, wide open. Mr. James G. Blaine [unsuccessful Republican presidential candidate in 1884], after, as well as before, he failed of his election, pointed out the evil which now besets us as a party and a nation. Senator John Sherman knows full well that the Solid South must be broken, that the colored citizen must not be cheated out of his vote any longer and that the Constitution must be obeyed in all parts of the country alike; that individual states are great, but that the United States are greater. He has said the right word, and said it calmly but firmly, in the face of the South itself, and I thank him and honor him for it. I am naming no candidate for the presidency. Any one of the dozen statesmen whose names are in the air and many whose names are not, would suit me and gain my best word and vote. There is one who has not been named and not likely to be named, who would suit me and who would fulfill the supreme demand of the hour, and that man is a Southern man. I refer to the Honorable John M. Harlan, Justice of the Supreme Court of the United States, who, true to his convictions, stood by the plain intention of the Fourteenth Amendment of the Constitution of the United States in opposition to all his brothers on the bench. The man who could do that in the circumstances in which he was placed, if made President of the United States, could be depended upon in any emergency to do the right thing.

But, as I have said, I am not naming candidates. The candidate of the Republican party will, in all the likelihoods of the case, be my candidate. I am no partisan. I have no ambition to be the first to name any man or make any man obliged to me for naming him for the high office of President. Other men may do this, and I have no disposition to find fault with them for doing it. If, however, John A. Logan [former U.S. senator from Illinois] were living I might name him. I am sure he would not allow himself to be trifled with or allow the Constitution to be defied or trampled in the dust. I have faith also, in Roscoe Conkling [U.S. senator from New York], whose dangerous illness we all deplore and whose recovery we profoundly and anxiously desire. With such a man in the Presidential chair the red shirt and rifle, horseback and tissue-ballot plan of South Carolina and the Mississippi bulldozing plan would receive no encouragement.

I am, however, not here to name men. My mission now, as all along during nearly fifty years, is to plead the cause of the dumb millions of our countrymen against injustice, oppression, meanness and cruelty, and to hasten the day when the principles of liberty and humanity expressed in the Declaration of Independence and the Constitution of the United States shall be the law and the practice of every section, and of all the people of this great country without regard to race, sex, color or religion.

SOURCES

Blassingame, John W., editor, *The Frederick Douglass Papers: Series One—Speeches, Debates, and Interviews,* Yale University Press, Volume 1: *1841-46,* 1979, Volume 2: *1847-54,* 1982, Volume 3: *1855-63,* 1985, Volume 4: *1874-80,* 1991.

Bontemps, Arna, *Free at Last: The Life of Frederick Douglass,* Dodd, Mead, 1971.

Douglass, Frederick, *My Bondage and My Freedom* (reprint), University of Illinois Press, 1987.

Foner, Philip S., editor, *The Voice of Black America: Major Speeches by Negroes in the United States, 1797-1971,* Simon & Schuster, 1972.

Foner, Philip S., *The Life and Writings of Frederick Douglass,* five volumes, International Publishers Company, 1975.

Hill, Roy L., *Rhetoric of Racial Revolt,* Golden Bell Press, 1964.

Huggins, Nathan Irvin, *Slave and Citizen: The Life of Frederick Douglass,* Little, Brown, 1980.

Martin, Waldo E., Jr., *The Mind of Frederick Douglass,* University of North Carolina Press, 1984.

O'Neill, Daniel J., editor, *Speeches by Black Americans,* Dickenson, 1971.

Meltzer, Milton, editor, *The Black Americans: A History in Their Own Words, 1619-1983,* Crowell, 1984.

Smith, Arthur L., *Rhetoric of Black Revolution,* Allyn & Bacon, 1969.

Smith, Arthur L., and Stephen Robb, editors, *The Voice of Black Rhetoric: Selections,* Allyn & Bacon, 1971.

Rita Dove

1952–

African American poet

On May 18, 1993, Pulitzer Prize-winning poet Rita Dove became the first black American woman and the youngest person ever to be named United States poet laureate. Because this honor is usually reserved for those in the twilight of their careers, her selection by the Librarian of Congress came as a surprise to most people. But during her tenure, the youthful and energetic Dove vowed to inject new vitality into the position, driven by what she described as a desire to end the perception that poetry "exist[s] in a parallel universe outside daily life in America."

Although Dove, a native of Akron, Ohio, had been composing poetry, plays, and stories since childhood, she intended to become a lawyer when she first entered Miami University. But almost immediately she realized that she lacked both the aptitude and the desire to excel in that profession. Instead, she found herself drawn to creative writing, and by her junior year she had made up her mind to become a poet. After graduating from Miami with honors in 1973, Dove spent time in Germany as a Fulbright scholar before continuing her course work at the University of Iowa Writers' Workshop, from which she received her master's degree in creative writing in 1977. She then divided her time between writing, traveling, and teaching, most recently (since 1989) as a professor in the English department at the University of Virginia in Charlottesville.

Dove's goal as a poet has been to take a commonplace incident or ordinary person and, through the magic of verse, give them a beauty and significance not readily apparent from a mere recitation of the facts at hand. These events and characters around which she constructs her poems are often drawn from her own life or from history and legend. She has been very successful at her craft, earning praise from critics and winning a number of awards, including the 1987 Pulitzer Prize for her third poetry collection, Thomas and Beulah. *Very loosely based on the lives of her maternal grandparents,* Thomas and Beulah *consists of short poems that skillfully combine biography and social history spanning a period of nearly fifty years. Dove is also the author of several other volumes of poetry, a book of short stories* (Fifth Sunday), *a novel* (Through the Ivory Gate), *and a verse drama* (The Darker Face of the Earth).

As poet laureate—a largely ceremonial role—Dove was charged with fostering the appreciation of poetry through various programs of the Library of Congress. Eager to capitalize on the burgeoning public interest in verse following Maya Angelou's creation of a special poem to commemorate the inauguration of President Bill Clinton, she launched an ambitious schedule of readings that attracted audiences with innovative and unusual presentations combining poetry with other media such as music and photography. She also "visited" classrooms across the nation via interactive video to stimulate interest in poetry among children and even lobbied television executives about airing public service announcements consisting of a brief poem and some animation.

On March 17, 1994, Dove shared her thoughts on poetry and the poet laureate position with members of the National Press Club in Washington, D.C. Dove furnished a transcription of her remarks.

Thank you, Mr. President. Ladies and gentlemen, friends and colleagues: It's a great pleasure for me—nearly a "perverse pleasure"—to be here today, a poet standing before the distinguished members of the Fourth Estate. The media coverage since my appointment has been tremendous; it's exhilarating to think that poetry has become news.

As poet laureate I am continually being asked to clarify my position—to list my duties, to elaborate on my plans for promoting the arts. I am usually asked to define poetry as well. Rarely does a journalist ask about poems themselves. In fact, one television reporter confessed afterwards he had been so nervous about our interview that he had solicited advice from his colleagues before venturing over to the Poetry Room at the Library of Congress. The consensus in his office was: "Ask her how she started writing and who her favorite poets are . . . but don't ask her about poems!" So what I want to do today, in the manner of St. Patrick, who charmed the snakes out of Ireland, is to chase some of the bugaboos about poetry out of this room and, hopefully, from the hearts of those on the receiving end of the radio waves traversing America.

Rita Dove

"Poetry—merely whispering its name frightens it away," said Jean Cocteau. Today, in our country, we could change that remark to: Poetry—merely whispering its name frightens everyone away. It can send grown men scurrying to the other end of the reception hall or plunge a pleasant airplane conversation into thunderous silence. There are a thousand and one myths about artists in general, and poets in particular: poets are eccentric, poets are not quite of this world; poets are blessed with imagination that the rest of the population can never hope to approach, poets lead wild—or at the very least, wildly disorganized—lives, and enjoy saying outrageous things in polite company. The prevailing notions our society harbors about the creative arts makes it difficult for all artists, and especially that lofty breed of poets, to be taken seriously, or even to be taken into account.

There was a time when I would hide behind less than the whole truth when asked what I "did" in life. As long as I was a student, it was easy: I was an English major, then, a graduate student. After graduation, I satisfied the curiosity of casual acquaintances by timidly saying: I'm working on a book. Later, after I'd begun to teach at a university, I shied away from the easy partial truth of my official designation; although I was an English professor, it sounded fraudulent to me, for I had nothing to do with the brilliant second-guessing of dead writers that one associates with English professors, instead I was myself a poet and very much alive, thank you. So I fudged by slurring all my occupations together: I'm a writer and teach creative writing. Then about twelve years ago, a young woman started up a conversation at a bus stop and posed the inevitable question. I hedged, saying, "I write," to which she replied cheerfully, "Oh, I do calligraphy, too!" That day I made a vow to tell the uncompromised truth. So now when asked what I do for a living, I answer: I'm a poet; I write poetry—and endure one of two reactions caused by my confession: either they grab my sleeve and regale me with the story of great-aunt Maud whose delightful verses brought such joy to family festivities and yet, as hard as she tried, poor soul, could never get her wonderful manuscript published. Then they might look at me as if I, as a published poet, was part of the conspiracy of the modern language mafia who had deprived their great-aunt Maud of her deserved recognition as a master wordsmith in the Mother Goose tradition. Or my confession might cause confusion, embarrassment, a kind of bumbling discomfort. The more damaging of the two notions is this one—that poetry is hermetic, cerebral stuff, impossible for mere mortals to comprehend.

So where does poetry reside? Where does it begin? When the painter Edgar Degas claimed to be full of ideas for poems, his friend Mallarmé said, "My dear Degas, poems are not made out of ideas; they're made out of *words.*" But Emerson reminds us: "Words are also actions, and actions are a kind of words." Although it turns upon the action of words, poetry roots in the acts of life. It springs from inner sources that are at the very core of our humanness—it resides in the interstices between the world and the inarticulated emotions circumscribing our souls.

Instead of sliding deeper into philosophical discourse, I'd like to offer an example from my own work.

My third poetry book, *Thomas and Beulah,* is based on the lives of my maternal grandparents, but it rapidly became an amalgam of biographical fact, imagination, and creative scholarship. *Thomas and Beulah* began, though, with a real event—one that was insignificant in the grand context of history but indispensable within the confines of personal biography (an incident time had condensed into an anecdote).

My grandfather died when I was thirteen years old. The family took turns keeping Grandma company; since I wasn't old enough to date, I was the prefect candidate for the weekend slot. One Saturday morning at breakfast, Grandma fixed me the one permitted cup of sweetened coffee, sat down, and related an incident from my grandfather's life before he met her, just as he must have told it to her countless times.

In his late teens, my grandfather worked the Mississippi riverboats as part of a song-and-dance duo. Late one night on the boat, my grandfather dared his mandolin-playing friend to swim across the river to an island where a chestnut tree was growing. The friend dove into the Mississippi and headed for the tree—when the island sank and the maelstrom sucked him down.

This "true story," as you can see, was pretty unbelievable. Chestnut trees in the middle of the Mississippi—okay. But islands that sink? As my daughter would say: Come on; get real.

My grandmother, however, stuck to her story, with an obstinance that made the anecdote undeniable. Many years later, I recognized it as the crucial point in my grandfather's life—that moment when Fate steps in and your life takes a sickening ninety-degree-turn and plops you down facing the wilderness. We've all had those moments, and the events surrounding it, recalled later, seem surreal, with the slow-motion over-magnification of anything worried over, obsessed over time and time again. Here's the poem:

THE EVENT

Ever since they'd left the Tennessee ridge
with nothing to boast of
but good looks and a mandolin,

the two Negroes leaning
on the rail of a riverboat
were inseparable: Lem plucked

to Thomas's silver falsetto.
But the night was hot and they
were drunk.
They spat where the wheel

churned mud and moonlight,
they called to the tarantulas
down among the bananas

to come out and dance.
You're so fine and mighty; let's see
what you can do, *said Thomas, pointing*

to a tree-capped island.
Lem stripped, spoke easy: Them's
chestnuts,
I believe. *Dove*

quick as a gasp. Thomas, dry
on deck, saw the green crown shake
as the island slipped
under, dissolved
in the thickening stream.
At his feet,

a stinking circle of rags,
a half-shell mandolin.
Where the wheel turned the water

gently shirred.

Now this story was my own; it haunted me. I wanted to know how to go on after that sickening turn. I asked myself: What are you going to do now, Rita?, and the answer came like an echo: Pick up the mandolin!

I don't know if my grandfather picked up his friend's mandolin or not. (Actually, my mother corrected me when I "interviewed" her for "material" for *Thomas and Beulah*—my grandfather had played the guitar when he was young, not mandolin. I had remembered incorrectly. Or did I? As Stravinsky said: "One lives by memory . . . and not by truth.") Well, my Thomas picks up that mandolin and the scraps of his partner's life, and he learns his double-stringed song. He gives up the riverboat life, continues north, and finally settles down in Akron, Ohio, the rubber-baron city built on the banks of the crooked Cuyahoga River, which was then forced underground to service man's factories, man's dreams of industry and wealth. Today that river, rich with chemicals and waste products, has burned more than once, inspiring that Randy Newman song which goes:

Now the Lord can make you tumble
The Lord can make you turn;
The Lord can make you overflow,
But the Lord can't make you burn.

When Thomas lands in Akron in 1921, however, it's still a city "on the up and up," the American Dream in full flower beneath the gritty stench of vulcanized rubber and the ever-present time clock. And there I got stuck. For what did I know about this town in 1921? How could I begin to follow Thomas through those streets if I didn't know what they looked like—how many black people he would see in passing, what a black working-class man could or couldn't do in 1921, what his hopes for the future might have been grounded on?

So I went to the library and amassed notes on working conditions in the factories, census reports, demographical charts. I learned how rubber is vulcanized and the times of the factory shifts; how many white workers from West Virginia were recruited in proportion to black southerners. I learned that the Goodyear Aerospace airdock was, around 1930, the largest structure of its time without interior supports, and that it was so vast, it had its own weather system; occasionally lightning would spark or fog accumulate under the dome.

And how much of this material did I actually use? Next to nothing. The process was very much like interviewing: Ask probing questions, talk to the subject for as long as you can before you get thrown out. And since you've only got a limited space—say 750 words, give or take a few—you look for an angle. I call it the "hinge"—that which swings open the door into the world of that poem—the color of a scarf, or the number of upholstery studs in a leather-backed office chair.

Frustrated, I interrupted my writing long enough to bake some oatmeal cookies—and as usual burned the first tray. That stench stopped me right in my tracks. Because I knew this smell, and not just from other failed batches. I had lived in it. Walked in it.

You see, the Akron where I grew up was governed by two scents: the smell of the rubber factories, and the smell of burning oats from the Quaker Oats silos. They were so prevalent that they had become normal, a part of life. Neither was pleasant, but both aroused the imagination of children. The rubber brought to mind huge truck tires rolling anywhere as long as it was out of Akron; later, in geography class, we dreamed of the massive, implacable rubber trees in India whose lashed sides streamed white latex. And the Quaker Oats smell brought a feeling of security, the comfort of the kitchen and its warm oven. It was a delicious push-pull I had forgotten.

So I entered my grandfather's Akron again through smell.

QUAKER OATS

The grain elevators have stood empty for years.
They used to feed an entire nation of children.
Hunched in red leatherette breakfast-nooks,
fingers dreaming, children let their spoons clack

on the white sides of their bowls. They stare at the carton on the table, a miniature silo with a kindly face smiling under a stiff black hat.

They eat their oats with milk and butter and sugar. They eat their oats in their sleep, where horsedrawn carts jolt along miry roads, past cabins where other children wait, half-frozen under tattered counterpanes. The man with the black hat, a burlap sack tucked under his arm, steps down from the wagon whispering come out, don't be afraid.

And they come, the sick and the healthy; the red, the brown, the white; the ruddy and the sallow; the curly and the lank. They tumble from rafters and crawl out of trundles. He gives them to eat. He gives them prayers and a good start in the morning. He gives them free enterprise; he gives them the flag and PA systems and roller skates and citizenship. He gives them a tawny canoe to portage overland, through the woods, through the midwestern snow.

The first half of *Thomas and Beulah* is Thomas's story; the second half is determined by his wife. Beulah is a self-taught milliner who picked up the skill while working in a dress shop, so she is very aware of color and texture. Thomas's favorite color, blue, becomes the memory trigger in the poem "Wingfoot Lake," becoming the perfect blue of a forbidden, because segregated, swimming pool, and also the blue of redemption, giving equal time to the blue sky of a Fourth of July picnic as well as the blue sky over the heads of the civil rights demonstrators marching through Washington, D.C., on August 28, 1963:

WINGFOOT LAKE

(Independence Day, 1964)

On her 36th birthday, Thomas had
shown her
her first swimming pool. It had been
his favorite color, exactly—just
so much of it, the swimmers' white
arms jutting
into the chevrons of high society.
She had rolled up her window
and told him to drive on, fast.

Now this act of mercy: four daughters
dragging her to their husbands' company picnic,
white families on one side and them
on the other, unpacking the same
squeeze bottles of Heinz, the same
waxy beef patties and Salem potato
chip bags.

So he was dead for the first time
on Fourth of July—ten years ago

had been harder, waiting for something
to happen,
and ten years before that, the girls
like young horses eyeing the track.
Last August she stood alone for hours
in front of the T.V. set
as a crow's wing moved slowly through
the white streets of government.
That brave swimming

scared her, like Joanna saying,
Mother, we're Afro-Americans now!
What did she know about Africa?
Were there lakes like this one
with a rowboat pushed under the pier?
Or Thomas' Great Mississippi
with its sullen silks? (There was
the Nile but the Nile belonged

to God.) Where she came from
was the past, 12 miles into town
where nobody had locked their
back door,
and Goodyear hadn't begun to dream of
a park
under the company symbol, a white foot
sprouting two small wings.

Although that poem revolves around recognizable historical events, the world arena is peripheral to the details of the picnic. Human beings do not live for history; they may live under its thrall or in spite of it, even in it—but not because of history.

Why does poetry affect us differently than, say, a newspaper feature, or a documentary, or even a miniseries? Let me read to you one woman's reaction, one from what are now well over a thousand letters I've received since assuming the poet laureateship. Dinny Moses from Putney, Vermont, writes:

> *I am not a poet, formal or learned. And I certainly don't understand it intellectually. However, the musician in me and the healer are very drawn to it as a medicine of expression. Maybe because it can have a quality of intimacy that I feel comfortable with. And in the past three years I find myself at times flooding with words that demand to be put to paper, unbidden by me consciously. But this outpouring is a kind of therapy, I suppose. I call it poetry.*

I am always astonished when people claim that poetry is "intellectual" or "elitist", that it has to do with "books and flowers and stuff."

To me, a poem is so firmly rooted in the world—or rather, the juncture between the world and the individual spirit—that I find poems more useful for negotiating the terms of our identities, more efficacious in providing a stay against extinction than the mass media. Mass media can provide us with the news but they can't tell us what to do with it. Of course, it is not the task of the news media to crank out solutions; but with no instructions on how to incorporate what's happening close to home or far away—how to locate our private emotions in the public sentiment—we feel helpless and betrayed.

It is a pity that large segments of our society regard the creative arts with some degree of apprehension, even suspicion—that they do not expect the arts, especially the arts created by their contemporaries, to be accessible, nor do they see any reason to incorporate the arts into their everyday or professional lives.

Who's afraid of poetry is not as interesting a question as *why* one is afraid, or maybe just apprehensive. Many of those who profess an aversion to poetry have not read a poem since being forced to memorize "Invictus" in the eighth grade—hardly a fair sampling of the field.

A reason that keeps recurring, in an infinite number of variations is: I don't understand it. Other variations on this theme include: It's not about real life. It's old-fashioned. The language is weird. It's too serious, too hermetic, too self-indulgent. You need a PhD to decipher that stuff. It makes me feel stupid. Well, many of us have suffered a classroom experience where our brave interpretation of a teacher's treasured poem was declared "wrong." Poems, then, became coded texts, something you were supposed to decipher, not enjoy. (And for many of us, unfortunately, that was the end of poetry.)

In one of the most popular poems in the English language, one-fifth of the words cannot be found in Webster's dictionary—cannot be found in any dictionary, in fact, because they are nonsense words. That poem is, of course, the "Jabberwocky" by Lewis Carroll, which begins:

'Twas brillig, and the slithy toves
Did gyre and gimble in the wabe:
All mimsy were the borogoves,
And the mome raths outgrabe.

Precocious seven-year-old Alice's tentative response shows that she is both befuddled and intrigued:

"It seems very pretty," she said when she had finished it, "but it's rather hard to understand! Somehow it seems to fill my head with ideas—only I don't exactly know what they are!"

Alice then goes on, in spite of her reservations, to give an accurate gloss of the narrative, saying "However, *somebody* killed *something:* that's clear at any rate—" That is exactly what happens in the poem. Alice got that part right. But the part that fills Alice's head with ideas—that, my friends, is poetry.

SOURCES

Books

Dictionary of Literary Biography, Volume 120: *American Poets Since World War II,* Gale, 1992.

Dove, Rita, *Thomas and Beulah,* Carnegie-Mellon University Press, 1986.

———, *Grace Notes,* Norton, 1989.

Periodicals

Detroit Free Press, "Unexpected Turn Yields Poet Laureate," June 24, 1993, p. 5A.

Detroit News, "A 'Poet of Distinction' Assumes Laureate Post," May 19, 1993, p. 5A.

Ebony, "Introducing: Pulitzer Prize-Winning Poet Rita Dove," October, 1987, pp. 44-46.

Grand Rapids Press, "Writers See Craft Revival with New Poet Laureate," May 19, 1993, p. A3.

Ms., "Bold Type: Rita Dove, People's Poet," November/December, 1993, p. 66.

New York Review of Books, "In the Zoo of the New," October 23, 1986, pp. 47-52.

New York Times, "Rita Dove Named Next Poet Laureate; First Black in Post," May 19, 1993; June 20, 1993.

People, "Lovely Meter, Rita-Made: Pulitzer Prize-Winner Rita Dove Puts a New Face on the Poet Laureate's Job," May 31, 1993, p. 92.

Time, "Poetry in Motion," May 31, 1993, p. 73; "Rooms of Their Own," October 18, 1993, pp. 88-89.

Washington Post, April 17, 1987; May 19, 1993.

W.E.B. Du Bois

1868–1963

African American educator, writer, and human rights activist

Although Booker T. Washington became known as the spokesman for black America after his 1895 address urging blacks to set aside their desire for equality and work toward economic advancement instead, he did not by any means represent the views of all African Americans. One of his harshest critics was the brilliant scholar W.E.B. Du Bois, who insisted that blacks had a right and a duty to demand their political, social, and civil rights as American citizens.

Born and raised in Massachusetts, Du Bois was educated at Fisk University, the University of Berlin, and Harvard University. During his long professional association with Atlanta University, he developed black sociology as a legitimate field of study and directed a series of annual conferences on the problems facing black Americans that cemented his academic reputation and brought him national recognition. He was also a major figure in the Pan-African movement, which fostered the concept of international unity among all black people.

During the 1950s, his embrace of communism and outspoken admiration of the Soviet Union made Du Bois the target of police and FBI harassment. Convinced that black Americans would never know freedom in their native land, he left the United States in 1961 to settle in Ghana. He died there two years later on the eve of the historic March on Washington.

In 1903, Du Bois published a collection of essays entitled The Souls of Black Folk *that examined many different social and political issues of importance to blacks. But it was a chapter entitled "On Booker T. Washington and Others" that made him the center of controversy. In that particular piece, Du Bois argued against the Tuskegee president's accommodationist philosophy, insisting that it was foolhardy and even dangerous for blacks to remain submissive in the belief that whites would ever voluntarily grant them equal rights. The book touched off a bitter feud between the two men that intensified as Du Bois delivered his message across the country on the lecture circuit. In one of his addresses, "The Training of Negroes for Social Power," he explained how vital it was to the future of black America that its young people—especially those with superior intellects, whom he referred to as "the Talented Tenth"—receive an education that included more than just training in the industrial arts. The speech is reprinted from Volume 1 of* W.E.B. Du Bois Speaks, *edited by Philip S. Foner (Pathfinder Press, 1970).*

The responsibility for their own social regeneration ought to be placed largely upon the shoulders of the Negro people. But such responsibility must carry with it a grant of power; responsibility without power is a mockery and a farce. If, therefore, the American people are sincerely anxious that the Negro shall put forth his best efforts to help himself, they must see to it that he is not deprived of the freedom and power to strive. The responsibility for dispelling their own ignorance implies that the power to overcome ignorance is to be placed in black men's hands; the lessening of poverty calls for the power of effective work, and one responsibility for lessening crime calls for control over social forces which produce crime.

Such social power means, assuredly, the growth of initiative among Negroes, the spread of independent thought, the expanding consciousness of manhood; and these things today are looked upon by many with apprehension and distrust, and there is systematic and determined effort to avoid this inevitable corollary of the fixing of social responsibility. Men openly declare their design to train these millions as a subject caste, as men to be thought for, but not to think; to be led, but not to lead themselves. Those who advocate these things forget that such a solution flings them squarely on the other horn of the dilemma; such a subject child-race could never be held accountable for its own misdeeds and shortcomings; its ignorance would be part of the nation's design, its poverty would arise partly from the direct oppression of the strong and partly from thriftlessness which such oppression breeds; and, above all, its crime would be the legitimate child of that lack of self-respect which caste systems engender. Such a solution of the Negro problem is not one which the saner sense of the nation for a moment contemplates; it is utterly foreign to American institutions, and is unthinkable as a future for any self-respecting race of men. The sound afterthought of the American people must come to realize that the responsibility for dispelling ignorance and poverty and uprooting crime among Negroes cannot be put upon their own shoulders unless they are given such independent leadership in intelligence, skill, and morality as will inevitably lead to an independent manhood which cannot and will not rest in bonds.

Let me illustrate my meaning particularly in the matter of educating Negro youth.

The Negro problem, it has often been said, is largely a problem of ignorance—not simply of illiteracy, but a deeper ignorance of the world and its ways, of the thought and experience of men; an ignorance of self and the possibilities of human souls. This can be gotten rid of only by training; and primarily such training must take the form of that sort of social leadership which we call education. To apply such leadership to themselves, and to profit by it, means that Negroes would have among themselves men of careful training and broad culture, as teachers and teachers of teachers. There are always periods of educational evolution when it is deemed proper for pupils in the fourth reader to teach those in the third. Such a method, wasteful and ineffective at all times, is peculiarly dangerous when ignorance is widespread and when there are few homes and public institutions to supplement the work of the school. It is, therefore, of crying necessity among Negroes that the heads of their educational system—the teachers in the normal schools, the heads of high schools, the principals of public systems, should be unusually well-trained men; men trained not simply in common-school branches, not simply in the technique of school management and normal methods, but trained beyond this, broadly and carefully, into the meaning of the age whose civilization it is their peculiar duty to interpret to the youth of a new race, to the minds of untrained people. Such educational leaders should be prepared by long and rigorous courses of study similar to those which the world over have been designed to strengthen the intellectual powers, fortify character, and facilitate the transmission from age to age of the stores of the world's knowledge.

Not all men—indeed, not the majority of men, only the exceptional few among American Negroes or among any other people—are

W.E.B. Du Bois

adapted to this higher training, as, indeed, only the exceptional few are adapted to higher training in any line; but the significance of such men is not to be measured by their numbers, but rather by the numbers of their pupils and followers who are destined to see the world through their eyes, hear it through their trained ears, and speak to it through the music of their words.

Such men, teachers of teachers and leaders of the untaught, Atlanta University and similar colleges seek to train. We seek to do our work thoroughly and carefully. We have no predilections or prejudices as to particular studies or methods, but we do cling to those time-honored sorts of discipline which the experience of the world has long since proven to be of especial value. We sift as carefully as possible the student material which offers itself, and we try by every conscientious method to give to students who have character and ability such years of discipline as shall make them stronger, keener, and better for their peculiar mission. The history of civilization seems to prove that no group or nation which seeks advancement and true development can despise or neglect the power of well-trained minds; and this power of intellectual leadership must be given to the talented tenth among American Negroes before this race can seriously be asked to assume the responsibility of dispelling its own ignorance. Upon the foundation stone of a few well-equipped Negro colleges of high and honest standards can be built a proper system of free common schools in the South for the masses of the Negro people; any attempt to found a system of public schools on anything less than this—on narrow ideals, limited or merely technical training—is to call blind leaders for the blind.

The very first step toward the settlement of the Negro problem is the spread of intelligence. The first step toward wider intelligence is a free public-school system; and the first and most important step toward a public-school system is the equipment and adequate support of a sufficient number of Negro colleges. These are first steps, and they involve great movements: first, the best of the existent colleges must not be abandoned to slow atrophy and death, as the tendency is today; secondly, systematic attempt must be made to organize secondary education. Below the colleges and connected with them must come the normal and high schools, judiciously distributed and carefully manned. In no essential particular should this system of common and secondary schools differ from educational systems the world over. Their chief function is the quickening and training of human intelligence; they can do much in the teaching of morals and manners incidentally, but they cannot and ought not to replace the home as the chief moral teacher; they can teach valuable lessons as to the meaning of work in the world, but they cannot replace technical schools and apprenticeship in actual life, which are the real schools of work. Manual training can and ought to be used in these schools, but as a means and not as an end—to quicken intelligence and self-knowledge and not to teach carpentry; just as arithmetic is used to train minds and not to make skilled accountants.

Whence, now, is the money coming for this educational system? For the common schools, the support should come from local communities, the state governments, and the United States government; for secondary education, support should come from local and state governments and private philanthropy; for the colleges, from private philanthropy and the United States government. I make no apology for bringing the United States government in thus conspicuously. The general government must give aid to southern education if illiteracy and ignorance are to cease threatening the very foundations of civilization within any reasonable time. Aid to common-school education could be appropriated to the different states on the basis of illiteracy. The fund could be administered by state officials, and the results and needs reported upon by United States educational inspectors under the Bureau of Education. The states could easily distribute the funds so as to encourage local taxation and enterprise and not result in pauperizing the communities. As to higher training, it must be remembered that the cost of a single battleship like the *Massachusetts* would endow all the distinctively college work necessary for Negroes during the next half century; and it is without doubt true that the unpaid balance from bounties withheld from Negroes in the Civil War would, with interest, easily supply this sum.

But spread of intelligence alone will not solve the Negro problem. If this problem is largely a question of ignorance, it is also scarcely less a problem of poverty. If Negroes are to assume the responsibility of raising the standards of living among themselves, the power of intelligent work and leadership toward proper industrial ideals must be placed in their hands. Economic efficiency depends on intelligence, skill, and thrift. The public-school system is designed to furnish the necessary intelligence for the ordinary worker, the secondary school for the more gifted worker, and the college for the exceptional few. Technical knowledge and manual dexterity in learning branches of the world's work are taught by industrial and trade schools, and such schools are of prime importance in the training of colored children. Trade-teaching cannot be effectively combined with the work of the common schools because the primary curriculum is already too crowded, and thorough common-school training should precede trade-teaching. It is, however, quite possible to combine some of the work of the secondary schools with purely technical training, the necessary limitations being matters of time and cost: the question whether the boy can afford to stay in school long enough to add parts of a high school course to the trade course, and particularly the question whether the school can afford or ought to afford to give trade-training to high-school students who do not intend to become artisans. A system of trade schools, therefore, supported by state and private aid, should be added to the secondary-school system.

An industrial school, however, does not merely teach technique. It is also a school—a center of moral influence and of mental discipline. As such it has peculiar problems in securing the proper teaching force. It demands broadly trained men: the teacher of carpentry must be more than a carpenter, and the teacher of the domestic arts more than a cook; for such teachers must instruct, not simply in manual dexterity, but in mental quickness and moral habits. In other words, they must be teachers as well as artisans. It thus happens that college-bred men and men from other higher schools have always been in demand in technical schools, and it has been the high privilege of Atlanta University to furnish during the thirty-six years of its existence a part of the teaching force of nearly every Negro industrial school in the United States, and today our graduates are teaching in more than twenty such institutions. The same might be said of Fisk University and other higher schools. If the college graduates were today withdrawn from the teaching force of the chief Negro industrial schools, nearly every one of them would have to close its doors. These facts are forgotten by such advocates of industrial training as oppose the higher schools. Strong as the argument for industrial school is—and its strength is undeniable—its cogency simply increases the urgency of the plea for higher training-schools and colleges to furnish broadly educated teachers.

But intelligence and skill alone will not solve the southern problem of poverty. With these must go that combination of homely habits and virtues which we may loosely call thrift. Something of thrift may be taught in school, more must be taught at home; but both these agencies are helpless when organized economic society denies to workers the just reward of thrift and efficiency. And this has been true of black laborers in the South from the time of slavery down through the scandal of the Freedman's Bank to the peonage and crop-lien system of today. If the southern Negro is shiftless, it is primarily because over large areas a shiftless Negro can get on in the world about as well as an industrious black man. This is not universally true in the South, but it is true to so large an extent as to discourage striving in precisely that class of Negroes who most need encouragement. What is the remedy? Intelligence—not simply the ability to read and write or to sew—but the intelligence of a society permeated by that larger division of life and broader tolerance which are fostered by the college and university. Not that all men must be college-bred, but that some men, black and white, must be, to leaven the ideals of the lump. Can any serious student of the economic South doubt that this today is her crying need?

Ignorance and poverty are the vastest of the Negro problems. But to these later years have added a third—the problem of Negro crime. That a great problem of social morality must have become eventually the central problem of emancipation is as clear as day to any student of history. In its grosser form as a problem of serious crime it is already upon us. Of course it is false and silly to represent that white women in the South are in daily danger of black assaulters. On the contrary, white womanhood in the South is absolutely safe in the hands of ninety-five percent of the black men—ten times safer than black womanhood is in the hands of white men. Nevertheless, there is a large and dangerous class of Negro criminals, paupers, and outcasts. The existence and growth of such a class, far from causing surprise, should be recognized as the natural result of that social disease called the Negro problem; nearly every untoward circumstance known to human experience has united to increase Negro crime: the slavery of the past, the sudden emancipation, the narrowing of economic opportunity, the lawless environment of wide regions, the stifling of natural ambition, the curtailment of political privilege, the disregard of the sanctity of black men's homes, and above all, a system of treatment for criminals calculated to breed crime far faster than all other available agencies could repress it. Such a combination of circumstances is as sure to increase the numbers of the vicious and outcast as the rain is to wet the earth. The phenomenon calls for no delicately drawn theories of race differences; it is a plain case of cause and effect.

But, plain as the causes may be, the results are just as deplorable, and repeatedly today the criticism is made that Negroes do not recognize sufficiently their responsibility in this matter. Such critics forget how little power today Negroes have over their own lower classes. Before the black murderer who strikes his victim today, the average black man stands far more helpless than the average white, and, too, suffers ten times more from the effects of the deed. The white man has political power, accumulated wealth, and knowledge of social forces; the black man is practically disfranchised, poor, and unable to discriminate between the criminal and martyr. The Negro needs the defense of the ballot, the conserving power of property, and, above all, the ability to cope intelligently with such vast questions of social regeneration and moral reform as confront him. If social reform among Negroes be without organization or trained leadership from within, if the administration of law is always for the avenging of the white victim and seldom for the reformation of the black criminal, if ignorant black men misunderstand the functions of government because they have had no decent instruction, and intelligent black men are denied a voice in government because they are black—under such circumstances to hold Negroes responsible for the suppression of crime among themselves is the cruelest of mockeries.

On the other hand, a sincere desire among the American people to help the Negroes undertake their own social regeneration means, first, that the Negro be given the ballot on the same terms as other men, to protect him against injustice and to safeguard his interests in the administration of law; secondly, that through education and social organization he be trained to work, and save, and earn a decent living. But these are not all; wealth is not the only thing worth accumulating; experience and knowledge can be accumulated and handed down, and no people can be truly rich without them. Can the Negro do without these? Can this training in work and thrift be truly effective without the guidance of trained intelligence and deep knowledge—without that same efficiency which has enabled modern peoples to grapple so successfully with the problems of the submerged tenth? There must surely be among Negro leaders the philanthropic impulse, the uprightness of character and strength of purpose, but there must be more than these: philanthropy and purpose among blacks as well as among whites must be guided and curbed by knowledge and mental discipline—knowledge of the forces of civilization that make for survival, ability to organize and guide those forces, and realization of the true meaning of those broader ideals of human betterment which may in time bring heaven and earth a little nearer. This is social power—it is gotten in many ways—by experience, by social contact, by what we loosely call the chances of life. But the systematic method of acquiring and imparting it is by the training of the youth to thought, power, and knowledge in the school and college. And that group of people whose mental grasp is by heredity weakest, and whose knowledge of the past is for historic reasons most imperfect, that group is the very one which needs above all, for the talented of its youth, this severe and careful course of training; especially if they are expected to take immediate part in modern competitive life, if they are to hasten the slower courses of human development, and if the responsibility for this is to be in their own hands.

Three things American slavery gave the Negro—the habit of work, the English language, and the Christian religion; but one priceless thing it debauched, destroyed, and took from him, and that was the organized home. For the sake of intelligence and thrift, for the sake of work and morality, this home life must be restored and regenerated with newer ideals. How? The normal method would be by actual contact with a higher home life among his neighbors, but this method the social separation of white and black precludes. A proposed method is by schools of domestic arts, but, valuable as these are, they are but subsidiary aids to the establishment of homes; for real homes are primarily centers of ideals and teaching and only incidentally centers of cooking. The restoration and raising of home ideals must, then, come from social life among Negroes themselves; and does that social life need no leadership? It needs the best possible leadership of pure hearts and trained heads, the highest leadership of carefully trained men.

"Three things American slavery gave the Negro—the habit of work, the English language, and the Christian religion; but one priceless thing it . . . took from him . . . was the organized home."

Such are the arguments for the Negro college, and such is the work that Atlanta University and a few similar institutions seek to do. We believe that a rationally arranged college course of study for men and women able to pursue it is the best and only method of putting into the world Negroes with ability to use the social forces of their race so as to stamp out crime, strengthen the home, eliminate degenerates, and inspire and encourage the higher tendencies of the race not only in thought and aspiration, but in everyday toil. And we believe this, not simply because we have argued that such training ought to have these effects, or merely because we hoped for such results in some dim future, but because already for years we have seen in the work of our graduates precisely such results as I have mentioned: successful teachers of teachers, intelligent and upright ministers, skilled physicians, principals of industrial schools, businessmen, and, above all, makers of model homes and leaders of social groups, out from which radiate subtle but tangible forces of uplift and inspiration. The proof of this lies scattered in every state of the South, and, above all, in the half-unwilling testimony of men disposed to decry our work.

Between the Negro college and industrial school there are the strongest grounds for cooperation and unity. It is not a matter of mere emphasis, for we would be glad to see ten industrial schools to every college. It is not a fact that there are today too few Negro colleges, but rather that there are too many institutions attempting to do college work. But the danger lies in the fact that the best of the Negro colleges are poorly equipped, and are today losing support and countenance, and that, unless the nation awakens to its duty, ten years will see the annihilation of higher Negro training in the South. We need a few strong, well-equipped Negro colleges, and we need them now, not tomorrow; unless we can have them and have them decently supported, Negro education in the South, both common-school and the industrial, is doomed to failure, and the forces of social regeneration will be fatally weakened, for the college today among Negroes is, just as truly as it was yesterday among whites, the beginning and not the end of human training, the foundation and not the capstone of popular education.

Strange, is it not, my brothers, how often in America those great watchwords of human energy—"Be strong!" "Know thyself!" "Hitch your wagon to a star!"—how often these die away into dim whispers when we face these seething millions of black men? And yet do they not belong to them? Are they not their heritage as well as yours? Can they bear burdens without strength, know without learning, and aspire without ideals? Are you afraid to let them try? Fear rather, in this our common fatherland, lest we live to lose those great watchwords of liberty and opportunity which yonder in the eternal hills their fathers fought with your fathers to preserve.

In 1905, Du Bois was one of about thirty blacks whose opposition to Washington led to the founding of the Niagara Movement. It was a forerunner of the National Association for the Advancement of Colored People (NAACP), which Du Bois also helped organize. (Despite his many philosophical disagreements with fellow NAACP leaders, he maintained an on-again, off-again relationship with the group for nearly forty years, serving a long stint as editor of its official publication, the Crisis.*) At their second annual meeting in 1906, members of the Niagara Movement gathered in Harpers Ferry, Virginia, to pay tribute to martyred abolitionist John Brown. At dawn on the morning of August 16, they heard Du Bois deliver one of the most significant speeches in the history of the black struggle for equality. It is reprinted from Volume 1 of* W.E.B. Du Bois Speaks, *edited by Philip S. Foner (Pathfinder Press, 1970).*

The men of the Niagara Movement coming from the toil of the year's hard work and pausing a moment from the earning of their daily bread turn toward the nation and again ask in the name of ten million the privilege of a hearing. In the past year the work of the Negro-hater has flourished in the land. Step by step the defenders of the rights of American citizens have retreated. The work of stealing the black man's ballot has progressed and the fifty and more representatives of stolen votes still sit in the nation's capital. Discrimination in travel and public accommodation has so spread that some of our weaker brethren are actually afraid to thunder against color discrimination as such and are simply whispering for ordinary decencies.

Against this the Niagara Movement eternally protests. We will not be satisfied to take one jot or tittle less than our full manhood rights. We claim for ourselves every single right that belongs to a freeborn American, political, civil and social; and until we get these rights we will never cease to protest and assail the ears of America. The battle we wage is not for ourselves alone but for all true Americans. It is a fight for ideals, lest this, our common fatherland, false to its founding, become in truth the land of the thief and the home of the slave—a byword and a hissing among the nations for its sounding pretensions and pitiful accomplishment.

Never before in the modern age has a great and civilized folk threatened to adopt so cowardly a creed in the treatment of its fellow citizens born and bred on its soil. Stripped of verbiage and subterfuge and in its naked nastiness, the new American creed says: Fear to let black men even try to rise lest they become the equals of the white. And this is the land that professes to follow Jesus Christ. The blasphemy of such a course is only matched by its cowardice.

In detail, our demands are clear and unequivocal. First, we would vote; with the right to vote goes everything: freedom, manhood, the honor of your wives, the chastity of your daughters, the right to work, and the chance to rise, and let no man listen to those who deny this.

We want full manhood suffrage, and we want it now, henceforth and forever.

Second. We want discrimination in public accommodation to cease. Separation in railway and street cars, based simply on race and color, is un-American, undemocratic, and silly. We protest against all such discrimination.

Third. We claim the right of freemen to walk, talk, and be with them that wish to be with us. No man has a right to choose another man's friends, and to attempt to do so is an impudent interference with the most fundamental human privilege.

Fourth. We want the laws enforced against rich as well as poor; against capitalist as well as laborer; against white as well as black. We are not more lawless than the white race: we are more often arrested, convicted and mobbed. We want justice even for criminals and outlaws. We want the Constitution of the country enforced. We want Congress to take charge of Congressional elections. We want the Fourteenth Amendment carried out to the letter and every state disfranchised in Congress which attempts to disfranchise its rightful voters. We want the Fifteenth Amendment enforced and no state allowed to base its franchise simply on color.

The failure of the Republican Party in Congress at the session just closed to redeem its pledge of 1904 with reference to suffrage conditions at the South seems a plain, deliberate, and premeditated breach of promise, and stamps that party as guilty of obtaining votes under false pretense.

Fifth. We want our children educated. The school system in the country districts of the South is a disgrace, and in few towns and cities are the Negro schools what they ought to be. We want the national government to step in and wipe out illiteracy in the South. Either the United States will destroy ignorance or ignorance will destroy the United States.

And when we call for education we mean real education. We believe in work. We ourselves are workers, but work is not necessarily education. Education is the development of power and ideal. We want our children trained as intelligent human beings should be, and we will fight for all time against any proposal to educate black boys and girls simply as servants and underlings, or simply for the use of other people. They have a right to know, to think, to aspire.

These are some of the chief things which we want. How shall we get them? By voting where we may vote, by persistent, unceasing agitation, by hammering at the truth, by sacrifice and work.

We do not believe in violence, neither in the despised violence of the raid nor the lauded violence of the soldier, nor the barbarous violence of the mob, but we do believe in John Brown, in that incarnate spirit of justice, that hatred of a lie, that willingness to sacrifice money, reputation, and life itself on the altar of right. And here on the scene of John Brown's martyrdom we reconsecrate ourselves, our honor, our property to the final emancipation of the race which John Brown died to make free.

Our enemies, triumphant for the present, are fighting the stars in their courses. Justice and humanity must prevail. We live to tell these dark brothers of ours—scattered in counsel, wavering and weak—that no bribe of money or notoriety, no promise of wealth or fame, is worth the surrender of a people's manhood or the loss of a man's self-respect. We refuse to surrender the leadership of this race to cowards and trucklers. We are men; we will be treated as men. On this rock we have planted our banners. We will never give up, though the trump of doom find us still fighting.

And we shall win. The past promised it, the present foretells it. Thank God for John Brown! Thank God for Garrison and Douglass! Sumner and Phillips, Nat Turner and Robert Gould Shaw, and all the hallowed dead who died for freedom! Thank God for all those today, few though their voices be, who have not forgotten the divine brotherhood of all men, white and black, rich and poor, fortunate and unfortunate.

We appeal to the young men and women of this nation, to those whose nostrils are not yet befouled by greed and snobbery and racial narrowness: stand up for the right, prove yourselves worthy of your heritage and whether born North or South dare to treat men as men. Cannot the nation that has absorbed ten million foreigners into its political life without catastrophe absorb ten million Negro Americans into that same political life at less cost than their unjust and illegal exclusion will involve?

Courage, brothers! The battle for humanity is not lost or losing. All across the skies sit signs of promise. The Slav is rising in his might, the yellow millions are tasting liberty, the black Africans are writhing toward the light, and everywhere the laborer, with ballot in his hand, is voting open the gates of opportunity and peace. The morning breaks over blood-stained hills. We must not falter, we may not shrink. Above are the everlasting stars.

During the late 1910s and 1920s, Du Bois was a vocal opponent of Marcus Garvey and the black separatist movement. While he supported the idea of promoting unity among blacks all over the world, he was a firm believer in integration and urged African Americans to keep up the fight for their rights at home. During the 1930s, however, as he observed the Depression's catastrophic effects on blacks, Du Bois reconsidered his position and instead began advocating what he called "voluntary segregation"—blacks banding together in their own organizations to help each other, free of dependence on or interference from whites. (In many ways, his plan foreshadowed that of the Black Power movement during the 1960s.) This put him at odds with the NAACP, which condemned segregation in any form, and was eventually a factor in his decision to leave the group in June 1934. Du Bois then made his call for establishing "a Negro nation within the nation"; a major theme of his speeches, including the following, which originally appeared in the June 1935, issue of Current History. *It was later reprinted in Volume 2 of* W.E.B. Du Bois Speaks, *edited by Philip S. Foner (Pathfinder Press, 1970).*

No more critical situation ever faced the Negroes of America than that of today—not in 1830, nor in 1861, nor in 1867. More than ever the appeal of the Negro for elementary justice falls on deaf ears.

Three-fourths of us are disfranchised; yet no writer on democratic reform, no third-party movement says a word about Negroes. The Bull Moose crusade in 1912 refused to notice them; the La Follette uprising in 1924 was hardly aware of them; the Socialists still keep them in the background. Negro children are systematically denied education; when the National Educational Association asks for federal aid to education it permits discrimination to be perpetuated by the present local authorities. Once or twice a month Negroes convicted of no crime are openly and publicly lynched, and even burned; yet a National Crime Convention is brought to perfunctory and unwilling notice of this only by mass picketing and all but illegal agitation. When a man with every qualification is refused a position simply because his great-grandfather was black there is not a ripple of comment or protest.

Long before the Depression Negroes in the South were losing "Negro" jobs, those assigned them by common custom—poorly paid and largely undesirable toil, but nevertheless life-supporting. New techniques, new enterprises, mass production, impersonal ownership and control have been largely displacing the skilled white and Negro worker in tobacco manufacturing, in iron and steel, in lumbering and mining, and in transportation. Negroes are now restricted more and more to common labor and domestic service of the lowest paid and worst kind. In textile, chemical and other manufactures Negroes were from the first nearly excluded, and just as slavery kept the poor white out of profitable agriculture, so freedom prevents the poor Negro from finding a place in manufacturing. The worldwide decline in agriculture has moreover carried the mass of black farmers, despite heroic endeavor among the few, down to the level of landless tenants and peons.

The World War and its wild aftermath seemed for a moment to open a new door; two million black workers rushed North to work in iron and steel, make automobiles and pack meat, build houses and do the heavy toil in factories. They met first the closed trade union which excluded them from the best-paid jobs and pushed them into the low-wage gutter, denied them homes and mobbed them. Then they met the Depression.

Since 1929 Negro workers, like white workers, have lost their jobs, have had mortgages foreclosed on their farms and homes, have used up their small savings. But, in the case of the Negro worker, everything has been worse in larger or smaller degree; the loss has been greater and more permanent. Technological displacement, which began before the Depression, has been accelerated, while unemployment and falling wages struck black men sooner, went to lower levels and will last longer.

Negro public schools in the rural South have often disappeared, while southern city schools are crowded to suffocation. The Booker Washington High School in Atlanta, built for one thousand pupils, has three thousand attending in double daily sessions. Above all, federal and state relief holds out little promise for the Negro. It is but human that the unemployed white man and the starving white child should be relieved first by local authorities who regard them as fellowmen, but often regard Negroes as subhuman. While the white worker has sometimes been given more than relief and been helped to his feet, the black worker has often been pauperized by being just kept from starvation. There are some plans for national rehabilitation and the rebuilding of the whole industrial system. Such plans should provide for the Negro's future relations to American industry and culture, but those provisions the country is not only unprepared to make but refuses to consider.

"The colored people of America are coming to face the fact quite calmly that most white Americans do not like them, and are planning neither for their survival, nor for their definite future if it involves free, self-assertive modern manhood."

In the Tennessee Valley beneath the Norris Dam, where do Negroes come in? And what shall be their industrial place? In the attempt to rebuild agriculture the southern landholder will in all probability be put on his feet, but the black tenant has been pushed to the edge of despair. In the matter of housing, no comprehensive scheme for Negro homes has been thought out and only two or three local projects planned. Nor can broad plans be made until the nation or the community decides where it wants or will permit Negroes to live. Negroes are largely excluded from subsistence homesteads because Negroes protested against segregation, and whites, anxious for cheap local labor, also protested.

The colored people of America are coming to face the fact quite calmly that most white Americans do not like them, and are planning neither for their survival, nor for their definite future if it involves free, self-assertive modern manhood. This does not mean all Americans. A saving few are worried about the Negro problem; a still larger group are not ill-disposed, but they fear prevailing public opinion. The great mass of Americans are, however, merely representatives of average humanity. They muddle along with their own affairs and scarcely can be expected to take seriously the affairs of strangers or people whom they partly fear and partly despise.

For many years it was the theory of most Negro leaders that this attitude was the insensibility of ignorance and inexperience, that white America did not know of or realize the continuing plight of the Negro. Accordingly, for the last two decades, we have striven by book and periodical, by speech and appeal, by various dramatic methods of agitation, to put the essential facts before the American people. Today there can be no doubt that Americans know the facts; and yet they remain for the most part indifferent and unmoved.

The main weakness of the Negro's position is that since emancipation he has never had an adequate economic foundation. Thaddeus Stevens recognized this and sought to transform the emancipated freedmen into peasant proprietors. If he had succeeded, he would have changed the economic history of the United States and perhaps saved the American farmer from his present plight. But to furnish fifty million acres of good land to the Negroes would have cost more money than the North was willing to pay, and was regarded by the South as highway robbery.

The whole attempt to furnish land and capital for the freedmen fell through, and no comprehensive economic plan was advanced until the advent of Booker T. Washington. He had a vision of building a new economic foundation for Negroes by incorporating them into white industry. He wanted to make them skilled workers by industrial education and expected small capitalists to rise out of their ranks. Unfortunately, he assumed that the economic development of America in the twentieth century would resemble that of the nineteenth century, with free industrial opportunity, cheap land and unlimited resources under the control of small competitive capitalists. He lived to see industry more and more concentrated, land monopoly extended and industrial technique changed by wide introduction of machinery.

As a result, technology advanced more rapidly than Hampton or Tuskegee could adjust their curricula. The chance of an artisan's becoming a capitalist grew slimmer, even for white Americans, while the whole relation of labor to capital became less a matter of technical skill than of basic organization and aim.

Those of us who in that day opposed Booker Washington's plans did not foresee exactly the kind of change that was coming, but we were convinced that the Negro could succeed in industry and in life only if he had intelligent leadership and far-reaching ideals. The object of education, we declared, was not "to make men artisans but to make artisans men." The Negroes in America needed leadership so that, when change and crisis came, they could guide themselves to safety.

The educated group among American Negroes is still small, but it is large enough to begin planning for preservation through economic advancement. The first definite movement of this younger group was toward direct alliance of the Negro with the labor movement. But white labor today as in the past refuses to respond to these overtures.

For a hundred years, beginning in the thirties and forties of the nineteenth century, the white laborers of Ohio, Pennsylvania and New York beat, murdered and drove away fellow workers because they were black and had to work for what they could get. Seventy years ago in New York, the center of the new American labor movement, white laborers hanged black ones to lamp posts instead of helping to free them from the worst of modern slavery. In Chicago and St. Louis, New Orleans and San Francisco, black men still carry the scars of the bitter hatred of white laborers for them. Today it is white labor that keeps Negroes out of decent low-cost housing, that confines the protection of the best unions to "white" men, that often will not sit in the same hall with black folk who already have joined the labor movement. White labor has to hate scabs; but it hates black scabs not because they are scabs but because they are black. It mobs white scabs to force them into labor fellowship. It mobs black scabs to starve and kill them. In the present fight of the American Federation of Labor against company unions it is attacking the only unions that Negroes can join.

Thus the Negro's fight to enter organized industry has made little headway. No Negro, no matter what his ability, can be a member of any of the railway unions. He cannot be an engineer, fireman, conductor, switchman, brakeman or yardman. If he organizes separately, he may, as in the case of the Negro Firemen's Union, be assaulted and even killed by white firemen. As in the case of the Pullman Porters' Union, he may receive empty recognition without any voice or collective help. The older group of Negro leaders recognize this and simply say it is a matter of continued striving to break down these barriers.

Such facts are, however, slowly forcing Negro thought into new channels. The interests of labor are considered rather than those of capital. No greater welcome is expected from the labor monopolist who mans armies and navies to keep Chinese, Japanese and Negroes in their places than from the captains of industry who spend large sums of money to make laborers think that the most worthless white man is better than any colored man. The Negro must prove his necessity to the labor movement and that it is a disastrous error to leave him out of the foundation of the new industrial state. He must settle beyond cavil the question of his economic efficiency as a worker, a manager and controller of capital.

The dilemma of these younger thinkers gives men like James Weldon Johnson a chance to insist that the older methods are still the best; that we can survive only by being integrated into the nation, and that we must consequently fight segregation now and always and force our way by appeal, agitation and law. This group, however, does not seem to recognize the fundamental economic bases of social growth and the changes that face American industry. Greater democratic control of production and distribution is bound to replace existing autocratic and monopolistic methods.

In this broader and more intelligent democracy we can hope for progressive softening of the asperities and anomalies of race prejudice, but we cannot hope for its early and complete disappearance. Above all, the doubt, deep-planted in the American mind, as to the Negro's ability and efficiency as worker, artisan and administrator will fade but slowly. Thus, with increased democratic control of industry and capital, the place of the Negro will be increasingly a matter of human choice, of willingness to recognize ability across the barriers of race, of putting fit Negroes in places of power and authority by public opinion. At present, on the railroads, in manufacturing, in the telephone, telegraph and radio business, and in the larger divisions of trade, it is only under exceptional circumstances that any Negro no matter what his ability, gets an opportunity for position and power. Only in those lines where individual enterprise still counts, as in some of the professions, in a few of the trades, in a few branches of retail business and in artistic careers, can the Negro expect a narrow opening.

Negroes and other colored folk nevertheless, exist in larger and growing numbers. Slavery, prostitution to white men, theft of their labor and goods have not killed them and cannot kill them. They are growing in intelligence and dissatisfaction. They occupy strategic positions, within nations and beside nations, amid valuable raw material and on the highways of future expansion. They will survive, but on what terms and conditions? On this point a new school of Negro thought is arising. It believes in the ultimate uniting of mankind and in a unified American nation, with economic classes and racial barriers leveled, but it believes this is an ideal and is to be realized only by such intensified class and race consciousness as will bring irresistible force rather than mere humanitarian appeals to bear on the motives and actions of men.

"If the leading Negro classes cannot assume and bear the uplift of their own proletariat, they are doomed for all time."

The peculiar position of Negroes in America offers an opportunity. Negroes today cast probably two million votes in a total of forty million, and their vote will increase. This gives them, particularly in northern cities, and at critical times, a chance to hold a very considerable balance of power, and the mere threat of this being used intelligently and with determination may often mean much. The consuming power of 2,800,000 Negro families has recently been estimated at $166,000,000 a month—a tremendous power when intelligently directed. Their manpower as laborers probably equals that of Mexico or Yugoslavia. Their illiteracy is much lower than that of Spain or Italy. Their estimated per capita wealth about equals that of Japan.

For a nation with this start in culture and efficiency to sit down and await the salvation of a white God is idiotic. With the use of their political power, their power as consumers, and their brainpower, added to that chance of personal appeal which proximity and neighborhood always give to human beings, Negroes can develop in the United States an economic nation within a nation, able to work through inner cooperation, to found its own institutions, to educate its genius, and at the same time, without mob violence or extremes of race hatred, to keep in helpful touch and cooperate with the mass of the nation. This has happened more often than most people realize, in the case of groups not so obviously separated from the mass of people as are American Negroes. It must happen in our case, or there is no hope for the Negro in America.

Any movement toward such a program is today hindered by the absurd Negro philosophy of Scatter, Suppress, Wait, Escape. There are even many of our educated young leaders who think that because the Negro problem is not in evidence where there are few or no Negroes, this indicates a way out! They think that the problem of race can be settled by ignoring it and suppressing all reference to it. They think that we have only to wait in silence for the white people to settle the problem for us; and finally and predominantly, they think that the problem of twelve million Negro people, mostly poor, ignorant workers, is going to be settled by having their more educated and wealthy classes gradually and continually escape from their race into the mass of the American people, leaving the rest to sink, suffer and die.

Proponents of this program claim, with much reason, that the plight of the masses is not the fault of the emerging classes. For the slavery and exploitation that reduced Negroes to their present level or at any rate hindered them from rising, the white world is to blame. Since the age-long process of raising a group is through the escape of its upper class into welcome fellowship with risen peoples, the Negro intelligentsia would submerge itself if it bent its back to the task of lifting the mass of people. There is logic in this answer, but futile logic.

If the leading Negro classes cannot assume

and bear the uplift of their own proletariat, they are doomed for all time. It is not a case of ethics; it is a plain case of necessity. The method by which this may be done is, first, for the American Negro to achieve a new economic solidarity.

There exists today a chance for the Negroes to organize a cooperative state within their own group. By letting Negro farmers feed Negro artisans, and Negro technicians guide Negro home industries, and Negro thinkers plan this integration of cooperation, while Negro artists dramatize and beautify the struggle, economic independence can be achieved. To doubt that this is possible is to doubt the essential humanity and the quality of brains of the American Negro.

No sooner is this proposed than a great fear sweeps over older Negroes. They cry "No segregation"—no further yielding to prejudice and race separation. Yet any planning for the benefit of American Negroes on the part of a Negro intelligentsia is going to involve organized and deliberate self-segregation. There are plenty of people in the United States who would be only too willing to use such a plan as a way to increase existing legal and customary segregation between the races. This threat which many Negroes see is no mere mirage. What of it? It must be faced.

If the economic and cultural salvation of the American Negro calls for an increase in segregation and prejudice, then that must come. American Negroes must plan for their economic future and the social survival of their fellows in the firm belief that this means in a real sense the survival of colored folk in the world and the building of a full humanity instead of a petty white tyranny. Control of their own education, which is the logical and inevitable end of separate schools, would not be an unmixed ill; it might prove a supreme good. Negro schools once meant poor schools. They need not today; they must not tomorrow. Separate Negro sections will increase race antagonism, but they will also increase economic cooperation, organized self-defense and necessary self-confidence.

The immediate reaction of most white and colored people to this suggestion will be that the thing cannot be done without extreme results. Negro thinkers have from time to time emphasized the fact that no nation within a nation can be built because of the attitude of the dominant majority, and because all legal and police power is out of Negro hands, and because large-scale industries, like steel and utilities, are organized on a national basis. White folk, on the other hand, simply say that, granting certain obvious exceptions, the American Negro has not the ability to engineer so delicate a social operation calling for such self-restraint, careful organization and sagacious leadership.

In reply, it may be said that this matter of a nation within a nation has already been partially accomplished in the organization of the Negro church, the Negro school and the Negro retail business, and, despite all the justly due criticism, the result has been astonishing. The great majority of American Negroes are divided not only for religious but for a large number of social purposes into self-supporting economic units, self-governed, self-directed. The greatest difficulty is that these organizations have no logical and reasonable standards and do not attract the finest, most vigorous and best educated Negroes. When all these things are taken into consideration it becomes clearer to more and more American Negroes that, through voluntary and increased segregation, by careful autonomy and planned economic organization, they may build so strong and efficient a unit that twelve million men can no longer be refused fellowship and equality in the United States.

SOURCES

Books

Du Bois, W.E.B., *In Battle for Peace: The Story of My 83rd Birthday* (reprint), Kraus Reprint, 1976.

———, *The Autobiography of W.E.B. Du Bois* (reprint), Kraus Reprint, 1976.

———, *The Souls of Black Folk: Essays and Sketches* (reprint), Random House, 1990.

Duffy, Bernard K. and Halford R. Ryan, editors, *American Orators of the Twentieth Century: Critical Studies and Sources*, Greenwood Press, 1987.

Foner, Philip S., editor, *W.E.B. Du Bois Speaks*, Pathfinder Press, 1970, Volume 1: *Speeches and Addresses, 1890-1919*, Volume 2: *Speeches and Addresses, 1920-1963*.

Hamilton, Virginia, *W.E.B. Du Bois: A Biography*, Crowell, 1972.

Lewis, David, *W.E.B. Du Bois: Biography of a Race, 1868-1919*, Holt, 1993.

Smith, Arthur L., *Rhetoric of Black Revolution*, Allyn & Bacon, 1969.

Stafford, Mark, *W.E.B. Du Bois*, Chelsea House, 1989.

Periodicals

Ebony, "Ten Greats of Black History," August, 1972, pp. 35-42.

Marian Wright Edelman

1939–

African American lawyer and children's rights activist

As founding president of the Children's Defense Fund (CDF), a nonpartisan research and lobbying group based in Washington, D.C., Marian Wright Edelman has achieved national prominence as an ardent and outspoken advocate for children. Her crusade embraces the young of all races and of all economic backgrounds, but especially those who spend their lives in a struggle against poverty, racism, violence, substandard education and health care, unemployment, and a host of other evils that plague contemporary society. Her goal, as she has stated many times, is to ensure that every American child enjoys "a healthy start, a head start and a fair start" in life.

Edelman, the daughter of a Baptist preacher and his wife, grew up as part of a loving and secure family in a small South Carolina town. Thanks to her parents and a supportive network of teachers and other members of the local black community, she developed a strong sense of self-respect and self-confidence that helped her cope with racial injustice she encountered as an African American in the segregated South. These same people also instilled in her the notion that service to others was an important part of everyday life.

After completing her secondary education, Edelman left her hometown in 1956 to attend Spelman College in Atlanta, where she prepared for a career in the U.S. foreign service. But her plans soon changed when she became involved in the fledgling civil rights movement. Determined to help in the struggle, she decided to go to law school after receiving her bachelor's degree in 1960. Upon her graduation from Yale three years later, Edelman joined the staff of the NAACP Legal Defense and Educational Fund. Her first assignment was in Mississippi, where she initially spent much of her time working on behalf of white student demonstrators from the North who had been jailed for trying to register black voters. Later, after becoming the first black woman admitted to the state bar, she turned her attention to other issues, most often those that involved improving the economic situation for blacks in Mississippi. Around this same time, she developed a particular interest in the plight of the desperately poor children she met during the course of her work. Before long, she had made up her mind to head to Washington, where she hoped to focus more national attention on the problems associated with extreme poverty in Mississippi and elsewhere.

In 1968, Edelman established the Washington Research Project, a research and advocacy organization devoted to making existing laws and programs work for the poor. From these efforts sprang the Children's Defense Fund, which she founded in 1973 specifically to provide a voice for the group she calls the true "silent majority" in America—children (especially poor, minority, and handicapped children) who cannot vote or speak up for themselves. She has served as its president ever since, lobbying tirelessly in Washington and throughout the country to make sure the needs of the country's youngest citizens are taken into account when legislators fashion public policy.

Under Edelman's leadership, the CDF has become known nationwide for its unwavering commitment to improving the lives of children and their families. It has investigated and reported on issues such as health care, teenage pregnancy, education, the juvenile justice system, homelessness, substance abuse, and violence, to name only a few. Edelman herself keeps in close contact with members of Congress to help craft new legislation or make the group's position known on bills that have a direct impact on children. She also contributes regularly to magazines and newspapers, grants frequent interviews, and fulfills numerous speaking engagements during the course of a typical year in order to "get the message out" to as many people as possible that America's children face an increasingly bleak future unless steps are taken now to reverse years of indifference.

On September 26, 1987, for example, Edelman addressed some three thousand members of the Congressional Black Caucus and their supporters at their annual weekend banquet. Held in Washington, its theme that year was "Educating the Black Child." In her typically intense and rapid-fire style—forceful but never angry or bitter—Edelman clearly defined for her audience what she felt their responsibilities were as leaders of the black middle class. Her remarks are reprinted here from Representative American Speeches, 1987-1988, *(Wilson, 1988).*

It was the best of times, it was the worst of times, it was the age of wisdom, it was the age of foolishness, it was the epoch of belief, it was the epoch of incredulity, it was the season of light, it was the season of darkness, it was the spring of hope, it was the winter of despair.

—A Tale of Two Cities, *Book 1, Chapter 1*

You have no right to enjoy a child's share in the labors of your fathers unless your children are to be blest by your labors.

—Frederick Douglass

For many of you sitting in this room, it is the best of times. Black per capita income is at an all-time high, and many of you have moved up the corporate ladder even if the ladders you are on frequently don't reach towards the pinnacle of corporate power. Black purchasing power, now at $200 billion, exceeds the gross national product of Australia and New Zealand combined. But it has not yet been translated into commensurate black economic influence and benefit. Black elected officials are more numerous than ever (6,681 in 1987, a 350 percent increase since 1970). But white economic power still controls our city tax bases. The amassing of committee and subcommittee chairmanships (8 full House committee chairs including the Select Committee, and 18 subcommittee chairs) by members of this Congressional Black Caucus is impressive by any standard, although the main political game in town is cutting the budget deficit. Spelman College, my alma mater, looks towards its future with a stronger endowment and student body than ever before while many other black colleges are struggling mightily to survive.

Bill Cosby is America's favorite daddy and Michael Jackson and Whitney Houston dot the top ten charts. Black leadership has permeated a range of mainstream institutions. Bill Gray chairs the House Budget Committee, Frank Thomas heads the Ford Foundation, and Cliff Wharton heads TIAA-CREF. A. Barry Rand is in charge of marketing at Xerox. Anita De Frantz is America's representative to the Olympic Committee, and Richard Knight is the city manager of Dallas.

I am proud of these and many similar accomplishments and applaud the black middle class for whom the times are good tonight. We've worked hard to get where we are. However, we have to work harder still to stay there and to move ahead.

But there is another black community that is not riding high tonight and that is going down and under. If you and I don't build a bridge back to them and throw out some strong lifelines to our children and youths and families whom poverty and unemployment and hopelessness are engulfing, they're going to drown, pull many of us down with them, and undermine the black future that our forebears dreamed, struggled, and died for.

I am grateful, therefore, that the Congressional Black Caucus has focused attention this year on educating the black child. Just as Martin Luther King, Jr., and others accepted the challenge of their time, so the challenge of our time is educating all of our children in mind, in body, and in soul if we are to preserve and strengthen the black future.

It is the worst of times for poor black babies born within a mile of this hotel and in many inner cities around the country who have less of a chance of living to the first year of life than a baby born in Costa Rica. Black babies are still twice as likely to die in the first year of life than white babies.

It is the worst of times for black youth and young adults trying to form families without decent skills or jobs and without a strong value base. Young marriages have essentially stopped in the black community. Sixty percent of all black babies today are born to never married single mothers; 90 percent of those born to black teens are born to unmarried mothers. One out of two children in a female-headed household is poor. Two out of three (67.1 percent) children in black female-headed households are poor. If that household is headed by a mother younger than 25, three out of four are poor. Even when teen pregnancy results in marriage, young two-parent families are almost three times as likely to be poor as those with parents 25 to 44 years of age.

A significant cause of this black family problem lies in young black men's eroding employment and wage base. Only 26.5 percent of all black male teens were employed in 1986 and 61.3 percent of those 20 to 24 years old. And even when they are lucky enough to work they frequently can't earn enough to lift a family out of poverty. Between 1973 and 1984, the average real (inflation-adjusted) annual earnings among males ages 20 through 24 fell by nearly 30 percent (from $11,572 to $8,072 in 1984 dollars). This sharp drop affected virtually all groups of young adult males—whether white, black, or Hispanic—although young black men suffered the most severe losses (nearly 50 percent). So the links between teen pregnancy and poverty are related not just to age and single parenthood but also to the poor skills and employment experience young parents seek to bring to the work force and to the lower wages young workers are paid.

To combat the poverty which is engulfing half of the black babies born today—half of our future as a black community—we must all work to prevent too early sexual activity and pregnancy and encourage our boys and girls to wait until they have the education and economic stability to form lasting families. If the share of single births in the black community grows at the rate of the last decade, by the year 2000, only one black baby in five will be born to a married woman. And if you don't care about these babies unselfishly you'd better care selfishly, for the future black voting and economic base upon which much of our leadership status rests resides in the health and education of the black child and the strength of the black family.

Not only are too many black babies and youths fighting poverty and sickness and homelessness and too little early childhood stimulation and weak basic skills preparation, they are also fighting AIDS and other sexually transmitted diseases; drug, tobacco, and alcohol addiction and crime which hopelessness and the absence of constructive alternatives and support systems in their lives leave them prey to. A black baby is seven or eight times more likely to be an AIDS victim than a white baby and minority teens (15 to 19) are the highest risk group for a range of sexually transmitted diseases. A black youth is five times more like-

Marian Wright Edelman

ly than a white youth to end up in an institution and is nearly as likely to be in prison as he is to be in college. Between 1979 and 1985 the number of black youth in juvenile detention facilities rose by 40 percent while the number of black youth entering college immediately after high school graduation fell by four percent. More black males go to prison each year than go to college. There are more black drug addicts than there are black doctors or lawyers.

Now some of you sitting here will ask what this has to do with you. You struggled and beat the odds and those folks who haven't made it could do the same. Others of you will rightfully say you're already doing your bit for the race by achieving yourself and by contributing to black organizations. Still others place the blame for growing black family poverty and weakening community bonds and support systems on urbanization and the continuing racial discrimination in national life which devalues black talent and curbs black opportunity.

As many nuggets of truth as each of these views may contain, I will simply say that unless the black middle class begins to exert more effective and sustained leadership with and without the black community on behalf of black children and families both as personal role models and value instillers and as persistent advocates for national, state and local policies—funded policies—that assure our children the health and child care, education, housing, and jobs they need to grow up into self sufficient adults, to form healthy families, and to carry on the black tradition of achievement, then all of our Mercedes and Halston frocks will not hide our essential failure as a generation of black haves who did not protect the black future during our watch.

Just as our nation is committing moral and economic suicide by permitting one in four of its preschool children to be poor, one in five to be at risk of being a teen parent, one in six to have no health insurance, and one in seven to face dropping out of school at a time when the pool of available young people to support an aging population and form a strong workforce is shrinking, so we are committing racial suicide by not sounding the alarm and protecting our own children from the poverty that ravages their dreams. For America will not treat our children fairly unless we make it.

We must recapture and care about our lost children and help them gain the confidence, self-esteem, values, and real world opportunities—education, jobs, and higher education which they need to be strong future guardians of the black community's heritage.

How do we do this? There are nine steps we must take if we are to help our children.

The first step is to remember and teach them that black folk have never been able to take anything for granted in America and we had better not start in these waning Reagan years of budget deficits and looming economic recession. Frederick Douglass put it bluntly: "Men may not get all they pay for in this world, but they must certainly pay for all they get." So you make sure that you are ready to do your part to help yourself and black children and to hold public and private sector officials accountable for doing their part in fostering health, education, and fair employment policies that are essential to black family survival.

Tell our children they're not going to jive their way up the career ladder. They've got to work their way up—hard and continuously. Too many young people want a fast elevator straight to the top floor and resist walking up the stairs or stopping on the floors of achievement between the bottom and top. Tell them to do their homework, pay attention to detail, and take care and pride in their work. People who are sloppy in little things tend to be sloppy in big things. Tell them to be reliable, to stick with something until they finish and resist jumping from pillar to post. And tell them to take the initiative in creating their own opportunity. They can't wait around for other people to discover them or to do them a favor.

The second step is to teach them the importance of getting a good education. While not a guarantee of success, education is a precondition to survival in America today. At a time when a smaller proportion of black high school graduates go on to college than ten years ago, we need to tell all of our children that college pays. In 1986, the average unemployment rate among black college graduates under 25 was 13.2 percent—more than one in every eight. Among young black high school graduates, it was 26.6 percent—more than one in four. College doubles their chance of getting a job. And we need to insist that they get a liberal education and learn how to think so that they can navigate an ever-changing job market.

The third step is to tell them that forming families is serious business and requires a measure of thoughtful planning and economic stability. In 1986, one in every five black families with children under 18 had someone unemployed. Of those 44 percent were single parents with no one at work. Among black married couples with children, only 18 percent had no one working.

That is the crucial point. Education alone, although of enormous value in itself, cannot guarantee a young black adult the income needed to raise children in economic safety today. But two black adults, both working, have the safety net of the second income when unemployment strikes. Remember, that's the only safety net President Reagan hasn't found a way to cut yet.

All these figures are from 1986, the fourth year of a long period of economic recovery. When the next recession arrives—and it will—the black unemployment rates will soar. Since this recession will come at a time when we have an extraordinary budget deficit, there is a great danger that the American voters will buy the argument that we must cut government spending in order to reduce interest rates and stimulate the economy. If this happens, there will be many unemployed teachers, nurses, employment counselors, and government workers of all sorts.

There is a warning here that relates to steps one and two. Just as black penetration into civil and social service professional jobs occurs, the growth and security of such jobs fall. Just as blacks rise to senior ranks in industrial and industrial union jobs, steel and auto manufacturing industries enter a steep decline. The economic goal posts keep shifting. How, then, do we work towards a full share in the power to set the goals in place, and not just the right to run the race?

The fourth step is to set goals and work quietly and systematically towards them. So often we feel we have to talk loud rather than act effectively. So often we get bogged down in our ego needs and lose sight of our broader community goals. T.S. Eliot in his play *The Cocktail Party* said that "half the harm that is done in this world is due to people who want to feel important." Wanting to feel important is good, but not at the expense of doing important deeds—even if we don't get the credit. You can get a mighty lot done in this world if you don't mind doing the work and letting other people take the credit. You know what you do and the Lord knows what you do and that's all that matters.

> ***"You can get a mighty lot done in this world if you don't mind doing the work and letting other people take the credit."***

The fifth step is knowing the difference between substance and style. Too many of us think success is a Saks Fifth Avenue charge card or a "bad" set of wheels or coming to this Black Caucus dinner. Now these are things to enjoy, but they are not life goals. I was watching one of President Johnson's inaugural balls on television with a black college president's wife in Mississippi when Mrs. Hamer, that great lady of the Mississippi civil rights movement who lacked a college degree, but certainly not intelligence or clear purpose, came onto the screen. The college president's wife moaned: "Oh my, there's Miz Hamer at the president's ball and she doesn't even have a long dress." My response was: "That's alright. Mrs. Hamer with no long gown is there and you and I with our long gowns are not." So often we miss the real point—we buy BMWs and fur coats before we think about whether where we're going to drive and wear them is worthwhile. Nobody ever asks about what kind of car Ralph Bunche drove or designer suit Martin Luther King, Jr., bought. Don't confuse style with meaning. Get your insides in order and your direction clear first and then worry about your clothes and your wheels. You may need them less.

The sixth step is valuing family life. We must build on the strong black tradition of family and teach our children to delay family formation until they are economically and emotionally stable and ready to raise the new generation of black children and leaders. Black and white men must support their children as best they can and not have them until they are ready to take responsibility for them. We must strengthen family rituals: prayers if we are religious, regular family meals, and participation in school work and in non-school activities. Our children need constructive alternatives to the street. We must do things with our children. Listen to them. Be moral examples for them. If we cut corners, they will too. If we lie, they will too. If we spend all our money on our backs and wheels and tithe no portion of it for our colleges, churches, and civic causes, they won't either.

We must join together as an entire community to establish an ethic of achievement and self-esteem in poor and middle class black children. They can do science and math as well as basketball and football, computers as well as cotillions, reading along with reggae. If we expect these accomplishments of them, support them in their learning processes, and help them in setting priorities. They need strong consistent adult buffers to withstand the negative messages of the external world that values them less than white or middle class children.

When I, like many of you, was growing up in my small segregated southern town, the whole outside world, the law of the land, local officials, the media, almost everybody outside our own community told black children we weren't worth much or were second rate. But we didn't believe it because our parents said it wasn't so. Our preachers said it wasn't so. Our caring teachers said it wasn't so. And they nurtured us as a community, shielded us against the constant psychological battery of our daily environment and made us understand that we could make it—had to make it—but in order to do so, we had to struggle to make our own opportunities in order to help change America. And we went on to college—poor and black—and tried to carry out their other lesson to give some of what they gave us back in service to others left behind. Service, they taught, is the rent you pay for living. Where is our buffer today for the black and poor children who are daily wounded by a national administration who would rather judge than help the poor? Where are the strong local officials and community voices and hands shielding and fighting for the poor children in our city streets against the ravages of drugs and crime? Where are the role modelling, mentoring, and tutoring programs that help black children overcome the pernicious undercurrents of many, even our purported friends, who really think black children lack the potential of other children? What activities are your churches and sororities and fraternities sponsoring to keep children busy and off the streets?

The seventh step is to vote and use our political and economic power. Only 51 percent of all voting age blacks voted in the 1980 election and only 56 percent in the 1984 election. Seventy percent of 18- to 25-year-old black youths did not vote in the last election. People who do not vote have no line of credit with people who are elected and pose no threat to those who act against our interests. Don't even pretend that you care about the black community, about poor children, about your nation, even about your own future, if you don't exercise the political leverage Medgar Evers and others died to make sure we had. And run for political office. And when you win don't forget that you are the means to serve others well and not the end.

No one running for president or any office should get black community support unless they have a well thought-out set of policies designed to lift the black child and family. Similarly, we need to use our economic power for the benefit of black families, particularly in industries where we constitute a large market share.

Two last steps and I'm done.

Remember your roots, your history, and the forebears' shoulders on which you stand. And pass them on to your children and to other black children whose parents may not be able to. As a black community today there is no greater priority than assuring the rootedness of all our children—poor, middle class, and Ivy League. Young people who do not know where they come from and the struggle it took to get them where they are now will not know where they are going or what to do for anyone besides themselves if and when they finally arrive somewhere. And if they run into bad weather on the way, they will not have the protective clothing to withstand the wind and the rain, lightning and thunder that have characterized the black sojourn in America. They need the anchor and rightful pride of a great people that produced a Harriet Tubman and Sojourner Truth and Frederick Douglass from slavery, a Benjamin Mays and Martin Luther King, Jr., and Fannie Lou Hamer from segregation, people second to none in helping transform America from a theoretical to a more living democracy.

The last step is to keep dreaming and aiming high. At a time when so many in public and private life seem to be seeking the lowest common denominator of public and personal conduct, I hope you will dream and set new examples of service and courage.

Dr. Benjamin Mays, a former president of Morehouse College and role model for me said: "It must be borne in mind that the tragedy of life doesn't lie in not reaching your goal. The tragedy lies in having no goal to reach. It is not a calamity to die with dreams unfulfilled, but it is a calamity not to dream. It is not a disaster to be unable to capture your ideal, but it is a disaster to have no ideal to capture. It is not a disgrace not to reach the stars, but it is a disgrace to have no stars to reach for. Not failure, but low aim, is sin." We must aim high for our children and teach them to aim high.

I'd like to end with part of a prayer for children written by Ina Hughes of South Carolina:

We pray for children
Who spend all their allowance before Tuesday,
Who throw tantrums in the grocery store and pick at their food,
Who like ghost stories,
Who shove dirty clothes under the bed, and never rinse out the tub,
Who get visits from the tooth fairy,
Who don't like to be kissed in front of the carpool,
Who squirm in church and scream in the phone,
Whose tears we sometimes laugh at and whose smiles can make us cry.

And we pray for those
Whose nightmares come in the daytime,
Who will eat anything,
Who have never seen a dentist,
Who aren't spoiled by anybody,
Who go to bed hungry and cry themselves to sleep,
Who live and move, but have no being.

We pray for children who want to be carried and for those who must,

For those we never give up on and for those who don't get a second chance.

For those we smother . . . and for those who will grab the hand of anybody kind enough to offer it.

Please offer your hands to them. Let your Amen be in your committed actions to help black children when you leave here. They desperately need your help on a one-to-one basis and in the political arena. We must all work to redirect the nation's foolish priorities which favor bombs and missiles over babies and mothers upon whom our real national and community security rest.

On June 9, 1994, Edelman spoke to graduates of the Harvard Medical School. In her talk, one of many such commencement addresses she has given over the years, she focused on one of the most pressing issues of the 1990s—violence and its impact on children. Displaying a characteristic passion for her subject that often leaves listeners in tears, she decried the "total breakdown in American values, common sense, and parent and community responsibility to protect and nurture children" and called upon all adults to "change ourselves, our hearts, our

personal priorities, and our neglect of any of God's children . . . to see that no child is left behind." The Children's Defense Fund furnished the copy of the speech that follows.

For what shall it profit a man, if he shall gain the whole world, and lose his own soul?

—Mark 8:36

Not by might, nor by power, but by my spirit, says the Lord of hosts.

—Zachariah 4:6

Whoever receives one such child in my name receives me: but whoever causes one of these little ones which believe in me to sin, it would be better for him to have a great millstone fastened round his neck, and to be drowned in the depth of the sea.

—Matthew 18:5-6

On April 5, 1968, in Cleveland, Ohio, following Dr. King's assassination, Robert F. Kennedy spoke "about the mindless menace of violence in America which again stains our land and every one of our lives." "It is not," he said, "the concern of any one race. The victims of the violence are black and white, rich and poor, young and old, famous and unknown. No one—no matter where he lives or what he does—can be certain who will suffer from some senseless action of bloodshed. And yet it goes on and on and on in this country of ours."

> **"The morally unthinkable has become normal as the killing of innocent children has become routine not only in Bosnia and Brazil but in Boston and Baltimore."**

Since Robert Kennedy spoke these words, he and 800,000 American men, women, and children have been killed by guns. Another 520,000 Americans have died violent deaths by other means in America's undeclared twentieth-century civil war.

Between 1979 and 1991 almost 50,000 American children were killed by guns. More American children died from firearms on the killing fields of America than American soldiers died on the killing fields of Vietnam.

From 1968 through 1991, when more than 1.3 million Americans died violently at home, 31,000 American soldiers died in military conflicts in other countries. Americans were 42 times more likely to kill each other than to be killed by an external enemy.

This quarter-century death toll of American against American—and of Americans who, unable to face life or find love, hope, purpose, or safe haven in their family, community, faith, or democratic civic life, took their own life—is almost three times the number of reported American battle deaths in all of the wars in the twentieth century.

Gun violence is not just an inner-city Black problem. Approximately half of the 316,496 gun homicide victims between 1968 and 1991 were White (158,738) and half were Black (157,738) and 93 percent of the 346,225 gun suicide victims were White. Most murders are committed not by strangers but by family members, neighbors, or acquaintances.

The morally unthinkable has become normal as the killing of innocent children has become routine not only in Bosnia and Brazil but in Boston and Baltimore. Twenty-five American children—the equivalent of a classroomful—are murdered every two days as the crisis of children having children has become the greater tragedy of children killing children. An American child is 15 times as likely to be killed by gunfire as a child growing up in Northern Ireland.

Homicide is now the third leading cause of death among children 5 to 14 years old, the second leading cause of death among youths and young adults 10 to 24, and the leading cause of death among Black teen males. More young Black males are killed by guns each year than from all the lynchings throughout American history.

Escalating violence against and by children

and youth is no coincidence. It is the cumulative, convergent, and heightened manifestation of a range of serious and too-long neglected problems. Epidemic child and family poverty, increasing economic inequality, racial intolerance and hate crimes, pervasive drug and alcohol abuse and violence in our homes and popular culture, and growing numbers of out of wedlock births and divorces have all contributed to the disintegration of the family, community, and spiritual values and supports all children need. Add to these crises easy access to deadlier and deadlier firearms; hordes of lonely and neglected children and youths left to fend for themselves by absentee parents in all race and income groups; gangs of inner city and minority youths relegated to the cellar of American life without education, jobs or hope; and political leadership over the 1980s that paid more attention to foreign than domestic enemies and to the rich than the poor, and you face the social and spiritual disintegration of American society that confronts us today.

Where are the family values in the richest nation on earth when one in five or 14.6 million of its children lived in poverty in 1992—5 million more than in 1973? What does national security mean to the estimated 3 million children who witness parental violence every year and the children reported abused and neglected every 13 seconds? How can we expect the 100,000 children who are homeless every night to respect the homes and property of others?

I wonder how many of the 15-year-old murderers today are children who were born without adequate prenatal care and nutrition because our nation said we could not afford to give them a Healthy Start? How many 16-year-old teen mothers having babies today entered school not ready to learn because we would not insist on a quality Head Start for them? How many 18-year-old murderers witnessed and suffered abuse and neglect at home from parents who themselves never were nurtured, taught to parent, or enabled to work? How many 19-year-old youths abusing and pushing drugs today are children who saw the adults in their lives abusing or pushing drugs and who lacked positive community alternatives to dysfunctional families and dangerous streets after school, on weekends, and during idle summer months?

We have not valued millions of our children's lives and so they do not value ours in a society in which they have no social or economic stake or sense of community. Countless youths are imprisoned by lack of skills in inner-city neighborhoods where "the future" means surviving the day and living to 18 is a triumph. Their neglect, abuse, and marginalization by parents, schools, communities, and our nation turned them first to and against each other in gangs and then against a society that would rather imprison than educate and employ them. Our market culture tells them they must have designer sneakers, gold chains, and fancy cars to be somebody while denying them the jobs to buy them legally. So they are easy marks for drug dealers and profit-driven gun manufacturers and sellers in pursuit of new markets for their lethal products. While the number of children and youths victimized by violence has soared, so has the number of youthful offenders. For murder and non-negligent manslaughter between 1982 and 1991, juvenile arrests rose 92.7 percent.

There is no excuse for youth or adult crime. Perpetrators must be swiftly and fairly punished. We must stop the ridiculous and simplistic political extremes and deal with our communal complexities—supporting both early investment in children, mentoring and counseling programs, and measures to control guns and ensure safe streets. But there also is no excuse for the unbridled trafficking in nonsporting handguns, assault weapons, and ammunition. A gun is produced in America every 10 seconds and is available to almost anybody who wants to own or rent one, including children. One ad encouraging parents to buy guns for children asks: "How old is old enough?" and concludes: "Age is not the major yardstick. Some youngsters are ready to start at 10, others at 14. The only real measures are those of maturity and individual responsibility. Does your youngster follow directions well? Is he conscientious and reliable? Would you leave him alone in the house for two or three hours? Would you send him to the grocery store with a list and a $20 bill? If the answer to these questions or similar ones are 'yes' then the answer can also be 'yes' when your child asks for his first gun."

More than 200 million guns are legally in the hands of Americans. There are more gun dealers than gas station owners in America. You often can get a license to sell guns easier than a driver's license and can buy a gun as readily as a toaster across the counters of some of our largest chain stores. Although our nation regulates the safety of countless products including children's teddy bears, blankets, toys, and pajamas, it does not regulate the safety of a product that kills and injures tens of thousands of children and other citizens each year.

Our failure to control the proliferation of arms and to confront the plague of violence which transcends all racial, geographic and income boundaries has contributed to escalating community and domestic violence and to its lethality. All the moral thresholds of war have disappeared in Rwanda, Sarajevo, and San Francisco as innocent civilians—old and young alike—are slaughtered by indiscriminate gun violence. Even a mother's womb no longer shields babies against violent assault. A Detroit pediatrician wrote: "We have seen 22 pregnant adolescents with gun shot wounds in two small inner-city hospitals in Detroit in 1993."

Violence romps through our children's playgrounds, invades their bedroom slumber parties, terrorizes their Head Start centers and schools, frolics down the streets they walk to and from school, dances through their school buses, waits at the stop light and bus stop, lurks at McDonald's, runs them down on the corner, shoots through their bedroom windows, attacks their front porches and neighborhoods, strikes them or their parents at home, and tantalizes them across the television screen every six minutes. It snatches away their family members at work, and at random saps their energy and will to learn, and makes them forget about tomorrow. It nags and picks at their minds and spirits day in and day out, snuffing out the promise and joy of childhood and of the future which becomes just surviving today.

> ***"Never have we experienced such a numbing and reckless reliance on violence to resolve problems, feel powerful, or be entertained."***

Inner-city children as young as 10, psychiatrists and social workers report, think about death all the time and even plan their own funerals. Young Black and Brown men speak longingly of reaching the ripe old age of 20 in their bullet-ravaged, job-destitute, politically forsaken neighborhoods. Some speak wistfully of prison with "three hots and a cot" as a safer haven than their dead-end streets and empty, jobless futures in a society that has decreed them expendable. Dr. James Garbarino, president of the Erikson Institute, says American inner-city children are exposed to such heavy doses of extreme violence they exhibit symptoms of post-traumatic stress disorder like children in war-torn countries such as Mozambique, Cambodia, and Palestine.

At least 13 children die daily from guns, at least 30 other children are injured every day, adding billions to our out-of-control public health costs. The National Association of Children's Hospitals and Rehabilitation puts the average child gun injury hospitalization cost at $14,434.

Although the threat of violence hovers most heavily over inner cities, it respects no boundaries as the madmen shootings on the Long Island commuter train, downtown San Francisco office building, and Waco tragedy attest. Violence was the top worry of parents and children, according to a 1993 Newsweek-CDF poll of 10- to 17-year-olds and their parents.

What do we do?

First, recognize that we face a total breakdown in American values, common sense, and parent and community responsibility to protect and nurture children.

Never has America permitted children to rely on guns and gangs rather than parents and neighbors for protection and love or pushed so many children onto the tumultuous sea of life without the life vests of nurturing families and communities, challenged minds, job prospects, and hope.

Never have we exposed children so early and relentlessly to cultural messages glamorizing violence, sex, possessions, alcohol, and tobacco with so few mediating influences from responsible adults. And never have we experienced such a numbing and reckless reliance on violence to resolve problems, feel powerful, or be entertained. A single trip to the movies often results in the witnessing of multiple deaths on a scale that makes them seem irrelevant. *New York Times* movie critic Vincent Canby counted 74 dead in *Total Recall,* 81 in *Robocop 2,* 106 in *Rambo III,* and 264 in *Die Hard II.* It's time to say enough. While I am sick of record companies profiting from the violent rap they find a ready market for among white suburban and inner-city youths alike, I am just as sick of Rambos and Terminators, and of video games like "Mortal Kombat" and "Night Trap" that portray decapitation, murder, and violence as fun and entertainment.

The average preschool child watches over

eight-and-one-half months of television before entering school. The lines between make believe and real life blur in rudderless child lives unpeopled by enough caring adults transmitting positive values or helping them interpret what they see. Is it any wonder that a teenaged boy in Boston responded to the murder of an MIT student with: "What's the big deal? People die every day."

Second, let's stop the adult hypocrisy and double standards. Today, two out of every three Black and one fifth of all White babies are born to never-married mothers. And if it's wrong for 13-year-old inner-city girls to have babies without the benefit of marriage, it's wrong for rich celebrities and we ought to stop putting them on the cover of *People* magazine. It is adults who have engaged in epidemic abuse of children and of each other in our homes. It is adults who have taught children to kill and disrespect human life. It is adults who manufacture, market, and profit from the guns that have turned many neighborhoods and schools into war zones. It is adults who have financed, produced, directed, and starred in the movies, television shows, and music that have made graphic violence ubiquitous in our culture. It is adults who have borne children and then left millions of them behind without basic health care, quality child care and education, or moral guidance. It is adults who have taught our children to look for meaning outside rather than inside themselves, teaching them in Dr. King's words "to judge success by the index of our salaries or the size of our automobiles, rather than by the quality of our service and relationship to humanity." And it is adults who have to stand up and be adults and accept our responsibility to parent and protect the young.

Step three is to mount a massive moral witness and mobilization against the violence of guns, poverty, and child neglect in American life. The NRA, powerful firearms and ammunition manufacturers and sellers, the military-industrial complex, wealthy corporations and individuals who gained most from the unjust economic priorities of the past 12 years, and their political allies, will not untie the noose from our children's necks and nation's future unless a massive movement swells up from every nook and cranny of America. Parent by parent, youth by youth, doctor by doctor, religious congregation by congregation, school by school, and neighborhood by neighborhood, we'll breathe life and security again into our democracy if we are willing to risk our comfort and status today for our children's and nation's tomorrow.

We must begin by taking guns out of the hands of children and those who kill children. Whether you are a hunter, NRA member, gun owner, or not, I hope you will agree that child gun deaths must stop and join in calling for a cease fire and responsible regulation of guns as the dangerous products they are. And I hope you will help spread the message that guns endanger rather than protect. A *New England Journal of Medicine* study found that a handgun in the home is 43 times more likely to be used to kill a family member or friend than for justifiable homicide. Suicide victims are two and a half times more likely to have guns at home. Over half of youth and child suicides involved guns.

But crucial gun control is not enough alone to prevent violence and reestablish peace, love and mutual respect in our homes, neighborhoods and society. We must also address the breakdown of spiritual, family, and community norms and just opportunity in America. Whether the focus is on random shootings or the drug epidemic or too early and out-of-wedlock childbearing, we are drawn back to the limited opportunities that lead too many children and adolescents to conclude that they have nothing to gain and little to lose. When our young lack a stake in our dominant values and norms, both we and they face a perilous road ahead.

Finally, determine that you will never become cynical or despondent about your capacity to help transform America and build nurturing families and caring communities.

Let me end with a story by Elizabeth Ballard about one school teacher, Jean Thompson, and one boy, Teddy Stollard.

On the first day of school, Jean Thompson told her students, "Boys and girls, I love you all the same." Teachers sometimes lie. Little Teddy Stollard was a boy Jean Thompson did not like. He slouched in his chair, didn't pay attention, his mouth hung open in a stupor, his clothes were mussed, his hair unkempt, and he smelled. He was an unattractive boy and Jean Thompson didn't like him.

Teachers have records. And Jean Thompson had Teddy's.

"First grade: Teddy's a good boy. He shows promise in his work and attitude. But he has a poor home situation.

Second grade: Teddy is a good boy. He does

what he is told. But he is too serious. His mother is terminally ill.

Third grade: Teddy is falling behind in his work; he needs help. His mother died this year. His father shows no interest.

Fourth grade: Teddy is in deep waters; he is in need of psychiatric help. He is totally withdrawn."

Christmas came, and the boys and girls brought their presents and piled them on her desk. They were all in brightly colored paper except for Teddy's. His was wrapped in brown paper and held together with scotch tape. And on it, scribbled in crayon, were the words, "For Miss Thompson from Teddy." She tore open the brown paper and out fell a rhinestone bracelet with most of the stones missing and a bottle of cheap perfume that was almost empty. When the other boys and girls began to giggle she had enough sense to put some of the perfume on her wrist, put on the bracelet, hold her wrist up to the other children and say, "Doesn't it smell lovely? Isn't the bracelet pretty?" And taking their cue from the teacher, they all agreed.

At the end of the day, when all the children had left, Teddy lingered, came over to her desk and said, "Miss Thompson, all day long, you smelled just like my mother. And her bracelet, that's her bracelet, it looks real nice on you too. I'm really glad you like my presents." And when he left, she got down on her knees and buried her head in the chair and she begged God to forgive her.

The next day when the children came, she was a different teacher. She was a teacher with a heart. And she cared for all the children, but especially those who needed help. Especially Teddy. She tutored him and put herself out for him.

"*It takes just one person to change a child's life. . . .*"

By the end of that year, Teddy had caught up with a lot of the children and was even ahead of some.

Several years later, Jean Thompson got this note:

Dear Miss Thompson:

I'm graduating from high school. I wanted you to be the first to know. Love, Teddy.

Four years later she got another note:

Dear Miss Thompson:

I wanted you to be the first to know. The university has not been easy, but I liked it. Love, Teddy Stollard.

Four years later there was another note:

Dear Miss Thompson:

As of today, I am Theodore J. Stollard, M.D. How about that? I wanted you to be the first to know. I'm going to be married in July. . . . I want you to come and sit where my mother would have sat, because you're the only family I have. Dad died last year.

And she went and she sat where his mother should have sat because she deserved to be there. She had become a decent and loving human being.

There are millions of Teddy Stollards all over our nation—children we have forgotten, given up on, left behind. How many Teddys will never become doctors, lawyers, teachers, police officers, or engineers because there was no Jean Thompson? No you? How many children will never learn enough now to earn a living later because you and I did not reach out to them, speak up for them, vote, lobby, and struggle for them?

How many times will you plead no time when a child seeks your attention, or refuse to serve the poor child because of the paperwork burden, or write off the unruly and unresponsive child in your classroom, agency, or neighborhood because you don't want to expend the energy or simply decide it isn't your job or responsibility?

Any one of us can become a Jean Thompson and everyone of us must if we are to feel and heal our children's pain and nation's divisions. It takes just one person to change a child's life and to ensure that children like Teddy are not left behind, have a safe haven from the street, a voice at the end of the phone, time with an attentive Big Sister, Brother, or mentor.

The most important step each of us can take to end the violence and poverty and child neglect that is tearing our country apart is to change ourselves, our hearts, our personal priorities, and our neglect of any of God's children, and add our voice to those of others in a new movement that is bigger than our individual efforts to see that no child is left behind.

Do not be overwhelmed or give up because problems seem so hard or intractable. Abraham Lincoln kept going through depression and war and never gave up. And so the American Union was preserved. Martin Luther King, Jr., did not give up when he was scared and depressed and tired and didn't know what next step to take. And so the walls of racial segregation crumbled from his labors and that of countless unsung Black and Brown and White citizens. Elizabeth Glaser hasn't stopped fighting despite being affected by AIDS for 13 years and the loss of a child to AIDS. Her dogged and urgent persistence has contributed to greater attention to this killer disease. Sarah and Jim Brady refused to give up despite setback after setback and opposition from the powerful NRA, and the Brady Bill was signed into law in 1993. Millions of children are still beating the odds every day and are staying in school and becoming law-abiding citizens despite the violence and poverty and drugs and family decay all around them. And so you and I can keep on keeping on until we change the odds for all American children by making the violence of guns, poverty, preventable disease, and family neglect unAmerican.

God speed.

The Republican takeover of Congress following the 1994 elections has given Edelman occasion to speak out forcefully against the party's "Contract with America" and its various reform measures, which she insists will be devastating for children. While she supports what she terms "responsible change," she has vowed to create a bipartisan campaign aimed at opposing "any foe of children whose proposals and actions will make more children destitute, hungry, homeless, uneducated, uncared for or unsafe."

SOURCES

Books

Edelman, Marian Wright, *Families in Peril: An Agenda for Social Change* (W.E.B. Du Bois Lectures), Harvard University Press, 1987.

———, *The Measure of Our Success: A Letter to My Children and Yours,* Beacon Press, 1992.

Peterson, Owen, editor, *Representative American Speeches, 1987-1988,* Wilson, 1988.

Periodicals

Detroit Free Press, "Advocate Calls Contract a Disaster for Kids," January 12, 1995; "Advocates for Young Will Need New Strategy," January 22, 1995.

Harper's Bazaar, "Saint Marian," February, 1993.

Mother Jones, "Kids First!" May/June, 1991.

Ms., "Marian Wright Edelman," July/August, 1987.

Newsweek, "A Mother's Guiding Message," June 8, 1992, p. 27.

New Yorker, "A Sense of Urgency," March 27, 1989.

New York Times, October 8, 1992.

New York Times Book Review, August 23, 1992.

People, "Save the Children," July 6, 1992, pp. 101-102.

Redbook, "The Woman Behind the First Lady," June, 1993.

Rolling Stone, "Marian Wright Edelman: On the Front Lines of the Battle to Save America's Children," December 10, 1992.

Time, "They Cannot Fend for Themselves," March 23, 1987, p. 27.

Joycelyn Elders

1933–

African American physician and former U.S. government official

From the moment President-elect Bill Clinton announced that she was his choice for the post of U.S. Surgeon General, Dr. Joycelyn Elders faced a barrage of criticism and even death threats for her unwavering liberal views on such hot-button issues as abortion, birth control, sex education, and drug use. While her backers pointed out that what she said just makes common sense in today's society, her opponents charged her with encouraging dangerous and immoral behavior. But the brash and blunt-spoken physician refused to back down and adopt a less confrontational and more conciliatory attitude. As she saw it, the very health and well-being—if not the future—of the entire country was at stake. It was a stance that eventually cost Elders her job.

Elders—originally named Minnie Lee Jones—was the oldest of eight children born to impoverished black sharecroppers. By virtue of her own hard work as well as the support of her parents and younger siblings, she was able to leave her rural Arkansas home after graduating from high school to fulfill her dream of attending college. (She later made it possible for five of her brothers and sisters to do the same.) At all-black Philander Smith College in Little Rock, she discovered her love for science and made plans to become a lab technician, one of the few fields she thought would be open to her. But a campus visit by Edith Irby Jones, the first black woman to attend the University of Arkansas Medical School, convinced Elders that she, too, could become a doctor.

So, after completing her undergraduate degree in 1952, Elders joined the U.S. Army, trained as a physical therapist, and then took advantage of the GI Bill to finance her medical education at the University of Arkansas, from which she graduated in 1960. Elders then went on to specialize in pediatric endocrinology (the study of various growth and hormone-related disorders), and by the end of the 1970s her research had established her as one of the country's foremost experts in the field. Beginning in 1967 and for the next twenty years, she also taught pediatrics at her alma mater.

Elders traces her interest in sex education and preventing teenage pregnancies directly to her work with young female diabetic patients. Because she knew that they risked potentially severe and permanent damage to their health if they became pregnant, Elders frankly discussed birth control options with them and their parents as part of an overall plan to keep them as healthy as possible. The success of this approach convinced her that a similar plan might work with the general public to stem the tide of teen pregnancies.

In 1987, the new young governor of Arkansas, Bill Clinton, appointed Elders to head the state department of health, making her the first black and the first woman to hold the job. From the day of her very first press conference, when she advocated distributing contraceptives to students through the schools, she angered many with her outspoken liberalism. Her efforts to establish school-based health clinics, for example, raised the ire of conservative Christian groups and pro-life activists who felt she was just trying to promote abortion. The opposition she encountered frequently forced her to lock horns with Arkansas state legislators over support for her programs and led to frequent calls for her resignation.

When Bill Clinton was elected president of the United States, he again turned to Elders, this time for the position of surgeon general, the highest-ranking public health official in the country. Opponents immediately seized upon her controversial record as Arkansas's so-called "Condom Queen" as reason enough to derail her nomination. But after a series of sometimes contentious hearings before the U.S. Senate during the summer of 1993, Elders was at last confirmed in September, thus making her only the second woman and the first African American to serve as surgeon general. In 1994, she also returned to academic life as adjunct professor of pediatrics at George Washington University Medical Center, rated as one of the nation's best medical schools.

After assuming her government post, Elders continued her crusade against teen pregnancy, which she felt had to be addressed through better and earlier sex education and easier availability of contraception and abortion. She also spoke out on AIDS, homosexuality, alcohol abuse, smoking and the tobacco industry, the legalization of certain drugs, domestic violence, gun control, and health care reform. Although her public statements sparked outrage in some quarters (including demands that she resign) and occasional dismay even among her fans, she did not curb her often fiery rhetoric.

The following address, peppered with statistics and delivered in the sonorous tones and rolling rhythms of a gospel preacher, is typical of the many speeches she made across the country during her term as surgeon general. In this particular instance, the date was January 24, 1994, and the place was Butler University in Indianapolis, Indiana. Her remarks were transcribed from a videotape made available by WTBU-TV, a broadcast service of Butler University.

I thank the university for inviting me to be a part of your visiting African American scholars program. It is indeed a pleasure. And I'm delighted to be here, because every one of us in this room shares a common agenda—the health and well-being of the future of America.

We all want *all* children to grow up healthy, educated, motivated, and to have hope for the future. Yet you've already heard [enough] from your attorney general, your health director, your prosecutor, and others in your community to know that not all children are having the opportunity of meeting that wonderful goal that we've set for them.

When we began to look and think about the problems that are going on in our community, we find that first of all, that our children are increasingly poor. That from 1970 to 1990, we went from one in seven children being poor to one in five.

Joycelyn Elders

We know that children that grow up in poverty are far more likely to be members of what we call the "Five-H Club." The Five-H Club are children that go to bed hungry. Every night in the richest country in the world, we have three to five million children who go to bed hungry.

You've heard some talk about health care, and we know that we've all talked more about health care the past year than we've ever talked about health care before. We're concerned because we have thirty-eight million Americans who have no health care. That is, a third of those are children. We spend more on health care than any other country. And that would be wonderful if we could look around and say that we have the healthiest country in the world. But we know that that's not true.

When we look at the measures of health care like infant mortality, I'm ashamed of what ours was in Arkansas, and I know Dr. Caine [the director of the Marion County, Indiana, Department of Health] is ashamed of what it is in Indianapolis. And we all should be ashamed of what it is in this country, because we're behind nineteen other industrialized countries. And when we look at our black infant mortality rate, we're dead last. When we look at our problems related to teen pregnancies, how we care for our elderly, we're not very proud.

It's said that if you want to save a society, you've got to control the three Ps. The three Ps are poverty—and I just told you our children are getting poorer; in fact, from 1990 to 1992, we went from one in five to one in four, and if they were minorities, it was one in two. So obviously we're not doing very well.

We have to control population. And all of you know that too many of our children in our society are being born to children. Children who'll graduate to the Five-H Club—the hungry, healthless, homeless, hugless, and hopeless. We have too many of our children that are graduating into that club. We have more than a million children every year who become parents, who become pregnant. More than 500,000 become parents before they become adults.

Dr. Caine was telling you about the violence in our country. Our children are killing our children. We had more children between 1979 and 1991 kill children than there were people killed in the Vietnam War. Our rate of homicide among our young men is the most common cause of death, and we're *four* times above any other country. But if we look at our young black males, we are *forty-seven times* above that of any other country.

We look at what's happening to our young black men, and we discover that we're eating up our seed corn. This is our best and our brightest. Only *one* out of five—*one* out of five!—young black men will ever grow up and earn enough money to raise a family. Two out of five will be lost to drugs and alcohol. One out of the five will be killed by black-on-black crime. (Ninety-three percent of all the homicides among young black men in America were black-on-black crime.) And one out of the five will be in prison. We have more young black men in prison than we have in institutions like Butler University. And the average cost of keeping a young man in prison for a year in this country is $35,600. I bet—I don't know what it costs, but I bet you could send them to Butler for less than that!

We have got to start investing in our children, the most valuable resource we'll ever have. We look at the problem of HIV/AIDS, and it's ever increasing. We're having our children engaging in sexual activities at a younger and younger age. We have more than a million people in this country who are HIV-positive, and the most rapid increase is [among] our young people. That's one in every two-hundred-fifty Americans. In *your* nation's capital, one in every seventy-seven high school students is HIV-positive. That's a major problem that we've got to begin to deal with and address.

"We look at what's happening to our young black men, and we discover that we're eating up our seed corn."

Well, what are some of the things that I feel we need to do about it? You've heard already about the problem of drugs. We know that it's far easier for many of our children to find drugs than it is to find hugs. We know that fifty-plus percent of our young people have tried illicit drugs; many use them regularly. Fifty percent of our twelve- to seventeen-year-olds—those are babies to me—drink more than a six-pack of beer a week. Thirty percent of our high-schoolers are involved in binge drinking more than five drinks at one time.

Well, now what can we do? What should we be doing about it, and how can we make a difference? You heard your attorney general and prosecutor say, well, you know we can talk about building bigger and better prisons, but that's not an answer. We've already tripled our prison population, and I told you what it costs per prisoner. So that means that we've got to start looking at other means.

We've got to *prevent* the problems that we're going into. We've got to *prevent* the number of children having children at a cost of twenty-six *billion* dollars just for AFDC, WIC, and Medicaid for children born to children. And you often hear when we start talking about prevention programs, and when we talk about health care reform, we said, well, you know, we talk about how much it's going to *cost?!?* Well, out of all the money we're talking about spending on health care that we're spending now, less than one percent of it is paid or spent on health. What we spend it on is very expensive *dying*. When I say less than one percent, I'm talking about for health education, I'm talking about immunizations, I'm talking about prenatal care—the things that everybody in this room will agree make an important difference and are very important.

So the things that I recommend we do, is first of all, we've got to start early. We've been doing too little, too late. We've got to have early childhood education, especially for our children that we know are at risk. Eighty-five percent of middle- and upper-income children have early childhood education. Only eighteen percent of your Medicaid children have early childhood education—the poorest of the poor. So if I would ask this group, what group do you think needs it the most? You'd all agree that [it would be] the children of thirteen- and fourteen-year-old mothers who don't know how to parent.

The second thing I feel we've got to do is we've got to invest in comprehensive health education programs, from kindergarten through twelfth grade. You know, everybody said, well, I say sex education. I say *comprehensive health education programs!* That is, we've got to teach our children. We've got to teach them how to feel good about themselves. We've got to teach them how to say "no." We've got to teach them that there are certain places on their body that *nobody* is supposed to touch; if they do, they need to tell somebody. *Those* are the kinds of things that we need to start early, it has to be age-appropriate, and we have to build on it.

People tell me, well, Dr. Elders, let the *parents* do it! The parents don't know how; nobody ever taught the parents. They say, Dr. Elders, let the *church* do it! Fifty-two percent of the children are unchurched; they don't go to *anybody's* church. So how are we going to teach them?

When I've talked to the ministers—and I'm very happy to say that the ministers in Arkansas are my most wonderful, ardent supporters, and if you don't believe that they're powerful, if you get the elderly and the ministers out there carrying signs in front of your legislature—watch how they vote! Because they know those are the people that vote. They vote for their children and their grandchildren, so we have got to make sure that we do the things we need to do for our children. People said, I told the ministers, I said, "I'm tired of you moralizing from the pulpit and preaching to the choir! I want you to get out in the streets and start helping with the children!"

The third thing we've got to do is we've got to educate our parents. We've got to teach them how to be parents. We've got to use all of those hundreds of years of experience that our AARP has invested in it and ask them to help us with the children. You may think, well, I've raised my children and I've done my job. Well, I want you to know that all of these are your children. They don't eat at your table, they don't sleep in your bed, but they're your children just the same.

The fourth thing we've got to do is we've got to teach our young men to be responsible, that there is more to being a father than donating sperm. So we've got to make *them* responsible. And one of the things that I feel that is an important part of the president's health care reform is his initiative on children to have health education and make full services available where children are. Twenty percent of our population is in school every day, and we need to take the services to our children rather than having them running around hunting us. We've got to make sure we have all the services we need.

And last but not least, we've got to offer our bright young people hope—hope for the future. You see, if you have nothing to look forward to, what difference does it make how long it takes you to get there or how many detours you get? Sometimes, the best life that a young man has ever had is the day he goes to prison. He knows that he's got a place to sleep, food to eat, and he's got health care. We've got to offer our children more than that. We can do better than that.

You've heard that word "prevention" mentioned lots of times. So how do we do it? We've got to *prevent* the problem. How do we prevent the problem? First of all, we get developed and focus on programs and policies that focus on prevention. We each in our own way, in our own community, we have to reach out and be responsible, wherever we are. This university has to become a part of this community and reach out to that community and help do the things we need to do. We can't start—you can legislate all kinds of important programs, but if the community, and the family, the school, the church, the health department, the judge, are not involved, I'll tell you, it won't work.

We've got to educate. We've got to educate our children. Educate our teachers. Educate our ministers. Educate this entire community.

And for the "v" in "prevention," I've often said that I want to be the voice and the vision for the poor and the powerless. And I've told many groups that I've said I don't mind being the lightning rod as long as I know that my thunder is behind me.

So we've got to move on and do what we need to do to make a difference for the children of America. We've got to empower our children, empower ourselves. When we sit around and talk about what's going on with the children, it's *us,* what are *we* going to do? Not what the federal government's going to do, not what the state's going to do, but what am *I* going to do to make a difference?

And I'm going to go out, and I'm going to fight as long as I can. The only reason I left Arkansas to go to Washington is to fight for the most valuable resource we'll ever have—our children.

> ***"The only reason I left Arkansas to go to Washington is to fight for the most valuable resource we'll ever have—our children."***

We've got to build networks—we've got a lot of coalitions going on, but we've got to start networking. And the best-connected network I know is the church. And I'm going to Atlanta tomorrow to talk and work with the churches again, because I feel that they need to get out there in the community and start doing some of the things that they have the power, the prestige, and the resources to get done. And I'm going to ask them to use it in their communities. It's not good enough to be a haven for the saved; I'm going to ask them to be a hospital for the sick and the sinners.

We've got to use the tools of commitment. And the tools of commitment—we've got to be willing to give of our time, our talent, and yes, we have to give of our treasures. We have to biopsy our pocketbooks if we are going to get it done.

And we've got to be involved. We've *all* got to be involved. It's not one person's job, it's *all* of our jobs.

For the "o" in "prevention" I chose opportunity. We have to use every opportunity we get. Opportunities are like a hair on a bald-headed man—they only go around once, and we have to grab them when they're there. And I think we're having a wonderful opportunity now to make a real commitment on behalf of children.

Well, when are we going to do this? We've got to do it *now*. Our children can't wait while we debate. We've got to do it *now*.

I know that many of you have been out there working for a very long time. But I want to tell you my old story about dancing with a bear. A United Methodist bishop tells this in Arkansas and we use it a lot. What it says is that when you're dancing with a bear, you can't get tired and sit down. You have to wait until the *bear* gets tired, and *then* you sit down. Well, I want you to know that I go day and night trying to recruit some more partners to help me dance with this bear so we can wear him down, so we can recapture our community, recapture our bright young people and have more of them in institutions of learning like this fine university. Thank you very much.

On December 1, 1994, Elders attended the World AIDS Day Conference in New York City. Responding to a reporter's question regarding her views on masturbation, she said that she favored teaching students about it as a natural part of human sexuality and as a way to curb the spread of sexually transmitted diseases. The resulting public furor over her comments—which were widely taken to mean that she advocated teaching schoolchildren how to masturbate—proved to be the last straw for President Clinton. On December 9, he abruptly fired Elders, noting that their views differed on too many issues for them to continue working together. She reacted without bitterness but with typical candor. "Joycelyn Elders was Joycelyn Elders," she said. "I've tried to always speak what I knew to be a truth." She has since returned to teaching and conducting research at the University of Arkansas Medical School in her field of expertise, pediatric endocrinology.

SOURCES

Detroit Free Press, "Even Fans Wonder How Many Storms Elders Can Endure," September 5, 1994; "Elders' Last Straw Is Our Lost Chance," December 13, 1994.

Detroit News, "Respect Your Elders," March 16, 1993.

Ebony, "In the Eye of the Storm: Surgeon General Joycelyn Elders Challenges the Status Quo," February, 1994.

Grand Rapids Press, "Clinton Fires Surgeon General Elders," December 10, 1994; "Elders Doesn't Regret Talk That Earned Her a Pink Slip," December 12, 1994, p. D7; "Former Surgeon General Returns to Arkansas Payroll," December 13, 1994, p. D3.

Harper's Bazaar, "An Uncompromising Woman," July, 1993.

Journal of the American Medical Association (JAMA), "'Health of Nation at Stake' Says Elders," May 19, 1993.

New York Times, September 14, 1993.

New York Times Magazine, "The Crusade of Dr. Elders," October 15, 1989; "Joycelyn Elders," January 30, 1994, p. 16.

People, "Ready for Combat," July 26, 1993.

Redbook, "Tough Talk from the Top," August, 1994.

Time, "Prognosis: Controversy," July 19, 1993, p. 52.

USA Weekend, "Listening to Elders," June 3-5, 1994, pp. 4-6.

U.S. News and World Report, "The Prescription of Dr. Yes," July 26, 1993.

Washington Post, February 16, 1993.

Jaime Escalante

1931–

Bolivian American educator and motivational speaker

"Ganas—that's all I need." Driven by his belief in the tremendous power of that single Spanish word, which loosely translates as "desire," Jaime Escalante has taken classrooms full of young people others wrote off as losers and turned them into winners. Nowadays, this near-legendary high school math teacher shares his formula for success with audiences of all ages and backgrounds via the lecture circuit. At every stop, the message is the same: believe in yourself, and you can do anything.

Escalante left his native Bolivia for the United States in 1964 to escape political turmoil. He and his wife and son settled in Pasadena, California, where Escalante's inability to speak English made it impossible for him to pursue his previous career as a calculus teacher. Instead, he took a job in a coffee shop and worked on his English, becoming fluent enough within a relatively short time to secure a position in the parts department of the Burroughs Corporation.

Despite the fact that he had soon made a good life for his family, Escalante desperately missed teaching. So he returned to class himself, attending seven years of night school at California State University to earn a math degree. In 1974, he joined the faculty of Garfield High School in East Los Angeles, a tough, predominantly Hispanic neighborhood known more for gangs and drugs than academic excellence. His first day on the job was an eye-opening experience; his unruly students straggled into the room without supplies and seemingly unable to perform the simplest math problems without counting on their fingers—"total chaos" is how he later described it. Sensing immediately that a traditional approach was doomed to fail in such an atmosphere, Escalante decided to try something different. Appearing before his class in a chef's hat and apron, he placed an apple on his desk, pulled out a meat cleaver, and chopped the apple in half. Smiling broadly at the startled group, he declared, "Let's talk about percentages."

Thus marked the beginning of an extraordinary partnership between Escalante and his students. Gradually, he captured not only their interest but their respect and affection with his blend of strict discipline laced with offbeat humor and generous doses of praise. He papered the walls of his room with inspirational messages and posters of people he admired as outstanding examples of success in their fields. Behind the scenes, he clashed with his fellow teachers over his unorthodox methods and badgered school administrators for more and better equipment and supplies. He also fought for money to furnish the most disadvantaged of his students with decent breakfasts and summer scholarships.

Perhaps his best-known accomplishment, however, is helping so many of his top students pass the advanced placement exam in calculus. Overcoming the skepticism of his colleagues, most of whom thought it was a waste of time to try to teach such a difficult subject to kids who probably wouldn't be going on to college, Escalante held his first calculus class in 1979; five people signed up, and four of them ended up passing the advanced placement exam. Over the next few years, he enjoyed similar success with an increasing number of students "by creating the aura of a winning football team preparing for the Big Game," as his biographer observes.

In 1982, however, this remarkable record was threatened when Escalante had to take a brief medical leave from his job after suffering a minor heart attack. He encouraged his eighteen calculus students to continue their studies without him, and fourteen of them passed the advanced placement exam. But officials with the testing service accused the entire group of cheating after noting that the errors they had made looked too similar to be just a coincidence. They gave the students two choices—either agree to take a new and more difficult version of the test or accept having their original scores declared invalid. Escalante was furious and tried to appeal the ruling with no luck; his students, hurt as well as angry, vowed to master the material they had missed and re-take the test. Two of them later reconsidered and went to work instead of enrolling in college, but the remaining twelve who took the test a second time passed.

Escalante's story has proven inspirational to others both inside and outside the field of education, thanks in part to the 1987 release of a movie version of his life, Stand and Deliver. *The critically-acclaimed drama, which stars Edward James Olmos in a riveting portrayal of Escalante, highlights the teacher's unique classroom style and burning intensity. These same qualities are also evident in the motivational speeches he regularly gives to audiences across the nation. One such occasion was during the summer of 1992 in Chicago, Illinois, when he spoke to those attending the annual meeting of the Million Dollar Round Table (MDRT), a group of life insurance agents who are among their industry's top performers in terms of sales and service. Peppering his talk with examples of "tricks" a person can use to help solve basic math problems, Escalante explained his teaching philosophy in rapid-fire, heavily-accented English that conveyed much of the passion he feels for his profession. The address he delivered at the convention has been transcribed from an audiotape available through the MDRT.*

Assume we have fifty-two times eleven. Easy! Anybody could do it! I know you can do it! One times two—two. One times five—five. One times two—two. One times five—five. Then you have a two over here, seven, five. Don't do that! Just take the fifty-two and add these two numbers, five plus two—seven, put in the middle. I know you can do it! Anybody could do it!

A student came up to me and said this: "How come? How come I'm getting only a D on this paper that you marked down 'good and original'?" So I looked at the kid, and I said this, "The part that was good was not original, and the part that was original is no good."

Teaching is fun. Teaching is fun. But I would like to speak—I would prefer to teach the kids in the classroom, educate our kids. Educating our kids of a powerful change in their personality. I should say, what we teach in the classroom will be played in our society. So, you can do it!

Four, one—let's see—three times eleven. Easy! Bring around—three. Add the neighbor—four. Add the neighbor—four. Add the neighbor—seven. Add the neighbor—four. That's it! We got it! Don't copy!

I said to my kids, the only thing you need in this class is *ganas*. *Ganas*. *G-A-N-A-S*. Which means "desire." And you can do it! Anybody could do it! Don't copy!

The other day when a student came up to me and said, "We had finals at Garfield High," and he said this to me, "How come I'm failing your class and my friend Johnny is getting a C?"

I looked at the kid, and I said, "You copied the test."

"I did *not* copy. You don't *like* me. I'm gonna bring my mom!" he said.

So I thought he was joking. The next day his mom came with the same question. "Why is it that my son is failing your class and his friend Johnny's getting a C?"

I gave her the same explanation—that he copied the test.

"No, he did *not* copy, you don't *like* him—and, by the way, you cannot prove it," she said.

So I went to my desk and I pulled out a test and explained to her, I said, "This is Johnny's test, and this is your son's test. Question number one—Johnny, well done; your son, correct. Question number two—Johnny, perfect; your son, I have no objection."

"That's what I'm getting—you don't like my son!" she said.

"Okay, let's go to question number three—Johnny, perfect; your son, neatly done. Question number four—Johnny says, 'I don't know,' and your son wrote, 'Me, either.'"

Teaching is fun, but I don't like to speak. I would prefer to teach in a classroom and speak to the kids. "Look, you can do it, Johnny, anybody could do it! Just fill the hole."

One, two, three, four, five, six, seven, eight, nine—eh!—times, times, times, times, times, times, times, times. Easy! Okay, one times nine—nine. Nine, nine, nine, nine, nine, nine—and we could put ten, if you wish—times nine, times nine. Equal, equal, equal, equal, equal, equal. You can do it! Anybody could do it, Johnny! So let's see—one times nine, yup! Nine times ten—easy! Now let's see what's left—one, two, three, four, five, six, seven, eight. Are you sure there's eight? Check! One, two, three, four, five, six, seven, eight.

"*Ganas*—that's all I need" is the motto I give to my students. When you have *ganas*, learning is easy. *Ganas* translated into English means "desire," although it is *much* more than that. It suggests a powerful urge to get ahead, a willingness to sacrifice and have the work done. And you can do it!

I say to my kids, "The power of your dreams could overcome any obstacle you have in life." And I teach my kids to play cool under the pressure. Pressure is a great teacher. It's an *energizer*. And I say to them, "With *ganas*, you will learn to use that energy to your advantage. You can do it! The only thing I need from you is *ganas*. I *know* you can do it!"

"'Ganas—that's all I need' is the motto I give to my students. When you have ganas, learning is easy."

The skills and expertise of a nation's work force are the foundations of its economic success. At this stage, this foundation is getting weak. High schools have *not* produced the students to stand and deliver for the challenges for the twenty-first century. Youngsters will be facing significant turning points. Kids between ten to fifteen years old will have a chance to choose a part toward a productive and fulfilling life. Others, perhaps, will have the last chance to avoid a diminished future. Ten to fifteen years old is the critical age. Ten to fifteen years old is the initial period of puberty and develops more rapidly than any phase of life except when the kid's five to ten. So this is the period in which kids bring new capacity to think in one way—a more abstract and complex way—and high schools should take advantage of this situation.

Unfortunately, a high percentage of kids have a risk. We know the variables. Some of the kids, say, drop out; teen pregnancy, adolescent suicide, AIDS, and so on. The problem is we do not recognize the fundamental breakdown in the human relationship—you know, the working relationship between the parents and the child. When the parent keeps a good relationship with the kid, it's gonna create a frame of understanding, affectingness, and love.

In order to obtain this, what I do is I invite the parents of my students and I say, "We're gonna have a potluck. You have to bring an extra dish." That day, the only thing we do is we socialize. We know each other, nothing else.

Then the next week, I call on the phone and I say this, "We are going to have another potluck. But this time, don't bring your kid, because the deal is between you and me." That's when I say to the parents, "I want you to follow three steps of advice. Number one: every time you talk to your kid, talk with love, without limits, unconditional love. Don't tell your kid, 'If you do this, you do that, you're gonna get this'. No! You spoil your kid. Remember, that kid does *not* belong to the park or the street or the school. He belongs to you.

"The second advice is this: When you tuck your kid in this hand you have to use love, affection. In the other, you have to use discipline. This way, this kid's going to learn what I call responsibility. I know you can do it! I need your help. School alone cannot educate. I need you.

> ***"Winners always look for solutions while losers search for excuses."***

"And the last step of advice, maybe, is the most difficult for you. You must understand your teenager. You can't? Easy. The two of us, you and I together, are going to help this child reach the highest possibility of personal development. He can do it! Anybody could do it! I need your help."

Then, in the classroom, when I don't remember the name of the kid, I call "Johnny." So Johnny could be the good, the bad, or the ugly. So I say, "Johnny," when the mind is not calm, and sometimes I say, "Johnny, you see, for instance, two, four—ah—make six, eight, times, times, times, times, six, six, six, six." Simple! You just copy this number from here. Two, four, six, and eight. Now, cut in half. Half of two—one. Half—two. Half—three. Half—four. You could do it! Anybody could do it!

At the beginning of the school year I begin each of my classes telling my students this: "I came to the United States in 1964, and I was not exposed to the language, and I couldn't communicate with others. Now, at this stage, I understand, I speak the language. However, I must apologize for my heavy British accent!" Now, please, my apologies for my Chicano accent. I picked up this in East Los Angeles from the students with whom I work.

As soon as I get in the class, I say to the kids, "One of the important aspects in life for all of us to remember is that no one person has the final authority over your destiny but yourself. You may honor, respect, a parent, a teacher, a friend. But the closest friend you will ever have is yourself. You must be a friend with yourself first. You must also be a success with yourself before to be a success with others. The greatest station you will ever have in your life is your self-image—a good opinion of yourself—and keep it that way, Johnny! You must never let *anybody* take away from you!. . . . School is the site where your dreams, your opportunities—this is the place in which you're gonna learn responsibility and build character and also develop your personal "I"—*I am*.

"Of course, you may listen to words of advice from mom, dad, friends, teachers, but in the final analysis, you must make a decision of what you want to be in life. Be a winner! Be a winner, Johnny! Enjoy your niche in life doing the good things. Scrap, reject, scratch evil things! Stay away from the negative influence! You are the best, Johnny. You can do it! Be a winner!

"Go, go toward your goals aggressively, refusing to let *anyone* steer you into drinking, smoking, pornography, or becoming a dropout. I know you can do it! Be a winner, Johnny! Believe in your goals. And you must strive toward them. You see, your parents' goals, your friends' goals, are different than your goals. Use your power! And the richest power is respect! Respect the integrity about this and respect your intelligence. . . . And you can do it! Be a winner!

"Go forward, go forward! If you go backward, you lose ground, Johnny. I know you can do it! You can do it! If you graduate from this school, it's a *big* plus for you, a *big* plus for your last name, and a pride of achievement. There is still the possibility to get a good education in high school, but you have to go to college to get it. You can do it, Johnny! Anybody could do it! I know, I know. Remember, be a winner! Winners always look for solutions while losers search for excuses. I know you can do it! Anybody could do it!"

I say to my kids, "Take a good look—two,

four, six, eight. Times, times, times, times. Seven, seven, seven, seven. Equal, equal, equal. It's easy! Simple! Double the number! Double the number! Four—half one. Double the number! Eight—half two. Double the number! Twelve—return one. Double the number! Sixteen! It's simple! You can do it! You continue the rest. You're gonna make it, Johnny! It's simple! Double—cut in half! Double—cut in half! But notice over here—six plus six, twelve. You carry one. Half is three. Plus one, four. And you can do it! Anybody could do it! Don't copy!"

The other day, a reporter came up to me and asked me this question: "What's the secret of your success?" I looked at him, and I said, "Simple. One day a pig and a chicken were walking down the road when they saw a sign that read 'Ham and Eggs for $1.85.' The chicken looked at the pig and said this, 'Is it not that great how you and I together give America a full, nutritious meal?' The pig looked at the chicken and responded, 'Yup. To me it's a tougher commitment, while you only participate.'"

That's what I expect from my students—a tougher commitment. And I know you can do it! And I make them believe, "You are gifted, Johnny, you are gifted."

A teacher does not need a whole semester to find out who is gonna be the comedian. So I just give an easy quiz, just for a test, and I call one by one, and I say, "I'm looking over your final test, and I'm really impressed with you and I'm proud of you. Have you heard this about the IQ in someplace?"

"Yup."

"When?"

"When I was in elementary school."

"Oh, yeah. You know what? I'm the only one who has the right equation to calculate correctly the IQ. *That's* why they made *Stand and Deliver!* You understand that? And people're after me trying to get this equation, and I found out you are gifted. Your IQ is 200."

"200?"

"Yes. Keep this secret. Don't tell anybody—it's just between you and me. You understand?"

Then comes the next kid, and I said—the troublemaker—same procedure. "Your IQ is 220, you are gifted."

"But they said that—"

"They don't know what they're saying! I'm the only one who knows how to calculate correctly the IQ, and you're gifted. Don't tell anybody—it's a secret between you and me. You understand?"

Perfect. No objection.

Then when the subject gets a little difficult or hard, the kid comes to me and says, "I'm gonna drop the class." I look at the kid and say, "You can't. You are gifted. You have to go all the way. Prove it, and you can do it. Anybody could do it."

The other day, a friend of mine in school who teaches told me this: "During my first year of teaching, two boys, each named Johnny, were in my class. One was a happy child, an excellent student, no finer school citizen. The second Johnny spent much of his time goofing off, . . . and I knew he was going to be a problem all year.

"Then, toward the end of September, the PTA held the first meeting of the year, and a woman came up to me and said, 'How is my son, Johnny, getting along?' For some reason, I assumed that she was the good Johnny's mother, and I responded, 'Oh, I can't tell you how much I enjoy him! I'm so glad he's in my class!'

"The next day, my problem kid came to me and said this: 'My mom told me what you said about me. I didn't know any teacher ever wanted me.' And that day, my problem kid did the class work. Then the next day, brought the homework. A few weeks later, he became one of my best friends. And later on, one of the good students."

I'm just wondering if some times we mistake the identity of a person and we think, "Nah, this guy's not gonna make it. This guy's not gonna do it. I'm not gonna be able to make business with this guy."

That's why I said to my kids, "You must combine your . . . intuition and intelligence with a great deal of hard work if you wish to be a success. Next, I will suggest to you, demand the best from yourself! You will be ahead or at least equal to the expectations of your teachers. You are the best, Johnny, you could do it! Anybody could do it!

"And don't be afraid. Don't be afraid to make mistakes. You know what? Successful people make lots of mistakes, but they learn from them. Remember by our history, Abraham Lincoln lost several elections before he won the presidency. And you can do it! Never stop testing your challenge or going on investigations beyond your limits! You could go beyond whatever you want to. The only thing you need is *ganas.* And you can do it! Anybody could do it!"

Students, when they walk into my room, I never ask them, "Who was your teacher last year?" Or I never ask, "Where are you coming from?" You know, the only thing I know is that when the kids walk into the room, they see posters of famous players decorating the classroom. Those are my principal teachings. In the back of the room, I have Wilt Chamberlain, Jerry West. Maybe not in the way for you, but I use them.

And I said to the kids, "Wilt Chamberlain, the only one in the NBA who scored 4,000 points. This guy used to pull lots of rebounds, used to intimidate the other team, and also used to block a great number of shots. The relationship between the Lakers and this team is simple: don't let the word 'algebra' or 'calculus' intimidate you. In this class, you have to pull lots of rebounds because only As and Bs are accepted. But you can do it! Anybody could do it, Johnny! And also, don't let any assignment, any homework, block your mind. You are the best, Johnny. People are watching you, looking at you, learning from you. They feel you can do it. Prove it."

Then I use, the next week, my favorite player, the famous 44—Jerry West. And I say to the kids, "You know what? Fans used to call him 'Mr. Clutch.' Simple. When the team needed a point during the last seconds of the game, they turned the ball over to him, positive that he will come through. *That*'s why he was called 'Mr. Clutch.' And I expect from you the same reflexes. If I ask you a question, I expect the answer right away. And you can do it! The only thing I need from you is the desire, the *ganas*. You can do it, Johnny!"

You know what? I do not call Jerry West "Mr. Clutch"—I call him "Mr. Consistency." I spoke with him one day. I asked this question: "Why is it that fans call you 'Mr. Clutch'?" And this is what he said: "Even if I don't have any game on the schedule, I take my basketball and shoot the ball at least five hundred times." *That's* why he was . . . a superstar!

"I expect from you the same thing, Johnny. When you go to college, you don't sit in the back, you sit in the front, people watching you, looking at you. But don't feel too comfortable! Remember what that famous pitcher Satchel Paige said: 'Don't look back—maybe something's gaining on you.' You can do it, Johnny. Anybody could do it!"

I have posters only to decorate the classroom and motivate the kids. But under the clock, I have an equation that reads: "Determination plus discipline plus hard work equals the way to success." And I put it under the clock because my kids have the tendency to look at the clock during the class time. So as soon as I see the kid doing that, I say, "Did you read that, Johnny?"

Jaime Escalante

"I-I-I-I—I was not looking at the clock."

"Read it, then! What does it say?"

"'Determination'."

"That means you refuse to quit, you don't give up! And then, what is this?"

"I-i-i-it says 'discipline.'"

"Follow the instruction from your mom, your dad, and your coach. I'm just your coach."

And I keep reminding him a coach is only as good as the entire team. But to insure that, the players make insinuations or suggestions and the coach makes decisions. And you could do it! Anybody could do it!

"What else does it say?"

"It says 'hard work.'"

"Hard work means the future. *You* are the future. What else?"

"'Equals the way to success.'"

"Success means victory. To obtain success, you must put a lot of *ganas,* work hard. And the first thing I ever ask you is believe in yourself. If you believe in yourself, that means you're thinking positively. If you believe in yourself, that means you're building confidence in yourself. If you believe in yourself, that means a giant step to success. And you can do it, Johnny. Anybody could do it! Just follow the instructions from your teacher."

Dreams accomplish wonderful things. Edison dreamed and the light came on. Mozart dreamed with that beautiful music—*visualize* that music!—and composed beautiful melodies. And Einstein dreamed challenging an action, and he came through. And the only thing I'm doing is a small amount in contribution to the dreams of my students. We lead by dreams.

And I say to my kids, "Everybody likes the baseball. One of the historic events in the baseball history took place in Chicago, and it had to do with Babe Ruth. This guy hit two home runs in that game. But the home run that *everybody* remembers is when Babe Ruth took his bat and held it out toward the outfield fence, suggesting his intention of hitting a home run.

The things were exciting because Babe Ruth in that game had two strikes on him, and this guy struck out many times—in fact, I think by history, he struck out at least 1,500 times. What would be the difference this time?

The point is, the pitch came, Babe Ruth extended his arm, took his swing, flicked his wrist, and the ball went flying over the outfield fence. . . . His teammates came carrying him literally across the field—they picked him up, let him down so he can tag the first base, and took him to second base, third base, and finally got home. For twenty minutes the game was stopped. And it was only the fourth inning.

At the end of the game, reporters were questioning Babe Ruth. And one of the reporters had this question: "What would you have done if you did not hit that home run? What would you have done if you struck out?" People who were there said that Babe Ruth kind of shrugged like the guy was completely out of his mind. And he looked at the reporter and he said this, "Mr. Reporter, it never entered my mind to do anything else but to hit that home run!"

That's what I expect from my kids. "Johnny, hit that home run or at least take the risk. . . ." I expect my kids to be winners. If you expect kids to be losers, they *will* be losers. If you expect more, hold them accountable for whatever they do—they will amaze you. A young life can change. I have seen it. I have done it through high school—many lives. Young members, oriented now, are doctors. That's a *big* plus for education. That's a *big* plus for the last name. It's a *big* plus for the country.

I believe in my students. I believe in God. I believe in education. We depend on education to prepare an educated work force, to transmit our cultural heritage to succeeding generations. School is the site of our dreams, our opportunities. As individuals, we seek the best school for our kids, recognizing with that how important education is in their future.

Talking about the future, the teacher—the teacher is the critical point. And the testimony of this claim lies among these collected memories. Each of us remembers a great teacher, the one that touched our lives, pressed us to do our best, counted our interests.

"If you expect kids to be losers, they will be losers. If you expect more, hold them accountable for whatever they do—they will amaze you."

As a teacher, the only thing I do is I exhibit deep, caring love for my students. I can be passionate with the subject I teach—with that, I capture the mind of my students. I create, innovate, my teaching constantly. I'm still making mistakes. But believe me, I'm proud to be a teacher. Thank you.

SOURCES

Books

Mathews, Jay, *Escalante: The Best Teacher in America,* Holt, 1988.

Periodicals

Mother Jones, "Reel Life," April, 1988, pp. 24-26.

Newsweek, "Escalante Still Stands and Delivers," July 20, 1992, pp. 58-59.

People, "Beating Long Odds, Jaime Escalante Stands and Delivers, Helping to Save a Faltering High School," April 11, 1988, pp. 57-58.

Other

Ganas . . . That's All I Need (audio recording), Million Dollar Round Table Tape Cassette Program, 1992.

Stand and Deliver (film), 1987.

Joseph A. Fernandez

1935–

Puerto Rican educator and organization executive

In January 1990, Joseph A. Fernandez accepted what many consider to be the toughest assignment in U.S. public education—chancellor of the massive New York City school system. Known as an energetic, strong-willed, no-nonsense reformer with an unusual degree of political savvy, he relished the chance to tame the behemoth that is responsible for educating nearly a million students in a city plagued by many social ills. The feeling both inside and outside New York was that if anyone could succeed at such a daunting task, Fernandez could. Although he was ultimately defeated following a struggle that had more to do with politics than education, he has since taken his quest for reform nationwide as president of the Council of the Great City Schools, an advocacy organization devoted to improving large urban school districts.

Fernandez, the son of Puerto Rican immigrants, is a native New Yorker who was born and raised in Harlem. During his own youth, he was an indifferent student at best; expelled from parochial school after the tenth grade for chronic truancy, he soon dropped out of the public school to which he had transferred. He then began hanging around with a gang of neighborhood toughs who pursued a life of drugs, petty crime, and street brawls.

It wasn't long, however, before Fernandez realized that he had to find a way out of East Harlem or risk ending up in jail or even dead. So he joined the Air Force at the age of seventeen and spent the next four years in Japan and Korea, during which time he earned his high school equivalency diploma. After his discharge in 1956, Fernandez married his childhood sweetheart and continued his education at Columbia University, where he studied mathematics. When his infant son developed respiratory problems in the late 1950s and doctors suggested a change in climate might help, he moved his family to Miami, Florida. There he worked his way through the University of Miami and finally obtained his bachelor's degree in 1963.

Fernandez's first teaching job was as a math instructor at a suburban Miami high school; within just a year, he was chairman of the department. His ultimate goal was to move into administration, however, so he began studying for his master's degree at Florida Atlantic University and taking on extra assignments whenever he could. His efforts soon paid off; in 1971, Fernandez became a high school assistant principal, and in 1975, he was named principal of Miami Central Senior High, a predominantly black school located in a slum area. Besides imposing a sense of order and discipline in corridors and classrooms where students had previously felt free to smoke and blast their radios, he hired several black teachers and administrators, fostered personal contacts with parents and the members of the community at large, and even had some trees planted around the building to improve its appearance.

In 1977, Fernandez was named director of community services for Dade County schools. He continued to move up the ranks, becoming an assistant superintendent in 1985 (the same year he earned his doctorate degree in education) and chief deputy to the superintendent the following year. Finally, in May 1987, the former dropout realized his dream when he was offered the superintendent's job, a promotion that put him in charge of the nation's fourth-largest public school system.

Over the next two years, Fernandez set out to transform the face of public education in Dade County and sell his vision of what it should and could be. He removed or transferred nearly fifty principals he felt were not performing up to his standards. He launched special Saturday classes in computers and music and established "magnet schools" in the arts, computers, broadcasting, and other professional fields. He set up satellite schools near several major employers in Miami (in space he persuaded several companies to donate) so that children could attend classes not far from where their parents worked. He repaired broken equipment and spruced up buildings inside and out. Above all, Fernandez championed the concept of "school-based management," a decentralization program that empowered committees of teachers, principals, and parents at each school (rather than just the bureaucrats at district headquarters) to make decisions regarding personnel, curriculum, and expenditures that best suited their particular needs.

Before long, Fernandez and his ambitious Dade County experiment had attracted national attention. In mid-1989, New York City public school officials approached him about the chancellor's job there. After some initial hesitation, Fernandez accepted their offer in late September and then hit the ground running.

Over the next three months, Fernandez maintained a whirlwind schedule of meetings with state and local leaders not only from the field of education but also from business, politics, labor, and other areas in the belief that their input and support were critical to his success. He also devoured stacks of reports to familiarize himself with the New York City system and issued periodic public statements on his findings. By the time he officially took office in January 1990, Fernandez had hammered out a reform agenda that he was ready to begin implementing. And New Yorkers had a new hero—a blunt, tough-talking guy who truly seemed capable of delivering on a promise to shake things up. As Fernandez himself remarked to a reporter for New York *magazine, "I'm very impatient with people . . . who say things can't be done because we've never tried them that way before. To move a large bureaucracy, sometimes you've got to kick people in the ass."*

In his first year or so on the job, Fernandez did just that. Among his many undertakings, he trimmed and reorganized the bureaucracy at Board of Education headquarters; abolished the practice of "building tenure," which had made it impossible to transfer a principal to another school without his or her consent; dismantled the Board of Examiners, a teacher certification agency long regarded as inept and inefficient; challenged the independence of the city's notoriously corrupt local school boards by threatening to take them over if they did not cooperate with him; tackled the huge backlog in building maintenance projects; and campaigned to curb the power of the custodians' union, whose labor contract strictly limited the off-hours use of school buildings. In addition, Fernandez was able to institute his school-based management program in about ten percent of the city's schools.

At the classroom level, too, Fernandez plunged right in. For example, he set up panels to recommend curriculum changes and figure out ways of dealing with overcrowding. He also took steps to have schools play a bigger role in combatting drugs, violence, racial tension, and other social problems. He even managed to overcome objections and win approval for a condom distribution plan he hoped would help decrease the teenage pregnancy rate and slow down the spread of AIDS and other sexually-transmitted diseases.

But by 1992, Fernandez's power struggles with school-board officials over these and other issues had escalated into an all-out war that threatened to overshadow his considerable achievements. Tensions finally came to a head over his proposed "Rainbow Curriculum," a teacher's guide for elementary grades that emphasized multiculturalism and promoted tolerance of gays and lesbians. All but one of the city's thirty-two local school boards eventually accepted it (or a modified version of it) without too much controversy, but a group of angry parents from the Queens district—backed by the Roman Catholic Church—labeled it "propaganda" and specifically condemned the section on homosexuality as an affront to their religious and moral values. Fernandez fought back, but in February 1993, at the end of a day-long public hearing during which dozens of people stood up to defend the chancellor, the central board voted not to renew his contract. Afterward, Fernandez told reporters, "Yes, I have made mistakes. But I have fought for children. I will always put their welfare ahead of political or special interests."

In July 1993, Fernandez assumed the presidency of the Council of the Great City Schools, a Washington, D.C.-based advocacy organization that assists some of the nation's largest urban school districts in their efforts to initiate change and advance the cause of education. Later that same year, on September 7, Fernandez shared his views on the state of American public education and discussed the Council's goals in a speech before the National Press Club in Washington, D.C. Fernandez furnished a copy of his remarks.

Thank you very much for that kind introduction and for the generous invitation you have extended to me and the Council of the Great City Schools to appear before such an esteemed group of national journalists.

For those of you who do not know us—though many of you do—the Council of the Great City Schools is a national coalition of the nation's largest urban public school systems. It is the only national organization whose sole mission is the improvement of education in our inner cities. I would like to introduce Michael Casserly, the Council's Executive Director, and Henry Duvall, its Director of Communications. Please feel free to call on any of us should you need information on our schools.

I hope my job here today will be easier than the one I had for three years as chancellor of the New York City Public Schools and as superintendent before that in Dade County, Florida. My successor in New York, Ray Cortines, will not have an easy time of it—like all of us in urban education—but he is superbly qualified for the job and I wish him well.

I have been asked to speak to you today about the state of American education and what it will take to pull our nation's schools up to a point at which we are justifiably proud—a point at which you have no choice but to write glowing reports about our conduct and our results.

I cannot come at this topic of American education by any other direction than through the cities. There is no American education—now or in the future—without its Great City Schools.

Nowhere does the national resolve to strengthen our children's education face a tougher test than in our inner cities. Every problem is more pronounced there, every solution harder to implement. The litany is now familiar to you: poverty, drug abuse, family instability or no families at all, aging buildings and facilities, dropouts, teen pregnancy, poor health care, violence, racism and bigotry, AIDS, limited-English language proficiency, disabilities and malnutrition. And efforts to address these must be conducted in an atmosphere of enormous political, demographic, economic, cultural, social and religious complexity and diversity—usually with precious few dollars or backing.

It is often asked, however, why anyone should care. Why should the larger community want to help solve problems that are so daunting, so complex, remote, costly, entrenched and divisive? The reasons are actually uncomplicated.

> ***"Nowhere does the national resolve to strengthen our children's education face a tougher test than in our inner cities."***

First, it is in America's best self-interest to care. Urban children take up too large a portion of America's total children to expect that the country can survive without them. Of the nation's 15,000 school districts, our largest 50 city school systems educate about 38 percent of the nation's limited-English proficient children, 25 percent of the nation's poor children and 14 percent of its disabled children. About 40 percent of our nation's African American, Latino and Asian American children are educated each day in our major city schools. Our total enrollment—not population—would qualify us as the 80th largest of the 160 countries in the United Nations.

Consider this: if the graduation rate for urban schools equaled the national average, the Great City Schools would have graduated 295,521 students in 1990-91 instead of 214,253. At the current 28 percent tax rate, the federal tax on the total *additional* lifetime earnings of those extra 81,268 individuals, *had they graduated,* is large enough annually to double the present congressional appropriation for elementary and secondary education, increase federal AIDS research five-fold, or boost federal drug prevention efforts by a factor of ten—efforts that benefit the entire nation, not just the cities.

Second, unless action is taken to meet the challenges of urban education, our problems will soon enough become prevalent in all but the most elite of the nation's schools. Finally, the country has a moral imperative, grounded in our own Constitution, to strive for individual justice and equality for its citizens, and education is the soundest way of endowing those rights.

The nation cannot afford to play a game of containment with us, hoping that our problems will stay inside the city limits. It is already too late for that and besides, we are too large a portion of the country and its future for such a strategy to work. And for our part, we cannot continue to pretend that we can do the job alone. The problems we face in our schools are so immense and so entangled with the problems of our nation and its cities, that we cannot hope to meet them ourselves. Nor can the nation realistically hope to meet its own goals and stay economically competitive without us.

It is how I come at the state of American education and what must be done to save it—through the cities.

Let me take a minute to describe where we are in urban education, let you draw your own conclusions about where American schools must be given what I have just described, then talk about what I think should be done and what we are doing specifically. It is a good news/bad news story. Let me give it to you in equal measure, goal by goal.

First is *preschool education* and readiness for school. Despite the national consensus about the importance of early development, the statistics are frightening:

-Some 15-20 percent of all babies in the country are born exposed to illegal drugs;

-Some 7 percent of all babies and 13 percent of African American babies are born with low birth weight;

-Some 20 percent of all pre-kindergarten students are not vaccinated against polio;

Joseph A. Fernandez

-Only 33 percent of eligible children receive Head Start services; and

-Some 25 percent of pregnant women receive no prenatal care during the first trimester.

It is an area, however, where urban schools may be doing better than America's schools, in general, in developing solutions. There are promising signs in our city schools:

-Some 58 percent of our urban school districts now assess the readiness of children for school using a combination of measures of cognitive development, immunizations, health, social development, weight and age; and

-Some 53.1 percent of our first-graders had a full-day kindergarten in the same school where they are now in first grade.

The bad news, though, is that some 20 percent of our urban school districts still use only a birth certificate to assess school readiness. We should do better than that. And we should do better at placing health services, family support programs, and child care services directly in our schools. Few efforts would provide greater payoff, in addition, than efforts by us to coordinate our social, family and health activities with those of other public and private agencies and groups throughout the cities. It is an area where urban schools are already doing better than most schools but where we could be models for the nation. The Council will be attempting to put together efforts to do just that, and applauds the Clinton administration for pushing so consistently for full funding of Head Start.

Second is the area of *dropouts* where urban schools have considerably more difficulty. Here the statistics are also troubling nationally but getting better:

-Only 69 percent of students entering high school in 1986 graduated in 1990;

-Pregnancy still leads the list of reasons why girls drop out, with over 1 million teen pregnancies a year; and

-The dropout gap between African American students and whites appears to be closing but remains wide with Hispanic students.

While our urban schools continue to have serious problems in this area there are positive signs that suggest that we are doing something right:

-The median annual dropout rate in our urban schools dropped from 10.6 percent in 1988-89 to 8.8 percent in 1990-91; and

-The median four-year dropout rate in urban schools declined from 32.1 percent in 1988-89 to 26.1 percent in 1990-91.

The bad news is that our rates still are about twice as high as the national average. And the dropout rates particularly of our Hispanic youngsters are not budging much. The rates for these youngsters are in the neighborhood of 10-15 percent annually. One of the promising trends nationally, however, is that the dropout rates among our African American youngsters is declining to a level that is nearly comparable to white students. My guess is that this positive development nationally can be traced directly to urban schools and the efforts they have been making over the last ten years, and is a clear indication of the link between the cities and how the nation fares. One thing we have clearly learned over the years is to tailor our programs better to the myriad reasons why youngsters drop out of school.

Third is *achievement*. The national figures here are also not good and are obviously now driving much of the current debate on standards and assessments:

-The U.S. ranks approximately 12th of 14 on international tests of math and science knowledge among 13-year-olds;

-Some 58 percent of 13-year-old U.S. students display only moderate reading ability; and

-Only 18 percent of U.S. 8th graders meet new national standards in mathematics.

There is evidence that our urban schools are making some progress here too, although the bad news continues to outstrip the good:

-About 67 percent of urban school districts showed increasing achievement test scores in reading and math between 1988-89 and 1990-91 at the elementary grade levels, and about half did in the secondary grades;

-The average urban student scored at about the 50th percentile in math in 1990-91, although lower in reading; and

-Urban public school students were completing advanced placement or international baccalaureate course in reading, math and science at about twice the national average.

These are obviously promising indicators but there are discouraging ones too. Only one-third of our urban students have completed a first-year course in algebra by the end of the 10th grade. And the achievement of our African American and Hispanic students is way too low. Only 10 percent of our African American students score in the top quartile in math by the 10th grade, although a full 25 percent had in second grade. We enroll 32 percent of the nation's Hispanic youth, yet produce fewer than 1000 Hispanic students each year who score in the top quartile in math.

We should do better than this in urban America. The new standards development process may help in this regard, but we as urban educators can make more headway on our own with more cooperative learning models, less tracking and remedial skills efforts, more intensive instructional approaches.

Fourth is *teachers* and teaching. While we have some of the most dedicated and talented teachers in the world teaching in U.S. schools, there are danger signs:

-A substantial portion of the nation's teachers are expected to retire in the next ten years;

-Fewer African Americans and Hispanics are pursuing careers in teaching; and

-The nation's schools spend precious little of their resources on professional development and training for teachers.

Urban schools, by and large, reflect national trends in this area, although there are positive indicators as well, including:

-Some 98.6 percent of our urban secondary-grade English teachers are certified to teach in English and 96.9 percent of our secondary-grade math teachers are certified to teach in math; and

-Urban teachers are more likely to be more experienced than the average teacher.

The bad news is that we are now not able to pay our teachers much more than the national average, thereby cutting our ability to attract individuals willing to work in our most difficult schools. In addition, the demographics of our teachers is almost the exact opposite of our students and the shortage of teachers in urban areas is about 2.5 times higher than national averages. Our ability to correct these trends will rest largely on our willingness to spend more on professional development, our ability to improve working conditions in our inner-city schools, and our aggressiveness in reaching out to the African American, Hispanic and Asian American communities to encourage more individuals from there to seek teaching in our schools as a career. Like the area of preschool education, it is an area in which urban schools can easily serve as national models.

Fifth is our *postsecondary opportunities*. Here we are now paying the price for years of underinvestment in education and literacy, and shifting demographics:

-Some 27 million Americans are judged to be illiterate;

-The average youth unemployment rate is about 15-20 percent, although about 30 percent in the inner cities; and

-About 75 percent of all new jobs between now and the year 2000 will be in the suburbs.

Urban schools are showing some positive signs here over which they have some control but there are many aspects of what happens here that our schools have trouble affecting:

-Some 41.8 percent of our graduates entered or planned to enter four-year colleges or universities, a rate higher than the national average.

But our good news here may be an artifact of our high dropout rates. The numbers do show, however, that if you stay in school—even an urban public school—your chances of going to college are as good as anybody from anywhere.

Finally are the challenges of *safety, drug abuse and facilities*. These are areas where schools nationally are facing serious problems but where the public has a difficult time investing resources to correct the problems, as the recent asbestos situation in New York City illustrates. The national statistics are troubling:

- -Each day there is estimated to be about 16,000 crimes on or near school property;
- -Some 100,000 students bring weapons to school each day;
- -Drug use among teens continues to be high despite promising trends recently; and
- -There is some $50-$100 billion in capital needs across the nation for our school facilities.

There are some promising indications, however, that urban schools continue to be a safe haven for inner-city youth:

- -There were only 2.0 incidents of drug or alcohol abuse on urban school premises for every 1,000 9-12 grade students in 1990-91;
- -Urban students continue to be safer in their schools than almost anywhere else—including home.

But the promising signs cannot mask a serious problem, not just for urban schools but for the American society. I think we need to keep squarely in mind that these are not problems of kids—these are problems of adults. It is adults who manufacture and distribute the guns, who produce and show the violence on television, and who abuse and beat our children—kids don't do this, adults do.

What does all this add up to? What should we be doing to save our schools? My hunch is that we as a nation are doing better with our public school system than most people realize and what most critics suggest. But even if the critics are entirely wrong, there is no reason to think that our schools nationally shouldn't be substantially improved. Our economic global competitiveness certainly rests on it, as does our domestic tranquility.

And here is where I am brought back to urban schools and their centrality to our national purpose and our desire to lead the world educationally.

Let me start at home base with urban schools themselves and what they could be doing better. And I do want to be up front about our thinking that we can do better in lots of areas. I have talked about some already but let me suggest a few more. Some of them actually cost surprisingly little money. Here is my "Top Ten List" for improving urban schools and improving the nation:

1. *Urban schools not only need to be more open to educational reform but actually lead it.* There are many cases where they have, including the schools in New York, Houston, San Diego, Dade County, Pittsburgh, Rochester, Chicago, Milwaukee, Cleveland and others. In fact, much of the reform movement that has now been somewhat co-opted by the states grew out of initiatives and experiments in city schools. Yet, urban education is often viewed as entrenched, immovable, self-protective and sluggish with bureaucracy. In too many instances this is the case, but the reformers among us can easily serve as models to the rest. It is, in fact, good for us to reform and it is better yet for us to reform ourselves—urban schools are in the best position to do that—and we do want to.

2. *Urban schools need to increase their collaborative arrangements with the community at large.* I said earlier that I thought that closer collaboration with other public and community agencies was necessary to deliver comprehensive services to our children. I will expand that here to include the churches, business, the media, the suburbs, the mayors and others. It also means keeping our facilities open to the community and designing our programs around the schedules and needs of the community, not our own. As far as I am concerned, urban education cannot solve the problems faced by society alone. That does not mean that we shouldn't be involving ourselves in issues no one else will touch; it does mean that we are asking for help from all quarters now that we have accepted the challenge.

3. *Urban schools need to stop treating parents as the enemy.* Urban education has amazingly few friends. Not only can it not afford to alienate anyone, it must develop better strategies to reach out to parents on whatever terms or grounds they find themselves. We should not only be treating them as our number-one customer but also our number-one ally. It is for that reason that the Council supports legislation to add another national goal on parental involvement.

4. *Urban school leaders need to stop chewing themselves up on political agendas.* I am not sure how to do this but there are examples galore in every city where the fractured and desperate nature of the community is leading educational leadership into gridlock that makes Washington seem pale in comparison. Part of what is going on can be traced to the extreme poverty and needs of the urban community badly wanting a quality education and a future, but

the desperation has begun to turn inward in the form of bureaucratic cannibalism.

5. *Urban schools need to do everything they can to stop sorting and tracking kids, and to raise the standards and expectations for their children.* Too much of schooling, not just in the cities but everywhere, is caught up in the unwitting sorting and tracking of students by ability or perceived ability. Too often the results lead only to sorting by race, sex and income and have nothing to do with the abilities or efforts of our children.

6. *Urban school boards, administrators and teachers should think more positively of their work.* People working in urban schools have listened so long to people bashing them and their work that I think they have started to believe and act on it. It has led to a defensiveness about what we do and a corresponding reflex instinct when we are criticized. In fact, most of the people I know in urban education are some of the most talented, dynamic and intelligent people working anywhere.

> *"The disparity in funding between rich and poor schools is a national disgrace."*

7. *Urban schools need to downsize anything that touches children.* When I was in New York, I started a process that has led to a series of smaller high schools. I think it is important that we reduce the size of our urban schools, particularly the high schools—even if they are only schools-within-schools. Children need warmth and individual attention to thrive and it is too hard to give it to them with schools the size of factories.

8. *Urban schools need to help break down the artificial barriers between managers and teachers.* Outside of students and parents, teachers should be our best friends in education but often they are not and we sometimes ensure it by how we act. Business has developed some very interesting models for how to establish more collaborative work settings and there is no reason why we shouldn't be looking at testing those in our settings. Education is, after all, a human endeavor where the merits of all our people need to be respected.

9. *Urban schools need to devote more time and effort to professional development, research and strategic planning.* So much of our work in urban education is crisis-oriented that we devote precious little time to planning for anything more than the next board meeting. Because education is a long-term endeavor, we need to plan and think long-term.

10. *Urban schools need to increase, not shy away from, their commitment to and emphasis on multiculturalism.* Urban schools often take a lot of heat for their efforts to celebrate and enhance the diversity of their students and teachers. But urban schools, in fact, are well ahead of a nation that will need to do the same thing very shortly. The nation could take a lesson from us here.

There are also things that I think that the states and the federal government could do to help us. Some of it has to do with money. While I don't think money cures all, I am a firm believer that money matters in schools like it does everywhere else. I saw it everyday in my work from the time I was a math teacher in Miami through the time I was chancellor of the New York City Public Schools. Part of that belief rests on the fact that urban schools just don't have the resources of other school systems. Our data indicates that the average large-city school system spent about $5,200 per student in 1990-91 while the average suburban school system spent $6,073 and the average suburban district spent about $5,476. That $873 disparity between urban schools and the suburbs amounts to nearly $22,000 more for a class of 25 children whose needs are not as high as their peers in the [cities].

The long and short of it is that America is getting what it's paying for in urban education. I repeat: There is no future for America that fails to include its Great City Schools.

The disparity in funding between rich and poor schools is a national disgrace. To date the states have been slow to move to correct the situation without court intervention. But besides pressing to correct these inequities, I would urge the states and the governors to urge Congress to help on this front by enacting legislation that makes the federal government an actor in education that reflects the national need. The governors should be pressing Congress for a major new education spending initiative or trust fund to help equalize the disparities and to deliver on the opportunity standards that many in Congress are calling for as part of the administration's reform bill.

And Congress, for its part, should not complete the process of reauthorizing the federal Elementary and Secondary Education Act without approving a sizable new initiative to help poor schools, particularly in urban and rural areas, to meet the national goals. This is the last reauthorization before the year 2000. Both Congress and the Clinton administration should want to leave a legacy that includes more than setting standards and reforming current programs.

Let me begin to wind this up by taking a minute to talk about what urban schools as a group, as a coalition, are doing to improve ourselves. And let me underscore that urban schools are not sitting back waiting to be reformed, broken up, taken over, privatized or left alone.

Just last September, the Council of the Great City Schools completed the first phase of its long-term efforts to improve urban schools which included the development of a set of National Urban Education Goals that are derived from the national ones set by the president and the governors, the convening of a National Urban Education Summit Conference that ratified the Urban Goals along with some eighty other national organizations and groups and the urban schools themselves, development of federal legislation (the Urban Schools of America USA bill) to lay out what we needed from Congress to meet those goals, and published a set of baseline statistical indicators on where urban schools stood on those goals.

The next phase for the Council will be devoted to meeting the goals and will include the following, amongst many others:

-First, the Council is naming a new National Urban Education Task Force to begin the process of designing a national urban school blueprint for meeting the goals.

-Second, the Council will be naming a National Commission on Urban Education to assist in the development of the blueprint and to serve as outside validators of what we are attempting to do.

-Third, the Council will be convening a second National Urban Education Summit Conference to ratify the blueprint with our urban goal partners.

-Fourth, the Council is developing a new set of discrete initiatives in each one of the National Urban Education Goal areas to help our schools deliver on what they have committed to and what the blueprint suggests, including efforts on preschool education, dropouts, achievement and standards, postsecondary opportunities, health and school safety.

-Fifth, the Council is designing a multilayer training collaborative with the nation's major corporations and public sector managers to improve our expertise in efficiently managing our large-scale responsibilities. Components will include urban school boards, managers and administrators, and urban school principals.

-Sixth, the Council is designing a major new collaborative between our urban schools and the colleges of education and historically black colleges and universities to work together on issues of teacher recruitment, pre-service and in-service training, teacher support and curricula development.

-Seventh, the Council is designing a new initiative to improve parental participation in our schools and to recognize the achievements of urban schools and students.

Ladies and gentlemen, America's schools have traditionally been at the heart of the communities they serve. As one of our fundamental institutions, public schools have been one of the few places where rich meet poor, the advantaged mingled with the disadvantaged, and where ideally, political, religious, and ethnic boundaries would not exist. As a nation, America has literally entrusted its future to our public schools.

This investment is doubly important in our urban schools, for they form one of the crucibles of American democracy. They are, in fact, one of the last frontiers of our democratic ideal. The nation cannot afford to survey our urban landscape—with its difficult terrain—and conclude that conquering our troubles is a lost cause. The year 2000 looms large and near. We—as a nation—cannot arrive there intact without [our] city kids. The alternatives are too bleak to imagine.

Thank you very much and I would be happy to take questions.

SOURCES

Books

Fernandez, Joseph A., with John Underwood, *Tales Out of School: Joseph Fernandez's Crusade to Rescue American Education*, Little, Brown, 1993.

Periodicals

Detroit Free Press, "NYC Schools Chief Ousted Over Sex

Education Policy," February 11, 1993, p. 3A; "For School Systems in Big Cities, the Top Job Is a Revolving Door," March 7, 1993, p. 6F.

Detroit News, "Angry New York Parents Protest First Grade Class on Gay Lifestyle," December 8, 1992.

Grand Rapids Press, "NYC Won't Renew School Chief's Contract," February 11, 1993, p. A5.

Hispanic, "King of the Blackboard Jungle," August, 1990.

Nation, "Over the Rainbow," May 10, 1993, pp. 631-636.

Newsweek, "If He Could Make It Here . . . ," December 21, 1992, p. 57; "Who Would Want This Job?" February 22, 1993, pp. 54-56.

New York, "The Report Card on Joe Fernandez," January 22, 1990, pp. 40-46.

New Yorker, "The End of the Rainbow," April 12, 1993, pp. 43-54.

New York Times Magazine, "Fernandez Takes Charge," June 17, 1990.

Reader's Digest, "Can a Former Dropout Save New York's Schools?" October, 1990, pp. 78-82.

Time, "Bracing for Perestroika," January 8, 1990, p. 68.

U.S. News and World Report, "Rebel Without a Pause," October 1, 1990, pp. 76-78.

Hiram L. Fong

1907–

Chinese American attorney, businessman, and former member of the U.S. Senate

Hiram L. Fong has played a role in more than a few important "firsts" in his life—founder of the first multiethnic law firm in Honolulu; first Chinese American to serve in Congress; senior member of the first three legislators to represent Hawaii when it was proclaimed the fiftieth state in 1959. (In fact, Fong was instrumental in the drive to secure statehood for Hawaii.) These remarkable achievements take on an added luster when considered against the backdrop of his impoverished childhood and struggle to obtain the best education possible. But as one of his Senate colleagues once noted, his is "a true Horatio Alger story," a rags-to-riches saga that "exemplifies those deeply held, genuinely American beliefs in hard work, perseverance, and opportunity."

Home for Fong was a tough slum neighborhood of Honolulu, where he was born the seventh of eleven children of parents who had come to Hawaii from China to work as indentured servants on a sugar plantation. The family was so poor that young Yau, as he was then known (he took the name Hiram in college), went to work picking beans at the age of four to help out financially. He continued doing odd jobs throughout his entire childhood, including shining shoes, selling newspapers, catching fish and crabs, and caddying at a local golf course.

Fong was a very good student who showed much promise, but his dream of going on to college after graduating from high school had to wait until he could earn enough money to pay his own way. For three years, he worked as a clerk at the Pearl Harbor Naval Shipyard, then enrolled at the University of Hawaii. He completed the course work necessary for his bachelor's degree in only three years, earning highest honors in the process. This he managed to accomplish while holding a variety of part-time jobs and participating in many outside activities such as editing the school newspaper, participating on the debate team, and competing in various sports.

Following his graduation from college in 1930, Fong went back to work full-time as an employee of suburban Honolulu's water department to finance his next step up the ladder—law school. In 1932, he went off to Harvard, returning home to Honolulu three years later completely broke but with his law degree in hand. After a brief stint as a municipal clerk, Fong then formed a partnership with several other *local attorneys of Japanese, Korean, and Caucasian ancestry to establish Honolulu's first multiethnic law firm. The venture proved to be extremely successful, enabling Fong to make a series of lucrative investments in real estate, insurance and finance firms, shopping centers, and a plantation. Within just a few years, the man who had once picked beans to supplement his father's meager wages was a millionaire.*

With his financial independence assured, Fong then turned his attention to public service. He worked as deputy attorney for both the city and county of Honolulu until 1938, at which time he won election as a Republican to the territorial House of Representatives. There he served for the next fourteen years (including three terms as speaker and two as vice-speaker) and made achieving statehood for Hawaii one of his top priorities. His efforts were finally rewarded on June 27, 1959, when islanders voted to join the United States. A month later, on July 28, they elected Fong to one of the new state's two seats in the U.S. Senate; the other went to a Democrat, Oren E. Long. On August 21, Hawaii was officially proclaimed the fiftieth state, and on August 24, a lucky coin toss and draw determined that Fong rather than Long would be considered Hawaii's "senior" senator and that he would also enjoy a longer term—five-and-a-half years as opposed to Long's three-and-a-half years.

Once in office, Fong—a self-described liberal on social issues and a conservative on fiscal and military ones—worked hard to make sure the country's newest state received fair and equitable treatment from the federal government. (In the case of national highway construction funds, for example, federal officials decided that since Hawaii didn't have any roads connecting it to other states, it wasn't entitled to any money for roads. Fong successfully disputed that judgment.) At the national level, he supported major civil rights and antidiscrimination legislation, including the landmark Civil Rights Bill of 1964. The following year, he played a key role in drafting immigration reform laws that eliminated the old quota system based on race and national origin and opened the door for larger numbers of Asians to enter the United States.

Perhaps most notably, however, Fong served as a living bridge between East and West. He fostered numerous cultural and economic exchanges between nations of the Asia-Pacific region and the United States, including helping to establish and secure funding for the East-West Center, an internationally respected think-tank based at the University of Hawaii. He was extremely proud of Hawaii's multiracial and multiethnic mix of residents, and he frequently held up his beloved home state as an example of how harmony and brotherhood were not beyond reach for the peoples of the world, no matter what their race, color, or creed.

In 1960, Fong's devotion to this ideal prompted members of the National Conference of Christians and Jews to name him the recipient of their National Brotherhood Award for his outstanding service and leadership. At a special gathering held in Providence, Rhode Island, on May 5 of that year, the senator formally accepted the honor and then delivered a speech in which he reflected on the factors that had contributed to Hawaii's uniqueness among the nations of man. On May 11, a Senate colleague asked that Fong's remarks be entered into the Congressional Record, *86th Congress, 2nd Session, Volume 106, Part 8, U.S. Government Printing Office, 1960, and it is from that version that the following is reprinted.*

It is indeed a great honor and a great privilege for my wife Ellyn and me to be with you this evening—to sit down with you and to break bread with you and to make your friendship.

To receive from you, friends I have just come to know, through your national president, Dr. Louis Webster Jones, this bronze award signifying service to the cause of brotherhood, moves me very, very deeply. I am doubly thankful for your kindness and for selecting me for this honor which I know I do not deserve.

My father and mother were Taoists. Were they living and here tonight amidst your warmth and friendliness, witnessing the receipt by their son of this very coveted service award from the National Conference of Christians and Jews they would undoubtedly have remarked, "This is truly in accord with what Confucius has said, 'Under heaven all men are brothers.'"

That we should be meeting here in historic Providence, one of the queen cities of New England, pleases me greatly. I feel very much at home, for you see New England is a part of me. Three long, hard, but rewarding years of my formative life between 1932 and 1935 were spent not far from here, at Cambridge, Massachusetts, as a Harvard Law School student. But even before Harvard, I was acquainted with New England. Its influence has been felt in my native Hawaii for 140 years—since the arrival in 1820 of the first group of 12 communities of Christian Congregational missionaries from New England.

It is amazing how tremendous was their and their children's contribution to the development and stability of Hawaii and how their Puritan philosophy has influenced Hawaii's outlook and life.

Through their influence, the Hawaiian language was reduced to writing, the Bible was translated, and schools were established. Through their influence, the first written constitution was approved in 1840, creating a supreme court and a representative body of legislators elected by the people.

Through their influence, prohibition was placed on immorality, gambling, drunkenness, theft, and violation of the Sabbath, much to the resistance of foreign sailors who, on several occasions, demonstrated by armed riots, not against the natives, but against the missionaries. Into

Hiram L. Fong

the home of one of them several cannon shots were fired.

Architecturally, too, New England has left its visible mark on Hawaii. Even today, it is not unusual to see a Cape Cod cottage on any one of the seven inhabited islands.

New England's influence on me has been quite personal. Besides being a graduate of Harvard Law School, I am a graduate of the public school system which the Congregational missionaries inaugurated. My name of Hiram is taken from the Reverend Hiram Bingham, leader of the first group of missionaries. My religion is Congregational.

So, it is indeed a distinct honor and a great privilege for me to be speaking here tonight in New England, for to me it is in a sense in more ways than one, like returning home.

Your regional director, Mrs. Rozella Switzer, has asked me to discuss Hawaii's role in human relationships and I am happy to accede to her wishes.

Hawaii, it is claimed by historians, was discovered by Captain James Cook, an Englishman. This claim, however, is disputed by the Chinese who relate this very plausible story. Ten years prior to Captain Cook's visit a Chinese junk left the harbor of Hong Kong and sailed eastward across the vast Pacific. Dropping anchor at Waikiki, the captain pulled out his spyglass and scanned the shore. This is what he saw—beautiful Hawaiian maidens, dressed in grass skirts, dancing to the tune of ukuleles. Putting his spyglass down, he turned to his men and said, "Men, we must sail on, there is no laundry to be done here." And this is the reason there are so many Chinese laundries in New England.

The cook on the ship, however, was not convinced. He, too, picked up the spyglass and scanned the shore. What he saw, he liked. Putting down his spyglass, he jumped overboard and swam to shore. As he was a good cook, the captain would not sail without him.

After a whole week of search, he was found in the loving arms of a very amorous Hawaiian maiden. Yanking him from her charms, the crew took him down to the beach where, to make an example of him before all the men, the captain made him put on heavy boots and marched him up and down. With every step he took, the captain gave him a kick. After many kicks, the cook turned around and said, "Why kickee me?" And that is how Waikiki got its name.

Essential to a deeper understanding of Hawaii is a knowledge of its history, its geographical location, and of the peoples who settled there. Situated in the vast Pacific Ocean which covers one-third of our globe the Hawaiian Islands number just eight out of the thousands of islands comprising Malaysia, Melanesia, Micronesia, and Polynesia. Archaeologists, anthropologists, and historians of these oceanic people and their culture virtually agree that stone-age Caucasian people in successive waves of migration from the Indochina Peninsula pushed eastward into Malaysia, then from there to Melanesia, then to the islands off and surrounding Tahiti, the heart of Polynesia. From Tahiti in great single and double canoes, they dispersed 2,500 miles north to Hawaii, southwest to New Zealand, and southeast to Mangareva, Pitcairn, and Easter Island.

Charcoals recently discovered in fireplaces used by the early settlers of Hawaii have been determined by the radio carbon method to date back a thousand years.

It is generally conceded that the first Polynesians landed on Hawaii some 1,200 years ago.

Little is known of the history of Hawaii until Captain James Cook, of Great Britain, discovered the islands in 1778, and brought to a close the period of Hawaiian isolation which had existed for ten centuries. Thereafter, fur traders of the Northwest and California, on their way to sell their furs in China, together with the demand for Hawaiian sandalwood and the outfitting of whaling fleets, made Hawaii an important port of commerce.

The strategic significance of Hawaii as a Pacific outpost became apparent in the middle of the nineteenth century, when a power struggle for dominance of the islands took place between England, France, and the United States.

Hawaii today could easily have been an English colony by right of discovery or by cession, or a French colony by force of arms.

A British naval force seized Hawaii and for five months the British flag flew over the islands in 1843. However, by that time, the influence of Americans in the islands and the gaining strength of the United States in the Pacific, assured the Hawaiian kingdom of its independence.

From 1795 when Kamehameha, a Hawaiian chieftain, took control of Hawaii, Maui, and Oahu, to 1893, a period of almost 100 years, the Hawaiian Islands were under the rule of seven kings and one queen. In 1893, Queen Liliuokalani was dethroned and a provisional government was formed. The Republic of Hawaii was established the following year.

Hawaii was annexed by the United States in 1898 and from 1900 to nine months ago, it was an incorporated territory of the United States with a representative legislature elected by the people but with an appointed governor.

Ethnically, Hawaii is composed of many nationalities. The early settlers were the Polynesians. Caucasian sailors, adventurers, whalers, traders, and missionaries were second comers. Then followed Chinese contract laborers recruited to work the sugar plantations as the Hawaiians were not inclined to hard labor.

With the annexation of the islands to the United States in 1898, Chinese labor immigration was completely prohibited as the laws, which were then in force excluding Chinese laborers to the United States, were made applicable to Hawaii.

Japanese contract laborers in great numbers were also imported from 1885 until their exclusion in 1924.

Portuguese, Swedes, Germans, Koreans, South Sea Islanders, Puerto Ricans, and Filipinos also comprised immigrant groups brought in for the cultivation and the processing of sugar.

From these heterogeneous and diverse ethnic groups has evolved a homogeneous community—a community which has been termed by students of sociology as a "twenty-first-century society" where racial harmony and cooperation are normal and accepted conditions of life. This spirit of working together pervades civic, business, political, and cultural endeavors. There is sincere respect for, rather than mere toleration of, each other's nationality, traits, characteristics, and cultures.

Living in an island paradise, tropical and balmy, with high standards of health and livelihood; with a good, free educational system; a stable, democratic government; where no group constitutes a racial majority; with peoples on one hand steeped in Christian Puritan outlook and justice, and on the other, imbued with Buddhist and Confucian philosophies stressing human and moral conduct; cemented together and mellowed by the generous open-heartedness and carefree *aloha* spirit of its native Hawaiian people, we in Hawaii would like to believe that we are giving life to a community approaching the ideal of a world at peace and in concord.

President Eisenhower said to the people of India during his recent trip, "Hawaii cries insistently to a divided world that all our differences of race and origin are less than the grand and indestructible unity of our common brotherhood. The world should take time to listen with attentive ear to Hawaii."

Hawaii is indeed a showcase for true brotherhood. Elsewhere, even as in ancient days, massive discrimination continues to blight human relationships. Our news media carry daily evidence of man's inhumanity to man, evidenced by oppression, fear, hatred, bias, and discrimination in all quarters of our globe.

Behind the Iron and Bamboo Curtains, religious and political persecution persist. In Tibet, the Red Chinese regime continues mass genocide of the civilian population. Large numbers of people still flee East Germany and Red China, at risk of life and limb, to seek sanctuary in more tolerant oases. Anti-Semitism and anti-Christianity erupt as atheistic communism seeks to wipe out religious worship.

Belligerent nationalism is more the rule than not in modern struggles to throw off the yoke of colonialism. Too often such nationalism provokes wholesale bloodletting, with guns replacing ballots as the means of attaining parity and settling disputes.

Unmindful of man's growing yearning for equal status, many cling to senseless caste systems of the discredited past. As in South Africa, the ruling race shocked the world with its brutal methods to enforce apartheid.

There is something barbaric in today's repression of man's natural passion for equity.

Here in the United States we are not yet purged of intolerance and prejudice. Denial of voting rights; desecration of churches, schools, and public buildings; discrimination in employment and in public accommodations point up the urgent need for further progress in learning to live peaceably together. In connection with recent sit-down demonstrations at lunch counters, it is significant to note that many whites who object to Negroes sitting as customers on one side of the counter do not object to Negroes on the other side of the counter cooking and serving the food they eat. Irrational from a standpoint of logic, this attitude is bewildering from a standpoint of emotion as well.

> *"[In Hawaii] there is sincere respect for, rather than mere toleration of, each other's nationality, traits, characteristics, and cultures."*

In our glasshouse that is America, our discrimination and bigotry are in full view of a critical world. We receive considerable adverse comment for our shortcomings—and perhaps not enough recognition for the undeniable progress we are making. Unlike some of our critics, we are not sweeping our problems of civil rights under the rug. We are facing up to them.

This year, in the Senate of the United States, 100 representatives of 179 million Americans aired our civil rights disagreements in public over a period of eight weeks. If ever opinions were thoroughly ventilated, these were. And when all the smog had lifted, what was the outcome?

Of the 100 senators, 82 supported passage of corrective and progressive civil rights legislation. Only 18 voted for the status quo.

In school, we usually consider 70 a "passing" grade. While 82 may not elevate us to honor roll, it certainly is a very respectable score.

In terms of public sentiment, the 82 percent of the Senate favoring this year's civil rights bill represents a sizable majority of American people. Without such widespread approval, this civil rights milestone would not have been achieved. Although the bill does not go far enough to suit some people and goes too far to suit others, it does denote real progress.

To those who are impatient with our speed in achieving true brotherhood, let me point out that, until 1957, more than eighty years elapsed without passage of a single significant civil rights law. Now, just three years later, we have enacted a second major civil rights statute. Unquestionably, this reflects significant transformation in American attitudes.

In many areas of the United States, of course, we still have not matched the tolerance found in Hawaii where acceptance, without regard to race, color, or creed, and based on individual merit and standing is the general rule—the unwritten rule. Acceptance comes from the heart. It is not superimposed by such means as legislation, judicial process, or promotional campaigns.

For example, discrimination does not exist in government employment. The Department of Public Instruction, administered by seven commissioners, has for its chairman, an American of Japanese descent, a commissioner of Chinese descent, and one of part-Hawaiian descent and four of Caucasian descent.

The University of Hawaii, with more than eight thousand full-time students is under the control of a board of regents of nine members—four of whom are of Caucasian ancestry, two of Japanese, two of Chinese, and one of Hawaiian ancestry.

The nine Public Housing Authority commissioners are composed of five of Caucasian, two of Chinese, one of Korean, and one part-Hawaiian ancestry operating dwellings housing more than four thousand families.

Intermarriage between members of different ethnic groups has been and is common and has produced fine, outstanding people, many of whom are leaders in the business, professional, political, and religious life of the Islands.

In the matter of voting, Dr. Andrew W. Lind, professor of sociology at the University of Hawaii, states that "racial bloc voting, in the mainland sense of the vigorous control over an entire bloc of voters of a common race, does not occur in Hawaii, and even in the more restricted sense of voting exclusively for members of one's own ethnic group, it is so slight as to be inconsequential." He observed that "any politician of the slightest sagacity soon learns, if he does not already know, that the surest route to political suicide is an appeal on a racial basis."

I must confess there is some racial discrimination practiced by some social groups in Hawaii but in recent years, more and more private groups are opening their memberships to persons of all races. It may not be too long before racial bars are lifted altogether.

In the field of public accommodations, all of our restaurants, theaters, hotels, public parks, public beaches, public swimming pools, golf courses, tennis courts, and transportation facilities are free of any discrimination based on race, color, religion or national origin.

Justice is dispensed with equity. There has been no reported case in which any question of discrimination in the administration or justice appears to have been raised.

Even though racial harmony prevails in Hawaii, there are groups dedicated to furthering interracial relations such as the Hawaii Chapter of World Brotherhood, the Honolulu Council of Churches, and the Pacific and Asian Affairs Council. While we do not have a chapter of the National Conference of Christians and Jews in Hawaii, efforts in behalf of racial and religious understanding are carried on by the Council of Churches and World Brotherhood.

In addition, business organizations such as the Chamber of Commerce, Board of Underwriters, Commercial Club, Employers Council, Home Builders Association and the Retail Board are comprised of individuals of varying racial extractions.

This is also true of civic, political, educational, fraternal, health, medical, veterans, and welfare groups.

Again this is true of the more than one dozen service organizations for young people.

The Honolulu Symphony Orchestra and the Community Theater include in their membership individuals of many races. I recall Community Theater productions that have had a Filipino Anna in the musical version of *Anna and the King of Siam,* better known as *The King and I.* Another time a young lady of Japanese extraction as Kate in *Kiss Me Kate.*

To bridge the gap between the two hemispheres, Hawaii has done many things. For instance, Hawaii sponsored an Afro-Asian student leader seminar where three dozen talented young college men and women from nearly as many countries on three continents conferred for four weeks on the place of higher education in society today.

Hawaii held an International Conference on Race Relations to discuss the conflicts and tensions which exist throughout the world between imperialistic powers and peoples imbued with the spirit of self-determination, with emphasis on the effect of economic change and nationalism on race relations in Africa, Asia, and the Western Hemisphere.

Hawaii held three East-West philosopher's conferences where an Asian conferee remarked that these meetings were the only ones in which Asians had felt free to express themselves frankly and did so.

For six years, the University of Hawaii has conducted an Asian Orientation Center for Mundt-Smith and Fulbright grantees headed for graduate study at mainland U.S. universities.

Last month, three prominent citizens of Hawaii accompanied by their wives began a tour of southeast Asia and India. Their mission is to meet and mingle informally with the peoples of the Pacific area. Each of the group represents a different race of the Pacific. Each has prospered through his individual merit in Hawaii's climate of racial understanding and harmony. In turn, each has contributed to Hawaii's growth and stature.

Chairman of the group is a Chinese attorney and businessman who served as the president of the senate in the last legislature of Hawaii before statehood.

Another is a Polynesian, Duke P. Kahanamoku, world-renowned sheriff of Honolulu County and former Olympic swimming champion. He is accompanied by his wife, a Caucasian.

The third is a state senator of Japanese extraction who had been a county judge.

As representatives of the State of Hawaii, they have vital information to impart on their tour. They can speak from personal experience of America's growing feeling of racial understanding so well in evidence in Hawaii. They can cite specific accomplishments in Hawaii resulting from this understanding.

A group of three University or Hawaii students, one a mother of three, last week launched a statewide fund-raising campaign to finance scholarships for Asian students. They hope to expand the program eventually to include an undergraduate student exchange program. By September, these students have scheduled to operate a cultural exchange with Asian universities, beginning with Keio University, one of the largest private schools in Japan.

Nearly two thousand elementary schoolchildren are participating in a "neighbor" language program to promote understanding through better communication. They are learning languages of the Far East under a program sponsored and conducted by the Hawaii Department of Public Instruction.

To promote better relations and understanding among the United States and the Nations of Asia and the Pacific, the Senate of the United States last week authorized a three-year expenditure of $30 million to establish in Hawaii a Center for Cultural and Technical Interchange between the East and the West. I hope that the House of Representatives will concur and make it a reality.

The Center is to have two major divisions: an International College where students from overseas and the United States can study together and an international training facility to provide technical instruction through on-the-job and in-service training for participants from other nations. It is expected to start off with 125 scholarship students and is to be increased to 2,000 after five years. Three-fourths will be from overseas and one-fourth from the United States.

The reason cited for the establishment of the Center in Hawaii was the uniquely favorable atmosphere there; a physical and a cultural climate in which students from the Orient can be at their ease; a community eager to participate in the program by opening its offices and homes to these students; and a community which itself displays the best qualities of East and West.

It is therefore manifestly evident that Hawaii, with its rich multiracial human resource, long and amicable history of ethnic integration, happy cultural interchange and strategic geography, has not in self-contentment and with detachment withdrawn herself into her own island sanctuary, but has diligently pursued numerous ways to contribute her good fortune and know-how to bring closer cooperation among her neighbors.

Clothed with the dignity of a sovereign state, she is confident that her people, few as they are, can effectively help to hasten the millennium of the brotherhood of man.

This we have accepted as the ultimate unfolding of our destiny, our great contribution to America. This we know is our transcendent mission. We live brotherhood, we believe in it, and we know it has real prospect for success nationally and internationally, for it satisfies the soul and has the force of logic.

We in Hawaii do feel a sense of history—not just of a dramatic past, great as it may be, but of a dynamic future with its promise of richer achievement benefiting humanity and auguring peace.

What we have accomplished in Hawaii in so short a period can well be duplicated by all communities. Many and propitious may have been the factors for Hawaii to so quickly attain a happy homogeneous community. Yet the lack of some of these factors should not render that attainment impossible elsewhere. It may perhaps take longer.

All communities are endowed with the substantive factors for success in human relationship. All they need is to catalyze and to synthesize them. In Hawaii we have found it. You, I know in a great measure, have also found it. Surprisingly so, it is everywhere in some measure. In the Old Testament, a book so dear to Christians as well as to Jews, third chapter of First Kings, we are told that the Lord appeared to Solomon in a dream and asked him what he would want and Solomon replied, "O Lord, my God, give thy servant therefor an understanding heart to judge thy people, that I may discern between good and evil; for who is able to judge this thy so great a people?"

It pleased the Lord, that Solomon had asked this thing and God said unto him, "Because thou hast asked this thing and hast not asked for thyself long life or riches or the life of thine enemies but hast asked for thyself understanding to discern what is right, behold, I have done according to thy words. Lo, I have given thee a wise and an understanding heart and I have also given thee that which thou hast not asked, both riches and honor."

I thank you.

Fong was re-elected to the U.S. Senate two more times, once in 1964 and again in 1970. He retired in January 1977, and since then has devoted himself to his many business interests. As a gift to the people of Hawaii, he also established a 725-acre plantation and botanical garden so that everyone has a "place of fragrance and tranquility" to visit. In recognition of Fong's business success and philanthropic contributions, Junior Achievement of Hawaii named him to the organization's "Hall of Fame" in 1995.

SOURCES

Books

Congressional Record, 86th Congress, 2nd Session, Volume 106, Part 8, U.S. Government Printing Office, 1960, pp. 9971-9974; 94th Congress, 2nd Session, Volume 122, Part 25, U.S. Government Printing Office, 1976, pp. 32817-32838.

Zia, Helen, and Susan Gall, eds., *Notable Asian Americans,* Gale Research, Detroit, 1995.

Periodicals

Hawaii Business, "Hall of Fame," January, 1995.

T. Thomas Fortune

1856–1928

African American journalist and civil rights activist

Around the turn of the century, the New York Age was the leading black newspaper in the United States. As its founder and editor, T. Thomas Fortune ranked as the country's most distinguished black journalist. His views on the racial situation—which he expressed both in print and on the speaker's platform—in some ways bridged the gap between the two main currents of thought at the time. An uncompromising radical who denounced racism and demanded complete equality for African Americans, he was nevertheless a staunch defender of his friend Booker T. Washington, who counseled blacks to set aside their dreams of civil and social equality and concentrate instead on making educational and economic gains. In essence, Fortune developed a philosophy that blended a call for militant agitation with an appeal to racial unity and support for the idea of self improvement. Although his ideas fell in and out of favor during his lifetime, they resurfaced again later in the twentieth century to serve as the foundation for many different civil rights organizations.

Fortune, the son of slaves, was born and raised in Florida. After the Civil War, his father became active in state politics, and young Thomas briefly attended a Freedmen's Bureau school. But his formal education ended after less than three years, at which time he apprenticed in the printer's trade and soon mastered the art of setting type. Unable to pursue his dream of becoming a lawyer due to a lack of funds, Fortune instead entered the newspaper business, first in Washington, D.C., where he had been taking some classes at Howard University, and then in New York City, his home beginning in 1879. Within two years, he was part owner and editor of a weekly tabloid entitled the Globe. After it ceased publication in 1884, Fortune started his own newspaper, the New York Freeman, which was renamed the New York Age in 1887.

Before long, thanks in large part to Fortune's fiery editorials, the New York Age was the nation's best-known black newspaper, and Fortune himself was recognized as a spokesman for what was then the far-left wing of African American thought. (He was also one of only a handful of black journalists invited to contribute to several major white newspapers.) In the pages of the New York Age, he demanded free public schools for all and crusaded against separate educational *facilities for black and white students; he condemned lynching and provided a forum to others who wanted to speak out against it; he criticized the Republican party for abandoning Southern blacks and urged African Americans to take a politically independent position; he blasted the capitalist economic system, particularly for the way it kept Southern black sharecroppers in a state of virtual slavery; and he condemned state and federal legislatures and courts for stripping away the rights blacks had won after the Civil War. In addition, Fortune was the first to champion the use of "Afro-American" instead of "Negro" or "Black" in the New York press.*

In 1890, Fortune established the Afro-American League, a nonpartisan organization that he hoped would advance the cause of civil rights and voting rights for blacks. At the group's founding meeting, he gave a speech in which he outlined his philosophy and how he proposed securing these rights for African Americans. Excerpts from his address, which was originally included in the official proceedings of the convention, are reprinted here from Black Nationalism in America *(Bobbs-Merrill, 1970).*

Ladies and Gentlemen of the Afro-American League—We are here today, as representatives of eight million freemen, who know our rights and have the courage to defend them. We have met here today to emphasize the fact that the past condition of dependence and helplessness upon men who have used us for selfish and unholy purposes, who have murdered and robbed and outraged us, must be reversed. . . .

Fellow members of the League, I congratulate you upon your presence here. I congratulate you upon the high resolve, the manly inspiration, which impelled you to this spot. I congratulate you that you have aroused from the lethargy of the past, and that you now stand face to face, brave men and true, with the awful fact that "Who would be free must themselves strike the first blow." I congratulate you that you now recognize the fact that a great work remains for you to do, and that you are determined, with the countenance of Jehovah, to do it. And, finally, I congratulate myself that I have been chosen as the humble spokesman to voice at this time and in this manner the high resolves which move you as one man to perfect an organization which shall secure to ourselves and to our children the blessings of citizenship so generally denied us.

The spirit of agitation which has brought us together here comprehends in its vast sweep the entire range of human history. The world has been rocked in the cradle of agitation from Moses to Gladstone. . . .

Apathy leads to stagnation. The arsenal, the fort, the warrior are as necessary as the school, the church, the newspapers and the public forum of debate. It is a narrow and perverted philosophy which condemns as a nuisance agitators. It is this sort of people who consider nothing to be sacred which stands in the pathway of the progress of the world. Like John crying in the wilderness, they are the forerunners of change in rooted abuses which revolutionize society.

Demosthenes, thundering against the designs of Philip of Macedon upon the liberties of Greece; Cicero, holding up to scorn and ridicule the schemes of Cataline against the freedom of Rome; Oliver Cromwell, baring his sturdy breast to the arrows of royalty and nobility to preserve to Englishmen the rights contained in Magna Charta; Patrick Henry, fulminating against the arrogant and insolent encroachments of Great Britain upon the rights of the American colonies; Nat Turner, rising from the dust of slavery and defying the slave oligarchy of Virginia, and John Brown, resisting the power of the United States in a heroic effort to break the chains of the bondsman—these are some of the agitators who have voiced the discontent of their times at the peril of life and limb and property. Who shall cast the stone of reproach at these noblest children of the race? Who shall say they were not heroes born to live forever in the annals of song and story?

Revolutions are of many sorts. They are either silent and unobservable, noiseless as the movement of the earth on its axes, or loud and destructive, shaking the earth from center to circumference, making huge gaps in the map of earth, changing the face of empires, subverting dynasties and breaking fetters asunder or riveting them anew.

Jesus Christ may be regarded as the chief spirit of agitation and innovation. He himself declared, "I come not to bring peace, but a sword."

St. Paul, standing upon Mars Hill, read the death sentence of Greek and Roman mythology in the simple sentence, "Whom ye ignorantly worship him I declare unto you."

A portion of mankind remains always conservative, while the other portion is moved by the spirit of radicalism; and no man can predict where the conflict may lead when once the old idea and the new one conflict, and must needs appeal to the logic of revolution to arbitrate between them. Few Romes are large enough to hold a Caesar and a Brutus. The old idea and the new idea, the spirit of freedom and the spirit of tyranny and oppression cannot live together without friction. The agitator must never be in advance of his times. The people must be prepared to receive the message he brings them. The harvest must be ripe for the sickle when the reaper enters the field.

As it was in ancient Greece and Rome, so it is in modern Europe and America. The just cause does not always prevail. The John Browns and the Nat Turners do not always find the people ready to receive the tidings of great joy they bring them. . . .

Fellow members of the League, it is matter of history that the 'abolition of slavery' was the fruit of the fiercest and most protracted agitation in the history of social reforms. Begun practically in 1816 by Benjamin Lundy, having been the chief bone of contention at the very birth of the republic, the agitation for the emancipation of the slave did not cease until Abraham Lincoln issued the Emancipation Proclamation in 1863. When emancipation was an established fact, when the slave had been made a freeman and the freeman had been made a citizen, the nation reached the conclusion that its duty was fully discharged. A reaction set in after the second election of General Grant to the presidency in 1872, and terminated after the election of Mr. Hayes in 1876, when the Afro-American citizen was turned over to the tender mercies of his late masters—deserted by the nation, deserted by the party he had served in peace and in war, left poor and defenseless to fight a foe who had baffled the entire nation through four years of bloody and destructive war. . . .

Ladies and gentlemen, we have been robbed of the honest wages of our toil; we have been robbed of the substance of our citizenship by murder and intimidation; we have been outraged by enemies and deserted by friends; and because in a society governed by law, we have been true to the law, true to treacherous friends, and as true in distrust of our enemies, it has been charged upon us that we are not made of the stern stuff which makes the Anglo-Saxon race the most consummate masters of hypocrisy, of roguery, of insolence, of arrogance, and of cowardice, in the history of races.

"The John Browns and the Nat Turners do not always find the people ready to receive the tidings of great joy they bring them. . . ."

Was ever race more unjustly maligned than ours? Was ever race more shamelessly robbed than ours? Was ever race used to advance the political and pecuniary fortunes of others as ours? Was ever race so patient, so law abiding, so uncomplaining as ours?

Ladies and gentlemen, it is time to call a halt. It is time to begin a fight fire with fire. It is time to stand shoulder to shoulder as men. It is time to rebuke the treachery of friends in the only way that treachery should be rebuked. It is time to face the enemy and fight him inch by inch for every right he denies us.

We have been patient so long that many believe that we are incapable of resenting insult, outrage and wrong; we have so long accepted uncomplainingly all that injustice and cowardice and insolence heaped upon us, that many imagine that we are compelled to submit and have not the manhood necessary to resent such conduct. When matters assume this complexion, when oppressors presume too far upon the forbearance and the helplessness of the oppressed, the condition of the people affected is critical indeed. Such is our condition today. Because it is true; because we feel that something must be done to change the condition; because we are tired of being kicked and cuffed by individuals, made the scapegoats of the law, used by one party as an issue and by another as a steppingstone to place and power, and elbowed at pleasure by insolent corporations and their minions, corporations which derive their valuable franchises in part by consent of these very people they insult and outrage—it is because of the existence of these things that we are assembled here today—determined to perfect an organization whose one mission shall be to labor by every reasonable and legal means to right the wrongs complained of, until not one right justly ours under the constitution is denied us.

Ladies and gentlemen, I stand here today and assert in all soberness that we shall no longer accept in silence a condition which degrades our manhood and makes a mockery of our citizenship. I believe I voice the sentiments of each member of the League here assembled when I assert that from now and hence we shall labor as one man, inspired with one holy purpose, to wage relentless opposition to all men who would degrade our manhood and who would defraud us of the benefits of citizenship; guaranteed alike to all born upon this soil or naturalization, by the Constitution which has been cemented and made indestructible by our blood in every war, foreign or domestic, waged by this grand Republic. . . .

There come periods in the history of every people when the necessity of their affairs makes it imperative that they take such steps as shall show to the world that they are worthy to be free, and therefore entitled to the sympathy of all mankind and to the cooperation of all lovers of justice and fair play. To do this they must unequivocally show that while they may solicit the sympathy and cooperation of mankind, they have the intelligence and courage to know what are their rights and to manfully contend for them, even though that sympathy and cooperation be ungenerously denied them.

I am in no sense unmindful of the vastness of the undertaking; but this, instead of being a drawback, is rather an incentive to prosecute the matter with more earnestness and persistence.

I now give in consecutive order the reasons which, in my opinion, justify the organization of the National Afro-American League, to wit:

1. *The almost universal suppression of our ballot in the South, and consequent "taxation without representation," since in the cities, counties and states where we have undisputed preponderating majorities of the voting population we have, in the main, no representation, and therefore no voice in the making and enforcing the laws under which we live.*

2. *The universal and lamentable reign of lynch and mob law, of which we are made the victims, especially in the South, all the more aggravating because all the machinery of the law making and enforcing power is in the hands of those who resort to such outrageous, heinous and murderous violations of the law.*

3. *The unequal distribution of school funds, collected from all taxpayers alike, and to the equal and undivided benefits of which all are alike entitled.*

4. *The odious and demoralizing penitentiary system of the South, with its chain gangs, convict leases and indiscriminate mixing of males and females.*

5. *The almost universal tyranny of common carrier corporations in the South—railroad, steamboat and other—in which the common rights of men and women are outraged and denied by the minions of these corporations, acting under implicit orders in most cases, as well as by common passengers, who take the matter in their own hands as often as they please, and are in no instances pursued and punished by the lawful authorities.*

6. *The discrimination practiced of those who conduct places of public accommodation, and are granted a license for this purpose, such as keepers of inns, hotels and conductors of theaters and kindred places of amusement, where one man's money, all things being equal, should usually be as good as another's.*

7. *The serious question of wages, caused in the main by the vicious industrial system in the South, by the general contempt employers feel for employees, and by the overcrowded nature of the labor market.*

These matters reach down into the very life of our people; they are fundamentally the things which in all times have moved men to associate themselves together in civil society for mutual benefit and protection, to restrain the rapacious and unscrupulous and to protect the weak, the timid and the virtuous; and whenever and wherever a condition of affairs obtains when these principles are disregarded and outraged, it becomes the imperative duty of the aggrieved to take such steps for their correction as the condition of affairs seems to warrant.

I know, ladies and gentlemen of the league, that those who are looking to this organization, loyal people in every section of the country, for some sensible action which shall assist in solving the great problems which confront us, as well as the croaking, skeptical few, who do not expect that we shall be able to advance or to accomplish anything which shall survive the hour of our adjournment, have their eyes upon us. I have confidence in the great race of which I am proud to be a member. I have confidence in its wisdom and its patriotism, and in its self-sacrifice for the common good. I have faith in the God who rules in the affairs of men, and who will not leave us alone to our own devices if we shall make an honest effort to assist ourselves. Thus fortitude in my faith, what have I to propose as remedies for some if not all of the evils against which we have to contend? It shall not be said that I have called you here to a barren feast; it shall not be said by friend or foe that I am an impracticable visionary, a man chasing shadows—a man who denounces the fearful structure in which we abide and would tear it down without offering at least a substitute to replace it. I have pondered long and seriously on the evils which beset us, and I have sought, as light was given me, for an antidote to them, if such there be. I lay them before you, and you are here to adopt or reject them. I propose, then,

1. *The adoption by this league of an Afro-American Bank, with central offices in some one of the great commercial centres of the republic and branches all over the country. We need to concentrate our earnings, and a bank is the proper place to concentrate them. And I shall submit a bank scheme which I have devised in the hope to meet the requirements of the situation.*

2. *I propose the establishment of a Bureau of Emigration. We need to scatter ourselves more generally throughout the republic.*

3. *I propose the establishment of a committee on legislation. We need to have a sharp eye upon the measures annually proposed in the federal and state legislatures affecting us and our interests, and there are laws everywhere in the republic the repeal of which must engage our best thought and effort.*

4. *I propose the establishment of a bureau of technical industrial education. We need trained artisans, educated farmers and laborers more than we need educated lawyers, doctors, and loafers on the street corners. The learned professions are overcrowded. There is not near so much room at the top as there was in the days of Daniel Webster.*

5. *And I propose lastly the establishment of a bureau of cooperative industry. We need to buy the necessaries of life cheaper than we can command them in many states. We need to stimulate the business instinct, the commercial predisposition of the race. We not only want a market for the products of our industry, but we want and must have a fair, and a living return for them.*

To my mind the solution of the problems which make this league a necessity is to be found in the five propositions here stated. Their successful execution will require the very highest order of executive ability and the collection and disbursement of a vast sum of money. Have we brains and the necessary capital to put these vast enterprises into successful motion? I think we have. There are eight million of us in this country. Some of us are rich and some of us are poor. Some of us are wise and some of us are foolish. Let us all—the rich and the poor, the wise and the foolish—resolve to unite and pull together, and the results will speak for themselves. Let us destroy the dead weight of poverty and ignorance which pulls us down and smothers us with the charity, the pity, and the contempt of mankind, and all other things will be added unto us. . . .

The people suffer in silence. This should not be. They should have a voice.

The grievances they are forced to suffer should be known of all the world and they must be. An organization national in its ramification, such as we propose, would be such a voice, so loud that it would compel men to hear it; for if it were silenced in the South, it would be all the louder in the North and the West.

"The people suffer in silence. This should not be. They should have a voice."

Whenever colored men talk of forming anything in which they are to be the prime movers and their grievances are to be the subjects to be agitated, a vast array of men, mostly politicians, and newspaper editors, more or less partisan, and therefore interested in keeping colored voters in a helpless state as far as disorganization and absence of responsible leadership can affect this, cry aloud that "colored men should be the last persons to draw the color line." So they should be; so they have been; and they would never have drawn any such line, or proposed that any such should be drawn, if white men had not first drawn it, and continue to draw it now in religion, in politics, in educational matters, in all moral movements, like that of temperance for instance. We have not drawn the color line. The A.M.E. Church did its founders establish it because they did not care to worship with their white co-religionists? Not a bit of it. They established that magnificent religious organization as a rebuke and a protest to the peanut gallery accommodations offered by white Christians, so-called, to colored Christians. The same spirit actuated the founders of the Zion A.M.E. Church and the colored M.E. Church.

It was not the colored Christians, but the white Christians, who, to their eternal shame and damnation, drew the color line, and continue to draw it, even unto this hour. Turn to the Masonic, the Odd Fellows and the Knights of Pythias orders—did colored men draw the line in these? Did they set up colored lodges all over the country because they did not care to fraternize with the white orders? The answer can be inferred when it is stated that white Masons, white Odd Fellows and white Knights of Pythias even at this hour refuse to fraternize with or to recognize the legality or regularity of the orders their actions caused Afro-Americans to establish. . . .

Ladies and gentlemen, let us stand up like men in our own organization where color will not be a brand of odium. The eternal compromises of our manhood and self-respect, true of the past, must cease. Right is right, and we should at no time or under any circumstances compromise upon anything but absolute right. If the white man cannot rescue our drunkards and evangelize our sinners except by insulting us, let him keep away from us. His contamination under such conditions does us more harm than good. It is not we who have drawn the color line. That is pure nonsense.

Take our public schools—take the schools and colleges throughout the land; who draw the color line in these? Is there an Afro-American school of any sort in the South where a white applicant would be refused admission on account of his color? Not one! Is there a white school in the South where a colored applicant would not be refused admission on account of his color? Not one! The thing is plain. The white man draws the color line in everything he has anything to do with. He is saturated with the black mud of prejudice and intolerance.

Leadership must have a following, otherwise it will run to seed and wither up, be of no benefit to the race or to the persons possessing the superior capacity. An army without a general is a mob, at the mercy of any disciplined force that is hurled against it; and a disorganized, leaderless race is nothing more than a helpless, restless mob.

All those men who have profited by our disorganization and fattened on our labor by class and corporate legislation, will oppose this Afro-American League movement. In the intensity of their opposition they may resort to the coward argument of violence; but are we to remain forever inactive, the victims of extortion and duplicity on this account? No, sir. We propose to accomplish our purposes by the peaceful methods of agitation, through the ballot and the courts, but if others use the weapons of violence to combat our peaceful arguments, it is not for us to run away from violence. A man's a man, and what is worth having is worth fighting for. It is proudly claimed that "the blood of the martyrs is the seed of the church." Certainly the blood of anti-slavery champions was the seed of Garrison's doctrine of "the genius of universal emancipation." Certainly the blood of Irish patriots has been the seed of Irish persistence and success; certainly the blood of Negro patriots was the seed of the independence of Hayti and San Domingo; and in the great revolution of our own country the cornerstones of American freedom were cemented with the blood of black patriots who were not afraid to die; and the refrain which celebrates the heroism and martyrdom of the first men who died that the American colonies might be free will reverberate down the ages.

Long as in freedom's cause the
wise contend
Dear to your country shall your
fame extend;
While to the world the lettered stone
shall tell
Where Caldwell, Attucks, Gray and Maverick fell.

Attucks, the black patriot—he was no coward! Toussaint L'Ouverture—he was no coward! Nat Turner—he was no coward! And the two hundred thousand black soldiers of the last war—they were no cowards! If we have a work to do, let us do it. And if there come violence, let those who oppose our just cause "throw the first stone." We have wealth, we have intelligence, we have courage; and we have a great work to do. We should therefore take hold of it like men, not counting our time and means and lives of any consequence further than they contribute to the grand purposes which call us to the work....

Despite Fortune's high hopes, within just a few years the Afro-American League succumbed to financial pressures and a lack of interest. In 1898, however, it was revived as the National Afro-American Council. This time, it was able to attract a substantial following of some of the best-known black leaders in the country, including Booker T. Washington. It was through the Council, in fact, that Washington secretly carried out a campaign against discriminatory voting practices in the South while maintaining a public position that was far more moderate.

Although Fortune and Washington strongly disagreed with each other on many topics, they were good friends whose personal and professional relationship was closely intertwined. Fortune, for example, served as one of Washington's advisors and even did some ghostwriting and publicity work for him, while Washington quietly helped subsidize the New York Age. *(For all its success as an outlet for African American protest, the paper never made much money, and its editor always had to seek out additional writing assignments to supplement his income). Fortune also defended his friend against fierce opponents such as W.E.B. Du Bois and William Monroe Trotter, leaders of an up-and-coming group of young black intellectuals who challenged Washington's accommodationist philosophy.*

In 1905, Du Bois, Trotter, and others who favored more of a more militant approach to securing civil rights broke away from the National Afro-American Council to launch the Niagara Movement, the forerunner of the National Association for the Advancement of Colored People (NAACP). A year later, having been greatly weakened by several years of tension between the Du Bois and Washington camps, the National Afro-American Council folded. But Fortune's legacy lived on; both the Niagara Movement and the NAACP fashioned their principles on those he had advocated in his opening statement to the Afro-American League.

SOURCES

Books

Bracey, John H., Jr., August Meier, and Elliott Rudwick, editors, *Black Nationalism in America*, Bobbs-Merrill, 1970.

Dictionary of Literary Biography, Volume 23: *American Newspaper Journalists, 1873-1900*, Gale, 1983.

Foner, Philip S., editor, *The Voice of Black America: Major Speeches by Negroes in the United States, 1797-1971*, Simon & Schuster, 1972.

Golden, James L., and Richard D. Rieke, *The Rhetoric of Black Americans*, Charles E. Merrill, 1971.

Thornbrough, Emma Lou, *T. Thomas Fortune: Militant Journalist*, University of Chicago Press, 1972.

Periodicals

Black Scholar, "Black Activists and Nineteenth-Century Radicalism," February, 1974, pp. 19-25.

Crisis, "T. Thomas Fortune: Dean of Black Journalists," October, 1976, pp. 285-287.

Henry Highland Garnet

1815–1882

African American clergyman and abolitionist

Among the many prominent figures in the antislavery movement, Henry Highland Garnet ranks as one of the most radical, and his speeches are among the most emotional ever delivered on the subject. The child of slaves (his father was an African chief who had been kidnapped and sold into bondage), he was only nine years old when he escaped with his family from a Maryland plantation and settled in New York City. He then enrolled in a private school maintained by the black community. It was there that Garnet first attracted attention for his public-speaking ability.

Invited to continue his studies at the Canaan Academy in Canaan, New Hampshire, Garnet headed north in 1835. But when he arrived on campus, an angry mob opposed to the education of blacks burned down the school rather than see its doors opened to him. He then went back to New York to prepare for a career in the ministry, graduating in 1840 from the Oneida Institute in Whitestown. Garnet subsequently held a number of pastorates (including ones in Troy, New York, and at several locations in the West Indies) before accepting a position at New York City's Shiloh Presbyterian Church, where he remained for more than forty years.

At Shiloh, Garnet's fiery antislavery sermons soon made him the best-known black clergyman in the city. Besides blasting white Northerners for their complacency, he repeatedly urged Southern slaves to revolt against their masters, no matter what the cost. Garnet delivered what is undoubtedly his most militant call-to-arms in Buffalo, New York, on August 22, 1843, at the National Convention of Colored Citizens. His extremism alarmed this group of rather moderate abolitionists, which included such up-and-coming public figures as Frederick Douglass and William Wells Brown. So controversial was Garnet's "Address to the Slaves of the United States of America" that delegates voted against publishing and distributing it as an official document of the convention. It was left to the author himself to have copies printed several years later, in 1848, which he bound with David Walker's famous Appeal*, an equally inflammatory piece that originally appeared in 1829. Garnet's speech was later reprinted in* The Voice of Black Rhetoric: Selections *(Allyn & Bacon, 1971), from which the following was taken.*

Brethren and fellow citizens: Your brethren of the North, East, and West have been accustomed to meet together in National Conventions, to sympathize with each other, and to weep over your unhappy condition. In these meetings we have addressed all classes of the free, but we have never, until this time, sent a word of consolation and advice to you. We have been contented in sitting still and mourning over your sorrows, earnestly hoping that before this day your sacred liberties would have been restored. But, we have hoped in vain. Years have rolled on, and tens of thousands have been borne on streams of blood and tears to the shores of eternity. While you have been oppressed, we have also been partakers with you; nor can we be free while you are enslaved. We, therefore, write to you as being bound with you.

Many of you are bound to us, not only by the ties of a common humanity, but we are connected by the more tender relations of parents, wives, husbands, and sisters, and friends. As such we most affectionately address you.

Slavery has fixed a deep gulf between you and us, and while it shuts out from you the relief and consolation which your friends would willingly render, it afflicts and persecutes you with a fierceness which we might not expect to see in the fiends of hell. But still the Almighty Father of mercies has left to us a glimmering ray of hope, which shines out like a lone star in a cloudy sky. Mankind are becoming wiser, and better—the oppressor's power is fading, and you, every day, are becoming better informed, and more numerous. Your grievances, brethren, are many. We shall not attempt, in this short address, to present to the world all the dark catalogue of the nation's sins, which have been committed upon an innocent people. Nor is it indeed necessary, for you feel them from day to day, and all the civilized world looks upon them with amazement.

Two hundred and twenty-seven years ago the first of our injured race were brought to the shores of America. They came not with their own consent, to find an unmolested enjoyment of the blessings of this fruitful soil. The first dealings they had with men calling themselves Christians exhibited to them the worst features of corrupt and sordid hearts: and convinced them that no cruelty is too great, no villainy and no robbery too abhorrent for even enlightened men to perform, when influenced by avarice and lust. Neither did they come flying upon the wings of Liberty to a land of freedom. But they came with broken hearts, from their beloved native land, and were doomed to unrequited toil and deep degradation. Nor did the evil of their bondage end at their emancipation by death. Succeeding generations inherited their chains, and millions have come from eternity into time, and have returned again to the world of spirits, cursed and ruined by American slavery.

Henry Highland Garnet

The propagators of the system, or their immediate successors, very soon discovered its growing evil, and its tremendous wickedness, and secret promises were made to destroy it. The gross inconsistency of a people holding slaves, who had themselves "ferried o'er the wave" for freedom's sake, was too apparent to be entirely overlooked. The voice of Freedom cried, "Emancipate your slaves." Humanity supplicated with tears for the deliverance of the children of Africa. Wisdom urged her solemn plea. The bleeding captive plead his innocence, and pointed to Christianity who stood weeping at the cross. Jehovah frowned upon the nefarious institution, and thunderbolts, red with vengeance, struggled to leap forth to blast the guilty wretches who maintained it. But all was vain. Slavery had stretched its dark wings of death over the land, the Church stood silently by—the priests prophesied falsely, and the people loved to have it so. Its throne is established, and now it reigns triumphant.

Nearly three millions of your fellow citizens are prohibited by law and public opinion (which in this country is stronger than law) from reading the Book of Life. Your intellect has been destroyed as much as possible, and every ray of light they have attempted to shut out from your minds. The oppressors themselves have become involved in the ruin. They have become weak, sensual, and rapacious—they have cursed you—they have cursed themselves—they have cursed the earth which they have trod.

The colonies threw the blame upon England. They said that the mother country entailed the evil upon them, and they would rid themselves of it if they could. The world thought they were sincere, and the philanthropic pitied them. But time soon tested their sincerity. In a few years the colonists grew strong, and severed themselves from the British Government. Their independence was declared, and they took their station among the sovereign powers of the earth. The declaration was a glorious document. Sages admired it, and the patriotic of every nation reverenced the Godlike sentiments which it contained. When the power of Government returned to their hands, did they emancipate the slaves? No; they rather added new links to our chains. Were they ignorant of the principles of Liberty? Certainly they were not. The sentiments of their revolutionary orators fell in burning eloquence upon their hearts, and with one voice they cried, Liberty or Death. Oh, what a sentence was that! It ran from soul to soul like electric fire, and nerved the arms of thousands to fight in the holy cause of Freedom. Among the diversity of opinions that are entertained in regard to physical resistance, there are but a few found to gainsay the stern declaration. We are among those who do not.

Slavery! How much misery is comprehended in that single word. What mind is there that does not shrink from its direful effects? Unless the image of God be obliterated from the soul, all men cherish the love of liberty. The nice discerning political economist does not regard the sacred right more than the untutored African who roams in the wilds of Congo. Nor has the one more right to the full enjoyment of his freedom than the other. In every man's mind the good seeds of liberty are planted, and he who brings his fellow down so low, as to make him contented with a condition of slavery, commits the highest crime against God and man. Brethren, your oppressors aim to do this. They endeavor to make you as much like brutes as possible. When they have blinded the eyes of your mind—when they have embittered the sweet waters of life—when they have shut out the light which shines from the word of God—then, and not till then, has American slavery done its perfect work.

TO SUCH DEGRADATION IT IS SINFUL IN THE EXTREME FOR YOU TO MAKE VOLUNTARY SUBMISSION. The divine commandments you are in duty bound to reverence and obey. If you do not obey them, you will surely meet with the displeasure of the Almighty. He requires you to love Him supremely, and your neighbor as yourself—to keep the Sabbath day holy—to search the Scriptures—and bring up your children with respect for His laws, and to

"Slavery! How much misery is comprehended in that single word."

worship no other God but Him. But slavery sets all these at nought, and hurls defiance in the face of Jehovah. The forlorn condition in which you are placed does not destroy your obligation to God. You are not certain of heaven, because you allow yourselves to remain in a state of slavery, where you cannot obey the commandments of the Sovereign of the universe. If the ignorance of slavery is a passport to heaven, then it is a blessing, and no curse, and you should rather desire its perpetuity than its abolition. God will not receive slavery, nor ignorance, nor any other state of mind, for love and obedience to Him. Your condition does not absolve you from your moral obligation. The diabolical injustice by which your liberties are cloven down, NEITHER GOD NOR ANGELS, OR JUST MEN, COMMAND YOU TO SUFFER FOR A SINGLE MOMENT. THEREFORE, IT IS YOUR SOLEMN AND IMPERATIVE DUTY TO USE EVERY MEANS, BOTH MORAL, INTELLECTUAL, AND PHYSICAL, THAT PROMISES SUCCESS. If a band of heathen men should attempt to enslave a race of Christians, and to place their children under the influence of some false religion, surely Heaven would frown upon the men who would not resist such aggression, even to death. If, on the other hand, a band of Christians should attempt to enslave a race of heathen men, and to entail slavery upon them, and to keep heathenism in the midst of Christianity, the God of heaven would smile upon every effort which the injured might make to disenthral themselves.

Brethren, it is wrong for your lordly oppressors to keep you in slavery as it was for the man thief to steal our ancestors from the coast of Africa. You should therefore now use the same manner of resistance as would have been just in our ancestors when the bloody footprints of the first remorseless soul-thief was placed upon the shores of our fatherland. The humblest peasant is as free in the sight of God as the proudest monarch that ever swayed a sceptre. Liberty is a spirit sent out from God, and like its great Author, is no respecter of persons.

Brethren, the time has come when you must act for yourselves. It is an old and true saying that, "if hereditary bondmen would be free, they must themselves strike the blow." You can plead your own cause, and do the work of emancipation better than any others. The nations of the Old World are moving in the great cause of universal freedom, and some of them at least will, ere long, do you justice. The combined powers of Europe have placed their broad seal of disapprobation upon the African slave-trade. But in the slaveholding parts of the United States the trade is as brisk as ever. They buy and sell you as though you were brute beasts. The North has done much—her opinion of slavery in the abstract is known. But in regard to the South, we adopt the opinion of the *New York Evangelist*—"We have advanced so far, that the cause apparently waits for a more effectual door to be thrown open than has been yet." We are about to point you to that more effectual door. Look around you, and behold the bosoms of your loving wives heaving with untold agonies! Hear the cries of your poor children! Remember the stripes your fathers bore. Think of your wretched sisters, loving virtue and purity, as they are driven into concubinage and are exposed to the unbridled lusts of incarnate devils. Think of the undying glory that hangs around the ancient name of Africa—and forget not that you are native-born American citizens, and as such you are justly entitled to all the rights that are granted to the freest. Think how many tears you have poured out upon the soil which you have cultivated with unrequited toil and enriched with your blood; and then go to your lordly enslavers and tell them plainly, that you are determined to be free. Appeal to their sense of justice, and tell them that they have no more right to oppress you than you have to enslave them. Entreat them to remove the grievous burdens which they have imposed upon you, and to remunerate you for your labor. Promise them renewed diligence in the cultivation of the soil, if they will render to you an equivalent for your services. Point them to the increase of happiness and prosperity in the British West Indies since the Act of Emancipation. Tell them in language which they cannot misunderstand of the exceeding sinfulness of slavery, and of a future judgment, and of the righteous retributions of an indignant God. Inform them that all you desire is FREEDOM, and that nothing else will suffice. Do this, and forever after cease to toil for the heartless tyrants, who give you no other reward but stripes and abuse. If they then commence work of death, they, and not you, will be responsible for the consequences. You had far better all die—die immediately, than live slaves, and entail your wretchedness upon your posterity. If you would be free in this generation, here is your only hope. However much you and all of us may desire it, there is not much hope of redemption without the shedding of blood. If you must bleed, let it all come at once—rather die freemen than live to be the slaves. It is impossible, like the children of Israel, to make a grand exodus from the land of bondage. The Pharaohs are on both sides of the blood-red waters! You cannot move en masse to the dominions of the British Queen—nor can you pass through Florida and overrun Texas, and at last find peace in Mexico. The propagators of American slavery are spending their blood and treasure that they may plant the black flag in the heart of Mexico and riot in the halls of the Montezumas. In language of the Reverend Robert Hall, when addressing the volunteers of Bristol, who were rushing forth to repel the invasion of Napoleon, who threatened to lay waste the fair homes of England, "Religion is too much interested in your behalf not to shed over you her most gracious influences."

You will not be compelled to spend much time in order to become inured to hardships. From the first moment that you breathed the air of heaven, you have been accustomed to nothing else but hardships. The heroes of the American Revolution were never put upon harder fare than a peck of corn and few herrings per week. You have not become enervated by the luxuries of life. Your sternest energies have been beaten out upon the anvil of severe trial. Slavery has done this to make you subservient to its own purposes; but it has done more than this, it has prepared you for any emergency. If you receive good treatment, it is what you can hardly expect; if you meet with pain, sorrow, and even death, these are the common lot of the slaves.

Fellowmen! Patient sufferers! Behold your dearest rights crushed to the earth! See your sons murdered, and your wives, mothers and sisters doomed to prostitution. In the name of the merciful God, and by all that life is worth, let it no longer be a debatable question, whether it is better to choose liberty or death.

In 1822, Denmark Veazie, of South Carolina, formed a plan for the liberation of his fellowmen. In the whole history of human efforts to overthrow slavery, a more complicated and tremendous plan was never formed. He was betrayed by the treachery of his own people, and died a martyr to freedom.

Many a brave hero fell, but history, faithful to her high trust, will transcribe his name on the same monument with Moses, Hampden, Tell, Bruce, and Wallace, Toussaint L'Ouverture, Lafayette, and Washington. That tremendous movement shook the whole empire of slavery. The guilty soul-thieves were overwhelmed with fear. It is a matter of fact that at this time, and in consequence of the threatened revolution, the slave states talked strongly of emancipation. But they blew but one blast of the trumpet of freedom, and then laid it aside. As these men became quiet, the slaveholders ceased to talk about emancipation: and now behold your condition today! Angels sigh over it, and humanity has long since exhausted her tears in weeping on your account!

The patriotic Nathaniel Turner followed Denmark Veazie. He was goaded to desperation by wrong and injustice. By despotism, his name has been recorded on the list of infamy, and future generations will remember him among the noble and brave.

Next arose the immortal Joseph Cinque, the hero of the *Amistad*. He was a native African, and by the help of God he emancipated a whole shipload of his fellowmen on the high seas. And he now sings of liberty on the sunny hills of Africa and beneath his native palm trees, where he hears the lion roar and feels himself as free as the king of the forest.

Next arose Madison Washington, that bright star of freedom, and took his station in the constellation of true heroism. He was a slave on board the brig *Creole,* of Richmond, bound to New Orleans, that great slave mart, with a hundred and four others. Nineteen struck for liberty or death. But one life was taken, and the whole were emancipated, and the vessel was carried into Nassau, New Providence.

Noble men! Those who have fallen in freedom's conflict, their memories will be cherished by the true-hearted and the God-fearing in all future generations; those who are living, their names are surrounded by a halo of glory.

Brethren, arise, arise! Strike for your lives and liberties. Now is the day and the hour. Let every slave throughout the land do this, and the days of slavery are numbered. You cannot be more oppressed than you have been—you cannot suffer greater cruelties than you have already. Rather die freemen than live to be slaves. Remember that you are FOUR MILLIONS!

It is in your power so to torment the God-cursed slaveholders that they will be glad to let you go free. If the scale was turned, and black men were the masters and white men the slaves, every destructive agent and element would be employed to lay the oppressor low. Danger and death would hang over their heads day and night. Yes, the tyrants would meet with plagues more terrible than those of pharaoh. But you are a patient people. You act as though your daughters were born to pamper the lusts of your masters and overseers. And worse than all, you tamely submit while your lords tear your wives from your embraces and defile them before your eyes. In the name of God, we ask, are you men? Where is the blood of your fathers? Has it all run out of your veins? Awake, awake; millions of voices are calling you! Your dead fathers speak to you from their graves. Heaven, as with a voice of thunder, calls on you to arise from the dust.

Let your motto be resistance! resistance! RESISTANCE! No oppressed people have ever secured their liberty without resistance. What kind of resistance you had better make you must decide by the circumstances that surround you, and according to the suggestion of expediency. Brethren, adieu! Trust in the living God. Labor for the peace of the human race, and remember that you are FOUR MILLIONS!

While the Emancipation Proclamation of 1863 declared free all slaves in states then at war against the Union, it was not until the Thirteenth Amendment to the Constitution was ratified in December 1865, that slavery was truly abolished throughout the entire country. Earlier in the year, shortly after the House of Representatives followed the Senate's lead and voted in favor of the amendment, Garnet was invited to preach a sermon in the halls of Congress to commemorate its passage. Thus it was that on February 12, 1865, he became the first African American to speak in the nation's Capitol. His words were recorded in an 1865 pamphlet entitled A Memorial Discourse by the Rev. Henry Highland Garnet, Delivered in the Hall of the House of Representatives, Washington, D.C., on Sabbath, February 12, 1865, with an Introduction by James McCune Smith, M.D., *and later reprinted in the book* Masterpieces of Negro Eloquence, *(Bookery Publishing Co., 1914; reprinted, Johnson Reprint, 1970).*

In this chapter, of which my text is a sentence, the Lord Jesus addressed his disciples, and the multitude that hung spellbound upon the words that fell from his lips. He admonished them to beware of the religion of the Scribes and Pharisees, which was distinguished for great professions, while it succeeded in urging them to do but a little, or nothing that accorded with the law of righteousness.

In theory they were right; but their practices were inconsistent and wrong. They were learned in the law of Moses, and in the traditions of their fathers, but the principles of righteousness failed to affect their hearts. They knew their duty but did it not. The demands which they made upon others proved that they themselves knew what things men ought to do. In condemning others they pronounced themselves guilty. They demanded that others should be just, merciful, pure, peaceable, and righteous. But they were unjust, impure, unmerciful—they hated and wronged a portion of their fellowmen, and waged a continual war against the government of God.

Such was their conduct in the Church and in the State. We have modern Scribes and Pharisees, who are faithful to their prototypes of ancient times.

With sincere respect and reverence for the instruction, and the warning given by our Lord, and in humble dependence upon him for his assistance, I shall speak this morning of the Scribes and Pharisees of our times who rule the State. In discharging this duty, I shall keep my eyes upon the picture which is painted so faithfully and lifelike by the hand of the Saviour.

Allow me to describe them. They are intelligent and well informed, and can never say, either before an earthly tribunal or at the bar of God, "We knew not of ourselves what was right." They are acquainted with the principles of the law of nations. They are proficient in the knowledge of Constitutional law. They are teachers of common law, and frame and execute statute law. They acknowledge that there is a just and impartial God, and are not altogether unacquainted with the law of Christian love and kindness. They claim for themselves the broadest freedom. Boastfully they tell us that they have received from the court of heaven the Magna Charta of human rights that was handed down through the clouds, and amid the lightnings of Sinai, and given again by the Son of God on the Mount of Beatitudes, while the glory of the Father shone around him. They tell us that from the Declaration of Independence and the Constitution they have obtained a guaranty of their political freedom, and from the Bible they derive their claim to all the blessings of religious liberty. With just pride they tell us that they are descended from the Pilgrims, who threw themselves upon the bosom of the treacherous sea, and braved storms and tempests, that they might find in a strange land, and among savages, free homes, where they might build their altars that should blaze with acceptable sacrifice unto God. Yes! They boast that their fathers heroically turned away from the precious light of Eastern civilization, and taking their lamps with oil in their vessels, joyfully went forth to illuminate this land, that then dwelt in the darkness of the valley of the shadow of death. With hearts strengthened by faith they spread out their standard to the winds of heaven, near Plymouth rock; and whether it was stiffened in the sleet and frosts of winter, or floated on the breeze of summer, it ever bore the motto, "Freedom to worship God."

But others, their fellow men, equal before the Almighty, and made by him of the same blood, and glowing with immortality, they doom to lifelong servitude and chains. Yes, they stand in the most sacred places on earth, and beneath the gaze of the piercing eye of Jehovah, the universal Father of all men, and declare, "that the best possible condition of the Negro is slavery."

In the name of the Triune God I denounce the sentiment as unrighteous beyond measure, and the holy and the just of the whole earth say in regard to it, Anathema-maranatha.

What is slavery? Too well do I know what it is. I will present to you a bird's-eye view of it; and it shall be no fancy picture, but one that is sketched by painful experience. I was born among the cherished institutions of slavery. My earliest recollections of parents, friends, and the home of my childhood are clouded with its wrongs. The first sight that met my eyes was a Christian mother enslaved by professed Christians, but, thank God, now a saint in heaven. The first sounds that startled my ear, and sent a shudder through my soul, were the cracking of the whip and the clanking of chains. These sad memories mar the beauties of my native shores, and darken all the slave-land, which, but for the reign of despotism, had been a paradise. But those shores are fairer now. The mists have left my native valleys, and the clouds have rolled away from the hills, and Maryland, the unhonored grave of my fathers, is now the free home of their liberated and happier children.

Let us view this demon, which the people have worshipped as a God. Come forth, thou grim monster, that thou mayest be critically examined! There he stands. Behold him, one and all. Its work is to chattelize man; to hold property in human beings. Great God! I would as soon attempt to enslave Gabriel or Michael as to enslave a man made in the image of God, and for whom Christ died. Slavery is snatching man from the high place to which he was lifted by the hand of God, and dragging him down to the level of the brute creation, where he is made to be the companion of the horse and the fellow of the ox.

It tears the crown of glory from his head, and as far as possible obliterates the image of God that is in him. Slavery preys upon man, and man only. A brute cannot be made a slave. Why? Because a brute has not reason, faith, nor an undying spirit, nor conscience. It does not look forward to the future with joy or fear, nor reflect upon the past with satisfaction or regret. But who in this vast assembly, who in all this broad land, will say that the poorest and most unhappy brother in chains and servitude has not every one of these high endowments? Who denies it? Is there one? If so, let him speak. There is not one; no, not one.

But slavery attempts to make a man a brute. It treats him as a beast. Its terrible work is not finished until the ruined victim of its lusts, and pride, and avarice, and hatred, is reduced so

"Slavery is snatching man from the high place to which he was lifted by the hand of God, and dragging him down to the level of the brute creation. . . ."

low that with tearful eyes and feeble voice he faintly cries, "I am happy and contented—I love this condition."

Proud Nimrod first the bloody chase began,
A mighty hunter he; his prey was man.

The caged lion may cease to roar, and try no longer the strength of the bars of his prison, and lie with his head between his mighty paws and snuff the polluted air as though he heeded not. But is he contented? Does he not instinctively long for the freedom of the forest and the plain? Yes, he is a lion still. Our poor and forlorn brother whom thou hast labelled "slave," is also a man.

He may be unfortunate, weak, helpless, and despised, and hated, nevertheless he is a man. His God and thine has stamped on his forehead his title to his inalienable rights in characters that can be read by every intelligent being. Pitiless storms of outrage may have beaten upon his defenseless head and he may have descended through ages of oppression, yet he is a man. God made him such, and his brother cannot unmake him. Woe, woe to him who attempts to commit the accursed crime.

Slavery commenced its dreadful work in kidnapping unoffending men in a foreign and distant land, and in piracy on the seas. The plunderers were not the followers of Mahomet, nor the devotees of Hindooism, nor benighted pagans, nor idolaters, but people called Christians, and thus the ruthless traders in the souls and bodies of men fastened upon Christianity a crime and stain at the sight of which it shudders and shrieks.

It is guilty of the most heinous iniquities ever perpetrated upon helpless women and innocent children. Go to the shores of the land of my forefathers, poor bleeding Africa, which, although she has been bereaved, and robbed for centuries, is nevertheless beloved by all her worthy descendants wherever dispersed. Behold a single scene that there meets your eyes. Turn not away neither from shame, pity, nor indifference, but look and see the beginning of this cherished and petted institution. Behold a hundred youthful mothers seated on the ground, dropping their tears upon the hot sands, and filling the air with their lamentations.

Why do they weep? Ah, Lord God, thou knowest!

Their babes have been torn from their bosoms and cast upon the plains to die of hunger, or to be devoured by hyenas or jackals. The little innocents would die on the "Middle Passage," or suffocate between the decks of the floating slave-pen, freighted and packed with unparalleled human woe, and the slavers in mercy have cast them out to perish on their native shores. Such is the beginning, and no less wicked is the end of that system which Scribes and Pharisees in the Church and the State pronounce to be just, humane, benevolent and Christian. If such are the deeds of mercy wrought by angels, then tell me what works of iniquity there remain for devils to do?

It is the highly concentrated essence of all conceivable wickedness. Theft, robbery, pollution, unbridled passion, incest, cruelty, cold-blooded murder, blasphemy, and defiance of the laws of God. It teaches children to disregard parental authority. It tears down the marriage altar, and tramples its sacred ashes under its feet. It creates and nourishes polygamy. It feeds and pampers its hateful handmaid, prejudice.

It has divided our national councils. It has engendered deadly strife between brethren. It has wasted the treasure of the Commonwealth, and the lives of thousands of brave men, and driven troops of helpless women and children into yawning tombs. It has caused the bloodiest civil war recorded in the book of time. It has shorn this nation of its locks of strength that was rising as a young lion in the Western world. It has offered us as a sacrifice to the jealousy and cupidity of tyrants, despots, and adventurers of foreign countries. It has opened a door through which a usurper, a perjured, but a powerful prince, might stealthily enter and build an empire on the golden borders of our southwestern frontier, and which is but a stepping-stone to further and unlimited conquests on this continent. It has desolated the fairest portions of our land, "until the wolf long since driven back by the march of civilization returns alter the lapse of a hundred years and howls amidst its ruins."

It seals up the Bible, and mutilates its sacred truths, and flies into the face of the Almighty, and impiously asks, "Who art thou that I should obey thee?" Such are the outlines of this fearful national sin, and yet the condition to which it reduces man, it is affirmed, is the best that can possibly be devised for him.

When inconsistencies similar in character, and no more glaring, passed beneath the eye of the Son of God, no wonder he broke forth in language of vehement denunciation. Ye Scribes, Pharisees, and hypocrites! Ye blind guides! Ye compass sea and land to make one proselyte, and when he is made ye make him twofold more the child of hell than yourselves. Ye are like unto whited sepulchres, which indeed appear beautiful without, but within are full of dead men's bones, and all uncleanness!

Let us here take up the golden rule, and adopt the self-application mode of reasoning to those who hold these erroneous views. Come, gird up thy loins and answer like a man, if thou canst. Is slavery, as it is seen in its origin, continuance, and end the best possible condition for thee? Oh, no! Wilt thou bear that burden on thy shoulders, which thou wouldest lay upon thy fellow man? No. Wilt thou bear a part of it, or remove a little of its weight with one of thy fingers? The sharp and indignant answer is no, no! Then how, and when, and where, shall we apply to thee the golden rule, which says, "Therefore all things that ye would that others should do to you, do ye even so unto them, for this is the law and the prophets."

Let us have the testimony of the wise and great of ancient and modern times:

"Sages who wrote and warriors who bled."

Plato declared that "Slavery is a system of complete injustice."

Socrates wrote that "Slavery is a system of outrage and robbery."

Cyrus said, "To fight in order not to be a slave is noble."

If Cyrus had lived in our land a few years ago he would have been arrested for using incendiary language, and for inciting servile insurrection and the royal fanatic would have been hanged on a gallows higher than Haman. But every man is fanatical when his soul is warmed by the generous fires of liberty. Is it then truly noble to fight in order not to be a slave? The chief magistrate of the nation, and our rulers, and all truly patriotic men think so; and so think legions of black men, who for a season were scorned and rejected, but who came quickly and cheerfully when they were at last invited, bearing a heavy burden of proscriptions upon their shoulders, and having faith in God, and in their generous fellow countrymen, they went forth to fight a double battle. The foes of their country were before them, while the enemies of freedom and of their race surrounded them.

Augustine, Constantine, Ignatius, Polycarp, Maximus, and the most illustrious lights of the ancient church denounced the sin of slave-holding.

Thomas Jefferson said at a period of his life, when his judgment was matured, and his experience was ripe, "There is preparing, I hope, under the auspices of heaven, a way for a total emancipation."

The sainted Washington said, near the close of his moral career, and when the light of eternity was beaming upon him, "It is among my first wishes to see some plan adopted by which slavery in this country shall be abolished by law. I know of but one way by which this can be done, and that is by legislative action, and so far as my vote can go, it shall not be wanting."

The other day, when the light of liberty streamed through this marble pile, and the hearts of the noble band of patriotic statesmen leaped for joy, and this our national capitol shook from foundation to dome with the shouts of a ransomed people, then methinks the spirits of Washington, Jefferson, the Jays, the Adamses, and Franklin, and Lafayette, and Giddings, and Lovejoy, and those of all the mighty, and glorious dead, remembered by history, because they were faithful to truth, justice, and liberty, were hovering over the august assembly. Though unseen by mortal eyes, doubtless they joined the angelic choir, and said, Amen.

Pope Leo X testifies, "That not only does the Christian religion, but nature herself, cry out against a state of slavery."

Patrick Henry said, "We should transmit to posterity our abhorrence of slavery." So also thought the Thirty-Eighth Congress.

Lafayette proclaimed these words: "Slavery is a dark spot on the face of the nation." God be praised, that stain will soon be wiped out.

Jonathan Edwards declared "that to hold a man in slavery is to be every day guilty of robbery, or of man stealing. "

Rev. Dr. William Ellery Channing, in a Letter on the Annexation of Texas in 1837, writes as follows: "The evil of slavery speaks for itself. To state is to condemn the institution. The choice which every freeman makes of death for his child and for every thing he loves in preference to slavery shows what it is.

"Every principle of our government and religion condemns slavery. The spirit of our age condemns it. The decree of the civilized world has gone out against it."

Moses, the greatest of all lawgivers and legislators, said, while his face was yet radiant with the light of Sinai: "Whoso stealeth a man, and selleth him, or if he be found in his hand, he shall surely be put to death." The destroying angel has gone forth through this land to execute the fearful penalties of God's broken law.

The representatives of the nation have bowed with reverence to the Divine edict, and laid the axe at the root of the tree, and thus saved succeeding generations from the guilt of oppression, and from the wrath of God.

Statesmen, jurists, and philosophers, most renowned for learning, and most profound in every department of science and literature, have testified against slavery; while oratory has brought its costliest, golden treasures, and laid them on the altar of God and of freedom, it has aimed its fiercest lightning and loudest thunder at the strongholds of tyranny, injustice, and despotism.

From the days of Balak to those of Isaiah and Jeremiah, up to the times of Paul, and through every age of the Christian church, the sons of thunder have denounced the abominable thing. The heroes who stood in the shining ranks of the hosts of the friends of human progress, from Cicero to Chatham, and Burke, Sharp, Wilberforce, and Thomas Clarkson, and Curran, assaulted the citadel of despotism. The orators and statesmen of our own land, whether they belong to the past, or to the present age, will live and shine in the annals of history, in proportion as they have dedicated their genius and talents to the defence of justice and man's God-given rights.

All the poets who live in sacred and profane history have charmed the world with their most enchanting strains, when they have tuned their lyres to the praise of liberty. When the muses can no longer decorate her altars with their garlands, then they hang their harps upon the willows and weep.

From Moses to Terence and Homer, from thence to Milton and Cowper, Thomson and Thomas Campbell, and on to the days of our own bards, our Bryants, Longfellows, Whittiers, Morrises, and Bokers, all have presented their best gifts to the interests and rights of man.

"Let the gigantic monster perish. Yes, perish now, and perish forever!"

Every good principle, and every great and noble power, have been made the subjects of the inspired verse, and the songs of poets. But who of them has attempted to immortalize slavery? You will search in vain the annals of the world to find an instance. Should any attempt the sacrilegious work, his genius would fall to the earth as if smitten by the lightning of heaven. Should he lift his hand to write a line in its praise, or defence, the ink would freeze on the point of his pen.

Could we array in one line, representatives of all the families of men, beginning with those lowest in the scale of being, and should we put to them the question, Is it right and desirable that you should be reduced to the condition of slaves, to be registered with chattels, to have your persons, and your lives, and the products of your labor, subjected to the will and the interests of others? Is it right and just that the persons of your wives and children should be at the disposal of others, and be yielded to them for the purpose of pampering their lusts and greed of gain? Is it right to lay heavy burdens on other men's shoulders which you would not remove with one of your fingers? From the rude savage and barbarian the negative response would come, increasing in power and significance as it rolled up the line. And when those should reply, whose minds and hearts are illuminated with the highest civilization and with the spirit of Christianity, the answer deep-toned and prolonged would thunder forth, no, no!

With all the moral attributes of God on our side, cheered as we are by the voices of universal human nature—in view of the best interests of the present and future generations—animated with the noble desire to furnish the nations of the earth with a worthy example, let the verdict of death which has been brought in against slavery, by the Thirty-Eighth Congress, be affirmed and executed by the people. Let the gigantic monster perish. Yes, perish now, and perish forever!

It is often asked when and where will the demands of the reformers of this and coming ages end? It is a fair question, and I will answer.

When all unjust and heavy burdens shall be removed from every man in the land. When all invidious and proscriptive distinctions shall be blotted out from our laws, whether they be constitutional, statute, or municipal laws. When emancipation shall be followed by enfranchisement, and all men holding allegiance to the government shall enjoy every right of American citizenship. When our brave and gallant soldiers shall have justice done unto them. When the men who endure the sufferings and perils of the battlefield in the defence of their country, and in order to keep our rulers in their places, shall enjoy the well-earned privilege of voting for them. When in the army and navy, and in every legitimate and honorable occupation, promotion shall smile upon merit without the slightest regard to the complexion of a man's face. When there shall be no more class-legislation, and no more trouble concerning the black man and his rights, than there is in regard to other American citizens. When, in every respect, he shall be equal before the law, and shall be left to make his own way in the social walks of life.

We ask, and only ask, that when our poor frail barks are launched on life's ocean—

Bound on a voyage of awful length
And dangers little known,

that, in common with others, we may be furnished with rudder, helm, and sails, and charts, and compass. Give us good pilots to conduct us to the open seas; lift no false lights along the dangerous coasts, and if it shall please God to send us propitious winds, or fearful gales, we shall survive or perish as our energies or neglect shall determine. We ask no special favors, but we plead for justice. While we scorn unmanly dependence; in the name of God, the universal Father, we demand the right to live, and labor, and to enjoy the fruits of our toil. The good work which God has assigned for the ages to come, will be finished, when our national literature shall be so purified as to reflect a faithful and a just light upon the character and social habits of our race, and the brush, and pencil, and chisel, and lyre of art, shall refuse to lend their aid to scoff at the afflictions of the poor, or to caricature, or ridicule a long-suffering people. When caste and prejudice in Christian churches shall be utterly destroyed, and shall be regarded as totally unworthy of Christians, and at variance with the principles of the gospel. When the blessings of the Christian religion, and of sound, religious education, shall be freely offered to all, then, and not till then, shall the effectual labors of God's people and God's instruments cease.

If slavery has been destroyed merely from necessity, let every class be enfranchised at the dictation of justice. Then we shall have a Constitution that shall be reverenced by all: rulers who shall be honored, and revered, and a Union that shall be sincerely loved by a brave and patriotic people, and which can never be severed.

Great sacrifices have been made by the people; yet, greater still are demanded ere atonement can be made for our national sins. Eternal justice holds heavy mortgages against us, and will require the payment of the last farthing. We have involved ourselves in the sin of unrighteous gain, stimulated by luxury, and pride, and the love of power and oppression; and prosperity and peace can be purchased only by blood, and with tears of repentance. We have paid some of the fearful installments, but there are other heavy obligations to be met.

The great day of the nation's judgment has come, and who shall be able to stand? Even we, whose ancestors have suffered the afflictions which are inseparable from a condition of slavery, for the period of two centuries and a half, now pity our land and weep with those who weep.

Upon the total and complete destruction of this accursed sin depends the safety and perpetuity of our Republic and its excellent institutions.

Let slavery die. It has had a long and fair trial. God himself has pleaded against it. The enlightened nations of the earth have condemned it. Its death warrant is signed by God and man. Do not commute its sentence. Give it no respite, but let it be ignominiously executed.

Honorable Senators and Representatives! Illustrious rulers of this great nation! I cannot refrain this day from invoking upon you, in God's name, the blessings of millions who were ready to perish, but to whom a new and better life has been opened by your humanity, justice, and patriotism. You have said, "Let the Constitution of the country be so amended that slavery and involuntary servitude shall no longer exist in the United States, except in punishment for crime." Surely, an act so sublime could not escape Divine notice; and doubtless the deed has been recorded in the archives of heaven. Volumes may be appropriated to your praise and renown in the history of the world. Genius and art may perpetuate the glorious act on canvass and in marble, but certain and more lasting monuments in commemoration of your decision are already erected in the hearts and memories of a grateful people.

The nation has begun its exodus from worse than Egyptian bondage; and I beseech you that you say to the people, "that they go forward." With the assurance of God's favor in all things done in obedience to his righteous will, and guided by day and by night by the pillars of cloud and fire, let us not pause until we have reached the other and safe side of the stormy and crimson sea. Let freemen and patriots mete out complete and equal justice to all men, and thus prove to mankind the superiority of our Democratic, Republican Government.

Favored men, and honored of God as his instruments, speedily finish the work which he has given you to do. Emancipate, enfranchise, educate, and give the blessings of the gospel to every American citizen.

Then before us a path of prosperity will open, and upon us will descend the mercies and favors of God. Then shall the people of other countries, who are standing tip-toe on the shores of every ocean, earnestly looking to see the end of this amazing conflict, behold a Republic that is sufficiently strong to outlive the ruin and desolations of civil war, having the magnanimity to do justice to the poorest and weakest of her citizens. Thus shall we give to the world the form of a model Republic, founded on the principles of justice, and humanity, and Christianity, in which the burdens of war and the blessings of peace are equally borne and enjoyed by all.

SOURCES

Books

Aptheker, Herbert, editor, *A Documentary History of the Negro People in the United States,* Volume 1: *From Colonial Times through the Civil War,* Citadel Press, 1965.

Bracey, John H., Jr., August Meier, and Elliott Rudwick, *Black Nationalism in America,* Bobbs-Merrill, 1970.

Dunbar, Alice Moore, editor, *Masterpieces of Negro Eloquence,* Bookery Publishing Company, 1914, reprinted, Johnson Reprint, 1970.

Foner, Philip S., editor, *The Voice of Black America: Major Speeches by Negroes in the United States, 1797-1971,* Simon & Schuster, 1972.

Golden, James L., and Richard D. Rieke, *The Rhetoric of Black Americans,* Charles E. Merrill, 1971.

Ofari, Earl, *"Let Your Motto Be Resistance": The Life and Thought of Henry Highland Garnet,* Beacon, 1972.

Smith, Arthur L., and Stephen Robb, editors, *The Voice of Black Rhetoric: Selections,* Allyn & Bacon, 1971.

Periodicals

Central States Speech Journal, "Henry Highland Garnet: Black Revolutionary in Sheep's Vestments," summer, 1970, pp. 93-98.

Journal of Black Studies, "The Rhetoric of Black Violence in the Antebellum Period: Henry Highland Garnet," September, 1971, pp. 45-56.

South Speech Journal, "Nineteenth Century Black Militant: Henry Highland Garnet's Address to the Slaves," fall, 1970, pp. 11-21.

Marcus Garvey

1887–1940

African American nationalist leader

During the late 1910s and early 1920s, Marcus Garvey became the first man to speak for millions of blacks all over the world as the founder and head of the Universal Negro Improvement Association (UNIA). The UNIA blended the self-help teachings of Booker T. Washington and Garvey's own dreams of an "Africa for Africans" in a message that had special appeal to the frustrated and disappointed black veterans of World War I. They had returned to the United States in triumph only to find that their sacrifices on the battlefield did not mean they had achieved equality at home. Garvey acknowledged that discontent by calling on blacks to take pride in their racial heritage and look to Africa as the place to establish a new homeland free of inequality and prejudice.

The UNIA first took root in Garvey's native Jamaica, where blacks had long suffered under British colonial rule. Well aware that people of African descent faced similar difficulties on neighboring Caribbean islands and in Latin America, Garvey began to contemplate the fate of blacks in other parts of the world. A period of study in England during which Garvey read extensively on Africa and colonialism widened his perspective even more. Returning to Jamaica in 1914, he founded the Universal Negro Improvement and Conservation Association and African Communities League and announced his intention to "lift the race" and establish a black nation in Africa.

In 1916, eager to launch his ideas internationally, Garvey settled in New York City and set up a UNIA branch there. Eventually it became the center of his ever-widening empire, which included several publications and numerous businesses, including the Black Star Line of steamships. In 1925, however, Garvey was sent to jail for mail fraud and then deported upon his release two years later. Without his strong personal leadership, the UNIA soon lost its influence and fell apart. But many of Garvey's ideas—especially about black pride—lived on in the philosophies of future black nationalists such as Malcolm X (whose father had been a UNIA activist) and the Black Panthers.

On November 25, 1922, Garvey spoke to a gathering in New York City about the principles of the UNIA and what it hoped to accomplish. His speech is reprinted from Philosophy and Opinions of Marcus Garvey *(Universal Publishing House, 1923-25; reprinted, Arno, 1969).*

Over five years ago the Universal Negro Improvement Association placed itself before the world as the movement through which the new and rising Negro would give expression of his feelings. This Association adopts an attitude not of hostility to other races and peoples of the world, but an attitude of self-respect, of manhood rights on behalf of 400,000,000 Negroes of the world.

We represent peace, harmony, love, human sympathy, human rights and human justice, and that is why we fight so much. Wheresoever human rights are denied to any group, wheresoever justice is denied to any group, there the U.N.I.A. finds a cause. And at this time among all the peoples of the world, the group that suffers most from injustice, the group that is denied most of those rights that belong to all humanity, is the black group of 400,000,000. Because of that injustice, because of that denial of our rights, we go forth under the leadership of the One who is always on the side of right to fight the common cause of humanity; to fight as we fought in the Revolutionary War, as we fought in the Civil War, as we fought in the Spanish-American War, and as we fought in the war between 1914-18 on the battle plains of France and Flanders. As we fought up the heights of Mesopotamia; even so under the leadership of the U.N.I.A., we are marshaling the 400,000,000 Negroes of the world to fight for the emancipation of the race and for the redemption of the country of our fathers.

We represent a new line of thought among Negroes. Whether you call it advanced thought or reactionary thought, I do not care. If it is reactionary for people to seek independence in government, then we are reactionary. If it is advanced thought for people to seek liberty and freedom, then we represent the advanced school of thought among the Negroes of this country. We of the U.N.I.A. believe that what is good for the other fellow is good for us. If government is something that is worth while; if government is something that is appreciable and helpful and protective to others, then we also want to experiment in government. We do not mean a government that will make us citizens without rights or subjects without consideration. We mean the kind of government that will place our race in control, even as other races are in control of their own governments.

Marcus Garvey

That does not suggest anything that is unreasonable. It was not unreasonable for George Washington, the great hero and father of the country, to have fought for the freedom of America giving to us this great republic and this great democracy; it was not unreasonable for the Liberals of France to have fought against the Monarchy to give to the world French Democracy and French Republicanism; it was no unrighteous cause that led in giving to the world the social democracy of Russia, an experiment that will probably prove to be a boon and a blessing to mankind. If it was not an unrighteous cause that led Washington to fight for the independence of this country, and led the Liberals of France to establish the Republic, it is therefore not an unrighteous cause for the U.N.I.A. to lead 400,000,000 Negroes all over the world to fight for the liberation of our country.

Therefore the U.N.I.A. is not advocating the cause of church building, because we have a sufficiently large number of churches among us to minister to the spiritual needs of the people, and we are not going to compete with those who are engaged in so splendid a work; we are not engaged in building any new social institutions, and Y.M.C.A.'s or Y.W.C.A.'s because there are enough social workers engaged in those praise-worthy efforts. We are not engaged in politics because we have enough local politicians, Democrats, Socialists, Soviets, etc., and the political situation is well taken care of. We are not engaged in domestic politics, in church building or in social uplift work, but we are engaged in nation building.

In advocating the principles of this Association we find we have been very much misunderstood and very much misrepresented by men from within our own race, as well as others from without. Any reform movement that seeks to bring about changes for the benefit of humanity is bound to be misrepresented by those who have always taken it upon themselves to administer to, and lead the unfortunate, and to direct those who may be placed under temporary disadvantages. It has been so in all other movements whether social or political; hence those of us in the Universal Negro Improvement Association who lead, do not feel in any way embarrassed about this misrepresentation, about this misunderstanding as far as the Aims and Objects of the Universal Negro Improvement Association go. But those who probably would have taken kindly notice of this great movement, have been led to believe that this movement seeks, not to develop the good within the race, but to give expression to that which is most destructive and most harmful to society and to government.

I desire to remove the misunderstanding that has been created in the minds of millions of peoples throughout the world in their relationship to the organization. The Universal Negro Improvement Association stands for the Bigger Brotherhood; the Universal Negro Improvement Association stands for human rights, not only for Negroes, but for all races. The Universal Negro Improvement Association believes in the rights of not only the black race, but the white race, the yellow race and the brown race. The Universal Negro Improvement Association believes that the white man has as much right to be considered, the yellow man has as much right to be considered, the brown man has as much right to be considered as well as the black man of Africa. In view of the fact that the black man of Africa has contributed as much to the world as the white man of Europe, and the brown man and yellow man of Asia, we of the Universal Negro Improvement Association demand that the white, yellow and brown races give to the black man his place in the civilization of the world. We ask for nothing more than the rights of 400,000,000 Negroes. We are not seeking, as I said before, to destroy or disrupt the society or the government of other races, but we are determined that 400,000,000 of us shall unite ourselves to free our motherland from the grasp of the invader. We of the Universal Negro Improvement Association are determined to unite 400,000,000 Negroes for their own industrial, political, social and religious emancipation.

We of the Universal Negro Improvement Association are determined to unite the 400,000,000 Negroes of the world to give expression to their own feeling; we are determined to unite the 400,000,000 Negroes of the world for the purpose of building a civilization of their own. And in that effort we desire to bring together the 15,000,000 of the United States, the 180,000,000 in Asia, the West Indies and Central and South America, and the 200,000,000 in Africa. We are looking toward political freedom on the continent of Africa, the land of our fathers.

The Universal Negro Improvement Association is not seeking to build up another government within the bounds or borders of the United States of America. The Universal Negro Improvement Association is not seeking to disrupt any organized system of government, but the Association is determined to bring Negroes together for the building up of a nation of their own. And why? Because we have been forced to it. We have been forced to it throughout the world; not only in America, not only in Europe, not only in the British Empire, but wheresoever the black man happens to find himself, he has been forced to do for himself.

"In advocating the principles of [the U.N.I.A.] we find we have been very much misunderstood and very much misrepresented by men from within our own race, as well as others from without."

To talk about Government is a little more than some of our people can appreciate just at this time. The average man does not think that way, just because he finds himself a citizen or a subject of some country. He seems to say, "Why should there be need for any other government?" We are French, English or American. But we of the U.N.I.A. have studied seriously this question of nationality among Negroes—this American nationality, this British nationality, this French, Italian or Spanish nationality, and have discovered that it counts for nought when that nationality comes in conflict with the racial idealism of the group that rules. When our interests clash with those of the ruling faction, then we find that we have absolutely no rights. In times of peace, when everything is all right, Negroes have a hard time, wherever we go, wheresoever we find ourselves, getting those rights that belong to us, in common with others whom we claim as fellow citizens; getting that consideration that should be ours by right of the constitution, by right of the law; but in the time of trouble they make us all partners in the cause, as happened in the last war, when we were partners, whether British, French or American Negroes. And we were told that we must forget everything in an effort to save the nation.

We have saved many nations in this manner, and we have lost our lives doing that before. Hundreds of thousands—nay, millions of black men, lie buried under the ground due to that old-time camouflage of saving the nation. We saved the British empire; we saved the French empire; we saved this glorious country more than once; and all that we have received for what we have done, even in giving up our lives, is just what you are receiving now, just what I am receiving now.

You and I fare no better in America, in the British Empire, or in any other part of the white world; we fare no better than any black man wheresoever he shows his head. And why? Because we have been satisfied to allow ourselves to be led, educated, to be directed by the other fellow, who has always sought to lead in the world in that direction that would satisfy him and strengthen his position. We have allowed ourselves for the last 500 years to be a race of followers, following every race that has led in the direction that would make them more secure.

The UNIA is reversing the old-time order of things. We refuse to be followers any more. We are leading ourselves. That means, if any saving is to be done, later on, whether it is saving this one nation or that one government, we are going to seek a method of saving Africa first. Why? And why Africa? Because Africa has become the grand prize of the nations. Africa has become the big game of the nation hunters. Today Africa looms as the greatest commercial, industrial and political prize in the world.

The difference between the Universal Negro Improvement Association and the other movements of this country, and probably the world, is that the Universal Negro Improvement Association seeks independence of government, while the other organizations seek to make the Negro a secondary part of existing governments. We differ from the organization in America because they seek to subordinate the Negro as a secondary consideration in a great civilization, knowing that in America the Negro will never reach his highest ambition, knowing that the Negro in America will never get his constitutional rights. All those organizations which are fostering the improvement of Negroes in the British Empire know that the Negro in the British Empire will never reach the height of his constitutional rights. What do I mean by constitutional rights in America? If the black man is to reach the height of his ambition in this country—if the black man is to get all of his constitutional rights in America—then the black man should have the same chance in the nation as any other man to become president of the nation, or a street cleaner in New York. If the black man in the British Empire is to have all his constitutional rights it means that the Negro in the British Empire should have at least the same right to become premier of Great Britain as he has to become street cleaner in the city of London. Are they prepared to give us such political equality? You and I can live in the United States of America for 100 more years, and our generations may live for 200 years or for 5000 more years, and so long as there is a black and white population, when the majority is on the side of the white race, you and I will never get political justice or get political equality in this country. Then why should a black man with rising ambition, after preparing himself in every possible way to give expression to that highest ambition, allow himself to be kept down by racial prejudice within a country? If I am as educated as the next man, if I am as prepared as the next man, if I have passed through the best schools and colleges and universities as the other fellow, why should I not have a fair chance to compete with the other fellow for the biggest position in the nation? I have feelings, I have blood, I have senses like the other fellow; I have ambition, I have hope. Why should he, because of some racial prejudice, keep me down and why should I concede to him the right to rise above me, and to establish himself as my permanent master? That is where the U.N.I.A. differs from other organizations. I refuse to stultify my ambition, and every true Negro refuses to stultify his ambition to suit any one, and therefore the U.N.I.A. decides if America is not big enough for two presidents, if England is not big enough for two kings, then we are not going to quarrel over the matter; we will leave one president in America, we will leave one king in England, we will leave one president in France and we will have one president in Africa. Hence, the Universal Negro Improvement Association does not seek to interfere with the social and political systems of France, but by the arrangement of things today the U.N.I.A. refuses to recognize any political or social system in Africa except that which we are about to establish for ourselves.

We are not preaching a propaganda of hate against anybody. We love the white man; we love all humanity, because we feel that we cannot live without the other. The white man is as necessary to the existence of the Negro as the Negro is necessary to his existence. There is a common relationship that we cannot escape. Africa has certain things that Europe wants, and Europe has certain things that Africa wants, and if a fair and square deal must bring white and black with each other, it is impossible for us to escape it. Africa has oil, diamonds, copper, gold and rubber and all the minerals that Europe wants, and there must be some kind of relationship between Africa and Europe for a fair exchange, so we cannot afford to hate anybody.

The question often asked is what does it require to redeem a race and free a country? If it takes man power, if it takes scientific intelligence, if it takes education of any kind, or if it takes blood, then the 400,000,000 Negroes of the world have it.

It took the combined man power of the Allies to put down the mad determination of the Kaiser to impose German will upon the world and upon humanity. Among those who suppressed his mad ambition were two million Negroes who have not yet forgotten how to drive men across the firing line. Surely those of us who faced German shot and shell at the Marne, at Verdun, have not forgotten the order of our Commander-in-Chief. The cry that caused us to leave America in such mad haste, when white fellow citizens of America refused to fight and said, "We do not believe in war and therefore, even though we are American citizens, and even though the nation is in danger, we will not go to war." When many of them cried out and said, "We are German-Americans and we can not fight," when so many white men refused to answer to the call and dodged behind all kinds of excuses, 400,000 black men were ready without a question. It was because we were told it was a war of democracy; it was a war for the liberation of the weaker peoples of the world. We heard the cry of Woodrow Wilson, not because we liked him so, but because the things he said were of such a nature that they appealed to us as men. Wheresoever the cause of humanity stands in need of assistance, there you will find the Negro ever ready to serve.

He has done it from the time of Christ up to now. When the whole world turned its back upon the Christ, the man who was said to be the Son of God; when the world cried out "Crucify Him," when the world spurned Him and spat upon Him, it was a black man, Simon, the Cyrenian, who took up the cross. Why? Because the cause of humanity appealed to him. When the black man saw the suffering Jew, struggling under the heavy cross, he was willing to go to His assistance, and he bore that cross up to the heights of Calvary. In the spirit of Simon, the Cyrenian, 1900 years ago we answered the call of Woodrow Wilson, the call of a larger humanity, and it was for that that we willingly rushed in to the war from America, from the West Indies, over 100,000; it was for that that we rushed into the war from Africa, 2,000,000 of us. We met in France, Flanders and in Mesopotamia. We fought unfalteringly. When the white men faltered and fell back on their battle lines, at the Marne and at Verdun, when they ran away from the charge of the German hordes, the black hell fighters stood before the cannonade, stood before the charge, and again they shouted, "There will be a hot time in the old town to-night."

"We are not preaching a propaganda of hate against anybody. We love the white man; we love all humanity, because we feel that we cannot live without the other."

We made it so hot a few months after our appearance in France and on the various battle fronts, we succeeded in driving the German hordes across the Rhine, and driving the Kaiser out of Germany, and out of Potsdam into Holland. We have not forgotten the prowess of war. If we have been liberal minded enough to give our life's blood in France, in Mesopotamia and elsewhere, fighting for the white man, whom we have always assisted, surely we have not forgotten to fight for ourselves, and when the time comes that the world will again give Africa an opportunity for freedom, surely 400,000,000 black men will march out on the battle plains of Africa, under the colors of the red, the black and the green.

We shall march out, yes, as black American citizens, as black British subjects, as black French citizens, as black Italians or as black Spaniards, but we shall march out with a greater loyalty, the loyalty of race. We shall march out in answer to the cry of our fathers, who cry out to us for the redemption of our own country, our motherland, Africa.

We shall march out, not forgetting the blessings of America. We shall march out, not forgetting the blessings of civilization. We shall march out with a history of peace before and behind us, and surely that history shall be our breastplate, for how can man fight better than knowing that the cause for which he fights is righteous? How can man fight more gloriously than by knowing that behind him is a history of slavery, a history of bloody carnage and massacre inflicted upon a race because of its inability to protect itself and fight? Shall we not fight for the glorious opportunity of protecting and forever more establishing ourselves as a mighty race and nation, never more to be disrespected by men? Glorious shall be the battle when the time comes to fight for our people and our race.

We should say to the millions who are in Africa to hold the fort, for we are coming 400,000,000 strong.

Two years later, Garvey argued even more strongly in favor of black nationalism at the Fourth International Convention of the Negro Peoples of the World. In this address, delivered August 1, 1924, in New York City, he stressed that the very survival of the black race was at stake. It was a common theme in many of his speeches, as were his blunt language and emotional appeal to his audience. The following is taken from Volume 2 of Philosophy and Opinions of Marcus Garvey *(Universal Publishing House, 1925; reprinted, Arno, 1969).*

Delegates to the Fourth International Convention of the Negro Peoples of the World, Ladies and Gentlemen:

The pleasure of addressing you at this hour is great. You have re-assembled yourselves in New York, coming from all parts of the world to this annual convention, because you believe that by unity you can alleviate the unfortunate condition in which racially we find ourselves.

We are glad to meet as Negroes, notwithstanding the stigma that is placed upon us by a soulless and conscienceless world because of our backwardness.

As usual, I am not here to flatter you, I am not here to tell you how happy and prosperous we are as a people, because that is all false. The Negro is not happy, but, to the contrary, is extremely miserable. He is miserable because the world is closing fast around him, and if he does not strike out now for his own preservation, it is only a question of a few more decades when he will be completely out-done in a world of strenuous competition for a place among the fittest of God's creation.

NEGRO DYING OUT

The Negro is dying out, and he is going to die faster and more rapidly in the next fifty years than he has in the past three hundred years. There is only one thing to save the Negro, and that is an immediate realization of his own responsibilities. Unfortunately we are the most careless and indifferent people in the world! We are shiftless and irresponsible, and that is why we find ourselves the wards of an inherited materialism that has lost its soul and its conscience. It is strange to hear a Negro leader speak in this strain, as the usual course is flattery, but I would not flatter you to save my own life and that of my own family. There is no value in flattery. Flattery of the Negro for another quarter of a century will mean hell and damnation to the race. How can any Negro leader flatter us about progress and the rest of it, when the world is preparing more than ever to bury the entire race? Must I flatter you when England, France, Italy, Belgium and Spain are all concentrating on robbing every square inch of African territory—the land of our fathers? Must I flatter you when the cry is being loudly raised for a white America, Canada, Australia and Europe, and a yellow and brown Asia? Must I flatter you when I find all other peoples preparing themselves for the struggle to survive, and you still smiling eating, dancing, drinking and sleeping away your time, as if yesterday were the beginning of the age of pleasure? I would rather be dead than be a member of your race without thought of the morrow, for it portends evil to him that thinketh not. Because I cannot flatter you I am here to tell, emphatically, that if we do not seriously reorganize ourselves as a people and face the world with a program of African nationalism our days in civilization are numbered, and it will be only a question of time when the Negro will be as completely and complacently dead as the North American Indian, or the Australian Bushman.

PROGRESS ON SAND

You talk about the progress we have made in America and elsewhere, among the people of our acquaintance, but what progress is it? A progress than can be snatched away from you in forty-eight hours, because it has been built upon sand.

You must thank God for the last two generations of whites in our western civilization; thank God that they were not made of sterner stuff, and character and a disposition to see all races their rivals and competitors in the struggle to hold and possess the world, otherwise, like the Indian, we would have been nearly all dead.

The progress of the Negro in our civilization was tolerated because of indifference, but that indifference exists no longer. Our whole civilization is becoming intolerant, and because of that the whole world of races has started to think.

Can you blame the white man for thinking, when red and yellow men are knocking at his door? Can you blame the tiger for being on the defensive when the lion approaches? And thus we find that generations ago, when the Negro was not given a thought as a world competitor he is now regarded as an encumbrance in a civilization to which he has materially contributed little. Men do not build for others, they build for themselves. The age and our religion demand it. What are you going to expect, that white men are going to build up America and elsewhere and hand it over to us? If we are expecting that we are crazy, we have lost our reason.

If you were white, you would see the rest in hell before you would deprive your children of bread to give it to others. You would give that which you did not want, but not that which is to be the sustenance of your family, and so the world thinks; yet a [W.E.B.] Du Bois and the National Association for the Advancement of Colored People will tell us by flattery that the day is coming when a white President of the United States of America will get out of the White House and give the position to a Negro, that the day is coming when a Mr. Hughes will desert the Secretaryship of State and give it to the Negro, James Weldon Johnson; that the time is just around the corner of constitutional rights when the next Ambassador to the Court of Saint James will be a black man from Mississippi or from North Carolina. Do you think that white men who have suffered, bled and died to make America and the world what it is, are going to hand over to a parcel of lazy Negroes the things that they prize most?

Stop flattering yourselves, fellowmen, and let us go to work. Do you hear me? Go to work! Go to work in the morn of a new creation and strike, not because of the noonday sun, but plod on and on, until you have succeeded in climbing the hills of opposition and reached the height of self-progress, and from that pinnacle bestow upon the world a civilization of your own, and hand down to your children and posterity of your own a worthy contribution to the age of human materialism.

We of the Universal Negro Improvement Association are fair and just. We do not expect the white man to rob himself, and to deprive himself, for our racial benefit. How could you reasonably expect that, in an age like this, when men have divided themselves into racial and national groups, when the one group has its own interest to protect as against that of the other?

The laws of self-preservation force every human group to look after itself and protect its own interest; hence so long as the American white man or any other white man, for that matter, realizes his responsibility, he is bound to struggle to protect that which is his and his own, and I feel that the Negro today who has been led by the unscrupulous of our race has been grossly misguided, in the direction of expecting too much from the civilization of others.

THE CARPETBAGGER

Immediately after emancipation, we were improperly led in the South by this same group and ultimately lost our vote and voice. The carpetbagger and the thoughtless, selfish Negro politician and leader sold the race back into slavery. And the same attempt is now being made in the North by that original group, prompted by the dishonest white political boss and the unscrupulous Negro politician. The time has come for both races to seriously adjust their differences and settle the future of our respective peoples. The selfish of both races will not stop to think and act, but the responsibility becomes more so ours who have the vision of the future.

CRIMINALS OUT OF JAIL

Because of my attempt to lead my race into the only solution that I see would benefit both groups, I have been maliciously and wickedly maligned, and by members of our own race. I have been plotted against, framed up, indicted and convicted, the story which you so well know. That was responsible for our not having a convention last year. I thank you, however, for the tribute you paid me during that period in postponing the convention through respect to my enforced absence. Last August I spent three months in the Tombs in New York but I was as happy then as I am now. I was sent there by the evil forces that have always fought and opposed reform movements, but I am as ready now to go back to the Tombs or elsewhere as I was when I was forced to leave you. The jail does not make a criminal, the criminal makes himself. There are more criminals out of jail than in jail, the only difference is that the majority of those who are out, are such skillful criminals that they know how to keep themselves out. They have tried to besmirch my name so as to prevent me doing the good that I desire to do in the interest of the race. It amuses me sometimes to hear the biggest crooks in the Negro Race referring to me as a criminal. As I have said before, Negro race leaders are the biggest crooks in the world. It is because of their crookedness that we have not made more progress. If you think I am not telling the truth in this direction you may quiz any of the white political bosses, and those who will tell the truth will reveal a tale most shocking as far as our Negro leaders are concerned. This is true of the group of fellows of our race that lead universally as well as nationally. They will sell the souls of their mothers and their country into perdition. That is why the Universal Negro Improvement Association has to make such a fight, and that is why the opposition is as hard and marked. You can pay the Negro leader to hang his race and block every effort of self-help. This is not commonly so among other races. We must give credit to the great white race, to the extent that they will fight among themselves, that they will cheat each other in business, but when it approaches the future and destiny of the race, a halt is immediately called. Not so with the Negro. he does not know when and where to stop in hurting himself.

REORGANIZING THE RACE

I repeat that we must reorganize ourselves as a people, if we are to go forward, and I take this opportunity, as you assemble yourselves here from all parts of the world, to sound the warning note.

To review the work of our Association for the past two years is to recount the exploits of a continuous struggle to reach the top. Our organization has been tested during the past two years beyond that of any other period in the history of Negro movements. I am glad to say, however, that we have survived all the intrigues, barriers, and handicaps placed in the way. Some of our enemies thought that they would have been able to crush our movement when I was convicted and sentenced to prison. They had depended upon that, as the trump card in their effort to crush the new spirit of freedom among Negroes, but like all such efforts, it was doomed to failure. I will bring to your recollection a similar effort made a little over nineteen hundred years ago when on Calvary's Mount, the Jews after inspiring the Romans, attempted to crucify the man, Christ, the leader of the Christian religion. They thought that after the crucifixion, after he was buried, that they would have silenced the principles of Christianity forever, but how successful they were, is made manifest today when we find hundreds of millions of souls the world over professing the principles for which the man died on Calvary's cross.

As in the rise of Christianity, so do we have the spiritual rise of the Universal Negro Improvement Association throughout the world. They tried to crucify it in America, and it has arisen in Africa a thousand fold. They tried to crucify it on the American continent, and it is now sweeping the whole world. You cannot crucify a principle; you cannot nail the souls of men to a cross; you cannot imprison it; you cannot bury it. It will rise like the spirit of the Great Redeemer and take its flight down the ages, until men far and near have taken up the cry for which the principle was crucified.

We of the Universal Negro Improvement Association are stronger today than we ever were before. We are strong in spirit, strong in determination; we are unbroken in every direction; we stand firm facing the world, determined to carve out and find a place for the four hundred millions of our suffering people. We call upon humanity everywhere to listen to the cry of the new Negro. We ask the human heart for a response, because Africa's sun cannot be downed. Africa's sun is rising, gradually rising, and soon shall take its place among the brilliant constellations of nations. The Negro wants a nation, nothing less, nothing more; and why shouldn't we be nationally free, nationally independent, nationally unfettered? We want a nationality similar to that of the English, the French, the Italian, the German, to that of the white American, to that of the yellow Japanese; we want nationality and government because we realize that the American nation in a short while will not be large enough to accommodate two competitive rivals, one black and the other white.

BLACK MAN'S ASPIRATIONS

There is no doubt about it that the black man of America today aspires to the White House, to the Cabinet, and to the Senate, and the House. He aspires to be head of State and municipal governments. What are you going to do with him? He cannot be satisfied in the midst of a majority group that seeks to protect its interest at all hazards; then the only alternative is to give the Negro a place of his own. That is why we appeal to the sober white minds of America, and not the selfish ones. The selfish ones will see nothing more than the immediate present, but the deep thinking white man will see the result of another fifty or one hundred years, when these two peoples will be brought together in closer contact of rivalry. As races we practically represent a similar intelligence today. We have graduated from the same schools, colleges and universities. What can you do with men who are equally and competently fitted in mind, but give them an equal chance, and if there is no chance of equality, there must be dissatisfaction on the one hand. That dissatisfaction we have in our midst now. We have it manifested by W.E.B. Du Bois, by James Weldon Johnson; we have it manifested by the organization known as the National Association for the Advancement of Colored People, that seeks to bring about social equality, political equality, and industrial equality, things that are guaranteed us under the Constitution, but which, in the face of a majority race, we cannot demand, because of the terrible odds against us. In the midst of this, then, what can we do but seek an outlet of our own, unless we intend to fight a losing game. Reason will dictate that there is no benefit to be derived from fighting always a losing game. We will lose until we have completely lost our stand in America.

THE PERIOD OF SELF-PROTECTION

To repeat myself, we talk about progress. What progress have we made when everything we do is done through the good will and grace of the liberal white man of the present day? But can he always afford to be liberal? Do you not realize that in another few decades he will have on his hands a problem of his own—a problem to feed his own children, to take care of his own flesh and blood? In the midst of that crisis, when he finds not even enough to feed himself, what will become of the Negro? The Negro naturally must die to give way, and make room for others who are better prepared to live. That is the danger, men; and that is why we have the Universal Negro Improvement Association. The condition that I have referred to will not only be true of America and of continental Europe; it will be true wherever the great white race lives. There will not be room enough for them, and others who seek to compete with them. That is why we hear the cry of Egypt for the Egyptians, India for the Indians, Asia for the Asiatics, and we raise the cry of Africa for the Africans; those at home and those abroad. That is why we ask England to be fair, to be just and considerate; that is why we ask France, Italy, Spain and Belgium to be fair, just and considerate; that is why we ask them to let the black man restore himself to his own country; and that is why we are determined to see it done. No camouflage, and no promise of good-will, will solve the problem. What guarantee have we, what lease have we on the future that the man who treats us kindly today will perpetuate it through his son or his grandson tomorrow?

Races and peoples are only safeguarded when they are strong enough to protect themselves, and that is why we appeal to the four hundred million Negroes of the world to come together for self-protection and self-preservation. We do not want what belongs to the great white race, or the yellow race. We want only those things that belong to the black race. Africa is ours. To win Africa we will give up America, we will give up our claim in all other parts of the world, but we must have Africa. We will give up the vain desire of having a seat in the White House in America, of having a seat in the House of Lords in England, of being President of France, for the chance and opportunity of filling these positions in a country of our own.

That is how the Universal Negro Improvement Association differs from other organizations. Other organizations, especially in America, are fighting for a political equality which they will never get, and never win, in the face of a majority opposition. We win so much today and lose so much tomorrow. We will lose our political strength in the North in another few years, as we lost it in the South during Reconstruction. We fill one position today, but lose two tomorrow, and so we will drift on and on, until we have been completely obliterated from western civilization.

> ***"Races and peoples are only safeguarded when they are strong enough to protect themselves . . ."***

CHANGES AMONG NEGROES

You may ask me what good has the Universal Negro Improvement Association done, what has it accomplished within the last six years? We will point to you the great changes that have taken place in Africa, the West Indies and America. In the West Indies, black men have been elevated to high positions by the British Government, so as to off-set and counteract the sweeping influence of the Universal Negro Improvement Association. Several of the Colonies have been given larger constitutional rights. In Africa, the entire West Coast has been benefitted. Self-government has been given to several of the African Colonies, and native Africans have been elevated to higher positions, so as to off-set the sweeping spirit of the Universal Negro Improvement Association throughout the Continent of Africa. In America, several of our men have been given prominent positions; Negro commissions have been appointed to attend to affairs of state; Negro Consuls have also been appointed. Things that happened in America within the last six years to advance the political status, the social and industrial status of the Negro were never experienced before. All that is traceable to the Universal Negro Improvement Association within the last six years. In the great game of politics you do not see the immediate results at your door, but those who are observant will be able to trace the good that is being done from the many directions whence it comes. If you were to take a survey of the whole world of Negroes you will find that we are more highly thought of in 1922 than we were in 1914. England, France and the European and Colonial powers regard the Universal Negro Improvement Association with a certain amount of suspicion because they believe that we are antagonistic. But we are not. We are not antagonistic to France, to England or Italy, nor any of the white Powers in Europe. We are only demanding a square deal for our race. Did we not fight to help them? Did we not sacrifice our blood, give up our all to save England, to save France, Italy and America during the last war? Then why shouldn't we expect some consideration for the service rendered? That is all we ask; and we are now pressing that claim to the throne of white justice. We are told that God's throne is white, although we believe it to be black. But if it is white, we are placing our plea before that throne of God, asking Him to so touch the hearts of our fellow-men as to let them yield to us the things that are ours, as it was right to yield to Caesar the things that were Caesar's.

As we deliberate on the many problems confronting us during the month of August, let us not lose control of ourselves; let us not forget that we are the guardians of four hundred millions; let us not forget that it is our duty to so act and legislate as to help humanity everywhere, whether it be black or white. We shall be called upon during this month to take up certain matters that are grave, but dispassionately we shall discuss them; and whenever the interest of the different race groups clash, let it be our duty to take the other fellow's feelings into our consideration. If we must be justly treated, then we ourselves must treat all men similarly. So, let no prejudice cause us to say or do anything against the interest of the white man, or the yellow man; let us realize that the white man has the right to live, the yellow man has the right to live, and all that we desire to do is to impress them with the fact that we also have the right to live.

SOURCES

Boulware, Marcus H., *The Oratory of Negro Leaders: 1900-1968,* Negro Universities Press, 1969.

Clarke, John Henrik, editor, *Marcus Garvey and the Vision of Africa,* Vintage, 1974.

Cronon, Edmund David, *Black Moses: The Story of Marcus Garvey and the Universal Negro Improvement Association,* revised edition, University of Wisconsin Press, 1987.

Duffy, Bernard K., and Halford R. Ryan, editors, *American Orators of the Twentieth Century: Critical Studies and Sources,* Greenwood Press, 1987.

Foner, Philip S., editor, *The Voice of Black America: Major Speeches by Negroes in the United States, 1797-1971,* Simon & Schuster, 1972.

Garvey, Amy Jacques, compiler, *Philosophy and Opinions of Marcus Garvey,* Universal Publishing House, Volume 1, 1923, Volume 2, 1925, both volumes reprinted, Arno, 1969.

Hill, Robert A., editor, *The Marcus Garvey and the Universal Negro Improvement Association Papers,* three volumes, University of California Press, 1975.

Hill, Roy L., *Rhetoric of Racial Revolt,* Golden Bell Press, 1964.

Meltzer, Milton, editor, *The Black Americans: A History in Their Own Words, 1619-1983,* Crowell, 1984.

O'Neill, Daniel J., editor, *Speeches by Black Americans,* Dickenson, 1971.

Smith, Arthur L., *Rhetoric of Black Revolution,* Allyn & Bacon, 1969.

Smith, Arthur L., and Stephen Robb, editors, *The Voice of Black Rhetoric: Selections,* Allyn & Bacon, 1971.

Stein, Judith, *The World of Marcus Garvey: Race and Class in Modern Society,* Louisiana State University Press, 1986.

Dan George

1899–1981

Native American actor and chief of the Salish tribe

Best known to American film audiences as Old Lodge Skins in the 1970 movie Little Big Man, *Dan George used the roles he played on stage and screen to challenge the popular image of Indians, particularly in his native Canada. His ability to convey a sense of dignity and spirituality was unique in its day and therefore made a profound impression on people accustomed to Hollywood's view of the Native American. In fact, it was the prospect of being able to demolish those very stereotypes that eventually motivated George to give acting a try at an age when many people are looking forward to retirement.*

Born on the Burrard Indian Reserve near Vancouver, British Columbia, George was a member of a small band of Coast Salish people known as the Tell-lall-watt. (He would later become the seventh generation of his family to serve as chief of the band; he also was an honorary chief of the Squamish and Sushwap tribes.) As a boy, he helped his father cut and sell timber, a profession young Dan also expected to follow after he left school at the age of sixteen. But by the time he was in his early twenties, the timber supply had dwindled to the point where he could no longer earn a living as a logger. So he became a longshoreman, working the docks for more than twenty-five years until an injury forced him to give up his job around 1947. He then worked at various construction jobs and even did some more logging before one of his sons urged him to take up acting at the age of sixty.

Recalling his decision to embark on a new career, George once told an interviewer, "I didn't like the cowboy-and-Indian movies one bit. . . . I watched those white men playing the parts of Indians and it always looked so phony to me. I wanted to show that an Indian, if he had talent, could play an Indian better than a white simply because he was playing his own nationality." He also saw it as a way to "build up Indian morale," as he phrased it. "I'm only going to take roles that will bring acceptance of the Indian," he declared. "There's no room for any kind of bad will. We're all human beings on this earth."

Under the name Chief Dan George, he appeared in a number of Canadian television programs and theater productions and over a half-dozen feature films, among them Smith! *(1969),* Harry and Tonto *(1974), and* The Outlaw—Josey Wales *(1976). It was in* Little Big Man, *however, that he made the strongest impression. His portrayal of a venerable Cheyenne elder opposite Dustin Hoffman as a colorful frontier character earned him an Academy Award nomination and best supporting actor honors from the New York Film Critics as well as from the National Society of Film Critics. (Reviewers were virtually unanimous in their praise of the chief's solemn grace and gentle humor, which they felt gave him an almost biblical presence on the screen.) Later in life, he also wrote two books of prose-poetry,* My Heart Soars *and* My Spirit Soars.

Although he did not personally become involved in any particular political cause, Chief Dan George was an eloquent defender of native rights and the environment. In 1967, for example, at a celebration in Vancouver marking Canada's one hundredth birthday, he lamented how much life had changed for his people and for his home during the previous century. His words are reprinted here from T.C. McLuhan's Touch the Earth: A Self-Portrait of Indian Existence *(Outerbridge & Dienstfrey, 1971).*

How long have I known you, oh Canada? A hundred years? Yes, a hundred years. And many many "seelanum" more. And today, when you celebrate your hundred years, oh Canada, I am sad for all the Indian people throughout the land.

For I have known you when your forests were mine; when they gave me my meat and my clothing. I have known you in your streams and rivers where your fish flashed and danced in the sun, where the waters said come, come and eat of my abundance. I have known you in the freedom of your winds. And my spirit, like the winds, once roamed your good lands.

But in the long hundred years since the white man came, I have seen my freedom disappear like the salmon going mysteriously out to sea. The white man's strange customs which I could not understand, pressed down upon me until I could no longer breathe.

When I fought to protect my land and my home, I was called a savage. When I neither understood nor welcomed this way of life, I was called lazy. When I tried to rule my people, I was stripped of my authority.

Dan George

My nation was ignored in your history textbooks—they were little more important in the history of Canada than the buffalo that ranged the plains. I was ridiculed in your plays and motion pictures, when I drank your fire-water, I got drunk—very, very drunk. And I forgot.

Oh Canada, how can I celebrate with you this centenary, this hundred years? Shall I thank you for the reserves that are left to me of my beautiful forests? For the canned fish of my rivers? For the loss of my pride and authority, even among my own people? For the lack of my will to fight back? No! I must forget what's past and gone.

Oh, God in Heaven! Give me back the courage of the olden chiefs. Let me wrestle with my surroundings. Let me again, as in the days of old, dominate my environment. Let me humbly accept this new culture and through it rise up and go on.

Oh, God! Like the thunderbird of old I shall rise again out of the sea; I shall grab the instruments of the white man's success—his education, his skills, and with these new tools I shall build my race into the proudest segment of your society. Before I follow the great chiefs who have gone before us, oh Canada, I shall see these things come to pass.

I shall see our young braves and our chiefs sitting in the houses of law and government, ruling and being ruled by the knowledge and freedom of our great land. So shall we shatter the barriers of our isolation. So shall the next hundred years be the greatest in the proud history of our tribes and nations.

As he made clear in the closing lines of the previous speech, Chief Dan George—despite his sadness over the loss of the old ways—supported Indian assimilation. "In the beginning I resented the adoption of the white man's ways," he once explained, "but I realize that if our children are to survive, they have to live and work in white society." In the following talk, delivered on an unknown occasion during the early 1970s, he reflected on the need for brotherhood and understanding between his people and the dominant white culture. His observations are reprinted from Contemporary Native American Address, *edited by John R. Maestas (Brigham Young University Press, 1976).*

I am a native of North America. In the course of my lifetime I have lived in two distinct cultures. I was born into a culture that lived in communal houses. My grandfather's house was eighty feet long. It was called a smoke house, and it stood down by the beach along the inlet. All my grandfather's sons and their families lived in this large dwelling. Their sleeping apartments were separated by blankets made of bull rush reeds. But one open fire in the middle served the cooking needs of all. In houses like these, throughout the tribe, people learned to live with one another; learned to serve one another; learned to respect the rights of one another, and children shared the thoughts of the adult world and found themselves surrounded by aunts and uncles and cousins who loved them and did not threaten them. My father was born in such a house and learned from infancy how to love people and be at home with them.

And beyond this acceptance of one another there was a deep respect for everything in nature that surrounded them. My father really loved the earth and all its creatures. The earth was his second mother. The earth and everything it contained was a gift from See-see-am . . . and the way to thank this great spirit was to use his gifts with respect.

I remember, as a little boy, fishing with him up Indian River and I can still see him as the sun rose above the mountain top in the early morning. I can see him standing by the water's edge with his arms raised above his head while he softly moaned . . . "Thank you, thank you." It left a deep impression on my young mind.

And I shall never forget his disappointment when once he caught me gaffing for fish "just for the fun of it."

"My son," he said, "The Great Spirit gave you those fish to be your brothers, to feed you when you are hungry. You must respect them. You must not kill them just for the fun of it."

This then was the culture I was born into and for some years the only one I really knew or tasted. This is why I find it hard to accept many of the things I see around me.

I see people living in smoke houses hundreds of times bigger than the one I knew. But the people in one apartment do not even know the people in the next and care less about them.

It is also difficult for me to understand the deep hate that exists among people. It is hard to understand a culture that justifies the killing of millions in past wars, and is at this very moment preparing bombs to kill even greater numbers. It is hard for me to understand a culture that spends more on wars and weapons to kill, than it does on education and welfare to help and develop.

It is hard for me to understand a culture that not only hates and fights his brothers but even attacks nature and abuses her. I see my white brothers going about blotting out nature from his cities. I see him strip the hills bare leaving ugly wounds on the face of mountains. I see him tearing things from the bosom of mother earth as though she were a monster, who refused to share her treasures with him. I see him throw poison in the waters, indifferent to the life he kills there, and he chokes the air with deadly fumes.

My white brother does many things well for he is more clever than my people, but I wonder if he knows how to love well. I wonder if he has ever really learned to love at all. Perhaps he only loves the things that are his own but never learned to love the things that are outside and beyond him. And this is, of course, not love at all, for man must love all creation or he will love none of it. Man must love fully or he will become the lowest of the animals. It is the power to love that makes him the greatest of them all . . . for he alone of all animals is capable of love.

"It is hard for me to understand a culture that not only hates and fights his brothers but even attacks nature and abuses her."

My friends, how desperately do we need to be loved and to love. When Christ said that man does not live by bread alone, he spoke of a hunger. This hunger was not the hunger of the body. It was not the hunger for bread. He spoke of a hunger that begins deep down in the very depths of our being. He spoke of a need as vital as breath. He spoke of our hunger for love.

Love is something you and I must have. We must have it because our spirit feeds upon it. We must have it because without it we become weak and faint. Without love our self-esteem weakens. Without it our courage fails. Without love we can no longer look out confidently at the world. Instead we turn inwardly and begin to feed upon our own personalities and little by little we destroy ourselves.

You and I need the strength and joy that comes from knowing that we are loved. With it we are creative. With it we march tirelessly. With it, and with it alone, we are able to sacrifice for others.

There have been times when we all wanted so desperately to feel a reassuring hand upon us. There have been lonely times when we so wanted a strong arm around us. I cannot tell you how deeply I miss my wife's presence when I return from a trip. Her love was my greatest joy, my strength, my greatest blessing.

I am afraid my culture has little to offer yours. But my culture did prize friendship and companionship. It did not look on privacy as a thing to be clung to, for privacy builds up walls and walls promote distrust. My culture lived in big family communities, and from infancy people learned to live with others.

My culture did not prize the hoarding of private possessions, in fact, to hoard was a shameful thing to do among my people. The Indian looked on all things in nature as belonging to him and he expected to share them with others and to take only what he needed.

Everyone likes to give as well as receive. No one wishes only to receive all the time. We have taken much from your culture. I wish you had taken something from our culture. For there were some beautiful and good things in it.

Soon it will be too late to know my culture for integration is upon us and soon we will have no values but yours. Already so many of our young people have forgotten the old ways. And many have been shamed of their Indian ways by scorn and ridicule. My culture is like a wounded deer that has crawled away into the forest to bleed and die alone.

The only thing that can truly help us is genuine love. You must truly love us, be patient with us and share with us. And we must love you with a genuine love that forgives and forgets . . . a love that forgives the terrible sufferings your culture brought ours when it swept over us like a wave crashing along a beach . . . with a love that forgets and lifts up its head and sees in your eyes an answering love of trust and acceptance.

This is brotherhood. . . . Anything less is not worthy of the name.

I have spoken.

SOURCES

Books

Maestas, John R., editor, *Contemporary Native American Address,* Brigham Young University, 1976.

McLuhan, T.C., *Touch the Earth: A Self-Portrait of Indian Existence,* Outerbridge & Dienstfrey, 1971.

Periodicals

New Republic, "Little Big Man," December 26, 1970, p. 18.

Newsweek, "How the West Was Lost," December 21, 1970, pp. 98-100; "The Chief," January 25, 1971, p. 80.

New York Times, "Film: Seeking the American Heritage," December 15, 1970, p. 53; September 24, 1981, p. D27.

Time, "The Red and the White," December 21, 1970, pp. 56-57; "The Noble Non-Savage," February 15, 1971, pp. 76-79.

Geronimo
(Goyathlay)

1829–1909

Native American war chief of the Chiricahua Apache tribe

A near-legendary symbol of Indian resistance to the white man, Geronimo was the wily war chief of a group of Apaches whose homeland was near the Chiricahua mountain range in what is now southwestern Arizona. The Apaches were primarily a nomadic tribe that hunted buffalo and did a little farming in the desert climate. Beginning in the late 1500s, they encountered the first major threat to their way of life when the Spanish arrived in Mexico and began to expand their influence north. Clashes between the two groups were still very common by the time the United States acquired the territory during the mid-1800s. Squeezed in between the Mexicans and an ever-growing number of Americans, the Apaches—well known for their skill and ferocity as warriors—struck back intermittently on both sides of the border.

Geronimo was born into this hostile atmosphere in 1829, near the headwaters of New Mexico's Gila River. After Mexicans killed his mother, wife, and children in 1858, he participated in a series of raids against white settlers in the region, then retreated peacefully to a reservation in Arizona for a while. In 1876, however, the U.S. government tried to move the Chiricahua Apaches to a reservation in New Mexico. Geronimo refused to leave, and over the next ten years, he and his followers—despite being vastly outnumbered by the troops sent in to subdue them—effectively waged guerrilla warfare against both the Mexicans and the Americans.

Although Geronimo himself was captured several times during this period, he always managed to escape and launch still more surprise attacks, after which he and his warriors would then vanish into the safety of the mountains. Occasionally, the Apaches tried to break the cycle by settling down to pursue ranching and farming. But the restrictions of such an existence left them unhappy and bored, and soon the raids would begin again. Meanwhile, the press offered up distorted accounts of Geronimo and the Apaches, enthralling readers with tales that depicted them as nothing more than brutal savages.

Geronimo's days as a warrior finally came to an end in 1886. That spring, U.S. troops once again cornered the Apaches and warned their most famous war chief that if the raids did not stop, the tribe would be sent to live on a reservation in

Florida. Realizing that perhaps the time had indeed come to surrender, Geronimo delivered the following defense of himself and his actions to U.S. Army General George Crook at a meeting between the two men in New Mexico. (Some historians have dismissed Geronimo's protest of innocence as a creative manipulation of the truth.) He and Crook were already well acquainted; they had been at odds with each other ever since 1883, the year Crook was first assigned to deal with the Chiricahua Apaches. Geronimo's speech is reprinted from W.C. Vanderwerth's Indian Oratory: Famous Speeches by Noted Indian Chieftains *(University of Oklahoma Press, 1971).*

I want to talk first of the causes which led me to leave the reservation. I was living quietly and contented, doing and thinking of no harm, while at the Sierra Blanca. I don't know what harm I did to those three men, Chato, Mickey Free, and Lieutenant Davis. I was living peaceably and satisfied when people began to speak bad of me. I should be glad to know who started those stories. I was living peaceably with my family, having plenty to eat, sleeping well, taking care of my people, and perfectly contented. I don't know where those bad stories first came from. There we were doing well and my people well. I was behaving well. I hadn't killed a horse or man, American or Indian. I don't know what was the matter with the people in charge of us. They knew this to be so, and yet they said I was a bad man and the worst man there; but what harm had I done? I was living peaceably and well, but I did not leave on my own accord. Had I left it would have been right to blame me; but as it is, blame those men who started this talk about me.

Geronimo

Some time before I left an Indian named Wodiskay had a talk with me. He said, "They are going to arrest you," but I paid no attention to him, knowing that I had done no wrong; and the wife of Mangus, Huera, told me that they were going to seize me and put me and Mangus in the guardhouse, and I learned from the American and Apache soldiers, from Chato, and Mickey Free, that the Americans were going to arrest me and hang me, and so I left.

I would like to know now who it was that gave the order to arrest me and hang me. I was living peaceably there with my family under the shade of the trees, doing just what General Crook had told me I must do and trying to follow his advice. I want to know now who it was ordered me to be arrested. I was praying to the light and to the darkness, to God and to the sun, to let me live quietly with my family. I don't know what the reason was that people should speak badly of me. I don't want to be blamed. The fault was not mine. Blame those three men. With them is the fault, and find out who it was that began that bad talk about me.

I have several times asked for peace, but trouble has come from the agents and interpreters. I don't want what has passed to happen again. Now, I am going to tell you something else. The Earth-Mother is listening to me and I hope that all may be so arranged that from now on there shall be no trouble and that we shall always have peace. Whenever we see you coming to where we are, we think it is God—you must come always with God. From this on I do not want that anything shall be told you about me even in joke. Whenever I have broken out, it was always been on account of bad talk. From this on I hope that people will tell me nothing but the truth. From this on I want to do what is right and nothing else and I do not want you to believe any bad papers about me. I want the papers sent you to tell the truth about me, because I want to do what is right. Very often there are stories put in the newspapers that I am to be hanged. I don't want that any more. When a man tries to do right, such stories ought not to be put in the newspapers.

There are very few of my men left now. They have done some bad things but I want them all rubbed out now and let us never speak of them again. There are very few of us left. We think of our relations, brothers, brothers-in-law, father-in-law, etc., over on the reservation, and from this on we want to live at peace just as they are doing, and to behave as they are behaving. Sometimes a man does something and men are sent out to bring in his head. I don't want such things to happen to us. I don't want that we should be killing each other.

What is the matter that you don't speak to me? It would be better if you would speak to me and look with a pleasant face. It would make better feeling. I would be glad if you did. I'd be better satisfied if you would talk to me once in a while. Why don't you look at me and smile at me? I am the same man; I have the same feet, legs, and hands, and the sun looks down on me a complete man. I want you to look and smile at me.

I have not forgotten what you told me, although a long time has passed. I keep it in my memory. I am a complete man. Nothing has gone from my body. From here on I want to live at peace. Don't believe any bad talk you hear about me. The agents and the interpreter hear that somebody has done wrong, and they blame it all on me. Don't believe what they say. I don't want any of this bad talk in the future. I don't want those men who talked this way about me to be my agents any more. I want good men to be my agents and interpreters; people who will talk right. I want this peace to be legal and good. Whenever I meet you I talk good to you, and you to me, and peace is soon established; but when you go to the reservation you put agents and interpreters over us who do bad things. Perhaps they don't mind what you tell them, because I do not believe you would tell them to do bad things to us. In the future we don't want these bad men to be allowed near where we are to live. We don't want any more of that kind of bad talk. I don't want any man who will talk bad about me, and tell lies, to be there, because I am going to try and live well and peaceably. I want to have a good man put over me.

While living I want to live well. I know I have to die sometime, but even if the heavens were to fall on me, I want to do what is right. I think I am a good man, but in the papers all over the world they say I am a bad man; but it is a bad thing to say so about me. I never do wrong without a cause. Every day I am thinking, how am I to talk to you to make you believe what I say; and, I think, too, that you are thinking of what you are to say to me. There is one God looking down on us all. We are all children of the one God. God is listening to me. The sun, the darkness, the winds, are all listening to what we now say.

To prove to you that I am telling you the truth, remember I sent you word that I would come from a place far away to speak to you here, and you see us now. Some have come on horseback and some on foot. If I were thinking bad, or if I had done bad, I would never have come here. If it has been my fault, would I have come so far to talk to you? I have told you all that has happened. I also had feared that I should never see Ka-e-te-na again, but here he is, and I want the past to be buried. I am glad to see Ka-e-te-na. I was afraid I should never see him again. That was one reason, too, why I left. I wish that Ka-e-te-na would be returned to us to live with his family. I now believe what I was told. Now I believe that all told me is true, because I see Ka-e-te-na again. I am glad to see him again, as I was told I should. We are all glad. My body feels good because I see Ka-e-te-na, and my breathing is good. Now I can eat well, drink well, sleep well, and be glad. I can go everywhere with good feeling. Now, what I want is peace in good faith. Both you and I think well and think alike.

Well, we have talked enough and set here long enough. I may have forgotten something, but if I remember it, I will tell you of it tonight, or tomorrow, or some other time. I have finished for today, but I'll have something more to say bye and bye.

After their surrender, Geronimo's band of Chiricahua Apaches—who by this time numbered only a few dozen men, women, and children—were sent to live at a succession of army bases, first in Florida, then in Alabama, and, finally, at Fort Sill in Oklahoma Territory, where they turned to farming. Geronimo himself eventually became quite a celebrity and tourist attraction. In 1905, he visited Washington, D.C., and attended the inauguration ceremonies of President Theodore Roosevelt. He died of pneumonia in 1909 at Fort Sill and is buried on the grounds there.

SOURCES

Brown, Dee, *Bury My Heart at Wounded Knee: An Indian History of the American West*, Holt, 1970.

Debo, Angie, *Geronimo: The Man, His Time, His Place*, University of Oklahoma Press, 1982.

Dugan, Bill, *War Chiefs: Geronimo*, HarperCollins, 1991.

McLuhan, T.C., *Touch the Earth: A Self-Portrait of Indian Existence*, Outerbridge & Dienstfrey, 1971.

Roberts, David, *Once They Moved Like the Wind: Cochise, Geronimo, and the End of the Indian Wars*, Simon & Schuster, 1993.

Rosenstiel, Annette, *Red and White: Indian Views of the White Man, 1492-1982*, Universe Books, 1983.

Schwartz, Melissa, *Geronimo*, Chelsea House, 1992.

Sonnichsen, C.L., editor, *Geronimo and the End of the Apache Wars*, University of Nebraska Press, 1990.

Vanderwerth, W.C., *Indian Oratory: Famous Speeches by Noted Indian Chieftains*, University of Oklahoma Press, 1971.

Witt, Shirley Hill, and Stan Steiner, *The Way: An Anthology of American Indian Literature*, Knopf, 1972.

Henry B. Gonzalez

1916–

Mexican American member of the U.S. House of Representatives

Throughout his long and often colorful political career, Henry B. Gonzalez—or simply "Henry B.," as he is affectionately known—has earned a reputation as a champion of the underdog and an outspoken critic of government skulduggery and abuse of power. Feisty, independent, and unpredictable, this liberal Democrat enjoys tremendous popularity among his Texas constituents and looks back with pride at his more than thirty years of service in the U.S. House of Representatives. Beholden to no special interests, he is, in the words of Harper's magazine writer Christopher Hitchens, "one of the few just men to have spent any time at all on the Hill."

Gonzalez was born in San Antonio, Texas, to parents who came to the United States from Mexico to escape the bloody revolution of 1911. The elder Gonzalez had been a successful politician and businessman in his home state of Durango, but once in America, he became a journalist and eventually served as the editor of what was then the only Spanish-language newspaper in the country, La Prensa. Young Henry thus grew up in a stimulating household that was rich in ideas but not in money. As a result, he had to work part-time throughout his entire childhood to help support his five brothers and sisters. He spent any spare time he had reading at the local public library. Gonzalez also became familiar with racial prejudice at an early age; he was the target of slurs and insults because of his heritage and remembers being barred from "whites only" facilities such as restaurants and swimming pools.

After graduating from high school, Gonzalez attended San Antonio Junior College and then the University of Texas at Austin. His studies in engineering were interrupted, however, when he could not find a job to help pay his expenses and had to return home. He completed his education at St. Mary's University in San Antonio, earning a bachelor's degree and then, in 1943, a law degree.

During the rest of the 1940s, Gonzalez worked at a variety of jobs, including running his father's Spanish-English translation bureau, acting as a public relations advisor for an insurance firm, and serving first as assistant chief probation officer and then as chief probation officer for the county juvenile court system. (He later resigned after being denied permission to add a black person to his *staff.) In 1950, he was appointed to the post of deputy family relocation director for the city of San Antonio's housing authority, a job that required him to help relocate families displaced by slum clearance projects.*

Gonzalez' first try at politics was in 1950, when he ran for a seat in the Texas House of Representatives and lost. In 1953, however, he won election to the San Antonio City Council, where one of his most notable accomplishments was sponsoring a law that abolished segregation in the city's recreational facilities. Three years later, he moved to Austin to take his place in the Texas Senate—the first Mexican American to do so in more than one hundred years. There he quickly established himself as one of the more liberal legislators with his strong and very vocal opposition to a series of bills that were intended to preserve racial segregation.

On the heels of unsuccessful bids for governor of Texas (1958) and U.S. senator (1961), Gonzalez was at last victorious in a special 1961 election to fill a vacant seat in the U.S. House of Representatives, making him the first Mexican American from Texas ever to serve in that national legislative body. He has represented San Antonio and its environs ever since, easily winning reelection each time. Perhaps even more remarkable is the fact that over the course of sixteen campaigns, he has never faced an opponent in the Democratic primary and has run unopposed in the general election six times. Furthermore, he has done so by consistently downplaying his ethnicity, noting that he has attracted support from all kinds of voters, not just Hispanics, and is therefore responsible for acting on the needs and wishes of his entire constituency. This has frequently led to tensions between Gonzalez and some Mexican Americans of a more radical bent who would have preferred him to take a stand on their behalf.

During his early years in the U.S. House, Gonzalez carved out a niche for himself as a fiery advocate of minority interests. Although he sponsored legislation reflecting a broad array of concerns, including civil rights, adult education and job training, the minimum wage, Puerto Rican rights, and the poll tax, he reserved his most vigorous efforts for the battle against extending Public Law 78, a controversial piece of farm labor legislation better known as the "Bracero Bill."

During World War II, by agreement between the governments of Mexico and the United States, Mexican contract workers known as braceros *were brought into the United States to help ease a chronic manpower shortage, especially on farms. These day laborers quickly became an integral part of the agricultural economy in the Southwest and West, so much so that growers repeatedly persuaded Congress to extend the life of the program and even expand it. In 1963, it was up for yet another renewal. This time around, however, it ran into fierce opposition from Mexican Americans, organized labor, and members of various religious and civic groups who protested that because* braceros *were unprotected under most federal and state laws regulating wages, working conditions, and other employment-related matters, they were often underpaid and otherwise mistreated by growers and labor contractors.*

Leading the charge in Congress against extending Public Law 78 was Gonzalez. Time and time again, he took to the floor to denounce it as a "slave labor" bill that perpetuated the oppression of farm workers, whom he said toiled under conditions "somewhere between civilization and medievalism." His impassioned words helped defeat the measure in early 1964, but as he and others well knew, the end of Public Law 78 did not mean the end of exploitation for America's migrant workers; in fact, the years that followed saw a tremendous increase in unionization efforts among farm workers to combat ongoing abuses. Gonzalez therefore continued to bring the issue before his colleagues and demand improve-

ments in employment recruitment, wages, and working conditions. One such occasion was on April 5, 1965, in response to attempts by growers to resurrect the bracero *program via new legislation. His remarks are reprinted here from the* Congressional Record, *89th Congress, 1st Session, Volume III, Part 5, U.S. Government Printing Office, 1965.*

Mr. Speaker, any reasonable and literate person ought to be able at this late date to read the congressional handwriting on the wall. The 88th Congress, in its wisdom, decided that time had run out on the "temporary" bracero program, and that it should expire at the end of 1964. The president, in his wisdom, signed into law that decision and thereby obligated himself and his administration to carry it out. The 89th Congress, in its wisdom, is not going to buckle under the pressures that have been generated to revive the discredited bracero program. The president is not going to buckle under those pressures, and the secretary of labor is not going to buckle under those pressures.

The bracero program is as dead as the dodo bird. It is time for the leadership in the farm industry to stop looking for cheap, captive sources of labor. It is time for the leadership in the farm industry to exert itself in a positive and constructive and progressive manner in order to help solve the farm labor problem. It is time to look forward to the day when the farmworker can share in the fruits of his labors. Today, for the sweat off his brow that he leaves in the rich and abundant fields and orchards which he harvests he receives for his part a pittance, a pat on the back, and a passport to nowhere. Justice, decency, and humanity demand that progress not pass him over for yet another generation.

Farmworkers under state and federal labor laws are relegated to a second-class citizenship. Millions of Americans are protected by minimum wage, maximum hours, and child-labor laws. Millions of Americans are protected by workmen's compensation and unemployment compensation. Millions of Americans are assured decent housing for their families, good schools for their children, health and medical facilities. Not so the farmworker.

Historically, labor laws were designed to regulate and set a floor under the working conditions of employees in industry and trade. At first these laws were limited to specific types or places of employment or to certain industries. Some of these laws have been extended to cover employment generally, but usually agricultural employment is expressly excluded. Even where no specific exclusion exists and the laws could cover farmworkers, they often are not applied.

For example, in only eight states and Puerto Rico are there laws or regulations which specifically regulate farm labor contractors and crew leaders. Only a few states—California, Colorado, Connecticut, New York, North Carolina, Oregon, Pennsylvania, and West Virginia—have laws setting safety standards for vehicles used in the transportation of farmworkers, and for the operation of such vehicles. Farm labor camps are regulated as to housing, location, and construction of the camp in thirty states. But in twenty states there is no such regulation. And even in the states where there are laws on this subject, the standards are very limited in most.

Only eleven states, Puerto Rico, and the District of Columbia provide a minimum age for employment of children on farms. This age is fourteen in Connecticut, Alaska, Hawaii, Missouri, Texas, the District of Columbia, and Puerto Rico. In four states the minimum age is twelve. In one state, Utah, the minimum age is ten. Compulsory school attendance requires children to attend school, usually to age sixteen, in most states. But in many states the laws permit children under sixteen or even under fourteen to be excused from school in order to work on farms.

In only four states and Puerto Rico do workmen's compensation laws cover all farm employment. Only seventeen states have any specific coverage for farmworkers at all. Only Hawaii and Puerto Rico provide any minimum wage coverage for all farmworkers. Hawaii requires a minimum of $1.25 an hour. Six states have wage payment laws and wage collection laws for farmworkers. Only Hawaii and Puerto Rico

Henry B. Gonzalez

specifically cover farmworkers in their unemployment insurance laws. In one state, California, farmworkers are covered by a temporary disability law.

Federal laws supplement these deficiencies somewhat. The 88th Congress enacted more laws for the protection of farmworkers than perhaps any other Congress. The Economic Opportunity Act contains provisions for the assistance of migrant farmworkers and for low-income rural families. The Housing Act of 1964 provides for grants to states or its political subdivisions, or private nonprofit organizations, to assist in providing housing and related facilities for domestic farm labor.

Have these laws been utilized for the benefit of farmworkers? What are we doing now to implement them and to pass additional legislation in the area of minimum wages and workmen's compensation? There are the fruitful areas of work and inquiry where the time and energy of the people and the Congress could be well spent.

The farmworker is the forgotten man in the industrial revolution that has benefited almost every other class of worker. Part of the evil inherent in the bracero program was that it served to keep the farm industry in a constant state of depression, as far as the workers were concerned. Braceros were a cheap source and a captive source of labor. They stifled competition and formed a crutch on which farmers and growers became accustomed to lean. That crutch is gone. It is now time for the farmer and the grower to walk without it, to seek his labor needs in the competitive market, and to give decent wages and working conditions to their employees.

Since the 1970s, Gonzalez has turned his attention to other domestic matters, including evaluating various conspiracy theories in the assassinations of President John F. Kennedy and Martin Luther King, Jr., fighting the administration of President Ronald Reagan for more low-cost housing, and—as chairman of the powerful House Banking, Finance, and Urban Affairs Committee from 1988 until the Republican takeover of Congress in 1995—leading the investigation into the savings and loan crisis of the late 1980s.

Gonzalez was particularly effective in the latter role, enhancing his reputation as a strong consumer advocate. His tenacious probing during hearings of his committee exposed the flawed practices and fraudulent dealings in the thrift industry that resulted in the collapse of hundreds of financial institutions and the loss of billions of depositors' dollars. In the aftermath of those hearings, Gonzalez was instrumental in the drafting of a "bailout bill" that tightened regulations governing savings and loan operations and provided funds to prosecute those suspected of wrongdoing in the wide-ranging scandal. His findings ultimately led him to take a closer look at the banking industry, too, with an eye toward reforms that would head off a similar crisis.

Gonzalez has also spearheaded a few initiatives over the years that have prompted some people to characterize him as cantankerous and more than a little eccentric. For example, he twice introduced resolutions calling for the impeachment of President Reagan, once in 1983 over the U.S. invasion of Grenada and again in 1987 for his alleged role in the Iran-Contra scandal. In 1991, he resorted to the same tactic against President George Bush. Not only did Gonzalez condemn Bush for going to war against Iraq without congressional approval, he also claimed that the administration had demonstrated gross misjudgment in the months and even years prior to the invasion for making advanced weapons technology and materials available to Iraqi leader Saddam Hussein.

Not everyone, however, has been inclined to dismiss his actions as frivolous. In 1993, for instance, Gonzalez received the Philip Hart Public Service Award from the Consumer Federation of America for his "willingness to stand up for the American consumer regardless of the odds." Cited in particular were his efforts to reform the banking and savings and loan industries and to improve enforcement of laws against the practice of redlining, or denying mortgages to buyers seeking housing in neighborhoods that are considered poor economic risks. And in 1994, he captured the John F. Kennedy Profile in Courage Award for the many times in his career he has chosen to take an unpopular position and hold firm despite criticism or ridicule.

Gonzalez's commitment to banking, consumer protection, and anti-discrimination legislation is evident in the following keynote address, delivered in his hometown of San Antonio on August 24, 1993. Speaking at a conference on community investment sponsored by the Federal Reserve Bank of Dallas, the congressman encouraged bankers, government agencies, and community groups to take a fresh look at the Community Reinvestment Act (CRA), a law that requires banks to serve the communities in which they do business. Gonzalez provided a copy of his remarks.

Welcome to San Antonio. I am glad to see so many people of different backgrounds come together to discuss community investment. It is especially fitting to hold this forum in San Antonio, not only because it is my hometown, but also because the city exemplifies the road community development has travelled over the past few decades.

Like the ancient Gaul of Caesar's *Commentaries,* San Antonio has always been divided into three economic and racial parts. When the city received its first municipal charter in 1837—the year following the Texas-Mexican War—the city's first mayor was not named Garcia, or Sanchez, or Gonzalez. He was John Smith. And not unlike other cities, the Anglo or Creole elite had the power to allocate development resources in a town comprised largely of poor Mexicans.

For example, when former mayor Bryan Callaghan II brought municipal progress to San Antonio, he paved and lighted the streets, brought water lines in, built the city's first jail and later courthouse, and set up a modern transit system. However, Callaghan's improvements existed mainly to facilitate the interests of the upper crust. Everybody else got attention only when it made good business sense; in other words, only when the well-off saw a larger benefit—that is, a benefit to their own interests. I remember all too well arriving on the City Council at a time when the Water Board didn't have the slightest concern about whole downtown neighborhoods with no water supply at all. Those in control simply did not find it necessary to serve everyone equally, and as a result, some were not served at all.

> ***"Many [lending] institutions see the only sound 'business decisions' as those that benefit mainly certain classes of people."***

Our banking system unfortunately works in much the same way. Like San Antonio's old elite, many institutions see the only sound "business decisions" as those that benefit mainly certain classes of people. Commercial office building developers, especially in Texas, found a plethora of willing lenders during the 1980s, even when there was no demonstrated demand for more office space. But small business owners here in San Antonio often could not locate working capital to finance their enterprises; minorities had an extremely difficult time borrowing money for a house; and low-income people had no easy access to places to deposit their savings. The same story exists everywhere, be it Los Angeles, New York, Atlanta, Washington, D.C., or Dallas.

The most direct measure of this phenomenon now available, while imperfect, is the Home Mortgage Disclosure Act (HmDA) data. HmDA data gathered over the past few years suggests that the primary factor in qualifying for a home loan is not how much you make, or whether you have other large debts. What seems to matter most to many financial institutions is where you live—a factor completely unrelated to the safety and soundness of a mortgage loan. Study after study confirms this, which points to redlining.

As a result, our country now faces the sad prospect of dying neighborhoods, communities where demand for credit and other basic financial services is met by "fringe bankers," such as pawn shops, check cashing outlets, liquor stores and loan sharks. These expensive financial intermediaries consume a large proportion of the resources of low-income neighborhoods, leaving fewer dollars for development and pushing neighborhoods into further decline.

In case after case, what we have is a phenomenon where credit is choked off, and areas become less capable of absorbing credit. Thus, these neighborhoods are seen as less desirable, and credit gets tighter still—until you reach the point of devastation. One way of looking at it is that redlining leads to a self-fulfilling prophecy: things are thought to be bad, resources are cut off, and sure enough, things are bad.

The federal government has tried many policies to arrest and reverse patterns of urban decline. However, none of these policies work unless there is private capital available to enable sustained growth to occur. For example, HemisFair made it possible to rebuild downtown San Antonio. This downtown area has benefitted from urban renewal, from Economic Development Administration grants, from UDAG [Urban Development Action Grant] programs, CDBG [Community Development Block Grant] programs, mass transit grants and many other forms of federal investment dating back to the CCC [Civilian Conservation Corps] of

Depression days. But if private capital in the form of credit had not been available, none of this would have made any difference.

A UDAG investment in the water feature that you will see connecting Alamo Plaza to the Hyatt Hotel and Riverwalk would not have made any difference if the hotel had not been built. Nor would it have made any difference if the river had been relocated with another grant—if credit had not been available to build the Marriott hotels and River Center Mall.

Here is a case in point. The federal government poured millions into land assembly and redevelopment a few blocks west of here. But in that area, credit and investment never materialized, and the result is a disappointing wasteland. I would not say that this failure was the result of redlining, but what it does prove is that federal urban policy cannot work unless it is complemented by private capital.

And that is where CRA comes in. If CRA means anything, it means making sure that banks do all they can to serve their communities; it means making sure that loan decisions are fairly evaluated; it means making sure that banks understand there are opportunities in their own backyards. While it might be easier to participate in a multimillion-dollar project in some distant place, it is absolutely essential to provide credit to the small businesses, homeowners and entrepreneurs who exist in great numbers within a few blocks of any bank or any branch.

President Clinton has proposed a kind of financial bridge that would connect the shores of the dispossessed to credit facilities, in the form of community development financial institutions. This legislation, H.R. 2666, would provide modest financial help to a wide range of community development institutions—microenterprise loan funds, community development corporations, community revolving loan funds, and others. But this legislation takes only a modest step, and will result in no real impact unless existing lenders weigh in with their resources.

That will happen only if we have an effective urban policy that addresses the whole range of problems that afflict declining neighborhoods. Community development—whether it's called urban renewal, CDBG, UDAG, or anything else—does not work unless we accurately understand what needs to be done and set out to correct problems in a systematic way. And even then, we can only achieve success when credit flows into the enterprises that alone make a neighborhood viable.

For example, you can turn a street into a very attractive pedestrian mall—but it will remain dead, a mass of empty concrete buildings and gleaming new streets, unless the credit is available to finance the shops and restaurants that will bring people to the area. A community development financial institution can perhaps provide some seed money, but nothing like the quantity of credit needed to make the ultimate difference between a viable area and one that is dying.

CRA is the tool that, properly used, enables institutions to understand not just the problems and challenges, but the real opportunities that exist in neighborhoods that today get little or no credit, and as a result have little or no chance.

The CRA is very simple: it says that banks must do what they are chartered to do, namely serve the convenience and needs of the community where they are located. It means redlining is unacceptable.

Unfortunately, despite its simplicity, enforcement of the CRA has been lacking. Today, here in San Antonio and in every other city, we see substantial evidence of disinvestment. The proliferation of more expensive "fringe bankers" like pawn shops and check cashers shows that insured financial institutions are ignoring a large part of the demand for financial services. Incredibly, and despite data showing redlining, more than ninety percent of financial institutions still receive at least satisfactory CRA ratings. And CRA ratings make little practical difference for the majority of institutions because they do not wish to expand. As a result of passive enforcement, community groups have taken the lead in enforcement, using the CRA process to bring bankers to the table to discuss community lending.

I receive complaints about this "CRA challenge" process from all sides. Bankers protest that radical community groups are holding them hostage, keeping them from expanding their empires. Further, when community groups and bankers enter into negotiations to avoid a CRA challenge, the law is being enforced not by regulators, but by third parties. This process creates weak and uneven enforcement because promises can be broken. But a merger or acquisition is permanent. In fact, I recently asked the regulatory agencies whether they checked up on community lending agreements made by expanding institutions. They all responded basically that they do not enforce deals that they had no part in making. In effect, the challenge process can force an institution to make a "deal" to make community loans, but there is no way to be certain these deals will be honored.

Sadly, this imperfect process continues because CRA challenges at least seem to move dollars into communities better than any other method tried thus far. Perhaps it is time to look behind this success. Meaningful, effective bank/community partnerships ultimately work because community-based organizations know there are good loans to be made in their neighborhoods. They also know the people who need basic banking services, or those who could start a small business with a little technical assistance. It has been demonstrated over and over that community lending done right yields results, not only in rebuilt neighborhoods, but in rebuilt markets for banking services and profits for banks.

The Clinton administration is currently undertaking a long overdue review of CRA enforcement. At the end of this process, there must be a clearer focus on getting banks to reach out to new parts of their communities, getting them to provide actual loans, and getting them to take an active part in economic development.

Unfortunately, not many banks currently see CRA as a process of useful self-examination. Most see it as a pestilential requirement to have so many community meetings and document such and such outreach effort—a kind of file-stuffing requirement. The new comptroller of the currency wants to make the process less paper-intensive and more results-oriented. Industry trade associations, on the other hand, want a law the essentially exempts banks from the process: small banks altogether, and big banks that score well on any given examination. To benefit everyone, CRA regulation must be reformed so that banks devise and carry out a sound business plan in their communities.

I am not talking about credit allocation. I am not talking about using CRA to force banks to make bad loans—for a bad loan does nobody any good. I am, however, suggesting that CRA properly used will identify real opportunities with real benefits for everyone concerned.

For this to happen, regulators must see CRA as something more than assembling impressive stacks of paper, and banks must see it as a useful business tool. If CRA can be turned into a program that is something more than file-stuffing and something beyond regulatory challenge and banker response, it can become the strongest tool possible for revitalizing distressed communities.

Banks today face an unprecedented array of challenges. Some see banks as dinosaurs unable to compete in the extremely efficient capital markets that are now capturing more and more of the core business of banks. Some point to laws that prevent banks from being efficient, and claim they are regulated to death. Still others herald bank safety as paramount, because banks are the source of all financial stability.

I see banks as the cornerstone of the economy. If we have a banking system that is sound and efficient, we will have a sound and efficient economy. It is that simple.

Part of that fundamental soundness is communities that have access to reasonable credit on reasonable terms. CRA is a little watchdog on the corner that reminds us all that the cornerstone of sound banking is the humble, hard toil of working with your neighbors, to see how best to serve the community.

And that is why we are here. To see how CRA can work better, as I believe it can. It is not only possible, but necessary. For in the final analysis, a banking system that cannot serve local communities is not a banking system at all.

Community reinvestment is a necessity—not just for those who are asking for better banking opportunities and services—but ultimately for banks as well. After all, if the community a bank draws its funds from implodes, the bank ultimately must fail too.

I hope this conference results in a vision of CRA as an opportunity, not merely an irritating requirement. If this happens, all of us will benefit. In my view, this not only *can* happen, but *must,* if we have any hope of arresting the process of neighborhood disinvestment, decline and bank weakness. Banks can—should—and must—be part of the answer. Not just as a social responsibility, but as an economic reality.

Credit is as essential as rainfall. If the rain fails, there is no crop. If the rain fails long enough, the rivers do not run and the springs do not flow. And if the rivers do not run and springs do not flow, the towns suffer and die.

We cannot make it rain. But community groups, federal and local governments, and the private sector should be able to figure out a way to irrigate, so that communities receive the greatest essential of growth—credit. That is what CRA asks us to do—quite simply, a better job of providing the most essential of all economic services. I will do everything I can to achieve this end, and I expect your help.

Thank you.

SOURCES

Books

Congressional Record, 89th Congress, 1st Session, Volume III, Part 5, U.S. Government Printing Office, 1965, pp. 6908-6909.

Periodicals

Harper's, "No Fool on the Hill," October, 1992, pp. 84-96.

Hispanic, "The Paradox of Henry B.: A Look at a Man Who Pulls No Punches, Yet Surprises People Who've Known Him for Years," October, 1989.

Mother Jones, "Give 'em Hell, Henry," July/August, 1991, pp. 12-13.

Nation, "Beltway Bandits," June 1, 1992, pp. 740-741.

New Republic, "Disregarding Henry," April 11, 1994, pp. 14-17.

Texas Monthly, "The Eternal Challenger," October, 1992.

Time, "'A Bunch of Delinquents,'" January 21, 1991, p. 57.

Stella G. Guerra

1945–

Mexican American federal government official

Although she has spent most of her time since 1980 working in various capacities for the federal government in Washington, D.C., Stella G. Guerra was born, raised, and educated in Texas. She grew up in the home of her maternal grandparents, who passed along to her a love of education and a drive to succeed. One of the first challenges she faced as a youngster was when she went off to school unable to speak English. (Her grandparents spoke only Spanish at home.) The difficulties and occasional embarrassment this caused through the years made a profound impression on Guerra and underscored for her the importance of good communication in all human relationships.

Guerra was an energetic and popular student by the time she reached her teens and was even voted first runner-up in the Miss Texas High School Pageant. Taking advantage of her prize—a free cosmetology course—she gained enough knowledge of hairdressing to go to work in the field after graduating from high school and then used the money she earned to help pay for her college education. Guerra eventually received a bachelor's degree from Texas A & I University, where she majored in education, art, and history. Soon thereafter she earned a master's degree in communication disorders from Our Lady of the Lake University in San Antonio, and an associate's degree in business from Del Mar College in her hometown.

In 1967, Guerra went to work for the Northeast Independent School District in San Antonio. She remained with the district for thirteen years, beginning as a teacher in a regular classroom, then moving into special education, and ending up as an administrator of testing programs. During part of this same period, from 1974 through 1980, she also owned and managed a successful chain of record and tape stores.

Guerra left Texas in 1980 for Washington, D.C., where she joined the Department of State as a staff assistant to the White House Chief of Protocol. The following year, she switched to the Department of Education and a position as special assistant for international affairs. Among her responsibilities in this particular job was representing the department at a number of conferences that attracted officials from all over the world to discuss such topics as cultural policy, aging, women's issues, and human intelligence.

In 1983, Guerra became acting deputy assistant secretary of civilian person-

nel policy and Equal Employment Opportunity (EEO) for the U.S. Air Force. In this role, she was responsible for making sure that civilian employees were not discriminated against because of their race, color, religion, sex, national origin, age, or disability; she was also charged with promoting equal employment opportunities for those seeking civilian jobs with the Air Force. As Guerra pointed out to an interviewer from Airman *magazine, such a program does not single out any particular group for special treatment; it is "simply a matter of management officials doing what is morally and legally correct." Her job was to make sure everyone got "a fair shot," but it was then up to each individual "to be prepared to take advantage of it"—words she herself has lived by throughout her entire life.*

Guerra's government position, along with her flair for public speaking (which has garnered her several awards), has created a demand for her services as a lecturer before various groups. In July 1986, for example, she addressed the opening session of the Federal Employed Women 17th National Training Program, held that year in Las Vegas. Her remarks focused on the gains women have made and will continue to make in the workplace and the critical role of self-development and good self-esteem in making those gains possible. Guerra's speech is reprinted here from Vital Speeches of the Day, *September 15, 1986.*

Let me begin by telling you what an honor it is for me to be participating in the opening session of the Federally Employed Women (FEW) 17th National Training Program. Accepting the invitation without a moment's hesitation, a year ago, reaffirms my belief that commitment is easy when it involves something that you truly love and respect.

Stella G. Guerra

Through my years in federal service I have come to recognize and respect FEW as a leading force in strengthening the careers of women.

FEW—I salute you for the leadership you provide to all of us in federal service. I encourage you to continue providing the direction which makes and government world of work, an environment of progress, pride and growth.

As the date approached, I began to give serious thought to what I would share with you today. Several topics came to mind—two were quickly cast aside, considering we were in Las Vegas—risk-taking and Gramm-Rudman.

Finally, I decided to talk about women—the progress we've made in the past and the strides we are making today. Most importantly, I want to share some thoughts with you about how each one of us here today can truly hitch our wagon to a star and chart our own course for tomorrow. A course that will let us share in the fruits of this great nation's success and fuel new generations of achievers for many years to come.

First, let's take a trip back to the past and take a brief glimpse at the road we have traveled. Rocky, and at times filled with a pothole or two, our path has been similar to a newborn baby. Like a newborn struggling to focus with blurry vision on those admiring parents that hold her aloft for all to see, we have strived to focus on our personal objectives as well as worked to help America achieve its present-day global status as the most prosperous country in the world.

Dating back to our forebears who first stepped foot on American soil, we have been a part of our nation's progress. In what some have called the toddler years of our country—the 1800s—we helped America take its first steps towards world prominence. We moved west, we worked in the fields tilling the soil, and in the factories to produce the food and goods that our country needed to prosper and grow.

Moving on—in the 1900s, during what some have affectionately referred to as "the Rosie the Riveter period," working in shipyards and steel mills, we helped our nation meet labor shortages in a time of national crisis. Afterwards, many of us who had entered the workforce returned home—but not for long. By the midpoint of the twentieth century, virtually no aspect of American society had been left untouched by our eager rush into the labor force.

Like a child that is anxious to learn about the world and all its opportunities, we began to stretch, to grow and expand our horizons. In a span of less than fifty years, our numbers in the labor force doubled. Our unbridled innocence and energy altered forever the way we lived and worked in this country. In the second half of the 1970s more of us were enrolled in college than ever before, and we began to move rapidly into business, industry, the federal sector, the teaching fields and other professions such as law and medicine.

The early years of America were indeed a time of challenge and a time of change. As women, we were a "spitting image" of that challenge and change. When America dreamed—we dreamed. When our nation stretched to achieve, we stretched. When America laughed, we shared in that laughter. Collectively, like that great universal symbol that stands off the shores of New York—*Lady Liberty*—we too stand as clear examples that in this country our dreams are achievable because we have the freedom to work toward change and to pursue our success-oriented goals. Yes, relying on inner strength, American women have made remarkable and magnificent strides.

Today, we are in a time like no other period in our nation's history, under the leadership of a president who has profoundly affected the way Americans think about themselves. We are moving ahead with great vigor and a national commitment not experienced in quite some time. Today we see a spirit of accomplishment and a sense of pride seldom seen on the national level.

With that same belief in achievement and success, we have moved with America from the so-called "smokestack" industries of years past to an economy where three out of every four jobs are located in the service industry. In this industry, on an average, we've created one million new jobs each year for the past twenty years; of these, two out of every three have gone to women. Right now more than fifty-four percent of our country's women are working and our percentage in the overall workforce has increased to forty-four percent. In short, we are continuing to help America forge an environment that says—opportunities are abundant.

In this environment of prosperity we've seen many *firsts:*

-The first female brigadier general

-The first female astronaut

-The first female sky marshall

-The first female ambassador to the United Nations

-The first female justice of the Supreme Court

-The first female director of Civil Service

-The first female U.S. Customs rep in a foreign country

-The first female to graduate at the very top of the class in a service academy—Navy '84; Air Force '86.

The list goes on and on—and this same progress can be seen in all sectors of our society.

In business there's been a sharp increase in the number of women who own their own businesses. The number of self-employed women from 1980-84 alone jumped 22 percent to 2.6 million people.

Three key factors have contributed to this significant upswing.

First, we are gaining experience in positions of leadership in both corporate America and the federal sector. We are moving into middle and upper level management at a record pace.

-In the federal government, in the past very few of us were found at the senior executive level. According to recent figures from the Office of Personnel Management, government-wide, in the last ten years, women have gone from 180 to 598 in the senior executive service.

-Additionally, at the GS-13 through GS-15 level, we have approximately 26,000 federally employed women involved in the decision-making process.

In the Air Force, we've experienced this same upswing.

-Between 1974-84 we went from 29.9 percent to 35.6 percent women in the civilian workforce.

-By 1990 the number of women in blue are expected to climb to a record high of 84,000. And in the past eight years, 30,000 new positions have been opened to Air Force women in uniform. This same trend holds true in our sister services. With initiatives by the Office of Personnel Management and the Department of Defense such as their Executive Leadership Demonstration Program, we expect those numbers to climb even higher.

The *second* factor pushing us on and upward has been education. Across the land, numbers increased twofold in the past twenty-one years for those of us entering the halls of higher education.

-In the same period, our numbers in law, medicine, and architectural schools have gone from five to thirty-two percent. Now we account for more than half of all college enrollment, earn one-third of all PhDs, and

-We are awarded fifty percent of all bachelor's and master's degrees.

-Today more of us are going to college than ever before. Our search for knowledge and quest for excellence has certainly opened up the doors of opportunity.

These opportunities have led us down paths previously untraveled. As our visions were broadened, women began to move into nontraditional areas—the third major factor for our success. Federal women were on the cutting edge of this movement. As Betty Harragan pointed out in her book, *Games Mother Never Taught You,* "Women have the potential to stagger the imagination." Our movement into presidential cabinet-level positions, into missile silos as crew commanders, aircraft mechanics and into the officer and enlisted ranks have indeed staggered the imagination. It also serves as a glistening example that in the past and in the present our hopes and dreams are interwoven into the very fiber of America. A fiber that will preserve opportunities and chart the course for a new generation of achievers.

During the next decade, almost two-thirds of the female population will enter the workforce and stay longer. Like the population at large in the teen years of America, we'll see our life span increase. At the start of the twentieth century, we were expected to live on an average of forty-eight years; now it's seventy-two years. And as remarkable as it seems, children born today are expected to live into their eighties.

As attitudes toward working careers change, so too will the structure of jobs. People like Patricia Aburdene and John Nesbitt, authors of *Reinventing the Corporation,* tell us an increase in knowledge power will create major changes in the way we work, live and relax. It's expected that by 1990 our work week will average thirty-two hours and by year 2000, it will be twenty-five hours. Flexible work schedules will be the norm with two or three people sharing jobs.

The great impact of high technology will shape and mold the jobs of tomorrow. Advances in technology, attitudes about work, and the increase in life spans will demand a change in the way we are educated and trained. More people will have college degrees or have had some sort of on-the-job training.

Yet, some jobs will not require as much formal education. Recently, sixty of the fastest-growing occupations in this country were singled out by the Labor Department. Few require a four-year college degree.

Job performance and pay for performance will continue to provide opportunities for our professional growth and financial gain. Various alternate personnel systems both in and outside of the federal government will be developed that specifically addresses pay for performance. In conjunction with these changes, in demographics and values, Federally Employed Women will do much to help continue to close the gap for America.

With vision and a sense of direction, we will continue to do what's right for America. We will continue to discuss and help explore ways to resolve concerns such as paternity leave and the use of sick leave to care for our families at times of illness. Like the years of "Rosie the Riveter" we'll continue to do our part to keep America strong, prosperous and upward bound.

Whether we are in the home rearing children or soaring towards the stars in outer orbit, women—and especially federally employed women—will help set a standard that will be hard to surpass. We will do this by helping to answer the tough questions and by facing the critical challenges ahead. James Baldwin once said, "Not everything that is faced can be changed; but nothing can be changed until it is faced."

As we turn toward the future, we've already begun to face the challenges of tomorrow. Within the departments of agriculture, commerce, defense, housing and labor to name a few, daycare programs have been established to help with the influx of two-wage-earner families. Additionally, the Office of Personnel Management (OPM), the Department of Defense, and other agencies are rapidly developing programs to move our best and brightest into the upper GS and senior executive ranks.

I can say with confidence that the senior leadership within the Air Force, Secretary Aldridge, and Assistant Secretary for Manpower, Tidal McCoy, certainly are concerned and committed to ensuring we continue on our positive track. From ensuring the number of women in the SES and GS ranks increase to providing appropriate joint spouse assignments where possible, the senior leadership of the Air Force is committed to helping us move onward and upward. Let's not forget other organizations such as the Department of Labor, Department of Justice or the Equal Employment Opportunity Commission (EEOC) who have not only seen the need but have spearheaded actions for implementation and compliance of equal opportunity laws. It is this type of collective action that go a long way toward keeping our nation on its track of progress and merit.

As we enter America's early adulthood we find that our hopes and dreams have been uplifted toward achievement. Yes, we are living in a time of change but the future holds exciting changes, challenges and opportunities that will tax our abilities, test our skills, and require a total commitment from you and I to keep us charging towards the stars.

We are living at a time when commitment, a spirit of achievement, and an overriding belief in oneself will help to prepare ourselves for what lies ahead. Looking back to our childhood days, perhaps you may recall a time when we really did not have many inhibitions about life, or the possibilities which existed for us. We dreamed that we could climb Mount Everest and swim across the mighty Mississippi to accomplish our goals—and we set out to do just that.

But sometimes as we travel along the road of life, perhaps we encounter those times when we lose some of that vigor, that drive and carefree spirit that encourages us on. Perhaps on occasion we lose our ability to smile and to turn dreams into reality. Along with the rest of America, now is the time to rekindle that spirit and dream. Now is the time for you and me to look at our commitment and the belief in self.

What is commitment?

It has been said that:

-Commitment is what transforms a promise into reality.

-It is the word that speaks boldly of our intentions and action which speaks louder than our words.

-It is making the time when there is none—coming through time after time—year after year after year.

-Commitment unlocks the doors of imagination, allows vision and gives us the "right stuff" to turn our dreams into reality.

Now is the time to review and perhaps change our mind-set about commitment; it is also time to take a fresh look at ourselves and how we view the world around us. We need to update our strategic road maps and recharge our batteries as we continue on the road to success. Changes to come in the years ahead dictate that we get and remain in step with innovative and new ways of doing things. Along with that burning commitment to achieve our individual goals, we'll need an astute ability to look within ourselves and project the positive outward to help our organizations achieve their national objectives.

"We are living at a time when commitment, a spirit of achievement, and an overriding belief in oneself will help to prepare ourselves for what lies ahead."

Back in the '60s, prominent sociologist of the day, David Reisman, wrote about inner-directed and outer-directed types of personalities and their approaches to setting criteria for success. Basically, he said that an outer-directed person was perhaps too sensitive to the outside world and relied too heavily on external criteria for success. The inner-directed person was said to be self-confident and approached success by carving out their own niche in life. In this time of change, in and out of the government work world, we need to ask: what type of criteria are we setting for ourselves as we begin to carve out our own niches in business, industry and within the federal government?

To meet the challenges ahead and move along on the road of progress, we must continue to take charge of our destinies and take responsibility for our own self-development. There are so many factors important to our self-development. However, none is more important that self-esteem. Some scholars have defined self-esteem as the integrated sum of self-confidence, self-respect and self-dignity. I would like to add to that definition—"as we see ourselves so do we act." It is the conviction gained through experience that we are competent to live and be worthy of living.

For all of us self-esteem exists on a continuum; it's not a case of "either you have it or you don't." Self-esteem comes in different doses and different degrees, and its potential is limitless. Scholars also claim, "character determines action." I hasten to add—self-concept determines destiny. As federally employed women, if we continue to put faith in ourselves, and strive to develop to our fullest potential, then our boundaries will be truly limitless.

I strongly believe that inner strength and a glowing concept of self carried us through early developmental years. That positive self-concept has helped us along with America to stretch and grow. It has brought us many firsts and promises much more.

Reflecting on my own youth, I can remember a time when there was little in the way of material things. What I did have was plenty of those simple teachings, later to be appreciated as my "building blocks."

-You are a child of God—equal to everyone.

-No one will do for you what you must do for yourself.

-You must get your education, a never-ending process. It is your right and something no one can ever take away from you.

In closing, I want to share a favorite song with a message which best sums it up. A message which we should often use to remind ourselves and most importantly, pass on.

GREATEST LOVE OF ALL

I believe the children are our future
Teach them well and let them lead
the way
Show them all the beauty they possess inside
Give them a sense of pride to make
it easier
Let the children's laughter remind us
how we used to be.
Everybody's searching for a hero
People need someone to look up to
I never found anyone to fulfill my needs
A lonely place to be
And so I learned to depend on me.
I decided long ago, never to walk in
anyone's shadow
If I fail, if I succeed
At least I'll live as I believe
No matter what they take from me
They can't take away my dignity
Because the greatest love of all
Is happening to me
I found the greatest love of all inside
of me
The greatest love of all
Is easy to achieve
Learning to love yourself
Is the greatest love of all.

I leave you with a question. What better wagon to hitch to a star than:

Your dreams

Your vision

Your being?

And if we fail, if we succeed, at least we'll live as we believe; no matter what they take from us, they can't take away our *dignity.*

In 1989, President George Bush appointed Guerra assistant secretary of the interior for territorial and international affairs. This job involved coordinating federal policies, programs, and funds in the territories of American Samoa, Guam, the U.S. Virgin Islands, and the Trust Territory of the Pacific Islands (Palau) as well as the freely-associated states of the Republic of the Marshall Islands and the Federated States of Micronesia. She left that post following the 1992 election, when Bill Clinton assumed the presidency.

SOURCES

Books

Telgen, Diane, and Jim Kamp, eds., *Notable Hispanic American Women,* Gale Research, Detroit, 1993.

Periodicals

Airman, September, 1985, p. 39.

Vital Speeches of the Day, "Women in American Shooting for the Stars," September 15, 1986, pp. 726-729.

Lani Guinier

1950–

African American lawyer and educator

On April 29, 1993, President Bill Clinton nominated University of Pennsylvania law professor Lani Guinier to be his assistant attorney general in charge of civil rights—the most powerful civil rights post in the Justice Department. Within days, those opposed to the innovative voting strategies she had once proposed for remedying racial discrimination in the U.S. political system fired the first shots in an often vicious battle that raged on throughout the entire month of May. Guinier emerged from that experience without the job that might well have been the crowning achievement of her career. In the process, however, she became a hero to many who believe she displayed uncommon dignity and courage during what some called a campaign to "demonize" her in the eyes of the American public.

Born and raised in New York City, Guinier credits her African American father and Jewish mother with instilling in her a devotion to civil rights, equality, and the possibility of achieving interracial understanding. Her father's struggle against prejudice made an especially strong impression; denied a scholarship to Harvard University on account of his race, he eventually worked his way through New York's City College and New York University Law School instead. (He later became the first head of the Afro-American studies department at Harvard.)

Guinier's outstanding academic record earned her a scholarship to Harvard-Radcliffe College upon her graduation from high school in 1967. Her interest in the ongoing efforts of civil rights activists to help African Americans achieve true equality within the U.S. political system ultimately influenced her decision to pursue a career in law after she received her bachelor's degree in 1971. While attending Yale Law School, she met and became friends with two fellow students who would figure prominently in her future—Bill Clinton and Hillary Rodham.

Guinier received her law degree in 1974 and then spent the next few years in Detroit, Michigan, first as a clerk for a U.S. Court of Appeals judge and then as a juvenile court referee for Wayne County. She then headed to Washington, D.C., as a special assistant to Drew Days, who was then serving in the very position she would one day be asked to fill—that of assistant attorney general in the civil rights division of the Justice Department. She remained there for four years, during which time she specialized in cases involving enforcement of the Voting Rights Act at the state and local level.

With the change in administrations following the 1980 presidential election, Guinier left government service and returned to New York City to take a job as assistant counsel with the NAACP Legal Defense and Educational Fund. There she enjoyed tremendous success as a litigator devoted to protecting the civil rights gains of the 1960s against a series of court challenges mounted by the Reagan administration.

In 1988, Guinier launched her academic career as a professor in the school of law at the University of Pennsylvania. It was there that she began to theorize about new ways to address racial discrimination in the voting process. Of particular concern to Guinier was the fact that while the law has made it possible for blacks to gain representation in various legislative bodies, it has done little to ensure that those representatives will not always be outvoted by their white colleagues. This "tyranny of the majority," as she calls it, makes it difficult for black legislators to enact policies that reflect the interests and needs of their black constituents.

Among Guinier's proposed solutions to the problem were several that conservatives and some moderates later seized upon as evidence of her "radicalism." For example, she suggested the idea of giving black legislators a "minority veto"—the power to block bills they oppose. She also considered the possibility of adopting a system of "cumulative voting." Under this plan, in an election to fill seven seats, for instance, each voter would receive seven ballots that they could split among several candidates or give to just one, thus increasing the power of minorities to elect a minority or special-interest candidate. Her critics offered these ideas as proof that she had no qualms about further polarizing the nation along racial lines. Guinier, however, thought that such changes would de-emphasize the significance of race in a way that the current practice of creating special "minority districts" does not. Ultimately, she hoped her plan would help foster the growth of cross-racial coalitions.

When her old friend Bill Clinton approached her about serving as his assistant attorney general for civil rights, Guinier looked forward to the opportunity to influence government policy on such issues as the Voting Rights Act. But on April 30, 1993—the day after her nomination became public—the first of many newspaper articles appeared that portrayed her as a dangerous left-wing extremist and "quota queen" who was determined to subvert democracy and the U.S. Constitution. The media scrutiny reached saturation levels during the month of May as countless journalists and talk-show hosts discussed—and often misinterpreted—her scholarly writings. Lost in the frenzy were comments from a number of other academics who pointed out that such articles are usually exercises in creative thinking, not blueprints for actual policy.

On orders from Clinton administration officials, however, Guinier remained silent throughout most of the debate, even when it descended (as it sometimes did) into the realm of personal insults about the "madwoman" with the "strange" name and "wild" hair. Only toward the end of May were she and her supporters finally allowed to respond to the charges against her. Although they made significant progress in a very short time by convincing key senators and members of the public that she at least deserved a fair hearing, it was too little, too late. On June 3, Guinier was called to the White House, where President Clinton told her that he would have to withdraw her nomination because he had belatedly discovered that he disagreed with her on some fundamental civil-rights issues. His decision provoked an angry reaction from black leaders and women's groups across the United States, many of whom felt he had sacrificed Guinier to appease political conservatives inside and outside the government.

A little over two months later, in one of her first public appearances since the nomination furor, Guinier attended the national NAACP convention in Indianapolis, Indiana. On July 13, surrounded by members of the civil rights community who had offered her their support, she accepted the organization's 1993 "Torch of Courage" award amid a round of thunderous applause and chants of "Lani! Lani! Lani!" She then addressed the enthusiastic audience with a fiery speech charging that her experience was "a metaphor for the way black people and the issues of race and racism are viewed in this society." Guinier's remarks are reprinted here from a copy of her speech furnished by the NAACP.

It is a wonderful honor to be among real friends—to be recognized by the president of *Crisis* magazine and to be given the chance to address a plenary session of the NAACP.

When I was an attorney for the NAACP Legal Defense Fund, I represented many NAACP plaintiffs, and with the support of the NAACP local branches, I won legal victories in thirty-one of approximately thirty-three voting cases I litigated.

In the most recent civil rights case in which I was involved, I followed the example set by these NAACP plaintiffs and other black people who refused to suffer quietly the indignity of unfairness. I endured the personal humiliation of being vilified as the "madwoman" with the strange name, strange hair and strange writings. The national media condemned me. My critics drove me from Washington as a "race-obsessed radical" whose views were so out of the mainstream that I did not even deserve the fundamental fairness of being allowed to defend myself and my reputation under oath before a Senate hearing.

But lest any of you feel sorry for me, according to press reports, the president still "loves" me. He just won't give me a job! But don't worry. The same press reports that Reverend Chavis has offered me a job with the NAACP, and I can understand Reverend Chavis's desire to have me work for him again. After all, when I was at the Justice Department in the Carter administration, I helped write the brief that ultimately persuaded the court to overturn Reverend Chavis's conviction.

But the issue here is not about a job. I have a job for life as a tenured law professor. My nomination was merely a metaphor. It was a metaphor for the way black people and the issue of race and racism are being defined by and characterized by others who are not sympathetic to the cause of civil rights and misrepresented history because, according to one Democratic staffer, I had a "strange name, strange hair and strange writings." Likewise, civil rights issues have been consigned to a similar fate—issues of race and racism are "history." They once were important but, unless we want to be known as race-obsessed, we are no longer permitted to discuss race in polite conversation or law review articles.

Well, what does it mean to be black? If you ask the United States Supreme Court, it means white people now have inherent standing to challenge a redistricting plan which integrates white voters in a fifty-four percent black district.

Now, again, we're talking about metaphors. And like my nomination, the recent Supreme Court case about Representative Mel Watt's congressional district in North Carolina tells us a lot about who they think we are.

They are practicing exclusion in a state that is almost one quarter black. And this exclusion is not ancient history. In a 1986 voting case in North Carolina, I was able to show on average that eighty-one percent of white voters would not vote for a black candidate, even if their choice was to vote for no one at all.

The district may have looked funny, but then the way black people are segregated and discriminated against in this society "looks off" too. If you want to draw a district that recognizes residential segregation and also takes into account the similarity of interests that black and white urban dwellers may have in a primarily rural state like North Carolina, you may have to link up several cities in one district. And what's wrong with that? If we link people by telephone, by satellite, by television, by fax, by market niche, then why is it not logical to fol-

Lani Guinier

low a major highway that links the only big cities in North Carolina? Indeed, the Bush Justice Department thought the district was OK and approved the district under the Voting Rights Act.

Even more importantly, though, this was the most integrated district in North Carolina—roughly fifty percent black and fifty percent white. Yet the Court acted as if this district was drawn to stigmatize voters based on an unusual view of what constitutes racial stereotypes. The Court said it was concerned that black voters, as a result of a common history and common experience and common residentially segregated living patterns, are subject to stereotypes when black and white legislators, in response to a Justice Department voting rights act objection, draw a district that allows those same blacks to act on a common set of political interests. The mere idea that black voters may have something in common is now, in and of itself, stigmatizing. Indeed, the Anti-Defamation League filed a brief in a similar case railing against even calling black people 'African American' because using a common name, in and of itself, is a racial stereotype.

We no longer get to define ourselves. We have been rendered neutered by others. Just like my nomination, we are not allowed to define ourselves.

As Justice O'Connor told us, "Appearances matter." Exactly what did she mean by appearances? In *Shaw v. Reno,* O'Connor tells that simply looking at a district which has a barely black majority, you can tell that the district appearance stigmatizes, segregates, and creates political apartheid. And this appearance gives you all this information only in the context of race. In other words, appearances are controlling only in districts with a black majority. If the district looks funny but was drawn to protect a white Republican in a contest with a white Democrat, white voters cannot complain on the basis of appearances. It the district looks funny and it was drawn to comply with one person/one vote, white voters cannot complain simply on the basis of appearances. It is only if the district creates a black majority that its appearance alone is the basis for a law suit.

Appearance apparently means: If you are white you are all right; if you are black, get back.

The Court here simply created out of whole cloth an independent, free-floating constitutional right to aesthetic correctness. This new constitutional right to aesthetic correctness apparently belongs to those who, because of their commitment to a racial neutrality, are more offended by the funny shape of a district than by the awful shape of racial prejudice which still defines reality in North Carolina.

Like the district it is designed to remedy, this new constitutional right is, indeed, funny, meaning in this instance peculiar, because it is essentially an obligation to correct subjective aesthetics rather than remedy substantive racial discrimination. The Court tells us that the creation of the first two majority black districts in over a century is more offensive than the creation and maintenance of an entire white legislative delegation for over one hundred years.

Now this district may not have been the best way to remedy a century of racial exclusion. And, indeed, ironically it was arguments that I made in law review articles suggesting alternatives to these kinds of districts that got me into so much trouble, that labeled me "anti-democratic."

I suggested, for example, that by giving all voters in North Carolina twelve votes, the same number of votes in any combination, black voters could use all twelve of their votes to vote for one black; or they could use six votes on one black and six on an environmentalist. But any way you looked at it, blacks could—if they chose—elect representatives of their choice and North Carolina could send an integrated delegation to Congress.

This alternative remedy, called cumulative voting, did not offend one person/one vote because all voters had the same, the exact same number of voters. This was not anti-democratic because, indeed, cumulative voting maximizes the opportunity of all voters to choose who represented them. This was not radical because the Reagan and Bush Justice Department had approved similar plans in over thirty cases. This was not separatist because it promoted cross-racial coalitions; whites could vote for blacks and vice versa. No, this was just plain old interest-group politics, but because I advocated innovative remedies like cumulative voting—a remedy currently used in corporate governance in thirty states in this country—I was condemned for strange ideas, anti-democratic ideas.

What is the lesson? The lesson is that in the name of race neutrality, we get excluded on the subjective ground of shape, not substance. My nomination was withdrawn not on the merits but on the appearance; it was controversial, so therefore it was problematic. The inference is clear—white hegemony, indifference, fear, and/or aesthetics are more important than remedying a century of exclusion.

And the focus on appearance only extends as far as race. It is apparently still permissible to draw odd and irregular boundaries to provide adequate representation, to Justice Stevens, "for rural voters, for union members, for Hasidic Jews, for Polish Americans, or Republicans." It is, however, not permissible to draw exactly the same shaped boundaries for the one group whose history gave birth to the constitutional amendment under which whites now have a right to aesthetic correctness. As Justice Stevens recognizes in dissent, "for members of the very minority group whose history in the United States gave birth to the Equal Protection Clause" the Court's conclusion can only be described as "perverse," because the opinion suggests that African Americans may now be the only group to which it is unconstitutional to offer specific benefits from redistricting.

If the Court's decision were an aberration, we might be shocked but not alarmed. However, the Court's reasoning now permeates our political discourses as well. In the name of race neutering, traditional Democrats do not want to talk about race anymore. Instead, they talk in euphemisms—drugs, welfare, crime. Republicans are not supposed to talk about race anymore either, or about jobs or health care. Instead, they just talk about cutting entitlement programs and building more prisons. And New Democrats—those Southern moderates who like black people as individuals and who "don't have a person to waste"—they can't talk about race either, especially if it appears that they are giving in to black demands or allowing black people too much power.

This is why I was not allowed to speak for myself about my innovative ideas such as cumulative voting, ideas for remedying racial discrimination without drawing funny-shaped districts. The censorship imposed against me means that officially there should be no serious debate or discussion about race, racism, and the value of fundamental fairness and justice to a true democracy.

Appearances do matter, just as Justice O'Connor said. But she got it wrong. It is not the appearance of being neutral that matters. It is the appearance of being fair.

> ***"My nomination was withdrawn not on the merits but on the appearance; it was controversial, so therefore it was problematic."***

Fairness requires that we identify the racial cleavages that exist in our society in order to remedy them. Fairness means we cannot be indifferent to racial exclusion, ignorant about racial difference, or too tired to engage in a conversation in which all voices are represented.

As W.E.B. Du Bois said at the dawning of this century, "The problem of the twentieth century is the problem of the color line." At the close of this century, unfortunately, Du Bois is still right. But most unfortunately, somehow, because white decision-makers are preoccupied with the appearance of being neutral, we are no longer permitted even to worry about being fair.

So let me conclude with a special plea for a national conversation about racial justice and fairness. At least, at the very least, let's insist that we have a meaningful dialogue about race, racism, and justice in which we do not silence anyone but in which we insist on our right to speak effectively, in which we insist on our right to speak for ourselves and to be represented by people we choose to represent our interests, in which we challenge our decision-makers to be fair, not just neutral. And above all, we must insist on defining ourselves.

Make no mistake about it, if this Supreme Court decision in *Shaw v. Reno* defines the mainstream of our political process, the mainstream is polluted by ignorance and indifference. If this means that those of us who challenge a dysfunctional definition of neutrality, who are committed instead to fairness, who are committed to empowering voters—all voters, who are committed instead to making our legislative bodies truly representative so as to legitimate political outcomes in the name of all of the people, who are committed to give American citizens a reason to work inside the political system outside the mainstream, then we must change the mainstream.

Because if appearance defines the mainstream, the American political system has little room in it for us "with strange hair" and strange ideas. And it has even less space in it to develop a true, fair, and legitimate democracy.

Since delivering her speech to the NAACP, Guinier has remained busy on the lecture circuit, taking her case directly to the American public in an effort to dispel the media's image of her as a "madwoman" with dangerously radical ideas. Indeed, she has called for a national discussion of the racial issues dividing the country in the hope that such dialogue will lead to greater interracial harmony. To that end, she founded a nonprofit organization known as Commonplace. She has also published a book, The Tyranny of the Majority, *and is at work on another to be published in late 1995.*

SOURCES

Books

Guinier, Lani, *The Tyranny of the Majority: Fundamental Fairness in Representative Democracy,* Free Press, 1994.

Periodicals

Crisis, "Lani Guinier: The Making of a Cause Célèbre," August/September, 1993.

Detroit Free Press, "Guinier Tells NAACP That Racism Thrives on Indifference," July 14, 1993, p. 5A.

Detroit News, "Guinier Calls Clinton Coward for Withdrawing Nomination," July 14, 1993, p. 5A.

Esquire, December, 1984, pp. 488-492.

Grand Rapids Press, "Spurned 'Quota Queen' Pens Her Defense," March 20, 1994, p. A9.

Ms., "Lani Guinier: The Anatomy of a Betrayal," September/October, 1993, pp. 51-57.

Newsweek, "Crowning a 'Quota Queen'?" May 24, 1993, p. 67; "So Long, Lani," June 14, 1993, pp. 26-28; "Guinier: The Rewards of Martyrdom," August 23, 1993, p. 25.

New York Times, "Guerrilla Fighter for Civil Rights," May 5, 1993, p. A19; "Senate Democrats Urge Withdrawal of Rights Nominee," June 2, 1993; "Aides Say Clinton Will Drop Nominee for Post on Rights," June 3, 1993; "Clinton Abandons His Nominee for Rights Post Amid Opposition," June 4, 1993; "President Blames Himself for Furor Over Nominee," June 5, 1993; "Abandoned by Clinton, She Finds Acceptance," July 14, 1993, p. A12; "At the Bar," September 3, 1993, p. A17.

New York Times Magazine, "Who's Afraid of Lani Guinier?" February 27, 1994.

New Yorker, "Idea Woman," June 14, 1993.

Progressive, "Lani Guinier," September, 1993, pp. 28-32.

Time, "Tailor-Made to Be Used Against Her," June 14, 1993.

U.S. News and World Report, "A Controversial Choice at Justice," May 17, 1993, p. 19; "The Trials of Lani Guinier," June 7, 1993, p. 38.

Alex Haley

1921–1992

African American writer

As the author of the award-winning 1976 bestseller Roots: The Saga of an American Family, *which inspired two equally popular television miniseries adaptations, Alex Haley has often been credited with reviving widespread interest in genealogy, particularly black genealogy. The dramatic yet folksy story of his quest to document his family history—recounted in his books and articles as well as on the lecture circuit—inspired countless Americans, black and white, to take up the search for their own "roots" and experience the thrill of discovering a familiar name among the dusty records of the past. And as more than a few observers noted, Haley's efforts paid off in another and far more important way. By reaching an audience now numbered in the tens (if not hundreds) of millions,* Roots *has made it possible for black and white Americans to reach a deeper understanding of the extent to which the histories of both races in this country are forever intertwined.*

Although he was born in Ithaca, New York, and grew up in various college towns throughout the South (his father was a professor), Haley spent a great deal of his youth at his maternal grandparents' home in Henning, Tennessee. It was there that he first heard the stories about his African ancestor, Kunta Kinte, that would later form the basis of Roots. *Long before that project ever took shape, however, Haley spent many years trying to establish himself as a writer while actually earning a living as a member of the U.S. Coast Guard. He met with just enough success to keep his dream alive, and upon his retirement from the service in 1959, he decided to pursue a free-lance career in earnest.*

The first few years on his own were tough ones for Haley. He then began to publish fairly regularly in the Reader's Digest *and several other major magazines. But his biggest break came when editors at* Playboy *approached him about developing a new interview feature. His first subject was jazz trumpeter Miles Davis, and the piece proved so popular that Haley was asked to do additional interviews, including one with Nation of Islam spokesman Malcolm X. That in turn led Malcolm to choose Haley as his collaborator on* The Autobiography of Malcolm X, *which has been a steady bestseller in the years since its publication in 1965.*

It was around that same time that Haley first began accumulating the material on his family's history that would eventually find its way into Roots. *For some twelve years, he devoted whatever time he could spare between writing assignments to visit libraries, archives, and other research centers; he also made a trip to a village in Gambia, the African homeland of his ancestors, where he listened to the local* griot, *or oral historian, spin a tale of a young man named Kinte that echoed much of what he had heard on his grandmother's front porch back in Henning, Tennessee. Haley then spent several years weaving all he had learned into a semifictional drama that vividly brought to life as never before the realities of slavery and its impact on several generations of a black American family.*

Roots *enjoyed tremendous success with readers as well as critics, zooming to the top of the bestseller list and snaring a number of prestigious honors, including a special Pulitzer Prize and a National Book Award. Its first television adaptation, broadcast in 1977, captured a then-record two-thirds of the possible viewing audience, and a sequel broadcast in 1979 also proved to be immensely popular. Its compelling and unprecedented portrait of what it felt like to be a slave from a black rather than a white perspective touched off a nationwide period of soul-searching and debate that many observers credited with opening some eyes to the state of race relations in America.*

Overwhelmed by the attention lavished upon him as the author of Roots, *Haley found it difficult for a while to return to his writing. He eventually did so, however, and also enjoyed an extremely busy second career appearing on television and radio programs and lecturing to all kinds of audiences throughout the world. One such occasion was on January 30, 1992, at Hope College in Holland, Michigan, where he shared with more than a thousand listeners one of his favorite stories—how* Roots *came to be. The following is a transcription of his speech taken from a tape recording provided by the Hope College Collection of the Joint Archives of Holland.*

It kind of tickles me—and I often sit in this position, or back of the stage curtains, or sit up on a dais or different places where you're preparing to speak—and I hear myself being introduced, and I sit there thinking to myself, God, I wish I could have known a little bit of that back then! It's like people often ask me, "Did you have any idea, did you know *Roots* was going to do so well?" And I think to myself, if I would, I would have typed a lot faster!

And another thing that sort of tickles me is that I was saying at dinner this evening, before *Roots,* nobody ever paid me a bit of attention, could care less what I had to say about anything. And ever since then, there are interviews, and there are opinions being expressed, and questions asked, and really it's kind of like your life becomes—mine certainly had become—what was *before Roots* and then *after Roots.*

I think that maybe the best thing I could do this evening is try to share with you, as I often do, really how this book came into being. The impression generally about me and other writers is that one day we just sat down and sort of decided and said, "I shall write a book, and it'll be the following," or something like that. That's not the case *at all.* I was talking night before last with a dear friend many of you would know about, Danielle Steel, and we were just sort of sharing how the rejection slips were so long a part of our lives. You write your head off, and you mail it out with prayer. And it comes back as quickly as the mails can get it back with a little card that'll say, "Thank you for thinking of us" or something, and you just keep on and keep on somehow.

But anyway, that's not getting at how *Roots* actually began. I was in a little town, I was raised in a little town called Henning, Tennessee. H-E-double N-I-N-G. It's in the western part of the state, about fifty miles north of Memphis.

Alex HALEY

Alex Haley

The population when I was there—as a boy, anyway—was about 470 people, about half and half white and black. It was another little typical farming town, and it was a town where the church and the school just about ran the town, really. And it was [a] very strongly Protestant community, it was Bible Belt, South. In Henning, you were either white or black, you were either Methodist or Baptist, or you were regarded as a sinner. Children all went to Sunday school, and we were pretty much stamped out like cookies.

And in this town, in this time, I was just raised, as we say in the South, by my grandparents. I had a particular love for my grandparents. Not that I didn't love my parents—they both were teachers, but their being teachers had them away from the home more than normally might have been the case, and my grandmother and my grandfather did the raising of me.

I have to just sort of divert a little bit. They put such a stamp on me that to this day I have a very special affection for grandparents, *anybody's* grandparents. If somebody tells me that's somebody's grandma, my inclination is just hug that lady because of what grandmas stand for.

Since *Roots* happened—to jump again ahead—I got very deeply involved in genealogy. And one of the things I discovered in the world of genealogy is that families often—and it's a marvelous thing—are trying to build their family history. And if you are setting out to do that, the most immediate thing you've got to try to do if you are blessed enough to have family elders living is to go interview the family elders who can tell you things in five minutes that you will spend years trying to find if you haven't asked them before they've passed away.

One of the things that is found to be absolutely the case is that when grandparents are to be interviewed, by all means the ideal interviewers are grandchildren. It is known absolutely that there is a particular interrelationship between grandparents—in fact, it's almost like a conspiracy—between grandparents and grandchildren. It is known, it is certainly viewed, that the reason that there is this strict bond between grandparents and grandchildren is that both of them seem to kind of perceive that they share a common enemy, and that's *parents*. And that's what makes them so tight together.

I had that with my grandfather, who owned a little lumberyard in this little town, which was unusual [in] that there would be a black owner of a lumberyard. But that was just sort of a side story—it happened. And he was very highly respected. For me, he was just the utter end of macho, and utter end of somebody to be proud of, and [a] role model. He was tall, straight, black.

Every afternoon about sundown, in the summers particularly, I would go out on the front porch, or in the front yard if the weather was particularly good, and I would watch toward downtown. And after a while, I would see Grandpa walking with his long strides, coming up toward our house. And I'd watch him, and then he'd be kind of blotted out from view by the white Baptist church for a while, and then by its parsonage. And he'd make a left turn down the dirt road coming toward our house. It was agreed that when he got at the corner by our house, I could charge out and tackle him around the knees. And part of the pageantry was that Grandpa would act as if he was unaware he was being tackled. And with all this flurry going on, I would keep my eye on his right hand. If he extended his right index finger straight down rigidly, the signal was I could grab it with my little fat fist and it meant he was just going to take us walking somewhere.

I never will forget how we would go, striding along, and I remember how I would look down and I would just marvel that for every stride Grandpapa took, I took three little skipping steps to keep up. We would go by the house, and by this time my grandmother was standing in the screen door, the front door, looking at us. And I would just kind of throw a little sideways wave at her as if to say, "Don't mess with us, we're busy," and Grandma would kind of make a little fist at me. It was all in love. And it just knocked me out that my grandfather could do anything he pleased, and he didn't have to ask Grandma *anything*. I just thought that was the height of macho! It was being raised like this, by loving grandparents whom I loved in turn—and then all of a relative sudden, my beloved grandfather died. It was as if the bottom fell out of everything. Nobody could *believe* that Will Palmer was gone.

Afterwards, Grandma sat like a zombie on the front porch in a white wicker rocking chair. People would pass on the road, and they would speak to her, "How're you, Miz Sis?"—her name was Cynthia, and people called her Sis—and Grandma often wouldn't even acknowledge the greetings. Nobody seemed to mind, because people knew how grief-stricken she was. And then, even I, a little boy of five, could tell that Grandma was going under if she didn't do *something*.

And after a while, she *did* do something. She began to write letters, more letters that I ever had known her to write—a total of five. And she wrote them in one week, one per afternoon. And she was writing them to her sisters, who lived in various very exotic places like East St. Louis; like Detroit; Inkster, Michigan, was another one. She was asking her sisters if they would come and spend the next summer there with us. One by one, the sisters answered, and they said they would be coming, and they would say whether or not they were coming on the train, the IC—Illinois Central train—or by the Greyhound bus. In subsequent letters, they told the exact date they would be coming. And on those dates, we would be dressed up, go downtown, meet train or bus, whoever was due would get off, and there'd be all kinds of hugging and screeching and carrying on, and then we'd come back up to the house. In this way, within the space of about ten days, five sisters came from all these glamorous, exotic places.

They spent the days, for the better part, visiting people around in Henning whom they had known growing up there as young girls before they got married and went away. Then in the evening, we would all come together and we would have what they called supper. It was a very—not much of a meal, you could even have something cold for supper, it wasn't much. And then the sisters would just kind of trickle toward the front porch. By now, it would be early night.

There were a number of rocking chairs on the front porch. Around three sides of the porch were thick honeysuckle vines. Do you know what honeysuckle is up here? You know—OK. And then over the honeysuckle were thousands, I guess, of what we called lightning bugs, fireflies, flicking on and off. And the sisters would get in the rocking chairs, and I would get behind my grandmother's rocking chair. There was an expression I haven't heard much since I was a boy called "scrounch down"—you just crouched down with your back against something solid, in this case the wall there on the porch.

And there would occur two things that the sisters all did that I know they never once thought about. It was purely involuntary, just automatic; it was what you did on front porches in the South at that time. The first thing there in the early dark, they would take maybe five minutes to get their rocking together. You know, you don't just sit down and start rocking. You've got to get that chair at just the right angle for you, and then you've got to get the cadence just right. You can tell a whole lot about people's personalities by how they rock. Nervous people have a jerky, quick rock, and others a more languid, slow rock.

And once they got their rocking kind of synchronized, every single one of them—without thinking about it, I know, they just did it—would run their hand in their apron pocket and come up with a little cylindrical tin can of sweet

. . . snuff. And they would pull out this lower lip and kind of load it up, and then they would start taking little practice shots out over the honeysuckle vine. The champion in that group among the sisters without any question was my Great-Aunt Liz, who had come from somewhere called Okmulgee, Oklahoma, where she'd been teaching for more than twenty-five years. Aunt Liz, when she was in good form, could drop a lightning bug at four yards. She was just incredible!

This was really what kind of established what might be called the ambience of the evening. They would start now laughing, there in the dark, me listening, ears like saucers. Not that I felt there was any particular value—it was just fascinating to listen. And they would talk about their girlhood. One of the things that got to me was how they would sort of slap each other on the thigh or the shoulder, and they'd say, "Oh, girl!" I remember thinking to myself, "These are gray-haired women calling each other 'girl,' it's terrible!" I didn't have the insight, of course, to know that they were reminiscing and as such they *were* girls again. And they would sort of segue out of the mischief that they used to do. And something else that just got to me was hearing them talk about the things they did! My own dear grandmother telling about things she did for which she would have choked me had I done it!

And then they'd begin to talk about their parents. They loved to talk about their father—strict, strong, blacksmith Tom Murray, who had been a slave blacksmith and who had vowed during slavery that come freedom he would own his own shop, as he in fact later had there in the town of Henning. And they talked about their mother, her name Arrena. They used to love to talk about how she would get upset if anybody called her "Irene" as people would sometimes do. And she would make certain that they understood her name was properly spelled A-R-R-E-N-A, and that she was one-fourth Cherokee Indian.

And then they would eventually start waggling their heads and cluck-clucking and saying something like, "Oh, he was just scandalous!" And when I began to hear this, I knew they were getting ready now to lay into their daddy's daddy. And this was the one that they talked about who fought roosters who was called Chicken George. They loved to talk about what a sinner he was. He drank whiskey, which was sinful, and when he drank he would curse (that was the first time I ever heard the expression "taking the Lord's name in vain"), and then there was another sin of his that I gathered—I didn't know what it meant, but from the way they acted I gathered it must have been worse than the other two combined—and that was womanizing, and they said he was doing that all the time.

And then their whole manner would change. All these people up to this time they had talked about had lived in somewhere called Alamance County, North Carolina. Now they became quiet, all but reverent, as they talked about Chicken George's mother. And they said she lived not in Alamance County, North Carolina, but in Spotsylvania County, Virginia. She lived on the plantation of her master, who was a medical doctor. His name, Dr. William Waller, and he was called Mas' Waller. And they told how he had a cook named Bell who was the mother of Miss Kizzy, who was the mother of Chicken George.

> ***"There were a number of rocking chairs on the front porch. . . . The sisters would get in the rocking chairs, and I would get behind my grandmother's rocking chair. . . . And they would talk about their girlhood."***

The father of Miss Kizzy was this African [Kunta Kinte] who was a buggy driver for the master. They told how the African drove the master both on his medical rounds and his social rounds. And then they told how when Miss Kizzy was coming up as a little girl, the African, when he got a chance taking her around, would hold her hand and he would, as best he could, convey to his little daughter sounds. He would point out tree, rock, cow—things, simple things like that, and he would say to her the African word, the word from his country and his people that meant that thing. And Miss Kizzy began to learn a few phonetic sounds.

She grew on up, building a little bit better repertoire of these sounds and eventually a few stories that he could tell her, in a very halting way with what little English he had commanded, about his country, where he came from, things like that. And then when Miss Kizzy was fifteen she was sold away. She was sold to a man whose name was Tom Lea, L-E-A. And as it would turn out, it was Tom Lea who became the father of Miss Kizzy's first child, a boy who was given the name George. And it was George who grew up into the rooster fighter, the gamecock fighter Chicken George.

Chicken George, for all his womanizing, did marry—or, in slave terms, he jumped the broom, that was the practice at that time for marrying among them—with Matilda, and in time, Matilda gave birth to eight children. The youngest of them, the second youngest of them, a boy named Tom, when he got to be fifteen, was apprenticed to a Dutch blacksmith. And Tom became an outstanding young slave blacksmith. In time, Tom met a young slave maid named Arrena, who was at the Holt plantation in Alamance County. And they jumped the broom. And in time, Arrena gave birth to seven children, all girls.

And now, two generations later, there were the five remaining ones of those girls sitting on the front porch of my grandmother, whom they called—and I couldn't understand that, they called her "the baby," and I couldn't figure how in the world is anybody's grandma "the baby"—and they were talking and they were reminiscing and they were telling the stories and I was listening. None of us had any idea that what we really were participating in was something which nowadays in more informed circles we call "oral history"—the passing down of the story from the elder to the younger. But I grew up hearing those stories, learning them through repetitive hearing.

In the same community there was another set of stories that I was exposed to. And that was, as I say—it was a very church-going community. All children went to Sunday school, and you learned there the biblical parables. And I guess by the time I was about eleven, my head in story terms was a jumble of such as David and Goliath, and Chicken George, and Moses, and Miss Kizzy. It was all mixed up in there.

And thus, I grew up. I got into other interests. I was in school; I was not a good student. Teachers used to tell my parents that I was a daydreamer, and they could not have been more correct. I used to love to get a seat over by the window where I could look out at the clouds and think to myself, "That cloud's shaped like a kangaroo, and that one looks like a cow" or something. And my grades used to kind of reflect this. And my father, who was a teacher, a dean of agriculture, was distressed no end that I was not being a role model for my two younger brothers.

Our father was determined that we were all going to be professors as he was. And when I got such bad grades, I got a good deal of what we'd call corporal punishment, and that didn't change too much anyway. Finally—I had the kind of dad who when he got something on his mind you heard a lot about it, and he began to talk about maturing. I had needed, he said, to go somewhere which was safe and mature to get enough sense to come back and finish college, then get a master's, get a doctorate, and become a professor as he was. And so my father went shopping in the military for me. He thought that was the best place. The Army, the Marine Corps, the Navy—all had four-year enlistments. And then he found one we didn't know much of anything about called the United States Coast Guard which had a three-year enlistment, and dad thought three years ought to do it. So with his recommendations, to put it charitably, I jumped into the Coast Guard.

I soon discovered that my father had done the best favor he ever could have done for me, because there was no comparison between being a student on a campus with your father bird-dogging your every move and being a sailor. I *loved* it, absolutely! I was on a ship. We called them weather-patrol ships. They would go out and do thirty-day patrols on grids in the ocean—Ocean Station Able, Ocean Station Baker, Ocean Station Charlie, Dog, and so on.

It was lonely out there. It was a time when if you were black and you went into any of the naval services, you automatically went into what was called a steward's department. You did menial, domestic-type things—wait on the officers' tables, shine shoes, make up their bunks, stuff life that—and when you would advance you would advance to cook or steward or in advance of that, cook's helper.

I did pretty well, and I had gotten rather quickly up to the area of cook's helper when I began to find a way to bear through the long thirty days at sea. I just began to write letters to people I'd known back in school. I wrote students, I wrote some of my father's faculty colleagues. I would write about what we were doing, and I would make it sound much more dramatic and exciting than it was. My hope was that they would simply go to bed and say, "Well, it looks like the boy is doing alright" or something. I couldn't write dad and tell him, "Look, I'm sorry. I wish I'd done better." But I hoped they might sort of suggest that to him.

As it turned out, something was happening that I had no dream about in the way of a future. I didn't even *think* about a future at that time. But sailors began to notice that I both wrote and received more mail than anybody else on the ship. And so some of them began to come up with sailor's things in mind, and they suggested it might be nice if I could help them write a letter to a girl. I thought it'd be kind of fun. It was known that I had been to a "college," and I don't think anybody else on the ship except the officers had been *near* a college. So they thought that might help me write a letter to a girl, and I thought that was great.

So it got to be every night, I would help the cooks all day, I'd come down below, get me a little nap, get me a shower, and go down in the mess deck. I would sit at a little table in the mess deck with some three-by-five index cards, and my clients would literally line up, and guys would sit over here to kibitz. Almost all my clients were white. We had on that ship 250 of us, I think. There were eight blacks, eight Filipinos, four Samoans, and the rest were white. And when the guys would come to me as I'm sitting here with my little index cards, taking tight little notes, I would interview them. I'd say, OK, what's her name, what's she look like—hair, eyes, mouth, nose, whatnot, anything—what special thing do you want me to say, anything like that. They would be pretty candid about whatever, and the fellows over here would be rather earthy in making commentary about whatever. And I would make my little cards with tight little notes.

The next day, up in the galley—in cooking, you didn't have to be cooking or stirring or frying all of the time, and I had good little periods of time, and I had a portable typewriter. My father, in his zeal to see me as a professor, had put me in typing class at age eight, and I could type well. So I would take a card with these little pieces of data about this young lady and take my typewriter and some paper, and I would write in double space the best I could create to help my buddy, and he would then write it in his own handwriting later. It would be something like, say, if a guy told me (as a number did) that the young lady's hair was blond. Well, out in the middle of the ocean I'd get in some fit of creativity and come up with something like, "Your hair is like the moonlight reflected on the rippling waves" and such as like that.

These letters would be mailed, and I never will forget—it took two trips at sea for the cycle to come full. We came back after the second trip at sea to where our ship our ship tied up, Portsmouth, Virginia. And the captain gave, as he usually did, what was called port-and-starboard liberty. And that meant half the crew was off the first night, and the next half would be off the next night, and would alternate like that. I was in the second night's liberty group.

Around about 1:00, 1:30 that first night after we got in, such a bedlam! Guys rushing back on the ship, and they were testifying to the top of their lungs what astounding successes they had met behind these letters when they got to shore. In the world of sailors, it was wonderful. I became heroic in one night. And the thing that happened was something I would never have dreamed—that the fellows were so happy and so grateful that they began to pay me fifty cents a letter. That was what accidentally—I always like to say *accidentally*—put me in the interest of trying to write.

I began then as a young sailor to try to write articles for magazines. I would send them out, the best I could write, and they would come straight back, as I already have said, with the little card that said, "Thank you for thinking of us." But that was what was important—I had started trying to write. Then I wrote almost every day, or every night (I became a night writer because I had more time at night), and particularly when I was at sea I would write.

It was years, literally eight years, before the first piece sold. It was a little piece to a magazine called *This Week* which no longer exists; it was a Sunday supplement like *Parade* magazine today. It was a piece about the Coast Guard, and they paid one hundred dollars. I got the check cashed into one hundred one-dollar bills and put fifty in each pocket and went down the street squeezing the tactile feeling of money earned by writing.

And that was what got me on to, ultimately, by the time I was out of the service—I stayed in twenty years because I loved the sea—and I began to sell to what used to be men's adventure magazines. Some of the older men in here could remember magazines like *Saga,* and *True,* and *Bluebook* and such as that which no longer exist. Television has killed off [an] incredible lot of magazines. It's almost impossible to imagine that there's no more *Collier's,* no more *Liberty,* that the *Saturday Evening Post*—once the greatest—is now sort of a, I don't know how often, but once in a while.

Anyway, by the time I got out of the military, I was selling not a lot, but some, and I was determined to make my living as a writer. The first assignment I got was from the *Reader's Digest,* conservative *Reader's Digest,* to do an article about the group colloquially called the Black Muslims. (They called themselves the Nation of Islam.) I did that article, and I met in the process the man who was their spokesman. His name was Malcolm X.

Then it wasn't too long afterwards when I got an offer from another magazine, a very exciting new magazine, and they asked me if I would start a new feature for them—interviews, because I'd done a lot of interviews. This was a magazine called *Playboy,* and I jumped at the chance. Everybody was—it was an exciting magazine. It paid more, and that's what moves writers deeply! It was kind of funny there, that I was for a little while working for two magazines, neither of which wanted the name of the other mentioned in their offices. That was *Reader's Digest* and *Playboy.*

Then I got a job working for a publisher, and the publisher asked Malcolm X if he would be willing to tell his life in book-length detail. Malcolm finally agreed he would, and then he—Malcolm—asked me if I would do the writing. I was pleased, honored, flattered at the opportunity. I had never written a book. It was kind of frightening to think of the length of a book versus magazine articles.

I started into what would turn out to be two years. I lived in Greenwich Village at the time in a little basement, one room, 92 Grove Street. Malcolm would come down there about twice a week, 9:30 maybe, and stay until midnight. And we would interview. I would ask him about his life, and he would tell little by little.

After a year, I had a pretty good overall picture, and it was then a thing of sort of fitting the pieces in in a chronological way like a quilt—pieces, patches of a quilt, or quilting pieces, they called them. And then I started writing the book, first person, as if I were he. And Malcolm periodically would say, "Brother, I'm not going to live to read this in print."

As it turned out, in the process of writing about him I would do other interviews, and I interviewed two other people, both of whom also predicted correctly that they would die by violence. One was Dr. King, and the other was the Nazi party leader George Lincoln Rockwell, who predicted he, also, would die violently, and they all did.

I finished Malcolm's book, the manuscript, turned it in to a publisher on a Thursday afternoon. Sunday morning, he was shot to death. The next week, I wrote like a dervish, trying to pull together everything I could into that one book so that within the two covers of the book would be the total of a man's life. As a matter of fact, the book had begun, I think—I've got to look at that opening line and see—but it's something like, "When my mother was pregnant with me, I was told later . . . ," and so it went from Malcolm as a fetus to in the grave.

When I finished that book—there's a saying in the business that when you've finished a big book, you're kind of like a lady who's just had a baby. Something you were full of, and all of a sudden it's gone, and you don't know what to do with yourself. And in that circumstance, of sorts, I was in Washington one Saturday morning. I had interviewed someone—I can't remember who nor for what—and I was walking down the sidewalk about 1:30 in the afternoon, and I saw ahead of me this tall, imposing building. Across the top of the columns was inscribed into the concrete, "Archives of the United States."

I don't know what, I never will know really what impelled me to go up the steep steps, unless it was that I have always had this innate thing about history. It always has kind of been like a magnet to me. I went up the steps, and in the main reading room, people were kind of moving around among the card indexes that we don't have anymore—I don't think we do have card indexes anymore. A young fellow, a young white fellow, came up to me, and he really kind of startled me, because I hadn't expected anybody to say anything or pay any attention to me. And he said, "Could I be of help to you?" (I later learned he was one of the young—what do they call them? Interns.) I don't know why, I just opened my mouth, and out of my mouth came something I don't understand really why it did to this day. I just said to him, "I wonder if I could see the census records for Alamance County, North Carolina, 1870."

Now why that gives me the goosebumps in a way is because I don't believe I had heard or read the words "Alamance County" since I was a boy. I said that much the same as I might have said the locale of Bethlehem or Jerusalem, which I had learned in the same time frame. And I said "1870" because somewhere in the interim I had learned that the first time black people were named in the census was after the Civil War, which would have been 1870.

The young man was not taken aback. He said

I should go up into the microfilm room, and I did. And he caused to be sent up eight boxes of microfilm. For the first time ever I threaded one of those reels, started one of those reels into one of the viewing machines—we've all seen them, where you view down on what the film shows. And I'm looking, as I turn the handle slowly, at this old-fashioned handwriting, where the "F"s look like "S"s and vice versa. Here was household number one—head of household, his wife, children. And I was struck by, as I got going, how many children died so early, like *months* old. It would have something like "child's name" and then say, "one-fourth," meaning it had lived three months, or stuff like that.

And I remember looking at the shape of the sheets—long, oblong sheets which were torn, ripped out of a book on the left side, so I knew it had been a ledger, a thick ledger. And I was thinking, this thing was heavy, and the man who was the census enumerator undoubtedly had a horse with a saddlebag to carry this. It's funny, you know, if you're into history, you're always kind of piecing things together to try to recreate one way or another, even if it's just for your own mind to better perceive something.

I went through four reels, looking. It was like standing on a hot, dusty road in wherever was Alamance County, North Carolina, looking at the people pass. And then I looked down, and what in the world am I looking at! There is "Murray, Thomas." His age, color—"b" for "black", occupation—blacksmith. For pete's sake! How many times had I heard Grandma, Aunt Liz, Aunt Plus, all of them talk about their daddy, Tom Murray the blacksmith, Alamance County! Could it possibly be that there had been more than one? And then I looked underneath his name, and there is his wife, and what do I see? A-R-R-E-N-A. How many times had I heard them say that mama spelled her name that way?

By now, I'm galvanized. And I'm looking at the names of the children. It wasn't that the names surprised me, because I'd sat on the front porch with these ladies of these names. But what astounded me was the ages—twelve, ten, nine, seven—Aunt Liz, the one I told you about from Oklahoma, the snuff-dipper, no way in the world she could have ever been six years old!—and then I was going down and all of a sudden I just was *enraged!* Where was Cynthia? Where was Grandma? How could they *possibly* have done this and not have Grandma? If it hadn't been for her, I wouldn't be there! I felt like taking the chair I'd been in and smashing the machine!

I remember then—I don't know why, from where, it just kind of trickled up in my head like a bubble might rise in this pitcher of water—*she wasn't born yet.* And when I look back upon it, that had to have been my first bite of what is colloquially called the genealogical bug from which there is no cure. Once you have been bitten by it, for the rest of your born days you'll be digging in old musty, dusty piles of records looking for a name, looking for a date, looking for a clue of any sort that will help you reach back with a family that doesn't even have to be your family.

> ***"Once you have been bitten by [the genealogical bug], for the rest of your born days you'll be digging in old musty, dusty piles of records looking for a . . . clue of any sort that will help you reach back. . . ."***

That was the beginning of what would become nine years of researching—not steadily researching, but doing what I could in between doing magazine articles to make a living by. And then, after that was done, three years of writing.

Finally, there was this book. I didn't know what to call it. I always liked one-word titles. I was for a long time, about five years, the title I had in my head was *Before This Anger*. The reason I came on that title was, it was in the sixties, and it was the civil rights struggles and all kinds of upheavals in that interest, and I had met quite a number of what I perceived to be really good, sincere, well-minded, and sympathetic, empathetic white people who had kind of said to me in one or another way, "What happened? Your people have been, you know, so peaceful, and all of a sudden all this upset. What is the trouble?" And so I had kind of thought, well, if I can write a book which would give these and other people some better perception of the history of us, of how we got to be here, and how we developed into whatever we are now, it might give them a better picture. Hence I had come up with this title of *Before This Anger*.

And then it was when I had been writing *The Autobiography of Malcolm X* that just by accident, different chapters—I had a thing about, you know, you write the chapter and then somewhere in the course of it, of that chapter, there is *a* word that seems to you to capture what that chapter's about.

Like Malcolm X one night told me the story of his mother trying to keep seven children together with the state trying to break up the family and give them to foster homes. Their father had been drawn under a streetcar and killed; he was a Baptist minister. And that just somehow seemed to be properly titled "Nightmare."

And then there was another where he went to Boston or Roxbury, Massachusetts, and he met a fellow from the area where he was who began to teach him how to be a hustler. How to make—when you shine shoes, don't just shine the shoes, but put a lot of slack in the rag and make it pop, and people would tip you another dime at least for a popping rag as opposed to a quiet shine. And that just seemed, because this man called Malcolm "Homeboy," that became that chapter.

Anyway, it was in that way I had gotten to like one word. And I kept thinking word, what word? And somehow by Providence, the word "roots" came to me, and so I changed the title. And I really, truly think that that word has had a lot to do with, for some reason, the success of the book, because it has meaning for everybody. The word "roots" has come to be used since the publication of the book in many, many ways that have nothing to do with the book, but it applies to all of us.

When the book came out, it was like falling over Niagara Falls. The thing of what is called "success" was just physically hard to try to live up to, to keep up with. I have since gone, traveled much of the world because the book was translated into thirty-one languages, and almost every time it's translated the publisher in that country wants you to be there for their big publication date or something, and you go. And you have all kinds of experiences. The film came out, it was received like the book. . . . More recently, just last week, it ran again, the first part of *Roots,* on cable, the Family Channel. I don't know the exact figures, but I've heard that it's something into the hundreds times more audience than they ever had before, which is pleasing, needless to say.

And I think that, probably, keeping an eye on my watch, . . . I think it might be a good time to make the most of whatever time we have left.

Alex Haley's talk at Hope College was one of his last public appearances; less than two weeks later, while in Seattle, Washington, to fulfill yet another speaking engagement, he suffered a fatal heart attack. He was buried on the grounds of his grandparents' home in Tennessee, not far from the front porch where he first heard the story of Kunta Kinte.

About a year before his death, Haley donated most of his papers, at least those related to his family history research and Roots, *to the University of Tennessee in Knoxville. After his death, his Malcolm X material was auctioned off to help pay estate debts. Other memorabilia, including his Pulitzer Prize, his Emmy Award, his typewriter, and various African artifacts, are in storage at the Tennessee State Museum in Nashville. Friends and family hope one day to secure the funding necessary to turn his grandparents' home in Henning into a more complete and permanent memorial.*

SOURCES

Books

Dictionary of Literary Biography, Volume 38: *Afro-American Writers After 1955: Dramatists and Prose Writers,* Gale Research, 1985.

Haley, Alex, with Malcolm X, *The Autobiography of Malcolm X,* Grove, 1965.

Haley, Alex, *Roots: The Saga of an American Family,* Doubleday, 1976.

Haley, Alex, with David Stevens, *Alex Haley's "Queen": The Story of an American Family,* Morrow, 1993.

Periodicals

Detroit News, "Friends Try to Help Museum in Alex Haley's Hometown Take Root," February 11, 1993, p. 7C.

Ebony, "Alex Haley: The Man Behind *Roots,*" April, 1977, pp. 33-41; "We Must Honor Our Ancestors," August, 1986, reprinted in special issue, November, 1990, pp. 152-156.

Grand Rapids Press, "Author Laments Loss of Family Ties," January 31, 1992; "Haley's *Roots* Manuscripts Go on Public View," February 23, 1993, p. D4.

New Republic, "Roots of Victory, Roots of Defeat," March 12, 1977, pp. 27-28.

Newsweek, "In Search of a Heritage," September 27, 1976, pp. 94-96; "After Haley's Comet," February 14, 1977, pp. 97-98; "Uncle Tom's Roots," February 14, 1977, p. 100.

New York Times, October 14, 1976; February 11, 1992, p. B8.

People, March 28, 1977; "Having Left LA to Settle in His Native Tennessee, Alex Haley Turns Out His First Book Since *Roots,*" December 12, 1988, pp. 126-128; "Deep Roots," February 24, 1992; "Torn Up by the Roots: An Estate Auction Threatens to Scatter the Precious Possessions of Alex Haley's Lifetime," October 5, 1992.

Playboy, "In Memoriam," July, 1992.

Publishers Weekly, "Alex Haley," September 6, 1976, pp. 8-12.

Reader's Digest, "My Search for Roots: A Black American's Story," April, 1977, pp. 148-152; "What *Roots* Means to Me," May, 1977, pp. 73-76.

Time, October 18, 1976; "Why *Roots* Hit Home," February 14, 1977, pp. 69-77; "*Roots'* Roots," December 25, 1978, p. 30; February 24, 1992, p. 68.

Fannie Lou Hamer

1917–1977

African American civil rights activist

To most people, the act of registering to vote is not an especially momentous event. But in the case of Fannie Lou Hamer, it was that and more. The year was 1962, the place was Mississippi, and blacks interested in exercising their constitutional right to the ballot faced open hostility—or worse. In a display of uncommon courage, Hamer and several other volunteers set out to improve the desperate conditions under which they lived by registering black voters and urging them to support changes in the political leadership. What they had to overcome to achieve their goal is one of the lesser-known chapters of the civil rights movement. And as their leader, Hamer is an often-overlooked figure in that struggle.

Hamer was the youngest of twenty children born to impoverished sharecroppers in Montgomery County, Mississippi. She began helping in the cotton fields at the age of six, and by the age of twelve she had dropped out of school to work full-time with the rest of her family. Her marriage in 1942 to a man who worked as a tractor driver on a neighboring plantation seemed to insure that she would remain mired in the only kind of life she had ever known, a life characterized by substandard housing, inadequate food, and little hope for a better future. Yet even then she felt the first stirrings of dissatisfaction and a yearning to do something to help her family and other African Americans who found themselves in similar circumstances.

But for the next two decades or so Hamer continued to eke out a meager existence, first as a field worker and then in the less back-breaking (but still low-paying) position of timekeeper. In August 1962, however, she attended her first civil rights meeting—a joint rally sponsored by the Southern Christian Leadership Conference (SCLC) and the Student Nonviolent Coordinating Committee (SNCC), held in her hometown of Ruleville. There she listened to a series of rousing speeches encouraging blacks to challenge Mississippi's unjust voting laws. Inspired by the notion that she just might be able to make a difference, she volunteered along with seventeen others to try to register at the county courthouse in Indianola.

On August 31, the group piled into an old school bus and set off on their historic journey. Upon their arrival in Indianola, Hamer, the group's spokesperson, explained their intentions to the clerk, who made them fill out a lengthy application form and take a literacy test that required them to read and interpret sections of the *state constitution. On the way back home, they were stopped by police who claimed that the color of their bus was "too yellow," which might lead people to believe it was a real school bus. The driver, who also owned the bus, was fined $100 and ordered to pay up immediately. The riders took up a collection among themselves and managed to gather together about $30, which a local judge accepted as payment. (Later, they learned that they had all failed the literacy test; Hamer finally passed it on her third try in January 1963.)*

Hamer had not seen the end of her troubles, however. Upon returning home, she was fired by her angry boss and ordered off the plantation when she refused to stop trying to register. A few days later, the house in which she was staying with a friend was riddled with gunfire; on another occasion, she was shot at from a speeding car. In the months that followed, both Hamer's husband and daughter were arrested and lost their jobs, and police barged into the family home and searched it without a warrant. Even the local water department tried to complicate their lives by sending them a bill for $9,000—this despite the fact that they did not have running water.

Hamer, who eventually found a new job with the SCLC and the SNCC working on welfare and voter registration programs, stood up to the intimidation and harassment. In fact, the woman who later declared that she was "sick and tired of being sick and tired" vowed never to give up, "even if they shoot me down." Her resolve nearly cost her her life after a 1963 incident when she defied a "whites only" policy at a bus terminal in the town of Winona, Mississippi. Arrested and charged with disorderly conduct, she was taken to jail, where guards ordered two black male prisoners to beat her or face severe punishment themselves. They complied, and the injuries she received at their hands left her with permanent physical damage.

More determined than ever to resist the system that fostered such brutality, Hamer became involved in politics. In 1964, she co-founded the Mississippi Freedom Democratic Party (MFDP), a group that sought to challenge the right of the so-called "regular" state Democratic Party—an all-white organization dedicated to upholding segregation laws in the South—to represent Mississippians at that summer's Democratic National Convention in Atlantic City, New Jersey. At a credentials committee hearing on August 22, the first day of the convention, an often-tearful Hamer spoke on behalf of the MFDP. Her straightforward yet poignant account of what she had been forced to endure as a result of her activism is reprinted here from Proceedings of the Democratic National Convention: 1964—Credentials Committee, *Democratic National Committee, 1964.*

Mr. Chairman, and the Credentials Committee, my name is Mrs. Fannie Lou Hamer, and I live at 626 East Lafayette Street, Ruleville, Mississippi, Sunflower County, the home of Senator James O. Eastland, and Senator Stennis.

It was the 31st of August in 1962 that eighteen of us traveled twenty-six miles to the county courthouse in Indianola to try to register to try to become first-class citizens.

We was met in Indianola by Mississippi men, Highway Patrolmens, and they only allowed two of us in to take the literacy test at the time. After we had taken this test and started back to Ruleville, we was held up by the City Police and the State Highway Patrolmen and carried back to Indianola where the bus driver was charged that day with driving a bus the wrong color.

After we paid the fine among us, we continued on to Ruleville, and Reverend Jeff Sunny carried me four miles in the rural area where I

Fannie Lou Hamer

had worked as a timekeeper and sharecropper for eighteen years. I was met there by my children, who told me the plantation owner was angry because I had gone down to try to register.

After they told me, my husband came, and said the plantation owner was raising Cain because I had tried to register, and before he quit talking the plantation owner came, and said, "Fannie Lou, do you know—did Pap tell you what I said?"

And I said, "Yes, sir."

He said, "I mean that," he said, "If you don't go down and withdraw your registration, you will have to leave," said, "Then if you go down and withdraw," he said, "You will—you might have to go because we're not ready for that in Mississippi."

And I addressed him and told him and said, "I didn't try to register for you. I tried to register for myself."

I had to leave that same night.

On the 10th of September, 1962, sixteen bullets was fired into the home of Mr. and Mrs. Robert Tucker for me. That same night two girls were shot in Ruleville, Mississippi. Also Mr. Joe McDonald's house was shot in.

And in June, the 9th, 1963, I had attended a voter registration workshop, was returning back to Mississippi. Ten of us was traveling by the Continental Trailway bus. When we got to Winona, Mississippi, which is Montgomery County, four of the people got off to use the washroom, and two of the people—to use the restaurant—two of the people wanted to use the washroom.

The four people that had gone in to use the restaurant was ordered out. During this time I was on the bus. But when I looked through the window and saw they had rushed out I got off of the bus to see what had happened, and one of the ladies said, "It was a State Highway Patrolman and a Chief of Police ordered us out."

I got back on the bus and one of the persons had used the washroom got back on the bus, too.

As soon as I was seated on the bus, I saw when they began to get the four people in a highway patrolman's car, [so] I stepped off of the bus to see what was happening and somebody screamed from the car that the four workers was in and said, "Get that one there," and when I went to get in the car, when the man told me I was under arrest, he kicked me.

I was carried to the county jail, and put in the booking room. They left some of the people in the booking room and began to place us in cells. I was placed in a cell with a young woman called Miss Ivesta Simpson. After I was placed in the cell I began to hear sounds of licks and screams. I could hear the sounds of licks and horrible screams, and I could hear somebody say, "Can you say, 'Yes, sir,' nigger?" Can you say, 'Yes, sir?' "

And they would say other horrible names.

She would say, "Yes, I can say, 'Yes, sir.'"

"So, say it."

She says, "I don't know you well enough."

They beat her, I don't know how long, and after a while she began to pray, and asked God to have mercy on those people.

And it wasn't too long before three white men came to my cell. One of these men was a State Highway Patrolman and he asked me where I was from, and I told him Ruleville, [and] he said, "We are going to check this."

And they left my cell and it wasn't too long before they came back. He said, "You are from Ruleville all right," and he used a curse word, and he said, "We are going to make you wish you was dead."

I was carried out of that cell into another cell where they had two Negro prisoners. The State Highway Patrolmen ordered the first Negro to take the blackjack.

The first Negro prisoner ordered me, by orders from the State Highway Patrolman for me, to lay down on a bunk bed on my face, and I laid on my face.

The first Negro began to beat, and I was beat by the first Negro until he was exhausted, and I was holding my hands behind me at that time on my left side because I suffered from polio when I was six years old.

After the first Negro had beat until he was exhausted the State Highway Patrolman ordered the second Negro to take the blackjack. The second Negro began to beat and I began to work my feet, and the State Highway Patrolman ordered the first Negro who had beat to set on my feet to keep me from working my feet. I began to scream and one white man got up and began to beat me in my head and tell me to hush.

One white man—my dress had worked up high, he walked over and pulled my dress down and he pulled my dress back, back up.

I was in jail when Medgar Evers was murdered.

All of this is on account we want to register, to become first-class citizens, and if the Freedom Democratic Party is not seated now, I question America, is this America, the land of the free and the home of the brave where we have to sleep with our telephones off of the hooks because our lives be threatened daily because we want to live as decent human beings, in America?

Thank you.

Hamer's emotional plea—"Is this America?"—struck a chord with many of the millions who watched news accounts of her testimony on national television that evening. As Mamie E. Locke noted in an essay on Hamer published in Women in the Civil Rights Movement, *"In that one question, Fannie Lou Hamer . . . brought America face to face with itself—its racism, bigotry, intolerance, hatred, and hypocrisy." Despite attempts to reach a compromise, members of the MFDP, the regular Mississippi Democrats, and the national party were unable to agree on who should be allowed to represent the state at the convention. The regular Mississippi Democrats walked out in protest, and the MFDP delegation, led by Hamer, repeatedly tried to take over their empty seats only to be escorted out of the hall. They finally left Atlantic City in frustration after failing to make their case that the regular Mississippi Democrats should not be acknowledged as legitimate representatives of the state party.*

Later that same year, Hamer ran unsuccessfully as an MFDP candidate for the U.S. House of Representatives. In 1965, she challenged the election victories of all five of Mississippi's congressmen, arguing that blacks had been illegally prevented from voting as a result of poll taxes and literacy requirements; after reviewing the evidence, the House administration rejected her claims. Despite these and other setbacks, Hamer and the MFDP kept up the political fight in Mississippi with little help from activists outside the state. At the same time, they had to deal with numerous attempts to discredit them as advocates of race hatred and revolution.

Although the MFDP slowly faded into obscurity, it managed to make a lasting impression on national party politics. And Hamer herself emerged as a role model for other poor blacks who had felt abandoned by the system. Strong and seemingly invincible, she remained a much-loved figure in the civil rights movement and was in demand as a grassroots organizer and as a speaker. On May 7, 1971, for example, she delivered a dynamic address at the NAACP Legal Defense Fund Institute on the role and responsibility of black women in the struggle. Excerpts of her remarks are reprinted here from Black Women in White America: A Documentary History *edited by Gerda Lerner (Pantheon Books, 1972).*

The special plight and the role of black women is not something that just happened three years ago. We've had a special plight for 350 years. My grandmother had it. My grandmother was a slave. She died in 1960. She was 136 years old. She died in Mount Bayou, Mississippi.

It's been a special plight for the black woman. I remember my uncles and some of my aunts—and that's why it really tickled me when you talked about integration. Because I'm very black, but I remember some of my uncles and some of my aunts was as white as anybody in here, and blue-eyed, and some kind of green-eyed—and my grandfather didn't do it, you know. So what the folks is fighting at this point is what they started. They started unloading the slave ships of Africa, that's when they started.

And right now, sometimes, you know I work for the liberation of all people, because when I liberate myself, I'm liberating other people. But you know, sometimes I really feel more sorrier for the white woman than I feel for ourselves because she been caught up in this thing, caught up feeling very special, and folks, I'm going to put it on the line, because my job is not to make people feel comfortable.... [At this point, Hamer was drowned out by applause]. You've been caught up in this thing because, you know, you worked my grandmother, and after that you worked my mother, and then finally you got hold of me. And you really thought, people—you might try and cool it now, but I been watching you, baby. You thought that you was *more* because you was a woman, and especially a white woman, you had this kind of angel feeling that you were untouchable. You know that? There's nothing under the sun that made you believe that you was just like me, that under this white pigment of skin is red blood, just like under this black skin of mine. So we was used as black women over and over and over.

You know, I remember a time when I was working around white people's house, and one thing that would make me mad as hell, after I would be done slaved all day long, this white woman would get on the phone, calling some of her friends, and said, "You know, I'm tired, because *we* have been working," and I said, "That's a damn lie." You're not used to that kind of language, honey, but I'm gone tell you where it's *at*. So all of these things was happening because you *had* more. You had been put on a pedestal, and then not only put on a pedestal, but you had been put in something like a ivory castle. So what happened to you, we have busted the castle open and [are] whacking like hell for the pedestal. And when you hit the ground, you're gone have to fight like hell, like we've been fighting all this time.

"I work for the liberation of all people, because when I liberate myself, I'm liberating other people."

In the past, I don't care how poor this white woman was, in the South she still felt like she was more than us. In the North, I don't care how poor or how rich this white woman has been, she still felt like she was more than us. But coming to the realization of the thing, her freedom is shackled in chains to mine, and she realizes for the first time that she is not free until I am free. The point about it, the male influence in this country—you know the white male, he didn't go and brainwash the black man and the black woman, he brainwashed his wife too. . . . He made her think that she was a angel. You know the reason I can say it, folks, I been watching. And there's a lot of people been watching. That's why it's such a shock wherever we go throughout this country, it's a great blow. White Americans today don't know what in the world to do because when they put us *behind* them, that's where they made their mistake. If they had put us in front, they wouldn't have *let* us look back. But they put us behind them, and we watched every move they made. . . .

And this is the reason I tell the world, as I travel to and fro, I'm not fighting for equal rights. What do I want to be equal to [Senator] Eastland for? Just tell me that. But we are not only going to liberate ourselves. I think it's a

> ***"Whether you have a PhD, DD, or no D, we're in this bag together. And whether you're from Morehouse or Nohouse, we're still in this bag together."***

responsibility. I think we're special people, God's children is going to help in the survival of this country if it's not too late. We're a lot sicker than people realize we are. And what we are doing now in the South, in politics, in gaining seats for black people and concerned whites in the state of Mississippi, is going to have an effect on what happens throughout this country.

You know, I used to think that if I could go North and tell people about the plight of the black folk in the state of Mississippi, everything would be all right. But traveling around, I found one thing for sure: it's up-South and down-South, and it's no different. The man shoot me in the face in Mississippi, and you turn around he'll shoot you in the back here [in New York]. We have a problem, folks, and we want to try to deal with the problem in the only way that we can deal with the problem as far as black women. And you know, I'm not hung up on this about liberating myself from the black man, I'm not going to try that thing. I got a black husband, six feet three, two hundred and forty pounds, with a fourteen shoe, that I don't want to be liberated from. But we are here to work side by side with this black man in trying to bring liberation to all people.

Sunflower County is one of the poorest counties, one of the poorest counties on earth, while Senator James 0. Eastland—you know, people tells you, don't talk politics, but the air you breathe is polluted air, it's political polluted air. The air you breathe is politics. So you have to be involved. You have to be involved in trying to elect people that's going to help do something about the liberation of all people.

Sunflower County, the county where I'm from, is Senator Eastland's county that owns 5,800 acres of some of the richest black fertile soil in Mississippi, and where kids, there in Sunflower County, suffer from malnutrition. But I want to tell you one of the things that we're doing, right now in Sunflower County. In 1969 I founded the Freedom Farm Co-op. We started off with 40 acres of land. Nineteen-seventy in Sunflower County, we fed 1,500 people from this 40 acres of land. Nineteen-seventy I've become involved with YWD —Young World Developers. On the 14th of January 1971, we put $85,400 on 640 acres of land, giving us the total of 680 acres of land. We also have 68 houses. We hope sometime in '71 we will build another hundred houses on a hundred of the 640 acres.

This coming Saturday . . . young people will be walking throughout the world against hunger and poverty. It will be forty countries walking, millions of people throughout the world. In the United States it will be over 377 walks. These walkers are young people that really care about what's going on. . . . And out of this walk—people will pay so much per mile for the kids that'll be walking—and out of this walk we hope to get a million dollars for Sunflower County. . . . If we get the kind of economic support that we need in Sunflower County, in two more years . . . we'll have the tools to produce food ourselves.

A couple of weeks ago, we moved the first poor white family into Freedom Farm in the history of the state of Mississippi. A white man came to me and said, "I got five children and I don't have nowhere to live. I don't have food. I don't have anything. And my children, some of them, is sick." And we gave this man a house. . . .

We have a job as black women, to support whatever is right, and to bring in justice where we've had so much injustice. Some people say, well, I work for $24 per week. That's not true in my case, I work sometimes for $15 per week. I remember my mother working for 25 and 30 cents per day. But we are organizing ourselves now, because we don't have any other choice. Sunflower County is one of the few counties in the state of Mississippi where in that particular area we didn't lose one black teacher. Because . . . I went in and told the judge, I said, "Judge, we're not going to stand by and see you take a man with a master's degree and bring him down to janitor help. So if we don't have the principal . . . there ain't gonna be no school, private or public." These are the kinds of roles.

A few years ago throughout the country the middle-class black woman—I used to say not really black women, but the middle-class colored women, c-u-l-l-u-d, didn't even respect the kind of work that I was doing. But you see now, baby, whether you have a PhD, DD, or no D, we're in this bag together. And whether you're from Morehouse or Nohouse, we're still in this bag together. Not to fight to try to liberate ourselves from the men—this is another trick to get us fighting among ourselves—but to work together with the black man, then we will have a better chance to just act as human beings, and to be treated as human beings in our sick society.

I would like to tell you in closing a story of an old man. This old man was very wise, and he could answer questions that was almost impossible for people to answer. So some people went to him one day, two young people, and said, "We're going to trick this guy today. We're going to catch a bird, and we're going to carry it to this old man. And we're going to ask him, 'This that we hold in our hands today, is it alive or is it dead?' If he says 'Dead,' we're going to turn it loose and let it fly. But if he says, 'Alive,' we're going to crush it." So they walked up to this old man, and they said, "This that we hold in our hands today, is it alive or is it dead?" He looked at the young people and he smiled. And he said, "It's in your hands."

SOURCES

Books

Crawford, Vicki L., Jacqueline Anne Rouse, and Barbara Woods, *Women in the Civil Rights Movement: Trailblazers and Torchbearers, 1941-1965,* Indiana University Press, 1990.

Lerner, Gerda, editor, *Black Women in White America: A Documentary History,* Pantheon Books, 1972.

Mills, Kay, *This Little Light of Mine: The Life of Fannie Lou Hamer,* Dutton, 1993.

Proceedings of the Democratic National Convention: 1964—Credentials Committee, Democratic National Committee, 1964.

Sewell, George A., *Mississippi History Makers,* University Press of Mississippi, 1977.

Williams, Juan, *Eyes on the Prize: America's Civil Rights Years, 1954-1965,* Viking-Penguin, 1987.

Wright, Nathan, Jr., *What Black Politicians Are Saying,* Hawthorn, 1972.

Periodicals

Ebony, "Black Voices of the South," August, 1971, p. 51.

Freedomways, "Life in Mississippi: An Interview with Fannie Lou Hamer," second quarter, spring, 1965, pp. 231-242.

Ms., "The Woman Who Changed the South: A Memory of Fannie Lou Hamer," July, 1977, p. 98.

Nation, "'Tired of Being Sick and Tired,'" June 1, 1964, pp. 548-551.

Michael Haney

1949–

Native American activist of the Seminole and Sioux tribes

Although his activist roots go back to the late 1960s, Michael Haney has only recently begun to garner widespread attention for his efforts on behalf of Native Americans. His confrontational tactics and often unpopular views on issues ranging from the display of Indian remains in museums to the use of Indian names for sports teams have prompted some to regard him as nothing more than a troublemaker. But Haney—who cuts an imposing figure at 6'5" and 240 lbs., with long braided hair and dark sunglasses—insists that such practices denigrate native peoples and trivialize their history. He shrugs off attempts to intimidate him (which have included threats, beatings, and shootings) and makes it clear that he has no intention of withdrawing from the fray. As he once observed in an interview with Chicago Tribune *reporter Wes Smith, "All the scared Indians are dead."*

Haney grew up on a reservation in Seminole County, Oklahoma, of mixed Seminole and Sioux heritage. As a youngster, he experienced very little anti-Indian prejudice and enjoyed friendships with many of the whites he played with as star pitcher on his high school baseball team. After graduation, he briefly attended Oklahoma State University before playing a year of minor-league baseball with a farm club of the San Francisco Giants. Drafted into the U.S. Army in 1968, he spent most of the next two years in Germany.

Haney emerged from his time in the service far more politically aware than he had been back home in Oklahoma. Before long, he became caught up in the spirit of activism then taking hold among many young Native Americans. He began taking part in various protests, including the famous occupation of Alcatraz Island (the site of a former federal prison) in San Francisco Bay, where a group of Indians took up residence from November 1969, until June 1971, to dramatize their opposition to the U.S. government's policies regarding Native Americans. It was there that he rediscovered his own roots and a sense of spirituality that motivated him to dedicate his life to fighting for change.

Soon after, Haney joined the fledgling American Indian Movement (AIM) and was eventually named state coordinator for Oklahoma, which at the time made him one of AIM's youngest leaders. He participated in most of the group's major *demonstrations during the 1970s, including the Trail of Broken Treaties march and subsequent takeover of the Bureau of Indian Affairs offices in Washington, D.C. (1972), the siege at Wounded Knee (1973), and the Longest Walk (1978). His reputation was that of a "warrior," a defiant, hot-tempered, and impatient young man who was quick to question and criticize his elders.*

Nowadays, a somewhat mellower Haney directs his energies toward activities that he feels will make a difference in the lives of his children and grandchildren. He is convinced that many of the problems Native Americans face—such as high rates of alcoholism, unemployment, and suicide—can be attributed to the fact that white society still looks at Indians as mere "museum pieces" who are not quite human. This in turn leads to low self-esteem among young Indians in particular, he insists, and it is that sense of worthlessness that he has vowed to combat.

To that end, Haney has fought against those seeking to establish landfills or dispose of hazardous materials on tribal property. He has also challenged non-Indian artists who try to sell their works as "authentic" Native American creations. In addition, he has crusaded on behalf of Indian religious freedom, especially regarding the use of peyote in traditional rituals.

But among his most-publicized battles are those that have centered around the treatment of Indian remains and artifacts. To Haney, digging up and displaying the bones and sacred objects of his ancestors is not only a physical violation of their graves but a spiritual one as well. In an effort to educate as many people as possible about the Indian point of view on what is termed "repatriation," or restoring items to their place of origin, he has traveled across the United States lecturing to a wide range of groups. He has also vigorously challenged scientists and museum officials (including ones at the Smithsonian in Washington, D.C.) to take a closer look at their practices and surrender pieces in their collections that are important to Native Americans.

Haney addressed these and other issues in testimony he delivered on March 30, 1991, before the United Nations Subcommission on the Prevention of Discrimination Against Minorities. His appearance at the special session (held at the American Indian Community House in New York City) was on behalf of the International Indian Treaty Council, which monitors the status of various agreements between Indian nations and government bodies. The following was transcribed from an audiotape provided by Haney.

I want to thank the International Indian Treaty Council for all the work that they have done since their founding. I was at part of the founding conference in 1974 in Mobridge, South Dakota, and it has come a long way. It's certainly a credit to the perseverance of the people that have been involved in this organization [that they have gotten] a consultive status to the United Nations.

We've learned throughout the history of our peoples that we *belong* in that international community. That treaties that were entered into with our governments and the United States were ratified by the Senate [and] signed into law by the president of the United States, just as treaties with NATO and treaties with the Soviet Union and treaties with Panama and other countries that are still valid and in full force and effect. It's no secret that the United States, in our opinion, has reneged on many of the provisions that were stipulated in those agreements.

I would like to point out the conspicuous absence of Dr. Miguel Alfonso Martínez and hope that he is able to join [us at] the other hearing sites as soon as possible. I also want to thank Robert Cruz, the director of the International Indian Treaty Council, for being here. He came a long way—from Scottsdale, Arizona—to be here.

As Robert said, I am a Seminole, born in Oklahoma. However, my mother's a Sioux woman, a Santee Sioux from the Niobara area, Nebraska. And I'm an Alligator Clan. We have a clan system there [that] we still recognize and work within. It's a system that our society has been based on for tens of thousands of years. It's in this role as an Alligator Clan member that I'm chairman of the repatriation committee for these twenty-six tribes and nations in Oklahoma.

Today there are approximately thirty-nine federally recognized tribes in Oklahoma. Almost three hundred thousand Indians are in Oklahoma, all the way from the Seneca, Cayuga, Delaware, Wyandotte, Ottawa, Comanche, Kiowa, Apache, [and] Seminole. We even have an Aztec reservation there.

It seems like almost every tribe that warred against the United States ended up in Oklahoma, like one big huge concentration camp. And at one point, it was called Indian Territory, up until 1906. . . . It was meant and destined to be the Indian state, a part of the union of the United States. But then they discovered salt, something very needed during that period [as a] preservative. Shortly after that, they discovered oil. And as the Kuwaitis have found out, white people are very thirsty for oil. And we suffered.

Our people were removed during the 1830s, in spite of the treaties. [In] 1832, the U.S. Supreme Court, in referring to treaties made with native governments, describes them as "dependent, domestic nations." In a suit that the state of Georgia attempted in order to pass laws over the Cherokee nations, the Supreme Court says they are equal and on par with the state. And these treaties are equal and on par to the Constitution. . . . That theory has been of help continually in Supreme Court decisions. Most recently, a Potawatomi decision was issued a month ago dealing with sovereign immunity and jurisdiction and [the] ability to levy taxes, collect money to provide services to citizens.

In Oklahoma, when Congress passed an alien act that allowed Oklahoma to become a state in 1906, they created a congress similar to the Continental Congress—the founding papers [of which], along with the Iroquois Confederacy's great law of peace, the U.S. Constitution is loosely based on. Our people were protected by the Supreme Court under the Supreme Court ruling. Of course, the famous quote by then-President Andrew Jackson was that "Justice Marshall has made his decision—now let him enforce it." [Jackson] promptly ordered the military to remove all Indians east of the Mississippi, which included the tribe I belonged to (Seminole), Creek, Cherokee, Choctaw, Chickasaw. We ended up in Oklahoma. At one time, all of Oklahoma belonged to [these] five tribes. They called us the "Five Civilized Tribes" because we were, I think, easier to steal from than some of our western brothers and cousins.

We walked to Oklahoma. It was called the Trail of Tears. We lost approximately one-third of our people along the way. The old, the very young perished. And when we got to Oklahoma, we settled in new land there. Some of it was very harsh. Remember those Woody Guthrie songs about the dustbowl days there in Oklahoma? That's where we were sent to. Can you imagine being sent from Florida, where there's a tropical setting? We were hunters and gatherers—didn't know how to plant. A lot of our Creek brothers were planters. But we survived. Still surviving today.

"Almost every tribe that warred against the United States ended up in Oklahoma, like one big huge concentration camp."

I'm very proud of that. [It's] very hard to be an Indian. [I'm] very proud of my ancestors for keeping our religion together. We have what we call Stomp Dances. A mother fire was brought, at great hardship, all the way from the southeast. It was really coveted, what we called the Mother Ground. Our medicine people carried that all the way to Oklahoma. And then from this we had what we call a *tookabatchee* ground, a Mother Ground. And then our different tribes—the Cayuga, the Hitchiti, the Miccosukee, the Alabama, the Koasati—those people took from that a coal and took it back to their grounds and made a fire. And then the camps from those grounds made their fire. So we kept that continual touch with that very important fire.

Then it was outlawed—our stick ball games, our fires. They said, "You're heathens 'cause you dance around a fire all night [and] you sing."

Well, we reminded them that the message of the Creator came to these white people through a burning bush, to their Moses. You came here seeking religious freedom and tolerance. Then you outlaw *ours!* It wasn't until 1970—*1970,* a brief twenty years ago!—that my people were allowed to fully elect our leaders (they were appointed before) and exercise our religious rights, traditional customs. This is why we need help from other sovereign governments, from other indigenous peoples across the world because we feel and we know that we're not alone in this political and religious oppression, and that today, our peoples have survived.

Next year the white people are going to celebrate five hundred years of being here since Columbus. [We've been] asked to take part in that. There's a lot of money for Indians to take to do powwow's, do art shows, to participate in this celebration. Well, we really thought about that. How can we do this? We like to have powwows and we're going to have them whether [they're in] conjunction [with Columbus Day ceremonies] or not. We're going to have them. So we finally decided that we would honor our ancestors by celebrating five hundred years of survival [under] colonialism.

Do you remember when those hostages were in Iran under that student group in the American embassy? We have a brother name John Thomas from the International Indian Treaty Council. He was sitting in one of the student's offices waiting to meet with some of them because we had one Indian in there. He was a quarter Kiowa, a man named Richard Kupke. He wanted help! So John Thomas, representing the Treaty Council, went there. (They trusted the Indians, those students.) He was sitting there, so he looked on the wall and there was a picture of Chief Gall. Have you ever seen that picture . . . ? It's wild! . . . That was a real odd place to find a poster like that, [under those] circumstances. So he asked them about it. "How come you've got a picture like that?" And they said, "American Indians are the symbol of resistance for us, because you exist in the belly of the beast, so to speak—right in the heart of Western civilization, right in the heart of colonial tyranny. And today, you still exist. You still speak your languages. You still enjoy and practice your customs and traditions. You give us hope [with] what you're doing."

I'm really proud. I'm really proud of our ancestors, and I'm proud of Robert and others that are here today and others that are out standing up for sovereign rights and standing up for their freedoms and standing up for the right to practice those older ways [and] provide alternatives for their children.

We are told by our elders that it is very important for us to pass on these things to our children. Our elders tell us that we are in danger of becoming the link that is broken between tens of thousands of years of instructions. That's how important *our* responsibility is. That's how important *our* role is. I don't want to be that generation, that link, that breaks the continuity between the original instructions that were given to our ancestors and our children. [We] have to continue [to] provide a basis for their spiritual foundation, something they can embrace and come home to.

I tell [that to] these Christians that want so much to save our souls, with good intentions. Often they're the largest landowners amongst our reservations and communities. In earlier times, the 1860s, they passed what they called the Comitty Act [under] which every tribe was assigned one religion. "The Jesuits, you can have the Mohawks. The Episcopalians, you can have the Oglalas over there. You Baptists, you can have the Creeks." There were holy wars back then over our souls. Of course, there were other wars over our lands and mineral rights, too, and timber and all that. This is what our ancestors faced and these are the conditions they lived under. What's so surprising [is] that we exist in such strength today. Because it wasn't meant [to be] so.

I tell [the Christians], if you want to look to help us when we're standing up in Oka [a Mohawk reservation in Canada] up there, when we're standing up for Dave Sohappy over here [in the] fishing rights struggle—*there's* where we need your help. We don't really suffer from a lack of religion, because it's been our religion that's kept us intact all these years. So don't look toward our spiritual needs, look toward our physical needs. I want to see you right alongside of me with your Bible—*that's* where we can use help.

It's really hard for me to understand missionary people. We didn't have—Cheyennes didn't go over to the Crows and try to convert them. Just like the beaver didn't go over to the coyote to try to convert him to be the beaver religion, either. This is how outrageous it seemed to us and still does. That's why it's important.

I want to focus in on what my role is with the tribes in Oklahoma [where] religious freedoms [continue to be] under attack. . . . In 1978, they passed the American Indian Religious Freedom Act. [It] sounded really good, but it didn't have much teeth in it. It doesn't protect the ancestral homelands. It doesn't protect the burial sites. I'll give you an idea of how important it is for this to take place.

In Nashville, Tennessee, today—as we speak—there is a landfill that's going to be [established] on top of five thousand Cherokee graves or mounds, right along the Cumberland River. . . . It makes a loop, there's a little peninsula around there, and those are mounds.

Our ancestors used these rivers as interstates. Those were our first highways, these waterways. And we traveled up and down and visited one another, traded. These dentalium shells that you see on these northern [plains] dresses? We found those in the tar pits down in Florida. There's only one way that you could have gotten those, and that's by physically, intentionally trading. All that comes from one spot, and that's the Pacific Northwest. They found gorgets like this and these crescent-shaped ones there, too.

Michael Haney

My people traded—the Seminole people—we navigated the Gulf, we went down in the Yucatán Peninsula, we went to Colombia. But you don't hear about that. White people don't tell you about that in your history books. Even some of our Indians don't learn that because they go to a public school, and that's where they get the basics of their education. (There is a gap we need, of course, to address ourselves—to control our schools, our educational systems.) But they were great navigators and travelers.

My people are Seminole. The beautiful vests and the patchwork that you see, only Seminoles have this. Have you ever seen the patchwork done [by] those people from Ecuador or Colombia [with] those birds and so forth? That's where we got this design, from them. We traded with them. You know what we gave them in return? Feathers. We had beautiful feathers down in the Florida Everglades. We traded for metals with the Aztec people, Montezuma's people. We traded for metals because [they're] not indigenous to our area. So we got tin and gold and silver from the Aztec people. We navigated the Gulf to come up around to what's New Orleans, to the Mississippi, and then down to Texas and down that way. We navigated that, but you don't learn about [it].

I went up to the Long House [on the Onondaga Reservation] one time and danced in their social dances—shake the bush, where you kind of dance backwards, and that one bean dance where you kind of dance with the girl. (I kind of like those!) But they did one kind of alligator dance, and that kind of got me. I said, "Alligator dance? Where do you guys get alligators at up here? The only ones I know of around here are in the sewers of New York City, and I know you're not going to be singing about *those!*" They've got a tiger dance, too. That's because we traded, we traveled.

Our ancestor Tecumseh, that Shawnee chief, [whom] I consider one of the very first AIM people, [tried] to unite all the tribes up and down the Ohio River. [He came] down to Creek country. We listened to him, too. We formed what we called the Red Sticks, or the Miccosukees. We warred against the United States.

When someone passed away, or we wanted to winter or summer along some beautiful valley, we dug mounds—burials—one on top of the other. Now those mounds belong to white people. Now the lands that those mounds are on are individual property in most cases. And they sell them—if you saw that film earlier, and I hope we get to see it later again—as grave robbers. "Artifact hunters," they call them. We buried pots with [the dead], drinking vessels, vessels with food in them, for [their] journey. It's our belief and understanding, as it is of Christian people, that the spirit is immortal, never dying. That when they leave this world, they continue on with what they call a spirit journey. [If] you interrupt their final resting places it interrupts them [and] causes a big friction.

I tell this to archaeologists: "You're getting yourself in trouble, you know. Spirits—they'll get you one of these days! Sooner or later, you're gonna join them, too, and you're gonna have a lot to answer for. A lot to answer for. I'm not trying to frighten you, but those are the things that you can consider before you excavate a mound or unearth a remain just to study. If you want to study, you want to learn about us, ask us! We'll be *really* glad to tell you."

I'm really happy to share the teachings of my people with non-Indians, because I think that we have a lot to talk about. I know a lot about white people—speak your language, been to your colleges, schools, churches. I should have a doctorate of Caucasian studies, [I] know so much about them. But you know very little about my people. Very, very little. I've seen people go spend a couple of years hanging around the res, and the next time you see them they've got a PhD after their name and [a] dissertation about two inches thick sitting around. [But] they know very little about us.

And that's a shame. Because the people that you should learn from are our elders, like Fools Crow, like Henry Crow Dog, Mad Bear Anderson. These people are a wealth of knowledge, and they're passing away. *There's* where you "archs" [archaeologists] ought to go. You sociologists and anthropologists and archaeologists and all you "ologists" ought to go talk to these people. Because when they pass away, they take a whole wealth of knowledge with them, never to be brought again on the face of this earth. Lost forever. It's been said that when one of these elders passes away, it's like a whole library burning completely down to the ground. Gone! And they're passing away at a real rapid rate.

It's important to get to them. Not only you lose, but we lose. It's important that we, too, as young men and women—Indian men and women—we have the responsibility to go to them and learn, too.... So if you want to learn about our ancient Cherokees, go talk to Cherokees. They'll be glad to talk with you about it.

From the burials that I have seen, they buried the people very much like we do today. Our people, we build a little house over the graves. And instead of putting it in the earth with them, we put it outside now. I guess it makes it so [that] you won't disturb the body when you come to steal the artifacts. They must have seen it coming. We give them this and maybe their favorite tool to work with, whether it's a scraper or an axe or something. These are what these pot-hunters are looking for.

Last year, at the Opryland Hotel in Nashville, Tennessee, they had an artifacts show. We came and stopped it. We started taking pictures of their license plates and taking pictures of those people.... [They were] trying to hide. But one of those pots ... went for sixty thousand dollars.

That Slack farm site you saw there, it looked like a bombing range where they had in excess of four hundred and sixty holes in the earth. They rented that site from a farmer. Ten of them paid fifteen hundred dollars each—fifteen thousand dollars they gave to him for two months to excavate it. You saw what they did. They rented a backhoe and just started throwing them up when they saw pots. They threw bones everywhere. They got a big three-inch hose, ran it down to the river [with] a pump, and they just started squirting all that. Bones are sticking out, skulls, everything. But they find a pot—one pot—and they've got all their money back plus some. They got literally hundreds of artifacts. So we need protection from [them].

The state feels that it's their property—"finder's keepers," regardless of who they belong to. The individual landowners are saying, "I bought it, it's mine, and no one's going to tell me how to live or what to do with it."

Our arguments to protect our ancestors were really falling on deaf ears. So we went to the U.S. Congress and lobbied a bill through last year. It's called Public Law 101-601, the Native American Grave Protection and Repatriation Act. We were [trying] to provide protection for burial sites and for remains that are in museums and in vaults across the nation, whether [at] the Smithsonian Museum or the Heye Center right here in Manhattan—they have a huge collection of remains and bones and sacred objects. We want those back. We want them back. We want them back out of those plastic bags and out of those paper sacks and out of those wooden boxes and out of those steel boxes. We want them back into the earth.

We feel—and we've been told—that we, as men and women (particularly men) have a responsibility to protect the defenseless, the youth and elders and those that have passed on before us. A lot of things we attempt to do today are unsuccessful because we ignore and we're not addressing our responsibility to our ancestors. [We must] get those ancestors out of the display cases, out of those vaults, and back into the ground so that they can continue that natural process of decomposing, becoming one with the earth, so that their bodies can provide nutrients for new life. Animals come by and eat that grass, and the whole cycle of life continues. That's why you see us wear things in a circle—to recognize the sacred hoop, the cycle of life. And when it's interrupted by these things being coated or being stuffed or formaldehyded in museums and in medical schools, particularly when they butcher them up by cutting them up for what they call scrapings or marrow testing, it's a desecration to us. It's not educational opportunities. It's not medical science. We're not finding a cure for cancer by digging up twelve-hundred-year-old remains of our ancestors.

I challenge those archaeologists to show me *one* study—*one!*—where you have benefitted nationally, medically, scientifically, or educationally from excavating the remains or the burials of my ancestors. They never have. They come up with, "Well, we found that you guys ate a lot of corn and you had arthritis." Well, we still eat corn. And we die from arthritis at about the same age these days, with the Indian Health Service and their budget. So very little has changed.

What we need is help from the United Nations to get the remains from other countries, too. It was really fashionable in the 1700s and 1800s to take Indians back to Europe, to have Indian skulls as ash trays, to have Indian artifacts in the castles in Europe and England.... It was a fad. Well, we think that's a very morbid fad, and we think that it's important to our spiritual health that these things be returned to us, that they be reburied so that they can continue that spirit journey. One of my jobs is to do whatever is necessary to get those remains back, whether it's speaking at forums, introducing legislation (state or national), or confronting state officials or archaeologists. I've been working with Robert a couple of times, very successfully, doing just that. But it's a long way to go.

Robert was with me in 1988 [when] we addressed the Society for American Archaeology. In [its] fifty-eight-year existence, [that was] the first time they'd ever heard from Indians. Can you imagine that? Here's a whole community of scientists. Their sole goal in life is to dig up the remains of my people—Indians—here in the United States, and they've never heard from the Indians!

They were really shocked when we appeared. I had on my name tag, "Michael Haney, Living Artifact." They were scared.... They all had beards and [were] dressed in khakis, and they had that Indiana Jones syndrome.... When we walked through there, it was like parting the Red Sea, like [in the movie] *The Ten Commandments*. Boy, they got out of our way! They were afraid to touch us. They were afraid of the Indians! You know [the saying] "the only good Indian is a dead Indian"? Well, they've got a saying that "the only good Indian is an unburied one." Tom Emerson [an archaeologist] from the historical society in Illinois said that. And they believe that! They compare repatriating remains and artifacts to book burning. They call us "anti-intellectual." [I told them,] "We'll see who's dumb [and] who's intellectual when you meet the Creator and you have to answer for all these desecrations that you've done. It'll make you sick."

I'm an Alligator Clan, and like I said earlier, we handle the burials for our people. We dig the grave, but when we do so, we protect ourselves. We sing songs. We take sweat. We have a medicine that we wash off us when we get finished because we're told that dealing with that earth, especially this time of year—spring—life comes from the earth, a very powerful thing. When we plant, as when we dig a grave, we open the earth, the fresh earth. We have to wash off because that earth will draw power from you. It'll make you weak. Sometimes it'll give you a leg cramp or something like that, or it'll make you a little restless. Or maybe [you'll] gripe at your wife or something....

I keep telling [the archaeologists] that. Compare it to handling uranium. It wasn't that long ago they had these Pueblo people digging in uranium mines with no clothing on. Then they found out there's radioactivity there. Of course, it was too late for those Laguna people. They've got a high rate of infant mortality and a high rate of birth defects and a high rate of cancer in that area disproportionate to others that didn't come in contact with that mining. We tell [the archaeologists], this is what you should treat remains like—like it's uranium. Because it'll get you. [They] may be unseen, those spiritual forces, but they're there.

And this is what we do. Our people, we wash off and we pray. But you guys don't do that. And at that Slack farm site that you saw earlier, I was there and I saw some archaeologists in those graves, and they were sitting there with their feet dangling off the edge like kids do. They were drinking a can of beer and they had their lunch over here, just some food, and it was sitting on those graves! I saw that and I told this guy, Chico Dulak, to go in there and run them out of there. They ran them out and, of course, *we* got charged with obstructing justice. And I said, "Well, they were drinking beer in there!" And they said, "Well, it was after hours, you know—after five o'clock."

Desecration is desecration. I don't care if you do it in the name of science or education or in the name of curiosity. But for the most part, it's money. Most of these people who are guilty of looting these graves are artifact hunters, are grave robbers and looters. They call themselves "amateur archaeologists" or "para-archaeologists." But that's just a cover-up for grave robbers.

There's so much money that is paid on the black market for those artifacts that they become reckless. They'll go in the middle of the night, and they'll get these miner's hats, and they'll come along in boats to those mounds and dig them up, find something, take off, and sell it the next day. And they're not prosecuted. You never hear of anyone being prosecuted for desecrating a grave.

"Desecration is desecration. I don't care if you do it in the name of science or education or in the name of curiosity."

We're particularly concerned about that one in Lewistown, Illinois, called the Dixon Mounds Museum. It's the only major museum in the United States today that displays human skeletal remains. They display two hundred thirty-seven American Indian remains there.

If you'll look [at] the aerial view of it, you'll see what they did is excavate into a mound, into a burial pit, and then they built a museum on top of it. Well, from an aerial view you'll see that that's the temple around there, and there's a plaza. At one time, that area—along with Cahokia Mounds, south around St. Louis—was the third-largest city in the world. Nine hundred years ago, around a hundred thousand people lived there. We had temples, we had plazas, we had corn fields, we had wheat fields—a very high level of civilization existed there. These were when Europeans were living in caves, hanging around trees and stuff. Our people were going through a copper period. The copper period of the Mayan people lasted longer than the entire Roman Empire.

Our civilization has a *lot* to offer here. Eighty percent of the foods that are used today are indigenous to the western hemisphere. The marketable cotton comes from here. The beans, the squashes, even "Irish" potatoes came from here. Where would the Russians be without their vodka? It came from here.

The United States is now embarking on a restructuring. Did you know that? They're trying to reorganize the BIA. We call it "Boss Indians Around." They call it the Bureau of Indian Affairs. It was first created in the 1700s, and it was in the department of the Army. That was shortly after the surgeon general issued a letter saying that he wanted to find out why Indians blindly followed or were so loyal to their leaders. Archaeology being a new science, they thought it was because they had large brains. So to study that, the Army ordered that all Indian leaders would be decapitated [if it could be learned] where they were buried. (I hope none were killed just for the science, but I suspect this could have happened.) They were decapitated and all their heads sent to Washington. That's true. We found that memo, and we confronted the Smithsonian Institution with this irrefutable, overwhelming evidence. They finally admitted that they did have a collection of heads from that period [of] Native American people. They were studying the cranium, measuring from ear to ear and from here to here, because they thought they had huge brains. What they didn't realize, it was the heart that was important. It was the love for their people that was important. That's immeasurable by their standards. They still get to measure that.

The Bureau underwent two major reformations. One in 1928, called the Meriam Report, and another one in 1975, called the American Indian Policy Review Commission. It was chaired by the senator from South Dakota at that time, James Abourezk. Last year, the BIA snuck in their appropriations a clause that would have [allowed] them to reorganize without consulting the tribes. One of the tribal organizations—the National Congress of American Indians—caught it, called it to the attention of the chairman of the Senate Select Committee on Indian Affairs, Daniel Inouye (the Democrat from Hawaii, a very powerful senator these days), and they got it stopped with the clause that they would consult with the tribes.

I'd like to submit to this body [an outline of] the structure of the BIA. I didn't know that they *had* a structure! The people are down here. That's the white people up here. Here's us, down here. I'd like to submit that as evidence to Robert. Also, the tribes have come up with what they call a laundry list of issues they would like to see addressed and kept in this BIA relationship. And here is this year's allocation for the Bureau of Indian Affairs.

Of course, they spent in one day the entire BIA budget during this Mideast crisis [the Persian Gulf War]. I thought it was pretty odd that they would send and spend thousands of troops, billions of dollars, all the way to the Mideast to protect the sovereignty of the Kuwaiti government. Sovereignty!—when they trample on the sovereignty every day of the American Indians here in the United States. They don't have to go far to find sovereign abuses.

We only wish that they would spend some of their attention here addressing the needs of the American Indians, the first Americans. Five hundred years is a long time to conduct an undeclared war. And we feel that that's exactly what has happened. We've had an undeclared war for five hundred years against our people. We think that it's time to stop. We think it's time they left us alone. That instead of self-administration, we should [have] self-determination. That the Bureau of Indian Affairs should be streamlined to the point that all they do is just transfer money to us. Today, eighty-five percent of every dollar is eaten up in administration costs. Only fifteen cents gets to the people. That's outrageous! White people wouldn't allow it, but it's okay for us because we employ a lot of white people in the BIA. Most of the people [who] get kicked out of the Defense Department or get washed out of the Department of Education all come to the BIA to retire. That's okay. These Indians—they're used to being trampled on. It's not going to reduce health care, it's not going to reduce educational opportunities for them because they're at a low. [There's] no place up but up for us, anyway. So they're after a major revision. We're concerned about that.

I want to give Robert one example. The University of Tennessee at Knoxville recently sent me a fax from the Department of Conservation. They said that they have 5,043 human skeletal remains. We *did* pass a law last year that caught these people by surprise. They didn't think we could do it, but we lobbied for it. We got a lot of church groups and a lot of people that were helpful, and we passed a law in Tennessee that said that no human skeletal remains will cross the state line unless they're going to be buried.

So we caught them. They were loaning our remains out to Oxford University! "I'll trade you a few Indians for some Africans. I'll trade you a few Indians for some people from Tibet or from Asia." They trade them like you do baseball trading cards! To me, that's very sacrilegious, and it's very disheartening to us. We want that to cease. We also want those five thousand-plus remains from the University of Tennessee. Now we're going to have to sue them to get [them] back.

I have a letter from the Cheyenne Sand Creek descendants [in] Oklahoma. You know, along with Wounded Knee, [there was] another large massacre called Sand Creek. [I think] it was highlighted in that movie called *Little Big Man*. Well, those descendants now live in Oklahoma. The Army went and dug up all those people that they murdered there and put them in a museum. These people want them back. I have a [letter], signed by the chairman, asking your assistance in getting their remains back. They want them back. They want to put them back in the earth.

I would also like to comment on a couple of pieces of legislation now in the draft stages with several organizations. [In] this new legislation we're going to introduce this year, we're trying to address sacred sites. Last year, we had to compromise in the final stages of the 101st session [of Congress] by [keeping] private lands exempt. We had to do this. The farm lobby just said that they were going to kill it, other groups said that they'd kill it. We had to drop private land, so the bill—the Great Protection Act, or Public Law 601—only covers public land and tribal, federal land. This bill that we're introducing April 15 is going to address sacred sites. So when we find burial mounds and village sites on public *or* private property, this is a mechanism that we can [use to] declare them sacred, and we can go in and take care of them. Now we realize there are times when we are going to have to excavate them, because if we leave them there the looters will be there anyway. So we want to set up a national, federal cemetery for Indians that are indigent or Indians that are like this that need a final resting place.

The second part of this [legislation]—there are four parts to it—the second part is dealing with peyote. Last year, they called the Smith decision, *Oregon v. Smith*. Basically, what it said was that the states can regulate the criminal code on the possession of this sacrament by American Indians—that we're not covered under the First Amendment of religious freedom, that states can pass laws to include Indians as criminals.

We feel that what caused this is a couple of groups called the Peyote Way Church. Back in the '60s, some of these—what do you call them? Hippies? We had a little hope for them because they sounded like Hopis a little bit. They called themselves hippies and said, "Oh, we *like* you, Indians," and they had beads all over the place. And then they asked us for peyote. Well, they started their own church and said that Indians have a special privilege because they're Indians. And that's discriminatory, [the hippies said,] because they have a right that's not afforded all Americans. And they sued. A lot of these suits reached the federal courts, of course, as they were preempted by state decisions. And now the Oregon case came, where the Smith decision is still a precedent. We need that sacrament protected. We're writing legislation now that would exempt American Indians from criminal prosecution for just the mere possession [of certain items,] including the ceremonial fans like eagle feathers and hawk and scissor tail—those are considered migratory birds [and are therefore protected].

They tried this in Oklahoma about ten years ago. They came in and they busted up ceremonies. They came into the tepees and confiscated fans [and] eagle feathers, [and] they arrested ten people. They prosecuted them for violation of the migratory bird act when, actually, these were fans that were used in ceremonies. They went after the very heart of the religion and arrested some medicine people as well.

Thirdly, [our proposed legislation] deals with political prisoners. Almost every Indian family in North America is affected in one way or another, either directly or indirectly, by the policies of state and federal prisons. We have friends or relatives or acquaintances or people we used to go to school with, go to church with, or dance with, or pray with [who at] one time or another are incarcerated. If you're a Methodist or Protestant or Presbyterian or Catholic, you can readily have access to ministers and clergymen, priests. But if you're a traditional American Indian, they say, "We're not gonna let those heathens in here. We're not gonna be building any sweat lodge over here. We're *certainly* not gonna hold a Sun Dance in here."

But our people really *need* the counseling. It's a very tough time for an Indian. It's like caging up a wild animal—this is how our people feel [behind] those bars, in those cages. They need all the strength that they can possibly derive from their own being. They need access to these spiritual people so they can pray with them, ask for help from the Creator during this real hardship time in their life. Federal law needs to provide the national standard for all the states to look at, sort of a backdrop. Because in Oklahoma, there's three hundred thousand of us. We still make up thirty-six percent of the prison population [even though] we make up around five percent of the total population in Oklahoma. And we're *not* all criminals. It's the judicial system—we can't afford it. We can't afford lawyers. Often, we can't afford bail bondsmen. I know of a couple of instances where people were exonerated, but they still spent six months in prison or in county jail waiting for their case to come up, depending on the public [defender who] was like Monty Hall—"let's make a deal" all the time. So they need help, and this piece of legislation that we're introducing will do that.

The fourth provision [of our legislation] is a legal cause of action, a vehicle for [gaining] access to the federal courts to provide remedies for these issues.

I realize that the United Nations is a very important body and that there are a lot of human rights violations all over the world and that addressing this is certainly a full-time job. But since this is the first time that they've ever come to the United States—and I know this man will come, this Dr. Martínez, because in five hundred years, this is the first time you've addressed *our* human rights. In an era when this country is looking toward economic development, I think they ought to pay some attention to human development as well. I think they ought to pay attention to the rights of minority people. I think they ought to realize that we all pray to the same holy being, whether we call him Jehovah, Hezaketameze, Wakantanka.... They're all the same. And that we're going to have a lot—I know *I'm* going to have a lot to talk about when *I* get up there! So I don't want anyone messing with my bones down here while I'm up there talking about my case, pleading my case! So I really want some protection for these final resting places.

If the United States can be embarrassed into seriously addressing the concerns of the Native American people, I hope that this hearing, and others like it, will be the beginning of that effort. If President Bush is very serious about sovereignty—and he points to human rights violations of the Soviet Union, the sovereignty of the country of Georgia, the sovereignty of the Balkan areas, the sovereignty of the Soviet nations within them, the sovereignty of the Kurdish people that are locked in war as we speak with the Iraqi people—then he, too, should be concerned about the sovereignty of American Indian nations and governments here in the United States. It's very hard to take him seriously, very hard to read his lips, when he's talking out of both sides of his mouth at the same time.

Our people want very much to co-exist with all other peoples. The four colors is not just a color scheme that we enjoy looking at. The four colors signifies all of mankind that we've always known existed. The hoop of life is something that we recognized when we were first put on this earth. Our people never felt that the world was flat. Next year, when they celebrate five hundred years of finding that lost Italian on our shores, they [should] remember this—they pay tribute to this navigator that was half a world off. You know, that's the most you can be, a half a world off. But there are going to be all sorts of celebrations. And I'd like for some of these energies to be focused on the right of self-determination, the right to protect our religious freedoms and to exercise our traditional ways of worshipping and paying tribute to the Creator and to all those living things. This is important for us, as American Indian people, for our future, for the future of our children, and for the future of our nations.

I'd like to close by expressing my gratitude to the American Indian Community House for providing the facilities here for this hearing and to commend the International Indian Treaty Council for the years of perseverance. I know it's really hard to talk about sovereign rights and international agreements when you've got an overwhelming phone bill to pay and you've got to decide, do I go to this conference or do I pay the rent? We shouldn't have to be faced with those kinds of decisions. But they've made them, and they still are existing and continuing to do the work their elders say *has* to be done in order for us to survive. And I want to thank them for that on behalf of all the tribes in Oklahoma.

I go to a lot of ceremonies back home. Often, I'm in those ceremonies and I hear these elders pray. They'll pray, "I've got a niece in Oklahoma City, got a nephew in Los Angeles, Chicago, New York. Be with them, Creator, because it's so very hard, it's hard to be Indian there. Be with them because they're exposed to a lot of detrimental things. Help them to make the right choice."

I want you to know, you that are here, the Treaty Council and those of the officials of this community house, before I left we had a peyote meeting, the Black Legging Society of the Kiowa nation, a warrior society. They prayed for you.

> ***"In an era when this country is looking toward economic development, I think they ought to pay some attention to human development as well."***

They prayed for the success of this hearing. I want you to know that sometimes when you're faced with these hardships—maybe it's [having] to scramble to pay the rent, pay that phone bill, [or someone saying], "I don't want to hear about another Indian program, I don't want to hear about another Indian project"—that these people are praying for you, are grateful. They're grateful for those organizations that are in Tennessee and Georgia and places that we came from, Chicago, Los Angeles, Seattle, Milwaukee, Twin Cities. Wherever they're protecting sovereignty, these people are praying for me. I want you to know that you're not alone in this.

We've always found strength through unity, strength through spirituality. And this spirituality, this camaraderie that we have amongst all of our Indian people is the strength that has kept us going for all these years, and it's the very thing that's going to keep us going for our future. If there's anything that we can do from Oklahoma, we'd be glad to do that. I extend an invitation for you to come. Let me know when you come. We're very proud. Tonight, in Oklahoma, there are at least three or four powwows. Every weekend—they've got so many tribes, Indian clubs. I'll be glad to take you there. Or come to our Stomp Dances. I'd like to dance with you and pray. I'm very proud of the ways of our people and how they've existed throughout these times.

And with that, I want to end the testimony. . . . Thank you very much.

More recently, Haney has spoken out forcefully against the use of Indian names for sports teams. As in the case of the reburial issue, he maintains that it comes down to a matter of respect. No one, he says, would think of naming a team the "New York Negroes" or the "Chicago Caucasians," yet names like the Cleveland Indians, Atlanta Braves, and Washington Redskins are deemed perfectly acceptable. Furthermore, observes Haney, the cartoonish mascot figures (which may be plastered on souvenirs as humble as toilet paper and underwear), along with stadium cheers and dance routines that feature "Indian" war whoops, tomahawk chops, feathered costumes and so on perpetuate old, racist stereotypes "that tend to keep our people locked in the past."

To address these concerns, Haney founded a protest organization, the National Coalition Against Racism in Sports and Media. It has demonstrated at a number of major events, including the 1992 Super Bowl in Minneapolis between the Buffalo Bills and the Washington Redskins. The group has also sued or threatened to sue several teams to force them to drop their traditional names. While he has yet to persuade any professional teams to see things his way, Haney has enjoyed some success at the college and university level. Despite the uphill climb, it is not a fight he has any intention of abandoning. "We [Indians] have a hard enough time without promoting racism with mascots," he told Wes Smith of the Chicago Tribune. *"Our effort is part of a spiritual and holistic approach toward alleviating problems that keep our people from reaching their potential."*

SOURCES

Books

Johnson, Sandy, compiler, *The Book of Elders: The Life Stories and Wisdom of Great American Indians*, Harper, 1994.

Periodicals

Chicago Tribune, "Fighting for His People," March 28, 1993; "Homecoming," March 5, 1995.

Detroit Free Press, "Cartoon Basher," April 5, 1993.

Peoria Journal Star, " 'I Feel a Sense of Accomplishment,' " April 4, 1993.

Lorraine Hansberry

1930–1965

African American writer and activist

Although she is best remembered as the author of the classic black drama A Raisin in the Sun, *Lorraine Hansberry was also a political and social activist whose concerns ranged from racism and homophobia to Pan-Africanism, McCarthyism, and global issues of war and peace. Her links to such groups as the Student Non-Violent Coordinating Committee (SNCC), the Communist party, and various black nationalist groups made her the target of FBI surveillance, as did her outspokenness—in print as well as at the podium. But only death was finally able to silence the woman who had so aptly defined what it meant "to be young, gifted and black."*

Hansberry, a native of Chicago, was raised in an upper-class black neighborhood on the city's South Side. As a member of a family that was well known in the African American community both at a local and a national level for their commitment to the fight for black liberation, she grew up believing in the value of challenging the status quo. By the time she was in her mid-twenties, Hansberry had already decided to combine a life of activism with her desire to write for the stage. Her debut effort, A Raisin in the Sun, *opened in New York in March 1959; directed by and starring African Americans, it was the first play by a black woman ever to run on Broadway. Its enthusiastic reception by critics as well as by the public at large—black and white—made the young playwright famous almost overnight. A subsequent film version of her play, based on a script she adapted from her own work, brought her even more acclaim. This in turn provided Hansberry with numerous opportunities to take her message to an even wider audience.*

One such occasion was on October 27, 1962, in New York City, when Hansberry was one of the invited speakers at a rally calling for the abolishment of the House Un-American Activities Committee (HUAC). Established in 1938, HUAC had been busy throughout the 1940s and 1950s investigating labor unions, peace groups, and various liberal organizations it accused of being subversive or disloyal to the U.S. government. Beginning in the late 1940s, HUAC's attention shifted to Hollywood, allegedly the home of numerous writers and performers with communist sympathies. Those who came under suspicion quickly found themselves shut out of the industry; eventually, the blacklist spread to include people outside Hollywood who were involved in radio, television, and the theater. In a speech entitled "The Challenge to Artists," Hansberry addressed this troubling situation from the perspective of an activist with ties to several unpopular groups and causes. Her remarks were later published in the winter, 1963, issue of Freedomways.

I am afraid that I haven't made a speech for a very long time and there is a significance in that fact which is part of what I should like to talk about this evening.

A week or so ago I was at my typewriter working on a scene in a play of mine in which one character, a German novelist, is trying to explain to another character, an American intellectual, something about what led the greater portion of the German intelligentsia to acquiesce to Nazism. He says this, "They (the Nazis) permitted us to feel, in return for our silence, that we were non-participants; merely irrelevant if inwardly agonized observers who had nothing whatsoever to do with that which was being committed in our names."

Lorraine Hansberry

Just as I put the period after that sentence, my own telephone rang and I was confronted with the voice of Dr. Otto Nathan asking this particular American writer if she would be of this decade and this nation and appear at this rally this evening and join a very necessary denunciation of a lingering *American* kind of travesty.

It is the sort of moment of truth that dramatists dearly love to put on the stage but find as uncomfortable as everyone else in life. To make it short, however, I am here.

I mean to say that one can become detached in this world of ours; we can get to a place where we read only the theatre or photography or music pages of our newspapers. And then we wake up one day and find that the better people of our nation are still where they were when we last noted them: in the courts defending *our* constitutional rights for us.

This makes me feel that it might be interesting to talk about where our artists our in the contemporary struggles. Some of them, of course, are being heard and felt. Some of the more serious actresses such as Shelley Winters and Julie Harris and a very thoughtful comedian such as Steve Allen have associated themselves with some aspect of the peace movement and Sidney Poitier and Harry Belafonte have made significant contributions to the Negro struggle. But the vast majority—where are they?

Well, I am afraid that they are primarily where the ruling powers have always wished the artist to be and to stay: in their studios. They are consumed, in the main, with what they consider to be larger issues—such as "the meaning of life," etc.... I personally consider that part of this detachment is the direct and indirect result of many years of things like the House Committee and concurrent years of McCarthyism in all its forms. I mean to suggest that the climate of fear, which we were once told, as I was coming along, by wise men, would bear a bitter harvest in the culture of our civilization, has in fact come to pass. In the contemporary arts, the rejection of this particular world is no longer a mere grotesque threat, but a fact.

Among my contemporaries and colleagues in the arts the search for the roots of war, the exploitation of man, of poverty and of despair itself, is sought in any arena other than the tone which has shaped these artists. Having discovered that the world is incoherent they have, some of them, also come to the conclusion that it is also unreal and, in any case, beyond the corrective powers of human energy. Having determined that life is in fact an absurdity, they have not yet decided that the task of the thoughtful is to try and help impose purposefulness on that absurdity. They don't yet agree, by and large, that simply being against life as it is is not enough; that simply *not* being a "rhinoceros" is not enough. That, moreover, replacing phony utopianisms of one kind with vulgar and cheap little philosophies of accommodation is also not enough. In a word, they do not yet agree that it is perhaps the task, I should think certainly the joy, of the artist to chisel out some expression of what life can conceivably be.

The fact is that this unwitting capitulation really does aim to be a revolt; really does aim to indict—*something*. Really does aim to be partisan in saying no to a world which it generally characterizes as a "brothel." I am thinking now, mainly, of course, of writers of my generation. It is they, upon whom we must depend so heavily for the refinement and articulation of the aspiration of man, who do not yet agree that if the world is a brothel—then someone has built the edifice and that if it was the hand of man then the hand of man can reconstruct it. That whatever man renders, creates, imagines—he can render afresh, re-create and even more gloriously re-imagine. But, I must repeat, that anyone who can even think so these days is held to be an example of unparalleled simple mindedness.

Why? For this is what is cogent to our meeting tonight; the writers what I am presently thinking of come mainly from my generation. That is to say that they come from a generation which was betrayed in the late forties and fifties by the domination of McCarthyism. We were ceaselessly told, after all, to be everything which mutilates youth: to be silent, to be ignorant, to be without unsanctioned opinions, to be compliant and, above all else, obedient to all the ideas which are in fact the dregs of an age. We were taught that agitational activity in behalf of changing this world was nothing but an expression, among other things, of our "neurotic compulsions" about our own self-dissatisfactions because our mothers dominated our fathers or some such as that. We were told in an age of celebrated liberations of repressions that the repression of the *urge* to protest against war was surely the only *respectable* repression left in the universe.

As for those who went directly into science or industry it was all even less oblique than any of that. If you went to the wrong debates on campus, signed the wrong petitions, you simply didn't get the job you wanted and you were forewarned of this early in your college career.

And, of course, things are a little different than in my parents' times, I mean with regard to the candor with which young people have been make to think in terms of money. It is the only single purpose which has been put before them. That which Shakespeare offered as a curse, "Put money in thy purse"—is now a boast. What makes me think of that in connection with what we are speaking of tonight? Well, I hope that I am wise enough to determine the nature of a circle. If, after all, the ambition in life is merely to be rich, then all which might threaten that possibility is much to be avoided, is it not? This means, therefore, not incurring the disfavor of employers. It means that one will not protest war if one expects to draw one's livelihood from, say, the aircraft industry if one is an engineer. Or, in the arts, how can one write plays which have either implicit or explicit in them a quality of the detestation of commerciality if in fact one is beholden to the commerciality of the professional theatre? How can one protest the criminal persecution of political dissenters if one has already discovered at nineteen that to do so is to risk a profession? If all one's morality is wedded to the opportunist, the expedient in life how can one have the deepest, most profound moral outrage about the fact of the condition of the Negro people in the United States? Particularly, thinking of expediency, when one has it dinned into one's ears day after day that the only reason why, perhaps, that troublesome and provocative group of people must some day be permitted to buy a cup of coffee or rent an apartment or get a job—is NOT because of the recognition of the universal humanity of the human race but because it happens to be extremely expedient international politics to now *think* of granting these things!

As I stand here I know perfectly well that such institutions as the House Committee, and all the other little committees, have dragged on their particular obscene theatrics for all these years not to expose "communists" or do anything really in connection with the "security" of the United States but merely to create an atmosphere where, in the first place, I should be afraid to come here tonight at all and, secondly, to absolutely guarantee that I will not say what I am going to say, which is this:

I think that my government is wrong. I would like to see them turn back our ships from the Caribbean. The Cuban people, to my mind, and I speak only for myself, have chosen their destiny and I cannot believe that it is the place of the descendants of those who did not ask the Monarchists of the eighteenth century for permission to make the United States a republic, to interfere with the twentieth century choice of another sovereign people.

I will go further, speaking as a Negro in America, and impose a little of what Negroes say all the time to each other on what I am saying to you. And that is that it would be a great thing if they would not only turn back the ships from the Caribbean but turn to the affairs of our country that need righting. For one thing empty and legislative and judicial chambers of the victims of political persecution so we know why that lamp is burning out there in the Brooklyn waters. And, while they are at it, go on and help fulfill the American dream and empty the Southern jails of the genuine heroes, practically the last vestige of dignity that we have to boast about at this moment in our history—those students whose imprisonment for trying to insure what is already on the book is our national disgrace at this moment.

And I would go so far, perhaps with an over sense of drama, but I don't think so, to say that maybe without waiting for another two men to die, that we sent those troops to finish the Reconstruction in Alabama, Georgia, Mississippi and every place else where the fact of our federal flag flying creates the false notion that what happened at the end of the Civil War was the defeat of the slavocracy at the political as well as the military level. And I say this not merely in behalf of the black and oppressed but, for a change, and more and more thoughtful Negroes must begin to make this point, also for the white and disinherited of the South; those poor whites who, by the millions, have been made the tragic and befuddled instruments of their own oppression at the hand of the most sinister political apparatus in our country. I think perhaps that if our government would do that it would not have to compete in any wishful way for the respect of the new black and brown nations of the world.

Finally, I think that all of us who are thinking about such things, who wish to exercise these rights that were are here defending tonight, must really exercise them. Speaking to my fellow artists in particular, I think that we must paint them, sing them, write about them. All these matters which are not currently fashionable. Otherwise, I think, as I have put into the mouth of my German novelist, we are indulging in a luxurious complicity—and no other thing.

I personally agree with those who say that from here on in, if we are to survive, we, the people, still an excellent phrase, we the people of the world must oblige the heads of all governments to become responsible to us. I personally do not feel that it matters if it be the government of China presently engaging in incomprehensible and insane antics at the border of India or my president, John F. Kennedy, dismissing what he knows to be in the hearts of the American people and engaging in overt provocation with our sister people to the South. I think that it is imperative to say "NO" to all of it; no to war of any kind, any where. And I think, therefore, and it is my reason for being here tonight, that it is imperative to remove from the American fabric any and all such institutions or agencies such as the House Committee on Un-American Activities which are designed expressly to keep us from saying—"NO!"

Lorraine Hansberry died of cancer a little more than two years later, on January 12, 1965.

SOURCES

Books

Foner, Philip S., *The Voice of Black America: Major Speeches by Negroes in the United States, 1797-1971,* Simon & Schuster, 1972.

Hansberry, Lorraine, *To Be Young, Gifted and Black: Lorraine Hansberry in Her Own Words,* edited by Robert Nemiroff, Prentice-Hall, 1969.

Periodicals

Crisis, "Lorraine Hansberry: Portrait of an Angry Young Writer," April, 1979, pp. 123-128.

Freedomways, "The Challenge to Artists," winter, 1963, pp. 31-35; "Lorraine Hansberry at the Summit," Number 19, 1979, pp. 269-272.

Washington Post, "Raisin in the Sun's Enduring Passion," November 16, 1986.

Other

Lorraine Hansberry Speaks Out: Art and the Black Revolution (recording), Caedmon, 1972.

Suzan Shown Harjo

1945–

Native American writer, political analyst, and activist of the Cheyenne and Muscogee Nations

As president and executive director of the Washington, D.C.-based Morning Star Institute, Suzan Shown Harjo directs her varied talents toward the goal of defending and preserving Native American rights. Her activities run the gamut from lobbying for religious freedom and the recovery of ancestral remains, sacred objects, and cultural property to challenging sports teams' use of names or mascots that ridicule or degrade Indians. Underlying all that she undertakes is the belief that existing prejudices or stereotypes about Native Peoples make it easier to deny their humanity and thus ignore them. As Harjo explained to an interviewer for the Los Angeles Times, *"Public policy is not done in any positive way for cartoons, or for people who are already dead, or people who don't have a future."*

Harjo was born in Oklahoma and spent her childhood there, helping her family scratch out a meager living on reservation land they farmed. During her early teens, however, she moved to Naples, Italy, where her father—a disabled veteran of World War II—was stationed with the U.S. Army after he re-enlisted during the 1950s. While life there was very different from what she had known back home, Harjo was able to relate to the warm, tribal-like relationships she observed between Italian families of her acquaintance, some of whom had known each other for generations.

The roots of Harjo's activism date back to struggles of the mid-1960s for religious freedom and civil rights. She and her late husband, Frank Ray Harjo, co-produced "Seeing Red," a bi-weekly radio program on WBAI-FM in New York City that was the first regularly-scheduled Indian news and analysis show in the United States. In addition to her duties as a journalist, she served as the station's director of drama and literature and produced hundreds of plays and other programs for broadcast. During this same period, Harjo also indulged her love of the theater by directing and performing on stage. She also was a co-founder of an Indian women's improvisational troupe called the Spiderwoman Theatre Company.

Harjo moved to Washington, D.C., in 1974, to begin work as news director of the American Indian Press Association. The Capitol has since served as the base of operations for her advocacy efforts on behalf of Native Americans. One of her first jobs was with the National Congress of American Indians (NCAI), an organization devoted to safeguarding the rights of Native Americans and preserving their culture. (Established in 1944 with a membership that cut across all tribal affiliations, it is the largest group of its kind in the United States.) Harjo served as the NCAI's communications director, legislative assistant, and coordinator of the National Indian Litigation Committee.

In 1978, Harjo joined the administration of President Jimmy Carter as special assistant in the Office of the Secretary of the Interior. In this role, she planned and drafted legislation concerning issues of interest to Native Americans and served as one of the administration's links to Congress on such topics as Indian religious freedom and the U.S. government's compliance with internationally-recognized principles of human rights and self-determination.

When the 1980s ushered in a new president whose Republican agenda was far different than that of his predecessor, Harjo's activities shifted to battling proposed budget cuts in Indian programs and attempts to turn over control of tribal and federal schools to the states. She also continued to champion legal cases involving treaty rights, individual civil liberties, land claims, environmental protection, and restoring federal recognition to tribes that lost their official status as Indians as a result of the government's termination policies of the 1950s.

In 1984, Harjo returned to the NCAI, this time as the organization's executive director. Over the next six years, she provided the leadership for the NCAI's national policy activities, focusing in particular on legislative and litigation efforts and cultural concerns. The year 1984 also marked the beginning of her current role as president of The Morning Star Institute. In addition, Harjo is the co-founder and vice president of Native Children's Survival, dedicated to "the healing of Mother Earth and her children."

Under the auspices of these and many other groups with which she is affiliated in one capacity or another, Harjo has emerged as a key player in a number of major Native American cultural initiatives. In 1989, for example, she was a leading force behind the law establishing the National Museum of the American Indian, a branch of the Smithsonian; she was also one of the chief negotiators in an agreement with Smithsonian officials regarding the return and reburial of Indian remains and sacred objects. (This agreement in turn prompted new congressional legislation in 1990, the Native American Grave Protection and Repatriation Act, which she also negotiated and co-authored.) She has also worked with a national coalition of Indian tribes and organizations as well as various environmental, human rights, and religious groups to secure legal protection for sacred sites through legislation and an Executive Order she drafted in 1994. She also is developing new policy on Native Peoples' cultural property rights.

Harjo has also taken up the fight against the use of Indian names and mascots for sports teams, which she and her supporters believe are demeaning and contribute to the problem of low self-esteem among young Native Americans in particular. In 1992, she became the lead petitioner in an ongoing lawsuit filed with the U.S. Patent and Trademark Office that would force the Washington Redskins football team to drop its name, logo, and mascot.

Harjo is a strong proponent of the arts and is herself a published author of numerous essays, articles, and poems. To showcase the talents of other Native American artists and writers, she organizes exhibitions and performances throughout the country. Through Native Children's Survival, she is involved in a series of music videos featuring Indian performers who combine traditional tribal and rock music.

A frequent lecturer at events across the nation, Harjo reflected on some of the issues and interests that preoccupy her most in an address she delivered to open the fourth annual "Seeds of Change" Conference in Santa Fe, New Mexico, on September 18, 1992. The following was transcribed from an audiotape provided by Harjo.

Good evening. Thank you.

Kenny [Asubel of Seeds of Change] said everything I wanted to say—and very well. Especially about relationships, and who we are, and who we are to each other. And not just to each other as human beings, but each other as every form of life that exists on this Mother Earth and that exists beyond her.

Many of the people in the world think they know about Native Peoples. And most of the things they know are wrong. They know things about us and associate things with us that have nothing to do with us. "Woo-woo-woo!" That's what drunken white people do at closing time at bars. But that's very much identified with Native People. "Boom-boom-boom-boom-boom" is just an unimaginative musical director for a Western film and his successors. Scalping. You know who introduced commercial scalping in this hemisphere? The French and British fur trappers. That's also where the term "redskin" came from. In commerce.

The French and British fur trappers used to drag in gunnysacks full of skulls of Native People for bounty. It was the way they made a living. And they would bring in the wagons full of Indian bodies. Well, that got to be right cumbersome, 'cause they were killing more and more Indians and had to bring in greater gunnysacks and bigger wagons. So the people who were paying the bounties agreed to pay bounty for the scalps, rather than the skulls, and for the red skins, rather than the whole bodies. Eighty cents for the men, sixty cents for the women, and forty cents for the children.

Now you don't even have to know that to know that there is something wrong with identification of anyone from outside that group. That's name-calling. "Redskins," despite what Jack Kent Cooke says—does everyone know who Jack Kent Cooke is? The owner of the Redskins. Oh, it's so wonderful to talk to people who don't know who Jack Kent Cooke is! See, I'm from Oklahoma and you can't be from Oklahoma without having been born on or near a football. . . . I really am a fan and probably would have been a player, but I wasn't *that* dumb.

Indians got rid of a mascot called "Little Red," who used to parade around and do stupid things at football games of the University of Oklahoma. I guess "Little Red" was the counterpart to the "Sooners," the "Sooners" representing what was stolen from the Indians in Oklahoma when the lands were opened up—other peoples' lands, by the way, called "freelands." And then what remained of the Indians? The stereotypes—the chicken feathers and the woo-woo-woos and the boom-boom-booms, and all of the things that Indians *just don't do*.

Jack Kent Cooke has said the name of the Redskins "is not derogatory." Well, he said two things. He said, "There's not a jot, whittle, chance in hell" that the name of the Redskins is going to be changed "because it would cost too much money." Well, he's wrong. It would make him a fortune. The name-change contest, which myself and six other petitioners before the U.S. Patent and Trademark Board have offered to conduct for Jack Kent Cooke—I think it would be great fun.

My personal favorite is "Wild Hogs." For those of you—well, it's in keeping with the line. They wouldn't have to give up their little pig faces; they're kind of cute. And it's perfectly in keeping with the Washington real sport of pork barreling. But that's just my opinion.

Anyway, I'm sure everyone can come up with wonderful names for this team that don't single out living human beings. Native People are the only living human beings singled out for abuse in the sports arena. Think about it.

Now, I made this point at a college in North Carolina two nights ago where the team name is the Fighting Christians. When the Bureau of Indian Affairs franchised out the Native Peoples to the various Christian denominations, the Cheyenne people got the Quakers, and it was sort of a wash. It was a good thing, because they thought very much like we did—they were peaceful and had meetings where you didn't speak unless the Spirit moved you. And you listened to every person and every voice, no matter how small, of the Creation, because it was a part of the Creation. So we had these great meetings for several generations, not talking to each other at all and gaining some understanding.

So, my idea of the Christians is not so much the Crusades—which I only found out about later and all the barbarism and the Spanish Inquisition and all that stuff. Just a few things wrong. I always thought that the Christians were people of peace and love and brotherhood and sisterhood and—well, maybe not sisterhood, until much later. But, certainly brotherhood. And so to hear the "Fighting Christians" is kind of odd to me. But I don't ask that names in sports make sense. We'd have to go one by one. The LA Lakers—are you kidding? The Utah Jazz? We're just asking that Native Peoples not be singled out for this treatment.

Suzan Shown Harjo

This young man, one of the Fighting Christian players from this small college in North Carolina the other night, said, "Oh, yeah, what about the Cowboys?" I said, "Well, my point exactly. They're an era." And that leads us to what's wrong with names of football teams and in other areas in sports being called "Indians." Just that. A misnomer to begin with, but we're sort of stuck with it for awhile.

Right now we're trying to reclaim our personal names, reclaim our Indian nations' names, because everyone's called something that we weren't called. Tsistsistas is the name of the Cheyenne People. The Lakota People had two words for us, Shyhela and Shyhanna—"the Red People" and "the People who talk so fast and funny you can't understand them." Or, if they're talking directly to us, "the People who speak and lead beautifully with their words." So, you be the judge.

And the French couldn't pronounce, they seemed to—Europeans had a lot of difficulty pronouncing names that are really quite simple. So they couldn't say "Shyhela," and they couldn't say "Shyhanna," and they couldn't say "Tsistsistas" for some reason, so they said "Cheyenne," and that stuck.

The Muscogees, that's our name for ourselves—that's my dad's People. And the British came in, and you may know the Muscogees by another name—Creek. And that's because the British were so imaginative that they said, "These people live around creeks. Let's call them. . . ."

So, when we are identified as an era, as in cowboys and Indians, and when we are identified by the color of our skin or what any dictionary will tell you is the most derogatory or disparaging or demeaning word you can call a Native American—there is one dictionary definition our attorneys found out in legal research on the word "redskin" that simply says, "not the preferred word for Native Americans." The collective name for us—don't worry about Native Americans, Indians, Indigenous People (which is much too long), Native Peoples—everything is wrong and inadequate. So just mix it up, use every term interchangeably and try to find out what our real names are and refer to us as that. That's the best thing.

Tohono O'odham, for example—the People in Arizona who have a reservation that's larger than the state of Connecticut—went to the Bureau of Indian Affairs in the mid-80s and said, "We want you to change your paper on us. You keep writing to us as Papago, and we don't like that term."

The woman at the BIA said, "Well, we have too much paper on you. We can't change this name."

They said, "Well, our name is the Tohono

O'odham. It's not too difficult. Call us that, write to us."

And she said, "Well, why don't you like Papago?"

"Well, it means 'bean-eater.' It was just something that someone said, 'You're a bean-eater, we'll call you that,' and it was just a way of stripping us of our identity." And so on and so forth.

And she said, "Well, I wouldn't mind being called a bean-eater myself."

And they said, "Okay, every time we write to you, we'll write to you as Papago. And when you write to us, address us as Tohono O'odham."

It's very difficult—I mean, that took several years of negotiating with the Bureau of Indian Affairs. I don't mean to always rag on the BIA. It *is* one of the worst federal agencies, no doubt about it. And it will not improve as long as it's in the Interior Department, divorced from other people. And as long as it has to compete with the Bureau of Land Management and the Bureau of Reclamation and Fish and Wildlife Service and so forth. And is run by people who see as their jobs the management of Indian People.

The BIA pretty much is a losing battle on most Indian reservations because the families are pretty strong at home and they don't have much of a foothold. They don't do much good, but anymore they don't do much that's bad. As long as you're not seeking kidney dialysis or something that they can stand in between you and a needed service. The Bureau of Indian Affairs is the agency that—it's one of the oldest federal agencies, and it's the one that Custer said to line up all the employees on his way out to Little Big Horn and said, "Now, don't do *nothin'* til you hear from me." Well, orders is orders!

I'm really pleased to have been able to, with my Cheyenne brother, Ben Nighthorse Campbell—the only Indian in Congress and the only producing artist in Congress of 535 members, who's going to be the next junior senator from Colorado (. . . twenty-six points ahead in the polls, that's good, not bad for a Cheyenne boy)—I was really happy to, because of his family and because of mine (my great-great-grandfather, Bull Bear, and his cousin, Two Moons, were two of the leaders of the Cheyenne at Little Big Horn), to be able to not only get a memorial honoring our Indian heroes from that place and time, but to get rid of the name of Custer. And on this October 12, many of our People whose ancestors were there—of the Lakota and the Blue Clouds, the Arapahos, and the Cheyennes—will gather on the Greasy Grass at Little Big Horn, and that's when there will be dedicated the national battlefield that's just called simply Little Big Horn National Battlefield.

It didn't make any sense that it was called "Custer" anyway. It was anomalous—it was the only battlefield in the park system that was named after an individual. And you wouldn't think the United States would name it after a loser. It shows you how far people will go to find heroes. I agree that we all need our heroes, but it's important to look at the kind of people we're propping up and shaking the dust off.

Columbus, really? If there are any Italian people here, *mi dispiace, paisano*. I would, were I Italian, want as a hero someone who could at least have written to his mother in Italian. He couldn't do that. Not a very bright guy. Certainly lost, we all know that. What did he write, day one, in his journal? About "the Indios." Guess where he thought he was? He kept four separate journals, each at variance with the other, so we know that, at best, he told the truth one-quarter of the time.

He and his tiny men and their rats brought gifts of civilization here. Here, to this place that Columbus wrote about as "Paradise on earth." Well, they couldn't have that in Europe, could they? What was the system that was there? The Spanish Inquisition was not confined to Spain. It was a system that had fed upon itself, of economic and religious slavery that meant no individual, no inherent, sovereignty. This is where governance forms based on inherent sovereignty were and so intrigued the founding fathers—Morgan, Jefferson, Franklin.

What was going on in Europe? There was top-down sovereignty. Divine right of kings. So, sovereignty flowed from God to kings to some of the people some of the time, and most of the people none of the time.

What happened? What kept it all together? The promise of Paradise. Or, like Eugene O'Neill wrote in a play earlier this year, "There's peace in the green fields of Eden, but you've gotta die to get there." Well, that was the punchline of the economic and religious system in Europe. Things might be lousy here, but don't worry about it. And they might get worse, but don't worry about it. Because, when you die, you will be glorified.

I have great respect for every person's religion. That was the missing ingredient from the other direction, by the way—respect. The only way to make the next five hundred years different from the past five hundred years is to begin with that single word—respect.

I do question the spiritual base of religions that would dictate that my children are going to a nightmare of a hell because they don't believe in the way of people who came from Europe. I don't know where they're going. I wish them well.

I don't understand a religion and its spiritual base that can, as Kenny was referring to, state in its basic document that "man shall have dominion over the beasts and the birds."

That is what's happened here. It began with

"The only way to make the next five hundred years different from the past five hundred years is to begin with that single word—respect."

Columbus and his men and his rats. And their diseases that were imported and that killed, by 1500, eight million people, in the Caribbean area, who had been alive in 1492. It was not simply a mowing down of people and this residual, coincidental, accidental disease. It was an ecocide of unimaginable proportions which is still going on, as so many of you know and are working to halt.

But, it's taken us a long time to be able to talk to each other in our own lifetime about things like people existing in the rain forest, as well as trees. People existing, thriving, gloriously at Taos Blue Lake, as well as the water there. We have much to do together.

What we need to begin—a different course of action—is to forget about the kinds of heroes that we've been propping up. And to start celebrating those small and large acts of courage that exist within ourselves and our families and our neighbors, each one of us, and *celebrate* that, *applaud* it. How wonderful when someone acts in a courageous way! Give them encouragement so they *might* do it again. Learn from it.

But, if we constantly prop up false heroes—and heroes who are not going to be one-hundred-percent perfect, because nobody's one-hundred-percent—we're constantly going to be disappointed in those individuals or make mythic beings out of pitiful people. We need to begin with that respect within ourselves and look for the essence of your own culture.

One thing that Native Peoples still have is very powerful belief systems. One thing I like about the fairly recent movie *Thunderheart* was that it showed the practical, everyday nature of magic and power—that it's not the stuff that you should be misty-eyed about. It happens as a matter of course. You drink water in the day, you do a little magic during the day (or a lot, depending on the situation). You just have to train yourself for it. And the best way to train yourself for it is by exploring whatever routes you have, whatever clues you have to your own character and identity and culture. And then come to us as whole people so we can talk, so we can share, so we can enhance each other.

I'd like to commit some poetry, which I always try to do when I get outside of Washington, D.C. I live on a terrible reservation there—abject poverty, rampant alcoholism, checks bouncing everywhere, cutthroat politics. So I always feel like I'm getting away with something when I'm outside of Washington and can do something as seditious—hear me, Jesse Helms—as commit poetry.

One I'd like to read because it's about gathering together and gathering rites (both spellings of that word). In this new world that we're going to all strive for we need to look at common things that exist all around us.

Over dinner, Tom [Hayden, California assemblyman and another keynote speaker at the conference] was asking about the buffalo movement, is that for real, and it is. It's such a terrific thing that we have enough bingo money to be able to buy some Indian things!

The Buffalo are really different kinds of beings, different kinds of People. One of these stereotypes about Indians that you see in all the Western movies is the Indian getting down on the ground, ear to the ground to hear how many leagues away the horses or the buffalo or the bad men or the good men might be. Well, that comes from something very real. Not Indians putting their ears to the ground, but there's a beetle that exists in the plains (only where there are buffalo) that points its antenna in the exact direction that the buffalo will appear from a day away. So the Indian People always look for that beetle. Do you know how long it must have taken to figure that out? And how interrelated the people had to be to understand that, simply that?

In *Dances with Wolves*—oh, I know, you probably liked it. To me, it's the same old Western. The Volvo of Westerns? Yes. *Out of Africa* for panoramas, *Cry Freedom* for regressive politics. The good-looking, good-hearted white guy who always has to tell our story had to tell the Lakota People (who could not have been that dumb) that the buffalo and a couple of hundred thousand tons of beef were on the hoof, just over the hill. Now isn't that arrogant to put in a film in this century, at this time, on the verge of a new century, something so Eurocentric?

It would have been nice if they had added some little girl kids. And they got the boy kids right. They should have added some little girl kids. Should have added some women who can talk in more than a whisper, when prone in bed, in the ear of a chief. Ninety-five percent of our Indian nations are matrilineal in the United States, not patrilineal. So, that really doesn't occur in just that way. That's a white man's notion of what happens in Indian country.

This is called "Gathering Rites":

the women gathered
from Cape Fox to Xingu
to mid-points of mystery
changing history
in unnoticed ways
in unrecorded parts
of red mother earth
timing their ceremonies
to grandmother moon
setting places for Creation's faces:
Corn Woman, Pipe Woman
Buffalo-Calf Woman
Morning Star Woman
Spirit Bird Woman
and the Old Stone Woman,
whose wrinkles are canyons

the women gathered
berries, roots, fruits of the season
bypassing the poison,
the bitter, the green
digging snake root and ironwood
for good sweats and sleep
wild onions, just tender,
for healing and feasting
clouds and smoke and moonlight
and sunrays
and sighs and death rattles and ba-
by's breath
and woman's sage
just the color of dawn
sharp-eyed, strong-armed
dirt under nails work.

the women gathered
poles and nets and wetweeds
for fishing
jumping salmon over salmon
struggling upstream
running the short run against the tide
with hemp and seaweed
and soft rope, no hooks
hard work of holding and clubbing
and landing
the long walk back to the river's
mouth
longer and slower
when empty-handed
professional women's work
this hunting and fishing

the women gathered
'round graves in the ground,
'neath the trees, near the water
dancing in circles
describing their grief
wailing, remembering, laughing
and singing
songs of the first and finest deeds
songs of condolence and duty and life
songs of forgive me, I want to live
songs so sweet
that the rocks shake and weep
songs so strong,
they are buried,
forgotten

the women gathered
to weave a rug, a roof, a hammock,
a blanket
spiderwomen spinning
memories and visions
with wool and wise words
and the sexiest of stories
explosions of patterns and local color
for regal occasions,
some for the tourists
birch bark for baskets and sweet grass
and ash
and bad-tasting berries for hang-
downs and paints
and horse hair and seaweed
and mourner's braids
and eagle-bone whistles
and porcupine quills
and tiger's teeth
and red driftwood cedar
with secret sea faces
and feathers and fluffs and sashes
and leggings

for dancing, for praying,
for praising, for giving
the women gathered
much from hushed conversations
in corridors of power
where their presence was strange
the constrained responses to
open questions
answering more
than answers would say
they gathered news from the radio,
from gun shots, from screams
stories from headlines and frontlines
between and behind lines.

they gathered the children
and sisters and mothers
their faces told more than they meant
to reveal

the women gathered
women gathered men gathered
children
gathered mothers gathered fathers
gathered pasts
gathered futures
gathered strength
gathered women
gathered time
in a bundle
and hurled it
at the sun
and the sun rained time
for the women
to gather
together
time
after
time

While the men are drumming, the women need to gather. And among the things that Native women still know how to do is live with each other and gather. It's an important lesson.

One nifty thing about ancient cultures is we got a lot of stuff right just by virtue of being around a long time and by trial and error. Just like that little beetle, noticing that.

The buffalo really are different. They do a ceremony with sunflowers. Wherever you find sunflowers, you will find buffalo gathering. And they do a dance. They always go to the left, they always circle the largest sunflower and rub up against it until every petal's gone. And it's an extraordinary thing.

One of the things that is going to be very helpful for the Native People—those of us who are going to reintegrate the buffalo on a daily basis into our lives—is that we're going to understand what some of our songs mean. 'Cause there are words that we use in our Indian languages that we don't understand. There are songs that we sing that we don't understand. We know they have some relationship to something important, otherwise they wouldn't still be around. So that's really going to help us in our understanding about ourselves, and perhaps we can help you.

I wrote a poem last year, and I notice a few people here who were at the P.E.N. conference earlier this year, and so you might want to take a little break so you don't have to hear this one again. This one's called "Jumping Through the Hoops of History."

I wrote it—it's dedicated to Columbus and Custer (and we've talked about them), Sheridan, who was the other great military man in U.S. history who said, "The only good Indian's a dead one." And then his protégé was Colonel Chivington, and they—both together with Custer—had a lot to do with the massacres of my relatives at Sand Creek and the Washita, where the two battle cries, if you will, as the men were cutting babies out of the wombs of the mothers, were "the only good Indian's a dead one" and "nits make lice." 'Cause Colonel Chivington, a week before the Sand Creek Massacre, had been asked at a public meeting, "When you say that we should all kill all the hostile Cheyennes"—I mean, that's how we were known, just "hostileCheyennes," one word—"Do you mean the babies, too?" And he answered, "Nits make lice."

This is also dedicated to John Wayne—well, you know why—and to all such heroes of yesteryear. I wrote it to get it off my chest, for one thing, and knowing that this would be a time of a lot of public stupidness, in addition to the funny hats and the parades and everything. And that some things had to be put in some sort of perspective.

The real push behind it was—the day I started to write this was the day I found out that, for the third decade in a row, our Indian teenagers took the prize. We're still the population in the country with the highest rate of teenage suicide. Most of that comes from low self-esteem. Most of that comes from the constant bombardment of negative imaging and having either ourselves written out of existence or written about wrongly.

Also, someone sent me a box of hollowed-out 45/70s. I don't know, are you hunters or gatherers? I'm both. So, anyway, this is a

45/70. It is a big bullet, folks. A little bitty bullet like this will drop a deer. This one—which was, oh, about that big actually before being hollowed out—had a special little treat, a little magnesium load. It was sort of the precursor of napalm, and it would explode on contact and just burn holes in you. And it was known to cut people in half. This was made especially for the Cheyenne, the Lakota, and the Arapaho people *and* the buffalo—this 45/70. So all of that together made me think, "This is a heck of a day."

I had just finished a major battle, too, in Washington and around the country, just getting new law so we could get back our dead relatives from museums and educational institutions and federal agencies, and our religious items. We had been successful in 1989, with the Smithsonian first and then with everyone else who receives federal funding or is a federal entity.

And one thing that gave me a little added push in 1989 to say, "No more kidding around. We've had it with talk and let's try forty lawsuits on your door, Smithsonian, unless we can come to an *entente cordiale,*" which we were able to do. One thing that gave me that little extra push was finding out, in the Anthropological Archives in the Smithsonian's National Museum of Natural History, the bills of lading for the heads of my relatives from the Massacre at Sand Creek. So, not only were they mutilated and mowed down—people who are not abstract and not just numbers, but people who we have oral history about, who are family people. Some of whom were known by my grandparents. Several my mother remembered as a child. Not abstract and ancient history. This is *real, new* stuff to us. So, that kind of plays in here, too.

Anyway, I'm going to read this and then one final one and then I am outta here.

10 little, 9 little, 8 little Indians
7 little, sick little, live baby Indians
poor little, me little, you little Indians
the only good Indian's a dead 1

a lot of young Indians got dead in
the '80s
just like the '70s and '60s
both 19 and 18 hundreds
and all the other 00s since 1492
a sucker's #s game over the sale of
the centuries
with 99-year leases and 1¢-treaties
with disappearing ink on the bottom line
signed by gilt-eyed oddsmakers
whose smart $ bet on 0 redskins by
half-time

in the 4th quarter, when this century
turned on us,
we were down to 250k in the u.s.
from the 50m who were here
but who just didn't hear about
the lost italian, lurching his way
from spain
with scurvy-covered sailors and yellow-fevered priests
at least 1,000 points of blight
and plague
in 3 wooden boxes marked "india or bust"
and "in gold we trust"

columbus washed up on our shores,
praising paradise on earth
and kinder, gentler people
who fixed them dinner, but laughed
so hard
at these metal-headed, tiny whitemen
that they fell to their knees
we please them, dear diary, columbus
wrote home
they think we're gods
so the knights of the lost boats
spread syphilis and The word of the 1
true gods
and planted 00s of flags of the 1
true kings
and sang their sacred 3-g song

"a, b, c, d, g, g, g
glory, god and gold, gold, gold"

rub-a-dub-dub, a niña tub
rub-a-dub-dub, a pinta tub
rub-a-grub-grub, Native gold
and lands
rub-a-chop-chop, Native ears
and hands
rub-a-dub-dub, santa maria sub
rub-a-rub-rub, Indians out
8m by 1500, or thereabout

meanwhile, back in the land of wicked
queens and fairy tales
serfs were sewing and owing
the churches
and paying dues to the papal store
all for the promise of the kingdom
of heaven
starving and dying to make it to that
pearly door
the inquisition kings reaped peasant
blood$, but wanted more

than those in robes could rob from
the poor
so the captains of invention
designed the missions to go forth
and mine
with tools of destruction to kill
the time
so cristobal colon led the chorus in the
same old song
kyrie, kyrie, kyrie eleison
a new world beat for average savages
who didn't change their tune
and were bound by chains of office
and staked out to pave the yellow
brick road
at invasion's high noon
and wizards in satin read their rights
in latin
kyrie, kyrie, kyrie requiremento
and a lot of Indians got dead
as was, by god, their right
to the sound of death songs in
the night
kyrie, kyrie, kyrie requiremento

and amerigo begat the beautiful
and the bibles grew and the bul-
lets flew
and the pilgrims gave thanks
and carved up turkeys and other
peoples' lands
and mrs. governor stuyvesant bowled
with 10 bloody skulls
and begat up against the wall streets
and shopping mauls on 00s of
mounds
and the 7th cavalry prayed and passed
the ammunition
and loaded gatling guns 100k times
and shot off extra special 45/70s
for any Indians or buffalo
between europe and manifest destiny
meanwhile, in most of Indian country
no one heard about the ironhorse or
the goldwhores
or the maggots in the black hills
with no-trespassing signs
or what's yours is homestake mine's
but that's what they called ballin'
the jack

then it was 2 late, about a 25¢
to midnight
and us without a second hand to tell
the times were a changin'
so, we jumped through the hoops
of history
on mile-high tightropes without a net
with no time to look back or back out
with no time to show off or cry out

look, ma, no hands
no hands
no hands

and the calendar was kept by #s of
sand creeks
and washitas and wounded knees and
acoma mesas
and 00s of army blankets of wool
and smallpox
and a lot of chiefs who made
their marks
no longer able to thumb their
way home
where x marked the spots on
their babies
and pocahantas haunted england

singing ring-a-ring-a-rosy
ashes, ashes, all fall dead

and a lot of fences got built
around a lot of hungry people
who posed for a lot of catlins
who shot their fronts
and snapped their backs

just say commodity cheese, please

and a lot of Indians got moved
and removed
relocated and dislocated
from c to shining c
from a 2 z
from spacious skies to fort renos
from purple mountains to oklahoma
from vision quests to long walks
from stronghold tables to forks in
the road
from rocks to hard places
from high water to hell
from frying pans to melting pots
from clear, blue streams to coke

and we got beads
and they got our scalps
and we got horses
and they got our land
and we got treaties
and they got to break them
and we got reservations
and they got to cancel them
and we got christian burials
and they got to dig us up
and they got america
and america got us

and they got a home where Indians
don't roam
(now follow the bouncing cannon ball)

and they got a home where Indians
don't roam
and a lot of young Indians got dead
and those were the glory daze
and we learned the arts of civilization
reciting the great white poets

(oh, little sioux or japanee
oh, don't you wish that you were me)

singing the great white songs

(onward christian soldiers
marching as to war
to save a wretch like me
amazin' race, amazin' race)

sailing down the mainstream

(with land o' lakes butter maiden
and kickapoo joy juice role models
for good little Indian girls and boys)

and we got chopped meat
and we got buffaloed
and we got oil-well murders
and they got black-gold heirs
and they got museums
and we got in them
and they got us under glass
and we got to guide them
and they got the kansas city chiefs
and we got a 14,000-man b.i.a.
and we got pick-up trucks
and they got our names for campers
and they got rubber tomahawks
and we got to make them
and they got to take us to lunch
and we got to eat it
and they got richer
and we got poorer
and we got stuck in their cities
and they got to live in our countries
and they got our medicines
and we got to heal them
and we got sick
and they got, well, everything
and we got to say please and thank you
and good morning, america
you're welcome, y'all come
and have a nice hemisphere

then, all of a sudden, a new day dawned
and america yawned
and the people mumbled
something about equality and the
quality of life
some new big deal to seal the
bargain
and jack and jill went to the hill
to fetch some bills to save us
and the united snakes of america
spoke in that english-only forked-
tongue way
about cash-on-the-barrelhead,
hand-over-fist
in exchange for Indian homes on
the termination list
and bankers and lawyers and other
great white sharks
made buyers-market killings
when more chiefs made their marks
and lots of Indians packed their
bags and old-pawn
for fun with dick and jane and
busing with blondes
for a bleeched-out, white-washed
american morn
while we were just trying to live and
get born

and a lot of young Indians got dead
in america's 2 big wars
and the little ones they tried to hide
like the my-lais
and other white lies
and the millions on the grate-nation's
main streets
with holes in their pockets
and tombstones for eyes
you see, america was busy lunching
and punching clocks
(and each other, don't tell)
and pushing paper
(and each other, do tell)
and loving and leaving cabbage-
patch/latch-key kids
in the middle of the road and
nowhere
(where everything got touched but
their hearts
where $ bought the love they were worth)
and America's daddy and mommy
looked
up from their desks
out from their ovens
over their shoulders
behind the times
down their noses
and right before their eyes
but just out of sight
behind flashlights in abandoned
buildings
through crack in the walls
and in the halls of boarding schools
a lot of young Indians got dead, too
girls with bullets, booze and lysol
for boyfriends
boys with nooses and razor blades
for cold comfort

and a few grandmas and grandpas
on their last legs anyway
and we who were left behind
sang songs for the dead and dying
for the babies to stop crying
for the burned-out and turned-out
for the checked-out and
decked-out
ain't that just like 'em
we said over cold coffee and hot tears
for getting themselves dead
forgetting to tell us goodbye
for giving america no 2-week notice
forgiving america with their bodies
ain't that just their way
to gather us up and put us down
gee, kids really do the darndest things
like get themselves dead
like a lot of them did
just yesterday and today
and a lot of young Indians got dead
faster than they could say
tomorrow

oh, say, can't you see
they learned america's song and dance
from the rockets' red glare
to god shed his light on thee
they read america's history
where they weren't
or were only bad news
they laughed when president rip
van reagan
told the russians the u.s.
shouldn't have humored us
they passed when senator slender
reed said
this is the best deal for your land
find another country or play
this hand
they learned the lessons about
columbus
in child-proof, ocean-blue rhymes
along with other whiteboy-hero
signs of the times
they saw the ships sailing, again
and a future as extras
in movies where Indians don't win
they knew they were about to be
discovered, again
in someone else's lost and
found mind
in an old-world/bush-quayle
new age/snake-oil
re-run as much fun
as the first scent of those sailors
fresh from the hold
exhaling disease, inhaling gold
and a lot of young Indians escaped
just in time
to miss the good wishes and cheer
have a happy, have a merry
have a very nice columbus year

10 little, 9 little, 8 little Indians
7 little, sick little, live baby Indians
poor little, me little, you little Indians
the only good Indian's a dead 1

I want to conclude with a shorter one. Never forget that it's worth a pout, but that we have many ways of thinking about everything. There's something that, when you find it in the books of ancient Native Peoples' poetry, there's something called "White Antelope's Chant." You know, even when you're talking in English the words are not the same for Indians. We don't have songs, we have "chants." We don't have religions, we have "belief systems," "ceremonies." We never ate corn, only "maize." Indians and buffalo "roam," we never walk, we never run. Do *any* of you do that in your writings? Nah! Well, this is a song called "White Antelope's Chant," and it's about one thing that unites us and one thing that we must struggle mightily to do, which is to heal this earth, our Mother.

White Antelope had a song
it was a Tsistsistas song
it was his song
because he sang it

Clouding Woman had a song
it was a Tsistsistas song
it was her song
because she sang it

Bull Bear had a song
it was a Tsistsistas song
it was his song
because he sang it

The Song that sang itself
had a Tsistsistas sound
and a truth for all who heard it
at the hour of the end

The Song that sang itself
had no language
it was a heartbeat that thundered
through the canyons of time

The Song that sang itself
had no chorus
its voice was the Morning Star
and the rain at the edge of time

The Song that sang itself
had no time
knew no season

it sounded with the power of the end
The Song sang a Tsistsistas Man
in the prayers in the sun
in the sighs on the wind
in the power of the end
The Song sang a Tsistsistas Woman
in the offerings at dawn
in the sighs of the wind
in the power of the end
The Song sang a Tsistsistas Child
in the cries in the night
in the sighs in the wind
in the power of the end
The Song sang a Tsistsistas sound
in the peace before dark
in the sighs on the wind
in the power of the end
Only Mother Earth Endures
sang the man
Only Mother Earth Endures
sang the woman
Only Mother Earth Endures
sang the child
Only Mother Earth Endures
sang the song
Only Mother Earth Endures

I love you all. Thank you for listening. Aho.

SOURCES

Dallas Morning News, "Columbus: Discoverer or Despoiler?" October 11, 1992.

Lear's, "An American Crusader: Suzan Shown Harjo of Washington, D.C.," July/August, 1989, pp. 135-136.

Los Angeles Times, "Suzan Shown Harjo: Fighting to Preserve the Legacy—and Future—of Native Americans," November 27, 1994, p. M3.

Native Peoples Magazine, "Guest Essay," winter, 1994, p. 5.

New York Times, "Working Profiles: Suzan Harjo, Lobbying for a Native Cause," April 2, 1986.

Washington Post, "Bury My Heart at RFK," November 6, 1994.

Frances Ellen Watkins Harper

1825–1911

African American writer, lecturer, abolitionist, and women's rights activist

Dubbed the "Bronze Muse" in honor of her skills as both a writer and lecturer, Frances Ellen Watkins Harper is regarded as one of the most extraordinarily accomplished black women of the nineteenth century. She was, for example, a respected poet whose ten volumes of verse sold well enough to provide her with a modest income. In 1859, she became the first black woman to publish a short story. And her only novel, Iola Leroy; or Shadows Uplifted, *was the first book by a black writer to depict the life of African Americans in the Reconstruction-era South. (Many colleges and universities across the United States still feature it as part of their women's studies and black literature courses.) But it was as a lecturer that Harper had her greatest impact, beginning in the antebellum period as an antislavery activist and ending up as a crusader for women's rights and moral reform.*

Harper was born of free parents in Baltimore, Maryland, and was raised there by an aunt and uncle after being orphaned at an early age. She attended a private school run by her uncle until she was thirteen, when she went to work as a housekeeper for a family that owned a bookstore. Harper's employer encouraged her to spend her free time reading and writing, and before long the young woman was composing her first poems and essays.

After leaving Maryland in 1850, Harper taught school for a while in Ohio and Pennsylvania. She also launched her career as an antislavery lecturer during this period, traveling extensively throughout New England, New York, Ohio, and eastern Canada to speak as often as three or four times a day. On May 13, 1857, for example, she addressed the New York Antislavery Society. The following piece, reprinted here from Outspoken Women: Speeches by American Women Reformers, 1635-1935 *by Judith Anderson (Kendall/Hunt, 1984), is believed to be the only surviving example of one of Harper's antislavery lectures.*

Could we trace the record of every human heart, the aspirations of every immortal soul, perhaps we would find no man so imbruted and degraded that we could not trace the word liberty either written in living characters upon the soul or hidden away in some nook or corner of the heart. The law of liberty is the law of God, and is antecedent to all human legislation. It existed in the mind of Deity when He hung the first world upon its orbit and gave it liberty to gather light from the central sun.

Some people say, set the slaves free. Did you ever think, if the slaves were free, they would steal everything they could lay their hands on from now till the day of their death—that they would steal more than two thousand millions of dollars? [applause] Ask Maryland, with her tens of thousands of slaves, if she is not prepared for freedom, and hear her answer: "I help supply the coffee-gangs of the South." Ask Virginia, with her hundreds of thousands of slaves, if she is not weary with her merchandise of blood and anxious to shake the gory traffic from her hands, and hear her reply: "Though fertility has covered my soil, though a genial sky bends over my hills and vales, though I hold in my hand a wealth of waterpower enough to turn the spindles to clothe the world, yet, with all these advantages, one of my chief staples has been the sons and daughters I send to the human market and human shambles." [applause] Ask the farther South, and all the cotton-growing states chime in, "We have need of fresh supplies to fill the ranks of those whose lives have gone out in unrequited toil on our distant plantations."

A hundred thousand newborn babes are annually added to the victims of slavery; twenty thousand lives are annually sacrificed on the plantations of the South. Such a sight should send a thrill of horror through the nerves of civilization and impel the heart of humanity to lofty deeds. So it might, if men had not found out a fearful alchemy by which this blood can be transformed into gold. Instead of listening to the cry of agony, they listen to the ring of dollars and stoop down to pick up the coin. [applause]

But a few months since a man escaped from bondage and found a temporary shelter almost beneath the shadow of Bunker Hill. Had that man stood upon the deck of an Austrian ship, beneath the shadow of the house of the Hapsburgs, he would have found protection. Had he been wrecked upon an island or colony of Great Britain, the waves of the tempest-lashed ocean would have washed him deliverance. Had he landed upon the territory of vine-encircled France and a Frenchman had reduced him to a thing and brought him here beneath the protection of our institutions and our laws, for such a nefarious deed that Frenchman would have lost his citizenship in France. Beneath the feebler light which glimmers from the Koran, the Bey of Tunis would have granted him freedom in his own dominions. Beside the ancient pyramids of Egypt he would have found liberty, for the soil laved by the glorious Nile is now consecrated to freedom. But from Boston harbor, made memorable by the infusion of three-penny taxed tea, Boston in its proximity to the plains of Lexington and Concord, Boston almost beneath the shadow of Bunker Hill and almost in sight of Plymouth Rock, he is thrust back from liberty and manhood and reconverted into a chattel. You have heard that, down South, they keep bloodhounds to hunt slaves. Ye bloodhounds, go back to your kennels; when you fail to catch the flying fugitive, when his stealthy tread is heard in the place where the bones of the revolutionary sires repose, the ready North is base enough to do your shameful service. [applause]

Francis Ellen Watkins Harper

Slavery is mean, because it tramples on the feeble and weak. A man comes with his affidavits from the South and hurries me before a commissioner; upon that evidence *ex parte* and alone he hitches me to the car of slavery and trails my womanhood in the dust. I stand at the threshold of the Supreme Court and ask for justice, simple justice. Upon my tortured heart is thrown the mocking words, "You are a Negro; you have no rights which white men are bound to respect"! [loud and long-continued applause] Had it been my lot to have lived beneath the Crescent instead of the Cross, had injustice and violence been heaped upon my head as a Mohammedan woman, as a member of a common faith, I might have demanded justice and been listened to by the Pasha, the Bey or the Vizier; but when I come here to ask for justice, men tell me, "We have no higher law than the Constitution." [applause]

But I will not dwell on the dark side of the picture. God is on the side of freedom; and any cause that has God on its side, I care not how much it may be trampled upon, how much it may be trailed in the dust, is sure to triumph. The message of Jesus Christ is on the side of freedom, "I come to preach deliverance to the captives, the opening of the prison doors to them that are bound." The truest and noblest hearts in the land are on the side of freedom. They may be hissed at by slavery's minions, their names cast out as evil, their characters branded with fanaticism, but O, *"To side with Truth is noble when we share her humble crust Ere the cause bring fame and profit and it's prosperous to be just."*

May I not, in conclusion, ask every honest, noble heart, every seeker after truth and justice, if they will not also be on the side of freedom. Will you not resolve that you will abate neither heart nor hope till you hear the death knell of human bondage sounded, and over the black ocean of slavery shall be heard a song, more exulting than the song of Miriam when it floated o'er Egypt's dark sea, the requiem of Egypt's ruined hosts and the anthem of the deliverance of Israel's captive people? [great applause]

After the Civil War, Harper continued to lecture on behalf of the women's movement and the Women's Christian Temperance Union. Her top priority, however, was the race issue; while on a lengthy tour across the South during the late 1860s and early 1870s, she saw firsthand that former slaves endured conditions nearly as intolerable as those that had existed before the war. (And as lynchings and other forms of racial intimidation became more commonplace, the lives of Southern blacks took on an increased sense of desperation.) Consequently, like many of her fellow black activists, she felt that securing rights for women could wait until African Americans were guaranteed certain basic freedoms. Harper addressed this very topic on February 23, 1891, at a meeting of the National Council of Women. Her remarks were originally published in 1891 in Transactions *and later reprinted in* Black Women in Nineteenth-Century American Life: Their Words, Their Thoughts, Their Feelings, *edited by Gerda Lerner (Pantheon Books, 1972), from which this version is taken.*

I deem it a privilege to present the negro, not as a mere dependent asking for northern sympathy or southern compassion, but as a member of the body politic who has a claim upon the nation for justice, simple justice, which is the right of every race, upon the government for protection, which is the rightful claim of every citizen, and upon our common Christianity for the best influences which can be exerted for peace on earth and goodwill to man.

Our first claim upon the nation and government is the claim for protection to human life. That claim should lie at the basis of our civilization, not simply in theory but in fact. Outside of America, I know of no other civilized country, Catholic, Protestant, or even Mahometan, where men are still lynched, murdered, and even burned for real or supposed crimes. As long as there are such cases as moral irresponsibility, mental imbecility; as long as Potiphar's wife stands in the world's pillory of shame, no man should be deprived of life or liberty without due process of law. A government which has power to tax a man in peace, and draft him in war, should have power to defend his life in the hour of peril. A government which can protect and defend its citizens from wrong and outrage and does not is vicious. A government which would do it and cannot is weak; and where human life is insecure through either weakness or viciousness in the administration of law, there must be a lack of justice, and where this is wanting nothing can make up the deficiency.

The strongest nation on earth cannot afford to deal unjustly towards its weakest and feeblest members. A man might just as well attempt to play with the thunderbolts of heaven and expect to escape unscathed, as for a nation to trample on justice and right and evade the divine penalty. The reason our nation snapped asunder in 1861 was because it lacked the cohesion of justice; men poured out their blood like water, scattered their wealth like chaff, summoned to the field the largest armies the nation had ever seen, but they did not get their final victories which closed the rebellion till they clasped hands with the negro, and marched with him abreast to freedom and to victory. I claim for the negro protection in every right with which the government has invested him. Whether it was wise or unwise, the government has exchanged the fetters on his wrist for the ballot in his right hand, and men cannot vitiate his vote by fraud, or intimidate the voter by violence, without being untrue to the genius and spirit of our government, and bringing demoralization into their own political life and ranks. Am I here met with the objection that the negro is poor and ignorant, and the greatest amount of land, capital, and intelligence is possessed by the white race, and that in a number of States negro suffrage means negro supremacy? But is it not a fact that both North and South power naturally gravitates into the strongest hands, and is there any danger that a race who were deemed so inferior as to be only fitted for slavery, and social and political ostracism, has in less than one generation become so powerful that, if not hindered from exercising the right of suffrage, it will dominate over a people who have behind them ages of dominion, education, freedom, and civilization, a people who have had poured into their veins the blood of some of the strongest races on earth? More than a year since Mr. Grady said, I believe, "We do not directly fear the political domination of blacks, but that they are ignorant and easily deluded, impulsive and therefore easily led, strong of race instinct and therefore clannish, without information and therefore without political convictions, passionate and therefore easily excited, poor, irresponsible, and with no idea of the integrity of suffrage and therefore easily bought. The fear is that this vast swarm, ignorant, purchasable, will be impacted and controlled by desperate and unscrupulous white men and made to hold the balance of power when white men are divided." Admit for one moment that every word here is true, and that the whole race should be judged by its worst, and not its best members, does any civilized country legislate to punish a man before he commits a crime?

It is said the negro is ignorant. But why is he ignorant? It comes with ill grace from a man who has put out my eyes to make a parade of my blindness—to reproach me for my poverty when he has wronged me of my money. If the negro is ignorant, he has lived under the shadow of an institution which, at least in part of the country, made it a crime to teach him to read the name of the ever-blessed Christ. If he is poor, what has become of the money he has been earning for the last two hundred and fifty years? Years ago it was said cotton fights and cotton conquers for American slavery. The negro helped build up that great cotton power in the South, and in the North his sigh was in the whir of its machinery, and his blood and tears upon the warp and woof of its manufactures.

But there are some rights more precious than the rights of property or the claims of superior intelligence: they are the rights of life and liberty, and to these the poorest and humblest man has just as much right as the richest and most influential man in the country. Ignorance and poverty are conditions which men outgrow. Since the sealed volume was opened by the crimson hand of war, in spite of entailed ignorance, poverty, opposition, and a heritage of scorn, schools have sprung like wells in the desert dust. It has been estimated that about two millions have learned to read. Colored men and women have gone into journalism. Some of the first magazines in the country have received contributions from them. Learned professions have given them diplomas. Universities have granted them professorships. Colored women have combined to shelter orphaned children. Tens of thousands have been contributed by colored persons for the care of the aged and infirm. Instead of the old slave-pen of former days, imposing and commodious are edifices of prayer and praise. Millions of dollars have flowed into the pockets of the race, and freed people have not only been able to provide for themselves, but reach out their hands to impoverished owners.

Has the record of the slave been such as to warrant the belief that permitting him to share citizenship with others in the country is inimical to the welfare of the nation? Can it be said that he lacks patriotism, or a readiness to make common cause with the nation in the hour of peril? In the days of the American Revolution some of the first blood which was shed flowed from the veins of a colored man [Crispus Attucks], and among the latest words that died upon his lips before they paled in death was, "Crush them underfoot," meaning the British guards. To him Boston has given a monument. In or after 1812 they received from General Jackson the plaudit, "I knew you would endure hunger and thirst and all the hardships of war. I knew that you loved the land of your nativity, and that, like ourselves, you had to defend all that is most dear; but you have surpassed my hopes. I have found in you, united to all these qualities, that noble enthusiasm which impels to great deeds." And in our late civil conflict colored men threw their lives into the struggle, rallied around the old flag when others were trampling it underfoot and riddling it with bullets. Colored people learned to regard that flag as a harbinger of freedom and bring their most reliable information to the Union army, to share their humble fare with the escaping prisoner; to be faithful when others were faithless and help turn the tide of battle in favor of the nation. While nearly two hundred thousand joined the Union army, others remained on the old plantation; widows, wives, aged men, and helpless children were left behind, when the master was at the front trying to put new rivets in their chains, and yet was there a single slave who took advantage of the master's absence to invade the privacy of his home, or wreak a summary vengeance on those whose "defenceless condition should have been their best defence?"

Instead of taking the ballot from his hands, teach him how to use it, and to add his quota to the progress, strength, and durability of the nation. Let the nation, which once consented to his abasement under a system which made it a crime to teach him to read his Bible, feel it a privilege as well as a duty to reverse the old processes of the past by supplanting his darkness with light, not simply by providing the negro, but the whole region in which he lives, with national education. No child can be blamed because he was born in the midst of squalor, poverty, and ignorance, but society is criminal if it permits him to grow up without proper efforts for ameliorating his condition.

Some months since, when I was in South Carolina, where I addressed a number of colored schools, I was informed that white children were in the factories, beginning from eight to ten years old, with working hours from six to seven o'clock; and one day, as a number of white children were wending their way apparently from the factory, I heard a colored man say, "I pity these children." It was a strange turning of the tables to hear a colored man in South Carolina bestowing pity on white children because of neglect in their education. Surely the world does move. When parents are too poor or selfish to spare the labor of their children from the factories, and the State too indifferent or short-sighted to enforce their education by law, then let the Government save its future citizens from the results of cupidity in the parents or short-sightedness in the State. If today there is danger from a mass of ignorance voting, may there not be a danger even greater, and that is a mass of "ignorance that does not vote"? If there is danger that an ignorant mass might be compacted to hold the balance of power where white men are divided politically, might not that same mass, if kept ignorant and disfranchised, be used by wicked men, whose weapons may be bombs and dynamite, to dash themselves against the peace and order of society? Today the hands of the negro are not dripping with dynamite. We do not read of his flaunting the red banners of anarchy in the face of the nation, nor plotting in beer-saloons to overthrow existing institutions, nor spitting on the American flag. Once that flag was to him an ensign of freedom. Let our Government resolve that as far as that flag extends every American-born child shall be able to read upon its folds liberty for all and chains for none.

And now permit me to make my final claim, and that is a claim upon our common Christianity. . . .It is the pride of Caste which opposes the spirit of Christ, and the great work to which American Christianity is called is a work of Christly reconciliation. God has heaved up your mountains with grandeur, flooded your rivers with majesty, crowned your vales with fertility, and enriched your mines with wealth. Excluding Alaska, you have, I think, nearly three hundred millions of square miles. Be reconciled to God for making a man black, permitting him to become part of your body politic, and sharing one rood or acre of our goodly heritage. Be reconciled to the Christ of Calvary, who said, "And I, if I be lifted up, will draw all men to me," and "It is better for a man that a millstone were hanged about his neck, and he were drowned in the depths of the sea, than that he should offend one of these little ones that believe in me." Forgive the early adherents of Christianity who faced danger and difficulty and stood as victors by the side of Death, who would say, "I perceive that God is no respecter of persons." "If ye have respect of persons ye commit sin." "There is neither Greek nor Jew, circumcision nor uncircumcision, Scythian nor Barbarian, bond nor free, but Christ is all, and in all."

What I ask of American Christianity is not to show us more creeds, but more of Christ; not more rites and ceremonies, but more religion glowing with love and replete with life—religion which will be to all weaker races an uplifting power, and not a degrading influence. Jesus Christ has given us a platform of love and duty from which all oppression and selfishness is necessarily excluded. While politicians may stumble on the barren mountains of fretful controversy and ask in strange bewilderment, "What shall we do with weaker races?" I hold that Jesus Christ answered that question nearly two thousand years since. "Whatsoever ye would that men should do to you, do you even so to them."

At the Columbian Exposition in Chicago in 1893, Harper delivered a speech entitled "Women's Political Future." In it, she reiterated her belief in the ability of women to exert a strong moral force for social change. Her address originally appeared in May Wright Sewall's 1894 book entitled The World's Congress of Representative Women *(Rand, McNally).*

If before sin had cast its deepest shadows or sorrow had distilled its bitterest tears, it was true that it was not good for man to be alone, it is no less true, since the shadows have deepened and life's sorrows have increased, that the world has need of all the spiritual aid that woman can give for the social advancement and moral development of the human race. The tendency of the present age, with its restlessness, religious upheavals, failures, blunders, and crimes, is toward broader freedom, an increase of knowledge, the emancipation of thought, and a recognition of the brotherhood of man; in this movement woman, as the companion of man, must be a sharer. So close is the bond between man and woman that you can not raise one without lifting the other. The world can not move without woman's sharing in the movement, and to help give a right impetus to that movement is woman's highest privilege.

If the fifteenth century discovered America to the Old World, the nineteenth is discovering woman to herself. Little did Columbus imagine, when the New World broke upon his vision like a lovely gem in the coronet of the universe, the glorious possibilities of a land where the sun should be our engraver, the winged lightning our messenger, and steam our beast of burden. But as mind is more than matter, and the highest ideal always the true real, so to woman comes the opportunity to strive for richer and grander discoveries than ever gladdened the eye of the Genoese mariner.

Not the opportunity of discovering new worlds, but that of filling this old world with fairer and higher aims than the greed of gold and the lust of power, is hers. Through weary, wasting years men have destroyed, dashed in pieces, and overthrown, but today we stand on the threshold of woman's era, and woman's work is grandly constructive. In her hand are possibilities whose use or abuse must tell upon the political life of the nation, and send their influence for good or evil across the track of unborn ages.

As the saffron tints and crimson flushes of morn herald the coming day, so the social and political advancement which woman has already gained bears the promise of the rising of the full-orbed sun of emancipation. The result will be not to make home less happy, but society more holy; yet I do not think the mere extension of the ballot a panacea for all the ills of our national life. What we need today is not simply more voters, but better voters. Today there are red-handed men in our republic, who walk unwhipped of justice, who richly deserve to exchange the ballot of the freeman for the wristlets of the felon; brutal and cowardly men, who torture, burn, and lynch their fellow men, men whose defenselessness should be their best defense and their weakness an ensign of protection. More than the changing of institutions we need the development of a national conscience, and the upbuilding of national character. Men may boast of the aristocracy of blood, may glory in the aristocracy of talent, and be proud of the aristocracy of wealth, but there is one aristocracy which must ever outrank them all, and that is the aristocracy of character; and it is the women of a country who help to mold its character, and to influence if not determine its destiny; and in the political future of our nation woman will not have done what she could if she does not endeavor to have our republic stand foremost among the nations of the earth, wearing sobriety as a crown and righteousness as a garment and a girdle. In coming into her political estate woman will find a mass of illiteracy to be dispelled. If knowledge is power, ignorance is also power. The power that educates wickedness may manipulate and dash against the pillars of any state when they are undermined and honeycombed by injustice.

I envy neither the heart nor the head of any legislator who has been born to an inheritance of privileges, who has behind him ages of education, dominion, civilization, and Christianity, if he stands opposed to the passage of a national education bill, whose purpose is to secure education to the children of those who were born under the shadow of institutions which made it a crime to read.

Today women hold in their hands influence and opportunity, and with these they have already opened doors which have been closed to others. By opening doors of labor woman has become a rival claimant for at least some of the wealth monopolized by her stronger brother. In the home she is the priestess, in society the queen, in literature she is a power, in legislative halls lawmakers have responded to her appeals, and for her sake have humanized and liberalized their laws. The press has felt the impress of her hand. In the pews of the church she constitutes the majority; the pulpit has welcomed her, and in the school she has the blessed privilege of teaching children and youth. To her is apparently coming the added responsibility of political power; and what she now possesses should only be the means of preparing her to use the coming power for the glory of God and the good of mankind; for power without righteousness is one of the most dangerous forces in the world.

Political life in our country has plowed in muddy channels, and needs the infusion of clearer and cleaner waters. I am not sure that women are naturally so much better than men that they will clear the stream by the virtue of their womanhood; it is not through sex but through character that the best influence of women upon the life of the nation must be exerted.

I do not believe in unrestricted and universal suffrage for either men or women. I believe in moral and educational tests. I do not believe that the most ignorant and brutal man is better prepared to add value to the strength and durability of the government than the most cultured, upright, and intelligent woman. I do not think that willful ignorance should swamp earnest intelligence at the ballot box, nor that educated wickedness, violence, and fraud should cancel the votes of honest men. The unsteady hands of a drunkard can not cast the ballot of a freeman. The hands of lynchers are too red with blood to determine the political character of the government for even four short years. The ballot in the hands of woman means power added to influence. How well she will use that power I can not foretell. Great evils stare us in the face that need to be throttled by the combined power of an upright manhood and an enlightened womanhood; and I know that no nation can gain its full measure of enlightenment and happiness if one-half of it is free and the other half is fettered. China compressed the feet of her women and thereby retarded the steps of her men. The elements of a nation's weakness must ever be found at the hearthstone.

More than the increase of wealth, the power of armies, and the strength of fleets is the need of good homes, of good fathers, and good mothers.

The life of a Roman citizen was in danger in ancient Palestine, and men had bound themselves with a vow that they would eat nothing until they had killed the Apostle Paul. Pagan Rome threw around that imperiled life a bulwark of living clay consisting of four hundred and seventy human hearts, and Paul was saved. Surely the life of the humblest American citizen should be as well protected in America as that of a Roman citizen was in heathen Rome. A wrong done to the weak should be an insult to the strong. Woman coming into her kingdom will find enthroned three great evils, for whose overthrow she should be as strong in a love of justice and humanity as the warrior is in his might. She will find intemperance sending its flood of shame, and death, and sorrow to the homes of men, a fretting leprosy in our politics, and a blighting curse in our social life; the social evil sending to our streets women whose laughter is sadder than their tears, who slide from the paths of sin and shame to the friendly shelter of the grave; and lawlessness enacting in our republic deeds over which angels might weep, if heaven knows sympathy.

How can any woman send petitions to Russia against the horrors of Siberian prisons if, ages after the Inquisition has ceased to devise its tortures, she had not done all she could by influence, tongue, and pen to keep men from making bonfires of the bodies or real or supposed criminals?

O women of America! into your hands God has pressed one of the sublimest opportunities that ever came into the hands of the women of any race or people. It is yours to create a healthy public sentiment; to demand justice, simple justice, as the right of every race; to brand with everlasting infamy the lawless and brutal cowardice that lynches, burns, and tortures your own countrymen.

To grapple with the evils which threaten to undermine the strength of the nation and to lay magazines of powder under the cribs of future generations is no child's play.

Let the hearts of the women of the world respond to the song of the herald angels of peace on earth and good will to men. Let them throb as one heart unified by the grand and holy purpose of uplifting the human race, and humanity will breathe freer, and the world grow brighter. With such a purpose Eden would spring up in our path, and Paradise be around our way.

SOURCES

Anderson, Judith, *Outspoken Women: Speeches by American Women Reformers, 1635–1935,* Kendall/Hunt, 1984.

Foner, Philip S., editor, *The Voice of Black America: Major Speeches by Negroes in the United States, 1797–1971,* Simon & Schuster, 1972.

Lerner, Gerda, editor, *Black Women in White America: A Documentary History,* Pantheon Books, 1972.

Loewenberg, Bert James, and Ruth Bogin, editors, *Black Women in Nineteenth-Century American Life: Their Words, Their Thoughts, Their Feelings,* Pennsylvania State University Press, 1976.

Sewall, May Wright, editor, *The World's Congress of Representative Women,* Rand, McNally, 1894.

LaDonna Harris

1931–

Native American activist of the Comanche tribe

For the past thirty years, LaDonna Harris has been a strong advocate of Indian self-determination, first on a statewide basis as the founder of Oklahomans for Indian Opportunity and later at the national level as the founder and president of Americans for Indian Opportunity. While the primary focus of both groups has been on achieving full employment in Indian communities and on fostering economic development, Harris's own interests range well beyond that to include feminism, the rights of children and the mentally ill, the world peace movement, and multicultural education. The underlying principle that guides her in all these endeavors is the same, however—accepting and encouraging the diversity of human existence can go a long way toward eliminating racism, poor self-image, and many of the other problems that plague society today. "We are all needed for the great balance," declares Harris. "We all have something to contribute. . . . That is what my entire life has been about, finding a way in which the small cultures of the world can participate in and contribute to the global system."

Born LaDonna Crawford in Oklahoma to a Comanche mother and an Irish-American father, Harris spent most of her childhood in the care of her maternal grandparents. They were traditionalists who spoke only Comanche, so when young LaDonna went off to school for the first time, she had to learn English as a "foreign" language. She now looks back on that experience as the key to her own appreciation of different cultures and ethnic backgrounds.

In 1965, as she watched the civil rights struggle of African Americans unfold across the South, Harris made up her mind to work against the segregation of Indians that existed in her very own state. Making use of the political know-how and contacts she had acquired as the wife of Oklahoma state senator Fred Harris, she established Oklahomans for Indian Opportunity. The state's first intertribal organization, it united sixty tribes behind the common goal of achieving equality and eliminating racism through economic development.

After her husband won a seat in the U.S. Senate and they relocated to Washington, D.C., Harris took her concept national and started Americans for Indian Opportunity (AIO) in 1970. Like its Oklahoma version, AIO has focused its efforts on helping Indian tribes achieve economic self-sufficiency within what

Harris terms "the context of traditional tribal and cultural values." Through the years, it has expanded that mission to encompass various political and social goals as well, such as showing Native Americans how to set up and run self-help programs at the local level, improving communications among Indians and non-Indians, and educating the public at large about Native American achievements and needs. AIO also supports various projects related to health, housing, and the environment. Even more recently, the group has become involved in issues affecting native peoples worldwide.

In addition to her work with AIO, Harris has been active on a number of other fronts. While living in Washington during the late 1960s and early 1970s, she worked with a number of private and government-affiliated organizations concerned with mental health, housing, discrimination, economic opportunity, and women's issues. (For example, she was a founding member of the National Women's Political Caucus and has served as a representative of the Inter-American Indigenous Institute, an agency created by the Organization of American States.) During the last half of the 1970s, although she had moved to New Mexico with her husband (they have since divorced), Harris was still in demand in the nation's capital as a special advisor to Carter administration officials.

Harris frequently lectures about the difficulties Native Americans face as they try to retain their traditional values and identity in a society that places a higher value on assimilation and overcoming differences in the name of "progress." One such occasion was on February 27, 1988, at the Wingspread Conference in Racine, Wisconsin. This event took place shortly after the release of a report updating the twenty-year-old findings of the Kerner Commission, a special investigative team that had looked into the causes of the riots that erupted in the nation's black ghettos during the summer of 1967. (Harris's husband, then a U.S. senator, was a member of the team.) The Kerner Commission concluded in its 1968 report that "white racism" was behind the disturbances and that it was slowly splitting the United States into distinctly separate and unequal communities.

Twenty years later, the authors of the new report arrived at much the same conclusion as their predecessors—American society was moving ever closer to total racial polarization due to poverty, unemployment, crime, and segregation in housing and schools. In her speech, reprinted here from a book edited by Jerry D. Blanche entitled Native American Reader: Stories, Speeches and Poems *(Denali Press, 1990), Harris evaluated the impact of such "institutional racism" on Native Americans.*

The ultimate dilemma of tribal peoples in the United States is that our situation is usually analyzed in inappropriate conceptual frameworks. If one formulates the wrong question, one arrives at the wrong answer.

Basically, the dominant society in the United States does not believe in the continued existence of tribal peoples, societies and governments. The assumption continues to be that Indians, belonging, as it were, to societies at a more primitive stage of evolution than Euro-American society, will eventually be absorbed in the Euro-American "melting pot." Somehow, it is anathema to the dominant U.S. psyche for a person to choose to maintain his or her group identity. Differentness, perhaps because of the fear of "mixed loyalties" generated by the country's immigrant history, is seen almost as unpatriotic, as un-American. Perhaps it is because many immigrant Americans gave up their group identities, they gave up who they were, that they have this messianic need for tribal people to give up who they are, to give up their group identity.

The tribal concept as regards differences is quite contrastive to the Euro-American one. Differentness, rather than being seen as a problem to be eradicated, is seen as a contribution to the whole. In tribal society the group does not dominate the individual, it nurtures individuals, so that strong, idiosyncratic individuals contribute to the strength of the group. Each person's understanding, each person's perception from his or her place in the universe enables the group to make better decisions. Difference does not equate to good/bad, better/best, hierarchy, domination and conflict. Difference is coordinated in terms of contributions made toward the good of the whole.

One cannot be "an Indian." One is a Comanche, an Oneida, a Hopi. One can be self-determining, not as "an Indian," but as a Comanche, and Oneida, etc. We progress as communities, not as individuals. We want to maintain ourselves as communities, according to our group identity, not just as mere individuals or as amorphous "Indians." We want to maintain ourselves as who we are so we can contribute our differentness, our particular understanding, to both the national community and to global society. To do this we must operate out of our own complexity as individuals, as tribal members and as citizens of a larger society. One cannot be a universalist without being a particularist.

The dominant society starts with the premise that tribal governments are bad. Yet what distinguishes Indian communities from other ethnic communities in the U.S. is that they are sovereign dependent nations, they are units of government which exercise internal sovereignty and have a government-to-government relationship with the federal government and do not come under state jurisdiction. This special relationship resonates well with traditional forms of relating which was usually done in terms of reciprocal obligations.

As for the dysfunction and inefficiency of tribal governments, as Felix Cohen, author of the *Handbook of Indian Law,* wrote,

> *. . . self-government is that form of government in which decisions are made not by the people who are wisest, or ablest, or closest to some throne in Washington or in Heaven, but, rather by the people who are most directly affected by the decisions. . . .*
>
> *Indian self-government is not a new or radical policy but an ancient fact. It is not something friends of the Indians can confer upon Indians. Nobody can grant self-government to anybody else. . . . The Federal Government . . . cannot give self-government to an Indian community. All it can really do is get out of the way.*
>
> *However, much of the dysfunction and inefficiency that do exist are due to the imposition of foreign, majoritarian forms of decision-making on traditionally consensus-based communities. The IRA Constitutions adopted by the tribes in the 1930s were never adapted to the cultural realities of particular tribes, especially as regards opinion aggregation. The existing village, clan and lineage leadership structures were completely overlooked and had no place in the "new order."*

Majoritarian forms of discourse emphasize adversarial relationships and consist of debates where each person argues their own position and tries to persuade other people to come over to their position. Consensus-building discourse occurs in a learning environment in which points of view are shared in order for a mutual vision to emerge. Participants in the discourse strive to articulate their understanding of the situation as clearly as possible and at the same time to listen carefully to everyone else's understanding. It is only after incorporating all these perceptions that a decision adequate to a total comprehension of the issue at hand and appropriate to the community can be made.

Many are disappointed with the progress tribal people have made over the last twenty years. However, evaluation of "progress" in "Indian Country" is a very complex process. Once again, we are not a homogeneous group, and tribal ideas of progress may be radically different from Euro-American ideas. For example,

"One cannot be 'an Indian.' One is a Comanche, an Oneida, a Hopi. . . . We want to maintain ourselves as communities, according to our group identity, not just as mere individuals or as amorphous 'Indians.'"

LaDonna Harris

the Northern Cheyenne count as "progress" their ability to maintain environmental quality, rather than the development of their coal resources.

At the moment there is a veritable renaissance going on in tribal America as we come to terms with who we are as tribal people in contemporary society. We are bringing tradition along with us into the future rather than "going back to tradition" and maintaining ourselves like rigid museum pieces. We have incredible success stories. Our infant mortality rate for the first time since contact is below the national average. Our old people are living longer. This has been largely due to the utilization of Community Health Representatives in the promotion of health and delivery of services. The Alabama Creeks have re-emerged as a recognized, culturally and economically viable group of people after a century and a half of being disappeared (like Poland was from the map of Europe for three hundred years.) The Mississippi Choctaw have created economic success, not only for themselves, but for blacks and poor whites around Philadelphia, Mississippi. They are now the fourteenth-largest employer in the entire state. These people were veritable serfs on their own land twenty years ago. The Winnebago of Nebraska have created a Winnebago Self-Sufficiency Plan for the Year 2000. Zuni has addressed its diabetes problem providing a health and wellness model for the nation as a whole, a model which has been adopted by the State of New Mexico. The Council of Energy Resource Tribes has been created followed by organizations bringing together lumber and fishery tribes. These new multitribal organizations have given tribal people control over their natural resources.

Another success story is the development of the Indian Community College system. There are over twenty such colleges. These institutions have emerged in response to the need for post-secondary, continuing education in the communities and to the need to create roles for educated Indians in the communities. In addition, an unexpected benefit of the development of these institutions has been a political one. The administration and faculty of these institutions have led the fight against the historic gerrymandering of school board election districts. They have fought for redistricting so that often for the first time in history in school districts with large numbers of Indian students, Indians are finally being elected to local school boards.

These success stories, while utilizing the special relationship of the tribes with the federal government, do not depend on the BIA for implementation. In fact, these successes are in the process of transforming the function of the BIA from being a provider of services to being a regulator of the institutional process through which Indian affairs is conducted. In addition, these "successes" have created entirely new institutional structures, for example, new relationships with states, certain kinds of international investment, etc.

It is in the institutional realm, however, and in the area of institutional racism that there remains much "progress" to be made. During the Johnson, Nixon, Ford and Carter administrations progress, regardless of which political party was in office, was made, especially in making institutions more responsive to tribal needs. For instance, there was an Indian desk in every federal agency. However, twenty years now after the Kerner Commission Report, during the Reagan administration, after two decades of bipartisan institutional progress, the cutbacks (which in themselves reflect institutional racism at all levels), not only brought to a screeching halt further progress, but eliminated much of the institutional progress already made. In this case it is not the tribes which have failed, but rather it is U.S. institutions which have failed the tribes.

Another specific example of institutional racism has been extensively explored by Kathryn Tijerina, Executive Director of the Indian Resource Development Center at New Mexico State University, and this is the decline in the enrollment of Indian students in higher education. There has been a steady decline since a high water mark in 1972. In the most recent years for which there are figures available the decline went from 87,700 enrolled in 1982 to 82,672 in 1984.

The reasons for this are the cutbacks in programs specifically designed to recruit Indian students (for example, the Tribal Management Program at the University of Oklahoma and Penn State's Indian Leadership Program) and the decline in funds ($300,000 in one program over the last three years) available for scholarships for Indian students. For Indian students who come from families who are three times as likely to live at or below the national poverty level, the lack of these funds is devastating.

In addition, there is the question of opportunity costs in terms of wages lost to the family of the Indian student if he or she is in school instead of working. Plus, the cost of an education has to be weighed against the opportunities for getting a job after graduation. With unemployment rates averaging seventy-five percent for adults on some reservations at an acute lack of jobs for the educated, having a college degree may provide no increased job opportunities on or near the reservation.

However, in those states (for example, New Mexico and Arizona) which have maintained their Indian college recruitment and retention programs with state funds, enrollments have continued to increase. New Mexico enrolled two times as many Indian college students in 1980 as in 1972. Also, the work of organizations like the American Indian Science and Engineering Society have resulted in increased Indian enrollment in the engineering field since 1982.

Rigid institutions in turn exacerbate our pockets of extreme dysfunction. The Dakotas, Montana, portions of the Navajo, and places in the Alaskan bush are rural analogs to the black phenomenon of the urban underclass. These are the areas of most recent contact and of, historically, the greatest oppression. These are the places where change has been most rapid and most extreme.

Particular local realities also have much to do with the function or dysfunction of particular tribal communities, especially as regards local racism and discrimination. Some of the Plains states are to Indians as Mississippi and Georgia have historically been to Blacks.

However, wherever dysfunction occurs in tribal America, the root cause seems to be the same. It emerges from a lack of awareness of and/or the inability to articulate for ourselves and then for others our particular, complex reality. The history we learn in school is always from a Euro-American, outsider's perspective. Our great task, as individual (multitribal/multicultural) people and as particular communities is to articulate first for ourselves, then for the larger society, the patterns of our own histories: national, tribal, village, clan, lineage, family and individual histories from our own perspective.

Understanding the differences between functional tribal communities and those that are dysfunctioning will also provide another way of looking at the inner city underclass. The differences hinge most often on a community's having the institutional structures, especially those that facilitate participation in decision-making, which permit self-determination to take place.

In the tribal sense we have made great "progress." The ultimate criterion on which decisions were made for most tribal groups was a single concept. Would such a decision allow the people to continue, not just in the present generation, but to the children's children's children's generation? Today tribal people are the fastest-growing community in the United States. Most of the people in our communities are below the age of sixteen. We have finally overcome the infectious diseases which decimated us during the last five centuries. That done and with growing awareness of the dynamics of our own survival, cultural and political, we can begin now to envision our futures as tribal peoples continuing into the twenty-first century.

SOURCES

Books

Blanche, Jerry D., editor, *Native American Reader: Stories, Speeches and Poems,* Denali Press, 1990.

Maestas, John R., editor, *Contemporary Native American Address,* Brigham Young University, 1976.

Periodicals

Redbook, "LaDonna Harris: A Woman Who Gives a Damn," February, 1970.

S.I. Hayakawa

1906–1992

Japanese American educator, university administrator, and member of the U.S. Senate

One of the most colorful—and controversial—public figures in recent American history was Samuel Ichiye Hayakawa, a noted educator and university administrator who burst onto the national scene in the late 1960s and later entered the realm of politics. Known as "Don" to family and friends, he was born in Vancouver, British Columbia, Canada, to parents who had emigrated from Japan. His father ran an import-export business and frequently moved his wife and four children from one Canadian city to another until he finally returned to his native country in 1929. Hayakawa completed his high school education in Winnipeg, Manitoba, and then went on to earn his bachelor's degree from the University of Manitoba in 1927 and his master's in English literature from Montreal's McGill University in 1930. Then he was off to the United States, where in 1935 he obtained his doctorate in English and American literature from the University of Wisconsin in Madison.

Unable to secure a teaching position in Canada, Hayakawa remained in Madison after completing his degree and taught adult students in the university's extension division. He left there in 1939 to take a job as instructor in English at the Illinois Institute of Technology in Chicago. He remained at the school throughout the 1940s, moving up to the rank of assistant professor of English in 1940 and associate professor in 1942.

At the same time he was advancing his academic career, Hayakawa was also making a name for himself outside the classroom. During the late 1930s, after observing Adolf Hitler and other totalitarian leaders of Europe skillfully manipulate words and symbols to seize and maintain political control, he began working on a book that he hoped would explain this deliberate misuse of language to students as well as to a general audience. Based on the theories of Alfred Korzybski, considered the founder of general semantics (the study of how people evaluate words and how that evaluation in turn influences their behavior), Hayakawa's Language in Action *(entitled* Language in Thought and Action *in subsequent editions) was published in 1941. With its blend of humor and clear explanations of a difficult yet fascinating subject, it became a bestseller and a staple in many high-school and college courses from the 1940s through the present day.*

Hayakawa soon was recognized as one of the leading experts in the field and went on to establish the International Society for General Semantics and serve for nearly thirty years as editor of its quarterly journal, ETC. *He went on to write seven other books on language and communication, including* Language, Meaning and Maturity *(1954),* Our Language and Our World *(1959),* Symbol, Status and Personality *(1963), and* Through the Communication Barrier *(1979). All were written in a way that was understandable to a popular audience, an approach that led some in the academic community to reject Hayakawa as not "scholarly" enough. He shrugged off the criticism and continued to do as he pleased, which was to find ways of enhancing appreciation for his teachings by relating them to situations people might encounter in everyday life.*

In 1955, after a five-year stint as an instructor in semantics at the University of Chicago, Hayakawa joined the faculty of San Francisco State College (later University) on a part-time basis, which allowed him the freedom to lecture elsewhere (which he did frequently) and write. He was still there when growing student unrest at San Francisco State thrust him into the unexpected role of college president near the end of 1968.

Hayakawa's sudden promotion came after an especially turbulent year on campuses across the nation. Demonstrations, sit-ins, and strikes had become popular means of protest by students as well as faculty members at many institutions, and San Francisco State was no exception. There, a relatively small group of radical students demanded that the school eliminate the ROTC program, relax admission standards to make it possible for more members of minority groups to enroll, establish a separate black studies department, and reinstate a suspended black instructor. When officials refused to agree to these "non-negotiable" demands, some students proceeded to disrupt classes, vandalize buildings, and launch a strike. Local police were called in to restore order, but the turmoil continued for weeks throughout 1968 and led to the resignations of two San Francisco State presidents within seven months.

Into this chaotic atmosphere stepped Hayakawa. Although he sympathized with some of the demonstrators' demands, including the need to expand and improve the black studies program and reassess admission standards, he felt the school's primary obligation should be to the vast majority of students who were not *on strike. In fact, he was one of the few faculty members who had supported the idea of resuming classes by any means necessary—even if it meant resorting to force.*

Hayakawa's feistiness and no-nonsense attitude caught the attention of Governor Ronald Reagan, who appointed him acting president of San Francisco State in late November 1968. (When asked later about how he came to be selected for the position, Hayakawa remarked, "I guess they dug down to the bottom of the barrel.") He immediately banned all student demonstrations and speeches and announced that classes would begin again right after the Thanksgiving break. When school reopened on December 2, angry students responded with violent attacks on classroom and administration buildings in an attempt to shut down classes once again. That same day, an equally outraged Hayakawa (outfitted in his trademark tam o' shanter hat) became a hero to all those exasperated by campus unrest when national news footage showed him confronting the protesters, climbing on their sound truck, and ripping out the wires connected to their loudspeaker.

By mid-December, Hayakawa's firmness and the presence of hundreds of police officers on campus appeared to have had the desired effect; the majority of students had returned to school, and many protesters had been arrested or suspended. But in January 1969, the American Federation of Teachers local that represented some San Francisco State faculty members called for a strike that again halted classes and heightened tensions.

On February 3, 1969, Hayakawa testified on Capitol Hill in connection with the San Francisco State situation. Concerned about the unrest plaguing so many colleges and universities across the nation, Congress had begun to discuss several ways of dealing with the problem, including cutting off federal financial aid to any student convicted of use of force, disruption, or seizure of a school's property. Legislators were very interested in hearing from the man who had taken such a strong stand against protesters and welcomed him warmly. Hayakawa's testimony that day is reprinted here from the official report Campus Unrest: Hearings Before the Special Subcommittee on Education of the Committee on Education and Labor, House of Representatives, *91st Congress, 1st Session, U.S. Government Printing Office, 1969.*

Madam Chairman and members of the subcommittee, San Francisco State College, earlier known as San Francisco State Teachers' College, began as a teacher's training institution just before the turn of the century. It began to offer bachelor's degrees in primary, elementary, and junior high school teaching in the 1920s. Since 1935, the institution has been called San Francisco State College, with broad programs in the liberal arts and sciences to supplement the professional work in education. In 1945, the state authorized a five-year program for the general secondary credential and by 1949 the graduate program was extended to grant the master's degree.

The majority of our liberal arts students come from the San Francisco Bay area. Our creative arts school, with an excellent reputation in drama, film, television, and music, draws from the entire country and abroad. Our education school draws from a wide area of the state.

Our students are not rich. Seventy-five percent or more work full or part time to pay their way through college. The average age is between twenty-four and twenty-five years, with a substantial number of married students who carry full loads and work at outside jobs. Of our 18,000 undergraduate and graduate students only 800 live in the two campus dormitories. An additional 800 will be housed when the third dormitory is available later this year.

About 3,500 students received money under federal aid programs. Dr. Helen Bedesem, the college financial aids officer, has detailed information on the entire aid picture. This is one area I cannot discuss with any great degree of competence since my major effort in eight weeks as president has been to restore order and to keep classrooms open for those who wish to teach and to study.

The ethnic composition, unfortunately, does not reflect either the statewide or the area figure. It includes something in the area of 3.6 percent Negro and a total of 15 to 17 percent nonwhite. The Negro percentage is down from an estimated 11 percent a decade ago, in part because of the growth of the junior colleges and in part because the college entrance standards worked to the disadvantage of many nonwhite young people whose earlier education suffered deficiencies. I do not believe there is any social or educational justification for trying to maintain a student ethnic composition in direct proportion to that of the area or the state, but I do believe that we must do more to increase opportunities for minority and disadvantaged groups, even at the expense of additional teachers and counselors to assist these young people.

San Francisco State College has long been known for its liberal and interesting faculty. It is a college that operated successfully for years with fewer rules and regulations than most any institution of higher education. Academic freedom has been a way of life and an incentive to attract exciting students and professors. This atmosphere may have had something to do with the rise of faculty militancy and the close relationship between some extremely liberal faculty members and students who became leaders of militant or ultraliberal groups.

The faculty is represented in many ways

through professional groupings and by a senate which sets academic policy for the institution. Our senate is only about five years old and still experiencing growing pains.

Generally, administrative control over the faculty cannot be described as dictatorial in the least, despite the present clamor over the state law which says that anyone who absents himself without leave for five consecutive days is considered to have resigned. The faculty has autonomy in essential matters, such as hiring, retention, tenure, and promotion. The president cannot even fire a faculty member. He can only recommend action to the chancellor.

"I do not believe there is any social or educational justification for trying to maintain a student ethnic composition in direct proportion to that of the area or the state, but I do believe that we must do more to increase opportunities for minority and disadvantaged groups. . . ."

Basically, the turnover rate is low. For the last few years our faculty turnover rate has been below the rate of the state college system as a whole.

A relatively small segment of the faculty is close to the small segment of the students who are the militant or dissident leadership. This is a strange alliance. I believe that some faculty may be radicals and may develop close association with radical students because of professional inadequacies. For example, a faculty member who is not considered to be a strong scholar among his peers may seek recognition from students. Then there are at least a few, I am sure, who are dedicated revolutionaries. We do know that there is a certain amount of coaching of radical students by radical faculty but I think we have reached the point where the students have much to teach their tutors.

The relationship of the faculty to the administration is one of those strange bureaucratic arrangements. Some teachers are professional politicians within the institution, very close to administrators at all levels, influencing decisions, carrying messages, and frequently contributing worthwhile feedback of general faculty opinion. Then there are some on our campus, and every other campus, who ignore the administration completely as they come and go from home to the classroom, laboratory, and library. Our strongest ties between the administration and the faculty stem from the council of academic deans, which includes all school deans and administrative deans working under the academic vice president. This is the body of experience, reason, intelligence, and total college concern that any president will rely on for sound advice and good counsel. The deans are close to their department chairmen who, in most cases, are close to their departmental faculty members.

Our administration is one of the problems in the sense that it needs additional manpower. We have excellent men in every key position, but the budget does not allow for assistance of equal caliber. Thus, when a crisis develops, our firstline men are completely occupied. Their routine work suffers and in the case of a prolonged episode like our recent thirteen weeks, fatigue eventually takes its toll. I imagine the same is true in most other urban colleges and universities and I look for the day when we have time to consider some basic reorganization to add strength in numbers at the top. Our administrative turnover is exceedingly low considering what the college has experienced in recent years—low except in the office of president. As you may know, I am the third president in less than twelve months, the eighth in ten years. This is another story and one that probably has had some effect on administration functions. I have not had time to analyze the effects of frequent presidential changes.

A portrait of student unrest groups: We have several white radical or ultraliberal groups. Their numbers total something around 300 when their allies are mobilized. Their central control is probably vested in less than 50 people. These 50 or so are dedicated, experienced, and effective in the field of organizing or disruption. And to answer a question in advance, we cannot eliminate any of these people without exercising due process, which includes finding them guilty of offenses. Recent events may have helped to solve our problem since most, if not all of the white activity leaders have been arrested at least once each.

Of our 800 or 900 black students, I would

estimate that less than 100 have been involved in the recent disruptions, although many more attend rallies under pressure from their leaders. The bravest young people on our campus are the nonviolent young black students who keep on attending classes at the risk of physical attack from black militants and in the face of distrust on the part of the majority of white students. I have praised these young people before in public and appreciate the opportunity to repeat my feelings of admiration for them today.

There is an important difference between black and white activists. Generally speaking, the black students are fighting for a place in society. White activists, such as the Students for a Democratic Society [SDS], are fighting to destroy the society, even though they have nothing better to propose as a substitute. It is only during periods of particular kinds of strife that both groups find enough in common to join forces as they have on our campus this year. And when they do join together the bonds are weak. The alliance is to execute tactics, not to achieve common objectives.

The Third World Liberation Front is relatively new. It was meant to include all the nonwhite and nonblack minorities. It is supposed to unite the oppressed peoples of the world; it is said to be the rallying point for victims of both capitalism and communism. Since its formation on our campus last April, the Third World has been dominated by a handful of Spanish-speaking students who claim to represent the much larger Latin and Oriental population of the campus and the community. There is little evidence to substantiate this claim.

We have some off-campus agitators involved in the present affair. But actually our homegrown brand need little outside help, except in numbers at those senseless rallies and endless marches. We have all the militant leadership that is needed for a first-class revolt and I understand that we have also exported some talent for disruptions at other campuses on both coasts.

Dissidents of all colors have worked exceedingly hard to build sympathy in ethnic communities throughout the year, with the objective of turning a campus problem into a much larger community problem. But their efforts have failed miserably. They have been able to attract as many as 100 students from other campuses for a one-day rally and march. But they have failed completely to attract any large numbers of citizens from the Spanish-speaking, black, or Oriental communities of San Francisco. From these facts, it is clear that the majority of the ethnic minority population is more interested in education as conducted or proposed by the college than in the wild plans for education by mob rule as proposed by our dissident students.

Some militants are genuine in their desire to improve the educational system. But it is also clear that some militants, especially in the Black Students Union, are more concerned with personal power than with education. We saw evidence of this in the very first press conference the BSU conducted on November 6, the first day of the strike. The leaders said boldly that their real objective was to seize power. They have never wavered from this plan. They have never attempted to hide their real purposes. What is unfortunate is that so many well-meaning supporters of increased opportunity for black students have attached different meanings to the struggle. The people on the fringes are the ones saying the noble things about opportunity and progress. The BSU leaders keep saying they want absolute control, with no accountability to anyone except their constituents, constituents ruled by force, intimidation, and gangster tactics.

> ***"Some militants are genuine in their desire to improve the educational system. But it is also clear that some militants . . . are more concerned with personal power than with education. . . ."***

The white militants are as explicit as the blacks. Their story is now familiar on every major campus. They believe our society is so corrupt that there is no hope except to destroy the entire structure and rebuild from the ground up. But their idea of rebuilding along the lines of a participatory democracy is to deny the very freedoms they claim are sacred. We have seen them in action. In their system, there is no more room for debate than at a Nazi rally in the days of Adolf Hitler. If you doubt this, try defending the American commitment in Vietnam at an SDS meeting.

We are asked frequently whether channels of communication are open to students. I cannot think of a college or university in this country where the channels are more open. Many imaginative proposals for changes in education and administration have resulted from the ability of our students to present new ideas to their professors, departments, schools, and presidents. We have supported a large experimental program for years, allowing for experimental courses within the regular structure of the departments and additionally through the experimental college operated on the campus, usually in the evenings, with unlimited opportunities for either students or faculty to try new modes of teaching or to experiment with new subject matter. Most of the courses now included in the black studies program were first tested through the cooperation of willing faculty and administrators.

The people we are forced to deal with in the present crisis—people trying to seize power or to destroy the institution—have used every device to corrupt the channels of communication. Their style of confrontation to achieve ends does not allow for free and open communication because communication in that sense might lead to reason and negotiation, which are the last things they want.

Our present difficulties were not triggered by a specific event, even though the temporary suspension of Black Panther George Murray, part-time instructor and graduate student, is often cited as the reason for the BSU action. The crisis was not triggered at all. It was planned very carefully over a long period of time. To illustrate, the strike started on the anniversary of the date in 1967—November 6—when nine black students attacked the campus newspaper editor and his staff in their offices. Many of those nine are the present student strike leaders. Many are out on parole.

From the very first day, our present strike has been characterized by planned violence. The objective was to cripple instruction. There was no attempt to seize buildings or to disrupt the administration. The first actions were directed toward the classroom. At first, bands of black students entered academic buildings to terrorize instructors and students by shouting, overturning furniture, and just pushing people around. Then we had a rash of minor bombing attempts and arson intended to frighten rather than to damage. For example, on one day we had fifty fires, all in waste baskets, on desk tops or in rest rooms, so the results would disrupt classes rather than to destroy buildings.

S.I. Hayakawa

After the white and Third World militants joined the BSU, which was only a matter of a few days, the action took on more massive proportions and for a time we had a combination of guerrilla tactics and mob action. Every midday in December there was an outdoor rally, usually resulting in attacks on one or more of the classroom buildings.

The people who deplore the use of police on campus seem to forget that the first days of this strike saw violence introduced by the students themselves as essential to their plan. The college use of police was a response to violence, not the cause. What we have succeeded in doing is to move the action from the classroom to the space between buildings and from there to the streets surrounding the campus. For weeks now the classrooms and the inner campus have been quiet and safe.

I believe that we have introduced something new to this business of preserving order on campuses. At most institutions the use of police is delayed as long as possible and when assistance is finally requested, the force is usually too small to handle the situation and new troubles develop. I went the other way. I had ample force available and demonstrated a willingness to use it quickly to protect people and property from attack. The opposition has received my message. I think we have communicated successfully.

During my eight weeks in office, my principal action has been to restore order. But I would not want anyone to believe that I think this is the solution for campus unrest. It is merely a first step. This is where my beliefs vary from those of many of the conservative supporters who have communicated with me. Several things must be accomplished if we are to end the present trend toward confrontation and violence. First, we must reassess many of our educational objectives and administrative systems. We must modernize quickly and on a vast scale to make the entire system more responsive to the times and to the needs of our young people.

Second, we must look realistically at problems of discipline and devise systems that will work without resorting to outside help. We must eventually put campus discipline in the hands of responsible faculty and student groups who will work cooperatively with administrations for the greater good of institutions. Our faculty and student disciplinary systems are not geared for today's problems.

In a sense, the issues behind most present troubles are valid. As a nation, we have said that education is vital for success for every citizen. Yet we still have an overwhelming number of elementary and secondary school systems that are crippling the poor and the minorities educationally. What we see now is a body of Negro, Spanish-speaking, and other young hammering on the door for an opportunity to obtain the education we have told them is so important to their future.

If we were dealing with hunger instead of education—you can imagine what would happen if we had a walled city in which the citizens had all the food they needed while outside there were hordes of starving people. We could not open the gates just a little to admit handsful of the starving and expect the rest to remain patiently outside. No. We would have to be prepared to open the gates wide and admit everyone, or be prepared for a riot. That is the situation now with higher education. We have opened the doors just a little with special programs that serve hundreds while thousands are clamoring for education. I believe we should open the gates fully, even at enormous expense, to provide educational opportunity at every level—in high schools, adult schools, junior colleges, state colleges, and the universities—for our entire minority and poor populations. We should mobilize the best brains available, just as we did when the nation attacked our problems of modern science to solve an educational crisis that means as much to our national welfare as our efforts in outer space.

The relationship of unrest to federal aid programs. Generally, students under aid programs are not the ones who have caused the troubles. Dr. Bedesem is better qualified to discuss this matter than I. But from what I understand after a preliminary study of records still being assembled there may be upward of 100 students receiving aid under one of the many federal programs among those 500 or 600 arrested for all causes during the past thirteen weeks. All people arrested are not necessarily troublemakers. Some, as in the large group arrested at the recent illegal rally, were just too close and failed to leave when ordered to do so. They are violators of the law, but their crime is far different than being plotters, planners, attackers, or arsonists.

Of the hundreds arrested since November 6, only one has so far been tried by civil authorities. He was not an aid recipient. Our college disciplinary system proved inadequate for the situation and is being revised to provide better, and I can say also quicker, procedures. During the next few weeks we will begin hearings on the people who have been arrested as well as on others who have been involved or cited by college officials. I can assure this committee that the provisions of federal law applying to students receiving financial aid will be observed faithfully.

Prognosis: It is not easy at this point to predict the course of events on our campus or elsewhere. I feel that the danger to the nation and to higher education has been vastly underestimated by a majority of people. Most of the news and much of the commentary deals with the action rather than the underlying causes of dissent and the methods to correct obvious ills.

If we are to end campus rebellion without destroying the educational institutions, we must redirect our energies. We must look beyond the day-to-day combat to the reasons underlying this deadly attack on higher education. We must learn to deal both with the dedicated revolutionary leaders and the unsolved problems that enable those leaders to enlist followers. The solution to these problems will take time, brains, and money. This nation is amply endowed with those resources. But we must act promptly and decisively.

During the question-and-answer period that followed, Hayakawa expressed his belief that the pattern of student violence was similar enough from campus to campus that it appeared to be part of a plan by the SDS to disrupt the educational system nationwide. He then drew a comparison between Adolf Hitler and his "fascism from the right" and this new "fascism from the left," noting:

I have said before and I am willing to say again that a fundamental purpose of a revolutionary group is to create doubt in the general public, doubt in the ability of administrations to administer and governments to govern. One of the important ways in which Nazism rose to power in Germany in the 1930s was by creating doubt in the administration of the courts of justice and the Reichstag. The ordinary processes of education and of government, and so on, were disrupted until the people became quite disillusioned in the ability of government to govern. When enough people are disillusioned with the ability of governments to govern, then the place is wide open for tyranny and dictatorship.

There is no incipient SDS dictator waiting in the wings that I know of, but certainly there is no question that the general attempt to create doubt in the ability of governments to govern and administrations to administer is a very important goal of the SDS.

Hayakawa was also critical of the way the mass media were covering the demonstrations. As he remarked:

It is a very tempting thing to have a noon rally and then get home in time to see yourself on the 6 o'clock news. In a sense, this very much magnifies a student's sense of his own importance and the justice of his cause when, let us say, this relatively trivial protest on cafeteria prices of something is blown up into a statewide or nationwide event because it gets on the 6 o'clock news.

Television, in other words, has had the influence of sharpening the sense of urgency and immediacy of about all sort of events. Of course, with the idealization of the young, and so on, I am afraid that it inevitably gets blown up out of all proportion.

The media have something to do with it. It is not their fault, you understand, but the fact that they exist has something to do with the unrest.

Finally, he shared his views on the meaning of academic freedom:

I earnestly believe in academic freedom; the freedom to teach that which you regard as the truth, especially in the field of your own competence and training. The freedom always to seek the truth and to pass it on as you see it. I think that our profession needs to defend that right down the line.

I think there is also freedom to learn. We have a fantastic degree of freedom to learn in this country in this sense, that, if you don't like one course, you can take another. We have a fantastic array of electives. You can major in German or Spanish or ceramics or mathematics. There are all those freedoms, and then there is freedom of discussion within the campus itself, so that we are all free to argue with each other about Marxism or social credit or free love or anything we want.

But one very important thing about academic freedom is, it is academic freedom. It is not freedom of action. No society gives us complete freedom of action. It is not freedom to interfere with the academic freedom of others. So if, let us say, in the exercise of your own academic freedom you have to disrupt somebody else's course in political science, you are interfering with other people's academic freedom at the same time you are exercising your own. . . .

Most of our defense of academic freedom which we have carefully built into our system were geared for previous emergency. The last great attacks on academic freedom, particularly those in the era of Senator Joe McCarthy, those attacks came from the right wing; they came from above, and they came from outside the colleges and universities.

Now the attacks on academic freedom come from the left and from below and from within our own ranks in students and faculty, and so our defenses to protect academic freedom are like the guns at Singapore. They were pointed the wrong way, and while they were pointed this way, those dirty old Japanese came in from behind. This is why we seem so totally unprotected.

Hayakawa eventually prevailed in the battle between San Francisco State and some of its students and faculty; agreements were worked out in March 1969, that settled the disputes mostly on the president's terms, and things slowly returned to normal on campus over the following weeks. Although some who disagreed with him left the university, many others in California and around the country applauded his decisiveness and his willingness to assert his authority over rebellious militants. Supporters urged him to seek political office but Hayakawa declined, citing his interest in remaining at his job to finish what he had started. In July 1969, he was named permanent president of the college.

In 1973, feeling that he had at last accomplished his goals, Hayakawa retired from the presidency of San Francisco State, switched his official party affiliation from Democrat to Republican, and announced his intention to seek a seat in the U.S. Senate. Under California law, however, he turned out to be ineligible to run because he did not change parties at least twelve months before becoming a candidate. Undaunted, Hayakawa tried again in 1976 and won on a platform that emphasized conservative measures such as decentralized government, lower taxes, and fewer regulations on business.

Although he preferred to describe himself as a "Republican unpredictable," Hayakawa quickly revealed himself to be one of the most conservative members of the Senate. He opposed busing to achieve racial integration in public schools, tried to withhold public funds from universities with affirmative action programs, supported reducing the minimum wage for younger workers, and proposed a constitutional amendment making English the country's official language. He also was known for his eccentricities, among them his habit of nodding off during Senate proceedings—a practice that earned him the nickname "Sleepin' Sam." (He claimed that he only fell asleep when a speaker took twenty minutes to say something that could have been said in two.) What was not generally known, however, was that Hayakawa suffered from the sleeping disorder narcolepsy, which quite suddenly plunges its victims into brief periods of deep sleep.

By the time he was up for re-election in 1982, Hayakawa had lost the backing of wealthy California conservatives, so he quickly withdrew from the race. But he did not completely desert politics or abandon the spotlight. From 1983 until 1990, for example, he served as special advisor to the U.S. Secretary of State for East Asian and Pacific Affairs. He also caused an uproar in the Japanese American community during the 1980s when he opposed efforts to seek redress for those who had been uprooted from their homes and sent to internment camps during World War II because they were perceived as a threat to national security. (Hayakawa was a Canadian citizen at the time and living in Chicago, so he was spared the fate of many West Coast Japanese Americans.) He argued that it was a reasonable course of action for the U.S. government to take given the bombing of Pearl Harbor and the well-known ferocity of Japanese soldiers and that he was "embarrassed" by the "ridiculous" attempts of some to seek an apology and compensation for their imprisonment.

Because Hayakawa himself had experienced racial prejudice—he was denied citizenship until the mid-1950s on account of his race, and his longtime marriage to a white woman was not considered legal in many states—many people, especially other Japanese Americans, found his conservative stance on such issues puzzling if not infuriating. Although he later reversed his position on the redress question, he created yet another stir with his outspoken opposition to making the United States a bilingual society, declaring that "the most rapid way of getting out of the ghetto is to speak good English."

In an expression of support for this cause, Hayakawa helped establish and then served as honorary chairman of U.S. English, a private lobbying organization based in Washington, D.C., that is dedicated to making English the country's official language and abolishing bilingual education programs in public schools. He also founded the California English Campaign, which in 1986 succeeded in persuading voters to have English declared the official language of that particular state. (Several other states—mostly those with large Hispanic populations—have since followed suit.)

On April 23, 1982, in an appearance in the nation's capital before the Subcommittee on Education, Arts and Humanities of the Senate Committee on Labor and Human Resources, Hayakawa (who was then still a member of the Senate) outlined the reasons behind his opposition to fostering bilingualism in the United States. He also used the occasion to urge support for his proposed constitutional amendment as well as for a pending bilingual education bill. His comments are reprinted here from Vital Speeches of the Day, *June 15, 1982.*

Thank you, Mr. Chairman. I am honored to follow the testimony of my good friend Secretary Terrel Bell of the Department of Education. He has described in detail the Bilingual Education Improvement Act, S. 2412, which I introduced in the Senate this past Wednesday. I am pleased to work with Secretary Bell on this issue, as we are both committed to giving school districts more flexibility in their teaching methods while targeting the immigrant population in greatest need of English instruction.

Today I would like to address bilingual education as it relates to a much broader issue: the question of what language will be used in the United States. As most of you know I have proposed a constitutional amendment, Senate Joint Resolution 72, which declares as the law of the land what is already a social and political reality: that English is the official language of the United States. This amendment is needed to clarify the confusing signals we have given in recent years to immigrant groups. For example the requirements for naturalization as a U.S. citizen say you must be able to "read, write and speak words in ordinary usage in the English language." And though you must be a citizen to vote, some recent legislation has required bilingual ballots in certain locations. This amendment would end that contradictory, logically conflicting situation.

Our immigration laws already require English for citizenship. The role of bilingual education is then to equip immigrants with the necessary English language skills to qualify them for this requirement. The problem is that all too often, bilingual education programs have strayed from their original intent of teaching English. A related issue is the full scale of interpretations for the term "bilingual education." Chances are that when one asks five people for a definition, five very different answers will be given. According to one interpretation, it simply means the teaching of English to non-English-speakers. This is the method I prefer and is usually called English-as-a-Second-Language or ESL. On the opposite side of the scale bilingual education is a more or less permanent two-track education system involving the maintenance of a second culture and an emphasis on ethnic heritage. This method is called transitional bilingual education and involves teaching academic subjects to immigrants in their own language coupled with English language instruction. This is the definition used to determine eligibility for Title VII funding.

We all grew up with the concept of the American melting pot, that is the merging of a multitude of foreign cultures into one. This melting pot has succeeded in creating a vibrant new culture among peoples of many different cultural backgrounds largely because of the widespread use of a common language, English. In this world of national strife, it is a unique concept. I believe every member of this committee will agree that it had a fundamental impact on our nation's greatness. In light of the growing emphasis on maintaining a second culture and instruction in the native languages, I ask myself what are we trying to do? Where do we want to go? Demographic research tells us that in some of our states, ten or twenty years from now there will be a majority of individuals with Spanish background. It seems to me that we are preparing the ground for permanently and officially bilingual states. From here to separatist movements à la Quebec would be the final step. Is this the development which we want to promote?

"All too often, bilingual education programs have strayed from their original intent of teaching English."

I believe that my constitutional amendment as well as my Title VII amendments will prevent a crisis similar to the separatist movement of French Canadians. That confused state of affairs is a result of controversy about which language shall be the official one used in Canada. I want to avoid a similar situation here in America where use of another language is encouraged to the point that it could become an official language alongside English. This would perpetuate differences between English-speaking and non-English-speaking citizens and isolate one group from the other. There can be no doubt that recent immigrants love this country and want to fully participate in its society. But well-intentioned transitional bilingual education programs have often inhibited their command of English and retarded their full citizenship.

Congress recognized the importance of teaching English to immigrants in 1968 when it passed Title VII of the Elementary and Secondary Education Act. This Act permitted the development of pilot projects to teach English to underprivileged immigrant children. In 1978 Congress expanded the bilingual education program, dropped the poverty qualification and required appreciation for the cultural heritage of the students served by federal funds. These amendments also introduced the option of providing academic instruction in the native languages of the students, coupled with English classes. This method of instruction, transitional bilingual education, has been interpreted by Title VII regulations as the only acceptable method of instruction for bilingual education. The unfortunate result of Congress' 1978 action was to deprive local schools of their flexibility to determine the best method of instruction for their particular non-English-speaking students.

I agree wholeheartedly that we need to do all we can to teach the English language to non-English-speaking students. However, I cannot support a rigid mandate prescribing a single method of instruction. I believe that given the flexibility to choose their own program, local schools will emphasize English instruction. Without the expensive requirement of a full academic curriculum in foreign languages, schools will be able to teach more non-English-speaking students for the same cost. I have met with many school boards who are struggling to maintain high quality education in the midst of reduced budgets. Through my personal communications studies, I have observed that the more academic instruction children get in their immigrant parents' language, the less quickly they learn English. I personally believe that ESL and immersion techniques allow non-English-speaking students to master our language so they can join the mainstream of society more quickly than through transitional bilingual education. My legislation broadens the range of instructional approaches for serving children of limited English proficiency. I expect school boards to welcome this opportunity to provide more efficient and cost effective instruction to their immigrant students while maintaining their eligibility for Title VII funds.

What the learning of a new language requires, as is well known in U.S. military language schools, is total immersion in the new language, or as close to total immersion as possible. Though I personally support intensive methods of English instruction, I must point out that even my proposed constitutional amendment does not prohibit the use of minority languages to assist non-English-speaking students. On the contrary, it specifically states that it "shall not prohibit educational instruction in a language other than English as required as a transitional method of making students who use a language other than English proficient in English." My bilingual education proposal follows the same line of reasoning by allowing local schools the freedom to choose the teaching method that will best serve their immigrant population and maintain their eligibility for federal bilingual education funds.

Some immigrant groups argue that transitional bilingual education is necessary to preserve equal educational rights for non-English-speaking students while they are learning English. I believe that this requirement can actually result in discrimination in the administration of Title VII programs. The cost of providing academic subjects in a language other than English can exclude many of our recent immigrant groups such as the Indochinese who speak a variety of languages. Many local districts educating these students simply cannot afford to provide academic instruction in the many Indochinese languages which are often represented in one school. Imagine the cost of providing academic instruction in Cambodian, Hmong, Laotian, and Vietnamese in several grades. These students are no more fluent in English than the traditional immigrant groups funded under Title VII. However, because local schools often use intensive English instruction for Indochinese students, they will not qualify for Title VII money. Section 2, subsection 2 of the Bilingual Education Improvement Act would correct this by allowing funding for projects which use a variety of methods for teaching children with limited English proficiency including but not limited to transitional bilingual education, ESL, or immersion. Section 2, subsection B insures educational quality for students served by requiring applicant schools to show that they have selected instruction methods that will complement the special needs and characteristics of the Title VII students.

The acquisition of a new language is far easier for children than for adults. Children at the ages of four to six are at the height of their language-learning powers. In families where the father speaks to the children in one language, the mother in another, and the maid in a third, the children grow up trilingual with no difficulty. From the age of six onward, there is a gradual decline in a child's language-learning powers, so that learning a new language as an adolescent is a more difficult and self-conscious process than it is for a child. For anyone over twenty, it is a much more difficult process, involving conceptualization, like learning rules of grammar. A child picks up unfamiliar grammar without conscious effort. Because of these differences in the rates and methods of language learning among different age groups, school children, especially under the age of ten, should be exposed to English constantly through contact with English-speaking classmates and playmates. They will learn English effortlessly, without the sense of undergoing a difficult experience.

The second provision of the Bilingual Education Improvement Act would give priority funding to Title VII projects which serve children who are both of limited English proficiency and whose usual language is not English. In our current period of limited federal resources in education, both Secretary Bell and I agree that it is imperative to target Title VII funds to this particular group of immigrant children. It is clear that the proposed Fiscal Year 1983 budget of $94.5 million cannot serve the approximately 3.6 million students who are technically eligible for Title VII aid. This provision of my legislation will target those who are most limited in their ability to speak English without tampering with the current definition of eligibility for Title VII funding. During our discussions, Secretary Bell and I have agreed that this effort to channel Title VII funds to the students who are least proficient in English is not to be interpreted as a federal mandate which will intrude in the local schools' determinations about their immigrant students. It is an incentive to local school officials to set priorities for using limited federal bilingual education funds. We agree that this new provision will be immensely helpful in clarifying a target population of students who are the *most* limited in their ability to speak English.

The third provision in this legislation would authorize several programs under Title VII which were previously under the Vocational Education Act. Vocational training for immigrant adults and out-of-school youth, training funds for teachers of immigrant students, and bilingual materials development have all proved to be small but effective programs. This provision would remove the set-aside for each program required under the Vocational Education Act and would allow the Department of Education to set priorities for the use of these funds. The focus of this funding will be for demonstration projects which will identify successful teaching methods rather than service projects which merely maintain the status quo. I am very encouraged by Secretary Bell's interest in using these programs as catalysts of research and development which will encourage state and local education agencies to share in the formulation of new training methods.

Another small, but extremely important provision of my legislation would require English proficiency for instructors in bilingual education programs. I was shocked to learn that Title VII currently places greater importance on its teachers knowing the native language of their students than on knowing English. My legislation will amend Section 721 (B) of the 1978 Act to fund programs "including only those teachers who are proficient in English, and, to the extent possible, in any other language used to provide instruction." The emphasis is reversed from knowledge of the immigrant language to English, which Secretary Bell and I agree reflects the true intent of federally-funded bilingual education.

The issue of English as our official language and bilingual education for immigrants is especially timely in light of the Census Bureau figures released this past Tuesday. The 1980 census found that 23 million people in the United States aged 5 or older speak a language other than English at home. We as Americans must reassess our commitment to the preservation of English as our common language. Learning English has been the primary task of every immigrant group for two centuries. Participation in the common language has rapidly made the political and economic benefits of American society available to each new group. Those who have mastered English have overcome the major hurdle to participation in our democracy. Passage of my English language amendment, as well as my bilingual education proposal, will insure that we maintain a common basis for communicating and sharing ideas.

SOURCES

Books

Campus Unrest: Hearings Before the Special Subcommittee on Education of the Committee on Education and Labor, House of Representatives, 91st Congress, 1st Session, U.S. Government Printing Office, 1969.

Hayakawa, S.I., and Alan Hayakawa, *Language in Thought and Action,* 5th edition, Harcourt, 1989.

Zia, Helen, and Susan Gall, eds., *Notable Asian Americans,* Gale Research, Detroit, 1995.

Periodicals

America, "Echoes of Nativism," December 10, 1988, p. 483.

English Journal, "From Pearl Harbor to Watergate to Kuwait: *Language in Thought and Action,*" February, 1991, pp. 28-35; "A Conversation with the Hayakawas," February, 1991, pp. 36-40.

Forbes, "Do We Want Quebec Here?" June 11, 1990, pp. 62-64.

National Review, "S.I. Hayakawa, RIP," March 30, 1992, pp. 15-16.

New York Times, "S.I. Hayakawa Dies at 85; Scholar and Former Senator," February 28, 1992, p. B6.

Time, March 9, 1992, p. 64.

USA Today, "Bilingualism in America: English Should be the *Only* Language," July, 1989, pp. 32-34.

Vital Speeches of the Day, "Bilingual Education Improvement Act: A Common Basis for Communication," June 15, 1982, pp. 521-523.

Antonia Hernández

1948–

Mexican American civil rights attorney

In her role as president and general counsel of the Mexican American Legal Defense and Educational Fund (MALDEF), a national organization devoted to protecting the civil rights of Latinos, Antonia Hernández is one of the country's most prominent activists. Monitoring the impact of laws and public policy on Hispanic Americans and challenging inequities through the courts have formed the basis of MALDEF's mission, and these same concerns have been of paramount importance to Hernández since she took over the reins of the organization in 1985. Of particular interest to her are immigration issues, perhaps because she herself is a native of Mexico and is therefore well acquainted with the problems many newcomers face.

Hernández was born in the town of Torreón in the state of Coahuila, which is located in the north central part of Mexico. She moved to the United States with her family when she was eight years old, settling in predominantly Hispanic East Los Angeles. There she and her five brothers and sisters grew up poor but secure in the love of their parents, who urged all of their children to seek higher education and find ways to make their lives meaningful in service to others.

With that goal in mind, young Antonia pursued a career in education at the University of California in Los Angeles (UCLA), earning a bachelor's degree in 1970 and a teaching certificate in 1971. She was teaching English as a second language to ghetto youngsters and taking graduate classes when she came to the realization that she might be able to do more to help her community if she switched professions and worked for change through the court system. So Hernández enrolled in UCLA's law school and earned her degree in 1974.

After graduation, Hernández hired on as a staff attorney with the Los Angeles Center for Law and Justice, where her duties included handling civil and criminal cases. Three years later, she became directing attorney of a Los Angeles-area Legal Aid office, working once again on civil and criminal cases as well as fighting for bills in the state legislature. Hernández left there in 1979 for a job in Washington, D.C., as staff counsel to the U.S. Senate Committee on the Judiciary, which required her to keep committee members informed on issues involving human rights and immigration. It also gave her valuable experience in drafting bills for consideration by Congress.

Hernández lost her job after Senate control shifted from the Democrats to the Republicans following the 1980 election, but it wasn't long before MALDEF approached her about becoming a staff attorney in the group's Washington office. (MALDEF's national headquarters are located in Los Angeles, with regional offices not only in Washington but in Chicago, San Francisco, and San Antonio as well.) Working her way up through the ranks, which included a transfer to national headquarters to serve as employment litigation director in 1983, she was offered the top post in 1985.

At MALDEF, Hernández directs all litigation and advocacy programs and plans the organization's long-range goals and objectives. She has been instrumental in a number of MALDEF's major initiatives, such as defeating a bill in Congress that would have required Latinos to carry identification cards, promoting affirmative action in both the public and private employment sectors, and challenging questionable school and voting district boundaries.

Hernández is often called upon to articulate MALDEF's view on issues of particular importance to Latinos, among them discrimination, bilingual education, voting rights, and even U.S. Census Bureau policies and statistics. Immigration remains a major concern, too, especially in the wake of recent trends that indicate more and more Americans are ready to deal with the problem of illegal immigrants in ways that some people view as unduly harsh and punitive.

In elections held during the fall of 1994, for example, Californians were asked to vote on Proposition 187, a controversial measure that would have barred illegal immigrants from attending public schools and receiving welfare and nonemergency health-care services, among other things. Proposition 187 sparked intense debate throughout the nation but was naturally a much hotter issue in California, where the rhetoric reached a fever pitch in the weeks before the election. On several occasions that fall, Hernández was asked to explain Proposition 187 and its implications to groups of interested voters. One such instance was on October 5, 1994, when she spoke at Temple Isaiah in Los Angeles. Her remarks that evening are reprinted from a copy of her speech provided by MALDEF.

I want to thank Mr. Levine for inviting me to speak to you this evening. I commend both Mr. Levine and Rabbi Gann for their concern over Proposition 187.

Immigration—legal and illegal—is an inherently difficult and complex issue that defies simplistic and reactionary solutions like 187.

On the one hand, I know all too well that it is easier to "crack down" on the undocumented worker, easier to punish the children of undocumented immigrants, easier to assume that aggressive posture than to deal with the root economic causes of the migration north.

There is no question that the influx has changed the dynamics of cities like Los Angeles, and its impact has been felt in Washington as surely as Sacramento.

We cannot ignore that fact.

Yet, despite all the rhetoric about undocumented immigrants living off the system, the fact is that they come to work and build a better life for themselves and their children, not to take advantage of our educational, medical, and public services. They come to share in our great American work ethic.

We know that many immigrants come from the lowest socioeconomic strata of Mexico and Central America. We know that the immigrant is no longer a male looking to work seasonally and then return to his native country. Entire families are migrating north and settling permanently.

It is therefore critical that we approach undocumented immigration with the facts.

In 1993, only 1.5 percent of immigrants received Social Security.

In 1992 the INS [Immigration and Naturalization Service] reported that 0.5 percent of undocumented immigrants received food stamps or AFDC and about half had private health insurance while only 21 percent used any government health services.

According to the Urban Institute, when all levels of government are considered together, immigrants contribute more in taxes paid than in services received.

Yet in the past few years, public discourse over immigration policy, shaped by misinformation, has shifted dangerously toward extremism. The by-product of that movement has created a rise in xenophobia and the scapegoating of immigrants.

Indeed, in the past several months, we have seen the federal government approve such proposals as banning emergency aid to undocumented immigrants who were victims of the earthquake in Los Angeles, funding the unemployment benefits extension program by cutting off benefits to legal permanent residents, and consider cutting off educational benefits to undocumented children in the public schools.

So taken by the effort to deny aid to undocumented immigrants who had been victimized by the earthquake, Secretary of Housing and Urban Development Henry Cisneros was compelled to say: "It is sad that the circumstances of a disaster would result in making these kinds of distinctions about human suffering."

In California, the Department of Motor Vehicles on March 1 began requiring proof of citizenship or legal status in order to obtain a driver's license or identification card. And now, California faces an extremist immigration policy under Proposition 187, one that could cost California taxpayers $15 billion and do nothing to address any immigration concerns.

All of these efforts are extreme and retrograde and speak to the virulence of the anti-immigrant sentiment that has gripped the state and nation.

I will tell you that I have always been averse to extremism and no less so when it comes to immigration policy.

For me, the answer lies in compassion, moderation and—above all—reason.

While we all have legitimate concerns about illegal immigration, the truth is that Proposition 187 is intended to save money and solve problems but will only make the situation worse and create a host of new problems—expensive ones.

Proposition 187 does nothing to enforce the laws we already have, nor does it beef up enforcement at the borders.

Recklessly drafted, 187 violates federal laws that control federal funding to our schools and hospitals. The independent analysis of 187 in the voter pamphlet shows passage of the proposition could cost our schools and hospitals $15 billion in lost federal funds.

Let's put that staggering amount in a context that every Californian can understand. Replacing that money would necessitate a $1,600 annual tax increase for the average California family.

Proponents of the proposition claim that the state will save hundreds of millions of dollars by denying "nonemergency" medical care to the undocumented. First of all, the estimated undocumented immigrant use of the medical services that 187 would prohibit is very low, just a fraction of one percent of California's budget.

"I will tell you that I have always been averse to extremism and no less so when it comes to immigration policy."

Also, refusal to provide fundamental health care is a severe danger to public interest. If 187 is successful in denying these basic services, undocumented persons will not be treated even if their medical problems are serious, even if they have communicable diseases, even if a low-cost dose of preventive medicine or an immunization could keep them from ending up in county emergency rooms with far more serious ailments that will cost the state even more to treat.

In this country, we long ago recognized that health is a community concern. Volumes of treatises on public health recognized the danger to all of society if certain diseases and injuries are left untreated. The trend toward health care reform shows above all that we believe illnesses are not confined solely to one segment of our population. Yet, under this provision,

Antonia Hernández

children would not be immunized and persons in desperate need of medical attention will not seek such care for fear of being reported to the INS. This constitutes not just a threat to the individual but a threat to our public health. As a society, we are best protected by treating the disease, not by turning away the individual in need of care.

By imposing yet another bureaucratic procedure in providing services, the provision will increase escalating costs of publicly-funded health services. Moreover, requiring verification and denying benefits or services on the basis of suspicion could cause unnecessary, and potentially life-endangering, delays and denials of care to citizens and legal residents who are otherwise entitled to medical assistance.

Finally, requiring health providers to notify the INS of their suspicion that someone may be undocumented compromises the patient-doctor confidentiality privilege. And, to the extent that the undocumented participate in drug abuse programs, the proposition may violate federal law that prohibits such providers from issuing information regarding the identity, diagnosis or treatment of any patient.

When you get beyond all the misinformation, you realize that undocumented immigrants are already ineligible for the vast majority of public social services such as state welfare or food stamps. One-eighty-seven's provision to deny such services to the undocumented merely creates a costly, enormous and unnecessary bureaucratic burden. Because existing federal verification procedures already prevent and discourage the undocumented from applying for public social services, the administrative costs of implementing this provision would offset, and most likely exceed any potential savings.

One-eighty-seven's public services provision also violates federal privacy protections for applicants under the Systematic Alien Verification of Eligibility (SAVE) system that already requires computerized verification of eligibility for such services but prohibits the use of immigration status information for enforcement purposes.

Additionally, the proposition violates federal law which prohibits the state from denying or delaying eligibility for benefits until the applicant has been given the opportunity to rebut any determination by the agency that he or she is undocumented. The proposition lacks the due process protections Congress created when it recognized that the INS verification system is not only time-consuming, but often inaccurate, and therefore could result in wrongful denial of services to United States citizens and legal residents.

One-eighty-seven is opposed by the California PTA and the entire education community because it will cost our schools more than it could ever save them. Even the U.S. Secretary of Education has informed state officials that 187 would violate federal laws and will force a cutoff of federal funds to California schools. At a time when California is working to improve educational quality, Proposition 187 would reduce the educational opportunities for all California children.

The provision to deny an education to undocumented children violates the United States Constitution under *Plyler v. Doe,* a 1982 United States Supreme Court case which recognized the right of all children to public education. [In *Plyler v. Doe,* the Supreme Court ruled that the state of Texas could not bar the children of illegal immigrants from attending public school.] It would also violate the state constitution's right to education.

Requiring schools to report to the INS any pupil or parent suspected of being undocumented violates the federal Family Educational Rights and Privacy Act (FERPA), which prohibits the release of information about public school students except in the most limited circumstances. FERPA is enforced by the federal government through the denial of federal funding. Thus, the proposition puts at serious risk the federal money that supports the education of all California children. Federal monies may also be denied to California colleges, and universities that violate FERPA.

Moreover, this provision would officially establish our public schools as agencies of family investigation and arms of government law enforcement. School officials, teachers, and other school employees would become immigration officials, responding to rumors and suspicions instead of educating our children. Fear of being reported to the INS may also cause undocumented parents to withdraw their United States citizen children from school—creating an underclass of uneducated United States citizens.

Finally, the cost to implement such a verification system could exceed tens of millions of dollars annually. Exclusion of undocumented students from California colleges and universities would result in loss of revenue and would take those students who may be the best and brightest of our communities and relegate them, perhaps permanently, to the underclass.

One-eighty-seven will mean more crime, not less, because it will kick an estimated three hundred thousand kids out of school and onto our streets, with no supervision. For this reason, LA County Sheriff Sherman Block and the state's largest law enforcement association of rank and file police officers and deputy sheriffs, the Peace Officers Research Association of California (PORAC), have spoken out against 187.

Additionally, 187's law enforcement provisions duplicate current law which encourages, and in some cases requires, local law enforcement to notify the INS of certain arrestees' immigration status. In fact, through a computerized booking system, police in several counties—including Los Angeles County—effectively report all suspected undocumented arrestees to the INS. These counties have established a booking system that allows the INS access to information regarding all foreign-born criminal arrestees.

Aside from duplicating already-existing practices, these provisions of the proposition would severely endanger the public safety. An increased distrust of the police would develop in many communities, leading to reduced cooperation with law enforcement agencies, increased criminal behavior because many witnesses and victims would not report crime for fear of being reported to the INS, and the undermining of efforts to implement community policing and other models of police-community cooperation.

There are additional disturbing questions about 187 that have been documented in recent press accounts. The people behind 187 are bankrolled by the Pioneer Fund, which is a secretive group that funds white supremacy research.

Alan Nelson, coauthor of 187, wrote the proposition while he was a paid lobbyist for the Federation for American Immigration Reform (FAIR). FAIR has received one million dollars from the Pioneer Fund, one of the longest and most consistent financial supporters of Nelson's FAIR. FAIR has also been the recipient of some of the Pioneer Fund's largest contributions in recent years. The Internal Revenue Service reports a long-standing financial relationship between the two groups.

FAIR has even admitted to the relationship. On March 30 of this year, FAIR's executive director Dan Stein admitted in the *San Francisco Chronicle:* "I think they support our work because the [Pioneer] trustees agree with what we're doing."

Despite Nelson's attempts to publicly distance himself from FAIR by starting a new organization this past May, the fact remains that he was FAIR's lobbyist when he authored 187.

Incorporated in 1937 by strict immigration, eugenics and sterilization advocates who saw selective breeding as a means of improving the quality of race, the Pioneer Fund remains an active, but secretive organization based in New

York. In addition to FAIR, the Pioneer Fund supports a number of controversial research projects and organizational efforts. Among them are the much-criticized works of Dr. William Shockley, who called for the sterilization of individuals with lower than average IQs; the well-known Minnesota Twins Study; researchers claiming to prove the inferiority of blacks with the use of gonad and cranium size studies; organizations promoting the notion that the "purity" of the white race is endangered by "inferior genetic stock"; and the editor of the neo-Nazi "mouthpiece" *Mankind Quarterly,* with its close ties to the mentor of Joseph Mengele of Auschwitz.

The ties of Nelson to these white supremacist supporters raise some very serious and fundamental concerns about 187 and sheds a whole new light on the "SUSPECT" reporting requirements of the proposition. I urge voters to read the 187 provisions which require that authorities report to the INS and the attorney general ANYONE they MERELY "SUSPECT" to be here illegally—in other words, anyone with "foreign" features, an accent or ethnic last name.

And 187 provides no protections for citizens or legal residents, particularly those with such attributes, against false accusations. Unlike current law, the proposition eliminates the required due process by not requiring an arrest to be lawful or that "suspicion" of undocumented status be "reasonable." The absence of "reasonableness" means there is little to protect immigrant witnesses and victims of crime from being falsely arrested and turned over to the INS. In effect, the provision turns police officers into INS agents, with all of the attendant fear that such status generates in immigrants, both legal residents and undocumented persons.

In summary:

One-eighty-seven punishes innocent children by denying them health care and education.

According to the state legislative analyst's offices, 187 will cost California taxpayers in excess of fifteen billion dollars in lost federal funds and in the development and administration of elaborate verification and notifications systems, and training of all state and local agencies.

One-eighty-seven will severely endanger the public safety by kicking three hundred thousand unsupervised kids out of school.

One-eighty-seven jeopardizes the privacy of Californians—forcing government employees, teachers, doctors, and other health care providers to act as INS agents, responding to rumors and suspicions instead of doing their jobs.

The people behind one 187 have close ties to a white supremacist group. By requiring all "suspects" to be reported to the authorities 187 would create a police-state mentality.

One-eighty-seven is unconstitutional, blatantly violating a clear ruling of the United States Supreme Court, and will force a cut in federal funds for our schools.

Finally, 187 does nothing to curb unlawful immigration into the state.

As a nation, we have been too apt to forget the benefits immigrants bring. We have also been given the opportunity to heed the lessons of our immigration history, and to this day we have squandered that opportunity. Instead, we have found ourselves in a desultory discourse that appeals to our worst nature as Americans, that plays to our darkest fears of "the foreigner."

Perhaps the saddest part of it all is that in so doing we have victimized not only voiceless immigrants but ourselves. For as I look upon this room and all the many faces, I am reminded again of this nation's great good fortune—that blessing—to be inheritor of such wealth, a true common wealth.

William Saroyan once wrote: "This is America, and the only foreigners here are those who forget it is America."

There has been all too much forgetting and not enough acknowledgment of our own immigrant stories, and the debate over immigration policy must be refracted through such a multicolored prism.

For if we are unable to bring some reason and decency to this debate, what is at stake is nothing less than who we are as a people, and how we define ourselves as a nation.

In the end, however, I remain optimistic that we will find our way to dealing compassionately and thoughtfully with immigrants. We will begin to move beyond the rhetoric and misinformation and posit the solutions to an issue that defies simplistic and reactionary approaches. I am optimistic because it is not our nature as Americans to turn our backs on those in need in the wake of a disaster—undocumented immigrants or not. It is not our nature to punish children and blame the ills of a nation on a small sector of our society. It is not our nature to turn away from issues that must be dealt with.

We will find our way to a reasoned and dignified policy by adhering to the sense of humanity that has made this country great, and acknowledges the role of the government controlling our borders. I know that we are a good and decent people—that is our nature and our franchise as Americans.

Thank you.

Proposition 187 was approved by California voters in November 1994, but opponents immediately launched various court challenges that have prevented its provisions from going into effect.

Just a couple of weeks after the election, on November 18, Hernández was in Albuquerque to attend a celebration marking the twenty-fifth anniversary of the founding of MALDEF. In her address that evening, she reflected on the past and speculated on what the future might hold, especially in light of increasing voter support for measures such as Proposition 187. Her remarks are reprinted from a copy of her speech provided by MALDEF.

Buenas noches. Welcome to this wonderful event celebrating the twenty-fifth anniversary of MALDEF. As I reflect on our accomplishments and continued challenges, I realize how appropriate it is that we should have this celebration in Albuquerque.

As the Latino population continues to grow throughout this country, the Latinos of New Mexico can be proud to know that, through their struggles and through their responsible participation in the civil rights movement, they have laid important groundwork for others.

Since so many of you are longtime friends and supporters of MALDEF, I do not need to go into all the details of our beginnings. Suffice it to say it began in San Antonio when Pete Tijerina, one of our founders and our first executive director, and a handful of other Mexican American attorneys decided to use the law to eliminate educational, economic, and political disparities—to use the law to open doors for a community that was shut out from the basic rights enjoyed by the larger society.

In the quarter-century that has transpired, we have cleared many hurdles. And while we sometimes find ourselves going back, having to clear the same hurdles that we confronted years ago, we cannot see this as regression. Rather, it is a crucial part of our mission: to protect and promote the civil rights of Latinos living in the United States.

Protect and promote. Two very different responsibilities.

Protecting is a defensive measure. It is a shielding from injury or damage. When we protect civil rights, therefore, we make sure these rights are secured in their current state.

Promoting, on the other hand, is a moving forward. When we promote the civil rights of Latinos, we take them to a higher level.

It is no wonder that we find ourselves simultaneously looking back and moving forward. It is our mission to do so. To protect and to promote.

In both areas, we have so much to be proud of. Our accomplishments in the area of political access have led to a tremendous increase in the number of Latino elected officials, as eligible Latino voters have had the opportunity to elect candidates of their choice. And due in large part to our advocacy efforts, the recently passed National Voter Registration Act will ensure that fewer bureaucratic hurdles stand between an eligible voter and the voting booth.

In the area of employment, we have fought English-only workplace rules, an endeavor that has opened up a new area of work for us: language rights. We also have protected immigrant workers through our challenges to city ordinances that attempted to restrict street vendors. It is not surprising that these cases so often cross programs. A language rights case is often an employment case. And both are often immigrants' rights cases.

The civil rights of Latinos are challenged in so many areas. But perhaps the most poignant area is education. Because in this area, our very youngest family members are being threatened. And if we do not come to their defense, and if we do not strive to take their situation to a higher level, who will?

As you all know, the recent passage of California's Proposition 187 is threatening the right to education of hundreds of thousands of children in California. Our 1982 Supreme Court victory in *Plyler v. Doe* is now one of those hurdles that we will have to clear again, twelve years later.

But before I discuss the implications of California's Proposition 187, I'd like to touch on the groundwork that has been laid quite recently by MALDEF, and I'd like to recognize the Latino community of *this* state for their role in establishing our capacity to serve.

Across the country, MALDEF is working tirelessly to protect and promote the civil rights of Latino school children. Our San Antonio office continues to litigate its landmark *Edgewood* case, which was originally filed a decade ago and which continues to seek an equitable legislative remedy for the inadequate Texas public school finance system.

In Chicago, our staff continue to challenge the misuse of Chapter 1 funds, which we allege have been wrongly allocated to cover administrative costs and to remedy the school board's budget crisis.

In Los Angeles, where Latinos comprise the majority of public school students, we prevailed in *Rodriguez v. Los Angeles Unified School District,* winning a settlement that will, among other things, ultimately equalize per-pupil expenditures.

And finally, in the San Francisco bay area, we were successful just last February in winning the approval of a consent decree in *Vasquez v. San Jose Unified School District,* a desegregation case that was first filed as far back as 1971. The settlement mandates a genuinely dedicated bilingual education program, a program that will serve as a model for districts nationwide.

In reflecting on these victories, I also need to touch on the work at our fifth regional office because we cannot underestimate the importance of our presence in Washington, D.C. Were we not to have that primarily legislative arm, were we not to have an established position among the coalitions that exist on Capitol Hill, we might not have had the opportunity brought to us last year by the Congressional Hispanic Caucus when they asked us to draft reauthorization legislation for the Elementary and Secondary Education Act. The centerpiece of this legislation is the Chapter 1 program, which determines how several billion dollars will be spent. Chapter 1 funding has the potential to make a huge and positive difference in the education of Latino and other underserved children, and so the opportunity to draft this legislation was one we embraced. Last month we proudly witnessed its passage.

As a funding measure, this legislation ensures vastly increased eligibility of economically disadvantaged and limited-English-proficient students. But this bill is also a reform measure because it targets the professional development of educators to make them more effective in the education of these children. It is a reform measure because it alters student assessment standards and coordinates health and other social services. It is a reform measure because it increases parent involvement.

I must confess, though, that I find it somewhat ironic to refer to the concept of parent involvement as a "reform". Because it was a group of Latino parents in New Mexico whose involvement, more than twenty years ago, helped put MALDEF on the map. If the rest of the country is just catching on to the value of parent involvement, then those individuals who initiated *Judy Serna v. Portales Municipal Schools* are truly pioneers.

I am sure many of you remember the conditions here in New Mexico in the late 1960s, early 1970s: discrimination evidenced by unequal application of suspension and expulsion rules; summary whippings of students; prohibition on speaking Spanish; failure to employ Mexican American teaching and administrative personnel; and the failure to integrate educational material on Mexican American history, language, and culture in the school curriculum on any level.

And those of you who were directly involved remember José Armas, who came to New Mexico in 1968 as a training director for the Vista program and who worked closely with the grassroots community. He inspired the parents and students to work together and to take their complaints to the schools. When this course of action did not pan out, the group decided to contact MALDEF in San Antonio.

We were a new, struggling organization then, but we took the case. And we pursued it because the community was so committed. Led by José and by Frank Sánchez, the parents and students were the ones who did the research and discovery. And even though they were physically attacked, threatened and intimidated by police, by school officials, and by non-Latino community leaders, they persevered. And because of them, we all won a tremendous victory.

The *Serna* decision provided MALDEF and all Spanish-speaking people in this country with a golden opportunity to pursue the right of bilingual education as a remedy for providing equal education opportunity to those children of the Spanish-speaking who cannot learn efficiently or effectively in classrooms where Spanish is neither used nor encouraged.

Twenty years later, we are still pursuing that right. And we are pursuing it with even greater fervor. We must. Between 1986 and 1991—a five-year period—total student enrollment in the nation's schools increased by four percent while schools' limited-English-proficient student population rose by fifty percent.

We also are still finding ourselves having to explain our rationale. The subject of bilingual education for non-English-speaking children is so frequently misunderstood. Sadly, there are people who think that providing the opportunity to learn in one's native language encourages the children (and by implication their parents) not to learn English. The truth, however, is that even a motivated child has extreme difficulty following lessons in an unfamiliar language; if they cannot learn what they need to know in the classroom, where are they to learn? If they cannot be provided with basic curriculum in their native language while simultaneously acquiring English proficiency, when will they learn the basics?

And so the battle continues. New faces, new names. But the battle continues. And thanks to our parent leadership program, which is implemented in both Los Angeles and San Antonio, we still have the assistance of parents, parents who would look to the *Serna* group as heroes, and who would be correct in doing so.

The battle continues on other fronts as well. In the area of immigrants' rights, it is all too clear that the cyclical nature of immigrant bashing has not yet been curbed. As I mentioned a few moments ago, California's ballot initiative, Proposition 187, did indeed pass last week—in spite of community education efforts undertaken by MALDEF and others.

And while we are saddened by this tragic decision, we are not necessarily surprised. As civil rights advocates, we are all too aware of the realities faced by the immigrant community.

Just last year, our San Antonio office litigated against the INS following the discovery of severe civil rights violations on the campus of El Paso's Bowie High School. On one occasion, the school's coach was driving two football players to a game when the border patrol stopped the car, pointed a pistol at the coach, forced the people our of the car, and subjected them to search and interrogation.

Another incident in El Paso involved two students who were stopped on their walk home from graduation exercises at the school. Despite the students' identifying themselves as U.S. citizens, the border patrol interrogated them, forcibly took belongings out of their hands, verbally and physically abused them.

Within two months of our filing suit, the federal judge granted an injunction against the INS prohibiting the agents from violating Fourth Amendment search-and-seizure rights of Latino persons traveling through the Bowie High School attendance area. The suit sought, among other remedies, injunctive relief from the INS, including better training of the border patrol agents and an improved complaint procedure for reporting abuses.

Settlement was finalized and today, the staff, participants, and alumni of our El Paso leadership development program are actively assisting MALDEF's legal staff in San Antonio as we continue to monitor the settlement to ensure compliance.

This collaborative effort—which involves the community, MALDEF's legal staff, our program staff, and former participants of MALDEF programs—is the key to the movement that is also taking place in California.

On the day following the election, opponents of Proposition 187 held a press conference. While we were all quite dismayed by the result of the election, and while we were particularly saddened to reflect on the percentage that voted in favor of Proposition 187, we also recognized something very positive. And as I stood on the platform with other community leaders, it became apparent that a strong coalition has been created. It is not a Latino coalition; it is not a minority coalition; it is not an anti-Republican coalition or an anti-Pete Wilson coalition. It is a civil rights coalition.

Formed at a time when we needed to defend our rights, this new civil rights coalition will grow and it will ultimately take our rights to a higher level. Again, MALDEF's mission surfaces: to protect and to promote.

So that is where we are: back in the courts revisiting *Plyler v. Doe,* and simultaneously looking ahead.

We are also looking east. Because we know that the battle fought in California does not just belong to California. It is the nation's battle. And the organizations that are instigating it, such as the Federation of Americans for Immigration Reform [FAIR], are not going to stop with their Prop 187 victory. They'll continue across the country, trying wherever they can to turn people's fears and frustrations into regressive policy dictated by poorly written and unfair laws.

I encourage you to recognize this trend and to be prepared to make something positive of it. Yes, I am disappointed by my state, by California, but I am so very proud of my community. I am proud of the sense of civic participation that was demonstrated by the students, particularly those who did not march for marching's sake but rather saw this as a time to become responsible members of a democracy. I am proud of the many diverse groups who united to bring reason to a heated debate. I am proud that when the votes were counted, the people most threatened by its outcome did not let their emotions lead to volatile behavior. Their leaders asked for calm, and calm prevailed. And now justice will prevail.

I encourage you to recognize the strength in your community and the strength in yourselves. Certainly MALDEF recognized it over twenty years ago when you worked so hard to ensure a victory in *Serna v. Portales.* For your assistance and your perseverance then, and for the leadership you have continued to demonstrate, I am thankful and I am proud. And I look forward to your continued support as we unite in our struggle, protecting those rights we have attained so far and moving forward to the next level.

SOURCES

Books

Telgen, Diane, and Jim Kamp, eds., *Notable Hispanic American Women,* Gale Research, Detroit, 1993.

Periodicals

Hispanic, "Antonia Hernández: MALDEF's Legal Eagle," December, 1990.

NEA Today, "Meet: Antonia Hernández," November, 1990, p. 9.

Parents, "Law in the Family," March, 1985.

Anita Hill

1956–

African American attorney and educator

In October 1991, millions of Americans were glued to their television sets to witness some of the most dramatic moments in the nation's political and social history—the confirmation hearings of U.S. Supreme Court nominee Clarence Thomas, charged with sexual harassment by a former co-worker named Anita Hill. Few such events have had the same ability to hold so many spellbound; few also have so polarized the country. To many, the enduring legacy of those hearings is that they awakened an entire nation to the idea of sexual harassment, forced employers to become more responsive to potential problems, and made it easier for women to lodge complaints against their harassers. To some African Americans, however, the Thomas-Hill confrontation was not eye-opening but disturbing because it involved accusations by a black woman that threatened to destroy the career and reputation of a black man. In either case, at the center of the controversy is Anita Hill, whose explosive testimony is still reverberating throughout the land.

Hill, the youngest of thirteen children born to a rural farm couple in Oklahoma, grew up in an atmosphere where both education and Baptist religious traditions figured prominently. A popular and hard-working student, she graduated at the top of her high school class and from there went on to Oklahoma State University, where she majored in psychology and received her bachelor's degree (with honors) in 1977. Partly with the help of a scholarship from the NAACP, Hill continued her studies at Yale University Law School, again graduating with honors upon completion of her degree in 1980.

In 1981, after a brief stint at a Washington, D.C., law firm, Hill then made the decision that would have such a tremendous impact on her future: she joined the civil rights division of the U.S. Department of Education, where her supervisor was a recent Reagan administration appointee named Clarence Thomas. A few months later, when Thomas was chosen to head the Equal Employment Opportunity Commission (EEOC)—which investigates job discrimination complaints involving sex, race, color, religion, or national origin—Hill continued to work for him as his special assistant. She left government service in 1983 and headed back to Oklahoma, where she taught for a short time at Oral Roberts University. In 1986, she became a law professor at the University of Oklahoma.

Meanwhile, Thomas remained with the EEOC throughout the rest of the

1980s. In late 1989, President George Bush nominated him for a federal appeals court judgeship, and, after his confirmation, he assumed his new post in March 1990. Thomas had served on the bench for little more than a year in relative anonymity when Bush named him to replace retiring Supreme Court justice Thurgood Marshall in July 1991. Despite protests from some civil rights organizations and women's groups who opposed his conservative politics, Thomas appeared to be headed for confirmation until October 6. It was on that day that the first media reports surfaced describing Anita Hill's confidential testimony before the Senate Judiciary Committee in early September in which she accused her former boss of sexual harassment while they worked together at the Department of Education and the EEOC.

The revelation sent shock waves across the country. Within days, the Senate Judiciary Committee—bowing to intense public pressure to look into Hill's charges—reluctantly agreed to reopen the hearings and give her a chance to speak publicly about the alleged harassment. On October 11, as a national television audience watched with rapt attention, Hill calmly recounted to the committee the details of Thomas's behavior, including that fact that he had made numerous sexual overtures to her and that he had repeatedly tried to involve her in lewd conversations about pornographic movies. Later that same day, an angry and somewhat perplexed Thomas vehemently denied Hill's accusations and declared that no job was worth what he and his family had had to endure.

Faced with the dilemma of having to choose between two respected, credible people with very different stories to tell, Americans hotly debated the issue of sexual harassment in the workplace; for many, it was the first time they had really looked at the dynamics of male-female relationships on the job. And for blacks, especially black women, it was as much a question of racial politics as it was sexual politics; Hill's accusations against Thomas meant having to decide which was more important—loyalty to one's race or to one's gender. On October 16, 1991, after hearing additional testimony from various witnesses for both sides, the Senate narrowly voted 52-48 to confirm Thomas. But the debate did not end. It rages on, still cutting across lines of class, race, gender, and political persuasion.

An extremely private person, Hill has kept a fairly low profile since the hearings. For much of that time, she was on leave from her teaching position at the University of Oklahoma; she submitted her resignation in March 1995. She is reportedly at work on her autobiography as well as on a book dealing with sexual harassment.

Hill has granted few interview requests and has chosen her public appearances carefully, accepting only occasional invitations to speak to legal groups, women's organizations, and student audiences. Most of the time, she makes few if any references to her own personal experience with sexual harassment in the workplace, preferring instead to look at the problem from a strictly legal standpoint or to discuss the difficulties women in general face if they choose to confront their harassers. In recognition of the courage it took for her to do so in such a public way, Hill has been showered with honors. On August 9, 1992, for example, the American Bar Association Commission on Women in the Profession presented her with a special Margaret Brent Women of Achievement Award. In her acceptance speech, reprinted here from an American Bar Association Commission pamphlet entitled Women Lawyers of Achievement 1992 Award Speeches, *Hill reflected on why women from all walks of life should be concerned about sexual harassment.*

Thank you very much. I am very honored to be here.

My family, who were here with me earlier today, had to leave. But I have, over the last few months, developed an extended family and, fortunately for this group, they are attorneys. I would like to introduce some people who have been very special to me not only during the hearings, but since the hearings. Professor Emma Jordan, Professor Charles Ogletree, my classmate Ronald Allen, Judge Susan Hoerchner, and her husband, Fred Gray. And I would like to thank all of you.

I would like to thank you for this opportunity to speak to you today. I first spoke before the American Bar Association a few years ago at the UCC Committee meeting, and I have some friends here from the UCC Committee. I spoke at the UCC Committee on the limitations conventions on international law and, I dare say, my colleagues from the [Business Law] Section, having heard that presentation once, did not come here to hear it again. And I know that the rest of you did not come here for that reason either.

But, I am here today. And I believe that you expect me to talk about sexual harassment, to explore what it is about the hearings, the aftermath, and the very issue of harassment itself that has touched a nerve in so many of us.

Many of us consider ourselves to be successful and productive in our fields. Many of us are well thought of by our colleagues, and our personal acquaintances consider that we have made it. Why do we, who have so much, have to be concerned about the women who experience sexual harassment? And why are so many of us even angry today?

Today, in briefly exploring the issue, I ask a series of questions and, in an approach which may seem very unacademic, I attempt to answer them and even suggest some modest proposals, responses to the issue for those of us who are members of the legal profession.

The first question is when we have made it, why do we care that perhaps as many as ninety-two percent of the working women in this country will be victimized by harassment? Is it that we know that the behavior is centuries old? Is it that we are simply offended by the appalling nature of the behavior that harassers exhibit toward their targets? Is it the references to women as sluts and whores? Or the prohibitions of newspapers on job sites where erotic material is openly read and displayed? Or is it the extortion of sex for a job or promotion or raise that we find patently offensive?

If not these things, surely it is the rape and assault that ten percent of the complainants of sexual harassment endure which cause us to reject harassment. Maybe it is our reaction to our own experiences of sexual harassment that cause us to bristle when we hear the term. Some may recall the self-scrutiny which we exhibited, perhaps even to the point of self-blame, when we were exposed to harassment.

"What is it about sexual harassment that . . . we can experience it, be absolutely frightened and offended by it, and then seemingly act as though it did not happen in one swift motion?"

Perhaps it was the societal reaction to the hearings that causes us to consider, even ten months afterward, the issues that were raised—the reactions of silencing and denial that were so common, and continue to be common, when claims of harassment are raised and as those in charge attempted to minimize the significance of the behavior and re-victimized its targets.

And finally, perhaps explanation lies in the response by some jurists who see the behavior as the harmless reflection of popular culture against which there are no prescriptions at law.

What is it about sexual harassment that has become so incorporated into our functioning that we can experience it, be absolutely frightened and offended by it, and then seemingly act as though it did not happen in one swift motion? I propose that it is all of the above, the repulsive behavior, the internalization of it and the social rejection of its victims, that strike a chord with so many of us.

I suggest, however, for those of us who have

made it, there is more, as we are forced to examine two premises underlying the hearings in particular and sexual harassment claims in general.

The first is the premise that no woman can be presumed to be telling the truth about her experiences of sexual abuse. Even without apparent motives, women will lie, fantasize or delude themselves. These premises date back to Freudian psychology where, as you may recall from your college psychology classes, women who complained of incest were presumed to be repressing fantasies about their fathers.

The second premise is that a women's contribution to the workplace never outweighs that of the man. As one writer put it, "A man's career is assumed to be the equivalent of a woman's life. A setback to his ambition will be taken as a threat to his very existence. A woman's career, on the other hand, is just a job." Wrapped up neatly in the harassment issue as it is presented to us are questions about our integrity and our professional work. And the burden of proof in the court of popular opinion seems always to be on us.

Anita Hill

Typical responses of incredulity are supported by myths that hold that women make up stories that wrongly characterize natural behavior as sexual abuse. We have seen the myth used before in cases involving allegations of rape. Lingering in everyone's thought is the almost always used and not easily rebutted suggestion that "she wanted it" or that "she made it up to get even with him." Thus, in a leap of reasoning, the victim's sexual history is presumed prohibitive of the issue of whether she consented to sex with the defendant.

The presumption that she made it up to get even was vividly realized in a New York jury's reaction in what has been dubbed the "LaCross Rape Case." That jury concluded that the sexual assault of a twenty-one-year-old was consensual on her part. The jury reached this conclusion even though several of the defendants corroborated the complaining witness's story that she had been given several drinks which, without her knowledge, had been laced with vodka, that she could hardly walk, and had passed out during the time that she was with the accused. In the face of this evidence and other evidence, one juror summed up the witness's claim with these words: "Hell hath no fury like a woman scorned." Such is the force of the presumption against those who allege acquaintance rape.

One must certainly be careful in analyzing society's reaction to criminal cases, and I firmly believe that in a criminal proceeding the rights of the accused must always be protected with the burden on the state to make its case. Yet in the court of public opinion this burden is extended to a more onerous one, not on the state but on the person claiming sexual misconduct. In the court of popular opinion she is often asked to defend her behavior not just as it relates to the act complained of, but she is often asked to defend her entire social history. We are often more concerned about what she wore and where she was at the time than the nature of the acts alleged.

Jurors and sometimes judges confuse the burden in the criminal proceeding with the burden of the court in popular opinion.

We as women who have made it may comfortably distance ourselves from these experiences of the victims and their plight. We may bolster our distancing with assumptions about ages and level of education and, thus, our wisdom. After all, we may reason, the burdens placed on these individuals went to their personal lives, not to professional competency, which defines so many and is universalized to all women. Thus, we can conclude that we are different.

We have managed to avoid facing attacks on women as professionals as well. And thus, we fail to internalize the challenges raised in *Price Waterhouse v. Hopkins,* or *Hishon v. King &*

Spaulding by women who were not appropriately feminine or who did not make partner. After all, we dress and act appropriately. We wear the right amount of makeup and we subscribe to the tenets of the culture and we do make partner. We dismiss the fact that the Supreme Court upheld a state's rights to exclude women from the Bar. Even though we know from the Commission's own study that women are underrepresented in all areas of the profession, but particularly in higher echelon positions. We reason that exclusion of women from the profession is a historic relic, an idea that is absent in today's legal and cultural climate, even though a lawyer may be referred to by opposing counsel in the courtroom as "little lady" or "dear" or "honey."

But when the issue is sexual harassment we must face it squarely, for it is neither removed from us culturally and socially nor is it a historic relic. It is real in our lives and in the lives of others. We recall our own lived experiences or threats of such. We recall stories told to us by our friends or colleagues that date back perhaps to high school and certainly to college. We hear the recent news stories of women who are breaking the silence for the first time. We even hear stories of girls in grade schools and junior high schools whose daily experience seems to be survival training rather than academic education.

From the slave to the domestic servant, from factory worker to construction worker, from law professor to neurosurgeon, we are each the potential target of this kind of abuse of power.

In sum, we have seen the victim of sexual harassment, and it is us. We are angry and with good cause. Whether we wear a suit to work or blue jeans, we must know that the injury to any of us is a threat to us all.

Harassment not only becomes a symbol of the questions of our integrity, our sanity and our dignity, but as well it becomes a metaphor for questions of our contributions to the workplace. Just as our harasser's word is preferred to ours, his contributions are often deemed more significant. So many times we hear the question, "Even if what she claims is true, is it worth ruining his career?" The question, of course, ignores the fact that her career and even her life is often destroyed in a process which denies the truth and the significance of her complaint.

The question for us translates to, why sacrifice his career when hers is so much more expendable? In the business culture, victims who are not believed often suffer economic, social and psychological losses when their complaints are ignored. Even victims who are believed are often transferred or ostracized and labeled troublemakers and thus suffer economic, social, and psychological losses even when their complaints are addressed. Moreover, once that one woman complains, each of us becomes suspect. At once, the personal and individual complaint becomes professional and universalized in our minds and the culture in which we function.

Now, how do we respond? We respond in a number of ways. We seek political office, we support political candidates, we withdraw support from others. But the issue exceeds elected politics. As members of a profession, we must see the professional implications. We must even, at some individual risk, participate in the education of our colleagues. At the same time, we must look out for other potential victims among our colleagues. Mentoring is important. Above all, as members of the legal profession, we must see the legal implications. We, after all, write the law and the policy which guide how the issue will be viewed in the workplace. We supply the rhetoric reflected in legal opinions, we craft the charges which assist the juries in rendering verdicts. As far as we have come on this issue, we are now only at a metaphase—a midpoint in our reaction. Whether we move forward to change or revert back to status quo is most assuredly up to us as a profession.

> ***"From the slave to the domestic servant, from factory worker to construction worker, from law professor to neurosurgeon, we are each the potential target of this kind of abuse of power."***

Charles Hamilton Houston, the great civil rights attorney, law professor and activist, opined that the lawyer is either a social engineer or a social parasite. And I was fortunate enough last night to be at a dinner where Justice Thurgood Marshall was honored. To hear him speak of Charles Hamilton Houston as his mentor and as his instructor was truly inspiring. And after hearing those words and reading the words of

Charles Hamilton Houston, it is clear to me that we only have one choice. Clearly, we must be social engineers.

Our engineering will be brought about through our rhetoric and deed. But it must be for positive change. It must move our profession and our society away from the presumptions that make possible the perpetuation of harassment and other forms of sexualized victimization. It must move us forward toward a solution to the problem of harassment and the inequities for which it has come to stand.

The passion which we feel for our careers and our lives is felt by many others regardless of their profession, regardless of their economic class, regardless of their position in life. Translate that passion into action that will benefit not only ourselves but others as well. Many do not have the opportunities to speak out as we do.

What we do with our voices can affect all.

It is with great honor and humility that I stand with these distinguished recipients of the Margaret Brent Award. In accepting it, I want to remind you that in 1990, eighty-five percent of thirteen thousand female lawyers witnessed or experienced some form of sexual harassment. I remind each of you of the thousands of women whose appointments in academic and work life will include meetings with their harassers. On behalf of those women and in hope that those encounters will be less frequent, less severe, and more readily redressed, I accept this award.

SOURCES

Books

Chrisman, Robert, and Robert L. Allen, editors, *Court of Appeal: The Black Community Speaks Out on the Racial and Sexual Politics of Clarence Thomas vs. Anita Hill*, Ballantine, 1992.

Mayer, Jane, and Jill Abramson, *Strange Justice: The Selling of Clarence Thomas*, Houghton, 1994.

Morrison, Toni, editor and author of introduction, *Race-ing Justice, En-Gendering Power: Essays on Anita Hill, Clarence Thomas, and the Construction of Social Reality*, Pantheon, 1992.

Nomination of Judge Clarence Thomas to Be Associate Justice of the Supreme Court of the United States: Hearings Before the Committee on the Judiciary, United States Senate, 102nd Congress, 1st session, Part 4 of 4 parts, October 11, 12, and 13, 1991.

Phelps, Timothy M., and Helen Winternitz, *Capitol Games: Clarence Thomas, Anita Hill, and the Story of a Supreme Court Nomination*, Hyperion, 1992.

Simon, Paul, *Advice and Consent: Clarence Thomas, Robert Bork, and the Intriguing History of the Supreme Court's Nomination Battles*, National Press Books, 1992.

Periodicals

Detroit Free Press, "Anita Hill's Impact Showing a Year Later," October 9, 1992, p. 3A; "Family Quarrel: Black Women Are Challenged for Bringing Charges Against Black Men," September 23, 1994.

Essence, "A House Divided," January, 1992; "Anita Hill: No Regrets," March, 1992.

Glamour, "Women of the Year," December, 1991.

Interview, "Anita Hill: Law Professor," January, 1992, p. 55.

Ms., "The Nature of the Beast," January/February, 1992; ". . . And the Language Is Race," January/February, 1992.

Newsweek, "Supreme Mystery," September 16, 1991; "Hearing But Not Speaking," September 16, 1991, p. 23; "Court Charade," September 23, 1991, pp. 18-20; October 21, 1991 (special section containing a variety of articles related to confirmation hearings); October 28, 1991 (special section containing a variety of articles related to confirmation hearings); "Who Lied?," November 14, 1994, pp. 52-54.

New York, "Tabloid Government," October 28, 1991, pp. 28-31; "Men on Trial II," December 16, 1991.

New York Times Book Review, "One Year Later, the Debate Goes On," October 25, 1992.

New York Times Magazine, "Taking Sides Against Ourselves," November 17, 1991.

People, "She Could Not Keep Silent," October 28, 1991; "Breaking Silence," November 11, 1991.

Time, October 21, 1991 (special section containing a variety of articles related to confirmation hearings); "Truths in the Ruins," October 28, 1991, p. 104; "Anita Hill's Legacy," October 19, 1992.

U.S. News and World Report, "Judging Thomas," October 21, 1991, pp. 32-36; "Thomas and Hill: Once More with Feeling," June 8, 1992, p. 10.

Other

Women Lawyers of Achievement 1992 Award Speeches (pamphlet), American Bar Association Commission on Women in the Profession, c. 1992.

John Hope

1868–1936

African American educator

An outspoken opponent of Booker T. Washington, John Hope was one of the few black college officials of his era to take a stand against the Tuskegee leader's accommodationist philosophy. In 1905, for example, he was the only college president to join the Niagara Movement. Four years later, he was the only college president to attend the founding meeting of the NAACP. In 1919, he co-founded the South's first biracial reform group, the Commission on Interracial Cooperation, forerunner of the Southern Regional Council. Hope's militant independence often made his role as an educator more difficult, particularly during the early years of his career, but it eventually won him respect and admiration both inside and outside the academic world.

The roots of Hope's militancy stretch back to his childhood in Georgia. Born to a Scottish father and a mother of mixed racial heritage, he enjoyed a happy and secure existence until the death of his father in 1876. The elder Hope's fairly substantial estate was then depleted by unscrupulous (and prejudiced) white executors, leaving the family to face financial hardship. That same year, young John witnessed a series of violent racial clashes in Hamburg, South Carolina, that led to the deaths of many blacks at the hands of angry white mobs. It made a profound impression on him, as did the infamous Atlanta riot of 1906, which he also witnessed.

Hope attended school in the North, working his way through Worcester Academy in Massachusetts and then Brown University in Rhode Island. Turning down a job offer from Booker T. Washington to teach at Tuskegee, he instead took a position at Nashville's Roger Williams University, a small liberal arts college for blacks. There he quickly began to make a name for himself as an exceptionally bright and skillful young teacher.

In September 1895, Hope attended the Cotton States Exposition in Atlanta to hear Booker T. Washington deliver his celebrated "Atlanta Compromise" address. Returning to Nashville, he spent the next few months reflecting on what the Tuskegee president had said and how his message had been received across the country by both blacks and whites. On February 22, 1896, Hope shared his thoughts on the subject with members of an African American debating society in Nashville. While not all of the remarks he made that day have survived, his very brief but impassioned conclusion still ranks among the sharpest rebukes ever directed at Washington and accommodationism. The following text is taken from The Story of John Hope *by Ridgely Torrance (Macmillan, 1948).*

If we are not striving for equality, in heaven's name for what are we living? I regard it as cowardly and dishonest for any of our colored men to tell white people or colored people that we are not struggling for equality. If money, education, and honesty will not bring to me as much privilege, as much equality as they bring to any American citizen, then they are to me a curse, and not a blessing. God forbid that we should get the implements with which to fashion our freedom, and then be too lazy or pusillanimous to fashion it. Let us not fool ourselves nor be fooled by others. If we cannot do what other freemen do, then we are not free. Yes, my friends, I want equality. Nothing less. I want all that my God-given powers will enable me to get, then why not equality? Now, catch your breath, for I am going to use an adjective: I am going to say we demand *social* equality. In this republic we shall be less than freemen, if we have a whit less than that which thrift, education, and honor afford other freemen. If equality, political, economic, and social, is the boon of other men in this great country of ours, of *ours,* then equality, political, economic, and social, is what we demand. Why build a wall to keep me out? I am no wild beast, nor am I an unclean thing.

Rise, Brothers! Come let us possess this land. Never say: "Let well enough alone." Cease to console yourselves with adages that numb the moral sense. Be discontented. Be dissatisfied. "Sweat and grunt" under present conditions. Be as restless as the tempestuous billows on the boundless sea. Let your discontent break mountain-high against the wall of prejudice, and swamp it to the very foundation. Then we shall not have to plead for justice nor on bended knee crave mercy; for we shall be men. Then and not until then will liberty in its highest sense be the boast of our Republic.

Hope later went on to serve as the first black president of Morehouse College, where during his long tenure he launched a very successful effort to improve the institution and its reputation by developing many new programs. (His accomplishments in this regard are even more remarkable in light of the fact that his opposition to Washington cost him badly-needed financial support from wealthy whites. At the Tuskegee president's insistence, philanthropists shut off funds to Morehouse to punish Hope for his independence.) In 1929, Hope assumed the presidency of newly-established Atlanta University, a co-educational graduate school. He also established the Atlanta University Center, which encompassed Atlanta University as well as the undergraduate colleges of Morehouse (for men) and Spelman (for women). In 1936, Hope was honored by the NAACP with its Spingarn Medal for his achievements as a leader in the fields of education and civil rights.

SOURCES

Foner, Philip S., editor, *The Voice of Black America: Major Speeches by Negroes in the United States, 1797-1971,* Simon & Schuster, 1972.

Meltzer, Milton, editor, *The Black Americans: A History in Their Own Words, 1619-1983,* Crowell, 1984.

Torrance, Ridgely, *The Story of John Hope,* Macmillan, 1948.

Dolores Huerta

1930–

Mexican American labor leader and activist

Co-founder, along with César Chávez, of the United Farm Workers (UFW), Dolores Huerta has been at the forefront of the American labor movement for well over thirty years. Her goal has always been to secure fair wages and decent living and working conditions for a group of people who not only rank among the most exploited workers in the world but also among the most difficult to organize. Huerta's tireless efforts on their behalf have made her a hero in the Hispanic American community at large and a near-legendary figure to those who pick the grapes, vegetables, and citrus fruits consumers enjoy here in the United States and in several foreign countries as well.

Born in New Mexico to parents whose families originally came from Mexico, Huerta grew up in Stockton, California. Her mother and father divorced when she was very young, so she and her brother and sister were raised mostly by their mother and maternal grandfather in a loving and happy household. But she also maintained sporadic contact with her father, a miner and migrant worker whose own political and labor activism later proved inspirational to his daughter.

While the Depression years of the 1930s were often a struggle for Huerta's family, the 1940s brought a new prosperity that made it possible for them to enjoy a more middle-class existence. Young Dolores was even able to go on to Stockton College after graduating from high school. A brief and unsuccessful marriage that produced two daughters prompted her to abandon her studies for a while, but after divorcing her husband, she returned to college and earned her associate's degree. Dissatisfied with the kinds of jobs available to her, she eventually resumed her education and obtained a provisional teaching certificate. Once in the classroom, however, she quickly grew frustrated by how little she could really do for those students who didn't have proper clothing or enough to eat.

Huerta's frustration eventually found an outlet in the Community Service Organization (CSO), a Mexican American self-help group that first took shape in Los Angeles in the years after World War II and then spread across California and the Southwest. She joined up during the mid-1950s and became very active in the CSO's many civic and educational programs, including registering voters, setting up citizenship classes, and lobbying local government officials for neighborhood improvements. Huerta showed particular talent for the latter, so much so that the

CSO soon hired her to handle similar duties for the group at the state level in Sacramento.

During the late 1950s, Huerta found herself particularly affected by the plight of Mexican American farm workers and subsequently joined a northern California-based community interest group, the Agricultural Workers Association. It later merged with a similar union-affiliated group known as the Agricultural Workers Organizing Committee, for which Huerta worked as secretary-treasurer. It was around this same time that she first met César Chávez, a fellow member of the CSO who had also taken an interest in migrant laborers. When they could not persuade the CSO to expand its urban focus and address the concerns of farm workers, too, they left the group and began their own organizing efforts among this overlooked segment of society. Thus was born the National Farm Workers Association or NFWA (later known as the United Farm Workers, or UFW) in September 1962.

The task Chávez, Huerta, and the others who joined them set out to accomplish was especially difficult given the nature of the migrant worker—most were illiterate, desperately poor, easily intimidated by the growers, and constantly on the move in search of the next farm that needed help in the fields. But with Chávez as president and Huerta as vice-president, the NFWA slowly managed to attract people to their evening meetings across the agricultural heart of the state with talk of an aggressive but nonviolent "revolution." Throughout the 1960s and 1970s, the union staged a series of successful strikes, marches, and boycotts that focused national attention on the low wages and often horrendous living and working conditions migrant laborers endured. While Chávez became identified with fasting as a method of protest, Huerta led countless picket lines and served as the union's chief contract negotiator, holding her own against hostile Anglo growers who resented the fact that any Mexican American—and a woman, *no less—would dare challenge the status quo.*

Huerta was a talented speaker, too, as the following text demonstrates. In September 1965, the fledgling NFWA—which by then claimed about two thousand members—voted to join Filipino grape pickers in their strike against growers in California's San Joaquin Valley. To reinforce the impact of the strike, César Chávez also called for a national boycott of table grapes. It was a move that quickly made headlines across the country and launched the movement that popularly came to be known as La Causa. *Later, in the spring of 1966, the NFWA organized a march of nearly three hundred miles from Delano to the state capital at Sacramento to dramatize the farm workers' resolve and keep media attention focused on their efforts. On April 10, as demonstrators rallied to mark the end of the march, Huerta addressed the crowd. Her speech is reprinted here from the* Delano Record *newspaper of April 28, 1966.*

This is the first time in [the] history of the United States that farm workers have walked three hundred miles to their state capitol; and the governor of this state is not here to greet them.

But this is not surprising. This is in keeping with the general attitude that the governor and the people have had toward farm workers. I can assure you that had doctors, lawyers, auto workers or any other organized labor group marched three hundred miles, the governor would be here to meet them.

We hope that the governor will not follow

Dolores Huerta (center).

the example of Harlan Hagen, who has reciprocated the continual loyalty of the Mexican-American voter and the work of the CSO in registering voters among the Spanish-speaking people in Kern, Kings and Tulare counties, with an unprecedented attack against the National Farm Workers Association and the Delano grape strikers and the efforts of the farm workers to uplift their cause.

The governor's indifference to our pilgrimage, Congressman Hagen's vicious slurs on our union both demonstrate that we should not be taken for granted by any political party. As of this moment we wish to inform the Democratic party of this state that we will be counted as your supporters, only when we can count you among ours. The Democratic party does not have us in its hip pocket.

The leaders of this association do not want to meet with the governor in a closed-door session. We have met with the governor and his secretaries before in a closed-door session. We are no longer interested in listening to the excuses the governor has to give in defense of the growers, to his apologies for them not paying us decent wages or why the growers can not dignify the workers as individuals with the right to place the price on their own labor through collective bargaining.

The governor maintains that the growers are in a competitive situation. Well, the farm workers are also. We must also compete—with the standard of living to give our families their daily bread.

In 1959, the CSO and organized labor tried the first legislative efforts to give the farm workers minimal social legislation needed to ameliorate their terrible oppression. At that time the farm workers were not aware these attempts were being made and were therefore not there to testify and lobby in their own behalf, except for a delegation that César Chávez brought up from Oxnard.

In 1961 and 1963 through efforts of the CSO, National Farm Workers Association and the herculean efforts of then Assemblyman—now Congressman—Phil Burton, we were able to obtain welfare legislation that would ameliorate some of the terrible suffering of the farm workers in the off-season.

And the growers are still complaining and fighting adequate administration of that law. Gus Hawkins also passed disability insurance for farm workers. That was eight years ago and we still have yet to see the needed legislation for a minimum wage enacted in this state.

But this is 1966.

Farm workers have not been driven down to a small closed-door session to see what the state can dole out to us in welfare legislation. The grape strikers of Delano after seven months of extreme hardship and deprivation have walked step by step through the San Joaquin Valley—the valley that has been their "Valley of Tears" for them and their families. Not to beg, but to insist on what they think is needed for them.

The difference between 1959 and 1966 is highlighted by the peregrination, it is revolution—the farm workers have been organized.

In 1959 a small group of people who had been influenced by a great man, Fred Ross, who organized the CSO, met to discuss and digest the previous efforts of organizing work. We analyzed these attempts and found certain principles that had been used time and again and we thought undesirable for organizing farm workers and striking. We decided that a strong nucleus of workers had to be organized before striking, then they could progress into the actual struggle of economic sanctions.

César Chávez began, as the *Corrido del Campesino* states, going through the San Joaquin Valley as a pilgrim inspiring the workers to organize; giving the confidence they needed through inspiration and hard work and educating them through the months to realize that no one was going to win their battle for them,

> ***"You cannot close your eyes and ears to our needs any longer, you cannot pretend that we do not exist, you cannot plead ignorance to our problem because we are here . . . ."***

that their condition could only be changed by one group—themselves.

He refused contributions and did not solicit money from any area. César felt that outside money was no good, and that the workers had to pay for their own organization and this was accomplished.

The National Farm Workers Association prior to the strike was supported entirely by its membership through the dues they paid. Furthermore, the members of the National Farm Workers Association put forth the programs that they felt were needed immediately, such as a credit union, a service program, a group life insurance plan—the credit union so they could save their money and borrow when necessary, a group life insurance plan for their families that would take care of emergencies that arise from sudden deaths, and the service program for their complaints of nonunion wages, injury and disability cases, etc., and other daily problems in which they are exposed and undefended.

Each worker that was helped by the association's program became an organizer and the movement has grown in this manner with each worker bringing in other members to make the union stronger. The foundation was built by César Chávez through his dedicated efforts and the successive sacrifices of his wife, Helen Chávez, and their eight children, and their relatives who assisted them during this crucial organizing period when financial aid was not forthcoming.

April 10, 1966, marks the fourth year of the organizing efforts of the National Farm Workers Association. And today our farm workers have come to the capitol of Sacramento.

To the governor and the legislature of California we say: You cannot close your eyes and ears to our needs any longer, you cannot pretend that we do not exist, you cannot plead ignorance to our problem because we are here and we embody our needs for you.

And we are not alone. We are accompanied by many friends. The religious leaders of the state, spearheaded by the California Migrant Ministry, the student groups and civil rights groups that make up the movement that has been successful in securing civil rights for Negroes in this country, right-thinking citizens, and our staunchest ally, organized labor, are all in the revolution of farm labor.

This support has been highlighted by the people who have joined us today. Furthermore, they have committed themselves to help until total victory is achieved.

The developments of the past seven months are only a slight indication of what is to come. The workers are on the rise. There will be strikes all over the state and throughout the country because Delano has shown what can be done, and the workers know now they are no longer alone.

The agricultural workers are not going to remain static. The towns that have been reached by the pilgrimage will never be the same. On behalf of the National Farm Workers Association, its officers and its members, on behalf of all the farm workers of this state, we unconditionally demand the governor of this state, Edmund G. Brown, to call a special session of the legislature to enact a collective bargaining law for the farm workers of the state of California.

We will be satisfied with nothing less. The governor cannot and the legislature cannot shrug off their responsibilities to the Congress. We are the citizens and residents of the state of California and we want to have rules set up to protect us in this state.

If the rules to settle our economic problems are not forthcoming, we will call a general strike to paralyze the state's agricultural economy, to let the legislators and the employers know we mean business. We will take economic pressures, strikes and boycotts to force recognition and obtain collective bargaining rights.

The social and economic revolution of the farm workers is well under way and will not be stopped until they receive equality.

During the late 1960s, after directing the table grape boycott in the New York City area, Huerta coordinated similar activities all along the east coast and its major distribution points for California produce. Her leadership was instrumental in taking the struggle national by involving activists of all kinds—religious, political, student, union, consumer—in the drive to secure decent wages and conditions for migrant workers. Their efforts finally paid off in 1970 when the Delano growers agreed to contracts that ended the five-year-old strike.

Huerta spent much of the early 1970s back in New York overseeing UFW boycotts against other grape-growers, including the makers of Gallo wine, as well as lettuce farmers. Again, the emphasis was on maintaining nationwide pressure to force changes in California. This required Huerta to travel extensively and share the UFW message anywhere she found an audience willing to listen, from college campuses to union halls.

One such trip took her to New Orleans, where she delivered the keynote address at the annual convention of the American Public Health Association. In her remarks, delivered October 21, 1974, Huerta focused on a topic she thought might be of particular interest to those in attendance—the unique health problems facing migrant workers and steps the union had taken to address them. She also briefly touched on the problems the UFW was then having with another union, the Teamsters, which was trying to conduct its own organizing efforts among the farm workers. This bitter (and sometimes violent) battle was not resolved until 1977, when the two reached a settlement granting the UFW sole bargaining rights. Huerta's speech is reprinted here from a copy in the archives of the Walter P. Reuther Library of Wayne State University in Detroit, Michigan.

Thank you very much Dr. Kerr and Mr. McBeath, executive director of this conference, and to all of you delegates.

I wish to tell you that Mr. Chávez's illness is his recurring illness that he has had over the years, which is that of his back. [By this time, frequent and often lengthy fasting—as well as the years he had spent stooped over doing farm work—had permanently damaged Chávez's health.] And he had just come back from a three-week tour of Europe, had been in Washington to testify about the use of illegal aliens in the government committee, went to a board meeting. We traveled all the way to Yuma, Arizona, where there are two thousand farm workers on strike, and he was unable to get out of the car and address a rally of workers who had waited for him for four hours. We don't know how long he is going to be laid up. He's in a hospital right now in San Jose, and we hope it won't be too long before he will be able to be back on his feet.

I wish to bring you greetings and a hope for a very successful convention . . . to all of you who have dedicated your lives to making life better for the world, for America. I think that your goals are very much like the goals of our union. We got into the business of organizing farm workers for mainly health reasons. It is no accident that farm workers have an average life span of forty-nine years of age. And those of you who have worked in rural communities I think know the reasons. Those of you that don't, I just want to give you a little picture of what health is like for a farm worker in a place where he does not have the United Farm Workers to represent him.

In Delano, California, I remember three specific instances. One, a worker who had his hand broken on the job . . . was sent to his local doctor, who, by the way, is also a grape-grower. The doctor prescribed some ointment to put on his hand. The worker's hand started swelling. He came later to use our x-ray machine, which at that time was just a small trailer. We had this old x-ray machine from the year one, and we found out that his hand was broken. There was another farm worker [who was ill], Chala Savala, who another local grape-grower doctor said . . . , "Why, you're pregnant." About six months later she found out she wasn't pregnant—she had tuberculosis. But by that time she had to have a lung removed. Farm workers who are poisoned with pesticides are told they have sunstroke. And it's always the same thing—you have no money, the doctor can't see you.

> ***"It is no accident that farm workers have an average life span of forty-nine years of age."***

When we first won our contracts as a result of our first strike and our first grape boycott, we made some very fantastic changes. I'd just kinda like to ask, how many of you didn't eat grapes between 1965 and 1970? Raise your hands. Well, I'm glad to see that there were a lot of you. And I'm going to tell you some of the changes that you brought about in health for farm workers in Delano, California, this very same place that I'm talking about.

The first thing that we got when we got our contracts was a medical plan. And we named it the Robert F. Kennedy Medical Plan after our good friend Robert Kennedy. The plan was paid for by the growers. We made them pay ten cents an hour for every hour that the workers worked. And the workers—we took the plan to the workers so that they could vote on it, so that they could decide what kind of medical care they wanted. And the workers decided that they wanted doctor's visits paid for, they wanted maternity benefits, they wanted hospitalization benefits, they wanted x-ray [and] lab, they wanted prescriptions paid for under their medical plan.

And so we developed a really fantastic medical plan. Because every migrant worker, his wife, and all of his children are covered under our medical plan. If they only work fifty hours for the migrant medical plan they were covered for a nine-month period. Nine months, no matter where, they can make a medical claim and get paid for it. And the money goes directly to the worker. Our major medical plan is two hundred and fifty hours. Under this plan they get hospitalization, and surgical benefits, ambulance benefits, a minimum dental and eyeglass prescription care. Again, no matter where they are at.

See, the beautiful thing about our medical plan and the reason that we were able to do this fantastic medical plan for ten cents an hour is because we did not go through an insurance company. Now when we first tried to get this plan passed, many of the growers were very upset about it. They said you have to go through an insurance company. We are very lucky that César Chávez is a grammar-school dropout and he hasn't been educated to think that insurance is a way of life. He said he wasn't going to give any of his money to an insurance company, any of the workers' money.

So the way that our medical plan works is that the money comes in and it goes out directly to the workers. It's a nonprofit plan, and it's administered by the farm workers themselves. The person who administers our RFK Medical Plan is out of the first grape strike, Maria Saludado-Magaña. When she first came into the union, she couldn't read or write English. She now administers the full medical plan. She's been audited many times, and our plan is perfect.

But once we got the medical plan, we found that that really didn't stop the abuses, because the doctors were still not giving the workers good health care. So the next step was then to build a clinic. So the workers started to build their clinics. During the period of the last three years we have built five clinics. Five clinics. Four of those were in the state of California, one of them is in Mexico, and we are building another one in Florida which will be opening soon.

I think our clinics are unique in that we call them people's clinics. The people built them, we raised the money for them. There is no government money at all in our clinics. And the kind of work that the clinic does is primarily, first of all, educational. And we don't have Mickey-Mouse clinics. Our clinics are really beautiful. I mean there is good medicine in our clinics. The workers are taught about nutrition, to combat diabetes, which is very common among farm workers. They are given prenatal instruction to have healthier babies and healthier mothers. They are taught about inoculations. You know, it's really a funny experience to go into the waiting room of our clinic, and you will see a group of farm workers sitting around talking. And one worker will say to the other one, "Well, I came in to get a shot." And the other worker will say, "Why, you shouldn't get a shot if you just have a cold, because you know you can build up an immunity to penicillin." And these are farm workers teaching each other about health.

Our health workers go into the labor camps. They've done a vast service on tuberculosis and on other diseases that are contagious. And when we find a sick farm worker, someone that has tuberculosis, someone that has another disease that shouldn't be in the labor force, we take that farm worker out of the labor force. And he is put on some kind of disability compensation so that he doesn't have to work until he becomes well again. We do home visits. We have a team approach with the doctor, the health worker, the nurse, and we go right into the homes of the farm workers.

Needless to say, this kind of preventative medicine that we are now undertaking has saved so many lives that the statistics of Tulare County in California have changed. Last year I had my tenth baby in a hospital in Tulare County, and the doctor who was delivering my baby—who happened to be a specialist—along with our own doctor from our clinic told me that our health care was so good that we had actually changed the statistics of Tulare County. I think that's pretty fantastic, because our doctors are so dedicated, and because their medicine is so good.

Now, some of you might wonder how come I have ten children, right? One of the main reasons is because I want to have my own picket line. But all kidding aside, it's really nice to be able to go to a clinic when you are pregnant with your tenth baby and not have people look at you like you are kind of crazy, or like you don't know where they come from, or put pressure on you not to have any more children. Because after all, you know, Mexicans are kind of poor people, and you shouldn't have all that many kids. So that's another good thing about our clinics. Because unfortunately, that pressure not to have children translates itself in county hospitals and places where people have no power into dead babies because those babies aren't taken care of, and into very hard labor for mothers because they are trying to make it as hard on the mother as they can to have another one. And I guess I feel a little bit strongly about that because I've been in situations where I've seen children die, babies die, because somebody there thought they shouldn't have been born in the first place.

Now another great thing about our clinics is that we train farm workers as lab assistants, lab technicians, nurse's aides, we train farm workers to do the administration of the clinic. The receptionist is a farm worker. We have two of our clinics right now being administered by farm workers. One of them, the Delano Clinic, is administered by Esther Uranday, who was a grape striker from the first grape strike. Juanita Ortega from Calexico administers the other clinic that we have. So what we're doing is we're not only just giving good health care—fantastic health care—but we are training our own people to be able to do the health work and to administer the program.

The amazing reason that we have been able to build these clinics in such a short period of time is because our clinics are nonprofit. The doctors that come to work with us work the way that we do. We work for no wages. Our doctors get a little bit more for some of you out there that might be interested. But nevertheless it is a sacrifice. And that's important. Because you can't help poor people and be comfortable. You know, the two things are just not compatible. If you want to really give good health care to poor people you've got to be prepared to be a little uncomfortable and to put a little bit of sacrifice behind it.

Now there [are] other ways that the union has changed things in terms of health care. And I'm going to talk a little bit about the pesticides, because . . . we raised the issue many years ago and a lot of people have been concerned about [it], but it was sort of a no-no. Nobody could talk about it openly. What we have in our union are ranch committees. Where we have a contract we elect a ranch committee. The workers elect their own committee. That committee is responsible [for making] sure that no pesticides that can be harmful to them or harmful to the consumers can be used in that ranch. They check out to see what kind of pesticides are going to be used, what the antidotes are, what the re-entry periods are, everything that there is possible to know about that pesticide.

Do you know that we were amazed to find out you can get all kinds of information about what's harmful to a pet, but you can't get any information about what's harmful to a farm worker? Because there has been very little research done in this area. And when we were negotiating contracts—I was in charge of the contract negotiations for the union—we called up a friend of ours who worked with the Los Angeles County Health [Department], and he gave us some information on one of the organic phosphates that we wanted to know. Well, one of the growers who was in on the negotiations tried to get him fired for giving us that information. And this man worked for the Los Angeles County Health Department. But this shows you—and I'm going to talk about that a little bit more—about the kind of repression that I know a lot of you are faced [with] when you do try to make real changes or when you try to get into those controversial areas where you have conflicts of power.

In our contracts, we banned DDT, Aldrin, Endrin, 2,4-D, 2,4-T, Tep and many of the other—Monitor 4—many of these other pesticides. We banned these pesticides in our contracts starting from 1970. It is interesting that just recently, the government has come out against Aldrin and Endrin. And the Farm Workers Union banned these pesticides many years ago. We find that the only way that you can be sure that the so-called laws are administered, that the so-called laws are carried out, is when you have somebody right there on the ranch, a steward, a ranch committee, somebody that can't get fired from the job, somebody that has the protection of a union contract to make sure that these things are carried out.

All of these great things that we were able to do—and all of you that didn't eat grapes helped us to accomplish—are being wiped out now. And they are being wiped out because last year, as many of you know, we lost our contracts. The growers brought in the Teamsters union, they signed backdoor contracts with them, fourteen thousand farm workers went out on strike. Four thousand farm workers—this was not a war, this was a strike—four thousand farm workers were jailed for picketing, two hundred farm workers were beaten and injured by Teamsters and police, and two farm workers were killed. It is sad for us to report this, but the clock has been turned back and California agriculture, with the exception of a handful of contracts that we still hold, we now have the labor contractor, the crew leader system back again, we now have child labor back again.

There was a bus accident—to talk to you about health standards and safety standards—there was a bus accident in Blythe, California, on January 15. This was under a Teamster contract. Nineteen farm workers were drowned when their bus turned over into an irrigation ditch. This was a school bus. It had no business transporting people seventy miles to work. The seats of that bus were not fastened to the floor. The people got tangled in the bus. They couldn't get out of the bus. They were crushed to death and they were drowned. Among those that were drowned was a thirteen-year-old child and his fifteen-year-old brother. There were four women that were drowned. The labor contractor who owned that bus got a fifty-dollar fine for the deaths of nineteen farm workers. I'm sure that many of you didn't read about it in your local newspapers because this is common among farm workers, these kinds of accidents. Twenty-five farm workers have been killed because of [the] lack of safety precautions in the fields since the Teamsters took over the contracts.

We now have a return to pesticides—forty thousand acres of lettuce were poisoned with Monitor 4. This lettuce was shipped to the market. In California, it was sold as shredded lettuce in Safeway stores. That's nice to have Monitor 4 with your shredded salad, huh?

And we have a return back to the archaic system that we had, [a] primitive system that existed before and still exists, where we don't have United Farm Workers contracts. People working out there in those fields without a toilet, people working out there in those fields without any hand-washing facilities, without any cold drinking water, without any kind of first-aid or safety precautions. All of this has come back again.

The California Rural Legal Assistance just did a spot survey of about twenty ranches in the Salinas and the Delano area just a couple of months ago. And [in] every single instance they found either no toilet or a dirty toilet, and you can imagine. And this is something consumers don't understand—that that lettuce, those grapes are being picked right there in that field. If there's a dirty toilet, it's right next to the produce, and that produce is picked and packed in that field and shipped directly to your store. The way you see grapes in your market, the way you see the lettuce in that market, it comes directly from the field. It doesn't go through any cleansing process. It's direct.

I remember talking to the head of the Food and Drug Administration in San Francisco. You know, I found out that there was a law that says no produce can be shipped for interstate commerce if it has been picked or packed in a way that it might become contaminated. Well, if you've got a field where you've got several hundred people or a thousand people working, and there's no toilet, that produce can be contaminated. You know what he told me? He said, "I've got to enforce the Food and Drug Administration law in four states. I can't go out there and check every field to see if there is a toilet or not, or hand-washing facilities." You know, these are these little tiny things that are kind of overlooked. And they're so serious. But I'll bet that if any public health person brings this up, there are going to be repercussions because they bring it up.

The Teamsters have brought back illegal aliens. And now when I say this, I want to tell you what's happening to these people. Today, President Ford is meeting with Echeverría in Mexico. And they're going to talk about a *bracero* program, which is a slave program for workers, for Mexican workers. And Mexico needs this because they've got a fifty percent inflation rate in Mexico, and they've got a thirty or forty percent unemployment rate. So they want to get rid of the people. They want to get rid of the problem.

But what does it do to people over here? They want to bring in one million Mexicans from Mexico. We've already got close to a million people here illegally. And how are they being treated? They are paying three hundred dollars each to come over the border. They are being put in housing where you have thirty or forty people in a room without any kind of a sanitary facility. We have one report of an illegal alien who was picking peaches on a ladder; the ladder was shaky, [and] it broke. The ladder went right through his anus. And they didn't give him any medical attention. Luckily, one of our members found out about it and brought him to one of our clinics for treatment. We're having illegal aliens who are coming in, who are being blinded by pesticides, for treatment. This is slavery. And it's wrong. And we've got to see what way we can stop this.

We can't really wait for legislation. You know, there's a lot of things that we can do right away. I think that the one thing that we've learned in our union is that you don't wait. You just get out and you start doing things. And you do things in such a way that you really help people to lay the foundations that you need.

We don't have to talk about a charitable outlook. You know, people come in with a lot of money and they give people charity. We've got to talk about ways to make people self-sufficient in terms of their medical health. Because when they go in there with charity and then they pull out, then they leave the people worse off than they ever were before. We've got to use government money to help people. And I don't think that this is so radical. Lord knows that the growers are getting billions of dollars not to grow cotton, all kinds of supports and subsidies. Well, if any money is given for medical health, it should stay in that community. It shouldn't just come in there at the pleasure of the local politicians and be pulled out at the pleasure of the local politicians.

> ***"I think that the one thing that we've learned in our union is that you don't wait. You just get out and you start doing things."***

And I don't think that public health people should be repressed. It worries me when I see a clinic in a farm-worker community that is afraid to put out a Farm Worker flag or put up César's picture because they are afraid that they are going to get their money taken away from them. And yet this has happened. And this is wrong. But the only reason it happens is because we let it happen. We've got to take the side of the people that are being oppressed. And if we can't do that, then we're not doing our job, because the people in that minority community or in that community are not going to have any faith in the medical program that is in there if you can't take their side. They're going to suspect you. We've got to be able to stand up and fight for our rights. We can't any longer cooperate with any kind of fear, any kind of bigotry, any kind of racism, anything that is wrong. We've got to be able to stand up and say, "That is wrong." And it's going to take that kind of courage, I think, the same kind of courage that César has taught the farm workers, to make the kind of changes that are needed.

Health, like food, has got to be to cure people, to make people well. It can't be for profit. Food should be sacred to feed people, not for profit. Health has got to be a right for every person and not a privilege. You would be sad to know that many farm workers—before we had our clinics—had never been to a doctor. And I'm sure like farm workers, there are many, many other people who have never been to a clinic or to a doctor. And many times that is even out of fear because they see the doctor or they see the medical person not as their friend but they see that person as their enemy.

Now I hope that what we have done, our experience, will serve some use to what you're interested in and what you're doing. I hope that you will help us get back what we have lost, which are our union contracts, so that we can continue this fantastic health program that we have that we started in California. And you can do this very easily just by not eating any grapes until we win, by not eating any lettuce until we win, and by not drinking any Gallo wine. And I'm saying that lightly. It's not light. It's a very serious situation.

Within the next year they are spending millions of dollars to destroy the United Farm Workers. They are spending millions of dollars to tell what a bad administrator César Chávez is. Have you seen these articles in the *New York Times* and *Time* magazine? They say César Chávez is a bad administrator. What they really mean is he is the wrong color. And if he were a good administrator.... Can you imagine five clinics, a medical plan, a credit union, a retirement center for farm workers, fantastic increases in wages, the removal of the labor contract system—all of this César did in a few short years. What would he do if he was a good administrator?

We have a booth here, booth 1020, where we're giving out information about our clinic. I implore all of you, if you can give up a year of your life or two years of your life, drop out and come and help us. The only reason we haven't got more clinics is because we need doctors. In our Delano clinic right now, we only have one doctor working. Please come and join the people and help us build health care for everybody, and we will give you a little bit of money, not too much. But we all work for five dollars a week. None of us gets paid. Even César gets five dollars a week for his personal benefit. We get five dollars a week for food. We live off of donations. All of the money that we need to run our boycott and our strikes. We have a button table where we invite you to buy a button. And please wear our button. As I say, all the contributions that you can give will be greatly, greatly appreciated, because we do need money very desperately.

We're also going to be showing a film, the film of our strike, of the bloody strike that we had in California last summer. It will be shown at one and two o'clock in the auditorium. I'd invite all of you to come and see the film. You'll never forget it. And you will really see—when we talk about the principle of nonviolence, you will see it in action. Because you will see farm workers getting beaten and killed, and you will see that the farm workers do not fight back with violence. We are using a nonviolent action of the boycott, so we really need your help in that.

Let's say a few *vivas* now, OK? You know what *viva* means? That's what you're all about—long life. Long life. And we always say that in the Spanish community, we say *viva,* which means "long life." So we're going to say a few *vivas,* and we're going to say some *abajos*. You know what *abajos* are? That means "down." And then we will say one other thing—*Si se puede*. Can we have this dream that we are talking about? Health for everyone, brotherhood, peace? "It can be done"—*si se puede*. And we'll all do the farm workers' handclap together to show that we're united in thought and action and in love. The farm workers' handclap starts out very slow, and then it goes very fast.

So let's try it. We're going to say first *"Viva la Causa,"* which is the cause of labor, peace, and health, *"Viva la justicia,"* which is justice, and then we will say *"Viva Chávez,"* for César, may God give him long life. And then we'll say "down with fear," *abajo,* and "down with lettuce and grapes," *abajo,* and "down with Gallo wine." Because Gallo is on the boycott, too. *Abajo.* By the way, Gallo has some other labels like Ripple, Thunderbird, Madria Madria Sangria, Joe Steuben. Anything that says Modesto, California, is Gallo wine.

OK, let's try it now. All together! I'll say, *"Viva la Causa!"* and everybody yells *"Viva!"* really, really loud, OK? *Viva la Causa! Viva!* Ugh—that was very weak. This is very important. This is like kind of praying together in unison, so it's really important. Let's try it again: *Viva la Causa! Viva! Viva la justicia! Viva!* Now—so César can hear us in the hospital where he's at and the growers can hear us where they're at: *Viva Chávez! Viva!* OK, now we'll try *abajo.* Down with fear! *Abajo!* Down with lettuce and grapes! *Abajo!* Down with Gallo! *Abajo!* You know, this really works. We did that at the impeachment rally in Washington, D.C., and we said, "Down with Nixon! *Abajo!"* and it worked. Can we live in a world of brotherhood and peace without disease and fear and oppression? *Si se peude,* right? OK, let's all do it together. *Si se puede.* [Clapping.] *Si se puede, si se puede,. . . .* [Clapping.]

Thank you very much.

In 1975, Huerta played a key role in yet another UFW triumph when California passed the Agricultural Labor Relations Act, the first law to recognize the right of farm workers to engage in collective bargaining. During the last half of the decade, she then turned her attention to running the union's political department, which once again called upon her talents as a legislative lobbyist. Although the UFW has seen its influence decline throughout the 1980s and 1990s due in part to changes in the economic and political climate at both the state and national levels, it still has a fighter in Huerta, who remains active in the ongoing struggle to achieve justice for migrant laborers.

SOURCES

Books

Day, Mark, *Forty Acres: César Chávez and the Farm Workers,* Praeger, 1971.

Dunne, John Gregory, *Delano: The Story of the California Grape Strike,* Farrar, 1976.

Levy, Jacques, *César Chávez: Autobiography of La Causa,* Norton, 1975.

Matthiessen, Peter, *Sal Si Puedes: César Chávez and the New American Revolution,* Random House, 1969.

Telgen, Diane, and Jim Kamp, eds., *Notable Hispanic American Women,* Gale Research, Detroit, 1993.

Periodicals

Delano Record, "Text of Mrs. Huerta's Speech at Capitol Rally," April 28, 1966, p. 1.

Ms., "Dolores Huerta: La Pasionaria of the Farmworkers," November, 1976, pp. 11-16.

Nation, " 'You Find a Way': The Women of the Boycott," February 23, 1974, pp. 232-238.

Progressive, "Stopping Traffic: One Woman's Cause," September, 1975, pp. 38-40.

David Henry Hwang

1957–

Chinese American playwright and screenwriter

David Henry Hwang was only twenty-three when he first saw his name on the marquee of a New York City theater and was barely past thirty when he picked up his first Tony Award for best play. Since then, he has continued to craft a number of plays, screenplays, and even a multimedia dramatic piece that examine various juxtapositions that intrigue him—appearance and reality, cultural "outsiders" and "insiders," and, perhaps most notably, the East and the West and what happens when they blend (or don't blend, as the case may be). In the process, Hwang has earned praise as one of today's most talented playwrights for his thought-provoking views on the Asian American experience.

Hwang was born in Los Angeles and grew up in the well-to-do suburban community of San Gabriel. Both of his parents were immigrants who arrived in the United States during the early 1950s. His father, a native of Shanghai, China, established the first Asian American-owned bank in the country. His mother, who was also of Chinese ancestry but who grew up in the Philippines, was a pianist and music teacher.

Theirs was a very westernized household, and the three Hwang children (David was the oldest and the only boy) were strongly encouraged to "be American." As a result, Hwang gave little thought to his heritage most of the time, considering it just another interesting but inconsequential personal characteristic, "like having red hair," as he once remarked in a New York Times Magazine *interview. But the many hours he spent as a little boy listening to his grandmother tell stories—ancient Chinese myths and fables as well as family lore—left a profound impression that later influenced his own work. So enthralled was he by her tales that he began writing them down when he was about twelve years old, producing a novel of sorts that he then copied and passed around to other relatives.*

After graduating from a local college prep school in 1975, Hwang entered Stanford University with the intention of pursuing a law degree. Before long, however, he found himself drawn to other interests, including music and writing. He was particularly fascinated with drama as a means of expression and began studying the art of writing plays, first at Stanford and then under the guidance of Sam Shepard and several other playwrights at a special workshop held during the summer of 1978 in Claremont, California.

College also proved to be a time of self-discovery in other ways for Hwang, who had begun to get in touch with his identity as a Chinese American. At the Claremont workshop, he tried his hand at writing a play he entitled FOB *that examined the cultural conflicts between a newly-arrived immigrant from China—known by the insulting term "FOB" for "Fresh Off the Boat"—and his very westernized Chinese American cousin. Hwang continued revising and polishing the text of his play once he returned to school that fall, and in March 1979, he directed a cast of fellow students in its first performance, which was held in a Stanford dormitory lounge.*

Hwang received his bachelor's degree in English that same spring and shortly afterward left for Waterford, Connecticut, where FOB *was being featured at the prestigious National Playwrights Conference. At this annual workshop, he was able to see his play acted by a professional cast before an audience of theater critics and other playwrights who then offered their suggestions.*

Back home in California, Hwang began teaching creative writing at a Los Angeles-area high school and worked on his own writing whenever he could. Meanwhile, FOB *captured the interest of Joseph Papp, the artistic director of the New York Shakespeare Festival. He ended up staging a full-scale production of Hwang's work Off-Broadway at the famous Public Theater during the 1980-81 season that garnered fairly good reviews and went on to win an Obie Award for best play of the year.*

While attending the Yale School of Drama during the 1980-81 school year, Hwang wrote his second play, The Dance and the Railroad. *This story of Chinese railroad workers in the United States during the mid-nineteenth century is told from the perspective of two of the workers, both of whom dream of returning to China one day to perform in the Beijing Opera. It also was staged Off-Broadway, where it enjoyed a long and successful run. Hwang soon followed up with another play,* Family Devotions, *a farcical look at a very prosperous Chinese American family very much like the author's own. In it, though, he makes some very serious points, noting, for example, how his mother's Christian fundamentalist beliefs had made it difficult for him to learn about his Chinese heritage.*

*Hwang wrote two more plays—*The House of Sleeping Beauties *and* The Sound of a Voice*—before the burdens of being a successful young playwright and a media-appointed spokesperson for Asian Americans took their toll. Unable and unwilling to produce any more of what he dismissed as "Orientalia for the intelligentsia," he stopped writing, traveled extensively, and considered enrolling in law school.*

Within a couple of years, however, Hwang had started writing again. When his first effort, Rich Relations, *did not do well, he finally felt free to tackle other kinds of projects, including some work for films and television. Meanwhile, another play was slowly taking shape in his mind. In 1986, he learned of the bizarre true story of a French diplomat who had carried on a twenty-year affair with a beautiful and intriguing Chinese opera singer yet insisted he had no idea she was really a spy—and a man. Hwang took this idea and spun his own tale around it, exploring the nature of imperialism and how racism and sexism can blind people to the truth.* M. Butterfly *opened on Broadway in 1988 to somewhat mixed reviews from the critics but enthusiastic acclaim from audiences. It went on to win a number of awards, including a Tony for best play, and was nominated for a 1989 Pulitzer Prize. Hwang later wrote the 1993 movie adaptation as well, though he was not entirely pleased with the results on screen. One of his future goals, in fact, is to move into directing the films of his screenplays so that he can exercise more control over the finished product.*

Since the success of M. Butterfly, *Hwang has been involved in a variety of creative endeavors. In addition to writing more plays, among them* Bondage *and* Face Value, *the latter a farce examining the controversy that erupted when a white actor was cast to play the lead role of a Eurasian pimp in the blockbuster musical* Miss Saigon, *he has completed several screenplays. One, an original entitled* Golden Gate, *was made into a movie in 1994; two others are adaptations of novels by A.S. Byatt Booker* (Possession) *and Caleb Carr* (The Alienist). *In collaboration with avant-garde music composer Philip Glass and stage designer Jerome Sirlin, Hwang has also created a multimedia drama entitled* 1000 Airplanes on the Roof *in which a single character tells the story of his terrifying abduction by visitors from outer space. Since then, Hwang has worked with Glass on a number of other projects, including the libretto for Glass's opera* The Voyage.

While he has branched out to work on these and other "non-Asian" projects, Hwang nevertheless continues to be preoccupied with the notion of what it means to be Asian American, especially in a country where people are trying to forge a common identity out of many different cultures yet maintain a sense of their own cultural identity as well. One aspect of the debate over multiculturalism that is of particular interest to him concerns "authenticity"—a hot-button, highly political issue that often surfaces in connection with works by or about minorities, women, or homosexuals. In the theater, for instance, it sparks discussions about nontraditional casting, such as having a non-Asian play an Asian role. In education, it may take the form of disagreements over how to interpret history or whether a particular literary work is "worthy" of study.

Hwang addressed these and other related topics during a talk he gave on April 15, 1994, while serving as artist-in-residence at the Massachusetts Institute of Technology (MIT) in Cambridge. His appearance as the 1994 William L. Abramowitz Lecturer came at the end of his three-day stay, during which time he had observed a rehearsal of his play FOB, *worked with students in MIT theater classes, and spoken to high school students in the Cambridge Public Schools. His lecture is reprinted from a copy provided by the MIT Office of the Arts.*

Thank you, and I'd also like to thank the Abramowitz Lecture Series for having me here. I've had a really great three days interacting with the students. It's often noted that the lecturer comes and gives something to the university, and while that may or may not be true, I think it's certainly equally true that the students give a great deal to whoever is invited. That person has the privilege to come and interact with them and get out of the isolation, if only for a short time, of the literary world, the theatrical world, the Hollywood world. Particularly I'd like to thank Maureen Costello and Mary Haller, as well as Alan Brody and Kim Mancuso from the Theater Arts department, all of whom who have really helped make my stay here something.

In 1990 I found myself in a room on a hot summer day, and on one side of the table was Cameron Mackintosh, who was going to bring a new musical to town called *Miss Saigon,* as well as Bernie Jacobs, who was one of the owners of the Shubert Theater chain where *Miss Saigon* was going to show. On the other side of the table were myself and Alan Eisenberg, who's the executive secretary of Actor's Equity, the actor's union, as well as their president, the late Colleen Dewhurst. We were arguing about the topic of Jonathan Pryce.

Jonathan Pryce is a British actor of Welsh descent who was cast in the role of the Engineer, ostensibly a character of Eurasian descent. He had played the role in London to great acclaim and now was being invited to repeat the role on Broadway, and several Asian Americans, including myself, had started to raise a bit of a fuss over this. And so we all met and the insults really flew. I think that Bernie Jacobs from the Shubert was very strong in pointing at me and saying, "Oh, he's a liar. You can't trust him."

At another point in the afternoon when I think Cameron was yelling at somebody else, I looked at Bernie Jacobs and he looked at me and he sort of shrugged as if to say, "Well, kid, what a way to make a living!" And I shrugged. And then our conversation went on. I think that the shrug, to me, is a representation of the fact that both of us realized that we were sort of players in a larger drama here. There is a sort of series of surprise reversals that's taking place in America right now, and it stems largely from a change in demographics that's taking place.

Most of us know that in another thirty, fifty years, Caucasians, European Americans—whatever you want to call them—will be a plurality rather than a majority. In other words, this country will not have a single majority race, and that leads to a great number of cultural and societal changes. The very definition of what it means to be an American is changing, and therefore the culture of America also is being reexamined. Two places where this battle is felt very strongly are one, in the arts, and two, in academia.

In the arts there is, for instance, the whole issue of what's called non-traditional casting—that is, who should get to play what parts, of what races. And it works kind of both ways, this battle. Nick Hytner, who directed *Miss Saigon,* I think is in a really interesting position because he directed *Miss Saigon* and initially cast Jonathan Pryce as this Eurasian and got a lot of flak from Asian Americans. This season he's directed a production of *Carousel* on Broadway and cast a lot of African Americans in parts that were normally considered Caucasian, and he's gotten a lot of criticism from the other side. (John Simon, for instance, has attacked him for being too PC.) So Nick Hytner is sort of catching it both ways, and I think that similarly the battle rages both ways. It's one of the topics that I'm interested in examining today.

In academia, of course, the battle's over curriculum—what works are in the canon, what constitutes quality in literature as well as history, how do we interpret history from a "Eurocentric" point of view, from an "Afrocentric" point of view. The whole notion of history as objective has always been somewhat doubtful, but it's particularly being called into question now as it relates to the experiences of different cultural groups—women, gays, whatever—and

David Henry Hwang

there is the charge that all this is leading to a lowering of standards, that by the inclusion of the voices of diverse groups, we compromise some sort of objective standard of excellence which previously had existed in the academy.

So we have this sort of battle between what might be called the multiculturalists and what might be called the politically incorrect. Political incorrectness, by the way, I think has become very trendy lately. There was recently a battle fought in court between a cable network and Jackie Mason. Comedy Central had a show called "Politically Incorrect" and Jackie Mason in his show on Broadway wanted to call his show *Politically Incorrect,* and they were battling to see who could be the most politically incorrect.

So today I've chosen to address the subject of authenticity, because a lot of these debates come down to some sort of struggle over whether we can reach a definition of objective truth, whether or not we can define a universal standard of excellence. I think that those of us who write about minorities, women, gays, whatever, are often criticized for being inauthentic by our own group and in turn, some of us (like myself) also go and criticize other people for being inauthentic. So I feel like I've been on both sides of that fence, and I'm going to frame this a little bit in terms of my own artistic journey. I'm coming to you to talk about issues that are sort of sociopolitical and all that, but I'm basically a playwright and my journey is essentially a personal one. I think I've been searching for authenticity in my work and contradicting myself at certain points and struggling with these issues, and I think that's the best way for me to go over this journey for you.

The subtitle [of my lecture], "It's OK to Be Wrong"—which some of the Asian students suggested I could say "It's OK to Be Hwang"—has to do with the recognition that all this is an evolution. I look at myself now, and I'm not exactly the same person as I was ten years ago, and I don't exactly have the same beliefs that I had ten years ago, and I don't expect that I will ten years from now. When I was younger, I used to feel that it was important to be completely consistent. Now I feel that it's a good idea to be consistent at least at any given time, but that I may contradict myself from the past. I think Oscar Wilde's notion that consistency is the hobgoblin of small minds has become more significant to me as the years have gone by.

I'm sort of encouraged by the example of people I admire, whether it's Malcolm X or Gandhi or whoever, who also contradicted themselves at different points in their lives. I've tried to make a virtue out of this by now believing that contradiction is sort of an antidote to nostalgia. So I hope you'll bear with me, and I hope that also a lot of my changes will encourage you to continue thinking and continue growing and not be afraid of evolving.

My parents were immigrants. My father comes from Shanghai, my mother's [from] a Chinese group in the Philippines. They both came to the states in the early 1950s to go to school. They met at a foreign students' dance at USC on Halloween and subsequently got married and tried to move to a suburb of Los Angeles called Monterey Park, but they were denied housing there because people wouldn't sell to Chinese at the time. This is interesting, because any of you who know Los Angeles know that Monterey Park now is almost completely Chinese. I think it's an example of the old saying that fear creates the thing feared.

Anyway, I ended up growing up instead in a neighboring suburb called San Gabriel with basically Anglos and Latinos, some African Americans, and a few Asians. I thought of my ethnicity, at the time, as sort of like having red hair—that is, it was a sort of interesting feature, part of my total makeup, but not of any intrinsic significance in and of itself. To this day, if people ask me (as people sometimes do in interviews) what sort of racism I encountered as a child, I'm not able to really recall a single racial incident. But circumstantial evidence I think to some extent contradicts my memory, because I do remember one time my mother telling me that if people teased me about my race that I should just consider them ignorant. I don't know why she would have to have told me that if I hadn't run into some trouble on that score.

Similarly, some of my earliest memories about being Asian American have to do with a certain aversion to Asian American characters in movies and television, and perhaps this was the beginning of why I ended up doing what I do today. But frankly, I remember feeling ashamed and changing the channel or not going to a particular movie. We'd talk about these sort of blatantly evil Asian American characters like Fu Manchu or the various soldiers in Japanese or Vietnam war movies, or we'd talk about sort of the benign obsequious version, the Charlie Chan or the guy in the Calgon commercial that said "ancient Chinese secret." All of those were a source of great embarrassment to me, and I think that, in the final analysis, I felt that these people were not me. And yet because of the way we looked, I was expected to have some sort of identification with them. Perhaps this was the first encounter with the issue of inauthenticity—that to me these characters were not inauthentic and yet I was being lumped in with them because of my race.

> *". . . those of us who write about minorities, women, gays, whatever, are often criticized for being inauthentic by our own group . . ."*

That leads to a discussion of the whole issue of the tyranny of appearances and how it is that the way we look establishes to a large extent the way that we're perceived, at least on first notice. Every minority group, I think, and every group in general, has their particular burden to bear. I think that among Asians, we have to deal with the idea of being perpetual foreigners. One's family can have been in this country five or six generations, but people still go, "Oh, you speak really good English," whereas it's not necessarily assumed that someone of Swedish descent speaks Swedish.

Similarly, if I'm walking on Christopher Street, for instance, and someone yells, "Go back to where you came from," I assume that they're not expressing a distaste for Californians. The perpetual-foreigner status, I think, leads to various harms. Some of them are minor irritants, but others are more significant. Certainly the internment of Japanese-Americans in World War II concentration camps here in America is a testament to the fact that these people were not really considered American, whereas people of German or Italian descent were rightly considered to be loyal.

Similarly, a few years ago, a Chinese-American named Vincent Chin was murdered in Detroit by unemployed autoworkers who were sort of mad at Hondas and Toyotas. In fact, as the trade tensions increased between the US and Japan in the '80s, incidents of anti-Asian violence rose at a sharper rate than that for any other ethnic group.

The perpetual-foreigner idea was especially ironic given my parents' desire to be Americans. They were not particularly traditional in terms of wanting to hold onto the root culture. They were very interested in blending into or assimilating into this culture, and they were trying to really create a new identity for themselves. In that sense, they were, in their own way, saying that their appearance was not an authentic representation of who they were inside.

Even as a boy, I think I began to try to search for some sort of authenticity behind the Fu Manchus and the Vietnamese generals that I saw on television. The only experience that I really had with writing before I got to college was when I was about twelve. We thought that my grandmother was going to die, and she was the only one who knew all of the family history. I thought it was really important that this sort of stuff be preserved, so I spent a summer with her and did a lot of oral histories and eventually wrote this into a kind of one-hundred-page nonfiction novel which was Xeroxed and distributed among my family and got very good reviews. I think that what I was trying to do was find a context for myself, find some way in which my identity, my existence as an Asian American could be validated, could be made authentic. I was trying to find something more real than the images that were around me.

Writing for me continued to be a search for authenticity. When I began wanting to write plays in college, I didn't actually have any idea I was going to focus on Asian American subjects. I was merely interested in the theater and in trying to become a playwright. I wrote a lot of plays about a lot of other subjects. I found a professor at Stanford who told me they were really horrible (which they were) and that my problem was I was trying to write theater in a vacuum—that is, I didn't know anything about the theater.

So I spent the next couple years trying to read as many plays and see as many plays as I could. Eventually I went to the Padua Hills Writers Workshop in southern California between my junior and senior years and studied there with playwrights like Sam Shepard and Maria Irene Fornes and Murray Mednick. I began to deal with the unconscious—how it is that we can begin to write and begin to make our art come alive with ideas that go beyond simply what the rational mind can manipulate.

As I began to write with free association, with speed writing, with all sorts of Dadaist collage techniques, I found that my work was leading me in a very unexpected place. It was leading me back to when I was twelve years old, back to the stories of my grandparents, things that I would hear as a child, back to the images that haunted me of Fu Manchu and Charlie Chan and all those things that I'd turn off on the television.

This was happening within a larger political context. There was an Asian American "yellow power" movement which was a child of the black power movements that had begun in the '60s. I lived in an Asian American theme house for a year and began to absorb various literary influences that were also Asian American. When I read *The Woman Warrior* by Maxine Hong Kingston, for instance, it was sort of a personal and artistic revelation to me, because the juxtaposition of almost a hyper-realistic view of growing up Chinese American in Stockton, California, with the ghosts of some imagined or mythological past seemed to feel very real to me. After all, I'd run for student-body president at the same time that my grandmother was telling me stories about her aunt casting out demons in Fukien.

At the same time, I was also very drawn to Frank Chin's work. Now Frank really hates me right now and thinks I'm a white racist and all that, but tough—he gave birth to me, too, and his works really inspired me to think that. He was the first Chinese American to be produced Off-Broadway professionally, and he inspired me to think that this was possible. There's a character in one of his plays, Gwan Gung, who represents a sort of Chinese American spirit, as it were, the spirit of the early immigrants.

I began to think about the juxtaposition of Fa Mu Lan, the woman warrior character from Maxine's book, and Gwan Gung, the character from Frank Chin's plays, and I began to think what would happen if they met in a Chinese restaurant in Torrance. Was there a way to synthesize these two traditions?

That led to my first play, *FOB,* which was the play that I wrote to be done in my dorm. In it, Dale, who's the ABC, or American Born Chinese character, is trying to deal with his own identity and the irritation he feels from Steve, an FOB, or Fresh Off the Boat immigrant. Steve is the sort of nightmare version of Dale's self. Dale has spent a lifetime trying to fit in, trying to be hip, trying to be white, basically, and Steve brings out the fact that he may be something different. There's a monologue where Dale tries to describe his own life, which I'd like to read. He says:

> *I am much better now. I go out now. Lots. I can, anyway. Sometimes I don't ask anyone, so I don't go out. But I could. I am much better now. I have friends now. Lots. They drive Porsche Carreras. Well, one does. He has a house up in the Hollywood Hills where I can stand and look down on the lights of LA. I guess I haven't really been there yet. But I could easily go. I'd just have to ask. My parents—they don't know nothing about the world, about watching Benson at the Roxy, about ordering* hors d'oeuvres *at Scandia's, downshifting onto the Ventura Freeway at midnight. They're yellow ghosts and they've tried to cage me up with Chinese-ness when all the time we were in America. So, I've had to work real hard—real hard—to be myself. To not be a Chinese, a yellow, a slant, a gook. To be just a human being, like everyone else, I've paid my dues. And that's why I am much better now. I'm making it, you know? I'm making it in America.*

So Dale is sort of the perpetual other, doomed to live forever on the outside. Steve and Grace, who were born in Asia and have immigrated to the States, are relative newcomers to America, but they have access to dramatic sequences where they metamorphose into Gwan Gung and Fa Mu Lan, accessing which sort of unconscious treasure trove of memories and cultures. Dale may also have these myths buried somewhere in his genes, but he's really alienated from them and can only watch kind of in silent confusion while her cousin and his friend play out stories that he either doesn't know or won't learn.

I think the idea of this rich cultural treasure trove, for instance, that's inherent in *FOB* is an interesting place to start looking at the notion of authenticity. Clearly, I was trying to search for something authentic beyond the stereotypes. And I was reaching out to a Chinese American literature as well as a root-culture Chinese tradition, and through this I thought that I was touching something authentic. Now was I touching something authentic? I think [there] are arguments to be made both ways. The argument can be made, for instance, that *FOB* is not historically accurate, that Fa Mu Lan and Gwan Gung, in Chinese literature, exist in different times and there's just no way that they would have met. Besides the fact that they're in a Chinese restaurant in Torrance, there's no way that they would have met even in the original literature.

Similarly, I think the question can be raised, are Gwan Gung and Fa Mu Lan really part of my past? These aren't stories that I grew up listening to. In order to find out who Gwan Gung was, I had to go to read *The Romance of the Three Kingdoms,* which is the sort of *Iliad*-like work in which Gwan Gung appears. To what extent do the appropriation of these mythical figures really constitute some sort of authenticity? To what extent can we say there is a rich cultural unconscious treasure trove? Hold onto that because I'm going to come back to it.

During this period I began what I was calling my "isolationist/nationalist phase." I think that when you begin to deal with your ethnicity when you haven't all your life, there's almost kind of a religious conversion quality to it, and you realize that certain things that you might have felt that are painful are not necessarily unique to you. For instance, if you're completely isolated and you don't know a lot of other Asian Americans and you don't share the experience, then if you're walking down the street and someone goes "Ching Chang Chong" or whatever, you might think, was I doing something too Oriental? Whereas if you are with a number of other people and you realize that this is a fairly common occurrence, then you realize that it's not you that is the problem, that there are certainly difficulties in the society itself. Your anger becomes refocused on change for the society.

And so it was a very exciting time. I wrote a lot of Chinese American plays—*The Dance and the Railroad,* where I was trying to reclaim an authentic history as well as deal with kind of an East-West fusion in terms of trying to combine Chinese opera with western naturalism and hoping that this was some sort of authentic Asian American form. Similarly, *Family Devotions* was a play that was largely autobiographical, and in it there's a character named Chester who is a violinist who's about to go off and play (with the Boston Symphony, as a matter of fact). He meets an uncle, Di-Gou, who's just arrived from the PRC [People's Republic of China] and is not part of the fundamentalist Christian tradition that he was brought up in.

They have a discussion which I think is very much about the issue of authenticity. Chester says, "I'm leaving here. Like you did." And Di-

"We who are born in America absorb our images of self and culture basically through western eyes. . . . Under such circumstances, how can we possibly discover who we really are?"

Gou says, "But, Chester, I've found that I cannot leave the family. Today—look!—I follow them across an ocean." Chester says, "You know, they're gonna start bringing you to church." Di-Gou, "No. My sisters and their religion are two different things. . . . There are faces back further than you can see. Faces long before the white missionaries arrived in China. Here. Look here. At your face. Study your face and you will see—the shape of your face is the shape of faces back many generations—across an ocean, in another soil. You must become one with your family before you can hope to live away from it. . . . Chester, you are in America. If you deny those who share your blood, what do you have in this country?"

In some sense you can read this debate in *Family Devotions* as an argument over the issue of authentic culture versus Orientalism. For instance, we who are born in America absorb our images of self and culture basically through western eyes, through the mainstream point of view, and even if we decide to, say, read original Chinese literature, we're often looking at translations that were made by western scholars with their own sets of idiosyncrasies or prejudices or preconceptions.

Under such circumstances, how can we possibly discover who we really are? How can we discover the reality, or the authentic Asian or Asian American culture? The questions of authenticity continue to haunt me. For instance, the use of Chinese opera in my work—what is the significance of Chinese opera in my life? I hadn't actually grown up with a lot of Chinese opera. It was something that I kind of appropriated as a cultural symbol.

Similarly, in this scene between Di-Gou and Chester, there's the issue of the face and the face as a repository of culture, the face as a repository of who you really are. The stories written in your face are the ones that you must believe. The notion of there being sort of a rich unconscious treasure trove is an interesting notion that again I'm going to file away and we'll get back to in a sec.

Because of all these questions, I just didn't write anything for two years. I hit a period of writer's block, and I wondered if I was sort of just creating Orientalia for the intelligentsia. That is, I looked at my work, and some of it had more dragons and gongs and stuff, and some of those seemed to be the more popular. I was wondering if I was repackaging the old stereotypes in more intellectually hip forms.

Authenticity is an extremely heated debate among Asian Americans and among people in general. The most common criticism an Asian American author hears is that his or her work reinforces stereotypes. I criticized *Miss Saigon* for reinforcing the stereotype of submissive Asian women. *M. Butterfly* was criticized for reinforcing the stereotype of Asian men being effeminate. *The Joy Luck Club* was criticized for reinforcing the notion that Asian men are not very nice. Frank Chin criticized both *The Woman Warrior* and *FOB* for inauthentic use of mythology. And Frank Chin's own plays, when first staged in Seattle, were picketed by Asian Americans for reinforcing stereotypes of broken-English-speaking Chinatown tour guides.

Now by and large, I have to say that I think these are really healthy debates. I mean, I don't like being criticized. Who does? But to some extent, it's a corollary for what I call the official Asian American Syndrome: when there's only one who's in the spotlight at a given time, everything we say is expected to represent the entire culture. I think that it's actually rather similar to—if you listen to lawyers talk about "LA Law," they have a very specific opinion about whether or not that would actually happen in a legal office.

Essentially of course, one has to come to the conclusion that only the community of artists

can represent the community, that no one artist can speak for an entire people as if those people were completely monolithic. But it does lead to what's called the "political correctness" debate right now. I think, personally, that political correctness has been a bit overplayed by the media. Certainly there's a lot of stressed charges, and some of the charges are exaggerated and perhaps overly emotional, but the fact is we've always accepted the legitimacy of aesthetic judgment. Critics, aesthetic critics, are free to blast works of art for being banal or poorly put together, only fit for kindling, without being accused of censorship.

The question is, therefore, do criticisms become inherently more dangerous when they focus on a work of art's content as opposed to the aesthetics? Personally, I think not. I think that as Americans we should be intellectually rigorous enough to promote healthy debate on both fronts. I think it's particularly true at a time in our history like now, when the definition of who is an American and what does it mean to be an American is in flux, because art has always served as one means by which people define themselves and define their vision of themselves. I don't think that political criticism necessarily equals censorship.

Empirically, that turns out to be true. I mean, I criticized *Miss Saigon* and it's still running, and Jonathan Pryce won a Tony—so there. People criticized *M. Butterfly* and it did very well, at least in the theater. If anything, the debates over political correctness usually, from a practical standpoint, just increase the number of people who decide to go see the work.

I do think, though, that there's an argument to be made that traditional criticism or traditional correctness, if you will, has existed as a type of censorship. I think it was Arthur Miller who once said that there is no single person in the old Soviet Union who has more authority over what people do or do not see in the theater than does the head critic of the *New York Times*. I think also if you look at, for instance, Bruce Lee, who developed the "Kung Fu" series but was replaced by David Carradine because the executives felt that an Asian American actor couldn't carry the lead in a series. We would have to say, I think, that this is not an example of best man for the job. Therefore, to me, the people who are very hysterical over political correctness seem to be a little disingenuous and a little nostalgic. To say that the political criticisms are inherently more damaging or censorious than aesthetic criticisms is to say that Susan Sontag's criticism of something based on content is less important, or less valid than say, Siskel and Ebert. I think that's a difficult case to make.

So essentially, I had to go through this period by reinvestigating the notion of nationalism and the isolationism that I was interested in at the time. I felt a need to—having addressed a lot of the problems and difficulties that I felt growing up as an Asian American—I now felt the need to kind of go beyond and continue to expand my circle. To choose one's associates on the basis of race seems a little arbitrary and limiting. People who continue to do so for many years on end—sometimes I'm tempted to compare them to people who spend a little too much time hanging around their old high school.

I think ethnic isolationism also runs the risk of reinforcing a larger prejudice in society—that ethnic minorities are defined primarily by their race. This can lead to the ghettoization of writers. Certainly those who choose to write about a particular ethnic group are really falling into a great literary tradition of writers like Tennessee Williams or Fitzgerald or August Wilson, whose work stems from its cultural specificity. That's certainly legitimate.

But there is this notion in Hollywood oftentimes that, okay, we should hire some African American, but they basically would write African American stuff. And women would write romantic comedies. Whereas in reality, if you look at, for instance, England—Kazuo Ishiguro, an Anglo-Japanese writer, wrote a beautiful novel, *Remains of the Day,* about an English butler. I think that we see that the ability of art to cross racial lines exists, and therefore ghettoization is a kind of knee-jerk reaction which may have been progressive at one point in the '60s but since has calcified.

I came out of this period by writing a play called *Rich Relations* which had no Asian characters. Basically, my thought on *Rich Relations* is good theory, lousy execution. I basically wrote an autobiographical play about my family and then just made them all white. That wasn't the way to do it.

Then I was at a party and somebody told me the story of the French diplomat who had a twenty-year affair with a Chinese actress who turned out to be A) a spy and B) a man. I thought that was interesting. I began to think of the real diplomat (whose name is Bernard Bouriscot) and what did he think he was getting when he met the spy. The answer came to me—he probably thought he was meeting some version of Madame Butterfly.

I'd like to just read the scene where Gallimard, the French diplomat, and Song, the Chinese spy, meet for the first time.

Gallimard says: "They say in opera the voice is everything. That's probably why I'd never before enjoyed opera. Here . . . here was a Butterfly with little or no voice—but she had the grace, the delicacy—I believed this girl. I believed her suffering. I wanted to take her in my arms—so delicate, even I could protect her, take her home, pamper her until she smiled."

Song, the spy, says: "Excuse me. Monsieur . . . ?"

Gallimard: "Oh! Gallimard. Mademoiselle . . . ? A beautiful . . ."

"Song Liling."

"A beautiful performance."

"Oh, please."

"I usually—"

"You make me blush. I'm no opera singer at all."

Gallimard says: "I usually don't like *Butterfly*."

"I can't blame you in the least."

"I mean, the story—"

"Ridiculous."

"I like the story, but . . . what?"

Song says: "Oh, you like it?"

"I . . . What I mean is, I've always seen it played by huge women in so much bad makeup."

"Bad makeup is not unique to the West."

"But, who can believe them?"

"And you believe me?"

Gallimard says: "Absolutely. You were utterly convincing. It's the first time—"

"Convincing? As a Japanese woman? The Japanese used hundreds of our people for medical experiments during the war, you know. But I gather such an irony is lost on you."

"No! I was about to say, it's the first time I've seen the beauty of the story."

"Really?"

"Of her death. It's a . . . a pure sacrifice. He's unworthy, but what can she do? She loves him . . . so much. It's a very beautiful story."

"Well, yes, to a Westerner."

"Excuse me?"

"It's one of your favorite fantasies, isn't it? The submissive Oriental woman and the cruel white man."

"Well, I didn't quite mean . . ."

"Consider it this way: what would you say if a blonde homecoming queen fell in love with a short Japanese businessman? He treats her cruelly, then goes home for three years, during which time she prays to his picture and turns down marriage from a young Kennedy. Then, when she learns he has remarried, she kills herself. Now, I believe you would consider this girl to be a deranged idiot, correct? But because it's an Oriental who kills herself for a Westerner—ah!—you find it beautiful."

"Yes . . . well . . . I see your point. . . ."

"I will never do Butterfly again, Monsieur Gallimard. If you wish to see some real theatre, come to the Peking Opera sometime. Expand your mind."

And Gallimard says: "So much for protecting her in my big Western arms."

In some sense, *M. Butterfly* allowed me to explore the very issues of authenticity which had caused the writer's block. I created a French diplomat who was caught up in an Orientalist fantasy, and in so doing, I was exploring both the pervasiveness and the seductiveness of these stereotypes. Through the juxtaposition of fantasy and reality that's in the play, I'm asking whether it's really possible to see the truth, to see the authenticity about a culture, a loved one, or even ourselves. Are we always going to be imprisoned within the realm of our own subjectivity and forced to perceive meaning through our own prejudices?

As Song says to Gallimard in their second meeting, "You're a Westerner. How can you objectively judge your own values?"

Gallimard says, "I think it's possible to achieve some distance."

Song says, "Do you?"

In Act Three, Song undresses before Gallimard and confronts the diplomat with the obvious fact of his self-delusion.

Gallimard says, "You, who knew every inch of my desires—how could you, of all people, have made such a mistake?"

Song says: "What?"

"You showed me your true self. When all I loved was the lie. A perfect lie, which you let fall to the ground, and now, it's old and soiled."

Song says: "So—you never really loved me? Only when I was playing a part?"

Gallimard says: "I'm a man who loved a woman created by a man. Everything else—simply falls short. . . . Tonight, I've finally learned to tell fantasy from reality. And, knowing the difference, I choose fantasy."

And so I'm bringing into the discussion of authenticity the question of subjectivity. There is a certain point where I felt that political activism would rescue me from subjectivity, that trying to see things from a point of view that took into account sociological perspective, history would therefore allow me to look at culture and look at identity in an objective fashion.

I question whether that's the case. I ask whether political activism is not subject to the same degree of subjectivity and prejudice and self-servingness that other activities are. This doesn't make it invalid, it only means that it, too, has to be looked at as rigorously as the arts and as the academic curricula that we may be criticizing. If we say that the personal is the political, then to some extent we have to accept the responsibilities of the converse, which is that the political sometimes gets wrapped up in the personal.

There was a fight between two really right-on Asian American activists when I was in college. At the time, I was just sort of beginning my journey to consciousness, and so I wasn't quite aware what it was all about. I just knew that they hated each other and it was a very political dispute. I bumped into one of these guys about five months ago at a benefit for the Asian American theater in San Francisco, and I said, now, will you explain to me what exactly was the root of your dispute with X? He said, "Well, actually, I think it was that we both wanted the same woman." So for the past fifteen years I've been scratching my head trying to figure out the political import of this debate when actually it was a personal debate.

Face Value, which was my play that previewed here in Boston to not much acclaim, was a lot about this as well. The plot basically hinged off of the *Miss Saigon* affair. It was about two Asian Americans who go in whiteface to disrupt the opening night of a musical in which the lead actor is a Caucasian playing an Asian. The plot is complicated with the arrival of two white supremacists who then kidnap the Caucasian actor, believing he actually is Asian and is stealing jobs from white people.

This is where we get back to some of the issues that I said to put on hold for a second. Because to some extent, what *Face Value* is about, and what I will try to make it more about in future rewrites, is the value or the lack of value of faces. True, we all come from different cultures, or many of us come from different cultures. There are, therefore, certain behavioral predispositions that exist with culture, but the face, the race, the skin color, does not necessarily equal the culture.

I often use the example of Chinese Americans who were born in the Deep South. They come from a particular culture, but it's not necessarily the culture you would associate with their faces. I think that in the future we are going to be seeing more and more examples of how it is not possible to predict behavior simply from race. Therefore the disunion of face and culture becomes more and more pronounced. So when I go back to some of my early work and the issues that I was exploring, I, for instance, ask about the rich cultural treasure trove that Grace and Steve had access to in *FOB,* I ask about Di-Gou in *Family Devotions* telling Chester that the stories he must believe are the stories written in your faces, and I ask myself, what is the power in faces? Is there an inherent spiritual or identity objectivity that we can hold on to from looking into the mirror? At this point in my life, I think the answer for me is no, there is not. . . .

". . . authenticity should be flexible enough to encompass change. What is authentic in 1960 is not necessarily authentic in 1990 and will not necessarily be authentic in 2020."

I think it's important to envision futures which are more just and inviting. I guess I'm arguing for a non-fundamentalist approach to the issue of authenticity—that authenticity should be flexible enough to encompass change. What is authentic in 1960 is not necessarily authentic in 1990 and will not necessarily be authentic in 2020.

What this means is we will have to write about each other and about ourselves, and we will continue to expect criticism and be subject to criticism. We will learn from one another, and that is simply the socialization process which I think is going to be taking place as the country struggles to redefine itself. Those of us who are minorities often talk about this change—Caucasians will no longer be a majority. White males, in particular, need to get it together and realize that the world is changing.

I think that's true, but I think the world is changing for us, too. There are a lot of certainties that we could depend on in the past that are not necessarily going to be there in the future. For instance, in the '70s many of us condemned assimilation as a pathetic attempt to ape European Americans. But after the Rodney King verdicts in Los Angeles, I think we also learned that the fact that we neglected to build certain bridges to other communities meant that we'd also neglected to build certain bridges to African Americans, to Latino Americans. For those of us who believe in sort of Third-World solidarity and took that as a state of grace, reality taught us that we'd become lost in self-delusion.

Now we have polls which show a sharp increase in the number of African Americans who characterize Asians as the most racist of all ethnic groups. Even the term "Asian American" itself, which was invented to identify a common sociopolitical group, faces some degree of redefinition, I think, in the light of intermarriage and the wide diversity of new immigrants. So we can't rest on the assumptions of the past. We have to realize that as America changes, all of us are going to be involved in change and all of us are going to be involved in investigating the authentic.

I've been quoted as saying that to have a honest discussion about race between people of different races is more intimate than sex. It was a little flip but I believe that, because to some extent it's very difficult for us to believe one another right now. It's very difficult for us to trust one another enough to be honest. It's easier to be defensive or not communicate or be polite—anything but really express whatever anger or frustrations that it is that we feel.

I think that if there is a certain degree of subjectivity to the debate over authenticity, then a corollary of that is that we may not necessarily have to like one another. We may not necessarily have to trust one another at this stage. But I think it might be nice to take the step to believe one another.... I don't believe it's constructive to dismiss [the subjectivity of personal experience] as simply delusional.

Also perhaps something that's more difficult for us. If a white man says, "I feel that I didn't get into X University because of quotas, reverse racism, and I feel that I'm qualified"—well, I have to believe that that's how he feels. I may then try to have a discussion and point to statistics and whatever, but I have to start with the assumption that he actually does have that feeling. That's somewhat more complicated than it sounds, because I think it's just as easy for us to slip into denial from all sides and to want to tell the white man, "You're crazy. Don't you realize that you're one of the most privileged people that ever walked the face of the planet?"

But I don't know that that's actually going to help us figure out what kind of society we're going to have in the future. So, in the final analysis, authenticity to me is a debate over the quest to validate the humanity of various peoples, of all the people in this country. I know a couple who's—gosh, he's Irish and Jewish and Japanese and she's Haitian and Filipino and something else. Anyway, they had a child, and someone whose business it is to know such things informed them that their child had never existed before. I began to wonder if this child grows up and becomes a writer—let's say it's a woman—what do we call her? Is she an African American writer or an Asian American writer, European American or is she basically a woman's writer, or etc.? And I think that when the day comes that we can simply call her an American writer, then we will have gone a long way to claiming the humanity and the authenticity of all our experiences as Americans.

Thank you.

SOURCES

Books

Hwang, David Henry, *Broken Promises: Four Plays,* Avon, 1983.

———, *M. Butterfly,* New American Library, 1989.

Street, Douglas, *David Henry Hwang,* Boise State University Press, 1989.

Zia, Helen, and Susan Gall, editors, *Notable Asian Americans,* Gale Research, Detroit, 1995.

Periodicals

Boston Globe, "Hwang's Political Stage," April 15, 1994.

Christian Science Monitor, "For Playwright Hwang, Mediums Change While Themes Stay the Same," April 13, 1994, p. 15.

Detroit News, "Myth Saigon," October 8, 1994.

New York Times Magazine, March 13, 1988.

People, January 9, 1984, p. 88.

U.S. News and World Report, March 28, 1988.

Daniel K. Inouye

1924–

Japanese American member of the U.S. Senate

A hero of World War II and the first Japanese American to serve in the U.S. Congress, Daniel K. Inouye has served the people of Hawaii since their island home became the fiftieth state in 1959. Initially a member of the House of Representatives, he was elected to the Senate in 1962, and there he has wielded considerable power and influence for the Democrats in a characteristically low-key fashion that emphasizes compromise over confrontation. It is an approach that has brought Inouye the respect of his colleagues within the government and the support of his constituents, who have re-elected him to national office a total of seven times.

Inouye is a member of the generation known by the Japanese term nisei, *which describes the U.S.-born children of parents who emigrated from Japan. His father was just a young boy when he arrived in Hawaii with his own parents. Later, as an adult, he worked in Honolulu as a file clerk to support his family, earning just enough for him, his wife, and four children to live in a state of genteel poverty. But as his son Dan later recalled, his childhood was a happy one, and he grew up with the feeling that a better future awaited him if he were willing to work for it.*

By the time he had reached his senior year of high school, Inouye's dream was to become a surgeon. But those plans changed forever on the morning of December 7, 1941, as he and his family were getting ready to go to church. Over the radio came news of the Japanese air raid then in progress at Pearl Harbor. Inouye, who had been teaching first aid at the local Red Cross station, rushed there to help and stayed on duty for nearly a week. He ended up spending much of the rest of his senior year attending classes during the day and working a twelve-hour shift for the Red Cross at night—a manic schedule he felt compelled to observe out of guilt over the fact that the attack had been carried out by the Japanese. Meanwhile, in the streets of Honolulu, he and other Hawaiians of Japanese descent endured taunts, insults, and sometimes outright hatred from whites.

In the fall of 1942, Inouye enrolled in the pre-med program at the University of Hawaii. He also added his voice to those of many other young nisei *men who were petitioning the U.S. government to allow them to serve in the armed forces and thus demonstrate their loyalty to the country. Finally, in January 1943, the War Department announced that it would accept fifteen hundred* nisei *volunteers for a new unit, the 442nd Regimental Combat Team. Inouye quit school and immediately joined up.*

The 442nd went on to become the most decorated unit in U.S. military history; its four thousand members—who adopted "Go for Broke!" as their motto—received more than eighteen thousand medals for bravery. Inouye earned fifteen of them himself as one of the 442nd's most heroic leaders. Fighting in Italy during the last few months of the war, he was critically wounded while directing a difficult uphill assault against a heavily-fortified German position on a high ridge. He spent the next two years in the hospital recovering from multiple bullet wounds to his abdomen and leg and the amputation of his right arm.

Upon returning home in 1947, Inouye resumed his education at the University of Hawaii. No longer interested in pursuing a career in medicine, he opted instead to study law with an eye toward one day entering public life. So, after receiving his bachelor's degree in 1950, he headed to Washington, D.C., where he attended George Washington University Law School. Following his 1952 graduation, he returned to Honolulu and became involved in politics as a Democrat, winning election to the Territorial House in 1954 and serving two terms as majority leader. In 1958, his bid for a seat in the Territorial Senate met with success, and there, too, he assumed the role of majority leader.

By the time Hawaii was admitted to the union as the fiftieth state in 1959, Inouye was so popular with his fellow islanders that he easily captured the new state's first seat in the U.S. House of Representatives. Three years later, he decided to run for the U.S. Senate seat being vacated by one of Hawaii's first senators and ended up beating his Republican opponent by more than a two-to-one margin.

From the very beginning of his congressional career, Inouye has tended to hold a liberal opinion on social issues but a more moderate or even conservative one on economic and defense issues. He has, for example, consistently supported civil rights legislation through the years, including the landmark Civil Rights Act of 1964, and also backed the "Great Society" social welfare programs of President Lyndon Johnson. As a loyal Democrat, he sided with the president on the conduct of the Vietnam War but aligned himself with the forces in his party calling for peace once Republican Richard Nixon took office.

Inouye's loyalty was rewarded during the 1960s with his appointment to a number of high-ranking positions in the party, including assistant majority whip and vice-chairman of the Democratic Senatorial Campaign Committee. He was also mentioned several times as a possible vice-presidential candidate, particularly after he delivered the following keynote address to delegates attending the Democratic National Convention in Chicago on August 29, 1968. At the time, the country was in turmoil—race riots had exploded in many major cities over several previous summers, shock waves still reverberated from the recent assassinations of Martin Luther King, Jr., and Robert F. Kennedy, and antiwar demonstrations were erupting on university and college campuses across the nation (and even right outside the convention hall). Inouye won widespread acclaim for a stirring speech in which he criticized the forces threatening to tear apart the United States and urged concerned citizens to take positive rather than negative action to correct political and social ills. It is reprinted here from Vital Speeches of the Day, *September 15, 1968.*

My fellow Americans: This is my country. Many of us have fought hard for the right to say that. Many are struggling today from Harlem to Danang so that they may say it with conviction.

This is our country.

And we are engaged in a time of great testing—testing whether this nation, or any nation conceived in liberty and dedicated to opportunity for all its citizens, can not only endure but continue to progress. The issue before all of us in such a time is how shall we discharge, how shall we honor our citizenship.

The keynote address at a national political convention traditionally calls for rousing oratory. I hope to be excused from this tradition tonight. For I do not view this occasion as one for either flamboyance or levity.

I believe the real reason we are here is that there is a word called "commitment," because we are committed to the future of our country and all our people, and because for that future, hope and faith are more needed now than pride in our party's past.

For even as we emerge from an era of unsurpassed social and economic progress, Americans are clearly in no mood for counting either their blessings or their bank accounts.

We are still embarked on the longest unbroken journey of economic growth and prosperity in our history. Yet we are torn by dissension, and disrespect for our institutions and leaders is rife across the land.

In at least two of our greatest universities, learning has been brought to a halt by student rebellions; others of the student revolution have publicly burned draft cards and even the American flag.

Crime has increased so that we are told one out of every three Americans is afraid to walk in his own neighborhood after dark.

Riot has bludgeoned our cities, laying waste our streets, our property and, most important, human lives. The smoke of destruction has even shrouded the dome of our Capitol, and in Washington the task of restoring order drew more than twice as many federal troops as were involved in the defense of Khesanh in Vietnam.

Voices of angry protest are heard throughout the land, crying for all manner of freedoms. Yet our political leaders are picketed and some who cry loudest for freedom have sought to prevent our president, our vice president and cabinet officers from speaking in public.

None go so far as publicly to condone a politics of assassination. Yet assassins' bullets have robbed our country of three great leaders within the last five years.

Why? . . . Why—when we have at last had the courage to open up an attack on the age-old curses of ignorance and disease and poverty and prejudice—why are the flags of anarchism being hoisted by leaders of the next generation? Why, when our maturing society welcomes and appreciates art as never before, are poets and painters so preponderantly hostile? Some conveniently blame all our ills and agonies on a most difficult and unpopular commitment overseas. The Vietnam war must end, they say, because it is an immoral war.

Of course, the war in Vietnam must be ended. But it must be ended, as President Johnson said last March, by patient political negotiation rather than through the victorious force of arms—even though this may be unpalatable for those raised in the tradition of glorious military victories.

But like our other complex problems, this one must also be solved responsibly. Just as we shun irresponsible calls for total and devastating military victory, so must we guard against the illusion of an instant peace that has no chance of permanence.

Of course, the Vietnam war is immoral. Whether by the teachings of Moses or by the teachings of Christ or by the teachings of Buddha, I believe that wars are immoral. During the Crusades, Christians in the name of Jesus Christ slaughtered innocent men, women and children and plundered their cities—because they were of another faith. These were immoral wars.

In Vietnam we build schools across the countryside and feed the hungry in the cities. And our president has pledged massive sums in aid to all Vietnamese as an incentive to peace. And yet this is an immoral war.

Perhaps by the time my four-year-old son is grown, men will have learned to live by the Ten Commandments. But men have not yet renounced the use of force as a means to their objectives.

And until they do, are we more immoral—if there be such a degree—to fracture our solemn commitments and then see our word doubted, not only by our friends abroad, but by our enemies?

Knowing that this could lead to tragic miscalculations, is it less immoral now to take the easier course, and gamble the lives of our sons and grandsons on the outcome?

These are not easy questions and perhaps there are no certain answers.

But when young people have rioted in China and Czechoslovakia as well as at Columbia, and in Paris and Berlin as well as in Berkeley, I doubt that we can blame all the troubles of our time on Vietnam.

Other critics tell us of the revolution of rising expectations. They charge that it has reached such proportions that men now take it as an insult when they are asked to be reasonable in their desires and demands.

If this is too often true as a generalization, it is all too frequently aimed particularly at our fellow citizens of African ancestry, whose aspirations have burst full-blown on us after more than one hundred years of systematic racist deprivation.

As an American whose ancestors came from Japan, I have become accustomed to a question most recently asked by a very prominent businessman who was concerned about the threat of riots and the resultant loss in life and property. "Tell me," he said, "why can't the Negro be like you?"

First, although my skin is colored, it is not black. In this country, the color of my skin does not ignite prejudice that has smoldered for generations.

Second, although my grandfather came to this country in poverty, he came without shackles; he came as a free man enjoying certain constitutional rights under the American flag.

Third, my grandfather's family was not shattered as individual members of it were sold as chattel or used as security on loans. And fourth, although others of my ancestry were interned behind barbed wires during World War II, neither my parents nor I were forced by covenants and circumstances to live in ghettos.

Unlike those of my ancestry, the Negro's unemployment rate is triple the national average. The mortality rate of his children is twice that of white children.

He often pays more for his miserable tenement than comparable space will cost in the white suburbs. He is likely to pay more for his groceries, more for his furniture, more for his liquor and more for his credit.

And, my fellow Americans, today many thousands of black Americans return from Vietnam with medals of valor, some of them have been crippled in the service of their country. But too often they return to economic and social circumstances that are barely, if at all, improved over those they left.

Daniel K. Inouye

Is it any wonder that the Negro questions whether his place in our country's history books will be any less forgotten than were the contributions of his ancestors? Is it any wonder that the Negroes find it hard to wait another one hundred years before they are accepted as full citizens in our free society?

Of course, expectations are rising—and they are rising faster than we in our imperfect world can fulfill them.

The revolution we in the United States are experiencing was born of Democratic processes that not only accommodate economic progress and social mobility, but actively encourage them.

But it is important to remember that these expectations are the children of progress and that today's restlessness has been nurtured by our very real achievements. Out of these should emerge a brighter and better society than we have known.

Nowhere is this clearer than in the situation of our young people today. The success of our economic system has freed them in ever-increasing numbers from the tragedies of premature mortality and early labor.

It has built the schools in which they are being educated to higher levels than ever in our nation's history. And this progress has been achieved in a political system that not only admits but safeguards the right of dissent.

So it should hardly surprise us when the children of such progress demand to be heard when they become aware of inequities still to be corrected. Neither should we fear their voices. On the contrary, whether we know it or not, the marching feet of youth have led us into a new era of politics and we can never turn back.

But what should concern us is something far more fundamental. The true dimension of the challenge facing us is a loss of faith. I do not mean simply a loss of religious faith, although this erosion is a major contributor to our unease. I mean a loss of faith in our country, in its purposes and its institutions. I mean a retreat from the responsibilities of citizenship.

The plain fact is that in the face of complexity and frustration, too many Americans have drifted into the use of power for purely destructive purposes. Too many Americans have come to believe it is their right to decide as individuals which of our laws they will obey and which they will violate.

I do not mean to say that all our laws are just. They're not, and I don't mean to suggest that protest against unjust laws is not proper. Performed in an orderly manner, the right to protest is a cornerstone of our system.

Men must have the opportunity to be heard even when their views are extreme and in a lesser democratic country, dangerous. I, too, have spoken against laws which I considered wrong and unjust, and I am sure I will speak—and vote—against many, many more.

But my fellow Americans, I have not burned my birth certificate, and I will not renounce my citizenship.

Those who would do such things are relatively few. But there is a much larger number who in the face of change and disorder have retreated into disengagement and quiet despair. Less destructively but not less surely, such men are also retreating from the responsibilities of citizenship.

Now let us not deceive ourselves about the consequences of such abdication. It is anarchy. It is a state in which each individual demands instant compliance with his own desires, and from there it is but a short step to the assumption by each individual of the right to decide which of his neighbors shall live and which shall not, and so accelerate the sickening spiral of violence which has already cost us our beloved John F. Kennedy, our great leader Martin Luther King Jr. and the voice of this decade, Senator Robert F. Kennedy.

We have been told that the revolts are against the system, and that Establishment must be torn down. But my fellow Americans, in Paris recently, students cut down hundred-year-old trees to erect temporary street barricades. Those trees had lived through two world wars. Some of them had even survived the revolution of 1848.

Were the goals of these students served by the destruction of those trees? How long will it take for their beauty and the vitality they symbolized to grow again? What trees did the students plant in their place?

> ***"Too many Americans have come to believe it is their right to decide as individuals which of our laws they will obey and which they will violate."***

If we cut down our institutions, public and private, and with indifference starve the systems which have given us our achievements, who will feed the hungry? Who will train the unskilled?

Who will supply the jobs that mean opportunity for the generation whose voices are not yet heard? And who will launch the much-needed Marshall Plan to rebuild our cities and open opportunity for all Americans? These undertakings are too great for individuals going their separate ways.

Finally, my fellow Americans, let us remember that even anarchy is only a way station. Man, the social animal, has always craved order. He has made the most essential function of his government the maintenance of some level of order.

Chaos and anarchy have never been more than preludes to totalitarianism. Tyrants like Adolph Hitler have taught this before.

So, my fellow Americans, let us reject violence as a means of protest, and let us reject those who preach violence. But let us not tempt those who would hide the evil face of racism behind the mask of law and order.

To permit violence and anarchy to destroy our cities is to spark the beginning of a cancerous growth of doubt, suspicion, fear and hatred that will gradually infect the whole nation.

Poverty, discrimination, deprivation, as evil as they are, do not justify violence or anarchy, do not justify looting or burning and do not justify murder or assassination. Law and order must be respected and maintained to protect the rights—yes, the civil rights—of all our citizens.

But let us resist also the temptation to apathy because we can never cure the causes of violence with indifference. And, my fellow Americans, in the last analysis law and order can only rest securely with justice and its foundation.

So let's look at how much we have already built and then get on with the work.

At a time when guns are still heard in some areas of the world, we have laid in place such building blocks of mankind's survival as the nuclear test ban treaty of 1963, the banning of atomic weapons in space of 1967, and the nuclear nonproliferation treaty of 1968. These are vital foundations, vital foundations of peace and we must build on them.

Under the health measures first proposed by the presidency of our most beloved Harry S Truman and passed during the remarkable administration of Lyndon B. Johnson, twenty million older Americans are now protected under Medicare.

Our elder Americans can now live their autumn years in dignity and in security. And infant mortality has declined to a new low, and federally-funded community health centers are now serving nearly fifty million Americans. These too are vital foundations and on them we must build fuller lives for our citizens.

And since 1963, President Johnson has proposed and Congress has enacted more than forty major new laws to foster education in our country. Since 1963, our government has tripled its investment in education and in the past four years alone we have invested twice as much as was spent in the previous one hundred years. These are the foundations from which towers of human achievement can soar.

The last eleven years have seen the passage of the five civil rights laws passed during the entire history of the United States, and I might note in passing that Lyndon Baines Johnson is the author, chief architect or primary sponsor of each of the civil rights laws.

When all summers are long and hot, it is well to remember that the one hundred years of the Emancipation Proclamation is finally but slowly but becoming a reality, and the occupants of some of our highest offices are testimony that black talent is just as important as white talent.

Working together, we have done much. We can and we must do much, much more.

Fellow Democrats, we are here tonight because in large part we share our faith in our country and in its processes of orderly, humanistic change. Change and challenge should not deter us now—we have long been a party of change and challenge.

The need for new ideas and improved institutions should not deter us now—we have long been a party of new ideas.

That today's crisis is one of the human spirit should not deter us—we have long been a party which gave priority to the needs of human beings.

So let us go forward with programs responsive to the needs of today and responsive to the needs of tomorrow.

Fellow Americans, this is our country. Its future is what we, its citizens, will make it.

And as we all know, we have much to do. Putting aside hatred on the one hand and timidity on the other, let us grow fresh faith in our purpose and new vigor in our citizenship.

Let us welcome the ideas and energies of the young and the talents and participation of all responsible people.

Let us plant trees and grow new opportunity. And, my fellow Americans, let us build not only new buildings but new neighborhoods and then let us live in them, all as full citizens and all as brothers.

In closing I wish to share with you a most sacred word of Hawaii. It is "aloha." To some of you who visited us it may have meant hello. To others "aloha" may have meant good-bye. But to those of us who have been privileged to live in Hawaii, "aloha" means "I love you."

So to all of you, my fellow Americans, aloha.

During the administrations of presidents Richard Nixon, Gerald Ford, Jimmy Carter, Ronald Reagan, George Bush, and Bill Clinton, Inouye continued to favor liberal causes such as abortion rights, gun control, organized labor, and consumer protection laws while voting to support some Cold War-era military measures, including funding for development of a neutron bomb. He has also been a longtime champion of Israel.

Inouye's influence in a number of these areas has been considerable thanks to the high-ranking positions he has held on key Senate committees—assignments that have occasionally put him in the national spotlight. In 1973, for example, Inouye served as a member of the Senate Watergate Committee, a role in which he won over many fans for his patient yet tenacious questioning of less-than-cooperative witnesses. He again found himself in the public eye in 1987, when he chaired the Iran-contra hearings.

But Inouye's most significant and enduring work has probably been carried out behind the scenes. In 1976, for instance, he served as chairman of the Senate Select Committee on Intelligence, which drafted rules governing the covert operations of U.S. intelligence organizations at home and abroad in an effort to curb some of their more flagrant abuses of power. As a longtime member of the Senate Appropriations Committee and former chairman of its Foreign Operations Subcommittee, Inouye has wielded a great deal of clout in foreign policy matters by determining which countries will receive aid and how much they will receive. More recently, he played an important role in overseeing developments in cable television, telephone communications, and the "Information Superhighway" as former chairman of the Science, and Transportation Subcommittee on Communications of the Senate Commerce Committee.

Because of his own experience with racial prejudice during World War II, Inouye has always been especially sensitive to discrimination against minorities. Of particular interest to him through the years have been the concerns of Native Americans, and as chairman of the Senate Committee on Indian Affairs he earned their trust and respect for his strong support of tribal sovereignty and self-determination. On December 2, 1991, Inouye addressed some of the major issues facing Native Americans and his Senate Committee in a speech he delivered at the annual convention of the National Congress of American Indians, held that year in San Francisco. Inouye provided a copy of his remarks.

Good morning. I am pleased to be with you again to address the theme of the 48th annual convention of the National Congress of American Indians—"protecting sovereignty, defending our rights, preserving our culture."

As most of you know, there are three principles that guide our work in the committee. These principles are sovereignty, self-determination and self-governance.

Together, we have accomplished much over the course of the past year, in preserving the sovereignty of tribal governments and defending tribal rights. As we gather here today, we can proudly celebrate two major achievements that directly affect the sovereignty of tribal governments.

The first, of course, is the action of the Congress to overturn the ruling of the Supreme Court in *Duro v. Reina*, and to recognize the inherent sovereignty of tribal governments to exercise criminal jurisdiction over all Indian people on their reservations.

The second major achievement in preserving the sovereignty of tribal governments grows out of a significant vote in the United States

Senate on June 25 of this year, in which members of the Senate took up a bill of considerable volume—245 pages in length—known as the Violent Crime Control Act. This act proposes to address a wide range of issues related to the control of violent crime—from safer streets and neighborhoods to the prevention and punishment of terrorist acts.

Buried within the hundreds of pages and the hundreds of provisions in this bill are 86 words—86 words that for Indian tribal governments, go to the very foundation of their status as sovereigns within our constitutional system.

These 86 words would accord to tribal governments a status which state governments have come to take for granted—the right to develop and shape the laws that will apply within the scope of their jurisdiction.

These 86 words became the subject of Senate debate for over two hours—86 words that affect Indian Country in a dramatic and demonstrable fashion.

Those 86 words confirm that tribal governments are sovereign, and that like state governments, they have the sovereign right to elect whether the death penalty will apply to crimes committed by Indians on Indian lands.

While there were some in the Senate who argued strongly against the recognition of tribes as sovereign governments—some who refused to acknowledge the governmental status of Indian nations and argued that Indians were only another "special-interest ethnic group"—in the end, the Senate elected, by a vote of 69 to 29, to confirm the sovereignty of tribal governments.

This morning, I have just come from a press conference that focused upon a new force in Indian Country—a unifying force that is bringing the leaders of diverse indian nations to work together and to speak with one voice.

In one short year, we have seen what you have accomplished with your collective energy and commitment. You have called upon the Congress to overturn the *Duro* decision—you spoke with one voice and with strong consensus—and the Congress acted upon your mandate.

You came to the Congress on the death penalty issue—you made members aware of the disproportionate impact such a federal penalty would have on Indian people, and you presented the issue in the context of sovereignty.

You urged the Congress to understand this issue as one that is fundamental to the sovereignty of your nations, and the Congress responded.

In April of this year, your representatives went to the White House, and you called upon the president to reaffirm the government-to-government relationship between the United States and Indian nations, and you asked him to reaffirm the federal policy of Indian self-determination.

On June 14 of this year, the president signaled that he had heard your message, and that he recognized your sovereignty. He reaffirmed the official policy of the United States of Indian self-governance and self-determination, he acknowledged the trust responsibility of the United States, and he underscored the government-to-government relationship and the status of tribal governments in the American family of governments.

Earlier this year, you brought your heartfelt message to the American people—that you would no longer tolerate the appropriation of Native American human remains, sacred and funerary objects, by museums and scientific institutions.

You communicated your message in every form of media, and slowly but surely you built a momentum of public opinion that carried your message to the halls of the Congress and to the living rooms of the American people.

You found that you had friends and supporters across the country who were sensitive to your cause, and who joined their voices with yours in calling upon the Congress to enact a federal law that would assure the repatriation of the remains of your ancestors.

Yes, you have achieved much in a very short time, by recognizing and focusing upon those concerns that you have in common.

By working together to address the problems that confront many of your communities, you have been able to make a substantial and real difference.

You have changed the laws, you have shaped new laws, you have caused law that was detrimental to your sovereignty to be rejected.

You have begun to explore your great power to communicate your concerns, your issues, to communicate your objectives and ideals. And you have found that there are many who are listening to your message.

I am pleased that you have chosen this path, because I have long thought that there are many positive stories in Indian Country to be told, and that a focus on communicating your successes could have a significant effect on the self-esteem of the younger generations of Indian people.

For instance, as I have stated before, I don't believe that it is generally known that American Indians have fought and died in the service of this country in numbers far greater than their proportion in the population.

This is a compelling statement about the patriotism and the commitment of Indian people to a nation that has not always dealt with them in an honorable fashion.

Given the history of efforts to exterminate the Indian people, to remove them from their homelands, and then to terminate their sovereign status, I think it is a wonder that thousands of Indian people would take up arms in the defense of the United States.

But Indian men and women have served the nation in every military action in which our country has been involved, and this is a story that should be told.

When we speak of unity, we must also be conscious of the lack of unity, and accordingly, I feel that I must take this opportunity to share with you my concerns over recent events related to the action of the committee to recognize the Lumbee tribe of North Carolina.

First, we must always be mindful that the forces which are arrayed against you are massive and powerful. Numerically, you are outnumbered. Economically, you are dwarfed. Politically, it is no contest.

Therefore, to get your message across, your voice must be a loud, unified voice—a voice representing the combined voices of two million Native American Indians.

Knowing this, I am all too often saddened to note the divisions among Native Americans—to note the divisions in Indian Country.

And in this particular case, I was deeply saddened to note the opposition—voiced not by non-Indian people, but opposition voiced by brother and sister Indians.

I am certain there were many sitting on the sidelines, smiling over this development and pleased with the division in the ranks.

If the opposition was based upon facts, such as a perception that the Lumbees are not Indians, but rather people masquerading as Indians, that would be understandable.

But the opposition, at least that which is publicly stated, was based upon the fact that the Lumbees were many in number, and thereby, as such, may take away what little is now being distributed in Indian Country.

This is not opposition based upon principle. This is not opposition based upon fact. This is opposition based upon a concept which I have been told is foreign among Native Americans—materialism.

If there is not enough to go around, let's do what we have been doing for the last five years—join hands and work towards getting more.

Because if the rationale of the argument of the opponents is carried to the ultimate, one way to get *more* for Indian Country is to reduce its numbers.

There will be *more* for the *few* remaining.

Let us not fall into the trap that your opponents and detractors have been laying out throughout these ages. Do not become the victims of the old ploy of "divide and conquer."

There is another matter that I wish to address today, and I will touch on it only briefly, because I believe that most of you may know that of which I speak.

When the Congress enacted the Indian Gaming Regulatory Act, there was a balance that was carefully struck to assure that the sovereignty of the state governments and the sovereignty of the tribal governments would be mutually respected.

> ***"Given the history of efforts to exterminate the Indian people . . . I think it is a wonder that thousands would take up arms in the defense of the United States."***

The act contemplates that both governments will negotiate in good faith, and that both governments will abide by the terms of the law.

The act provides that tribal governments must have management contracts approved, and background checks are to be conducted to assure that tribal gaming activities are operated by honest people.

The act is clear about the kinds of activities and the kinds of machines that fall within the

Class III category, and for those activities and machines, there must be a tribal-state compact in place.

If there is no compact, there is a violation of federal law that carries with it criminal penalties.

Recently, we have received reports of activities that are clearly not allowed under the law, and as many of you know, there has already been action taken in some states to bring a halt to such activities.

My message is this. Tribal governments must abide by the terms of the federal law, just as tribes expect state governments to do.

If you don't monitor and enforce the law as it relates to your own activities, there are many who are just waiting on the sidelines, who are *eager* to do so.

Ten days ago, I joined some of you in presenting testimony to the House Interior Committee on the idea of an American Indian university.

This is not a new idea—it has been around for some twenty years. It is an idea that is approached with some caution, as well it should be.

But it is also an idea to which many members of the Select Committee are committed, if you but signal the course of action.

As you discuss strategies of achieving the goals which are the theme of this conference I hope that you will consider a national Indian university—if well-designed in full consultation with Indian Country—as a strategy that is likely to be beneficial.

In my testimony ten days ago on Delegate Faleomavaega's bill to establish such an institution, I reflected what I had heard from tribal leaders and Indian educators—that the first step should be an analysis of the need for and the purpose of an Indian university within the framework of existing tribal colleges and other postsecondary education opportunities.

Further, I urged careful formulation of a statement of purpose for such an institution. If the purpose urged by one Indian nation at the hearing—*to help assure the future vitality of Indian communities*—were to be adopted, an Indian university could certainly become part of a strategy to achieve the goals of this conference.

I await your guidance and direction on this matter, but I want to underscore that if it is your wish to proceed with the planning for an American Indian university, there are several members of the Select Committee who are poised to act to assure that this idea becomes a reality, because they believe that the time is ripe for action.

Finally, I want to address the matter of preserving your culture, for without your sovereignty and without your culture, none of us would be here today.

I am committed to two major undertakings in the coming year, at a minimum. One is to work with you to begin the planning for hearings and meetings that will be held across Indian Country on the issue of sovereignty.

This may be, perhaps, the first opportunity that Indian Country has had to define sovereignty, to develop a definitive record on the historical and legal developments that have established the sovereign status of tribal governments in the United States Constitution and in the law.

I would anticipate that these hearings and meetings would begin in 1993 and would go on for at least three years. And so, I want to begin work with you now to plan where these hearings will be conducted and the issues that they will address.

Secondly, over the course of the coming year, I am committed to holding hearings on the draft bill that most of you know as the American Indian Religious Freedom Resolution.

There is nothing more sacred than the protection and preservation of your languages, your culture and your traditions. Your religious freedom must be guaranteed. I pledge my time and support to this effort.

It will not be an easy road to travel. There will need to be much education of the American Public and the members of the Congress. But in the end, I know that we will be successful.

It is my hope and my goal to assure that the American Indian Religious Freedom Resolution becomes part of the body of federal Indian law in 1993.

Another subject of intense personal interest for Inouye is his wartime service and the strong bond he has maintained through the years with his fellow members of the 442nd Regimental Combat Team. In March 1993, hundreds of survivors met in Honolulu to mark the fiftieth anniversary of the founding of their unit, the bravery they displayed overseas, and their triumph over bigotry at home. One of the two featured speakers at the reunion was Inouye, who delivered a poignant keynote address on March 24. The senator supplied a copy of his speech.

This gathering is an important one—it will be a gathering of nostalgia . . . a gathering of sad memories . . . a gathering of laughter and fun . . . a gathering of goodbyes, for this may be our last roll call of the regiment.

We have travelled vast distances—from every state and from many foreign lands—to be together in Honolulu. We have travelled a lifetime together for this meeting in Honolulu. When did this journey to Honolulu begin?

Although this is our 50th reunion, our journey began before that date. Our fate was decided 52 years, 3 months and 2 weeks ago on that tragic Sunday in December. Our journey began on December 7, 1941.

Soon after that tragic Sunday morning, we who were of Japanese ancestry were considered by our nation to be citizens without a country. I am certain all of us remember that the Selective Service system of our country designated us to be unfit for military service because we were "enemy aliens." Soon after that, on February 19, 1942, the White House issued an extraordinary Executive Order—Executive Order 9066. This dreaded Executive Order forcibly uprooted our mainland brothers and their families and their loved ones from their homes with only those possessions that they were able to carry themselves and were granted forty-eight hours to carry out this order.

Our mainland brothers were not charged or indicted or convicted for the commission of any crime—because no crime was committed. Their only crime, if any, was that they were born of Japanese parents and for that crime, they were incarcerated in internment camps surrounded by barbed-wire fences, guarded by machine-gun towers. They were sent to strange places with strange names—Manzanar, Tule Lake, Rohwer, Gila, Topaz. Although a few members of Hawaii's Japanese community were interned in Honouliuli (a rather well-kept secret), very few, if any of us in Hawaii, were aware of the mass internment of our mainland brothers and their families.

Although we were separated by a vast ocean and mountain ranges, we from the mainland and Hawaii shared one deep-seated desire—to rid ourselves of that insulting and degrading designation, "enemy alien." We wanted to serve our country. We wanted to demonstrate our love for our country.

After many months of petitions and letters,

"Their only crime, if any, was that they were born of Japanese parents and for that crime, they were incarcerated in internment camps. . . ."

another Executive Order was issued with the declaration that ". . . Americanism is a matter of mind and heart; Americanism is not, and never was, a matter of race or ancestry." By this Executive Order, the formation of the special combat team made up of Japanese Americans was authorized.

More than the anticipated numbers volunteered; in fact, in Hawaii, about eighty-five percent of the eligible men of Japanese Americans volunteered. Those who were selected assembled in Schofield Barracks to prepare for our departure from Hawaii. That was fifty years ago. In early April, we boarded railway flatbeds in Wahiawa and rode to Iwilei. There we got off the trains with our heavy duffel bags to march to Pier 7. But keep in mind that most of us had less than two weeks of military training and many of us were yet to be toughened and hardened. And so we found ourselves struggling with those heavy bags on a march of over a mile. This was the farewell parade of the 442nd. For many parents this was the last sight of their sons. I cannot understand why the Army did not place those duffel bags in trucks and permit us to march heads up and tall as we said goodbye to Hawaii. For many, the last look of their sons must have been a rather sad one because we looked like a ragtag formation of prisoners of war. I will never forget our sad departure from Hawaii.

But after several weeks, we from Hawaii and the mainland gathered in Camp Shelby in Hattiesburg, Mississippi, the home of chiggers and ticks, sweat and dirt.

All of us were of the same ancestry, but somehow our first encounter was an unhappy one. In a few days, violent arguments and fights erupted within our area and these fights became commonplace. The men of the regiment found themselves segregated into two camps, one from Hawaii and the other from the mainland. This relationship was so bad that senior Army officers seriously considered disbanding the regiment.

Many projects were initiated and many lectures were delivered to bring about unity, but all failed except the Rohwer experiment. Our regimental records will not disclose the name of the author of this experiment, but history will show that we owe much to him.

Whoever he was, [he] suggested that the internees of Rohwer send an invitation to the regiment inviting young enlisted men from Hawaii to join them for a weekend of fun and festivities in the camp. As I recall, each company selected ten enlisted men. I was fortunate to be one of those selected by E Company. On the appointed day, these men from Hawaii, all cleanly showered, smelling of after-shave lotion, with their guitars and ukuleles, boarded trucks for this journey to Rohwer. Rohwer was an internment camp in Arkansas.

From the time we left Shelby in the early morning hours, this special convoy was a convoy of laughter and music. All were anticipating happy times with the young ladies of Rohwer.

Suddenly, this fantasy was shattered. We came in sight of the Rohwer internment camp. In the distance, we could see rows of barracks surrounded by high barbed-wire fences with machine-gun towers. The music stopped and there was no laughter.

Keep in mind that very few, if any of us, were aware of these camps. Our mainland brothers never spoke of them, never complained, and so we did not know.

When we finally came to the gate, we were ordered to get off the trucks. We were in uniform and were confronted by men in similar uniforms but they had rifles with bayonets. For a moment, I thought that there would be a tragic encounter, but fortunately nothing happened as we were escorted through the gate. There we were greeted by the people of Rohwer who were all persons of Japanese ancestry—grandparents, parents, children, grandchildren. Although a dance was held that evening, I doubt if any of us really enjoyed ourselves. But it was an unforgettable evening.

When we left Rohwer the following morning, the singing and the laughter and music that filled our trucks when we left Camp Shelby was replaced by grim silence. The atmosphere was grim and quiet, and I believe that all of us, as we reflected upon that strange visit, asked ourselves the question, "Would I have volunteered from a camp like Rohwer?" To this day, I cannot give an answer because I really do not know if I would have volunteered to serve our nation if I had been interned in one of those camps.

So suddenly, our respect, admiration, and love for our Kotonk brothers rose to phenomenal heights. They suddenly became our blood brothers and overnight a new, tough, tightly united military fighting machine was formed. It was a regiment made up of blood brothers and we were ready to live up to our motto, "Go for Broke." And thus the 442nd Infantry Regimental Combat Team was formed.

There are too many battles to recall—from Belvedere to Bruyeres, from Hill 140 to the Po Valley. But there is one we will never forget and one hopefully that our nation will always remember—the Battle of the Lost Battalion.

This battle began during the last week of October, 1944. The members of the First Battalion of the 141st Infantry Regiment of the 36th Texas Division found themselves surrounded by a large number of enemy troops. This "lost battalion" was ordered to fight its way back, but could not do so. The Second and Third Battalions of the Texas Regiment were ordered to break through but they were thrown back, and so on October 26, the 442nd was ordered to go into the lines to rescue the "lost battalion." On November 15, the rescue was successfully concluded.

Two days later, we were ordered to assemble in formal retreat parade formation to personally receive the commendation of the 36th Division from the commanding general of the Texas unit. The men of the regiment assembled in a vast field of a French farm. I can still hear the company commanders making their reports—A Company, all present and accounted for; B Company, all present and accounted for; E Company, all present and accounted for. It was an eerie scene. It has been reported that General Dahlquist, who had ordered this formation, was at first angered by the small attendance and reprimanded our commander, who in reply is reported to have said, "Sir, this *is* the regiment." As a result of the Battle of the Lost Battalion, two thousand men were in hospitals and over three hundred had died. The price was heavy. Although we did not whimper or complain, we were sensitive to the fact that the rescuers of the Texas Battalion were not members of the Texas Division. They were Japanese Americans from Hawaii and from mainland internment camps. They were "enemy aliens."

I can still hear the proud and defiant voices of the company commanders as they made their reports. I can still see the company commander of E Company making his report. E Company had forty-two men, and though we were less than a quarter of the authorized company strength, E Company was the largest company at that retreat parade. K Company was led by a staff sergeant. K Company was made up of twelve men. When I heard the last commander shout out his report, "All present and accounted for," like many of you, I could almost feel the insulting and degrading designation that was placed on our shoulders long ago in December, 1941—the designation of "enemy alien"—fall crashing to the ground in that faraway French farm. And we knew that from that moment on, no one could ever, ever, question our loyalty and our love for our country. The insulting stigma was finally taken away.

Years later, the United States Army called upon a special commission of military historians, analysts and strategists to select the ten most important battles of the U.S. Army Infantry from the Revolutionary War to the Korean War. The Battle of the Lost Battalion was selected as one of the honored ten. Our battle is listed together with our nation's most glorious and historic battles, such as the Battle of Vicksburg during the Civil War, the Battle at Meuse-Argonne in France during World War I, and the Battle of Leyte in the Philippines during World War II. Today, specially commissioned paintings of these ten most important battles are proudly displayed in the Pentagon.

Over the years, many have asked us—"Why?" "Why did you fight and serve so well?" My son, like your sons and daughters, has asked the same question—"Why?" "Why were you willing and ready to give your life?" We have tried to provide answers to these questions and I hope that my answer to my son made sense.

I told my son it was a matter of honor. I told him about my father's farewell message when I left home to put on the uniform of my country. My father was not a man of eloquence but he said, "Whatever you do, do not dishonor the family and do not dishonor the country." I told my son that for many of us, to have done any less than what we had done in battle would have dishonored our families and our country.

Second, I told my son that there is an often-used Japanese phrase—*Kodomo no tame ni*. Though most of us who went into battle were young and single, we wanted to leave a legacy of honor and pride and the promise of a good life for our yet-to-be-born children and their children.

My brothers, I believe we can assure ourselves that we did succeed in upholding our honor and that of our families and our nation. And I respectfully and humbly believe that our service and the sacrifices of those who gave their all on the battlefield assure a better life for our children and their children.

Yes, I believe we can stand tall this evening in knowing that our journey together, a journey that began on that tragic Sunday morning, was not in vain. And so tonight, let us embrace with our hearts and minds the memory of those brothers who are not with us this evening and let us do so with all of our affection and gratitude. Let us embrace with deep love our loved ones for having stood with us and walked with us on our journey. Let us embrace with everlasting gratitude and Aloha the many friends and neighbors who supported us throughout our journey. Let us embrace with everlasting love our great nation.

And finally, let us embrace our sons and daughters with full pride and with the restful assurance that the story of our journey of honor will live on for generations to come.

And so, my brothers, let us this evening, in the spirit of our regiment, stand tall with pride, have fun, and let's "Go for Broke."

SOURCES

Books

Inouye, Daniel K., and Lawrence Elliott, *Journey to Washington,* Prentice-Hall, 1967.

Zia, Helen, and Susan Gall, editors, *Notable Asian Americans,* Gale Research, Detroit, 1995.

Periodicals

Congressional Quarterly Weekly Report, "The Quiet Insider: Hawaii's Daniel Inouye Wields a Private, Personal Power," April 16, 1988, p. 979.

Grand Rapids Press, "442nd Unit Marks 50th Anniversary," March 22, 1993, p. D11.

Newsweek, August 10, 1959, pp. 22-24; April 9, 1962, pp. 39-40.

Time, "New Faces in Congress," August 10, 1959, p. 13; August 27, 1973, p. 18.

Vital Speeches of the Day, "Commitment" (keynote address at 1968 Democratic National Convention), September 15, 1968, pp. 709-711.

Jesse Jackson

1941–

African American clergyman and political and civil rights leader

From the days when he marched alongside Martin Luther King, Jr., through his present crusade against black-on-black violence, Jesse Jackson has been at or near the forefront of the civil rights struggle in the United States. His message of hope and promise of justice has found an audience among a veritable "rainbow coalition" of disadvantaged and disenchanted whites, blacks, Hispanics, Native Americans, Asian Americans, and others who have felt alienated from and abandoned by the current two-party political system. While this audience has often fluctuated in size and strength over the past decade or so, it remains Jackson's core constituency. And his ability to lead and inspire his followers has to a large extent flowed from his considerable skills as a public speaker with a fiery yet poetic oratorical style.

The South Carolina-born Jackson grew up amid poverty, but even from an early age he projected a sense of the dignity and drive that would characterize his adult life. Thanks to his skills on the football field as a high school student, he earned a scholarship to the University of Illinois. But when he was denied the position of team quarterback on account of his race, he left Illinois and headed instead to North Carolina Agricultural and Technical College in Greensboro. There Jackson excelled on the football field as well as in the classroom. On the civil rights front, he took a leading role in the burgeoning student sit-in movement that fought to desegregate the town of Greensboro. It was during this same period that he also seriously began to contemplate entering the ministry rather than pursue a career in law, which had been his initial plan.

In 1963, after obtaining his bachelor's degree, Jackson enrolled in the Chicago Theological Seminary. In addition, he remained active in the battle for civil rights, and in 1965, while participating in the famous Selma-to-Montgomery March, he finally met his hero, Martin Luther King, Jr. Soon after, Jackson became a member of King's Southern Christian Leadership Conference (SCLC) staff. Returning to Chicago, he helped plan King's ambitious 1966 campaign to challenge Mayor Richard Daley's policies and wipe out discrimination in the Windy City. Later that same year, he was named head of the SCLC's local Operation Breadbasket organization. Under Jackson's direction, it carried out many successful boycotts against Chicago-area companies that practiced racial discrimination and ultimately forced them to hire more African Americans and purchase goods and services from more black-owned businesses.

Jackson, who was ordained a Baptist minister shortly after King's assassination in 1968, maintained his affiliation with the SCLC and Operation Breadbasket until 1971, when he quit to establish Operation PUSH (People United to Save Humanity). Dedicated to furthering the cause of human rights on an international scale, it has exercised the most impact at the national level in its efforts to improve the economic status of African Americans. To that end, it has used boycotts and other means to encourage large corporations (such as Burger King, Coca-Cola, and Anheuser-Busch) to hire more black workers at every level, set up black distributorships, and advertise in black publications; it has also led the fight to involve more blacks in professional sports not on the playing field but as managers and part of the front-office personnel. Some more recent offshoots of Operation PUSH, such as PUSH for Excellence, which stresses the importance of obtaining a good education and avoiding self-destructive life choices, are specifically aimed at young people.

Some of Jackson's most memorable speeches, in fact, have been delivered to young people. It is during these motivational "pep rallies" that he clearly demonstrates his rhetorical roots in black culture (particularly the black church) and the impact of his close association with Martin Luther King, Jr., who is considered one of the twentieth century's greatest orators. Other distinctive characteristics of Jackson's speeches include his strikingly effective use of alliteration, repetition, and contrasts; his appeals for audience participation; and his frequent references to religion and the Bible. Up until the mid-1970s or so, he also incorporated into his language words and grammatical constructions common in black English. Once he began reaching out beyond the black community, however, he stopped this practice.

All of these elements are very much on display in the following talk, delivered to a conference of teenagers gathered in Atlanta, Georgia, on June 19, 1978. Reprinted from Straight from the Heart, *by Jesse L. Jackson (Fortress Press, 1987), it is fairly typical of his early public appearances, particularly those before groups of young African Americans.*

Good morning. I'm grateful for this privilege to participate in this youth congress, this fantastic national meeting with so many implications. This morning I want to speak on the subject, "It's Up to You," for it is important for you to get involved and to be a part of what's happening as you move toward making these decisions.

I want this area to my left to be Section A, and this area to my right, Section B. There are four steps in this ritual. Once we rehearse it one time, we will stand and do it all together.

The first part is called, "I Am Somebody." That is significant because if you don't feel that you're somebody, you won't act as if you're somebody, and you won't treat other people as if they are somebody. You must feel that you count in order to appreciate yourself and develop yourself in relation to other people.

People to my right, I am

[Answer] "I am"

Now don't sound all scared and timid. I know better. I am

[Answer] "I am"

Somebody.

[Answer] "Somebody."

I am

[Answer] "I am"

Jesse Jackson

Somebody.

[Answer] "Somebody."

That's kind of mediocre. Try it, to my left. I am

[Answer] "I am"

I am

[Answer] "I am"

Somebody.

[Answer] "Somebody."

That's a little better. Give them a hand. That part deals with the question of self-appreciation and self-reliance: "I am somebody." The other is that it does not matter if we have the opportunity to live if we choose death. And so we say, "Down with dope; up with hope" because we cannot be what we ought to be if we push dope in our veins rather than hope in our brains.

Repeat this: Down with dope.

[Answer] "Down with dope."

Up with hope.

[Answer] "Up with hope."

Down with dope.

[Answer] "Down with dope."

Up with hope.

[Answer] "Up with hope."

You're kind of alive. I'm going to give you another hand. Now the third phase of it—and all of us are going to get involved with this—is that you must believe in your mind that you can do it. You must believe that you can do it. Don't let anybody convince you that you can't learn anything necessary for you to survive.

Repeat this: My mind

[Answer] "My mind"

Is a pearl.

[Answer] "Is a pearl."

I can learn anything

[Answer] "I can learn anything"

In the world.

[Answer] "In the world."

My mind

[Answer] "My mind"

Is a pearl.

[Answer] "Is a pearl."

I can learn anything

[Answer] "I can learn anything"

In the world.

[Answer] "In the world."

Now, take this last one. This is a very big one, maybe the biggest of all. Repeat this: Nobody

[Answer] "Nobody"

Will save us

[Answer] "Will save us"

For us

[Answer] "For us"

But us.

[Answer] "But us."

This means that nobody is going to register you for you. Nobody is going to protect your body for you but you. Nobody is going to develop your mind for you but you. And if you don't develop your mind, you'll just be in bad shape, pitiful for the rest of your life.

Nobody

[Answer] "Nobody"

Will save us

[Answer] "Will save us"

For us

[Answer] "For us

But us.

[Answer] "But us."

Everybody stand. Give yourselves a big hand. Everybody stand. Now let's do the whole thing:

I am somebody. I may be poor, But I am somebody. I may be unskilled, But I am somebody. Respect me. Protect me. Never neglect me. I am somebody.

Down with dope. Up with hope.

My mind is a pearl. I can learn anything in the world.

Nobody will save us for us but us.

Excel!

Excel!

Excel!

Right on!

As you gather for this most important conference here in Atlanta, there are several points I want to wrestle with. The first point is that all of us cannot be famous because all of us cannot be well known. But all of us can be great because all of us can serve. Every now and then, I hear people brag about the new generation. It's not really anything to brag about being in the new generation because you didn't do anything to become the new generation. Your parents did something to make the new generation. You are the new generation without effort. So why brag about being new, when it's not the result of your work? Why brag about being black or being white? It's not the result of your work. You are a new generation without putting forth any effort. Your challenge is to become a greater generation, and you become a greater generation because you serve. If you feed more hungry people, you are a greater generation. If more people of this generation are educated, it's a greater generation. If the racial lines that separate us are overcome, we are a greater generation. And so our challenge is to be not just a new generation, based upon birth, but to be a greater generation based upon work and effort.

Second, there's always the challenge of concentration. We used to have a saying some years ago in the freedom struggle, "Keep your eyes on the prize." If your prize is to develop your mind; if your prize is to develop your body; if your prize is to develop spiritual depth; if your prize is to grow up healthy, marry, and develop a family—if that is your prize, then don't let any activity divert you from your prize. When we are traveling, sometimes there are bumps in the road. Sometimes there are potholes in the road. Sometimes nails and broken glass may puncture our tire and delay us and divert us from the prize.

One of the challenges of this generation is the threat of mass media as diversion. This is the first generation that, by age eighteen, has watched eighteen thousand hours of television and listened to more radio than that, compared with eleven thousand hours of school and less than three thousand hours of church. There's nothing that you need that you will ever achieve by being a mass-media addict. You will not learn to read, write, count, or think better simply by being a mass-media addict. And so you cannot become a victim of mass-media diversion. The same time you spend at night being entertained, you must commit to becoming educated. But that is a choice you must make. Part of my challenge is to lay before you what that decision is.

The other side of it, of course, is moral decadence, social decadence. In some real sense, premature pregnancy threatens this generation. Intercourse without discourse threatens this generation. Grabbing fire that's too hot for you to hold threatens this generation. There are two hallmarks of every champion: discipline and character. Sex is too beautiful to be made ugly by ignorance, greed, or lack of self-control. Sex as pleasure, sex as procreation, sex as fulfillment has its place. But sex is too beautiful to be made ugly by ignorance, greed, and lack of self-control.

On the other hand, not only is sex too beautiful to be made ugly by greed and ignorance and lack of self-control, sex is too powerful to stay in the realm of superstition. Our parents and teachers and preachers teach us about electrical wires because electrical wires are important, and they're dangerous. They teach us about cars because cars are important, and cars are dangerous. And we go to school and we learn who the presidents are, and that is important. We learn where the states are and what the capitals of the states are, and that is important. But in all of our studying, we must study ourselves, because we are more powerful than that car. We're more important than that state. We are more important than that car. We're more important than that electrical wire. So in all of our studying of the nation and of the states and of the presidents, we must study ourselves because sex is too beautiful to be made ugly by ignorance, greed, and lack of self-control, and sex is too powerful to be left to the realm of superstition.

One of the charges in this conference is to challenge you to make decisions. One decision I urge you to make today is that sex is not the only thrill in life. Sex is a thrill. But sex is not the only thrill in life. Twenty-five years ago when Senator Joseph McCarthy and the McCarthy movement were threatening free speech, a generation of youth rebelled and protested, fighting for free speech—and that was a thrill. When Rosa Parks sat down on the bus in Montgomery and Dr. King came to her rescue and then a whole generation fought to get a public accommodations bill, that was a thrill. When a group of students went to Selma, Alabama, and fought for the right to vote, that was a thrill.

One of the resolutions I want you to pass here today has to do with voter registration. Virtually all of you will be eighteen when you become seniors in high school. Seniors are eligible to vote. A few years ago, we fought for the right to vote. When you go back across this nation, you should lobby at the various boards of education and make it mandatory that they teach you, during your senior year, how to use a voting machine; teach you who your alderman is; teach you where your precinct is; teach you who your elected officials are. Last year, 3.1 million high school students graduated. All of them should have been registered to vote. The reason most of them did not register and vote was because they were not taught in school to register and vote. People are not born voting. People don't vote by instinct. People vote because they're taught to vote. You three or four thousand students here today, when you come across that stage and graduate, if you have a diploma in one hand (symbolizing knowledge and wisdom) and a voter registration card in the other hand (symbolizing power and responsibility), you will not only be a new generation, you will be a powerful generation, a generation to be respected, a generation that will get a response!

Now some of us get confused because sometimes we measure our manhood and our womanhood by violence and sex. In other words, if I can knock somebody down because I've got muscles, I am a man. I am tough. Or if I can engage in sex as often as I want to, I am a man; I am a woman. But I want you to know today that if someone is sick with fever and about to die, if someone stands there, 6'6" and cannot even give the person an aspirin, that person is not manly enough or adult enough or tough enough to make a difference. Somebody 5'3" might show up with a medicine bag under his or her arm. That person has the ability to save the person who is sick. You are not a man because you can kill somebody; you are a man because you can heal somebody. A man must be able to function. You're not a man because you can make a baby. Test tubes can make babies. You are a man because you can raise a baby and provide for a baby and develop a baby's life. A man is a man by a functioning definition. "I am a man if I can produce, protect, and provide."

> *"The same time you spend at night being entertained, you must commit to becoming educated."*

In the same way, you are a woman by a functioning definition. Girls can make babies, but it takes women to raise them. The emotional maturity required to raise a baby means that babies really shouldn't have babies. If you cannot handle that load, then don't pick it up in the first place. You must make that decision!

Brothers, I want you to repeat this after me.

"I am a man. I will produce; I will protect; I will provide."

Sisters, repeat this: "I am a woman. I will produce; I will protect; I will provide."

Now let me raise this next point with you. There's a scripture I used to read when I was much younger, but I didn't quite understand it then. "God causes it to rain on the just and the unjust alike." I didn't understand that too well because I knew that God was merciful and he helped people who couldn't help themselves. But the older I got, I finally learned what that verse meant. It meant that even though God loves you, you must live with the consequences of your decisions. In other words, if a little baby falls in a bathtub full of water, that baby will drown and must live with the consequences of that decision. If a six-year-old innocent, wonderful little child steps in front of a moving car, that child will most likely be killed because that child must live with the consequences of that decision. You who make the decision to put dope in your veins rather than hope in your brains or fill up your nose with cocaine or float around in angel dust—you may be black or white or rich or poor, but you must live with the consequences of your decisions. And that is why it is important that the church, the home, and the school teach us our options so we can know what decisions to make, whether to choose the high road or whether to choose the low road.

I repeat: sex is too beautiful to be made ugly by ignorance, greed, and lack of control, and sex is too important for us to be ignorant of it. We need to learn sex education in the first grade, second grade, third grade, fourth grade, and fifth grade! We need to learn about our sex organs just as soon as we learn about our other organs. We learn that if something is hot, it'll burn you. So don't touch it. We learn that if something is cold not to stay up against it too long—you'll freeze. We learn that if something tastes bitter, to spit it out of our mouths. We learn about our senses at ages two, three, four, five, and six. There's no reason why we should cut ourselves off to the reality of our sex. We need to remove the superstition and the taboo and the foolishness. Sex is too powerful for us to leave in the realm of superstition.

"You who make the decision to put dope in your veins rather than hope in your brains—you may be black or white or rich or poor, but you must live with the consequences of your decisions."

Finally, I want to challenge you on this question of philosophy. I was listening not too long ago to a song that is an interesting kind of song to me. "You Light Up My Life" is beautiful. And for a long time, I was merely impressed with the melody. And there were some other songs that I had argued were damaging. Songs like "Shake Your Booty," "It's All Right to Make Love on the First Night," and "Let's Do It the French Way" because I knew what that implied. And this song eventually closes on this line: it talks about "How can it be wrong when it feels so right?" Now that's an interesting proposition, because a whole lot can be wrong with something even though it feels right. That's just like saying how can not doing homework be so wrong when it feels so right? How can not developing my mind be so wrong when it feels so right?

If you go further in school, you will learn the philosophy called "hedonism." It deals with short-term pleasure and long-term pain. You remember this: the laws of convenience lead to collapse, but the laws of sacrifice lead to greatness. Those who sacrifice for the Olympics get the gold medal. Those who sacrifice and go to medical school get the medical degree. Those who sacrifice and go to law school get the law degree. Those who are able to live with the laws of sacrifice are able to settle for short-term pain but enjoy long-term pleasure. Too many of us, unfortunately, end up with short-term pleasure and long-term pain.

We must make a decision. You can either use willpower on the inside and cope with or use pill power and cop out. If you've got willpower, just because it rains, you don't have to drown. If you have willpower, just because a mountain is high, it doesn't mean you can't climb it. If you've got willpower, just because it's cold, it doesn't mean you will freeze. We must develop willpower and cope with, rather than pill power and cop out. We must know the difference between sweat and tears. Sweat is wet; tears are wet. Sweat is salty; tears are salty. But progress comes through sweat. Progress never came through tears. When life gets

difficult, there's nothing like reaching down on the inside, sweating for that which you believe.

Finally, I want you to know that there's nothing more dangerous than to be trapped with a shrinking mind and an expanding behind. You must develop your mind to protect your behind, your body, and your soul. You must make that decision. Nobody can make it for you. You must make that decision. I want all of you to repeat this now:

If my mind can conceive it, and my heart can believe it, I know I can achieve it.

Down with pill power. Up with willpower. Down with dope. Up with hope.

It's not my aptitude but my attitude that determines my altitude, with a little intestinal fortitude.

My mind is a pearl. I can learn anything in the world.

I am somebody.

Nobody will save us for us but us.

Right on!

During the late 1970s and early 1980s, while repeatedly sounding the call for African Americans to flex their power in the voting booth, Jackson began to attract a wider following as a champion of economic and social justice. Around this time he also became a highly visible presence in international affairs, mostly in an attempt the mediate the conflict in the Middle East between Jews, Arabs, Palestinians, and other warring factions.

By 1983, Jackson was a major figure on the U.S. political scene, and in November of that year he announced his intention to seek the 1984 Democratic nomination for president. He was not the first African American to do so; Congresswoman Shirley Chisholm had given it a try a dozen years earlier. But Jackson was the first black candidate to mount a full-scale effort and win an impressive amount of support, especially among blacks, Hispanics, women, the poor, and other groups—the so-called "Rainbow Coalition"—who felt that no one else was bothering to pay attention to them. Of concern to some voters, however, were his overtures to the Palestinians and his friendship with Nation of Islam leader Louis Farrakhan. The situation worsened when it was widely reported that in a private conversation he had referred to Jews as "Hymies" and to New York City as "Hymietown." Jackson eventually apologized for his remarks and began to distance himself from Farrakhan, but to no avail. The controversy damaged his campaign beyond repair.

Although Jackson ultimately finished third (with about eleven percent of the vote) in the delegate tally behind Walter Mondale and Gary Hart at the 1984 Democratic National Convention in San Francisco, he was asked to give a major address. On July 17, before a prime-time television audience larger than any that tuned in that year to hear his fellow candidates from both political parties, Jackson delivered what still ranks as one of the most electrifying speeches of his career. Several slightly different versions of this address exist; the following one is reprinted from Straight from the Heart, *by Jesse L. Jackson (Fortress Press, 1987.)*

Tonight we come together, bound by our faith in a mighty God, with genuine respect and love for our country, and inheriting the legacy of a great party—the Democratic party—which is the best hope for redirecting our nation on a more humane, just, and peaceful course. This is not a perfect party. We are not a perfect people. Yet we are called to a perfect mission: to feed the hungry, to clothe the naked, to house the homeless, to teach the illiterate, to provide jobs for the jobless, and to choose the human race over the nuclear race. We are gathered here this week to nominate a candidate and write a platform which will expand, unify, direct, and inspire our party and the nation to fulfill this mission.

My constituency is the damned, the disinherited, the disrespected, and the despised. They are restless and seek relief. They've voted in record numbers. They have invested faith, hope, and trust in us. The Democratic party must send them a signal that we care. I pledge my best not to let them down.

Leadership must heed the call of conscience—redemption, expansion, healing, and unity—for they are the keys to achieving our mission. Time is neutral and does not change things. With courage and initiative, leaders change things. No generation can choose the age or circumstances in which it is born, but through leadership it can choose to make the age in which it is born an age of enlightenment—an age of jobs, peace, and justice. Only leadership—that intangible combination of gifts, discipline, information, circumstance, courage, timing, will, and divine inspiration—can lead us out of the crisis in which we find ourselves. Leadership can mitigate the misery of our nation. Leadership can part the waters and lead our nation in the direction of the Promised Land. Leadership can lift the boats stuck at the bottom.

I have had the rare opportunity to watch seven men, and then two, pour out their souls, offer their service, and heed the call of duty to direct the course of our nation. There is a proper season for everything. There is a time to sow, and a time to reap. There is a time to compete, and a time to cooperate. I ask for your vote on the first ballot as a vote for a new direction for this party and this nation—a vote of conscience and conviction. But I will be proud to support the nominee of this convention for the presidency of the United States. I have watched the leadership of our party grow and develop. My respect for both Mr. Mondale and Mr. Hart is great. I have watched them struggle with the crosswinds and cross fires of being visible public servants, and I believe that they will both continue to try to serve us faithfully. I am elated by the knowledge that, for the first time in our history, a woman, Geraldine Ferraro, will be recommended to share our ticket.

Throughout this campaign, I have tried to offer leadership to the Democratic party and the nation. If, in my high moments, I have done some good, offered some service, shed some light, healed some wounds, rekindled some hope, stirred someone from apathy and indifference, or in any way helped someone along the way, then this campaign has not been in vain. For friends who loved and cared for me, for a God who spared me, and for a family who understood me, I am eternally grateful.

If, in my low moments, in word, deed, or attitude, through some error of temper, taste, or tone, I have caused anyone discomfort, created pain, or revived someone's fears, that was not my truest self. If there were occasions when my grape turned into a raisin and my joy bell lost its resonance, please forgive me. Charge it to my head and not to my heart. My head is so limited in its finitude, but my heart is boundless in its love for the human family. I am not a perfect servant. I am a public servant, doing my best against the odds. As I grow, develop, and serve, be patient. God is not finished with me yet.

This campaign has taught me much: that leaders must be tough enough to fight, tender enough to cry, human enough to make mistakes, humble enough to admit them, strong enough to absorb the pain, and resilient enough to bounce back. For leaders, the pain is often intense. But you must smile through tears and keep moving with the faith that there is a brighter side somewhere.

I went to see Hubert Humphrey three days before he died. He had just called Richard Nixon from his dying bed, and many people wondered why. I asked him. He said, "Jesse, from this vantage point, with the sun setting in my life, all of the speeches, the political conventions, the crowds, and the great fights are behind me now. At a time like this, you are forced to deal with your irreducible essence, forced to grapple with that which is really important to you. What I have concluded is this: when all is said and done, we must forgive each other, redeem each other, and move on."

Our party is emerging from one of its most hard-fought battles for the Democratic party's presidential nomination in our history. But our healthy competition should make us better, not bitter. We must use the insight, wisdom, and experience of the late Hubert Humphrey as a balm to heal the wounds in our party, this nation, and the world. We must forgive each other, redeem each other, regroup, and move on.

Our flag is red, white, and blue, but our nation is a rainbow—red, yellow, brown, black, and white—and all are precious in God's sight. America is not like a blanket, one piece of unbroken cloth—the same color, the same texture, the same size. It is more like a quilt—many patches, many pieces, many colors, many sizes, all woven and held together by a common thread. The white, the Hispanic, the black, the Arab, the Jew, the woman, the Native American, the small farmer, the businessperson, the environmentalist, the peace activist, the young, the old, the lesbian, the gay, and the disabled make up the American quilt. Even in our fractured state, all of us count and fit in somewhere. We have proven that we can survive without each other. But we have not proven that we can win or make progress without each other. We must come together.

From Fannie Lou Hamer in Atlantic City in 1964 to the Rainbow Coalition in San Francisco today, from the Atlantic to the Pacific, we have experienced pain, but progress, as we obtained open housing; as young people got the right to vote; as we lost Malcolm, Martin, Medgar, Bobby, John, and Viola. The team that got us here must be expanded, not abandoned. Twenty years ago, tears welled up in our eyes as the bodies of Schwerner, Goodman, and Chaney were dredged from the depths of a river in Mississippi. Twenty years later, our communities, black and Jewish, are in anguish, anger, and pain. Feelings have been hurt on both sides. There is a crisis in communications. Confusion is in the air, but we cannot afford to lose our way. We may agree to agree, or agree to disagree on issues, but we must bring back civility to the tensions. We are copartners in a long and rich religious history—the Judeo-Christian traditions. Many blacks and Jews have a shared passion for social justice at home and peace abroad. We must seek a revival of the spirit, inspired by a new vision and new possibilities. We must return to higher ground. We are bound by Moses and Jesus, but also connected with Islam and Muhammad. We are bound by Dr. Martin Luther King, Jr., and Rabbi Abraham Heschel crying out from their graves for us to reach common ground. We are bound by shared blood and shared sacrifices. We are much too intelligent; much too bound by our Judeo-Christian heritage; much too victimized by racism, sexism, militarism, and anti-Semitism; much too threatened as historical scapegoats to go on divided one from another. We must turn from finger-pointing to clasped hands. We must share our burdens and our joys with each other once again. We must turn to each other and not on each other.

Twenty years later, we cannot be satisfied by just restoring the old coalition. Old wineskins must make room for new wine. We must heal and expand. The Rainbow Coalition is making room for Arab Americans. They too know the pain and hurt of racial and religious rejection. They must not continue to be made pariahs. The Rainbow Coalition is making room for Hispanic Americans who this very night are living under the threat of the Simpson-Mazzoli immigration bill and farm workers in Ohio who are fighting the Campbell Soup Company with a boycott to achieve legitimate worker rights.

The Rainbow is making room for the Native Americans, the most exploited people of all and a people with the greatest moral claim among us. We support them as they seek to preserve their ancestral homelands and the beauty of a land that once was all theirs. They can never receive a fair share for all that they have given, but they must finally have a fair chance to develop their great resources and to preserve their people and their culture.

> ***"Our flag is red, white, and blue, but our nation is a rainbow—red, yellow, brown, black, and white—and all are precious in God's sight."***

The Rainbow includes Asian Americans, now being killed in our streets—scapegoats for the failures of corporate, industrial, and economic policies. The Rainbow is making room for young Americans. Twenty years ago, our young people were dying in a war for which they could not even vote. Twenty years later, young America has the power to stop a war in Central America and the responsibility to vote in great numbers. Young America must be politically active in 1984. The choice is war or peace. We must make room for young America.

The Rainbow includes disabled Americans. The color "chrome" fits in the rainbow. The disabled have their handicap revealed and their genius concealed, while the able-bodied have their genius revealed and their disability concealed. But ultimately we must judge people by their values and their contribution. Don't leave anybody out. I would rather have Roosevelt in a wheelchair than Reagan on a horse.

The Rainbow is making room for small farmers. They have suffered tremendously under the Reagan regime. They will either receive ninety percent parity or one hundred percent charity. We must address their concerns and make room for them. The Rainbow includes lesbians and gays. No American citizen ought to be denied equal protection under the law.

We must be unusually committed and caring as we expand our family to include new members. All of us must be tolerant and understanding as the fears and anxieties of the rejected and of the party leadership express themselves in so many different ways. Too often what we call hate—as if it were deeply rooted in some philosophy or strategy—is simply ignorance, anxiety, paranoia, fear, and insecurity. We must be long-suffering as we seek to right the wrongs of our party and our nation. We must expand our party, heal our party, and unify our party. That is the means to our mission in 1984.

We are often reminded that we live in a great nation—and we do. But it can be greater still. The Rainbow is mandating a new definition of greatness. We must not measure greatness from the mansion down but from the manger up. Jesus said that we should not be judged by the bark we wear but by the fruit we bear. Jesus said that we must measure greatness by how we treat the least of these.

President Reagan says the nation is in recovery. Those ninety thousand corporations that made a profit last year but paid no federal taxes are recovering. The thirty-seven thousand military contractors who have benefited from Reagan's more than doubling the military budget in peacetime are surely recovering. The big corporations and rich individuals who received the bulk of the three-year multi-billion-dollar tax cut from Mr. Reagan are recovering. But no such comparable recovery is under way for the least of these. Rising tides don't lift all boats, particularly those stuck on the bottom.

For the boats stuck at the bottom, there is a rising misery index. This administration has made life for the poor miserable. Its attitude toward poor people has been contemptuous. Its policies and programs have been cruel and unfair to working people. It must be held accountable in November for an increasing infant-mortality rate among the poor. In Detroit, one of the great cities of the Western world, babies are dying at the same rate as in Honduras, the most underdeveloped nation in our hemisphere. This administration must be held accountable for policies that contribute to the growing poverty in America. Under President Reagan, there are eight million more people in poverty. Currently fifteen percent of our nation is in poverty, thirty-four million people. Of the thirty-four million poor people, twenty-three million are white, eleven million are black, Hispanic, Asian, and others. More and more of the poor are children. By the end of this year, there will be forty-one million people in poverty—more people than at any time since the inadequate War on Poverty program began in 1965. We cannot stand by idly. We must fight for change, now.

Under President Reagan, the misery index has increased.

Social Security. The 1981 budget cuts included 9 permanent Social Security benefit cuts totaling 20 billion dollars over five years. Now he says we may need more.

Small Businesses. Approximately 98 percent of all businesses in America can be considered "small"—employing fewer than 500 workers. Yet under the Reagan tax cuts, only 18 percent of total business tax cuts went to them—82 percent went to big business.

Health Care. Reagan sharply cut funding for screening children for lead poisoning—which can lead to retardation, behavioral difficulties, and learning disabilities—from 9.1 million dollars in 1981 to 5.8 million dollars in 1983. Estimates for 24 states indicate that the number of children screened dropped from 1.1 million to 600,000.

Education. He cut real spending for education by 6 billion dollars, or 25 percent. Four million three hundred thousand handicapped children are receiving delayed or reduced services. One hundred twenty-four thousand fewer college students receive Pell Grant assistance from the federal government.

Women. There are now 9.7 million female-headed families. They represent 16 percent of all families, but half of all poor families. Seventy percent of all poor children live in a household headed by a woman. Working women make less than men in every job category, at every educational level, yet Mr. Reagan sees no need for the Equal Rights Amendment.

Environmental Protection. This administration has cleaned up only 6 of 546 priority toxic-waste dumps in 3 years.

Farmers. In 1983, real net farm income was only about half its level of 1979 and was lower than at any time since the Great Depression.

Many say that the race in November will be decided in the South. President Reagan is depending on the conservative South to return him to office. But the South, I tell you, is unnaturally conservative. The South is the nation's poorest region and therefore has the least to conserve. In his appeal to the South, Mr. Reagan is trying to substitute flags and prayer clauses for jobs, food, clothing, education, health care, and housing. But apparently President Reagan is not even familiar with the structure of a prayer. We must watch false prophecy. He has cut energy assistance to the poor, he has cut food stamps, children's breakfast and lunch programs, the Women, Infants, and Children (WIC) program for pregnant mothers and infants, and job training for children; and then says, "Let us pray." In a prayer, you are supposed to thank God for the food you are about to receive, not for the food that just left. I take prayer very seriously—I've come this way by the power of prayer. So we need to pray. But we need to pray to remove the man that removed the food. We need a change in November.

Poor people and working people—black, white, and brown—all across America, but especially in the South, must resist the temptation to go for Mr. Reagan's social placebo as a substitute for jobs and economic justice. Cotton candy may taste good, it may even go down smoothly, but it has no substance and it's not good for you.

Under President Reagan, the misery index has increased dramatically for the poor, but the danger index for everyone has escalated. The military budget has been doubled to protect us from the Russians, yet today Soviet submarines are closer to our shores, and their missiles are more accurate. Tonight we live in a world that is more miserable and dangerous.

The Reagan administration has failed to achieve any agreed-upon nuclear arms reductions whatsoever. The Reagan administration's attempts to regain military superiority, to achieve a first-strike capability, its plans and preparations to launch and win a limited nuclear war, and its commitment to "Star Wars" have left the world a much more unstable and dangerous place in which to live. We are at a nuclear standoff in Europe. We are mining the harbors of Nicaragua and attempting to covertly overthrow a legitimate government there—actions which have been condemned by many of our allies and by the World Court. Under this administration we have been at war and lost the lives of American boys in Lebanon, Honduras, and Grenada. Under this administration, one-third of America's children have come to believe that they will die in a nuclear war. The danger index for everybody is increasing—and it is frightening.

But it is not enough simply to react to the effects—a growing misery and danger index. We must dig deeper and comprehend the underlying cause of the growing misery and danger index—Reaganomics. We must distinguish between Mr. Reagan's political appeal and his economic deal. Mr. Reagan's economic program is a combination of cyanide and Kool-Aid, jelly beans and poison. It may taste good, but the results are disastrous. We must distinguish between Reaganism and Reaganomics.

While Reaganism is largely subjective, supply-side economics is more objective. Reaganism was used to impose Reaganomics. Reaganism is the perception. Reaganomics is the reality. We are fatter now, but less secure. Many who were once basking in the sun of Reaganism have now been burned to a crisp with Reaganomics. In 1980 many thought they saw a light at the end of the tunnel in Reaganism. But in 1984 we now know it was not sunshine, but a train coming this way.

In 1980 then-candidate George Bush called Mr. Reagan's economic plan to get America back on track "voodoo economics." Third-party candidate John Anderson said that the combination of massive military spending, tax cuts, and a balanced budget by 1984 could only be accomplished with blue smoke and mirrors. We now know they were both right.

President Reagan declares that we are having a dynamic economic recovery. And we are having a recovery of sorts. After three and a half years, unemployment has inched just below where it was when he took office in 1981. But there are still 8.1 million people officially unemployed, and 11 million working only part-time jobs. Make no mistake about it, inflation has come down, but let's examine how and at whose expense this was achieved—and how long it is likely to last.

President Reagan's 1984 economic recovery has come after the deepest and longest recession since the Great Depression. President Reagan curbed inflation by cutting consumer demand. He cut consumer demand with conscious and callous fiscal and monetary policies. He used the federal budget deliberately to induce unemployment and curb social spending. He then urged and supported the tight monetary policies of the Federal Reserve Board deliberately to drive up interest rates—again to curb consumer demand created through borrowing.

Unemployment reached 10.7 percent; we experienced skyrocketing interest rates; our dollar inflated abroad; there were record bank failures, record farm foreclosures, record business bankruptcies, record budget deficits, record trade deficits, and more. President Reagan brought inflation down by destabilizing our economy, disrupting family life, and wreaking havoc on the poor.

Remember President Reagan's central promise of the 1980 campaign—to balance the budget by 1984? Instead of balancing the budget, in 1984 we are having record budget deficits and looking at record budget deficits for as far as the eye can see. Under President Reagan, the cumulative budget deficits for just his four years in office will be virtually equal to the total budget deficits from George Washington to Jimmy Carter—equal to all past presidents' budget deficits combined. I tell you, we need a change. Reagan's economic recovery is being financed by deficit spending—nearly $200 billion a year. Yet military spending, a major cause of the deficit, is projected over the next five years to be nearly $2 trillion and will cost about $40,000 for every taxpaying family.

When the government borrows $200 billion annually to finance the deficit, this encourages the private sector to make money off of interest rates rather than investing in economic development and growth. Even worse, we don't have enough domestically to finance the debt, so we are borrowing money abroad from foreign banks, governments, and financial institutions—$40 billion in 1983; $70 to $80 billion in 1984 (40 percent of our total); over $100 billion in 1985 (50 percent of the total); and rising. By 1989, it is projected that 50 percent of all individual income taxes will be going just to pay for the interest on the debt. The U.S. used to be the largest exporter of capital, but under President Reagan we soon will become the largest debtor nation. About two weeks ago, on July 4, we celebrated our Declaration of Independence and our freedom. Yet every day supply-side economics is making our nation more economically dependent and less economically free. Five to six percent of our gross national product is now being eaten up with President Reagan's budget deficit.

To depend on foreign military powers to protect our national security would be foolish and make us less secure. Yet Reaganomics is increasingly making us more dependent. By increasing our economic dependency, Reaganomics decreases our ability to control our own economic future and destiny, decreases our security, and decreases our self-respect. A great nation must be measured by its ability to produce, not just its ability to consume. We are negotiating away our independence. Freedom and independence are the result of self-determination, self-reliance, self-discipline, and self-respect. Under President Reagan, America is less economically free and more dependent.

President Reagan's consumer-led, but deficit-financed, recovery is unbalanced, artificial, and will be short-lived. President Reagan's recovery is an economic "quick fix" that is based on foreign borrowing and will end in another recession. The boom of '84 will become a boomerang. If we continue down the road of supply-side—with a "dead-end" sign in front of us, with no brakes, and a cliff behind the sign—we will deserve our inevitable fate.

Reaganomics is economic opium that is destroying us from within. President Reagan's recovery is like Santa Claus's wish list at Christmas time—buy now and pay later. President Reagan's recovery may bring the joy of Christmas morning in 1984, but there will be sadness, sacrifice, and suffering when the generation of your children, and your children's children, have to pay for it. Our adult generation should not be so selfish and self-centered as to burden our children with our indulgent and short-lived behavior. It is short-term pleasure, but it's leading to long-term pain.

Yet an artificial recovery is merely the beginning of our problems. The record Reagan budget deficits drive up interest rates. High interest rates overvalue the dollar abroad. Because of an overvalued dollar, our prices have increased relative to all of our competitors by about thirty-five percent over the last three years. We cannot give our competitors a thirty-five-percent subsidy, or give ourselves a thirty-five-percent tax, and remain competitive in the world market. An overvalued dollar is good for the American consumer because it subsidizes imports, but it is bad for American exports (farm products and machinery in particular) because it taxes Americans out of jobs and competition. The trade imbalance this year is projected to be close to $120 billion. For every $1 billion of trade imbalance, it costs Americans about 25,000 jobs. Thus President Reagan's record trade imbalance alone will cost Americans nearly 3 million jobs. We need a balance of trade, because another four years of Reaganomics will bring on the greatest tide of protectionism in American history.

Record budget deficits, high interest rates, and an overvalued dollar are contributing to the international debt crisis in the Third World. The greatest threat to our national security in Central America is not the East-West conflict. It is the international debt crisis, created principally by President Reagan's record budget deficits. They are threatening to destabilize the world economy, including the U.S. economy. In light of the international debt crisis, the International Monetary Fund and the big multinational banks are imposing austerity programs on the developing nations. Some developing nations cannot even pay the interest on their debt. These governments are unable to meet the basic needs of their citizens, and the people are rebelling. The buildup of our large interventionary forces is mainly for the purpose of putting down these economic and social rebellions in the name of stopping communism, but it is largely of our own making—and heightened under Reaganomics.

Democracy guarantees opportunity; it does not guarantee success. Democracy guarantees the right to participate; it does not give a license to either a majority or a minority to dominate. The victory for the Rainbow Coalition in the platform debates today was not whether we won or lost the vote but that we raised the right issues. We could afford to lose the vote. Issues are negotiable. We could not afford to avoid raising the right questions. Our self-respect and our moral integrity were at stake. Our heads are perhaps bloody but unbowed. Our backs are straight, and our vision is clear. We can go home and face our people. And when we think, in this journey from slave ship to championship, that we have gone from the planks of the boardwalk in Atlantic City in 1964 to fighting to help to write the planks in the Democratic party platform in San Francisco in 1984, there is a deep and abiding sense of joy in our soul, in spite of the tears in our eyes. Although there are missing planks, there is a solid foundation upon which we can build.

The real challenge to our individual and collective Democratic leadership is to do three things: (1) provide hope, which will inspire people to struggle and achieve, (2) provide a plan that shows the people a way out of our dilemma, and (3) courageously lead the way out.

There is a way out. Justice. The requirement for rebuilding America is justice. The linchpin of progressive politics in America is not new programs in the North but new power in the South. That is why I argue over and over again, that from Lynchburg, Virginia, around to Texas, there is only one black congressperson out of 115. Nineteen years after passage of the Voting Rights Act, we're locked out of the House, the Senate, and the governor's mansion. The key to unlocking Southern power is getting the Voting Rights Act enforced and ending the new forms of political disenfranchisement.

The key to a Democratic victory in 1984 is enfranchisement of the progressive wing of the Democratic party. They are the ones who have been devastated by Reaganomics, and, therefore, it is in their self-interest to vote in record numbers to oust their oppressor. Those already poor and those who are being impoverished do not simply want a change in leaders, they want a change in direction. The poor are not looking to be embellished, they have a need to be empowered. The key to political enfranchisement is enforcement of the Voting Rights Act. Gerrymandering, annexations, at-large elections, inaccessible registrars, roll purges, dual registrations, and second primaries—these are the schemes that continue to disenfranchise the locked-out. Why do I fight these impediments? Because you cannot hold someone in the ditch without lingering there with them. If the Voting Rights Act is enforced, we'll get twelve to twenty black, Hispanic, female, and progressive congresspersons from the South. We can save the cotton, but we've got to fight the boll weevils. We've got to make a judgment.

It's not enough to hope ERA will pass. How can we pass ERA? If blacks vote in great numbers, progressive whites win. It's the only way progressive whites win. If blacks vote in great numbers, Hispanics win. If blacks, Hispanics, and progressive whites vote, women win. When women win, children win. When women and children win, workers win. We must all come up together. We must come up together I tell you, with all of our joy and excitement, we must not save the world and lose our souls. We should never short-circuit enforcement of the Voting Rights Act at every level. If one of us rises, all of us must rise. Justice is the way out.

There is a way out. Peace. The only way we can have jobs at home is to have peace abroad. We should not act as if nuclear weaponry is negotiable and debatable. In 1984, other nations have nuclear weapons too. Now if we drop the bomb, six to eight minutes later, we, too, will be destroyed. The issue now is not about dropping the bomb on somebody; it's about dropping the bomb on everybody. We must choose developed minds over guided missiles and think our way out, not fight it out. We must develop a coherent strategic nuclear strategy. We used nuclear weapons once before on Japan. But we must declare that never again will we be the ones to engage in the "first use" of nuclear weapons. Our real security is in developed minds, not guided missiles.

Our foreign policy must be demilitarized. We must choose mutual respect, talk, negotiations, diplomacy, trade, and aid, and measure human rights by one yardstick as the way of resolving international conflicts. We should support a legitimate Solidarity labor movement and oppose martial law in Poland. But then we cannot become the number-one trading partner with South Africa when they impose martial law and violently crush a black solidarity labor movement—especially while they are developing a nuclear capability. The U.S. must apply a new formula in assisting South African liberation—enfranchisement, investment; disenfranchisement, disinvestment. Our present relationship with South Africa is a moral disgrace.

Beyond the liberation of South Africa, we must fight for trade and aid for development in all of Africa, as well as in Europe and the Middle East. We must be as concerned about the preservation of democracy in Africa as we are in Europe. We've turned our heads and our backs when democracy has been dealt blows in Africa. This indifference must not be allowed to happen in the future.

Our present formula for peace in the Middle East is inadequate and will not work. There are twenty-two nations in the Middle East, and we must be able to talk, act, influence, and reconcile all of them. Currently we have too many interests and too few friends. We must have a mutual recognition policy, built on the Camp David agreement, which was a good first step, and measure human rights by one yardstick.

We should not be mining the harbors of Nicaragua and trying to covertly overthrow that government. Military aid and military advisors (who will give military advice) should be withdrawn from El Salvador. We should use our strength to get FDR-FMLN and President Duarte to agree to a cease-fire and negotiations. We should not be establishing military bases in Honduras and militarizing the nation of Costa Rica. It was wrong for our nation to invade tiny Grenada. And if we can have diplomatic relations with the Soviet Union and China, as we should, we can have diplomatic relations with Cuba. Just this week, we have seen progress as a result of our moral appeal. In addition to the Americans returned, the political prisoners released (and more to be released), negotiations, at this very moment, are being conducted over the Mariel prisoners, a Cuban family-reunification program, and President Castro has agreed to exchange ambassadors without preconditions. Let's give peace a chance.

There is a way out. Jobs. If we enforce the Voting Rights Act as a way of achieving justice; and if we achieve peace through cutting the defense budget without cutting our defense, respect other nations of the world, and resolve conflicts through negotiations instead of confrontations; then we will have enough power and money to rebuild America. We can use the money we are currently squandering on the arms race to save the human race. We can use that money to build millions of new houses, to build hospitals, to train and pay our teachers and educate our young people, to provide health care and health-care training, to rebuild our cities and end rural poverty; use that money to rebuild two hundred and fifty thousand bridges, rebuild our railroads, and build mass-transit systems; use that money to put steelworkers back to work; use that money to rebuild the infrastructure of our country: repair our roads, our ports, our riverbeds, our sewer systems, and stop soil erosion; use that money to clean up our environment: our land, our water, and our air; use that money to make "America the Beautiful." We could put America back to work.

Ronald Reagan claims the votes of the South. I say to you this night that the soil is too rich and the people are too poor for Ronald Reagan to have the votes of the South. The South is going to rise up and move from racial battlegrounds to economic common ground and moral higher ground. We love our God, and we love our country too, but we want moral values with material substance. Black and white together, men and women, we will take the South.

We have fought hard to build our Rainbow

Coalition of the rejected over the last eight months. We have fought hard for party justice and for our minority planks because we believe that expanding our party to include the locked-out is the key to victory in November and to developing the progressive politics of the future.

What this campaign has shown above all else is that the key to our liberation is in our own hands and in our dream and vision of a better world. It is the vision that allows us to reach out to each other and to redeem each other. It is the dream that sustains us through the dark times and the dark realities. It is our hope that gives us a why for living when we do not see how to live.

In the final analysis, however, we must be driven not by a negative—the fear of Reagan—but by the positive leadership and programs of the Democratic party. It is not enough motivation just to vote against Reagan, we must inspire our constituency to vote for us. We must offer our people the vision of a just society and the dream of a peaceful world. We must inspire the American people with hope. We must put forth the vision of a government that cares for all of its people, the vision of a people at work rebuilding its nation. We must not be forced to choose between the two valid principles of seniority and affirmative action. We must put all of America back to work.

With courage and conscience, conviction and vision, we can win. If we don't raise the issues, if the truth is locked away, the people won't get excited. But when the truth is lifted up, they'll come running. Across lines of race and sex, they'll come running to vote for us. If we lift up before this nation a plan to wipe out cheese and bread lines, to feed our hungry and malnourished people, they'll come running. If we lift up a plan to house the homeless and educate the illiterate, they'll come running. If we reach out to the Vietnam veteran, to the disabled, to the poor, to the widow, to the orphan, and tell them that help is on the way, they'll come running.

When I was a child in Greenville, South Carolina, the Reverend James Hall used to preach a sermon, every so often, about Jesus. He would quote Jesus as saying, "If I be lifted up, I'll draw all men unto me." When I was a child I didn't quite understand what he meant. But I understand it a little better now. If you raise up truth, it's magnetic. It has a way of drawing people. With all this confusion in the convention—bright lights, parties, and big fun—we must raise up a simple proposition: feed the hungry, and the poor will come running; study war no more, and our youth will come running. If we lift up a program to put America back to work as an alternative to welfare and despair, the unemployed will come running. If we cut the military budget without cutting our defense and use that money to rebuild bridges and put steelworkers back to work; use that money to provide jobs for our citizens; use that money to build schools and train teachers and educate our children; use that money to build hospitals and train doctors and nurses—the whole nation will come running to us.

As I lived in the ghettos, in barrios, on reservations, and in the slums, I had a message for our youth. Young America, I know you face a cutback in jobs, large reductions in housing and food, inferior health care and education, and a general environment that tries to break your spirit. But don't put dope in your veins; put hope in your brains. Don't let them break your spirit. There is a way out. Our party must not only have the courage and the conscience to expose the slummy side. We must have the conviction and vision to show America the sunny side, the way out. When I see urban decay I see a sunny side and a slummy side. A broken window is the slummy side. Train that youth to be a carpenter. That's the sunny side. A missing brick? That's the slummy side. Train that youth to be a brick mason. That's the sunny side. The hieroglyphics of destitution on the walls? That's the slummy side. Train that youth to be a painter or an artist. That's the sunny side. Then unions must open up, embrace, and train our youth so they can help to rebuild America.

> *". . . the key to our liberation is in our own hands and in our dream and vision of a better world."*

I am more convinced than ever that we can win. We'll vault up the rough side of the mountain—we can win. But I just want the youth of America to do me one favor Exercise the right to dream. You must face reality—that which is. But then dream of the reality that ought to be, that must be. Live beyond the pain of reality with the dream of a bright tomorrow. Use hope and imagination as weapons of survival and progress. Use love to motivate you and obligate you to serve the human family.

Young people, dream of peace. Choose the human race over the nuclear race. We must bury the weapons and not burn the people. We are the first generation that will either freeze the weapons or burn the people and freeze the planet.

Young people, dream of a new value system. Dream of teachers, but teachers who will teach for life, not just for a living. Dream of doctors, but doctors who are more concerned with public health than personal wealth. Dream of lawyers, but lawyers who are more concerned with justice than a judgeship. Dream of artists, but artists who will convey music and message, rhythm, rhyme, and reason. Dream of priests and preachers, but priests and preachers who will prophesy and not profiteer. Dream of writers, but writers who will ascribe, describe, prescribe, not just scribble. Dream of authentic leaders who will mold public opinion against a headwind, not just ride the tailwinds of opinion polls. Dream of a world where we measure character by how much we share and care, not by how much we take and consume. Preach and dream. Our time has come.

We must measure character by how we treat the least of these, by who feeds the most hungry people, by who educates the most uneducated people, by who cares and loves the most, by who fights for the needy and seeks to save the greedy. We must dream and choose the laws of sacrifice, which lead to greatness, and not the laws of convenience, which lead to collapse.

In your dreaming you must know that unearned suffering is redemptive. Water cannot wash away the blood of martyrs. Blood is thicker than water. Water makes grass and flowers grow, but blood makes sons and daughters of liberation grow. No matter how difficult the days and dark the nights, there is a brighter side somewhere. In Angola, Mozambique, Nicaragua, El Salvador, South Africa, Greenville, South Carolina, and Harlem, there is a brighter side.

Jesus was rejected from the inn and born in the slum. But just because you were born in the slum does not mean that the slum was born in you. With a made-up mind, which is the most powerful instrument in the world, you can rise above your circumstances. No mountain is too high, and no valley is too low; no forest is too dense, and no water is too deep—if your mind is made up. With eyesight, you may see misery. But with insight, you can see the brighter side.

Suffering breeds character, character breeds faith, and in the end faith will not disappoint. Faith, hope, and dreams will prevail. Weeping may endure for a night, but joy is coming in the morning. Troubles won't last always. Our time has come. No graves can hold our bodies down. Our time has come. No lie can live forever. Our time has come. We must leave our racial battlegrounds, come to economic common ground, and rise to moral higher ground. America, our time has come. Give me your tired, your poor, your huddled masses yearning to breathe free. And come November, there will be a change, because our time has come.

Despite this impassioned plea from the Democrats, Republican Ronald Reagan won re-election in a landslide. Jackson spent the next four years enlarging his base of support to include more whites and making overtures to those who had been uncomfortable with some of his prior affiliations. In 1988, he made another attempt to capture the Democratic nomination for president of the United States and did even better than he had in 1984; of the seven candidates who started the race, only he and Michael Dukakis remained by the time of the convention in July. Even though he failed to win the nomination, he posted a strong second-place finish, demonstrating that Americans were indeed willing to consider electing a black president.

Since then, Jackson has moved in and out of the national political limelight as other issues have demanded his attention. (While he sat out the 1992 election, he has not ruled out a future run for the presidency.) A strong supporter of statehood for the District of Columbia, he has served as its "shadow senator" since 1990. And when Benjamin Hooks retired as head of the NAACP in 1993, Jackson's name was frequently mentioned as a possible replacement, and he made no secret of his interest in the job. (He eventually withdrew his name from consideration when it appeared he lacked enough support to win over the NAACP board, and Benjamin Chavis got the nod instead.)

Despite the fact that the Republicans vacated the White House in January 1993, Jackson has not remained silent about what he sees as the failure of the Democrats to make good on their promises. On August 28, 1993, for example, he attended a celebration marking the thirtieth anniversary of the March on Washington. Some seventy-five thousand people assembled in the nation's capital to commemorate the historic event and listen to a variety of speakers reflect on what had and had not changed since Martin Luther King, Jr., shared his dream with America from the steps of the Lincoln Memorial. One of those speakers was Jesse Jackson, and in his remarks he focused on how much—and how little—actual progress had been made since 1963. The following text is reprinted from Historic Documents of 1993, *Congressional Quarterly Inc., 1994.*

To the faithful remnant who have kept the Covenant and returned thirty years later to the spot where our forefathers and foremothers sighed and to a new generation of freedom fighters—welcome.

We gather today—ardent messengers of an urgent petition, crying out with our very bodies for jobs, for justice, for equal opportunity and equal protection. Many despair. The day is hot. The road is long. The mountain too steep. The people too tired. The powerful too distant. But do not despair. We have come a long way.

When we came there thirty years ago, we had no right to vote. We could not stop along the road and find room in an inn for sleep or to relieve our bodies. In every valley at every stop, there was a prevailing terrorism against blacks and browns sanctioned by the government. In every valley, there were Bull Connors to avoid, Klan to fear.

But we did not stop. We won our civil rights. We won the right to vote.

We helped lift a people from segregation, and a nation from shame. We have come a long way. But we can't stop now.

Thirty years ago, we came seeking jobs and justice. We sought to redeem a check that had bounced, Dr. King told us, marked "insufficient funds." We urged America to honor the sacred obligation to all Americans. Sorry, we were told, "there was a Cold War to fight." The Soviet bear was in the woods. The conservative Congress would not help. A young president could not help.

But Dr. King did not stop. With the younger generation fired up with a passion for justice and a will to suffer and sacrifice for an authentic new world order, young America changed the course of the world with human rights as its centerpiece.

Now thirty years later, there are more poor people, more working poor people than thirty years ago. The ghettos and barrios of our cities are more abandoned and more endangered than thirty years ago. Jobs have gone. Drugs and guns have spread. Hope is down; violence is up.

We come down this road again. The need is there. The opportunity is clear. The Soviet bear is gone. A new administration promised a Covenant to rebuild America, to put people back to work.

Once again, the check has bounced. Insufficient funds they say. The deficit must be addressed. The military must police the world. A conservative Congress will not help. A young president cannot deliver.

So just as thirty years ago—the march was a beginning, not an end, so this march is a beginning, too. We cannot sit on our hands when so many of our brothers and sisters are forced to their knees. And so we march.

We march to challenge despair, and raise up hope. We march to challenge the moral and ethical collapse that engulfs our society. Our young lost to despair, to drugs and guns, to a culture that puts a price on everything and a value on nothing. This is not a racial or an urban problem only—it is as true in the suburbs as the city, among the affluent young as among the poor, among white as well as black and brown. We need a moral movement to help regenerate hope, to renew the will to live, the desire to struggle.

We must end the killing. The fruits of despair. If death has merely changed its name from rope to dope, from genocide to fratricide to homicide; that's retrogression. Brothers and sisters, we must go forward by hope and life, not backward by fear and death. We must reclaim, project and secure our youth. And so we march.

> ***"We cannot sit on our hands when so many of our brothers and sisters are forced to their knees."***

We march to demand a program to rebuild America, to save our children, to put people back to work. Fulfill the Covenant. Put people first. No more broken promises. And so we march.

We march to demand justice. We've come a long way. But, today, justice is still not colorblind. Black males are arrested and jailed at four times the rate of white. There are four times as many young black males in US jails than in South African prisons. More black men in jail than in college. Black, brown and poor people receive more time for less crime than those who are affluent or white. Forty-six thousand cases of police brutality reported to the Justice Department since 1986. Fewer than two hundred prosecuted. Injustice abounds, so we march. Too often, it seems the more things change the more they stay the same.

In an attempt to gain the conscience and attention of the nation, I left jail, thirty years ago, to come here fighting for public accommodations. This week along with other citizens of the nation's capital, we had to face jail again while urging the president to honor his Covenant and the Congress to be as committed to democracy here at home as it is in the world.

We march to demand the right to vote. DC remains the last colony. Its citizens pay more taxes than forty-eight states. It has more residents than five states. Its citizens pay taxes in dollars that are green. Its soldiers shed blood that is red. But we are taxed and serve without the right to vote largely because our skin color is black. We demand DC statehood.

We march to reverse the assault on equal protection and equal opportunity laws. Attempts to turn back the clock abound. A conservative Supreme Court has challenged reapportionments that gave long-excluded minorities some measure of representation. And yet today, neither a Democratic Congress nor a Democratic president has spoken clearly on the continuing wounds caused by racism and the need for affirmative action if this nation is to remain one. Indifference and cynical posturing abounds. And, so we march.

We march for jobs, for an economic plan that puts people first. For a trade accord with Mexico that lifts their workers up, not an investor's treaty like NAFTA that will drag our workers down, and drain our jobs South.

For a single payer national health care plan that makes health care a right for everyone; not a plan that sacrifices care for some to protect profits for a few. In order to achieve these ends, politics as we know it is not working for us. Too often, we're rounding up votes to empower people to humiliate us and be indifferent to our legitimate interest. We must see more clearly from this mountain than we saw from the valley.

We must unleash the strength of our freedom struggle in new political forms. Our legitimate needs and interests are beyond the reach and boundaries of concern for both parties. But, the waters of justice must not be dammed up and become stagnant while urban Americans and family farmers perish in valleys of neglect. The levee is breaking. We must unleash the flood gates, waters of deep passion yearning to break free roll over the rocks of broken Covenants and deceit. We must become free political agents bound only by principles not limited by party. There were twelve million African Americans alone who voted for change and legal protection, yet we do not have an attorney general for civil rights that we can call on to fight our cause.

Through it all, don't let them break your spirit. Though the tide of fascist racism is on the rise, though the arrogant forces of indifference expand jails, underfund our schools, and warehouse our youths as they languish unemployed and unskilled with broken dreams. Don't let them break your spirit. KEEP HOPE ALIVE! Though the media stereotypes us as less worthy, less intelligent, less hardworking, less universal, less patriotic, and more violent. Don't let them break your spirit. KEEP HOPE ALIVE!

Though the plant gates are closing and jobs are shifting to cheap labor markets subsidized by our own government. Though the White House and the Congress offer a crime bill to contain the people rather than an economic stimulus plan to develop the people. Don't let them break your spirit. KEEP HOPE ALIVE! It's tough but thirty years ago, it was tougher. The sun was hotter and there was no shade. The winters were colder and there was no place of warm refuge. When torrential rains poured, we were trapped in the lowlands. Yet, we did not let it break our spirits. We must be caring not callous, loving not rejecting, putting character over color, ethics over ethnicity. We must trust in God's word.

Let's go forward back to our towns and hamlets to build new structures for freedom, new vehicles for hope in our quest to redeem the soul of America and make our world more secure. From Angola to Alabama, New York to Nigeria, Birmingham to Brazil, let the world know that we will stand fast and never surrender.

Hear this biblical admonition and promise: If my people were called by my name, will humble themselves and pray, and seek my face and turn from their wicked ways, God will forgive their sins and they will hear from heaven. Then, God will heal their land.

KEEP HOPE ALIVE!!!

Of particular concern to Jackson over the past few years is the sharp increase in violent crimes committed by blacks against other blacks, especially among young people. In 1993, he launched what he calls the Rainbow Crusade for Moral and Academic Excellence with a blunt message to the black community: "The premier civil rights issue of this day is youth violence in general and black-on-black crime in particular. It's clear now that we must look inward in order to go onward."

As part of his plan to convince blacks to assume more personal responsibility for the state of their neighborhoods, Jackson tells young people it is their moral obligation to turn in dealers of drugs and guns. He also urges ministers to get out from behind their pulpits and serve as mentors to children at risk from the violence of the streets. And he says that parents must take charge of their children's lives by accompanying them to school, staying in close contact with their teachers, and turning off the television set at night.

Jackson was sharply critical of the 1994 crime bill, however, particularly the so-called "three strikes and you're out" provision that would send three-time offenders to prison for life. Speaking to a National Press Club audience in February of that year, he characterized it as nothing more than "a mock tough crime bill, filled with bumper-sticker gimmicks that will waste money and that have no effect on crime." He went on to declare: "We already lock up more of our young people per capita than any other nation in the world. We must go another way."

Following the major Republican victory in the November 1994, elections, Jackson stepped forward to lead a coalition of liberals opposed to the so-called "Contract with America." Describing many of its initiatives as "mean-spirited and evil," he and his colleagues have pledged to seek common ground with President Clinton and the Republicans wherever possible but fight against those agen-

da items that threaten to "impact negatively on millions of ordinary American families." As an alternative, they have proposed a ten-point "covenant" that emphasizes prevention programs instead of prisons and calls for improvements in education and job creation.

To some observers, Jackson's outspoken criticism of both the Democratic leadership (embodied by President Clinton) and the Republican Congress hint that he may be contemplating another run at the presidency in 1996, perhaps as a third-party candidate. With that prospect in mind, Jackson took steps in July 1995 to retire the debt remaining from his 1988 campaign. He also has had researchers investigating state ballot access laws for third-party candidates. Yet he has declined to say for sure what his future plans include.

SOURCES

Books

Carson, Clayborne and others, editors, *The Eyes on the Prize Civil Rights Reader,* Penguin, 1991.

Chaplik, Dorothy, *Up with Hope: A Biography of Jesse Jackson,* Dillon, 1986.

Collins, Sheila D., *The Rainbow Challenge: The Jackson Campaign and the Future of U.S. Politics,* Monthly Review Press, 1986.

Colton, Elizabeth O., *The Jackson Phenomenon: The Man, the Power, the Message,* Doubleday, 1989.

Duffy, Bernard K., and Halford R. Ryan, editors, *American Orators of the Twentieth Century: Critical Studies and Sources,* Greenwood Press, 1987.

Haskins, James, *I Am Somebody!: A Biography of Jesse Jackson,* Enslow, 1992.

Historic Documents of 1993, Congressional Quarterly Inc., 1994.

House, Ernest R., *Jesse Jackson and the Politics of Charisma: The Rise and Fall of the PUSH/Excel Program,* Westview, 1988.

Jackson, Jesse L., *Straight from the Heart,* edited by Roger D. Hatch and Frank E. Watkins, Fortress Press, 1987.

———, *A Time to Speak: The Autobiography of the Reverend Jesse Jackson,* Simon & Schuster, 1988.

Kosof, Anna, *Jesse Jackson,* F. Watts, 1987.

Quinn, Richard, and Thomas Landess, *Jesse Jackson and the Politics of Race,* Green Hill, 1985.

Reed, Adolph L., Jr., *The Jesse Jackson Phenomenon: The Crisis of Purpose in Afro-American Politics,* Yale University Press, 1986.

Periodicals

Detroit Free Press, "Jackson Quits Race for Top Job at NAACP," April 8, 1993; "Jackson Crusade Against Violence," November 7, 1993.

Detroit News, "Jackson in Hunt for Top NAACP Post," February 21, 1993, p. 3A; "Jesse Jackson Denounces Black-on-Black Violence," January 6, 1994, p. 15A; "Jackson Leads Coalition to Fight 'Contract with America,'" January 6, 1995, p. 5A; "Presidential Politics of a Third Kind," June 18, 1995.

Grand Rapids Press, "Summit Urges Blacks to Take 'Moral Offensive' Against Violence," January 9, 1994, p. A17; "Jackson Will Weigh 'Mood Factor' Before Making Candidacy Decision," February 28, 1995, p. A5; "Jackson Retiring Debt with an Eye on Presidency," July 1, 1995, p. D6; "Jackson's Plans a Serious Threat to Clinton," July 2, 1995, p. A4.

Nation, "For Jesse Jackson and His Campaign," April 16, 1988, p. 517; "Jesse Is History," June 20, 1988, pp. 15-18; "Creating a Democratic Majority," December 26, 1988, p. 705.

New Republic, "Anything He Wants," April 25, 1988, pp. 10-11; "The Curse of Jesse," December 5, 1988, p. 705.

New Statesman and Society, "America's Great Black Hope," July 10, 1992.

Newsweek, "Does Jackson Want the Job?" June 27, 1988, p. 72; "The Jesse Primary," June 22, 1992, p. 37; "Breaking the 'Code of Silence,'" January 10, 1994; "An Older, Grimmer Jesse," January 10, 1994, p. 24; " 'Run, Jesse, Run' Redux?" April 17, 1995, p. 76.

New Yorker, February 3, 1992; February 10, 1992; February 17, 1992.

People, "Stand and Deliver," April 11, 1994.

Time, "The Jackson Problem," December 12, 1988, p. 29; "He Just Can't Resist the Spotlight," July 8, 1991, p. 9; "And the New Head of the NAACP Is . . . ," April 5, 1993, p. 13; "Process of Elimination," April 19, 1993, p. 17; "Rumblings on the Left," December 13, 1993, p. 40; "White House to Jesse: Please Be Our Friend," May 16, 1994, p. 34.

U.S. News and World Report, "A New Civil Rights Frontier," January 17, 1994.

Vital Speeches of the Day, "The Rainbow Coalition," 1984.

Daniel "Chappie" James, Jr.

1920–1978

African American military officer

In September 1975, veteran combat pilot Daniel "Chappie" James made history when he became the first black four-star general in U.S. military history. The youngest of seventeen children, he was born and raised in Pensacola, Florida, at a time when rigid racial segregation was the norm. With his mother's encouragement, however, he vowed to make a better life for himself. Leaving behind his job pushing a coal cart in a local gas plant, James went off to Tuskegee Institute in 1937 and graduated from the U.S. Army Air Corps program there. (He was one of the original black pilots to serve in this predecessor of today's Air Force.) Commissioned a second lieutenant in 1943, he was stationed at bases in Michigan and Indiana before being assigned to duty in the Philippines. He later distinguished himself as a pilot in over 100 combat missions during the Korean War.

After the war, James held various staff assignments around the world and in 1957 graduated from the Air Command and Staff College at Alabama's Maxwell Air Force Base. Beginning in 1966, he served as deputy commander for operations of the 8th Tactical Fighter Wing, a unit based in Thailand. Once again he demonstrated his skills as a pilot by flying in numerous combat missions during the Vietnam War. James's next assignment took him to Libya, where he was made commander of the 7272nd Flying Training Wing at Wheelus Air Base. He continued to rise through the ranks, becoming a brigadier general in 1970 and a lieutenant general in 1973. Two years later, after being named head of the North American Air Defense Command (NORAD), James received his historic promotion to four-star general.

A dynamic and persuasive orator with a forceful physical presence, James was widely known for his patriotic, upbeat speeches extolling the "American Dream" and asserting that racial harmony was indeed possible. On February 14, 1975, he touched on this theme during a Black History Week appearance before students at Escambia High School in his hometown of Pensacola. The text that follows is reprinted from the Congressional Record; *it originally appeared as an article in the February 15, 1975, issue of the* Pensacola Journal.

Thank you very much. It's always a pleasure to come home; especially to come home to that kind of reception from my fellow Pensacolians.

It is fitting that I should return here a year later after having spoken to the other half of Escambia High School. It is remarkable that knowing that I'm a Washington High alumnus that you'd ask me back here because I understand that when you folks meet on the basketball court it's quite a scrimmage out there, but then, we always beat everybody in town anyway so nothing's changed. I had to slide that in.

But I come to you at a time when we are commemorating a gain. A week where we stop to take stock of a certain segment of history.

A young lady who sat here changed it, took a paragraph out of my speech and she hadn't even seen my speech. But it is exactly what I was going to express—that these things that are colored different shades of black or white or red or gray will pass with time and understanding of the various races of this great melting pot that is the United States of America.

As people reach out to one another and I, like she, I look forward to that great day when Black History Week will just become a part of American history week. And that will be its name, American History Week, where we take special time to look at the whole of what we are and where we came from.

Now we have various things, various songs, various poems, various art, figments of art, other parts of our culture that will be preserved as coming from the days when things were not really quite all right, but they will be used for just what they were intended, to mark those times.

And so we can assess the progress that we've made from back there to right here. The songs that we sang many times when I was in school here had a central chorus that really remarked on history and it was known as the Negro national hymn.

And it said:

Stony the road we trod, bitter the chastening rod felt in the days when hope unborn had died; yet with the steady beat had not our weary feet come to the place for which our fathers sighed? We have come over a way that with tears has been watered, we have come treading our path through the blood of the slaughtered, out of the gloomy past till now we stand at last where the white gleam of our bright star is cast.

Daniel "Chappie" James, Jr.

Now that song was written over a hundred years ago, and even at that time black people in this country were assessing the progress that they had made since the days of bondage and slavery and they said we have come to the place "where the white gleam of our bright star is cast" and they were not indeed anywhere near where they are today and where they can go tomorrow, if we proceed to that place together, all of us, not looking for black achievement or white achievement or red achievement but American progress, the kind that has a chance only in our country and countries like ours but in our country to the greatest degree of all.

To get there, though, we've got to cast out some old hang-ups. We've got to be big enough no matter what our color to take the lead in making sure that that progress doesn't get staggered or slowed by retreats back to that path in the blood of the slaughtered.

We have marched enough, we have said enough, we have set out, we have walked out, we have copped out, we've sat in, the tune is go get it together.

You kids used to sing a song that I thought was very hopeful. It said, "It's going to take a little more time to get it together." There's been a whole lot of people been working to get it together, like you and me, we're determined that every man and woman is going to be free but it's just going to take a little more time to get it together.

And that's what we should be about, getting it together. Do not fall into the tracks of our elders who still practice their biases. You indeed will inherit this earth. The meek will not inherit this earth, unfortunately or fortunately, because this earth is governed by the strong, not only the strong physically, but the strong morally and mentally who are willing to put down that bias, that bias of hatred based on race, creed, religion, social arts and the what-else-have-you.

Stop finding so many ways to hate each other because of race, creed, religion, social structure, section of the block, political party, falling on somebody else's scandal and picking at the bones of the fallen.

Get it together. That's the only way to move mountains. You, the young people of Pensacola, will inherit this land and the positions of leadership in it.

There are possibilities now for young black people to go that were never possible during my time except for the few of us who had the courage and the preparation and the guidance that I fortunately was given by my mother, who told me some of the things that I'm telling you today, who in spite of the serious biases that existed in that day fought our way to the top by building what she called the greatest weapon on earth and the greatest power on earth.

She said, "My son, don't you dare sacrifice your ability on the dubious altar of despair. You take advantage of every opportunity that's offered you right here in this town, in Pensacola, Florida, in the Deep South," where the benches were labeled "colored" and "white" in the parks at that time and the latrine doors "colored" and "white" and the buses "white—colored to the rear."

All of those signs that gave a built-in inferiority complex to young black lads growing up.

She said, "Don't pay any attention to that now. Because those will be later removed as a by-product of what you achieve and don't you make a profession of being black. You take advantage of every opportunity that's offered to you and build for yourself the greatest power on earth.

"The power is called the power of excellence, and that's the only power worth investing in, the power of your own individual excellence, and you develop it. And you display it, and you use it to vault yourself to the top of your chosen field whatever it is, because you'll find that the power of excellence is a staple that doesn't decrease in value and it's in demand throughout the world and nobody questions its color."

And she was right. Nobody does question its color. And I entered the Air Force feeling that I was going to shoot for the top and I was going to try to be the greatest in my field, to vault with my power of excellence to the top of my chosen field because she said when you get up there with authority, you can do more to solve the ills that beset your people.

"You can't rise from the bottom with a brick or a torch or a harsh sign led on by some idiot who wants to make a profession of racism."

And you can't rise from the bottom with a brick or a torch or a harsh sign led on by some idiot who wants to make a profession of racism.

She was right—and I listened to her and I'm at the top of my field.

When I came into the Air Force I was determined to be a general officer and a leader of men, all men, not just black men, Americans, and I've got news for you—I am.

It is possible only here that these barriers have fallen as fast as they have. You can't stand there banging on that door of opportunity yelling, "Let me in! Let me in! Let me in!"

And all of a sudden, somebody opens that door and you say, "Wait a minute, I've got to go get my bags." You stand there armed with your bags of knowledge and your bags of intelligence and your bags of tolerance and your bags of understanding and your bags of Americanism and when they crack that door you walk in and take charge and that's possible for anybody in this room at the sound of my voice here.

Don't trip on the stumbling blocks of reverse racism. I say to my young black friends, "Reach out your hands." There are a lot of hands out there reaching out to you in friendship and in help and many of these hands are white, but they find it pretty hard to grasp ahold if your hand is balled tightly into a fist of hate.

Togetherness, pride, yes. Hatred, separatism, never.

Bigotry is ugly no matter what its color, no matter from which direction it's beamed. The human dignity of a person must be respected and we must always remember that our race ends where another man or woman's begins. And we must practice that.

And I say to my young black friends all over the world to reach out because the opportunity is more equal now and it's going to be even more equal as we go along that those hands will be stretched out there and that that hand of friendship might be any color.

And I tell the white majority in the same voice, don't you make me a liar. Make sure your hand is stretched out there, because that's the only way we can go about it: with the strength that would make it possible for us to study war no more. Because if we have that internal strength that is born of togetherness, nobody will dare attack our nation.

Our internal strength is a bargaining chip that we must have in the international family of nations. So I ask you today to reach out to each other, not just during Black History Week, not just on "I Am an American Day" but every day. Get it together.

Make sure that you invest in the biggest weapon we have ever had in our arsenal.

Now this isn't a physical weapon, mind you, it's a psychological one. It's a weapon called unity. Unity in the principles of democracy of the law and the letter of the Constitution of the United States of America.

That is the greatest piece of paper in the world and the words are great. You just have to make sure they work. It's up to you. You are the back that must provide the up-to-date modification of that weapon called unity.

We've come a long way in Pensacola. Assess that progress that black kids don't have to walk two-and-a-half miles all the way across town to an all-black school anymore in this town.

There are no segregated public schools in this city, I'm proud to see. And we have solved most of the problems: those benches in the park are now painted green like the grass. And all of the citizens of my town sit on them and discuss other ways to improve it, I hope. We don't bother to get hung up, I hope, on little arguments that recall the evils of the past. When we get down to the point that all we've got to worry about is the flag and the song, then I think we've got it mostly whipped.

There was a lot more wrong with it when I was here. Long time ago. Let's not go back there. Over something as stupid and minor as a song, or a flag.

I want to tell you something that's ironic. When I was in the Philippines I went to the first all-white squadron that I was ever in because that's when we integrated the Air Force. And I made light of this and all of the rest of the members of my flight were white and the former flight leader was from Texas. And the symbol of our flight was the rebel flag. And we sang "Dixie" in the club every Friday night. And when I took over the flight they said, "Well, Chappie, I guess you want to change that symbol. We'll get our razor blades out and scrape it off ourselves."

For what? I am from Dixie and I sang "Dixie" just as loud as anybody else and we defused the whole thing because the connotation of what some people were putting on "Dixie" ceased to be the connotation. It did not represent racial hatred, it represented our rallying cry, of what we were all about and we were indeed Americans, no matter what our color.

Now I will admit to you of all colors and races in here, that there are some people who cannot stand progress and truths and a call for unity, but I ask you to assume the kind of dignity and the kind of attitude that you will be brave enough to not only make constructive change but to be a part of it and when the hang-up gets to be something non-remarkable that you will resist that by being an American first and everything else secondary.

And so I ask you to by the way you live your daily lives build for yourselves your link in that chain that is the unity that has always preceded the States of America, the United States of America, and make her strong and show that unity to the world and they won't stand against us and maybe they will listen to us when we say we don't want to study war no more.

And maybe they'll stand with us as we try to reach out to each other and get it altogether and then, and only then, standing together as Americans all, we'll all truly overcome.

Thank you very much.

Poor health forced James to retire from the Air Force in January 1978. A month later, he died of a heart attack. On his portrait at the Pentagon appear the following words, which he himself inscribed there: "I fought three wars and three more wouldn't be too many to defend my country. . . . I love America and as she has weaknesses or ills, I'll hold her hand."

SOURCES

Books

Braden, Waldo W., editor, *Representative American Speeches: 1974-1975,* Wilson, 1975.

Congressional Record, 94th Congress, 1st session, March 6, 1975, Vol. 121, pt. 5, pp. 5558-5560.

Periodicals

Pensacola Journal, February 15, 1975.

Leonard Jeffries

1937–

African American educator and historian

A self-described "African conspiracy theorist," Leonard Jeffries is one of the leading proponents of Afrocentrism, a controversial theory that emphasizes the African roots of history and civilization. Afrocentrists believe that whites of European origin have deliberately falsified or obscured the record of black achievement through the centuries. They also believe that whites are still actively plotting ways to oppress the African peoples of the world and ultimately bring about their destruction. Jeffries has personally provoked the ire of many for insisting that Jews financed the slave trade, for characterizing George Washington, Thomas Jefferson, and the other founding fathers of the United States as "slavemaster bastard[s]," and for declaring that AIDS was manufactured in a German laboratory and then injected into Africans by medical personnel linked to the World Health Organization.

A native of Newark, New Jersey, Jeffries attended Pennsylvania's Lafayette College, from which he graduated with honors in 1959. He then studied abroad for two years at the University of Lausanne in Switzerland. Upon returning to the United States, he enrolled in Columbia University's School of International Affairs to pursue a master's degree. It was during this period—the early 1960s—that Jeffries became fascinated with Africa. He began spending his summer vacations helping run community-development programs in several different West African nations. He also read extensively in the fields of black history and philosophy. This pattern continued while he worked on his PhD in political science at Columbia. And as he watched Africans and African Americans struggle to advance and prosper, Jeffries grew increasingly radical and bitter. The student protests and burgeoning black studies movement of the late 1960s intensified his desire to bring about changes in the academic system.

In 1972, after brief teaching stints at New York's City College and California's San Jose State College, Jeffries was offered a choice assignment back at City College: chairman of the new black studies department and full professor of black studies (with immediate tenure, which guaranteed him job security). He has spent the years since then establishing the black studies program, conducting research as part of a group of scholars, traveling throughout Africa, and lecturing in high schools, colleges, and even some corporations. He has, however, done almost no original research of his own and has published no books and only a couple of articles. Instead, he relies almost exclusively on the work of others to bolster his theories.

Jeffries was not widely known outside City College and Afrocentrist academic circles until around 1988, when he served as consultant to a multicultural task force charged with revamping the public school curriculum in New York State to reflect the contributions of minorities. The group's final report, written after several months of study and debate in which Jeffries played a major role, was sharply criticized for its harsh tone and anti-European bias; it was later shelved and the state education department convened another task force made up of more moderate voices. But Jeffries and his supporters kept the issue alive with relentless attacks on those who had condemned the report and anyone else who opposed Afrocentrism.

The controversy came to a head on July 20, 1991, at the Empire State Black Arts and Cultural Festival in Albany, New York. There Jeffries delivered a nearly two-hour-long speech that attracted widespread attention after it was broadcast on the state-run cable channel and reported on in several New York newspapers. Besides accusing government officials of trying to undermine efforts to establish a multicultural education program, Jeffries made other statements that many regarded as racist and anti-Semitic. The following represents the full text of his speech as it appeared in the August 19, 1991, edition of New York Newsday.

Last year I was here, and it was very good. I appreciated the opportunity to come because the storm around the curriculum was hot then. This has been going on now for almost two years, and it continues—and continues because the existing educational system is not isolated from the existing cultural-social-political-economic system of the United States. It is part and parcel. If the social, economic, political and cultural system of the United States is racist, there's no way you can insulate and isolate the educational system. So racism in the educational system has to be dealt with. That's the number-one item that has to be removed before we can have true education.

So I think that if we see this enormous struggle against us, it is just another manifestation of racism and white supremacy, and we have to deal with it as that. It seems more vicious because you would think these are not Ku Klux Klan—because they've got PhDs or other things behind their name. But they operate in much the same way, and as far as I'm concerned they have the same VIP: values, interests and principles—the values, interests and principles of white supremacy.

So, I will proceed forthwith with the presentation. For those who are up here and over there—are going to be at a disadvantage because if I do—one of my favorite things is to say, "Let's go to the videotape," and that might mean I might try to show something, you know, like this *Newsweek* article; and if you're way up in the boondocks or over there, you won't be able to see it. Or if I might want to show you an image of the black Statue of Liberty, you know, you would not be able to see it.

But I think we have to understand that although we like to think of education as race-neutral and politically neutral, education is part of racism, and the fact that some of its worst manifestations—and it's a part of politics. So I think that what we're doing must be correct because of the storm that we've raised and created. I'm surprised, however, at the reaction, because when I was asked to evaluate the curriculum of the state of New York two years ago—and I was virtually begged to help bail the state and the commissioner and the task force that had been put in place to work with the curriculum—they really needed our help. And they asked me to suspend what I'm doing—and no one is busier than I at City College, and Vivian [Gordon, a professor of African American studies at the State University of New York in Albany] knows that. But I virtual-

Leonard Jeffries

ly suspended my activities, running a chairmanship and doing all the other activities we had—to set aside this work. They asked four of us to evaluate the curriculum of the state of New York.

The way the misinformation campaign—the defamation of my character—has gone, it's as if only one person was involved in evaluating the curriculum of the state of New York. There were four of us—four scholars. We looked at over one hundred documents from the state of New York Department of Education. There may have been a hundred and fifty documents, covering every area of education. And I thought this could be done, you know, communally, cooperatively and collectively. That's the African value system—the three Cs, I call it: communal, cooperative and collective—working together in a spiritual dimension. So I pulled together a team of people—other PhDs—Dr. Shashi McIntyre, Professor Edward Scobie, Dr. Douglas Davis, Dr. Kamuti Kiteme from Kenya—to help me in this endeavor.

But when I realized how serious this thing was—and you had to actually go line by line through these documents—I said I'd better take firm control of this thing to make sure that the importance of it is fully realized. I spent six months reviewing documents. Some documents I had to read over ten times because I could not believe what it was I was seeing. Ten times.

The social studies document which dealt with Africa I had to read over and over again because I said this is not happening in 1987, '89. I can't believe that this curriculum was revised in '87 and this is what they have. The social studies document actually took Egypt out of Africa; took the Nile Valley out of Africa. Now, of course, they explained it in European-American—very common rational terms: they were going to deal with it in another part of the world. You know? You can always look for it—you know? They were gonna deal with the Nile Valley in another part of the world. So that was supposed to be the Near East, Middle East or whatever other part of the world they like to call that. And in that area they were going to deal with Mesopotamia, Tigris, Euphrates, the ancient Hebrews and the Nile Valley, Egypt.

And I read this over and over again; I couldn't believe my eyes. There was no content to the Nile Valley unit. No content. No mentioning of the literature of the ancients of Africa. The first literature of the world—of significance—is the literature of the Africans of the Nile Valley. No mention of the science of the Africans of the Nile. No people have built more in a more dynamic fashion—a more meaningful and technological fashion—than Africans of the Nile. No mention of the philosophy and the ethos and ethics, the morality that's carved in their tombs and temples, built into the designs of their cities, even how they structured their society: one side of the river being the place of the living, the other side being the preserve of the dead. And the two are opposites that are complementary: that the living and the dead beget each other and there is life after death.

No concept that the Africans had put in place the concept of the oneness of God before the ancient Hebrews. There was no content.

And I had to say to myself after reading it ten times, unbelieving what I was reading, that this was not an accident. This was by design, by people who know what they were doing. Stripping Africa of its significance in its place in the world. And the people who are doing it are very nice, friendly white folks and some of their achieving Negro partners. That's the tragedy. These are not Ku Klux Klan people. These are some very nice white folks—your neighbors, your colleagues, the people that you work with. They go to church and the synagogue, think highly of themselves; but they didn't hesitate at all to distort history in what I call racial pathology.

They say they were upset with me with terms like that. "Ohhhh. Jeffries, the tone! You know. . . ." Racial pathology. Well, how else do you describe something as diabolical as that? How else do you describe the attack on me, as if I was the lone person reviewing the curriculum?

And there were four of us. Dr. [Shirley] Hune, an Asian scholar from Hunter University, reviewed—and our task force was not to look at white history; our task force was to look at the—we had a charge; it was written down. It was to look at the hundred and fifty volumes to see which of those volumes effectively dealt with people of color and which did not; and which were strong and which needed revision. We weren't asked to look at what Thomas Jefferson was doing; I brought that in as a—part of my own understanding of what was happening. They said we weren't positive about white folks. That's not what the charge was. We were to look to see what white folks had done about black folks. And they had done nothing about black folk in any significant way. And they had done nothing about Asian Americans or Asians, and Dr. Hune said that in her report. And Dr. [Carlos Rodriguez-]Fraticelli, who handled the Puerto Rican-Latino part, said they had done nothing in reference to the Latino and Puerto Rican. And the person who—Professor [Lincoln C.] White, who handled Native Americans—said they had done nothing in reference to the Native American.

In fact, the three special volumes on our particular groups—one on the black experience, one on the Puerto Rican experience and one on the Native American experience—were inadequate. We gave them their plusses, but they were inadequate. The volume—the only volume on blacks in the state of New York—was done by a schoolteacher and her students. That's what was submitted. It wasn't good enough. The volume on the Puerto Ricans focused mainly on mainland Puerto Rico and not the enormous migrant community of Puerto Ricans along the East Coast of the United States. The volume on the Native Americans dealt with the one tradition—the long house tradition—not the other traditions. It wasn't good enough. And we mentioned that.

All of us never had met—we never met. To this day I have not seen Professor Hune, Dr. Fraticelli I met one time, after all of this occurred. Professor White I never met; we never even communicated on the telephone. I received their reports and synthesized them, pulled out what we had collectively stated and sent them as part of the general report—but their complete reports went as the appendices. And then the task force, which included white folks, Native Americans, Asians, blacks, et cetera, African peoples—took our recommendation, took our reports, and they put their analysis to it and presented it.

It's as if one person took over the state of New York educational system, Len Jeffries, controlled the commissioner and beat up this committee and imposed himself upon—for his own reasons. The little bit of money that they paid me to do it, I get in some speaking engagements in an hour. I don't have to spend six months out of my life for a couple of thousand dollars.

But once I saw what the problem was and what the test was, I realized it was part of the sacred mission that we as black folk have: to try to right things that are wrong. And those of us who have carved out education as our area realize that we have to do a major job; major surgery has to take place in the educational arena because the educational arena was designed to support the system of white supremacy that was institutionalized in this nation. That's what education was for.

The legal system was designed to support the system of white supremacy in this nation. The economic system was the heart of this system of white supremacy in this nation. And the cultural system went along with that—movies, all the rest of it. For years—and I grew up as a youngster just like you did, going to movies where the African peoples were completely denigrated. That was a conspiracy planned and plotted and programmed out of Hollywood, where people called Greenberg and Weisberg and Trigliani and whatnot—it's not anti-Semitic to mention who developed Hollywood. Their names are there—MGM: Metro-Goldwyn-Mayer, Adolph Zukor, Fox. Russian Jewry had a particular control over the movies, and their financial partners, the Mafia, put together a system of destruction of black people. Talk about self-image and self-esteem? This was an important part of the cultural development of any youth. We went to the movies every Saturday and saw the Native Americans being wiped out and Africans being denigrated: Sambo images, Beaulah, Stepin Fetchit. That's what they put up there. It was by design. It was calculated.

So we have to see that there is a war against the African. Now, I knew it before, but I didn't know how devilish it was gonna get or could be. They're nice white people. You don't feel so bad if you got to go up against someone who is really down-and-out devilish and doggish. But if you get the smiling people like [former Columbia University professor and assistant U.S. education secretary] Diane Ravitch—"I'm trying to do the right thing"—deedeedee—"and I have done the right thing all these years." Read Diane Ravitch's record; look at her track record. This is the ultimate, supreme, sophisticated, debonair racist—pure and simple. And when they say, "Hey, you and the others called her Miss Daisy"—they did it right. And Asa said: "We're gonna let Miss Daisy drive her own damn car from now on." [Laughter and applause from audience.]

And Miss Daisy and her several partners. Albert Shanker has been holding her hand for some time, and now he's at the door of the governor, beating him up, saying you've got to go against this latest report. They went against our report, using me as the scapegoat—that some nasty person has gotten control of the educational system. So then they put in place a sanitized committee; they check these people out on the computers. Ran the computer. "Good, sound, qualified achieving Negro. No problem." "Good, sound Native American. No problem." And they used their computers.

But, see, they don't know—and don't you all tell them—the power of the African Holy Ghost. See, once that African Holy Ghost starts moving around, whatever their calculations was is thrown off. And that African Holy Ghost started working and that committee with only a few blacks, which was supposed to be not only sanitized but it was supposed to be dominated and led by rich white men with property and power—[historian] Arthur Schlesinger, distinguished professor at City University, and had been with the Kennedys and had been at Harvard. And then the melting pot man—what was his name?—Glazer. Nathan Glazer. Dr. Nathan Glazer. Melting pot Glazer. And then Dr. Kenneth Jackson. Now these three were supposed to dominate the other twenty. But, see, they underestimated the African Holy Ghost. And once Dr. Elleni Tedla felt that Holy Ghost—because she's from Ethiopia—now you know the Holy Ghost has been roaming around Ethiopia for a long time. Ethiopia's the oldest Christian nation; that Holy Ghost is there. And Lalibela built the new Jerusalem in the twelfth century—twelve stone churches—not from the ground up: wonders of the world. Lalibela in Ethiopia.

> ***"Once I saw what the problem was . . . I realized it was part of the sacred mission that we as black folk have: to try to right things that are wrong."***

From the ground down: to protect them from the Muslim invasions. Holy Ghost in Ethiopia.

So Elleni Tedla got herself together and brought it to the table. And then little Diane Glover—she's just a schoolteacher. But she found the strength—talking to the African Holy Ghost—that she was a dynamite—looked Glazer and Schlesinger in the eye and said, "You're not correct. I do not agree, Dr. Glazer." Here's a little schoolteacher out in Long Island looking these big white men with property, power and prestige—they knew they had met their match.

So Schlesinger, being a weakling and not prepared to learn and grow, stepped off of the committee. This is how slick and devilish they are. He refused to be in the committee because he saw the learning process that these sisters and brothers bring that material to the table—that they all had to digest—was changing the committee. The truth was manifesting itself. So he said: "I'm going to step off, but not really step off." That's how slick and devilish and dirty and dastardly they are. He said, "I just want to be a consultant." Be a consultant. So he's privy to all the material and what they're doing but not a part of what it is, so that he could go out and contact Federal Express and produce a devilish volume such as this, called the *Disuniting of America*—a political trap passing off as a scholarly document [published by Whittle Publishing Company].

This is why the unconscionable—he refused to sit down with any of us and discuss any of these matters. They let the newspaper people jump up with these articles. Here's a book that's supposed to be the definitive book on the reflections on a multicultural society. And it's really reflections on the African. Nobody else is mentioned in this book except African people. No Asians are mentioned; they're not attacked. No Native Americans, no Latinos are attacked. The Africans are attacked, and our pictures are put in here—pictures of Asa Hilliard, pictures of [others]—in the margin. And I've never seen a book like this. How could they put this out? Between every chapter there's an advertisement for Federal Express—an advertisement for Federal Express.

And this is the book that's going to be talked about—*The Disuniting of America*. You talk about primps and pimps and prostitutes parading. I mean, I hate to be—I mean, you see my reaction. I'm trying to be very cool, calm and collected. And he even had to put one of us—"Provides immediate relief from stress and anxiety" Federal Express advertisement, in between the chapter on "The New Race"—this is a chapter on "New Race"—and then they have this black fella there.

History the weapon—and then they have some of our pictures. But, you know, "Battle for the Schools" . . . what this reveals is that what we're—and then they have—look, Diane Ravitch. They just gave her a little picture in the corner. Miss Daisy. Adjunct professor at City College—I mean at Columbia. Not a professor. Miss Daisy has not passed muster to be a professor. Dr. Gordon and I have passed muster to be a professor. Miss Daisy was there as an adjunct because she brought in a grant. She's hooked up with the grants—with the Heritage Foundation and these other conservative foundations—because she's doing the work of these devilish folks.

In fact, she is the new standard. The old standard was a Bible Belt Texas rural family. That's the standard for the textbooks that went into the schools for generations. Now the new standard is not a Bible Belt Texas family but a sophisticated Texas Jew. And that standard is not good enough either—because many people, such as the Ravitches, who happen to be Jewish, have blinded us on the attack coming from the Jewish community—systematic, unrelenting. And until we can look at it and deal with it, there's no efforts we can make that're going to be successful. Not anti-Semitic to raise the issue—but if you do not deal with it, you're fooling yourself.

There's an orchestrated attack by the Schlesingers and the Shankers, working with the white conservatives (the George Wills, the Heritage Foundation)—we're pinpointing their relationship; we're putting it to our African computer: the document is being prepared.

And they know who to point to: so the largest photo in the darned book is Len Jeffries. He doesn't get in the margin. He's got a whole big thing there. And so the people around me say, "Len, they're targeting you for death." I said, "That's cool. That means I must be doing something right." I live forty-five, forty-four years on this plane, and if I hadn't done what I should do by then, then, you know, there's not much more I'm going to do. Malcolm only had thirty-nine. Martin only had thirty-nine. So death is not a thing. I'm not gonna back down, no matter what. They just—they picked on the right person at the right time, and they're not going to win this one.

And, in fact, I called the *New York Times* after they attacked me last year, and I told them: "Thank you for making me a folk hero among my people wherever I go. And thank you for introducing me to scholars around the world."

Most of you don't realize that when the *New York Times* put in the paper that Jeffries said rich Jews were involved in the enslavement process, they put that in there to paint me as an anti-Semitic. An anti-Semitic does not stay at City College for twenty years as chairman of a department and have friends (even those who do not like him) and his enemies respect him at City College. And the head Jew at City College, Dr. Bernard Somer, saw me after the article in the *Times,* said: "Len, everybody knows rich Jews helped finance the slave trade." If everybody knows it, then let's put it in the classroom.

Miss Ravitch says that black people sold black people into slavery. She don't hesitate to say that. Schlesinger says black people sold black people into slavery.

Let's talk about who financed, planned, operated, maintained the slave system. Let's talk about every slave ship being blessed by a Protestant minister or Catholic priest. Let's talk about the Catholic Church initiating this. Let's talk about the Danes, the Dutch, the Portuguese, the French, the Scots, the Swedes, the Brandenberg Germans that were involved in the slavery for hundreds of years—Jews and Gentiles, Arabs and Christians. Let's deal with the whole ball of wax. Let's not just say that Africans sold Africans into slavery.

But I don't do anything unless I'm backed up with some documentation. So—the Ravitches and whatnot don't have documentation—they don't want to come by me.

They sent their leading emissary, Edward I. Koch—and Eddie called me up, wrote me a letter: "Dr. Jeffries, I'd like you to come down to my office so we can discuss your documentation and what these things are you're dealing with." I thought he wasn't serious. But I realized he had been on TV the week before and said, "Jeffries is wrong because he's teaching racism in his class. [Professor Michael] Levin is right because he's not teaching it in his class." This is this convoluted logic and rationality of white folk who are pathological—affected by racism.

So most people tell me: "Don't be bothered with him." Dr. Adelaide Sanford said: "You can't deal with him. The man will distort anything you say." Dr. Clark said: "Don't worry about him."

But the African Holy Ghost said: When you're with your truth, you can go anywhere and deal with anybody. And since he is the biggest and the baddest that they got, you got to take on their best so you don't have to worry about the rest.

And so Dr. J. called them up and said, "I'm interested in your proposition, but I have a condition: I'm not coming; I want you to come up to my office."

"Oh, no. I couldn't come up to your office."

I said, "I have all the books and everything up here."

"Oh, no, no. I couldn't do that because that would cause—you know, too much publicity."

So I said: "Well, I'll come down to your office but first you've got to give up my pyramid."

He said: "What?"

I said, "I would not even consider a dialogue unless you are prepared to give up my pyramid." I said, "We have a picture of you riding on a camel around the pyramids several years ago talking about your ancestors built them thousands of years ago. We got another picture of Menachem Begin dancing in front of the pyramids that his ancestors built thousands of years ago. We want our pyramids back, and there's no need to even dialogue unless you are prepared to give them up."

So you have to operate from some strength. If you operate from weakness, doubt, and you don't know what you're doing, there's no need to be in the ball park. Let the Gordons, Jeffries and others do the shooting, because you will all be shooting the wrong people and using the wrong ammunition. What I'm saying is you've got to master the understanding of your own experience and your history and have this knowledge. It's there; it's available; it's in the books. You've got to study. You set up study groups; put the study groups in your homes, in your churches, in your apartment houses, on your jobs; and study this material. It's there. Then you can be as firm and sure as the others of us are—the Wade Nobles and the Haki Madhubutis and the Na'im Akbars, Frances Cress Welsing. Because the material is there; we haven't produced any magic to get this material. We just want discipline, hard work and more persistence than others.

So once he was prepared to give up my pyramid—and I always carry an image of the pyramids around—once he was prepared to give them up, I said I would come down. And he called in from Hong Kong to tell his people, "Tell Jeffries he can have his pyramids back."

So my brother said, "Look, I can't allow you to go down there by yourself." This is my little brother; he's into heavy African martial arts. And that's why it's good to have these little brothers. He said, "I'm going down with you because my aura will protect you."

So the Jeffries boys from Newark, New Jersey, went down to Rockefeller Plaza to meet Edward I. Koch. I rolled down—just as I rolled this stuff here in all these books—I don't go nowhere without your ammunition. There's no need to begin a war and you ain't armed, you're just mouthin' and wolfin'. Take your ammunition. And so we rolled into Koch's office with all this stuff. First thing I saw—and he wants to know, "Where is your documentation?"

I say, "We have it all here."

Well, before he could say anything, I said, "Look. That thing over there on the cabinet—we're going to have to deal with—before we do anything."

He said, "What? What?"

I said, "That. That Statue of Liberty."

"What do you mean?"

"Well, well, uh, uh, you're not familiar with the Statue of Liberty?"

"Yes. The Statue of Liberty's in the harbor."

"No, no. Its background. The reason for it being." I said, "The Statue of Liberty has not a darned thing to do with your immigrant forebears. It has to do with my forebears fighting for liberty in these United States."

He tried to act cool, but it was clear he was becoming discombobulated.

When I showed him some of the documentation, he knew he was in a war for control of the mind, and so he left and said, "I'll be right back." And he brought in his Dr. Clark, attorney [Dan] Wolf, and sat him in the room.

So here was my brother and I—the Jeffries boys—with attorneys Wolf and Koch. We presented the information and Koch, after an hour, got what I called cognitive dissonance. That's what happens when this new information is brought before the folks. Cognitive dissonance is a much nicer term—a psychological term, when imbalanced disharmony occurs when the information is—but I like to call it racial pathology, but cognitive dissonance is good enough for those who cannot digest racial pathology. Well, cognitive dissonance started to set in; and after a while he got so uncomfortable, he asked me about—"Well, what is this about you had said something about rich Jews involved in the enslavement of Africans?"

So I said, "Where do you want us to start? What period of history? You want us to start in the Spanish-Portuguese period of the starting of the slave trade in the 1400s and 1500s? Do you want us to move it from Seville and Lisbon on to Amsterdam and Hamburg, where the new Jewish community in those areas continued the slave trade for the Dutch, the Germans and the English? Or do you want us to move it to Brazil and the Caribbean and Curaçao, which became a new Amsterdam, the new center of the slave trade in the western world centered around the Jewish immigrants that moved into Curaçao? Or do you want us to move it to New York and Newport, Rhode Island? Where do you want us to start?"

Newport, Rhode Island, at the time of the American Revolution was the leading legal slaving center in America, and that was the home of the largest Jewish community and most active, wealthy Jewish community in America. Newport, Rhode Island.

"Where do you want to start, man?"

"Well, uh, babababbababba. Well, what books do you have?"

"Well, we have a book here, Aaron Lopez, *Lopez of Newport.*"

In 1750s and '60s: one of the largest slavers out of Newport, Rhode Island, a community that had a number of outstanding, wealthy Jews who not only controlled a couple hundred of the slave ships—and Lopez himself controlling a couple dozen—but they controlled most, if not all, of the thirty distilleries that processed molasses from the Caribbean into rum, to be sold to the native Americans as "fire water" and to be sold to Africa, for enslaved Africans.

"Where do you want to start? You want to go back into the Spanish Sephardic Jewish community? Then get Stephen Birmingham's *The Grandees.*"

The grandees: the Jewish rich that supported the Spanish throne and helped lay the foundation for the enslavement in the 1400s and 1500s. Even after the Jewish community was persecuted in Spain with the Inquisition in 1492, many of them that converted to Christianity stayed in Spain and helped the Spanish king and queen, who was anti-Semitic (Queen Isabella)—helped her maintain the slave system against the Africans and native Americans.

"Where do you want to start? Do you want to go to Amsterdam? Then get a book by Jonathan Israel on *European Jewry in the Age of Mercantilism, 1550-1750.*"

And there's a picture of the Amsterdam synagogue, which was the center of slave trading for the Dutch. Amsterdam became a leading port in this period of time for slaving. And it was around this synagogue that the slaving system was established.

Now, we're not talking about most Jews. Most Jews were being beat—up and down Europe—persecuted for being Jewish. We're talking about rich Jews, and we specifically make that distinction. We're not talking about white folks in general when we talk about oppression; we're talking about the wealthy white folks, the powerful white folks that make the decision.

So let's make some decisions, some clarity, when we talk about these things. But the documentation is there. We are now preparing the ten volumes dealing with the Jewish relationship with the black community in reference to slavery, so we can put it in the school system, so there'll be no question about Miss Daisy, Arthur Schlesinger—Schlesinger in his book said, "Dr. Jeffries said something about the Jews involved in enslavement"—and then just leaves it there.

I had to ask this man who called me from California. I said, "What is the reference that he cites?"

"The *New York Times.*"

I said, "That's not a reference to cite."

"Well, they quote you being quoted from some other newspaper."

I said, "That original quote was not correct, and so anything else after that is not correct. Whey didn't he contact me and find out what it is that we're saying? Everybody was involved in the enslavement of Africans."

But if you want to deal with slavery, let's deal with it. And I'm going to lay this down. That's why we're being attacked. You see, if they had just let us put a few black folks in the curriculum and been satisfied with that, then there would be no problem, and we would have been satisfied. But they didn't want us to do that. So our intellectual abilities and capacities and our sacred mission has pushed us into serious study and analysis. No one has studied more than myself in the last couple of years and the people around me.

Producing documents, position papers—Dr. Carruthers, Dr. Asanti, Dr. Hilliard, Dr. Shashi McIntyre, my wife—we have been in a heavy study, and what has been revealed is a mind-boggling process. We'll have the ten major books relating to the Jewish community (the wealthy Jewish community) and enslavement.

In Spain there were the grandees, managing the money of the Spanish throne. In Germany, in the 16- and 1700s, there were the court Jews, managing the political and economic apparatus of Europe, the Hapsburg empire, the German states, et cetera. We have the names. We know who they were, what they were, what they controlled. We know when they set up the Dutch East Indian Company, Dutch West Indian Company, the Portuguese company, the Brazilian company. We know who and what documents. We know the family connections. We know that even when they converted to Christianity, they maintained links with their Jewish community brothers who had not converted; and that's why they had a network around the world.

But even more than that, if you keep digging on and—as quiet as it's kept, a number of Jewish scholars from around the country sent me documentation on the Jews' involvement in slave trade. Not one wrote to me contesting what they thought I had said. A dozen sent me information, including a SUNY professor.

And then we discovered—in my copy room—I don't know. The African Holy Ghost works in wondrous ways. The African Holy Ghost put a book in my copy room called *The Jews of Germany* by [Marvin] Lowenthal. And it details the movement of the Jewish community into Europe after the fall of the Roman Empire, along with the Syrians and Lebanese; and they became the lifeline of the fallen Roman Empire in the 15- and 1600s. And they began to institutionalize a trade link with the Middle East. A trade link dealt with:

Number One—

Number Two: Furs.

And Number One: it dealt with humans, the humans that it dealt with for hundreds of years, with the Slavic peoples of central, eastern and southern Europe, the Czechs, the Poles, the Yugoslavs, the Russians—an alliance between the Catholic Church and rich Jews selling white central, eastern and southern Europeans into Arab slavery.

The truth will set you free.

Did you hear what I said? The white slave trade in Europe—because the central and eastern Europeans were pagans; they were not Christians. Catholic Church had no allegiance to them. And the Jewish community didn't care either which way. So rich Jews and the Catholic Church had an alliance for hundreds of years, selling white folks from central, eastern and southern Europe into slavery in the Arab world—the white slave trade, which is the precursor of enslavement later.

In fact, the term "slavery" is rooted in the word "slavs." You see why we're in trouble?

If they had just let us alone and let us put Lewis Latimer, Granville Woods and [names unclear]—if they just let us alone, we would have been so worried about putting these people in the curriculum that we wouldn't have to dig up these truths. But we might as well go for the whole ball of wax, getting ourselves prepared for the twenty-first century. It's in the works; it's in the material. You just have to grab hold of it.

Let me quickly say what I'm trying to say. I had to deal with that because, see, if Schlesinger had let me alone—I had not touched the Jewish question for the past year. I had made an agreement with my Jews at City College that I would not deal with it. Koch, after he'd met me in May, had nothing to say about Dr. Jeffries for a year. He has never said anything about me since that last May. Once he saw the documentation and information, there was nothing to be said. In fact, his—his senior—attorney Wolf—when I called him—because I wanted my [word unclear] documents back, and I called him and I told him I wanted to apologize for being a little rough on attorney Wolf—because he did say something, and I said in the African tradition, you know, we respect elders and, you know, you just got in the way of my bullets for Koch. Attorney Wolf said he was so glad and delighted to see the encounter. He has known Koch for years, and he has never seen him sit, listen and learn. Even Koch, after the meeting, when he—he got up and said, "I have a meeting to go to." After an hour he didn't have a meeting to go to—he just couldn't take it anymore. And I kept going for—for another half an hour. But even he, after the encounter, said that "Uh, uh, you know, he's an interesting chap." That's the best he could come up with, but that's a compliment coming from him. But I had brought two hundred dollars' worth of books, these books, for them to purchase. I thought they were seriously interested in what it is that we are saying and what it is we're basing it upon. But they were not. They wanted to destroy me, to make a spectacle of me, to ridicule me. And I knew they weren't going to buy the books, so I said: "I brought two hundred dollars' worth of books but since"—I see Koch had set in—"you're not prepared to buy the books, I'm going to give you one of the key books that I think you should have." And that was *Black Athena* by Martin Bernal.

One of your own has written an enormous book on the experience of Africans in relationship to Greece. Now Martin Bernal has come out with a second book, and we're not raising Martin Bernal up higher than anybody else; but at least he's an individual who has talked about the falsification of history and how they created a false Greece at the time of the American Revolution to create the Aryan model of white supremacy that has been perpetuated for the last couple of hundred years; that the Greeks worshipped the Africans and acknowledged the Africans and revered the Africans, went to learn at the foot of the Africans in the greatest buildings of the ancient world, the Luxor university temple. This is where the great Greeks wanted to learn. This is the symbol of the pillared temples everywhere in the world. If there's a pillared temple on the Acropolis in Greece called the Parthenon, it was inspired by this great pillared temple. If you have a pillared temple in Washington, D.C., called the Lincoln Memorial, it was inspired by this great pillared temple. If you have a pillared temple at Forty-second Street in New York, which is the New York Public Library, and outside of it you have two lions, you'd better believe it has been inspired by the African—because those lions are the sphinx. Wouldn't you think that they'd put lions outside the Bronx Zoo and not outside of a library? Except they've been inspired by the African tradition; the lions are the guardian forces of the temples of learning.

They've taken your traditions because you haven't tapped into them fully enough. You cannot even articulate them because you're culturally illiterate. So it's not a question of putting something in school for the five- and six-year-old; it's putting something in the homes for the parents. It's putting something in the studies for the teachers who need help, who have to refashion themselves—even those of us with these PhDs and BBDs. You need to tap into a whole other level of knowledge that is available to you so that when someone talks about this symbol, and they take you down to Washington, D.C., and you take your little kiddies and say, "Look, Sammy! Look, Mary Jo!, Look at the monument they built for George Washington!"—and you don't have the knowledge, critical understanding or cultural literacy to say, "Look, Sammy!" and "Look, Mary Jo!" at the African monument of resurrection that was refashioned for George Washington, the slave master bastard Founding Father.

But there's a new ballgame. We have the information on the Statue of Liberty. When it first came out, it was a student who gave it to me—I'm going to run for these next few minutes. There was a student that gave me the information because a black chemist, Jack Felder, had compiled an information sheet with the date of information, where you could find it. And when we put our information out there, we need to put at the end of it the documentation source, where we can discover this information. And so when he put the documentary data, et cetera, I followed it up, being the consummate scholar. I grabbed some of the sons of Africa. We jumped in a couple cars, went down to the New York City Museum, 106th Street and Fifth Avenue, looking for this black Statue of Liberty. The first model was of a—image of a black woman holding the broken chains of enslavement, with the broken chains of enslavement at her feet. Nobody there knew anything about it. All the people there were black. Five or six blacks—ain't nobody knew nuthin'. I refused to leave. Black folks got cognitive dissonance; they didn't want to understand, didn't want to do nothing. But when I refused to leave, then they got—start to thinking. There was a Haitian guard who was there. So they said, "Go get him. Maybe he knows something." He was there in '86 when they had the celebrations. So they go get the Haitian guard. And he said, "Of course. The model of the Statue of Liberty is downstairs."

I said, "Can we see it?"

"No. The director has the key. Locked up. Ain't nobody can see it."

So I said, "Well, is there any other information about the Statue of Liberty?"

He went off, came back with a book by Marvin Trachtenberg called *The Statue of Liberty*. And in it—he opened it up and showed the various models of the Statue of Liberty with the chains at the feet.

Then the brother—Felder—said, "You can go down to the French Cultural Center." That's further down on Fifth Avenue—Eighty-third Street, Eighty-second Street at Fifth Avenue. I went there, knocked on the door, just got in there just in time. I had called them before and asked them did they have any information on the Statue of Liberty. And they gave me a large magazine called *Liberty*, the anniversary edition of the magazine *France*. And that dealt with the founding of the Statue of Liberty. It had a picture of Edouard-Rene [Lefebvre de Laboulaye], the Frenchman who came up with the idea of the Statue of Liberty. He was a political scientist; he was a French leader; he was a French parliamentarian; he wrote a three-volume history of the United States. But more important than that, Edouard-Rene Lefebvre de Laboulaye, who came up with the idea of the Statue of Liberty in 1865, was head of the French anti-slave society.

In 1865 people were not interested in immigration into the United States. In fact, the United States in the 1850s and 1860s had established a Know-Nothing Party; they did not want immigrants; they were against immigrants; and the immigrants that they were against were Papists, German and Irish Catholics. There was no prospect of bringing in immigrants from central, eastern and southern Europe; these were the unwashed masses. Eighteen-sixty-five was our period. Eighteen-sixty-five was when half a million black people, a quarter-million of them official Union army, navy troops—participated in the Civil War. [Word unclear] four million of their—four million of their compatriots—and then saving this nation.

The question of black folks getting into their history, starting to fight for liberty and struggling for what is right is not the question of disuniting America. It has been our struggle that has kept America united. It has been our struggle that has raised anew the liberties that this nation professes. It has been our struggle that has created the Fourteenth Amendment that became the amendment that the women could use and others could use, when they talk about the expansion of liberty in America.

America was founded by rich white men with property and power. It was founded on an affirmative-action program for rich white men with property and power. From the very beginning of the founding of these colonies, rich white men with property and power were given affirmative action and set-asides—whole land set aside for them to develop and whole people set aside to work it for free, including white folks who came as virtual slaves under indentured servitude. There was a set-aside and affirmative action for rich white folks with property and power in the beginning of this nation, and that tradition under the British and under the Dutch was maintained. And when independence was established, the independence was established, and the Constitution put in place in 1787 is a document of affirmative action for rich white folks with property and power.

Because we do not have the critical analysis we need—and that's why we need study groups, serious study groups for the adults and for the teachers—we continue to go around talking about there was a three-fifths clause put in the Constitution and we have three-fifths the rights of white folks. You have no rights in the American constitutional frame of reference. Women have no significant rights. The Constitution does not speak to them and poor whites, men, did not have any significant rights in the Constitution. The Constitution speaks to rich white

"America was founded by rich white men with property and power. . . . The Constitution . . . is a document of affirmative action for rich white folks with property and power."

men with property and power. It is there for you to read with your eyes open and put on to it.

Three-fifths clause and affirmative action are set aside for the slave owners. A slave owner who had two hundred of our peoples enslaved, had three-fifths more votes, voting power for them, than a normal rich white man. That's democracy? That's oligarchy. But we still posture our position of democracy as part of the founding process. Democracy came as we struggled to widen the American process to include the most deprived and dispossessed of the people in the system. Our struggle has been the heroic struggle. It's an enormous struggle and you can only tap into it, if you only knew it. This struggle of our people collectively, for freedom, justice. We have been the liberating people force in this nation. From day one when we arrived.

And that Constitution: read it again, two places where it mentions black folks is the three-fifths clause. And then you've got this question of 1808. Eighteen-hundred-eight is the set-aside for rich white men of property and power, the Jeffersons, the Washingtons and the Monroes. A set aside, instead of ending slavery in 1787, which they could have done, if they were lovers of freedom, justice and equality. Instead of ending the slave trade in 1787, which they could have done, if the Declaration of Independence meant anything to them, we are all men created, endowed by their Creator with certain inalienable rights, among these rights, liberty, pursuit of happiness. If they really believed that they could have instituted a constitution that destroyed these things as the French did. But they did not believe that, because the nation was founded by rich white men of property and power. They put the Constitution and Bill of Rights and everything together, so they set aside twenty years so they continued the slave trade, up until 1808. Set aside so rich white men with property and power to become what has been the basis of this nation. And then they beat up on us about affirmative action and set asides for what we contribute to Vietnam.

So you've got to have an analysis. That's what we're saying. Just let me give you this one frame of reference to show how this enormity of material can be processed in a way to make it work for you. And then we'll have the question-answer period.

I've come up with a formulation which I call "pyramid analysis." And I put this available to the committee, the committee wanted it and that pyramid analysis, that you've got to be able to process the enormity of information about human experience. Using a pyramid as a model. It allows us to deal with the basic rule and understanding of human life and life on the planet and life in the universe and that's duality. Duality and polarity is a basic concept that has to be understood. The pyramidal framework gives us a chance to deal with that.

One polarity is what I call the thesis, the other polarity is what I call the antithesis. Between the polarities you have search for truth and knowledge which relates to duality and polarity. As you deal with the knowledge, breaking it down and analyzing between the polarities, then you synthesize it and you come up with critical thinking. You put a circle around it, it represents systems, external system. You put a circle inside the pyramid, you deal with internal system. Dealing with biology, basic simple biology, basic simple life. You have the female principle, the male principle. Interaction between the male principle and the female principle and this is what? The child. The synthesis becomes the child. In the human development, of the human process, you have the duality. Two hemispheres of the brain, two eyes, two nostrils, two lips, two lungs, two arms, two ova, two testes and so that question of duality is in our own existence. Then the question of the brain. The left side of the brain interacts with the right side of the brain and the synthesis becomes thinking. So the basic understanding of duality, polarity, is what we are talking about. When we see the human family and you don't have the worry about the information based.

We stand on science and history, science and history is on our side. Our secret weapon has arrived. And the secret weapon is books such as this: *Civilization or Barbarism.* Everybody should have that. It's a must. This was a book of a scholar, dealing with scholarship. Taking on the whole tradition of western European scholarship and he won the battle. Establishing what? Number one, the African origin of humanity. Number two, millions of years ago. In fact Dr. [Cheikh] Diop says there is only one human race and it's the African race. Everything else is a mutation off African genes. That's the scientific and historical data. That's what we stand on. Number two, you have the African evolution of science. A hundred thousand years ago when humankind wanted to disrupt the evolutionary process, developing fire, settle communities, learn to use tools, domesticating animals, domesticating plants. And it is that evolution that took place largely in the sun belt that produced: number three, the cradle of civilization in the Nile River valleys and the other river valleys of the world. When the ecology of the sun produces the ingredients for positive development. As so [Dr. Diop] has a concept which he has in his book, called the *Unity of Africa,* that you have a southern cradle, around what we can call "sun people," and you have the northern cradle, around what we can call "ice people." And the people [word unclear] around the world.

People are terribly upset. Dr. Jeffries has this theory of "ice people," "sun people." People call me from all around the world, Scotland, Australia. Dr. Jeffries, can we have some material on your "ice people, sun people"? Some woman called me from Kentucky or Tennessee, obviously a white Southerner. "Dr. Jeffries, I heard about your 'ice people, sun people,' and I think it's an interesting theory. In fact, I believe it. Can I get a copy of your work?"

Now, there's no "ice people, sun people" theory. What we had was a framework of analysis. We had a paradigm to organizing information. The white boy has given us a paradigm. Haves and have-nots. The haves is white folks. The have-nots is anybody that's not white. And that's ironic. Because even if the Africans have the gold, the diamonds, uranium, the platinum, the plutonium, the oil, they are considered the have-nots. Even if the white folks ain't got a pot to pee in, they are considered the haves. So, I mean, that paradigm doesn't hold water.

We have another paradigm, which is okay, nobody's criticizing it: First World and Third World. We don't even know what the Second World is. You know that the First World, the First World is white folks. And everything else comes after that. The first people, the First World were African people, people of color, sun peoples, and we stand on that. Everybody else comes after that. And we are the haves. We have had the beginning of the march of humankind. We are the mothers and fathers of civilization. We developed science, mathematics, philosophy. And we stand on that. All of that is in the work of Dr. Diop, Dr. Chester Williams, John Jackson's book. And this particular book.

So these are the things that you need to tap into. Now don't think you are going to get it and read it on a weekend. I'm telling you, you have to have some special processes to take place. This is a scientific document. This was designed to view with all of the B.S. that white folks have put up, the falsifications that they have put up. So you've got to take this slowly but surely. And over the years it may make sense to you. I'm telling people, take it and put in on your night table. Either put it on top of your Bible or move the Bible over. Or the Koran. Put it on the top of your night table. And then, the knowledge and information we have is such now that you are going to have to deal with the Bible in an African way. Most of you have been reluctant. But we are developing study groups and whatnot all around the country, in the churches. I came from Ft. Lauderdale, where they have study groups in the churches.

And one of the things that, we just had a visitor or house guest this past weekend. This is a brother who has produced this book that you

> ***"The first people . . . were African people, people of color, sun peoples, and we stand on that. Everybody else comes after that."***

have to get a hold of—I brought a number of them. We have them available for you. And you know, I know you save your money to buy some shirts and some, you know, and some patent leather shoes. But these are some of the things that you need to get. Now, this is a two-volume study. Expensive, but well worth it: *The Black Presence in the Bible,* by Rev. Walter McCray. The brother's very beautiful. A member of an organization, based in Chicago. Put a lot of work into putting the truth of the people of the Bible. The people of the Bible were not European. They were African or people of mixed African blood. And you have to begin to deal with that. In our lessons we will put the ten major historical figures in the Bible and all of their ten African wives. Each of them had an African wife. Now it's ironic that in Jewish tradition, in the orthodoxy that if you are an orthodox Jew, you cannot be a true Jew unless you pass through the woman's line. But isn't it ironic that in the Biblical text most of the great historic Jewish figures had African wives? So we've got to know that. And know what the implications are. And know it critically.

So we're talking about recapturing the truth of people. And it's not a question of negative self-esteem. Isn't it ironic that Miss Daisy and her people are running around talking about that "this is just self-esteem and feel-good curriculum"? What the hell do they have in place for white people now? And it's ironic because if you read the documents of the state of New York, and we have some of the documents for you and a sister has had, Jackie, has some of the documents coming from the state that you need to write to the state, the department of education, and get these documents and if you live in this area, you can walk right across the street and get them. They have these documents. In the Board of Regents, it says that there is, one of the goals is to develop the self esteem of each student, so that they can be motivated to be achievers. So how the hell can you be beating on us about our self-esteem? Particularly when in the culture of white racism, there is such a negative image of African people? Feel-good curriculum. What the hell do you think the existing curriculum is?

We learn about Washington and the cherry tree. I don't want to feel good or feel bad about Washington, I want to know about Washington and the enslavement process. I don't want to know about Jefferson and his Declaration of Independence in 1776. Let me know about the first draft in 1775 when he compromised and took out the indictment against slavery. And then let me know some more about Jefferson, his character and whatnot. Because when you talk about education you're talking about, again the dual process. Education is a dual process. One, the foundation of education is socializing function. In the socializing function you're talking about what? Character development. Africans understood that, so the educational process for the African started in the mind of the woman as she was a young girl growing up into womanhood. Being prepared to being the teachers of her, the product of her womb. So from zero to five the first foundations of education are established in the home. And so that's where character development has to be instilled—the socializing function.

And our value system is centered around what I call the "three Cs". Communal, cooperative and collective spiritual development. Seeing a unity spiritual in the universe. That's the value system of some people. Whether you talk about Native Americans or southern Asian. But next to this polarity, you have the polarity of tooling. The tooling function. So you have the socializing function, character development, in relationship to the tooling function which is skills development. And the tooling function is where you get the knowledge from the mathematics and the techniques, etc. But you need the two of them together in order to have a synthesized true education.

What the white boy has said is that the only thing significant is the skills function. So he tests on the skills function and then he decides whether we've had an education or not. Based upon tests. I'm here to tell you that test taking is no more than anything but testing test taking. I was in a Jewish fraternity in college. Most of you may not have known that. I spoke with one of my fraternity brothers Monday, Billy Rothchild, for dinner. I was the president of the Jewish fraternity. One hundred Jews and me and a couple of Christians. And the president of the Jewish fraternity was called a "rex." So I had to go through college as the rex, the King of the Jews. Now I managed it. But the most important thing about the fraternity was they had a system: that they knew how to take tests, they know how to put a system of support in place. They had the records of all the professors, they had the tests, they analyzed how they changed their questions from year to year to try to fool the students, we left nothing to chance. The Jewish fraternity won the scholarship trophy fourteen semesters in a row. The whole average of the fraternity was a Dean's List average, even dumb Jews made it, because there was a system of support.

My roommate was a black youngster from the football team, Dan Wooten from Cape May, New Jersey, he was the vice president. So in the 1950s at Lafayette College, the president of this Jewish fraternity was black, vice-president was black, two boys from New Jersey. Dan Wooten is now a medical doctor surgeon, UCLA Medical School, King Hospital in Los Angeles. And, of course, you know about Dr. J.

But people, other people have a system. The important thing I'm saying is that other people have a system. We have to put a system in place. It begins in the home. It should be in our communities, our fraternal orders, in our clubs. But we don't have that type of understanding. We are not playing the game of politics and education the way they should. As you look at this polarity again let me give you three things and I got to step into the wing.

The first and foremost principle is economics. Economics is basic, if you don't have economics you can't survive. Economics is related to ecology, because your economics is the gear to your ecology. The ecology of the river valleys of the world produced the first economic systems of plenty that allowed for civilizations and culture. The economy of the northern cradle, the economy of the ice, could not produce the type of surplus needed to survive. It produced barbarism.

That's why Diop's book, *Civilization or Barbarism,* makes some sense. In the river valleys of the world, civilization occurred. In the northern regions and other regions like the desert where the environment was negative and the ecology was difficult, then you had barbarity. This is a *Newsweek* article, November 10, 1986. Where you are beating on me about "ice people, sun people," what do they say here? Our ice age heritage, language, arts, fashion and the family. So we're trying to say that it's clear that what we've done is to synthesize the information. We have not created any concept of ice and sun. Ice and sun are very real and very scientific. We are sun people, people of color because of the sun. The melanin factor. Europeans have a lack of melanin and have lost a great deal of it because much of the European development has been in the caves of Europe where you do not need melanin. So the factor of the ice is a key factor in the development of the European biologically, culturally, economically, socially.

And what we are talking about is the values that are transmitted from ecologies. So this is the last thing that I want to leave with you: that your economy which is related to your ecology begets your sociology which is related to your politics. Economics is the productive capacity, politics is the management capacity. The ecological systems are related to your sociological systems. This duality of economics and politics, ecology and sociology has to be related and then you synthesize them and you have culture, the psychological dimension. The cement that keeps things together. Economics, politics and culture relate; as ecological and sociological and psychological dimensions relate. It is this relationship that we as African peoples have to work at and make work for us.

They have it all divided up. In fact, they tell us, don't worry about the economics, we'll take care of it. In fact, they bring people in our community to take care of it. Arabs, Vietnamese and other people. Don't worry about the economics, we'll even have some others to take care of it, when we can't take care of it. Then the politics. You get involved in politics. But just come at election time. We'll take care of who you should vote for, give you a little bit of money to work on the polls, but, you know, don't waste too much time to become involved in politics. But you can have culture. Become as black as you want. But if you only have culture and you've not hooked the economics and it's not related to your politics, then you do not have a system of development. You only have a system of survival. And what our educational omission tells us is, that we have to develop a system of development. And that means that we have to take our schools and make them work for us.

But we have to put the educational process in the community, in the homes. We have to tap into this enormity of knowledge and then you have to be prepared to tell the truth. We have to be prepared to say that we are not going to celebrate Columbus. That no African or Native American youngster should celebrate Columbus. You Italians, you Spanish can celebrate it if you will. But we are not prepared to deal with the devilishness of Columbus. And Mario Cuomo is not going to like it. But you going have the courage to have to tell him the truth.

So that's what it's all about. It's a political struggle; it's not just an economic struggle; it's not just economic cultural struggle; it's not just an educational struggle. It's economics because they want to keep that money. New York's budget, New York City's budget is seven to eight billion dollars. They don't want black folks messin' with that budget. So when they thought we were getting into the curriculum, they thought we were also talking about teacher training and other things, which we were. So immediately they said that's not your realm.

> ***"No African or Native American youngster should celebrate Columbus. . . . We are not prepared to deal with the devilishness of Columbus."***

And across the country, Bush wants to put in a new order, a new world order. That means they've got to have mind controls in the schools. And here we come with African-centered education and that's blown up their plans for mind control in the schools. Because African-centered education does not allow for the concept of rich white men with property and power dominating the world view of this planet. So what we have prepared for you and we have it in this packet here, and, unfortunately, I couldn't bring enough of them, but it includes some of the materials you need in terms of historical mentions of the struggle for an African-centered education. It includes the report, *Curriculum of Inclusion,* it's the new report. It includes the course outline by Dr. Clark, dealing with African history. Includes Noble's analysis of African-centered educational practice. It includes the multi-culture of the city of New York. And it includes documents such as the statement by our brother on educating the African child. So, this type of document and the books we do have available for you.

What we're saying is tap into them from the study groups. Start breaking the things down. See the connection between things. This book here by Diop has to be related to the book by Jackson. Do not try to even deal with Diop if you have not related to Jackson. And then you need to see the generations of resistance and struggle in Van Sertima's book, *Egypt Revisited.* [Edited by Ivan Van Sertima.] It's the new generation coming up. Dr. Asa Hilliard, and others that are complementing the work of Dr. Diop. We have to see generations of African resistance and scholarship. We stand on scholarship and science, we make no excuses about it.

But the beauty of our experience is no matter where you start, your history is like nobody else's history. If you deal with Africans and science and technology after the slavery period. And that's what we are trying to say. And just to give it to you in one sentence. This is what we're trying to say. They've B.S.'d up and down the world about what we are saying. What we are saying: take this system again. The thesis would be the founding of America. The Anglo-Saxon elite model. The antithesis would be the other America, all the rest of us. You have to relate the Anglo-Saxon elite model with the multi-culture pluralistic model to get the synthesis of what truly was America. And that's what we're calling for in the curriculum of inclusion.

We also said you can apply it into the science area. For example, at this polarity you might have an elite Anglo-Saxon model: Benjamin Franklin, he was dealing with science, he had an almanac. But over in the pluralistic multicultural model, African centered you have: Benjamin Banneker, living at the same time, knowing each other, dealing with inventions and almanacs. And Banneker being part of that contribution of Africa to the unity of this nation which led to the building of Washington, D.C. When the Frenchmen got disgusted and left, they had to tap into Benjamin Banneker. Benjamin Banneker represents more than Franklin. He represents a principal struggle for freedom, justice and equality. And he challenged Thomas Jefferson in his beliefs in the inferiority of African peoples, even though Thomas Jefferson never had a white woman by his side after the white wife died in 1782 and for the next twenty years as he was ambassador to France, secretary of state, president of the United States, Jefferson only had a black woman by his side, Sally Hemmings. And we need to understand the principled stand that our people represent as opposed to a Thomas Jefferson, because Thomas Jefferson never freed any of the children that he had with Sally Hemmings or Sally Hemmings herself and that's not a principled liberator or freedom lover in my book. When a Banneker challenged Jefferson, so that, what we said, put that in the history books. That's a fantastic dialogue. Of someone up from an enslaved population, although Banneker's parents were free, challenging the greatest of American spiritician, etc.

But more than that. Put it in the books that the people who really fought for freedom, justice and equality in the revolutionary war on the principle basis were black folks. They fought on both sides. They fought on the British side; they fought on the American side. They answered the call for freedom. Washington, Jefferson and others were writing about it and trying to protect the slave system. Black folks were fighting for freedom.

But then you not only have the Bannekers, you have the situation when you have Thomas Edison on the Anglo side. And on the pluralistic side you have Lewis Latimer, who was his partner. And Latimer, carbon-filament invention helped to make the light bulb functional. Plus they were together for twenty or thirty years. So you have to have a relationship with Latimer, it's legitimate, it's very real.

Then you can put Granville Woods, on the black side and put Alexander Graham Bell on the white side. They were involved with communications. But Granville Woods was a principled black man, who said, "I'm not going to be bought off by a white man," and him and his brother set up the Woods Electric Company out in Ohio.

In other words, this is the story. This is pre-slavery. The waves of immigrants ain't come in yet. You ain't got the waves of Jews, the waves of Italians, the waves of Greeks, waves of Russians. This is us dealing with the Anglos, trying to establish the foundation of America's technology and its industrial development. And here you have an interesting development that is very real. Lewis Latimer worked with Edison. Granville Woods took Edison to court two times for stealing his patents and won. Now that's got to be in everybody's history book. That that black man took the white leader of American industrial development to court and won.

And these are the type of things we're saying you need to put in the history book. That's what real inclusion is. But for us the real inclusion has to be to put this stuff in our homes, in our communities. And then walk it into the schools. And then we don't have to worry about Miss Daisy.

The uproar that followed Jeffries's speech included demands that he resign or that City College take action against him. Eventually, college officials removed him as chairman of the black studies department, ostensibly for being a poor administrator. (As a tenured professor, he could not be dismissed from the faculty without a major battle.) Jeffries responded with a lawsuit against the school claiming that his removal from the chairmanship really stemmed from his comments about Jews and whites. A New York City jury agreed, and in May 1993, it ordered City College to pay him $400,000 in damages for violating his constitutional right to free speech. He was reinstated as head of the black studies department in the fall of 1993.

But in November 1994, the United States Supreme Court—citing a ruling it had made the previous May that gave public employers greater freedom to fire employees for what they say—overturned the decision in Jeffries' case and referred it back to a U.S. Appeals Court in New York City for further consideration. In April 1995, the Appeals Court upheld his dismissal from the chairmanship of the black studies department. Jeffries has said that he will appeal.

SOURCES

Commentary, "The Jeffries Affair," March, 1992, pp. 34-38.

Detroit Free Press, "Justices Reopen Case on the Cost of Speech," November 15, 1994, p. 6A; "Today's Lecture, Tomorrow's Court Case," May 21, 1995.

Detroit News, "Appeals Court Must Reconsider Case of Black Professor Demoted for Anti-Semitic Remarks," November 15, 1994, p. 8A.

Nation, "Bitter History," September 9, 1991, pp. 251-252; "Blacks and Jews," September 9, 1991, pp. 252-253.

New Republic, "Dr. Uncool J," March 2, 1992, pp. 11-12; "Speech Defect," June 14, 1993.

New York, "Doctor J," September 2, 1991, pp. 32-37; "He's Back!," May 24, 1993, pp. 10-11.

New York Newsday, "Suspicion on Racism Rift," August 19, 1991.

New York Times, "CUNY Professor Criticizes Jews," August 6, 1991, p. B1; "For Jeffries, a Penchant for Disputes," September 7, 1991.

Time, "The Provocative Professor," August 26, 1991, pp. 19-20.

James Weldon Johnson

1871–1938

African American writer, educator, diplomat, and civil rights activist

Although he is probably best remembered as the author of the lyrics to "Lift Every Voice and Sing," James Weldon Johnson was a man whose interests and talents spanned many different fields. In addition to his noteworthy contributions as a writer of both poetry and prose, for example, he served his country as a diplomat, helped shape the size and agenda of the National Association for the Advancement of Colored People (NAACP) during a critical decade in its history, and ended his career in the company of a number of distinguished scholars as a professor at Fisk University. Neither a radical nor a conservative, he adopted a moderate approach to improving the lot of African Americans that acknowledged and condemned the existing inequities while advocating realistic and practical ways to overcome them.

Johnson was born and raised in Jacksonville, Florida, one of two sons of a resort hotel waiter and his schoolteacher wife. He received both his secondary and college education at Georgia's Atlanta University, then returned to his hometown in 1894 to serve for the next seven years as principal of the local grammar school for black children. During this same period, he also studied law and in 1898 became the first black admitted to the county bar.

When he was not busy with his duties as a principal and a practicing attorney, Johnson devoted himself to writing, focusing mainly on prose pieces such as the series of editorials that appeared in a short-lived newspaper he launched in 1895. He tried his hand at poetry, too, and in 1900 produced "Lift Every Voice and Sing." Set to music by his younger brother, J. Rosamond Johnson, it eventually achieved renown as "the Negro National Anthem."

In 1902, the Johnson brothers escaped from the increasingly repressive atmosphere in the South and headed to New York City. There they enjoyed great success as composers of a number of popular songs, many of which were featured in some of the notable musical comedies of the day. Their fame brought both men into social and professional contact with many influential people, and James Weldon Johnson in particular took advantage of every opportunity that came his way. He immersed himself in literary studies, attending classes at Columbia University to learn more about the literature of the theater. He also became involved in

Republican politics as a supporter of presidential candidate Teddy Roosevelt and allied himself with an old acquaintance, Booker T. Washington, who was at that time the best-known and most respected black leader in America. This relationship in turn led to Johnson's selection for the diplomatic post of U.S. consul to Venezuela in 1906, thus marking the beginning of yet another phase of his career.

Johnson served as consul in Venezuela and then in Nicaragua until 1913, when he resigned from the diplomatic service following the victory of Democrat Woodrow Wilson in the 1912 presidential election. During his tenure, however, he was able to devote a fair amount of his time to writing. In 1912 came the first publication of his novel The Autobiography of an Ex-Colored Man, *which met with only modest success until it was re-released to greater acclaim in 1927. On January 1, 1913, his poem "Fifty Years" appeared in the* New York Times *and was highly regarded by readers and critics alike.*

In 1914, Johnson became editor of the New York Age *newspaper. Over the next ten years, he produced a number of much-praised editorials that revealed his ability to bridge the competing ideologies of the day: On the one hand, he took a rather militant stance on racial pride and urged African Americans to use the press to help in the fight for civil rights. On the other hand, he supported the conservative view that blacks needed to shoulder most of the responsibility for overcoming their inferior position in U.S. society and improve their mental and moral fitness in order to achieve equality with whites.*

During this same period, Johnson also became involved with the National Association for the Advancement of Colored People (NAACP), first as an organizer of new branches in the South and then as the group's general secretary beginning in 1920. Under his direction, the NAACP dramatically increased its membership and effectiveness as a champion of civil rights for African Americans. Johnson personally took up the fight against lynching and repeatedly denounced the policies of a nation that saw no hypocrisy in calling on its black citizens to fight for democracy overseas while subjecting them to hostility and increasingly restrictive conditions at home. One such occasion was in New York City on March 10, 1923, at a dinner honoring then-Congressman Fiorello La Guardia. In his address, reprinted here from Negro Orators and Their Orations *(Association for the Study of Negro Life and History, 1925; reprinted, Russell & Russell, 1969), Johnson specifically attacked the practice of making it difficult or impossible for African Americans to exercise their right to vote.*

Ladies and gentlemen: For some time since I have had growing apprehensions about any subject—especially the subject of a speech—that contained the word "democracy." The word "democracy" carries so many awe-inspiring implications. As the keyword of the subject of an address it may be the presage of an outpour of altitudinous and platitudinous expressions regarding "the most free and glorious government of the most free and glorious people that the world has ever seen." On the other hand, it may hold up its sleeve, if you will permit such a figure, a display of abstruse and recondite theorizations or hypotheses of democracy as a system of government. In choosing between either of these evils it is difficult to decide which is the lesser.

Indeed, the wording of my subject gave me somewhat more concern than the speech. I am not sure that it contains the slightest idea of what I shall attempt to say; but if the wording of my subject is loose it only places upon me

James Weldon Johnson

greater reason for being more specific and definite in what I shall say. This I shall endeavor to do; at the same time, however, without being so confident or so cocksure as an old preacher I used to listen to on sundry Sundays when I taught school one summer down in the backwoods of Georgia, sometimes to my edification and often to my amazement.

On one particular Sunday, after taking a rather cryptic text, he took off his spectacles and laid them on the pulpit, closed the Bible with a bang, and said, "Brothers and sisters, this morning I intend to explain the inexplainable, to find out the indefinable, to ponder over the imponderable, and to unscrew the inscrutable."

It is one of the commonplaces of American thought that we have a democracy based upon the free will of the governed. The popular idea of the strength of this democracy is that it is founded upon the fact that every American citizen, through the ballot, is a ruler in his own right; that every citizen of age and outside of jail or the insane asylum has the undisputed right to determine through his vote by what laws he shall be governed and by whom these laws shall be enforced.

I could be cynical or flippant and illustrate in how many ways this popular idea is a fiction, but it is not my purpose to deal in *cleverisms*. I wish to bring to your attention seriously a situation, a condition, which not only runs counter to the popular conception of democracy in America but which runs counter to the fundamental law upon which that democracy rests and which, in addition, is a negation of our principles of government and a menace to our institutions.

Without any waste of words, I come directly to a condition which exists in that section of our country which we call "the South," where millions of American citizens are denied both the right to vote and the privilege of qualifying themselves to vote. I refer to the wholesale disfranchisement of Negro citizens. There is no need at this time of going minutely into the methods employed to bring about this condition or into the reasons given as justification for those methods. Neither am I called upon to give proof of my general statement that millions of Negro citizens in the South are disfranchised. It is no secret. There are the published records of state constitutional conventions in which the whole subject is set forth with brutal frankness. The purpose of these state constitutional conventions is stated over and over again, that purpose being to exclude from the right of franchise the Negro, however literate, and to include the white man, however illiterate.

The press of the South, public men in public utterances, and representatives of those states in Congress, have not only admitted these facts but have boasted of them. And so we have it as an admitted and undisputed fact that there are upwards of four million Negroes in the South who are denied the right to vote but who in any of the great northern, midwestern or western states would be allowed to vote or would at least have the privilege of qualifying themselves to vote.

Now, nothing is further from me than the intention to discuss this question either from an anti-South point of view or from a pro-Negro point of view. It is my intention to put it before you purely as an American question, a question in which is involved the political life of the whole country.

Let us first consider this situation as a violation, not merely a violation but a defiance, of the Constitution of the United States. The Fourteenth and Fifteenth Amendments to the Constitution taken together express so plainly that a grammar school boy can understand it that the Negro is created a citizen of the United States and that as such he is entitled to all the rights of every other citizen and that those rights, specifically among them the right to vote, shall not be denied or abridged by the United States or by any state. This is the expressed meaning of these amendments in spite of all the sophistry and fallacious pretense which have been invoked by the courts to overcome it.

There are some, perhaps even here, who feel that it is no more serious a matter to violate or defy one amendment to the constitution than another. Such persons will have in mind the Eighteenth Amendment. This is true in a strictly legal sense, but any sort of analysis will show that violation of the two Civil War Amendments strikes deeper. As important as the Eighteenth Amendment may be, it is not fundamental; it contains no grant of rights to the citizen nor any requirement of service from him. It is rather a sort of welfare regulation for his personal conduct and for his general moral uplift.

But the two Civil War Amendments are grants of citizenship rights and a guarantee of protection in those rights, and therefore their observation is fundamental and vital not only to the citizen but to the integrity of the government.

We may next consider it as a question of political franchise equality between the states. We need not here go into a list of figures. A few examples will strike the difference:

In the elections of 1920 it took 82,492 votes in Mississippi to elect two senators and eight representatives. In Kansas it took 570,220 votes to elect exactly the same representation. Another illustration from the statistics of the same election shows that one vote in Louisiana has fifteen times the political power of one vote in Kansas.

> ***"... the argument is still made that the Negro is ignorant, illiterate, venal, inferior; and, therefore ... he must be debarred from the polls."***

In the Congressional elections of 1918 the total vote for the ten representatives from the State of Alabama was 62,345, while the total vote for ten representatives in Congress from Minnesota was 299,127, and the total vote in Iowa, which has ten representatives, was 316,377.

In the presidential election of 1916 the states of Alabama, Arkansas, Georgia, Louisiana, Mississippi, North Carolina, South Carolina, Tennessee, Texas and Virginia cast a total vote for the presidential candidates of 1,870,209. In Congress these states have a total of 104 representatives and 126 votes in the electoral college. The State of New York alone cast a total vote for presidential candidates of 1,706,354, a vote within 170,000 of all the votes cast by the above states, and yet New York has only 43 representatives and 45 votes in the electoral college.

What becomes of our democracy when such conditions of inequality as these can be brought about through chicanery, the open violation of the law and defiance of the Constitution?

But the question naturally arises, What if there is violation of certain clauses of the Constitution; what if there is an inequality of political power among the states? All this may be justified by necessity.

In fact, the justification is constantly offered. The justification goes back and makes a long story. It is grounded in memories of the Reconstruction period. Although most of those who were actors during that period have long since died, and although there is a new South and a new Negro, the argument is still made that the Negro is ignorant, the Negro is illiterate, the Negro is venal, the Negro is inferior; and, therefore, for the preservation of civilized government in the South, he must be debarred from the polls. This argument does not take into account the fact that the restrictions are not against ignorance, illiteracy and venality, because by the very practices by which intelligent, decent Negroes are debarred, ignorant and illiterate white men are included.

Is this pronounced desire on the part of the South for an enlightened franchise sincere, and what has been the result of these practices during the past forty years? What has been the effect socially, intellectually and politically, on the South? In all three of these vital phases of life the South is, of all sections of the country, at the bottom. Socially, it is that section of the country where public opinion allows it to remain the only spot in the civilized world—no, more than that, we may count in the blackest spots of Africa and the most unfrequented islands of the sea—it is a section where public opinion allows it to remain the only spot on the earth where a human being may be publicly burned at the stake.

And what about its intellectual and political life? As to intellectual life I can do nothing better than quote from Mr. H.L. Mencken, himself a Southerner. In speaking of the intellectual life of the South, Mr. Mencken says:

> *It is, indeed, amazing to contemplate so vast a vacuity. One thinks of the interstellar spaces, of the colossal reaches of the now mythical ether. One could throw into the South France, Germany and Italy, and still have room for the British Isles. And yet, for all its size and all its wealth and all the 'progress' it babbles of, it is almost as sterile, artistically, intellectually, culturally, as the Sahara Desert. . . . If the whole of the late Confederacy were to be engulfed by a tidal wave tomorrow, the effect on the civilized minority of men in the world would be but little greater than that of a flood on the Yang-tse-kiang. It would be impossible in all history to match so complete a drying-up of a civilization. In all that section there is not a single poet, not a serious historian, not a creditable composer, not a critic good or bad, not a dramatist dead or alive.*

In a word, it may be said that this whole section where, at the cost of the defiance of the Constitution, the perversion of law, the stultification of men's consciousness, injustice and violence upon a weaker group, the "purity" of the ballot has been preserved and the right to vote restricted to only lineal survivors of Lothrop Stoddard's mystical Nordic supermen—that intellectually it is dead and politically it is rotten.

If this experiment in super-democracy had resulted in one one-hundredth of what was promised, there might be justification for it, but the result has been to make the South a section not only in which Negroes are denied the right to vote, but one in which white men dare not express their honest political opinions. Talk about political corruption through the buying of votes, here is political corruption which makes a white man fear to express a divergent political opinion. The actual and total result of this practice has been not only the disfranchisement of the Negro but the disfranchisement of the white man. The figures which I quoted a few moments ago prove that not only Negroes are denied the right to vote but that white men fail to exercise it; and the latter condition is directly dependent upon the former.

The whole condition is intolerable and should be abolished. It has failed to justify itself even upon the grounds which it is claimed made it necessary. Its results and its tendencies make it more dangerous and more damaging than anything which might result from an ignorant and illiterate electorate. How this iniquity might be abolished is, however, another story.

I said that I did not intend to present this subject either as anti-South or pro-Negro, and I repeat that I have not wished to speak with anything that approached bitterness toward the South.

Indeed, I consider the condition of the South unfortunate, more than unfortunate. The South is in a state of superstition which makes it see ghosts and bogeymen, ghosts which are the creation of its own mental processes.

With a free vote in the South the specter of Negro domination would vanish into thin air. There would naturally follow a breaking up of the South into two parties. There would be political light, political discussion, the right to differences of opinion, and the Negro vote would naturally divide itself. No other procedure would be probable. The idea of a solid party, a minority party at that, is inconceivable.

But perhaps the South will not see the light. Then, I believe, in the interest of the whole country, steps should be taken to compel compliance with the Constitution, and that should be done through the enforcement of the Fourteenth Amendment, which calls for a reduction in representation in proportion to the number of citizens in any state denied the right to vote.

And now I cannot sit down after all without saying one word for the group of which I am a member.

The Negro in the matter of the ballot demands only that he should be given the right as an American citizen to vote under the identical qualifications required of other citizens. He cares not how high those qualifications are made whether they include the ability to read and write, or the possession of five hundred dollars, or a knowledge of the Einstein Theory—just so long as these qualifications are impartially demanded of white men and black men.

In this controversy over which have been waged battles of words and battles of blood, where does the Negro himself stand?

The Negro in the matter of the ballot demands only that he be given his right as an American citizen. He is justified in making this demand because of his undoubted Americanism, an Americanism which began when he first set foot on the shores of this country more than three hundred years ago, antedating even the Pilgrim Fathers; an Americanism which has woven him into the woof and warp of the country and which has impelled him to play his part in every war in which the country has been engaged, from the Revolution down to the late World War.

Through his whole history in this country he has worked with patience, and in spite of discouragement he has never turned his back on the light. Whatever may be his shortcomings, however slow may have been his progress, however disappointing may have been his achievements, he has never consciously sought the backward path. He has always kept his face to the light and continued to struggle forward and upward in spite of obstacles, making his humble contributions to the common prosperity and glory of our land. And it is his land. With conscious pride the Negro can say :

This land is ours by right of birth,
This land is ours by right of toil;
We helped to turn its virgin earth,
Our sweat is in its fruitful soil.

Where once the tangled forest stood,—
Where flourished once rank weed and thorn,—
Behold the path-traced, peaceful wood,
The cotton white, the yellow corn.

To gain these fruits that have been earned,
To hold these fields that have been won,
Our arms have strained, our backs have burned
Bent bare beneath a ruthless sun.

That banner which is now the type
Of victory on field and flood—
Remember, its first crimson stripe
Was dyed by Attucks' willing blood.

And never yet has come the cry—
When that fair flag has been assailed—
For men to do, for men to die,
That we have faltered or have failed.

The Negro stands as the supreme test of the civilization, the Christianity and the common decency of the American people. It is upon the answer demanded of America today by the Negro that there depends the fulfillment or the failure of democracy in America. I believe that that answer will be the right and just answer.I believe that the spirit in which American democracy was founded, though often turned aside and often thwarted, can never be defeated or destroyed but that ultimately it will triumph.

If American democracy cannot stand the test of giving to any citizen who measures up to the qualifications required of others the full rights and privileges of American citizenship, then we had just as well abandon that democracy in name as in deed. If the Constitution of the United States cannot extend the arm of protection around the weakest and humblest of American citizens as around the strongest and proudest, then it is not worth the paper it is written on.

Throughout the 1920s, Johnson maintained an extremely busy work schedule that left him ill from exhaustion on several occasions. In addition to his efforts on behalf of the NAACP, he continued to write magazine articles, pamphlets, poems, and several well-regarded nonfiction books, such as The Book of American Negro Spirituals, The Second Book of American Negro Spirituals, God's Trombones: Seven Negro Sermons in Verse, *and* Black Manhattan. *In 1930, not long after a health-related leave of absence, Johnson decided to retire from the NAACP and accept a professorship in creative literature and writing at Fisk University. While he had looked upon his appointment as an opportunity to pursue a more relaxed lifestyle, he remained almost as busy as ever; he not only taught, he continued to write, lecture, and participate in the civil rights movement. He died in 1938 as a result of injuries received in an automobile accident.*

SOURCES

Books

Boulware, Marcus H., *The Oratory of Negro Leaders, 1900–1968,* Negro Universities Press, 1969.

Foner, Philip S., editor, *The Voice of Black America: Major Speeches by Negroes in the United States, 1797–1971,* Simon & Schuster, 1972.

Johnson, James Weldon, *Along This Way* (autobiography), Viking, 1933, reprinted, Da Capo, 1973.

———, *Negro Americans, What Now?,* Viking, 1934, reprinted, Da Capo, 1973.

Levy, Eugene, *James Weldon Johnson: Black Leader, Black Voice,* Chicago University Press, 1973.

Tolbert-Rouchaleau, Jane, *James Weldon Johnson,* Chelsea House, 1988.

Wilson, Sondra Kathryn, editor, *The Selected Writings of James Weldon Johnson,* two volumes, Oxford University Press, 1995.

Woodson, Carter G., editor, *Negro Orators and Their Orations,* Association for the Study of Negro Life and History, 1925, reprinted, Russell & Russell, 1969.

Periodicals

Christian Century, July 13, 1938, p. 860.

Nation, July 2, 1938, p. 4; July 9, 1938, p. 44.

New York Times, June 28, 1938, p. 18.

Newsweek, July 4, 1938, p. 2.

Time, July 4, 1938, p. 43.

Mordecai Wyatt Johnson

1890–1976

African American minister, educator, and human rights activist

Mordecai Wyatt Johnson's stature in African American history rests largely on his thirty years of service to Howard University as its first black president. A native of Tennessee, he was the son of a Baptist minister. He received his education at Morehouse College, the University of Chicago, Rochester Theological Seminary, and Harvard University. After leaving the seminary, Johnson served as a pastor for nine years at a Baptist church in Charleston, West Virginia, and also taught at Morehouse and Howard before assuming the presidency of the latter in 1926.

When Johnson took on his new role, he faced a formidable task; the struggling institution was little more than a cluster of unaccredited departments and programs that commanded virtually no respect in the academic world. Under his leadership, however, Howard quickly shed its old image and came to be recognized as one of the country's finest universities. Only two years into his tenure, his spectacular success at raising funds, revamping the curriculum, and attracting students and faculty earned him the NAACP's highest award, the Spingarn Medal. At the same time, Johnson was gaining a reputation as an outstanding orator. He probably reached his peak during the 1930s and 1940s when, as a fervent supporter of Franklin D. Roosevelt, he took every opportunity to urge black audiences to support their president's New Deal programs. Later, after World War II, Johnson was one of several prominent African Americans who attended the conference at which the United Nations charter was drawn up and approved. Through the years, he made the same demand—racial justice for minorities, not only those living in the United States but oppressed people all over the world.

Of the many speeches Johnson gave throughout his career, the one that is without a doubt his most famous dates back to June 22, 1922. On that day, he stepped up to the podium to deliver the commencement address for the graduating class of Harvard University Divinity School. In his speech, entitled "The Faith of the American Negro," Johnson discussed the profound sense of disappointment, betrayal, and frustration many blacks felt as a result of their experiences both during and after World War I. As both soldiers and defense-plant workers, they faced outright discrimination, hostility, and prejudice. Consequently, the years *immediately following the war were some of the bloodiest and most chaotic in American history as race riots rocked the country and many blacks found hope in the words of separatist leaders such as Marcus Garvey and his back-to-Africa movement. Johnson's remarks on the situation were hailed at the time as the most notable comments by an African American since Booker T. Washington's "Atlanta Compromise" address of 1895. They were published in* Nation *magazine of July 19, 1922.*

Since their emancipation from slavery the masses of American Negroes have lived by the strength of a simple but deeply moving faith. They have believed in the love and providence of a just and holy God; they have believed in the principles of democracy and in the righteous purpose of the federal government; and they have believed in the disposition of the American people as a whole and in the long run to be fair in all their dealings.

In spite of disfranchisement and peonage, mob violence and public contempt, they have kept this faith and have allowed themselves to hope with the optimism of Booker T. Washington that in proportion as they grew in intelligence, wealth and self-respect they should win the confidence and esteem of their fellow white Americans, and should gradually acquire the responsibilities and privileges of full American citizenship.

In recent years, and especially since the Great War, this simple faith has suffered a widespread disintegration. When the United States government set forth its war aims, called upon Negro soldiers to stand by the colors and Negro civilians, men, women and children, to devote their labor and earnings to the cause, and when the war shortage of labor permitted a quarter million Negroes to leave the former slave states for the better conditions of the North, the entire Negro people experienced a profound sense of spiritual release. For the first time since emancipation they found themselves comparatively free to sell their labor on the open market for a living wage, found themselves launched on a great world enterprise with a chance to vote in a real and decisive way, and, best of all, in the heat of the struggle they found themselves bound with other Americans in the spiritual fellowship of a common cause.

When they stood on the height of this exalted experience and looked down on their prewar poverty, impotence and spiritual isolation, they realized as never before the depth of the harm they had suffered, and there arose in them a mighty hope that in some way the war would work a change in their situation. For a time indeed it seemed that their hope would be realized. For when the former slave states saw their labor leaving for the North, they began to reflect upon the treatment they had been accustomed to give the Negro, and they decided that it was radically wrong. Newspapers and public orators everywhere expressed this change of sentiment, set forth the wrongs in detail, and urged immediate improvement. And immediate improvement came. Better educational facilities were provided here and there, words of appreciation for the worth and spirit of the Negro as a citizen began to be uttered, and public committees arose to inquire into his grievances and to lay out programs for setting these grievances right. The colored people in these states had never experienced such collective goodwill, and many of them were so grateful and happy that they actually prayed for the prolongation of the war.

At the close of the war, however, the Negro's hopes were suddenly dashed to the ground. Southern newspapers began at once to tell the Negro soldiers that the war was over and the sooner they forgot it the better. "Pull off your uniform," they said, "find the place you had before the war, and stay in it." "Act like a Negro should act," said one newspaper, "work like a Negro should work, talk like a Negro should talk, study like a Negro should study. Dismiss all ideas of independency or of being lifted up to the plane of the white man. Understand the necessity of keeping a Negro's place." In connection with such admonitions there came the great collective attacks on Negro life and property in Washington, Chicago, Omaha, Elaine and Tulsa. There came also the increasing boldness of lynchers who advertised their purpos-

Mordecai Wyatt Johnson

es in advance and had their photographs taken around the burning bodies of their victims. There came vain appeals by the colored people to the president of the United States and to the houses of Congress. And finally there came the reorganization and rapid growth of the Ku Klux Klan.

The swift succession and frank brutality of all this was more than the Negro people could bear. Their simple faith and hope broke down. Multitudes took weapons in their hands and fought back violence with bloody resistance. "If we must die," they said, "it is well that we die fighting." And the Negro American world, looking on their deed with no light of hope to see by, said, "It is self-defense, it is the law of nature, of man, and of God; and it is well."

From those terrible days until this day the Negro's faith in the righteous purpose of the federal government has sagged. Some have laid the blame on the parties in power. Some have laid it elsewhere. But all the colored people, in every section of the United States, believe that there is something wrong, and not accidentally wrong, at the very heart of the government.

Some of our young men are giving up the Christian religion, thinking that their fathers were fools to have believed it so long. One group among us repudiates entirely the simple faith of former days. It would put no trust in God, no trust in democracy, and would entertain no hope for betterment under the present form of government. It believes that the United States government is through and through controlled by selfish capitalists who have no fundamental goodwill for Negroes or for any sort of laborers whatever. In their publications and on the platform the members of this group urge the colored man to seek his salvation by alliance with the revolutionary labor movement of America and the world.

"All the colored people, in every section of the United States, believe that there is something wrong . . . at the very heart of the government."

Another and larger group among us believes in religion and believes in the principles of democracy, but not in the white man's religion and not in the white man's democracy. It believes that the creed of the former slave states is the tacit creed of the whole nation, and that the Negro may never expect to acquire economic, political and spiritual liberty in America. This group has held congresses with representatives from the entire Negro world, to lay the foundations of a black empire, a black religion, and a black culture; it has organized the provisional Republic of Africa, set going a multitude of economic enterprises, instituted branches of its organization wherever Negroes are to be found, and binds them together with a newspaper ably edited in two languages.

Whatever one may think of these radical movements and their destiny, one thing is certain: they are homegrown fruits, with roots deep sprung in a world of black American suffering. Their power lies in the appeal which they make to the Negro to find a way out of his trouble by new and self-reliant paths. The larger masses of the colored people do not belong to these more radical movements. They retain their belief in the Christian God, they love their country, and hope to work out their salvation within its bounds. But they are completely disillusioned. They see themselves surrounded on every hand by a sentiment of antagonism which does not intend to be fair. They see themselves partly reduced to peonage, shut out from labor unions, forced to an inferior status before the courts, made subjects of public contempt, lynched and mobbed with impunity, and deprived of the ballot, their only means of social defense. They see this antagonistic sentiment consolidated in the places of power in the former slave states and growing by leaps and bounds in the North and West. They know that it is gradually reducing them to an economic, political and social caste. And they are now no longer able to believe with Dr. Booker T. Washington, or with any other man, that their own efforts after intelligence, wealth, and self-respect can in any wise avail to deliver them from these conditions unless they have the protection of a just and beneficent public policy in keeping with American ideals. With one voice, therefore, from pulpit and from press, and from the humblest walks of life, they are sending up a cry of pain and petition such as is heard today among the citizens of no other civilized nation in the world. They are asking for the protection of life, for the security of property, for the liberation of their peons, for the freedom to sell their labor on the open market, for a human being's chance in the courts, for a better system of public education, and for the boon of the ballot. They ask, in short, for public equality under the protection of the federal government.

Their request is sustained by every sentiment of humanity and by every holy ideal for which this nation stands. The time has come when the elemental justice called for in this petition should be embodied in a public policy initiated by the federal government and continuously supervised by a commission of that government representing the faith and will of the whole American people.

The Negro people of America have been with us here for three hundred years. They have cut our forests, tilled our fields, built our railroads, fought our battles, and in all of their trials until now they have manifested a simple faith, a grateful heart, a cheerful spirit, and an undivided loyalty to the nation that has been a thing of beauty to behold. Now they have come to the place where their faith can no longer feed on the bread of repression and violence. They ask for the bread of liberty, of public equality, and public responsibility. It must not be denied them.

We are now sufficiently far removed from the Civil War and its animosities to see that such elemental justice may be given to the Negro with entire goodwill and helpfulness toward the former slave states. We have already had one long attempt to build a wealth and culture on the backs of slaves. We found that it was a costly experiment, paid for at last with the blood of our best sons. There are some among our citizens who would turn their backs on history and repeat that experiment, and to their terrible heresy they would convert our entire great community. By every sacred bond of love for them we must not yield, and we must no longer leave them alone with their experiment. The faith of our whole nation must be brought to their support until such time as it is clear to them that their former slaves can be made both fully free and yet their faithful friends.

Across the seas the darker peoples of the earth are rising from their long sleep and are searching this Western world for light. Our Christian missionaries are among them. They are asking these missionaries: Can the Christian religion bind this multicolored world in bonds of brotherhood? We of all nations are best prepared to answer that question, and to be their moral inspiration and their friend. For we have the world's problem of race relationships here in crucible, and by strength of our American faith we have made some encouraging progress in its solution. If the fires of this faith are kept burning around that crucible, what comes out of it is able to place these United States in the spiritual leadership of all humanity. When the Negro cries with pain from his deep hurt and lays his petition for elemental justice before the nation, he is calling upon the American people to kindle anew about the crucible of race relationships the fires of American faith.

SOURCES

Books

Boulware, Marcus H., *The Oratory of Negro Leaders: 1900-1968,* Negro Universities Press, 1969.

Foner, Philip S., editor, *The Voice of Black America: Major Speeches by Negroes in the United States, 1797-1971,* Simon & Schuster, 1972.

Woodson, Carter G., *Negro Orators and Their Orations,* Associated Publishers, 1925.

Periodicals

Nation, "The Faith of the American Negro," July 19, 1922, pp. 64-65.

Barbara Jordan

1936–

African American politician and educator

A native of Houston, Texas, Barbara Jordan was the youngest of three daughters in a poor family. Both of her parents expected her to work hard and excel academically, thus instilling in her a determination to be the best. She first exercised her considerable oratory skills as a member of her high school debate team. She continued her involvement in public speaking at Texas Southern University, where she studied political science, and later at Boston University, from which she obtained a law degree in 1959. She then returned to Houston and began to practice law from the dining room of her parents' house. Three years passed before she was able to save enough money to open up a real office in partnership with another lawyer.

Jordan entered politics in 1960 as a behind-the-scenes worker for the county branch of the Democratic party. She decided to seek a more public role when she successfully filled in for the scheduled guest at a presidential campaign rally. Jordan lost in her first two tries at elected office—she ran for the Texas House of Representatives in 1962 and again in 1964—but in 1966, she earned a seat in the Texas State Senate, thus becoming the first black since Reconstruction and the first black woman ever to serve in that particular legislative body. Jordan was re-elected in 1968, then ran for the U.S. Congress in 1972 and easily triumphed over her opponent.

The rookie congresswoman first captured national attention as a member of the House Judiciary Committee, which had been conducting an investigation into the Watergate affair since the fall of 1973. By mid-1974, hearings were under way to consider the impeachment of President Richard Nixon for his role in the scandal. Each of the thirty-eight members of the committee had been promised fifteen minutes to give a statement outlining their views and concerns. On the evening of July 25, in front of a television audience that numbered in the millions, Jordan made her case for impeachment with an impressive discourse on the Constitution. Her remarks are taken from the official government publication entitled Debate on Articles of Impeachment: Hearings of the Committee on the Judiciary, House of Representatives, *93rd Congress, 2nd session, U.S. Gov't Printing Office, 1974.*

Mr. Chairman, I join my colleague, Mr. Rangel, in thanking you for giving the junior members of this committee the glorious opportunity of sharing the pain of this inquiry. Mr. Chairman, you are a strong man and it has not been easy but we have tried as best we can to give you as much assistance as possible.

Earlier today we heard the beginning of the Preamble to the Constitution of the United States, "We, the people." It is a very eloquent beginning. But when that document was completed on the seventeenth of September in 1787 I was not included in that "We, the people." I felt somehow for many years that George Washington and Alexander Hamilton just left me out by mistake. But through the process of amendment, interpretation and court decision I have finally been included in "We, the people."

Today, I am an inquisitor. I believe hyperbole would not be fictional and would not overstate the solemnness that I feel right now. My faith in the Constitution is whole, it is complete, it is total. I am not going to sit here and be an idle spectator to the diminution, the subversion, the destruction of the Constitution.

"Who can so properly be the inquisitors for the nation as the representatives of the nation themselves?" (Federalist, number 65) The subject of its jurisdiction are those offenses which proceed from the misconduct of public men. That is what we are talking about. In other words, the jurisdiction comes from the abuse or violation of some public trust. It is wrong, I suggest, it is a misreading of the Constitution for any member here to assert that for a member to vote for an article of impeachment means that that member must be convinced that the president should be removed from office. The Constitution doesn't say that. The powers relating to impeachment are an essential check in the hands of this body, the legislature, against and upon the encroachment of the executive. In establishing the division between the two branches of the legislature, the House and the Senate, assigning to the one the right to accuse and to the other the right to judge, the framers of this Constitution were very astute. They did not make the accusers and the judges the same person.

We know the nature of impeachment. We have been talking about it awhile now. "It is chiefly designed for the president and his high ministers" to somehow be called into account. It is designed to "bridle" the executive if he engages in excesses. "It is designed as a method of national inquest into the conduct of public men." (Hamilton, Federalist, number 65) The framers confined in the Congress the power if need be, to remove the President in order to strike a delicate balance between a president swollen with power and grown tyrannical; and preservation of the independence of the executive. The nature of impeachment is a narrowly channeled exception to the separation of powers maxim, the federal convention of 1787 said that. It limited impeachment to high crimes and misdemeanors and discounted and opposed the term, "maladministration." "It is to be used only for great misdemeanors," so it was said in the North Carolina ratification convention. And in the Virginia ratification convention: "We do not trust our liberty to a particular branch. We need one branch to check the others."

The North Carolina ratification convention: "No one need be afraid that officers who commit oppression will pass with immunity."

"Prosecutions of impeachments will seldom fail to agitate the passions of the whole community," said Hamilton in the Federalist Papers, number 65. "And to divide it into parties more or less friendly or inimical to the accused." I do not mean political parties in that sense.

The drawing of political lines goes to the motivation behind impeachment; but impeachment must proceed within the confines of the constitutional term, "high crime and misdemeanors."

Of the impeachment process, it was Woodrow Wilson who said that "nothing short of the grossest offenses against the plain law of the land will suffice to give them speed and effectiveness. Indignation so great as to overgrow party interest may secure a conviction; but nothing else can."

Common sense would be revolted if we engaged upon this process for petty reasons. Congress has a lot to do. Appropriations, tax reform, health insurance, campaign finance reform, housing, environmental protection, energy sufficiency, mass transportation. Pettiness cannot be allowed to stand in the face of such overwhelming problems. So today we are not being petty. We are trying to be big because the task we have before us is a big one.

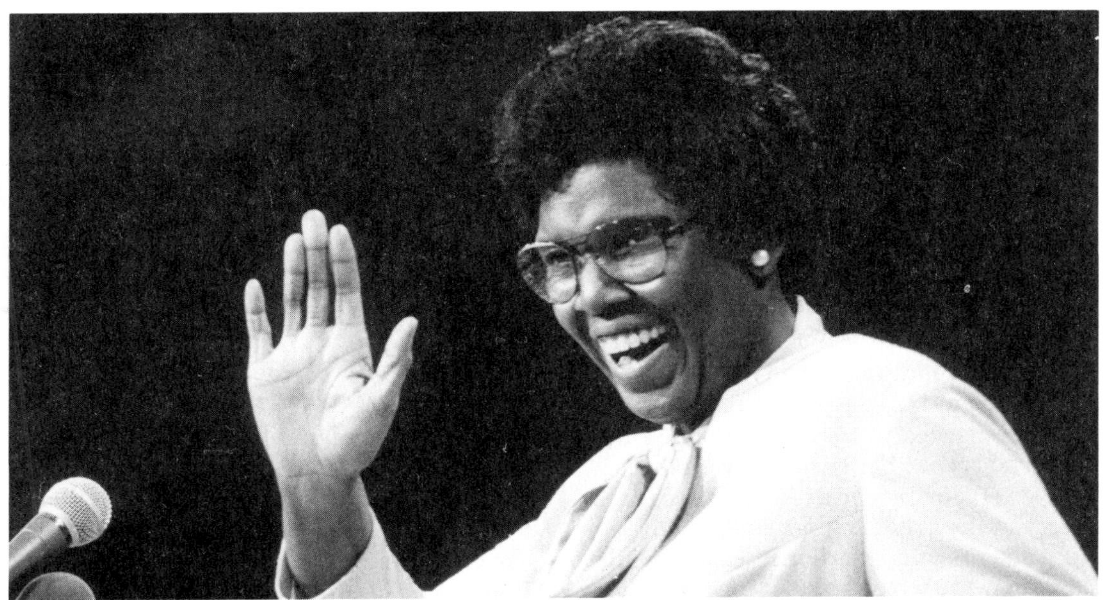

Barbara Jordan

This morning in a discussion of the evidence we were told that the evidence which purports to support the allegations of misuse of the CIA by the president is thin. We are told that that evidence is insufficient. What that recital of the evidence this morning did not include is what the president did know on June 23, 1972. The president did know that it was Republican money, that it was money from the Committee for the Re-election of the President, which was found in the possession of one of the burglars arrested on June 17.

What the president did know on June 23 was the prior activities of E. Howard Hunt, which included his participation in the break-in of Daniel Ellsberg's psychiatrist, which included Howard Hunt's participation in the Dita Beard ITT affair, which included Howard Hunt's fabrication of cables designed to discredit the Kennedy administration.

We were further cautioned today that perhaps these proceedings ought to be delayed because certainly there would be new evidence forthcoming from the president of the United States. There has not even been an obfuscated indication that this committee would receive any additional materials from the president. The committee subpoena is outstanding and if the president wants to supply that material, the committee sits here.

The fact is that on yesterday, the American people waited with great anxiety for eight hours, not knowing whether their president would obey an order of the Supreme Court of the United States.

At this point I would like to juxtapose a few of the impeachment criteria with some of the president's actions.

Impeachment criteria: James Madison, from the Virginia ratification convention. "If the president be connected in any suspicious manner with any person and there be grounds to believe that he will shelter him, he may be impeached."

We have heard time and time again that the evidence reflects payment to the defendants of money. The president had knowledge that these funds were being paid and that these were funds collected for the 1972 presidential campaign.

We know that the president met with Mr. Henry Petersen twenty-seven times to discuss matters related to Watergate and immediately thereafter met with the very persons who were implicated in the information Mr. Petersen was receiving and transmitting to the president. The words are, "If the President be collected in any suspicious manner with any person and there be grounds to believe that he will shelter that person, he may be impeached."

Justice Story: "Impeachment is intended for occasional and extraordinary cases where a superior power acting for the whole people is put into operation to protect their rights and rescue their liberties from violations."

We know about the Huston plan. We know

about the break-in of the psychiatrist's office. We know that there was absolute complete direction in August 1971 when the president instructed Ehrlichman to "do whatever is necessary." This instruction led to a surreptitious entry into Dr. Fielding's office.

"Protect their rights." "Rescue their liberties from violation."

The South Carolina ratification convention impeachment criteria: Those are impeachable "who behave amiss or betray their public trust."

Beginning shortly after the Watergate break-in and continuing to the present time the president has engaged in a series of public statements and actions designed to thwart the lawful investigation by government prosecutors. Moreover, the president has made public announcements and assertions bearing on the Watergate case which the evidence will show he knew to be false.

These assertions, false assertions, impeachable, those who misbehave. Those who "behave amiss or betray their public trust."

James Madison again at the constitutional convention: "A president is impeachable if he attempts to subvert the Constitution."

The Constitution charges the president with the task of taking care that the laws be faithfully executed, and yet the president has counseled his aides to commit perjury, willfully disregarded the secrecy of grand jury proceedings, concealed surreptitious entry, attempted to compromise a federal judge while publicly displaying his cooperation with the processes of criminal justice.

"A president is impeachable if he attempts to subvert the Constitution."

If the impeachment provision in the Constitution of the United States will not reach the offenses charged here, then perhaps that eighteenth century Constitution should be abandoned to a twentieth century paper shredder. Has the president committed offenses and planned and directed and acquiesced in a course of conduct which the Constitution will not tolerate? That is the question. We know that. We know the question. We should now forthwith proceed to answer the question. It is reason, and not passion, which must guide our deliberations, guide our debate, and guide our decision.

Largely on the strength of this performance before a national television audience, Jordan was invited to deliver one of two keynote addresses at the 1976 Democratic National Convention in New York City. Until she stepped up to the podium on the evening of July 12, the convention had been a rather lackluster affair; Ohio Senator John Glenn, who spoke immediately before Jordan, had generated very little enthusiasm with his remarks. But when Jordan began to address the gathering, she quickly won over the delegates as well as a large number of the approximately 75 million viewers across the country. Her rousing speech was frequently interrupted with cheers and applause, and by the next day, there was a serious effort in progress to nominate her for the vice-presidency. Jordan's remarks were reprinted in Representative American Speeches: 1976-1977 *(Wilson, 1977), from which the following was taken.*

One hundred and forty-four years ago, members of the Democratic party first met in convention to select a presidential candidate. Since that time, Democrats have continued to convene once every four years and draft a party platform and nominate a presidential candidate. And our meeting this week is a continuation of that tradition.

But there is something different about tonight. There is something special about tonight. What is different? What is special? I, Barbara Jordan, am a keynote speaker.

A lot of years passed since 1832, and during that time it would have been most unusual for any national political party to ask that a Barbara Jordan deliver a keynote address . . . but tonight here I am. And I feel that notwithstanding the past that my presence here is one additional bit of evidence that the American Dream need not forever be deferred.

Now that I have this grand distinction what in the world am I supposed to say?

I could easily spend this time praising the accomplishments of this party and attacking the Republicans but I don't choose to do that.

I could list the many problems which Americans have. I could list the problems which cause people to feel cynical, angry, frustrated: problems which include lack of integrity in government; the feeling that the individual no longer counts; the reality of material and spiritual poverty; the feeling that the grand American experiment is failing or has failed. I could recite these problems and then I could sit down and offer no solutions. But I don't choose to do that either.

The citizens of America expect more. They deserve and they want more than a recital of problems.

We are a people in a quandary about the present. We are a people in search of our future. We are a people in search of a national community.

We are a people trying not only to solve the problems of the present: unemployment, inflation . . . but we are attempting on a larger scale to fulfill the promise of America. We are attempting to fulfill our national purpose; to create and sustain a society in which all of us are equal.

Throughout our history, when people have looked for new ways to solve their problems, and to uphold the principles of this nation, many times they have turned to political parties. They have often turned to the Democratic party.

What is it, what is it about the Democratic party that makes it the instrument that people use when they search for ways to shape their future? Well I believe the answer to that question lies in our concept of governing. Our concept of governing is derived from our view of people. It is a concept deeply rooted in a set of beliefs firmly etched in the national conscience, of all of us.

Now what are these beliefs?

First, we believe in equality for all and privileges for none. This is a belief that each American regardless of background has equal standing in the public forum, all of us. Because we believe this idea so firmly, we are an inclusive rather than an exclusive party. Let everybody come.

I think it no accident that most of those emigrating to America in the nineteenth century identified with the Democratic party. We are a heterogeneous party made up of Americans of diverse backgrounds.

We believe that the people are the source of all governmental power; that the authority of the people is to be extended, not restricted. This can be accomplished only by providing each citizen with every opportunity to participate in the management of the government. They must have that.

"I feel that notwithstanding the past that my presence here is one additional bit of evidence that the American Dream need not forever be deferred."

We believe that the government which represents the authority of all the people, not just one interest group, but all the people, has an obligation to actively underscore, actively seek to remove those obstacles which would block individual achievement . . . obstacles emanating from race, sex, economic condition. The government must seek to remove them.

We are a party of innovation. We do not reject our traditions, but we are willing to adapt to changing circumstances, when change we must. We are willing to suffer the discomfort of change in order to achieve a better future.

We have a positive vision of the future founded on the belief that the gap between the promise and reality of America can one day be finally closed. We believe that.

This, my friends, is the bedrock of our concept of governing. This is a part of the reason why Americans have turned to the Democratic party. These are the foundations upon which a national community can be built.

Let's all understand that these guiding principles cannot be discarded for short-term political gains. They represent what this country is all about. They are indigenous to the American idea. And these are principles which are not negotiable.

In other times, I could stand here and give this kind of exposition on the beliefs of the Democratic party and that would be enough. But today that is not enough. People want more. That is not sufficient reason for the majority of the people of this country to vote Democratic. We have made mistakes. In our haste to do all things for all people, we did not foresee the full consequences of our actions. And when the people raised their voices, we didn't hear. But our deafness was only a temporary condition, and not an irreversible condition.

Even as I stand here and admit that we have made mistakes I still believe that as the people

"It is hypocritical for the public official to admonish and exhort the people to uphold the common good if we are derelict in upholding the common good."

of America sit in judgment on each party, they will recognize that our mistakes were mistakes of the heart. They'll recognize that.

And now we must look to the future. Let us heed the voice of the people and recognize their common sense. If we do not, we not only blaspheme our political heritage, we ignore the common ties that bind all Americans.

Many fear the future. Many are distrustful of their leaders, and believe that their voices are never heard. Many seek only to satisfy their private work wants. To satisfy private interests.

But this is the great danger America faces. That we will cease to be one nation and become instead a collection of interest groups; city against suburb, region against region, individual against individual. Each seeking to satisfy private wants.

If that happens, who then will speak for America?

Who then will speak for the common good?

This is the question which must be answered in 1976.

Are we to be one people bound together by common spirit sharing in a common endeavor or will we become a divided nation?

For all of its uncertainty, we cannot flee the future. We must not become the new puritans and reject our society. We must address and master the future together. It can be done if we restore the belief that we share a sense of national community, that we share a common national endeavor. It can be done.

There is no executive order; there is no law that can require the American people to form a national community. This we must do as individuals and if we do it as individuals, there is no President of the United States who can veto that decision.

As a first step, we must restore our belief in ourselves. We are a generous people so why can't we be generous with each other? We need to take to heart the words spoken by Thomas Jefferson: "Let us restore to social intercourse that harmony and that affection without which liberty and even life are but dreary things."

A nation is formed by the willingness of each of us to share in the responsibility for upholding the common good.

A government is invigorated when each of us is willing to participate in shaping the future of this nation.

In this election year we must define the common good and begin again to shape a common good and begin again to shape a common future. Let each person do his or her part. If one citizen is unwilling to participate, all of us are going to suffer. For the American idea, though it is shared by all of us, is realized in each one of us.

And now, what are those of us who are elected public officials supposed to do? We call ourselves public servants but I'll tell you this: we as public servants must set an example for the rest of the nation. It is hypocritical for the public official to admonish and exhort the people to uphold the common good if we are derelict in upholding the common good. More is required of public officials than slogans and handshakes and press releases. More is required. We must hold ourselves strictly accountable. We must provide the people with a vision of the future.

If we promise as public officials, we must deliver. If we as public officials propose, we must produce. If we say to the American people it is time for you to be sacrificial; sacrifice. If the public official says that, we (public officials) must be the first to give. We must be. And again, if we make mistakes, we must be willing to admit them. We have to do that. What we have to do is strike a balance between the idea that government should do everything and the idea, the belief, that government ought to do nothing. Strike a balance.

Let there be no illusions about the difficulty of forming this kind of a national community. It's tough, difficult, not easy. But a spirit of harmony will survive in America only if each of us remembers that we share a common destiny. If each of us remembers when self-interest and bitterness seem to prevail, that we share a common destiny.

I have confidence that we can form this kind of national community.

I have confidence that the Democratic party can lead the way. I have that confidence. We cannot improve on the system of government handed down to us by the founders of the Republic, there is no way to improve upon that. But what we can do is to find new ways to implement that system and realize our destiny.

Now, I began this speech by commenting to you on the uniqueness of a Barbara Jordan making the keynote address. Well I am going to close my speech by quoting a Republican President and I ask you that as you listen to these words of Abraham Lincoln, relate them to the concept of a national community in which every last one of us participates: "As I would not be a slave, so I would not be a master."

This expresses my idea of Democracy. Whatever differs from this, to the extent of the difference is no democracy.

SOURCES

Books

Blue, Rose, and Corinne Naden, *Barbara Jordan,* Chelsea House, 1992.

Braden, Waldo W., editor, *Representative American Speeches: 1974–1975,* Wilson, 1975.

———, *Representative American Speeches: 1976–1977,* Wilson, 1977.

Debate on Articles of Impeachment: Hearings of the Committee on the Judiciary, House of Representatives, 93rd Congress, 2nd Session, U.S. Gov't Printing Office, 1974.

Duffy, Bernard K., and Halford R. Ryan, editors, *American Orators of the Twentieth Century: Critical Studies and Sources,* Greenwood Press, 1987.

Haskins, James, *Barbara Jordan,* Dial Press, 1977.

Jordan, Barbara, and Shelby Hearon, *Barbara Jordan: A Self-Portrait,* Doubleday, 1979.

Kennedy, Patricia Scileppi, and Gloria Hartman O'Shields, *We Shall Be Heard: Women Speakers in America, 1828–Present,* Kendall/Hunt, 1983.

Roberts, Naurice, *Barbara Jordan: The Great Lady from Texas,* Childrens Press, 1984.

Periodicals

New York Times, "Black Woman Keynoter: Barbara Charline Jordan," July 13, 1976, p. 24.

Vernon Jordan

1935–

African American lawyer and civil rights leader

Although he has remained out of the spotlight since retiring from his position as head of the National Urban League in 1981, Vernon Jordan was at one time one of the country's most vocal and articulate advocates for minority rights. During his decade with the organization famous for championing the cause of the urban poor in particular, he worked tirelessly behind the scenes to secure the support of business and government leaders in his quest to improve the lives of black Americans. At the same time, he used his considerable skills as a speaker to keep an increasingly apathetic and often hostile public focused on the problems of the underclass. As Jordan once noted in a speech delivered near the end of his tenure, his goal was a simple one—"the creation of a society in which black people and white people share equally in the rewards and responsibilities of our nation."

A native of Atlanta, Georgia, Jordan grew up enjoying the benefits of a middle-class lifestyle while enduring the strict racial segregation of the South. A good student and athlete in the all-black public schools he attended as a youth, he headed north to attend college at DePauw University in Greencastle, Indiana. One of only five blacks on campus, he led a busy life, pursuing studies in political science and involving himself in numerous other activities, including playing basketball, writing and appearing in plays, and holding political office. He also excelled at oratory and won several collegiate competitions.

After graduating from DePauw in 1957, Jordan headed to Washington, D.C., and Howard University Law School, from which he obtained his degree in 1960. Turning down job offers from several corporate law firms, he then returned to his hometown of Atlanta to work on behalf of the civil rights movement, initially as a law clerk in the office of famed civil rights attorney Donald Hollowell. Two years later, Jordan took on additional responsibilities as Georgia field secretary for the NAACP, a position in which his speech-making talents were put to the test as he established new local branches and organized demonstrations and boycotts.

Jordan left Georgia in 1964 for Arkansas, where he entered into a private partnership with a fellow civil rights lawyer and also became director of the Voter Education Project. In the latter post, he traveled all over the South coordinating voter registration drives and educating new black voters about the importance of electing black officials to represent them. As a result of his successes, which included acting as a cool-headed yet forceful mediator between the various groups competing to register black voters, Jordan was soon acknowledged as a major figure on the national civil rights scene.

In 1970, about the same time he was considering making his own bid for political office, Jordan was approached about heading the United Negro College Fund (UNCF), an organization devoted to providing financial support to some three dozen predominantly black colleges nationwide. As a firm believer in the need to foster the development of a black intellectual elite that could serve as a role model for all African Americans while helping lead the drive for changes to benefit the less fortunate, he embraced the challenge with gusto and quickly proved himself to be an effective fund-raiser.

Jordan's affiliation with the UNCF was brief, however. In March 1971, Whitney Young, the dynamic director of the National Urban League, suffered a heart attack and drowned while in Nigeria attending a conference of black leaders. Just a couple of months later, the Urban League governing board unanimously chose Jordan to succeed Young as head of the venerable civil rights organization. After fulfilling his commitment to the UNCF, he officially assumed the post in January 1972.

Jordan took over the reins of the Urban League at a time when the gains of the 1950s and early 1960s were threatened by a federal government that seemed increasingly indifferent to the economic and social problems facing black Americans. It was a theme he touched upon time and time again in his many speeches, particularly during the Republican administration of President Richard Nixon. One such occasion was on March 16, 1973, at an appearance before the National Press Club in Washington, D.C. In the following address, reprinted here from Representative American Speeches: 1972–1973, *edited by Waldo W. Braden (Wilson, 1973), Jordan blasted the Nixon administration's proposed budget as one that would guarantee a life of greater hardship for those still seeking a share in the "American Dream."*

In his budget message to the Congress, the president once again called for "a new American Revolution to return power to the people." But the message itself, and the provisions of a federal budget that hacks away at social spending with ruthless intensity, can only be seen as the first shots of a counterrevolution designed to destroy the social reforms of the 1960s.

Indeed, the proposed budget is the blueprint for the conversion of a national policy of "benign neglect" into a policy of active hostility to the hopes, dreams and aspirations of black Americans.

I do not believe this policy is intentional, nor do I believe that it is the product of conscious, anti-black, anti-poor reasoning. Rather it is the by-product of a view of society and of the proper role of government that is incompatible with the implementation of the precious rights won by minorities in recent years. The yawning gap between the philosophy of decentralized government marked by a passive domestic role for the federal administration, and the effects of such a system on poor people and minorities vividly illustrates how honorable intentions can have disastrous results.

I am reminded of the famous lines by T.S. Eliot: "Between the idea and the reality/Between the motion and the act/Falls the shadow." Today that shadow falls on black Americans, minorities, and on the overwhelming numbers of poor people who are white. It is they who are being asked to carry the burdens imposed by the impending massive federal withdrawal from moral and programmatic leadership in the domestic arena. The shadow that falls upon them is deep and its darkness spreads a blight across our land.

The administration's domestic policy, as revealed in its budget proposals and in a flurry of public statements, encompasses on the one hand, sharp cuts in spending on social services, and on the other, a massive shift in resources and responsibility from Washington to local governments. These are the two prongs of a pincer movement that entraps millions of Americans.

A brief examination of just a few of the federal actions both proposed and already taken, are enough to indicate that urban America is well on the way to becoming a free fire zone doomed to destruction by the very forces it looks to for salvation.

In employment, the Emergency Employment Act will be phased out, ending public service jobs for about 150,000 state and city employees, some forty percent of whom had been classified as disadvantaged. Job-creation and -training programs already crippled by the refusal to spend appropriated funds, will be cut sharply. A wide variety of federally backed summer and youth employment programs will be dropped, and special programs for high-unemployment areas will be eliminated.

In housing, a freeze has been imposed on federally subsidized housing affecting hundreds of thousands of low-income families and robbing construction workers of jobs.

In education, federal programs to provide compensatory educational services to disadvantaged children, and important vocational education programs will be dismantled, while day care, student loans, special school milk programs and aid to libraries will be eliminated or reduced to a small fraction of their former size.

In health, twenty-three million aged and handicapped people will have an extra billion dollars torn from them in higher Medicare charges and lessened coverage, while funds for the successful community mental health centers and for new hospitals will be eliminated.

In addition to this listing of horror stories, there are further atrocities—the dismantling of the Office of Economic Opportunity and abolition of its over nine hundred community action programs; the end of the Model Cities program, and the effective end of urban renewal and a host of other federal programs of community development.

A number of arguments have been advanced to justify the far-reaching changes the new American counterrevolution seeks to establish. Taken together, they recall Horace Walpole's comment about the world: that it "is a comedy to those that think, a tragedy to those that feel."

It is said, for example, that the budget cuts are necessary to avoid new taxes and to control inflation. This neatly avoids mention of the imposition of a sharply increased Social Security payroll tax that falls disproportionately on the same low-income families that will be hurt most by social service cutbacks. I accept the need for a ceiling on federal expenditures, but I cannot accept the faulty priorities that raise military expenditures by just under five billion dollars while slicing funds for the poor and for the cities. The cost of one Trident submarine would pay for the public service employment program. The requested increase in funds for the F-15 fighter is about equal to the amounts cut from manpower training funds. Federal disinvestment in human resources reflects an irrational choice of priorities.

Another reason for the cuts is the overly optimistic view that many of the federal programs are no longer needed. The president himself seemed to be making this point in his human resources message when he said: "By almost any measure life is better for Americans in 1973 than ever before in our history, and better than in any other society of the world in this or any earlier age." And the theme was repeated in the message dealing with cities, which declared that "the hour of crisis has passed."

I cannot agree. I believe, instead, that the hour of crisis is upon us, and is intensified by the federal withdrawal from urban problems. I would hate to have to explain to a poor black family in Bedford-Stuyvesant that's chained to an overcrowded slum apartment because of the housing subsidy freeze that this is really the best of all possible worlds. I would hate to have to explain to a poor black farm worker in Mississippi that the record gross national product means he's living in a golden era. And I would hate to have to explain to an unemployed Vietnam veteran who can no longer enter a federal manpower training program that he is being adequately repaid for his sacrifices.

Life in 1973 may be better for some people, but it is not better for black Americans. We are afflicted with unemployment rates more than double those for white workers. Black teenage unemployment is near forty percent. Unemployment and underemployment in the ghettos of America is from one third to one half of the work force. The total number of poor people in this country has risen sharply in the past several years. No. This is no Eden in which we live and we cannot complacently agree that there is no longer a need for federal social service programs.

Another justification for ending some programs is arrived at by a method of reasoning I confess I am unable to comprehend. Such programs, it is said, have proved their worth and therefore the government should no longer operate them. Since they are so good, someone else should do them. I can only suppose that the next step will be to tell the Joint Chiefs of Staff that the armed forces have done such a good job that the federal government will stop funding them.

Another argument—a serious one of some substance—is that some programs have not worked and therefore should be abandoned. Such programs fall into two categories—those that appear to neutral observers to have accomplished their goals, and those that clearly have not been as effective as they should have been.

> ***"For years, the agony of the Vietnam war was justified on the grounds that we had made a moral commitment to the people there. Can we now abandon the moral commitment to our own cities and to our own people?"***

It is inaccurate and unfair to suggest that the community action programs or the Model Cities programs, to take two important examples, have failed. There is every indication that they have brought a new sense of spirit and accomplishment to many hundreds of cities. By fully involving poor people in the decision-making process they have contributed significantly to urban stability and to individual accomplishment. Federal evaluation studies endorse this view. Local political leadership has also insisted that the programs are successful. For years, the agony of the Vietnam war was justified on the grounds that we had made a moral commitment to the people there. Can we now abandon the moral commitment to our own cities and to our own people?

Some federal programs have been clear disappointments. Some of the housing subsidy programs, for example, were sabotaged not by poor people seeking a decent home, but by some speculators in league with some federal employees. Thus, although thousands of families have been sheltered by these programs; although scandal-free housing has been produced by effective nonprofit organizations and although the need for low- and moderate-income housing is pressing, federal housing subsidies have been frozen and appear on their way to an early death. The victims of federal housing failures are being punished doubly—once by ineffective program control, and again by the moratorium on all housing subsidies. Ending all housing programs because some have shown signs of failure makes about as much sense as eliminating the Navy because some new ships have had cost overruns.

The final justification of the administration's policies, and the core of the new American counterrevolution, is that federal funds will be transferred to local governments in the form of bloc grants in four major areas—community development, education, manpower and law enforcement. It is proposed that the federal government end its categorical grant programs administered, financed and monitored by federal agencies and that local governments should now decide whether to spend federal monies on job training or on roads, on compensatory education in the ghetto or on a new high school in the suburbs. This has been called "returning power to the people."

To black Americans, who historically had no choice but to look to the federal government to correct the abuses of state and local governments, that is very much like hiring the wolf to guard the sheep. It is axiomatic in American political life, with some exceptions, that the lower the level of government, the lower the level of competence and the higher the margin for discrimination against the poor and the powerless.

The power that has accrued to the central government is due to the failure of localities to be responsive to the needs of all but a handful of their constituents. Black Americans have looked to the federal government to end slavery, to end peonage, to restore our constitutional rights and to secure economic progress in the face of discrimination. Yes, we looked to Washington because we could not look to Jack-

Vernon Jordan

son, to Baton Rouge or to Montgomery. White people looked to Washington too, for the federal programs that helped many of them survive the Depression, helped them move to suburbia and helped them to prosper economically. Now that Washington has finally embarked on programs that hold out some hope for minorities, we are told instead to look to local governments notorious for their historic insensitivity to the needs and aspirations of blacks and the poor.

Before falling prey to the siren song of local infallibility, the administration should examine the use local governments are making of general revenue-sharing grants already distributed. News reports from across the country repeat the same dismal story—federal money used to build new city halls, to raise police salaries, and to cut local taxes. All this is taking place at a time when school systems are falling apart, housing is being abandoned, and health needs are unmet. The record does not inspire confidence that lost federal social service programs will be replaced with effective local ones.

General revenue sharing is a fact. It is a reality. Thirty billion dollars is in the pipeline for state and local governments. Rather than throw still more money at local governments at the expense of federal programs with proven track records, the administration should be developing performance standards and effective compliance mechanisms that assure these local programs will work. Folding—or rather, crumbling—federal social service programs into no-strings-attached special revenue-sharing packages seems to me to be a prescription for disaster.

Black Americans have been assured that antidiscrimination regulations will prevent local abuses. While the Treasury Department's guidelines have been revised and strengthened, we still cannot take heart from such assurances. They come just a few weeks after the Civil Rights Commission reported the persistence of "inertia of agencies in the field of civil rights," and after the government was subjected to a federal court order to enforce the laws against school segregation. It is hard to imagine that the politically charged decision to withhold funds from states or cities that discriminate will be made. And without federal standards assuring that funds will be used in behalf of poor people in need of job training, public housing, and special school and health programs, the money will once again find its way into the pockets of entrenched local interests.

The proposed special revenue-sharing approach breaks faith not only with poor people, but with local governments as well. What Washington gives with one hand it takes with the other. Mayors who once hungered for no-strings-attached bloc grants are now panicked by the realization that the funds they receive will be inadequate to meet the needs of their communities and will be less than their cities get in the current categorical-aid programs. In addition, there is the probability that future special revenue-sharing funds will continue to shrink. Rather than shifting power to the people, the new American counterrevolution creates a vacuum in responsible power.

We must not forget, as so many have, that federal programs today do embody local initiatives and local decision making. The myth of the Washington bureaucrat making decisions for people three thousand miles away is false. The money often comes from the federal treasury. The broad program goals and definitions of national needs come, as they should, from the Congress. But the specific program proposals, their implementation, and their support come from local governments, citizens and agencies. Those federal dollars that are now deemed tainted actually enable local citizens to meet local problems under the umbrella of national financial and moral leadership. To shift the center of gravity away from national leadership is to compound the drift and inertia that appear to categorize our society today.

It is in this context that the blast of white silence is so puzzling. Far more white people than blacks will be hurt by the budget cuts. Yet the responsibility for calling attention to their impact falls increasingly on black leadership. There are three times as many poor white families as there are poor black families. The majority of people on welfare are white. Of the black poor, more than half don't get one devalued dollar from welfare. Two thirds of the families who got homes through the now-frozen 235 subsidy program were white. The majority of trainees in manpower programs, and three fourths of the people who will lose their jobs under the public employment program are white.

But because black Americans have been the most vocal segment of the population in urging social reforms, there is the mistaken impression that only blacks benefit from them. The Battle of the Budget is a larger-scale replay of the fight for welfare reform waged—and lost—last year. Then, as now, black leadership was out front in favor of a living guaranteed income for all. But we had few white supporters, although many more white people than black would have benefited. It is reasonable to ask, had we won that struggle would all of those poor white people have returned their income supplement checks? And it is fair to ask today that white people join us in the struggle to preserve the social services of the federal government that enable them, too, to survive.

The silent white majority that has been the prime beneficiary of the programs of the 1960s and is today the group most in need of further federal services will have to speak up. They are not stigmatized, as are blacks, by charges of special pleading by special Americans looking for special treatment. And their representatives in the Congress will have to act, too. They cannot complacently watch their constituents' welfare being trampled on, nor can they accept the shrinkage of their rightful constitutional role in our system of government.

Already, there have been signs that some congressmen whose votes helped to pass progressive legislation a few short years ago are now of a mind to compromise with administration power, to compromise the jobs and livelihood and needs of their constituents, to compromise the power of the Congress to control the purse and to influence domestic policies, and finally, to compromise their own principles. If this is so, it will be tragic for the Constitution, tragic for the country, tragic for the poor people, and tragic for the heritage of liberalism.

The gut issues of today—better schools, jobs and housing for all, personal safety and decent health care—are issues that transcend race. So long as they are falsely perceived as "black issues," nothing constructive will be done to deal with them. White America must come to see that its cities, its needs and its economic and physical health are at stake. The needs of blacks and whites are too strongly entwined to separate. As Whitney Young used to say, "We may have come here on different ships, but we're in the same boat now."

So white Americans must join with black people to rekindle the American Dream, and to sing, in the words of Langston Hughes:

O, let America be America again—
The land that never has been yet—
and yet

Jordan continued his attack on what he saw as the federal government's lackluster performance on issues of particular concern to minorities throughout the rest of the 1970s. He reserved his sharpest rhetoric for the Republicans but was also highly critical of Democrat Jimmy Carter, whose administration he characterized as a "disappointment," mostly because of its failure to bring about economic growth and appoint more African Americans to government office.

Jordan closed out the decade with a fiery speech delivered at the 1979 National Urban League annual convention in which he warned leaders of both political parties that they would have to earn the black vote in the 1980 presidential election. "The black community will be harsh judges," he warned. "Black people will be examining your record, evaluating your performance, and checking your positions. . . . We don't have the wealth. We don't have the power. But we do have the numbers."

On May 29, 1980, Jordan was in Fort Wayne, Indiana, to speak to the local Urban League chapter when he was critically wounded in an assassination attempt; despite an extensive investigation, his assailant was never caught. (At one point, authorities arrested a white supremacist, but he was later released for lack of evidence.) The following year, he announced his retirement from active leadership of the organization, declaring that ten years in office was enough for anyone. Others speculated that his brush with death as well as the frustrating prospect of battling the conservative tide ushered in by the new Reagan administration also influenced his decision.

Jordan has kept a very low profile since leaving the Urban League, signing on as a partner for a Dallas, Texas-based law firm and serving on the boards of several major corporations, including American Express, Xerox, and RJR Nabisco. After the 1992 presidential election, he co-chaired his friend Bill Clinton's transition team and then assumed the role of unofficial advisor to the president.

SOURCES

Books

Braden, Waldo W., editor, *Representative American Speeches: 1971-1972,* Wilson, 1972.

———, *Representative American Speeches: 1972-1973,* Wilson, 1973.

———, *Representative American Speeches: 1975-1976,* Wilson, 1976.

———, *Representative American Speeches: 1979-1980,* Wilson, 1980.

Peterson, Owen, editor, *Representative American Speeches: 1980-1981,* Wilson, 1981.

———, *Representative American Speeches: 1985-1986,* Wilson, 1986.

Periodicals

Ebony, "Vernon Jordan," December, 1980.

Newsweek, "Who Shot Vernon Jordan?" June 9, 1980; "Break in the Vernon Jordan Case?" October 13, 1980, p. 48; "The Transition: Setting the Tone," November 16, 1992.

New York Times, June 16, 1971; June 17, 1971.

People, "For All His Differences with Ronald Reagan, Vernon Jordan Shares the Kinship of Survival," April 27, 1981; "Mr. Inside," November 23, 1992.

Time, "Man at the Bridge," June 28, 1971; "Ambush in the Night," June 9, 1980; "Jordan Riddle," June 16, 1980.

U.S. News and World Report, "Reminder of Racial Unrest," June 9, 1980, p. 12.

Vanity Fair, "Clinton's Mr. Inside," March, 1993.

Wall Street Journal, July 24, 1991.

Vital Speeches of the Day, "End of the Second Reconstruction?," July 1, 1972; "The Second Reconstruction Period," September 15, 1972; "Black People on the Economic Front," September 15, 1975; "The New Negativism," September 15, 1978.

Chief Joseph
(In-mut-too-yah-lat-lat)

1840(?)–1904

Native American leader of the Nez Perce tribe

Among the most poignant stories of Indian resistance against the westward migration of white settlers was that of Chief Joseph and his tribe, a small group known as the Nez Perce. (French explorers gave them that name, which means "pierced nose," after observing their custom of wearing nose rings.) Their ancestral home was a large tract of land that stretched across what is now southeastern Washington, northeastern Oregon, and central Idaho. For the most part, they lived peacefully with neighboring tribes and the few white farmers and trappers they encountered while hunting and fishing. When the Pacific Northwest came under U.S. control in 1848, however, a surge in the number of white settlers attracted to the area led to tensions that eventually destroyed the Nez Perce way of life.

Joseph, who was born around 1840 in Oregon's Wallowa Valley, grew up during this troubled time as the son of a chief who repeatedly cautioned his people to be careful in their dealings with whites. In 1855, however, some of the Nez Perces signed a treaty giving up most of their land; in return, U.S. government officials assured them that the Wallowa Valley could serve as their reservation. Eight years later, even this land was ceded to the whites in a treaty not sanctioned by all the Nez Perces, including the band led by Joseph's father.

By the time Joseph assumed the title of chief from his father around 1871, his band of Nez Perces was waging a war of passive resistance against further white encroachment and attempts to move them to a reservation in Lapwai, Idaho. But before long, the discovery of gold in the Wallowa Valley increased pressure on U.S. authorities to make the Indians leave the area. Finally, in the spring of 1877, General Oliver O. Howard issued an ultimatum: either the Nez Perces agreed to give up all of their lands and relocate to Lapwai within thirty days, or the Army would see to it that they did.

Chief Joseph was not a warrior and had no desire to do battle with the whites. Viewing himself primarily as a protector of the aged, the weak, and the helpless among his people, he advised them to obey General Howard's order. His plea for patience and peace did not find favor with everyone, however; while the Nez Perces were in the process of making their way to their new home, several young male members of the tribe who bitterly resented the way they were being treated attacked and killed some white settlers over the course of several days in mid-June 1877. The incident touched off a series of skirmishes between the Nez Perces and the U.S Army in which Chief Joseph showed unexpected military skill by defeating the better-equipped and more numerous federal troops. Yet he knew that he could not continue to do so indefinitely (more soldiers were already on the way from other Western outposts), so he made a fateful decision: he and his people would try to escape into Canada.

Over the next eleven weeks, Chief Joseph led a band of several hundred Nez Perce men, women, and children on a retreat of well over a thousand miles through the rugged terrain of the Pacific Northwest, hoping to evade the U.S. government forces and enemy Indians on their trail. On at least a dozen occasions, they directly engaged their pursuers in battle and in most cases defeated them or fought to a stalemate. Throughout the well-documented campaign, Chief Joseph never failed to impress his opponents with his courage and his steady determination. They were also impressed with the fact that he did not harm the white settlers his band encountered along the way.

By late September, the Nez Perces at last found themselves within about thirty miles of the Canadian border at a place in Montana known as Eagle Creek. The price they had paid to get that far was a steep one; in addition to those who had fallen in battle, there were many others who died from exhaustion, hunger, and disease. For all who had managed to survive, the coming winter promised severe weather and probable starvation. Surrounded and vastly outnumbered by a well-armed contingent of U.S. troops, Chief Joseph finally surrendered on October 5, 1877. His brief remarks to General Howard and General Nelson A. Miles are among the best-known and most heart-wrenching words ever spoken by a Native American. They are reprinted here from W.C. Vanderwerth's Indian Oratory: Famous Speeches by Noted Indian Chieftains *(University of Oklahoma Press, 1971).*

Tell General Howard I know his heart. What he told me before, I have in my heart. I am tired of fighting. Our chiefs are killed. Looking Glass is dead. Toohoolhoolzote is dead. The old men are all dead. It is the young men who say yes and no. He [Ollokot, Joseph's own brother] who led on the young men is dead. It is cold and we have no blankets. The little children are freezing to death. My people, some of them, have run away to the hills and have no blankets, no food; no one knows where they are—perhaps freezing to death. I want to have time to look for my children and see how many I can find. Maybe I shall find them among the dead. Hear me, my chiefs. I am tired; my heart is sick and sad. From where the sun now stands I will fight no more forever.

While some of the Nez Perces did manage to slip away to Canada, Chief Joseph and his followers were sent to live in Indian Territory in what is now Oklahoma. There they still faced tremendous hardship; many of them (including five of Chief Joseph's children) succumbed to illness. Chief Joseph did his best to bring their desperate condition to the attention of authorities. In 1879, for example, he

was allowed to go to Washington, D.C., where on January 14 he testified before a special gathering of cabinet members, congressmen, and other government officials. His eloquent description of how the Nez Perces came to be at odds with the whites is reprinted here from W.C. Vanderwerth's Indian Oratory: Famous Speeches by Noted Indian Chieftains *(University of Oklahoma Press, 1971).*

My friends, I have been asked to show you my heart. I am glad to have a chance to do so. I want the white people to understand my people. Some of you think an Indian is like a wild animal. This is a great mistake. I will tell you all about our people, and then you can judge whether an Indian is a man or not. I believe much trouble and blood would be saved if we opened our hearts more. I will tell you in my way how the Indian sees things. The white man has more words to tell you how they look to him, but it does not require many words to speak the truth. What I have to say will come from my heart, and I will speak with a straight tongue. Ah-cum-kin-i-ma-me-hut [the Great Spirit] is looking at me, and will hear me.

My name is In-mut-too-yah-lat-lat [Thunder Traveling Over the Mountains]. I am chief of the Wal-lam-wat-kin band of Chute-palu, or Nez Perces. I was born in eastern Oregon, thirty-eight winters ago. My father was chief before me. When a young man, he was called Joseph by Mr. [Henry H.] Spaulding, a missionary. He died a few years ago. He left a good name on earth. He advised me well for my people.

Our fathers gave us many laws, which they had learned from their fathers. These laws were good. They told us to treat all men as they treated us; that we should never be the first to break a bargain; that it was a disgrace to tell a lie; that we should speak only the truth; that it was a shame for one man to take from another his wife, or his property without paying for it. We were taught to believe that the Great Spirit sees and hears everything, and that he never forgets; that hereafter he will give every man a spirit-home according to his desserts: if he has been a good man, he will have a good home; if he has been a bad man, he will have a bad home. This I believe, and all my people believe the same.

We did not know there were other people besides the Indian until about one hundred winters ago, when some men with white faces came to our country. They brought many things with them to trade for furs and skins. They brought tobacco, which was new to us. They brought guns with flint stones on them, which frightened our women and children. Our people could not talk with these white-faced men, but they used signs which all people understand. These men were Frenchmen, and they called our people "Nez Perces," because they wore rings in their noses for ornaments. Although very few of our people wear them now, we are still called by the same name. These French trappers said a great many things to our fathers, which have been planted in our hearts. Some were good for us, but some were bad. Our people were divided in opinion about these men. Some thought they taught more bad than good. An Indian respects a brave man, but he despises a coward. He loves a straight tongue, but he hates a forked tongue. The French trappers told us some truths and some lies.

The first white men of your people who came to our country were named [Meriwether] Lewis and [William] Clark. They also brought many things that our people had never seen. They talked straight, and our people gave them a great feast, as a proof that their hearts were friendly. These men were very kind. They made presents to our chiefs and our people made presents to them. We had a great many horses, of which we gave them what they needed, and they gave us guns and tobacco in return. All the Nez Perces made friends with Lewis and Clark, and agreed to let them pass through their country, and never to make war on white men. This promise the Nez Perces have never broken. No white man can accuse them of bad faith, and speak with a straight tongue. It has always been the pride of the Nez Perces that they were the friends of the white men.

When my father was a young man there came to our country a white man [Spaulding] who talked spirit law. He won the affections of our people because he spoke good things to them. At first he did not say anything about white men wanting to settle on our lands. Nothing was said about that until about twenty winters ago, when a number of white people came into our country and built houses and made farms. At first our people made no complaint. They thought there was room enough for all to live in peace, and they were learning many things from the white men that seemed to be good. But we soon found that the white men were growing rich very fast, and were greedy to possess everything the Indian had. My father was the first to see through the schemes of the white men, and he warned his tribe to be careful about trading with them. He had suspicion of men who seemed anxious to make money. I was a boy then, but I remember well my father's caution. He had sharper eyes than the rest of our people.

Next there came a white officer [Governor Isaac I. Stevens of the Washington Territory], who invited all the Nez Perces to a treaty council [in 1855]. After the council was opened he made known his heart. He said there were a great many white people in our country, and many more would come; that he wanted the land marked out so that the Indians and white men could be separated. If they were to live in peace it was necessary, he said, that the Indians should have a country set apart for them, and in that country they must stay. My father, who represented his band, refused to have anything to do with the council, because he wished to be a free man. He claimed that no man owned any part of the earth, and a man could not sell what he did not own.

Mr. Spaulding took hold of my father's arm and said, "Come and sign the treaty." My father pushed him away, and said: "Why do you ask me to sign away my country? It is your business to talk to us about spirit matters and not to talk to us about parting with our land." Governor Stevens urged my father to sign his treaty, but he refused. "I will not sign your paper," he said; "you go where you please, so do I; you are not a child, I am no child; I can think for myself. No man can think for me. I have no other home than this. I will not give it up to any man. My people would have no home. Take away your paper. I will not touch it with my hand."

My father left the council. Some of the chiefs of the other bands of the Nez Perces signed the treaty, and then Governor Stevens gave them presents of blankets. My father cautioned his people to take no presents, for "after a while,"

Chief Joseph

he said, "they will claim that you have accepted pay for your country." Since that time four bands of the Nez Perces have received annuities from the United States. My father was invited to many councils, and they tried hard to make him sign the treaty, but he was firm as the rock, and would not sign away his home. His refusal caused a difference among the Nez Perces.

Eight years later [1863] was the next treaty council. A chief called Lawyer, because he was a great talker, took the lead in this council, and sold nearly all the Nez Perces country. My father was not there. He said to me: "When you go into council with the white man, always remember your country. Do not give it away. The white man will cheat you out of your home. I have taken no pay from the United States. I have never sold our land." In this treaty Lawyer acted without authority from our band. He had no right to sell the Wallowa [winding water] country. That had always belonged to my father's own people, and the other bands had never disputed our right to it. No other Indians ever claimed Wallowa.

In order to have all people understand how much land we owned, my father planted poles around it and said: "Inside is the home of my people—the white man may take the land outside. Inside this boundary all our people were born. It circles around the graves of our fathers, and we will never give up these graves to any man."

The United States claimed they had bought all the Nez Perces country outside the Lapwai Reservation, from Lawyer and other chiefs, but we continued to live on this land in peace until eight years ago, when white men began to come inside the bounds my father had set. We warned them against this great wrong, but they would not leave our land, and some bad blood was raised. The white men represented that we were going upon the warpath. They reported many things that were false.

The United States government again asked for a treaty council. My father had become blind and feeble. He could no longer speak for his people. It was then that I took my father's place as chief. In this council I made my first speech to white men. I said to the agent who held the council: "I did not want to come to this council, but I came hoping that we could save blood. The white man has no right to come here and take our country. We have never accepted any presents from the government. Neither Lawyer nor any other chief had authority to sell this land. It has always belonged to my people. It came unclouded to them from our fathers, and we will defend this land as long as a drop of Indian blood warms the hearts of our men."

The agent said he had orders, from the Great White Chief at Washington, for us to go upon the Lapwai Reservation, and that if we obeyed he would help us in many ways. "You must move to the agency," he said. I answered him: "I will not. I do not need your help; we have plenty, and we are contented and happy if the white man will let us alone. The reservation is too small for so many people with all their stock. You can keep your presents; we can go to your towns and pay for all we need; we have plenty of horses and cattle to sell, and we won't have any help from you; we are free now; we can go where we please. Our fathers were born here. Here they lived, here they died, here are their graves. We will never leave them." The agent went away, and we had peace for a little while.

Soon after this my father sent for me. I saw he was dying. I took his hand in mine. He said: "My son, my body is returning to my mother earth, and my spirit is going very soon to see the Great Spirit Chief. When I am gone, think of your country. You are the chief of these people. They look to you to guide them. Always remember that your father never sold this country. You must stop your ears whenever you are asked to sign a treaty selling your home. A few years more, and white men will be all around you. They have their eyes on this land. My son, never forget my dying words. This country holds your father's body. Never sell the bones of your father and your mother." I pressed my father's hand and told him I would protect his grave with my life. My father smiled and passed away to the spirit land.

I buried him in that beautiful valley of winding waters. I love that land more than all the rest of the world. A man who would not love his father's grave is worse than a wild animal.

For a short time we lived quietly. But this could not last. White men had found gold in the mountains around the land of winding water. They stole many horses from us, and we could not get them back because we were Indians. The white men told lies for each other. They drove off a great many of our cattle. Some white men branded our young cattle so they could claim them. We had no friend who would plead our cause before the law councils. It seemed to me that some of the white men in Wallowa were doing these things on purpose to get up a war. They knew that we were not strong enough to fight them. I labored hard to avoid trouble and bloodshed. We gave up some of our country to the white men, thinking that then we could have peace. We were mistaken. The white man would not let us alone. We could have avenged our wrongs many times, but we did not. Whenever the government has asked us to help them against other Indians, we have never refused. When the white men were few and we were strong we could have killed them all off, but the Nez Perces wished to live at peace.

If we have not done so, we have not been to blame. I believe that the old treaty has never been correctly reported. If we ever owned the land we own it still, for we never sold it. In the treaty councils the commissioners have claimed that our country had been sold to the government. Suppose a white man should come to me and say, "Joseph, I like your horses, and I want to buy them." I say to him, "No, my horses suit me, I will not sell them." Then he goes to my neighbor, and says to him: "Joseph has some good horses. I want to buy them, but he refuses to sell." My neighbor answers, "Pay me the money, and I will sell you Joseph's horses." The white man returns to me, and says, "Joseph, I have bought your horses, and you must let me have them." If we sold our lands to the government, this is the way they were bought.

On account of the treaty made by the other

bands of the Nez Perces, the white men claimed my lands. We were troubled greatly by white men crowding over the line. Some of these were good men, and we lived on peaceful terms with them, but they were not all good.

Nearly every year the agent came over from Lapwai and ordered us on to the reservation. We always replied that we were satisfied to live in Wallowa. We were careful to refuse presents or annuities which he offered.

Through all the years since the white men came to Wallowa we have been threatened and taunted by them and the treaty Nez Perces. They have given us no rest. We have had a few good friends among white men, and they have always advised my people to bear these taunts without fighting. Our young men were quick-tempered, and I have had great trouble in keeping them from doing rash things. I have carried a heavy load on my back ever since I was a boy. I learned then that we were but few, while the white men were many, and that we could not hold our own with them. We were like deer. They were like grizzly bears. We had a small country. Their country was large. We were contented to let things remain as the Great Spirit Chief made them. They were not; and would change the rivers and mountains if they did not suit them.

Year after year we have been threatened, but no war was made upon my people until General Howard came to our country two years ago and told us he was the white war-chief of all that country. He said: "I have a great many soldiers at my back. I am going to bring them up here, and then I will talk to you again. I will not let white men laugh at me the next time I come. The country belongs to the government, and I intend to make you go upon the reservation."

"We were contented to let things remain as the Great Spirit Chief made them. [White men] were not; and would change the rivers and mountains if they did not suit them."

I remonstrated with him against bringing more soldiers to the Nez Perces country. He had one house full of troops all the time at Fort Lapwai.

The next spring the agent at Umatilla agency sent an Indian runner to tell me to meet General Howard at Walla Walla. I could not go myself, but I sent my brother and five other head men to meet him, and they had a long talk.

General Howard said: "You have talked straight, and it is all right. You can stay in Wallowa." He insisted that my brother should go with him to Fort Lapwai. When the party arrived there General Howard sent out runners and called all the Indians in to a grand council. I was in that council. I said to General Howard, "We are ready to listen." He answered that he would not talk then, but would hold a council next day, when he would talk plainly. I said to General Howard: "I am ready to talk today. I have been in a great many councils, but I am no wiser. We are all sprung from a woman, although we are unlike in many things. We can not be made over again. You are as you were made, and as you were made you can remain. We are just as we were made by the Great Spirit, and you can not change us; then why should children of one mother and one father quarrel—why should one try to cheat the other? I do not believe that the Great Spirit Chief gave one kind of men the right to tell another kind of men what they must do."

General Howard replied: "You deny my authority, do you? You want to dictate to me, do you?"

Then one of my chiefs—Too-hool-hool-suit—rose in the council and said to General Howard: "The Great Spirit Chief made the world as it is, and as he wanted it, and he made a part of it for us to live upon. I do not see where you get authority to say that we shall not live where he placed us."

General Howard lost his temper and said: "Shut up! I don't want to hear any more of such talk. The law [the treaty] says you shall go upon the reservation to live, and I want you to do so, but you persist in disobeying the law. If you do not move, I will take the matter into my own hand, and make you suffer for your disobedience."

Too-hool-hool-suit answered: "Who are you, that you ask us to talk, and then tell me I sha'n't talk? Are you the Great Spirit? Did you make the world? Did you make the sun? Did you make the rivers to run for us to drink? Did you make the grass to grow? Did you make all these things, that you talk to us as though we were boys? If you did, then you have the right to talk as you do."

General Howard replied, "You are an impudent fellow, and I will put you in the guard house," and then ordered a soldier to arrest him.

Too-hool-hool-suit made no resistance. He asked General Howard: "Is that your order? I don't care. I have expressed my heart to you. I have nothing to take back. I have spoken for my country. You can arrest me, but you can not change me or make me take back what I have said."

The soldiers came forward and seized my friend and took him to the guard house. My men whispered among themselves whether they should let this thing be done. I counseled them to submit. I knew if we resisted that all the white men present, including General Howard, would be killed in a moment, and we would be blamed. If I had said nothing, General Howard would never have given another unjust order against my men. I saw the danger, and, while they dragged Too-hool-hool-suit to prison, I arose and said: "I am going to talk now. I don't care whether you arrest me or not." I turned to my people and said: "The arrest of Too-hool-hool-suit was wrong, but we will not resent the insult. We were invited to this council to express our hearts, and we have done so." Too-hool-hool-suit was prisoner for five days before he was released.

The council broke up for that day. On the next morning General Howard came to my lodge, and invited me to go with him and White-Bird and Looking-Glass, to look for land for my people. As we rode along we came to some good land that was already occupied by Indians and white people. General Howard, pointing to this land, said: "If you will come on to the reservation, I will give you these lands and move these people off."

I replied: "No. It would be wrong to disturb these people. I have no right to take their homes. I have never taken what did not belong to me. I will not now."

We rode all day upon the reservation, and found no good land unoccupied. I have been informed by men who do not lie that General Howard sent a letter that night, telling the soldiers at Walla Walla to go to Wallowa Valley, and drive us out upon our return home.

In the council, next day, General Howard informed me, in a haughty spirit, that he would give my people thirty days to go back home, collect all their stock, and move on to the reservation, saying, "If you are not here in that time, I shall consider that you want to fight, and will send my soldiers to drive you on."

I said: "War can be avoided, and it ought to be avoided. I want no war. My people have always been the friends of the white man. Why are you in such a hurry? I can not get ready to move in thirty days. Our stock is scattered, and Snake River is very high. Let us wait until fall, then the river will be low. We want time to hunt up our stock and gather supplies for winter."

General Howard replied: "If you let the time run over one day, the soldiers will be there to drive you on to the reservation, and all your cattle and horses outside of the reservation at that time will fall into the hands of the white men."

I knew I had never sold my country, and that I had no land in Lapwai; but I did not want bloodshed. I did not want my people killed. I did not want anybody killed. Some of my people had been murdered by white men, and the white murderers were never punished for it. I told General Howard about this, and again said I wanted no war. I wanted the people who lived upon the lands I was to occupy at Lapwai to have time to gather their harvest.

I said in my heart that, rather than have war, I would give up my country. I would give up my father's grave. I would give up everything rather than have the blood of white men upon the hands of my people.

General Howard refused to allow me more than thirty days to move my people and their stock. I am sure that he began to prepare for war at once.

When I returned to Wallowa I found my people very much excited upon discovering that the soldiers were already in the Wallowa Valley. We held a council and decided to move immediately, to avoid bloodshed.

Too-hool-hool-suit, who felt outraged by his imprisonment, talked for war, and made many of my young men willing to fight rather than be driven like dogs from the land where they were born. He declared that blood alone would wash out the disgrace General Howard had put upon him. It required a strong heart to stand up against such talk, but I urged my people to be quiet, and not to begin a war.

We gathered all the stock we could find, and made an attempt to move. We left many of our horses and cattle in Wallowa, and we lost several hundred in crossing the river. All of my people succeeded in getting across in safety. Many of the Nez Perces came together in Rocky Canyon to hold a grand council. I went with all my people. This council lasted ten days. There was a great deal of war talk, and a great deal of excitement. There was one young brave present whose father had been killed by a white man five years before. This man's blood was bad against white men, and he left the council calling for revenge.

Again I counseled peace, and I thought the danger was past. We had not complied with General Howard's order because we could not, but we intended to do so as soon as possible. I was leaving the council to kill beef for my family, when news came that the young man whose father has been killed had gone out with several other hot-blooded young braves and killed four white men. He rode up to the council and shouted: "Why do you sit here like women? The war has begun already."

I was deeply grieved. All the lodges were moved except my brother's and my own. I saw clearly that the war was upon us when I learned that my young men had been secretly buying ammunition. I heard then that Too-hool-hool-suit, who had been imprisoned by General Howard, had succeeded in organizing a war party. I knew that their acts would involve all my people. I saw that the war could not be prevented. The time had passed. I counseled peace from the beginning. I knew that we were too weak to fight the United States. We had many grievances, but I knew that war would bring more. We had good white friends, who advised us against taking the war path. My friend and brother, Mr. [Arthur I.] Chapman, who has been with us since the surrender, told us just how the war would end. Mr. Chapman took sides against us, and helped General Howard. I do not blame him for doing so. He tried hard to prevent bloodshed. We hoped the white settlers would not join the soldiers. Before the war commenced we had discussed this matter all over, and many of my people were in favor of warning them that if they took no part against us they should not be molested in the event of war being begun by General Howard. This plan was voted down in the war council.

There were bad men among my people who had quarreled with white men, and they talked of their wrongs until they roused all the bad hearts in the council. Still I could not believe that they would begin the war. I know that my young men did a great wrong, but I ask, who was first to blame? They had been insulted a thousand times; their fathers and brothers had been killed; their mothers and wives had been disgraced; they had been driven to madness by whisky sold to them by white men; they had been told by General Howard that all their horses and cattle which they had been unable to drive out of Wallowa were to fall into the hands of white men; and, added to all this, they were homeless and desperate.

I would have given my own life if I could have undone the killing of white men by my people. I blame my young men and I blame the white men. I blame General Howard for not giving my people time to get their stock away from Wallowa. I do not acknowledge that he had the right to order me to leave Wallowa at any time. I deny that either my father or myself ever sold that land. It is still our land. It may never again be our home, but my father sleeps there, and I love it as I love my mother. I left there, hoping to avoid bloodshed.

If General Howard had given me plenty of time to gather up my stock, and treated Too-hool-hool-suit as a man should be treated, there would have been no war.

My friends among white men have blamed me for the war. I am not to blame. When my young men began the killing, my heart was hurt. Although I did not justify them, I remembered all the insults I had endured, and my blood was on fire. Still I would have taken my people to the buffalo country without fighting, if possible.

I could see no other way to avoid a war. We moved over to White Bird Creek, sixteen miles away, and there encamped, intending to collect our stock before leaving; but the soldiers attacked us, and the first battle was fought. We numbered in that battle sixty men, and the soldiers a hundred. The fight lasted but a few minutes, when the soldiers retreated before us for twelve miles. They lost thirty-three killed, and had seven wounded. When an Indian fights, he only shoots to kill; but soldiers shoot at random. None of the soldiers were scalped. We do not believe in scalping, nor in killing wounded men. Soldiers do not kill many Indians unless they are wounded and left upon the battlefield. Then they kill Indians.

Seven days after the first battle, General Howard arrived in the Nez Perces country, bringing seven hundred more soldiers. It was now war in earnest. We crossed the Salmon River, hoping General Howard would follow. We were not disappointed. He did follow us, and we got back between him and his supplies, and cut him off for three days. He sent out two companies to open the way. We attacked them, killing one officer, two guides, and ten men.

We withdrew, hoping the soldiers would follow, but they had got fighting enough for that day. They entrenched themselves, and next day we attacked them again. The battle lasted all day, and was renewed next morning. We killed four and wounded seven or eight.

About this time General Howard found out that we were in his rear. Five days later he attacked us with three hundred and fifty soldiers and settlers. We had two hundred and fifty warriors. The fight lasted twenty-seven hours. We lost four killed and several wounded. General Howard's loss was twenty-nine men killed and sixty wounded.

The following day the soldiers charged upon us, and we retreated with our families and stock a few miles, leaving eighty lodges to fall into General Howard's hands.

Finding that we were outnumbered, we retreated to Bitter Root Valley. Here another body of soldiers came upon us and demanded our surrender. We refused. They said, "You can not get by us." We answered, "We are going by you without fighting if you will let us, but we are going by you anyhow." We then made a treaty with these soldiers. We agreed not to molest any one, and they agreed that we might pass through the Bitter Root country in peace. We bought provisions and traded stock with white men there.

We understood that there was to be no more war. We intended to go peaceably to the buffalo country, and leave the question of returning to our country to be settled afterward.

With this understanding we traveled on for four days, and, thinking that the trouble was all over, we stopped and prepared tent poles to take with us. We started again, and at the end of two days we saw three white men passing our camp. Thinking that peace had been made, we did not molest them. We could have killed them or taken them prisoners, but we did not suspect them of being spies, which they were.

That night the soldiers surrounded our camp. About daybreak one of my men went out to look after his horses. The soldiers saw him and shot him down like a coyote. I have since learned that these soldiers were not those we had left behind. They had come upon us from another direction. The new white war-chief's name was [General John] Gibbon. He charged upon us while some of my people were still asleep. We had a hard fight. Some of my men crept around and attacked the soldiers from the rear. In this battle we lost nearly all our lodges, but we finally drove General Gibbon back.

Finding that he was not able to capture us, he sent to his camp a few miles away for his big guns [cannons], but my men had captured them and all the ammunition. We damaged the big guns all we could, and carried away the powder and lead. In the fight with General Gibbon we lost fifty women and children and thirty fighting men. We remained long enough to bury our dead. The Nez Perces never make war on women and children; we could have killed a great many women and children while the war lasted, but we would feel ashamed to do so cowardly an act.

We never scalp our enemies, but when General Howard came up and joined General Gibbon, their Indian scouts dug up our dead and scalped them. I have been told that General Howard did not order this great shame to be done.

We retreated as rapidly as we could toward

> ***"The Nez Perces never make war on women and children . . . we would feel ashamed to do so cowardly an act."***

the buffalo country. After six days General Howard came close to us, and we went out and attacked him, and captured nearly all his horses and mules (about two hundred and fifty head). We then marched on to the Yellowstone Basin.

On the way we captured one white man and two white women. We released them at the end of three days. They were treated kindly. The women were not insulted. Can the white soldiers tell me of one time when Indian women were taken prisoners, and held three days and then released without being insulted? Were the Nez Perces women who fell into the hands of General Howard's soldiers treated with as much respect? I deny that a Nez Perce was ever guilty of such a crime.

A few days later we captured two more white men. One of them stole a horse and escaped.

We gave the other a poor horse and told him he was free.

Nine days' march brought us to the mouth of Clarke's Fork of the Yellowstone. We did not know what had become of General Howard, but we supposed that he had sent for more horses and mules. He did not come up, but another new war chief [General Samuel D. Sturgis] attacked us. We held him in check while we moved all our women and children and stock out of danger, leaving a few men to cover our retreat.

Several days passed, and we heard nothing of General Howard, or Gibbon, or Sturgis. We had repulsed each in turn, and began to feel secure, when another army, under General Miles, struck us. This was the fourth army, each of which outnumbered our fighting force, that we had encountered within sixty days.

We had no knowledge of General Miles' army until a short time before he made a charge upon us, cutting our camp in two, and capturing nearly all of our horses. About seventy men, myself among them, were cut off. My little daughter, twelve years old, was with me. I gave her a rope, and told her to catch a horse and join the others who were cut off from the camp. I have not seen her since, but I have learned that she is alive and well.

I thought of my wife and children, who were now surrounded by soldiers, and I resolved to go to them or die. With a prayer in my mouth to the Great Spirit Chief who rules above, I dashed unarmed through the line of soldiers. It seemed to me that there were guns on every side, before and behind me. My clothes were cut to pieces and my horse was wounded, but I was unhurt. As I reached the door of my lodge, my wife handed me my rifle, saying: "Here's your gun. Fight!"

The soldiers kept up a continuous fire. Six of my men were killed in one spot near me. Ten or twelve soldiers charged into our camp and got possession of two lodges, killing three Nez Perces and losing three of their men, who fell inside our lines. I called my men to drive them back. We fought at close range, not more than twenty steps apart, and drove the soldiers back upon their main line, leaving their dead in our hands. We secured their arms and ammunition. We lost, the first day and night, eighteen men and three women. General Miles lost twenty-six killed and forty wounded. The following day General Miles sent a messenger into my camp under protection of a white flag. I sent my friend Yellow Bull to meet him.

Yellow Bull understood the messenger to say that General Miles wished me to consider the situation; that he did not want to kill my people unnecessarily. Yellow Bull understood this to be a demand for me to surrender and save blood. Upon reporting this message to me, Yellow Bull said he wondered whether General Miles was in earnest. I sent him back with my answer, that I had made up my mind, but would think about it and send word soon. A little later he sent some Cheyenne scouts with another message. I went out to meet them. They said they believed that General Miles was sincere and really wanted peace. I walked on to General Miles' tent. He met me and we shook hands. He said, "Come, let us sit down by the fire and talk this matter over." I remained with him all night; next morning Yellow Bull came over to see if I was alive, and why I did not return.

General Miles would not let me leave the tent to see my friend alone.

Yellow Bull said to me: "They have got you in their power, and I am afraid they will never let you go again. I have an officer in our camp, and I will hold him until they let you go free."

I said: "I do not know what they mean to do with me, but if they kill me you must not kill the officer. It will do no good to avenge my death by killing him."

Yellow Bull returned to my camp. I did not make any agreement that day with General Miles. The battle was renewed while I was with him. I was very anxious about my people. I knew that we were near Sitting Bull's camp in King George's land, and I thought maybe the Nez Perces who had escaped would return with assistance. No great damage was done to either party during the night.

On the following morning I returned to my camp by agreement, meeting the officer who had been held a prisoner in my camp at the flag of truce. My people were divided about surrendering. We could have escaped from Bear Paw Mountain if we had left our wounded, old women, and children behind. We were unwilling to do this. We had never heard of a wounded Indian recovering while in the hands of white men.

On the evening of the fourth day General Howard came in with a small escort, together with my friend Chapman. We could now talk understandingly. General Miles said to me in plain words, "If you will come out and give up your arms, I will spare your lives and send you to your reservation." I do not know what passed between General Miles and General Howard.

I could not bear to see my wounded men and women suffer any longer; we had lost enough already. General Miles had promised that we might return to our own country with what stock we had left. I thought we could start again. I believed General Miles, or I never would have surrendered. I have heard that he has been censured for making the promise to return us to Lapwai. He could not have made any other terms with me at that time. I would have held him in check until my friends came to my assistance, and then neither of the generals nor their soldiers would have ever left Bear Paw Mountain alive.

On the fifth day I went to General Miles and gave up my gun, and said, "From where the sun now stands I will fight no more." My people needed rest—we wanted peace.

I was told we could go with General Miles to Tongue River and stay there until spring, when we would be sent back to our country. Finally it was decided that we were to be taken to Tongue River. We had nothing to say about it. After our arrival at Tongue River, General Miles received orders to take us to Bismarck. The reason given was, that subsistence would be cheaper there.

General Miles was opposed to this order. He said: "You must not blame me. I have endeavored to keep my word, but the chief who is over me has given the order, and I must obey it or resign. That would do you no good. Some other officer would carry out the order."

I believe General Miles would have kept his word if he could have done so. I do not blame him for what we have suffered since the surrender. I do not know who is to blame. We gave up all our horses—over eleven hundred—and all our saddles—over one hundred—and we have not heard from them since. Somebody has got our horses.

General Miles turned my people over to another soldier, and we were taken to Bismarck. Captain Johnson, who now had charge of us, received an order to take us to Fort Leavenworth. At Leavenworth we were placed on a low river bottom, with no water except river water to drink and cook with. We had always lived in a healthy country, where the mountains were high and the water was cold and clear. Many of my people sickened and died, and we buried them in this strange land. I cannot tell how much my heart suffered for my people while at Leavenworth. The Great Spirit Chief who rules above seemed to be looking some other way, and did not see what was being done to my people.

During the hot days [July 1878] we received notice that we were to be moved farther away from our own country. We were not asked if we were willing to go. We were ordered to get into railroad cars. Three of my people died on the way to Baxter Springs [Kansas]. It was worse to die there than to die fighting in the mountains.

We were moved from Baxter Springs to the Indian Territory, and set down without our lodges. We had but little medicine, and we were nearly all sick. Seventy of my people have died since we moved there.

We have had a great many visitors who have talked many ways. Some of the chiefs [General Fish and Colonel William Stickney] from Washington came to see us, and selected land for us to live upon. We have not moved to that land, for it is not a good place to live.

The Commissioner Chief [E.A. Hayt, the Commissioner of Indian Affairs] came to see us. I told him, as I told everyone, that I expected General Miles' word would be carried out. He said it "could not be done; that white men now lived in my country and all the land was taken up; that, if I returned to Wallowa, I could not live in peace; that law-papers were out against my young men who began the war, and that the government could not protect my people." This talk fell like a heavy stone upon my heart. I saw that I could not gain anything by talking to him. Other law chiefs [members of a congressional committee] came to see me and said they would help me to get a healthy country. I did not know who to believe. The white people have too many chiefs. They do not understand each other. They do not all talk alike.

The Commissioner Chief [Hayt] invited me to go with him and hunt for a better home than we have now. I like the land we found [west of the Osage Reservation] better than any place I have seen in that country; but it is not a healthy land. There are no mountains and rivers. The water is warm. It is not a good country for stock. I do not believe my people can live there. I am afraid they will all die. The Indians who occupy that country are dying off. I promised Chief Hayt to go there, and do the best I could until the government got ready to make good General Miles' word. I was not satisfied, but I could not help myself.

Then the Inspector Chief [General John O'Neil] came to my camp and we had a long talk. He said I ought to have a home in the mountain country north, and that he would write a letter to the Great Chief at Washington. Again the hope of seeing the mountains of Idaho and Oregon grew up in my heart.

At last I was granted permission to come to Washington and bring my friend Yellow Bull and our interpreter with me. I am glad we came. I have shaken hands with a great many friends, but there are some things I want to know which no one seems able to explain. I cannot understand how the government sends a man out to fight us, as it did General Miles, and then breaks his word. Such a government has something wrong about it. I cannot understand why so many chiefs are allowed to talk so many different ways, and promise so many different things. I have seen the Great Father Chief [President Rutherford B. Hayes], the next Great Chief [Secretary of the Interior Carl Schurz], the Commissioner Chief [Hayt], the Law Chief [General Butler], and many other law chiefs [congressmen], and they all say they are my friends, and that I shall have justice, but while their mouths all talk right I do not understand why nothing is done for my people. I have heard talk and talk, but nothing is done.

Good words do not last long unless they amount to something. Words do not pay for my dead people. They do not pay for my country, now overrun by white men. They do not protect my father's grave. They do not pay for all my horses and cattle. Good words will not give me back my children. Good words will not make good the promise of your War Chief General Miles. Good words will not give my people good health and stop them from dying. Good words will not get my people a home where they can live in peace and take care of themselves. I am tired of talk that comes to nothing. It makes my heart sick when I remember all the good words and all the broken promises. There has been too much talking by men who had no right to talk. Too many misrepresentations have been made, too many misunderstandings have come up between the white men about the Indians.

"I am tired of talk that comes to nothing. It makes my heart sick when I remember all the good words and all the broken promises."

If the white man wants to live in peace with the Indian he can live in peace. There need be no trouble. Treat all men alike. Give them the same law. Give them all an even chance to live and grow. All men were made by the same Great Spirit Chief. They are all brothers. The earth is the mother of all people, and all people should have equal rights upon it. You might as well expect the rivers to run backward as that any man who was born a free man should be contented when penned up and denied liberty to go where he pleases. If you tie a horse to a stake, do you expect he will grow fat? If you pen an Indian up on a small spot of earth, and compel him to stay there, he will not be contented, nor will he grow and prosper. I have asked some of the great white chiefs where they get their authority to say to the Indian that he shall stay in one place, while he sees white men going where they please. They cannot tell me.

I only ask of the government to be treated as all other men are treated. If I cannot go to my own home, let me have a home in some country where my people will not die so fast. I would like to go to Bitter Root Valley. There my people would be healthy; where they are now they are dying. Three have died since I left my camp to come to Washington.

When I think of our condition my heart is heavy. I see men of my race treated as outlaws and driven from country to country, or shot down like animals.

I know that my race must change. We can not hold our own with the white men as we are. We only ask an even chance to live as other men live. We ask to be recognized as men. We ask that the same law shall work alike on all men. If the Indian breaks the law, punish him by the law. If the white man breaks the law, punish him also.

Let me be a free man—free to travel, free to stop, free to work, free to trade where I choose, free to choose my own teachers, free to follow the religion of my fathers, free to think and talk and act for myself—and I will obey every law, or submit to the penalty.

Whenever the white man treats an Indian as they treat each other, then we will have no more wars. We shall all be alike—brothers of one father and one mother, with one sky above us and one country around us, and one government for all. Then the Great Spirit Chief who rules above will smile upon this land, and send rain to wash out the bloody spots made by brothers' hands from the face of the earth. For this time the Indian race are waiting and praying. I hope that no more groans of wounded men and women will ever go to the ear of the Great Spirit Chief above, and that all people may be one people. In-mut-too-yah-lat-lat has spoken for his people.

Chief Joseph and his people were never allowed to return to their home in the Wallowa Valley. Instead, they were moved to the Colville Reservation in northern Washington during the mid-1880s, and it is there that Chief Joseph died in 1904.

SOURCES

Aly, Bower, and Lucile Folse Aly, *American Short Speeches: An Anthology,* Macmillan, 1968.

Armstrong, Virginia Irving, compiler, *I Have Spoken: American History Through the Voices of the Indians,* Sage Books, 1971.

Beal, Merrill D., *"I Will Fight No More Forever:" Chief Joseph and the Nez Perce War,* University of Washington Press, 1963.

Brown, Dee, *Bury My Heart at Wounded Knee: An Indian History of the American West,* Holt, 1970.

Haines, Francis, *The Nez Perces: Tribesmen of the Columbia Plateau,* University of Oklahoma Press, 1955.

Jones, Louis Thomas, *Aboriginal American Oratory: The Tradition of Eloquence Among the Indians of the United States,* Southwest Museum (Los Angeles), 1965.

Josephy, Alvin M., Jr., *The Nez Perce Indians and the Opening of the Northwest,* Yale University Press, 1965.

McLuhan, T.C., *Touch the Earth: A Self-Portrait of Indian Existence,* Outerbridge & Dienstfrey, 1971.

Nabokov, Peter, editor, *Native American Testimony: A Chronicle of Indian-White Relations from Prophecy to the Present, 1492-1992,* Penguin Books, 1991.

Rosenstiel, Annette, *Red and White: Indian Views of the White Man, 1492-1982,* Universe Books, 1983.

Sanders, Thomas E., and Walter W. Peek, *Literature of the American Indian,* Glencoe Press, 1973.

Vanderwerth, W.C., *Indian Oratory: Famous Speeches by Noted Indian Chieftains,* University of Oklahoma Press, 1971.

Witt, Shirley Hill, and Stan Steiner, editors, *The Way: An Anthology of American Indian Literature,* Knopf, 1972.

Coretta Scott King

1927–

African American civil rights activist

For more than twenty-five years, Coretta Scott King—the widow of slain civil rights leader Martin Luther King, Jr.—has labored tirelessly to keep the spirit of her husband's life and work alive. Her efforts have taken her throughout the world on a mission to promote justice and harmony, not only between the races but between individuals and even entire nations. Through the written and the spoken word and by her own example as head of the Martin Luther King, Jr., Center for Nonviolent Social Action, she has pledged to "keep the dream alive" so that a future generation might one day achieve the goals of racial equality that still seem out of reach as the twentieth century draws to a close.

Coretta Scott King's life began on the family farm in rural Alabama. Although her parents had not attended school beyond the elementary grades, they placed a high value on education and managed to send all three of their children to college. Singing was the first great love of Coretta's life, and in 1951 she graduated from Ohio's Antioch College with a degree in music and elementary education. After that, she pursued advanced studies in voice at the New England Conservatory in Boston, where she met a young minister named Martin Luther King, Jr., who was then at work on his doctorate degree at Boston University. Romance blossomed, and in June 1953, the couple was married. A little more than a year later, with Coretta having earned her degree in voice and Martin having completed all but his dissertation, they moved to Montgomery, Alabama, where Martin had accepted a position as pastor of the Dexter Avenue Baptist Church.

The Kings barely had time to settle into their new home before Martin was drawn into what would become one of the landmark events of the fledgling civil rights movement, the 1955 Montgomery bus boycott. From that moment on, Coretta was almost always at her husband's side, lending him her support and encouragement at demonstrations and marches across the South and accompanying him on his travels throughout the rest of the nation and the world. (During the early years, she also handled much of the administrative work connected with his activities.) As the years went by, she began making more and more solo appearances at various civil rights functions, a number of which were benefit concerts at which she sang and lectured. While Coretta often functioned as Martin's representative at these affairs, she was also becoming a respected leader in her own right.

On April 4, 1968, Martin Luther King, Jr., was in Memphis, Tennessee, to participate in a rally on behalf of striking sanitation workers. As he stood on the balcony of his motel room that evening around dinnertime, he was struck by an assassin's bullet and died a couple of hours later. Coretta, who was home in Atlanta recuperating from surgery, arrived in Memphis early the next morning to accompany her husband's body on the flight back to Georgia. On April 8, she and her family and other civil rights leaders headed back to Memphis to lead a massive demonstration Martin had planned to participate in before his death. Later that day at city hall, Coretta—obviously grieving yet quietly composed—addressed the crowd. Her speech is reprinted here from her autobiography, My Life with Martin Luther King, Jr., *Holt, 1969.*

To my dear friends in Memphis and throughout this nation:

I come here today because I was impelled to come. During my husband's lifetime I have always been at his side when I felt that he needed me, and needed me most. During the twelve years of our struggle for human rights and freedom for all people, I have been in complete accord with what he stood for.

I came because whenever it was impossible for my husband to be in a place where he wanted to be, and felt that he needed to be, he would occasionally send me to stand in for him. And so today, I felt that he would have wanted me to be here.

I need not say to you that he never thought in terms of his personal welfare, but always in terms of the cause which he dedicated his life to, and that cause we shared with him. I have always felt that anything I could do to free him to carry on his work, that I wanted to do this, and this would be the least that I could do.

Three of our four children are here today, and they came because they wanted to come. And I want you to know that in spite of the times that he had to be away from his family, his children knew that Daddy loved them, and the time that he spent with them was well spent. And I always said that it's not the quantity of time that is important but the quality of time.

I have been deeply gratified, and my spirit has been uplifted, because so many thousands of persons and followers of my husband, like you, have done so many wonderful things and said so many kind things to lift my spirit and that of our family. Your presence here today indicates your devotion, and I would say your dedication to those things which he believed in, and those things that he gave his life for.

My husband was a loving man, a man who was completely devoted to nonviolence, and I don't need to say that. And he, I think, somehow was able to instill much of this into his family. We want to carry on the best we can in the tradition in which we feel he would want us to carry on.

And this hour to me represents much more than just a time to talk about and to eulogize my husband, who I can say was a great man, a great father and a great husband. We loved him dearly, the children loved him dearly. And we know that his spirit will never die.

And those of you who believe in what Martin Luther King, Jr., stood for, I would challenge you today to see that his spirit never dies and that we will go forward from this experience, which to me represents the crucifixion, on toward the resurrection and the redemption of the spirit.

How many times have I heard him say, that with every Good Friday there comes Easter. When Good Friday comes these are the moments in life when we feel that all is lost, and there is no hope. But then Easter comes as a time of resurrection, of rebirth, of hope and fulfillment.

We must carry on because this is the way he would have wanted it to have been. We are not going to get bogged down. I hope in this moment we are going to go forward; we are going to continue his work to make all people truly free and to make every person feel that he is a human being. His campaign for the poor must go on.

Twelve years ago in Montgomery, Alabama,

Coretta Scott King

we started out with the bus protest, trying to get a seat, the right to sit down on the bus in any seat that was available. We moved through that period on to the period of desegregating public accommodations and on through voting rights, so that we could have political power. And now we are at the point where we must have economic power.

He was concerned about the least of these, the garbage collectors, the sanitation workers here in Memphis. He was concerned that you have a decent income and protection that was due you. And this was why he came back to Memphis to give his aid.

We are concerned about not only the Negro poor, but the poor all over America and all over the world. Every man deserves a right to a job or an income so that he can pursue liberty, life, and happiness. Our great nation, as he often said, has the resources, but his question was: Do we have the will? Somehow I hope in this resurrection experience the will will be created within the hearts, and minds, and the souls, and the spirits of those who have the power to make these changes come about.

If this can be done, then I know that his death will be the redemptive force that he so often talked about in terms of one giving his life to a great cause and the things that he believed in.

He often said, unearned suffering is redemptive, and if you give your life to a cause in which you believe, and which is right and just—and it is—and if your life comes to an end as a result of this, then your life could not have been lived in a more redemptive way. And I think that this is what my husband has done.

But then I ask the question: How many men must die before we can really have a free and true and peaceful society? How long will it take? If we can catch the spirit, and the true meaning of this experience, I believe that this nation can be transformed into a society of love, of justice, peace, and brotherhood where all men can really be brothers.

In the years since her husband's death, Coretta Scott King has taken a leading role in the effort to create "a society of love, of justice, peace, and brotherhood." In May 1968, just weeks after the assassination, she journeyed to Washington to participate in the Poor People's Campaign, a project of her husband's that had been postponed while he devoted himself to the cause of the striking sanitation workers in Memphis. In 1969, she announced plans to establish the Martin Luther King, Jr., Center for Nonviolent Social Change in Atlanta, which carries on its namesake's quest for better interracial relations through nonviolent action. (Today she serves as the center's president, raising funds and helping to develop and direct the many different seminars, training programs, and workshops it offers.) During the 1970s, she was active in the movement to have the neighborhood around the center designated a National Historic Site, a status it achieved in 1980. Another major victory came in January 1986, when—after years of intense lobbying by black leaders from all walks of life—the country observed the first legal celebration of the national Martin Luther King, Jr., holiday.

Coretta Scott King has spread her late husband's message in other ways as well. Her syndicated weekly newspaper column has provided her with the opportunity to comment on various social, political, and economic issues from a "Kingian" perspective. She also travels extensively throughout the United States and the world, offering her support to political and human rights movements and speaking to a wide variety of audiences, always emphasizing her unwavering commitment to nonviolence.

On April 8, 1993, for example, she appeared before the National Press Club in Washington, D.C., to assess the state of black America twenty-five years after the release of the Kerner Report. (The Kerner Report sprang from a landmark government investigation into the racial unrest that plagued the nation's cities during the summer of 1967. The authors of the report had concluded that "white racism" was the principal cause of the riots and that the United States was quickly splitting into two distinct communities, "one white, one black, separate and unequal.") As King makes clear in her speech (furnished by the Center for Nonviolent Social Change), much remains to be done in the quest for equality and justice for all Americans.

Thank you for your very gracious introduction. It is a great pleasure to be here today and address this forum. My thanks to the board of governors of the National Press Club for sponsoring my participation today.

I have been asked to speak about civil rights in America twenty-five years after the Kerner Report was issued to the nation on March 1, 1968.

To commemorate the twenty-fifth anniversary of the report of the National Advisory Commission on Civil Disorders, the Milton Eisenhower Foundation has issued a report of its own, entitled "Investing in Children and Youth, Reconstructing Our Cities." I am in general agreement with the Eisenhower Foundation assessment that the famous prophesy of the Kerner Commission of "two societies, one black, one white—separate and unequal—is more relevant today than in 1968, and more complex, with the emergence of multiracial disparities and growing income segregation."

The cancer of racism flourished during the last decade as a climate of hostility to civil rights was permitted to fester in America, including the Supreme Court and the Justice Department. Working people of different races were forced to compete for scarce jobs and opportunities. With the shattering intensity of a lightning bolt, the violence in Los Angeles, Atlanta and other cities a year ago revealed the deep racial divisions that frustrate our hopes for national unity.

In this new era of hope and optimism for the future, let us remember that racism not only remains a major problem in American society; it is the single most destructive force in American life.

African Americans have probably made more progress in politics than in any other arena of American society, as evidenced by the election of the nation's first black governor and first black woman U.S senator. According to the Joint Center for Political Studies, there are more than seventy-five hundred black elected officials in the U.S. today, compared with less than one thousand when the Kerner Commission report was released in 1968. Yet seventy-five hundred black office holders is still less than two percent of all the elected officials in the nation, even though we are twelve percent of the population of the U.S. Clearly, we have to do better before we can say we have achieved political empowerment.

In the social sphere, we have desegregated public accommodations, such as hotels, restaurants and public transportation. We see more interracial friendships today, but all too often a vast gulf of distrust and hostility has stifled prospects for interracial brother and sisterhood America. This is a great disappointment. As Martin Luther King, Jr., said, "We have to *be* together before we can learn to *live* together."

Equal *economic* opportunity has remained an elusive goal. There has been little progress for African American executives in the highest echelons of corporate management. Today no black American heads a Fortune 500 company and few can be found in the higher levels of decision-making in multinational corporations. Black businesses and entrepreneurs are still being redlined by banks, and black home buyers are still being steered away from neighborhoods by realtors and experiencing discrimination in securing home loans.

The average median income for African American families has been holding at about sixty percent of the figure for white families. Nearly half of African American children are still living in poverty. The unemployment rate for black workers today is about double the rate for white workers. As Andrew Young has said, "The struggle of the 1990s is to integrate the money."

The key to economic self-sufficiency for black Americans who are living in poverty is jobs and education. Parents who have decent jobs are providers for their children and models for their behavior. But they are also a force for community stability. Other social goals, like clean and safe streets, decent housing, adequate medical care and positive race relations can only come from a base of full employment.

Nothing less than the future of America is at stake. Right now a new generation is growing up, all too many in homes where the parent is without work. The unemployment rate for black teenagers is about forty percent nationwide and much higher in cities like Los Angeles.

With no role models at home, where will these children learn about the "work ethic"? With declining educational and training opportunities, where will they learn job skills and work habits that are essential for productive employment?

After the violence in Los Angeles last year, Congress and the president enacted a 1.3 billion-dollar aid package and a 500 million-dollar summer jobs program to employ young people across the country. I don't know how many jobs were actually created or how long these jobs have lasted. But this appropriation is in keeping with the pattern of acting after a crisis has erupted. What we need instead is a more sustained, cost-efficient and pro-active investment in job training, which has been lacking since the Kerner Report was issued.

> ***"Let us remember that racism not only remains a major problem in American society; it is the single most destructive force in American life."***

President Clinton, to his credit, wants to create another 200,000 jobs and invest an additional 14 billion dollars in tax incentives for job creation. This would be a good beginning, but Senate Republicans want to kill even this modest investment. They claim to be concerned about its effect on the federal deficit, but many of them voted for huge deficits under presidents Reagan and Bush.

Yet, government statistics indicate that every one percent of unemployment costs the federal government 50 billion dollars, according to the economist Woodrow Ginsburg. If we achieved something close to full employment, the entire federal deficit would be eliminated.

We know that government can't accept the entire burden of educating and training the unemployed and putting them to work. Management and labor must also join together to expand their job training programs for minorities. As consumers, we have to press banks and corporations to invest in projects that provide jobs, instead of corporate mergers and real estate deals. As far as tax policy goes, the rule should be incentives for companies that create jobs, but disincentives for those that export jobs.

We have to challenge government, business and labor to create a social contract to fulfill the dream of a nation free from poverty and deprivation, a nation where every willing worker can find a job at a decent wage. This is an ambitious vision, to be sure. But surely it is possible in a nation with the wealth and resources of the U.S.

On top of worsening economic conditions and declining educational opportunities for African Americans, we have to add the fifty million guns, which the Bureau of Alcohol, Tobacco and Firearms estimates have been added to American society since 1968. As a result, the annual death toll from handgun homicides has about tripled since 1968, from about five thousand when the Kerner Report was published to fifteen thousand today.

In the four years after the Kerner Commission report was first published, firearm production doubled in the U.S. I think we should be very concerned about a sharp increase in handgun homicides in the months and years ahead, considering that gun sales reportedly went off the charts in Los Angeles after the violence last year.

I am much encouraged that prospects for enacting the Brady Bill in this session of Congress are good. But I think we need more gun control legislation if we want to stop the mayhem that is destroying our society. Representative Mel Reynolds has introduced legislation that would raise taxes on firearm production and earmark the revenues for medical care related to firearm violence. I would support this approach, as well as legislation to ban automatic weapons and other handgun control measures.

We can simply no longer afford the lax gun control policies that have led to more than 730,000 gun deaths since 1968. I think this is a matter of the most immediate national security to the American people, and it requires strong action from Congress and the White House.

As we call on our federal state and local governments to do more to fight discrimination, let us not forget the private sector. Corporate social responsibility means more than simply obeying affirmative action laws. It means going beyond the letter of the law to make the spirit of equality a part of corporate policy.

In the newspaper industry, for example, racial minorities, who are now about 20 percent of the general population, were only about 9.4 percent of newsroom employees in 1992, according to a survey by the American Society of Newspaper Editors. The percentage of minority supervisors in the nation's newsrooms was only about 6.3 percent. Such statistics help explain why a black crack addict has a better chance of being subjected to a feature profile than a black national merit scholar.

Discrimination in media employment has an impact far beyond just one industry. It has much to do with negative stereotyping that perpetuates racial polarization. Many white reporters do a good job of reporting about minority communities, but I think that their lack of experience-based understanding often leads to cultural myopia. There has to be a better balance between reporting on the very real problems of disadvantaged minorities and their many positive achievements and role models.

If both the print and electronic media will rise to the challenge of making newsrooms look more like America, I think it could help reduce racism throughout the nation.

Another key institution that has a special responsibility to provide leadership for better race relations is organized religion. I believe strongly that the religious community is the front line of the struggle against racism. More than anywhere else it is in our churches and temples and mosques, where most Americans look for moral leadership. As my husband said in his "Letter from a Birmingham Jail," which he wrote thirty years ago this April 16, "the church must be a headlight, not a taillight" in the struggle against racism.

Many white religious leaders have demonstrated courageous leadership in speaking out against racism and some of them marched alongside Martin Luther King, Jr., in every campaign of the civil rights movement. But it is still true, as Martin said, that "the most segregated hour in America is 11:00 A.M. Sunday morning." In addition, all too many white clergy have been silent on the issue of racism. I still wait for the day when a televangelist with millions of viewers tells his flock that racism is unchristian and immoral.

Meanwhile, there must be stronger affirmative action, set asides and other government programs to help the disadvantaged have a decent life. I'm hopeful that President Clinton will restore balance in the U.S. Supreme Court and throughout the federal court system.

Surely creating of society of full economic opportunity for women and men of all races is not an unrealistic goal for a great democracy. For too long we have allowed political leaders and economists tell us why we can't afford full employment and educational opportunities for all of our citizens. We need some political leadership that won't take no for an answer.

In a great democracy the highest standards of equality and tolerance should be observed as part of the obligations of citizenship. But we have learned that there is nothing automatic about good race relations. Instead we must work unceasingly to foster interracial trust and cooperation, and the nation's schools should take the lead in this effort.

It is my hope that the Martin Luther King, Jr., holiday will help to heal the wounds and breach the divisions that have polarized Americans for these two centuries. No other government agency or program has done a more effective job of promoting better race relations with fewer resources than the Martin Luther King, Jr., Federal Holiday Commission, not just on the holiday, but all year long. The commission's contributions will be even more significant in the future, if Congress will see the wisdom and benefits in providing full funding for this unique and invaluable federal agency.

Equal rights can be legislated, but genuine brotherhood can not, for it comes from the heart. But it can be taught by example and by study. Young people of different races, beginning in preschool and continuing on through graduate school, if necessary, should be taught that tolerance and interracial cooperation are patriotic as well as moral obligations. Such a commitment to improving race relations can help prevent further racial conflict.

My husband once said that "we must work passionately and indefatigably to bridge the gulf between our scientific progress and our moral progress. One of the great problems of mankind is that we suffer from a poverty of the spirit which stands in glaring contrast to our scientific and technological abundance. The richer we have become materially, the poorer we have become morally and spiritually."

He believed that "there is another kind of power that America can and should be. It is a moral power, a power harnessed to the service of human beings. If we decide to become a moral power," he said, "we will be able to transform the jangling discords of this world into a beautiful symphony of brotherhood. . . . This will be a glorious day. In reaching it we can fulfill the noblest of American dreams."

Through intensive workshops and educational programs, the King Center in Atlanta, which I serve as president, is providing a unique kind of moral education and training for leadership development. The center has trained thousands of people, including teachers, law enforcement personnel and particularly young people in applying Martin Luther King, Jr.'s philosophy and methods of nonviolence as a way of life, as well as in social conflicts.

"Equal rights can be legislated, but genuine brotherhood can not, for it comes from the heart."

Last year we trained young people from gangs, including the "Crips" and "Bloods" of Los Angeles, Atlanta and other cities. We just finished training over seven hundred Detroit teenagers in kingian nonviolence, which is the term we use for Martin Luther King, Jr.'s philosophy and methods of nonviolent social change and conflict resolution. We have already provided training and orientation in kingian nonviolence for several thousand Detroit youth this year and we plan to have trained twenty thousand Detroit youngsters by the time this project is completed. We believe that this training will not only reduce violence in Detroit, but will also help energize and organize the young people as an active force for social and economic progress and better race relations.

We are teaching young people that nonviolence is a powerful force for moral transformation. We are empowering them to rise above the bitter cycle of revenge, retaliation and retribution that poisons human relationships and create instead a climate of cooperation that can confront and rectify injustice in a more loving way. We are teaching them how to engage their adversaries, not with anger, hatred and revenge, but with unconditional love, respect and courtesy.

My husband, Martin Luther King, Jr., challenged us to make America a more loving community. He called on people of all races, religions and ethnic groups to put an end to poverty, racism and violence. He called us to have the vision and courage to create a beloved community of caring and compassion, where *all* people can live together in peace and justice.

Like Martin Luther King, Jr., we were not put here in this greatest of nations to dream small dreams and perform insignificant deeds. The struggle to fulfill his dream of the beloved community will demand courage, dedication, and yes, sacrifice.

This is why we are going back to the Lincoln Memorial on August 28, which is the thirtieth anniversary of the great March on Washington, where Martin Luther King, Jr., told the world about his dream. We will come to Washington in great numbers, Americans of all races—black, white, red, brown and yellow—in a new coalition of conscience, united in our challenge to the nation's leadership to take action to fulfill the dream, for now is *not* the time for hesitation. Now is *not* the time for uncertainty. Now is *not* the time for indecision.

But now *is* the time to move forward in a unified nonviolent coalition to fulfill the promise of democracy. *Now* is the time to make real the dream of freedom and justice. And *now* is the time to stand up against racism and to rise up in a great new movement for national unity, peace and brotherhood.

Thank you and God bless you.

Every year as part of the Martin Luther King, Jr., national holiday celebration, Coretta Scott King delivers a "State of the Dream" speech that focuses on a specific aspect of American life and society and its impact on the drive to achieve racial harmony. In her 1994 speech, delivered on January 17 at Atlanta's Ebenezer Baptist Church, she discussed a problem then uppermost on many people's minds—youth violence. King's speech provided by the Center for Nonviolent Change.

Thank you, Chairman Jesse Hill, Jr., for your generous introduction. Congressman Lewis, Secretary Shalala, Governor Miller, Governor Voinovich, Mayor Campbell, Mrs. Tambo, Ambassador Young, Mrs. Farris, members of the clergy, distinguished guests, it is a great pleasure and an honor to share this day and be with all of you today.

Dr. Roberts, I especially want to thank you and all the members of Ebenezer for hosting this beautiful service of commemoration marking the ninth annual Martin Luther King, Jr., holiday.

This year we mark the holiday with an urgent concern about the tidal wave of violence that has engulfed our nation. With all of the assaults, rapes, homicides, drive-by shootings, armed robberies, kidnappings, carjackings, spouse and child abuse, our cities and towns have become war zones. Hospital emergency rooms now treat three times as many gunshot wounds as they did six years ago. There is an arms race *within* America that is a direct and immediate threat to our national security. What we are facing is a *national emergency* that is destroying the soul of America and our hopes for the future.

Yet, amid all of this suffering and tragedy, I bring you a message of hope today. The American people are beginning to rise up. All across the nation people are starting to demand action to *stop the violence*.

This uprising against violence has already won impressive victories few thought possible when we met here last year. The passage of the Brady Bill was a significant first step toward getting some sanity in our handgun policy.

A new anticrime legislative package includes $400 million for antiviolence programs. From the Atlantic to the Pacific, communities in crisis have begun to organize citizens patrols, antidrug hotlines and gun turn-in programs, such as the pioneering effort being conducted here in Atlanta by SCLC. Conflict-resolution programs are springing up in schools and workplaces.

Even more encouraging, the news media and political leaders have begun to earnestly examine the *systemic injustices* of poverty, deprivation and exploitation which contribute to the destructive violence in our society. All of these efforts, and many more, are needed to end the bloodshed in our communities.

Somehow, millions of America's young people have lost their faith and their self-esteem. We can blame the demoralizing effects of poverty and the destabilization of families that so often goes with it. We can blame the seductive culture of materialism that leaves so many young people feeling shallow and empty.

But let us be clear. Poverty and systemic injustice are *never* justification for violence and brutality. *No* injustice, no matter how great, can excuse even a single act of violence against another human being.

If you are driving on a wet and slippery road, that's no excuse to drive recklessly. On the contrary, you have a moral obligation to drive even more carefully. In the same way, we have a moral obligation to challenge poverty, racism and systemic injustice with a carefully thought-out plan of nonviolent action, not with mindless acts of violence.

Poverty and injustice can *never* excuse violence. And violence must *never* be accepted as an excuse for tolerating poverty and injustice.

There are many causes of the explosion of youth violence, but I feel strongly that the root cause is spiritual and moral decay. Wherever you find violence, you find people who have lost their spiritual bearings.

We have to keep working for a more just society, but we can't afford to wait for the day when it finally becomes a reality, because we are losing too many young people to the war in our streets. We have to restore faith in God, faith in the power within us to change and make a positive difference in our lives and the world. We have to set an irresistible example of decency and truthful living for young people so that they will be strong enough to resist violence and poverty and materialism.

If we dare to call ourselves followers of Martin Luther King, Jr., if we dare to be worthy of the dream, *now* is the time to follow the rhetoric of concern with the force of *action*. We have to do more, much more to provide young people with a moral education and a spiritual foundation that will empower them to resist this culture of violence. This is the meaning of the 1994 birthday theme; "Nonviolence: Empowering to Make a Difference." Our more than thirty King Week events and all of the King Center's programs and projects are designed to serve this purpose.

We have to teach young people about the importance of personal responsibility, that life has moral obligations as well as privileges. With more and more homes broken or headed by a single parent, we have to organize more mentoring and big brother and sister programs to give young people every opportunity to get the moral and spiritual guidance that will empower them to become productive citizens and decent parents.

> ***"No injustice, no matter how great, can excuse even a single act of violence against another human being."***

It's time for us to demand that public schools become partners in moral development. We're not asking that they get involved in religious controversy or engaged in church and state conflict. But we must insist that they create programs to teach young people the same virtues that empowered Martin Luther King, Jr. These virtues are honesty, tolerance for diversity, self-respect and respect for others, love, forgiveness, compassion, sharing and most of all, the moral courage to resist peer group pressure and to stand up for what is right.

We have to instill in American youth a passion for justice and peace and the strength to embrace the philosophy and strategies of nonviolence that Dr. King taught, preached and lived. We have to teach them by *example* that nonviolence is the most revolutionary force for social and personal transformation ever applied. This is what we are about at the King Center, and we need your help more than ever to meet this challenge.

We must also demand more from young people themselves. At this point I want to take a moment to address the young people who are here with us today and those who are watching on television.

I ask the young people of America to make Martin Luther King, Jr., Day a day of service. Whether you are African American, Hispanic or Native American, whether you are caucasian or Asian American, you are part of the great dream Martin Luther King, Jr., had for America. This is not a black holiday; it is a *peoples'* holiday. And it is the young people of all races and religions who hold the keys to the fulfillment of his dream.

I know many of you are having a difficult time. No other generation in history has been more challenged by temptations that lead to human destruction. It requires an almost heroic effort on your part to resist the drug pushers, to say no to guns, to say no to irresponsible sex, to say no to greed and dishonesty. To say no to prejudice and hatred. The people who submit to these temptations end up feeling empty, lost and alienated. But, those who resist evil find greater self-esteem and stronger character.

> ***"[Martin Luther King, Jr., Day] is not a black holiday; it is a peoples' holiday."***

Young people, don't let yourselves be used by the purveyors of violence and moral depravity. *Make no more deals with the devil.* Make yourselves strong and righteous, make yourselves drum majors for justice and peace and freedom. No one else can do that for you. There is no better way to honor Martin Luther King, Jr.

How do you become a drum major? Start by getting fed up about drug pushers destroying your community, and decide to do something about it. You could also begin by getting angry about violence in the media—as well as in the street, and decide not to support violent movies, music or television. You can start by getting fired up about the national disgrace of poverty and neglected children, and organizing some action to eliminate it. You can speak out against bigotry and hatred. You can channel your anger into a positive, creative and powerful force for change. And the way you do this is study and commit to the teachings of Martin Luther King, Jr., and apply them with a vigorous spirit of determination.

Remember that the most important tool for your empowerment is the force of your will. *You* have to decide that nobody is going to lead you to destruction, that *you* are going to be a person of high moral and spiritual standards. *You* have to decide that *you* are going to be a person who demands excellence from yourself, as well as from others.

Martin Luther King, Jr., was not a physically large man. His strength did not come from his ability to hurt anyone. He never held political office, he never had a lot of money. Yet he was one of the most powerful leaders of this century. His power came from faith in God and love for all humanity, including his most violent and hate-filled adversaries.

He was empowered by love, the greatest power of all—a power that cannot be taken away by threats, abuse or violence. His love was so powerful that it is still a motivating force long after his death. That's why people in more than one hundred countries are celebrating his birthday with a magnificent outpouring of love and service and healing.

I call on you on this holiday to say *yes* to the power of love. Say yes to nonviolence, so you will be encouraged and empowered to carry forward his unfinished work. Get involved in the nonviolent movement against injustice. Come out from the shadows of apathy and indifference.

Young people, yours is the chosen generation, the generation which must lead a nonviolent revolution for a better world. America needs your contributions. We need your energy, your courage and your creativity to create a truly great society. The King Center is here to provide you with training that can help you be more effective. If you accept this challenge with courage, determination and dedication, some future historian will write that yours was the generation that fulfilled the dream of Martin Luther King, Jr.

This is not an easy road to travel. There will be times when it seems unbearably difficult. When these times come, I hope you will remember these words from a sermon by Martin Luther King, Jr. He said, "I would urge you to give priority to the search for God," said Dr. King. "Allow His spirit to permeate your being. Before the ship of your life reaches its last harbor, there will be long, drawn-out storms, howling and jostling winds and tempestuous seas that make the heart stand still.... Without God all of our efforts turn to ashes and our sunrises to darkest nights.... But with Him we are able to rise from tension-packed valleys to the sublime heights of inner peace, and find radiant stars of hope against the nocturnal bosom of life's most depressing nights."

Building moral character is important. But I don't believe it is the only problem. We must also identify and challenge the external forces behind this epidemic violence.

We must be aware of many factors, alcohol and drug abuse, handguns, unemployment, disintegrating families, inadequate educational opportunities and media glorification of violence all contribute to pervasive alienation, despair and hopelessness among young people. All of these problems are interconnected. All reinforce each other to create a destructive mix of conditions that make frustration, anger and violence all but inevitable.

Studies show that abuse of drugs and alcohol plays a part in the majority of all homicides. Simultaneous with this influx of drugs there has been a huge increase in handgun violence. Since 1970 the number of guns circulating in America has more than doubled to over two hundred million today, including sixty-seven million handguns. *Time* magazine reports that about one hundred thousand students carry guns to school every day.

To stop this war in our communities, we should support legislation that is being introduced in Congress to require further controls on handguns and assault weapons. But, as followers of Martin Luther King, Jr., we must never lose sight of the larger goal of *domestic disarmament.* We must remember that our charge is to create a society free from the threat of these deadly weapons, the *nonviolent* society Martin Luther King, Jr., envisioned and worked to achieve.

In addition to the fragmentation of families, the role of guns, drugs and economic deprivation, we have to recognize that the saturation of American culture with violence has had a *devastating* effect. Our films and television, music videos and even video games for children have gone way too far in glorifying a sick, depraved subculture of violence.

Dr. King expressed a prophetic concern about the growth of violence in entertainment. Back in 1963 he said, "By our readiness to allow arms to be purchased at will and fired at whim; by allowing our movie and television screens to teach our children that the hero is one who masters the art of shooting and the technique of killing . . . we have created an atmosphere in which violence and hatred have become popular pastimes." If this was a concern thirty years ago, it is a crisis today.

A 1990 study of American films revealed that one out of every eight Hollywood movies depicts at least one rape. A survey of pre-teenagers done about the same time found that more of them could identify "slasher" film characters "Jason" and "Freddy" than could identify Martin Luther King, Jr., or Abraham Lincoln.

Young people often look to performing artists for moral guidance and inspiration, as well as entertainment. When these artists glorify guns, beatings and contempt for women, they are injecting poison into the veins of America's future.

I feel strongly that there is an unspoken conspiracy between those who profit from violence. The gun and drug pushers, the producers of violent films, videos and music. Even if they never speak to each other, they depend on each other to reinforce and promote a poisonous culture of violence for monetary gain.

These profiteers are merchants of death. We have given them a free ride for too long, and the time has come for us to put an end to it. We have to create a great American coalition to *take the profit out of violence.*

We must do everything in our power to overthrow their reign of death and destruction. We must become more aggressive lobbyists for antiviolence reforms in our federal, state and local legislative bodies. We must become better-organized consumers, so we can launch boycotts against those who are subsidizing and profiting from the culture of violence. I have to say it again: *we must take the profit out of violence.*

We have to press federal, state and local governments, foundations, corporations and other funding agencies to support those artists who promote a culture of nonviolence. We have to make sure that performing artists and producers of entertainment programs begin to take more responsibility for the consequences of their work.

I am encouraged that President Clinton has challenged the entertainment industry to promote a culture of nonviolence. Today I call on everyone who believes in the dream of Martin Luther King, Jr., to join together in an all-out nonviolent campaign against this culture of violence and materialism, which is so ruthlessly undermining decency in our society.

Let this campaign begin on this day when we honor America's great prophet of peace. Today I call on the followers of Martin Luther King, Jr., here in America and all over the world to observe a *moratorium on violence.* Use *this* day to plant the seeds of a peaceful resolution of divisive conflicts in the family, the community, the nation and world.

Let this moratorium signal a new beginning for America. Let this moratorium set an example of peace and healing and service to humanity. And if we can create just one day of peace, and one day of service, then maybe we can create another . . . and another . . . and another.

We have an historic opportunity for a great national healing. If we will accept these challenges with courage and determination, I can see a great nation being reborn in justice and brotherhood. I see a nation where every child is safe and secure from the mayhem of deadly weapons and the scourge of drugs. I see a nation that nurtures its children and protects their precious innocence with compassion and caring. I see a nation where every child is enrolled in a good school that has all of the resources needed to teach them to love learning.

I see a nation where young people can get as much education as their minds can absorb and a full range of cultural opportunities to enrich their spirits. I see a nation where families are once again restored to wholeness, where parents can find employment adequate to create a decent living for their children. I see a beloved community where children need look no further for positive role models than the faces of their own mothers and fathers.

We *can* bring this great vision into reality. We *can* put an end to epidemic drug abuse and create the beloved community that Martin Luther King, Jr., envisioned, if we work and pray and struggle together in the spirit of nonviolence.

Martin Luther King, Jr., often reminded us that the human family transcends race, religion and national boundaries. His dream was not confined to America, but is a global dream. This is why more than one hundred nations commemorate his birthday in some way. They know that he had a vision of a worldwide beloved community, where every child could have a decent life free from war and violence.

In his last book, entitled *Where Do We Go from Here?: Chaos or Community?,* He challenged his followers to embrace "a new revolution of values."

"A true revolution of values," he said, "will soon look uneasily on the glaring contrast of poverty and wealth . . . and say: 'this is not just.' . . . A true revolution of values will lay hands on the new world order and say of war: 'this way of settling differences . . . cannot be reconciled with wisdom, justice and love."

"A genuine revolution of values," he said, "means in the final analysis that our loyalties must become ecumenical rather than sectional. Every nation must now develop an overriding loyalty to mankind as a whole in order to preserve the best in their individual societies."

We have seen how his philosophy and methods have been used to empower freedom struggles and peace movements all over the world. We are encouraged by the breakthroughs in peace talks between Israelis and Palestinians. We welcome the progress toward reconciliation of the Vatican and Israel, Northern Ireland and Great Britain, the U.S. and Vietnam.

In South Africa, Nelson Mandela and President F.W. De Klerk have been awarded the Nobel Peace Prize for negotiating an agreement for South Africa's transition from apartheid to a nonracial democracy. The King Center has worked long and hard to help the South African people win their freedom. We lobbied Congress for years to pass sanctions against apartheid. We picketed the embassy and some of us went to jail in anti-apartheid protests. At this very moment King Center staff and board members are in South Africa helping with voter education projects in support of their first free elections.

Yet, we are also keenly aware of new threats to peace and stability—the unholy mix of ethnic violence and aggressive nationalism that is shattering hopes for peace in so many regions of our world.

As followers of Martin Luther King, Jr., we can't express concern about what is happening to the children of America and remain silent about the oppression of children around the world. We must find a way to do more to help the suffering children of strife-torn nations, such as Haiti and Bosnia and Somalia. We have to demand international action to help the homeless children on the streets of cities like Rio de Janeiro, the children who have been virtually enslaved in Bangladesh sweatshops or sold into prostitution in Thailand. We have to support the relief agencies that serve these children and other development programs that can help sow the seeds of self-sufficiency throughout Asia, Africa, Latin America and Eastern Europe.

So what is the state of the dream? My brothers and sisters, the dream is very much alive in those people and places we are reaching through the King Center's nonviolence workshops, our community empowerment initiative, our training of law enforcement officers, the mediation we are taking with street gangs—Kingfest, the archives and King papers project. And we'll continue to educate, motivate, mediate, and yes, even agitate when we need to. But until the dream has meaning for all of us, it can not have full meaning for any of us. Help us to share the dream. Help us to reach wider, higher, further, deeper. Help us to touch all humanity when this service concludes, we will begin to assemble downtown for a march commemorating the Martin Luther King, Jr., holiday.

We will march today to signal a vigorous new era of nonviolent protest against poverty, racism and violence.

We call you to join our march for jobs and educational opportunities, for drug- and gun-free zones in our schools, homes and communities.

Join our call for the moral and spiritual renewal of our society.

Help us demand decent health care for everyone.

Support our protest against child abuse and neglect.

Work with us to insure that every American has a decent home and food to eat.

Express your support for the people of South Africa.

Stand up for the war-ravaged children of Bosnia, Burundi and the Middle East, and the millions of hungry children of Africa, Asia and Latin America.

Rise up and help us take the profit out of violence.

Have faith, stand up and march on with a renewed sense of moral and spiritual empowerment.

Rise up and march on with unstoppable courage for the dream of a world aglow with the blessings of peace and prosperity, where the human family can live together as brothers and sisters, a world where love, justice and brotherhood will reign supreme. Keep the dream alive.

SOURCES

King, Coretta Scott, *My Life with Martin Luther King, Jr.*, Holt, 1969.

Martin Luther King, Jr.

1929–1968

African American minister and civil rights activist

Considered one of the outstanding orators of the twentieth century, Martin Luther King, Jr., used his skills as a communicator to become the intellectual and spiritual guiding force of the civil rights movement during the years of its greatest triumphs. His words—both written and spoken—powerfully linked his cause to America's social, political, and religious consciousness. By combining his Christian-influenced ideals with the techniques of nonviolence as practiced by India's Mohandas Gandhi, he infused the civil rights struggle with a sense of urgency and high moral purpose that no one else before him had seemed to be able to convey.

King was born in Atlanta, Georgia, to Martin Luther King, Sr., a prominent black minister, and Alberta Williams King, a teacher. After attending local primary and secondary schools, he continued his education in his hometown at Morehouse College. At first, he felt no particular calling to the religious life, but with the encouragement and support of Morehouse's president, Dr. Benjamin Mays, King came to realize that he could achieve personal and professional fulfillment as a minister. Therefore, after earning his bachelor's degree, he went on to attend Crozer Theological Seminary and then Boston University, from which he received his doctorate degree in 1955.

By then, King was already working in Montgomery, Alabama, as pastor of the Dexter Avenue Baptist Church. It was there, in December 1955, that he first gained national attention for spearheading the black community's famous citywide bus boycott in response to Rosa Parks's arrest for refusing to give up her seat to a white person. Two years later, King co-founded and was chosen first president of the Southern Christian Leadership Conference (SCLC), which had as its chief goal securing equal rights for blacks through assertive but nonviolent action such as protest marches and voter-registration drives.

In 1960, King and his family moved back to Atlanta, where he became copastor (with his father) of Ebenezer Baptist Church. It was not long, however, before he had given up the responsibilities of the pulpit to devote all of his time to the SCLC and its fight for justice. It was a crusade that would occupy him until April 1968, when an assassin's bullet ended his life. Time and time again, King braved hostile crowds and the possibility of arrest and jail to focus attention on the immorality of racial discrimination and also to give blacks a more positive self-image and sense of direction. He was, for example, at the head of the anti-discrimination protests in Birmingham, Alabama, in 1963, led the Selma-to-Montgomery Freedom March in 1965, and rallied blacks in Chicago to challenge segregation in 1966. King also made use of every opportunity to take his message to America and the world through his writings and speeches. It was a message he always delivered with emotion and drama, relying on words and rhythms shaped by his southern background and religious training to touch and inspire his listeners.

On December 5, 1955, King made what qualifies as his first public speech on civil rights. The occasion was a mass meeting at Holt Street Baptist Church in Montgomery, Alabama. Local black leaders had called the meeting to map out a course of action following the arrest of Rosa Parks for violating segregation laws on a city bus. Turning to the new, young minister in town—he was just twenty-six years old—they asked him to deliver the keynote address. Working without notes or a manuscript, King obliged and was met with great enthusiasm. Most of what he said that evening follows; it is reprinted from The Eyes on the Prize Civil Rights Reader *(Penguin, 1991).*

We are here this evening for serious business. We are here in a general sense because first and foremost we are American citizens, and we are determined to apply our citizenship to the fullness of its means. We are here because of our love for democracy, because of our deep-seated belief that democracy transformed from thin paper to thick action is the greatest form of government on earth. But we are here in a specific sense, because of the bus situation in Montgomery. We are here because we are determined to get the situation corrected.

This situation is not at all new. The problem has existed over endless years. For many years now Negroes in Montgomery and so many other areas have been inflicted with the paralysis of crippling fear on buses in our community. On so many occasions, Negroes have been intimidated and humiliated and oppressed because of the sheer fact that they were Negroes. I don't have time this evening to go into the history of these numerous cases.... But at least one stands before us now with glaring dimensions. Just the other day, just last Thursday to be exact, one of the finest citizens in Montgomery—not one of the finest Negro citizens but one of the finest citizens in Montgomery—was taken from a bus and carried to jail and arrested because she refused to get up to give her seat to a white person.... Mrs. Rosa Parks is a fine person. And since it had to happen I'm happy it happened to a person like Mrs. Parks, for nobody can doubt the boundless outreach of her integrity. Nobody can doubt the height of her character, nobody can doubt the depth of her Christian commitment and devotion to the teachings of Jesus....

And just because she refused to get up, she was arrested.... You know my friends there comes a time when people get tired of being trampled over by the iron feet of oppression. There comes a time my friends when people get tired of being flung across the abyss of humiliation where they experience the bleakness of nagging despair. There comes a time when people get tired of being pushed out of the glittering sunlight of life's July and left standing amidst the piercing chill of an Alpine November.

We are here, we are here this evening because we're tired now. Now let us say that we are not here advocating violence. We have overcome that. I want it to be known throughout Montgomery and throughout this nation that we are Christian people. We believe in the Christian religion. We believe in the teachings of Jesus. The only weapon that we have in our hands this evening is the weapon of protest. And secondly, this is the glory of America, with all of its faults. This is the glory of our democracy. If we were incarcerated behind the iron curtains of a Communistic nation we couldn't do this.

Martin Luther King, Jr.

If we were trapped in the dungeon of a totalitarian regime we couldn't do this. But the great glory of American democracy is the right to protest for right.

My friends, don't let anybody make us feel that we ought to be compared in our actions with the Ku Klux Klan or with the White Citizens' Councils. There will be no crosses burned at any bus stops in Montgomery. There will be no white persons pulled out of their homes and taken out to some distant road and murdered.

There will be nobody among us who will stand up and defy the Constitution of this nation. We only assemble here because of our desire to see right exist.

My friends, I want it to be known that we're going to work with grim and firm determination to gain justice on the buses in this city. And we are not wrong, we are not wrong in what we are doing. If we are wrong, then the Supreme Court of this Nation is wrong. If we are wrong, the Constitution of the United States is wrong. If we are wrong, God Almighty is wrong. If we are wrong, Jesus of Nazareth was merely a utopian dreamer and never came down to earth. If we are wrong, justice is a lie. And we are determined here in Montgomery to work and fight until Justice runs down like water and righteousness like a mighty stream.

I want to say that with all of our actions we must stick together. Unity is the great need of the hour. And if we are united, we can get many of the things that we not only desire but which we justly deserve. And don't let anybody frighten you. We are not afraid of what we are doing, because we are doing it within the law. There is never a time in our American democracy that we must ever think we're wrong when we protest. We reserve that right. . . .

We, the disinherited of this land, we who have been oppressed so long are tired of going through the long night of captivity. And we are reaching out for the daybreak of freedom and justice and equality. . . . In all of our doings, in all of our deliberations . . . whatever we do, we must keep God in the forefront. Let us be Christian in all of our action. And I want to tell you this evening that it is not enough for us to talk about love. Love is one of the pinnacle parts of the Christian faith. There is another side called justice. And justice is really love in [application]. Justice is love correcting that which would work against love. . . . Standing beside love is always justice. And we are only using the tools of justice. Not only are we using the tools of persuasion but we've got to use the tools of coercion.

Not only is this thing a process of education but it is also a process of legislation.

And as we stand and sit here this evening, and as we prepare ourselves for what lies ahead, let us go out with a grim and bold determination that we are going to stick together. We are going to work together. Right here in Montgomery when the history books are written in the future, somebody will have to say, "There lived a race of people, black people, fleecy locks and black complexion, of people who had the moral courage to stand up for their rights." And thereby they injected a new meaning into the veins of history and of civilization. And we're gonna do that. God grant that we will do it before it's too late.

King delivered one of the pivotal addresses in his career on November 16, 1961, at the annual meeting of the Fellowship of the Concerned, an interracial, nondenominational organization of southern church leaders. Commonly known by the title "Love, Law, and Civil Disobedience," it explained the philosophy behind the student protests and nonviolent resistance to an audience that was for the most part sympathetic to the aims of the civil rights movement but not yet fully convinced that there was a legitimate moral justification for its existence. In his remarks, King sought to make this point clear, not just to those in attendance, but, by extension, to the country at large. His speech is reprinted from Rhetoric of Racial Revolt *(Golden Bell Press, 1964).*

Members of the Fellowship of the Concerned, of the Southern Regional Council, I need not pause to say how very delighted I am to be here today, and to have the opportunity of being a little part of this very significant gathering. I certainly want to express my personal appreciation to Mrs. Tilly and the members of the Committee, for giving me this opportunity. I would also like to express just a personal word of thanks and appreciation for your vital witness in this period of transition which we are facing in our Southland, and in the nation, and I am sure that as a result of this genuine concern, and your significant work in communities all across the South, we have a better South today and I am sure will have a better South tomorrow with your continued endeavor and I do want to express my personal gratitude and appreciation to you of the Fellowship of the Concerned for your significant work and for your forthright witness.

Now, I have been asked to talk about the philosophy behind the student movement. There can be no gain-saying of the fact that we confront a crisis in race relations in the United States. This crisis has been precipitated on the one hand by the determined resistance of reactionary forces in the South to the Supreme Court's decision in 1954 outlawing segregation in the public schools. And we know that at times this resistance has risen to ominous proportions. At times we find the legislative halls of the South ringing loud with such words as interposition and nullification. And all of these forces have developed into massive resistance. But we must also say that the crisis has been precipitated on the other hand by the determination of hundreds and thousands and millions of Negro people to achieve freedom and human dignity. If the Negro stayed in his place and accepted discrimination and segregation, there would be no crisis.

But the Negro has a new sense of dignity, a new self respect, and new determination. He has re-evaluated his own intrinsic worth. Now this new sense of dignity on the part of the Negro grows out of the same longing for freedom and human dignity on the part of the oppressed people all over the world; for we see it in Africa, we see it in Asia, and we see it all over the world. Now we must say that this struggle for freedom will not come to an automatic halt, for history reveals to us that once oppressed people rise up against that oppression, there is no stopping point short of full freedom. On the other hand, history reveals to us that those who oppose the movement for freedom are those who are in privileged positions who very seldom give up their privileges without strong resistance. And they very seldom do it voluntarily. So the sense of struggle will continue. The question is how will the struggle be waged.

Now there are three ways that oppressed people have generally dealt with their oppression. One way is the method of acquiescence, the method of surrender; that is, the individuals will somehow adjust themselves to oppression, they adjust themselves to discrimination or to segregation or colonialism or what have you. The other method that has been used in history is that of rising up against the oppressor with corroding hatred and physical violence. Now of course we know about this method in western civilization, because in a sense it has been the hallmark of its grandeur, and the inseparable twin of western materialism. But there is a weakness in this method because it ends up creating many more social problems than it solves. And I am convinced that if the Negro succumbs to the temptation of using violence in his struggle for freedom and justice, unborn generations will be the recipients of a long and desolate night of bitterness. And our chief legacy to the future will be an endless reign of meaningless chaos.

But there is another way, namely the way of nonviolent resistance. This method was popularized in our generation by a little man from India, whose name was Mohandas K. Gandhi. He used this method in a magnificent way to free his people from the economic exploitation and the political domination inflicted upon them by a foreign power.

This has been the method used by the student movement in the South and all over the United States. And naturally whenever I talk about the student movement I cannot be totally objective. I have to be somewhat subjective because of my great admiration for what the students have done. For in a real sense they have taken our deep groans and passionate yearnings for freedom, and filtered them in their own tender souls, and fashioned them into a creative protest which is an epic known all over our nation. As a result of their disciplined, nonviolent, yet courageous struggle, they have been able to do wonders in the South, and in our nation. But this movement does have an underlying philosophy, it has certain ideas that are attached to it, it has certain philosophical precepts. These are the things that I would like to discuss for the few moments left.

I would say that the first point or the first principle in the movement is the idea that means must be as pure as the end. This movement is based on the philosophy that ends and means must cohere. Now this has been one of the long struggles in history, the whole idea of means and ends. Great philosophers have grappled with it, and sometimes they have emerged with the idea, from Machiavelli on down, that the end justifies the means. There is a great system of thought in our world today, known as Communism. And I think that with all of the weakness and tragedies of Communism, we find its greatest tragedy right here, that it goes under the philosophy that the end justifies the means that are used in the process. So we can read or we can hear the Lenins say that lying, deceit, or violence, that many of these things justify the ends of the classless society.

This is where the student movement and the nonviolent movement that is taking place in our nation would break with Communism and any other system that would argue that the end justifies the means. For in the long run, we must see that the end represents the means in process and the ideal in the making. In other words, we cannot believe, or we cannot go with the idea that the end justifies the means because the end is pre-existent in the means. So the idea of nonviolent resistance, the philosophy of nonviolent resistance, is the philosophy which says that the means must be as pure as the end, that in the long run of history, immoral destructive means cannot bring about moral and constructive ends.

"The first point or the first principle in [our] movement is the idea that the means must be as pure as the end."

There is another thing about this philosophy, this method of nonviolence which is followed by the student movement. It says that those who adhere to or follow this philosophy must follow a consistent principle of noninjury. They must consistently refuse to inflect injury upon another. Sometimes you will read the literature of the student movement and see that, as they are getting ready for the sit-in or stand-in, they will read something like this, "if you are hit do not hit back, if you are cursed do not curse back." This is the whole idea, that the individual who is engaged in a nonviolent struggle must never inflict injury upon another. Now this has an external aspect and it has an internal one. From the external point of view it means that the individuals involved must avoid external physical violence. So they don't have guns, they don't retaliate with physical violence. If they are hit in the process, they avoid external physical violence at every point. But it also means that they avoid internal violence of spirit. This is why the love ethic stands so high in the student movement. We have a great deal of talk about love and nonviolence in this whole thrust.

Now when the students talk about love, certainly they are not talking about emotional bosh, they are not talking about merely a sentimental outpouring; they're talking something much deeper, and I always have to stop and try to define the meaning of love in this context. The Greek language comes to our aid in trying to deal with this. There are three words in the Greek language for love, one is the word *Eros*. This is a beautiful type of love, it is an aesthetic love. Plato talks about it a great deal in his *Dialogue,* the yearning of the soul for the realm of the divine. It has come to us to be a sort of romantic love, and so in a sense we have read about it and experienced it. We've read about it in all the beauties of literature. I guess in a sense Edgar Allan Poe was talking about *Eros* when he talked about his beautiful Annabelle Lee, with the love surrounded by the halo of eternity. In a sense Shakespeare was talking about *Eros* when he said "Love is not love which alters when it alteration finds, or bends with the remover to remove; O' no! it is an ever fixed mark that looks on tempests and is never shaken, it is the star to every wandering bark." (You know, I remember that because I used to quote it to this little lady when we were courting; that's *Eros*.) The Greek language talks about *Philia* which was another level of love. It is an intimate affection between personal friends, it is a reciprocal love. On this level you love because you are loved. It is friendship.

Then the Greek language comes out with another word which is called the *Agape*. *Agape* is more than romantic love, agape is more than friendship. *Agape* is understanding, creative, redemptive, good will to all men. It is an overflowing love which seeks nothing in return. Theologians would say that it is the love of God operating in the human heart. So that when one rises to love on this level, he loves men not because he likes them, not because their ways appeal to him, but he loves every man because God loves him. And he rises to the point of loving the person who does an evil deed while hating the deed that the person does. I think this is what Jesus meant when he said "love your enemies." I'm very happy that he didn't say like your enemies, because it is pretty difficult to like some people. Like is sentimental, and it is pretty difficult to like someone bombing your home; it is pretty difficult to like somebody threatening your children; it is difficult to like congressmen who spend all of their time trying to defeat civil rights. But Jesus says love them, and love is greater than like. Love is understanding, redemptive, creative, good will for all men. And it is this idea, it is this whole ethic of love which is the idea standing at the basis of the student movement.

There is something else: that one seeks to defeat the unjust system, rather than individuals who are caught in that system. And that one goes on believing that somehow this is the important thing, to get rid of the evil system and not the individual who happens to be misguided, who happens to be misled, who was taught wrong. The thing to do is to get rid of the system and thereby create a moral balance within society.

Another thing that stands at the center of this movement is another idea: that suffering can be a most creative and powerful social force. Suffering has certain moral attributes involved, but it can be a powerful and creative social force. Now, it is very interesting at this point to notice that both violence and nonviolence agree that suffering can be a very powerful social force. But there is this difference: violence says that suffering can be a powerful social force by inflicting the suffering on somebody else; so this is what we do in war, this is what we do in the whole violent thrust of the violent movement. It believes that you achieve some end by inflicting suffering on another. The nonviolent say that suffering becomes a powerful social force when you willingly accept that violence on yourself, so that self-suffering stands at the center of the nonviolent movement and the individuals involved are able to suffer in a creative manner, feeling that unearned suffering is redemptive, and that suffering may serve to transform the social situation.

Another thing in this movement is the idea that there is within human nature an amazing potential for goodness. There is within human nature something that can respond to goodness. I know somebody's liable to say that this is an unrealistic movement if it goes on believing that all people are good. Well, I didn't say that. I think the students are realistic enough to believe that there is a strange dichotomy of disturbing dualism within human nature. Many of the great philosophers and thinkers through the ages have seen this. It caused Ovid the Latin poet to say, "I see and approve the better things of life, but the evil things I do." It caused even St. Augustine to say, "Lord, make me pure, but not yet." So that is in human nature. Plato, centuries ago, said that the human personality is like a charioteer with two headstrong horses, each wanting to go in different directions, so that within our own individual lives we see this conflict and certainly when we come to the collective life of man, we see a strange badness. But in spite of this there is something in human nature that can respond to goodness. So that man is neither innately good nor is he innately bad; he has potentialities for both. So in this sense, Carlyle was right when he said that "there are depths in man which go down to the lowest hell, and heights which reach the highest heaven, for are not both heaven and hell made out of him, everlasting miracle and mystery that he is?" Man has the capacity to be good, man has the capacity to be evil.

And so the nonviolent resister never lets this idea go, that there is something within human nature that can respond to goodness. So that a Jesus of Nazareth or a Mohandas Ghandi, can appeal to human beings and appeal to that element of goodness within them, and a Hitler can appeal to the element of evil within them. But we must never forget that there is something within human nature that can respond to goodness, that man is not totally depraved, to put it in theological terms, the image of God is never totally gone. And so the individuals who believe in this movement and who believe in nonviolence and our struggle in the South, somehow believe that even the worst segregationist can become an integrationist. Now sometimes it is hard to believe that this is what this movement says, and it believes it firmly, that there is something within human nature that can be changed, and this stands at the top of the whole philosophy of the student movement and the philosophy of nonviolence.

It says something else. It says that it is as much a moral obligation to refuse to cooperate with evil as it is to cooperate with good. Non-cooperation with evil is as much a moral obligation as the cooperation with good. So that the student movement is willing to stand up courageously on the idea of civil disobedience. Now I think this is the part of the student movement that is probably misunderstood more than anything else. And it is a difficult aspect, because on the one hand the students would say, and I would say, and all the people who believe in civil rights would say, obey the Supreme Court's decision of 1954 and at the same time, we would disobey certain laws that exist on the statutes of the South today.

This brings in the whole question of how can you be logically consistent when you advocate obeying some laws and disobeying other laws. Well, I think one would have to see the whole meaning of this movement at this point by seeing that the students recognize that there are two types of laws. There are just laws and there are unjust laws. And they would be the first to say obey the just laws, they would be the first to say that men and women have a moral obligation to obey just and right laws. And they would go on to say that we must see that there are unjust laws. Now the question comes into being, what is the difference, and who determines the difference, what is the difference between a just and an unjust law?

Well, a just law is a law that squares with a moral law. It is a law that squares with that which is right, so that any law that uplifts human personality is a just law. Whereas that law which is out of harmony with the moral is a law which does not square with the moral law of the universe. It does not square with the law of God, so for that reason it is unjust and any law that degrades the human personality is an unjust law.

Well, somebody says that that does not mean anything to me; first, I don't believe in these abstract things called moral laws and I'm not too religious, so I don't believe in the law of God; you have to get a little more concrete, and more practical. What do you mean when you say that a law is unjust, and a law is just? Well, I would go on to say in more concrete terms that an unjust law is a code that the majority inflicts on the minority that is not binding on itself. So that this becomes difference made legal. Another thing that we can say is that an unjust law is a code which the majority inflicts upon the minority, which that minority had no part in enacting or creating, because that minority had no right to vote in many instances, so that the legislative bodies that made these laws were not democratically elected. Who could ever say that the legislative body of Mississippi was democratically elected, or the legislative body of Alabama was democratically elected, or the legislative body even of Georgia has been democratically elected, when there are people in Terrell County and in other counties because of the color of their skin who cannot vote? They confront reprisals and threats and all of that; so that an unjust law is a law that individuals did not have a part in creating or enacting because they were denied the right to vote.

Now the same token of just law would be just the opposite. A just law becomes saneness made legal. It is a code that the majority, who happen to believe in that code, compel the minority, who don't believe in it, to follow, because they are willing to follow it themselves, so it is saneness made legal. Therefore the individuals who stand up on the basis of civil disobedience realize that they are following something that says that there are just laws and there are unjust laws. Now, they are not anarchists. They believe that there are laws which must be followed; they do not seek to defy the law, they do not seek to evade the law. For many individuals who would call themselves segregationists and who would hold on to segregation at any cost seek to defy the law, they seek to evade the law, and their process can lead on into anarchy. They seek in the final analysis to follow a way of uncivil disobedience, not civil disobedience. And I submit that the individual who disobeys the law, whose conscience tells him it is unjust and who is willing to accept the penalty by staying in jail until that law is altered, is expressing at the moment the very highest respect for law.

This is what the students have followed in their movement. Of course there is nothing new about this, they feel that they are in good company and rightly so. We go back and read the *Apology* and the *Crito,* and you see Socrates practicing civil disobedience. And to a degree academic freedom is a reality today because Socrates practiced civil disobedience. The early Christians practiced civil disobedience in a superb manner, to a point where they were willing to be thrown to the lions. They were willing to face all kinds of suffering in order to stand up for what they knew was right even though they knew it was against the laws of the Roman Empire.

We could come up to our own day and we see it in many instances. We must never forget that everything that Hitler did in Germany was "legal." It was illegal to aid and comfort a Jew, in the days of Hitler's Germany. But I believe that if I had the same attitude then as I have now I would publicly aid and comfort my Jewish brothers in Germany if Hitler were alive today calling this an illegal process. If I lived in South Africa today in the midst of the white supremacy law in South Africa, I would join Chief Luthuli and others in saying break these unjust laws. And even let us come up to America. Our nation in a sense came into being through a massive act of civil disobedience, for the Boston Tea Party was nothing but a massive act of civil disobedience. Those who stood up against the slave laws, the abolitionists, by and large practiced civil disobedience. So I think these students are in good company, and they feel that by practicing civil obedience they are in line with men and women through the ages who have stood up for something that is morally right.

Now there are one or two other things that I want to say about this student movement, moving out of the philosophy of nonviolence, something about what it is a revolt against. On the one hand it is a revolt against the negative peace that has encompassed the South for many years. I remember when I was in Montgomery, Alabama, one of the white citizens came to me one day and said—and I think he was very sincere about this—that in Montgomery for all of these years we have been such a peaceful community, we have had so much harmony in race relations and then you people have started this movement and boycott, and it has done so much to disturb race relations, and we just don't love the Negro like we used to love them, because you have destroyed the harmony and the peace that we once had in race relations. And I said to him, in the best way I could say and I tried to say it in nonviolent terms, we have never had peace in Montgomery, Alabama, we have never had peace in the South. We have had a negative peace, which is merely the absence of tension; we've had a negative peace in which the Negro patiently accepted his situation and his plight, but we've never had true peace, we've never had positive peace, and what we're seeking now is to develop this positive peace. For we must come to see that peace is not merely the absence of some negative force, it is the presence of a positive force. True peace is not merely the absence of tension, but it is the presence of justice and brotherhood. I think this is what Jesus meant when he said, I come not to bring peace but a sword. Now Jesus didn't mean he came to start war, to bring a physical sword, and he didn't mean, I come not to bring positive peace. But I think what Jesus was saying in substance was this, that I come not to bring an old negative peace, which makes for stagnant passivity and deadening complacency, I come to bring something different, and whenever I come, a conflict is precipitated, between the old and the new, whenever I come a struggle takes place between justice and injustice, between the forces of light and the forces of darkness. I come not to bring a negative peace, but a positive peace, which is brotherhood, which is justice, which is the Kingdom of God.

And I think this what we are seeking to do today, and this movement is a revolt against a negative peace and a struggle to bring into being a positive peace, which makes for true brotherhood, true integration, true person-to-person relationships. This movement is also revolt against what is often called tokenism. Here again many people do not understand this, they feel that in this struggle the Negro will be satisfied with tokens of integration, just a few students and a few schools here and there and a few doors open here and there. But this isn't the meaning of the movement and I think that honesty impels me to admit it everywhere I have an opportunity, that the Negro's aim is to bring about complete integration in American life. And he has come to see that token integration is little more than token democracy, which ends up with many new evasive schemes and it ends up with new discrimination, covered up with such niceties of complexity. It is very interesting to discover that the movement has thrived in many communities that had token integration. So this reveals that the movement is based on a principle that integration must become real and complete, not just token integration.

It is also a revolt against what I often call the myth of time. We hear this quite often, that only time can solve this problem. That if we will only be patient, and only pray—which we must do, we must be patient and we must pray—but there are those who say just do these things and wait for time, and time will solve this problem. Well the people who argue this do not themselves realize that time is neutral, that it can be used constructively or destructively. At points the people of ill will, the segregationists, have used time much more effectively than the people of good will. So individuals in the struggle must come to realize that it is necessary to aid time, that without this kind of aid, time itself will become an ally of the insurgent and primitive forces of social stagnation. Therefore, this movement is a revolt against the myth of time.

There is a final thing that I would like to say to you, this movement is a movement based on faith in the future. It is a movement based on a philosophy, the possibility of the future bringing into being something real and meaningful. It is a movement based on hope. I think this is very important. The students have developed a theme song for their movement, maybe you've heard it. It goes something like this, "we shall overcome, deep in my heart, I do believe, we shall overcome," and then they go on to say another verse, "we are not afraid, we are not afraid today, deep in my heart I do believe, we shall overcome." So it is out of this deep faith in the future that they are able to move

> *"We must come to see that peace is not merely the absence of some negative force, it is the presence of a positive force."*

out and adjourn the councils of despair, and to bring new light in the dark chambers of pessimism. I can remember the times that we've been together, I remember that night in Montgomery, Alabama, when we had stayed up all night, discussing the Freedom Rides, and that morning came to see that it was necessary to go on with the Freedom Rides, that we would not in all good conscience call an end to the Freedom Rides at that point. And I remember the first group got ready to leave, to take a bus for Jackson, Mississippi, we all joined hands and started singing together. "We shall overcome, we shall overcome." And something within me said, now how is it that these students can sing this, they are going down to Mississippi, they are going to face hostile and jeering mobs, and yet they could sing, "We shall overcome." They may even face physical death, and yet they could sing, "We shall overcome." Most of them realized that they would be thrown into jail, and yet they could sing, "We shall overcome, we are not afraid." Then something caused me to see at that moment the real meaning of the movement. That students had faith in the future. That the movement was based on hope, that this movement had something within it that says somehow even though the arc of the moral universe is long, it bends toward justice. And I think this should be a challenge to all others who are struggling to transform the dangling discords of our Southland into a beautiful symphony of brotherhood. There is something in this student movement which says to us, that we shall overcome. Before the victory is won some may have to get scarred up, but we shall overcome. Before the victory of brotherhood is achieved, some will maybe face physical death, but we shall overcome. Before the victory is won, some will lose jobs, some will be called Communists, and reds, merely because they believe in brotherhood, some will be dismissed as dangerous rabblerousers and agitators merely because they're standing up for what is right, but we shall overcome. That is the basis of this movement, and as I like to say, there is something in this universe that justifies Carlyle in saying no lie can live forever. We shall overcome because there is something in this universe which justifies William Cullen Bryant in saying truth crushed to earth shall rise again. We shall overcome because there is something in this universe that justifies James Russell Lowell in saying, truth forever on the scaffold, wrong forever on the throne. Yet that scaffold sways the future, and behind the dim unknown standeth God within the shadows, keeping watch above His own. With this faith in the future, with this determined struggle, we will be able to emerge from the bleak and desolate midnight of man's inhumanity to man, into the bright and glittering daybreak of freedom and justice. Thank you.

Without a doubt, the most stirring and memorable of King's many public addresses is the one he gave in Washington, D.C., on August 28, 1963. The occasion was the single largest protest demonstration in U.S. history, an event that saw some 250,000 people gather in front of the Lincoln Memorial to demand that Congress pass sweeping civil rights legislation. Facing that massive crowd as well as a national television audience and members of the press from all over the world, King delivered his strikingly intense and dramatic "I Have a Dream" speech, reprinted here from the book Rhetoric of Racial Revolt *(Golden Bell Press, 1964). In it, he erased all doubt that the civil rights struggle was anything less than a moral crusade of the highest order.*

I am happy to join with you today in what will go down in history as the greatest demonstration for freedom in the history of our nation.

Five score years ago, a great American, in whose symbolic shadow we stand today, signed the Emancipation Proclamation. This momentous decree came as a great beacon of light of hope to millions of Negro slaves who had been seared in the flames of withering injustice. It came as a joyous daybreak to end the long night of their captivity.

But one hundred years later, the Negro still is not free. One hundred years later, the life of the Negro is still sadly crippled by the manacles of segregation and the chains of discrimination.

One hundred years later, the Negro lives on a lonely island of poverty in the midst of a vast ocean of material prosperity. One hundred years later, the Negro is still languished in the corners of American society and finds himself an exile in his own land. So we have come here today to dramatize a shameful condition.

In a sense we have come to our nation's capital to cash a check. When the architects of our republic wrote the magnificent words of the

Constitution and the Declaration of Independence, they were signing a promissory note to which every American was to fall heir. This note was a promise that all men, yes, black men as well as white men, would be granted the unalienable rights of life, liberty, and the pursuit of happiness.

It is obvious today that America has defaulted on this promissory note insofar as her citizens of color are concerned. Instead of honoring this sacred obligation, America has given the Negro people a bad check; which has come back marked "insufficient funds."

But we refuse to believe that the bank of justice is bankrupt. We refuse to believe that there are insufficient funds in the great vaults of opportunity of this nation. So we have come to cash this check—a check that will give us upon demand the riches of freedom and the security of justice.

We have also come to this hallowed spot to remind America of the fierce urgency of now. This is no time to engage in the luxury of cooling off or to take the tranquilizing drug of gradualism. Now is the time to make real the promises of democracy. Now is the time to rise from the dark and desolate valley of segregation to the sunlit path of racial justice. Now is time to lift our nation from the quick sands of racial injustice to the solid rock of brotherhood. Now is the time to make justice a reality for all of God's children.

It would be fatal for the nation to overlook the urgency of the movement and to underestimate the determination of the Negro. This sweltering summer of the Negro's legitimate discontent will not pass until there is an invigorating autumn of freedom and equality; 1963 is not an end but a beginning. Those who hope that the Negro needed to blow off steam and will now be content will have a rude awakening if the nation returns to business as usual.

There will be neither rest nor tranquility in America until the Negro is granted his citizenship rights. The whirlwinds of revolt will continue to shake the foundations of our nation until the bright day of justice emerges.

But there is something that I must say to my people who stand on the warm threshold which leads into the palace of justice. In the process of gaining our rightful place we must not be guilty of wrongful deeds.

Let us not seek to satisfy our thirst for freedom by drinking from the cup of bitterness and hatred. We must forever conduct our struggle on the high plane of dignity and discipline. We must not allow our creative protest to degenerate into physical violence. Again and again we must rise to the majestic heights of meeting physical force with soul force.

The marvelous new militancy which has engulfed the Negro community must not lead us to a distrust of all white people, for many of our white brothers, as evidenced by their presence here today, have come to realize that their destiny is tied up with our destiny and they have come to realize that their freedom is inextricably bound to our freedom. This offense we share mounted to storm the battlements of injustice must be carried forth by a biracial army. We cannot walk alone.

And as we walk, we must make the pledge that we shall always march ahead. We cannot turn back. There are those who are asking the devotees of civil rights, "When will you be satisfied?" We can never be satisfied as long as the Negro is the victim of the unspeakable horrors of police brutality.

We can never be satisfied as long as our bodies, heavy with the fatigue of travel, cannot gain lodging in the motels of the highways and the hotels of the cities. We cannot be satisfied as long as the Negro's basic mobility is from a smaller ghetto to a larger one.

We can never be satisfied as long as our children are stripped of their selfhood and robbed of their dignity by signs stating "for whites only." We cannot be satisfied as long as a Negro in Mississippi cannot vote and a Negro in New York believes he has nothing for which to vote. No, we are not satisfied, and we will not be satisfied until justice rolls down like waters and righteousness like a mighty stream.

I am not unmindful that some of you have come here out of excessive trials and tribulation. Some of you have come fresh from narrow jail cells. Some of you have come from areas where your quest for freedom left you battered by the storms of persecution and staggered by the winds of police brutality. You have been the veterans of creative suffering. Continue to work with the faith that unearned suffering is redemptive.

Go back to Mississippi; go back to Alabama; go back to South Carolina; go back to Georgia; go back to Louisiana; go back to the slums and ghettos of the Northern cities, knowing that somehow this situation can, and will be changed. Let us not wallow in the valley of despair.

So I say to you, my friends, that even though

we must face the difficulties of today and tomorrow, I still have a dream. It is a dream deeply rooted in the American dream that one day this nation will rise up and live out the true meaning of its creed—we hold these truths to be self evident, that all men are created equal.

I have a dream that one day on the red hills of Georgia, sons of former slaves and sons of former slaveowners will be able to sit down together at the table of brotherhood.

> ***"I have a dream my four little children will one day live in a nation where they will not be judged by the color of their skin but by content of their character. I have a dream today!"***

I have a dream that one day, even the state of Mississippi, a state sweltering with the heat of injustice, sweltering with the heat of oppression, will be transformed into an oasis of freedom and justice.

I have a dream my four little children will one day live in a nation where they will not be judged by the color of their skin but by content of their character. I have a dream today!

I have a dream that one day, down in Alabama, with its vicious racists, with its governor having his lips dripping with the words of interposition and nullification, that one day, right there in Alabama, little black boys and black girls will be able to join hands with little white boys and white girls as sisters and brothers. I have a dream today!

I have a dream that one day every valley shall be exalted, every hill and mountain shall be made low, the rough places shall be made plain, and the crooked places shall be made straight and the glory of the Lord will be revealed and all flesh shall see it together.

This is our hope. This is the faith that I go back to the South with.

With this faith we will be able to hear out of the mountain of despair a stone of hope. With this faith we will be able to transform the jangling discords of our nation into a beautiful symphony of brotherhood.

With this faith we will be able to work together to pray together, to struggle together, to go to jail together, to stand up for freedom together, knowing that we will be free one day. This will be the day when all of God's children will be able to sing with new meaning—"my country 'tis of thee; sweet land of liberty; of thee I sing; land where my fathers died, land of the pilgrim's pride; from every mountain side, let freedom ring"—and if America is to be a great nation, this must become true.

So let freedom ring from the prodigious hilltops of New Hampshire.

Let freedom ring from the mighty mountains of New York.

Let freedom ring from the heightening Alleghenies of Pennsylvania.

Let freedom ring from the snow-capped Rockies of Colorado.

Let freedom ring from the curvaceous slopes of California.

But not only that.

Let freedom ring from Stone Mountain of Georgia.

Let freedom ring from Lookout Mountain of Tennessee.

Let freedom ring from every hill and molehill of Mississippi, from every mountainside, let freedom ring.

And when we allow freedom to ring, when we let it ring from every village and hamlet, from every state and city, we will be able to speed up that day when all of God's children—black men and white men, Jews and Gentiles, Catholics and Protestants—will be able to join hands and to sing in the words of the old Negro spiritual, "Free at last, free at last; thank God Almighty, we are free at last."

In 1964, King became the youngest person—and only the second black man—to win the Nobel Peace Prize. On December 10 of that year, he delivered the following acceptance speech in Oslo, Norway. It is reprinted here from A Testament of Hope: The Essential Writings of Martin Luther King, Jr. *(Harper & Row, 1986).*

Your Majesty, your Royal Highness, Mr. President, excellencies, ladies and gentlemen:

I accept the Nobel Prize for Peace at a moment when twenty-two million Negroes of the United States of America are engaged in a creative battle to end the long night of racial injustice. I accept this award in behalf of a civil rights movement which is moving with determination and a majestic scorn for risk and danger to establish a reign of freedom and a rule of justice.

I am mindful that only yesterday in Birmingham, Alabama, our children, crying out for brotherhood, were answered with fire hoses, snarling dogs and even death. I am mindful that only yesterday in Philadelphia, Mississippi, young people seeking to secure the right to vote were brutalized and murdered.

I am mindful that debilitating and grinding poverty afflicts my people and chains them to the lowest rung of the economic ladder.

Therefore, I must ask why this prize is awarded to a movement which is beleaguered and committed to unrelenting struggle: to a movement which has not won the very peace and brotherhood which is the essence of the Nobel Prize.

After contemplation, I conclude that this award which I received on behalf of that movement is profound recognition that nonviolence is the answer to the crucial political and moral question of our time—the need for man to overcome oppression and violence without resorting to violence and oppression.

Civilization and violence are antithetical concepts. Negroes of the United States, following the people of India, have demonstrated that nonviolence is not sterile passivity, but a powerful moral force which makes for social transformation. Sooner or later, all the people of the world will have to discover a way to live together in peace, and thereby transform this pending cosmic elegy into a creative psalm of brotherhood.

If this is to be achieved, man must evolve for all human conflict a method which rejects revenge, aggression and retaliation. The foundation of such a method is love.

From the depths of my heart I am aware that this prize is much more than an honor to me personally.

Every time I take a flight I am always mindful of the many people who make a successful journey possible, the known pilots and the unknown ground crew.

So you honor the dedicated pilots of our struggle who have sat at the controls as the freedom movement soared into orbit. You honor, once again, Chief (Albert) Luthuli of South Africa, whose struggles with and for his people, are still met with the most brutal expression of man's inhumanity to man.

You honor the ground crew without whose labor and sacrifices the jet flights to freedom could never have left the earth.

Most of these people will never make the headlines and their names will not appear in *Who's Who.* Yet the years have rolled past and when the blazing light of truth is focused on this marvelous age in which we live—men and women will know and children will be taught that we have a finer land, a better people, a more noble civilization—because these humble children of God were willing to suffer for righteousness' sake.

I think Alfred Nobel would know what I mean when I say that I accept this award in the spirit of a curator of some precious heirloom which he holds in trust for its true owners—all those to whom beauty is truth and truth beauty—and in whose eyes the beauty of genuine brotherhood and peace is more precious than diamonds or silver or gold.

The tortuous road which has lead from Montgomery, Alabama, to Oslo bears witness to this truth. This is a road over which millions of Negroes are travelling to find a new sense of dignity. This same road has opened for all Americans a new era of progress and hope. It has led to a new civil rights bill, and it will, I am convinced, be widened and lengthened into a superhighway of justice as Negro and white men in increasing number create alliances to overcome their common problems.

I accept this award today with an abiding faith in America and an audacious faith in the future of mankind. I refuse to accept the idea that the "isness" of man's present nature makes him morally incapable of reaching up for the eternal "oughtness" that forever confronts him.

I refuse to accept the idea that man is mere flotsam and jetsam in the river of life which surrounds him. I refuse to accept the view that mankind is so tragically bound to the starless midnight of racism and war that the bright daybreak of peace and brotherhood can never become a reality.

I refuse to accept the cynical notion that nation after nation must spiral down a militaristic stairway into hell of thermonuclear destruction. I believe that unarmed truth and unconditional love will have the final word in reality. That is why right temporarily defeated is stronger than evil triumphant.

I believe that even amid today's mortar bursts and whining bullets, there is still hope for a brighter tomorrow. I believe that wounded justice, lying prostrate on the blood-flowing streets of our nations, can be lifted from this dust of shame to reign supreme among the children of men.

I have the audacity to believe that peoples everywhere can have three meals a day for their bodies, education and culture for their minds, and dignity, equality and freedom for their spirits. I believe that what self-centered men have torn down men other-centered can build up. I still believe that one day mankind will bow before the alters of God and be crowned triumphant over war and bloodshed, and nonviolent redemptive good will will proclaim the rule of the land. "And the lion and the lamb shall lie down together and every man shall sit under his own vine and fig tree and none shall be afraid." I still believe that we shall overcome.

This faith can give us courage to face the uncertainties of the future. It will give our tired feet new strength as we continue our forward stride toward the city of freedom. When our days become dreary with low-hovering clouds and our nights become darker than a thousand midnights, we will know that we are living in the creative turmoil of a genuine civilization struggling to be born.

Today I come to Oslo as a trustee, inspired and with renewed dedication to humanity. I accept this prize on behalf of all men who love peace and brotherhood.

King then returned to the United States to continue his work, launching a voter registration drive in Selma, Alabama, just a few weeks after accepting his Nobel Prize. Over the next few months, as angry whites stiffened their resistance, civil rights activists intensified their efforts. Before long, the protest had captured national attention as participants were subjected to brutal violence and mass arrests. Beginning March 21, 1965, thousands of King's supporters staged a fifty-mile-long "Freedom March" from Selma to Montgomery to dramatize their struggle. On March 25, about fifty thousand people gathered in front of the state capitol building to listen to their leaders criticize Alabama officials for interfering with their voting rights. King, of course, was one of those speakers. His triumphant words—reprinted here from A Testament of Hope: The Essential Writings of Martin Luther King, Jr. *(Harper & Row, 1986)—brought the protest to an end.*

My dear and abiding friends, Ralph Abernathy, and to all the distinguished Americans seated here on the rostrum, my friends and co-workers of the state of Alabama and to all of the freedom-loving people who have assembled here this afternoon, from all over our nation and from all over the world.

Last Sunday, more than eight thousand of us started on a mighty walk from Selma, Alabama. We have walked on meandering highways and rested our bodies on rocky byways. Some of our faces are burned from the outpourings of the sweltering sun. Some have literally slept in the mud. We have been drenched by the rains.

Our bodies are tired, and our feet are somewhat sore, but today as I stand before you and think back over that great march, I can say as Sister Pollard said, a seventy-year-old Negro woman who lived in this community during the bus boycott and one day she was asked while walking if she wanted a ride and when she answered, "No," the person said, "Well, aren't you tired?" And with her ungrammatical profundity, she said, "My feets is tired, but my soul is rested."

And in a real sense this afternoon, we can say that our feet are tired, but our souls are rested.

WE ARE HERE

They told us we wouldn't get here. And there were those who said that we would get here only over their dead bodies, but all the world today knows that we are here and that we are standing before the forces of power in the state of Alabama saying, "We ain't goin' let nobody turn us around."

The Civil Rights Act of 1964 gave Negroes some part of their rightful dignity, but without the vote it was dignity without strength.

Once more the method of nonviolent resistance was unsheathed from its scabbard and once again an entire community was mobilized to confront the adversary. And again the brutality of a dying order shrieks across the land. Yet Selma, Alabama, became a shining moment in the conscience of man.

There never was a moment in American history more honorable and more inspiring than the pilgrimage of clergymen and laymen of every race and faith pouring into Selma to face danger at the side of its embattled Negroes.

Confrontation of good and evil compressed in the tiny community of Selma generated the massive power to turn the whole nation to a new course. A president born in the South had the sensitivity to feel the will of the country, and in an address that will live in history as one of the most passionate pleas for human rights ever made by a president of our nation, he pledged the might of the federal government to cast off the centuries-old blight. President Johnson rightly praised the courage of the Negro for awakening the conscience of the nation.

On our part we must pay our profound respects to the white Americans who cherish their democratic traditions over the ugly customs and privileges of generations and come forth boldly to join hands with us. From Montgomery to Birmingham, from Birmingham to Selma, from Selma back to Montgomery, a trail wound in a circle and often bloody, yet it has become a highway up from darkness. Alabama has tried to nurture and defend evil, but the evil is choking to death in the dusty roads and streets of this state.

So I stand before you this afternoon with the conviction that segregation is on its deathbed in Alabama and the only thing uncertain about it is how costly the segregationists and [Governor George] Wallace will make the funeral.

Our whole campaign in Alabama has been centered around the right to vote. In focusing the attention of the nation and the world today on the flagrant denial of the right to vote, we are exposing the very origin, the root cause, of racial segregation in the Southland.

The threat of the free exercise of the ballot by the Negro and the white masses alike resulted in the establishing of a segregated society. They segregated southern money from the poor whites; they segregated southern mores from the rich whites; they segregated southern churches from Christianity; they segregated southern minds from honest thinking, and they segregated the Negro from everything.

We have come a long way since that travesty of justice was perpetrated upon the American mind. Today I want to tell the city of Selma, today I want to say to the state of Alabama, today I want to say to the people of America and the nations of the world: We are not about to turn around. We are on the move now. Yes, we are on the move and no wave of racism can stop us.

WE ARE ON THE MOVE

We are on the move now. The burning of

our churches will not deter us. We are on the move now. The bombing of our homes will not dissuade us. We are on the move now. The beating and killing of our clergymen and young people will not divert us. We are on the move now. The arrest and release of known murderers will not discourage us. We are on the move now.

Like an idea whose time has come, not even the marching of mighty armies can halt us. We are moving to the land of freedom.

Let us therefore continue our triumph and march to the realization of the American dream. Let us march on segregated housing, until every ghetto of social and economic depression dissolves and Negroes and whites live side by side in decent, safe and sanitary housing.

Let us march on segregated schools until every vestige of segregated and inferior education becomes a thing of the past and Negroes and whites study side by side in the socially healing context of the classroom.

"... today I want to say to the people of America and the nations of the world ... we are on the move and no wave of racism can stop us."

Let us march on poverty, until no American parent has to skip a meal so that their children may march on poverty, until no starved man walks the streets of our cities and towns in search of jobs that do not exist.

Let us march on ballot boxes, march on ballot boxes until race baiters disappear from the political arena. Let us march on ballot boxes until the Wallaces of our nation tremble away in silence.

Let us march on ballot boxes, until we send to our city councils, state legislatures, and the United States Congress men who will not fear to do justice, love mercy, and walk humbly with their God. Let us march on ballot boxes until all over Alabama God's children will be able to walk the earth in decency and honor.

For all of us today the battle is in our hands. The road ahead is not altogether a smooth one. There are no broad highways to lead us easily and inevitably to quick solutions. We must keep going.

MY PEOPLE, LISTEN!

My people, my people, listen! The battle is in our hands. The battle is in our hands in Mississippi and Alabama, and all over the United States.

So as we go away this afternoon, let us go away more than ever before committed to the struggle and committed to nonviolence. I must admit to you there are still some difficulties ahead. We are still in for a season of suffering in many of the black belt counties of Alabama, many areas of Mississippi, many areas of Louisiana.

I must admit to you there are still jail cells waiting for us, dark and difficult moments. We will go on with the faith that nonviolence and its power transformed dark yesterdays into bright tomorrows. We will be able to change all of these conditions.

Our aim must never be to defeat or humiliate the white man but to win his friendship and understanding. We must come to see that the end we seek is a society at peace with itself, a society that can live with its conscience. That will be a day not of the white man, not of the black man. That will be the day of man as man.

I know you are asking today, "How long will it take?" I come to say to you this afternoon however difficult the moment, however frustrating the hour, it will not be long, because truth pressed to earth will rise again.

How long? Not long, because no lie can live forever.

How long? Not long, because you still reap what you sow.

How long? Not long. Because the arm of the moral universe is long but it bends toward justice.

How long? Not long, 'cause mine eyes have seen the glory of the coming of the Lord, trampling out the vintage where the grapes of wrath are stored. He has loosed the fateful lightning of his terrible swift sword. His truth is marching on.

He has sounded forth the trumpets that shall never call retreat. He is lifting up the hearts of man before His judgment seat. Oh, be swift, my soul, to answer Him. Be jubilant, my feet. Our God is marching on!

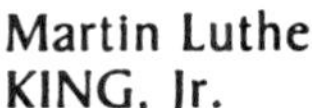

By 1967, however, it was clear to King and others in the mainstream civil rights movement that their message of Christian brotherhood and peaceful protest was making little headway among young, angry blacks in the urban ghettoes of the North. Also, the Vietnam War was beginning to claim an increasingly larger share of funds and attention that used to be devoted to the fight against poverty and racial injustice. Although he had often voiced his belief in world peace, King had been reluctant to reveal his strong personal opposition to the Vietnam War out of fear that he would antagonize too many of his supporters. But in early 1967, he allied himself publicly for the first time with the antiwar movement, hoping to encourage those who were committed to both peace in Vietnam and civil rights for blacks to form a new coalition. On April 4, King outlined his position at a meeting of Clergy and Laity Concerned in New York City in a speech commonly titled "A Time to Break Silence." Published in the spring 1967, issue of Freedomways, *it was later reprinted in* A Testament of Hope: The Essential Writings of Martin Luther King, Jr. *(Harper & Row, 1986).*

I come to this magnificent house of worship tonight because my conscience leaves me no other choice. I join with you in this meeting because I am in deepest agreement with the aims and work of the organization which has brought us together: Clergy and Laymen Concerned about Vietnam. The recent statement of your executive committee are the sentiments of my own heart and I found myself in full accord when I read its opening lines: "A time comes when silence is betrayal." That time has come for us in relation to Vietnam.

The truth of these words is beyond doubt but the mission to which they call us is a most difficult one. Even when pressed by the demands of inner truth, men do not easily assume the task of opposing their government's policy, especially in time of war. Nor does the human spirit move without great difficulty against all the apathy of conformist thought within one's own bosom and in the surrounding world. Moreover when the issues at hand seem as perplexed as they often do in the case of this dreadful conflict we are always on the verge of being mesmerized by uncertainty: but we must move on.

Some of us who have already begun to break the silence of the night have found that the calling to speak is often a vocation of agony, but we must speak. We must speak with all the humility that is appropriate to our limited vision, but we must speak. And we must rejoice as well, for surely this is the first time in our nation's history that a significant number of its religious leaders have chosen to move beyond the prophesying of smooth patriotism to the high grounds of a firm dissent based upon the mandates of conscience and the reading of history. Perhaps a new spirit is rising among us. If it is, let us trace its movements well and pray that our own inner being may be sensitive to its guidance, for we are deeply in need of a new way beyond the darkness that seems so close around us.

Over the past two years, as I have moved to break the betrayal of my own silences and to speak from the burnings of my own heart, as I have called for radical departures from the destruction of Vietnam, many persons have questioned me about the wisdom of my path. At the heart of their concerns this query has often loomed large and loud: Why are *you* speaking about war, Dr. King? Why are *you* joining the voices of dissent? Peace and civil rights don't mix, they say. Aren't you hurting the cause of your people, they ask? And when I hear them, though I often understand the source of their concern, I am nevertheless greatly saddened, for such questions mean that the inquirers have not really known me, my commitment or my calling. Indeed, their questions suggest that they do not know the world in which they live.

In the light of such tragic misunderstanding, I deem it of signal importance to try to state clearly, and I trust concisely, why I believe that the path from Dexter Avenue Baptist Church—the church in Montgomery, Alabama, where I began my pastorate—leads clearly to this sanctuary tonight.

I come to this platform tonight to make a passionate plea to my beloved nation. This speech is not addressed to Hanoi or to the National Liberation Front. It is not addressed to China or to Russia.

Nor is it an attempt to overlook the ambiguity of the total situation and the need for a collective solution to the tragedy of Vietnam. Neither is it an attempt to make North Vietnam or the National Liberation Front paragons of virtue, nor to overlook the role they can play in a successful resolution of the problem. While they both may have justifiable reason to be suspicious of the good faith of the United States, life and history give eloquent testimony to the fact that conflicts are never resolved without trustful give and take on both sides.

Tonight, however, I wish not to speak with Hanoi and the NLF, but rather to my fellow Americans who, with me, bear the greatest responsibility in ending a conflict that has exacted a heavy price on both continents.

IMPORTANCE OF VIETNAM

Since I am a preacher by trade, I suppose it is not surprising that I have seven major reasons for bringing Vietnam into the field of my moral vision. There is at the outset a very obvious and almost facile connection between the war in Vietnam and the struggle I, and others, have been waging in America. A few years ago there was a shining moment in that struggle. It seemed as if there was a real promise of hope for the poor—both black and white—through the poverty program. There were experiments, hopes, new beginnings. Then came the buildup in Vietnam and I watched the program broken and eviscerated as if it were some idle political plaything of a society gone mad on war, and I knew that America would never invest the necessary funds or energies in rehabilitation of its poor so long as adventures like Vietnam continued to draw men and skills and money like some demonic destructive suction tube. So I was increasingly compelled to see the war as an enemy of the poor and to attack it as such.

Perhaps the more tragic recognition of reality took place when it became clear to me that the war was doing far more than devastating the hopes of the poor at home. It was sending their sons and their brothers and their husbands to fight and to die in extraordinarily high proportions relative to the rest of the population. We were taking the black young men who had been crippled by our society and sending them eight thousand miles away to guarantee liberties in Southeast Asia which they had not found in southwest Georgia and East Harlem. So we have been repeatedly faced with the cruel irony of watching Negro and white boys on TV screens as they kill and die together for a nation that has been unable to seat them together in the same schools. So we watch them in brutal solidarity burning the huts of a poor village, but we realize that they would never live on the same block in Detroit. I could not be silent in the face of such cruel manipulation of the poor.

My third reason moves to an even deeper level of awareness, for it grows out of my experience in the ghettos of the North over the last three years—especially the last three summers. As I have walked among the desperate, rejected and angry young men I have told them that Molotov cocktails and rifles would not solve their problems. I have tried to offer them my deepest compassion while maintaining my conviction that social change comes most meaningfully through nonviolent action. But they asked—and rightly so—what about Vietnam? They asked if our own nation wasn't using massive doses of violence to solve its problems, to bring about the changes it wanted. Their questions hit home, and I knew that I could never again raise my voice against the violence of the oppressed in the ghettos without having first spoken clearly to the greatest purveyor of violence in the world today—my own government. For the sake of those boys, for the sake of this government, for the sake of the hundreds of thousands trembling under our violence, I cannot be silent.

For those who ask the question, "Aren't you a civil rights leader?" and thereby mean to exclude me from the movement for peace, I have this further answer. In 1957 when a group of us formed the Southern Christian Leadership Conference, we chose as our motto: "To save the soul of America." We were convinced that we could not limit our vision to certain rights for black people, but instead affirmed the conviction that America would never be free or saved from itself unless the descendants of its slaves were loosed completely from the shackles they still wear. In a way we were agreeing with Langston Hughes, that black bard of Harlem, who had written earlier:

O, yes,
I say it plain,
America never was America to me,
And yet I swear this oath—
America will be!

Now, it should be incandescently clear that no one who has any concern for the integrity and life of America today can ignore the present war. If America's soul becomes totally poisoned, part of the autopsy must read Vietnam. It can never be saved so long as it destroys the deepest hopes of men the world over. So it is that those of us who are yet determined that America *will* be are led down the path of protest and dissent, working for the health of our land.

As if the weight of such a commitment to the life and health of America were not enough, another burden of responsibility was placed upon me in 1964; and I cannot forget that the Nobel Prize for Peace was also a commission—a commission to work harder than I had ever worked before for "the brotherhood of man." This is a calling that takes me beyond national allegiances, but even if it were not present I would yet have to live with the meaning of my commitment to the ministry of Jesus Christ. To me the relationship of this ministry to the making of peace is so obvious that I sometimes marvel at those who ask me why I am speaking against the war. Could it be that they do not know that the good news was meant for all men—for communist and capitalist, for their children and ours, for black and for white, for revolutionary and conservative? Have they forgotten that my ministry is in obedience to the one who loved his enemies so fully that he died for them? What then can I say to the "Vietcong" or to Castro or to Mao as a faithful minister of this one? Can I threaten them with death or must I not share with them my life?

Finally, as I try to delineate for you and for myself the road that leads from Montgomery to this place I would have offered all that was most valid if I simply said that I must be true to my conviction that I share with all men the calling to be a son of the living God. Beyond the calling of race or nation or creed is this vocation of sonship and brotherhood, and because I believe that the Father is deeply concerned especially for his suffering and helpless and outcast children, I come tonight to speak for them.

This I believe to be the privilege and the burden of all of us who deem ourselves bound by allegiances and loyalties which are broader and deeper than nationalism and which go beyond our nation's self-defined goals and positions. We are called to speak for the weak, for the voiceless, for victims of our nation and for those it calls enemy, for no document from human hands can make these humans any less our brothers.

STRANGE LIBERATORS

And as I ponder the madness of Vietnam and search within myself for ways to understand and respond to compassion my mind goes constantly to the people of that peninsula. I speak now not of the soldiers of each side, not of the junta in Saigon, but simply of the people who have been living under the curse of war for almost three continuous decades now. I think of them too because it is clear to me that there will be no meaningful solution there until some attempt is made to know them and hear their broken cries.

They must see Americans as strange liberators. The Vietnamese people proclaimed their own independence in 1945 after a combined French and Japanese occupation, and before the communist revolution in China. They were led by Ho Chi Minh. Even though they quoted the American Declaration of Independence in their own document of freedom, we refused to recognize them. Instead, we decided to support France in its reconquest of her former colony.

Our government felt then that the Vietnamese people were not "ready" for independence, and we again fell victim to the deadly Western arrogance that has poisoned the international atmosphere for so long. With that tragic decision we rejected a revolutionary government seeking self-determination, and a government that had been established not by China (for whom the Vietnamese have no great love) but by clearly indigenous forces that included some communists. For the peasants this new government meant real land reform, one of the most important needs in their lives.

For nine years following 1945 we denied the people of Vietnam the right of independence. For nine years we vigorously supported the French in their abortive effort to recolonize Vietnam.

Before the end of the war we were meeting eighty percent of the French war costs. Even before the French were defeated at Dien Bien Phu, they began to despair of the reckless action, but we did not. We encouraged them with our huge financial and military supplies to continue the war even after they had lost the will. Soon we would be paying almost the full costs of this tragic attempt at recolonization.

After the French were defeated it looked as if independence and land reform would come again through the Geneva agreements. But instead there came the United States, determined that Ho should not unify the temporarily divided nation, and the peasants watched again as we supported one of the most vicious modern dictators—our chosen man, Premier Diem. The peasants watched and cringed as Diem ruthlessly routed out all opposition, supported their extortionist landlords and refused even to discuss reunification with the north. The peasants watched as all this was presided over by U.S. influence and then by increasing numbers of U.S. troops who came to help quell the insurgency that Diem's methods had aroused. When Diem was overthrown they may have been happy, but the long line of military dictatorships seemed to offer no real change—especially in terms of their need for land and peace.

The only change came from America as we increased our troop commitments in support of governments which were singularly corrupt, inept and without popular support. All the while the people read our leaflets and received regular promises of peace and democracy—and land reform. Now they languish under our bombs and consider us—not their fellow Vietnamese—the real enemy. They move sadly and apathetically as we herd them off the land of their fathers into concentration camps where minimal social needs are rarely met. They know they must move or be destroyed by our bombs. So they go—primarily women and children and the aged.

They watch as we poison their water, as we kill a million acres of their crops. They must weep as the bulldozers roar through their areas preparing to destroy the precious trees. They wander into the hospitals, with at least twenty casualties from American firepower for one "Vietcong"-inflicted injury. So far we may have killed a million of them—mostly children. They wander into the towns and see thousands of the children, homeless, without clothes, running in packs on the streets like animals. They see the children degraded by our soldiers as they beg for food. They see the children selling their sisters to our soldiers, soliciting for their mothers.

What do the peasants think as we ally ourselves with the landlords and as we refuse to put any action into our many words concerning land reform? What do they think as we test out our latest weapons on them, just as the Germans tested out new medicine and new tortures in the concentration camps of Europe? Where are the roots of the independent Vietnam we claim to be building? Is it among these voiceless ones?

We have destroyed their two most cherished institutions: the family and the village. We have destroyed their land and their crops. We have cooperated in the crushing of the nation's only non-communist revolutionary political force—the unified Buddhist church. We have supported the enemies of the peasants of Saigon. We have corrupted their women and children and killed their men. What liberators!

Now there is little left to build on—save bitterness. Soon the only solid physical foundations remaining will be found at our military bases and in the concrete of the concentration camps we call fortified hamlets. The peasants may well wonder if we plan to build our new Vietnam on such grounds as these? Could we blame them for such thoughts? We must speak for them and raise the questions they cannot raise. These too are our brothers.

Perhaps the more difficult but no less necessary task is to speak for those who have been designated as our enemies. What of the National Liberation Front—that strangely anonymous group we call VC or communists? What must they think of us in America when they realize that we permitted the repression and cruelty of Diem which helped to bring them into being as a resistance group in the south? What do they think of our condoning the violence which led to their own taking up of arms? How can they believe in our integrity when now we speak of "aggression from the north" as if there were nothing more essential to the war? How can they trust us when now we charge them with violence after the murderous reign of Diem and charge them with violence while we pour every new weapon of death into their land? Surely we must understand their feelings even if we do not condone their actions. Surely we must see that the men we supported pressed them to their violence. Surely we must see that our own computerized plans of destruction simply dwarf their greatest acts.

How do they judge us when our officials know that their membership is less than twenty-five percent communist and yet insist on giving them the blanket name? What must they be thinking when they know that we are aware of their control of major sections of Vietnam and yet we appear ready to allow national elections in which this highly organized political parallel government will have no part? They ask how we can speak of free elections when the Saigon press is censored and controlled by the military junta. And they are surely right to wonder what kind of new government we plan to help form without them—the only party in real touch with the peasants. They question our political goals and they deny the reality of a peace settlement from which they will be excluded. Their questions are frighteningly relevant. Is our nation planning to build on political myth again and then shore it up with the power of new violence?

Here is the true meaning and value of compassion and nonviolence when it helps us to see the enemy's point of view, to hear his questions, to know his assessment of ourselves. For from his view we may indeed see the basic weaknesses of our own condition, and if we are mature, we may learn and grow and profit from the wisdom of the brothers who are called the opposition.

So, too, with Hanoi. In the north, where our bombs now pummel the land, and our mines endanger the waterways, we are met by a deep but understandable mistrust. To speak for them is to explain this lack of confidence in Western words, and especially their distrust of American intentions now. In Hanoi are the men who led the nation to independence against the Japanese and the French, the men who sought membership in the French commonwealth and were betrayed by the weakness of Paris and the willfulness of the colonial armies. It was they who led a second struggle against French domination at tremendous costs, and then were persuaded to give up the land they controlled between the thirteenth and seventeenth parallel as a temporary measure at Geneva. After 1954 they watched us conspire with Diem to prevent elections which would have surely brought Ho Chi Minh to power over a united Vietnam, and they realized they had been betrayed again.

When we ask why they do not leap to negotiate, these things must be remembered. Also it must be clear that the leaders of Hanoi considered the presence of American troops in support of the Diem regime to have been the initial military breach of the Geneva agreements concerning foreign troops, and they remind us that they did not begin to send in any large number of supplies or men until American forces had moved into the tens of thousands.

Hanoi remembers how our leaders refused to tell us the truth about the earlier North Vietnamese overtures for peace, how the president claimed that none existed when they had clearly been made. Ho Chi Minh has watched as America has spoken of peace and built up its forces, and now he has surely heard of the increasing international rumors of American plans for an invasion of the north. He knows the bombing and shelling and mining we are doing are part of traditional pre-invasion strategy. Perhaps only his sense of humor and of irony can save him when he hears the most powerful nation of the world speaking of aggression as it drops thousands of bombs on a poor weak nation more than eight thousand miles away from its shores.

At this point I should make it clear that while I have tried in these last few minutes to give a voice to the voiceless on Vietnam and to understand the arguments of those who are called enemy, I am as deeply concerned about our troops there as anything else. For it occurs to me that what we are submitting them to in Vietnam is not simply the brutalizing process that goes on in any war where armies face each other and seek to destroy. We are adding cynicism to the process of death, for they must know after a short period there that none of the things we claim to be fighting for are really involved. Before long they must know that their government has sent them into a struggle among Vietnamese, and the more sophisticated surely realize that we are on the side of the wealthy and the secure while we create a hell for the poor.

Somehow this madness must cease. We must stop now. I speak as a child of God and brother to the suffering poor of Vietnam. I speak for those whose land is being laid waste, whose homes are being destroyed, whose culture is being subverted. I speak for the poor of America who are paying the double price of smashed hopes at home and death and corruption in Vietnam. I speak as a citizen of the world, for the world as it stands aghast at the path we have taken. I speak as an American to the leaders of my own nation. The great initiative in this war is ours. The initiative to stop it must be ours.

This is the message of the great Buddhist leaders of Vietnam. Recently one of them wrote these words: *Each day the war goes on the hatred increases in the heart of the Vietnamese and in the hearts of those of humanitarian instinct. The Americans are forcing even their friends into becoming their enemies. It is curious that the Americans, who calculate so carefully on the possibilities of military victory, do not realize that in the process they are incurring deep psychological and political defeat. The image of America will never again be the image of revolution, freedom and democracy, but the image of violence and militarism.*

If we continue there will be no doubt in my mind and in the mind of the world that we have no honorable intentions in Vietnam. It will become clear that our minimal expectation is to occupy it as an American colony and men will not refrain from thinking that our maximum hope is to goad China into a war so that we may bomb her nuclear installations. If we do not stop our war against the people of Vietnam immediately the world will be left with no other alternative than to see this as some horribly clumsy and deadly game we have decided to play.

The world now demands a maturity of America that we may not be able to achieve. It demands that we admit that we have been wrong from the beginning of our adventure in Vietnam, that we have been detrimental to the life of the Vietnamese people. The situation is one in which we must be ready to turn sharply from our present ways.

In order to atone for our sins and errors in Vietnam, we should take the initiative in bringing a halt to this tragic war. I would like to suggest five concrete things that our government should do immediately to begin the long and difficult process of extricating ourselves from this nightmarish conflict:

1. End all bombing in North and South Vietnam.

2. Declare a unilateral cease-fire in the hope that such action will create the atmosphere for negotiation.

3. Take immediate steps to prevent other battlegrounds in Southeast Asia by curtailing our military buildup in Thailand and our interference in Laos.

4. Realistically accept the fact that the National Liberation Front has substantial support in South Vietnam and must thereby play a role in any meaningful negotiations and in any future Vietnam government.

5. Set a date that we will remove all foreign troops from Vietnam in accordance with the 1954 Geneva agreement.

Part of our ongoing commitment might well express itself in an offer to grant asylum to any Vietnamese who fears for his life under a new regime which included the Liberation Front. Then we must make what reparations we can for the damage we have done. We must provide the medical aid that is badly needed, making it available in this country if necessary.

PROTESTING THE WAR

Meanwhile we in the churches and synagogues have a continuing task while we urge our government to disengage itself from a disgraceful commitment. We must continue to raise our voices if our nation persists in its perverse ways in Vietnam. We must be prepared to match actions with words by seeking out every creative means of protest possible.

As we counsel young men concerning military service we must clarify for them our nation's role in Vietnam and challenge them with the alternative of conscientious objection. I am pleased to say that this is the path now being chosen by more than seventy students at my own alma mater, Morehouse College, and I recommend it to all who find the American course in Vietnam a dishonorable and unjust one. Moreover I would encourage all ministers of draft age to give up their ministerial exemptions and seek status as conscientious objectors. These are the times for real choices and not false ones. We are at the moment when our lives must be placed on the line if our nation is to survive its own folly. Every man of humane convictions must decide on the protest that best suits his convictions, but we must all protest.

There is something seductively tempting about stopping there and sending us all off on what in some circles has become a popular crusade against the war in Vietnam. I say we must enter the struggle, but I wish to go on now to say something even more disturbing. The war in Vietnam is but a symptom of a far deeper malady within the American spirit, and if we ignore this sobering reality we will find ourselves organizing clergy and laymen-concerned committees for the next generation. They will be concerned about Guatemala and Peru. They will be concerned about Thailand and Cambodia. They will be concerned about Mozambique and South Africa. We will be marching for these and a dozen other names and attending rallies without end unless there is a significant and profound change in American life and policy. Such thoughts take us beyond Vietnam, but not beyond our calling as sons of the living God.

In 1957 a sensitive American official overseas said that it seemed to him that our nation was on the wrong side of a world revolution. During the past ten years we have seen emerge a pattern of suppression which now has justified the presence of U.S. military "advisors" in Venezuela. This need to maintain social stability for our investments accounts for the counterrevolutionary action of American forces in Guatemala. It tells why American helicopters are being used against guerrillas in Colombia and why American napalm and Green Beret forces have already been active against rebels in Peru. It is with such activity in mind that the words of the late John F. Kennedy come back to haunt us. Five years ago he said, "Those who make peaceful revolution impossible will make violent revolution inevitable."

Increasingly, by choice or by accident, this is the role our nation has taken—the role of those who make peaceful revolution impossible by refusing to give up the privileges and the pleasures that come from the immense profits of overseas investment.

I am convinced that if we are to get on the right side of the world revolution, we as a nation must undergo a radical revolution of values. We must rapidly begin the shift from a "thing-oriented" society to a "person-oriented" society. When machines and computers, profit motives and property rights are considered more important than people, the giant triplets of racism, materialism, and militarism are incapable of being conquered.

A true revolution of values will soon cause us to question the fairness and justice of many of our past and present policies. On the one hand we are called to play the Good Samaritan on life's roadside; but that will be only an initial act. One day we must come to see that the whole Jericho Road must be transformed so that men and women will not be constantly beaten and robbed as they make their journey on life's highway. True compassion is more than flinging a coin to a beggar; it is not haphazard and superficial. It comes to see that an edifice which produces beggars needs restructuring. A true revolution of values will soon look uneasily on the glaring contrast of poverty and wealth. With righteous indignation, it will look across the seas and see individual capitalists of the West investing huge sums of money in Asia, Africa and South America, only to take the profits out with no concern for the social betterment of the countries, and say: "This is not just." It will look at our alliance with the landed gentry of Latin America and say: "This is not just." The Western arrogance of feeling that it has everything to teach others and nothing to learn from them is not just. A true revolution of values will lay hands on the world order and say of war: "This way of settling differences is not just." This business of burning human beings with napalm, of filling our nation's homes with orphans and widows, of injecting poisonous drugs of hate into veins of peoples normally humane, of sending men home from dark and bloody battlefields physically handicapped and psychologically deranged, cannot be reconciled with wisdom, justice and love. A nation that continues year after year to spend more money on military defense than on programs of social uplift is approaching spiritual death.

America, the richest and most powerful nation in the world, can well lead the way in this revolution of values. There is nothing, except a tragic death wish, to prevent us from reordering our priorities, so that the pursuit of peace will take precedence over the pursuit of war. There is nothing to keep us from molding a recalcitrant status quo with bruised hands until we have fashioned it into a brotherhood.

> *"A nation that continues to spend more money on military defense than on programs of social uplift is approaching spiritual death."*

This kind of positive revolution of values is our best defense against communism. War is not the answer. Communism will never be defeated by the use of atomic bombs or nuclear weapons. Let us not join those who shout war and through their misguided passions urge the United States to relinquish its participation in the United Nations. These are days which demand wise restraint and calm reasonableness. We must not call everyone a communist or an appeaser who advocates the seating of Red China in the United Nations and who recognizes that hate and hysteria are not the final answers to the problem of these turbulent days. We must not engage in a negative anti-communism, but rather in a positive thrust for democracy, realizing that our greatest defense against communism is to take offensive action in behalf of justice. We must with positive action seek to remove those conditions of poverty, insecurity and injustice which are the fertile soil in which the seed of communism grows and develops.

THE PEOPLE ARE IMPORTANT

These are revolutionary times. All over the globe men are revolting against old systems of exploitation and oppression and out of the wombs of a frail world new systems of justice and equality are being born. The shirtless and barefoot people of the land are rising up as never before. "The people who sat in darkness have seen a great light." We in the West must support these revolutions. It is a sad fact that, because of comfort, complacency, a morbid fear of communism, and our proneness to adjust to injustice, the Western nations that initiated so much of the revolutionary spirit of the modern world have now become the arch anti-revolutionaries. This has driven many to feel that only Marxism has the revolutionary spirit. Therefore, communism is a judgment against our failure to make democracy real and follow through on the revolutions that we initiated. Our only hope today lies in our ability to recapture the revolutionary spirit and go out into a sometimes hostile world declaring eternal hostility to poverty, racism, and militarism. With this powerful commitment we shall boldly challenge the status quo and unjust mores and thereby speed the day when "every valley shall be exalted, and every mountain and hill shall be made low, and the crooked shall be made straight and the rough places plain."

> ***"We can no longer afford to worship the god of hate or bow before the altar of retaliation."***

A genuine revolution of values means in the final analysis that our loyalties must become ecumenical rather than sectional. Every nation must now develop an overriding loyalty to mankind as a whole in order to preserve the best in their individual societies.

This call for a worldwide fellowship that lifts neighborly concern beyond one's tribe, race, class and nation is in reality a call for an all-embracing and unconditional love for all men. This oft misunderstood and misinterpreted concept—so readily dismissed by the Nietzsches of the world as a weak and cowardly force—has now become an absolute necessity for the survival of man. When I speak of love I am not speaking of some sentimental and weak response. I am speaking of that force which all of the great religions have seen as the supreme unifying principle of life. Love is somehow the key that unlocks the door which leads to ultimate reality. This Hindu-Moslem-Christian-Jewish-Buddhist belief about ultimate reality is beautifully summed up in the first epistle of Saint John:

> *Let us love one another: for love is God and everyone that loveth is born of God and knoweth God. He that loveth not knoweth not God; for God is love. If we love one another God dwelleth in us, and his love is perfected in us.*

Let us hope that this spirit will become the order of the day. We can no longer afford to worship the god of hate or bow before the altar of retaliation. The oceans of history are made turbulent by the ever-rising tides of hate. History is cluttered with the wreckage of nations and individuals that pursued this self-defeating path of hate. As Arnold Toynbee says: "Love is the ultimate force that makes for the saving choice of life and good against the damning choice of death and evil. Therefore the first hope in our inventory must be the hope that love is going to have the last word."

We are now faced with the fact that tomorrow is today. We are confronted with the fierce urgency of now. In this unfolding conundrum of life and history there is such a thing as being too late. Procrastination is still the thief of time. Life often leaves us standing bare, naked and dejected with a lost opportunity. The "tide in the affairs of men" does not remain at the flood; it ebbs. We may cry out desperately for time to pause in her passage, but time is deaf to every plea and rushes on. Over the bleached bones and jumbled residue of numerous civilizations are written the pathetic words: "Too late." There is an invisible book of life that faithfully records our vigilance or our neglect. "The moving finger writes, and having writ moves on. . . ." We still have a choice today; nonviolent coexistence or violent co-annihilation.

We must move past indecision to action. We must find new ways to speak for peace in Vietnam and justice throughout the developing world—a world that borders on our doors. If we do not act we shall surely be dragged down the long, dark and shameful corridors of time reserved for those who possess power without compassion, might without morality, and strength without sight.

Now let us begin. Now let us rededicate ourselves to the long and bitter—but beautiful—struggle for a new world. This is the calling of the sons of God, and our brothers wait eagerly for our response. Shall we say the odds are too great? Shall we tell them the struggle is too hard? Will our message be that the forces of American life militate against their arrival as full men, and we send our deepest regrets? Or will there be another message, of longing, of hope, of solidarity with their yearnings, of commitment to their cause, whatever the cost? The choice is ours, and though we might prefer it otherwise we *must* choose in this crucial moment of human history.

As that noble bard of yesterday, James Russell Lowell, eloquently stated:

Once to every man and nation,
Comes the moment to decide
In the strife of truth and falsehood
For the good or evil side;
Some great cause God's new Messiah
Offering each the gloom or blight
And the choice goes by forever
Twixt that darkness and that light.

Though the cause of evil prosper
Yet 'tis truth along is strong
Though her portion be the scaffold
And upon the throne be wrong
Yet that scaffold sways the future
And behind the dim unknown
Standeth God within the shadow
Keeping watch above his own.

On August 16, 1967, King gave his final presidential address at the tenth anniversary convention of the Southern Christian Leadership Conference in Atlanta, Georgia. Entitled "Where Do We Go from Here?," it revealed that he was beginning to look beyond the immediate goals of the civil rights movement to a more radical restructuring of American society. His remarks were later reprinted in A Testament of Hope: The Essential Writings of Martin Luther King, Jr. *(Harper & Row, 1986).*

Now, in order to answer the question, "Where do we go from here?" which is our theme, we must first honestly recognize where we are now. When the Constitution was written, a strange formula to determine taxes and representation declared that the Negro was sixty percent of a person. Today another curious formula seems to declare that he is fifty percent of a person. Of the good things in life, the Negro has approximately one half those of whites. Of the bad things of life, he has twice those of whites. Thus half of all Negroes live in substandard housing. And Negroes have half the income of whites. When we view the negative experiences of life, the Negro has a double share. There are twice as many unemployed. The rate of infant mortality among Negroes is double that of whites and there are twice as many Negroes dying in Vietnam as whites in proportion to their size in the population.

In other spheres, the figures are equally alarming. In elementary schools, Negroes lag one to three years behind whites, and their segregated schools receive substantially less money per student than the white schools. One-twentieth as many Negroes as whites attend college. Of employed Negroes, seventy-five percent hold menial jobs.

This is where we are. Where do we go from here? First, we must massively assert our dignity and worth. We must stand up amidst a system that still oppresses us and develop an unassailable and majestic sense of values. We must no longer be ashamed of being black. The job of arousing manhood within a people that have been taught for so many centuries that they are nobody is not easy.

Even semantics have conspired to make that which is black seem ugly and degrading. In Roget's *Thesaurus* there are 120 synonyms for blackness and at least sixty of them are offensive, as for example, blot, soot, grim, devil and foul. And there are some 134 synonyms for whiteness and all are favorable, expressed in such words as purity, cleanliness, chastity and innocence. A white lie is better than a black lie. The most degenerate member of a family is a "black sheep." Ossie Davis has suggested that maybe the English language should be reconstructed so that teachers will not be forced to teach the Negro child sixty ways to despise himself, and thereby perpetuate his false sense of inferiority, and the white child 134 ways to adore himself, and thereby perpetuate his false sense of superiority.

The tendency to ignore the Negro's contribution to American life and to strip him of his personhood is as old as the earliest history books and as contemporary as the morning's newspaper. To upset this cultural homicide, the Negro must rise up with an affirmation of his own Olympian manhood. Any movement for the Negro's freedom that overlooks this necessity is only waiting to be buried. As long as the mind is enslaved, the body can never be free. Psychological freedom, a firm sense of self-esteem, is the most powerful weapon against the long night of physical slavery. No Lincolnian emancipation proclamation or Johnsonian civil rights bill can totally bring this kind of freedom. The Negro will only be free when he reaches down to the inner depths of his own being and signs with the pen and ink of assertive manhood his own emancipation proclamation. And, with a spirit straining toward true self-esteem, the Negro must boldly throw off the manacles of self-abnegation and say to himself and to the world, "I am somebody. I am a person. I am a man with dignity and honor. I have a rich and noble history. How painful and exploited that history has been. Yes, I was a slave through my foreparents and I am not ashamed of that. I'm ashamed of the people who were so sinful to make me a slave." Yes, we must stand up and say, "I'm black and I'm beautiful," and this self-affirmation is the black man's need, made compelling by the white man's crimes against him.

Another basic challenge is to discover how to organize our strength in terms of economic and political power. No one can deny that the Negro is in dire need of this kind of legitimate power. Indeed, one of the great problems that the Negro confronts is his lack of power. From old plantations of the South to newer ghettos of the North, the Negro has been confined to a life of voicelessness and powerlessness. Stripped of the right to make decisions concerning his life and destiny, he has been subject to the authoritarian and sometimes whimsical decisions of this white power structure. The plantation and ghetto were created by those who had power, both to confine those who had no power and to perpetuate their powerlessness. The problem of transforming the ghetto, therefore, is a problem of power—confrontation of the forces of power demanding change and the forces of power dedicated to the preserving of the status quo. Now power properly understood is nothing but the ability to achieve purpose. It is the strength required to bring about social, political and economic change. Walter Reuther defined power one day. He said, "Power is the ability of a labor union like the UAW to make the most powerful corporation in the world, General Motors, say 'Yes' when it wants to say 'No.' That's power."

Now a lot of us are preachers, and all of us have our moral convictions and concerns, and so often have problems with power. There is nothing wrong with power if power is used correctly. You see, what happened is that some of our philosophers got off base. And one of the great problems of history is that the concepts of love and power have usually been contrasted as opposites—polar opposites—so that love is identified with a resignation of power, and power with a denial of love.

It was this misinterpretation that caused Nietzsche, who was a philosopher of the will to power, to reject the Christian concept of love. It was this same misinterpretation which induced Christian theologians to reject the Nietzschean philosophy of the will to power in the name of the Christian idea of love. Now, we've got to get this thing right. What is needed is a realization that power without love is reckless and abusive, and love without power is sentimental and anemic. Power at its best is love implementing the demands of justice, and justice at its best is power correcting everything that stands against love. And this is what we must see as we move on. What has happened is that we have had it wrong and confused in our own country, and this has led Negro Americans in the past to seek their goals through power devoid of love and conscience.

This is leading a few extremists today to advocate for Negroes the same destructive and conscienceless power that they have justly abhorred in whites. It is precisely this collision of immoral power with powerless morality which constitutes the major crisis of our times.

We must develop a program that will drive the nation to a guaranteed annual income. Now, early in this century this proposal would have been greeted with ridicule and denunciation, as destructive of initiative and responsibility. At that time economic status was considered the measure of the individual's ability and talents. And, in the thinking of that day, the absence of worldly goods indicated a want of industrious habits and moral fiber. We've come a long way in our understanding of human motivation and of the blind operation of our economic system. Now we realize that dislocations in the market operations of our economy and the prevalence of discrimination thrust people into idleness and bind them in constant or frequent unemployment against their will. Today the poor are less often dismissed, I hope, from our consciences by being branded as inferior or incompetent. We also know that no matter how dynamically the economy develops and expands, it does not eliminate all poverty.

The problem indicates that our emphasis must be twofold. We must create full employment or we must create incomes. People must be made consumers by one method or the other. Once they are placed in this position we need to be concerned that the potential of the individual is not wasted. New forms of work that enhance the social good will have to be devised for those for whom traditional jobs are not available.

In 1879 Henry George anticipated this state of affairs when he wrote in *Progress and Poverty:*

> *The fact is that the work which improves the condition of mankind, the work which extends knowledge and increases power and enriches literature and elevates thought, is not done to secure a living. It is not the work of slaves driven to their tasks either by the task, by the taskmaster, or by animal necessity. It is the work of men who somehow find a form of work that brings a security for its own sake and a state of society where want is abolished.*

Work of this sort could be enormously increased, and we are likely to find that the problems of housing and education, instead of preceding the elimination of poverty, will themselves be affected if poverty is first abolished. The poor transformed into purchasers will do a great deal on their own to alter housing decay. Negroes who have a double disability will have a greater effect on discrimination when they have the additional weapon of cash to use in their struggle.

Beyond these advantages, a host of positive psychological changes inevitably will result from widespread economic security. The dignity of the individual will flourish when the decisions concerning his life are in his own hands, when he has the means to seek self-improvement. Personal conflicts among husbands, wives and children will diminish when the unjust measurement of human worth on the scale of dollars is eliminated.

> ***"What is needed is a realization that power without love is reckless and abusive, and love without power is sentimental and anemic."***

Now our country can do this. John Kenneth Galbraith said that a guaranteed annual income could be done for about twenty billion dollars a year. And I say to you today, that if our nation can spend thirty-five billion dollars a year to fight an unjust, evil war in Vietnam, and twenty billion dollars to put a man on the moon, it can spend billions of dollars to put God's children on their own two feet right here on earth.

Now, let me say briefly that we must reaffirm our commitment to nonviolence. I want to stress this. The futility of violence in the struggle for racial justice has been tragically etched in all the recent Negro riots. Yesterday, I tried to analyze the riots and deal with their causes. Today I want to give the other side. There is certainly something painfully sad about a riot. One sees screaming youngsters and angry adults fighting hopelessly and aimlessly against impossible odds. And deep down within them, you can see a desire for self-destruction, a kind of suicidal longing.

Occasionally Negroes contend that the 1965 Watts riot and the other riots in various cities represented effective civil rights action. But those who express this view always end up with stumbling words when asked what concrete gains have been won as a result. At best, the riots have produced a little additional antipoverty money allotted by frightened government officials, and a few water sprinklers to cool the children of the ghettos. It is something like improving the food in the prison while the people remain securely incarcerated behind bars. Nowhere have the riots won any concrete improvement such as have the organized protest demonstrations. When one tries to pin down advocates of violence as to what acts would be effective, the answers are blatantly illogical. Sometimes they talk of overthrowing racist state and local governments and they talk about guerrilla warfare. They fail to see that no internal revolution has ever succeeded in overthrowing a government by violence unless the government had already lost the allegiance and effective control of its armed forces. Anyone in his right mind knows that this will not happen in the United States. In a violent racial situation, the power structure has the local police, the state troopers, the National Guard and, finally, the army to call on—all of which are predominantly white. Furthermore, few if any violent revolutions have been successful unless the violent minority had the sympathy and support of the nonresistant majority. Castro may have had only a few Cubans actually fighting with him up in the hills, but he could never have overthrown the Batista regime unless he had the sympathy of the vast majority of Cuban people.

It is perfectly clear that a violent revolution on the part of American blacks would find no sympathy and support from the white population and very little from the majority of the Negroes themselves. This is no time for romantic illusions and empty philosophical debates about freedom. This is a time for action. What is needed is a strategy for change, a tactical program that will bring the Negro into the mainstream of American life as quickly as possible. So far, this has only been offered by the nonviolent movement. Without recognizing this we will end up with solutions that don't solve, answers that don't answer and explanations that don't explain.

And so I say to you today that I still stand by nonviolence. And I am still convinced that it is the most potent weapon available to the Negro in his struggle for justice in this country. And the other thing is that I am concerned about a better world. I'm concerned about justice. I'm concerned about brotherhood. I'm concerned about truth. And when one is concerned about these, he can never advocate violence. For through violence you may murder a murderer but you can't murder murder. Through violence you may murder a liar but you can't establish truth. Through violence you may murder a hater, but you can't murder hate. Darkness cannot put out darkness. Only light can do that.

And I say to you, I have also decided to stick to love. For I know that love is ultimately the only answer to mankind's problems. And I'm going to talk about it everywhere I go. I know it isn't popular to talk about it in some circles today. I'm not talking about emotional bosh when I talk about love, I'm talking about a strong, demanding love. And I have seen too much hate. I've seen too much hate on the faces of sheriffs in the South. I've seen hate on the faces of too many Klansmen and too many White Citizens Councilors in the South to want to hate myself, because every time I see it, I know that it does something to their faces and their personalities and I say to myself that hate is too great a burden to bear. I have decided to love. If you are seeking the highest good, I think you can find it through love. And the beautiful thing is that we are moving against wrong when we do it, because John was right, God is love. He who hates does not know God, but he who has love has the key that unlocks the door to the meaning of ultimate reality.

I want to say to you as I move to my conclusion, as we talk about "Where do we go from here," that we honestly face the fact that the movement must address itself to the question of restructuring the whole of American society. There are forty million poor people here. And one day we must ask the question, "Why are there forty million poor people in America?" And when you begin to ask that question, you are raising questions about the economic system, about a broader distribution of wealth. When you ask that question, you begin to question the capitalistic economy. And I'm simply saying that more and more, we've got to begin to ask questions about the whole society. We are called upon to help the discouraged beggars in life's marketplace. But one day we must come to see that an edifice which produces beggars needs restructuring. It means that questions must be raised. You see, my friends, when you deal with this, you begin to ask the question, "Who owns the oil?" You begin to ask the question, "Who owns the iron ore?" You begin to ask the question, "Why is it that people have to pay water bills in a world that is two-thirds water?" These are questions that must be asked.

Now, don't think that you have me in a "bind" today. I'm not talking about communism.

What I'm saying to you this morning is that communism forgets that life is individual. Capitalism forgets that life is social, and the kingdom of brotherhood is found neither in the thesis of communism nor the antithesis of capitalism but in a higher synthesis. It is found in a higher synthesis that combines the truths of both. Now, when I say question the whole society, it means ultimately coming to see that the problem of racism, the problem of economic exploitation, and the problem of war are all tied together. These are the triple evils that are interrelated.

If you will let me be a preacher just a little bit—One night, a juror came to Jesus and he wanted to know what he could do to be saved. Jesus didn't get bogged down in the kind of isolated approach of what he shouldn't do. Jesus didn't say, "Now Nicodemus, you must stop lying." He didn't say, "Nicodemus, you must stop cheating if you are doing that." He didn't say, "Nicodemus, you must not commit adultery." He didn't say, "Nicodemus, now you must stop drinking liquor if you are doing that excessively." He said something altogether different, because Jesus realized something basic—that if a man will lie, he will steal. And if a man will steal, he will kill. So instead of just getting bogged down in one thing, Jesus looked at him and said, "Nicodemus, you must be born again."

He said, in other words, "Your whole structure must be changed." A nation that will keep people in slavery for 244 years will "thingify" them—make them things. Therefore they will exploit them, and poor people generally, economically. And a nation that will exploit economically will have to have foreign investments and everything else, and will have to use its military might to protect them. All of these problems are tied together. What I am saying today is that we must go from this convention and say, "America, you must be born again!"

So, I conclude by saying again today that we have a task and let us go out with a "divine dissatisfaction." Let us be dissatisfied until America will no longer have a high blood pressure of creeds and an anemia of deeds. Let us be dissatisfied until the tragic walls that separate the outer city of wealth and comfort and the inner city of poverty and despair shall be crushed by the battering rams of the forces of justice. Let us be dissatisfied until those that live on the outskirts of hope are brought into the metropolis of daily security. Let us be dissatisfied until slums are cast into the junk heaps of history, and every family is living in a decent sanitary home. Let us be dissatisfied until the dark yesterdays of segregated schools will be transformed into bright tomorrows of quality, integrated education. Let us be dissatisfied until integration is not seen as a problem but as an opportunity to participate in the beauty of diversity. Let us be dissatisfied until men and women, however black they may be, will be judged on the basis of the content of their character and not on the basis of the color of their skin. Let us be dissatisfied. Let us be dissatisfied until every state capitol houses a governor who will do justly, who will love mercy and who will walk humbly with his God. Let us be dissatisfied until from every city hall, justice will roll, down like waters and righteousness like a mighty stream. Let us be dissatisfied until that day when the lion and the lamb shall lie down together, and every man will sit under his own vine and fig tree and none shall be afraid. Let us be dissatisfied. And men will recognize that out of one blood God made all men to dwell upon the face of the earth. Let us be dissatisfied until that day when nobody will shout "White Power!"—when nobody will shout "Black Power!"—but everybody will talk about God's power and human power.

I must confess, my friends, the road ahead will not always be smooth. There will be still rocky places of frustration and meandering points of bewilderment. There will be inevitable setbacks here and there. There will be those moments when the buoyancy of hope will be transformed into the fatigue of despair. Our dreams will sometimes be shattered and our ethereal hopes blasted. We may again with tear-drenched eyes have to stand before the bier of some courageous civil rights worker whose life will be snuffed out by the dastardly acts of bloodthirsty mobs. Difficult and painful as it is, we must walk on in the days ahead with an audacious faith in the future. And as we continue our charted course, we may gain consolation in the words so nobly left by that great black bard who was also a great freedom fighter of yesterday, James Weldon Johnson:

Stony the road we trod,
Bitter the chastening rod
Felt in the days
When hope unborn had died.

Yet with a steady beat,
Have not our weary feet
Come to the place
For which our fathers sighed?
We have come over the way
That with tears hath been watered.
We have come treading our paths
Through the blood of the slaughtered,

Out from the gloomy past,
Till now we stand at last
Where the bright gleam
Of our bright star is cast.

Let this affirmation be our ringing cry. It will give us the courage to face the uncertainties of the future. It will give our tired feet new strength as we continue our forward stride toward the city of freedom. When our days become dreary with low-hovering clouds of despair, and when our nights become darker than a thousand midnights, let us remember that there is a creative force in this universe, working to pull down the gigantic mountains of evil, a power that is able to make a way out of no way and transform dark yesterdays into bright tomorrows. Let us realize the arc of the moral universe is long but it bends toward justice. Let us realize that William Cullen Bryant is right: "Truth crushed to earth will rise again." Let us go out realizing that the Bible is right: "Be not deceived, God is not mocked. Whatsoever a man soweth, that shall he also reap." This is for hope for the future, and with this faith we will be able to sing in some not too distant tomorrow with a cosmic past tense, "We have overcome, we have overcome, deep in my heart, I did believe we would overcome."

In April 1968, King journeyed to Memphis, Tennessee, to show his support for striking city garbage workers and help in the effort to unionize them. It was there, on the evening of April 3, that he delivered what was to be his final speech, reprinted here from A Testament of Hope: The Essential Writings of Martin Luther King, Jr. *(Harper & Row, 1986). With its references to having seen the promised land that he might never get to visit, it was perhaps his most eerily prophetic address. The next day, King was felled by an assassin's bullet as he stood on the balcony of his motel room.*

Thank you very kindly, my friends. As I listened to Ralph Abernathy in his eloquent and generous introduction and then thought about myself, I wondered who he was talking about. It's always good to have your closest friend and associate say something good about you. And Ralph is the best friend that I have in the world.

I'm delighted to see each of you here tonight in spite of a storm warning. You reveal that you are determined to go on anyhow. Something is happening in Memphis, something is happening in our world.

As you know, if I were standing at the beginning of time, with the possibility of general and panoramic view of the whole human history up to now, and the Almighty said to me, "Martin Luther King, which age would you like to live in?"—I would take my mental flight by Egypt through, or rather across the Red Sea, through the wilderness on toward the promised land. And in spite of its magnificence, I wouldn't stop there. I would move on by Greece, and take my mind to Mount Olympus. And I would see Plato, Aristotle, Socrates, Euripides and Aristophanes assembled around the Parthenon as they discussed the great and eternal issues of reality.

But I wouldn't stop there. I would go on, even to the great heyday of the Roman Empire. And I would see developments around there, through various emperors and leaders. But I wouldn't stop there. I would even come up to the day of the Renaissance, and get a quick picture of all that the Renaissance did for the cultural and esthetic life of man. But I wouldn't stop there. I would even go by the way that the man for whom I'm named had his habitat. And I would watch Martin Luther as he tacked his ninety-five theses on the door at the church in Wittenberg.

But I wouldn't stop there. I would come on up even to 1863, and watch a vacillating president by the name of Abraham Lincoln finally come to the conclusion that he had to sign the Emancipation Proclamation. But I wouldn't stop there. I would even come up to the early thirties, and see a man grappling with the problems of the bankruptcy of his nation. And come with an eloquent cry that we have nothing to fear but fear itself.

But I wouldn't stop there. Strangely enough, I would turn to the Almighty, and say, "If you allow me to live just a few years in the second half of the twentieth century, I will be happy." Now that's a strange statement. But I know, somehow, that only when it is dark enough, can you see the stars. And I see God working in this period of the twentieth century in a way that men, in some strange way, are responding—something is happening in our world. The masses of people are rising up. And wherever they are assembled today, whether they are in Johannesburg, South Africa; Nairobi, Kenya; Accra, Ghana; New York City; Atlanta, Georgia; Jackson, Mississippi; or Memphis, Tennessee—the cry is always the same—"We want to be free."

And another reason that I'm happy to live in this period is that we have been forced to a point where we're going to have to grapple with the problems that men have been trying to grapple with through history, but the demands didn't force them to do it. Survival demands that we grapple with them. Men, for years now, have been talking about war and peace. But now, no longer can they just talk about it. It is no longer a choice between violence and nonviolence in this world; it's nonviolence or nonexistence.

That is where we are today. And also in the human rights revolution, if something isn't done, and in a hurry, to bring the colored peoples of the world out of their long years of poverty, their long years of hurt and neglect, the whole world is doomed. Now, I'm just happy that God has allowed me to live in this period, to see what is unfolding. And I'm happy that he's allowed me to be in Memphis.

I can remember, I can remember when Negroes were just going around as Ralph has said, so often, scratching where they didn't itch, and laughing when they were not tickled. But that day is all over. We mean business now, and we are determined to gain our rightful place in God's world.

And that's all this whole thing is about. We aren't engaged in any negative protest and in any negative arguments with anybody. We are saying that we are determined to be men. We are determined to be people. We are saying that we are God's children. And that we don't have to live like we are forced to live.

Now, what does all of this mean in this great period of history? It means that we've got to stay together. We've got to stay together and maintain unity. You know, whenever Pharaoh wanted to prolong the period of slavery in Egypt, he had a favorite, favorite formula for doing it. What was that? He kept the slaves fighting among themselves. But whenever the slaves get together, something happens in Pharaoh's court, and he cannot hold the slaves in slavery. When the slaves get together, that's the beginning of getting out of slavery. Now let us maintain unity.

Secondly, let us keep the issues where they are. The issue is injustice. The issue is the refusal of Memphis to be fair and honest in its dealings with its public servants, who happen to be sanitation workers. Now, we've got to keep attention on that. That's always the problem with a little violence. You know what happened the other day, and the press dealt only with the window-breaking. I read the articles. They very seldom got around to mentioning the fact that one thousand, three hundred sanitation workers were on strike, and that Memphis is not being fair to them, and that Mayor Loeb is in dire need of a doctor. They didn't get around to that.

Now we're going to march again, and we've got to march again, in order to put the issue where it is supposed to be. And force everybody to see that there are thirteen hundred of God's children here suffering, sometimes going hungry, going through dark and dreary nights wondering how this thing is going to come out. That's the issue. And we've got to say to the nation: we know it's coming out. For when people get caught up with that which is right and they are willing to sacrifice for it, there is no stopping point short of victory.

We aren't going to let any mace stop us. We are masters in our nonviolent movement in disarming police forces; they don't know what to do. I've seen them so often. I remember in Birmingham, Alabama, when we were in that majestic struggle there we would move out of the

16th Street Baptist Church day after day; by the hundreds we would move out. And Bull Connor would tell them to send the dogs forth and they did come; but we just went before the dogs singing, "Ain't gonna let nobody turn me round." Bull Connor next would say, "Turn the fire hoses on." And as I said to you the other night, Bull Connor didn't know history. He knew a kind of physics that somehow didn't relate to the transphysics that we knew about. And that was the fact that there was a certain kind of fire that no water could put out. And we went before the fire hoses; we had known water. If we were Baptist or some other denomination, we had been immersed. If we were Methodist, and some others, we had been sprinkled, but we knew water.

That couldn't stop us. And we just went on before the dogs and we would look at them; and we'd go on before the water hoses and we would look at it, and we'd just go on singing "Over my head I see freedom in the air." And then we would be thrown in the paddy wagons, and sometimes we were stacked in there like sardines in a can. And they would throw us in, and old Bull would say, "Take them off," and they did; and we would just go in the paddy wagon singing, "We Shall Overcome." And every now and then we'd get in the jail, and we'd see the jailers looking through the windows being moved by our prayers, and being moved by our words and our songs. And there was a power there which Bull Connor couldn't adjust to; and so we ended up transforming Bull into a steer, and we won our struggle in Birmingham.

Now we've got to go on to Memphis just like that. I call upon you to be with us Monday. Now about injunctions: We have an injunction and we're going into court tomorrow morning to fight this illegal, unconstitutional injunction. All we say to America is, "Be true to what you said on paper." If I lived in China or even Russia, or any totalitarian country, maybe I could understand the denial of certain basic First Amendment privileges, because they hadn't committed themselves to that over there. But somewhere I read of the freedom of assembly. Somewhere I read of the freedom of speech. Somewhere I read of the freedom of the press. Somewhere I read that the greatness of America is the right to protest for right. And so just as I say, we aren't going to let any injunction turn us around. We are going on.

We need all of you. And you know what's beautiful to me, is to see all of these ministers of the Gospel. It's a marvelous picture. Who is it that is supposed to articulate the longings and aspirations of the people more than the preacher? Somehow the preacher must be an Amos, and say, "Let justice roll down like waters and righteousness like a mighty stream." Somehow, the preacher must say with Jesus, "The spirit of the Lord is upon me, because he hath anointed me to deal with the problems of the poor."

And I want to commend the preachers, under the leadership of these noble men: James Lawson, one who has been in this struggle for many years; he's been to jail for struggling; but he's still going on, fighting for the rights of his people. Rev. Ralph Jackson, Billy Kyles; I could just go right on down the list, but time will not permit. But I want to thank them all. And I want you to thank them, because so often, preachers aren't concerned about anything but themselves. And I'm always happy to see a relevant ministry.

It's alright to talk about "long white robes over yonder," in all of its symbolism. But ultimately people want some suits and dresses and shoes to wear down here. It's alright to talk about "streets flowing with milk and honey," but God has commanded us to be concerned about the slums down here, and his children who can't eat three square meals a day. It's alright to talk about the new Jerusalem, but one day, God's preacher must talk about the New York, the new Atlanta, the new Philadelphia, the new Los Angeles, the new Memphis, Tennessee. This is what we have to do.

Now the other thing we'll have to do is this: Always anchor our external direct action with the power of economic withdrawal. Now, we are poor people, individually, we are poor when you compare us with white society in America. We are poor. Never stop and forget that collectively, that means all of us together, collectively we are richer than all the nations in the world, with the exception of nine. Did you ever think about that? After you leave the United States, Soviet Russia, Great Britain, West Germany, France, and I could name the others, the Negro collectively is richer than most nations of the world. We have an annual income of more than thirty billion dollars a year, which is more than all of the exports of the United States, and more than the national budget of Canada. Did you know that? That's power right there, if we know how to pool it.

We don't have to argue with anybody. We don't have to curse and go around acting bad with our words. We don't need any bricks and bottles, we don't need any Molotov cocktails, we just need to go around to these stores, and to these massive industries in our country, and say, "God sent us by here, to say to you that you're not treating his children right. And we've come by here to ask you to make the first item on your agenda—fair treatment, where God's children are concerned. Now, if you are not prepared to do that, we do have an agenda that we must follow. And our agenda calls for withdrawing economic support from you."

And so, as a result of this, we are asking you tonight, to go out and tell your neighbors not to buy Coca-Cola in Memphis. Go by and tell them not to buy Sealtest milk. Tell them not to buy—what is the other bread?—Wonder Bread. And what is the other bread company, Jesse? Tell them not to buy Hart's bread. As Jesse Jackson has said, up to now, only the garbage men have been feeling pain; now we must kind of redistribute the pain. We are choosing these companies because they haven't been fair in their hiring policies; and we are choosing them because they can begin the process of saying, they are going to support the needs and the rights of these men who are on strike. And then they can move on downtown and tell Mayor Loeb to do what is right.

But not only that, we've got to strengthen black institutions. I call upon you to take your money out of the banks downtown and deposit your money in Tri-State Bank—we want a "bank-in" movement in Memphis. So go by the savings and loan association. I'm not asking you something that we don't do ourselves at SCLC. Judge [Benjamin] Hooks and others will tell you that we have an account here in the savings and loan association from the Southern Christian Leadership Conference. We're just telling you to follow what we're doing. Put your money there. You have six or seven black insurance companies in Memphis. Take out your insurance there. We want to have an "insurance-in."

Now these are some practical things we can do. We begin the process of building a greater economic base. And at the same time, we are putting pressure where it really hurts. I ask you to follow through here.

Now, let me say as I move to my conclusion that we've got to give ourselves to this struggle until the end. Nothing would be more tragic than to stop at this point, in Memphis. We've got to see it through. And when we have our march, you need to be there. Be concerned about your brother. You may not be on strike. But either we go up together, or we go down together.

Let us develop a kind of dangerous unselfishness. One day a man came to Jesus; and he wanted to raise some questions about some vital matters in life. At points, he wanted to trick Jesus, and show him that he knew a little more than Jesus knew, and through this, throw him off base. Now that question could have easily ended up in a philosophical and theological debate. But Jesus immediately pulled that question from mid-air, and placed it on a dangerous curve between Jerusalem and Jericho. And he talked about a certain man, who fell among thieves. You remember that a Levite and a priest passed by on the other side. They didn't stop to help him. And finally a man of another race came by. He got down from his beast, decided not to be compassionate by proxy. But with him, administered first aid, and helped the man in need. Jesus ended up saying, this was the good man, this was the great man, because he had the capacity to project the "I" into the "thou," and to be concerned about his brother. Now you know, we use our imagination a great deal to try to determine why the priest and the Levite didn't stop. At times we say they were busy going to church meetings—an ecclesiastical gathering—and they had to get on down to Jerusalem so they wouldn't be late for their meeting. At other times we would speculate that there was a religious law that "One who was engaged in religious ceremonials was not to touch a human body twenty-four hours before the ceremony." And every now and then we begin to wonder whether maybe they were not going down to Jerusalem, or down to Jericho, rather to organize a "Jericho Road Improvement Association." That's a possibility. Maybe they felt that it was better to deal with the problem from the causal root, rather than to get bogged down with an individual effort.

But I'm going to tell you what my imagination tells me. It's possible that these men were afraid. You see, the Jericho road is a dangerous road. I remember when Mrs. King and I were first in Jerusalem. We rented a car and drove from Jerusalem down to Jericho. And as soon as we got on that road, I said to my wife, "I can see why Jesus used this as a setting for his parable." It's a winding, meandering road. It's really conducive for ambushing. You start out in Jerusalem, which is about 1,200 miles, or rather 1,200 feet above sea level. And by the time you get down to Jericho, fifteen or twenty minutes later, you're about 2,200 feet below sea level. That's a dangerous road. In the days of Jesus it came to be known as the "Bloody Pass." And you know, it's possible that the priest and the Levite looked over that man on the ground and wondered if the robbers were still around. Or it's possible that they felt that the man on the ground was merely faking. And he was acting like he had been robbed and hurt, in order to seize them over there, lure them there for quick and easy seizure. And so the first question that the Levite asked was, "If I stop to help this man, what will happen to me?" But then the Good Samaritan came by. And he reversed the question: "If I do not stop to help this man, what will happen to him?"

That's the question before you tonight. Not, "If I stop to help the sanitation workers, what will happen to all of the hours that I usually spend in my office every day and every week as a pastor?" The question is not, "If I stop to help this man in need, what will happen to me?" "If I do not stop to help the sanitation workers, what will happen to them?" That's the question.

Let us rise up tonight with greater readiness. Let us stand with a greater determination. And let us move on in these powerful days, these

"I've seen the promised land. I may not get there with you. But I want you to know tonight, that we, as a people will get to the promised land."

days of challenge to make America what it ought to be. We have an opportunity to make America a better nation. And I want to thank God, once more, for allowing me to be here with you.

You know, several years ago, I was in New York City autographing the first book that I had written. And while sitting there autographing books, a demented black woman came up. The only question I heard from her was, "Are you Martin Luther King?"

And I was looking down writing, and I said yes. And the next minute I felt something beating on my chest. Before I knew it I had been stabbed by this demented woman. I was rushed to Harlem Hospital. It was a dark Saturday afternoon. And that blade had gone through, and the x-rays revealed that the tip of the blade was on the edge of my aorta, the main artery. And once that's punctured, you drown in your own blood—that's the end of you.

It came out in the *New York Times* the next morning, that if I had sneezed, I would have died. Well, about four days later, they allowed me, after the operation, after my chest had been opened, and the blade had been taken out, to move around in the wheelchair in the hospital. They allowed me to read some of the mail that came in, and from all over the states, and the world, kind letters came in. I read a few, but one of them I will never forget. I had received one from the president and the vice-president. I've forgotten what those telegrams said. I'd received a visit and a letter from the governor of New York, but I've forgotten what the letter said. But there was another letter that came from a little girl, a young girl who was a student at the White Plains High School. And I looked at that letter, and I'll never forget it. It said simply, "Dear Dr. King: I am a ninth-grade student at the White Plains High School." She said, "While it should not matter, I would like to mention that I am a white girl. I read in the paper of your misfortune, and of your suffering. And I read that if you had sneezed, you would have died. And I'm simply writing you to say that I'm so happy that you didn't sneeze."

And I want to say tonight, I want to say that I am happy that I didn't sneeze. Because if I had sneezed, I wouldn't have been around here in 1960, when students all over the South started sitting-in at lunch counters. And I knew that as they were sitting in, they were really standing up for the best in the American dream. And taking the whole nation back to those great walls of democracy which were dug deep by the Founding Fathers in the Declaration of Independence and the Constitution. If I had sneezed, I wouldn't have been around in 1962, when Negroes in Albany, Georgia, decided to straighten their backs up. And whenever men and women straighten their backs up, they are going somewhere, because a man can't ride your back unless it is bent. If I had sneezed, I wouldn't have been here in 1963, when the black people of Birmingham, Alabama, aroused the conscience of this nation, and brought into being the Civil Rights Bill. If I had sneezed, I wouldn't have had a chance later that year, in August, to try to tell America about a dream that I had had. If I had sneezed, I wouldn't have been down in Selma, Alabama, to see the great movement there. If I had sneezed, I wouldn't have been in Memphis to see a community rally around those brothers and sisters who are suffering. I'm so happy that I didn't sneeze.

And they were telling me, now it doesn't matter now. It really doesn't matter what happens now. I left Atlanta this morning, and as we got started on the plane, there were six of us, the pilot said over the public address system, "We are sorry for the delay but we have Dr. Martin Luther King on the plane. And to be sure that all of the bags were checked, and to be sure that nothing would be wrong with the plane, we had to check out everything carefully. And we've had the plane protected and guarded all night."

And then I got into Memphis. And some began to say the threats, or talk about the threats that were out. What would happen to me from some of our sick white brothers?

Well, I don't know what will happen now. We've got some difficult days ahead. But it doesn't matter with me now. Because I've been to the mountaintop. And I don't mind. Like anybody, I would like to live a long life. Longevity has its place. But I'm not concerned about that now. I just want to do God's will. And He's allowed me to go up to the mountain. And I've looked over. And I've seen the promised land. I may not get there with you. But I want you to know tonight, that we, as a people will get to the promised land. And I'm happy, tonight. I'm not worried about anything. I'm not fearing any man. Mine eyes have seen the glory of the coming of the Lord.

SOURCES

Books

Bosmajian, Haig A. and Hamida Bosmajian, *The Rhetoric of the Civil Rights Movement,* Random House, 1969.

Boulware, Marcus H., *The Oratory of Negro Leaders: 1900-1968,* Negro Universities Press, 1969.

Branch, Taylor, *Parting the Waters: America in the King Years 1954-1963,* Simon & Schuster, 1989.

Carson, Clayborne and others, editors, *The Eyes on the Prize Civil Rights Reader,* Penguin, 1991.

Carson, Clayborne, and Ralph E. Luker, editors, *The Papers of Martin Luther King, Jr.,* Volume 1: *Called to Serve, January 1929-June 1951,* University of California, 1992. [Set is projected to run fourteen volumes when completed.]

Duffy, Bernard K., and Halford R. Ryan, editors, *American Orators of the Twentieth Century: Critical Studies and Sources,* Greenwood Press, 1987.

Foner, Philip S., editor, *The Voice of Black America: Major Speeches by Negroes in the United States, 1797-1971,* Simon & Schuster, 1972.

Hill, Roy L., *Rhetoric of Racial Revolt,* Golden Bell Press, 1964.

Holland, DeWitte, editor, *America in Controversy: History of American Public Address,* William C. Brown Company, 1973.

King, Coretta Scott, *My Life with Martin Luther King, Jr.,* Holt, 1969.

King, Martin Luther, Jr., *Stride toward Freedom: The Montgomery Story,* Harper & Row, 1958.

———, *Strength to Love,* Harper & Row, 1963.

Lewis, David L., *King: A Biography,* second edition, University of Illinois Press, 1978.

Oates, Stephen B., *Let the Trumpet Sound: The Life of Martin Luther King, Jr.,* New American Library, 1982.

O'Neill, Daniel J., editor, *Speeches by Black Americans,* Dickenson Publishing Company, 1971.

O'Neill, William L., *Coming Apart: An Informal History of America in the 1960s,* Quadrangle, 1971.

Scott, Robert L., and Wayne Brockriede, *The Rhetoric of Black Power,* Harper & Row, 1969.

Smith, Arthur L., and Stephen Robb, editors, *The Voice of Black Rhetoric: Selections,* Allyn & Bacon, 1971.

Washington, James Melvin, *A Testament of Hope: The Essential Writings of Martin Luther King, Jr.,* Harper & Row, 1986.

Periodicals

Commonweal, "Doctor King's Legacy," April 19, 1968, pp. 125-126.

Detroit News, "King Legacy Was More Than Just His 'Dream,' " January 16, 1995.

Ebony, "I've Been to the Mountaintop," May, 1968; "Prince of Peace Is Dead," May, 1968.

Freedomways, spring, 1967, pp. 103-117.

Liberation, January, 1965, pp. 28-29.

Newsweek, April 15, 1968, pp. 34-38; "King's Last March: We Lost Somebody," April 22, 1968, pp. 26-31.

New York Times, April 5, 1968.

Time, April 12, 1968, pp. 18-21; "King's Last March," April 19, 1968, pp. 18-19.

Worldview, "New Sense of Direction," April, 1972.

Susette LaFlesche

(Bright Eyes, Inshta Theamba)

1854–1903

Native American activist and writer of the Omaha tribe

During the late nineteenth and early twentieth centuries, several of the most prominent Native Americans in the country were members of a single family, the LaFlesches. Chief Joseph LaFlesche, also known as Iron Eye, presided over the Omaha reservation in Nebraska and was a major force in encouraging them to embrace Christianity and other traditions of dominant white society. His son Francis documented Omaha customs in detail as the first Native American to become a professional anthropologist. The chief's daughter Susan was the first Native American woman to graduate from a U.S. medical school and set up a Western-style practice; she was also a temperance crusader, health care activist, and political advocate on behalf of the Omaha. Perhaps the best known of Iron Eye's offspring, however, was his daughter Susette, whose efforts as both a lecturer and a writer focused public attention on the often tragic consequences of Indian resettlement policies.

Susette LaFlesche was born on the Omaha reservation of mixed Native American and white heritage. She attended a Presbyterian mission school there until it closed when she was in her early teens. A couple of years later, on the recommendation of one of her former teachers, Susette enrolled in the Elizabeth Institute for Young Ladies in New Jersey. There she distinguished herself as a student of both literature and writing. Upon her graduation, she returned to Nebraska, where she studied art at the university and eventually obtained a teaching position at the Omaha reservation school.

Around this same time—the late 1870s—the Omahas watched with concern and fear as members of a neighboring tribe, the Poncas, were forcibly removed from their land in northern Nebraska by U.S. Army troops and relocated to Indian Territory in present-day Oklahoma. On a personal level, the action was upsetting because many of the Omahas (including the LaFlesches) had family ties to the Poncas. But the broader implications were even more disturbing; might they be the next ones ordered to move?

Before long, the controversy began to generate national headlines. During the winter of 1878–79, Chief Standing Bear of the Poncas defied government regulations requiring him to seek official permission to leave the reservation and led a group of his people back to their ancestral home in Nebraska. There he was arrested and brought to trial in April 1879. One of those who testified on his behalf was Susette LaFlesche, who had taken up the Poncas' cause in response to her own anger and sadness at their plight. Thanks in part to the information she assembled and presented in court, Standing Bear received a favorable ruling from the federal judge presiding over the case, and the Poncas were eventually granted new reservation lands in Nebraska.

From then on, LaFlesche devoted herself to investigating and publicizing conditions among resettled Indians and lobbying for Indian rights. In late 1879, she and her half-brother, Francis, accompanied by Standing Bear, went on a six-month lecture tour of the eastern United States. Appearing before civic groups, literary clubs, and various organizations concerned with Indian welfare, LaFlesche—billed as Bright Eyes, her Indian name—served as Standing Bear's interpreter and also spoke on her own as an advocate for him and his people. On November 25, she faced an audience in Boston, Massachusetts, and delivered the following speech, reprinted here from Judith Anderson's Outspoken Women: Speeches by American Women Reformers, 1635-1935, *Kendall/Hunt Publishing Company, 1984. Her remarks were originally published in the* Boston Daily Advertiser *on November 26, 1879.*

I have lived all my life, with the exception of two years, which I spent at school in New Jersey, among my own tribe, the Omahas, and I have had an opportunity, such as is accorded to but few, of hearing both sides of the "Indian question." I have at times felt bitterly toward the white race, yet were it not for some who have shown all kindness, generosity and sympathy toward one who had no claims on them but that of common humanity, I shudder to think what I would now have been. As it is, my faith in justice and God has sometimes almost failed me but, I thank God, only almost.

Susette LaFlesche

It crushed our hearts when we saw a little handful of poor, ignorant, helpless, but peaceful people, such as the Poncas were, oppressed by a mighty nation, a nation so powerful that it could well have afforded to show justice and humanity if it only would. It was so hard to feel how powerless we were to help those we loved so dearly when we saw our relatives forced from their homes and compelled to go to a strange country at the point of the bayonet. The whole Ponca tribe were rapidly advancing in civilization; cultivated their farms, and their schoolhouses and churches were well filled, when suddenly they were informed that the government required their removal to Indian Territory. My uncle said it came so suddenly upon them that they could not realize it at first, and they felt stunned and helpless. He also said if they had had any idea of what was coming, they might have successfully resisted; but as it was, it was carried rigidly beyond their control. Every objection they made was met by the word "soldier" and "bayonet." The Poncas had always been a peaceful tribe, and were not armed, and even if they had been they would rather not have fought. It was such a cowardly thing for the government to do! They sold the land which belonged to the Poncas to the Sioux, without the knowledge of the owners, and, as the Poncas were perfectly helpless and the Sioux well armed, the government was not afraid to move the friendly tribe.

The tribe has been robbed of thousands of dollars' worth of property, and the government shows no disposition to return what belongs to them. That property was lawfully theirs; they had worked for it; the annuities which were to be paid to them belonged to them. It was money promised by the government for land they had sold to the government. I desire to say that all annuities paid to Indian tribes by the government are in payment for land sold by them to the government, and are not charity. The government never gave any alms to the Indians, and we all know that through the "kindness" of the "Indian ring" they do not get the half of what the government actually owes them. It seems to us sometimes that the government treats us with less consideration than it does even the dogs.

For the past hundred years the Indians have had none to tell the story of their wrongs. If a white man did an injury to an Indian he had to suffer in silence, or being exasperated into revenge, the act of revenge has been spread abroad through the newspapers of the land as a causeless act, perpetrated on the whites just because the Indian delighted in being savage. It is because I know that a majority of the whites have not known of the cruelty practiced by the "Indian ring" on a handful of oppressed, helpless and conquered people, that I have the courage and confidence to appeal to the people of the United States. I have said "a conquered people." I do not know that I have the right to say that. We are helpless, it is true; but at heart we do not feel that we are a conquered people. We are human beings; God made us as well as you; and we are peculiarly his because of our ignorance and helplessness. I seem to understand why Christ came upon the earth and wandered over it, homeless and hated of all men. It brings him so much nearer to us to feel that he has suffered as we suffer, and can understand it all—suffered that we might feel that we belonged to him and were his own.

I will relate a single instance out of many, given me by my father, who knows the individuals concerned in it. I do not select it because it exceeds in horrors others told me by my Indian friends, but because it happens to be freshest in my memory. My father said there was in the Pawnee tribe a warrior holding a prominent position and respected by all the Indians. A white man was given the position on the reservation of government farmer for the Pawnee tribe. The Pawnees expected, of course, that he would go around among them and teach them how to plough and plant. Instead of doing that, he had fenced in a large piece of land, and had that sown and planted with grain and produce of all kinds. The Indians planted it and thought they would receive a part, at least, of the harvest. They never got any of it.

The warrior mentioned above was one day in the field killing the blackbirds which had alighted in the field in large numbers. While engaged in doing this the powder gave out. He went to the government farmer's house to ask for more. He saw a jewelled flask hanging up in the outside of the door, and as the farmer came to the door he pointed to his gun to show that it was empty, and motioned to the flask to make known that he wanted some more powder. The government farmer shook his head and refused. The Indian, thinking he had misunderstood, raised his arm to take the flask to show him what he wanted. The government farmer, I suppose, thinking he, the Indian, intended to take the flask without his permission, raised a broadax lying on the ground, swung it in the air, and at one blow chopped the man's arm and cut into his side. The farmer then fled.

The Pawnee Indians gathered around the dying warrior, and were making preparations for war on the white people in revenge for the deed, but the dying man made them promise him that they would do nothing in return. He said, "I am dying, and when I am dead you cannot bring me back to life by killing others. The government will not listen to you, but will listen to the farmer and send its soldiers and kill many of you, and you will all suffer for my sake. Let me die in peace and know you will not have to suffer for me." They promised him, and none but the Indian people ever knew anything about it.

It is wrongs such as these which, accumulating, exasperate the Indians beyond endurance and prompt them to deeds of vengeance, which, to those who know only one side of the story, seem savage barbarism, and the Indians are looked upon with horror as beings whose thirst for blood is ever unslaked. I tell you we are human beings, who love and hate as you do. Our affections are as strong, if not stronger, than yours; stronger in that we are powerless to help each other, and can only suffer with each other.

Before the tribal relations were voluntarily broken up by the Omahas, my father was a chief. He helped make some of the treaties with the government. He had been acquainted with the last eighteen agents who have transacted the business for one tribe on the part of the government, and out of those eighteen agents four only were good and honest men.

The following instance will show how these agents squandered the money of the tribe: About four years ago one of them, without counselling the tribe, had a large handsome house built at a cost of about five thousand dollars, at the expense of the Omaha tribe. The building was intended by the agent, he said, for an infirmary, but he could not get any Indian to go into it, and it has never been used for anything since. It is of no use to the tribe, but it was a good job for the contractors. The tribe is now endeavoring to have it altered, to use it as a boarding school for the Indian children.

I have been intimately acquainted with the affairs of the Poncas. The Poncas and Omahas speak the same language and have always been friends, and thus I have known all their sorrows and troubles. Being an Indian, I, of course, have a deep interest in them. So many seem to think that Indians fight because they delight in being savage and are bloodthirsty. Let me relate one or two instances which serve to show how powerless we are to help ourselves. Some years ago an Omaha man was missed from one of our tribes. No one could tell what had become of him. Some of our people went to look for him. They found him in a pigpen, where he had been thrown to the hogs after having been killed by the white men.

Another time a man of our tribe went to a settlement about ten miles distant from our reserve to sell potatoes. While he stood sorting them out two young men came along. They were white men, and one of them had just arrived from the East; he said to his companion, "I should like to shoot that Indian, just to say that I had shot one." His companion badgered him to do it. He raised his revolver and shot him.

Four weeks ago, just as we were starting on this trip, a young Indian boy of sixteen was stabbed by a white boy of thirteen. The stabbing took place near my house. The white people in the settlements around wondered that the Indian allowed the white boy to stab him, when he was so much older and stronger. It was because the Indian knew, as young as he was, that if he struck a blow to defend himself, and injured the boy in defending himself, the whole tribe would be punished for his act; that troops might be sent for and war made on the tribe. I think there was heroism in that boy's act.

For wrongs like these we have no redress whatever. We have no protection from the law. The Indians all know that they are powerless. Their chiefs and leading men had been to Washington, and have returned to tell their people of the mighty nation which fill the land once theirs. They know if they fight that they will be beaten, and they only fight when they are driven to desperation or are at the last extremity; and when they do at last fight, they have none to tell their side of the story, and it is given as a reason that they fight because they are bloodthirsty.

I have come to you to appeal for your sympathy and help for my people. They are immortal beings, for whom Christ died. They asked me to appeal to the churches, because they had heard that they were composed of God's people, and to the judges because they righted all wrongs. The people who were once owners of this soil ask you for their liberty, and law is liberty.

LaFlesche's words made a profound impression on her audience, some of whom—such as poet Henry Wadsworth Longfellow—were among the most celebrated public figures of the day. Having thus established herself as an Indian rights activist, she spent most of the next few years on the road, lecturing extensively and even testifying on several occasions before the United States Congress on condi-

tions among the Omaha and Ponca tribes. In 1887, she took her message about the need for reform in Indian policy to overseas audiences during a ten-month speaking tour throughout England and Scotland. Upon returning to America, LaFlesche settled once again in Nebraska. There she began a second career as a successful writer, publishing numerous articles and stories in a variety of midwestern newspapers and magazines.

SOURCES

Anderson, Judith, *Outspoken Women: Speeches by American Women Reformers, 1635-1935,* Kendall/Hunt Publishing Company, 1984.

Armstrong, Virginia Irving, *I Have Spoken: American History Through the Voices of the Indians,* Sage Books, 1971.

Brown, Marion M., *Susette LaFlesche: Advocate for Native American Rights,* Children's Press, 1992.

Clifton, James A., editor, *On Being and Becoming Indian: Biographical Studies of North American Frontiers,* Dorsey Press, 1989.

Nabokov, Peter, editor, *Native American Testimony: A Chronicle of Indian-White Relations from Prophecy to the Present, 1492-1992,* Penguin Books, 1991.

Wilson, Dorothy Clarke, *Bright Eyes: The Story of Susette LaFlesche,* McGraw-Hill, 1974.

John Mercer Langston

1829–1897

African American lawyer, politician, educator

John Mercer Langston, great-uncle of Harlem Renaissance poet Langston Hughes, was a noted educator and orator who was also among the last blacks to serve in the Reconstruction-era Congress. Born in Virginia to a white plantation owner and a slave woman of mixed African and Indian heritage, he was raised by a close family friend after the deaths of both his parents in 1834. In keeping with his father's wishes, Langston received a good education. He attended public and private schools in Chillicothe and Cincinnati, Ohio, then went on to Oberlin College, where he earned his bachelor's degree in 1849 and his master's degree in 1852. Denied admission to law school, he studied on his own under a judge in Elyria, Ohio, and was admitted to the state bar in 1854.

Langston remained in Ohio for another ten years. There he practiced law, entered local politics (in 1855 he became the first African American ever voted into public office in the United States when he was elected clerk of Brownhelm Township), and participated in the antislavery movement as well as the Conventions of Colored Citizens. During the Civil War, he also helped recruit black soldiers for the Union Army. It was during this period of activism that Langston first made a name for himself as a public speaker. His strong support for freedom and increased educational and occupational opportunities for blacks soon attracted attention outside his home state, and in 1864 he was elected president of the National Equal Rights League, a forerunner of the Niagara Movement and the National Association for the Advancement of Colored People (NAACP).

After the war, Langston went to work as an inspector-general for the Freedmen's Bureau. Two years later, in 1869, he was named head of the new law department at Howard University; he subsequently served as the university's vice-president and acting president. From 1877 until 1885 he lived and worked abroad for the U.S. government as minister to Haiti and chargé d'affaires to the Dominican Republic. Upon his return home, he became president of Virginia Normal and Collegiate Institute.

In 1888, Langston decided to run for Congress as the Republican candidate in Virginia's fourth district. Thanks to some election-day trickery, however, his Democratic opponent was declared the winner. Langston challenged the results for nearly two years until the U.S. House of Representatives finally voted to seat him in

September 1890. With only six months remaining in his term, he tried to accomplish as much as possible before the end of the session. As a member of the education committee, for example, he pushed for legislation to create a National Industrial University for Colored Youth. In addition, he closely monitored voting practices that had an impact on African Americans, criticizing efforts to intimidate black voters in the South and warning his colleagues about the imminent collapse of Reconstruction policies there. One such warning came in a speech he delivered in Congress on January 16, 1891, reprinted here from the Congressional Record *51st Congress, 2nd Session, U.S. Gov't Printing Office, 1891. Though basically an optimist about the future of the United States in general and African Americans in particular, Langston was nevertheless deeply disturbed by the attempts of Southern Democrats to undermine the Constitution.*

If there is anything that I would gladly see, it is "Our country first on land, and first on sea," and it is natural for me, coming into this body, as I do, from the Old Dominion that gave life to Washington and birth to Jefferson to come with the sentiment I have just expressed. I have seen American masters of ships wronged in foreign countries, and finally successfully defended by the government through the vigorous and manly efforts of our representatives abroad. I recollect among the very last things that occurred when I had the honor of representing this government abroad was this fact, first, that an old shipmaster said to me in our legation, "When you go home, if you ever have the opportunity to say a word for us, say it, say it freely and say it positively, and so emancipate us, that on the great sea, as well as at home, we may feel the consciousness that we are Americans."

John Mercer Langston

I promised that shipmaster that if ever I had the opportunity of speaking for our shipping I would do it, and do it fearlessly and thoroughly. One of these days, in this august body, I trust that I shall have the opportunity of saying a word. But how can we make our land and our government great in the estimation of others, except as finally we plant ourselves as a nation on those fundamental, far-reaching, eternal principles underlying all democracies and perpetuating all republics?

I would speak today to you, not in any other wise than as I would defend the Constitution of my country, planting myself a those doctrines of the Declaration so clearly and forcibly enunciated in these words:

We hold these truths to be self-evident; that all men are created equal; that they are endowed by their Creator with certain unalienable rights; that among these are life, liberty and the pursuit of happiness. That to secure these rights governments are instituted among men, deriving their just powers from the consent of the governed.

Ah, Mr. Chairman, the day has come to us now when we are to recur in our thoughts and reach in our purposes those olden times of this Republic when our fathers built, as Christ did, "on the rock," that His church might stand, and now that our government may stand.

Why, the feeling in the country seems to be today that silver is the thing; and a man said to me the other day, when the silver bill had been laid aside for the time being, "Ah, sir, your cause has been sold for thirty pieces of silver."

[Langston was at this point interrupted by Representative Joseph P. Taylor of Ohio, who wanted to clarify that Langston was referring to the fact that the elections bill had been laid aside.]

Yes; I mean when the election bill was laid aside. But I said: "Not so, sir, for we live in the United States of America, in the midst of schoolhouses, in the midst of schools, in the midst of churches, in the midst of Christians, and we have built our nation on other material than that which shall find any class of our population, politicians or statesmen, finally willing to sell the cause of liberty, the rights of the humblest citizen of our government, for anything like a compromise, even in silver." [Applause on the Republican side.]

Why, on what are we built and where do we go? Our nation is built first on those fundamental laws given in the midst of the flame and smoke of Sinai, and across the gateway of the old Mosaic system it was written, "He that stealeth a man and selleth him, or if he be found in his hands, he shall surely die"; and in the light of this law slavery has gone. We find that there was in the same law, enunciated so clearly and so beautifully by Him "who spake as never man spake," the maxim that "Whatever you would that men should do unto you, do ye even so unto them." And we built on that afterwards. But here is the declaration which we have built on, and that is this Constitution, which we have amended, not because it needed amendment, but that there might be no mistake as to the question of whether a black man might be free or slave; whether he should continue ignorant and a discredit to you by having been born in this country. In his nativity, he finds the fact that he is an American, and the law must protect him in that character. [Loud applause on the Republican side.]

But my friend on the other side of the House the other day referred to what was done in 1815. He alluded to the fact that great men moved in that day, and I watched for him to come down to the position of General Jackson on the Negro question, because I wanted to hear him on that; but he tarried at the Hartford convention and did not come on down to the victory that was won at New Orleans, when the great general of that day called his troops about him and gave utterance to sentiments that the Negro loves and some men hate even up to this hour. [Applause on the Republican side.] Ah, General Jackson was not a bad man, although he was a Democrat in some senses of the word. [Laughter.]

I would that the Democrats of the United States would accept the doctrines of that great and venerable man who, firm and true to the last, was able to see, beyond the curl of a man's hair and beyond the color of his face, the fact that he was a man and the fact that he could be a patriotic American. [Applause on the Republican side.] Now, if you will permit me I will read a few words from the utterance of that distinguished man on this subject, to show that he could call us citizens of the United States, American citizens, and, in addressing us, could use language which became the lips of a brave and valiant American general:

Soldiers—

He says, in addressing his black troops after the war—

Soldiers, when on the banks of the Mobile I called you to take up arms, inviting you to partake in the perils and glory of your white fellow-citizens—

Ah, my white fellow-citizens on the other side of the House [laughter], and my white fellow-citizens on every side of the House, and my white fellow-citizens in every section of the country, black as we are no man shall go ahead of us in devotion to this country, in devotion to its free institutions, for we hold our lives, our property, and our sacred honor in pledge to the welfare of our country and of all our fellow-citizens. [Applause on the Republican side.] Do you want men to fight; call us and we will come. Do you want men to tarry at home and take care of your wives, take care of your children, take care of your homes and protect your interests; call on us. And when the time is past, if you can find a Negro who has betrayed you in a single case put your finger on him and we will aid you in lynching him. [Applause.] But he cannot be found.

Oh, no. What a wonderful chapter that is, that the men who lived near where General Jackson uttered these words, in the state of Louisiana, and in the states of the South, all along the line of battle, could go away leaving everything in the hands of the Negro and come back and find that it had been guarded, thoroughly protected. For that alone, if for no other reason, the Negro might well be accorded the freedom and justice that are his right, and he would be if those men had only been fair and true to him. Now, you see, General Jackson calls us your "fellow-citizens" by referring to the white man as our "white fellow-citizens." [Laughter.] That certainly is legal and logical. He says further:

> *I expected much from you, for I was not ignorant that you possessed qualities most formidable to an invading enemy. I knew with what fortitude you could endure hunger and thirst and the fatigues of the campaign. I knew well how you loved your native country—*

"Your native country." Oh, yes; this is our native country. We do not have to go abroad to find our native country, for Jackson has told us we need not go. Some men want us to go to Africa and to the isles of the sea, but, blessed be the name of this grand old Democrat, he has taught us another lesson; he has taught us that this is our home; and in the name of Jackson, whose shade is about me now, I declare in this sacred place that we are here to stay and never will go away. [Laughter.] Why, we cannot go. How can I get out of this country?

I undertook to leave Virginia, and the first thing I knew I was back there. I moved away and located in Ohio, but I could not stay. I came to the District of Columbia, but I could not stay here. I went abroad, but I could not stay there. When I returned and undertook to go away again, by a curious adjustment of Providence, I found myself in Virginia; and today, by a curious adjustment of Providence, I find myself standing in this august and wonderful presence. We cannot control ourselves in these things.

Do you think that the Negro would have come to this country to find slavery when the white man came here to find liberty? Yet, when the white men were landing on the eastern shores of the continent and beginning to build our nationality, the Negro came in chains to the southward; and, as the white men became great in numbers, the Negroes multiplied, until finally, in the great struggle for liberty, when, in its far-reaching and broad sweep slavery had stricken down the liberties of the people, and the fight had to come, the Negro, in the midst of the thunder of the great contest, is called from his slumbers, comes forth from his rags a free man, and enters upon real life the equal of his white fellow-citizen. [Applause on the Republican side.] Here we are and here we are to stay. And I give my Democratic friends a warning that they may oppress us as much as they will, but still we shall remain. Abuse us as you will, gentlemen, we will increase and multiply until, instead of finding every day five hundred black babies turning up their bright eyes to greet the rays of the sun, the number shall be five thousand and shall still go on increasing. [Laughter and applause.]

There is no way to get rid of us. [Laughter.] It is our native country.

> *And that you as well as ourselves had to defend what man holds most dear, parents, wife, children, and property. You have done more than I have expected. In addition to the previous qualities I before knew you to possess, I found among you a noble enthusiasm which leads to the performance of great things.*

And we will not disappoint you in that.

> *Soldiers! The president of the United States shall hear how praiseworthy was your conduct in the hour of danger, and the representatives of the American people will give you the praise your exploits entitle you to. Your general anticipates them in applauding your noble ardor.*

We are simply fellow-citizens. We have always been fellow-citizens. We are nothing but fellow-citizens today, and fellow-citizens in permanent residence in this our native country.

But this is not the only testimony. I can offer on this subject Southern testimony which goes further than this. Gentlemen are very timid about us; not only timid, but anxious. But where do you find the very first judicial opinion, broad and comprehensive, recognizing the Negro of this country not only as a citizen, but as an elector? Suppose I should state here, Mr. Chairman, that in this matter we must follow the lead of the South? Suppose I should say that as a matter of fact the enunciation in that behalf, clear and distinct, was made not by a Northern judge, but by a Southern judge, and that this judge was the first lawyer of the state of North Carolina ? I will say so; and I will astonish you by reading (if you have not read it) from the learned opinion of Chief Justice Gaston, as given in the case of the State vs. Manuel. A Negro boy, having assaulted a white boy, was brought to trial and found guilty; the punishment adjudged was thirty-nine lashes at the whipping post.

A young white lawyer said to gentlemen of Fayetteville, N.C.: "Raise a little purse and I will take this case before the supreme court of the state; I will ask Judge Gaston to pass on the case, and I believe he will decide that no colored man, even though born a slave, if subsequently emancipated, as Manuel has been, can be punished at the whipping post, because by reason of his nativity he is an American citizen." The money was raised and the case carried to the supreme court. Judge Gaston sat in that case and delivered the opinion. Now, what do my Democratic friends think he said? Mark you, I read from the opinion of a North Carolina judge. Listen:

According to the laws of this state (North Carolina) all the human beings within it who are not slaves fall within one of two classes. Whatever distinctions may have existed in the Roman laws between citizens and free inhabitants, they are unknown to our institutions. Before our Revolution all free persons born within the dominions of the king of Great Britain, whatever their color or complexion, were native-born British subjects; those born out of his allegiance were aliens. Slavery did not exist in England, but it did in the British colonies. Slaves were not, in legal parlance, persons, but property. The moment the incapacity, the disqualification of slavery was removed, they became persons, and were then either British subjects or not British subjects, according as they were or were not born within the allegiance of the British king.

Upon the Revolution no other change took place in the laws of North Carolina than was consequent on the transition from a colony dependent on a European king to a free and sovereign state; slaves remained slaves; British subjects in North Carolina become North Carolina freemen; foreigners, until made members of the state, remained aliens; slaves manumitted here became freemen; and therefore, if born within North Carolina, are citizens of North Carolina, and all free persons born within the state are born citizens of the state. The Constitution extended the elective franchise to every freeman who had arrived at the age of twenty-one and paid a public tax, and it is a matter of universal notoriety that under it free persons, without regard to color, claimed and exercised the franchise until it was taken from freemen of color a few years since by our amended constitution.

North Carolina started this doctrine and we accept it.

And on this question of citizenship, allow me to read the opinion of Honorable Edward Bates, given by him as attorney general of the United States, in 1862, in response to the question propounded by the then secretary of the Treasury, Salmon P. Chase, "Are colored men citizens of the United States, and therefore competent to command American vessels?"

1. In every civilized country the individual is born to duties and rights, the duty of allegiance and the right to protection; and these are correlative obligations, the one the price of the other, and they constitute the all-sufficient bond of union between the individual and his country, and the country he is born in is prima facie *his country.*

2. And our Constitution in speaking of natural-born citizens uses no affirmative language to make them such, but only recognizes and reaffirms the universal principle, common to all nations and as old as political society, that the people born in the country do constitute the nation, and, as individuals, are natural members of the body politic.

3. In the United States it is too late to deny the political rights and obligations conferred and imposed by nativity, for our laws do not pretend to create or enact them, but do assume and recognize them as things known to all men, because pre-existent and natural, and therefore things of which the laws must take cognizance.

4. It is strenuously insisted by some that "persons of color," though born in the country, are not capable of being citizens of the United States. As far as the Constitution is concerned, this is a naked assumption, for the Constitution contains not one word upon the subject.

5. There are some who, abandoning the untenable objection of color, still contend that no person descended from Negroes of the African race can be a citizen of the United States. Here the objection is not color, but race only. The Constitution certainly does not forbid it, but is silent about race as it is about color.

6. But it is said that African Negroes are a degraded race, and that all who are tainted with that degradation are forever disqualified for the functions of citizenship. I can hardly comprehend the thought of the absolute incompatibility of degradation and citizenship; I thought that they often went together.

7. Our nationality was created and our political government exists by written law, and inasmuch as that law does not exclude persons of that descent, and as its terms are manifestly broad enough to include them, it follows inevitably that such persons born in the country must be citizens unless the fact of African descent be so incompatible with the fact of citizenship that the two cannot exist together.

Being citizens, being electors, we are confronted today as distinctly as in 1861-65 with the question of slavery or freedom, with the question whether every American citizen may wield the ballot in this country freely and according to his own judgment in the interest of the welfare of our common country. It does not matter how black we are; it does not matter how ignorant we are; it does not matter what our race may be; it does not matter whether we were degraded or not; the question presented today under our amended Constitution, as under the Constitution without amendment, is, shall every freeman, shall every American citizen, shall every American elector in the North and in the South, everywhere in the country, be permitted to wield a free ballot in the interests of our common country and our free institutions? [Applause.]

Here lies the difference: The old Democratic party used to maintain that this right should be accorded to every American citizen; the new Democratic party is fighting it. But, thank God, the genuine Americans—mainly found in the Republican party—some few in the Democratic party, but through mistake [laughter]—are standing up bravely and truly today to meet this question intelligently and patriotically.

"Oh," but the Democrats say, "you got beaten at the last election." In one sense we did and in one sense we did not. "Whom the Lord loveth he chasteneth." [Laughter.] We have only been chastened a little to make us more firm, and more solid, and the more certain in the high march that is before us to the "promised land" in the midst of our own homes to which God would lead us in the establishment of an all-comprehensive freedom and equality of right.

How dark it was in 1861! How dark it was in 1850! Ah! Compromises were made; the great orators spoke; the great parties resolved; and the friends of freedom came well-nigh to despair. But the voice of the faithful and the true was still heard; and finally in the thunder of great guns, in the midst of terrible smoke as of the Mountain of Sinai, and in the flashes of light that made every slave in the land glad, emancipation was declared and the country was saved. [Applause.]

But, Mr. Chairman, it is sneeringly said that the Republican party laid aside the elections bill in the Senate. But it was only for a little while; it was only to take it up again; that was all. And they have taken it up now in earnest. And if the elections shall come around shortly you will see the change when the people have been forgotten who failed to do their duty in connection with the matter. Yes, they have taken up the elections bill again, and those people who yielded it for awhile, who laid it aside to address themselves to other matters, have gone back to the solid, patriotic conviction that at last liberty is the whitest and brightest jewel in the firmament, and that the greatest heritage of American citizenship is to be free. [Applause.]

Why, sir, the Democrats talk of carrying the election in 1892. How could they carry it? They could not do it by any fair means. But our Democratic friends do not talk of fair means any more. They avoid all that. [Laughter.] A gentleman who spoke the other day, and talked of free ballots and all that sort of thing, was asked against whom he made the charges. He said "The Democratic party." Why should we not so charge it under the circumstances? I would like to see somebody put his finger on something that the Democratic party has done from the beginning that looks like favoring freedom or favoring the colored men in this country, at whose friends on this floor strange words have been hurled. How peculiarly our friends are characterized! You can hardly believe the language that is used towards them. I have some of it here before me, studied, selected, written, and rewritten it must have been, but yet very peculiar language. I have read it a good many times, but I never saw anything like it before. Here is a specimen:

> *Mr. Speaker, I am heartily tired and sick of this eternal cant and hypocrisy. I think the time has come to tear off the thin veil which covers it, and to express our opinions about this business and the fellows who are engaged in it.*
>
> *What is this bill, anyhow? It is urged on the pretense that it is necessary to secure fair elections. But every honest man of intelligence knows that that is a mere subterfuge. It originates in a section of the Union which has grown enormously rich at the expense of the West and South. It observes the development and rapid growth in political power of the West and South with ever-increasing alarm. Conscious that unity of interest will, as a matter of self-defense, ultimate inevitably in bringing about some unity of action between the West and South, this bill is thrown as a firebrand into our politics, with the hope of passing it under the spur of partisan prejudice and pressure, thereby delaying that political adhesion already approaching in*

other sections, and using it to perpetuate as long as possible a local advantage.

Fair elections! Sir, it will be a sad day for this Republic when the people can be no longer trusted with the ballot box. Virtue is the very essence of popular liberty; but equally so is liberty the essence of public virtue. These gentlemen say they can no longer trust the states and the people with their own ballot box. They hold it has become necessary to have an army of officials, without direct responsibility to the voters, to watch, to supervise, and, if need be, to punish them. If, indeed, it be true that patriotism and public sentiment and public morals have come to this low ebb, then are we approaching that starless night into whose eternal shadows has disappeared nearly every effort at popular government which mankind, striving for higher and nobler ideas of liberty, have ever made in the history of the world. I do not believe it.

I can still trust with perfect confidence the people of all or any of the states of the American Union. I had rather confide the ballot box to the plain people of the land, risk its purity to their patriotism and its safety to their hands, than trust it to any band of partisan mercenaries, with badges on their lapels and batons or bayonets in their hands, appointed by any federal administration that ever was or shall be.

Against whom, specially and professedly, is this haughty insolence directed? Against whom are these charges of fraud and crime, these burning and intolerable insults, leveled? The Democratic party. Forget not, gentlemen, that that party represents a large majority of all the people of the whole country, and a full round million majority of the white voters of the United States, the sons of the warriors and matrons who won the battles of the Revolution and laid broad and deep the foundations of the Republic. They can not be intimidated by a threat nor overawed by a menace.

There is no need to continue this. It is found on every page of the *Record*.

In this connection I wish to quote in contrast what is said so ably by the president [Benjamin Harrison] in his last annual message:

But it is said that this legislation will revive race animosities, and some have even suggested that when the peaceful methods of fraud are made impossible they may be supplanted by intimidation and violence. If the proposed law gives to any qualified elector, by a hair's weight, more than his equal influence, or detracts by so much from any other qualified elector, it is fatally impeached. But if the law is equal and the animosities it is to evoke grow out of the fact that some electors have been accustomed to exercise the franchise for others as well as for themselves, then these animosities ought not to be confessed without shame and can not be given any weight in the discussion without dishonor. No choice is left to me but to enforce with vigor all laws intended to secure to the citizen his constitutional rights, and to recommend that the inadequacies of such laws be promptly remedied. If to promote with zeal and ready interests every project for the development of its material interests, its rivers, harbors, mines, and factories, and the intelligence, peace, and security under the law of its communities and its homes, is not accepted as sufficient evidence of friendliness to any state or section, I can not add connivance at election practices that not only disturb local results, but rob the electors of other states and sections of their most priceless political rights.

Eight millions of people who stand behind me today, a few in the West and all over the South, command me to say to you that so long as there is a name akin to that of Hoar in New England we will honor and revere it because that man has been true to us in the Senate. [Applause on the Republican side.] But it would not have made any difference. We do not forget our friends.

You recollect that there was a Hoar who went South once, and he went to Charleston, South Carolina, going there as the agent of the great state of Massachusetts. He appeared in the name of the sovereignty of that great state as a lawyer, not to "steal Negroes," but to inquire in the courts of that state as to whether it was legal for a colored citizen of the state of Massachusetts, sailing into the harbor of Charleston on a Northern vessel, to be arrested and imprisoned and adjudged a free Negro and sold into interminable slavery. He was accompanied by his sweet, elegant, charming daughter, a young lady of Boston. He appeared, and very soon a committee of gentlemen of property waited on him. "What is your business here, sir?" He said, "I have come," as I have described, "in the name of the Commonwealth in which I live, to look after matters of interest to the great body of the people of our state."

"We give you, sir, one hour's notice to take your trunk and leave this city, and if you are not gone within that time we will tar and we will feather you." And at the end of that time the committee waited on him again. He was a little behind time. And, Mr. Chairman, it is recorded in history that the presence of his daughter alone saved him from their clutches.

[Representative Elijah A. Morse of Massachusetts interrupted at this point to declare that what Langston had said was "as true as Gospel."]

And coming around to Philadelphia, a Whig national convention was in session, and this noble man of Massachusetts, this grand man, was called on for a speech. How do you think he opened his address?

> *Fellow-citizens, having escaped the bloody clutches of the slaveholders of the South, I take a great deal of pleasure in addressing you.*

Ah, Mr. Chairman, this spirit does not know white man or black man. All stand equal before it, as they should stand equal before the law. When I stand here today speaking for the cause of the people of my state, my native state, the state of Virginia, I am pleading for her people, both white and black. I am speaking for white men as well as for Negroes; for white men in my state are proscribed, and they are denied a free ballot, though their "locks be flaxen and their eyes blue." I might cite you the case of a man, a friend of mine, residing in Chase City, the postmaster at that place, appointed through my efforts. He writes me:

> *I cannot go to the polls on election day to vote for you because I was proscribed already for my support of you. My family were proscribed, my children at the school, and we are all hated because I vote the Republican ticket.*

And that is no uncommon or isolated case. But go into another county, if you will. Go with me to my beautiful city of Petersburgh. They sometimes say I do not live there, but if you will go with me down there I will show you that I do live there and live at home. [Laughter.] One man said, "I do not believe you live in Petersburgh, because you have a house in Washington." Well, unfortunately, I have got a house in Washington, because it sometimes happens that a colored man can have two houses, one in which he lives and one where he does not live. [Laughter.] White men, of course, may have three or four without question.

[Representative George W. Atkinson of West Virginia then remarked, "Some do not have any."]

That is true. But most Negroes now have their own homes.

Come down there with me. Let me introduce you to a fine-looking man with splendid hair, noble face, fine bearing, the picture of intelligence. He leaves his table on election day and gets to the door of his office, where he is met and asked:

"Where are you going?"

"Going to vote."

"Are you going to vote for that fellow?"

"What do you mean?" he asks.

"Why, are you going to vote for Langston?"

"Yes, I am. Langston is a Republican. There is only one Republican running, and I always vote the Republican ticket. Here is my ticket. I am on the way to vote for him."

He went and voted. What was the result? The next morning at five o'clock, when he stepped out of his door, he found it all draped with crape. What was going to be done? Why, he voted for a Republican yesterday, and this crape was significant. What was the result? He was proscribed, his children were proscribed. They point their fingers at his children as they are on the way to school, and when they get to the school they call his children names. And I plead the cause here today, Mr. Chairman, not only of seven million Negroes of the South, but of the white men in all the South who have accepted the principles of the fathers and dedicated their faith to Republican doctrine. [Applause on the Republican side.] And I do not apologize for it.

I appeal to any and every Democrat on this floor, if it is not true, that I state hastily here, too hastily to make myself well understood, the doctrine, first, that the white men of the South have maintained that Negroes are citizens upon their nativity; secondly, the decision of Judge Gaston, who ruled that we are entitled to the elective franchise upon a property qualification in North Carolina; and then, thirdly and lastly, if it is not true today in the South that white men may not vote the Republican ticket with greater facility or larger freedom from proscription than Negroes themselves? Oh, you ought to come down there and see it. You ought to see an intelligent, fine-looking white girl, well dressed, well behaved, bearing herself like a lady, passing along the street with a rabble of white men saying, "Your father voted for a damned Negro and we will show you," and frightening that sweet American girl.

Do you like that spirit? I do not. I will never be the coward to say that I do. And I would pass bills and pile up penalties and put behind every bill soldiers until they rose to the top of the mountains and kissed the stars, to put these women and these men in the sure consciousness of their protection by law. [Applause on the Republican side.]

Now, oppress Negroes if you must, but for God's sake stop oppressing white voters. [Applause on the Republican side.] Deny to the Negro the ballot if you will, but for God's sake do not take the ballot from your own brothers with flaxen hair and blue eyes! And yet that is done.

Now, another speaker says, "Why don't you make Bruce president? Why don't you make Langston president?" I want to plead guilty to some things here. I think we have honored Mr. Bruce a good deal. He is a splendid gentleman. He is one of the class of good-looking colored men on this continent, and you will excuse me if I tell you we have got some of the finest looking Negroes on this continent that you ever saw. And then we have got so many. You think you have got millions in the United States, but go with me where I used to live when I was your representative, and let me show you hundreds of thousands there, so black on one side of the island and so light on the other, and let me introduce you to that living monument of fine appearance and culture and magnificent appointments in every respect, the man who used to be president of the Republic of Hayti.

When Rear Admiral Cooper visited me on his ship, the *Tennessee,* I said, "Admiral, do not you want to see a splendid man; do not you want to see the best-looking black man in the world; do not you want to see a great man, the impersonation of learning and culture, a man who many a day escorted Mrs. Dix to dinner in Paris, who towered up there in all his beauty as a gentleman admired by every representative of every foreign country?" The old admiral said, "I would like to see him." And I made arrangements whereby on the next morning, at ten o'clock, we went to the national palace, the White House of that country, where we were received in fine style, the national band playing what they thought was our national air:

John Brown's body lies moldering in
the grave,
But his soul is marching on.

[Applause and laughter on the Republican side.]

That will be your national air one of these days, in the good time coming. Our bands shall play it, our choristers shall sing it, and we as a Christian nation shall march on under the banner of the Republican party to national and local victory under the impulse and purpose which that song will awaken in our souls.

We entered the palace, and very soon we were in the presence of this magnificent man of more than three hundred pounds' weight. His hair was as white as the snow, his face as black as the night, his face the face of Webster, his manner polite, genteel, and elegant, like the manner of Wendell Phillips. He was the impersonation of culture. And when I said to him in French: "Mr. President, I have the honor to present to you a rear admiral of the American Navy," the bow he made, out of his high regard for our free institutions and our noble country and our magnificent nation, was charming in the extreme.

And shortly we took the usual elegant drink of magnificent champagne without ice, as is the custom in this country. [Laughter.] When the rear admiral was about ready to go he said, "Now, minister, make my speech to the president. Tell the president that my goodly ship, the *Tennessee,* has carried me into the waters of every civilized nation; that I have looked into the faces of kings and queens, emperors and empresses, and the executives of all sorts of men and governments; and say to him that I seem now, in the presence of this president, to stand in the presence of the man whom we call the Father of Our Country, 'First in war, first in peace, and first in the hearts of his countrymen.' I feel that I stand in the presence of Washington himself." I threw it into French, as I could then, and then these great men advanced with tears in their eyes and gave each other the warm palm; and I said to them, "Ah! Gentlemen, this is the Great Republic of the North extending her warm palm in sympathy to this Negro republic."

It is prophetic of what? That American influences shall prevail with reference to the Negro race of this country on the continent and in the isles of the sea. We are here on the continent; we are here living on the continent as a part of a great nation. God is with us; the people are with us, and we are with you, and we are in the South to remain; coming gently towards the North, increasing day by day, to wield the ballot, the free ballot, given to us by the government that we defended in its possession, and we will wield it to make our country great on the land and great on the sea, matchless in the ship, and matchless in industry, with mankind to applaud our magnificent pride of country, emulating the white man in our endeavors to realize the glory and distinction which the fathers knew this country would attain in the future; and to that end may God help us. [Loud applause on the Republican side.]

SOURCES

Books

Congressional Record, 51st Congress, 2nd session, January 16, 1891, U.S. Gov't Printing Office, 1891, pp. 1479-1482.

Langston, John Mercer, *Freedom and Citizenship: Selected Lectures and Addresses,* Rufus H. Darby, 1883, reprinted, Mnemosyne Publishing, 1969.

———, *From the Virginia Plantation to the National Capitol* (autobiography), original edition, 1894, reprinted, Johnson Reprint, 1968.

Smith, Arthur L., and Stephen Robb, editors, *The Voice of Black Rhetoric: Selections,* Allyn & Bacon, 1971.

Periodicals

Civil War History, "John Mercer Langston: Black Protest Leader and Abolitionist," June, 1970, pp. 101-120.

Bette Bao Lord

1938–

Chinese American writer and pro-democracy/human rights activist

The path Bette Bao Lord traveled to become a best-selling author and respected activist can best be described as circuitous, perhaps even a bit serendipitous. She was born in Shanghai, China, to Dora and Sandys Bao, an electrical engineer who worked for the Nationalist Chinese government. Shortly after the end of World War II, Sandys Bao left for an extended trip to the United States on behalf of his country, which was in the market for equipment to help rebuild China. As his assignment stretched from months into a year, he grew lonesome for his family. In 1946, he was finally given permission to send for his wife and two of his three daughters, including eight-year-old Bette. (An infant daughter, Sansan, stayed behind with relatives because her parents felt she was too young to make the long journey.) The Baos settled briefly in Brooklyn, New York, where Bette enrolled in public school. Later, they moved to Teaneck, New Jersey.

The family was still in the United States when civil war erupted in China between the Nationalist government and communist rebels led by Mao Zedong. By the time the communists claimed victory over the Nationalists in 1949, the Baos knew that they could not return home and that trying to spirit Sansan out of China would be dangerous if not impossible. So they remained in New Jersey, and it was there that Bette grew up.

An excellent student who was well-liked by her classmates, Bao graduated from high school in 1954 and went on to college at Tufts University in Boston. Although her intention was to major in chemistry because "every Chinese child is supposed to grow up to be an '-ist,' as in scientist," as she explained to a Chicago Tribune reporter, both she and her professors agreed that she would probably be happier in another field. So she switched to history and earned her bachelor's degree in 1959. The following year, she obtained her master's degree in international relations from the Fletcher School of Law and Diplomacy (also at Tufts).

Bao then headed to the University of Hawaii, where she began as an assistant to the director of the school's East-West Center and within a short time headed her own department. She left in 1961 for a job in Washington, D.C., as an advisor to the director of the Fulbright Exchange Program. There she became reacquainted *with a former Tufts classmate, Winston Lord, who was then working in the U.S. Foreign Service. They married in 1963.*

Meanwhile, Sansan Bao—separated from her family for more than fifteen years—was finally allowed to leave China, ostensibly to visit her ailing mother in Hong Kong. The "illness" was just a ruse, however, that enabled the Baos to help Sansan escape to America. Friends who were familiar with her lifetime of hardship under the communist regime in China and eventual reunion with her family thought the story would make fascinating reading, and her sister agreed. When Bette couldn't find anyone else to take on the project (the fact that Sansan spoke no English was a major obstacle), she quit her job and tackled it herself. The result was Eighth Moon: The True Story of a Young Girl's Life in Communist China, *published by Harper in 1964 to wide commercial and critical success.*

From 1965 until 1967, Bette taught and performed modern dance in Geneva, Switzerland, where her husband had been sent as a member of the U.S. negotiating team involved in international tariff discussions. Not long after their return home, Winston joined President Richard Nixon's administration as a top aide to foreign policy advisor Henry Kissinger. In this capacity, Winston was very much involved in the events leading up to official U.S. recognition of Red China in 1972. The following year, Bette accompanied her husband on a journey to the land of her birth—her first visit since she had left there as a child. Her impressions of modern China eventually found their way into a historical novel she worked on during the late 1970s entitled Spring Moon. *Like her first book, it was a hit with both readers and critics and was even nominated for a National Book Award.*

In 1985, the Lords returned to China when Winston was named U.S. ambassador. There Bette once again devoted herself to cultural pursuits, becoming active in local theater and turning the American Embassy in Beijing into a meeting place for writers and artists. She also provided valuable assistance to her husband as an unofficial diplomat of sorts, guiding him through what proved to be an especially tumultuous time in Chinese history. Just as his term was coming to an end during the spring of 1989, student-led pro-democracy demonstrations erupted in at least twenty major cities, including Beijing. Although Winston had to return to Washington in April, Bette stayed behind and provided commentary on the unfolding events for CBS News and Newsweek *magazine. She left China just days before exhilaration gave way to tragedy in Beijing's Tiananmen Square on June 6, when Army troops opened fire on the unarmed demonstrators, killing an estimated five thousand people and injuring thousands more. Hundreds of students and workers were subsequently arrested, and many were executed or imprisoned.*

The horror of what occurred in Tiananmen Square to so many of those with whom she had talked and shared dreams of a brighter future compelled Lord to take action. Shortly after her return to the United States, she wrote the nonfiction book Legacies: A Chinese Mosaic, *a selection of oral histories she had gathered while living in China that she hoped would "put faces and stories with what happened there [in Tiananmen Square]." Like her previous works, it was very well received.*

The events of Tiananmen Square also catapulted Lord into the human rights movement. In 1991, she joined the board of directors of Freedom House, a New York City-based organization (co-founded by Eleanor Roosevelt) that monitors and works for human rights around the world while promoting democracy as the key to preserving those rights. Two years later, she became its chairwoman.

It was in connection with her role at Freedom House that Lord appeared in Washington, D.C., before the foreign affairs committee of the U.S. House of Representatives on March 10, 1993, to offer her views on the role of U.S. foreign policy in strengthening human rights and democracy around the world. As she made clear in both her testimony and in the written statement that accompanied it, she regards American-style democracy as "the most successful model for nurturing a vibrant society, responsive government, a free press, effective unions, domestic harmony and global cooperation." At the same time, she condemns "neo-isolationism and disengagement from world affairs" now that communism no longer appears to pose a threat as "precisely the wrong prescriptions at the wrong time. . . . In the end, the true power of America is its ideas." Lord's statement is reprinted here from The Future of U.S. Foreign Policy (Part II): Functional Issues—Hearings Before the Committee on Foreign Affairs, House of Representatives, *103rd Congress, 1st Session, U.S. Government Printing Office, 1993.*

As an immigrant, I have a singular honor to testify before this committee. As the chairman of Freedom House, I have the opportunity to speak on behalf of a bipartisan, nonprofit organization founded fifty years ago by Eleanor Roosevelt and Wendell Wilkie, on the subject that is our reason for being, promoting democracy and human rights.

While my written statement addresses your important questions in a more orthodox way, permit me to speak personally. I do so to provide a different perspective, one that native-born Americans cannot offer naturally. Taught to question every premise, they do not flinch from dissecting America's failings. It is a most admirable trait. But such clinical probes overlook the intangibles through which people living in distant lands discern America. I know. I am able to disappear among them and eavesdrop.

To the masses denied dignity by their rulers, America is not just another country with material goods that they covet. It is the embodiment of intangibles—liberty, conscience, hope. The sun we enjoy blithely, they behold as a beacon from afar.

I recall how curious my Chinese friends were watching our presidential debates, but what they viewed as an earth-shaking phenomenon totally escaped even me. They were awestruck by the fact that a lowly TV journalist—apologies to Dan, Tom, and Peter—could politely, but in no uncertain terms, tell the paramount leader of the most powerful nation in the world that his time was up.

How confounding, just when technology and humanity's newest trials mock walls, borders, and oceans, some extol the efficacy of withdrawing to our shores or, worse, ethnically correct enclaves. Just when human rights, however mislabeled or mangled, must be given lip service by even the most repressive regimes, some Americans balk at invoking them at all. Just when there is but one superpower left, some question America's need to stay engaged.

How ironic, just when totalitarian states have imploded and democracy holds sway among more peoples than ever before, Americans are losing faith in the wisdom of promoting freedom and human rights abroad.

> ***"To the masses denied dignity by their rulers, America is not just another country with material goods that they covet. It is the embodiment of intangibles—liberty, conscience, hope."***

Some wonder if certain peoples will always be incapable or averse to ruling themselves. They fail to acknowledge that no man or woman has ever aspired to be a pawn. On the contrary, regardless of culture and history, everyone years to be the master of his or her own fate.

Some consider it culturally chauvinistic to project our own values elsewhere. They fail to understand that freedom is not a matter of

"Westernization," it is the core of modernization. They also fail to recognize that human rights are not made in America, that they are universal, that every nation belonging to the United Nations has pledged to honor them, that international organizations from the CSCE to the OAS invoke them in their work.

Some fret that promoting democracy and human rights is a luxury we can ill afford. They fail to understand that this pursuit not only serves our values but interests. Spreading democracy not only warms American hearts but cools foreign threats. What hundreds of billions worth of arms failed to do, rallies of converts did. Gone, the Berlin Wall, gone, the Warsaw Pact. Democracies do not war against one another, democracies make better partners. Democracies do not ignore the environment, shelter terrorists, or spawn refugees. Democracies honor human rights.

Now, for the third time in this century, destiny calls. America must step forth. We must earn the right to enjoy our myriad blessings. I speak about only two. First, the vitality of Americans. Where does it come from? From everywhere. Apologies to Michael Jackson; We are the world. Second, the stature of America. Believe me, despite all the venom the most arrogant dictators may spew they care profoundly where Uncle Sam points a finger, shakes hands, or pats them on the back. They hate losing face, but they crave respectability.

Thus, vitality and stature endow America with extraordinary gifts for making a difference in the world. Like liberty, conscience, hope, they are intangibles. To be true to our legacy, to enrich our future, America must invest in freedom.

Bette Bao Lord

SOURCES

Books

Fox, Mary Virginia, *Bette Bao Lord: Novelist and Chinese Voice for Change*, Children's Press, 1993.

The Future of U.S. Foreign Policy (Part II): Functional Issues—Hearings Before the Committee on Foreign Affairs, House of Representatives, 103rd Congress, 1st Session, U.S. Government Printing Office, 1993, pp. 260-261, 312-319.

Lord, Bette Bao, *Legacies: A Chinese Mosaic*, Knopf, 1990.

Newsmakers: 1994 Cumulation, Gale Research, Detroit, 1995.

Zia, Helen, and Susan Gall, eds., *Notable Asian Americans*, Gale Research, Detroit, 1995.

Periodicals

Chicago Tribune, June 3, 1990.

Newsweek, "These People Have No Fear," May 29, 1989, p. 29; "'Warn Americans Not to Be Fooled,'" June 12, 1989, p. 28; "Walking in Lucky Shoes," July 6, 1992, p. 10.

New York Times, February 5, 1993.

Malcolm X

1925–1965

African American religious leader

From a life marked by endless turmoil, brutal violence, and ever-shifting identities emerged one of the most charismatic and controversial figures of the twentieth century—Malcolm X. As a youth, he embarked down a path of crime that eventually landed him in prison, where he converted to Elijah Muhammad's Black Muslim faith. Within just a few short years of his release, he had become Muhammad's closest disciple and a nationally recognized spokesman for the Nation of Islam. But his reign was brief; in 1965, assassins linked to the Muslim organization gunned him down as he spoke to a gathering of followers in Harlem. Yet Malcolm X endures today as a powerful symbol of black pride, and his words continue to inspire a new generation.

Malcolm X's first identity was as Malcolm Little, one of eight children of Louise Norton Little and Earl Little, a Baptist minister and fervent supporter of black nationalist leader Marcus Garvey. Earl Little's beliefs made him the target of various white vigilante groups, who forced the family to leave Omaha, Nebraska, where Malcolm was born, and flee to Milwaukee, Wisconsin, and eventually to Lansing, Michigan. There the Littles encountered even more harassment; in 1929, their house was burned to the ground by a white terrorist group, and in 1931, Earl Little himself was found dead on some streetcar tracks. The police called it an accident, but the family was convinced it was murder.

By the late 1930s, the Littles had fallen victim to the years of upheaval and tragedy. Louise Little was committed to a mental hospital, and her children were parceled out to foster homes and state institutions. Young Malcolm, who was an excellent student and class leader despite his tumultuous home life, dreamed one day of becoming a lawyer. But after a teacher pointed out to him that as a black he should aim for a profession more in keeping with his place in society—such as being a carpenter—he lost interest in school and soon dropped out. Malcolm then headed to Boston and worked at a series of menial jobs and committed a few petty crimes. From there he moved to Harlem, where as a streetwise hustler nicknamed "Detroit Red" he became involved in gambling, selling drugs, and prostitution. Malcolm then returned to Boston and headed a burglary ring, an activity that landed him in prison in 1946.

While in prison, the inmate known as "Satan" to his fellow convicts because he was so consumed by anger and hate took steps to turn his life around through a process of self-education. He also embraced the Muslim faith, and by the time he was paroled in 1952, he was determined to seek out Elijah Muhammad to express in person his gratitude and devotion. (By this time, he had also dropped the "slave name" Little, taking on the surname "X" as a symbol of the unknown African name of his ancestors.) Upon meeting the earnest and intelligent young man, Muhammad was so impressed he quickly accepted him into the Nation of Islam and made him a minister.

Throughout the rest of the 1950s and into the early 1960s, Malcolm X served at mosques in Detroit, Philadelphia, and Harlem and frequently traveled throughout the country helping to establish new congregations. His forceful personality and riveting oratory were responsible for transforming the Muslims from a relatively insignificant religious sect into a nationwide force (mostly urban in nature) of perhaps ten thousand official members and countless more sympathizers. He was by far the movement's most visible and effective spokesman and was a popular guest on college campuses, at meetings of various associations, and on radio and television programs. But Malcolm's fiery rhetoric, which condemned integration (and, by extension, the mainstream civil rights movement) and urged blacks to take up arms in self-defense against hostile whites, inspired hate and fear among most whites and many blacks. To them, his words seemed likely to provoke a violent race war. This perception was reinforced by the media, which again and again depicted Malcolm as a dangerous outlaw and rabble-rouser.

Typical of one of his early speeches—before he had attracted widespread national attention—is the following address, delivered in 1960 at a Muslim rally in Harlem. It was originally published in the September 1960, issue of Muhammad Speaks *and later reprinted in* Black Nationalism in America *(Bobbs-Merrill, 1970). In keeping with the doctrines of his spiritual guide, Elijah Muhammad, Malcolm the minister denounced the white race as "devils" and predicted the imminent end of the white world. He also condemned integration, interracial marriage, and mainstream political and social movements and extolled black nationalism (including a demand for land), black self-discipline and self-determination, and black unity.*

AS-SALAAM-ALAIKUM, Beloved Brothers and Sisters

WELCOME TO OUR HARLEM FREEDOM RALLY

When we say "our" we do not mean Muslim nor Christian, Catholic nor Protestant, Baptist nor Methodist, Democrat nor Republican, Mason nor Elk. By "our" Harlem Freedom, we mean the Black people of Harlem, the Black people of America, and the Black people all over this earth.

The largest concentration of Black people on earth is right here in Harlem, so we are gathered here today in Harlem Square to a Freedom Rally, of Black people, by Black people, and for the benefit of Black people.

We are not here at this Rally because we have already gained freedom. No!!! We are gathered here rallying for the freedom which we have long been promised, but have as yet not received. This Rally is for that perfect freedom which up until now this government has not granted us. There would be no need to protest to the government if we were already free.

Freedom is essential to life itself. Freedom is essential to the development of the human being. If we don't have freedom we can never expect justice and equality. Only after we have freedom do justice and equality become a reality.

Malcolm X

Today we are gathered at this Rally to hear from our leaders who have been acting as our spokesmen, and representing us to the white man downtown. We want to know how our leaders really think, how they talk, how they feel . . . and most important of all, we want them to know how we feel.

Many of these leaders have suddenly become "experts on Harlem" and as such are often regarded by the white man as the "voice of Harlem." If this must be the case, then we want the voice of these leaders to ring sometimes in Harlem too.

Leaders have differences, and these differences offtimes cause serious division among the masses. But the HOUR is too short today for Black people to afford the luxury of "differences."

Again I repeat, we are not gathered here today because we are Muslims or Christians, Protestants or Catholics, Baptists or Methodists, Democrats or Republicans, Masons or Elks . . . but, because as a collective mass of Black people we have been colonized, enslaved, lynched, exploited, deceived, abused, etc.

As a collective mass of Black people we have been deprived, not only of civil rights, but even our human rights, the right to human dignity . . . the right to be a human being!

This Freedom Rally is to be a united effort by all our leaders. We have set aside all petty differences, and in the Spirit of Bandung we have come together on this same platform, wherein each one can voice his personal feelings and his personal solution to this grave crisis we face.

The Western World today faces a great catastrophe. It stands on the brink of disaster. Mr. Muhammad says the only way our people can avoid the fiery destruction that God Himself will soon unleash upon this wicked world, is for our people to come together among themselves in unity and practice true brotherhood. Mr. Muhammad says God is with us to unite our people into one brotherhood, and to aid those that are oppressed, and to uplift those who are downtrodden.

The Western World, filled with evil and wickedness, is groping and stumbling blindly through spiritual darkness toward its inevitable doom. Mr. Muhammad says we must qualify ourselves so that God's Spiritual Light will guide us past the pitfalls of destruction.

The Western World is filled with drunkedness, dope addiction, lying, stealing, gambling, adultery, fornication, prostitution and hosts of other evils. These evils must be removed if the world is to have peace. These evils are the primary cause of troubles all over the earth. These evils promote greed and lust, increase wickedness and unrest, and destroy all hopes for peace.

You want peace. I want peace. Everyone craves for a world of peace. Mr. Muhammad says anyone who will submit to the God of Peace will have peace. Even the white man himself can prolong his time today if he will submit to the God of Peace, and give Freedom, Justice and Equality to the "people of God" . . . the so-called Negroes here in America.

The city of Nineveh in the Bible to whom Jonah was sent to warn is a good prophetic example of today. They were actually spared because they repented when the warning came to them from God. God will spare our slavemaster today too if he will repent.

The whole Dark World wants peace. When I was in Africa last year I was deeply impressed by the desire of our African Brothers for peace, but even they agree that there can be no peace without freedom from colonialism, foreign domination, oppression and exploitation.

The God of Peace and Righteousness is about to set up His Kingdom of Peace and Righteousness here on this earth. Knowing that God is about to establish His Righteous Government, Mr. Muhammad is trying to clean up our morals and qualify us to enter into this new Righteous Nation of God.

The American so-called Negroes must recognize each other as Brothers and Sisters . . . stop carrying guns and knives to harm each other, stop drinking whiskey, taking dope, reefers, and even cigarettes. No more gambling! Save your money. Stop fornication, adultery and prostitution. Elevate the Black woman; respect her and protect her. Let us rid ourselves of immoral habits and God will be with us to protect and guide us.

Then, we must form a platform that will be good for all of our own people, as well as for others. As Black people we must unite. We must recognize and give intelligent active support to our political leaders who fight for us unselfishly, sincerely, and fearlessly.

But, to prove their sincerity and their right for the support of the Black Masses, these leaders must first display fearlessness, intelligence, and unity among themselves. They must stop their public bickering with each other. They must stop attacking each other in front of the white man, and for the benefit of the white man.

If the Black leaders must have differences of opinion, learn to go into the closet with each other, but when you come from behind closed doors, show a united front in the face of the one who is a common enemy to all of us.

> ***"They call us racial extremists. . . . [But] if it were not for the extremists, the white man would ignore the moderates."***

Mr. Muhammad has invited all of the leaders here today for that purpose. He wants our people united, but unity will never exist among the Black masses as long as our leaders are not united.

We want to get behind leaders who will fight for us . . . leaders who are not afraid to demand freedom, justice, and equality. We do not want leaders who are handpicked for us by the white man. We don't want any more Uncle Toms. We don't want any more leaders who are puppets or parrots for the white man.

We want brave leaders as our spokesmen, who are not afraid to state our case, who can intelligently demand what we need, what we want, and what is rightfully ours. We don't want leaders who are beggars, who feel they must compromise with the enemy. And we don't want leaders who are selfish or greedy . . . who will sell us out for a few pieces of silver.

A big election is coming up this year. What kind of leaders do we want in office? Which ones will the Black masses get behind? Mr. Muhammad has thousands of followers, and millions of sympathizers. He will place his weight behind any fearless Black leaders who will stand up and help the so-called American Negroes get complete and immediate freedom.

If these Black leaders are afraid that to be identified with us they will irk the white man, or lose the white man's favor or his support, then they can no longer expect the support of the Black masses.

They call us racial extremists. They call Jomo Kenyatta also a racial extremist and Tom Mboya a moderate. It is only the white man's fear of men like Kenyatta that make him listen to men like Mboya. If it were not for the extremists, the white man would ignore the moderates. To be called a "moderate" in this awakening Dark World today, that is crying for freedom, is to receive the "kiss of death" as spokesman or leader of the masses . . . for the masses are ready to burst the shackles of slavery whether the "moderates" will stand up or not.

We have many Black leaders who are unafraid, especially when they know the Black masses stand behind them. Many of them are qualified to represent us not only in this United States government, but could also represent us in this government if we are given one hundred percent citizenship and the opportunity for FIRST CLASS participation . . . or else we can get behind these same leaders in setting up an independent government of our own.

We, the Black masses, don't want these leaders who seek our support coming to us representing a certain political party. They must come to us today as Black Leaders representing the welfare of Black people.

We won't follow any leader today who comes on the basis of political party. Both parties (Democrat and Republican) are controlled by the same people who have abused our rights, and who have deceived us with false promises every time an election rolls around.

Mr. Muhammad grieves over the disunity that exists even among the intellectual and professional so-called Negroes. It is these "educated" so-called Negroes who should be leading us out of this maze of misery and want. They possess the academic knowhow, great amounts of technical skills . . . but they can't use it for the benefit of their own kind simply because they themselves are also disunited. If these intellectuals and professional so-called Negroes would unite, not only Harlem would benefit, but it will benefit our people all over the world.

Mr. Muhammad says disunity is our number one stumbling block, and this disunity exists only because we lack knowledge of SELF (our own kind). So-called Negro "intellectuals" seem to think integration is the answer. But, is it? "Integrate" means to become as one unit. How can these "intellectuals" expect the white man to accept us into his social unit, political unit, or economic unit when we are not yet in unity (as a unit) among our own kind?

We, the Muslims, are for "Brotherhood," but not for integration! What is the difference? Brotherhood is based on love, which automatically produces voluntary acts of "sincere benevolence." But integration produces hypocrisy. It forces the white man to pose as a "liberal," to be pretensive and false. Thus, "benevolent" acts which are "forced by integration laws" are producing white hypocrites, and reducing chances of creating a "mutual-working-agreement" between the two races.

Your thirst for integration makes the white man think you want only to marry his daughter. We (Muslims) who follow Mr. Muhammad don't think God ever intended for Black men to marry white women. Mr. Muhammad and his followers are violently opposed to intermarriage.

This is conveniently and purposely misinterpreted by our enemies to mean that we are anti-white, anti-Christian, and anti-American (simply because we refuse to chase after the white man's women!). Let the white man keep his women, and let us keep ours.

Some Negroes who love race-mixing, and want white women, are angry at Mr. Muhammad because he teaches against race-mixing . . . so they slip around and make the white man think we are anti-white. (I'm surprised that the white man is dumb enough to believe these Uncle Toms, who stoop so low, like JUDAS, to be stool pigeons against their own kind.)

We have oceans of Dark People on this earth: in Africa, Asia, and even here in America. Our women are the most beautiful, like a bouquet of flowers. Why should we chase white women?

In this "changing" world today, what would we do married to a white woman? Her people don't want you in their neighborhood around them, and our fast awakening people don't want you to bring her back into our neighborhood any more to live around us. Thus, you both become a "misfit" . . . unwelcomed and unwanted in either society . . . where can you go?

Because we Muslims look at this as it is and face reality does not mean we are anti-white. We don't want his white mother, his white sister, nor his white daughter. We want only an equal chance on this earth, but to have an equal chance we must have the same thing the white man himself needed before he could get this nation started . . . WE MUST HAVE SOME LAND OF OUR OWN!

Why do we want some land of our own? Because land is essential to freedom. How else can twenty million Black people who now constitute a nation in our own right, a NATION WITHIN A NATION, expect to survive forever in a land where we are the last ones hired and the first ones fired . . . simply because we have no land of our own?

For over four hundred years we have been very faithful to our American slave masters. Now God is warning them through Mr. Muhammad that they should be nice enough to give us some land so we can separate ourselves from them and get started for ourselves.

This is no more than what the white man should do. It is in complete accord with the Christian religion. Their bible says that when a slave is set free, his slave master should give him something to help him get started on his own . . . never send him away empty-handed.

If the Hebrews in the bible numbered only six hundred thousand in the land of their bondage, and God was concerned with giving them freedom in a land of their own, a land "flowing with milk and honey," . . . then what about twenty million so-called Negroes here in America, who have the "freedom" only to look for a job?

Can you not see that our former "leaders" have been fighting for the wrong thing . . . the wrong kind of freedom? Mr. Muhammad says we must have some land where we can work hard for ourselves, make ourselves equal, and live in dignity. Then and only then we won't have to beg the white man for the crumbs that fall occasionally from his table. No one respects or appreciates a beggar.

Since we say Lincoln freed us, let us avail ourselves of that freedom by uniting together and doing something for our own kind. But, we must have some of this earth. We have been in America over four hundred years. We have been so-called "free" a hundred years, and yet he still calls us "the white man's burden."

We Muslims don't want to be a burden on America any longer. God has given Mr. Muhammad a Divine Message, Program, and Solution. WE MUST HAVE SOME LAND! The white man should be glad to give his loyal "slaves" some land so we can get out of his way and go for ourselves.

We will then set up our own farms, factories, business, and schools . . . and show him how much we appreciate the education he has given us, by using it to become self-sustaining . . . economically and otherwise.

We want some land where we can create unity, harmony and brotherhood . . . and live together in peace. Since America now sees that this false show of integration and intermarriage will not work, she should make immediate steps to set aside a few of these states for us, and put us there to ourselves.

If America will repent and do this, God will overlook some of her wicked deeds (as in the days of Nineveh) . . . but if America refuses to give Mr. Muhammad what God instructed him to ask for, . . . then, like the biblical houses of Egypt and Babylon (slave empires of the Bible), God will erase the American government and the entire race that it favors and represents, from this planet . . . and God will then give the whole earth back to the Original Owners, The Black Man!

As Malcolm X's audience broadened and he began to attract national attention, his rhetoric also changed. He spent less time paraphrasing Elijah Muhammad and explaining Muslim theology, choosing instead to devote more time to the secular concerns that were of greater interest to him personally—racism, politics, economics, justice, human rights. His tone became angrier and more militant, his wit more acidic. By 1963, Malcolm's persuasive powers were approaching their peak. Speaking in Detroit on November 10 of that year, he delivered a "message to the grass roots" at a special leadership conference attended by an almost all-black, predominantly non-Muslim audience that interrupted his talk numerous times with enthusiastic applause and laughter. What follows is about half of the speech he gave that evening; it is reprinted from Malcolm X Speaks: Selected Speeches and Statements *(Pathfinder Press, 1965).*

We want to have just an off-the-cuff chat between you and me, us. We want to talk right down to earth in a language that everybody here can easily understand. We all agree tonight, all of the speakers have agreed, that America has a very serious problem. Not only does America have a very serious problem, but our people have a very serious problem. America's problem is us. We're her problem. The only reason she has a problem is she doesn't want us here. And every time you look at yourself, be you black, brown, red or yellow, a so-called Negro, you represent a person who poses such a serious problem for America because you're not wanted. Once you face this as a fact, then you can start plotting a course that will make you appear intelligent, instead of unintelligent.

What you and I need to do is learn to forget our differences. When we come together, we don't come together as Baptists or Methodists. You don't catch hell because you're a Baptist, and you don't catch hell because you're a Methodist. You don't catch hell because you're a Methodist or Baptist, you don't catch hell because you're a Democrat or a Republican, you don't catch hell because you're a Mason or an Elk, and you sure don't catch hell because you're an American; because if you were an American, you wouldn't catch hell. You catch hell because you're a black man. You catch hell, all of us catch hell, for the same reason.

So we're all black people, so-called Negroes, second-class citizens, ex-slaves. You're nothing but an ex-slave. You don't like to be told that. But what else are you? You are ex-slaves. You didn't come here on the *Mayflower*. You came here on a slave ship. In chains, like a horse, or a cow, or a chicken. And you were brought here by the people who came here on the *Mayflower*, you were brought here by the so-called Pilgrims, or Founding Fathers. They were the ones who brought you here.

We have a common enemy. We have this in common: We have a common oppressor, a common exploiter, and a common discriminator. But once we all realize that we have a common enemy, then we unite—on the basis of what we have in common. And what we have foremost in common is that enemy—the white man. He's an enemy to all of us. I know some of you all think that some of them aren't enemies. Time will tell.

In Bandung back in, I think, 1954, was the first unity meeting in centuries of black people. And once you study what happened at the Bandung conference, and the results of the Bandung conference, it actually serves as a model for the same procedure you and I can use to get our problems solved. At Bandung all the nations came together, the dark nations from Africa and Asia. Some of them were Buddhists, some of them were Muslims, some of them were Christians, some were Confucianists, some were atheists. Despite their religious differences, they came together. Some were communists, some were socialists, some were capitalists—despite their economic and political differences, they came together. All of them were black, brown, red or yellow.

The number-one thing that was not allowed to attend the Bandung conference was the white man. He couldn't come. Once they excluded the white man, they found that they could get together. Once they kept him out, everybody else fell right in and fell in line. This is the thing that you and I have to understand. And these people who came together didn't have nuclear weapons, they didn't have jet planes, they didn't have all of the heavy armaments that the white man has. But they had unity.

They were able to submerge their little petty differences and agree on one thing: That there one African came from Kenya and was being colonized by the Englishman, and another African came from the Congo and was being colonized by the Belgian, and another African came from Guinea and was being colonized by the French, and another came from Angola and was being colonized by the Portuguese. When they came to the Bandung conference, they looked at the Portuguese, and at the Frenchman, and at the Englishman, and at the Dutchman, and learned or realized the one thing that all of them had in common—they were all from Europe, they were all Europeans, blond, blue-eyed and white skins. They began to recognize who their enemy was. The same man that was colonizing our people in Kenya was colonizing our people in the Congo. The same one in the Congo was colonizing our people in South Africa, and in Southern Rhodesia, and in Burma, and in India, and in Afghanistan, and in Pakistan. They realized all over the world where the dark man was being oppressed, he was being oppressed by the white man; where the dark man was being exploited, he was being exploited by the white man. So they got together on this basis—that they had a common enemy.

"What you and I need to do is learn to forget our differences. . . . And what we have foremost in common is [an] enemy—the white man."

And when you and I here in Detroit and in Michigan and in America who have been awakened today look around us, we too realize here in America we all have a common enemy, whether he's in Georgia or Michigan, whether he's in California or New York. He's the same man—blue eyes and blond hair and pale skin—the same man. So what we have to do is what they did. They agreed to stop quarreling among themselves. Any little spat that they had, they'd settle it among themselves, go into a huddle—don't let the enemy know that you've got a disagreement.

Instead of airing our differences in public, we have to realize we're all the same family. And when you have a family squabble, you don't get out on the sidewalk. If you do, everybody calls you uncouth, unrefined, uncivilized, savage. If you don't make it at home, you settle it at home; you get in the closet, argue it out behind closed doors, and then when you come out on the street, you pose a common front, a united front. And this is what we need to do in the community, and in the city, and in the state. We need to stop airing our differences in front of the white man, put the white man out of our meetings, and then sit down and talk shop with each other. That's what we've got to do.

I would like to make a few comments concerning the difference between the black revolution and the Negro revolution. Are they both the same? And if they're not, what is the difference? What is the difference between a black revolution and a Negro revolution? First, what is a revolution? Sometimes I'm inclined to believe that many of our people are using this word "revolution" loosely, without taking careful consideration of what this word actually means, and what its historic characteristics are. When you study the historic nature of revolutions, the motive of a revolution, the objective of a revolution, the result of a revolution, and the methods used in a revolution, you may change words. You may devise another program, you may change your goal and you may change your mind.

Look at the American Revolution in 1776. That revolution was for what? For land. Why did they want land? Independence. How was it carried out? Bloodshed. Number one, it was based on land, the basis of independence. And the only way they could get it was bloodshed. The French Revolution—what was it based on? The landless against the landlord. What was it for? Land. How did they get it? Bloodshed. Was no love lost, was no compromise, was no negotiation. I'm telling you—you don't know what a revolution is. Because when you find out what it is, you'll get back in the alley, you'll get out of the way.

The Russian Revolution—what was it based on? Land; the landless against the landlord. How did they bring it about? Bloodshed. You haven't got a revolution that doesn't involve bloodshed. And you're afraid to bleed. I said, you're afraid to bleed.

As long as the white man sent you to Korea, you bled. He sent you to Germany, you bled. He sent you to the South Pacific to fight the Japanese, you bled. You bleed for white people, but when it comes to seeing your own churches being bombed and little black girls murdered, you haven't got any blood. You bleed when the white man says bleed; you bite when the white man says bite; and you bark when the white man says bark. I hate to say this about us, but it's true. How are you going to be nonviolent in Mississippi, as violent as you were in Korea? How can you justify being nonviolent in Mississippi and Alabama, when your churches are being bombed, and your little girls are being murdered, and at the same time you are going to get violent with Hitler, and Tojo, and somebody else you don't even know?

If violence is wrong in America, violence is wrong abroad. If it is wrong to be violent defending black women and black children and black babies and black men, then it is wrong for America to draft us and make us violent abroad in defense of her. And if it is right for America to draft us, and teach us how to be violent in defense of her, then it is right for you and me to do whatever is necessary to defend our own people right here in this country.

The Chinese Revolution—they wanted land. They threw the British out, along with the Uncle Tom Chinese. Yes, they did. They set a good example. When I was in prison, I read an article—don't be shocked when I say that I was in prison. You're still in prison. That's what America means: prison. When I was in prison, I read an article in *Life* magazine showing a little Chinese girl, nine years old; her father was on his hands and knees and she was pulling the trigger because he was an Uncle Tom Chinaman. When they had the revolution over there, they took a whole generation of Uncle Toms and just wiped them out. And within ten years that little girl became a full-grown woman. No more Toms in China. And today it's one of the toughest, roughest, most feared countries on this earth—by the white man. Because there are no Uncle Toms over there.

Of all our studies, history is best qualified to reward our research. And when you see that you've got problems, all you have to do is examine the historic method used all over the world by others who have problems similar to yours. Once you see how they got theirs straight, then you know how you can get yours straight. There's been a revolution, a black revolution, going on in Africa. In Kenya, the Mau Mau were revolutionary; they were the ones who brought the word "Uhuru" to the fore. The Mau Mau, they were revolutionary, they believed in scorched earth, they knocked everything aside that got in their way, and their revolution also was based on land, a desire for land. In Algeria, the northern part of Africa, a revolution took place. The Algerians were revolutionists, they wanted land. France offered to let them be integrated into France. They told France, to hell with France, they wanted some land, not some France. And they engaged in a bloody battle.

So I cite these various revolutions, brothers and sisters, to show you that you don't have a peaceful revolution. You don't have a turn-the-other-cheek revolution. There's no such thing as a nonviolent revolution. The only kind of revolution that is nonviolent is the Negro revolution. The only revolution in which the goal is loving your enemy is the Negro revolution. It's the only revolution in which the goal is a desegregated lunch counter, a desegregated theater, a desegregated park, and a desegregated public toilet; you can sit down next to white folks—on the toilet. That's no revolution. Revolution is based on land. Land is the basis of all independence. Land is the basis of freedom, justice, and equality.

The white man knows what a revolution is. He knows that the black revolution is worldwide in scope and in nature. The black revolution is sweeping Asia, is sweeping Africa, is rearing its head in Latin America. The Cuban Revolution—that's a revolution. They overturned the system. Revolution is in Asia, revolution is in Africa, and the white man is screaming because he sees revolution in Latin America. How do you think he'll react to you when you learn what a real revolution is? You don't know what a revolution is. If you did, you wouldn't use that word.

Revolution is bloody, revolution is hostile, revolution knows no compromise, revolution overturns and destroys everything that gets in its way. And you, sitting around here like a knot on the wall, saying, "I'm going to love these folks no matter how much they hate me." No, you need a revolution. Whoever heard of a revolution where they lock arms, as Reverend Cleage was pointing out beautifully, singing "We Shall Overcome"? You don't do that in a revolution. You don't do any singing, you're too busy swinging. It's based on land. A revolutionary wants land so he can set up his own nation, an independent nation. These Negroes aren't asking for any nation—they're trying to crawl back on the plantation.

When you want a nation, that's called nationalism. When the white man became involved in a revolution in this country against England, what was it for? He wanted this land so he could set up another white nation. That's white nationalism. The American Revolution was white nationalism. The French Revolution was white nationalism. The Russian Revolution too—yes, it was—white nationalism. You don't think so? Why do you think Khrushchev and Mao can't get their heads together? White nationalism. All the revolutions that are going on in Asia and Africa today are based on what?—black nationalism. A revolutionary is a black nationalist. He wants a nation. I was reading some beautiful words by Reverend Cleage, pointing out why he couldn't get together with someone else in the city because all of them were afraid of being identified with black nationalism. If you're afraid of black nationalism, you're afraid of revolution. And if you love revolution, you love black nationalism.

To understand this, you have to go back to what the young brother here referred to as the house Negro and the field Negro back during slavery. There were two kinds of slaves, the house Negro and the field Negro. The house Negroes—they lived in the house with master, they dressed pretty good, they ate good because they ate his food—what he left. They lived in the attic or the basement, but still they lived near the master; and they loved the master more than the master loved himself. They would give their life to save the master's house—quicker than the master would. If the master said, "We got a good house here," the house Negro would say, "Yeah, we got a good house here." Whenever the master said "we," he said "we." That's how you can tell a house Negro.

"Whoever heard of a revolution where they lock arms . . . singing 'We Shall Overcome'? You don't do that in a revolution. You don't do any singing, you're too busy swinging."

If the master's house caught on fire, the house Negro would fight harder to put the blaze out than the master would. If the master got sick, the house Negro would say, "What's the matter, boss, we sick?" We sick! He identified himself with his master, more than his master identified with himself. And if you came to the house Negro and said, "Let's run away, let's escape, let's separate," the house Negro would look at you and say, "Man, you crazy. What you mean, separate? Where is there a better house than this? Where can I wear better clothes than this? Where can I eat better food than this?" That was that house Negro. In those days he was called a "house nigger." And that's what we call them today, because we've still got some house niggers running around here.

This modern house Negro loves his master. He wants to live near him. He'll pay three times as much as the house is worth just to live near his master, and then brag about "I'm the only Negro out here." "I'm the only one on my job." "I'm the only one in this school." You're nothing but a house Negro. And if someone comes to you right now and says, "Let's separate," you say the same thing that the house Negro said on the plantation. "What you mean, separate? From America, this good white man? Where you going to get a better job than you get here?" I mean, this is what you say. "I ain't left nothing in Africa," that's what you say. Why, you left your mind in Africa.

On that same plantation, there was the field Negro. The field Negroes—those were the masses. There were always more Negroes in the field than there were Negroes in the house. The Negro in the field caught hell. He ate leftovers. In the house they ate high up on the hog. The Negro in the field didn't get anything but what was left of the insides of the hog. They call it "chitt'lings" nowadays. In those days they called them what they were—guts. That's what you were—gut-eaters. And some of you are still gut-eaters.

The field Negro was beaten from morning to night; he lived in a shack, in a hut; he wore old, castoff clothes. He hated his master. I say he hated his master. He was intelligent. That house Negro loved his master, but that field Negro—remember, they were in the majority, and they hated the master. When the house caught on fire, he didn't try to put it out; that field Negro prayed for a wind, for a breeze. When the master got sick, the field Negro prayed that he'd die. If someone came to the field Negro and said, "Let's separate, let's run," he didn't say "Where we going?" He'd say, "Any place is better than here." You've got field Negroes in America today. I'm a field Negro. The masses are the field Negroes. When they see this man's house on fire, you don't hear the little Negroes talking about "our government is in trouble." They say, "The government is in trouble." Imagine a Negro: "Our government"! I even heard one say "our astronauts." They won't even let him near the plant—and "our astronauts"! "Our Navy"—that's a Negro that is out of his mind, a Negro that is out of his mind.

Just as the slavemaster of that day used Tom, the house Negro, to keep the field Negroes in check, the same old slavemaster today has Negroes who are nothing but modern Uncle Toms, twentieth-century Uncle Toms, to keep you and me in check, to keep us under control, keep us passive and peaceful and nonviolent. That's Tom making you nonviolent. It's like when you go to the dentist, and the man's going to take your tooth. You're going to fight him when he starts pulling. So he squirts some stuff in your jaw called novocaine, to make you think they're not doing anything to you. So you sit there and because you've got all of that novocaine in your jaw, you suffer—peacefully. Blood running all down your jaw, and you don't know what's happening. Because someone has taught you to suffer—peacefully.

The white man does the same thing to you in the street, when he wants to put knots on your head and take advantage of you and not have to be afraid of your fighting back. To keep you from fighting back, he gets these old religious Uncle Toms to teach you and me, just like novocaine, to suffer peacefully. Don't stop suffering—just suffer peacefully. As Reverend Cleage pointed out, they say you should let your blood flow in the streets. This is a shame. You know he's a Christian preacher. If it's a shame to him, you know what it is to me.

There is nothing in our book, the Koran, that teaches us to suffer peacefully. Our religion teaches us to be intelligent. Be peaceful, be courteous, obey the law, respect everyone; but if someone puts his hand on you, send him to the cemetery. That's a good religion. In fact, that's that old-time religion. That's the one that Ma and Pa used to talk about: an eye for an eye, and a tooth for a tooth, and a head for a head, and a life for a life. That's a good religion. And nobody resents that kind of religion being taught but a wolf, who intends to make you his meal.

This is the way it is with the white man in America. He's a wolf—and you're sheep. Any time a shepherd, a pastor, teaches you and me not to run from the white man and, at the same time, teaches us not to fight the white man, he's a traitor to you and me. Don't lay down a life all by itself. No, preserve your life, it's the best thing you've got. And if you've got to give it up, let it be even-steven.

The slavemaster took Tom and dressed him well, fed him well and even gave him a little education—a little education; gave him a long coat and a top hat and made all the other slaves look up to him. Then he used Tom to control them. The same strategy that was used in those days is used today, by the same white man. He takes a Negro, a so-called Negro, and makes him prominent, builds him up, publicizes him, makes him a celebrity. And then he becomes a spokesman for Negroes—and a Negro leader.

I would like to mention just one other thing quickly, and that is the method that the white man uses, how the white man uses the "big guns," or Negro leaders, against the Negro revolution. They are not a part of the Negro revolution. They are used against the Negro revolution.

When Martin Luther King failed to desegregate Albany, Georgia, the civil rights struggle in America reached its low point. King became bankrupt almost, as a leader. The Southern Christian Leadership Conference was in financial trouble; and it was in trouble, period, with the people when they failed to desegregate Albany, Georgia. Other Negro civil rights leaders of so-called national stature became fallen idols. As they became fallen idols, began to lose their prestige and influence, local Negro leaders began to stir up the masses. In Cambridge, Maryland, Gloria Richardson; in Danville, Virginia, and other parts of the country, local leaders began to stir up our people at the grass-roots level. This was never done by these Negroes of national stature. They control you, but they have never incited you or excited you. They control you, they contain you, they have kept you on the plantation.

As soon as King failed in Birmingham, Negroes took to the streets. King went out to California to a big rally and raised I don't know how many thousands of dollars. He came to Detroit and had a march and raised some more thousands of dollars. And recall, right after that Roy Wilkins attacked King. He accused King and CORE [Congress Of Racial Equality] of starting trouble everywhere and then making the NAACP [National Association for the Advancement of Colored People] get them out of jail and spend a lot of money; they accused King and CORE of raising all the money and not paying it back. This happened; I've got it in documented evidence in the newspaper. Roy started attacking King, and King started attacking Roy, and [James] Farmer started attacking both of them. And as these Negroes of national stature began to attack each other, they began to lose their control of the Negro masses.

The Negroes were out there in the streets. They were talking about how they were going to march on Washington. Right at that time Birmingham had exploded, and the Negroes in Birmingham—remember, they also exploded. They began to stab the crackers in the back and bust them up 'side their head—yes, they did. That's when Kennedy sent in the troops, down in Birmingham. After that, Kennedy got on the television and said "this is a moral issue." That's when he said he was going to put out a civil rights bill. And when he mentioned civil rights bill and the Southern crackers started talking about how they were going to boycott or filibuster it, then the Negroes started talking—about what? That they were going to march on Washington, march on the Senate, march on the White House, march on the Congress, and tie it up, bring it to a halt, not let the government proceed. They even said they were going out to the airport and lay down on the runway and not let any airplanes land. I'm telling you what they said. That was revolution. That was revolution. That was the black revolution.

It was the grass roots out there in the street. It scared the white man to death, scared the white power structure in Washington, D.C., to death; I was there. When they found out that this black steamroller was going to come down on the capital, they called in Wilkins, they called in Randolph, they called in these national Negro leaders that you respect and told them, "Call it off." Kennedy said, "Look, you all are letting this thing go too far." And Old Tom said, "Boss, I can't stop it, because I didn't start it." I'm telling you what they said. They said, "I'm not even in it, much less at the head of it." They said, "These Negroes are doing things on their own. They're running ahead of us." And that old shrewd fox, he said, "If you all aren't in it, I'll put you in it. I'll put you at the head of it. I'll endorse it. I'll welcome it. I'll help it. I'll join it."

A matter of hours went by. They had a meeting at the Carlyle Hotel in New York City. The Carlyle Hotel is owned by the Kennedy family; that's the hotel Kennedy spent the night at, two nights ago; it belongs to his family. A philanthropic society headed by a white man named Stephen Currier called all the top civil rights leaders together at the Carlyle Hotel. And he told them, "By you all fighting each other, you are destroying the civil rights movement. And since you're fighting over money from white liberals, let us set up what is known as the Council for United Civil Rights Leadership. Let's form this council, and all the civil rights organizations will belong to it, and we'll use it for fund-raising purposes." Let me show you how tricky the white man is. As soon as they got it formed, they elected Whitney Young as its chairman, and who do you think became the co-chairman? Stephen Currier, the white man, a millionaire. [Adam Clayton] Powell was talking about it down at Cobo Hall today. This is what he was talking about. Powell knows it happened. Randolph knows it happened. Wilkins knows it happened. King knows it happened. Every one of that Big Six—they know it happened.

Once they formed it, with the white man over it, he promised them and gave them $800,000 to split up among the Big Six; and told them that after the march was over they'd give them $700,000 more. A million and a half dollars—split up between leaders that you have been following, going to jail for, crying crocodile tears for. And they're nothing but Frank James and Jesse James and the what-do-you-call-'em brothers.

As soon as they got the setup organized, the white man made available to them top public-relations experts; opened the news media across the country at their disposal, which then began to project these Big Six as the leaders of the march. Originally they weren't even in the march. You were talking this march talk on Hastings Street, you were talking march talk on Lenox Avenue, and on Fillmore Street, and on Central Avenue, and 32nd Street and 63rd Street. That's where the march talk was being talked. But the white man put the Big Six at the head of it; made them the march. They became the march. They took it over. And the first move they made after they took it over, they invited Walter Reuther, a white man; they invited a priest, a rabbi, and an old white preacher, yes, an old white preacher. The same white element that put Kennedy into power—labor, the Catholics, the Jews, and liberal Protestants; the same clique that put Kennedy in power, joined the march on Washington.

It's just like when you've got some coffee that's too black, which means it's too strong. What do you do? You integrate it with cream, you make it weak. But if you pour too much cream in it, you won't even know you ever had coffee. It used to be hot, it becomes cool. It used to be strong, it becomes weak. It used to wake you up, now it puts you to sleep. This is what they did with the march on Washington. They joined it. They didn't integrate it, they infiltrated it. They joined it, became a part of it, took it over. And as they took it over, it lost its militancy. It ceased to be angry, it ceased to be hot, it ceased to be uncompromising. Why, it even ceased to be a march. It became a picnic, a circus. Nothing but a circus, with clowns and all. You had one right here in Detroit—I saw it on television—with clowns leading it, white clowns and black clowns. I know you don't like what I'm saying, but I'm going to tell you anyway. Because I can prove what I'm saying. If you think I'm telling you wrong, you bring me Martin Luther King and A. Philip Randolph and James Farmer and those other three, and see if they'll deny it over a microphone.

No, it was a sellout. It was a takeover. When James Baldwin came in from Paris, they wouldn't let him talk, because they couldn't make him go by the script. Burt Lancaster read the speech that Baldwin was supposed to make; they wouldn't let Baldwin get up there, because they know Baldwin is liable to say anything. They controlled it so tight, they told those Negroes what time to hit town, how to come, where to stop, what signs to carry, what song to sing, what speech they could make, and what speech they couldn't make; and then told them to get out of town by sundown. And every one of those Toms was out of town by sundown. Now I know you don't like my saying this. But I can back it up. It was a circus, a performance that beat anything Hollywood could ever do, the performance of the year. Reuther and those other three devils should get an Academy Award for the best actors because they acted like they really loved Negroes and fooled a whole lot of Negroes. And the six Negro leaders should get an award too, for the best supporting cast.

This "message to the grass roots" proved to be Malcolm's last major address as a member of the Nation of Islam; just a few weeks later, Elijah Muhammad silenced Malcolm after he publicly described the assassination of President John

F. Kennedy as an example of "chickens coming home to roost" in a society that tolerated white violence against blacks. But tensions between the two men had been building for months before this particular incident. Muhammad and other Muslim leaders had grown jealous of Malcolm's fame and suspicious of his growing desire to distance himself from certain cultish aspects of the movement. The standoff continued until March 12, 1964, when Malcolm announced his intention to quit the Nation of Islam and form a new group of his own, the Muslim Mosque, Inc. A short time later, he established the secular Organization of Afro-American Unity, which was open to all blacks, regardless of their religious beliefs.

That same spring, while in Cleveland, Ohio, on April 3, Malcolm X delivered what is perhaps his most famous speech, one he himself titled "The Ballot or the Bullet." It incorporated many of the themes he had been developing for some time, and with only slight variations, it soon became his standard speech. The following version is taken from Malcolm X Speaks: Selected Speeches and Statements *(Pathfinder Press, 1965).*

Mr. Moderator, Brother Lomax, brothers and sisters, friends and enemies: I just can't believe everyone in here is a friend and I don't want to leave anybody out. The question tonight, as I understand it, is "The Negro Revolt, and Where Do We Go From Here?" or "What Next?" In my little humble way of understanding it, it points toward either the ballot or the bullet.

Before we try and explain what is meant by the ballot or the bullet, I would like to clarify something concerning myself. I'm still a Muslim, my religion is still Islam. That's my personal belief. Just as Adam Clayton Powell is a Christian minister who heads the Abyssinian Baptist Church in New York, but at the same time takes part in the political struggles to try and bring about rights to the black people in this country; and Dr. Martin Luther King is a Christian minister down in Atlanta, Georgia, who heads another organization fighting for the civil rights of black people in this country; and Reverend Galamison, I guess you've heard of him, is another Christian minister in New York who has been deeply involved in the school boycotts to eliminate segregated education; well, I myself am a minister, not a Christian minister, but a Muslim minister; and I believe in action on all fronts by whatever means necessary.

Although I'm still a Muslim, I'm not here tonight to discuss my religion. I'm not here to try and change your religion. I'm not here to argue or discuss anything that we differ about, because it's time for us to submerge our differences and realize that it is best for us to first see that we have the same problem, a common problem—a problem that will make you catch hell whether you're a Baptist, or a Methodist, or a Muslim, or a nationalist. Whether you're educated or illiterate, whether you live on the boulevard or in the alley, you're going to catch hell just like I am. We're all in the same boat and we all are going to catch the same hell from the same man. He just happens to be a white man. All of us have suffered here, in this country, political oppression at the hands of the white man, economic exploitation at the hands of the white man, and social degradation at the hands of the white man.

Now in speaking like this, it doesn't mean that we're anti-white, but it does mean we're anti-exploitation, we're anti-degradation, we're anti-oppression. And if the white man doesn't want us to be anti-him, let him stop oppressing and exploiting and degrading us. Whether we are Christians or Muslims or nationalists or agnostics or atheists, we must first learn to forget our differences. If we have differences, let us differ in the closet; when we come out in front, let us not have anything to argue about until we get finished arguing with the man. If the late President Kennedy could get together with Khrushchev and exchange some wheat, we certainly have more in common with each other than Kennedy and Khrushchev had with each other.

If we don't do something real soon, I think you'll have to agree that we're going to be forced either to use the ballot or the bullet. It's one or the other in 1964. It isn't that time is running out—time has run out! 1964 threatens to be the most explosive year America has ever witnessed. The most explosive year. Why? It's also a political year. It's the year when all of the white politicians will be back in the so-called Negro community jiving you and me for some votes. The year when all of the white political crooks will be right back in your and my community with their false promises, building up our hopes for a letdown, with their trickery and their treachery, with their false promises which they don't intend to keep. As they nourish these dissatisfactions, it can only lead to one thing, an explosion; and now we have the type of black man on the scene in America today—I'm sorry, Brother Lomax—who just doesn't intend to turn the other cheek any longer.

Don't let anybody tell you anything about the odds are against you. If they draft you, they send you to Korea and make you face eight hundred million Chinese. If you can be brave over there, you can be brave right here. These odds aren't as great as those odds. And if you fight here, you will at least know what you're fighting for.

> ***"I'm speaking as a victim of this American system. And I see America through the eyes of the victim. I don't see any American dream; I see an American nightmare."***

I'm not a politician, not even a student of politics; in fact, I'm not a student of much of anything. I'm not a Democrat, I'm not a Republican, and I don't even consider myself an American. If you and I were Americans, there'd be no problem. Those Hunkies that just got off the boat, they're already Americans; Polacks are already Americans; the Italian refugees are already Americans. Everything that came out of Europe, every blue-eyed thing, is already an American. And as long as you and I have been over here, we aren't Americans yet.

Well, I am one who doesn't believe in deluding myself. I'm not going to sit at your table and watch you eat, with nothing on my plate, and call myself a diner. Sitting at the table doesn't make you a diner, unless you eat some of what's on that plate. Being here in America doesn't make you an American. Being born here in America doesn't make you an American. Why, if birth made you American, you wouldn't need any legislation, you wouldn't need any amendments to the Constitution, you wouldn't be faced with civil rights filibustering in Washington, D.C., right now. They don't have to pass civil rights legislation to make a Polack an American.

No, I'm not an American. I'm one of the twenty-two million black people who are the victims of Americanism. One of the twenty-two million black people who are the victims of democracy, nothing but disguised hypocrisy. So, I'm not standing here speaking to you as an American, or a patriot, or a flag-saluter, or a flag-waver—no, not I. I'm speaking as a victim of this American system. And I see America through the eyes of the victim. I don't see any American dream; I see an American nightmare.

These twenty-two million victims are waking up. Their eyes are coming open. They're beginning to see what they used to only look at. They're becoming politically mature. They are realizing that there are new political trends from coast to coast. As they see these new political trends, it's possible for them to see that every time there's an election the races are so close that they have to have a recount. They had to recount in Massachusetts to see who was going to be governor, it was so close. It was the same way in Rhode Island, in Minnesota, and in many other parts of the country. And the same with Kennedy and Nixon when they ran for president. It was so close they had to count all over again. Well, what does this mean? It means that when white people are evenly divided, and black people have a bloc of votes of their own, it is left up to them to determine who's going to sit in the White House and who's going to be in the dog house.

It was the black man's vote that put the present administration in Washington, D.C. Your vote, your dumb vote, your ignorant vote, your wasted vote put in an administration in Washington, D.C., that has seen fit to pass every kind of legislation imaginable, saving you until last, then filibustering on top of that. And your and my leaders have the audacity to run around clapping their hands and talk about how much progress we're making. And what a good president we have. If he wasn't good in Texas, he sure can't be good in Washington, D.C. Because Texas is a lynch state. It is in the same breath as Mississippi, no different; only they lynch you in Texas with a Texas accent and lynch you in Mississippi with a Mississippi accent. And these Negro leaders have the audacity to go and have some coffee in the White House with a Texan, a Southern cracker—that's all he is—and then come out and tell you and me that he's going to be better for us because, since he's from the South, he knows how to deal with the Southerners. What kind of logic is that? Let Eastland be president, he's from the South too. He should be better able to deal with them than Johnson.

In this present administration they have in the House of Representatives 257 Democrats to only 177 Republicans. They control two-thirds of the House vote. Why can't they pass something that will help you and me? In the Senate, there are 67 senators who are of the Democratic Party. Only 33 of them are Republicans. Why, the Democrats have got the government sewed up, and you're the one who sewed it up for them. And what have they given you for it? Four years in office, and just now getting around to some civil rights legislation. Just now, after everything else is gone, out of the way, they're going to sit down now and play with you all summer long—the same old giant con game that they call filibuster. All those are in cahoots together. Don't you ever think they're not in cahoots together, for the man that is heading the civil rights filibuster is a man from Georgia named Richard Russell. When Johnson became president, the first man he asked for when he got back to Washington, D.C., was "Dicky"—that's how tight they are. That's his boy, that's his pal, that's his buddy. But they're playing that old con game. One of them makes believe he's for you, and he's got it fixed where the other one is so tight against you, he never has to keep his promise.

So it's time in 1964 to wake up. And when you see them coming up with that kind of conspiracy, let them know your eyes are open. And let them know you got something else that's wide open too. It's got to be the ballot or the bullet. The ballot or the bullet. If you're afraid to use an expression like that, you should get on out of the country, you should get back in the cotton patch, you should get back in the alley. They get all the Negro vote, and after they get it, the Negro gets nothing in return. All they did when they got to Washington was give a few big Negroes big jobs. Those big Negroes didn't need big jobs, they already had jobs. That's camouflage, that's trickery, that's treachery, window-dressing. I'm not trying to knock out the Democrats for the Republicans, we'll get to them in a minute. But it is true—you put the Democrats first and the Democrats put you last.

Look at it the way it is. What alibis do they use, since they control Congress and the Senate? What alibi do they use when you and I ask, "Well, when are you going to keep your promise?" They blame the Dixiecrats. What is a Dixiecrat? A Democrat. A Dixiecrat is nothing but a Democrat in disguise. The titular head of the Democrats is also the head of the Dixiecrats, because the Dixiecrats are a part of the Democratic Party. The Democrats have never kicked the Dixiecrats out of the party. The Dixiecrats bolted themselves once, but the Democrats didn't put them out. Imagine, these lowdown Southern segregationists put the Northern Democrats down. But the Northern Democrats have never put the Dixiecrats down. No, look at that thing the way it is. They have got a con game going on, a political con game, and you and I are in the middle. It's time for you and me to wake up and start looking at it like it is, and trying to understand it like it is; and then we can deal with it like it is.

The Dixiecrats in Washington, D.C., control the key committees that run the government. The only reason the Dixiecrats control these committees is because they have seniority. The only reason they have seniority is because they come from states where Negroes can't vote. This is not even a government that's based on democracy. It is not a government that is made up of representatives of the people. Half of the people in the South can't even vote. Eastland is not even supposed to be in Washington. Half of the senators and congressmen who occupy these key positions in Washington, D.C., are there illegally, are there unconstitutionally.

I was in Washington, D. C., a week ago Thursday, when they were debating whether or not they should let the bill come onto the floor. And in the back of the room where the Senate meets, there's a huge map of the United States, and on that map it shows the location of Negroes throughout the country. And it shows that the Southern section of the country, the states that are most heavily concentrated with Negroes, are the ones that have senators and congressmen standing up filibustering and doing all other kinds of trickery to keep the Negro from being able to vote. This is pitiful. But it's not pitiful for us any longer; it's actually pitiful for the white man, because soon now, as the Negro awakens a little more and sees the vise that he's in, sees the bag that he's in, sees the real game that he's in, then the Negro's going to develop a new tactic.

These senators and congressmen actually violate the constitutional amendments that guarantee the people of that particular state or county the right to vote. And the Constitution itself has within it the machinery to expel any representative from a state where the voting rights of the people are violated. You don't even need new legislation. Any person in Congress right now, who is there from a state or a district where the voting rights of the people are violated, that particular person should be expelled from Congress. And when you expel him, you've removed one of the obstacles in the path of any real meaningful legislation in this country. In fact, when you expel them, you don't need new legislation, because they will be replaced by black representatives from counties and districts where the black man is in the majority, not in the minority.

If the black man in these Southern states had his full voting rights, the key Dixiecrats in Washington, D.C., which means the key Democrats in Washington, D.C., would lose their seats. The Democratic Party itself would lose its power. It would cease to be powerful as a party. When you see the amount of power that would be lost by the Democratic Party if it were to lose the Dixiecrat wing, or branch, or element, you can see where it's against the interests of the Democrats to give voting rights to Negroes in states where the Democrats have been in complete power and authority ever since the Civil War. You just can't belong to that party without analyzing it.

I say again, I'm not anti-Democrat, I'm not anti-Republican, I'm not anti-anything. I'm just questioning their sincerity, and some of the strategy that they've been using on our people by promising them promises that they don't intend to keep. When you keep the Democrats in power, you're keeping the Dixiecrats in power. I doubt that my good Brother Lomax will deny that. A vote for a Democrat is a vote for a Dixiecrat. That's why, in 1964, it's time now for you and me to become more politically mature and realize what the ballot is for; what we're supposed to get when we cast a ballot; and that if we don't cast a ballot, it's going to end up in a situation where we're going to have to cast a bullet. It's either a ballot or a bullet.

In the North, they do it a different way. They have a system that's known as gerrymandering, whatever that means. It means when Negroes become too heavily concentrated in a certain area, and begin to gain too much political power, the white man comes along and changes the district lines. You may say, "Why do you keep saying white man?" Because it's the white man who does it. I haven't ever seen any Negro changing any lines. They don't let him get near the line. It's the white man who does this. And usually, it's the white man who grins at you the most, and pats you on the back, and is supposed to be your friend. He may be friendly, but he's not your friend.

So, what I'm trying to impress upon you, in essence, is this: You and I in America are faced not with a segregationist conspiracy, we're faced with a government conspiracy. Everyone who's filibustering is a senator—that's the government. Everyone who's finagling in Washington, D.C., is a congressman—that's the government. You don't have anybody putting blocks in your path but people who are a part of the government. The same government that you go abroad to fight for and die for is the government that is in a conspiracy to deprive you of your voting rights, deprive you of your economic opportunities, deprive you of decent housing, deprive you of decent education. You don't need to go to the employer alone, it is the government itself, the government of America, that is responsible for the oppression and exploitation and degradation of black people in this country. And you should drop it in their lap. This government has failed the Negro. This so-called democracy has failed the Negro. And all these white liberals have definitely failed the Negro.

So, where do we go from here? First, we need some friends. We need some new allies. The entire civil rights struggle needs a new interpretation, a broader interpretation. We need to look at this civil rights thing from another angle—from the inside as well as from the outside. To those of us whose philosophy is black nationalism, the only way you can get involved in the civil rights struggle is give it a new interpretation. That old interpretation excluded us. It kept us out. So, we're giving a new interpretation to the civil rights struggle, an interpretation that will enable us to come into it, take part in it. And these handkerchief-heads who have been dillydallying and pussyfooting and compromising—we don't intend to let them pussyfoot and dillydally and compromise any longer.

How can you thank a man for giving you what's already yours? How then can you thank him for giving you only part of what's already yours? You haven't even made progress, if what's being given to you, you should have had already. That's not progress. And I love my Brother Lomax, the way he pointed out we're right back where we were in 1954. We're not even as far up as we were in 1954. We're behind where we were in 1954. There's more segregation now than there was in 1954. There's more racial animosity, more racial hatred, more racial violence today in 1964, than there was in 1954. Where is the progress?

And now you're facing a situation where the young Negro's coming up. They don't want to hear that "turn-the-other-cheek" stuff, no. In Jacksonville, those were teenagers, they were throwing Molotov cocktails. Negroes have never done that before. But it shows you there's a new deal coming in. There's new thinking coming in. There's new strategy coming in. It'll be Molotov cocktails this month, hand grenades next month, and something else next month. It'll be ballots, or it'll be bullets. It'll be liberty, or it will be death. The only difference about this kind of death—it'll be reciprocal. You know what is meant by "reciprocal"? That's one of Brother Lomax's words, I stole it from him. I don't usually deal with those big words because I don't usually deal with big people. I deal with small people. I find you can get a whole lot of small people and whip hell out of a whole lot of big people. They haven't got anything to lose, and they've got everything to gain. And they'll let you know in a minute: "It takes two to tango; when I go, you go."

The black nationalists, those whose philosophy is black nationalism, in bringing about this new interpretation of the entire meaning of civil rights, look upon it as meaning, as Brother Lomax has pointed out, equality of opportunity. Well, we're justified in seeking civil rights, if it means equality of opportunity, because all we're doing there is trying to collect for our investment. Our mothers and fathers invested sweat and blood. Three hundred and ten years we worked in this country without a dime in return—I mean without a dime in return. You let the white man walk around here talking about how rich this country is, but you never stop to think how it got rich so quick. It got rich because you made it rich.

You take the people who are in this audience right now. They're poor, we're all poor as individuals. Our weekly salary individually amounts to hardly anything. But if you take the salary of everyone in here collectively it'll fill up a whole lot of baskets. It's a lot of wealth. If you can collect the wages of just these people right here for a year, you'll be rich—richer than rich. When you look at it like that, think how rich Uncle Sam had to become, not with this handful, but millions of black people. Your and my mother and father, who didn't work an eight-hour shift, but worked from "can't see" in the morning until "can't see" at night, and worked for nothing, making the white man rich, making Uncle Sam rich.

This is our investment. This is our contribution—our blood. Not only did we give of our free labor, we gave of our blood. Every time he had a call to arms, we were the first ones in uniform. We died on every battlefield the white man had. We have made a greater sacrifice than anybody who's standing up in America today. We have made a greater contribution and have collected less. Civil rights, for those of us whose philosophy is black nationalism, means: "Give it to us now. Don't wait for next year. Give it to us yesterday, and that's not fast enough."

I might stop right here to point out one thing. Whenever you're going after something that belongs to you, anyone who's depriving you of the right to have it is a criminal. Understand that. Whenever you are going after something that is yours, you are within your legal rights to lay claim to it. And anyone who puts forth any effort to deprive you of that which is yours, is breaking the law, is a criminal. And this was pointed out by the Supreme Court decision. It outlawed segregation. Which means segregation is against the law. Which means a segregationist is breaking the law. A segregationist is a criminal. You can't label him as anything other than that. And when you demonstrate against segregation, the law is on your side. The Supreme Court is on your side.

Now, who is it that opposes you in carrying out the law? The police department itself. With police dogs and clubs. Whenever you demonstrate against segregation, whether it is segregated education, segregated housing, or anything else, the law is on your side, and anyone who stands in the way is not the law any longer. They are breaking the law, they are not representatives of the law. Any time you demonstrate against segregation and a man has the audacity to put a police dog on you, kill that dog, kill him, I'm telling you, kill that dog. I say it, if they put me in jail tomorrow, kill—that—dog. Then you'll put a stop to it. Now, if these white people in here don't want to see that kind of action, get down and tell the mayor to tell the police department to pull the dogs in. That's all you have to do. If you don't do it, someone else will.

If you don't take this kind of stand, your little children will grow up and look at you and think "shame." If you don't take an uncompromising stand—I don't mean go out and get violent; but at the same time you should never be nonviolent unless you run into some nonviolence. I'm nonviolent with those who are nonviolent with me. But when you drop that violence on me, then you've made me go insane, and I'm not responsible for what I do. And that's the way every Negro should get. Any time you know you're within the law, within your legal rights, within your moral rights, in accord with justice, then die for what you believe in. But don't die alone. Let your dying be reciprocal. This is what is meant by equality. What's good for the goose is good for the gander.

When we begin to get in this area, we need new friends, we need new allies. We need to expand the civil rights struggle to a higher level—to the level of human rights. Whenever you are in a civil rights struggle, whether you know it or not, you are confining yourself to the jurisdiction of Uncle Sam. No one from the outside world can speak out in your behalf as long as your struggle is a civil rights struggle. Civil rights comes within the domestic affairs of this country. All of our African brothers and our Asian brothers and our Latin American brothers cannot open their mouths and interfere in the domestic affairs of the United States. And as long as it's civil rights, this comes under the jurisdiction of Uncle Sam.

"When you drop that violence on me, then you've made me go insane, and I'm not responsible for what I do. And that's the way every Negro should get."

But the United Nations has what's known as the charter of human rights, it has a committee that deals in human rights. You may wonder why all of the atrocities that have been committed in Africa and in Hungary and in Asia and in Latin America are brought before the UN, and the Negro problem is never brought before the UN. This is part of the conspiracy. This old, tricky, blue-eyed liberal who is supposed to be your and my friend, supposed to be in our corner, supposed to be subsidizing our struggle, and supposed to be acting in the capacity of an adviser, never tells you anything about human rights. They keep you wrapped up in civil rights. And you spend so much time barking up the civil rights tree, you don't even know there's a human rights tree on the same floor.

When you expand the civil rights struggle to the level of human rights, you can then take the case of the black man in this country before the nations in the UN. You can take it before the General Assembly. You can take Uncle Sam before a world court. But the only level you can do it on is the level of human rights. Civil rights keeps you under his restrictions, under his jurisdiction. Civil rights keeps you in his pocket. Civil rights means you're asking Uncle Sam to treat you right. Human rights are something you were born with. Human rights are your God-given rights. Human rights are the rights that are recognized by all nations of this earth. And any time any one violates your human rights, you can take them to the world court. Uncle Sam's hands are dripping with blood, dripping with the blood of the black man in this country. He's the earth's number-one hypocrite. He has the audacity—yes, he has—imagine him posing as the leader of the free world. The free world!—and you over here singing "We Shall Overcome." Expand the civil rights struggle to the level of human rights, take it into the United Nations, where our African brothers can throw their weight on our side, where our Asian brothers can throw their weight on our side, where our Latin American brothers can throw their weight on our side, and where eight hundred million Chinamen are sitting there waiting to throw their weight on our side.

Let the world know how bloody his hands are. Let the world know the hypocrisy that's practiced over here. Let it be the ballot or the bullet. Let him know that it must be the ballot or the bullet.

When you take your case to Washington, D.C., you're taking it to the criminal who's responsible; it's like running from the wolf to the fox. They're all in cahoots together. They all work political chicanery and make you look like a chump before the eyes of the world. Here you are walking around in America, getting ready to be drafted and sent abroad, like a tin soldier, and when you get over there, people ask you what are you fighting for, and you have to stick your tongue in your cheek. No, take Uncle Sam to court, take him before the world.

By ballot I only mean freedom. Don't you know—I disagree with Lomax on this issue—that the ballot is more important than the dollar? Can I prove it? Yes. Look in the UN. There are poor nations in the UN; yet those poor nations can get together with their voting power and keep the rich nations from making a move. They have one nation—one vote, everyone has an equal vote. And when those brothers from Asia, and Africa and the darker parts of this earth get together, their voting power is sufficient to hold Sam in check. Or Russia in check. Or some other section of the earth in check. So, the ballot is most important.

Right now, in this country, if you and I, twenty-two million African Americans—that's what we are—Africans who are in America. You're nothing but Africans. Nothing but Africans. In fact, you'd get farther calling yourself African instead of Negro. Africans don't catch hell. You're the only one catching hell. They don't have to pass civil rights bills for Africans. An African can go anywhere he wants right now. All you've got to do is tie your head up. That's right, go anywhere you want. Just stop being a Negro. Change your name to Hoogagagooba. That'll show you how silly the white man is. You're dealing with a silly man. A friend of mine who's very dark put a turban on his head and went into a restaurant in Atlanta before they called themselves desegregated. He went into a white restaurant, he sat down, they served him, and he said, "What would happen if a Negro came in here?" And there he's sitting, black as night, but because he had his head wrapped up the waitress looked back at him and says, "Why, there wouldn't no nigger dare come in here."

So, you're dealing with a man whose bias and prejudice are making him lose his mind, his intelligence, every day. He's frightened. He looks around and sees what's taking place on this earth, and he sees that the pendulum of time is swinging in your direction. The dark people are waking up. They're losing their fear of the white man. No place where he's fighting right now is he winning. Everywhere he's fighting, he's fighting someone your and my complexion. And they're beating him. He can't win any more. He's won his last battle. He failed to win the Korean War. He couldn't win it. He had to sign a truce. That's a loss. Any time Uncle Sam, with all his machinery for warfare, is held to a draw by some rice-eaters, he's lost the battle. He had to sign a truce. America's not supposed to sign a truce. She's supposed to be bad. But she's not bad any more. She's bad as long as she can use her hydrogen bomb, but she can't use hers for fear Russia might use hers. Russia can't use hers, for fear that Sam might use his. So, both of them are weaponless. They can't use the weapon because each's weapon nullifies the other's. So the only place where action can take place is on the ground. And the white man can't win another war fighting on the ground. Those days are over. The black man knows it, the brown man knows it, the red man knows it, and the yellow man knows it. So they engage him in guerrilla warfare. That's not his style. You've got to have heart to be a guerrilla warrior, and he hasn't got any heart. I'm telling you now.

I just want to give you a little briefing on guerrilla warfare because, before you know it, before you know it—It takes heart to be a guerrilla warrior because you're on your own. In conventional warfare you have tanks and a whole lot of other people with you to back you up, planes over your head and all that kind of stuff. But a guerrilla is on his own. All you have is a rifle, some sneakers and a bowl of rice, and that's all you need—and a lot of heart. The Japanese on some of those islands in the Pacific, when the American soldiers landed, one Japanese sometimes could hold the whole army off. He'd just wait until the sun went down, and when the sun went down they were all equal. He would take his little blade and slip from bush to bush, and from American to American. The white soldiers couldn't cope with that. Whenever you see a white soldier that fought in the Pacific, he has the shakes, he has a nervous condition, because they scared him to death.

The same thing happened to the French up in French Indochina. People who just a few years previously were rice farmers got together and ran the heavily-mechanized French army out of Indochina. You don't need it—modern warfare today won't work. This is the day of the guerrilla. They did the same thing in Algeria. Algerians, who were nothing but Bedouins, took a rifle and sneaked off to the hills, and de Gaulle and all of his highfalutin' war machinery couldn't defeat those guerrillas. Nowhere on this earth does the white man win in a guerrilla warfare. It's not his speed. Just as guerrilla warfare is prevailing in Asia and in parts of Africa and in parts of Latin America, you've got to be mighty naive, or you've got to play the black man cheap, if you don't think some day he's going to wake up and find that it's got to be the ballot or the bullet.

I would like to say, in closing, a few things concerning the Muslim Mosque, Inc., which we established recently in New York City. It's true we're Muslims and our religion is Islam, but we don't mix our religion with our politics and our economics and our social and civil activities—not any more. We keep our religion in our mosque. After our religious services are over, then as Muslims we become involved in political action, economic action and social and civic action. We become involved with anybody, anywhere, any time and in any manner that's designed to eliminate the evils, the political, economic and social evils that are afflicting the people of our community.

The political philosophy of black nationalism means that the black man should control the politics and the politicians in his own community; no more. The black man in the black community has to be re-educated into the science of politics so he will know what politics is supposed to bring him in return. Don't be throwing out any ballots. A ballot is like a bullet. You don't throw your ballots until you see a target, and if that target is not within your reach, keep your ballot in your pocket. The political philosophy of black nationalism is being taught in the Christian church. It's being taught in the NAACP. It's being taught in CORE meetings. It's being taught in SNCC [Student Nonviolent Coordinating Committee] meetings. It's being taught in Muslim meetings. It's being taught where nothing but atheists and agnostics come together. It's being taught everywhere. Black people are fed up with the dillydallying, pussyfooting, compromising approach that we've been using toward getting our freedom. We want freedom now, but we're not going to get it saying "We Shall Overcome." We've got to fight until we overcome.

The economic philosophy of black nationalism is pure and simple. It only means that we should control the economy of our community. Why should white people be running all the stores in our community? Why should white people be running the banks of our community? Why should the economy of our community be in the hands of the white man? Why? If a black man can't move his store into a white community, you tell me why a white man should move his store into a black community. The philosophy of black nationalism involves a reeducation program in the black community in regards to economics. Our people have to be made to see that any time you take your dollar out of your community and spend it in a community where you don't live, the community where you live will get poorer and poorer, and the community where you spend your money will get richer and richer. Then you wonder why where you live is always a ghetto or a slum area. And where you and I are concerned, not only do we lose it when we spend it out of the community, but the white man has got all our stores in the community tied up; so that though we spend it in the community, at sundown the man who runs the store takes it over across town somewhere. He's got us in a vise.

So the economic philosophy of black nationalism means in every church, in every civic organization, in every fraternal order, it's time now for our people to become conscious of the importance of controlling the economy of our community. If we own the stores, if we operate the businesses, if we try and establish some industry in our own community, then we're developing to the position where we are creating employment for our own kind. Once you gain control of the economy of your own community, then you don't have to picket and boycott and beg some cracker downtown for a job in his business.

The social philosophy of black nationalism only means that we have to get together and remove the evils, the vices, alcoholism, drug addiction, and other evils that are destroying the moral fiber of our community. We ourselves have to lift the level of our community, the standard of our community to a higher level, make our own society beautiful so that we will be satisfied in our own social circles and won't be running around here trying to knock our way into a social circle where we're not wanted.

So I say, in spreading a gospel such as black nationalism, it is not designed to make the black man re-evaluate the white man—you know him already—but to make the black man reevaluate himself. Don't change the white man's mind—you can't change his mind, and that whole thing about appealing to the moral conscience of America—America's conscience is bankrupt. She lost all conscience a long time ago. Uncle Sam has no conscience. They don't know what morals are. They don't try and eliminate an evil because it's evil, or because it's illegal, or because it's immoral; they eliminate it only when it threatens their existence. So you're wasting your time appealing to the moral conscience of a bankrupt man like Uncle Sam. If he had a conscience, he'd straighten this thing out with no more pressure being put upon him. So it is not necessary to change the white man's mind. We have to change our own mind. You can't change his mind about us. We've got to change our own minds about each other. We have to see each other with new eyes. We have to see each other as brothers and sisters. We have to come together with warmth so we can develop unity and harmony that's necessary to get this problem solved ourselves. How can we do this? How can we avoid jealousy? How can we avoid the suspicion and the divisions that exist in the community? I'll tell you how.

I have watched how Billy Graham comes into a city, spreading what he calls the gospel of Christ, which is only white nationalism. That's what he is. Billy Graham is a white nationalist; I'm a black nationalist. But since it's the natural tendency for leaders to be jealous and look upon a powerful figure like Graham with suspicion and envy, how is it possible for him to come into a city and get all the cooperation of the church leaders? Don't think because they're church leaders that they don't have weaknesses that make them envious and jealous—no, everybody's got it. It's not an accident that when they want to choose a cardinal [as Pope] over there in Rome, they get in a closet so you can't hear them cussing and fighting and carrying on.

Billy Graham comes in preaching the gospel of Christ, he evangelizes the gospel, he stirs everybody up, but he never tries to start a church. If he came in trying to start a church, all the churches would be against him. So, he just comes in talking about Christ and tells everybody who gets Christ to go to any church where Christ is; and in this way the church cooperates with him. So we're going to take a page from his book.

Our gospel is black nationalism. We're not trying to threaten the existence of any organization, but we're spreading the gospel of black nationalism. Anywhere there's a church that is also preaching and practicing the gospel of black nationalism, join that church. If the NAACP is preaching and practicing the gospel of black nationalism, join the NAACP. If CORE is spreading and practicing the gospel of black nationalism, join CORE. Join any organization that has a gospel that's for the uplift of the black man. And when you get into it and see them pussyfooting or compromising, pull out of it because that's not black nationalism. We'll find another one.

And in this manner, the organizations will increase in number and in quantity and in quality, and by August, it is then our intention to have a black nationalist convention which will consist of delegates from all over the country who are interested in the political, economic and social philosophy of black nationalism. After these delegates convene, we will hold a seminar, we will hold discussions, we will listen to everyone. We want to hear new ideas and new solutions and new answers. And at that time, if we see fit then to form a black nationalist party, we'll form a black nationalist party. If it's necessary to form a black nationalist army, we'll form a black nationalist army. It'll be the ballot or the bullet. It'll be liberty or it'll be death.

It's time for you and me to stop sitting in this country, letting some cracker senators, Northern crackers and Southern crackers, sit there in Washington, D.C., and come to a conclusion in their mind that you and I are supposed to have civil rights. There's no white man going to tell me anything about my rights. Brothers and sisters, always remember, if it doesn't take senators and congressmen and presidential proclamations to give freedom to the white man, it is not necessary for legislation or proclamation or Supreme Court decisions to give freedom to the black man. You let that white man know, if this is a country of freedom, let it be a country of freedom; and if it's not a country of freedom, change it.

> ***"You let that white man know, if this is a country of freedom, let it be a country of freedom; and if it's not a country of freedom, change it."***

We will work with anybody, anywhere, at any time, who is genuinely interested in tackling the problem head-on, nonviolently as long as the enemy is nonviolent, but violent when the enemy gets violent. We'll work with you on the voter-registration drive, we'll work with you on rent strikes, we'll work with you on school boycotts—I don't believe in any kind of integration; I'm not even worried about it because I know you're not going to get it anyway; you're not going to get it because you're afraid to die; you've got to be ready to die if you try and force yourself on the white man, because he'll get just as violent as those crackers in Mississippi, right here in Cleveland. But we will still work with you on the school boycotts because we're against a segregated school system. A segregated school system produces children who, when they graduate, graduate with crippled minds. But this does not mean that a school is segregated because it's all black. A segregated school means a school that is controlled by people who have no real interest in it whatsoever.

Let me explain what I mean. A segregated district or community is a community in which people live, but outsiders control the politics and the economy of that community. They never refer to the white section as a segregated community. It's the all-Negro section that's a segregated community. Why? The white man controls his own school, his own bank, his own economy, his own politics, his own everything, his own community—but he also controls yours. When you're under someone else's control, you're segregated. They'll always give you the lowest or the worst that there is to offer, but it doesn't mean you're segregated just because you have your own. You've got to control your own. Just like the white man has control of his, you need to control yours.

You know the best way to get rid of segregation? The white man is more afraid of separation than he is of integration. Segregation means that he puts you away from him, but not far enough for you to be out of his jurisdiction; separation means you're gone. And the white man will integrate faster than he'll let you separate. So we will work with you against the segregated school system because it's criminal, because it is absolutely destructive, in every way imaginable, to the minds of the children who have to be exposed to that type of crippling education.

Last but not least, I must say this concerning the great controversy over rifles and shotguns. The only thing that I've ever said is that in areas where the government has proven itself either unwilling or unable to defend the lives and the property of Negroes, it's time for Negroes to defend themselves. Article number two of the constitutional amendments provides you and me the right to own a rifle or a shotgun. It is constitutionally legal to own a shotgun or a rifle. This doesn't mean you're going to get a rifle and form battalions and go out looking for white folks, although you'd be within your rights—I mean, you'd be justified; but that would be illegal and we don't do anything illegal. If the white man doesn't want the black man buying rifles and shotguns, then let the government do its job. That's all. And don't let the white man come to you and ask you what you think about what Malcolm says—why, you old Uncle Tom. He would never ask you if he thought you were going to say, "Amen!" No, he is making a Tom out of you.

So, this doesn't mean forming rifle clubs and going out looking for people, but it is time, in 1964, if you are a man, to let that man know. If he's not going to do his job in running the government and providing you and me with the protection that our taxes are supposed to be for, since he spends all those billions for his defense budget, he certainly can't begrudge you and me spending $12 or $15 for a single-shot, or double-action. I hope you understand. Don't go out shooting people, but any time, brothers and sisters, and especially the men in this audience—some of you wearing Congressional Medals of Honor, with shoulders this wide, chests this big, muscles that big—any time you and I sit around and read where they bomb a church and murder in cold blood, not some grownups, but four little girls while they were praying to the same god the white man taught them to pray to, and you and I see the government go down and can't find who did it.

Why, this man—he can find Eichmann hiding down in Argentina somewhere. Let two or three American soldiers, who are minding somebody else's business way over in South Vietnam, get killed, and he'll send battleships, sticking his nose in their business. He wanted to send troops down to Cuba and make them have what he calls free elections—this old cracker who doesn't have free elections in his own country. No, if you never see me another time in your life, if I die in the morning, I'll die saying one thing: the ballot or the bullet, the ballot or the bullet.

If a Negro in 1964 has to sit around and wait for some cracker senator to filibuster when it comes to the rights of black people, why, you and I should hang our heads in shame. You talk about a march on Washington in 1963, you haven't seen anything. There's some more going down in '64. And this time they're not going like they went last year. They're not going singing "We Shall Overcome." They're not going with white friends. They're not going with placards already painted for them. They're not going with round-trip tickets. They're going with one-way tickets.

And if they don't want that non-nonviolent

army going down there, tell them to bring the filibuster to a halt. The black nationalists aren't going to wait. Lyndon B. Johnson is the head of the Democratic Party. If he's for civil rights, let him go into the Senate next week and declare himself. Let him go in there right now and declare himself. Let him go in there and denounce the Southern branch of his party. Let him go in there right now and take a moral stand—right now, not later. Tell him, don't wait until election time. If he waits too long, brothers and sisters, he will be responsible for letting a condition develop in this country which will create a climate that will bring seeds up out of the ground with vegetation on the end of them looking like something these people never dreamed of. In 1964, it's the ballot or the bullet. Thank you.

Shortly after giving this speech, Malcolm X made a pilgrimage to the holy city of Mecca. He then spent several months traveling and studying in the Middle East and Africa, where he marveled at the sight of people from all different races coming together in the name of Islam. Upon his return to the United States in late 1964, he proclaimed himself to be a changed man. He announced his conversion to orthodox Islam and said that from then on he wanted to be known by the name of El-Hajj Malik El-Shabazz. Blending elements of his religious faith with socialism, anticolonialism, and what came to be known as "black consciousness," he developed a new, more conciliatory philosophy that acknowledged the necessity of forging ties with the very people and movements he had condemned in the past, including moderate blacks and progressive whites. He also softened his views on a variety of other issues, including separatism, and tried to downplay his fierce image.

But the conflict between Malcolm and Elijah Muhammad still raged; Malcolm had become increasingly critical of his former mentor and the Nation of Islam, and Muhammad's spokesmen shot back with insults and accusations of their own. The dispute took on a more sinister aspect after Malcolm reported that he had received several death threats. During the middle of the night on February 14, 1965, he and his family were forced to flee from their home in the wake of a firebomb attack. Later that same day, a still-shaken Malcolm delivered what would prove to be one of his last speeches to an audience in Detroit. It is taken from Malcolm X Speaks: Selected Speeches and Statements *(Pathfinder Press, 1965).*

Attorney Milton Henry, distinguished guests, brothers and sisters, ladies and gentlemen, friends and enemies: I want to point out first that I am very happy to be here this evening and I am thankful to the Afro-American Broadcasting Company for the invitation to come here this evening. As Attorney Milton Henry has stated—I should say Brother Milton Henry because that's what he is, our brother—I was in a house last night that was bombed, my own. It didn't destroy all my clothes but you know what fire and smoke do to things. The only thing I could get my hands on before leaving was what I have on now.

It isn't something that made me lose confidence in what I am doing, because my wife understands and I have children from this size on down, and even in their young age they understand. I think they would rather have a father or brother or whatever the situation may be who will take a stand in the face of reaction from any narrow-minded people rather than to compromise and later on have to grow up in shame and disgrace.

So I ask you to excuse my appearance. I don't normally come out in front of people without a shirt and tie. I guess that's somewhat a holdover from the Black Muslim movement which I was in. That's one of the good aspects of that movement. It teaches you to be very careful and conscious of how you look, which is a positive contribution on their part. But that positive contribution on their part is greatly offset by too many liabilities.

Also, last night, when the temperature was about twenty above and when this explosion took place, I was caught in what I had on—some pajamas. In trying to get my family out of the house, none of us stopped for any clothes at that point, so we were out in the twenty-degree cold. I got them into the house of the neighbor next door. I thought perhaps being in that condition for so long I would get pneumonia or a cold or something like that, so a doctor came today, a nice doctor, and shot something in my arm that naturally put me to sleep. I've been back there asleep ever since the program started in order to get back in shape. So if I have a tendency to stutter or slow down, it's still the effect of that drug. I don't know what kind it was, but it was good; it makes you sleep, and there's nothing like sleeping through a whole lot of excitement.

Tonight one of the things that has to be stressed, which has not only the United States very much worried but also has France, Great Britain and most of the powers who formerly were known as colonial powers worried, and that is the African revolution. They are more concerned with the revolution that is taking place on the African continent than they are with the revolution in Asia and in Latin America. And this is because there are so many people of African ancestry within the domestic confines or jurisdictions of these various governments.... There is an increasing number of dark-skinned people in England and also in France.

When I was in Africa in May, I noticed a tendency on the part of the Afro-Americans to—what I call lollygag. Everybody else who was over there had something on the ball, something they were doing, something constructive. Let's take Ghana as an example. There would be many refugees in Ghana from South Africa.... Some were being trained in how to be soldiers but others were involved as a pressure group or lobby group to let the people of Ghana never forget what happened to the brother in South Africa. Also you had brothers there from Angola and Mozambique. All of the Africans who were exiles from their particular country and would be in a place like Ghana or Tanganyika, now Tanzania—they would be training. Their every move would be designed to offset what was happening to their people back home where they had left.... When they escaped from their respective countries that were still colonized, they didn't try and run away from the family; as soon as they got where they were going, they began to organize into pressure groups to get support at the international level against the injustices they were experiencing back home.

But the American Negroes or the Afro-Americans, who were in these various countries, some working for this government, some working for that government, some in business—they were just socializing, they had turned their back on the cause over here, they were partying, you know. When I went through one country in particular, I heard a lot of their complaints and I didn't make any move. But when I got to another country, I found the Afro-Americans there were making the same complaints. So we sat down and talked and we organized a branch in this particular country of the Organization of Afro-American Unity. That one was the only one in existence at that time. Then during the summer when I went back to Africa, I was able in each country that I visited to get the Afro-American community together and organize them and make them aware of their responsibility to those of us who are still here in the lion's den.

They began to do this quite well, and when I got to Paris and London—there are many Afro-Americans in Paris, and many in London—in November, we organized a group in Paris and within a very short time they had grown into a well-organized unit. In conjunction with the African community, they invited me to Paris Tuesday to address a large gathering of Parisians and Afro-Americans and people from the Caribbean and also from Africa who were interested in our struggle in this country and the rate of progress that we have been making. But the French government and the British government and this government here, the United States, know that I have been almost fanatically stressing the importance of the Afro-Americans uniting with the Africans and working as a coalition, especially in areas which are of mutual benefit to all of us. And the governments in these different places were frightened....

I might point out here that colonialism or

imperialism, as the slave system of the West is called, is not something that is just confined to England or France or the United States. The interests in this country are in cahoots with the interests in France and the interests in Britain. It's one huge complex or combine, and it creates what's known not as the American power structure or the French power structure, but an international power structure. This international power structure is used to suppress the masses of dark-skinned people all over the world and exploit them of their natural resources, so that the era in which you and I have been living during the past ten years most specifically has witnessed the upsurge on the part of the black man in Africa against the power structure.

He wants his freedom and now. Mind you, the power structure is international, and its domestic base is in London, in Paris, in Washington, D.C., and so forth. The outside or external phase of the revolution which is manifest in the attitude and action of the Africans today is troublesome enough. The revolution on the outside of the house, or the outside of the structure, is troublesome enough. But now the powers that be are beginning to see that this struggle on the outside by the black man is affecting, infecting the black man who is on the inside of that structure—I hope you understand what I am trying to say. The newly awakened people all over the world pose a problem for what is known as western interests, which is imperialism, colonialism, racism and all these other negative isms or vulturistic isms. Just as the external forces pose a grave threat, they can now see that the internal forces pose an even greater threat. But the internal forces pose an even greater threat only when they have properly analyzed the situation and know what the stakes really are.

Just advocating a coalition of African, Afro-Americans, Arabs, and Asians who live within the structure automatically has upset France, which is supposed to be one of the most liberal countries on earth, and it made them expose their hand. England is the same way. And I don't have to tell you about this country that we are living in now. When you count the number of dark-skinned people in the Western hemisphere you can see that there are probably over one hundred million. When you consider Brazil has two-thirds what we call colored, or non-white, and Venezuela, Honduras and other Central American countries, Cuba and Jamaica, and the United States and even Canada—when you total all these people up, you have probably over one hundred million. And this one hundred million on the inside of the power structure today is what is causing a great deal of concern for the power structure itself. . . .

We thought that the first thing to do was to unite our people, not only internally, but with our brothers and sisters abroad. It was for that purpose that I spent five months in the Middle East and Africa during the summer. The trip was very enlightening, inspiring, and fruitful. I didn't go into any African country, or any country in the Middle East for that matter, and run into any closed door, closed mind, or closed heart. I found a warm reception and an amazingly deep interest and sympathy for the black man in this country in regards to our struggle for human rights. . . .

I hope you will forgive me for speaking so informally tonight, but I frankly think it is always better to be informal. As far as I am concerned, I can speak to people better in an informal way than I can with all of this stiff formality that ends up meaning nothing. Plus, when people are informal, they are relaxed. When they are relaxed, their mind is more open, and they can weigh things more objectively. Whenever you and I are discussing our problems we need to be very objective, very cool, calm and collected. That doesn't mean we should always be. There is a time to be cool and a time to be hot. See—you got messed up into thinking that there is only one time for everything. There is a time to love and a time to hate. Even Solomon said that, and he was in that book too. You're just taking something out of the book that fits your cowardly nature when you don't want to fight, and you say, "Well, Jesus said don't fight." But I don't even believe Jesus said that. . . .

Before I get involved in anything nowadays, I have to straighten out my own position, which is clear. I am not a racist in any form whatsoever. I don't believe in any form of racism. I don't believe in any form of discrimination or segregation. I believe in Islam. I am a Muslim and there is nothing wrong with being a Muslim, nothing wrong with the religion of Islam. It just teaches us to believe in Allah as the God. Those of you who are Christians probably believe in the same God, because I think you believe in the God who created the universe. That's the one we believe in, the one who created the universe—the only difference being you call him God and we call him Allah. The Jews call him Jehovah. If you could understand Hebrew, you would probably call him Jehovah too. If you could understand Arabic, you would probably call him Allah. But since the white man, your friend, took your language away from you during slavery, the only language you know is his language. You know your friend's language, so when he's putting the rope around your neck, you call for God and he calls for God. And you wonder why the one you call on never answers....

Elijah Muhammad had taught us that the white man could not enter into Mecca in Arabia and all of us who followed him, we believed it.... When I got over there and went to Mecca and saw these people who were blond and blue-eyed and pale-skinned and all those things, I said, "Well," but I watched them closely. And I noticed that though they were white, and they would call themselves white, there was a difference between them and the white ones over here. And that basic difference was this: In Asia or the Arab world or in Africa, where the Muslims are, if you find one who says he's white, all he's doing is using an adjective to describe something that's incidental about him, one of his incidental characteristics; there is nothing else to it, he's just white.

> ***"I don't believe in any form of racism. I don't believe in any form of discrimination or segregation. I believe in Islam."***

But when you get the white man over here in America and he says he's white, he means something else. You can listen to the sound of his voice—when he says he's white, he means he's boss. That's right. That's what white means in this language. You know the expression, "free, white and twenty-one." He made that up. He's letting you know that white means free, boss. He's up there, so that when he says he's white he has a little different sound in his voice. I know you know what I'm talking about....

Despite the fact that I saw that Islam was a religion of brotherhood, I also had to face reality. And when I got back into this American society, I'm not in a society that practices brotherhood. I'm in a society that might preach it on Sunday, but they don't practice it on any day. America is a society where there is no brotherhood. This society is controlled primarily by the racists and segregationists who are in Washington, D.C., in positions of power. And from Washington, D.C., they exercise the same forms of brutal oppression against dark-skinned people in South and North Vietnam, or in the Congo, or in Cuba or any other place on this earth where they are trying to exploit and oppress. That is a society whose government doesn't hesitate to inflict the most brutal form of punishment and oppression upon dark-skinned people all over the world.

Look right now what's going on in and around Saigon and Hanoi and in the Congo and elsewhere. They are violent when their interests are at stake. But for all that violence they display at the international level, when you and I want just a little bit of freedom, we're supposed to be nonviolent. They're violent in Korea, they're violent in Germany, they're violent in the South Pacific, they're violent in Cuba, they're violent wherever they go. But when it comes time for you and me to protect ourselves against lynchings, they tell us to be nonviolent.

That's a shame. Because we get tricked into being nonviolent, and when somebody stands up and talks like I just did, they say, "Why, he's advocating violence." Isn't that what they say? Everytime you pick up your newspaper, you see where one of these things has written into it that I am advocating violence. I have never advocated any violence. I have only said that black people who are the victims of organized violence perpetrated upon us by the Klan, the Citizens Councils, and many other forms, should defend ourselves. And when I say we should defend ourselves against the violence of others, they use their press skillfully to make the world think that I am calling for violence, period. I wouldn't call on anybody to be violent without a cause. But I think the black man in this country, above and beyond people all over the world, will be more justified when he stands up and starts to protect himself, no matter how many necks he has to break and heads he has to crack....

The Klan is a cowardly outfit. They have perfected the art of making Negroes be afraid. As long as the Negro is afraid, the Klan is safe. But the Klan itself is cowardly. One of them never come after one of you. They all come together. They're scared of you. And you sit there when they're putting the rope around your neck saying, "Forgive them, Lord, they know not what they do." As long as they've been doing it, they're experts at it, they know what they're doing. No, since the federal government has shown that it isn't going to do anything about it but *talk,* then it is a duty, it's your and my duty as men, as human beings, it is our duty to our people, to organize ourselves and let the government know that if they don't stop that Klan, we'll stop it ourselves. *Then* you'll see the government start doing something about it. But don't ever think that they're going to do it just on some kind of morality basis. No. So I don't believe in violence—that's why I want to stop it. And you can't stop it with love, not love of those things down there. No! So, we only mean vigorous action in self-defense, and that vigorous action we feel we're justified in initiating by any means necessary.

Now, for saying something like that, the press calls us racist and people who are "violent in reverse." This is how they psycho you. They make you think that if you try to stop the Klan from lynching you, you're practicing violence in reverse. Pick up on this, I hear a lot of you parrot what the man says. You say, "I don't want to be a Ku Klux Klan in reverse." Well, if a criminal comes around your house with his gun, brother, just because he's got a gun and he's robbing your house, and he's a robber, it doesn't make you a robber because you grab your gun and run him out. No, the man is using some tricky logic on you. I say it is time for black people to put together the type of action, the unity, that is necessary to pull the sheet off of them so they won't be frightening black people any longer. That's all. And when we say this, the press calls us "racist in reverse." "Don't struggle except within the ground rules that the people you're struggling against have laid down." Why, this is insane, but it shows how they can do it. With skillful manipulating of the press they're able to make the victim look like the criminal and the criminal look like the victim.

Right now in New York we have a couple of cases where the police grabbed a brother and beat him unmercifully—and charged him with assaulting them. They used the press to make it look like he is the criminal and they are the victims. This is how they do it, and if you study how they do it here then you'll know how they do it over there. It's the same game going all the time, and if you and I don't awaken and see what this man is doing to us, then it will be too late. They may have the gas ovens built before you realize that they're already hot.

One of the shrewd ways that they project us in the image of a criminal is that they take statistics and with the press feed these statistics to the public, primarily the white public. Because there are some well-meaning persons in the white public as well as bad-meaning persons in the white public. And whatever the government is going to do, it always wants the public on its side—whether it is the local government, state government or federal government. At the local level, they will create an image by feeding statistics to the public through the press showing the high crime rate in the Negro community. As soon as this high crime rate is emphasized through the press, then people begin to look upon the Negro community as a community of criminals.

And then any Negro in the community can be stopped in the street. "Put your hands up," and they pat you down. Might be a doctor, a lawyer, a preacher or some other kind of Uncle Tom, but despite your professional standing, you'll find that you're the same victim as the man who's in the alley. Just because you're black and you live in a black community which has been projected as a community of criminals. And once the public accepts this image, it also paves the way for police-state type of activity in the Negro community—they can use any kind of brutal methods to suppress blacks because they're criminals anyway. And what has given us this image? The press again, by letting the power structure or the racist element in the power structure use them in that way.

A very good example was the riots that took place during the summer. I was in Africa, I read about them over there. If you noticed, they referred to the rioters as vandals, hoodlums, thieves, and they skillfully took the burden off the society for its failure to correct these negative conditions in the black community. They took the burden completely off the society and put it right on the community by using the press to make it appear that the looting and all of this was proof that the whole act was nothing but vandals and robbers and thieves, who weren't really interested in anything other than that which was negative. And I hear many dumb, brainwashed Negroes who parrot the same old party line that the man handed down in his paper.

It was not the case that they were just knocking out store windows ignorantly. In Harlem, for instance, all of the stores are owned by white people, all of the buildings are owned by white people. The black people are just there—paying rent, buying the groceries; but they don't own the stores, clothing stores, food stores, any kind of stores; don't even own the homes that they live in.

These are all owned by outsiders, and for these run-down apartment dwellings, the black man in Harlem pays more money than the man down in the rich Park Avenue section. It costs us more money to live in the slums than it costs them to live down on Park Avenue. Black people in Harlem know this, and that the white merchants charge us more money for food in Harlem—and it's the cheap food, the worst food; we have to pay more money for it than the man has to pay for it downtown. So black people know that they're being exploited and that their blood is being sucked and they see no way out.

When the thing is finally sparked, the white man is not there—he's gone. The merchant is not there, the landlord is not there, the one they consider to be the enemy isn't there. So, they knock at his property. This is what makes them knock down the store windows and set fire to things, and things of that sort. It's not that they're thieves. But they [the newspapers] are trying to project the image to the public that this is being done by thieves, and thieves alone. And they ignore the fact that it is not thievery alone. It's a corrupt, vicious, hypocritical system that has castrated the black man, and the only way the black man can get back at it is to strike it in the only way he knows how.

"You're in a society that's just as capable of building gas ovens for black people as Hitler's society was."

[When I say] they use the press, that doesn't mean that all reporters are bad. Some of them are good, I suppose. But you can take their collective approach to any problem and see that they can always agree when it gets to you and me. They knew that the Afro-American Broadcasting Company was giving this affair—which is designed to honor outstanding black Americans, is it not? But you find nothing in the newspapers that gives the slightest hint that this affair was going to take place—not one hint, though there are supposed to be many sources of news. If you don't think that they're in cahoots, watch. They're all interested, or none of them are interested. It's not a staggering thing. They're not going to say anything in advance about an affair that's being given by any black people who believe in functioning beyond the scope of the ground rules that are laid down by the liberal elements of the power structure.

When you start thinking for yourselves, you frighten them, and they try and block your getting to the public, for the fear that if the public listens to you then the public won't listen to them anymore. And they've got certain Negroes whom they have to keep blowing up in the papers to make them look like leaders. So that the people will keep on following them, no matter how many knocks they get on their heads following them. This is how the man does it, and if you don't wake up and find out how he does it, I tell you, they'll be building gas chambers and gas ovens pretty soon—I don't mean those kind you've got at home in your kitchen—[and] . . . you'll be in one of them, just like the Jews ended up in gas ovens over there in Germany. You're in a society that's just as capable of building gas ovens for black people as Hitler's society was. . . .

Now what effect does [the struggle over Africa] have on us? Why should the black man in America concern himself since he's been away from the African continent for three or four hundred years? Why should we concern ourselves? What impact does what happens to them have upon us? Number one, you have to realize that up until 1959 Africa was dominated by the colonial powers. Having complete control over Africa, the colonial powers of Europe projected the image of Africa negatively. They always project Africa in a negative light: jungle savages, cannibals, nothing civilized. Why then naturally it was so negative that it was negative to you and me, and you and I began to hate it. We didn't want anybody telling us anything about Africa, much less calling us Africans. In hating Africa and in hating the Africans, we ended up hating ourselves, without even realizing it. Because you can't hate the roots of a tree, and not hate the tree. You can't hate your origin and not end up hating yourself. You can't hate Africa and not hate yourself.

You show me one of these people over here who has been thoroughly brainwashed and has a negative attitude toward Africa, and I'll show you one who has a negative attitude toward himself. You can't have a positive attitude toward yourself and a negative attitude toward Africa at the same time. To the same degree that your understanding of and attitude toward Africa become positive, you'll find that your understanding of and your attitude toward yourself will also become positive. And this is what the white man knows. So they very skillfully make you and me hate our African identity, our African characteristics.

You know yourself that we have been a people who hated our African characteristics. We hated our heads, we hated the shape of our nose, we wanted one of those long dog-like noses, you know; we hated the color of our skin, hated the blood of Africa that was in our veins. And in hating our features and our skin and our blood, why, we had to end up hating ourselves. And we hated ourselves. Our color became to us a chain—we felt that it was holding us back; our color became to us like a prison which we felt was keeping us confined, not letting us go this way or that way. We felt that all of these restrictions were based solely upon our color, and the psychological reaction to that would have to be that as long as we felt imprisoned or chained or trapped by black skin, black features and black blood, that skin and those features and that blood holding us back automatically had to become hateful to us. And it became hateful to us.

It made us feel inferior; it made us feel inadequate; made us feel helpless. And when we fell victims to this feeling of inadequacy or inferiority or helplessness, we turned to somebody else to show us the way. We didn't have confidence in another black man to show us the way, or black people to show us the way. In those days we didn't. We didn't think a black man could do anything except play some horns—you know, make some sound and make you happy with some songs and in that way. But in serious things, where our food, clothing, shelter and education were concerned, we turned to the man. We never thought in terms of bringing these things into existence for ourselves, we never thought in terms of doing things for ourselves. Because we felt helpless. What made us feel helpless was our hatred for ourselves. And our hatred for ourselves stemmed from our hatred for things African. . . .

After 1959 the spirit of African nationalism was fanned to a high flame and we then began to witness the complete collapse of colonialism. France began to get out of French West Africa, Belgium began to make moves to get out of the Congo, Britain began to make moves to get out of Kenya, Tanganyika, Uganda, Nigeria and some of these other places. And although it looked like they were getting out, they pulled a trick that was colossal.

When you're playing ball and they've got you trapped, you don't throw the ball away—you throw it to one of your teammates who's in the clear. And this is what the European powers did. They were trapped on the African continent, they couldn't stay there—they were looked upon as colonial and imperialist. They had to pass the ball to someone whose image was different, and they passed the ball to Uncle Sam. And he picked it up and has been running it for a touchdown ever since. He was in the clear, he was not looked upon as one who had colonized the African continent. At that time, the Africans couldn't see that though the United States hadn't colonized the African continent, it had colonized twenty-two million blacks here on this continent. Because we're just as thoroughly colonized as anybody else.

When the ball was passed to the United States, it was passed at the time when John Kennedy came into power. He picked it up and helped to run it. He was one of the shrewdest backfield runners that history has ever recorded. He surrounded himself with intellectuals—highly educated, learned and well-informed people. And their analysis told him that the government of America was confronted with a new problem. And this new problem stemmed from the fact that Africans were now awakened, they were enlightened, they were fearless, they would fight. This meant that the Western powers couldn't stay there by force. Since their own economy, the European economy and the American economy, was based upon their continued influence over the African continent, they had to find some means of staying there. So they used the friendly approach.

They switched from the old openly colonial imperialistic approach to the benevolent approach. They came up with some benevolent colonialism, philanthropic colonialism, humanitarianism, or dollarism. Immediately everything was Peace Corps, Operation Crossroads, "We've got to help our African brothers." Pick up on that: Can't help us in Mississippi. Can't help us in Alabama, or Detroit, or out here in Dearborn where some real Ku Klux Klan lives. They're going to send all the way to Africa to help. I know Dearborn; you know, I'm from Detroit, I used to live out here in Inkster. And you had to go through Dearborn to get to Inkster. Just like driving through Mississippi when you got to Dearborn. Is it still that way? Well, you should straighten it out.

So, realizing that it was necessary to come up with these new approaches, Kennedy did it. He created an image of himself that was skillfully designed to make the people on the African continent think that he was Jesus, the great white father, come to make things right. I'm telling you, some of these Negroes cried harder when he died than they cried for Jesus when he was crucified. From 1954 to 1964 was the era in which we witnessed the emerging of Africa. The impact that this had on the civil rights struggle in America has never been fully told.

For one thing, one of the primary ingredients in the complete civil rights struggle was the Black Muslim movement. The Black Muslim movement took no part in things political, civic—it didn't take too much part in anything other than stopping people from doing this drinking, smoking, and so on. Moral reform it had, but beyond that it did nothing. But it talked such a strong talk that it put the other Negro organizations on the spot. Before the Black Muslim movement came along, the NAACP was looked upon as radical; they were getting ready to investigate it. And then along came the Muslim movement and frightened the white man so hard that he began to say, "Thank God for old Uncle Roy, and Uncle Whitney and Uncle A. Philip and Uncle"—you've got a whole lot of uncles in there; I can't remember their names, they're all older than I so I call them "uncle." Plus, if you use the word "Uncle Tom" nowadays, I hear they can sue you for libel, you know. So I don't call any of them Uncle Tom anymore. I call them Uncle Roy.

One of the things that made the Black Muslim movement grow was its emphasis upon things African. This was the secret to the growth of the Black Muslim movement. African blood, African origin, African culture, African ties. And you'd be surprised—we discovered that deep within the subconscious of the black man in this country, he is still more African than he is American. He *thinks* that he's more American than African, because the man is jiving him, the man is brainwashing him every day. He's telling him, "You're an American, you're an American." Man, how could you think you're an American when you haven't ever had any kind of an American treat over here? You have never, never. Ten men can be sitting at a table eating, you know, dining, and I can come and sit down where they're dining. They're dining; I've got a plate in front of me, but nothing is on it. Because all of us are sitting at the same table, are all of us diners? I'm not a diner until you let me dine. Just being at the table with others who are dining doesn't make me a diner, and this is what you've got to get in your head here in this country.

Just because you're in this country doesn't make you an American. No, you've got to go farther than that before you can become an American. You've got to enjoy the fruits of Americanism. You haven't enjoyed those fruits. You've enjoyed the thorns. You've enjoyed the thistles. But you have not enjoyed the fruits, no sir. You have fought harder for the fruits than the white man has, you have worked harder for the fruits than the white man has, but you've enjoyed less. When the man put the uniform on you and sent you abroad, you fought harder than they did. Yes, I know you—when you're fighting for them, you can fight.

The Black Muslim movement did make that contribution. They made the whole civil rights movement become more militant, and more acceptable to the white power structure. He would rather have them than us. In fact, I think we forced many of the civil rights leaders to be even more militant than they intended. I know some of them who get out there and "boom, boom, boom" and don't mean it. Because they're right on back in their corner as soon as the action comes.

John F. Kennedy also saw that it was necessary for a new approach among the American Negroes. And during his entire term in office, he specialized in how to psycho the American Negro. Now, a lot of you all don't like my saying that—but I wouldn't ever take a stand on that if I didn't know what I was talking about. By living in this kind of society, pretty much around them, and you know what I mean when I say "them," I learned to study them. You can think that they mean you some good ofttimes, but if you look at it a little closer you'll see that they don't mean you any good. That doesn't mean there aren't some of them who mean good. But it does mean that most of them don't mean good.

Kennedy's new approach was pretending to go along with us in our struggle for civil rights. He was another proponent of rights. But I remember the expose that *Look* magazine did on the Meredith situation in Mississippi. *Look* magazine did an expose showing that Robert Kennedy and Governor Barnett had made a deal, wherein the Attorney General was going to come down and try to force Meredith into school, and Barnett was going to stand at the door, you know, and say, "No, you can't come in." He was going to get in anyway, but it was all arranged in advance and then Barnett was supposed to keep the support of the white racists, because that's who he was upholding, and Kennedy would keep the support of the Negroes, because that's who he'd be upholding. It was a cut-and-dried deal. And it's not a secret; it was written, they write about it. But if that's a deal, how many other deals do you think go down? What you think is on the level is crookeder, brothers and sisters, than a pretzel, which is most crooked.

So in my conclusion I would like to point out that the approach that was used by the administration right up until today was designed skillfully to make it appear they were trying to solve the problem when they actually weren't. They would deal with the conditions, but never the cause. They only gave us tokenism. Tokenism benefits only a few. It never benefits the masses, and the masses are the ones who have the problem, not the few. That one who benefits from tokenism, he doesn't want to be around us anyway—that's why he picks up on the token. . . .

The masses of our people still have bad housing, bad schooling and inferior jobs, jobs that don't compensate with sufficient salaries for them to carry on their life in this world. So that the problem for the masses has gone absolutely unsolved. The only ones for whom it has been solved are people like Whitney Young, who is supposed to be placed in the cabinet, so the rumor says. He'll be the first black cabinet man. And that answers where he's at. And others have been given jobs, like Carl Rowan, who was put over the USIA, and is very skillfully trying to make Africans think that the problem of black men in this country is all solved.

The worst thing the white man can do to himself is to take one of these kinds of Negroes and ask him, "How do your people feel, boy?" He's going to tell that man that we are satisfied. That's what they do, brothers and sisters. They get behind the door and tell the white man we're satisfied. "Just keep on keeping me up here in front of them, boss, and I'll keep them behind you." That's what they talk when they're behind closed doors. Because, you see, the white man doesn't go along with anybody who's not for him. He doesn't care are you for right or wrong, he wants to know are you for him. And if you're for him, he doesn't care what else you're for. As long as you're for him, then he puts you up over the Negro community. You become a spokesman.

In your struggle it's like standing on a revolving wheel; you're running, but you're not going anywhere. You run faster and faster and the wheel just goes faster and faster. You don't ever leave the spot that you're standing in. So, it is very important for you and me to see that our problem has to have a solution that will benefit the masses, not the upper class—so-called upper class. Actually, there's no such thing as an upper-class Negro, because he catches the same hell as the other class Negro. All of them catch the same hell, which is one of things that's good about this racist system—it makes us all one. . . .

"There's no such thing as an upper-class Negro, because he catches the same hell as the other class Negro. All of them catch the same hell, which is one of things that's good about this racist system—it makes us all one."

If you'd tell them right now what is in store for 1965, they'd think you crazy for sure. But 1965 will be the longest and hottest and bloodiest year of them all. It has to be, not because you want it to be, or I want it to be, or we want it to be, but because the conditions that created these explosions in 1963 are still here; the conditions that created explosions in 1964 are still here. You can't say that you're not going to have an explosion when you leave the conditions, the ingredients, still here. As long as those explosive ingredients remain, then you're going to have the potential for explosion on your hands.

And, brothers and sisters, let me tell you, I spend my time out there in the streets with people, all kinds of people, listening to what they have to say. And they're dissatisfied, they're disillusioned, they're fed up, they're getting to the point of frustration where they begin to feel, "What do we have to lose?" When you get to that point, you're the type of person who can create a very dangerously explosive atmosphere. This is what's happening in our neighborhoods, to our people.

I read in a poll taken by *Newsweek* magazine this week, saying that Negroes are satisfied. Oh, yes, *Newsweek,* you know, supposed to be a top magazine with a top pollster, talking about how satisfied Negroes are. Maybe I haven't met the

Negroes he met. Because I know he hasn't met the ones that I've met. And this is dangerous. This is where the white man does himself the most harm. He invents statistics to create an image, thinking that that image is going to hold things in check. You know why they always say Negroes are lazy? Because they want Negroes to be lazy. They always say Negroes can't unite because they don't want Negroes to unite. And once they put this thing in the Negro's mind, they feel that he tries to fulfill their image. If they say you can't unite black people, and then you come to them to unite them, they won't unite because it's been said that they're not supposed to unite. It's a psycho that they work, and it's the same way with these statistics.

When they think that an explosive era is coming up, then they grab their press again and begin to shower the Negro public, to make it appear that all Negroes are satisfied. Because if you know you're dissatisfied all by yourself and ten others aren't, you play it cool; but if you know that all ten of you are dissatisfied, you get with it. This is what the man knows. The man knows that if these Negroes find out how dissatisfied they really are—even Uncle Tom is dissatisfied, he's just playing his part for now—this is what makes the man frightened. It frightens them in France and frightens them in England, and it frightens them in the United States.

And it is for this reason that it is so important for you and me to start organizing among ourselves, intelligently, and try to find out: "What are we going to do if this happens, that happens or the next thing happens?" Don't think that you're going to run to the man and say, "Look, boss, this is me." Why, when the deal goes down, you'll look just like me in his eyesight; I'll make it tough for you. Yes, when the deal goes down, he doesn't look at you in any better light than he looks at me. . . .

I point these things out, brothers and sisters, so that you and I will know the importance in 1965 of being in complete unity with each other, in harmony with each other, and not letting the man maneuver us into fighting one another. The situation I have been maneuvered into right now, between me and the Black Muslim movement, is something that I really deeply regret, because I don't think anything is more destructive than two groups of black people fighting each other. But it's something that can't be avoided because it goes deep down beneath the surface, and these things will come up in the very near future.

I might say this before I sit down. If you recall, when I left the Black Muslim movement, I stated clearly that it wasn't my intention to even continue to be aware that they existed; I was going to spend my time working in the non-Muslim community. But they were fearful if they didn't do something that perhaps many of those who were in the [Black Muslim] mosque would leave it and follow a different direction. So they had to start doing a takeoff on me, plus, they had to try and silence me because of what they know that I know. I think that they should know me well enough to know that they certainly can't frighten me. But when it does come to the light—excuse me for keeping coughing like that, but I got some of that smoke last night—there are some things involving the Black Muslim movement which, when they come to light, will shock you.

The thing that you have to understand about those of us in the Black Muslim movement was that all of us believed one hundred percent in the divinity of Elijah Muhammad. We believed in him. We actually believed that God, in Detroit by the way, that God had taught him and all of that. I always believed that he believed it himself. And I was shocked when I found out that he himself didn't believe it. And when that shock reached me, then I began to look everywhere else and try and get a better understanding of the things that confront all of us so that we can get together in some kind of way to offset them.

I want to thank you for coming out this evening. I think it's wonderful that as many of you came out, considering the blackout on the meeting that took place. Milton Henry and the brothers who are here in Detroit are very progressive young men, and I would advise all of you to get with them in any way that you can to try and create some kind of united effort toward common goals, common objectives. Don't let the power structure maneuver you into a time-wasting battle with others when you could be involved in something that is constructive and getting a real job done. . . .

I say again that I'm not a racist, I don't believe in any form of segregation or anything like that. I'm for brotherhood for everybody, but I don't believe in forcing brotherhood upon people who don't want it. Let us practice brotherhood among ourselves, and then if others want to practice brotherhood with us, we're for practicing it with them also. But I don't think that we should run around trying to love somebody who doesn't love us. Thank you.

Exactly one week later, while preparing to address some of his followers in Harlem's Audubon Ballroom, Malcolm X was assassinated by three black gunmen with ties to the Nation of Islam. All were convicted of his murder and sent to prison; two have since been paroled.

In January 1995, one of Malcolm X's daughters, Qubilah Shabazz, was arrested and charged with trying to hire someone to kill the current head of the Nation of Islam, Louis Farrakhan. Malcolm X and Farrakhan had been bitter rivals, and members of the slain black leader's family had long suspected Farrakhan of somehow being involved in the assassination.

Farrakhan has steadfastly denied that he was behind any plot to do away with Malcolm X but admits that his inflammatory rhetoric at the time created an "atmosphere" that encouraged the real killers to act. He claims that continued attempts to link him to Malcolm X's assassination are part of a government conspiracy to discredit black leaders, and he has defended Shabazz—who was only four years old when she watched her father die in a hail of bullets—as a confused young woman who was manipulated by federal authorities into trying to destroy him.

Indeed, as events unfolded during the early months of 1995, it became clear that the government's case against Shabazz was a rather shaky one. It was based on secretly taped telephone conversations between the troubled Qubilah Shabazz and a government informant of dubious credibility, as well as on a statement she gave to FBI agents in December 1994. The evidence indicated that while she did bear a definite grudge against Farrakhan and was afraid that he still represented a threat to her mother, she may well have been lured into the murder-for-hire scheme by the government informant.

In May 1995, just as the case was scheduled to go to trial, Shabazz and government prosecutors reached a surprise settlement. Under the terms of the agreement, Shabazz accepted responsibility for (but did not actually admit to being guilty of) participating in a murder plot against Farrakhan and agreed to stop accusing the FBI of trying to frame her. She also pledged to seek drug and psychiatric treatment. If she fulfills these conditions and remains out of further trouble with the law, the federal indictment against her will be dismissed in two years.

SOURCES

Books

Bosmajian, Haig A., and Hamida Bosmajian, editors, *The Rhetoric of the Civil-Rights Movement*, Random House, 1969.

Bracey, John H., Jr., August Meier, and Elliott Rudwick, editors, *Black Nationalism in America*, Bobbs-Merrill, 1970.

Breitman, George, editor, *Malcolm X Speaks: Selected Speeches and Statements*, Pathfinder Press, 1965.

———, editor, *By Any Means Necessary: Speeches, Interviews and a Letter by Malcolm X*, Pathfinder Press, 1970.

Clarke, John Henrik, editor, *Malcolm X: The Man and His Times*, Collier, 1969.

Duffy, Bernard K., and Halford R. Ryan, editors, *American Orators of the Twentieth Century: Critical Studies and Sources*, Greenwood Press, 1987.

Dyson, Michael Eric, *Making Malcolm*, Oxford University Press, 1995.

Golden, James L., and Richard D. Rieke, editors, *The Rhetoric of Black Americans*, Charles E. Merrill, 1971.

Goldman, Peter, *The Death and Life of Malcolm X*, Harper, 1973, revised edition, 1979.

Hill, Roy L., editor, *The Rhetoric of Racial Revolt*, Golden Bell Press, 1964.

Holland, DeWitte, editor, *America in Controversy: History*

of American Public Address, William C. Brown Company, 1973.

Lomax, Louis, *When the Word Is Given . . . : A Report on Elijah Muhammad, Malcolm X, and the Black Muslim World,* World Publishing, 1963.

Malcolm X (as told to Alex Haley), *The Autobiography of Malcolm X,* Grove, 1965.

Myers, Walter Dean, *Malcolm X: By Any Means Necessary,* Scholastic, 1993.

Perry, Bruce, *Malcolm X: The Last Speeches,* Pathfinder Press, 1989.

———, *Malcolm: The Life of a Man Who Changed Black America,* Station Hill Press, 1991.

Rummell, Jack, *Malcolm X: Black Militant Leader,* Chelsea House, 1989.

Scott, Robert L., and Wayne Brockriede, *The Rhetoric of Black Power,* Harper, 1969.

Smith, Arthur L., *Rhetoric of Black Revolution,* Allyn & Bacon, 1969.

Smith, Arthur L., and Stephen Robb, editors, *The Voice of Black Rhetoric: Selections,* Allyn & Bacon, 1971.

Periodicals

Detroit Free Press, "Woman Charged with Plotting to Kill Farrakhan," January 13, 1995; "Farrakhan Death Plot Charges Dropped," May 2, 1995, p. 5A.

Detroit News, "Malcolm X's Daughter Accused of Plotting to Kill Farrakhan," January 13, 1995; "Malcolm X's Daughter Pleads Not Guilty in Murder Plot," January 19, 1995, p.5A; "Feds Drop Charges Against Daughter of Malcolm X," May 2, 1995, p. 1A.

Grand Rapids Press, "Malcolm X's Daughter Held in Farrakhan Death Plot," January 13, 1995, p. A1; "Informant Is Called 'Set-Up Artist,' " January 14, 1995, p. A1; "Innocent Plea," January 18, 1995, p. A3; "Murder Plot Case Turns on FBI; Blacks Suspicious of Government," January 19, 1995, p. A4; "Prosecution: Malcolm X's Daughter Obsessed with Killing Farrakhan," February 28, 1995, p. A6; "Witness to Farrakhan Plot Says He Talked to Get Money," March 24, 1995, p. A7; "Settlement Reached in Plot to Murder Islam's Farrakhan," May 1, 1995, p. A3; "Shabazz on Plot: 'I Fell for It Out of Love,' " May 2, 1995, p. A5.

Newsweek, "Back in the Line of Fire," January 23, 1995, pp. 20-22; "A Tale of Two Lonely Lives," January 30, 1995, pp. 46-48; " 'I Was in It to Save Lives,' " May 15, 1995, pp. 29-30.

Wilma Mankiller

1945–

Native American leader of the Cherokee tribe

In 1987, Wilma Mankiller made history when she became the first woman elected chief of a major Native American tribe. Her victory capped a life plagued by poverty, racism, sexism, and several close brushes with death—heavy burdens even for a person whose family name harks back to an old Indian military title meaning "one who safeguards the village." As leader of the Cherokee Nation, which is second in size only to the Navajo Nation, Mankiller has worked tirelessly to bring economic prosperity to her people while seeing to their many social and cultural needs as well. In the process, she has become a near-legend in the Native American community for her dedication and compassion.

Born in Tahlequah, Oklahoma (the capital of the Cherokee Nation), to a Cherokee father and a mother of Dutch and Irish descent, Mankiller was one of eleven children. She spent the first decade of her life not far from her birthplace, happily close to her family but barely getting by on what meager crops her father was able to raise and sell. When the struggle finally proved too great, the Mankillers accepted the federal government's offer to move them to California, where they settled in a San Francisco ghetto as part of a Bureau of Indian Affairs program to "urbanize" Native Americans. Life did not improve, however; the children were desperately homesick and cringed at the racist insults of their classmates, and Charlie Mankiller, Wilma's father, had trouble landing steady employment.

Eventually, however, the Mankillers adjusted to living in the city. Wilma finished high school and went on to college at San Francisco State, where throughout the 1960s she pursued studies in sociology with an eye toward becoming a social worker. It was during this same period that she arrived at a new appreciation of her heritage when she began associating with a group of young Native American activists. In 1969, some of them occupied Alcatraz Island in San Francisco Bay to protest the U.S. government's mistreatment of Indian people and reassert their treaty rights. Mankiller's subsequent efforts to round up support for the demonstrators led her into the fledgling American Indian Movement, and by 1975 she had left California to return to Oklahoma and what she hoped would be an opportunity to work on behalf of the Cherokee people.

Mankiller spent the next few years developing and implementing a number of economic and social self-help programs in the community under the auspices of the

Cherokee Nation. She also resumed her education, this time at the University of Arkansas in Fayetteville. While driving back home after class one morning in late 1979, she was involved in a car accident that killed her best friend and left Mankiller critically injured. Not long afterward, she was diagnosed with a serious muscle disease, myasthenia gravis. All of this was in addition to the kidney problems she had been suffering from since the early 1970s—problems severe enough that she would later undergo surgery and eventually a transplant.

Mankiller struggled for nearly a year to overcome the physical and emotional trauma of the accident and its aftermath. Once she was able to work again, she took up where she had left off, setting up programs to help her people help themselves (primarily in the areas of health care and housing) as director of the Cherokee Nation Community Development Department. Her success soon attracted the attention of tribal leaders, including Principal Chief Ross Swimmer, who asked her to be his running mate (for the post of deputy chief) in his 1983 re-election campaign. Despite facing opposition from some male members of the tribe who felt that a woman had no business being in the race, Swimmer and Mankiller managed to win by a narrow margin. Two years later, when Swimmer resigned to accept a job with the administration of President Ronald Reagan, Mankiller assumed the role of principal chief, making her the first woman ever to hold the position.

In 1987, Mankiller decided to seek election as principal chief in her own right. Once again, she faced some resistance; not all of the men were convinced that a woman was suited for the post. Also, Mankiller's continuing health problems were of concern. But with the encouragement and support of her husband, Charlie Soap, who works on rural development projects for the Cherokee Nation, she was able to summon the strength and the will to prevail over her opponent.

On August 14, 1987, Mankiller faced her people as their newly-elected principal chief and voiced her hopes and plans for the future. Her historic inaugural address, delivered in the Cherokee Nation capital of Tahlequah, is reprinted here from Native American Address: Stories, Speeches and Poems, *edited by Jerry D. Blanche (Denali Press, 1990).*

Good afternoon. I'd like to tell you how truly delighted I am to be here today. There's no greater honor I've ever had than to be chosen by my own people to lead them and I think that feeling is shared by Deputy Chief John Ketcher and members of the Tribal Council.

I heard someone say this week, "How are all these 'ordinary' people elected to the tribal council going to make the weighty decisions for the Cherokee Nation?" I can tell you quite frankly that "ordinary" people take very seriously the responsibility and trust that has been given them. I think you'll see a change in these people who have been elected to make decisions for you, merely from the weight of that responsibility. People say that crisis changes people and turns ordinary people into wiser or more responsible ones. As crises develop within the Cherokee Nation and we begin to resolve those crises, you will see many changes.

I'd like to talk just a little about the Cherokee Nation, where I see us today and where I see us going in the future. I think I can say without the tiniest bit of false pride that we are one of the most progressive tribes in the U.S. today. That progress we enjoy today, the Cherokee Nation that you see today—a very progressive, large, diverse organization—is not the result of the work of one person. It's the work of many, many people. There are a lot of people who laid the foundation for the work we're doing today, beginning principally in this latest revitalization, with Chief Milam, moving to

Wilma Mankiller

Chief Keeler, to Chief Swimmer, who was my immediate predecessor, and myself.

The tribal council members who have become more active and assumed more responsibility within the tribal government are responsible for much of that work. I don't ever forget that much of the good work at the Cherokee Nation and much of our success can be attributed directly to the hundreds of tribal citizens who become involved in our work, as well as the tribal employees who carry out the policies established by the tribal government. Many people only see the employees. They rarely get to see the inner workings of the tribal government, so I would also like to thank all the tribal employees who make our government what it is today.

We've grown very rapidly in the past fifteen years, just in the past ten years that I've been associated with the tribe. That growth has been phenomenal, and the manifestation of the growth over the past fifteen years is all around you. You can see the new Hastings Hospital, Cherokee Nation Industries, Cherokee Gardens, rural health clinics, the Head Start centers and many other examples of this growth. When I came to the Cherokee Nation ten years ago, there were two hundred or three hundred tribal employees. There are now well over seven hundred permanent employees, and several hundred more have seasonal employment.

That growth has not occurred without problems. Growth is a painful process. I'd like everybody to remember that we're still growing, we're still young. In the totality of Cherokee history, fifteen years isn't very long. And we've got many more painful processes to work through before we reach a point where we will level off.

Our overall goal determined by the last tribal council and the last chief and deputy chief was a goal of self-sufficiency as total independence from federal aid. That's not at all what we mean. I personally think that the U.S. government owes us much in federal aid. We paid for much of what we receive today in lost lives and lost land. Our interpretation of self-sufficiency could simply be described as capability—the capability to do things for ourselves . . . the capability to do things with some assistance from the BIA [Bureau of Indian Affairs], but basically running the tribe ourselves . . . with some assistance from the IHS [Indian Health Service], but making the decisions ourselves. If you'll look where we are today, we're well on our way to self-sufficiency. Many people talk about self-sufficiency, self-reliance and self-determination in a rhetorical sense, but to translate that into reality is a very difficult task that I think the Cherokee Nation is doing fairly well.

"I think I can say without the tiniest bit of false pride that we are one of the most progressive tribes in the U.S. today."

We have an excellent group of elected officials, a very diverse group of people from various areas throughout the Cherokee Nation, from various backgrounds. We have some very serious challenges ahead of us. I will talk very briefly about one related to the constitution. Because the rest of the United States is talking about the U.S. Constitution, I'm going to talk about the Cherokee constitution.

In this election of 1987, the Cherokee voters overwhelmingly passed an amendment to our Constitution which would allow the council members to be elected by districts. One of the major tasks of this newly elected tribal council, the legislative body of the tribe, is to develop a plan for districting. That is a monumental undertaking. The voters have said "we want districting," but the details have to be worked out during the next four years.

I also think there's a need for a constitutional convention. In fact, our constitution requires us to have one within the next fifteen years. The reason we review our constitution is the same reason the U.S. government reviews its Constitution—it should reflect the collective values of the Cherokee people. As time changes our values and needs, the constitution needs a new look and some amendments. This amendment we just passed is the first to our constitution, but I certainly don't think it's the last. The Cherokee constitution, as you heard in our oaths, basically provides a legal infrastructure for our government. That's our Bible, everything we do follows that so that's one of the very important challenges we have to undertake in the next four years. It's principally the task of the tribal council.

Another important task we face is that of protecting tribal rights. By tribal rights, I mean the protection of those rights that are afforded us because we are tribal government. This is something that I, the deputy chief, and the tribal council are going to have to spend a great deal of time on. There are powerful anti-Indian lobbyists who are constantly trying to diminish tribal rights, and I think that what we have to do is constantly protect our tribal rights. Many of the services and programs we enjoy today are a direct result of the special government-to-government relationship with the U.S. government that has to be protected.

I also believe that we need to concentrate on the stimulation and development of the economy in this area. As I've told many of you before, we can't do economic development in a vacuum. We don't have the resources to do that by ourselves. We have to work in a team effort with the Oklahoma Chamber of Commerce, state government, local bankers, and the business community to develop the economy of this area. Oklahoma in general is suffering from a depressed economy. I believe the Cherokees are suffering even more. Our people are very hardworking. That's a well known fact. You can look at Cherokee Gardens, Cherokee Nation Industries, many of the industries in Arkansas that recruit and bus Cherokees across the border into Arkansas because they are good workers. We have hardworking people, but many of them don't have a place to work. One of our priorities is searching for ways to develop the economy of this area. That's critical.

We also must continue to move our health care system outward. When we proposed this eight or nine years ago, it seemed like a radical idea. At that time we didn't have rural health clinics and we were only developing a tribal-specific health plan and talking about moving services closer to the people. Today that's a reality. We have many clinics in outlying areas and are looking at developing more. We should look very closely at our whole health care system and begin to place more emphasis on prevention and education.

With all of the progressive work we do in economic development, protection of tribal rights and in running a very complex organization, we must not forget who we are. We must pay attention to the protection and preservation of tribal culture. There are many definitions of tribal culture but we must sit down and define for ourselves those things we consider important to protect for future generations. In the past, promotion of tribal culture has been viewed as a function of the community and family, not of tribal government. But we've reached a point where we need to assume a leadership role. We need to explore what we as a government can do to promote and protect our culture.

I don't think that anybody, anywhere can talk about the future of their people or of an organization without talking about education. Whoever controls the education of our children controls our future, the future of the Cherokee people and of the Cherokee Nation. There are many new programs I'm going to propose and I'm sure the council will propose regarding education. We're doing a lot of innovative things in education but there's more we can do. We have always placed a great deal of importance on education and that has helped us as a people. We must continue to do that.

In our education programs, I would like to incorporate education about tribal government and tribal history. If we know where we've been as a people, our history, our culture and our ancestry we have a better sense of where we are today, and certainly, a better sense of where we're going.

I've talked about some of the battles we face in terms of education, economic development. It is easy to talk about these problems but it takes the teamwork of many people to address them.

Finally, while there are a lot of external threats to the Cherokee Nation, the really great threat is one that is internal.

As any young organization and as officials elected to tribal government, we must develop an environment where dissent and disagreement can be handled in a respectful way. Dissent is natural and good. Out of respectful dissent and disagreement comes change that is usually positive. As tribal officials we can set an example how to disagree in a respectful and good way. We all have many goals for our tribe that will require myself, the deputy chief, the tribal council, the tribal citizens and tribal employees working together to reach.

We certainly can't do it if we focus on our disagreements. If we begin to focus on the things that we agree, we can forge ahead. We come from different backgrounds and certainly we're going to disagree. We must figure a way to balance that and the things we can work. The darkest pages in Cherokee history, the greatest tragedies that occurred to us as a people came when we were divided internally.

People say I'm a positive person, that I focus on positive things. I do. We've done a lot. I'm very proud of the Cherokee Nation, I'm very proud of the many people in our communities, I'm very proud of our history, I'm proud to be Cherokee. But that doesn't mean I don't know there are a lot of serious problems in our organization, that there are a lot of serious problems we still face in the communities and that I don't realize how much work remains to be done. As we continue to work on these problems, we need to be aware that the things we do will have a profound effect on the future of the Cherokee Nation, its government and the Cherokee people.

We take our responsibility extremely seriously. We work very hard and we welcome your input. As I said, we didn't acquire instant wisdom by being elected but we do take our jobs seriously and I think you'll see that over the next four years.

This is a very exciting time for me, for all these people. I hope that in the next four years we return in a very real sense to the golden era of the Cherokee Nation where we have economic prosperity, where we begin to do some really innovative things in education, where we do more in the health care field and continue the revitalization of our communities.

With that, I ask for your continued support throughout the next four years. You have certainly been supportive during this time, during the election and during the eighteen months I served as principal chief prior to the election. I thank all of those who helped me. I wouldn't want to start thanking everyone from my kindergarten teacher on up, but I would like to thank my husband. Without his support, I could not have run for office, nor could I continue in this position. I won't ask him to stand up but I would like to thank my husband, Charlie Soap, for all his help and all his work. I, too, would like to recognize the family of Clarence Sunday, because Clarence Sunday helped me an awful lot, not only in the campaign but by talking through a lot of issues.

So with that, again, I'd like to thank you for your attention, hope you'll stay very involved in the Cherokee Nation and continue to give us your ideas, your support and your prayers.

Thank you very much.

Since taking office, Mankiller has remained true to her promise to stress economic development and various social welfare programs, especially those having to do with education, housing, and health care. She has also taken steps to bolster the self-esteem of her people and help them make the transition from the old ways to the new while preserving what is best about their culture and value system. At the same time, Mankiller is working to overcome white society's stereotypes about Indians.

Her efforts have been rewarded with widespread recognition and acclaim, including being named to the National Women's Hall of Fame in 1993. The typically modest Mankiller downplays her accomplishments, however, preferring to share the glory with those she believes are most responsible—namely, the employees, tribal council, and citizens of the Cherokee Nation. As she once declared,

"It's up to all of us, every tribal member, to take part in making sure that we survive into the twenty-first century as a culturally distinct group of people. Every Cherokee, whether full-blood or mixed-blood, whether rich or poor, whether liberal or conservative, has a responsibility to honor our ancestors by helping to keep our government, our communities, and our people very strong."

Perhaps the most personally gratifying aspect of Mankiller's success is that she has seen the opposition to her as a female chief gradually fade over time until it has become a non-issue. "People are used to me," she once remarked. "I don't get treated differently than anybody else. If I do a good job, people are happy; if I do something they don't like, they let me know they are unhappy." In 1991, their confidence in her ability to govern was made clear when they re-elected her as principal chief of the Cherokee Nation with over eighty percent of the vote.

In April 1994, noting that "my season here is coming to an end," Mankiller announced that she would not seek re-election to a third term, confident that she had paved the way for other women to follow in her footsteps. She also felt that, despite the "daunting" problems still facing the Cherokee people, she had indeed made some progress. "When I was younger, I was full of anger," she told an NEA Today *interviewer. "But you can't dwell on problems if you want to bring change, you must be motivated by hope, by the feeling you can make a difference." In her final "State of the Nation" address, delivered in Tahlequah on September 3, 1994, Mankiller reflected on the accomplishments of her administration and expressed gratitude for the support many had offered her. The Cherokee Nation provided a copy of her remarks.*

I would like to thank John Ketcher [and] the tribal council for joining us here today as they do every year. I can't tell you enough of the things about John Ketcher. He is a gentleman. He's unfailingly diplomatic and polite and good to people. If you've ever heard me talk about people—Cherokee people—having a good life, John Ketcher is a personification of that, [and] I wanted to publicly thank him for his work. Also, this council and every council I've had to work with in the last three terms have been superb. We don't always agree, but we feel that our disagreements are conflicts of ideas rather than personal kinds of dislikes among and between one another. Every single person who runs for public office or the tribal council gives a lot of their own time, and they always act [in] what they perceive to be the best interest of the Cherokee Nation, so I also wanted to formally thank them. And I also wanted to ask your prayers for Mige Glory, who's in the hospital very seriously ill. Mige has been a very active member of the tribal council.

As it has been for the past twelve years, it's an honor and a privilege to give a report on the state of the Cherokee Nation. Before coming home, when I lived in California, my family was a product of a relocation program. I once saw a photo of people giving addresses right here in this very same place under these same trees on the state of the Nation and talking to Cherokee people about issues that were very important to them. It never occurred to me when looking at that photo that I would someday be able to stand here and report to you on the state of the Nation.

What I remember [about] the very first time I came up here in 1983 as deputy chief was after the program was over, I asked Ross Swimmer (who was the chief then) if he had any comment on my very brief comments. And the only comment he had was that someone in the audience complained that I wore cowboy boots. When I ran for election in 1983, 1987, and 1991, I never promised anybody I'd be a fashion plate. I promised you that I would work very hard to try to revitalize the Cherokee Nation, and I've done what I could to do that.

Usually my remarks here are very brief. I'm going to take a little more time to touch on a few more things that I usually do here just because I want you to understand the broad spectrum of work that we do. Let me just briefly remind you that the current period of revitalization of the Cherokee Nation just began a little more than twenty years ago right here in Tahlequah. It's interesting because [since] we've done so much in such a short period of time people assumed that this effort has been going on for much longer that it has. But it really was in just 1971 that we began this process all over again . . . as we've done time and time again throughout history. When we opened the Cherokee Nation again—the great Cherokee Nation again—in 1971, we opened it in a store front, with no marketable resources or much other kind of leg up. . . . So in that relatively short period of time, we've managed to do some very aggressive redevelopment. During this twenty years there's no way that we can undo over a century of injustice and dishonor to the Cherokees, but during that period of time, I think all of us—my predecessors and I—have done what we could.

The 1970s, if you recall, was a decade of organization, and there was a time when . . . the people ratified a new constitution, the first tribal elections since statehood were held, and we literally began to put together a kind of an administrative filter and enabling center—something I'm very proud of.

Most people are surprised [with] my active background how much emphasis that I put on having what I call an "enabling center" that has a solid accounting system, a solid purchasing system, a solid personnel system, and all those support services. I call it an "enabling center" because I think without that central instrument core, the people who want to go out and provide services are unable to do that.

I'm always proud to report every single year for the past nine years that our accounting department has received nine consecutive certificates of achievement for financial excellence, one of the few tribes that receives that. There are lots of people who help me and work with me that you never see that really keep the central core of the Cherokee Nation support services flowing—Dwayne Couch, T.J. Stand, Juanita Riles, George Bearpaw. People like Becky Mitchell, George Long, Allen Harder, [and] many others that are there working in this enabling center so that we can all do our work.

In the 1970s, we all saw the beginning of many new programs for the Cherokee Nation. I had the privilege of joining the Cherokee Nation as a staff person in 1977 at a point when program development was just beginning to accelerate. I got to personally write the first WIC program grant, the first elderly program grant, the first Indian child welfare grant, the first grant for the youth help shelter, and be involved in the building of the foundation for many of the programs we have today.

The 1980s and the 1990s were periods of phenomenal growth and very rapid development. The membership has grown [since] 1980 from around 56,000 to today over 150,000. Our employment has grown from around 500 to just under 1,300 (and that's just for the Cherokee Nation) and over 700 more in tribal businesses owned and operated by the Cherokee Nation. [As for] the employment [statistics], eighty-five percent of the Cherokee Nation employees are Cherokee, thirteen percent are other tribes, and two percent are non-Indian. In the full spectrum of employees [are] the lawyers, the accountants, computer software specialist, social workers, paramedics, and many other people who help make the Cherokee Nation work.

> *"I promised you that I would work very hard to try to revitalize the Cherokee Nation, and I've done what I could to do that."*

In the past decade, I think we've had a tremendous impact on the economy of our area. We have through the Community Development Department built many miles of basic infrastructure, like water systems and housing. We work with the BIA on the construction of roads.

We have an annual payroll of more that $22 million, which has an enormous impact on this area. We also purchase many millions of dollars worth of goods and services in this area, which also has an impact on the economy.

We've created a countless number of jobs in construction and many support services, manufacturing, and other areas. We've trained and placed hundreds of Cherokee people during the past decade.

We've helped develop businesses ranging from an individually-owned masonry business to . . . a furniture manufacturing company called the Cherokee Nation Industry. Cherokee Nation Industry has spawned Cherokee Nation Distributing and, most importantly, has provided an incredible downtrend in the kind of business that we do at Cherokee Nation Industries, including wire and cable harness work under the able leadership of Ross Swimmer, our former chief. The gift shop, taxation revenue, the Arkansas Riverbed leases and the Outpost revenue exceed two million dollars a year.

We [also] have a small project here which I'm very proud of. In the totality of the things we do with an $86 million budget, this is a relatively small program, but it's a program that helps around ten people every year for welfare to get into self-employment. That program is simply called the EARN program—one of the single most rewarding programs that we have. The participants in that program which are starting individually-owned businesses are responsible for organizing and putting on the parade today, and I commend them for a job well done.

In [the] area of governmental services, this has been an area—particularly in the last five years—where we've had a very aggressive period of development. We've had to redevelop from scratch basic governmental services like law enforcement [and] the tribal tax commission, re-establish a court system. We've put together a very sophisticated computerized land system to help us identify where our lands are and the status of the land.

I can rattle off all these things like the tax commission and the court system and the law enforcement system and other areas of the government. But each and every one requires an awful lot of development for us to make that happen. [In] law enforcement, I'm particularly proud of the job that Pat Ragsdale has done in having our marshals move into our community precincts. . . . In fact, we've provided training for other law enforcement agencies on [the] effective enforcement of laws against domestic violence and crimes against children. I'm very proud of that professional group of people.

Speaking of children, in the last eight years, we've had a tremendous amount of growth in the area of services to children and youth. In 1988, I appointed a Cherokee Children Commission headed by Gwen Grayson. [A] thirteen-member task force studied the state of Cherokee children and recommended initiative for change. Since 1988, we've developed a unique children's village on the Sequoyah High School campus which brings the tribe child development center, teen pregnancy prevention program, Head Start, day care, and adult literacy program together. The combination of these programs allows us to go out and provide services on a holistic basis. The children's village was featured in a national early childhood magazine as a showcase site.

When we began the Indian Child Welfare Program in the late seventies, it was an extremely modest program. I think there was one staff person there, and we added another one. Now we have a full staff of social workers and child advocates working to see that the rights and needs of children are met. So, as you know, we now license our own foster care centers and have placed more than 150 Cherokee children in Cherokee homes since 1992. Last year we began providing adoption services and have now placed over 100 children with new families. We built a youth shelter, a youth treatment center, we offer a youth fitness camp, and we are still in the process of developing a juvenile justice system. We have a tribal youth council, a child care subsidy program, and a summer gifted and talented program, just to name a few new programs we have for children and youth. This past summer, we were able to provide summer employment to over 550 young people. This year we will be able to provide weekend and after-school employment to a number of youth.

In education we have placed a lot of emphasis on Cherokee language retention. The staff, led by longtime Cherokee Nation employee Victor Lance, developed the Cherokee language work book called *See, Say, Write*. In addition, Sandy Long, Durbin Feeling, and others are working on the development of a Cherokee language curriculum for first-graders in public schools. In addition, the Cherokee Nation has offered Cherokee language classes at community schools throughout the Cherokee Nation, including Stilwell, Kansas, and Fort Gibson. We also provide specialized instructors who teach the reading and writing of Cherokee. The Cherokee syllabary invented by Sequoyah remains the only written native language created independently by an Indian tribe.

The Johnson O'Malley program, which is an in-school support program, has grown from 25 sites with 3,000 students to 75 sites serving over 16,000 students. The Head Start program has grown from 256 students in 5 states to 11 centers serving more than 680 children. [As for Sequoyah school, every year] the enrollment was declining, and it was on the verge of closing. . . . [They were also] operating with a very severe budget problem. In 1984 . . . student enrollment was less than 125, so in 1985 we contracted the program. The beginning enrollment this year for Sequoyah school was 320 students. Ten years ago the student body for Sequoyah school was primarily from outside the Cherokee Nation. Today sixty-five percent of the students come from the fourteen-county area of the Cherokee Nation.

In 1988 we applied for and received accreditation [for Sequoyah] from the North Central Accreditation Association, and recently we were successful in convincing Congress to help us to provide two million dollars for a new series of construction projects at Sequoyah. We also—through a series of efforts by the tribal council and private fund raising—have now completed plans to build an ecumenical, non-denominational chapel at Sequoyah which will be built in late 1994 or early 1995. By the end of this year, we will build a new thirteen-million-dollar state-of-the-art vocational education facility (Talking Leaves Job Corps) here in Tahlequah. To help us with this expanded effort, we have acquired a new Job Corps center director. We also just received word yesterday [that] Sequoyah school will be a GED testing site, probably the only tribal school in the country that has that honor.

In the health department, we've had the most growth of any other department in the entire Cherokee Nation. When I came to the Cherokee Nation [in 1977] we had, I think, a CHR program [that] was the only health program that we were operating at that time. We soon added the WIC program and other programs and then began to develop a tribal-specific health plan that we're involved in today.

In 1984 we had two health clinics; we now operate five rural health centers in key locations throughout the Cherokee Nation. [When] the state hospital went bankrupt, we bought that hospital in 1991 and renovated it [as] the Sam Hider Community Clinic and four sub-offices in Delaware County. The Nowatta clinic was added in 1989 and is due for expansion soon. The Red Bird Smith Health Center in Sallisaw was dedicated in 1992, and in 1994, before the end of this year, we'll have a 37,000-square-foot health center in Stilwell which will provide a large array of services. We have purchased the land and are getting ready to build a new clinic in Salina as well.

In 1984 the Indian Health Services operated two of the four clinics for the Cherokees. Today the Cherokee Nation operates all five, all of which are rural health certified. In the area of health we have more toward self-governance. We have placed a lot more emphasis on decentralizing services—moving them closer to people rather than having them come in to receive services, and [we] have [a] mobile health care unit as well.

I've spent a quite lot of my time—in fact, one-third of all my time over the past two years—in trying to find some kind of settlement of the Arkansas Riverbed case. [I] spent many months putting together what I thought was a good settlement proposal. The settlement proposal would have allowed all the Cherokees [to] retain our mineral rights, exchange Arkansas Riverbed land that we have no access to for land that we could use in the fourteen counties, and receive a one-hundred-million-dollar settlement for the Arkansas Riverbed. If you recall, the beds and banks of the Arkansas were given to us in exchange for lands that we lost in the Southeast. The land was taken from us without compensation at the turn of the century.

One of the few times when I've been very angry is being in Washington and trying to talk with senators and congressman and members of the administration about getting some type of justice for the Cherokees. We have lost every time we've taken the Riverbed case to court because the courts keep saying the United States government can take property if it needs to be used for navigation. So they filed a principle called "navigation servitude" that allows them to take our land without compensation. So my argument to them this past year has been—in countless meetings and trips to Washington—that that's just a legal mechanism. I am talking [about] dealing with the Cherokees fairly and honorably and compensating for a resource that was taken from us.

It is interesting to sit at the Justice Department across the table from Justice lawyers and have them talk to me about why they can't do that and act like what they do is more productive. I can tell you from my own experience in working with the Justice Department it is going to be very difficult to get justice for the Cherokees, whether they are Republican or Democrat. It has been a very difficult process. Bill Keeler, my predecessor, Ross Swimmer, and I have all spent a great deal of energy trying to get this resolved. One of the few champions that we have had in the Congress has been Mike

Synar, who went out and really battled for us. But we have not had the rest of the delegation and administration on board with us. So what we've done basically [is] because we could not get this settled.... They wanted to settle but not for what I thought the Riverbed was worth. We have backed out on that now. What we are doing at this point is trying to remove the trespassers and working on other kinds of issues. I had hoped to leave as a legacy a settlement of this case so we could [give] you the proceeds to re-purchase some of that land we lost and many other things.

One of the things that I have tried to do is spend time resolving some of the longstanding issues. I remember when I first came into office in 1983, there was this problem with the Delawares, a problem with the UKB, and I thought I'd solve this. So I went off to speak with various elders and asked their advice and was told that this would not be taken care of quickly [because] there are a lot of complex issues that have to be resolved beforehand. I am sorry to say that I have not been able to resolve those issues, but I have given it my best effort.

We have aggressively decentralized services in the last ten years. Ten years ago we had five offices, and today we have twelve field offices throughout the Cherokee Nation and will soon add another in Claremore.

So that's kind of a summary of where we are at this particular point with regards to the Cherokee Nation. And I think I can safely say that the Cherokee Nation is good. At the end of this year we will complete twenty million dollars of construction, and I always think that new construction is a good sign of economic progress.

[As for] the other programs that I will be working on, we're going to have an environmental summit. There is a crisis [that] is not the most exciting thing to work on, but in government we work on these things, which is solid waste management. Frank Ferrell, Fran Robison, and others have been working on it this year for quite sometime. So the Community Development Department, along with the Cherokee Nation, will host an environmental summit to talk about the solid waste problem in Oklahoma, hopefully this fall or early spring.

We also are beginning plans to open centers to take care of the frail elderly [and] to help them stay in their homes.... We have a planning grant to work on that.

I've talked to a lot of people here that have asked me an interesting question, which is, "What are we going to do about new leadership? What if we get someone in who's not going to carry on programs and lead us well?" I thought that was an interesting question because that's not up to me—that's up to you to make sure that we do. You have control of that. It's not just an idea or thing floating out there that we might not end up with responsible leadership. You have control over that in your hands—you educate yourself about people, and you vote.

When people come up to me and say, "I am real glad for what you've done, I've always wanted to work with Cherokee people," then I say, "Why haven't you?" That's a good question for someone who just pops up out of nowhere and decides they want to lead the Cherokee Nation. Most people who have gotten in and managed to fight—those are the kind of people we need to look for when we are looking for new leadership for the Cherokee Nation. Positive people, people that are willing to work.

I guess I just wanted to thank all of you for your support, friendship, and for electing me for three terms. I'll be here for a while longer, until next June. When the new election occurs, I am sure I will see many of you again and again. So I won't say good-bye, but in my final state of the Nation [I'd like to tell] you all how much I appreciate all of you staying with me. That's what I always liked—even if you didn't agree with me, you stayed.... I have never overestimated my importance to the Cherokee Nation and Cherokee history. I don't think I leave any great legacy. I hope when I leave you will remember that I did what I said.

SOURCES

Books

Blanche, Jerry D., editor, *Native American Reader: Stories, Speeches and Poems*, Denali Press, 1990.

Malinowski, Sharon, ed., *Notable Native Americans*, Gale Research, Detroit, 1995.

Mankiller, Wilma, and Michael Wallis, *Mankiller: A Chief and Her People*, St. Martin's, 1993.

Periodicals

Grand Rapids Press, "Outgoing Cherokee Chief Likes Nation's Direction," October 21, 1994, p. A9.

Ms., "Wilma Mankiller: Harnessing Traditional Cherokee Wisdom," August, 1986, p. 32; January, 1988, pp. 68-69.

NEA Today, "Wilma Mankiller: Destined to Lead," October, 1994, p. 7.

News from Indian Country, "The Very Human Side of Cherokee Nation Chief Wilma Mankiller," January 31, 1994.

Parade, "She Leads a Nation," August 18, 1991, pp. 4-5.

People, "Activist Wilma Mankiller Is Set to Become the First Female Chief of the Cherokee Nation," December, 1985, pp. 91-92.

Southern Living, "Chief of the Cherokee," November, 1986, p. 190.

Time, "To Each Her Own: Combining Talent and Drive, Ten Tough-Minded Women Create Individual Rules for Success," fall, 1990 (special issue); April 18, 1994, p. 27.

U.S. News and World Report, "'People Expect Me to Be More Warlike,' " February 17, 1986, p. 64.

Thurgood Marshall

1908–1993

African American justice of the U.S. Supreme Court and civil rights activist

Known as "Mr. Civil Rights" for his lifelong commitment to overturning the laws that for so many years sanctioned racial discrimination in the United States, Thurgood Marshall achieved prominence not only as a leading civil rights attorney but also as the nation's first black Supreme Court justice. His name will forever be associated with what ranks as perhaps the NAACP's greatest legal victory—the 1954 ruling in Brown v. Board of Education, *which saw the nation's highest court strike down public school segregation. Thirteen years later, Marshall himself became a member of the very group before which he had argued his landmark case. As the Supreme Court's only black and one of its most liberal justices, he worked for nearly twenty-five years to preserve and defend hard-won civil rights gains in all areas of American life.*

Marshall was born and raised in Baltimore, except for a five-year period during his infancy and early childhood when he lived in Harlem. A good student known for his fun-loving ways and rebellious spirit, he graduated with honors from Lincoln University in 1929. He then tried to enroll in the University of Maryland Law School, but was turned down on account of his race. Marshall attended Howard University Law School instead, graduating (once again with honors) in 1933 and going into private practice with a specialty in civil rights and criminal law. (One of his early cases pitted him against the University of Maryland Law School on behalf of a black man who had been denied admittance for racial reasons; Marshall won, and the school was forced to enroll its first black student.) Around the same time, he also began handling some legal work for the local chapter of the National Association for the Advancement of Colored People (NAACP). In 1936, this led to an invitation to become the assistant to the organization's chief counsel at national headquarters in New York City. Two years later, Marshall himself was named chief counsel, and in 1940, he was named head of the newly-created NAACP Legal Defense and Educational Fund.

Under his leadership, the NAACP devised a strategy to defeat racial discrimination through the courts by proving that scores of restrictive laws then in place (especially in the South) were unconstitutional. Working on a case-by-case basis, he and his staff challenged the unjust treatment experienced by African

Americans who tried to vote, make full use of public transportation and public facilities, rent or buy real estate, or serve on a jury or in the armed forces. Marshall personally argued thirty-two cases before the Supreme Court and won twenty-nine of them.

By far the most famous of the cases he took before the Supreme Court was Brown v. Board of Education, *the collective title of a group of lawsuits that all challenged the practice of segregating public school students by race. Supporters of "separate-but-equal" facilities insisted that the Supreme Court's decision in the* Plessy v. Ferguson *case of 1896 upheld the right of states to allow segregation in the schools. (In* Plessy v. Ferguson, *the Supreme Court had ruled that the Fourteenth Amendment to the Constitution guaranteed political but not social equality and that the state of Louisiana thus had the power to segregate railroad cars.) On the other hand, Marshall maintained that the "separate-but-equal" doctrine was unconstitutional because "separate educational facilities are inherently unequal."*

On May 17, 1954, the Supreme Court ruled unanimously that the segregation of black and white students in the public schools was indeed unconstitutional. Earlier that spring, when it appeared that victory might be near, an upbeat Marshall addressed an audience at Dillard University in New Orleans on the great strides that had been made toward achieving integration in the United States and what still remained to be done. An excerpt of his lecture follows; it is reprinted from The Voice of Black America: Major Speeches by Negroes in the United States, 1797–1971 *(Simon & Schuster, 1972).*

... There has been much discussion during recent years concerning the question of the removal in this country of dual citizenship based solely on race and color. The primary emphasis has been on the elimination of racial segregation. No one denies that progress is being made. There are, however, some who say that the progress is too slow and others who say that the progress is too rapid. The important thing to remember is that progress is being made. We are moving ahead. We have passed the crossroads. We are moving toward a completely integrated society, North and South.

Those who doubt this and those who are afraid of complete integration are victims of a background based upon long indoctrination of only one side of the controversy in this country. They know only of one side of the controversy in this country. They know only of one side of slavery. They know only the biased reports about Reconstruction and the long-standing theory which seems to support the "legality" of the separate-but-equal doctrine.

In order to adequately appraise the situation, we must first understand the problem in relation to our history—legal and political. Secondly, we must give proper weight to progress that has been made with and without legal pressure, and thirdly, we must look to the future.

Our government is based on the principle of the equality of man the individual, not the group. All of us can quote the principle that "All men are created equal." Our basic legal document, the Constitution of the United States, guarantees equal protection of the laws to all of us. Many state constitutions have similar provisions. We even have a "Bill of Rights" in the Constitution of Louisiana. These high-sounding principles we preach and teach. However, in the eyes of the world we stand convicted of violating these principles day in and day out.

Today, 177 years after the signing of the Declaration of Independence and 86 years after the Fourteenth Amendment was adopted, we have a society where, in varying degrees throughout the country, but especially in the South, Negroes, solely because they are Negroes, are segregated, ostracized and set apart from all other Americans. This discrimination extends from the cradle to the graveyard. (And I emphasize graveyard, rather than grave.) Or, to put it even more bluntly, in many areas of this country, a white paroled murderer would be welcome in places which would at the same time exclude such people as Ralph Bunche, Marian Anderson, Jackie Robinson, and many others. Constitutionally protected individual rights have been effectively destroyed by outmoded theories of racial or group inferiority. Why is this true? How long can we afford the luxury of segregation and discrimination?

One reason this condition of dual citizenship exists is because we have been conditioned to an acceptance of this theory as a fact. We are the products of a misunderstanding of history. As a matter of fact, only in recent years have accurate studies of the pre-Civil War period and the Reconstruction period of our history been published.

Our position today is tied up with our past history—at least as far back as the 1820s. At that time the antislavery movement was beginning to take permanent form. It should be borne in mind that those people in New England, Ohio and other areas, who started this movement became dedicated to a principle which has become known as the Judeo-Christian ethic. This principle was carried forth in their determination to remove slavery from our society, and to remove the badges of caste and inferiority whereby an American could be ostracized or set apart from fellow Americans solely because of race. Of course, slavery per se was the immediate objective—the abolition of slavery—but the ultimate goal was the same as the unfinished business we have before us today, namely, to remove race and caste from the American life.

These people in the 1820 period—1820 to 1865—sought to translate their moral theories and principles into law. They started by pamphleteering and speechmaking. They recognized that equal protection of the laws must always be, in part, an ethical and moral concept, rather than a law. They sought to constitutionalize this moral argument or ideal. Slavery—with its theories of racial damnation, racial inferiority and racial discrimination—was inherently repugnant to the American creed and Christian ethics. They sought to support their moral theories by use of the Declaration of Independence and certain sections of the Constitution as it existed at that time. In so far as public meetings were concerned, speakers were barred from such meetings in the South—brutally beaten or killed, and many were run out of similar meetings in Northern cities and towns. It was, therefore, impossible to get behind the original iron curtain to get public support for much of the program.

In their legal attack they were thwarted by the decision of the United States Supreme Court in the Dred Scott case, which held that no person of African descent, slave or free, had any rights that a white man was bound to respect. The important thing to remember throughout this period is that the opponents of slavery were seeking a Constitutional basis—a legal platform—for the democratic principle of the equality of man.

After the Emancipation Proclamation was signed, many states passed Black Codes and other infamous statutes, effectively returning the emancipated slaves to their inferior status. Consequently, the same people who fought to abolish slavery had to take the lead in Congress in writing the thirteenth, fourteenth and fifteenth amendments.

This short period of intense legislation was followed by the Reconstruction period. Much of that which we have read concerning this period has emphasized, overstated and exaggerated the errors of judgment made in trying to work out the "Negro problem" in such fashion as to give real meaning to these Civil War amendments [but these amendments] were actually thwarted by the conspiracy between Northern capitalists and others to bring "harmony" by leaving the Negro and his problem to the tender mercies of the South. This brought about the separate-but-equal pattern, which spread not only throughout the South but extended and now exists in many Northern and Western areas.

Despite the distortion of this historical background, which has become firmly embedded in our minds, is the "understanding" that racial segregation is legal and valid even if in violation of our moral principles. The fallacy of this reasoning is that the equal protection of the laws was intended to be the constitutionalization of the ethic and moral principle of the absolute equality of man—the right of an individual neither to be circumscribed or conditioned by group, race or color.

It should, therefore, be remembered that our society is the victim of the following periods of history: the period of slavery, when the slaveholders defended slavery by repeating over and over again the myth that slavery was not only a positive good for the nation but was absolutely beneficial and necessary for the Negroes themselves. Consequently, even free Negroes were denied the right of citizenship and subjected to all manner of abuse without legal redress. Immediately following the Civil War, and indeed up to the 1930s, is the period when Negroes were no longer slaves but were certainly not yet full citizens. Having passed through this laissez-faire period in so far as asserting our Constitutional rights is concerned, Negroes began in the thirties the all-out fight to secure the right to vote and at the same time to break down discrimination and segregation.

In so far as securing the right to vote, beginning with the registration cases and the white-primary cases and others, much progress has been made to the end that as of the 1948 national elections, at least 1,300,000 Negroes voted in the deep South. We have seen Negroes elected to the city council in Richmond, Virginia, Nashville, Tennessee, and many cities in North Carolina. We have seen Negroes elected to the governing board of the Democratic party in Atlanta, Georgia. We have also seen Negroes elected to school boards in cities such as Atlanta, Georgia, Lynchburg, Virginia, and Winston-Salem, North Carolina. There are still, however, several small areas in Alabama, Mississippi, and at least four parishes in Louisiana where Negroes are still prevented from registering as qualified voters. (But these are distinctly local problems, which are being attended to and can be pushed aside on that basis.)

In the North we have seen the drive for protection of the right to work without regard to race and color—the drive for FEPC [Fair Employment Practices Committee] legislation. We have seen such legislation passed in at least eight states in the North, leaving forty states and the District of Columbia to go, before we have the necessary safeguards to protect man's right not to be deprived of an opportunity to earn a livelihood because of race, religion or ancestry.

Thurgood Marshall

We have also seen the breaking-down of the legal barriers to owning and occupying real property without regard to race or color. Today, as a result of several Supreme Court decisions, any American any place in the United States, regardless of race or color, may own and occupy property wherever he can find a willing seller, has the money to purchase the property and courage to live on it. We still, however, have residential segregation throughout the country, not by law, not by the courts, but by a combination of circumstances, such as, the reactionary policies of mortgage companies and real-estate boards, public-housing agencies, including FHA, and other governmental agencies. We also find an unwillingness on the part of many Negroes to exercise their rights in this field. In recent years instead of progress toward an integrated community, we find that the Negro ghetto is merely expanding into a larger and more glorified and gilded ghetto. This unwillingness to exercise our own rights is due in part to the long indoctrination that we are different from or inferior to others and therefore should voluntarily segregate ourselves.

As of the present time, the paramount issue in so far as Americanism is concerned is the ending of all racial distinctions in American life. The reasons for this are many. A weighty factor, of course, is the recognition by more and more people in high places that the world situation in regard to the sensitive areas throughout the world depends on how well we can handle our race problem in this country. Our country can no longer tolerate an Achilles heel of discriminatory practices toward its darker citizens. Even more important is the realization that the equality of man as a principle and the equal protection of the laws as a Constitutional concept are both based upon the moral principle of individual responsibility rather than racial identity.

Racial segregation in our country is immoral, costly, and damaging to the nation's prestige. Segregation and discrimination violate the Judeo-Christian ethic, and the democratic creed on which our national morality is based is soundly established in the minds of most men. But in addition, it has been shown that the costs of segregation and discrimination to the nation are staggering. Elmo Roper, social scientist and pollster of American public opinion, has stated, "The resultant total of the cost of discrimination comes to roughly $10 out of every $75 paycheck, or, in total, $30 billion lost every year." This figure alone would amount to a cost of $2,000 per year to every individual in America. But perhaps even more damaging to the nation is the current effect of America's racial practices on America's role in international affairs and world leadership. According to a recent statement by our State Department experts, nearly half of the recent Russian propaganda about America has been concentrated on race, linking Communist germ-warfare charges with alleged racial brutality in this country. In addition, Americans returning from abroad consistently report having been questioned over and over about racial problems in this country.

This concern about American racial practices seems especially strong among the two thirds of the world that is darker-skinned. Our former ambassador to India, Chester Bowles, wrote the following statement, after attending an Indian press conference: "As I later discovered is almost invariably the case in any Asian press conference or forum, the Number One question was, 'What about America's treatment of the Negro?'"

Shortly after returning from a tour of Asian and Pacific areas, Vice President Nixon made this statement:

Americans must create a better understanding of American ideals abroad by practicing and thinking tolerance and respect for human rights every day of the year. Every act of racial discrimination or prejudice in the United States hurts Americans as much as an espionage agent who turns over a weapon to a foreign enemy.

Historically, we have to ask whether or not, even as we stand today, our country can afford to continue in practicing *not* what they preach. Historically, the segregation patterns in the United States are carry-overs from the principles of slavery. They are based on the exploded theory of the inferiority of the minority group. Segregation is recognized as resulting from the decision of the majority group without even consulting, less known in seeking, the consent of the segregated group. All of us know that segregation traditionally results in unequal facilities for the segregated group. Duplication of facilities is expensive, diverts funds from the economy which could be utilized to improve facilities for all groups. Finally, segregation leads to the blockage of real communication between the two groups. In turn, this blockage increases mutual suspicion, distrust, hostility, stereotypes and prejudice; and these, all together, result in a social climate of tension favorable to aggressive behavior and social disorganization which sometimes culminate in race riots. Even where we do not have race riots, the seeds of tension are ever present in a segregated system.

> ***"Our country can no longer tolerate an Achilles heel of discriminatory practices toward its darker citizens. . . . Racial segregation in our country is immoral, costly, and damaging to the nation's prestige."***

The harm done to the individual begins with the child's earliest years, when he becomes aware of status differences among groups in society and begins to react to patterns of segregation. Prejudice and discrimination are potentially damaging to the personalities of all children.

The children of the majority group are affected differently from those of the minority group. This potential psychological damage is crystallized by segregation practices sanctioned by public law—and it is the same whether in the North, the East, the West, or the South. Damage to the immediate community is inevitable. This is followed by damage to the state, our federal government and, finally, the world today. The only answer is the complete removal of all racial distinctions that lay at the basis of all this.

And now for the future. Everyone in and out of government must understand that the future of our government and indeed the world depends on the recognition of the equality of man—the principle which is inherent in the theory of our government and protected by our Constitution.

Of course, we have made progress, but instead of gloating over this progress, we should get renewed courage to tackle the next job. Let us not listen to the rantings of politicians like governors Byrnes and Talmadge. Governor Byrnes has declared:

> *Should the Supreme Court decide this case against our position, we will face a serious problem. Of only one thing can we be certain. South Carolina will not now, nor for some years to come, mix white and colored children in our schools. . . . If the Court changes what is now the law of the land, we will, if it is possible, live within the law, preserve the public school system, and at the same time maintain segregation. If that is not possible, reluctantly we will abandon the public school system.*

That statement is made by a governor who was formerly a member of the Supreme Court which he is now talking about. Governor Herman Talmadge announces that if the decision comes down opposed to what he thinks it should be, that *he,* Governor Talmadge, will get together as much of his militia as he can find and challenge the whole United States Army.

Instead of listening to people like this, why not listen to people who speak for the South like Ralph McGill of the *Atlanta Constitution* who writes:

> *An end to segregation—when it comes—will not, of course, force people to associate socially. That will remain, as now, personal choice. But it will bring on change—and this is what state legislatures in South Carolina, Georgia, Mississippi, Virginia and Alabama are, or will be, considering. They consider not how to retain legal segregation—which they see soon ending—but how to effect it without legal compulsion. . . . Segregation is on the way out and he who tries to tell the people otherwise does them great disservice. The problem of the future is how to live with the change.*

There are still those who will continue to tell us that law is one thing and ethics another. However, I prefer to follow what one legal historian has stated—"Laws and ethics, some men bluntly tell us are separate fields. So indeed they are. But spare America the day when both together do not determine the meaning of equal protection of the laws."

We must understand the slavery background of segregation and we must understand the complete lack of any scientific support for racial superiority or inferiority. We must understand that racial segregation is violative of every religious principle, as I said before. We must never forget what racial segregation did to our parents and is doing to us, and how it will affect our children. We must turn from misunderstanding and fear to intelligent planning, courage and determination.

Psychologists acknowledge that to achieve a well-balanced, well-adjusted personality, all human beings require a sense of personal dignity and worth, acknowledged not only within themselves but by the society in which they live—the total society. Not every child reacts to personality conflict in the same way. Behavior patterns depend on such interrelated factors as family relations, social and economic class, general personality patterns and other factors. In the final analysis, however, each segregated child is forced to adjust to conflicts not faced by members of the majority group.

Studies published in the *Journal of Social Psychology* indicate that members of the lower economic class may react to racial frustrations by overaggressive behavior, hostility toward the minority group and/or the majority group, and by antisocial behavior. These reactions are self-destructive inasmuch as society not only punishes the offenders but often interprets such behavior as justification for continuing segregation practices against all members of the group. These studies further indicate that members of the middle upper class may react by withdrawal, submissive behavior or rigid conformity to the expected pattern of segregation. Psychologically, this is equally bad.

Generally, however, children of all classes react by adopting an overall defeatist attitude, a lowering of personal ambitions, hypersensitivity and anxiety about relations in a larger society, and a tendency to see hostility or rejection even where it might not exist. This may result in the development and perpetuation of generally sensitive, conflicting personalities.

Although the range of individual reaction in terms of behavior and personality patterns is very wide, there is no question that all minority children are necessarily affected adversely by enforced segregation—and there is not a single scientific study to the contrary.

While the effects of enforced segregation on majority-group children are more obscure, they are, nevertheless, real. Children who are taught prejudice, directly or indirectly, are also taught to gain and evaluate themselves on a totally unrealistic basis. Perceiving minority-group members as inferior does not permit a member of the majority group to evaluate himself in terms of actual ability or achievement but permits and encourages self-deception—that is, "I am at least better than a Negro."

A culture which permits and encourages enforced segregation motivates feelings of guilt and necessitates an adjustment to protect against recognizing the injustice of racial fears and hatreds.

The contradiction between moral, religious, democratic principles of the brotherhood of man, the importance of justice or fair play and the actuality of the prejudiced, discriminatory practices of individuals and institutions inevitably results in confusion, conflict, moral cynicism and guilt feelings in the majority group. This conflict, supported by pressure to conform to existing patterns, may result in disrespect for authority, unwholesomeness of ideals of all authorities (parents, political leaders) and a determination to run roughshod over everyone not in the conforming group. Some persons may attempt to resolve this conflict by intensifying hostility toward the minority group or to express self-hatred in aggressive behavior.

Of the large number of social scientists who replied to a questionnaire concerning the probable effect of enforced segregation under conditions of equal facilities, ninety percent replied that, regardless of the equality of the facilities provided, enforced segregation is psychologically harmful to the *minority*-group members; eighty percent stated it was their opinion that enforced segregation would have damaging effects also on the majority-group members. (M. Deutscher and I. Chein, "The Psychological Effects of Enforced Segregation: A Survey of Social Science Opinion," *Journal of Psychology,* 1948, Volume 26, pp. 259-87.)

Enforced segregation appears to have the same general and psychological effect regardless of the quality of facilities available. (That is to answer any of you who believe that the building of a new Jim Crow high school will solve the problem.)

Enforced-segregation public schools offer official recognition, sanction and perpetuation to the assumption of inferiority, a myth which has already been exploded.

The results of an effort to get a full picture

> ***"Enforced-segregation public schools offer official recognition, sanction and perpetuation to the assumption of inferiority. . . ."***

of desegregation in American communities are now available. And it is hoped that these results can be passed on to every American and to our friends and critics overseas. For these results clearly show that in the past ten years, America has undergone a startling, dramatic and completely unprecedented change in race relations—and all for the better. Racial desegregation has been attempted successfully in literally hundreds of instances, in all regions, and in all walks of life. In addition to the more noticeable areas of schools and the armed forces, complete success has been reported in desegregating public-housing projects, labor unions, Catholic and Protestant churches, public and private swimming pools, professional organizations, some YMCAs and many YWCAs, Southern industries, notably the Southern plants of International Harvester Company, officers' and enlisted men's clubs and housing areas on Army posts, hospitals, summer camps, and many other areas—even cemeteries.

An impressive part of these great changes is the way that the "unthinkables" of ten years ago have become the "taken-for-granteds" of today. Ten years back, it was unthinkable that Negroes would participate in the white professional baseball leagues. Today, Negroes are on the teams in Dallas, Texas, Atlanta, Georgia, Savannah, Georgia, and other areas. During World War II, it was unthinkable that Negro and white children would ever attend the same schools on Southern Army posts. As of 1953, the last federally operated Army school on a Southern military post was desegregated; and a recent announcement from the office of the Secretary of Defense states that segregation will be abolished in all schools of every Southern military post by September, 1955, in all states, including Mississippi. Before the war, Negroes traveling by train in Southern regions had great difficulty in getting Pullman berths, and risked embarrassment every time they sought to use the dining car. Since that time, legal action and voluntary adjustments made by some railroads have resulted in a shifting pattern in dining cars in the South—from complete exclusion, to being put behind a curtain, to seating at separate tables without a curtain, and, finally to a completely integrated seating pattern. Interstate travel patterns have been liberalized on railroads, buses and planes, but this has just barely dented the surface. Southern airports are not progressive.

One of the most impressive signs of change may be seen in the area of schools. In 1943, as far as is known, no Negroes were attending Southern white institutions of higher learning. But today, the Sweatt and McLaurin cases have opened the doors of previously all-white graduate schools in every Southern state except five—Mississippi, Alabama, Georgia, Florida, and South Carolina. It is now estimated that around two thousand Negroes are now attending Southern white institutions of higher learning. As of September, 1953, Negroes were attending the graduate or professional schools of twenty-three Southern white state-supported institutions, attending the undergraduate levels of ten Southern white state and municipal schools, and attending forty-two Southern white private schools. And, according to the *Journal of Negro Education,* "what is more important, there has not been reported a single untoward incident of any kind as a result of this change."

Private institutions of higher learning have admitted Negro students in eight Southern states, and, in one school, there are now two hundred fifty-one Negro students and five Negro teachers. Several Southern Negro colleges have admitted white students, and in Northern areas there are now over one hundred professors and instructors teaching in predominantly white schools.

Some specific incidents stand out. School authorities in Louisville, Kentucky, closed its Negro Municipal College, admitted Negro students to the white college, and hired one Negro teacher. In that same city, a young female Negro doctor is now teaching pediatrics in the previously all-white medical school. In St. Louis, Missouri, Washington, D.C., and Wilmington, Delaware, the Catholic parochial schools have admitted Negro students. In Tennessee, all but one member of a white theological seminary turned in their resignations to the president when the Board of Trustees refused to admit a Negro student. The Town Council of Oak Ridge, Tennessee, has asked the Atomic Energy Commission to end segregation in the public school system. The Council passed a resolution to that effect by a 4-2 vote, and sent a copy of it to President Eisenhower.

In elementary and secondary schools outside the South, successful desegregation has been effected in fifty-nine separate communities in such states as Arizona (two communities), California (one), Delaware (three), Illinois (twelve), Kansas (three), Indiana (four), Maryland (one), New Jersey (sixteen), New Mexico (two), New York (three), Ohio (seven), and Pennsylvania (five)—fifty-nine known instances in the past four years of the breaking-down of segregation. Researchers suspect that there are many other instances of desegregation.

A special and informative example of successful school desegregation is found in the state of New Jersey. In 1947, the people of New Jersey adopted a new constitution, containing a provision that no person in the state shall be segregated in the public schools "because of religious scruples, race, color, ancestry or national origin." One year later a survey revealed that there were fifty-three New Jersey school districts containing one or more all-Negro schools, and that in forty-three of these, the all-Negro facilities were the result of deliberate segregation rather than geographical factors.

As a result of efforts by the state Commissioner of Education, it was announced in late August, 1948, that thirty of these forty-three school districts would open school in September on a completely integrated basis. Of the remaining thirteen, eight had taken partial steps, aiming for integration by September, 1949. In the other five districts, the situation remained unsettled. As of September, 1951, forty of the forty-three districts had undertaken complete elimination of the racially separated schools. Racial segregation still remained in the other three schools, though "progress was being made."

An especially interesting aspect of New Jersey school desegregation was what happened to the Negro teachers. In many circles, great fears have been expressed that Negro teachers will lose their jobs if the schools are desegregated. New Jersey offers an interesting testing ground for this fear. In 1945, New Jersey had 479 Negro teachers, and 415 of them were employed in the nine counties that maintained separate schools. A recent study of this situation shows that in these nine formerly segregated counties, there are 425 Negro teachers, and in the whole state, a total of 645 Negro teachers, a statewide gain of 166 Negro teachers. One community reported to have desegregated its Negro school, placed one Negro teacher in the high school and placed the Negro principal in charge of five white teachers.

Perhaps the most noticeable and the most complete example of desegregation involving millions of persons is found in the armed forces. At the beginning of World War II, the Army policy was one of almost complete segregation of Negro troops, the Air Force was just beginning an "experiment" in the training of Negro flyers in the face of a widespread belief that Negroes could not be taught to fly airplanes, the Navy confined Negroes almost exclusively to the Messmen's Branch, and the Marines excluded Negroes entirely. But soon cracks began to appear in the wall. The Army's Officers Candidate School and a few other service schools became integrated; the Air Forces regarded its experiment with a Negro pursuit squadron as a success and expanded it to a fighter group; the Navy in 1942 allowed Negroes to enlist in branches other than the messmen's service (although they were still segregated and barred from seagoing vessels); and, in 1942, the Marine Corps admitted its first Negroes, in strictly segregated units, as laborers, anti-aircraft gunners and ammunition handlers.

Subsequently, the pressures for integration increased. The armed forces found that they had serious morale problems in some of the segregated Negro units. They also found that the picture of a segregated American Army of Occupation, attempting to teach democracy to the people of Germany and Japan, was a ridiculous experiment. So, in a series of careful and unpublicized moves, the armed forces began a gradual program of racial desegregation. In 1953, the Secretary of the Army reported that at least ninety percent of the Negroes in the Army were serving in nonsegregated units (the number continues to increase), and added: "The Army policy is one of complete integration, and it is to be accomplished as soon as possible."

In the European Army Command, a battalion commander from the deep South is quoted as saying: "We got the order. We got detailed instructions for carrying it out and a time limit to do it in. And that was it."

And in our armed forces all over the globe, Negro servicemen were brought into previously all-white units rapidly and with no trouble by officers who gave white servicemen such terse instructions as these: "Some Negro men are joining our unit. These men are soldiers. Treat them as such."

This is the problem that everybody says is such a "horrible" thing to face up to.

What is the picture today? According to Lee Nichols' exciting new book *Breakthrough on the Color Front,* the Army reports that less than 10,000 Negroes are still serving in all-Negro units out of some 200,000 Negroes in the Army. Assistant Defense Secretary John A. Hannah estimates that by June, 1954, there will be no remaining segregated Army units. The Air Force, which had moved more rapidly, stated that Negro servicemen who were in the Air Force in August, 1953, had been integrated into all of its units throughout the world. Of the 23,000 Negroes serving in the Navy in 1953, about half were still in the Messmen's or Steward's Branch. The rest were integrated and scattered through nearly every job classification that the Navy has. The Marine Corps, last of all the services to take Negroes, reports that its last two all-Negro units were integrated "some time" before the summer of 1952.

Today, Negro and white draftees from the most poverty-stricken parts of the deep South, as well as the rest of the nation, are inducted into a completely integrated command, and the typical report from commanders who had previously held fears was that "the frictions and antagonisms that lay behind previous race conflicts have been substantially reduced, and that so far there has not been a single major incident traceable to integration."

What about segregation in the nation's capital? Many Americans have expressed disgust, and foreign visitors have stated their amazement, at the fact that public and private facilities in the capital of our democracy were almost completely segregated—restaurants, schools, housing projects, theaters, and so forth. Though there is still much to be done in Washington, there have been several recent examples of progress. On June 3, 1953, the National Capital Housing Authority announced the adoption of a policy of opening all present and future public low-rent housing properties in the District of Columbia to low-income families, without regard to race. Around that same time, the Supreme Court handed down a decision preventing discrimination in Washington restaurants. All the restaurants have abided by the decision, and no incident of any kind has been reported. Hotel accommodations now are available to Negroes in most of the larger hotels, although the policy of many smaller hotels is still uncertain. Negroes are now admitted to the three legitimate theaters of Washington, and to at least four—and probably more—of the downtown movie theaters. The majority of the city's private schools have opened their doors to Negroes, and the Catholic parochial schools have also become integrated. A recent bulletin reports that the nation's capital has even agreed to desegregate the jails. Washington is slowly moving toward a position where it can command the respect of the world where race relations are involved.

Why have people decided to desegregate? Members of American communities have tried to integrate their institutions for an extremely varied number of reasons. The pressures to desegregate have come from several forces—sometimes from an aroused Negro community, sometimes from administrative rulings of local authorities, sometimes from rulings by a national body, sometimes from voluntary decision by a majority of concerned community members. It now appears that the success or failure of the desegregation effort is not related to the reason for desegregating, since the reasons are so varied.

The success of racial desegregation has been shown to be related not so much to the type of community that is involved or the prejudice of its members as to the close adherence to a set of specific principles. We have reached the stage where scientists, sociologists and others, have agreed upon rules which when followed bring about smooth desegregation whether in Illinois or Louisiana. The main point is that once the state law preventing intergroup communication in institutional life is removed, it is then up to the local community to work out its own salvation, with the understanding that it must be done within the American framework.

The accomplishment of effective and efficient desegregation with a minimum of social disturbance depends on the following five things:

1. There must be a clear and unequivocal statement of policy by leaders with prestige, and by authority officials.

2. There must be firm enforcement and persistent execution of the nonsegregation policy in the face of initial resistance.

3. Authorities and law enforcement officials must show a willingness to deal with violations, attempted violations or incitement to violations, by applying the law and backing it up with strong enforcement action.

4. Authorities must refuse to employ, engage in or tolerate subterfuges, gerrymandering or other devices for evading the principle and the fact of desegregation.

5. The accomplishment of desegregation must be accompanied by continual interpretation of the reasons for the action, and appealing to the democratic and moral values of all persons involved.

In conclusion, racial segregation is grounded upon the myth of inherent racial superiority. This myth has been completely exploded by all scientific studies. It now stands exposed as a theory which can only be explained as a vehicle for perpetuating racial prejudice. History reveals that racial segregation is a badge of slavery, is just as unscientifically supported, immoral and un-American as slavery. Recent history shows that it can be removed, and that it can be done effectively when approached intelligently.

There is no longer any justification for segregation. There is no longer any excuse for it. There is no longer any reason under the sun why intelligent people should continue to find excuses for not ending segregation in their own community, in the South as well as in the North.

Marshall's career took a different turn in 1961, when President John F. Kennedy nominated him to a federal judgeship on the U.S. Court of Appeals. Despite fierce opposition from Southern segregationists who stalled the process for nearly a year, he was at last confirmed. In 1965, President Lyndon Johnson named him

solicitor general, a position in which he argued cases before the Supreme Court on behalf of the government. Two years later, declaring it was "the right thing to do, the right time to do it, the right man, and the right place," the president again turned to Marshall, this time to fill a vacancy on the U.S. Supreme Court. As before, a group of Southern congressmen who criticized his liberal views and activist past tried to derail the nomination. But they quickly met with defeat, thus paving the way for Marshall to make history as the first African American to serve on the nation's highest court.

During the more than twenty years he was an associate justice, Marshall stood firm against a rising tide of conservatism that influenced many of the Supreme Court's rulings throughout the 1970s and 1980s. Pervading all of his decisions was his belief that the rights of the individual took precedence over the rights of the state. He was an outspoken opponent of the death penalty, for example, on the grounds that it is an "excessive" punishment that unfairly discriminates against certain classes of people; he also supported defendants' rights regarding questionable searches and interrogation practices. In addition, Marshall was a fierce champion of the right to privacy and of First Amendment provisions guaranteeing freedom of speech and freedom of religion. Above all, he never failed to remind his colleagues—often with a pointed or folksy anecdote—of the human consequences of their actions.

Marshall's philosophy is evident in the following commencement address, delivered on May 21, 1978, to the graduating class of the University of Virginia. In it, he explains that a well-educated and well-informed populace is the foundation of a government that truly honors the principles of democracy and equality. His speech is reprinted here from "I Am Honored to Be Here Today . . .": Commencement Speeches by Notable Personalities *(Oceana Publications, 1985).*

It is customary on giving speeches to say how honored and pleased the speaker is at being invited to stand before the invariably august body that is present. Sometimes this is a mere convention, and the speaker would rather be in any of a hundred other places. For several reasons, however, I am truly honored and pleased to be here today.

The University of Virginia is of course one of the outstanding universities of this country. It was conceived in grandeur, and has, more than most other institutions, fulfilled the ambitions and ideals of its founder, Thomas Jefferson. Jefferson started planning this great University over twenty years before it was chartered in 1819. His conception was, at the time, revolutionary—as befitted the man. He believed that a university should be an "academical village," a small democracy in action; it should consist of different schools devoted to different disciplines, with a curriculum that expressed the most modern ideas in scientific and liberal thought. He scandalized some of his contemporaries by proposing to omit instruction in "religious divinity"; in his view was such instruction at a state institution was inconsistent with the great constitutional principles of religious freedom and separation of church and state. And Jefferson insisted on getting only the best in their fields as instructors, even if that meant going to European colleges and, to use a modern word, "raiding" their faculties.

Thomas Jefferson, in short, conceived and executed in the early nineteenth century a plan for a very modern university. This university today stands as a testament to the enduring nature of what some at the time thought was a wild vision. His road to this achievement was no easy one—it took twenty years of planning, perseverance and vision. It also took a willingness to engage in the inevitable compromises of politics, for it was quite a battle to get the state legislature of the time to authorize the funds for this suspicious experiment. But Jefferson did not disdain the hurly-burly of political negotiation, compromise and argument; he thrived on it.

Jefferson believed as deeply as anything that an educated citizenry could make rational and responsible decisions on almost any matter. Indeed, this belief in the intelligence and wisdom of a well-educated people not only drove him to promote public education, at the primary as well as higher levels, but it also informs many of his most eloquent political passages.

I don't know how many of you graduating from the College of Arts and Sciences studied politics and government in your four years at this university. I do know that one innovation that Jefferson favored strongly was that of "electives." A favorite grandson of his had groaned under the rigidities of a set curriculum at another college of the day, and Jefferson was convinced that permitting students to choose their areas of study would improve the quality of their educational experience. There are educators in this country who believe this trend has gone too far, that students are not trained in the core aspects of what an educated person should know. The way the world looks to me, it seems awfully difficult to say what "core" knowledge should be; and it may be that the last person in this country who could really claim to have mastered the whole of human knowledge was Jefferson himself.

"For me, [the Constitution's] cardinal principle is that all persons stand in a position of equality before the law."

But there are certain core values, embodied in Thomas Jefferson's handiwork in the Declaration of Independence and the Constitution, as well as in setting up this university, of which I hope you are all aware—those of you graduating with advanced degrees as well as the undergraduates. And these core values, tried and trite as they may appear, are in my judgment worthy of continued reflection, so that they may be better realized in this country, just as your university so well realized the values of its founder.

I can best introduce them by telling you of a brief incident. At one argument in a United States District Court, an attorney representing a city was arguing in support of an ordinance challenged as being unconstitutional. The details of the case are unimportant, but at one point in his argument, this attorney told the Court that there was "something higher than the Constitution of the United States." I asked him what he could be thinking of; and the poor man had no answer.

My first reaction, and probably that of many other listeners, was that his failure to answer illustrated that his assertion was wrong, and in a way it was; but in another, equally important way, the lawyer simply failed to come up with the right answer.

His assertion is wrong because our system is perhaps uniquely characterized by adherence to the proposition that this is a government of laws, and not merely of men and women—and the United States Constitution is the supreme law of the land. The Constitution is binding on federal judges and municipal courts, on governors of the states and on presidents of the United States—in short, on all governmental decisionmakers in the state and federal systems. There simply is no "higher law" in this country.

The democratizing aspects of the Constitution cannot be overstated. For me, its cardinal principle is that all persons stand in a position of equality before the law. The Constitution gives to each and every one of you an equal right to your own opinions and to participate in the process of your own governance. These are precious rights that we must continually strive to preserve, and whose promise we must seek to attain. There are still far too many persons in this country who cannot participate as equals in the processes of government—persons too poor, too ignorant, persons discriminated against by other people for no good reason. But our ideal, the ideal of our Constitution, is to eliminate these barriers to the aspirations of all Americans to participate fully in our government and society. We have realized it far better than most countries, but we still have a long way to travel and we must continue to strive in that direction.

This brings me to my second point about my poor lawyer's assertion. As I said a moment ago, his statement was profoundly true in a way, for there *is* something "higher" than the Constitution—that is, quite simply, the people. I do not mean that "the people" are not bound to live under our system of laws—any other proposition could lead to violence and from there to anarchy. But what I do mean is what Thomas Jefferson said in the Declaration of our Independence—that just governments derive their authority from the consent of the governed. And because of this, you have not only a right but a responsibility to the government of this country.

Let me elaborate. Governments derive their *power* from many sources—the military or police are instruments of power and may in the short run enforce the government's directives against an unwilling people. But *authority* is a different question—and no government can govern long, or well, without the authority that comes from a shared consensus among the governed. They must believe that theirs is a rightful, and lawful, and just government.

But in order to preserve this power in the people—the power of defining and limiting the authority of their government—it is first and foremost essential that the people be well informed. Jefferson's commitment to this university was only part of a larger commitment to the value of public education. That vision accounts for the primacy of public schools in the American community, for it was Jefferson's guiding hand that helped draft the Northwest Ordinance, which resulted in public lands being dedicated across the new territories for public schools. Today, however, just as in Jefferson's times, we still see students of less privileged backgrounds than your own, or people who are just less lucky, being denied quality education at all levels. Voters turn down school financing referenda, legislatures oppose integration of school systems. There is appalling ignorance even among some of the supposedly well-educated youth of our country, and the extent of illiteracy remains staggering. Education towards the goal of an informed citizenry requires all of the qualities that Jefferson embodied: commitment to difficult projects, confidence in the soundness of one's own vision and perseverance in working through a problem.

As the areas of human knowledge have expanded, so have the aspirations of the American people. It is vitally important that the aspirations of our government keep pace with the knowledge and expectations of our people. With the explosion in human knowledge and expertise, it sometimes seems very difficult to understand what the government is doing, to understand what our problems are, and to keep up. Yet the duty to keep up, to be informed, to be knowledgeable in some area of human endeavor, is an essential one, not only for the continued survival of our government but in the long run for our civilization. It is hard work being well-informed; but it is essential work for the citizens of a democracy.

It is a work, moreover, for which people in your position have been specially prepared. The privilege of attending so fine a university as this one must bear with it an unceasing responsibility to use your knowledge and training for improving the lives of others. Whether you pursue this as a lawyer dedicated to the public interest; a doctor serving those in pain and sickness; a scholar adding to the store of human knowledge and sharing that knowledge with others; an engineer applying new technologies to serve human needs; an artist improving the quality of life by creative efforts; or just by seeking to be a good person who values helping others—matters not. What matters is to remember always the obligation you bear to the society that has placed you in a position where you could afford to spend four years of your lives—and for many of you, there have been and will be several more—in an institution of learning.

I said at the beginning of my talk that there were several reasons why I was truly honored to be here today. I have already mentioned the first—that this university represents something special in the American tradition. The second one is because you are young, you are a new generation just starting out. Those of us who are a bit older (like myself—and I said, just a bit), no matter how hard we may have worked to serve humanity—our time is coming to a close. I don't for a moment mean our *lives,* since I for one intend to keep on plugging at my present job for many years to come. But I recall to you now Thomas Jefferson's answer to the pleas of a friend in 1814. His friend begged Jefferson to take a stand then and there as a leader in the fight against slavery. Jefferson's answer, though hardly commendable, shows a human truth; he said, "No, I have outlived the generation with which mutual labors and perils begat mutual confidence and influence. This enterprise is for the young—for those who can follow it up, and bear it through to its consummation."

You people here today, about to use your degrees, it is for you now to undertake the projects of this age—in Jefferson's words, to follow them up and bear them through. It is not for me to tell you what these are—each generation must find its own calling. But you have the energies of youth—and while you have them, use them, that you may look back on your lives with as much of a sense of accomplishment as Jefferson no doubt did.

This is a great country, but fortunately for you it is not perfect. There is much to be done to bring about complete equality. Remove hunger. Bring reality closer to theory and democratic principles.

Each of you as an individual must pick your own goals. Listen to others but do not become a blind follower. Do not wait for others to move out—move out yourself—where you see wrong or inequality or injustice speak out, because this is your country. This is your democracy—make it—protect it— pass it on. You are ready. Go to it.

In 1990, Marshall retired from the Supreme Court, citing as reasons his advancing age and failing health. Reportedly quoted as saying he would not die until the Democrats once again occupied the White House, he succumbed to heart failure on January 24, 1993, just days after the inauguration of President Bill Clinton.

SOURCES

Books

Aldred, Lisa, *Thurgood Marshall,* Chelsea House, 1990.

Broderick, Francis L., and August Meier, editors, *Negro Protest Thought in the Twentieth Century,* Bobbs-Merrill, 1965.

Davis, Michael D., and Hunter R. Clark, *Thurgood Marshall: Warrior at the Bar, Rebel on the Bench,* Carol Publishing, 1992.

Foner, Philip S., editor, *The Voice of Black America: Major Speeches by Negroes in the United States, 1797–1971,* Simon & Schuster, 1972.

Golden, James L., and Richard D. Rieke, *The Rhetoric of Black Americans,* Charles E. Merrill, 1971.

Goldman, Roger, and David Gallen, *Thurgood Marshall: Justice for All,* Carroll & Graf, 1992.

Grunewald, Donald, editor, *"I Am Honored to Be Here Today . . .": Commencement Speeches by Notable Personalities,* Oceana Publications, 1985.

Rowan, Carl T., *Dream Makers, Dream Breakers: The World of Thurgood Marshall,* Little, Brown, 1992.

Williams, Jamye Coleman, and McDonald Williams, editors, *The Negro Speaks: The Rhetoric of Contemporary Black Leaders,* Noble & Noble, 1970.

Periodicals

Ebony, "The Thurgood Marshall Nobody Knows," May, 1990, pp. 68-76; "Forty-Five Years in Law and Civil Rights," November, 1990, pp. 80-86.

Newsweek, "A Great Original's Lives at the Law: Thurgood Marshall Made as Much History in Front of the Supreme Court as He Did Serving It," July 8, 1991.

People, "Justices Marshall and Brennan Battle to Keep Liberalism Alive at the U.S. Supreme Court," July 7, 1986, pp. 53-54; "A Warrior Retires: The Son of a Black Steward in an All-White Club Rewrote the Rules about Race," July 15, 1991.

Time, "Negro Justice," June 23, 1967, pp. 18-19; "The First Negro Justice," September 8, 1967, p. 16; "A Lawyer Who Changed America," July 8, 1991.

U.S. News and World Report, "With Mr. Marshall on the Supreme Court," June 26, 1967, pp. 12-13; "With Another 'Liberal' on High Court," September 11, 1967, p. 21; "Embracing a Great Man's Gift to America," July 8, 1991.

José Martí

1853–1895

Cuban American writer and revolutionary

Revered throughout Latin America as a symbol of the fight for independence from foreign domination, José Martí was the architect of the revolution that finally drove Spain out of Cuba. He was also a writer of significance whose originality of expression, especially in his poetry and essays, ushered in a new era in Spanish letters. Yet it was his death in the heat of battle—before he could see his dream of a free Cuba come true—that vaulted Martí to the status of hero and martyr, a place he still holds today among Latin Americans at both ends of the political spectrum.

A native of Havana, Cuba, Martí was one of eight children of parents who had been born in Spain. His father was a sergeant in the Spanish Royal Artillery at the time of José's birth and later worked as a guard, a policeman, and a minor civil servant. Except for a period of about two years when his family moved back to Spain to live, Martí spent all of his childhood in Havana. There he was taken under the wing of one of his teachers, who saw to it that he was allowed to continue his education past the age when his father wanted him to quit school and find a job to help support the family.

Martí's mentor was of a decidedly liberal bent, and young José grew up steeped in the patriotic notion that Cuba, then a colony of Spain, deserved independence. This was at a time when the political situation on the island was very tense and revolution was definitely in the air, particularly after a rebellion that erupted in late 1868 touched off a decade of guerrilla warfare between Cuban insurgents and the Spanish military known as the Ten Years' War. Martí was barely in his teens when he began writing pieces that were critical of the colonial regime, and in October 1869, at the age of only sixteen, he was arrested and charged with treason. Five months later, in March 1870, he was sentenced to six years in prison, a sentence that came to an end in January 1871, when he was deported to Spain, where Cuban authorities hoped he would be too far away to cause any trouble.

But Martí soon hooked up with other Cuban exiles in Spain and continued his activities on behalf of the independence movement. He also resumed his education, first at Central University in Madrid and then at the University of Zaragoza, from which he received both a law degree and a liberal arts degree in

1874. After a brief visit to Paris, he left Europe for Mexico, where his parents had settled. Working out of the capital, Mexico City, he contributed articles and poems to a leading local newspaper, some under his own name and some under a pseudonym. He also wrote a play, Amor con amor se paga, *that was well received upon its first public performance in December 1875.*

In 1877, Martí returned to Havana under an assumed name, but conditions there were so dismal he soon left for Guatemala. With a friend's help, he was able to secure a position as a high school teacher. In mid-1878, however, after running afoul of government officials there who took offense at his criticisms, he went back to Cuba. This time, Martí was able to take advantage of the amnesty granted to political exiles in the wake of an agreement that ended the so-called Ten Years' War. He then clerked in a law office while trying to obtain permission to practice law himself, an effort that ultimately proved futile.

Despite this disappointing turn of events, Martí was still very much involved in the Cuban independence movement. His weapon of choice was the word—both written and spoken—and he again allied himself with others who shared his goal of freedom for their island home. In September 1879, his activism led colonial officials to charge him with conspiracy and quickly deport him to Spain, where he remained only until December. By January 3, 1880, he had made his way to New York City, which became his base of operations for the next fifteen years. There he found a sizable community of fellow exiles, many of whom had left Cuba during the Ten Years' War. He immediately joined the Cuban Revolutionary Committee, a group that had been organized some two years earlier by a veteran of the war with Spain, General Calixto García.

While Martí's obsession was Cuban independence, his years in New York were a time of remarkable creative output as well. He actually earned his living (meager though it was) contributing articles to some of the leading newspapers in Latin America and top Spanish-language publications in the United States; his work also appeared in several English-language newspapers based in New York. In his spare time, he wrote poetry (most notably contained in the collections Ismaelillo, Versos libres, *and* Versos sencillos*), fiction (including the novel* Amistad Funesta*), and children's stories. He also translated a variety of literary works, sometimes for pay and sometimes just for his own pleasure. In addition, Martí was an exceptionally prolific essayist, pamphleteer, and reviewer.*

Before long, by virtue of his extensive writings, political activism, and personal charisma, Martí was a major force in the liberation movement and a respected figure throughout all of Latin America. He even served for a time as the official representative in New York of the governments of Uruguay, Argentina, and Paraguay until Spain's ambassador to Madrid questioned the propriety of a Cuban revolutionary acting as a diplomat for other nations. Martí's response was to resign from his posts, ostensibly to devote more of his time to the efforts to liberate Cuba.

One of the subjects that Martí frequently addressed during this period as both a speechmaker and a writer was the lack of understanding that characterized relations between North Americans and Latin Americans. In his work, he often functioned as a cultural "interpreter" of sorts and tried to resolve the differences that existed between the two—although the longer he remained in New York, the less impressed he was with the United States and the less inclined he was to extol its virtues. He was especially critical of racial oppression and the emphasis on achieving material wealth, a goal he considered shallow. It soon became clear to him that any war waged for Cuba's independence also had to incorporate a struggle for social justice, democracy, and an end to slavery.

Martí was also disturbed by signs that the United States was seriously contemplating annexing Cuba. Gradually, he came to believe that U.S. imperialism posed a dangerous threat to Latin America and that an independent Cuba could serve as a barrier. Martí also embraced the idea of a united Latin America he often referred to as "Our America" (Nuestra America), an entity forged out of the historical, political, social, and economic experiences shared by the former colonies of Spain that would stand in opposition to the overwhelming presence of the United States in the hemisphere.

These sentiments were at the heart of the following speech, delivered in New York and subsequently published in La revista ilustrada (The Illustrated Review) *on January 10, 1891. It is reprinted here from a version that appears in* The Hispanic-American Almanac, *Gale, 1993. Martí's analysis of sociopolitical conditions in Latin America and encroaching U.S. imperialism firmly established for all time the concept of two separate Americas.*

The conceited villager believes the entire world to be his village. Provided that he can be mayor, or humiliate the rival who stole his sweetheart, or add to the savings in his strong-box, he considers the universal order good, unaware of those giants with seven-league boots who can crush him underfoot, or of the strife in the heavens between comets that streak through the drowsy air-devouring worlds. What remains of the village in America must rouse itself. These are not the times for sleeping in a nightcap, but with weapons for a pillow, like the warriors of Juan de Castellanos weapons of the mind, which conquer all others. Barricades of ideas are worth more than barricades of stone.

There is no prow that can cut through a cloudbank of ideas. A powerful idea, waved before the world at the proper time, can stop a squadron of iron-clad ships, like the mystical flag of the Last Judgment. Nations that do not know one another should quickly become acquainted, as men who are to fight a common enemy. Those who shake their fists, like jealous brothers coveting the same tract of land, or like the modest cottager who envies the squire his mansion, should clasp hands and become one. Those who use the authority of a criminal tradition to lop off the lands of their defeated brother with a sword stained with his own blood, ought to return the lands to the brother already punished sufficiently, if they do not want the people to call them robbers. The honest man does not absolve himself of debts of honor with money, at so much a slap. We can no longer be a people of leaves living in the air, our foliage heavy with blooms and crackling or humming at the whim of the sun's caress, or buffeted and tossed by the storms. The trees must form ranks to keep the giant with seven-league boots from passing! It is the time of mobilization, of marching together, and we must go forward in close order, like silver in the veins of the Andes.

Only those born prematurely are lacking in courage. Those without faith in their country are seven-month weaklings. Because they have no courage, they deny it to others. Their puny arms—arms with bracelets and hands with painted nails, arms of Paris or Madrid—can hardly reach the bottom limb, and they claim the tall tree to be unclimbable. The ships should be loaded with those harmful insects that gnaw at the bone of the country that nourishes them. If they are Parisians or from Madrid, let them go to the Prado under lamplight, or to Tortoni's for a sherbet. Those carpenters' sons who are ashamed that their fathers are carpenters! Those born in America who are ashamed of the mother who reared them, because she wears an Indian apron, and who disown their sick mother, the scoundrels, abandoning her on her sickbed! Then who is a real man? He who stays with his mother and nurses her in her illness, or he who puts her to work out of sight, and lives at her expense on decadent lands, sporting fancy neckties, cursing the womb that carried him, displaying the sign of the traitor on the back of his paper frockcoat? These sons of

Our America, which will be saved by its Indians and is growing better; these deserters who take up arms in the armies of a North America that drowns its Indians in blood and is growing worse! These delicate creatures who are men but are unwilling to do men's work! The Washington who made this land for them, did he not go to live with the English, to live with the English at a time when he saw them fighting against his own country? These "iconoclasts" of honor who drag that honor over foreign soil, like their counterparts in the French Revolution with their dancing, their affectations, their drawling speech!

For in what lands can men take more pride than in our long-suffering American republics, raised up from among the silent Indian masses by the bleeding arms of a hundred apostles, to the sounds of battle between the book and the processional candle? Never in history have such advanced and united nations been forged in so short a time from such disorganized elements.

The presumptuous man feels that the earth was made to serve as his pedestal because he happens to have a facile pen or colorful speech, and he accuses his native land of being worthless and beyond redemption because its virgin jungles fail to provide him with a constant means of traveling over the world, driving Persian ponies and lavishing champagne like a tycoon. The incapacity does not lie with the emerging country in quest of suitable forms and a utilitarian greatness; it lies rather with those who attempt to rule nations of a unique and violent character by means of laws inherited from four centuries of freedom in the United States and nineteen centuries of monarchy in France. A decree by Hamilton does not halt the charge of the plainsman's horse. A phrase by Sieyes does nothing to quicken the stagnant blood of the Indian race. To govern well, one must see things as they are. And the able governor in America is not the one who knows how to govern the Germans or the French; he must know the elements that compose his own country, and how to bring them together, using methods and institutions originating within the country, to reach that desirable state where each man can attain self-realization and all may enjoy the abundance that Nature has bestowed on everyone in the nation to enrich with their toil and defend with their lives. The government must originate in the country. The spirit of the government must be that of the country. Its structure must conform to rules appropriate to the country. Good government is nothing more than the balance of the country's natural elements.

> ***"The spirit of the government must be that of the country. . . . Good government is nothing more than the balance of the country's natural elements."***

That is why the imported book has been conquered in America by the natural man. Natural men have conquered learned and artificial men. The native halfbreed has conquered the exotic Creole. The struggle is not between civilization and barbarity, but between false erudition and Nature. The natural man is good, and he respects and rewards superior intelligence as long as his humility is not turned against him, or he is not offended by being disregarded—a thing the natural man never forgives, prepared as he is to forcibly regain the respect of whoever has wounded his pride or threatened his interests. It is by conforming with these disdained native elements that the tyrants of America have climbed to power, and have fallen as soon as they betrayed them. Republics have paid with oppression for their inability to recognize the true elements of their countries, to derive from them the right kind of government, and to govern accordingly. In a new nation a governor means a creator.

In nations composed of both cultured and uncultured elements, the uncultured will govern because it is their habit to attack and resolve doubts with their fists in cases where the cultured have failed in the art of governing. The uncultured masses are lazy and timid in the realm of intelligence, and they want to be governed well. But if the government hurts them, they shake it off and govern themselves. How can the universities produce governors if not a single university in America teaches the rudiments of the art of government, the analysis of elements peculiar to the peoples of America? The young go out into the world wearing Yankee or French spectacles, hoping to govern a people they do not know. In the political race entrance should be denied to those who are ignorant of the rudiments of politics. The prize in literary contests should not go for the best ode, but for the best study of the political fac-

José Martí

tors of one's country. Newspapers, universities, and schools should encourage the study of the country's pertinent components. To know them is sufficient, without mincing words; for whoever brushes aside even a part of the truth, whether through intention or oversight, is doomed to fall. The truth he lacks thrives on negligence, and brings down whatever is built without it. It is easier to resolve our problem knowing its components than to resolve it without knowing them. Along comes the natural man, strong and indignant, and he topples all the justice accumulated from books because he has not been governed in accordance with the obvious needs of the country. Knowing is what counts. To know one's country and govern it with that knowledge is the only way to free it from tyranny. The European university must bow to the American university. The history of America, from the Incas to the present, must be taught in clear detail and to the letter, even if the archons of Greece are overlooked. Our Greece must take priority over the Greece which is not ours. We need it more. Nationalist statesmen must replace foreign statesmen. Let the world be grafted onto our republics, but the trunk must be our own. And let the vanquished pedant hold his tongue, for there are no lands in which a man may take greater pride than in our long-suffering American republics.

With the rosary as our guide, our heads white and our bodies mottled, both Indian and Creole, we fearlessly entered the world of nations. We set out to conquer freedom under the banner of the virgin. A priest, a few lieutenants, and a woman raised the Republic of Mexico onto the shoulders of the Indians. A few heroic students, instructed in French liberty by a Spanish cleric, made Central America rise in revolt against Spain under a Spanish general. In monarchic garb emblazoned with the sun, the Venezuelans to the north and the Argentineans to the south began building nations. When the two heroes clashed and the continent was about to rock, one of them, and not the lesser, handed the reins to the other. And since heroism in times of peace is rare because it is not as glorious as in times of war, it is easier for a man to die with honor than to think with logic. It is easier to govern when feelings are exalted and united than after a battle, when divisive, arrogant, exotic, or ambitious thinking emerges. The forces routed in the epic struggle with the feline cunning of the species, and using the weight of realities were under-mining the new structure which comprised both the rough-and-ready, unique regions of our halfbreed America and the silk-stocking and frockcoated people of Paris beneath the flag of freedom and reason borrowed from nations skilled in the arts of government. The hierarchical constitution of the colonies resisted the democratic organization of the republics. The clavated capitals left their country boots in the vestibule. The bookworm redeemers failed to realize that the revolution succeeded because it came from the soul of the nation; they had to govern with that soul and not without it or against it. America began to suffer, and still suffers, from the tiresome task of reconciling the hostile and discordant elements it inherited from a despotic and perverse colonizer, and the imported methods and ideas which have been retarding logical government because they are lacking in local realities. Thrown out of gear for three centuries by a power which denied men the right to use their reason, the continent disregarded or closed its ears to the unlettered throngs that helped bring it to redemption, and embarked on a government based on reason—a reason belonging to all for the common good, not the university brand of reason over the peasant brand. The problem of independence did not lie in a change of forms but in a change of spirit.

It was imperative to make common cause with the oppressed, in order to secure a new system opposed to the ambitions and governing habits of the oppressors. The tiger, frightened by gunfire, returns at night to his prey. He dies with his eyes shooting flames and his claws unsheathed. He cannot be heard coming because he approaches with velvet tread. When the prey awakens, the tiger is already upon it. The colony lives on in the republic, and Our America is saving itself from its enormous mistakes the pride of its capital cities, the blind triumph of a scorned peasantry, the excessive influx of foreign ideas and formulas, the wicked and un-politic disdain for the aboriginal race because of the higher virtue, enriched with necessary blood, or a republic struggling against a colony. The tiger lurks behind every tree, lying in wait at every turn. He will die with his claws unsheathed and his eyes shooting flames.

But "these countries will be saved," as was announced by the Argentinean Rivadavia, whose only sin was being a gentleman in these rough-and-ready times. A man does not sheathe a machete in a silken scabbard, nor can he lay aside the short lance in a country won with the short lance merely because he is angered and stands at the door of Iturbide's Congress, "demanding that the fairhaired one be named Emperor." These countries will be saved because a genius for moderation, found in the serene harmony of Nature, seems to prevail on the continent of light, where there emerges a new realistic man schooled for these realistic times in the critical philosophy which in Europe has replaced the philosophy of guess-work and phalanstery that saturated the previous generation.

We were a phenomenon with the chest of an athlete, the hands of a dandy, and the brain of a child. We were a masquerader in English breeches, Parisian vest, North American jacket, and Spanish cap. The Indian hovered near us in silence, and went off to the hills to baptize his children. The Negro was seen pouring out the songs of his heart at night, alone and unrecognized among the rivers and wild animals. The peasant, the creator, turned in blind indignation against the disdainful city, against his own child. As for us, we were nothing but epaulets and professors' gowns in countries that came into the world wearing hemp sandals and headbands. It would have been the mark of genius to couple the headband and the professors' gown with the founding fathers' generosity and courage, to rescue the Indian, to make a place for the competent Negro, to fit liberty to the body of those who rebelled and conquered for it. We were left with the judge, the general, the scholar, and the sinecure. The angelic young, as if caught in the tentacles of an octopus, lunged heavenward, only to fall back, crowned with clouds, in sterile glory. The native, driven by instinct, swept away the golden staffs of office in blind triumph. Neither the European nor the Yankee could provide the key to the Spanish American riddle. Hate was attempted, and every year the countries amounted to less. Exhausted by the senseless struggle between the book and the lance, between reason and the processional candle, between the city and the country, weary of the impossible rule by rival urban cliques over the natural nation tempestuous or inert by turns, we begin almost unconsciously to try love. Nations stand up and greet one another.

"What are we?" is the mutual question, and little by little they furnish answers. When a problem arises in Cojimar, they do not seek its solution in Danzig. The frockcoats are still French, but thought begins to be American. The youth of America are rolling up their sleeves, digging their hands in the dough, and making it rise with the sweat of their brows. They realize that there is too much imitation, and that creation holds the key to salvation. "Create" is the password of this generation. The wine is made from plantain, but even if it turns sour, it is our own wine! That a country's form of government must be in keeping with its natural elements is a foregone conclusion. Absolute ideas must take relative forms if they are not to fail because of an error in form. Freedom, to be viable, has to be sincere and complete. If a republic refuses to open its arms to all, and move ahead with all, it dies. The tiger within sneaks in through the crack; so does the tiger from without. The general holds back his cavalry to a pace that suits his infantry, for if the infantry is left behind, the cavalry will be surrounded by the enemy. Politics and strategy are one. Nations should live in an atmosphere of self-criticism because criticism is healthy, but always with one heart and one mind. Stoop to the unhappy, and lift them up in your arms! Thaw out frozen America with the fire of your hearts! Make the natural blood of the nations course vigorously through their veins. The new Americans are on their feet, saluting each other from nation to nation, the eyes of the laborers shining with joy. The natural statesman arises, schooled in the direct study of Nature. He reads to apply his knowledge, not to imitate. Economists study the problems at their point of origin. Speakers begin a policy of moderation. Playwrights bring native characters to the stage. Academies discuss practical subjects. Poetry shears off its romantic locks and hangs its red vest on the glorious tree. Selective and sparkling prose is filled with ideas. In the Indian republics, the governors are learning Indian.

America is escaping all its dangers. Some of the republics are still beneath the sleeping octopus, but others, under the law of averages, are draining their lands with a sublime and furious haste, as if to make up for centuries lost. Still others, forgetting that Juarez went about in a carriage drawn by mules, hitch their carriages to the wind, their coachmen soap bubbles. Poisonous luxury, the enemy of freedom, corrupts the frivolous and opens the door to the foreigner. In others, where independence is threatened, an epic spirit heightens their manhood. Still others spawn an army capable of devouring them in voracious wars. But perhaps Our America is running another risk that does not come from itself but from the difference in origins, methods, and interests between the two halves of the continent, and the time is near at hand when an enterprising and vigorous people who scorn or ignore Our America will even so approach it and demand a close relationship. And since strong nations, self-made by law and shotgun, love strong nations, and them alone; since the time of madness and ambition from which North America may be freed by the predominance of the purest elements in its blood, or on which it may be launched by its vindictive and sordid masses, its tradition of expansion, or the ambitions of some powerful leader is not so near at hand, even to the most timorous eye, that there is no time for the test of discreet and unwavering pride that could confront and dissuade it; since its good name as a republic in the eyes of the world's perceptive nations puts upon North America a restraint that cannot be taken away by childish provocations or pompous arrogance or parricidal discords among Our American nations the pressing need of Our America is to show itself as it is, one in spirit and intent, swift conqueror of a suffocating past, stained only by the enriching blood drawn from hands that struggle to clear away the ruins, and from the scars left upon us by our masters. The scorn of our formidable neighbor who does not know us is Our America's greatest danger. And since the day of the visit is near, it is imperative that our neighbor know us, and soon, so that it will not scorn us. Through ignorance it might even come to lay hands on us. Once it does know us, it will remove its hands out of respect. One must have faith in the best in men and distrust the worst. One must allow the best to be shown so that it reveals and prevails over the worst. Nations should have a pillory for whoever stirs up useless hates, and another for whoever fails to tell them the truth in time.

There can be no racial animosity, because there are no races. The theorists and feeble thinkers string together and warm over the bookshelf races which the well-disposed observer and the fair-minded traveler vainly seek in the justice of Nature where man's universal identity springs forth from triumphant love and the turbulent hunger for life. The soul, equal and eternal, emanates from bodies of various shapes and colors. Whoever foments and spreads antagonism and hate between the races, sins against humanity. But as nations take shape among other different nations, there is a condensation of vital and individual characteristics of thought and habit, expansion and conquest, vanity and greed which could from the latent state of national concern, and in a period of internal disorder, or the rapidity with which the country's character has been accumulating be turned into a serious threat for the weak and

"The scorn of our formidable neighbor who does not know us is Our America's greatest danger. . . . Once it does know us, it will remove its hands out of respect."

isolated neighboring countries, declared by the strong country to be inferior and perishable. The thought is father to the deed. And one must not attribute, through a provincial antipathy, a fatal and inborn wickedness to the continent's fairskinned nation simply because it does not speak our language, or see the world as we see it, or resemble us in its political defects, so different from ours, or favorably regard the excitable, dark-skinned people, or look charitably from its still uncertain eminence upon those less favored by history, who climb the road of republicanism by heroic stages. The self-evident facts of the problem should not be obscured, because the problem can be resolved, for the peace of centuries to come, by appropriate study, and by tacit and immediate unity in the continental spirit. With a single voice the hymn is already being sung. The present generation is carrying industrious America along the road enriched by their sublime fathers; from the Rio Grande to the Straits of Magellan, the Great Sem, astride his condor, is sowing the seed of the new America through-out the Latin nations of the continent and the sorrowful islands of the sea!

Martí's efforts to lay the groundwork for a future invasion of Cuba involved more than just writing articles and giving speeches, however. By 1884, he had persuaded two heroes of the Ten Years' War, General Máximo Gómez and General Antonio Maceo, to lend their expertise to the movement. But the relationship between the three men was fraught with conflict from the very beginning; while Martí made it clear that he favored a civilian government for Cuba and could not support any operation that resulted in a military dictatorship, Gómez and Maceo felt quite differently. The disagreement led to a parting of the ways that lasted until Martí made peace with Gómez in 1892 and Maceo a year later.

In late 1891 and early 1892, Martí spent a fair amount of time in Florida, where he met with Cuban insurrectionist groups in Tampa and Key West and worked with them to produce a statement of the aims of the liberation movement. In April 1892, all of the various exile groups came together to form the official Cuban Revolutionary Party and elected Martí the delegate, which was the equivalent of president. Around the same time, he also became publisher and editor of the newspaper Patria, *a weekly out of New York that served as the voice of the party.*

Martí spent much of 1893 on the road between New York and Florida coordinating preparations for the revolution, raising funds for supplies, and rallying his fellow exiles behind the cause. By the end of 1894, everything was in place to launch a three-pronged invasion from Costa Rica, the Dominican Republic, and Key West. But then one of the conspirators tipped off U.S. authorities, who confiscated all the rebels' ships and arms before they could make it to Cuba. Martí was devastated, but with the encouragement of his friends, he developed a new strategy. In the meantime, he passed along orders to his supporters within Cuba to launch the uprising there. When news came in late February 1895, that the revolution had indeed begun, Martí's invasion plans shifted into high gear.

General Gómez, one of the operation's military commanders, urged Martí to return to New York and oversee events from there. But Martí, who was unwilling to send other men to die without risking his own life as well, insisted on accompanying the invasion force to Cuba. He finally set foot on the island on April 12, 1895, accompanied by a small expedition of five men, including Gómez. Their intention was to meet up with General Maceo and his men, which they did on May 5. As the rebels moved slowly westward across the island, they came under attack by Spanish forces. Although Gómez had ordered Martí to stay behind in their camp, Martí defied the general and rode into the thick of the battle astride a white horse. There he was recognized by one of the Spanish soldiers, who shot and killed him.

The revolution did not die with Martí, however. Gómez and Maceo continued the guerrilla war against the Spanish; after Maceo died in action in late 1896, Gómez carried on with the help of General Calixto García and was still fighting when the United States intervened in April 1898, on the side of the rebels, launching the so-called Spanish-American War. The conflict ended eight months later with Spain giving up its sovereignty over Cuba. A U.S. military government ruled the island until May 1902, at which time the Cuban republic was officially established. Yet as Martí had feared, the United States more or less dominated Cuban economic and social affairs for almost the next sixty years, until Fidel Castro seized control in 1959.

SOURCES

Books

Abel, Christopher, and Nissa Torrents, editors, José Martí, Revolutionary Democrat, Duke University Press, 1986.

Appel, Todd M., *José Martí,* Chelsea House, 1992.

Gray, Richard Butler, *José Martí, Cuban Patriot,* University of Florida Press, 1962.

Kanellos, Nicolás, editor, *The Hispanic-American Almanac,* Gale Research, Detroit, 1993.

Kirk, John M., *José Martí, Mentor of the Cuban Nation,* University Presses of Florida, 1983.

Mañach, Jorge, *Martí, Apostle of Freedom* (translated from the Spanish), Devin-Adair, 1950.

Martí, José, *Inside the Monster: Writings on the United States and American Imperialism,* edited by Philip S. Foner, Monthly Review Press, 1975.

———, *Our America: Writings on Latin America and the Struggle for Cuban Independence,* edited by Philip S. Foner, Monthly Review Press, 1977.

Periodicals

American History Illustrated, "Who Was José Martí?" July/August, 1990.

Vilma S. Martinez

1943–

Mexican American civil rights attorney

In 1965, the U.S. Congress passed the Voting Rights Act, a landmark bill that outlawed schemes such as the poll tax and literacy tests that had been used mostly in the South to prevent blacks from registering to vote. Ten years later, legislators tackled the matter of extending the provisions of the act and broadening its scope to include not only blacks but Hispanic Americans, who themselves often encountered many obstacles on their way to the polls. The woman charged with convincing Congress to take that historic step was Vilma S. Martinez, the president and general counsel of the Mexican American Legal Defense and Educational Fund, or MALDEF, a national civil rights organization.

A native of San Antonio, Texas, Martinez earned a bachelor's degree from the University of Texas in 1964 and then headed to New York City's Columbia University, from which she obtained a law degree in 1967. Because she was personally well acquainted with the kind of prejudice that Mexican Americans often face, Martinez had made up her mind while she was still quite young that she wanted to devote her life to fighting injustice and unfair treatment. It was this strong commitment that led her into civil rights work right after graduation.

Her first job was as a staff attorney with the Legal Defense and Educational Fund of the National Association for the Advancement of Colored People (NAACP). In this role, she argued cases on behalf of minorities and poor people who were victims of illegal discrimination. In 1970 Martinez moved on to a position with the New York State Division of Human Rights, where she offered counsel on drafting and implementing new regulations and administrative procedures having to do with equal employment opportunity rights. She then spent two years, from 1971 until 1973, as a labor lawyer with a private New York law firm. During this same period, she became one of the first two women invited to serve on the board of MALDEF.

In 1973, Martinez was named president and general counsel of MALDEF, which monitors the impact of laws and public policy on Hispanic Americans and challenges inequities through the courts. As head of the fledgling organization (it was founded in 1969), Martinez divided her time between fund-raising activities, forging links with other groups interested in civil rights, and handling actual legal cases. Many of these cases—too many, it seemed to her—involved voting rights issues that she felt violated the spirit if not the actual letter of the existing law. (The

Voting Rights Act of 1965 technically applied only to blacks and Puerto Ricans.) MALDEF had recorded instances of tactics that were similar to those used to disenfranchise African Americans, including outright threats and polling places that suddenly "ran out" of ballots whenever Mexican Americans tried to vote. In addition, the failure to furnish ballots printed in Spanish excluded Latino voters who were not fluent in English.

When the Voting Rights Act came up for extension in 1975, Martinez led MALDEF's efforts to make sure that Hispanic Americans were also protected. With the support of other groups such as the Congressional Black Caucus, organized labor, and Japanese Americans, she was able to persuade members of Congress that much more remained to be done if they truly wanted to eliminate the problem of voter discrimination in the United States. On March 24, 1975, Martinez delivered the opening statement of her lengthy testimony on the abuses she was aware of through her work with MALDEF. That summary of her observations is reprinted here from Hearings Before the Subcommittee on Civil and Constitutional Rights of the Committee on the Judiciary, House of Representatives, 94th Congress, 1st Session, on H.R. 939, H.R. 2148, H.R. 3247, and H.R. 3501, Extension of the Voting Rights Act, *Serial No. 1, Part 1, U.S. Government Printing Office, 1975.*

Ms. Martinez: I would like to introduce Mr. Al Perez, an associate counsel of the Mexican American Legal Defense and Educational Fund, MALDEF, and Mr. Tom Reston of the law firm of Hogan & Hartson who has helped us with this testimony today.

As you may know, the Mexican American Legal Defense and Educational Fund, MALDEF, is a nonprofit organization which works to redress the grievances and vindicate the legal and constitutional rights of over six million United States citizens of Mexican ancestry. Today our community constitutes the second largest minority in America. It is predicted that within the next decade and a half the Spanish-surnamed community—and we are 65 percent of the Spanish-surnamed community—will become the largest minority in this country. Its needs, gentlemen, are enormous. The barriers it faces are legion. The discrimination it has endured and continues to endure is pervasive. But I should like to believe that its hope and its ultimate faith in this country are abiding and deep-sprung. Today we are calling on this committee and this Congress to vindicate that hope and that faith.

Vilma S. Martinez

I will not be reading my entire statement because you do have a copy of it. I would like to highlight certain of the aspects here. I know how boring it is to sit and listen to statistics, but I do want you to know that the statistics tell a lot here. In terms of the poverty level you will see that in Texas over 35 percent of our people are at the poverty level. In terms of representation to elective office in California as well as Texas, you will see that in Texas Mexican Americans comprise 18 percent of the population and only 6.2 percent of the 4,070 elected offices are held by Chicanos. In California it is even worse, and I wish that Representative Edwards were here to hear that.

Mr. Butler: He has heard it.

Ms. Martinez: In 1970, of 15,650 major elected and appointed positions at all levels of government, federal, state, and local, only 310, or 1.98 percent were held by Mexican Americans. This result is no mere coincidence. It is the result of manifold discriminatory practices which have the design and effect of excluding Mexican Americans from participation in their own government and maintaining the status quo.

I would like to share with this committee, at some length, two things: First, is that what we have found through the work of the U.S. Commission on Civil Rights to be extant today in Uvalde County, Texas; and second, to share with you what the Mexican American Legal Defense Fund has had to litigate over the past seven years in the voting rights area.

What the Commission found in Uvalde exists all across the state of Texas. The pattern of abuses in Uvalde County is strikingly reminiscent of the Deep South of the early 1960s. The Civil Rights Commission's study documents that duly registered Chicano voters are not being placed on the voting lists; that election judges are selectively and deliberately invalidating ballots cast by minority voters; that election judges are refusing to aid minority voters who are illiterate in English; that the tax assessor-collector of Uvalde County, who is responsible for registering voters, refuses to name members of minority groups as deputy registrars; that the Uvalde County tax assessor repeatedly runs out of registration application cards when minority voter applicants ask for them; that the Uvalde County tax assessor-collector refuses to register voter applicants based on the technicality that the application was filed on a printed card bearing a previous year's date.

Other abuses were uncovered by the study of the Civil Rights Commission in Uvalde County, and elsewhere in Texas: Widespread gerrymandering with the purpose of diluting minority voting strength; systematic drawing of at-large electoral districts with this same purpose and design; maintenance of polling places exclusively in areas inaccessible to minority voters; excessive firing fees to run for political office; numbered paper ballots which need to be signed by the voter, thus making it possible to discover for whom an individual cast his ballot.

The Civil Rights Commission field investigation in Uvalde also uncovered widespread economic threats and coercion directed at citizens who became involved with insurgent political forces. Again and again, interviewees express fear of reprisals as one reason for low voter registration and turn out. As one woman put it bluntly, "Jobs are at stake." The Uvalde County school system fires teachers who attempt to run for office. Local officials in Uvalde County have shown ingenuity and determination in depriving Mexican Americans of their right to vote. The city council of the town of Uvalde, for example, met and unilaterally decided in secret not to print on the ballot the name of a Chicano candidate for the council, even though he had duly qualified to stand for election.

Mr. Butler: May I interrupt just there? That is a flagrant violation of the law, I would think, to keep a qualified candidate off the ballot. What was done about that in that instance?

Ms. Martinez: He filed suit. The court found that his constitutional rights had in fact been violated; but the court refused to call another election. It was in the state court.

Mr. Butler: You did not think that you had any grievance in the federal court under section 3.

Ms. Martinez: That was all that was done at that time. There are no private remedies under section 3 of the Voting Rights Act. The operation of section 3 is entirely within the discretion of the attorney general. The attorney general has never seen fit to use his section 3 powers to enforce the voting rights of Mexican Americans.

Mr. Butler: I thank you.

Ms. Martinez: To better acquaint you with Uvalde, Texas, I would like to point out that last December I argued before the fifth circuit in New Orleans a school desegregation case coming out of Uvalde, Texas. In Texas, as many of you know, children were required to be educated in either the white or the colored school. Officials in Texas, and I have in mind Pecos County and Nueces County, which have large percentages of Mexican American people, could not decide whether Mexican Americans were white or colored, so we got no schools. In most other schools, as in Uvalde, we were in fact put into a third category of school, called the Mexican school. In order to prevail in Texas, we have to argue what is now known as the northern *de jure* segregation cases. We culled through the school board minutes going back to 1919. We traced the development of their school construction policies, their school assignment policies. We noticed that even toys were provided on the basis of race; twice the amount was spent for children in the Anglo schools as for children in the Mexican school, even though there were double the number of children in the Mexican schools as in the Anglo schools.

This, then, is the situation in at least one of the 254 Texas counties. As the Civil Rights Commission found, the processes by which this country conducts its elections are riddled with subtle, and not so subtle, discriminatory devices, which have the effect of excluding minorities. The atmosphere in which those elections are conducted is heavy with the clouds of discrimination and coercive control. Consider, if you will, the multitude of suits which would have to be filed by private parties to remedy each of these separate abuses which the Civil Rights Commission uncovered there. Consider the enormous pressure to which the suing party would be subjected. Consider the time which such litigation would consume. Consider the cost. And then consider that these problems by no means are found in Uvalde County alone. They exist all across the great swath of Texas where Chicanos are attempting to share in decisions affecting their county, their city, and their schools, decisions which are crucial to their daily lives. It is thus crucial that the constitutional rights of these citizens be enforced.

"The processes by which this country conducts its elections are riddled with subtle, and not so subtle, discriminatory devices, which have the effect of excluding minorities."

But it is simply not possible to guarantee to these people a meaningful right to vote with private litigation alone. There is an alternative remedy, an expansion as well as extension of the Voting Rights Act.

I would now like to share with you the experience of the Mexican Legal Defense Fund with case-by-case litigation to date, in order to show the committee the artificial barriers and obstacles which have been placed in our people's path. It will also demonstrate, I believe, the enormity and perhaps ultimate impossibility of dealing with these abuses one suit at a time.

One of the most severe problems we face is the at-large election or the multimember-district election. Such an election effectively operates to cancel out minority voting strength where a Chicano, if running from a single-member district, might otherwise hope to win. We have sued to strike down such schemes in California for the San Fernando city council; in Texas for the state house of representatives, the city council of San Antonio, and school board elections in Corpus Christi, Lubbock, Waco, and Hondo; in Arizona for school board elections in Tucson; in Washington State, for school board elections in Yakima County.

Another tool employed by those who wish to exploit minority participation and block Chicano access to elective office is the gerrymander. In California we have attacked a flagrant gerrymander of the Los Angeles city council; in Texas, we have sought to strike down gerrymandered congressional redistricting in El Paso, and gerrymandered county commissioner districts in Bexar, Kleberg, and Val Verde counties. In El Paso, we moved to force reapportionment of justice of the peace precincts.

Language has been a recurrent problem in qualifying to vote and in voting itself. MALDEF has brought actions alleging the unconstitutionality of English-language literacy tests in Arizona and the state of Washington. We have attacked the state of California statute which prohibited use of the Spanish language at the polling place. And in Texas, we overturned that state's prohibition on assistance to voters who could not read the ballot.

We have waged battles against unduly restrictive voting procedures. In Texas, we brought a suit which overturned that state's annual voting registration requirements. In another action, we challenged Texas statutes which required a student to intend to reside indefinitely at his student domicile in order to vote there. In California we attacked that state's early closing date for registration.

I would like to quote from the Supreme Court decision in *White v. Register* regarding the Chicano political experience in Texas, and I am quoting at page 768 of 412 U.S.:

A cultural incompatibility conjoined with the poll tax and the most restrictive voter registration procedures in the nation have operated to effectively deny Mexican American access to the political process in Texas even longer than blacks were formally denied access by the white primary.

Qualifying a candidate to stand for office has proved enormously burdensome in some areas. In New Mexico, we attempted to set aside a requirement that third-party candidates for the state legislature from multicounty districts collect signatures of three percent of the registered voters in the entire state. In Carrizo Springs, Texas, we discovered and sought to hold unconstitutional a requirement that one had to be a property owner to run for city council.

Finally, we have attacked refusals by local election officials to set up a polling place in a Chicano neighborhood of Villa Coronado, Texas, where seventy-five percent of the district's population resided, thus forcing those voters to travel seven miles in order to cast their ballots.

This list of voting abuses, Mr. Chairman, is by no means exhaustive. It does show, however, the persistence, determination, and the resources of local officials bent on making it as difficult as possible, and in some cases actually impossible, for minorities to exercise their right to an effective vote.

Mr. Chairman, members of the committee, most, if not all, of the types of abuses that I have outlined for you this morning would be routinely objectionable under section 5 of the Voting Rights Act. These abuses, which would be susceptible to swift administrative remedy under the attorney general's section 5 preclearance powers, demand legal resources which are simply too great for private litigants like MALDEF to bear. In our suit attacking Texas discriminatory use of multimember districts, for instance, we have gone through one district court proceeding which resulted in extensive findings of discrimination and mandated single-member districts for Bexar County. Texas appealed that to the Supreme Court, and our position was affirmed. On remand, the district court struck down additional multimember districts in the state reapportionment plan. Texas again appealed, and just this past January we were again in the Supreme Court defending that appeal. It has now been over three years, and the matter of Texas reapportionment is still not yet finally resolved.

In reading the Supreme Court's decision in *South Carolina v. Katzenbach*, upholding the constitutionality of the Voting Rights Act, I noted that at page 314 of the opinion of the Court, they said voting suits are unusually onerous to prepare, sometimes requiring as many as 6,000 man-hours. I am sure some of them were women-hours spent combing through registration records in preparation for trial. At page 315, the House Committee on the Judiciary was quoted, and the Court noted the House Committee's concern that the voting rights litigation in Dallas County, Alabama, had taken four years to open the door to the exercise of constitutional rights conferred almost a century ago. This committee said, "Four years is too long; the burden is too heavy; the wrong to our citizens is too serious; the damage to our national conscience is too great not to adopt more effective measures than exist today." My question to you today is: do you feel that way about Mexican Americans? Basically, this is a senseless waste of legal resources by both private attorneys and the courts; and it points up the need for a more rational approach to the problems we encounter, certainly in Texas, but also in many other parts of the Southwest, including California.

More importantly, a privately funded organization like MALDEF does not have the resources to litigate against discriminatory voting procedures in every county in Texas or even to identify exhaustively where discriminatory voting procedures are being employed. Only the Justice Department with its public resources, its expertise in this field gained over the past ten years, and with the aid of the presumptions set forth in the statutory language of section 5 can effectively insure that minority voters' rights in the Southwest are secured.

That is why MALDEF earlier this year petitioned the attorney general to determine that Texas, because less than 60 percent of the eligible voters there voted in 1964 and 1968, and because Texas maintained a test or device by conducting elections only in the English language, should already be covered pursuant to the existing section 4(b) trigger. We believe the judicial authority supporting our position is overwhelming and dispositive. I ask the permission of the committee to insert in the record a copy of our petition to the attorney general with related supplementary materials.

Mr. Edwards (presiding): Without objection, so ordered.

Ms. Martinez: However, since the attorney general has refused to grant our petition, we come before you as the final forum for redress of our grievances.

This committee should clarify for the Justice Department its responsibilities under the Voting Rights Act of 1965. By amending the statutory definition of test or device, the Congress will only write into law what we believe the Supreme Court has already held, but what the attorney general refuses to enforce.

The Congress should pass amendatory language which would afford Mexican Americans in Texas and elsewhere in the Southwest the powerful protections of section 5 of the Voting Rights Act.

In all this there lies only the fervent desire to be heard, to participate in our own government, and to insure that electoral rules and procedures foster, not foreclose, our opportunity for self-expression at the polls. And ultimately, if this legislation is passed by the Congress and enforced by the Justice Department, it will mean better local government, it will mean better education for our children, it will mean better street lighting and police protection, and other vital services. It will mean the beginnings of a fair share for Mexican Americans. I sincerely hope this committee will help us make that new beginning here today.

Thank you.

The following month, Martinez delivered a similar message to members of the Senate Subcommittee on Constitutional Rights of the Committee on the Judiciary, who were considering their own versions of the Voting Rights Act extension. Finally, on July 28, 1975, Congress approved the extension and agreed with Martinez that the act should be broadened to include Spanish-speaking Americans and others the legislators defined as "language minorities."

Martinez scored a number of other significant victories while with MALDEF, including the case of Plyler v. Doe, *which challenged a Texas law denying free public school education to the children of illegal immigrants. In 1982, feeling that it was time to move on both personally and professionally, she left the organization for a partnership in a large Los Angeles law firm, Munger, Tolles & Olson. There she has specialized in handling commercial litigation as well as federal and state court civil litigation involving issues such as wrongful termination and employment discrimination. She has also become active on several corporate and institutional boards (including MALDEF's) and was a longtime member of the University of California Board of Regents. It was in this latter capacity that Martinez addressed a special all-university faculty gathering on February 8, 1990, at California's Pala Mesa Conference Center on the subject of achieving greater cultural diversity in higher education. The following is reprinted from a copy of the speech provided by Martinez.*

During the last fifteen to twenty years we have witnessed much greater participation by women and ethnic and cultural minorities in our university. But the completion of the task is a long way off, in spite of the massive efforts by so many university people. We still face the problem of a low UC eligibility rate for underrepresented minorities, and this at a time when their share of the general population is increasing. One of the reasons for this is that we have barely begun to attack one of the root causes of this problem, student preparation and retention for the years K-12. Another reason is that we have not expanded our horizon of recruitment and analysis of those minority students who might not meet certain traditional norms but who would be a credit to the university.

I am concerned that some members of the university community do not share the belief that failure to make the university more culturally diverse not only represents a loss to the institution but indeed threatens its very existence as a major world university. Many such people hold that standards of excellence can be maintained while being insulated from the society which nurtures it. For many of them the very use of the term "affirmative action" tempts them into a logical fallacy: that where the recruitment method includes an element of affirmative action, anyone recruited in this manner is necessarily less qualified or able to secure the university's excellence.

This conclusion—which is shared by both detractors and supporters of affirmative action—is wrong because it is based on two erroneous assumptions: first, that the pre-affirmative action traditional process and standards were sophisticated and thoughtful and guaranteed continued excellence; and, second, that there is a generally accepted, immutable definition of what constitutes a great university and what we should be doing to build and to strengthen it.

In the first place, it seems clear that the traditional process was not as sophisticated or thoughtful as it should have been. All it generated was more of the same. Was this—is this—enough to secure a future of greatness for our university?

Much more important, the traditional process, even without its flaws, failed to address what must be our most important goals, the nurturing of a great university; and it failed to do so because there has been an inadequate understanding of just what such a university is.

What does it take to build a great university? One must start from the premise that a great university is much more than a campus which provides a home to a group of professional schools. The courses which it chooses to offer, the people it chooses to employ and to teach, and the questions it chooses for research ultimately derive not exclusively from discussions in faculty meetings, *but from society:* society's demands, its questions, its dreams. The university is both the creation of and the intellectual force for the society in which it lives. A university flourishes as it examines and teaches the intellectual questions arising from the society of that time and place. It is in terms of these goals that many of the customary, pre-affirmative action processes may be wanting.

This university, the greatest of its kind and one of the greatest of any kind, traces its beginnings back nearly a thousand years to the great centers of learning in Italy. I speak only of the Western stream; sources in other civilizations and cultures are far more ancient. In subsequent centuries Western universities grew enormously; they built buildings, granted degrees and employed full-time faculty, and by the mid-eighteenth century the university as an institution existed in most areas of the West and Middle East. But the most significant growth was reflected in the number and variety of courses of study offered to students. By the mid- nineteenth century universities in the United States offered courses in business, architecture, public administration and modern languages, and these institutions were populated by students and faculty committed to these courses of study.

The point is that the subjects themselves were not new. Modern languages had always existed, as had business skills and architectural theory. The reason that they had become part of a regular university curriculum was an understanding that they were part of the intellectual definition of the culture—or cultures—in which the university lived.

"The university of the twenty-first century would be irrelevant if it did not take account of the most striking changes in our world: rapid communications, enormous increases in literacy, and, most importantly, greater mixing of cultures in all aspects of our lives."

The university of the twenty-first century would be irrelevant if it did not take account of the most striking changes in our world: rapid communications, enormous increases in literacy, and, most importantly, greater mixing of cultures in all aspects of our lives.

This challenge to respond to the complex cultural and ethnic mix of our state also constitutes our greatest opportunity.

Traditionally, students have been most stimulated in those environments providing the greatest diversity of curriculum, students and faculty. And the universities which could most easily provide such a mix were often quite small, but located in countries with diverse populations. Regardless of levels of teaching skills, the universities in Geneva and Zurich, just because of where they are, have always provided a fertile environment to the student.

One would think that university administrators would make efforts to maintain a continuous infusion of students and faculty from our various cultures for no other reason than to enrich and strengthen the institution.

But we don't. Our efforts are sporadic, frequently grudging. This does not mean that our university leaders are racist or xenophobic; but it frequently means that they have an insufficient understanding of the role of a great university in the history of our civilization.

We must develop this diversity. This is where many throw up their hands and say they cannot accomplish this goal without failing in their other goal of maintaining "academic excellence." To this there are answers. First, many university people, again not racist but perhaps not very thoughtful, measure academic excellence in a relatively narrow way, one more suitable to one of the ancient academies than to a university in the twenty-first century. Second, many people of good will simply do not try very hard or very well, to do what is necessary to nurture and learn from the diversity.

We do not fulfill our role as a university when we, effectively, abdicate our charge to foster and maintain diversity in the university environment.

What does this mean? Does it mean active and vigorous recruiting of people from all our different cultural and ethnic groups? Yes, and it might even mean aggressive recruiting through use of both standard linear measurements and measures not yet fully articulated if we are to be a great university in this multicultural world.

While we can easily attract professors of Chinese, Korean, Arabic, Swahili or Spanish, this alone would not distinguish us from the University of Nebraska or other similarly situated institutions.

What this state offers us are resources which few other states can match: first, a mix of cultures unmatched in our country; and second, an economy which includes a myriad of trade, investment, family, and financial ties with all parts of the globe.

The challenge for us is to recognize and to treat these people not as problems, but as the great resources that they are. Together the university and these resource-people can create centers of learning the likes of which this country has never before seen.

It means requiring all students to study the history, culture, and contributions of these people whom we call "minorities."

It means encouraging all our faculty to mentor these students and to urge them to pursue graduate studies.

It means strengthening all the affirmative action programs which work.

It means fighting for bigger budgets for financial assistance for graduate students and affirmative action programs.

Finally, it means intervening in all of the educational systems and policies for pre-university students. It means educating teachers and administrators in these systems what we, as a university, want in our students and telling these students how to achieve it.

This is a great university, one of the greatest in the world; but greatness is not something that once attained lives on forever. It is an ideal, the path toward which is not always clear. Together, we can keep the University of California on this path of greatness.

It means that your role as a university requires you to participate in, to shape, our educational system as a whole.

The only alternative is to sit back, sift those students who make it through whatever pre-university structure happens to be in place, and let events shape you. That is not the role of a great university.

In sum, if the goal of this great university is excellence, and it is and should be, the attainment of that excellence requires diversity as a fundamental element. Anything less is mere pretension.

I know that we will meet this challenge and continue to build this university as one of which all Californians, indeed all the world, can be proud.

SOURCES

Extension of the Voting Rights Act of 1965: Hearings Before the Subcommittee on Constitutional Rights of the Committee on the Judiciary, United States Senate, 94th Congress, 1st Session, on S. 407, S. 903, SD. 1297, S. 1409, and S. 1443, U.S. Government Printing Office, 1975.

Hearings Before the Subcommittee on Civil and Constitutional Rights of the Committee on the Judiciary, House of Representatives, 94th Congress, 1st Session, on H.R. 939, H.R. 2148, H.R. 3247, and H.R. 3501, Extension of the Voting Rights Act, Serial No. 1, Part 1, U.S. Government Printing Office, 1975.

Telgen, Diane, and Jim Kamp, eds. *Notable Hispanic American Women,* Gale Research, Detroit, 1993.

Jorge Mas Canosa

1939–

Cuban American businessman and activist

One of the most influential—and controversial—members of Miami's Cuban-exile community is Jorge Mas Canosa, longtime chairman of the Cuban American National Foundation (CANF). Under his forceful leadership, CANF stands poised to help Cuba make the transition to democracy and a free-market economy once Fidel Castro is no longer in the picture. "Castro's days are numbered," declared Mas in a "60 Minutes" interview that first aired in 1992 and then again in 1994. "Castro is going to fall, and he's going to fall in the immediate future, and we must be prepared to bring freedom and democracy back to Cuba, but most important, prosperity."

The son of a Cuban army veterinarian, Mas was born in the port city of Santiago de Cuba. As a student activist in his native country during the late 1950s, he ran afoul of authorities after denouncing the corrupt regime of military dictator Fulgencio Batista on the radio. Mas's parents then sent him to the United States to attend school at Presbyterian Junior College in Maxton, North Carolina.

Following the Castro-led coup that ousted Batista from power in 1959, there was some hope among Cubans that their new leader would temper his radicalism and follow a more moderate course. But it soon became clear that the country had merely traded one authoritarian leader for another. Mas, who had returned home a week after the revolution to enroll in law school at the University of Oriente, soon became active in the anti-Castro movement and once again found himself facing arrest. So, in 1960 he fled to Miami.

In the city's Little Havana neighborhood, Mas made contacts with other Cuban exiles and joined the famous 2506 Brigade, which participated in the disastrous Bay of Pigs invasion of Cuba in 1961. Like the rest of the veterans of that unsuccessful U.S.-backed attempt to overthrow Castro, he was then offered a commission as a lieutenant in the U.S. Army, which he accepted in the belief that he and his fellow exiles would be called on to lead another invasion some day. But as soon as he realized that no such plans were under consideration, he resigned his commission and returned to Miami.

Mas then worked at a series of jobs—dishwasher, shoe salesman, milkman—to support himself and his growing family. (He and his wife eventually had three sons.) He also became active in an organization of militant anti-Castro Cuban exiles with ties to the U.S. Central Intelligence Agency (CIA). Their goal was to oust the hated dictator in any way possible, even if it meant resorting to terrorism and violence. During this same period, Mas also worked as a commentator on a CIA-backed radio station that broadcast anti-Castro messages to Cuba.

Later in the 1960s, Mas secured financial assistance that enabled him to enter the business world as a partner in a local contracting firm, Iglesias y Torres. It was a time of tremendous growth in the Greater Miami area, and Mas's company prospered doing construction work for utilities and other public service corporations throughout South Florida. By the end of the decade, he had bought out his partners and anglicized the firm's name to Church & Tower. (In 1994, it merged with another company, and the combined firm now goes by the name MasTec.) As a result of the tremendous success he continued to enjoy throughout the 1970s, Mas began to branch out into other businesses as well, including one that supplies light and heavy equipment to the construction industry. Before long, the once-impoverished immigrant was a multimillionaire.

At the same time he was making his fortune in business, Mas was becoming involved in politics. He forged close relationships with local and state government officials who were sympathetic to the anti-Castro exiles and encouraged them to adopt a tough, uncompromising approach toward Cuba. Following the election of staunch anti-communist Ronald Reagan to the presidency of the United States in 1980, Mas felt the time was right for Cuban Americans "to stop the commando raids and concentrate on influencing public opinion and governments." So he and fourteen other wealthy members of the Miami exile community who shared his views established the Cuban American National Foundation (CANF) to disseminate information to the public on conditions in Cuba and promote the idea of fostering political change there.

As CANF's chairman, Mas immediately began cultivating contacts in the nation's capital to drum up support for the organization's first big undertaking—a private radio station along the lines of Radio Free Europe that would counter Castro's monopoly on the news and other information. The battle over Radio Martí, as it was known (in honor of Cuban patriot José Martí), raged for a couple of years while Congress debated the need for it and the State Department warned of possible repercussions from Castro. Finally, in 1982, Radio Martí became a reality when Congress passed a bill placing it under the umbrella of the U.S. Information Agency; its first broadcast was in 1985. After overcoming similar obstacles, TV Martí followed several years later. Mas heads the advisory boards for both stations.

Throughout the 1980s, Mas built CANF into one of the most powerful lobbying organizations in Washington by successfully persuading important members of both political parties—including presidents Ronald Reagan and George Bush—that Fidel Castro represents a continuing threat to democracy in the Western Hemisphere. (This perception in turn helped shape U.S. foreign policy during the period, especially in Central America and the Caribbean.) He also made overtures to a couple of dozen world leaders as well, including Russian President Boris Yeltsin, urging them to isolate Castro and Cuba. One of Mas's greatest triumphs, in fact, came when Russia ended all economic and military aid to Cuba in 1993.

Domestically, CANF has supported legislation and other measures aimed at making life difficult for Cubans and therefore for Castro, such as limiting the amount of money Cuban exiles can send back home to help out their families, cutting off flight service from Miami to Cuba for family members, and detaining those who attempt to flee Cuba by boat at the U.S. military base at Cuba's

Guantánamo Bay. Mas has also worked out a special arrangement with the U.S. Immigration and Naturalization Service allowing Cuban exiles living in other countries to enter the United States if they are sponsored by CANF.

Looking ahead to the future, Mas has cultivated contacts with major multinational corporations, banks, brokerage firms, and wealthy individuals who are eager to offer post-Castro Cuba billions of dollars in investment capital. Meanwhile, CANF has worked with lawyers to draft a new constitution for Cuba. And the group's version of the Peace Corps, Misión Martí, has trained volunteers who are ready to head to Cuba and provide guidance on easing the transition to a capitalist economy.

In late 1991, Mas played a key role in drafting the Cuban Democracy Act (S. 2918), a bill that proposed strengthening the decades-old trade embargo against Cuba. While opponents of the measure argued that it was unduly harsh and punitive and would only result in more suffering among the Cuban people, CANF and its supporters viewed it as a way to intensify the internal pressures on Castro and thus hasten his downfall. Those against it—including the United Nations and most major allies of the U.S.—also criticized the continuing embargo as a violation of international trade law and a relic of Cold War-era politics.

When first introduced in February 1992, the bill garnered little support. The State Department opposed it as a "self-destructive" move guaranteed to anger our allies because it banned trade with Cuba by U.S. subsidiaries located in third world countries. Even Mas's close friend and ally, President George Bush, did not want to back a measure that was so unpopular both at home and abroad. But during a visit to Miami in April 1992, presidential candidate Bill Clinton announced his support of the Cuban Democracy Act and subsequently pocketed over a million dollars in campaign contributions from South Florida donors. Bush soon reversed himself, and suddenly the future looked considerably brighter for S. 2918.

As he had done several times in the past for other pending legislation regarding Cuba, Mas personally appeared before members of the House and Senate to present the case in favor of the Cuban Democracy Act. His testimony occurred on August 5, 1992, before the Subcommittee on Western Hemisphere and Peace Corps Affairs of the Senate Committee on Foreign Relations. The following reprint of his remarks is taken from the official report entitled The Cuban Democracy Act of 1992, S. 2918: Hearing Before the Subcommittee on Western Hemisphere and Peace Corps Affairs of the Committee on Foreign Relations, United States Senate, *102nd Congress, 2nd Session, U.S. Government Printing Office, 1992.*

Thank you, Mr. Chairman. It is my honor to appear before you and the distinguished members of the Senate Foreign Relations Committee to talk about U.S. policy toward Cuba. I sincerely hope that our discussion today will lead to decisions that in some way can bring an end to the suffering of the Cuban people, including the tragedy taking place in the Straits of Florida where thousands of Cubans are dying while trying to escape Fidel Castro's tyranny in unseaworthy rafts and boats.

Mr. Chairman, Fidel Castro's trip to Spain two weeks ago for the Ibero-American summit served as a telling indicator of the current state of his regime. Everywhere he went, he was heckled and jeered, the Spanish press criticized him, and all Latin American heads of state in Madrid openly criticized him in public. It was such a setback for Castro that he cut his visit several days short, and even shorter still when mere rumors about troop movements on the island caused him to flee back to Cuba.

Mr. Chairman, this growing global intolerance of Fidel Castro, evident in numerous meetings I have had with heads of state around the world, demonstrates that a policy of isolating Fidel Castro is not simply a United States position, but it is one that is gaining the increasing support of the world community.

If Castro is a pariah, it is the Cuban people who continue to bear the very heavy burden of his arrogance and intransigence in the face of the global march toward freedom and democracy. Press reports out of Cuba and personal testimonies describe an ever more depressing situation on the island; an economy grinding to a halt, pervasive rationing, a skyrocketing underground economy, widespread discontent and alienation, and widespread repression of human rights.

Just in case any Cuban citizen gets the idea that they may want to publicly disagree with the regime, rapid action brigades—thugs reminiscent of Hitler's brown shirts—have been organized to torment and physically abuse anyone considering such action. These measures, Mr. Chairman, actually are desperate reactions to a growing phenomenon in Cuba today: increasing numbers of Cubans who will not accept socialism or death, who are moving decisively beyond dissident activity to outright open opposition to the regime.

This leads me into the topic of today's discussion—U.S.-Cuba relations and specifically, S. 2918, the Cuban Democracy Act of 1992, which forty-seven of your colleagues, Mr. Chairman, have signed on as co-sponsors. I am grateful that we have moved beyond the sterile debate over whether to engage in dialogue with Fidel Castro to a more promising discussion on options for accelerating Castro's departure from power and building a foundation for a new and democratic Cuba.

Mr. Chairman, we believe the current situation, both inside and outside Cuba, mandates a new approach to promoting a peaceful transition to democracy in Cuba. That is why we in the Cuban American Foundation support the Cuban Democracy Act, which applies the stick to Castro by tightening U.S. sanctions against his regime, and extends a carrot to the Cuban people by facilitating humanitarian assistance and expanding lines of communication.

I might add that a recent poll of Cuban Americans showed sixty-nine percent of the community also supports the bill. More importantly, so do numerous peaceful opposition groups on the island, including the Cuban Democratic Coalition, the largest opposition organization on the island, several groups of the Cuban Democratic Convergence, and twelve more independent opposition groups. In fact, one jailed dissident, Pablo Reyes, was told by Cuban security forces the reason he was arrested was because of his public support for the Cuban Democracy Act. He is now facing a sixteen-year sentence.

The Cuban Democracy Act is reminiscent of the U.S. approach toward South Africa, where a comprehensive policy of economic and political isolation made a very real contribution toward fostering change in that society. The political and economic isolation of Fidel Castro must remain the cornerstone of U.S. policy as long as Castro continues to reject any meaningful reform and refuses to surrender power. Why? Number one, it sends a message to those in leadership positions around Castro that he, Castro, is the obstacle to Cuba's reintegration into the family of nations.

Also, engagement with Castro does not work, Mr. Chairman. Just look at the former Soviets; they were engaged with Castro for thirty years and they have no influence over his behavior whatsoever. Two days ago, in the *Washington Post* a former United Nations Ambassador, Jeane Kirkpatrick, observed that in the current crises in Iraq, Yugoslavia, and Cambodia, Saddam Hussein and the others like him used peace negotiations and other agreements as tactics to buy short-range advantages. She writes it is standard practice for cutthroats to make agreements when the heat is on and to break them later. That could be used as a preview of coming attractions should we travel that road with Castro, Mr. Chairman. The Cuban American Foundation also supports the measures in the Cuban Democracy Act to tighten the U.S. embargo of Cuba, especially at this time when Fidel Castro's functionaries are roaming the world in a desperate search for alternative sources of aid.

When you provide resources to Cuba, all of those resources go in the hands of Fidel Castro, and him alone. He has used the roughly $100 billion in aid received from the Soviet Union, not to help the Cuban people, who have been issued rationing books since 1960, but to buy the loyalty of those around him to sustain himself in power. The embargo deprives Fidel Castro of those resources and will continue to shrink his inner circle.

Indeed, to see who would benefit from trade relations with Cuba Mr. Chairman, follow the money. The Cuban American National Foundation has obtained from sources inside Cuba a financial audit of a Cuban front company in Panama called CIMEX, one of many he uses to circumvent the U.S. embargo to get U.S. products into Cuba and to get Cuban products into the United States.

CIMEX was cited, incidentally, in the recent letter made public from former General Patricio de la Guardia, who is serving thirty years in a Cuban jail for his part in the Ochoa affair, as one holding 500 kilos of cocaine for shipments to the United States. These financial records show, Mr. Chairman, that at a time of outrageous austerity measures being imposed on the Cuban people, Fidel Castro is hoarding $300 million in total assets in CIMEX, one of his personal piggy banks, including $100 million in cash, twice the amount of the total reported cash reserves held by the Castro regime.

These are the types of activities Fidel Castro continues to be engaged in, and it is why we want to make the U.S. embargo more effective. One measure in the Cuban Democracy Act that does so is what is known as the Mack Amendment, which you, Mr. Chairman, have supported in the past, a provision that would restore the embargo to its original language by closing the loophole opened in 1975 that allows foreign subsidiaries of U.S. companies to trade with Cuba.

It is truly distressing that at a time when Russia has radically reduced trade relations and eliminated subsidies to Castro, U.S. companies are extending a trade lifeline to Fidel Castro through their foreign subsidiaries. Even more so when subsidiary trade is not allowed with any other nation embargoed under the Trade With the Enemy Act.

Equally important to increasing economic pressure on the Castro regime is the idea of improving communications with the Cuban people. We support the elements of the Cuban Democracy Act that would institute careful and direct openings to the Cuban people quite apart from the regime, to contribute to the opening up of Cuban society. What can we communicate to the Cuban people? That there is life after Castro and that the international community is in solidarity with them.

In every available forum, the U.S. must reiterate that the Cuban people face no threat from the United States, that they should not fear a change in government, and that the United States is eager to restore traditional ties of economic and diplomatic cooperation with a free Cuba. We should not let Castro get away with the fear and hysteria over an American invasion that never seems to come.

We can also go a long way in rebutting the ludicrous charges made regularly in certain media circles that sinister Cuban exiles are plotting to return to Cuba and seize property and resources once Castro is gone from power. Indeed, if one were to believe his reporting, you would think that people on the island are vehemently anti-American, fearful of an invasion by Cuban exiles and foreign capitalists, and repulsed by the free-market system.

This cartoon caricature of the Cuban people could not be more inaccurate. Cubans on the island are painfully aware that communism does not work and that Cuban Americans enjoy tremendous opportunities that are denied [them]. Let us not delude ourselves by automatically equating Cuban nationalism with anti-Americanism. It is not that simple. Let me also state for the record that Cuban exiles have no intention of going back to Cuba to buy the island, to conquer the island, to hold people in Cuba accountable for the actions in Cuba during the last thirty-three years.

We must reassure the Cuban citizens on the island that we, the Cuban people, are one nation divided by one man, this outdated dictator, Fidel Castro. The only one who fears the reunification of the Cuban people is Castro. Finally, Mr. Chairman, the last dimension of the Cuban Democracy Act, stating what the U.S. is prepared to do to help Cuba, once Castro is out of power and free and fair elections are held. This includes, among other measures, removing the U.S. embargo.

I cannot overestimate the symbolic importance of this for the Cuban people. It says that this powerful nation is waiting to help and will do what it can to alleviate the inevitable and tremendous difficulties of transforming a country decimated economically and spiritually by thirty-three years of Marxist dictatorship. It will also make a positive contribution to ensuring that those positions of power in Cuba, around the Castro brothers, support a peaceful, nonviolent transition.

Fidel Castro has attempted to crush the Cuban people's hopes for the future and the future of their children. I believe the Cuban Democracy Act will restore that hope. We must not let the Cuban people down. The Cuban people are going to decide for themselves their own destiny.

It is our responsibility to do what we can to hasten the demise of the Castro regime and the advent of a free democratic and prosperous Cuba. All that is needed is the vision and the will to seize this opportunity to help eliminate, once and for all, a bizarre political experiment that has plagued our era. Then, and only then, can the suffering of the Cuban people be replaced by a new golden age of national self-determination and economic revival. Thank you very much.

No longer faced with any significant opposition by the fall of 1992, the Cuban Democracy Act sailed through both the House and the Senate and was signed into law by President Bush at an October ceremony in Miami. As predicted by some, it has led to a greatly reduced standard of living for the Cuban people, who once enjoyed plenty of food and a health-care system widely acknowledged as the best in the Third World. It has also triggered periodic refugee crises as desperate Cubans take to makeshift boats to escape across the Straits of Florida and the promise of freedom in the United States.

This hardline approach has also served to reveal a growing split in the Cuban American community. On the one hand are Mas and CANF, still devoted to squeezing Cuba until it explodes in revolution, which they feel will pave the way for democracy and capitalism to triumph. More moderate voices favor ending the trade embargo and opening a dialogue with Castro to put an end to the inhumane suffering of the Cuban people. There are disagreements as well over the role the exile community should play in any transition period once Castro is gone. CANF, of course, sees itself as instrumental in bringing about a new Cuban government based on capitalist free-market principles, while others insist that such decisions are Cuba's affair and that everyone else should stay out.

Meanwhile, Castro shows no sign of losing his grip on Cuba. More significantly, the anti-Castro Cuban exiles who arrived during the early 1960s—generally well-educated and prosperous—are getting up in years, and few have an interest in returning to live in the country they left more than thirty years ago. They have little in common with the younger generation of exiles (those who have arrived since 1980 or so), most of whom have less education and are from a working-class background.

Mas, however, is a member of the older generation who still dreams of the day when he can once again live in the town where he was born and grew up. As he declared to a reporter for the Los Angeles Times, *as quoted in an* Esquire *article: "I am a Cuban first. I have never assimilated. I love America, and I would die for it. I'd never been so successful in Cuba. But people like me need to be fed with more than success. I have all the money I'll ever need. I don't do this for the money. I do this because I feel like a tree without roots."*

SOURCES

Books

The Cuban Democracy Act of 1992, S. 2918: Hearing Before the Subcommittee on Western Hemisphere and Peace Corps Affairs of the Committee on Foreign Relations, United States Senate, 102nd Congress, 2nd Session, U.S. Government Printing Office, 1992.

Periodicals

Christian Century, "U.S. Cuba Policy Is Obsolete," September 7-14, 1994, pp. 803-804.

Common Cause, "Mr. Mas Goes to Washington," January/February, 1991, pp. 37-40.

Esquire, "Who Is Jorge Mas Canosa?" January, 1993.

Nation, "Will Congress Kill TV Marti?" August 22-29, 1994, pp. 194-196; "Minority Report," December 26, 1994, p. 787.

New Leader, "Mas Canosa vs. Betancourt: Struggle Among the Cuban Exiles," March 19, 1990, pp. 9-11.

New Republic, "Our Man in Miami," October 3, 1994, pp. 20-25.

Newsweek, "How Can We Say No?" September 5, 1994, pp. 28-29.

Progressive, "The Cuban Obsession," July, 1993, pp. 18-22.

Time, "The Man Who Would Oust Castro," October 26, 1992, pp. 56-57.

U.S. News and World Report, "Castro's New Revolution," June 24, 1991, pp. 38-41; "After Castro Moves Out," May 4, 1992, pp. 42-44.

Other

"60 Minutes" (transcript of television news program), Volume 26, Number 51, September 4, 1994, Burrelle's Information Services.

Robert T. Matsui

1941–

Japanese American attorney and member of the U.S. House of Representatives

One of the most powerful and respected politicians in Washington, D.C., Democrat Robert T. Matsui has represented his Sacramento, California-area district in the House of Representatives since 1978. Born in Sacramento to parents who were also American-born but of Japanese ancestry, Matsui was only a few months old when Japan and the United States went to war after the bombing of Pearl Harbor on December 7, 1941. Just a couple of months later, on February 19, 1942, President Franklin Roosevelt issued Executive Order 9066. This infamous decree called for the evacuation of some 120,000 Japanese Americans—ostensibly for their own "protection"—from the West Coast to "relocation centers" in remote areas of nearly two dozen states, including Arizona, Arkansas, inland California, Colorado, Idaho, Utah, and Wyoming. About two-thirds of those interned were U.S. citizens; Japanese Americans in other parts of the country were not affected by the order, and no similar action was taken against German Americans or Italian Americans.

Like most others in their situation, the Matsuis were given very little time to prepare for their evacuation. In the space of forty-eight hours, Mr. Matsui had to abandon his small produce business and sell the family home so that he, his wife, and infant son could leave for their assigned camp in northern California. They later were transferred to a farm labor area in Idaho and forbidden to return to Sacramento until the war ended. Although Matsui himself was too young to have many memories of his incarceration, he vividly recalls his parents' reluctance to discuss their experiences and their enduring sense of shame at having had their loyalty questioned. It was those same feelings of shame at having been imprisoned that subsequently motivated Matsui to seek redress for all who had been treated so unjustly.

Inspired by the example of Clarence Darrow to pursue a career in law so that he could "protect the underdog," Matsui—who received his bachelor's degree in political science from the University of California at Berkeley in 1963—fulfilled his dream in 1966 when he graduated from the Hastings College of Law. He then established a private practice in his hometown and involved himself in various civic and cultural activities.

In 1971, Matsui fulfilled yet another dream when he ran for and won a seat on the Sacramento City Council. (He had contemplated entering public service ever since hearing John F. Kennedy's 1961 inaugural address in which the new president encouraged Americans to "ask not what your country can do for you—ask what you can do for your country.") He was re-elected in 1975 and became vice-mayor of Sacramento in 1977. A year later, he decided to run for the U.S. House of Representatives when the incumbent from his local district declined to seek another term. Matsui trailed two other Democratic candidates early in the game, but calling upon the same networking skills and grassroots support that had earned him his city council position, he was able to overtake his opponents in the primary and subsequently defeat his Republican challenger in the general election. As of 1995, the voters have returned him to office eight more times by wide margins.

Since arriving in Washington, Matsui has distinguished himself as one of the most respected and powerful legislators on Capitol Hill. In general, he tends to favor a liberal social agenda and a more conservative approach to business issues. He is an acknowledged leader in such areas as trade, taxes, social security, health care, and welfare reform, mostly by virtue of his membership on the House Ways and Means Committee (specifically its subcommittees on trade and human resources). He has played key roles in formulating policy regarding U.S.-Japan trade negotiations, Most Favored Nation (MFN) trade status for China, and the General Agreement on Tariffs and Trade (GATT).

In 1993, President Bill Clinton designated Matsui as his point man in the battle over the controversial North American Free Trade Agreement (NAFTA), a measure designed to reduce trade barriers between the United States, Canada, and Mexico. In this high-profile position, Matsui pulled together a diverse, bi-partisan team of fellow legislators, past and present cabinet secretaries, scholars, business leaders, and environmentalists to "sell" NAFTA to a doubt-filled Congress. The representative himself made numerous appearances on television news shows to present arguments in favor of the agreement to the American public. His efforts ultimately paid off when he was able to secure congressional approval for NAFTA—a significant victory for the fledgling Clinton administration and further confirmation of Matsui's well-honed political skills.

Matsui is also recognized as a champion of issues that have a particular impact on children, especially those living in poverty. He has, for example, fought to include money in the federal budget for programs intended to prevent child abuse and neglect and help keep families together. He has also introduced major welfare reform legislation that encourages recipients to move from welfare to work. And he has been outspoken on the need to make health insurance for children a national priority.

Before NAFTA elevated his profile in Washington and around the country, however, Matsui was already known for his staunch support of the movement to obtain redress for Japanese Americans whose constitutional rights were ignored in the rush to round up "enemy aliens" during World War II. On September 28, 1979, along with fellow Japanese American congressman Norman Y. Mineta and others, he became one of the co-sponsors of H.R. 5499, a House bill that proposed creating a commission to investigate the wartime relocation of Japanese Americans and determine what, if any, compensation was owed to them for the losses they had suffered both emotionally and economically. A Senate version of the bill, S. 1647, eventually passed in mid-1980. A year later, the Commission on Wartime Relocation and Internment of Civilians (CWRIC) began holding hearings to gather testimony; eventually, more than seven hundred people went on the record with their recollections and opinions, including Matsui.

In 1983, the CWRIC published a report of its findings entitled Personal Justice Denied *in which members condemned the relocation of Japanese Americans as a measure undertaken not for military reasons but out of "race prejudice, war hysteria and a failure of political leadership." It later issued several recommendations for redress, including an apology from Congress and the president acknowledging the injustice done to Japanese Americans as a result of the order and a payment of $20,000 to each of the estimated sixty thousand survivors of the camps.*

Several years of occasional debate followed, with most of the discussion centering on the controversial notion of awarding monetary damages to former internees. Matsui and others repeatedly argued that cash compensation was an absolutely essential part of the plan given the well-established legal tradition of awarding damages to stress accountability.

Matsui presented his case on several occasions during the 1980s at various hearings on the issue of redress. On June 20, 1984, for example, he appeared before the Subcommittee on Administrative Law and Governmental Relations of the House Committee on the Judiciary, which was considering legislation to adopt CWRIC's recommendations. His testimony is reprinted from the official government transcript Japanese-American and Aleutian Wartime Relocation: Hearings Before the Subcommittee on Administrative Law and Governmental Relations of the Committee on the Judiciary, House of Representatives, *98th Congress, 2nd Session, U.S. Government Printing Office, 1985.*

Mr. Chairman and Mr. Shaw, I would like to thank both of you and other members of the subcommittee, and also members of the staff, for holding these hearings on H.R. 4110. The topic before us is of tremendous importance for our system of constitutional liberty, and I thank all of you for your very excellent leadership.

William Howard Taft reminded us that "constitutions are checks on the hasty actions of the majority." Today we are faced with the memory of a time when our system failed to provide the necessary checks, when hasty actions trampled over the rights of 120,000 people, most of whom were citizens of this country.

But today we have the opportunity to restore the system to its proper balance. With legislative action, we can at last provide redress to Americans of Japanese ancestry who were deprived of their basic civil rights during World War II.

For me, and I know this is true for many others here, this issue is endowed with strong personal memories. I was a mere ten months old when I entered the internment camp at Tule Lake with my family. Like so many of those interned, my parents were proud citizens of the United States, a country they had known to be just and ruled by a reasoned constitutional law.

But with Executive Order 9066, my parents' citizenship and loyalty suddenly meant nothing. The exclusion and detention order recognized ancestry and only ancestry. That they were born in this country—my mother in 1920 and my father in 1916, in Sacramento, California—upheld its laws and were loyal to its principles, was discarded as irrelevant.

What was the experience of that camp? It's interesting, because my parents, prior to the formation of the Commission that the Congress set up, refused to talk about it. I never could understand why. It was not until the last twenty-four months that I became appreciative of their own situation. For my parents, there was the discouraging loss of business, home, and other possessions.

My father had just begun a private produce business with his brother. Of course, that was lost. They had a home in which they had been living for about six months. That was lost. They sold their refrigerator and other worldly possessions for $5 or $10, whatever they could receive from the person who would knock on their door and say, "I know you have to leave within a short period of time and, therefore, I'll give you $5 for the refrigerator" or whatever it happened to be.

They also have visions of barbed-wire fences and sentry dogs, of loss of privacy and lack of adequate sanitation, and memories of the heart-wrenching divisions that occurred as families were separated by physical distance and the emotional distress of the camps.

I might add, however, that my family was somewhat fortunate. After nine months at Tule Lake, we were able to move on to a farm labor area in Idaho. Although there were no soldiers or watchtowers, we remained within restricted boundaries, unable to return to our home in California for three more years.

But what is most striking about all of these internment camp stories that I have learned to grow up with is the faith and hope that remained, faith in the law of the land, pride in this country, and most of all, a sincere desire to prove loyalty to this great nation and be allowed to serve its ideals and principles. All this, despite the fact that basic constitutional and civil rights were being denied to then and others in their position.

Robert T. Matsui

"I am convinced that monetary compensation must be a part of any redress effort."

It is the spirit of this faith that brings me here before you today, for I firmly believe that our actions here are essential for giving credibility to our constitutional system and reinforcing our traditional sense of justice.

As you will hear today from the Commission on Wartime Relocation and Internment of Civilians, there is no question that basic, civil rights were denied. There was no review of individual cases and no exceptions or considerations of personal service. The basic concept of habeas corpus was forgotten. I guess that I, being a nine-month-old child, can attest to the fact that I had no due process personally given to me.

As you hear more from the witnesses in the next few days, it will be clear that constitutional rights were just simply ignored. For my part, I would like to leave the subcommittee with one simple thought: because justice was denied, there certainly is a need for redress. The question before us must be to provide the most appropriate form of redress for this tragic episode in our nation's history.

As a lawmaker involved in framing the redress legislation, I will not accept monetary reparations, because to do so would lead some to suggest my actions are motivated by self-interest. They certainly are not. I am convinced that monetary compensation must be a part of any redress effort. Estimates of losses from income and property alone would account for the sum requested by the bill. Such estimates do not include disruption of careers, long-term loss of opportunity, and the tremendous personal losses from the denial of freedom and the stigma of being interned and being considered disloyal to one's country. These are the types of issues considered when awarding damages.

But the logic of compensation goes far beyond simple economics. Our legal tradition provides us with the system of damage compensation to stress the notion of accountability. If we make it absolutely clear that people will be held accountable for their actions, we can hope to deter such actions in the future. When the actions are taken by our government, it is particularly important to stress that we will hold it accountable for its actions.

Some will argue that there were extenuating circumstances, that our government acted in what is believed to be in everyone's best interest. But I must contend that nothing a government does is inherently above the law. All actions, including those of our leaders, must be subject to the constraints established by our U.S. Constitution.

War is a period of extreme national stress. It is during such periods of stress that the survival of liberty is at its most fragile point. We must try to tailor our safeguards to fit these treacherous moments.

Our task now is to provide the final legal redress and reinforce our system of justice and equity. We must remind future generations that such a tragic denial of rights must not and will not be tolerated ever again.

Mr. Chairman and Mr. Shaw, I personally would like to thank you for holding these hearings. I know, from some of the mail I have received, the kind of situation you have placed yourselves in just by merely holding these hearings—the fact that there are some people who have attempted to equate what happened to me and my family and others in my position with what happened at Pearl Harbor during World War II, which has no relationship and no causal connection. I know that you are probably receiving a lot of hate type mail. But the mere fact that you have decided to hold these hearings indicates to me that our system does work and that there are opportunities for all Americans, irrespective of our race, our color, creed, or religious background.

I would be happy to answer questions, and I thank you again very much for giving me this opportunity.

While H.R. 4110 did not make it to the House floor in 1984, a version of it known as H.R. 442 finally did come up for a vote on September 17, 1987. It proposed that the CWRIC's recommendations be adopted, including the provision for awarding monetary damages—a major sticking point for some legislators. In particular, Republican Congressman Dan Lungren of California, who had been a member of the CWRIC, questioned the fairness of holding present-day taxpayers liable for wrongs committed decades earlier and raised the prospect that approving such payments would open the door to similar claims from African Americans and other groups.

Along with his colleague Norman Y. Mineta, who delivered an emotional plea in favor of the bill, Matsui spoke movingly of his reasons for supporting H.R. 442 and urged his fellow legislators to approve it in its entirety, including the provision awarding compensation to former Japanese American prisoners of the United States. His remarks during that debate are reprinted here from the Congressional Record, *100th Congress, 1st Session, U.S. Government Printing Office, 1988.*

I would like to first of all thank the leadership of both the majority and minority for holding this bill on the 17th of September.

I would also like to thank both the Republican-Democratic caucus members for being here on a day when this is the only issue before us.

I realize many members would like to get back to their home districts or their home states for celebrations in their various areas, and that to be here on this day is somewhat of an imposition on the membership.

I would also like to state that this is a very difficult issue for me to speak on today, mainly because it is, I guess, so personal and perhaps some of you may think that I may lack objectivity. That may very well be the case. But I will try to be objective.

I would like if I may for a moment, however, to indicate to all of you perhaps what it was like to be an American citizen in 1942 if you happened to be of Japanese ancestry.

My mother and father, who were in their twenties, were both born and raised in Sacramento, California, so they were American citizens by birth. They were trying to start their careers. They had a child who was six months old. They had a home like any other American. They had a car. My father had a little produce business with his brother.

"How could I, as a six-month-old child born in this country, be declared by my own government to be an enemy alien?"

For some reason, because of Pearl Harbor, in 1942 their lives and their futures were shattered. They were given seventy-two hours' notice that they had to leave their home, their neighborhood, abandon their business, and show up at the Memorial Auditorium, which is in the heart of Sacramento, and then be taken—like cattle—in trains to the Tule Lake Internment Camp.

My father was not able to talk about this subject for over forty years, and I was a six-month-old child that they happened to have. So I really did not even understand what had happened until the 1980s. It was very interesting, because when he finally was able to articulate, he said, "You know what the problem is, why I can't discuss this issue, is because I was in one of those internment camps, a prisoner of war camp, and if I talk about it the first thing I have to say is look, I wasn't guilty, I was loyal to my country, because the specter of disloyalty attaches to anybody who was in those camps."

And that stigma exists today on every one of those 60,000 Americans of Japanese ancestry who happened to have lived in one of those camps.

They were in that camp for three and a half years of their lives and, yes, they have gotten out and they have made great Americans of themselves, and I think if my mother were alive today she would be very proud of what the U.S. Congress hopefully is about to do. Because the decision we make today really is not a decision to give $20,000 to the 66,000 surviving Americans, the decision today is to uphold that beautiful, wonderful document, the Constitution of the United States.

You know, because this is the 200th celebration, we have been talking about those fifty-five individuals who put together that document, and I do not think there is any question that there was some Supreme Being that gave them the inspiration to put that document together. I will also say if you took that same document and put it in the Soviet Union there would be no way that the people of that country would understand what it truly means and the spirit behind it. It is only because of the American people that that document is a living document with meaning, not only 200 years ago, but for 200 years in the future as well. The real issue here today is an issue of fundamental principle. How could I, as a six-month-old child born in this country, be declared by my own government to be an enemy alien? How can my mother and father, who were born in this country, also be declared a potential enemy alien to their country? That is the underlying issue here. They did not go before a court of law, they did not know what charges were filed against them. They were just told, "You have three days to pack and be incarcerated." That is the fundamental issue here.

Now I would like to just, if I may, discuss some of the principles that were raised by the proponents of the Lungren amendment just for a moment.

The gentleman from Minnesota said, "Why should today's generation pay for the tragedies of the past generation?" I do not look upon America in terms of generations. We must look upon this country as a continuous flow and ebb. We are not talking about a generation in the 1940s and a generation today. We are talking about fundamental principles because the Constitution does not change from generation to generation. It is a living document that exists forever, for eternity. So it is not a question of generations. I know that some would say, "Well, we as Americans in time of war have responsibilities, and everybody suffers in time of war." You know, that is true. Ron Packard from California gave an eloquent presentation of the fact that his father had been incarcerated during World War II by the Japanese government, a prisoner of war. Many families lost their husbands and their sons and many families were broken because of tragedies like divorce because of the separations. Everybody suffers during times of war, so why should not the Japanese Americans also share in that suffering? Let me say this: every one of us, if war were declared today, would volunteer to fight on behalf of our country and our democracy; that is a fundamental principle.

[The Chairman then interrupted to note that Matsui's time had expired, but by the unanimous consent of his fellow legislators, he was allowed to proceed for an additional three minutes.]

That is a fundamental responsibility of a democracy, a fundamental responsibility of our government, that if our security is jeopardized we have a responsibility to defend it.

We have a responsibility to die for our country, but I tell you one thing, that in a democracy—this democracy with our Constitution—a citizen does not have a responsibility . . . to be incarcerated by our own government without charges, without trial, merely because of our race. That is what our constitutional fathers meant 200 years ago when they wrote the Bill of Rights. That is not a responsibility and an inconvenience of a democracy.

I hope that each and every one of the members will find it in their hearts to look at this issues not as an individual tragedy for 60,000 Americans of Japanese ancestry but look at it in terms of the real meaning of this country. We are celebrating 200 years of a great democracy, and I think we can today uphold and renew that democracy with a vote in favor of this bill and a vote against the pending amendment.

Thanks in large measure to the pleadings of Matsui and his colleague, Norman Y. Mineta, H.R. 442 was approved in a landslide vote, with the provision awarding monetary damages to survivors of the concentration camp left intact. The Senate went on to pass its version of the proposal in April 1988, and President Ronald Reagan signed it into law that August.

SOURCES

Books

Bosworth, Allan R., *America's Concentration Camps*, Norton, 1967.

Congressional Record, 100th Congress, 1st Session, U.S. Government Printing Office, 1988.

Daniels, Roger, *Asian America: Chinese and Japanese in the United States Since 1850*, University of Washington Press, 1988.

———, *Concentration Camps USA: Japanese Americans and World War II*, Holt, 1972.

———, *The Politics of Prejudice: The Anti-Japanese Movement in California and the Struggle for Japanese Exclusion*, University of California Press, 1962.

Girdner, Audrie, and Anne Loftis, *The Great Betrayal: The Evacuation of the Japanese Americans During World War II*, Macmillan, 1969.

Grodzins, Morton M., *Americans Betrayed: Politics and the Japanese Evacuation*, University of Chicago Press, 1949.

Hosokawa, Bill, *JACL: In Quest of Justice*, Morrow, 1982.

———, *Nisei: The Quiet Americans*, Morrow, 1969.

Japanese-American and Aleutian Wartime Relocation: Hearings Before the Subcommittee on Administrative Law and Governmental Relations of the Committee on the Judiciary, House of Representatives, 98th Congress, 2nd Session, U.S. Government Printing Office, 1985.

Personal Justice Denied: Report of the Commission on Wartime Relocation and Internment of Civilians, U.S. Government Printing Office, 1983.

tenBroek, Jacobus, Edward N. Barnhart, and Floyd W. Matson, *Prejudice, War and the Constitution*, University of California Press, 1954.

Uyeda, Clifford I., editor, *The Japanese American Incarceration: A Case for Redress* (booklet), 3rd edition, National Committee for Redress of the Japanese American Citizens League, 1980.

Periodicals

A. Magazine, "Power Brokers," fall, 1993, pp. 25-34; "The Power of Two," fall, 1993.

Christian Science Monitor, "Japanese Americans Detained in WWII Have Hope of Redress," September 16, 1987.

Los Angeles Times, "House Votes to Pay Japanese WWII Internees," September 18, 1981.

New York Times, "Seeking Redress for an Old Wrong," September 17, 1987; "House Votes Payments to Japanese War Internees," September 18, 1987.

San Francisco Examiner, "House OKs Reparations for Internees," September 18, 1987.

Time, "The Burden of Shame," September 28, 1987, p. 31.

Washington Post, "House Votes Apology, Reparations for Japanese Americans Held During War," September 18, 1987.

Spark M. Matsunaga

1916–1990

Japanese American member of the U.S. Senate

As one who was well acquainted with the devastating effects of war, Spark Matsunaga made peace the focus of his career in the United States Senate. For nearly two decades, he lobbied his colleagues to establish a National Academy of Peace and Conflict Resolution, which he envisioned as a place young Americans could go to learn how to resolve domestic and international disputes without resorting to violence. He also championed the creation of a cabinet-level Department of Peace. While Matsunaga knew full well that his dream faced an uphill climb, he pursued it until the end of his days. "This is a nation which is built upon men who have dared to do the impossible," he once declared. "I feel that we must show the world that peace can be a way of life. . . ."

Born in Hawaii to parents who had emigrated from Japan, Matsunaga and his five siblings grew up amid extreme poverty. Yet their parents instilled in them the belief that hard work would bring them success. Indeed, Matsunaga held a variety of jobs while still in high school and also worked his way through the University of Hawaii, graduating with honors in 1941. Postponing his plans to go on to law school, he joined the U.S. Army and was commissioned a second lieutenant. But fate soon intervened; on December 7 of that year, the Japanese bombed Pearl Harbor and brought the United States into World War II.

In the weeks and months following the attack, Japanese Americans—even those who were U.S. citizens—became targets of prejudice, fear, and hatred by those who questioned their loyalty to America. On February 19, 1942, President Roosevelt issued Executive Order 9066, which called for the evacuation of some 120,000 Japanese Americans (about two-thirds of whom were U.S. citizens) from the West Coast to large "relocation centers" in isolated areas of Arizona, Arkansas, inland California, Colorado, Idaho, Utah, and Wyoming. (A number of smaller camps were also set up in about fourteen other states.) By and large, Japanese Americans living elsewhere in the United States and in Hawaii were not affected by the order. But as a member of the military, Matsunaga was considered suspect, even though he had given no cause for anyone to doubt his allegiance. So he, too, was shipped off to an internment camp in Wisconsin.

But many young Japanese American men wanted the chance to fight for their country and prove their loyalty. Before long, a number of them (including internees such as Matsunaga) began petitioning the U.S. government to allow them to serve in the armed forces. Finally, in January 1943, the War Department announced that it would accept fifteen hundred Japanese American volunteers for a new unit, the 442nd Regimental Combat Team. Matsunaga joined up and fought for the 100th Infantry Battalion in Italy, where he was wounded twice. The now-legendary 442nd went on to become the most decorated unit in U.S. military history; Matsunaga himself returned home as a captain with many medals and commendations.

After the war, Matsunaga earned his law degree from Harvard University in 1951. He then headed back to Hawaii, where he worked as a prosecutor in Honolulu until 1954 and then entered politics as a member and later majority leader in the Territorial House of Representatives. He was also active in the administrative ranks of the Democratic party, serving as an executive board member of the state organization and a delegate to county and state conventions. When Hawaii became a state in 1959, the immensely popular and personable Matsunaga was elected to its new senate.

In 1962, Matsunaga made the leap to national office when he was elected to the U.S. House of Representatives. He went on to serve seven consecutive terms in that body before being elected to the U.S. Senate in 1976. While his impact on legislation was not as great as that of his fellow senator from Hawaii, Daniel K. Inouye, Matsunaga's devotion to his causes—peace, nuclear arms control, safeguarding the environment, securing redress for Japanese Americans interned during World War II—was never in doubt, and he fought tirelessly to bring them to the attention of his colleagues and solicit their support for pending legislation.

One such instance was in connection with his efforts to establish a National Academy of Peace and Conflict Resolution. Envisioned as a place where young Americans could go to master "the art of peace," it was a cherished dream of Matsunaga's that surfaced time and time again from the moment he arrived in Washington. On January 25, 1978, he appeared before the Subcommittee on International Operations of the House Committee on International Relations to plead his case yet again. His remarks are reprinted here from the official report entitled National Academy of Peace and Conflict Resolution: Hearings Before the Subcommittee on International Operations of the Committee on International Relations, House of Representatives, *95th Congress, 2nd Session, U.S. Government Printing Office, 1978.*

I am here, of course, to offer testimony in support of H.R. 10192, a bill to establish a commission on proposals for a U.S. Academy for Peace and Conflict Resolution. This measure as you know embodies a concept that has long been of great importance to me—the institutionalization at the federal level of our nation's commitment to the goal of global peace.

As you may be aware, Mr. Chairman, since being first elected to the Congress in 1962, I have introduced legislation to establish a cabinet-level Department of Peace. The idea of such a department did not originate with me, but I believe that no other objective deserves greater priority. Others have striven to achieve this elusive goal, dating back to the first men who proposed a Peace Department shortly after the Revolutionary War, down to my present distinguished colleague in the Senate, Senator Jennings Randolph of West Virginia, who first introduced such a measure in 1945 and has been doing so ever since. I am greatly honored that Senator Randolph, along with Senator Mark Hatfield, have joined me as co-sponsors of the

Department of Peace bill which I have introduced in the 95th Congress.

One of the major duties assigned to the proposed Department of Peace would be the establishment and maintenance of a National Academy of Peace. H.R. 10192 and its companion measure, S. 469, co-sponsored by Senator Randolph and myself and passed by the Senate on June 17, 1977, would set up a commission to study proposals for the establishment of an Academy of Peace and Conflict Resolution.

Three centuries ago the Dutch philosopher Spinoza captured the subtleties of the meaning of the word "peace" in one short sentence. He said, and I quote: "Peace is not an absence of war, it is a virtue, a state of mind, a disposition for benevolence, confidence, justice."

This nation's concern over this situation is not entirely altruistic.

The bills before this subcommittee seek in the final analysis the creation of an institution that will embody, in Spinoza's words again, "a disposition for benevolence, confidence, justice."

The United States wields all economic, social, cultural, and political power over the world that is unequaled in history. I believe that this legislation will enable our nation to bring this power to bear directly on the problems of war and on those related problems that plague the lesser developed countries. Some of the programs, both national and international, that must be undertaken in this effort have already been conceptualized and some have been implemented. Others still need to be invented. The needs vastly exceed the solutions.

An Academy of Peace and Conflict Resolution could provide the trained personnel with the solutions—the negotiators behind international agreements, such as a Law of the Sea Treaty, which are so crucial to food and natural resources problems.

The Academy could provide the trained staffs for international development institutions such as agricultural improvements organizations. Obviously, Academy graduates could fill these same positions in bilateral American efforts, both public and private, to better the lot of the world's poor.

Finally, the Academy could provide the diplomats, and widen the foreign policy community in the United States and the rest of the free world, to bring about an end to the arms race and even bring about a degree of disarmament.

I am reminded that in January of each year we members of Congress participate in the process by which the finest of our young men and women are chosen to enter the military service academies. These academies and their insistence on high standards both academically and physically are an important part of the reason the United States has the best armed forces in the world. I cannot help but think what an impact an Academy of Peace could have on the fate of not only our own nation but the fate of nations in every part of the globe.

It was Albert Einstein, whose genius was the catalyst for a revolution in scientific thought which resulted in the creation of the atomic bomb and who later—perhaps as a result of this fact—became a renowned pacifist, who said, "Peace cannot be kept by force; it can only be achieved by understanding."

I submit that peace, like war, is an art which must be studied and learned before it can be waged well. . . .

I might add a Confucius saying here although not stated in writing. He said, "We can never know peace unless every individual citizen will want it."

Surely one task that lies before the Peace Academy Commission is that of convincing the American people and peoples of other nations that we must want peace and that we must work to maintain it. However, the most convincing proof of this argument will be the example of the achievement of graduates of the Peace Academy as they begin their work in the United States and the world.

I ask you today to report H.R. 10192 or S. 469 favorably to the House so that this great endeavor in peace can be set in motion. I ask you to launch our nation on a course that may well become the accomplishment for which we will be known in future world history because no other nation dared to do it—the pursuit of peace as an art.

Thank you very much.

It was not until 1984 that Matsunaga was successful in persuading his colleagues to establish such a program (minus the creation of a Department of Peace within the cabinet), which awards graduate degrees to those who help resolve disputes in the national and international arena.

Perhaps the most significant achievement of Matsunaga's legislative career, however, was the key role he played in obtaining redress for those Japanese Americans who were victims of injustice during World War II as a result of the infamous Executive Order 9066. Ostensibly imprisoned for their own "protection," these men, women, and children of all ages and backgrounds had not been accused of any crime, yet they spent as long as three years imprisoned in tar-paper shacks behind barbed wire and guarded by armed military police. Many had been forced to give up everything they owned. But the greatest blow was to their dignity and sense of security; they could not comprehend why their loyalty was being questioned and why the government they respected and admired was so willing to cast aside their constitutional rights.

On August 2, 1979, Matsunaga co-sponsored a bill known as S. 1647 that proposed creating a commission to investigate the wartime relocation of Japanese Americans and determine what, if any, compensation was owed to them for the losses they had suffered both emotionally and economically. In the months before the bill finally came up for consideration in the Senate, hearings were held to debate its merits. Appearing at one of those sessions on March 18, 1980, was Matsunaga, who very clearly stated his reasons for supporting S. 1647. His testimony is reprinted here from the official report entitled Commission on Wartime Relocation and Internment of Civilians Act: Hearing Before the Committee on Governmental Affairs, United States Senate, *96th Congress, Second Session, U.S. Government Printing Office, 1980.*

Mr. Chairman, I welcome this opportunity to join such a distinguished panel of witnesses in urging that early and favorable consideration of S. 1647. S. 1647 provides for the establishment of a federal commission to study, in an impartial and unbiased manner, the detention of civilians under the provisions of Executive Order 9066 during World War II.

Some of those who are here today will recall with great clarity the atmosphere which prevailed in the United States following the attack on Pearl Harbor on December 7, 1941. Rumors were rampant that Japanese warplanes had been spotted off the west coast, and erroneous reports of followup attacks on the U.S. mainland abounded. A great wave of fear and hysteria swept the United States, particularly the west coast.

Some two months after the attack on Pearl Harbor, in February 1942, President Franklin D. Roosevelt issued Executive Order 9066. The Executive Order gave to the Secretary of War the authority to designate "military areas" and to exclude "any or all" persons from such areas. Penalties for the violation of such military restrictions were subsequently established by Congress in Public Law 77-503, enacted in March of that year.

Also in March, the military commander of the western district—General John L. DeWitt—issued four public proclamations, and it was under those proclamations that the first civilian order was issued by the general on March 24 1942, which marked the beginning of the evacuation of some 120,000 Japanese Americans and their parents from the west coast.

It is significant to note that the military commander of the then-territory of Hawaii, which had actually suffered an enemy attack, did not feel it was necessary to evacuate all individuals of Japanese ancestry from Hawaii—although it is true that a number of leaders in the Japanese American community in Hawaii were sent to detention camps on the mainland.

Moreover, no military commander felt that it was necessary to evacuate from any area of the country all Americans of German or Italian ancestry, although the United States was also at war with Germany and Italy.

FBI Director J. Edgar Hoover, who could hardly be accused of being soft on suspected seditionists, opposed the evacuation of Japanese Americans from the west coast, pointing out that the FBI and other law enforcement agencies were capable of apprehending any suspected saboteurs or enemy agents.

I might point out that whenever I criticized the FBI, the late J. Edgar Hoover was quick on the telephone to remind me that he opposed the evacuation of Japanese Americans from the west coast.

Indeed, martial law was never declared in any of these western states, and the federal courts and civilian law enforcement agencies continued to function normally.

You will be interested to know, Mr. Chairman, as a senator from the state of Washington, that one of the real strong defenders of the Japanese Americans during this distressing period in their lives was the mayor of Tacoma, Washington, the Honorable Harry Cain. One western governor, the Honorable Ralph Carr of Colorado, was willing to accept Americans of Japanese ancestry as residents of his state and undertook to guarantee their constitutional rights.

Of the 120,000 Americans of Japanese ancestry and their parents who were evacuated from the west coast and placed in detention camps, about one-half were under the age of twenty-one; about one-quarter were young children; many were elderly immigrants prohibited by law from becoming naturalized citizens, who had worked hard to raise their American-born children to be good American citizens. Not one, I repeat, not one, was convicted or tried for or even charged with the commission of a crime.

As a consequence of their evacuation, they lost their homes, jobs, businesses, and farms. More tragically the American dream was snuffed out of them and their faith in the American system was severely shaken. Reportedly, one of the evacuees, a combat veteran of World War I, who fervently believed that his own U.S. government would never deprive him of his liberty without due process of law, killed himself when he discovered that he was wrong.

In retrospect, the evacuation of Japanese Americans from the west coast and their incarceration in what can only be properly described as concentration camps is considered by many historians as one of the blackest pages in American history. It remains the single most traumatic and disturbing experience in the lives of many Nisei.

Some, now middle-aged and older, still weep when they think about it. Some become angry. And some still consider it such a degrading experience that they refuse to talk about it. More importantly, their children have started to ask questions about the internment of their parents and grandparents. Why didn't they "protest?" Did they commit any crimes that they are ashamed of? If the government was wrong, why hasn't the wrong been admitted and laid to rest forever?

> ***"Of the 120,000 Americans of Japanese ancestry and their parents who were . . . placed in detention camps . . . not one, I repeat, not one, was convicted or tried for or even charged with the commission of a crime."***

No branch of the federal government has ever undertaken a comprehensive examination of the actions taken under Executive Order 9066. In 1943 and 1944, the U.S. Supreme Court did hear three cases involving the violation of the Executive Order. In *Hirabayashi v. United States* (1943) and *Korematsu v. United States* (1944), the Court ruled that an American citizen could be restrained by a curfew and could be excluded from a defined area.

However, in *Ex parte Endo* (1944), the Court held that neither the Executive Order nor act of Congress authorized the detention of an American citizen against her will in a relocation camp.

In 1972, the Congress repealed the Emergency Detention Act, a repugnant law enacted in 1950 which provided a procedural means of incarcerating Americans suspected of espionage or sabotage during an internal security emergency in camps similar to those established for Japanese Americans in World War II.

In 1975, President Ford revoked Executive Order 9066, and Congress repealed Public Law 77-503, and a host of other outmoded emergency war powers granted to the president on a temporary basis since the Civil War.

Despite these commendable actions, many unanswered questions remain about the detention of Japanese Americans during World War II, and there remains an unfinished chapter in our national history.

In recent years, the issue of how to write "The End" to this sad and unsavory episode has been widely discussed in the Japanese American community. From time to time, reports that the Japanese Americans might be preparing to request monetary reparations have been floated in the national press.

Some members of the Japanese American community do believe that the federal government should provide some form of monetary compensation to redress them for the injustice they suffered. However, members of this committee ought to know that an almost equal number maintain that no amount of money can ever compensate them for the loss of their inalienable right to life, liberty, and the pursuit of happiness, or the loss of their constitutional rights.

The proposed bill is not a redress bill. Should the Commission authorized to look into the matter decide that some form of compensation should be provided, the Congress would still be able to consider the question and make the final decision. Whether or not redress is provided, the study undertaken by the Commission will be valuable in and of itself, not only for Japanese Americans, but for all Americans.

Passage of S. 1647 will be just one more piece of evidence ours is a nation great enough to recognize and rectify its mistakes.

Thank you.

S. 1647 sailed through the Senate on May 22, 1980, and, after the House and Senate reached agreement on a final version, it was signed into law by President Jimmy Carter on July 31. On July 14, 1981, the Commission on Wartime Relocation and Internment of Civilians (CWRIC) began gathering testimony from others with something to say about this dark episode in American history. In all, more than seven hundred people appeared before the CWRIC, which in 1983 published a report of its findings entitled Personal Justice Denied. *In this document, members of the commission condemned the relocation of Japanese Americans, insisting it was done not out of military necessity but as a result of "race prejudice, war hysteria and a failure of political leadership." The CWRIC later issued several recommendations for redress, including an apology from Congress and the president acknowledging the injustice done to Japanese Americans and a payment of $20,000 to each of the estimated sixty thousand survivors of the camps.*

Finally, on April 19, 1988, a bill known as S. 1009 proposing that the CWRIC's recommendations be adopted made it to the floor. Matsunaga, who had shepherded the measure through the Senate with a number of impassioned speeches urging its approval, faced his colleagues yet again, this time to head off attempts by opponents to eliminate cash compensation to former internees. (Few legislators had a problem with the idea of apologizing to Japanese Americans, but some questioned the fairness of holding present-day taxpayers responsible for wrongs committed decades earlier and raised the prospect that approving such payments would open the door to similar claims from African Americans and other groups.) Matsunaga's speech is reprinted from the Congressional Record, *100th Congress, Second Session, U.S. Government Printing Office, 1988.*

Mr. President, as of September 17 of last year, we have been observing the bicentennial of the greatest human document ever written—the U.S. Constitution. With pride in our unique heritage, we Americans should reaffirm our commitment to the proposition that the United States is one nation with liberty and justice for all.

I am, therefore, extremely grateful to the chairman of the Governmental Affairs Committee, Senator Glenn, for expediting the reporting of this bill to the floor, and I thank the chairman for his most generous remarks. I assure him that the admiration is mutual. I do appreciate all the help he has given me on this piece of legislation. I thank him very much.

I also wish to thank the ranking member of the committee, Senator Roth, and the distinguished majority and the distinguished minority leader for scheduling for floor action S. 1009, a bill which I introduced with seventy-three co-sponsors, to provide a long overdue remedy for one of the worst violations of individual civil liberties in our nation's history—the evacuation, relocation, and detention of American citizens and resident aliens of Japanese ancestry during World War II.

In the life of every individual, and every nation, there are certain events which have a lasting, lifelong impact and which change the shape of their future. For some Americans, the October 1987 stock market decline brought back frightening memories of the Crash of 1929 and the Great Depression which followed it. For others, the image or words of a slain president or civil rights leader remind them of a turning point in their lives.

For Americans of Japanese ancestry who are over the age of forty-five years, the single, most traumatic event, the one which shaped the rest of their lives, is the wholesale relocation and incarceration in American-style concentration camps of some 120,000 Americans of Japanese ancestry and their parents and grandparents, who were legal resident aliens barred by United States law from becoming naturalized American citizens.

All Americans of that generation no doubt recall with great clarity where they were and what they were doing on December 7, 1941, the day that Japan attacked the American naval base at Pearl Harbor. I myself was in active military service on the Hawaiian Island of Molokai as an Army officer in temporary command of an infantry company. In fact, I was one of 1,565 Americans of Japanese ancestry who had volunteered for and were in active military service before Pearl Harbor, and who, with other Americans, stood in defense of the Territory of Hawaii against the enemy.

We remember vividly the atmosphere which prevailed in this country immediately after the bombing of Pearl Harbor. Rumors of a Japanese attack on the West Coast of the United States were rampant and numerous false sightings of enemy war planes off the coast were reported. A great wave of fear and hysteria swept the United States, particularly along the West Coast, where a relatively small population of Japanese Americans had, even before the outbreak of war, been subjected to racial discrimination and often violent attacks.

Two months after the attack on Pearl Harbor, in February 1942, President Franklin D. Roosevelt issued Executive Order 9066. The Executive Order gave to the Secretary of War the authority to designate restricted military areas and to exclude any or all persons from such areas. Penalties for violation of the restrictions were subsequently established by Congress in Public Law 77-503, enacted in March 1942.

At about the same time, the military commander of the western district, Lieutenant General John DeWitt, issued public proclamations establishing restricted military zones in eight western states, instituting a curfew applicable to enemy aliens and persons of Japanese ancestry, and restricting the travel of Americans of Japanese ancestry and enemy aliens. The first "civilian exclusion order" was issued by General DeWitt on March 24, 1942, and marked the beginning of the relocation and internment of the Japanese American population on the West Coast.

Significantly, the military commander of the then-Territory of Hawaii, which was under martial law, did not believe that it was necessary to order the wholesale evacuation of all Americans or resident aliens of Japanese ancestry, although about 1,400 leaders of the Japanese American community in Hawaii were rounded up immediately after the attack and sent to detention camps on the mainland.

J. Edgar Hoover, then director of the Federal Bureau of Investigation, opposed the mass incarceration of Japanese Americans, pointing out that the FBI was capable of apprehending and arresting any spies or saboteurs. Japanese diplomats, consular officials and military attachés who were in this country at the outbreak of war between the United States and Japan were not incarcerated in detention camps. On Hoover's orders, they were confined to house arrest and treated courteously, because the FBI director hoped that American citizens in Japan would be treated in a similar manner. The Office of Naval Intelligence had also informed President Roosevelt that the wholesale incarceration of Japanese Americans was unnecessary, pointing to the lack of evidence of any acts of espionage or sabotage by Americans of Japanese ancestry or their parents, before, during or after the attack on Pearl Harbor.

Of the 120,000 individuals who were ordered on seventy-two hours' notice to pack, leave their homes, and report to assembly centers prior to being moved to camps in the interior United States, about eighty percent were native-born American citizens—many of them young children and teenagers. The remainder, including many elderly people, were legal alien residents of the United States who were prohibited by the Oriental Exclusion Act of 1924 from becoming naturalized American citizens regardless of how much they wanted to be, like my father and mother. All of them, citizens and alien residents alike, were entitled to the protection of the U.S. Constitution, but their constitutional rights were summarily denied. Without being charged or indicted, without trial or hearing, without being convicted of a single crime, they were en masse ordered into what can only be described as American-style concentration camps surrounded by barbed-wire fences with searchlights, watchtowers and armed guards—and there they remained, many for over three years.

In 1980, thirty-eight years after the beginning of the relocation and internment of Japanese Americans, Congress authorized a thorough study of the circumstances surrounding the event. A distinguished nine-member commission, appointed by the president of the United States, was mandated to examine the facts surrounding the issuance of Executive Order 9066 and the subsequent relocation and internment of Japanese Americans. In addition, the commission was authorized to study the circumstances surrounding the evacuation of the Aleutian and Pribilof Islands in Alaska and the relocation of Native American Aleuts. The commissioners were Joan Z. Bernstein, a Washington, D.C., attorney, chairman; Daniel E. Lungren, a member of Congress from California, vice chairman; Edward W. Brooke, a former U.S. Senator from Massachusetts; Robert F. Drinan, a former member of Congress from Massachusetts; Arthur S. Flemming, formerly chairman of the U.S. Commission on Civil Rights; Arthur J. Goldberg, a former justice of the U.S. Supreme Court; Ishmael V. Gromoff of Alaska; William M. Marutani of Pennsylvania; and Hugh B. Mitchell of Washington State.

In 1983, following twenty days of public hearings which included more than 750 witnesses, and extensive review of federal records, contemporary writings, personal accounts and historical analyses, the commission filed its report, entitled "Personal Justice Denied." See how thick a volume it is.

The commission's comprehensive report was welcomed by Americans of Japanese ancestry who had lived through the relocation and internment. It revealed publicly for the first time what they had always known: the relocation and internment of Japanese Americans was not justified by military necessity or national security but was the result of racial prejudice, wartime hysteria and the failure of political leadership.

The commission found that the precipitous action had been taken under the leadership of men like General DeWitt, who believed, and stated to the U.S. House of Representatives Naval Affairs Subcommittee on April 13, 1943:

> *A Jap's a Jap. They are a dangerous element, whether loyal or not. There is no way to determine their loyalty. . . . It makes no difference whether he is an American; theoretically, he is still a Japanese, and you can't change him. . . . You can't change him by giving him a piece of paper.*

Moreover, the commission found that the exclusion of Japanese Americans from the west coast and their detention continued long after the initial panic following the attack on Pearl Harbor had abated. In a meeting with Justice Department officials in 1944, Assistant Secretary of War John J. McCloy is reported to have remarked that:

> *It was curious how the two major cases in which the Army had interfered with civilians had started out for serious military reasons and had ended being required by wholly non-military considerations. For example, the Japanese were evacuated back in the dark days before Mid-*

way when an attack on the Pacific Coast was feared. Now the exclusion is being continued by the president for social reasons.

The Battle of Midway, a great American naval victory, took place in June 1942, at the very beginning of the government's relocation and detention of Japanese Americans. It ended the threat of a Japanese attack on the continental United States.

While revelation of the truth at last by a congressionally-created commission is a great relief to Americans of Japanese ancestry who were victims of this grave wartime mistake, the public report alone is not enough to provide them with justice too long denied—any more than it would be for any other American falsely imprisoned for years on trumped-up charges. In our great society, the victims of such errors in justice are entitled to more tangible relief.

What kind of relief is appropriate? The commission recommended and S. 1009 provides, first, for an official acknowledgement of the injustice and an apology to the surviving internees. Second, the bill establishes a civil liberties education fund which would conduct educational research and fund projects designed to inform the public of the events surrounding the relocation and internment of Japanese Americans, to ensure that such a thing never happens again. S. 1009 also provides that court cases wherein Japanese Americans were convicted of violating curfew and travel restrictions imposed by the western military district be reviewed by the U.S. Department of Justice, and that presidential pardons be recommended where appropriate. Finally, S. 1009 provides for the payment of $20,000 to each of the approximately 60,000 former internees who are still alive.

This last provision is perhaps the most controversial in the bill, Mr. President, and I would like to take a few minutes to address it.

Opponents of the individual payments provision often ask why the commission picked the seemingly arbitrary figure of $20,000 and why there was not an effort to base the compensatory payments on actual losses.

In 1983, the commission asked the firm of ICF, Inc. to estimate the value of losses sustained by Japanese Americans because of their evacuation, relocation, and incarceration during World War II. Michael C. Barth, the president of ICF, Inc., testifying before the House Judiciary Subcommittee on Administrative Law and Governmental Relations, on April 28, 1987, stated that:

We were asked in the late winter of 1983 to estimate the economic losses in the aggregate of American citizens of Japanese descent and resident aliens as a result of their exclusion and detention during the Second World War.

My firm, ICF, Inc., then endeavored to determine what information was available and to determine the concepts of losses that could be estimated. Economic losses were divided into two categories—income losses and property losses.

Two other important categories of losses were not either susceptible of estimation or able to be estimated. The first were what are called human capital losses, which are no doubt of immense importance. These are losses resulting from losses in education, training, and experience during exclusion and detention. We were unable to come up with any estimate of these.

The report also does not address concepts such as pain and suffering. Therefore I will concentrate on our estimates of income losses and property losses.

Income losses were defined to be the amount of income that might have been earned by excludees had they not been in the detention camps during the period 1942–46. These were adjusted for the actual income that was earned by excludees—by detainees while they were in the camps since modest amounts of pay was paid.

This analysis yielded an estimate of the income losses, and we produced a range estimate, in 1945 dollars, of between $108 million and $164 million for that concept. Adjusting that to 1983 dollars yielded an amount of between roughly $600-$900 million, and we further adjusted that for illustrative purposes because it's possible that had this money been available to the detainees they might have been able to invest it as other citizens might have, and that yielded an amount between $900 million and $1.4 billion.

Property losses were particularly difficult to estimate because of the lack of information. We were given access to all of the claims files available for the 1947 Japanese American Evacuation Claims Act (which has been referred to earlier), as well as the private files of some citizens who were involved in litigation at that time.

Based on this information, we estimated ranges of the amounts of losses per claimant. Now it's possible that not all persons who had property losses filed under the 1947 Evacuation Claims Act. Accordingly then, in order to ensure that we were not grossly underestimating claims, we conducted various analyses of the amounts of claims that might have been claimed for had people not been ignorant or unaware or otherwise unable to make claims for which they could not provide adequate justification.

We also then adjusted our estimates for the fact that $37 million was in fact paid by the U.S. government to claimants, and between 1947 and 1958 when the final claim was paid (sic). These estimates, because of the substantial data problems, resulted in a large range, but putting together the income and the property loss estimates and adjusting that for inflation to 1983 yielded a range of $810 million to $2 billion. Adjusting for the foregone interest that might have been earned yielded a range of $1.2-$3.1 billion.

It's my understanding that the commission then used our range of losses in the aggregate to develop what they thought was the appropriate amount of restitution per claimant. . . .

Those who contend that token payments are an inappropriate way to redress this injustice overlook the basic fact that compensatory remedies are deeply rooted in American jurisprudence. It has long been considered proper for our courts to award monetary damages to individuals who have been unjustifiably injured. In tort law, for example, there are virtually thousands of reported cases in which substantial damages have been awarded to persons who were falsely arrested or imprisoned, on nonracially motivated grounds.

> ***"Japanese Americans were deprived of their freedom through the actions of their own government . . . not the enemy."***

The amounts of damages in such cases vary considerably, ranging from several hundred dollars to well over $100,000. The vast majority of reported awards stem from detentions lasting no more than a few days in duration, as compared to three years in the case of Japanese Americans. In many jurisdictions, an award for false arrest or imprisonment can include an amount for mental suffering. Humiliation, shame, and fright are elements that are considered in determining mental suffering. In addition, many jurisdictions include punitive damages where the conduct of the wrongdoer was particularly egregious or outrageous. Mr. President, I ask unanimous consent that I may append to my remarks examples of false arrest and false imprisonment cases in which monetary damages were awarded, including the factors upon which the judge relied in upholding the award. . . .

These examples are contained in the appendix of testimony by Mr. Angus Macbeth, former special counsel to the Commission on Wartime Relocation and Internment of Civilians.

When one considers the fact that most of the internees were detained for three years or more, the $20,000 lump-sum payments simply cannot be considered excessive. The funds authorized for these payments are allocated over a period of five years and will constitute but a tiny fraction of our trillion-dollar federal budget. In addition, as was pointed out several times during the House debate on this legislation, the $20,000 lump-sum payments are equivalent to less that $3,000 in 1945 dollars, a very small amount of compensation considering the degree of economic, social, and emotional injury incurred by the internees during their three-year confinement.

In addition, opponents of S. 1009 often express the concern that enactment of the bill will set a dangerous precedent and invite similar claims by other minority groups.

It should be noted that under the provisions of S. 1009, payments are to be made only to those living individuals who were victims of the federal government's wartime policy. No payments are to be made to heirs or descendants of the former internees. S. 1009 would, therefore, not open the door for claims by descendants of former slaves or the descendants of Native American victims of the federal government's nineteenth-century policies with respect to American Indians. When we look for cases of people alive today who were themselves directly injured by the federal government because of their race or ethnicity, the incarceration of Japanese Americans is unprecedented.

Finally, I am often asked about the case of American citizens who were held captive by Japan during World War II. The War Claims Act of 1948 compensated each civilian American citizen who was held by the Imperial Japanese Government in the amount of $60 per month. The act was later extended to cover civilians captured by North Korea during the Korean conflict. Later still, it was extended to cover American civilians captured by North Vietnam during the war in Vietnam. Civilians captured in Vietnam were compensated in the amount of $150 for each month they were imprisoned. Like the Japanese Americans, these Americans suffered a loss of liberty; the difference is that Japanese Americans were deprived of their freedom through the actions of their own government—the United States of America, not the enemy.

Federal courts have also addressed constitutional violations and false imprisonment in individual or class-action settings. In *Dellums v. Powell,* 566 F. 2d 167 (D.C. Cir. 1977), the case which grew out of the mass arrests of demonstrators at the 1972 May Day demonstration in Washington, D.C., damages for false imprisonment were awarded in amounts ranging from $120 for twelve hours or less to $1,800 for forty-eight to seventy-two hours of detention.

Individual payments have also been made to Americans held hostage as a consequence of terrorism. Of the fifty-two Americans held hostage in Iran for 444 days, all but one were U.S. government employees. Congress voted each of these fifty-one a special bonus of $50 per day for that period—a total of $22,200 for each former hostage.

So it is clear that Congress can act to provide appropriate compensation to individuals who were the victims of such a grave injustice. Such compensation is long overdue. Since the end of World War II, many who were directly or indirectly involved in the mass evacuation and detention of Japanese Americans and resident aliens of Japanese ancestry have acknowledged the wrong inflicted on the evacuees.

President Roosevelt, in approving the induction of Japanese Americans into the U S. Army, observed that "Americanism is a matter of the mind and heart—not race or ancestry." Henry L. Stimson, then Secretary of War, recognized that "to loyal citizens, this forced evacuation was a personal injustice." Francis Biddle, then the attorney general of the United States, expressed his belief that "the program was ill-advised, unnecessary, and unnecessarily cruel." Milton Eisenhower, the first director of the War Relocation Authority, described the evacuation and detention of Japanese Americans as "an inhuman mistake." The late chief justice of the U.S. Supreme Court, Earl Warren, who, as attorney general of the state of California, urged evacuation of Japanese Americans, stated, "I have since deeply regretted the removal order and my own testimony advocating it, because it was not in keeping with our American concept of freedom and the rights of citizens."

S. 1009 also has the strong support of a large number of contemporary individuals and organizations, and I ask unanimous consent that such a list may be printed in the *Record* following my statement. . . .

Mr. President, it is time that Congress, too, recognized the grave injustice inflicted by the federal government on American citizens of Japanese ancestry and move to make amends. Passage of S. 1009 would remove a longstanding blot on our national Constitution—a most appropriate way to commemorate its bicentennial. It would also remove a cloud which has hung over the heads of innocent Americans of Japanese ancestry since World War II.

When the Japanese American 442nd Regimental Combat Team, described by General Mark Clark as the "most fightingest and most highly decorated military unit in the history of the United States," marched up Pennsylvania Avenue to the White House, upon its return from the European Theater at the end of World War II, President Harry S Truman, in presenting the team with its seventh Presidential Unit Citation said, "You fought not only the enemy, but prejudice—and won."

Mr. President, as a twice-wounded veteran of the 100th Infantry Battalion, which is the first battalion of the 442nd Regimental Combat Team, I plead with my colleagues to make that victory complete and meaningful by passage of S. 1009.

The debate over S. 1009 continued the next day, April 20. Matsunaga again rose to speak in support of the bill and against any attempts to remove provisions that awarded monetary damages to former internees. Shortly before a vote was taken, Matsunaga made the following speech, also reprinted here from the Congressional Record. *Newspaper accounts noted that he wept and momentarily fal-*

tered as he recalled the suffering of some prisoners, especially that of an elderly man whose innocent moment of fun with his grandson ended in tragedy.

Mr. President, I rise in opposition to the amendment offered by the senator from Nevada [Mr. Hecht].

The Hecht amendment would delete from the bill funds provided to compensate each of about 60,000 surviving former internees and would also delete funds provided for the establishment of a "civil liberties education fund." Further, the Hecht amendment would delete title III of the bill, pertaining to compensation for Aleuts, in its entirety.

Those who contend that monetary compensation is an inappropriate way to redress this longstanding injustice overlook the fact that monetary compensatory remedies are an integral part of our system of jurisprudence. It has long been regarded as proper for the courts to award monetary damages to individuals who have been unjustifiably injured. The amounts of damages vary widely, of course, ranging from several hundred dollars to well over $100,000, and the vast majority of such awards are for wrongful detentions of only a few days. To cite only a few examples, in the case of *Bucher v. Krause* (200 F. 2d 576, 7th Cir., 1952), a man wrongfully arrested following a barroom scuffle and held in jail for just one day was awarded $50,000 in compensatory damages; in *Globe Shopping v. Williams* (Tex. Civ. App. 1976), a shopper falsely arrested and imprisoned for only six hours was awarded $35,000 in compensatory damages; and in *Skillern v. Stewart* (379 S.W. 2d 687, Tex. Civ. App. 1964), a woman who was falsely charged with shoplifting by her employer, detained for several hours, and assaulted, was awarded $10,000 in compensatory damages plus $10,000 in punitive damages. In *Dellums v. Powell,* the case stemming from the arrest and detention of demonstrators during the antiwar demonstration in Washington, D.C. on May 1, 1972, compensatory damages in amounts ranging from $120 to $1,800 were awarded to those detained for a few hours up to three days.

> ***"The stigma of disloyalty has haunted Japanese Americans for the past forty-five years, and it is one of the principal reasons that they are seeking congressional action to remove that cloud over their heads."***

In addition to these actions by the courts, Congress has acted to redress the claims of civilians and military personnel held captive by the enemy in World War II, the Korean conflict, and the war in Vietnam. Civilian federal employees who were held hostage in Iran for less than eighteen months were awarded compensation in the amount of $22,000 per person by act of Congress.

Mr. President, the American citizens of Japanese ancestry who were the victims of the federal government's wartime policy were imprisoned for three years or more not by an enemy, but by their own government, the United States of America. It seems to me that it is equally important, if not more important, that we provide monetary compensation as was done in cases I just cited. To do any less would demean the serious injustice which they suffered; $20,000, equal to $3,000 in 1945 dollars, is truly not too much for individuals who were falsely incarcerated for three years or longer.

During hearings of the Commission on Wartime Relocation and Internment of Civilians, which came out with that excellent report which all members have in their offices, former internees, many telling their stories for the first time, told of infants, young mothers, and elderly persons who died for lack of adequate medical care and facilities; of families who were separated, with elderly parents or in-laws going to one camp while their married children were sent to another; of large families forced to live together in one small room; of the constant, nagging uncertainty about the future, both near and long term; of the strains which this placed on their

Spark Matsunaga

families and on the close-knit Japanese American community as a whole; and, most dramatically, of internees who were shot and killed by camp guards because they inadvertently wandered too close to the camp barbed wire fences. In one such incident, an elderly man and his grandson were playing pitch-catch ball near the fence late one afternoon. Under the camp rules, one was never to be seen between the two barbed-wire fences after six p.m. Although it was after six o'clock, on this day it was a bright summer day and it was still broad daylight. The grandfather, having missed the ball, chased after it, and when he got in between the two fences the guard up on the watchtower yelled, "Get back," and the elderly gentleman said, "Oh, I am only going for the ball," and continued his chase; whereupon the guard up on the watchtower fired the machine gun, killing the elderly man instantly. His grandson and members of his family still bear the scars of that incident.

And I myself become overly emotional when I think about it even to this day.

It is also reported, Mr. President, that an elderly American veteran of World War I committed suicide because he was so ashamed of being branded as "disloyal" to the United States. Indeed, the stigma of disloyalty has haunted Japanese Americans for the past forty-five years, and it is one of the principal reasons that they are seeking congressional action to remove that cloud over their heads. . . .

Mr. President, the sponsors of the bill do not pretend that history can be erased, but the measure would provide for the first time an official acknowledgement of the grave injustice which was done, and it would provide token monetary compensation to those who suffered irreparable losses. Without such compensation the bill would be meaningless.

Mr. President, perhaps of greater significance, as I stated yesterday, is that S. 1009 would remove forever a longstanding blot on that great Constitution of the United States, and its passage, as reported by the committee, will prove that our beloved country is great enough to acknowledge and correct its past mistakes.

Later that same day—April 20, 1988—the Senate voted 69 to 27 in favor of S. 1009, including the provision awarding a $20,000 payment to former internees. President Ronald Reagan signed it into law in August.

SOURCES

Books

Bosworth, Allan R., *America's Concentration Camps,* Norton, 1967.

Commission on Wartime Relocation and Internment of Civilians Act: Hearing Before the Committee on Governmental Affairs, United States Senate, 96th Congress, Second Session, U.S. Government Printing Office, 1980.

Congressional Record, 100th Congress, 1st Session [and] 2nd Session, U.S. Government Printing Office, 1988.

Daniels, Roger, *Asian America: Chinese and Japanese in the United States Since 1850,* University of Washington Press, 1988.

———, *Concentration Camps USA: Japanese Americans and World War II,* Holt, 1972.

———, *The Politics of Prejudice: The Anti-Japanese Movement in California and the Struggle for Japanese Exclusion,* University of California Press, 1962.

Girdner, Audrie, and Anne Loftis, *The Great Betrayal: The Evacuation of the Japanese Americans During World War II,* Macmillan, 1969.

Grodzins, Morton M., *Americans Betrayed: Politics and the Japanese Evacuation,* University of Chicago Press, 1949.

Hosokawa, Bill, *JACL: In Quest of Justice,* Morrow, 1982.

———, *Nisei: The Quiet Americans,* Morrow, 1969.

National Academy of Peace and Conflict Resolution: Hearings Before the Subcommittee on International Operations of the Committee on International Relations, House of Representatives, 95th Congress, 2nd Session, U.S. Government Printing Office, 1978.

Personal Justice Denied: Report of the Commission on Wartime Relocation and Internment of Civilians, U.S. Government Printing Office, 1983.

tenBroek, Jacobus, Edward N. Barnhart, and Floyd W. Matson, *Prejudice, War and the Constitution,* University of California Press, 1954.

Uyeda, Clifford I., editor, *The Japanese American Incarceration: A Case for Redress* (booklet), 3rd edition, National Committee for Redress of the Japanese American Citizens League, 1980.

Periodicals

Christian Science Monitor, "Japanese Americans Detained in WWII Have Hope of Redress," September 16, 1987.

New York Times, "Senate Votes to Compensate Japanese-American Internees," April 21, 1988; "Spark M. Matsunaga Dies at 73; Senator Led Fight for Reparations," April 16, 1990, p. D10.

Russell Means

1940–

Native American activist of the Sioux tribe

One of the most vocal and visible Native American activists today is Russell Means, who has worked on behalf of indigenous peoples throughout the world for more than twenty-five years. He first rose to prominence during the early 1970s as one of the leaders of the American Indian Movement (AIM), a Minneapolis-based civil rights organization founded in 1968. Eloquent and charismatic with a striking physical presence and flair for drama, he quickly became the symbol of what many admired—and some feared—about AIM and its activities. Although he withdrew from the organization during the late 1980s to pursue other personal and professional interests, Means remains devoted to his original cause. "My ultimate aim," he has said, "is the reinstitution of pride and self-dignity of the Indian in America."

An Oglala Sioux, Means was born in Porcupine, South Dakota, on the Pine Ridge Reservation, but grew up in and around Oakland, California. Trained as an accountant, he also worked as a rodeo rider, Indian dancer, and ballroom dance instructor before returning to his midwest roots in the late 1960s. There he found a job in the tribal office on the Rosebud Reservation. He left South Dakota for Cleveland, Ohio, in 1970, where he headed the city's Indian Center. Around this same time, Means was introduced to the American Indian Movement when he attended an Indian conference in Minneapolis. Founded by activist Clyde Bellecourt and others, AIM operated on the belief that the federal government's supervision of Native American affairs would eventually lead to the total destruction of the Indian people unless they themselves took action to ensure their survival.

This message greatly appealed to the aggressively outspoken Means, who bitterly resented the fact that white society had forced him and his ancestors to give up their culture and their language. Upon his return to Cleveland, he established a local AIM chapter and immediately became involved in major AIM demonstrations across the country, including the establishment of a camp at Mount Rushmore to symbolize Sioux claims to the Black Hills and the observance of a "national day of mourning" at Plymouth, Massachusetts, on Thanksgiving Day.

Around 1972, Means, who had grown tired of living in the city, moved back to the Pine Ridge Reservation. There he gained personal fame as well as increased respect for AIM when he led a caravan of supporters across the state line into

Nebraska to protest the brutal death of an Indian named Raymond Yellow Thunder. Two young white brothers had beaten up Yellow Thunder "just for fun" and then paraded him around at a dance in the town of Gordon while inviting onlookers to kick him. They then stuffed him in a car trunk, where he later died. When it appeared local authorities had no plans to charge the brothers with any serious crime, AIM became involved at the request of the victim's family. Means successfully reached a settlement that resulted in the resignation of the police chief and a promise to address the rampant racism that had led to Yellow Thunder's death.

Means went on to play key roles in many other AIM protests, among them the Trail of Broken Treaties march to Washington, D.C., in 1972 and the famous Wounded Knee siege in 1973. In the latter incident, which took place on the Pine Ridge Reservation, several hundred AIM members and sympathizers rebelled against the reservation's head administrator, Dick Wilson, whom some of the tribal elders accused of corruption and strong-arm tactics. In a symbolic gesture of defiance, they occupied the hamlet of Wounded Knee, the site of an 1890 massacre of more than two hundred Sioux men, women and children by U.S. Army troops who had been ordered to crush the Ghost Dance spiritual movement. Federal marshals and FBI agents immediately stepped in to re-establish government control, provoking an armed standoff between the Indians and the U.S. government. Means served as one of the major spokesmen for the Native Americans during the seventy-one-day occupation and also helped negotiate with authorities. Afterwards, he and a number of other AIM leaders were arrested on various civil disobedience charges. The eight-month trial ended when the presiding judge threw the case out of court for prosecutorial misconduct.

By then, Means had become an international celebrity. With his solemn and somewhat menacing looks—enhanced by his rough denim clothes, Indian jewelry, and long dark braids—he was indeed an imposing figure. He remained controversial both on and off the reservation, partly because some people felt he enjoyed being in the limelight a bit too much. In 1974, he lost a close (and hotly disputed) election for tribal chairman to Dick Wilson that intensified hostilities between pro-AIM and anti-AIM forces. He also became a target; over the next six years or so, Means survived five shootings, was brought up on criminal charges four times, and spent a year in a South Dakota state prison, where he was stabbed by a fellow inmate.

Means nevertheless continued his efforts to keep the concerns of Native American people in the forefront of the overall struggle for human rights. To that end, in September 1977, he was one of the principal speakers at a special United Nations conference on discrimination against indigenous people of the Americas. Held in Geneva, Switzerland, the conference brought together more than one hundred delegates from over thirty countries. More than fifty years had passed since Native Americans had been given the opportunity to air their grievances before a similar world audience, so each speaker was well aware of the import of his words. On September 20, the opening day of the four-day meeting, Means delivered the following assessment of the Indian's standing in the international community. His words are reprinted here from Native American Reader: Stories, Speeches and Poems, *edited by Jerry D. Blanche (Denali Press, 1990).*

We come here as one people to once again tell you that for centuries since the invader came to our shores that we have shown the world mutual respect. And we are again here today as a people, as one people, to show that mutual respect.

However, I talk for a people who live in the belly of the monster. The monster being the United States of America and every country in the Western Hemisphere and in the Western world who follows the lead of that monster. I come not to turn the other cheek because my people are tired of turning the other cheek. We have turned it now for almost five hundred years, and we realize that here in Geneva this is our first small step into the international community.

And we talk about human rights. The president of the United States, to show you what a racist he is, can talk about human rights when my people are suffering genocide not only in the United States but in the entire hemisphere. Planned genocide by the governments of the Western Hemisphere. We have brought documentation to Geneva that substantiates this charge.

Twenty-five years ago in the UN there was a conference on human rights and twenty-five years later, today, nothing has changed. The world community is talking about Latin America, Southern Africa, the Mediterranean, the same issues. There is one difference. Twenty-five years ago, what they called at that time tribal people, what they are calling us, tribes from Africa approached the UN for a hearing. Twenty-five years ago. The only thing that has changed is that now there are other tribes, this time they are from the Western Hemisphere.

And we are approaching the international community this first time and every time after this for support and assistance not only to stop the rape of our sacred Mother Earth, but also to stop the genocide of a whole people. A people with international rights backed up specifically in North America by treaties. The treaties made between Canada and the United States with the Indian Nations of those so-called countries.

Now, United States is a monster and its multinational corporations have manifested into dictating foreign policy in this world. They no longer care about the future, as witnessed by the Dene, as witnessed by my people, as witnessed by South and Central Americans. We all know if we have common sense and can read that the multinational corporations of Western Europe are investing heavily and are increasing their investments ten-fold in the last four years, thirty-fold in the Western Hemisphere. We also have documentation about the secret activities between the CIA and the multinational corporations that are now in Brazil, Ecuador, Peru, Colombia, and Venezuela. The activities do exploit that because everyone knows that the next major exploitation will be in South America.

Now you have heard some of our spirituality, our mutual respect for all of life because it is our relatives. Well, let me put it to you in the white man's terms. Instead of asking you to respect life we are going to ask you to respect capital. Look upon the natural resources of this world as capital. No longer look upon them as income that has to be flushed out immediately because if you continue to look at our relatives and our sacred Mother as income you will waste all the non-renewable resources in this country, in this world. But if you look on them as capital then you might find some respect. Because you see capital, you do not want to lose your capital, because once the capital is gone, of course, the income is gone. Our oil, our petroleum, our uranium, our coal, our timber, all of these natural resources are capital. And if you look on them as capital, then maybe you will think of the future. Because you see that capital is about to be wasted by the multinational corporations and the monster and its tail. Now we know that the United States of America and every country in the Western Hemisphere cannot afford to address itself to the original people because to do so they would then have to admit they have no respect.

Now also, there is another reason I am here to talk about. It's liberation, liberation of our people as separate entities, separate nations, our right as the Red people of the Western Hemisphere to join in the family of nations. There is only one color of mankind that is not allowed to participate in the international community. And that color is the red. The black, the white, the brown, the yellow all participate in one form or another. We no longer until this day have had a voice within the international community. As someone once said, "You can tell the power of a country by the oppression its people will tolerate." Well, no longer are we going to tolerate the monster. I wonder if we are wise enough to understand that we need the cooperation of the international community. And believe me, I hope, I foresee, that maybe with the cooperation of the international community, just maybe, twenty-five years from now, the Red people will be helping other indigenous peoples gain their liberation. Thank you.

Means left AIM in early 1988 but has remained much in demand around the world as a lecturer and spokesman for various Indian causes. (As he once declared, "Only Indians help Indians.") He has also testified before numerous governmental bodies, including a special U.S. Senate committee investigating the federal government's relationship with Native Americans. As the following speech makes clear, time has not dimmed his radicalism—or his bluntness. Delivered September 28, 1988 (the place and occasion are unknown), it is reprinted here from Native American Reader: Stories, Speeches and Poems, *edited by Jerry D. Blanche (Denali Press, 1990). Means began with an Oglala Lakota greeting, which he then proceeded to translate for his audience.*

What I said is, "Hello, my relatives. I am an ally, and I come from Yellow Thunder Camp in our very sacred holy land, the Black Hills."

Back in 1968-70, the state of the American Indian nations in the Americas of the Western Hemisphere was unchanged from 1492. That's in 1968, 1969, and 1970. This is now 1988, and it still remains unchanged from 1492. In 1492 we were considered an "expendable peoples" by Columbus and the governments of Europe, including the Roman Catholic Church. It wasn't until 1897, thirty-two years after the conclusion of the Civil War, that the Catholic Church declared us to be human beings. Until then, the Marine Corps of the Catholic Church, the Jesuits and the Franciscans, considered us to be "beasts of burden." And now they're going to canonize, make into a saint, Father Serra, a slaveowner, a murderer. That is the state of the American Indian nations. The pope is going to canonize an Indian murderer, an Indian slaveowner, Father Serra, who established these missionary outposts for the Marine Corps, I mean the Catholic Church, along the western coast of Mexico and California.

We are an "expendable people." Go down to Brazil and you will see the government forcibly relocating and allowing miners and forestry employees to massively murder Indian people. Go to Paraguay where they still have bounties on the Aiche. Go to Chile, where Pinochet is officially starving the Mapuche to get their remaining lands. Go to Costa Rica, where Weyerhauser is removing Indian people so they can get at their forests. Go to Nicaragua, where the entire government effort has not only relocated but mass murdered, and it continues to this day, the Indian people. Both the left or the right excuse it and would rather deal with dope dealers. Go to Mexico. Go to Alaska. Go to Canada. Come right here to the United States of America, where this government right here today, at this very moment, is relocating and starving to death and completely destroying an Indian nation, the Navajo, in Arizona. Forced relocation, the same thing the Sandinistas are doing.

Welcome to the Americas. Welcome to the Americas, my home, where the dust that you kick up as you walk is made up of the bones of my ancestors. Welcome. For what you have appropriated and for what we have given to you, I will tell you.

Sixty percent of the world's foodstuffs comes from us. Eighty percent of what the average American eats every day comes from us. Non-Indians are continually asking me, "What's some traditional Indian food?" What did you eat today? Did you go to a salad bar? That's all ours."

Russell Means

We domesticated and developed, for instance, over ten thousand species of potatoes. So when the Europeans came over here, what did they take back? One species. So when the blight hit their potato crop, they had nothing to fall back on, and consequently, we got a lot of Kennedys coming over here. When the blight hit one of our potato crops, we had 9,999 to fall back on. And they call me primitive!

Sewage systems we gave to the Europeans. When Cortez and Pizarro and Coronado and all the rest of the conquistadors were over here destroying Indian people and our records, some of the people with them recognized that, hey, these Indians have sewage systems. Let's take it back to Europe and clean up Berlin and Rome and London and Madrid and Brussels, Paris. And voilà! In less than a generation the amount of disease and the plague that was rampant in Europe dramatically was reduced to less than one percent than what it had been before. Because of the introduction of sewage systems that we gave to the world.

I could go on and on and on. The medicines, the advent of pasteurization, named after Louis Pasteur. B.S.! In his own writings he credits the Indians!

Welcome to natural childbirth. The Lamaze method. A Frenchman comes over here, studies the Indian way of giving birth, goes back to France, writes it up, and you call it the Lamaze method.

Welcome to the Americas. Welcome. The finest medicines in the world developed here. Developed here! Welcome to the Americas. From quinine to penicillin. Welcome. Codeine.

Welcome to the Americas. But instead of the Europeans, the Asians, the Africans, the Middle Easterners, the Far Easterners, instead of saying "thank you," we are still an "expendable people." Does anyone talk about majority rule in Ecuador or Bolivia or Peru or Panama or the Northwest Territories of Canada or Guatemala? No. You don't hear about majority rule. Because those are Indians, campesinos, peasants. Do you see at the family of nations a red person sitting around the table with the family of nations? We are the only color of the human race not allowed to participate in the international community. That's an insult to your own humanity! Think about it! Look around! Your own humanity is being insulted! You live in this modern day and age when an entire people is not even considered to be a part of the international community.

Welcome to the Americas. The states of the American Indian peoples. You blithely continue on in life without an acknowledgement of Colorado or of any of the forty states whose names are derived from the origin of the Indian language. It's amazing how people are not saying "thank you."

> ***"[Native Americans] are the only color of the human race not allowed to participate in the international community."***

[In] 1968 and 1969, 1970, Indians that protested back east were wearing Plains Indians outfits. American Indian people were attending conferences in ties, shined shoes and suits and bouffant hairdos, with pearl earrings on the women. They were afraid to wear beadwork, afraid to wear silver and turquoise. They were embarrassed to announce to the world that they are proud of who they are. I was fortunate to be in the vanguard of a cultural revolution that took place in the late 1960s and 1970s. That cultural revolution enabled our pride and self-dignity to once again become the criteria of what the American Indian nations are all about. It succeeded beyond our wildest plans and expectations, hopes or dreams.

When I sat in Minneapolis with Clyde Bellecourt and Dennis Banks in 1969 and we took the American Indian movement into a national and then international organization, I remember when we attended Indian conferences and they wouldn't allow us to speak because we looked "ridiculous" in headbands and beadwork and moccasins and we had a drum with us. Our own people. When Dr. Alfonso Ortiz, a Pueblo Indian from New Mexico, who is a doctor of anthropology at the University of New Mexico, was up in his three-piece suit at the National Indian Education Association, of which I was on the board at the time, he was giving the keynote address at a banquet. The American Indian Movement. We came in. I was sitting up there on the dais with him, and the American Indian Movement came in with all their headbands and all their beadwork and their drum, and we stood, Indian people, at each exit, and wouldn't allow these other Indians in their ties and gowns to leave because they tried to leave. We sang Indian at that conference, the National Indian Education Association, NIEA, which now is somehow wallowing in the left-brain, right-brain arguments. That was the state of the American Indian nations in 1970. The Indian people embarrassed about who they are.

It's changed that cultural revolution. We had to challenge the United States government militarily, and we won again! Again! Because we were right and we're still right.

But understand the state of the American Indian nations. Because we know. You see, at the advent of the opening up of half the world to the rest of the world, we allowed disease and overpopulation of Europe to dramatically decrease, as I said, in the matter of a generation. There were diseases that were rampant and incurable in Europe: the plague, everything. They instituted sewage systems and the population density went from thirty-five per square mile in 1492 down to seven in less than a century because of the opening of the Western Hemisphere and the cleaning up of the environment.

What happened? The disease was contained. The diseases were contained. But have you all learned? What's the disease today that's incurable? AIDS. The revolution comes around again, but this time there is no more Western Hemisphere, no more Indians. Because we already told those moon Indians, "Watch out, they're coming." There's no other place to go.

The message is the same: clean up. You want to cure AIDS? Clean it up. You want to cure all the other diseases, the cancers, every one that pops up every day? Clean up. As Chief Seattle said, "Continue to contaminate your bed and one night you will suffocate in your own waste."

The state of the American Indian nations, that cultural revolution I was talking about of the 1970s. Here's the beauty of that experience: our traditional people gained respect. Our culture gained respect. And we're still struggling. We're now embarking on an economic revolution. The Red Nations of the Western Hemisphere.

But let me tell you something about the state of the American Indian nations. There is Indian activism in virtually every Indian community. Wherever there's more than one Indian, there's activism. That goes whether it's Seattle University, the Navajo, Nicaragua, Argentina, Chile, Alaska, Canada—everywhere we live. And it's infected the world. Because of our cultural revolution the onslaught and attack on indigenous peoples worldwide is now pervasive.

They're getting our own people to call themselves "Native American." They're getting our own people to teach in universities like this about "we come from China." Understand that we do not come from China. That is a racist, a very racist concept that began with Thomas Jefferson, and he only wrote about it in passing, because of our physical characteristics. In fact, the reverse is true. Geologists know it's impossible for us to have migrated from the Western Hemisphere west. Because during the Ice Ages, the ice corridors that were formed along the northwest coasts of the Western Hemisphere made it impossible to migrate from here to the west, or, as the Europeans call it, the Far East. I could never figure that one out. In fact, those same ice corridors made migration from here going west possible. Geologists know this.

Where are the anthropologists around here? Don't they ever visit with geologists? The archaeologists, the official grave robbers of intellectual institutions such as this? Any high school students that have aspirations towards robbing graves, I would suggest that it is one of the most disrespectful professions and dishonorable professions, if you want to call it that, in the world today. There are federal laws protecting grave robbers. What kind of ghouls are archaeologists?

I live at Canyon de Chelly, on the Navajo for aeons. Canyon de Chelly is part of a whole tourist route to go see where Indians used to live. Cliff-dwellers, they're called. The Anasazi people, they're called by "anthros" and "archies." And these peoples, the Diné, the Hopi, all indigenous peoples of that area, the Zuni, the Pueblos, the Apache, those ruins that are in the sides of the cliffs. We never go there. We have respect for that. We have respect. But day in and day out tourists, non-Indian tourists are trampling all over those cliff dwellings. Every day of the year. They call them cliff-dwellers. They want to know what happened. But you know that archaeologists and anthropologists will not consult with Indian people because that would prejudice their findings. So they have come to the conclusions by robbing some of our graves, and this is the most recent, that we were cannibals because these bones were all broken up and in mass graves in a mass area.

Of course, these graves are about six or seven thousand years old. They didn't take into account any earthquakes or a coyote or two hanging around digging up the earth or moles or worms, etc. They didn't even go over to the Hopi and say, "Hey, guys, how do you bury your people?" They came to the conclusion we're cannibals. I retorted that if I used the same criteria as anthropologists and archaeologists of these learned institutions, I will go to a Christian gravesite, dig up a grave, find a body in a coffin, and say, "Aha! Aha! The white man is saving his dead for future famines! They have found a way to preserve food." That's how ridiculous this grave-robbing has become in the alleged intellectual community. We have our own people believing this. In the same institutions not even protesting it!

I am sick and tired of the state of the American Indian. We had a beautiful cultural revolution, but you know what happens? The government and all institutions are making it even harder for us to know who we are. You see, in this country, the United States of America, the Indian people, we can be anything we want to be. Anything. We can even become archaeologists. But we can't be Indian. It's against the law in this country to be Indian. We can't pray. The last six decisions of the Supreme Court concerning our freedom of religion all denied it. The last Rehnquist decision totally obliterated our right to freedom of religion. In the name of "progress."

We do not have the right to pray in the Black Hills. I know. We are still in court. I have argued. I'm the only non-lawyer ever to argue before a U.S. Court of Appeals. I argued on behalf of the Yellow Thunder Camp against the Black Hills National Forest for their refusal to allow us to pray in the Black Hills according to our ways. But we as Indian people are not allowed, and I'm going to give you a view of what American Indian people are doing to themselves, because we've become our own worst enemy.

Understand this about the U.S. government: they practice and perfect their colonialism on us, here, in the backyard of America, and then export it to the world. If you don't believe it, look at the West Bank, look at South Africa, look at Borneo, look at the Philippines, etc. Then look at yourselves, look in the mirror. What do we think? We cannot, we do not have self-determination. It's called "self-administration," and that's my term. We get to administer someone else's policies.

> ***"In this country, the United States of America, the Indian people, we can be anything we want to be. . . . But we can't be Indian."***

Do you think Indian people are standing up? No. Do you know who they consider our leaders? The ones who suck off of Uncle Sam. Those are our alleged leaders, who are leaders by permission from the federal government. They're not my leader. Understand colonialism, where you're not allowed a choice of who your leaders are going to be. In fact, it insults your intelligence so much you refuse to participate in the society. Is that why only forty-five percent of Americans vote? Because they refuse opportunity, they refuse choices?

We still have a lot to give to the world. To be independent. We're not allowed to know who our heroes are. Our Indian children, every day, are bombarded with white and black heroes on TV and in school. And that's good, for the white children and the black children, and that didn't come without struggle. But our children, and you think our fancy, educated Indians are doing anything about making sure that their heroes are known to our own children? No. The only heroes they know, and that's because of us, AIM, are the ones from the last century.

What about our heroes from the first decade of this century? Or the second decades? Or the twenties? We had heroes, local and national heroes. And in the thirties, and the forties, and the fifties and the sixties and the seventies and the eighties. Our children don't know the names. In 1950 all the sports media in this country got together and they voted on who was the finest athlete in the first half century. You think they voted Jesse Owens? No! Jim Thorpe. They did it again in 1975.

Who was the finest athlete America produced in the first three-quarters of the twentieth century? Jim Thorpe won again, overwhelmingly so, both times. I go around the Indian nation. I ask Indian teenagers and I ask Indian little kids. Just last week, I asked my daughter, who's in the third grade, "Who's Jim Thorpe?" "I don't know." And yet, one of the high schools on my reservation is called the Thorpes. Nobody on my reservation knows who Jim Thorpe is. None of the children.

I said, "Who's Billy Mills?" He won the 10,000 meters at Tokyo. He's from my reservation. None of the kids know who Billy Mills is. That was just in 1964, for crying out loud.

I say, "Who's the first Indian ever to run for president of the United States?" First I ask, "Who was the first Indian to become vice president of the United States of America?" Charles Curtis. [Curtis served with Herbert Hoover from 1929 until 1933.] Everybody knows that, right? My own kids, other Indian kids don't know that.

I said, "Who's the first Indian ever to run for president of the United States?" I asked my daughter. She didn't know. I said, "It's your dad." [During the 1980s, Means ran for president on two different occasions, once as the Libertarian candidate.]

But you see? I tell my own people: "Quit your complaining. You want to complain to somebody? Look in the mirror. And be a little bit independent."

But Indians and non-Indians: You're penalized today for being independent. If you're not part of the masses, you're penalized. Think about it. In every aspect of your life. Just look at the tax structure if you don't believe.

The state of the American Indian nations. I'm sick and tired of our own people. There's an entire people now in North Carolina who have Indian blood in their veins and want to be federally recognized. To me that's the abomination of what Indian people are. They actually believe that if you're federally recognized by the United States government, that somehow is a positive development. To me it is the most negative.

The Mikasukis, the Seminoles, the ones who defeated the United States of America not once, but twice, the ones that had every Indian killed by the United States of America in that Seminole war, who have never been defeated by the United States government, cost the United States government then a million dollars. This is back in the early 1800s, when a million dollars was a million dollars. Now a million dollars in those terms is about 120 million, OK?

Imagine, in a war where for every death you cause it cost you 120 million dollars. Those Seminoles, the Mikasukis, who still live in the Everglades, back in the 1960s, when Buffalo Tiger was looking for federal recognition and got it, half of his nation refused to be enrolled in the federal government, refused to go along with him. They said, "No, that would legitimize the United States government. The United States government isn't legal."

These primitives, who refuse to be enrolled with their national ID number, refuse to recognize the United States of America, that is who our Indian leaders are. Not somebody funded by the federal government, funded by you all. You're the taxpayers. Funded by you. That's not my leader.

One thing about Indian people, and I just want to give you a small glimpse of who we are. Indian people are not tourists. We have homes that we never leave, and those that do are no longer Indian because they have no more connection.

Understand what that connection is. It's that dust I talked about earlier, that dust that comes from our Mother Earth. And only out of respect can you regain that. The Indian people are fooling themselves, not only in their culture, they've dropped their culture so they can call it a "powwow circuit," and they can dress any way they want to be, to the point where they fight their own people and are dependent on the federal government.

I come from the poorest county in the United States of America, the Pine Ridge Indian Reservation. The poorest county. I moved away from there last year to the home of my wife, a Navajo, Diné. Because that culturally is the way we do things. The man always moves to where the woman is from.

In fact, because we are a matrilineal society, if we had the disrespect enough to take another's last name, it would be the woman's last name, not the man's. Because the male lives a shorter life than the female. So it's a natural sense that the man would go where the woman is from so that because the man, when we leave this earth, then our wife and children are around their relatives and friends. So they'll always be in friendly society, never be alone.

But we have a home. We don't have to look for zen. We don't have to look for Franciscans, you know. We have a way of life. We do not have a religion, we have a way of life. Our way of life is made up of one word: it's called "respect." But it means a lot more. Respect for our relatives' visions. When you understand that everything lives and that everything is sacred and the further you get away from what is natural the less important life becomes.

When you get yourselves locked into the asphalt jungles and there is no life, then even the human being's life is no longer important. My son, who is three years old, we live out on the Diné land in the desert, and I take him to the anthills and I show him and we sit there and we watch the ant people and I tell him about the ant people: "Have respect. Don't walk on their homes." He says, "Well, Reba does it." Reba's our horse. I say, "Reba's part of the earth. We know better."

If you have respect for the ant people then you'll have respect for people in Hiroshima. If you have respect for the ant people then you will have respect for people in Nicaragua or South Africa or anywhere else in the world.

The state of the Indian nation. Do you know the names of these mountains that are so beautiful right here, that you're so proud of you even put them on your license plates? When I moved down to Navajo, my wife didn't take me around. Just every time we traveled around she'd tell me the name of that mountain and that mountain and its history and whose land this is and what family has lived on that land and why.

This is the state of the Indian nations, but we're losing that because our educated Indians who have bought the white man's way will not allow our children to know our own heroes, our contemporary heroes, and what is beautiful and natural and respectful.

The state of the Indian nations. It's important that you know that you cannot break a branch when you're a child because you're breaking the arm of a living being. It's important to understand and be thankful for rain and not curse it because you have to walk in it. And to love the winter, not because you can ski on it, but because it makes you strong as a person, as an individual.

If you know who you are I know who we are because I know the sacred colors. I know that pink stands for medicine. So I ask why? So my elders tell me. You go into the medicinal plants, all the plants that are good for you, inside the bud, not available to the naked eye. It's pink. Poisonous plants do not have that pink. Remember that when you're out around here at the rivers, because there's some poisonous plants that'll kill you just like that. It's good to know.

Have respect for colors. I know why orange is the color of water. And they say we primitives are not capable of abstract thought? I say, "Now wait a minute. How do you get orange the color of water? Why does that denote water?" Well, according to my nation, we live in the middle of a plains area. Orange is because when the moon comes up it's orange, and the moon controls water. Voilà.

> *"Our way of life is made up of one word: it's called 'respect.'"*

I know what orange means. To me it means the feminine power of birth. I know what it is to respect life because my grandfather told me my role in life, and I didn't know what he was talking about. I finally figured it out. Unfortunately, it took me thirty-seven years to figure it out. Because I had to go through sixteen years of white man education before I went back to school among my own people.

What I found out is that a long time ago, when the Lakota were sitting around the campfire, the men began to see the women grow with child. As they watched, they witnessed the miracle of life: birth. They watched a little longer and they saw that new life, that birth, being taken in the arms of woman and nurtured at her breast. They watched the child grow and become strong. Then they looked at one another. That was the end of my grandfather's story. I add this: The men looked at one another and said, "What are we doing here?"

So we look for the balance in life, the male-female balance of life which is in the universe, which is trapped in these trees, those grasses. All of life has a male-female balance, even you. If you understand the male-female balance then you don't have to worry about your rights, because every individual has a right.

In the 1970s, when I was younger and a militant and I wanted to change the world today, I went around to my people, advocating they pick up the gun. I said, "If we can't win let's get it over with. It's not worth watching the rape of our mother. It's not worth watching the massacre of her children. Let's get it over with."

But the old people would say, "Have patience, young man. Look around you. Understand who you are, where you come from, and why and where you are going. Understand that time is on your side and just because someone has invented a clock does not mean you have to hurry through life. Clocks are for those who are going to be trained to do the bidding of the master. Time is on your side. If you understand that you'll know how to utilize time. Therefore life is no longer a problem. Today is no longer a problem. Your teenage years is no longer a problem. Nothing is a problem because you understand that there is no time."

The state of the American Indian nation. It's all good, and we don't have to pick up the gun because we understand about life. We understand that we don't need the gun because if that was true then all the grasshoppers in the world would get together and jump on you all. That doesn't happen. We understand immortality. The next world.

And immortality is today. You don't have to worry about tomorrow for peace of mind. That's why we're not tourists.

The old people will not travel for just any reason. I'll give you an example. [In] 1982, the Bertrand Russell Tribunal, a very formidable, very prestigious international forum put together by intellectuals the world over, "anthros," and "archies," and all the alleged social scientists. They did a heck of a thing for the Palestinians in the 1970s. They decided to have a forum on the American Indians of the Western Hemisphere in Rotterdam in 1982. So they invited us. And they came to us, the Indian people.

I was part of that. We wanted to get the issue of the 1868 Fort Laramie treaty with the Lakota Nation before this international tribunal, and we wanted our elders, our most revered elders, the traditional chiefs of our nation, to take our message over there.

So we arranged for our oldest chief, Fool's Crow, and his interpreter and another chief, Matthew King, a noble red man, to go over. We arranged a first class passage on an airplane. We got the St. Mark's Hotel in New York City to give them a three-bedroom suite free.

I was in our international affairs office at the UN arranging last minute details. I got a call from my home in South Dakota. There were Indians coming from all over the Americas; this is just one story, going to Rotterdam. I got a call and they said, "Fool's Crow and Matthew King, they don't want to go."

So I call and I go around and I get the police to go after Matthew King and get him to a telephone and they get him on a telephone, and I said, "Look, your flight leaves early tomorrow morning. You get into New York City. We have first class. We have everybody ready. The airlines, the hostesses, everybody's going to treat you great. I've got you a suite in Rotterdam, and it's going to be first class passage back."

He said, "Nephew, understand this. We're old people. That's a long way away. We might die over there. We don't want to go there. But you tell those Russell people that if they ever come to the United States and have a meeting, maybe we will attend."

Understand the beauty of that. Talk about individual sovereignty, independence. That was the ultimate statement. Here were all these educated Indians in the United States, Canada and the rest of the hemisphere, all the ones with their degrees, all the ones that like this kind of thing, we're hopping, including myself. I wasn't going, but I was all excited about it.

That really sat me down to look at what we are. All of that materialism, all of that ego tripping, didn't mean a thing to these old people. All of these fancy titles after all of these fancy people that were putting on this tribunal. If they ever decide, they'll never have a tribunal over here.

"If those Russell people ever have a meeting over here, then maybe we'll come." I think that is the ultimate statement of sovereignty, individual sovereignty.

The state of the American Indian nations is an exciting state. I see that what goes around comes around. I understand that, because everything that is holy and sacred and good is round. Understand that also. That's part of the male-female balance. The sun is round, the moon is round. Walk up on a hill and you'll see that our sacred grandmother, the Mother Earth, is round. Everything sacred is round. So what goes around comes around.

Our people accomplished a socioeconomic phenomenon in the 1970s, in one decade, in less than fifteen years, not only in the United States of America but in Canada and the rest of the Western Hemisphere.

It's an exciting time to live, and we're fighting, but I'm sick and tired of the educated Indian, because to me they're not educated. They've educated their wisdom out. It's good. I have confidence in people who have education. I have one; my children are getting theirs. I advocate Indians to go on to institutions of higher learning. I hold seminars on it to those that will listen. Drug abuse and alcohol abuse.

But understand that I know what oppression is. I know what sacrifice is. Understand that peoples who come from the barrio, the reservation, the ghetto, we know oppression. So we know how to struggle. We know what sacrifice is. Ask any mother. It's really that simple. Any mother.

So it's an exciting time. And I see it's time now to go to my own people, slap them in the face and hear them say, "Thank you. I needed that."

Because we did it once before, as I told you, at that convention at the NIEA. Understand that we're not through yet.

The sanctity of life is too precious to allow this society to continue to be disrespectful. I have grandchildren, nine grandchildren, and I fought so that my sons and my daughters would have a better way. And I'm not going to allow my sons and daughters to be satisfied so that their sons and daughters get back in the same old rut.

I'm not going to allow these pseudo-Indians who call themselves leaders, who the white man calls leaders. They're an insult to you and to me and to your government to allow these tribal governments to continue.

Understand that you are the next tribal peoples. You're going to be the new Indians of the twenty-first century. You're already feeling the squeeze. Understand. I know the beauty of the male-female balance. I know my creation story, and those that continue to suck off of Uncle Sam are my enemy and the enemy of everyone. It's not just limited to Indians. Maybe to all Native Americans, huh? The state of the Native American.

So I'll leave you with the words of Chief Seattle, and I quote part of his letter and speech to the then-president of the United States of America. He said, "Wave follows wave, and tribe follows tribe. It's the order of nature, and regret is useless. Your time of decay may be distant, but it will surely come. For even the white man's god who walked and talked with him as friend with friend could not escape our common destiny. We may be brothers after all. We shall see."

Thank you.

Means has more recently branched out into yet another field of endeavor—acting. He launched his new career with a well-received performance as Chingachgook in the 1992 version of The Last of the Mohicans. *In 1995, he gave voice to the character of Chief Powhatan in Disney's animated feature* Pocahontas *and also served as a consultant on the project. Future goals include producing and directing his own films that would help educate the American people about Indians. "In America," says Means of his new willingness to enter the mainstream, "you achieve visibility through entertainment or the arts."*

SOURCES

Books

Blanche, Jerry D., editor, *Native American Reader: Stories, Speeches and Poems,* Denali Press, 1990.

Matthiessen, Peter, *In the Spirit of Crazy Horse,* Viking, 1983, new edition, 1991.

Means, Russell, *Where White Men Fear to Tread: The Autobiography of Russell Means,* St. Martin's Press, 1995.

Voices from Wounded Knee, 1973: In the Words of the Participants, Akwesasne Notes, 1974.

Periodicals

Detroit News, "Russell Means' Acting Hasn't Cooled His Activism," October 12, 1992.

Grand Rapids Press, "A People's Man," March 21, 1993, p. A3.

Other

Incident at Oglala: The Leonard Peltier Story (documentary film), Carolco International, 1992.

Thunderheart (film), 1992.

Norman Y. Mineta

1931–

Japanese American member of the U.S. House of Representatives

Although his area of expertise in Congress centers around public works and transportation issues, Norman Y. Mineta has also served as a voice of conscience on the subject of redress for Japanese Americans who were forced to leave their homes and relocate to concentration camps during World War II. It is a painful episode from America's past with which he is personally familiar, for as a ten-year-old boy, he was one of those imprisoned for the "crime" of being of Japanese ancestry.

A native of San Jose, California, Mineta was one of five children born to Japanese immigrants. His father, who had arrived in the United States in 1902 at the age of fourteen, worked as a farm laborer for a number of years before he opened his own insurance agency. The Mineta family's life was comfortable and fairly uneventful until December 7, 1941—the day the Japanese bombed Pearl Harbor, an action that brought the United States into World War II.

A little more than two months later, on February 19, 1942, President Franklin Roosevelt issued Executive Order 9066. This infamous decree mandated the evacuation of some 120,000 Japanese Americans—about two-thirds of whom were U.S. citizens—from the West Coast to "relocation centers" in remote areas of nearly two dozen states, including Arizona, Arkansas, inland California, Colorado, Idaho, Utah, and Wyoming. The move was ostensibly for their own "protection," yet Japanese Americans in other parts of the country were not affected by the order, and no similar action was taken against German Americans or Italian Americans.

The Minetas, like most others under orders to relocate, were given just a short time to make arrangements for their evacuation. Government officials shut down the family insurance business and confiscated their bank savings; Norman's older sister had to quit her job and his older brother had to leave school; Norman himself had to give away his dog. On May 29, 1942, the Minetas were loaded on to a train with what few personal possessions they could carry and sent to a camp established at the Santa Anita racetrack in suburban Los Angeles. Later that year, they were transferred to a camp in Wyoming complete with barbed wire, guard towers, and armed military police.

The family remained in the camp until late 1943. Mr. Mineta was then offered a job in Chicago teaching Japanese to U.S. Army personnel enrolled in a special program. After the war, the Minetas were allowed to return to California, where they tried to resume their lives.

Following his graduation from high school in his hometown of San Jose, Mineta went on to the University of California at Berkeley, from which he received his bachelor's degree in business in 1953. He then served in the U.S. Army as a military intelligence officer before heading back to San Jose, where his father had reopened the family insurance agency. Mineta worked in the business throughout the rest of the 1950s and into the 1960s while also becoming involved in community affairs. From memberships in civic groups such as the Chamber of Commerce, the Rotary Club, and the Japanese American Citizens League (JACL), he moved into politics, joining the city's Human Relations Commission in 1962 and then serving on the Housing Authority. In 1967, Mineta became San Jose's first minority councilman when he was appointed to fill a vacancy; two years later, he was elected to the position in his own right.

Mineta's political career shifted into higher gear in the 1970s. In 1971, he successfully ran for mayor of San Jose, a victory that made him the first Japanese American to preside over the government of a major city. One of the major hurdles he faced was managing the tremendous growth then under way in the area, located in the heart of the booming Silicon Valley. After completing his mayoral term in 1974, he aimed for a seat in the U.S. Congress. Voters were anxious for change in that post-Watergate era, and Mineta—who campaigned as a reform-minded Democrat—was able to capitalize on their sentiments and emerge the winner in a district that had long been dominated by Republicans.

Once in Washington, Mineta quickly made his way up the ranks, serving as deputy whip for the House Democratic leadership and as a member of the Budget Committee, the Policy and Steering Committee, and the Post Office and Civil Service Committee. He has also chaired several subcommittees of the Public Works and Transportation Committee and chaired the committee itself from 1992 until the Republicans gained control of the House after the 1994 elections. Known as a consensus-builder, he is, according to a former colleague, "always nice and always tactful, but can be tough as nails."

In addition, Mineta holds the distinction of being the only Asian American offered a seat in the cabinet of President Bill Clinton, as Secretary of Transportation. He declined, however, explaining that he felt he could be of more use in Congress, where he helps shape the nation's policy on numerous construction and environmental projects involving highways, railroads, federal buildings, airports, clean water and wetlands regulation, and other infrastructure concerns.

But it is in the role of spokesman for Japanese Americans who were wronged by their country that Mineta has gained the most recognition from the public at large. As he once remarked to an interviewer, those who lived through the concentration-camp experience emerged "without any rancor or bitterness, but with a very strong conviction that this should never, ever happen again to anybody else." With that goal in mind, on September 28, 1979, he became one of the co-sponsors of H.R. 5499, a House bill that proposed creating a commission to investigate the wartime relocation of Japanese Americans and determine what, if any, compensation was owed to them for the losses they had suffered both emotionally and economically. A Senate version of the bill, S. 1647, eventually passed in mid-1980, and beginning in mid-1981, the Commission on Wartime Relocation and Internment of Civilians (CWRIC) gathered testimony from over seven hundred people.

In 1983, the CWRIC published a report of its findings entitled Personal Justice Denied *in which members condemned the relocation of Japanese Americans as a measure undertaken not for military reasons but out of "race prejudice, war hysteria and a failure of political leadership." It later issued several recommendations for redress, including an apology from Congress and the president acknowledging the injustice done to Japanese Americans as a result of the order and a payment of $20,000 to each of the estimated sixty thousand survivors of the camps.*

Finally, on September 17, 1987, a bill proposing that the CWRIC's recommendations be adopted came to the floor of the House of Representatives for debate. To those who opposed H.R. 442, as it was known, awarding monetary damages was the sticking point. Republican Congressman Dan Lungren of California, who had been a member of the CWRIC, questioned the fairness of holding present-day taxpayers liable for wrongs committed decades earlier and raised the prospect that approving such payments would open the door to similar claims from African Americans and other groups. Standing before his colleagues that day, Mineta—his voice often quavering with emotion, his hand occasionally brushing away a tear—delivered an impassioned plea in favor of the bill, including the provision awarding compensation to former Japanese American prisoners of the United States. His remarks that day are reprinted here from the Congressional Record, *100th Congress, 1st Session, U.S. Government Printing Office, 1988.*

Mr. Chairman, I say to my colleagues that I would like to first express my deep appreciation of thanks to the leadership on both sides of the aisle for the opportunity to have this bill brought up on the 17th of September, 1987.

Congressman Jim Wright, the Speaker of the House of Representatives, has been involved in this issue right from the beginning. He was the original author of the bill that created the Presidential Commission on Wartime Relocation and Internment of Civilians. That Commission was appointed in 1981, and it worked on this for eighteen months in order to complete its report. Then Congressman Jim Wright went ahead and produced the work product, the legislative recommendations of that Commission, and he has been a strong supporter of this effort ever since. In the 100th Congress, with Congressman Jim Wright becoming the Speaker of the House and unable to sponsor legislation, our majority leader, the gentleman from Washington, Mr. Tom Foley, has been the author of it, and we have had good, strong bipartisan leadership on behalf of this bill all the way through.

But to me this is a very, very emotional day, in sharp contrast to May 29, 1942, when, as a ten-and-a-half-year-old boy wearing a Cub Scout uniform, I was herded onto a train under armed guard in San Jose, California, to leave for Santa Anita, a race track in southern California. And here, on the 17th of September, 1987, we are celebrating the 200th anniversary of the signing of that great document, the Constitution of our great land. It is only in this kind of a country, where a ten-and-a-half-year-old can go from being in a Cub Scout uniform to an armed-guard-guarded train to being a Member of the House of Representatives of the greatest country in the world.

Mr. Chairman, I rise now to urge my colleagues' opposition to the amendment offered by our fine friend, the gentleman from California [Mr. Lungren]. Today we can truly celebrate the bicentennial of our great Constitution by passing this legislation without any weakening amendments. H.R. 442, including compensation, will reaffirm and strengthen this very, very vital document that we are celebrating today.

H.R. 442 may not deal with events either as distant or as proud as those in Philadelphia two hundred years ago, but the bill does address events just as central and just as fundamental to our rights and to our laws.

The gentleman's amendment would eliminate a key provision of this bill, the payment of monetary compensation to the present-day survivors of a shameful episode in our nation's long and proud history. Beginning in 1942, the federal government ordered and sent 120,000 Americans of Japanese ancestry to isolated camps scattered throughout the Western United States, and those who were interned and evacuated had but days, sometimes only hours, to dispose of their property and set their affairs in order, and then, carrying only what their arms could hold, these Americans were summarily shipped off to parts unknown for up to three years.

Because the government of the United States was responsible for the violation of the rights of 120,000 lives, that government, our government, has a legal and moral responsibility to compensate the internees for the abrogation of their civil and human rights.

Now, some are saying that these payments are inappropriate, that liberty is priceless and we cannot put a price on freedom. That is an easy statement to make when you have your freedom, but it is absurd to argue that because constitutional rights are priceless, they really have no value at all. Would you sell your civil and constitutional rights for $20,000? Of course not. But when those rights are ripped away without due process, are you entitled to compensation? Absolutely.

Norman Y. Mineta

"Some are saying that . . . liberty is priceless and we cannot put a price on freedom. That is an easy statement to make when you have your freedom. . . ."

I served on our House Budget Committee for six years. I was a member of the conference committee which wrote Gramm-Rudman-Hollings, so I understand and appreciate our budget constraints. But we all know that the funds authorized by H.R. 442 will be appropriated over several years and are but a tiny fraction of our trillion-dollar federal budget. But the most important considerations in our actions today must be merit and justice, and this authorization is not only just but long, long overdue. If we reject this amendment, history will show that on this bicentennial day, the House of Representatives could not rest until it had redressed the wrong of 1942.

[The Chairman then interrupted to note that Mineta's time had expired, but by the unanimous consent of his fellow legislators, he was allowed to proceed for an additional three minutes.]

Mr. Chairman, those wrongs will not be righted, those injured will not have been redressed until we have acted to prove, not only in word but in word and in deed, that the evacuation and the internment were tragic mistakes that our government will never repeat. By keeping compensation in H.R. 442, the House will tell the world that this body is genuine in its commitment to the Constitution and we will be putting our money where our mouth is.

One night in early 1942, when we did not know what events were to come, my father called our family together. I had one sister in San Francisco, but the rest of us, the four of us, were still in San Jose. He said he did not know what the war would bring to my mother and to him since they were resident aliens, my dad having come in 1902 and my mother in 1912, but with the Oriental exclusion law of 1924 they were not able to become citizens because they were prohibited by that racial exclusion law from becoming U.S. citizens. However, he was confident that his beloved country would guarantee and protect the rights of his children, American citizens all. But his confidence, as it turned out, was misplaced.

I was born in this country, as were most of those who were interned, yet at that time even citizenship was not enough if your parents or grandparents had come from Japan. So on May 29, 1942, my father loaded his family upon that train under armed guard which was taking us from our home in San Jose to an unknown distant barracks. He was later to write to friends in San Jose, and he wrote in that letter about his experience and his feelings as our train pulled out of the station. I quote from the letter:

> *I looked at Santa Clara's streets from the train over the subway. I thought this might be the last look at my loved home city. My heart almost broke, and suddenly hot tears just came pouring out, and the whole family cried out, could not stop, until we were out of our loved county.*

We lost our homes, we lost our businesses, we lost our farms, but worst of all, we lost our most basic human rights. Our own government had branded us with the unwarranted stigma of disloyalty which clings to us still to this day.

So the burden has fallen upon us to right the wrongs of forty-five years ago. Great nations demonstrate their greatness by admitting and redressing the wrongs that they commit, and it has been left to this Congress to act accordingly.

Injustice does not dim with time. We cannot wait it out. We cannot ignore it, and we cannot shrug our shoulders at our past. If we do not refute the shame of the indictment here and now, the specter of this tragedy will resurface just as surely as I am standing here before you, and the injustice will recur.

This bill is certainly about the specific injury suffered by a small group of Americans, but the bill's impact reaches much deeper into the very soul of our democracy. Those of us who support this bill want not just to close the books on the sad events of 1942, we want to make sure that such blatant constitutional violations never occur again.

I must confess that this is a moment of great emotion for me. Today we will resolve, if we can finally lift the unjust burden of shame which 120,000 Americans have carried for forty-five painful years.

It is a day that I will remember for the rest of my life. I hope the members will help me, too, to remember it as a day when justice was achieved, and so with all my heart, I urge the members to oppose this amendment and to support H.R. 442, the Civil Liberties Act of 1987, and in so doing, to reaffirm our Constitution on this very historic day.

Mr. Chairman, I urge my colleagues to vote for H.R. 442.

Mineta's impassioned appeal, along with that of another Japanese American in the House, Robert Matsui, helped secure passage of H.R. 442 in a landslide vote. The Senate went on to pass its version of the proposal in April 1988, and President Ronald Reagan signed it into law that August.

Several years later, on February 15, 1992, Mineta spoke to an audience gathered in San Francisco to commemorate the fiftieth anniversary of Executive Order 9066, the decree signed by President Franklin Roosevelt that sent Japanese Americans to relocation camps during World War II. His reflections on that event, however, prompted a warning that the United States must continue to be on guard against future acts of discrimination. Mineta provided a copy of his speech.

I am proud to join you here today. Very proud. And as I stand before you—my friends and neighbors here in San Francisco—I feel a great sadness, but I also feel an even greater hope.

I know my sadness is shared throughout this center, throughout this city, and throughout the Japanese American community here in the United States. Our sadness is not for ourselves, but for our parents and grandparents who did not live to see this day. These pioneers and survivors would have been proud of this moment, and proud of us. Proud of us all.

There would have been a time, not all that many years ago, when I would have wondered if anyone other than Americans of Japanese ancestry would—or could—feel the power of this anniversary, as we do. Some would say that no one could truly know the tragedy of our internment by the United States government as we know it. And this is true. But today, the difference is that people from all across the country—and indeed, from around the world—*want* to know.

Earlier this year, my Washington office got a call from representatives of Czechoslovak President Vaclav Havel, requesting information about redress so that they might try to redress injustices done to that nation's Hungarian minority. This is our legacy to the world.

"Why should an American, who happens to be of Asian ancestry, have to face the prospect of being beaten with a baseball bat, or have his car spray painted with the words 'Die Nip'?"

The fact that our nation—the United States of America—has now apologized to us for our internment fifty years ago tells me how much this nation has changed, and that the changes have been for the better. With those changes have come understanding, reflection, and the recognition that basic human rights either apply to us all—or they belong to no one. *However,* there is no escaping another truth: that the specter of racism is lurking in us all.

In times of acute economic hardship or jingoistic pressures, this evil can surface all too easily. We've seen that when Vincent Chin was beaten to death in Detroit by unemployed auto workers. We've seen that during the war in the Middle East, when Arab Americans were the target of bigotry and suspicion. And we see it today as a result of Japan-bashing.

Why should an American, who by accident of birth happens to be of Asian ancestry, have to face the prospect of being beaten with a baseball bat, or have his car spray painted with the words "Die Nip"? The answer is, there is no answer. No one should have to face such crimes of hate. So, too, was it in 1942.

It was here in California and the West Coast fifty years ago that this standard was put to the test. Our life as a community was forever transformed by an attack that struck at the heart of the U.S. Constitution. This was an attack not of our making. But three thousand miles away in Washington, D.C., the government of the United States—our government—decided that Americans of Japanese ancestry were a categorical threat to the United States.

No matter that these threats were unproven, or that we were either American citizens or permanent resident aliens. All were tarred with the same indiscriminate brush of racial hatred and fear.

We were all scared, those of us who were alive at the time. The entire world was at war. The United States had been brought into this war—the Second World War—after the Empire of Japan had attacked Pearl Harbor, Hawaii, on December 7, 1941. One of the first casualties of that attack was faith and trust within our American nation.

America quickly saw little value in distinguishing between the attackers that Sunday morning and loyal Japanese Americans who were every bit as much the target of that dawn air raid in Hawaii. All too much effort was invested, instead, in expedience. And the search was on for scapegoats.

Headlines told this story. And by February of 1942, those headlines had reached a fevered pitch.

Wednesday, February 18. The *San Francisco Chronicle.* Headline: "Enemy Aliens: Demand for State Martial Law Sent to General DeWitt by Impatient Congressmen."

Thursday, February 19. Headline: "Enemy Aliens: Congressmen Demand All American-Born Japs Be Moved from Coastal Areas."

Friday, February 20. Headline: "Enemy Aliens: Second Generation Japs to be Evacuated from Coast, War Department Predicts. Civil Liberties May Go by the Boards."

And finally, on Saturday, February 21. Headline: "Drive Against Enemy Aliens: FDR Orders Army Rule for All Strategic Areas. Even Citizen Japs May be Cleared from Coast."

And the story in the *Chronicle* read, in part: "Bringing California only a step short of martial law, the president slashed through a web of legal entanglements, directed military commanders to mark whatever zones they need, and to oust immediately any unwanted aliens and citizens."

And the story continued: "His orders smashed directly at 60,000 American-born Japanese on the West Coast, all hitherto protected under a cloak of U.S. citizenship."

Think about that for a moment. "A cloak of U.S. citizenship." When you came down to it in 1942, that was all the illusory protection we had: a cloak.

When the signs went up telling us, as Americans of Japanese ancestry, that we would have to leave our homes, the signs said, "ATTENTION: ALIENS AND NONALIENS." Our own government wouldn't even acknowledge us as citizens.

In a way, that was not surprising. Our parents and grandparents had not even that much, since they were forbidden by racial exclusion laws from becoming American citizens. So, with the stroke of a pen at the White House, even that illusory cloak—which my father thought would protect his children—was stripped away.

One by one, Japanese American communities along the West Coast disappeared: removed into stark, barren camps scattered throughout some of the most inhospitable regions of the United States. The myth that this forced relocation was being done for our protection was a lie exposed by the first sight of camp guard towers with their machine guns pointed in at us, instead of out.

Tens of thousands of us spent up to four long years in these camps. The vast majority of us cooperated with our government, determined to prove our loyalty in the long run by sacrificing peacefully in the short run our most basic rights as Americans. And we served this country well. Far above and beyond the call of duty.

The all-Nisei 442nd Regimental Combat Team and its 100th Battalion were volunteers from the camps, enlistees fighting Nazi Germany and fascist Italy while their families remained behind barbed wire. These men became the most-decorated Army fighting force in all of American history. They gave of themselves, they gave of their blood, and they gave of their lives to protect America even though America did not see fit to protect their rights.

In the Pacific, a top-secret war was fought by Japanese Americans in the Military Intelligence Service—a story untold for decades. But it was they, these volunteers, who cracked code after code—saving countless American lives. And yet, after the war, the stigma of shame born of the internment lived on in all of us.

Internment drained and crippled many Japanese American families. Homes, farms, and businesses were lost. Lives were ruined. The hot brand of disloyalty hung over our heads like a thundercloud ready to burst at the mention of our subjugation as second-class citizens.

The result was that once the war had ended and the camps were closed, we tried to forget the internment.

Parents never spoke of it to their children. But here there was an inescapable contradiction: How can you prove your loyalty once and for all, as we had tried to do, if you allow personal justice denied to stand silently in a specter of shame? The answer is, you can't.

And the lesson I learned was that wronged individuals must stand up and fight for their rights if our nation is to be true to its principles, without exception. That's what our successful effort to redress the internment was meant to do.

For me, that ten-year struggle in Congress won back for us our dignity. In the Civil Liberties Act of 1988, there is a passage that is more everlasting a testament than any I know to our national ethic. I am proud that this legislation was written in my office, put together by a brilliant legislative director I had at the time, Glenn Roberts. It says, and I quote:

> *The Congress recognizes that, as described by the Commission on Wartime Relocation and Internment of Civilians, a grave injustice was done to both citizens and permanent resident aliens of Japanese ancestry by the evacuation, relocation, and internment of civilians during World War II.*
>
> *As the Commission documents, these actions were carried out without adequate security reasons and without any acts of espionage or sabotage documented by the Commission, and were*

motivated largely by racial prejudice, wartime hysteria, and a failure of political leadership.

The excluded individuals of Japanese ancestry suffered enormous damages, both material and intangible, all of which resulted in significant human suffering for which appropriate compensation has not been made.

For these fundamental violations of the basic civil liberties and constitutional rights of these individuals of Japanese ancestry, the Congress apologizes on behalf of the Nation.

That last sentence means more to me than perhaps any other in law, for it represents everything that our government is designed to do when it works at its best. And today, fifty years after Executive Order 9066 was signed, the successful effort to redress that wrong stands as a reminder of what ultimate accountability can and should mean in the United States.

"Those who prefer not to learn from the mistakes of the past, those who prefer a jingoism of hate, those who prefer to seek scapegoats continue to pose a threat."

It should mean truth. It should mean justice. And it should mean universality of the rights guaranteed by the U.S. Constitution.

But today, we must remain vigilant to ensure that these truths hold true for our children and grandchildren. The most recent wave of Japan-bashing and America-bashing holds for us a special danger. Those who prefer not to learn from the mistakes of the past, those who prefer a jingoism of hate, those who prefer to seek scapegoats continue to pose a threat.

We have seen these latest headlines, and experienced these latest hate crimes. And the specter of tragedy remains all too real. But today, unlike fifty years ago, we have the political strength to bear witness—and to protect ourselves and our neighbors from more senseless tragedies.

The war in the Middle East last year demonstrated how genuine a concern this is for every minority community. In 1942, Japanese Americans were threatened and interned. But in 1991, when Arab Americans were threatened, there were voices within government and without to bear witness. We helped stop history from repeating itself.

None of us can predict who might next fall target to hysteria, racism, and weak political leadership. But with our strength of conviction, and witness to history, I do believe that we can ensure that such a tragedy as our internment never befalls anyone ever again here in the United States.

SOURCES

Books

Bosworth, Allan R., *America's Concentration Camps*, Norton, 1967.

Congressional Record, 100th Congress, 1st Session, U.S. Government Printing Office, 1988.

Daniels, Roger, *Asian America: Chinese and Japanese in the United States Since 1850*, University of Washington Press, 1988.

———, *Concentration Camps USA: Japanese Americans and World War II*, Holt, 1972.

———, *The Politics of Prejudice: The Anti-Japanese Movement in California and the Struggle for Japanese Exclusion*, University of California Press, 1962.

Girdner, Audrie, and Anne Loftis, *The Great Betrayal: The Evacuation of the Japanese Americans During World War II*, Macmillan, 1969.

Grodzins, Morton M., *Americans Betrayed: Politics and the Japanese Evacuation*, University of Chicago Press, 1949.

Hosokawa, Bill, *JACL: In Quest of Justice*, Morrow, 1982.

———, *Nisei: The Quiet Americans*, Morrow, 1969.

Personal Justice Denied: Report of the Commission on Wartime Relocation and Internment of Civilians, U.S. Government Printing Office, 1983.

tenBroek, Jacobus, Edward N. Barnhart, and Floyd W. Matson, *Prejudice, War and the Constitution*, University of California Press, 1954.

Uyeda, Clifford I., editor, *The Japanese American Incarceration: A Case for Redress* (booklet), 3rd edition, National Committee for Redress of the Japanese American Citizens League, 1980.

Periodicals

A. Magazine, "Power Brokers," fall, 1993, pp. 25-34.

AsianWeek, "Remembering a Painful Era: Honoring the Strength of Japanese Americans," February 28, 1992, p. 16.

Business Journal, "Norman Mineta: World War II Injustice Drives His Political Life," May 2, 1994, p. 12.

Christian Science Monitor, "Japanese Americans Detained in WWII Have Hope of Redress," September 16, 1987.

ENR (Engineering News-Record), "The Main Men on Public Works," September 6, 1993, pp. 24-26.

Los Angeles Times, "House Votes to Pay Japanese WWII Internees," September 18, 1981.

New York Times, "Seeking Redress for an Old Wrong," September 17, 1987; "House Votes Payments to

Japanese War Internees," September 18, 1987; "The Heat of War Welds a Bond That Endures Across Aisles and Years," April 26, 1988. p. A22.

San Francisco Examiner, "House OKs Reparations for Internees," September 18, 1987.

Time, "The Burden of Shame," September 28, 1987, p. 31.

Washington Post, "House Votes Apology, Reparations for Japanese Americans Held During War," September 18, 1987.

Patsy Takemoto Mink

1927–

Japanese American attorney and member of the U.S. House of Representatives

A fiercely independent politician who has often gone against the grain to remain true to her beliefs, Patsy Takemoto Mink is a third-generation Hawaiian who has battled discrimination both as a woman and as an Asian American to succeed in the world of politics. She was born on the island of Maui, the daughter of a civil engineer and his wife, both of whom were of Japanese descent. From the time she was just a little girl, she dreamed of becoming a doctor so that she could be of service to others. In fact, that remained her goal throughout most of her undergraduate years at the University of Hawaii until she realized that she was drawn more to the humanities than to science. So, after spending several semesters on the mainland at Pennsylvania's Wilson College and the University of Nebraska, Mink earned her bachelor's degree in zoology and chemistry in 1948 and eventually headed to the University of Chicago School of Law.

Returning to Hawaii in 1953 with her law degree in hand, Mink went into private practice in Honolulu. During this same period, she also began teaching business law at the University of Hawaii and served as house attorney for the Hawaii House of Representatives. In 1954, Mink became involved in Democratic politics at the local level and by 1956 was heading Hawaii Young Democrats. That same year, she was elected to the Hawaii House of Representatives; in 1958, she won a seat in the Hawaii Senate. Mink's growing prominence as a liberal party activist led to her selection for a spot on the platform committee at the 1960 Democratic National Convention, where she helped negotiate adoption of the civil rights plank. That year's general election saw her win a second term in the Hawaii Senate.

After Hawaii became a state in 1959, Mink was one of several contenders in the primary election to choose who would represent Hawaiians in the U.S. House of Representatives. While her bid proved unsuccessful, a second try in 1964 ended in victory, making her the first Asian American woman to serve in Congress. Once in Washington, Mink pursued an agenda that revealed her concern for issues involving equal rights for women and minorities, children, the elderly, education, health care, housing, and the war against hunger and poverty. She favored normalizing relations with the People's Republic of China and even testified before the United Nations on the subject. She also was one of her party's most outspoken opponents to the military draft and the Vietnam War and strongly defended the right of people to protest against it without fear of being labeled "un-American."

In June 1967, for example, a controversy erupted in Congress over the burning of an American flag in New York's Central Park during an antiwar demonstration. Angry legislators, eager to punish the perpetrators, proposed a bill making it a federal crime to show "contempt" for the flag by "publicly mutilating, defacing, defiling or trampling upon it." In the heated debate that ensued, Mink stood up to voice her anger at the notion that patriotism is somehow linked to how one looks or behaves. Her impassioned defense of the right of all Americans to engage in dissent is reprinted here from the Congressional Record, *90th Congress, 1st Session, Volume 113, Part 12, U.S. Government Printing Office, 1967.*

Mr. Chairman, I rise on a matter of personal privilege for myself and for my constituents in the state of Hawaii, to call to the attention of this House a defamatory and highly insulting letter which was placed in the record on page 48 of the hearings on H.R. 271, before the subcommittee of the Judiciary. This was a letter submitted by one Aaron E. Koota, district attorney of Kings County, Brooklyn, New York. His letter referred to a recent court decision by a distinguished jurist in my state, a Harlan Fiske scholar and graduate of Columbia University Law School, a former legislator, a much-decorated veteran of World War II, and a member of the famous 442nd Infantry Battalion, which has been acclaimed as the most decorated unit in all of American military history.

Patsy Takemoto Mink

This case involved a student from the state of New York attending the University of Hawaii's East-West Center who had drawn a large caricature of the flag with dollar signs for stars and the stripes dripping as with blood. The student was arrested under state law which makes it a crime to show contempt for the flag of the United States. The judge after reviewing the case ruled that the drawing was symbolic of the defendant's feeling about certain policies of his country, but that he did not intend by his drawing to dishonor the flag which to him still symbolized everything that he loved and honored about America.

Mr. Koota in trying to dismiss the legal significance of this case said in his letter:

Although it is true that the act in the latter case was condoned by the court as symbolic speech, we must realize that the background of the state of Hawaii is not as steeped in the same spirit of Americanism as are the other states of the Union. Hawaii has a foreign ideology as its background and that is probably explanatory of the Court's attitude.

By this outrageous statement the loyalty, patriotism, and Americanism of my entire state has been impugned, as well as that of my esteemed friend the Honorable Masato Doi, the

judge in this case whose learned opinion took tremendous courage and conviction to write.

This is precisely the outrage that will be perpetrated by this bill on all Americans who do not conform in ideas or beliefs or color of skin or shape of their eyes or nose.

A disagreement on what we believe to be the real meaning of our Constitution will lead to emotional, irrational accusations like Koota's that the reasons for disagreement is due to lack of love of our country or lack of Americanism.

According to Attorney Koota, I wonder how many generations must we be Americans to be steeped with this spirit of Americanism with which he believes he is possessed? Can it be said that only Hawaii has a foreign ideology as its background and not Brooklyn, New York, or any city in this country where its people are of immigrant stock?

We feel that same pride when our colors are presented, our skin like yours rises in goose pimples at the playing of the national anthem, our eyes like yours wept as many tears over the death of our late President Kennedy, our blood as been shed in three wars for the defense of our country and is now being shed again in Vietnam.

I am willing to match the love and devotion to our country of the people of my state whose only difference is the color of their skins, with any group of people anywhere in America.

The greatness of our country lies in our people, diverse and of all possible immigrant backgrounds, who are bound together by their common love of freedom and liberty. No law is needed to require this loyalty; no punishment, not even confinement in wartime relocation camps with complete denial of due process, can obliterate this loyalty.

The love for our country cannot be destroyed; the nation cannot be injured by the mere burning or defiling of one flag. America stands for too much that is a tribute to freedom that no few foolish acts of contempt can dishonor its greatness. Rather these childish tantrums now cast only ridicule upon the perpetrators of this insane and irrational behavior.

I cannot believe that these few extremists in our society endanger the honor of this country; if they truly do, then no mere $1,000 fine or year in jail would be punishment enough.

Ramsey Clark, the Attorney General of the United States, in commenting on this bill states:

> *Particular care should be exercised to avoid infringement of free speech. To make it a crime if one "defies" or "casts contempt . . . either by word or act" upon the national flag is to risk invalidation. This broad language may be too vague under standards of constitutional law to constitute the basis of a criminal action. Such language reaches toward conduct which may be protected by First Amendment guarantees, and the courts have found vagueness in this area.*

I stand four-square behind our attorney general and more particularly behind the honored jurist of my state whose Americanism has been questioned because he chose to place the Constitution above his own popularity and to ignore the passionate demands of people who seek to punish all offbeat conduct without regard for the true meaning of liberty and freedom.

America is not a country which needs to punish its dissenters to preserve its honor. America is not a country which needs to banish its atheists to preserve its religious faith. America is not a country which needs to demand conformity of its people, for its strength lies in all our diversities converging in one common belief, that of the importance of freedom as the essence of our country and the real honor and heritage of our nation, which no trampled flag can ever symbolically desecrate.

I did not intend to speak against or even vote against this bill, but when my Americanism has been challenged and that of the people of my state, by persons who see only disloyalty in dissent, then I must rise to voice my faith and my belief that America is too great to allow its frenetic fringes to curb the blessings of freedom and liberty, which are the cornerstones of our democracy.

When the flag desecration bill came up for a vote, Mink was one of only 16 legislators who voted against it; 387 voted for it. A revised version of the bill that specifically added the word "burning" to the list of acts it banned passed in the Senate in 1968.

Mink has spoken out on intolerance—especially racial intolerance—on numerous other occasions as well. On November 6, 1971, for example, she gave the keynote address at the Thirtieth Anniversary and Installation Banquet of the West Los Angeles Japanese American Citizens League (JACL). In her speech, reprinted here from Representative American Speeches: 1971-1972, *edited by Waldo W. Braden (Wilson, 1972), Mink reflected on the anger and frustration then driving many young people to protest in ways their elders often found disturbing.*

I would like to thank President Ranegai and the other officers and members of the West Los Angeles Japanese American Citizens League for this opportunity to be with you at your thirtieth anniversary banquet and installation.

I am delighted to participate in this memorable occasion. It must be difficult to look back thirty years to 1941 and relive the pains and agonies that were inflicted upon you; as citizens, unloved and unwanted in their own country of their birth. Loving this land as much as any other citizen, it is difficult to fathom the despair and fury which many must have felt, yet who fought back and within a few years had reestablished their lives and their futures. Most of us remember these years vividly. Our faith in justice was tested many times over. Our patriotism was proven by blood of our sons upon the battlefields.

Yet today, thirty years later to many even in this room, it is only a part of our history. Our children, thirty years old and younger, cannot follow with us these memories of the forties. They tire of our stories of the past. Their life is now, today ... tomorrow. Their youthful fervor was poured into the symbolism of the repeal of Title II of the Internal Security Act of 1950, portrayed by its title, Emergency Detention Act. That act became law nearly ten years *after* the Japanese were evacuated from the West Coast into "relocation camps." Yet, it stood as a reminder of what could happen again. Of course, despite the successful repeal, it could happen again, as it did indeed to the Japanese Americans who were rounded up without any statutory authority whatsoever. It was not until 1950 that Title II became law.

It is quite evident that I am standing before an affluent group whose surface appearance does not reveal the years of struggle and doubt that have ridden behind you.

Sociologists have generally described the Japanese Americans as an easily acculturated people who quickly assimilated the ways of their surroundings. This has always been in my view a friendly sort of jab at our cultural background, for what it has come to mean for me is a description of a conformist which I hope I am not!

I still dream that I shall be able to be a real participant in the changing scenario of opportunity for all of America. In this respect, I share the deep frustration and anguish of our youth as I see so much around us that cries out for our attention and that we continue to neglect.

Many factors have contributed towards a deepening sense of frustration about our inability to solve our problems of poverty and racial prejudice. Undoubtedly the prolonged, unending involvement in Vietnam has contributed to this sense of hopelessness. At least for our youth who must bear the ultimate burden of this war, it seems unfair that they should be asked to serve their country in this way when there are so many more important ways in which their youth and energy can be directed to meet the urgent needs at home. They view our government as impotent to deal with these basic issues.

It is true that Congress has passed a great many civil rights laws. The fact that new, extra laws were found necessary to make it easier for some people to realize their constitutional guarantees is a sad enough commentary on the American society, but what is even worse is the fact that the majority of our people are still unready, personally, to extend these guarantees to all despite the Constitution and all the civil rights laws, and despite their protestations to the contrary.

Certainly, no one will admit his bigotry and prejudice—yet we always find ways to clothe such feelings in more presentable forms—and few will openly advocate suppression or oppression of other men, but nevertheless, it exists.

Although Congress has repealed the Emergency Detention Act, the fight for freedom is not over. We now see a new witch hunt proclaimed in which all government employees will be examined for their memberships and organizations. It seems that we have not yet succeeded in expunging the notion that "dangerous" persons can be identified by class or group relationships and punished accordingly.

I believe that nobody can find safety in numbers—by huddling with the larger mass in hopes of being overlooked. Those who seek to suppress will always find ways to single out others. Instead, we must change the basic attitude that all must conform or be classed as renegades and radicals. Our nation was founded on the idealistic belief in individualism and pioneering spirit, and it would be tragic for our own generation to forswear that ideal for the false security of instant assimilation.

It seems to me that our society is large enough to accept a wide diversity of types and opinions, and that no group should be forced to try to conform to the image of the population as a whole. I sometimes wonder if our goal as Japanese Americans is to be so like the white Anglo-Saxon Protestant population as to be indistinguishable from it. If so, we will obviously never succeed!

There has been and continues to be prejudice in this country against Asians. The basis of this is the belief that the Oriental is "inscrutable." Having such base feelings, it is simple to stir up public outrage against the recognition of the People's Republic of China in the United Nations, for instance, even though reasoned judgment dictates otherwise, unless of course a yellow communist is really worse than a red one!

The World War II detention overnight reduced the entire population of one national origin to an enemy, stripped of property, rights of citizenship, human dignity, and due process of law, without so much as even a stifled voice of conscience among our leading scholars or civil libertarians. More recently, the Vietnam War has reinforced the view of Orientals as something less than fully human. All Vietnamese stooping in the rice fields are pictured as the enemy, subhuman without emotions and for whom life is less valuable than for us.

During the trial of Lieutenant Calley, we were told about "MGR," the "Mere Gook Rule" which was the underlying basis for Calley's mindless assertion that the slaughter of defenseless women and children, our prisoners of war, was "no big thing." The "Mere Gook Rule" holds that life is less important, less valuable to an Oriental.

Laws that protect other human beings do not apply to "gooks." One reporter noted before the verdict became known that the essence of the Calley case was to determine the validity of this rule. He described it as the "unspoken issue" at the trial.

The issue was not as unspoken as most would prefer to believe. The indictment drawn up by the Army against Lieutenant Calley stated in six separate charges that he did at My Lai murder four "Oriental human beings" . . . murder not less than thirty "Oriental human beings" . . . murder three "Oriental human beings" . . . murder an unknown number of "Oriental human beings" not less than seventy . . . and so on numbering 102. Thus, the Army did not charge him with the murder of human beings as presumably would have been the case had Caucasians been involved, but instead charged the apparently lesser offense of killing mere "Oriental human beings."

The Army's definition of the crime is hardly surprising inasmuch as the Army itself could have been construed as on trial along with Calley for directing a genocide against the Vietnamese. Indeed, the lieutenant pleaded he was only doing what he thought the Army wanted. It seems clear to me that the Army recognized the "Mere Gook Rule" officially by distinguishing between the murder of human beings and "Oriental human beings." When Calley was convicted, the resulting thunder of criticism verified that many in the public also went along with the concept of differing scales of humanity.

Somehow, we must put into perspective Dean Rusk's dread of the "yellow peril" expressed as justification for a massive antiballistic missile system on the one hand, and on the other, a quest for improved relations with Peking. This latter event could have a great meaning in our own lives as Japanese Americans. We could help this country begin to deal with Asians as people. Just the other day in a beauty parlor, I heard a congressional secretary discuss China and say, "An Asian is different, you can never figure out what he's really thinking. He has so little value for life!"

Instead of seeking refuge, we should seek to identify as Asians, and begin to serve America as the means by which she can come to understand the problems of the East. Our talents have not been used in American diplomacy, I suspect, largely because we are still not trusted enough.

We must teach our country that life is no less valuable, and human dignity no less precious, in Asia than elsewhere. Our detractors point to the large-scale killings that have occurred in China, Vietnam, Pakistan, and elsewhere in Asia, but we hear remarkably few references to the mass slaughter of six million Jews in Nazi gas chambers in World War II—that was done by Aryans, not Asians, and the total

"We must teach our country that life is no less valuable, and human dignity no less precious, in Asia than elsewhere."

far exceeds the loss of life in the Orient that has been used to justify the debasement of "mere gooks." I am not trying to compare one group against another, but merely to point out that a lack of appreciation for the value of human life can occur wherever totalitarian government exists. This makes it more than vital for us to oppose such influences within our own country wherever they may occur. The war in Vietnam has lasted for seven years. If Americans believed there was the same worth in the life of an Asian, this war would have ended long ago. If Americans were willing to concede that the Asian mind was no different than his, a peace would have been forged in Paris long ago. I am convinced that racism is at the heart of this immoral policy.

I know that many of you are puzzled and even dismayed by actions of some of your sons and daughters who have insisted on a more aggressive role in combating the war and other evils that exist in our society. I plead with you for understanding of this Third World movement in which not only young Japanese Americans but many minority groups are so deeply involved.

We are confronted with what seem to be many different revolutions taking place all over the world . . . the black revolution, the revolution of emerging nations, the youth revolution here and in other countries as well—and something that was even more unheard of, the priests challenging the Vatican on the most basic issues of celibacy and birth control. It is no accident that these things are all happening at the same time, for they all stem from the same great idea that has somehow been rekindled in the world, and that is the idea that the individual is important.

All of the systems of the world today have this in common: for they are mainly concerned with industrialization, efficiency, and gross national product; the value of man is forgotten.

The children of some of you here tonight are involved in the great protests of today—are they chronic malcontents and subversives? I think not—I think they are probably fairly well-educated, thoughtful people who see certain conditions they don't like and are trying to do something about it. I'm not sure they know exactly what they want to do. I do know they are clearly dissatisfied with the way their world has been run in the past.

So, the problem is not what to do about dissent among our young people—the problem is what to do about the causes of this dissent. The question is not "how to suppress the dissent" but how to make it meaningful . . . how to make it productive of a better society which truly places high value on individual human beings as human beings and not merely as so many cogs in the great, cold and impersonal machinery of an industrialized society.

I, for one, believe that the grievances of our youth are real and that they are important. Merely because the majority of students are not involved . . . merely because the dissidents are few . . . should not minimize the need for serious efforts to effectuate change. Our eighteen-year-olds now have the right to vote. Whether we like it or not, we will have to take better account of their wishes. Their acceptance as adults will bring into policy making eleven million new voters next year. Their cause for identity must be encouraged.

Our sons and daughters seek to establish a link with the past. They want to discover who they are, why they are here, and where their destinies are to take them. So many of our children are growing up in complete isolation in a society that places a premium on conformity, in middle-class homes where parents still want to play down their differences, and prefer to homogenize with society. Some of these children are rebelling and are seeking ways to preserve their uniqueness and their special heritage. I see pride and strength in this.

One of the most promising avenues for this renewed search for one's heritage is in our school systems—the logical place for instructing children in the knowledge they need. Programs of ethnic heritage studies are needed in our schools. I feel that this would be particularly valuable in Hawaii, California, and other areas where there are large numbers of children of Oriental descent.

It seems to me that we as Asians have a large stake in encouraging and promoting such a program. We cannot and must not presume knowledge about Asia merely because we are Asians. This requires concentrated study and dedicated determination. Of course, we do not need to become scholars cloistered in the ivory tower of some campus. We need to become aware of the enormous history of Asia and through our daily lives, regardless of what our profession, translate it to all the people with whom we deal. We have not fully met our responsibility to educate the public about Asia and its people.

I hope that all Japanese American organizations and others with strong beliefs in the magnificent history and culture of the Orient will now help lead the way to a more enlightened America. We have an immense story to tell, for as I have said the public at large too often assumes that all civilization is Western and no worth is given to the human values of the East. As long as this belief persists, we will have future Vietnams. The way to counteract it is to build public knowledge, through school courses, travel, and dedicated emphasis on increased communications, so that our people will know and appreciate all that is Asian.

Last Thursday night in a display of utter ignorance and contempt for diversity, the House of Representatives killed the ethnic heritage studies program by a vote of 200 ayes to 159 noes. And so you see, I speak of an urgent matter. We are so few and they who do not care to understand us are so numerous.

It is fine for all citizens to pursue the good life and worldly goods on which our society places such emphasis, but there is increasing recognition that all will be ashes in our mouths unless our place as individuals is preserved. This is what the young are seeking—and I am among those who would rejoice in their goals.

They need the guidance and support of their parents to succeed, but in any event with or without us, they are trying. It behooves us to do all we can to accept their aspirations, if not all of their actions, in the hope that this new generation will be able to find a special role for themselves in America, to help build her character, to define her morality, to give her a depth in soul, and to make her realize the beauty of our diverse society with many races and cultures of which we are one small minority.

In 1972, Mink mounted a campaign for the presidency of the United States but could not muster enough delegate support to be taken seriously. Four years later, she opted not to run for a seventh term in the House and instead decided to try for a seat in the U.S. Senate. After losing in the Democratic primary to Spark Matsunaga, Mink remained active in government and politics in other positions. In 1977 and 1978, for example, she served in the administration of President Jimmy Carter as assistant secretary of state for oceans and international environmental and scientific affairs. She then spent three years as president of Americans for Democratic Action. Returning home to Hawaii, she was elected to the Honolulu City Council, spending two years (1983 to 1985) as chair, and remained a member of that body until 1987. (A 1986 bid for the governor's chair and a 1988 run for mayor of Honolulu were not successful, however.) She also resumed her law practice and lectured at the University of Hawaii.

Mink returned to the U.S. House of Representatives in 1990 as the winner of a special election held to fill the vacancy created when Daniel Akaka resigned to take the late Spark Matsunaga's place in the Senate. There she once again serves as an advocate for civil rights and equal opportunity, as well as universal health care, and family and medical leave.

SOURCES

Braden, Waldo W., editor, *Representative American Speeches: 1971–1972*, Wilson, 1972.

Congressional Record, 90th Congress, 1st Session, Volume 113, Part 12, U.S. Government Printing Office, 1967, pp. 16491-16492.

Zia, Helen, and Susan Gall, editors, *Notable Asian Americans*, Gale, Detroit, 1995.

Toni Morrison

1931–

African American writer

On October 7, 1993, Toni Morrison made history as the first African American (and only the second American woman) to win the Nobel Prize in literature. It was the latest and most prestigious in a string of accolades she has received during her career. Often described as the foremost black American female writer of her generation, Morrison has won particular praise for her novels Song of Solomon, Beloved, and Jazz. In announcing their choice for the Nobel Prize, members of the Swedish Academy also singled out those works, noting that they have given "life to an essential aspect of American reality" through their "visionary force and poetic import." Indeed, it is with her imaginative and lyrical language that Morrison has so vividly brought to life a cast of strong black characters—most of them women—to help fill what she has called "huge silences in literature . . . silences about black girls, black women, contemporary stories."

Born Chloe Anthony Wofford in Lorain, Ohio (she changed her given name to Toni as a young adult), Morrison grew up in an integrated, working-class community as part of a tight-knit family that included not only her parents but also her maternal grandparents. Their life was often beset with financial difficulties, which made storytelling an inexpensive and popular form of entertainment. Through her father's stories in particular, Morrison was exposed from a very early age to black folklore and superstition. She also gained an understanding of black history and black-white relations by listening to her parents and grandparents discuss their personal experiences with racial prejudice and how they had chosen to deal with it. All of these elements, many of which later emerged as themes in her fiction, combined to give Morrison a strong sense of racial identity and self-worth.

After graduating from high school with honors, Morrison earned a bachelor's degree in English from Howard University in 1953. She then pursued graduate studies at Cornell University and received her master's degree in 1955. Following a two-year teaching stint at Texas Southern University, she joined the Howard faculty, married, and gave birth to two sons. Dissatisfaction with her marriage prompted Morrison to turn to writing as an escape. After she and her husband divorced in 1964, writing became a means of coping with the isolation she felt as a single mother with a new job (as an editor for Random House publishers) living in a new city (Syracuse, New York).

Morrison's first project was an expanded version of a story she had originally written for a writers' group she belonged to at Howard. Entitled The Bluest Eye, *it tells the story of a young black girl who prays for blue eyes so that others will think she is beautiful. It was published in 1969 to mixed reviews. Her second novel,* Sula, *which appeared four years later, met with greater critical success for its poetic prose and strong characterizations of two very different black women and their stormy friendship.*

In 1977, Morrison vaulted into the ranks of major contemporary black writers with the novel Song of Solomon. *It represents a significant departure from her previous works in that its central character is not a girl or a woman but a man, Malcolm "Milkman" Dead. His mythic search for both personal and ethnic identity proved to be a critical and commercial breakthrough for Morrison, who earned respect and acclaim as a writer capable of broadening her fictional world in terms of both character and theme. She followed it in 1981 with* Tar Baby, *which was more of a popular success than a critical one with its look at relationships between black men and women as well as between blacks and whites.*

By far Morrison's most famous novel to date is the 1987 novel Beloved, *for which she won the 1988 Pulitzer Prize for fiction. Inspired by a true story, it is the horrific account of a runaway slave woman who slashes her baby daughter's throat just as they are about to be recaptured because she cannot bear to see the child doomed to a lifetime of bondage. Critics were lavish in their praise of this brutally powerful and haunting work peopled by characters who struggle against the physical and spiritual cruelties of slavery. Another ambitious undertaking was Morrison's 1992 novel,* Jazz. *Written in a style that mimics the rhythms of jazz music, it tells a story of love and obsession in 1920s Harlem.*

The news that Morrison had won the 1993 Nobel Prize came as a complete surprise to the author as well as to the literary world; for a variety of reasons, she was not believed to be in contention for the honor that year. But most observers agreed that the Swedish Academy's historic choice was also a well-deserved one. Exactly two months after the announcement, on December 7, 1993, Toni Morrison stood in the Grand Hall of the Swedish Academy in Stockholm to deliver her Nobel Prize lecture, a complex and thought-provoking reflection on the vital importance and magic of language that one listener later described as a "prose poem." Her address is reprinted here from Historic Documents of 1993, *Congressional Quarterly Inc., 1994.*

"Once upon a time there was an old woman. Blind but wise." Or was it an old man? A guru, perhaps. Or a griot soothing restless children. I have heard this story, or one exactly like it, in the lore of several cultures. "Once upon a time there was an old woman. Blind. Wise."

In the version I know the woman is the daughter of slaves, black American, and lives alone in a small house outside of town. Her reputation for wisdom is without peer and without question. Among her people she is both the law and its transgression. The honor she is paid and the awe in which she is held reach beyond her neighborhood to places far away; to the city where the intelligence of rural prophets is the source of much amusement.

One day the woman is visited by some young people who seem to be bent on disproving her clairvoyance and showing her up for the fraud they believe she is. Their plan is simple: they enter her house and ask the one question the answer to which rides solely on her difference from them, a difference they regard as a profound disability: her blindness. They stand before her, and one of them says, "Old woman, I

Toni Morrison

hold in my hand a bird. Tell me whether it is living or dead."

She does not answer, and the question is repeated. "Is the bird I am holding living or dead?"

Still she doesn't answer. She is blind and cannot see her visitors, let alone what is in their hands. She does not know their color, gender or homeland. She only knows their motive.

The old woman's silence is so long, the young people have trouble holding their laughter.

Finally she speaks and her voice is soft but stern. "I don't know," she says. "I don't know whether the bird you are holding is dead or alive, but what I do know is that it is in your hands. It is in your hands."

Her answer can be taken to mean: if it is dead, you have either found it that way or you have killed it. If it is alive, you can still kill it. Whether it is to stay alive, it is your decision. Whatever the case, it is your responsibility.

For parading their power and her helplessness, the young visitors are reprimanded, told they are responsible not only for the act of mockery but also for the small bundle of life sacrificed to achieve its aims. The blind woman shifts attention away from assertions of power to the instrument through which that power is exercised.

Speculation on what (other than its own frail body) that bird-in-the-hand might signify has always been attractive to me, but especially so now, thinking as I have been, about the work I do that has brought me to this company. So I choose to read the bird as language and the woman as a practiced writer. She is worried about how the language she dreams in, given to her at birth, is handled, put into service, even withheld from her for certain nefarious purposes. Being a writer she thinks of language partly as a system, partly as a living thing over which one has control, but mostly as agency—as an act with consequences. So the question the children put to her: "Is it living or dead?" is not unreal because she thinks of language as susceptible to death, erasure; certainly imperiled and salvageable only by an effort of the will. She believes that if the bird in the hands of her visitors is dead the custodians are responsible for the corpse. For her a dead language is not only one no longer spoken or written, it is unyielding language content to admire its own paralysis. Like statist language, censored and censoring. Ruthless in its policing duties, it has no desire or purpose other than maintaining the free range of its own narcotic narcissism, its own exclusivity and dominance. However, moribund, it is not without effect for it actively thwarts the intellect, stalls conscience, suppresses human potential. Unreceptive to interrogation, it cannot form or tolerate new ideas, shape other thoughts, tell another story, fill baffling silences. Official language smitheryed to sanction ignorance and preserve privilege is a suit of armor, polished to shocking glitter, a husk from which the knight departed long ago. Yet there it is: dumb, predatory, sentimental. Exciting reverence in schoolchildren, providing shelter for despots, summoning false memories of stability, harmony among the public.

She is convinced that when language dies, out of carelessness, disuse, and absence of esteem, indifference or killed by fiat, not only she herself, but all users and makers are accountable for its demise. In her country children have bitten their tongues off and use bullets instead to iterate the voice of speechlessness, of disabled and disabling language, of language adults have abandoned altogether as a device for grappling with meaning, providing guidance, or expressing love. But she knows tongue-suicide is not only the choice of children. It is common among the infantile heads of state and power merchants whose evacuated language leaves them with no access to what is left of their human instincts for they speak only to those who obey, or in order to force obedience.

The systematic looting of language can be recognized by the tendency of its users to forgo its nuanced, complex, mid-wifery properties for menace and subjugation. Oppressive language does more than represent violence; it is violence; does more than represent the limits of knowledge; it limits knowledge. Whether it is obscuring state language or the faux-language of mindless media; whether it is the proud but calcified language of the academy or the commodity driven language of science; whether it is the malign language of law-without-ethics, or language designed for the estrangement of minorities, hiding its racist plunder in its literary cheek—it must be rejected, altered and exposed. It is the language that drinks blood, laps vulnerabilities, tucks its fascist boots under crinolines of respectability and patriotism as it moves relentlessly toward the bottom line and the bottomed-out mind. Sexist language, racist language, theistic language—all are typical of the policing languages of mastery, and cannot, do not permit new knowledge or encourage the mutual exchange of ideas.

"Oppressive language does more than represent violence; it is violence; does more than represent the limits of knowledge; it limits knowledge."

The old woman is keenly aware that no intellectual mercenary, nor insatiable dictator, no paid-for politician or demagogue; no counterfeit journalist would be persuaded by her thoughts. There is and will be rousing language to keep citizens armed and arming; slaughtered and slaughtering in the malls, courthouses, post offices, playgrounds, bedrooms and boulevards; stirring, memorializing language to mask the pity and waste of needless death. There will be more diplomatic language to countenance rape, torture, assassination. There is and will be more seductive, mutant language designed to throttle women, to pack their throats like paté-producing geese with their own unsayable, transgressive words; there will be more of the language of surveillance disguised as research; of politics and history calculated to render the suffering of millions mute; language glamorized to thrill the dissatisfied and bereft into assaulting their neighbors; arrogant pseudoempirical language crafted to lock creative people into cages of inferiority and hopelessness.

Underneath the eloquence, the glamour, the scholarly associations, however, stirring or seductive, the heart of such language is languishing, or perhaps not beating at all—if the bird is already dead.

She has thought about what could have been the intellectual history of any discipline if it had not insisted upon, or been forced into, the waste of time and life that rationalizations for and representations of dominance required—lethal discourses of exclusion blocking access to cognition for both the excluder and the excluded.

The conventional wisdom of the Tower of Babel story is that the collapse was a misfortune. That it was the distraction, or the weight of many languages that precipitated the tower's failed architecture. That one monolithic language would have expedited the building and heaven would have been reached. Whose heaven, she wonders? And what kind? Perhaps the achievement of Paradise was premature, a little hasty if no one could take the time to understand other languages, other views, other narratives. Had they, the heaven they imagined might have been found at their feet. Complicated, demanding yes, but a view of heaven as life; not heaven as postlife.

She would not want to leave her young visitors with the impression that language should be forced to stay alive merely to be. The vitality of language lies in its ability to limn the actual, imagined, and possible lives of its speakers, readers, writers. Although its poise is sometimes in displacing experience it is not a substitute for it. It arcs toward the place where meaning may lie. When a president of the United States thought about the graveyard his country had become, and said "The world will little note nor long remember what we say here. But it will never forget what they did here." His simple words are exhilarating in their life-sustaining properties because they refused to encapsulate the reality of six hundred thousand dead men in a cataclysmic race war. Refusing to monumentalize, disdaining the "final word," the precise "summing up," acknowledging their "poor power to add or detract," his words signal deference to the uncapturability of the life it mourns. It is the deference that moves her, that recognition that language can never live up to life once and for all. Nor should it. Language can never "pin down" slavery, genocide, war. Nor should it yearn for the arrogance to be able to do so. Its force, its felicity is in its reach toward the ineffable.

Be it grand or slender, burrowing, blasting, or refusing to sanctify; whether it laughs out loud or is a cry without an alphabet, the choice word, the chosen silence, unmolested language surges toward knowledge, not its destruction. But who does not know of literature banned because it is interrogative; discredited because it is critical; erased because alternative? And how many are outraged by the thought of a self-ravaged tongue?

Word-work is sublime, she thinks, because it is generative; it makes meaning that secures our difference, our human difference—the way in which we are like no other life.

We die. That may be the meaning of life. But we do language. That may be the measure of our lives.

"Once upon a time, . . ." visitors ask an old woman a question. Who are they, these children? What did they make of that encounter? What did they hear in those final words: "The bird is in your hands?" A sentence that gestures toward possibility or one that drops a latch? Perhaps what the children heard was "It's not my problem. I am old, female, black, blind. What wisdom I have now is in knowing I can not help you. The future of language is yours."

They stand there. Suppose nothing was in their hands? Suppose the visit was only a ruse, a trick to get to be spoken to, taken seriously as they have not been before? A chance to interrupt, to violate the adult world, its miasma of discourse about them, for them, but never to them? Urgent questions are at stake, including the one they have asked: "Is the bird we hold living or dead?" Perhaps the question meant: "Could someone tell us what is life? What is death?" No trick at all; no silliness. A straightforward question worthy of the attention of a wise one. An old one. And if the old and wise who have lived life and faced death cannot describe either, who can?

But she does not; she keeps her secret; her good opinion of herself; her gnomic pronouncements; her art without commitment. She keeps her distance, enforces it and retreats into the singularity of isolation, in sophisticated, privileged space.

Nothing, no word follows her declarations of transfer. That silence is deep, deeper than the meaning available in the words she has spoken. It shivers, this silence, and the children, annoyed, fill it with language invented on the spot.

"Is there no speech," they ask her, "no words you can give us that help us break through your dossier of failures? Through the education you have just given us that is no education at all because we are paying close attention to what you have done as well as to what you have said? To the barrier you have erected between generosity and wisdom?

"We have no bird in our hands, living or dead. We have only you and our important question. Is the nothing in our hands something you could not bear to contemplate, to even guess? Don't you remember being young when language was magic without meaning? When what you could say, could not mean? When the invisible was what imagination strove to see? When questions and demands for answers burned so brightly you trembled with fury at not knowing?

"Do we have to begin consciousness with a battle heroines and heroes like you have already fought and lost leaving us with nothing in our hands except what you have imagined is there? Your answer is artful, but its artiness embarrasses us and ought to embarrass you. Your answer is indecent in its self-congratulation. A made-for-television script that makes no sense if there is nothing in our hands.

"Why didn't you reach out, touch us with your soft fingers, delay the sound bite, the lesson, until you knew who we were? Did you so despise our trick, our *modus operandi* you could not see that we were baffled about how to get your attention? We are young. Unripe. We have heard all our short lives that we have to be responsible. What could that possibly mean in the catastrophe this world has become; where, as a poet said, "nothing needs to be exposed since it is already barefaced." Our inheritance is an affront. You want us to have your old, blank eyes and see only cruelty and mediocrity. Do you think we are stupid enough to perjure ourselves again and again with the fiction of nationhood? How dare you talk to us of duty when we stand waist deep in the toxin of your past?

"You trivialize us and trivialize the bird that is not in our hands. Is there no context for our lives? No song, no literature, no poem full of vitamins, no history connected to experience that you can pass along to help us start strong? You are an adult. The old one, the wise one. Stop thinking about saving your face. Think of our lives and tell us your particularized world.

Make up a story. Narrative is radical, creating us at the very moment it is being created. We will not blame you if your reach exceeds your grasp; if love so ignites your words they go down in flames and nothing is left but their scald. Or if, with the reticence of a surgeon's hands, your words suture only the places where blood might flow. We know you can never do it properly—once and for all. Passion is never enough; neither is skill. But try. For our sake and yours forget your name in the street; tell us what the world has been to you in the dark places and in the light. Don't tell us what to believe, what to fear. Show us belief's wide skirt and the stitch that unravels fear's caul. You, old woman, blessed with blindness, can speak the language that tells us what only language can: how to see without pictures. Language alone protects us from the scariness of things with no names. Language alone is meditation.

"Tell us what it is to be a woman so that we may know what it is to be a man. What moves at the margin. What it is to have no home on this place. To be set adrift from the one you knew. What it is to live at the edge of towns that cannot bear your company.

"Tell us about ships turned away from shorelines at Easter, placenta in a field. Tell us about a wagonload of slaves, how they sang so softly their breath was indistinguishable from the falling snow. How they knew from the hunch of the nearest shoulder that the next stop would be their last. How, with hands prayered in their sex they thought of heat, then suns. Lifting their faces, as though it was there for the taking. Turning as though there for the taking. They stop at an inn. The driver and his mate go in with the lamp leaving them humming in the dark. The horse's void steams into the snow beneath its hooves and its hiss and melt is the envy of the freezing slaves.

"The inn door opens: a girl and a boy step away from its light. They climb into the wagon bed. The boy will have a gun in three years, but now he carries a lamp and a jug of warm cider. They pass it from mouth to mouth. The girl offers bread, pieces of meat and something more: a glance into the eyes of the one she serves. One helping for each man, two for each woman. And a look. They look back. The next stop will be their last. But not this one. This one is warmed."

It's quiet again when the children finish speaking, until the woman breaks into the silence.

"Finally," she says, "I trust you now. I trust you with the bird that is not in your hands because you have truly caught it. Look. How lovely it is, this thing we have done—together."

SOURCES

Books

Dictionary of Literary Biography, Gale, Volume 6: *American Novelists Since World War II*, 1980, Volume 33: *Afro-American Fiction Writers After 1955*, 1984.

Dictionary of Literary Biography Yearbook: 1981, Gale, 1982.

Harris, Trudier, *Fiction and Folklore: The Novels of Toni Morrison*, University of Tennessee Press, 1991.

Historic Documents of 1993, Congressional Quarterly Inc., 1994.

Jones, Bessie W., and Audrey L. Vinson, *The World of Toni Morrison: Explorations in Literary Criticism*, Kendall-Hunt, 1985.

Morrison, Toni, *Playing in the Dark: Whiteness and the Literary Imagination* (essays based on the 1990 William E. Massey, Sr., Lectures in the History of American Civilization), Harvard University Press, 1992.

Periodicals

Detroit Free Press, "Nobel Prize Spotlights Overlooked Perspective," October 8, 1993.

Detroit News, "There's a New Chapter in Toni Morrison's Life—A Nobel Prize," October 8, 1993.

Ebony, "The Magic of Toni Morrison," July, 1988, pp. 100-106.

Essence, "Toni Morrison Now," October, 1987.

Grand Rapids Press, "Laughter Helps Morrison Survive, Succeed," October 10, 1993, p. A5.

Ms., "Toni Morrison," January, 1988, pp. 60-61.

Nation, "Travels with Toni," January 17, 1994, pp. 59-62.

New Republic, "The Toni Award," June 19, 1989, pp. 9-10.

Newsweek, "Toni Morrison's Black Magic," March 30, 1981, pp. 52-57; "Keep Your Eyes on the Prize," October 18, 1993, p. 89.

New York Times, "Toni Morrison Is '93 Winner of Nobel Prize in Literature," October 8, 1993; "In Sweden, Proof of the Power of Words," December 8, 1993.

New York Times Book Review, September 13, 1987.

New York Times Magazine, "The Song of Toni Morrison," May 20, 1979.

Time, "The Pain of Being Black," May 22, 1989, pp. 120-122; "Rooms of Their Own," October 18, 1993, pp. 86-87.

Carol Moseley-Braun

1947–

African American member of the U.S. Senate

In November 1992, Carol Moseley-Braun made history when she became the first black woman (and the first black Democrat) to be elected to the United States Senate. Her victory in the Illinois race came in a year that saw many voters register their disgust with "politics-as-usual" by supporting a record number of female and minority candidates for office at the local, state, and national level. But none of those campaigns generated as much interest as that of Moseley-Braun, an underdog who was not expected to survive the primary election let alone triumph in the general election.

Moseley-Braun, the daughter of a police officer and a medical technician, was born and raised in Chicago. She received her bachelor's degree from the University of Chicago in 1967 and her law degree from same in 1972. Her first try at elective office came in 1978 when she ran for the Illinois state legislature and beat eleven other candidates despite her lack of political experience. Four years later, she was made assistant majority leader (the first woman to serve in that post); she also functioned as Chicago Mayor Harold Washington's official spokesperson in the legislature. In 1987, a year after an unsuccessful bid to win her party's nomination for lieutenant governor, Moseley-Braun ran for the position of Cook County recorder of deeds and easily defeated her Republican opponent.

Her decision to enter national politics took shape during the fall of 1991, in the wake of Anita Hill's experiences with the all-male, all-white Senate Judiciary Committee during confirmation hearings for Supreme Court hopeful Clarence Thomas. Illinois Senator Alan Dixon was one of those who voted to confirm Thomas even though Hill claimed he had sexually harassed her at work years earlier. Convinced by what she had seen and heard that government officials had "lost touch" with the people, Moseley-Braun made up her mind to challenge Dixon, a two-term veteran, in the March 1992, primary. Against tremendous odds—Dixon had never lost a race in a forty-year-long political career, and he had considerable funds at his disposal—she pulled off a stunning upset over Dixon and millionaire lawyer Albert Hofeld. Both men had ferociously battled each other while virtually ignoring the low-key but personable Moseley-Braun.

Her unexpected victory, which seemed destined to lead to the historic senate seat, made Moseley-Braun an overnight star on the national political scene. For the next six months or so she ran a somewhat leisurely and disorganized campaign that was very nearly derailed in its final weeks by rumors of staff problems and hints of ethics violations in her personal financial affairs. But in the end, voter worries over the shaky economy helped propel her to victory over her Republican opponent, a wealthy lawyer from suburban Chicago named Richard Williamson who had served as a senior aide in the Reagan administration.

After weathering several post-election controversies that prompted questions about her conduct and judgment, Moseley-Braun eventually settled into her new role. She accepted three committee assignments, including the Judiciary, which had been the target of so much criticism during the Clarence Thomas hearings, and early on established herself as a highly visible advocate of various liberal causes.

On July 22, 1993, Moseley-Braun spoke out as she had never spoken out before and experienced what is without a doubt one of the greatest moments of her political career. On that day, Jesse Helms, the Republican senator from North Carolina, proposed an amendment to the National and Community Service Act that would have granted a congressional design patent to the emblem of the United Daughters of the Confederacy. With a design featuring the original Confederate flag encircled by a wreath, the emblem struck the freshman senator from Illinois as an unacceptable and offensive tribute to slavery and racism. After South Carolina Senator Strom Thurmond spoke up in support of Helms's amendment, Moseley-Braun asked for the opportunity to respond. In a voice that often shook with emotion, she passionately argued against putting the Senate's stamp of approval on such a painful symbol of the past. Her words are taken from the Congressional Record, *103'd Congress, 1st Session, U.S. Gov't Printing Office, 1993.*

Mr. President, I would like to respond to this amendment and to suggest that it is absolutely ill-founded and to oppose the amendment.

Mr. President, I understand that we do not have a germaneness rule here in the Senate. But I would submit that, in the first instance, this amendment is not germane, either to this bill, or, frankly, to anything else.

The real bottom line with regard to this amendment and to the request for a design patent extension by the United Daughters of the Confederacy is that it is not needed. This was recognized by the Judiciary Committee when, on the 12th of May of this year, it considered the extension of design patents and, by a vote of 13 to 2, I believe, rejected the appeal of the United Daughters of the Confederacy for renewal and extension of this particular design patent.

I think it is important to note what a design patent is. It is not just a matter of simple recognition. It is a rare honor given to an organization. There are very few of them given. In fact, design patents have only been conferred on fewer than ten organizations in this century. They are given for a period of some fourteen years. And it just is rarely done, in any event, for any organization.

There are a number of fine organizations throughout this country that are well known that do not enjoy or do not have design patents. But this organization, by a matter of oversight or whatever, has—this last year, as was brought to the attention of the Judiciary Committee, and the design patent was refused or withheld. Now the Senator from South Carolina has come to the floor attempting to undo the work of the Judiciary Committee, attempting to undo the decision of that committee that a design patent was not necessary in this case.

I submit further that the design patent is not needed in terms of the work of the organization. The Senator from South Carolina has gone on at great length to talk about the charitable work of the United Daughters of the Confederacy. The fact of the matter is the refusal to extend this extraordinary honor by this body does not stop them from doing whatever it is they do, from continuing their work in the community and the like.

The Senator has not explained, however, why the Daughters need this extraordinary congressional action to continue the work of their organization or protect against the unauthorized use of their insignia. He has not addressed at all the conclusions that have been set forth from the Treasury, which were addressed in the committee, that say it is not only extraordinary but probably inappropriate to have a design patent issued in this regard.

When members of the United Daughters of the Confederacy came to my office to discuss this issue when we were involved with consideration of the issue before the Judiciary Committee, they could not even then answer the question why it was necessary to have a design patent. They can continue to fundraise. They can continue to exist. They can continue to use the insignia. Nothing changes in terms of what it is they do. The only issue is whether or not this body is prepared to put its imprimatur on the Confederate insignia used by the United Daughters of the Confederacy.

I submit to you, Mr. President, and the members who are listening to this debate, as I did in the Judiciary Committee, that the United Daughters of the Confederacy have every right to honor their ancestors and to choose the Confederate flag as their symbol if they like. However, those of us whose ancestors fought on a different side in the Civil War, or who were held, frankly, as human chattel under the Confederate flag, are duty bound to honor our ancestors as well by asking whether such recognition by the U.S. Senate is appropriate.

The United Daughters of the Confederacy did not require this action to either conduct the affairs of their organization or to protect their insignia against unauthorized use. As the Patent Commissioner, Mr. Kirk, wrote in a letter issued April 30:

> *In the absence of design patent protection and regardless of statutory protection nonprofit organizations have still other options for obtaining protection for their badges, insignias, logos, and names.*

So this is not an issue about protecting the insignia of the United Daughters of the Confederacy, nor is it an issue about whether or not they do good works in the community, nor is it an issue of whether or not the organization has a right to use this insignia. I think the answer in all those cases is they have a right to use whatever insignia they want, they have a right to organize in any way they want, they have a right to conduct whatever business they want. But at the same time it is inappropriate for this Senate, this U.S. Congress, to grant a special, extraordinary imprimatur, if you will, to a symbol which is as inappropriate to all of us as Americans as this one is.

I have heard the argument on the floor today with regard to the imprimatur that is being sought for this organization and for this symbol, and I submit this really is revisionist history. The fact of the matter is the emblems of the Confederacy have meaning to Americans even one hundred years after the end of the Civil War. Everybody knows what the Confederacy stands for. Everybody knows what the insignia means. That matter of common knowledge is not a surprise to any of us. When a former governor stood and raised the Confederate battle flag over the Alabama State Capitol to protest the federal government support for civil rights and a visit by the attorney general at the time in 1963, everybody knew what that meant. Now, in this time, in 1993, when we see the Confederate symbols hauled out, everybody knows what that means.

So I submit, as Americans we have an obligation, Number 1, to recognize the meaning, not to fall prey to revisionist history on the one hand; and also really to make a statement that we believe the Civil War is over. We believe that as Americans we are all Americans and have a need to be respectful of one another with regard to our respective histories, just as I would.

Whether we are black or white, northerners or southerners, all Americans share a common history and we share a common flag. The flag which is behind you right now, Mr. President, is our flag. The flag, the Stars and Stripes forever, is our flag, whether we are from the North or South, whether we are African Americans or not—that is our flag. And to give a design patent, that even our own flag does not enjoy, to a symbol of the confederacy seems to be just to create the kind of divisions in our society that are counterproductive, that are not needed.

So I come back to the point I raised to begin with. What is the point of doing this? Why would we give an extraordinary honor to a symbol which is counter to the symbol that we as Americans, I believe, all know and love, which would be a recognition of the losing side of the war, a war that I hope—while it is a painful part of our history—I hope as Americans we have all gotten past and we can say as Americans we come together under a single flag? And this organization, if it chooses to honor the losing side of the Civil War, that is their prerogative. But it is inappropriate for that organization to call on the rest of us, on everybody else, to give our imprimatur to the symbolism of the Confederate flag.

Symbols are important. They speak volumes to the people in our country. They speak volumes to the people outside of our country who follow and who care about what happens in this, the greatest nation in the world. It seems to me the time has long passed when we could put behind us the debates and arguments that have raged since the Civil War, that we get beyond the separateness and we get beyond the divisions and we get beyond fanning the flames

Carol Moseley-Braun

"The flag, the Stars and Stripes forever, is our flag, whether we are from the North or South, whether we are African Americans or not. . . ."

of racial antagonism. I submit that to use the insignia of the United Daughters is their prerogative. However, it is not their prerogative to force me and other members of this body to assent to an extraordinary honor of their own revisionist history. That is the purpose of the design patent.

[A few minutes later, the Senate voted on a motion to reject the amendment; forty-eight were in favor of doing so, but fifty-two were not. An angry Moseley-Braun once again asked to be heard.]

Madam President, I really had not wanted to have to do this because in my remarks I believe that I was restrained and tempered. I talked about the committee procedure. I talked about the lack of germaneness of this amendment. I talked about how it was not necessary for this organization to receive the design patent extension, which was an extraordinary extension of an extraordinary act to begin with. What I did not talk about and what I am constrained now to talk about with no small degree of emotion is the symbolism of what this vote—[Moseley-Braun was at this point interrupted by the presiding officer, who called the Senate to order.] That is what this vote really means.

I started off—maybe—I do not know—it is just my day to get to talk about race. Maybe I am just lucky about that today.

I have to tell you this vote is about race. It is about racial symbolism. It is about racial symbols, the racial past, and the single most painful episode in American history.

I have just gone through—in fact in committee yesterday I leaned over to my colleague Dianne Feinstein and I said, "You know, Dianne, I am stunned about how often and how much race comes up in conversation and debate in this general assembly." Did I not say that?

[Moseley-Braun was again interrupted while the Senate was called to order.]

So I turned to my colleague, Dianne Feinstein. You know, I am really stunned by how often and how much the issue of race, the subject of racism, comes up in this U.S. Senate, comes up in this body and how I have to, on many occasions, as the only African American here, constrain myself to be calm, to be laid back, to talk about these issues in very intellectual, nonemotional terms, and that is what I do on a regular basis, Madam President. That is part and parcel of my daily existence.

But at the same time, when the issue of the design patent extension for the United Daughters of the Confederacy first came up, I looked at it. I did not make a big deal of it. It came as part of the work of the Judiciary Committee. I looked at it, and I said, well, I am not going to vote for that.

When I announced that I was not going to vote for it, the chairman, as was his due, began to poll the members. We talked about it, and I found myself getting drawn into a debate that I frankly never expected.

Who would have expected a design patent for the Confederate flag? And there are those in this body who say this really is not the Confederate flag. The other thing we did know was a Confederate flag.

I did my research, and I looked it up as I am wont to do, and guess what? That is the real Confederate flag. The thing we see all the time and are accustomed to is the battle flag. In fact, there is some history on this issue. I would like to read the following quote from the *Flag Book of the United States.*

The real flower in the southern flag began in November 1860, when the election of Lincoln to the president caused widespread fear the federal government will try to make changes in the institution of slavery. The winter of 1860 to 1861, rallies and speeches were held throughout the South and, frankly, the United States flag was replaced by a local banner.

This flag is the real flag of the Confederacy. If there is anybody in this chamber, anybody, indeed anybody in this world, that has a doubt that the Confederate effort was around preserving the institution of slavery, I am prepared and I believe history is prepared to dispute them to the nth. There is no question but that battle was fought to try to preserve our nation, to keep the states from separating themselves over the issue of whether or not my ancestors could be held as property, as chattel, as objects of commerce and trade in this country.

And people died. More Americans died in the Civil War than any war they have ever gone through since. People died over the proposition that indeed these United States stood for the proposition that every person was created equal without regard to race, that we are all American citizens.

I am sorry, Madam President. I will lower my voice. I am getting excited, because, quite frankly, that is the very issue. The issue is whether or not Americans, such as myself, who believe in the promise of this country, who feel strongly and who are patriots in this country, will have to suffer the indignity of being reminded time and time again, that at one point in this country's history we were human chattel. We were property. We could be traded, bought, and sold.

Now, to suggest as a matter of revisionist history that this flag is not about slavery flies in the face of history, Madam President.

"To suggest as a matter of revisionist history that this [Confederate] flag is not about slavery flies in the face of history."

I was not going to get inflammatory. In fact, my staff brought me this little thing earlier, and it has been sitting here. I do not know if you noticed it sitting here during the earlier debate in which I was dispassionate and tried my level best not to be emotional and lawyering about and not get into calling names and talking about race and racism. I did not use it to begin with. I do want to share it now. It is a speech by the Vice President of the Confederate States of America, March 21, 1861, in Savannah, Georgia.

"Slavery, the Cornerstone of the Confederacy," and this man goes on to say:

The new Confederate constitution has put to rest forever all agitating questions relating to our peculiar "institution," which is what they called it. African slavery as it exists among us, the proper status of a Negro in our form of civilization. This was the immediate cause of the late rupture and present revolution.

The prevailing ideas entertained by Thomas Jefferson and most of the leading statesmen at the time of the formation of the old Constitution were that the enslavement of the African was in violation of the laws of nature, that it was wrong in principle, socially, morally, and politically.

And then he goes on to say:

Our new government is founded upon exactly the opposite idea. Its foundations are laid, its cornerstone rests upon the great truth that the Negro is not equal to the white man, that slav-

ery, subordination to the superior race is his natural and moral condition.

This was a statement by the Vice President of the Confederate States of America.

Madam President, across the room on the other side is the flag. I say to you it is outrageous. It is an absolute outrage that this body would adopt as an amendment to this legislation a symbol of this point of view and, Madam President, I say to you that it is an important issue. It is a symbolic issue up there. There is no way you can get around it.

The reason for my emotion—I have been here almost seven months now, and my colleagues will tell you there is not a more congenial, laid back, even person in this entire body who makes it a point to try to get along with everybody. I make it a point to try to talk to my colleagues and get beyond controversy and conflict, to try to find consensus on issues.

But I say to you, Madam President, on this issue there can be no consensus. It is an outrage. It is an insult. It is absolutely unacceptable to me and to millions of Americans, black or white, that we would put the imprimatur of the United States Senate on a symbol of this kind of idea. And that is what is at stake with this amendment, Madam President.

I am going to continue—I am going to continue because I am going to call it like I see it, as I always do. I was appalled, appalled at a segment of my own Democratic Party that would go take a walk and vote for something like this.

I am going to talk for a minute first about my brethren, my close-in brethren, and then talk about the other side of the aisle and the responsibility of the Republican Party.

The reason the Republican Party got run out on a rail the last time is the American people sensed intolerance in that party. The American people, African Americans sensed there was not room for them in that party. Folks took a look at the convention and said, my God, what are these people standing for? This is not America. Andy they turned around and voted for change. They elected Bill Clinton president and the rest of us to this chamber. The changes they were speaking out for was a change that said we have to get past racism, we have to get past sexism, the many issues that divide us as Americans, and come together as Americans so we can make this country be what it can be in the twenty-first century.

That is the real reason, Madam President, that I am here today. My state has less than twelve percent African Americans in it, but the people of Illinois had no problem voting for a candidate that was African American because they thought they were doing the same thing.

Similarly, the state of California sent two women, two women to the U.S. Senate, breaking a gender barrier, as did the state of Washington. Why? Because they felt it was time to get past the barriers that said that women had no place in the conduct of our business.

And so, just as our country is moving forward, Madam President, to have this kind of symbol shoved in your face, shoved in my face, shoved in the faces of all the Americans who want to see a change for us to get beyond racism, is singularly inappropriate.

I say to you, Madam President, that this is no small matter. This is not a matter of little old ladies walking around doing good deeds. There is no reason why these little old ladies cannot do good deeds anyway. If they choose to wave the Confederate flag, that certainly is their right. Because I care about the fact that this is a free country. Free speech is the cornerstone of democracy. People are supposed to be able to say what they want to say. They are supposed to be able to join associations and organizations that express their views.

But I daresay, Madam President, that following the Civil War, and following the victory of the United States and the coming together of our country, that that peculiar institution was put to rest for once and for all; that the division in our nation, the North versus the South, was put to rest once and for all. And the people of this country do not want to see a day in which flags like that are underwritten, underscored, adopted, approved by this U.S. Senate.

That is what this vote is about. That is what this vote is about.

I say to you, Madam President, I do not know—I do not want to yield the floor right now because I do not know what will happen next.

I will yield momentarily to my colleague from California, Madam President, because I think that this is an issue that I am not going—if I have to stand here until this room freezes over, I am not going to see this amendment put on this legislation which has to do with national service.

[After the presiding officer confirmed that Moseley-Braun had agreed to give up the floor briefly to allow someone else to speak, the senator concluded her remarks.]

If I have to stand here until this room freezes over, Madam President, I am going to do so. Because I will tell you, this is something that has no place in this body. It has no place in the Senate. It has no place in our society.

And the fact is, Madam President, that I would encourage my colleagues on both sides of the aisle—Republican and Democrat; those who thought, "Well, we are just going to do this, you know, because it is no big deal"—to understand what a very big deal indeed it is—that the imprimatur that is being sought here today sends a sign out to the rest of this country that that peculiar institution has not been put to bed for once and for all; that, indeed, like Dracula, it has come back to haunt us time and time and time again; and that, in spite of the fact that we have made strides forward, the fact of the matter is that there are those who would keep us slipping back into the darkness of division, into the snake pit of racial hatred, of racial antagonism and of support for symbols—symbols of the struggle to keep African Americans, Americans of African descent, in bondage.

After some debate, another vote was taken on the motion to table the amendment. This time, seventy-five senators voted yes, and twenty-five voted no. An emotional Moseley-Braun thanked her colleagues "for having the heart, having the intellect, having the mind and the will to turn around what, in my mind, would have been a tragic mistake." She ended with the following observation: "As a student of history and mathematics, I have said this to people before. There is something called factor addition in mathematics that says you add forces working together, you subtract forces working against each other, and that, Madam President, is the message and the lesson of things like what happened here today, the lesson that if we work together as Americans, we will be the great country that this Constitution defines and our Declaration of Independence set out and that so many people hold so dear in their heart. We will be able to find pride and real meaning to that flag, the flag of the United States, that is the flag that we all love because we love this country and because we know that in its diversity is its strength."

SOURCES

Congressional Record, 103rd Congress, 1st session, July 22, 1993, U.S. Gov't Printing Office, 1993, pp. S9252-S9270.

Jet, "Carol Moseley-Braun Makes Victorious Stand in Senate Against Confederate Flag," August 9, 1993, pp. 4-6.

Time, "Nixing Dixie," August 2, 1993, p. 30.

Elijah Muhammad

1897–1975

African American religious leader

During the 1930s—at the depth of the Depression—a new black separatist movement took root in the United States. Established by an enigmatic peddler named W.D. Fard or Wallace Fard Muhammad, it was known as the Lost-Found Nation of Islam, or, more commonly, the Black Muslims. Fard urged his followers to shun Christianity as a white man's religion and embrace the tenets of Islam instead. He also condemned whites as an inferior race of "devils" whose main purpose on earth was to make life miserable for blacks, whom he characterized as a superior race descended from the Muslims of Africa and Asia.

One of Fard's most ardent disciples was a man named Elijah Poole. A native of Georgia who had moved north to seek a better life, Poole was a devout Baptist and very race-conscious man who deeply resented the insults and economic hardships he had been forced to endure as an African American. Eventually, he was attracted to the message of the Black Muslims. Before long, he had become one of Fard's closest associates and had changed his name to Elijah Muhammad. In 1934, after Fard mysteriously disappeared, Muhammad assumed the role of the group's new spiritual leader, a position he held for more than forty years. Like his predecessor, he advocated a blend of Islam and black nationalism. Besides expecting his followers to abide by strict prohibitions against dancing, gambling, stealing, and extramarital sex, Muhammad urged them to show respect for black women and work for economic self-reliance.

Until Malcolm X arrived on the scene in the late 1950s, the Black Muslims probably numbered less than ten thousand (although they claimed many more adherents), concentrated mostly in larger urban areas. They were not afraid to incite controversy, however. During World War II, for example, they created quite a stir when they refused to fight for the United States and came out in support of Japan instead. (Muhammad even served a federal prison term for encouraging his followers to resist the military draft.) And while many other blacks joined in the fight for integration during the 1950s and 1960s, the Black Muslims held firmly to their belief in separatism. In fact, in 1960 Muhammad proposed creating an economically, politically, socially, and culturally independent black nation within the borders of the United States.

At a rally in Atlanta, Georgia, in 1961, Elijah Muhammad explained the

Black Muslim doctrine to a crowd that had braved the prospect of a confrontation with the Ku Klux Klan to hear him speak. His five-hour speech—only part of which follows—was introduced by Malcolm X, his most famous pupil and soon to become his chief rival. Malcolm's fiery and impassioned style contrasted sharply with that of his teacher, a small, delicate-looking man with a formal air and a rather soft speaking voice. Muhammad's remarks are reprinted from When the Word Is Given . . . : A Report on Elijah Muhammad, Malcolm X, and the Black Muslim World *(World Publishing, 1963).*

As-Salaam-Alaikum: In the name of Allah, the most Merciful God, to whom all holy praises are due, the Lord of all the worlds; the most Merciful Finder (of) and Lifegiver to the Lost-found, mentally dead so-called Negroes here in the Wilderness of North America.

My Beloved Brothers and Sisters:

I am more than honored by your presence here this afternoon and your sincere welcome to me and to my followers here in this great city of Atlanta.

I thank Allah for Minister Jeremiah, my faithful minister here whose tireless efforts in Atlanta and throughout the South have made this great gathering here today possible. The work that Minister Jeremiah has been doing here in the South has pleased Allah, and it has pleased me too.

Year after year I receive letters from many converts here in Atlanta, and I know that the Word of Allah is spreading rapidly among our people here in the South because of the ever increasing volume of your letters to me.

And, my beloved people, I want you to know that those of you here in Atlanta and in other parts of the South who accept Islam, which is the true religion of Almighty God, are not alone. Not only do you have a fast-growing number of brothers and sisters in all of the Northern cities, but you have 725 million more brothers and sisters in the World of Islam.

I am also thankful to my followers who have traveled here to Atlanta to be with me today from my various temples throughout America, and especially the caravan of young Muslims who motored over two thousand miles all the way from Los Angeles, California, to be here on this grand occasion.

My followers are with me wherever I go, and it is wonderful to have such sincere people who will follow you all around the country like this because it shows unity, and it also shows there is no religion that can produce unity like the unity produced by Islam. Yes, today the Muslims are in all the major cities of America, and if you look around in the smaller cities you will find us there also. Just walk around saying, "As-Salaam-Alaikum," and pretty soon someone will reply, "Wa-Alaikum-Salaam."

Beloved brothers and sisters, again I must thank Allah for permitting me to be in your presence here in Atlanta this afternoon. I am thankful also to the Atlanta Police Department for the courtesies they have shown us here in this city, and I want everyone to know we are a people who are grateful to anyone who is nice to us, and peaceful toward us. We are a people of peace. We are seeking to spread brotherly love among the so-called Negroes for it is they who have been deprived of brotherly love. We (Muslims) have come through the same trials and tribulations as they have, and now we want them to see and share the brotherhood that Islam has given us.

Islam is not a new religion. Islam is not a religion that has been organized by the white man. Islam is the religion of God Himself, and Islam is the religion of all the prophets of God, from Adam to Muhammad (the last). Islam was the religion of Moses, Noah, Abraham, and Jesus. Islam will be the last of the three great religions (Buddhism, Christianity, and Islam) that now dominate the earth.

Islam must be the last of these three great religions because God Himself is the Author of Islam, and Islam is to bring peace and contentment after this war and trouble-making world which you now know has been destroyed . . . and you can see that this trouble-making world is already on its way out.

Islam has not made great progress for the

Elijah Muhammad

past six thousand years because this is the religion that God Himself would spread in the "last days." If Islam had been forced upon all the people of the earth during the past six thousand years there would not have been any "World of Christianity," there would not have been any "World of Buddhism" . . . and there would never have been anything like the "Caucasian World." Islam would have prevented their progress. God Himself has held Islam "in check" to give these other "worlds" free reign during the past six thousand years.

But, Islam was the religion of the black people who lived before Adam was made, as far back as sixty-six trillion years ago when the earth and the moon were together and formed one and the same planet . . . and which at that time was called "moon" instead of earth.

According to the word of Allah to me, one of our wise black scientists was upset over the dialect the people were speaking, and he wanted to change the language and make all of the people speak the same dialect. He became angry because he could not get the others to go along with him, and when he saw that he could not accomplish what he wanted, he drilled a huge shaft into this planet for about four or five thousand miles deep, and filling that hole with high explosives he set it off, with the intention of destroying all civilization. He thought he would get rid of us.

That part of the planet which we call "moon" today was blasted twelve thousand miles from its original pocket that it had been rotating in at the time of the explosion, and this part that we call "earth" today dropped thirty-six thousand miles from that pocket and found another pocket and started rotating again . . . (it all happened in the twinkling of an eye) . . . and that part (moon) that was blasted away dropped all of its water upon this part (earth), and this is why three-fourths of the earth's surface today is covered by water, and also why there is no life on the moon.

We are the people who devised that great destruction of our planet. That part (moon) that you see up there in the sky shining at night was once joined with this part (earth) that we now live on. Before the explosion the entire planet was then called "moon." (Not really by the word "moon" that we use today, but by a word in Arabic that means practically the same thing.) We will have another great destruction, and we will provide that one too. We ourselves (the black nation) are a people who can never be destroyed. There never was a time when we (the black nation) didn't exist. We don't have any birth record of the black nation. We have no beginning and we have no ending. So don't talk about getting rid of the Black Man, because you cannot do it.

Again I say, we are happy to be in Atlanta today, the capital of Georgia . . . my birth state. I was born in this state, and grew up in this state. I was a grown man, married and the father of children even before I left this state. So don't try and make me acquainted with Georgia. I am already acquainted with Georgia.

This great city of Atlanta with its five colleges, institutions of learning, is one of America's most important cities, and is even the gateway to the South. We thank the city for permitting us to enter it, and the courtesy of the police department, and the mayor of this great city, and the governor of the state. We are happy to be called one of your own state-borned sons.

My beloved people, I am one of your brothers; I am not a foreigner, but I have a Divine Message from the Lord of the Worlds that sounds foreign to you because you have not heard it before.

I want you to know that we so-called Negroes are the people who have been on this

"There is no such thing as a race of Negroes. This is a false name given you during slavery by your slave master . . ."

planet for trillions of years. I say so-called Negro because you are not a Negro. You are members of the Asiatic Nation, from the Tribe of Shabazz. There is no such thing as a race of Negroes. This is a false name given you during slavery by your slave master, who, after robbing you completely of your knowledge of your homeland, your parents, and your culture, called you "Negro" or Nigger because that word means something that is "NEUTER" or "NEUTRAL." Therefore you are now a little group of people on this earth who stand out because you have become neutralized by ignorance of yourself and your own kind, and of your enemy. You are "neutral" . . . not united with yourselves, among yourselves, nor are you united with your own people of your own world.

Since ignorance of self and hatred of self makes you reluctant to unite with your own kind, and despite your love and worship of your slave master he will not let you unite with him . . . thus you are in the middle, standing alone, neutralized by your own lack of knowledge, unacceptable to either friend or foe . . . NEGROES!!!

This is why you are called NEGRO. The slave master gave you this name because he understood the meaning of it, although Webster has cunningly kept you away from the true meaning of it by saying it refers to black people . . . and especially the black African who has no education or independence.

My dear brothers and sisters, and distinguished educators of Atlanta, you have often wondered why you had to call yourselves by this name "Negro." It has been due to the fact that you didn't know its origin and you didn't know your origin. You have been asleep. You don't know whom you are from, where you are from, where you are going, how you should stand, how you should sit . . . you know nothing at all but what your slave master chooses to tell you, and since he tells you only that which will benefit himself and his own kind, you have been made into a NEUTRAL person . . . a shiftless, helpless NEGRO.

If the white man says to you, "Johnny, go back home, I have no work for you today," you go back home and sit down and wait for the white man to send for you (when he sees fit) to come back and work on his job. You don't try to create a job for yourself. You are shiftless because the lack of "proper" education and self-knowledge has left you lifeless (mentally, economically, and otherwise).

I am not making fun of you. I am trying to lead you to the point where you can see the basic cause of your condition. I am one of you. I came through the same trials and tribulation and the same hell that you did. What I say about you I am also saying it about myself. I am your brother; I am here, if necessary, to give my life to save yours. I am not running from death. I am running to save your life. So take me for a friend and not an enemy.

You must learn to make jobs for yourselves so that the next time "boss" tells you he does not have any work for you, you can tell him that you are going to do some work for yourself.

Three hundred years under the persecution of your slave master has made you into a blind, deaf, and dumb . . . and an absolutely "dead" people. He has taught you to eat the rotten and worse type of foods, even the flesh of that poisonous animal, the swine (pork) . . . filling your stomach with this poison meat (pork) has deteriorated you physically, mentally as well as morally. The Arab word for the pig is "Khainsuer." ("khain" means "I see," and "suer" means "very foul.") This word thus means "I see something that is very foul, filthy, diseased" . . . something that is not fit to be eaten by intelligent, civilized people.

Your slave master reared you on this poisonous meat, which has dulled your brains, and you ceased to think about your past history, and then you were deprived easily of the knowledge of your own God and your own religion. Thus it became easy for the slave master to deprive you also of the knowledge of your own kind, and the knowledge of his kind. Now you don't know the way back to your own kind, and his kind won't accept you . . . so they call you Nigger or Negro, which means deaf, dumb, and blind . . . neutral, dead, lifeless.

We, the Nation of Islam, who believe in freedom, justice and equality stand not only before you today, but before the entire world as we declare this truth about the American so-called Negroes. The nations of earth are faced today with a worse problem than has ever presented itself in the history of mankind, and the primary ingredient of this great "world problem" involves the condition and position of the so-called Negro here in America . . . twenty million ex-slaves who have become a nation within a nation and who are now crying out for something that they can call their own. This is creating a problem not only for America, but for the entire world, and that problem is: how to give you a knowledge and understanding of yourself, teach you the knowledge of your own God and your own religion, and to teach you the knowledge of your own nation so that you can make a stand for yourselves as other nations are making for themselves.

This problem is so delicate and complicated that only God Himself can solve it. I am not a man who has grabbed a suitcase with a Bible in it upon my own impulses. No! I stand before you as a man who has been chosen for you by God Himself. I did not choose myself. This must be made clear! The Divine Revelation which I have received and which I am preaching to you and to the entire world came to me from the Mouth of God.

I did not see Him in a vision and receive my mission in a vision as others before me received theirs. I was in the Presence of God for over three years, and I received what I am teaching you directly from His Mouth.

Let the infidels curse and swear at me. Let the infidels go on the warpath of propaganda against Elijah, but I warn you: "You better listen today to him who has received his instructions directly from the Mouth of Almighty God." I did not receive this gospel from a paper, nor a book, nor from a vision, nor from an angel, but directly from the Mouth of Almighty God Himself.

My beloved people: I know your problems and your burdens; I know your problems and your burdens; I know what you go through; you don't have to tell me . . . for I have the ABSOLUTE CURE for all your problems and ailments. All you have to do is listen to what I say, and then jump up on your feet and follow me.

I don't want you to be too proud, as others were in former times; they were too proud to follow the words of the prophets. I don't want you to be like that. I want you to place more value on your life than they did. Think something of your future, and your children, and your people. Accept Allah and His religion and follow me and I will lead you to Him and to a heaven right here on this earth. Come and follow me, and you will not have to wait until after you die to see God, nor will you have to wait until after you die to enjoy a heaven somewhere up in the sky.

Beloved brothers and sisters: after receiving this Divine Revelation that I am teaching you from the Mouth of God, I have not stopped one day for the last twenty-nine years. I have been standing, preaching to you throughout these past twenty-nine years, while I was free and even while I was in bondage. I spent three and one-half years in the federal penitentiary and also over a year in the city jail for teaching this truth. I was also deprived of a father's love for his family for seven long years while I was running from hypocrites and other enemies of this word and revelation of God, and which will give life to you and put you on the same level with all other civilized and independent nations of this earth . . . and this is the greatest desire of Almighty God Allah and Elijah Muhammad. This afternoon I want to teach the so-called American Negroes the true knowledge of themselves that will lift them from the bottom and place them back at the top of civilization.

I know how you feel. I know how you think. You think as Ezekiel says of you. Ezekiel says, "This whole House of Israel, they say their hope was lost and they were cut off from their fathers." You are a people who are all hopeless because you think there is no hope for you. You think that because you have been cut off from your own people for so long there is no chance of you ever uniting or of ever becoming anything but what you now are. I say you are wrong. The God of your Fathers, whose proper name is Allah, will strengthen you and cause you to stand upon your own feet as an independent people in the eyes of other people on this earth.

This Truth that I am teaching will raise you up from the grave, not out of the earthly grave, but out of the "grave of ignorance." You just need the knowledge of yourself, your own God and your own religion. God has missioned me to give you this Truth: freedom, justice, and equality.

These are the things I must teach you about: freedom first, because you have never been free here in America. You know nothing about the pleasures or happiness of a free person. You know nothing about justice. You know nothing about equality, or being equal with other civilized nations of earth.

I know you and your thoughts about me and what I teach. Inwardly, some of you are with me one hundred percent, but outwardly you are not. Why? Because you have the greatest enemy over you a man can have, and that is "FEAR." Fear is your greatest enemy. You were filled with fear of your slave master when you were little babies, over four hundred years ago when our fathers were brought in chains to the Western Hemisphere on a slave ship that was named "The Good Ship Jesus." The captain of that ship was an English Christian named John Hawkins.

The American white people had come to this country from Europe and had already begun to subdue the Indians. We were brought here to a people who could not speak our language nor could we speak theirs. Thus the language of our forefathers was soon destroyed, and you know nothing about it today. The language of the slave master was forced upon our foreparents, and they were brought up also wearing the names of the slave masters. Today, you are still speaking their language and wearing their names.

During three hundred long years of slavery you were deprived of the privilege of even going to church, and there were no such things as schools for you in those days. Besides depriving you of education the slave master did not teach you about God, Jesus, and the Holy Ghost that he is now teaching you about today. You were never allowed to sit with them in their churches until just a few years ago.

Beloved brothers and sisters, think over this: for over four hundred years you had no knowledge of yourselves, no knowledge of your own religion, and no knowledge of the biblical prophecies and predictions pertaining to the "lost people" who would be on this planet until the last days, and whom God Himself would have to search for and then save them from the clutches of their enemies. You have never been given a knowledge of that because your slave master knew those prophecies were speaking about you (the American so-called Negroes).

For less than one hundred years now a little bit of the Christian religion has been taught to you in a diluted form, but never the full text of it. You have never learned the prophetic fate of Christianity, nor do you know anything about the Caucasian people who have translated the Bible into their language. Yet, you are a people who think you know all about the Bible, and all about Christianity, and you are even foolish enough to believe that nothing is right but Christianity.

Your slave master tampered with the words of the Bible; he "translated" it; he "revised" it; he fixed the reading of it to make you a worse slave than your foreparents were. The slave master is the "god" who "sent" some of your fellow slaves to preach to you. Their favorite text was, "Servant, obey your master." But he didn't really have to preach that because the lashes of the whip upon the backs of your parents for three hundred years had beaten them into obedient submission.

But, my beloved brothers and sisters, the Christian religion you now are believing in so strongly came down to you from your slave masters. They kept that religion and its secrets guarded from your parents' ears for three hundred years. What was then so sacred in Christianity? What was so sacred in the Bible which they kept locked away from the slaves? What was so sacred about these things that the slave master did not want his slaves to read or even hear preached? If it was so good, why didn't he want his slave to hear this good then? Why didn't he want his slave to believe in God then?

First of all, the slave master did not want the slaves to know the truth about God nor about His true religion, fearing that the slave would then begin looking for his God to deliver him from his white oppressors.

I know some of you are afraid to listen to this truth but I am going to preach it to you until you are free of that fear. A man told me a few years ago that I would be wasting my time to come to Georgia. He said that the Negroes in Georgia were more afraid of white people than you will find anywhere else on this earth. I told him that I myself was born in Georgia and did not see why they should be afraid of the white man. I told him that I was a grown man, married and with two children when I left Georgia. I also told him that they need not fear the white man; the only thing they need to fear is the fear within themselves.

I say to you that your fear of the white man is THE GREAT EVIL. Fear is of such nature that it will make you deprive yourself of your own salvation. Fear is the enemy that will make you stoop and bring yourself to disgrace before the world. Fear is the real enemy that you and I should throw into the garbage can.

My beloved brothers and sisters, how could you accept of God, Jesus and the Holy Ghost. How do you know? I am not asking you to answer these questions, because God has missioned me to answer them for you. You don't know the answers. All you know is what you have heard your slave master say.

You say Christianity is the right religion and that you believe in God the Father, God the Son, and God the Holy Ghost. You believe that this Jesus is God's son, and that He gave His son to save you. You say that the Holy Ghost "overpowered" a virgin girl named Mary, yet you don't call the child the son of the Holy Ghost, you call the child "the son of God." You charge God with being the father of this virgin girl's child.

My beloved brothers and sisters, how could you accept a religion that teaches you to believe the God of Righteousness was responsible for making a virgin girl in Palestine pregnant with a child two thousand years ago, called this child his "son," and let this "son" die for the sins of the wicked world?

When a man is not married to a woman and he commits such a sinful act it is called adultery. God is not married to a woman, and if He commits such a sinful act that produces a child out of wedlock, which actually opens the gateway of adultery to the entire world, then it is a shame to ask me to believe in that god.

We in Islam do not ascribe "sonship" to Almighty God, because He has no son. All of us are His "spiritual" children, but He has no physical son. To say that God has produced a physical son out of wedlock (without being married to the mother of that son), and then placed this son before our eyes and said, "This is my beloved son; all who believe in him and follow him shall be saved," actually opens the gateway for all kinds of adultery and other indecent acts.

God had already told His prophet Moses that the people should be stoned to death for adultery. Now if God had come two thousand years after giving the law against adultery to Moses, and after "courting" or"overpowering" Mary, and she was a virgin girl who had never been touched by any man, and yet she became pregnant with His child, and that child is the flesh and blood "son" of God . . . then the Christians are charging God Himself with having committed adultery with Mary.

This just could not have been done if God was a spirit. If He was a spirit He could not father a flesh and blood son. He would have to have a son like Himself. If He was a spirit, then His son would have to be a spirit too. And, if He did beget a son by Mary, then all other women would be justified in producing sons that same way, by committing adultery and then blaming it on the "spirit."

The Western World is always defending Christianity and they mock me and other Islamic teachers. They do not want Islam preached to you, but the reason you are hearing it today is because it is time. This preaching of Islam to you today cannot be stopped; it is like the rising of the sun . . . right on time.

Here in America there are also three and one-half million indirect believers in Islam, in the secret order called Shriners, or Higher Masons. When you take the thirty-third degree in masonry you are no longer called a Mason; you are then called a Moslem Son, and in that order (or degree) you are taught the prayers of the Moslems and you come under the teachings of Islam. In that High Degree you are taught to turn your face Eastward, toward the Holy City of Mecca in Arabia. All of this is part of the Moslem religion, Islam.

Today, Islam must be taught to the so-called American Negroes. You must learn about this religion, because there can be no judgment of the devil and his wicked world until after you (the lost people of God) have heard the truth about God and the truth about the devil as I am teaching you today. It is only after you have heard the teachings of Islam that you can make a wise choice between God and the devil.

We are not trying to force you to accept Islam, but we are trying to make you realize that we know what is in store for the world; we know what tomorrow will bring. Therefore, we are not in fear of losing our lives, but we will lay down our lives this very minute for the truth. We are not running from death; we are running only to save lives . . . YOUR LIVES!!!

You must have freedom, justice, and equality. You cannot be free as long as you are calling yourselves by your slave master's name; you cannot be free as long as you do not know who you are; you cannot be free as long as you do not know your own people; you cannot be free as long as you don't know how to even ask for freedom.

Beloved brothers and sisters, God has given me the key that will open the door of freedom, justice, and equality that has been locked against you. You must be taught a knowledge of your own God. My mission is to make you acquainted with Him, to prepare you to meet Him face to face.

"You cannot be free as long as you are calling yourselves by your slave master's name; you cannot be free as long as you do not know who you are . . ."

God is not a mystery today; He is not something invisible. He is not a spirit. He is not something other than flesh and blood; He is in the flesh and in the blood. God is a human being! God would have no joy or pleasure in humans (us) if He Himself were something other than a human being. God would have no joy or pleasure in the material universe if He Himself were other than material.

The devil is also a flesh and blood human being. The devil is not an invisible spirit. The Bible and the Holy Quran both plainly state that God is going to destroy the devil in a Lake of Fire in "the last days." If the devil was an invisible spirit he could not be destroyed. You can destroy a man but you cannot destroy a spirit. So I repeat to you, my beloved brothers and sisters, God and the devil both are flesh and blood human beings.

There is no such thing as seeing God or the devil after you die. There is no such thing as a heaven up in the sky or a hell down in the ground. All of that is fantasy, false stories made up by your slave master to further enslave you. God is a man! The devil is a man! Heaven and hell are two conditions, and both are experienced in this life right here on this earth. You have already suffered the worse kind of hell in the hands of the only real devil!

It is the devil who did not want you to know this truth that God has missioned me to teach my people. He is afraid that when you learn his real identity you will then separate yourselves from him and thereby escape the fiery destruction God has prepared for him. He wants to keep you from your salvation in the hereafter. He knows that without this truth that I am teaching you, you could never avoid the fire that God has ordained for him and enter into the Hereafter. And by HEREAFTER, we mean the Kingdom of Righteousness that God will establish "here" on this earth "after" the devil has been destroyed in the Divine Lake of Fire.

Beloved brothers and sisters, it has been predicted by all the prophets that God is coming. Well, if God is coming (and He must be coming because the whole world claims to be *"looking"* for Him), then He must be something visible. If He is an invisible spirit then the world wouldn't be *"looking"* for Him to come. The world couldn't say, "We will *see* Him" . . . because we don't *"look"* for a spirit, we *feel* for a spirit.

If God is a spirit and He says He made Adam in His own image and likeness, then I say to you Adam would have been a spirit. But God did not make a spirit; He made a man like Himself. Man looks like God and God looks like man because God is a man.

Man acts like God; he acts with power. Man does not just sit down and wait for the wheat to grow itself, harvest itself, make itself into flour, bake itself, and then bring itself to him to eat, does he? No!!!

Man plants the wheat, man cultivates it, man threshes it, man grinds it into flour, man bakes the bread, and then man eats it. If man sits all day in the house waiting for a spirit to produce that bread he would starve to death. No spirit in heaven or in hell will bring you bread . . . and no spirit in heaven or in hell will bring you freedom, justice, or equality.

I say to you, my beloved brothers and sisters, your slave master and his imps (the Negro preachers) have blinded you by such ignorant teachings and today you are still foolishly sending your praises and your prayers to an invisible God who is supposed to be somewhere out in space, and who cannot be found by you until after you die. And, this same ignorant doctrine has you believing there is an invisible devil down in the earth somewhere beneath your feet . . . while in reality the devil is right here on top of the earth, walking around on two feet like you are, and you are looking at him every day.

God is a man, a flesh and blood being, but He is a Divine Being. Why do we call God a Divine Being? Because He is a being like we are but His wisdom, power, and other capabilities and attributes are Supreme . . . making Him the Highest Power, the Supreme in Power, or Supreme Power. He is a being like ourselves, but He has the Divine Capacity of exercising His Power or to project through His Power the powers of the Universe . . . and therefore we call Him the Supreme Being and the God of the Universe. He has the Divine Power to will whatever He wishes and to bring it into existence with His Divine Will. But He is not an invisible spirit somewhere up in the sky. His home is right here on this earth.

I would defy any spirit outside the spirit that is in a man to do anything for me or to me. I would defy any devil that is outside of a man to do anything for me or to me. But I do recognize the devil in these that can do us harm and have done us harm. No spirit independent of man can do us harm or good.

Beloved brothers and sisters, let us bring our minds out of the sky; let us stop being spooky; let us learn to face reality; let us look around here on this earth as other intelligent and civilized people are doing. Here in Atlanta is the seat of education for the so-called Negroes in this country. Yet most Negroes here are still locked into the most crowded and undesirable areas. Therefore, I would like to know what are our educated people doing with this education to elevate the living standards of your own people, and to eliminate the misery and poverty yet suffered by the so-called Negro masses who do not have education?

You who are college graduates, and you who are educators and instructors here in Atlanta, Georgia: I would like for you to tell me what you are doing with this education you have received from the white man toward making your own people more independent? What are you doing for your people with your education? Should not you take that education to unite your people and bring them up out of the "mud of ignorance," and make them an independent people? But with all your education you yourself are still dependent upon your slave master for a job, and for your food, clothing and shelter. With your education, you have enough land and farmers to do something about the condition of the so-called American Negro.

But you must first agree that the most important ingredient has been omitted from your education, and that is the knowledge of God, the devil, of yourself, and of your enemy. Accept Allah and His true religion (Islam), and come and follow me. I am God's Messenger to you. I have the keys to your salvation. Come and follow me and I will show you how to use your education, your skills and talents, for the good of your own people and yourself.

In the unity and harmony and Brotherhood created by the religion of Islam, it is easy for us to pool our knowledge and finance to set up farms and grow food to feed our people; we can set up factories to manufacture our own necessities, and other businesses with which we can establish trade and commerce and become independent as other civilized people are. Then, in this way you will be using your education to bring your people out of the slums and the breadlines. They will cease to be the "last hired and the first fired," when you use your education to make jobs for them.

I thank you, my beloved brothers and sisters, for being here this afternoon, and listening so attentively to this truth. I am God's last Messenger to you. You must accept Allah as God. You must know that Islam is your religion. Come and follow me; let me teach you, and I will put twenty million so-called American Negroes overnight on the road to success . . . on the road toward complete independence in a home of your own, where you will never any more have to beg anyone for freedom, justice, or equality.

Thank you, my beloved brothers and sisters. May Allah forever bless you, as I leave you with the greetings of the peaceful and the righteous: As-Salaam-Alaikum . . . which means, "Peace be unto you."

SOURCES

Boulware, Marcus H., *The Oratory of Negro Leaders: 1900-1968,* Negro Universities Press, 1969.

Lomax, Louis E., *When the Word Is Given . . . : A Report on Elijah Muhammad, Malcolm X, and the Black Muslim World,* World Publishing, 1963.

Foner, Philip S., editor, *The Voice of Black America: Major Speeches by Negroes in the United States, 1797-1971,* Simon & Schuster, 1972.

Luis Muñoz-Marín

1898–1980

Puerto Rican journalist and political leader

Described by a New York Times *reporter as a man with "the mind of a politician and the soul of a poet," Luis Muñoz-Marín was instrumental in achieving for Puerto Rico its current status as a freely associated commonwealth of the United States. His strong and charismatic leadership also helped transform the island colony once dubbed "the poorhouse of the Caribbean" into one of Latin America's few economic and political success stories. While Puerto Ricans are now inching closer to opting for statehood, they have Muñoz-Marín to thank for instilling in them a sense of self-respect and an appreciation for democratic traditions.*

Muñoz-Marín may well have inherited the skills that made him such an effective leader. His father, Luis Muñoz-Rivera, was a journalist and politician fondly known as "the George Washington of Puerto Rico" for his efforts to secure his country's independence, first from Spain and then from the United States. In 1897, for example, Muñoz-Rivera successfully pressured Spain into granting its Caribbean colony some measure of home rule. A year later, the island was turned over to U.S. control following Spain's defeat in the Spanish-American War, but Muñoz-Rivera's commitment to independence remained firm. In 1910, he became Puerto Rico's resident commissioner in Washington, D.C., where he held a non-voting seat in the House of Representatives. Although he died in office in 1916, Muñoz-Rivera is also credited with paving the way for Congress to extend U.S. citizenship to Puerto Ricans in 1917.

Luis Muñoz-Marín, Muñoz-Rivera's only son, was born in San Juan just a few months before American troops occupied Puerto Rico at the close of the Spanish-American War. He spent much of his youth in the company of his father, first in New York City and later in Washington. An indifferent student who bounced from school to school, he quit for good following his father's death and decided to work on establishing himself as a writer. He spent most of the next fifteen years in New York, contributing articles to various newspapers and magazines on topics ranging from U.S. foreign policy to the latest Broadway show. Muñoz-Marín also translated the poetry of such luminaries as Walt Whitman, Carl Sandburg, and Robert Frost into Spanish and edited a magazine on Latin American culture.

But Muñoz-Marín could not quite turn his back on his heritage; he returned to Puerto Rico several times during this same period and dabbled in politics a bit, embracing a philosophy that was decidedly less conservative than his father's. He worked on behalf of Latin American labor and unity movements, for instance, and was briefly a member of the Socialist party until joining Puerto Rico's newly-formed Liberal party in 1926. In the pages of La Democracia, *the newspaper his late father had founded, Muñoz-Marín demanded complete independence for his native land and increased attention to the needs of its poorest citizens, the landless peasants known as* jibaros.

It was not until he settled permanently in Puerto Rico in 1931, however, that Muñoz-Marín was able to shake the image many had of him as just a dilettante who played at politics now and then. The country he saw at that particular time was still reeling from the devastating effects of two hurricanes; there was no sugar cane, coffee, or tobacco to harvest, and the jibaros *had crowded into the island's few major cities. Poverty, disease, and illiteracy were widespread.*

In 1932, Muñoz-Marín ran for and won a seat in the Puerto Rican House of Representatives. Through his Washington connections, he scored points almost immediately by obtaining some New Deal money for the island from President Franklin Roosevelt. Muñoz-Marín's popularity soared to even greater heights after he played a key role in the fight to oust an unpopular governor (who at that time was appointed by the United States, not elected by the Puerto Rican people) and in pushing through legislation that broke up some of the larger sugar plantations and redistributed the land among the peasants.

In 1937, after a falling out with the Liberal party over how best to help the peasants, Muñoz-Marín established a new party of his own, the Popular Democrats. By this time, his political beliefs had undergone a shift as well; he no longer felt Puerto Rico was quite ready politically or economically to stand completely on its own as a state or nation. So armed with the slogan "Bread, Land, and Liberty," he began to campaign vigorously throughout the island's cities and villages against independence and for continued support from the United States to help the island deal with its many problems. In the 1940 elections, the Popular Democrats did surprisingly well, winning control of the Senate (where Muñoz-Marín, who had received more votes than any other candidate, was elected president) but falling two votes short of actually controlling the House. But due to skillful politicking, Muñoz-Marín was able to form a coalition that essentially gave him control over the House, too.

Over the next few years, Muñoz-Marín launched some ambitious land reforms and industrial and farm development plans that counted heavily on government supervision and aid. These programs, which his critics referred to as "socialist experiments," often put him at odds with the island's appointed governor and with the U.S. Congress, not to mention some of his fellow legislators. But he charged ahead anyway with the overwhelming support of the Puerto Rican people, who regarded him as their hero.

On quite a few occasions, both in print and from the podium, Muñoz-Marín took his case directly to the American people in an effort to win their backing as well. One such instance was on May 26, 1945, when he spoke to a national radio audience tuned to the CBS network about the future of Puerto Rico in the post-World War II era and the role of the United States in that future. At the time, he was beginning to advance the notion that perhaps it was time to re-evaluate the relationship between the two—not exactly with an eye toward independence, but certainly toward increased autonomy. His remarks are reprinted here from Vital Speeches of the Day, *August 1, 1945.*

The future peace of the world depends to an important degree on the solution or solutions that may be found to the colonial problem. It also depends, to a still greater degree, on the prestige of the United States among the peoples of the world—on the confidence that the common man everywhere shall continue to have in the human understanding and the democratic sincerity of the American people.

It is of the utmost importance to democracy that the United States shall not cease to be the champion of democratic rights in the minds of men and women everywhere. It is clear that our great ally Russia is making a bid for the confidence and that trust which have been the traditional heritage of the United States. Of course, Russia's attitude in this respect should not be unwelcome. There is no such thing as too much good will, as too much recognition of rights and liberties. The world certainly needs as much of that as it can get from all possible sources. But certainly Russia's attitude should not be allowed to displace and substitute the traditional American attitude, but only to complement it and support it. Russia's developing international liberalism would appear best in its proper place, that is, as a follower of the tradition that the United States has made its own these many years.

In the treatment of colonies and of otherwise dependent peoples, the United States has an eminent field for sustaining, strengthening, and developing its policy for a good, for a confidence inspiring, for a lasting peace under the principles that have reared the national greatness of the American people.

I am proud to say that in this respect my own country, Puerto Rico, which has contributed without stint to the war effort, is now making what is perhaps a still more important contribution to the peace effort. Puerto Rico is a Caribbean island country of two million people which came under the jurisdiction of the United States as a result of the Spanish-American War almost half a century ago. Puerto Rico is a colony of the United States. It is a colony, it is true, that has been administered in a mild, though not always intelligible, way, by the United States government. But it is a colony. It is what each of the original thirteen states were before 1776; basically its government does not derive its powers from the consent of the governed. That is, by the time-honored definition written by Jefferson, what colonialism means to the American mind; and by that definition, Puerto Rico is a colony of the United States. Puerto Rico is also a very poor country in its economic geography. It has but 3,500 square miles of territory. Half of its land is not arable, much of the rest is not of very good quality; there is not much mineral wealth under that land, and two million people, that is 560 persons per square mile, must make their living from the top of that land. In order for so many people to subsist on such a scarcity of resources, the bulk of production must be of intensive cash-crops that can be sold in extensive markets at reasonably good prices.

It is this same people of Puerto Rico, to whom nature has been so harsh, who have reached their political maturity, according to a message of the late President Roosevelt to the Congress. They have given proof of this maturity. Eighty-five percent of the registered voters vote on the basis of universal adult suffrage. Although political passions frequently run high, elections are absolutely peaceful and orderly. Defeated candidates recognize their defeat and the fairness of the electoral process. The buying of votes has been unheard of for quite some time. The people vote on the clear understanding that they are giving a mandate for certain laws to be enacted and certain policies to be carried out insofar as their elected legislators have the legal authority to do so, and they are vigilant as to whether their clear-cut democratic mandates are carried out or not. The Puerto Rican people, in fact, are more than just a politically mature people. I sincerely and proudly believe that in their hinterland of the world they constitute the best rural school of democracy in America today, and that there is profit in looking to its poverty-stricken electorate as an example of sound democratic practice.

It is these people, so politically sound and so economically harassed, that are now contributing to the peace effort, as they are contributing to the war effort. They are now proposing to the Congress and the government of the United States a plan for self-determination. This plan may well serve as a basis for dealing with the colonial problem in many other parts of the world as well as in Puerto Rico. It should also help the United States in clarifying, maintaining, strengthening, and developing that leadership of hard-pressed mankind everywhere

Luis Muñoz-Marín (right)

which is of such decisive importance to world justice and world peace.

The legislature of Puerto Rico has unanimously proposed to the Congress of the United States a clear-cut, straightforward method of solving the colonial problem, on the basis of self-determination, in democratic terms, and in the fiber of American policy and tradition. The Puerto Rican proposal is as follows:

At the request, the unanimous request, of the legislature of Puerto Rico, all political parties concurring, a bill has been introduced in the Senate by United States Senator Millard E. Tydings, of Maryland, and in the United States House of Representatives by Resident Commissioner Pinero, of Puerto Rico. This bill contains four titles and offers three alternative forms of government to the people of Puerto Rico. Title 1 provides that there shall be a referendum in which the people of Puerto Rico shall decide whether they want independence under certain economic conditions necessary for their survival, or statehood, or dominion status similar to that of Australia or Canada in the British Commonwealth of Nations. Title 2 describes independence. Title 3 describes statehood. Title 4 describes dominion status. If a majority of the people of Puerto Rico vote for independence, then Title 2 shall go into effect. If they vote for statehood, then Title 3 shall go into effect. If they vote for dominion status, then Title 4 shall go into effect. In this manner, if the bill is approved, the people of Puerto Rico themselves will choose their own future, on the basis of an offer by the American Congress, and in choosing it they will have before them the fullest possible picture of what they are voting about.

It is worthy of note that the proposal provides that the United States shall have in perpetuity all the military and naval bases and rights that they may need in Puerto Rico for the defense of the United States and the Western Hemisphere. This is of very great importance, as Puerto Rico constitutes one of the chief military protections of the Panama Canal, and has been called by military authorities "the Gibraltar of the Caribbean." Parallel with these perpetual rights of the United States, under any form of government that the people of Puerto Rico may choose, certain minimum economic conditions are established, also under any form of government that the people of Puerto Rico may choose. These minimum economic conditions are considered necessary if the people are to survive in the face of the difficult economic circumstances that confront them. I should call attention to the fact that these minimum economic conditions do not represent any increase in economic facilities. Therefore the granting of them would not in any way increase the commitments of the United States, but would rather decrease them. What is, therefore, proposed is to wipe out political discontent without intolerably increasing economic suffering and discontent. This is of importance, not only as a matter of justice and of American leadership in democracy but also as a means of surrounding important military defenses with the greatest possible democratic good will.

Let us look at what the colonial problem means in broad terms. Obviously, the United States will have need of military and naval establishments in many parts of the world. But just as obviously these establishments are a second line of defense. The need for military establishments is predicated upon the sensible provision that all good-will means of keeping the peace may fail. The first line of defense is the maintenance of peace, the creation of conditions that, so far as human understanding and good sense can make it so, will tend to keep the world at peace with itself. For that reason, the need for military establishments—the second line of defense—should not contradict the need for democratic procedure in the maintenance of world confidence in American leadership. Neither, of course, should the need to maintain this leadership weaken in any way America's maximum ability to defend itself if peace should fail. The Puerto Rican proposal is made in the clear recognition of these two paramount factors.

Military and naval establishments may be needed in two broadly different kinds of places. They may be needed in small places scantily populated, and they may be needed, as they are in Puerto Rico for instance, among large populations with a developed civilization, with a recognized political maturity, and an acute consciousness that the principles of freedom are applicable to them also. The United States is making this distinction clear at the San Francisco Conference. Military and naval bases and establishments, of course, must be where strategy says they must be, whether on small rocks of the sea where the problems of the population are at a minimum or in developed communities where the problems of the people are of great significance and importance with relation to the general democratic principles and policies at stake.

In offering its proposal for self-determination, Puerto Rico is bearing in mind these considerations. The United States, at San Francisco, are standing for self-government to colonies, which may include independence. The Puerto Rican proposal is a specific proposal for self-government on the basis of an alternative offer by Congress of different forms of self-government, which may include independence, and an acceptance by the people of Puerto Rico, in referendum, of one of the forms of self-government offered by Congress.

The proposal that the legislature of Puerto Rico has unanimously presented to the Congress of the United States is a self-determination proposal as embodied in Senate bill 1002 and in House bill 3237. We make this proposal both as a claim of justice for Puerto Rico and as a contribution to American leadership—a leadership so completely necessary for the prevention of future wars—in the minds and hearts of average men and women the world over. For both reasons we hope to receive for our proposal the support of the American people.

In 1947, the U.S. Congress voted to make the post of governor of Puerto Rico an elected position instead of an appointed one. Muñoz-Marín was the runaway winner in the following year's election, and under his leadership, the "Operation Bootstrap" program began. With its emphasis on investment (mostly on the part of U.S. firms attracted by generous tax incentives) in light industry and manufacturing, Operation Bootstrap resulted in lower unemployment rates and improved housing, schools, and health care. It also fostered the growth of a conservative Puerto Rican middle class that favored maintaining close ties with the United States. While the program was not entirely successful in eradicating poverty (many of the island's poorest citizens fled to America—especially to New York City and other areas of the Northeast—in search of jobs and higher wages), it did raise the standard

of living overall, especially in comparison with many of Puerto Rico's Latin American neighbors.

At the urging of Muñoz-Marín, the U.S. Congress tentatively granted Puerto Rico limited self-government in 1950 when it approved commonwealth status for the island and called on Puerto Ricans to write their own constitution and subject it to a popular vote. After months of work, the measure passed and received the backing of Congress as well, making Puerto Rico a commonwealth as of July 25, 1952. (Under this new status, Puerto Ricans would enjoy home rule, receive federal funds, and be exempt from paying federal taxes, but they would not be able to vote in mainland elections and would have only a non-voting presence in the U.S. Congress.) Later that same year, Muñoz-Marín won re-election to his second term as governor; he was returned to office for two more four-year terms, bowing out of the race for a fifth term in 1964 over the objections of his many supporters within the Popular Democratic party. In 1968, he was elected to the Senate and served a four-year term.

Muñoz-Marín remained active in politics for the rest of his life, keeping a particularly close eye on the shifts in power between those who wanted to continue Puerto Rico's commonwealth status and those who favored statehood. (Members of a much smaller third group advocate complete independence and have occasionally tried to further their agenda through violence and terrorism, including a 1950 assassination attempt on President Harry Truman.) When the statehood movement gained momentum in the 1970s with the election of a pro-statehood governor, Muñoz-Marín—by then nearly eighty years old and in failing health—again traveled throughout the cities and villages of Puerto Rico to ask the people to side with the backers of commonwealth status. As before, he believed it was the best way to preserve the island's Hispanic culture while taking advantage of the security and economic aid offered by the United States.

Muñoz-Marín died in 1980, but the commonwealth versus statehood battle still rages in Puerto Rico. In a special referendum held in November 1993, forty-eight percent of islanders approved a measure to retain commonwealth status, forty-six percent favored statehood, and four percent chose independence.

SOURCES

Grand Rapids Press, "Puerto Rico Votes to Stay U.S. Commonwealth," November 15, 1993, p. A3.

New York Times, "Luis Muñoz Marín Is Dead at 82; Began Puerto Rico's Fight on Poverty," May 1, 1980, p. D19; "Adios to a Democrat," May 2, 1980, p. 26.

Vital Speeches of the Day, "The Future of Puerto Rico," August 1, 1945, pp. 619-620; "The Substance of Freedom," November 1, 1956, pp. 40-42.

Irene Natividad

1948–

Filipino American activist, feminist, and educator

"The one constant in my life is that . . . I could get people together to fight a cause." Thus observed Irene Natividad about herself in an International Examiner *article discussing her activism on behalf of women and minorities, particularly Asian Americans. It is a path she has followed for over twenty-five years and one that has seen her rise to top posts in several major organizations, including the National Women's Political Caucus, the National Commission on Working Women, and the Philippine American Foundation. The common goal that links these endeavors is Natividad's commitment to making sure those who are often overlooked or ignored gain power and influence through political action. "The price of citizenship is political involvement," she asserts. "To be silent is to not be counted, and we can't afford not to be counted."*

A native of Manila, the capital and largest city of the Philippines, Natividad is the oldest of four children born to a chemical engineer whose job took him around the world. She thus spent her childhood in a number of different countries, including Japan, Iran, Greece, and India, and is fluent in a half-dozen languages. To this day, Natividad credits her family's frequent moves with making it easier for her to work with people from other cultures. It also made her especially sensitive to the limited opportunities afforded to women in many nations where they were not allowed to hold jobs outside the home.

Natividad completed her high school education in Greece, and from there she went on to attend New York's Long Island University, from which she graduated in 1971 at the top of her class. She then enrolled at Columbia University, earning her master's in American literature in 1973 and her master's in philosophy in 1976. She has since completed the course work toward her doctorate but increasing demands on her time have made it impossible for her to finish her dissertation.

During the early 1970s, Natividad taught at Lehman College of the City University of New York and Columbia University. The late 1970s and early 1980s saw her move into the administrative ranks as director of continuing education at Long Island University and then at New Jersey's William Paterson College.

Her first brush with activism was while she was working as a waitress. Exercising her natural talent for organizing, she rallied her fellow waiters and waitresses to demand higher wages. Although she lost her job as a result, Natividad was not discouraged. She subsequently became active politically, distributing campaign leaflets for 1968 presidential candidate Eugene McCarthy. Later, as her interest in women's issues grew, she became involved in a number of organizations devoted to their concerns. For example, in 1980, she founded and headed a group known as Asian American Professional Women and was a founding director of both the National Network of Asian-Pacific American Women and the Child Care Action Campaign.

Natividad became active on the national political scene in the early to mid-1980s. After a two-year stint as chair of the New York State Asian Pacific Caucus early in the decade, she went on to serve as deputy vice-chair of the Asian Pacific Caucus of the Democratic National Committee. During the 1984 presidential campaign of Walter Mondale, she was chosen by Democratic party officials to act as liaison between the Asian American community and Mondale's choice for vice-president, Geraldine Ferraro—the first woman ever selected for the post by a major U.S. political party. Even Mondale and Ferraro's loss in the election to Republicans Ronald Reagan and George Bush could not completely dampen Natividad's spirits, however, for as she later declared to a reporter for the Honolulu Star-Bulletin, *Ferraro "broke the credibility gap for all women candidates. . . . I don't consider '84 a loss. I consider it a win."*

In 1985, Natividad made history herself when she became the first minority woman to head a mainstream political organization—the National Women's Political Caucus, based in Washington, D.C. Founded in 1971 by a small group of prominent feminists, including congresswomen Shirley Chisholm, Patsy Mink, and Bella Abzug, the National Women's Political Caucus is a bipartisan group that concentrates its efforts on electing more women to public office.

During her four-year tenure, Natividad took steps to ensure the flow of potential women candidates for national office would continue by emphasizing the need for them to gain political experience at the local level first. To that end, the Caucus conducted training sessions throughout the country for women candidates and their staffs (including the first-ever program for minority women) on the ins and outs of running a successful campaign. Members of the Caucus also collected and analyzed data to help them understand the influential factors in congressional races involving women. In addition, the Caucus monitored political appointments of women at the state and national level and promoted women candidates for such posts.

In a keynote address delivered in 1991 at a symposium held in Washington, D.C., at the National Museum of American History (part of the Smithsonian Institution), Natividad reflected on the many achievements of women in American political life over the past few decades. Natividad provided a transcript of her remarks.

When the scribes of history sit down to write a chapter on the past three decades, they ought to call it "The Wonder Years." ... From the first shaky steps out of our kitchens in the late fifties, to the fortifying sessions of consciousness-raising groups formed in our own parlors during the sixties, and the growing pains of entering the work world in the seventies and eighties, women in the nineties have indeed come of age. Unquestionably, we are now enjoying the largest measure of personal and political freedom in this country's history. There

Irene Natividad

are those among you in this audience who will agree that the path to progress has been a bumpy one, but no one doubts that indeed we have moved forward.

As we have come of age, from the very basic and revolutionary struggles of our early foremothers who are celebrated by this exhibit, through the seasoning experience of our more recent fights for equality, we have all learned that the personal is indeed the political. You might say we have gone public over the years, and the world has not been the same. The result today is that we are in the fortunate position of having power, serious power, within our reach—power to win our rights, to fulfill our dreams, and to assume full partnership in the public business of this nation.

Today we are fortunate to have Ann Richards serving as the governor of the third-largest state in this country, Texas. The nation's capital is governed by a woman, Sharon Pratt Dixon. And she is joined by many other women mayors: in Houston, for instance, with Kathy Whitmire; in Dallas with Annette Strauss; in Charlotte, North Carolina, with Sue Myrick. Kansas distinguishes itself by being the only state that has a woman governor, Joan Finney, a woman senator, Nancy Kassebaum, and a woman congressional representative, Jan Meyers, all serving at the same time. Equally important, women of color have broken through the dual barriers of race and gender, so that for the first time, there are four African American women serving in Congress—Cardiss Collins, Eleanor Holmes Norton, Barbara Rose Collins, and Maxine Waters—as well as one Asian American, Patsy Mink, who was there long before, and one Hispanic American, Ileana Ros-Lehtinen.

The leadership breakthroughs in business and the professions are legion. Mickey Siebert's history-making feat in the early seventies—being the first woman to buy a seat in the New York Stock Exchange—no longer confounds us, as a series of firsts have happened in rapid succession: the first woman on the Supreme Court, Sandra Day O'Connor; the first woman astronaut, Sally Ride; most recently, the first woman surgeon general, Antonia Novello, and so on.

We have come to accept that certain notoriety that comes with being the first woman to enter the rooms of power, be they economic, political or social. Men have entered those rooms in the past, assuming their rightful place as if they had been expected. Well, we are not yet expected in large numbers, for the time being, but as more women enter the room the spotlight will dim and not focus exclusively on the newest member of the club. Instead, the focus will shift to our numbers. Women are now the majority of students in colleges and graduate schools all across this nation. Large numbers of women are studying in medical schools, law schools, and business schools. Women are projected to be the majority of workers in the next century, and the majority of new small businesses are now started by women.

> *"[Women] are now enjoying the largest measure of personal and political freedom in this country's history."*

But the most important numerical fact, which underscores our power to shape the forces of twenty-first century America, is that women are the majority of voters in every state of the United States. That means that no one can get elected without our votes, not to the House, not to the Senate, not to the presidency, let alone to school boards. The gender gap—or the women's vote, as I prefer to call it—provided the margin of victory for Ann Richards in the last election, for Governor Doug Wilder in Virginia, and for Mayor David Dinkins in New York City in the 1989 elections.

Equally important, the threat of the women's vote propelled the issue of child care into the 1988 presidential campaign. And we saw candidates for the first time tripping over themselves at child care centers. It's not that they had discovered children lately. It's just that the mediagenic politics of the last decade dictates that you go to a child care center because it resonates among women voters.

Lastly, the large female electorate has encouraged officeholders interested in re-election to make record numbers of women's appointments at both the state and the federal levels. Right now, President Bush's record stands at twenty-two percent of all senior-level positions held by women, beating all prior presidents' records. I don't think it's an accident that President Bush suffered a gender gap against him prior to being elected.

The successes of the past three decades that I've been recounting to you were the result of efforts from the early suffrage movement to the modern women's movement. These extraordinary gains challenge us to reach yet another plateau in history—to top our gains, so to speak. But I didn't come here tonight merely to sing the praises of women's achievements of these past thirty years. I came to provide, if I can, a frank assessment.

The organized women's movement is far from being a small band of feminists doing consciousness-raising, or "hell-raising," as some would have said a few decades ago. Over the years the movement has acquired sophisticated, grass-roots organizing, coalition-building, political skills that have helped to win many a victory. The quest for equality in employment, education, in all areas of public life, has been embraced by this nation. The pioneers of women's freedom of the late sixties have been transformed into the largest mainstream movement of the late eighties.

Yet the test that confronts this movement is one of durability. It is, in effect, a dare—a dare to continue to thrive when powerful vehicles, such as the presidency and the courts, are no longer available to support basic rights won earlier in the struggle for social reform along gender lines. All successful movements must face the fact that with successes come failures. To live beyond the moment of ascendancy, to live to get the whole job done, great movements must reinvest themselves. To sustain themselves, movements must not only grow, they must change. That great feminist theorist, Simone de Beauvoir, phrased it well when she titled one of her last essays "Feminism: Alive, Well, and in Constant Danger." The fact of the matter is that, ironically, women have created enough change to be significant, but too little change to be sufficient. This uncomfortable dichotomy makes it difficult to chart a future course as definitive as that pursued during the seventies, when equal rights, embodied in the fight for the Equal Rights Amendment [ERA], made the mission so clear and seemingly so simple.

The contradictions to women's successes have proved most frustrating. The public consensus we had for women's equality has had little effect on the wage gap. Today women still earn only two-thirds of what men earn, no matter what area or level of employment. As Jesse Jackson said so well, the loaf of bread does not cost the woman any less, so why pay her less? It seems so clear, but no one is listening. The consensus for women's equality has not produced a coherent and caring system of child care for families and for the women that society has encouraged to work. The equal rights majority has not been able to gain recognition and protection for the rights of women in the nation's most basic legal document, the Constitution of the United States. Reproductive choice has been won and now is threatened state by state.

These mixed results confuse and confound. So while women are buoyed by their successes, they are simultaneously bedeviled by the inability to sustain the fast pace they had set for themselves in the sixties and seventies. The result is frustration. Frustration is inevitable for a country in which we still must reargue the basics of reproductive choice, affirmative action, and civil rights as a whole. Frustration is justified when a group that is fifty-three percent of the population numbers as its representatives only two percent of the Senate, only six percent of the House, only sixteen percent of the state legislatures, and only nine percent of the federal district court judges. Frustration is justified when there seems to be an inverse relationship between the number of women in public life and the degree of power that they exercise. The higher you go, the less accessible it seems. Frustration is justified when a majority of the poor are still women and children and women workers are still clustered, for the most part, in low-paying clerical, sales, and service jobs.

Frustration is justified when the largest industrialized nation in the world is unable to pass a family and medical leave bill at a time when two-earner families are the norm in this country.

These frustrations make the organized women's movements' efforts seem sisyphean at times. For every step up the hill, we roll back a few times. But women are resilient and persistent, and so are our organizations. Women's groups didn't fold up their tents and go home when the ERA failed or when the Supreme Court handed down the Webster decision almost two years ago. Instead, they learned to coalesce, not just among themselves, but with civil rights groups, labor groups, and, in some instances, even business groups to fight for issues demanding their attention. The results are palpable: the passage of a child care bill (many of us do not deem it to be sufficient but, at least, a significant first step); the passage of the Civil Rights Restoration Act, which restored institution-wide coverage of civil rights bills for minorities, women, the aging, and the handicapped; the defeat of judicial nominations deemed to be contrary to the interests of the disadvantaged in this society. In addition, women have become experts in using the media to reach the majority of Americans, so that more than any one piece of legislation, the women's movement's best achievement of late is the creation of a growing constituency for a family support system in a society where women's disproportionate responsibilities for work at home and work at work often make time more valuable than money.

The threat to women's reproductive rights actually proved to be a boon to a movement that had not been able to attract young adherents in large numbers prior to the Supreme Court's Webster decision. For the first time, women leaders were able to make a direct connection for young women—as they had never been able to do before—between politics and their daily lives, between the act of voting and preserving a right. Young women understood, all of a sudden, that indeed the personal is the political. The challenge, of course, is how to maintain the commitment of these young women, energized and politicized by an issue that is no longer on the front pages of the nation's newspapers, and, equally important, how to extend that commitment to choice to the other issues affecting women.

The women's vote remains the most powerful tool for social change in the coming decades. Not always voting as a bloc, except recently on the issue of choice, women have increasingly come to view their vote as the expression of their hopes and dreams for a better world. The candidate who makes direct appeals to this vote wins, as Governor Doug Wilder discovered. Women are also much more likely to cross party lines to vote their interests.

The enlightened, self-interest dimension of the women's vote is, to a large extent, a product that we might call an economic gender gap. Focus groups of infrequent women voters were asked in 1988 what the issues were that propelled them to vote. The results were not surprising. "Not earning as much as a man" was the number-one answer—not pay equity, not comparable worth, but "not earning as much as a man." Crime, or personal vulnerability as a whole, was the second most important issue. Employment. Environment. And the prism through which women saw all of these issues—children.

"The women's vote remains the most powerful tool for social change in the coming decades."

It is important to note that there is a strong correlation between the increasing number of women in the workplace and the increasing number of women voters. The more women become charged with their economic destiny, the more likely they are to vote. Shirley Chisholm phrased it well when she said that women vote according to their pocketbooks. The truly liberating issue for women is economic security.

The task that remains, however, is how to mobilize that vote. Like most Americans, women are still voting only half their strength—a fact which I find personally frustrating. I have told women all across this country that if they do not vote, then they have not earned the right to complain about crime, about education, about discrimination, about the environment. I remind them that in other countries—in Latin America, for instance—people get shot for exercising their right to vote. But in this country, we take that right for granted. On election day, many of us go shopping, which is all right as long as we shop as well for a candidate who represents our interests. I tell them the story of my friend who lost a state legislative race in South Dakota by one vote, even after a recount. And most recently, in that same state, an anti-choice bill was defeated in the senate, again by one vote.

There is no substitute, however, for promoting social reform through our own leaders, our own representatives. The impact of one Pat Schroeder, who pushes for a child care bill, the impact of one Claudine Schneider, who sponsors an environmental bill, one Connie Morella, who pushes for legislation for the aging, one Marge Roukema, who fights for family and medical leave, would be even more dramatic if there were 290 of them in Congress out of 435 instead of 29 out of 435. Clearly, token numbers of us on the inside cannot speak for the millions of us who are out here. And it remains the most challenging task of the women's movement to make those numbers grow bigger. It is not an easy task. It is an effort that's a little bit like carving a woman's face on Mount Rushmore. It will take years to chip away at stubborn rock before a woman's face begins to emerge. But trust me, emerge it will.

A 1987 survey of voters' attitudes towards women candidates, commissioned by the National Women's Political Caucus, revealed that the future of women candidates is positive. From school board to Congress to the presidency, the poll showed that the bias against women candidates is eroding. In part, this is due to the public's becoming more accustomed to the notion of women holding office. Madeleine Kunin so eloquently articulated this when she said, "I couldn't have been elected governor of the State of Vermont . . . without Dixie Lee Ray, without Martha Layne Collins. In a very real way we create public confidence through one another."

Given the changing demographics of the United States, which project a next century when minorities will be the majority, the Madeleine Kunins of the future will come from various ethnic groups. The next plateau for the women's movement, which so far has been largely white and middle class, is how to embrace pluralism in its maturity. How to arrive at consensus in the future—given the possibility of emerging political tensions between the ethnic groups that will come into ascendance—will pose a difficult challenge for many of us.

Where the women's movement will be in the new political mosaic of the coming decades will be interesting to see, as Hispanics conflict with Asian or African Americans, or vice versa, in carving out new districts. How do you coalesce the interests of the young with the interests of the old? Will it be child care versus Medicare at a time when twenty-five percent of the American population will be older Americans, the majority of whom will vote, when children can't?

Clearly the task before us is enormous. But we women are more than up to it. Like Wonder Woman, we are smart, we are patient, we are persevering. There are more of us and we live longer. The hurdles that we face are real. But we cannot move forward if we spend our time bemoaning our fate and the foibles and arrogance of the other gender.

Nancy Astor, the first woman to sit in the British House of Commons, said it best when she said, "Mercifully, women have no political past. We have all the mistakes of one-sex legislation with its appalling failures to guide us. We should know what to avoid. It is no use blaming the men. We made them and now it's up to us, the makers of men, to be a little more responsible."

Thank you very much.

Since stepping down as head of the National Women's Political Caucus, Natividad has remained busy with a number of other endeavors on both the national and international level. In 1991, for example, she became chair of the National Commission on Working Women, which is devoted to improving the economic status of working women in the United States. The following year, she served as co-chair of the Women of Color Committee for Clinton/Gore. She maintains affiliations with many Asian American organizations as well, among them the Philippine American Foundation, which she serves as executive director; its efforts to reduce poverty in her native Philippines include fostering grassroots rural de-

velopment. In addition, Natividad heads her own consulting firm, Natividad & Associates, which provides services to groups that are trying to reach specific segments of the voting population.

Natividad's activities often take her outside the United States as well. Besides organizing and leading political workshops on an international scale, she also directs the Global Forum of Women, a biennial gathering of women from around the world who meet to discuss and develop leadership strategies. (Dublin, Ireland, hosted the 1992 session, followed by Taiwan in 1994.) And in 1995, Natividad was involved in planning a meeting on political leadership that ran in conjunction with the United Nations Fourth World Conference on Women.

SOURCES

Books

Zia, Helen, and Susan Gall, eds., *Notable Asian Americans,* Gale Research, Detroit, 1995.

Periodicals

AsianWeek, "Women Shape the Course of Their Future During Conference," October 23, 1992, p. 12.

Honolulu Star-Bulletin, "Leading the Fight to Give Women Political Might," July 9, 1985.

International Examiner, "Activist Natividad Wants APIs to Make Themselves Heard," November 3, 1993, p. 1.

USA Today, "Asian-American Leads National Group," July 1, 1985; "Women's Caucus Loses Cornerstone," August 2, 1989, p. 2A.

Huey Newton

1942–1989

African American political and social activist

In October 1966, black revolutionaries Huey Newton and Bobby Seale formed the Black Panther Party in Oakland, California. Inspired by the teachings of Malcolm X and, later, those of Karl Marx, Friedrich Engels, Vladimir Lenin, Mao Tse-tung, Ho Chi Minh, and Che Guevara, Newton and Seale called for radical economic and social change to combat the effects of white oppression in the black community. They also insisted on an end to police brutality and announced that blacks would take up arms in self-defense against such unwarranted violence. Outfitted in black berets and black leather jackets with guns and ammunition clips in clear view, the Panthers provoked fear among most white Americans with their menacing look and fierce rhetoric. And few of them attracted as much attention as Newton, whose 1967 arrest for the shooting death of an Oakland policeman made "Free Huey" a popular rallying cry for the Panthers and their supporters.

A native of Louisiana, Newton was only a year old when he and his family moved to California. He met Bobby Seale in 1960 while both were attending Merritt Junior College in Oakland. There they became active in a black nationalist organization but dropped out after concluding that the group paid too little attention to the urban black community and its problems. Their solution was to form the Black Panther Party instead. Almost immediately, they became the focus of intense police hostility and resentment. In October 1967, tensions came to a head when Newton was charged with killing an Oakland policeman, wounding a second one, and kidnapping a black motorist. His subsequent trial became a cause célèbre, *attracting more than 2,500 demonstrators who chanted their support for Newton and the Panthers.*

On February 16, 1969, a huge rally was held in Oakland in honor of Newton's birthday the next day and to raise money for his defense fund. The occasion was also notable in that it made official a loose merger of the Black Panthers and the Student Nonviolent Coordinating Committee (SNCC, headed by Stokely Carmichael). In addition, the Panthers announced it was forming a coalition with the Peace and Freedom Party, a group of white radicals opposed to the war in Vietnam and committed to the idea of black liberation. Held in jail without bond, Newton himself could not attend the rally. But he taped a brief message that was played to the crowd in which he urged them to accept the party's new direction. His speech was published in the March 3, 1969, issue of The Black Panther.

REVOLUTIONARY BROTHERS AND SISTERS, WHITE RADICALS WHO ARE BECOMING BROTHERS AND SISTERS:

I'm very happy that we are all here together today, not because it's my birthday, but because we should be together on any and every occasion that we possibly can in the name of solidarity.

February 17 fortunately is also the Tet of the lunar new year. So we're celebrating the lunar new year with our brothers in Viet Nam. We're daily making the people more and more aware of the need for unity among all revolutionary people and also that it's impossible for us to overcome the treacherous bureaucratic class without an organized force.

The students at the many universities across the nation are challenging the reactionary authority of the schools and are also pointing out very vividly that it's impossible to have a free university, free schools, or a free society, in a society that's ruled by a fascist military-industrial complex. The community is now seeing that our fight on the campuses is more than just a fight for "freedom of speech" on the campus, or Blacks gaining a knowledge of our heritage; it's also showing the direct relationship between the reactionary government and the agencies and institutions that are only an arm of these reactionaries. Until we penetrate the community and make them aware, and plant the seed of revolution, we will never have freedom at our schools. The community now is being mobilized by the Black revolutionary forces and along with them are our white revolutionary comrades.

It seems that the time has come for an escalation of our offensive. Just as our brothers in Viet Nam had the Tet offensive last year, this celebration today will only be a prelude or celebration to the offensive that we are going to wage in the not-too-far future. "In the near future a colossal event will occur where the masses of the people will rise up like a mighty storm and a hurricane, sweeping all evil gentry and corrupt officials into their graves." Brother Mao put that quite well, and we will follow the pattern and follow the thoughts of Chairman Mao.

Huey Newton

Today it should mark a new time [for] the TWO-REVOLUTIONARY force in the country. The TWO-REVOLUTIONARY force I'm speaking of is the alienated white group and the masses of Blacks in the ghettos, who for years sought freedom and liberation from a racist, reaction-system. After approximately three years now that the Panthers have been organized, we have gained even closer relationship with our Latin American brothers, our Chicano brothers in the United States, and the Cuban people, and every other people who are striving for freedom.

I would like to thank everyone very much for coming, and we must remember that we must never make excuses for such gatherings as this. Today we'll use the excuse of my birthday; but the real issue is the need to come together in unity and brotherhood.

Our Minister of Information Eldridge Cleaver is with us in spirit, and I'm very sure that this decadent fascist society wasn't worthy of him and couldn't tolerate his presence because he acted as a guide flag for the people. So we must make a society that will welcome people like our Minister of Information.

The Oakland Seven are now standing trial for resisting the fascist system, and we would like to let them know and would like to rally the community for support. They have a very able representative in court with them, Charles Garry, who is very capable and truly a revolutionary. Brother Eldridge Cleaver has said on more than one occasion that he would go into any court in the world with an attorney like Charles Garry. I would like to bear witness to that from a personal experience. With a representative like Charles Garry we're sure that we would have victory as long as the community supports us. We have, with the support of the community and with the fine attorney such as Charles Garry, we have nothing to fear.

A short time ago we suffered a very tragic experience in that two of our very talented and gifted and dedicated brothers were assassinated in LA: Brother "Bunchy" and Brother Huggins. This was only an escalation of the oppression against us. The assassins were agents of the establishment, and they took the occasion to eliminate the people's fighters, or fighters for the people. Knowing that the people have no recourse, the institutions and the court institutions give us no recourse because they're only representatives of the reactionary system. The community will have to erect revolutionary courts and also a community militia to protect the community and see that the community gets justice.

Brother Ruben has suffered many investigations, and now he's under investigation. He's going to trial on or about four or five different alleged crimes, and the crimes are SEEKING JUSTICE. The society views any person who's striving after justice and freedom and to end exploitation as a "criminal." We know that if we are criminals, the criminals have received their ultimate revenge when Karl Marx indicted the bourgeoisie of grand theft. We realize that it's they who are criminals and it's they who will have to be brought to justice. We will have to go on fighting in spite of the losses and in spite of the hardships that we're bound to suffer, until the final downfall of the reactionary power structure.

So, POWER TO THE PEOPLE, BLACK POWER TO BLACK PEOPLE, AND PANTHER POWER TO THE VANGUARD!

Newton was eventually convicted of manslaughter and sentenced to prison. In 1970, however, the conviction was overturned, and two subsequent retrials both ended in mistrials when jurors could not reach a decision. In December 1971, the charges against Newton were dropped.

On August 15, 1970, in Oakland, Newton—who was at that time out of jail—delivered the eulogy at the funeral of Jonathan Jackson and William Christmas. Both men had died in the infamous Marin County (California) Courthouse gun battle, a botched attempt to take hostages who could be exchanged for the state's most celebrated prisoners, the Soledad Brothers. (Jackson's real-life brother George was one of the three so-called Soledad Brothers, inmates of California's Soledad Prison who had been charged with killing a white guard; the Panthers and other radicals such as Angela Davis considered them victims of racism and political repression rather than criminals.) More of an exhortation than a eulogy, Newton's remarks appeared in the August 21, 1970, edition of The Black Panther.

While it is viewed as a tragedy, and many would weep for Jonathan Jackson and William A. Christmas, the Black Panther Party serves notice that it is not brothers Jonathan Jackson and William A. Christmas for whom we should weep. They have achieved freedom and we remain slaves. If we must weep let it be for those of us who remain in bondage.

The Black Panther Party will follow the example that was set forth by these courageous revolutionaries. The people refuse to submit to the slavery and bondage that is required in order for us to live a few more years on the planet earth. IF THE PENALTY FOR THE QUEST FOR FREEDOM IS DEATH—THEN BY DEATH WE ESCAPE TO FREEDOM.

Without freedom life means nothing. We have nothing to lose but our shackles and freedom to gain. We have gathered today not only to give respect to Comrades Jonathan Jackson and William Christmas, but also to pledge our lives to the accomplishment of the goals exemplified in the actions of brothers Jonathan Jackson and William Christmas.

THERE ARE NO LAWS THAT THE OPPRESSOR MAKES THAT THE OPPRESSED ARE BOUND TO RESPECT.

Laws should be made to serve people. People should not be made to serve laws. When laws no longer serve the people, it is the people's right and the people's duty to free themselves from the yoke of such laws.

Oppressed people in general, and Black people in particular, have suffered too long and we must draw the line somewhere. There is a big difference between thirty million unarmed Black people and thirty million Black people armed to the teeth.

We are not alone. We have allies everywhere. We find our comrades wherever in the world we hear the oppressor's whip. People all over the world are rising up, the high tide of revolution is about to sweep the shores of America—sweeping away the evil gentry and corrupt officials.

Our comrades Jonathan Jackson and William A. Christmas have taught us a revolutionary lesson. They have intensified the struggle and placed it on a higher level.

A picture is worth a thousand words but action is supreme. Comrades Jonathan Jackson and William A. Christmas have made the ultimate sacrifice. They have given the revolution their lives.

Newton later drifted away from the Panthers and the Black Power Movement and had several more run-ins with police for various offenses, including assault, drug possession, and murder. On August 22, 1989, he was shot to death by a known drug dealer who claimed he had fired at the former Panther in self defense.

SOURCES

Books

Foner, Philip S., editor, *The Black Panthers Speak*, Lippincott, 1970.

Holland, DeWitte, editor, *America in Controversy: History of American Public Address*, William C. Brown Company, 1973.

Seale, Bobby, *Seize the Time: The Story of the Black Panther Party and Huey P. Newton*, Black Classic, 1991.

Periodicals

The Black Panther, "Message from Huey," March 3, 1969, p. 2; "Eulogy Delivered by Huey P. Newton, Supreme Commander, Black Panther Party, at the Revolutionary Funeral of Comrades Jonathan Jackson and William Christmas," August 21, 1970, p. 12.

Eleanor Holmes Norton

1937–

African American lawyer, educator, and government official

As a lawyer and government official who has been in the public eye for more than thirty years, Eleanor Holmes Norton has demonstrated an unwavering commitment to the pursuit of justice and equality. Her sympathies have always been with those she feels have received unfair treatment on the basis of sex or race. In addition, she has often defended unpopular positions and people in the belief that certain principles—such as freedom of speech—are worth fighting for. Most recently, as an elected public official who represents the District of Columbia in the United States Congress, Norton has spearheaded the D.C. statehood movement, insisting that taking such action will serve to right a grievous wrong that has endured for more than two hundred years.

Born and raised in Washington, D.C., Norton grew up as part of a close-knit, middle-class family that stressed the importance of education and achievement. Her first inclination upon entering Ohio's Antioch College was to major in science, but by her sophomore year she had switched to history instead. After receiving her bachelor's degree in 1960, she left for Yale University, where in 1963 she obtained her master's degree in American studies. Then this self-described "natural advocate" made up her mind to pursue a career in law and went on to graduate from Yale Law School in 1964.

Following a year spent clerking for a federal judge in Philadelphia, Norton accepted the position of assistant legal director for the American Civil Liberties Union (ACLU) in New York City. Over the next five years, she represented a wide variety of clients, from Vietnam war protesters and civil rights activists to white supremacists and even Alabama governor George Wallace, who sued the city for not granting him a permit to hold a campaign rally in Shea Stadium during the 1968 presidential campaign. (A passionate defender of freedom of speech, she specialized in standing up for those she felt were being denied their First Amendment rights—no matter what their political leanings.) Norton also handled charges of discrimination against women and minorities and tackled occasional criminal cases as well.

In 1970, Norton left the ACLU to become chairman of the New York City Commission on Human Rights. Once again, she assumed the role of advocate, this time for all those who felt that they had been unfairly judged on the basis of sex, race, religion, or national origin. She devoted a great deal of her efforts to eliminating discrimination against women in the workplace and in other settings. She also took steps to remedy inequalities in wage structures and workmen's compensation and fought for improvements in day care and maternity leave programs. In addition, Norton led the charge against discrimination in housing, in the public school system, and in city government.

Norton's aggressive approach to weeding out inequality in New York City eventually attracted attention throughout the country, and as a result she was often asked to speak on the topic before various groups. On March 7, 1976, for example, she appeared at the opening session of the National Conference on Higher Education, held that year in Chicago, Illinois. The theme of her address, given that her audience was made up primarily of college and university administrators, focused on how the academic world was in an ideal position to take the lead in resolving issues of quality and equality in society at large. Her remarks are reprinted from Representative American Speeches: 1976-1977, *edited by Waldo W. Braden (Wilson, 1977).*

Ladies and Gentlemen: I knew I was speaking before a group of hardy academic souls when I learned that you unfailingly come to Chicago each March for this conference, apparently willingly, choosing it out of all the more gentle places in other parts of the country. Were you from some other sectors of our society, you might not be so hipped on Chicago. You would alternate between Puerto Rico and Miami. Anyway, I am pleased as a dyed-in-the-wool New Yorker to welcome you to Chicago.

A new equality has emerged during the past twenty years. It has been very much discussed but too little analyzed. It has been negatively associated with everything from the development of permissiveness to the demise of law and order. Its positive accreditations have sometimes been similarly exaggerated, as the use of the language of liberation to describe significant but modest moves toward equality would suggest. It has annoyed or exhilarated every significant and most insignificant parts of our society, not the least of them higher education.

Eleanor Holmes Norton

The emergence of black people out of the shadows as darkies and into the light as blacks is of course the throbbing center of the newest impulse toward equality. But the nation is still unraveling its oldest, most torturous, most redundant riddle—the settlement of its black people. For they, alone among America's immigrants, remain unsettled after three hundred years. Over these centuries they moved from slave plantations to rural hovels until they emerged in the twentieth century as a profoundly urban people still searching for their place in America. What changed slowest about them was their status in America. In a land where mobility seemed mandated and came to all but the damned, America's dark-skinned immigrants remain at the bottom. Only in the past two decades, beginning with the *Brown* decision, has there been any serious challenge to the permanency of the subterranean status of America's blacks and its other people of color.

So elastic was this new equality that it readily reached to accommodate women, the nation's unequal majority, as well. Following the pattern of the black revolution, women began rapidly redefining the meaning of equality for themselves and thus for all of us in the 1970s. Should they fully succeed they could by the force of their numbers and the inherent radicalism of their demands cause society itself to make fundamental alterations.

But the open struggle of blacks for equality influenced many more than those who saw themselves as similarly situated. The original social energy of the period in which we still live derives from the civil rights movement. The antiwar movement, the women's rights movement, the antipoverty movement, the struggles of other minorities—all patterned themselves in one fashion or another on the extraordinarily fertile civil rights struggle.

Most of the developments toward deeper equality took shape and substance from the 1960s, a period characterized by the upset of social convention and injustice. The decade of the sixties was in deep reaction to the spirit of the fifties, a decade rooted more in the notion that all men should be alike than that they should be equal. The young people of the sixties were a quintessential movement generation. They were as shaped by social movements as the generation of the fifties was shaped by none.

Some changes that characterize the new equality appear fairly permanent. The black struggle for equality has changed America as much as it has changed the status of blacks. White Americans today are the first white people in the nation's history to be decisively influenced in their values by the experience, aspirations, and actions of black Americans. Martin Luther King, Jr., influenced America as much as John F. Kennedy. Aretha Franklin and James Brown shaped the style of this period in the way that Dinah Shore and Bing Crosby influenced their parents' youth.

Such changes may be new, but they emerge from a special historic context. The recent vintage of changes in matters of equality sometimes serves to obscure the fact of a much longer American obsession with this subject. Historians may differ as to when to date its beginnings. But the nationalization of the antislavery controversy with the Missouri Compromise surely demarks a point when slavery and thus equality became truly national concerns tied to the destiny of the nation itself. At least since 1820, then, I think it fair to say that Americans have had an unparalleled and unceasing struggle with themselves over the meaning and the virtue of equality.

For no other people has equality required such sustained attention for so long a time. Nowhere else in the world has the struggle over this single question been so intense, so dynamic, so costly.

I would include within this more than 150-year period not only the perplexing and omnipresent struggle of black men and women. For mounted on the same canvas are the collages of others, including the old women's-suffrage movement, the women's-equality movement of today, and the largely successful struggle of European immigrants for inclusion on terms of equality and mobility. The very diversity of the actors who have played out equality themes in America has contributed to the preoccupation of Americans with this subject.

The American experience with equality has been both tortured and exhilarating. At the most promising end of the scale, successive waves of poor immigrants—most entering as illiterate peasants—found spectacular economic success in one or two generations, a phenomenal mobility unprecedented in world history. Somewhere in between are white women who, with the right to vote, won a new sense of themselves after a long struggle. While their transformation in equality terms is incomplete and disappointing, no one can doubt what the past fifty years have done to make the American woman more equal, both in her home and in her transformed role as member of the workforce. At the low end of the scale, the national experience with black people has been a unique tragedy, characterized first by sustained oppression and then by furtive progress. Still the past two decades have raised uncommon hopes and produced unprecedented gains. At the very least, black people have come from psychological depths to which it would seem impossible to return.

In any case Americans have had more diverse and concentrated experience with the dynamics of equality than any other people in the world. This has given America the opportunity to disproportionately influence the very meaning of the word. The American experience has done as much to define equality for the world as the Russian Revolutionary period did to give reality to Marxism.

Examples of American leadership on matters of equality, leadership often carved out of painful experience, are legion. The choice of Martin Luther King, Jr., for world recognition as recipient of the Nobel Peace Prize in 1964 did not come because of his leadership of an indigenous freedom movement in the United States. King's world status derives from the same process that made world and not merely national leaders of Gandhi and Lenin. All staged essentially national movements with such universal force and applicability, that they moved men and women across the face of the earth. King made the idea of racial equality plainer to millions than it had ever been before, just as Gandhi moved peasants everywhere to demand freedom from colonialism.

One could cite other examples of American

> ***"The American experience has done as much to define equality for the world as the Russian Revolutionary period did to give reality to Marxism."***

pace setting in the conception of equality. The women's movement appears better developed in this country than in most others. The French have a new cabinet post for the *condition féminine* but underdeveloped notions of feminism and no strong activist movement. Russian and other East European women have won significant access to male jobs but very little change in sex roles. By contrast, American women, with historically better developed notions of equality to work with, are pursuing change in magnificent proportions from carefully circumscribed issues such as equal employment and universal child care to weighty philosophical issues whose resolution could virtually redefine womanhood and remake entire areas of human experience.

All of these developments toward greater equality in America have been influenced in no small measure by American higher education, both in its functional educational role and in its role as a social force. But academe, like most other sections of our society, is experiencing some difficulty today, when pressure for equality implementation has succeeded the simple demand for common justice. New and more complicated equality themes have replaced easier notions of simple justice from the days of "Freedom Now."

Thus, you do well to hold a conference concerned with equality and quality in what appears to be a congenial and truly searching atmosphere. I think it fair to say that in a very real sense the country has traditionally depended on American higher education, more than on most others, for leadership on issues of equality. But in recent years there have been some uncharacteristically discordant chords emanating from academe on matters of equality, seeming to challenge the applicability of equality principles to the university setting. These arguments have been made in such a way as to undermine the preeminent place of the American university as a locus for pushing the society toward the realization of its own highest ideals.

I do not fault academic voices for their criticism of this or that government approach to affirmative action in university employment, for example. There is, I assure you, much room for criticism. Moreover the university is in a position to offer the most useful of criticism, because of its own research and scholarly functions. Affirmative action should not be exempt from criticism from academe simply because the university is affected.

Rather I would argue just the opposite: that the academic community is in a unique position to contribute to the perfection of techniques for achieving equality but has inexplicably hung back from this natural function in recent years. This can be seen both in areas where the university has some self-interest and in areas where it does not.

Let me cite just one where universities themselves are not implicated, simply for the purpose of making my point about the university lag in contributing to the resolution of increasingly difficult equality issues in America today. Consider busing, a technique encountering deepening trouble and unpopularity throughout the country. When Professor James Coleman recently suggested that busing had spurred white flight from the cities and had thus hurt school integration, something of a furor developed. This deepened when it was learned that the cities he had studied had indeed experienced flight but not busing. Many who believe in school integration now simply discount Dr. Coleman's view as that of just one more turncoat liberal adversary to integration. This, of course, is unfair to Professor Coleman. Busing, like any controversial technique, needs criticism if we are to have any hope of making improvements. But in the context of today's chilled climate for racial equality, a finding that comes out of a decidedly negative context will only contribute to controversy. The need is not so much for less criticism of the mechanisms of integration as it is for a more forthright search for answers to complicated new issues that arise as we untangle our tortured racial past.

Indeed the need for clear analysis suggesting pathways to permanent equality solutions is especially great today, particularly in light of the inadequacy of a number of techniques in use. But when the thrust is one of complaint, rather than of searching—that a technique, busing for example, is not working, without more—many hear only the sound of retreat. If not busing, what is proposed? In a country where racial degradation and separation have been the rule, few blacks are prepared to consider arguments based on the utility of various approaches to equality—not when whites have so often found the entire exercise of equality unuseful. This may not be a wholly rational response, but it is understandable. Professor Coleman's conclusions concerning busing might have been received differently had they arisen within a more balanced study. In the absence of a committed search for alternatives, civil rights advocates feel they will be a part of their own undoing if they acquiesce in doubts about busing or other integration techniques.

Who is in the best position to search for alternatives to this troublesome issue? Politicians who find the issue especially treacherous in the political marketplace? The government which feels the day-by-day pressure from both sides? Judges sworn to expand constitutional principle and ignore popular reaction? None is in a better position than the university where detachment and time are afforded to think through society's most difficult problems—from cures for diseases to, yes, school integration. How are we to account therefore for the scant study of the actual experience of children in integrated settings, except for the search for magical improvement in test scores many somehow expected school integration to produce? There is a danger that one hopeful technique, the magnet school—one with special features or additional resources designed to attract a balanced role-mix—will fall by the way because of lack of study of what specific features make a school able to attract white students in this way. I have seen such magnets thrown together so carelessly that they fail, giving the hopeful magnet concept a bad name as just one more failed integration technique. And I have seen others that succeed brightly.

One would think that some professor would be busily cataloging success and failure factors in magnet schools and by this time would be well on his way to developing a success model. My own Commission, hard pressed by budget cutbacks, is considering undertaking such a study in the absence of this kind of assistance from the academic community to meet urgent problems of school integration.

Busing is only one of a litany of issues produced by the new complexities of race, ethnicity, and sex in America where the need for thoughtful study is as clear as the neglect of scholarly attention. Just to mention two others among the most serious: The conflict between the values of seniority and affirmative action, a most difficult question, is greatly in need of the best conceptual treatment. Another is the awesomely complicated question of encouraging racially and economically diverse cities in the face of white flight, the flight of other middle income people, and the resulting catastrophic effect on the viability of the American city itself. Both of these are issues on which my small government agency, without a single PhD, has been struggling without federal or academic leadership.

Why problems of such magnitude have inspired so little academic attention is not altogether clear. But this failure on large issues of equality has not helped to create an affirmative and hospitable atmosphere once these issues have come closer to home.

And they have come home to roost in academe on both faculty and student selection. The faculty discrimination issues have provoked much more hostile reaction from administrators and faculty than student selection matters, although the issues are at least of equal moment. The society has at least as great a stake in fair student selection as in fair faculty selection. Of course, the matter of self-interest is, I think you will agree, a bit clearer in one than in the other. In any case, the cries from college and university presidents and professors, almost all of them white men, have not been received by the public as disinterested laments.

I do not mean to imply that their points of criticism are totally without merit. What I am saying is that they have no right to ask what amounts to an exemption for the university from many of the procedures of the civil rights laws. While today most academic institutions have found their way toward a posture of compliance, the early outcries, especially from the university presidents, called for a virtual exemption of colleges and universities from many of the only effective procedures that have been developed, all of which apply to every other large employer in the country. These techniques include an evaluation of confidential personnel records, a matter not without difficulty, but one also not beyond the reach of those interested in compliance with the civil rights laws. And goals and timetables for rectifying exclusion within universities have also been subject to special displeasure. This issue, which continues to plow discord in academe, is also capable of resolution if compliance rather than avoidance is the goal.

The fact is that the blame for the way the controversy between the universities and HEW [U.S. Department of Health, Education, and Welfare] developed belongs with both sides. When compliance was first attempted, the universities responded like wounded deer, the victims of a predator that did not understand the sensitivity of the beast. Its traditional strong concern for equality was not summoned in this, its own personal equality crisis. No galaxy of professors presented themselves as a technical task force to bring some reason into the process. The university chose noncompliance until persistence by the federal government appeared to destroy that option.

In the same way HEW, which had seen the face of recalcitrance before, identified this as just another garden variety. The agency was mindful that women professors had filed a massive class action against the entire university community, to prod the Department into a more forthright discharge of its antidiscrimination duties. In this atmosphere the question of whether some serious work might be done by the Department to adapt its procedures to college and university employment systems did not arise until negotiations occurred, often only after painful confrontation and then, at least until recently, on an *ad hoc* rather than a systematic and comprehensive basis.

I believe that a sound case can be made that universities constitute a special case when it comes to antidiscrimination enforcement and therefore are in need of special assistance and perhaps even a system of race and sex analysis and implementation of remedies attuned to the peculiar contours of the university work place. As a technician with some experience in this field, I accept the view that factors which in other situations must be rigidly controlled, such as credentialism and broad discretion to evaluate a candidate, must have fuller sway in the selection of faculty. Moreover, I believe this need not lead to more lenient application of the antidiscrimination laws to universities than to other employers, a wholly unfair and unacceptable result. By not looking at the university system in this particularized way, HEW may have sown the seeds that have made enforcement so tough and controversial in colleges and universities.

But if the government should have developed and provided better technical assistance to the universities, it is universities themselves, which, ironically are the richest resource for creating the appropriate technology. No other employer in the nation was in a position to influence government equal opportunity policy in the way the university was and is. By merely playing the role society expects of it, academe had within its hands the power to shut down the controversy over the procedures of compliance and, through research and scholarly study, submit alternatives.

I am not suggesting that the university might have designed its own mode of compliance to equal opportunity laws. I am saying that by regarding the matter of compliance adversarially and not as an honest question of considerable technical difficulty, the university defaulted in its commitment to equality and encouraged needless and harmful controversy. No group of professors undertook to look at these as serious questions for study. Instead some formed themselves into a committee to oppose affirmative action.

One professor has authored a recent book designed to show that court decisions and other government actions to enforce the civil rights laws have themselves discriminated against the majority, a work whose deficiencies begin with the author's failure to read and digest the relevant court decisions or to understand the basic law of remedies in our system of jurisprudence. Nowhere in all of corporate America, with its historic lack of identification with equality and association with prejudice, has so negative a development toward equality emerged. It has fallen to the university to speak for the recalcitrant employer.

Problems of equality in the university promise to accentuate, not diminish in the years ahead. While faculties doubled in the 1960s, with 30,000 new hires a year, in the 1980s only 6,000 new hires annually are expected, a replacement rate that itself may diminish, as the years of fantastic expansion are followed not even by stabilization, but, as likely as not, by retrenchment. Last month the U.S. Office of Education reported that in 1975 faculty women lost ground in both salary increase and rank. According to the report, "The average salaries of men continue to exceed the average salaries of women at every academic rank and at every institutional level, in both publicly and privately controlled institutions." If the university is to avoid becoming a haven for racial and sex discord, it must summon its own best traditions, marshall its decided skill, and absorb itself in designing strategies for genuine equality in academe.

In the same way student selection policies need urgent attention. If student admission procedures have upset administrators and professors less than faculty selection, they have been of considerable concern in the society-at-large. Again, part of the blame rests squarely with government. Colleges and universities have been left almost totally to their own devices in designing techniques for the admission of disadvantaged minority students. The government encouraged the opening of opportunities but, as in the case of university affirmative action, provided no technical assistance.

The result was the *DeFunis* case and a number of others like it. These cases demonstrate that universities had considerably more good will than expertise in criteria for evaluating disadvantaged minority students, who have been historically excluded from their student population. That good will has substantially diminished in the face of budgetary cutbacks and the controversy emanating from these very cases. But the problem will remain until someone decides to consider it an issue worthy of serious research and study. As with affirmative action technology, I cannot avoid asking again, who is in a better position than academicians themselves.

Neither the university nor the government has chosen to move toward rational problem solving here either. Instead court cases continue to make this explosive issue more so. The adversarial route has been chosen over the scholarly search.

Here the government is particularly at fault, for there has been a persuasive appeal for help on this matter before HEW for almost two years. After the inconclusive Supreme Court decision in the *DeFunis* case I talked with the heads of six national racial and ethnic organizations, all with headquarters in New York, who had been on opposite sides of the case. The following letter to then HEW Secretary Caspar Weinberger resulted:

Dear Dr. Weinberger:

While the undersigned organizations have taken varying positions on the DeFunis *case, we have, over the years worked closely in support of civil rights and human freedom.*

We all recognize that the process of creating affirmative action is not an exact science. It is only in the past few years that the nation has begun the development of procedures for dismantling discrimination.

All of us wish to avoid polarization. We agree that a primary goal for all of us is the elimination of all forms of discrimination and the establishment of affirmative actions and processes that will provide equal opportunity within our constitutional framework.

Since the issues raised by the DeFunis *case remain, we believe that an early response from HEW, within whose jurisdiction such matters lie, is indicated. We are therefore requesting that you direct the issuance of nondiscriminatory guidelines clarifying how educational institutions can best develop appropriate tools for special efforts to recruit persons from previously excluded groups.*

This letter was signed by the heads of the Anti-Defamation League of B'nai B'rith, the American Jewish Committee, the American Jewish Congress, the NAACP, the National Urban League, and the Puerto Rican Legal Defense and Educational Fund.

"If the university is to avoid becoming a haven for racial and sex discord, it must . . . absorb itself in designing strategies for genuine equality in academe."

Mr. Weinberger reacted immediately and a departmental study and letter of guidelines to college and university presidents were promised. Over a year later, when Dr. Weinberger was about to resign, I wrote to remind him that all were awaiting the promised guidance and was assured that the matter would be carried on by his successor in the department. Now almost another year has passed with no resolution of these issues.

This is inexcusable neglect from the federal government. The standards are theirs to give. Still government default need not have been decisive on the question. The knowledge and skills to develop the fair admission devices are found in special abundance among various disciplines in the very universities that now must commit resources instead to fighting court cases. Once again academe has lost its way on issues that were thought to be of special concern.

In a very special way the country needs you who teach and administer higher education today. Rearrangements among the races and sexes and classes appear too complicated for many. The swirling events of our time seem to many not the inevitable content of modern change but a signal of endemic instability in American life. The line between rapid, dynamic change and meandering, perplexing instability has always been thin. But that line is not drawn entirely by events. It is drawn also by those who shape and react to events.

At such times, education is or should be a valuable hedge against bewilderment and panic. More than most Americans, educational leaders understand the reasons for the fear of change. After all, until the twentieth century most of the world's people lived virtually changeless lives. Change was a matter of the seasons or of youth mellowing into old age, which often came by forty. Change itself is a twentieth century phenomenon. Change has made all our lives more difficult. But it has also made them more rewarding. We are richer but we are also more burdened.

I would be the first to agree that higher education cannot and should not always pursue the utilitarian. You are not society's anointed problem-solvers. But you have always ventured special concern for equality in America. It is time to step forward once again. Someone needs to stand with both reason and justice. If not you, who?

In 1977, Norton left New York City for Washington, D.C., and a presidential appointment as chairperson of the Equal Employment Opportunity Commission (EEOC). She remained in that position until 1983 while also teaching in the law school at Georgetown University. An active participant in Jesse Jackson's 1988 presidential campaign, Norton decided to run for office herself in 1990 as the District of Columbia delegate to the U.S. Congress, a special nonvoting position. She won easily and has also been victorious in subsequent reelection campaigns. Since taking office, Norton has served on the subcommittee that oversees compensation for all federal employees as well as subcommittees on District law enforcement, education, public works, and transportation; she was also appointed to a joint committee of Congress assigned the task of finding ways to eliminate "gridlock" between the political parties and the legislative and executive branches of the government.

Norton's top priority in Congress, however, has been working toward achieving statehood for the District of Columbia, which enjoys only limited self-rule. (For example, Congress retains control over D.C.'s budget and has the power to overturn laws decided on by the mayor and city council.) The idea of creating a fifty-first state that would be overwhelmingly Democratic does not have great appeal for Republicans, and even a number of Democrats have voiced objections. But noting that the District's residents have been taxed for two hundred years without true representation, Norton declares that it's time "to correct a historic anomaly that has become a profound injustice."

To that end, on May 29, 1991, during her first term in Congress, Norton introduced the "New Columbia Admission Act" (known officially as H.R. 2482) for consideration by her colleagues. It proposed creating the fifty-first state—to be named New Columbia—out of all but the immediate area around the White House and most government buildings and federal monuments, which would then constitute the new District of Columbia.

At congressional hearings held in late 1991 and early 1992, Norton took the floor on several occasions and argued strongly in favor of her bill. Perhaps her most impassioned plea came on April 2, 1992, when she emphasized her own very personal interest in the issue. The testimony that follows, which Norton addressed to retiring Congressman Mervyn M. Dymally of California, the chairman of the Subcommittee on Judiciary and Education and a longtime supporter of D.C. statehood, is taken from a government report entitled Admission of State of New Columbia into the Union: Hearing and Markup before the Subcommittee on Judiciary and Education and the Committee on the District of Columbia, House of Representatives, *Volume 2, U.S. Government Printing Office, 1992.*

Mr. Chairman, when my great-grandfather, Richard Holmes, crossed the District line before the Civil War, a fugitive slave from Virginia, Washington, D.C., represented freedom. Today for Richard's great-great-grandchildren, John Holmes Norton and Katherine Felicia Norton, Washington is the place in our country where there is the least freedom. Less freedom than the fifty states to be sure but also less freedom than the territories, none of which have ever petitioned for statehood. Guam, Puerto Rico, the Virgin Islands, and American Samoa do not have voting representation in the Congress, Mr. Chairman, but at least the Congress does not undermine its own professed democratic ideals by reviewing and overturning the official enactments of their democratic elected local governments.

I am grateful, therefore, Mr. Chairman, for your extraordinary leadership for twenty-one years to right this wrong. Yours has been a service to your country and not to Washingtonians alone, for in bringing us to this historic day you have moved to wipe away a conspicuous blemish on American democracy. From your first year in the Congress, you have worked for full and undiluted democracy for the District and have been an architect who has perfected and protected the home rule we have achieved. For all your rank and importance in the Congress, you will surely be remembered by history for your unique work in making American democracy more perfect.

In the same way, the subcommittee chairman, Mervyn Dymally, who, against, our protestations, has announced that he will retire at the conclusion of this session, will go with the applause, yes, and with the cheers of all who felt or watched his years of outstanding service on this committee and to the District. His principled, patient, and eloquent leadership was especially important in guiding the New Columbia Statehood Act through subcommittee.

While my good friends of the minority will almost surely vote against us today, each and every one of them has approached my bill with the dignity and seriousness its subject matter deserves. Their criticisms have always been thoughtful and have even led to improvements in the bill itself. Mr. Bliley, the ranking minority member of the full committee, and Mr. Lowery, the ranking minority member of the subcommittee, have led their side with comments that were always substantive and never pejorative or deprecating of the District or its people.

Nevertheless, the careful consideration given H.R. 2482 has probably not altered the party-line vote that will probably result today. Thus has it always been. Whenever a state has sought admission to the Union, the political considerations of the moment have always been the deciding factor; whether the state was slave or free before the Civil War; or whether its residents are Democrats or Republicans today.

Opposition to D.C. statehood has been couched in two major ways. First, and perhaps most prominently, in constitutional terms and then in economic terms, up to and including questions of viability.

The constitutional issues raise matters of first impression because the District itself is unique. Yet precedent is surely on the side of statehood. Congress reduced the size of the District to meet the request of the people of Virginia for return of their land over a matter of slavery. It can do so to meet the request of the people of the District for Statehood. Article 4, section 3 of the Constitution cannot be interpreted to require the United States of America to receive permission from the State of Maryland to reduce the size of federally owned land. Maryland gave the land in absolute fee simple to the United States, retaining no claims. It is too late in the century and too many years after countless interpretations of the supremacy clause to argue that the sovereign Government of the United States of America cannot do as it pleases with the land on which its Capital is located and over which it has now had sovereign control for 201 years.

Constitutional lawyers, of course, disagree about this and other points. Where no definitive constitutional answer is available, Congress must err on the side of democracy. No harm can be done by granting statehood. Rank, palpable injustice will be done by denying it.

> ***"No harm can be done by granting [the District of Columbia] statehood. Rank, palpable injustice will be done by denying it."***

Arguments concerning the financial viability of the District are far easier to rebut because they are manifestly groundless. District residents who pay higher taxes than all but two states must wonder whether to laugh or cry when they hear the economic viability of the District questioned.

First, most of the discussion of viability we have heard would hold the District to a higher standard than other states which have gained admission to the Union. Many entered with little population and scant development. One of the most recent examples was Alaska, but the House committee report used as the test of viability that a state have "sufficient population and resources to support a state government and to provide its share of the cost of the federal government." The District far surpasses this standard.

The District raises most of its own $3.8 billion budget, and as with most states, it does so through income, property and sales taxes, in that order. Looking only at locally raised revenues, discounting federal funds altogether, the District raised more revenue than eleven states in the fiscal years 1989-90. These were Delaware, Idaho, Maine, Montana, Nevada, New Hampshire, North Dakota, Rhode Island, South Dakota, Vermont and Wyoming.

The D.C. economy would surely be the envy of most states today. Until recently, the District was described as recession-proof and even now its diverse white-collar employment base gives it more protection from cyclical episodes than most states. The District's per capita income is the third highest in the nation and our per capita contribution to the federal treasury is likewise third in rank. The average earnings of our workers is $32,106; forty-two percent above the national average. The District is counted among the leading states in just those upscale areas where most states seek to lead their economies. Business services, where we outrank thirty states. Communications, where we outrank twenty-five states. Finance, insurance and real estate, where we outrank fourteen states. Hotels and lodging, where we outrank twenty-seven states. Legal services, where we outrank forty-one states. Moreover, Mr. Chairman, the great majority of our work force, almost seventy percent, is employed in the nongovernmental sector.

It is difficult to believe that any state came into the Union with greater financial viability. Indeed statehood would make the District more viable. Today, fifty-five percent of D.C. land is exempted from taxation. Statehood would place much of the federal land in the National Capital service area, and New Columbia would then have only thirty percent of its land exempted from taxation.

Mr. Chairman, Washingtonians have always tried to make up for their disabilities, whether of citizenship, of economics or of race, by working harder. We have the largest middle class of any large city in the country and the largest black middle class in the world. No state or major city has population the equal of ours in years of college education.

But what we in the District are most proud of is our record of self-governance. No state has had to earn statehood and yet we have earned it. We have earned it through eighteen hundred enactments since home rule, only three of which have been overturned by the Congress. We have earned it by paying our own way and subsidizing less wealthy jurisdictions with an unusually high contribution in federal taxes, without representation in the Congress, and with only limited democracy at home. We earned it with immediate desegregation of our schools when I was in high school without massive resistance or other forms of resistance of southern jurisdictions like ourselves. We continue to earn it with a highly responsible government and local officials who have faced up to the hard issues which in recent years have left crippling problems throughout the United States, including our neighboring states and cities.

The District has tried the other alternatives, Mr. Chairman, and is left with none but statehood. Only sixteen states ratified the voting rights amendment, and if all fifty had, the District's local governance would still have been left under the undemocratic control of Congress. Retrocession is impossible because neither jurisdiction desires it and thus retrocession itself would be undemocratic and unconstitutional. After two hundred years, the District has acquired a distinctive culture and demography. To ask the District to retrocede to Maryland is like asking West Virginia to return to Virginia.

Mr. Chairman, my great-grandfather found a better life and greater democracy in the District than he had known. His great-great-grandchildren want to continue on the route he started when he walked away from slavery. Katherine Felicia and John Holmes, who trace our family back generations before their great-grandfather, want to be full American citizens. This is the time. Statehood is the only way.

Despite Norton's persuasive powers, H.R. 2482 died in the House without ever coming up for a vote. Its supporters did not give up, however; on January 5, 1993, led again by the representative from the District of Columbia, they proposed H.R. 51, essentially the same bill as H.R. 2482 under a new name honoring the potential fifty-first state. This time, the bill made it out of committee and was put to a vote in the House in November 1993, where it lost by a margin of 277 to 153. Despite going down to defeat, Norton and others who favor D.C. statehood were overjoyed that their bill picked up as many votes as it did on its first try. "I'm ready to declare a victory right now," she said afterwards. "The vote has surpassed my greatest expectations." She has vowed to keep striving in the quest to achive D.C. statehood in the immediate future.

SOURCES

Books

Admission of State of New Columbia into the Union: Hearing and Markup before the Subcommittee on Judiciary and Education and the Committee on the District of Columbia, House of Representatives, two volumes, U.S. Government Printing Office, 1992.

Braden, Waldo W., editor, *Representative American Speeches: 1976-1977,* Wilson, 1977.

Periodicals

Black Enterprise, "Freshmen on the Hill," April, 1991, p. 25.

Ebony, "Defender of Unpopular Causes," January, 1969; "Eleanor Holmes Norton Takes D.C. Seat," January, 1991, pp. 104-106.

Essence, "What Have They Done for Us Lately?" May, 1990, pp. 66-68.

Grand Rapids Press, "D.C. Statehood Backers Promise to Try Again," November 22, 1993, p. A3.

McCall's, "I Hope I'm Not a Token," October, 1971, p. 51.

New Republic, "Gaining Ground," June 5, 1989, pp.10-11.

Antonia C. Novello

1944–

Puerto Rican physician and public official

In 1990, Antonia C. Novello made history as not only the first woman but the first Hispanic American to hold the post of United States Surgeon General. Her appointment put her in charge of the Public Health Service, the government agency responsible for protecting and improving the health of the nation's citizens. And while she was not quite as outspoken as her predecessor, C. Everett Koop, or as combative as her successor, Joycelyn Elders, Novello nevertheless used her high-profile position to focus attention on what she identified as the special health-related needs of women, children, and minorities—speaking up, as she once said, "for the people who are not able to speak for themselves."

A native of Fajardo, Puerto Rico, Novello was inspired to enter the medical profession as a result of her own childhood experiences with chronic illness, the result of a painful congenital deformity of her large intestine that was not repaired surgically until she was in her early twenties. She began her studies at the University of Puerto Rico, earning her bachelor's degree in 1965 and her medical degree in 1970. She then completed her internship and residency in pediatrics at the University of Michigan Medical Center from 1970 until 1973, earning a reputation as a caring and well-respected physician who became the first woman to receive her department's "Intern of the Year" award.

Novello remained in Ann Arbor, Michigan, throughout the rest of 1973 and 1974, serving as a fellow in the university hospital's pediatric nephrology unit. While caring for young patients awaiting kidney transplants, she was saddened by those who had "fallen through the cracks" at some point in their lives and had not received proper treatment when they needed it. The realization made her think that she might one day like to pursue a career in government service, where she hoped to find solutions to the kinds of problems (such as AIDS and inadequate health care) that have an especially profound impact on children.

In 1978, after serving two years as a fellow in the pediatric nephrology unit at Georgetown University Hospital in Washington, D.C., and two years in private practice, Novello took the first step toward fulfilling her dream when she went to work for the U.S. Public Health Service at the National Institutes of Health (NIH), an agency consisting of several separate divisions that each conduct research on the causes, cure, and prevention of various diseases. Her first post was as a project officer at the National Institute of Arthritis, Metabolism and Digestive Diseases, where she was affiliated with the artificial kidney and chronic uremia program. She then served as a staff physician at NIH before taking a job as the executive secretary in the Division of Research and Grants beginning in 1981. (During this same period, she also obtained a master's degree in public health from Johns Hopkins University.) In 1986, Novello became deputy director of the National Institute on Child Health and Human Development. It was there that she took a particular interest in pediatric AIDS, not only as a medical problem but also as a social one.

In late 1989, the pending retirement of C. Everett Koop as U.S. Surgeon General prompted Bush administration officials to search for a replacement. After several candidates withdrew their names from consideration because they could not support the White House's stand against abortion and fetal tissue research, Novello emerged as a favorite—a caring, dedicated physician whose views were in sync with the administration and who had a proven track record in working cooperatively with others. She was quickly confirmed for the post and took office in March 1990.

While some may have hoped for a less outspoken surgeon general after the tenure of the often controversial Dr. Koop, they did not always get it in Novello, who caused a stir more than once during her three years in office. She did not shy away from the truth as she saw it and expressed particular concern about the health problems of minorities, children, teens, and women, including AIDS, domestic violence, decreasing rates of immunization against common infectious diseases, injury prevention, and lack of insurance coverage among Hispanic Americans. On more than one occasion, she declared that ignoring those problems put the very future of the nation at risk.

But Novello reserved her harshest words for advertisers who glamorize activities such as smoking cigarettes and drinking alcohol and make them appear totally harmless. She was especially disgusted and angered by ads that were designed to appeal to children and teens, even though the products themselves are ostensibly for adults only. (Her favorite targets were the cartoon character "Joe Camel" of Camel cigarettes and beverages with a high alcohol content that nevertheless enjoyed a "soda pop" image.) In fact, condemning such tactics became one of the major themes of her administration and a constant source of friction between her and those who manufacture and promote cigarettes and alcohol.

On April 21, 1992, Novello addressed a Town Hall audience in Los Angeles during which she discussed many of these issues as part of an overall look at health priorities for the 1990s. Her speech is reprinted from Vital Speeches of the Day, *August 15, 1992.*

Good afternoon. I am delighted to be here in Los Angeles. It is a wonderful city, and I am honored to be here. It is a long way from the town center of Fajardo to Los Angeles, California.

I come here with two messages: first, that for most of us our health status is molded and shaped one decision at a time and, second, that women and minorities are threatened by a large number of serious health concerns, which we can only address one decision at a time. Unless we make every effort to provide the attention, recognition, respect, empathy and care necessary for each of our citizens, then we fail as policy makers and as a community.

I accepted the job as Surgeon General because our citizens must have the facts—as Cervantes said, we cannot "Mince the matter." I am dedicated to the proposition that we must give our people the health information they need to make vital healthy choices and decisions that will ripple out for years to come.

As the Surgeon General of the U.S. Public Health Service, I serve as the Surgeon General for all the people of these United States. When I was appointed, I didn't focus on being a woman or a minority—although I realized that in terms of an appointment, each of these characteristics was symbolic.

In my efforts to protect our nation's health, I have spoken out especially about the dangers associated with illegal underage drinking, smoking, AIDS, and violence. What I have learned since taking on this task has alarmed me, but at the same time, it has also taught me that my efforts cannot let up.

I promised myself when I accepted this position that my job would not be complete until I truly felt that I had "touched" the young people of this country by teaching them what I knew. I believe that our kids are smart—perhaps smarter than we were at their age—and if we will give them honest and factual information and treat them with respect, they will make good decisions. I know that I'm *far from finished,* and I will continue to speak out about these issues whenever and wherever possible. But I am here today to enlist your help.

Gathering together in forums such as this accomplishes my first important goal—*we learn from one another, and education is our most valuable tool* to get us where we need to go.

One phrase I have continued to recite during my tenure as Surgeon General is that *our young people are our nation's most valuable resource*—I say it over and over again because I believe it myself so fervently. When we say we have hope for the future, what we are really saying is that we have hope for our children. The work we do now can ensure that our hope becomes a reality.

In the work that we do—as legislators, educators, business leaders, health care providers, and most importantly, *as parents*—our focus must be on our young people.

The America of today is far different from what it was when we were young. The challenges are different, the pressures greater, the poverty and despair more rampant, and the availability of drugs and alcohol more widespread. These things are tragic—and we must do everything we can to turn them around.

ALCOHOL

One pressure young people face that inherently makes my job and our hopes for the future that much more difficult to guarantee, is the pressure to *drink alcohol,* or abuse other substances.

Illegal underage drinking is one issue which I have identified to be a cornerstone of my agenda as Surgeon General.

I speak out about it whenever and wherever possible. And today, I would like to outline the problem for you as I see it, and then I'm going to *ask for your help.*

I have been working on this issue since September, 1990, when I launched "fact finding" mission on this issue. I toured the country talking to community leaders, to teachers, and to young people about the problem of illegal underage drinking.

I learned that this issue is *more pervasive than I originally realized*—and that it is truly the mainstream drug abuse issue plaguing most communities and families in America today.

I also learned that, in order to realize any success, we need to strengthen our prevention efforts—I've learned that *prevention works best if the message the young person gets at home is the one he gets at school, and at church, and is the one reinforced by his community and his peers.*

I began to learn then—and I relearn it every day—how confusing the *mixed messages* are that we send to our children about alcohol. Assistant Secretary for Health James Mason says, and I agree, that we've made progress in the illicit drug war because our youth have gotten consistent messages from their families, their schools, their churches, their communities, their nation—and their media.

However, we're losing the war on the underage use of alcohol because our youth receive some very mixed messages, like the advertisements and other media images that tell them "drink me and you will be cool. Drink me and you will be glamorous. Drink me and you will have fun!" Or even worse, "Drink me and there will be no consequences."

Our health message is clear—"use of alcohol by young people can lead to serious health consequences—not to mention absenteeism, vandalism, date rape, random violence, and even death." But how can that be expected to compete with the Swedish bikini team or the Bud Man?

I have released, as part of my campaign against illegal underage drinking, the invaluable series of reports done for me by the HHS [Health and Human Services] Inspector General.

Let me talk about those reports for a moment. In June 1991, I released *Youth and Alcohol: Drinking Habits, Access, Attitudes and Knowledge* and *Do They Know What They Are Drinking?*

These studies showed that:

-*At least 8 million American teenagers use alcohol every week and almost half a million go on a weekly binge (or 5 drinks in a row)*—confirming earlier surveys by the National Institute on Drug Abuse.

-Junior and senior high school students drink 35 percent of all wine coolers sold in the U.S. (31 million gallons), and 1.1 billion cans of beer (102 million gallons) consumed each year.

-Many teenagers who drink are using alcohol to *handle stress and boredom*. And many of them *drink alone*, breaking the old stereotype of party drinking.

-*Labeling is a big problem*. Two out of three teenagers cannot distinguish alcoholic from non-alcoholic beverages because they appear similar on store shelves.

-Teenagers lack essential knowledge about alcohol. Very few are getting clear and reliable information about alcohol and its effects—some nine million to be exact, learn the facts from their peers, and close to two million do not even know a law exists pertaining to illegal underage drinking.

In September 1991, we released the second set of IG reports, this one on enforcement of underage drinking laws called, *Laws and Enforcement: Is the 21-year-old Drinking Age a Myth?* Also, we made available a *Compendium of State Laws on Youth and Alcohol*.

This report showed that:

-The National Minimum Drinking Age Act of 1984 started out with five exemptions that in some states, have become loopholes.

-The federally-mandated 21-year-old minimum drinking law is largely a myth—and it is riddled with loopholes. As I said, *two-thirds of teens who drink, almost 7 million kids, simply walk into a store and buy booze*.

Police also point out that parents do not like their children arrested for "doing what everyone else does." One official described enforcement of alcohol laws as "a no-win" situation. And another commented, "Local police have another priority—[illicit] drugs. They ignore alcohol."

And by and large, there are only nominal penalties against vendors and minors when they violate these laws. While vendors may have fines or their licenses suspended, license revocations are rare. The penalties against the youth who violate the laws are often not deterrents. Even when strict penalties exist, courts are lenient and do not apply them.

Antonia C. Novello

We are seeing over and over again the potential for the kind of tragedy that occurred last year on Maryland's eastern shore where Brian Ball, 15 years old, drank 26 shots of vodka at an "all you can drink" party and died two days later—parties where underage drinking gets out of hand, and no adult is held liable. *Only ten states* have adopted so-called "social host" laws that hold the host adult or parent liable for any consequences of underage drinking on their property, and only 23 states have adopted dram shop laws.

Finally, on November 4, I released the Inspector General's final report entitled, *Youth and Alcohol: Controlling Alcohol Advertising That Appeals to Youth*.

-Concern over alcohol advertising arises because much alcohol advertising goes beyond describing the specific qualities of the beverage. It creates a glamorous, pleasurable image that may mislead youth about alcohol and the possible consequences of its use.

-In a September 1991 poll done by the Wirthlin Group, *73 percent of respondents agreed that alcohol advertising is a major contributor to underage drinking.*

Additionally, the majority of Americans think the alcohol industry is "on the wrong track," with one of the reasons being that alcohol "ads target the young." This finding bolsters a 1988 BATF [Bureau of Alcohol, Tobacco, and Firearms] poll in which 80 percent of respondents believe that alcohol advertising influences underage youth to drink alcoholic beverages.

Last week, as honorary chair of Alcohol Awareness Month, I released the fourth report which deals with those usually unreported consequences of teen drinking that we often do not attribute to alcohol.

Drinking and driving certainly puts many lives at risk, but an alcohol-impaired person doesn't need to get behind the wheel of a car to do harm to himself and to others. Depression, suicides, random violence, and criminal acts—such as date rape, battery, other forms of assault and abuse, and homicide—all have strong links to alcohol use. So do the unintentional alcohol-related injuries that result from falls, drownings, shootings, residential fires, and the like.

This study shows that there is much more to drinking than dying. Crime is one major consequence of alcohol consumption. Approximately one-third of our young people who commit serious crimes have consumed alcohol just prior to the commission of these illegal actions.

According to figures from the Department of Justice, alcohol consumption is associated with almost 27 percent of all murders, almost 33 percent of all property offenses, and more than 37 percent of robberies committed by young people. In fact, nearly 40 percent of the young people in adult correctional facilities reported drinking before committing a crime.

Alcohol has also shown itself to be a factor in being a *victim* of crime. Intoxicated minors were found to provoke assailants, to act vulnerable, and to fail to take normal, commonsense precautions. Among college student crime victims, for example, 50 percent admitted using drugs and/or alcohol at the time the crime was committed.

Rape and sexual assault are also closely associated with alcohol misuse by our youth. Among college age students, 55 percent of perpetrators were under the influence of alcohol, and so were 53 percent of the victims. Administrators at one U.S. university found that 100 percent of sexual assault cases during a specific year were alcohol related. Who can honestly tell me that alcohol is not adversely affecting the future of these young people?

I want to share with you another finding I find particularly shocking and revolting: among high school females, 18 percent—nearly one in five—said it was okay to force sex if the girl was drunk, and among high school males, almost 40 percent—two out of every five—said the same thing.

We found other startling links, such as:

-70 percent of attempted suicides involved the frequent use of drugs and/or alcohol.

-And water activities—of special interest and concern with summer rapidly approaching—often result in alcohol use and danger.

-40 to 50 percent of young males who drown used alcohol prior to drowning.

-40 to 50 percent of all diving injury victims had consumed alcoholic beverages.

Clearly, something *must* be done about this pervasive problem confronting our youth. In focusing my efforts and those of my office on this issue of illegal underage drinking, several things are clear.

First, we all have a role to play in solving this problem. And secondly, by working together, we *can* solve it.

I have urged the alcohol industry to come to the table, to work with us, to become *a part of the solution*. I have also urged schools to make alcohol education a central part of the health curriculum from the earliest grades all the way through—and I must add, this curriculum must include teaching resistance education and risk avoidance techniques.

And, finally, I have urged families—parents and children—to talk to each other about alcohol, about distinguishing truth from fiction.

AIDS

Now, let me outline briefly for you another dangerous situation we face with regard to the issues of sexual behavior, HIV/AIDS and substance abuse, and their associated problems.

To be Surgeon General in the United States today is to be deeply involved with AIDS. In this, its second decade, AIDS is a disease that is increasingly female, increasingly heterosexual, and increasingly young.

Let me start out by highlighting some statistics for you:

-According to the World Health Organization's latest figures, *10-12 million people* have become infected with the HIV virus since the beginning of the epidemic. *Over 1 million of those infections have occurred since April, 1991, and well over 90 percent of infected adults acquired their infection from heterosexual intercourse.*

-World Health Organization figures state that 484,148 cases of AIDS have been reported as of April, 1992. More than half of these cases are reported from the Americas and more than one-fourth are from African countries. WHO estimates that at least 9-11 million adults and 1 million children are infected with HIV worldwide.

-The World Health Organization estimates that up to *5,000 people are infected with HIV each day and predicts that the number of worldwide HIV infections will increase four-fold by the end of the decade.*

Looking a little closer to home, we find that in the United States there has been a rapid increase in HIV incidence in the past decade; the number of deaths from AIDS has continued to increase each year, from 165 by 1981 to more than 27,000 in 1990—a 166-fold increase in one decade. This means that more than 75 people die in the United States every day of AIDS—one every 19 minutes.

Sadly, we also expect the number of AIDS cases to continue to climb over the next several years. By the end of 1994, the cumulative total of AIDS cases in the United States is projected to reach 415,000-535,000 and result in 325,000-390,000 deaths.

CDC [Centers for Disease Control] estimates that approximately 1 million people are currently infected with HIV in this country alone, which represents about 1 in 250 Americans.

The HIV epidemic has been particularly devastating to young Americans. In 1989, HIV infection/AIDS was the second leading cause of death among U.S. men 25-44 years of age (who compromise 34 percent of the adult male population)—surpassing heart disease, cancer, suicide, and homicide, in fact all causes except unintentional injuries.

For men 25-44 years of age in New York City, San Francisco, and Los Angeles, HIV infection/AIDS has been the leading cause of death since the mid- to late 80s.

For women 25-44 years of age (46 percent of all women), HIV infection/AIDS was the eighth leading cause of death in 1988; by 1989, HIV/AIDS had become the sixth leading cause of death for women in this age group. In New York City and New Jersey, HIV infection/AIDS is already the leading cause of death in African American women of childbearing age.

As many of you know, we recently passed an unfortunate milestone of 200,000 reported AIDS cases. It took 8 years to reach the first 100,000 cases in August 1989—100,000 more cases were reported in the next 26 months.

The patterns and trends of the epidemic have changed during its first decade. The number of AIDS cases among injecting drug users and men who have sex with men appears to be leveling somewhat; however, cases are rising among women and perinatal infected children. There is also increasing concern about the vulnerability of adolescents, since many young people with AIDS were infected with HIV as teenagers.

Specifically, if we compare the characteristics of the first 100,000 reported AIDS cases with those of the second 100,000, we can get a clearer picture of these changing trends:

-Of the first 100,000 cases, 61 percent occurred among homosexual or bisexual men with no history of injecting drug use (IDU), and 20 percent occurred among female or heterosexual male drug injectors. Among the second 100,000 cases, 55 percent occurred among homosexual or bisexual men with no history of drug injection, and 24 percent among female or heterosexual male IDUs.

-Of the first 100,000 persons reported with AIDS, 5 percent reportedly acquired HIV through heterosexual transmission, compared with 7 percent among the second 100,000—a 44 percent increase.

A recent analysis of expected trends in U.S. AIDS cases suggests that by 1995, the infection rate among non-drug-injecting heterosexual men and women may be associated with a doubling of AIDS cases acquired through heterosexual transmission. The increase in cases among women will also be reflected in growing numbers of cases in children resulting from perinatal transmission.

This trend of increasing HIV infection and AIDS cases among women is deeply disturbing. CDC estimates that 100,000 women in the United States are infected with HIV. Although many and perhaps most of these women do not even know they are infected, women with the end stage of HIV disease—AIDS—are being reported to CDC at ever-increasing rates.

More than 22,000 women in the United States have been reported with AIDS, almost half of them in the past 2 years. This total represents 11 percent of the cumulative adult/adolescent cases reported, although women represented 13 percent of all reported AIDS cases among adults and adolescents in 1991. It also represents a 17 percent increase in cases among women over the previous year, compared with a 4 percent increase in cases among men for the same time period. Although most of the reported cases of AIDS in the United States are still among men, women and perinatal infected children represent the fastest growing groups of people reported, with 1990 AIDS cases in these latter groups increasing 34 percent and 21 percent, respectively, over the previous year.

A recent CDC study also found that 50 percent of U.S. adolescent females who were diagnosed with AIDS in 1990 contracted the virus through heterosexual contact. The ratio of males to females reported with AIDS is 8:1 in adults and 2.7:1 among teenagers. Findings from serosurveillance among Job Corps applicants indicates that HIV infection is more prevalent among young female than male applicants.

And let me paint the local picture more specifically by giving you some statistics from here in California.

In the communities of Los Angeles, Long Beach and Pasadena alone, there are over 16,000 AIDS cases, and 11,357 people have died. If you add in San Diego, the total number of cases exceeds 19,000, and the number of deaths reaches 13,392.

If San Francisco—one of the cities in this country hit the hardest by the AIDS epidemic—is included, the total cases will reach nearly 30,000, and the death toll climbs to 21,256.

Specifically, this is how the picture looks for your entire state:

-Total number of cases in California, as of April 1: 41,527

-Total number of deaths in California as of April 1: 28,640

-Pediatric cases (under 13): 278 (1 percent)

-Adolescent cases (13-19): 86 (<1 percent)

-Young Adult cases (20-29): 6822 (16 percent)

Quite simply, in the second decade of this disease, our focus must also include adolescents, young adults, women, and families. HIV/AIDS has changed its focus—it is no longer a disease of "them," it is now a disease of all of "us." And especially, with our young people, *HIV/AIDS is like an accident waiting to happen*—it is like putting a match next to a can of gasoline. Let me put these figures in context:

-The median latency period—or the period between being infected with HIV and the onset of AIDS—is estimated to be about 10 years. Which means that *most persons under age 29 with AIDS were infected with HIV when they were adolescents.*

-Sexually-Transmitted Diseases—STDs—are particularly alarming for young people. *In the U.S., an adolescent gets an STD every 30 seconds,* with 8 million STD cases in persons under age 25—and the highest rates of gonorrhea and chlamydia of any age group! I am particularly concerned about this information *because non-HIV STDs and open sores may make a person more susceptible to HIV infection.*

-And let me give you another fact. In testimony before the National AIDS Commission in March, 1991, Dr. Robert Johnson of Adolescent Medicine at the University of Medicine and Dentistry of New Jersey stated that the *last four cases of heterosexually-transmitted AIDS in New Jersey were in adolescents*—and that they were *adolescents who, interestingly enough, had been drinking the highly-potent alcoholic beverage, Cisco, and did not use any protection.*

> ***"HIV/AIDS has changed its focus—it is no longer a disease of 'them,' it is now a disease of all of 'us.'"***

Let me talk about the two avenues of HIV infection in young people—drug use and unprotected sex. First, some information about drug use and HIV.

With young people, sexual transmission is the usual route of infection. The role of drug use in HIV is usually not injection drug use, or getting infected from dirty needles and works.

Instead, the role of drug use here is that *it leads to risk taking, to more frequent sexual activity, and to unprotected sex.*

Let us look at the epidemiology of drug use in high school and college students, as a snapshot of the general pattern for young adults, and let me remind you that when we talk of drug abuse, we are talking here about the abuse of alcohol and other drugs:

-It is estimated that 3 *percent of high school students use intravenous drugs, including cocaine or heroin—a direct avenue to HIV infection* through infected needles and works.

-*Nearly half of high school seniors have used an illicit drug* (48 percent). Two percent of students have used crack in the past year. And *trading sex* for drugs is frequently the way kids get crack.

-*Over half (57 percent) of senior high school students drink alcohol and one-third (33 percent) of seniors drink 5 or more drinks in a row.* Nearly one-half million college students, or 4 percent, drink every day. And college students get drunk more often than their counterparts not in college.

With regard to sex, let me tell you what we do know about the sexual activity of our youth and how that relates to HIV and AIDS:

-The majority of adolescents have engaged in sexual intercourse. Among adolescents aged 15-19 surveyed in 1988, 52 *percent of women and 60 percent of men had engaged in premarital sexual intercourse.* The proportion of women who are sexually active increased between 1970 and 1988. Recent CDC data states that 54 percent of our youth are sexually active before they graduate from high school.

-The average age of the *first sexual experience is 16 years* among adolescents in the U.S. However, in some urban areas it may be 12 years of age.

-Approximately 21 percent of high school students in 1989 said they had engaged in sex with *four or more partners* during their lifetime.

-Many adolescents know how HIV is transmitted; however, *63 percent of those who are sexually active do not consistently use condoms*—for example, 9 percent of adolescents surveyed in Massachusetts in 1990 knew that HIV can be contracted through heterosexual and homosexual transmission.

However, in a recent survey, 40 percent of sexually-active adolescents reported "sometimes" using a condom, and 23 percent reported "never" using a condom.

-A substantial proportion of adolescents engage in anal intercourse, a principle risk factor for HIV. One review indicated that *between 10 percent and 26 percent of adolescents practice anal intercourse,* often to protect virginity or avoid pregnancy. Moreover, a recent study conducted among University of Puerto Rico students found that 31 percent of women and 40 percent of men practiced anal sex.

-*Heterosexual contact has surpassed homosexual contact as the major mode of sexual transmission for adolescent AIDS since 1990.* Among adolescent AIDS cases reported in 1990, 51 percent of women and 4 percent of men contracted HIV through heterosexual contact—29 percent of adolescent men were exposed to AIDS through homosexual/bisexual contact.

As Surgeon General, I cannot just sit and wait for accidents such as these to occur. I *must* act. We must teach people that first, *abstinence is the only sure way to protect yourself* from acquiring an STD or HIV. But we must also be realistic, and we must educate our youth *and their parents* about methods of protecting themselves when they are sexually active.

And when we do, *we must provide the education, the instructions, and alert them of their responsibility.* Condom availability, just for condom sake and devoid of education and instructions, is not only bad public health policy, it is a dangerous endeavor.

The need to address the issue of HIV infection among young people is immediate. The legal, ethical, social and medical challenges that you young people present to our current legal and health care systems, however, makes this a cumbersome process.

AIDS in young people presents many more *social* issues than I ever would have imagined. As all of you can attest, adolescence is a period of profound physiological, psychological and social change.

Many young people often feel alienated from the rest of society, and society, in turn, often finds it difficult to understand their emotions and behaviors, which are often impulsive or risky. This alienation is heightened in the presence of HIV.

The behaviors that lead to HIV infection in adolescents are often deemed socially unacceptable, and there is a temptation to stigmatize most of the adolescent population as "high risk," or "hard to reach." It is crucial for us as adults to understand—to remember—that *most* young people find themselves at times in situations that are risky for acquiring HIV, even if these situations are encountered only infrequently, for only a few minutes, a few hours, or a few weeks.

This situation demands immediate action—

action which therefore needs to build on existing systems of health care services. Given that *40 percent of recent adolescent AIDS cases are linked to sexual contact,* and because there are behavioral and physiologic relationships between HIV and other sexually transmitted diseases (STDs), *we must provide HIV prevention education and services* at the same time we give care and information about other STDs.

More broadly, the HIV/AIDS services we provide must make sense, and they must be provided in the places where health care is sought. I often say that what we need is to provide good medicine combined with good sense, and I believe it more every day.

Also, *young people must be treated with respect,* and we need to *foster an atmosphere of trust* between them and the health care provider.

We must work to provide HIV prevention education immediately—and not in isolation, but as an integral element of a comprehensive health curriculum that also provides education about sexuality and drug abuse. A dialogue between young people and their parents is critical to such education, and all views should be acknowledged and accommodated.

SMOKING

Allow me now to discuss smoking. The Office of the Surgeon General will always be involved in trying to convince the American public of the dangers of tobacco. Some of the things we have been saying for years now, are:

-Each year, smoking causes *over 434,000 deaths from lung and other kinds of cancer, heart disease, emphysema, chronic bronchitis, and strokes.*

-The Environmental Protection Agency estimates that more than *3,700 nonsmokers will die every year from lung cancer.* It is estimated that passive smoke now causes 22,000 new cancers of all types annually, *including 7,000 in people who never smoked.*

-*Nonsmokers married to smokers have a 30 percent greater risk of heart attack* than do nonsmokers married to nonsmokers.

According to the EPA, *9 to 12 million children* in the United States are exposed to passive or sidestream smoke from their parents. These children suffer from more ear infections and have *a 200 to 400 percent greater risk for deep chest infections.*

Of special concern to me is the new generation of smokers—our young people who are not receiving an honest picture of what smoking actually does to their lives.

I believe in the power of a free market and the importance of advertising in making a free market operate. Advertising that is honest and gives the facts about a product is not only necessary, but good for consumers and producers alike. However, there are times when the power of advertising must be voluntarily restrained because of its great potential to influence.

Young people are flooded with images of the strong, independent Marlboro man, and told that smoking Camels will give them a "smooth character." What they aren't told is that there's nothing smooth about lung cancer and emphysema, and that your independence is restricted when you can't breathe without a respirator.

Calling for the voluntary withdrawal of a successful advertising campaign is not a traditional role of the Surgeon General, yet, it is the only responsible position that I can take regarding advertisements that mislead our youth into making decisions that will adversely affect their health.

Let me tell you about some recent research published in the Journal of the American Medical Association and the CDC's MMWR. This research has shown that: approximately *30 percent of 3-year-olds, and 91 percent of 6-year-olds correctly identified "Old Joe" with a picture of a cigarette.* This is a shocking finding, indicating the power of advertising has reached the very young. Did you even imagine that 6-year-olds—yes, even 6-year-olds—are as familiar with "Old Joe" as with Mickey Mouse?

As a pediatrician, public health official, and responsible citizen, I am appalled at these findings.

Let's look at these findings more closely. The researchers found that, by 3 years of age, children understand both the content, and for whom, commercials are made. Of course, R.J. Reynolds and the other tobacco companies stubbornly insist that they don't want children to smoke ... that their advertising does not target kids ... that their ads are aimed only at making adults switch brands.

While cigarette companies claim that they do not intend to market directly to children, the reality is that this argument is irrelevant if advertising affects what children know and believe.

Old Joe Camel recognition results from ubiquitous everyday exposure—from billboards, to movies, T Shirts, posters, promotional activities during sporting events, video arcade games, toys and candy.

Even many in the advertising industry recognize that these ads go too far. A recent *Advertising Age* editorial argued that "Old Joe Must Go." These ads are deplorable—they have to stop. If we do not push for this marketing tactic to change, then our tolerance might open the floodgates for a tide-wave of media campaigns that will attempt to duplicate these tactics—not just for cigarettes, but alcohol and other products as well.

These copy-cat antics are already prevalent. For example, Camel is not the only brand to prey upon our susceptible youth—it has just become the most obvious one. The strong, rough, independent Marlboro cowboy is another, earlier example. His appeal to young people is obvious. In fact, a national survey shows that seven in 10 adolescents between ages 12 and 18 buying their own cigarettes choose to smoke Marlboro.

Of course, in one way or another all cigarette manufacturers promote images of youth and fun, glamour and affluence, independence and achievement, and rugged spiritedness. They promote these images with the full knowledge that nearly 90 percent of smokers become regular smokers before they turn 21.

That is why tobacco manufacturers spend incredible amounts of money—3.6 billion dollars each year in advertisement and promotion to be exact—to expose children and adolescents to their messages touting peer acceptance and the social rewards of smoking.

Surveys before 1988 indicated little preference for Camels among young people. Recent surveys show that in some communities in America, one-fourth or more of young smokers are now buying Camel. Indeed, the major source of Camel's recent market-share increase appears to have come from younger smokers.

It's time for the tobacco industry to stop preying on our nation's youth. It's time that cigarette companies act—voluntarily and responsibly—to help the nation achieve a key Healthy People 2000 objective: to eliminate or severely restrict all forms of tobacco product advertising and promotion to which youth younger than 18 are likely to be exposed.

So I have been making this appeal on behalf of the very future of this country: our youth. In years past, R.J. Reynolds would have had us walk a mile for a Camel. The time has come that we all invite "Old Joe" Camel himself to take a hike!

VIOLENCE

Another critical issue I want to address today on which I focus the energies of my office is violence. Violence is a major public health problem in America, and has an enormous impact on our nation as a whole. *Violence takes the lives of 50,000 persons each year.* For the United States as a whole, the homicide rate was 9 per 100,000 in 1988. For African-American youth, however, *homicide was the leading cause of death.* The homicide rate was more than nine times the rate for white youth and *17 to 283 times the rate for all young men in Western Europe.* Although violence affects all communities, it affects low income, minority, and the disadvantaged communities at much higher rates than the general population.

The need to address the issue of violence in our society grows daily. *Violence has an impact on all of our citizens,* regardless of where they are located. It permeates our lives and fear is the increasingly prevalent result.

The seriousness of the problem is measured not only in human terms, but also by the impact of violence on health care costs. In a very recent study, the District of Columbia Hospital Association estimated that *treating victims of interpersonal violence cost D.C. hospitals $20 million in 1989, and an additional $20 million in non-hospital health care costs.* Because 68 percent of the D.C. victims lacked health insurance, treating these persons places considerable burden on the health care system.

The study *estimated total health care costs of criminal violence for the nation in 1989 at $3.5 billion.*

Then there is the ever-growing problem of domestic violence.

-The FBI has estimated that domestic violence touches as many as *one-fourth of all American families. Every 12 seconds a woman is battered in the United States.*

-One survey of married Americans showed that up to *six out of ten couples have experienced violence* at some time during the marriage.

Studies of homeless families in communities throughout the nation consistently find that between 25 and 50 percent of these homeless families left the home to escape domestic violence.

What can be done to prevent domestic violence?

The use of *standardized protocols to screen trauma patients* in a hospital emergency room has been found to substantially increase the ability of health care provides to identify battered women. Once identified, victims need to be referred to appropriate service providers. In addition to arrest, perpetrators can also be referred to counseling programs.

The productive interactions of public health, social service, and criminal justice agencies is necessary for the ultimate success of efforts to prevent this pointless violence.

-Another form of violence, *suicide, is the third leading cause of death among youth aged 15 through 24*. We need to help these youths see that they have so much to live for.

-2.2 million people are victimized annually by violent injury.

Violence is affecting our youth in ways we never imagined:

-Seven percent of youth account for: 79 percent of all serious violent offenses, 72 percent of all drug sales, 56 percent of all delinquent offenses.

-Alcohol alone plays a role in 50 percent of all homicides, suicides, assaults, and sex-related crimes.

For too many, violence is becoming the response of first recourse in cases of emotional and mental distress and interpersonal conflict.

Physicians must play a vital role in reporting and fighting all kinds of violence. I have worked closely with and applaud the American Medical Association in their efforts to establish uniform reporting procedures and interventions to help stop domestic violence at the first sign, but we must do more.

Families and educators most get involved. We need to teach our children that *violence is not acceptable* and stop the problems before the first incident ever occurs.

The children of today will be the adults of tomorrow—the leaders of our country, the scientists, the teachers, and parents themselves. The choices they make today regarding their health will affect them for the rest of their lives. It is our responsibility to help them see this, and to help them recognize the many potential consequences of their choices.

Just as so many people made a difference with me, I ask you to make a difference for those around you. Service and commitment are the hallmark of any truly successful life.

The need for prevention underlines our mutuality. We live, study and work together in a community. No man is an island. Perhaps the best lesson revealed by these statistics is that we truly cannot live well without empathy, patience and love for each other. I hope we all may learn these valuable lessons.

Thank you for sharing this time with me, and God bless.

With the change in presidential administrations after the 1992 election, Novello left her post as U.S. Surgeon General in June 1993. Since then, she has served as UNICEF's special representative for health and nutrition.

SOURCES

Books

Telgen, Diane, and Jim Kamp, eds., *Notable Hispanic American Women*, Gale Research, Detroit, 1993.

Periodicals

Hispanic, "Dr. Antonia Novello: The Right Stuff," January/February, 1990, p.20; "Beyond Nursing," October, 1991, p. 15.

Newsweek, "Surgeon General: Abortion Foe," October 30, 1989. p. 84.

New York Times, November 5, 1991, p. A16; November 6, 1991, p. A25.

People, "Butt Out, Guido Sarducci! Surgeon General Antonia Novello, Your Sister-in-Law, Wants Everyone to Quit Smoking," December 17, 1990, pp. 109-110.

Saturday Evening Post, "Antonia Novello: A Dream Come True," May/June, 1991.

Vital Speeches of the Day, "Health Priorities for the Nineties: The Quest for Prevention," August 15, 1992, pp. 666-672.

Harry P. Pachon

1945–

Hispanic American political scientist and educator

As a founding member and former executive director of the National Association of Latino Elected and Appointed Officials (NALEO) Educational Fund, Harry P. Pachon has devoted a substantial portion of his career to research and analysis of issues important to the Hispanic community. Based in Los Angeles with additional offices in New York, Chicago, Houston, and Washington, D.C., NALEO was established in 1975 to provide a network of support and guidance for Hispanic Americans elected or appointed to positions in government. As part of its mission to serve as an advocate for Latino people, it also keeps track of Hispanic American participation in the voting process and acts as a clearinghouse for information on obtaining U.S. citizenship.

Pachon is a native of Miami, Florida. He received his education in California, receiving his bachelor's degree in 1967 and his master's degree in 1968, both from California State University in Los Angeles. He then went on to earn a doctorate in politics from the Claremont Graduate School in 1973.

Pachon's first job was in the academic world as an assistant professor at Michigan State University. Following his two-year stint, which ended in 1976, he worked until 1981 as an administrative assistant to the Appropriations Committee of the U.S. House of Representatives. He then resumed teaching, this time at the City University of New York, holding the rank of associate professor there until 1986. The year 1987 marked Pachon's return to California, where he joined the faculty of Pitzer College (one of the Claremont Colleges) as Kenan Professor of Politics, a post he still holds. More recently, he assumed the presidency of the Tomás Rivera Center, a national institute for policy studies on Latino issues that is affiliated with the Claremont Graduate School and Trinity University in San Antonio, Texas.

Pachon contributes regularly to social science journals and is the author of two books, Mexican Americans (1975) and, with Joan Moore, Hispanics in the United States. He has also acted as a consultant to the U.S. Agency for International Development and the U.S. Department of Health and Human Services.

Concurrent with the teaching positions he held during the 1980s and early 1990s, Pachon served as executive director of NALEO, where he initiated a U.S. citizenship project that has received national acclaim for its numerous community-

based drives aimed at encouraging those eligible to become citizens to take the first steps toward doing so. As he made clear in the following speech, reprinted here from Vital Speeches of the Day, *May 15, 1988, this has always been of special concern to NALEO because noncitizens cannot vote, thus limiting their ability to participate in the democratic process.*

In his address, delivered on February 14, 1988, in Albany, New York, before the 1988 Black and Puerto Rican Legislative Caucus, Pachon made two other key points that reflected his interests at NALEO. First of all, he emphasized to his listeners the need for more and better statistical record-keeping on Latinos to ensure that public policy analysts such as himself can accurately identify and track the problems facing their community. This plea sprang in part from his experiences in trying to assess the extent of poverty among Hispanic children, an issue he helped bring to the nation's attention. Secondly, he warned of a troubled future ahead if nothing is done to reverse current trends regarding the high-school dropout rate among minorities and the failure of colleges and universities to recruit more minority students.

It's truly a pleasure to be here with so many honored guests and distinguished speakers and to have been asked to share some thoughts on the issues of Hispanic politics. Before I address these issues, however, I think it's important to discuss two political myths that continue to surround the Hispanic community in 1988. Myths are like stereotypes. They belie the complexity of political reality. Unfortunately, believing these myths has political consequences for the community's political future and for the strategies it adopts.

The first of these myths—and by far the common—is that Hispanic political power is still at the stage of "potential." We've all heard versions of this. As recently as three weeks ago, the *New York City Tribune* ran its political analysis of the 1988 Hispanic vote under the banner headline: "Votes of 20 Million Hispanics Called a Sleeping Giant." A sleeping giant. Imagine the image this conveys—a dormant community about to wake up from its afternoon siesta. So much of our discourse on Latino politics involves this image.

Yet the facts present a different picture: there are now more than 3,300 Hispanic elected officials in this county; there are one and a half times as many Hispanic elected officials in California as any other minority group in that state; there are seven times as many Hispanic elected officials in Texas as any other minority; the number of Hispanic elected officials has doubled in size in a decade; growing number of Hispanics are entering voting age years. In two years the size of the potential Hispanic electorate grew by twenty-five percent. That, ladies and gentlemen, is ten times the growth of the electorate as a whole.

This growth in electoral power was already demonstrated in the 1986 elections. Based on the actual vote in 1986, it took only 10.1 percent of the Puerto Rican/Latino vote to make a point shift in a statewide election in New York. In California, the state with the most electoral votes, 6 percent of the Latino population shifting its votes makes a 1-point difference. In Texas, a presidential or statewide candidate has only to reach 3.4 percent of the Hispanic vote to shift the statewide results by 1 percent. Based on figures like this, the myth of the sleeping giant is seen for what it is. Images need to change. Hispanic political power is not simply a potential but instead is an emerging reality. Hispanic political gains are real.

The Hispanic vote is real. It is no longer necessary to speak of "mañana" but we do with what we have today.

Yet we have to be cautious because there is another myth that can trap us. This myth, unfortunately, we *want* to believe. Again, many of you have heard it. It goes like this. Given the dramatic, if not spectacular, growth in the Hispanic community, there is a hidden Latino electoral force out there. All we have to do is reach out and mobilize the Hispanic electorate. This myth is persuasive. Eleven percent of the adults in New York State are Puerto Rican/Hispanic. In New Jersey, this figure is 7.4 percent; in California, 19 percent.

Yet, the numbers are deceptive. Forty percent of our community in 1980 was below voting age. Even though the Hispanic community's average age has increased to 24 years old, consider the implications of being the youngest age group in American society today. Disproportionate numbers of Hispanics are precisely in those age ranges that vote the least (18 to 24 years). We know this because as a country we were unable to get high voting participation of the vast majority of baby boomers in the late 1960s and 1970s. How can we expect Hispanic youth to be so different than their majority counterparts? The positive side to this, however, is that the Hispanic vote is nowhere near to reaching its true potential. In fact it may be in the late 1990s when we see the full magnitude of the *present* Hispanic vote.

Besides youth, however, there is another hidden factor that affects the Hispanic electorate. This factor is invisible and, by and large, has no counterpart in the black community. This factor is U.S. citizenship. While the media tends to look at Hispanics as either being native-born citizens or illegal foreign-born aliens, there is another large group Hispanics who are neither—neither illegals nor native born. This third group of people numbers close to four million. One of three adult Hispanics fits into this category. And that category is legal resident immigrants.

Here in New York you are familiar that in, or adjacent to, Puerto Rican communities there are other Latin American enclaves. In New York City, it's the Dominicans in Manhattan; the Colombians in Queens; in New Jersey it's Cuban. While Puerto Ricans are U.S. citizens by birth, forty percent of the Hispanics in New York are from other parts of Latin America. Approximately one quarter of a million Hispanics in this state cannot vote, cannot serve on grand juries, cannot work in the police department or the federal government. This large body of noncitizens explains why fifty-two percent of all Hispanics who did not vote in 1986 gave as their reason "noncitizenship." In the presidential elections this November, there will be nearly as many Hispanics who can't vote due to noncitizenship as there will be Hispanic registered voters.

Let's keep this clearly in mind next time we find ourselves being swayed by the myth that our large number should automatically and unequivocally be linked to voters going to the polls.

Yet, the political future is bright. As our community's youth matures they will become increasingly involved in politics. Every two years in this decade a new cohort of 200,000 potential Hispanic voters enters voting age. More and more Latin Americans are becoming U.S. citizens. If U.S. citizenship projects like NALEO's—which is now in progress—succeed, millions of Hispanics will become eligible to vote. And ladies and gentlemen, there is something curious about the naturalized U.S. citizens. He or she tends to vote more than their native-born counterparts. It is for this reason that one of the major political challenges faced by the Hispanic community is how to overcome this hidden obstacle to political empowerment.

The problem is straightforward. There are "no stand-alone, off-the-shelf" models for U.S. citizenship campaigns. We are just beginning to realize the magnitude of the task ahead of us. There are issues to be addressed in our communities in this regard. How, for example, do we make the benefits of U.S. citizenship apparent to Hispanic immigrants who are already working and have no real idea of the benefits of naturalization? How do we overcome the perceived, and sometimes very real, fear of the federal agency in charge of naturalization—the Immigration and Naturalization Service? How do we overcome the abuses that are made by anonymous INS bureaucrats who have the nerve to ask such questions during the citizenship exam as:

-How many pilgrims landed at Plymouth Rock?

-What is the governor of California's wife's first name?

-Who won the 1966 world series?

The citizenship exam, ladies and gentlemen, is the closest equivalent we have to the literacy tests of yesteryear. Every year more than 100,000 citizenship applicants are rejected and we do

> ***"Hispanic political power is not simply a potential but instead is an emerging reality."***

not know for what reason or from what country they are from. Are Haitians and Dominican immigrants rejected at higher rates than Italians or German immigrants? We don't know now, but we will know, thanks to a NALEO initiated amendment passed by the Senate that mandates INS to investigate why more than a million people have been turned down from becoming Americans in the 1980s. These challenges, however, are for the future.

For the present we have to combat blind acceptance of myths that simplistically portray the Hispanic community. Instead we have to consider the implications that the political gains the Hispanic community has made in the past ten years have been achieved while more than fifty percent of the Hispanic population in this country has not been franchised to vote.

From this perspective, we see that the Hispanic community has done much in the political arena. Much more remains to be done. In 1988, with the last presidential election of this decade just ahead, perhaps it is appropriate to reflect on those issues that will continue to affect the Hispanic community. Let me say at this point, however, that many of you in this audience deal with the pressing issues our community faces on a day-to-day basis. Rather than reciting the familiar litany of poverty, education, housing, drug abuse, employment and other issues that you know so well, let me address two other—and not so frequently discussed—issues where the Hispanic and black communities face common interests.

> ***". . . today's problems of low levels of education and inadequate employment training for black and Hispanic youth are tomorrow's economic problems for Anglo middle-class America."***

The first of these issues is a technical one that those of us who have been in government encounter on recurring basis. I refer to the current practices that government agencies engage in when collecting statistics on minority populations. Statistics—the word brings to mind dreary columns of numbers that are the concern of academics and social scientists. Yet eighty years ago, H.G. Wells said that statistical literacy will be as necessary in the modern world as traditional literacy. The word itself, after all, refers to "numbers of the state." H.G. Wells may have been overstating the case, but we in minority communities can well take heed. Let me offer a few examples.

All too often we hear populations in need being described in terms of "white" and "nonwhite" categories. In cases like this we assume that "white" means Anglo and that "nonwhite" means black, Hispanics and Asian. It's a wrong assumption since the "white" category includes Hispanics. Even more frequently, we hear social issues in terms of "white" and "black" populations. This continuing practice also hurts both the black and Hispanic populations. It obviously affects Hispanics by making them invisible to government policymakers. "If you can't see them, you can't serve them." This probably describes why Hispanics' social conditions are so often overlooked. In 1987, for example, some states still do not keep death records based on ethnicity. As a consequence we are lacking vital health information on the leading causes of death among Hispanics in key states throughout the nation. Illinois, for example, just this year changed its record-keeping procedures.

The more prevalent area where we do not keep adequate information on Hispanics is in government benefit programs. We still don't fully know how Hispanics underutilize Social Security, Medicare or participate in other programs. This continuing practice of excluding Hispanics as a separate category when describing social problems in the country also directly affects black Americans. It hurts the black community by reducing the difference in the conditions between white and black America. Thus when we describe the income gap between blacks and whites, and we include all the low-income Hispanics among the white population, it obviously makes the differences more narrow. Imagine that the same reporting goes on for describing white and black children in poverty, for describing health care access, educational achievement and the list goes on. We, as minority communities, need to realize the continuing nature of this problem and attack it head-on when anyone, whether from the executive branch, private sector or from a university, adopts it as a means of telling us about our communities.

Yet this is a small issue in comparison to another issue of which we are becoming increasingly aware. All of us know that the high school dropout rates and the failure of colleges to recruit black and Hispanic youths are problems of major proportions in this country. There are schools in East and Central Los Angeles that have improved so that their dropout rates are only about 40 percent. Only five of every 100 Hispanic youths beginning elementary school will complete a college education today. Most of us know these figures.

There is, however, a consequence of these education problems that will not become apparent until several decades from now. If you combine the extreme youth of the black and Hispanic populations—remember that the average age of Hispanics is 24 years—with the low levels of education they are receiving, then we as a country face the long-term dilemma that ever-increasing segments of our labor force will be ill equipped to handle the increasing demands of a post-industrial economy.

Consider, 50 percent of the minority workers of today will be still working 40 years from now. In other words, in the year 2028 one-half of the present Hispanic workers will be in the work force. This is not solely a minority problem. Because coupled with increasing minority representation in the work force, you also have the aging of the American population. Today's baby boomers range from 25 to 41 years of age. In the beginning part of next century, they will begin to retire. As they leave the work force a change is projected in the American economy. Whereas at the present there are 18.6 elderly people supported by every 100 workers, this number will double—to 37 elderly people being supported by every 100 workers—by the year 2030. This great "dependency ratio" will come at a time when black and Hispanic workers will be at the peak of their economically productive years. An immediate challenge we as minority communities face is to frame the dialogue of the minority educational and employment crisis as part of the long-range problems of an American economy that is undergoing vast transformations. In other words, the bottom line is that today's problems of low levels of education and inadequate employment training for black and Hispanic youth are tomorrow's economic problems for Anglo middle-class America.

Unity on issues between blacks and Hispanics on these common problems is natural. In my opinion, coalitions are made on issues—not ideology. The facts are that there are many common issues we face together. If we could work together, think of the political force blacks and Hispanics could represent. In three of five largest states, blacks and Hispanics now represent 1 out of every 4 adults. blacks and Hispanics represent, today—not tomorrow—powerful numbers of the total vote in the states with the largest electoral vote delegations. For example, the combined actual vote of blacks and Hispanics in 1986 was as follows:

-In New York, 14 percent;

-In New Jersey, 12 1/2 percent;

-In Texas, 25 percent;

-In California, 14 percent.

These are crucial numbers to consider. Yet all of us know that coalitions and unity are difficult goals to achieve. The famous revolutionary leader of South America, Simon Bolívar, after unsuccessfully attempting to promote unity among South American countries, is reputed to have said: "I have sown upon the oceans." One hundred and fifty years later we know that unity is a still difficult goal.

You are all laboring on its behalf since the stakes are so high. Every 80 seconds another black and Hispanic child is born into poverty. During the course of this evening another 100 minority children have been born into the ranks of the poor. Your efforts and dedication on behalf of these children and our communities are to be commended and supported.

Thank you.

SOURCES

Hispanic, "On the Fringes," June, 1991, p. 48; "Fiesta Politics," January/February, 1992, p. 124; "The '94 Elections and the Latino Community," January/February, 1995, p. 140.

Vital Speeches of the Day, "Politics and Public Policy: The Hispanic Community," May 15, 1988, pp. 464-466.

Leonard Peltier

1944–

Native American activist of the Chippewa and Sioux tribes

In 1977, one of the most controversial trials in American history came to an end with a guilty verdict against Leonard Peltier, an American Indian Movement member accused in the shooting deaths of two FBI agents on South Dakota's Pine Ridge Reservation in June 1975. Sentenced to two consecutive life terms, he now spends his days in the federal penitentiary at Leavenworth, Kansas. In the opinion of more than a few observers, however, Peltier is not a murderer but a political prisoner—convicted for his beliefs and affiliations rather than for any crime.

Born in Grand Forks, North Dakota, Peltier had a rather unsettled and unhappy childhood as part of a large extended family that was often on the move in search of whatever work they could find. After his parents separated when he was four, he lived mostly with his paternal grandparents. But his beloved grandfather's death in 1952 left his grandmother nearly destitute, and the following year, at the suggestion of Bureau of Indian Affairs officials, young Leonard was shipped off to an Indian school. There he endured very harsh conditions until his mother arrived to claim him. He later went to live with his father for a while but left home at the age of fourteen to head out west, where his mother was a migrant laborer in Oregon and Washington. Leonard learned the welding trade and eventually found work in the shipyards of Portland. By the age of twenty, he was co-owner of an auto body shop in Seattle.

Peltier first became involved with the American Indian Movement (AIM) in 1970 when he joined some Seattle-area Indians in a dispute with the federal government over land claims. (AIM had been established about two years earlier in Minneapolis by Clyde Bellecourt and others to help Native Americans living in urban areas deal with police harassment and obtain education, job training, housing, and health care.) Heading back home to the Midwest, Peltier quickly rose into AIM's upper ranks and traveled extensively raising funds for the group. He also participated in a number of its major demonstrations, including the Trail of Broken Treaties in 1972 and the subsequent takeover of the Bureau of Indian Affairs office in Washington.

By the summer of 1975, Peltier was living on the Pine Ridge Sioux Reserva-

tion in South Dakota. Two years earlier, it had been the site of the infamous Wounded Knee siege in which Indian activists squared off for seventy-one days against a veritable army of federal officials. Conditions had deteriorated even more since then; tensions were running high not only between Indians and whites but also between Indian activists and Indians who worked for (or sided with) the U.S. government. To many of the people at Pine Ridge, a virtual state of civil war existed.

The incident that would ultimately land Peltier in jail occurred near the town of Oglala on June 26, 1975. While most of the specifics are in dispute, what is known without a doubt is that two FBI agents who had gone to Pine Ridge to arrest a young Indian man for theft and assault exchanged gunfire with some Indians and ended up dead. Later that same day, after more FBI agents and Indian police reinforcements arrived on the scene and another gun battle erupted, an Indian was killed.

According to the scenario suggested by government officials, a group of Indians—including Peltier—had brutally ambushed the agents when they pursued a suspect into the makeshift compound that served as the informal headquarters of a number of AIM members and other tribal activists. The Indians, on the other hand, maintained that it was the sound of gunfire nearby that had originally prompted them to leave their compound and investigate. After spotting the agents' cars and noting that the two men were wounded but still alive, they cautiously began to move in closer. But before they could reach the vehicles, someone else in a red pickup truck drove up, got out, and fired in the direction where the agents' bodies were later found, both were shot several times at point-blank range through the head.

In November 1975, Peltier—who had by then fled to Canada—and two other Indians were indicted for murder in the agents' deaths. (Charges against a fourth man were later dropped.) Arrested and returned to the United States in early 1976, Peltier went on trial in Fargo, North Dakota, in the spring of 1977. At the conclusion of the highly controversial proceedings, which saw the government mount a case based on questionable evidence while excluding most of the testimony favorable to the defense, Peltier was convicted and sentenced to two life terms in prison; the other two Indians were acquitted.

At his sentencing on June 1, 1977, Peltier read a statement to the presiding judge in which he sharply criticized the conduct of the trial and the treatment of Indian activists at the hands of the United States government. His words are reprinted here from Native American Reader: Stories, Speeches and Poems, *edited by Jerry D. Blanche (Denali Press, 1990.)*

There is no doubt in my mind or my peoples' minds you are going to sentence me to two consecutive life terms. You are, and have always been prejudiced against me and any Native Americans who have stood before you. You have openly favored the government all through this trial, and you are happy to do whatever the FBI would want you to do in this case.

I did not always believe this to be so! When I first saw you in the courtroom in Sioux Falls, your dignified appearance misled me into thinking that you were a fair-minded person who knew something of the law and who would act in accordance with the law! Which meant that you would be impartial and not favor one side or the other in this lawsuit. That has not been the case and I now firmly believe that you will impose consecutive life terms solely because that's what you think will avoid the displeasures of the FBI. Neither my people nor myself know why you would be so concerned about an organization that has brought so much shame to the American people. But you are! Your conduct during this trial leaves no doubt that you will do the bidding of the FBI without any hesitation!

You are about to perform an act which will close one more chapter in the history of the failure of the United States courts and the failure of the people of the United States to do justice in the case of a Native American. After centuries of murder of millions of my brothers and sisters by white racist America, could I have been wise in thinking that you would break that tradition and commit an act of justice? Obviously not! Because I should have realized that what I detected was only a very thin layer of dignity and surely not of fine character. If you think my accusations have been harsh and unfounded, I will explain why I have reached these conclusions and why I think my criticism has not been harsh enough:

Leonard Peltier

First, each time my defense team tried to expose FBI misconduct in their investigation of this lawsuit and tried to present evidence of this you claimed it was irrelevant to this trial. But the prosecution was allowed to present their case with evidence that was in no way relevant to this lawsuit—for example, an automobile blowing up on a freeway in Wichita, Kansas; an attempted murder in Milwaukee, Wisconsin, for which I have not been found innocent or guilty; or a van loaded with legally-purchased firearms, and a policeman who claims someone fired at him in Oregon state. The Supreme Court of the United States tried to prevent convictions of this sort by passing into law that only past convictions may be presented as evidence if it is not prejudicial to the lawsuit, and only evidence of said case may be used. This court knows very well I have no prior convictions, nor am I even charged with some of these alleged crimes; therefore, they cannot be used as evidence in order to receive a conviction in this farce called a trial. This is why I strongly believe you will impose two life terms, running consecutively, on me.

Second, you could not make a reasonable decision about my sentence because you suffer from at least one of three defects that prevent a rational conclusion: you plainly demonstrated this in your decision about the Jimmy Eagle and Myrtle Poor Bear aspects of this case. In Jimmy's case, for some unfounded reason that only a judge who consciously and openly ignores the law, would call it irrelevant to my trial; in the mental torture of Myrtle Poor Bear you said her testimony would shock the conscience of the American people, if believed! But you decided what was to be believed and what was not to be believed—not the jury! Your conduct shocks the conscience of what the American legal system stands for—the search for the truth by a jury of citizens. What was it that made you so afraid to let that testimony in? Your own guilt of being part of a corrupted pre-planned trial to get a conviction no matter how your reputation would be tarnished? For these reasons, I strongly believe you will do the bidding of the FBI and give me two consecutive life terms.

Third, in my opinion, anyone who failed to see the relationship between the undisputed facts of these events surrounding the investigation used by the FBI in their interrogation of the Navajo youths: Wilford Draper, who was tied to a chair for three hours and denied access to his attorney; the outright threats to Norman Brown's life; the bodily harm threatened to Mike Anderson; and finally, the murder of Anna Mae Aquash, must be blind, stupid, or without human feelings so there is no doubt and little chance that you have the ability to avoid doing today what the FBI wants you to do—which is to sentence me to two life terms running consecutively.

Fourth, you do not have the ability to see

that the conviction of an AIM activist helps to cover up what the government's own evidence showed: that large numbers of Indian people engaged in that fire fight on June 26, 1976.

You do not have the ability to see that the government must suppress the fact that there is a growing anger amongst Indian people and that Native Americans will resist any further encroachments by the military forces of the capitalistic Americans, which is evidenced by the large number of Pine Ridge residents who took up arms on June 27, 1975, to defend themselves. Therefore, you do not have the ability to carry out your responsibility towards me in an impartial way and will run my two life terms consecutively.

Fifth, I stand before you as a proud man; I feel no guilt! I have done nothing to feel guilty about! I have no regrets of being a Native American activist—thousands of people in the United States, Canada, and around the world have and will continue to support me to expose the injustices which have occurred in this courtroom. I do feel pity for your people that they must live under such an ugly system. Under your system, you are taught greed, racism, and corruption—and most serious of all, the destruction of Mother Earth. Under the Native American system, we are taught all people are brothers and sisters, to share the wealth with the poor and needy. But the most important of all is to respect and preserve the Earth, who we consider to be our Mother. We feed from her breast; our Mother gives us life from birth and when it's time to leave this world, who again takes us back into her womb. But the main thing we are taught is to preserve her for our children and our grandchildren, because they are the next who will live upon her.

"I stand before you as a proud man; I feel no guilt! . . . I have no regrets of being a Native American activist . . ."

No, I'm not the guilty one here; I'm not the one who should be called a criminal—white racist America is the criminal for the destruction of our lands and my people; to hide your guilt from the decent human beings in America and around the world, you will sentence me to two consecutive life terms without any hesitation.

Sixth, there are less than 400 federal judges for a population of over 200 million Americans. Therefore, you have a very powerful and important responsibility which should be carried out impartially. But you have never been impartial where I was concerned. You have the responsibility of protecting the constitutional rights and laws, but where I was concerned, you neglected to even consider mine, or Native Americans', constitutional rights. But, the most important of all—you neglected our human rights.

If you were impartial, you would have had an open mind on all the factual disputes in this case. But, you were unwilling to allow even the slightest possibility that a law enforcement officer would lie on the stand. Then, how could you possibly be impartial enough to let my lawyers prove how important it is to the FBI to convict a Native American activist in this case? You do not have the ability to see that such a conviction is an important part of the efforts to discredit those who are trying to alert their brothers and sisters to the new threat from the white man, and the attempt to destroy what little Indian land remains in the process of extracting our uranium, oil, and other minerals. Again, to cover up your part in this, you will call me a heartless, cold-blooded murderer who deserves two life sentences consecutively.

Seventh, I cannot expect a judge who has openly tolerated the conditions I have been jailed under to make an impartial decision on whether I should be sentenced to concurrent or consecutive life terms. You have been made aware of the following conditions which I had to endure at the Grand Forks County Jail, since the time of the verdict:

(1) I was denied access to a phone to call my attorneys concerning my appeal;

(2) I was locked in solitary confinement without shower facilities, soap, towels, sheets or pillow;

(3) the food was inedible, what little there was of it;

(4) my family—brothers, sisters, mother and father—who travelled long distances from the reservation, were denied visitation.

No human being should be subjected to such treatment; and while you parade around pretending to be decent, impartial, and law-abiding, you knowingly allowed your fascist chief deputy marshal to play stormtrooper. Again, the only conclusion that comes to mind is that you know and always knew that you would sentence me to two consecutive life terms.

Finally, I honestly believe that you made up your mind long ago that I was guilty and that you were going to sentence me to the maximum sentence permitted under the law. But this does not surprise me, because you are a high-ranking member of the white racist American establishment which has consistently said, "In God We Trust," while they went about the business of murdering my people and attempting to destroy our culture.

Peltier's trial and conviction attracted worldwide attention and generated support among millions of sympathizers; the human-rights organization Amnesty International considers him a political prisoner and has called for clemency. Since 1977 he has launched numerous appeals, basing his request for a new trial on claims that government prosecutors suppressed and falsified evidence and relied on "witnesses" who really were not present or whose testimony was coerced. Despite the fact that newly-uncovered evidence (including the confession of a man known only as Mr. X who insists he shot the agents in self-defense) does indeed cast doubt on Peltier's involvement in the Pine Ridge shootout, he has been repeatedly denied a new trial.

SOURCES

Books

Blanche, Jerry, editor, *Native American Reader: Stories, Speeches and Poems,* Denali Press, 1990.

Matthiessen, Peter, *In the Spirit of Crazy Horse,* Viking, 1983, new edition, 1991.

Periodicals

Esquire, "The Trials of Leonard Peltier," January, 1992, pp. 55-57.

Nation, "Free Peltier!" July 18, 1994, pp. 76-77.

People, "A Question of Justice," May 4, 1992, pp. 36-39.

Other

Incident at Oglala: The Leonard Peltier Story (documentary film), Carolco International, 1992.

Thunderheart (film), 1992.

Federico Peña

1947–

Mexican American attorney, politician, and U.S. government official

In January 1993, Federico Peña joined President Bill Clinton's cabinet as Secretary of Transportation. Established in the mid-1960s, the Department of Transportation (DOT) coordinates and administers federal transportation policy. As head of the department, Peña oversees highway planning and construction, urban mass transit, railroads, aviation, oil and gas pipelines, and the waterways of the United States. The DOT is also responsible for ensuring the safety of these various forms of transportation through agencies such as the Federal Aviation Administration (FAA), the National Highway Traffic Safety Administration (NHTSA), and the U.S. Coast Guard.

A native of Laredo, Texas, Peña is a member of a family whose roots in the state go back some two hundred years. His father earned a good living as a broker for a cotton manufacturer, enabling the six Peña children to enjoy a comfortable existence growing up in the city of Brownsville. After graduating with honors from high school, Federico—or Fred, as he was known to his peers—attended the University of Texas at Austin, from which he received his bachelor's degree in 1969. He then went on to the University of Texas School of Law and received his law degree in 1972.

Later that same year, Peña moved to Denver, Colorado, home of his older brother, Alfredo, who was also a lawyer; in 1973, they formed their own partnership. During this same period, Federico also became involved in issues of particular interest to the Hispanic community through other positions he held, including staff attorney for the Mexican American Legal Defense and Educational Fund (MALDEF) and legal advisor to the Chicano Education Project.

Peña's first foray into politics was in 1978, when he ran for and won a seat in the Colorado House of Representatives. There he served with distinction for two terms, garnering praise from the Colorado Social Action Committee as outstanding Democratic freshman during his first term and winning election to the minority speaker's post during his second term.

In 1982, Peña decided not to pursue a third term in the legislature so that he would be free to take on a new challenge: running for mayor of Denver. Observers *initially wrote off his candidacy, which pitted him against a fourteen-year incumbent in a city without a large Hispanic voting bloc to turn to for support. (At the time, only about eighteen percent of Denver's population identified themselves as Hispanic.) But Peña successfully appealed to a wide variety of people, fashioning a coalition that included not only Hispanics but also blacks and Asian Americans as well as labor groups, environmentalists, feminists, gays, and young white professionals. Thanks to a team of several thousand volunteers who conducted massive voter registration drives on his behalf and a campaign that stressed an exciting new future for Denver under his leadership, he came out on top in both the primary election in May 1983, and in the regular election a month later.*

Not long after Peña first took office, he was forced to reevaluate his ambitious plans for the city when a sharp downturn in the oil, mining, and high-technology industries wreaked havoc with Denver's economy. Unemployment soared, real estate prices took a nosedive, and the thirty-one-percent vacancy rate in downtown office buildings was the highest in the nation. By the time the 1987 election rolled around, Peña's popularity had taken a beating, too, and he was not expected to win. But in the last month or so of the campaign, he slowly managed to edge up in the polls when he adopted a harder line against his opponent. On election day, he emerged victorious with fifty-one percent of the vote.

Peña's second term got off to a shaky start when Denver was hit with a blizzard and ice storm in December 1987, that crippled the city. With some streets still difficult and dangerous to maneuver well into February 1988, some outraged residents launched a recall effort that fell just a couple of thousand signatures short of the total needed to force a special election.

In time, however, Peña was able to make some headway with his plans to turn Denver into a "world-class" hub for commerce and trade. Over the course of a few years, he secured approval for and supervised the construction of a new convention center (this after the public had overwhelmingly rejected a similar initiative during his first term); improved local parks and recreation areas; attracted a new major league baseball franchise, the Colorado Rockies; obtained funding to build and repair roads, bridges, libraries, and other public facilities; spruced up aging neighborhoods; and significantly reduced air pollution by actively promoting the use of alternative fuels.

Without a doubt Peña's biggest project was building the new airport he envisioned as one of the largest and most technologically innovative and efficient complexes of its kind in the entire world. He managed to win approval for it over the objections of many who thought it was too expensive, too fancy, and too far from downtown (eighteen miles) by assuring Coloradans that it was necessary "to create jobs, stimulate the local economy and meet future air transportation needs." But major problems surfaced during its construction (most notably with a computerized baggage-handling system that just didn't work), delaying its opening from late 1993 until early 1995 and more than tripling its original estimated cost.

Peña was not in office throughout much of the controversy, however; despite the fact that he had regained his popularity with the people of Denver and was at last comfortable in his role as mayor, he declined to run for re-election in 1991 in order to spend more time with his growing family (he has two young daughters) and earn a higher income than was possible as a public servant. He then founded Peña Investment Advisors, a corporate pension fund investment company, and served as counsel to a major local law firm. He also was a member of a state commission that formulated a long-term transportation plan for Colorado.

In 1992, however, public life beckoned once again. A diligent campaigner for Bill Clinton in that year's presidential election, Peña was subsequently named to head the president-elect's transition team for transportation issues. While he had told friends that he did not want a job with the new administration, he accepted Clinton's offer to stay on after the transition period as Secretary of Transportation to help fulfill the president's goal of repairing and rebuilding the country's troubled infrastructure, from its crumbling highway bridges to its airline companies on the brink of bankruptcy. Peña made it through his confirmation hearings with no trouble and was sworn into office in January 1993.

On July 15, 1993, Peña appeared before an audience at the National Press Club in Washington, D.C., to discuss his plans for the nation as a member of the Clinton cabinet. His remarks are reprinted here from a copy of his speech furnished by the Office of the Secretary for Public Affairs of the U.S. Department of Transportation.

I'd like to thank Clayton Boyce very much for that kind introduction. I am delighted to be here with all of you to talk about my priorities and the role that the Department of Transportation plays in President Clinton's goals for our country.

Interestingly, there are two current events that underscore for me the crucial role that transportation plays in our economy and in people's lives.

The first is the flood now devastating the Midwest—disrupting trucking, railroads, and river traffic. We have been engaged in helping right from the beginning. I have surveyed 300 miles of the Mississippi River and remain in close touch with the affected industries and states and the Federal Emergency Management Agency. Our Coast Guard's rescue and relief missions have saved dozens of lives and all elements of the Department are poised to get the Midwest's transportation system up and running as soon as possible.

I think we can all see how the severing of transportation systems through the spine of our country threatens industrial production, affects food prices and disrupts lives. The just-in-time delivery systems that many factories now use, for example, are far more efficient, yet far more fragile, more dependent on a national transportation system that actually works.

But even as the rivers overflow their banks, we are also seeing the great strengths of our transportation system. There are miracles of improvisation as shippers adapt to the worst flood in centuries, and the system is coping through most of the region. There are a lot of unsung heroes on those roads and rails and rivers.

To me, this underscores our need to remove transportation bottlenecks and make even more and better intermodal connections between our highways, our ports, our rail and air traffic networks so that they reinforce each other in ordinary commerce as well as in emergencies.

There's another event, beginning today, with major implications for our transportation system and for our nation. I'm referring, of course, to the budget reconciliation talks in Congress. The stakes are very, very high.

Many will naturally focus on the details and the political disputes. But I trust we won't get so bogged down in these details as to miss the essential story—that after a decade of drift and neglect we finally have a president who is actually grappling with our deficit, a president committed to getting this economy moving, creating jobs and making America more globally competitive.

The plan President Clinton proposes will be the largest deficit reduction in our history—$500 billion in reductions. It is a fair plan, placing the bulk of the burden on those most able to pay—wealthy Americans—and raising millions of working people out of poverty. It will protect older Americans from the huge cuts in Social Security, Medicare, and Veterans' benefits that the Republicans have proposed. It will create millions of jobs through tax incentives, investments, and the lower interest rates we're seeing that only a credible deficit reduction plan can guarantee.

Finally, our nation has a president who's willing to take responsibility and to take the heat. And as we saw in Tokyo, the whole world is watching and hoping that America has the courage to change.

I am very, very proud to be a member of President Clinton's cabinet. We share the same philosophy of government and the same vision of why investment in transportation is central to our people's future. And much of the investment we need depends on passing the president's budget. That's obviously one reason why I support it. Another is that I understand—in my bones—what the president is trying to do.

I recall that back in 1983, when I was elected mayor of Denver, our economic boom had peaked and we were slipping into deep recession. After a long-running boom based on high oil prices, real estate development, and a flood of foreign investment, the bottom just fell out. Our unemployment rate soared to two percent above the national average; office vacancies hit thirty-one percent; foreclosures were skyrocketing. So were bankruptcies. Property values started to plummet. Our economy essentially imploded. Public morale was at rock bottom. The only thing Denver was "Number 1" in was in air pollution—sixty-five "bad air days" a year.

Much of this was the legacy of a philosophy that had been content to ride the oil boom, failing to invest in needed infrastructure like our roads and bridges. My predecessors practiced the kind of "don't-worry-be-happy" politics that were so popular in the 1980s. Those same political forces from the national level also cost Denver millions of federal dollars for housing, community development and other urban programs just as I was taking office. I found myself in a position like a famous French general in the First World War, who said: "My right is collapsing, my center will not hold.... Situation excellent.... We attack!"

And that's just what we did. We were forced to both cut spending and raise taxes in the teeth of the recession. Believe me, I learned a lot about bad poll numbers—fast.

But we also embarked on a whole series of investments in Denver's future. We invested in neighborhoods and small businesses; we set out to build a new convention center and a new multibillion dollar airport, both in partnership with the private sector. We passed two large new bond issues that I proposed and that the people of Denver supported, to pay for viaducts, bridges, roads, new parks and a new library.

Federico Peña

We did it at a time when our people were suffering. They were scared. And we did it in the face of skepticism from some in Denver who were simply afraid of change. Others just didn't believe anymore that government could do anything right, let alone get the city's economy moving again. Our critics could always cite some reason why we shouldn't act: "We can't afford it.... We'll never finish all the jobs we set out to do." These were those who preferred gridlock and the status quo to taking action and bring change.

Now, does that sound familiar?

I know you might be amazed to hear that we even ran into some doubts and criticism from members of the press!

But we brought that convention center in on time and on budget. Our new airport will open this winter. People are moving back into central Denver. Office vacancies are down to twenty percent and falling; Denver's unemployment rate is now below the national average. There are more and better jobs to be had, and the number of bad air days is down from sixty-five a year to six. And most importantly, people feel more hopeful and upbeat about their city. Maybe that's why our Colorado Rockies are setting the all-time attendance record for major league baseball this year.

I just want to make two things clear to you.

The first is that investments in our people, our transportation system and our infrastructure were all crucial to Denver's turnaround.

The second is that I am not running again for mayor. I love the job I have right now.

I believe—and I know President Clinton does, too—that if we have a clear vision of the future, a willingness to make partnerships and the courage to confront tough issues (even if that's not immediately popular), we can overcome and succeed beyond our fondest hopes.

Right from the beginning, President Clinton has stressed the central role that transportation and infrastructure investment can play in stimulating lasting growth, creating jobs, and reviving our national spirit. Investing in our people requires investing in transportation, because nothing touches all of our daily lives more or has a greater impact on our economy. The health of America's economy in the future depends on our making the right strategic investments now in partnership with state and local governments and the private sector—what I call "public-private-public" partnerships. If we invest wisely, we can spur the development of new technologies, even whole new industries, and contribute to a cleaner American environment at the same time.

My goals for DOT are straightforward.

First, our highest priority—this whole administration's first target—is to get our economy moving and create jobs, both immediately and in the long term, by making strategic transportation investments.

Second, these investments should be made in ways that will help clean up and even beautify our environment.

Third, we must integrate all modes of transportation into a seamless system for moving goods and people from coast to coast and within metropolitan communities.

Fourth, we must develop and apply new technologies that will create whole new industries.

And, fifth, we must ensure that all of our investments improve daily life by making travel safer, more convenient and more "human."

This is a vision that goes far beyond the traditional bricks-and-mortar image of the Department of Transportation.

In the brief time that we have today, I would like to focus only on two of these five goals: the application of new technologies and the "humanization" of transportation.

We are already in the midst of a revolution in transportation technologies that will transform our economy and our daily lives as much as the arrival of railroading and commercial aviation did. I can foresee American companies leading the world in a range of transportation technologies, and exporting super-sophisticated air traffic control systems, non-polluting vehicles, high-tech safety devices and components ranging from ceramic engine blocks to bridging systems made from composite fibers. The truth is—and most Americans are unaware of this—the early stages of this revolution are already underway. I've seen and touched and taken test drives on some of these new wonders as I've traveled around the country.

Let me cite just a few examples.

We are already beginning to use the Global Positioning System based on satellites in space to track trains and trucks here on earth and guide ships and airplanes more accurately and safely than ever before.

> *"Investing in our people requires investing in transportation, because nothing touches all of our daily lives more or has a greater impact on our economy."*

Texas Instruments in Dallas is developing infrared vision devices—used by our military in Desert Storm—to enhance safety on our roads at night.

The first of a new generation of computerized collection devices are being used now in Oklahoma to eliminate toll booth delays.

We are well advanced on research into "intelligent" highway systems that will speed traffic flows and enhance safety. In Oakland County, Michigan, I've seen "intelligent" traffic lights that adjust to actual traffic flows and speed commuters to work while reducing pollution at the same time.

The Department of Transportation is now part of the Technology Reinvestment Project led by ARPA which will provide over $500 million in assistance to companies promoting dual-use technologies. I sought full DOT participation in this effort precisely because of the great potential for using technologies developed for defense in the transportation arena. It's only a small stretch of the imagination, for example, to conceive new composite materials like those used for the Stealth bomber being applied to coming generations of vehicles and even bridges. In fact, there is a company in California now working on a "Stealth bus."

The Department of Transportation is also leading the administration's push for a $1.3 billion investment in new high-speed rail corridors and technical research, including the design of a world-class, American prototype of a magnetic levitation train. We hope to "leverage" this initial federal stake to a total investment of over $2.5 billion by encouraging partnerships with cities, states, and private industries. Together, we will develop new high-speed rail corridors far beyond Amtrak's Northeast Corridor. In the longer term, we envisage growth of a new U.S. industry based on manufacturing and maintaining high-speed rail systems. Our nation, which builds the world's most advanced planes, can also build the fastest trains.

Or the best subway cars, for that matter. We are exploring the coordination of equipment purchases by local transit authorities across the United States so that we can achieve the economies of scale that would permit American manufacturers to compete with foreign suppliers for transit car contracts.

And we are forging an R & D partnership with Detroit for a new generation of safe, nonpolluting automobiles.

All of these technologies are real. They're being deployed now, and they will be the seedbeds for new American industries, employing American workers, earning American wages.

New as they are, I believe these technologies are crucial to reviving an old American tradition—winning. We are determined not to repeat the mistakes of the past. We will not fail again to support the creative genius of our nation and forfeit technological advances to other nations.

As we Americans ride the exciting X-2000 tilt train from Sweden or the Talgo from Spain, let's remember that this technology was invented by Americans who sold their patents to the Europeans. As we focus on a Mag-Lev prototype system for America, let's recall that this technology was invented by Americans—and tested in Pueblo, Colorado, over fifteen years ago—but we lost it to Japan and Germany because our government could not afford to support it.

I am committed to forming partnerships with U.S. scientists, U.S. engineers, and U.S. companies to develop and manufacture the new transportation technologies of the next century.

But as exciting as these technologies are, as promising for our economy's future, they must also meet another standard—humanizing our transport system and improving peoples' daily lives. We have to remember *why* we're investing in new technologies. We must remember who we serve and what values we believe in. We need to see transportation as more than the engine of economic growth and technology, but as an integral part of all our policy goals—even welfare and health-care reform and urban redevelopment.

When my good friend Henry Cisneros spoke to you in April he suggested that one reason that "our cities are smoldering" is sheer isolation. Clearly, gaps in transportation have a lot to do with that.

Let me suggest to you, for example, that we won't succeed in putting any real "power" in any new "empowerment zone" unless we see that workers can get to work there and back home and that raw materials and finished goods can get in and out efficiently. Nor will we succeed in moving people off of welfare unless we ensure that single parents can get their kids to day-care centers on the way to work without having to take three different buses. When inner-city residents have to travel miles to shop at major supermarkets, when they cannot easily get to health clinics, then they are trapped in ways few of us can even imagine.

If we're serious about a new national health system that works, we're also going to need to find ways to bring rural people (like the senior citizens I met in Montana this spring) to health clinics. That's the only way they can get preventive care instead of being forced to turn to expensive emergency rooms for help.

Speaking of health care, how can we ignore the human agony and sheer cost of highway crashes—the fourth-leading cause of death in our country? We lost more than 39,000 lives on our highways last year. There were 300,000 hospitalizations, more than 3 million injuries in all. The total cost to our society was over $137 billion—two percent of our gross national product.

Thanks to safer vehicles, seat belts, air bags, tougher drunk driving laws and other measures, those casualties were the lowest in recent decades. So we have made progress. But can anybody doubt that to build an effective health care system we must do much, much better?

Let me assure you. We will never let up on safety in any of our transportation systems. Our roads, our airways are the safest in the world, but we will make them safer. Too many precious lives are at stake.

Another part of "humanizing" transportation is simply taking account of the views of the people most effected by the decisions that we make. I was delighted earlier this week to meet with a coalition of community groups in Boston who are supporting the Central Artery/Harbor Tunnel project there. They're backing it because it will reunite the historic heart of that great city with beautiful new parks and walkways. But they're also backing it because they have had a say in designing it—their voices are being heard.

We are long past the day when "experts" or "technocrats" can devise transportation projects and ram them through neighborhoods without peoples' consent. We need to weigh human needs for convenience, for quiet, for clean air, even for beauty, in all our transportation decisions. And we will. Those are just a few examples of why we need to blend human needs with the technological revolution that's underway in transportation.

Today, our country needs the vision and determination to take bold steps, some of which won't show payoffs until the next century. We must rekindle the American entrepreneurial zeal to take risks, even to make mistakes. We need what Franklin Roosevelt called "a bold spirit of experimentation."

President Clinton has challenged Americans to "make change our friend." I am up for that challenge.

To be sure, there will always be doubters and naysayers. There will be some who are simply too scared of change. And the worst of it is, they won't all be Republicans!

But we must begin. We will win people over the only way we can—not only with beautiful visions, but with tangible, step-by-step progress. The place to start is with the passage of the first—and the only—deficit-cutting, job-creating budget in nearly a generation.

We can and will revive America's can-do spirit. And we will build a transportation system that will enhance Americans' safety and prosperity as we carry on the pursuit of happiness.

Thank you all very much.

Since taking office, Peña has faced a number of crises and controversies. In October 1994, he caused a stir when—for the first time in history—he overruled a National Highway Traffic Safety Administration (NHTSA) recommendation not to recall as many as six million General Motors (GM) pickup trucks some consumer advocates had charged with a tendency to burst into flames following side-impact collisions. Because the NHTSA's findings suggested that the overall risk of death in a pickup crash was no greater in GM models than in those manufactured by Ford or Chrysler, critics charged that Peña's decision had more to do with politics than science.

Airline troubles have taken up much of his time as well. He has been forced to defend the rights of American carriers at airports overseas and find ways to help companies on shaky financial ground to secure tax relief and loan guarantees to head off foreign investors. Airline safety—particularly that of planes belonging to regional commuter lines—also loomed large in 1994, the worst year for deaths in U.S. air crashes since 1988. In response to the disturbing increase, Peña called for a safety audit of the nation's airlines and declared a "zero accident" goal. His boldest move, however, was to propose privatizing the Federal Aviation Administration's air traffic control operation in an effort to improve efficiency and reduce costs.

Another problem Peña has had to deal with is a shrinking budget. In February 1995, he submitted a plan that would cut his department's workforce in half and slash billions of dollars in spending from highway, rail, and aviation programs. His aim, he declared, was to "build bridges, not bureaucracy, and move people, not paper."

SOURCES

Detroit News, "GM Loses Plea on Pickup Trucks," November 16, 1994, p. 1C; "Peña Offers Restructuring Plan," February 3, 1995, p. 5A.

Hispanic, "Federico Peña: Quick Study," June, 1993, pp. 16-21.

Nation's Cities Weekly, "Secretary Peña Promises to Bring 'New Perspective' to DOT Role," March 15, 1993, p. 6.

New Republic, "Cabinet Losers," February 28, 1994, pp. 22-29.

Newsweek, "Forget About the Experts," October 31, 1994, p. 42; "How Safe Is This Flight?" April 24, 1995, pp. 18-29.

U.S. News and World Report, "A Taj Mahal in the Rockies," February 13, 1995, pp. 48-53.

P.B.S. Pinchback

1837–1921

African American politician and businessman

One of the best-known black political leaders of the Reconstruction period was Pinckney Benton Stewart Pinchback, who also had the distinction of serving (albeit briefly and under unusual circumstances) as the nation's first African American governor. He spent most of his adult life fighting for civil and political rights for blacks, especially the right to vote. Eventually, the increasingly hostile and repressive atmosphere African Americans faced in the waning years of the nineteenth century led him down another path, namely the one proposed by Booker T. Washington and his accommodationist philosophy. Yet Pinchback's legacy remains that of a man who did not hesitate to stand up for the rights he felt blacks deserved.

P.B.S. Pinchback was the free-born son of a white Mississippi planter, William Pinchback, and a former slave of African, Native American, and white ancestry named Eliza Stewart. (William Pinchback had taken Stewart to Philadelphia and freed her shortly before their son—the eighth of their ten children—was born, probably near Macon, Georgia.) When he was about ten, young Pinckney was sent north to attend school in Cincinnati, Ohio. But the death of his father in 1848 left the family in dire financial straits and threatened with reenslavement by their white relatives. So his mother and siblings joined him in Cincinnati, and he went to work, first as a cabin boy on canal boats in Ohio and later as a steward on Mississippi riverboats.

During the Civil War, Pinchback volunteered to serve with the Union Army and was assigned to recruit other African Americans. However, he soon quit in protest over the discrimination faced by both black officers (he himself was a captain) and regular soldiers. It was around this same time that he began speaking out on the subject of political rights for blacks, insisting that they should not be drafted unless they also had the right to vote.

After the war, Pinchback helped establish the Louisiana Republican party and served as one of its key organizers. In 1867, he also participated in the state constitutional convention. In that forum he urged his fellow delegates to approve universal suffrage, civil rights for all, and free tax-supported schools. The following year, he was elected to the state Senate, where he introduced legislation banning discrimination in public accommodations. Three years later, by virtue of the fact that he had recently been voted president pro tempore *of the state Senate, Pinchback moved into the lieutenant governor's position upon the death of Oscar Dunn, a fellow black legislator who had held the post since 1868. This in turn led to Pinchback's brief stint (December 9, 1872, through January 13, 1873) as acting governor of Louisiana after the white governor was impeached.*

It was during this period of upheaval in Louisiana politics that the state legislature named Pinchback congressman-at-large and also elected him to a six-year term in the U.S. Senate. As was so often the case at that time with black elected officials, however, both elections were contested. The battle went on for several years before Pinchback's white opponents were finally seated.

By this time, Louisiana had a new Democratic governor, and Republicans—especially black Republicans—were becoming discouraged about the future of African Americans in the South. Pinchback himself, alarmed by the course of events, began to believe that some type of accommodation with white Southerners was essential if blacks were to survive. Yet he remained adamant on the subject of voting rights, as evidenced by the following address. Delivered in Indianapolis, Indiana, during the presidential campaign of 1880, Pinchback's speech condemned the intimidation of African American voters in the South and warned of dire consequences to the entire nation if such practices were not stopped. His remarks are reprinted from Masterpieces of Negro Eloquence *(Bookery Publishing Co., 1914; reprinted, Johnson Reprint, 1970).*

Mr. President and Fellow Citizens:

The founders of the Republican party were aggressive men. They believed in the Declaration of Independence and the great truths it contains; and their purpose was to make these truths living realities. Possessing the courage of their convictions and regarding slavery as the archenemy of the Republic—the greatest obstruction to its maintenance, advancement and prosperity—they proclaimed an eternal war against it and, marshalling their forces under the banner of freedom and equality before the law for all men, boldly and defiantly met the enemy at every point and fairly routed it all along the line. Those men believed in and relied upon the conscience of the people. To touch and arouse public conscience and to convince it of the justice of their cause, they felt was all that was necessary to enlist the people on their side. Ridiculed, threatened, ostracized, and assaulted, they could not be turned from their purpose, and their achievements constitute the grandeur and glory of the Republican party. There were no apologists for wrongdoers among those men, and there ought to be none in the Republican party today. The South was the great disturbing element then as it is now; and the causes which rendered it so are, in a large measure, the same. The people were divided into three classes—slaveholders, slaves, and poor whites, or "poor white trash" as the latter were called by the colored people because of their utter insignificance in that community. Its peculiar condition established in the large land and slaveowning portion of the people a sort of privileged class who claimed and exercised the right not only to rule the South, but the nation; and for many years that class controlled both. Gorged with wealth and drunk with power, considering themselves born to command and govern, being undisputed rulers, almost by inheritance in their states, the Southern politicians naturally became aggressive, dictatorial, and determined to ruin the country and sever the Union rather than consent to relinquish power, even though called upon to do so by constituted methods. Hence it was that, when the people of the great North and Northwest concluded to assert their rights and choose a man from among themselves for president, they rebelled and forced upon the country so far as they were concerned, the most causeless and unnatural war recorded in history.

I shall not dwell upon the history of the war or attempt to detail its horrors and sum up its cost. I leave that task to others. If the wounds made by it have been healed, which I do not concede, far be it from my purpose to reopen

P.B.S. Pinchback

them. My sole reason for referring to the war at all is to remind the Northern people of some of the agencies employed in its successful prosecution. When it commenced, the principal labor element of the South—the source of its production and wealth—was the colored race. Four millions and a half of these unfortunate people were there, slaves and property of the men who refused to submit to the will of the people lawfully expressed through the ballot box. They were the bone and sinew of the Confederacy, tilling its fields and producing sustenance for its armies, while many of the best men of the North were compelled to abandon Northern fields to shoulder a musket in defense of the Union. As a war measure and to deprive the South of such a great advantage, your president, the immortal Lincoln, issued a proclamation in September, 1862, in which he gave public notice that it was his purpose to declare the emancipation of the slaves in the States wherein insurrection existed on January 1, 1863, unless the offenders therein lay down their arms. That notice, thank God, was disregarded, and the proclamation of January 1, 1863, proclaiming universal emancipation followed. Had the requirements of the first proclamation been observed by the people to whom it was addressed who can doubt what would have been the fate of the colored people in the South? It is reasonable to assume, inasmuch as the war was waged to perpetuate the Union and not to destroy slavery—that they would have remained in hopeless bondage. On more than one occasion President Lincoln officially declared that he would save the Union with slavery if he could, and not until it became manifest that slavery was the mainstay of the Confederacy, and the prosecution of the war to a successful close would be difficult without its destruction, did he dare touch it. I do not think that President Lincoln's hesitancy to act upon the question arose from sympathy with the accursed institution, for I believe every pulsation of his heart was honest and pure and that he was an ardent and devoted lover of universal liberty; but he doubted whether his own people would approve of his interference with it. Assured by the manner in which the people of the North received his first proclamation that they appreciated the necessity of destroying this great aid of the enemy, he went forward bravely declaring that, "possibly for every drop of blood drawn by the lash one might have to be drawn by the sword, but if so, as was said over eighteen hundred years ago, the judgments of the Lord are just and righteous altogether," and abolished human slavery from the land forever.

That this great act was a Godsend and an immeasurable blessing to the colored race, I admit, but I declare in the same breath that it was dictated and performed more in the interest of the white people of the North and to aid them in conquering the rebellion than from love of or a disposition to help the Negro. The enfranchisement of the colored race also sprang from the necessities of the nation. At the close of the war the Southern states had to be rehabilitated with civil governments and readmitted into the Union. The men who had plunged the country into war and had tried to destroy the government were about to resume their civil and political rights, and, through the election of representatives and senators in Congress, regain influence and power in national councils. Apprehending danger from the enormous power they would possess if reinstated in absolute control of eleven states, some means had to be devised to prevent this. A political element, loyal to the Union and the flag, must be created; and again the ever faithful colored people were brought into requisition, and without their asking for it, the elective franchise was conferred upon them. There was no question about the loyalty of these people, and the supposition that they would be a valuable political force and form the basis of a loyal political party in the South was both natural and just, and the wisdom of their enfranchisement was demonstrated by the establishment of Republican governments in several of the states, and the sending of mixed delegations of Republican and Democratic members of Congress therefrom so long as the laws conferring citizenship upon the colored man were enforced.

If the South is to remain politically Democratic as it is today, it is not the fault of the colored people. Their fealty to the North and the Republican party is without parallel in the world's history. In Louisiana alone more than five thousand lives attest it. While in nearly every other Southern state fully as many lie in premature graves, martyrs to the cause. Considering themselves abandoned and left to the choice of extermination or the relinquishment of the exercise of their political rights, they have, in large districts in the South, wisely preferred the latter. Kept in a constant condition of suspense and dread by the peculiar methods of conducting canvasses and elections in that section, who can blame them? It is my firm conviction that no other people under God's sun, similarly situated, would have done half so well. The fault is attributable to the vicious practice, which obtains largely even here in the civilized North, of apologizing for and condoning crimes committed for political purposes. Men love power everywhere and Southern Democrats are no exception. On the contrary, deeming themselves "born to command," as I have already remarked, and knowing that there is no power to restrain or punish them for crimes committed upon the poor and defenseless colored citizens, of course they have pushed them to the wall. The inequality between the two races in all that constitutes protective forces was such as to render that result inevitable as soon as federal protection was withdrawn, and I do not hesitate to affirm that unless some means are devised to enforce respect for the rights of the colored citizens of the South, their enfranchisement will prove a curse instead of a benefit to the country. Emancipated to cripple the South and enfranchised to strengthen the North, the colored race was freed and its people made citizens in the interest of the Republic. Its fundamental law declares them citizens, and the Fifteenth Amendment expressly states that: "The right of citizens of the United States to vote shall not be denied or abridged by the United States or by any state on account of race, color, or previous condition of servitude." The faith and honor of the nation are pledged to the rigid enforcement of the law in this, as in every other respect, and the interests of the forty million white people in the Republic demand it. If the law, both constitutional and statutory, affecting the rights and privileges of the colored citizens can be defiantly ignored and disobeyed in eleven states of the Union in a matter of such grave import as this—a matter involving the very essence of republican government, i.e., the right of the majority to rule—who can tell where it will end and how long it will be before elections in all of the states will be armed conflicts, to be decided by the greatest prowess and dexterity in the use of the bowie knife, pistol, shotgun and rifle?

". . . unless some means are devised to enforce respect for the rights of the colored citizens of the South, their enfranchisement will prove a curse instead of a benefit to the country."

White men of the North, I tell you this practice of controlling elections in the South by force and fraud is contagious! It spreads with alarming rapidity and unless eradicated, will overtake and overwhelm you as it has your friends in the South. It showed its horrid head in Maine, and came very near wresting that state from a lawful majority. Employed in the South first to drive Republicans from a few counties, it has grown from "autumnal outbreaks" into an almost perpetual hurricane and, gathering force as it goes, has violently seized state after state, mastered the entire South, and is even now thundering at the gates of the national capital. Whether it shall capture it too, and spread its blighting influence all over the land, is the question you must answer at the polls in this election.

It was the intention of the great men who founded this Republic that it should be "A government of the people, for the people, and by the people"; that its citizens, from the highest to the lowest, should enjoy perfect equality before the law. To realize this idea the rule of the majority, to be ascertained through the processes provided by law, was wisely adopted, and the laws providing for and regulating elections are respected and obeyed in the Northern, Eastern, and Western states. The Democracy of the South alone seems privileged to set at defiance the organic as well as every statutory enactment, national and state, designed to secure this essential principle of free government. Those men must be taught that such an exceptional and unhealthy condition of things will not be tolerated; that the rights of citizens of every nationality are sacred in the eyes of the law, and their right to vote for whom they please and have their ballots honestly counted shall not be denied or abridged with impunity; that the faith of the nation is pledged to the defense and maintenance of these obligations, and it will keep its pledge at whatever cost may be found necessary.

Pinchback remained active in the Republican party for the rest of his life, holding several political appointments during the 1880s and 1890s. He was also a successful businessman with a share in a cotton brokerage and a shipping company that operated along the Mississippi River. In addition, he took up the study of law when he was in his late forties and was admitted to the bar but apparently never actually practiced. Pinchback spent his final years as an ally of Booker T. Washington and saw his own influence wane after the Tuskegee president's death in 1915.

SOURCES

Bennett, Lerone, Jr., *Black Power U.S.A.: The Human Side of Reconstruction, 1867-1877,* Johnson, 1967.

Christopher, Maurine, *America's Black Congressmen,* Crowell, 1971.

Dunbar, Alice Moore, editor, *Masterpieces of Negro Eloquence,* Bookery Publishing Company, 1914, reprinted, Johnson Reprint, 1970.

Foner, Philip S., editor, *The Voice of Black America: Major Speeches by Negroes in the United States, 1797-1971,* Simon & Schuster, 1972.

Haskins, James, *Pinckney Benton Stewart Pinchback: A Biography,* Macmillan, 1973.

Alvin F. Poussaint

1934–

African American psychiatrist and child-rearing expert

Harvard Medical School psychiatrist Dr. Alvin F. Poussaint is one of today's foremost experts on the family, particularly the black family. A passionate advocate for children, he has devoted his career to examining the ways American parents raise and nurture their offspring and the many forces—such as racism, poverty, violence, and even pop culture—that disrupt or undermine those efforts. In Poussaint's view, the entire nation must first acknowledge that children are one of its most valuable resources if it ever hopes to solve the current crisis. As he proclaims in his lectures as well as on his stationery, "raising a child is everybody's business."

Poussaint, the grandson of Haitian immigrants, was born and raised in New York City. A serious bout with rheumatic fever when he was nine prevented him from participating in the more boisterous activities of his seven siblings and their friends, so he filled the time during his long convalescence by reading and studying instead. He soon discovered that he had a special knack for mathematics and science. With a teacher's encouragement, he tried out for and was admitted to a program for gifted students at one of the city's public schools. After graduating in 1952, he went on to Columbia University and then to Cornell Medical College, where he was the only black in a class of nearly ninety. The prejudice Poussaint encountered there on a daily basis strongly influenced his decision to specialize in psychiatry with an emphasis on the emotional effects of racism.

Poussaint fulfilled his medical internship and residency requirements at the University of California at Los Angeles (UCLA) during the early 1960s, first at the Center for Health Sciences and later at the Neuropsychiatric Institute. He then worked briefly in the South for the Student Nonviolent Coordinating Committee (SNCC) providing medical care to civil rights workers. In 1966, he returned to the northeast as assistant professor of psychiatry at Tufts University in Massachusetts. Three years later, he joined the faculty of Harvard Medical School as associate professor of psychiatry; he remains there today as clinical professor of psychiatry and associate dean for student affairs. In addition, he maintains a private psychiatric practice at a center affiliated with Children's Hospital in Boston.

During his early years at Harvard, Poussaint developed an "aggression-

rage" theory to explain what he saw as a basic difference between the white psyche and the black psyche. In his view, blacks and whites experience life in different ways and therefore do not suffer the same kinds of emotional illnesses. He rejected the commonly-held belief that racial self-hatred is at the root of most of the psychological and social problems in the black community, maintaining instead that repressed rage stemming from years of having been robbed of all sense of self respect was to blame. (Nowadays, he feels that economic and social frustration have compounded the effects of racial oppression.) According to Poussaint, while blacks may find release for this rage in positive actions, they often express it in negative ways such as underachievement in school or at work, alcohol and drug abuse, or unwed parenthood.

It was his conviction that black parents need to learn how to instill their children with self-esteem from the very beginning *to counteract these destructive forces that eventually led Poussaint to focus on child-rearing techniques. He has written extensively on the subject for both professional and popular publications and in 1975 co-authored the book* Black Child Care, *a revised version of which came out in 1992 under the title* Raising Black Children.

His name and his ideas gained even wider exposure during the 1980s when he served as a consultant to one of television's most popular series, "The Cosby Show." While some (including a number of blacks) criticized its portrait of an upper-middle-class African American family as idealistic and unreal, Poussaint insists that it did indeed represent one aspect of black "reality"—just not the stereotypical version most television viewers were accustomed to seeing in shows such as "Good Times" or "The Jeffersons."

Partially as a result of his connection to "The Cosby Show," Poussaint is much in demand as a speaker and social critic on topics ranging from the influence of rap music to black-on-black violence. Yet his primary concern is still how parents—especially black parents—should raise their children to survive and thrive in a difficult world. On October 29, 1987, he shared his thoughts on that topic with a group of students and educators at the University of Michigan School of Social Work. The following speech was provided by Poussaint.

Thank you for inviting me to the University of Michigan, known to many as the Yale of the Midwest; and thanks also to the Fauri family for this lecture which makes it possible for people like myself to come to the University to talk about issues of child welfare.

This will not be a heavy or scholarly talk, but I want to discuss with you some ideas about Black children and the institutional process—the things that affect them and things that have become fixed in our culture without our really recognizing or understanding how they have come to have such a strong effect upon us. One of the most difficult things I do, in reviewing scripts for television shows, is to deal with some of the irrational and untrue assumptions of our society. Sometimes people are not really being racist; they are just not able to understand our (Black) cultural context because they have been so conditioned to see things in one particular way.

I think that it will become apparent how this process works if we start by considering Native Americans. We condition all American children in their earliest youth to look down on Native Americans; this is deeply implanted in our history and our culture. If you do not believe me, go to any preschool and ask the three- and four-year-olds what they know about Indians. You will see how very effective the conditioning process is in laying the groundwork for bigotry in American children.

When children are very young, one of the first acting-out games they play is "Cowboys and Indians"; they do not play Irish, or Italian, or Negro—they play Indian. And "playing Indian" involves jumping up and down and acting in what kids imagine is savage or "wild Indian" behavior. Then, they go to nursery school where they learn to sing, "One little, two little, three little Indians." If those kids came home singing, "One little, two little, three little Italians," or "One little, two little, three little Jews," you would think their teacher was crazy! You would know something was very wrong, and you would certainly question why children were being taught such songs. But, we accept it with Native Americans.

Then, the kids go on to elementary school and we teach them that the Indians sold Manhattan Island to the colonists for beads and trinkets worth $24—so the kids conclude, as they are intended to, that Indians were stupid and childish. No wonder, then, that these children, particularly white children, develop negative attitudes and view people of color as inferior to themselves. Even Black kids will develop these attitudes. And, these prejudices are easily transferred to other minority populations.

Do you know that the Declaration of Independence refers to "merciless Indian savages"? What do you do about slanders like that? Should Native Americans demand a rewriting of the United States Declaration of Independence? Or accept forevermore such stereotypes as part of the basic nature of this country? What does it mean to the Native American population if we accept that, and what does it say about this country? How do you suppose, for example, that Indians feel about our celebration of Columbus Day and the explorers' "discovery" of America?

This kind of thing escalates rapidly. It starts out as nursery songs and works itself right into what we think of as academic science. There is a question on the Wechsler IQ Test asking who discovered America. Until recently, when Native American children answered that their people were here first, they were marked down for a wrong answer. Now, we are more enlightened and the examiner is supposed to ask, "Yes, but who came across the ocean to discover America?" The question is racist in wording and concept, and it should be eliminated. But, it remains because Indians do not have enough power to fight against institutionalized racism.

Two years ago I picked up a copy of the *New York Times* with a headline, "Uncle Sam Indian Giver." I called someone I know who is influential at the *New York Times*. I told him that the headline was the equivalent of saying "he works like a nigger" or "Jew them down." The term "Indian giver" is not only derogatory; it is a lie. It accuses the Indians of doing what the white man did—giving something and then taking it back. The United States government broke the treaties, not the Indians; but the term remains in our language as a slur against Native Americans. The editor I spoke to said he could not understand how that term had gotten past all his editors and into a headline. But, we know how it got past them all. It got past them because racism against Native Americans is so institutionalized that they do not even consider it derogatory—and if it is, they do not care. It tells you clearly how little we value the lives and feelings of Native Americans, doesn't it?

That kind of thinking is what racism is all about. Ultimately, as we institutionalize it, when we build it into the system, it is about genocide. That is when you begin to hear expressions like, "The only good Indian is a dead Indian." You may have heard, too, that "The only good nigger is a dead nigger," or "The only good Jew is a dead Jew," referring to any group which is judged to be inferior. It is no wonder that Native Americans are having such a terrible time surviving in this country. We put them on reservations, laid down laws for them, and told them what they could and could not do on their own land—bad land at that. With that kind of history of oppression and the history of Black slavery, we may never be able to really rid this country of racism, because the norms and definitions are so firmly established and the process is so firmly institutionalized.

Let me now move to an issue we are all familiar with, though perhaps we are unaware how deeply embedded it is in the culture and in our psyches. What would you answer if I were to ask you the definition of a Black person? Who defined Blackness, and by what criteria, and for what purpose? First of all, Black people did not create the definition—whites did. It is a definition that makes no scientific sense. It is anthropological nonsense and biological nonsense; it is absurd. Its sole purpose is to victimize and to oppress people, to perpetuate racism in the minds and hearts of all Americans for all time.

Here is how our society defines a Black person: if there is any known Black ancestry, you are Black. If you have ninety-nine percent white blood or white genes (whatever they are) and only one percent Black blood, you are Black. One drop of the stuff does it to you! Very strong stuff, that Black blood. Now, why is it that one percent of white blood does not make you white? Because the definition is set up to tell you every day you wake up that white is superior and that Black is inferior. That definition says that if you take white purity and dilute it with so much as a drop of Black impurity, you have "spoiled" the pure whiteness forever. It is a very effective way of perpetuating the notion of white supremacy; and, it is one that we accept, and live with. Even Black folks are going around policing people to catch the one with the taint of Blackness—and if you have the taint, you are considered inferior until you prove yourself otherwise.

When Vanessa Williams became Miss America, some people questioned how she could be "Black" and still have blonde hair and blue eyes. Well, by the white definition of Blackness, Vanessa Williams is Black, and she was raised Black by that definition. That seemed like a victory for Black people because, in spite of the taint of Blackness, it was possible for her to become Miss America. So, Blacks claimed her proudly; but, when she fell from grace, Blacks turned on her as fast as whites did.

No matter on what level you operate, and I am telling you that this is universal—you can be a student here or at Harvard, or a corporate vice-president—in your interactions with white people and in the white system, you will be treated as suspect until you have proved yourself over and over. This is a burden of stress and anxiety for Blacks, as for any oppressed group. In Nazi Germany they operated on the same principal to decide who should be persecuted and sent to a concentration camp—any amount of Jewish ancestry was enough to soil the purity of the Aryan race.

It applies to crosscultural discrimination as well: people with Afro-Asian blood are regarded as inferior to those with Eurasian blood. Ask the soldiers who served in Japan and Vietnam. Young people who are Asian-Black tend to identify more with Blacks than with Asians because there is so much pressure on them to do so. Their Black ancestry makes them Black, more than their Asian ancestry makes them Asian.

People with that taint feel pressure to represent the whole race all the time. Other people relate to you in the context of your being Black, and we Blacks do it as well. If someone looks white, we relate to him/her one way; if we find out he or she is really Black, we change our attitudes toward that person. Remember that during and after slavery, light-skinned Blacks were segregated along with darker ones. Though there was a social advantage to being lighter skinned, some of the psychology was the same.

So much for the ways we are affected by the definitions not of our own making. Suppose that, as a political exercise, we Blacks were to challenge the whole thing. We could convene a national conference here at the University of Michigan to reconsider the issue of racial definition. And, suppose we decided that anyone with one drop of white blood is white. From then on, we would all be white—because we have declared that to be true. It certainly makes as much sense as what they have been doing to us.

When psychologists say that they are doing studies comparing Black people with white people, they are not telling the truth. They cannot be studying the IQs of Black and white people because the definition is inaccurate. What they are doing is studying people with the taint in our culture and people without the taint, and making comparisons. What they are also studying are the psychological and socioeconomic effects of carrying that taint with us. Remember that most Black/white comparisons are intended to demoralize Blacks. Most of the time we lose, but the system is set up for us to lose. They will tell you that on SATs, Black students score much lower than whites. That is no surprise. More important, the comparison makes no sense and has no validity because it compares different socioeconomic groups. Whites in this society have had three to four hundred years to accumulate wealth and privilege, and now they are comparing whites and Blacks as simple racial categories. Thirty to thirty-five percent of the Black community right now is below the poverty line, and anyone who works with SATs can tell you that scores are strongly related to class. Leaving aside immigrant groups for a moment, what that means is that the richer you are, the better you will do on the SATs, with some exceptions. So, the comparisons are socioeconomic, not racial. But, these negative comparisons increase our self-doubts and negative self-image, eat away at our confidence. Even within the Black community, there is much diversity; and, family and other influences can affect our outlook, so we must be cautious about sweeping generalizations. But, it is too often true that when you lump everything together and make Black/white comparisons, Blacks are going to be the losers most of the time.

Black people are the victims of the genetic definitions accepted by our culture. They do not like it when whites say that Blacks have "natural rhythm"; but, when they are alone with other Blacks, they say, "Yeah, we got it!" Rhythm is not genetic: there are lots of Blacks who cannot dance, and lots of whites who can. But, the multirhythmic style of many Black dancers appears wild and savage to whites who do not realize how difficult it is to do that well. And, Blacks contribute to it by pretending that it "comes naturally."

Isiah Thomas got into trouble by correctly observing that when white basketball players do well, sports writers talk about how hard the players work and how intelligently they study the game; but, when Black players do well, they say it is natural and instinctive. A lot of coaches believe this—that is why some are over in Africa trying to recruit basketball players. We have to rid ourselves of these misconceptions. We need to realize that the environment and cultural surroundings determine that Blacks become good basketball players, but not because of any genetic proficiency.

Al Campanis appeared on "Nightline" and suggested to Ted Koppel and the television audience that racial genetics is one reason there are no Black managers in professional baseball. The inferior people are supposed to be good for the muscle work; the superior race is presumed to be suited for the head work, the executive functions. Campanis said we were fleet of foot; we fly through the air with the greatest of ease. He also said we could not float. You have heard that before—that Blacks do not swim because they cannot float. People who believe that are really blind. They choose not to see that Blacks might not swim because we were frequently barred from beaches and swimming pools—also, some do not want to get suntanned or get their hair wet! Once we get over those obstacles, we swim just fine.

Black kids are good at basketball because they practice it. The media and the community have taught them that sports can provide a way out of the ghetto—they are going to get rich and be able to buy their mothers a house. So, after school every day, they grab the basketball and practice for five hours because that is a sport that they can afford to play—they do not need a lot of expensive equipment. Go to any inner city, and you will find Black kids playing basketball, even at night in the dark; and, you know how good they will be when they turn on the lights. Any educator will tell you that practice and the will to succeed accounts for eighty percent of any student's success at anything. There is no question in my mind that if those Black kids came home and someone put science and math on their agenda for four or five hours a day, they would be good at science and math. Anyone who believes otherwise is falling into the genetic trap.

The next argument put forth is that achievement is mostly or partly innate in terms of what Blacks put on their agendas—what our priorities are. It is true that there are certain expectations, many of them associated with the heritage of racism. For example, even during slavery, we were allowed and expected to be entertainers; and, this image has been perpetuated, even when it is untrue, because whites liked the image. Blacks behaving like clowns and fools, the Stepin Fetchit or the Amos and Andy thing. But, that was what was allowed, and Blacks fell into it. Then, we got into sports because we were told we were good at that. Part of the problem is that we tend to believe what we are told about ourselves, if we are told it often enough.

"Black people are the victims of the genetic definitions accepted by our culture."

What, then, are we doing to help our Black children? There are all kinds of reasons for the problems our children are having. Some of it relates to environment, some to parents, some to schools and teachers, and some of it to the whole institutional system.

Among the biggest problems I think we are coping with, maybe even overshadowing racial problems, are the socioeconomic issues facing our families and our communities. We can blame ourselves, but that is part of the game, too. We, as a people, were freed from slavery only 120 years ago—and we started with nothing, we owned nothing. We were not truly out of bondage until the Voting Rights Law of 1965. Not having the vote perpetuated the segregated order of things where Blacks had access only to the most menial jobs. And, this whole country was involved in racism, not just the South. The United States Army was still segregated during World War II. That was not just the South—that was the whole country. We were freed from bondage twenty-three years ago, but we are still struggling to be free.

I mean this next statement symbolically: when they freed us from bondage, all the beachfront property was already taken. We may never get the beachfront property, and that is part of the frustration of what we hope to accomplish. There may always be certain things that we will never get, because they are already taken. There will always be relatively few of us who get to the top. Do you think there can ever be a Black General Motors? The days of creating that kind of power, that kind of empire, are "like history," as the kids say. It is reflected in the fact that the average net worth of a white family, including all the immigrants, is $39,000. The average Black family has a net worth—meaning all assets, things you can leave to your children—of $3,400. We are talking about some economic discrepancies that are going to be expressed in all kinds of ways.

The Black unmarried teenage birth rate is rising, and not just because young Black women are having more pregnancies. The reason it is going up, even as the overall rate goes down a bit, is that they are not getting married. They are not getting married because there is a very high rate of unemployment in Black communities, whether the economic cycle is on an upswing or a downturn. In 1985, about forty-six percent of the adult Black males were not in the work force. The last thing you want to do, if you do not have any money or a job or the prospects of a job, is to get married. There are reasons we can explore for the high rate of unemployment—having to do with the system, the changing economy, women in the work force—but, we must understand that the socioeconomic facts of life are critical in the raising of Black children.

"'Family' is just too narrow a concept to consider for our purposes. We need to think 'children' first . . ."

There is a constant stream of literature about child development, but most of the people exposed to these concepts are in the middle class. The new ideas have not reached the poor who are still using strategies and techniques that are no longer appropriate or effective in a society which has changed dramatically in the past thirty years. Whatever happened to the nuclear family? In the United States, as a whole, there are now about twenty-five percent single-parent households; in the Black community, the figure is fifty percent. That in itself is a great disadvantage. Not that the single parent (usually a single mother) is a bad parent, but that there is only one person there. Research has shown that the presence of a grandmother or other family member in the home improves the situation greatly. It does not have to be a father; it is the support of an extended family that matters.

The extended family has declined with the increase of individualism and personal mobility. Many social and psychological concepts are value-laden, and so we cling to them even when they have become dysfunctional. We pass along to our children the virtues of independence and self-reliance, going out on your own; but, in fact, people may be getting too individualistic. We should realize that these values are culturally determined, and we can determine anything that is useful for our survival. Right now, the extended family and interdependence is a more appropriate model to seek.

Perhaps the social scientists should not focus on the problems of the single-parent family; maybe they should be trying to get single-parent families to join forces. If two single-parent families live together, we might eliminate some issues of welfare; one adult could be in the work force, while the other maintains a stable home. Often, problems can be solved by changing the way we look at them and the way we deal with the issues—bring people together instead of perpetuating policies that separate them.

Some of it has to do with our psychology. If a single, young working man lives with his parents, our value system suggests that there is something wrong with him. In another culture with a different value system, if that young man went out and got an apartment, people would wonder why a young man wanted to move away from his family. But, we do not realize that these judgments are part of a value system; we say that such separation is necessary for maturity, as though it were a scientific certainty. In fact, these ideas exist in a cultural context.

Sometimes, we can learn a lot about what is happening in our society by observing the middle class. Right now, the middle class is buying a lot of child-care and family services. They understand that the family has changed, and they are acting accordingly. We have dual-career families, and who is caring for the children? Studies tell us that children are not necessarily being shortchanged; but, the studies are measuring specific things, not the quality of life. So, we feel guilty and we start talking about spending quality time with our children—some people get home so rarely, they are making quality telephone calls to their kids.

We all know, in our hearts, that it does not work that way. The fact is that "family" is just too narrow a concept to consider for our purposes. We need to think "children" first: if we do that, we can consider all the other possibilities of what needs to happen for our children, especially for Black children. Given the current structures of the family and society, parents cannot do it alone anymore; we are going to have to create alternative institutions for helping to raise our children. High on the political agenda should be issues of daycare and preschool programs as a necessary supplement to family life—we have to fight for this in the workplace, as well as in school and churches. Both the public and private sector must accept responsibility for this.

We have to start even earlier. We stress prenatal care because we want healthy babies; now we have to talk about postnatal care. There is a journal published by the National Association for Infant Mental Health, and in it I read studies about things determined in infancy which will be projected into the child's future. There is some data to suggest that at twelve or eighteen months, they can predict what the child's IQ will be at age six or seven years. Now, I am not sure that this is true, but it is possible—and that makes it important that we get in there and start early. It is not easy to provide the postnatal care to give Black children the mental and emotional skills they will need to survive in the world; but it is important to try, because others will have an enormous head start on them if we do not.

Finally, one of the things that you can do politically, as educators and students, is to fight for recognition of the dilemma we face and to require training for parenthood. We have training courses for almost everything else; now we should begin parenthood training with courses in junior high and extending through high school. A certain percentage of those students will become parents during those years anyway; we must begin to teach them what it means to be a parent and what they should do for their children right from birth. A lot of people really do not know, and some of them do not even know how much they do not know! One nice side effect might be that after three years of parenting courses, teenagers will change their minds about wanting to have children.

In some of the middle-class communities in Boston, when a baby is born, a public health nurse visits the home, unsolicited, to help these mostly affluent parents in caring for their child—to show them the ropes. So, this free service—paid for out of town taxes—gets a lot of families off on the right foot, but not necessarily those who need the help most.

Parents need this sort of training before they even have children. It is too late when parents come in and tell you that they beat their four-month-old because the baby was crying, and they had to keep it from being spoiled. They think that is responsible parenting, and you have to tell them that it is wrong. They need to be told before they harm the baby, because no one is there to stop them at the time. Somehow we have to reach these young people.

We have to remove the use of physical force from childrearing practice. Politically and sociopsychologically, Black organizations should take a stand against spanking. That will not end spanking, but it will establish a public stance that will put pressure on families to use other techniques to discipline children. It would make people begin to question the old behavior patterns that so many studies show can mess up a kid. Of course, what one parent calls spanking is not spanking to another parent: one child may get an electrical cord; one a light tap on the bottom; some a paddle; and, some kids get punched out. They all call it spanking, and some defend it by saying, "My parents spanked me and I turned out all right." Maybe they did, but you have to consider the overall effects on the community of the use of physical force because it makes kids defiant.

"Do you want to know why a lot of Black kids are violent? Because they get treated violently."

Do you want to know why a lot of Black kids are violent? Because they get treated violently. On the streets you can see Black kids as young as six or seven and they are filled with rage. Their anger is not at racism; they do not know about that. They are enraged at the way they are being treated in the community and in their families. Sometimes, parents distance their kids, and the kids get treated with a lot of physical force. They may become more independent, but they also become more defiant. They move away from their family to their peer group more frequently and more quickly. I hope you will talk and think about this; it may be a critical item.

We could write a book called *Nonviolent Parenting,* and give examples of what parents should do. Watch a young mother in a supermarket with a one-and-a-half-year-old toddler as they approach the checkout counter. The marketing people have arranged for candy and gum to be placed on the lower shelves so that kids can reach it—and you have a crisis with your kid every time you are in line at the checkout. This is no exaggeration—there are these parent-child fights at every checkout counter in America. The kid picks up the package of bubblegum, and the mother treats it as a discipline issue: "I told you not to touch that!" or she slaps the kid. But this is not a discipline issue; it is a learning issue. That gum is put there for him to pick up. We ought to worry about the kid if he does not respond to the stimulus, not if he does. If parents understand the marketing strategy, then they can treat it as an event of that type and teach a useful lesson. You say to the kid: "Yes, that is a pretty package. It is purple and there is gum in it. Do you know what you do with gum? You chew it. And, do you know where this package of bubblegum goes? It goes right here." You have taught the child something without hitting him and messing him up. If you hit him, he feels that his curiosity is something bad. You sabotage his desire to learn if you use an inappropriate response.

> ***"On the streets you can see Black kids as young as six or seven and they are filled with rage. Their anger is not at racism. . . . They are enraged at the way they are being treated in the community and in their families."***

A final point. One aspect of being a "suspect" person and questioning ourselves too much is that we sometimes work ourselves too much into a minority status. It is possible to develop a minority personality. Think about what it means to be in the minority—it can involve a lot of self-doubt and the feeling of being always a victim. It makes you feel that you are not in charge of your life, that your position is rather tentative: "Do I have the ability? Can I do that? May I; can I; will you accept me?" If you persist in thinking like a minority personality, you are less able to take control of your life and your environment.

Being in charge is one of the things that help you to learn and to develop. It has to do with all those theories and studies about locus of control, fate control, and so forth. People who understand how that works in society instill that kind of in-charge attitude in their children. If you visit one of those fancy prep schools, you will see eleven-year-old kids walking around as though they own the place—white kids, mostly, in training to become chairman of the board. We have to make Black kids feel that they too can be chairman of the board, that they can be in charge; and, that in itself will propel them to learn. But, we cannot do this for our kids if we do not feel in charge ourselves. Reverend Jackson says, "I am somebody!" and the kids repeat back to him, "I am somebody!" That is good, but it is also sad that so many Black children in 1988 have to have someone tell them that they are somebody. And that is only the first stage. We have to move ahead from the "I am somebody" mode, and we have to do it quickly. We do not have to start with a "May I, can I?", which is the "I am somebody" stage. Instead, we should start with "Yes, I can; yes, you can," and particularly, "Together, yes we can."

SOURCES

Books

Comer, James P., and Alvin F. Poussaint, *Raising Black Children,* Plume, 1992.

Periodicals

Detroit Free Press, "Guiding Black Parents," February 16, 1993; "'Cosby Show' Advisor Brings Parenting Tips to Workshops," March 18, 1994.

Ebony, August, 1970; December, 1972; February, 1973; "The Huxtables: Fact or Fantasy?," October, 1988, pp. 72-74.
Grand Rapids Press, "Caring: The Coz Way," April 14, 1993; "Children One of Nation's Valued Assets, Expert Says," April 20, 1993, p. B3.
New York Times Magazine, "A Negro Psychiatrist Explains the Negro Psyche," August 20, 1967.

Adam Clayton Powell, Jr.

1908–1972

African American politician and minister

A colorful and controversial figure on the American political scene for nearly thirty years, Adam Clayton Powell, Jr., left behind a decidedly mixed legacy. To some, he was a hard-working civil rights advocate who courageously challenged the status quo. To others, he was an immoral playboy and deal-maker who excelled at the art of self-promotion. In truth, Powell was both—a man of sharp contrasts whose flamboyant personal excesses prevented him from achieving true greatness of the type enjoyed by his contemporaries Malcolm X and Martin Luther King, Jr.

Powell was born in New Haven, Connecticut, but grew up in New York City's Harlem district. There his father, Adam Clayton, Sr., served as pastor of the venerable Abyssinian Baptist Church, the oldest black congregation in the North and at the time one of the largest Protestant congregations in the entire United States. After earning his undergraduate degree from Colgate University in 1930 and his master's degree from Columbia University in 1932, the younger Powell returned to Abyssinian Baptist Church as an assistant and took over as pastor upon his father's retirement in 1936. Two years later, he received his Doctor of Divinity degree from Shaw University.

From the very beginning, the scrappy and sharp-tongued Powell combined his ministry with community activism and quickly earned a reputation as a fearless rabble-rouser. In an effort to force big businesses and government offices that operated in Harlem to hire more blacks, for example, he organized and led picket lines, boycotts, strikes, and other demonstrations that met with great success. He also developed a number of social and welfare programs at Abyssinian Baptist Church, including a vocational guidance clinic, a soup kitchen, and a distribution center that provided food, clothing, and fuel to impoverished Harlem residents.

In 1941, Powell was elected to the New York City Council, and three years later, as a result of reapportionment, he became the first person to hold the newly-created seat in the U.S. House of Representatives that included Harlem. In Washington as in New York, he continued his fight against racial injustice, vowing that his only goal was to secure the total integration of blacks into the political and economic fabric of the United States. He boldly defied the many unwritten rules barring him from certain public places such as dining rooms and barber shops. On the House floor he furiously challenged Southern segregationists, denounced racism in public transportation, and introduced legislation that would have denied federal funds to projects that tolerated discrimination. As chairman of the House Committee on Education and Labor, a position he held from 1960 until 1967, Powell was perhaps the most powerful African American in the country. During his tenure, the committee passed nearly fifty significant pieces of social legislation dealing with such issues as the minimum wage, juvenile delinquency, and vocational education.

Not surprisingly, Powell's confrontational style often brought him into conflict with his colleagues in both political parties and with other government officials (including the president) as well as with labor leaders and educators. And his personal lifestyle—which as the years went by increasingly featured expensive clothes and cars, long vacations, and a bevy of beautiful female "associates"—only served to arouse anger and prompt charges of irresponsibility and financial mismanagement. In characteristically blunt fashion, Powell responded that he was only doing "right out in the open" all of the "things other congressmen try to hide."

By the 1960s, a particular irritation to many both inside and outside government was Powell's outspoken support for the black power movement at a time when mainstream civil rights activists were cool if not downright hostile on the subject. Thumbing his nose at those he referred to as "ceremonial Negro leaders," the congressman from Harlem delivered the following important address at Chicago's Ebenezer Baptist Church on May 28, 1965, reprinted here from The Negro Speaks: The Rhetoric of Contemporary Black Leaders, *(Noble & Noble, 1970). A fiery orator who could hold an audience spellbound, Powell was deliberately provocative and dramatic in this and in most of his other public speeches, including those he gave in Congress.*

Periodically in the conduct of American foreign policy, an important and comprehensive document is published outlining the official position of our government on a particular problem of foreign affairs.

This document is known as a "White Paper."

It is, in effect, a position paper, a statement of high purpose setting forth the historical reasons why the United States intends to alter its existing policy and pursue a new course in that area of foreign affairs.

An example was the famous White Paper on China in 1950.

Tonight, I would like to submit for your thoughtful consideration the topic: "Marching Blacks, 1965: A Black Position Paper for America's Twenty Million Negroes."

Twenty years ago, back in 1945—before the United States Supreme Court decision outlawing racial segregation in public schools, before the Montgomery bus boycott, before Birmingham or the March on Washington—I wrote a book called *Marching Blacks.*

Marching Blacks was the result of fifteen years of victories—victories in the picket lines on the sidewalks of New York City, victories at the bargaining table, victories in opening up new jobs for black people.

For a while, these victories continued and were repeated around the country. Then, a debilitating lull set in. Black people suffering from molting Uncle Tom leadership weakened in the fervor of their crusade as the white-conceived doctrine of "gradualism" took over the civil rights movement.

Then, without warning, the explosive force of the black revolt thundered into reality. The black masses displaced our so-called Negro leaders. And a new battle cry was framed by two words: "Freedom now!"

Victories were many in the black revolt, but still, no radical changes occurred in America's social structure.

Adam Clayton Powell, Jr.

Why? Because a revolt is only an interlude of social protest, a temporary resistance of authority.

To sustain these victories, to radically alter the face of white America and complete its cycle, the Negro revolt must change into a black revolution. As the Negro revolt was our Sunday of protests, so the black revolution must become our week of production.

This can only be done by black people seeking power—audacious power.

Audacious power belongs to that race which believes in itself, in its heroes, and its successes, its deeds, and yes, even its misdeeds.

Audacious power begins with the stand-up-and-be-counted racial pride in being black and thinking black—"I am black, but comely, oh ye daughters of Jerusalem."

Audacious power is the determination of black people to be mayors, United States senators, presidents of companies, members of stock exchanges; to have the power to decide elections and the capability to alter the course of history.

But one word blocks the realization of these goals: *How?*

Once black people have decided to pursue audacious power in the building of the Great Society, what steps do we take?

Tonight, I offer these steps, and this is my Black Position Paper.

1. Black organizations must be black-led. The extent to which black organizations are led by whites, to that precise extent are they diluted of their black potential for ultimate control and direction.

2. The black masses must finance their own organizations, or at least such organizations must derive the main source of their funds from black people. No other ethnic or religious group in America except Negroes permits others to control their organizations. This fact of organizational life is the crucible for black progress. Jews control Jewish organizations (there are no Italians or Irish on the board of directors of B'nai B'rith). Poles control Polish-American organizations. But the moment a black man seeks to dominate his own organization, he's labeled a "racist." And frightened, black Uncle Toms quickly shun him and cuddle up to Mr. Charlie to prove their sniveling loyalty to the doctrine that "white must be right."

3. The black masses must demand and refuse to accept nothing less than that proportionate percentage of the political spoils, such as jobs, elective offices, and appointments, which are equal to their proportion of the population and their voting strength. They must reject the shameful racial tokenism that characterizes the political life of America today. Where Negroes provide twenty percent of the vote, they should have twenty percent of the jobs.

This is not true of other ethnic groups who usually obtain political favors far in excess of their proportion. A good example for comparison are Chicago's Negroes and Polish Americans. According to the 1960 census, there were 223,255 Polish-Americans and 812,637 Negroes in Chicago. There are now three Polish-American congressmen from Chicago and only one Negro congressman. Thus, with approximately one-fourth as many persons as Negroes, Polish-Americans nonetheless have three times as many congressmen. That kind of inequity is not due to racial discrimination. It is due to racial apathy and stupidity.

4. Black people must support and push black candidates for political office first, operating on the principle of "all other things being equal." This is a lesson you Chicago Negroes might well learn. In last April's primary in the heavily black Sixth Congressional District, you Chicago black people actually elected a dead white man over a live black woman. Only a few days ago, a young white candidate who only had going for him the fact that he was young and white, defeated an intelligent, dedicated black woman backed by all major civil rights groups for alderman in a predominantly black ward.

5. Black leadership in the North and the South must differentiate between and work within the two-pronged thrust of the black revolution: economic self-sufficiency and political power. The Civil Rights Act of 1964 has absolutely no meaning for black people in New York, Chicago, or any of the northern cities. *De jure* school segregation, denial of the right to vote, or barriers to public accommodations are no longer sources of concern to northern Negroes. Civil rights in the North means more jobs, better education, manpower retraining, and development of new skills. As chairman of the House Committee on Education and Labor, I control all labor legislation, such as minimum wage, all education legislation, including aid to elementary schools and higher education, the manpower training and redevelopment program, vocational rehabilitation, and of greater importance today, the "War on Poverty." This is legislative power. This is political power. I use myself as an example because this is the *audacious power* I urge every black woman and man in this audience to seek—the kind of political clout needed to achieve greater economic power and bring the black revolution into fruition.

6. Black masses must produce and contribute to the economy of the country in the proportionate strength of their population. We must become a race of producers, not consumers. We must rid ourselves of the welfare paralysis which humiliates our human spirit.

7. Black communities of this country—whether it is New York's Harlem, Chicago's South and West sides, or Philadelphia's North side—must neither tolerate nor accept outside leadership—black or white. Each community must provide its own local leadership, strengthening the resources within its own local community.

8. The black masses should only follow those leaders who can sit at the bargaining table with the white power structure as equals and negotiate for a share of the loaf of bread, not beg for some of its crumbs. We must stop sending little boys whose organizations are controlled and financed by white businessmen to do a man's job. Because only those who are financially independent can be men. This is why I earlier called for black people to finance their own organizations and institutions. In so doing, the black masses guarantee the independence of their leadership.

9. This black leadership—the ministers, politicians, businessmen, doctors, and lawyers—must come *back* to the Negroes who made them in the first place or be *purged* by the black masses. Black communities all over America today suffer from *"absentee black leadership."* The leaders have fled to the suburbs and, not unlike their white counterparts in black communities, use these communities to make their two dollars, then reject those who have made them in the first place as neighbors and social equals. This kind of double-dealing must stop.

10. Negroes must reject the white community's carefully selected *"ceremonial Negro leaders"* and insist that the white community deal instead with the black leadership chosen by black communities. For every *"ceremonial Negro leader"* we permit to lead us, we are weakened and derogated just that much.

11. Negroes must distinguish between desegregation and integration. Desegregation removes all barriers and facilitates access to an open society. Integration accomplishes the same thing but has a tendency to denude the Negro of pride in himself. Negroes must seek desegregation, thereby retaining pride and participation in their own institutions just as other groups—the Jews, Irish, Italians, and Poles—have done. Negroes are the only group in America which has utilized the word "integration" in pursuing equality.

12. Demonstrations and all continuing protest activity must always be *nonviolent*. Violence,

even when it erupts recklessly in anger among our teenagers, must be curbed and discouraged.

13. No black person over twenty-one must be permitted to participate in a demonstration, walk a picket line, or be part of any civil rights or community activity unless he or she is a registered voter.

14. Black people must continue to defy the laws of man when such laws conflict with the law of God. The law of God ordains that "there is neither Jew nor Greek, there is neither bond nor free, there is neither male nor female: for ye are all one in Christ Jesus." Equal in the eyes of God, but unequal in the eyes of man, black people must press forward at all times, climbing toward that higher ground of the harmonious society which shapes the laws of man to the laws of God.

15. Black people must discover a new and creative total involvement with ourselves. We must turn our energies inwardly toward our homes, our churches, our families, our children, our colleges, our neighborhoods, our businesses and our communities. Our fraternal and social groups must become an integral part of this creative involvement by using their resources and energy toward constructive fund-raising and community activities. *This is no time for cotillions and teas.*

These are the steps I would urge all of America's twenty million black people to take as we begin the dawn of a new day by walking together. And as we walk together hand in hand, firmly keeping the faith of our black forebears, let us glory in what we have become and are today. Glory in the golden legacy of our shackled and tortured past.

Glory in the remembered greatness of black civilizations which built civilizations when white men huddled in caves.

Glory in the proud heritage of black heroes like Crispus Attucks, Sojourner Truth, Dorie Miller, and millions of black men whose blood, spilled all over the world in America's eight wars, has watered the lush foliage of American democracy and given it the beauty of everlasting life.

Glory in that mighty fortress of our strength—the Christian faith—"on Christ the solid rock I stand, all other ground is sinking sand!"

Brothers and sisters, I bring history up to date tonight. In closing, let me reach back again to those twenty years—1945—to my book, *Marching Blacks*. Written in 1945, *Marching Blacks* survives in the potency of its message for black people twenty years later. All of you sitting out there this evening, in the glittering majesty of your black skins, are the "Marching Blacks" of 1965.

As a call to new greatness, as a call to the timelessness of our culture in the catalogues of human existence, as a call to cling together in the building of the Great Society, I leave the following words from *Marching Blacks*, written in 1945, with you on this evening of 1965:

> *This is what I am a product of—the sustained indignation of a branded grandmother, the disciplined resentment of my father and mother and the power of mass action of the church. I am a new Negro—a marching black.*
>
> *America has come upon easy days. We have grown soft. We need to return to the radicalism that made us what we were. Here the* new Negro *stands. That is why he is misunderstood. The* new Negro *is as radical—no more, no less—as Jefferson, Clay, Webster, and Tom Paine. . . .*
>
> *He will not stop until out of the rubble of present-day religion there rises an edifice that includes all races, all creeds, and all classes.*
>
> *He will not stop until a people's democracy is born out of the rotten decaying political life of America.*
>
> *The black man is out to save America, to salvage its best, and to take his position in the vanguard of those building an international order of brotherhood.*
>
> *What will the white man's world do? Continue on its suicidal way to end ingloriously in a form of mass hara-kiri? Try to stand outnumbered against the "fresh might" of a billion and a half non-Western people? If it does, the white man is finished—that is the old white man. . . . The white voice that will trumpet in the South and call the people from their shame and decay will not echo from the vaulted corridors of the capital in Montgomery, Alabama. Somewhere along a back road turning the wearily exhausted red clay with a broken plow, shoeless and in blue jeans, some white will catch a glimpse of the Glory Road that the blacks have gone up. He will sound the call, answering which men will find a new world waiting for them.*
>
> *The trumpet call that will summon the new white man from the standards of "white man's civilization" may not be heard in gilded halls, but it will be heard across the fields and through the valleys in sharecroppers' shacks, in mines and mills, on heaving seas—wherever the com-*

mon man precariously seeks out his meager existence.

The black man continues on his way.

He plods wearily no longer—*he is striding freedom road with the knowledge that if he hasn't got the world in a jug at least he has the stopper in his hand!*

He is ready to throw himself into the struggle to make the dream of America become flesh and blood, bread and butter, freedom and equality. He walks conscious of the fact that he is no longer alone—no longer a minority.

He does not want the day of victory to be obtained through violence and bloodshed.

But of one thing he is positive. In the words of Sherwood Eddy, writing in his *Pilgrimage of Ideas*—"in the wrong way or the right way, through violence or nonviolence, it will surely come!"

Glory Hallelujah!

A year later, as guest speaker at Howard University's commencement exercises, Powell delivered what is considered to be his most famous speech on the subject of black power. His address to the students took place on May 29, 1966, in Washington, D.C.; the version that follows is taken primarily from Rhetoric of Black Revolution *with some additional text from a version that appeared in* The Voice of Black America: Major Speeches by Negroes in the United States, 1797-1971, *(Simon & Schuster, 1972).*

Can there any good thing come out of Nazareth?

Almost two thousand years ago, that question was a contemptuous inquiry in the book of John.

"And Nathanael said unto Philip, 'Can there any good thing come out of Nazareth?' Philip saith, 'Come and see.'" Nazareth was the Mississippi of Galilee. There were no great artists or philosopher-kings or musicians. There was no center of learning such as Howard University. In this commencement of your life, the world will ask: Can there any good thing come out of Howard?

As black students educated at America's finest black institution of higher learning, you are still second-class citizens. A mere one hundred years in the spectrum of time separates us from the history of slavery and a lifetime of indignities. Next year, on March 2, 1967, Howard will celebrate the centennial of its founding. Next year, on March 21, 1967, the Committee on Education and Labor of which I am the chairman will also celebrate its one-hundredth anniversary.

How ironic that the Committee on Education and Labor which was formed immediately after the Civil War to help black slaves make the transition into freedom should have a black man one hundred years later as its chairman. One of the purposes of the Committee's founding was to take care of Howard University. It is too late for you who are graduating to know this unless you plan to pursue graduate work here, but it is not too late for the faculty to know it: the Education and Labor Committee is in charge of Howard University. Howard, along with other federal institutions such as St. Elizabeth's and Gallaudet College, is under the jurisdiction of my committee. While both Howard and I as chairman of this committee will celebrate our one hundred years together, joy of our success is tempered by the sobering fact that our status as black people has been denied first-class acceptance.

Keith E. Baird, writing in the spring edition of *Freedomways,* gives eloquent voice to these thoughts in his poem, "Nemesis":

You snatched me from my land,
Branded my body with your irons

And my soul with the slave-
name, 'Negro'
(How devilish clever to spell it up-
per case
And keep me always lower!)

To possess a black skin today in America means that if you are in Los Angeles driving your pregnant wife to a hospital, you'll be shot to death by a white policeman.

A black skin means that if your family lives in Webster County, Mississippi, your average family income will be $846 a year—$16.30 a week for an entire family.

A black skin today is an unemployment rate twice that of whites, despite a skyrocketing gross national product of $714 billion and an unprecedented level of employment.

A black skin means you are still a child, that all the white liberals who have helped you to take your first steps toward freedom and manhood now believe they own your soul, can manage your lives and control your civil rights organizations. Only SNICK [SNCC—the Student Nonviolent Coordinating Committee] has been able to resist the seductive blandishments of white liberals.

So beware not only of Greeks bearing gifts, but colored men seeking loans and Northern white liberals!

At this graduation today, this is the reality of self you must face. Your graduation comes at a particularly critical period of the black man's searching reassessment of who he is, what he should become and how he should become IT. The history of the last twenty-five years of the freedom struggle has been capsuled in only two concepts: integration and civil rights.

During those years, our leaders—and black people are the only people who have "leaders"; other groups have politicians, statesmen, educators, financiers and businessmen—but during those years, our leaders drugged us with the LSD of integration. Instead of telling us to seek audacious power—more black power—instead of leading us in the pursuit of excellence, our leaders led us in the sterile chase of integration as an end in itself in the debasing notion that a few white skins sprinkled amongst us would somehow elevate the genetics of our development.

As a result, ours was an integration of intellectual mediocrity, economic inferiority and political subservience. Like frightened children, we were afraid to eat the strong meat of human rights and instead sucked the milk of civil rights from the breasts of white liberals, black Uncle Toms and Aunt Jemimas. From the book of Hebrews, a diet of courage is offered to black people:

For every one that useth milk is unskillful in the word of righteousness: for he is a babe. But strong meat belongeth to them that are of full age, even those who by reason of use have their senses exercised to discern both good and evil.

Historically, strong meat was too risky for most black people for it would have enabled them to discern both good and evil, the difference between civil rights and human rights.

Human rights are God-given. Civil rights are manmade. Civil rights has been that grand deception practiced by those who have not placed God first, who have not believed that God-given rights can empower the black man with superiority as well as equality.

Our life must be purposed to implement human rights:

-The right to be secure in one's person from the excessive abuses of the state and its law-enforcing officials.

-The right to freedom of choice of a job to feed one's family.

-The right to freedom of mobility of residence.

-The right to the finest education man's social order can provide.

-And most importantly, the right to share fully in the governing councils of the state as equal members of the body politic.

To demand these God-given human rights is to seek black power, what I call audacious power—the power to build black institutions of splendid achievement.

Howard University was once well on its way toward becoming a lasting black institution of splendid achievement when it struggled to contain the intellectual excitement and dynamic creativity of such black scholars as Alain Locke, Sterling Brown, E. Franklin Frazier, Sam Dorsey, Eugene Holmes, James Nabrit and Rayford Logan—all on the campus at the same time. What glorious symbols they were of black creativity!

But where are the black symbols of creativity of 1966? Where is the greatness of our yesteryears? Where are the sonnets black poets once sung of the black man's agony of life? Can any good thing come out of Howard today?

There can and there must. I call today for a black renaissance at Howard University. Resurrect black creativity, not only in literature, history, law, poetry and English, but more so in mathematics, engineering, aerodynamics and nuclear physics. Like Nicodemus, Howard must be born again—born again in the image of black greatness gone before.

Will one black woman here today dare to come forth as a pilgrim of God, a Sojourner Truth—as a black Moses, Harriet Tubman, or a Nannie Burroughs? Will one black man here today dare be a Denmark Vesey, a Nat Turner, a Frederick Douglass, a Marcus Garvey, a W.E.B. Du Bois or a Malcolm X?

One with God is a majority.

This divine oneness can restore Howard to the Glory of Charlie Houston whose classrooms were the womb of the civil rights movement—a womb that birthed a Thurgood Marshall. But the womb has aborted and the good thing which must come out of Howard must also come out of black people. Ask yourselves that higher question: Can any good thing come of black people?

We are the last revolutionaries in America—the last transfusion of freedom into the blood stream of democracy. Because we are, we must mobilize our wintry discontent to transform the cold heart and white face of this nation.

Indeed, we must "drop our buckets" where we are. We must stop blaming "Whitey" for all our sins and oppressions and deal from situations with strength. Why sit down at the bargaining table with the white man when you have nothing with which to bargain? Why permit social workers and various leagues and associations to represent us when they are representing the decadent white power structure which pays their salaries, their rent and tells them what to say? Such men cannot possess the noble arrogance of power that inspires men, moves nations and decides the fate of mankind.

I call for more arrogance of power among black people, but an arrogance of power that is God-inspired, God-led and God-daring. As Cassius said: "The fault, dear Brutus, is not in our stars, but in yourselves, that we are underlings. So, every bondman in his own hand bears the power to cancel his captivity."

We can cancel the captivity of our souls and destroy the enslavement of our minds by refusing to compromise any of our human rights. The era of compromise for the black man is gone! Birmingham, Harlem and Watts have proved this. You cannot compromise man's right to be free, nor can you sit down and "reason together" whether man should have some rights today and full rights tomorrow.

Let somebody reason with Mrs. Barbara Deadwyler in Los Angeles that a white policeman really did not intend to kill her black husband. Let somebody tell her that the passion of her love for her husband should bow to the reason of diaphanous official alibis. Only God can reason with her and soothe her grief. And there is a "God who rules above with a hand of power and a heart of love, and if I'm right He'll fight my battle and I shall be free this day."

This same God calls us first to the conference table, and His Son, when the word of reason was no longer heeded, went into the temple and "began to cast out those that sold." Those that sell black people down the river must be cast out. Those conference tables which defile the human spirit must be overturned.

Conferences are for people who have time to contemplate the number of angels dancing on a civil rights pin. Conferences are for people who seek a postponement until tomorrow of a decision which screams for a solution today. Conferences are an extravagant orgy of therapy for the guilt-ridden and a purposeless exercise in dialectics for the lazy. America has been holding too many conferences, conducting too many seminars; writing too many books and articles about the black man and his right to freedom for over a century.

This week, three thousand black and white people will gather once again in our nation's capital to whisper words of futility into the hurricane of massive indifference. Certainly the federal government should cease to be a partner in this cruel, historic charade with the black man's rights.

To fulfill these rights? Let us begin with first things first. The largest single employer in the United States is the federal government—2,574,000 employees. Yet, racial discrimination within the government—more subtle, more sophisticated, more elegantly structured—continues almost as rampant as yesterday. The times have changed, but the system hasn't.

Though racial persecution presses its crown of thorns on our brows, our faith in God must never falter. We must sustain that faith which helps us to cast off the leprosy of self-shame in our black skins and lift us up to the glorious healing power of belief in the excellence of black power. We must have the faith to build mighty black universities, black businesses and elect black men as governors, mayors and senators. Our faith must be sustained by our passion for dignity and our trust in God, not man's faithless reason in himself.

What is easier—"to say to the sick of the palsy Thy sins be forgiven thee; or to say, Arise and take up thy bed and walk?"

Black children of Howard, take up thy beds and walk into the new era of excellence.

Arise, and walk into a new spirit of black pride.

"Can there any good thing come out of Nazareth? Come and see, said Philip."

Nathanael came and saw Jesus and the world felt, as he did, the power of his love and the beauty of his words.

Can there any good thing come out of Howard University here today?

"Come and see," you Howard graduates must say. "Come and see" us erect skyscrapers of economic accomplishment, scale mountains of educational excellence and live among the stars of audacious political power.

"Come and see" us labor for the black masses—not the black leaders—but the black masses who have yearned for audacious leadership.

In March 1967, following an investigation into Powell's reported misbehavior in both his public and private life, members of the House of Representatives voted to expel him. His Harlem constituents stood behind him, however, and in a special election held that summer, they voted him back into office. After he agreed to give up his seniority and pay a fine for misuse of funds, he was finally allowed to take his seat again in January 1969. Six months later, the U.S. Supreme Court ruled that the House decision to expel him had been unconstitutional.

But Powell's career was nevertheless hurtling toward an end; after being hospitalized for cancer in 1969, he was defeated in the 1970 Democratic primary. His death in 1972 sparked a few final headlines when two different women battled over his funeral arrangements and his estate. His body was ultimately cremated and his ashes were scattered over the island of Bimini in the Bahamas, one of Powell's favorite vacation spots.

SOURCES

Books

Boulware, Marcus H., *The Oratory of Negro Leaders: 1900-1968,* Negro Universities Press, 1969.

Foner, Philip S., editor, *The Voice of Black America: Major Speeches by Negroes in the United States, 1797-1971,* Simon & Schuster, 1972.

Hamilton, Charles V., *Adam Clayton Powell, Jr.: The Political Biography of an American Dilemma,* Atheneum, 1991.

Haskins, James, *Adam Clayton Powell: Portrait of a Marching Black,* Dial, 1979.

Haygood, Wil, *Kings of Cats: The Life and Times of Adam Clayton Powell, Jr.,* Houghton, 1993.

Powell, Adam Clayton, Jr., *Keep the Faith, Baby!,* Trident, 1967.

———, *Adam by Adam: The Autobiography of Adam Clayton Powell, Jr.,* Dial, 1971.

Williams, Jamye Coleman, and McDonald Williams, editors, *The Negro Speaks: The Rhetoric of Contemporary Black Leaders,* Noble & Noble, 1970.

Periodicals

Ebony, "Harlem Bids Farewell to Keeper of the Faith,", June 1972; "Adam Lives: Forever!," June, 1972, pp. 150-151.

Newsweek, "Black Revolution's Adam," April 17, 1972, p. 32.

New York Times, April 5, 1972.

Time, "Playboy Politician," April 17, 1972, p. 24.

Washington Post, April 6, 1972.

Colin Powell

1937–

African American military and political leader

One of the most intriguing—and enduring—heroes to emerge from the Persian Gulf War was General Colin Powell, chairman of the Joints Chiefs of Staff and the mastermind behind operations Desert Shield and Desert Storm. Americans who had lost nearly all faith in the military found a new reason to be proud as they became acquainted with this man who emerged from humble beginnings to earn the trust of presidents. Today, more than five years later, Powell (who retired from the Army in 1993) remains the most respected public figure in the United States, with a personal-approval level one analyst described as "somewhere close to Mother Teresa."

The son of Jamaican immigrants who came to New York City in search of a better life, Powell was born in Harlem and grew up in the South Bronx. He was an indifferent student in both high school and at City College, from which he received a degree in geology in 1958. Outside the classroom, however, Powell excelled as a member of the college's Reserve Officer Training Corps (ROTC) unit; he served as commander of the precision drill team and rose to the highest possible rank, that of cadet colonel. Consequently, upon graduation he went into the Army, figuring he would put in his two years and then look for a "real" job.

Little did Powell know that his decision marked the beginning of a distinguished thirty-five-year-long career that would eventually lead him into the upper echelons of the United States government as an advisor to several presidents. Along the way came a series of increasingly important military assignments at home and abroad as well as political appointments in Washington that cemented his reputation as a skilled and efficient organizer and an intermediary of uncommon integrity, candor, and level-headedness.

Most of Powell's early accomplishments occurred out of the public eye, either at various army bases or behind the scenes at the Pentagon. It was not until 1986, when he was personally summoned to Washington by President Ronald Reagan, that he moved into a higher-profile position—that of assistant to National Security Council (NSC) director Frank Carlucci, who had been charged with cleaning up the NSC and restoring its credibility in the wake of the Iran-Contra scandal. So impressive was Powell's performance that he was chosen to succeed his boss when Carlucci left to head the Department of Defense in late 1987. As further testimony of Powell's high standing in the capital, his nomination received the enthusiastic approval of virtually every top government official.

Powell served as head of the NSC throughout the rest of Reagan's term, then returned to military duty in early 1989. Later that same year, however, President George Bush nominated him over dozens of more senior candidates to become chairman of the Joint Chiefs of Staff, the chief advisor to the president on military affairs and thus one of the most powerful positions in the U.S. government. Congress quickly confirmed him for the job, and in October 1989, General Powell became the first black and the youngest man ever to serve as chairman of the Joint Chiefs.

In August, 1990, the Iraqi invasion of Kuwait catapulted Powell into the public eye as never before. Drawing on his skills as a soldier, a politician, and a diplomat, he planned the land, sea, and air campaigns the allies used to force Iraq to retreat and also helped shape policy regarding non-military matters, sold the overall strategy to the president and to Congress, and explained it to the American people at a couple of televised press briefings. His calm and confident demeanor—a display of firmness without bombast—as well as his unapologetic patriotism won him widespread respect and admiration. To many, Powell radiated a sense of decency and trust lacking in many public figures and seemed to personify the military ideal that had taken such a battering during the post-World War II era. Equally appealing was the impression he gave of having completely transcended society's many racial and political divisions.

As a result of his tremendous popular appeal, which many observers feel could translate into votes, Powell has spent much of his time since the Persian Gulf War fending off persistent questions about his political ambitions. He has carefully avoided saying anything that would suggest he is seriously contemplating a run for office, however, even to the point of keeping his party affiliation a mystery. (The speculation is that he is an independent with moderate-to-conservative views.) Instead, he finished out his term as chairman of the Joint Chiefs of Staff toward the end of Bill Clinton's first year as president and then retired from the military, having served both Democratic and Republican administrations with distinction.

On September 28, 1993, just two days before his retirement was due to take effect, Powell addressed an audience at the National Press Club for the third time in six years. In his speech, which was very warmly received, the general reflected on his career, the U.S. armed forces, and the changing world scene.

Thank you very much, ladies and gentlemen.

Thank you very much for that kind introduction, and let me say that we will not be discussing politics. [Laughter.] And I am, once again, delighted to be back at the National Press Club. And before beginning my talk on the role of the military and some of the things we have been doing in recent months and years, let me take this final opportunity perhaps to express my appreciation to the members of the press for the relationship that I've enjoyed with you over the last six years. It's been tough, and you've ripped me apart a lot, but I think I've managed to survive it. But there's still two days left to go. [Laughter.]

We haven't always agreed on every issue that's come along during my four years as chairman and my two years as national security advisor. When you have agreed with me, I've been amazed at your brilliance. When you've disagreed with me, I have been dismayed by your ignorance. [Laughter.] But it has always been for the single purpose of making sure that the American people got the best information. We always had the same mission: to keep the American people informed and to do it in an adversarial way, where the government tries to put out a point of view and it's the purpose of a free and aggressive press to attack and to come at us and to make sure that we were always on the mark, that we were serving the American people.

And so I thank you for the relationship that we've had over the last several years. And I think the people who have benefitted from it the most are the people that we treasure the most, the American people. And I once again express my appreciation to you for that relationship.

It's a pleasure for me to be here for my third appearance. My first appearance was five years ago, and it was a final appearance in a sense, because it was the last major speech I gave as national security advisor to President Reagan. It was in the fall of 1988 when we were within a few months of the end of the Reagan-Bush administration. I realized the other day that by coincidence this, of course, is my last major speech as chairman of the Joint Chiefs of Staff. It is a coincidence, but, of course, if I ever appear here again giving a last major speech in some capacity, by then it will become a tradition. Who knows what might happen? [Laughter.]

But five years ago when I was here, the theme of my speech was to talk about what the Reagan presidency had been about with respect to foreign policy. It was a proud record, and we could take credit for a number of things. I talked about the historic summit meetings that had been held between President Reagan and President Gorbachev, and I talked at some length about the historic results that had flowed from those meetings. I suggested conservatively five years ago that we might be entering a fundamentally new era in our relationship with the Soviet Union.

I also noted a number of other things that were happening in the world. The cease-fire in that terrible, eight-year-old Iran-Iraq war. The Soviet withdrawal from Afghanistan was underway. The flourishing of democracy under Mrs. Aquino in Manila. I touched on the INF treaty, a marvelous treaty that had been concluded which for the first time would begin the process of destroying nuclear weapons and not building them anymore. And I noted at that time that we were on the verge of perhaps having a mandate to begin work on a CFE treaty, conventional forces in Europe, where we could do with conventional forces what we were doing with nuclear weapons, start at disassemble the huge armies that had been created during the course of the Cold War.

I also shared some disappointments. I noted that Panama was still under the heel of General Manuel Noriega, and noted that in due course, something would have to be done about that. The world, as I would report to President Reagan a few months later on his last day in office, was relatively quiet. There was a feeling of hope. There was a feeling of anticipation. Yes, there was smoldering and bubbling, but overall, the world seemed quiet and very hopeful. Little did I know, nor did anyone else here at that time know what really was in front of us, what was in store for us for the five years between that appearance and my appearance today.

Yes, it was quiet for a while, and then the lid blew. Eleven months after I spoke here as national security adviser, President Bush appointed me to be chairman of the Joint Chiefs of Staff on the first of October, 1989. In the first ninety days, the Berlin Wall fell. My old friend, Manuel Noriega, was dealt with. Mrs. Aquino got in trouble, and American armed forces very surgically and precisely came to her assistance one night in December of 1989. The Warsaw Pact started to crumble. Russian Jews were finally being allowed to emigrate in significant numbers. We saw a free government arise in Hungary. Honecker was out in East Germany, Ceausescu out in Romania. We invaded Panama, as I noted, and in that particular operation, we allowed an elected president to assume office.

And after those first ninety days, things really began to pick up. [Laughter.] Total collapse of the Warsaw Pact. The freeing of Eastern Europe and the rise of democratic institutions and nations and movements around the world. The reunification of Germany, something we thought might take years, suddenly burst upon the world stage in a matter of months. Then we saw the end of communism, the end of communism as a political system, the end of communism as an economic system, the end of communism, more importantly, as a value system, the end of communism as something for people to believe in. We watch now patiently months ahead for those few remaining aging starlets in Havana and Pyongyang and one or two other places to catch up with history and realize that their time is past. And we defeated communism by the strength of our economy, our political system, our value system, our military forces, but ultimately it was a contest between ideas. And the idea of communism failed. We saw the end of the Soviet Union, and Mr. Gorbachev, that great reformer, who did so much, was replaced by a great revolutionary by the name of Boris

Colin Powell

Yeltsin, who we watch on the stage in Moscow today, pushing that revolution forward.

Gorbachev, however, unlike old Soviet leaders, did not disappear and go into oblivion. I discover that, among other things, he has become an environmentalist, and he is setting up his office at a United States Army base, in the Presidio in San Francisco. Is this a great world or what? [Laughter.]

CFE that we talked about in 1988 actually became a treaty, and the armies that once glowered at each other in Europe began to fall back and shrink. Elsewhere in the world, we saw Nelson Mandela freed to join South Africa's turbulent political process. We saw elections in Namibia and Angola. Even in Cambodia, we saw in our newspapers this week how that UN operation has achieved a brilliant success and the UN was able to turn Cambodia back over to its people. In our hemisphere, we saw the end of conflict in El Salvador and Nicaragua. The democratically-elected civilian president in South Korea completed the transition from military rule.

We have marveled at the emergence of the United Nations, assuming responsibilities dreamed of by its founders but only now realizable. There will be difficulties ahead, but we shouldn't allow these UN difficulties to overshadow the immensity of this development. Old enemies becoming new friends and partners. Old alliances, such as NATO, adapting to new roles and realities. Shortly after I became chairman in 1989 and early '90, there was much debate about NATO. "Whither NATO?" was the question that all the Europe think tanks were talking about. Now, in 1993, it's not "Whither NATO?"; it's "How can I get in? Where do I find an application card? How can I join this solid alliance?"

In the aftermath of the Gulf war, our hostages in Lebanon were released. The major aggressor in the region, Iraq, was neutralized and made irrelevant, even though Saddam Hussein and the Iraqi regime is still very annoying. And the Middle East peace process re-energized, leading ultimately to the historic ceremony that we all saw just a few weeks ago, where President Clinton presided on the White House lawn over the signing of those agreements between Prime Minister Rabin and Chairman Arafat, where they shook hands in that memorable picture on an agreement to recognize each other.

Chairman Arafat, who was also a guest here, wasn't even wearing his trademark pistol that day, but he was turned out in a smartly tailored uniform, and a little while later, that afternoon or the next day, he was asked by an inquisitive reporter why he wore a uniform. And he remarked, "Why not? Chairman Powell wears a uniform." [Laughter.] So even in my declining days I find myself a fashion role model. [Laughter and applause.]

But who—if I had come to this audience three months ago and told you that on Friday, the 24th of September, 1993, the two lead stories combined on the front page of the *New York Times* would be the Israeli Knesset approving an agreement to recognize the PLO and right underneath it the South African Parliament agreeing to integrate blacks into the political process—amazing times, historic times, unprecedented times.

And the United States' armed forces have been incredibly busy dealing with these historic events. Panama—but that's not all—we rescued United States' embassies in Liberia and Somalia. We had to send troops, regretfully, to Los Angeles, to deal with a riot that shocked us, and we sent our troops to rescue our fellow Americans in south Florida after a terrible hurricane. We rescued Haitians at sea and ran a camp for them at Guantanamo while working for a restoration of their democracy, a restoration that we hope is almost at hand. We undertook humanitarian operations on a scale never seen before in Bosnia and Bangladesh, in Guam and Somalia, in northern Iraq, in Russia, and a dozen other places.

And of course, the highlight of all of these activities of the last four years can best be characterized as Desert Storm and Norm. Saddam Hussein reminded us, in case we needed any reminding, that there was still evil in the world, and President Bush and Secretary Cheney sent 541,000 Americans 8,000 miles to join a massive coalition to deal with this particular brand of evil. Led by General Schwarzkopf, whose performance—brilliant performance—electrified a nation and a world. Those troops under his command did well and made America proud of its armed forces again in a way that we had not seen since VJ and VE days back in 1945.

We were engulfed in parades. It got so bad that by July I was getting calls from commanders saying, "Chairman, we've got to stop the parades. The troops are getting tired of parades. [Laughter.] Their feet are getting flat, they are getting fat from all of this food that they get at these parade parties. When can we go back to training?" I said, "Not till the American people have had their fill." Those parades bonded us again—people's Army, Navy, Air Force, Marine Corps, Coast Guard—bonded us again with the American people in a way that bridged the estrangement of the post-Korea and post-Vietnam periods. We included in those parades our Vietnam veterans and our Korean buddies, and shared with them so that they finally had the parades that they didn't get before. GI Joe—[applause]—GI Joe and GI Jane again became terms of endearment and not derision.

Almost thirty times in the past four years our armed forces have been called on to fight wars, to restore and preserve peace, to relieve pain, to provide hope, to deter aggression, to show the flag, to back up diplomacy, to show the American will, to stand watch quietly in places like Korea, to reassure friends and to sober enemies. In every instance, they've gone about their job with a competency and with a spirit too rarely seen in our country—proud, patriotic, selfless, drug-free, the best and brightest of American youth. And the American people responded. Perhaps that's why now as an institution we are polled as perhaps one of the most highly regarded institutions in the nation.

Now, ladies and gentlemen, I won't bother comparing the polling data on the American armed forces with any groups that might perhaps be represented in this room today. [Laughter.] Of this record of accomplishment on the part of the armed forces, I am enormously proud, and I am, of course, enormously proud to have been a member of this group.

And yet, for all that has happened in these five years, it is probably only a foretaste of the revolutionary events that are just ahead. History seems to be taking two paths. On one path, some nations are moving forward to new democratic futures with hope for their people. President Yeltsin and what he's doing in Russia is a good example. The other path, however, is a little more confused, a little more dangerous. Some have yet to step on other paths, but others have taken this second path and have returned to 1914 to fight out old hatreds and grudges that had been put on hold by the superpower Cold War pause button.

So we enter a time of hope and promise and a time still of great danger and uncertainty. It will take all of our best wisdom to navigate through these troubled times. It will take American leadership. The debates that we're seeing now about unilateralism or multilateralism or isolationism and interventionism and the other "isms" are somewhat silly and they miss the point. The point is that history and destiny have made America the leader of the world that would be free. And the world that would be free is looking to us for inspiration. The world that would be free trusts America, trusts our values, trusts our people, trusts what we stand for.

We must play that role in whatever form it presents itself. It means political leadership. It means diplomatic leadership. It means economic leadership. And it means leadership of all kinds backed up by a strong military. This isn't to say we will go everywhere and do everything or be the world's policemen. We will have to make choices, and there will be limits. But we cannot step back away from this position of leadership. Where we can make a difference, we must try to make that difference. And so I expect our armed forces to be busier in the days ahead than they have been in the nice static garrison days of the Cold War.

In this torrent of history over the past four years, I have had two primary goals as chairman. The first one was to make sure that we accomplished successfully every operational mission assigned to us by the secretary of defense and the president and the American people. Second, to begin the process of restructuring and downsizing all of our armed forces in response to this new changed environment, the absence of the Cold War and to do it in a way that preserved the capability and the quality of our armed forces. No demobilization, no breaking apart this superb aggregation of young men and women.

> ***"History and destiny have made America the leader of the world that would be free. And the world that would be free is looking to us for inspiration."***

Others will make the final evaluation, but I feel pretty good about both of these goals. The more difficult of the two was the downsizing and restructuring. The first thing we did a few years ago was to drop the Cold War as a planning assumption. In the absence of a Soviet Union, in the absence of an empire of communism to orchestrate all of this, cold war was over. World War III was unthinkable. We no longer had to be prepared to fight everywhere in the world at once against an empire. And the new strategic assumption which was adopted by President Bush and Secretary Cheney in 1990 was to concentrate on fighting two regional conflicts that might emerge. Why two? Because you don't want to be so occupied with one that you don't have a capacity to handle another one and thereby tempt another one. It's as simple as that.

I'm pleased that President Clinton and Secretary Aspin have now built on that rather simple strategic principle and we are allowed to move forward with our restructuring of the armed forces. We used first the concept of the base force to control our descent from our Cold War highs. President Clinton has now approved Secretary Aspin's bottom-up review force, which allows us to go down even lower, but a controlled descent. I am not concerned about the name of the force or the name of the process. I am driven of a need to preserve for future presents, for future secretaries, for future chairmen, for future generations a force capable of executing any future strategy of successfully dealing with a future crisis, a crisis that nobody today can predict, but most assuredly will arrive at 2:00 one morning some time in the future. And I am confident, hopeful—my prayer is—there'll be a force ready to deal with that crisis when it comes.

What we had to do to avoid this rapid demobilization was to begin it in a sensible, prudent manner. We decided to go down about twenty-five percent, and now we have accelerated that to go down even further. This hasn't been an easy process. It's been one of the most difficult management challenges ever presented to the Department of Defense. Six hundred thousand to seven hundred thousand troops are in the process of being discharged. We've cut the size of the Army and the Navy and the Air Force forty percent, twenty-five percent of the Marine Corps. We've eliminated or will eliminate in the course of the next several years seventy percent of the nuclear weapons that were in our inventory when I became chairman just four years ago. That'll be done shortly after the turn of the century.

Hundreds of hardware programs have been cut. Hundreds of bases being closed. Reserves and civilian employees being reduced by the hundreds of thousands. In the last several years alone, 200,000 troops have been brought home with their families from Europe—a major contraction of the defense industry. So the armed forces, ladies and gentlemen, are paying and will continue to pay a peace dividend. But we have also seen that the peace dividend has temporarily hurt the economy. That will sort itself out in time as our free economic system and the conversion practices of the Department of Defense allow the economy to move into this new direction and away from too much of a reliance on defense spending.

And through it all, the force remains ready. The force remains of extremely high quality with high morale, ready to perform missions and performing difficult missions around the world today. In some ways, the force of today is even better than a few years ago. We have gone a long way toward operating as a team, rather than just four separate services. You saw that in Desert Storm, where we all came together under a single commander, General Schwarzkopf, and service preferences and parochial considerations was secondary to the needs of the team.

But we learned a lot about ourselves in Desert Storm. We found that we had to make improvements. And we've been hard at work for the last two years making those improvements. We worked hard then to come up with a joint doctrine for all services, joint procedures for all services. We don't want to unify the services, however. Some critics of mine have suggested that in the roles and missions work I've done I didn't go far enough with respect to merging the activities of the services. Some people would even take it to the extreme, and I'm rather critical of these views. I'm not interested in creating the Aeroflot model in the armed forces of the United States.

We need each and every one of our services. They bring forward from the past proud traditions. I have yet to find a combat capability in any of those four services we did not have a need for at some time over the last four years. So we could do better. We can get rid of redundancy, but let's not get rid of complementarity where it serves the nation's purpose.

We have to remember also that we're warriors. We're not a church picnic group. We're warriors. And I want every Air Force fighter pilot to go into the sky believing he's the best fighter pilot in the world, he's a top gun alongside his Navy counterpart. I want them to believe each one is better than the other. I want an American Marine infantryman to believe there is no infantryman better on the face of the earth. And I want an Army American infantryman to be sure that that Marine is wrong because he's better than he is. That kind of competition serves our interests well. It gives you the kind of proud force that we have now. But when it's time to do a mission, when it's time to go to war, all of that gets set aside and there has to be one team going to war. On any one crisis, one service might get the game ball, but it takes the team to win.

Tomorrow in Norfolk, Virginia, or later this week in Norfolk, Virginia—probably Friday—we're going to take this one step forward when we re-designate the United States Atlantic Command with a new mission. Traditionally, all of our forces in overseas theaters worked for a single commander. Thus, everybody in Europe worked for General Shalikashvili. Everybody in the Pacific works for Admiral Larson. But here in the United States the services maintain control over the operational training of units here in the United States. So that the Army had principal responsibility for large unit training of Army units; similarly with the other services.

What we are going to do with this Atlantic Command—we're going to give the Atlantic Command the operational control of all of the available, deployable active forces here in the United States, and the responsibility of that command will be to train them as joint teams, train them so that when the whistle blows and a General Schwarzkopf needs troops in the future or a General Thurman needs troops in Panama, what they will receive are forces that have been trained jointly by a single commander whose headquarters is in Norfolk. No more pickup games. You're going to get forces ready to go to combat right away. And since it is no longer just a Navy command with a focus on the Russian navy—no longer a problem—the commander of our Atlantic Command may be a Naval officer or an Army officer or a Marine officer or an Air Force officer. From now on, best person gets the job; no longer service-oriented.

So we're going to be doing more and more things like that. We are starting to send Navy instructor pilots to Air Force schools and Air Force instructor pilots to Navy schools so we can ultimately integrate the training of all of our pilots. We have done quite a bit in terms of integrating our strategic forces. We're going into the common development of aircraft components. More will follow as this team concept really becomes imbedded within the Department of Defense.

And I want to give great credit to my colleagues on the Joint Chiefs of Staff—brilliant military leaders, dedicated military leaders—for their efforts to bring this about. They are not what you all refer to all the time as the "Pentagon brass," a term I absolutely detest. And if you're going to give me a gift—[laughter]—as a result of this luncheon, do not give me some cheap mug. [Laughter.] What I want you to do is go back to your computers—[laughter and applause]—what I want you to do is to go back to your computers and get rid of the term "Pentagon brass." Is that too much to ask? Probably, but I make the case anyway. We have some of the most distinguished leaders in the Armed Forces of the United States, and that's what you ought to call them, and not the "Pentagon brass." But, alas, I know I dream. [Laughter.]

You see how proud I am of this force. One of the questions that is always on everybody's mind is how and when do we use that force, what are the circumstances under which you commit the Armed Forces of the United States? And I am usually characterized in this debate as the reluctant warrior and someone who always seeks decisive results. I'm guilty. I'm guilty. Because the fact of the matter is that one of the most important decisions that a president has to make is to commit the Armed Forces of the United States in combat. And the single most important job, the legal job, of the chairman of the Joint Chiefs of Staff and the other chiefs of staff—members of the Chiefs—Joint Chiefs of Staff have is to advise the president and the secretary of defense on issues relating to the commitment of those armed forces.

> ***"[Sending troops into combat] is nothing less than sending young American sons and daughters off to a foreign land to fight other sons and daughters . . ."***

This is not an abstract intellectual exercise. It is nothing less than sending young American sons and daughters off to a foreign land to fight other sons and daughters, perhaps to kill them and to be killed. And sometimes it does end tragically, as we saw again this past weekend in Somalia, where we lost three of our youngsters in that terrible tragedy with the helicopter. But it's what they are trained to do. They're warriors. That's why we have armed forces. But it is never a decision to be taken lightly. We are not committing mercenaries. We are committing sons and daughters.

And committing forces of the United States also means that you're committing the will and the strength of the American people. We must go into battle with the support and understanding of the American people. Frequently a president has to make a quick decision and to go into battle before he really knows what the American people might think about his action. But in due course the American people will indicate their support of a particular decision, and that decision should always be made, in my view, with a clear purpose in mind. And if it isn't possible to come up with a clear purpose, if the situation, as is too often the case, is murky, then you should understand its murkiness and know that, as you go into this, you have to find the clarity that you will eventually need.

Reluctance to use military force is an American military tradition. I can trace it back from Washington to Grant to Eisenhower. Since war is ultimately a political act, not a military act, give political tools the opportunity to work first. Military power can back up political tools and make them credible. We saw that in the Cold War, which we prevailed in without firing a shot. And it is the responsibility of military leaders to ensure that political leaders have an analysis of all the options—the good, the bad, the popular, the unpopular, the fashionable, the unfashionable. And only then, when the candid advice of the military leaders are provided to our political leaders, can they then make proper decisions, make that political decision that the Constitution only gives them the right to do, and then we, the military leaders, execute.

And my view is we should always execute for decisive results. Decisive doesn't mean overwhelming. Decisive means decisive. It means committing the force needed to achieve the political objective. If the political objective is very, very limited, very circumscribed, the force should still be decisive in order to achieve that limited objective. The Philippines is one of my favorite examples. On the 1st of December, I think it was, 1989, late at night we got a call for help from the Philippine government. Rebellion was underway. "We want you to come bomb a Philippine air base" where Philippine planes were taking off to attack Mrs. Aquino.

We examined it quickly. We made some judgments and decided that in this case we didn't need to apply overwhelming force. We thought that just sending some F-4 fighters with great young Air Force pilots aboard buzzing the airfield would be enough to keep those planes on the ground without us having to kill a single person. Precise application of military force for a very limited objective. And we made it all up within about two hours, and the mission was over in . . . hours. And the instructions we gave to the pilots were very simple and clear: go over the airfield and demonstrate extreme hostile intent. [Laughter.] They did. Mission completed.

My philosophy in all this is rather simple: match political expectations to military means in a wholly realistic way. Don't slide in, don't mislead yourself. This isn't some syndrome I'm suffering from. It comes from thirty-five years of experience. As a first lieutenant, I saw what doing otherwise was—results were in the Bay of Pigs—President Kennedy. As a major and a captain and a lieutenant colonel, I saw what doing otherwise produced in Vietnam. And in Beirut as a major general in 1983, I saw what doing otherwise can result in.

In the case of places like Somalia where the mission was nice and clear cut when we went in, but it's becoming a little more difficult now. We will have to continue our calculus of political objectives, means applied to that objective, and sort them out. But because things get difficult, you don't cut and run. You work the problem and try to find a correct solution.

I'm pleased that the philosophy I've just espoused has seen favor with the two presidents and the two secretaries of defense that I have worked for in the past four years. We've learned our lesson, I think. At the end of the day, though, strategy and force structure and matters such as I have been talking about kind of go by the wayside. At the end of the day, all of our plans, the missions we have in mind, rest on the shoulder of the individual GI, be he a soldier, a sailor, an airman, a Marine or Coast Guardsman, he or she is at the heart and soul of our armed forces—cold, tired, frightened, away from home, a soldier of the nation willing to go anywhere, to do anything, to sacrifice whatever is required for the mission. Hundreds of thousands of such wonderful young men and women, trained and bonded together, make up the armed forces of the United States. They are a treasure. And they count on us—all of us here today—for leadership, for support, and for caring for them.

I am so very proud to have been one of them for the past thirty-five years, and for the last four years to have represented them. It all ends for me on Thursday. I've been a soldier all my life. I've never wanted to be anything else. I have loved every single minute of it, and I thank the nation for having given me the opportunity to serve in the proud armed forces of the United States. Thank you. [Extended applause.]

Since retiring from the military, Powell has kept busy writing his memoirs (which are scheduled to be published in late 1995) and fulfilling numerous speaking engagements. While he appears before many different kinds of audiences, he is especially drawn to young people, whom he advises to get a good education, persevere even in the face of adversity, hold fast to a strong value system, and take personal responsibility for their lives and their actions. One such appearance came on May 14, 1994, when Powell received an honorary degree and delivered the commencement address at Howard University in Washington, D.C.

Thank you for your very warm reception.

Mr. President, Mr. Chairman, members of the board of trustees, fellow honorees, alumni, faculty members, family members, the great Howard class of 1994.

I am so pleased to be with you on this very beautiful spring morning. I am deeply honored to be the recipient of an honorary degree alongside two gentlemen as distinguished as Dr. Cheek and Ambassador Annenberg. For that, I thank the university and the board of trustees.

Let me also take this opportunity to extend my thanks to President and Mrs. Jennifer for their service to Howard University and to wish them every success at the University of Texas as they begin a new phase in their life of service to American youth. I also congratulate Dr. Ladner on her elevation to acting president.

I am especially pleased to be the commencement speaker for the class of 1994. I have wanted to be the commencement speaker for a number of years, and this is my lucky year.

Because you know, these days you get a lot of attention being a speaker at Howard University. Is Connie Chung here today so I can get on her "Eye to Eye" television show? [Note: Earlier in the school year, a controversy had erupted on campus when a Nation of Islam official was invited to speak to students.]

The real challenge in being a commencement speaker is figuring out how long to speak.

The graduating students want a short speech, five to six minutes and let's get it over. They are not going to remember who their commencement speaker was anyway. P-o-w-e-l-l.

Parents are another matter. Arrayed in all their finery, they have waited a long time for this day, some not sure it would ever come, and they want it to last. So go on and talk for two or three hours. We brought our lunch and want our money's worth.

The faculty member who suggested the speaker hopes the speech will be long enough to be respectable, but not so long that he has to take leave for a few weeks beginning Monday.

So the poor speaker is left figuring out what to do. My simple rule is to respond to audience reaction. If you are appreciative and applaud a lot early on, you get a nice short speech. If you make me work for it, we're liable to be here a long time.

You know, the controversy over Howard's speaking policy has its positive side. It has caused the university to go through a process of self-examination, which is always a healthy thing to do. Since many people have been giving advice about how to handle this matter, I thought I might as well, too.

First, I believe with all my heart that Howard must continue to serve as an institution of learning excellence where freedom of speech is strongly encouraged and rigorously protected. That is at the very essence of a great university, and Howard is a great university.

And freedom of speech means permitting the widest range of views to be presented for debate, however controversial those views may be. The First Amendment right of free speech is intended to protect the controversial and even outrageous word and not just comforting platitudes, too mundane to need protection.

Some say that by hosting controversial speakers who shock our sensibilities, Howard is in some way promoting or endorsing their message. Not at all. Howard has helped put their message in perspective while protecting their right to be heard. So that the message can be exposed to the full light of day.

I have every confidence in the ability of the administration, the faculty and the students of Howard to determine who should speak on this campus. No outside help needed, thank you. I also have complete confidence in the students of Howard to make informed, educated judgments about what they hear.

But for this freedom to hear all views, you bear a burden to sort out wisdom from foolishness. There is great wisdom in the message of self-reliance, of education, of hard work, and of the need to raise strong families. There is utter foolishness, evil and danger in the message of hatred, or of condoning violence, however cleverly the message is packaged or entertainingly it is presented. We must find nothing to stand up and cheer about or applaud in a message of racial or ethnic hatred.

I was at the inauguration of President Mandela in South Africa earlier this week. You were there, too, by television and watched that remarkable event. Together, we saw what can happen when people stop hating and begin reconciling. De Klerk the jailer became De Klerk the liberator and Mandela the prisoner became Mandela the president.

Twenty-seven years of imprisonment did not embitter Nelson Mandela. He invited his three jail keepers to the ceremony. He used his liberation to work with his former tormentors to create a new South Africa and to eliminate the curse of apartheid from the face of the earth. What a glorious example! What a glorious day it was!

Last week you also saw Prime Minister Rabin and PLO Chairman Arafat sign another agreement on their still difficult, long road to peace, trying to end hundreds of years of hatred and two generations of violence. Palestinian authorities have now begun entering Gaza and Jericho.

In these two historic events, intractable enemies of the past have shown how you can join hands to create a force of moral authority more powerful than any army and which can change the world. Although there are still places of darkness in the world where the light of reconciliation has not penetrated, these two beacons of hope show what can be done when men and women of good will work together for peace and for progress.

There is a message in these two historic events for us assembled here today. As the world goes forward, we cannot start going backward.

African Americans have come too far and we have too far yet to go to take a detour into the swamp of hatred. We—as a people who have suffered so much from the hatred of others—must not now show tolerance for any movement or philosophy that has at its core the hatred of Jews or of anyone else. Our future lies in the philosophy of love and understanding and caring and building. Not of hatred and tearing down.

We know that. We must stand up for it and speak up for it! We must not be silent if we would live up to the legacy of those who have gone before us from this campus.

I have no doubt that this controversy will pass and Howard University will emerge even stronger, even more than ever a symbol of hope, of promise and of excellence. That is Howard's destiny!

Ambassador Annenberg, one of your honorees today, is a dear friend of mine and is one of America's leading businessmen and greatest philanthropists. You have heard of his recent contributions to American education and his generous gift to Howard.

A few years ago, I told Mr. Annenberg about a project I was involved in to build a memorial to the Buffalo Soldiers, those brave black cavalrymen of the west whose valor had long gone unrecognized. Ambassador Annenberg responded immediately, and with his help the memorial now stands proudly at Fort Leavenworth, Kansas.

The Buffalo Soldiers were formed in 1867, at the same time as Howard University. It is even said that your mascot, the bison, came from the bison, or Buffalo, Soldiers.

Both Howard and the Buffalo Soldiers owe their early success to the dedication and faith of white military officers who served in the Civil War. In Howard's case, of course, it was your namesake, Major General Oliver Howard. For the Tenth Cavalry Buffalo Soldiers, it was Colonel Benjamin Grierson who formed and commanded that regiment for almost twenty-five years. And he fought that entire time to achieve equal status for his black comrades. Together, Howard University and the Buffalo Soldiers showed what black Americans were capable of when given the education and opportunity, and when shown respect and when accorded dignity.

I am a direct descendent of those Buffalo Soldiers, of the Tuskegee Airmen, and of the Navy's "Golden Thirteen," the Montfort Point Marines, and all the black men and women who served this nation in uniform for over three hundred years—all of whom served in their time and in their way and with whatever opportunity existed then to break down the walls of discrimination and racism to make the path easier for those of us who came after them. I climbed on their backs and stood on their shoulders to reach the top of my chosen profession to become chairman of the American JCS. I will never forget my debt to them and to the many white Colonel Greirsons and General Howards who helped me over the thirty-five years of my life as a soldier. They would say to me now, "Well done. And now let others climb up on your shoulders."

> *"African Americans have come too far and we have too far yet to go to take a detour into the swamp of hatred."*

Howard's "Buffalo Soldiers" did the same thing and on their shoulders now stand governors and mayors and congressmen and generals and doctors and artists and writers and teachers and leaders in every segment of American society. And they did it for the class of 1994. So that you can now continue climbing to reach the top of the mountain; while reaching down and back to help those less fortunate.

You face "great expectations." Much has been given to you and much is expected from you. You have been given a quality education, presented by a distinguished faculty who sit here today in pride of you. You have inquiring minds and strong bodies given to you by God and by your parents, who sit behind you and pass on to you today their still unrealized dreams and ambitions. You have been given citizenship in a country like none other on earth, with opportunities available to you like nowhere else on earth—beyond anything available to me when I sat in a place similar to this thirty-six years ago.

What will be asked of you is hard work. Nothing will be handed to you. You are entering a life of continuous study and struggle to achieve your goals. A life of searching to find

> ***"... continue climbing to reach the top of the mountain; while reaching down and back to help those less fortunate."***

that which you do well and love doing. Never stop seeking.

I want you to have faith in yourselves. I want you to believe to the depth of your soul that you can accomplish any task that you set your mind and energy to.

I want you to be proud of your heritage. Study your origins. Teach your children racial pride and draw strength and inspiration from the cultures of our forebearers, not as a way of drawing back from American society and its European roots, but as a way of showing that there are other roots as well—African and Caribbean roots that are also a source of nourishment for the American family tree. To show that African Americans are more than a product of our slave experience. To show that our varied backgrounds are as rich as that of any other American; not better or greater, but every bit as equal. Our black heritage must be a foundation stone we can build on, not a place to withdraw into.

I want you to fight racism. But remember, as Dr. King and Dr. Mandela have taught us, racism is a disease of the racist. Never let it become yours. White South Africans were cured of the outward symptoms of this disease by President Mandela's inauguration, just as surely as black South Africans were liberated from apartheid.

Racism is a disease you can help cure here by standing up for your rights and by your commitment to excellence and to performance. By being ready to take advantage of your rights and the opportunities that will come from those rights. Never let the dying hand of racism rest on your shoulder, weighing you down. Let racism always be someone else's burden to carry.

As you seek your way in the world, never fail to find away to serve your community. Use your education and your success in life to help those still trapped in cycles of poverty and violence.

Above all, never lose faith in America. Its faults are yours to fix, not to curse.

America is a family. There may be differences and disputes in the family but we must not allow the family to be broken into warring factions. From the diversity of our people, let us draw strength and not cause weakness.

Believe in America with all your heart and soul and mind. It remains the "last best hope of earth." You are its inheritors and its future is today placed in your hands.

Go forth from this place today inspired by those who went before you.

Go forth with the love of your families and the blessings of your teachers.

Go forth to make this a better country and society. Prosper, raise strong families, remembering that all you will leave behind is your good works and your children.

Go forth with my humble congratulations. And let your dreams be your only limitations, now and forever.

Thank you and God bless you. Have a great life!

In September 1994, Powell played a key role in a special three-member delegation President Bill Clinton sent to Haiti to persuade that country's ruling generals to step down and thus avoid an American invasion. His success touched off another round of speculation that he might be gearing up for a presidential bid in 1996. As usual, Powell declined to comment on his future plans but hinted that he would probably make an announcement sometime in late 1995.

SOURCES

Books

Landau, Elaine, *Colin Powell: Four-Star General,* F. Watts, 1991.

Powell, Colin, *My American Journey: An Autobiography,* Random House, 1995.

Roth, David, *Sacred Honor: The Biography of Colin Powell,* Zondervan, 1993.

Woodward, Bob, *The Commanders,* Simon & Schuster, 1991.

Periodicals

Atlantic, "President Powell?" October, 1993.

Detroit Free Press, "Four-Star Candidate," October 25, 1994; "General Ambition," February 8, 1995, p. 5A.

Detroit News, "Presidential Politics of a Third Kind," June 18, 1995.

Ebony, "Black General at the Summit of U.S. Power," July, 1988, pp. 136-146; "The World's Most Powerful Soldier," February, 1990, pp. 136-142.

Esquire, "A Confederacy of Complainers," July, 1991.

Grand Rapids Press, "Colin Powell Teases Crowds with Hints of '96 Campaign," April 30, 1995, p. A4.

Newsweek, "'The Ultimate No. 2' for NSC," November 16, 1987, p. 63; "Pragmatist at the Pentagon," August 21, 1989, p. 20; "Bush's Maximum Force," September 3, 1990, pp. 36-38; "The Reluctant Warrior," May 13, 1991, pp. 18-22; "Everybody's Dream Candidate," August 23, 1993, p. 21; "Here We Go Again," September 26, 1994, pp. 20-24; "Can Colin Powell Save America?," October 10, 1994, pp. 20-26.

People, "Colin Powell, America's Top Soldier, Has Taken His Influence from Harlem to the White House," September 10, 1990, pp. 52-55; "Colin Powell," December 31, 1990-January 7, 1991, pp. 60-61; "Colin Powell," spring/summer, 1991, pp. 38-39.

Reader's Digest, "'It's Not My Fault!'" October, 1991.

Time, "The General Takes Command," November 16, 1987, p. 22; "A 'Complete Soldier' Makes It," August 21, 1989, p. 24; "Five Who Fit the Bill," May 20, 1991, pp. 18-20; "The Rebellious Soldier," February 15, 1993, p. 32; "Colin Powell, the Reluctant Candidate," June 20, 1994, p. 15. *U.S. News and World Report,* "The Right Stuff," February 4, 1991; "What's Next, General Powell?," March 18, 1991, pp. 50-53; "Colin Powell, Superstar: Will America's Top General Trade His Uniform for a Future in Politics?" September 20, 1993.

Hugh B. Price

1941–

African American head of the National Urban League

In May 1994, a new figure appeared on the national civil rights scene when Rockefeller Foundation senior officer Hugh B. Price was named president and chief executive officer of the Urban League. Founded in 1910, the Urban League has traditionally focused its efforts on economic and employment issues and their impact on the black community. By the 1990s, however, it was facing a number of serious challenges to its very existence, including dwindling financial support and a growing sense that it had become irrelevant and ineffective. Charged with reversing this trend, Price has vowed to breathe new life into the Urban League with ambitious yet practical goals—preparing children academically and socially for the twenty-first century, enabling families to become economically self-sufficient, and fostering "racial inclusion" rather than racial separation.

A native of Washington, D.C., Price grew up in a middle-class family that was actively involved in efforts to secure voting and civil rights for black citizens of the nation's capital. After receiving his bachelor's degree from Amherst College in 1963 and his law degree from Yale University in 1966, he pursued his own interest in social justice as an attorney with the New Haven Legal Assistance Association, where his specialties were criminal law and representing new community organizations. He also served as the first executive director of the Black Coalition of New Haven, a group that formed in the late 1960s to promote racial cooperation and restore vitality to neighborhoods that had been plagued with civil unrest.

In 1970, Price joined an urban affairs consulting firm, rising to the rank of partner. Beginning around 1975, he went to work for the City of New Haven as human resources administrator; he also supervised the local Head Start program and other special services for children and senior citizens. In 1978, Price took on a new challenge when he became a member of the editorial board of the New York Times*, a position in which he regularly produced editorials on a wide variety of public policy issues. He remained with the* Times *until 1982, then served for six years as senior vice president of WNET/Thirteen, New York City's public television station. He left there in 1988 to become vice president of the Rockefeller Foundation, where he managed educational programs for at-risk young people before accepting the presidency of the Urban League.*

On July 24, 1994, Price gave the keynote address at the National Urban League convention in Indianapolis, Indiana. It was his first major public appearance as the group's new president, and by all accounts it was a triumphant debut. As New York Times *columnist Bob Herbert observed, Price's speech was "a welcome breeze" delivered "without a lot of flamboyant rhetoric. It spoke the truth, unadorned, without crude appeals to prejudice. It was courageous, intelligent and important." The text that follows was furnished by the National Urban League.*

This is a thrilling moment for me, as you can well imagine. Seeing the Urban League movement arrayed before me, several thousand strong, spanning four generations and primed for action, is a stunning sight to behold.

To the veterans who have built and sustained the movement through decades of adversity and triumph, to our allies of all complexions and religious faiths who have coalesced with us, and to the next generation of Urban League leaders—especially the NULITES students who have journeyed here from Bloomington—I salute each of you for making the Urban League the venerable and revered movement that it is. And I salute you for your collective determination to carry our cause of social, economic and legal justice for all into the twenty-first century.

The thrill I feel is tempered, I must admit, by a profound sense of humility. For I am following in the awesome footsteps of the likes of George Edmund Hayes; Eugene Kinckle Jones; Lester Granger, who led the movement with such a steady hand for so many years; Whitney Young, who expanded it and ushered it into the civil rights arena; Vernon Jordan, who positioned the League as a forceful advocate for justice; and John Jacob, who sustained it through excruciatingly difficult times with dignity and compassion.

Assuming the helm of the National Urban League is also humbling because the movement so much resembles family, with all the love, support and lofty expectations typically associated with that term.

Though I admittedly am a stranger to many of you, rest assured that the Urban League is no stranger to me. In fact, I've been part of your extended family my entire life.

As a child growing up in Washington, D.C., I often heard my uncle, Dr. R. Frank Jones, speak of the League in reverent tones. Early in my career as head of the Black Coalition of New Haven, Connecticut, Bob Bowles, director of the Urban League chapter there, served on my board and as a trusted mentor.

June Branche, another dear friend in Westchester County, is the niece of Lester Granger. And I learned just the other day that Eugene Kinckle Jones was the godfather of my cousin, Winifred Norman.

Now that I'm graduating from the extended family to the immediate Urban League family, let me introduce you to several members of my own who are here this evening. First and foremost my wife, Marilyn Lloyd Price, who I love even more today than the day we married, which we're both reluctant to admit was almost thirty-one years ago. Those physicians and dentists here who attended Howard may remember "Mama" Lloyd from the anatomy department. She's Marilyn's mother.

Our youngest daughter, Lauren, is here. She graduated from college a year ago and now works at the Washington-based Center for Youth Development, a field that's dear to many of us. Our two other daughters are globe-trotting today and thus couldn't join us. Traer, a designer and choreographer of water fountains, is on assignment in Taiwan. Janeen, a second-year law student, has just wrapped up a summer internship in Washington and arrived earlier today in Mexico City to begin a second internship there.

My own mother, Charlotte Schuster Price, has come from Cape Cod to share this moment with me. She and my late father, Dr. Kline A. Price, lived in Washington for nearly forty years.

My brother, Dr. Kline Price, Jr., and his wife, Bebe Drew Price, are with us. Bebe, by the way, stands for "Blood Bank". Yes, she's the daughter of the late Dr. Charles Drew, an authentic African American and American hero. My cousins, Al and Sandi Brothers, have journeyed here from Ft. Wayne, where Sandi is active in the Urban League.

Occasionally I am asked by friends and colleagues how long I agonized over whether to accept the board's offer to become president of the National Urban League. I usually pause for a moment or three, and then reply that it took about that long. The decision was easy for several reasons.

For starters, service runs in my family. Like many physicians of his era who graduated from Howard and stayed in D.C., my father tithed with his time by volunteering many weekday mornings in the clinic for poor folk at Freedman's Hospital.

My mother was active in the movement to win Washingtonians the right to vote. Also, my parents were among the families who helped finance Charles Houston's early litigation efforts for the NAACP Legal Defense Fund that laid the legal foundation for *Brown vs. Board of Education.*

Reared in this tradition of service, I've devoted virtually my entire professional career to the cause of social and economic justice for our people. While it's true that I'm not an alumnus of the traditional civil rights movement, I have served our folk, effectively I would like to think, in other ways.

Indeed, I feel as though I have been apprenticing for the presidency of the League my entire professional life.

Another reason the decision was easy is because this isn't just a terrific job, it's a calling. By that I mean that we—you and I—who are this movement have little choice but to be in it.

Seven years ago, I yearned to become president of the public television station where I worked. It didn't happen and I was crestfallen for months. I possessed all the right credentials, or so I thought, and had run the key divisions of the station. Yet I smacked my head squarely against that glass ceiling before I'd even heard of the term.

It took my daughter Traer, who is rather spiritual, to pull me out of the funk. One day that I'll never forget, she said, "Dad, don't worry about not getting that job. You're being saved for something more important." This, obviously, is what she'd foreseen that I could not. Thank heavens that daughter always knows best.

Before charting the course for the Urban League through the remainder of this century and into the next, let me briefly describe the changing and challenging seas that we'll be navigating together. We who are African American live, alongside all other Americans, in a world which bears little resemblance to that of a mere half-decade ago, much less a generation ago.

Communism has crumbled, falling victim to its own oppressiveness and inefficiency. Market economies now reign supreme. Nations are redefining themselves with stunning rapidity. Immigrants and refugees stream almost unchecked across borders, radically and rapidly altering the ethnic make-up of nations.

This ruthlessly competitive world waits for no nation, no ethnic group and no individual. Should any competitor falter, there is always an emerging country, an enterprising people or an eager immigrant waiting in the wings or, more likely, already seizing the opportunity to fill the void.

Technological change, "rightsizing," industrial outmigration and structural unemployment are now familiar phrases throughout the developed world. Statistically speaking, the unemployment problems of Canada, the U.K., France and Germany are twice as bad as ours.

Closer to home, America is enduring its own economic upheavals, with cities and the urban poor feeling the severest aftershocks. For millions of black folk who, thanks to the civil rights movement, have flooded into higher education, big corporations and their own mainstream businesses, these clearly are the best of times.

But for millions more of us stranded in violent, hopeless, poverty-stricken inner cities, only slavery and the half century that followed it could have been worse.

When the landmark *Brown vs. Board of Education* decision was handed down forty years ago this spring, I think it's fair to say we all assumed that the defeat of Jim Crow laws would fling open the doors of opportunity to the robust, post-World War II mainstream economy from which we'd by and large been excluded.

What no one foresaw back in '54 and even through the '70s was that urban economies would slowly yet steadily erode. The manufacturing jobs that once enabled blue-collar workers to purchase their own homes and occasional new cars have all but vanished from the inner city.

Take my uncle Edgar Royster. Though not a college man, he was a provider in the noblest sense of the term. He worked for years at the Winchester arms plant in New Haven and held a second job at Yale University. Both were within walking distance of his home in the Dixwell neighborhood.

Uncle Edgar's earnings enabled his family to save enough money to move out of public housing into a new home that they built in nearby West Haven. They actually lived out the American dream almost exactly as the script was written back then.

Now, the Winchester plant is history, along with the decent-paying jobs that provided access for people like my uncle Edgar to the economic mainstream. Those service jobs that have replaced them often pay so miserably that the full-time employees who hold them still cannot work their way out of poverty.

I recite these global and domestic trends because it's essential that we place our circumstances in a larger context. Yes, racism is still abroad in the land. Though subtler and somewhat less pervasive now, it's still a well-documented and undeniable reality in employment, housing, lending and the like.

Even so, we must not let ourselves and, especially, our children fall into the paranoid trap of thinking that racism accounts for all that plagues us. The global realignment of work and wealth is, if anything, the bigger culprit. We who serve must be clear-eyed about these color-blind economic trends if we're to be genuinely helpful to our folk.

"We must not let ourselves and, especially, our children fall into the paranoid trap of thinking that racism accounts for all that plagues us."

Lest we and our children forget, the civil rights movement was a huge success in many respects. It unquestionably placed those of us with solid educations, ample family support, personal drive and a healthy dose of luck on the up escalator economically.

Yet millions of our people remain stuck on the down escalator, headed nowhere or worse. Their dire circumstances must dwell in our consciences because of the tragic loss of human potential and the mounting drain on societal resources and compassion.

It is their fate, then, that must be the primary focus of the Urban League movement. This renewed emphasis on our sisters and brothers and children in greatest need honors our original mission, which was to serve those of us in meager circumstances who are seeking access to mainstream society.

How will we pursue this ambitious goal? Given our limited resources, we must concentrate with laser-like focus on those critical areas where we can leverage our unique strengths for greatest impact. I see three areas of concentration for the Urban League:

-The first is the education and development of our children growing up in the inner city so that they have the academic and social skills to be successful.

-The second is to enable their families to become economically self-sufficient.

-Finally, we should encourage racial inclusion so that our folk can participate fully in the mainstream economy.

Let me elaborate on each priority. First, and foremost, our children, for all the obvious reasons. How easy it is to forget, in the flood of awful articles and newscasts about youth violence, that they are our future.

Look around you at the five hundred smart and committed NULITES students. They, too, are our future, though we seldom read or see anything about them in the media. Let's make certain these young leaders know how much we love and appreciate them by giving them a rousing round of applause.

Children growing up in the inner city are being cheated of many supports that are crucial for their success. The Urban League intends to do something about two of them—education and social development.

There's little mystery about how to do a better job of educating poor children. School reformers, like James Comer, Jeff Howard, Bob Slavin and Ted Sizer, and dedicated teachers across the country have shown convincingly that it can be done. Among the key ingredients are high expectations, challenging academic material and flexible instructional techniques.

Unfortunately, effective teaching and learning for poor children occurs mostly in isolated classrooms led by motivated teachers. It seldom permeates entire schools and school districts. That's largely because districts still aren't genuinely committed to reform or prepared to invest adequately in retooling teachers and principals to take it on in earnest.

What's missing, therefore, is not the way to change, but the will. It'll take concerted outside pressure from parents and community groups to prevail upon school systems to improve the education of inner-city children.

That's precisely where the Urban League comes in. I see us mobilizing and equipping parents and community leaders to become sophisticated and insistent consumers of education for their children.

Let's go house-by-house, living room-by-living room in the inner-city neighborhoods we serve. Let's help parents understand, in layman's terms, exactly what their children must know and be able to do in order to meet twenty-first-century standards of competency.

If their kids are off course, then encourage them to inquire, constructively yet insistently, exactly what the teachers intend to do about it, by when, and what they, the parents, can do concretely to be supportive.

I repeat. Concerted pressure from sophisticated consumers—namely parents—is a major missing ingredient in urban school reform. That's the Urban League's natural niche, our unique contribution to improving the education of our children.

But we cannot stop there. What happens after class is equally important since children spend most of their waking hours outside of school. In the home, of course. But also in extracurricular programs, settlement houses and boys clubs, and organized sports.

Ideally, this is where social development of children occurs. Where their values are shaped. Where they learn to collaborate with others in teams. Where they learn social graces. Where they are exposed to new horizons through visits to museums and such.

That's the theory anyway. The trouble is that in all too many inner-city neighborhoods, this so-called developmental infrastructure has virtually vanished. Many parents these days, especially single moms, are stringing together several low wage jobs just to get by. They simply aren't home in mid-afternoon when their children arrive from school.

Most urban school systems are too strapped financially to provide the rich array of extracurricular clubs that many of us enjoyed as teenagers. Many inner-city settlement houses, assuming they're even still on the scene, are too underfunded and dilapidated physically to provide safe havens and constructive activities for all the children who need them. Municipal park and recreation departments are but a shadow programmatically of their former selves.

But I'll tell you who is well-financed and omnipresent, however. The gangs that are growing everywhere. They've filled the void left by we supposedly responsible adults and have built their own anti-social developmental infrastructure which ensnares youngsters in search of identity and companionship.

Just listen to this chillingly perceptive analysis by a Los Angles gang leader, one Tee Rogers, of why adolescents join gangs:

> *What I think is formulating here is that human nature wants to be accepted. A human being gives less of a damn what he is accepted into. At that age—eleven to seventeen—all kids want to belong. They are unpeople.*

Politicians talk incessantly these days about taking back the streets from criminals. I say we take back our children from the streets and from the gangs, and the streets will take care of themselves.

It's high time that society at large and, especially, we of the African American community muster the will and the wherewithal to ensure that each inner-city child who needs attention, support and direction has a caring adult in his or her life every day.

We African Americans who have made it must tithe with our time and, more importantly, our money to see to it that those of our children whom the civil rights movement hasn't yet touched also have a real chance to succeed. Volunteer mentors are wonderful. But given their often unpredictable schedules, even the most well-meaning of them aren't reliable enough to provide the continuity of caring needed by these kids.

Let's get right down to cases. I propose that each Urban League affiliate establish a Youth Development Fund and formulate, in conjunction with others in the community, a master plan for delivering youth services after school and over the summer in churches, schools, settlement houses, community centers, safe homes, museums, even National Guard armories.

Mind you, the idea isn't to run our own programs with this money. That would undercut our credibility because people might think it's merely a money grab by us. For the same reason, we probably need a credible, representative panel of community people to disburse the funds. Our goal is to be of service in the broadest sense of the term.

I also see us monitoring the performance of those who receive the funds and connecting contributors with the kids. We should be flexible so that donor groups, like sororities, can retain their identity while giving to the fund.

Where would the money come from? From our young, well-heeled professionals who don't yet have family obligations. From older folk like me whose children are now out of college. From everyone else—of all races, I hasten to add—who can afford to give. From those who cannot but are willing to stage fundraisers instead. From groups like the Elks, the frats, and so forth.

How much have I in mind? I belong to a black men's organization, called the Westchester Clubmen. We partner with the White Plains YMCA in providing an after-school program for adolescent African American boys from the local middle school.

A few Sundays ago, the twenty-five of us put up $17,000—yes $17,000—for this year's program. Our grant pays the salaries of the three part-time youth workers who are there with the seventeen or so youngsters every weekday afternoon during the school year.

In other words, for a mere $1,000 annually per child, we can put a caring adult in the daily life of a youngster throughout the school year. Given the frightening realities facing our kids today, how can we afford not to make certain this happens? How can we in good conscience buy that luxury car when a less expensive model would serve our needs plus those of an inner-city youngster as well? Think about it, sisters and brothers.

Our mission, then, is to raise $500 to $1000 each year from every African American who can possibly afford it so we can put a caring adult regularly in the life of every child who needs one. If we're successful, we can then turn the tables on the majority community—business, government and foundations—and challenge it to match us for a change.

If we personally buy into this prevention strategy, we'll then be in a better position to say to our elected officials who are obsessed with crime, and legitimately so, that there's a smarter way to spend tax dollars to combat it.

Those 100,000 cops we're about to add under the federal anti-crime bill are the rough equivalent, cost-wise, of 300,000 part-time youth workers. Working at a ratio of 1 of them to every 6 or 7 youngsters, we could, with the same money, put a caring youth worker in the daily lives of 2 million inner-city youngsters.

Which anti-crime strategy—100,000 cops or 2 million inner-city kids tended by a caring adult every day—do you think would work best? I know which bet I'm prepared to place as a taxpayer.

Back now to our own youth development fund. We obviously need an army of fundraisers to extract this money from our folks. My friends, we've actually got one already enlisted in our cause. We simply need to give them new marching orders with the instruction that there is no more important mission for the Urban League. If need be, tell them: "Uncle Hugh wants you—now."

And who's that standing army, you might ask? It's the 3000 local Urban League board members, the 3000 members of our local guilds, the thousands of other volunteers who pitch in from time to time, the 2000-plus executives in BEEP (the Black Executive Exchange Program), the 500-strong NULITES students and, yes, the thousands of clients we've helped locally over the years through our training and other programs.

My friends, this mobilization campaign to take back our children from the streets is the manifest destiny of the Urban League movement. Who else has the credibility and the capacity and the connections to pull it off all across the country? If not us, then who? If not now, when? Our children urgently await our answer.

Let me turn now to our second focus area—economic self-sufficiency for poor families. As I said earlier, the economies of cities have undergone profound changes which have undermined the ability of marginally skilled and low skilled workers of all races adequately to support their families.

Just a generation ago, these blue-collar workers were the backbone of the American economy, and celebrated in the media as such. With the destruction of their livelihoods has come the rapid deterioration of their neighborhoods, the onset of despair, the break-up of families whose fathers can no longer be proud providers like my Uncle Edgar, the escalation of violent crime, and the ascendancy of the code of the streets.

Make no mistake, it's all of a piece. Each

breakdown begets or exacerbates another. To break the cycle, we must go back to the source of the problem, namely the growing inability of inner-city adults to find legitimate jobs that enable their families to live in dignity with a decent standard of living.

Marvelous as the market economy works for most Americans, it has all but collapsed for inner-city folk. There are fewer and fewer jobs for low-skilled workers, especially males. And the wages for those jobs that exist are just plain lousy, all too often at or below the poverty line.

In my view, many politicians and economists are in denial about the depth of this problem. Some blame its victims, saying they don't want to work anyway, despite convincing evidence to the contrary.

Others say high unemployment and low wages for low-skilled workers are the natural order of things in modern market economies and that government ought not interfere. Still others argue, optimistically, that there will be a happy ending when technology eventually replaces the lost jobs with more highly skilled and highly paid new ones.

The trouble is that none of these scenarios holds out much hope for inner-city people trapped in poverty today. It's unrealistic to expect all of them to upgrade themselves overnight from laborers and welfare recipients to office workers and small entrepreneurs.

Yet society these days expects everyone to support themselves. And the poor, not unreasonably, expect work to be worthwhile economically. Otherwise, why bother? Only the independently wealthy toil for therapeutic reasons alone.

Government invests lots of money in job training, but largely avoids the ideologically uncomfortable question of whether the market economy is actually creating enough jobs for everyone in the inner city who wants to or is expected to work.

The Urban League will join this crucial issue at several levels. Our bottom line goal, as Brother Herman Ewing of Memphis puts it, is to help dependent people become independently productive. Obviously we must continue our successful job training and placement programs. We'll also encourage entrepreneurship education for our young people and economic development for African American firms. In this vein, we welcome our partnership with the U.S. Small Business Administration, which has the Small Business Resource Center here.

We will pressure private and public employers to cut poor people in on the local job action, so that everyone has a shared stake in the overall community's quality of life. For instance, what if employers reserved training slots and real jobs for residents of neighborhoods or census tracts with high unemployment rates?

The way I see it, this wouldn't be a politically contentious race-based approach. Instead, it's a more palatable alternative which recognizes that poor people of all races need decent jobs.

But even these local measures may not be enough to employ everyone. There simply may be no alternative to government action if legitimate work is to be reintroduced as the prevailing way of life in poor neighborhoods.

I call upon government to create a new labor-intensive public enterprise to perform services valued by taxpayers. We taxpayers all know there's plenty of infrastructure work to do. Schools are crumbling. Subway and bus stations are strewn with graffiti and railroad rights-of-way are littered with trash. Public parks in cities and suburbs alike are poorly maintained.

> *"Marvelous as the market economy works for most Americans, it has all but collapsed for inner-city folk."*

Critics of governments jobs programs usually say it's the private sector's responsibility to create jobs. I agree in principle. But when the private labor market comes up woefully short, as it does today in the inner city, then government must step in if people are to work.

How quickly we forget in this post-Perestroika era that the military once was what I've just proposed—a labor-intensive public enterprise employing thousands of marginally skilled workers who helped produce goods and services (namely the national defense) that taxpayers really wanted.

Let's elevate America's infrastructure to the same valued status and alleviate urban unemployment in the bargain. What's several billion in new public dollars invested in schools, parks and people when compared with the billions more now spent much less productively on public assistance for the able-bodied and extra policemen and prisons?

That brings me to my third and final focus area—helping our racially diverse society work more harmoniously. Belief in racial inclusion goes to the marrow of my bones. My great-great-grandfather was a slave named George Latimer. He escaped from his master in Virginia. Latimer fled to Massachusetts, where white abolitionists rallied around him and prevented his recapture.

The incident inspired John Greenleaf Whittier to write a poem about it, entitled "From Massachusetts to Virginia." By the way, Latimer was the father of the celebrated inventer, Lewis Latimer, and the grandfather of the cousin I mentioned earlier, Winifred Norman, who is the goddaughter of Eugene Kinckle Jones.

I fully understand the instinct to separate when we are incessantly under economic siege. When we're still discriminated against some forty years after the *Brown* decision. And when, thanks to those recurring images on evening newscasts of black youngsters being hauled off to jail, even our honor students are trailed like common thieves when they enter stores.

Even so, it's suicidal economically to become so bitter that we isolate ourselves from others. America is a robustly multicultural society. So is its labor market. For example, I read recently of a small manufacturing firm in Southern California which has two hundred workers representing thirty nationalities. That's the new U.S. labor market. We deny this reality at our—and our children's—peril.

For all our suffering, we cannot become so fixated on our problems that we ignore our commonality of interest with others. All of the problems I've addressed this evening—inadequate schooling, idle and alienated youngsters, and chronic unemployment—cut across racial lines. If we're ever to deal with them on a scale remotely equal to their size, we must coalesce with people of other complexions who feel the same pain, even if it isn't yet as acute.

For instance, the expanded Earned Income Tax Credit and, soon I hope, universal health care would never happen were they seen solely as our issues. Yet both are of enormous benefit to our people.

Whites of all religions have oppressed us at one time or another. Mormons, Catholics, Jews, Episcopalians, Baptists. We've even been oppressed by our own on occasion. It's a form of reverse racism to single out any specific group of whites for vilification.

Many whites of good will have accompanied us on our long journey for racial, social and economic justice. None has matched the Jewish community as long-distance runners in the civil rights movement.

Just as we denounce misleading media stereotypes of African Americans, it is morally repugnant as well to impugn an entire people, especially long-standing allies, like Jews, because of the unconscionable behavior of some of them.

What constructive purpose is served by driving deeper wedges between races? Of course we must root out any vestiges of racism. But let's not wallow forever in real or perceived grievances lest we become Bosnia some day.

I say, let's get on with making our gloriously multicultural society work. If Nelson Mandela and F.W. De Klerk can bury the hatchets of hatred and oppression in the sand, instead of one another's heads, and get on with South Africa's future, then surely so can we.

At the same time, our allies should understand that serious-minded African Americans must be free to discuss the acute pain afflicting our community. Even if that means conferring with those with whom we vehemently disagree on other issues.

Dialoguing, even arguing, with those who hold abhorrent views is difficult yet sometimes necessary. Otherwise, opposing sides remain at loggerheads to the detriment of progress. How would U.S. relations with arch-enemy China ever have been normalized had Richard Nixon never met with Mao Zedong?

Would there ever have been a Camp David accord had Begin refused to dialogue with Sadat? Did Yitzhak Rabin compromise his moral integrity by meeting with Yassar Arafat as a prelude to today's Middle East peace? Would apartheid ever have ended had Mandela adamantly refused to negotiate with his people's brutal and hated oppressors?

As Churchill once said, "it's better to jaw, jaw, than to war, war." The time-honored role of the Urban League is to build bridges, not just between poverty and plenty, but between peoples of all races and persuasions.

The challenges I've outlined tonight are formidable. But seeing the thousands of Urban League faithful out there and feeling the energy emanating from you, I'm even more confident than when I took office that we're equal to them.

Why am I optimistic? Because Americans are beginning to see the connection between the nation's economic competitiveness and their own quality of life, on the one hand, and the decline of cities and the persistence of urban poverty, on the other.

They're finally connecting the dots between these phenomena. That's due in no small part to a President and First Lady who really understand and genuinely care about these issues, about our issues. That's a rare and welcome combination in elected officials these days.

I see a greater sense of shared risk, which is the necessary prelude to shared responsibility for finding solutions to our problems. And there's a growing sense that the social compact between society and the individual needs strengthening on both sides.

One side defines what people owe society—personal responsibility, nurturing their children, supporting themselves and their families, and abiding by society's laws. The other side defines what society owes its citizens—the opportunity to be self-reliant and protection from anarchy at home and invasion from abroad.

In recent decades, important elements of both sides of the social compact have eroded due to the profound economic changes sweeping the developed world, including our own country.

Many individuals are shirking responsibility and wreaking havoc on fellow citizens. Meanwhile, society has reneged on its obligation of providing reasonable access to opportunity for all. The result is the chaos we now see in cities.

We of the Urban League must work with our own in restoring personal responsibility—taking family obligations, child-rearing, education, self-reliance and citizenship seriously.

But society must update and then uphold its end of the bargain. What use is talk of opportunity when poor people see so little of it? The social compact must be revised so that self-reliance, with dignity and a decent standard of living, is an everyday reality instead of empty rhetoric.

To pursue the ambitious agenda I've outlined tonight, the Urban League must become a force to be reckoned with, not merely another minority face at the table.

That means reinvigorating and focusing our movement for maximum effectiveness. That means creating a state-of-the-art organization that's equipped today for the twenty-first century.

That means speaking once again with the authority that derives from our own research, our own innovative yet realistic ideas, and our own thorough critiques of the policies and approaches of others.

And that means backing our intellectual credibility with the clout of a vast network of influential and effective affiliates which are deeply rooted in their communities.

This is a tall order, but I'm absolutely confident that we're equal to it. Why? Because of the firm foundation that you in this vast audience have built over eighty-four years of service to our folk. Because of our unparalleled strengths—a proud history, a treasured household name, a terrific track record, a vast army of volunteers, and an affiliate network that delivers the goods every day for our people.

> ***"The Urban League must become a force to be reckoned with, not merely another minority face at the table."***

I'm often asked in interviews whether the Urban League has lost touch, whether we're relevant any longer to the needs of ordinary, as opposed to affluent, African Americans. What's my reply?

Just come with me, I say, to Africa Square Park in Liberty City and listen to T. Willard Fair tell you how the Miami Urban League recaptured that park from drug dealers and transformed it into a safe haven for children, complete with constructive programs after school and over the summer.

Come to Memphis and talk, as I did, to the public housing mother of five who told me how she's on her way to economic self-sufficiency thanks to the Urban League's Skill Center training.

Come with me to the Chicago Urban League to see Jim Compton's impressive research department which prepared the definitive statewide study of school finance inequities that cheat poor children of better educations.

That's the impressive and relevant work that skeptics would see in the field today were they actually to take a look.

Still, to those of us in this remarkable and respected movement, I say, that's great, but not yet good enough. Together we must take the Urban League to an entirely new plateau of effectiveness and impact for our people.

That's "the something more important" that my daughter predicted I was being saved for. That is your charge to me as I take office, And that is my challenge to you tonight. That is the manifest destiny of this great movement.

Ladies and gentlemen, it's time we get on with our calling. Let this 84th Annual Conference of the Urban League begin.

SOURCES

Detroit News, "Urban League Chief Spells Out Goals," September 23, 1994, p. 3B.

Jet, "Hugh Price Named President and Chief Executive of National Urban League," June 13, 1994, p. 26.

Newsweek, "A Tale of Two Cities," August 15, 1994, p. 57.

New York Times, "A Rights Leader Minimizes Racism as a Poverty Factor," July 24, 1994, p. A18; "Blacks' Problems, Seen Plain" (column), July 27, 1994, p. A21.

Wall Street Journal, "Urban League Chief Offers Ambitious, Practical Proposals," July 27, 1994.

Deborah Prothrow-Stith

1954–

African American physician and educator

One of the most passionate and respected voices speaking out on the subject of violence—especially violence against children—as a public health crisis is Dr. Deborah Prothrow-Stith, associate dean of the Harvard School of Public Health. In her many speeches (an average of three per week) as well as in her 1991 book, Deadly Consequences, *she paints a grim portrait of a country whose youngest citizens are at tremendous risk of injury or worse because so many adults glorify violence and teach that force is an acceptable way to resolve conflicts. Hers is a powerful message that often brings tears to the eyes of those who come to hear her decry the fact that "a significant portion of our children are withering on the vine before they have even bloomed a little."*

A native of Texas, Prothrow-Stith received her bachelor's degree from Spelman College in 1975 and went on to attend Harvard Medical School, from which she received her MD in 1979. It was while she was completing a routine internship in the emergency room of a Boston hospital in 1978 that the problem of youth violence began to trouble her deeply. Her medical training had prepared her to tend to the sick and the injured, and her background in public health education had predisposed her to thinking in terms of prevention as well as treatment. Yet she soon realized that while public health officials emphasized prevention in campaigns to reduce smoking and drug abuse, for example, they were silent on the subject of violent behavior and its impact. "I wanted to understand the forces that sent so many [young men] to the emergency room—cut up, shot up, bleeding, and dead," she explained in a Detroit Free Press *article. "Why were so many young males striking out with knives and guns? What could be done to stop the carnage? These questions motivated me to learn about violence."*

Prothrow-Stith's search for answers to her questions eventually led her to become an activist in violence prevention, which she insists is indeed a public health issue because it involves putting an end to behavior that causes harm to children. Adolescent health is, in fact, her area of specialty. During the late 1980s, she worked for the city of Boston as co-director of its Health Promotion Center for Urban Youth, for the Harvard Street Neighborhood Health Center as clinical chief, and for the state of Massachusetts as the first woman (and only the second African American) commissioner of public health. Prothrow-Stith has also served as an investigator on numerous adolescent violence projects. Since 1990, she has been affiliated with the Harvard School of Public Health, most recently as associate dean of government and community programs.

As a public health professional, Prothrow-Stith argues that the way to eliminate the climate of violence that exists in disadvantaged neighborhoods in particular is to get the message out through every means possible—government, schools, churches, community organizations, businesses, the media—that there are ways other than violence to deal with feelings of anger and aggression. In this way, she hopes to end the cycle of child abuse and spouse abuse that often prompts victims to one day become perpetrators themselves, either within the family or outside it.

Prothrow-Stith touches on these and related issues in many of her public appearances. In early May 1993, for example, she headed to Chicago to address the United Methodist National Youth Ministry Organization conference on youth and violence. An edited version of her keynote speech to an audience made up mostly of young adults is reprinted here from Christian Social Action, *a publication of the United Methodist Church.*

I am a physician. During my training, I got a little tired of stitching people up and sending them out knowing that they were at risk of subsequent episodes of violence. In fact, the most painful thing I ever had to do was to go out and tell a family, who had sent their son off to school that morning expecting that he would return as usual that evening, that he was now dead. I got a little tired of this problem of violence and responding to it but not feeling as if, as a society, we were trying to do anything about it.

Then one morning about three a.m., a young man who had gone to a party came in because he had been in a fight, and he needed stitches just over his eyebrow. I put in the stitches and as he was about to leave, he turned to me and said, "Now look, don't go to bed because the person who did this to me is going to be in this emergency room in about an hour, and you are going to get all the practice you need putting in stitches."

Deborah Prothrow-Stith

I was struck by that because while I knew people were going out to fight again, they never really said that to me, and this night, this early morning, that young man told me what he was going to do. I did not have a response, because I wasn't trained as a physician to have a response.

It dawned on me that if he had made a suicide attempt, if he had taken pills, and we had cleaned out his stomach, and he said to us, "Don't go to bed because I'm going to go home and take some more pills, so I'll be back in this emergency room and you'll get all the practice you need cleaning out my stomach," we would have responded very differently. In fact, we wouldn't have waited on him to volunteer that information. If somebody is depressed or has made a suicide attempt, we are obligated to ask about his or her intentions.

The more I thought about it the more I realized that in almost every aspect of health care we were concerned about prevention. If somebody has heart disease, we might do surgery, or offer medicine. However, you know we also get involved in issues of behavior—diet, exercise, smoking, stress reduction—all to prevent future heart disease. With lead poisoning, a children's problem, we get the lead out of the blood. We do that, but we also make sure that the house has been de-leaded before the child goes home. That involves economic, political, and social issues. In the name of prevention, in almost every aspect of medicine, we are involved in those kinds of issues—behavioral, psychological, political, economic—except with this problem of violence, for which we were content to stitch people up and send them out.

I really started thinking about this problem of violence, and it dawned on me that part of the problem is that we don't think we can prevent violence. As a society, we act like violence is a natural part of the human mission, as if there is nothing we can do about it except get tough when it happens. So I started studying this problem of violence, and I learned a couple of things that I want to share with you.

The first thing I learned surprised me a little bit. I learned we have a very big problem in the United States. I guess I knew that because I read the newspapers and I watch television, but I was surprised at how we compared to other industrialized countries when it came to homicide rates. The homicide rate for young men in the United States is at about twenty-two per hundred thousand. We are four times higher than Scotland, the next highest industrialized country. We are seventy times higher than Austria, found at the bottom of the list. In the middle are Portugal, Greece, France, Canada, Israel—countries to which we usually compare ourselves, industrialized countries, not at war, with stable governments.

This information said to me that violence isn't a natural problem. If this was a natural or inevitable part of the human condition, you would expect the homicide rate from country to country to be very similar. Everybody would have the problem. This kind of wide discrepancy in homicide rates suggested that we are doing something that we shouldn't be doing, or there are some things we ought to be doing that we are not doing, or both. Either way, this is a preventable problem; it is a problem we don't have to have.

I also learned that some people in the United States are at higher risk for this problem. The homicide rate for white men in the United States is over two times higher than Scotland and thirty-five times higher than Austria. You see, we think of this problem of violence as a problem of Black urban poor men, Hispanic men or "other" people, but we've got a US problem. We have grown to tolerate a level of violence in the United States as normal that is so much higher than the rest of the world. However, there are some people who are more at risk. The homicide rate for young Black men in the United States is eighty-five per hundred thousand, four times higher than the rate that's already seventy times higher than the rate in Austria. We've got a problem in America and some people are at greater risk.

I need to tell you something about this. These data come from the FBI. That agency collects them regularly. They are labeled "Black," "white," and "other." So if you are a Latino man, for instance, you might be labeled "Black, " you might be labeled "white," you might be labeled "other." So there is a lot that this doesn't tell us.

Another thing that this doesn't tell us is about the problem of poverty. You read a lot of newspaper reports, a lot of social science reports, a lot of medical reports, that say Blacks have a higher problem of violence, but unless you consider the problem of poverty, you won't know what's race and what's poverty. All the studies that have been done that look at poverty say this problem is not race. It is labeled race, but young Black men are overrepresented among the poor. This is really poverty.

One study shows the homicide rate for young Black men in the military. That rate is lower than the homicide rate for white men in the United States, suggesting that being in the military affords some economic, structural and support systems that affect this problem of violence.

Another study out of Atlanta looked at overcrowding in houses as a factor of poverty. Overcrowded whites had the same high homicide rates as did overcrowded Blacks, and less crowded Blacks had the same lower homicide rate as did less crowded whites. So [these studies] suggest that, while data are labeled race, what we are really looking at is poverty.

The second thing I learned shocked me.

Again, using the FBI numbers, about half of the homicides occur between friends and families—people who know each other and get into an argument. Half of the murders in the United States occur among friends and families.

That shocked me because watching the news, reading the newspaper, gives a sense that stranger bad-guy stuff is the bulk of the problem of violence and other felonies—that's drug trafficking, robbery, burglary, all that stranger bad-guy stuff—that's fifteen percent of the homicides, and half occur between friends and family who get into an argument. Think about it. More police, more street lights, stiffer sentences, trying teenagers as adults—all of those responses to crime will not have an impact on two people who know each other who get into an argument.

We also know that they are often drinking alcohol, or using another drug, and we know they have a gun. Think about it. Two people who know each other, who are drinking alcohol, or using another drug, who get into an argument, and who have a gun, a handgun. That is the typical homicide setting. Family is twenty percent, and friends and acquaintances represent another forty percent, that's half of the time. People who know each other. We've got a growing problem with violence in part because our response to violence has little to do with the problem. We respond aggressively to that stranger bad-guy stuff, but we do very little to prevent people who know each other who get into an argument from getting into a fight and from having homicide as an outcome.

> ***"From your very first cartoon, all the way through the latest superhero movie, we have taught you that violence is funny. . . . It is not funny."***

Half the time hand guns are the weapon. When you think about the difference between the United States and all those other countries, think about guns. That is part of the problem. A very interesting study compared Seattle, Washington, to Vancouver, British Columbia—cities in two different countries, with two different sets of gun laws. In Vancouver, you cannot get a handgun legally. They are there, but much more difficult to get. In Seattle, as in the case in most of our cities, you can get a gun; and they are very accessible.

Look at the assault rate. In Seattle and Vancouver, assaults by sticks and bats and fists are about the same [numbers]; also about the same are assaults by knives. However, the assault by guns is about four times greater in Seattle than in Vancouver. People ask the question, "Do guns kill people, or do people kill people?" This study suggests that, in fact, guns play a big role.

The same study reported on homicides, not just assault, but homicides. In Seattle, homicides are five times higher than in Vancouver. Two people who know each other who get into an argument who don't have a gun don't seem to find another way to kill each other. Guns seem to be a major risk factor for this problem of homicide.

Think about the United States compared to other countries. Guns are part of the [violence] problem, but they're not all of the problem. Some countries with guns don't have our very high homicide rate. Scandinavian countries have two or three guns in almost every household because of the way people are enrolled in the military. Sweden is a country like that, and it doesn't have our high homicide rates.

What about poverty? Homicide rates are higher in poor communities in the United States, but this is not the poorest country in the world. Lots of countries are poorer and don't have our high homicide rates. The Atlanta study [indicates that] overcrowding is part of the problem. But if any of you have been to Hong Kong or plan to travel through the major cities in Japan, you'll see there are lots of places much more overcrowded than any US city, and they don't have our high homicide rate. It's guns, and it's poverty, and it's overcrowding, and it is what I call our "make my day" ethic.

From your very first cartoon, all the way through the latest superhero movie, we have taught you that violence is funny, it's entertaining, it's the hero's first choice, it's successful, it's painless, it's guiltless, it's interesting. Some of you have been to enough funerals to know that it's not. It is not funny. It doesn't solve problems. It is certainly not a first choice. It is interesting because all of that hype in the movies about violence is just that—hype, not real. A lot of people make a lot of money making us think it is funny when somebody falls down or gets hit across the head or gets shot.

"Boys in the Hood" was a movie that showed violence, but the violence didn't solve a problem. In actuality, "Boys in the Hood" was kind of a sad movie, probably one of the few movies that told you the truth about violence.

In "Total Recall" not only did [the husband] shoot his wife, but after he shot her, he cracked a joke on the way out the door. In the escalator scene in that movie, he grabbed a man's body who had been shot and used that body to shield himself against the bullets as he went up the escalator. We were all thinking, "Wow, that is so smart." When he gets to the top of the escalator, he tosses that man to the side and said something like, "Buddy, you had a bad day." No funeral, no tears, no kids wondering why Daddy didn't come home, none of the pain of violence.

Part of our problem is this "make my day ethic." Movies and television are just part of it. We have had a "kick butt" president, and we have had a "make my day" president. Adults in our society have gotten kind of confused on this issue. Sometimes parents tell kids, "You go back outside and you beat him up or I'm going to beat you." Nobody wants a wimp for a child.

It's not just the adults who are confused on this issue; teenagers put pressure on each other to fight. Somebody starts talking about somebody else. Somebody else tells somebody else, and somebody else tells somebody else, and then a whole bunch of somebodies want to know what's going on, what's going down, what's going to happen. Somebody says three o'clock on the corner and everybody's there. Everybody wants to see. With these whetted appetites for violence, we set our friends up to fight. Then we all go to see.

Something is really wrong with us as a country. Almost every message at almost every level of communication encourages violence. If our problem was stranger bad-guy violence, then maybe I wouldn't care. But our problem is that we don't know how to get along with each other. We don't know how to get along with friends and family. Handling anger is not so easy, and right now we either beat people up or we do nothing.

I'm involved with a number of people across the country working to change this problem—change our attitudes about it, change our thinking on it. We are using some of what we used to change our attitudes about smoking. When I was about eight years old, I used to buy those candy cigarettes, and I would stand in front of the television and imitate all the beautiful people on television smoking. Movie stars smoked, everybody smoked. It was really a glamorous thing to do. Now, in Boston, people are standing outside in some very cold weather smoking cigarettes. You know why? Because it is offensive and it is unhealthy. Some of them work in smoke-free buildings. They can't smoke inside. That's a big change in attitude. It requires education, working with the media, doing lots of stuff to change our attitudes.

Two public service announcements now say, "Fighting is a lousy way to loose a friend. Friends for life. Don't let friends fight."

That's a part of this whole effort. It comes with t-shirts, billboards, posters, education in the classroom about handling anger. Probably the thing that keeps me most optimistic is how many students and parents have gotten involved in this. On the order of Mothers Against Drunk Driving (MADD), and Students Against Drunk Driving (SADD), there are organizations in Detroit called SOSAD (Save Our Sons and Daughters), in Atlanta called MOMS (Mothers of Murdered Sons) and in Nebraska, out of Omaha, called MAD DADS. These people are getting ready to say this is a problem that we don't have to have.

SOURCES

Books

Prothrow-Stith, Deborah, with Michaele Weissman, *Deadly Consequences*, HarperCollins, 1991.

Periodicals

Christian Social Action, "Fighting Is a Lousy Way to Lose a Friend," June, 1993.

Detroit Free Press, "A Bloody Turning Point," January 3, 1993, p. 6H; "Stop Glorifying Violence, Doctor Says," May 29, 1993, p. 10A.

Essence, January, 1992, p. 42.

People, June 14, 1993, p. 54.

A. Philip Randolph

1889–1979

African American labor leader and civil rights activist

As founder of the Brotherhood of Sleeping Car Porters and a lifelong activist on behalf of black workers, A. Philip Randolph ranks as one of the twentieth century's most prominent labor leaders. He battled discrimination in industry, in unions, and in the military at a time when African Americans typically found themselves among the "last hired, first fired." As a result of his efforts, he was branded a radical and a troublemaker, even by some of his fellow blacks who advocated a more conservative approach. But Randolph remained at the forefront of both the labor and civil rights movements for nearly forty years, from the 1920s through the 1960s.

A native of Crescent City, Florida, Randolph attended high school at Cookman Institute (now Bethune-Cookman College) in Daytona Beach before heading north to New York City. There he worked at a series of low-paying jobs while taking political science classes at City College. It was also during this same period that he first began organizing efforts on behalf of various unions, including the American Federation of Labor (AFL)-affiliated Elevator and Starters Union, the Negro Motion Pictures Operators of New York, the Negro Garment Workers of New York, and the Philadelphia Longshoremen. These activities proved unpopular with many of his employers and often prompted them to fire him.

Equally unpopular with employers were Randolph's other causes: socialism and antiwar activism. Beginning around 1915 and for the next dozen years or so, he served as editor and publisher of the Messenger, *a radical black journal that endorsed socialism as the answer to the economic problems facing African Americans. In 1921, he entered the political arena, running unsuccessfully for the office of secretary of state in New York on the socialist ticket. A committed pacifist, Randolph also vehemently protested America's entry into World War I and blasted the hypocritical notion that the United States had an obligation to "make the world safe for democracy" when its black citizens faced discrimination and death by lynching in their own hometowns. He angered many by urging blacks to refuse to serve in the armed forces as long as such bias was allowed to continue.*

His special area of concern, however, was the lot of the sleeping car (Pullman) porters on the nation's railroads—black men who worked from 300 to 400 hours *per month (traveling a distance of some 11,000 miles) for an average wage of less than $70, out of which they had to buy their own uniforms, shoe polish, and meals. Job security was nonexistent, and the treatment each man received varied from one supervisor to another.*

Randolph announced his plan to organize the porters in August 1925, vowing to secure for them the right to collective bargaining, higher pay, shorter hours, and improved working conditions. While he won the support of the AFL (which granted the Brotherhood an international charter, its first ever to a black union), the NAACP, and the National Urban League, he faced strong opposition from Pullman Company officials, who branded him a dangerous radical. Nevertheless, by 1928 over half the sleeping car porters in the country were members of the Brotherhood, and by 1937, the Pullman Company had at last consented to give the union full recognition and negotiate a new contract—thanks to Randolph's persistence. Even more remarkable was the fact that he achieved this without resorting to any strikes, violence, or political pressure.

In 1936, Randolph was named president of the newly-formed National Negro Congress, an organization that united diverse groups of progressive-minded African Americans in the hope that together they could find solutions to the many difficult economic and social problems blacks faced as a consequence of the Depression. While he did not prohibit whites from participating and in fact encouraged cooperation with people of other races who shared the goals of the Congress, he tried to make it a mostly-black organization and stressed that its aim was strength through unity, self-direction, and self-sufficiency. As such, it was the most significant black nationalist movement in America between the decline of Marcus Garvey in the 1920s and the emergence of the black power advocates during the 1960s.

Illness kept Randolph from delivering the keynote address in person that first year, but he was able to attend the second meeting of the Congress in 1937. There he gave a stirring opening speech in honor of the 150th anniversary of the U.S. Constitution, a particularly fitting subject since fascism and totalitarianism were then threatening to engulf Europe and the Far East. In his remarks, he touched on some of the high and low points in African American history and summarized the progress made by the National Negro Congress during its brief existence. His speech, which originally appeared in the official proceedings of the conference, is taken here from Negro Protest Thought in the Twentieth Century, *(Bobbs-Merrill, 1965).*

In this hour of crisis in the nation, in the whole wide world, in governments, in industry, in trade union movements and among oppressed minorities everywhere, the Second National Negro Congress, representing hundreds of thousands of Negroes in America, hails the Constitution on its 150th birthday. We hail it as a Magna Charta of human rights. The Negro people, oppressed and persecuted, especially look to the Constitution as an impregnable citadel of their liberties.

Caught between the powerful forces of the southern plantation economy, on the one hand, and the rising financial and industrial power of the north, on the other, the Constitution was a compromise on the question of slavery, but the Thirteenth, Fourteenth, and Fifteenth Amendments sought to chart and establish the guarantees of their full citizenship rights of the Negro people.

Sinister tendencies toward the re-enslavement of the freedmen manifested themselves soon after the Civil War had ended, and the

A. Philip Randolph

uncompromising Sumner, and the valiant band of Abolitionists had lost their memorable fight to protect the newly emancipated slaves with federal troops in the South. This unhappy chapter in American history tells of the tragic loss of the liberty of an entire race following the breakdown of the great and inspiring experiment of Reconstruction, rendering the bourbon plantation owners and the former slave-masters free to use the shotgun, the tissue ballot and the Ku Klux Klan terror, to drive the Negro back into a semi-caste status. Indeed, the conditions calculated to achieve the full citizenship for the former slaves were never fulfilled by the Civil War, though the beginning was challenging. Verily, the Constitution, without the force of enlightened public opinion back of it, could not itself effect what a bourgeois revolution did not accomplish.

While the new South with its lumber, turpentine and cotton magnates, went out for cheap labor as its major interest, to pile up high profits, it also attacked the civil rights of the Negro with a view to breaking his hope and faith in the inner redemptive forces of the race so that they would undervalue their human worth and economic role in Southern industry and planting. This created the need and demand for the Fourteenth and Fifteenth Amendments to th Constitution. They were passed. But the d process clause has been employed more as a weapon for defending corporate wealth rather than the human rights of the Negro people.

Now, it has become a commonplace that Black America is not only concerned with the Thirteenth, Fourteenth and Fifteenth Amendments that grew out of the Civil War and the Reconstruction period, a period which though maligned, condemned and misrepresented by historians, with more of the Nordic bias than of the scientific spirit, will ever live as a glorious record of the capacity and genius of the Negro people for orderly, enlightened and the constructive administration of government, but Afro-Americans are, too, interested in the Bill of Rights of the Constitution which provides the framework and basis of civil and political liberties within and upon which alone as free people or rather may seek to secure and maintain their freedom, and build those institutions that help preserve freedom.

It is well nigh a truism that without the freedom of speech, of habeas corpus, of the freedom of worship, of the right to vote and be voted for, the basic institutions of modern society, such as the home, family, church, school, press, free business enterprise, trade union movements and associations seeking the liberation of all oppressed minority groups, could hardy exist and enjoy a healthy growth and development.

The Constitution stands as an imposing bulwark of these rights. But the Constitution is not an end in itself. Nor is it a perfect document. It possesses many grave limitations, and needs some fundamental and permanent change so as to make possible reforms for the protection and advancement of the workers. This worthy objective is now courageously sought by President Roosevelt, without the method of constitutional change, in his Supreme Court reorganization plan. Any such change through the method of legislation only, though desirable and timely, may not be so enduring as if wrought through change of the Constitution itself. But let us back the president's fight for judicial justice.

In very truth, the Constitution is a means to an end. The end is the attainment of an enlightened and humane government, and an economic order that will invest the people with the right and the power to live the good life, the more abundant life.

And today, in a world of storm and stress, of confusion and uncertainty, of arrogant cynicism and deadly pessimism, of war and fascism, the American Constitution proudly reveals its deeper moorings of stability, assurance and hope for democracy.

> ***"Freedom is never given; it is won. And the Negro people must win their freedom. . . . This involves struggle, continuous struggle."***

While the Negro people, under the Constitution, because of nullification by the spirit of the Lost Cause, are still without the full measure of citizenship in the former Confederate States, the Constitution, at least, vouchsafes complete citizenship rights and provides the grounds of principle and promises to secure it.

Albeit, it is more and more becoming correctly understood that the task of realizing full citizenship for the Negro people is largely in the hands of the Negro people themselves. Assuring full citizenship rights to [the] Afro-American is the duty and responsibility of the State, but securing them is the task of the Negro; it is the task of labor and the progressive and liberal forces of the nation. Freedom is never given; it is won. And the Negro people must win their freedom. They must achieve justice. This involves struggle, continuous struggle.

True liberation can be acquired and maintained only when the Negro people possess power; and power is the product and flower of organization—organization of the masses, the masses in the mills and mines, on the farms, in the factories, in churches, in fraternal organizations, in homes, colleges, women's clubs, student groups, trade unions, tenants' leagues, in cooperative guilds, political organizations and civil rights associations.

Organization is the purpose and aim of the Second National Negro Congress. While it does not seek, as its primary program, to organize the Negro people into trade unions and civil rights movements, it does plan to integrate and coordinate the existing Negro organizations into one federated and collective agency so as to develop greater and more effective power. The Congress does not stress or espouse any political faith or religious creed, but seeks to formulate a minimum political, economic and social program which all Negro groups can endorse and for which they can work and fight.

The Congress supports the fight of the National Association for the Advancement of Colored People for a federal anti-lynching bill, for around this issue there is no basic difference of opinion among Negroes. All Negro people desire and seek fair opportunities for work and the right to join trade unions. No one can object to a proposal for more and better jobs, the abolition of Jim Crow labor unions, and for equal educational chances in public schools and universities.

It may not be amiss to add also, in this connection, that the Congress is not Communist or Republican, Democratic or Socialist. It is not Methodist, Baptist or Christian Scientist. It avoids control by any single religion or political party. It shuns the Scylla and Charybdis of the extreme left and the extreme right. But, in the true spirit of the united front, and in the pattern and purpose of integration and coordination, for mass strength, [it] embraces all sections of opinion among the Negro people. It does not seek to impose any issue of philosophy upon any organization or group, but rather to unite varying and various organizations, with various and varying philosophies, left, center, and right among the Negro people upon a simple, minimum program so as to mobilize and rally power and mass support behind vital issues affecting the life and destiny of the race.

Be it also known that the Congress does not seek to change the American form of government, but rather to implement it with new and rugged morals and spiritual sinews to make its democratic traditions, forms and ideals more permanent and abiding and a living force.

Startling changes, economic, political and social, have come upon the world. The empire of the Kaiser, apparently rock-ribbed and as steadfast as the sun, has been replaced by the totalitarian Third Reich. The Italian democratic state has given way to a corporate, fascist system. And the Czar, of all the Russias, has been relegated to oblivion by the Soviets of the workers.

And even if the honored democracies of the United States, England and France, have not succumbed and capitulated to the drastic and dangerous pattern of the dictator, they are under constant, menacing stress and strain of tendencies toward the rule of fascist force. Deadlocked, withal, in a mighty struggle for supremacy are the governments by the rule of "the man on horseback" and governments by rule of a free people.

Add to our existing political disorder reflected in the amazing and rapid transformation of the structure and direction of modern governments, economic maladjustments as seen in worldwide chronic and permanent unemployment, monetary fluctuations and industrial instability, the ever rising threat of a widening sweep of the wave of war, then optimism and hope are shattered and replaced by pessimism and fear.

Already, large areas of the world are in the flames of war. The "little brown men" of militaristic Nippon are raining fire and destruction upon the land of Confucius, but the Chinese people, proud in their noble heritage, are defending their country with matchless courage and resolve, yielding no single inch of territory except under the imperative of superior force.

And when we turn our eyes to the West, to the Mediterranean, we witness the vile and vicious efforts of Mussolini and Hitler, in accordance with the terms of a Berlin-Rome axis seeking to encompass by open murder the destruction of democracy. Lulled and solaced in conscience by the non-intervention sham, the democratic nations, England, France and the United States, are observing defenseless women and children of the legitimate Loyalists government of Spain massacred in shocking barbarism by the hoards [hordes] of Franco, backed by the money and men in Italy and Germany. Whither doth it lead, comes the query?

It is well nigh accepted quite generally by the thoughtful peoples everywhere that if the dykes of democracy break in the land of the little Iberian peninsula, a world flood of fascism may not be far behind, and imperil free peoples everywhere.

This may be the tragic price that mankind must pay for its complacent and timid spirit before the brutal and ruthless aggression by Japan upon China in creating the puppet kingdom of Manchukuo, and the cruel and savage invasion of the ancient kingdom of Ethiopia by the fascist legions of Italy. The independence of Ethiopia has been sold down the river by the League of Nations, while winked at by England and France.

And when we return to our shores, we find closer at home that all is not well. Despite signs of some recovery from the Depression, unemployment trenches hard upon eight million. Unemployment has taken on the picture of permanency. Production in certain industries increases while the workers decrease. The development of the machine, the refinements in management and the concentration and centralization of economic power in trusts and holding companies make this possible. With grave warning, President Roosevelt has declared that one-third of the population is in ill health, underfed, underhoused and underclothed. Relief needs have not appreciably lessened, for jobs are still scarce for the workers.

Civil rights, in industrial areas, where conflict between labor and capital is on, are arrogantly disregarded and broken down by pliant municipal representatives, and extra-governmental organizations such as the Ku Klux Klan, the Black Legion and other vigilante movements.

But not only are the rights of the workers assailed by vigilante mobs at the behest of the Liberty League and the organized open-shop business interests of America, but in state legislatures and Congress, diehard tories, such as Senator Vanderberg [Vandenberg] and others, are seeking to enact legislation, forcing upon trade unions and corporations, compulsory arbitration and the elimination of strikes.

And as we look to labor we find its house divided. Thus it is obvious that the great problem of the workers in America today is the problem of unity. . . . Craft and industrial unionism can and must go side by side in the struggle of the workers for industrial democracy. These forms of organization must develop and function in one house of labor. Now, what of the Negro in relation to these problems?

The Negro people are an integral part of the American commonwealth. They, like our white brothers, bleed and die in war. They suffer and hunger in the depression. Thus, theirs is the task of consolidating their interests with the interest of the progressive forces of the nation. Collective bargaining brings power to black as well as to white workers. The abolition of the company union frees the Negro workers from economic bondage and enables them to express their voice in the determination of wage rates, hours and working conditions the same as it does for white workers. Thus, the strengthening of the labor movement, the improvement of labor standards, brings comfort, health and decency to black as well as to white workers.

But there are other problems that the Negro people face. In the South there is a blight of Jim Crowism, segregation, disfranchisement through grandfather clauses and lily-white primaries and the terror of the Ku Klux Klan.

Peonage, a form of involuntary servitude, in utter nullification of the Thirteenth Amendment, holds the Negro in many Southern states in a condition of virtual slavery. Negro tenant farmers are browbeaten, persecuted and driven, when they evince any semblance of independence[,] out of their miserable and squalid shacks onto the highway. Civil and political rights for them are virtually unknown. Differentials in wages and hours of work are a common practice. Relief, though given by the federal government is administered by whim of Southern prejudice in the mood of arrogant superiority. What can be done about this? The answer is: Let us build a united front of all Negro organizations, of varying strata, purpose and outlook. Let us build a united front in cooperation with the progressive and liberal agencies of the nation whose interests are common with Black America.

With the spirit and strategy of the United Front, the five remaining Scottsboro Boys can be released from their dark dungeon in Alabama. With it peonage in the South can be wiped out and the sharecropper and tenant farmers, black and white, can organize and improve their economic status through collective bargaining. With it the horror of lynching in America may be eliminated and mob terror relegated to oblivion.

Thus, on the occasion of the 150th anniversary of the American Constitution, and the 2nd anniversary of the National Negro Congress, the Negro peoples face the future, with heads erect and souls uncurbed, resolved to march forward in the van of progress, with hope and faith in the creation of a new and better world. And the Congress shall help to guide them, to lead them on!

What now of the stewardship of the Congress since its memorable bow to black and white America?

Can more be said than that it has fought a good fight? It has kept the faith. It has worked and not grown weary for a happier humanity.

On the far-flung battle lines of steel, it marshalled militant black men to march in the van with the CIO to chalk up an enviable record in bringing workers into the field of industrial organization. And it has worked with the American Federation of Labor. Our men did not fail or faint before blood or bullets—in South Chicago, Detroit, Michigan, Ohio and Pennsylvania.

The Congress has brought eager and aggressive black youth to grapple with the problem of the organization of the tobacco workers in Virginia. And these youth are winning their spurs.

To the laundry workers in Washington, D.C., the Congress is carrying the message of trade union organization. And it enlisted Negro organizers to join CIO forces to organize the automobile industry.

On the civil and political rights' front, the Congress joined the fighting forces of the National Association for the Advancement of Colored People, to battle for the Wagner-Gavagan federal anti-lynching bill.

And to the rescue of Herndon and the Scottsboro Boys, the Congress has carried its unflagging fighting spirit.

But not only has it fought in the front for the defense of the rights of the Negro people, the Congress has also thrown its might with the progressive forces in the land to aid in the cause of Spanish democracy, the independence of China from the domination of Japan, and the restoration of Hailie Selassie to an independent kingdom of Ethiopia.

Yes it has joined the great demonstration of the nation against war and fascism. And, too, it is stirring the women and youth of the Negro people to join and struggle with the national and world agencies of their groups for a better world.

Therefore, with humble pride we cry out of the depths of our souls to mankind everywhere: forward with the destruction of the imperialist domination and oppression of the great peoples of Africa! Forward to the abolition of the fascist rule of Italy over the noble independent, and unconquerable men of Ethiopia! Forward to the creation of a united, free and independent China! Forward to victory of the valiant loyalist armies over the fascist brigands of Franco! Long live the cause of world peace! Long live the spirit of world democracy! Long live the memory and love of the black revolutionist of the eighteenth century, led by Denmark Vesey, Nat Turner, Gabriel, Harriet Tubman, Sojourner Truth, and Frederick Douglass! Long live the valor of those black regiments of slaves and freedom [freedmen] whose blood and courage made . . . Lincoln's Emancipation Proclamation a living reality!

Forward to the unity of the workers! Forward to democracy and freedom, progress and plenty! Forward with the torch of education, the instrument of agitation, the weapon of organization to a day of peace on earth and toward men, good will!

Randolph's affiliation with the National Negro Congress was short-lived; he resigned the presidency in 1940 after it became clear that some communist members—who had played key roles in the group's formation—were determined to advance an agenda of their own. Still convinced of the need for an all-black, action-oriented organization, Randolph formed the March on Washington Movement in 1941. Its immediate goal was to challenge discrimination and segregation in the defense industry and the armed forces, both of which were gearing up to respond to the first rumblings of World War II. His plan was to rally tens of thousands of African Americans in the nation's capital on July 1, 1941, to demand equal opportunities for African Americans.

Fearful that such a demonstration would undermine the image of national unity he was trying to project to a world then at war, President Franklin Roosevelt repeatedly urged Randolph to call off the march. The labor leader adamantly refused to do so until the president finally agreed to take action. On June 25, Roosevelt issued Executive Order 8802, which prohibited racial discrimination in the hiring of defense industry workers and established the Fair Employment Practices Committee to monitor any abuses. Randolph responded by canceling the demonstration, but not until almost the very last minute. The march that had required no one to take a single step was a tremendous victory and made a hero out of its leader, already widely respected among blacks for his work with the Brotherhood of Sleeping Car Porters.

Even though the protest itself had been called off, Randolph kept the March on Washington Movement intact so that it could continue to press for equal rights for African Americans.

On September 27, 1942, he addressed supporters at a special policy conference in Detroit. In his speech, which was originally published in pamphlet form, Randolph outlined the goals of the movement, which clearly foreshadow those of the civil rights struggle of the 1960s. The version of his remarks that follows combines excerpts from The Voice of Black America: Major Speeches by Negroes in the United States, 1797-1971, *and* Black Protest: History, Documents, and Analyses, 1619 to the Present, *(Ballantine, 1983).*

Fellow marchers and delegates to the Policy Conference of the March on Washington Movement and friends: We have met at an hour when the sinister shadows of war are lengthening and becoming more threatening. As one of the sections of the oppressed darker races, and representing a part of the exploited millions of the workers of the world, we are deeply concerned that the totalitarian legions of Hitler, Hirohito and Mussolini do not batter the last bastions of democracy. We know that our fate is tied up with the fate of the democratic way of life. And so, out of the depth of our hearts, a cry goes up for the triumph of the United Nations. But we would not be honest with ourselves were we to stop with a call for a victory of arms alone. We know this is not enough. We fight that the democratic faiths, values, heritages and ideals may prevail.

Unless this war sounds the death knell to the old Anglo-American empire systems, the hapless story of which is one of exploitation for the profit and power of a monopoly-capitalist economy, it will have been fought in vain. Our aim, then, must not only be to defeat Nazism, fascism and militarism on the battlefield but to win the peace, for democracy, for freedom and the Brotherhood of Man without regard to his pigmentation, land of his birth or the God of his fathers.

We therefore sharply score the Atlantic Charter as expressing a vile and hateful racism and a manifestation of the tragic and utter collapse of an old, decadent democratic political liberalism which worshiped at the shrine of a world-conquering monopoly capitalism. This system grew fat and waxed powerful off the flesh, blood, sweat and tears of the tireless toilers of the human race and the sons and daughters of color in the underdeveloped lands of the world.

When this war ends, the people want something more than the dispersal of equality and power among individual citizens in a liberal, political, democratic system. They demand with striking comparability the dispersal of equality and power among the citizen-workers in an economic democracy that will make certain the assurance of the good life—the more abundant life—in a warless world.

But, withal this condition of freedom, equality and democracy is not the gift of the Gods. It is the task of men—yes, men—brave men, honest men, determined men.

This is why we have met in Detroit in this Policy Conference of the March on Washington Movement. We have come to set forth our goals, declare our principles, formulate our policies, plan our program and discuss our methods, strategy, and tactics. This is the job of every movement which seeks to map out clearly the direction in which it is going as well as build up and strengthen the motivations.

Now our goals are what we hope to attain. They are near and remote, immediate and ultimate. This requires the long and short range program.

Thus our feet are set in the path toward equality—economic, political and social and racial. Equality is the heart and essence of democracy, freedom and justice. Without equality of opportunity in industry, in labor unions, schools and colleges, government, politics and before the law, without equality in social relations and in all phases of human endeavor, the Negro is certain to be consigned to an inferior status. There must be no dual standards of justice, no dual rights, privileges, duties or responsibilities of citizenship. No dual forms of freedom.

If Negroes are not the equal of white citizens, then they are unequal, either above or below them. But if they are to set the standards, Negroes will be below them. And if Negroes are considered unequal on a sub-standard basis, then they will receive unequal or inferior treatment.

Justice for the slave is not the same justice for the freeman. Treatment of a thoroughbred is not the same as the treatment of a workhorse.

But our nearer goals include the abolition of discrimination, segregation and Jim Crow in the government, the Army, Navy, Air Corps, U.S. Marine, Coast Guard, Women's Auxiliary Army Corps and the Waves, and defense industries; the elimination of discrimination in hotels, restaurants, on public transportation conveyances, in educational, recreational, cultural, and amusement and entertainment places such as theaters, beaches and so forth.

We want the full works of citizenship with no reservations. We will accept nothing less.

But goals must be achieved. They are not secured because it is just and right that they be possessed by Negro or white people. Slavery was not abolished because it was bad and unjust. It was abolished because men fought, bled and died on the battlefield in the Union Army and conquered the Confederate forces in the Civil War. Of course slavery was uneconomic and would have disappeared in time but this economic axiom involves no moral judgment.

Therefore, if Negroes secure their goals, immediate and remote, they must win them and to win them they must fight, sacrifice, suffer, go to jail and, if need be, die for them. These rights will not be given. They must be taken.

Democracy was fought for and taken from political royalists—the kings. Industrial democracy, the rights of the workers to organize and designate the representatives of their own choosing to bargain collectively is being won and taken from the economic royalists—big business.

Now the realization of goals and rights by a nation, race or class requires belief in and loyalty to principles and policies. Principles represent the basic and deep human and social convictions of a man or a people such as democracy, equality, freedom of conscience, the deification of the state, protestantism. Policies rest upon principles. Concretely, a policy sets forth one's position on vital public questions such as political affiliations, religious alliances. The March on Washington Movement must be opposed to partisan political commitments, religious or denominational alliances. We cannot sup with the communists, for they rule or ruin any movement. This is their policy. Our policy must be to shun them. This does not mean that Negro communists may not join the March on Washington Movement.

As to the composition of our movement. Our policy is that it be all-Negro, and pro-Negro but not anti-white, or anti-Semitic or anti-labor, or anti-Catholic. The reason for this policy is that all oppressed people must assume the responsibility and take the initiative to free themselves. Jews must wage their battle to abolish anti-Semitism. Catholics must wage their battle to abolish anti-Catholicism. The workers must wage their battle to advance and protect their interests and rights.

But this does not mean that because Jews must take the responsibility and initiative to solve their own problems that they should not seek the cooperation and support of Gentiles, or that Catholics should not seek the support of Negroes, or that the workers should not attempt to enlist the backing of Jews, Catholics, and Negroes in their fight to win a strike; but the main reliance must be upon the workers themselves. By the same token because Negroes build an all-Negro movement such as the March, it does not follow that our movement should not call for the collaboration of Jews, Catholics, trade unions and white liberals to help restore the President's Fair Employment Practice Committee to its original status of independence, with responsibility to the President. That was done. William Green, President of the AF of L and Philip Murray, President of CIO were called upon to send telegrams to the President to restore the Committee to its independence. Both responded. Their cooperation had its effects. Workers have formed citizens committees to back them while on strike, but this does not mean that they take those citizens into their unions as members. No, not at all.

And while the March on Washington Movement may find it advisable to form a citizens

> *"We want the full works of citizenship with no reservations. We will accept nothing less."*

committee of friendly white citizens to give moral support to a fight against the poll tax or white primaries, it does not imply that these white citizens or citizens of any racial group should be taken into the March on Washington Movement as members. The essential value of an all-Negro movement such as the March on Washington is that it helps to create faith by Negroes in Negroes. It develops a sense of self-reliance with Negroes depending on Negroes in vital matters. It helps to break down the slave psychology and inferiority complex in Negroes which comes and is nourished with Negroes relying on white people for direction and support. This inevitably happens in mixed organizations that are supposed to be in the interest of the Negro.

Now, in every community there are many and varied problems. Some are specialized and others are generalized. For instance the problem of anti-Semitism is a specialized one and must be attacked by the Jews through a Jewish organization which considers this question its major interest. The organization of the unorganized workers and the winning of wage increases, shorter hours, and better working conditions, is a specialized problem of workers which must be handled through a trade union composed of workers, not lawyers, doctors, preachers, or business men or by an organization of Catholics or Negroes.

The problem of lynching is a specialized one and Negroes must take the responsibility and initiative to solve it, because Negroes are the chief victims of low wages and must act to change and raise them.

But the problems of taxation, sanitation, health, a proper school system, an efficient fire department, and crime are generalized problems. They don't only concern the workers or Jews or Negroes or Catholics, but everybody and hence it is sound and proper social strategy and policy for all of these groups in the community to form a generalized or composite movement, financed by all, to handle these problems that are definitely general in nature. Neither group can depend upon the other in dealing with a general social problem. No one group can handle it properly. But this same general organization could not be depended upon to fight for the abolition of segregation of Negroes in the government, or to abolish company unionism in the interest of the workers, or to fight anti-Semitism. Its structure is too general to qualify it to attempt to solve a special problem. And, by the same logic, the Zionist Movement, or the Knights of Columbus, or the Longshoremen's Union is too special in structure and purpose to be qualified to deal with such a general problem as crime, or health, or education in a community.

Therefore, while the March on Washington Movement is interested in the general problems of every community and will lend its aid to help solve them, it has as its major interest and task the liberation of the Negro people, and this is sound social economy. It is in conformity with the principle of the division of labor. No organization can do everything. Every organization can do something, and each organization is charged with the social responsibility to do that which it can do, is built to do.

I have given quite some time to the discussion of this question of organizational structure and function and composition, because the March on Washington Movement is a mass movement of Negroes which is being built to achieve a definite objective, and is a departure from the usual pattern of Negro efforts and thinking. As a rule, Negroes do not choose to be to themselves in anything, they are only to themselves as a result of compulsive segregation. Negroes are together voluntarily for the same reason the workers join voluntarily into a trade union. But because workers only join trade unions, does not mean that the very same workers may not join organizations composed of some nonworkers, such as art museums or churches or fraternal lodges that have varying purposes. This same thing is true of Negroes. Because Negroes only can join the March on Washington Movement, does not indicate that Negroes in the MOWM may not join an interracial golf club or church or Elks Lodge or debating society or trade union.

No one would claim that a society of Filipinos is undemocratic because it does not take in Japanese members, or that Catholics are anti-Jewish because the Jesuits won't accept Jews as members or that trade unions are illiberal because they deny membership to employers. Neither is the March on Washington Movement undemocratic because it confines its members to Negroes. Now this reasoning would not apply to a public school or a Pullman car, because these agencies are public in nature and provide a service which is necessary to all of the people of a community.

Now, the question of policy which I have been discussing involves, for example, the March on Washington Movement's position on the war. We say that the Negro must fight for his democratic rights now, for after the war it may be too late. This is our policy on the Negro and the war. But this policy raises the question of method, programs, strategy and tactics—namely, how is this to be done. It is not sufficient to say that Negroes must fight for their rights now, during the war. Some methods must be devised, program set up, and strategy outlined.

This Policy Conference is designed to do this very thing. The first requirement to executing the policies of the March on Washington Movement is to have something to execute them with. This brings me to the consideration of organization. Organization supplies the power. The formulation of policies and the planning process furnish direction. Now, there is organization and organization. Some people say, for instance, Negroes are already organized, and they cite the Sisters of the Mysterious Ten, the Sons and Daughters of I Will Arise, the Holy Rollers, the social clubs, and so forth. But these organizations are concerned about the individual interest of helping the sick and funeralizing the dead or providing amusement and recreation. They deal with no social or racial problem which concerns the entire people. The Negro people as a whole is not interested in whether Miss A. plays contract bridge on Friday or not, or whether the deacon of the Methodist Church has a 200- or 500-dollar casket when he dies. These are personal questions. But the Negro race is concerned about Negroes being refused jobs in defense plants, or whether a Negro can purchase a lower in a Pullman car, or whether the United States Treasury segregates Negro girls. Thus, while it is true Negroes are highly organized, the organizations are not built to deal with and manipulate the mechanics of power. Nobody cares how many whist clubs or churches or secret lodges Negroes establish, because they are not compulsive or coercive. They don't seek to transform the socioeconomic racial milieu. They accept and do not challenge conditions with an action program.

Hence, it is apparent that the Negro needs more than organization. He needs mass organization with an action program, aggressive, bold and challenging in spirit. Such a movement is our March on Washington.

Our first job, then, is actually to organize millions of Negroes, and build them into block systems, with captains, so that they may be summoned to action overnight and thrown into physical motion. Without this type of organization, Negroes will never develop mass power, which is the most effective weapon a minority people can wield. Witness the strategy and maneuver of the people of India with mass civil disobedience and noncooperation and the marches to the sea to make salt. It may be said that the Indian people have not won their freedom. This is so, but they will win it. The central principle of the struggle of oppressed minorities like the Negro, labor, Jews, and others is not only to develop mass-demonstration maneuvers, but to repeat and continue them. The workers don't picket firms today and quit. They don't strike today and fold up. They practice the principle of repetition. . . .

We must develop huge demonstrations, because the world is used to big dramatic affairs. They think in terms of hundreds of thousands and millions and billions. Millions of Germans and Russians clash on the Eastern Front. Billions of dollars are appropriated at the twinkling of an eye. Nothing little counts.

Besides, the unusual attracts. We must develop a series of marches of Negroes at a given time in a hundred or more cities throughout the country, or stage a big march of a hundred thousand Negroes on Washington to put our cause into the mainstream of public opinion and focus the attention of world interests. This is why India is in the news.

Therefore, our program is in part as follows:

1. A national conference for the integration and expression of the collective mind and will of the Negro masses.

2. The mobilization and proclamation of a nationwide series of mass marches on the city halls and city councils to awaken the Negro masses and center public attention upon the grievances and goals of the Negro people and serve as training and discipline of the Negro masses for the more strenuous struggle of a March on Washington, if, as, and when an affirmative decision is made thereon by the Negro masses of the country through our national conference.

3. A march on Washington as an evidence to white America that black America is on the march for its rights and means business.

4. The picketing of the White House following the March on Washington and maintaining the said picket line until the country and the world recognize the Negro has become of age and will sacrifice his all to be counted as men, free men.

This program is drastic and exacting. It will test our best mettle and stamina and courage. Let me warn you that in these times of storm and stress, this program will be opposed. Our Movement, therefore, must be well knit together. It must have moral and spiritual vision, understanding, and wisdom.

"The central principle of the struggle of oppressed minorities like the Negro, labor, Jews, and others is not only to develop mass-demonstration maneuvers, but to repeat and continue them. . . . We must develop huge demonstrations, because the world is used to big dramatic affairs."

How can we achieve this?

Our Movement must be blueprinted. Our forces must be marshaled, with block captains to provide immediate and constant contact. Our block captains must hold periodic meetings for their blocks to develop initiative and the capacity to make decisions and move in relation to direction from the central organization of the division.

Our educational program must be developed around the struggle of the Negro masses.

This can be done by developing mass plans to secure mass registration of the Negro people for the primaries and elections. Through this program the Negro masses can be given a practical and pragmatic view of the mechanics and function of our government and the significance of mass political pressure.

Plans should be mapped by the various divisions to fight for Negro integration in the public utilities as motormen and conductors. During the war women may be placed on these jobs. We must make a drive now to see to it that Negro men and women receive their appropriate consideration in every important field of American industry from which Negroes are now generally barred.

Our day-to-day exercise of our civil rights is a constant challenge. In theaters, hotels, restaurants, amusement places, even in the North, now there is discrimination against Negroes. This is true in every large city. Negroes have the moral obligation to demand the right to enjoy and make use of their civil and political privileges. If we don't, we will lose the will to fight for our citizenship rights, and the public will consider that we don't want them and should not have them. This fight to break down these barriers in every city should be carefully and painstakingly organized. By fighting for these civil rights the Negro masses will be disciplined in struggle. Some of us will be put in jail, and court battles may ensue, but this will give the Negro masses a sense of their importance and value as citizens and as fighters in the Negro liberation movement and the cause for democracy as a whole. It will make white people in high places and the ordinary white man understand that Negroes have rights that they are bound to respect.

The giant public protest meetings must continue. They are educative and give moral strength to our movement and the Negro masses.

For this task we need men and women who will dedicate and consecrate their life, spirit, mind and soul to the great adventure of Negro freedom and justice.

Our divisions must serve as Negro mass parliaments where the entire community may debate the day-to-day issues such as police brutality, high rents, and other questions and make judgments and take action in the interest of the community. These divisions should hold meetings at least twice a month. In them every Negro should be made to feel his importance as a factor in the Negro liberation movement. We must have every Negro realize his leadership ability, the educated and uneducated, the poor and wealthy. In the March on Washington Movement the highest is as low as the lowest and the lowest is as high as the highest. Numbers in mass formation is our key, directed, of course, by the collective intelligence of the people.

Let us put our weight behind the fight to abolish the poll tax. This will give the black and white workers of the South new hope. But the Negro people are not the only oppressed section of mankind. India is now waging a world-shaking, history-making fight for independence. India's fight is the Negro's fight.

Now, let us be unafraid. We are fighting for big stakes. Our stakes are liberty, justice and democracy. Every Negro should hang his head in shame who fails to do his part now for freedom. This is the hour of the Negro. It is the hour of the common man. May we rise to the challenge to struggle for our rights. Come what will or may, let us never falter.

More than twenty years passed before Randolph's dream of a massive March on Washington came true. On August 28, 1963, hundreds of thousands of blacks and whites gathered in the nation's capital for the largest single protest demonstration in American history. Organized and directed by Randolph, by then in his mid-seventies, the march dramatized the need for sweeping civil rights legislation

and ended with the memorable words of Martin Luther King, Jr.'s "I Have a Dream" speech. It was the highlight of Randolph's lifelong struggle to secure equal opportunity and equal treatment for black Americans.

Another cause with which he was closely identified was the fight against segregation and discrimination in the U.S. armed forces. Randolph—who personally opposed war—found it especially galling that African Americans were expected to defend a country that treated them with such disdain. He tempered his criticism somewhat during World War II, but afterwards he stepped up his campaign to pressure the government to eliminate Jim Crowism. On March 30, 1948, he testified on the subject before the U.S. Senate Committee on Armed Services, stunning those in attendance by declaring that he was ready to advise African Americans to resist the military draft as long as segregation and discrimination were sanctioned. Randolph's angry opening statement to the committee is reprinted from a government publication entitled Universal Military Training: Hearings Before the Committee on Armed Services, United States Senate.

Mr. Grant Reynolds, national chairman of the Committee Against Jim Crow in Military Service and Training, has prepared for you in his testimony today a summary of wartime injustices to Negro soldiers, injustices by the military authorities and injustices by bigoted segments of the police and civilian population.

The fund of material on this issue is endless, and yet, three years after the end of the war, as another crisis approaches, large numbers of white Americans are blissfully unaware of the extent of physical and psychological aggression against and oppression of the Negro soldier.

Without taking time for a thorough probe into these relevant data, a probe which could enlighten the nation, Congress may now heed Mr. Truman's call for universal military training and selective service, and in the weeks ahead enact a Jim Crow conscription law and appropriate billions for the greatest segregation system of all time.

In a campaign year, when both major parties are playing cynical politics with the issue of civil rights, Negroes are about to lose the fight against Jim Crowism on a national level. Our hard-won local gains in education, fair employment, hospitalization, housing are in danger of being nullified, being swept aside, Mr. Chairman, after decades of work, by a federally enforced pattern of segregation.

I am not beguiled by the Army's use of the word "temporary." Whatever may pass in the way of conscription legislation will become permanent, since the world trend is toward militarism. The Army knows this well. In such an eventuality, how could any permanent Fair Employment Practices Commission dare to criticize job discrimination in private industry if the federal government itself were simultaneously discriminating against Negro youth in military installations all over the world?

There can be no doubt of my facts. Quite bluntly, Chairman Walter G. Andrews of the House Armed Services Committee told a delegation from this organization that the War Department plans segregated white and Negro battalions if Congress passes a draft law.

The *Newark Evening News* of March 26, 1948, confirmed this in a Washington dispatch based on official memoranda sent from Secretary Forrestal's office to the House Armed Services Committee. Nine days ago when we called this to the attention of the Commander-in-Chief in a White House conference, he indicated that he was aware of these plans for Jim Crow battalions. This despite his civil rights message to Congress.

We have released all of this damaging information to the daily press, to leaders of both parties in Congress, and to supposedly liberal organizations. But we, a relative handful of exceptions, we have found our white "friends" silent, indifferent, even hostile.

Justice Roberts, who provided you last week

with vigorous testimony in behalf of the president's draft recommendations, is a trustee of Lincoln University in Pennsylvania, a prominent Negro institution. Yet for nearly four months, Mr. Roberts has not shown us the courtesy to reply to letters asking his support for antisegregation and civil rights safeguards in any draft law.

Three days after the *Newark Sunday News* embarrassed Congressman Harry L. Towe in his home district by exposing his similar failure to acknowledge our correspondence, Mr. Towe, author of the universal military training bill in the House, suddenly found time to answer letters which had been on his desk since December.

This situation, this conspiracy of silence, shall I say?—has naturally commanded wide publicity in the Negro press. I submit for the record a composite of newspaper clippings. In my travels around the country I have sounded out Negro public opinion and confirmed for myself the popular resentment as reflected by the Negro press.

I can assure members of the Senate that Negroes do put civil rights above the high cost of living and above every other major issue of the day, as recently reported by the *Fortune* opinion poll, I believe.

Even more significant is the bitter, angry mood of the Negro in his present determination to win those civil rights in a country that subjects him daily to so many insults and indignities.

With this background, gentlemen, I reported last week to President Truman that Negroes are in no mood to shoulder a gun for democracy abroad so long as they are denied democracy here at home. In particular, they resent the idea of fighting or being drafted into another Jim Crow Army. I passed this information on to Mr. Truman not as a threat, but rather as a frank, factual survey of Negro opinion. Today I should like to make clear to the Senate Armed Services Committee and through you, to Congress and the American people that passage now of a Jim Crow draft may only result in a mass civil disobedience movement along the lines of the magnificent struggles of the people of India against British imperialism. I must emphasize that the current agitation for civil rights is no longer a mere expression of hope on the part of Negroes. On the one hand, it is a positive, resolute out-reading for full manhood. On the other hand, it is an equally determined will to stop acquiescing in anything less. Negroes demand full, unqualified, first-class citizenship. In resorting to the principles and direct-action techniques of Gandhi, whose death was publicly mourned by many members of Congress and President Truman, Negroes will be serving a higher law than any passed by a national legislature in an era which racism spells our doom.

They will be serving a law higher than any decree of the Supreme Court which in the famous Winfred Lynn case evaded ruling on the flagrantly illegal segregation practiced under the wartime Selective Service Act. In refusing to accept compulsory military segregation, Negro youth will be serving their fellow men throughout the world. I feel qualified to make this claim because of a recent survey of American psychologists, sociologists, and anthropologists. The survey revealed an overwhelming belief among these experts that enforced segregation on racial or religious lines has serious and detrimental psychological effects both on the segregated groups and on those enforcing segregation. Experts from the South, I should like to point out, gentlemen, were as positive as those from other sections of the country as to the harmful effects of segregation. The views of these social scientists were based on scientific research and their own professional experience. So long as the Armed Services propose to enforce such universally harmful segregation not only here at home but also overseas, Negro youth have a moral obligation not to lend themselves as worldwide carriers of an evil and hellish doctrine. Secretary of the Army Kenneth C. Royall clearly indicated in the New Jersey National Guard situation that the armed services do have every intention of prolonging their anthropologically hoary and untenable policies. For 25 years now the myth has been carefully cultivated that Soviet Russia has ended all discrimination and intolerance, while here at home the American Communists have skillfully posed as champions of minority groups. To the rank-and-file Negro in World War II, Hitler's racism posed a sufficient threat for him to submit to the Jim Crow Army abuses. But this factor of minority-group persecution in Russia is not present, as a popular issue, in the power struggle between Stalin and the United States. I can only repeat that this time Negroes will not take a Jim Crow draft lying down. The conscience of the world will be shaken as by nothing else when thousands and thousands of us second-class Americans choose imprisonment in preference to permanent military slavery.

While I cannot with absolute certainty claim results at this hour, I personally will advise Negroes to refuse to fight as slaves for a democracy they cannot possess and cannot enjoy.

Let me add that I am speaking only for myself, not even for the Committee Against Jim Crow in Military Service and Training, since I am not sure that all its members would follow my position. But Negro leaders in close touch with GI grievances would feel derelict in their duty if they did not support such a justified civil disobedience movement, especially those of us whose age would protect us from being drafted. Any other course would be a betrayal of those who place their trust in us. I personally pledge myself to openly counsel, aid, and abet youth, both white and Negro, to quarantine any Jim Crow conscription system, whether it bear the label of universal military training or selective service.

I shall tell youth of all races not to be tricked by any euphonious election-year registration for a draft. This evasion, which the newspapers increasingly discuss as a convenient way out for Congress, would merely presage a synthetic "crisis" immediately after November 2d when all talk of equality and civil rights would be branded unpatriotic while the induction machinery would move into high gear. On previous occasions I have seen the "national emergency" psychology mow down legitimate Negro demands.

From coast to coast in my travels I shall call upon all Negro veterans to join this civil disobedience movement and to recruit their younger brothers in an organized refusal to register and be drafted.

Many veterans, bitter over Army Jim Crow, have indicated that they will act spontaneously in this fashion, regardless of any organized movement. "Never again," they say with finality.

I shall appeal to the thousands of white youth in schools and colleges who are today vigorously shedding the prejudices of their parents and professors. I shall urge them to demonstrate their solidarity with Negro youth by ignoring the entire registration and induction machinery.

And finally I shall appeal to Negro parents to lend their moral support to their sons, to stand behind them as they march with heads high to federal prisons as a telling demonstration to the world that Negroes have reached the limit of human endurance, that, in the words of the spiritual, we will be buried in our graves before we will be slaves.

May I, in conclusion, Mr. Chairman, point out that political maneuvers have made this drastic program our last resort. Your party, the party of Lincoln, solemnly pledged in its 1944 platform a full-fledged congressional investigation of injustices to Negro soldiers. Instead of that long overdue probe, the Senate Armed Services Committee on this very day is finally hearing testimony from two or three Negro veterans for a period of twenty minutes each. The House Armed Services Committee and Chairman Andrews went one step further and arrogantly refused to hear any at all.

Since we cannot obtain an adequate congressional forum for our grievances, we have no other recourse but to tell our story to the peoples of the world by organized direct action. I do not believe that even a wartime censorship wall could be high enough to conceal news of a civil disobedience program.

> ***"In resisting the insult of Jim Crowism to the soul of black America, we are helping to save the soul of America."***

If we cannot win your support for your own party commitments, if we cannot ring a bell in you by appealing to human decency, we shall command your respect and the respect of the world by our united refusal to cooperate with tyrannical injustice. Since the military, with their southern biases, intend to take over America and institute total encampment of the populace along Jim Crow lines, Negroes will resist with the power of nonviolence, with the weapons of moral principles, with the good-will weapons of the spirit; yes, with the weapons that brought freedom to India. I feel morally obligated to disturb and keep disturbed the conscience of Jim Crow America. In resisting the insult of Jim Crowism to the soul of black America, we are helping to save the soul of America.

And let me add that I am opposed to Russian totalitarian communism and all its works. I consider it a menace to freedom. I stand by democracy as expressing the Judean-Christian ethic. But democracy and Christianity must be boldly and courageously applied for all men regardless of race, color, creed, or country. We shall wage a relentless warfare against Jim Crow without hate or revenge for the moral and spiritual progress and safety of our country, world peace, and freedom. Finally let me say that Negroes are just sick and tired of being pushed around and we just do not propose to take it, and we do not care what happens.

Thank you very much.

On July 26, 1948, less than four months after Randolph testified at the Senate hearing, President Harry Truman issued an executive order calling for an end to segregation and discrimination in the U.S. armed forces.

SOURCES

Books

Anderson, Jervis, *A. Philip Randolph: A Biographical Portrait*, Harcourt, 1973.

Aptheker, Herbert, editor, *A Documentary History of the Negro People in the United States, 1933-1945*, Citadel Press, 1974.

Bontemps, Arna, *One Hundred Years of Negro Freedom*, Dodd, 1961.

Boulware, Marcus H., *The Oratory of Negro Leaders: 1900-1968*, Negro Universities Press, 1969.

Broderick, Francis L., and August Meier, editors, *Negro Protest Thought in the Twentieth Century*, Bobbs-Merrill, 1965.

Bracey, John H., Jr., August Meier, and Elliott Rudwick, editors, *Black Nationalism in America*, Bobbs-Merrill, 1970.

Cook, Roy, *Leaders of Labor*, Lippincott, 1966.

Davis, Daniel S., *Mr. Black Labor: The Story of A. Philip Randolph, Father of the Civil Rights Movement*, Dutton, 1972.

Foner, Philip S., editor, *The Voice of Black America: Major Speeches by Negroes in the United States, 1797-1971*, Simon & Schuster, 1972.

Grant, Joanne, editor, *Black Protest: History, Documents, and Analyses, 1619 to the Present*, second edition, Ballantine, 1983.

Smith, Arthur L., and Stephen Robb, editors, *The Voice of Black Rhetoric: Selections*, Allyn & Bacon, 1971.

Universal Military Training: Hearings Before the Committee on Armed Services, United States Senate, 80th Congress, 2nd session, March 30, 1948, pp. 685-689.

Periodicals

Newsweek, "Stately Radical," May 28, 1979, p. 43.

New York Times, "A. Philip Randolph Is Dead; Pioneer in Rights and Labor," May 17, 1979.

Time, "Most Dangerous Negro," May 28, 1979, p. 18.

Red Jacket
(Sa-Go-Ye-Wat-Ha)

1750–1830

Native American chief of the Seneca tribe

One of the most prominent figures of the Iroquois confederation during the colonial era was Red Jacket, whose colorful English-language name was inspired by the bright red British military coat he always wore. (The Iroquois confederation was a powerful coalition of six different Indian tribes whose original territory spanned present-day New York State and much of southeastern Ontario.) He was a contemporary—and rival—of other major Iroquois leaders such as Cornplanter, a fellow Seneca, and Joseph Brant, a Mohawk. Unlike them, however, he considered himself first and foremost an orator rather than a warrior. Red Jacket's fame, in fact, rests almost entirely on his legendary way with words.

Red Jacket was born near Lake Geneva, New York, around 1750. (Some sources place his year of birth later in the decade.) Although he was an ally of the British, he only reluctantly pledged his support to them during the Revolutionary War and actually did very little fighting on their behalf, prompting some Indians to denounce him as a coward. Afterward, Red Jacket became the principal spokesman for the Senecas, serving as their representative at numerous councils and treaty sessions as well as before various government officials. It was around this same time that he first began to voice his opposition to Christianity and urge his fellow Iroquois to reject European ways and preserve their own beliefs and traditions before it was too late. Red Jacket sounded this warning for the rest of his days, with varying degrees of success.

His most famous statement on the subject came in 1805. Sometime that summer, a Protestant missionary from Boston by the name of Cram arrived in Buffalo, New York, seeking permission from Seneca tribal leaders to preach among their people. After the Reverend Mr. Cram delivered a patronizing speech in which he promised to "enlighten" his pagan audience about the one true way to worship, Red Jacket stood up and recounted in angry detail what he and his people had already observed about the difference between Christian words and not-so-Christian deeds. It is reprinted here from W.C. Vanderwerth's Indian Oratory: Famous Speeches by Noted Indian Chieftains *(University of Oklahoma Press, 1971).*

Friend and Brother! It was the will of the Great Spirit that we should meet together this day. He orders all things, and he has given us a fine day for our council. He has taken his garment from before the sun and has caused the bright orb to shine with brightness upon us. Our eyes are opened so that we see clearly. Our ears are unstopped so that we have been able to distinctly hear the words which you have spoken. For all these favors we thank the Great Spirit and him only.

Brother! This council fire was kindled by you. It was at your request that we came together at this time. We have listened with attention to what you have said. You have requested us to speak our minds freely. This gives us great joy, for we now consider that we stand upright before you, and can speak what we think. All have heard your voice and all speak to you as one man. Our minds are agreed.

Brother! You say that you want an answer to your talk before you leave this place. It is right that you should have one, as you are a great distance from home, and we do not wish to detain you. But we will first look back a little, and tell you what our fathers have told us, and what we have heard from the white people.

Brother! Listen to what we say. There was a time when our forefathers owned this great island [meaning the continent of North America—a common belief among the Indians]. Their seats extended from the rising to the setting of the sun. The Great Spirit had made it for the use of Indians. He had created the buffalo, the deer, and other animals for food. He made the bear and the deer, and their skins served us for clothing. He had scattered them over the country, and had taught us how to take them. He had caused the earth to produce corn for bread. All this he had done for his red children because he loved them. If we had any disputes about hunting grounds, they were generally settled without the shedding of much blood. But an evil day came upon us. Your forefathers crossed the great waters and landed on this island. Their numbers were small. They found friends and not enemies. They told us they had fled from their own country for fear of wicked men, and had come here to enjoy their religion. They asked for a small seat. We took pity on them, granted their request and they sat down amongst us. We gave them corn and meat. They gave us poison [alcohol] in return. The white people had now found our country. Tidings were carried back and more came amongst us. Yet we did not fear them. We took them to be friends. They called us brothers. We believed them and gave them a large seat. At length their numbers had greatly increased. They wanted more land. They wanted our country. Our eyes were opened, and our minds became uneasy. Wars took place. Indians were hired to fight against Indians, and many of our people were destroyed. They also brought strong liquors among us. It was strong and powerful and has slain thousands.

Red Jacket

Brother! Our seats were once large, and yours were very small. You have now become a great people, and we have scarcely a place left to spread our blankets. You have got our country, but you are not satisfied. You want to force your religion upon us.

Brother! Continue to listen. You say that you are sent to instruct us how to worship the Great Spirit agreeably to his mind; and if we do not take hold of the religion which you white people teach we shall be unhappy hereafter. You say that you are right, and we are lost. How do you know this to be true? We understand that your religion is written in a book. If it was intended for us as well as for you, why has not the Great Spirit given it to us; and not only to us, but why did he not give to our forefathers the knowledge of that book, with the means of understanding it rightly? We only know what you tell us about it. How shall we know when to believe, being so often deceived by the white people?

Brother! You say there is but one way to worship and serve the Great Spirit. If there is but one religion, why do you white people differ so much about it? Why not all agree, as you can all read the book?

Brother! We do not understand these things. We are told that your religion was given to your forefathers and has been handed down, father to son. We also have a religion which was given to our forefathers, and has been handed down to us, their children. We worship that way. It teaches us to be thankful for all the favors we received, to love each other, and to be united. We never quarrel about religion.

Brother! The Great Spirit has made us all. But he has made a great difference between his white and red children. He has given us a different complexion and different customs. To you he has given the arts; to these he has not opened our eyes. We know these things to be true. Since he has made so great a difference between us in other things, why may not we conclude that he has given us a different religion, according to our understanding? The Great Spirit does right. He knows what is best for his children. We are satisfied.

Brother! We do not wish to destroy your religion, or to take it from you. We only want to enjoy our own.

Brother! You say you have not come to get our land or our money, but to enlighten our minds. I will now tell you that I have been at your meetings and saw you collecting money from the meeting. I cannot tell what this money was intended for, but suppose it was for your minister; and if we should conform to your way of thinking, perhaps you may want some from us.

Brother! We are told that you have been preaching to the white people in this place. These people are our neighbors. We are acquainted with them. We will wait a little while, and see what effect your preaching has upon them. If we find it does them good and makes them honest and less disposed to cheat Indians, we will then consider again what you have said.

Brother! You have now heard our answer to your talk, and this is all we have to say at present. As we are going to part, we will come and take you by the hand, and hope the Great Spirit will protect you on your journey, and return you safe to your friends.

According to accounts of this exchange, the Reverend Mr. Cram refused to shake hands with the Indians, proclaiming that there could be "no fellowship between the religion of God and the devil." The Indians reportedly just smiled and left the meeting.

Red Jacket was also critical of other activities that threatened the foundations of Indian culture. In the following speech, the date and place of which are unknown, he reiterates his objections to white attempts to acculturate the Senecas and assures his listener that Indian ways work best for Indian people—and that perhaps white people might actually learn something from them. *His words are taken from* American Indian Literature: An Anthology, *edited by Alan R. Velie (University of Oklahoma Press, 1979).*

Brother, I rise to return you the thanks of this nation and to return them back to our ancient friends—if any such we have—for their good wishes toward us in attempting to teach us your religion. Inform them we will look well into this matter. We have well weighed your exertions, and find your success not to answer our expectations. But, instead of producing that happy effect which you so long promised us, its introduction so far has rendered us uncomfortable and miserable. You have taken a number of our young men to your schools. You have educated them and taught them your religion. They have returned to their kindred and color neither white men nor Indians. The arts they have learned are incompatible with the chase, and ill adapted to our customs. They have been taught that which is useless to us. They have been made to feel artificial wants, which never entered the minds of their brothers. They have imbibed, in your great towns, the seeds of vices which were unknown in the forest. They become discouraged and dissipated, despised by the Indians, neglected by the whites, and without value to either—less honest than the former, and perhaps more knavish than the latter.

Brother, we were told that the failure of these first attempts was attributable to miscalculation, and we were invited to try again, by sending others of our young men to different schools, to be taught by different instructors. Brother, the result has been invariably the same. We believe it wrong for you to attempt further to promote your religion among us or to introduce your arts, manners, habits, and feelings. We believe that it is wrong for us to encourage you in so doing. We believe that the Great Spirit made the whites and the Indians but for different purposes.

Brother, in attempting to pattern your example, the Great Spirit is angry, for you see he does not bless or crown your exertions. But, Brother, on the other hand we know that the Great Spirit is pleased that we follow the traditions and customs of our forefathers, for in so doing we receive his blessing, we have received strength and vigor for the chase. The Great Spirit has provided abundance; when we are hungry we find the forest filled with game, when thirsty, we slake our thirst in the pure streams and springs that spread around us.

When weary, the leaves of the trees are our bed; we retire with contentment to rest, we rise with gratitude to the Great Preserver. Renovated strength in our limbs, and bounding joy in our hearts, we feel blessed and happy. No luxuries, no vices, no disputed titles, no avaricious desires, shake the foundations of our society, or disturb our peace and happiness. We know the Great Spirit is better pleased with his red children than with his white, when he bestows upon us a hundredfold more blessings than upon you.

Perhaps, Brother, you are right in your religion—it may be peculiarly adapted to your condition. You say that you destroyed the Son of the Great Spirit. Perhaps this is the merited cause of all your troubles and misfortunes. But, Brothers, bear in mind that we had no participation in this murder. We disclaim it—we love the Great Spirit—and as we never had any agency in so unjust, so merciless an outrage, he therefore continues to smile upon us, and to give us peace, joy and plenty.

Brother, we pity you—we wish you to bear to our good friends our best wishes. Inform them that in compassion toward them, we are willing to send them missionaries to teach them our religion, habits and customs. We would be willing they should be as happy as we are, and assure them that if they should follow our example, they would be more, far more happy than they are now. We cannot embrace your religion; it renders us divided and unhappy. But by your embracing ours, we believe that you would be more happy and more acceptable to the Great Spirit. Here [pointing his finger to several whites present who had been captured when children and been brought up among them], here, Brother [with an animation and exulting triumph which cannot be described], here is the living evidence before you. Those young men have been brought up with us. They are contented and happy. Nothing would be an inducement with them to abandon their enjoyments and adopt yours, for they are too well aware of the blessings of our society, and the evils of yours. But, as you have our good will, we would gladly know that you have relinquished your religion, productive of so much disagreement and inquietude among yourselves, and instead thereof that you should follow ours.

Accept of this advice, Brother, and take it back to your friends as the best pledge of our wishes for your welfare. Perhaps you think we are ignorant and uninformed. Go, then and teach the whites. Select, for example, the people of Buffalo. We will be spectators and remain silent. Improve their morals and refine their habits—make them less disposed to cheat Indians. Make the whites generally less inclined to make Indians drunk, and to take them from their lands. Let us know the tree by the blossoms, and the blossoms by the fruit. When this shall be made clear to our minds we may be more willing to listen to you. But until then we must be allowed to follow the religion of our ancestors.

Brother, Farewell!

Red Jacket continued his efforts to keep the white man's religion and customs at bay, even after many Senecas—including members of his own family—embraced Christianity. In 1824, he succeeded in having all missionaries temporarily expelled from tribal territory. But the resulting tensions between the traditionalists and the converts led to a bitter split in the Seneca nation, a split exacerbated by Red Jacket's own problems with alcohol and accusations of witchcraft against his followers. In 1827, he was ousted as a Seneca chief. He managed to win reinstatement shortly before he died and spent his last months sounding a final warning to all who would listen. In her book I Have Spoken: American History Through the Voices of the Indians *(Sage Books, 1971), compiler Virginia Irving Armstrong recounts Red Jacket's parting words to the Senecas.*

I am about to leave you, and when I am gone and my warning shall no longer be heard or regarded, the craft and avarice of the white man will prevail. Many winters I have breasted the storm, but I am an aged tree, and can stand no longer. My leaves are fallen, my branches are withered, and I am shaken by every breeze. Soon my aged trunk will be prostrated, and the foot of the exulting foe of the Indian may be placed upon it with safety; for I leave none who will be able to avenge such an injury. Think not I mourn for myself. I go to join the spirits of my fathers, where age cannot come; but my heart fails when I think of my people, who are soon to be scattered and forgotten.

SOURCES

Armstrong, Virginia Irving, compiler, *I Have Spoken: American History Through the Voices of the Indians,* Sage Books, 1971.

Jones, Louis Thomas, *Aboriginal American Oratory: The Tradition of Eloquence Among the Indians of the United States,* Southwest Museum (Los Angeles), 1965.

McLuhan, T.C., *Touch the Earth: A Self-Portrait of Indian Existence,* Outerbridge & Dienstfrey, 1971.

Nabokov, Peter, editor, *Native American Testimony: A Chronicle of Indian-White Relations from Prophecy to the Present, 1492–1992,* Penguin Books, 1991.

Rosenstiel, Annette, *Red and White: Indian Views of the White Man, 1492–1982,* Universe Books, 1983.

Sanders, Thomas E., and Walter W. Peek, *Literature of the American Indian,* Glencoe Press, 1973.

Stone, William L., *The Life and Times of Sa-Go-Ye-Wat-Ha,* [New York], 1866.

Vanderwerth, W.C., *Indian Oratory: Famous Speeches by Noted Indian Chieftains,* University of Oklahoma Press, 1971.

Velie, Alan R., editor, *American Indian Literature: An Anthology,* University of Oklahoma Press, 1979.

Witt, Shirley Hill, and Stan Steiner, editors, *The Way: An Anthology of American Indian Literature,* Knopf, 1972.

Syngman Rhee

1875–1965

Korean political activist and founding president of South Korea

Although he was not an American, Syngman Rhee was educated in the United States, found inspiration for his political beliefs in American-style democracy, and spent much of the three decades he was in exile from his native land on American soil. A descendant of the family that had ruled Korea since 1392, Rhee was born in Hwanghae Province, located in present-day North Korea. Because his country had enjoyed close cultural ties with China for centuries, Rhee's father saw to it that his son received a classical Chinese education to prepare him for a high-level career in government service. (He subsequently placed first in the annual national examinations held in the capital city of Seoul.) English was not part of his instruction, however, and since Rhee felt that learning it would be important to his future, he remained in Seoul and enrolled in a school run by Methodist missionaries.

There Rhee was introduced to the concept of democracy, and in 1894—to the dismay of his father—he joined a group of young reform-minded student activists known as the Independence Club. This organization not only demanded changes in the ancient Korean monarchy but also insisted on an end to the growing Japanese influence in the government. (Since the mid-1870s, Japan had been trying to undermine Korea's relationship with China and force Korea to deal with it instead.) Rhee founded and edited a newspaper devoted to their cause (Korea's first daily newspaper as well as the first published solely by a Korean) and became head of the reform movement in 1895 after the leader of the Independence Club was forced to flee the country.

Two years later, Rhee himself was arrested and jailed after leading a massive student demonstration in Seoul. He then suffered through seven months of torture in prison, during which time he converted to Christianity. Later, he was sentenced to a life term and moved to another prison. There he organized classes for his fellow prisoners in religion, economics, and English, conducted religious services, translated several books from English into Korean and vice versa, and wrote a book of his own entitled The Spirit of Independence.

In 1904, Rhee gained his freedom when the Korean monarchy unexpectedly declared a general amnesty for all political prisoners. He then headed to the United

States and spent the next six years pursuing his education, earning a bachelor's degree from George Washington University, a master's degree from Harvard University, and a doctorate from Princeton University. It was at Princeton that he came to admire the school's president, Woodrow Wilson, whose philosophy of international justice strongly influenced Rhee. (This was just a few years before Wilson became president of the United States and advanced the concept of the League of Nations, forerunner of the United Nations.)

Returning to Korea around 1911, Rhee worked as an official for the YMCA, established and led the Korean Christian Student Movement, and served as a teacher for the Methodist Mission Board. His return came on the heels of Japan's formal occupation of Korea (which the Japanese renamed Choson) and takeover of all major government functions, including foreign relations, the armed services, police, currency and banking, and communications. From 1910 until 1918 the Japanese sought to tighten their grip on the country by getting rid of nationalists, gaining control of the land system, and instituting strict administrative changes. In 1919, millions of Koreans demanding an end to Japanese domination (including Rhee) took to the streets in a series of nonviolent demonstrations for independence known as the March First Movement. The uprising was quickly crushed, however, and Rhee was again forced to flee.

From a base he established in Hawaii (but with frequent visits to China, home to a substantial community of others who had also left Korea), Rhee spent the next twenty-two years as president of the Korean Provisional Government in Exile. (He also established the Korean Methodist Church and the Korean Christian Institute there.) He had been the unanimous choice for the position among his fellow dissidents, and as such he emerged as the voice and inspiration of the Korean independence movement. Inside Korea, these rebels used a combination of passive-resistance techniques and guerrilla warfare to harass and de-stabilize their Japanese occupiers. Meanwhile, Rhee worked tirelessly on the outside to achieve international recognition for his government (concentrating his efforts on the United States in particular) and to locate a forum where he could present their case before the western democracies. His pleas fell largely on deaf ears, however; Japanese propagandists successfully persuaded world leaders throughout the 1920s and 1930s that Korea was not worth their attention.

Rhee was regularly re-elected president of the government-in-exile until 1941, at which time the post went to another independence leader. But Rhee continued to wage his campaign on behalf of his country throughout World War II as head of the Korean Commission, an agency he set up in Washington, D.C., to serve as a sort of diplomatic arm of the provisional Korean government.

Ultimately, it took the surrender of the Japanese in August 1945, to bring about Korea's liberation. Two months later, Rhee returned to his homeland amid widespread popular support and began the second phase of the battle for its independence. Over the next three years, as the United States and the Soviet Union negotiated the fate of the country they occupied jointly (U.S. troops presided over a zone south of the 38th parallel, and Soviet troops held the territory north of that), Rhee argued that the only acceptable solution was to hold immediate elections so that the Korean people could determine their own future. He totally opposed any compromises that would have divided Korea even on a temporary basis and feared that allowing the Soviets to remain in the north would eventually cause the entire region to fall under communist control. Watching in frustration as the two emerging superpowers haggled over his country, Rhee often went over the heads of U.S. government officials to take his case directly to the American people and win their support.

Despite power struggles within the independence movement itself that saw several rivals challenge his leadership, Rhee emerged triumphant in United Nations-supervised elections held throughout the U.S. zone during the spring of 1948, winning the right to represent Seoul in the National Assembly. That body in turn named him president of the newly-formed Republic of Korea. (Leftists had boycotted the elections and therefore were not represented in the government, which consisted almost entirely of right-wing anti-communists such as Rhee.) On August 15, a ceremony was held marking the formal transfer of sovereign authority from the U.S. Military Government of South Korea to the fledgling regime of Syngman Rhee. On that solemn yet joyous occasion, he briefly reflected on the past before laying out the challenges of the future. His words are reprinted here from Vital Speeches of the Day, *September 15, 1948.*

The ceremonies of this day mark the third anniversary of the liberation of our nation from the Japanese Empire. As we receive, in the name of the whole Korean people, our sovereign government once more into our own hands, our national independence is solemnly and fatefully restored. This day is the culmination of four decades of hopes, dreams, struggles, and sacrifices. To stand in this hour in my own country as a free citizen under our own government is the greatest moment of my life. I speak to you on this occasion as your duly elected president, but speak in greatest humbleness as the servant of all our people.

But, my fellow citizens, the final destination toward which we are bound lies yet ahead, at the end of a road that may be both long and rough. We have answered the doubters who questioned our ability to govern our own destinies—even though we had already so governed them for more than forty-two hundreds of years—with an overwhelming and spontaneous demonstration of democratic self-determination in the election of May 10. We have answered the doubters with patience and with deeds, rather than with cries of anger or distress. We must continue in this same spirit to meet the critical problems that overshadow our rejoicing today. This is no time to relax and take our ease. Rather than to brood upon the past, or to rejoice in the present, we must plan and work for the future.

Ours is now the task to forge in labor, in love, and in loyal devotion the foundations upon which our Republic can rise securely and in peace. From you who have given so much and endured so much there must come yet greater sacrifices and an even stronger determination. Wearied and distraught though we may be from the struggles of the past, we can face the future with renewed strength, in the proud realization that we labor not only for ourselves but also for the peace and security of all mankind.

As we turn our thoughts ahead, there are certain strong foundations upon which we must build anew the structure of our national life.

We should place our full trust and faith in democracy.

It is my greatest regret that among our people are some who believe that only a dictatorship can guide us through the troubles that beset our way. Still others, shuddering at the destructive tactics of communism, and fearing

"To stand in this hour in my own country as a free citizen under our own government is the greatest moment of my life."

that the people have not within themselves the strength and wisdom to meet the needs of the time, have reluctantly come to believe that a dictatorship may be necessary for the immediate future at least. But we must not permit temporary doubts or uneasiness to prevent our laying the basis of fundamental principles that will stand the test of time.

History has proved that dictatorships cannot establish peace and prosperity. The democratic way will be slow and hard, but we must hold to the faith that only righteousness can defeat evil. If we would make a mountain, we know from experience that we must carry every load of earth. Democracy is the faith of our friends in every part of the world. Dictatorship is the method of government against which our friends have fought. Democracy is the only form of government under which the liberties of the people will be secure.

We must protect civil rights and fundamental freedom.

The essence of democracy is the protection of the fundamental freedom of individuals. Both citizens and government must be alert to protect freedom of speech, of assembly, of religion, and of thought, by all proper means. Any who try to buy food at the price of freedom will end by losing both. We have endured a generation of tyranny in which not only our words and our deeds but our very thoughts were subject to the harsh restraints of an alien police. But this is not the native habit of our historic experience. In the strength of our local government, in the justice of our courts, in the responsibility of the police to the people, in the principle that he who would lead must serve, and most of all, in the unshakable integrity of our own hearts there lies the fundamental guarantee we seek and demand.

Liberalism must be understood, respected, and protected.

Liberals, certain intellectuals, and progressive-minded youth are often critical of the necessary processes of establishing an organized state. Many patriots, judging too quickly of their words and deeds, have condemned such critics as dangerous and destructive. Actually, freedom of thought is the basic foundation of a democratic state. Such people must be protected in their right to disagree. If we seek to overwhelm them, it must be with embarrassment from the fullness of our respect and tolerance for their views. In the eternal struggle between right and wrong, we must stand firm in the faith that truth eventually will prevail.

Generosity and cooperation should be the keystones of our new government.

The greatest need of our new national life, to establish its stability at home and its dignity abroad, is that it be a government of, by, and

Syngman Rhee

for all the people. Our country needs the active support of every citizen, whatever his former beliefs may have been. We must start our new government in the hope that our people from every political group will stand together behind the ideals and the program set forth in our Constitution. Like all true democracies everywhere in the world, we must close ranks after an election is held and unite not in partisanship but in patriotism.

We must strive to unite our divided nation.

We await with hope and determination the missing third of our representatives from the north. The 38th parallel division is no part of our choice and is wholly foreign to our destiny. Nothing must be neglected to keep wide open the door to reunion of the whole nation. The Everwhite Mountains are as surely our boundary to the north as are the Straits of Korea to the south. No temporary international situation can obscure what has been established through the centuries as historic fact.

We must not allow ourselves to be hurried into any conviction that we have a duty to conquer and reclaim the north. Instead, we must be content to proceed slowly and carefully, in accord with the program already laid down by the United Nations. This program can never be complete until the provinces of the north are enabled to hold an election internationally approved and to unite with us fully in the formation of a truly national government. No matter what the obstacles to this program may be, it is our duty and our strong determination to give to the people in the north every opportunity to join with us in common and equal brotherhood. A peacefully united nation is the only kind of nation we have known or wish to know. We shall never rest until this goal has been achieved.

Our foreign policy is devoted to world peace.

In all our dealings with foreign nations, our solemn endeavor is to further the cause of world peace and international cooperation. It is in this spirit that we gratefully accept the aid tendered us by the United States. We have known a time when foreign aid was deeply distrusted, as meaning in effect foreign control. It is true that our request for such aid must always reflect the most careful consideration of potential effects. However, the old conception has given way to a new concept of the relationship of all nations, both great and small, recognizing the independence of all nations and the inseparability of the problems of peace and war. The freedom of small nations has come to be of concern to the great powers both individually and through the United Nations. Experience has shown and we believe the future will continue to show that it is to the interest of the entire free world that the largest possible portion should remain free. Therefore, aid is not given to entrench selfish imperialism but in the hope of maintaining world peace.

Today the American Military Government in south Korea is ending, and the Republic of Korea is beginning. This day marks a fresh renewal of the friendship commenced between Koreans and Americans two generations ago. We owe our liberty to the destruction of the enemy by the armed forces of our friends. During the occupation of our country by American troops, the United States has proved its devotion to the principles of humanity and justice on which that great nation was founded. We wish to express the thanks of every Korean to the individuals who have participated in the Military Government, and to the commanding General, John R. Hodge, a fine soldier and true friend of our people.

Our relations with the United States of America are especially cordial. We are proud also of the close ties maintained with our neighboring government of China for millenniums. We shall never forget the participation of the United Kingdom in the Cairo pledge guaranteeing our independence. We are especially happy for the fine speech by Dr. Luna, of the Philippine Republic, Chairman of the United Nations Temporary Commission on Korea. Our deep gratitude is extended to all the nations that sent delegates to assist in the free and democratic elections from which this government is derived. Considering the particular problems that still confront us, we express our earnest wish to live at peace with the Union of Socialist Soviet Republics.

We realize that without the good will and assistance of free nations, the many problems before us might be insuperable. But we know we have their good will and feel we can count on their assistance. Above all, we need and we count upon the loyalty, the devotion to duty, and the determination of all Korean citizens. With hopeful hearts and minds alert we take into our own hands today a sovereign republican government that will long endure.

The hopeful tone of Rhee's address soon gave way to the realities of the situation in Korea. As he struggled to set up a working democracy, he not only faced political conflicts from his opponents within South Korea but also escalating tensions between the Soviet Union and the United States over the Soviets' continuing domination of North Korea, which had declared itself the Democratic People's Republic of Korea in August, 1948. On June 25, 1950, following months of border skirmishes, troops from the North—with the support of their Soviet ally—invaded the South. The United Nations condemned the aggression, and within a week, U.S. ground forces arrived on the scene, joined later by troops from other countries who were also members of the United Nations. Before long, the communist government of China intervened on the side of the North.

The war lasted three years and ended in a stalemate, with armed troops on both sides of the old border at the 38th parallel. South Korea, meanwhile, was in state of complete social and economic turmoil. Although he retained his popular appeal and easily won re-election to the presidency in both the 1952 and 1956 elections, the fiercely anti-communist Rhee adopted an increasingly authoritarian posture toward his political opponents, some of whom he threw in jail. The aging leader also fell under the influence of a number of corrupt friends and advisors who isolated him from the deteriorating conditions in South Korea throughout the 1950s.

Following Rhee's victory in the 1960 presidential election amid widespread charges that the vote had been rigged, violent student demonstrations erupted in Seoul and spread throughout the country. Within just a couple of months, the government collapsed and Rhee once again sought refuge in Hawaii. There he lived out his life in exile, succumbing to complications from a stroke in 1965. His body was returned to South Korea for a state funeral, an acknowledgment of what one official described as his "great contribution to national independence."

SOURCES

Books

Zia, Helen, and Susan Gall, eds., *Notable Asian Americans,* Gale Research, Detroit, 1995.

Periodicals

New York Times, "Syngman Rhee Dies an Exile from Land He Fought to Free," July 20, 1965.

Vital Speeches of the Day, "The Goal We Seek: We Must Establish Our Own Government Ourselves," October 15, 1947, pp. 27-28; "Re-establishment of Korean Nation: We Must Plan and Work for the Future," September 15, 1948, pp. 709-710; "Where Do We Stand Today: United Resistance of Free Countries of Asia," March 15, 1950, pp. 346-348; "Korea Cannot Live Divided and Half-Occupied: Our Cause of Freedom Is the World's Cause of Freedom," September 1, 1952, pp. 703-704; "Death Is Scarcely Closer to Seoul Than to Washington: Destruction of the U.S. the Prime Objective of Kremlin," August 15, 1954, pp. 643-644; "America, Trust Yourselves a Little More: Have Faith in Your Own Ideals," April 1, 1955, pp. 1138-1140.

Paul Robeson

1898–1976

African American singer and actor

An entertainer by profession, Paul Robeson was probably the only black of his generation who combined singing and acting with protest oratory to focus attention on racial and economic injustice at home and abroad. He paid a steep price for his activism, however; labeled a communist during the "Red Scare" of the late 1940s and 1950s, he found it impossible to earn a living in the United States and yet was prevented by the government from traveling overseas, where his long-established popularity would have assured him steady work. Robeson's insistence on his right to freedom of speech ultimately cost him his career and reputation, leaving him to die in virtual obscurity. Yet this man with the striking bass-baritone voice that thrilled audiences all over the world with its power and passion left an indelible mark on his own and subsequent generations.

Born and raised in New Jersey, Robeson was the youngest of eight children of a well-respected minister and his schoolteacher wife. He excelled in both academics and athletics at Rutgers University, from which he graduated in 1919, then went on to Columbia University Law School. While there, he occasionally took a break from his studies to act in community theater productions; one such appearance led to a brief stint on Broadway and a tour of England. Robeson still felt his future was in the legal profession, however, and not long after receiving his degree, he accepted a job with a New York firm. Faced with a lack of opportunities and the resentment of his white colleagues, he soon quit in frustration.

Despite the fact that he had had no formal training in dramatic arts, Robeson made up his mind to pursue an acting career in earnest. As a member of playwright Eugene O'Neill's Provincetown Players, he first earned acclaim on the New York stage in 1924 for his starring roles in The Emperor Jones *and* All God's Chillun Got Wings. *From there Robeson went on to do other plays and even a silent film. With the encouragement of family and friends who admired his voice, he also launched a singing career with a program of African American folk music. Following his triumphant debut in New York in early 1925, Robeson went on tour throughout the United States, Great Britain, and Europe and became an instant celebrity. So warm was the reception he received abroad that he and his family settled in London in 1928 and remained there for the next eleven years.*

Robeson's stature as both an actor and singer increased throughout the rest of the 1920s, the 1930s, and well into the 1940s. As Joe in the musical Show Boat, *for example, he achieved fame for his rendition of "Ol' Man River," the song with which he was most closely identified for the rest of his life. In 1930, a virtuoso performance in the title role of Shakespeare's* Othello *on the London stage brought him widespread acclaim. Thirteen years later, his interpretation of the same part on Broadway was equally well received. (It was also remarkable in that it was the first time a black actor had worked with a white supporting cast before an American audience.) In addition, Robeson made nearly a dozen films during this period, in some instances recreating roles he had originated on stage.*

As Robeson's popularity grew, so, too, did his interest in speaking out on racial and economic issues that had been troubling him for some time. His worldwide travels had helped convince him that the Soviet Union's brand of socialism offered the best hope for international peace and justice. At the same time, his extensive studies of various musical forms had awakened in him a strong sense of pride in African culture. Before long, his political activism had become completely intertwined with his professional life.

By the end of the 1940s, however, many Americans were looking at Robeson with suspicion and even anger. His lavish praise for the Soviet Union—which he usually coupled with fierce criticism of the United States—alienated many of his fans during the anti-communist hysteria that followed World War II. For some of them, the final blow came during the spring of 1949. On April 20, while attending the World Congress of the Defenders of Peace in Paris, Robeson was quoted as saying that he found it "inconceivable" that black Americans would consider going to war against the Soviet Union on behalf of a country that had oppressed them for so many generations. The remark created a tremendous uproar in the United States, leading to violence at two of his concerts that summer and sparking a nationwide boycott against him. At a "Welcome Home" rally in New York City on June 19, 1949, an angry and defiant Robeson publicly responded to his critics. The version of his speech that appears here was originally published as a pamphlet by the Council on African Affairs and reprinted in Paul Robeson Speaks: Writings, Speeches, Interviews, 1918-1974, *(Brunner/Mazel, 1978).*

Thanks for the welcome home. I have traveled many lands and I have sung and talked to many peoples. Wherever I appeared, whether in professional concert, at peace meetings, in the factories, at trade union gatherings, at the mining pits, at assemblies of representative colonial students from all over the world, always the greeting came: "Take back our affection, our love, our strength to the Negro people and to the members of the progressive movement of America."

It is especially moving to be here in this particular auditorium in Harlem. Way back in 1918, I came here to this very hall from a football game at the Polo Grounds between Rutgers and Syracuse. There was a basketball game between St. Christopher and Alpha. Later I played here for St. Christopher against the Alphas, against the Spartans, and the Brooklyn YMCA, time and time again. This was a home of mine. It is still my home.

I was then, through my athletics and my university record, trying to hold up the prestige of my people; trying in the only way I knew to ease the path for future Negro boys and girls. And I am still in there slugging, yes, at another level, and you can bet your life that I shall battle every step of the way until conditions around these corners change and conditions change for the Negro people all up and down this land.

The road has been long. The road has been hard. It began about as tough as I ever had it—

Paul Robeson

in Princeton, New Jersey, a college town of Southern aristocrats, who from Revolutionary time transferred Georgia to New Jersey. My brothers couldn't go to high school in Princeton. They had to go to Trenton, ten miles away. That's right—Trenton, of the "Trenton Six." My brother or I could have been one of the "Trenton Six."

Almost every Negro in Princeton lived off the college and accepted the social status that went with it. We lived for all intents and purposes on a Southern plantation. And with no more dignity than that suggests—all the bowing and scraping to the drunken rich, all the vile names, all the Uncle Tomming to earn enough to lead miserable lives.

My father was of slave origin. He reached as honorable a position as a Negro could under these circumstances, but soon after I was born he lost his church and poverty was my beginning. Relatives from my father's North Carolina family took me in, a motherless orphan, while my father went to new fields to begin again in a corner grocery store. I slept four in a bed, ate the nourishing greens and cornbread. I was and am forever thankful to my honest, intelligent, courageous, generous aunts, uncles and cousins, not long divorced from the cotton and tobacco fields of eastern North Carolina.

During the [Henry A.] Wallace [presidential] campaign [of 1948], I stood on the very soil on which my father was a slave, where some of my cousins are sharecroppers and unemployed tobacco workers. I reflected upon the wealth bled from my near relatives alone, and of the very basic wealth of all this America, beaten out of millions of the Negro people, enslaved, freed, newly enslaved until this very day.

And I defied—and today I defy—any part of an insolent, dominating America, however powerful; I defy any errand boys, Uncle Toms of the Negro people, to challenge my Americanism, because by word and deed I challenge this vicious system to the death; because I refuse to let my personal success, as part of a fraction of one percent of the Negro people, explain away the injustices to fourteen million of my people; because with all the energy at my command, I fight for the right of the Negro people and other oppressed labor-driven Americans to have decent homes, decent jobs, and the dignity that belongs to every human being!

Somewhere in my childhood these feelings were planted. Perhaps when I resented being pushed off the sidewalk, when I saw my women being insulted, and especially when I saw my elder brother answer each insult with blows that sent would-be slave masters crashing to the stone sidewalks, even though jail was his constant reward. He never said it, but he told me day after day: "Listen to me, kid." (He loved me very dearly.) "Don't you ever take it, as long as you live."

I realized years after how grateful I was for

that example. I've never accepted any inferior role because of my race or color. *And, by God, I never will!*

That explains my life. I'm looking for freedom, *full freedom,* not an inferior brand. That explains my attitude to different people, to Africa, the continent from which we came. I know much about Africa, and I'm not ashamed of my African origin. I'm *proud* of it. The rich culture of that continent, its magnificent potential, gives me plenty of cause for pride. This was true of the deep stirrings that took place within me when I visited the West Indies in January. This explains my feeling toward the Soviet Union, where in 1934 I for the first time walked this earth in complete human dignity, a dignity denied me at the Columbia University of Medina,

"I defied—and today I defy—any part of an insolent, dominating America, however powerful; I defy any errand boys, Uncle Toms of the Negro people, to challenge my Americanism. . . ."

denied me everywhere in my native land, despite all the protestations about freedom, equality, constitutional rights, and the sanctity of the individual.

And I say to the *New York Times* that personal success can be no answer. It can no longer be a question of an Anderson, a Carver, a Robinson, a Jackson, or a Robeson. It must be a question of the well-being and opportunities not of a few but for *all* of this great Negro people of which I am a part.

There, in my childhood, I saw my father choose allies. To him, it was the Taylor Pineses of the Wall Street millionaires. They helped the church. They spread around a little manna now and then—that was an age of philanthropy. But I recall that my father could never think of attacking these men for the conditions of those times. Always one had to bend and bow.

That was forty years ago. These present-day sycophants of big business, these supposed champions of Negro rights, can't grow up to the knowledge that the world has gone forward. Millions and millions of people have wrung their freedom from these same Taylor Pineses, these same Wall Street operators, these traders in the lives of millions for their greedy profits. There is no more Eastern Europe to bleed; no more Russia, one-sixth of the earth's surface, to enslave; no more China at their disposal.

They can't imagine that our people, the Negro people—40 millions in the Caribbean and Latin America, 150 millions in Africa, and 14 million here, today, up and down this America of ours—are also determined to stop being industrial and agricultural serfs. They do not understand that a new reconstruction is here, and that this time we will not be betrayed by any coalition of Northern big finance barons and Southern bourbon plantation owners. They do not realize that the Negro people, with their allies, other oppressed groups, the progressive sections of labor, millions of the Jewish and foreign-born of former white indentured labor, north, south, east and west, in this day and time of ours are determined to see some basic change.

Roosevelt foreshadowed it. We are going to realize it! We were fooled in 1948. We aren't going to be fooled in 1949, 1950, and '51 and '52. We are going to fight for jobs and security at home, and we are going to join the forces of friendship and cooperation with advanced peoples and move on to build a decent world.

And you stooges try to do the work of your white bourbon masters, work they have not the courage to do. You try to play the role of cowardly labor leaders who are attempting to do the same job in the ranks of labor. Try it, but the Negro people will give you your answer! They'll drive you from public life! The Negro people know when they're being sold down the river. They've been watching a long, long time. It's good the challenge has come. Keep on, and you'll have no magazines in which to publish your viciousness. You'll not have many more opportunities to sell into a new slavery our cousins in Liberia, our relatives in South Africa, our brothers in the West Indies. You'll get your answer—and soon! The Negro people are smoldering. They're not afraid of their radicals who point out the awful, indefensible truth of our degradation and exploitation.

What a travesty is this supposed leadership of a great people! And in this historic time, when their people need them most. How Sojourner Truth, Harriet Tubman, Fred Douglass must be turning in their graves at this spectacle of a craven, fawning, despicable leadership, able to be naught but errand boys, and—at the lowest level—stooges and cowardly renegades, a disgrace to the Negro people and to the real and true America of which they so glibly talk. Let them get their crumbs from their Wall Street masters. Let them snatch their bit of cheese and go scampering rat-like into their holes, where, by heaven, the Negro people will keep them, left to their dirty consciences, if any they have.

Now, let's get out the record. In 1946, I declared in St. Louis on the picket line against segregation of Negro people that I would give up my professional career, then at its height, to devote my time and energy to the struggle for the liberation of the Negro people. I appeared everywhere, north, south, east, and west, for Negro colleges, churches, organizations.

I led an anti-lynch crusade to Washington. There I heard our president declare that it was not politically expedient to take any federal action against lynching. You may remember that I said that perhaps the Negro people would have to do something about it themselves. But a committee stepped in—one of those committees to stop the militant Negro struggle. And lynch law is still in committee, while Negroes continue being lynched.

I entered the struggle for peace and freedom with Wallace in 1948, talking at street corner meetings four and five times a day. Without that struggle of the Progressive party the issues before the people would not have been clarified, and we might now be at war. Wallace made a tremendous contribution time and again to the cause of peace, to Negro freedom, and to American freedom. He said peace was the issue. *Peace was, and is, the issue.* He said a war economy was an economy of scarcity and unemployment. *That it was, and is.* He said it meant the loss of civil liberties, the loss of the freedom of European countries. *It has meant just that.* He said it meant slavery for colonial people. *That it is fast becoming.* He said it meant domestic fascism. *That is just around the corner.*

Negroes rallied to Wallace's banner, the banner of their freedom. Then their trusted leaders stepped in to confuse and to frighten them. They sold them a hollow bill of goods in the Democratic party, and a nominee that even these leaders did not trust. Remember, they wanted Eisenhower. But they were afraid of any militant struggle for our people. Where is the civil rights program? Are we still subject to terror? Ask Mrs. Mallard, ask the boys in Virginia, ask the Trenton Six: "Where are our liberties?"

As a consequence of my activities for Negro freedom, I had eighty-six concerts cancelled out of eighty-six. Of course, these were very special concerts. I don't blame auto barons in Detroit for not wanting to pay to hear me when I was in Cadillac Square fighting for the auto workers. I don't blame the iron-ore owners of the Michigan and Minnesota iron-ore ranges for not wanting to hear me when I was on picket lines for the steel workers in these regions. And so with the packinghouse owners of Chicago, or the ship owners of the east and west coasts, or the sugar plantation owners of Hawaii.

Well, they can have their concerts! I'll go back to their cities to sing for the people whom I love, for the Negro and white workers whose freedom will insure my freedom. I'll help, together with many other progressive artists, whenever I can get the time from freedom's struggle, to show how culture can be brought back to the people. We created it in the first place, and it's about time it came back to us!

Today the fight is still on for peace and freedom. Concerts must wait. There is a fierce political struggle which must be won. However, I decided to go to Europe to resume my professional concerts for a very short period, in order to make it perfectly clear that the world is wide and no few pressures could stop my career. Let's go to the record: Albert Hall (London) with its 8,000 seats sold out twice with a five dollar top; 10,000 in the Harringay Arena; thousands turned away all over Europe—the most successful concert tour of my career.

Why? Because I came to the English people from *progressive* America, from the America of Wallace and the Progressive party, from the America of the twelve great Communist leaders who are on trial for their devotion to the Negro people and to the American working class; because I came from Negro America whose struggle had become known to the English during the war when a folk saying grew up: "We love those American soldiers, the black and the brown ones."

I finished my professional tour at its height and announced that never again would I sing at a five dollar top, that I would sing at prices so that workers could come in comfort and dignity. I did this because I belonged to working people. I struggled as a boy in the brickyards, on the docks, in the hotels to get a living and an education. Ninety-five per cent of the Negro people are workers. So I said that my talents would henceforth belong to my people in their struggle. And I acted on this. Thousands and thousands came. That's my answer to the bourbons who think they can end my career!

Later I toured England in peace meetings for British-Soviet friendship, did a series of meetings on the issues of freedom for the peoples of Africa and the West Indies, and on the question of the right of colored seamen and colored technicians to get jobs in a land for which they had risked their lives. Ten thousand people turned out to a meeting in Liverpool on this latter issue.

I stood at the coal pits in Scotland and saw miners contribute from their earnings $1,500 to $2,000 for the benefit of African workers. I helped build up a substantial fund in England to help the cause of African freedom, saw this whole question of the relation of English and colonial peoples raised to a new level as English workers came to understand that if cheap labor could be obtained in Africa or the West Indies or in Southeast Asia, their living standards in England would suffer accordingly. This is a lesson white workers in America must increasingly learn. For the tentacles of American imperialism are stretched far and wide into colonial countries: Cuba, Haiti, Puerto Rico, Hawaii, Trinidad, Panama; down through Latin America; in the Philippines and some parts of the East; and all over the continent of Africa. White workers in America must be aware of this and watch it closely.

Then I moved into Scandinavia. Through a stroke of circumstance, I was booked through *Politiken*. This was an old liberal newspaper in years gone by, but the pressures of present-day American imperialism, exerted mainly through the Marshall Plan, had caused all pretense of liberalism to vanish. I read an editorial of *Politiken* in England supporting the Atlantic Pact, attacking the eastern democracies and the Soviet Union. I immediately asked that my contracts be cancelled. I explained to the press that it was unthinkable that I could appear under the sponsorship of a paper which had allied itself with an imperialism which had enslaved my father and forefathers and was in the process of enslaving my brothers and sisters in Africa, Latin America, the West and East Indies, and which was trying to work up a war against the greatest champion of the rights of colonial and exploited peoples—the Union of Soviet Republics.

The contracts cancelled, I sang for the newspapers of the progressive and Communist forces of Scandinavia (papers like the *Daily Worker*). All the other press had gone the way of the Reuthers, Murrays, Careys, Townsends, et al, who have betrayed American workers and the Negro people to American, British, Dutch, French, Belgian and Japanese imperialists.

Thousands upon thousands in the Scandinavian countries turned out in support of peace and against the Atlantic Pact. These countries of Scandinavia had been freed by Soviet armies, had erected monuments to Soviet heroes. It was unthinkable that they would join the fascist elements of Western Germany and Vichy France against their natural friend and ally. It was clear from the meetings that the great majority of Scandinavian people did not support their governments. I am sure American imperialism is aware of this.

My role was in no sense personal. I represented to these people Progressive America, fighting for peace and freedom, and I bring back to you their love and affection, their promise of their strength to aid us, and their gratefulness for our struggles here. They beg us to send more progressive Americans—Wallace, Marcantonio, trade unionists Negro and white. And they all sent special messages to the Negro people, assuring them of their support of the liberation of Negro peoples everywhere.

Our allies stretch far and wide and they beg us for information and for collective united action. If the originators of the vicious Atlantic Pact can get in a huddle to plot joint action against us, one by one, let us get together to see that nobody can ever take us one by one, that they will have to engage us as a strong, unbending, united force for the peace and freedom of all oppressed peoples.

Why did I take this stand on the Atlantic Pact—the Arms Pact—and its forerunner, the Marshall Plan? Let us examine the results of the Marshall Plan. We don't need to guess and theorize. Western European countries have completely lost their freedom. This was honestly acknowledged everywhere. American big business tells all of Western Europe what to do, what it can produce, where it must buy, with whom it can trade. And finally, with the Atlantic Pact, the western Europeans are told that they must be ready to die to the last man in order to defend American Big Business.

The Eisler case illustrated the European people's revolt against American domination. For the English people decided this was too much. They still have some respect for their judicial law, extending from Magna Charta days—different from us as yet here in America with our Foley Square travesties. The English people move from below—it was a mass movement which forced their government to retreat on Eisler and tell the United States, "Nothing doing." And the Communists of Great Britain started the defense which soon involved great sections of the British people—another important lesson for us. For British people knew that if Eisler was not freed, no longer could they themselves be protected under British law and the whole structure of British freedom would be in danger.

That is just as true here. If the twelve Communists are not freed, all Americans can say goodbye to their civil liberties. *Especially* will we Negro people be forced to say goodbye to any attempts to add to the few civil liberties we as yet have. Just as a mass movement in a few days won this tremendous victory for peace and freedom in London—I was there at the time—so we here in New York and America can do the same if we act with speed and courage in the cause of our freedoms, not just those of the "Twelve."

But beyond this strangling of Western Europe, the real meaning of the Marshall Plan is the complete enslavement of the colonies. For how can British, French and other Western European bankers repay Wall Street? Only in raw materials—in gold, copper, cocoa, rubber, uranium, manganese, iron ore, ground nuts, oils, fats, sugar, bananas. From where? Why, from South Africa, Nigeria, East Africa, French Africa, Belgian Congo, Trinidad, Jamaica, Cuba, Honduras, Guatemala, Viet Nam, Malaya. The Marshall Plan means enslavement of our people all over the earth, including here in the United States on the cotton and sugar plantations and in the mines of the North and South.

And the Atlantic Pact means legal sanction for sending guns and troops to the colonies to insure the enslavement and terrorization of our people. They will shoot our people down in Africa just as they lynch us in Mississippi. That's the other side of the same coin.

For who owns plantations in the South? Metropolitan Life—yes, the same Metropolitan Life Insurance Company that owns and won't let you live in the Stuyvesant Town flats in New York. It is such giant financial interests that are getting millions from the Marshall Plan. They enslave us, they enslave Western Europe, they enslave the colonies.

Many of our Negro leaders know this. But some of these so-called distinguished leaders are doing the dirty work for Stettinius, aiding his scheme for the exploitation of Liberia and its people, or are serving as errand boys for Forrestal's cartel interests, even though the chief has now departed. And there are a few other of these so-called Negro leaders who are too low and contemptible to give the courtesy of mention.

Are these financial big boys America? No! They are the former enemies of Roosevelt. They were the ones who were glad when Roosevelt died. They are the same ones who Roosevelt said were the core of American fascism. They are the allies of the remains of the Hitler entourage, that Hitler who burned up eight million of a great Jewish people and said he would like to burn up fourteen million of us. They are the friends of Franco, the living representatives of the Spanish Conquistadores who enslaved us and still enslave us in Latin America. They are the ones who hate American democracy as did the enemies of Jefferson and Lincoln before them. *They are no part of America!* They are the would-be preservers of world fascism and the enemies of progressive America!

And they are in the government, too—you saw them deny your civil rights on the floors of Congress; you saw them throw our promised civil rights right into our teeth, while our supposed chief defender enjoyed the sun down in Florida, a state that is the symbol, of course, of the freedom and equality of the Negro people.

And now this greedy section of democratic America, by corrupting our leaders, by shooting us as we attempt to vote, by terrorizing us as in the case of the "Trenton Six," has the gall to try to lure us into a war against countries where the freedoms that we so deeply desire are being realized, together with a rich and abundant life, the kind of life that should be ours also, because so much of America's wealth is realized from our blood and from our labor.

My last weeks abroad were spent in these countries to the East, Czechoslovakia, Poland, and finally the Soviet Union. Here thousands of people—men, women, children—cried to me to thank progressive America for sending one of its representatives, begged me so to take back their love, their heartfelt understanding of the suffering of their Negro brothers and sisters, that I wept time and time again. Whole nations of people gave me a welcome I can never forget—a welcome not for me, Paul Robeson, but in your name, the name of the Negro people of America, of the colonies; in the name of the progressive America of Wallace and the Progressive party; and in the name of the twelve Communist leaders. Outstanding people in the government treated me with the greatest respect and dignity because I represented you (but there were no calls from the American embassies).

Here in these countries are *the people,* their

spokesmen are in the forefront of our struggle for liberation—on the floor of the United Nations, in the highest councils of world diplomacy. Here in the Soviet Union, in Czechoslovakia, in battered but gallant Warsaw with its brave saga of the ghetto, are the nations leading the battle for peace and freedom. They were busy building, reconstructing; and the very mention of war caused one to look at you as if you were insane.

I was in Stalingrad. I saw a letter from President Roosevelt—no equivocation there. It said that in Stalingrad came the turning point in the battle for civilization. I stood in the little rectangle where the heroic people of Stalingrad fought with their backs to the mighty Volga—and saved us—saved you and me from Hitler's wrath. We loved them then. What has happened to us? For they are the same, only braver. Midst their ruins, they sing and laugh and dance. Their factories are restored—fifty percent above prewar. I sang at their tractor factory and saw a tractor—*not a tank*—coming off the line every fifteen minutes. It was a factory built by Soviet hands, Soviet brains, Soviet know-how.

"I am born and bred in this America of ours. I want to love it. I love a part of it. But it's up to the rest of America when I shall love it with the same intensity that I love the Negro people from whom I spring. . . ."

They want peace and an abundant life. Freedom is already theirs. The children cried, "Take back our love to the Negro children and the working class children." And they clasped and embraced me literally and symbolically for you. I love them.

Here is a whole one-sixth of the earth's surface, including millions of brown, yellow and black people who would be Negroes here in America and subject to the same awful race prejudice that haunts us. In this Soviet Union, the very term "backward country" is an insult, for in one generation former colonial peoples have been raised to unbelievable industrial and social levels. It is, indeed, a vast new concept of democracy. And these achievements make completely absurd the solemn pronouncements that it will take several generations, maybe hundreds of years, before we Negro people in the West Indies, Africa and America can have any real control over our own destiny.

Here is a whole nation which is now doing honor to our poet Pushkin—one of the greatest poets in history—the Soviet people's and our proud world possession. Could I find a monument to Pushkin in a public square of Birmingham or Atlanta or Memphis, as one stands in the center of Moscow? No. One perhaps to Goethe, but not to the dark-skinned Pushkin.

Yes, I love this Soviet people more than any other nation, because of their suffering and sacrifices for us, the Negro people, the progressive people, the people of the future in this world.

At the Paris Peace Conference I said it was unthinkable that the Negro people of America or elsewhere in the world could be drawn into war with the Soviet Union. I repeat it with hundredfold emphasis. THEY WILL NOT.

And don't ask a few intellectuals who are jealous of their comfort. Ask the sugar workers whom I saw starving in Louisiana, the workers in the cotton lands and the tobacco belts in the South. Ask the sugar workers in Jamaica. Ask the Africans in Malan's South Africa. Ask them if they will struggle for peace and friendship with the Soviet people, with the peoples of China and the new democracies, or if they will help their imperialist oppressors to return them to an even worse slavery. The answer lies there in the millions of my struggling people, not only the 14 million in America, but the 40 million in the Caribbean and Latin America and the 150 million in Africa. No wonder all the excitement! For one day this mighty mass will strike for freedom, and a new strength like that of gallant China will add its decisive weight to insuring a world where all men can be free and equal.

I am born and bred in this America of ours. I want to love it. I love a part of it. But it's up to the rest of America when I shall love it with the same intensity that I love the Negro people from whom I spring—in the way that I love progressives in the Caribbean, the black and Indian peoples of South and Central America, the peoples of China and Southeast Asia, yes suffering people the world over—and in the way that I deeply and intensely love the Soviet Union. That burden of proof rests upon America.

Now these peoples of the Soviet Union, of the new eastern democracies, of progressive Western Europe, and the representatives of the Chinese people whom I met in Prague and Moscow, were in great part Communists. They were the first to die for our freedom and for the freedom of all mankind. So I'm not afraid of Communists; no, far from that. I will defend them as they defended us, the Negro people. And I stand firm and immovable by the side of that great leader who has given his whole life to the struggle of the American working class, Bill Foster; by the side of Gene Dennis; by the side of my friend, Ben Davis; Johnny Gates, Henry Winston, Gus Hall, Gil Green, Jack Stachel, Carl Winter, Irving Potash, Bob Thompson, Johnny Williamson—twelve brave fighters for my freedom. Their struggle is *our* struggle.

But to fulfill our responsibilities as Americans, we must unite, especially we Negro people. We must know our strength. We are the decisive force. That's why they terrorize us. That's why they fear us. And if we unite in all our might, this world can fast be changed. Let us create that unity now. And this important, historic role of the Negro people our white allies here must fully comprehend. This means increasing understanding of the Negro, his tremendous struggle, his great contributions, his potential for leadership at all levels in the common task of liberation. It means courage to stand by our side whatever the consequences, as we the Negro people fulfill our historic duty in Freedom's struggle.

If we unite, we'll get our law against lynching, our right to vote and to labor. Let us march on Washington, representing 14,000,000 strong. Let us push aside the sycophants who tell us to be quiet.

The so-called western democracies—including our own, which so fiercely exploits us and daily denies us our simple constitutional guarantees—can find no answer before the bar of world justice for their treatment of the Negro people. Democracy, indeed! We must have the courage to shout at the top of our voices about our injustices and we must lay the blame where it belongs and where it has belonged for over three hundred years of slavery and misery: right here on our own doorstep—not in any far away place. This is the very time when we can win our struggle.

And we cannot win it by being lured into any kind of war with our closest friends and allies throughout the world. For any kind of decent life we need, we want, and *we demand* our constitutional rights—RIGHT HERE IN AMERICA. We do not want to die in vain any more on foreign battlefields for Wall Street and the greedy supporters of domestic fascism. If we must die, let it be in Mississippi or Georgia! Let it be wherever we are lynched and deprived of our rights as human beings!

Let this be a final answer to the warmongers. Let them know that we will not help to enslave our brothers and sisters and eventually ourselves. Rather, we will help to insure peace in our time—the freedom and liberation of the Negro and other struggling peoples, and the building of a world where we can all walk in full equality and full human dignity.

Despite ongoing attempts to silence him professionally and personally, Robeson continued to perform and speak out whenever and wherever he could. More and more as time went on, his appearances were limited to gatherings of union members and various peace and social or political action groups. He also spoke frequently at events sponsored by the Council on African Affairs, an organization he himself had established to support African independence efforts. In every instance, Robeson clearly demonstrated that for him, at least, the roles of activist and artist were completely intertwined. In late 1951, for example, he addressed the opening session of the Conference for Equal Rights for Negroes in the Arts, Sciences and Professions, which was held in New York City. In a speech entitled "The Negro Artist Looks Ahead," he noted that African American artists faced two major hurdles—widespread ignorance regarding their past accomplishments and discrimination that limited their opportunities to excel. His remarks, slightly abridged

from the original text of his speech, are reprinted here from Masses and Mainstream *magazine, January 1952.*

We are here today to work out ways and means of finding jobs for colored actors and colored musicians, to see that the pictures and statues made by colored painters and sculptors are sold, to see that the creations of Negro writers are made available to the vast American public. We are here to see that colored scientists and professionals are placed in leading schools and universities, to open up opportunities for Negro technicians, to see that the way is open for colored lawyers to advance to judgeships—yes, to the Supreme Court of these United States, if you please.

It is not just a question of jobs, of positions, of commercial sales. No—the questions at hand cannot be resolved without the resolution of deeper problems involved here. We are dealing with the position in this society of a great people—of fifteen million closely-bound human beings, of whom ten millions in the cotton and agricultural belt of the South form a kind of nation based upon common oppression, upon a magnificent common heritage, upon unified aspiration for full freedom and full equality in the larger democratic society.

The Negro people today are saying all up and down this nation (when you get on the streets, into the churches, into the bars to talk to them): "We will not suffer the genocide that might be visited upon us. We are prepared to fight to the death for our rights."

Yes, we are dealing with a great people. Their mere survival testifies to that. One hundred millions sacrificed and wasted in the slave ships, on the cotton plantations, in order that there might be built the basic wealth of this great land. It must have been a tremendously strong people, a people of tremendous stamina, of the finest character, merely to have survived. Not only have the Negro people survived in this America, they have given to these United States almost a new language, given it ways of speech, given it perhaps the only indigenous music.

One great creation, modern popular music, whether it be in theatre, film, radio, records—wherever it may be—is almost completely based upon the Negro idiom. There is no leading American singer, performer of popular songs, whether it be a Crosby, a Sinatra, a Shore, a Judy Garland, an Ella Logan, who has not listened (and learned) by the hour to Holliday, Waters, Florence Mills, to Bert Williams, to Fitzgerald, and to the greatest of all, Bessie Smith. Without these models, who would ever have heard of a Tucker, a Jolson, a Cantor?

Go into the field of the dance. Where could there have come an Astaire, an Eleanor Powell and a James Barton without a Bill Robinson, a Bert Williams, an Eddie Rector, a Florence Mills? How could Artie Shaw and Benny Goodman have appeared but for a Teddy Wilson, Turner Latan, Johnny Dunn, Hall Johnson, Will Marion Cook? Whence stems even Gershwin? From the music of Negro America joined with the ancient Hebrew idiom. Go and listen to some of the great melodies. Here again is a great American composer, deeply rooted, whether he knew it or not, in an African tradition, a tradition very close to his own heritage.

I speak very particularly of this popular form. This is very important to the Negro artists, because billions, literally billions of dollars, have been earned and are being earned from their creation, and the Negro people have received almost nothing.

At another stage of the arts there is no question, as one goes about the world, of the contribution of the Negro folk songs, of the music that sprang from my forefathers in their struggle for freedom—not songs of contentment—but songs like "Go Down, Moses" that inspired Harriet Tubman, John Brown, and Sojourner Truth to the fight for emancipation.

I think of Larry Brown who went abroad, heard Moussorgsky, heard the great folk music of other lands and dedicated himself, as did Harry Burleigh before him, to showing that this was a great music, not just "plantation songs."

One perhaps forgets my own career, and that for five years I would sing nothing but the music of my people. Later, when it was established as a fine folk music, I began to learn of the folk music of other peoples. This has been one of the bonds that have drawn me so close to the peoples of the world, bonds through this likeness in music that made me understand the political growth of many peoples, the struggles of many peoples, and brought me back to you to fight here in this land, as I shall continue to do.

I remember in England in the old days (incidentally, I just heard from Kingsley Martin, of the *New Statesman and Nation,* who is concerned about my inability to travel and to function as an artist in this land, and who is beginning a campaign in England on this basis)—I remember writing several articles for the *New Statesman and Nation,* going to the whole root of this matter. I think back now—the deep pride that I had and still have in the creations of my people and in seeing the links here with Africa, and with the other peoples of Asia, and taking issue with the view that Western music was the only great music in the world and that everything else was so backward.

I remember writing: "Mr. Beethoven, yes, he is a great composer, but he deals with themes. He has to develop them a bit, but he starts with a very simple theme. . . ." And I was interested in reading a book the other day on the thematic process which takes the whole Ninth Symphony and proves that in every movement it begins and stems from a kernel that really in the end is a few bars. In those days I didn't quite know it technically, but had a feeling, and I listened to all the music and I still am looking to find anywhere greater themes to start with than "Deep River" or "Go Down, Moses," or "I'm a Poor Wayfaring Stranger."

So we are dealing with a people who come from great roots. There is no need to quote the names of an Anderson or a Hayes and many more; or of the great scientists—of a Julian, of a Carver. No need today for the Negro people to prove any more that they have a right to full equality. They have proven it again and again.

The roots of this great outpouring we are talking about today in the cultural expression of my people, is a great culture from a vast continent. If these origins are somewhat blurred in this America of ours, they are clear in Brazil, where Villa-Lobos joins Bach with African rhythms and melodies; in Cuba and Haiti a whole culture, musical and poetic, is very deep in the Africa of its origins—an African culture quite comparable to the ancient culture of the Chinese—similar in religious concepts, in language, in poetry, in its sculpture, in its whole aesthetic; a culture which has deeply influenced the great artists of our time—a Picasso, a Modigliani, a Brancusi, an Epstein, a de Falla, a Milhaud. So we are today discussing the problems of a proud people, rich in tradition, a people torn from its ancient homeland but who in three hundred years have built anew, have enriched this new continent with its physical power, with its intellect, with its deep, inexhaustible spirit and courage.

As I have said, in spite of all these contributions to our culture, the fruits have been taken from us. Think of Handy, one of the creators of the blues; think of Count Basie, playing to half-filled houses at the Apollo; colored arrangers receiving a pittance while white bands reap harvests. What heartbreak for every Negro composer! Publishing houses taking his songs for nothing and making fortunes. Theatres in the heart of the Negro communities dictating to Negro performers what they shall act . . . arrogantly telling Negro audiences what they shall see.

I went to a whole group of my Negro friends. I wanted them to put down some of the things in which they were interested this morning. What did they want you to know? Here are some things that I will read:

Negroes have carried on an important struggle in the United States throughout the history of this country, even before there was any significant progressive movement in the U.S.: this is a lesson progressives must learn—and accept it as a privilege and duty to join in the struggle. The progressive movement must understand with crystal clarity that the Negro people of the United States have never retreated or compromised in their aspirations, and progressives must follow a dynamic path with them. For if they do otherwise, they will find themselves conscious or unconscious allies of reactionaries and pseudo-liberals. Progressives must re-orient themselves to the qualitative change that has come about in the unalienable and rightful demand of the United States Negro. The Negro men and women of the United States want equality for everybody, in everything, everywhere, now.

This is awfully good, I must say.

Whites must come forward and put up a struggle, no matter what the repercussions; struggle must be constant in unions, housing organizations and not only where Negroes are involved—whites must take action every day and not wait for Negroes to raise issues in order to come in on the struggle. . . . Peace is crucial in this question. Its maintenance depends on whether or not democracy is extended to the Negro. Support must be twofold. In order to show support politically, there must be an understanding and appreciation of Negro culture. There must be a willingness to learn. If present U.S. cultural patterns do not permit the utilization of Negro talent, then independent means must be found.

Another comment:

The U.S. theatre must show the totality of Negro life, thereby eliminating stereotypes in either extreme. To offset the so-called objective reporting in the white press, all positive accomplishments by Negro cultural workers should be designated as such. Every Negro artist needs and must now demand free and equal opportunity to develop in fields of his or her endeavor. White progressives must recognize that in joining the Negro struggle, they join on the Negro people's terms.

Mr. Hood, in Cincinnati, put it very sharply: We must work together. We are a unit—certainly we are, but to the trade union leader (we say) we seek your cooperation; we no longer ask your permission.

Let us touch for a moment on radio and television. We all know the difficulties—no major hours with Negro talent, an occasional guest appearance eagerly awaited by the Negro audience. Why this discrimination? Well, these mass media are based on advertising, commercialism at its worst, and the final answer is very simple. It goes to the root of all that has been said. The final answer is: "The South won't take it."

Now, I had a program myself in the forties, all set up by one of the biggest advertising agencies, a very fine program, a dignified program in which I would have been doing Othello and many other things. One morning they said, "We made some inquiries and the South just won't have it. You can come on once in a while and sing with Mr. Voorhees, and so forth, but no possibility of a Negro artist having his own program." Not *that* dignity. And so we have allowed the South with its patterns to determine for all America how, when and where the Negro will be denied an opportunity.

"... all pronouncements of our wonderful democracy ring hollow as soon as one points the finger at the oppression of 15 million second- and third-class citizens of this land."

I think that public opinion could be aroused on this issue. This is a matter of national protest, of national pressure. These media happen to be under the control of Federal Communications. We are dealing here with matters as serious as the passage of an anti-lynch bill, anti-poll tax and free voting legislation, of FEPC, of the whole issue of federal and states' rights. We can demand a change in the public interest in the pursuance of democratic procedures. Added to this, of course, can be pressure on the advertisers who wax fat today from the purchases of Negro customers. These latter, plus their allies, could have very decisive influence.

The films today are of vast significance and influence. Here, too, the South determines the attempts to camouflage, to pass off so-called progressive films, to find new approaches to the treatment of the Negro. They have been very thoroughly analyzed and exposed for what they are by V.J. Jerome in his exhaustive pamphlet on *The Negro in Hollywood Films*. Here, too, the mounting of the right kind of campaign could shake Hollywood to its foundations, and help would be forthcoming from all over the world. Their markets everywhere in the world could be seriously affected, if the lead came from here.

The struggle on this front could have been waged with some real measure of success at any time, but today conditions insure the careful heeding of the collective wrath of the Negro people and their allies. For today, in the struggle extending all over the world, all pronouncements of our wonderful democracy ring hollow and clearly false as soon as one points the finger at the oppression of fifteen million second- and third-class citizens of this land.

There is no way to cover that up. One day, Willie McGee; the next, Martinsville; the next, Cicero; the next, Groveland, Florida. Behind these horrors is the mounting anger of a long-suffering people, of a people that has its Denmark Veseys, its Frederick Douglasses, its Sojourner Truths, its Harriet Tubmans, its Du Boises, its Benjamin Davises—a people that fought for its freedom in the great Civil War and buried the hated Confederate flags in the dust.

Behind these people and their allies here in the U.S. are the tens and tens of millions of advanced workers through the world, west and east, bulwarked by the overwhelming millions of a fast-emerging colonial world hastening to final and complete control of their destinies, inspired by the events of a November 7th, thirty-four years ago, by the victories of many new people's democracies, by the world-shattering creation of the new People's Republic of China. This world in change makes possible here new levels of action, insures victories hitherto unsuspected. The millions of India watch and Mr. Bowles will have his hands and his mouth full to convince these people that the civilization extolled by Byrnes of South Carolina, Smith of Georgia, Connally of Texas, is just the thing to bring new vistas of freedom and individual liberty to that ancient continent. I often get letters from India. They seem to be somewhat doubtful.

The government can be pressured in this time and it certainly can be pressured on this issue. Most important for us here is the recognition of the Negro's rights to all kinds of jobs in the arts, not only the rights of the artists, but technical jobs for engineers, all sorts of opportunities in production, in scenic design, at all levels. I am very much interested in that: I've got a son, Paul, who studied engineering at Cornell, majored in communications. I'd like to see him get a good job in television.

And so in the case of Actors Equity—we who are members of Equity must fight not only for the rights of Negro actors, we must see that the stagehands are there. We must fight within the AFL, Equity's parent organization, for the right of Negroes to work in *every* field. And so in the American Guild of Musical Artists and in the American Federation of Radio Artists—they are shouting an awful lot these days about how democratic and American they are. Let them show it!

The final problem concerns new ways, new opportunities based upon a deep sense of responsibility in approaching the problem of the Negro people in its totality. There are despoilers abroad in our land, akin to these who attempted to throttle our Republic at its birth. Despoilers who would have kept my beloved people in unending serfdom, a powerful few who blessed Hitler as he destroyed a large segment of a great people. Today they would recreate the image of Hitler, stifle millions of the hitherto oppressed as they struggle forth for their emancipation, destroy the people's republics where life has been created anew, where the forces of nature have been turned to man's prosperity and good.

All these millions of the world stand aghast at the sight and the very name of *that* America—but they love *us;* they look to *us* to help create a world where we can all live in peace and friendship, where we can exchange the excellences of our various arts and crafts, the manifold wonders of our mutual scientific creations, a world where we can rejoice at the unleashed powers of our innermost selves, of the potential of great masses of people. To them *we* are the real Americans. Let us remember that.

And let us learn how to bring to the great masses of the American people *our* culture and *our* art. For in the end, what are we talking about when we talk about American culture today? We are talking about a culture that is restricted to the very, very few. How many workers ever get to the theatre? I was in concerts for twenty years, subscription concerts, the two thousands seats gone before any Negro in the community, any worker, could even hear about a seat. Even then, the price was $12.00 for six concerts. How could working people ever hear these concerts? Only by my going into the trade unions and singing on the streets and on the picket lines and in the struggles for the freedom of our people—only in this way could the workers of this land hear me.

We are talking about a culture which as yet has no relationship to the great masses of the American people. I remember an experience in England. I sang not only in Albert Hall, the concert halls, but also in the picture theatres, and one night I came out and a young woman was standing there with her mother, an aged lady. "My grandmother wants to thank you very much. She always wanted to hear you in person. She heard you tonight and she's going home. She just had sixpence above her bus fare." So she was able to hear me. Later, that was so in the Unity Theatre in London—now a theatre which has stretched all over England. Here in America, in 1948 in the deep South, I remember standing singing to white workers in Memphis, workers who had come out on strike that Negro workers might get equal wages.

In the theatre I felt this years ago and it would interest you to know that the opening night of *Othello* in New York, in Chicago, in San Francisco (I never told this to the Guild), I told Langner he could have just one-third of the house for the elite. I played the opening night of *Othello* to the workers from Fur, from Maritime, from Local 65.

Just the other night I sang at the Rockland Palace in the Bronx, to this people's audience.

We speak to them every night. To thousands. Somewhere, with the impetus coming from the arts, sciences and professions, there are literally millions of people in America who would come to hear us, the Negro artists. This can be very important. Marian Anderson, Roland Hayes, all of us started in the Baptist churches. I'm going right back there very soon. If you want to talk about audiences, I defy any opera singer to take those ball parks like Sister Tharpe or Mahalia Jackson. It is so in the Hungarian communities (I was singing to the Hungarian-Americans yesterday), the Russian-Americans, the Czech-Americans . . . all of them have their audiences stretching throughout this land.

The progressive core of these audiences could provide a tremendous base for the future, a tremendous base for our common activity and a necessary base in the struggle for peace. These people must be won. We can win them through our cultural contributions. We could involve millions of people in the struggle for peace and for a decent world.

But the final point. This cannot be done unless we as artists have the deepest respect for these people. When we say that we are people's artists, we must mean that. I mean it very deeply. Because, you know, the people created our art in the first place.

Haydn with his folk songs—the people made it up in the first place. The language of Shakespeare—this was the creation of the English-speaking people; the language of Pushkin, the creation of the Russian people, of the Russian peasants. That is where it came from—a little dressed up with some big words now and then which can be broken down into very simple images.

So, in the end, the culture with which we deal comes from the people. We have an obligation to take it back to the people, to make them understand that in fighting for their cultural heritage they fight for peace. They fight for their own rights, for the rights of the Negro people, for the rights of all in this great land. All of this is dependent so much upon our understanding the power of this people, the power of the Negro people, the power of the masses of America, of a world where we can all walk in complete dignity.

In 1950, the U.S. State Department revoked Robeson's passport and declined to issue him a new one until he signed an oath stating that he was not a communist. The government also insisted that he stop criticizing American foreign and domestic policy in speeches delivered overseas. As a result of his repeated refusals to comply with these demands, he spent most of the rest of the decade mired in a frustrating legal battle to regain the right to travel abroad, where he was still immensely popular.

Perhaps the most public airing of his dispute with federal officials came in July 1956, when Robeson was called before the infamous House Un-American Activities Committee to explain his political affiliations and activities. Committee members finally adjourned the hearing when it became clear that he had no intention of answering their questions. In an angrily eloquent statement he was not allowed to read to his accusers (but which was released later to the press), Robeson observed:

"It is a sad and bitter commentary on the state of civil liberties in America that the very forces of reaction . . . who have denied me access to the lecture podium, the concert hall, the opera house, and the dramatic stage, now hale me before a committee of inquisition in order to hear what I have to say. It is obvious that those who are trying to gag me here and abroad will scarcely grant me the freedom to express myself fully in a hearing controlled by them. . . . It is my firm intention to continue to speak out against injustices to the Negro people, and I shall continue to do all within my power in behalf of independence of colonial peoples of Africa. It is for [Secretary of State John Foster] Dulles to explain why a

Negro who opposes colonialism and supports the aspirations of Negro Americans should for those reasons be denied a passport. My fight for a passport is a struggle for freedom—freedom to travel, freedom to earn a livelihood, freedom to speak, freedom to express myself artistically and culturally. . . . My travels abroad to sing and act and speak cannot possibly harm the American people. In the past I have won friends for the real America among the millions before whom I have performed. . . . By continuing the struggle at home and abroad for peace and friendship with all of the world's people, for an end to colonialism, for full citizenship for Negro Americans, for a world in which art and culture may abound, I intend to continue to win friends for the best in American life."

As a result of a related court case, Robeson finally regained his passport in 1958. But by then, his income and popularity had plummeted to almost nothing. After giving a few farewell concerts in the United States, he embarked on an extended overseas tour. Poor health soon forced him to retire from the stage, however. He spent the next few years in and out of foreign hospitals and nursing homes before returning to New York to live in the mid-1960s. On April 22, 1965, at a combination "Welcome Home"/birthday party that turned out to be his last appearance at a public event, the ailing Robeson reflected on his often troubled past and looked toward the future with a sense of optimism. The following is an excerpt from his speech, which was published in the summer 1965, issue of Freedomways.

Well, I am certainly proud and happy to be with you tonight. I've never had a reception anything like this at any time that I can remember. And there are friends in the audience, people who went to school with me, back in New Jersey. They seem to come from many sections of our land to say hello. And I certainly want to thank you all for being here, for what we just heard. I know that all of you understand the struggles that are going on and it's been a wonderful evening to be sitting out there and listening to the beautiful singing, to the understanding of what our struggle means in this country today, and in other lands. I was also very happy to have Mr. Billy Taylor here; I felt like "getting in the jive."

I want to thank *Freedomways* for making this evening possible. This particular magazine is one which many of us have followed from the beginning. It is significant to note that *Freedomways* came into being along with the thrust of the Negro freedom movement, to express, to record, and to contribute in this history-making activity in our country. This magazine is of particular importance to all American writers, and especially to the Negro writers who are playing such a splendid role in interpreting the struggle which is going on in our lives today in Harlem, in the deep South, all over the country, and also in Africa. Negro American writers in Africa, and Africans themselves give us direct and welcome insight into the activities on that continent. The magnificent special issues of *Freedomways,* for example, the one devoted to the people of the Caribbean and notably the most recent one devoted to the life and contributions of our great teacher, Dr. W.E.B. Du Bois, already serve as points of reference as well as giving deep artistic satisfaction. We hope that the quality and scope of this magazine will be appreciated by growing numbers of people in all groups in our country and in other parts of the world.

I want to especially thank the artists who have taken time out from their busy lives to come here this evening. It has been very moving to see so many of the actors that I came up with (now a little older, maybe), down in the Village long ago, in the twenties. And someone is here who was at one of the first concerts way back in 1925. It is a great joy, certainly, to see the tremendous talent and the development of the growing numbers of our artists reaching, as they are, the highest levels. I would like for a moment to call your attention to an artist who has been closely associated with me in my career. I hope Larry is still here, my friend and colleague, Mr. Lawrence Brown, an authority on Negro and classical music who has been my partner in concerts for forty years. And I want to say, Larry, if you are still here, that when I came in and heard your protege take off there and sing, he sounded pretty good to me. Larry is teaching, and I felt when he came in, I'd better go on singing, "I'm gonna lay down my sword and shield down by the riverside, ain't gonna study war no more."

Recalling my own work in music and the theatre, as I said back in the twenties and thirties, it is encouraging today to see the ever-increasing opportunities and widening horizons

> ***"Our languages may be different, the political, economic and social systems under which we live may be different, but art reflects a common humanity."***

for our Negro playwrights, actors and actresses in theatre, films, radio and TV, for our musicians in concert and in opera, and for our artists in almost every aspect of the cultural life of our country. It is also most interesting to see that these artists are becoming known all over the world, by records, TV and personal appearances. It is equally interesting to note that audiences all over the world understand and respond to the best of our art and our artists, even as we here appreciate the visiting artists who come from abroad.

Yes, our languages, our idioms, our forms of expression may be different, the political, economic and social systems under which we live may be different, but art reflects a common humanity. And further, much of the contemporary art reflecting our times has to do with the struggles for equality, human dignity, freedom, peace and mutual understanding. The aspirations for a better life are similar indeed all over the world and when expressed in art, are universally understood. While we become aware of great variety, we recognize the universality, the unity, the oneness of the many people in our contemporary world. In relation to this, in our travels we visited many peoples in socialist countries. Today we know that hundreds of millions of people (a majority of the world's population) are living in socialist countries or are moving in a socialist direction. Likewise newly emancipated nations of Africa and Asia are seriously considering the question as to which economic system best fits their needs. Some of their most outstanding leaders agree that the best road to the people's goals is through a socialist development, and they point to the advances made by the Soviet Union, the People's Republic of China, Cuba and the other socialist countries as proof of their contention.

The large question as to which society is better for humanity is never settled by argument. The proof of the pudding is in the eating. *Let the various social systems compete with one another under conditions of peaceful coexistence, and the people can decide for themselves.* It is very interesting to note the support which comes from the socialist countries for the freedom struggles everywhere. At this historic moment, it is certainly wonderful and heartwarming to see the participation of our artists, Negro and white, in the freedom struggle, and to note their brilliant contributions to the understanding so necessary for all sections of our American community. Yes, it's good to be back again!

Since we've been away, we've been to many countries: Britain, Hungary, France, the Soviet Union, Czechoslovakia, Rumania, the German Democratic Republic and as far away as Australia and New Zealand. Everywhere we found a warm welcome for our music, and especially for the songs expressing a deep desire for friendship, equality and peace. There was an opportunity to appear at the birthplace of Shakespeare in Stratford-on-Avon in a warmly received production of *Othello;* also to appear on television in music and drama to sing in St. Paul's Cathedral in London, and with miners in Wales and in Scotland; and in many cities to sing for and with students from various parts of Africa. There was also occasion to participate in great rallies for peace in Paris, Moscow, in London's famous Trafalgar Square and in many other capitals of the world. All the while that we were abroad we kept in touch with the remarkable progress of the freedom struggle here at home. The struggle for "Freedom Now" in the South and all over this land is a struggle uniting many sections of the American people, as evidenced in that great march from Selma to Montgomery, where thousands of black and white citizens of this country marched for the freedom of our people in the deep South and for a new kind of America. Also uniting many sections of our people is the struggle for peace, this demand to avoid any chance of nuclear war, rather to live in peace and friendship. This was evidenced by the recent march to the United Nations and the students' March on Washington. It is clear that large sections of the American people are feeling and accepting their responsibility for freedom and peace. It also is clear that from the Negro people has come a tremendous initiative and dynamic power in the forward thrust of our march toward freedom. It is clear that the Negro people are claiming their rights and they are in every way determined to have those rights and nothing can turn us back!

Most important is the recognition that achieving these demands in no way lessens the democratic rights of white American citizens. On the contrary, it will enormously strengthen the base of democracy for all Americans. So, the initiative, the power and independence of the Negro movement are all factors which strengthen the alliance between the Negro people and the white citizens of our country at every level in our society. Now we must find and build a living connection, deeper and stronger, between the Negro people and the great mass of white Americans who are indeed our natural allies in the struggle for democracy. In fact, the interests of the overwhelming majority of the American people as a whole demand that this connection be built and that the "Negro question" be solved. It is not simply a matter of justice for a minority. Just as in Lincoln's time the basic interests of the American majority made it necessary to strike down the system of Negro enslavement so today these interests make it necessary to abolish the system of Negro second-class citizenship.

In all of our struggles (on the marches, in the demonstrations, at the mass meetings) we see and feel that the part played by *music* is of extraordinary importance. How wonderful to hear these songs tonight and to hear the songs that serve to inspire, encourage, sustain and unite the thousands of participants, particularly the beautiful old songs which were a part of the Negro's long struggle during slavery and Reconstruction. Today these old songs, sometimes with new words, serve the same high purpose as do the beautiful songs newly composed in the heat of the day. Songs like "We Shall Not Be Moved," "Freedom," "Ain't Gon' Study War No More" and "This Little Light of Mine, I'm Gon' Let It Shine, Let It Shine, Let It Shine, Let It Shine . . ." and "We Are Climbing Jacob's Ladder." I remember always being taken by that song as a boy. We *are* climbing "Jacob's Ladder," rung by rung, higher and higher, until we find our freedoms, our complete equality in the lands of our birth. I could go on with many songs from other parts of the world. They liked our music (as our artists have found out when they went), so we sang in many of the languages in the countries we visited. We saw the unity of the struggles. There is one song that I have always said comes from struggles of the peoples, like we sang "Go Down Moses," there is another song from these great peoples that goes:

Never say that you have reached the
very end,
When leaden skies a bitter future
may portend:
For sure the hour for which we yearn
will yet arrive
And our marching steps will thunder
'We Survive!'

And for all of my family I want to thank you again, Ossie, Ruby, all who have been so kind. I'm happy to be with you and hope that we can act again (can't tell), sing, move again.

Be sure that you are subscribing to this wonderful magazine, *Freedomways*. I certainly go home knowing and feeling more and more deeply, *"We shall overcome, deep in my heart I do believe, We Shall Overcome some day."*

SOURCES

Books

Boulware, Marcus H., *The Oratory of Negro Leaders: 1900-1968,* Negro Universities Press, 1969.

Ehrlich, Scott, *Paul Robeson,* Chelsea House, 1988.

Foner, Philip S., editor, *Paul Robeson Speaks: Writings, Speeches, Interviews, 1918-1974,* Brunner/ Mazel, 1978.

Graham, Shirley, *Paul Robeson: Citizen of the World,* Messner, 1946.

Hamilton, Virginia, *Paul Robeson: The Life and Times of a Free Black Man,* Harper, 1974.

Robeson, Paul, *Here I Stand,* Othello Associates, 1958, reprinted, Beacon Press, 1971.

Periodicals

Black Scholar, "Paul Robeson: Beleaguered Leader," December, 1973, pp. 25-32.

Commonweal, September 9, 1949, p. 524.

Crisis, March, 1976, pp. 77-80; "Paul Robeson: A Remembrance," pp. 81-83.

Ebony, "Paul Robeson: Farewell to a Fighter," April, 1976, pp. 33-42.

Freedomways, "It's Good to Be Back" (part of a special multi-article salute to Robeson), Volume V, no. 3, summer, 1965, pp. 373-377; Volume XI, no. 1, 1971 (entire issue devoted to Robeson); Volume XVI, no. 1, 1976, pp. 8-24.

Masses and Mainstream, "The Negro Artist Looks

Ahead," January, 1952, pp. 7-14; "Voting for Peace," August, 1952, pp. 9-14.

Newsweek, January 1, 1951, p. 13; "Tragic Hero," February 2, 1976, p. 73.

New York Times, April 21, 1949, p. 6; July 18, 1949, p. 17; January 24, 1976.

Time, June 27, 1949, p. 36; February 2, 1976, p. 55.

John Ross

(Coowescoowe)

1790–1866

Native American chief of the Cherokee tribe

John Ross led the Cherokees for some forty years during the mid-nineteenth century, a period that coincided with some of the darkest days in their history. The most tragic episode was without a doubt the "Trail of Tears," a forced march that saw thousands of Cherokee and other tribes of the southeastern United States removed from their homelands and resettled in what is now Oklahoma. It is there that John Ross lived out his days working for unity not only among the Cherokee themselves but among all those who had been uprooted by government edict and sent to live among strangers in a strange land.

Born near Lookout Mountain, Tennessee, of a Scottish father and a part-Cherokee mother, Ross was still a young man when he first began to resist efforts to relocate eastern Indians out west in order to make room for the growing white population. During the very early 1800s, a few thousand Cherokees did migrate across the Mississippi (where they became known as the tribe's western band), but most remained behind in present-day North and South Carolina, Tennessee, and northern portions of Georgia and Alabama. There this so-called eastern band of the Cherokees and members of four other tribes made an effort to adopt and adapt to American ways, soon earning recognition as "civilized" tribes for their accomplishments as landowners, businessmen, and scholars. But it was not enough; by 1819—the year John Ross assumed the presidency of the National Council of the Cherokee—Georgia officials had begun to pressure the federal government to relocate the tribe elsewhere.

In 1828, Ross became principal chief of the eastern band of the Cherokees. That same year, Andrew Jackson became president of the United States, ushering in a period of official government policy sanctioning the forced removal of Indians from state lands in defiance of treaty guarantees and Supreme Court decisions rendering such actions unconstitutional. In 1838, his fight against relocation having failed, Ross led his people on the Trail of Tears to their new home. About twenty thousand people made the three-hundred-mile march; some four thousand of them died along the way of hunger, disease, and exposure.

Once settled in Indian Territory, the Cherokees reorganized their government under Ross, who became head of both the eastern and western bands of the tribe. It proved to be a difficult adjustment, especially for those who had known relative prosperity and stability back east. Of utmost importance to the new chief, however, was the question of unity. Ross made many attempts to forge closer bonds between the Cherokees and other tribes who had suffered a similar fate, often to no avail. One such occasion was in June 1843, when a special council was held in Tahlequah, Oklahoma, headquarters of the Cherokee Nation. At the opening session of the council, Ross delivered the following plea in the hope that those present would set aside their differences and pursue their common interests. His speech is reprinted from W.C. Vanderwerth's Indian Oratory: Famous Speeches by Noted Indian Chieftains, *University of Oklahoma Press, 1971.*

Brothers: The talk of our forefathers has been spoken, and you have listened to it. You have also smoked the pipe of peace, and shaken the right hand of friendship around the Great Council Fire, newly kindled at Tahlequah, in the west, and our hearts have been made glad on the interesting occasion.

Brothers: When we look into the history of our race, we see some green spots that are pleasing to us. We also find many things to make the heart sad. When we look upon the first council fire kindled by our forefathers, when the pipe of peace was smoked in brotherly friendship between the different nations of red people, our hearts rejoice in the goodness of our Creator in having thus united the heart and hand of the red man in peace.

For it is in peace only that our women and children can enjoy happiness and increase in numbers.

By peace our condition has been improved in the pursuit of civilized life. We should, therefore, extend the hand of friendship from tribe to tribe, until peace shall be established between every nation of red men within the reach of our voice.

Brothers: When we call to mind the only associations which endeared us to the land which gave birth to our ancestors, where we have been brought up in peace to taste the benefits of civilized life; and when we see that our ancient fire has there been extinguished, and our people compelled to remove to a new and distant country, we cannot but feel sorry; but the designs of Providence, in the course of events, are mysterious—we should not, therefore, despair of once more enjoying the blessings of peace in our new homes.

John Ross

Brothers: By this removal, tribes that were once separated by distance have become neighbors, and some of them, hitherto not known to each other, have met and become acquainted. There are, however, numerous other tribes to whom we are still strangers.

Brothers: It is for reviving here in the west the ancient talk of our forefathers, and of perpetuating forever the old fire and pipe of peace brought from the east, and of extending them from nation to nation, and for adopting such international laws as may be necessary to redress the wrongs which may be done by individuals of our respective nations upon each other, that you have been invited to attend the present council.

Brothers: Let us so then act that the peace and friendship which so happily existed between our forefathers, may be forever preserved; and that we may always live as brothers of the same family.

Despite many setbacks, Ross continued his quest for unity among the Cherokees and other tribes living in Indian Territory. Beginning in the 1850s, however, a newly-emerging issue threatened the group's cohesiveness—the growing antagonism between the North and the South over slavery and other issues. Cherokee sympathies were divided (some members of the tribe owned black slaves, for example), and the conflict over which side to support escalated once civil war broke out in April 1861. Finally, at a meeting of the Cherokee National Assembly in Tahlequah on October 9, 1861, Ross announced the tribe's official position. His remarks are reprinted here from W.C. Vanderwerth's Indian Oratory: Famous Speeches by Noted Indian Chieftains, *University of Oklahoma Press, 1971.*

Friends and Fellow Citizens: Since the last meeting of the National Council, events have occurred that will occupy a prominent place in the history of the world. The United States have been dissolved and two governments now exist. Twelve of the states composing the late Union have erected themselves into a government under the style of the Confederate States of America, and as you know, are now engaged in a war for their independence. The contest thus far has been attended with success, almost uninterrupted on their side, and marked by brilliant victories. Of its final result there seems to be no ground for a reasonable doubt. The unanimity and devotion of the people of the Confederate States must sooner or later secure their success over all opposition and result in the establishment of their independence and a recognition of it by the other nations of the Earth.

At the beginning of the conflict, I felt that the interests of the Cherokee people would be best maintained by remaining quiet and not involving themselves in it prematurely. Our relations had long existed with the United States government and bound us to observe amity and peace alike with all the states. Neutrality was proper and wise so long as there remained a reasonable probability that the difficulty between the two sections of the Union would be settled, as a different course would have placed all our rights in jeopardy and might have led to the sacrifice of the people.

But when there was no longer any reason to believe that the Union of the states would be continued, there was no cause to hesitate as to the course the Cherokee Nation should pursue. Our geographical position and domestic institutions allied us to the South, while the developments daily made in our vicinity and as to the purposes of the war waged against the Confederate States clearly pointed out the path of interest. These considerations produced a unanimity of sentiment among the people as to the policy to be adopted by the Cherokee Nation, which was clearly expressed in their general meeting held at Tahlequah on the 21st day of August last. A copy of the proceedings of that meeting is submitted for your information.

In accordance with the declarations embodied in the resolutions then adopted, the executive council deemed it proper to exercise the authority conferred upon them by the people there assembled. Messengers were dispatched to General Albert Pike, the distinguished Indian commissioner of the Confederate States, who, having negotiated treaties with the neighboring Indian nations, was then establishing relations between his government and the Comanches and other Indians in the Southwest, who bore a copy of the proceedings of the meeting referred to, and a letter from the executive authorities, proposing on behalf of the Nation to enter into a treaty of alliance, defensive and offensive, with the Confederate States. In the exercise of the same general authority and to be ready as far as practicable to meet any emergency that might spring upon our northern border, it was thought proper to raise a regiment of mounted men and tender its service to General McCulloch.

The people responded with alacrity to the call, and it is believed the regiment will be found as efficient as any other like number of men. It is now in the service of the Confederate States for the purpose of aiding in defending their homes and the common rights of the Indian nations about us. This regiment is composed of ten full companies, and in addition to the force previously authorized to be raised to operate outside of the Nation by General McCulloch, will show that the Cherokee people are ready to do all in their power in defense of the Confederate cause which has now become their own. And it is to be hoped that our people will spare no means to sustain them, but contribute liberally to supply any want of comfortable clothing for the approaching season.

In years long since past, our ancestors met undaunted those who would invade their mountain homes beyond the Mississippi; let not their descendants of the present day be found unworthy of them, or unable to stand by the chivalrous men of the South by whose side they may be called to fight in self defense.

The Cherokee people do not desire to be involved in war, but self-preservation fully justifies them in the course they have adopted, and they will be recreant to themselves if they do no sustain it to the utmost of their humble abilities.

A treaty with the Confederate States has been entered into and is now submitted for your ratification. In view of the circumstances by which we are surrounded, and the provisions of the treaty, it will be found to be the most important ever negotiated on behalf of the Cherokee Nation, and will mark a new era in its history. Without attempting a recapitulation of all its provisions, some of its distinguishing features may be briefly enumerated.

The relations of the Cherokee Nation are changed from the United to the Confederate States, with guarantees of protection and a recognition in future negotiations only of its constitutional authorities. The metes and boundaries as defined by patent from the United States are continued and a guaranty given for the neutral land, or a fair consideration in case it should be lost by war or negotiation, and an advance thereon to pay the national debt, and to meet other contingencies. The payment of all our annuities and the security of our investment are provided for. The jurisdiction of the Cherokee courts over all members of the Nation, whether by birth, marriage, or adoption is recognized.

Our title to our lands is placed beyond dispute. Our relation with the Confederate States is that of a ward; theirs to us that of a protectorate with powers restricted. The district court, with limited civil and criminal jurisdiction, is admitted into the country instead of being located in Van Buren as was the United States Court. This is, perhaps, one of the most important provisions of the treaty and secures to our own citizens the great constitutional right of trial by a jury of their own vicinage, and releases them from the petty abuses and vexations of the old system before a foreign jury and in a foreign country. It gives us a delegate in Congress on the same footing with delegates from the territories by which our interests can be represented—a right which has long been withheld from the Nation and which has imposed upon it a large expense and great injustice. It also contains reasonable stipulation in regard to the appointment powers of the agent, and in regard to licensed traders. The Cherokee Nation may be called upon to furnish troops for the defense of the Indian country, but is never to be taxed for the support of any war in which the states may be engaged.

The Cherokee people stand upon new ground. Let us hope that the clouds which overspread the land will be dispersed, and that we shall prosper as we have never before done. New avenues to usefulness and distinction will be opened to the ingenuous youth of the country. Our rights of self-government will be more fully recognized, and our citizens be no longer dragged off upon flimsy pretexts to be imprisoned and tried before distant tribunals. No just cause exists for domestic difficulties. Let them be buried with the past and only mutual friendship and harmony be cherished.

Our relations with the neighboring tribes are of the most friendly character. Let us see that the white path which leads from our country to theirs be obstructed by no act of ours, and that it be open to all those with whom we may be brought into intercourse.

Amid the excitement of the times, it is to be hoped that the interests of education will not be allowed to suffer and that no interruption be brought into the usual operations of the government. Let all its officers continue to discharge their appropriate duties. As the services of some of your members may be required elsewhere and all unnecessary expense should be avoided, I respectfully recommend that the business of the session be promptly discharged.

SOURCES

Moulton, Gary E., *John Ross: Cherokee Chief,* University of Georgia Press, 1986.

Rosenstiel, Annette, *Red and White: Indian Views of the White Man, 1492-1982,* Universe Books, 1983.

Ross, John, *The Papers of Chief John Ross,* two volumes, University of Oklahoma Press, 1985.

Vanderwerth, W.C., *Indian Oratory: Famous Speeches by Noted Indian Chieftains,* University of Oklahoma Press, 1971.

Bayard Rustin

1910–1987

African American civil rights activist, and labor and economic reformer

A man of many causes—civil rights, socialism, and the antiwar movement, to name but a few—Bayard Rustin firmly believed that only within the context of wider economic and social reform could African Americans expect to achieve true justice and equality. During his long association with black labor leader A. Philip Randolph, including more than twenty years spent as executive director of the A. Philip Randolph Institute, he focused his considerable energies on formulating and proposing many rather radical solutions to the problems of unemployment, wages, education, housing, and health. Yet Rustin was no wild-eyed revolutionary; in his view, "revolution" had nothing to do with how people dressed or wore their hair, or with how many black studies classes they took and how many slogans they knew. Rather, he insisted, it was by exercising their right to participate in the political process, by joining and supporting labor unions, and by forming coalitions with white liberals that African Americans could bring about real change in their communities.

Rustin was born in West Chester, Pennsylvania, and raised there by his grandparents. He faced both economic hardship and racial prejudice, but young Bayard excelled at his studies as well as in athletics. He was also deeply influenced by the teachings of his grandmother's Quaker faith, especially regarding war and violence.

After studying literature and history at Cheyney State College in Pennsylvania and at Wilberforce College in Ohio, Rustin headed to New York City during the mid-1930s. There he supported himself by singing with such noted entertainers as Leadbelly and Josh White while taking classes at City College and working as a political organizer with the Young Communist League. In 1941, however, he left the League over the brewing war crisis and embraced socialism instead. That same year, he became race relations secretary for the Fellowship of Reconciliation, an antiwar group, and helped recruit young people to participate in A. Philip Randolph's March on Washington. A year later, Rustin was named the first field secretary of the newly-formed Congress of Racial Equality (CORE).

During World War II, Rustin spent over two years in a federal prison as a conscientious objector. After his release, he worked in the United States and abroad on behalf of India's independence movement. He was also a key member of A. Philip Randolph's Committee Against Discrimination in the Armed Forces. Although both Randolph and Rustin were ardent pacifists, they found it intolerable that African Americans were expected to fight and possible die for a country that denied them basic freedoms and stripped them of their dignity and the chance for advancement.

On April 11, 1948, Rustin explained his views on the "Jim Crow Army" in an address he delivered at a meeting of the Council Against Intolerance in America. At this point, he and Randolph had been pressuring the federal government for several years to take action against discrimination in the armed forces, and their lack of success had prompted them to adopt a more radical tactic—they began advising young black men to refuse to serve in the military if drafted. The text of his remarks is taken from Down the Line: The Collected Writings of Bayard Rustin, *(Quadrangle Books, 1971).*

It is a real opportunity to speak with American citizens who seriously seek to remove racial and religious intolerance from our national life, for recent history amply reveals that America cannot gain moral leadership in the world until intolerance of minority groups has been eliminated at home. The Journey of Reconciliation was organized not only to devise techniques for eliminating Jim Crow in travel, but also as a training ground for similar peaceful projects against discrimination in such major areas as employment and in the armed services.

The use of these methods against Jim Crow military service is a regrettable necessity. Today no single injustice more bitterly stands out in the hearts and minds of colored people the world over, or continues more successfully to frustrate the United States' efforts abroad, than the continuation of discrimination and segregation in our military forces.

As a follower of the principles of Mahatma Gandhi, I am an opponent of war and of war preparations and an opponent of universal military training and conscription; but entirely apart from that issue, I hold that segregation in any part of the body politic is an act of slavery and an act of war. Democrats will agree that such acts are to be resisted, and more and more leaders of the oppressed are responsibly proposing nonviolent civil disobedience and noncooperation as the means.

On March 22, 1948, A. Philip Randolph and Grant Reynolds, trusted Negro leaders, told President Truman that Negroes "do not propose to shoulder another gun for democracy abroad while they are denied democracy here at home." A few days later, when Mr. Randolph testified before the Senate Armed Services Committee, he declared that he openly would advise and urge Negro and white youth not to submit to Jim Crow military institutions. At this statement, Senator Wayne Morse interrupted and warned Mr. Randolph that "the Government would apply the legal doctrine of treason to such conduct."

This is a highly regrettable statement for a United States senator to make. Certainly throughout Asia and Africa millions must have agreed with the lovers of freedom here who reasoned that if treason is involved, it is the treason practiced by reactionaries in the North and South who struggle to maintain segregation and discrimination and who thus murder the American creed. The organizers and perpetuators of segregation are as much the enemy of America as any foreign invader. The time has come when they are not merely to be protested. They must be resisted.

The world and the United States should know that there are many younger leaders, both black and white, in positions of responsibility who, not wishing to see democracy destroyed from within, will support Mr. Randolph and Mr. Reynolds.

We know that men should not and will not fight to perpetuate for themselves caste and second-class citizenship. We know that men cannot struggle for someone else's freedom in the same battle in which they fasten semi-slavery more securely upon themselves. While there is

Bayard Rustin

a very real question whether any army can bring freedom, certainly a Jim Crow army cannot. On the contrary, to those it attempts to liberate, it will bring discrimination and segregation such as we are now exporting to Europe and to South America. To subject young men at their most impressionable age to a forced caste system, as now outlined in the Universal Military Training and Selective Service bills, is not only undemocratic but will prove to be suicidal.

Segregation in the military must be resisted if democracy and peace are to survive. Thus civil disobedience against caste is not merely a right but a profound duty. If carried out in the spirit of good will and nonviolence, it will prick the conscience of America as Gandhi's campaigns stirred the hearts of men the world over.

Therefore, in the future I shall join with others to advise and urge Negroes and white people not to betray the American ideal by accepting Jim Crow in any of our institutions, including the armed services. Further, I serve notice on the government that, to the extent of my resources, I shall assist in the organization of disciplined cells across the nation to advise resistance and to provide spiritual, financial, and legal aid to resisters.

If Senator Morse and the government believe that intimidation, repression, prison, or even death can stop such a movement, let them examine past struggles for freedom. If the government continues to consider such action treason, let it recall the advice that Justice Jackson gave the German people at the opening of the Nuremberg trials: "Men," he said, "are individually responsible for their acts, and are not to be excused for following unjust demands made upon them by governments." Failure of the German citizens to resist antisocial laws from the beginning of the Hitler regime logically ended in their placing Jews in gas furnaces and lye pits. Justice Jackson indicated in conclusion that individual resistance to undemocratic laws would have been a large factor in destroying the unjust Nazi state.

I believe that American citizens would do well to ponder Mr. Jackson's remarks. Civil disobedience is urged not to destroy the United States but because the government is now poorly organized to achieve democracy. The aim of such a movement always will be to improve the nature of the government, to urge and counsel resistance to military Jim Crow in the interest of a higher law—the principle of equality and justice upon which real community and security depend.

I sincerely hope that millions of Negroes and white people who cherish freedom will pledge themselves now to resist Jim Crow everywhere, including the military establishments. Thereby the United States may, in part, achieve the moral leadership in world affairs for which we so vigorously strive. I urge you to register this intention now with your Senators and Congressmen.

It is my supreme desire that those who resist will do so in that spirit which is without hatred, bitterness, or contention. I trust that all resisters will hold firm to the true faith that only good-will resistance, in the end, is capable of overcoming injustice.

A little more than three months later, on July 26, 1948, President Truman issued an executive order calling for an end to unequal treatment and opportunity in the U.S. armed forces.

Throughout the rest of the 1940s until the mid-1950s, Rustin devoted himself primarily to antiwar activities (including nuclear disarmament) and to various African independence movements. But in 1955, the emergence of Martin Luther King, Jr., as a civil rights leader and champion of nonviolent protest once again focused Rustin's attention on domestic issues. He helped the young minister organize the Montgomery bus boycott in 1955 and for the next seven years served as King's special assistant in the Southern Christian Leadership Conference. Perhaps his greatest achievement during this period was the key role he played in organizing the 1963 March on Washington. Although his longtime friend and mentor A. Philip Randolph received much of the credit for its success, Rustin was the man he had relied on to serve as his behind-the-scenes coordinator and logistics expert.

In 1964, Rustin became director of the A. Philip Randolph Institute, a lobbying group that focused on social and economic reform. But because he remained a strong advocate of nonviolence and rejected black separatist and nationalist philosophies as naive and simplistic, he was not popular among those African Americans who had begun to take a more radical stance. Rustin nevertheless continued to speak out in favor of peaceful coalition-building with white liberals as a long-term solution to the problems in the black community, even as a series of race riots exploded across the United States during the mid- and late 1960s. During the summer of 1967, for example, shortly after riots rocked the city of Detroit, he addressed a gathering in that city about the causes behind such disturbances and the steps the federal government should take to avoid future trouble. His talk, entitled "A Way Out of the Exploding Ghetto," is reprinted here from Down the Line: The Collected Writings of Bayard Rustin, *(Quadrangle Books, 1971); it originally appeared in the* New York Times Magazine.

There is no longer any denying that this country is in the throes of a historic national crisis. Its ramifications are so vast and frightening that even now, shocked into numbness and disbelief, the American people have not yet fully grasped what is happening to them.

The grim data are clear enough and still coming in. Since this summer began, thirty of our cities, big and small, have been wracked by racial disorder; scores of citizens, almost all of them black, have been killed, thousands injured, and even more arrested. Property damage has exceeded a billion dollars; total income loss is incalculable.

As a people, we are not unaccustomed to violence. Frontier lawlessness, Southern vigilante-ism, Chicago gangsterism: these are images and themes embedded in the American tradition. We have only just lost a president to an assassin's bullet. But, having escaped the bombs of two world wars, we are not familiar with the horror of burned-out buildings, smoking rubble, tanks in our streets, the blasts of Molotov cocktails, the ring of snipers' bullets from rooftops. Today we look at sections of Detroit and think of war-torn Berlin. We see rampaging, looting mobs and think of the unstable politics of underdeveloped countries. A nation's identity has been overturned.

In our own history we can find no precedent in this century for the massive destruction the past three years have brought to our cities—no precedent since the Civil War. But the greatest toll is not in property damage or even in lives lost. Nor is the greatest danger that the violence will go on indefinitely, any more than the Civil War did. It is that the aftermath of that war will be repeated, that as in the Compromise of 1877 the country will turn its back on the Negro, on the root causes of his discontent, on its own democratic future.

Not since the Great Depression have social policy, our national institutions, our political order been more severely tested than at present. The coming months will shape the character of America in the remainder of the twentieth century—and I am trying to speak with the utmost sobriety, precision, and restraint.

Why does the republic find itself at a crossroads? What has actually happened?

The term "race riot" is unilluminating and anachronistic. It describes the Detroit disorders of 1943, when the Negro and white communities were locked in combat. White mobs invaded the ghetto. Negroes forayed downtown. Men were beaten and murdered for the color of their skins. In the upheavals of the last four summers, destruction has been confined to the ghetto; nor, discounting the police, were black and white citizens fighting each other. In fact, in Detroit whites joined in the looting and sniping. And I am told that whites were free to walk through the embattled ghetto without fear of violence from Negroes.

This is not to deny the importance of anti-white hostility. One has only to hear the sick racial epithets "honkey" and "whitey" to recognize the deep and bitter hatred that is loose on the streets of the ghettos. But if white blood was what the rioters thirsted for, they didn't go very far to get it. What they assaulted were the symbols of white power—police and property, the latter embracing the entire ghetto. These are traditional targets of rebellions and in that sense the riots can be called rebellions.

That sense, however, must be sharply qualified. Is it correct to speak of "race rebellion" or "Negro rebellion"? Are America's Negroes on the verge of revolution? More than one newspaper and television commentator has already begun to draw comparisons between the ghetto uprisings and the French, Russian, Algerian, Irish, and Black African independence revolutions. Some black power advocates have proclaimed the beginnings of guerrilla warfare and see the urban Negro as a counterpart to the Viet Cong. And in Paris it has become fashionable to speak of the *"révolution des noires"* in the U.S.

The reality is that the revolutionary rhetoric now employed by some young Negro militants cannot create the preconditions for successful, or even authentic, revolution. The independence movements in colonial territories provide no model for the simple reason that American Negroes can have no geographical focus for nationalist sentiment.

Moreover, American Negroes do not constitute a popular majority struggling against a relatively small white colonial ruling group—the ideal condition for guerrilla warfare. Whatever separatist impulses exist among American Negroes cannot find appropriate models in the colonial world.

If independence revolutions are no model, what of social revolutions? This is a more interesting subject because the phrase "social revolution" has been widely used by the civil rights and liberal movements generally. But in this sense—and the sense in which I have been using it for thirty years—the phrase designates fundamental changes in social and economic class relations resulting from mass political action. Such action would be democratic. That is, it would aim to create a new majority coalition capable of exercising political power in the interest of new social policies. By definition the coalition has to be interracial.

As a minority, Negroes by themselves cannot bring about such a social revolution. They can participate in it as a powerful and stimulating force, or they can provoke a counterrevolution. In either case the decisive factor will be the political direction in which the majority will move.

Numbers are not the only issue. Also important is the class content of revolt. At least in the French and Russian revolutions, revolutionary leaders and parties sought to mobilize fairly definable and cohesive socioeconomic classes—workers, peasants, the middle class—which, though oppressed or aggrieved, were part of the society they sought to transform. Upon what classes do the advocates of rioting, the voices of the apocalypse, base their revolutionary perspective? This is another way of posing the question I left hanging earlier: Who is rioting?

Daniel Patrick Moynihan is correct in locating the riots in the "lower class" or, in the words of another controversial man, Karl Marx, in the "*lumpenproletariat*" or "slum proletariat." Lower class does not mean working class; the distinction is often overlooked in a middle-class culture that tends to lump the two together.

The distinction is important. The working class is employed. It has a relation to the production of goods and services; much of it is organized in unions. It enjoys a measure of cohesion, discipline, and stability lacking in the lower class. The latter is unemployed or marginally employed. It is relatively unorganized, incohesive, unstable. It contains the petty criminal and antisocial elements. Above all, unlike the working class, it lacks the sense of a stake in society. When the slum proletariat is black, its alienation is even greater.

From the revolutionist point of view, the question is not whether steps could be taken to strengthen organization among the *lumpenproletariat* but whether that group could be a central agent of social transformation. Generally, the answer has been no.

The black slum proletariat has been growing in numbers and density. As agricultural mechanization and other factors continue pushing Negroes out of the South, the urban ghettos expand each year by half a million; only 40,000 Negroes annually find their way into the suburbs. This trend has not been affected at all by any antipoverty or Great Society programs.

When the migration of Negroes to Northern and Western cities was at its height during World War II, factory jobs were available at decent wages. With the advent of advanced technology eliminating many semi-skilled and unskilled jobs, and with the movement of plants from the central cities to the suburbs (New York lost 200,000 factory jobs in a decade), urban Negroes suffered rising joblessness or employment in low-paying service jobs.

The depth of the unemployment problem in the slum ghettos is indicated in a recent U.S. Department of Labor report on "subemployment" in cities and slums. While the traditional unemployment rate counts only those "actively looking" but unable to find work, the subemployment index reflects in addition: (1) those who have dropped out of the labor market in despair, (2) those who are working part time but want full-time jobs, (3) heads of households under sixty-five working full time but earning poverty wages (less than $60 a week), (4) individuals under sixty-five who are not heads of households and earn less than $56 a week in full-time jobs, and (5) a conservatively estimated portion of males known to be living in the slums but who somehow do not show up in employment or unemployment counts.

The report states: "If the traditional statistical concept of 'unemployment' (which produced the nationwide average of 3.7 per cent unemployment rate for January, 1967) is applied to the urban slum situation, the *'unemployment rate' in these areas is about 10 percent . . . three times the average for the rest of the country.*" [Original italics.] The figure for Detroit's Central Woodward area, incidentally, is 10.1 percent.

The subemployment rate in the 10 cities surveyed yields an average figure of almost 35 percent. Though possibly in need of further refining, the subemployment rate is the more meaningful figure. Not only does it include the categories listed above, but it also tends to reflect the number of people who experience unemployment over a period of time. By contrast, the official rate counts those unemployed at a point in time (i.e., the time the survey is taken).

High unemployment and low income are not the only problems afflicting the black slum proletariat, but they are the crucial ones. Without adequate income, there is no access to the decent housing market, educational opportunity, even proper health care. (In 1964, East and Central Harlem, comprising 24 percent of Manhattan's population, accounted for 40 percent of its TB deaths, 33 percent of its infant deaths; in Bedford-Stuyvesant, which contains 9 percent of Brooklyn's population, the respective figures were 24 and 22 percent.)

The tendency of much current antipoverty rhetoric to create a multitude of disparate problems out of a central multifaceted one is a mistake. It is precisely in the expansion of public facilities and social services that new employment opportunities can be generated, at varying skill levels. High subemployment rates and the lack of decent housing in the slums are two sides of the same coin.

Meanwhile, within the slum proletariat, youth constitutes a subdivision of increasing economic and political importance. While according to the official unemployment rates the joblessness gap between Negro and white men over 20 has been narrowing since 1961, even this official rate records a widening of the gap between Negro and white teenagers since 1957. Right now the Negro unemployment rate is 25 percent nationally, but for 16-19-year-olds in the 10 slum areas surveyed, it is over 38 percent! Moreover, this rate was unaffected by the downward trend of the nation's overall unemployment rate late last year. For white teenagers, on the other hand, unemployment since 1957 never went beyond 15 percent and is now at 10 percent.

Nor is there any evidence that Negro teenagers do not want to work. Whenever job programs have been announced, they have turned out in large numbers, only to find that the jobs weren't there. In Oakland, a "Job Fair" attracted 15,000 people; only 250 were placed. In Philadelphia, 6,000 were on a waiting list for a training program.

What Negro teenagers are not inclined to accept are dead-end jobs that pay little and promise no advancement or training. Many would prefer to live by their wits as hustlers or petty racketeers, their version of the self-employed businessman or salesman. That their pursuit of this distorted entrepreneurial ideal only mires them deeper in the slum proletariat is not the point. They want to be part of the white-collar organization man's world that is America's future, not trapped behind brooms and pushcarts.

Nor can they fairly be blamed by a society which has itself produced these yearnings, reveled in its affluence, encouraged the consumption of trivia, and proclaimed the coming of computerized utopias. The middle classes may nostalgically extol their immigrant parents' fortitude and perseverance in manual labor, but they do not steer their own children toward the construction gang or the garment district. They show them the push buttons, not the pushcart. Might they not then show some compassionate understanding of black youngsters who dream of better things, even when crippled by poor education, broken families, and the disabilities bred by slum life? If it is true that a Negro boy is nobody unless he owns alligator shoes and an alpaca sweater, who created these symbols? Who whetted this appetite? Who profited from the sale of these commodities, and who advertised them? And who is victimized?

The ghetto youth who is out of school, unemployed, and rejected even by the draft (as 52 percent are in Harlem) is the extreme embodiment of the bitter frustration in the slum proletariat. He is utterly propertyless, devoid of experience in the productive process, and without a stake in existing social arrangements. At the same time, because he is young and not beaten down, he is irreverent, filled with bravado, hostile to the alien authority of the police, and determined to "make it" in any way that he can. He is at the core of the rioting.

In Detroit, the riot begins when pimps and prostitutes taunt police who are raiding a "blind pig" at 5 a.m. In Minneapolis, two women fight over a wig, the police try to break it up, and a riot erupts in an atmosphere already charged by delays in the mailing of Federal Youth Opportunity Program pay checks to youths in the ghetto area. In Cairo, Illinois, a Negro soldier dies in the city jail; police say it was suicide but order the body embalmed without an autopsy, and fire bombings and shooting follow.

In these cases, the police figure prominently in the incidents that triggered the rioting. Sometimes they are not directly involved, but rumors of police brutality flood through the ghetto. Although it may be of some interest to search for a pattern, no very profound purpose is served by concentrating on who struck the match. There are always matches lying around. We must ask why there was also a fuse and why the fuse was connected to a powder keg.

To pursue this analogy: Whether the match is struck by police misconduct or by an "extremist" exhorting his listeners to violence, the fuse is the condition of life among the black slum proletariat—hostile, frustrated, and with nothing to lose. The powder keg is the social background against which the riots break out and which extends their scope. They become more than riots pure and simple, yet less than politically coherent rebellions. They are *riotous manifestations of rebellion.*

The social background is defined by the fact that the black slum proletariat is part of a larger community of oppressed and segregated citizens—the overwhelming majority of the Negro population. Were it not for this the riots could be dismissed merely as wild, inchoate sprees of looting and violence, the expressions of criminal greed, a carnival of destruction to be suppressed by police force. Such actions, detached from political policies, programs, and goals—and, make no mistake about it, the riots were not on behalf of the black power ideology; the latter is an after-the-fact justification employed by people in search of a constituency—do not properly constitute a rebellion.

But because of the social background, the riots, while not *the rebellion* of the Negro people, are charged with manifestations of rebellion.

It is because of this background that the riots can set off a chain reaction, fan out from the slum proletariat and, as Detroit showed, involve people who ordinarily would not be found looting stores. It is because of this background that snipers and the most violent elements can feel that their actions are in some sense heroic. And it is because of this background that the riots have enormous implications for the future of all Negroes.

As Martin Luther King, A. Philip Randolph, Roy Wilkins, and Whitney Young pointed out in their recent statement, the most severe and immediate damage has been to the Negro community itself. In addition to those who lost their lives, thousands lost their homes, food supplies, access to schools. There is danger of a counterreaction enlisting the most bigoted, vigilante-minded elements in the white community. Ammunition has been given to the reactionaries in an already backlash-dominated Congress. Many whites sincerely in favor of integration will be silenced out of fear and confusion. Riots do not strengthen the power of black people; they weaken it and encourage racist power.

"Riots do not strengthen the power of black people; they weaken it and encourage racist power."

But why, asks white America, do the Negroes riot now—not when conditions are at their worst but when they seem to be improving? Why now, after all of the civil rights and antipoverty legislation? There are two answers.

First, progress has been considerably less than is generally supposed. While the Negro has won certain important legal and constitutional rights (voting, desegregation of public accommodations, etc.), his relative socioeconomic position has scarcely improved. There simply has not been significant, visible change in his life.

Second, if a society is interested in stability, it should either not make promises or it should keep them. Economic and social deprivation, if accepted by its victims as their lot in life, breeds passivity, even docility. The miserable yield to their fate as divinely ordained or as their own fault. And, indeed, many Negroes in earlier generations felt that way.

Today, young Negroes aren't having any. They don't share the feeling that something must be wrong with them, that they are responsible for their own exclusion from this affluent society. The civil rights movement—in fact, the whole liberal trend beginning with John Kennedy's election—has told them otherwise.

Conservatives will undoubtedly seize the occasion for an attack on the Great Society, liberalism, the welfare state, and Lyndon Johnson. But the young Negroes are right: the promises made to them were good and necessary and long, long overdue. The youth were right to believe in them. The only trouble is that they were not fulfilled. Prominent Republicans and Dixiecrats are demanding not that the promises be fulfilled, but that they be revoked.

What they and the American people absolutely must understand now is that the promises cannot be revoked. They were not made to a handful of leaders in a White House drawing room; they were made to an entire generation, one not likely to forget or to forgive. If Republican leaders Everett Dirksen and Gerald Ford, hand in glove with the diehards of the Confederacy, continue their contemptible effort to exploit the nation's tragedy for partisan political advantage, they will sow the dangerous seeds of race hate and they will discredit themselves morally in the eyes of the coming generations and of history. This is not a wise policy for a party that only yesterday reduced itself to a shambles by catering to the most backward and reactionary elements in the country.

It is ironic that in a nation which has not undertaken a massive social and economic reform since the New Deal one now hears even liberal voices asking: "Don't the causes of the riots go deeper than economics, than jobs, housing, schools? Aren't there profound moral, cultural, psychological, and other factors involved—powerlessness, an identity crisis?"

Of course, but in the present context such questions smack of a trend toward mystification which, if it gains ascendancy, will paralyze public policy. Then, too, I cannot help suspecting that they are rationalizations for the yearning of some white liberals to withdraw. "Obviously," they are saying, "there seems to be nothing we can do. We're not even wanted. Why not give the ghettos over to the black power people?"

I have no hesitation in saying that this recommendation simply aids and abets the congressional reactionaries, who would have no objection to letting Negroes run their own slum tenements, dilapidated schools, and tax-starved communities. Isn't this in the best tradition of rugged self-help, Horatio Alger and all that? Haven't Barry Goldwater and William F. Buckley endorsed this notion of black power? Just so long as white people are left alone. Just so long as the total society is not forced to examine its own inner contradictions. Just so long as the federal government isn't challenged to launch radical and massive programs to rebuild our cities, end poverty, guarantee full employment at decent wages, clear our polluted air and water, and provide mass transportation.

This is just the challenge posed by A. Philip Randolph's $185 billion "Freedom Budget for All Americans"—a carefully designed, economically feasible program for the obliteration of poverty in ten years. Unless the nation is prepared to move along these lines—to rearrange its priorities, to set a timetable for achieving them, and to allocate its resources accordingly—it will not be taking its own commitments seriously. Surely it cannot then turn amazedly to responsible Negro leaders, whose pleas for large-scale programs it has failed to heed, for an explanation of the consequences.

The present administration has a grave responsibility. It is very well for it to proclaim that we can have guns *and* butter, that we can pursue our course in Vietnam and still make progress at home. We do have the economic capacity for both, as the Freedom Budget itself shows. But we are not doing both. Let us stop proclaiming that we *can* do what we *don't* do and start *doing* it.

If administration actions are not to mock its own rhetoric, the president must now take the lead in mobilizing public opinion behind a new resolve to meet the crisis in our cities. He should now put before Congress a National Emergency Public Works and Reconstruction bill aimed at building housing for homeless victims of the riot-torn ghettos, repairing damaged public facilities, and in the process generating maximum employment opportunities for unskilled and semiskilled workers. Such a bill should be the first step in the imperative reconstruction of all our decaying center cities.

Admittedly, the prospects for passage of such a bill in the present Congress are dismal. Congressmen will cry out that the rioters must not be rewarded, thereby further penalizing the very victims of the riots. This, after all, is a Congress capable of defeating a meager $40 million rat extermination program the same week it votes $10 million for an aquarium in the District of Columbia!

But the vindictive racial meanness that has descended upon this Congress, already dominated by the revived coalition of Republicans and Dixiecrats, must be challenged—not accommodated. The president must go directly to the people, as Harry Truman did in 1948. He must go to them, not with slogans, but with a timetable for tearing down every slum in the country.

There can be no further delay. The daydreamers and utopians are not those of us who have prepared massive Freedom Budgets and similar programs. They are the smugly "practical" and myopic philistines in the Congress, the state legislatures, and the city halls who thought they could sit it out. The very practical choice now before them and the American people is whether we shall have a conscious and authentic democratic social revolution or more tragic and futile riots that tear our nation to shreds.

In late June and early July of 1968, at a four-day meeting of the National Jewish Community Relations Advisory Council in New York City, Rustin participated in a debate on the question of separatism versus integration. His opponent was Robert S. Browne, an economics professor at Fairleigh Dickinson University

and an executive of the Black Power Conference. After Browne spoke in favor of separation, Rustin responded to his arguments from the point of view of a committed integrationist. His rebuttal is reprinted from Representative American Speeches: 1968-1969, *(Wilson, 1969).*

Dr. Browne dealt with the concept of separation in psychological rather than sociological terms. The proposition that separation may be the best solution of America's racial problems has been recurrent in American Negro history. Let us look at the syndrome that has given rise to it.

Separation, in one form or another, has been proposed and widely discussed among American Negroes in three different periods. Each time, it was put forward in response to an identical combination of economic and social factors that induced despair among Negroes. The syndrome consists of three elements: great expectations, followed by dashed hopes, followed by despair and discussion of separation.

The first serious suggestion that Negroes should separate came in the aftermath of the Civil War. During that war many Negroes had not only been strongly in favor of freedom but had fought for the Union. It was a period of tremendous expectations. Great numbers of Negroes left the farms and followed the Union Army as General Sherman marched across Georgia to the sea; they believed that when he got to the sea they would be not only free but also given land—"forty acres and a mule." However, the compromise of 1876 and the withdrawal of the Union Army from the South dashed those expectations. Instead of forty acres and a mule all they got was a new form of slavery.

Out of the ruins of those hopes emerged Booker T. Washington, saying in essence to Negroes: "There is no hope in your attempting to vote, no hope in attempting to play any part in the political or social processes of the nation. Separate yourself from all that, and give your attention to your innards: that you are men, that you maintain dignity, that you drop your buckets where they are, that you become excellent of character."

Of course, it did not work. It could not work. Because human beings have stomachs, as well as minds and hearts, and equate dignity, first of all, not with caste, but with class. I preached the dignity of black skin color and wore my hair Afro style long before it became popular; I taught Negro history in the old Benjamin Franklin High School, where I first got my teaching experience, long before it became popular. But in spite of all that it is my conviction that there are three fundamental ways in which a group of people can maintain their dignity: one, by gradual advancement in the economic order; two, by being a participating element of the democratic process; and three, through the sense of dignity that emerges from their struggle. For instance, Negroes never had more dignity than when Martin Luther King won the boycott in Montgomery or at the bridge in Selma.

This is not to say that all the values of self-image and identification are not important and should not be stimulated; but they should be given secondary or tertiary emphasis; for, unless they rest on a sound economic and social base, they are likely only to create more frustration by raising expectation or hopes with no ability truly to follow through.

The second period of frustration and the call for separation came after World War I. During that war, 300,000 Negro troops went to France—not for the reason Mr. Wilson thought he was sending them, but because they felt that if they fought for their country they would be able to return and say: "We have fought and fought well. Now give us at home what we fought for abroad."

Again, this great expectation collapsed in total despair, as a result of postwar developments: lynchings in the United States reached their height in the early twenties; the Palmer raids did not affect Negroes directly but had such a terrifying effect on civil liberties that no one paid any attention to what was happening to Negroes; the Ku Klux Klan moved its headquarters from Georgia to Indianapolis, the heart of the so-called North; and unemployment among Negroes was higher at that period than it had ever been before. It was at that time, too, the Negroes began their great migration to the North, not from choice but because they were being driven off the land in the South by changed economic conditions.

The war having created great expectations, and the conditions following the war having shattered them, a really great movement for separation ensued—a much more significant movement than the current one. Marcus Garvey organized over two million Negroes, four times the number the NAACP has ever organized, to pay dues to buy ships to return to Africa.

Today, we are experiencing the familiar syndrome again. The Civil Rights Acts of 1964 and 1965 and the Supreme Court decisions all led people seriously to believe that progress was forthcoming, as they believed the day Martin Luther King said, "I have a dream." What made the march on Washington in 1963 great was the fact that it was the culmination of a period of great hope and anticipation.

But what has happened since? The ghettos are fuller than they have ever been, with 500,000 people moving into them each year and only some 40,000 moving out. They are the same old Bedford-Stuyvesant, Harlem, Detroit, and Watts, only they are much bigger, with more rats, more roaches, and more despair. There are more Negro youngsters in segregated schoolrooms than there were in 1954—not all due to segregation or discrimination, perhaps, but a fact. The number of youngsters who have fallen back in their reading, writing, and arithmetic since 1954 has increased, not decreased, and unemployment for Negro young women is up to 35, 40, and 50 percent in the ghettos. For young men in the ghettos, it is up to 20 percent, and this is a conservative figure. For family men, the unemployment is twice that of whites. Having built up hopes, and suffered the despair which followed, we are again in a period where separation is being discussed.

I maintain that, in all three periods, the turn to separation has been a frustration reaction to objective political, social, and economic circumstances. I believe that it is fully justified, for it would be the most egregious wishful thinking to suppose that people can be subjected to deep frustration and yet not act in a frustrated manner. But however justified and inevitable the frustration, it is totally unrealistic to divert the attention of young Negroes at this time either to the idea of a separate state in the United States, or to going back to Africa, or to setting up a black capitalism (as Mr. Nixon and CORE are now advocating), or to talk about any other possibility of economic separation, when those Negroes who are well off are the two million Negroes who are integrated into the trade union movement of this country.

This is not to belittle in any way the desirability of fostering a sense of ethnic unity or racial pride among Negroes or relationships to other black people around the world. This is all to the good, but the ability to do this in a healthy rather than a frustrated way will depend upon the economic viability of the Negro community, the degree to which it can participate in the democratic process here rather than separate from it, and the degree to which it accepts methods of struggle that are productive.

I would not want to leave this subject without observing that while social and economic

"What made the march on Washington in 1963 great was the fact that it was the culmination of a period of great hope and anticipation."

conditions have precipitated thoughts of separation, it would be an oversimplification to attribute the present agitation of that idea exclusively to those causes. A good deal of the talk about separation today reflects a class problem within the Negro community.

I submit that it is not the *lumpenproletariat,* the Negro working classes, the Negro working poor, who are proclaiming: "We want Negro principals, we want Negro supervisors, we want Negro teachers in our schools." It is the educated Negroes. If you name a leader of that movement, you will put your finger on a man with a master's or a Ph.D. degree. Being blocked from moving up, he becomes not only interested in Negro children, but in getting those teaching jobs, supervisory jobs, and principal jobs for his own economic interest. While this is understandable, it is not true that only teachers who are of the same color can teach pupils effectively. Two teachers had an effect upon me; one was black, and the other was white, and it was the white teacher who had the most profound effect, not because she was white, but because she was who she was.

Negroes have been taught that we are inferior, and many Negroes believe that themselves, and have believed it for a long time. That is to say, sociologically we were made children. What is now evident is that the entire black community is rebelling against that concept in behalf of manhood and dignity. This process of rebellion will have as many ugly things in it as beautiful things. Like young people on the verge of maturity many Negroes now say, "We don't want help; we'll do it ourselves. Roll over, Whitey. If we break our necks, okay."

Also, while rebelling, there is rejection of those who used to be loved most. Every teenager has to go through hating mother and father, precisely because he loves them. Now he's got to make it on his own. Thus, Martin Luther King and A. Philip Randolph and Roy Wilkins and Bayard Rustin and all the people who marched in the streets are all finks now. And the liberals, and the Jews who have done most among the liberals, are also told to get the hell out of the way.

The mythology involved here can be very confusing. Jews may want now to tell their children that they lifted themselves in this society by their bootstraps. And when Negroes have made it, they will preach that ridiculous mythology too. That kind of foolishness is only good after the fact. It is not a dynamism by which the struggle can take place.

"... true self-respect and a true sense of image are the results of a social process and not merely a psychological state of mind."

But to return to separation and nationalism. We must distinguish within this movement that which is unsound from that which is sound, for ultimately no propaganda can work for social change which is not based in absolute psychological truth.

There is an aspect of the present thrust toward black nationalism that I call reverse-ism. This is dangerous. Black people now want to argue that their hair is beautiful. All right. It is truthful and useful. But, to the degree that the nationalist movement takes concepts of reaction and turns them upside down and paints them glorious for no other reason than that they are black, we're in trouble—morally and politically. The Ku Klux Klan used to say: "If you're white, you're right; if you're black, no matter who you are, you're no good." And there are those among us who are now saying the opposite of the Ku Klux Klan: "He's a whitey, he's no good. Those white politicians, they both stink, don't vote for either of them. Go fishing because they're white."

The Ku Klux Klan said: "You know, we can't have black people teaching," and they put up a big fight when the first Negro was hired in a white school in North Carolina. Now, for all kinds of "glorious" reasons, we're turning that old idea upside down and saying: "Well, somehow or other, there's soul involved, and only black teachers can teach black children." But it is not true. Good teachers can teach children. The Ku Klux Klan said: "We don't want you in our community; get out." Now there are blacks saying: "We don't want any whites in our community for business or anything; get out." The Ku Klux Klan said: "We will be violent as a means of impressing our will on the situation." And now, in conference after conference a small number of black people use violence and threats to attempt to obstruct the democratic process.

What is essential and what we must not lose sight of is that true self-respect and a true sense of image are the results of a social process and not merely a psychological state of mind.

It is utterly unrealistic to expect the Negro middle class to behave on the basis alone of color. They will behave, first of all, as middle-class people. The minute Jews got enough money to move off Allen Street, they went to West End Avenue. As soon as the Irish could get out of Hell's Kitchen, they beat it to what is now Harlem. Who thinks the Negro middle classes are going to stay in Harlem? I believe that the fundamental mistake of the nationalist movement is that it does not comprehend that class ultimately is a more driving force than color, and that any effort to build a society for American Negroes that is based on color alone is doomed to failure.

Now, there are several possibilities. One possibility is that we can stay here and continue the struggle; sometimes things will be better, sometimes they will be worse. Another is to separate ourselves into our own state in America. But I reject that because I do not believe that the American government will ever accept it. Thirdly, there is a possibility of going back to Africa, and that is out for me, because I've had enough experience with the Africans to know that they will not accept that.

There is a kind of in-between position—stay here and try to separate, and yet not separate. I tend to believe that both have to go on simultaneously. That is to say there has to be a move on the part of Negroes to develop black institutions and a black image, and all this has to go on while they are going downtown into integrated work situations, while they are trying to get into the suburbs if they can, while they are doing what all other Americans do in their economic and social grasshopping. That is precisely what the Jew has done. He has held on to that which is Jewish, and nobody has made a better effort at integrating out there and making sure that he's out there where the action is. It makes for tensions, but I don't believe there's any other viable reality.

Furthermore, I believe that the most important thing for those of us in the trade union movement, in the religious communities, and in the universities is not to be taken in by methods that appeal to people's viscera but do not in fact solve the problems that stimulated their viscera.

We must fight and work for a social and economic program which will lift America's poor, whereby the Negro who is most grievously poor will be lifted to that position where he will be able to have dignity.

Secondly, we must fight vigorously for Negroes to engage in the political process, since there is only one way to have maximum feasible participation—and that is not by silly little committees deciding what they're going to do with a half million dollars, but by getting out into the real world of politics and making their weight felt. The most important thing that we have to do is to restore a sense of dignity to the Negro people. The most immediate task is for every one of us to get out and work between now and November so that we can create the kind of administration and the kind of Congress which will indeed bring about what the Freedom Budget and the Poor People's Campaign called for.

If that can happen, the intense frustration around the problem of separation will decrease as equal opportunities—economic, political, and social—increase. And that is the choice before us.

SOURCES

Books

Rustin, Bayard, *Down the Line: The Collected Writings of Bayard Rustin,* Quadrangle Books, 1971.

Rustin, Bayard, *Strategies for Freedom: The Changing Patterns of Black Protest,* Columbia University Press, 1976.

Thonssen, Lester, editor, *Representative American Speeches: 1968-1969,* Wilson, 1969.

Periodicals

Newsweek, September 7, 1987.

New York Times, August 25, 1987.

New York Times Magazine, "A Way Out of the Exploding Ghetto," August 13, 1967; "A Strategist without a Movement," February 16, 1969.

Time, September 7, 1987.

Satank

(Sitting Bear)

1810(?)–1871

Native American chief of the Kiowa tribe

A prominent war chief and medicine man among the Kiowa Indians, a tribe that lived in the grassy flatlands of what is now Oklahoma, Colorado, and New Mexico, Satank led his people's resistance efforts against white expansion into the southern plains of North America during the mid-nineteenth century. The Kiowas were a nomadic people that relied on buffalo hunting to survive, and they deeply resented new settlements and the coming of the railroad into territory they were accustomed to roaming freely. They also balked at attempts to Christianize them and turn them into farmers. Satank stood out as an especially fierce—and fearsome—presence in a tribe known for being more warlike than many others in the same region.

Satank was born in the Black Hills area of present-day South Dakota, perhaps as early as 1800 but probably no later than 1810. He later moved with his tribe into the southern plains. Around 1840, he served as a principal spokesman for the Kiowas in peace negotiations with the Cheyenne, thus uniting two major tribes into a force that effectively challenged white settlers and soldiers across a broad stretch of the continent. In 1853, he worked out a similar agreement with the Comanches, another Plains tribe noted for its ferocity. Along with his fellow Kiowa chiefs Satanta and Kicking Bird, Satank launched many predatory raids on U.S. encampments over the years, often in violation of various treaty agreements. In 1864, he very nearly touched off a full-fledged war when he shot a soldier at Fort Larned, Kansas. The resulting commotion stampeded the fort's horses, and nearby Indians were forced to flee until tensions eased.

In October 1867, Satank attended the famous Medicine Lodge Council, held at Medicine Lodge Creek in Kansas. The largest such gathering of whites and Indians ever convened, its focus was on President Ulysses S. Grant's peace policy, particularly in light of an incident that had taken place in Sand Creek, Colorado, in 1864, when U.S. troops massacred a peaceful group of Cheyenne men, women, and children. (The attack came after several years of escalating conflicts between the Cheyenne and white prospectors who had flocked to Colorado during the 1850s in search of gold.) Satank was called upon to speak on behalf of the Kiowas. His words are reprinted here from W.C. Vanderwerth's Indian Oratory: Famous Speeches by Noted Indian Chieftains, *University of Oklahoma Press, 1971.*

It has made me glad to meet you, who are the commissioners of the Great Father. You no doubt are tired of the much talk of our people. Many of them have put themselves forward and filled you with their sayings. I have kept back and said nothing, not that I did not consider myself still the principal chief of the Kiowa nation, but others, younger than I, desired to talk, and I left it to them. Before leaving, however, as I now intend to go, I come to say that the Kiowas and Comanches have made with you a peace, and they intend to keep it. If it brings prosperity to us, we, of course, will like it better. If it brings poverty and adversity we will not abandon it. It is our contract and it shall stand.

Our people once carried on war against Texas. We thought the Great Father would not be offended, for the Texans had gone out from among his people and become his enemies. You now tell us they have made peace and returned to the great family. The Kiowa and Comanche will now make no bloody trail in their land. They have pledged their word, and that word shall last unless the whites shall break their contract and invite the horrors of war.

We do not break treaties. We make but few contracts, and them we remember well. The whites make so many they are able to forget them. The white chief seems not to be able to govern his braves. The Great Father seems powerless in the face of his children. He sometimes becomes angry when he sees the wrongs of his people committed on the red man, and his voice becomes loud as the roaring winds. But, like the wind, it soon dies away, and leaves the sullen calm of unheeded oppression. We hope now that a better time has come.

If all would talk and then do as you have done, the sun of peace would shine forever. We have warred against the white man, but never because it gave us pleasure. Before the day of oppression came, no white man came to our villages and went away hungry. It gave us more joy to share with him than it gave him to partake of our hospitality. In the far-distant past there was no suspicion among us. The world seemed large enough for both the red man and the white man. Its broad plains seem now to contract, and the white man grows jealous of his red brother. He once came to trade; he comes now to fight. He once came as a citizen; he now comes as a soldier. He once put his trust in our friendship, and wanted no shield but our fidelity, but now he builds forts and plants big guns on their walls. He once gave us arms and powder, and bade us hunt the game. We then loved him for his confidence. He now suspects our plighted faith, and drives us to be his enemies. He now covers his face with a cloud of jealousy and anger, and tells us to begone, as the offended master speaks to his dog.

Satank

We thank the Great Spirit that all these wrongs are now to cease, and the old day of peace and friendship to come again. You came as friends. You talked as friends. You have patiently heard our many complaints. To you they have seemed trifling; to us they are everything.

You have not tried, as many do, to get from us our lands for nothing. You have not tried to make a new bargain merely to get the advantage. You have not asked to make our annuities smaller; but, unasked, you have made them larger. You have not withdrawn a single gift, but voluntarily you have provided new guarantees for our education and comfort.

When we saw these things we then said, "These are the men of the past." We at once gave your our hearts. You now have them. You know what is best for us. Do for us what is best.

Teach us the road to travel, and we will not depart from it forever. For your sakes the green grass shall not be stained with the blood of the whites. Your people shall again be our people, and peace shall be our mutual heritage. If wrong comes, we shall look to you for the right. We know you will not forsake us, and tell your people to be as you have been. I am old and will soon join my father, but those who come after me will remember this day. It is now treasured up by the old, and will be carried by them to the grave, and then handed down to be kept as a sacred tradition by their children and their children's children.

There is not a drop of my blood in the veins of any creature living, and when I am gone to the happy land, who will mourn for Satank? And now the time has come that I must go. Good by! You may never see me more, but remember Satank as the white man's friend!

The treaty that eventually resulted from this council gave the Kiowas land on a reservation in present-day Oklahoma. Despite Satank's assurances that he only wanted peace—or perhaps because he was not able to exercise as much control over his young warriors as he thought he could—his people continued to wage war against the whites. In May 1871, for example, Satank joined with fellow Kiowa chiefs Satanta and Kicking Bird and attacked an army wagon train making its way through Texas, killing eight of the twelve white men driving the wagons and stealing their cargo. Satank and Satanta were later arrested for their part in leading the raid. While being returned to Texas to stand trial, Satank tried to escape from the soldiers guarding him and was shot and killed.

SOURCES

Brown, Dee, *Bury My Heart at Wounded Knee: An Indian History of the American West,* Holt, 1970.

Jones, Louis Thomas, *Aboriginal American Oratory: The Tradition of Eloquence Among the Indians of the United States,* Southwest Museum (Los Angeles), 1965.

Wanderwerth, W.C., *Indian Oratory: Famous Speeches by Noted Indian Chieftains,* University of Oklahoma Press, 1971.

Satanta
(White Bear)

1830(?)–1878

Native American chief of the Kiowa tribe

Known among the Americans he dealt with as the "Orator of the Plains" in recognition of his eloquence, Satanta was a warrior and chief of the Kiowa Indians, whose lands stretched across the southern flatlands of the United States. Along with his fellow chiefs Satank and Kicking Bird, he led his tribe's resistance against white settlements and acculturation to white ways during the mid-nineteenth century. In both word and deed, Satanta made it clear that the idea of abandoning their nomadic hunting existence was completely incomprehensible and unacceptable to the Kiowas.

Satanta was born around 1830 somewhere in the northern plains but later moved south with the rest of his tribe. He spent most of his life at war with white settlers and soldiers, participating in and later leading countless raids. In addition to his reputation as a brave and aggressive fighter, however, he was also famous as a speaker.

On May 1, 1867, for example, Satanta addressed a gathering of whites and Indians at a meeting in Fort Larned, Kansas. This meeting had been called to gauge the concerns of area tribes in anticipation of the upcoming Medicine Lodge Council. (See below.) Among those in attendance were Major Generals W.S. Hancock and A.J. Smith, to whom Satanta directed his remarks, reprinted here from W.C. Vanderwerth's Indian Oratory: Famous Speeches by Noted Indian Chieftains, *University of Oklahoma Press, 1971.*

I look upon you [General Hancock] and General Smith as my fathers. I want friends, and I say, by the sun, and the earth I live on, I want to talk straight and tell the truth. All other tribes are my brothers, and I want friends, and am doing all I can for peace. If I die first, it is all right. All of the Indians south of here are my friends. When I first started out as a warrior I was a boy; now I am a man, and all men are my friends.

I want the Great Father at Washington, and all the soldiers and troops to hold on. I don't want the prairies and country to be bloody, but just hold on for a while. I don't want war at all. I want peace. As for the Kiowas talking war, I don't know anything about it. Nor do I know anything about the Comanches, Cheyennes, and Sioux talking about war. The Cheyennes, Kiowas, and Comanches are poor. They are all of the same color. They are all red men. This country here is old, and it all belongs to them. But you are cutting off the timber, and now the country is of no account at all. I don't mean anything bad by what I say.

I have nothing bad hidden in my breast at all; everything is all right there. I have heard that there are many troops coming out in this country to whip the Cheyennes, and that is the reason we were afraid, and went away. The Cheyennes, Arapahos, and Kiowas heard that there were troops coming out in this country; so also the Comanches and Apaches, but do not know whether they were coming for peace or for war. They were on the lookout, and listening, and hearing from down out of the ground all the time. They were afraid to come in.

I don't think the Cheyennes wanted to fight, but I understand you burned their village. I don't think that was good at all. To you, General, and to all these officers sitting around here, I say that I know that whatever I tell you will be sent to Washington, and I don't want anything else but the truth told. Other chiefs of the Kiowas, who rank below me, have come in to look for rations, and to look about, and their remarks are reported to Washington, but I don't think their hearts are good.

[At this point, a Colonel Leavenworth interrupted to explain that what Satanta meant was that other chiefs often made speeches just to get something to eat. Satanta then continued.]

Lone Wolf, Stumbling Bear, and Kicking Bird all came in with that object, and their speeches amount to nothing. The Cheyennes, the Arapahos, the Comanches, Kiowas, Apaches, and some Sioux, all sent to see me, for they know me to be the best man, and sent information that they wanted peace. They do not work underhanded at all, but declare plainly that they want peace. I hope that you two generals, and all these officers around here, will help me, and give me heart, and help the Cheyennes, and not destroy them, but let them live. All of the Indians south of this desire the same, and when they talk that way to me I give them praise for it.

Whatever I hear in this council, and whatever you tell me, I will repeat when I reach my

Satanta

villages, and there are some Cheyennes over there whom I will tell, and will induce them to preserve peace. But if they will not listen to me, all my men and myself will have nothing more to do with them. I want peace, and will try to make them keep peaceful. The Kiowa braves have grown up from childhood, obtaining their medicine from the earth. Many have grown old, and continue growing old, and dying from time to time, but there are some remaining yet.

I do not want war at all, but want to make friends, and am doing the best I can for that purpose. There are four different bands of Comanches camped at different points in the south, along on the streams, and there are five different bands of Kiowas, those of Lone Wolf, Heap of Bears, Timber Mountain, Black Bird, and Stumbling Bear, and they profess to be chiefs, although they have but two or three lodges each. They are waiting, however, to hear what they can learn before taking the warpath. The Kiowas do not say anything, and whatever the white man says is all right for them. The Kiowas and the white men are in council today, but I hope no mistake will be made about what the Indians say here, and that nothing will be added to it because I know that everything is sent right to Washington.

[General Hancock broke in to assure Satanta that there were several interpreters on hand to make sure that his words were properly recorded. Satanta then asked for a copy of the proceedings so that he would have one to show to other U.S. officials if necessary. General Hancock promised him a copy as soon as one was available, and Satanta continued his speech.]

As for this Arkansas wagon road, I have no objection to it, but I don't want any railroad here, but upon the Smoky Hill route a railroad can run there, and it is all right. On the Arkansas and all those northern streams, there is no timber; it has all been cut off; but, nevertheless, if anybody knows of anything bad being done, I do not like it.

There are no longer any buffaloes around here, nor anything else we kill to live on; but I am striving for peace now, and don't want anything construed to be bad from what I say, because I am simply speaking the plain truth. The Kiowas are poor. Other tribes are very foolish. They make war and are unfortunate, and then call upon the Kiowas to aid them, and I don't know what to think about it. I want peace, and all these officers around this country know it. I have talked with them until now I am tired. I came down here, and brought my women with me, but came for peace.

If any white men steal our stock, I will report it openly. I continue to come often and am not tired. Now I am doing the best I can, and the white man is looking for me. If there were troops in this country, and the citizens only lived around here, that would be better. But there are so many troops coming in here that I fear they will do something bad to me.

When Satank shot the sentinel here at the post, some two or three years since, there was then war, and that was bad. I came near losing my life then. The Kiowas have now thrown him [Satank] away. If the Indians up north wish to act foolishly, that is not any of my business, and is no reason why we should do so down here. If the Indians further south see the white men coming, they will not come up on the warpath, nor fight. They will not do so if they want to fight, but will call a council, to come and talk as they do here now. Today it is good and tonight it is good, and when the grass comes it will be good; and this road which runs up to the west is good also. Everything is all right now.

If you keep the horses herded around here close to the fort, they will never be good. Let them run away off on the prairies; there is no danger. Let them get grass, and they will get fat; but do not let the children and boys run away off on the hills now. That is not good. I don't do it, nor do the Cheyennes. I think that is a very good idea. You are a big chief, but when I am away over to the Kiowas, then I am a big chief myself.

Whenever a trader comes to my camp I treat him well, and do not do anything out of the way to him. All the traders are laughing and shaking hands with me. When the Indians get a little liquor they get drunk and fight sometimes, and sometimes they whip me; but when they get sober they are all right, and I don't think anything about it. All the white men around here can look at me, and hear what I say. I am doing all I can to keep my men down, and doing the best I can to have peace. Down at the mouth of the Little Arkansas, where a treaty was made, Colonel Leavenworth was present, and I was the first man who came in there to make peace with Colonel Leavenworth, and I did it all by my word.

Little Mountain, the former chief of the tribe,

> ***"The prairie is large and good, and so are the heavens above, and I do not want them stained by the blood of war."***

is now dead. He did all he could to make peace, and kept talking and talking, but the white man kept doing something bad to him, and he was in so much misery that he died. The white men and Indians kept fighting each other backward and forward, and then I came in and make peace myself. Little Mountain did not give me my commission. I won it myself. These three braves [pointing to some Indians around him] are chiefs also, and are not afraid of soldiers, and the sight of them does not frighten them at all. The prairie is large and good, and so are the heavens above, and I do not want them stained by the blood of war. I don't want you to trouble yourself and have fear about bringing out too many trains in this country, for I don't want to see any wagons broken or destroyed by war.

Now, I want to find out what is the reason Colonel Leavenworth did not give me some annuity goods. I have never talked bad, and I don't want to talk bad, but I want to find out the reason I did not get my annuity goods. There are Lone Bear, Heap of Bears, Stumbling Bear, and

Little Heart, and others, six chiefs with very small bands, and they all received annuity goods, while those of my tribe are as plenty as the grass, and I came in for my goods and did not see them. You can look upon us all, and see if we have any of those goods. All that we have we have bought and paid for. We are all poor men; and I think others have got all the goods; but let them keep them. I want peace, and I don't want to make war on account of our goods. I expect to trade for what I get, and not get anything for making speeches.

My heart is very strong. We can make robes and trade them. That is what we live upon. I have no mules, horses, nor robes to give Colonel Leavenworth for my goods. I am a poor man, but I am not going to get angry and talk about it. I simply want to tell this to these officers here present. Such articles of clothing as the white man may throw away we will pick up and brush off and use, and make out the best we can; and, if you throw away provisions, we will clean and use them also, and thus do the best we can.

I see a great many officers around here with fine clothing, but I do not come to beg. I admire fine clothes, although I never did beg, or anything of that sort. I have no hat, and am going about without one, the same as all the other Kiowas. Colonel Bent used to come over often to my tent, and the Kiowas went there to him very often, and were glad and shook hands with him; and Mr. Curtis went there, and he was treated the same way. All were treated the same. But I am not poor enough to die yet. I think my women can make enough to live upon, and can make something yet.

When Colonel Bent was our agent, and brought our goods to us, he brought them out and kept them in a train; and when he arrived he unloaded all our goods to us, and that was the way to do it. But now there is a different way of doing things. At my camp I waited and sent for the agent, and did not see him; but other chiefs mounted their horses, and went there and claimed to be principal men.

I heard that the railroad was to come up through this country, and my men and other tribes objected to it; but I advised them to keep silent. I thought that by the railroad being built through here, we would get our goods sure, but they do not come. I would like to get some agent who is a good and responsible man—one who would give us all our annuities. I do not want an agent who will steal half of our goods and hide them, but an agent who will get all my goods and bring them out here, and give them to me.

I am not talking any thing badly or angrily, but simply the truth. I don't think the great men at Washington know anything about this, but I am now telling your officers to find it out.

Now I am done and whatever you [General Hancock] have to say to me I will listen to, and those who are with me will listen, so that when we return to camp we can tell others the same as you tell us.

Later that same year, in October, Satanta spoke at the Medicine Lodge Council. This ceremonial gathering—the largest of its kind, attended by Indians as well as a number of white observers—convened at Medicine Lodge Creek in Kansas. Many chiefs stood up to protest their treatment at the hands of whites. Among them was Satanta, whose words (originally delivered in Spanish) were widely quoted, including in the New York Times. *Their simple eloquence led the Americans present to dub him the "Orator of the Plains." His speech is reprinted from W.C. Vanderwerth's* Indian Oratory: Famous Speeches by Noted Indian Chieftains, *University of Oklahoma Press, 1971.*

You, the commissioners, have come from afar to listen to our grievances. My heart is glad and I shall hide nothing from you. I understood that you were coming down to see us. I moved away from those disposed for war, and I also came along to see you. The Kiowas and Comanches have not been fighting. We were away down south when we heard you were coming to see us.

The Cheyennes are those who have been fighting with you. They did it in broad daylight so that all could see them. If I had been fighting I would have done it by day and not in the dark. Two years ago I made peace with Generals Harney, Sanborn and Colonel Leavenworth at the mouth of the Little Arkansas.

That peace I have never broken. When the grass was growing in the spring, a large body of soldiers came along on the Santa Fe road. I had not done anything and therefore I was not afraid. All the chiefs of the Kiowas, Comanches, and Arapahos are here today; they have come to listen to good words. We have been waiting here a long time to see you and are getting tired. All the land south of the Arkansas belongs to the Kiowas and Comanches, and I don't want to give away any of it. I love the land and the buffalo and will not part with it. I want you to under stand well what I say. Write it on paper. Let the Great Father see it, and let me hear what he has to say. I want you to understand, also, that the Kiowas and Comanches don't want to fight, and have not been fighting since we made the treaty. I hear a great deal of good talk from the gentlemen whom the Great Father sends us, but they never do what they say. I don't want any of the medicine lodges [schools and churches] within the country. I want the children raised as I was. When I make peace, it is a long and lasting one—there is no end to it. We thank you for your presents.

All the headmen and braves are happy. They will do what you want them, for they know you are doing the best you can. I and they will do our best also. When I look upon you, I know you are all big chiefs. While you are in this country we go to sleep happy and are not afraid. I have heard that you intend to settle us on a reservation near the mountains. I don't want to settle. I love to roam over the prairies. There I feel free and happy, but when we settle down we grow pale and die.

I have laid aside my lance, bow, and shield, and yet I feel safe in your presence. I have told you the truth. I have no little lies hid about me, but I don't know how it is with the commissioners. Are they as clear as I am?

A long time ago this land belonged to our fathers; but when I go up to the river I see camps of soldiers on its banks. These soldiers cut down my timber; they kill my buffalo; and when I see that, my heart feels like bursting; I feel sorry. I have spoken.

Unhappy with the treaty resulting from the Medicine Lodge Council that assigned the Kiowa to a reservation in present-day Oklahoma, Satanta—despite his professed desire for peace—continued to lead raids across the prairie, killing white settlers and soldiers and stampeding livestock. The beginning of the end came in May 1871, when he and Satank and Kicking Bird ambushed an army wagon train traveling through Texas, killing eight of the twelve men driving the wagons and stealing their freight. Eventually arrested and convicted, Satanta was sentenced to death but paroled in 1873 on the condition that he not set foot outside the Kiowa reservation. The following year, when war broke out between the U.S. and the Comanches, he turned himself in to authorities hoping to demonstrate that he was not involved. Satanta was nevertheless sent off to a state prison in Huntsville, Texas, where he committed suicide in 1878 after learning he would never be set free.

SOURCES

Armstrong, Virginia Irving, *I Have Spoken: American History Through the Voices of the Indians,* Sage Books, 1971.

Brown, Dee, *Bury My Heart at Wounded Knee: An Indian History of the American West,* Holt, 1970.

Jones, Louis Thomas, *Aboriginal American Oratory: The Tradition of Eloquence Among the Indians of the United States,* Southwest Museum (Los Angeles), 1965.

Vanderwerth, W.C., *Indian Oratory: Famous Speeches by Noted Indian Chieftains,* University of Oklahoma Press, 1971.

Chief Seattle

(Seathl)

1788(?)–1866

Native American leader of the Duwamish and Suquamish tribes

Some of the most famous—and most controversial—words ever spoken by a Native American leader are those of Chief Seattle, who lived with his people in the area of Puget Sound where the city of Seattle, Washington, now thrives. Thanks to a speech of somewhat murky origin, Seattle is known for his poignant eloquence and extraordinary foresight regarding the major environmental concerns of the twentieth century. As a result, he has become a powerful symbol of the ecology movement both in the United States and abroad—even though it is doubtful that he ever expressed the sentiments with which he is most closely identified.

Seattle was a young man when white settlers began arriving in greater numbers in the Pacific Northwest. Like his father before him, he was friendly to the newcomers and encouraged his people to be helpful and accommodating to them as well. Seattle himself willingly embraced many of their traditions; during the 1830s, for example, he converted to Catholicism at the urging of French missionaries. He continued to counsel peace and patience well into the 1850s despite increasing tensions between Indians and whites. (Much of this hostility was prompted by the discovery of gold in the region, which in turn attracted hordes of miners who did not always honor established boundaries and customs.) When war finally did break out in the middle of the decade, Seattle refused to participate, and in January 1855, he became the first to sign the Fort Elliot Treaty. Under the terms of this document, he and his people gave away most of their land and agreed to relocate to a reservation with several other Washington tribes.

It was supposedly at the signing of the Fort Elliot Treaty that Chief Seattle addressed territorial Governor Isaac Stevens and uttered the words that have so endeared him to champions of the environment. This image has proven to be especially popular in Europe, where American Indians have long been viewed as very spiritual beings who live in mystical harmony with nature. A similar perception began to emerge in the United States in the late 1960s and early 1970s with the rapid growth of the ecology movement.

Rudolf Kaiser, a professor affiliated with the University of Hildesheim in Germany, has made a thorough study of the Chief Seattle speech (which is sometimes described instead as a letter to President Franklin Pierce) and has identified a number of different versions, none of which resembles the texts of two short speeches the Indian leader was actually known to have given at the treaty ceremony. (These are both stored among government documents in the National Archives in Washington, D.C.) Kaiser reported his findings in the book Recovering the Word: Essays on Native American Literature, *edited by Brian Swann and Arnold Krupat, University of California Press, 1987. Four major versions of Chief Seattle's speech that Kaiser tracked down and analyzed in detail are reprinted here from his essay, entitled "Chief Seattle's Speech(es): American Origins and European Reception."*

According to Kaiser, the first version of Chief Seattle's speech to appear in print was published in the Seattle Sunday Star *on October 29, 1887. In the accompanying article, a physician named Henry Smith reported that he had been present when Chief Seattle gave a memorable speech in late 1853 or early 1854 at a reception for the newly-arrived commissioner of Indian affairs for Washington Territory, Isaac Stevens. Impressed by the chief's dignity and the solemnity of his message, Smith took detailed notes on the speech for his diary (which has since been lost) and later reconstructed it for the piece in the* Star. *In Kaiser's opinion, it is this account that has served as the basis for the many subsequent versions of the same speech.*

Yonder sky has wept tears of compassion on our fathers for centuries untold, and which, to us, looks eternal, may change. To-day it is fair, to-morrow it may be overcast with clouds. My words are like the stars that never set. What Seattle says the great chief, Washington, can rely upon, with as much certainty as our pale-face brothers can rely upon the return of the seasons [the Indians in early times thought that Washington was still alive. They knew the name to be that of a president, and when they heard of the president at Washington they mistook the name of the city for the name of the reigning chief. They thought, also, that King George was still England's monarch, because the Hudson Bay traders called themselves "King George men." This innocent deception the company was shrewd enough not to explain away for the Indians had more respect for them than they would have had, had they known England was ruled by a woman.]. The son of the white chief says his father sends us greetings of friendship and good-will. This is kind, for we know he has little need of our friendship in return, because his people are many. They are like the grass that covers the vast prairies, while my people are few, and resemble the scattering trees of a wind-swept plain.

The great, and I presume also good, white chief sends us word that he wants to buy our lands but is willing to allow us to reserve enough to live on comfortably. This indeed appears generous, for the red man no longer has rights that he need respect, and the offer may be wise, also, for we are no longer in need of a great country. There was a time when our people covered the whole land as the waves of a wind-ruffled sea cover its shell-paved floor. But that time has long since passed away with the greatness of tribes almost forgotten. I will not mourn over our untimely decay, nor reproach my pale-face brothers with hastening it, for we, too, may have been somewhat to blame.

When our young men grow angry at some real or imaginary wrong and disfigure their faces with black paint, their hearts, also, are disfigured and turn black, and then their cruelty is relentless and knows no bounds, and our old men are not able to restrain them.

But let us hope that hostilities between the red man and his pale-face brothers may never return. We would have everything to lose and nothing to gain.

Chief Seattle

True it is that revenge, with our young braves, is considered gain, even at the cost of their own lives, but old men who stay at home in times of war, and old women who have sons to lose, know better.

Our great father Washington, for I presume he is now our father as well as yours, since [King] George has moved his boundaries to the north; our great and good father, I say, sends us word by his son, who, no doubt, is a great chief among his people, that if we do as he desires, he will protect us. His brave armies will be to us a bristling wall of strength, and his great ships of war will fill our harbors so that our ancient enemies far to the northward, the Simsiams and Hydas, will no longer frighten our women and old men. Then he will be our father and we will be his children. But can this ever be? Your God loves your people and hates mine; he folds his strong arms lovingly around the white man and leads him as a father leads his infant son, but he has forsaken his red children; he makes your people wax strong every day, and soon they will fill the land; while our people are ebbing away like a fast-receding tide, that will never flow again. The white man's God cannot love his red children or he would protect them. They seem to be orphans and can look nowhere for help. How then can we become brothers? How can your father become our father and bring us prosperity and awaken in us dreams of returning greatness?

Your God seems to be partial. He came to the white man. We never saw Him; never even heard His voice; He gave the white man laws but He had no word for His red children whose teeming millions filled this vast continent as the stars fill the firmament. No, we are two distinct races and must ever remain so. There is little in common between us. The ashes of our ancestors are sacred and their final resting place is hallowed ground, while you wander away from the tombs of your fathers seemingly without regret.

Your religion was written on tables of stone by the iron finger of an angry God, lest you might forget it. The red man could never remember nor comprehend it.

Our religion is the traditions of our ancestors, the dreams of our old men, given them by the great Spirit, and the visions of our sachems, and is written in the hearts of our people.

Your dead cease to love you and the homes of their nativity as soon as they pass the portals of the tomb. They wander off beyond the stars, are soon forgotten and never return. Our dead never forget the beautiful world that gave them being. They still love its winding rivers, its great mountains and its sequestered vales, and they ever yearn in tenderest affection over the lonely hearted living and often return to visit and comfort them.

Day and night cannot dwell together. The red man has ever fled the approach of the white man, as the changing mists on the mountain side flee before the blazing morning sun.

However, your proposition seems a just one, and I think my folks will accept it and will retire to the reservation you offer them, and we will dwell apart and in peace, for the words of the great white chief seem to be the voice of nature speaking to my people out of the thick darkness that is fast gathering around them like a dense fog floating inward from a midnight sea.

It matters but little where we pass the remainder of our days. They are not many. The Indian's night promises to be dark. No bright star hovers about the horizon. Sad-voiced winds moan in the distance. Some grim Nemesis of our race is on the red man's trail, and wherever he goes he will still hear the sure approaching footsteps of the fell destroyer and prepare to meet his doom, as does the wounded doe that hears the approaching footsteps of the hunter. A few more moons, a few more winters and not one of all the mighty hosts that once filled this broad land or that now roam in fragmentary bands through these vast solitudes will remain to weep over the tombs of a people once as powerful and as hopeful as your own.

But why should we repine? Why should I murmur at the fate of my people? Tribes are made up of individuals and are no better than they. Men come and go like the waves of the sea. A tear, a tamanamus, a dirge, and they are gone from our longing eyes forever. Even the white man, whose God walked and talked with him, as friend to friend, is not exempt from the common destiny. We may be brothers after all. We shall see.

We will ponder your proposition, and when we have decided we will tell you. But should we accept it, I here and now make this the first condition: That we will not be denied the privilege, without molestation, of visiting at will the graves of our ancestors and friends. Every part of this country is sacred to my people. Every hillside, every valley, every plain and grove has been hallowed by some fond memory or some sad experience of my tribe. Even the rocks that seem to lie dumb as they swelter in the sun along the silent seashore in solemn grandeur thrill with memories of past events connected with the late of my people, and the very dust under your feet responds more lovingly to our footsteps than to yours, because it is the ashes of our ancestors, and our bare feet are conscious of the sympathetic touch, for the soil is rich with the life of our kindred.

"Every part of this country is sacred to my people. . . . [Even] the very dust under your feet responds more lovingly to our footsteps than to yours, because it is the ashes of our ancestors, and our bare feet are conscious of the sympathetic touch. . . ."

The sable braves, and fond mothers, and glad-hearted maidens, and the little children who lived and rejoiced here, and whose very names are now forgotten, still love these solitudes, and their deep fastnesses at eventide grow shadowy with the presence of dusky spirits. And when the last red man shall have perished from the earth and his memory among white men shall have become a myth, these shores shall swarm with the invisible dead of my tribe, and when your children's children shall think themselves alone in the field, the shop, upon the highway or in the silence of the woods they will not be alone. In all the earth there is no place dedicated to solitude. At night when the streets of your cities and villages shall be silent, and you think them deserted, they will throng with the returning hosts that once filled and still love this beautiful land. The white man will never be alone. Let him be just and deal kindly with my people, for the dead are not altogether powerless.

In 1969, American poet and writer William Arrowsmith published what he called a "translation" of Chief Seattle's speech in the journal Arion. *(Six years later, it was reprinted in an issue of the* American Poetry Review.) *In his notes at the end of the speech, Arrowsmith explained that his "translation" was actually a revision or modernization of Smith's account that eliminated "the dense patina of nineteenth-century literary diction and syntax." As a result, the versions differ somewhat in vocabulary but not significantly in content.*

Brothers: That sky above us has pitied our fathers for many hundreds of years. To us it looks unchanging, but it may change. Today it is fair. Tomorrow it may be covered with cloud.

My words are like the stars. They do not set. What Seattle says, the great chief Washington can count on as surely as our white brothers can count on the return of the seasons.

The White Chief's son says his father sends us words of friendship and goodwill. This is kind of him, since we know he has little need of our friendship in return. His people are many, like the grass that covers the plains. My people are few, like the trees scattered by the storms on the grasslands.

The great—and good, I believe—White Chief sends us word that he wants to buy our land. But he will reserve us enough so that we can live comfortably. This seems generous, since the red man no longer has rights he need respect. It may also be wise, since we no longer need a large country. Once, my people covered this land like a flood-tide moving with the wind across the shell-littered flats. But that time is gone, and with it the greatness of tribes now almost forgotten.

But I will not mourn the passing of my people. Nor do I blame our white brothers for causing it. We too were perhaps partly to blame. When our young men grow angry at some wrong, real or imagined, they make their faces ugly with black paint. Then their hearts too are ugly and black. They are hard and their cruelty knows no limits. And our old men cannot restrain them.

Let us hope that the wars between the red man and his white brothers will never come again. We would have everything to lose and nothing to gain. Young men view revenge as gain, even when they lose their own lives. But the old men who stay behind in time of war, mothers with sons to lose—they know better.

Our great father Washington—for he must be our father now as well as yours, since George has moved his boundary northward—our great and good father sends us word by his son, who is surely a great chief among his people, that he will protect us if we do what he wants. His brave soldiers will be a strong wall for my people, and his great warships will fill our harbors. Then our ancient enemies to the north—the Haidas and Tsimshians—will no longer frighten our women and old men. Then he will be our father and we will be his children.

But can that ever be? Your God loves your people and hates mine. He puts his strong arm around the white man and leads him by the hand, as a father leads his little boy. He has abandoned his red children. He makes your people stronger every day. Soon they will flood all the land. But my people are an ebb tide, we will never return. No, the white man's God cannot love his red children or he would protect them. Now we are orphans. There is no one to help us.

So how can we be brothers? How can your father be our father, and make us prosper and send us dreams of future greatness? Your God is prejudiced. He came to the white man. We never saw him, never even heard his voice. He gave the white man laws, but he had no word for his red children whose numbers once filled this land as the stars filled the sky.

No, we are two separate races, and we must stay separate. There is little in common between us.

To us the ashes of our fathers are sacred. Their graves are holy ground. But you are wanderers, you leave your fathers' graves behind you, and you do not care.

Your religion was written on tables of stone by the iron finger of an angry God, so you would not forget it. The red man could never understand it or remember it. Our religion is the ways of our forefathers, the dreams of our old men, sent them by the Great Spirit, and the visions of our sachems. And it is written in the hearts of our people.

Your dead forget you and the country of their birth as soon as they go beyond the grave and walk among the stars. They are quickly forgotten and they never return. Our dead never forget this beautiful earth. It is their mother. They always love and remember her rivers, her great mountains, her valleys. They long for the living, who are lonely too and who long for the dead. And their spirits often return to visit and console us.

No, day and night cannot live together.

The red man has always retreated before the advancing white man, as the mist on the mountain slopes runs before the morning sun.

So your offer seems fair, and I think my people will accept it and go to the reservation you offer them. We will live apart, and in peace. For the words of the Great White Chief are like the words of nature speaking to my people out of great darkness—a darkness that gathers around us like the night fog moving inland from the sea.

It matters little where we pass the rest of our

days. They are not many. The Indians' night will be dark. No bright star shines on his horizons. The wind is sad. Fate hunts the red man down. Wherever he goes, he will hear the approaching steps of his destroyer, and prepare to die, like the wounded doe who hears the steps of the hunter.

A few more moons, a few more winters, and none of the children of the great tribes that once lived in this wide earth or that roam now in small bands in the woods will be left to mourn the graves of a people once as powerful and as hopeful as yours.

But why should I mourn the passing of my people? Tribes are made of men, nothing more. Men come and go, like the waves of the sea. A tear, a prayer to the Great Spirit, a dirge, and they are gone from our longing eyes forever. Even the white man, whose God walked and talked with him as friend to friend, cannot be exempt from the common destiny.

We may be brothers after all. We shall see.

We will consider your offer. When we have decided, we will let you know. Should we accept, I here and now make this condition: we will never be denied the right to visit, at any time, the graves of our fathers and our friends.

Every part of this earth is sacred to my people. Every hillside, every valley, every clearing and wood, is holy in the memory and experience of my people. Even those unspeaking stones along the shore are loud with events and memories in the life of my people. The ground beneath your feet responds more lovingly to our steps than yours, because it is the ashes of our grandfathers. Our bare feet know the kindred touch. The earth is rich with the lives of our kin.

The young men, the mothers, and girls, the little children who once lived and were happy here, still love these lonely places. And at evening the forests are dark with the presence of the dead. When the last red man has vanished from this earth, and his memory is only a story among the whites, these shores will still swarm with the invisible dead of my people. And when your children's children think they are alone in the fields, the forests, the shops, the highways, or the quiet of the woods, they will not be alone. There is no place in this country where a man can be alone. At night when the streets of your towns and cities are quiet, and you think they are empty, they will throng with the returning spirits that once thronged them, and that still love these places. The white man will never be alone.

So let him be just and deal kindly with my people. The dead have power too.

Without a doubt the most famous version of Chief Seattle's speech is one that many people throughout the world became familiar with thanks to a film entitled Home. *Around 1970, a man named Ted Perry was teaching at the University of Texas when he attended a rally on the environment and heard a colleague named William Arrowsmith recite his "translation" of Seattle's speech. Later, the Southern Baptist Radio and Television Commission approached Perry about doing a film on the effects of pollution. Recalling the Chief Seattle speech, Perry contacted Arrowsmith and asked for permission to use it as the basis for his script. Arrowsmith agreed, and Perry then spun an original work of fiction that depicted Seattle as an angry, resentful Indian who chastises the white man for his carelessness toward the environment.*

Around 1972, Perry saw the completed film for the first time when it was broadcast on television. As the credits rolled, he was surprised to see that the producer had failed to give him credit as the author of the script. Instead, viewers were left with the impression that the material was authentic—that it represented the exact words of Chief Seattle. Thus, despite the fact that it is almost entirely the product of another man's imagination, the following version of "Seattle's" speech is the one that has stirred the souls of ecology-minded people throughout America and Europe.

The Great Chief in Washington sends word that he wishes to buy our land.

The Great Chief also sends us words of friendship and goodwill. This is kind of him, since we know he has little need of our friendship in return. But we will consider your offer. For we know that if we do not sell, the white man may come with guns and take our land.

How can you buy or sell the sky, the warmth of the land? The idea is strange to us.

If we do not own the freshness of the air and the sparkle of the water, how can you buy them from us.

We will decide in our time.

What Chief Seattle says, the Great Chief in Washington can count on as truly as our white brothers can count on the return of the seasons. My words are like the stars. They do not set.

Every part of this earth is sacred to my people. Every shining pine needle, every sandy shore, every mist in the dark woods, every clearing, and humming insect is holy in the memory and experience of my people. The sap which courses through the trees carries the memories of the red man.

The white man's dead forget the country of their birth when they go to walk among the stars. Our dead never forget this beautiful earth, for it is the mother of the red man.

We are part of the earth and it is part of us. The perfumed flowers are our sisters the deer, the horse, the great eagle, these are our brothers. The rocky crests, the juices in the meadows, the body heat of the pony, and man—all belong to the same family.

So, when the Great Chief in Washington sends word that he wishes to buy our land, he asks much of us.

The Great Chief sends word he will reserve us a place so that we can live comfortable to ourselves. He will be our father and we will be his children.

But can that ever be? God loves your people, but has abandoned his red children. He sends machines to help the white man with his work, and builds great villages for him. He makes your people stronger every day. Soon you will flood the land like the rivers which crash down the canyons after a sudden rain. But my people are an ebbing tide, we will never return.

No, we are separate races. Our children do not play together and our old men tell different stories. God favors you, and we are orphans.

So we will consider your offer to buy our land. But it will not be easy. For this land is sacred to us. We take our pleasure in these woods. I do not know. Our ways are different from your ways.

This shining water that moves in the streams and rivers is not just water but the blood of our ancestors. If we sell you land, you must remember that it is sacred, and that each ghostly reflection in the clear water of the lakes tells of events and memories in the life of my people. The water's murmur is the voice of my father's father.

The rivers are our brothers, they quench our thirst. The rivers carry our canoes, and feed our children. If we sell you our land, you must remember, and teach your children, that the rivers are our brothers, and yours, and you must henceforth give rivers the kindness you would give any brother.

The red man has always retreated before the advancing white man, as the mist of the mountain runs before the morning sun. But the ashes of our fathers are sacred. The graves are holy ground, and so these hills, these trees, this portion of the earth is consecrated to us. We know that the white man does not understand our ways. One portion of land is the same to him as the next, for he is a stranger who comes in the night and takes from the land whatever he needs. The earth is not his brother but his enemy, and when he has conquered it, he moves on. He leaves his father's graves behind, and

> ***"The earth is not [the white man's] brother but his enemy, and when he has conquered it, he moves on. . . . his appetite will devour the earth and leave behind only a desert."***

he does not care. He kidnaps the earth from his children. He does not care. His father's graves and his children's birthright are forgotten. He treats his mother, the earth, and his brother, the sky, as things to be bought, plundered, sold like sheep or bright beads. His appetite will devour the earth and leave behind only a desert.

I do not know. Our ways are different from your ways. The sight of your cities pains the eyes of the red man. But perhaps it is because the red man is a savage and does not understand.

There is no quiet place in the white man's cities. No place to hear the unfurling of leaves in spring or the rustle of insect's wings. But perhaps it is because I am a savage and do not understand. The clatter only seems to insult the ears. And what is there to life if a man cannot hear the lonely cry of the whippoorwill or the arguments of the frogs around a pond at night? I am a red man and do not understand. The Indian prefers the soft sound of the wind darting over the face of a pond, and the smell of the wind itself, cleansed by a midday rain, or scented with the pinon pine.

The air is precious to the red man, for all things share the same breath—the beast, the tree, the man, they all share the same breath. The white man does not seem to notice the air he breathes. Like a man dying for many days, he is numb to the stench. But if we sell our land, you must remember that the air is precious to us, that the air shares its spirit with all the life it supports. The wind that gave our grandfather his first breath also receives his last sigh. And the wind must also give our children the spirit of life. And if we sell you our land, you must keep it apart and sacred, as a place where even the white man can go to taste the wind that is sweetened by the meadow's flowers.

So we will consider your offer to buy our land. If we decide to accept, I will make one condition: The white man must treat the beasts of this land as his brothers.

I am a savage and I do not understand any other way. I have seen a thousand rotting buffalos on the prairie, left by the white man who shot them from a passing train. I am a savage and I do not understand how the smoking iron horse can be more important than the buffalo that we kill only to stay alive.

What is man without the beasts? If all the beasts were gone, men would die from a great loneliness of spirit. For whatever happens to the beasts, soon happens to man. All things are connected.

Whatever befalls the earth, befalls the sons of the earth.

You must teach your children that the ground beneath their feet is the ashes of our grandfathers. So that they will respect the land, tell your children that the earth is rich with the lives of our kin. Teach your children what we have taught our children, that the earth is our mother. Whatever befalls the earth, befalls the sons of the earth. If men spit upon the ground, they spit upon themselves.

This we know. The earth does not belong to man; man belongs to the earth. This we know. All things are connected like the blood which unites one family. All things are connected.

Whatever befalls the earth befalls the sons of the earth. Man did not weave the web of life; he is merely a strand in it. Whatever he does to the web, he does to himself.

No, day and night cannot live together.

Our dead go to live in the earth's sweet rivers, they return with the silent footsteps of spring, and it is their spirit, running in the wind, that ripples the surface of the ponds.

We will consider why the white man wishes to buy the land. What is it that the white man wishes to buy, my people ask me. The idea is strange to us. How can you buy or sell the sky, the warmth of the land?—the swiftness of the antelope? How can we sell these things to you and how can you buy them? Is the earth yours to do with as you will, merely because the red man signs a piece of paper and gives it to the white man? If we do not own the freshness of the air and the sparkle of the water, how can you buy them from us.

Can you buy back the buffalo, once the last one has been killed? But we will consider your offer, for we know that if we do not sell, the white man may come with guns and take our land. But we are primitive, and in his passing moment of strength the white man thinks that he is a god who already owns the earth. How can a man own his mother?

But we will consider your offer to buy our land. Day and night cannot live together. We will consider your offer to go to the reservation you have for my people. We will live apart, and in peace. It matters little where we spend the rest of our days. Our children have seen their fathers humbled in defeat. Our warriors have felt shame, and after defeat they turn their days in idleness and contaminate their bodies with sweet foods and strong drink. It matters little where we pass the rest of our days. They are not many. A few more hours, a few more winters, and none of the children of the great tribes that once lived on this earth or that roam now in small bands in the woods will be left to mourn the graves of a people once as powerful and hopeful as yours.

But why should I mourn the passing of my people? Tribes are made of men, nothing more. Men come and go, like the waves of the sea.

Even the white man, whose God walks and talks with him as friend to friend, cannot be exempt from the common destiny. We may be brothers after all; we shall see. One thing we know, which the white man may one day discover—our God is the same God.

You may think now that you own Him as you wish to own our land; but you cannot. He is the God of man, and His compassion is equal for the red man and the white. This earth is precious to Him, and to harm the earth is to heap contempt on its Creator. The whites too shall pass; perhaps sooner than all other tribes. Continue to contaminate your bed, and you will one night suffocate in your own waste.

But in your perishing you will shine brightly, fired by the strength of the God who brought you to this land and for some special purpose gave you dominion over this land and over the red man. That destiny is a mystery to us, for we do not understand when the buffalo are all slaughtered, the wild horses are tamed, the secret corners of the forest heavy with the scent of many men, and the view of the ripe hills blotted by talking wires. Where is the thicket? Gone. Where is the eagle? Gone. And what is it to say goodbye to the swift pony and the hunt? The end of living and the beginning of survival.

God gave you dominion over the beasts, the woods, and the red man, and for some special purpose, but that destiny is a mystery to the red man. We might understand if we knew what it was that the white man dreams—what hopes he describes to his children on long winter nights—what visions he burns onto their minds so that they will wish for tomorrow. But we are savages. The white man's dreams are hidden from us. And because they are hidden, we will go our own way. For above all else, we cherish the right of each man to live as he wishes, however different from his brothers. There is little in common between us.

So we will consider your offer to buy our land. If we agree, it will be to secure the reservation you have promised. There, perhaps, we may live out our brief days as we wish.

When the last red man has vanished from this earth, and his memory is only the shade of a cloud moving across the prairie, these shores and forests will still hold the spirits of my people. For they love this earth as the newborn loves its mother's heartbeat.

If we sell you our land, love it as we've loved it. Care for it as we've cared for it. Hold in your mind the memory of the land as it is when you take it. And with all your strength, with all your mind, with all your heart, preserve it for your children, and love it . . . as God loves us all.

One thing we know. Our God is the same God. This earth is precious to Him. Even the white man cannot be exempt from the common destiny. We may be brothers after all. We shall see.

Another fairly well-known version of Chief Seattle's speech that Kaiser analyzed in his essay was part of a display in the United States pavilion at the 1974 world exposition held in Spokane, Washington. Its author is unknown, but it is essentially a shorter and somewhat more poetic adaptation of Ted Perry's film script version. As such, it no doubt enhanced the increasingly popular image of Chief Seattle as a nineteenth-century visionary with strong spiritual links to the ecology movement of the late twentieth century.

The President in Washington sends word that he wishes to buy our land.

Buy our land! But how can you buy or sell the sky? The land? The idea is strange to us. If we do not own the freshness of the air and the sparkle of the water, how can you buy them?

Every part of this earth is sacred to my people. Every shining pine needle, every sandy shore, every mist in the dark woods, every meadow, every humming insect. All are Holy in the memory and experience of my people.

We know the sap which courses through the trees as we know the blood that courses through our veins. We are part of the earth and it is part of us.

The perfumed flowers are our sisters. The bear, the deer, the great eagle, these are our brothers.

The rocky crests, the juices in the meadow, the body heat of the pony—and man, all belong to the same family.

This shining water that moves in the streams and rivers is not just water, but the blood of our ancestors.

If we sell you our land you must remember that it is sacred. Each ghostly reflection in the clear water of the lakes tells of events and memories in the life of my people. The water's murmur is the voice of my father's father.

The rivers—they are our brothers. They quench our thirst. They carry our canoes, they feed our children. So, you must give to the rivers the kindness you would give to any brother.

If we sell you our land, remember that the air is precious to us, that the air shares its spirit with all life it supports. It is the wind that gave our grandfather his first breath. It is the wind that receives his last sigh.

The wind also gives our children the spirit of life. So, if we sell you our land, you must keep it apart as a place where man can go and experience the Sacred.

Keep the land as a place where man can go to taste the wind that is sweetened by the meadow flowers.

Will you teach your children what we have taught our children? That the earth is our mother?

Whatever befalls the earth, befalls all the sons of the earth.

This we know: The earth does not belong to man, man belongs to the earth. All things are connected like the blood which unites us all.

Man did not weave the web of life, he is merely a strand in it. Whatever he does to the web, he does to himself.

One thing we know: Our God is also your God. We both know that the earth is precious to Him and to harm the earth is to heap contempt upon its Creator.

Your destiny is a mystery to us. What will happen when the buffalo are all slaughtered? The wild horses tamed? What will happen when the secret corners of the forest are heavy with the scent of many men?

What will happen when the view of the ripe hills is blotted by talking wires? Where will the thicket be? Gone. Where will the eagle be? Gone. And what is it to say goodbye to the swift pony and the hunt? That would be the end of living and the beginning of surviving.

When the last red man has vanished with his wilderness and his memory is only the shadow of a cloud moving across the prairie, will these shores and forests still be here? Will there be any of the spirit of my people left?

We love this earth as a newborn loves its mother's heartbeat. So, if we sell you our land, love it as we have loved it. Care for it as we have cared for it. Hold it in your mind. Keep forever the memory of the land as it is when you receive it. Preserve the land for all children and love it.

As we are part of the land, you too are part of the land. This earth is precious to us. It is also precious to you.

No man, be he red man or white man can be apart. One thing we know: There is only one God. We are all brothers.

The real Chief Seattle and his people, who maintained friendly relations with the whites, eventually settled on the Port Madison Reservation near what is now Bremerton, Washington.

SOURCES

Armstrong, Virginia Irving, compiler, *I Have Spoken: American History Through the Voices of the Indians,* Sage Books, 1971.

Jones, Louis Thomas, *Aboriginal American Oratory: The Tradition of Eloquence Among the Indians of the United States,* Southwest Museum (Los Angeles), 1965.

McLuhan, T.C., *Touch the Earth: A Self-Portrait of Indian Existence,* Outerbridge & Dienstfrey, 1971.

Rosenstiel, Annette, *Red and White: Indian Views of the White Man, 1492-1982,* Universe Books, 1983.

Sanders, Thomas E., and Walter W. Peek, *Literature of the American Indian,* Glencoe Press, 1973.

Swann, Brian and Arnold Krupat, editors, *Recovering the Word: Essays on Native American Literature,* University of California Press, 1987.

Vanderwerth, W.C., *Indian Oratory: Famous Speeches by Noted Indian Chieftains,* University of Oklahoma Press, 1971.

Witt, Shirley Hill, and Stan Steiner, editors, *The Way: An Anthology of American Indian Literature,* Knopf, 1972.

Sitting Bull
(Tatanka Yotanka)

1831(?)–1890

Native American leader of the Sioux tribe

One of the best known and most colorful of the nineteenth century's Indian leaders was Sitting Bull, a legendary figure even during his own lifetime. A skilled warrior, statesman, and spiritual guide, he was a member of one of the many nomadic Sioux tribes of the Plains, whose lands stretched from central Canada to Mexico and from the Midwest to the Rocky Mountains. (His particular band, the Hunkpapa Sioux, hunted buffalo and lived mostly in what is now Montana, Wyoming, and the Dakotas.) His fame springs from the major role he played in the defeat of General George Armstrong Custer at the Battle of the Little Bighorn. Sitting Bull's stunning victory made him a symbol of Native American resistance against the United States government—an image that endures to this day—and secured for him a place in history as one of the greatest Indian leaders of all time.

Born near the Grand River in what is now South Dakota around 1831, Sitting Bull was in his early twenties when he first achieved prominence among his people as a leader of a warrior society called the "Strong Hearts"; by the time he reached his mid-twenties he was a respected chief. His rise coincided with the advance of white settlement westward, an invasion that threatened the very existence of the Sioux. Sitting Bull and his tribe managed to avoid the initial conflicts that erupted between Indians and whites on the Plains, particularly during the Civil War when the flow of settlers eased and the U.S. Army was preoccupied back east. But after the war ended, homesteaders, ranchers, railroad workers, and others began to pour into the region in ever-increasing numbers. They in turn pressured the federal government to send in troops to annex the Indians' lands and bring them under control on reservations.

Sitting Bull, however, had no intention of abandoning Sioux territory or traditions. He rejected the Fort Laramie Treaty of 1868 that negotiated a peace agreement between some Sioux and the United States because it restricted his people's freedom to travel and hunt. The situation grew even more tense in 1874, when the discovery of gold in the Black Hills attracted hordes of would-be miners, some of whom illegally entered Sioux lands while federal officials looked the other way. This touched off a series of confrontations between Sitting Bull's warriors and U.S. soldiers.

At a council held at the tribe's Powder River hunting grounds around 1875, Sitting Bull expressed his love for his native land and his contempt for the people who were trying to take it away. His words are reprinted here from T.C. McLuhan's Touch the Earth: A Self-Portrait of Indian Existence, *Outerbridge & Dienstfrey, 1971.*

Behold, my Brothers, the spring has come; the earth has received the embraces of the sun and we shall soon see the results of that love!

Every seed is awakened and so has all animal life. It is through this mysterious power that we too have our being and we therefore yield to our neighbors, even our animal neighbors, the same right as ourselves, to inhabit this land.

Yet, hear me, people, we have now to deal with another race—small and feeble when our fathers first met them but now great overbearing. Strangely enough they have a mind to till the soil and the love of possession is a disease with them. These people have made many rules that the rich may break but the poor may not. They take tithes from the poor and weak to support the rich who rule. They claim this mother of ours, the earth, for their own and fence their neighbors away; they deface her with their buildings and their refuse. That nation is like a spring freshet that overruns its banks and destroys all who are in its path.

We cannot dwell side by side. Only seven years ago we made a treaty by which we were assured that the buffalo country should be left to us forever. Now they threaten to take that away from us. My brothers, shall we submit or shall we say to them: "First kill me before you take possession of my Fatherland. . . ."

Finally, after months of escalating conflict between the Sioux and U.S. troops, exasperated government officials ordered all Sioux hunting bands to report to federal agencies attached to reservations by January 1876. This was completely unacceptable to Sitting Bull and his people, who dreaded the spiritual impoverishment of life spent rooted to one place as farmers. He prepared for all-out war with the whites, and as it turned out, he did not have to wait long. During the spring of 1876, three different U.S. military divisions moved into the Bighorn Valley area of eastern Montana. Their strategy was to launch a multi-pronged attack against the Sioux, one that would ultimately surround and subdue them. What the soldiers did not know, however, was that they were about to face one of the largest groups of Plains Indians ever to gather in a single place—about twelve to fifteen thousand people scattered in encampments along the Little Bighorn River.

On June 17, 1876, Sitting Bull and his warriors clashed with U.S. soldiers under the command of General George Crook in the Battle of the Rosebud. Forced into retreat, the Army made plans to strike again. On June 24, a regiment that had been sent out to do some scouting in advance of the main body of troops spotted an Indian village. The officer in charge, a cocky and flamboyant Civil War veteran by the name of General George Armstrong Custer, grossly underestimated the number of warriors nearby (which included members of both the Sioux and Cheyenne tribes) and attacked the next morning. This fateful—and foolish—decision led to the deaths of Custer and 264 of his men in the famous Battle of the Little Bighorn.

Ironically, "Custer's Last Stand" also represented the last major stand of Plains Indians against white expansion into their territory. Sitting Bull, who had helped mastermind the victory at Little Bighorn, was subsequently vilified in the newspapers and magazines of the day as a vicious savage who had cruelly massacred a courageous and heroic group of soldiers. He soon fled to Canada with some of his followers. The loose alliance of Plains tribes that he had fashioned fell apart, and many of the smaller bands of Sioux surrendered in the face of overwhelming U.S. military might.

Sitting Bull did not give up, however. Despite the hardships (including near starvation) he and his people endured in Canada, they refused to return home and accept life on a reservation. At one point, a group of U.S. government officials led by General Alfred Terry visited him in exile and urged him to surrender. Sitting Bull replied with a long summary of the white man's history of breaking promises and treaties. His concluding remarks, reprinted below from T.C. McLuhan's Touch the Earth: A Self-Portrait of Indian Existence *(Outerbridge & Dienstfrey, 1971), underscored his resolve not to become "a reservation Indian."*

For sixty-four years you have persecuted my people. I ask you what we have done to cause us to depart from our own country? I will tell you. We had no place to go, so we took refuge here. It was on this side of the boundary I first learned to shoot and be a man. For that reason I have come back. I was kept ever on the move until I was compelled to forsake my own lands and come here. I was raised close to, and today shake hands with, these people. [He strides toward Canadian Commissioner Macleod and Superintendent Walsh, shakes hands with them, then turns to the American commissioners.]

That is the way I came to know these people, and that is the way I propose to live. We did not give you our country; you took it from us. Look how I stand with these people [pointing to the Canadian North West Mounted Police]. Look at me. You think I am a fool, but you are a greater fool than I am. This house, the home of the English, is a medicine house [the abode of truth] and you come here to tell us lies. We do not want to hear them. Now I have said enough. You can go back. Say no more. Take your lies with you. I will stay with these people. The country we came from belonged to us; you took it from us; we will live here.

Finally, the hardships became too much to bear; on July 19, 1881, Sitting Bull and most of his followers crossed the border into the United States and surrendered to U.S. authorities. He spent much of the next two years as a prisoner and then was allowed to settle on the Standing Rock Indian Reservation, which straddles the border between the present-day states of North and South Dakota. It was there, in August 1883, that Sitting Bull testified before members of a special U.S. Senate committee that had been ordered to investigate conditions among Indians living in the former Sioux territory. His plea on behalf of the welfare of his people is reprinted here from W.C. Vanderwerth's Indian Oratory: Famous Speeches by Noted Indian Chieftains, *University of Oklahoma Press, 1971.*

I came in with a glad heart to shake hands with you, my friends, for I feel that I have displeased you. And here I am to apologize to you for my bad conduct and to take back what I said.

I will take it back because I consider I have made your hearts bad. I heard that you were coming here from the Great Father's house some time before you came, and I have been sitting here like a prisoner waiting for some one to release me. I was looking for you everywhere, and I considered that when we talked with you it was the same as if we were talking with the Great Father. And I believe that what I pour out from the heart the Great Father will hear.

What I take back is what I said to cause the people to leave the council, and want to apologize for leaving myself. The people acted like children, and I am sorry for it. I was very sorry when I found out that your intentions were good and entirely different from what I supposed they were.

"I feel that my country has gotten a bad name. . . . You are the only people now who can give it a good name, and I want you to take good care of my country and respect it."

Now I will tell you my mind and I will tell everything straight. I know the Great Spirit is looking down upon me from above, and will hear what I say, therefore I will do my best to talk straight. And I am in hopes that some one will listen to my wishes and help me to carry them out.

I have always been a chief, and have been made chief of all the land. Thirty-two years ago I was present at the councils with the white man, and at the time of the Fort Rice council I was on the prairie listening to it. And since then a great many questions have been asked me about it, and I always said, wait. And then the Black Hills council was held, and they asked me to give up that land, and I said they must wait. I remember well all the promises that were made about that land because I have thought a great deal about them since that time.

Of course, I know that the Great Spirit provided me with animals for my food, but I did not stay out on the prairie because I did not wish to accept the offers of the Great Father, for I sent in a great many of my people and I told them that the Great Father was providing for them and keeping his agreements with them. And I was sending the Indians word all the time I was out that they must remember their agreements and fulfill them, and carry them out straight.

When the English authorities were looking for me I heard that the Great Father's people were looking for me, too. I was not lost. I knew where I was going all the time. Previous to that time, when a Catholic priest called White Hair [meaning Bishop Marty] came to see me, I told him all these things plainly. He told me the wishes of the Great Father, and I made promises which I meant to fulfill, and did fulfill. And when I went over into the British possessions he followed me, and I told him everything that was in my heart, and sent him back to tell the Great Father what I told him.

And General [Alfred] Terry sent me word afterwards to come in, because he had big promises to make me. And I sent him word that I would not throw my country away; that I considered it all mine still, and I wanted him to wait just four years for me; that I had gone over there to attend to some business of my own, and my people were doing just as any other people would do. If a man loses anything and goes back and looks carefully for it be will find it, and that is what the Indians are doing now when they ask you to give them the things that were promised them in the past. And I do not consider that they should be treated like beasts, and that is the reason I have grown up with the feelings I have.

Whatever you wanted of me I have obeyed, and I have come when you called me. The Great Father sent me word that whatever he had against me in the past had been forgiven and thrown aside, and he would have nothing against me in the future, and I accepted his promises and came in. And he told me not to step aside from the white man's path, and I told him I would not, and I am doing my best to travel in that path.

I feel that my country has gotten a bad name, and I want it to have a good name. It used to have a good name, and I sit sometimes and wonder who it is that has given it a bad name. You are the only people now who can give it a good name, and I want you to take good care of my country and respect it.

When we sold the Black Hills we got a very small price for it, and not what we ought to have received. I used to think that the size of the payments would remain the same all the time, but they are growing smaller all the time.

I want you to tell the Great Father everything I have said, and that we want some benefits from the promises he has made to us. And I don't think I should be tormented with anything about giving up any part of my land until those promises are fulfilled. I would rather wait until that time, when I will be ready to transact any business he may desire.

I consider that my country takes in the Black Hills, and runs from the Powder River to the Missouri, and that all of this land belongs to me. Our reservation is not as large as we want it to be, and I suppose the Great Father owes us money now for land he has taken from us in the past.

You white men advise us to follow your ways, and therefore I talk as I do. When you have a piece of land, and anything trespasses on it, you catch it and keep it until you get damages, and I am doing the same thing now. And I want you to tell this to the Great Father for me. I am looking into the future for the benefit of my children, and that is what I mean, when I say I want my country taken care of for me.

My children will grow up here, and I am looking ahead for their benefit, and for the benefit of my children's children, too; and even beyond that again. I sit here and look around me now, and I see my people starving, and I want the Great Father to make an increase in the amount of food that is allowed us now, so that they may be able to live. We want cattle to butcher—I want to kill three hundred head of cattle at a time. That is the way you live, and we want to live the same way. This is what I want you to tell the Great Father when you go back home.

If we get the things we want, our children will be raised like the white children. When the Great Father told me to live like his people I told him to send me six teams of mules, because that is the way white people make a living, and I wanted my children to have these

Sitting Bull

things to help them to make a living. I also told him to send me two spans of horses with wagons, and everything else my children would need. I also asked for a horse and buggy for my children. I was advised to follow the ways of the white man, and that is why I asked for those things.

I never ask for anything that is not needed. I also asked for a cow and a bull for each family, so that they can raise cattle of their own. I asked for four yokes of oxen and wagons with them. Also a yoke of oxen and a wagon for each of my children to haul wood with.

It is your own doing that I am here. You sent me here, and advised me to live as you do, and it is not right for me to live in poverty. I asked the Great Father for hogs, male and female, and for male and female sheep for my children to raise from. I did not leave out anything in the way of animals that the white men have; I asked for every one of them. I want you to tell the Great Father to send me some agricultural implements, so that I will not be obliged to work bare-handed.

Whatever he sends to this agency our agent will take care of for us, and we will be satisfied because we know he will keep everything right. Whatever is sent here for us he will be pleased to take care of for us. I want to tell you that our rations have been reduced to almost nothing, and many of the people have starved to death.

Now I beg of you to have the amount of rations increased so that our children will not starve, but will live better than they do now. I want clothing, too, and I will ask for that, too. We want all kinds of clothing for our people. Look at the men around here and see how poorly dressed they are. We want some clothing this month, and when it gets cold we want more to protect us from the weather.

That is all I have to say.

Except for a brief period during the mid-1880s when he left to join Buffalo Bill Cody's Wild West Show, a traveling exhibition that was supposed to give audiences a taste of life on the Plains, Sitting Bull remained on the Standing Rock Reservation for the rest of his life. There he became a good farmer and rancher; he even sent his children to the reservation school. At the same time, Sitting Bull tried to keep as much of the Sioux culture alive as possible despite increasing pressure on the tribe to assimilate. He also continued to speak out forcefully against the corrupt practices of many Indian commissioners, particularly in light of their attempts to coerce more land from the Sioux. On one such occasion in 1889, Sitting Bull addressed a gathering of his fellow Indians and denounced the latest round of broken promises and worthless treaties. His speech to them is reprinted here from The Way: An Anthology of American Indian Literature, *edited by Shirley Hill Witt and Stan Steiner, Knopf, 1972.*

Friends and Relatives: Our minds are again disturbed by the Great Father's representatives, the Indian Agent, the squaw-men, the mixed-bloods, the interpreters, and the favorite-ration-chiefs. What is it they want of us at this time? They want us to give up another chunk of our tribal land. This is not the first time nor the last time. They will try to gain possession of the last piece of ground we possess. They are again telling us what they intend to do if we agree to their wishes. Have we ever set a price on our land and received such a value? No, we never did. What we got under the former treaties were promises of all sorts. They promised how we are going to live peaceably on the land we still own and how they are going to show us the new ways of living, even told us how we can go to heaven when we die, but all that we realized out of the agreements with the Great Father was, we are dying off in expectation of getting things promised us.

One thing I wish to state at this time is, something tells me that the Great Father's representatives have again brought with them a well-worded paper, containing just what they want but ignoring our wishes in the matter. It is this that they are attempting to drive us to. Our people are blindly deceived. Some are in favor of the proposition, but we who realize that our children and grandchildren may live a little longer must necessarily look ahead and flatly reject the proposition. I, for one, am bitterly opposed to it. The Great Father has proven himself an *unktomi* [trickster] in our past dealings.

When the white people invaded our Black Hills country our treaty agreements were still in force but the Great Father ignored it—pretending to keep out the intruders through military force, and at last failing to keep them out they had to let them come in and take possession of our best part of our tribal possession. Yet the Great Father maintains a very large standing army that can stop anything.

Therefore, I do not wish to consider any proposition to cede any portion of our tribal holdings to the Great Father. If I agree to dispose of any part of our land to the white people I would feel guilty of taking food away from our children's mouths, and I do not wish to be that mean. There are things they tell us sound good to hear, but when they have accomplished their purpose they will go home and will not try to fulfill our agreements with them.

My friends and relatives, let us stand as one family as we did before the white people led us astray.

Sitting Bull's words were spoken during a time of great turmoil among the Plains Indians. This restlessness sprang, in part, from the teachings of a Paiute prophet named Wovoka. During the late 1880s, he claimed that God had appeared to him in a vision and had told him of a dance ritual that would enable Indians to recover their lands, drive away the whites, reunite with their ancestors, and live in peace and prosperity. Known as the Ghost Dance, this ritual found much support among the Plains tribes, and by 1890 many of them were performing it nightly.

Such activities made U.S. authorities very nervous; they feared that the spiritual revival sparked by the Ghost Dance, combined with Sitting Bull's appeals for unity among the Sioux, might well lead to a violent new Indian uprising. On December 15, 1890, two tribal policemen arrived at Sitting Bull's home during a Ghost Dance ceremony with orders to arrest him. A melee erupted, and in the resulting confusion, the policemen shot and killed Sitting Bull, who had resisted being taken into custody.

The tragedy did not end there, however. On December 29, some two to three hundred Sioux followers of Sitting Bull and the Ghost Dance—unarmed men, women, and children who had fled from Standing Rock to seek refuge elsewhere—were massacred by U.S. troops at Wounded Knee, South Dakota. Their deaths quickly led to the decline of the Ghost Dance movement and also ended the Plains Indians' war of resistance against the whites.

SOURCES

Adams, Alexander B., *Sitting Bull: An Epic of the Plains,* Putnam, 1974.

Brown, Dee, *Bury My Heart at Wounded Knee: An Indian History of the American West,* Holt, 1970.

Manzione, Joseph, *I Am Looking to the North for My Life: Sitting Bull, 1876-1881,* University of Utah Press, 1990.

McLuhan, T.C., *Touch the Earth: A Self-Portrait of Indian Existence,* Outerbridge & Dienstfrey, 1971.

Rosenstiel, Annette, *Red and White: Indian Views of the White Man, 1492-1982,* Universe Books, 1983.

Utley, Robert, *The Lance and the Shield: The Life and Times of Sitting Bull,* Holt, 1993.

Vanderwerth, W.C., *Indian Oratory: Famous Speeches by Noted Indian Chieftains,* University of Oklahoma Press, 1971.

Vestal, Stanley, *Sitting Bull, Champion of the Sioux,* University of Oklahoma Press, 1957.

Witt, Shirley Hill, and Stan Steiner, editors, *The Way: An Anthology of American Indian Literature,* Knopf, 1972.

Smohalla

1815(?)–1907

Native American spiritual leader

Smohalla was the founder of the so-called "Dreamer Religion," a messianic philosophy that developed among the Indians of the northwest during the late 1800s in response to increasing white expansion into the territory. Born in eastern Washington State along the Columbia River, Smohalla (whose exact tribal affiliation is unknown) left there around 1850 after quarreling with a local chief. He then traveled for several years, distinguishing himself as a warrior until he was wounded and left for dead during a skirmish with members of another tribe. Upon returning to his homeland—where his sudden reappearance was deemed a miracle—Smohalla told of having visited the Spirit World. His claim that religious truths and supernatural powers had been revealed to him in dreams or in a trance-like state (eventually giving rise to the name of his movement) found a ready audience among those reduced to desperation by disease and the steady loss of land to white settlers.

Smohalla's message was a unique combination of the missionary teachings he had been exposed to as a youngster, Native American beliefs about nature and the environment, and his conviction that Indians should totally reject American culture and return to their own traditions. Although he did not sanction violence, he predicted that one day, with the help of the Great Spirit, all Indian people (both living and dead) would rise up and drive the whites from their lands. At the heart of Smohalla's teachings was his concept of a benevolent Earth Mother, as the following brief but impassioned statement attributed to him makes clear. This oft-quoted plea is reprinted from Literature of the American Indian, *by Thomas E. Sanders and Walter W. Peek (Glencoe Press, 1973.)*

Smohalla's words had a great impact on many Indians of the northwest and often landed him in trouble with U.S. authorities, who occasionally imprisoned him. One of his most notable followers was Chief Joseph of the Nez Perces, a convert from Christianity. He and other Dreamers strongly resisted all attempts to turn them into farmers, a decision that ultimately cost many of them their lives.

My young men shall never work. Men who work cannot dream, and wisdom comes in dreams.

You ask me to plow the ground. Shall I take a knife and tear my mother's breast? Then when I die she will not take me to her bosom to rest.

You ask me to dig for stone. Shall I dig under her skin for bones? Then when I die I cannot enter her body to be born again.

You ask me to cut grass and make hay and sell it, and be rich like the white men. But how dare I cut off my mother's hair?

It is a bad law, and my people cannot obey it. I want my people to stay with me here. All the dead men will come to life again. We must wait here in the house of our fathers and be ready to meet them in the body of our mother.

Smohalla

SOURCES

McLuhan, T.C., *Touch the Earth: A Self-Portrait of Indian Existence,* Outerbridge & Dienstfrey, 1971.

Ruby, Robert H., and John A. Brown, *Dreamer-Prophets of the Columbia Plateau: Smohalla and Skolaskin,* University of Oklahoma Press, 1989.

Sanders, Thomas E., and Walter W. Peek, *Literature of the American Indian,* Glencoe Press, 1973.

Standing Bear (Mochunozhi)

1829–1908

Native American chief of the Ponca tribe

In 1879, the sad plight of Standing Bear and his people captured national attention as a result of one of the most famous court cases in Native American history. At its heart was the debate over the "personhood" of Indians—that is, whether they were entitled to enjoy the same individual civil rights guaranteed to whites under the terms of the Constitution. By declaring that "an Indian is a 'person' within the meaning of the laws of the United States," the federal judge who presided over Standing Bear's fate became the first government official to recognize the rights of individual Indians to personal freedom and legal protection.

Standing Bear's story had begun some twenty years earlier when the Poncas, a peaceful tribe whose homeland was in what is now Nebraska, reached an agreement with the U.S. government that established their territorial boundaries. Ten years later, however, the U.S. government negotiated a treaty with the Sioux tribe (longstanding enemies of the Poncas) that effectively overturned the prior agreement by granting Ponca lands to the Sioux without the Poncas' knowledge or consent. This injustice was compounded in 1877 when, by order of Congress, the U.S. Army forcibly relocated the Poncas hundreds of miles away to Indian Territory in present-day Oklahoma. The journey was a heartbreaking one; of the nearly six hundred Poncas who made the trip, about one-third died of disease or starvation within months after their arrival, and many others were left sick and disabled.

Among the dead were two of Chief Standing Bear's children. Determined to return the bones of his son to the tribe's ancestral burial grounds, Standing Bear left Indian Territory during the winter of 1878-79, allegedly without asking permission from the local Indian agent as federal law required. In the company of thirty of his people, he slowly made his way back to Nebraska. There the Poncas took refuge with a tribe to whom they were closely linked by marriage and tradition, the Omahas. It was on the Omaha reservation that Standing Bear was arrested by U.S. Army officers in April 1879.

The arrest sparked disbelief and outrage among the Omahas. The story garnered even wider attention after Standing Bear recounted the Poncas' experiences to a reporter in Omaha and then repeated it to members of an Omaha church. His words, reprinted here from Peter Nabokov's Native American Testimony: A Chronicle of Indian-White Relations from Prophecy to the Present, 1492-

1992, (Penguin Books, 1991), paint a vivid and tragic picture of the impact of forced resettlement.

We lived on our land as long as we can remember. No one knows how long ago we came there. The land was owned by our tribe as far back as memory of men goes. We were living quietly on our farms. All of a sudden one white man came. We had no idea what for. This was the inspector. He came to our tribe with Reverend Mr. Hinman. These two, with the agent, James Lawrence, they made our trouble.

Standing Bear

They said the president told us to pack up—that we must move to the Indian Territory.

The inspector said to us: "The president says you must sell this land. He will buy it and pay you the money, and give you new land in the Indian Territory."

We said to him: "We do not know your authority. You have no right to move us till we have had council with the president."

We said to him: "When two persons wish to make a bargain, they can talk together and find out what each wants, and then make their agreement."

We said to him: "We do not wish to go. When a man owns anything, he does not let it go till he has received payment for it."

We said to him: "We will see the president first."

He said to us: "I will take you to see the new land. If you like it, then you can see the president, and tell him so. If not, then you can see him and tell him so." And he took all ten of our chiefs down. I went, and Bright Eyes' uncle went. [Bright Eyes, also known as Susette LaFlesche, was an Omaha who became an advocate for the Poncas; her uncle, White Swan, was a Ponca leader.] He took us to look at three different pieces of land. He said we must take one of the three pieces, so the president said. After he took us down there, he said: "No pay for the land you left."

We said to him: "You have forgotten what you said before we started. You said we should have pay for our land. Now you say not. You told us then you were speaking truth."

All these three men took us down there. The man got very angry. He tried to compel us to take one of the three pieces of land. He told us to be brave. He said to us: "If you do not accept these, I will leave you here alone. You are one thousand miles from home. You have no money. You have no interpreter, and you cannot speak the language." And he went out and slammed the door. The man talked to us from long before sundown till it was nine o'clock at night.

We said to him: "We do not like this land. We could not support ourselves. The water is bad. Now send us to Washington, to tell the president, as you promised."

He said to us: "The president did not tell me to take you to Washington; neither did he tell me to take you home."

We said to him: "You have the Indian money you took to bring us down here. That money belongs to us. We would like to have some of it. People do not give away food for nothing. We must have money to buy food on the road."

He said to us: "I will not give you a cent."

We said to him: "We are in a strange country. We cannot find our way home. Give us a pass, that people may show us our way."

He said: "I will not give you any."

We said to him: "This interpreter is ours. We pay him. Let him go with us."

He said: "You shall not have the interpreter. He is mine, and not yours."

We said to him: "Take us at least to the railroad; show us the way to that."

And he would not. He left us right there. It was winter. We started for home on foot. At night we slept in haystacks. We barely lived till morning, it was so cold. We had nothing but our blankets. We took the ears of corn that had dried in the fields; we ate it raw. The soles of our moccasins wore out. We went barefoot in the snow. We were nearly dead when we reached the Otoe Reserve. It had been fifty days. We stayed there ten days to strengthen up, and the Otoes gave each of us a pony. The agent of the Otoes told us he had received a telegram from the inspector, saying that the Indian chiefs had run away; not to give us food or shelter, or help in any way. The agent said: "I would like to understand. Tell me all that has happened. Tell me the truth. . . ."

Then we told our story to the agent and to the Otoe chiefs—how we had been left down there to find our way.

The agent said: "I can hardly believe it possible that anyone could have treated you so. The inspector was a poor man to have done this. If I had taken chiefs in this way, I would have brought them home; I could not have left them there."

In seven days we reached the Omaha Reservation. Then we sent a telegram to the president; asked him if he had authorized this thing. We waited three days for the answer. No answer came.

In four days we reached our own home. We found the inspector there. While we were gone, he had come to our people and told them to move.

Our people said: "Where are our chiefs? What have you done with them? Why have you not brought them back? We will not move till our chiefs come back."

Then the inspector told them: "Tomorrow you must be ready to move. If you are not ready you will be shot." Then the soldiers came to the doors with their bayonets, and ten families were frightened. The soldiers brought wagons, they put their things in and were carried away. The rest of the tribe would not move. . . .

Then, when he found that we would not go, he wrote for more soldiers to come.

Then the soldiers came, and we locked our doors, and the women and children hid in the woods. Then the soldiers drove all the people [to] the other side of the river, all but my brother Big Snake and I. We did not go; and the soldiers took us and carried us away to a fort and put us in jail. There were eight officers who held council with us after we got there. The commanding officer said: "I have received four messages telling me to send my soldiers after you. Now, what have you done?"

Then we told him the whole story. Then the officer said: "You have done no wrong. The land is yours; they had no right to take it from you. Your title is good. I am here to protect the weak, and I have no right to take you; but I am a soldier, and I have to obey orders."

He said: "I will telegraph to the president, and ask him what I shall do. We do not think these three men had any authority to treat you as they have done. When we own a piece of land, it belongs to us till we sell it and pocket the money."

Then he brought a telegram, and said he had received answer from the president. The president said he knew nothing about it.

They kept us in jail ten days. Then they carried us back to our home. The soldiers collected all the women and children together; then they called all the chiefs together in council; and then they took wagons and went round and broke open the houses. When we came back from the council, we found the women and children surrounded by a guard of soldiers.

They took our reapers, mowers, hay rakes, spades, ploughs, bedsteads, stoves, cupboards, everything we had on our farms, and put them in one large building. Then they put into the wagons such things as they could carry. We told them that we would rather die than leave our lands; but we could not help ourselves. They took us down. Many died on the road. Two of my children died. After we reached the new land, all my horses died. The water was very bad. All our cattle died; not one was left. I stayed till one hundred and fifty-eight of my people had died. Then I ran away with thirty of my people, men and women and children. Some of the children were orphans. We were three months on the road. We were weak and sick and starved. When we reached the Omaha Reserve the Omahas gave us a piece of land, and we were in a hurry to plough it and put in wheat. While we were working, the soldiers came and arrested us. Half of us were sick. We would rather have died than have been carried back; but we could not help ourselves.

Later that year, Standing Bear shared this same moving story with audiences in the eastern United States while on a lecture tour with Indian rights activist Susette LaFlesche. He usually appeared on stage in traditional Ponca attire while LaFlesche interpreted for him and offered an eloquent plea of her own. Once the true reasons behind his decision to leave Indian Territory became more widely known, many Americans who were appalled by his treatment at the hands of government officials bombarded Congress with angry letters. Federal authorities nevertheless decided to pursue the case against him in court, arguing that under the Constitution, Indians were not persons and therefore had no rights. Standing Bear, they insisted, had to return to Indian Territory despite reports that he had severed his ties to the Poncas, disbanded the tribe, and expressed a desire to blend into American society.

Federal Judge Elmer S. Dundy ultimately ruled in favor of Standing Bear, noting in his written opinion that in fifteen years on the bench, he had "never been called upon to hear or decide a case that appealed so strongly to my sympathy." He concluded that Indians were indeed persons under the laws of the nation and that no one therefore had the authority to hold Standing Bear in custody or force him to return to Indian Territory.

Standing Bear was at last allowed to complete the sad task that had brought him back to Nebraska in the first place. At the urging of Susette LaFlesche and others, Congress launched an investigation into the Poncas' claims against the government and in 1880 granted them land for a reservation in Nebraska. There Standing Bear lived out his remaining years.

SOURCES

Anderson, Judith, *Outspoken Women: Speeches by American Women Reformers, 1635–1935,* Kendall/Hunt Publishing Company, 1984.

Armstrong, Virginia Irving, *I Have Spoken: American History Through the Voices of the Indians,* Sage Books, 1971.

Brown, Dee, *Bury My Heart at Wounded Knee: An Indian History of the American West,* Holt, 1970.

Brown, Marion M., *Susette LaFlesche: Advocate for Native American Rights,* Children's Press, 1992.

Clifton, James A., editor, *On Being and Becoming Indian: Biographical Studies of North American Frontiers,* Dorsey Press, 1989.

Nabokov, Peter, editor, *Native American Testimony: A Chronicle of Indian-White Relations from Prophecy to the Present, 1492–1992,* Penguin Books, 1991.

Wilson, Dorothy Clarke, *Bright Eyes: The Story of Susette LaFlesche,* McGraw-Hill, 1974.

Maria W. Miller Stewart

1803–1879

African American journalist and women's rights activist

Although her career as an orator lasted less than two years, Maria W. Miller Stewart left an indelible mark on history. At a time when it was considered shocking for a woman to give a public speech, she was the first American-born woman to do so. (Even more shocking in those days was the fact that she appeared before a mixed audience of men and women.) In addition, she was probably the first black woman to lecture on women's rights. Blending religious zeal with reform-minded militancy (and a willingness to be a martyr to her cause), Stewart was one of the earliest advocates of black pride, racial unity, and self-reliance.

A freeborn native of Hartford, Connecticut, Stewart was orphaned at the age of five and was then bound to a minister's family. While she received virtually no formal schooling, she was able to acquire basic reading and writing skills (which she improved upon as an adult) as well as a knowledge of theology and religious rhetoric. At the age of fifteen, she left what had been her home to go to work as a domestic servant. In 1826, she married James W. Stewart, an independent shipping agent based in Boston, and settled into a comfortable life as part of the city's small black middle class. But her husband died just three years into the marriage, and Stewart was left impoverished after a group of dishonest white businessmen and lawyers cheated her out of a substantial inheritance. Depressed by her personal troubles as well as by the death in 1830 of prominent antislavery activist David Walker, she entered a period of introspection that culminated in a religious conversion. As a result of this "born again" experience, she vowed to devote the rest of her life to serving God and her race in the fight against oppression.

Stewart's first foray into activism was an essay she contributed to the Liberator, *a weekly paper founded by abolitionist William Lloyd Garrison. (He later published her speeches as well.) That was in late 1831; in April of 1832, she began her public speaking career with an appearance before the Afric-American Female Intelligence Society in Boston. As is clear from her words, Stewart felt that the task of strengthening the black community economically as well as morally rested with black people themselves—especially black women. Her remarks originally appeared in the April 28, 1832, issue of the* Liberator *and again in the*

1835 book Productions of Mrs. Maria W. Stewart. *The following version of her speech is taken from* Spiritual Narratives *(Oxford University Press, 1988) which contains a reprint of* Productions of Mrs. Maria W. Stewart.

The frowns of the world shall never discourage me, nor its smiles flatter me; for with the help of God I am resolved to withstand the fiery darts of the devil, and the assaults of wicked men. The righteous are as bold as a lion, but the wicked fleeth when no man pursueth. I fear neither men nor devils; for the God in whom I trust is able to deliver me from the rage and malice of my enemies, and from them that rise up against me. The only motive that has prompted me to raise my voice in your behalf, my friends, is because I have discovered that religion is held in low repute among some of us; and purely to promote the cause of Christ and the good of souls, in the hope that others more experienced, more able and talented than myself, might go forward and do likewise. I expect to render a strict, a solemn, and an awful account to God for the motives that have prompted me to exertion, and for those with which I shall address you this evening.

What I have to say, concerns the whole of us as Christians and as a people; and if you will be so kind as to give me a hearing this once, you shall receive the incense of a grateful heart.

The day is coming, my friends, and I rejoice in that day, when the secrets of all hearts shall be manifested before saints and angels, men and devils. It will be a great day of joy and rejoicing to the humble followers of Christ, but a day of terror and dismay to hypocrites and unbelievers. Of that day and hour knoweth no man, no not even the angels in heaven, but the Father only. The dead that are in Christ shall be raised first. Blessed is he that shall have a part in the first resurrection. Ah, methinks I hear the finally impenitent crying, "Rocks and mountains! fall upon us, and hide us from the wrath of the Lamb, and from him that sitteth upon the throne!

High on a cloud our God shall come,
Bright thrones prepare his way;
Thunder and darkness, fire and storm
Lead on the dredful day.

Christ shall descend in the clouds of heaven, surrounded by ten thousand of his saints and angels, and it shall be very tempestuous round about him; and before him shall be gathered all nations, and kindred, and tongues, and people; and every knee shall bow, and every tongue confess—they also that pierced him shall look upon him, and mourn. Then shall the King separate the righteous from the wicked, as a shepherd divideth the sheep from the goats, and shall place the righteous on his right hand, and the wicked upon his left. Then, says Christ, shall be weeping, and wailing, and gnashing of teeth, when ye shall see Abraham and the prophets sitting in the Kingdom of heaven, and ye yourselves thrust out. Then shall the righteous shine forth in the Kingdom of their Father as the sun. He that hath ears to hear, let him hear. The poor despised followers of Christ will not then regret their sufferings here; they shall be carried by angels into Abraham's bosom, and shall be comforted; and the Lord God shall wipe away their tears. You will then be convinced before assembled multitudes, whether they strove to promote the cause of Christ, or whether they sought for gain or applause. "Strive to enter in at the strait gait; for many, I say unto you, shall seek to enter in, and shall not be able. For except your righteousness shall exceed the righteousness of the Scribes and Pharisees, ye shall in no wise enter into the Kingdom of Heaven."

Ah, methinks I see the people lying in wickedness; and as the Lord liveth, and as your souls live, were it not for the few righteous that are to be found among us, we should become as Sodom, and like unto Gomorrah. Christians have too long slumbered and slept; sinners stumbled into hell, and still are stumbling, for the want of Christian exertion; and the devil is going about like a roaring lion, seeking whom he may devour. And I make bold to say, that many who profess the name of Christ at the present day, live so widely different from what becometh the Gospel of our Lord Jesus Christ, that they cannot and they dare not reason to the world upon righteousness and judgment to come.

Be not offended because I tell you the truth, for I believe that God has fired my soul with a holy zeal for his cause. It was God alone who inspired my heart to publish the *Meditations* thereof; and it was done with pure motives of love to your souls, in the hope that Christians might examine themselves, and sinners become pricked in their hearts. It is the word of God, though men and devils may oppose it. It is the word of God; and little did I think that any of the professed followers of Christ would have frowned upon me, and discouraged and hindered its progress.

Ah, my friends, I am speaking as one who expects to give account at the bar of God; I am speaking as a dying mortal to dying mortals. I fear there are many who have named the name of Jesus at the present day that strain at a gnat and swallow a camel; they neither enter into the kingdom of heaven themselves, nor suffer others to enter in. They would pull the motes out of their brother's eye, when they have a beam in their own eye. And were our blessed Lord and Saviour, Jesus Christ, upon the earth, I believe he would say of many that are called by his name, "O ye hypocrites, ye generation of vipers, how can you escape the damnation of hell."

I have enlisted in the holy warfare, and Jesus is my captain; and the Lord's battle I mean to fight, until my voice expire in death. I expect to be hated of all men, and persecuted even unto death for righteousness and the truth's sake.

A few remarks upon moral subjects, and I close. I am a strong advocate for the cause of God, and for the cause of freedom. I am not your enemy, but friend both to you and to your children. Suffer me, then, to express my sentiments just this once, however severe they may appear to be, and then hereafter let me sink into oblivion, and let my name die in forgetfulness.

Had the ministers of the gospel shunned the very appearance of evil; had they faithfully discharged their duty, whether we would have heard them or not; we should have been a very different people from what we now are; but they have kept the truth as it were, hid from our eyes, and have cried, "Peace! Peace!" when there was no peace; they have plastered us up with untempered mortar, and have been as it were blind leaders of their blind.

It appears to me that there are no people under the heavens, so unkind and so unfeeling towards their own, as are the descendants of fallen Africa. I have been something of a traveller in my day; and the general cry amongst the people is, "Our own color are our greatest opposers;" and even the whites say that we are greater enemies towards each other, than they are towards us. Shall we be a hissing and a reproach among the nations of the earth any longer! Shall they laugh us to scorn forever? We might become a highly respectable people; respectable we now consider ourselves, but we might become a highly distinguished and intelligent people. And how? In convincing the world, by our own efforts, however feeble, that nothing is wanting on our part but opportunity. Without these efforts, we shall never be a people, nor our descendants after us.

But God has said that Ethiopia shall stretch forth her hands unto him. True, but God uses means to bring about His purposes; and unless the rising generation manifest a different temper and disposition towards each other from what we have manifested, the generation following will never be an enlightened people. We this day are considered as one of the most degraded races upon the face of the earth. It is useless for us any longer to sit with our hands folded, reproaching the whites; for that will never elevate us. All the nations of the earth have distinguished themselves, and have shown forth a noble and a gallant spirit. Look at the suffering Greeks. Their proud souls revolted at the idea of serving a tyrannical nation, who were no better than themselves, and perhaps not so good. They made a mighty effort and arose; their souls were knit together in the holy bonds of love and union; they were united, and came off victorious. Look at the French in the late revolution! No traitors amongst them, to expose their plans to the crowned heads of Europe! "Liberty or Death!" was their cry. And the Haytians, though they have not been acknowledged as a nation, yet their firmness of character and independence of spirit have been greatly admired and highly applauded. Look at the Poles, a feeble people! They rose against three hundred thousand mighty men of Russia; and though they did not gain the conquest, yet

> *"It is useless for us any longer to sit with our hands folded, reproaching the whites; for that will never elevate us."*

they obtained the name of gallant Poles. And even the wild Indians of the forest are more united than ourselves. Insult one of them, and you insult a thousand. They also have contended for their rights and privileges, and are held in higher repute than we are.

And why is it, my friends, that we are despised above all the nations upon the earth? Is it merely because our skins are tinged with a sable hue, No, nor will I ever believe that it is. What then is it? Oh, it is because that we and our fathers have dealt treacherously one with another, and because many of us now possess that envious and malicious disposition, that we had rather die than see each other rise an inch above a beggar. No gentle methods are used to promote love and friendship amongst us, but much is done to destroy it. Shall we be a hissing and a reproach amongst the nations of the earth any longer? Shall they laugh us to scorn forever?

Ingratitude is one of the worst passions that reigns in the human breast: it is this that cuts the tender fibers of the soul; for it is impossible for us to love those who are ungrateful towards us. "Behold," says that wise man Solomon, counting one by one, "a man have I found in a thousand, but a woman among all these have I not found."

I have sometimes thought, that God had almost departed from among us. And why? Because Christ has said, if we say we love the Father, and hate our brother, we are liars, and the truth is not in us; and certainly if we were the true followers of Christ, I think we could not show such a disposition towards each other as we do: for God is all love.

A lady of high distinction among us, observed to me, that I might never expect your homage. God forbid! I ask it not. But I beseech you to deal with gentleness and godly sincerity towards me; and there is not one of you, my dear friends, who has given me a cup of cold water in the name of the Lord, or soothed the sorrows of my wounded heart, but God will bless, not only you, but your children for it. Cruel indeed, are those that indulge such an opinion respecting me as that.

Finally, I have exerted myself both for your temporal and eternal welfare, as far as I am able; and my soul has been so discouraged within me, that I have almost been induced to exclaim, "Would to God that my tongue hereafter might cleave to the roof of my mouth, and become silent forever!" and then I have felt that the Christian has no time to be idle, and I must be active, knowing that the night of death cometh, in which no man can work; and my mind has become raised to such as extent, that I will willingly die for the cause that I have espoused; for I cannot die in a more glorious cause than in the defence of God and his laws.

O woman, woman! upon you I call; for upon your exertions almost entirely depends whether the rising generations shall be any thing more than we have been or not. O woman, woman! your example is powerful, your influence great; it extends over your husbands and over your children, and throughout the circle of your acquaintance. Then let me exhort you to cultivate among yourselves a spirit of Christian love and unity, having charity one for another, without which all our goodness is as sounding brass, and as a tinkling cymbal. And O, my God, I beseech thee to grant that the nations of the earth may hiss at us no longer! O suffer them not to laugh us to scorn forever!

On September 21 of that same year (1832), also in Boston, came Stewart's historic lecture delivered to a so-called "promiscuous" audience—that is, one consisting of both men and women. Again, her deep religious beliefs are evident in her style, which relied heavily on biblical references and paraphrases. And while Stewart supported abolitionism, she did not make it her focus in this or any other speech. Instead, she identified racism, ignorance, and poverty as the greatest evils confronting both free and enslaved African Americans. The following version of her speech is taken from Productions of Mrs. Maria W. Stewart *as reprinted in* Spiritual Narratives *(Oxford University Press, 1988).*

Why sit ye here and die? If we say we will go to a foreign land, the famine and the pestilence are there, and there we shall die. If we sit here, we shall die. Come let us plead our cause before the whites: if they save us alive, we shall live—and if they kill us, we shall but die.

Methinks I hear a spiritual interrogation—"Who shall go forward, and take off the reproach that is cast upon the people of color? Shall it be a woman?" And my heart made this reply—"If it is thy will, be it even so, Lord Jesus!"

I have heard much respecting the horrors of slavery; but may Heaven forbid that the generality of my color throughout these United States should experience any more of its horrors than to be a servant of servants, or hewers of wood and drawers of water! Tell us no more of southern slavery; for with few exceptions, although I may be very erroneous in my opinion, yet I consider our condition but little better than that. Yet, after all, methinks there are no chains so galling as the chains of ignorance—no fetters so binding as those that bind the soul, and exclude it from the vast field of useful and scientific knowledge. O, had I received the advantages of early education, my ideas would, ere now, have expanded far and wide; but, alas! I possess nothing but moral capability—no teachings but the teachings of the Holy Spirit.

I have asked several individuals of my sex, who transact business for themselves, if providing our girls were to give them the most satisfactory references, they would not be willing to grant them an equal opportunity with others? Their reply has been—for their own part, they had no objection; but as it was not the custom, were they to take them into their employ, they would be in danger of losing the public patronage.

And such is the powerful force of prejudice. Let our girls possess what amiable qualities of soul they may; let their characters be fair and spotless as innocence itself; let their natural taste and ingenuity be what they may; it is impossible for scarce an individual of them to rise above the condition of servants. Ah! why is this cruel and unfeeling distinction? Is it merely because God has made our complexion to vary? If it be, shame to soft, relenting humanity! "Tell it not in Gath! publish it not in the streets of Askelon!" Yet, after all, methinks were the American free people of color to turn their attention more assiduously to moral worth and intellectual improvement, this would be the result: prejudice would gradually diminish, and the whites would be compelled to say, unloose those fetters!

Though black their skins as shades
of night,
Their hearts are pure, their souls
are white.

Few white persons of either sex, who are calculated for anything else, are willing to spend their lives and bury their talents in performing mean, servile labor. And such is the horrible idea that I entertain respecting a life of servitude, that if I conceived of there being no possibility of my rising above the condition of a servant, I would gladly hail death as a welcome messenger. O, horrible idea, indeed! to possess noble souls aspiring after high and honorable acquirements, yet confined by the chains of ignorance and poverty to lives of continual drudgery and toil. Neither do I know of any who have enriched themselves by spending their lives as house-domestics, washing windows, shaking carpets, brushing boots, or tending upon gentlemen's tables. I can but die but expressing my sentiments; and I am as willing to die by the sword as the pestilence; for I am a true born American; your blood flows in my veins, and your spirit fires my breast.

> ***"Methinks there are no chains so galling as the chains of ignorance—no fetters so binding as those that bind the soul . . ."***

I observed a piece in the *Liberator* a few months since, stating that the colonizationists had published a work respecting us, asserting that we were lazy and idle. I confute them on that point. Take us generally as a people, we are neither lazy nor idle; and considering how little we have to excite or stimulate us, I am almost astonished that there are so many industrious and ambitious ones to be found; although I acknowledge, with extreme sorrow, that there are some who never were and never will be serviceable to society. And have you not a similar class among yourselves?

Again. It was asserted that we were "a ragged set, crying for liberty." I reply to it, the whites have so long and so loudly proclaimed the theme of equal rights and privileges, that our souls have caught the flame also, ragged as we are. As far as our merit deserves, we feel a common desire to rise above the condition of servants and drudges. I have learnt, by bitter experience, that continual hard labor deadens the energies of the soul, and benumbs the faculties of the mind; the ideas become confined, the mind barren, and, like the scorching sands of Arabia, produces nothing; or, like the uncultivated soil, brings forth thorns and thistles.

Again, continual hard labor irritates our tempers and sours our dispositions; the whole system becomes worn out with toil and fatigue; nature herself becomes almost exhausted, and we care but little whether we live or die. It is true, that the free people of color throughout these United States are neither bought nor sold, nor under the lash of the cruel driver; many obtain a comfortable support; but few, if any, have an opportunity of becoming rich and independent; and the employments we most pursue are as unprofitable to us as the spider's web or the floating bubbles that vanish into air. As servants, we are respected; but let us presume to aspire any higher, our employer regards us no longer. And were it not that the King eternal has declared that Ethiopia shall stretch forth her hands unto God, I should indeed despair.

I do not consider it derogatory, my friends, for persons to live out to service. There are many whose inclination leads them to aspire no higher; and I would highly commend the performance of almost any thing for an honest livelihood; but where constitutional strength is wanting, labor of this kind, in its mildest form, is painful. And doubtless many are the prayers that have ascended to Heaven from Afric's daughters for strength to perform their work. Oh, many are the tears that have been shed for the want of that strength! Most of our color have dragged out a miserable existence of servitude from the cradle to the grave. And what literary acquirements can be made, or useful knowledge derived, from either maps, books, or charts, by those who continually drudge from Monday morning until Sunday noon? O, ye fairer sisters, whose hands are never soiled, whose nerves and muscles are never strained, go learn by experience! Had we had the opportunity that you have had, to improve our moral and mental faculties, what would have hindered our intellects from being as bright, and our manners from being as dignified as yours? Had it been our lot to have been nursed in the lap of affluence and ease, and to have basked beneath the smiles and sunshine of fortune, should we not have naturally supposed that we were never made to toil? And why are not our forms as delicate, and our constitutions as slender, as yours? Is not the workmanship as curious and complete? Have pity upon us, have pity upon us, O ye who have hearts to feel for others' woes; for the hand of God has touched us. Owing to the disadvantages under which we labor, there are many flowers among us that are

> *—born to bloom unseen,*
> *And waste their fragrance on the desert air.*

My beloved brethren, as Christ has died in vain for those who will not accept of offered mercy, so will it be vain for the advocates of freedom to spend their breath in our behalf, unless with united hearts and souls you make some mighty efforts to raise your sons and daughters from the horrible state of servitude and degradation in which they are placed. It is upon you that woman depends; she can do but little besides using her influence: and it is for her sake and yours that I have come forward and made myself a hissing and a reproach among the people; for I am also one of the wretched and miserable daughters of the descendants of fallen Africa. Do you ask, why are you wretched and miserable? I reply, look at many of the most worthy and interesting of us doomed to spend our lives in gentlemen's kitchens. Look at our young men, smart, active, and energetic, with souls filled with ambitious fire; if they look forward, alas! what are their prospects? They can be nothing but the humblest laborers, on account of their dark complexions; hence many of them lose their ambition, and become worthless. Look at our middle-aged men, clad in their rusty plaids and coats; in winter, every cent they earn goes to buy their wood and pay their rents; their poor wives also toil beyond their strength, to held support their families. Look at our aged sires, whose heads are whitened with the frosts of seventy winters, with their old wood-saws on their backs. Alas, what keeps us so? Prejudice, ignorance, and poverty. But ah! methinks our oppression is soon to come to an end; yea, before the Majesty of heaven, our groans and cries have reached the ears of the Lord of Sabaoth. As the prayers and tears of Christians will avail the finally impenitent nothing; neither will the prayers and tears of the friends of humanity avail us any thing, unless we possess a spirit of virtuous emulation within our breasts. Did the pilgrims, when they first landed on these shores, quietly compose themselves, and say, "The Britons have all the money and all the power, and we must continue their servants forever?" Did they sluggishly sigh and say, "Our lot is hard, the Indians own the soil, and we cannot cultivate it?" No; they first made powerful efforts to raise themselves, and then God raised up those illustrious patriots, WASHINGTON and LAFAYETTE, to assist and defend them. And, my brethren, have you made a powerful effort? Have you prayed the Legislature for mercy's sake to grant you all the rights and privileges of free citizens, that your daughters may rise to that degree of respectability which true merit deserves, and your sons above the service situations which most of them fill?

On September 21, 1833, Stewart delivered her farewell address to an audience in Boston. Her precise reason for withdrawing from public life is unclear; as she indicates in her speech (reprinted here from Spiritual Narratives, *Oxford University Press, 1988), it may have been because she was subjected to considerable criticism as an outspoken woman with strong religious views. In any event, before the end of the year she had left Boston for New York City, where she taught school for several years and associated with some of the city's black intellectuals as a member of two ladies' literary societies. Later, she moved to Baltimore and then to Washington, D.C., where she spent the rest of her life.*

Is this vile world a friend to grace,
To help me on to God?

Ah no! For it is with great tribulation that any shall enter through the gates into the holy city.

My respected friends, you have heard me observe that the shortness of time, the certainty of death, and the instability of all things here, induce me to turn my thoughts from earth to heaven. Borne down with a heavy load of sin and shame, my conscience filled with remorse; considering the throne of God forever guiltless, and my own eternal condemnation as just, I was at last brought to accept of salvation as a free gift, in and through the merits of a crucified Redeemer. Here I was brought to see,

'Tis not by works of righteousness
That our own hands have done,
But we are saved by grace alone,
Abounding through the Son.

After these convictions, in imagination I found myself sitting at the feet of Jesus, clothed in my right mind. For I before had been like a ship tossed to and fro, in a storm at sea. Then was I glad when I realized the dangers I had escaped; and then I consecrated my soul and body, and all the powers of my mind to his service, from that time, henceforth; yea, even for evermore, amen.

I found that religion was full of benevolence; I found there was joy and peace in believing, and I felt as though I was commanded to come our from the world and be separate; to go forward and be baptized. Methought I heard a spiritual interrogation, are you able to drink of that cup that I have drank of? And to be baptized with the baptism that I have been baptized with? And my heart made this reply: Yea, Lord, I am able. Yet amid these bright hopes, I was filled with apprehensive fears, lest they were false. I found that sin still lurked within; it was hard for me to renounce all for Christ, when I saw my earthly prospects blasted. O, how bitter was that cup. Yet I drank it to its very dregs. It was hard for me to say, thy will be done; yet I was made to bend and kiss the rod. I was at last made willing to be any thing or nothing, for my Redeemer's sake. Like many, I was anxious to retain the world in one hand, and religion in the other. "Ye cannot serve God and mammon," sounded in my ear, and with giant-strength, I cut off my right hand, as it were, and plucked out my right eye, and cast them from me, thinking it better to enter life halt and maimed, rather than having two hands or eyes to be cast into hell. Thus ended these mighty conflicts, and I received this heart-cheering promise, "That neither death, nor life, nor principalities, nor powers, nor things present, nor things to come, should be able to separate me from the love of Jesus Christ, our Lord."

And truly, I can say with St. Paul, that at my conversion, I came to the people in the fullness of the gospel of grace. Having spent a few months in the city of—, previous, I saw the flourishing condition of their churches, and the progress they were making in their Sabbath Schools. I visited their Bible Classes and heard of the union that existed in their Female Associations. On my arrival here, not finding scarce an individual who felt interested in these subjects, and but few of the whites, except Mr. Garrison, and his friend Mr. Knapp; and hearing that those gentlemen had observed that female influence was powerful, my soul became fired with a holy zeal for your cause; every nerve and muscle in me was engaged in your behalf. I felt that I had a great work to perform; and was in haste to make a profession of my faith in Christ, that I might be about my Father's business. Soon after I made this profession, the Spirit of God came before me, and I spake before many. When going home, reflecting on what I had said, I felt ashamed, and knew not where I should hide myself. A something said within my breast, "press forward, I will be with thee." And my heart made this reply, Lord, if thou wilt be with me, then will I speak for thee so long as I live. And thus far I have every reason to believe that it is the divine influence of the Holy Spirit operating upon my heart that could possibly induce me to make the feeble and unworthy efforts that I have.

But to begin my subject: "Ye have heard that it hath been said, whoso is angry with his brother without a cause, shall be in danger of the judgment; and whoso shall say to his brother, Raca, shall be in danger of the council. But whosoever shall say, thou fool, shall be in danger of hell-fire." For several years my heart was in continual sorrow. And I believe that the Almighty beheld from his holy habitation, the affliction wherewith I was afflicted, and heard the false misrepresentations wherewith I was misrepresented, and there was none to help. Then I cried unto the Lord in my troubles. And thus for wise and holy purposes, best known to himself, he has raised me in the midst of my enemies, to vindicate my wrongs before this people; and to reprove them for sin, as I have reasoned to them of righteousness and judgment to come. "For as the heavens are higher than the earth, so are his ways above our ways, and his thoughts above our thoughts." I believe, that for wise and holy purposes, best known to himself, he hath unloosed my tongue and put his word into my mouth, in order to confound and put all those to shame that have rose up against me. For he hath clothed my face with steel, and lined my forehead with brass. He hath put his testimony within me, and engraven his seal on my forehead. And with these weapons I have indeed set the fiends of earth and hell at defiance.

What if I am a woman; is not the God of ancient times the God of these modern days? Did he not raise up Deborah, to be a mother, and a judge in Israel? Did not queen Esther save the lives of the Jews? And Mary Magdalene first declare the resurrection of Christ from the dead? Come, said the woman of Samaria, and see a man that hath told me all things that ever I did, is not this the Christ? St. Paul declared that it was a shame for a woman to speak in public, yet our great High Priest and Advocate did not condemn the woman for a more notorious offence than this; neither will he condemn this worthless worm. The bruised reed he will not break, and the smoking flax he will not quench, till he send forth judgment unto victory. Did St. Paul but know of our wrongs and deprivations, I presume he would make no objections to our pleading in public for our rights. Again; holy women ministered unto Christ and the apostles; and women of refinement in all ages, more or less, have had a voice in moral, religious and political subjects. Again; why the Almighty hath imparted unto me the power of speaking thus, I cannot tell. "And Jesus lifted up his voice and said, I thank thee, O Father, Lord of heaven and earth, that thou hast hid these things from the wise and prudent, and hast revealed them unto babes: even so, Father, for so it seemed good in thy sight."

But to convince you of the high opinion that was formed of the capacity and ability of woman, by the ancients, I would refer you to "Sketches of the Fair Sex." Read to the fifty-first page, and you will find that several of the northern nations imagined that women could look into futurity, and that they had about them, an inconceivable something, approaching to divinity. Perhaps that idea was only the effect of the sagacity common to the sex, and the advantages which their natural address gave them over rough and simple warriors. Perhaps, also, those barbarians, surprised at the influence which beauty has over force, were led to ascribe to the supernatural attraction, a charm which they could not comprehend. A belief, however, that the Deity more readily communicates himself to women, has at one time or other, prevailed in every quarter of the earth; not only among the Germans and the Britons, but all the people of Scandinavia were possessed of it. Among the Greeks, women delivered the Oracles; the respect the Romans paid to the Sybils, is well known. The Jews had their prophetesses. The prediction of the Egyptian women obtained much credit at Rome, even under the Emperors. And in the most barbarous nations, all things that have the appearance of being supernatural, the mysteries of religion, the secrets of physic, and the rites of magic, were in the possession of women.

If such women as are here described have once existed, be no longer astonished then, my brethren and friends, that God at this eventful period should raise up your own females to strive, by their example both in public and private, to assist those who are endeavoring to stop the strong current of prejudice that flows so profusely against us at present. No longer ridicule their efforts, it will be counted for sin. For God makes use of feeble means sometimes, to bring about his most exalted purposes.

In the fifteenth century, the general spirit of this period is worthy of observation. We might then have seen women preaching and mixing themselves in controversies. Women occupying the chairs of Philosophy and Justice; women haranguing in Latin before the Pope; women writing in Greek, and studying in Hebrew; nuns were Poetesses, and women of quality Divines; and young girls who had studied Eloquence, would with the sweetest countenances, and the most plaintive voices, pathetically exhort the Pope and the Christian Princes, to declare war against the Turks. Women in those days devoted their leisure hours to contemplation and study. The religious spirit which has animated women in all ages, showed itself at this time. It has made them, by turns, martyrs, apostles, warriors, and concluded in making them divines and scholars.

Why cannot a religious spirit animate us now? Why cannot we become divines and scholars? Although learning is somewhat requisite, yet recollect that those great apostles, Peter and James, were ignorant and unlearned. They were taken from the fishing boat, and made fishers of men.

In the thirteenth century, a young lady of Bologne, devoted herself to the study of the Latin language, and of the Laws. At the age of twenty-three she pronounced a funeral oration in Latin, in the great church of Bologne. And to be admitted as an orator, she had neither need of indulgence on account of her youth or of her sex. At the age of twenty-six, she took the degree of Doctor of Laws, and began publicly to expound the Institutions of Justinian. At the age of thirty, her great reputation raised her to a chair, where she taught the law to a prodigious concourse of scholars from all nations. She joined the charms and accomplishments of a woman to all the knowledge of a man. And such was the power of her eloquence, that her beauty was only admired when her tongue was silent.

"It is not the color of the skin that makes the man or the woman, but the principle formed in the soul."

What if such women as are here described should rise among our sable race? And it is not impossible. For it is not the color of the skin that makes the man or the woman, but the principle formed in the soul. Brilliant wit will shine, come from whence it will; and genius and talent will not hide the brightness of its lustre.

But, to return to my subject; the mighty work of reformation has begun among this people. The dark clouds of ignorance are dispersing. The light of science is bursting forth. Knowledge is beginning to flow, nor will its moral influence be extinguished till its refulgent rays have spread over us from East to West, and from North to South. Thus far is this mighty work begun, but not as yet accomplished. Christians must awake from their slumbers. Religion must flourish among them before the church will be built up in its purity, or immorality be suppressed.

Yet, notwithstanding your prospects are thus fair and bright, I am about to leave you, perhaps, never more to return. For I find it is no use for me as an individual to try to make myself useful among my color in this city. It was contempt for my moral and religious opinions in private that drove me thus before a public. Had experience more plainly shown me that it was the nature of man to crush his fellow, I should not have thought it so hard. Wherefore, my respected friends, let us no longer talk of prejudice, till prejudice becomes extinct at home. Let us no longer talk of opposition, till we cease to oppose our own. For while these evils exist, to talk is like giving breath to the air, and labor to the wind. Though wealth is far more highly prized than humble merit, yet none of these things move me. Having God for my friend and portion, what have I to fear? Promotion cometh neither from the East or West, and as long as it is the will of God, I rejoice that I am as I am; for man in his best estate, is altogether vanity. Men of eminence have mostly risen from obscurity; nor will I, although a female of a darker hue, and far more obscure than they, bend my head or hang my harp upon willows; for though poor, I will virtuous prove. And if it is the will of my heavenly Father to reduce me to penury and want, I am ready to say, amen, even so be it. "The foxes have holes, and the birds of the air have nests, but the Son of man hath not where to lay his head."

During the short period of my Christian warfare, I have indeed had to contend against the fiery darts of the devil. And was it not that the righteous are kept by the mighty power of God through faith unto salvation, long before this I should have proved to be like the seed by the way-side. For it has actually appeared to me at different periods, as though the powers of earth and hell had combined against me, to prove my overthrow. Yet amidst their dire attempts, I have found the Almighty to be "a friend that sticketh closer than a brother." He never will forsake the soul that leans on him; though he chastens and corrects, it is for the soul's best interest. "And as a Father pitieth his children, so the Lord pitieth them that fear him."

But some of you have said, "do not talk so much about religion, the people do not wish to hear you. We know these things, tell us something we do not know." If you know these things, my dear friends, and have performed them, far happier, and more prosperous would you now have been. "He that knoweth his Lord's will and obeyeth it not, shall be beaten with many stripes." Sensible of this, I have, regardless of the frowns and scoffs of a guilty world, plead up religion, and the pure principles of morality among you. Religion is the most glorious theme that mortals can converse upon. The older it grows the more new beauties it displays. Earth, with its brilliant attractions, appears mean and sordid when compared to it. It is that fountain that has no end, and those that drink thereof shall never thirst; for it is, indeed, a well of water springing up in the soul unto everlasting life.

Again, those ideas of greatness which are held forth to us, are vain delusions, are airy visions which we shall never realize. All that man can say or do can never elevate us, it is a work that must be effected between God and ourselves. And, how? By dropping all political discussions in our behalf, for these, in my opinion, sow the seed of discord, and strengthen the cord of prejudice. A spirit of animosity is already risen, and unless it is quenched, a fire will burst forth and devour us, and our young will be slain by the sword. It is the sovereign will of God that our condition should be thus and so. "For he hath formed one vessel for honor, and another for dishonor." And shall the clay say to him that formed it, why hast thou formed me thus? It is high time for us to drop political discussions, and when our day of deliverance comes, God will provide a way for us to escape, and fight his own battles.

Finally, my brethren, let us follow after godliness, and the things which make for peace. Cultivate your own minds and morals; real merit will elevate you. Pure religion will burst your fetters. Turn your attention to industry. Strive to please your employers. Lay up what you earn. And remember, that in the grave distinction withers, and the high and low are alike renowned.

But I draw to a conclusion. Long will the kind sympathy of some much loved friend, be written on the tablet of my memory, especially those kind individuals who have stood by me like pitying angels, and befriended me when in the midst of difficulty; many blessings rest on them. Gratitude is all the tribute I can offer. A rich reward awaits them.

To my unconverted friends, one and all, I would say, shortly this frail tenement of mine will be dissolved and lie mouldering in ruins. O, solemn thought! Yet why should I revolt, for it is the glorious hope of a blessed immortality, beyond the grave, that has supported me thus far through this vale of tears. Who among you will strive to meet me at the right hand of Christ? For the great day of retribution is fast approaching, and who shall be able to abide his coming? You are forming characters for eternity. As you live so you will die; as death leaves you, so judgment will find you. Then shall we receive the glorious welcome, "Come, ye blessed of my Father, inherit the kingdom prepared for you from before the foundation of the world." Or, hear the heart-rending sentence, "Depart ye cursed into everlasting fire prepared for the devil and his angels." When thrice ten thousand years have rolled away, eternity will be but just begun. Your ideas will but just begin to expand. O, eternity, who can unfathom thine end, or comprehend thy beginning.

Dearly beloved: I have made myself contemptible in the eyes of many, that I might win some. But it has been like labor in vain. "Paul may plant, and Apollos water, but God alone giveth the increase."

To my brethren and sisters in the church, I would say, be ye clothed with the breast-plate of righteousness, having your loins girt about with truth, prepared to meet the Bridegroom at his coming; for blessed are those servants that are found watching.

Farewell. In a few short years from now, we shall meet in those upper regions where parting will be no more. There we shall sing and shout, and shout and sing, and make heaven's high arches ring. There we shall range in rich pastures, and partake of those living streams that never dry. O, blissful thought! Hatred and contention shall cease, and we shall join with redeemed millions in ascribing glory and honor, and riches, and power and blessing to the Lamb that was slain, and to Him that sitteth upon the throne. Nor eye hath seen, nor ear heard, neither hath it entered into the heart of man to conceive of the joys that are prepared for them that love God. Thus far has my life been almost a life of complete disappointment. God has tried me as by fire. Well was I aware that if I contended boldly for his cause, I must suffer. Yet, I chose rather to suffer affliction with his people, than to enjoy the pleasures of sin for a season. And I believe that the glorious declaration was about to be made applicable to me, that was made to God's ancient covenant people by the prophet, Comfort ye, comfort ye, my people: say unto her that her warfare is accomplished, and that her iniquities are pardoned. I believe that a rich reward awaits me, if not in this world, in the world to come. O, blessed reflection. The bitterness of my soul has departed from those who endeavored to discourage and hinder me in my Christian progress; and I can now forgive my enemies, bless those who have hated me, and cheerfully pray for those who have despitefully used and persecuted me.

Fare you well, farewell.

SOURCES

Anderson, Judith, *Outspoken Women: Speeches by American Women Reformers, 1635-1935,* Kendall/Hunt, 1984.

Campbell, Karlyn Kohrs, *Man Cannot Speak for Her,* Greenwood Press, 1989, Volume 1: *A Critical Study of Early Feminist Rhetoric,* Volume 2: *Key Texts of the Early Feminists.*

Golden, James L., and Richard D. Rieke, *The Rhetoric of Black Americans,* Charles E. Merrill, 1971.

Lerner, Gerda, editor, *Black Women in White America: A Documentary History,* Pantheon Books, 1972.

Loewenberg, Bert James, and Ruth Bogin, editors, *Black Women in Nineteenth-Century American Life: Their Words, Their Thoughts, Their Feelings,* Pennsylvania State University Press, 1976.

Richardson, Marilyn, *Maria Stewart: America's First Black Woman Political Writer* (contains reprints of *Productions of Mrs. Maria W. Stewart* and *Meditations from the Pen of Mrs. Maria W. Stewart;* see below), Indiana University Press, 1971.

Spiritual Narratives (contains reprint of *Productions of Mrs. Maria W. Stewart),* Oxford University Press, 1988.

Stewart, Maria W. Miller, *Productions of Mrs. Maria W. Stewart,* Friends of Freedom and Virtue [Boston], 1835.

———, *Meditations from the Pen of Mrs. Maria W. Stewart,* [Washington, D.C.], 1879.

Ross Swimmer

1943–

Native American leader of the Cherokee tribe

One of the most accomplished Native American leaders of the contemporary era is Ross Swimmer, an attorney and businessman who has served with distinction as principal chief of the Cherokee Nation and as head of the Bureau of Indian Affairs. Born and raised in Oklahoma City, he was the son of two lawyers; his father, who was half Cherokee, was in private practice, and his mother worked for the Federal Aviation Administration. Ross Swimmer followed in their footsteps, earning a bachelor's degree in political science from the University of Oklahoma in 1965 before pursuing his law degree there as well. After graduation, he went to work with a local firm, achieving partnership status in 1970.

Two years later, however, Swimmer left Oklahoma City and began his long affiliation with the Cherokee Nation when he accepted the position of general counsel at the Nation's headquarters in Tahlequah. In 1975, upon the retirement of his mentor, Chief W.W. Keeler, Swimmer himself decided to run for chief and was victorious. Re-elected in 1979 and again in 1983, he successfully led the Cherokee Nation through a period of significant changes as he pushed for more self-determination and self-sufficiency while coping with decreasing financial support from federal and state sources.

To realize his goals, Swimmer developed management and marketing programs designed to help Cherokee businesses flourish and thus boost employment rates. He also took on companies that had long been extracting minerals from Cherokee land without seeking permission or offering compensation, lobbying Congress in support of legislation that would give the tribe the right to sue the companies involved. In addition, during his tenure Swimmer obtained funding for a new Indian Health Service hospital in Tahlequah and spearheaded efforts to update the Cherokee constitution.

In 1983, as a result of the steps he had taken to improve his tribe's economic standing, Swimmer was named co-chairman of President Ronald Reagan's Commission on Indian Reservation Economies. His devotion to the ideals of self-determination and self-sufficiency for Native Americans so impressed administration officials that in 1985, halfway through his third term as chief, Swimmer was named Assistant Secretary of the Interior and assigned specifically to head the much-maligned Bureau of Indian Affairs. Thanks to strong bipartisan support and enthusiastic recommendations from several other prominent Native American leaders, his nomination sailed through the Senate.

Swimmer served the Bureau for four years, during which time he tried to apply the lessons he had learned as chief of the Cherokee Nation to Indian communities across the country. True to form, he promoted economic development and encouraged tribal governments to take a more active role in leading their people. He also made every effort to bring his business expertise to bear on the problems facing federal Indian programs.

Swimmer left his government post in 1989 and returned to Oklahoma, where he signed on as an attorney with a Tulsa firm and specialized in Indian law. In 1992, Cherokee principal chief Wilma Mankiller named him president and CEO of Cherokee Nation Industries (CNI), an electronics company owned by the Nation and based in the town of Stilwell. Founded in 1969, CNI—the tribe's largest business enterprise—manufactures wiring harness and electrical cable assembly for the U.S. military; it struggled for a number of years before Swimmer, then chief of the Cherokee Nation, helped make it a success. The major challenge facing him in the 1990s is ensuring CNI's survival in an era of cutbacks in defense spending, and to that end he has been actively seeking to expand into the private sector.

As a well-known Native American leader with many achievements to his credit, Swimmer is often asked to share with others his thoughts on self-determination and self-reliance. On several occasions in the 1990s, he has given a variation of the following speech, which he has entitled "An Indian Crossroad." It is reprinted here from a copy provided by Swimmer.

We have reached the proverbial crossroad of Indian affairs. The question remains, however, where to go from here? Information gleaned from reports over the past twenty years to the present investigation by the Senate Select Committee on Indian Affairs, leads to the conclusion that the federal government has helped Indians, literally, to death. Why?

Whether the policy was one of placing Indians on reservations to protect them from white society and vice versa; or the General Allotment Act of the 1880s, giving individual ownership of land to Indians so they could be competitive and self-reliant; or the reorganization days of the 1930s that would retribalize Indians to permit self-government; or the termination era of the 1950s that would encourage division of tribal resources and allow Indians to "become just like us"; or the self-determination days of the past twenty years, all of those policies were presented as a way of helping the Indians. Only one thing has been missing from each. That is Indian involvement in the development of the policy. My reference to Indian involvement means the men, women and children actually living on reservations or in Indian country, and is specifically meant to exclude those in Washington, D.C.

As principal chief of the Cherokees, I sometimes followed the blind lead of Washington bureaucrats. We built our share of ill-planned rural housing and industrial parks. We also operated numerous social programs that Washington bureaucrats told us would be good for the Cherokees. However, when we began listening to the rural Cherokee people about their problems and inviting them to participate in developing solutions, we also began to change the way the tribe did business.

Today, Indian people too often see their tribal governments as extensions of the Washington bureaucracy. People get good jobs at the tribes because that is where Washington puts the money first. The Bureau continues to act as trustee for the Indians' land, money and other resources, so it is not unusual for people to get confused about which entity is really in charge. In many cases, the Bureau is the only "bank" the people have ever known. The only

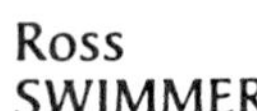

Ross Swimmer

distinction between the Bureau and the tribes is based on activities performed by the two groups. If the Bureau operated an employment assistance program in the 1960s, that program may now be operated by the tribe. If it was unsuccessfully operated by the Bureau then, it likely will be the same with tribes today.

Congress sees the tribes and Indian people in as many different ways as there are congressmen and senators. Senators on the Senate Select Committee for Indian Affairs state their unequivocal support for Indian sovereignty, yet are often the same ones who will not support tribal criminal jurisdiction over non-Indians, taxation by Indian tribes over non-Indians and their property, or exclusive rights to regulate, zone or otherwise manage all aspects of the reservations.

The administration sees Indian Affairs as an effort to preside over constant conflict. Often, The Bureau of Indian Affairs is pressured by a tribe and congressmen to make a loan or grant that has little chance of success. After the project fails, the BIA is blamed for making a bad decision. Within the Department of Interior, conflicts are the rule, rather than the exception.

So, what about this new crossroad? Do we keep helping Indians as we have or is it time for a change? The answer lies in Indian country, not Washington, D.C. Indian people have to answer that question. If they are satisfied with a maintenance program made up of three billion dollars of federal aid, that can be continued easily enough. Should we continue to expect Indians to be alcoholic, unemployed and at the bottom of the socioeconomic scale? Or should we expect Indian people to help themselves, stop drinking, find employment, get educated and share in the economic benefits this country offers? I sincerely believe Indians will rise to the latter expectations, but only if they are free to decide how to use the resources available to get there.

Do Indians want tribal government as we know it today? Yes and no. What they do want is the freedom to have the kind of tribal organization they desire and not be bound by rules for governing themselves set forth by the federal government. Some may desire to leverage their sovereignty and federal money to purchase needed governmental functions from other governments in their area and have money left over while supporting a much smaller tribal government.

Congress could solve unemployment on the reservations overnight—if the people want to go work. Simple amendments to the tax code or providing financial incentives to industry for creating jobs in Indian country could provide enough work to have full employment—if that is what people want. The cost would probably be no more than what we pay now to maintain people in a state of unemployment. There are now tribes with access to more jobs than tribal members, yet unemployment is high. Job creation alone won't reduce unemployment unless Indian people want to work, are able and capable, and sufficient incentives exist.

Congress could also address poverty in Indian country by authorizing the administration of social service programs through an incentive system for success instead of constantly rewarding failure. For instance, if money were provided to alcohol treatment centers, counseling programs, and others based on days, weeks, months, or years of sobriety achieved, instead of on total number of alcoholics counseled, treated or housed, we would see some dramatic successes. Particularly, if the money were then left on the table with the tribes to address other chronic social problems.

Teachers of Indian students at Bureau schools will soon be paid the highest salaries of any teachers in public or private education. Will test scores go up as a result? Likely not. Not until Indian parents agree to send their children to school, keep them there, and share in the responsibility for their education. Not until every teacher is held accountable for teaching students. Not until Bureau schools are used as places of learning and teaching instead of employment programs. Senators and congressmen can mandate and provide pay increases, but they cannot force parents to get involved in their children's education, make teachers teach or force school boards to hire competent people. Indian children can improve educationally if simply given the opportunity and a few incentives to make it all worthwhile.

I do not know if Indians will be allowed to answer the question about which road to take, but I suspect that if congressmen would visit Indian communities and talk to Indian people, the road taken would go in a far different direction than the one likely to be chosen for them.

SOURCES

Books

Maestas, John R., editor, *Contemporary Native American Address,* Brigham Young University, 1976.

Malinowski, Sharon, editor, *Notable Native Americans,* Gale Research, Detroit, 1995.

Periodicals

Cherokee Advocate, "Ross Swimmer Named President, Chief Executive of CNI," April 30, 1992.

Tecumseh

(Tecumtha)

1768(?)–1813

Native American leader of the Shawnee tribe

Tecumseh was a prominent spokesmen for midwestern Indians during the period of white expansion into the valleys of the Ohio, Allegheny, and Monongahela rivers. Born the son of a Shawnee chief near the present-day town of Springfield, Ohio, he was trained as a warrior from an early age and fought with the British against the American colonists during the Revolutionary War. Afterward, Tecumseh educated himself about the historical and legal standing of Native Americans and soon became known as a fiercely eloquent opponent of the treaties that ceded Indian lands to white settlers. He argued that the land belonged to all tribes, not just to one, and he therefore refused to recognize the legitimacy of any agreement that did not have the consent of all Indians.

On one occasion in August 1810, for example, Tecumseh angrily confronted William Henry Harrison, then the governor of Indiana Territory (and later president of the United States) with his objections to land sales that he felt violated the terms of a treaty dating back to 1804. Refusing to enter the governor's mansion, he delivered his remarks outside the residence in Vincennes. They are reprinted here from I Have Spoken: American History Through the Voices of the Indians, *compiled by Virginia Irving Armstrong, Sage Books, 1971.*

Houses are built for you to hold councils in; Indians hold theirs in the open air. I am a Shawnee. My forefathers were warriors. Their son is a warrior. From them I take my only existence. From my tribe I take nothing. I have made myself what I am. And I would that I could make the red people as great as the conceptions of my own mind, when I think of the Great Spirit that rules over us all. . . . I would not then come to Governor Harrison to ask him to tear up the treaty. But I would say to him, "Brother, you have the liberty to return to your own country."

You wish to prevent the Indians from doing as we wish them, to unite and let them consider their lands as the common property of the whole. You take the tribes aside and advise them not to come into this measure. . . . You want by your distinctions of Indian tribes, in allotting to each a particular, to make them war with each other. You never see an Indian endeavor to make the white people do this. You are continually driving the red people, when at last you will drive them onto the great lake, where they can neither stand nor work.

Since my residence at Tippecanoe, we have endeavored to level all distinctions, to destroy village chiefs, by whom all mischiefs are done. It is they who sell the land to the Americans. Brother, this land that was sold, and the goods that was given for it, was only done by a few.... In the future we are prepared to punish those who propose to sell land to the Americans. If you continue to purchase them, it will make war among the different tribes, and, at last I do not know what will be the consequences among the white people. Brother, I wish you would take pity on the red people and do as I have requested. If you will not give up the land and do cross the boundary of our present settlement, it will be very hard, and produce great trouble between us.

The way, the only way to stop this evil is for the red men to unite in claiming a common and equal right in the land, as it was at first, and should be now—for it was never divided, but belongs to all. No tribe has the right to sell, even to each other, much less to strangers.... Sell a country! Why not sell the air, the great sea, as well as the earth? Did not the Great Spirit make them all for the use of his children?

How can we have confidence in the white people?

When Jesus Christ came upon the earth you killed Him and nailed him to the cross. You thought he was dead, and you were mistaken. You have Shakers among you and you laugh and make light of their worship.

Everything I have told you is the truth. The Great Spirit has inspired me.

Tecumseh

When he was not personally engaged in battle against white settlers near his home in Indiana's Wabash River Valley, Tecumseh traveled extensively trying to convince other tribes of the need for a confederation of Indians to stop the advance of the white man. Joining him in this effort was his younger brother, Tenskwatawa, a mystical religious leader known as the Prophet. Together they launched a resistance movement based on the notion that Indians could achieve spiritual rebirth by rejecting European ways and once again embracing their own culture. (They were especially critical of the practice of drinking alcohol, which they blamed for many of the ills that had befallen their people.) Their ultimate goal, however, was to drive the whites back over the Appalachian Mountains. These ideas found favor among a number of other Indians who also felt threatened by the westward march of white civilization. Before long, Tecumseh and his brother had established a community of believers in a village they called Prophet Town (or Prophet's Town), located near the Wabash River and Tippecanoe Creek.

During 1810 and 1811, Tecumseh journeyed from the Great Lakes area across to the Plains and then down to the Gulf of Mexico in search of support for his Indian confederation. Appearing before the Osage in 1811, for example, he delivered the following speech, reprinted here from Literature of the American Indian, *by Thomas E. Sanders and Walter W. Peek, Glencoe Press, 1973.*

Brothers: We all belong to one family; we are all children of the Great Spirit; we walk in the same path; slake our thirst at the same spring; and now affairs of the greatest concern lead us to smoke the pipe around the same council fire!

Brothers: We are friends; we must assist each other to bear our burdens. The blood of many of our fathers and brothers has run like water on the ground, to satisfy the avarice of the white men. We, ourselves, are threatened with a great evil; nothing will pacify them but the destruction of all the red men.

Brothers: When the white men first set foot on our grounds, they were hungry; they had no place on which to spread their blankets, or to kindle their fires. They were feeble; they could do nothing for themselves. Our fathers commiserated their distress, and shared freely with them whatever the Great Spirit had given his red children. They gave them food when hungry, medicine when sick, spread skins for them to sleep on, and gave them grounds, that they might hunt and raise corn.

Brothers: The white people are like poisonous serpents: when chilled, they are feeble, and harmless, but invigorate them with warmth, and they sting their benefactors to death.

The white people came among us feeble; and now we have made them strong, they wish to kill us, or drive us back, as they would wolves and panthers.

Brothers: The white men are not friends to the Indians: at first, they only asked for land sufficient for a wigwam; now, nothing will satisfy them but the whole of our hunting grounds, from the rising to the setting sun.

Brothers: The white men want more than our hunting grounds; they wish to kill our warriors; they would even kill our old men, women and little ones.

Brothers: Many winters ago, there was no land; the sun did not rise and set; all was darkness. The Great Spirit made all things. He gave the white people a home beyond the great waters. He supplied these grounds with game, and gave them to his red children; and he gave them strength and courage to defend them.

Brothers: My people wish for peace; the red men all wish for peace; but where the white people are, there is no peace for them, except it be on the bosom of our mother.

Brothers: The white men despise and cheat the Indians; they abuse and insult them; they do not think the red men sufficiently good to live.

The red men have borne many and great injuries; they ought to suffer them no longer. My people will not; they are determined on vengeance; they have taken up the tomahawk; they will make it fat with blood; they will drink the blood of the white people.

Brothers: My people are brave and numerous; but the white people are too strong for them alone. I wish you to take up the tomahawk with them. If we all unite, we will cause the rivers to stain the great waters with their blood.

Brothers: If you do not unite with us, they will first destroy us, and then you will fall an easy prey to them. They have destroyed many nations of red men because they were not united, because they were not friends to each other.

Brothers: The white people send runners amongst us; they wish to make us enemies, that they may sweep over and desolate our hunting grounds, like devastating winds, or rushing waters.

Brothers: Our Great Father, over the great waters, is angry with the white people, our enemies. He will send his brave warriors against them; he will send us rifles, and whatever else we want—he is our friend, and we are his children.

Brothers: Who are the white people that we should fear them? They cannot run fast, and are good marks to shoot at: they are only men; our fathers have killed many of them; we are not squaws, and we will stain the earth red with their blood.

Brothers: The Great Spirit is angry with our

enemies; he speaks in thunder, and the earth swallows up villages, and drinks up the Mississippi. The great waters will cover their lowlands; their corn cannot grow; and the Great Spirit will sweep those who escape to the hills from the earth with his terrible breath.

Brothers: We must be united; we must smoke the same pipe; we must fight each other's battles; and more than all, we must love the Great Spirit; he is for us; he will destroy our enemies, and make his red children happy.

During the same trip, while visiting in the area of present-day Mississippi, Tecumseh took his case before a special council meeting of Choctaws and Chickasaws. His passionate plea for unity in the face of white expansion westward is reprinted here from W.C. Vanderwerth's Indian Oratory: Famous Speeches by Noted Indian Chieftains, *University of Oklahoma Press, 1971.*

In view of questions of vast importance, have we met together in solemn council tonight. Nor should we here debate whether we have been wronged and injured, but by what measures we should avenge ourselves; for our merciless oppressors, having long since planned out their proceedings, are not about to make, but have and are still making attacks upon our race who have as yet come to no resolution. Nor are we ignorant by what steps, and by what gradual advances, the whites break in upon our neighbors. Imagining themselves to be still undiscovered, they show themselves the less audacious because you are insensible. The whites are already nearly a match for us all united, and too strong for any one tribe alone to resist; so that unless we support one another with our collective and united forces; unless every tribe unanimously combines to give check to the ambition and avarice of the whites, they will soon conquer us apart and disunited, and we will be driven away from our native country and scattered as autumnal leaves before the wind.

But have we not courage enough remaining to defend our country and maintain our ancient independence? Will we calmly suffer the white intruders and tyrants to enslave us? Shall it be said of our race that we knew not how to extricate ourselves from the three most dreadful calamities—folly, inactivity and cowardice? But what need is there to speak of the past? It speaks for itself and asks, Where today is the Pequod? Where the Narragansetts, the Mohawks, Pocanokets, and many other once powerful tribes of our race? They have vanished before the avarice and oppression of the white men, as snow before a summer sun. In the vain hope of alone defending their ancient possessions, they have fallen in the wars with the white men. Look abroad over their once beautiful country, and what see you now? Naught but the ravages of the paleface destroyers meet our eyes. So it will be with you Choctaws and Chickasaws! Soon your mighty forest trees, under the shade of whose wide spreading branches you have played in infancy, sported in boyhood, and now rest your wearied limbs after the fatigue of the chase, will be cut down to fence in the land which the white intruders dare to call their own. Soon their broad roads will pass over the grave of your fathers, and the place of their rest will be blotted out forever. The annihilation of our race is at hand unless we unite in one common cause against the common foe. Think not, brave Choctaws and Chickasaws, that you can remain passive and indifferent to the common danger, and thus escape the common fate. Your people, too, will soon be as falling leaves and scattering clouds before their blighting breath. You, too, will be driven away from your native land and ancient domains as leaves are driven before the wintry storms.

Sleep not longer, O Choctaws and Chickasaws, in false security and delusive hopes. Our broad domains are fast escaping from our grasp.

Every year our white intruders become more greedy, exacting, oppressive and overbearing. Every year contentions spring up between them and our people and when blood is shed we have to make atonement whether right or wrong, at the cost of the lives of our greatest chiefs, and the yielding up of large tracts of our lands. Before the palefaces came among us, we enjoyed the happiness of unbounded freedom, and were acquainted with neither riches, wants nor oppression. How is it now? Wants and oppression are our lot; for are we not controlled in everything, and dare we move without asking, by your leave? Are we not being stripped day by day of the little that remains of our ancient liberty? Do they not even kick and strike us as they do their blackfaces? How long will it be before they will tie us to a post and whip us, and make us work for them in their cornfields as they do them? Shall we wait for that moment or shall we die fighting before submitting to such ignominy?

Have we not for years had before our eyes a sample of their designs, and are they not sufficient harbingers of their future determinations? Will we not soon be driven from our respective countries and the graves of our ancestors? Will not the bones of our dead be plowed up, and their graves be turned into fields? Shall we calmly wait until they become so numerous that we will no longer be able to resist oppression? Will we wait to be destroyed in our turn, without making an effort worthy of our race? Shall we give up our homes, our country, bequeathed to us by the Great Spirit, the graves of our dead, and everything that is dear and sacred to us, without a struggle? I know you will cry with me: Never! Never! Then let us by unity of action destroy them all, which we now can do, or drive them back whence they came. War or extermination is now our only choice. Which do you choose? I know your answer. Therefore, I now call on you, brave Choctaws and Chickasaws, to assist in the just cause of liberating our race from the grasp of our faithless invaders and heartless oppressors. The white usurpation in our common country must be stopped, or we, its rightful owners, be forever destroyed and wiped out as a race of people. I am now at the head of many warriors backed by the strong arm of English soldiers. Choctaws and Chickasaws, you have too long borne with grievous usurpation inflicted by the arrogant Americans. Be no longer their dupes. If there be one here tonight who believes that his rights will not sooner or later be taken from him by the avaricious American palefaces, his ignorance ought to excite pity, for he knows little of the character of our common foe.

And if there be one among you mad enough to undervalue the growing power of the white race among us, let him tremble in considering the fearful woes he will bring down upon our entire race, if by his criminal indifference he assists the designs of our common enemy against our common country. Then listen to the voice of duty, of honor, of nature and of your endangered country. Let us form one body, one heart, and defend to the last warrior our country, our homes, our liberty, and the graves of our fathers.

Choctaws and Chickasaws, you are among the few of our race who sit indolently at ease. You have indeed enjoyed the reputation of being brave, but will you be indebted for it more from report than fact? Will you let the whites encroach upon your domains even to your very door before you will assert your rights in resistance? Let no one in this council imagine that I speak more from malice against the paleface Americans than just grounds of complaint. Complaint is just toward friends who have failed in their duty; accusation is against enemies guilty of injustice. And surely, if any people ever had, we have good and just reasons to believe we have ample grounds to accuse the Americans of injustice; especially when such great acts of injustice have been committed by them upon our race, of which they seem to have no manner of regard, or even to reflect. They are a people fond of innovations, quick to contrive and quick to put their schemes into effectual execution no matter how great the wrong and injury to us; while we are content to preserve what we already have. Their designs are to enlarge their possessions by taking yours in turn; and will you, can you longer dally, O Choctaws and Chickasaws?

"Let us form one body, one heart, and defend to the last warrior our country, our homes, our liberty, and the graves of our fathers."

Do you imagine that that people will not continue longest in the enjoyment of peace who timely prepare to vindicate themselves, and manifest a determined resolution to do themselves right whenever they are wronged? Far otherwise. Then haste to the relief of our common cause, as by consanguinity of blood you are bound; lest the day be not far distant when you will be left single-handed and alone to the cruel mercy of our most inveterate foe.

Despite his eloquence, Tecumseh was no match for the Choctaw chief Pushmataha, who spoke before the same council and argued against the Shawnee's proposal, insisting that the Americans were their friends and that the Great Spirit would punish the Indians for breaking their treaties with the white man. (Tecumseh's prediction about what would happen to the Choctaws and Chickasaws proved true, however; during the early 1830s, they were forced off their land and sent west along the Trail of Tears to Indian Territory in present-day Oklahoma.)

When Tecumseh returned home to Prophet Town after his long journey, he found the community destroyed at the hands of Governor William Henry Harrison and U.S. Army troops in the so-called Battle of Tippecanoe. (Harrison later capitalized on his victory all the way to the White House.) Soon after, the British and Americans squared off against each other in what would become known as the War of 1812. Tecumseh, his dreams of an Indian confederation virtually in ruins, headed for Canada and joined the British forces. So impressive was he as a warrior—he distinguished himself in particular during the battle for the capture of Detroit—he was promoted to the rank of brigadier general.

Within just a short time, however, the tide began to turn against the British. In September 1813, a major naval battle took place on Lake Erie in which American forces led by Commodore Oliver Hazard Perry defeated the British fleet and effectively drove them from the Great Lakes region. As the British prepared to flee to Canada, Tecumseh, unaware of the battle's outcome and puzzled by this sudden retreat, reminded his allies of their promises to the Indians and urged them to stay and fight the Americans on land. His appeal to General Proctor, the British commander, appears in W.C. Vanderwerth's Indian Oratory: Famous Speeches by Noted Indian Chieftains, *University of Oklahoma Press, 1971.*

Father, listen to your children! You have them now all before you.

The war before this, our British father gave the hatchet to his red children, when our old chiefs were alive. They are now dead. In the war, our father was thrown on his back by the Americans, and our father took them by the hand without our knowledge; and we are afraid that our father will do so again this time.

Summer before last, when I came forward with my red brethren, and was ready to take up the hatchet in favor of our British father, we were told not to be in a hurry, that he had not yet determined to fight the Americans.

Listen! When war was declared, our father stood up and gave us the tomahawk and told us that he was then ready to strike the Americans; that he wanted our assistance; and that he would certainly get our lands back, which the Americans had taken from us.

Listen! You told us, at that time, to bring forward our families to this place; and we did so; and you promised to take care of them, and they should want for nothing, while the men would go out and fight the enemy; that we need

not trouble ourselves about the enemy's garrisons; that we knew nothing about them, and that our father would attend to that part of the business. You also told your red children that you would take good care of your garrison here, which made our hearts glad.

Listen! When we were last at the Rapids it is true we gave you little assistance. It is hard to fight people who live like groundhogs.

Father, listen! Our fleet has gone out. We know they have fought. We have heard the great guns, but we know nothing of what has happened to our father with that arm. Our ships have gone one way, and we are much astonished to see our father tying up everything and preparing to run away the other, without letting his red children know what his intentions are. You always told us to remain here and take care of our lands. It made our hearts glad to hear that was your wish. Our great father, the king, is the head, and you represent him. You always told us that you would never draw your foot off British ground; but now, father, we see you are drawing back, and we are sorry to see our father doing so without seeing the enemy. We must compare our father's conduct to a fat dog, that carries its tail upon its back, but when afrighted, it drops it between its legs and runs off.

Father, listen! The Americans have not yet defeated us by land. Neither are we sure that they have done so by water. We therefore wish to remain here and fight our enemy, should they make their appearance. If they defeat us, we will then retreat with our father.

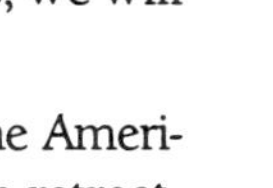

At the battle of the Rapids, last war, the Americans certainly defeated us, and when we retreated to our father's fort at that place the gates were shut against us. We were afraid that it would now be the case; but instead of that, we now see our British father preparing to march out of his garrison.

Father! You have got the arms and ammunition which our great father sent for his red children. If you have an idea of going away, give them to us, and you may go and welcome for us. Our lives are in the hands of the Great Spirit. We are determined to defend our lands, and if it be his will, we wish to leave our bones upon them.

Less than a month later, while fighting alongside British forces near Chatham, Ontario, Tecumseh was shot and killed in the Battle of the Thames. At the head of the victorious American troops was his old nemesis, William Henry Harrison.

SOURCES

Armstrong, Virginia Irving, compiler, *I Have Spoken: American History Through the Voices of the Indians,* Sage Books, 1971.

Eckert, Allan W., *A Sorrow in Our Heart: The Life of Tecumseh,* Bantam Books, 1992.

Edmunds, R. David, *Tecumseh and the Quest for Indian Leadership,* Harper, 1987.

Jones, Louis Thomas, *Aboriginal American Oratory: The Tradition of Eloquence Among the Indians of the United States,* Southwest Museum (Los Angeles), 1965.

McLuhan, T.C., *Touch the Earth: A Self-Portrait of Indian Existence,* Outerbridge & Dienstfrey, 1971.

Nabokov, Peter, editor, *Native American Testimony: A Chronicle of Indian-White Relations from Prophecy to the Present, 1492-1992,* Penguin Books, 1991.

Rosenstiel, Annette, *Red and White: Indian Views of the White Man, 1492-1982,* Universe Books, 1983.

Sanders, Thomas E., and Walter W. Peek, *Literature of the American Indian,* Glencoe Press, 1973.

Sugden, John, *Tecumseh's Last Stand,* University of Oklahoma Press, 1990.

Vanderwerth, W.C., *Indian Oratory: Famous Speeches by Noted Indian Chieftains,* University of Oklahoma Press, 1971.

Velie, Alan R., editor, *American Indian Literature: An Anthology,* University of Oklahoma Press, 1979.

Mary Church Terrell

1863–1954

African American educator and activist for women's rights and civil rights

An activist from the time she was in her twenties until almost her dying day at the age of ninety, Mary Church Terrell spoke out frequently about the problems blacks—especially black women—faced in American society. Her first crusade was against the crime of lynching, a cause she embraced in the wake of the very same incident that had prompted Ida Wells-Barnett to take action. Her final efforts were on behalf of the battle against racial segregation in Washington, D.C. In between, she worked tirelessly to advance the cause of women's rights.

Mary Church was the daughter of the South's first black millionaire, Robert Church, a former slave who had made his fortune in real estate, and his wife, Louisa Ayers, a successful businesswoman in her own right. Although her family was based in Memphis, Tennessee, young Mary attended school in Ohio. She went on to graduate from Oberlin College, earning a bachelor's degree in 1884 and a master's degree in 1888, then studied and traveled in Europe for two years. Against her father's wishes—he thought a young lady of her standing should not work—she insisted on pursuing a career as a teacher. Her first job was as an instructor at Wilberforce College; she later taught in the District of Columbia public schools.

Following her marriage to fellow educator Robert Terrell in 1891, however, she had to give up her dream because married women were legally barred from teaching. Instead, Terrell became active in the women's suffrage movement and served as a founder and first president of the National Association of Colored Women. She was also a charter member of the National Association for the Advancement of Colored People (NAACP) and a member of the District of Columbia board of education—the first black woman in the country to hold such a position. A poised and eloquent speaker who usually worked without a manuscript, Terrell was much in demand on the lecture circuit both in the United States and in Europe for nearly thirty years. Most often, she talked to white audiences about such topics as racial injustice, lynching, the progress of black women since Emancipation, women's suffrage, and black history and culture. In the belief that racism flourished where there was ignorance, her goal was to educate and enlighten her audiences.

In early 1904, Terrell was invited to speak before the Congregational Association of Maryland and the District of Columbia. In an address entitled "The Progress of Colored Women"—most of which follows—she detailed the many fine qualities and achievements they displayed despite facing prejudice against their sex and race. Her speech was published in the July 1904, issue of The Voice of the Negro *and later reprinted in* The Voice of Black America: Major Speeches by Negroes in the United States, 1797-1971 *(Simon & Schuster, 1972).*

... When one considers the obstacles encountered by colored women in their effort to educate and cultivate themselves, since they became free, the work they have accomplished and the progress they have made will bear favorable comparison, at least with that of their more fortunate sisters, from whom the opportunity of acquiring knowledge and the means of self-culture have never been entirely withheld. Not only are colored women with ambition and aspiration handicapped on account of their sex, but they are almost everywhere baffled and mocked because of their race. Not only because they are women, but because they are colored women are discouragement and disappointment meeting them at every turn. But in spite of the obstacles encountered, the progress made by colored women along many lines appears like a veritable miracle of modern times. Forty years ago for the great masses of colored women there was no such thing as home. Today in each and every section of the country there are hundreds of homes among colored people, the mental and moral tone of which is as high and as pure as can be found among the best people of any land.

Mary Church Terrell

To the women of the race may be attributed in large measure the refinement and purity of the colored home. The immorality of colored women is a theme upon which those who know little about them or those who maliciously misrepresent them love to descant. Foul aspersions upon the character of colored women are assiduously circulated by the press of certain sections and especially by the direct descendants of those who in years past were responsible for the moral degradation of their female slaves. And yet, in spite of the fateful heritage of slavery, even though the safeguards usually thrown around maidenly youth and innocence are in some sections entirely withheld from colored girls, statistics compiled by men not inclined to falsify in favor of my race show that immorality among the colored women of the United States is not so great as among women with similar environment and temptations in Italy, Germany, Sweden and France.

Scandals in the best colored society are exceedingly rare, while the progressive game of divorce and remarriage is practically unknown.

The intellectual progress of colored women has been marvelous. So great has been their thirst for knowledge and so Herculean their efforts to acquire it that there are few colleges, universities, high and normal schools in the North, East and West from which colored girls have not graduated with honor. In Wellesley, Vassar, Ann Arbor, Cornell and in Oberlin, my dear alma mater, whose name will always be loved and whose praise will always be sung as the first college in the country broad, just and generous enough to extend a cordial welcome to the Negro and to open its doors to women on an equal footing with the men, colored girls by their splendid records have forever settled the question of their capacity and worth. The instructors in these and other institutions cheerfully bear testimony to their intelligence, their diligence and their success.

As the brains of colored women expanded, their hearts began to grow. No sooner had the heads of a favored few been filled with knowledge than their hearts yearned to dispense blessings to the less fortunate of their race. With tireless energy and eager zeal, colored women have worked in every conceivable way to elevate their race. Of the colored teachers engaged in instructing our youth it is probably no exaggeration to say that fully eighty percent are women. In the backwoods, remote from the civilization and comforts of the city and town colored women may be found courageously battling with those evils which such conditions always entail. Many a heroine of whom the world will never hear has thus sacrificed her life to her race amid surroundings and in the face of privations which only martyrs can bear.

Through the medium of their societies in the church, beneficial organizations out of it and clubs of various kinds, colored women are doing a vast amount of good. It is almost impossible to ascertain exactly what the Negro is doing in any field, for the records are so poorly kept. This is particularly true in the case of the women of the race. During the past forty years there is no doubt that colored women in their poverty have contributed large sums of money to charitable and educational institutions as well as to the foreign and home missionary work. Within the twenty-five years in which the educational work of the African Methodist Episcopal Church has been systematized, the women of that organization have contributed at least five hundred thousand dollars to the cause of education. Dotted all over the country are charitable institutions for the aged, orphaned and poor which have been established by colored women. Just how many it is difficult to state, owing to the lack of statistics bearing on the progress, possessions and prowess of colored women.

Among the charitable institutions either founded, conducted or supported by colored women, may be mentioned the Hale Infirmary of Montgomery, Alabama, the Carrie Steel Orphanage of Atlanta, the Reed Orphan Home of Covington, and the Hains Industrial School of Augusta, all three in the state of Georgia; a home for the aged of both races in New Bedford, and St. Monica's Home of Boston, in Massachusetts, Old Folks Home of Memphis, Tennessee, and the Colored Orphan's Home of Lexington, Kentucky, together with others which lack of space forbids me to mention. Mt. Meigs Institute is an excellent example of a work originated and carried into successful execution by a colored woman. The school was established for the benefit of colored people on the plantations in the black belt of Alabama. In the township of Mt. Meigs the population is practically all colored. Instruction given in this school is of the kind best suited to the needs of the people for whom it was established. Along with some scholastic training, girls are taught everything pertaining to the management of the home, while boys are taught practical farming, wheelwrighting, blacksmithing, and have some military training. Having started with almost nothing, at the end of eight years the trustees of the school owned nine acres of land and five buildings in which several thousand pupils had received instructions, all through the energy, the courage and the sacrifice of one little woman.

Up to date, politics have been religiously eschewed by colored women, although questions affecting our legal status as a race is sometimes agitated by the most progressive class. In Louisiana and Tennessee colored women have several times petitioned the legislatures of their respective states to repel the obnoxious Jim-Crow-car laws. Against the convict-lease system, whose atrocities have been so frequently exposed of late, colored women here and there in the South are waging a ceaseless war. So long as hundreds of their brothers and sisters, many of whom have committed no crime or misdemeanor whatever, are thrown into cells whose cubic contents are less than those of a goodsize grave, to be overworked, underfed and only partially covered with vermin-infested rags, and so long as children are born to the women in these camps who breathe the polluted atmosphere of these dens of horror and vice from the time they utter their first cry in the world till they are released from their suffering by death, colored women who are working for the emancipation and elevation of their race know where their duty lies. By constant agitation of this painful and hideous subject they hope to touch the conscience of the country, so that this stain upon its escutcheon shall be forever wiped away.

Alarmed at the rapidity with which the Negro is losing ground in the world of trade, some of the farsighted women are trying to solve the labor question, so far as it concerns the women at least, by urging the establishment of schools of domestic science wherever means therefore can be secured. Those who are interested in this particular work hope and believe that if colored women and girls are thoroughly trained in domestic service, the boycott which has undoubtedly been placed upon them in many sections of the country will be removed. With so few vocations open to the Negro and with the labor organizations increasingly hostile to him, the future of the boys and girls of the race appears to some of our women very foreboding and dark.

The cause of temperance has been eloquently espoused by two women, each of whom has been appointed national superintendent of work among colored people by the Woman's Christian Temperance Union. In business, colored women have had signal success. There is in Alabama a large milling and cotton business belonging to and controlled by a colored woman, who has sometimes as many as seventy-five men in her employ. Until a few years ago the principal ice plant of Nova Scotia was owned and managed by a colored woman, who sold it for a large amount. In the professions there are dentists and doctors whose practice is lucrative and large. Ever since a book was published in 1773 entitled "Poems on Various Subjects, Religious and Moral by Phillis Wheatley, Negro Servant of Mr. John Wheatley," of Boston, colored women have given abundant evidence of literary ability. In sculpture we are represented by a woman upon whose chisel Italy has set her seal of approval; in painting by one of Bouguereau's pupils and in music by young women holding diplomas from the best conservatories in the land.

In short, to use a thought of the illustrious Frederick Douglass, if judged by the depths from which they have come, rather than by the heights to which those blessed with centuries of opportunities have attained, colored women need not hang their heads in shame. They are slowly but surely making their way up to the heights, wherever they can be scaled. In spite of handicaps and discouragements they are not losing heart. In a variety of ways they are rendering valiant service to their race. Lifting as they climb, onward and upward they go struggling and striving and hoping that the buds and blossoms of their desires may burst into glorious fruition ere long. Seeking no favors because of their color nor charity because of their needs they knock at the door of Justice and ask for an equal chance.

While Terrell condemned segregation wherever it existed, she was especially critical of the fact that Washington, D.C., was one of the most segregated cities in the country. In her view, the existence of such discrimination in the nation's capital was a disgrace to the ideals upon which the country had been founded. Consequently, she led the fight against Jim Crowism there for many years. On October 10, 1906, at a meeting of the United Women's Club of Washington, D.C., Terrell described what African Americans routinely had to deal with as residents of the city. Her remarks appeared in the January 24, 1907, issue of The Independent *and were later reprinted in Volume 2 of* Man Cannot Speak for Her *(Greenwood Press, 1989).*

Washington, D.C., has been called "The Colored Man's Paradise." Whether this sobriquet was given to the national capital in bitter irony by a member of the handicapped race, as he reviewed some of his own persecutions and rebuffs, or whether it was given immediately after the war by an ex-slave-holder who for the first time in his life saw colored people walking about like freemen, minus the overseer and his whip, history saith not. It is certain that it would be difficult to find a worse misnomer for Washington than "The Colored Man's Paradise" if so prosaic a consideration as veracity is to determine the appropriateness of a name.

For fifteen years I have resided in Washington, and while it was far from being a paradise for colored people, when I first touched these shores, it has been doing its level best ever since to make conditions for us intolerable. As a colored woman I might enter Washington any night, a stranger in a strange land, and walk miles without finding a place to lay my head. Unless I happened to know colored people who live here or ran across a chance acquaintance who could recommend a colored boarding-house to me, I should be obliged to spend the entire night wandering about. Indians, Chinamen [sic], Filipinos, Japanese and representatives of any other dark race can find hotel accommodations, if they can pay for them. The colored man alone is thrust out of the hotels of the national capital like a leper.

As a colored woman I may walk from the Capitol to the White House, ravenously hungry and abundantly supplied with money with which to purchase a meal, without finding a single restaurant in which I would be permitted to take a morsel of food, if it was patronized by white people, unless I were willing to sit behind a screen. As a colored woman I cannot visit the tomb of the Father of this country, which owes its very existence to the love of freedom in the human heart and which stands for equal opportunity to all, without being forced to sit in the Jim Crow section of an electric car which starts from the very heart of the city—midway between the Capitol and the White House. If I refuse thus to be humiliated, I am cast into jail and forced to pay a fine for violating the Virginia laws. Every hour in the day Jim Crow cars filled with colored people, many of whom are intelligent and well to do, enter and leave the national capital.

As a colored woman I may enter more than one white church in Washington without receiving that welcome which as a human being I have a right to expect in the sanctuary of God. Sometimes the color blindness of the usher takes on that peculiar form which prevents a dark face from making any impression whatsoever upon his retina, so that it is impossible for him to see colored people at all. If he is not so afflicted, after keeping a colored man or woman waiting a long time, he will ungraciously show these dusky Christians who have had the temerity to thrust themselves into a temple where only the fair of face are expected to worship God to a seat in the rear, which is named in honor of a certain personage, well known in this country, and commonly called Jim Crow.

Unless I am willing to engage in a few menial occupations, in which the pay for my services would be very poor, there is no way for me to earn an honest living, if I am not a trained nurse or a dressmaker or can secure a position

"For fifteen years I have resided in Washington, and while it was far from being a paradise for colored people, . . . it has been doing its level best ever since to make conditions for us intolerable."

as teacher in the public schools, which is exceedingly difficult to do. It matters not what my intellectual attainments may be or how great is the need of the services of a competent person, if I try to enter many of the numerous vocations in which my white sisters are allowed to engage, the door is shut in my face.

From one Washington theater I am excluded altogether. In the remainder certain seats are set aside for colored people, and it is almost impossible to secure others. I once telephoned to the ticket seller just before a matinee and asked if a neat-appearing colored nurse would be allowed to sit in the parquet with her little white charge, and the answer rushed quickly and positively thru [sic] the receiver—NO. When I remonstrated a bit and told him that in some of the theaters colored nurses were allowed to sit with the white children for whom they cared, the ticket seller told me that in Washington it was very poor policy to employ colored nurses, for they were excluded from many places where white girls would be allowed to take children for pleasure.

If I possess artistic talent, there is not a single art school of repute which will admit me. A few years ago a colored woman who possessed great talent submitted some drawings to the Corcoran Art School, of Washington, which were accepted by the committee of awards, who sent her a ticket entitling her to a course in this school. But when the committee discovered that the young woman was colored, they declined to admit her, and told her that if they had suspected that her drawings had been made by a colored woman, they would not have examined them at all. The efforts of Frederick Douglass and a lawyer of great repute who took a keen interest in the affair were unavailing. In order to cultivate her talent this young woman was forced to leave her comfortable home in Washington and incur the expense of going to New York. Having entered the Woman's Art School of Cooper Union, she graduated with honor, and then went to Paris to continue her studies, where she achieved signal success and was complimented by some of the greatest living artists in France.

With the exception of the Catholic University, there is not a single white college in the national capital to which colored people are admitted, no matter how great their ability, how lofty their ambition, how unexceptionable their character or how great their thirst for knowledge may be.

A few years ago the Columbian Law School admitted colored students, but in deference to the Southern white students the authorities have decided to exclude them altogether.

Some time ago a young woman who had already attracted some attention in the literary world by her volume of short stories answered an advertisement which appeared in a Washington newspaper, which called for the services of a skilled stenographer and expert typewriter. It is unnecessary to state the reasons why a young woman whose literary ability was so great as that possessed by the one referred to should decide to earn money in this way. The applicants were requested to send specimens of their work and answer certain questions concerning their experience and their speed before they called in person. In reply to her application the young colored woman, who, by the way, is very fair and attractive indeed, received a letter from the firm stating that her references and experience were the most satisfactory that had been sent and requesting her to call. When she presented herself there was some doubt in the mind of the man to whom she was directed concerning her racial pedigree, so he asked her point-blank whether she was colored or white. When she confessed the truth the merchant expressed great sorrow and deep regret that he could not avail himself of the services of so competent a person, but frankly admitted that employing a colored woman in his establishment in any except a menial position was simply out of the question.

Another young friend had an experience which, for some reasons, was still more disheartening and bitter than the one just mentioned. In order to secure lucrative employment she left Washington and went to New York. There she worked her way up in one of the largest dry goods stores till she was placed as saleswoman in the cloak department. Tired of being separated from her family, she decided to return to Washington, feeling sure that, with her experience and her fine recommendation from the New York firm, she could easily secure employment. Nor was she overconfident, for the proprietor of one of the largest dry goods stores in her native city was glad to secure the services of a young woman who brought such hearty credentials from New York. She had not been in this store very long, however, before she called upon me one day and asked me to intercede with the proprietor in her behalf, saying that she had been discharged that afternoon because it had been discovered that she was colored. When I called upon my young friend's employer he made no effort to avoid the issue, as I feared he would. He did not say he had discharged the young saleswoman because she had not given satisfaction, as he might easily have done. On the contrary, he admitted without the slightest hesitation that the young woman he had just discharged was one of the best clerks he had ever had. In the cloak department, where she had been assigned, she had been a brilliant success, he said. "But I cannot keep Miss Smith in my employ," he concluded. "Are you not master of your own store?" I ventured to inquire. The proprietor of this store was a Jew, and I felt that it was particularly cruel, unnatural and coldblooded for the representative of one oppressed and persecuted race to deal so harshly and unjustly with a member of another. I had intended to make this point when I decided to intercede for my young friend, but when I thought how a reference to the persecution of his own race would wound his feelings, the words froze on my lips. "When I first heard your friend was colored," he explained, "I did not believe it and said so to the clerks who made the statement. Finally, the girls who had been most pronounced in their opposition to working in a store with a colored girl came to me in a body and threatened to strike. 'Strike away,' said I, 'your places will be easily filled.' Then they started on another tack. Delegation after delegation began to file down to my office, some of the women my very best customers, to protest against my employing a colored girl. Moreover, they threatened to boycott my store if I did not discharge her at once. Then it became a question of bread and butter and I yielded to the inevitable—that's all. Now," said he, concluding, "if I lived in a great, cosmopolitan city like New York, I should do as I pleased, and refuse to discharge a girl simply because she was colored." But I thought of a similar incident that happened in New York. I remembered that a colored woman, as fair as a lily and as beautiful as a Madonna, who was the head saleswoman in a large department store in New York, had been discharged, after she had held this position for years, when the proprietor accidentally discovered that a fatal drop of African blood was percolating somewhere thru [sic] her veins.

Not only can colored women secure no employment in the Washington stores, department and otherwise, except as menials, and such positions, of course, are few, but even as customers they are not infrequently treated with discourtesy both by the clerks and the proprietor himself. Following the trend of the times, the senior partner of the largest and best department store in Washington, who originally hailed from Boston, once the home of William Lloyd Garrison, Wendell Phillips, and Charles Sumner, if my memory serves me right, decided to open a restaurant in his store. Tired and hungry after her morning's shopping a colored school teacher, whose relation to her African progenitors is so remote as scarcely to be discernible to the naked eye, took a seat at one of the tables in the restaurant of this Boston [sic] store. After sitting unnoticed a long time the colored teacher asked a waiter who passed her by if she would not take her order. She was quickly informed that colored people could not be served in that restaurant and was obliged to leave in confusion and shame, much to the amusement of the waiters and the guests who had noticed the incident. Shortly after that a teacher in Howard University, one of the best schools for colored youth in the country, was similarly insulted in the restaurant of the same store.

In one of the Washington theaters from which colored people are excluded altogether, members of the race have been viciously assaulted several times, for the proprietor well knows that colored people have no redress for such discriminations against them in the District courts. Not long ago a colored clerk in one of the departments who looks more like his paternal ancestors who fought for the lost cause than his grandmothers who were the victims of the peculiar institution, bought a ticket for the parquet of this theater in which colored people are nowhere welcome, for himself and mother, whose complexion is a bit swarthy. The usher refused to allow the young man to take the seats for which his tickets called and tried to snatch from him the coupons. A scuffle ensued and both mother and son were ejected by force. A suit was brought against the proprietor and the damages awarded the injured man and his mother amounted to the munificent sum of one cent. One of the teachers in the Colored High School received similar treatment in the same theater.

Not long ago one of my little daughter's bosom friends figured in one of the most pathetic instances of which I have ever heard. A gentleman who is very fond of children promised to take six little girls in his neighborhood to a matinee. It happened that he himself and five of his little friends were so fair that they easily passed muster, as they stood in judgment before the ticket seller and the ticket taker. Three of the little girls were sisters, two of whom were very fair and the other a bit brown. Just as this little girl, who happened to be last in the procession, went by the ticket taker, that argus-eyed sophisticated gentleman detected something which caused a deep, dark frown to mantle his brow and he did not allow her to pass. "I guess you have made a mistake," he called to the host of this theater party. "Those little girls," pointing to the fair ones, "may be admitted, but this one," designating the brown one, "can't." But the colored man was quite equal to the emergency. Fairly frothing at the mouth with anger, he asked the ticket taker what he meant, what he was trying to insinuate about that particular little girl. "Do you mean to tell me," he shouted in rage, "that I must go clear to the Philippine Islands to bring this child to the United States and then I can't take her to the theater in the National Capital?" The little ruse succeeded brilliantly, as he knew it would. "Beg your pardon," said the ticket taker, "don't know what I was thinking about. Of course she can go in."

"What was the matter with me this afternoon, mother?" asked the little brown girl innocently, when she mentioned the affair at home. "Why did the man at the theater let my two sisters and the other girls in and try to keep me out?" In relating this incident, the child's mother told me her little girl's question, which showed such blissful ignorance of the depressing, cruel conditions which confronted her, completely unnerved her for a time.

Altho [sic] white and colored teachers are under the same Board of Education and the system for the children of both races is said to be uniform, prejudice against the colored teachers in the public schools is manifested in a variety of ways. From 1870 to 1900 there was a colored superintendent at the head of the colored schools. During all that time the directors of the cooking, sewing, physical culture, manual training, music and art departments were colored people. Six years ago a change was inaugurated. The colored superintendent was legislated out of office and the directorships, without a single exception, were taken from colored teachers and given to the whites. There was no complaint about the work done by the colored directors, no more than is heard about every officer in every school. The directors of the art and physical culture departments were particularly fine. Now, no matter how competent or superior the colored teachers in our public schools may be, they know that they can never rise to the height of a directorship, can never hope to be more than an assistant and receive the meager salary therefor, unless the present regime is radically changed.

Not long ago one of the most distinguished kindergartners in the country came to deliver a course of lectures in Washington. The colored teachers were eager to attend, but they could not buy the coveted privilege for love or money. When they appealed to the director of kindergartens, they were told that the expert kindergartner had come to Washington under the auspices of private individuals, so that she could not possibly have them admitted. Realizing what a loss colored teachers had sustained in being deprived of the information and inspiration which these lectures afforded, one of the white teachers volunteered to repeat them as best she could for the benefit of her colored co-laborers for half the price she herself had paid, and the proposition was eagerly accepted by some.

> ***"Early in life many a colored youth is so appalled by the helplessness and the hopelessness of his situation that in a sort of stoical despair he resigns himself to his fate."***

Strenuous efforts are being made to run Jim Crow streetcars in the national capital. "Resolved, that a Jim Crow law should be adopted and enforced in the District of Columbia," was the subject of a discussion engaged in last January by the Columbian Debating Society of the George Washington University in our national capital, and the decision was rendered in favor of the affirmative. Representative Heflin, of Alabama, who introduced a bill providing for Jim Crow street cars in the District of Columbia last winter, has just received a letter from the president of the East Brookland Citizens' Association "indorsing [sic] the movement for separate street cars and sincerely hoping that you will be successful in getting this enacted into a law as soon as possible." Brookland is a suburb of Washington.

The colored laborer's path to a decent livelihood is by no means smooth. Into some of the trades unions here he is admitted, while from others he is excluded altogether. By the union men this is denied, altho [sic] I am personally acquainted with skilled workmen who tell me they are not admitted into the unions because they are colored. But even when they are allowed to join the unions they frequently derive little benefit, owing to certain tricks of the trade. When the word passes round that help is needed and colored laborers apply, they are often told by the union officials that they have secured all the men they needed, because the places are reserved for white men, until they have been provided with jobs, and colored men must remain idle, unless the supply of white men is too small.

I am personally acquainted with one of the most skilful laborers in the hardware business in Washington. For thirty years he has been working for the same firm. He told me he could not join the union, and that his employer had been almost forced to discharge him, because the union men threatened to boycott his store if he did not. If another man could have been found at the time to take his place he would have lost his job, he said.

When no other human being can bring a refractory chimney or stove to its senses, this colored man is called upon as the court of last appeal. If he fails to subdue it, it is pronounced a hopeless case at once. And yet this expert workman receives much less for his services than do white men who cannot compare with him in skill.

And so I might go on citing instance after instance to show the variety of ways in which our people are sacrificed on the altar of prejudice in the Capital of the United States and how almost insurmountable are the obstacles which block his [sic] path to success. Early in life many a colored youth is so appalled by the helplessness and the hopelessness of his situation in this country that, in a sort of stoical despair he resigns himself to his fate. "What is the good of our trying to acquire an education? We can't all be preachers, teachers, doctors and lawyers. Besides those professions, there is almost nothing for colored people to do but engage in the most menial occupations, and we do not need an education for that." More than once such remarks, uttered by young men and women in our public schools who possess brilliant intellects, have wrung my heart.

It is impossible for any white person in the United States, no matter how sympathetic and broad, to realize what life would mean to him if his incentive to effort were suddenly snatched away. To the lack of incentive to effort, which is the awful shadow under which we live, may be traced the wreck and ruin of scores of colored youth. And surely nowhere in the world do oppression and persecution based solely on the color of the skin appear more hateful and hideous than in the capital of the United States, because the chasm between the principles upon which this Government was founded, in which it still professes to believe, and those which are daily practiced under the protection of the flag, yawns so wide and deep.

Terrell's battle against segregation in Washington continued throughout the rest of her life. During the early 1950s, when she was nearly ninety, she headed a group of blacks who demanded that officials enforce an old law banning restaurants from discriminating against customers on the basis of race as long as they were "well behaved." In June 1953, the U.S. Supreme Court upheld the old law, thus paving the way for the integration of other public facilities in the capital. It was one of her last victories; Terrell died a little more than a year later.

SOURCES

Boulware, Marcus H., *The Oratory of Negro Leaders: 1900-1968,* Negro Universities Press, 1969.

Campbell, Karlyn Kohrs, editor, *Man Cannot Speak for Her,* Greenwood Press, 1989, Volume 1: *A Critical Study of Early Feminist Rhetoric,* Volume 2: *Key Texts of the Early Feminists.*

Foner, Philip S., editor, *The Voice of Black America: Major Speeches by Negroes in the United States, 1797-1971,* Simon & Schuster, 1972.

Jones, Beverly Washington, *Quest for Equality: The Life and Writings of Mary Church Terrell,* Carlson Publishers, 1990.

Terrell, Mary Church, *A Colored Woman in a White World* (reprint), Arno, 1980.

Clarence Thomas

1948–

African American associate justice of the U.S. Supreme Court

Clarence Thomas was an inexperienced and little-known appeals court judge when President George Bush nominated him on July 1, 1991, to replace retiring Justice Thurgood Marshall, a veteran of the civil rights struggle and the first African American ever to serve on the Supreme Court. But within a few short weeks, he found himself the target of widespread criticism for his conservative political views. And before his confirmation hearings finally ended in the fall, he had become tangled in an explosive national controversy involving what some have called the *workplace issue of the 1990s: sexual harassment.*

A native of the small Georgia town of Pin Point, Thomas grew up in what he has described as a "strong, stable, and conservative" household where the emphasis was on God, school, discipline, hard work, and "knowing right from wrong." The major influences in his early years were his maternal grandparents, with whom he and his younger brother lived after their family home burned down around 1955. (As a consequence of the same fire, his mother and an older sister moved in with a relative in Savannah; his father had left several years earlier to work in Philadelphia.) Later, Thomas received support and encouragement from the white nuns who ran the all-black Catholic school he attended.

After completing his secondary education at a Catholic boarding school in rural Georgia where he was one of only two black students, Thomas entered Missouri's Immaculate Conception Seminary with the goal of becoming a priest. The assassination of Martin Luther King, Jr., prompted him to reassess his plans, and in 1968 he left the seminary and transferred to Holy Cross College in Massachusetts. He earned his bachelor's degree from there in 1971 and then went off to Yale Law School. Following his graduation in 1974, Thomas went to work as an aide to John Danforth, then Missouri's attorney general. Three years later he left that job to serve as an attorney for the Monsanto Company in St. Louis. When Danforth was elected to the U.S. Senate in 1979, Thomas moved to Washington, D.C., and again went to work for his former boss.

Once in the nation's capital, Thomas slowly began to make a name for himself in Republican circles, mostly as a result of a speech he gave at a conference of black conservatives in December 1980. His strong denunciation of welfare dependency in particular, subsequently reported on at length in a Washington

Post *article, brought him to the attention of Reagan administration officials, and in May 1981, Thomas was appointed to the position of assistant secretary for civil rights in the Department of Education. He spent only eight rather turbulent months there before being named to head the Equal Employment Opportunity Commission (EEOC), which investigates job discrimination complaints involving race, sex, color, religion, or national origin. He remained in that post until 1990, drawing fire from many who felt his policies undermined the progress that had been made in several key areas during previous administrations. He also continued to make waves with speeches and articles that clearly defined him as a strong opponent not only of welfare but also of school desegregation, affirmative action, and abortion.*

In late 1989, President Bush nominated Thomas for a judgeship on the U.S. Circuit Court of Appeals for Washington, D.C. Easily confirmed by the Senate Judiciary Committee in March 1990, he had served for little more than a year and had ruled in only a couple of dozen routine cases when he received another call from the president. This time, Bush proposed him as a replacement for the Supreme Court's first black associate justice, Thurgood Marshall, who had just announced his retirement for health reasons. Reaction to Thomas's nomination was swift; in the weeks before the confirmation hearings began in September 1991, a number of civil rights organizations and women's groups expressed concern and sometimes outrage that an "ultraconservative" would be taking the place of one of the Court's most liberal members.

Despite the opposition he faced in certain quarters, Thomas won over the Senate Judiciary Committee and appeared to be headed for full Senate approval until October 6. On that day, a startling piece of information was leaked to the news media: about two weeks earlier, Anita Hill, a law professor at the University of Oklahoma who had once worked for Thomas at the Department of Education and the EEOC, had provided Judiciary Committee staff members with an affidavit stating that her former boss had sexually harassed her during the early 1980s. The public pressure to look into her charges soon forced the committee to resume the hearings.

On October 11, a nationwide television audience sat transfixed as Hill recounted calmly and in detail how Thomas had made repeated sexual overtures to her and how he had frequently tried to engage her in lewd conversations about pornographic movies. That same day, Thomas responded to her charges with a mixture of anger and bewilderment, speaking first at a morning session before Hill had testified and later at an evening session that followed her disturbing revelations. His remarks are reprinted from the official U.S. government transcript of the proceedings, a document entitled Nomination of Judge Clarence Thomas to Be Associate Justice of the Supreme Court of the United States: Hearings Before the Committee on the Judiciary, United States Senate.

Mr. Chairman, Senator Thurmond, members of the committee: as excruciatingly difficult as the last two weeks have been, I welcome the opportunity to clear my name today. No one other than my wife and Senator Danforth, to whom I read this statement at 6:30 a.m., has seen or heard the statement, no handlers, no advisers.

The first I learned of the allegations by Professor Anita Hill was on September 25, 1991, when the FBI came to my home to investigate her allegations. When informed by the FBI agent of the nature of the allegations and the person making them, I was shocked, surprised, hurt, and enormously saddened.

I have not been the same since that day. For almost a decade my responsibilities included enforcing the rights of victims of sexual harassment. As a boss, as a friend, and as a human being I was proud that I have never had such an allegation leveled against me, even as I sought to promote women, and minorities into nontraditional jobs.

In addition, several of my friends, who are women, have confided in me about the horror of harassment on the job, or elsewhere. I thought I really understood the anguish, the fears, the doubts, the seriousness of the matter. But since September 25, I have suffered immensely as these very serious charges were leveled against me.

I have been wracking my brains, and eating my insides out trying to think of what I could have said or done to Anita Hill to lead her to allege that I was interested in her in more than a professional way, and that I talked with her about pornographic or x-rated films.

Contrary to some press reports, I categorically denied all of the allegations and denied that I ever attempted to date Anita Hill, when first interviewed by the FBI. I strongly reaffirm that denial. Let me describe my relationship with Anita Hill.

In 1981, after I went to the Department of Education as an assistant secretary in the Office of Civil Rights, one of my closest friends, from both college and law school, Gil Hardy, brought Anita Hill to my attention. As I remember, he indicated that she was dissatisfied with her law firm and wanted to work in government. Based primarily, if not solely, on Gil's recommendation, I hired Anita Hill.

During my tenure at the Department of Education, Anita Hill was an attorney-adviser who worked directly with me. She worked on special projects, as well as day-to-day matters. As I recall, she was one of two professionals working directly with me at the time. As a result, we worked closely on numerous matters.

I recall being pleased with her work product and the professional, but cordial relationship which we enjoyed at work. I also recall engaging in discussions about politics and current events.

Upon my nomination to become chairman of the Equal Employment Opportunity Commission, Anita Hill, to the best of my recollection, assisted me in the nomination and confirmation process. After my confirmation, she and Diane Holt, then my secretary, joined me at EEOC. I do not recall that there was any question or doubts that she would become a special assistant to me at EEOC, although as a career employee she retained the option of remaining at the Department of Education.

At EEOC our relationship was more distant. And our contacts less frequent, as a result of the increased size of my personal staff and the dramatic increase and diversity of my day-to-day responsibilities.

Upon reflection, I recall that she seemed to have had some difficulty adjusting to this change in her role. In any case, our relationship remained both cordial and professional. At no time did I become aware, either directly or indirectly that she felt I had said, or done anything to change the cordial nature of our relationship.

I detected nothing from her or from my staff, or from Gil Hardy our mutual friend, with whom I maintained regular contact. I am certain that had any statement or conduct on my part been brought to my attention, I would remember it clearly because of the nature and seriousness of such conduct, as well as my adamant opposition to sex discrimination [and] sexual harassment.

But there were no such statements.

In the spring of 1983, Mr. Charles Cothey contacted me to speak at the law school at Oral Roberts University in Tulsa, Oklahoma. Anita Hill, who is from Oklahoma, accompanied me on that trip. It was not unusual that individuals on my staff would travel with me occasionally. Anita Hill accompanied me on that trip primarily because this was an opportunity to combine business and a visit to her home.

As I recall, during our visit at Oral Roberts University, Mr. Cothey mentioned to me the possibility of approaching Anita Hill to join the faculty at Oral Roberts University Law School. I encouraged him to do so. I noted to him, as I recall, that Anita Hill would do well in teaching. I recommended her highly and she eventually was offered a teaching position.

Although I did not see Anita Hill often after she left EEOC, I did see her on one or two subsequent visits to Tulsa, Oklahoma. And on one visit I believe she drove me to the airport. I also occasionally received telephone calls from her. She would speak directly with me or with my secretary, Diane Holt. Since Anita Hill and

Clarence Thomas

Diane Holt had been with me at the Department of Education they were fairly close personally and I believe they occasionally socialized together.

I would also hear about her through Linda Jackson, then Linda Lambert, whom both Anita Hill and I met at the Department of Education. And I would hear of her from my friend Gil.

Throughout the time that Anita Hill worked with me I treated her as I treated my other special assistants. I tried to treat them all cordially, professionally, and respectfully. And I tried to support them in their endeavors, and be interested in and supportive of their success.

I had no reason or basis to believe my relationship with Anita Hill was anything but this way until the FBI visited me a little more than two weeks ago. I find it particularly troubling that she never raised any hint that she was uncomfortable with me. She did not raise or mention it when considering moving with me to EEOC from the Department of Education. And she never raised it with me when she left EEOC and was moving on in her life.

And to my fullest knowledge, she did not speak to any other women working with or around me, who would feel comfortable enough to raise it with me, especially Diane Holt, to whom she seemed closest on my personal staff. Nor did she raise it with mutual friends, such as Linda Jackson, and Gil Hardy.

This is a person I have helped at every turn in the road, since we met. She seemed to appreciate the continued cordial relationship we had since day one. She sought my advice and counsel, as did virtually all of the members of my personal staff.

During my tenure in the executive branch as a manager, as a policymaker, and as a person, I have adamantly condemned sex harassment. There is no member of this committee or this senate who feels stronger about sex harassment than I do. As a manager, I made every effort to take swift and decisive action when sex harassment raised or reared its ugly head.

The fact that I feel so very strongly about sex harassment and spoke loudly about it at EEOC has made these allegations doubly hard on me. I cannot imagine anything that I said or did to Anita Hill that could have been mistaken for sexual harassment.

But with that said, if there is anything that I have said that has been misconstrued by Anita Hill or anyone else, to be sexual harassment, then I can say that I am so very sorry and I wish I had known. If I did know I would have stopped immediately and I would not, as I have done over the past two weeks, had to tear away at myself trying to think of what I could possibly have done. But I have not said or done the things that Anita Hill has alleged. God has gotten me through the days since September 25 and He is my judge.

Mr. Chairman, something has happened to me in the dark days that have followed since the FBI agents informed me about these allegations. And the days have grown darker, as this very serious, very explosive, and very sensitive allegation or these sensitive allegations were selectively leaked, in a distorted way to the media over the past weekend.

As if the confidential allegations, themselves, were not enough, this apparently calculated public disclosure has caused me, my family, and my friends enormous pain and great harm.

I have never, in all my life, felt such hurt, such pain, such agony. My family and I have been done a grave and irreparable injustice. During the past two weeks, I lost the belief that if I did my best all would work out. I called upon the strength that helped me get here from Pin Point, and it was all sapped out of me. It was sapped out of me because Anita Hill was a person I considered a friend, whom I admired and thought I had treated fairly and with the utmost respect. Perhaps I could have better weathered this if it were from someone else, but here was someone I truly felt I had done my best with.

Though I am, by no means, a perfect person, no means, I have not done what she has alleged, and I still do not know what I could possibly have done to cause her to make these allegations.

When I stood next to the president in Kennebunkport, being nominated to the Supreme Court of the United States, that was a high honor. But as I sit here, before you, 103 days later, that honor has been crushed. From the very beginning charges were leveled against me from the shadows—charges of drug abuse, anti-Semitism, wife-beating, drug use by family members, that I was a quota appointment, confirmation conversion and much, much more, and now this.

I have complied with the rules. I responded to a document request that produced over 30,000 pages of documents. And I have testified for 5 full days, under oath. I have endured this ordeal for 103 days. Reporters sneaking into my garage to examine books I read. Reporters and interest groups swarming over divorce papers, looking for dirt. Unnamed people starting preposterous and damaging rumors. Calls all over the country specifically requesting dirt. This is not American. This is Kafka-esque. It has got to stop. It must stop for the benefit of future nominees, and our country. Enough is enough.

I am not going to allow myself to be further humiliated in order to be confirmed. I am here specifically to respond to allegations of sex harassment in the work place. I am not here to be further humiliated by this committee, or anyone else, or to put my private life on display for a prurient interest or other reasons. I will not allow this committee or anyone else to probe into my private life. This is not what America is all about.

To ask me to do that would be to ask me to go beyond fundamental fairness. Yesterday, I called my mother. She was confined to her bed, unable to work and unable to stop crying. Enough is enough.

Mr. Chairman, in my forty-three years on this Earth, I have been able, with the help of others and with the help of God, to defy poverty, avoid prison, overcome segregation, bigotry, racism, and obtain one of the finest educations available in this country. But I have not been able to overcome this process. This is worse than any obstacle or anything that I have ever faced. Throughout my life I have been energized by the expectation and the hope that in this country I would be treated fairly in all endeavors. When there was segregation I hoped there would be fairness one day or some day. When there was bigotry and prejudice I hoped that there would be tolerance and understanding some day.

"My family and I have been done a grave and irreparable injustice. I lost the belief that if I did my best all would work out."

Mr. Chairman, I am proud of my life, proud of what I have done, and what I have accomplished, proud of my family, and this process, this process is trying to destroy it all. No job is worth what I have been through, no job. No horror in my life has been so debilitating. Confirm me if you want, don't confirm me if you are so led, but let this process end. Let me and my family regain our lives. I never asked to be nominated. It was an honor. Little did I know the price, but it is too high.

I enjoy and appreciate my current position, and I am comfortable with the prospect of returning to my work as a judge on the U.S. Court of Appeals for the D.C. Circuit and to my friends there.

Each of these positions is public service, and I have given at the office. I want my life and my family's life back and I want them returned expeditiously.

I have experienced the exhilaration of new heights from the moment I was called to Kennebunkport by the president to have lunch and he nominated me. That was the high point. At that time I was told eye-to-eye that, Clarence, you made it this far on merit, the rest is going to be politics and it surely has been. There have been other highs. The outpouring of support from my friends of long-standing, a bonding like I have never experienced with my old boss, Senator Danforth, the wonderful support of those who have worked with me.

"As far as I am concerned, [this] is a high-tech lynching for uppity blacks who in any way deign to think for themselves, to do for themselves, to have different ideas . . ."

There have been prayers said for my family, and me, by people I know and people I will never meet, prayers that were heard and that sustained not only me, but also my wife and my entire family. Instead of understanding and appreciating the great honor bestowed upon me, I find myself, here today defending my name, my integrity, because somehow select portions of confidential documents, dealing with this matter were leaked to the public.

Mr. Chairman, I am a victim of this process and my name has been harmed, my integrity has been harmed, my character has been harmed, my family has been harmed, my friends have been harmed. There is nothing this committee, this body or this country can do to give me my good name back, nothing.

I will not provide the rope for my own lynching or for further humiliation. I am not going to engage in discussions, nor will I submit to roving questions of what goes on in the most intimate parts of my private live or the sanctity of my bedroom. These are the most intimate parts of my privacy, and they will remain just that, private.

[Several hours later, Thomas opened the evening session with an even more emphatic statement denying all charges against him.]

I would like to start by saying unequivocally, uncategorically that I deny each and every single allegation against me today that suggested in any way that I had conversations of a sexual nature or about pornographic material with Anita Hill, that I ever attempted to date her, that I ever had any personal sexual interest in her, or that I in any way ever harassed her.

Second, and I think a more important point, I think that this today is a travesty. I think that it is disgusting. I think that this hearing should never occur in America. This is a case in which this sleaze, this dirt was searched for by staffers of members of this committee, was then leaked to the media, and this committee and this body validated it and displayed it in prime time over our entire nation.

How would any member on this committee or any person in this room or any person in this country would like sleaze said about him or her in this fashion or this dirt dredged up and this gossip and these lies displayed in this manner? How would any person like it?

The Supreme Court is not worth it. No job is worth it. I am not here for that. I am here for my name, my family, my life and my integrity. I think something is dreadfully wrong with this country, when any person, any person in this free country would be subjected to this. This is not a closed room.

There was an FBI investigation. This is not an opportunity to talk about difficult matters privately or in a closed environment. This is a circus. It is a national disgrace. And from my standpoint, as a black American, as far as I am concerned, it is a high-tech lynching for uppity blacks who in any way deign to think for themselves, to do for themselves, to have different ideas, and it is a message that, unless you kow-tow to an old order, this is what will happen to you, you will be lynched, destroyed, caricatured by a committee of the U.S. Senate, rather than hung from a tree.

On October 15, 1991, the full Senate voted to confirm Clarence Thomas as an associate justice of the Supreme Court by what proved to be the narrowest margin in history—fifty-two for and forty-eight against. Since then, he has shunned the limelight even more than is typical of his colleagues and has made few public comments on his nomination process. And as expected, his rulings have most often placed him in the camp of fellow justice Antonin Scalia, by far the most conservative member of the Court.

SOURCES

Books

Chrisman, Robert, and Robert L. Allen, editors, *Court of Appeal: The Black Community Speaks Out on the Racial and Sexual Politics of Clarence Thomas vs. Anita Hill*, Ballantine, 1992.

Danforth, John C., *Resurrection: The Confirmation of Clarence Thomas*, Viking, 1994.

Mayer, Jane, and Jill Abramson, *Strange Justice: The Selling of Clarence Thomas*, Houghton, 1994.

Morrison, Toni, editor, *Race-ing Justice, En-Gendering Power: Essays on Anita Hill, Clarence Thomas, and the Construction of Social Reality*, Pantheon, 1992.

Nomination of Judge Clarence Thomas to Be Associate Justice of the Supreme Court of the United States: Hearings Before the Committee on the Judiciary, United States Senate, 102nd Congress, 1st session, Part 4 of 4 parts, October 11, 12, and 13, 1991, pp. 5-10, 157-158.

Phelps, Timothy M., and Helen Winternitz, *Capitol Games: Clarence Thomas, Anita Hill, and the Story of a Supreme Court Nomination*, Hyperion, 1992.

Simon, Paul, *Advice and Consent: Clarence Thomas, Robert Bork, and the Intriguing History of the Supreme Court's Nomination Battles*, National Press Books, 1992.

Periodicals

Atlantic, "A Question of Fairness," February, 1987.

Grand Rapids Press, "Justice Says He's No 'Uncle Tom,' " October 28, 1994, p. A6.

National Review, "Trial by Zeitgeist," January 24, 1994, pp. 48-52.

Newsweek, "Where Does He Stand?" July 15, 1991, pp. 16-17; "How to Judge a Judge," July 15, 1991, p. 64; "Supreme Mystery," September 16, 1991; "Hearing But Not Speaking," September 16, 1991, p. 23; "Court Charade," September 23, 1991, pp. 18-20; October 28, 1991 (special section covering a variety of topics related to nomination fight).

New York, "Tabloid Government," October 28, 1991, pp. 28-31.

New Yorker, "The Burden of Clarence Thomas," September 27, 1993, pp. 38-51.

New York Times, July 3, 1991; July 16, 1991; "Two Years After His Bruising Hearing, Justice Thomas Can Rarely Be Heard," November 27, 1993, p. 7.

People, "The Making of a Judge," July 22, 1991; "Breaking Silence," November 11, 1991.

Policy Review, "No Room at the Inn: The Loneliness of the Black Conservative," fall, 1991, pp. 72-78.

Time, "Marching to a Different Drummer," July 15, 1991, pp. 18-21; "An Ugly Circus," October 21, 1991; "Truth in the Ruins," October 28, 1991, p. 104; "Judging Thomas," July 13, 1992, pp. 30-31.

U.S. News and World Report, "The Crowning Thomas Affair," September 16, 1991; "Judging Thomas," October 21, 1991, pp. 32-36.

Monroe Trotter

1872–1934

African American journalist and civil rights activist

Without a doubt, one of the most militantly aggressive members of the anti-Booker T. Washington movement that sprang up around the turn of the century was Monroe Trotter. As the founder and editor of the Guardian, a radical newspaper devoted to challenging the Tuskegee president's accommodationist philosophy, Trotter again and again demanded an immediate end to racial discrimination and championed black unity and what later came to be known as "black power." Yet his often flamboyant tactics and inability to get along with others who felt as he did ultimately deprived him of a more prominent place in the history of civil rights protest.

Although he was born on his grandparents' Ohio farm, Trotter (whose full name was William Monroe Trotter) grew up in a white suburb of Boston as part of a loving and fairly well-to-do family that experienced little in the way of overt racism. His early heroes—in addition to a father he revered—were the abolitionists who had made Massachusetts their base before and during the Civil War, and from them he gained a strong moralistic sense that influenced the choices he made later in his life. After graduating with honors from Harvard University (where he was the first black student to be elected to Phi Beta Kappa), Trotter went into the real estate business as a mortgage negotiator for a white-run firm. In 1899, he left there to establish his own company. But as he watched the racial situation deteriorate across the country and chafed under increasingly restrictive laws even in traditionally liberal Boston, the young man felt himself pulled in a direction other than business.

In 1901, after finding that Jim Crowism was making it difficult to pursue his once-promising career, Trotter launched the Guardian to counter what he described as Booker T. Washington's "betrayal" of African Americans. He bitterly characterized the Tuskegee president as a hypocrite who hobnobbed with the rich and powerful while telling his fellow blacks to accept the prevailing social conditions and concentrate on achieving economic success. Equally galling to Trotter was Washington's emphasis on the value of industrial education for all African Americans and his disdain for the type of classical instruction Trotter himself had received at Harvard. The antagonism between the two men finally *reached the boiling point in July 1903, when Trotter was arrested in Boston for heckling Washington while he was giving a speech in favor of segregation. As a result of the highly-publicized incident—dubbed the "Boston Riot"—he spent a month in jail.*

The popularity of the Guardian, *as well as its founder's love of confrontation, soon catapulted Trotter to the forefront of anti-Washington protesters. His fierce commitment to radical change also caught the eye of W.E.B. Du Bois, another Washington opponent, and convinced him to enter the fray. Together the two men began the Niagara Movement in 1905, which in turn led to the founding of the National Association for the Advancement of Colored People (NAACP) in 1909. It was at that point that Trotter parted ways with the mainstream civil rights movement; besides the fact that he and Du Bois were not getting along well, he simply could not bring himself to become involved with an organization that was funded and led mostly by whites, whom he thoroughly distrusted. He also felt the NAACP was not militant enough to suit him.*

Trotter's response was to form the all-black National Equal Rights League. But it never came close to rivaling the NAACP in numbers or influence, mostly because Trotter continued to operate somewhat erratically on the far-left fringe of the civil rights movement, albeit with good intentions. Typical of his behavior was an incident in November 1914, when he led a group of African Americans to the White House to meet with President Woodrow Wilson about ending segregation in government facilities. Trotter's opening statement—reprinted here from The Voice of Black America: Major Speeches by Negroes in the United States, 1797-1971 *edited by Philip S. Foner (Simon & Schuster, 1972)—created quite a stir at the time. According to some accounts, the two men argued for nearly an hour before the president ordered the group to leave his office; Wilson was reportedly so insulted by Trotter's abrasiveness that he refused to discuss anything with the group as long as Trotter was still a member.*

One year ago we presented a national petition, signed by Afro-Americans in thirty-eight states, protesting against the segregation of employees of the national government whose ancestry could be traced in whole or in part to Africa, as instituted under your administration in the Treasury and Post Office departments. We then appealed to you to undo this race segregation in accord with your duty as president and with your preelection pledges. We stated that there could be no freedom, no respect from others, and no equality of citizenship under segregation for races, especially when applied to but one of the many racial elements in the government employ. For such placement of employees means a charge by the government of physical indecency or infection, or of being a lower order of beings, or a subjection to the prejudices of other citizens, which constitutes inferiority of status. We protested such segregation as to working positions, eating tables, dressing rooms, rest rooms, lockers, and especially public toilets in government buildings. We stated that such segregation was a public humiliation and degradation, entirely unmerited and far-reaching in its injurious effects, a gratuitous blow against ever-loyal citizens and against those many of whom aided and supported your elevation to the presidency of our common country.

At that time you stated you would investigate conditions for yourself. Now, after the lapse of a year, we have come back, having found that all the forms of segregation of government employees of African extraction are still practiced in the Treasury and Post Office department buildings, and to a certain extent have spread into other government buildings.

Monroe Trotter

Under the Treasury Department, in the Bureau of Engraving and Printing, there is segregation not only in dressing rooms, but in working positions, Afro-American employees being herded at separate tables, in eating, and in toilets. In the Navy Department there is herding at desks and separation in lavatories; in the Post Office Department there is separation in work for Afro-American women in the alcove on the eighth floor, of Afro-American men in rooms on the seventh floor, with forbidding even of entrance into an adjoining room occupied by white clerks on the seventh floor, and of Afro-American men in separate rooms just instituted on the sixth floor, with separate lavatories for Afro-American men on the eighth floor; in the main Treasury Building in separate lavatories in the basement; in the Interior Department separate lavatories, which were specifically pointed out to you at our first hearing; in the State and other departments in separate lavatories, though there is but one Afro-American clerk to use it; in the War Department in separate lavatories; in the Post Office Department Building separate lavatories; in the sewing and bindery divisions of the Government Printing Office on the fifth floor there is herding at working positions of Afro-American women and separation in lavatories, and new segregation instituted by the division chief since our first audience with you. This lavatory segregation is the most degrading, most insulting of all. Afro-American employees who use the regular public lavatories on the floors where they work are cautioned and then warned by superior officers against insubordination.

We have come by vote of this league to set before you this definite continuance of race segregation and to renew the protest and to ask you to abolish segregation of Afro-American employees in the Executive Department.

Because we cannot believe you capable of any disregard of your pledges, we have been sent by the alarmed American citizens of color. They realize that if they can be segregated and thus humiliated by the national government at the national capital, the beginning is made for the spread of that persecution and prosecution which makes property and life itself insecure in the South; the foundation of the whole fabric of this citizenship is unsettled.

They have made plain enough to you their opposition to segregation last year by a national antisegregation petition, this year by a protest registered at the polls, voting against every Democratic candidate save those outspoken against segregation. The only Democrat elected governor in the eastern states was Governor Walsh of Massachusetts, who appealed to you by letter to stop segregation. Thus have the Afro-Americans shown how they detest segregation.

In fact, so intense is their resentment that the movement to divide this solid race vote and make peace with the national democracy, so suspiciously revived when you ran for the Presidency, and which some of our families for two generations have been risking all to promote, bids fair to be undone.

Only two years ago you were heralded as perhaps the second Lincoln, and now the Afro-American leaders who supported you are hounded as false leaders and traitors to their race. What a change segregation has wrought!

You said that your "colored fellow citizens could depend upon you for everything which would assist in advancing the interests of their race in the United States." Consider that pledge in the face of the continued color segregation! Fellow citizenship means congregation. Segregation destroys fellowship and citizenship. Consider that any passerby on the streets of the national capital, whether he be black or white, can enter and use the public lavatories in government buildings, while citizens of color who do the work of the government are excluded.

As equal citizens and by virtue of your public promises we are entitled at your hands to freedom from discrimination, restriction, imputation and insult in government employ. Have you a "new freedom" for white Americans and a new slavery for your "Afro-American fellow citizens"? God forbid!

The colored people object to the government undertaking to interpret this treatment of them in the way of sympathy and help and charity for the benefit of dependent wards. The colored American is a full-fledged, absolutely equal citizen under the law.

Segregation is in itself an injury and denial of the equality of citizenship. It is unfair to separate the Afro-American when there is no similar segregation of the Semitic, Teutonic, Latin, Celtic or Slavic government employees.

It is entirely contrary to the facts to say that segregation was instituted because of racial friction. White and colored employees have been working together in peace and harmony and friendship for years, even under a former Democratic president. Segregation was drastically introduced as soon as this administration came into being by John Skelton Williams, Secretary McAdoo and Postmaster General Burleson, because of their own racial prejudices.

It would be impossible for us, were we willing, to make the colored people of the United States to regard segregation as anything other than humiliating and degrading. We have been delegated to ask you to issue an executive order against any and all segregation of government employees because of race and color, and to ask whether you will do so. We await your reply, that we may give it to the waiting citizens of the United States of African extraction.

Trotter continued to challenge the status quo in very public and often provocative ways. In 1915, for example, he was arrested and jailed for picketing a showing of the anti-black film Birth of a Nation. *Four years later, just after the end of World War I, he found himself at the center of another major controversy. Eager to focus the world's attention on the plight of American blacks—especially black soldiers who had honorably served their country only to return to a worsening racial climate—Trotter applied for a passport to attend the Paris Peace Conference. His request was denied, however, an action he and his supporters "felt was extraordinary tyranny, flagrant enough to justify us in seeking to overcome it." Trotter then resolved to take his case to the world by clandestine means: posing as a ship's cook, he made his way to France and from there to the conference. Once in Paris, he tried unsuccessfully to meet with key delegates, hoping to persuade them to add a clause to the charter of the newly-formed League of Nations that would have outlawed racial discrimination. Although he won support among the Japanese in particular, the Western allies, including the United States, opposed the idea.*

Trotter remained true to his principles until he died in 1934, apparently by his own hand. While his stridency and independence had made it impossible for him to be a part of the mainstream civil rights movement of his day, his methods of nonviolent protest enjoyed a revival during the 1950s and 1960s.

SOURCES

Books

Foner, Philip S., editor, *The Voice of Black America: Major Speeches by Negroes in the United States, 1797-1971,* Simon & Schuster, 1972.

Fox, Stephen R., *The Guardian of Boston: William Monroe Trotter,* Atheneum, 1970.

Long, Richard A., and Eugenia Collier, editors, *Afro-American Writing: An Anthology of Prose and Poetry,* New York University Press, 1972.

Periodicals

Christian Science Monitor, "Negro Delegate Tells of His Work," July 25, 1919, p. 14.

Journal of Negro History, "William Monroe Trotter, 1872-1934," October, 1958, pp. 298-316.

John Trudell

1947–

Native American activist and musician of the Sioux tribe

Once a major spokesman of the American Indian Movement (AIM), John Trudell has more recently fused his activism with poetry and music to highlight the struggle for Native American rights. He was born and raised on the Santee Sioux Reservation, located on the border of South Dakota and northeastern Nebraska. He left there to serve in the U.S. Navy for four years during the Vietnam War, an experience that heightened his awareness of the racism directed at blacks, Asians, and other minorities such as himself.

After his tour of duty ended in the late 1960s, Trudell began associating with other young Native Americans who felt it was time to challenge the status quo. They struck their first major blow on November 20, 1969, when a group of about ninety Indians from a number of different tribes occupied Alcatraz Island (the site of a former federal prison) in San Francisco Bay to dramatize the government's seizure of Indian land and restrictions on Native American hunting and fishing rights. Ten days later, Trudell joined them, and there he remained for most of the next nineteen months until U.S. marshals removed the last of the demonstrators on June 11, 1971.

At the peak of the protest in mid-1970, as many as a thousand people assembled on Alcatraz to protest the mistreatment of Native Americans and to demand that the site be turned into an Indian educational and cultural center. Throughout the occupation, Trudell was the voice of "Radio Free Alcatraz," which broadcast the concerns of the occupiers from stations in Berkeley, Los Angeles, and New York City. He also traveled and lectured extensively, garnering support wherever he could for Indian land claims to the island. Although Alcatraz ultimately became a national park, it remains a powerful symbol of courage and solidarity to many Native Americans.

Trudell officially joined the American Indian Movement (AIM) during the spring of 1970, about two years after its founding in Minneapolis, and soon became the group's national spokesman. (AIM leaders believed that the federal government's supervision of the Indian people was slowly but surely destroying them and that they had to take charge of their own future in order to survive.) He participated in several more occupations of federal land and government buildings early in the decade, including one at an abandoned missile range in California in 1971 and another at the Bureau of Indian Affairs office in Washington, D.C., in 1972. The latter incident occurred in connection with the Trail of Broken Treaties, a demonstration that brought together thousands of Indians from throughout the country to present the U.S. government with a formal list of their demands.

In 1973, Trudell was elected co-chair of AIM. That same year, he took part in the much-publicized siege near the hamlet of Wounded Knee on South Dakota's Pine Ridge Sioux Reservation. (Wounded Knee had already earned a place in history as the site of an 1890 massacre of more than two hundred Sioux men, women, and children by U.S. Army troops intent on quashing the Ghost Dance spiritual movement.) The 1973 confrontation began in February when several hundred AIM members and sympathizers gathered at Pine Ridge to take a stand against the mistreatment of Indians. Their anger was focused in particular on the reservation's head administrator, Dick Wilson, whom some of the Sioux elders accused of corruption and strong-arm tactics. After AIM occupied Wounded Knee on February 27, federal marshals and FBI agents immediately moved in to re-establish government control. The resulting armed standoff lasted seventy-one days, ending only when federal negotiators promised to set up a meeting between Sioux elders and several White House representatives.

Within a year or so after the siege ended, Trudell delivered the following talk to a Native American audience in which he stressed the need for unity, sobriety, and commitment to the goals of AIM. (The exact date and occasion of his remarks are unknown.) Those who have heard him speak have described him as charismatic and rather "edgy"; in the words of singer and fellow activist Buffy Sainte-Marie, Trudell "was the orator who could make sense of a complicated situation and really move the individual listener on an intimate level. . . . [He was] a person in control of a powerful righteousness. He stood up for our native people. . . ." His speech is reprinted here from Contemporary Native American Address, *edited by John R. Maestas (Brigham Young University, 1976).*

I want to talk about commitment for our organization. I think commitment is the number one thing we should be thinking about. We've got to have commitment so strong that when we get mad at each other we can overlook it. We have got to have commitment so strong that we will never accept "no" for an answer. We have to have commitment so strong that we will not accept their excuses or lies as an answer. We have to have commitment so strong that we will live and we will die for our people.

We have got to start thinking in terms of love. You know we get caught up in hating the white man for what he's done to us and that hate shows. It shows in our own organization. We start playing the white man's games, and we start fighting each other. We're out for the good of Indian people but if we don't like something someone does, then we start backstabbing and calling names, and we criticize. We need to be open and talk to these individuals that the individuals are displeased with and confront them with how we feel. We go around trying to build support and try to advocate a home for ourselves. Sometimes I question that that white man affects us or that we affect ourselves. The white man manipulates and we react. It's ridiculous that he can coordinate our feelings.

I wonder about respect. We speak of respect. We study respect, and we use the word many times. But then we go and pour alcohol into our bodies. We do not respect our bodies when we do this. We rip off from each other. We do not respect our brothers when we do this. We do not respect our brothers when we talk about them behind their backs. These are things that we have to start thinking about.

John Trudell

We have heard many complaints about the grievances against the white man and against the Bureau of Indian Affairs and against the state. We have got to understand such things as colonialism. We've got to understand the methods the white man uses to put us under his thumb. *Colonialism*. That means the white man comes to our country and takes our lands away from our people and puts us into reservations and he continues to control three-fourths of the reservation and our lives. That is colonialism. When we have white landlords and white officials that sit there looking good and we go hungry and sit there without our rights—that is colonialism. Those in the Interior Department sit back and get rich and get fat, and they keep us from gaining the working knowledge and experience we need to control our lives again. That is colonialism. Colonialism is when the white man controls our land and he does our thinking for us, and then he continues to keep us disoriented and keep us at each other's throats. This is colonialism. Our enemy is not the United States, our enemy is not the individual white man. Our enemy is the collective white man. If the collective white man sits back and he allows this to happen—then he is our enemy. The white man is the one who has to accept this before there can be peace, love and understanding between the races. They have got to understand that he is in the wrong.

It was white people that made it capitalism. It was white people that created communism. It was white people that created jails, and it was white people that robbed our land. It was white people that sat back in the corner and allowed their government to do it. They come to us and talk to us of love and brotherhood. It was the white people that sold us guns, guns that got us killed. What would happen if the white man had to pick up these guns and go into the community and fight the white man himself? They sell us guns and make some money off of us. They use us. They've got it set up so that they can play off of our fears, emotionalism. You know what happened to South Dakota in the courtroom at Sioux Falls. They planned that. They wanted that to happen. That was not a spontaneous action. They planned it because they wanted to teach us a lesson. They still think they can teach us a lesson with their clubs and their guns and their Bible. But you look at the overall strategy that they've got, and we can see they are using intimidation because they want to isolate us like the SLA and the Black Panthers. They abuse us by calling us names, and they intimidate us by coming in with their clubs and beating us. They come in with their tear gas, and they shoot, and they make the communities afraid of us because they want to isolate us. They do not want us talking of freedom. They do not want the black man to think about freedom. They do not even want their own people to think about freedom.

They try to intimidate us and tell us that they have power, but the truth is that they have no power. They have guns, bombs, airplanes, laws and other methods of destruction, but that is not power. Power comes from the people. Power comes from love for the people. Power comes from not fighting each other. Power comes from standing together. Power comes from the right to live—that is power. We've got the power, and all we have to do is put it together. But we do not have to take this crap from the white people. We will have to continue to put up with it until we pull ourselves together. The biggest contradiction that I have seen within the American Indian Movement is that we don't respect each other. We say we do, but we don't act it.

There are two types of languages: the language of our mouths and the language of our actions. The language of what we do is separate as in the white man's world. They are separate. They will always be separate. Sometimes I see it happening to us. We think one thing, and then we do another. As long as we stay in this type of position and as long as we continue to do this, then we will always be disoriented.

I've heard a lot of talk about legal aid, about laws, and I don't see much hope of depending on the white man's laws. I don't see much hope in depending on the white man's understanding. Something that I firmly, honestly believe is that things aren't going to change. The technology has changed, but the civilization hasn't. The white man's civilization has always been one of creating a government and making that government stand. Always. The violence is the same. The corruption is the same. The manipulation of people's lives and his mind is the same. Their civilization is the same. Their technology is all that has changed, and this is something that we have got to expect. At any time, they come out and tell us these things take time, and I've heard that fifty thousand times in the last year. These things take time—1876 was when the American government was celebrating its first illegal anniversary. They had problems with the blacks. They had problems in the Grant administration. They had problems. What has changed from 1876 to 1974? Now you can see it on TV, now we come to a microphone and talk about it. The technology has changed but the system hasn't. We must not be fooled by them. We must put ourselves in their position, and we must condition our minds and condition them to say "no," becoming a collecting voice of "no" from the people. That is the only way that we are going to be able to correct them. We must have the courage to tell them NO, NO, NO!

We must stop becoming drunk. You don't know how many times we have tried to reason with you. Drunk, drunk—the biggest damn problem we have is being drunk. How much money do we make and spend on alcohol? Alcohol is the number one weapon against the Indian people. One hundred years ago they started pumping the alcohol through us and have used it against us since the first white man put his foot on this land. They have taken our religion, they have taken our children. They are taking our land and giving us alcohol, and alcohol is fast becoming the new God of the Indian people. Alcohol is becoming the new way of life. We hold our gatherings, and many people come. But first they go out and drink, and then they have to ask us for gas money to get home. You know the American Indian Movement has a hard time getting money—it's real hard. All the money we are getting now, they are taking it and wrapping it up in the courts. They are making us give the money back to them. Because we have to fight these legal hassles in the courts, we have to take the money right back into the court system.

"They are taking our land and giving us alcohol, and alcohol is fast becoming the new God of the Indian people."

No matter what the record happens to be, the actions are always different. It is only us that can change it. We oppress ourselves because we listen to them. Maybe we listen to their lies because we don't want to deal with the truth, but if we are going to talk about revolution, if we are going to talk about freedom, if we are going to talk about humanities and people's rights, we are going to have to deal with the truth. We are going to have to recognize it. We're going to have to understand it. We're going to have to learn to work with it. And when that truth hurts us, then we are going to have to sit down and evaluate ourselves too. We needn't worry about the truth or being criticized. We are not perfect, but too many times within our own organization, that is the biggest problem that we come up with. We are too good to be criticized and too good to be humble. We are too good to express love. We want to show that we are free by fighting each other, and that is getting us nowhere.

We need to start thinking. We need to start being ourselves. We need to stop being manipulated by the white man in his media and political systems, courtrooms, poolrooms, and by his alcohol industry. We've got to start taking action of our own. Things are getting serious, much more serious than they were two years ago. You've got rampant corruption going on in Washington, D.C. The white Americans are getting so corrupt that they no longer hide their illegal activities from the white people of this country. That is something to think about. When they no longer try to hide corruption, then that means that they have something up their sleeves.

We had better start preparing ourselves and pulling ourselves together. Let's start being a family. You know the American Indian Movement is the only family I've got. When I come into my family, I don't like to see name-calling and accusations. I don't like to see people shooting each other because when we do that we only please the white man.

You know, I don't buy this crap that Indians have always fought and can't get along. Too many times we listen to them. I would like to see all the white nations in the world sit down and form one way they could communicate with respect to everyone's language. They can't—English is the dominant language. We have the sign language, and it was more adept than anything they ever had because it respected the individual languages of the tribe. But these white people could not devise a language that would be universal. They come, and they tell us, and too many times we get sucked into believing it. All we've got to relate to is that we are the Indian people, and when the white persons came over here, we showed them how to live, we showed them how to survive, and they were peaceful toward us, and they were nice because they did not know how to live here. Once they found out how to live here, they then started killing us and stealing our land. Then they brought the black man in, and then started their history of oppression of the people of this land. They told us we were going to live in a free democracy. They told us we had human rights, and they got us to believe it. One politician will come up and say it, and then another will come up and say it, and they never say that we are losing our freedom. The people create the illusion of freedom because they create something like the civil rights bill that says that you've got these rights. We know we have these rights to create the illusion of freedom. They claim the American government fought a civil war all by itself so they could end slavery so there would be no more human bondage. And they tell us because this Civil War was fought, we are free. You know we believe it and we accept it, but the Civil War had nothing to do with human slavery. The real reason for the Civil War was because the industrial aids had come to America. It had nothing to do with humanity. Why are the black people still slaves in the ghetto?

We can't decide what our education will be. We cannot decide what our religion will be and can't get it recognized because we aren't free. Free? There is no freedom in this country unless you are extremely rich or unless you have liberated your own self. Which is our main concern—ourselves. What are we going to do with ourselves? Are we going to be able to accept criticism? Are we going to be able to recognize that the whole Indian community is a priority? Everybody has to start thinking about not spending all of our money on good ole booze and a fun time. We are going to have to start thinking about not stabbing others in the back because we don't agree with what they say. We've got to have open minds because we do not like the way things are being done. When our opinions are expressed and put down, we should not be mad and want to jump on each other's backs. We should accept the fact that we are all together and we all believe in the same thing, and this has got to be the number one priority.

Trudell remained co-chair of the American Indian Movement through the end of the 1970s, serving as coordinator of the group's defense efforts on behalf of Leonard Peltier, an Indian convicted of shooting to death two FBI agents on the Pine Ridge Reservation in June 1975. His outspoken support for Peltier may well have cost the activist the lives of his family; in February 1979, his wife, mother-in-law, and three children perished in a mysterious house fire that broke out only a few hours after Trudell burned an American flag on the steps of the FBI building in Washington, D.C., during a pro-Peltier demonstration.

In the aftermath of that tragedy, Trudell turned to writing poetry with a distinct social and political flavor. He also continued to make appearances at various benefits for Indian and environmental causes, reciting his verse and delivering fiery speeches that attracted the attention of notables such as musicians Jackson Browne and Bonnie Raitt. With their encouragement, Trudell began to set some of his thoughts to music, first to traditional Native American sounds and then to modern electric rock.

Since then, he has released two spoken-word albums, AKA Graffiti Man *(1992) and* Johnny Damas and Me *(1994), that strive to blend the personal with the political, and tribal voices and instruments with contemporary music. As Trudell explained to a* Billboard *reporter, "I'm trying to achieve a genuine fusion. . . . I'm not really trying to entertain or deliver a message. I'm trying to communicate. Politics will always be a part of me, but that's all it is—a part. I'm a whole person just trying to express my feelings, and hopefully others can relate to them."*

Trudell has also become involved in film. In 1992, for example, he served as a consultant to the makers of Incident at Oglala, *a documentary on the Leonard Peltier case, and appeared in on-camera interviews as well. That same year, he acted in the thriller* Thunderheart, *which incorporates in its storyline some of the events that took place on the Pine Ridge Reservation during the 1970s.*

SOURCES

Books

Maestas, John R., editor, *Contemporary Native American Address,* Brigham Young University, 1976.

Matthiessen, Peter, *In the Spirit of Crazy Horse,* Viking, 1983, new edition, 1991.

Voices from Wounded Knee, 1973: In the Words of the Participants, Akwesasne Notes, 1974.

Periodicals

Billboard, "Native American Song, Then and Now," May 9, 1992, p. 5; "Trudell Inspires Unusual Ryko Promo," January 29, 1994, pp. 13-14.

Interview, "Rocking a Difference and Rolling a Change," April, 1992, pp. 98-103.

Other

Incident at Oglala: The Leonard Peltier Story (documentary film), Carolco International, 1992.

Thunderheart (film), 1992.

Sojourner Truth

1797(?)–1883

African American abolitionist and women's rights activist

Born a slave named Isabella in upstate New York, Sojourner Truth spent her youth as a member of several different households after she was sold to a new master and separated from her parents at the age of nine. By that time, however, young Bell (as she was known) had already received from her mother the moral and spiritual education that formed the basis of her lifetime devotion to religion and reform.

In 1828, Isabella was freed as a result of changes in New York state laws. She then supported herself and her children (she was separated from her husband) by working as a domestic, often in New York City. (She also took a last name, Van Wagener, from one of her employers.) It was there that she became a follower of a self-proclaimed messenger from God. Isabella eventually grew disillusioned with him and his movement and left New York City on June 1, 1843. Only a few miles into her trip, she underwent a profound religious experience that prompted her to change her name to Sojourner Truth and commit herself to a life of urging others to accept Jesus and avoid sin.

For the next forty years, until her death in 1883, Truth lived up to her name as the traveler charged with bringing enlightenment to as many people as possible. She lectured throughout the Northeast and Midwest and soon broadened her topics to include not only religion but also the abolition of slavery (she was the first black woman antislavery speaker), women's rights, temperance, and prison reform. She was especially skilled at weaving together the concepts of freedom for blacks with freedom for women. But her unpopular views frequently made her the target of abuse and arrest.

Truth delivered her most famous speech, "Ain't I a Woman?," on May 29, 1851, to a women's rights convention in Akron, Ohio. Presiding over the gathering was Frances Gage, who recorded Truth's remarks in a substandard southern dialect that probably did not reflect her actual speaking style. In fact, she had grown up in the North speaking Dutch, did not learn English until after she was sold to a new master, and never even met a southerner—white or black—almost until she reached adulthood. This version of the speech, complete with Gage's bracketed notes about the audience's reaction, originally appeared in Volume 1 of the 1881 title History of Woman Suffrage, *edited by Elizabeth Cady Stanton and others; it was later reprinted in* We Shall Be Heard: Women Speakers in America, 1828–Present. *Following the speech as Gage wrote it down is a version without the southern dialect markers that was first published in the* Narrative of Sojourner Truth *and later reprinted in Volume 2 of* Man Cannot Speak for Her *(Greenwwod Press, 1989).*

[I rose and announced "Sojourner Truth," and begged the audience to keep silence for a few moments. The tumult subsided at once, and every eye was fixed on this almost Amazon form, which stood nearly six feet high, head erect, and eye piercing the upper air, like one in a dream. At her first word, there was a profound hush. She spoke in deep tones, which, though not loud, reached every ear in the house, and away through the throng at the doors and windows:]

"Wall, chilern, whar dar is so much racket dar must be somethin' out o' kilter. I tink dat twixt de niggers of de Souf and de woman at de Norf, all talkin' 'bout rights, de white men will be in a fix pretty soon.

"But what's all dis here talkin' 'bout? Dat man ober dar say dat woman needs to be helped into carriages, and lifted ober ditches, and to hab de best place everywhar. Nobody eber helps me into carriages, or ober mud-puddles, or gibs me any best place!" [And raising herself to her full height, and her voice to a pitch like rolling thunder, she asked,] "And ain't I a woman? Look at me! Look at my arm! [and she bared her right arm to the shoulder, showing her tremendous muscular power.] I have ploughed, and planted, and gathered into barns, and no man could head me! And ain't I a woman? I could work as much and eat as much as a man—when I could get it—and bear de lash as well! And ain't I a woman? I have borne thirteen chilern and seen 'em mos' all sold off to slavery, and when I cried out with my mother's grief, none but Jesus heard me! And ain't I a woman?

"Den dey talks 'bout dis ting in de head; what dis dey call it? ["Intellect," whispered some one near.] "Dat's it honey. What's dat got to do wid woman's rights or niggers' rights? If my cup won't hold but a pint, and yourn holds a quart, wouldn't ye be mean not to let me have my little half-measure full?" [And she pointed

Sojourner Truth

her significant finger, and sent a keen glance at the minister who had made the argument. The cheering was long and loud.]

"Den dat little man in black dar, he say women can't have as much rights as men, 'cause Christ wan't a woman! Whar did your Christ come from?" [Rolling thunder couldn't have stilled that crowd, as did those deep, wonderful tones, as she stood there with outstretched arms and eyes of fire. Raising her voice still louder, she repeated,] "Whar did your Christ come from? From God and a woman! Man had nothin' to do wid Him." [Oh, what a rebuke that was to that little man.]

[Turning again to another objector, she took up the defense of Mother Eve. I can not follow her through it all. It was pointed, and witty, and solemn: eliciting at almost every sentence deafening applause; and she ended by asserting:] "If de fust woman God ever made was strong enough to turn de world upside down all alone, dese women togedder [and she glanced her eye over the platform] ought to be able to turn it back, and get it right side up again! And now dey is asking to do it, de men better let 'em." [Long-continued cheering greeted this.]

"'Bleeged to Ye for hearin' on me, and now ole Sojourner han't got nothin' more to say."

[Amid roars of applause, she returned to her corner, leaving more than one of us with streaming eyes, and hearts beating with gratitude. She had taken us up in her strong arms and carried us safely over the slough of difficulty turning the whole tide in our favor. I have never in my life seen anything like the magical influence that subdued the mobbish spirit of the day, and turned the sneers and jeers of an excited crowd into notes of respect and admiration. Hundreds rushed up to shake hands with her, and congratulate the glorious old mother, and bid her God-speed on her mission of "testifyin' agin concerning the wickedness of this 'ere people."]

Without any southern dialect markers, the above reads as follows:

Well, children, where there is so much racket there must be something out o' kilter. I think that 'twixt the Negroes of the South and the women of the North all a-talking about rights, the white men will be in a fix pretty soon.

But what's all this here talking about? That man over there says that women need to be helped into carriages, and lifted over ditches, and to have the best place everywhere. Nobody ever helps me into carriages, or over mud puddles or gives me any best place, and aren't I a woman? Look at me! Look at my arm! I have plowed, and planted, and gathered into barns, and no man could head me—and aren't I a woman? I could work as much and eat as much as a man (when I could get it), and bear the lash as well—and aren't I a woman? I have borne thirteen children and seen them almost all sold off into slavery, and when I cried out with a mother's grief, none but Jesus heard—and aren't I a woman?

Then they talk about this thing in the head—what's this they call it? That's it honey. What's that got to do with woman's rights or Negroes' rights? If my cup won't hold but a pint and yours holds a quart, wouldn't you be mean not to let me have my little half-measure full?

Then that little man in black there, he says women can't have as much rights as man, 'cause Christ wasn't a woman. Where did your Christ come from? Where did your Christ come from? From God and a woman. Man had nothing to do with him.

"Nobody ever helps me into carriages, or over mud puddles or gives me any best place, and aren't I a woman?"

If the first woman God ever made was strong enough to turn the world upside down, all alone, these together ought to be able to turn it back and get it right side up again; and now they are asking to do it, the men better let them.

'Bliged to you for hearing on me, and now old Sojourner hasn't got anything more to say.

After the Civil War, Truth continued to speak out for women's rights. She was particularly concerned that in the push to secure voting privileges for newly-freed black men, black women were being ignored. At the first annual American Equal Rights Association Convention in May 1867, Truth delivered several speeches over the course of a couple of days in which she again linked the granting of rights to blacks with the granting of rights to women. Her opening address of May 9 set the tone for her later remarks. It is reprinted from Volume 2 of Man Cannot Speak for Her *(Greenwood Press, 1989).*

My friends, I am rejoiced that you are glad, but I don't know how you will feel when I get through. I come from another field—the country of the slave. They have got their rights—so much good luck: now what is to be done about it? I feel that I have got as much responsibility as anybody else. I have got as good rights as anybody.

There is a great stir about colored men getting their rights, but not a word about the colored women; and if colored men get their rights, and not colored women get theirs, there will be a bad time about it. So I am for keeping the thing going while things are stirring; because if we wait till it is still, it will take a great while to get it going again.

White women are a great deal smarter, and know more than colored women, while colored women do not know scarcely anything. They go out washing, which is about as high as a colored woman gets, and their men go about idle, strutting up and down; and when the women come home, they ask for their money and take it all, and then scold because there is no food. I want you to consider on that, chil'n [sic].

I want women to have their rights. In the Courts women have no right, no voice; nobody speaks for them. I wish woman to have her voice there among the pettifoggers. If it is not a fit place for women, it is unfit for men to be there.

I am above 80 years old; it is about time for me to be going. But I suppose I am kept here because something remains for me to do; I suppose I am yet to help break the chain.

I have done a great deal of work; as much as a man, but did not get so much pay. I used to work in the field and bind grain, keeping up with the cradler; but men never doing no more, got twice as much pay. So with the German women. They work in the field and do as much work, but do not get the pay. We do as much, we eat as much, we want as much.

I suppose I am about the only colored woman that goes about to speak for the rights of the colored woman. I want to keep the thing stirring, now that the ice is broken. What we want is a little money. You men know that you get as much again as women when you write, or for what you do. When we get our rights, we shall not have to come to you for money, for then we shall have money enough of our own. It is a good consolation to know that when we have got this we shall not be coming to you any more.

You have been having our right so long, that you think, like a slaveholder, that you own us. I know that it is hard for one who has held the reins for so long to give up; it cuts like a knife. It will feel all the better when it closes up again. I have been in Washington about five years, seeing about these colored people. Now colored men have a right to vote; and what I want is to have colored women have the right to vote. There ought to be equal rights more then ever, since colored people have got their freedom.

I am going to talk several times while I am here; so now I will do a little singing. I have not heard any singing since I came here.

[Accordingly, suiting the action to the word, Sojourner sang, "We are going home."]

There, children, we shall rest from all our labors; first do all we have to do here.

There I am determined to go, not to stop till I get there to that beautiful place, and I do not mean to stop till I get there.

SOURCES

Books

Campbell, Karlyn Kohrs, *Man Cannot Speak for Her,* Greenwood Press, 1989, Volume 1: *A Critical Study of Early Feminist Rhetoric,* Volume 2: *Key Texts of the Early Feminists.*

Foner, Philip S., editor, *The Voice of Black America: Major Speeches by Negroes in the United States, 1797–1971,* Simon & Schuster, 1972.

Kennedy, Patricia Scileppi, and Gloria Hartman O'Shields, *We Shall Be Heard: Women Speakers in America, 1828-Present,* Kendall/Hunt, 1983.

Lerner, Gerda, editor, *Black Women in White America: A Documentary History,* Pantheon Books, 1972.

Loewenberg, Bert James, and Ruth Bogin, editors, *Black Women in Nineteenth-Century American Life: Their Words, Their Thoughts, Their Feelings,* Pennsylvania State University Press, 1976.

Mabee, Carlton, and Susan Mabee Newhouse, *Sojourner Truth: Slave, Prophet, Legend,* New York University Press, 1993.

McKissack, Pat, and Fredrick McKissack, *Sojourner Truth: Ain't I a Woman?,* Scholastic, 1992.

Ortiz, Victoria, *Sojourner Truth: A Self-Made Woman,* Lippincott, 1974.

Stanton, Elizabeth Cady, and others, editors, *History of Woman Suffrage,* Volume 1, Fowler & Wells, 1881, reprinted, Arno, 1969.

Truth, Sojourner, and Olive Gilbert, *The Narrative of Sojourner Truth* (reprint of original 1878 edition), Oxford University Press, 1991.

Other

Great American Women's Speeches (sound recording; two cassettes), Caedmon, 1973.

Henry McNeal Turner

1834–1915

African American clergyman and politician

Between the end of Reconstruction and World War I, African Americans faced oppression so widespread and cruel it rivaled (and sometimes surpassed) that practiced under the old slavery system. Lynchings, disenfranchisement, discrimination, segregation, and race riots became commonplace as the U.S. Supreme Court struck down law after law that had guaranteed blacks certain civil rights and the federal government adopted a "hands-off" policy, especially toward the South. One of the many voices who challenged this grim state of affairs was Henry McNeal Turner, the most outspoken and militant black nationalist of his day. In his numerous articles and speeches, he repeatedly attacked racism and those blacks who hesitated to take radical action against it. As he watched conditions worsen around him, he became convinced that only by emigrating to Africa would American blacks be able to reclaim their self respect and enjoy the human rights they deserved.

A freeborn native of South Carolina, Turner was just a child when his parents bound him out to labor side-by-side with slaves on local plantations. He escaped that life at the age of fifteen, eventually reaching the town of Abbeville, where he worked as a janitor and then as a messenger for a law office. It was there that he learned to read and write, largely through his own efforts, and subsequently devoured every book and magazine he could find. His particular areas of interest were law, medicine, and theology.

As a young black man in the pre-Civil War South, Turner had few career options. A yearning to enter public life was satisfied in part when he became a traveling evangelist for the Southern Methodist Church and attracted large crowds of whites as well as blacks on tours throughout the southeastern states. But while on a visit to New Orleans in 1857, he heard about the black-run African Methodist Episcopal (AME) Church, which he immediately joined. Turner then settled in Baltimore to prepare for the ministry. He accepted his first pastorate in 1862 in Washington, D.C., where his flamboyant preaching captured the attention of federal government officials, who appointed him the first black chaplain in the U.S. Army. After the war, Turner worked briefly for the Freedmen's Bureau in Georgia and then entered state politics helping to recruit black votes for the Republican party. In early 1868, he served as a delegate to the Georgia state constitutional *convention. (The U.S. Congress had ordered all of the former Confederate states to hold such conventions before they could be readmitted to the Union.)*

Later that same year, Turner was one of twenty-seven African Americans elected as Republicans to the first Reconstructionist legislature of Georgia. But white Democrats—who were in the majority—then voted to deny them their seats on account of their race. On September 3, 1868, Turner stood before the group that had expelled him and his colleagues and angrily yet eloquently protested their decision. Most of what he said that day follows; it was later published in pamphlet form, with a few additional notes appearing in brackets. This version is taken from Respect Black: The Writings and Speeches of Henry McNeal Turner, *edited by Edwin S. Redkey (Arno, 1971).*

Mr. Speaker: Before proceeding to argue this question upon its intrinsic merits, I wish the Members of this House to understand the position that I take. I hold that I am a member of this body. Therefore, sir, I shall neither fawn nor cringe before any party, nor stoop to *beg* them for my rights. Some of my colored fellow members, in the course of their remarks, took occasion to appeal to the *sympathies* of Members on the opposite side, and to eulogize their character for magnanimity. It reminds me very much, sir, of slaves begging under the lash. I am here to demand my rights, and to hurl thunderbolts at the men who would dare to cross the threshold of my manhood. There is an old aphorism which says, "Fight the Devil with fire," and if I should observe the rule in this instance, I wish gentlemen to understand that it is but fighting them with their own weapon.

The scene presented in this House, today, is one unparalleled in the history of the world. From this day, back to the day when God breathed the breath of life into Adam, no analogy for it can be found. Never, in the history of the world, has a man been arraigned before a body clothed with legislative, judicial or executive functions, charged with the offence of being of a darker hue than his fellow men. I know that questions have been before the Courts of this country, and of other countries, involving topics not altogether dissimilar to that which is being discussed here today. But, sir, never, in all the history of the great nations of this world—never before—has a man been arraigned, charged, with an offence committed by the God of Heaven himself. Cases may be found where men have been deprived of their rights for crimes and misdemeanors; but it has remained for the State of Georgia, in the very heart of the nineteenth century, to call a man before the bar, and there charge him with an act for which he is no more responsible than for the head which he carries up on his shoulders. The Anglo-Saxon race, sir, is a most surprising one. No man has ever been more deceived in that race than I have been for the last three weeks I was not aware that there was in the character of that race so much cowardice, or so much pusillanimity. The treachery which has been exhibited by gentlemen belonging to that race has shaken my confidence in it more than anything that has come under my observation from the day of my birth.

What is the question at issue? Why, sir, this Assembly, today, is discussing and deliberating on a matter upon which Angels would tremble to sit in judgment; there is not a Cherubim that sits around God's Eternal Throne, today, that would not tremble—even were an order issued by the Supreme God himself—to come down here and sit in judgment on my manhood. Gentlemen may look at this question in whatever light they choose, and with just as much indifference as they may think proper to assume, but I tell you, sir, that this is a question which will not die today. This event shall be remembered by posterity for ages yet to come, and while the sun shall continue to climb the hills of heaven.

Whose Legislature is this? Is it a white man's Legislature, or is it a black man's Legislature? Who voted for a Constitutional Convention, in obedience to the mandate of the Congress of the United States? Who first rallied around the standard of Reconstruction? Who set the ball of loyalty rolling in the State of Georgia? And whose voice was heard on the hills and in the valleys of this State? It was the voice of the brawny-armed negro, with the few humanitarian-hearted white men who came to our assistance. I claim the honor, sir, of having been the instrument of convincing hundreds—yea, thousands—of white men, that to reconstruct under the measures of the United States Congress was the safest and the best course for interest of the State.

Let us look at some facts in connection with this matter. Did half the white men of Georgia vote for this Legislature? Did not the great bulk of them fight, with all their strength, the Constitution under which we are acting? And did they not fight against the organization of this Legislature? And further, sir, did they not *vote* against it? Yes, sir! And there are persons in this Legislature, today, who are ready to spit their poison in my face, while they themselves opposed, with all their power, the ratification of this Constitution. They question my right to a seat in this body, to represent the people whose legal votes elected me. This objection, sir, is an unheard of monopoly of power. No analogy can be found for it, except it be the case of a man who should go into my house, take possession of my wife and children, and then tell me to walk out. I stand very much in the position of a criminal before your bar, because I dare to be the exponent of the views of those who sent me here. Or, in other words, we are told that if black men want to speak, they must speak through white trumpets; if black men want their sentiments expressed, they must be adulterated and sent through white messengers, who will quibble, and equivocate, and evade, as rapidly as the pendulum of a clock. If this be not done, then the black men have committed an outrage, and their Representatives must be denied the right to represent their constituents.

The great question, sir, is this: Am I a man? If I am such, I claim the rights of a man. Am I not a man, because I happen to be of a darker hue than honorable gentlemen around me? Let me see whether I am or not. I want to convince the House, today, that I am entitled to my seat here. A certain gentleman has argued that the negro was a mere development similar to the orangutan or chimpanzee, but it so happens that, when a negro is examined, physiologically, phrenologically and anatomically, and, I may say, physiognomically, he is found to be the same as persons of different color. I would like to ask any gentleman on this floor, where is the analogy? Do you find me a quadruped, or do you find me a man? Do you find three bones less in my back than in that of the white man? Do you find less organs in the brain? If you know nothing of this, I do; for I have helped to dissect fifty men, black and white, and I assert that by the time you take off the mucous pigment—the color of the skin—you cannot, to save your life, distinguish between the black man and the white. Am I a man? Have I a soul to save, as you have? Am I susceptible of eternal development, as you are? Can I learn all the arts and sciences that you can—has it ever been demonstrated in the history of the world? Have black men ever exhibited bravery, as white men have done? Have they ever been in the professions? Have they not as good articulative organs as you? Some people argue that there is a very close similarity between the larynx of the negro and that of the orangutan. Why, sir, there is not so much similarity between them as there is between the larynx of the man and that of the dog, and this fact I dare any Member of this House to dispute. God saw fit to vary everything in Nature. There are no two men alike—no two voices alike—no two trees alike. God

"The great question, sir, is this: Am I a man? If I am such, I claim the rights of a man. Am I not a man, because I happen to be of a darker hue than honorable gentlemen around me?"

has weaved and tissued variety and versatility throughout the boundless space of His creation. Because God saw fit to make some red, and some white, and some black, and some brown, are we to sit here in judgment upon what God has seen fit to do? As well might one play with the thunderbolts of heaven as with that creature that bears God's image—God's photograph.

The question is asked: "What is it that the negro race has done?" Well, Mr. Speaker, all I have to say upon the subject is this: that if we are the class of people that we are generally represented to be, I hold that we are a very great people. It is generally considered that we are the Children of Canaan, and that the curse of a father rests upon our heads, and has rested all through history. Sir, I deny that the curse of Noah has anything to do with the negro. We are not the Children of Canaan; and if we were, sir, where should we stand? Let us look a little into history. Melchisedeck was a Canaanite; all the Phoenicians—*all* those inventors of the arts and sciences were the posterity of Canaan; but, sir, the negro is not. We are the children of Cush, and Canaan's curse has nothing whatever to do with the negro. If we belong to that race, Ham belonged to it, under whose instructions Napoleon Bonaparte studied military tactics. If we belong to that race, St. Augustine belonged to it. Who was it that laid the foundation of the great Reformation? Martin Luther, who lit the light of Gospel Truth—a light that will never go out until the sun shall rise to set no more; and long ere then, Democratic principles will have found their level in the regions of Pluto and of Proserpine.

The negro is here charged with holding office. Why, sir, the negro never wanted office. I recollect that when we wanted candidates for the Constitutional Convention, we went from door to door in the "negro belt," and begged white men to run. Some promised to do so; and yet, on the very day of election, many of them *first* made known their determination not to comply with their promises. They told black men, everywhere, that they would rather see *them* run; and it was this encouragement of the white men that induced the colored man to place his name upon the ticket as a candidate for the Convention. In many instances, these white men voted for us. We did not want them, nor ask them, to do it. All we wanted them to do was, to stand still and allow us to walk up to the polls and deposit our ballots. They would not come here themselves, but would insist upon sending us. Ben Hill told them it was a nigger affair, and advised them to stay away from the polls—a piece of advice which they took very liberal advantage of. If the "niggers" had "office on the brain," it was the white man that put it there—not carpetbaggers, either, nor Yankees, nor scalawags, but the high-bred and dignified Democracy of the South. And if any one is to blame for having negroes in these Legislative Halls—if blame attaches to it at all—it is the Democratic party. Now, however, a change has come over the spirit of their dream. They want to turn the "nigger" out; and, to support their argument, they say that the black man is debarred from holding office by the Reconstruction measures of Congress. Let me tell them one thing for their information. Black men have held office, and are now holding office, under the United States Government. Andrew Johnson, President of the United States, in 1865, commissioned me as United States Chaplain, and I would have been Chaplain today, had I not resigned—not desiring to hold office any longer. Let the Democratic party, then, go to Mr. Johnson, and ask him why he commissioned a negro to that position? And if they inquire further, they will ascertain that black men have been commissioned as Lieutenants, Captains, Majors, Brevet Colonels, Surgeons, and other offices of trust and responsibility, under the United States Government. Black men, today, in Washington City, hold positions as Clerks, and the only reason why Mr. Langston is not at this time a Consul Diplomat or Minister Plenipotentiary in some foreign country, is, because he would not be corrupted by President Johnson and made to subscribe to his wicked designs. Is not that an office, and is it not a great deal better office than any seat held in this body?

The honorable gentleman from Whitfield [Mr. Shumate], when arguing this question, a day or two ago, put forth the proposition that to be a Representative was not to be an officer—"it was a privilege that citizens had a right to enjoy." These are his words. It was not an office; it was a "privilege." Every gentleman here knows that he denied that to be a Representative was to be an officer. Now, he is recognized as a leader of the Democratic party in this House, and generally cooks victuals for them to eat; makes that remarkable declaration, and how are you, gentlemen on the other side of the House, to ignore that declaration? Are you going to expel me from this House, because I am an officer, when one of your great lights says that I am *not* an officer? If you deny my right—the right of my constituents to have representation here—because it is a "privilege," then, sir, I will show you that I have as many privileges as the whitest man on on this floor. If I am not permitted to occupy a seat here, for the purpose of representing my constituents, I want to know how white men can be permitted to do so? How can a white man represent a colored constituency, if a colored man cannot do it? The great argument is: "Oh, we have inherited" this, that and the other. Now, I want gentlemen to come down to cool, common sense. Is the created greater than the Creator? Is man greater than God? It is very strange, if a white man can occupy on this floor *a seat created by colored votes,* and a black man cannot do it. Why, gentlemen, it is the most short-sighted reasoning in the world. A man can see better than that with half an eye; and even if he had no eye at all, he could forge one, as the Cyclops did, or punch one with his finger, which would enable him to see through that.

It is said that Congress never gave us the right to hold office. I want to know, sir, if the Reconstruction measures did not base their action on the ground that no distinction should be made on account of race, color, or previous condition! Was not that the grand fulcrum on which they rested? And did not every reconstructed State have to reconstruct on the idea that no discrimination, in any sense of the term, should be made? There is not a man here who will dare say, "No." If Congress has simply given me merely sufficient civil and political rights to make me a mere political slave for Democrats, or anybody else—giving them the opportunity of jumping on my back, in order to leap into political power—I do not thank Congress for it. Never, so help me, God, shall I be a political slave. I am not now speaking for those colored men who sit with me in this House, nor do I say that they endorse my sentiments [cries from the colored Members, "We do!"], but I am speaking simply and solely for myself. Congress, after assisting Mr. Lincoln to take me out of servile slavery, did not intend to put me and my race into *political* slavery. If they did, let them take away my ballot—I do not want it, and shall not have it. [Several colored Members: "Nor we!"] I don't want to be a mere tool of that sort. I have been a slave long enough already.

I tell you what I would be willing to do: I am willing that the question should be submitted to Congress for an explanation as to what was meant in the passage of these Reconstruction measures, and of the Constitutional Amendment. Let the Democratic party in this House pass a Resolution giving this subject that direction, and I shall be content. I dare you, gentlemen, to do it. Come up to the question openly, whether it meant that the negro might hold office, or whether it meant that he should merely have the right to vote. If you are honest men, you will do it. If, however, you will not do that, I would make another proposition: Call together, again, the Convention that framed the Constitution under which we are acting; let them take a vote upon the subject, and I am willing to abide their decision.

In the course of this discussion, a good deal of reference has been made to the Constitution of the United States. I hold, sir, that, under that Constitution, I am as much a man as anybody else. I hold that that document is neither proscripted, or has it ever, in the first instance, sanctioned slavery.

The Constitution says that any person escaping from service in one State, and going to another, shall, on demand, be given up. That has been the clause under which the Democratic fire-eaters have maintained that that document sanctioned slavery in man. I shall show you that it meant no such thing. It was placed there, according to Mr. Madison, altogether for a different purpose. In the Convention that drafted the Constitution,

> *Mr. Madison declared, he "thought it wrong to admit in the Constitution the idea that there could be property in man." On motion of Mr. Randolph, the word "SERVITUDE" was struck out, and "service" unanimously inserted—the former being thought to express the condition of SLAVES, and the latter the obligation of free persons.—8D MAD. PAP., 1429 and 1569.*

Now, if you can, make anything out of that that you find in it. It comes from one of the fathers of the Constitution. Sir, I want the gentleman to know that the Constitution, as Mr. Alexander H. Stephens said, I think, in 1854, so far as slavery is concerned, is neutral. He said, that if slavery existed in Georgia, it existed under the Constitution and by the authority of the Constitution; that if slavery did not exist in Pennsylvania, or in New York, *it was equally under the Constitution.*

That is a distinct avowal that the Constitution was neutral, and it is the opinion of a man who is acknowledged to be a man of great mind and large acquaintance with political affairs. Again: the Constitution of the United States has the following clause:

> *This Constitution, and and* all laws made in pursuance thereof, *shall be the supreme law of the land.*

Every law, therefore, which is passed under the Constitution of the United States, is a portion of the supreme law of the land, and you are bound to obey it.

But gentlemen say that the Democrats did not pass the Reconstruction measures. I know they did not. Such Democrats as we are having in this State come pretty well under the description given of the Bourbons by Napoleon Bonaparte, who said that they never originated a new idea, nor ever forgot an old one. They certainly never would pass such measures. Did the Revolutionary Fathers intend to perpetuate slavery? Many say they did; I say they did not. What was meant by the clause which states that no bill of attainder or *ex-post facto* law shall be passed? I will tell you what I believe the Revolutionary Fathers meant: I believe it was intended to put a clause there which should eventually work out the emancipation of the slaves. It was not intended that because the father had served in slavery the curse should descend.

One of the strongest objections to the negro holding office is based upon the fact that he has been a slave, and had no rights; but the Fathers of this country framed a Constitution and Laws, whose spirit and letter condemn this everlasting proscription of the negro.

Let us take, for example, an extract from a memorial sent to Congress in 1794. It was written by a Committee of which Dr. Rush was Chairman, and is signed by such men as Samuel Adams, John Adams, Isaac Law, Stephen Hopkins, and a host of other prominent gentlemen. This memorial says:

> *Many reasons concur in persuading us to abolish slavery in our country. It is inconsistent with the safety of the liberties of the United States. Freedom and slavery cannot long exist together.*

Let it be remembered that some of the gentlemen who signed this memorial had been presidents of the United States. It is also well known that General Washington, in his will, earnestly expresses a desire that all his slaves should receive their freedom upon the death of his wife. He says:

> *Upon the decease of my wife, it is my will and desire that all the slaves held by me in my own right should receive their freedom. And I do most pointedly and solemnly enjoin on my Executors to see that the clause regarding my slaves, and every part thereof, be religiously fulfilled.*

Did *he* intend to perpetuate slavery or negro proscription? What says he, when writing to General Lafayette?—

> *There is not a man living who wishes more sincerely than I do, to seea plan adopted for the abolition of slavery, but there is only one plan by which it can be accomplished. That is by legislative authority, and this, so far as my suffrage will go, shall not be wanting.*

General Lafayette once said:

> *I never thought, when I was fighting for America, that I was fighting to perpetuate slavery. I never should have drawn my sword in her defence, if I suspected such a thing.*

Jefferson says:

> *And can the liberties of the nation be thought secure, when we have removed the only firm basis—the conviction of the minds of the people that liberty is the gift of God? Indeed, I tremble for my country, when I reflect that God is just, and that injustice cannot last forever.*

I could quote from such men for days and weeks together, to show the spirit that was in them upon this subject, if I thought it necessary to my cause.

We are told that we have no right to hold office, because it was never conferred upon us by "specific enactment." *Were we ever made slaves by specific enactment?* I hold, sir, that there never was a law passed in this country, from its foundation to the Emancipation, which enacted us slaves. Even the great Mr. Calhoun said: "I doubt whether there is a single State in the South that *ever enacted them slaves.*" If, then, you have no laws enacting me a slave, how can you question my right to my freedom? Judge Lumpkin, one of the ablest jurists that Georgia ever had, said that there never was any positive law in the State of Georgia that forbade negroes from testifying in Courts; "and they are," said he, "only debarred by their ignorance and ignoble status." Neither did Queen Elizabeth, when she gave to Sir John Hawkins a charter to bring negroes to this country, give him that right with any other understanding than that no violence or force should be used therefor; and she never intended that they should be anything more than apprentices. Mr. Madison, in speaking upon the subject of jury trials for negroes, says: "Proof would have to be brought forward that slavery was established by preexisting laws;" "and," said he, "it will be impossible to comply with such a request, *for no such law could be produced.*" Why, then, do gentlemen clamor for proof of our being free "by virtue of specific enactment?" Show me any specific law of Georgia, or of the United States, that enacted black men to be slaves, and I will then tell you that, before we can enjoy our rights as free men, such law must be repealed.

I stand here today, sir, pleading for ninety thousand black men—voters—of Georgia; and I shall stand and plead the cause of my race until God, in His providence, shall see proper to take me hence. I trust that He will give me strength to stand, and power to accomplish the simple justice that I seek for them.

Why did your forefathers come to this country? Did they not flee from oppression? They came to free themselves from the chains of tyranny, and to escape from under the heel of the Autocrat. Why, sir, in England, for centuries together, men—and *white* men at that—wore metal collars around their necks, bearing, in graven characters, the names by which they were known. Your great and noble race were sold in the slave-marts of Rome. The Irish, also, held many white slaves, until 1172; and even Queen Elizabeth, in her day, had to send a deputation to inquire into the condition of such white slaves as had been born in England. King Alfred the Great, in his time, provided that for seven years' work the slave should be set free. And, going back to more ancient and more valuable authority, did not God himself, when he had brought the Children of Israel out of Egypt, say unto them: "Remember that you were slaves in Egypt?" I say to you, white men, today, that the great deliverance of the recent past is not altogether dissimilar to the great deliverance of ancient times, Your Democratic party may be aptly said to represent Pharaoh; the North to represent one of the walls, and the South the other. Between these two great walls the black man passes out to freedom, while your Democratic party—the Pharaoh of today—follows us with hasty strides and lowering visage.

The gentleman from Floyd [Mr. Scott] went down amid the chambers of the dead, and waked up the musty decision of Judge Taney in the Dred Scott case. Why, the very right on which he denied citizenship to Dred Scott, was, that if he were a citizen, he would be a free man, and invested with all rights of citizenship. The Constitution says that

> *All persons born or naturalized in the United States, and resident in this State, are hereby declared citizens of this State; and no law shall be made or enforced that shall abridge the privileges or immunities of citizens of the United States, or of this State, or deny to any person within its jurisdiction the equal protection of its laws.*

For what purpose was this clause inserted in that Constitution? It was placed there, sir, to protect the rights of every man—the Heaven-granted, inalienable, unrestricted rights of mine, and of my race. Great God, if I had the voice of seven thunders, today, I would make the ends of the earth to hear me. The Code of Laws known as Irwin's Code of Georgia, clearly states the rights of citizens. Section 1648 is as follows:

> *Among the rights of citizens are the enjoyment of personal security, of personal liberty, private property and the disposition thereof, the elective franchise, the right to hold office, to appeal to the Courts, to testify as a witness, to perform any civil function, and to keep and bear arms.*

Section 1649 of the same Code says:

> *All citizens are entitled to the exercise of their right as such, unless specially prohibited by law.*

I would like to ascertain, Mr. Speaker, what prohibition has been put upon me, or upon my race, and what can be put upon it, under the

"I stand here today, sir, pleading for ninety thousand black men—voters—of Georgia; and I shall stand and plead the cause of my race until God, in His providence, shall see proper to take me hence."

provision of the Constitution, which would deprive us of holding office. The Constitution of Georgia, Article 2, Section 2, says that:

> *Every male person who has been born or naturalized, or who has legally declared his intention to become a citizen of thc United States, twenty years old or upward, who shall have resided in this State six months next preceding the election, and shall have resided thirty days in the county in which he offers to vote, and shall have paid all taxes which may have been required of him, and which he may have had an opportunity of paying, agreeably to law, for the year next preceding the election (except as hereinafter provided), shall be declared an elector; and every male citizen of the United States, of the age aforesaid (except as hereinafter provided), who may be a resident of the State at the time of the adoption of this Constitution, shall be deemed an elector, and shall have all the rights of an elector as aforesaid.*

Now let me read to you the meaning of the

word "citizen," as given by Mr. Bouvier in his Law Dictionary:

In American law, one who, under the Constitution and Laws of the United States has a right to vote for Representatives in Congress and other public officers, and who is qualified to fill offices in the gift of the people. Any white person born in the United States, or naturalized person born out of the same, who has not lost his right as such.

Now, sir, I claim to be a citizen, I claim to be an elector, and I claim to be entitled to hold office.

We have heard a good deal said about Greece and Rome, and the great nations of antiquity, and of such great men as Socrates, Seneca, Aristotle, Plato, Herodotus, Horace, and Homer. Well, I make a reference or two to these times and nations. A freedman among the Romans was nothing more than, in the time of slavery in this country, a free negro would be. He could not come in contact with the citizen upon an equal footing, but when the Empire came under the sway of Constantine, he provided that all slaves who were made free upon account of meritorious conduct should be franchised. Go back, then, Georgians, to the days of Constantine, and learn from him a lesson of wisdom. In the days of Justinian, too, provision was made that every slave who was made free should be enfranchised and made a full citizen of Rome. The celebrated Roman writer, Horace, boasted that he was the son of a freedman; and I would remind you, also, that one of the Emperors and rulers of Rome had a slave mother. Another provision of those times was, that a slave could become free and a citizen by the consent of six thousand other citizens. Now, sir, even following the example of Rome, am I not a citizen? Have not more than six thousand white citizens voted me my rights as such? And have not forty thousand white citizens voted for the Constitution which grants me my rights as such?

We learn some peculiar points in regard to slavery from many of the writers of ancient times. Tacitus, for instance, tells us that, amongst the ancient Germans, if, in gaming, the slave should win, the master became his property and slave, while he became master. Mohammed gave political rights to all slaves who defended his religion; and so, indeed, in general, did the Crusaders; and the Popes of Rome used to teach their flocks that all men were the Lord's freemen. St. Jerome once remarked that a man's right to enfranchisement existed in his knowledge of the truth. I might quote for hours from such authorities as these upon the rights which rested in, and were acquired by, the slaves of old, but I deem it unnecessary to do so at this time.

These colored men, who are unable to express themselves with all the clearness, and dignity, and force of rhetorical eloquence, are laughed at in derision by the Democracy of the country. It reminds me very much of the man who looked at himself in a mirror, and, imagining that he was addressing another person, exclaimed: "My God, how ugly you are!" [Laughter.] These gentlemen do not consider for a moment the dreadful hardships which these people have endured, and especially those who in any way endeavored to acquire an education. For myself, sir, I was raised in the cotton field of South Carolina, and, in order to prepare myself for usefulness, as well to myself as to my race, I determined to devote my spare hours to study. When the overseer retired at night to his comfortable couch, I sat and read, and thought, and studied, until I heard him blow his horn in the morning. He frequently told me, with an oath, that if he discovered me attempting to learn, he would whip me to death, and I have no doubt he would have done so, if he had found an opportunity. I prayed to Almighty God to assist me, and He did, and I thank Him with my whole heart and soul.

Personally, I have the highest regard for the gentleman from Floyd [Mr. Scott], but I need scarcely say that I heartily despise the political sentiments which he holds. I would pledge myself to do this, however: To take the Holy Bible and read it in as many different languages as he will. If *he* reads it in English, *I* will do it; if *he* reads it in Latin, *I* will do the same; if in Greek, *I* will read it in that language, too; and if in Hebrew, *I* will meet *him,* also there. It can scarcely, then, be upon the plea of ignorance that he would debar me from the exercise of political rights.

I must now direct your attention to a point which shows the intention of the framers of the Constitution of Georgia, which you have sworn to support. In the "Proceedings of the Constitutional Convention," which framed this Constitution, I find, under date of March 3d, 1868, that, on motion of Mr. Akerman, the report of the Judiciary Committee on the subject of the qualifications of persons for membership to the first General Assembly, after the ratification and adoption of the Constitution, was taken up, and, without amendment, adopted. That report is as follows:

Be it ordained by the people of Georgia, in Convention assembled, That the persons eligible as members of the General Assembly, at the first election held under the Constitution framed by this Convention, shall be citizens of the United States who shall have been inhabitants of this State for six months, and of the district or county for which they shall be elected for three months next preceding such election, and who, in the case of Senators, shall have attained the age of twenty-five years, and, in the case of Representatives, the age of twenty-one years, at the time of such election.

Gentlemen will observe the word "inhabitant" in the Ordinance; and it was put there especially, in order that no question could arise as to who were eligible to fill the positions of Senator and Representative.

So far as I am personally concerned, no man in Georgia has been more conservative than I. "Anything to please the white folks" has been my motto; and so closely have I adhered to that course, that many among my own party have classed me as a Democrat. One of the leaders of the Republican party in Georgia has not been at all favorable to me for some time back, because he believed that I was too "conservative" for a Republican. I can assure you, however, Mr. Speaker, that I have had quite enough, and to spare, of such "conservatism."

The "conservative" element has pursued a somewhat erratic course in the reconstruction of Georgia. In several instances—as, for instance, in Houston county—they placed negroes on their tickets for county offices, and *elected* them, too, and *they are holding office today.* And this policy is perfectly consistent with the doctrine taught, in public and in private, by the great lights of Democracy, all through the last canvass. They objected to the Constitution, "because," said they, "it confers upon the niggers the right to hold office." Even Mr. Alexander H. Stephens—one of the greatest men, if not the *greatest* man, in the South, today, and one for whom I have the utmost respect—in a conversation that I had with him before the Legislature convened (Governor Brown's Marietta speech being one of the topics under consideration very generally throughout the State at the time), said: "Governor Brown says that the black man cannot hold office under that Constitution, but he *knows* that he can."

But, Mr. Speaker, I do not regard this movement as a thrust at me. It is a thrust at the Bible—a thrust at the God of the Universe, for making a man and not finishing him; it is simply calling the Great Jehovah a fool. Why, sir, though we are not white, we have accomplished much. We have pioneered civilization here; we have built up your country; we have worked in your fields, and garnered your harvests, for two hundred and fifty years! And what do we ask of you in return? Do we ask you for compensation for the sweat our fathers bore for you—for the tears you have caused, and the hearts you have broken, and the lives you have curtailed, and the blood you have spilled? Do we ask retaliation? We ask it not. We are willing to let the dead past bury its dead; but we ask you, now, for our RIGHTS. You have all the elements of superiority upon your side; you have our money and your own; you have our education and your own; and you have our land and your own, too. We, who number hundreds of thousands in Georgia, including our wives and families, with not a foot of land to call our own—strangers in the land of our birth; without money, without education, without aid, without a roof to cover us while we live, nor sufficient clay to cover us when we die! It is extraordinary that a race such as yours, professing gallantry, and chivalry, and education, and superiority, living in a land where ringing chimes call child and sire to the Church of God—a land where Bibles are read and Gospel truths are spoken, and where courts of justice are presumed to exist; it is extraordinary, I say, that, with all these advantages on your side, you can make war upon the poor defenceless black man. You know we have no money, no railroads, no telegraphs, no advantages of any sort, and yet all manner of injustice is placed upon us. You know that the black people of this country acknowledge you as their superiors, by virtue of your education and advantages.

"We are willing to let the dead past bury its dead; but we ask you, now, for our RIGHTS."

There was a Resolution passed here at the early part of this session stating that all persons who were in their seats were eligible thereto. What are gentlemen going to do, with that Resolution staring them in the face? Your children and my children will read that Resolution, and they will be astonished that persons, claiming to be men, with souls and consciences, should, contrary to the express provision of that Resolution, turn the colored man out of his seat in this Hall. Another Resolution came before this House, a short time ago, praying Congress to remove all political disabilities from the white people of Georgia. I stand in my place here, sir, and advocate that Resolution, and advise all colored Members to do the same; and almost everyone of them voted for it. We were willing to give the white man every right which he ever rightfully possessed, and, were there forty negroes in this country to one white man, I would have precisely the same feeling, and act precisely the same way. The action of the House reminds me very much of a couple of lines of verse which we occasionally read:

When the Devil was sick, the Devil a
saint would be;
When the Devil was well, the Devil a
saint was he.

When this House was "sick" with fear for the safety of the seats of ineligible Democrats, they were all very gracious and polite. But, when the Resolution was passed, declaring, in the face of facts, that all who were in their seats were eligible, then the foot was raised which was to trample on the poor negro, and that, too, by those who claim bravery and chivalry.

You may expel us, gentlemen, but I firmly believe that you will some day repent it. The black man cannot protect a country, if the country doesn't protect him; and if, tomorrow, a war should arise, I would not raise a musket to defend a country where my manhood is denied. The fashionable way in Georgia, when hard work is to be done, is, for the white man to sit at his ease, while the black man does the work; but, sir, I will say this much to the colored men of Georgia, as, if I should be killed in this campaign, I may have no opportunity of telling them at any other time: Never lift a finger nor raise a hand in defence of Georgia, unless Georgia acknowledges that you are men, and invests you with the rights pertaining to manhood. Pay your taxes, however, obey all orders from your employers, take good counsel from friends, work faithfully, earn an honest living, and show, by your conduct, that you can be good citizens.

I want to take your memories back to 1862. In that year, the Emperor of Russia, with one stroke of his pen, freed twenty-two millions of serfs. What did Russia do, then? Did she draw lines of distinction between those who had been serfs and her other citizens? No! That noble Prince, upon whose realm the sun never sets, after having freed these serfs, invested them with all the political rights enjoyed by his other subjects. America boasts of being the most enlightened, intelligent and enterprising nation in the world, and many people look upon Russia as not altogether perfectly civilized. But, look at what Russia has done for her slaves; there were twenty-two millions of them, while there are but four millions of us in the whole South, and only half a million in Georgia. If the action is taken in this House that is contemplated today, I will call a colored Convention, and I will say to my friends: Let us send North for carpetbaggers and Yankees, and let us send to Europe and all over the world for immigrants, and when they come here, we will give them every vote we have, and send them to the Legislature, in preference to sending a Georgian there.

Go on with your oppressions. Babylon fell. Where is Greece? Where is Nineveh? And where is Rome, the mistress Empire of the World? Why is it that she stands, today, in broken fragments throughout Europe? Because oppression killed her. Every act that we commit is like a bounding ball. If you curse a man, that curse rebounds upon you; and when you bless a man, the blessing returns to you; and when you oppress a man, the oppression, also, will rebound. Where have you ever heard of four millions of freemen being governed by laws, and yet have no hand in their making? Search the records of the world, and you will find no example. "Governments derive their just powers from the consent of the governed." How dare you to make laws by which to try me and my wife and children, and deny me a voice in the making of these laws? I know you can establish a monarchy, an autocracy, an oligarchy, or any other kind of an "ocracy" that you please; and that you can declare whom you please to be sovereign; but tell me, sir, how you can clothe me with more power than another, where all are sovereigns alike? How can you say you have a Republican form of Government, when you make such distinction and enact such proscriptive laws?

Gentlemen talk a good deal about the negroes "building no monuments." I can tell the gentlemen one thing; that is, that we could have built monuments of fire while the war was in progress. We could have fired your woods, your barns and fences, and called you home. Did we do it? No, sir! And God grant that the negro may never do it, or do anything else that would destroy the good opinion of his friends. No epithet is sufficiently opprobrious for us now. I say, sir, that we have built a monument of docility, of obedience, of respect, and of self-control, that will endure longer than the Pyramids of Egypt.

We are a persecuted people. Luther was persecuted; Galileo was persecuted; good men in all nations have been persecuted; but the persecutors have been handed down to posterity with shame and ignominy. If you pass this Bill, you will never get Congress to pardon or enfranchise another rebel in your lives. You are going to fix an everlasting disfranchisement upon Mr. Toombs and the other leading men of Georgia. You may think you are doing yourselves honor by expelling us from this House; but when we go, we will do as Wickliffe and as Latimer did. We will light a torch of truth that will never be extinguished—the impression that will run through the country, as people picture in their mind's eye these poor black men, in all parts of this Southern country, pleading for their rights. When you expel us, you make us forever your political foes, and you will never find a black man to vote a Democratic ticket again; for so help me God I will go through all the length and breadth of the land, where a man of my race is to be found, and advise him to beware of the Democratic party. Justice is the great doctrine taught in the Bible. God's Eternal Justice is founded upon Truth and the man who steps from Justice steps from Truth, and cannot make his principles to prevail.

I have now Mr. Speaker, said all that my physical condition will allow me to say. Weak and ill, though I am, I could not sit passively here and see the sacred rights of my race destroyed at one blow. We are in a position somewhat similar to that of the famous "Light Brigade," of which Tennyson says, they had

Cannon to right of them,
Cannon to left of them,
Cannon in front of them,
Volleyed and thundered.

I hope our poor, downtrodden race may act well and wisely through this period of trial, and that they will exercise patience and discretion under all circumstances.

You may expel us, gentlemen, by your votes, today; but, while you do it, remember that there is a just God in Heaven, whose All-Seeing Eye beholds alike the acts of the oppressor and the oppressed, and who, despite the machinations of the wicked, never fails to vindicate the cause of Justice, and the sanctity of His own handiwork.

Turner's denunciation failed to move the white legislators, thus effectively shutting him out of the world of politics, at least in the South. After serving briefly as postmaster of Macon, Georgia, and as a customs official in Savannah, he devoted himself to increasing the membership of the AME Church. In 1880, he was made a bishop, and for the next thirty-five years he was one of the denomination's most active and influential leaders.

As the years went by, Turner also became deeply disillusioned by the failure of the United States and its white citizens to make good on their promises to the former slaves. Eventually, he began urging his followers to emigrate to Africa if they wanted true freedom and equality. Although his message appealed to quite a few blacks—especially those among the "common folk" who rejected the accommodationist philosophy of Booker T. Washington and the rather elitist views of W.E.B. Du Bois—it also encountered strong opposition and financial roadblocks. Some blacks resented his harsh attacks on those who disagreed with him on the emigration question, and the millions of dollars needed for transporting emigrants to Africa and establishing a new nation proved to be impossible to raise. Turner nevertheless continued his crusade and reigned as the chief advocate of emigration from about the mid-1870s until his death in 1915.

In August 1893, alarmed by the deteriorating racial situation in the United

States, Turner called for a national convention of blacks who supported the idea of seeking radical solutions to the problems they faced. His opening address to the gathering, which was held in Cincinnati, Ohio, that November, detailed his ongoing concerns and frustrations. Originally published in the December 1893, issue of Turner's own publication, Voice of Missions, *it is reprinted here in part from* Respect Black: The Writings and Speeches of Henry McNeal Turner, *edited by Edwin S. Redkey (Arno, 1971).*

Gentlemen of the National Council: In pursuance of a call issued September 30th, by the solicitation and endorsement of over three hundred prominent and distinguished members of our race, from every section of the United States, we have assembled in a national convention today. The circumstances that bring us together are of the most grave, serious and solemn character that could command attention and sober consideration. Our anomalous condition as a race and the increasing evils under which we exist have impressed me for the last four years that a national convention or council of our people should assemble and speak to the country, at least, or sue in some other respects for better conditions. . . .

You are here assembled to consider and pass upon our condition as a distinct and specific race, yet a part of the aggregated people of the United States of America. I use the term specific race because of the special or specific legislation which has been enacted by the states, and the judicial decisions which apply and affect our rights and privileges in contradistinction to every other portion of the American people, whether claiming citizenship or occupying a place here as temporary inhabitants. The scum of creation can come to this country and receive kinder and more just treatment than we who were born and reared here. Thus the black, yet patient, loyal and ever faithful children of the United States are individualized and made the victims of class legislation, and the subjects of close discrimination, class proscription and race prejudice in a manner and to an extent that the world at present offers no parallel; and it is a question if history furnishes another instance.

Let us, by way of premises, itemize a few facts connected with our career in this country. We have been inhabitants of this continent for 273 years, and a very limited part of that time were we citizens—I mean from the ratification of the XIV amendment of the national constitution until the Supreme Court of the United States, Oct. 15th, 1883, declared that provision of the constitution null and void, and decitizenized us. Now, what does history set forth relative to our conduct and behavior during this our long residence?

While it is true that we were brought here as captive heathens, through the greed and avarice of the white man, to serve him as a slave, I believe that as over-ruling Providence suffered it to be because there was a great and grand purpose to be subserved, and that infinite wisdom intended to evolve ultimate good out of a temporary evil, and that in the ages to come, the glory of God will be made manifest and that millions will thank heaven for the limited toleration of American slavery. All of you may not accept my sentiments upon this point, but I believe there is a God, and that he takes cognizance of human events; for such a stupendous evil could not have existed so long, affecting the destiny of the unborn, without a glorious purpose in view.

However, since our forced introduction into this land, willingly or unwillingly, mankind will accord to us a fidelity to every interest that will command the respect of the world forever.

As slaves, in the aggregate, we were obedient, faithful and industrious. We felled the forests, tilled the ground, pioneered civilization and were harmless. As far back as 1704, long before the establishment of an independent nation was ever dreamed of, we find the colonies enacting laws for the enlistment of black men to fight the Spanish and French invaders; and in 1708, a hundred years before the African slave trade was arrested by congressional enactments, we find black men being manumitted by colonial legislation for bravery and heroism in defending the territory of His Majesty, and in some instances, when maimed, provid-

Henry McNeal Turner

ed with a liberal pension. It was for this heroic integrity and incorruptible trustworthiness that Negro slaves acquired their freedom so early in the history of the institution, and laws were even enacted to protect them and their children in the enjoyment of the freedom thus conferred. History also informs us that during the early settlement of this country, the Negro would work for his master during the day and watch the skulking and murderous Indians by night, who sought his master's life and the lives of his wife and children. The first blood that crimsoned the soil for American independence was the blood of the Negro, Crispus Attucks, in the tea riot in the streets of Boston. Over five thousand Negro patriots fought in the revolutionary war for freedom from British domination and American independence. Peter Salem, a Negro though he was, turned the tide of victory in favor of the Americans at the battle of Bunker Hill by a shot from his gun which killed a British major. General Jackson issued an official proclamation complimenting the bravery and patriotism of black men in the war of 1812 at the battle of New Orleans. One hundred and eighty-five thousand Negro soldiers came to the defense of the stars and stripes in the late internecine war between the North and South, and forty-six thousand of them are now sleeping in bloody graves for the integral unity of a nation that cares nothing for them. On the other hand, respecting the powers that be, the Negro was as loyal to the Confederate flag as he was to the federal. For, while every available white man in the South was fighting for what would be regarded as his rights, the Negro, in the field and pursuing every form of industry, was the base of supply, and at the same time the virtual custodian of every white lady and child in the South, and nobody has proclaimed this fact louder and in more complimentary terms than the brave Confederate soldier. Singular and strange as it may appear to some present, a black man completed the Goddess of Liberty, which ornaments the dome of our national capitol; and it will stand there, heaven high, as a monument to his genius and industry for ages to come. Yet this same Goddess of Liberty has been transformed into a lying strumpet, so far as she symbolizes the civil liberties of the black man.

But why consume your valuable time in an attempt to particularize the characteristics and fidelity of the black man to every industry and patriotic emergency in the past as we are willing to be weighed in the balance with any other portion of humanity, under similar circumstances, who has ever lived.

I am willing to accord to the white man every meed of honor that ability, grit, backbone, sagacity, tact and invincibility entitle him to. For this Anglo-Saxon, I grant, is a powerful race; but put him in our stead, enslave him for 250 years, emancipate him and turn him loose upon the world without education, without money, without horse or mule or a foot of land, when passion engendered by war was most intense, to eke out a subsistence from nothing beyond the charity of an indignant people on the one hand, and a cold-shouldering and proscriptive people upon the other; and I do not believe he would have equaled us in respect, obedience, fidelity and accomplished results and maintained the pacific equilibrium we have. For our nation freed the black man as a war measure, I grant, but freedom entailed and left upon us a mendicancy that the unborn will ask the reason why. Even the usufruct claim, guaranteed to the serfs of Russia—a nation at that time regarded as semi-civilized—was denied the freedmen by this so-called enlightened and Christian nation.

The mule and forty acres of land, which has been so often ridiculed for being expected by the black man, was a just and righteous expectation, and had this nation been one-fiftieth part as loyal to the black man as he has been to it, such a bestowment would have been made, and the cost would have been a mere bagatelle, compared with the infinite resources of this Republic, which has given countless millions to foreigners to come into the country and destroy respect for the Sabbath, flood the land with every vice known to the ends of the earth, and form themselves into anarchal bands for the overthrow of its institutions, and venerated customs.

Nevertheless, freedom had been so long held up before us as man's normal birthright, and as the bas-relief of every possibility belonging to the achievements of manhood, that we received it as heaven's greatest boon and nursed ourselves into satisfaction, believing that we had the stamina, not only to wring existence out of our poverty, but also wealth, learning, honor, fame and immortality.

But through some satanic legerdemain, within the last three or four years, the most fearful crimes have been charged upon members of our race, known to the catalogue of villainy, and death and destruction have stalked abroad with an insatiable carnivoracity, that not only beggars description, but jeopardizes the life of every Negro in the land—as anyone could raise an alarm by crying rape, and some colored man must die, whether he is the right one or not, or whether it was the product of revenge or the mere cracking of a joke.

I stated in the call of Sept. 30th:

That owing to the dreadful, horrible, anamolous and unprecedented condition of our people in the United States, it would seem that some common action, move or expression on our part, as a race, is demanded. The revolting, hideous, monstrous, unnatural, brutal and shocking crimes charged upon us daily, on the one hand, and the reign of mobs, lynchers, and fire-fiends, and midnight and midday assassins on the other, necessitated a national convention on our part, for the purpose of crystalizing our sentiments and unifying our endeavors for better conditions in this country, or a change of base for existence.

The terms employed, you will observe, are the most severe that can be found in the English language, as applied both to our condition and to the daily charges made by the public press against our civilization as a race and our morality and humanity, and if true, stamps us as the most degraded race that ever existed. Almost every day the very lightning of heaven is made to flash these horrible deeds from one end of the continent to the other; the allegations being that we are outraging and raping white women to such an extent that an editor of the *Christian Advocate* proclaims to the world that "three hundred white women have been raped by Negroes within the preceeding three months." In other words, a high acclesiastical representative charges that the members of our race are perpetrating a hundred rapes a month upon the white women of the country. Another public daily paper tells the civilized world that Negroes raped seven hundred white women from the first day of last January up to October 10th, which is undoubtedly the most revolting and blood-curdling charge ever presented against a people since time began. Without, however, attempting to number the white women that black men have been charged with outraging, it is known to all present that not a week, and at times scarcely a day, has passed in the last three or four years but what some colored man has been hung, shot or burned by mobs of lynchers, and justified or excused upon the plea that they had outraged some white married or single woman, or some little girl going to or from school. These crimes alleged against us, whether true or false, have been proclaimed by the newspapers of the country in such horrific terms that it would seem like an amazing grace that has held back the curse of God and the vengeance of man, to enable us to meet here today. For if the accusations are even half true, we must be allied to a race of such incarnate fiends that no hopeful prospect illumines our future.

Now, gentlemen, I shall not presume to affirm or deny the monstrous imputations, but certainly as a specific and a race largely regarded as alien by the white people of the country, we owe it to ourselves and posterity to inquire into this subject and give it the most patient, thorough and impartial investigation that ever fell to the lot of man. If the charges are true, then God has no attribute that will side with us. Nature has no member, no potential factor, that will defend us, and while we may not all be guilty, nor one in ten thousand, it nevertheless shows, if true, that there is a libidinous taint, a wanton and lecherous corruption that is prophetic of a dreadful doom, as there must be a carnal blood poison in the precincts of our race that staggers the most acute imagination in determining its woeful results. Nor can we excuse it, palliate it or manifest indifference upon the postulation that it is a righteous retribution upon the white man for the way he treated our women for hundreds of years. For if the countercharge is true, we certainly did not visit swift vengeance upon the white man, as he is doing upon us by his lawless mobs. There is but one recourse left us that will command the respect of the civilized world and the approval of God, and that is to investigate the facts in the premises, and if guilty, acknowledge it, and let us organize against the wretches in our own ranks. Let us call upon the colored ministry to sound it from the pulpit, our newspapers to brand it with infamy daily, weekly, monthly and yearly. Let us put a thousand lecturers in the field and canvass every section of the land, and denounce the heinous crime. Let us organize ourselves into societies, associations and reforming bands, and let them hold public meetings, print circulars and awaken among our young men a better sentiment. And if nothing else will prevail, and lawlessness is to be the order of the day, it would be a thousand times more to our credit, as a race, to organize all over the land against our own rapers, and have passwords, grips and signs, and if we can find out that the act is even contemplated, that we catch the individual and severely punish him, even if the punishment should consist of the infliction of a thousand lashes, and if we can detect any one in the act, catch him and treat him as God did Cain of old—put a mark upon him, cut off his right ear, brand the letter R on his cheek or forehead, symbolic of raper, that his infamous deed may disgrace him through life and condemn his memory when dead.

And let us do everything within the bounds of human endeavor to arrest this flood tide of vice and redeem the good name which we have borne through all the ages, for the protection of female honor. For even among the heathen Africans, whatever else may be said about them, the world will have to admit that they are the purest people, outside of polygamy, in their connubial and virgin morals, upon the face of the globe. White women, to my personal knowledge, hundreds of miles interiorward in Africa, can remain in their midst and teach school for years without being insulted which proves to a demonstration that where our natures have not been distorted and abnormalized, that we are the most honorable custodians of female virtue now under heaven. I have been told by white ladies in Africa, from Louisiana, South Carolina, New York, Nebraska, England and Ireland, that no white lady would be improperly approached in Africa in a lifetime, unless she made herself unusually forward. . . .

[In the West Indian Islands] records show that only one rape has been charged upon a black man since 1832, and that occurred sixteen years ago while eleven rapes have been charged upon white men, nine of which were perpetrated upon black women and two upon white women. It may be, however, due to the fact that there the laws and institutions recognize the black man as a full-fledged citizen and a gentleman, and his pride of character and sense of dignity are not degraded and self-respect imparts a higher prompting and gentlemanly bearing to his manhood, and makes him a better citizen and inspires him with more gallantry and nobler principles. For like begets like. While in this country we are degraded by the public press, degraded by class legislation, degraded on the railroads after purchasing first-class tickets, degraded at the hotels and barber shops, degraded in many states at the ballot box, degraded in most of the large cities by being compelled to rent houses in alleys and the most disreputable streets. Thus we are degraded in so many respects that all the starch of respectability is taken out of the manhood of millions of our people, and as degradation begets degradation, it is very possible that in many instances we are guilty of doing a series of infamous things that we would not be guilty of, if our environments were different. Think of it! The great World's Fair, or exposition, at Chicago, out of more than ten thousand employees, gave no recognition to the colored race beyond taking charge of the toilet rooms.

"We are degraded in so many respects that all the starch of respectability is taken out of the manhood of millions of our people . . ."

I would not have you understand that I am denying, condoning or excusing the crime of rape, as is being charged to a greater or less extent upon the members of our race, nor must we, in convention assembled, jump at a hasty and rash conclusion; but I fear much of it, if true, is due to our unnatural and immethodical environments and ignoble status, nor do I for one believe that we will ever stand out in the symmetrical majesty of higher manhood, half free and half slave—hence my African preferences, of which you have so often heard, or Negro nationalization elsewhere, where we can cultivate the higher properties or virtues of our manhood.

But gentlemen, we are here, and for all I know we are here to stay for an indefinite time, at all events, and we must adjust ourselves to our surroundings and put forth the utmost endeavor to improve our behavior, and merit the favor of God and man. I appeal to this intelligent body of gentlemen, elected representatives of our people, from all parts of the country, while in Council assembled, to rigidly inquire into our condition and conduct, especially as it relates to the outraging of white ladies. . . . Let no spleenishness, or counter-prejudice, or spirit of revenge, or even the conviction that some have been put to death innocently, bar us from doing our whole duty. Let us do right, though others do wrong. Let us be cool-headed, calculating, and show the world that we wish to be fair and just.

Let us not convert this convention into another mob, nor prematurely denounce the black rapers or white lynchers until we shall appoint a committee or committees and let them sit day and night until every man present goes before them and testifies to all he may know personally, and presents all the documents he may be in possession of, bearing upon the question; and if, after a patient investigation, we find that we have been malignly misrepresented, let us have the manhood, courage to dare to say so in no uncertain terms and thus vindicate our good name before the world; but should we find that a part of the accusations are true, while even much may be false, let us say so. For honesty will be the best policy in dealing with this question, as it is in dealing with every other. We are a free people, North and South, East and West, so far as our locomotion and individualities are concerned, and we will have our own destiny to work out, and nobody cares anything about us particularly, and we had just as well be honest and true to God and the right, as to be insincere, and cater to any whim, whether it is popular among the whites or among the blacks.

The United States Congress and Supreme Court both have dumped the Negro. Our supposed constitutional rights have been nullified and the President of the United States can do nothing but give us a few second-hand positions, and those of us who are not dead are simply living by the grace of our representative communities and we had as well realize our situation and pander to no sentimentality, but that which involves our honor and manhood. Therefore, I submit the matter to your wise and prudent judgment.

But, gentlemen of the convention, there is another side to this question. Under the genius and theory of civilization throughout the world, no man is guilty of any crime, whatever, until he is arrested, tried by an impartial process of law and deliberately convicted. The Supreme Court of England, on one occasion, set aside the verdict of a lower court because a case had been tried too hastily to allow deliberation and sober thought to gain the ascendancy in the community. Lynching a man is an act of barbarism and cannot be justified by even what a distinguished bishop terms "emotional insanity." For even insanity has no authority to intrude its maddened vengeance upon the law and order of the public. Judge O'Neil, of South Carolina, many years ago, long before freedom was contemplated, sentenced two white men to the gallows for putting a slave Negro to death without legal process, and they were hung dead by the neck, and the militia of South Carolina turned out in regiments to see that the sentence was fully executed. This, too, was at a time when the theory prevailed that black men, especially slaves, had no rights that white men were bound to respect. But now, a quarter of a century after we are free, a mob can band themselves together and hang a Negro about perpetrating a rape upon some white woman, but rarely give the name of the individual, and when you visit the community and inquire as to who it was thus outraged, in many instances, nobody knows, and the mob is justified upon the plea that the Negro confessed it. Confessed it to whom? Confessed it to a set of bloody-handed murderers, just as though a set of men who were cruel enough to take the life of another were too moral to tell a lie. Strange, too, that the men who constitute these banditti can never be identified by the respective governors or the law officers, but the newspapers know all about them—can advance what they are going to do, how and when it was done, how the rope broke, how many balls entered the Negro's body, how loud he prayed, how piteously he begged, what he said, how long he was left hanging, how many composed the mob, the number that were masked, whether they were prominent citizens or not, how the fire was built that burnt the raper, how the Negro was tied, how he was thrown into the fire, and the whole transaction; but still the fiendish work was done by a set of "unknown men."

I fear that what I have been told in confidence by prominent white men, that a large number of associations are in existence, bound by solemn oaths and pledged to secrecy by the most binding covenants, to exterminate the Negro by utilizing every possible opportunity, has more truth in it than I was at first inclined to believe. For the white people all over the country have everything in their own hands, can do absolutely as they please in administering their own created laws to the Negro. They have all the judges, and all the juries, and virtually all the lawyers, all the jails, all the penitentiaries, all the ropes, all the powder, and all the guns; at least they manufacture them all, and why these hasty, illegal executions unless Negro extermination is the object desired? They evidently must fear a public trial, otherwise it is very singular that they should be so anxious to silence the tongue and close the lips of the only one who can speak in his own defense by putting him to death so hastily and without judge or jury. The white people of this country, almost without exception, claim to be constitutionally superior to the black man. Then why should a race so superior and so numerically, financially, and intellectually in advance of the colored man be so afraid of a raping wretch that they will not allow him a chance to open his inferior lips in his own defense? Gentlemen, it is a serious question, and this Council must consider and pass upon both of these grave issues—the black rapers on the one hand, and the exterminators of the blacks on the other.

I know it is held that if you give a Negro who is charged with outraging a white woman a fair trial, that the process of the law will be so long, tedious and so many technicalities are liable to be raised, that the time and expense would be worth more than the life of the victim. But rather than flood the land with blood, especially if it should be innocent blood, and the retributive vengeance of an angry God, we had far better ask for the old slave time trial before a justice of the peace, and abide by its consequences, for such as are accused of this revolting crime, or, vulgar and shocking as it would be, do the next best thing, and the thing that will effectually cure this evil, if you should find that it actually exists. Let the raper be castrated and let him live and remain as a monument of his folly and madness. Certainly he will never repeat the crime, and it would be far better than shedding so much of what may be innocent blood. So far as I am individually concerned, if there is no way to rid the country of these lynching mobs, I had rather for this convention to make a national request of all the law officers in the land when they capture a raper, or a so-called raper, to castrate him and turn him loose. It would be far better for the country and for its future than to be taking so much of human life.

Let us ask Congress for a law to banish them from the country. Thousands of white criminals were banished from England over here, all through the seventeenth century, and many of the offspring of these banished criminals are the lynchers of today. If Rome, Scotland and England could banish their irredeemable white criminals, surely this country can banish its black criminals. But spare the lives of the wretches. For there is but one deed that God permits the taking of human life for, anyway, and that is for the crime of murder. Horrible as the crime of raping may be, it is a grave question whether it merits the death penalty or not. I do not believe it does when there are so many other ways he can be adequately punished, unless the perpetration of the satanic deed involves the death of the outraged. Left to me individually, I would enact a law to cut off his ear or a part of his nose, or brand raper upon his forehead or his cheek, or castrate him. The old adage, so familiar to the ancients, is as true today in taking life as it was then: Blow for blow,/Blood for blood./Thou shalt reap/What thou hast sown.

And unless this nation, North and South, East and West, awakes from its slumbers and calls a halt to the reign of blood and carnage in this land, its dissolution and utter extermination is only a question of a short time. For Egypt went down; Greece went down; Babylon went down; Nineveh went down; Rome went down, and other nations numerically stronger than the United States, and the spirit of conquest, cruelty, injustice and domination was the death of them all and the United States will never celebrate another centennial of undivided states, without a change of programme. A Negro is a very small item in the body politic of this country, but his groans, prayers and innocent blood will speak to God day and night, and the God of the poor and helpless will come to his relief sooner or later, and another fratricidal war will be the sequence, though it may grow out of an issue as far from the Negro as midday is from midnight. For this is either a nation or a travesty. If it is a nation, every man East and West, North and South, is bound to the protection of human life and the institutions of the country; but if it is a burlesque or a national sham, then the world ought to know it. The North is responsible for every outrage perpetrated in the South, and the South is responsible for every outrage perpetrated in the North, and so of the East and West, and it is no use to blame the South and excuse the North, or blame the North and excuse the South. For any species of injustice perpetrated upon the Negro, every man in every portion of this nation, if it is a nation, is responsible.

The truth is, the nation as such, has no disposition to give us manhood protection anyway. Congress had constitutional power to pursue a runaway slave by legislation into any state and punish the man who would dare conceal him, and the Supreme Court of the United States sustained its legislation as long as slavery existed. Now the same Supreme Court has the power to declare that the Negro has no civil rights under the general government that will protect his citizenship, and authorize the states to legislate upon and for us, as they may like; and they are passing special acts to degrade the Negro by authority of the said high tribunal, and Congress proposes no remedy by legislation or by such a constitutional amendment as will give us the status of citizenship in the nation that is presumed we are to love and to sacrifice our lives, if need be, in the defense of. Yet Congress can legislate for the protection of the fish in the sea and the seals that gambol in our waters, and obligate its mien, its money, its navy, its army and its flag to protect, but the eight million or ten million of its black men and women, made in the image of God, possessing $265,000,000 worth of taxable property, with all their culture, refinement in many cases, and noble bearing, must be turned off to become the prey of violence, and when we appeal to the general government for protection and recognition, Justice, so-called, drops her scales and says, away with you.

I am abused as no other man in this nation because I am an African emigrationist, and while we are not here assembled to consider that question, nor do I mention it at the present time to impose it upon you, but if the present condition of things is to continue, I had not only rather see my people in the heart of Africa, but in ice-bound, ice-covered and ice-fettered Greenland. "Give me liberty or give me death!"

Other American Negroes may sing—"My country 'tis of thee,/Sweet land of liberty,/Of thee we sing." But here is one Negro whose tongue grows palsied whenever he is invited to put music to these lines.

Foreigners may come here from the ends of the earth, and corrupt the country with their vices and diseases, and there is no law or judicial decision to frown them down. John Chinaman, after feasting on opium, is of such exhalted consequences that the United States Congress declares by special enactment, that no Negro shall testify in the courts of the land about anything connected with his citizenship.

Even United States Senators literally gamble over us, if the reports of the Associated Press be true. For the senators of the Western states are represented as telling the Southern senators that we voted with you against the election bill, commonly known as the Force Bill, with the promise upon your part that you would vote with us on the silver question; and as an evidence that there might be some truth in the Associated Press dispatches, which were telegraphed over the country, we see that a large portion of the Southern senators really did stand by the Western senators and fought manfully.

As one, I feel grateful for many things that have been done for us within the last thirty years. I am thankful for Mr. Lincoln's manumitting Proclamation, for its ratification by Congress, for the Thirteenth, Fourteenth and Fifteenth Amendments to the Constitution, which were placed there by the American people for the benefit of our race, even if the United States Supreme Court has destroyed the Fourteenth Amendment by its revolting decision.

I am thankful to our generous-hearted friends of the North, who have given voluntarily millions upon millions to aid in our education. I am thankful to the South for the school laws they have enacted and for the generous manner they have taxed themselves in building and sustaining schools for our enlightenment and intellectual and moral elevation.

But if this country is to be our home, the Negro must be a self-controlling, automatic factor of the body politic or collective life of the nation. In other words, we must be full-fledged men; otherwise we will not be worth existence itself.

To passively remain here and occupy our present ignoble status, with the possibility of being shot, hung or burnt, not only when we perpetrated deeds of violence ourselves, but whenever some bad white man wishes to black his face and outrage a female, as I am told is often done, is a matter of serious reflection. To do so would be to declare ourselves unfit to be free men or to assume the responsibilities which involve fatherhood and existence. For God hates the submission of cowardice. But on the other hand, to talk about physical resistance is literal madness. Nobody but an idiot would give it a moment's thought. The idea of eight or ten million of ex-slaves contending with sixty million people of the most powerful race under heaven! Think of two hundred and sixty-five million of dollars battling with one hundred billion of dollars! Why we would not be a drop in the bucket. It is folly to indulge in such a thought for a moment.

Since I have called this convention, hundreds of letters have been written to me, but I will only refer to two, which were evidently written by men of prominence. One from New York says: "The colored people are such cowards is the reason they have so many things to complain of and until they fight and die a little it will continue to be the case." But another letter from Philadelphia says:

> *You Negroes had better not provoke a conflict with the white people at your convention in Cincinnati, for if you do, the whites, North and South, will join together and exterminate the last one of you from the face of the land. Take warning now, for I know the sentiment of the North, and the South justly hates you.*

Of the two letters referred to, the latter, I fear, deserves more attention than the former; for it appears to be the desire of some of the white people of the United States to provoke some kind of race war, as in every instance, when a race war is spoken of, it comes from some white quarter. The black man never thinks about it, much less speaks about it; for where individual conflicts take place between white and colored men, in a thousand cases to one they are provoked by the former. I know the Negro as well as any man that breathes the breath of life, and I affirm before earth and heaven today that no such project has ever been contemplated, nor do I believe it ever will be. We have been reared in this country to revere, honor and love the whites, and we delight to do it when they will give us half a chance.

I know that thousands of our people hope and expect better times for the Negro in this country, but as one I see no signs of a reformation in our condition; to the contrary, we are being more and more degraded by legislative enactments and judicial decisions. Not a thing has been said or done that contemplates our elevation or the promotion of our manhood in twelve or fifteen years outside of promoting our education in erecting schools for our general enlightenment; but a hundred things have been done to crush out the last vestige of self-respect and to avalanche us with contempt. My remedy, without a change, is, as it would be folly to attempt resistance, and our appeals for better conditions are being unheeded, for that portion of us, at least, who feel we are self-reliant, to seek other quarters. There are many propositions before the colored people of this country. Some favor a partial African emigration, and I am one of that number; others favor Mexican emigration, Canadian emigration, Central and South American emigration, while Hon. John Temple Graves, one of our profoundest thinkers, most brilliant orators and broadest humanitarians in the country, advocates the setting apart of a portion of the public domain as a separate and distinct state, where we can have our own governors, United States senators, members of the lower house of Congress, and all the machinery of state, and thereby have a chance to speak for ourselves, where we can be heard, and give evidence of statesmanship to show to the world that we are capable of self-government, and where our educated sons and daughters can practicalize the benefits of their culture. The position of Mr. Graves may not commend itself to the favorable consideration of all present, any more than my African sentiments or the Mexican, Canadian or Central American theories, but we must do something. We must agree upon some project. We must offer some plan of action to our people or admit that we are too ignorant and worthless to do anything. This nation justly, righteously and divinely owes us for work and services rendered, billions of dollars, and if we cannot be treated as American people, we should ask for five hundred million dollars, at least, to begin an emigration somewhere, for it will cost, sooner or later, far more than that amount to keep the Negro down unless they re-establish slavery itself. Freedom and perpetual degradation are not in the economy of human events. It is against reason, against nature, against precedent and against God. A people who read, attend schools, receive the instruction of the pulpits, write for the public press, think and furnish famous orators, cannot be chained to degrada-

"If this country is to be our home . . . we must be full-fledged men; otherwise we will not be worth existence itself."

tion forever. They will be a menace to the land, and God himself, with all the laws of nature, will help them fight the injustice, and no pomp or boast of heraldry can prevent it, yet it may involve horror to both races. Money to leave and build up a nation of our own, where we can respect ourselves at least, or justice at the hands of the American nation, should be the watch word of every Negro in the land.

I have been more or less all over the world, and have mingled among people of many tongues, but I have never found such a condition of things as there is here in the United States.

I was told in England by old, gray-haired, and baldheaded white men, that they had never known of a man being lynched or put to death without due process of law. Yet every nation upon the face of the globe was represented there, as British ships go everywhere and return with representatives of all people, while in this country, so many of us are killed, that dead bodies hanging to some tree limb and pierced with bullets are so common that they are regarded as current events. What would have horrorized our fathers and mothers is passed by in these degenerate days as a natural occurrence. The Negro may be exterminated, but in the accomplishment of the heaven-defying job, a crop of imbruted children will grow up, who will annihilate each other. "For whatsoever a man soweth, that shall he also reap," is the declaration of the word of God, and all history confirms its truth.

The Negro, at best, in this country, occupies a very low plane. Look at the Greek, Latin and mathematical scholars employed as Pullman car porters and other college-bred young men, restricted to the sphere of a scullion, because color prejudice bars them from employment in harmony with their culture. Yet the Negro is the nearest competitor in aptitude, physical endurance, industrial application and punctuality to business, the white man has on the face of the globe; and because this fact is well known, the moment some ignorant white man gets into some legislature, he is offering a bill to increase the degradation of the Negro. For you never find such bills or resolutions emanating from first-class white gentlemen. All of these discriminating and proscribing laws that have been enacted against the colored people on these railroads have originated with what we used to call in the slave time "poor white trash." True, some of them since freedom have climbed up a little and have got to be congressmen and even governors of states, but it is the same old second-class roughs who can find nothing else to think or talk about but the ghost of the Negro. Yet the first-class white men and the entire nation, North and South, are responsible and the God of nations will so hold them. I refer to these facts merely to show you that degradation or extermination appears to hold a prominent place in the minds of the ruling powers of this country, and I cannot believe that our freedom, which cost so much blood and treasure, was intended for any such ultimatum.

But some of you may think I am over-gloomy, too despondent, that I have reached the plane of despair, and should anyone present so presume you will not be much at fault. For I confess that I have seen so much and know so much about American prejudice that I have no hope in the future success of my race in our present situation.

But you will discover that in this address I have largely spoken for myself. You will have time enough, and I know you have the ability to speak for yourselves. Should we differ, as we naturally will, let us defend our respective positions and sentiments with the best logical arguments we are able to advance. Slurs, philippics, witty utterances, light anecdotes, innuendoes, cutting remarks, sarcasm, tirades and bitter invectives should not be indulged in in this convention. Men of ability will not do it; they will have too many other things to say. Moreover, if we cannot now, surrounded as we are by mobs, lynchers, ropes, bullets, fire, proscription, color prejudice, decitizenship, blood, carnage, death and extermination, present a united front of action, although we may differ in opinions, then there is no unity of action in us and our destiny is a hopeless one.

You evidently see from the points I have endeavored to raise, and many more that I have not touched, that our condition in this country inferiorates us, and no amount of book-learning, divested of manhood, respect and manhood promptings will ever make us a great people; for, underlying all school culture, must exist the consciousness that I am somebody, that I am a man, that I am as much as anybody else, that I have rights, that I am a creature of law and order, that I am entitled to respect, that every avenue to distinction is mine. For where this consciousness does not form the substratum of any people, inferioration, retrogression and ultimate degradation will be the result. And seeing that this is our status in the United States today, it devolves upon us to project a remedy for our condition, if such a remedy is obtainable, or demand of this nation, which owes us billions of dollars for work done and services rendered, five hundred million dollars to commence leaving it; or endorse the petition of the colored lawyers' convention which was held in Chattanooga, Tennessee, asking Congress for a billion dollars for the same purpose. For I can prove, by mathematical calculation, that this country owes us forty billion dollars for daily work performed. The one great desideratum of the American Negro is manhood impetus. We may educate and acquire general intelligence, but our sons and daughters will come out of college with all their years of training and drift to the plane of the scullion as long as they are restricted, limited and circumscribed by colorphobia. For abstract education elevates no man, nor will it elevate a race. What we call the heathen African will strut around his native land, three-fourths naked, and you can see by the way he stands, talks and acts, that he possesses more manhood than fifty of some of our people in this country, and any ten of our most distinguished colored men here; and until we are free from menace by lynchers, hotels, railroads, stores, factories, restaurants, barbershops, courthouses and other places, where merit and worth are respected, we are destined to be a dwarfed people. Our sons and daughters will grow up with it in their very flesh and bones.

Gentlemen of the National Council, I leave the grave, solemn and awful subject with you.

SOURCES

Books

Aptheker, Herbert, editor, *A Documentary History of the Negro People in the United States,* Volume 2: *From the Reconstruction Years to the Founding of the NAACP in 1910,* Citadel, 1964.

Bracey, John H., Jr., August Meier, and Elliott Rudwick, editors, *Black Nationalism in America,* Bobbs-Merrill, 1970.

Foner, Philip S., *The Voice of Black America: Major Speeches by Negroes in the United States, 1797-1971,* Simon & Schuster, 1972.

Redkey, Edwin S., *Black Exodus: Black Nationalist and Back-to-Africa Movements, 1890-1910,* Yale University Press, 1969.

Redkey, Edwin S., editor, *Respect Black: The Writings and Speeches of Henry McNeal Turner,* Arno, 1971.

Periodicals

Journal of American History, "Bishop Turner's African Dream," September, 1967, pp. 271-290.

Clifford I. Uyeda

1920(?)–

Japanese American physician and activist

Although his name may be unfamiliar to most people, Clifford I. Uyeda played a key role in two defining moments of recent Japanese American history—moments during the 1970s and 1980s when he and other members of his community finally began to come to grips with their painful memories of the World War II era. A longtime member of the Japanese American Citizens League (JACL), he spearheaded the group's efforts to obtain a pardon for "Tokyo Rose," a Japanese American woman convicted of treason for making English-language propaganda broadcasts to U.S. troops stationed in the Pacific. Uyeda subsequently headed the JACL committee that launched the campaign seeking redress for all those Japanese Americans evacuated from their homes and forced into concentration camps as potential threats to national security. For many Japanese Americans, these events were best forgotten. But to Uyeda, they were wrongs that deserved to be righted—not just for the benefit of Japanese Americans, but to underscore how truly vulnerable our freedom is in times of national stress and self-doubt.

A native of Washington's capital, Olympia, Uyeda grew up in the nearby city of Tacoma. After graduating from his local high school, he attended the University of Wisconsin, from which he received his bachelor's degree. He then went on to the Tulane University School of Medicine, where he earned his MD. Uyeda pursued additional specialized training in pediatrics at Harvard Medical School and Massachusetts General Hospital in Boston.

Following stints as a clinical and research fellow with the Harvard Pediatric Study and as a teaching fellow in pediatrics at Harvard Medical School, Uyeda moved to California. There he served as staff pediatrician with the Kaiser-Permanente Medical Group in San Francisco from 1953 until his retirement in 1975.

For Uyeda, however, "retirement" was when he at last had more time to devote to the causes that interested him most. The same year he left the medical field, for example, he became chairman of the JACL's National Committee for Iva Toguri, better known as "Tokyo Rose." Born in Los Angeles and educated at the University of California, Toguri happened to be in Japan visiting a critically ill aunt when war broke out between the United States and Japan. Unable to return home, *she was pressured by the Japanese to broadcast propaganda aimed at American troops stationed in the Pacific region. (She was just one of about a dozen women announcers soldiers dubbed "Tokyo Rose.") She would not agree to Japanese demands that she renounce her citizenship, however, a decision that later made it possible for U.S. authorities to charge her with treason when she re-entered the country after the war ended. Found innocent of overt acts of treason but convicted of trying to undermine American morale at her 1949 trial, Toguri was sentenced to ten years in prison and released on parole after serving a little more than six years.*

During and after Toguri's trial, the Japanese American community tried very hard to distance itself from her and her "crimes." In the early 1970s, however, Uyeda learned from someone who had closely studied the trial that Toguri's prosecution and conviction were based on evidence the government knew was false, mainly because officials had threatened and intimidated defense witnesses and bribed others to lie during their testimony. Determined to correct this injustice, he eventually overcame opposition within the JACL (mostly among older members who did not want to get involved) and led the group's nationwide efforts to obtain a pardon for Toguri. Marshalling support from politicians, the media, and the public at large, Uyeda finally met with success in January 1977, when outgoing President Gerald Ford pardoned Toguri as one of his last official acts.

But Uyeda faced a much tougher battle over the next issue that he championed—redress for Japanese Americans interned in concentration camps during World War II. While the idea had surfaced occasionally among Japanese Americans since the late 1960s or so, it always sparked so much controversy both inside and outside their community (far more than even the Toguri case had) that little action had been taken on the subject.

On February 19, 1942, just nine weeks after the bombing of Pearl Harbor catapulted the United States into World War II, President Franklin Roosevelt issued Executive Order 9066. This order called for the evacuation of some 120,000 Japanese Americans (about two-thirds of whom were U.S. citizens) from the West Coast to large "relocation centers" in isolated areas of Arizona, Arkansas, inland California, Colorado, Idaho, Utah, and Wyoming. (A number of smaller camps were also set up in about fourteen other states.) Japanese Americans in other parts of the country were not affected by the order, and no similar action was taken against German Americans or Italian Americans.

None of the internees—who included men, women, and children of all ages and backgrounds—had been accused of any crime, yet they spent as long as three years imprisoned in tar-paper shacks behind barbed wire and guarded by armed military police. Many lost their homes, their businesses, their land, and their possessions; some lost their minds or even their lives; nearly all lost their dignity, their self-esteem, and their sense of security.

It was not until February 19, 1976, that the U.S. government officially rescinded Executive Order 9066. Issuing a special proclamation on the thirty-fourth anniversary of the original order, President Ford apologized for the relocation and acknowledged that "Japanese Americans were and are loyal Americans."

Ford's statement convinced some JACL members that the time was right to mount a campaign seeking some sort of compensation from the U.S. government to help make up for the injustice of having been persecuted merely for being of Japanese ancestry. In 1977, Uyeda became chairman of the group's National Committee for Redress, which immediately began compiling the information necessary "to clarify the issue of reparations, then submit concrete alternative plans to the Japanese Americans for their review and comments," as he explained their purpose at the time. To foster a consensus on the issue among Japanese Americans, he contributed numerous articles on redress to the JACL's newspaper, Pacific Citizen, *throughout the rest of 1977 and into 1978. Five JACL districts also conducted a survey on redress among members to gauge reactions to the idea.*

In 1978, when Uyeda assumed the post of JACL national president, he shared the committee's recommendations with the rest of the organization. They included a controversial demand for $25,000 to be paid to each person relocated to a camp (or their heirs) as a result of Executive Order 9066 and the establishment of a $100 million-dollar trust fund to benefit Japanese Americans "to remind our nation of the continued need for vigilance and to render less likely the recurrence of similar injustice."

While Uyeda's proposal was unanimously adopted by the JACL's national council, it proved to be a harder sell elsewhere. As Roger Daniels notes in his book Asian America: Chinese and Japanese in the United States Since 1850, *"conservative forces within the organization, the community, and the nation were shocked that a 'model minority' should make such strident demands." Senator S.I. Hayakawa of California—a Japanese American who had been a Canadian citizen living in Chicago during the war and was therefore unaffected by the relocation—was sharply critical of the redress campaign and suggested that imprisoning Japanese Americans might actually have helped them in the long term because it pushed them out of their own little communities "to discover the rest of America." (He later reversed his position and supported redress.)*

While virtually no other Japanese American agreed with Hayakawa's view of their ordeal, many did object to redress on other grounds. Some looked at it as a form of welfare and refused to have anything to do with it. Others maintained that no amount of money could possibly make up for what they had suffered and lost. Still others just did not want to dredge up the past.

During the two years he headed the JACL, Uyeda often spoke to members of local chapters across the country to explain the reasons behind the fight for redress. One such occasion was on January 20, 1979, when he addressed the Twin Cities group at a dinner held in Minneapolis. Uyeda furnished a copy of his remarks.

I appreciate this opportunity to appear before you tonight. I believe you will want me to speak out on the subject of redress which Japanese Americans seek for the injustices suffered as an official act of our own United States government. It happened in our lifetime. It is not an ancient wrong of the dim past.

There was no evidence or record of sabotage or espionage. There was no charge or indictment made against us. The [Supreme] Court, however, upheld the proposition that all persons of Japanese ancestry were enemies, that the war was not directed against Japan but at the Japanese race.

Losses sustained by the evacuees were far reaching. Property losses alone were estimated by the Federal Reserve Bank of San Francisco to be in excess of $400 million in 1942.

For those who point to the Evacuation Claims Act of 1948, remind them that the amount returned was less than a single year's interest on the original sum. [That] $400 million would, in thirty-seven years, accumulate in interest alone billions of dollars.

For those who point to $25,000 per individual as too large a redress, ask them if they would be willing to be uprooted from their homes and without a charge be incarcerated in a desert camp for years with complete uncertainty about their future for a mere $25,000.

To some *Nikkei,* seeking redress is unacceptable, they say, because it is placing a price tag on our freedom and our rights.

Loss of freedom or injustice can never be equated monetarily. A meaningful redress, however, is a tangible expression of our own government's acknowledgment of the injustice and wrong committed against her own people.

Many fear backlash. It is fear of what their non-Japanese friends would say or think. There is also fear of reawakening in them their own feelings which had been so long suppressed.

Such fears may be well founded, but they are inappropriate in a responsible citizen. If we continue to ignore the past because it was unpleasant, and never even ask for a just restitution because it is not popular, then the experience emasculates the entire Japanese Americans as a group. To continue this submissive stance is tantamount to saying: "We prefer to be second class. Let someone else take the risk and the responsibility of a first-class citizenship."

If there are those amongst us who have achieved decent income, there are also others who have not. Let us not forget them.

Then there is the plight of the Japanese elderly. One out of five has income less than poverty level. According to the latest available national statistics, the Japanese 65 years and over have a lower median income than that of the total elderly population. It was $2400 a year for males and $1300 a year for females. Forty percent of the males and sixty-three percent of the females had income less than $2000 a year.

In spite of the lower income the elderly Japanese received lower Social Security benefits than families of other races.

Therefore, many elderly Japanese Americans have very low median income on which to subsist, many are below poverty level, and many live alone.

Much of this was due to their having been expelled from the West Coast at the height of their productive years. They not only could not save for old age, they had lost everything they worked for.

It is the height of insensitivity to ignore our own people who must live in poverty because some of us are not in want.

We hear that because there will be recipients who are not at poverty level, redress is not justified. Since when has wealth or poverty of an individual had anything to do with one's right to be free from false imprisonment, his right to constitutional safeguards, and his right to redress the wrong committed against him?

Clifford I. Uyeda

We are talking about the fundamental rights guaranteed all Americans by our own Constitution. Are the guarantees of the Bill of Rights absolute, or are we free to suspend them at anytime according to the whims of those in power or the mood of hysteria which may prevail? We must take responsibility for what we do as a nation. We readily take credit for what our past generations have accomplished in the name of humanity. Can we so easily exclude ourselves then from our past national mistakes? Japanese Americans were deprived of liberty and property without criminal charges, and without a trial of any kind.

We must not be intimidated by irrational statements from the public, or even by some amongst us. What are some of the major backlashes being heard in America?

1)That those other Americans drafted to fight in the war were also uprooted from their homes, lived in camps, suffered deprivations, pain and even death on the battlefields.

Japanese American soldiers—there were 33,000 of them during World War II—also went through the same sacrifices common to all citizens during wartime, and we seek no redress for such deprivations and sufferings.

Yes, there was a war going on. But to be regarded and treated as an enemy by one's own government without a shred of evidence, stripped of all constitutional and human rights, and then be told that your suffering is no different from those of any other American—any other American subjected to similar treatment by one's own government would have been equally outraged.

2) That if Japanese Americans seek redress, all Americans who suffered under enemy actions should be compensated. What about Americans who died at Pearl Harbor, and what about the sufferings of the POWs, they say.

The plain answer is that Japanese Americans had nothing to do with Pearl Harbor. We were also the victims on that tragic day. The POWs were under the control of the Japanese military government, not Japanese Americans.

These are the very reasons why we must speak about the evacuation and the need for redress. The very fact that so many Americans associate Japanese Americans with Pearl Harbor and the sufferings of the POWs clearly indicates that America still does not see us as Americans but as former enemies.

This was the myth the 442nd boys went out to destroy. They did a superb job, and paid for it in blood all out of proportion to a regiment of equal size. There is, however, much more to be done. This is the work of the redress campaign.

Thirty-five years ago it could be done only with sacrifices and more sacrifices on our own part, hoping against hope that these sacrifices would be recognized as a proof of our Americanism. When confronted with hostility from without, we punished ourselves to excel. We wanted the public to say, "Look, they're Americans after all." We were clearly a second-class citizen.

Today, as first-class citizens, we need no longer take just a submissive stance. We are ready to accept the responsibility and the risk of first-class citizens. We must claim our rights as Americans and claim the justice guaranteed us by our Constitution.

It is about time that Japanese Americans cut aside the second-class mentality with which we were forced to live.

On November 10, 1978, the West German Chancellor Helmut Schmidt and President Walter Scheel attended a memorial service to remember "Kristallnacht," the night 30,000 Jews were arrested and sent to concentration camps. It marked the beginning of the official anti-Semitism in Hitler's Germany exactly forty years ago.

Said Chancellor Schmidt: "Today's Germans are mostly innocent—yet we have to carry the political inheritance of the guilty and draw the consequences."

Germany can remember and make restitutions, but the United States cannot?

It took three hundred years before American blacks could demand to be treated with equality. It took thirty-five years for Japanese Americans to recover from the state of shock they were put into by the incarceration experience. And the American public is just beginning to understand that Japanese Americans were victims of gross injustice.

"Are the guarantees of the Bill of Rights absolute, or are we free to suspend them at anytime according to the whims of those in power? . . ."

Japanese Americans in 1945 were just out of concentration camps. They had lost everything. Mere survival was the major concern.

Today there is increasing concerns for human rights, both here and abroad.

Japanese Americans are, finally, overcoming their reluctance to express their feelings. They realize that if they don't speak out for themselves, no one else will.

For those who are afraid of the backlash, cringing at every criticism thrown our way, let me state that there are also friends out there whose sense of justice is keen and undaunted. They are also watching us.

We have received many heartwarming letters. Let me share a few with you. These are all from Caucasian Americans:

> Mamaroneck, New York, October 24, 1978: *I was one of the U.S. infantry privates ordered to serve eviction notices to Japanese Americans in Guadalupe, California. I have not forgotten the pain I suffered in helping to implement this unsavory and totally un-American order. I wish*

you to believe that the guilt has rested heavily with me. . . . I wish you would let me know in what manner I could be of help in your effort to obtain a redress from our government. J.C.W.

Honolulu, Hawaii, August 13, 1978: *I'm so glad the time is finally right for you to take on this challenge. The redress is long overdue, and America will learn a great lesson by meeting its obligations to the Japanese Americans involved. By rethinking this whole matter, and finally doing the right thing, the black mark on our history will at least have some sunlight shine on it.* C.M.G.

Seattle, Washington, July 24, 1978: *Only by a drastic measure can we bring the lesson home to make the Constitution mean what it says. . . . Even in Germany they found that an apology was not enough and that the victims had to be redressed. We should not do anything less.* G.O.

Wheat Ridge, Colorado, October 27, 1978: *I am a German American, but I was never blamed for what the Germans did to six million Jews during World War II. . . . I hope your efforts prove successful. . . . You have opened some eyes, and reminded thousands of one of the most embarrassing incidents in American history.* D.P.L.

And finally,

Walnut Creek, California, October 20, 1978: *I was captured on Bataan by the Japanese Army in April, 1942, and remained a prisoner of war for forty-two-and-a-half months. When the war was over and I returned to Chicago and was told that we sent our own American citizens of Japanese ancestry to American concentration camps, I could not believe that happened or could happen in America. Let me start off by saying $25,000 is too low a figure for compensation. It bothers me that there are those in your ranks that are still concerned about what their fellow white Americans will think. . . . Do not listen to the timid in your organization. Let the Hayakawas go their separate way. Let me assure you, there are thousands of white Americans who will stand behind you in this endeavor to right the great wrong. If I can be of some help to you or your organization, please be free to call on me. . . . I will pray for your organization's success.* E.A.F.

These are only few of the many letters of support we are receiving from fellow Americans. They're also expecting Japanese Americans to act like first-class citizens. Given the opportunity and the perfect case, let us not disappoint these concerned Americans. And most important of all, let us not disappoint ourselves.

I thank you.

Faced with continuing resistance inside and outside the JACL to the idea of pushing for redress, the group downplayed its original recommendations and instead supported bills introduced in both the U.S. Senate (S. 1647) and House of Representatives (H.R. 5499) in 1979 that proposed creating a commission to investigate the wartime relocation of Japanese Americans and determine what, if any, compensation seemed appropriate. The Senate version passed in mid-1980, and in mid-1981, the Commission on Wartime Relocation and Internment of Civilians (CWRIC) began hearings in Washington, D.C. (Commissioners later visited Los Angeles, San Francisco, Seattle, Anchorage, Chicago, New York, and Boston to gather additional testimony.) Over the course of several months, more than seven hundred people from all walks of life shared their often emotional recollections with members of the CWRIC. One of those who testified was Uyeda himself, who reiterated some of the reasons why redress was necessary. He spoke on August 11, 1981; his remarks are reprinted from a copy he furnished.

Clifford I. UYEDA

Mr. Chairman and members of the Commission: My name is Clifford Uyeda. I am the immediate past national president of the Japanese American Citizens League. During the Second World War I was working my way through medical school while my family members were incarcerated in detention camps, first at Tule Lake and then at Granada.

Today, I would like to address to an issue which has been of great concern to many former evacuees who have generally made successful adjustments following the incarceration experience.

To some of them the principle of monetary redress is most uncomfortable because it seems to place a price tag on our freedom and our rights—rights that should be regarded as priceless. To them demanding redress seems to diminish the grace and realism with which they and their parents made the best of the impossible situation. The patriotism and courage with which *Nisei* fought for America when given a chance, they believe, might be depreciated.

Others fear backlash. It is fear of what their non-Japanese friends would say and think. There is also a fear of reawakening their own feelings which had been so long suppressed.

It took us nearly forty years to recover from the state of shock we were put into by the incarceration experience. The wound would have to at least partially heal before victims can begin to address the problems.

A prevalent myth is that Japanese Americans by hard work have fully recovered from the losses suffered from the evacuation experience. Many, and especially the elderly, have never recovered. One out of five elderly Japanese have income less than poverty level.

Moreover, one's economic status has nothing to do with the dispensing of justice or the payment of redress when justice is not only denied but forcibly taken away from its own people in the absence of any charges or indictments. We are not asking for charity.

Japanese Americans during World War II have made all the sacrifices other Americans have made, including giving our lives for our country on the battlefield. Our losses we are speaking of today, however, were the result of the actions of the American government against American citizens and against our parents who were permanent residents of this country.

Today, right here in America, nearly forty years after the beginning of World War II, Japanese Americans still suffer the misconception in the public's mind: 1) that we were guilty of disloyalty to our country because of the actions taken against us by the United States government, and 2) that evacuation was both necessary and justified, a powerful belief upheld by the Supreme Court in the Korematsu case.

To many Americans the fact that no meaningful damages have been paid by the United States government is taken as a proof that no real injustice was done. Only a congressional action authorizing redress for the victims will ever erase this misconception from the public's mind and indelibly etch the incident into American history and conscience.

Mr. Chairman and members of the Commission, the issue is not for us to recover what cannot be recovered. The issue is to make tangible and meaningful restitution to the victims of injustice and thus discourage similar injustice from recurring in the future. Do not penalize the Japanese Americans for persevering and overcoming great handicaps by denying us redress for justified grievance. Denying us meaningful restitution is the same as assessing the damages at zero.

> ***"The United States cannot insist on human rights abroad and then refuse to acknowledge and correct the wrong committed against her own people."***

I hope this Commission's report will be most thorough and comprehensive, a report that will answer many questions which have been plaguing us for nearly forty years. I hope that your report will become an American human rights document that will boldly address restitutions for victims of gross injustice within our society, a report that will impact all Americans for generations to come.

The United States cannot insist on human rights abroad and then refuse to acknowledge and correct the wrong committed against her own people.

Thank you for this opportunity to appear before this Commission.

In 1983, the Commission published a report of its findings entitled Personal Justice Denied *in which members condemned Executive Order 9066 as a measure undertaken not for military reasons but out of "race prejudice, war hysteria and a failure of political leadership." It later issued several recommendations for redress, including an apology from Congress and the president acknowledging the injustice done to Japanese Americans as a result of the order and a payment of $20,000 to each of the estimated sixty thousand survivors of the camps. After some five years of debate over the issue of holding present-day taxpayers liable for wrongs committed decades earlier amid fears that approving such payments would open the door to similar claims from African Americans and other minorities, the Senate finally passed a bill in April 1988, enacting all of the Commission's recommendations, and President Ronald Reagan signed it into law in August.*

In addition to his activities on behalf of the redress campaign, Uyeda has embraced other causes and interests as well. For example, he has long been involved in supporting the moratorium on commercial whaling and served from 1974 until 1978 as chairman of the JACL's Whale Issue Committee, a group that seeks to educate the public—especially the people of Japan and Japanese Americans—"on the plight of the whales as symbolic of our need to save our oceans." From 1982 until 1986, he was also chairman of a special JACL committee set up to keep the Japanese American community informed about efforts to force the Navajo Indians off their ancestral land. And from 1988 until 1994, he served as president of the National Japanese American Historical Society in San Francisco and editor of its journal, Nikkei Heritage.

SOURCES

Books

Bosworth, Allan R., *America's Concentration Camps,* Norton, 1967.

Daniels, Roger, *Asian America: Chinese and Japanese in the United States Since 1850,* University of Washington Press, 1988.

———, *Concentration Camps USA: Japanese Americans and World War II,* Holt, 1972.

———, *The Politics of Prejudice: The Anti-Japanese Movement in California and the Struggle for Japanese Exclusion,* University of California Press, 1962.

Girdner, Audrie, and Anne Loftis, *The Great Betrayal: The Evacuation of the Japanese Americans During World War II,* Macmillan, 1969.

Grodzins, Morton M., *Americans Betrayed: Politics and the Japanese Evacuation,* University of Chicago Press, 1949.

Hosokawa, Bill, *JACL: In Quest of Justice,* Morrow, 1982.

———, *Nisei: The Quiet Americans,* Morrow, 1969.

Personal Justice Denied: Report of the Commission on Wartime Relocation and Internment of Civilians, U.S. Government Printing Office, 1983.

tenBroek, Jacobus, Edward N. Barnhart, and Floyd W. Matson, *Prejudice, War and the Constitution,* University of California Press, 1954.

Uyeda, Clifford I., *A Final Report and Review: The Japanese American Citizens League National Committee for Iva Toguri,* Asian American Studies Program of the University of Washington, 1980.

Uyeda, Clifford I., editor, *The Japanese American Incarceration: A Case for Redress* (booklet), 3rd edition, National Committee for Redress of the Japanese American Citizens League, 1980.

Periodicals

Detroit Free Press, "Painful History Lesson," March 16, 1995, p. 8A.

Pacific Citizen, "Reparations Committee," October 28, 1977, p. 6; "JACL Faces Stiff Redress Campaign," August 4, 1978; "Redress Campaign: A Brief Review," September 16, 1988, p. 5.

Booker T. Washington

1856–1915

Black American educator and statesman

Born into slavery on a Virginia plantation, Booker T. Washington later graduated from the Hampton Institute, a well-known black college that emphasized training in practical skills. In 1881, at the age of twenty-five, he was hired to establish and head a similar school in Tuskegee, Alabama. By the end of the decade, the Tuskegee Institute had earned national acclaim for its emphasis on achieving black economic advancement through self-help programs, and Washington himself was well on his way to becoming the best known and most respected black man in America.

On September 18, 1895, Washington delivered one of the opening speeches at the Cotton States and International Exposition in Atlanta. Reprinted here from the fifth edition of The Negro Almanac: A Reference Work on the African American *(Gale, 1989), his talk before the racially-mixed audience focused on his belief that it was time for African Americans to put aside their desire for civil and social equality and concentrate instead on making themselves a vital part of the nation's economy through education and productivity. Once they had demonstrated their ability to do so, he maintained, black Americans would most certainly be granted the rights that years of protests had not yet won.*

Greeted with polite applause when he was first introduced, Washington left the platform to the sound of a thunderous ovation. As a result of that single, fifteen-minute speech—later dubbed the "Atlanta Compromise"—Washington gained the enthusiastic support of whites and many blacks throughout the country and reigned for the next twenty years as the preeminent spokesman for black America. Yet he was scorned by more militant African Americans such as W.E.B. Du Bois, who thought it naive and potentially self-defeating to assume that whites would ever willingly grant blacks equality without a struggle.

Mr. President and Gentlemen of the Board of Directors and Citizens:

One-third of the population of the South is of the Negro race. No enterprise seeking the material, civil, or moral welfare of this section can disregard this element of our population and reach the highest success. I but convey to you, Mr. President and Directors, the sentiment of the masses of my race when I say that in no way have the value and manhood of the American Negro been more fittingly and generously recognized than by the managers of this magnificent Exposition at every stage of its progress. It is a recognition that will do more to cement the friendship of the two races than any occurrence since the dawn of our freedom.

Not only this, but the opportunity here afforded will awaken among us a new era of industrial progress. Ignorant and inexperienced, it is not strange that in the first years of our new life we began at the top instead of at the bottom; that a seat in Congress or the State Legislature was more sought than real estate or industrial skill; that the political convention or stump speaking had more attractions than starting a dairy farm or a truck garden.

A ship lost at sea for many days suddenly sighted a friendly vessel. From the mast of the unfortunate vessel was seen a signal: "Water, water; we die of thirst!" The answer from the friendly vessel at once came back: "Cast down your bucket where you are." A second time the signal, "Water, water; send us water!" ran up from the distressed vessel, and was answered, "Cast down your bucket where you are." And a third and fourth signal for water was answered: "Cast down your bucket where you are." The captain of the distressed vessel, at last heeding the injunction, cast down his bucket, and it came up full of fresh, sparkling water from the mouth of the Amazon River. To those of my race who depend on bettering their condition in a foreign land, or who underestimate the importance of cultivating friendly relations with the Southern white man, who is their next door neighbor, I would say: "Cast down your bucket where you are"—cast it down in making friends in every manly way of the people of all races by whom we are surrounded.

Cast it down in agriculture, mechanics, in commerce, in domestic service, and in the professions. And in this connection it is well to bear in mind that whatever other sins the South may be called to bear, when it comes to business, pure and simple, it is in the South that the Negro is given a man's chance in the commercial world, and in nothing is this Exposition more eloquent than in emphasizing this chance. Our greatest danger is, that in the great leap from slavery to freedom we may overlook the fact that the masses of us are to live by the production of our hands, and fail to keep in mind that we shall prosper in proportion as we learn to dignify and glorify common labor, and put brains and skill into the common occupations of life; shall prosper in proportion as we learn to draw the line between the superficial and the substantial, the ornamental gewgaws of life and the useful. No race can prosper till it learns that there is as much dignity in tilling a field as in writing a poem. It is at the bottom of life we must begin, and not at the top. Nor should we permit our grievances to overshadow our opportunities.

Booker T. Washington

To those of the white race who look to the incoming of those of foreign birth and strange tongue and habits for the prosperity of the South, were I permitted, I would repeat what I say to my own race, "Cast down your bucket where you are." Cast it down among the 8,000,000 Negroes whose habits you know, whose fidelity and love you have tested in days when to have proved treacherous meant the ruin of your firesides. Cast down your bucket among these people who have, without strikes or labor wars, tilled your fields, cleared your forests, builded your railroads and cities, and brought forth treasures from the bowels of the earth, and helped make possible this magnificent representation of the progress of the South. Casting down your bucket among my people, helping and encouraging them as you are doing on these grounds, and, with education of head, hand and heart, you will find that they will buy your surplus land, make blossom the waste place in your fields, and run your factories. While doing this, you can be sure in the future, as in the past, that you and your families will be surrounded by the most patient, faithful, law-abiding, and unresentful people that the world has seen. As we have proved our loyalty to you in the past, in nursing your children, watching by the sick bed of your mothers and fathers, and often following them with tear-dimmed eyes to their graves, so in the future, in our humble way, we shall stand by you with a devotion that no foreigner can approach, ready to lay down our lives, if need be, in defense of yours, interlacing our industrial, commercial, civil, and religious life with yours in a way that shall make the interests of both races one. In all things that are purely social we can be as separate as the fingers, yet one as the hand in all things essential to mutual progress.

There is no defense or security for any of us except in the highest intelligence and development of all. If anywhere there are efforts tending to curtail the fullest growth of the Negro, let these efforts be turned into stimulating, encouraging, and making him the most useful and intelligent citizen. Effort or means so invested will pay a thousand percent interest. These efforts will be twice blessed—"blessing him that gives and him that takes."

There is no escape through law of man or God from the inevitable:

The laws of changeless justice bind
Oppressor with oppressed;
As close as sin and suffering joined
We march to fate abreast.

Nearly sixteen millions of hands will aid you in pulling the load upwards, or they will pull against you the load downwards. We shall constitute one-third and more of the ignorance and crime of the South, or one-third its intelligence and progress; we shall contribute one-third to the business and industrial prosperity of the South, or we shall prove a veritable body of death, stagnating, depressing, retarding every effort to advance the body politic.

Gentlemen of the Exposition, as we present to you our humble effort at an exhibition of our progress, you must not expect over much. Starting thirty years ago with ownership here and there in a few quilts and pumpkins and chickens (gathered from miscellaneous sources), remember the path that has led from these to the invention and production of agricultural implements, buggies, steam engines, newspapers, books, statuary, carving, paintings, the management of drug stores and banks, has not been trodden without contact with thorns and thistles. While we take pride in what we exhibit as a result of our independent efforts, we do not for a moment forget that our part in this exhibition would fall far short of your expectations but for the constant help that has come to our educational life, not only from the Southern States, but especially from Northern philanthropists, who have made their gifts a constant stream of blessing and encouragement.

The wisest among my race understand that the agitation of questions of social equality is the extremist folly, and that progress in the enjoyment of all the privileges that will come to us must be the result of severe and constant struggle rather than of artificial forcing. No race that has anything to contribute to the markets of the world is long in any degree ostracized. It is important and right that all privileges of the law be ours, but it is vastly more important that we be prepared for the exercise of those privileges. The opportunity to earn a dollar in a factory just now is worth infinitely more than the opportunity to spend a dollar in an opera house.

> ***"No race can prosper till it learns that there is as much dignity in tilling a field as in writing a poem."***

In conclusion, may I repeat that nothing in thirty years has given us more hope and encouragement, and drawn us so near to you of the white race, as this opportunity offered by the Exposition; and here bending, as it were, over the altar that represents the results of the struggles of your race and mine, both starting practically empty-handed three decades ago, I pledge that, in your effort to work our the great and intricate problem which God has laid at the doors of the South, you shall have at all time the patient, sympathetic help of my race; only let this be constantly in mind that, while from representations in these buildings of the product of field, of forest, of mine, of factory, letters, and art, much good will come, yet far above and beyond material benefits will be that higher good, that let us pray God will come, in a blotting out of sectional differences and racial animosities and suspicions, in a determination to administer absolute justice, in a willing obedience among all classes to the mandates of law. This, coupled with our material prosperity, will bring into our beloved South a new heaven and a new earth.

In September 1906, after weeks of escalating racial tensions over a variety of issues, a major riot broke out in Atlanta, Georgia. When blacks organized themselves in defense against angry white mobs, the police intervened on the side of the whites. The disturbance resulted in at least twelve deaths, numerous arrests, and extensive property damage in the African American community. It also inflamed northern blacks, who urged their southern brothers to form self-defense groups. Not surprisingly, Washington vehemently rejected this suggestion. In a speech delivered in New York City before the Afro-American Council on October 11, he criticized blacks in the North for helping to stir up trouble and advised southern blacks to show that they were "a law-abiding and law-respecting people." His remarks, originally published in the October 20, 1906, issue of The Public, *are taken here from* The Voice of Black America: Major Speeches by Negroes in the United States, 1797–1971 *(Simon & Schuster, 1972).*

In the season of disturbances and excitement if others yield to the temptation of losing control of their judgment and give way to passion and prejudice, let us, as a race, teach the world that we have learned the great lesson of calmness and self-control; that we are determined to be governed by reason rather than by feeling. Our victories in the past have come to us through our ability to be calm and patient, often while enduring great wrong.

Again, I am most anxious—and I know that in this I speak the sentiment of every conservative member of our race—that our race everywhere bears the reputation of a law-abiding and law-respecting people. If others would break the law and trample it underfoot, let us keep and respect it, and teach our children to follow our example. In this connection I repeat what I have uttered on a recent occasion: that every iota of influence that we possess should be used to get rid of the criminal and loafing element of our people and to make decent, law-abiding citizens.

To the members of my race who reside in the Northern states let me utter the caution that in your enthusiastic desire to be of service to your brethren in the South you do not make their path more thorny and difficult by rash and intemperate utterances. Before giving advice to the Negro in the South, the Negro in the North should be very sure that what he advises is that which he himself would be willing to take into the heart of the South and put into practice. Be careful not to assist in lighting a fire which you will have no ability to put out.

Some may think that the problems with which we are grappling will be better solved by inducing millions of our people to leave the South for residence in the North, but I warn you that instead of this being a solution it will but add to the complications of the problem.

While condemning the giving of prominence to the work of the mob in the South, we should not fail to give due credit to those of the white race who stood manfully and courageously on the side of law and order during the recent trying ordeals through which this section of our country has been passing. During the racial disturbances the country very seldom hears of the brave and heroic acts of a certain element of Southern white people whose deeds are seldom heralded through the press.

The indiscriminate condemnation of all white people on the part of any member of our race is a suicidal and dangerous policy. We must learn to discriminate. We have strong friends, both in the South and in the North, and we should emphasize and magnify the efforts of our friends more than those of them who wish us evil.

I have said we must differentiate between white people at the South. We cannot afford to class all as our enemies, for there are many who are our friends. The country must also learn to differentiate among black people. It is a mistake to place all in the same class when referring to labor, morality or general conduct. There is a vicious class that disgraces us; there is also a worthy class which should always receive commendation. Further, we must frankly face the fact that the great body of our people are to dwell in the South, and any policy that does not seek to harmonize the two races and cement them is unwise and dangerous.

Creation—construction, in the material, civic, educational, moral and religious world—is what makes races great. Any child can cry and fret, but it requires a full-grown man to create, to construct. Let me implore you to teach the members of our race everywhere that they must become, in an increasing degree, creators of their own careers.

Toward the end of his career, although he was still influential among white Americans, Washington no longer enjoyed quite the same degree of power and prestige among African Americans. Younger and more liberal blacks in particular had begun to look elsewhere for leadership, turning to people such as W.E.B. Du Bois and others associated with the more militant NAACP. They had frequently denounced Washington and his accommodationist policies over the years, blaming them in part for the deterioration in black-white relations and increasingly oppressive racial atmosphere of the early 1900s. Washington, however, was not blind to the inequities that existed—especially in the area of education—and while he extolled the progress made thus far, he realized how much work remained to be done.

Washington died on November 14, 1915.

SOURCES

Books

Boulware, Marcus Hanna, *The Oratory of Negro Leaders: 1900-1968,* Negro Universities Press, 1969.

Foner, Philip S., editor, *The Voice of Black America: Major Speeches by Negroes in the United States, 1797-1971,* Simon & Schuster, 1972.

Harlan, Louis R., *Booker T. Washington: The Making of a Black Leader, 1856-1901,* Oxford University Press, 1972.

Harlan, Louis R., and others, editors, *The Booker T. Washington Papers,* fourteen volumes, University of Illinois Press, 1972-1989.

Hill, Roy L., *Rhetoric of Racial Revolt,* Golden Bell Press, 1964.

Meier, August, *Negro Thought in America, 1880-1915: Racial Ideologies in the Age of Booker T. Washington,* University of Michigan Press, 1963.

Meltzer, Milton, editor, *The Black Americans: A History in Their Own Words, 1619-1983,* Crowell, 1984.

Ploski, Harry A., and James Williams, editors, *The Negro Almanac: A Reference Work on the African American,* fifth edition, Gale, 1989.

Schroeder, Alan, *Booker T. Washington,* Chelsea House, 1992.

Smith, Arthur L., and Stephen Robb, editors, *The Voice of Black Rhetoric: Selections,* Allyn & Bacon, 1971.

Thornbrough, Emma Lou, editor, *Booker T. Washington,* Prentice-Hall, 1969.

Washington, Booker T., *The Story of My Life and Work* (reprint), Greenwood Press, 1970.
———, *Up from Slavery* (reprint), Viking Penguin, 1986.
———, *My Larger Education* (reprint), Mnemosyne Publishing, 1969.

Periodicals

Ebony, "Ten Greats of Black History," August, 1972, pp. 35-42.

New York Times, November 15, 1915.

Ida B. Wells-Barnett

1862–1930

African American journalist and anti-lynching activist

During the late nineteenth and early twentieth centuries, Ida B. Wells-Barnett launched and headed a virtual one-woman crusade against lynching. This vicious practice, which claimed more than 1,200 black lives (mostly men, but also some women and even children) from 1890 to 1900, was widely accepted—especially in the South—as a legitimate means of punishing black criminals. In many instances, however, these so-called "crimes" involved such offenses as arguing with whites, being disrespectful, or having intimate relationships with white women. To Wells-Barnett, this clearly proved that lynching was nothing more than a horrific form of racial prejudice that no decent human being could ignore or justify. She waged her war against it in the press as well as on the podium, earning a reputation for fearlessness and determination despite numerous efforts to intimidate her, including death threats.

Born into slavery in Holly Springs, Mississippi, Wells-Barnett received her education there following the Civil War at a high school and industrial college established by Methodist missionaries from the North. She went to work as a teacher at the age of sixteen to support herself and her five younger brothers and sisters after their parents died in a yellow fever epidemic.

In 1884, Wells-Barnett moved to Memphis, Tennessee, and taught there for several years. She also began writing for various local black newspapers and then for some national publications. In 1889, she was invited to become part owner and editor of the Free Speech *newspaper, and it was in those pages that her angry denunciations of lynching began to attract attention throughout the United States and even overseas. The brutal kidnapping and murder of three black grocers in 1892 prompted Wells-Barnett to publish a series of scathing editorials and urge blacks to boycott the city's new streetcar line and move out of Memphis if at all possible. Enraged whites responded by burning the* Free Speech *office. Realizing it was too dangerous for her to remain in town, she moved to New York City and continued her crusade as a columnist for T. Thomas Fortune's* New York Age *newspaper and as a lecturer in the North and in Europe and Great Britain. She later settled in Chicago and was a founding member of the Niagara Movement and the National Association for the Advancement of Colored People (NAACP).*

In February 1893, Frederick Douglass invited Wells-Barnett to talk about her campaign at the Metropolitan African Methodist Episcopal Church in Washington, D.C. She had recently published a booklet, Southern Horrors, *in which she analyzed various lynchings and challenged the myth that white men were only trying to protect white women from being raped by black men. Like many of her fellow African Americans, Wells-Barnett believed that if northern whites learned the extent of the slaughter in the South, they would take steps to put an end to it. Her speech follows; it is reprinted from Volume 2 of* Man Cannot Speak for Her *(Greenwood Press, 1989).*

Wednesday evening, May 24, 1892, the city of Memphis was filled with excitement. Editorials in the daily papers of that date caused a meeting to be held in the Cotton Exchange Building; a committee was sent for the editors of the *Free Speech,* an Afro-American journal published in that city, and the only reason the open threats of lynching that were made were not carried out was because they could not be found. The cause of all this commotion was the following editorial published in the *Free Speech* May 21, 1892, the Saturday previous.

Ida B. Wells-Barnett

> *Eight Negroes lynched since last issue of the* Free Speech, *one at Little Rock, Arkansas, last Saturday morning where the citizens broke (?) into the penitentiary and got their man; three near Anniston, Alabama, one near New Orleans; and three at Clarksville, Georgia, the last three for killing a white man, and five on the same old racket—the new alarm about raping white women. The same programme of hanging, then shooting bullets into the lifeless bodies was carried out to the letter.*
>
> *Nobody in this section of the country believes the old thread-bare lie that Negro men rape white women. If Southern white men are not careful, they will over-reach themselves and public sentiment will have a reaction; a conclusion will then be reached which will be very damaging to the moral reputation of their women.*

The *Daily Commercial* of Wednesday following, May 25, contained the following leader:

> *Those negroes who are attempting to make the lynching of individuals of their race a means for arousing the worst passions of their kind are playing with a dangerous sentiment. The negroes may as well understand that there is no mercy for the negro rapist and little patience with his defenders. A negro organ printed in this city, in a recent issue publishes the following atrocious paragraph: "Nobody in this section of the country believes the old thread-bare lie that Negro men rape white women. If Southern white men are not careful they will over-reach themselves, and public sentiment will have a reaction; and a conclusion will be reached which will be very damaging to the moral reputation of their women."*
>
> *The fact that a black scoundrel is allowed to live and utter such loathsome and repulsive calumnies is a volume of evidence as to the wonderful patience of Southern whites. But we have had enough of it.*

> *There are some things that the Southern white man will not tolerate, and the obscene intimations of the foregoing have brought the writer to the very outermost limit of public patience. We hope we have said enough.*

The *Evening Scimitar* of same date, copied the *Commercial*'s editorial with these words of comment:

> *Patience under such circumstances is not a virtue. If the negroes themselves do not apply the remedy without delay it will be the duty of those whom he has attacked to tie the wretch who utters these calumnies to a stake at the intersection of Main and Madison Streets, brand him in the forehead with a hot iron and perform upon him a surgical operation with a pair of tailor's shears.*

Acting upon this advice, the leading citizens met in the Cotton Exchange Building the same evening, and threats of lynching were freely indulged, not by the lawless element upon which the deviltry of the South is usually saddled—but by the leading business men, in their leading business center. Mr. Fleming, the business manager and owning a half interest [in] the *Free Speech,* had to leave town to escape the mob, and was afterwards ordered not to return; letters and telegrams sent me in New York where I was spending my vacation advised me that bodily harm awaited my return. Creditors took possession of the office and sold the outfit, and the *Free Speech* was as if it had never been.

The editorial in question was prompted by the many inhuman and fiendish lynchings of Afro-Americans which have recently taken place and was meant as a warning. Eight lynched in one week and five of them charged with rape! The thinking public will not easily believe freedom and education more brutalizing than slavery, and the world knows that the crime of rape was unknown during four years of civil war, when the white women of the South were at the mercy of the race which is all at once charged with being a bestial one.

Since my business has been destroyed and I am an exile from home because of that editorial, the issue has been forced, and as the writer of it I feel that the race and the public generally should have a statement of the facts as they exist. They will serve at the same time as a defense for the Afro-American Sampsons [sic] who suffer themselves to be betrayed by white Delilahs.

The whites of Montgomery, Alabama, knew J.C. Duke sounded the keynote of the situation—which they would gladly hide from the world, when he said in his paper, the *Herald,* five years ago: "Why is it that white women attract negro men now more than in former days? There was a time when such a thing was unheard of. There is a secret to this thing, and we greatly suspect it is the growing appreciation of white Juliets for colored Romeos." Mr. Duke, like the *Free Speech* proprietors, was forced to leave the city for reflecting on the "honah" of white women and his paper suppressed; but the truth remains that Afro-American men do not always rape (?) white women without their consent.

Mr. Duke, before leaving Montgomery, signed a card disclaiming any intention of slandering Southern white women. The editor of the *Free Speech* has no disclaimer to enter, but asserts instead that there are many white women in the South who would marry colored men if such an act would not place them at once beyond the pale of society and within the clutches of the law. The miscegnation [sic] laws of the South only operate against the legitimate union of the races; they leave the white man free to seduce all the colored girls he can, but it is death to the colored man who yields to the force and advances of a similar attraction in white women. White men lynch the offending Afro-American, not because he is a despoiler of virtue, but because he succumbs to the smiles of white women.

The *Cleveland Gazette* of January 16, 1892, publishes a case in point. Mrs. J.S. Underwood, the wife of a minister of Elyria, Ohio, accused an Afro-American of rape. She told her husband that during his absence in 1888, stumping the State for the Prohibition Party, the man came to the kitchen door, forced his way in the house and insulted her. She tried to drive him out with a heavy poker, but he overpowered and chloroformed her, and when she revived her clothing was torn and she was in a horrible condition. She did not know the man but could identify him. She pointed out William Offett, a married man, who was arrested and, being in Ohio, was granted a trial.

The prisoner vehemently denied the charge of rape, but confessed he went to Mrs. Underwood's residence at her invitation and was criminally intimate with her at her request. This availed him nothing against the sworn testimony of a minister's wife, a lady of the highest respectability. He was found guilty, and entered the penitentiary, December 14, 1888, for fifteen years. Some time afterwards the woman's remorse led her to confess to her husband that the man was innocent.

These are her words:

I met Offett at the Post Office. It was raining. He was polite to me, and as I had several bundles in my arms he offered to carry them home for me, which he did. He had a strange fascination for me, and I invited him to call on me. He called, bringing chestnuts and candy for the children. By this means we got them to leave us alone in the room. Then I sat on his lap. He made a proposal to me and I readily consented. Why I did so, I do not know, but that I did is true. He visited me several times after that and each time I was indiscreet. I did not care after the first time. In fact I could not have resisted, and had no desire to resist.

When asked by her husband why she told him she had been outraged, she said: "I had several reasons for telling you. One was the neighbors saw the fellows [sic] here; another was, I was afraid I had contracted a loathsome disease, and still another was that I feared I might give birth to a Negro baby. I hoped to save my reputation by telling you a deliberate lie." Her husband, horrified by the confession, had Offett, who had already served four years, released and secured a divorce.

There are thousands of such cases throughout the South, with the difference that the Southern white men in insatiate fury wreak their vengeance without intervention of law upon the Afro-Americans who consort with their women. A few instances to substantiate the assertion that some white women love the company of the Afro-American will not be out of place. Most of these cases were reported by the daily papers of the South.

In the winter of 1885-6 the wife of a practicing physician in Memphis, in good social standing whose name has escaped me, left home, husband and children, and ran away with her black coachman. She was with him a month before her husband found and brought her home. The coachman could not be found. The doctor moved his family away from Memphis, and is living in another city under an assumed name.

In the same city last year a white girl in the dusk of evening screamed at the approach of some parties that a Negro had assaulted her on the street. He was captured, tried by a white judge and jury, that acquitted him of the charge. It is needless to add if there had been a scrap of evidence on which to convict him of so grave a charge he would have been convicted.

Sarah Clark of Memphis loved a black man and lived openly with him. When she was indicted last spring for miscegenation, she swore in court that she was not a white woman. This she did to escape the penitentiary and continued her illicit relation undisturbed. That she is of the lower class of whites, does not disturb the fact that she is a white woman. "The leading citizens" of Memphis are defending the "honor" of all white women, demimonde included.

Since the manager of the *Free Speech* has been run away from Memphis by the guardians of the honor of Southern white women, a young girl living on Poplar Street, who was discovered in intimate relations with a handsome mulatto young colored man, Will Morgan by name, stole her father's money to send the young fellow away from that father's wrath. She has since joined him in Chicago.

The Memphis *Ledger* for June 8 has the following:

If Lillie Bailey, a rather pretty white girl seventeen years of age, who is now at the City Hospital, would be somewhat less reserved about her disgrace, there would be some very nauseating details in the story of her life. She is the mother of a little coon. The truth might reveal fearful depravity or it might reveal the evidence of rank outrage. She will not divulge the name of the man who has left such black evidence of her disgrace, and, in fact, says it is a matter in which there can be no interest to the outside world. She came to Memphis nearly three months ago and was taken in at the Woman's Refuge in the southern part of the city. She remained there until a few weeks ago, when the child was born. The ladies in charge of the Refuge were horrified. The girl was at once sent to the City Hospital, where she has been since May 30. She is a country girl. She came to Memphis from her father's farm, a short distance from Hernando, Mississippi. Just when she left there she would not say. In fact she says she came to Memphis from Arkansas, and says her home is in that State. She is rather good looking, has blue eyes, a low forehead and dark red hair. The ladies at the Woman's Refuge do not know anything about the girl further than what they learned when she was an inmate of the institution; and she would not tell much. When the child was born an attempt was made to get the girl to reveal the name of the Negro who had disgraced her, she obstinately refused and it was impossi-

ble to elicit any information from her on the subject.

Note the wording. "The truth might reveal fearful depravity or rank outrage." If it had been a white child or Lillie Bailey had told a pitiful story of Negro outrage, it would have been a case of woman's weakness or assault and she could have remained at the Woman's Refuge. But a Negro child and to withhold its father's name and thus prevent the killing of another Negro "rapist." A case of "fearful depravity."

The very week the "leading citizens" of Memphis were making a spectacle of themselves in defense of all white women of every kind, an Afro-American, M. Stricklin, was found in a white woman's room in that city. Although she made no outcry of rape, he was jailed and would have been lynched, but the woman stated she bought curtains of him (he was a furniture dealer) and his business in her room that night was to put them up. A white woman's word was taken as absolutely in this case as when the cry of rape is made, and he was freed.

What is true of Memphis is true of the entire South. The daily papers last year reported a farmer's wife in Alabama had given birth to a Negro child. When the Negro farm hand who was plowing in the field heard it he took the mule from the plow and fled. The dispatches also told of a woman in South Carolina who gave birth to a Negro child and charged three men with being its father, every one of whom has since disappeared. In Tuscumbia, Alabama, the colored boy who was lynched there last year for assaulting a white girl told her before his accusers that he had met her there in the woods often before.

Frank Weems of Chattanooga who was not lynched in May only because the prominent citizens became his body guard until the doors of the penitentiary closed on him, had letters in his pocket from the white woman in the case, making the appointment with him. Edward Coy, who was burned alive in Texarkana, January 1, 1892, died protesting his innocence. Investigation since, as given by the Bystander in the *Chicago Inter-Ocean,* October 1, proves:

1. The woman who was paraded as a victim of violence was of bad character; her husband was a drunkard and a gambler.

2. She was publicly reported and generally known to have been criminally intimate with Coy for more than a year previous.

3. She was compelled by threats, if not by violence, to make the charge against the victim.

4. When she came to apply the match, Coy asked her if she would burn him after they had "been sweethearting" so long.

5. A large majority of the "superior" white men prominent in the affair are the reputed fathers of mulatto children.

These are not pleasant facts, but they are illustrative of the vital phase of the so-called "race question," which should properly be designated an earnest inquiry as to the best methods by which religion, science, law and political power may be employed to excuse injustice, barbarity and crime done to a people because of race and color. There can be no possible belief that these people were inspired by any consuming zeal to vindicate God's law against miscegnationists [sic] of the most practical sort. The woman was a willing partner in the victim's guilt, and being of the "superior" race must naturally have been more guilty.

In Natchez, Mississippi, Mrs. Marshall, one of the crème de la crème of the city, created a tremendous sensation several years ago. She has a black coachman who was married, and had been in her employ several years. During this time she gave birth to a child whose color was remarked, but traced to some brunette ancestor, and one of the fashionable dames of the city was its godmother. Mrs. Marshall's social position was unquestioned, and wealth showered every dainty on this child which [sic] was idolized with its brothers and sisters by its white papa. In course of time another child appeared on the scene, but it was unmistakably dark. All were alarmed, and "rush of blood, strangulation" were the conjectures, but the doctor, when asked the cause, grimly told them it was a Negro child. There was a family conclave, the coachman heard of it and leaving his own family went West, and has never returned. As soon as Mrs. Marshall was able to travel she was sent away in deep disgrace. Her husband died within the year of a broken heart.

Ebenzer [sic] Fowler, the wealthiest colored man in Issaquena County, Mississippi, was shot down on the street in Mayersville, January 30, 1885, just before dark by an armed body of white men who filled his body with bullets. They charged him with writing a note to a white woman of the place, which they intercepted and which proved there was an intimacy existing between them.

Hundreds of such cases might be cited, but enough have been given to prove the assertion that there are white women in the South who love the Afro-American's company even as there are white men notorious for their preference for Afro-American women.

There is hardly a town in the South which has not an instance of the kind which is well known, and hence the assertion is reiterated that "nobody in the South believes the old threadbare lie that Negro men rape white women." Hence there is a growing demand among Afro-Americans that the guilt or innocence of parties accused of rape be fully established. They know the men of the section of the country who refuse this are not so desirous of punishing rapists as they pretend. The utterances of the leading white men show that with them it is not the crime but the class. Bishop Fitzgerald has become apologist for lynchers of the rapists of white women only. Governor Tillman, of South Carolina, in the month of June, standing under the tree in Barnwell, South Carolina, on which eight Afro-Americans were hung [sic] last year, declared that he would "lead a mob to lynch a negro who raped a white woman." So say the pulpits, officials and newspapers of the South. But when the victim is a colored woman it is different.

Last winter in Baltimore, Maryland, three white ruffians assaulted a Miss Camphor, a young Afro-American girl, while out walking with a young man of her own race. They held her escort and outraged the girl. It was a deed dastardly enough to arouse Southern blood, which gives its horror of rape as an excuse for lawlessness, but she was an Afro-American. The case went to the courts, an Afro-American lawyer defended the men and they were acquitted.

"The utterances of the leading white men show that with them it is not the crime but the class."

In Nashville, Tennessee, there is a white man, Pat Hanifan, who outraged a little Afro-American girl, and, from the physical injuries received, she has been ruined for life. He was jailed for six months, discharged, and is now a detective in that city. In the same city, last May, a white man outraged an Afro-American girl in a drug store. He was arrested, and released on bail at the trial. It was rumored that five hundred Afro-Americans had organized to lynch him. Two hundred and fifty white citizens armed themselves with Winchesters and guarded him. A cannon was placed in front of his home, and the Buchanan Rifles (State Militia) ordered to the scene for his protection. The Afro-American mob did not materialize. Only two weeks before Eph. Grizzard, who had only been charged with rape upon a white woman, had been taken from the jail, with Governor Buchanan and the police and militia standing by, dragged through the streets in broad daylight, knives plunged into him at every step, and with every fiendish cruelty a frenzied mob could devise, he was at last swung out on the bridge with hands cut to pieces as he tried to climb up the stanchions. A naked, bloody example of the blood-thirstiness of the nineteenth century civilization of the Athens of the South! No cannon or military was called out in his defense. He dared to visit a white woman.

At the very moment these civilized whites were announcing their determination "to protect their wives and daughters," by murdering Grizzard, a white man was in the same jail for raping eight-year-old Maggie Reese, an Afro-American girl. He was not harmed. The "honor" of grown women who were glad enough to be supported by the Grizzard boys and Ed Coy, as long as the liasion [sic] was not known, needed protection; they were white. The outrage upon helpless childhood needed no avenging in this case; she was black.

A white man in Guthrie, Oklahoma Territory, two months ago inflicted such injuries upon another Afro-American child that she died. He was not punished, but an attempt was made in the same town in the month of June to lynch an Afro-American who visited a white woman.

In Memphis, Tennessee, in the month of June, Ellerton L. Dorr, who is the husband of Russell Hancock's widow, was arrested for attempted rape on Mattie Cole, a neighbor's cook; he was only prevented from accomplishing his purpose, by the appearance of Mattie's employer. Dorr's friends says he was drunk and not responsible for his actions. The grand jury refused to indict him and he was discharged.

The appeal of Southern whites to Northern sympathy and sanction, the adroit, insiduous [sic] plea made by Bishop Fitzgerald for suspension of judgment because those "who condemn lynching express no sympathy for the white woman in the case," falls to the ground in the light of the foregoing.

From this exposition of the race issue in

lynch law, the whole matter is explained by the well-known opposition growing out of slavery to the progress of the race. This is crystalized in the oft-repeated slogan: "This is a white man's country and the white man must rule." The South resented giving the Afro-American his freedom, the ballot box, and the Civil Rights Law. The raids of the Ku-Klux and White Liners to subvert reconstruction government, the Hamburg and Ellerton, South Carolina, the Copiah County, Mississippi, and the Lafayette Parish, Louisiana, massacres were excused as the natural resentment of intelligence against government by ignorance.

Honest white men practically conceded the necessity of intelligence murdering ignorance to correct the mistake of the general government, and the race was left to the tender mercies of the solid South. Thoughtful Afro-Americans with the strong arm of the government withdrawn and with the hope to stop such wholesale massacres urged the race to sacrifice its political rights for the sake of peace. They honestly believed the race should fit itself for government, and when that should be done, the objection to race participation in politics would be removed.

But the sacrifice did not remove the trouble, nor move the South to justice. One by one the Southern States have legally (?) disfranchised the Afro-American, and since the repeal of the Civil Rights Bill nearly every Southern State has passed separate car laws with a penalty against their infringement. The race regardless of advancement is penned into filthy, stifling partitions cut off from smoking cars. All this while, although the political cause has been removed, the butcheries of black men at Barnwell, South Carolina, Carrolton, Mississippi, Waycross, Georgia, and Memphis, Tennessee, have gone on; also the flaying alive of a man in Kentucky, the burning of one in Arkansas, the hanging of a fifteen-year-old girl in Louisiana, a woman in Jackson, Tennessee, and one in Hollendale, Mississippi, until the dark and bloody record of the South shows 728 Afro-Americans lynched during the past 8 years. Not 50 of these were for political causes; the rest were for all manner of accusations from that of rape of white women, to the case of the boy Will Lewis who was hanged at Tullahoma, Tennessee, last year for being drunk and "sassy" to white folks.

These statistics, compiled by the Chicago *Tribune,* were given the first of this year (1892). Since then, not less than one hundred and fifty have been known to have met violent death at the hands of cruel bloodthirsty mobs during the past nine months.

To palliate this record (which grows worse as the Afro-American becomes intelligent) and excuse some of the most heinous crimes that ever stained the history of a country, the South is shielding itself behind the plausible screen of defending the honor of its women. This, too, in the face of the fact that only one-third of the 728 victims to mobs have been charged with rape, to say nothing of those of that one-third who were innocent of the charge. A white correspondent of the Baltimore *Sun* declares that the Afro-American who was lynched in Chesterton, Maryland, in May for assault on a white girl was innocent; that the deed was done by a white man who had since disappeared. The girl herself maintained that her assailant was a white man. When that poor Afro-American was murdered, the whites excused their refusal of a trial on the ground that they wished to spare the white girl the mortification of having to testify in court.

This cry has had its effect. It closed the heart, stifled the conscience, warped the judgment and hushed the voice of press and pulpit on the subject of lynch law throughout this "land of liberty." Men who stand high in the esteem of the public for Christian character, for moral and physical courage, for devotion to the principles of equal and exact justice to all, and for great sagacity, stand as cowards who fear to open their mouths before this great outrage. They do not see that by their tacit encouragement, their silent acquiescence, the black shadow of lawlessness in the form of lynch law is spreading its wings over the whole country.

Men who, like Governor Tillman, start the ball of lynch law rolling for a certain crime, are powerless to stop it when drunken or criminal white toughs feel like hanging an Afro-American on any pretext.

Even to the better class of Afro-Americans the crime of rape is so revolting they have too often taken the white man's word and given lynch law neither the investigation nor condemnation it deserved.

They forget that a concession of the right to lynch a man for a certain crime, not only concedes the right to lynch any person for any crime, but (so frequently is the cry of rape now raised) it is in a fair way to stamp us a race of rapists and desperadoes. They have gone on hoping and believing that general education and financial strength would solve the difficulty, and are devoting their energies to the accumulation of both.

The mob spirit has grown with the increasing intelligence of the Afro-American. It has left the out-of-the-way places where ignorance prevails, has thrown off the mask and with this new cry stalks in broad daylight in large cities, the centers of civilization, and is encouraged by the "leading citizens" and the press.

The *Daily Commercial* and *Evening Scimitar* of Memphis, Tennessee, are owned by leading business men of that city, and yet, in spite of the fact that there had been no white woman in Memphis outraged by an Afro-American, and that Memphis possessed a thrifty law-abiding, property owning class of Afro-Americans, the *Commercial* of May 17th, under the head of "More Rapes, More Lynchings" gave utterance to the following:

> *The lynching of three Negro scoundrels reported in our dispatches from Anniston, Alabama, for a brutal outrage committed upon a white woman will be a text for much comment on "Southern barbarism" by Northern newspapers; but we fancy it will hardly prove effective for campaign purposes among intelligent people. The frequency of these lynchings calls attention to the frequency of the crimes which causes lynching. The "Southern barbarism" which deserves the serious attention of all people North and South, is the barbarism which preys upon weak and defenseless women. Nothing but the most prompt, speedy and extreme punishment can hold in check the horrible and beastial [sic] propensities of the Negro race. There is a strange similarity about a number of cases of this character which have lately occurred.*
>
> *In each case the crime was deliberately planned and perpetrated by several Negroes. They watched for an opportunity when the women were left without a protector. It was not a sudden yielding to a fit of passion, but the consummation of a devilish purpose which has been seeking and waiting for the opportunity. This feature of the crime not only makes it the most fiendishly brutal, but it adds to the terror of the situation in the thinly settled country communities. No man can leave his family at night without the dread that some roving Negro ruffian is watching and waiting for this opportunity. The swift punishment which invariably follows these horrible crimes doubtless acts as a deterring effect upon the Negroes in that immediate neighborhood for a short time. But the lesson is not widely learned nor long remembered. Then such crimes, equally atrocious, have happened in quick succession, one in Tennessee, one in Arkansas, and one in Alabama. The facts of the crime appear to appeal more to the Negro's lustful imagination than the facts of the punishment do to his fears. He sets aside all fear of death in any form when opportunity is found for the gratification of his bestial desires.*
>
> *There is small reason to hope for any change for the better. The commission of this crime grows more frequent every year. The generation of Negroes which have grown up since the war have lost in large measure the traditional and wholesome awe of the white race which kept the Negroes in subjection, even when their masters were in the army, and their families left unprotected except by the slaves themselves. There is no longer a restraint upon the brute passion of the Negro.*
>
> *What is to be done? The crime of rape is always horrible, but [for] the Southern man there is nothing which so fills the soul with horror, loathing and fury as the outraging of a white woman by a Negro. It is the race question in the ugliest, vilest, most dangerous aspect. The Negro as a political factor can be controlled. But neither laws nor lynchings can subdue his lusts.*
>
> *Sooner or later it will force a crisis. We do not know in what form it will come.*

In its issue of June 4, the Memphis *Evening Scimitar* gives the following excuse for lynch law:

> *Aside from the violation of white women by Negroes, which is the outcropping of a bestial perversion of instinct, the chief cause of trouble between the races in the South is the Negro's lack of manners. In the state of slavery he learned politeness from association with white people, who took pains to teach him. Since the emancipation came and the tie of mutual interest and regard between master and servant was broken, the Negro has drifted away into a state which is neither freedom nor bondage. Lacking the proper inspiration of the one and the restraining force of the other he has taken up the idea that boorish insolence is independence, and the exercise of a decent degree of breeding toward white people is identical with servile submission. In consequence of the prevalence of this notion there are many Negroes who use every opportunity to make themselves offensive, particularly when they think it can be done with impunity.*
>
> *We have had too many instances right here in Memphis to doubt this, and our experience is not exceptional. The white people won't stand this sort of thing, and whether they be insulted*

as individuals are [sic] as a race, the response will be prompt and effectual. The bloody riot of 1866, in which so many Negroes perished, was brought on principally by the outrageous conduct of the blacks toward the whites on the streets. It is also a remarkable and discouraging fact that the majority of such scoundrels are Negroes who have received educational advantages at the hands of the white taxpayers. They have got just enough of learning to make them realize how hopelessly their race is behind the other in everything that makes a great people, and they attempt to "get even" by insolence, which is ever the resentment of inferiors. There are well-bred Negroes among us, and it is truly unfortunate that they should have to pay, even in part, the penalty of the offenses committed by the baser sort, but this is the way of the world. The innocent must suffer for the guilty. If the Negroes as a people possessed a hundredth part of the self-respect which is evidenced by the courteous bearing of some that the Scimitar *could name, the friction between the races would be reduced to a minimum. It will not do to beg the question by pleading that many white men are also stirring up strife. The Caucasian blackguard simply obeys the promptings of a depraved disposition, and he is seldom deliberately rough or offensive toward strangers or unprotected women.*

The Negro tough, on the contrary, is given to just that kind of offending, and he almost invariably singles out white people as his victims.

On March 9, 1892, there were lynched in this same city three of the best specimens of young since-the-war Afro-American manhood. They were peaceful, law-abiding citizens and energetic business men.

They believed the problem was to be solved by eschewing politics and putting money in the purse. They owned a flourishing grocery business in a thickly populated suburb of Memphis, and a white man named Barrett had one on the opposite corner. After a personal difficulty, which Barrett sought by going into the "People's Grocery" drawing a pistol and was thrashed by Calvin McDowell, he (Barrett) threatened to "clean them out." These men were a mile beyond the city limits and police protection; hearing that Barrett's crowd was coming to attack them Saturday night, they mustered forces and prepared to defend themselves against attack.

When Barrett came, he led a posse of officers, twelve in number, who afterward claimed to be hunting a man for whom they had a warrant. That twelve men in citizen's clothes should think it necessary to go in the night to hunt one man who had never before been arrested, or made any record as a criminal has never been explained. When they entered the back door the young men thought the threatened attack was on, and fired into them. Three of the officers were wounded, and when the defending party found it was officers of the law upon whom they had fired, they ceased and got away.

Thirty-one men were arrested and thrown in jail as "conspirators," although they all declared more than once they did not know they were firing on officers. Excitement was at fever heat until the morning papers, two days after, announced that the wounded deputy sheriffs were out of danger. This hindered rather than helped the plans of the whites. There was no law on the statute books which would execute an Afro-American for wounding a white man, but the "unwritten law" did. Three of these men, the president, the manager and clerk of the grocery—"the leaders of the conspiracy"—were secretly taken from jail and lynched in a shockingly brutal manner. "The Negroes are getting too independent," they say, "we must teach them a lesson."

"What lesson?[''] The lesson of subordination. "Kill the leaders and it will cow the Negro who dares to shoot a white man, even in self-defense."

Although the race was wild over the outrage, the mockery of law and justice which disarmed men and locked them up in jails where they could be easily and safely reached by the mob—the Afro-American ministers, newspapers and leaders counselled obedience to the law which did not protect them.

Their counsel was heeded and not a hand was uplifted to resent the outrage; following the advice of the *Free Speech,* people left the city in great numbers.

The dailies and associated press reports heralded these men to the country as "toughs," and "Negro desperadoes who kept a low dive." This same press service printed that the Negro who was lynched at Indianola, Mississippi, in May, had outraged the sheriff's eight-year-old daughter. The girl was more than eighteen years old, and was found by her father in this man's room, who was a servant on the place.

Not content with misrepresenting the race, the mob-spirit was not to be satisfied until the paper which was doing all it could to counteract this impression was silenced. The colored people were resenting their bad treatment in a way to make itself felt, yet gave the mob no excuse for further murder, until the appearance of the editorial which is construed as a reflection on the "honor" of the Southern white women. It is not half so libelous as that of the *Commercial* which appeared four days before, and which has been given in these pages. They would have lynched the manager of the *Free Speech* for exercising the right of free speech if they had found him as quickly as they would have hung [sic] a rapist, and glad of the excuse to do so. The owners were ordered not to return. The *Free Speech* was suspended with as little compunction as the business of the "People's Grocery" broken up and the proprietors murdered.

Henry W. Grady in his well-remembered speeches in New England and New York pictured the Afro-American as incapable of self-government. Through him and other leading men the cry of the South to the country has been "Hands off! Leave us to solve our problem." To the Afro-American the South says, "the white man must and will rule." There is little difference between the Antebellum South and the New South.

"There is little difference between the Antebellum South and the New South. Her white citizens are wedded to any method . . . for the subjugation of the young manhood of the race."

Her white citizens are wedded to any method however revolting, any measure however extreme, for the subjugation of the young manhood of the race. They have cheated him out of his ballot, deprived him of civil rights or redress therefor in the civil courts, robbed him of the fruits of his labor, and are still murdering, burning and lynching him.

The result is a growing disregard of human life. Lynch law has spread its insiduous [sic] influence till men in New York State, Pennsylvania, and on the free Western plains feel they can take the law in their own hands with impunity, especially where an Afro-American is concerned. The South is brutalized to a degree not realized by its own inhabitants, and the very foundation of government, law and order, are imperilled.

Public sentiment has had a slight "reaction" though not sufficient to stop the crusade of lawlessness and lynching. The spirit of Christianity of the great M[ethodist] E[piscopal] Church was aroused to the frequent and revolting crimes against a weak people, enough to pass strong condemnatory resolutions at its General Conference in Omaha last May. The spirit of justice of the grand old party asserted itself sufficiently to secure a denunciation of the wrongs, and a feeble declaration of the belief in human rights in the Republican platform at Minneapolis, June 7th. Some of the great dailies and weeklies have swung into line declaring that lynch law must go. The President of the United States issued a proclamation that it be not tolerated in the territories over which he has jurisdiction. Governor Northern and Chief Justice Bleckley of Georgia have proclaimed against it. The citizens of Chattanooga, Tennessee, have set a worthy example in that they not only condemn lynch law, but her public men demanded a trial for Weems, the accused rapist, and guarded him while the trial was in progress. The trial only lasted ten minutes, and Weems chose to plead guilty and accept twenty-one years sentence, than invite the certain death which awaited him outside that cordon of police if he had told the truth and shown the letters he had from the white woman in the case.

Col. A.S. Colyar, of Nashville, Tennessee, is so overcome with the horrible state of affairs that he addressed the following earnest letter to the Nashville *American*.

> *Nothing since I have been a reading man has so impressed me with the decay of manhood among the people of Tennessee as the dastardly submission to the mob reign. We have reached the unprecedented low level, the awful criminal depravity of substituting the mob for the court and jury, of giving up the jail keys to the mob whenever they are demanded. We do it in the largest cities and in the country towns; we do it in midday; we do it after full, not to say formal, notice, and so thoroughly and generally is it acquiesced in that the murderers have discarded the formula of masks. They go into the town where everybody knows them, sometimes under the gaze of the governor, in the presence of the courts, in the presence of the sheriff and his deputies, in the presence of the entire police force, take out the prisoner, take his life,*

often with fiendish glee, and often with acts of cruelty and barbarism which impress the reader with a degeneracy rapidly approaching savage life. That the State is disgraced but faintly expresses the humiliation which has settled upon the once proud people of Tennessee. The State, in its majesty, through its organized life, for which the people pay liberally, makes but one record, but one note, and that a criminal falsehood, "was hung by persons to the jury unknown." The murder at Shelbyville is only a verification of what every intelligent man knew would come, because with a mob a rumor is as good as a proof.

These efforts brought forth apologies and a short halt, but the lynching mania was [sic] raged again through the past three months with unabated fury.

The strong arm of the law must be brought to bear upon lynchers in severe punishment, but this cannot and will not be done unless a healthy public sentiment demands and sustains such action.

The men and women in the South who disapprove of lynching and remain silent on the perpetration of such outrages are particeps criminis, accomplices, accessories before and after the fact, equally guilty with the actual lawbreakers who would not persist if they did not know that neither the law nor militia would be employed against them.

In the creation of this healthier public sentiment, the Afro-American can do for himself what no one else can do for him. The world looks on with wonder that we have conceded so much and remain law-abiding under such great outrage and provocation.

To Northern capital and Afro-American labor the South owes its rehabilitation. If labor is withdrawn capital will not remain. The Afro-American is thus the backbone of the South. A thorough knowledge and judicious exercise of this power in lynching localities could many times effect a bloodless revolution. The white man's dollar is his god, and to stop this will be to stop outrages in many localities.

The Afro-Americans of Memphis denounced the lynching of three of their best citizens, and urged and waited for the authorities to act in the matter and bring the lynchers to justice. No attempt was made to do so, and the black men left the city by thousands, bringing about great stagnation in every branch of business. Those who remained so injured the business of the street car company by staying off the cars, that the superintendent, manager and treasurer called personally on the editor of the *Free Speech*, asked them to urge our people to give them their patronage again. Other business men became alarmed over the situation and the *Free Speech* was run away that the colored people might be more easily controlled. A meeting of white citizens in June, three months after the lynching, passed resolutions for the first time, condemning it. But they did not punish the lynchers. Every one of them was known by name, because they had been selected to do the dirty work, by some of the very citizens who passed these resolutions. Memphis is fast losing her black population, who proclaim as they go that there is no protection for the life and property of any Afro-American citizen in Memphis who is not a slave.

The Afro-American citizens of Kentucky, whose intellectual and financial improvement has been phenomenal, have never had a separate car law until now. Delegations and petitions poured into the Legislature against it, yet the bill passed and the Jim Crow Car of Kentucky is a legalized institution. Will the great mass of Negroes continue to patronize the railroad? A special from Covington, Kentucky, says:

> *Covington, June 13.—The railroads of the State are beginning to feel very markedly, the effects of the separate coach bill recently passed by the Legislature. No class of people in the State have so many and so largely attended excursion as the blacks. All these have been abandoned, and regular travel is reduced to a minimum. A competent authority says the loss to the various roads will reach $1,000,000 this year.*

A call to a State Conference in Lexington, Kentucky, last June had delegates from every county in the State. Those delegates, the ministers, teachers, heads of secret and other orders, and the head of every family should pass the word around for every member of the race in Kentucky to stay off railroads unless obliged to ride. If they did so, and their advice was followed persistently the convention would not need to petition the Legislature to repeal the law or raise money to file a suit. The railroad corporations would be so effected [sic] they would in self-defense lobby to have the separate car law repealed. On the other hand, as long as the railroads can get Afro-American excursions they will always have plenty of money to fight all the suits brought against them. They will be aided in so doing by the same partisan public sentiment which passed the law.

White men passed the law, and white judges and juries would pass upon the suits against the law, and render judgment in line with their prejudices and in deference to the greater financial power.

The appeal to the white man's pocket has ever been more effectual than all the appeals ever made to his conscience. Nothing, absolutely nothing, is to be gained by a further sacrifice of manhood and self-respect. By the right exercise of his power as the industrial factor of the South, the Afro-American can demand and secure his rights, the punishment of lynchers, and a fair trial for accused rapists.

Of the many inhuman outrages of this present year, the only case where the proposed lynching did not occur, was where the men armed themselves in Jacksonville, Florida, and Paducah, Kentucky, and prevented it. The only times an Afro-American who was assaulted got away has been when he had a gun and used it in self-defense.

> ***"The appeal to the white man's pocket has ever been more effectual than all the appeals ever made to his conscience."***

The lesson this teaches and which every Afro-American should ponder well, is that a Winchester rifle should have a place of honor in every black home, and it should be used for that protection which the law refuses to give. When the white man who is always the aggressor knows he runs as great risk of biting the dust every time his Afro-American victim does, he will have greater respect for Afro-American life. The more the Afro-American yields and cringes and begs, the more he has to do so, the more he is insulted, outraged and lynched.

The assertion has been substantiated throughout these pages that the press contains unreliable and doctored reports of lynchings, and one of the most necessary things for the race to do is to get these facts before the public. The people must know before they can act, and there is no educator to compare with the press.

The Afro-American papers are the only ones which will print the truth, and they lack means to employ agents and detectives to get at the facts. The race must rally a mighty host to the support of their journals, and thus enable them to do much in the way of investigation.

A lynching occurred at Port Jarvis, New York, the first week in June. A white and colored man were implicated in the assault upon a white girl. It was charged that the white man paid the colored boy to make the assault, which he did on the public highway in broad day time, and was lynched. This, too, was done by "parties unknown." The white man in the case still lives. He was imprisoned and promises to fight the case on trial. At the preliminary examination, it developed that he had been a suitor of the girl's. She had repulsed and refused him, yet had given him money, and he had sent threatening letters demanding more.

The day before this examination she was so wrought up, she left home and wandered miles away. When found she said she did so because she was afraid of the man's testimony. Why should she be afraid of the prisoner? Why should she yield to his demands for money if not to prevent him exposing something he knew? It seems explainable only on the hypothesis that a liason [sic] existed between the colored boy and the girl, and the white man knew of it. The press is singularly silent. Has it a motive? We owe it to ourselves to find out.

The story comes from Larned, Kansas, October 1, that a young white lady held at bay until daylight, without alarming any one in the house, "a burly Negro" who entered her room and bed. The "burly Negro" was promptly lynched without investigation or examination of inconsistent stories.

A house was found burned down near Montgomery, Alabama, in Monroe County, October 13, a few weeks ago; also the burned bodies of the owners and melted piles of gold and silver.

These discoveries led to the conclusion that the awful crime was not prompted by motives of robbery. The suggestion of the whites was that "brutal lust was the incentive, and as there are nearly two hundred Negroes living within a radius of five miles of the place the conclusion was inevitable that some of them were the perpetrators."

Upon this "suggestion," probably made by the real criminal, the mob acted upon the "conclusion" and arrested ten Afro-Americans, four of whom, they tell the world, confessed to the deed of murdering Richard L. Johnson and outraging his daughter, Jeanette. These four men,

Berrell Jones, Moses Johnson, Jim and John Packer, none of them twenty-five years of age, upon this conclusion, were taken from jail, hanged, shot, and burned while yet alive the night of October 12. The same report says Mr. Johnson was on the best of terms with his Negro tenants.

The race thus outraged must find out the facts of this awful hurling of men into eternity on supposition, and give them to the indifferent and apathetic country. We feel this to be a garbled report, but how can we prove it?

Near Vicksburg, Mississippi, a murder was committed by a gang of burglars. Of course it must have been done by Negroes, and Negroes were arrested for it. It is believed that two men, Smith Tooley and John Adams, belonged to a gang controlled by white men and, fearing exposure, on the night of July 4, they were hanged in the Court House yard by those interested in silencing them. Robberies since committed in the same vicinity have been known to be by white men who had their faces blackened. We strongly believe in the innocence of these murdered men, but we have no proof. No other news goes out to the world save that which stamps us as a race of cut-throats, robbers and lustful wild beasts. So great is Southern hate and prejudice, they legally (?) hung [sic] poor little thirteen-year-old Mildrey Brown at Columbia, South Carolina, October 7, on the circumstantial evidence that she poisoned a white infant. If her guilt had been proven unmistakably, had she been white, Mildrey Brown would never have been hung.

The country would have been aroused and South Carolina disgraced forever for such a crime. The Afro-American himself did not know as he should have known, as his journals should be in a position to have him know and act.

Nothing is more definitely settled than [that] he must act for himself. I have shown how he may employ the boycott, emigration and the press, and I feel that by a combination of all these agencies can be effectually stamped out lynch law, that last relic of barbarism and slavery. "The gods help those who help themselves."

SOURCES

Campbell, Karlyn Kohrs, *Man Cannot Speak for Her,* Greenwood Press, 1989, Volume 1: *A Critical Study of Early Feminist Rhetoric,* Volume 2: *Key Texts of the Early Feminists.*

Foner, Philip S., editor, *The Voice of Black America: Major Speeches by Negroes in the United States, 1797–1971,* Simon & Schuster, 1972.

Meltzer, Milton, editor, *The Black Americans: A History in Their Own Words, 1619–1983,* Crowell, 1984.

Wells-Barnett, Ida B., *On Lynchings: Southern Horrors, A Red Record, Mob Rule in New Orleans* (reprints of original pamphlets), Arno, 1969.

———, *Crusader for Justice: The Autobiography of Ida B. Wells,* edited by Alfreda M. Duster, University of Chicago Press, 1970.

Cornel West

1953–

African American philosopher, educator, writer, and social activist

One of today's most prominent black voices on the topic of race and class relations is Harvard University professor Cornel West, who brings to the discussion his unique perspective as a devout Christian, a pragmatist in the tradition of American philosopher John Dewey, and a self-described "non-Marxist socialist." In his view of the world, these three traditions can serve as especially powerful weapons against the forces that have contributed to the sense of despair and loss of hope and meaning he sees in the black community. It is a message the charismatic West shares with audiences both inside and outside the academic world, prompting a writer for the New Yorker *to dub him "a public intellectual"—a rare breed of contemporary philosopher who is "deeply involved with the social and political elements of his society."*

The son of a civilian administrator for the U.S. Air Force, West was born in Oklahoma but moved frequently as a child due to his father's job. The family finally settled in Sacramento, California, when young Corn (as he was known) was about five years old, and there he eventually became known as a bit of a troublemaker—defiant, sharp-tongued, and always ready for a fight. (He was, in fact, suspended from school once for punching a teacher who had slapped him because he refused to recite the Pledge of Allegiance in a protest against blacks' second-class status in America.)

This same child, however, found tremendous comfort and inspiration in the Baptist church his family attended. And he was very much drawn to the Black Panthers who operated in his neighborhood; it was through them that he became familiar with the teachings of Karl Marx and learned about the value of community activism. But while he admired the Panthers' racial militancy and charitable programs to benefit the black poor, he could not bring himself to accept their contemptuous rejection of Christianity.

West was an indifferent student until a forced transfer to another school landed him in an accelerated program. He then began to take his studies much more seriously and, as a result, received a scholarship to Harvard University upon his graduation from high school. Recalled by a number of his professors there as an unusually gifted and creative thinker, he earned his bachelor's degree (with honors) in only three years while working two outside jobs and then went on to Princeton for graduate courses in philosophy. After obtaining his master's degree in 1975, West was a Du Bois fellow at Harvard prior to accepting his first teaching assignment, that of assistant (later associate) professor of philosophy and religion at New York's Union Theological Seminary. He remained there from 1977 until 1984, during which time he also worked on his doctoral dissertation. (He received his PhD from Princeton in 1980.)

West's next move was to the Yale Divinity School, where he became professor of religion and philosophy in 1984. He left there three years later to return to Union Theological Seminary, fully expecting to spend the rest of his life there in the belief that, as he once wrote, it offered him "the perfect place to become a broadly engaged cultural critic with a strong grounding in the history of philosophy and criticism." But in 1988, he responded to a challenge from Princeton University officials to serve as professor of religion and director of the Afro-American studies program, which was badly in need of some energetic new leadership. Under his direction, the once-lackluster program achieved a level of distinction and intellectual excitement it had never known before. In 1994 West moved on once again, becoming professor of Afro-American studies and the philosophy of religion at Harvard University.

A man of eclectic interests that range well beyond his academic specialties, West takes an equally cosmopolitan approach to black studies that has not always met with the approval of his colleagues. He takes a rather dim view of Afrocentrism, for example, criticizing it as "a contemporary species of black nationalism" that ignores the distinctive cultural hybrid that is America. In his view, it is impossible to ground the African American sense of self only in African culture. West also refuses to "ghettoize" or marginalize the idea of black studies as a subject "added on to the discussion of what it means to be an American." Instead, he prefers to "put black subject matter, in all its forms, at the center of the wider cultural conversation, so that we can see it as a whole—the Afro-American relationship to all of the New World."

Until 1993, West's reputation as an insightful social critic was confined mostly to academic circles. That year, however, he published his seventh book, Race Matters, *a provocative collection of essays aimed at a general audience. In it he touches on a diverse assortment of topics such as the 1992 Los Angeles riots, the state of black-Jewish relations, the renewed popularity of Malcolm X, and the Clarence Thomas/Anita Hill hearings. West's unsparing look at the flaws of American society and the political and moral failures of today's liberal and conservative leaders—black as well as white—touched off a flurry of media attention that quickly landed* Race Matters *on the bestseller lists. It also created a demand for his services as a speaker before all kinds of audiences, from students and scholars to inner-city church congregations.*

On January 12, 1994, for example, West was in Grand Rapids, Michigan, to deliver a lecture at Calvin College as part of their acclaimed "January Series." Displaying oratorical skills that typically incorporate the fiery zeal of a Baptist preacher, the improvisations of a jazz musician, the rhymes and cadence of urban street talk, and the vocabulary of an Ivy League professor, he touched on some of the key points discussed in Race Matters. *His speech was transcribed from an audiotape furnished by Calvin College.*

What a wonderful introduction! . . . I would first like to thank each and every one of you for coming out this afternoon, and I look forward to our discussion. But I'd also like to thank Ms. June Hamersma. She is a dynamic citizen who constitutes these public forums on her own, projects her own vision, and I think it is appropriate for us to extend our gratitude to her, this labor of love.

So much of what I have to say today has to do with the degree to which public life in America seems barren and vacuous and empty. What it means to be a citizen and called a citizen in these very dark and difficult times.

I stand before you this afternoon less as an individual from New Jersey but rather a small part of a long and rich tradition. And it is a tradition that I consider to be the best of the democratic tradition. I take quite seriously what T.S. Eliot said in his essay of 1919, "Tradition and Individual Talent," where he writes, "Tradition is not something you inherit. If you want it, you must obtain it with great labor." One of the fundamental questions of our time is to what degree can the best of the democratic tradition be preserved and expanded under contemporary circumstances and conditions.

The black freedom struggle is but one species, one version, of this tradition. This notion, this precious notion, that ordinary people ought to live lives of decency and dignity, and hence they ought to have a say in the decision-making processes in those institutions that guide and regulate their lives. How precious! This notion that there are Promethean energies among ordinary folk, if unleashed, produce possibilities heretofore ignored, downplayed, overlooked.

And keep in mind that democracies are quite rare in the history of humankind. And usually short-lived—they usually don't last that long. When we look at what accounts for the unraveling of democracy since the beginning of the human adventure, we see, on the one hand, poverty producing escalating levels of despair, and paranoia producing escalating levels of distrust.

And to talk about race in America, in the USA, is to talk about poverty on the one hand and to talk about paranoia on the other. Which means to talk about race is to take us to the very core and center of the crisis of American democracy. It is not a marginal issue. It is not peripheral. We can't "ghettoize" it. We can't confine it to chocolate cities. It sits at the very center of the degree to which this experiment called America can continue with moral substance and ethical content. And it means then that it affects each and every one of us or, to put it more crudely, that in the end we hang together or we hang separately.

Democratic tradition represented by a Sojourner Truth or a Harriet Tubman or an Ida B. Wells-Barnett or an A. Phillip Randolph—these are just the icons, they're waves in an ocean, targeting one particular form of illegitimate authority. But of course, democracy is about, what, critiques of illegitimate authority, ensuring that there are institutional mechanisms such that arbitrary uses of power are checked and curtailed. And white supremacy is one particular kind of illegitimate authority—like male supremacy, like unchecked corporate elites or bank elites, or like homophobic authority.

Those who are serious about preserving the best of the democratic tradition, whoever you are, Christian, non-Christian, Buddhist, non-Buddhist, secular, whatever. I happen to be a Christian—we'll talk about that. But whoever it is, I believe the democratic tradition is the best that we featherless, two-legged, linguistically-conscious creatures born between urine and feces—that's us! Made in the image of God!—it's the best tradition that we've come up with. Whereas the great Reinhold Niebuhr used to say, "Democracy is a proximate solution to insoluble problems." The best we human beings have come up with.

> *"To talk about race . . . is to take us to the very core and center of the crisis of American democracy. . . . It sits at the very center of the degree to which this experiment called America can continue with moral substance and ethical content."*

What happens when it wanes, when citizens lose confidence in the ability of public institutions to do anything right? What happens when citizens feel helpless, many hopeless, impotent, feeling as if they don't make a difference? Can a democracy survive, as John Dewey put it in his classic of 1927, *The Public and Its Problems*? Can it survive when public life loses its vitality and vibrancy, and the private is cast as sacred, or close to sacred? It is not to say the private doesn't play a crucial role in the private's fears, not inescapable. But when it's cast in an idolatrous way, when we return to our cubbyholes and our cocoon-like views of the world, given the segregation and polarization and fragmentation and segmentation of our society, what happens to the best of the democratic tradition?

As I said before, black freedom struggle is one species of it. And so any time one is serious about a critique of white supremacy, one is serious about the various psychic scars and existential bruises and ontological wounds that are left by the white supremacist assaults on black beauty, on black intelligence, on black capacity and capability, on black humanity. Any time you raise the issue, it takes you at the very heart of trying to ensure that American democracy is thoroughly democratized.

It reminds you of David Walker's great appeal to colored citizens of the world. You all recall that text published in September of 1829, where he says, "My task is to out-Jeffersonianize Jefferson." Jefferson, the great democratic theorist, from whom I learned so much and yet a slaveholder. I need a dialectical reading of Jefferson.

Malcolm X's scientific definition of a nigger—"a victim of American democracy." Sounds oxymoronic or self-contradictory. What he was saying was here is a group of persons whose backs have served as one of the fundamental pillars for American democracy to flourish.

Why? Because one of the distinctive features of American civilization from the very beginning, in the sixteenth century, was the institutionalizing of ideologies of whiteness and blackness. So we're the most race-conscious society, except for South Africa. But a Sicilian peasant who, coming from the southern part of Italy, discovers he's white when he arrives at Ellis Island. 'Cause whiteness had no saliency, it had no potency in the discourse of southern Italy. He knows that the northern Italians have been exploiting him, or she knows. But show up in America and you're told you're white.

"What do you mean, I'm white?"

"Look at him."

"Oh, I'm getting the point. I'm in America."

In fact, you have something in common with those northern Italians that you abhor, in America. When an Irishman discovers that he or an

Cornel West

Irish woman discovers they have something in common with the English—given that vicious history of British imperialism in America—because of an ideology called whiteness.

For the twenty-one percent of the inhabitants of the United States in 1776 who were people of African descent can serve as one of the pillars for the beginning of this grand experiment in democracy—as they are enslaved, as they are experiencing natal alienation (meaning that they have no progeny or predecessors), meaning that they are subject to the brutish contingency of the slave auction. No right to read. Can't worship God without white supervision. You all know the history.

I don't invoke the history to paralyze anybody but to remind us of the ways in which white supremacy has served as a means of suffocating the democratic tradition. And therefore it is not just a matter of what one's views are about black people or brown people or yellow peoples or red peoples, but it has to do with your fundamental commitment to the democratic experiment called America. That's the challenge. It's not simply an appeal to self-interest, even though we know self-interest will play a role. But it's an appeal to our collective self-definition, our collective self-understanding of ourselves as inhabitants of, citizens of, a democratic republic. Very important to keep in mind.

I'm talking about the black freedom tradition and the black freedom struggle. So now we can find the black people.

This is so important for young people these days. There are so many young people who have lost track, or no longer are in tune, with the best of American history. Mention Lydia Maria Child—who is she? Towering figure of the nineteenth century. Wrote a book in 1833 called *Appeal and Favor of That Class of Americans Called Africans.*

One thinks of an Elijah Lovejoy who died on his roof in Alton, Illinois, defending the black freedom struggle as an abolitionist. Gave his life!

And one could go on and on with a whole host of white brothers and sisters who are part of the best of the democratic tradition in terms, in this case, of struggling for black freedom.

Now granted, one has to cut against the grain if you're going to be serious about a critique of white supremacy in the white community. I'm not naive. I know. You have to take a risk. And you pray God that martyrdom is not the requirement, as it was for Brother Elijah Lovejoy.

Think of a Wendell Phillips or a Charles Sumner. Or in the twentieth century, think of a Miles Horton . . . that would help train a Rosa Parks. Or Robert Moses. One could go on and on. You think of Jewish brothers and sisters like the late, great rabbi, Abraham Joshua Heschel, or Asian sisters. . . .

I'm talking about the black freedom struggle, I'm not just confining it to people of African descent. It's a moral issue. Can you get up in the morning and look at yourself, if you're a Christian, how do you understand the claims of the gospel in terms of "love one another" and still put up with the degree to which white supremacy dehumanizes? And as it is institutionalized, it imposes constraints on life chances which deforms the democratic tradition.

I believe that we are living in one of the most frightening and terrifying moments in the history of this country. Now often when I say that, people say, "Oh, come on, Brother West, we've had the Civil War. We've had the Depression. Those were frightening moments." And rightly so, that's true.

But . . . since November 9, 1989, when the Berlin Wall fell, America no longer has an external enemy to define itself against. And when we look closely—critically—at ourselves, it looks as if we are quietly threatened by internal decay on a number of different levels: the relative economic decline, the impact of that world process of de-industrialization in which manufacturing units left the United States and went elsewhere, resulting in the devastation of so many fellow citizens who worked (and of course, in the black community, this has been overwhelming). You think, for example, in 1960, where forty percent of young black men between sixteen and twenty-one had decent-paying industrial jobs. That figure today is seven percent. A slow-motion depression. Or as the economist Wallace Peterson says, "A silent depression ravaging certain pockets of America." Disproportionately black and brown but not solely so. We can look at white brothers and sisters in Appalachia. See the same social misery.

"I believe that we are living in one of the most frightening and terrifying moments in the history of this country."

But with it, the relative economic decline was not simply de-industrialization but also has so much to do with that escalating disparity between the rich and poor. The various ways in which levels of inequality not just expanded poverty but went hand-in-hand, as we shall see, with social breakdown and individual crack-up.

Like I was just reading F. Scott Fitzgerald's famous essay of the crack-up the other day, and I was thinking to myself, "My God, this sounds like not just F. Scott Fitzgerald at thirty-eight years old, it sounds so much like parts of America in 1994." Unable to cope, overwhelmed by dread and despair. Unable to project a sense of the future. Most importantly, I think, for most Americans, the relative economic decline takes the form of the downsizing of the American middle class.

One of the great achievements of the unprecedented economic boom in the United States between 1945 and 1973 was the creation of a social structure that looks like a diamond rather than a pyramid. Most societies look like a pyramid, don't they? Rich at the top, the majority—the poor—at the bottom. For the first time in the history of the modern world, we actually have a society in which it looks like a diamond mass, middle class. But since 1978 and on—this is why it's not a partisan affair, it's not just a matter of the Republican party or Democratic party, it's a question of the leadership of the country across the boards—our social structure begins to look like an hourglass. Downsizing of American middle class.

And you know and I know that any time human beings find themselves engaged in social slippage and downward mobility, it brings out the worst in them. They're looking for scapegoats.

I was just in Cairo, Illinois, just the other day. I had a white brother, very reactionary white brother, telling me I was responsible for the loss of his job. I said, "I didn't know I ran the factory. I didn't know black folk did." Hmmm, interesting. Scapegoating, very narrow projection, mediated by xenophobic sensibility. Blaming women. "Oh, if those women just had stayed in the kitchen and hadn't gone into the labor force, we would have a stable economy." Hmmm. We won't even *begin* to get into the economic motivation of women going into the labor force, given a decline of real wages, inflation-adjusted wages for over forty-two percent of American workers. And hence the need to have two persons in the family working in order to sustain the same standard of living that they were used to before. We won't even have to critique a patriarch, it's just wrong to deny other human beings access to positions simply because they represent fifty-two percent of humanity. Simply because they're women.

"Market moralities and market mentalities saturate and permeate every nook and cranny of our society. . . . A culture of consumption that tries to promote in us an addiction to stimulation, trying to convince us we're only alive and vibrant when we're buying and selling."

In other words, the moment is frightening when race plays a fundamental role, because given the relative economic decline—I know this sounds a bit strange to many fellow citizens because it's true that we've had these waves of economic recovery, twenty-one million jobs created, no doubt, and it's produced impressive income for the top twenty percent. Tremendous wealth for the top one percent. But so many of those jobs are part time. Very few benefits. Sometimes no pension. Which means when we look at the relative well-being of the majority of American people, economic recovery doesn't necessarily translate into the enhancement of the well-being of the majority of American people—even given the fact that the recovery did occur.

But it is not the relative economic decline that I think is most important at this moment, it's the undeniable cultural decay. And of course, this is something that all of us experience every day. Now granted, one may experience it a bit more in Detroit and New York than Grand Rapids, but I know it affects Grand Rapids, too.

What I mean by undeniable cultural decay is the degree to which a fully crystallized market culture has taken hold in which market moralities and market mentalities saturate and permeate every nook and cranny of our society. A whole culture evolving around buying and selling and promoting and advertising. A culture of consumption that tries to promote in us an addiction to stimulation, trying to convince us we're only alive and vibrant when we're buying and selling. You're down and out? Go to the mall. Feeling down and out? Turn on your television and engage in that spectatorial passivity. You're bombarded by those images—many of them degraded images of women. Be stimulated and titillated. And we won't even add the way in which sex, violence, sexual foreplay, orgiastic intensity, violent conquest serve as a major means by which we are titillated and stimulated. How spiritually impoverished a way of being in the world!

The ultimate conclusion is to simply hook up to a pleasure machine. Why have friendships? Why have conversation? Why have interaction? Just hook up! Be stimulated! High levels, all the time.

I wonder to what degree crack itself is a reflection of this culture of consumption that promotes stimulation given that, I'm told, it's the highest form of stimulation to the human brain known to humankind. Ten times more than orgasm, my God! Isn't that good enough? Don't want to get crude here, but you see the point.

What happens in a market culture is that non-market values are pushed to the margin.

Pushed to the peripheral. Love, care, concern, service to others, loyalty, commitment, trust. Even non-market values that affect us in so many intimate ways, like tenderness and kindness and gentleness and sweetness, they're pushed to the edges. Anybody walking around trying to be gentle and tender these days, you cuttin' against the grain. No, no.

Market culture has gone, hand-in-hand, with the creeping *zeitgeist* of coldheartedness and mean-spiritedness. This social Darwinian conception of the world—you better engage in the survival of the fittest, you better be rough and tough.

Note the patriarchal character of that discourse. Rough, tough, machismo. Even women who gain entree to this culture find that they have to become patriarchalized in order to survive oftentimes. How narrow a conception of the good life!

And keep in mind that justice and freedom and equality go far beyond a market culture. And *most* frightening is that a market culture in the end leads to what I call the "gangsterization" of culture. By gangsterization of culture, what I mean is the acceptance of the notion—and it's gaining every day in this nation—the acceptance of the notion, "I'm going to gain access the power and pleasure and property by any means. *Now.*" We used to call it "wilding" in New York City.

It is not just on the ground among disadvantaged citizens. Levels of lawlessness and corruption and graft in high places. The corporate world. Your government. Right across the board. Churches, my synagogues. This is this feeling that so many fellow citizens have that we're sliding down a slippery slope to chaos and anarchy.

What is at work? It's not just these various trials that Americans follow every day that are so far out, these lunatic fringe crimes or possible crimes. But we feel as if they speak to us, they say something about where this civilization is going. And those who are concerned about the best of the democratic tradition say, "Well, how then do we understand this? And how does it relate to—for—me?" This one problem that's always said is at the very center of the crisis of American democracy, which is race. Or the blackness/whiteness dichotomy. I'm not overlooking brownness, I'm not overlooking yellowness. But the blackness/whiteness dichotomy is the fundamental one in terms of the way in which Americans have come to understand themselves.

Why is it very difficult for black and brown to understand themselves? Because they tend to see each other through a white supremacist lens. They accept stereotypes about each other, and it makes it very difficult to communicate. Just as it is so very difficult to communicate between black and white because of our various stereotypes. And of course, both groups have the capacity for cruelty, barbarism—they're human beings. Like anyone else.

Undeniable cultural decay is exemplified most readily in the erosion of the nurturing system for children. Now, William O'Neill has said that one distinctive feature of the fall of every civilization going back to the Sumerians and Mesopotamia or the Egyptians of northern Africa is the erosion of the nurturing system for children. Another way of saying, "Young folk outta control." It's not an empirical claim, but it's a claim that one has to take quite seriously.

Alexis de Tocqueville came to America in the 1830s and he wrote, "Young people in America, outta control." He's talkin' about the tight controls, in France, of young people. Children speaking back to their parents and so forth and so on. He thought this was just *revolting*.

Nineteen-ninety-four. If they were *just* speaking back! Gun culture, drug culture, collapse—God bless you!—collapse of those institutions that transmit meaning and value. Decency and dignity, elegance and excellence, orientation and direction. Crisis in family, crisis in neighborhoods. . . .

[This] is not an attempt to trash the media, but it is an attempt to acknowledge the way in which media now plays such a fundamental role in socializing and acculturating young people. And yet so many of the values promoted by that media have to do with that hedonism and narcissism and privatism and materialism that go hand-in-hand with the market sensibility.

And what happens to young people? Well, they find themselves dangling, rootless, what I call socially deracinated and culturally denuded. By socially deracinated, I mean they find themselves adrift and unable to gain access to the necessary effective bonds that are requisite for gaining any cultural armor to deal with what we know are the ultimate facts of human existence—of dread and despair and disease and being able to confront death.

And the only way human beings have been able to do that is to accept certain stories and narratives and engage in certain rituals so that we're not culturally denuded or culturally naked. Because to be culturally naked means to put an accent on aggressive instinct. Of course, putting an accent on aggressive instinct is part and parcel to gangsterization of culture. And so many young people who are in many ways thoroughly creatures of a market culture find themselves culturally naked. I call it nihilism. Feelings of meaninglessness, hopelessness, lovelessness, touchlessness, we could go on and on. What a way to live! Defeated at twelve!

I was in Washington, D.C., the other day, and I heard the story about the city councilman there who had just had his car stolen and he wanted to find out which cars had high priority for car thieves. And so he went hanging around the corner to hear the young people describing the particular kinds of cars—he thought cars—so that he wouldn't buy the kind of car that would have high priority on their list. They were talking about the chrome, they were talking about the color, they were talking about the shape, and then he, he ended their conversation, "Is that the kind of car?" They said, "No, we're describing the coffins that we want for ourselves. 'Cause we're not going to be around that long. And we want to go out in style. We want people to remember us with the kind of coffin we had, the kind of material toy that we ended up with."

Keep in mind that these young brothers and sisters are on the same continuum with us. Even if we invest in an idolatrous way the material toys that we have as we live. That's the level of nihilism that we're talking about here.

"There can be no substantive democracy without public conversation."

It is difficult to speak to that without hitting head-on the political lethargy, as I mentioned before. By political lethargy, what I mean is the sense that ordinary citizens cannot make a significant difference. Which means that the public itself is associated with squalor. Squalor. Think of public education. "Oh, no, I'm keeping my distance. No, no." Think of public transportation. "No, those buses break down too often, subway's too unsafe." Think of public provisions. "Oh, those undeserved people, lazy, shiftless, receiving these handouts."

And I must say, of course, you can imagine the sense of rage that someone like myself would feel when I hear public provisions associated with welfare queens, associated with black women, and then I think of my mother and grandmother who worked in and out. My grandmother actually raised white kids in white households and raised my father and Aunt Tiny and Uncle Earl. Sixty-two percent of black women working in both households in the 1940s, and they become the example of *laziness*? Come on! Come on! Of *idleness*? Not deferring gratification? Were they not the most frugal? Were they not acting on the promise and ethic, giving their all? And they become the example of public provisions wasted? I'm getting a little carried away, aren't I? You see my point!

And I must say, it's not just public provision, not just public transportation, public education, not just public infrastructure—the bridges and railways and roads—but as I mentioned before, in relation to Sister June Hamersma, that we are in some ways losing the art of public conversation. Which means breakdown in communication. And there can be no substantive democracy without public conversation.

And by public conversation, what I mean is the precious activity of fellow citizens engaging in agreement and disagreement, mediated with mutual respect and civility. More and more name-calling, finger-pointing, pigeon-holing, premature conclusions drawn against flat sound bites. So one's identity, one's constituency, speaks for me. It's not a matter of good reason, it's not a matter of the substance of my vision, I just have identity or a group or a constituency whose demands and complaints and grievances ought to be addressed.

Nothing wrong with making demands, nothing wrong with making complaints or grievances, but it has to be cast in the form of how it relates to the common good, how it relates to public interests. If it's just a matter of constituency and group or identity, then it's a matter of the Balkanization of the body politic. And the Balkanization of the body politic ultimately leads again to not just conflicting cleavage—there'll always be conflicting cleavage. It leads toward distrust.

And one of the reasons why it is so very important for there to be a candid and critical discussion about race in America is precisely because there can be no such discussion without forging bonds of trust. And one of the reasons why we have such difficulty engaging in the candid and critical discussion about race is because there's few public spaces for us to come together to do it.

So many young people these days, I see they're hungry, they're thirsty for such a discussion, they're looking for new kinds of idealism, but they're inexperienced because they grew up in context where they didn't see any black or brown bodies. They saw a lot of black and brown bodies on television. Watch Arsenio every night. Oprah at 4:00. You know, Martin at 8:00. Michael Jordan—every possible chance. But when it really comes on the ground, flesh and blood black bodies—anxiety, fear. And it's understandable, but in the long run, it's inexcusable. Now granted that we have one of the highest levels of segregation—*de facto,* no longer *de jure*—segregation in housing, so it makes it very difficult for young people to actually grow up and interact with one another. You've got to either join a band or join some sporting activity in order to bump up against one another.

I was on the radio this morning, in fact, and I heard this fascinating fact about the level of segregation—higher now than in the 1950s in this particular region, Grand Rapids. I didn't know that. It might be wrong, but I heard it, it struck me. Hmmm. What's going on?

How do we talk about relearning the art of public conversation? The only way you do it, I think, is four-fold. I'm going to put this forward and then sit down.

First is we have to have something that's very un-American—that is, a sense of history. So many of us are running away from our history. Granted, it's understandable. America is, in fact, a land of mobility and individuality. Even Henry Ford said, "History is bunk," and went on to create that automobile that exemplifies mobility and individuality. Ralph Waldo Emerson said, "Everything good is on the highway." The cosmos is on wheels. Huck on the boat, Ahab's on the ship—don't wanna land for too long. Very American, no doubt.

But without acknowledging the degree to which we are indebted to those who came before, that we are embedded in webs of relationship that shape us into who and what we are, shot through with both prejudice as well as wonderful things. Love, care from parents, but also oftentimes, their limitations, their blindnesses, a sense of history. And I would even add a tragic sense of history. There can be no reconstruction of public conversation—which means reconstruction of public life—without a tragic sense of history.

And what I mean by tragic is not to be confused with the pathetic. The pathetic is to view yourself solely as a victim. But tragic is to be an agent against limits you know not of. Tragedy is the exploration of possibilities of human action against some limits, but limits you don't know. You don't know exactly where they exist, but you're going to hit up against them sooner or later, as with Antigone, or as with Lear, or as in the blues. There are limits. Which ought to be humbling, of course, for Christians looking at history through the lens of the cross and seeing what Hegel saw, a slaughterhouse with blood flowing. Or seeing what Gibbons saw, a register of human crimes and follies and misfortunes.

History. It's so un-American because so many Americans' perception of history is melodramatic. Good guys on one side, bad guys on the other. Virtue triumphs in the end. Very soap opera-like. It's not history at all. Ask Armenians, ask Jews, ask Poles, ask Southerners, ask black folk—history is the scar and bruises as well as the joys and pleasures.

Tragic sense of history is necessary. Why? Because then we will see that there are ambiguous legacies and hybrid cultures at work in history. *No* group has a monopoly on truth or virtue. That's how dialogue has to begin.

"So many Americans' perception of history is melodramatic. Good guys on one side, bad guys on the other. Virtue triumphs in the end. Very soap opera-like. It's not history at all. . . . History is the scar and bruises as well as the joys and pleasures."

Oftentimes, race relations, people talk about race, "Oh, I don't want to hear that again, that's going to make me feel guilty. I know white people often didn't do the right thing. I recognize black people were lynched every two and a half days for a half a century in America. I don't want to hear about it. Let me watch my television." We say, "No, we don't introduce the history in order to make you feel paralyzed. We note the history in order to provide some insights so you can be an agent."

That's what the tragic is about—agency, engagement, action. And maybe that tragic sense of history will generate some empathy and some sympathy and compassion. 'Cause as Simone Weil put it so well, "Love of thy neighbor in all of his fullness means being able to say to him or her, 'What are you going through?'" You can form empathetic linkages with other people when you have a sense of what they're going through.

Do you all remember the book *Black Like Me,* published in 1961? It was a bestseller at that time. It was a sign of the times. This white brother changed his epidermal, went down to Mississippi. Thousands and thousands and thousands of Americans read this book. What was it *really* like, John Griffin? And he would say, "Well, you see, I turned back to white rather soon, but I can describe it. It was tough beyond description. The level of humiliation. . . ," and so forth and so on. It was an empathetic link—an attempt to walk a mile in one's shoes. Someone else's shoes. And to identify with their frustrations and anxieties.

And of course it's got to be a mutual affair. Black folk have to be able to identify with the frustrations and anxieties of what it's like to be white in American society. Or what it's like to be perceived as a racist before you've gotten the argument out.

A tragic sense of history ought to go hand-in-hand with the expansion of empathy. And to me, a tragic sense of history and expansion of empathy has much to do with a self-critical courageous stance.

There can be no reviving of public conversation about race 'til we recognize none of us have the panacea or the authoritative solution, that we have to be critical of each other and ourselves. Try to make sense of what Socrates meant when he said, "The unexamined life is not worth living." But we can add that the examined life is painful beyond that comfort zone. . . . Taking a risk, cutting against the grain, or Nietzsche put it well when he said, "At times, it's a matter not simply of having the courage *of* one's convictions but having the courage to *attack* one's convictions." *That's* how you grow and mature and develop. That's what Malcolm X means when he says, "My life has been a chronology of changes. I've had to attack my most precious beliefs. The very things that held me together, I had to call into question at times."

If the white supremacy [is] seemingly holding you together too much, you need to attack it. Male supremacy, the same way. Sense of privilege, the same way. Becoming idolatrous. Self-critical, courageous stance—crucial, in this regard. But Charles Sanders Peirce, the great founder of American pragmatism—that indigenous form of philosophical reflection in this country—put it, he said, "One must never block the road to inquiry, but all travelers must be willing to put their neck in power or relative ignorance under the spotlight."

That's tough. That's difficult to do. But it's necessary. That is what it means to be an engaged citizen in a democracy.

Last, but not least, in this present moment, one often mentions race. People feel depressed, demoralized. Here we go again, are there any possibilities? We've got to enter the dialogue in such a way that we have a sense of audacious hope. Or what Abraham Joshua Heschel once called "radical amazement."

And by audacious hope, I don't mean optimism—I'm not optimistic. Hope and optimism are not the same thing. I don't believe that at present there is enough evidence out there to allow me to infer that things are going to get better. I make a leap of faith, a Pascalian leap of faith, beyond the evidence. Hope is about struggling *against* the evidence, *against* the grain, *against* the grain of history, fallen history. That impossible possibility the Christians talk about—hope. The sense of being able to look beyond the present, saying there is a vision and there is an analysis that I'm going to try to act on exemplifying my life in an imperfect and self-critical way such that I can leave the world a little better than when I found it.

Now audacious hope can energize and galvanize fellow citizens, so persons who once believed there was no possibility may believe there is, in fact, a possibility because you acted. It becomes contagious, and we're not talking about mass movements. We're talking about critical minorities, prophetic minorities in each and every respective community. It doesn't take mass movements. It takes about five or six percent of people with integrity and character to say, "I'm going to stand up and represent the best of democratic tradition. I'm going to hit white supremacy head-on, and I'm going to be consistent in my critiques of other forms of dehumanization."

That's the kind of audacious hope that I'm talking about, predicated on the notion that the world is incomplete, and that history is unfinished, and that the future is open-ended. As William James would put it, "The day breaks forever that it is always dawn, that somewhere above the eastern horizon, at this very moment, the sun is about to peak."

And we can seize that window of opportunity in such a way that in keeping our head to the sky and our hands on the plow and our eyes on the prize—not each other—we may be able to regenerate and rejuvenate democratic possibilities as it relates to race but is not confined to race.

Thank you all so very much.

SOURCES

Books

West, Cornel, *Prophesy Deliverance!: An Afro-American Revolutionary Christianity,* Westminster Press, 1982.

———, *Prophetic Fragments,* Eerdmans, 1988.

———, *The American Evasion of Philosophy: A Genealogy of Pragmatism,* University of Wisconsin Press, 1989.

———, *The Ethical Dimensions of Marxist Thought,* Monthly Review Press, 1991.

———, *Race Matters,* Beacon Press, 1993.

———, *Keeping Faith: Philosophy and Race in America,* Routledge, 1993.

———, *Beyond Eurocentrism and Multiculturalism,* Common Courage Press, 1993.

West, Cornel, and bell hooks, *Breaking Bread: Insurgent Black Intellectual Life,* South End Press, 1991.

Periodicals

Christian Century, "Black Politics, Black Leadership: An Interview with Cornel West," August 11-18, 1993, pp. 774-777.

Detroit Free Press, "Author Explains the Crisis for Blacks," August 22, 1994, p. 1B.

Dissent, "Nihilism in Black America: A Danger That Corrodes from Within," spring, 1991 (also see below).

Grand Rapids Press, "Author Calls for Race Discussion, New Commitment to Democracy," January 13, 1994, p. B2.

New Yorker, "The Public Intellectual," January 17, 1994, pp. 39-48.

New York Times Magazine, "Princeton's Public Intellectual," September 15, 1991, pp. 39-49.

Time, "Philosopher with a Mission," June 7, 1993, pp. 60-62.

U.S. News and World Report, "A Theology for the Streets," December 28, 1992, p. 94.

Utne Reader, "The Loss of Hope" (reprint of *Dissent* article entitled "Nihilism in Black America: A Danger That Corrodes from Within," spring, 1991), September/October, 1991, pp. 53-55.

George H. White

1852–1918

African American politician, lawyer, and businessman

The last African American to serve in the U.S. Congress during the Reconstruction period, George H. White was born into slavery in North Carolina and educated in the public schools of that state after the Civil War. He then attended Howard University, from which he received a teaching certificate in 1877. Returning to North Carolina, White spent several years teaching school and directing an educational facility for aspiring black teachers. In 1879, he was admitted to the state bar and quickly earned a reputation as a skillful lawyer. The following year he launched his political career with a victorious run for the state House of Representatives. He remained in office until the election of 1884, at which time he became one of just two blacks elected to the state Senate. Two years later, White easily won election as solicitor and prosecuting attorney of the Second Judicial District, a position he held for a decade before making the leap to national office in 1896.

During his two terms as the only black member of the U.S. House of Representatives, White was known as a vigorous defender of the rights of African Americans, especially regarding disenfranchisement, discrimination, military and private financial relief programs, and the Freedman's Bank. He frequently put his outstanding oratory skills to use to detail the notable qualities and positive achievements of blacks at a time when the national sentiment was becoming increasingly anti-black. His most significant act as a legislator occurred on February 23, 1900, when he introduced a bill—the first of its kind—that would have made lynching a federal crime. His impassioned argument in its favor follows; it is taken from the Congressional Record, *56th Congress, 1st session.*

Mr. Chairman, perhaps at no time in the history of our nation have there been more questions of moment before us for consideration than we have at this time. Our recent war with Spain and the result in acquisitions of territory by reason of that war, and the necessary legislation for the government of these new possessions in order that they may not work any harm with us, to establish rules, laws, and customs, require the most thoughtful consideration of all of our statesmen. Not only the question that we have before us tonight as to the character of the tariff to be imposed upon Puerto Rico, but the government that shall be established to perpetuate, elevate, and civilize and Christianize the Hawaiian Islands, the Philippine Islands, and, in my opinion at no very distant day, the Cuban Island, also require our very best effort.

The weightiness of the consideration of these questions is increased by the peculiar circumstances surrounding these new possessions. Their relative geographical position, their climate, their distance from our shores, their close proximity to other foreign powers, coupled with a heterogeneous composition of population of these islands, and their want in Christian and civil development all tend to increase the consideration and make more complex the solution of their future government.

But these responsibilities are ours, taken of our own motion, and our plain duty with reference to these people must not be shirked, but met and disposed of honestly, patriotically, in the spirit of justice between man and man.

As a humble representative of this House, I would like to feel free to discuss and aid in the disposition of these questions in the same way that my 355 colleagues on this floor do.

Mr. Chairman, it would be a great pleasure to me to know that fairness and justice would be meted out to all the constituent parts of our beloved country alike in such a way as to leave no necessity for a defense of my race in this House against the attacks and unfair charges from any source. The very intimation of this fact with reference to the surroundings of the colored people of this country at this time, naturally causes the inquiry, Should not a nation be just to all of her citizens, protect them alike in all their rights, on every foot of her soil—in a word, show herself capable of governing all within her domain before she undertakes to exercise sovereign authority over those of a foreign land—with foreign notions and habits not at all in harmony with our American system of government? Or, to be more explicit, should not charity first begin at home?

George H. White

There can be but one candid and fair answer to this inquiry, and that is in the affirmative. But, unfortunately for us, what should have been done has not been done, and to substantiate this assertion we have but to pause for a moment and make a brief survey of the manumitted Afro-American during the last thirty-five years. We have struggled on as best we could with the odds against us at every turn. Our constitutional rights have been trodden under foot; our right of franchise in most every one of the original slave states has been virtually taken away from us, and during the time of our freedom fully fifty thousand of my race have been ignominiously murdered by mobs, not one percent of whom have been made to answer for their crimes in the courts of justice, and even here in the nation's Capitol—in the Senate and House—senators and representatives have undertaken the unholy task of extenuating and excusing these foul deeds, and in some instances, they have gone so far as to justify them.

It was only a few days ago upon this floor that the gentleman from Mississippi [Mr. Williams] depicted one of these horrible butcheries and held it up to the public in the following language:

A man leaves his home—a farmer. He goes down to the little town of Canton to market and sell his crop. It is rumored in the neighborhood that he had brought money from the market town the week before and that it is in the house. That night six or seven Negro men break into that house, ravish his daughter and his wife, and then they manacle and tie them together, and not only them but the little children—one of them, I believe, four or five years of age—manacle them down in the center of that house and set it on fire and burn them all up, hoping that the fire had done away with all trace of the crime. One of the Negroes happened to have a peculiar foot, which led to tracking him. That led to crimination and recrimination among the criminals and to a confession. It led to confessions from others. The people arose and lynched those men, and while they were lynching them they burned one of them, a voice coming from the crowd that he ought to receive the punishment himself which he had meted out to this innocent, helpless woman, her helpless daughter, and her helpless little children.

This is entirely *ex parte;* nothing has been said of the other side. While I deprecate as much as any man can the fiend who commits an outrage upon any woman, and do not hesitate to say that he should be speedily tried and punished by the courts, yet I place but little credence in the statement of a mob hunting for an excuse for its crimes when the statement is made that the victim confessed with a rope perhaps around his neck. No court of justice anywhere in this broad land of ours would allow testimony under duress of this kind to be introduced against a defendant. A shoe track, a confession while being burned at the stake with the hope that life may be spared thereby, are very poor excuses for taking of a human life. A trial by jury is guaranteed to everyone by the Constitution of the United States, and no one should be deprived of this guaranty, however grave the charge preferred against him.

In order to fasten public sentiment against the Negro race and hold them up before the world in their entirety for being responsible for what some are pleased to call "the race crime"—rape—the gentleman from Georgia [Mr. Griggs] described in detail the other day the "fiendishness" of Sam Hose, late of his state, and I believe his district, and among other things he said:

But let me tell you of a case that happened in Georgia last year. A little family a few miles from the town of Newnan were at supper in their modest dining room. The father, the young mother, and the baby were seated at the table. Humble though it was, peace, happiness, and contentment reigned in that modest home. A monster in human form, an employee on the farm, crept into that happy little home and with an ax knocked out the brains of that father, snatched the child from its mother, threw it across the room out of his way, and then by force accomplished his foul purpose. . . . I do not seek to justify that, but I do say that the man who would condemn those people unqualifiedly under these circumstances has water instead of blood to supply his circulation. Not the limpid water that flows from the mountain streams, Mr. Chairman, but the fetid water found in the cesspools of the cities.

The other side of this horrible story portrays a very different state of affairs. A white man, with no interest in Hose or his victim, declares upon oath that Hose did not commit this atrocious crime charged against him, but was an employee of Cranford, and had importuned him for pay due him for labor. This incensed his employer, who rushed upon Hose with a gun. Hose seized an ax and killed Cranford instantly, in self-defense, and then fled to the woods with the greatest possible speed. I do not vouch for either side of this story, but only refer to it to show the necessity for trying all persons charged with crime, as the law directs.

The gentleman might have gone further and described the butchery in his district of six colored persons arrested upon suspicion of being guilty of arson, and while they were crouching in a warehouse, manacled with irons, and guarded by officers of the law, these poor victims, perhaps guilty of no crime whatever, were horribly shot to death by irresponsibles, no one of whom has ever been brought to justice.

He might have depicted also, if he had been so inclined, the miserable butchery of men, women, and children in Wilmington, N.C., in November, 1898, who had committed no crime, nor were they even charged with crime. He might have taken the minds of his auditors to the horrible scene of the aged and infirm, male and female, women in bed from childbirth, driven from their homes to the woods, with no shelter save the protecting branches of the trees of the forest, where many died from exposure, privation, and disease contracted while exposed to the merciless weather. But this description would not have accomplished the purpose of riveting public sentiment upon every colored man of the South as a rapist from whose brutal assaults every white woman must be protected.

Along the same line the senator from Alabama [Mr. Morgan], in a recent speech, used this language:

> *In physical, mental, social, inventive, religious, and ruling power the African race holds the lowest place, as it has since the world has had a history, and it is no idle boast that the white race holds the highest place. To force this lowest stratum into a position of political equality with the highest is only to clog the progress of all mankind in its march, ever strenuous and in proper order, toward the highest planes of human aspiration.*
>
> *Whoever has supposed or has endeavored to realize that free republican government has for its task the undoing of what the Creator has done in classifying and grading the races according to His will overestimates both the powers and the duties of its grand mission. It is a vain effort and is fatal to the spirit and success of free government to attempt to use its true principles as a means of disturbance of the natural conditions of the races of the human family and to reestablish them on the merely theoretical basis, which is not true, that, in political power, all men rust be equal in order to secure the greatest happiness to the greatest number.*
>
> *It is the experiences of the younger men, arising out of the effort to work Negro suffrage into our political system as a harmonious element, and not the prejudices or resentments of the former slaveholders, that have prompted this strong and decisive movement in the Southern states. It will never cease unless it is held down by military power. It is a social evil as well as political, and the cost of its suppression will not be counted by this and succeeding generations in connection with questions of material prosperity.*
>
> *No great body of white people in the world could be expected to quietly accept a situation so distressing and demoralizing as is created by Negro suffrage in the South. It is a thorn in the flesh and will irritate and rankle in the body politic until it is removed as a factor in government. It is not necessary to go into the details of history to establish the great fact that Negro suffrage in Louisiana and the other Southern states has been one unbroken line of political, social, and industrial obstruction to progress and a constant disturbance of the peace in a vast region of the United States.*

"It is easy for these gentlemen to taunt us with our inferiority, at the same time not mentioning the causes of this inferiority."

This language impliedly puts at naught and defies the fourteenth and fifteenth amendments to the Constitution of the United States, and from present indications it is only a matter of a short time when the abrogation of these constitutional provisions will be openly demanded.

It is easy for these gentlemen to taunt us with our inferiority, at the same time not mentioning the causes of this inferiority. It is rather hard to be accused of shiftlessness and idleness when the accuser of his own motion closes the avenues for labor and industrial pursuits to us. It is hardly fair to accuse us of ignorance when it was made a crime under the former order of things to learn enough about letters to read even the Word of God.

While I offer no extenuation for any immorality that may exist among my people, it comes with rather poor grace from those who forced it upon us for 250 years, to taunt us with that shortcoming.

We are trying hard to relieve ourselves of the bonds with which we were bound and over which we had no control, nothing daunted, however, like the skilled mariner who, having been overtaken by the winds and storms and thrown off his bearings, stops to examine the chart, the compass, and all implements of navigation, that he may be sure of the proper course to travel to reach his destination.

In our voyage of life struggle for a place whereon we can stand, speak, think and act as unrestricted American citizens, we have been and are now passing through political gales, storms of ostracism, torrents of proscription, waves and inundations of caste prejudice and hatred; and, like the mariner, it is proper that we should examine our surroundings, take our bearings, and devise ways and means by which we may pursue our struggle for a place as men and women as a part of this body politic.

Possibly at no time in the history of our freedom has the effort been made to mold public sentiment against us and our progress so strongly as it is now being done. The forces have been set in motion and we must have sufficient manhood and courage to overcome all resistance that obstructs our progress.

A race of people with the forbearance, physical development, and Christian manhood and womanhood which has characterized us during the past 285 years will not down at the bidding of any man or set of men, and it would be well that all should learn this lesson now.

As slaves we were true to our rulers; true to every trust reposed in us. While the white fathers and sons went forth to battle against us and the nation to perpetuate our bonds, the strong, brawny arms of the black man produced the food to sustain the wives, children and aged parents of the Confederate soldier, and kept inviolable the virtue and care of those entrusted to his keeping, and nowhere will anyone dare say that he was unfaithful to the helpless and unprotected over whom he kept a guardian watch.

How does this statement of facts compare with the frequent charges made against colored men for outraging white females? Is it a futile attempt to prove that an ignorant slave was a better man and more to be trusted than an intelligent freeman? But of these brutal murders, let us revert to a few facts and figures.

Since January 1, 1898, to April 25, 1899, there were lynched in the United States 166 persons, and of this number 155 occurred in the South. Of the whole number lynched, there were 10 white and 156 colored. The thin disguise usually employed as an excuse for these inhuman outrages is the protection of the virtue among white women.

I have taken the pains to make some little investigation as to the charges against the 166 persons killed, and find as a result of my efforts that 32 were charged with murder, 17 were charged with assault, criminal or otherwise, 10 with arson, 2 with stealing, 1 with being impudent to white women, and I am ashamed to acknowledge it, but this latter took place in North Carolina. Seventy-two of the victims were murdered without any specific charge being preferred against them whatever. Continuing this record of carnage, I give the record of the number of lynchings, with causes, from April 24, 1899, to October 20, 1899, inclusive:

Crime committed:

Murder 9

Talked too much 2

Barn burning 1

Trespass 1

Sheltering a murderer 3

Defending a colored man 3

Brother to murderer 1

Suspected of murder 1

Drowned a man 1

Innocent 2

Bad character 1

Wounded a white man 1

Mormonism 1

Assault, criminal and otherwise 16

Nothing 2

Church burning 2

No cause stated 3

Put hand on white woman 1

Shooting a man 2

Entered a lady's room drunk 1

Wanted to work 7

Spoke against lynching 2

Total 63

Of the 63 lynched there were 1 Italian, 1 Cuban, 4 white men, and 57 Negroes.

These facts and figures which I have detailed are reliable; still the same old, oft-repeated slander, like Banquo's ghost, will not down, but is always in evidence.

[White then quoted at length from several different newspaper articles on the subject of lynching that discussed how sensationalistic and inaccurate information had often led to mob violence against the innocent.]

Mr. Chairman, the sickening effect of these crimes is bad enough in degenerating and degrading the moral sensibilities of those who now play upon the arena of the nation, but this is nothing when compared with the degrading and morbid effect it must have upon the minds of children in communities where these murders are committed in open daylight with the flagrant defiance of all law, morals, the state and nation, and the actors are dubbed as the best citizens of the community.

I tremble with horror for the future of our nation when I think what must be the inevitable result if mob violence is not stamped out of existence and law once permitted to reign supreme.

If state laws are inadequate or indisposed to check this species of crime, then the duty of the national government is plain, as is evidenced by section 1 of the Fourteenth Amendment to the Constitution of the United States, to wit:

All persons born or naturalized in the United States, and subject to the jurisdiction thereof, are citizens of the United States and of the State wherein they reside. No state shall make or enforce any law which shall abridge the privileges or immunities of citizens of the United States; nor shall any state deprive any person within its jurisdiction the equal protection of the laws.

To the end that the national government may have jurisdiction over this species of crime, I have prepared and introduced the following bill, now pending before the Committee on the Judiciary, to wit:

A bill for the protection of all citizens of the United States against mob violence, and the penalty for breaking such laws.

Be it enacted by the Senate and House of Representatives of the United States of America in Congress assembled, *That all persons born or naturalized in the United States, and subject to the jurisdiction thereof, and being citizens of the United States, are entitled to and shall receive protection in their lives from being murdered, tortured, burned to death by any and all organized mobs commonly known as "lynching bees," whether said mob be spontaneously assembled or organized by premeditation for the purpose of taking the life or lives of any citizen or citizens in the United States aforesaid; and that whenever any citizen or citizens of the United States shall be murdered by mob violence in the manner hereinabove described, all parties participating, aiding, and abetting in such murder and lynching shall be guilty of treason against the Government of the United States, and shall be tried for that offense in the United States courts; full power and jurisdiction being hereby given to said United States courts and all its officers to issue process, arrest, try, and in all respects deal with such cases in the same manner now prescribed under existing laws for the trial of felonies in the United States courts.*

Sec. 2. That any person or persons duly tried and convicted in any United States court as principal or principals, aiders, abettors, accessories before or after the fact, for the murder of any citizen or citizens of the United States by mob violence or lynching as described in Section 1 hereof, shall be punished as is now prescribed by law for the punishment of persons convicted of treason against the United States Government.

Sec. 3. That all laws and parts of laws in conflict with this statute are hereby repealed.

I do not pretend to claim for this bill perfection, but I have prepared and introduced it to moot the question before the Congress of the United States with the hope that expedience will be set aside and justice allowed to prevail, and a measure prepared by the Committee on the Judiciary that will come within the jurisdiction of the Constitution of the United States, as above cited.

There remain now but two questions to be settled: first, perhaps, is it expedient for the American Congress to step aside from the consideration of economic questions, and all-absorbing idea of acquisition of new territory, and consider for a moment the rights of a portion of our citizens at home and the preservation of their lives? That question I leave for you to answer.

The second is: has Congress power to enact a statute to meet these evils? In my opinion, it has ample authority under the Constitution of the United States.

[White then quoted from a U.S. Supreme Court report and a long letter from the attorney general of Massachusetts to bolster his argument that Congress indeed had the authority to take such action.]

In concluding these remarks, Mr. Chairman, I wish to disclaim any intention of harshness or the production of any friction between the races or the sections of this country. I have simply raised my voice against a growing and, as I regard it, one of the most dangerous evils in our country. I have simply raised my voice in behalf of a people who have no one else to speak for them here from a racial point of view; in behalf of a patient and, in the main, inoffensive race which has often been wronged but seldom retaliated; in behalf of the people who—

Like birds, for others we have built the
downy nest;
Like sheep, for others we have worn the
fleecy vest;
Like bees, for others we have collected
the honeyed food;
Like the patient ox, we have labored for
others' good.

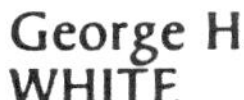

Although White's colleagues responded to his speech with prolonged applause, they balked at the idea of making lynching a federal crime subject to the same punishment as treason. A little more than a year later, having lost his seat to a white Democrat in the 1900 election, the nation's only black representative once again faced fellow members of the House, this time for a farewell address. His memorable speech, delivered January 29, 1901, is taken from the Congressional Record, *56th Congress, 2nd session.*

I want to enter a plea for the colored man, the colored woman, the colored boy, and the colored girl of this country. I would not thus digress from the question at issue and detain the House in a discussion of the interests of this particular people at this time but for the constant and the persistent efforts of certain gentlemen upon this floor to mold and rivet public sentiment against us as a people and to lose no opportunity to hold up the unfortunate few who commit crimes and depredations and lead lives of infamy and shame, as other races do, as fair specimens of representatives of the entire colored race. And at no time, perhaps, during the Fifty-sixth Congress were these charges and countercharges, containing, as they do, slanderous statements, more persistently magnified and pressed upon the attention of the nation than during the consideration of the recent reapportionment bill, which is now a law. As stated some days ago on this floor by me, I then sought diligently to obtain an opportunity to answer some of the statements made by gentlemen from different states, but the privilege was denied me; and I therefore must embrace this opportunity to say, out of season perhaps, that which I was not permitted to say in season.

In the catalogue of members of Congress in this House perhaps none have been more persistent in their determination to bring the black man into disrepute and, with a labored effort, to show that he was unworthy of the right of citizenship than my colleague from North Carolina, Mr. Kitchin. During the first session of this Congress, while the constitutional amendment was pending in North Carolina, he labored long and hard to show that the white race was at all times and under all circumstances superior to the Negro by inheritance if not otherwise, and the excuse for his party supporting that amendment, which has since been adopted, was that an illiterate Negro was unfit to participate in making the laws of a sovereign state and the administration and execution of them; but an illiterate white man living by his side, with no more or perhaps not as much property, with no more exalted character, no higher thoughts of civilization, no more knowledge of the handicraft of government, had by birth, because he was white, inherited some peculiar qualification, clear, I presume, only in the mind of the gentleman who endeavored to impress it upon others, that entitled him to vote, though he knew nothing whatever of letters. It is true, in my opinion, that men brood over things at times which they would have exist until they fool themselves and actually, sometimes honestly, believe that such things do exist.

I would like to call the gentleman's attention to the fact that the Constitution of the United States forbids the granting of any title of nobility to any citizen thereof, and while it does not in letters forbid the inheritance of this superior caste, I believe in the fertile imagination of the gentleman promulgating it, his position is at least in conflict with the spirit of that organic law of the land. He insists and, I believe, has introduced a resolution in this House for the repeal of the Fifteenth Amendment to the Constitution. As an excuse for his peculiar notions about the exercise of the right of franchise by citizens of the United States of different nationality, perhaps it would not be amiss to call the attention of this House to a few facts and figures surrounding his birth and rearing. To begin with, he was born in one of the counties in my district, Halifax, a rather significant name.

I might state as a further general fact that the Democrats of North Carolina got possession of the state and local government since my last election in 1898, and that I bid adieu to these historic walls on the fourth day of next March, and that the brother of Mr. Kitchin will succeed me. Comment is unnecessary. In the town where this young gentleman was born, at the general election last August for the adoption of the constitutional amendment, and the general election for state and county officers, Scotland Neck had a registered white vote of 395, most of whom of course were Democrats, and a registered colored vote of 534, virtually if not all of whom were Republicans, and so voted. When the count was announced, however, there were 831 Democrats to 75 Republicans; but in the town of Halifax, same county, the result was much more pronounced.

In that town the registered Republican vote was 345, and the total registered vote of the township was 539, but when the count was announced it stood 990 Democrats to 41 Republicans, or 492 more Democratic votes counted than were registered votes in the township. Comment here is unnecessary, nor do I think it necessary for anyone to wonder at the peculiar notion my colleague has with reference to the manner of voting and the method of counting these votes, nor is it to be a wonder that he is a member of this Congress, having been brought up and educated in such wonderful notions of dealing out fair-handed justice to his fellow man.

It would be unfair, however, for me to leave the inference upon the minds of those who hear me that all of the white people of the State of North Carolina hold views with Mr. Kitchin and think as he does. Thank God there are many noble exceptions to the example he sets, that, too, in the Democratic party; men who have never been afraid that one uneducated, poor, depressed Negro could put to flight and chase into degradation two educated, wealthy, thrifty white men. There never has been, nor ever will be, any Negro domination in that state, and no one knows it any better than the Democratic party. It is a convenient howl, however, often resorted to in order to consummate a diabolical purpose by scaring the weak and gullible whites into support of measures and men suitable to the demagogue and the ambitious office seeker, whose crave for office overshadows and puts to flight all other considerations, fair or unfair.

As I stated on a former occasion, this young statesman has ample time to learn better and more useful knowledge than he has exhibited in many of his speeches upon this floor, and I again plead for him the statute of youth for the wild and spasmodic notions which he has endeavored to rivet upon his colleagues and this country. But I regret that Mr. Kitchin is not alone upon this floor in these peculiar notions advanced. I quote from another young member of Congress, hailing from the State of Alabama [Mr. Underwood]:

> *Mr. Speaker, in five minutes the issues involved in this case can not be discussed. I was in hopes that this question would not come up at this session of Congress. When the Fourteenth Amendment was originally adopted it was the intention of the legislative body that enacted it and of the people who ratified it to force the Southern people to give the elective franchise to the Negro. That was the real purpose of the Fourteenth Amendment. It failed in that purpose. The Fifteenth Amendment was adopted for the same purpose. That was successful for the time being. It has proved a lamentable mistake, not only to the people of the South, but to the people of the North; not only to the Democratic party, but to the Republican party.*
>
> *The time has now come then the bitterness of civil strife has passed. The people of the South, with fairness and justice to themselves and fairness to that race that has been forced among them—the Negro race—are attempting to work away from those conditions; not to oppress or to put their foot on the neck of the Negro race, but to protect their homes and their property against misgovernment and at the same time give this inferior race a chance to grow up and acquire their civilization. When you bring this resolution before this House and thrust it as a firebrand into the legislation here, you do more injury to the Negro race of the South than any man has done since the Fifteenth Amendment was originally enacted. I tell you, sirs, there is but one way to solve this problem. You gentlemen of the North, who do not live among them and do not know the conditions, can not solve it.*
>
> *We of the South are trying, as God is our judge, to solve it fairly to both races. It can not be done in a day or a week; and I appeal to you, if you are in favor of the upbuilding of the Negro race, if you are in favor of honest governments in the Southern states, if you are willing to let us protect our homes and our property—yes, and the investments that you have brought there among us—then I say to you, let us send this resolution to a committee where it may die and never*

be heard of again. When we have done that, when we have worked out the problem and put it upon a fair basis, then if we are getting more representation than we are entitled to, five or six or ten years from now come to us with the proposition fairly to repeal both the Fourteenth and Fifteenth Amendments and substitute in their place a constitutional amendment that will put representation on a basis that we can all agree is fair and equitable. Do not let us drive it along party lines.

It is an undisputed fact that the Negro vote in the State of Alabama, as well as most of the other Southern states, has been effectively suppressed, either one way or the other—in some instances by constitutional amendment and state legislation, in others by cold-blooded fraud and intimidation, but whatever the method pursued, it is not denied, but frankly admitted in the speeches in this House, that the black vote has been eliminated to a large extent. Then, when some of us insist that the plain letter of the Constitution of the United States, which all of us have sworn to support, should be carried out, as expressed in the second section of the Fourteenth Amendment thereof, to wit:

Representatives shall be apportioned among the several states according to their respective numbers, counting the whole number of persons in each state, excluding Indians not taxed. But when the right to vote at any election for the choice of electors for president and vice-president of the United States, representatives in Congress, the executive and judicial officers of a state, or the members of a legislature thereof, is denied to any of the male inhabitants of such state, being twenty-one years of age, and citizens of the United States, or in any way abridged, except for participation in rebellion, or other crime, the basis of representation therein shall be reduced in proportion which the number of such male citizens shall bear to the whole number of male citizens twenty-one years of age in such state.

That section makes the duty of every member of Congress plain, and yet the gentleman from Alabama says that the attempt to enforce this section of the organic law is the throwing down of firebrands, and notifies the world that this attempt to execute the highest law of the land will be retaliated by the South, and the inference is that the Negro will be even more severely punished than the horrors through which he has already come.

Let me make it plain: The divine law, as well as most of the state laws, says, in substance: "He that sheddeth man's blood, by man shall his blood be shed." A highwayman commits murder, and when the officers of the law undertake to arrest, try, and punish him commensurate with the enormity of his crime, he straightens himself up to his full height and defiantly says to them: "Let me alone; I will not be arrested, I will not be tried, I'll have none of the execution of your laws, and in the event you attempt to execute your laws upon me, I will see to it many more men, women, or children are murdered."

Here's the plain letter of the Constitution, the plain, simple, sworn duty of every member of Congress; yet these gentlemen from the South say, "Yes, we have violated your Constitution of the nation; we regarded it as a local necessity; and now, if you undertake to punish us as the Constitution prescribes, we will see to it that our former deeds of disloyalty to that instrument, our former acts of disfranchisement and opposition to the highest law of the land will be repeated many fold."

Not content with all that has been done to the black man, not because of any deeds that he has done, Mr. Underwood advances the startling information that these people have been thrust upon the whites of the South, forgetting, perhaps, the horrors of the slave trade, the unspeakable horrors of the transit from the shores of Africa by means of the middle passage to the American clime; the enforced bondage of the blacks and their descendants for two and a half centuries in the United States. Now, for the first time perhaps in the history of our lives, the information comes that these poor, helpless, and in the main inoffensive people were thrust upon our Southern brethren.

Individually, and so far as my race is concerned, I care but little about the reduction of Southern representation, except in so far as it becomes my duty to aid in the proper execution of all the laws of the land in whatever sphere in which I may be placed. Such reduction in representation, it is true, would make more secure the installment of the great Republican party in power for many years to come in all its branches, and at the same time enable that great party to be able to dispense with the further support of the loyal Negro vote; and I might here parenthetically state that there are some members of the Republican party today—"lily whites," if you please—who, after receiving the unalloyed support of the Negro vote for over thirty years, now feel that they have grown a little too good for association with him politically, and are disposed to dump him overboard. I am glad to observe, however, that this class constitutes a very small percentage of those to whom we have always looked for friendship and protection.

I wish to quote from another Southern gentleman, not so young as my other friends, and who always commands attention in this House by his wit and humor, even though his speeches may not be edifying and instructive. I refer to Mr. Otey, of Virginia, and quote from him in a recent speech on this floor, as follows:

> *Justice is merely relative. It can exist between equals. It can exist among homogeneous people. Among equals—among heterogeneous people—it never has and, in the very nature of things, it never will obtain. It can exist among lions, but between lions and lambs, never. If justice were absolute, lions must of necessity perish. Open his ponderous jaws and find the strong teeth which God has made expressly to chew lamb's flesh! When the Society for the Prevention of Cruelty to Animals shall overcome this difficulty, men may hope to settle the race question along sentimental lines, not sooner.*
>
> *These thoughts on the Negro are from the pen, in the main, of one who has studied the Negro question, and it was after I heard the gentleman from North Carolina, and after the introduction of the Crumpacker bill, that they occurred to me peculiarly appropriate.*

I am wholly at sea as to just what Mr. Otey had in view in advancing the thoughts contained in the above quotation, unless he wishes to extend the simile and apply the lion as a white man and the Negro as a lamb. In that case we will gladly accept the comparison, for of all animals known in God's creation the lamb is the most inoffensive, and has been in all ages held up as a badge of innocence. But what will my good friend of Virginia do with the Bible, for God says that He created all men of one flesh and blood? Again, we insist on having one race—the lion clothed with great strength, vicious, and with destructive propensities, while the other is weak, good natured, inoffensive, and useful—what will he do with all the heterogeneous intermediate animals, ranging all the way from the pure lion to the pure lamb, found on the plantations of every Southern state in the Union?

I regard his borrowed thoughts, as he admits they are, as very inaptly applied. However, it has perhaps served the purpose of which he intended it—the attempt to show the inferiority of the one and the superiority of the other. I fear I am giving too much time in the consideration of these personal comments of members of Congress, but I trust I will be pardoned for making a passing reference to one more gentleman—Mr. Wilson of South Carolina—who, in the early part of this month, made a speech, some parts of which did great credit to him, showing, as it did, capacity for collating, arranging, and advancing thoughts of others and of making a pretty strong argument out of a very poor case.

If he had stopped there, while not agreeing with him, many of us would have been forced to admit that he had done well. But his purpose was incomplete until he dragged in the Reconstruction days and held up to scorn and ridicule the few ignorant, gullible, and perhaps purchasable Negroes who served in the state legislature of South Carolina over thirty years ago. Not a word did he say about the unscrupulous white men, in the main bummers who followed in the wake of the Federal Army and settled themselves in the Southern states, and preyed upon the ignorant and unskilled minds of the colored people, looted the states of their wealth, brought into lowest disrepute the ignorant colored people, then hied away to their Northern homes for ease and comfort the balance of their lives, or joined the Democratic party to obtain social recognition, and have greatly aided in depressing and further degrading those whom they had used as tools to accomplish a diabolical purpose.

These few ignorant men who chanced at that time to hold office are given as a reason why the black man should not be permitted to participate in the affairs of the government which he is forced to pay taxes to support. He insists that they, the Southern whites, are the black man's best friend, and that they are taking him by the hand and trying to lift him up; that they are educating him. For all that he and all Southern people have done in this regard, I wish in behalf of the colored people of the South to extend our thanks. We are not ungrateful to friends, but feel that our toil has made our friends able to contribute the stinty pittance which we have received at their hands.

I read in a Democratic paper a few days ago, the *Washington Times,* an extract taken from a South Carolina paper, which was intended to exhibit the eagerness with which the Negro is grasping every opportunity for educating himself. The clipping showed that the money for each white child in the State ranged from three to five times as much per capita as was given to each colored child. This is helping us some, but not to the extent that one would infer from the gentleman's speech.

If the gentleman to whom I have referred will pardon me, I would like to advance the statement that the musty records of 1868, filed away in the archives of Southern capitols, as to what the Negro was thirty-two years ago, is not a proper standard by which the Negro living on the threshold of the twentieth century should be measured. Since that time we have reduced the illiteracy of the race at least 45 percent. We have written and published nearly 500 books. We have nearly 800 newspapers, 3 of which are dailies. We have now in practice over 2,000 lawyers, and a corresponding number of doctors. We have accumulated over $12,000,000 worth of school property and about $40,000,000 worth of church property. We have about 140,000 farms and homes, valued in the neighborhood of $750,000,000, and personal property valued about $170,000,000. We have raised about $11,000,000 for educational purposes, and the property per capita for every colored man, woman and child in the United States is estimated at $75.

We are operating successfully several banks, commercial enterprises among our people in the Southland, including 1 silk mill and 1 cotton factory. We have 32,000 teachers in the schools of the country; we have built, with the aid of our friends, about 20,000 churches, and support 7 colleges, 17 academies, 50 high schools, 5 law schools, 5 medical schools and 25 theological seminaries. We have over 600,000 acres of land in the South alone. The cotton produced, mainly by black labor, has increased from 4,669,770 bales in 1860 to 11,235,000 in 1899. All this was done under the most adverse circumstances. We have done it in the face of lynching, burning at the stake, with the humiliation of "Jim Crow" cars, the disfranchisement of our male citizens, slander and degradation of our women, with the factories closed against us, no Negro permitted to be conductor on the railway cars, whether run through the streets of our cities or across the prairies of our great country, no Negro permitted to run as engineer on a locomotive, most of the mines closed against us. Labor unions—carpenters, painters, brick masons, machinists, hackmen and those supplying nearly every conceivable avocation for livelihood—have banded themselves together to better their condition, but, with few exceptions, the black face has been left out. The Negroes are seldom employed in our mercantile stores. At this we do not wonder. Some day we hope to have them employed in our own stores. With all these odds against us, we are forging our way ahead, slowly, perhaps, but surely. You may tie us and then taunt us for a lack of bravery, but one day we will break the bonds. You may use our labor for two and a half centuries and then taunt us for our poverty, but let me remind you we will not always remain poor. You may withhold even the knowledge of how to read God's word and learn the way from earth to glory and then taunt us for our ignorance, but we would remind you that there is plenty of room at the top, and we are climbing.

> ***"You may withhold the knowledge of how to read God's word . . . and then taunt us for our ignorance, but we would remind you that there is plenty of room at the top, and we are climbing."***

After enforced debauchery with many kindred horrors incident to slavery, it comes with ill grace from the perpetrators of these deeds to hold up the shortcomings of some of our race to ridicule and scorn.

"The new man, the slave who has grown out of the ashes of thirty-five years ago, is inducted into the political and social system, cast into the arena of manhood, where he constitutes a new element and becomes a competitor for all its emoluments. He is put upon trial to test his ability to be counted worthy of freedom, worthy of the elective franchise; and after thirty-five years of struggling against almost insurmountable odds, under conditions but little removed from slavery itself, he makes a fair and just judgment, not of those whose prejudice has endeavored to forestall, to frustrate his every forward movement, rather those who have lent a helping hand, that he might demonstrate the truth of 'the fatherhood of God and the brotherhood of man.'"

Mr. Chairman, permit me to digress for a few moments for the purpose of calling the attention of the House to two bills which I regard as important, introduced by me in the early part of the first session of this Congress. The first was to give the United States control and entire jurisdiction over all cases of lynching and death by mob violence. During the last session of this Congress I took occasion to address myself in detail to this particular measure, but with all my efforts the bill still sweetly sleeps in the room of the committee to which it was referred. The necessity of legislation along this line is daily being demonstrated. The arena of the lyncher no longer is confined to Southern climes, but is stretching its hydra head over all parts of the Union.

Sow the seed of a tarnished name—
You sow the seed of eternal shame.

It is needless to ask what the harvest will be. You may dodge this question now; you may defer it to a more seasonable day; you may, as the gentleman from Maine, Mr. Littlefield, puts it—

Waddle in and waddle out,
Until the mind was left in doubt,
Whether the snake that made the track
Was going south or coming back.

This evil peculiar to America, yes, to the United States, must be met somehow, some day.

The other bill to which I wish to call attention is one introduced by me to appropriate $1,000,000 to reimburse depositors of the late Freedman's Savings and Trust Company.

A bill making appropriation for a similar purpose passed the Senate in the first session of the Fiftieth Congress. It was recommended by President Cleveland, and was urged by the comptroller of the currency, Mr. Trenholm, in 1886. I can not press home to your minds this matter more strongly than by reproducing the report of the Committee on Banking and Currency, made by Mr. Wilkins on the Senate bill above referred to, as follows:

In March, 1865, the Freedman's Savings and Trust Company was incorporated by the Congress of the United States to meet the economic and commercial necessities of 7,000,000 colored people recently emancipated.

Its incorporators, 50 in number, were named in the act authorizing its erection, and embraced the names of leading philanthropic citizens of the United States, whose names, as was intended, commended the institution to those inexperienced, simple-minded people who are today its principal creditors.

The Freedman's Bank, as it is popularly called, was designed originally to perform for this trustful people the functions, as its name implies, of a savings bank, and none other than those hithertofore held in slavery or their descendants were to become its depositors.

Its purpose was (to quote the paragraph in the original law)—

To receive on deposit such sums of money as may from time to time be offered therefor, by or in behalf of persons hithertofore held in slavery in the United States, or their descendants, and investing the same in the stocks, bonds, and Treasury notes, or other securities of the United States.

The distinction provided in the bill in favor of the payment of "such persons in whole or in part of African descent" rests upon the foregoing paragraph of the original law, and no persons other than those named have the right to make use of this institution in any manner; neither have they the right to acquire by any means any interest in its assets.

For four years after the organization of the Freedman's Savings and Trust Company the laws seemed to have been honestly observed by its officers and the provisions in its charter faithfully recognized. Congress itself, however, seems to have been derelict in its duty. One section of the original grant provided that the books of the institution were to be open at all times to inspection and examination of officers appointed by Congress to conduct the same, yet it does not appear that Congress ever appointed an officer for this purpose, nor has an examination of the character contemplated by Congress ever been made. The officers of the bank were to give bonds. There is nothing in the records to show that any bond was ever executed. Any proper examination would have developed this fact, and probably great loss would have been prevented thereby. In 1870 Congress changed or amended the charter without the knowledge or consent of those who had entrusted their savings to its custody.

This amendment embodied a radical change in the investment of these deposits by providing that instead of the safe, conservative, and prudent provision in the original charter "that two-thirds of all the deposits should be invested exclusively in government securities," the dangerous privilege of allowing the irresponsible officers to loan one-half of its assets in bonds and mortgages and other securities, invest in and improve real estate without inspection, without examination, or responsibility on the part of its officers. The institution could only go on to a certain bankruptcy. In May, 1870, Congress amended the charter, and from that date began the speculative, dishonest transactions upon the part of those controlling the institution until resulting in ultimate suspension and failure, with consequent disastrous loss to this innocent and trustful people.

It is contended by your committee that there was a moral responsibility, at least, if not an equitable responsibility, assumed by the government when Congress changed the original charter of the company as the nature of its loans and investments, when it failed to have the consent of the depositors, because of which changes most of its losses were incurred. This ought to be regarded a very strong argument in favor of this bill.

Then, again, Congress undertook the supervision of the trust and failed, so far as your committee can ascertain, to carry out their undertaking.

[Representative White then quoted from President Cleveland's message to Congress in December, 1886, in which he reminded members of their duty to treat depositors in the Freedman's Bank with "equity and fairness." The congressman followed this with lengthy excerpts from the comptroller of the currency's 1886 report to Congress in which he, too, urged the government to act immediately to settle the claims of all depositors—out of a sense of honor, if for no other reason. After reading these excerpts aloud to his colleagues, White resumed his speech.]

May I hope that the Committee on Banking and Currency who has charge of this measure will yet see its way clear to do tardy justice, long deferred, to this much wronged and unsuspecting people. If individual sections of the country, individual political parties can afford to commit deeds of wrong against us, certainly a great nation like ours will see to it that a people so loyal to its flag as the black man has shown himself in every war from the birth of the Union to this day, will not permit this obligation to go longer uncanceled.

Now, Mr. Chairman, before concluding my remarks I want to submit a brief recipe for the solution of the so-called American Negro problem. He asks no special favors, but simply demands that he be given the same chance for existence, for earning a livelihood, for raising himself in the scales of manhood and womanhood, that are accorded to kindred nationalities. Treat him as a man; go into his home and learn of his social conditions; learn of his cares, his troubles and his hopes for the future; gain his confidence; open the doors of industry to him; let the word "Negro," "colored," and "black" be stricken from all the organizations enumerated in the federation of labor.

Help him to overcome his weaknesses, punish the crime-committing class by the courts of the land, measure the standard of the race by its best material, cease to mold prejudicial and unjust public sentiment against him, and, my word for it, he will learn to support, hold up the hands of, and join in with that political party, that institution, whether secular or religious, in every community where he lives, which is destined to do the greatest good for the greatest number. Obliterate race hatred, party prejudice, and help us to achieve nobler ends, greater results and become satisfactory citizens to our brother in white.

This, Mr. Chairman, is perhaps the Negroes' temporary farewell to the American Congress; but let me say, phoenix-like he will rise up some day and come again. These parting words are in behalf of an outraged, heartbroken, bruised, and bleeding, but God-fearing people, faithful, industrious, loyal people—rising people, full of potential force.

Mr. Chairman, in the trial of Lord Bacon, when the court disturbed the counsel for the defendant, Sir Walter Raleigh raised himself up to his full height and, addressing the court, said, "Sir, I am pleading for the life of a human being."

The only apology that I have to make for the earnestness with which I have spoken is that I am pleading for the life, the liberty, the future happiness, and manhood suffrage for one-eighth of the entire population of the United States.

More than twenty-five years would pass before another African American served in the United States Congress. After leaving office, White returned to practicing law, first in Washington, D.C., and later in Philadelphia. It was there that he opened and operated a bank that helped finance one of his dreams—the establishment of an all-black town. Known as Whitesboro, it was built on the grounds of a former plantation in Cape May County, New Jersey.

SOURCES

Congressional Record, 56th Congress, 1st session, February 23, 1900, pp. 2151-2154; 56th Congress, 2nd session, January 29, 1901, pp. 1635-1638.

Journal of Negro History, "Four in Black: North Carolina's Black Congressmen, 1874-1901," summer, 1979, pp. 229-243.

Negro History Bulletin, "George Henry White: A Militant Negro Congressman in the Age of Booker T. Washington," March, 1966.

Walter F. White

1893–1955

African American civil rights activist

As the head of the National Association for the Advancement of Colored People (NAACP) from 1931 until his death in 1955, Walter F. White presided over the civil rights organization at a time when it began to wield a significant amount of power in American society. He possessed remarkable enthusiasm and energy and displayed special talents as an administrator and public relations expert. An uncompromising advocate of social reform, he tackled injustice on many fronts—mob violence and lynching, disfranchisement, unfair labor practices, segregation in education and the armed forces, and racism in the arts, to name only a few of the areas in which he took action. Underlying all of his efforts was the belief that once people were taught to question and examine the conditions under which blacks (and other minorities) lived, they could overcome obstacles to change such as tradition and apathy. It was this role as both educator and agitator that White embraced with gusto.

A native of Atlanta, Georgia, White was a blue-eyed, blonde-haired, fair-skinned black who once noted that he never really knew what it meant to be African American until the Atlanta race riots of 1906. The brutal attacks he witnessed as well as his own family's frighteningly close brush with an angry white mob left him with a lifelong hatred of violence and a passion to seek out and expose those who practiced racial violence in particular.

Following his graduation from Atlanta University in 1916, White immediately became involved in efforts among members of the local black community to protest the racist policies of the Atlanta Board of Education. His leadership role in that campaign helped earn him the head position in the NAACP's Atlanta chapter when it began operating later that same year. His skills as an administrator and public speaker soon captured the attention of the group's regional director, James Weldon Johnson, who recommended the young man for a position at national headquarters. Thus it came to be that in 1918 White headed for New York City as the NAACP's new assistant secretary.

Ambitious and energetic, White quickly made a name for himself setting up new branches and making contacts with influential government officials. But it was his undercover investigation of lynchings in the South that will stand as the most enduring legacy of this part of his career. Relying on his looks as well as his *familiarity with Southern society, he passed as a white man and risked his life to ferret out important information on some of the most heinous incidents. White later shared his findings not only with the NAACP but with lecture audiences throughout the country. He also produced two novels based on his experiences during a period in his life when he was eager to try his hand at writing fiction.*

In 1920, James Weldon Johnson became head of the NAACP, and together he and White shepherded the organization through a decade of spectacular growth in terms of both numbers and prestige. While Johnson handled many of the public relations duties, White tended to a myriad of administrative details, including overseeing the activities of the NAACP's legal committee, which had already begun aggressively pursuing enforcement of African Americans' constitutional rights through the courts.

Upon Johnson's retirement in 1931, White took over as executive secretary. Besides continuing to direct the legal assault on segregation and disfranchisement, he also expertly guided the organization through the economic hardships of the Depression years. The NAACP emerged from that period with White more firmly in charge than ever and poised to lead the group through the battles of the 1940s and 1950s.

In addition to his high-profile NAACP responsibilities, White was involved in many other activities that made him a veritable celebrity. A tireless traveler who logged nearly half a million miles during his career, he was a delegate to several major international conferences, including the one in 1945 that organized the United Nations. During World War II, he regularly visited Europe, North Africa, Italy, the Middle East, and the Pacific theater of operations as a special correspondent for a wide variety of magazines and newspapers.

It was on July 16, 1944, shortly after he returned from a tour of several war zones, that White gave the following address in which he denounced the hypocrisy of a nation engaged in eliminating racial bigotry abroad while practicing it at home. Delivered in Chicago at the annual meeting of the NAACP, it is fairly typical of his speeches—aggressive but not emotional. As one journalist of the day observed, White most often sounded like "a lawyer presenting facts dispassionately in summation before a jury." Yet his words effectively inspired audiences to take a hard look at explosive issues and come up with solutions rather than slogans. His speech is reprinted here from A Documentary History of the Negro People of the United States, 1933-1945 *(Citadel Press, 1974).*

On this 952nd day of America's participation in a war to save the world from the military aggression and racial bigotry of Germany and Japan, the United Nations with a comparable master race theory of its own moves on to victory. The growing certainty of that victory intensifies determination to permit no fundamental change in the attitude of "white" nations toward the "colored" peoples of the earth.

This is the harsh reality of the report I must unhappily bring you from visits to battlefronts stretching from England to the Middle East. In that reality lies not only continued misery and exploitation for black and brown and yellow peoples who constitute two-thirds of the population of the world. In it exists as well the virtual certainty of another and bloodier and costlier world war in the not too distant future.

The white world has not yet learned the danger and folly of its racial greed and intransigence. The wholesome and becoming humility of the dark days of the early part of the war when Hitler seemed unstoppable has passed.

Walter F. White

The certainty of "white supremacy" is hastily wrapped again like a mantle about the shoulders of the United Nations as their citizens emerge from bomb shelters into the comforting light of victory, a little ashamed of the panic they had felt. Only a few wise men and women like Wendell Willkie and Henry Wallace, Edwin Embree and Sumner Welles, Marshall Field and Pearl Buck are discerning enough to see that the old world is gone and that a new one must take its place or else we all may perish.

Though the voices of the thousands here today may be only as one crying in the wilderness, nevertheless it is our duty to cry aloud unceasingly and, whatever the price we have to pay, doing so not for our own selfish interests but to save the world from destroying white and colored together.

But there is comfort in the fact that today ours is not a lone voice. The hundreds of millions of China and India, of Africa and South America and the Caribbean are neither silent nor inactive. A vast and unstoppable seething moves them. They take literally the shibboleths of the Four Freedoms. They intend to secure and enjoy those freedoms and to put an end to the old order in which men, solely because they are colored, can be worked to exhaustion, exploited, despised, spat upon and derided by those whose chief right to sovereignty is whiteness of skin. And Russia with a passion not only for economic equality but for racial and cultural equality is committed to the fight against prejudice and discrimination.

It is highly significant that the eyes that see and the voices that speak are not solely those of the oppressed. I was in England when four by-elections were held in which the people repudiated the old order of Winston Churchill and his class who would perpetuate imperialism for the benefit of the few. In North Africa and the Middle East I talked with *maquis* just escaped from Nazi-controlled France whose gaunt figures and tense faces bespoke the strain of the underground resistance movement, who are determined that the old order shall not be restored where a decadent class lives in luxury on the exploitation of colonials and working class white French men and women. In London and Algiers and Cairo I talked with men and women who had escaped from Balkan countries all the way from Estonia on the north down to the Black Sea and the Aegean. Almost without exception they favor—distrustful as they are of the old order which brought on the terrible misery of this and the last war—alliance with a steadily more powerful Russia than further reliance on an Anglo-Saxon capitalist world. Mind you, they do not wholly trust Russia. But they place slightly more hope in the Soviet as perhaps the lesser of two evils.

Meanwhile, a similar process proceeds with even greater speed to the east of Russia in Asia and the Pacific. This is less Russia's doing than it is England's and America's. A high official of the British Empire's India Office told me bluntly that Nehru and Gandhi and the other leaders of the fight for freedom of India's three hundred and fifty million people would never be freed from prison until they confessed guilt of treason and insurrection for daring to demand that India's millions receive as well as fight for freedom. Lest he be made a martyr by dying in prison, Gandhi has since been nominally freed. But the brilliant Nehru and other Indian leaders remain in jail to furnish the Japanese propagandists with superb material to convince the one thousand million colored peoples of the Pacific that the white nations of the world are liars and hypocrites when they say that this is a war for the freedom of all men everywhere.

In this shameful program, the United States is doing her full share to create cynicism and skepticism. Every lynching, every coldblooded shooting of a Negro soldier in Louisiana or Mississippi or Georgia, every refusal to abolish segregation in our armed forces, every filibuster against an anti-poll tax or anti-lynching bill, every snarling, sneering reference by a Mississippi senator like Eastland to "burr-headed niggers" in fulmination against an appropriation for the Fair Employment Practice Committee builds up a debit balance of hatred against America which may cost countless lives of Americans yet unborn.

Capitalist America and Great Britain fear and distrust communist Russia, despite all the oleaginous talk nowadays about "our Russian ally." If they hope to preserve a capitalist economy, would they not be wise enough to stop virtually forcing the oppressed of the world—white, black, brown and yellow—into desperate alliance with communism or a racial war which would destroy white and colored peoples? Would not such a course be dictated at least by enlightened self-interest?

Instead of such a course what has recently happened and what will likely happen right here in Chicago during the next week? Three weeks ago the Republicans adopted here a weasel-worded platform plank on postwar international relations which is so meaningless that even the isolationist *Chicago Tribune* approves it. The same platform favors increased international trade and "a fair protective tariff"; opposes government subsidies and favors grants to farmers; pledges reduction of taxes and at the same time a reduction in the public debt and an abundant income for everybody. Since the Congress voted only a two-and-a-half billion-dollar tax bill with the war and the running of the government costing us nearly one hundred billion dollars a year one wonders what feat of legerdemain the Republicans plan to perform to achieve such a miracle.

"We Negroes are finished with being treated as nitwits and dolts."

But the height of double talk was reached when the Republicans came to the Negro question. Painfully aware that they could not reoccupy the White House unless they can corral the 2,500,000 Negro voters who hold the potential balance of power in 17 or more states with a total of 281 or more votes in the Electoral College, the Republicans set about to lure the Negro back into the Republican fold. They included one plank pledging congressional establishment of a permanent Fair Employment Practice Committee which, on the surface, was fair and unequivocal. But elsewhere they pledged "the return of the public employment office system to the states at the earliest possible time...." Shades of consistency!!! Eight of the thirteen million Negro citizens of the United States still live in the South. Imagine—if you will subject yourself to such torture—the chances of a Negro getting a postwar job in a state-controlled employment system in a Mississippi controlled by Bilbo and Rankin!

Let's look at what the GOP proposes to do about housing—the direst of all needs of the ghetto-doomed Negro. They propose to stimulate "state and local plans to provide decent low-cost housing properly financed by the Federal Housing Administration"—the agency which has done more than any other body in the history of America to enforce restrictive covenants as a means of perpetuating, extending, and giving federal sanction to the unholy pattern of condemnation of Negroes to slums forever.

The Republicans say they favor "legislation against lynching," but they neglect to specify whether they mean federal, state or municipal legislation. If they mean state legislation their gesture is both silly and dishonest in the light of the number of Republicans in the states where lynchings are most frequent. If they mean federal legislation they are even more dishonest when they fail even to mention, much less pledge, to vote for cloture to stop filibusters by Southern Democratic senators. I speak from more than a quarter of a century of experience with Republican majority and minority leaders including the late Senator Charles McNary and the present minority leader, Senator Wallace A. White of Maine. Both of these men smiled sweetly but delivered a sufficient number of Republican votes to estop cloture. We Negroes are finished with being treated as nitwits and dolts.

The Republicans promise Negroes an "investigation" of "mistreatment, segregation and discrimination against Negroes who are in our armed forces ... and the adoption of corrective legislation." In 1941 the NAACP secured introduction of a resolution for a Senate investigation of mistreatment of Negroes in the armed services. It got little support from either Republicans or Democrats. Now three years later, on election eve, an investigation is promised. The Congress is in recess until August and, in effect, will be so until after the election. Only a miracle could effect the passage of a resolution for such an investigation by the end of the present Congress in January. Do the Republicans believe us to be completely stupid to think such an investigation will be put through by them in time to be effective in this war? Or are they thinking of World War III?

The whole procedure is redolent of the evasion practiced by Mr. Dewey in New York State in connection with the commission to investigate discrimination in war industries. The commission, composed of distinguished Negro and white New Yorkers, devoted eight months to its work and recommended remedial legislation. This was pocketed by Governor Dewey and a new commission appointed to traverse the same ground and report some time in 1945—well beyond the 1944 election day. Dewey could find but two Negroes in the whole of New York State to serve on his new commission—one of them a political appointee. The Negro's coming of age politically is evidenced by the courage of men like Channing Tobias who refused to be deluded or kidded.

But most shameful of all is the Republican proposal to abolish the poll tax by a constitutional amendment. Southern Democratic senators, aided by reactionary Northern Republicans, have time and again blocked by a filibuster a vote on federal legislation against the poll tax which required only a majority. How much more impossible will it be to pass a resolution for a constitutional amendment which requires a two-thirds vote of both houses of the Congress, and approval by thirty-six, or two-thirds of the state legislatures, of the amendment. After twenty years only twenty-eight state legislatures have approved the child labor amendment which most certainly is less venomously opposed than would be one to enfranchise ten million white and Negro Southerners whose disfranchisement perpetuates the Eugene Coxes and Rankins, the Bilbos and Tom Connallys in power. As a Negro I bitterly resent the Republican implication that we Negroes are as feeble-minded as they appear to believe us to be.

But if you think the GOP platform dishonest and stupid as I do, we "ain't seen nothin' yet" until the Democrats get going here Wednesday. Playing a brazen game of bluffing, the sub-Potomac Democrats have been "revolting" for the past three years. They threaten to throw the election into the House of Representatives, to "secede from the union," and to do a host of other dire things, not one of which they have the slightest intention of doing. Their strategy is not nearly as fantastic and bombastic as it seems. It is, instead, shrewdly and calculatingly conceived. They demand that Vice President Wallace be replaced as the president's running mate because his views on racial, social and economic questions are "fantastic" and "impractical." They conveniently forgot that what Wallace advocates today the president himself preached in 1933 but now no longer preaches—namely, a world of the common man.

But Wallace is only a pawn in the hardboiled game the Southern revolutionists play with more than a fair chance of succeeding. Their real goal and purpose is to force the nomination as vice president on the Democratic ticket of a reactionary Southerner. They count on the president not surviving another four years in the White House or, more likely, his resigning when the war ends to head some sort of international peace commission and thereby turning over to the vice president the reins and powers of office.

Let me solemnly warn the Democratic convention that if it nominates a Southerner as vice president it can kiss the Negro vote goodbye. This is not a sectional issue. There are a number of Southerners, white and Negro, who would make excellent vice presidents. But none of them has a ghost of a chance to be nominated by the ruthless political machines of the South which perpetuate themselves in power by disfranchisement of from ninety to ninety-seven percent of the voters, white and Negro.

Let me make crystal clear at this point that what I say today is not the opinion of a single individual or even of a single organization, even though it be the NAACP with 783 branches and a membership of 400,000. What I say is instead what is deep in the hearts and minds of thoughtful Negro citizens all over this country. As evidence I submit excerpts from the statement, drafted and adopted with striking unanimity on June 17th by the spokesmen of the twenty-five most important mass organizations of Negroes in the United States with a combined membership of six and a half million.

Here is what these men and women ask of their country:

In the coming November election, the Negro voter will judge political parties, as well as candidates, by their words and deeds as to whether they show a determination to work for full citizenship status for thirteen million American Negroes and to better the lot of all disadvantaged peoples. Political parties and candidates that seek the votes of Negroes must be committed to the wholehearted prosecution of the war to total victory, must agree to the elimination of the poll tax by act of Congress, the passage of antilynching legislation, the unsegregated integration of Negroes into the armed forces, the establishment of a permanent federal committee on fair employment practice, and a foreign policy of international cooperation that promotes economic and political security for all peoples.

The votes of Negroes cannot be purchased by distributing money to and through party hacks. They cannot be won by pointing to jobs given a few individual Negroes, although the recognition of the Negro as an integral part of the body politic through the selection of qualified Negroes for appointive or elective offices is included among the Negro's demands. Negroes are no longer persuaded by meaningless generalities in party platforms which are promptly forgotten on election day.

Later in the same statement, the twenty-five organizations declared:

In evaluating the merits of parties and candidates we must include all issues—those touching the life of Negroes as a group as well as those affecting the entire country. The party or candidate who refuses to help control prices, or fails to support the extension of social security, or refuses to support a progressive public program for full postwar employment, or opposes an enlarged and unsegregated program of government-financed housing, or seeks to destroy organized labor, is as much the enemy of Negroes as is he who would prevent Negroes from voting.

We insist upon the right to vote in every state, unrestricted by poll taxes, white primaries, or lily-white party conventions, the gerrymandering of districts, or any other device designed to disfranchise Negroes and other voters.

We hereby serve notice that if either major political party shall nominate for president or vice president a candidate of vacillating or reactionary character, or with an anti-Negro record, it will be vigorously opposed by Negro voters.

Let me emphasize here that what is asked is not asked solely of national political bodies nor of the South alone. It is directed as well at Northern Democratic and Republican organizations which have all too often played ball and made deals with Southern reactionaries, using the Negro vote as the vanishing plea in a political shell game.

Though the Republicans are little if any better—particularly in the recent years of the congressional coalition of death composed of reactionaries of both parties—we may have to submit to the temporary defeat of seeing Tweedledum replace Tweedledee. There are disturbing rumors that the Southern bluff is likely to succeed and that the president plans to "leave to the convention" the choice of a vice president. Negroes have reason to be grateful for much during the Roosevelt administrations. We have deep respect and affection for the courage and integrity of Mrs. Roosevelt. But we cannot run the risk—so desperate is our plight—of an anti-Negro figure as heir apparent to the most powerful position in the world today.

The South—or certain political elements in it like Senator "Cotton Ed" Smith of South Carolina and the Democratic state committees of Texas, Mississippi and South Carolina—declare that they will secede unless they have their way. Let me say here quite seriously that a far worse fate could come to America than to have this happen. Just as the proverbial one rotten apple spoiled the barrel of apples, so democracy itself is being destroyed by the anti-democratic forces in the South today. They utilize hatred of the Negro precisely as Hitler used prejudice against Jews, Catholics and Christians. Through disfranchisement and the seniority rule, they head or dominate more than sixty percent of the Senate and House committees which determine not only domestic legislation but foreign affairs and the shape of the postwar world. Southerners constitute twenty-eight percent of the nation's population but less than ten percent of them are permitted to vote. Thus approximately three percent of the population of America control, through the men they elect and who chair congressional committees, the destiny of America. Perhaps democracy in America can be saved only by letting the rebels secede until the South is ready to obey the Constitution and the laws of human decency. Our nation's plight is far too precarious not only now but even more in the years to come to risk being jeopardized even more by the racism and bigotry of the Rankins and Bilbos.

Permit me to put race aside for the moment and point out how much a menace this bloc is to the interests of Americans generally. Between eleven and twelve million American men and women are serving in the armed forces, nearly six million of them overseas. If any citizens are worthy of the privilege of participation by voting in a democracy, it should be those who are sacrificing most in defense of that democracy. But certain people in and outside of Congress feared that soldiers and sailors might upset their political apple carts by voting too intelligently and liberally. They got Eastland and Rankin of Mississippi, McClellan of Arkansas and McKellar of Tennessee to sponsor a substitute measure, shameless in its ineffectualness. Why did they select these four men to put over disfranchisement of men facing death? For the simple reason that these four legislators were invulnerable to the wrath of an aroused electorate because the overwhelming majority of that electorate is disfranchised.

Or consider another example from among many which could be cited—the Bankhead amendment to the price control act which would have added three hundred and fifty million dollars a year to the cost of clothing—not only, mind you, of the cost of clothing to the people of Senator Bankhead's state of Alabama but to the cost of clothing to the people of Illinois, California, New York and of every other state of the union. Fortunately, this barefaced attempt to add greater profits to the textile interests was blocked. But hamstringing amendments on the Office of Price Administration were affixed as the basis of compromise. How neatly Bankhead's amendment fits in with the Republican platform's pledge to "terminate rationing, price fixing and all other emergency powers." Inflation, thar she blows!

This kind of legislative sabotage of all that we are fighting for in the war illustrates an obligation upon American voters, particularly those who belong to racial, economic and religious minorities, which cannot possibly be stressed too strongly. Never forget that it is vitally important that we elect a president and vice president at this crucial stage of the world's history who by record and promise symbolize the march towards genuine democracy and freedom for all men everywhere. But it is equally important that we elect a Senate and a House of Representatives equally intelligent and liberal. In the October, 1943, and June, 1944, issues of the NAACP *Bulletin* we published the voting record of every member of both Houses of the Congress on issues which affect your interests. Study those records. Cast your ballot according to what that record shows; not by what candidates promise in some vague future. "By their fruits ye shall know them." Pay no attention to their party affiliations. Party labels, as we have seen in the congressional coalition of reactionary Southern Democrats and Northern Republicans, mean nothing to the enemies of progress. They should mean even less to us.

Continue to repudiate venal, slippery politicians who claim to be able to deliver—for a price—the Negro vote. Make this particularly true of Negro charlatans who jump from candidate to candidate, from party to party which has the largest campaign fund, who are able to fool only gullible white candidates because the latter know so little and take so little trouble to learn what the masses of Negroes really think. But while we repudiate purchasable politicians, we must also vigorously support those political leaders who fight for principle and the rights of all.

Permit me now to report tersely to you on my trip overseas since last we met in annual conference and to tell you how your sons and fathers and husbands and friends are faring. I

> *"Just as the proverbial one rotten apple spoiled the barrel of apples, so democracy itself is being destroyed by the anti-democratic forces in the South today."*

covered as a war correspondent more than twenty thousand miles in the European, North African, Italian and Middle East theaters of operations. I talked with many thousands of officers and soldiers, white and Negro, ranging in rank from GI's of engineering units who had just stepped off the boat from America to the supreme allied commander, General Eisenhower. I shared with them the unique fraternity of enemy bombs dropping nearby and the ultimate democracy where race or color do not count—when men huddle together in a slit trench as enemy planes strafe at the rate of thirty-two hundred fifty-caliber bullets per minute per plane.

I wish it were possible for me to tell you truthfully that the alchemy of war and fighting to destroy Nazism had transformed the racial behavior of Americans in the armed services overseas. I cannot do so.

We have merely transplanted to other lands the American pattern, both good and bad. As is true at home, there are some officers and enlisted men, from North and South, who are decent human beings who believe in and practice democracy. A decidedly encouraging note is the number of GI's who, brought face to face with death, are reexamining their racial and other opinions. Some of them are beginning to realize that race is a global question which must be faced and solved. Unfortunately, our War and Navy departments, threatened by congressional reactionaries and bigots, have manifested but slight and grudging recognition of the existence of this enlightened minority in the armed services. Basically, the root of all our difficulties overseas is in insistence on racial segregation.

As long as our government insists on segregation in an army, and navy allegedly fighting for democracy, the chasm between the races will be perpetuated and broadened with resultant bitterness on both sides. When ten or eleven million men return after the war is over, our government cannot escape responsibility for whatever happens since it is in large measure responsible for immature racial, political, economic and social thinking among these men whose every act they have directed for the period of their army and navy service.

What some of us like to believe is that a minority of American soldiers overseas have deliberately fomented brawls with colored soldiers, and spread malicious falsehoods about Negroes among the citizens of countries where these men have been stationed. Among them are that all Negroes have tails, that they are illiterate and diseased and inferior, and even that Negroes are so sub-human that they cannot speak English but communicate their thoughts, if any, by grunting and barking. It is fortunate for America that colored soldiers had self-control and sense enough to treat this campaign as a joke. In some areas Negro soldiers, learning on arrival of the fanciful tales about themselves which had been spread in advance of their coming, barked at the English people of the neighborhood. Belying their reputation of being slow to catch on to a joke, the English soon began to bark back in a kind of warm, friendly language of friendship.

In Italy I ran across a deliberate printed campaign of vilification of Negro American soldiers. Large green placards appeared mysteriously one day on billboards in Naples, allegedly put out by the "Comitate Italiano-Americano," whose full name, translated, is the Italian-American Committee for the Preservation of the Italian Race. The placard vilified Negroes, declaring them to be inferior because their skins were black and warned Italians that they would not receive much consideration or help if they treated American Negro soldiers as equals.

As your representative, I investigated these and other attempts to spread prejudice against the Negro and reported my findings to Major General David G. Barr, chief of the North African theater of operations. I am happy to read you the following excerpt from a letter recently received from General Barr:

> *As a result of your letter calling my attention to the conditions which you came across during your visit to Naples, I directed that an immediate investigation of the conditions . . . be instigated so as to enable us to take remedial action, if necessary. I have delayed answering you until such a time as I might have the benefit of the report submitted as the result of this investigation.*
>
> *The 'Comitate Italiano-Americano' poster referred to by you appeared in Naples on 12 January 1944. The investigation revealed that an American soldier of Italian extraction was fully responsible for its posting. This soldier, and two others who had assisted in financing and distributing the poster, have subsequently been tried and convicted by court martial under the 96th Article of War.*

General Barr's prompt and effective action in this instance is matched, fortunately, by some of the other high officers of the United States Army overseas. Lieutenant General John C.H. Lee, deputy theater commander of the European theater of operations, has recently written, "My staff has been instructed to implement wherever possible your many fine suggestions. It should be a source of great satisfaction to you to know that you have played a definite part in the preparation of our men for the primary mission—combat operations against the enemy. Suggestions such as promotion for Negro officers; the placing of certain officers in positions where they can be of most value are being gone into thoroughly, and, I know, will bring beneficial results."

In General Lee, I found a real friend of fair play and justice for the Negro. When the War Department published an excellent pamphlet, *The Command of Negro Troops,* General Lee had many thousands of copies printed in England for distribution to every officer in the European theater of operations.

When I was in England, virtually all of the Negro soldiers there were so-called service troops—members of quartermaster, engineer, port battalion and trucking units. It was strongly urged that Negro combat troops as well be brought to the European theater and given opportunity to participate in the invasion of the continent. You have recently seen Army photographs of Negro combat troops on the Normandy beachheads, and you heard at the opening session of this conference General Eisenhower's tribute to the part Negroes are playing with other Americans in beating Hitler.

One of the most galling practices to Negro soldiers overseas is the designation of certain towns and other places as "off limits." This practice sorely limited already greatly limited areas in which soldiers could find diversions while on leave. An order has been issued by General Eisenhower forbidding such practices.

Some prejudiced officers have utilized court martial to intimidate Negro soldiers. This has been true both here and overseas. It has been strongly urged upon the War Department that special boards of review of such cases be established and that on them shall serve able Negro lawyers, appropriately commissioned, to insure justice. It is our intention to follow up this recommendation to the end that no officer of the United States Army will dare utilize the machinery of the court martial to implement his prejudices.

Another source of dissatisfaction I found was the tendency to transform Negro combat units into service units. We have reason to believe that facts presented on this issue will check this process.

These are but some of the specific problems and the specific action which your Association attempted to take on them. There are others which are in process of correction. But all of these and other problems are but the surface manifestations of the basic evil—segregation. If I were asked to state my most fundamental criticism not only of our Army and Navy, but of our whole governmental attitude, it would be this—that white America has so little faith in the inherent decency of white Americans. Wherever I went overseas, I found many young, intelligent, decent Americans, both Northern and Southern, who are disturbed by the race problem. They would like to bring their practice of democracy into line with their profession of it. But they fear that to do so would get them into difficulties with their superior officers. I believe the time has come for our government and all its agencies to stop basing their racial patterns on the lowest common denominator of American thought and action on this question. Unless it does so, I predict broadening of the chasm between the races which can only result in greater hatred, more friction and a weakening of the whole democratic structure.

One final word regarding the framing of the peace and the postwar years. I am happy to announce that the distinguished American scholar, Dr. W.E.B. Du Bois, will return to your NAACP on September 1 as Director of Special Research. His first and chief responsibility will be the preparation of material, in cooperation with a distinguished committee of Negro and white Americans, for presentation of the Negro's cause to the peace conference or peace conferences. If the peace treaty is based on the perpetuation of white overlordship over the peoples of the earth, another war is inevitable. On behalf of the Negroes not only of America, but of Africa, the West Indies and other parts of the world, we shall make our voice heard in an effort to save the framers from the folly of another Versailles Treaty.

We have just completed the most active and successful year in the Association's history. Ahead of us lie tears and heartaches, problems and hard work. But also there lies ahead greater strength out of which will come inevitably greater victories. We must, in the wise words of C.C. Spaulding, teach America that "It cannot play the 'Star-Spangled Banner' without using both the black and the white keys."

White served as head of the NAACP until his death in 1955, not long after the organization's triumph in the landmark Brown v. Board of Education *case that struck down the concept of "separate but equal" educational facilities.*

SOURCES

Aptheker, Herbert, editor, *A Documentary History of the Negro People of the United States, 1933-1945,* Citadel Press, 1974.

Boulware, Marcus H., *The Oratory of Negro Leaders: 1900-1968,* Negro Universities Press, 1969.

Foner, Philip S., *The Voice of Black America: Major Speeches by Negroes in the United States, 1797-1971,* Simon & Schuster, 1972.

Hughes, Langston, *Fight for Freedom: The Story of the NAACP,* Norton, 1962.

White, Walter F., *A Rising Wind,* Doubleday, Doran, 1945, reprinted, Negro Universities Press, 1971.

———, *A Man Called White: The Autobiography of Walter White,* Viking, 1948, reprinted, Indiana University Press, 1970.

———, *How Far the Promised Land?,* Viking, 1955.

L. Douglas Wilder

1931–

African American politician

On November 7, 1989, Virginia lieutenant governor L. Douglas Wilder logged another first in African American history by capturing the governor's seat after an extremely close race. His triumph was significant in two respects—not only did it make him the first black governor of a state that had been at the heart of the Confederacy during the Civil War, it also made him the first elected *black governor in U.S. history. (In late 1872, Louisiana's African American lieutenant governor, P.B.S. Pinchback, served briefly as acting governor.) These "firsts" catapulted Wilder onto the national political scene virtually overnight and since then have helped fuel his ambition for higher office.*

Wilder, the grandson of slaves, was born and raised in Virginia's capital city, Richmond, amid conditions he has described as "gentle poverty." After graduating from high school at the age of sixteen, he tried to enlist in the Navy, but his mother—a firm believer in the benefits of a good education—refused to give her permission. So he enrolled at Virginia Union College, from which he received a bachelor's degree in chemistry in 1951. The arrival of a draft notice then forced him to postpone his plans to go on to law school; instead, he served honorably with the U.S. Army during the Korean War.

Returning home in 1953, Wilder worked as a chemist in the state medical examiner's office until 1956, when he headed off to Howard University Law School in Washington, D.C. (At the time, no law school in Virginia would admit blacks.) Following his graduation in 1959, he set up a practice in his old Richmond neighborhood, specializing in criminal cases and personal-injury lawsuits. With his flashy dress and a courtroom style that was at times breezy and at times combative, he also managed to raise a few eyebrows.

Wilder entered politics in 1969 as a Democratic candidate for the Virginia state senate. His victory made him the first African American to serve in the state legislature since the Reconstruction era. Once in office, he quickly demonstrated that he was not afraid to challenge the status quo. Even though he had never been active in the civil rights movement, for example, he immediately launched a fierce attack on the official state song, "Carry Me Back to Old Virginny," on the grounds that it celebrated slavery in sentimental terms. He also worked hard on a campaign to make the birthday of Martin Luther King, Jr., a state holiday. Among his other concerns were fair-housing legislation, voting rights, capital punishment, and minority hiring in both the public and private sector.

Wilder remained in the state senate until 1986, when he became the nation's only black lieutenant governor in an upset win that saw him tone down his image as a fiery liberal and adopt a more moderate approach. His run for governor three years later was also characterized by a decidedly moderate approach to the issues then facing Virginians; in fact, about the only subject he and his white Republican opponent disagreed on was abortion. (Wilder was pro-choice.) In addition, both candidates deliberately downplayed race as a factor in the contest. On election day, Wilder's margin of victory was less than seven thousand votes—about one-third of one percent—but it did nothing to diminish the historic significance of the occasion.

In the eloquent inaugural speech he delivered on January 13, 1990, before an exceptionally large and enthusiastic crowd, Wilder acknowledged his place in Virginia's long and distinguished history but urged his audience to look forward, not backward. His address is reprinted here from Representative American Speeches: 1989-1990 *(Wilson, 1991).*

Mr. Justice Powell, Mr. Justice Carrico, to the lieutenant governor, to the attorney general, members of the General Assembly, distinguished guests, family and friends, and my fellow Virginians, we gather here today for what is both a culmination and a continuation of the democratic process.

Four years ago, I stood on this spot to assume the second-highest office in the Commonwealth. Today, because of your faith in our efforts, I stand before you as chief executive of this state. And now, in keeping with the sanctioned privilege extended to all governors, it is my honor to address the people of this Commonwealth and to express to my fellow citizens the profound gratitude and deep sense of purpose that I feel in fulfilling your expectations.

Candor and honesty would have me admit to you that I was not blessed with the foresight to know that this moment was in the offing when I stood here in 1985. Having been tested in the political crucible of trial and cross-examination, I have been rendered a verdict by having had delivered unto me the greatest outpouring of votes ever accorded any candidate for this great office. For that, I shall be eternally grateful. And, be assured, I shall demonstrate that gratitude during the next four years by being a governor who will be beholden to but one special interest: the welfare of Virginians, all Virginians.

L. Douglas Wilder

But my gratitude is not of such recent origin. It is said, "To whom much is given, much shall be expected." I will be the first to admit that I have been the beneficiary of much through no endeavors of my own. While I have indeed worked hard and performed to the best of my abilities, I have also had a few breaks along the way.

Indeed, in every walk, in every period of my life, there have been many more deserving and justly entitled to the fruits that wholesome opportunities present. And yet, for many, those chances never came and the bell of fulfillment never tolled for them. Providence indeed has directed my course. And I shall remain ever mindful of my good fortune.

In recent years, Virginia too has been blessed with good fortune. The progress and the prosperity we have enjoyed during this period has enabled us to reclaim the respected achievements of times past. In looking to our accomplishments in education, economic development, the environment, employment, housing, or transportation, we find that Virginia ranks among those states in the vanguard of forward-looking movement.

Not surprisingly, the ensuing pride in seeing our state climb in rank among our sister states in the nation and in preeminence among the Southern states causes Virginians everywhere to feel good about our cause, our mission, and our success in forging Virginia's New Mainstream.

That commitment to looking ahead and not behind, of building rather than destroying, of bringing people together rather than pitting them against each other, also calls for me to address you with measured sobriety in facing conditions in the Commonwealth today, and I will comment further in that regard when I address the General Assembly on Monday.

But for this moment, let me assure you that I do not intend to participate in bringing to a halt the momentum to which people of Virginia have grown accustomed, supported, and enjoyed. Cicero, in a parting observation, noted that "A Commonwealth is not any collection of human beings . . . but an assembly of people joined in agreement on justice and partnership for the common good, and a community where civility must reign and all must live peacefully together." And we know what happened to Cicero's Rome, which could not pass on the heritage of its past to the people of its future. But we have done so; we can do so. And we shall do so.

These are times when the people of our state and of our country can feel the resurgence of the dominance of the individual spirit which proves daily to be unconquerable. Whirlwinds of rebellion shake all shores where tyranny once ruled, and we are redeemed in our deeply held and treasured beliefs in the development of the high possibility of every individual who breathes the sweetness of liberty's air.

At this time, and in the place where so many great names in American history have trod, we renew this celebration of freedom in the full and certain knowledge that with it comes great responsibility. Without question, much tighter economic times which loom in the days ahead will test to the fullest our ability to make hard decisions, to lead, and to govern. But progress will be possible. Opportunity can be expanded. Freedom can be increased.

Resources employed in the past for the finer things in life can be, and will have to be, deployed for the more serious of our needs. For we know that freedom is but a word for the man or woman who needs and cannot find a job. Freedom, as it has been written, is a dream deferred when it "Dries up like a raisin in the sun, and stinks like rotten meat."

Freedom is meaningless when a woman's right to choose is regulated outside the dictates of her own faith and conscience. Freedom is impotent when there is intolerance to those who hold moral and political beliefs different from our own. Freedom is restricted when labor and management cannot reach agreements. Freedom is impossible for the uneducated who try to live in today's complex world. Freedom is restrained for business and industry when our network of transportation is allowed to deteriorate. Freedom for the police is denied when their resources are unduly limited. Freedom for the people is assaulted when lawful authority is abused. Freedom for the next generation is mortgaged when we destroy our environment. And, as has been proven throughout recorded history, freedom is nowhere to be found when the people are overtaxed and over-regulated.

As we salute the idea of freedom today, let us pledge to extend that same freedom to others tomorrow. Let us fulfill the perfect promise of freedom and liberty left as a legacy for us by those who founded this Commonwealth. And let us likewise be thankful that, while our country gave birth to a freedom long denied and delayed for all who loved freedom, the belief in these dreams held by those forebears was passed from generation to generation, and spawned the seeds that propagated the will and the desire to achieve.

We are on hallowed ground today, and the steps we take from this place must be steps of honor. The words we issue must be words of wisdom. The laws we pass must be laws of mercy and justice. And the faith we possess must be true to the Almighty. In meeting these challenges, and they will be difficult, I ask your help and that of God.

I do not shrink from the enormity of the task. In six million Virginians, there is endless courage and enormous strength . . . in the coming years, we will need it all. As we all know, as complexities of human relationships increase, the power to govern them also increases. The proper use of that power must always be subordinated to the public good and that shall be uppermost in the hearts and minds of those to whom those powers are justly delegated by the people.

We shall not pause; we shall not rest upon laurels. For we have not fulfilled our destinies. In the coming years, we must persist and make every citizen of our Commonwealth the subject of our interest and concern. We must insist that every agency of our government utilize every proper and effective instrument to carry out the will of the people—for, as with any democracy, the will of the people is supreme.

An administration can only be effective when it works for the people, all of the people. Our prosperity can continue only if our leaders and private citizens alike stay constantly advised of all of the relevant facts. In turn, we can expect to receive your support, as well as your constructive criticism, when you receive true information from those of us who serve as your trustees.

I am undaunted by that which lies ahead, as we have shown at other points in our history what we can accomplish when we fearlessly face the future. We have, and we shall, shun the defects of destruction, and shall work to achieve the highest degree of improvement in our status of which we are capable. We have a common concern, and we share the responsibility.

"We mark today . . . the triumph of an idea. . . . The idea that all men and women are created equal, that they are endowed by their Creator with certain inalienable rights. . . ."

I see a Virginia of hope and happiness, of mothers and fathers building and nurturing families in those hearthstones where the cradle of childhood is rocked with wholesome expectation for the future, a future in which an education is within intellectual and financial reach; a future in which adequate and affordable housing is possible; a future in which nothing is impossible. I see a place where crime is not only reduced and our streets and neighborhoods are safe, but the root-causes thereof—illiteracy, poverty, joblessness are stamped out. I see a Virginia where the homeless can find shelter, where hunger cannot and does not stalk those unable to fend for themselves.

We must set priorities in the coming years. Specifically, we must be partners in working toward a revived economy, a healthy and thriving economy that provides equal opportunity for all Virginians. While the flow may have slowed, Virginia's New Mainstream is far from drying up. It shall be the task of this administration to ensure that a rising tide of prosperity and opportunity is possible in the future.

Some describe conditions in our Commonwealth today in dismal terms. And yet, one must question the resolve and the reserve of those who are not called upon to make sacrifices greater than those who have preceded us. Despite our economic slowdown, we are living in the best of times. And they can be even better. And they will be better.

If you will forgive me a moment of nostalgia, we mark today not a victory of party or the accomplishments of an individual, but the triumph of an idea, an idea as old as America, as old as the God who looks out for us all. It is the idea expressed so eloquently from this great Commonwealth by those who gave shape to the greatest nation ever known: Jefferson, Madison, Mason, and their able colleagues.

The idea that all men and women are created equal, that they are endowed by their Creator with certain inalienable rights: the right to life, liberty, and the pursuit of happiness. The idea that shows forth in the concepts of freedom and opportunity, not only in Virginia, but more recently in the fresh, new winds of Eastern Europe and the tumult of Panama.

If these words about freedom are to be heard at all today, I hope they will be heard by the young people of this Commonwealth. I want them to know that oppression can be lifted; that discrimination can be eliminated; that poverty need not be binding; that disability can be overcome; and that offer of opportunity in a free society carries with it the requirement of hard work, the rejection of drugs and other false highs, and a willingness to work with others whatever their color or national origin.

We have come far, but we have far to go. We have done much, but we have much to do. I ask for your energy, for your understanding, for your dedication, for your patience and, yes, for your prayers.

Four years ago, I said to the people of Virginia that I was proud to be a Virginian. I did not think then that my pride could possibly be greater. And, in theory, it isn't. But in reality, that pride does burst forth, and lifts my voice and my spirit to proclaim, "I am a son of Virginia."

I thank you all. And may God be ever with us.

Wilder's term as governor of Virginia was marked by a severe budget crisis that was fueled in part by the continuing national recession as well as decreases in federal defense spending. Wilder himself, who was in much demand as a speaker after his historic victory, spent a considerable amount of time out of the state during his first year in office. He then announced his intention to seek the 1992 Democratic presidential nomination. In January 1992, however, Wilder abruptly called a halt to his fledgling campaign, citing a need to devote his full attention to Virginia's fiscal problems.

In June 1993, Wilder decided to try again for higher office, this time as a candidate for the U.S. Senate. Seven months later, with his term as governor about to expire, he dropped out of the race and declared that it was time for him to leave politics. But in mid-1994, he re-entered the race as an independent, facing off against his longtime Democratic rival Senator Charles. S. Robb, Republican candidate Oliver North, and another independent, Marshall Coleman. Despite his pledge to remain in the race until the end, Wilder abruptly quit again in September 1994, after polls showed him lagging far behind Robb. "I have said that I was in this campaign for one reason only, and that was to win," explained Wilder in a statement announcing his withdrawl. "I am a realist. I know when to hold them and when to fold them." Robb went on to defeat North and Coleman in the November election.

SOURCES

Books

Peterson, Owen, editor, *Representative American Speeches: 1989-1990,* Wilson, 1991.

Yancey, Dwayne, *When Hell Froze Over: The Untold Story of Doug Wilder,* Taylor Publishing, 1990.

Periodicals

Detroit News, "Former Virginia Governor Wilder Ends His Independent Senate Race," September 16, 1994, p. 5A.

Ebony, "L. Douglas Wilder: Virginia's Lieutenant Governor," April, 1986; "Elected Governor," February, 1990.

Grand Rapids Press, "Wilder Bows Out of Senate Race in Virginia," September 15, 1994, p. A3.

Jet, "L. Douglas Wilder: 'I Claim the Governorship of Virginia,'" November 27, 1989, pp. 8-11.

Newsweek, "A Black Victory in Old Dominion," November 18, 1985, p. 46; "A 'Demolition Derby,'" June 24, 1991, pp. 16-17.

New York Times, November 8, 1989, p. 10; "Wilder Exits Virginia Politics with a Feisty Flourish," January 14, 1994, p. A12; "Wilder Hints He May Run for Senate as Independent," April 16, 1994, p. 6.

People, "Doug Wilder Carries Old Virginny, Making History as He Wins the Lieutenant Governorship,"

December 9, 1985; "Yes, Virginia, Doug Wilder Could Be America's First Elected Black Governor," November 6, 1989, pp. 54-55.

Time, "Battling an Old Bugaboo," April 17, 1989, pp. 26-27; "Breakthrough in Virginia," November 20, 1989, pp. 54-57; "Virginia's Demolition Derby," June 24, 1991, p. 23; "A Ghetto Kid Who Remembers His Roots," November 11, 1991, pp. 49-50; "Then There Were Five," January 20, 1992, p. 25.

U.S. News and World Report, "Governor-Elect Doug Wilder," November 20, 1989; "The Day of 'Man as Man,' " January 22, 1990, pp. 10-11.

Roy Wilkins

1901–1981

African American civil rights activist

As head of the National Association for the Advancement of Colored People (NAACP) from 1955 until 1977, Roy Wilkins played a major role in some of the most important battles of the civil rights movement. The tone he set for the organization during that period reflected his own quiet, low-key style of conservative yet efficient leadership. But it also made him the target of criticism from those who felt he lacked the proper "fire," especially after the struggle for racial justice took a more militant turn with the rise of the black power movement of the 1960s. Yet by the end of his tenure, most agreed that Wilkins had effectively steered the NAACP through an especially difficult time in its history.

Wilkins was born in St. Louis, Missouri, but grew up in St. Paul, Minnesota. He attended the University of Minnesota, earning a journalism degree and serving as editor of the school newspaper as well as editor of a local black weekly. Horrified by several local incidents of racial violence, including the mob lynching of a black man in the town of Duluth, he also joined the NAACP. After graduating from college, Wilkins took a job with a black weekly in Missouri, the Kansas City Call. *The rigid segregation and prejudice he encountered in Kansas City convinced him that African Americans had to take their fight for equality to the courts. So he stepped up his NAACP activities, which eventually brought him to the attention of the organization's national leaders. In 1931, they offered Wilkins a staff position. His acceptance marked the beginning of a forty-six-year-long career fighting for an end to discrimination through legal means.*

Wilkins held a variety of administrative positions before rising to the rank of NAACP executive secretary in 1955, including serving a fifteen-year stint as editor of the group's magazine, Crisis. *His investigative work often helped provide the evidence necessary to bring discrimination complaints to trial, and afterwards, he monitored efforts to make sure the intent of the law was observed. As executive secretary, Wilkins distinguished himself as a superb manager and one of the civil rights movement's best speakers and writers. Instead of drama and emotion, however, he relied on well-researched facts and a calm, controlled approach to persuade his audiences.*

One of his first major speeches as the new head of the NAACP came at the group's annual convention during the summer of 1955. Delegates were still savoring the legal victory of the previous year in the famous Brown v. Board of Education of Topeka, Kansas *case, which saw the U.S. Supreme Court declare racial segregation in public schools unconstitutional. But Wilkins, while praising the outcome of the trial, warned his listeners about the dangers of becoming complacent when it was clear that many people opposed to integration were prepared to defy the Court's ruling. Originally published by the NAACP in August 1955, as a pamphlet entitled* The Conspiracy to Deny Equality, *his speech was later reprinted in* The Voice of Black America: Major Speeches by Negroes in the United States, 1797-1971 *(Simon & Schuster, 1972).*

Last year at Dallas we had a celebration. The convention theme was victory, for we had just had the pronouncement of the United States Supreme Court that segregation in the public schools was unconstitutional.

Most of us knew that the victory was sweet, not because it immediately desegregated the Jim Crow schools, but because it gave us the prize we had been seeking for fifty-eight years: the declaration by the nation's highest court that such segregation was now unlawful. Hitherto, we had had the moral conviction that these schools were wrong and contrary to the guarantees of American citizenship; we had had outrage and frustration as our companions while we went up and down the land seeking recruits to our army of moral and spiritual devotees.

But we had not had the law. We had no means of enforcing our moral convictions except through preachment and persuasion. We secured converts, but they—and we—were helpless without the law. On May 17, 1954, we got the law. On May 31, 1955, we got the decree as to how the law would have to be carried out.

With the May 31 opinion, it has become apparent that we have entered a new era, an era where racial discrimination and segregation are to be not merely morally wrong, but contrary to the law and the Constitution. A description of this era has been given by an editorial writer for the Charlotte, North Carolina, *News,* in its issue of June 1, 1955. Under the heading, "End of an Era," its opening paragraph states:

> *The stark, elementary realities of the Supreme Court decision on segregation in the public schools can be avoided no longer. Racial barriers which have existed for generations must be dissolved. A massive change . . . is about to take place.*

I should like to borrow this for my general theme. We have come to the end of an era and the beginning of a new one. Our great Association, which has carried the fight thus far, is faced with new challenges, new responsibilities, new and more pressing calls to duty, to devotion, intelligence and skill. Each and every officer and member, wherever he may be, shares the heavy burden of the transition. None may shirk his duty, for that would be to betray the ones who come after. Let no one in tomorrow's world be able to say that in the years of decision, when destiny was in our hands, we failed to measure up. The people of 1903 had no such challenge and opportunity; nor did those of 1923, or 1943. This great day is ours. Upon us depend the speed, the order and the completeness of the victory.

We have emerged from more than a half-century of the doctrine of "separate but equal" set forth in the now-famous *Plessy v. Ferguson* case of 1896. We Negroes always knew the Plessy doctrine to be wrong and we fervently believed it to be unconstitutional. But it was not until our attorneys carried to the highest court the challenge to its legality that we finally shook off the shackles that had hobbled our progress since the turn of the century.

What did the Plessy era hold for us? To what kind of life were we committed by it? Discrimination and segregation were our lot. In his great dissenting opinion in the Plessy case, Mr. Justice Harlan said the result would be "mischievous." At another point he used the word "pernicious." He spoke also of state enactments regulating the enjoyment of civil rights as being "cunningly devised" to defeat the legitimate results of the Civil War.

It is pertinent to quote some of his words because they were so prophetically true, be-

Roy Wilkins

cause they described so accurately, that day in 1896, what we as a group were destined to suffer for more than fifty years. Said Mr. Justice Harlan:

> *In my opinion, the judgment this day rendered will, indeed, prove to be quite as pernicious as the decision made by this tribunal in the Dred Scott case. . . . I am of the opinion that the statute of Louisiana is inconsistent with the personal liberty of citizens, white and black, in that state and hostile to both the spirit and letter of the Constitution of the United States. If laws of like character should be enacted in the several states of the Union, the effect would be in the highest degree mischievous. Slavery as an institution tolerated by law would, it is true, have disappeared from our country, but there would remain a power in the states, by sinister legislation, to interfere with the full enjoyment of the blessings of freedom; to regulate civil rights common to all citizens, upon the basis of race; and to place in a condition of legal inferiority a large body of American citizens. . . .*

Mark well that last phrase—"to place in a condition of legal inferiority a large body of American citizens."

For us it was all this and more. We have been subject to the whims and fancies of white persons, individually and collectively. We went to back doors and were forced to live in hollows and alleys and back streets. We stepped off sidewalks and removed our hats and said "Sir" to all and sundry, if they were white. If schools were provided, our children went to shanties and whites to schools. We rode in the rear seats of buses and trolleys and in the dirty, dangerous front-end coaches of the trains. We could not vote. Our health and our recreation were of little or no concern to the responsible officials of government. In time of war we were called to serve, but were insulted, degraded and mistreated even as we fought to defend the flag that flew over every American. We were beaten, shot, lynched and burned, and no man was punished for what he did to us.

Slowly in this fifty-eight years, we have lifted ourselves by our own bootstraps. Step by halting step, we have beaten our way back. It has been a long and tortuous road since the Dred Scott decision of 1857, which branded us as noncitizens and which, by the Plessy decision, gave the states and the nation as a whole the green light to treat us as they pleased.

But we are here, through the grace of God, through our refusal to quit, through the strength and skill of our own right arms, and through the burning spirit from father to son, from mother to daughter, that persisted in hope and prayer to the precious goal of freedom.

We need only recall, not recount the victories along the way. We wiped out lynching. We knocked out the strongest barriers to voting, as well as the widely used restrictive covenants on housing. We have clothed our fighting men with dignity. Travel is no longer an ordeal of both the body and the spirit. The courts, in the South as well as in the North, are becoming places where color-blind justice is dispensed. Our men and women are working at more and better jobs and at better and better wages.

Now our children, at long last, are to have equality in education. They are to have a chance in the race of life without being penalized before they are born.

Truly, we are at the beginning of a new era. But just as the old order did not pass without prayer and struggle and sacrifice even unto death—so the new order will not come into being unless we accomplish it by our own efforts. This is the beginning, not the end. This is a time for action, not for resting. Some have complained that they thought May 17 settled everything and that now they could retire and enjoy. Freedom never came to any people in that fashion.

We cannot be complacent as we see before our eyes the outlines of a conspiracy to deny, in 1955, the equality we have won for ourselves. For this school decision heralds the death of all inequality in citizenship based upon race. The Richmond, Virginia, editor, Virginius Dabney, correctly stated in 1953 that public-school segregation was the keystone in the arch of segregation. It has been knocked out and the arch will fall.

The conspirators know this, hence the desperation of their tactics. To us who have known the refined as well as the brutal methods of persecution, the emerging pattern is not new.

"We cannot be complacent as we see before our eyes the outlines of a conspiracy to deny . . . the equality we have won for ourselves."

First they are organizing. Here and there, dotting the South, organizations have sprung up overnight, some with fancy names like Virginia's Defenders of State Sovereignty and Individual Liberty and others like the White Citizens' Councils in Mississippi, which frankly declare their anti-Negro purpose.

Terror and intimidation are the weapons being used. The Mississippi Councils—now spreading to Alabama—seek to freeze Negroes economically and frighten them bodily.

"We intend," said one organizer, "to see that no Negro who believes in equality has a job, gets credit, or is able to exist in our communities."

"Is able to exist"—that means agree and knuckle under, or flee, or die.

It is not strange that in such an atmosphere, Rev. George W. Lee was murdered by a shotgun blast on May 7 in his home town of Belzoni, Mississippi. The Reverend Mr. Lee's "crime" was that he was the first Negro to register to vote in his county, and he had refused orders from whites to remove his name from the voting list. The state headquarters of the White Citizens' Councils is a scant sixty miles from Belzoni, in Winona.

But naked terror alone will not do the job. Even murder will not guarantee victory to the conspirators.

They have a well-oiled system, rooted in politics, by which they hope to stave off defeat. All these years the system has worked. Today they are trying to use it still.

At the local and state levels they have enforced disfranchisement of Negroes, which in turn has permitted the election of local and state officers wholly indifferent to the plight, wishes and demands of our citizens. No better illustration of the effectiveness of this technique at this level can be found than the actions of the South Carolina, Georgia, Louisiana and Mississippi legislators during the past year in passing legislation frankly and brazenly labeled as efforts to deny the Negro equality and to prevent him from voting.

This same disfranchisement has permitted the election of congressmen and senators to Washington who are pledged to block any executive or legislative moves which recognize the needs of Negroes as citizens. These Southern Congressmen and Senators have used their committee posts to smother legislation and, in the Senate, the filibuster to kill legislation.

While hamstringing presidents and choking off legislation they have not had as much success in hampering the courts, although they have done their best through their power to confirm judicial appointees. With but few exceptions they are now in full cry against the courts and especially the Supreme Court. If they had a ghost of a chance they would emulate South Africa in making Supreme Court decrees subject to ratification by the Congress.

Thus we have had a two-pronged political

operation, one prong bottling up the Negro vote in the South at the ballot box level, and the other nullifying the Negro vote in the North by the use of blackjack tactics in both houses of the Congress.

This system has worked through the decades whether a Democratic or Republican president has been in office. The only chief executive to buck it was Harry S Truman, who split his party rather than keep silent on his recommendations as to civil rights for Negro Americans.

The system has been aided by Northern Democrats who seek "party unity" as they play poker politics with the civil rights of Negroes as the joker card.

The system is aided also by the Republicans, who seek support for their program and who also continue to hope that they will be able to build a permanent party structure in the South. It might be added here that if they continue to talk like Dixiecrats, act like Dixiecrats, and vote like Dixiecrats, they will not have to infiltrate the South; it will have taken them over.

One of our principal objectives as an Association is the smashing of this iniquitous network of political strangulation, which has its base in the choking off of Negro citizenship rights at the precinct or county level through denial of the ballot. During the past year we have stimulated increased registration by Negro citizens in many Southern states. Intensive campaigns have been underway in Virginia, Alabama, North Carolina and South Carolina. We expect to increase this activity in these and other states between now and the 1956 election.

Along with the effort to broaden the voting base in the South will go a campaign to use the northern Negro's voting strength to break the hold of the Dixiecrat system. Northern Democratic officeholders may continue to receive Negro votes on the basis of their individual records, and many, like Senator Herbert Lehman of New York, have most excellent records. But increasingly, Negro voters—as far as the Democratic party is concerned—are demanding less unity with the system that disfranchises, insults, terrorizes, and generally creates an atmosphere in which violence can flourish. They want no unity with the White Councils of Mississippi; no unity with areas that murder men as the Reverend Mr. Lee was murdered, for wanting to vote; no unity with the forces of slander, as exemplified by a nationwide radio talk of Senator Allen J. Ellender of Louisiana branding Negroes as ignorant, diseased and crime-ridden; no unity with those who defy the law of the land as laid down by the Supreme Court, as exemplified by the recent television broadcast of Senator James O. Eastland of Mississippi.

On the other hand, the Republicans, who hope and hope, cannot expect substantial support as long as they "play footsie" with southern Democrats on civil rights. They wonder why the Negro vote does not return to the G.O.P. fold. Well, thousands want to return because they are not comfortable in the party of Herman Talmadge, but they cannot see any percentage in changing as long as the Republicans play ball with the Dixiecrats.

These conspirators about whom I have been talking—the conscious as well as the unconscious ones—went so far as to enlist the prestige of the White House in their demands to maintain segregation and circumvent the national policy of no discrimination in the armed services. On June 8 the President in his press conference lashed out at those who seek antisegregation amendments to pending legislation including the military reserves bill.

We who seek such amendments were accused of placing our special desires above the security of the nation. We want to say here plainly and unmistakably that it is not we who seek our own way at the expense of the country. It is the southern Democratic bloc, which openly threatened to kill the military-reserves bill unless it contained their provision for segregation. The President has every right to demand the legislation he deems necessary for the welfare of the nation, but in all fairness the blame for the delay on that legislation should be placed at the doorstep of those who are guilty.

We love our country. We have fought for it in the past and we will fight for it in the future, but we do not relish our patriotism being called into question because we demand our rights as American citizens.

We feel the same way about the antisegregation amendment to the housing bill and to the bill which would provide aid to the states for the construction of public schools. We do not believe that housing which is provided out of the funds or the credit of all the people of the United States should be denied to any citizen because of his race or color. We do not believe that the tax funds of all the people of the United States should be given to any state or locality for the purpose of subsidizing these in defying the Supreme Court ruling on segregated schools.

Our legislative goals, of course, are not limited to amendments to pending bills. Although the president expressed the opinion in 1953 that the states should pass fair-employment-practice bills, only the states with Democratic administrations have so far complied, the latest being Minnesota and Michigan. Two state governments of the president's own party—Illinois and Pennsylvania—have defeated FEPC. Neither the 83rd nor the 84th Congress has done anything on FEPC, nor has the president made any recommendation on this or any other civil-rights bill.

"We do not relish our patriotism being called into question because we demand our rights as American citizens."

Our Department of Justice will remain almost impotent in prosecuting civil-rights crimes, such as the murders of Mr. and Mrs. Harry T. Moore of Florida, and the Reverend Mr. Lee of Mississippi, until Congress passes a bill to strengthen the civil-rights laws.

These and other bills to make secure the rights of all our citizens form the continuing objective of our members, who will make their likes and dislikes known in the polling booths.

Yes, in fashioning the new era we shall use all the weapons at our disposal. Thurgood Marshall, our general counsel, has outlined how we will use the courts. We shall continue to use education and persuasion and moral pressure. Heartened by the support of millions of our white fellow citizens in all sections of the country, we welcome their participation in the crusade, which is one not alone for us, but for our nation as a whole. And we shall use all the political power we can muster, for this is the most vital ingredient in a government of, by and for the people, not the white people, but all the people.

As the new era dawns there are those who say "it shall never be." The Richmond, Virginia, *News Leader,* a long-established and apparently responsible journal, declared in an angry editorial after the May 31 opinion:

> *When the court proposes that its social revolution be imposed upon the South "as soon as practicable" there are those of us who would respond that "as soon as practicable" means never at all.*

But my friends, the Richmond paper and others like it say "never" like the Romans before the coming of Christ; like King John before Magna Carta; like the emperors of France before 1789; like George III of England before the Declaration of Independence; like the Southern plantation owners before the Civil War.

We know them. How we know them! They are wicked, and wickedness shall not prevail, though for a time it shall spread itself like the green bay tree.

The time of the wicked is fast approaching. We shall never return to bondage, with or without shackles. We shall heed the word of God as set forth in Leviticus 26:13:

> *I am the Lord your God which brought you forth out of the land of Egypt, that you should not be their bondsmen; and I have broken the bands of your yoke, and made you go upright.*

We shall go upright. We shall go in faith, without hatred of any man, but with determination in the righteousness of our cause, armed with the weapons provided for us. We shall not—we cannot—fail. We shall, we will, be free men.

One of the most serious issues facing mainstream civil rights groups during the mid- and late 1960s was the growing influence of the black power movement, particularly among younger African Americans who had grown impatient with the slow pace of political, social, and economic change. In their view, organizations such as the NAACP were far too conservative. Indeed, Wilkins absolutely refused to endorse any part of the black power program, a decision that angered

some people both inside and outside the NAACP. On July 5, 1966, at the group's annual convention (held that year in Los Angeles), Wilkins explained his position. His speech is taken from The Rhetoric of the Civil Rights Movement *(Random House, 1969).*

In the transition period of the civil rights movement, 1966 is developing into a critical year. The 57th annual convention of our NAACP is thus a gathering of more than ordinary significance.

All about us are alarums and confusions as well as great and challenging developments. Differences of opinion are sharper. For the first time since several organizations began to function where only two had functioned before, there emerges what seems to be a difference in goals.

Heretofore there were some differences in methods and in emphases, but none in ultimate goals. The end was always to be the inclusion of the Negro American, without racial discrimination, as a full-fledged equal in all phases of American citizenship. The targets were whatever barriers, crude or subtle, which blocked the attainment of that goal.

There has now emerged, first, a strident and threatening challenge to a strategy widely employed by civil rights groups, namely, nonviolence. One organization, which has been meeting in Baltimore, has passed a resolution declaring for defense of themselves by Negro citizens if they are attacked.

This position is not new as far as the NAACP is concerned. Historically our Association has defended in courts those persons who have defended themselves and their homes with firearms. Extradition cases are not as frequent or as fashionable as they once were, but in past years we have fought the extradition of men who had used firearms to defend themselves when attacked.

We freed seventy-nine Arkansas sharecroppers in a four-year court battle beginning in 1919. They had returned gunfire directed at a meeting they were holding in a church.

We employed the late Clarence Darrow in 1926 to defend a man and his family when a member of a mob threatening his newly-purchased Detroit home was shot and killed. The NAACP has subscribed to nonviolence as a humane as well as a practical necessity in the realities of the American scene, but we have never required this as a deep personal commitment of our members. We never signed a pact either on paper or in our hearts to turn the other cheek forever and ever when we were assaulted.

But neither have we couched a policy of manly resistance in such a way that our members and supporters felt compelled to maintain themselves in an armed state, ready to retaliate instantly and in kind whenever attacked. We venture the observation that such a publicized posture could serve to stir counter-planning, counter-action and possible conflict. If carried out literally as instant retaliation, in cases adjudged by aggrieved persons to have been grossly unjust, this policy could produce—in extreme situations—lynchings, or, in better-sounding phraseology, private, vigilante vengeance.

Moreover, in attempting to substitute for derelict law enforcement machinery, the policy entails the risk of a broader, more indiscriminate crackdown by law officers, under the ready-made excuse of restoring law and order.

It seems reasonable to assume that proclaimed protective violence is as likely to encourage counter-violence as it is to discourage violent persecution.

But the more serious division in the civil rights movement is the one posed by a word formulation that implies clearly a difference in goals.

No matter how endlessly they try to explain it, the term "black power" means anti-white power. In a racially pluralistic society, the concept, the formation and the exercise of an ethnically-tagged power, means opposition to other ethnic powers, just as the term "white supremacy" means subjection of all nonwhite people. In the black-white relationship, it has to mean that every other ethnic power is the rival and the antagonist of "black power." It has to mean "going-it-alone." It has to mean separatism.

Now, separatism, whether on the rarefied debate level of "black power" or on the wishful level of a secessionist Freedom City in Watts, offers a disadvantaged minority little except the chance to shrivel and die.

The only possible dividend of "black power" is embodied in its offer to millions of frustrated and deprived and persecuted black people of a solace, a tremendous psychological lift, quite apart from its political and economic implications.

Ideologically it dictates "up with black and down with white" in precisely the same fashion that South Africa reverses that slogan.

It is a reverse Mississippi, a reverse Hitler, a reverse Ku Klux Klan.

If these were evil in our judgment, what virtue can be claimed for black over white? If, as some proponents claim, this concept instills pride of race, cannot this pride be taught without preaching hatred or supremacy based upon race?

"No matter how endlessly they try to explain it, the term 'black power' means anti-white power."

Though it be clarified and clarified again, "black power" in the quick, uncritical and highly emotional adoption it has received from some segments of a beleaguered people can mean in the end only black death. Even if, through some miracle, it should be enthroned briefly in an isolated area, the human spirit, which knows no color or geography or time, would die a little, leaving for wiser and stronger and more compassionate men the painful beating back to the upward trail.

We of the NAACP will have none of this. We have fought it too long. It is the ranging of race against race on the irrelevant basis of skin color. It is the father of hatred and the mother of violence.

It is the wicked fanaticism which has swelled our tears, broken our bodies, squeezed our hearts and taken the blood of our black and white loved ones. It shall not now poison our forward march.

We seek, therefore, as we have sought these many years, the inclusion of Negro Americans in the nation's life, not their exclusion. This is our land, as much so as it is any American's—every square foot of every city and town and village. The task of winning our share is not the easy one of disengagement and flight, but the hard one of work, of short as well as long jumps, of disappointments, and of sweet successes.

In our Fight for Freedom we choose:

1. The power and the majesty of the ballot, the participation of free men in their government, both as voters and as honorable and competent elected and appointed public servants. Year in and year out, the NAACP voter registration work has proceeded. No one except the Federal Government has registered more Negro voters in Mississippi than the NAACP. In six weeks last summer more than twenty thousand new names were added by our workers alone, with additional thousands during an intensive renewal last winter. That work is continuing under the leadership of our Mississippi state president, Dr. Aaron Henry, and of our state director, Charles Evers. Later this month a summer task force will be at work in Louisiana. Already our South Carolina NAACP is busy on registration, as is our Alabama organization.

We are aware that a Louisiana young man, born along the Mississippi border, has been named and confirmed as one of the seven governors of the Federal Reserve Bank. We know that his extraordinary ability finally tipped the scales, but we know also, that, without ballot power, he would not even have been on the scales ready to be tipped.

2. We choose employment for our people—jobs not hidden by racial labels or euphemisms, not limited by racial restrictions in access and promotion, whether by employers or organized labor. We commend a growing number of corporations for expanding their employment of Negro applicants in technical and professional posts, but we insist that only the surface has been scratched.

We commend the "good guys" among the trade unions for the improvement in opportunities and advancement for the Negro worker, but we condemn the policies of some unions which have either barred or heavily handicapped the Negro worker. Negro employment is in a crisis stage. The rate of unemployment ranges from twice that of whites to four and five times the white rate in some areas. The answer to the complaint of employers that workers are not trained is to institute in-plant training, just as they have in other shortages. The apprentice training stranglehold must be broken, the racially separate seniority lines, the still-persisting segregated local and the remaining crude segregation in plant facilities must be abolished. The demonstrations before the U.S. Steel Corporation offices and plants under the cooperative leadership of Dr. John Nixon, our Alabama president, and Henry Smith, our Pennsylvania president, had wide and beneficial impact.

The Negro migrant worker, the forgotten man in the employment picture, must have attention.

In the Watts district of Los Angeles last year the unemployment rate was more than 30 percent, a rate higher than that during the great, nationwide depression of the 1930s. The Negro teenage rate is nearly 25 percent as against 13 percent for white teenagers.

Negro employment is a disaster area demanding the strict enforcement of Title VII of the 1964 Civil Rights Act. The NAACP has filed more than one thousand complaints with the Equal Employment Opportunity Commission and will file more until the law accomplishes what it was enacted to do. As evidence of his continuing concern, Congressman Augustus Hawkins of Los Angeles succeeded in having his bill relating to Federal employment passed by the House as an amendment to Title VII of the 1964 Civil Rights Act.

3. We choose to combat the color line in housing. In one breath our opinion-makers decry the existence of the poverty and filth and crime and degradation of the slums, but in the next they decry low-cost housing and fair housing laws. Here in California the hysteria over whether Negro Americans should live in gullies or be pushed into the sea reached the Proposition 14 stage which the state's highest court has declared unconstitutional. But who cares about the Constitution when a Negro might be enabled to move into the neighborhood? One could think black Americans were men from Mars. Instead, we have been here, side by side with the white folks (some of whom just got here), for 345 years.

They tell us to work hard and save our money, to go to school and prepare ourselves, to be "responsible," to rear and educate our children in a wholesome and directed family atmosphere, to achieve, to "get up in the world."

After we do all this, they look us in the eye and bar us from renting or buying a home that matches our achievements and one in keeping with our aspirations for further advancement.

Some public officials, including mayors of cities, and many candidates for election to public office are not above public double talk and private single talk on this issue. Any candidate who orates about basic Americanism or "the American way," but who hems and haws over fair housing legislation, is no friend of the Negro citizen.

The Administration's civil rights bill of 1966 with its vital section barring discrimination in the rental or sale of housing must be enacted with the amendment, already inserted by the committee, providing for administrative redress as well as court action.

Your Congressmen and Senators are at home until July 11 celebrating Independence Day—Freedom Day for the United States. See them or have your branch officers back home see them in person. Urge them to rub some freedom off on twenty million loyal Americans by voting for a strong civil rights bill. Of course the section on punishing in the Federal courts those who attack civil rights workers must pass. And we must have indemnification for victims.

4. Most of all, we choose to secure unsegregated, high quality public education for ourselves and our children. A new report, made public only last week, is a jolt for anyone who thought the 1954 Supreme Court decision or subsequent legislation solved the problem.

The report says officially and professionally what we have contended all along: that predominantly Negro schools are inferior to those attended largely by whites. Also that the achievement gap widens between the first grade and the twelfth. In other words, the longer our children attend racially segregated schools, the farther they fall behind white children.

And, lest the non-southerners feel smug, the report found that segregation for both whites and Negroes is more complete in the South, but "is extensive in other regions where the Negro population is concentrated: the urban North, Midwest and West."

The federal government, whose Office of Education has made some strong statements, must follow up with a strong enforcement of Title VI of the 1964 law. The empty promises of school officials and the defiance of the whole State of Alabama must not be accepted meekly by Federal officials. The furor over the guidelines issued by HEW is another version of the Dixie bluff on race which has worked so well for so many decades. The guidelines are mild. They are legal and not illegal as Governor Wallace proclaimed to his state's educators. They ask the southerners to do what is for them a strange thing: obey the school desegregation law. On this point the federal government must not yield. The Attorney General and the Department of Justice must back up resolutely the legality of federal action. There can be no temporizing.

Outside the South the call is for unrelenting activity to wipe out de facto school segregation. Boston, Massachusetts, has proved to be the Mississippi of the North. In fact, in fairness to Mississippi and in consideration of the starting points and traditions of the two places, Boston is below Mississippi on this issue. The details, the traps, the methods and the progress will be covered in workshop discussions, but here it must be said that before we can get jobs to earn increased income to buy and rent better homes, before we can contribute to the enrichment of our nation, we must have free access to quality education.

The man who shoots and burns and drowns us is surely our enemy, but so is he who cripples our children for life with inferior public education.

5. We also choose to wrestle with the complex problems of urban life, all of which include an attitude toward and a treatment of millions of Negro citizens. The solution of urban problems will become the solution of living in the last third of our century since more than 70 percent of Americans now live in urban communities.

If it has been asked once, it has been asked a hundred times: Are we going to have a long, hot summer? The answer has many facets, some extremely complex and difficult. But one quick answer is that the police everywhere can make or break urban racial tensions by their conduct toward minority group citizens.

Last summer you had here an upheaval that shook the world. To many of us who looked from afar, it appeared to be a wild, senseless rampage of hate and destruction. But that was far from the whole truth.

There was powder in Watts, piled up and packed down through the years: wide-scale unemployment, both adult and teenage, slum housing, crowded schools, nonexistent health facilities, inadequate transportation and—the Parker police attitude. Everyone was suspect and everyone was subject to harassment in one form or another. The community smoldered under the peculiar brand that police place upon a whole section with their constant sirens, their contemptuous searches, their rough talk, their ready guns and their general "Godalmightiness."

The lesson they and city officials have learned from last year is to seek not correction and improvement, but still more repression. Mayor Yorty and whoever writes his scripts testified in Sacramento in support of a so-called riot-control bill.

The only thing one has to remember about this bill is that it would allow a policeman to judge whether an utterance or an act is an incitement to riot! On his own judgment he could arrest or club or otherwise deter—or shoot—a person whom he (not the law or the courts) deemed to be an inciter of riot. Down the drain goes freedom of speech and down, too, possibly, goes a life.

The McCone Report on the 1965 riot called for "costly and extreme" remedies for Watts, undertaken with a "revolutionary attitude." The answer of the City of Los Angeles was to vote down a hospital bond issue. The answer of Mayor Yorty and of his man, Chief Parker, is a trampling-tough riot-control bill which, if enacted, would loose the police, almost without restraint, upon a populace sick to death—literally—of race control. To blot out any remaining fitful light, one of the gubernatorial candidates, full of disavowals, is the darling of those ultra-conservatives who believe in iron control of what they call "violence in the streets"—their code name for Negroes.

If this is the best that a great city can bring to a hard urban problem, one largely of its own making, then God pity both the whites and the Negroes!

We have no panacea for all these problems. We do not proclaim that what we declare here this week is going to change the course of the whole civil rights movement. We do not know all the answers to the George Wallace problem in Alabama, the James Eastland problem in Mississippi, or to the Boston, Massachusetts, school committee and its Louise Day Hicks problem. We certainly don't know the answers to foreign policy and to tax and interest rate puzzlers.

But in this unsettled time when shifts are the order of the day and when change is in the air, we can sail our NAACP ship "steady as she goes," with more drive to the turbines, more skill at the wheel, but no fancy capers for the sake of capers.

We can follow down into each community the really advanced blueprint of the White House Conference "To Fulfill These Rights," which covered four principal areas: economic security and welfare, education, housing, and the administration of justice.

We can expand and point up the community services of our NAACP branches, each of which is, in reality, a citizenship clinic. Just as medical clinics need specialists to cure physical ills, so our branch clinics should recruit volunteer specialists to diagnose and minister to social ills.

We must involve people in the communities in the solution of our problem—not limiting ourselves to our church or lodge or club group.

We must keep the pressure on our local and state education systems through the employment of every legitimate technique: protests, surveys, discussions, demonstrations, picketing and negotiation. Nothing should be overlooked in fighting for better education. Be persistent and ornery; this will be good for the lethargic educational establishment and will aid the whole cause of public education.

Our branches are at work in their territories. In Baltimore, the NAACP won a case against the police commissioner which the Fourth Circuit Court of Appeals declared revealed the most flagrant police practices ever to come before the court. The Blair County, Pennsylvania, NAACP is busy rooting out the remaining discrimination in public accommodations in Clearfield, Pennsylvania.

The Wilmington, Ohio, NAACP has a program for tutoring adults and drop-outs and has recruited college professors and students and textbooks to make the project effective. The Bay City, Michigan, NAACP also has a tutorial program under way as well as continuous work on industrial employment practices and housing. The Stillwater, Oklahoma, NAACP is active on a child care center project and on high school desegregation.

And the Montgomery County, West Virginia, NAACP, bless its heart, is 112 percent above last year in membership and 500 percent above last year in funds raised.

Thirty-one branches found time and funds to be present at the Meredith march rally in Jackson, Mississippi, even though the Association, at the last minute, was insulted by the barring of Charles Evers as an NAACP spokesman.

This is only part of the chronicle of "steady as she goes." In a world where the Mayor of Los Angeles is yelling "riot control," where Rhodesia says "never!" to black representation while in America SNCC raises the chant of black power, where the federal government at long last is committed, but both the far right and the far left offer vocal and vicious objection, someone has to drive the long haul toward the group goal of Negro Americans and the larger ideal of our young nation.

> ***"In this unsettled time when shifts are the order of the day and when change is in the air, we can sail our NAACP ship 'steady as she goes. . . .'"***

Our objective is basically as it was laid down in 1909 by the interracial founders of our NAACP. Back there William Lloyd Garrison expressed the strong feeling that the first NAACP conference "will utter no uncertain sound on any point affecting the vital subject. No part of it is too delicate for plain speech. The republican experiment is at stake, every tolerated wrong to the Negro reacting with double force upon white citizens guilty of faithlessness to their brothers."

As it was then, so it is today. The republican experiment is at stake in 1966. More than that, the dream of a brotherhood in equality and justice is imperiled.

Our fraternity tonight, as it was then, is the fraternity of man, not the white, or brown, or yellow, or black man, but man.

SOURCES

Bosmajian, Haig A., and Hamida Bosmajian, editors, *The Rhetoric of the Civil Rights Movement,* Random House, 1969.

Boulware, Marcus H., *The Oratory of Negro Leaders: 1900-1968,* Negro Universities Press, 1969.

Foner, Philip S., editor, *The Voice of Black America: Major Speeches by Negroes in the United States, 1797-1971,* Simon & Schuster, 1972.

Smith, Arthur L., and Stephen Robb, editors, *The Voice of Black Rhetoric: Selections*, Allyn & Bacon, 1971.

Wilkins, Roy, with Tom Mathews, *Standing Fast: The Autobiography of Roy Wilkins*, Viking, 1982.

Williams, Jayme Coleman, and McDonald Williams, editors, *The Negro Speaks: The Rhetoric of Contemporary Black Leaders*, Noble & Noble, 1970.

Whitney M. Young, Jr.

1921–1971

African American social worker and civil rights leader

One of the titans of the civil rights movement of the 1960s was Whitney M. Young, Jr., who served for a tumultuous decade as executive director of the National Urban League. Within just a few years after taking over the reins of the venerable organization in 1961, he managed to change its image from that of a rather stodgy alliance of conservative blacks and white businessmen to one that reflected his own personal dynamism and impatience with the slow pace of improvement—especially economic improvement—in the status of African Americans. For maintaining close contacts with the white corporate and political leaders he felt were in the best position to help him achieve his ambitious agenda, Young endured the insults of more militant blacks who considered him an "Uncle Tom." Yet he was truly one of his generation's most forceful and outspoken advocates for changes that promised to reverse centuries of neglect and deprivation.

A native of Kentucky, Young was one of three children born to the director of a boarding high school for blacks and his wife, a teacher. After graduating from the school his father headed, he went on to Kentucky State College and earned his bachelor's degree in premed studies. A yearlong stint as a high school teacher and assistant principal ended around 1942 when Young entered the military and was sent to study engineering at the Massachusetts Institute of Technology before heading overseas with an anti-aircraft artillery group. His experiences—both positive and negative—as a black Army private under the command of a white Southern captain led him to consider pursuing a career other than medicine, and upon his return home he enrolled in the social work program at the University of Minnesota, from which he received his master's degree in 1947.

From 1947 until 1950, Young was director of industrial relations and vocational guidance for the St. Paul (Minnesota) branch of the National Urban League and a lecturer at the local College of St. Catherine. He then moved on to Omaha, Nebraska, to serve as head of that city's Urban League chapter. During this same period, he taught in the School of Social Work at the University of Nebraska and at Creighton University. As the civil rights movement took shape in the South, however, Young wanted very much to be a part of it, so in 1954 he headed to Atlanta University to become dean of its School of Social Work.

In 1961, while he was on leave from Atlanta University to study at Harvard on a Rockefeller Foundation grant, Young was appointed to succeed Lester Granger as head of the National Urban League, then at a crossroads in its fifty-year existence. Founded in New York City, it had functioned basically as a social-work agency devoted to the economic problems of urban blacks in the North, especially those who had migrated from rural areas of the South. By forging alliances with white businessmen, the conservative-leaning blacks of the Urban League hoped to secure job training and placement for African American industrial workers and thus improve their standard of living. With the dawn of the 1960s, however, the Urban League—never as large or as militant as the NAACP and some of the newer groups—seemed particularly out of step with the times. Young's mission thus became one of revitalization and renewal, of using the long-established ties with white decision-makers to formulate new plans of action and facilitate the changes other activists were demanding.

Outspoken and articulate, Young was an ideal choice to publicize the Urban League's new mission. To that end, he contributed numerous articles and columns to magazines and newspapers and spoke to audiences throughout the United States about his plans to fight unemployment, poverty, and hopelessness in the black community. One such occasion was in 1963 at the annual meeting of the Urban League when he discussed his so-called "domestic Marshall Plan," a reference to the post-World War II rebuilding program fashioned by Secretary of State George C. Marshall that provided massive amounts of aid to European countries. Young unveiled his proposal during an especially turbulent spring and summer that had already seen thousands of demonstrations and riots erupt in cities across the country. His controversial suggestion that African Americans deserved preferential treatment to make up for years of slavery and segregation thrust him into the national spotlight for the first (but certainly not the last) time. A lengthy excerpt from his address is reprinted here from Negro Protest Thought in the Twentieth Century *(Bobbs-Merrill, 1965).*

This year's National Conference of the Urban League convenes during a crucial period in America's race relations history....

Every major city in the United States has felt some manifestation of the unrest and burning desire of its Negro citizens for equality—now! And hundreds of smaller communities have had reflected in their mirror the discontent that has spread like wildfire and that has illuminated the land with the flames of a modern revolution the counterpart of which neither this nation or any nation has ever witnessed.

This revolution bears no similarity, however, to the American Revolution, or to the French Revolution, or to the Russian Revolution. There is no attempt here to overthrow a government. This is a revolution against historic injustice, against a way of life, against persons who maintain that the measure of achievement of man is determined by and related to the color of his skin. This is a revolution peculiarly characterized by a heroic drive and a courageous fight to gain the rights and respect that should be synonymous with the word "American." It is a revolution not by black people against white people, but by people who are right against those who are wrong.

This revolution is unlike any other also, because, after three hundred years of deprivation, the deprived seek redress for their grievances in an expression of faith in a nation that has done very little to develop and nurture such faith. Their demands are simple and elemental, and those who would describe them as difficult and complicated do a disservice to America and to Americans.

This revolution is what I chose last year at our National Conference to call a "Revolution

Whitney M. Young, Jr.

of Expectation." Today I would call it a "Revolution of Witnessing."

A review by me now of the events in this conflict as they have occurred since we met together last year is unnecessary. For there is not a person in this room tonight who cannot recall with his mind's eye, and with vividness and recurring horror, the photographs of brutality and barbarism. There is not a person in this room tonight who cannot remember with pride and humility the pictures of the bright-eyed children and courageous youth participants in the events of recent months.

For the Negro citizen, therefore, these are acts of bearing witness to his faith in democracy through peaceful nonviolent demonstration, and by channelling in constructive ways justified resentments and pent-up frustrated emotions that have been born out of age-old abuses and contemptuous indignities.

For the white citizen these events mean bearing witness to the fact that democracy is more than a convenient institution through which privileges and material products flow to him.

For both, democracy is a way of life, an ideal in which all share its rewards, as well as its responsibilities. Indeed, without this concept, democracy has no meaning and certainly no permanence.

For the church and its membership, this is a time of witnessing that piety rests not in credal affirmation, but in the confirmation of deeds.

For the public official—whether city, state or federal—witnessing means greater concern for broad, democratic promises and human rights, rather than preoccupation with technical, constitutional details and states' rights.

For the private sector of our society—whether business, labor, or health and welfare—this is a time for witnessing that the free enterprise system works equally well for *all* American citizens.

For the Urban League this is a time to express willingness to witness that while our past contributions need no defense or apology, our future challenges and opportunities are greater and more demanding than any we have ever faced. These are times that call for us to be frank, not only with the perpetuators of injustice as to their responsibilities, but equally frank and forthright with the victims of injustice as to their responsibilities in this new day that is full with promise of a brighter destiny for those whom we are committed to serve.

It is not enough to remind white Americans that for fifty-three years the Urban League has warned them of this inevitable consequence of indifference; neither is it necessary to boast of League contributions that now help to make it possible for Negro Americans to express their grievances so courageously.

The past is prologue. Today the nation and its Negro citizens ask of the Urban League: "What have you done for me recently? What will you be doing for me tomorrow?"

We in the Urban League are in the position of being able to answer these questions in language and with machinery possessed by no other agency. Our job is clear. Our job is to give meaning and reality to the revolution to which we all now serve as witnesses.

As we win the battle for civil rights, we can, and might well lose the war for human rights.

In this age of automation and urbanization, the demands on Americans differ. The victories so courageously won in the streets can easily become an empty, hollow mockery if we do not simultaneously equip ourselves with the skills, the values, and the sense of community responsibility and participation which the future will demand.

At the risk of being misunderstood by the currently immature; by those who are merely seeking to remove the symbols that disturb their consciences; or even by the naive who believe that equality is a condition automatically arrived at through the lowering of overt barriers, the League hereby announces its intent to pursue what we know to be a necessary program.

We have this year shared our identity with all others who struggle for the goal of equality, and we will continue to do so. But while we applaud and respect the victories which they have won, by the use of methods different from those of the Urban League, we will continue to seek their understanding and mutual respect for the long-range and vitally necessary programs and methods of the Urban League—programs and methods which can only be achieved by a professionally-structured agency, devoting itself full time to this problem.

This we see not as competitive or in any way discrediting but rather as complementing and supplementing. To put it bluntly: We say that while there must be those who in the interest of justice and equality must walk the picket line in front of restaurants, hotels, theaters, business establishments—these same persons, and others, with equal zest and determination, must walk to the libraries, to the adult education classes, and to the voting registrar's office. And they must take time to serve on policy-making bodies of agencies and institutions. For reality now dictates that we must recognize that those who would enter the new doors of opportunity must have the skills to qualify, the money to pay, and the confidence and security of knowing that they are, in fact, equal citizens.

"The real test . . . of the sincerity and the maturity of all of us now participating in this struggle will be our willingness to labor in the vineyards where we are not televised and photographed, and in those places where our contributions may not be popular news copy."

I am not offering a substitute, or an either/or suggestion. Both are necessary—both must be done. The real test, therefore, of the sincerity and the maturity of all of us now participating in this struggle will be our willingness to labor in the vineyards where we are not televised and photographed, and in those places where our contributions may not be popular news copy.

I feel very deeply that the increasing numbers of Negro women, as well as our allies among men and women of other racial groups, who are willing to volunteer a few hours a week to tutor youngsters who bear the scars of generations of deprivation, are making a lasting contribution to the struggle—a contribution as lasting as that made by the gallant heroes who go to jail, or those who lie in the streets.

The Urban League is challenged, therefore, to see that the barriers of yesterday—the barriers built by prejudice, fear and indifference which are now crumbling—are not replaced by new barriers of apathy, of underdeveloped skills, of lack of training. If this happens, our gains will be but temporary, our victories hollow.

Protest we must. Demonstrate if necessary. These are the time-tested weapons for correcting injustices and righting historic wrongs. But these alone are not enough. We will only have cleared the site. The next task is to build upon that site the new house of true democracy. This requires different skills—but equal commitment and equal energy. This we will do. This we must do. The same faith and determination that have been responsible for the Negro's survival in a hostile and cruel society will respond to the new challenge. That faith and determination will respond if given reasonable understanding and assistance from a total society more sympathetic and honest than heretofore. . . .

As George Bernard Shaw has said: "America has relegated the Negro citizen to be a bootblack, and now condemns him because his hands are dirty."

There is today great talk among our many new and self-appointed advisors about self-help and personal responsibility on the part of the Negro citizen himself. The curious, if not tragic aspect of this, is that this talk comes from so many white Americans who themselves have been passive participants in, or passive observers of the age-old denials responsible for the lacks which they now deplore.

If this is not done, then Negro America will have less need to be defensive, and its leadership will not run the risk of being misunderstood when it addresses itself to this aspect. Today nothing is more discouraging or inhibiting to responsible Negro leadership, and to discussion of self-help and self-responsibility, than the fact that this has become the chief theme song of many self-appointed advisors who would claim now to be our friends, but who for all these years have never raised their voices against the obvious racial injustices—those who even today say little about the real responsibilities of white Americans.

As President Kennedy noted recently—demonstrations would be minimized, if not eliminated, if there was as much concern and indignation about the injustices and the discrimination against Negro citizens to which these demonstrations are addressed, as there is to the demonstrations themselves.

The present and future test of the concern and sincerity of the responsible white leadership of America will be the degree to which they assume what seems to me clear-cut and obvious tasks. Let me indicate them.

1. White leadership must be honest about the fact that throughout the history of this country there has existed a special, privileged class of citizens who have received special preferential treatment over other citizens purely on the basis of an accident of birth. The problems of social disorganization and racial unrest which we face today are the direct result of this fact. Honesty and decency should compel our mass media and responsible majority leadership to admit a long-established sociological fact—that the high ratio of dependency, crime and social disorganization among Negro citizens which so many of them deplore, actually occurs in the same degree among white citizens of the same socio-economic class. Negro citizens representing the middle-income group have actually less social disorganization than white citizens in similar economic circumstances. These problems, therefore, are problems not of race, but of socio-economic condition.

2. Responsible white leadership and the mass media must, with honesty and sincerity, promote and teach the idea that integration should and can be viewed as an opportunity for all Americans, rather than an irritating and uncomfortable problem—that integration can provide for all of us the creative experience that flows from inclusiveness, rather than the stagnating and damaging effects that accompany exclusiveness.... It is poignantly tragic that American citizens debate the rights of fellow Americans to live in the same neighborhoods, attend the same schools, eat in the same restaurants, or attend the same houses of worship.

This is a time when great minds and great nations will reflect their true greatness by concentrating on the multitude of things we have in common. For the truth is, that today white Americans and black Americans are equally and mutually dependent upon each other.

3. Responsible white leadership in this nation can demonstrate the sincerity of its desire to accelerate constructive transition, by enthusiastic support of the Urban League's massive "domestic Marshall Plan," as the only fair and realistic way of closing the gap and correcting historic abuses. This is little indeed to ask of a great nation if it is to truly provide world leadership in the brief time allowed us by a fast-moving world society....

In broad terms this plan calls for a transitional period of intensified special effort of corrective measures in education, in training and employment, in housing and in health and welfare. It calls for the same kind of expression of generosity and understanding which motivated this country to spend twelve billion dollars under the original Marshall Plan in a four-year period to rehabilitate war-torn Europe. It calls for the same kind of concern that has motivated our nation more recently to spend millions of dollars in providing special help for Hungarian and Cuban refugees fleeing oppression. Should this nation—can this nation do less for its own citizens whose blood, sweat and tears have gone into building and preserving this great country which is ours?

4. Responsible white leadership must provide support—unprecedented support—both morally and financially, to existing responsible Negro agencies and their leadership. As Winston Churchill said so forthrightly to America during the moment of England's gravest crisis in World War II: "Give us the tools and we will do the job."

For fifty-three years the Urban League has valiantly endeavored to provide America with responsible leadership. But the League was forced to do so with token financial support offered with the subtle inference that even such meager support might be jeopardized if there was too close identification with the legitimate aspirations of the masses of Negro citizens for equality, dignity and first-class citizenship.

Today, however, there is strong evidence that a different and more mature point of view is now being adopted by corporations, government, labor and enlightened community funds. It is becoming clear now, that if the impatience and the heightened aspirations of the masses of Negro citizens are to be protected and to be channelled along constructive lines, then the Urban League must of necessity be involved in this feat of social engineering. To divorce ourselves from this would be an expression of irresponsibility; to isolate our organization from this activity would be to deny corporations, foundations and community funds a unique opportunity for representation and participation in a new era of social planning. The Urban League will be value-less to responsible institutions in our society if it does not maintain communication with and the respect of other responsible Negro organizations and the respect of the masses of Negro citizens.

The final aspirations of Negro citizens can never be realized unless they, too, respect the distinctive and vital role which the Urban League can play—a role which the Urban League is peculiarly and uniquely qualified for, and can perform. Only the Urban League has the professional equipment and the know-how for this role, and the contacts and machinery to implement. In this moment of grave racial crisis, the Urban League is gearing itself for accelerated activity in its traditional role; and girding itself to maintain identity with all other responsible groups in the struggle for human rights. In this process we will be enabled to understand motives and test the sincerity of our friends and supporters.

5. And finally, responsible white leadership must not permit itself to be drawn into anxiety around an increasingly popular phrase "reverse reactions." For to do so is to suggest that there are still degrees of citizenship to which society is committed to grant Negro Americans.

Our expression must be loud and clear. Once and for all we must state it: Human rights and civil rights in America are not negotiable. There does not exist in the hands of any one group of citizens either the divine right or the constitutional authority to give or to withhold from another, rights that are God-given and legally implemented.

Two years later, on August 1, 1965, Young again faced his Urban League colleagues at their annual convention. Speaking in Miami Beach, Florida, he shared with them an "agenda for the future" that addressed what he felt were some of the major problems left unresolved by several years of protest and progress. Excerpts from his speech are reprinted from The Negro Speaks: The Rhetoric of Contemporary Black Leaders *(Noble and Noble, 1970).*

This 1965 conference of the National Urban League finds us at an all-important midpoint of the 1960s, a decade which has been characterized as the "Decade of the Social Revolution," a decade which history will undoubtedly label as containing the most dramatic and provocative phase of the civil rights movement. This is not to imply that the revolution began at the end of 1959 or that it will end in 1970, for surely its seeds were sown many, many years earlier, during the era of slavery some three hundred years ago and refertilized in the 1860s with the Emancipation Proclamation—which decreed only in fact freedom for the Negro.

And whether or not it ends in 1970 will depend on how effective we have been in destroying the roots of despair and disillusionment and transplanting the seeds of hope and promise into the more fertile soil of plenty and prosperity.

Today, we recognize a new mood of the Negro. Many factors have contributed to bring this about: World War II; the media of mass communication which awakened the nation's conscience; legal gains too long delayed; and numerous other catalysts which helped the Negro citizen's determination for equality to burst into full bloom at the start of this decade.

Today, the Negro citizen—in all of his achievements, his gains, his plights, his miseries—

stands tall as never before; and it is our purpose at this National Urban League Conference—we who have contributed significantly to this new stature of the Negro—to fully survey our journey, to reassess our progress, and to outline an agenda for the future that will assure real, honest communication between all peoples. . . .

The year 1964 saw the fruition of many of our hopes and aspirations. The churches became more sensitized to the Judeo-Christian commitment. Business and industry began a more conscientious subscription to the principle of equal opportunity for all. The federal government passed the most comprehensive Civil Rights Act in history, and President Johnson launched a War on Poverty famous for its corrective measures and its commitments to expanded programs of education and retraining. Time after time he has matched these programs with strong words, calling for a clear and honest recognition of what America has historically done to the Negro and must, therefore, now do with the Negro—not only to correct the abuses of the past but also to provide America with the rich resources of that segment of our population too long denied the opportunity to contribute to the development of their country.

But lest we lapse into smug complacency because of these few gains—major though some may be—let us be reminded, and quickly, that a revolution is not a special moment in time; rather, it is made up of before and after, and there is still much to do to complete the before. The temper of a revolution is not tomorrow, but now; not part of the way, but all of the way. Wisdom must be developed to cope with obstacles and interim strategies, and action must be brought forth to guide it to its intended outcome. . . .

The Negro citizen wants racial peace, yes; but a peace based on justice. He wants order, yes; but, as Oliver Wendell Holmes, Jr., phrased it, an order based on law—the same law for black men as for white. We, as Negro citizens, stand for progress, yes—but a progress in which our role is that of equals and brothers—in which the progress of our nation is based on partnership, not on paternalism. . . .

If the apostles of violence are to be thwarted, then the answer is clear. More than intrepid police work and federal action will be required. Across the nation, the voices of discord and hate must be drowned under the crushing weight of enlightened public opinion. For it is public opinion—not the courts or the police—that is the final bulwark of our democratic institutions. A public that does not cherish its laws with an outspoken courage will soon see them trampled underfoot by those who strike in the dark.

To effect peaceful change, our allies in the civil rights movement have distinguished themselves by the character of their statesmanship in the past year. The NAACP is carrying forward an unrelenting battle in the courts and in the legislative halls. The Student Nonviolent Coordinating Committee and the Congress of Racial Equality continue to press their campaign for voter registration, political initiative, and education; and the Southern Christian Leadership Conference goes forward with its mass marches and its banners flying—from Selma, Alabama, to Chicago, Illinois.

As for the Urban League, our role was never more clear—never more necessary. For as we share with our courageous brothers the task of reducing the more visible barriers of race, our primary responsibility is to ensure that Negro citizens have the qualifications and the resources with which to take advantage of the opening doors.

> *"Let us be reminded, and quickly, that a revolution is not a special moment in time; rather, it is made up of before and after, and there is still much to do to complete the before."*

Jointly, we have created a glorious revolution to change the spirit, laws, and institutions of America. And we of the Urban League must focus on the next phase—one that is every bit as critical and as difficult as those that have gone before. This phase must be a revolution of fulfillment that will call forth all the grandeur and greatness that is in our people.

Our goal, therefore, must be to seek to establish a standard of life for all men in which such social pathologies are eliminated. Only this can lead to real fulfillment—to the achievement by each human being of his or her highest, God-given potential. And this can be a more powerful weapon in our international competition for the minds of men than atomic achievements or a successful landing on the moon. As the late novelist Albert Camus once wrote, the only true nobility lies not in being superior to others but in becoming superior to one's former self.

A comparison of the status of the Negro race with even the present inadequate level of the general society indicates how far we have to go to close the gap. And for those who assert they are tired of hearing these facts, I say we are tired of living these facts. We are tired of seeing every second colored family living in poverty, as compared with every fifth white family. We are tired of trying to live on an annual income of only fifty-five percent of that enjoyed by the majority of American families. We are tired of an unemployment rate more than twice that of white workers.

We can no longer endure a condition in which nearly twice as many Negro infants as whites die during their first year of life because of discriminatory medical care—an infant mortality rate of forty per one thousand live births, as compared with twenty-two for white babies.

We cannot bear witness to forty-four percent of our citizens living in slums, compared with thirteen percent of whites—and a rate of overcrowding three times as great.

We are gravely concerned that twenty-five percent of Negro women are separated or living apart from their husbands, as compared with eight percent of white women; that twenty-one percent of Negro families are headed by a female, as compared with nine percent of white families. We confess our tempers rise when we witness that fifty-six percent of all Negro children are at some time dependent upon public assistance, as compared with eight percent of white children, and that fifty percent of the unemployed and out-of-school youth in this country are Negro, when they represent only fifteen percent of the population in this age range. . . .

This is the Urban League's charge; this is our adventure; this is what Negro citizens and the nation expect of us. . . .

But before we move into identification of those items which must have priority on our agenda for the future, let us make it clear that we regard as basic to all we do the strengthening of the Negro family—and that we recognize that the key, the crucial element in any crusade designed to strengthen that family, is the Negro male! The matriarchal family, consciously and cruelly produced by a hostile society seeking first to enslave and second to exploit, must be dramatically changed. In the Negro family, as in all others, strength and stability must emerge from a father who can share the responsibilities within the family and who can act as a provider and as an appropriate role model.

Therefore, the Negro male becomes our target. No citizen in our society has suffered more. He has been punished for being aggressive and prevented from becoming responsible. His psychological castration has dealt a crippling, disastrous blow to his family unit—a unit which must be the cornerstone of our drive for fulfillment. We cannot use the results of injustices of the past as an excuse now for excluding the Negro male from the mainstream of American economic life. The youngster whose father has never held a steady job will lack the will to learn because he himself cannot believe he has the chance to earn. His need is for a home in which a working father is a daily fact of life—not a fantasy.

Therefore, with the future of the Negro family in mind, the National Urban League hereby submits a clarion call for—

1. An immediate program of economic improvement that will include retraining for those automated from their jobs, and a massive program of public works and urban rehabilitation designed not only to rehabilitate our land and urban centers but also, as a basic consideration, to assure gainful employment for every individual in the labor market of this country.

2. A more realistic meeting of the health and welfare needs of individuals and families. Guaranteed minimum income must be accompanied by maximum standards for health and medical care, corrective as well as preventive. We need to develop a nationwide network of community health and information centers. We need a national health insurance plan that would assure quality medical care for all our citizens.

We need a nationwide network of community clinics—urban and rural—where decentralized services can be taken practically to the doorstep of the ghetto resident.

We need a major effort to break the color line in child adoptions, such as we have been able to do in employment. The courts and the foundling homes today must abandon the use of racial factors in adoptions. Too many child welfare agencies are guilty of rank discrimination in preventing childless white couples from adopting Negro babies. And we need, at the same time, more concern on the part of Negro middle-class families and more responsiveness from them to the cries of the homeless. . . .

3. The improvement of our educational levels and our educational systems. We are all familiar with the failure of the American educational system to provide good schools for all—and particularly for Negro children and youth. I will not chronicle again the long list of abuses which Negro pupils must live with every day in the slum schools of America. Anyone who denies that our children are receiving the poorest education, the poorest instruction, that they are exposed to the poorest facilities, the poorest texts, is just plain out of touch with reality.

Underlying the Urban League's approach to this problem must be the conviction that education today is truly a national issue, and that we will rise or fall as a nation depending on whether we succeed in setting standards and providing resources so that we may educate the American people for living and working in—and contributing to—the national society, rather than merely a regional or local area. We have become a mobile nation. . . .

4. A broader and more realistic housing program that will disperse future public housing and permit low income families to purchase homes, and the establishment of a federal fair housing law to break up the immoral and restrictive covenants which have produced a system of intolerable and inhumane ghettos.

To deny Negroes a place to live because of their color is a conspiracy in restraint of trade. With few exceptions our appeals to the housing industry have been a monument to futility. We need a ringing national affirmation of our intention to do what is right not simply to refrain from doing what is wrong. We need a federal civil rights act for housing—an act which will open the doors for Negro families in today's existing market. . . .

The agenda for the future which I have outlined here tonight does not pretend to detail all of the various needs and remedies of our society. These needs will be met and remedies found—if we will them. The important consideration is whether or not we have the fortitude to enable Negro citizens to achieve fulfillment—as well as to help millions of white citizens.

The life of man is made up of two parts. He lives as a social animal in the larger world and as an individual within his own internal world. The movement for civil rights must grapple with both. It must ask Negro citizens to strive for excellence just as it demands of white citizens that they strive for equality.

Just as we press for equality without, we must prepare for excellence within. To win one without the other is to lead half a life, a dismal, stifling existence, devoid of meaning, usefulness, and fulfillment.

This knowledge is sure to be greeted by many without enthusiasm. Some of us will resent the standard of excellence as an imposition, just as inflexible whites regard equality as an affront.

Our pains and sorrows are by no means concluded. In a hundred Harlems, the grief of our people is great. But so is our hope, our fortitude, our courage, our faith, and our spirit. Once again we hear the roar of the mighty waters of which Frederick Douglass spoke—the steady and relentless drumming of the tides of change upon the shores of our national life. Beyond today's struggle, however, I believe there lies a tranquil sea upon which we may one day embark. Our vision must look forward toward it—the promise of a society of equality and excellence, of justice and of unity, undivided by distinctions of race, unshackled by issues of class, unbowed by fears of want.

"Just as we press for equality without, we must prepare for excellence within. To win one without the other is to lead half a life. . . ."

Toward this goal the revolution for equality is well begun—but the revolution of fulfillment has only just begun. It was Franklin D. Roosevelt who said "the only limits on our future are our doubts." I would paraphrase that by saying that the only limits to our realization of tomorrow will be our doubts of today.

May I close with the words of a great rabbi—uttered in a prayer, but which in this context could also be regarded as a plea:

> *Lord, give us men who are proud of their godliness, and yet humble in their humanity—men who know themselves, but who in knowing themselves do not ignore others . . .*
>
> *Lord, give us men—men like Abraham Lincoln, who did not stop at the cheap art of es-*

pousing causes, but who championed men amongst the anonymous mass of men; men like him whose piety lay not in credal affirmation, but rather in the confirmation of his deeds.

Lord, give us men—for our age needs men who can fight together not only for their physical preservation but for the potentialities of moral living. To this end we need Thy help, and with Thy help we may yet—all of us—become men, all of us brothers, all of us Thy children, all of us truly human.

One of the chief preoccupations of politicians, sociologists, business leaders, and others during the 1960s was the future of the American city. Congested streets, decaying buildings, pollution, crime, racial unrest, fiscal woes—all that and more clearly signaled that the nation's urban areas were facing a crisis of unprecedented proportions. As both a social worker and head of the Urban League, Young was deeply disturbed about the situation; he was convinced that the economic impact of this relentless downward spiral would eventually prove catastrophic not only to the black community but to the entire country. On February 28, 1967, he spoke in Cambridge, Massachusetts, to a meeting of the Joint Center for Urban Studies of the Massachusetts Institute of Technology and Harvard University. In his remarks, he outlined the major difficulties as he saw them and warned that unless some action was taken soon, many cities would succumb to a variety of destructive forces and descend into chaos. The text of his address is taken from Representative American Speeches: 1966-1967 *(Wilson, 1967).*

Here at the outset I may as well state my central thesis, which is that the central cities of this increasingly urban nation are not only threatened with collapse but are, in fact, collapsing, in large part due to the fiscal drain of the ghetto. As a consequence, what we are confronted with in the civil rights struggle is no longer a problem for the Negro alone, but for the whole society.

Throughout the country, the major cities are in trouble, scarred by slums and ghettos, threatened by racial strife and crippled by inadequate finances. Predictions are that the nation's urban population will double by the beginning of the next century and unless adequate steps are taken to avoid disaster, so will the problems of the big cities. Without radical action, our cities are destined to become centers of chaos.

One speaks of the possibility of violence with caution. Too often, to predict the possibility of violence is interpreted as an incitement to violence. But I infinitely prefer to be called an alarmist than to stand by, a silent witness to impending crisis. If what I say is interpreted as the message of an alarmist, then I can only say that Paul Revere was an alarmist.

I assume that what we are really talking about here, in talking about the crisis of the cities, are the problems of people—that we are not confining ourselves simply to questions of bricks and mortar in our consideration of the urban scene—and that we are concerned with the problems of people living in an urban environment, an environment to which mankind did not come naturally. Many of these problems derive from tangible factors, many from intangibles—from feelings of anonymity, of being nameless and faceless, a feeling of being lost in the great urban mass. Most of these latter derive from rootlessness and the lack of a personal stake in the community.

The questions before us become questions of how to provide the urban resident, and most particularly the slum and ghetto resident, with a stake in his own community, how to diminish the sense of anonymity he feels, how to reduce the impersonality of the urban environment, and, in the process, how to approach all the problems affecting the society-at-large.

Urbanization, first of all, causes severe stresses both for the community and the individual. Housing shortages are chronic in all our major cities. Educational facilities in our slums are inferior from the standpoint of social and welfare services. Urbanization perhaps has its most profound impact on the structure of family institutions. The old traditions and values of the original family unit disintegrate under the impact of urbanization. The problems of the ghetto invade every aspect of life. It is our responsibility, in this society, to insure that the same skills, genius and creative drive that have gone into brick-and-mortar progress throughout the world, into the building of bridges, highways and tunnels, and indeed into smashing the atom and flights into space, must and do, now, go into planning with people for their own social needs. Only in this way can our cities reflect viable functional modes of productive living rather than struggles for survival against despair, hopelessness and frustration. Children then are not walled off from grass and sky and adults need not be faced with a monotonous routine which, at best, becomes a matter of existing—and without much choice.

Man in the urban complex has more than just physiological needs—the needs for food, clothing and shelter. He also has psychological needs—the needs for attention, affection, status and a feeling of making a contribution to his community.

At one time a man was adequate and had status if he simply provided a roof over the head of his family and could give his children a piece of candy from time to time. To be able to perform these simple acts was sufficient to obtain physiological and psychological satisfaction and to provide him with status in the community where he lived.

But living in the city demands more in terms of skills and of sophistication and so, man, newly transplanted within the urban complex, faces, and feels, alienation, a sense of rejection and loneliness, which makes even more painful the vision of those who are more affluent than he in the affluent society he sees all about him; and he either reacts with hostility by concluding that he is being exploited by the forces that are making others affluent, or he is diminished in his own self-estimation and says to himself, "I'm a failure." Such self-devaluation carries over into his role as a husband and as a father and into his concept of his own status and dignity.

Under the burden of anxiety, individual urban man becomes apathetic, overwhelmed, withdrawn. Because he doesn't want to acknowledge that he himself is inadequate in a new setting, he must cite powers bigger than himself, and what he says to himself and the community is, "I don't care," "I don't want to succeed anyhow," "You can't beat the system," "You can't fight City Hall." Apathy is hopelessness, powerlessness and the forgetting of the most important fact, the fact that money is not power, that status is not power, that color can never be power. That the greatest power is to be right. And if you're right and believe in that right, you can get power. The Negro cause in America today is right and that's why it upsets those who refuse to accept change.

The question before us is how, given all the factors that make up reality, we can build into urban society the human institutions which will provide the experience of community. The problem is how to make the urban environment human and humane, how to make the geographical entity in which so many people reside livable, how to guarantee that people do not live as part of an amorphous mass, as impersonal cogs in the urban complex where the size and formality and the impersonal quality of the urban setting tend to deprive the individual man of his sense of identity.

I am prepared to say without hesitation that, in large measure, this country's success or failure will be gauged by the success or failure of Negro Americans in their struggle for existence in the urban environment, and on the success or failure of white Americans in meeting the challenges posed by the circumstances in which the bulk of American Negroes live. The real test of the urban structure will be whether or not the Negro within it benefits and succeeds on a par with his white peer in the larger society.

The simple fact is that despite all the frenzied activity, despite all the well intentioned efforts, and all the signs of real progress in the last decade and more, the gap between nonwhite citizens in the United States and white citizens has not been closed. In most instances it is not even narrowing—it is widening.

The time is clearly past for half way measures, token gestures, pilot programs and halfhearted, one-dimensional, small-scale efforts, no matter how well intentioned. The crisis of our cities defies any such simple solutions. The expanding ghettos are not only thoroughly destructive to the people who live in them, but they threaten the welfare of every major city with strangulation and dry-rot. As one mark of our urbanity today we now have more people living in slums than we have on farms. The United States Census shows twenty-one million on farms; twenty-two million in slums—and that was in 1960. There is little doubt but that current figures, if available as of today, would show a still more remarkable picture.

"We are using a slingshot for a job that calls for nuclear weapons [and] applying band-aids in the curious expectation of stopping the growth of an advanced cancer."

We are using a slingshot for a job that calls for nuclear weapons. We are applying band-aids in the curious expectation of stopping the growth of an advanced cancer.

Three things are obvious. First, it is obvious that, whatever specific approach to the problems of the cities, the job is too big for government alone. Success will require the fullest possible commitment from every segment of this society, from the private sector as well as the public sector, from industry, labor, federal, state and local government, as well as from the nonprofit sector as represented by the foundations.

Second, we cannot confine ourselves to any single approach, or to any one method. There must be concerted and coordinated action on many fronts at once, in education, in housing, in employment and in health and welfare. The job requires the full application of American genius and imagination.

It is also essential to realize that the debate now raging over whether to disperse the ghetto or to rebuild it is a debate without substance. Housing stock in the ghetto must be redeemed or replaced no matter who lives there—this year or next. The schools in the ghetto must be made excellent no matter who attends them—this year or next. And neither can wait on solutions to other problems before the beginnings are made there.

Third, it is obvious that within the federal sector, with many of the legislative battles now won, that the struggle in the immediate future will lie to a considerable extent in the struggle for appropriations massive enough to get the job done that must be done.

The overriding question is one of the *will* to achieve definitive solutions. The first imperative is that we devise programs appropriately scaled to the size and urgency of the problems we face.

Recently, we have seen a growing recognition of the need for a massive effort, as expressed in the "Freedom Budget," which calls for an expenditure of $185 billion over the next ten years to be derived from the nation's "economic growth dividend"—a plan which fleshes out, puts meat on the bones of the domestic Marshall Plan we in the Urban League enunciated several years ago. We support this, and other, proposals which actively serve the same ends. These are proposals properly scaled to the size and urgency of the urban problems we face. Only when the need is understood on this scale and long-range programming is undertaken along these lines, will we be able to assume that we are on the road to adequate solutions.

Nothing short of action on the scale indicated in the "Freedom Budget" will allow us to rescue the cities from the problems that now beset them, restore a viable tax base to major municipalities, create a full-employment economy, and provide every American with a decent home and a decent education, all of which are essential objectives if the crisis of the cities is to be overcome. Otherwise we will have to face all the implications of finding our central cities more and more fully occupied by a dispossessed, undereducated, underemployed, embittered, angry, impatient, low-income population.

New York City is a good case in point. What is happening in one degree or another in every major metropolitan area in the country. New York's annual budget crisis occurs with the regularity of clockwork. It did not begin with the Lindsay administration and it will not end with the Lindsay administration. Where it will end may well determine the fate of the Republic.

A year ago, New York, deep in its desperate annual search for funds to make up the difference between public revenues and the cost of essential public services, faced a budget deficit of $518 million. The mayor stated then "that without new revenues a major reduction of all city services will be necessary resulting in a drastic change in the quality of life in New York City." In the course of the crisis the New York

Stock Exchange threatened to leave the city; the City University was threatened with seriously cutting back on the number of students it could accept and city hospitals were threatened with a catastrophic mass resignation of nurses for want of adequate pay and for a time municipal hospital doors were closed to all but emergency patients. New taxes were enacted and the city survived.

Today one year later, of course, the city is in the grips of this year's budget crisis and the mayor has stated that "New York City is at a crossroads. We must find the revenues to keep city government financially viable or so cut back services that government provides that the city becomes less and less livable."

The New York Stock Exchange still has not resolved the question of where to settle, and this month Pepsico, the American Can Company, Corn Products Flintcote, and Olin-Mathieson have announced that they will move their operations out of the city. More disturbing, Leonard C. Yaseen, board chairman of the Fantus Company, the world's largest location consultants, has said that "six years ago we might have done six relocation studies in an entire year, but in 1967 we may conduct forty such studies."

This is the kind of disruption of the normal business and civic cycle that American cities are experiencing now in the present moment and it is symptomatic of the price we as a nation are paying for our failure to resolve the problems of the ghetto.

Put another way, HHFA [Housing and Home Finance Agency] figures show that the average cost per citizen for municipal services in a blighted area is $7 but the area pays back only $4.25; whereas in a good area, the average cost of essential services is $3.60 per citizen and the area pays back $11.30. Because of the distressed conditions under which they live, the number of Negroes on the public welfare rolls is increasing and one third of the $3.5 billion we spend today as a nation for public aid, education and housing goes to Negroes who constitute only eleven percent of the population. In light of these facts, the fiscal management of the cities becomes increasingly difficult and the plight of the ghetto resident becomes increasingly acute.

It is inconceivable to me that responsible legislators and leaders in industry and commerce should any longer deny strong support to all measures necessary to correct the evils that pervade ghetto life and drain the resources of American cities.

And yet, what, for instance, is the picture in Washington today, and what is the picture in the private sector? In both arenas, it is exceedingly mixed. In Washington, leadership in the executive branch is strong. You can give Johnson hell if you like on Vietnam, but the commitment of the executive to solutions to our number one domestic problem is beyond doubt. Added evidence accumulates every day. To talk to people at the policy-making levels in the executive departments is often immensely rewarding. The best of them are creative, sophisticated in the nature of the problem, passionately committed to solutions and imaginative in the use of legislative tools already at hand.

The picture in the Congress is, in large part, another story altogether and this is not just a result of the elections in November. The elections in November only serve to make matters worse. They can't be said to have been all that good prior to November.

For one thing the pace of implementation of domestic legislation is dependent upon manipulation of the fiscal machinery of government. Much worthy legislation languishes for lack of adequate appropriations. The Model Cities legislation enacted by the last Congress, for example, is conceived to put the full resources of the nation—federal, state and municipal, public and private—to work to achieve not only the physical, but the social, rehabilitation of the cities. To date, the total sum appropriated for Model Cities is $11 million and that is for planning. No monies have yet been appropriated for the implementation of the Model Cities legislation.

Moreover, it is interesting to ponder the fact that this appropriation is in the control of a subcommittee of the House Appropriations Committee which is composed of ten men, not one of whom comes from a major city. The chairman, Representative Joe L. Evins, is from Smithville, Tennessee, a town with a population of 2,348. The largest city represented on this committee is Springfield, Massachusetts, with a population of 174,463. Other members of the committee come from towns of 8,780; 2,428; and 5,699.

To the president's full credit, his budget message recommended appropriations for the implementation of the Model Cities legislation at the full level of departmental request. What the appropriations subcommittee will choose, in its wisdom, to recommend is anybody's guess.

A further part of the problem in the Congress is that, in general, the northern liberal representative in the Congress, the man who votes "right" on issues affecting the Negro, is neither as shrewd nor as committed to his objectives as the southern representative. In practice, the northern liberal tends to be completely outmaneuvered by the committed southerner and the key to effective implementation of legislation is inevitably tied to the federal purse strings which are firmly in the grip of the Congress.

Quite aside from the deliberations of the ten small-town men who, by virtue of their seniority, sit astride the appropriations for Model Cities, I greatly fear what the record of some members of northern congressional delegations, for example, may be when they are called upon to vote on massive appropriation rather than on say, the Civil Rights Bill of 1967. Many a northern congressman, whose heart isn't really in it, may find it thoroughly feasible to vote against an appropriations bill, which is poorly understood by his constituency, whereas he could never vote against a civil rights bill. As we enter into a new phase of the struggle, where appropriations massive enough to do the job under existing legislation are of the essence, the lack of commitment among many northern congressmen becomes a matter for serious concern.

It is further interesting to note that, at a time when it has become clear that dispersal of the ghetto is essential to the health of the central cities, that it was a congressman from New York City who required inclusion of language in the Model Cities bill which precludes use of the Model Cities program to effect dispersal of the ghetto. In the same vein, more than a decade after the Supreme Court decision desegregating the schools, the Elementary and Secondary Education Act was passed, but only after language was inserted which states that "desegregation shall not mean assignment to public schools in order to overcome racial imbalance."

The picture in the private sector is no less interesting. Hundreds of companies have voluntarily complied with the president's Plans for Progress, and many have proved imaginative and inventive in dealing with the problems of recruiting, training and motivating minority workers. But the job and the responsibility of the private sector does not stop there.

I like to cite the situation as it now exists in Hartford, Connecticut, where, I am informed, the most progressive element in the community is the Chamber of Commerce, and the most regressive elements are the two major political parties, the Democratic the more so in that it is the stronger. Now the reason for the progressivism of the Chamber of Commerce, I am told, is that being good Yankee businessmen, its members take the position that they don't care what color people are, they are concerned only with getting them back on the tax rolls. "If you have to educate them, educate them," these men say. "If you have to build them houses, build them houses. But let's get them back on the tax rolls." This is my idea of an enlightened outlook for business and businessmen, and I hope and pray that the business community generally rapidly accepts the wisdom of this approach—both for the welfare of the Negro community and for the sake of the future of the cities.

There are further encouraging signs on the horizon. Within the recent past, for example, the New York Board of Trade, which is a major business-civic organization in New York, has taken the position that it is deeply aware of the total environment in which business operates and that equal concern must be given in management's planning for environmental factors other than the purely economic. The Board of Trade has determined to take an active part in identifying management's rightful role in the solution of socioeconomic problems besetting New York City, including those of the ghetto. There are even rumblings from within the National Association of Manufacturers emanating from a deep urge to image-changing through a new examination of the role of the corporate structure in relation to the socioeconomic problems that haunt the entire society.

As the pressures of the urban crisis continue to mount, it is possible that the most significant pressures for change will come not from their accustomed sources but from a concerned, aware and affected private sector. It is also possible that the Model Cities program which requires the active cooperation of the private sector will effect the first happy marriage in the solution of the problems besetting urban areas between federal, state and local government and private interests.

To revert now to the coming struggle for massive appropriations as opposed to new legislation at the federal level. The need, of course, varies from area to area. In general, the necessary legislative tools already exist for a broadscale attack on the problems of housing and manpower training.

The Department of Housing and Urban Development has a battery of techniques available to it, prime among which are the Turnkey Housing formula for the rehabilitation and replacement of substandard housing stock, and the leasing program which makes it possible for local Public Housing Authorities to lease apartments at will for use as public housing units. Massive application of the Turnkey concept alone could serve to eradicate substandard housing, estimated at five million units nationally, within the next ten years, if a massive effort were undertaken, as indeed it must be.

In addition, HUD has the tools at hand to create broad opportunities for home ownership by low-income people, a proposition the Urban League stresses as essential to any plan for the physical and social redemption of the ghetto. Home ownership, and the pride of ownership, constitute the surest way to create a stake in the community for individual families and to guarantee the health and stability of the community over the long haul.

The Urban League has proposed that leases on all rehabilitated housing made available to low-income families be combined with an option to buy, either on a cooperative or a condominium basis. Under this proposal, as a family's income increases, the family could undertake purchase rather than being required to move. Present housing law contains a provision for private ownership of public housing in attached and semidetached houses, a device so far being utilized only in St. Louis.

We have also proposed that private ownership of low-cost housing be further encouraged through the introduction of a federally subsidized below-market interest rate of not more than three percent for the purchase of rehabilitated substandard housing by low-income families, a precedent for which currently exists in the Model Cities Act, which authorizes the purchase of such mortgages by the Federal National Mortgage Association under its special assistance program. In this connection, we would further urge the extension of such a below-market interest rate to all returning veterans.

Thirdly, we have proposed that one component in any program for the mass rehabilitation of slum housing be a provision whereby slum residents can obtain a "sweat equity" in ownership, through contributing physical labor to the rehabilitation and construction process, and that this provision for "sweat equity" be coupled with on-the-job-training in the construction trades. A precedent for "sweat equity" in low-cost housing exists in HUD's Mutual Help Program which so far has been applied on only a limited basis, and never yet in an urban setting.

It is not my purpose to discuss these proposals at length here. The point I wish to make is that in the field of housing the question now is largely one of the imaginative and, most importantly, the massive use of presently available housing tools. What must be developed within existing legislation is a basic framework for action consisting of the fullest possible use of the credit and subsidy powers of the federal government on a massive and coordinated basis and in a fashion designed to involve the initiative and incentives of competitive free enterprise.

Again, the debate about whether to "gild" the ghetto or disperse it is irrelevant. The housing stock in the ghetto has to be redeemed or replaced now no matter who is to live there now or at a later date.

As in housing, the laws on the books affecting manpower training are generally adequate. Programs have been written to cover most contingencies in this field and there is adequate leeway for experiment. What is essential, again, is that these tools be utilized on a scale commensurate with the problem, with the need to train all those who need training in order to become gainfully employed.

In both education and welfare there is a continuing need for legislation if, on the one hand, quality and integration are indeed to become the hallmarks of our public school system, and if, on the other, poverty is to be eradicated in this affluent society.

It is still very early to tell what the results to date have been of Title I of the Elementary and Secondary Education Act in contributing either to the quality of education in the schools or to the integration of the schools. Present indications are that while some schools have been able to make very good use of the monies provided by this act, many schools were unprepared to utilize the monies to full advantage and, in the eyes of concerned people, they have often resulted in what could be called "add-on" programs, programs which have just provided the schools with more of the same old uninspired and uninspiring materials, equipment and program they have had before.

As for the progress of integration, the United States Civil Rights Commission has just reported that thirteen years after the Supreme Court decision desegregating the schools, seventy-five percent of all Negro children and eighty-three percent of all white children still go to schools that are ninety percent or more segregated, whether the segregation be of Negro children or of white; that the achievement levels of Negro children have been only slightly affected by so-called "compensatory programs" in these segregated schools; and that they will continue to suffer academically unless legislation is enacted that requires racial balance in all the nation's public schools. Like the Supreme Court decision of 1954, the current report by the Civil Rights Commission holds that both Negro and white children suffer when isolated from the mainstream of society. It further states that even though state and local governments in the North do not decree segregated school systems, Negroes are nevertheless denied equal protection of the law through a subtle combination of assignment patterns, school board decisions and the selection of school sites, which affect them quite as severely as those practices which have permeated the South.

The problem, obviously, of desegregating the schools is not an easy one. No schoolman wants to turn his whole system inside out in order to desegregate, but, often, that's the only real solution. Some inspired efforts have been undertaken in cities and towns across the country including Xenia, Ohio, where white support was enlisted for desegregation with a demonstration school in the Negro neighborhood; in Irondequoit, New York, where Negro youngsters were successfully imported into the school system of an all-white community; in Evanston, Illinois, where a computer was used to redistrict school attendance areas and to redistribute white and Negro students in combination with a dynamic education improvement program for the whole district; in York, Pennsylvania, where Negro youngsters were gradually slipped into elementary schools, grade by grade, starting with kindergarten in combination with a human relations program for students, parents and teachers; in Teaneck, New Jersey, where developing *de facto* segregation was rooted out by converting an elementary school into a central school for all sixth-graders; and in Riverside, California, where a crisis situation paved the way for integration of the schools.

In Riverside, where schoolmen were committed to the concept of the neighborhood school, someone else in the community wasn't. So, he burned one of them down. With a Molotov cocktail. At midnight.

A crisis? Yes—and an opportunity, too, as it turned out. The school's destruction forced immediate integration of its students into other schools. And this integration went off so smoothly that, within a matter of months, the Riverside Superintendent of Schools was able to schedule integration of the city's remaining racially imbalanced schools and predict that "minority pupils will be as well received by staff members and other pupils as those who were integrated as a result of the fire."

Which is not to say that this school superintendent or any other sane schoolman recommends school burning as a desegregation catalyst. But the fact remains that, in this case, the fire stimulated fast and effective action. Within a month of the fire, Riverside's administration was able to announce a solid plan to desegregate totally within two years.

Or—consider the education plaza, or educational park, as it's being developed in Orange, New Jersey. The concept is simple enough. If small neighborhood grade schools are creating a *de facto* segregation problem, and the entire K-12 system is getting out of date to boot, the idea is to close the schools and consolidate. The first step toward an education plaza has already been taken in East Orange. A pilot group of 250 fifth- and sixth-graders is being introduced to nongraded, individualized instructional techniques which will be used in the projected school plant. Land purchase and construction of a $1.5 million base building is scheduled for completion in 1968. A large intermediate school, an upper school and a lower school, are scheduled to follow in that order. The base building will be used for new teaching programs for the plaza and will be integrated into that structure later. Total implementation time for the plaza, which will also include a resource tower and junior college, a "lively arts" center, gymnasiums, a covered stadium and a large parking lot—is pegged at fifteen years.

It has even been suggested that one way to desegregate the schools is to strip the ghetto of schools for a period of time. The rationale behind this suggestion is that given a situation where you have an all-black school here and an all-white school there and perhaps an integrated school in between, the logical movement of pupils would be from the all-black school to the all-white school, and vice versa, but that, in fact, this two-way movement doesn't work. You can get movement from the all-black school to the all-white school, but you can't get comparable movement from the all-white school to the all-black school as long as the latter is perceived by the white community as an all-Negro school. Hence the proposal is to strip the ghetto of schools by moving the student population out and leaving the buildings empty if need be until such time as the school in question is no longer perceived as an all-Negro school; at that time it can be reopened with an enriched curriculum designed to attract white students as well as black on the magnet theory. I am by no means facetious in seriously urging that this approach be explored fully where everything else seems to fail.

To be good, the schools of this nation have to be desegregated. Where the will to desegregate exists, the schools are being desegregated.

There are still other things that a given school district can do. The middle-school concept, or the 4-4-4 system can change perceptions of the all-Negro school so that schools attract a more representative student body. Shuttle lines can be established, so that kids can get to an integrated school in a ten-minute bus ride. Bussing, like the idea of federal control of the schools, is a false issue. White parents, who can afford to, have been bussing their children to private schools for generations. The rural consolidated school has depended on bussing for decades. And as far as federal control is concerned, out of the total spent on education in this country for education at all levels, including higher education, only eight percent comes from federal sources. At the elementary and secondary levels, the percentage is a mere four percent.

The legislative route to achieving integration of the schools might result from a happy marriage between certain provisions of bills introduced in the last session of the Congress by Senator Edward Kennedy and Representative Adam Clayton Powell. The Kennedy bill would amend Title IV of the Civil Rights Act of 1964 to authorize the Commissioner of Education to provide technical assistance and grants to school boards which have drawn up programs for overcoming racial imbalance in their public schools. In other words, it would provide monies, which present legislation does *not* do, to meet the costs of desegregation. There are no coercive provisions in this bill whatsoever. The Powell bill, on the contrary, provides that every school district shall report to the United States Commissioner of Education on the racial composition of its student population by building and if, by 1970, any building exceeds the minority population of the school district by more than twenty percent, it would get no more federal money. For instance, in New York City, where the minority public school population throughout the City is thirty-three percent of the total, any school with a minority population of fifty-four percent as of 1970 would be deprived of any further federal aid. Solutions are possible. It is not beyond the genius of America to find solutions.

The major needs for welfare legislation are threefold. One most important step is legislation requiring that by a given date, the states pay in full their own standards of assistance, which at this point, numbers of them do not. Further legislation is required in order to establish a major training component for people now receiving Aid for Dependent Children plus incentives to work. At present, we give the needy income. And we take away most of that income if the recipient gets the smallest job, causing needless waste and demoralization. Worse still, public assistance as presently written and administered encourages the disintegration of the family. In most states, the main assistance program, Aid for Dependent Children, is not available if there is an able-bodied man in the house, even if he is not working. All too often it is necessary for the father to leave his children so that they can eat. It is bad enough to provide incentives for idleness but even worse to provide legislative incentives for desertion.

Perhaps the best solution would be for the federal government to assume the cost of providing a minimum income. Nothing is quite so certain to provide an antidote for poverty as the provision of definite and dependable income. Ideally, such income would derive from expanded job opportunities, including jobs on needed public works, but in the absence of sufficient job opportunities, a minimum income is eminently desirable.

Numerous arguments are raised against this solution, the foremost among which is the assertion that it would destroy individual incentive. Yet, nothing is more certain than that we now have a welfare system that could not be better designed to destroy incentives if it had been planned for that specific purpose.

Perhaps the best solution to the crisis of the cities would be for the federal government to assume the cost of providing a minimum income, and thus freeing the cities from the present burden of welfare costs. In the years of the farm crisis, federal government did this for agriculture. In these years of urban crisis, we need a system that directs funds not by some formula to the country at large, but to the points of greatest need, in short, to the large cities. The

United States Conference of Mayors, for one, is convinced that the cities are being shortchanged in a period when their own taxing resources are manifestly too limited to halt urban decay.

To transfer income maintenance to the federal government, would be to free big city budgets of a large share of their welfare payments and would be an enormous step in the right direction, leaving the cities free to meet problems which can be met only on local terms.

Whatever the analysis of our urban problems, whatever combination of approaches are taken toward their solution, one point is clear and that is that there is no simple way. The problems that confront us are desperate problems, infinite in their complexity and interrelatedness, and we must use every tool in the social arsenal to achieve solutions.

As one additional tool, which requires no legislative action, just administrative decision in both the public and private sectors, I would draw your attention to the Urban League's proposal for Operation Urban Survival, first enunciated at our annual conference in Philadelphia last August and predicated on the following facts.

"... we now have a welfare system that could not be better designed to destroy incentives if it had been planned for that specific purpose."

The explosive increase of the Negro population in northern, central and western cities represents one of the most dramatic social changes in urban history. No other ethnic group has ever made up as large a proportion of the population as does the Negro today. In 1910, when the Urban League was founded, seventy-three percent of all Negroes lived in rural areas. Today, seventy-three percent of all Negroes live in cities. In just one decade, New York City lost a middle-class white population almost the size of Washington, D.C., and gained a nonwhite population almost the size of Pittsburgh.

The United States Civil Rights Commission has reported that if all of New York City were as jammed with people as several of the worst blocks in Harlem, the entire population of the United States could fit into three of the city's five boroughs, with two left over for expansion.

By 1970, it is estimated that there will be 18 million Negroes living in our urban centers and before long, ten of the major cities of the United States will be more than 50 percent Negro. Washington, D.C., already is and has been for nearly a decade. Newark, which was 34.4 percent Negro at the time of the 1960 census, is now over 50 percent Negro.

In Detroit, Baltimore, Cleveland and St. Louis, Negroes constitute a third or more of the population and in Chicago, Philadelphia, Cincinnati, Indianapolis and Oakland, they constitute more than one fourth of the population. The impact of the expanding ghetto is being felt in smaller cities like New Haven and Gary, San Diego, Buffalo and Rochester, Toledo and Akron, Fort Wayne and Milwaukee, Kansas City and Wichita. Not even the South is immune. New Orleans is 41 percent Negro, Memphis and Atlanta, 38 percent.

Whether you accept or reject the basic immorality inherent in the existence and growth of the racial ghetto, it is clear that the emerging picture in the central cities has implications which overshadow past social and economic revolutions and make them pale into insignificance. As long as the ghettos continue to swell, the welfare of American cities is in jeopardy.

The welfare of the American city depends upon the stability of its fiscal base; its ability to finance those collective necessities which make it possible for large numbers of people to live close together, allow commerce to thrive and create those public facilities and services which make urban life tolerable. Blighted areas—and all the ghettos of our major cities are blighted—work intolerable hardships on the people who live in them and drain the total community of its financial resources. Such areas are utterly unable to make a satisfactory contribution to the city treasury in return for services. Taxable income diminishes as the ghettos expand and the cost of public services mushrooms. This is the vise in which most of our major cities are caught.

In light of these facts, the Urban League's Operation Urban Survival represents a major additional measure for the alleviation of these conditions.

Operation Urban Survival calls, quite simply, for public and private institutional building in the ghetto, for a nationwide program of locating new commercial, governmental, industrial, cultural and educational buildings and developments in slum areas in order to spearhead the transformation of the ghettos into viable, integrated communities. *Where* such facilities are located can have as much social meaning as the purposes they are intended to house and social costs to the community can be vastly reduced by just such enlightened measures as this.

Widely implemented, Operation Urban Survival would mean a vast upgrading of ghetto areas. Just as location of the United Nations upgraded a blighted area of the East Side of New York, just as location of Lincoln Center upgraded a blighted area of the West Side, and just as Rockefeller Center upgraded a deteriorating section of midtown Manhattan, the location of major commercial, governmental, cultural and educational institutions designed to service the total community, black and white, in the ghetto, would not only upgrade blighted areas but would have a multitude of tangential, and eminently desirable, effects.

This proposal addresses itself to the social, commercial, civic and cultural vitality of areas now alienated from the larger community. A major, though intangible, side effect would be the improvement of communications between the races, an essential to progress which is largely lacking at present.

Operation Urban Survival means creating jobs within the ghetto that will command a mixed working population and is conceived in the belief that a mixed working population will lead to a mixed residential population. Dispersal of the ghetto, essential to the health of the central cities, requires not only that Negroes move out of the ghetto but that whites have good reason to move in.

In one stroke, Operation Urban Survival can bring new life and vitality to a decaying part of the city. It will generate new hope in the slums as adults find jobs and youngsters see that education can lead to tangible results. It will generate many kinds of peripheral enterprise and development, further adding to the vitality of the community. Such projects in the hearts of the ghettos will provide visible evidence that the city cares, that neglect and abuse are at an end, and that integration is a living force in city life. Most important of all, it will end the isolation of the ghetto from the rest of the community and is essential to achieving healthy traffic in both directions.

For example, if the two million square feet now planned for consolidation of New York State Office space in the World Trade Center on a site in downtown Manhattan, were consolidated instead in Harlem, we would have a facility in the Harlem community that would meet all the standards of Operation Urban Survival. It would employ a mixed working population, it would establish a healthy in-and-out traffic in the area, it would lead to the development of peripheral enterprise and would create a standing reservoir of jobs in the ghetto, and it could be expected to lead to a mixed residential pattern.

In addition, it is more than probable that construction of the two million square feet of office space now scheduled for the World Trade Center downtown would prove significantly cheaper to build in Harlem.

There is every reason for state and municipal governments to respond favorably to this proposal inasmuch as substantial portions of their funds go to bridge the gap caused by the economic conditions of the ghettos. The private sector has a comparable stake in this means to establishing the future fiscal health of the cities.

In conclusion, it is obvious that the urban crisis stems in large part from the failure to resolve the problems that confront the Negro and it is obvious what the Negro wants. He wants what white Americans are able to take for granted. He wants the same opportunity to earn a living, the same freedom of choice in the selection of housing and the same quality of education for his children. He wants dignity as well as opportunity, performance on the part of white Americans as well as pledge.

If there is no genuine conviction about the rightness of integration and human relations and no will to arrive at solutions—then laws alone cannot solve the problem—and the future welfare of our cities is in serious jeopardy.

I hope I have made it utterly clear that nothing less than massive effort will produce significant results. We must marshal all our available resources for the job at hand and proceed on a scale commensurate with the task. We are in terrible danger, and our cities in desperate peril, if any among us permit ourselves the luxury of "thinking small."

On March 11, 1971, while visiting Nigeria, Young suffered a heart attack and drowned while swimming. He and a group of black and white Americans had been in the African nation's capital of Lagos for a special conference intended to forge closer ties between blacks in Africa and the United States. Eight months earlier, on July 19, 1970, Young had addressed the Urban League annual convention in New York City for the last time. In his speech, he discussed in blunt yet moving terms what he felt had to be the strategy of the upcoming decade—a decade that, as he noted, clearly posed a new set of challenges. The following text is reprinted from the September 15, 1970, issue of Vital Speeches of the Day.

There comes a time in the life of every great nation when it finds itself at the crossroads—on one side, the path of division, decline, and oblivion; on the other, the path of progress, purpose, and decency. There is every indication that this nation, almost two centuries after its birth by fire, is at that crossroads.

At every hand we see chaos instead of concern, drift instead of decision, and hate instead of hope. It may well be that we are witnessing the exhaustion of the American spirit; the full-scale retreat by a people nurturing false dreams of superiority; a retreat from the responsibilities and decency that characterize true greatness.

Six renowned historians recently probed the confused spirit of our country in a national weekly. One called this "The Age of Rubbish." Another proclaimed "the end of the American era." Another said we are experiencing "a massive breakdown." Yet another said we suffer from "a case of hypochondria." All, Conservative and Marxist alike, agreed there is a crisis of confidence. The overwhelming impression one gets from their comments is doubt that the quality of national leadership today is adequate to the magnitude of the challenges faced.

The signs, then, are unmistakable that this unhappy land, this bitterly polarized society, seems incapable of living up to the ideals and dreams that it purportedly held for so long.

A hateful war that no one wants has spread to neighboring lands. A public inured to "body counts" and "enemy kills" has found that its own children—at Kent State and Jackson—form a new set of body count numbers.

A country whose very survival depends upon the reconstruction of its young, its poor, and its neglected nonwhite minorities seems only capable of hate rather than love, isolation rather than reclamation, and killing rather than saving.

Repression is rampant. Americans—for the first time in decades—now have their own "show" trials, political prisoners, and midnight police raids that kill people in their beds, people whose crime was dissent from a society that persecuted them.

And fanning the flames of repression have been the mindless pseudo-revolutionists of the left whose idea of changing society is to plant bombs where they might kill the innocent—and the mindless pseudo-conservatives of the right whose idea of standing up for the democracy they are sworn to protect is to destroy it through division and hate. Those super-patriots who yell "America, love it or leave it" ought to recognize the words of the great French philosopher Albert Camus who said: "I would like to be able to love my country and justice at the same time."

This is an America that generously supports a giant welfare subsidy program for the rich in the form of unbridled defense spending, space programs, and supersonic planes, while refusing funds to feed starving black kids in Mississippi or housing to shelter the poverty-stricken of the rural areas and cities.

It is a nation whose answer to a disturbing inflation is to create an even more dangerous recession. It tinkers with the economic system to artificially induce unemployment, to bring housing construction to a virtual end, and to drive all hope from the hearts of the poor. And in so doing, it may yet create the Depression that will rob it of the wealth it tries so hard to protect.

Beset by the twin evils of repression and recession, black people today are fearful that the limited gains of the sixties are in danger. We have seen that in spite of legal and legislative victories, racism is still alive in new and different forms.

We know all too well that the cost of liberty is less than the price of repression, and that the cost of economic justice is but a fraction of the price of racial privilege and exploitation.

It has become more clear than ever, that the black man's fight for respect and for manhood is also a fight to right the wrongs of a bloated, sick society, and to bring it back to its senses.

Our task at this conference will be to devise the strategies that will ensure that the cause of equality, for which so much blood and tears have been shed, will triumph in this land. In our sessions and workshops we will question the prevailing myths that entangle current thinking on economic and political problems afflicting blacks and other minorities, and we will continue to move beyond the narrow limits of debate to get at the roots of the problem of bringing power to the powerless.

I am hopeful that out of this conference will come strategies for the seventies; the framework for organizing for results, results that will have an impact upon the millions of victims of racism and neglect, a neglect sometimes called "benign" but more accurately called "callous."

The Urban League, at this stage of its history, has the responsibility to continue in its efforts to pull together America's minority communities in order to mobilize its enormous reservoir of talent and skills to win political, economic, and social victories.

The Urban League is in position to assert such leadership not only because of its historic strengths, its dedicated staff of full-time experts and the devoted cooperation of its thousands of volunteers, but also because of its own experience with change; its own success in developing a new thrust into the ghettos of America.

For, in this our sixtieth year, the Urban League has evolved far from the limited functions envisioned by its founders. The social services we once provided newcomers to the cities of the North have had to be supplemented and replaced by a much more comprehensive organization of the black community. Two years ago, we organized our New Thrust program to do just that. The Urban League moved into the ghetto—physically and spiritually—and is serving as an enabling vehicle for a black community determined to win unity, dignity, and power.

We responded to that need. We responded with vigor, and with the realization that we exist to serve the community, to identify with it, and to provide the technical assistance and know-how to enable the community itself to organize for successful action.

For we believe that "Power to the People" is but an empty phrase unless the people can be provided with the mechanism, technical assistance, and opportunities to make that power work for them in their own communities, on their own terms, under their own leadership. And a clenched fist is useless, if, when forced open, it is found to be empty of the resources of money, intellect, and the will to do the job.

New Thrust has proved itself. In city after city, local affiliates have become more relevant to the needs of the ghetto. In city after city, while continuing to keep vital channels of communication with the white community open, we have served as the catalyst that brought blacks together to win victories.

> ***"'Power to the People' is but an empty phrase unless the people can be provided with the mechanism, technical assistance, and opportunities to make that power work for them. . . ."***

The Urban League movement continues to be flexible, relevant, and vital. We have successfully shifted gears from treating the results of racism and poverty to mounting a full-scale attack on the *causes* of racism and poverty. The Urban League has taken on a commitment to change the institutions and the society that perpetuates injustice.

And that is not a short-term commitment. The New Thrust activities that started as a laboratory for community change are now part and parcel of our movement. New Thrust is no longer a separate program; it is structurally a part of our ongoing operations, and its spirit and thinking permeate every facet of our movement.

In order to insure our increased effectiveness, we have implemented structural changes within the national office, beginning with the addition of a competent deputy director, that will increase our accountability and provide better planning and operating procedures. Our new departments of research, personnel and training, and our strengthened Washington bureau—together with a redefining of our program planning and operating procedures—will make possible more effective services to our now-almost one hundred affiliates.

The past year also saw the Urban League initiate a broad coalition of groups to influence what we tried to make the first accurate census count of nonwhite peoples in the history of the nation. The "Make Black Count" campaign was founded on the realization that by undercounting the actual numbers of blacks and browns in America, the government, in effect, was withholding from them the federal aid distributed on a per capita basis. Black communities across the land were not getting their fair share of hospital and school monies, or even proper representation in Congress and state legislatures. The figures are not all in yet, but the "Make Black Count" staff will be "riding herd" on the Census Bureau to insure that blacks—blacks, for a welcome change—get a fair count.

But equal to the importance of the count itself was the way the campaign was able to bring black people together, making it possible to deal with the Census Bureau from a position of strength.

The "Make Black Count" campaign has been a unified effort of the black community. It has been a coalition of all representative groups—organized welfare mothers, street gangs, church members, sororities, civil rights organizations, and others. The Urban League was the catalyst, the enabler, the provider of resources and technical assistance. We were content to take a back seat in this. Our intent was not to hog headlines or be pictured on television. All literature, posters, publicity, etc., highlighted the coalition, not the Urban League. Our goal was to bring the community together on a vital issue, and to set in motion the national and local coalitions that will become the basis for further cooperation and unity. Our experience in this campaign convinces me that our purpose has been successful, and we shall build upon it in the coming months.

We joined, also, with others to mount campaigns to protest the willful murders of Black Panthers and black college students by our home-grown version of the SS, and to successfully protest the nomination of insensitive judges to the Supreme Court that protects our liberties from the very system of racism they represent.

The Urban League is active on a broad series of fronts:

At the request of key congressional leaders we are submitting to the Congress a detailed agenda for an updated domestic Marshall Plan which we first proposed in 1964 to do for the victims of American racism and the poor of all colors what America so willingly did for the European victims of World War II.

We have started the National Urban League Housing Foundation to expand the supply of low and moderate income housing and to give black people a share in the building and control of their own housing.

We took a giant step toward strengthening black colleges through the Black Executive Exchange Program that brings blacks who have made it in the competitive give-and-take of the professions and business to lecture and advise students and faculty at black institutions of higher education.

And we have served the needs of ghetto youth in a variety of ways, including consultation and assistance for Youth Organizations United, the national federation of over two hundred city street gangs that is helping to channel the energies of these youngsters into constructive action on behalf of their communities.

And, further serving youth, our summer student program brought one hundred college student leaders again into the ghettos of America in a constructive program to help organize the black community, and to place the talent and spirits of campus youth at the service of their brothers and sisters.

We moved to fill the nationwide vacuum in child care through a Day Care Center Corporation that promises to fill a crying need for neighborhood day care centers operated and controlled by the community.

Our new Consumer Protection Program is designed at organizing the exploited minority community to a new awareness of making the most effective use of their scarce dollars and ending the callous preying upon the poor that typifies so much of the economic life of the ghetto.

The Urban League's pioneering Street Academies will come to many more communities through the establishment of an Urban Education Institute that will provide the framework for planning and consulting with other institutions and the community in order to duplicate many times over our successes in helping deprived youngsters to recover from the failures of the heartless educational bureaucracies, and go on to higher educational goals.

Our Labor Education Advancement Program (LEAP) is responsible for the greatest breakthrough of black apprentices into the building trades in history, while at the same time creating and supporting black contractors.

Our On-the-Job Training programs are the most efficient in the country, with the highest retention rate at the lowest cost per trainee.

Other Urban League programs are helping to develop black businessmen, bring new opportunities to returning veterans, and family planning and mental retardation services to the black community under its own control for the first time. And our various job placement and training programs pumped $400 million of cool, green cash into the black community in new and added wages and salaries.

But we cannot be complacent about our successes, accomplished with limited resources. They represent a challenge for still greater efforts in the future; a base from which we must build the coalitions and unity without which racism will remain supreme, and poverty will possess the souls of the real forgotten Americans—the blacks, the browns, and the reds of the rural and urban ghettos.

This new decade could bring promise of a new era in the relations between the races. Just as the nation as a whole is at a crossroads, so, too, black people face a new turning point, a decisive strategic moment that may put us on a new path to freedom. Just as there is some doubt whether the nation will choose the right path to greatness there must be doubts, especially in the light of the historic racism of America, that the seventies will bring true equality for black people. But while we may question the future, it becomes our duty to mobilize and steel ourselves for a new phase of struggle.

Black Americans first pursued a *strategy of conciliation*. Fresh from the prison of slavery, the Freedmen and their sons tried to work with whites and convince them to act with decency. Whites remained in basic control of all matters affecting blacks, and the strategy of conciliation became, above all, a strategy of survival, a strategy to squeeze short-term gains under adversity.

Then there came a *strategy of organization*. Blacks created the institutions without which there can be no community and no progress in a hostile society. These were the years that saw the birth of the NAACP, the Urban League, and educational, civil, religious and business associations. The institutional structure of the black community took shape, and, abandoned by white society, blacks came together to build strength for the inevitable future confrontation with unbridled white power.

The next phase was the *strategy of confrontation,* in which the institutions of the black community staged a frontal assault on the pillars of racism. This was the era of the boycott, the sit-in, ride-ins, wade-ins, lie-ins and all the other disruptive tactics that confronted Americans not with the pliant, silent oppressed blacks they wanted, but with the proud, determined black men and women who insisted on equality.

We will be forever grateful for the dedicated, fearless warriors of CORE, SNCC, SCLC, the NAACP and the Urban League who fought the evils of racism on its home grounds—in the Southern Black Belt, and in the rigged courts and bigoted cities of the North.

And, basically, this strategy worked. To it we owe the destruction of the formal, legal structure of racism in America. To it we owe the passage of laws and the legal decisions that provide a framework from which we can pursue the goals of complete equality. To it we owe the worldwide realization that America is plagued by racism, and our country has won not the respect, not even the envy, of the world's peoples, but their pity that so great a nation can be so incapable of morality and action to end poverty and bigotry.

The suspicions harbored by black people of this [Nixon] Administration's intentions, suspicions that are supported by many of its actions, have led to intensified confrontations. Last year, at our annual conference in Washington, I recited a long list of administration actions and warned that black people would not stand for a reversion to official attitudes and actions directed against them. A few weeks ago Bishop Spottswood, chairman of the NAACP, reasserted the widespread black disillusionment with the administration in a forceful indictment that accurately reflected much of the mood of black people today. This mood was further reflected in the Gallup poll of last week which shows the overwhelming majority of black people dissatisfied with the current administration.

It is obvious that where blacks are concerned,

the administration faces a credibility gap of enormous proportions. But it persists in claiming that the record does not justify this suspicion; that progress is being made, and that it does not intend to abandon blacks to the evil expedient of a Southern strategy that tries to out-Wallace Wallace.

The record is sometimes muddied. As critical as I have been of administration actions, I do admit that there are some signs that elements of this administration are moving forward to bring about change. In recent weeks there have been indications that tax-exemptions for the South's private "Hate Academies" will be cut off; that school desegregation might be implemented; that the government proposes to move more strongly against job discrimination. And there are indications that agencies such as OEO and HEW will channel new funds and programs into black organizations that have the expertise and the community's respect to do the job that others failed to do. All these may be but straws in the wind, but it would be a mistake for us to fail to recognize that within every administration there are contending forces. To cease to fight for our victories and to fail to negotiate with those in power is to leave the field to the political Neanderthals that so far seem to have dominated decision-making in the past few years.

Early in his administration, the president asked black Americans to judge him by his deeds and not his words. We have done that—and we have been greatly disappointed. Both words and deeds have left a bitterness that must now be transcended. Black people have—with justification—always judged white America with suspicion and disappointment. Promises have rarely led to performance, and words as well as well-meaning deeds have often been traps to further ensnare us.

"Black people have—with justification—always judged white America with suspicion and disappointment."

We have been forced by this administration to react with defensive measures, if not actual confrontation, and perhaps now a new strategy would be more fitting. For these tactics were based on protest born of powerlessness. I believe that we have demonstrated that we do have some power now—power to make America sit and listen, and to negotiate with us as equal partners. America can no longer afford to ignore its awakened black masses. And no administration—unless it is willing to preside over the destruction of American democracy, can afford to refuse the just demands of its neglected minorities.

While we would hope that the nation's leadership would exercise the kind of determined, crusading sense of mission that is the hallmark of great leadership, it is a fact of life that there is developing a national stand-off between those of us who are fighting for justice and those who want to maintain the status quo.

This is an impasse that leads nowhere, unless it be to further polarization, further division, further bitterness. White society has shown that it lacks the courage and the imagination to break this impasse by moving constructively. It is up to the black community to show the way.

Our cause is just. But white America still possesses the power. We must forge the union of justice with power. In the words of Pascal: "Justice and power must be brought together, so that whatever is just may be powerful, and whatever is powerful may be just."

I propose that the just and the powerful deal with each other as equals in a *strategy of negotiation*.

White society has the trappings of power—its police, its army, its law. But blacks have demonstrated effectively that unless our just demands are dealt with, these trappings of power only make a society muscle-bound; only drive it into displays of raw, naked power, displays that solve nothing and tear apart everything.

The two Americas—black and white—need each other. Let us break the rigid confines of charges and countercharges, protest and neglect. Let us negotiate our way out of the impasse that threatens to split the country apart.

By all means, we must continue to confront injustice. A strategy of negotiation does not imply weakness; on the contrary, it implies strength—the strength a unified black community can demonstrate. In the words of John F. Kennedy: "Let us never negotiate out of fear; but let us never fear to negotiate." Such a strategy demands from white America that it face up to the realities of a situation in which black young men are sent thousands of miles from home to fight and die for a cause labeled democracy, while democracy is denied them in the swollen ghettos of New York and in the sullen farmlands of Mississippi.

It demands from white America that it implement a massive domestic Marshall Plan that will rescue all Americans from poverty and disease.

And above all, it demands from white America that it demonstrate the will, the honesty, and the sincerity to face its black brothers on equal terms, as peers in a joint effort to rid the nation of the cancer of racism.

A strategy of negotiation demands from black America the power to negotiate from a position of strength. I believe we have demonstrated that power. In one sense, we have amply demonstrated a power to disrupt. In another sense, we have demonstrated, through the election of black mayors and legislators, political strength, and through the relentless accomplishment of our people against great odds, a changing economic and educational strength. We have made the most of the limited opportunities available to the point where we have the pride, the strength, and the accomplishments which should compel white leadership to sit down with us as equals.

A strategy of negotiation demands of black leadership a sense of unity and purpose, without which we will be subject to the old divide-and-conquer tactics oppressors have always used. It will demand of us a discipline and a willingness to rise above differences of doctrine and personality for the greater good of all black people. We must, more than ever, impose upon ourselves and our organizations a community of spirit and a fraternal bond that will enable us to better negotiate from a base of strength and unity.

Because we believe so strongly in the need for a unified black community to negotiate from a position of strength, we here and now issue a *Call to Black Leadership* to meet and to discuss an agenda for change.

We want to arrive at a broad consensus of positions that can be negotiated with White America.

We call for a meeting of blacks that includes all points of view from all shades of the spectrum of opinion.

We would like to cooperate with our brothers and sisters of all persuasions. We seek peaceful dialogue, not only with those whose opinions we share, but with all representative elements of the black community.

In unity there is strength, and we seek to help to bring about a unified black position with which white society can be confronted and with which it must negotiate.

It will not be easy to achieve such unity, because there are those whose experiences have led them to despair of white America ever acting in a decent way. But I have confidence that black people will muster the courage and the strength to make one last effort, based on our common sufferings, to stand united against the system that oppresses us.

And for America, this may be the last opportunity she has to deal with black Americans and to negotiate with leaders responsible to their people, before the terrifying prospect of internal strife, armed suppression and needless destruction descend fully upon us all.

Black unity is essential for black progress. This is no time for divisions. This is no time for us to mimic the polarization of white society. Only by unified action can we break the bonds that chain us. Only by unified action can we force America to become moral. Only by unified action can we forge the alliances across racial lines that promise progress.

And only through unity can we cut through the undergrowth of myth and misunderstanding and unite with other minorities to forge a new coalition for a better tomorrow.

I know that blacks have often been suspicious of such alliances. We have become contemptuous of an America that has "discovered" its problems so recently, although we have struggled with them for so long. We sense that other causes have higher priority than our own—that the motives of others are not always the same as ours, and that our suffering is so much more intense, and has been so prolonged.

But we must not let ourselves become imprisoned by concepts of race that ignore the other causes of our misery. As W.E.B. Du Bois pointed out: "Back of the problem of race and color lies a greater problem which both obscures and implements it: and that is the fact that so many civilized persons are willing to live in comfort even if the price of this is poverty, ignorance, and disease of the majority of their fellow men."

The economic and power dimensions of the problems facing us can be met through alliances with others in this twisted society who are hurting, too.

The problems of poverty are not black alone. There is hunger in the tenements and shacks of whites and browns and reds as well. There is misery in Appalachian ghost towns, in the barrios of the West, in migrant labor camps, and in Indian reservations. And there is misery here in New York's Harlem, South Bronx, and Bedford Stuyvesant.

America has grown fat and heavy with the sweat and labor of all minorities, now she must grow proud and strong through an alliance based on our realism and sense of purpose. There is at hand the raw material for building the strong alliance for social justice that is essential if America is to be saved—and we must save her if we are not *all* to go down the drain. While it is an historic fact that we came here on different ships, it is imperative that we realize that we're in the same boat now.

Coalitions for action can be formed with those whose frustrations may be somewhat different from those of minorities and the poor. White workers are hurting economically—just as we are. The top five percent of the population makes twenty percent of the income, the bottom twenty percent makes only five percent of the income. And that hasn't changed despite the New Deal, the Fair Deal, and all the other efforts at reform in the past. The white working class must be helped to understand that they, too, are dying in Vietnam; they, too, are hurting from the recession; and that they, too, are plagued by many of the problems that plague black people.

> ***"The problems of poverty are not black alone. . . . While it is an historic fact that we came here on different ships, it is imperative that we realize that we're in the same boat now."***

The white working class can also unite with us to combat crime. For all the talk of crime in the streets, it is the black community that suffers disproportionately from crime. If you are black, the chances that you will be robbed are triple those if you are white; the chances you'll know burglary and car theft are almost double. If you make less than $3,000 your chances of being robbed are five times higher than if your income is over $10,000, your chances of being raped are four times as high; and your chances of being burglarized, double. Blacks and whites can join together to combat the fear that grips both our communities.

Moreover, the deep frustrations caused by the expanding war; the horror of the Jackson and Kent State killings; the growing unemployment and recession; the stock market's steep decline; and the dissatisfaction with the rampant materialism that poisons the environment have convinced millions of Americans that you cannot tolerate injustice to the few without encouraging the erosion of justice for the many. Affluent Americans are beginning to see these connections and they are beginning to listen to their children, who are not only concerned with the poverty of the ghetto, but also are angry at the poverty of the spirit that afflicts their elders.

I believe that the time is now for broad coalitions.

I believe that the many disparate and contending forces in our society today, the diverse people and groups trying to change some small corner of American life, can be brought to see how racism and mindless materialism work hand-in-hand to turn the American dream into a nightmare.

And I believe that—whether because they pursue their own self-interest or because they move their idealism to a higher, more realistic plane—a new coalition can be forged that will once more return America to a sense of purpose and a will to justice.

I believe the time has come when black people must unite, must create coalitions in order to negotiate a peace that will settle the issues that divide the country and, by so doing, bring us together.

The proud black spirit of today seeks justice and decency. It seeks to move beyond racism to a new era of progress and reconciliation. It seeks power not for its own sake, but in order to use it wisely and to prevent its misuse by racism. It seeks peace with honor, justice with respect. It seeks a newer world, and a better tomorrow.

And for that tomorrow,
God, give us men
Men who are proud of their Godliness,

Yet humble in their humanity;
Men who know themselves, but who in knowing themselves
Do not ignore others;
Men who are conscious of others, not only of what
They can derive from them, but also give to them;
God give us men,
Men like Abraham Lincoln, Frederick Douglass,
Franklin D. Roosevelt and John Brown
Who would not stop at the cheap art of espousing causes,
But who championed men among the anonymous mass of men;
Men like these whose piety
Lay not only in credal affirmation, but rather in the
Confirmation of their deeds.
To this end,
We need Thy help,
And with Thy help we may yet, all of us, become men,
All of us brothers,
All of us Thy children;
All of us truly human.

SOURCES

Books

Baraka, Imamu Amiri (LeRoi Jones), editor, *African Congress: A Documentary of the First Modern Pan-African Congress,* Morrow, 1972.

Boulware, Marcus H., *The Oratory of Negro Leaders: 1900–1968,* Negro Universities Press, 1969.

Broderick, Francis L., and August Meier, editors, *Negro Protest Thought in the Twentieth Century,* Bobbs-Merrill, 1965.

Foner, Philip S., editor, *The Voice of Black America: Major Speeches by Negroes in the United States, 1797–1971,* Simon & Schuster, 1972.

Hale, Frank W., Jr., *The Cry for Freedom: An Anthology of the Best That Has Been Said and Written on Civil Rights Since 1954,* A.S. Barnes, 1969.

Thonssen, Lester, editor, *Representative American Speeches: 1966–1967,* Wilson, 1967.

Weiss, Nancy J., *Whitney M. Young, Jr., and the Struggle for Civil Rights,* Princeton University Press, 1989.

Williams, Jamye Coleman, and McDonald Williams, *The Negro Speaks: The Rhetoric of Contemporary Black Leaders,* Noble & Noble, 1970.

Young, Whitney M., Jr., *To Be Equal,* McGraw-Hill, 1964.

———, *Beyond Racism: Building an Open Society,* McGraw-Hill, 1969.

Periodicals

Ebony, "America Mourns Whitney M. Young, Jr.," May, 1971.

Newsweek, "Whitney Young: He Was Doer," March 22, 1971, p. 29.

New York Times, March 12, 1971; March 13, 1971.

New York Times Magazine, "Whitney Young: Black Leader or 'Oreo Cookie'?" September 20, 1970.

Time, "Kind of Bridge," March 22, 1971, p. 20.

Vital Speeches of the Day, "The Intermingled Revolutions," September 1, 1964, pp. 692-694; "The Positive Side of the Racial Story," July 1, 1965, pp. 572-576; "A New Thrust Toward Economic Security," October 1, 1969, pp. 759-763; "A Strategy for the Seventies,' September 15, 1970; pp. 732-736.

Raul Yzaguirre

1939–

Mexican American civil rights activist and association executive

Although no single group can claim to represent the diverse interests of the entire Hispanic American community, the one that perhaps comes closest to fulfilling that role is the National Council of La Raza (NCLR), a Washington, D.C.-based network of more than 150 organizations working toward the common goal of securing civil and economic rights for Hispanics. For more than twenty years, Raul Yzaguirre has served as its president and chief spokesman. His leadership has helped make NCLR into the largest and one of the most respected Latino advocacy groups in the United States.

Yzaguirre's activism first took root amid the poverty and discrimination he knew as a youngster growing up in the Rio Grande Valley of south Texas. As he told a reporter for Hispanic, *"Back then we had no control over our schools, our cities, or our government. Unless you wanted to shut the world out . . . you had to get involved." He was only fifteen when he organized a youth auxiliary of the American G.I. Forum, a well-known Hispanic veterans group. In 1964, following a four-year stint in the U.S. Air Force Medical Corps, Yzaguirre founded the National Organization for Mexican American Services, or NOMAS. Out of a proposal he wrote for NOMAS sprang what is now the National Council of La Raza.*

At the same time he was active with NOMAS, Yzaguirre was also pursuing his education at George Washington University, from which he received his bachelor's degree in 1966. He then worked as a program analyst in the Migrant Division of the U.S. Office of Economic Opportunity for several years before establishing the nation's first Mexican American research association, Interstate Research Associates, and building it into a multimillion-dollar nonprofit consulting firm.

Although he had served as a consultant to the National Council of La Raza from its very beginnings in 1968, Yzaguirre officially joined the ranks of the organization in 1974 when he was asked to assume the post of executive director. (He was named president four years later.) Originally envisioned as a group that would assist primarily Mexican Americans ("La Raza" being the name they used to describe themselves), NCLR under Yzaguirre has embraced all the Hispanic people of the New World in its quest for strength through unity. Its network of affiliates, most of which are community-based, can take advantage of the technical assistance and training offered by the parent organization in the areas of economic and business development, housing, employment, health, and other areas; they also benefit from Yzaguirre's success at obtaining the necessary funds for their programs from foundations, private corporations, and government grants.

During Yzaguirre's tenure, NCLR has also become involved in issues of immigration policy, citizenship, and voter registration to ensure that Hispanic Americans are able to participate in the democratic process and have a voice in matters that affect their lives. In 1992, armed with statistics that showed even Hispanics who encountered blatant discrimination in the workplace or while house-hunting were unlikely to make an official complaint, the organization launched a "Know Your Rights" campaign to educate Latinos about their civil rights and how to deal with the various agencies that are supposed to resolve such problems.

Perhaps the most widely publicized of NCLR's recent efforts, however, has focused on the impact of negative stereotyping of Hispanics on television, in the movies, and in the news, both broadcast and print. The subject was discussed in depth in the group's third annual State of Hispanic America *report, issued in 1994, and also became the focus of Yzaguirre's remarks at the NCLR convention that same year. "More than hurt feelings are at stake," he declared. "Our inaccurate and poor media image has a devastating effect on virtually all aspects of the Hispanic policy agenda." Both Yzaguirre and the NCLR report blamed the problem on the lack of Latino journalists and sources in the major media. Besides encouraging various industry groups to adopt "Latino-specific hiring and promotion goals," he suggested that Congress and the Federal Communications Commission might consider taking steps to increase positive Hispanic visibility in broadcasting.*

This same topic was very much on Yzaguirre's mind when he addressed the graduating class of Mercy College in White Plains, New York, on May 31, 1994. Only a few weeks earlier—on the Mexican holiday Cinco de Mayo (May 5), in fact—a radio station in Lansing, Michigan, had aired a commercial parody informing listeners of a contest in which the "prize" was a Mexican servant. The incident prompted Yzaguirre to reflect on the new wave of immigrant-bashing in the United States. The following remarks are reprinted from a copy provided by Yzaguirre.

Thank you very much for that very kind introduction. What a big day! Allow me to add my congratulations to the graduating students, to your parents, spouses, relatives, and friends. I have just attended my own son's graduation ceremonies, and I know from first-hand the bittersweet emotions you are experiencing.

We are participating in a rite of passage, and as in all rites of passage, there are elements of both joy and sorrow. In these rites, society—indeed, all societies—ask the participants to leave the old behind and take on new responsibilities. For some of you, the so-called "non-traditional" students, responsibility is nothing new. You have been shouldering multiple roles and responsibilities for many, many years.

Yet all of you will be asked to help shape the destiny of this great nation of ours. As members of the college-educated "elite," in the best sense of that word, you will be expected to weigh in on the monumental issues of our time.

One of those issues will be the matter of immigration. Mercy College, because of its history, location, and inclination, has at a very practical level responded to the challenges and

Raul Yzaguirre

opportunities that newly-arrived immigrants present to us. Because of your experiences here at Mercy, you are in a position to lead the rest of us as we wrestle with this divisive question.

America is of two minds when it comes to immigrants. On the one hand, we are proud of our immigrant heritage, symbolized by that great American icon known as the Statue of Liberty. Yet public opinion, going back as far as the early 1800s, has been decidedly against each new wave of immigrants.

Every American, including American Indians, are immigrants or descendants of immigrants. Newcomers to our land are "Americans by choice"; indeed, our very existence as a nation is based on that heritage.

Yet we are witnessing a wave of immigrant-bashing that mimics the most shameful episodes in our history. During the 1850s and through the Civil War, the so-called Know-Nothing party campaigned successfully on an explicitly racist and anti-immigrant platform, and what is disconcerting is that *exactly* the same rhetoric used at that time is prevalent today.

Just this past month, the following "contest" played on a radio station in the state of Michigan. Now try to imagine all the bells and whistles and the appropriate jingles and background music and listen to this as you would be listening to a radio program:

Some are giving away trips to Mexico City, but we are bringing Mexico to *you!* That's right! We are giving away Mexicans—real, live Mexicans! Ay carramba!

We'll be smuggling illegal aliens across the border in the wheel-well of a station van, and then we'll give one to *you!* Imagine—your own personal Mexican! They'll wash your car, clean your house, pick your crops, anything you want. Because if they don't, you'll have them deported!

Adios, amigos. Be the fifth caller when you hear this sound (the sound of a mooing cow) and win a Mexican!

Bathing and delousing of Mexicans is winner's responsibility. Station assumes no liability for infectious diseases carried by Mexicans.

Celebrate Cinco de Mayo in your own home every day with your own Mexican!

How should we interpret these kinds of public remarks? Is it OK to talk about—even in jest—people owning people? Whatever the intent, we know from past history that the first step in oppressing a people is to dehumanize them and/or to demonize them.

And that is exactly what we did to the new Americans that came from Germany, from Ireland, from Italy, from China and Japan, from Hungary. And that is what we did to Jews who came from all over Europe. Anti-immigration legislation specifically aimed at these groups has either passed or nearly passed in our past.

I hasten to add that there are well-meaning Americans who believe in more restrictionist immigration policies who are neither racist nor xenophobic. Some Americans are honestly worried about the total population of this nation and about our collective ability to accommodate differences in culture and language. Others truly believe that immigrants cost the taxpayer additional burdens.

These are reasonable concerns that can be addressed by the facts. And the facts are that the number of foreign-born in the United States as a percentage of our population is not any higher than it has been in our past. The fact is that today's new Americans are assimilating *faster* than previous immigrants. The fact is that immigrants are *not* a net burden to the United States taxpayer but a net contributor, a significant contributor.

Yet we should all be worried about continued undocumented immigration and about exploitation of human beings—be they documented, undocumented, immigrant, or native-born.

We also know that economic security fuels our worst fears and brings out our meanest instincts. During every single recession, and especially during the Great Depression, the United States implemented policies that should bring shame to all of us. While precise figures are hard to come by, we can confidently estimate that well over one million legal immigrants and American citizens have been illegally and unjustly deported during economic downturns.

Today, we are witnessing a replay of history. Politicians from both parties are scapegoating immigrants for our economic and social problems. Apparently there is a great deal of political capital in demonizing immigrants.

Regretfully, there are few statesmen willing to stand tall and bring reason and decency to this debate.

We need leaders like my own personal hero, President Harry Truman. He stood up to Congress and vetoed a racist immigration bill, and he sent the following message to Congress and to the American people, and let me quote:

The idea behind this policy [referring to the quota system] was, to put it boldly, that Americans with English or Irish names were better people and better citizens than Americans with Italian or Greek or Polish names. . . . Such a concept is utterly unworthy of our traditions and our ideals. It violates the great political doctrine of the Declaration of Independence that "all men are created equal". . . . It is incredible to me that, in this year of 1952, we should again be enacting into law such a slur on the patriotism, the capacity, and the decency of a large part of our citizenry.

Well, now we're here in 1994, and today we are not only slurring the decency of people, we are questioning their very humanity.

In years to come, I hope to read about an alumnus of Mercy College who stood up and reminded us that America is and always will be a place of opportunity, a nation of liberties, and a beacon to the world.

Thank you, have a great life, and God bless.

The controversy over the image of Hispanics in the media erupted again during the fall of 1994. This time, the trigger was the release of a study by the Washington-based Center for Media and Public Affairs that found Hispanics represent only about one percent of all characters on television and that most are shown in criminal or stereotypical roles. Yzaguirre responded with anger, stating bluntly that "what we're seeing here is systematic slander of the entire Hispanic community." He specifically cited the television shows "Cops" and "America's Most Wanted" for their negative portrayals of Hispanics while praising "NYPD Blue," "The John Larroquette Show," and "Beverly Hills 90210" for depicting Latinos in a favorable light. While he stopped short of saying exactly what the NCLR might do in response to the study results, Yzaguirre warned that networks and sponsors could face economic consequences if they don't take steps to mend their ways.

SOURCES

Detroit Free Press, "Hispanic Civil Rights Group Accuses Shows of Slander," September 8, 1994.

Editor and Publisher, "State of Hispanic America," August 6, 1994, p. 11.

Hispanic, "Know Your Rights," May, 1992, p. 46; "Committed to Unity," July, 1992, pp. 11-14.

Helen Zia

1952–

Chinese American writer, media consultant, and activist

"I am not exactly sure when it happened, but somewhere during my childhood I decided I wasn't American." Thus observed Helen Zia in Essence *magazine, recalling her sense of feeling like an "outsider" among her friends because she "didn't match the national color scheme." In a society that only recognized white and black during the 1950s and 1960s, Asian Americans were the "forgotten minority," and their concerns were of little import to the rest of the country. Zia has devoted her life to countering that trend, not just as an activist on behalf of Asian Americans, but for* all *people whose rights to justice and equality have often been ignored by mainstream society.*

Born in Newark, New Jersey, of parents who immigrated from China, Zia grew up amid the traditions of two very different cultures. "I liked hot dogs, Kool-Aid, apple pie and the two-tone Chevy wagon my dad drove," she has said. "But I ate my Spam with rice and could use chopsticks as well as an abacus." By the time she was eight, however, she and her family had endured so much racial prejudice on account of their perceived "foreignness" that Zia concluded "America didn't want me, and in that case I didn't want to be a part of it." During her teenage years, she very much identified with the black civil rights movement and its leaders. But she was also slowly becoming aware of other battles waiting to be fought.

After receiving her bachelor's degree from Princeton University in 1973, Zia worked briefly for the U.S. Department of State as a public affairs specialist before enrolling in the Tufts University School of Medicine, which she attended until 1975. She then headed to Detroit, where she pursued graduate studies in industrial relations at Wayne State University and was a factory worker for Chrysler Corporation from 1977 until 1979. During this same period, she began her career in journalism, contributing pieces to local and national publications.

It was also in Detroit that Zia became involved in a landmark civil rights case stemming from the racially-motivated beating death of Vincent Chin, a Chinese American. In June 1982, the twenty-seven-year-old draftsman accompanied three friends to a bar to celebrate his upcoming marriage. Also in the bar that evening was an unemployed white autoworker named Ronald Ebens who blamed his joblessness on the shrinking market share of U.S. car manufacturers. Thinking

Chin was Japanese, Ebens made some racial slurs that led to a fight, and all the participants were forced to leave. Later that night, Ebens and his stepson, Michael Nitz (who had also been involved in the bar incident), spotted Chin at a fast-food restaurant. They waited for him to come out and then, while Nitz held Chin, Ebens beat him with a baseball bat. Chin died several days later. Although initially charged with second-degree murder, Ebens and Nitz bargained their way into pleading guilty to manslaughter instead, for which they were fined about $3,000 each and put on probation for three years.

Asian Americans everywhere reacted with outrage at this clearly unjust outcome. Zia was one of the founders of American Citizens for Justice, the organization that sprang up to seek justice for Vincent Chin and to counter anti-Asian prejudice. Members of this group circulated and helped raise funds for legal expenses to challenge the Chin decision. Zia served as the campaign's national spokesperson and was elected president of the group for two terms. Nationwide protests eventually forced federal authorities to investigate, and Ebens was indicted for depriving Chin of his civil rights. While he was tried and found guilty, he saw his conviction reversed on appeal. A civil suit against Ebens proved more successful, however, and Chin's estate was awarded $1.5 million. Despite this less-than-satisfying resolution to the case, Zia and other Asian Americans counted it as a partial victory because it marked the first time they were able to demonstrate a direct link between anti-Asian prejudice and increasing rates of violence against Asian Americans.

Zia moved into the field of journalism on a full-time basis in 1983 when she joined the staff of Metropolitan Detroit *magazine as an associate editor. She left in 1985 to become executive editor of* Meetings and Conventions *magazine, part of the Murdoch Magazines/NewsAmerica group located in Secaucus, New Jersey. She remained with the company for the next four years, serving as editorial director of* Travel Weekly *from 1986 to 1987 and then as editor-in-chief of* Meetings and Conventions *magazine from 1987 to 1989.*

In 1989, Zia moved to New York to become executive editor of Ms. *magazine, a post she held until 1992. She then headed to San Francisco, where she was vice president and editor-in-chief of WorldView Systems (an electronic publishing company) through 1994. She now works primarily as a free-lance writer, lecturer, and media consultant. Zia is also a contributing editor to* Ms. *magazine and is at work on her own books of fiction and nonfiction. In 1995, she served as co-editor of the reference book* Notable Asian Americans.

In addition to her efforts on behalf of Asian Americans, Zia is also active in the feminist and gay/lesbian movements as well as other social justice causes. All of these interests figure prominently in her speeches, of which she may give up to two dozen or so in the course of a typical year. On August 27, 1992, for example, Zia was in Washington, D.C., to deliver the keynote address at the annual convention of the Asian American Journalists Association (AAJA), a group to which she belongs. The subject of her talk was media coverage of Asian Americans—particularly by other Asian Americans. Zia provided a transcript of her remarks.

Welcome to AAJA's annual national convention. I've been given the task of saying something meaningful (and hopefully rousing) on our role as Asian American journalists today. You know—something about whether we are Asian Americans who happen to be journalists, or journalists who happen to be Asian Americans. I have only a short time to address this complete question, and this will be a challenge. It's been an amazing year in the news for Asian Americans; news events that involve and directly impact the Asian American community have figured prominently in the national headlines.

We've been on the front pages as crime victims. Who can forget the sweet, youthful face of Konerak Sinthasimphone, the Laotian boy who was raped, murdered, and cannibalized by serial killer Jeffrey Dahmer? Police said they thought the fourteen-year-old was an adult.

And what about front-page/front-cover/top-of-the-news image of the smiling, charming, victorious face of Olympic gold medal figure skater Kristi Yamaguchi, the fourth-generation Japanese American who defeated Midori Ito of Japan?

Then there was the media event of this half century—that is, of course, the fiftieth anniversary of the bombing of Pearl Harbor. Virtually every media outlet in the country played some special Pearl Harbor angle.

This was followed by very cursory coverage—if there was any coverage at all—of the fiftieth anniversary of the racist incarceration of 120,313 Japanese Americans into U.S. concentration camps.

We witnessed (in George Bush's infamous trip to Japan) the spectacle of a U.S. president going overseas to ask for economic relief, which—following the hype over Pearl Harbor—resulted in even greater anti-Asian fervor.

Two major reports on Asian Americans were released nationally, one by the U.S. Civil Rights Commission on the rise of anti-Asian prejudice, and one by AAJA—our media resource handbook on covering the Asian American community. Both reports were ridiculed by some national media (such as *U.S. News and World Report, New Republic,* and *Reader's Digest*) because they dared to discuss issues of sensitivity to Asian Americans.

But the most dramatic news involving Asian Americans this year took place during the LA rebellion—which, to Asian Americans, represents the selective targeting of an entire Asian nationality and implicates all other look-alike Asians. The riot coverage *also* represents the overall failure of our business to go beyond the surface in reporting on the Asian community. Not only was there inadequate reporting, but considerable mischaracterization and disinformation about Korean Americans disseminated in the name of news.

Helen Zia

Those are just some of the Asian American news highlights since our last convention. Pretty big visibility for a community that's used to being invisible in the national news—and I think this change reflects the dynamic period of history that we're in. We are on the verge of the next millennium, tagged the century of Asia and the Pacific Rim.

As Asian Americans, we find ourselves at the crossroads of two major trends. First, there is the decline of U.S. economic might while the nations of Asia are on the ascendancy. This trend involves major shifts in global power relationships. Does anyone here doubt that there will be fundamental repercussions of all kinds for Asian Americans?

Secondly, Asian America is changing. Our numbers have doubled every ten years for each of the last four census reports, making us the fastest-growing minority in the U.S. It wasn't so long ago that being Asian American meant being either Chinese or Japanese. But now we are so diverse that even many Asian Pacific

Americans know little about their fellow Asian brothers and sisters.

And we, as Asian American journalists, have a very big role to play during this historic period, precisely because we are at the crossroads and in a position to give shape to who this Asian American community is to a nation that really doesn't have a clue.

"Asian American journalists . . . [are] in a position to give shape to who this . . . community is to a nation that really doesn't have a clue."

I, like most of you, remember what it was like never to see people who looked like me in the world beyond my immediate circle. When I was growing up in the 1950s, Asians were nowhere to be found in the media, except occasionally in the movies. There, at the Saturday matinee, my brothers and I would sit with all the other kids in town watching old World War II movies—you know, where the evil zero pilots would be heading for their unsuspecting prey, only to be thwarted by the all-American heroes, who were, of course, always white. These movies would have their defining moment, that crescendo of emotion when the entire theater would rise up, screaming, "Kill them! Kill them! Kill them!" ("Them" being the Japanese.) When the movie was over and the lights came on, I wanted to be invisible so that my neighbors wouldn't direct their red-*white*-and blue fervor toward me.

When I was a little older, I was inspired by the civil rights movements of the 1960s. In my high school, the social unrest often took the form of bomb scares and other disruptions. One afternoon, as my classmates and I stood in the schoolyard talking about racism while waiting for the bomb squad, one of my black girlfriends turned to me and said somberly, "Helen, you've got to decide whether you're black or white."

These incidents took place many years ago. I wish I could say things have changed a lot since, but I can't. In spite of the news coverage this year and the relative visibility of Asian Americans, a closer look at the coverage shows that we're still rendered invisible.

Take the front-page coverage of Konerak Sinthasimphone. How much—or perhaps I should ask, how little—consideration was given to the fact that he was Laotian? What was the response of the Laotian community, which is a sizable and impoverished minority group in the Midwest? Does anybody know? Did any reporters bother to try to find out? Was there any mention made of the anti-Asian racism that was exhibited by the Milwaukee police, in addition to their homophobic and anti-black attitude?

What about the very interesting social/political implications of Kristi Yamaguchi's ancestry at this particular point in history, especially following all the Pearl Harbor hype? Not too many news organizations wanted to touch that one—or maybe it never occurred to them how. *Newsweek*'s long essay by Frank Deford described her physique down to the two "cute" little moles on her face, but not a bit of analysis about how her Japanese heritage might be playing in Peoria.

Speaking of Pearl Harbor, what news value is there really to have so many polls, in just about every media market, asking how much more do Americans hate the Japanese today than they did yesterday? (Of course, these "Americans" are presumed to be non-Asian.) And don't you agree that this is a strange question? Would we ever see such widespread polling on how much more we hate the Germans today than yesterday, or the Russians, or the Cubans? Somehow it is assumed to be accepted behavior to hate Japanese people—and this is biased, non-objective journalism coming from our news directors at some of our most esteemed news organizations. The *New York Times* runs this poll every few years, and both the *Wall Street Journal* and the *Los Angeles Times* asked, "Was America right in dropping the atom bomb on Hiroshima and Nagasaki?" (The surprise answer—a high proportion of respondents said yes.) Or their question, "Was America right to intern 120,313 Japanese Americans?" (Surprise again—a significant proportion said yes.) I mean, we might imagine a poll that asked, "Do you think Germany was right to try to exterminate the Jews?" and we might even get a considerable response that said yes. But what journalistic purpose would this question serve? And what assumptions are being made in even asking the question?

Many of you may be involved in the coverage of Soon-Yi Farrow, adopted daughter of

Mia Farrow, who was raised as a daughter of Woody Allen. Some of our colleagues (or even some of us) call it a "love triangle." But would we be more likely to call it "incest" if she looked more like she could be his biological daughter instead of an Asian female, with all those sexual connotations? What does this so-called affair mean for an entire generation of adopted Korean children? Soon-Yi's Asian face is all over the news, but her Asianness is ignored and invisible.

This kind of invisibility was never so apparent than in the national coverage of Los Angeles, the story in which the nation's news media discovered Korean Americans, but then could only fixate on the image of Korean men with guns. A demonstration involving thousands of Korean Americans calling for justice for Rodney King was barely covered. "Nightline" let only one Korean spokesperson, Angela Oh, appear for an abbreviated broadcast after days of prolonged interviews with African American gang members who made grossly incorrect statements about Korean people that largely went unchallenged, and only then after community protests. As John Lee and Dean Takahashi wrote in the AAJA newsletter, a *Los Angeles Times* post-riot survey reported only the responses of whites, blacks, and Latinos—and "other." As explanation, they said that Asians are not statistically significant enough to count, even though they comprise eleven percent of LA's population—and even when Asians were so strongly impacted by the rebellion.

At some points, the insurrection seemed to be portrayed as a black-Korean issue (forget about police brutality and economic injustice). There was virtually no news analysis on the potential impact on other Asian Americans, or the fact that several hundred stores owned by Cambodians, Chinese, Japanese, and South Asians were also looted and burned.

This stuff is simply poor journalism. It wouldn't get out of Reporting 101—you know, the section on how to ask the right questions. But when it comes to Asian Americans, some people just don't seem to know what questions to ask to get beyond the superficial stereotypes.

I know I'm making this sound a lot like "us versus them," even though as journalists, many of us are the "them." But the fact is that many of us—perhaps *most* of us—are still outsiders in our own newsrooms. Jimmy Breslin almost got away with calling Mary Ji-Yeon Yuh a "little yellow dog" . . . and when he didn't get away with it, many of his colleagues (*our* colleagues) rushed to his defense. We're just not in the newsrooms in sufficient numbers yet or in enough positions of authority to be taken seriously. How many Asian American journalists were sent to cover LA? Shockingly few. I've heard several accounts of experienced Asian American journalists who requested to go and cover the riots and were turned down, even if the organization had no other Asian reporters. Yet if she or he pushed too hard or criticized too loudly, the consequences could be harsh, including the ultimate insult—being labeled as "not objective."

Now I'd like to deal with this objectivity issue for a moment. Somewhere, somehow, we ourselves have started to buy into this backlash mythology that to be a professional journalist means we can have no point of view—and if that were possible, that it would be a virtue. This is a fiction and an hypocrisy that only serves to keep us doubting ourselves.

Last year at the Seattle convention, I sat in a workshop and listened to a young woman in her first journalism job as an education reporter questioning her own ability to cover issues like bilingual education simply because she is Asian and *that* might be a conflict in and of itself. Obviously *every* story has implicit assumptions that steer the reader or viewer to some kind of impression. The issue is who determines those assumptions? Who decides what questions to ask, or not to ask?

For example, so much media hype is made on the point of Japanese investment. Yet in the news media itself several of the largest companies are owned by British, German, Australian, Canadian, and French interests. Imagine how differently the news coverage would play if the late Robert Maxwell had been Japanese. Can you imagine the headlines? "Maxwell-san Says 'Sayonara' After Kamikaze Strike on Tribune Company." "Maxwell's Sons Make Sneak Attack on U.S. Workers' Pensions." But Maxwell was British, not Japanese, and instead we see very staid, very respectful coverage. Is this not an inherent bias?

Personally, I think the whole issue of objectivity is a smokescreen to make us and others think that *we* are somehow deficient for not fitting the mold that the traditional white male standard created in its own image. We of all groups should never forget that we work in an industry that was singularly responsible for the systematic vilification and exclusion of Asian immigrants. Some venerable newspapers played a key role in the incarceration of Japanese Americans. Radio helped spearhead the "red scares" of the McCarthy era that led to the persecution of many Chinese Americans. More recently, the Kerner Commission in 1968 outlined how the news media and its lack of diversity contributed to the civil disorders of the 1960s—and sadly, progress has been at a glacial pace.

So when we get accused of not being objective, we need to be able to stand our ground and point out the double standard that is being applied to us at the expense of good journalism.

I should also note that I do not believe these editors and news directors and colleagues of ours are necessarily being deliberately racist. I think they're just doing what they've been taught, acting out some of their own biases. Don't you know that some of them were sitting near me—or near you—shouting, "Kill them! Kill them! Kill them!" Or perhaps they were explaining to another kid in another schoolyard how you have to decide whether you're black or white.

It's a vicious cycle—news gets shaped by people who are not even aware of their own prejudices. Journalists produce news that often reinforces their own beliefs, thereby steering public opinion in a way that perpetuates the same crap. And so on and so on. That's what we saw in LA—*some* black people using their prejudices toward Asians in general Koreans in particular to justify their actions; and *some* Korean people using their prejudices toward blacks to justify their actions. And where did each group learn these prejudices? Mostly through news and entertainment media.

Indeed, this is our historic role at this historic time with the confluence of these trends. *We* can interrupt this crazy feedback loop of misinformation about our communities and cultural heritage. We are in a very powerful position to outline the public perception of who Asian Americans are—not only within our newsrooms but to build bridges with other communities through the various minority journalists organizations.

This is not an easy task. Look around in this room. What you see are pioneers in this effort. Every one of us is a pioneer. As you go through this convention picking up skills for professional development and networking for career advancement, remember that our collective development includes being role models for each other as part of this historic position we hold.

There will be times when an issue of fairness stands out so blatantly that you will be moved to act, and you will find strength in knowing that you don't have to act alone because there is an entire organization that stands with you. There's nothing radical about this—it's simply about trying to create the newsroom environment in which the Asian American journalists can reach their fullest potential without having to explain why they speak English so well, or having to deal with colleagues who try to second-guess if the color of their skin or the shape of their eyes had anything to do with a job, a promotion, or a story assignment.

As you look around this room and think how comfortable it is not to have a worry about such things, imagine being able to feel this way at a meeting of the Society of Professional Journalists, the American Society of Magazine Editors, the American Society of Newspaper Editors, and so on, or even your own newsroom. One day it will be that way for all of us, because of our pioneering efforts in AAJA. So enjoy the convention, be good role models to each other, and remember that history is on our side.

The following year, on March 6, 1993, Zia spoke at the "Equality and Harm Conference" at the University of Chicago Law School. Her focus that day was on hate crimes—specifically sexual assaults and murder—against women of color. Zia furnished a transcript of her address.

My remarks focus on a very specific intersecting area of racism, hate crimes, and pornography—that is, where race and gender overlap and where current civil rights law *can* but *fails* to address racially-motivated, gender-based crimes against women of color. I'm talking about the area of bias-motivated sexual assault against women of color, which has also been called "ethno-rape" and which I sometimes refer to as "hate rape."

Before I begin, I want to acknowledge a fact that is well known within the battered women's movement and the sexual assault movement—that most sexual assaults, probably some eighty percent, are perpetrated by men of the same race as the victim and most of whom were known by the victim. But a probe into the area of bias-motivated rape can offer some insight into the separate but sometimes parallel legal remedies for race- and gender-based crimes.

I started looking into this issue after years of organizing around hate killings of Asian Americans. After a while, I noticed that all the cases I could name involved male victims, and I wondered why. Maybe it was because Asian American men came into contact with perpetrator types more often. Maybe it's because Asian American men are more hated and therefore attacked by racists. But a feminist analysis of the subordination and vulnerability of Asian American women whose dominant stereotype is to be sexually exotic and subservient and passive conflicted with that argument. So where were the Asian American women victims of hate crimes?

Once I began looking, I found them through random news clippings, footnotes in books, word of mouth. Let me share with you some of what I consider to be examples of bias-motivated attacks and sexual assaults.

In February 1984, Ly Yung Cheung, a nineteen-year-old Chinese woman who was seven months pregnant was pushed in front of a New York City subway train and decapitated. Her attacker, a white male high-school teacher, claimed he suffered from "a phobia of Asian people" and he was overcome with the urge to kill this woman. He successfully pleaded insanity. If this case had been investigated as a hate crime, there might have been more information about his so-called phobia and whether there was a pattern of racism. But because she was Asian and because she was a woman, it was not investigated as a hate crime.

On December 7, 1984, fifty-two-year-old Japanese American Helen Fukui disappeared in Denver, Colorado; her decomposed body was found weeks later. The fact that she disappeared on Pearl Harbor day, when anti-Asian speech and incidents increased dramatically, was considered significant in the community. But the case was not investigated as a hate crime and no suspects were ever apprehended.

In 1985 an eight-year-old Chinese girl named Jean Har-Kaw Fewel was found raped and lynched in Chapel Hill, North Carolina—two months after *Penthouse* featured pictures of Asian women in various poses of bondage and torture, including hanging bound from trees, in deathlike poses. Were epithets or pornography used? No one knows—her rape and killing wasn't investigated as a possible hate crime.

Last year a serial rapist was convicted of kidnapping and raping a Japanese exchange student in Oregon, where he was also a student. He had also assaulted a Japanese woman in Arizona, and another in San Francisco. He was sentenced to jail time for these crimes, which were not pursued as hate crimes even though California has a hate statute. Was hate speech or race-specific pornography used? Who knows, since it wasn't investigated as a hate crime.

At Ohio State University, two Asian women were gang-raped by fraternity brothers in two separate incidents. One of the rapes was part of a racially-targeted "game" called the "Ethnic Challenge" in which the fraternity men followed an ethnic checklist indicating what kind of women to gang-rape—in this case, Asian women. Because the women feared humiliation and ostracism by their communities, neither woman reported the rapes. However, the attacks were known to a few campus officials, who did not take them up as hate crimes or anything else.

All of these incidents could have been investigated and prosecuted as state hate crimes and/or federal criminal civil rights cases. However, to do so would have required awareness and interest on the part of police investigators and the prosecutors, and we know they have a lousy track record on race and gender issues. Failing that, it would have helped to have awareness and support for civil rights charges by the Asian American community, which is also generally lacking when it comes to issues like women, gender, sex, and sexual assault. The result is a double-silencing effect in the assaults and deaths of these women—silencing and invisibility because of their gender and their race.

I would like to point out that although my empirical research centers on hate crimes toward Asian women, this silencing and what amounts to the failure to provide equal protection has its parallels in all of the other classes protected by federal civil rights and hate statutes. That is, all other communities of color, to my knowledge, also have a similar hate crimes prosecution rate for the women in their communities—in other words, zero. Zilch. This dismal record is almost as bad in the lesbian and gay anti-violence projects. The vast preponderance of hate crimes reported, tracked, and prosecuted involve gay men—very few lesbians. *So where are all these women?*

The answer to this question lies in what was said yesterday in many different ways—that this system of justice was not designed for women. In yet another way, we are mere shadows in the existing civil rights framework. But in spite of all this, I still think federal civil rights and state hate-crimes law offers a legal avenue for women to be heard.

Federal civil rights prosecutions, for example, are excellent platforms for high-visibility community education on the harmful impact of hate speech and behavior. When two white autoworkers in Detroit called Chinese American Vincent Chin racial slurs and said, "It's because of you . . . that we're out of work," the national civil rights campaign that followed launched a new social movement and raised the level of national discourse on what constitutes racism toward Asian Americans. When we began that campaign, constitutional law professors and members of the ACLU and NLG told us that we were wasting our time, that Asian Americans are not covered by civil rights law. We dealt with that misconception.

Hate-crimes remedies can be used to force the racist, sexist criminal justice bureaucracy to take on new attitudes. When Patrick Purdy went to an elementary school in Stockton, California, that was eighty-five percent Southeast Asian students, and when he selectively aimed his automatic weapon and killed five eight-year-olds and wounded thirty others, the first response by the police and the media was that this couldn't possibly be a bias-motivated crime. (Kind of reminiscent of the denial response by the Montreal officials in the femicide of fourteen women students.) But an outraged Asian American community forced a state investigation into the incident and uncovered hate literature in the killer's effects. As a result, the sense of the community was validated and empowered, and there was new level of understanding of the community as a whole, including the criminal justice system and the media.

Imagine if a federal criminal civil rights investigation were launched in the rape of the St. John's University student—the African American student who was raped and sodomized by white members of the school lacrosse team, who were later acquitted. Issues could be raised about those white men's attitudes toward the victim as a black woman, to see whether hate speech or race-specific pornography was involved, to investigate overall racial climate on campus, and to bring all of the silenced issues to the public eye. Perhaps it would lead to a guilty verdict this time for deprivation of her civil rights; but even if not, at a minimum the community discourse could be raised to a higher level, paving the way for other legislation, like the Dworkin-MacKinnon civil rights law, or the Violence Against Women Act.

This will not be an easy road. Hate-crimes efforts go for blatant cases, with high community consensus, not cases that bring up hard issues like gender-based violence. But these are the very issues we must give voice to.

There are a few serious issues in pushing for use of federal and state hate remedies. First and foremost is that some state statutes have already been used against men of color—specifically, on behalf of white rape victims against African American men. We know that the system, if left unchecked, will try to use anti-hate laws to enforce unequal justice.

At the same time, the state hate statutes could be used to prosecute men of color who are believed to have assaulted women of color of another race. Inter-minority assaults are increasing. Also, if violence against women were made into a general hate crime, Asian women could seek prosecutions against Asian men for their gender-based violence. This would make it even harder to win the support of men in communities of color, as well as women in those communities who would not want to be accused of dividing the community.

But at least within the Asian American anti-violence community, this discourse is taking place now. Asian American feminists in San Francisco have prepared a critique of the Asian anti-hate crimes movement and the men of that movement are listening. I hope what's happened in the Asian American community can be used by other communities to examine the nexus between race and gender for women of color, and by extension, all women.

This has been a very abbreviated, non-legal summary of a longer, more complex analysis. Please understand this strategy is not seen as a panacea. We know that civil rights cases can be lost; after five years in federal court, the Vincent Chin campaign for justice was ultimately lost, and as we all know, the outcome of the federal civil rights trial of Rodney King's attackers is far from certain. This is, however, another way to give voice to the experience of women, especially women of color who have been so silenced in our society.

I would like to challenge attorneys and theorists to push the boundaries of existing law and to include the most invisible women. There are hundreds and hundreds of cases involving women of color that are waiting to be taken on. I also challenge the activists in the violence against women movement to reexamine current views on gender-based violence, and not to view all sexual assaults as the same. They are not. Racism used in a sexual assault adds another complex wrinkle to the pain and harm that are inflicted on women.

By taking women of color out of the shadows of legal invisibility and moving toward personhood, all women gain status toward full human dignity and human rights.

In the following speech, delivered at the Sixth Annual Gay Asian Pacific Alliance (GAPA) conference in San Francisco on January 29, 1994, Zia weaves together several of her interests as she reflects on the issue of achieving visibility and empowerment for gay and lesbian Asian Americans. Zia provided a copy of her remarks.

I'm truly honored and proud to be a part of GAPA's celebration of the diversity of Gay and Bisexual Asian Pacific Islander Men. Even before I moved to San Francisco a year and a half ago, I had heard of this magazine called *Lavender Godzilla* published by a really right-on group called GAPA that was doing incredible work to increase visibility of gay and bisexual men of Asian Pacific ancestry, to provide support around issues of coming out, community and family, HIV/AIDS, and to build powerful role models.

Building role models for visibility and empowerment is no small task. When you look in this wide world around us, where can you find us, the Asian Pacific Islander gay/lesbian/bisexual/transgender people?

Will you find us in media portrayals and popular images of the gay and lesbian community? No, you won't find us there. The quintessential standard for who is queer is white and male.

Will you find us in the leadership of the national gay and lesbian organizations and institutions? With a few exceptions that you can count on one hand, you won't find us there, either.

If you go home to the diverse Asian American communities across the United States where many of our parents and families are, you won't find us there. After all, our aunties and uncles

> *"The quintessential standard for who is queer is white and male."*

and cousins watch TV, too, and have concluded that "homosexuality is white man's problem."

And this shouldn't come as a surprise either, because if we were each to trace our roots across the Pacific and visit one of our many sexually-repressive ancestral homelands in search of gays, lesbians and bisexuals, we'd again be very hard put to find our gay sisters and brothers—except perhaps in mental wards, prisons, or living as outcasts who are infected with the dreaded Western "disease" of homosexuality.

Speaking of sexual repression, when we think about the popular concept of Asian sexuality, what do we find? Asian men in general are viewed as asexual, so being "gay" and "Asian" is an impossible construct. Meanwhile, Asian women are viewed as supersexual exotic creatures who are hot for white men, so it's similarly not possible to think of us as lesbians.

All this negation makes it incredibly tough to be a queer API [Asian Pacific Islander]. When there isn't a group like GAPA around, where in the world can we find validation of ourselves, let alone find positive images that build our sense of self-esteem and self-respect?

I know the damage this can do from my own personal experience, as I suspect most of you do. When I first became aware of my attraction to the same sex as a kid, I didn't have a place for it in my consciousness. And coming from an immigrant Chinese family, we never spoke of sex—ever. I got my sex education from reading the *Encyclopaedia Britannica.* Having read the entry on reproduction several times, I can assure you that there was no mention of homosexuality.

When I finally got the courage to go to lesbian bars, it was great to be around women-loving women, but I didn't exactly feel like I had found my home, either. All the dykes I met were white and I didn't know of any Asian lesbians. That situation made me feel like I couldn't be a real lesbian. And because I didn't think I could be a real lesbian, I also didn't feel I could be attractive to real lesbians.

But the worst part was how my fellow Asian American community activists reacted when they realized I was hanging out with a lot of white lesbians. This was back in the early 70s, before "gay" was an accepted word yet, and it was at the height of the Asian American movement and the radical Third World liberation movements, the days when the revolution was right around the corner.

I was one of those Asian American movement activists, and my strongest sense of myself at that time was as an Asian American. But my Asian American comrades—my Asian community/family—had determined that homosexuality was "counterrevolutionary" and a "petit bourgeois degenerate deviation." They called a special meeting to investigate my sexual proclivities. I remember sitting through that difficult meeting in rolled-up t-shirt sleeves and a leather bomber jacket that was too big for me, already confused and anxious about my sexuality. As you can imagine, this didn't help my coming-out process.

Luckily for me, I finally found my way to those Sapphic pleasures, and over time have struggled through many issues like being out in the straight Asian Pacific Islander community. Coming out to Asian community groups has its lighter moments. A few years ago, I was delivering a speech to the Asian American Journalists Association national convention in Washington, D.C., and the speech was going to be carried on C-SPAN. I tried hard to write something into the speech about being a lesbian, but it just wasn't going to fit the topic of my speech. So I asked the person who was going to introduce me to be sure to include the fact that I was a lesbian in the introduction—you know, just to blend it in with the other stuff and not to make it a big deal. She said "Fine, no problem." But when it came time for her to stand in front of AAJA and the C-SPAN cameras to introduce me, here's what she said: "Helen Zia is a longtime feminist and Asian community activist and she's a l-l-l-lesbian. . . ." And then she sort of coughed, fiddled with the microphone, and said, "Is the microphone working? Did you all hear that, she's a l-l-l-lesbian. . . ."

I just thought, "Well, so much for subtlety." But if the alternative was invisibility, I'm glad she went the other way. Because the price we end up paying for this invisibility is far too high. We have all experienced our own forms of personal hell as a result of being invisible. But there are other costs, too.

We all know how bias-motivated crimes against gay men and lesbians have been increasing at frightening rates; in areas like Oregon and Colorado, where the anti-gay initiatives have been organized, it's open season against us. We also know that anti-Asian hate crimes have been increasing, especially as racist hysteria against Asian imports and Asian immigrants has heated up. Well, we—Asian Pacific queers—are directly in the fire for both hate trends.

Yet how can we effectively respond to and counter attacks when they happen? The unfortunate answer is that we can't when we're invisible to a community that is unable—or unwilling—to see us.

I'm sad to say that there have been several

incidents of hate violence against Asian American gays and lesbians as well as an ambivalent response by our Asian communities. Only last year we witnessed the near fatal beating of Loc Minh Truong by a group of teenage boys near a local gay bar in Laguna Beach, California. Truong, a Vietnamese refugee who was fifty-five years old at the time of the attack, was so badly beaten that authorities could not initially determine his race. His left eye was out of his socket and a rock was impaled nearly an inch into his skull. Truong was in critical condition for several days; police described the attack as one blow short of murder.

Truong's attackers were apprehended and two pleaded guilty to attempted murder, felonious aggravated assault, and committing a hate crime against Loc Minh Truong. The attackers admitted to saying to Truong, "You fucking faggot . . . we're going to get you!" and "If a fag approached me, I'd beat him on the spot." They denied that Truong's race was a factor in the beating. Asian community anti-Asian violence activists monitored the case, but *Truong's family and the local Vietnamese community denied that he is gay and did not want to associate him with being gay.* Much Asian community energy went into speculating whether Truong was gay and to try to establish a race-biased motive instead. In point of fact, Truong's actual sexual orientation is irrelevant, since his attackers perceived him to be gay, and since sexual orientation and race are both protected under the California hate crimes law.

Does this mean that our Asian Pacific Islander community would be less likely to support a hate crime victim because of his or her sexual orientation? Well, as long as we remain invisible to our API communities, we make it easy for homophobia to rule their reactions.

Homophobia may have been the reason that there was little community response to the 1988 murder of Paul Him Chow, a gay Chinese American who was killed in New York City's Greenwich Village. Homophobia and racism may explain the subsequent lack of aggressive police investigation.

And both anti-gay prejudice in the API community and racism came into play in the 1991 murder of Konerak Sinthasimphone, a fourteen-year-old Laotian boy, by serial killer Jeffrey Dahmer. Then, the racist and homophobic police were all too willing to turn a naked, bleeding fourteen-year-old [over] to Dahmer, accepting the word of a white man that this Asian child was his adult lover. And after the atrocities were exposed, our Asian communities were again silent.

Actually, the only time I recall hearing of a grassroots community discussion of homosexuals was in the context of a community-wide alert against child sexual molesters of Asian boys—and the public posters suggesting that homosexuals were lying in wait to molest their sons. Not only was this homophobic, but also a complete heterosexual fantasy, since it's a well-established fact that the vast majority of child sexual abuse is committed by heterosexual men, and mostly toward girls.

As we all know, this silence, coupled with ignorance, can only mean death when it comes to a community-based response to HIV/AIDS. At a time when API men and women of all sexual orientations are at extremely high risk of HIV infection—largely because of community denial—we cannot afford to live with this invisibility.

> ***"The price we end up paying for [our] invisibility is far too high. We have all experienced our own forms of personal hell as a result of being invisible."***

That's why GAPA and the handful of other Asian gay, lesbian, bi, and transgender organizations are playing such a critical historic role today. Fighting for a spot in the Chinatown Lunar New Year parade, for example, is exactly the kind of VISIBILITY that we need to take on the challenges of today *and* tomorrow.

Looking forward to the future, what do we see? In six short years, we will be entering a new century, already dubbed the "Century of Asia and the Pacific." There will be a tremendous transfer of economic and political might to the nations of the Asia and the Pacific Rim, with incredible ramifications for APIs in the U.S.

To the extent that national visibility and power gets transferred to a sense of individual esteem, think of all the Asian gay men and lesbians who will potentially become more empowered. How many more will find the courage to be true to themselves and come out?

Let's do the math. In the U.S. today, there are 3.4 million Asian Pacific Islanders. Within a decade, that should more than double to 8-10 million, or 800,000 to 1 million gay, lesbian, bi, transgender Asian Americans. Next, I challenge you to think globally. Looking across the Pacific, there's 1-plus billion people in China, 1 billion in India, plus several hundreds of millions more in other Asian nations. At least 3 billion Asian people in the world, and if 10 percent are gay, lesbian, and bi, that's 300 million Asian Pacific Islander queers! It's more than the entire population of the United States—that's a lot of invisible queer power looking to come out!

And where will all these 300 million Asian gays, lesbians, and bisexuals be turning to for role models on what their lives can be and how they can be recognized for who they are?

I believe they'll be looking right here at GAPA and other courageous Asian queers, at all of you to learn who they are, to get reassurance that they have a right to live and love in dignity and respect and that as proud Asian queers they have an important contribution to make to their communities. That is the historic role and responsibility we have to play *today*.

So while you go about your daily lives and do all the important programs that you do for GAPA, think about how we must each strive to be good role models for each other and all those many other APIs who are desperately seeking some affirmation of who they are so they can be out and proud too. And get ready for the day that you'll have to crank out 100 million-plus membership cards. Now that's Lavender Godzilla power!

SOURCES

Books

Daniels, Roger, *Asian America: Chinese and Japanese in the United States Since 1850,* University of Washington Press, 1988.

Periodicals

Essence, "Not Black, Not White," May, 1993.

Other

"Who Killed Vincent Chin?" (video documentary).

Keyword Index

A

D

E

F

I

J

M

N

O

P

Q

R

S

U

V

W

Y

Z

DATE			